BUSINESS LAW & THE REGULATORY ENVIRONMENT

PRINCIPLES & CASES

TWELFTH EDITION

RONALD A. ANDERSON
Professor Emeritus
Drexel University
Member of the Pennsylvania and Philadelphia Bars

IVAN FOX
Professor of Law
Pace University
Member of the New York Bar

DAVID P. TWOMEY
Professor of Law, Carroll School of Management
Boston College
Member of the Massachusetts and Florida Bars

SOUTH-WESTERN College Publishing

An International Thomson Publishing Company

Team Director: Scott D. Person
Acquisitions Editor: Christopher Will
Developmental Editor: Dr. Carol A. Cromer
Production Editor: Lois Boggs-Leavens
Production House: Navta Associates, Inc.
Cover and Interior Designer: Craig LaGesse Ramsdell
Marketing Manager: Denise Carlson
Manufacturing Coordinator: Karen Truman

LA70LA
Copyright © 1995
by South-Western Publishing
Cincinnati, Ohio

Anderson, Ronald Aberdeen
    Business law and the regulatory environment : principles and cases / Ronald A.
    Anderson, Ivan Fox, David P. Twomey. — 12th ed.
    p. cm.
    Rev. ed. of: Business law : principles, cases, legal environment. 11th ed. c1992
    Includes index.
    ISBN 0-538-84228-8 Y.
    Commercial law — United States—Cases. I. Fox, Ivan.
    II. Twomey, David P.   III. Anderson, Ronald Aberdeen
    Business law. IV. Title.
    KF888.A44 1995
    346.73'07—dc20
    [347.3067]

    345678 VH 1098765

Printed in the United States of America

 This book is printed on acid-free paper that meets Environmental Protection Agency standards for recycled paper.

I(T)P   International Thomson Publishing
    South-Western College Publishing is an ITP Company. The ITP trademark is used under this license.

About the Authors

Ronald A. Anderson, Professor of Law and Government, Drexel University, taught the subjects covered by this book for 40 years. He is the internationally renowned author of the definitive, 14-volume treatise, *Anderson on the Uniform Commercial Code*, published by Clark Boardman Callaghan. He has written many other well-respected professional works.

Professor Anderson was graduated from the University of Pennsylvania and also earned his Juris Doctor from that school. He is a member of the American Bar Association and is an active member of the legal community.

Ivan Fox, Professor of Law at Pace University, is widely known for his work with the Fox-Gearty CPA Review Course. He has lectured extensively to professional and banking groups on various business law topics.

Professor Fox was graduated from Pace University, earned his Juris Doctor from New York Law School, and received his LL.M. from New York University. He is a member of the New York Bar and the New York State Bar Association.

David P. Twomey is Professor of Law at Boston College Carroll School of Management. He has a special interest in curriculum development, having served three terms as chairman of his school's Educational Policy Committee. He is chairman of the Business Law Department at Boston College.

Professor Twomey was graduated from Boston College and earned his MBA at the University of Massachusetts at Amherst. After two years of business experience, he entered Boston College Law School and earned his Juris Doctor. He is a member of the Massachusetts,

Florida, and Federal Bars. Professor Twomey is a nationally known labor arbitrator and was elected to membership in the National Academy of Arbitrators. He has written a great number of books and articles on labor and employment law and other business law topics.

Preface

The 21st century is almost here. New technology and new methods of doing business are bringing new laws of business. It is with the present and the future in mind that we have written this Twelfth Edition of BUSINESS LAW AND THE REGULATORY ENVIRONMENT: PRINCIPLES AND CASES. Our objectives are to bring to readers the law they will face as human beings, citizens, and persons in business and to help readers develop the *critical thinking skills* necessary to be successful citizens and business persons. Our goals have been to make this book (1) accurate, (2) understandable, (3) balanced, (4) life- oriented, and (5) thought provoking.

By *accurate*, we mean that we have done everything possible to insure that the content of the book is as up-to-date as modern publishing technology will permit. Accurate also means that new doctrines and minority trends have been identified. Accordingly, we have endeavored to make this book anticipatory as well as retrospective. In the process of so doing, we hope to emphasize the dynamic character of the law.

Understandable means that legalistic jargon and words of art must be translated into ordinary English. We have replaced linguistic provincialisms and obscure words with ordinary language that can be understood by the modern student.

Balanced means that from the myriad discrete legal topics that might have some significance for undergraduate students of business law, those with the greatest relevance have been selected. If all the volumes of professional treatises relating to business were added together, the number would exceed

1,000. The business law student is given one book. Obviously, careful choice is necessary to bring the great mass of the law down into a one-volume text for beginners. In addition, great care must be exercised to treat all portions of the student's book with the appropriate degree of intensity.

Life-oriented requires the book to be devoted to those areas that the undergraduate student of today will most likely meet in future years. Consequently, it means avoiding the unusual, the bizarre, the headline cases that have no real value for the business person. Above all, life-oriented brings out the interrelationship between the law and life: the law is shaped by the environment, and the law gives direction to the environment. For the purpose of curriculum compartmentalization, "law" is a separate subject but as far as life is concerned it is an inseparable part of living. The more the student can appreciate this interrelationship, the better will be the student's understanding both of law and of life.

Thought provoking means the text, cases, and case questions throughout the book require students to develop critical thinking skills enabling them to analyze the positions of the parties, identify flaws in arguments, and evaluate the appropriateness of legal remedies. Moreover, the end-of-chapter materials ask students to identify basic questions, to apply existing principles to the solution of such basic questions, and to make intelligent decisions when there are no preexisting principles to govern the exact basic questions that are involved. This system not only brings the student back to the orientation of law to life but also assures the teaching of law a permanent place in the pattern of higher education.

Where appropriate throughout the book, ethical, public policy, and international dimensions are integrated into the text.

The objectives set forth above have guided the writing of this book for more than a third of a century. Though our focus on these objectives has never wavered, the specific content of the book has evolved to keep pace with changing times. The early 1960s witnessed the integration of the Uniform Commercial Code in the Seventh Edition as a result of the growth in the number of states adopting the UCC. In subsequent years that coverage has been continually updated to keep pace with amendments to the UCC and other uniform and model acts. Curriculum trends have us placing increasing emphasis upon environmental and regulatory topics.

THE LEGAL AND REGULATORY ENVIRONMENT OF BUSINESS

Part I of the book brings together various chapters relating to societal or public law that form the general background for individual business transactions. To borrow terms familiar to the economist, Part I deals with macro law while much of the balance of the book relates to micro law. It is important that the student see the background of macro law. It is also important that the student recognize that the legal environment of business is the sum total of the macro and micro areas.

More specifically, Part I deals with the regulatory environment in which business operates. The social forces behind the creation and evolution of the specific principles and substantive rules that govern disputes and transactions between individuals are explored. A comprehensive discussion of the federal and state court structure and the procedures involved in a lawsuit, from commencement to execution of the judgment, is included. The Constitution, as the foundation of the legal environment of business, is presented. The increasing role played by the administrative agencies in the government regulation of business is fully discussed.

This allocation of the indicated material to Part I is in harmony with the increased concern for an environmental approach to the teaching of business law. At the same time, this focusing on societal or public law is not made at the expense of the treatment of the areas of private law. There has been no lessening of attention to accuracy of content, clarity of expression, and thoroughness of subject matter coverage.

In addition to the topics discussed in Part I, other chapters throughout the book are appropriate for a course that focuses on public law. Although every chapter in the text possesses the potential for an environmental approach, some chapters lend themselves to this mode of teaching more readily than others. An outline of chapters emphasizing public law follows.

SUGGESTED LEGAL AND REGULATORY ENVIRONMENT OUTLINE

Chapters:
1. Law and Determination of Legal Rights
2. Ethics, Social Forces, and the Law
3. The Constitution as the Foundation of the Legal Environment
4. Government Regulation of Competition and Prices
5. Administrative Agencies
6. The Legal Environment of International Trade
7. Crimes
8. Torts
20. Personal Property (protection of intangible proprietary rights; trademarks, copyrights, patents, trade secrets)
29. Consumer Protection
37. Bankruptcy
42. Regulation of Employment
43. Equal Employment Opportunity Law
49. Securities Regulation
52. Environmental Law and Community Planning

An introductory course that emphasizes societal or public law may include the chapters above and other appropriate chapters selected for the course. An introductory course emphasizing private law may cover selected chapters from Part I, "The Legal, Social, and Regulatory Environment of Business," and chapters on contracts, personal property, or agency. The instructor may choose to cover additional topics in this introductory course, depending upon the ability level of the students and the time allotted to the course at the institution. The remainder of the book may be covered in advanced courses.

PREPARATION FOR CPA EXAM

As was true in previous editions, this Twelfth Edition provides strong preparation for the business law section of the CPA exam. This text is used as an authoritative source for the business law section of the exam.

The business law section of the CPA exam is now called "Business Law and Professional Responsibility" (LPR). Many new topics have been added and are covered in detail in this Twelfth Edition of BUSINESS LAW AND THE REGULATORY ENVIRONMENT: PRINCIPLES AND CASES. If you are preparing for the exam, note the highlighted sections in this text. The sections marked "CPA" are areas that are heavily tested by the CPA examiners.

The new content specifications of the LPR section of the CPA exam and their weights are set forth below. You will also note the chapter in this text where these areas are covered in detail.

LPR—CONTENT SPECIFICATION OUTLINE

Text Chapter
I. Professional Responsibilities (15 percent)
 A. Code of Conduct and Other Responsibilities
  1. Code of Professional Conduct
  2. Proficiency, Independence, and Due Care
  3. Responsibilities in Consulting Services
  4. Responsibilities in Tax Practice
Chapter 19
 B. The CPA and the Law
  1. Common Law Liability to Clients and Third Parties
  2. Federal Statutory Liability
  3. Working Papers, Privileged Communication, and Confidentiality
II. Business Organizations (20 percent)
Chapters 39-41
 A. Agency
  1. Formation and Termination

A. Real Property
1. Types of Ownership
2. Lessor-Lessee
3. Deeds, Recording, Title Defects, and Title Insurance

NEW TOPICS

New or expanded topics in this Twelfth Edition include: NAFTA (Chapter 6); arbitrating international business disputes (Chapter 6); U.S. laws on counterfeit goods and grey market goods (Chapter 6); bailments—court refusal to enforce explicit exclusions of liability in automobile rental contracts (Chapter 22); leases of personal property (Chapter 24); compensatory and punitive damages for insurer bad faith breach of the insurance contract (Chapter 38); negligent hiring and retention of employees (Chapter 41); regulation of employment and equal employment opportunity law (new Chapter 42 and 43); limited liability companies (Chapter 46); the SEC's new small business initiative and securities industry self-regulation (Chapter 49); the fiduciary duty of corporate directors-officers (Chapter 50).

UP-TO-DATE WITH THE CODE

Recently a wave to reform the UCC began. Thus far, five new articles or revisions have been adopted as official parts of the Code. The first footnote in Appendix 3 of this text lists the states that have adopted these new articles. This book is up-to-date with these changes in the Code. Selected sections of the statute are presented in Appendix 3. In addition, Article 2A, "Leases," is covered in Chapter 24; the 1990 versions of Articles 3 and 4 are covered in Part 5 of the text; Article 4A is covered in Chapter 34; and Article 6 is handled briefly in Chapter 24.

Part 5 of the text, on negotiable instruments and funds transfers, features a unique comparative discussion of both the old (1952) and the new (1990) Uniform Commercial Code, Articles 3 and 4. Readers in states adopting the new code Articles will of course

be interested in these up-to-date materials. But, in addition, the comparison of the new Articles with the former versions furnishes an excellent opportunity for the student to see how business practices and new technologies give rise to new situations that call for new law.

CASES

As in previous editions, this Twelfth Edition contains ample cases—including case questions—integrated with the text of each chapter. Popular, precedent-setting cases have been retained while at the same time adding many new decisions.

FEATURES

New to this edition are chapter objectives at the beginning of each chapter to identify main points to be learned. Another new feature is a "Law in Practice" section at the end of each chapter that presents several practical points related to the chapter content. Popular features continued in this edition include chapter-opening outlines, illustrations within the chapters, and end-of-chapter summaries designed to assist students in assimilating the material.

A section on "Analysis of Court Opinions" is presented on pages xiii - xv. This section includes a chart designed to assist students in identifying and analyzing ethical issues in the cases.

A glossary, a case index, and a subject index are included, as well as appendices "How to Find the Law," the U.S. Constitution, the Uniform Commercial Code, the United Nations Convention on Contracts for the International Sale of Goods (CISG), the Uniform Partnership Act, and the Revised Model Business Corporation Act.

STUDENTS' SUPPLEMENTS

Accompanying this Twelfth Edition is a student study guide authored by Ronald L. Taylor of Metropolitan State College of Denver. The study guide contains an outline of each chapter in the text expanded by general rules, limitations on these rules, and study hints. Review and application questions are given for each chapter. Answers are in a separate key.

The Legal Tutor™ on Contracts and The Legal Tutor™ on Sales, also authored by Ronald Taylor, provide the opportunity to develop analytical ability, improve academic performance, and expand knowledge through the use of interactive IBM-compatible software.

INSTRUCTOR'S MATERIALS

An instructor's manual was prepared by Kim Tyler of Shasta College in conjunction with the text authors. This manual contains a paragraph explaining the significance of each chapter, chapter outlines, suggested answers to chapter objectives, lecture notes, case briefs, and answers to end-of-chapter questions and case questions.

A printed test bank of over 2,850 questions, prepared by Arthur M. Magaldi of Pace University, is available. The test questions may also be obtained in an easy-to-use software package, MicroExam.

A set of color transparencies has been developed to enhance classroom presentation of text concepts.

Videos, custom-designed for use with this text, are available to adopters. Video topics include the UCC, employment law, and the business law portion of the CPA exam. A CNBC video is new to this edition.

ACKNOWLEDGMENTS

We thank the faculty and students who have provided valuable suggestions that have influenced this text. In particular we wish to thank the following reviewers:

E. Eugene Arthur, S. J.
Rockhurst College

Gregory W. Baxter
Southeastern Oklahoma State University

Thomas M. Branton
Alvin Community College

Thomas H. S. Brucker
University of Washington

George F. Conlin
Savannah State College

Frank P. Darr
The Ohio State University

Kenneth R. Davis
Fordham University

Gamewell Gantt
Idaho State University

Lula M. Goode
Angelo State University

Susan E. Grady
University of Massachusetts at Amherst

Ellen Harshman
Saint Louis University

James M. Highsmith
California State University Fresno

Madelyn M. Huffmire
The University of Connecticut

Richard J. Hunter, Jr.
Seton Hall University

Carey Kirk
University of Northern Iowa

Walter E. Lippincott
Naugatuck Valley Community-Technical College

Sal B. Marchionna
Triton College

Deborah Medlar
Central Washington University

Alan Moggio
Illinois Central College

Richard G. Muchow
Palomar College

Mary Anne Nixon
Western Carolina University

John M. Norwood
University of Arkansas

Jacqueline O'Neal
Northeast Louisiana University

Dianne S. Osborne
Broward Community College

William R. Parks, III
Orange Coast College

Laura B. Pincus
DePaul University

Richard W. Post
College of the Desert

Elinor Rahm
Central Missouri State University

Mitchell A. Sherr
Indiana University-Purdue University at Fort
Wayne

John W. Tiede
Missouri Southern State College

WRITE THE AUTHORS

Any instructor may write to any of the authors regarding any questions as to teaching methodology or specific rules of law. We represent in the aggregate over a century of teaching and will be happy to respond to your questions. Our addresses are:

Ronald A. Anderson
252 S. Van Pelt Street
Philadelphia, PA 19103

Ivan Fox
Business Law Department
Pace University
Pace Plaza
New York, NY 10038

David P. Twomey
Carroll School of Management
Boston College
Fulton Hall
Chestnut, MA 02167

Analysis of Court Opinions

Beginning with page 5, you will find opinions that were handed down by judges in actual cases. Some of these opinions show how the courts apply a rule of law that has been stated in the text. Other opinions extend or expand the rule stated in the text.

COMPONENTS OF A COURT OPINION

The information for each case is presented in three parts: (a) the heading, (b) the facts of the case, and (c) the opinion. In this explanation the case Manrique v Fabbri, beginning on page 10, will be used as an example.

(a) HEADING. The heading of the case consists of the title and the source.

(1) Title. The title of the case usually consists of the names of the parties to the action. In the illustrative case Manrique, as plaintiff, sued Fabbri as defendant.

The title of an appealed case may not reveal who the plaintiff was in the original or lower court or who the defendant was. When the action is begun in the lower court, the first party named is the plaintiff and the second is the defendant. When the case is appealed, the name of the party who takes the appeal may appear first on the records of the higher court, so that if the defendant takes the appeal, the original order of the names of the parties is then reversed.

(2) Source. The second part of the heading gives the source of the opinion. Manrique v Fabbri was decided by the Florida Supreme Court and is found in "493 So 2d 437."

This means that the opinion is found in the 493rd volume of the second series of the Southern (So) reporter[1] beginning at page 437.

(b) FACTS.   The paragraph following the heading is a summary of the facts of the case, which provides a background for an understanding and analysis of the opinion. Read the statement of facts. Keep in mind the principles of law that you studied in the chapter. Then read the opinion carefully to see how the court made its decision, what it decided, and whether it agrees with what you thought would be decided.

(c) OPINION.   The opinion of the court includes the name of the judge, excerpts from the reasoning of the court, and the judgment.

(1) Judge.   At the beginning of the opinion is the surname of the judge who wrote it. The opinion in the Manrique case was written by Judge Barkett.

The letter or letters following the name of the judge indicate the judge's rank or title. J. stands for Judge or Justice. (JJ. is the plural form.) Other abbreviations include C.J. for Chief Justice or Circuit Judge, D.J. for District Judge, P.J. for Presiding Judge or President Judge, A.J. for Associate Judge or less often Auditing Judge, and C. for Chancellor or Commissioner.

When a case is perfectly clear and obvious, the opinion will frequently be filed without naming the writing judge and will then have a heading of "memorandum" or "per curiam."

(2) Body of the Opinion.   The material following the judge's name is quoted from the opinion of the court. Words enclosed in brackets [ ] did not appear in the original opinion but have been added to explain a legal term, to identify a party, or to clarify a statement. Ellipses (three or four periods) are used to indicate that, for use in the textbook, something has been omitted that is not pertinent to the point of law with which we are concerned at this time.

Decisions vary in length from less than a page to more than a hundred pages, and opinions frequently involve several points of law. Each case in this book has been carefully edited so that the excerpts reprinted here will be convenient for student use.

Opinions do not follow a standard pattern of organization; but usually the well-written opinion will carefully examine the arguments presented by all parties and then explain why the court accepts or rejects those arguments in whole or in part. In this process the opinion may discuss the opinion of the lower court, the decisions in similar cases in other courts, and material from other sources.[2]

(3) Judgment.   The case is concluded with a statement of the court's decision. If the case has been appealed and if the court agrees with the lower court, the decision may simply be "Judgment affirmed" or a similar expression. If the appellate court disagrees, the decision may be expressed as "Judgment reversed." "Case remanded" means that the case is returned to the lower court to proceed further in harmony with the appellate court's decision. In lower court cases when the judgment is on a narrow issue, the judgment of the court may be limited to "Objection sustained" or "Objection dismissed."

A judge of the court who disagrees with the majority may file a dissenting opinion.

Checklist for Case Study

The questions in the following checklist will serve as a guide for the analysis of each case. It should be understood, however, that not every case will provide answers to all these questions.

(a) COURT.   In what court was the action brought originally, and which court filed the opinion being studied?

---

[1]   See Appendix, "How to Find the Law," footnote 1, for sectional reporters.
[2]   See Appendix, "How to Find the Law."

(b) PARTIES. Who were the parties to the action? Were they the parties to the original transaction, or were they strangers such as creditors?

(c) PURPOSE OF THE ACTION. What was the relief or remedy sought in the action?

(d) ACTION APPEALED FROM. What was done in the lower court that the appellant deemed wrong and from which the appeal was taken?

(e) ARGUMENTS OF THE PARTIES. What were the arguments made by the respective parties?

(f) DECISION OF THE COURT. What did the court decide?

(g) BASIS FOR DECISION. On what authority or ground did the court base its decision? Was it common law, decision, statute, Restatement of the Law, text, logic, or the personal belief of the court?

(h) APPRAISAL OF THE DECISION. What social objectives are advanced by the decision? What social objectives are hindered or defeated by the decision? What ethical principles are involved in the case? Is the decision socially desirable? Is it practical in application? Does it give rise to any dangers?

Figure 1 Guidelines To Business Ethics

Guidelines to Business Ethics	
Selected Ethical Principles or Issues to Discuss in Relation to Cases	**Elementary Guidelines for an Ethical Analysis of Contemplated Action**
1. Integrity and truthfulness.	1. Identify the ethical principle(s) involved in the case.
2. Promise-keeping.	2. Define the problem from the decision maker's point of view.
3. Loyalty.	3. Identify who could be injured by the contemplated action.
4. Fairness.	4. Define the problem from the opposing point of view.
5. Doing no harm.	5. Would you (as the decision maker) be willing to tell your family, your supervisor, your CEO, and the board of directors about the planned action?
6. Maintaining confidentiality.	
7. Avoiding conflict of interest.	
8. Whistleblowing.	6. Would you be willing to go before a community meeting, a congressional hearing, or a public forum to describe the action?
9. Efficiency and effectiveness (create new jobs and the products necessary for a humane life).	7. With moral common sense and full consideration of the facts and alternatives, reach a decision about whether the contemplated action should be taken.
10. Innovation.	

BRIEF
CONTENTS

CONTENTS

PART 1

The Legal and Social Environment of Business

CHAPTER 1

LAW AND DETERMINATION OF LEGAL RIGHTS

A. NATURE OF LAW AND LEGAL RIGHTS
1. Legal Rights
2. What Are Sources of the Law?
3. Uniform State Laws
4. Classifications of Law

B. DETERMINATION OF LEGAL RIGHTS
5. Contract Selection of Law or Forum
6. Courts
7. Administrative Agencies
8. Alternative Means of Dispute Resolution
9. Disposition of Complaints and Ombudsmen

LEARNING OBJECTIVES

After studying this chapter, you will be able to:
1. *Give two examples of the evolutionary character of legal rights.*
2. *List the agencies or bodies that interpret and apply law.*
3. *Name seven alternatives for resolving disputes without formal court action.*

Why have law? If you have ever been stuck in a traffic jam or jostled in a crowd leaving a stadium, you have been in a position to observe the need for order to keep things running smoothly and efficiently. What is true on a small scale for traffic jams and crowds is true on a large scale for society in general. The order, or pattern of rules, that society establishes to govern the conduct of individuals and the relationships among them we call "law." Law is society's way of keeping things running smoothly and efficiently.

A. NATURE OF LAW AND LEGAL RIGHTS

Law consists of the body of principles that govern conduct and that can be enforced in courts or by administrative agencies.

1. Legal Rights

What are legal rights? Who has them? In answering these questions, we tend to make the mistake of thinking of society as being unchanging. But consider the evolution of the concept of the "rights of the human being" and the right of privacy.

(a) THE "RIGHTS OF THE HUMAN BEING" CONCEPT. Our belief in the American way of life and in the concepts on which our society or government is based should not obscure the fact that at one time there was no American way of life. In the past, many religious leaders, philosophers, and poets spoke of the rights and dignity of people, but rulers disregarded such pretensions and governed people in a rigid system based on status. A noble had the rights of a noble. A warrior had the rights of a warrior. A slave had very few rights at all. In each case, the law saw only status; rights did not attach to the human beings, but to their status.

In the course of time, serfdom displaced slavery in much of the Western world. Eventually feudalism disappeared and, with the end of the Thirty Years War in 1648, the modern nation-state began to emerge. Surely one

might say that in such a "new order," a human being had legal rights. But the person had rights not as a human being; only as a subject. Even when the English colonists settled in America, they brought with them not the rights of human beings but the rights of British subjects. Even when the colonies were within one year of war, the Second Continental Congress presented to King George III the Olive Branch Petition asking the king to recognize the colonists' rights as English subjects. For almost a year the destiny of the colonies hung in the balance, with the colonists unable to decide between remaining loyal to the Crown, trying to obtain recognition of their rights as English subjects (a "status" recognition), or doing something else.

Finally, the ill-advised policies of George III and the eloquence of Thomas Paine's *Common Sense* tipped the scales. The colonists spoke on July 4, 1776, not in terms of the rights of English subjects but in terms of the rights of people existing independently of any government. Had the American Revolution been lost, the Declaration of Independence would have gone rattling down the corridors of time with many other failures. But the American Revolution was won, and the new government that was established was based on *human beings* rather than on *subjects* as the building blocks. The concept of rights of human beings replaced the concept of rights of subjects. With this transition, the obligations of a monarch to faithful subjects were replaced by the rights of human beings existing without regard to the will or authority of any king. Since then, America has been going through additional stages of determining what is embraced by the concept of "rights of human beings."

(b) THE RIGHT OF PRIVACY. One legal right recognized by all Americans today is the right of privacy. Before 1890, however, this right did not exist in American law. Certainly those who wrote the Declaration of Independence and the Bill of Rights were conscious of rights. How can we explain that the law did not recognize a right of privacy until a full century later?

The answer is that, at a particular time, people worry about the problems that then face them. Note the extent of the fears and concerns of the framers of the Bill of Rights. The Fourth Amendment states: "The right of the people to be secure in their persons, houses, papers, and effects, against unreasonable searches and seizures, shall not be violated, and no warrants shall issue, but upon probable cause, supported by oath or affirmation, and particularly describing the place to be searched and the persons or things to be seized." The people of 1790 were afraid of a recurrence of the days of George III.

The framers of the Fourth Amendment declared what we today would regard as a segment of privacy—protection from police invasion of privacy. The people of 1790 were simply not concerned with invasion of privacy by a private person. While a snooping person could be prosecuted to some extent under a Peeping Tom statute, this was a criminal liability. The victim could not sue for damages for invasion of privacy.

If we are honest in reviewing history, all we can say is that modern people think highly of privacy and want it to be protected. Knowing that the law is responsive to the wishes of society, we can also say that the right is protected by government. But note that we should go no further than to say that it is a right that society wishes to protect at the present time. If circumstances arise in our national life of such a nature that the general welfare is opposed to the right of privacy, we can expect that the right of privacy will be limited or modified. For example, the right of privacy prevents a bank from giving out information about a customer's bank account. However, the federal government, acting under a 1969 statute, can require such information to see if income taxes are due or if money has been paid or received in criminal transactions.

(c) ABOLITION OF RIGHTS. When not protected by a constitutional provision, rights may be abolished by statute. The *Strock*[1] case turned on whether a legislature could destroy a right to sue.

STROCK v PRESSNELL

38 Ohio 3d 207, 527 NE2d 1235 (1988)

Strock and his wife were unhappily married. Strock sued Pressnell for alienation of affections, claiming that it was Pressnell's fault that Strock's wife no longer loved him. Pressnell raised the defense that the action for alienation of affections had been abolished by state statute. Strock claimed that the statute was unconstitutional. The court held the statute was constitutional. Strock appealed.

WRIGHT, J. . . . The challenges to the constitutionality of [the statute] are that abolition of these common-law actions without providing an alternative remedy is violative of both state and federal Constitutions. The challengers contend that the statute denies due process and/or equal protection under the Fourteenth Amendment

---

[1] For an explanation of case references, see Appendix, How to Find the Law, section on Court Decisions.

to the United States Constitution and due course of law and equal protection under Sections 2 and 16, Article I of the Ohio Constitution. . . .

The United States Supreme Court has emphatically declared that no person has a vested right in any of the rules of the common law:

A person has no property, no vested interest, in any rule of the common law. . . . Rights of property which have been created by the common law cannot be taken away without due process; but the law itself, as a rule of conduct, may be changed at the will, or even at the whim, of the legislature, unless prevented by constitutional limitations. Indeed, the great office of statutes is to remedy defects in the common law as they are developed, and to adapt it to the changes of time and circumstances. Munn v Illinois (1876), 94 U.S. 113, 134, 24 L. Ed. 77; . . .

The federal Constitution does not forbid the abolition of common-law rights so long as it is to attain a permissible legislative objective. . . .

Similarly, we have consistently held that the legislative branch of state government, unless prohibited by constitutional limitations, may modify or entirely abolish common-law actions. . . . As we stated in . . . *Leis v Cleveland Ry. Co.* (1920), 101 Ohio St. 162, 128 N.E. 73: "Rights of property cannot be taken away or interfered with without due process of law. But there is no property or vested right in any of the rules of the common law, as guides of conduct, and they may be added to or repealed by legislative authority."

Thus, we hold that actions for alienation of affections and criminal conversation are not "property interests" and the General Assembly enacted [the statute] with a permissible legislative objective. This holding is consistent with virtually every other court decision that has addressed the constitutionality of these statutes. . . .

Therefore, we hold that . . . the statute that abolished amatory actions, is constitutional; it does not violate either . . . the Ohio Constitution, or the Equal Protection or Due Process Clauses of the Fourteenth Amendment to the United States Constitution.

[Judgment affirmed as to constitutionality of statute]

QUESTIONS

1. Did Strock claim that the legislature could not change the law? Explain.
2. How would the case have been decided if the court had held that the statute in question involved a property right?

2. What Are the Sources of Law?

The expression "a law" is ordinarily used to indicate a statute enacted by a state legislature or by the Congress of the United States. For example, an act of the federal Congress to provide old-age benefits is a law. However, the statutes enacted by legislative bodies are not the only source of law.

Constitutional law is the branch of law that is based on the constitutions in force in a particular area or territory. A **constitution** is a body of principles that establishes the structure of a government and the relationship of the government to the people who are governed. Constitutions are generally a combination of a written document and practices and customs that develop with the passage of time and the emergence of new problems. In each state, two constitutions are in force: the state constitution and the national constitution.

Statutory law includes legislative acts declaring, commanding, or prohibiting something. Each state has its own legislature, and the United States has the Congress; both of these bodies enact laws. In addition, every city, county, or other subdivision has some power to adopt ordinances that, within their sphere of operation, have the same binding effect as legislative acts.

Of great importance are **administrative regulations**, which are rules promulgated by state and national administrative agencies, such as the Securities and Exchange Commission and the National Labor Relations Board. The regulations generally have the force of statute and are therefore part of the law.

Law also includes principles that are expressed for the first time in court decisions. This is **case law**. For example, when a court decides a new question or problem, its decision becomes a **precedent**, which stands as the law for that particular problem in the future. This rule that a court decision becomes a precedent to be followed in similar cases is the doctrine of *stare decisis*.

Court decisions do not always deal with new problems or make new rules. In many cases, courts apply rules as they have been for many years, even centuries. These time-honored rules of the community are called the **common law**. Statutes will sometimes repeat or redeclare the common law rules. Many statutes depend on the common law for definition of the terms in the statute.

Law also includes treaties made by the United States and proclamations and orders of the president of the United States or of other public officials.

3. Uniform State Laws

To secure uniformity as far as possible, the National Conference of Commissioners on Uniform State Laws, composed of representatives from every state, has drafted statutes on various subjects for adoption by the states. The best example of such laws is the Uniform Commercial Code (UCC).[2] The UCC regulates the fields of sales and leasing of goods; commercial paper, such as checks; funds transfers; secured transactions in personal property; bulk transfers; and particular aspects of banking, letters of credit, warehouse receipts, bills of lading, and investment securities.

National uniformity has also been brought about in some areas of consumer protection by the adoption of the federal Consumer Credit Protection Act (CCPA).[3] Title I of the CCPA is popularly known as the Truth in Lending Act. A Uniform Consumer Credit Code (UCCC) has been proposed and is now before the states for adoption. To the extent that it is adopted, it

---

[2] The UCC or Code has been adopted in every state, except Louisiana has not adopted Article 2 on Sales. It has also been adopted for Guam, the Virgin Islands, and the District of Columbia. The National Conference of Commissioners on Uniform State Laws has adopted amendments to Article 8, Investment Securities (1977) and Article 9, Secured Transactions (1972). It has also adopted new articles: 2A, Leases; 4A, Funds Transfers; and 6, Bulk Sales. Revisions of Articles 3, Commercial Paper (now called Negotiable Instruments), and 4, Bank Deposits and Collections, were adopted in 1990. The states that have adopted these later articles are listed on the first page of Appendix 3 of this book.

Uniformity has also reached international scope. The United Nations Convention on Contracts for the International Sale of Goods (CISG) applies to contracts between parties in the United States and those in the other nations that have approved the convention. The provisions of this convention, or international agreement, have been strongly influenced by Article 2 of the Uniform Commercial Code.

[3] 15 United States Code (USC) Sections (§§) 1601 et seq. and 18 USC §§ 891 et seq.

will complement the Uniform Commercial Code.[4]

4. Classifications of Law

Law is classified in many ways. For example, **substantive law**, which creates, defines, and regulates rights and liabilities, is contrasted with **procedural law**, which specifies the steps that must be followed in enforcing those rights and liabilities. Law may also be classified in terms of its origin, as coming from the Roman (or civil) law, the English common law of principles based on customs and usages of the community,[5] or the law merchant. Law may be classified as to subject matter, such as the law of contracts, the law of real estate, and the law of wills.

Law is at times classified in terms of principles of law and principles of equity. The early English courts were very limited as to the kinds of cases they could handle. Persons who could not obtain relief in those courts would petition the king to grant them special relief according to principles of equity and justice. In the course of time, these special cases developed certain rules that are called principles of **equity**. In general, they require that the plaintiff be in a situation in which the law courts cannot grant relief. Equitable relief is denied unless the plaintiff will suffer a loss that cannot be compensated for by the payment of damages. At one time in the United States, there were separate law courts and separate equity courts. Except in a few states, these courts have been combined, so that one court applies principles of both law and equity. Even though administered by the same court, the two systems of principles remain distinct. That is, if the plaintiff seeks what historically would be equitable relief, the case is governed by equitable principles. If the plaintiff brings what historically would have been an action at law, the action is governed by law principles rather than equity.[6] To illustrate the difference, consider the case of a homeowner making a contract to sell the home to a buyer. If the owner refuses to go through with the contract, the rules of law will permit the buyer to sue the owner for damages. Rules of equity will go further and will compel the owner to actually transfer the ownership of the house to the buyer. This equitable remedy is called *specific performance*.

B. DETERMINATION OF LEGAL RIGHTS

Legal rights are meaningless unless they can be enforced. Government, therefore, provides a system by which the parties' legal rights can be determined and enforced. Generally, the instrumentality of government by which this is accomplished is a court, and the process involved is an action or a lawsuit. Administrative agencies have also been created to enforce law and to determine rights within certain areas. In addition, various alternative means have developed as out-of-court methods of dispute resolution.

5. Contract Selection of Law or Forum

The parties to a contract may to some extent control the determination of their legal rights by specifying (a) the law that should apply to the contract and (b) the **forum**, or the court in which any lawsuit should be brought.

(a) CHOICE OF LAW. To reduce the uncertainty of transactions or to further the convenience of the parties, it is customary for the

---

[4] As of June, 1993, the 1968 version of the UCCC has been adopted in Colorado, Indiana, Oklahoma, South Carolina, Utah, Wisconsin, and Wyoming. It has also been adopted for Guam. The 1968 version of the UCCC has been replaced by a 1974 version that has been adopted in Idaho, Iowa, Kansas, and Maine. In 1985, Idaho replaced the UCCC with the Idaho Credit Code.

[5] Samsel v Wheeler Transport Services, ___Kan___, 789 P2d 541 (1990).

[6] Gibbons v Stillwell, 149 Ill App 3d 411, 102 Ill Dec 864, 500 NE2d 965 (1986).

Figure 1-1   Dispute Resolution Procedures

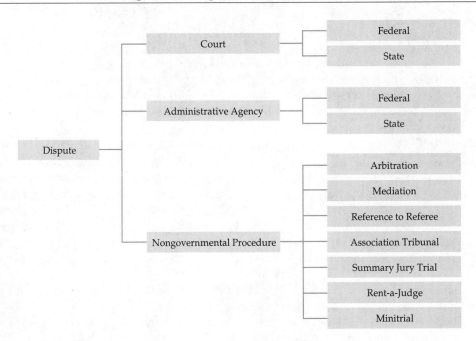

modern contract to state that the contract should be governed by the law of a particular state or nation. This becomes important for an enterprise that does business in many states. Such an enterprise will typically specify that all contracts are governed by the law of the state in which the home office is located. For example, a life insurance company may issue policies to people all across the country. These policies will ordinarily state that they are governed by the law of the home office state. This means the legal staff of the insurance company need only concern itself with the law of one state rather than the law of 50 different states. As long as the state whose law is selected bears a reasonable relationship to the transaction, and the selection is not contrary to a strong public policy, the designation by the contract will be followed.

(b) CHOICE OF FORUM. The parties to a contract may specify that any lawsuit must be brought in the court of a particular state or country. This will generally be done for the convenience of the stronger party, who will specify a local jurisdiction. If the choice is made in order to block lawsuits by the weaker party, the court-selection provision will be held invalid. Thus, a provision that if a consumer in state *A* would bring a lawsuit against the manufacturer located in state *B* the suit must be brought in a distant state *C*, is invalid because it sets up an unconscionable hurdle to the bringing of the lawsuit. If, however, there is a reasonable relationship between the parties or the transaction and the jurisdiction of the court selected, the forum-selection clause is valid and will be enforced.[7] In the *Manrique* case, the plaintiff claimed that he was not bound by the forum selection clause of the contract.

---

[7] Cal-State Business Products & Services, Inc. 12 Cal App 4th 1666, 16 Cal Rptr 2d 417 (1993).

MANRIQUE v FABBRI

(Fla) 493 So 2d 437 (1986)

> Fabbri made a contract to sell Florida land to Manrique. The contract speci-
> fied that any lawsuit should be brought in the courts of the Netherlands An-
> tilles. A dispute arose, and Manrique sued Fabbri in a Florida court. Fabbri
> raised the defense that suit could not be brought in Florida. An appeal was
> taken to the state supreme court.

BARKETT, J. . . . The Third District Court of Appeals has consistently held that contractual provisions requiring that future disputes be resolved in specified foreign jurisdictions are void as impermissible attempts to oust Florida of subject matter
jurisdiction. On the other hand, the Fourth District in *Maritime [Limited Partnership v
Greenman Advertising Associates, Inc.* (Fla App) 455 So 2d 1121] has held that parties
to a contract may agree to submit to the jurisdiction of a chosen forum provided that
(1) the forum was not chosen because of one party's overwhelming bargaining
power; (2) enforcement would not contravene public policy; (3) the purpose of such
an agreement is not to transfer a local dispute to a remote and alien forum in order
to inconvenience one or both of the parties.

In *Maritime*, the Fourth District relied upon and adopted the reasoning of the
United States Supreme Court in *The Bremen v Zapata Off-Shore Co.*, 407 U.S. 1 (1972).
In *Zapata*, a German corporation (Unterweser) contracted with Zapata, an American
Corporation, to tow an oil rig across the Atlantic Ocean to Italy. The contract pro-
vided: "Any dispute arising must be treated before the London Court of Justice."
The rig was damaged in transit and towed to Tampa. Zapata, notwithstanding such
provision, instituted proceedings for damages against Unterweser in the United
States District Court, Middle District of Florida. . . . The United States Supreme
Court . . . held that forum selection clauses are prima facie valid and should be enforced unless enforcement is shown by the resisting party to be unreasonable under
the circumstances. In *Zapata*, the Court rejected the same policy position adopted by
the Third District in the case presently before us, saying:

*The argument that such clauses are improper because they tend to "oust" a court of jurisdic-
tion is hardly more than a vestigial legal fiction. It appears to rest at core on historical judicial resistance to any attempt to reduce the power and business of a particular court and has
little place in an era when all courts are overloaded and when businesses once essentially local now operate in world markets. It reflects something of a provincial attitude regarding the
fairness of other tribunals. . . .*

The Supreme Court gave compelling reasons why a freely negotiated private
agreement unaffected by fraud, undue influence, or overweening bargaining power
should be given full effect. It noted that at the very least such clauses represent
efforts to eliminate uncertainty as to the nature, location, and outlook of the forum
in which parties of differing nationalities might find themselves. Moreover,
such clauses might be vital parts of agreements fixing monetary terms, with the
consequences of the forum clause figuring prominently in the parties' calculations.
The Court concluded:

The correct approach would have been to enforce the forum clause specifically unless [the party] could clearly show that enforcement would be unreasonable and unjust, or that the clause was invalid for such reasons as fraud or overreaching.

The view articulated by the Court in *Zapata* enables freely contracting parties to conduct their interstate and international business affairs more efficiently. . . . Because the *Zapata* rule is based on a realistic assessment of modern commercial culture, and because the rule enhances contractual predictability within the culture, it is not surprising that it is rapidly becoming a majority view. . . .

We reject the position espoused by the Third District and adopt the view enunciated in *Zapata* and *Maritime*. Florida courts should recognize the legitimate expectations of contracting parties. The trial courts of this state can effectively protect a party by refusing to enforce those forum-selection provisions which are unreasonable or result from unequal bargaining power. We hold that forum-selection clauses should be enforced in the absence of a showing that enforcement would be unreasonable or unjust. . . .

We remand with directions that the matter be returned to the trial court for proceedings consistent herewith.

[Action remanded]

QUESTIONS

1. What did the court hold?
2. Are there any limits on the power to specify the court in which suits are to be brought?
3. How does the court's opinion relate to freedom of contract and the predictability of contractual relations?

6. Courts

A **court** is a tribunal established by government to hear and decide matters properly brought before it, to give redress to the injured or enforce punishment against wrongdoers, and to prevent wrongs. A **court of record** is one in which the proceedings are preserved in an official record. In a **court not of record**, the proceedings are not officially recorded. In the United States, courts are organized into two distinct systems—the federal and state court systems.

(a) JURISDICTION. Each court is empowered to decide certain types or classes of cases. This power is called **jurisdiction**. A court may have original or appellate jurisdiction, or both. A court with **original jurisdiction** has the authority to hear a controversy when it is first brought into court. A court having **appellate jurisdiction**, on the other hand, has authority to review the judgment of a lower court.

The jurisdiction of a court may be general, as distinguished from limited or special. A court having **general jurisdiction** has power to hear and decide all controversies involving legal rights and duties. A court of **limited** or **special jurisdiction** has authority to hear and decide only those cases that fall within a particular class, such as cases in which the amounts are below a specified sum.

Courts are frequently classified in terms of the nature of their jurisdiction. A **criminal court** is one that is established for the trial of crimes, which are regarded as offenses against the public. A **civil court**, on the other hand, is authorized to hear and decide issues involving private rights and duties and also noncriminal public matters. In similar manner, courts are classified as equity courts, juvenile courts, probate courts, and courts of domestic relations, on the basis of their limited jurisdiction.

(b) JUDICIAL CONTROL OF PROCEDURE. Each court has inherent power to establish rules necessary to preserve order in the court or to transact the business of the court. Just as a police patrol watches over traffic, the judge of the court watches over the proceedings to be sure that everyone is following proper rules. To prevent abusive use of court actions or obstruction of their conduct, courts may impose a variety of penalties. These include imposing court costs on the wrongdoer, fining and imprisoning for contempt, barring a claim or a defense, or refusing to listen to evidence that had been improperly withheld earlier in the action.[8]

(c) DECLARATORY JUDGMENT. Declaratory judgment procedure is a court procedure, authorized by statute, for deciding disputes. Under **declaratory judgment procedure** a person, when confronted with the early stages of an actual controversy, may petition the court to decide the question or declare the rights of the parties before loss is actually sustained. A copy of the petition is served on all parties, and they may file answers. After all the pleadings have been filed, the court then decides the questions involved just as though a lawsuit had been brought.

(d) MOOTNESS AS A BAR TO COURT RELIEF. Courts have the power to determine controversies. Under declaratory judgment statutes, courts have the power to determine budding controversies that have not yet become full-blown disputes. However, courts do not have the power to decide matters after the dispute has disappeared. When this occurs, the case is described as being **moot**.

(e) IMMUNITY FOR WRONG DECISION. The fact that a judge, jury, or arbitrator makes a wrong decision does not impose any liability on the decision-maker. If the decision-maker is involved in a crime, such as bribery, the wrongdoer may be prosecuted for that offense. However, there is no liability for merely making a wrong decision. For example, the fact that a judge does not know the law and makes a mistake does not entitle the loser to sue the judge. Even if the decision is later reversed on appeal, the winning party cannot go back and sue the judge. That is, the judge has immunity from liability while acting within the scope of judicial authority.[9]

7. Administrative Agencies

It is difficult for courts to administer laws regulating all phases of the economy. This difficulty led Congress and the state legislatures to establish commissions or agencies of experts to make the rules and to pass judgment on violations of the rules. Thus, the Interstate Commerce Commission (ICC) now regulates interstate commerce and passes on whether conduct of a carrier is a violation of ICC regulations. The ICC acts as a lawmaker, an executive that enforces the law, and a court that interprets and applies the law. This is also true of the Federal Trade Commission, the Securities and Exchange Commission, the National Labor Relations Board, and many other federal and state administrative agencies.

8. Alternate Means of Dispute Resolution

Because of the rising costs, delays, and complexities of litigation, business people often seek to resolve disputes out of court.

---

[8] Dwyer v Crocker National Bank, 194 Cal App 3d 1418, 240 Cal Rptr 297 (1987).
[9] Grane v Grane, 143 Ill App 3d 979, 98 Ill Dec 91, 493 NE2d 1112 (1986).

(a) ARBITRATION. By **arbitration**, a dispute is settled by one or more arbitrators (disinterested persons selected by the parties to the dispute). Arbitration first reached extensive use in the field of commercial contracts. This procedure is encouraged as a means of avoiding expensive litigation and easing the workload of courts. Arbitration enables the parties to present the facts before trained experts familiar with the practices that form the background of the dispute.

A Uniform Arbitration Act has been adopted in a number of states.[10] Under this act and similar statutes, the parties to a contract may agree in advance that all disputes arising thereunder will be submitted to arbitration. In some instances, the contract will name the arbitrators for the duration of the contract. The Uniform Act requires a written agreement to arbitrate.[11]

The Federal Arbitration Act[12] declares that an arbitration clause in a contract relating to an interstate transaction is valid, irrevocable, and enforceable. When a contract subject to the Federal Arbitration Act provides for the arbitration of disputes, the parties are bound to arbitrate in accordance with the federal statute even if the agreement to arbitrate would not be binding under state law.

(1) Mandatory Arbitration. In contrast with statutes that merely regulate arbitration when selected voluntarily by the parties, some statutes require that certain kinds of disputes be submitted to arbitration. In some states, by rule or statute, the arbitration of small claims is required.

(2) Scope of Arbitration. When arbitration is required by the statute, the terms of the statute will define the scope of the arbitration. When the parties have voluntarily agreed to arbitrate, their agreement will control the scope. In such case, questions may arise as to what disputes are covered thereby. This was the issue involved in the *Gross* case.

GROSS v RECABAREN
206 Cal App 3d 771, 253 Cal Rptr 820 (1988)

In 1984, Gross went to Doctors Fister and Recabaren to have certain growths removed from his face. At that time, Gross signed a written agreement to submit to arbitration "any dispute as to medical malpractice." Two growths were removed and further treatment was not required. In 1986 Gross returned to these two doctors for the removal of other growths on his head and face. Gross was not satisfied with the result of the surgery. He sued the doctors for malpractice. The doctors raised the defense that Gross was bound by the 1984 agreement to arbitrate the claim. From a judgment for the defendants, Gross appealed.

---

[10] The 1955 version of the Uniform Arbitration Act has been adopted in Alaska, Arizona, Arkansas, Colorado, Delaware, Florida, Idaho, Illinois, Indiana, Iowa, Kansas, Kentucky, Maine, Maryland, Massachusetts, Michigan, Minnesota, Missouri, Montana, Nebraska, Nevada, New Mexico, North Carolina, North Dakota, Oklahoma, Pennsylvania, South Carolina, South Dakota, Tennessee, Texas, Utah, Vermont, Virginia, Wyoming, and the District of Columbia. The 1925 version of the act is in force in Wisconsin.

[11] Anderson v Federated Mu. Ins. Co. (Minn App) 465 MW2d 68 (1991).

[12] 9 USC §§ 114.

GATES, J. . . . This state has a strong public policy favoring arbitration over litigation as a speedy and relatively inexpensive means of dispute resolution which eases court congestion. . . .

Code of Civil Procedure section 1295 . . . "encourages and facilitates the *arbitration* of medical malpractice disputes by specifying uniform language to be used in binding arbitration contracts to assure that the patient knows what he is signing and what its ramifications are."* . . .

Because the scope of arbitration is a matter of agreement between the parties, the court should attempt to give effect to [their] intentions, in light of the usual and ordinary meaning of the contractual language and the circumstances under which the agreement was made. . . . Any doubts concerning the scope of arbitrable issues must be resolved in favor of arbitration. . . .

It is manifest that the contract signed by Steven Gross cannot, on its face, reasonably be said to be limited only to those services provided contemporaneous to its signing. . . . We are satisfied that . . . it was intended to encompass those situations where Gross, in the course of an ongoing doctor-patient relationship, sought treatment for a condition of the type which initially brought him to Dr. Fister's office. As we stressed in *Hilleary v Garvin* " . . . to impose upon a physician, during a continuous doctor-patient relationship, the extra burden of having to renew the arbitration agreement each time there is a variation in treatment or ailment would be impractical, and would frustrate the purpose of the statute, which is to facilitate, not emasculate, the arbitration process."

Although the course of treatment Gross received in 1984 and 1986 differed, in each instance he sought medical services for the treatment of similar problems, i.e., potentially malignant skin lesions on his face and head. . . .

There was simply no objective evidence from which a reasonable person could conclude either of the parties viewed their relationship as having terminated in 1984. The mere fact that they did not anticipate Gross would return in the absence of further dermatological problems requiring the attention of an oncologist does not demonstrate otherwise. Obviously, Gross *hoped* additional treatment would not be necessary. When it was, however, he once again sought Dr. Fister's services. This

---

* Section 1295 provides: "(a) Any contract for medical services which contains a provision for arbitration of any dispute as to professional negligence of a health care provider shall have such provision as the first article of the contract and shall be expressed in the following language: 'It is understood that any dispute as to medical malpractice, that is as to whether any medical services rendered under this contract were unnecessary or unauthorized or were improperly, negligently or incompetently rendered, will be determined by submission to arbitration as provided by California law, and not by a lawsuit or resort to court process except as California law provides for judicial review of arbitration proceedings. Both parties to this contract, by entering into it, are giving up their constitutional right to have any such dispute decided in a court of law before a jury, and instead are accepting the use of arbitration.'

"(b) Immediately before the signature line provided for the individual contracting for the medical services must appear the following in at least 10-point bold red type:

"'NOTICE: BY SIGNING THIS CONTRACT YOU ARE AGREEING TO HAVE ANY ISSUE OF MEDICAL MALPRACTICE DECIDED BY NEUTRAL ARBITRATION AND YOU ARE GIVING UP YOUR RIGHT TO A JURY OR COURT TRIAL. SEE ARTICLE I OF THIS CONTRACT.'

"(c) Once signed, such a contract governs all subsequent open-book account transactions for medical services for which the contract was signed until or unless rescinded by written notice within 30 days of signature. Written notice of such rescission may be given by a guardian or conservator of the patient if the patient is incapacitated or a minor...."

was persuasive evidence of an ongoing relationship. Likewise, the manner in which Steven Gross' medical and billing records were maintained by Dr. Fister was indicative of a continuing association. . . .

[Judgment affirmed]

QUESTIONS

1. What are the reasons for the California policy with regard to arbitration?
2. Was the decision in the *Gross* case inevitable?
3. When the patient signed the paper in 1984, do you think he read it with sufficient care to realize what it said about arbitration and that he remembered what it said when he came back for treatment in 1986?

(3) Finality of Arbitration. When arbitration is based on the agreement of the parties, it is generally agreed that the decision of the arbitrator shall be final. This is so even if the decision was wrong, unless there is clear proof of fraud, arbitrary conduct, or a significant procedural error.

In contrast, when arbitration is mandatory under statute or rule, it is generally provided that the losing party may appeal from such arbitration to a court.[13] The appeal will proceed just as though there never had been any prior arbitration. This is called a **trial** *de novo* and is required to preserve the constitutional right to a jury trial. As a practical matter, however, relatively few appeals are taken from arbitration decisions.

(b) MEDIATION. In mediation, a neutral person acts as a messenger between opposing sides of a dispute, carrying to each side the latest settlement offer made by the other. The mediator has no authority to make a decision, although in some cases the mediator may make suggestions that might ultimately be accepted by the disputing parties.

The use of mediation has the advantage of keeping discussions going when the disputing parties have developed such fixed attitudes or personal animosity that direct discussion between them has become impossible.

(c) REFERENCE TO THIRD PERSON. Many types of transactions provide for a third person or a committee to make an out-of-court determination of the rights of persons. Thus, employees and an employer may have agreed as a term of the employment contract that claims of employees under retirement plans shall be decided by a designated board or committee. The seller and buyer may have selected a third person to determine the price to be paid for goods. Construction contracts often include as a term of the contract that any dispute shall be referred to the architect in charge of the construction and that the architect's decision shall be final.

Ordinarily the parties agree that the decision of such a third person or board shall be final and that no appeal or review may be had in any court. In most cases, referral to a third person is used in situations that involve the determination of a particular fact. In contrast, arbitration seeks to end a dispute.

Fire insurance policies commonly provide that if the parties cannot agree on the amount of the loss, each will appoint an appraiser, the two appraisers will appoint a third appraiser, and the three will determine the amount of the

---

[13] Porreco v Red Top RV Center, 216 Cal App 3d 113, 264 Cal Rptr 609 (1989).

loss the insurer is required to pay. These appraisers must be independent and impartial.

The *Central Life Insurance* case raised the question whether the appraisers were impartial.

CENTRAL LIFE INS. CO. v
AETNA CAS. & SURETY CO.
(Iowa) 466 NW2d 257 (1991)

The Central Life Insurance Company insured its building against fire with the Aetna Casualty & Surety Company. There was a fire loss and both Central and Aetna agreed to submit the matter to appraisers to determine the extent of the loss. The appraiser selected by Aetna was paid a flat fee. Central agreed to pay its appraiser a percentage of the amount recovered by it. The assessment made by the Central appraiser was about three times the assessment made by the Aetna appraiser. Aetna applied to the court to set aside the assessment made by the appraisers. From a judgment for Central, Aetna appealed.

SCHULTZ, J. . . . An appraisal is a supplementary arrangement to arrive at a resolution of a dispute without a formal lawsuit. Provisions for appraisal of an insurance loss, whether under policy terms or pursuant to independent agreement, are valid and binding on the parties. . . . Appraisal awards do not provide a formal judgment and may be set aside by a court. When reviewed, the award is supported by every reasonable presumption and will be sustained even if the court disagrees with the result. . . . We have reasoned that private resolution of disputes is favored by the law because it serves as an inexpensive and speedy means of settling disputes over matters such as the amount of loss and value of the property in question. . . . The award will not be set aside unless the complaining party shows fraud, mistake or misfeasance on the part of an appraiser or umpire. . . .

Aetna urges that Central's agreement to pay its appraiser a contingent fee based on a percentage of the amount of loss recovered causes the appraiser to be interested, which . . . mandates setting aside the award. . . .

We have long recognized that the object and purpose of an appraisal is to secure a fair and just evaluation by an impartial tribunal. . . .

The appraisal procedure involves an adjudication of a dispute between parties; however, the selected participants must act fairly, without bias, and in good faith. The intent of the appraisal procedure is not to provide appraisers who possess the total impartiality that is required in a court of law. The appraisers do not violate their commitment by acting as advocates for their respective selecting parties. However, appraisers should be in a position to act fairly and be free from suspicion or unknown interest. . . .

An inherent qualification for a quasi-judicial decision-maker is disinterest in the result. . . . Furthermore, we have defined a disinterested person to be one without a pecuniary interest. . . . Due to the contingent fee arrangement, Central's appraiser was interested because he had a direct financial interest in the dispute. . . .

[Judgment reversed and action remanded]

QUESTIONS

1. Courts oppose provisions for the nonjudicial settlement of disputes because it takes business away from the courts and has the suggestion that the parties do not think that the courts can handle the matter. Appraise this statement.
2. Was there any evidence that the Central Life appraiser had acted improperly?
3. What underlies the decision of the court?

(d) ASSOCIATION TRIBUNALS. Many disputes never reach the law courts because both parties to the dispute belong to a group or association, and the tribunal created by the group or association disposes of the matter. Thus, a dispute between members of a labor union, a stockbrokers' exchange, or a church may be heard by some board or committee within the association or group. Courts will review the action of such tribunals to determine that a fair and proper procedure was followed, but generally the courts will not go any further. Courts will not examine the facts of the case to see if the association tribunal reached the same conclusion that the court would have reached.

Trade associations commonly require their members to employ out-of-court methods of dispute settlement. Thus, the National Association of Home Builders requires its member builders to employ arbitration. The National Automobile Dealers' Association provides for panels to determine warranty claims of customers. The decision of such panels is final as to the dealer, but the consumer is allowed to bring a regular lawsuit after losing before the panel.

Members of an association must make use of an association tribunal. This means that they cannot ignore the association tribunal and go directly to a law court.[14]

(e) SUMMARY JURY TRIAL. A summary jury trial is in effect a dry run or mock trial in which the lawyers present their claims before a jury of six persons. The object is to get the reaction of a sample jury. No evidence is presented before this jury, and it bases its opinion solely on what the lawyers state. The determination of the jury has no binding effect, but it has value in that it gives the lawyers some idea of what a jury might think if there were an actual trial. This has special value when the heart of a case is whether something is reasonable under all the circumstances. When the lawyers see how the sample jury reacts, the lawyers may moderate their positions and reach a settlement.

(f) RENT-A-JUDGE. Under the rent-a-judge plan, the parties hire a judge to hear the case. In many states, this is done by the parties voluntarily choosing the judge as a "referee," with the judge acting under a statute authorizing the appointment of referees.[15] Under such a statute, the referee hears all the evidence just as though there were a regular trial, and the judge's determination is binding on the parties unless reversed on appeal. In some jurisdictions,

---

[14] Canady v Meharry Medical College (Tenn App) 811 SW2d 902 (1991).

[15] See Section 8(b) of this chapter.

special provision is made for the parties to agree that the decision of the judge selected as referee shall be final.

(g) MINITRIAL.   When only part of a case is disputed, the parties may stay within the framework of a lawsuit but agree that only the disputed issues be submitted to a jury. For example, when there is no real dispute over the liability of the defendant but the parties disagree as to the damages, the issue of damages alone may be submitted to the jury.

In some states, instead of submitting the matter to a regular jury, attorneys will agree to hold a minitrial. Under this system, the parties agree that a particular person, frequently a retired judge, should listen to the evidence on the disputed issues and decide the case. The agreement of the parties for the minitrial may specify whether this decision is binding on the parties. As a practical matter, the evaluation of the case by a neutral person will often bring the opposing parties together to reach a settlement.

(h) CONTRACT PROVISIONS. The parties' contract may pave the way for the settlement of future disputes by containing clauses requiring the parties to make use of one of the procedures described above. In addition, contracts may provide that no action may be taken until after the expiration of a specified cooling-off period. Contracts may also specify that the parties shall continue in the performance of their contract even though there is a dispute between them.

9. Disposition of Complaints and Ombudsmen

In contrast with the traditional and alternative procedures for resolving disputes are the procedures aimed at removing the ground for complaint before it develops into a dispute that requires resolution. For example, the complaint department in a department store will often be able to iron out the difficulty before the customer and the store are locked in an adversary position that could end in a lawsuit. Grievance committee procedures will often be effective to bring about an adjustment or removal of grounds for complaint. A statute may create a government official for the purpose of examining complaints. Such an official is often called an **ombudsman**.[16] The few federal statutes that have created such an officer have not given the ombudsman any judicial power. Typically, the ombudsman is limited to receiving complaints, supervising the administration of the system, and making recommendations for improvements. Two of the federal statutes expressly declare that the creation of the office of ombudsman does not impair any right existing by law.[17] In addition, when the complaint involves a right that would require a jury trial at common law, the Seventh Amendment to the U.S. Constitution guarantees that right. An ombudsman could not be given the power to decide such a matter. Moreover, the trend in America is to create special tribunals or administrative agencies rather than to give the ombudsman greater power.

SUMMARY

Law consists of the pattern of rules established by society to govern conduct and relationships. These rules can be expressed as constitutional provisions, statutes, case decisions, and administrative regulations. Law can be classified as substantive or procedural, and it can be described in terms of its historical origins, by the subject to which it relates, or in terms of law or equity.

---

[16] This name is Swedish for commissioner.

[17] For example, see the Solid Waste Disposal Act of November 8, 1984, PL 98-616, §§ 703(a), 98 Stat 3225, 42 USC §§ 6917; and the Panama Canal Commission Act of September 17, 1979, PL 96-70, §§ 1113, 93 Stat 460, 22 USC 3623.

Courts have been created to hear and resolve legal disputes. A specific court's power is defined by its jurisdiction, which may be original or appellate, general or special, and criminal or civil. Courts in the United States are organized in two distinct systems, federal and state.

Because a formal trial can be time-consuming and costly, the parties sometimes agree to an alternative method of resolving the dispute. Common alternatives are arbitration, reference to a third person or association tribunal, the summary jury trial, the private judge or referee, and the minitrial.

LAW IN PRACTICE

1. Get the facts before you enter into any transaction or when becoming involved in any legal dispute.

2. Double-check all information regardless of its source. Some persons will unintentionally falsify the facts by a desire to build up their part as a witness. Information from a computer may be false because what was added to the database was false.

3. Think of the facts objectively. Do not be deceived by your expectations and desires of what you want the facts to be. Do not be blinded by an automatic reaction that the other person is wrong.

4. If you have reached the point of a legal dispute, consider whether an alternative dispute resolution procedure is available and practical.

5. If a dispute goes into litigation, keep your eye on the real issues involved and the cost of litigation in terms of time, money, and stress.

[At the end of each chapter, the heading of LAW IN PRACTICE will direct you to key points in the chapter that you have just studied. Careful thought on your part will introduce you to other points that could be included under this heading if space permitted.]

[In addition, bear in mind that surrounding circumstances may modify or cause you to ignore a point noted. For example, if you would buy a $25 million generator for your power plant, it is obvious that you would take many steps for your protection that you would ignore when you buy a can of soup at the supermarket. Similarly, if you and the other party are old friends or have been doing business for many years you will probably omit steps that you would take if dealing with a stranger or a person of unknown reputation. All of this means that every situation must be examined carefully and a thoughtful application made of the rules of law. Unfortunately, your mind cannot be programmed to meet all the situations that lie in your future. The only thing that can be done is to train your mind to think for you.]

[The foregoing words of caution will not be repeated in subsequent chapters but they should be borne in mind in reading the points noted under the heading of "LAW IN PRACTICE."]

QUESTIONS AND CASE PROBLEMS

1. Carlton and Ricardo had a dispute over building construction costs. They submitted the matter to a summary jury trial. The jury decided that Ricardo owed Carlton $60,000. Ricardo did not pay Carlton. After 60 days, Carlton directed the sheriff to seize and sell property of Ricardo in order to raise money to pay the debt of $60,000. Ricardo objected to this. Decide.

2. Tenton owes Orlando $1,000. Orlando has a friend, Helen, who is a judge in the Court of International Trade. Orlando wants to sue Tenton in that court. May he do so? Explain.

3. Carolyn, Elwood, and Isabella are involved in a real estate development. The development is a failure, and Carolyn, Elwood, and Isabella want to have their rights determined. They could bring a lawsuit, but they are afraid that the case is so complicated that a judge and jury not familiar with the problems of real estate development would not reach a proper result. What can they do?

4. How do you account for the rise of both law courts and equity courts?

5. Distinguish between mandatory and voluntary arbitration.

6. Shute lived in Washington. She and other persons who lived in Western states were passengers on a cruise ship operated by Carnival Cruise Lines on a seven-day trip from Los Angeles to Mexico and back. Carnival was a Panamanian corporation and had its principal office in Miami, Florida.

Shute was injured when she slipped on a deck mat while on the cruise. She sued Carnival in a Washington federal district court claiming that proper precautions had not been taken. Carnival raised the defense that the travel contracts with the passengers specified that any lawsuit had to be brought in Florida. Did this provision of the contracts bar suit in Washington? [*Carnival Cruise Lines, Inc. v Shute, 499 US 585*]

7. Tenried Furnace Company installs heating systems in many parts of the United States. It is a Washington corporation, and its only office is in Seattle, Washington. It installed a heating system for Rhoda in her home in Massachusetts. The contract stated that any lawsuit must be brought in the courts of Mississippi. Rhoda was not satisfied with the heating system and sued Tenried in a Massachusetts court. Tenried claimed that this action must be dismissed because it had been agreed that any lawsuit had to be brought in Mississippi. Decide.

8. Esmeralda sued Adolphus. She lost the lawsuit because the judge made a wrong decision. She then sued the judge who raised the defense that a judge is immune from liability for a wrong decision. Esmeralda claimed that this cannot be; no one should be above the law. Decide.

9. The right of privacy is a fundamental right that has always been recognized by American law. Appraise this statement.

10. The right to trial by jury is a fundamental procedure that must always be used whenever any issue of fact is to be determined. Appraise this statement.

11. Mostek Corporation, a Texas corporation, made a contract to sell computer-related products to the North American Foreign Trading Corporation, a New York corporation. North American used its own purchase order form, on which appeared the statement that any dispute arising out of this order shall be submitted to arbitration as provided in the terms set forth on the back of this order. Acting on the purchase order, Mostek delivered almost all of the goods but failed to deliver the final installment. North American then demanded that the matter be arbitrated. Mostek refused to do so. Was it required to arbitrate? [*Mostek Corporation, 120 App Div 2d 383, 502 NYS2d 181*]

12. Why is the law not the same everywhere in the United States?

13. Fabricator Corporation, a California company, purchased component parts from various suppliers in Europe, Asia, and the United States. These it assembled into systems for the production of electricity. Fabricator entered into a contract with SLM, a German manufacturer, for the purchase of a generator for $25 million. The terms of the contract were discussed in detail by the attorneys and executive officers of both Fabricator and SLM, meeting both in California and Germany over a period of several months. The contract finally agreed to by them specified that any lawsuit under the contract would be brought in a German court and would be subject to German law. SLM did not deliver the generator and Fabricator brought suit against it in New York. SLM claimed that suit could only be brought in Germany. Fabricator asserted that the requirement of suit in Germany was not binding because it imposed an unreasonable burden upon it. Decide and explain your decision.

14. The *Strock* case on pages 3–4 of this chapter was decided on the basis that the legislature can abolish a common law right. Could the court have decided that a common law right could not be abolished?

15. A young man purchased heavy farm equipment on credit. The sales contract specified that any dispute that would arise under the contract would be submitted to arbitration. In order to boost the buyer's credit rating so that the sale could be made, the buyer's father wrote the seller that the father would stand behind the buyer's contract. Difficulties appeared in the machinery, there was a dispute between the buyer and the seller, and the buyer stopped making payments. The seller insisted that the buyer and father arbitrate the dispute with the seller. Was the seller correct?

APPENDIX TO CHAPTER 1: COURT ORGANIZATION AND PROCEDURE

Courts are government tribunals for determining legal rights, giving redress to injured parties, or enforcing punishment against wrongdoers. Courts in the United States are organized in two distinct systems: the federal courts and the state courts. Although created under separate governments, the methods of operation and organization of these two systems are similar.

A. PERSONNEL OF COURTS

Both the federal and state court systems require the assistance of many people. These include not only those individuals in the direct employ of the court, but also those described as officers of the court and, in many cases, a jury as well.

1. Officers of the Court

The **judge** is the primary officer of the court. A judge is either elected or appointed. **Attorneys** or counselors at law are also officers of the court. They are usually selected by the parties to the controversy but, in some cases, by the judge to present the issues of a case to the court.

The **clerk** of the court is appointed in some of the higher courts but is usually elected to office in the lower courts. The principal duties of the clerks are to enter cases on the court calendar, to keep an accurate record of the proceedings, to attest the record of the proceedings, and, in some instances, to approve bail bonds and to compute the amount of costs involved.

The **sheriff** is the chief executive of a county. It is a sheriff's duty to maintain peace and order within the territorial limits of a county. In addition, the sheriff has many other duties in connection with the administration of justice in county courts of record. These duties include summoning witnesses, taking charge of the jury, preserving order in court, serving writs, carrying out judicial sales, and

executing judgments. The **marshals** of the United States perform these duties in the federal courts. In county courts not of record, such as the courts of justices of the peace, these duties, when appropriate, are performed by a **constable**. Some of the duties of the sheriff are now performed by persons known as **court criers**, or by deputy sheriffs, known as **bailiffs**.

2. The Jury

The **jury** is a body of citizens sworn by a court to determine by verdict the issues of fact submitted to them. The first step in forming a jury is to make a **jury list**. This involves the preparation by the proper officers or board of a list of qualified persons from which a jury may be drawn. Persons drawn from the jury list constitute the **jury panel**. A trial jury is selected from members of the panel.

B. FEDERAL COURTS

The Supreme Court of the United States is the highest court in the federal system. The courts of appeals are intermediate courts. The district courts and special courts are the lower courts.

3. Supreme Court of the United States

The Supreme Court is the only court expressly established by the Constitution. Congress is authorized by the Constitution to create other federal courts.

The Supreme Court has original jurisdiction in all cases affecting ambassadors, other public ministers, and consuls, and in those cases in which a state is a party. Except as regulated by Congress, the Supreme Court has appellate jurisdiction in all cases that may be brought into the federal courts in accordance with the terms of the Constitution. The Supreme Court also has appellate jurisdiction in certain cases that have been decided by the

Figure 1-2   American Courts

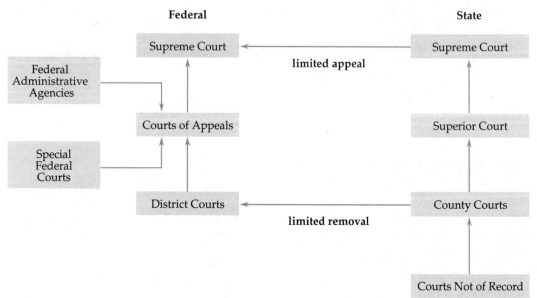

Note: This chart does not indicate the jurisdiction of the courts noted, whether appeal is of right or is discretionary, the scope of review, or local variations in the names of state courts.

supreme courts of the states. Thousands of cases are filed with the Court each year.

4. Courts of Appeals

The United States, including the District of Columbia, is divided geographically into 12 judicial circuits. Each of the circuits has a court of appeals. There is also a Court of Appeals for the Federal Circuit. It has nationwide jurisdiction for certain subject areas, such as patents and copyrights. These courts are courts of record.

A court of appeals has appellate jurisdiction only and is empowered to review the final decisions of the district courts, except in cases that may be taken directly to the Supreme Court. The decisions of the courts of appeals are final in most cases. An appeal may be taken as a matter of right on certain constitutional questions. Otherwise, review depends on the discretion of the Supreme Court and, in some cases, of the court of appeals.

5. District Courts

The United States, including the District of Columbia, is further divided into a number of judicial districts. Some states form a single district, whereas others are divided into two or more districts. District courts are also located in the territories.

The district courts have original jurisdiction in practically all cases that may be brought in the federal courts. They are the trial courts for civil and criminal cases.

Civil cases that may be brought in these district courts are (1) civil suits in which the United States is a party; (2) actions brought by citizens of the same state claiming land under grants by different states; (3) proceedings under the bankruptcy, postal, copyright, and patent laws; (4) civil cases of admiralty and maritime jurisdiction; (5) actions against national banking associations; (6) cases between citizens of different states or between citizens of one state and a foreign state involving $50,000 or more; and (7) cases that arise under the federal Constitution or laws and treaties made thereunder.

6. Other Federal Courts

In addition to the Supreme Court, the courts of appeals, and the district courts, the following tribunals have been created by Congress to determine other matters as indicated by their titles: Court of International Trade, Claims Court, Tax Court, Court of Military Appeals, and the territorial courts.

C. STATE COURTS

The system of courts in the various states is organized along lines similar to the federal court system, although differing in details such as the number of courts, their names, and jurisdiction.

7. State Supreme Court

The highest court in most states is known as the supreme court. In a few states it may have a different name, such as Court of Appeals in New York. The jurisdiction of a supreme court is ordinarily appellate, although in a few instances it is original. In some states, the supreme court is required to render an opinion on certain questions that may be referred to it by the legislature or by the chief executive of the state. The decision of a state supreme court is final in all cases not involving the federal Constitution, laws, and treaties.

8. Intermediate Courts

In some states, intermediate courts have original jurisdiction in a few cases, but in the main they have appellate jurisdiction of cases decided in the county or district courts. The intermediate courts are known as superior, circuit, or district appellate courts. As a general rule, their decisions may be reviewed by the highest state court.

9. County and District Courts

County and district courts of record have appellate jurisdiction of cases tried in the justice of the peace and police courts, as well as general original jurisdiction of criminal and civil cases. They also have jurisdiction of wills and guardianship matters except when, as in some states, the jurisdiction of such cases has been given to special orphans', surrogate, or probate courts.

10. Other State Courts

In addition to the foregoing, the following, which are ordinarily not courts of record, have jurisdiction as indicated by their titles: city or municipal courts, police courts, traffic courts, small claims courts, and justice of the peace courts.

D. COURT PROCEDURE

Detailed laws specify how, when, and where a legal dispute can be brought to court. Rules of procedure are necessary in order to achieve an orderly, fair determination of litigation and in order to obtain, as far as humanly possible, the same decision on the same facts. It is important to remember, however, that there is no uniform judicial procedure. While there are definite similarities, the law of each state may differ from that of the others and from federal procedure. For the most part, the uniform laws that have been adopted do not regulate matters of procedure.

E. STEPS IN A LAWSUIT

The following are the steps in a civil (non-criminal) lawsuit. Not every step is taken in every suit. The facts of a case may be such that the case ends before every possible step is taken. The parties may not want to fight it out to the very end or to raise every possible point.

11. Avoidance of Litigation

Typically, attorneys will seek to settle cases by compromise rather than run the risks and delays of litigation. A Federal Executive Order now requires attorneys handling U.S. cases to seek out-of-court settlements or the disposition of cases by alternative methods of dispute resolution.[1]

12. Commencement of Action

An action is begun by filing a **complaint** with the clerk of the appropriate court. The complaint generally consists of a description of the acts complained of by the plaintiff and a request for some sort of reparation or relief.

13. Service of Process

The defendant must be served with **process** (a writ, notice, or summons, or the complaint itself) to give notice that the action is pending and to subject the defendant to the power of the court.

14. Pleadings

After the plaintiff has filed a complaint and process has been served on the defendant, the defendant must make some reply to the complaint, generally within 15 or 20 days. If the defendant fails to do so, the plaintiff ordinarily wins the case by default.

Before answering the plaintiff's complaint, the defendant may make certain preliminary objections, such as that the action was brought in the wrong court or that service was not properly made. If the objection is sustained, the case may be ended, depending on the nature of the objection. The plaintiff may be allowed to correct the mistake if that is possible. The defendant may also raise the objection, sometimes called a **motion to dismiss** or **demurrer**, that even if the plaintiff's complaint is accepted as true, the plaintiff is still not entitled to any relief.

If the defendant makes an objection that is overruled or dismissed, or if the defendant makes no objection, the defendant must file an **answer**. An answer either admits or denies the facts asserted by the plaintiff. For example, if the plaintiff declared that the defendant made a contract on a certain date, the defendant may either admit making the contract or deny having done so. An admission of having made the contract does not end the case. The defendant may then be able to plead defenses, for example, that at a later date the plaintiff and defendant had agreed to set the contract aside.

Without regard to whether the defendant pleads a defense, the defendant may generally assert a **counterclaim** or **cross complaint** against the plaintiff. Thus, the defendant may contend that the plaintiff owes money or is liable for damages and that this liability should be offset against any claim the plaintiff may have.

After the defendant files an answer, the plaintiff may generally file preliminary objections to the answer. Just as the defendant could raise objections, the plaintiff may, in certain instances, argue that a counterclaim raised by the defendant could not be asserted in that action, that the answer is fatally defective in form, or that it is not legally sufficient. Again the court must pass upon the preliminary objections. When these are disposed of, the pleading stage is ordinarily over.

Generally, all of the pleadings in an action may raise only a few or perhaps one question of law, or a question of fact, or both. Thus, the entire case may depend on whether a letter admittedly written by the defendant amounted to an acceptance of the plaintiff's offer, thereby constituting a contract. If this question of law is answered in favor of the plaintiff, a judgment will be entered for the plaintiff; otherwise, for the defendant. By way of contrast, it may be that a certain letter would be an acceptance if it had been written by the defendant, but the defendant may deny having written it. Here the question is one of fact, and the judgment is entered for the plaintiff

---

[1] Executive order of October 23, 1991, No. 12778, 56 Fed. Reg. 55195.

if it is determined that the facts happened as claimed by the plaintiff. Otherwise, the judgment is entered for the defendant.

If the only questions involved are questions of law, the court will decide the case on the pleadings alone, since there is no need for a trial to determine the facts. If questions of fact are involved, there must be a trial to determine what the facts really were.

15. Pretrial Procedure

Many states and the federal courts have adopted other procedural steps that may be employed before the trial, with the purpose of eliminating the need for a trial, simplifying the issues to be tried, or giving the parties information needed for preparation for trial.

(a) MOTION FOR JUDGMENT ON THE PLEADINGS. After the pleadings are closed, many courts permit either party to move for a **judgment on the pleadings**. When such a motion is made, the court examines the record and may then enter a judgment according to the merits of the case as shown by the record.

(b) MOTION FOR SUMMARY JUDGMENT. In most courts, a party may shorten a lawsuit by showing that there is no substantial dispute as to the material facts relating to the claim or defense asserted by that party. This is ordinarily done by filing in court sworn statements and affidavits that show that the claim or defense of the adverse party is false or a sham. If the court concludes that there is no substantial dispute as to the material facts involved, it will enter such judgment as is proper on the actual facts of the case. If the court decides that there is a substantial dispute as to a material fact, it will dismiss the motion, and the case will then continue as though the motion had not been filed.

(c) PRETRIAL CONFERENCE. In many courts, either party may request the court to call a **pretrial conference**, or the court may take the initiative in doing so. This conference is a discussion by a judge of the court and the attorneys in the case. The object of the conference is to eliminate matters that are not in dispute and to determine what issues remain for litigation. Some cases are settled at this stage.

(d) DISCOVERY. The Federal Rules of Civil Procedure and similar rules in a large number of states permit one party to inquire of the adverse party and of all witnesses about anything relating to the action. This includes asking the adverse party the names of witnesses; asking the adverse party and the witnesses what they know about the case; examining, inspecting, and photographing books, records, buildings, and machines; and making an examination of the physical or mental condition of a party when it has a bearing on the action. These procedures are classed as **discovery**.

(e) DEPOSITIONS. Ordinarily, a witness testifies in court at the time of the trial. In some instances, it may be necessary or desirable to take such testimony out of court before the time of the trial. It may be that the witness is aged or infirm or is about to leave the state or country and will not be present when the trial is held. In this case, the interested party is permitted to have the witness's testimony, called a **deposition**, taken under oath outside of the court.

16. Determination of Facts

A legal system must provide for someone to determine the facts of a case when the parties do not agree on the facts.

(a) THE TRIER OF FACTS. If the legal controversy is one that under the common law would have been tried by a jury, either party to the action has the constitutional right today to demand that the action be tried before a jury. If all parties agree, however, the case may be tried by the court or judge alone without a jury, and in some instances it may be referred to a master or a referee appointed by the court to hear the matter.

In equity, there is no constitutional right to a jury trial, but a chancellor or equity judge may submit questions to a jury. There is the basic difference that in such cases the verdict or decision of the jury is only advisory to the chancellor; that is, the chancellor is not bound by the verdict. In contrast, the verdict of a jury in an action at law is binding on the court unless a basic error is present.

When new causes of action are created by statute, there is no constitutional right to a trial by jury. For example, an employee's right to obtain workers' compensation for an injury arising in the course of employment is not determined by a jury. When there is no jury, the trier of facts may be a judge, or a special administrative board or agency, such as a Workers' Compensation Board.

(b) BASIS FOR DECISION. The trier of facts, whether a jury, a judge, a referee, or a board, can only decide questions of fact on the basis of evidence presented before it. Each party offers evidence. The evidence usually consists of the answers of persons to questions in court. Their answers are called **testimony.** The evidence may also include **real evidence,** that is, tangible things, such as papers, books, and records. It is immaterial whether the records are kept in ordinary ledger books or stored in a computer, because a computer printout made for trial is admissible as evidence of the information contained in the computer. In some cases, such as a damage action for improper construction of a building, the trier of facts may be taken to view the building so that a better understanding of the evidence can be obtained.

The witness who testifies in court is usually a person who had some direct contact with the facts in the case, such as a person who saw the events occur or who heard one of the parties say something. In some instances, it is also proper to offer the testimony of persons who have no connection with the case, when they have expert knowledge and their opinions as experts are desired.

A witness who refuses to appear in court may be required to do so by a court order called a **subpoena**. The witness may also be compelled to bring relevant papers to the court by a **subpoena duces tecum**. If a witness does not obey a subpoena, the witness may be arrested for contempt of court. In some states, the names of the order upon the witness and the procedure for contempt have been changed, but the substance remains the same.

17. Conduct of the Trial

The conduct of a trial will be discussed in terms of a jury trial. Generally a case is one of several assigned for trial on a certain day or during a certain trial period. When the case is called, the opposing counsel seat themselves at tables in front of the judge, and the jury is selected. After the jury is sworn, the attorneys usually make **opening addresses** to the jury. Details vary in different jurisdictions, but the general pattern is that each attorney tells the jury what will be proven. When this step has been completed, the presentation of the evidence by both sides begins.

The attorney for the plaintiff starts with the first witness and asks any questions pertinent to the case. This is called the **direct examination** of the witness, since it is made by the attorney calling the witness. After the direct examination has been finished, the opposing counsel asks the same witness other questions in an effort to disprove the prior answers. This is called **cross-examination.**

After the cross-examination has been completed, the attorney for the plaintiff may ask the same witness other questions to overcome the effect of the cross-examination. This is called **redirect examination**. This step in turn may be followed by further examination by the defendant's attorney, called **recross-examination**.

After the examination of the plaintiff's witness has been concluded, the plaintiff's second witness takes the witness stand and is subjected to an examination in the same way as the first. This continues until all of the plaintiff's witnesses have been called. Then the plaintiff rests, and the defendant calls the first defense witness. The pattern of examination of witnesses is repeated, except that now the defendant is calling the witnesses, and the defendant's attorney conducts the direct and redirect examination. The questioning by the plaintiff's attorney is now cross- or recross-examination.

After the witnesses of both parties have been examined and all the evidence has been presented, each attorney makes another address to the jury. This is called a **summation**. It sums up the case and suggests that a particular verdict be returned by the jury.

18. Charge to the Jury and Verdict

The summation by the attorneys is followed by a charge of the judge to the jury. This **charge** is a resume of what has happened at the trial and an explanation of the applicable law. At its conclusion, the judge instructs the jury to retire and study the case in the light of the charge and then return a **verdict**, or a finding. By such instructions, the judge leaves to the jury the problem of determining the facts. However, the judge states the law that the jury must apply to such facts as they may find. The jury then retires to secret deliberation in the jury room.

19. Taking the Case from the Jury and Attacking the Verdict

At several points during the trial or immediately after it, a party may take a step to end the case or to set aside the verdict the jury has returned.

(a) VOLUNTARY NONSUIT. A plaintiff who is dissatisfied with the progress of the trial may wish to stop the trial and begin again at a later date. In most jurisdictions, this can be done by taking a **voluntary nonsuit**.

(b) COMPULSORY NONSUIT. After the plaintiff has presented the testimony of all witnesses, the defendant may request the court to enter a nonsuit on the ground that the case presented by the plaintiff does not entitle the plaintiff to recover. This is called a **compulsory nonsuit.**

(c) MISTRIAL. When necessary to avoid great injustice, the trial court may declare that there has been a **mistrial**. This terminates the trial and postpones it to a later date. While either party may move the court to enter a mistrial, it is discretionary with the court whether it does so. A mistrial is commonly entered when the evidence has been of a highly prejudicial character and the trial judge does not believe that the jury can ignore it even when instructed to do so. A mistrial may also be declared when a juror has been guilty of misconduct.

(d) DIRECTED VERDICT. After the presentation of all the evidence at the trial, either party may request the court to direct the jury to return a verdict in favor of the requesting party. When the plaintiff would not be entitled to recover, even if all of the testimony in the plaintiff's favor were believed, the defendant is entitled to have the court direct the jury to return a verdict for the defendant. The plaintiff is entitled to a directed verdict when, even if all the evidence on behalf of the defendant were believed, the jury would still be required to find for the plaintiff. In some states, the defendant may make a motion for a directed verdict at the close of the plaintiff's proof.

(e) NEW TRIAL. After the verdict has been returned by the jury, a party may move for a new trial if not satisfied with the verdict or with the amount of damages awarded. If it is clear that the jury made a mistake or if material evidence that could not have been discovered before the trial becomes available later, the court will award a new trial, and the case will be tried again before another jury.

(f) JUDGMENT N.O.V. If the verdict returned by the jury is clearly wrong as a matter of law, the court may set aside the verdict and enter a judgment contrary to the verdict. In some states, this is called a **judgment** *non obstante veredicto* (notwithstanding the verdict), or as it is abbreviated, a **judgment n.o.v.**

20. Judgment and Costs

The court enters a judgment conforming to the verdict unless a new trial has been granted, a mistrial declared after the return of the verdict, or a judgment n.o.v. entered. Generally the winning party will also be awarded costs in the action. In equity actions or those that had their origin in equity, and in certain statutory proceedings, the court has discretion to award costs to the winner or to divide costs between the parties.

Costs ordinarily include the costs of filing papers with the court, the cost of having the sheriff or other officers of the court take official action, statutory fees paid to witnesses, and the jury fee. Costs also include printing the record, when this is required on appeal. Costs do not include compensation for the time spent by the party in preparing the case or in being present at the trial, the time lost from work because of the case, or the fee paid to an attorney. Sometimes when a special statutory action is brought, the statute authorizes recovery of a small fee for the attorney. Thus, a mechanic's lien statute may authorize the recovery of an attorney's fee of 10 percent of the amount recovered, or a reasonable attorney's fee. As a general rule, the costs that a party recovers represent only a small part of the total expenses actually incurred in the litigation.

21. Appeal

After a judgment has been entered, any party who is aggrieved thereby may appeal. This means that a party who wins the judgment but is not awarded as much as had been hoped, as well as a party who loses the case, may appeal.

The appellate court does not hear witnesses. It examines the record of the proceedings before the lower court (that is, the file of the case containing all the pleadings, the testimony of witnesses, and the judges charge) to see if there was an error of law. To assist the court, the attorneys for the parties file arguments or briefs and generally make arguments orally before the court.

An appellate court may not agree with the application of the law made by the lower court. In such a case, the appellate court generally sets aside or modifies the action of the lower court and enters such judgment as it concludes the lower court should have

entered. It may set aside the action of the lower court and send the case back to the lower court with directions to hold a new trial or with directions to enter a new judgment in accordance with the opinion that is filed by the appellate court.

22. Execution

After a judgment has been entered or after an appeal has been decided, the losing party generally complies with the judgment of the court. If not, the winning party may then take steps to **execute**, or carry out, the judgment.

(a) MONEY JUDGMENT. If the judgment is for the payment of a sum of money, the plaintiff may direct the sheriff or other judicial officer to sell as much of the defendant's property as is necessary to pay the plaintiff's judgment and the costs of the proceedings and of the execution. Acting under this authorization, the sheriff may make a public sale of the defendant's property and apply the proceeds to the payment of the plaintiff's judgment. In most states, the defendant is allowed a limited monetary exemption and an exemption for certain articles, such as personal clothing and tools of trade.

(b) GARNISHMENT OF DEBT. When a money judgment is entered in favor of A against B, it may happen that B is owed money by C. A can garnish or attach this debt of C to B. To the extent that money paid by C then goes to A instead of B, both the debt of C to B and the judgment liability of B to A are reduced or discharged.

(c) NONMONEY JUDGMENT.   If the judgment is for the recovery of specific property, the judgment will direct the sheriff to deliver the property to the plaintiff.

If the judgment directs the defendant to carry out or to refrain from an act, it is commonly provided that failure to obey the order is a contempt of court punishable by fine or imprisonment.

ETHICS, SOCIAL FORCES, AND THE LAW

LEARNING OBJECTIVES

After studying this chapter, you will be able to:
1. *Describe how ethics and social forces make the law.*
2. *List the most common social forces that make the law.*
3. *Explain the way the social forces may sometimes conflict.*
4. *Show how a rule of law may be a synthesis of conflicting social forces.*
5. *Describe how law is an evolutionary process.*

In a democratic society, laws represent the expression of the collective desires of the people to encourage conduct that is right, good, and just. In this sense, the law has its underpinnings in the ethics of society.

This chapter takes you behind the rules of law, behind general labels of justice and ethics, to see the basic or underlying objectives of society in establishing the particular rules of law. These are the social forces that make the law.

A. ETHICS AND LAW

To what extent do ethical values affect the law?

1. What Is Ethics?

Ethics constitutes the branch of philosophy dealing with values relating to human conduct, with respect to the goodness and the rightness of motives and actions. Thus far, the matter is easy. The difficulty arises in defining *goodness*. Society's definition changes over time. Consider the Founding Fathers, who obtained our national independence and established our Constitution. We certainly respect, admire, and praise them. But they thought of inalienable rights as being the rights of man— white, free men over 21; women and slaves excluded. To them, labor unions were illegal conspiracies and employees could not strike or picket against their employers. It was to take almost a century after they lived, a civil war, and a constitutional amendment to delegalize the institution of slavery and abolish the concept that a slave was a thing or chattel owned by a master. It was to take the 20th century to give employees the right to unionize, strike, and picket and to recognize the legal rights of women.[1]

Further study of history and of different societies will emphasize that goodness, and therefore ethics, does not have the same meaning at all times to all peoples.

2. Why Ethical Concepts Change

If we look closely at why one society or one generation believes something is bad although another society or generation thought it was good, we come to the conclusion that there are certain underlying currents that run through the pages of history. These currents are described in this chapter as social forces. Depending on the importance attached to the different forces at different times, the content of the community's code of ethics changes. Thus, the underlying reason for changed ethics is the change in the value placed on the different social forces. Understanding why society's evaluation of social forces changes requires a thorough study of practically every field of knowledge and therefore lies beyond the scope of this book. It is sufficient for our purpose to recognize that there are social forces, that these forces give rise to the ethical patterns of the day, that the evaluation of the social forces changes, and that with such changes, there are corresponding changes in the field of ethics.

3. Ethics and Modern Law

The social forces considered in this chapter give rise to our ethical concepts. Ethical concepts in turn influence and give rise to the rules of law. The law existing at any one time is part of the social environment in which people live and work. The goals and objectives inspired by the environment will seek to advance certain social forces. Thus, there is an endless circle of interaction between social environment, social forces, ethics, and the law.

By their very nature, ethical concepts are broad and general. The law, as contrasted with ethical standards, must be more definite and

---

[1] One quotation will be sufficient to show that our views of what is right or good today are much different from views in former years. In 1869, a woman lawyer was refused admission to the bar of the state of Illinois because she was a woman. On appeal, the U.S. Supreme Court held that this was proper. Justice Bradley stated that "the paramount destiny and mission of woman are to fulfill the noble and benign office of wife and mother. This is the law of the Creator." [Bradwell v Illinois, 16 Wall 130 (1873), affirming 55 Ill 535]

Figure 2-1   The Endless Cycle of Societal Interaction

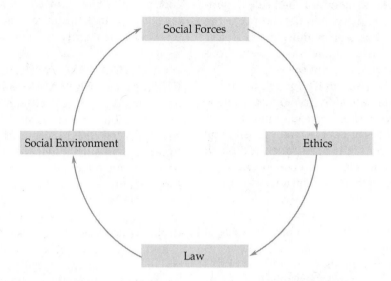

stable to be capable of consistent enforcement. Despite this distinction between law and ethics, it is clear that there is a strong relation between them. Laws are made and remade as notions of justice change. A society's sense of justice is in turn influenced by its laws. The interactions are unquestionably complex, but a few observations can still be made.

(a) LAW AS THE CRYSTALLIZATION OF ETHICS. Not all ethical values are capable of expression as laws, but certainly the more elemental ethical principles find their way into a society's legal framework. An ethical regard for the value of human life is crystallized in criminal codes detailing precisely defined degrees of offense—murder, manslaughter, negligent homicide. Similarly, an ethical obligation to look after the well-being of others takes the form of the legally enforceable duty of parents to care for their children. In these areas, the law approaches the attainment of ethical values of society and locks the ethical concepts into binding rules of conduct.

But the law cannot equal the reach of ethical values, at least partly because some things are better left to individual choice and initiative. Criminal penalties for behavior that actively or negligently endangers human life

stop short of imposing a general duty to intervene to save a life already in danger. Legal obligations to further the well-being of others are not extended to members of society generally, but only to those with a dependent relationship. In fact, it might be said that if a society's ethical codes constitute its concept of ideal behavior, then that society's law is its minimum standard of conduct.

(b) SOCIETAL ETHICS AS THE BLUEPRINT FOR FUTURE LAW. As was noted earlier, a society's ethical values change over time. The law similarly evolves to keep pace with changing technologies and values, though at a much more deliberate pace. Because of the close relationship between law and ethics, the ethical values of today's society can be regarded as a blueprint for the law of tomorrow.

(c) PARTICULAR APPLICATIONS. As you study business law, you will find many instances of established legal principles that became inadequate to serve society's changing notions of what was right or just. As public sentiment against a particular law or legal principle grew, a legal system that was otherwise resistant to change found various ways to relieve the pressure. The change sometimes took the form of a judicial decision that found a new exception to an established rule or simply overturned an earlier decision. Or the change may have been manifested as a new statute or a constitutional amendment. Consider the following illustrations.

As was discussed in Chapter 1, there has not always been a legally recognized right of privacy. The very rapid spread of information to great numbers of people made possible by the development of the newspaper, and much later by radio and television, created a need for enforceable protection against unwarranted intrusion in private lives. Privacy is now a constitutionally protected right.[2]

Another example of changes in societal ethics resulting in changes in the law involves consumerism. Beginning in the middle of this century, society began to feel that it was just not right to treat the consumer as the equal of the giant seller. The result—consumer protection laws—gave the consumer special protection because of this inequality. The Uniform Commercial Code placed special duties on merchants. Our American ideal of equality was modified in recognition of the fact that equality does not exist in the marketplace.

(d) IMPLICATIONS FOR BUSINESS. As the size, resources, and business patterns of society change, what seems right today may seem wrong in the future. While society's changing notions of what is right and just do not create binding obligations on businesses and businesspeople, they do constitute a force that will help to mold future law. Businesses that act irresponsibly and with disregard for society's view of what is right will speed the transition from ethical concept to enforceable law. Business can only avoid society's tendency toward more stringent regulation by acting responsibly and in harmony with societal ethics. Today, many companies have established codes of ethics as guides for their employees, requiring that company business be conducted not only in compliance with the law, but also in accordance with the standards of +business integrity and honest dealings.

(e) LIMITATIONS ON USE OF ETHICS IN JUDICIAL DECISION MAKING. The law and society seek justice—an ethical goal. However, it must be recognized that in many situations "ethics" does not furnish any guide to a court. In such situations we must delve deeper than ethics and examine the social forces that make both our ethics and our law.

(1) Which school of ethics? At the outset it would be necessary for a court to decide which school of ethics it should follow. This is vital because the choice of one school in preference to another could produce a different result. To illustrate, in the first quarter of this century "Let the buyer beware" was considered normal, moral, and ethical. Today that view is condemned as unethical, and the law now follows "Let the seller beware."[3]

(2) Commerical practicality. In the business world many rules of law are merely designed to establish a fixed rule to meet the business needs. For example, when the law fixes three days as the time in which notice must be given, can we say that "ethics" determined that it should be three and neither two nor four? Likewise is a check different than a contract because of ethics?

(3) Matters as to which society does not agree as to what is right and wrong. Modern technology, medicine, and internationalism give rise to the need for new rules of law. Ethics here provides little guidance because no one really knows what is right or wrong. Ethics cannot give the answers. Yet cases must be decided. This problem is illustrated by the case of *Re T. A. C. P.*[4] The court in that case was faced with the question of whether a child born with a fatally damaged brain could be

---

[2] Griswold v Connecticut, 381 US 479 (1965).

[3] The problem is all the more confusing because there are some 12 different schools of ethics and very few lawyers or judges have had any significant training in these areas.

[4] (Fla) 609 So 2d 588 (1992).

regarded as "dead" for the purpose of removing organs for transplanting. The court decided the case, as you will see in Chapter 3, but stated "We express no opinion today about who is right and who is wrong on these issues—if any 'right' or 'wrong' can be found here. The salient point is that no consensus exists as to: (a) the utility of organ transplants of the type at issue here; (b) the ethical issues involved; or (c) the legal and constitutional problems implicated."

B. SOCIAL FORCES AND THE LAW

Every rule of law seeks some goal or objective. General objectives are the creation and maintenance of order, stability, and justice.

4. Social Forces

The desires or forces that motivate society in making its laws can be called **social forces**. The social forces and objectives of the law are, in effect, the opposite sides of the same coin. Because certain forces are pushing society, society seeks certain objectives. Asking what is the objective of a law is thus another way of asking what social force in society seeks that result. The sum of these societal drives gives us the ethical pattern or environment of society.

(a) PROTECTION OF THE STATE. A number of laws are designed to protect the existing governments, both state and national. Laws condemning treason, sedition, and subversive practices are examples of society's taking measures to preserve governmental systems. Less dramatic are the laws that impose taxes to provide for the support of those governments. Under the national social security system, a number is assigned to each person. The same number is used by other government programs and agencies, such as the Internal Revenue Service and various relief programs. The numbering system solves the problem of distinguishing between two persons with the same name. Since the assigned numbers are shorter than the names of most people, the numbering system speeds up the process of storing and retrieving information. The use of the same identifying numbers by the various government programs makes it easier for the government to spot fraudulent claims. However, various attacks have been made on this numbering system on the ground that it is dehumanizing or violates religious principles. The *Bowen* case deals with a conflict between the plaintiff's religious beliefs and the governmental requirement of using a social security number in order to obtain financial assistance.

(b) PROTECTION OF THE PERSON. A second social force is protection of the person. At an early date, laws were developed to

BOWEN v ROY
476 US 693 (1986)

> Federal law provides financial assistance to poor families through the food stamp program and Aid to Families with Dependent Children. In order to obtain benefits under these programs, the federal law requires a recipient to give a social security number to any state welfare agency involved. Roy, a Native American, was refused federal benefits for his two-year-old daughter

because he would not furnish a social security number. He claimed that the use of a number was contrary to his religious belief and that freedom of religion gave him the right to refuse to furnish a social security number. From a decision against him, he appealed.

BURGER, C. J. . . . Roy is a Native American descended from the Abenaki Tribe, and he asserts a religious belief that control over one's life is essential to spiritual purity and indispensable to "becoming a holy person." Based on recent conversations with an Abenaki chief, Roy believes that technology is "robbing the spirit of man." In order to prepare his daughter for greater spiritual power, therefore, Roy testified to his belief that he must keep her person and spirit unique and that the uniqueness of the social security number as an identifier, coupled with the other uses of the number over which she has no control, will serve to "rob the spirit" of his daughter and prevent her from attaining greater spiritual power. . . .

Never to our knowledge has the Court interpreted the First Amendment to require the Government *itself* to behave in ways that the individual believes will further his or her spiritual development or that of his or her family. The Free Exercise Clause simply cannot be understood to require the Government to conduct its own internal affairs in ways that comport with the religious beliefs of particular citizens. Just as the Government may not insist that appellees engage in any set form of religious observance, so appellees may not demand that the Government join in their chosen religious practices by refraining from using a number to identify their daughter. "The Free Exercise Clause is written in terms of what the government cannot do to the individual, not in terms of what the individual can extract from the government." *Sherbert v Verner*, 374 US 398, 412 (1963) (Douglas, J., concurring). . . .

The statutory requirement that applicants provide a social security number is wholly neutral in religious terms and uniformly applicable. There is no claim that there is any attempt by Congress to discriminate invidiously or any covert suppression of particular religious beliefs. . . . It may indeed confront some applicants for benefits with choices, but in no sense does it affirmatively compel appellees, by threat of sanctions, to refrain from religiously motivated conduct or to engage in conduct that they find objectionable for religious reasons. Rather, it is [Roy and his daughter] who seek benefits from the Government and who assert that, because of certain religious beliefs, they should be excused from compliance with a condition that is binding on all other persons who seek the same benefits from the Government.

This is far removed from the historical instances of religious persecution and intolerance that gave concern to those who drafted the Free Exercise Clause of the First Amendment. . . .

Governments today grant a broad range of benefits; inescapably at the same time the administration of complex programs requires certain conditions and restrictions. Although in some situations a mechanism for individual consideration will be created, a policy decision by a government that it wishes to treat all applicants alike and that it does not wish to become involved in case-by-case inquiries into the genuineness of each religious objection to such condition or restrictions is entitled to substantial deference. Moreover, legitimate interests are implicated in the need to avoid any appearance of favoring religious over nonreligious applicants. . . .

The social security number requirement clearly promotes a legitimate and important public interest. No one can doubt that preventing fraud in these benefits programs is an important goal. . . .

[Judgment affirmed]

QUESTIONS

1. Does the court agree or disagree with the religious beliefs of Roy?
2. How does the decision affect Roy's religious freedom?
3. Who would be harmed if Roy were allowed to receive governmental benefits and still follow his beliefs?

protect the individual from being injured or killed. The field of criminal law is devoted to a large extent to the protection of the person. In addition, under civil law a suit can be brought to recover damages for the harm done by criminal acts. Over the course of time, the protection of personal rights has broadened to include protection of reputation and privacy, and protection of contracts and business relations from malicious interference by outsiders. A number of states have adopted statutes prohibiting insurance companies from disclosing, outside of judicial proceedings, any information they possess as to their policyholders or the amount of their insurance.[5]

In the *Rasmussen* case the privacy interest of blood donors and the public welfare interest were in conflict with the interest of an AIDS victim seeking to learn the identity of the donors.

In cases similar to *Rasmussen*, if the court has greater sympathy with the plaintiff than with the donors, discovery may be obtained. However, restrictions are imposed on such discovery to prevent the information from going beyond the parties to the action and their attorneys.[6]

It is a federal offense to knowingly injure, intimidate, or interfere with anyone who is exercising a basic civil right (such as voting),

RASMUSSEN v SOUTH FLORIDA BLOOD SERVICE, INC.
(Fla) 500 So 2d 533 (1987)

Donald Rasmussen was hit by an automobile. In the hospital he was given a number of blood transfusions. Some time thereafter it was determined that he had AIDS. He filed a petition for a court order against the blood bank that

---

[5] Griffith v State Farm Insurance Companies, ___ Cal App 3d ___, 281 Cal Rptr 165 (1991).

[6] Gulf Coast Regional Blood Center v Houston (Tex App) 745 SW2d 557 (1988). In some states, statutes or administrative regulations prohibit such discovery. Doe v American Red Cross (DC SC) 790 F Supp 590 (1992).

had furnished the blood to the hospital. He wanted to learn the names and addresses of all blood donors so that he could determine if any had AIDS. He hoped by this to prove that he had contracted AIDS as the result of one of the transfusions in the hospital. He died from AIDS, and his estate continued the proceeding. The court of appeals certified the question to the state supreme court.

BARKETT, J. . . . The court must balance the competing interests that would be served by granting discovery or by denying it. . . .

The Supreme Court first recognized a right of privacy based on the United States Constitution in *Griswold v Connecticut*, 381 U.S. 479 (1965). This right of privacy has been described as "the most comprehensive of rights and the right most valued by civilized man." *Stanley v Georgia*, 394 U.S. 557, 564 (1969). . . . In recent cases, the Court has discussed the privacy right as one of those fundamental rights that are "'implicit in the concept of ordered liberty' such that 'neither liberty nor justice would exist if [they] were sacrificed.'" *Bowers v Hardwick*, [478] U.S. [186], 106 S.Ct. 2841, 2844 (1986). . . .

In 1980, the voters of Florida amended our state constitution to include an express right of privacy. Art. V, Section 23, Fla Const. In approving the amendment, Florida became the fourth state to adopt a strong, freestanding right of privacy as a separate section of its state constitution, thus providing an explicit textual foundation for those privacy interests inherent in the concept of liberty which may not otherwise be protected by specific constitutional provisions.

Although the general concept of privacy encompasses an enormously broad and diverse field of personal action and belief, there can be no doubt that the Florida amendment was intended to protect the right to determine whether or not sensitive information about oneself will be disclosed to others. . . .

It is now known that AIDS is a major health problem with calamitous potential. At present, there is no known cure and the mortality rate is high. As noted by the court below, medical researchers have identified a number of groups which have a high incidence of the disease and are labeled "high risk" groups. . . .

The [court order requested] gives petitioner access to the names and addresses of the blood donors with no restrictions on their use. There is nothing to prohibit petitioner from conducting an investigation without the knowledge of the persons in question. We cannot ignore, therefore, the consequences of disclosure to nonparties, including the possibility that a donor's co-workers, friends, employers, and others may be queried as to the donor's sexual preferences, drug use, or general life-style.

The threat posed by the disclosure of the donors' identities goes far beyond the immediate discomfort occasioned by third party probing into sensitive areas of the donors' lives. Disclosure of donor identities in any context involving AIDS could be extremely disruptive and even devastating to the individual donor. If the requested information is released, and petitioner queries the donors' friends and fellow employees, it will be functionally impossible to prevent occasional references to AIDS. As the district court recognized:

AIDS is the modern day equivalent of leprosy. AIDS, or a suspicion of AIDS, can lead to discrimination in employment, education, housing and even medical treatment. . . .

We conclude, therefore, that the disclosure sought here implicates constitutionally protected privacy interests.

Our analysis of the interests to be served by denying discovery does not end with the effects of disclosure on the private lives of the fifty-one donors implicated in this case. Society has a vital interest in maintaining a strong volunteer blood supply, a task that has become more difficult with the emergence of AIDS. . . . It is clearly "in the public interest to discourage any serious disincentive to volunteer blood donation." Rasmussen, 467 So. 2d at 804. Because there is little doubt that the prospect of inquiry into one's private life and potential association with AIDS will deter blood donation, we conclude that society's interest in a strong and healthy blood supply will be furthered by the denial of discovery in this case.

In balancing the competing interests involved, we do not ignore Rasmussen's interest in obtaining the requested information. . . . However, we find that the discovery order requested here would do little to advance that interest. The probative value of the discovery sought by Rasmussen is dubious at best. The potential of significant harm to most, if not all, of the fifty-one unsuspecting donors in permitting such a fishing expedition is great and far outweighs the plaintiff's need under these circumstances. . . .

QUESTIONS

1. What social forces were involved in the *Rasmussen* case?
2. Assume that Rasmussen had obtained the names and addresses of the donors. If one of them had AIDS, would that prove that Rasmussen had contracted AIDS from the blood transfusions?

taking part in any federal governmental program, or receiving federal assistance. Interference with attendance in a public school or college, participation in any state or local governmental program, service as a juror in a state court, or the use of any public facility (common carrier, hotel, or restaurant) is prohibited when based on race, color, religion, or national origin discrimination.[7]

Protection of the person has expanded to protect economic interests. Laws prohibiting discrimination in employment, in furnishing hotel accommodations and transportation, and in commercial transactions in the sale of property are an extension of the concept of protecting the person. Because membership in a professional association, a labor union, or a trade or business group has economic importance to its members, an applicant can no longer be excluded arbitrarily from the membership or be expelled without notice of the charges made and an opportunity to be heard.[8]

(c) PROTECTION OF PUBLIC HEALTH, SAFETY, AND MORALS. The law seeks to protect the public health, safety, and morals in many ways. Laws relating to quarantine, food inspection, and compulsory inoculation protect the public health. Laws regulating highway

---

[7] Civil Obedience Act of 1968, PL 90-284, 18 USC § 245.

[8] Silver v New York Stock Exchange, 373 US 341 (1963); Cunningham v Burbank Board of Realtors, 262 Cal App 2d 211, 68 Cal Rptr 653 (1968).

Figure 2-2 Objectives of Social Forces Behind Laws

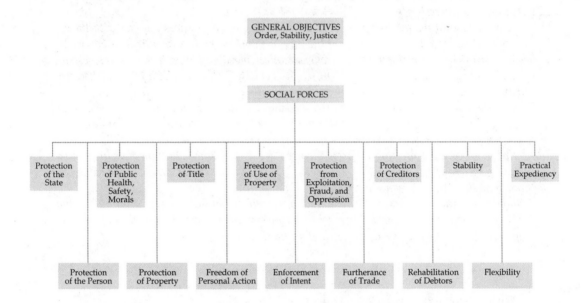

Note; The listing of some social forces at a higher level is not intended that such forces have superiority when in conflict with the forces shown at the lower level.

speeds and laws requiring fire escapes or guard devices around moving parts of factory machinery are for the safety of the public. Laws prohibiting the sale of liquor to minors and those prohibiting obscenity protect the morals of the public.

(d) PROTECTION OF PROPERTY. Just as laws have been developed to protect the individual's physical well-being, laws have been developed to protect one's property from damage, destruction, and other harmful acts. For example, a thief who steals an automobile is civilly liable to the owner of the automobile for its value and is criminally responsible to the state.

(e) PROTECTION OF TITLE. Because of the importance of ownership of property, one of the objectives of the law has been to protect the title of the owner of property. Thus, if property is stolen, the true owner may recover it from the thief, and even from a person who purchased it in good faith from the thief.

When a person claims ownership of property by sale or gift, the title of the original owner is protected by placing on the claimant the burden of proving that title had been acquired as claimed.[9]

(f) FREEDOM OF PERSONAL ACTION. In the Anglo-American stream of history, the desire for freedom from political domination gave rise to the American Revolution. The desire for freedom from economic domination gave rise to the free enterprise philosophy. Today, freedom is the dominant element in the constitutional provisions for the protection of free-

---

[9] Boyce v Murray, ___ Ga App ___, 395 SE2d 255 (1990).

dom of religion, press, and speech, and also in such laws as those against business combinations in restraint of trade by others.

Freedom of action is also given to a patient who is competent to choose to die—the person may refuse to take medical treatment that might prolong life. Moreover, many courts will give a guardian authority to carry out a patient's instructions as to termination of life-support systems when the patient is no longer mentally competent to act.[10]

This right of freedom of personal action, however, cannot be exercised by one person in such a way that it interferes to an unreasonable extent with the rights of others. Freedom of speech, for example, does not mean freedom to speak or write a malicious, false statement about another person's character or reputation. Neither freedom of speech nor freedom of religion enables the elders of a church to denounce the morality of a former church member who has left the church.[11]

(g) FREEDOM OF USE OF PROPERTY. Freedom of action is often stated in terms of freedom of use of property. For example, the owner of an automobile is free to drive the car or not, to say who shall ride in it, to sell or give it away, and so on.

It must be remembered, however, that there are often restrictions on the use of property. For example, there are speed laws governing the driving of automobiles, zoning laws regulating building on real property, and anti-pollution laws restricting the operation of factories.

(h) ENFORCEMENT OF INTENT. When persons voluntarily enter into a transaction, the law usually seeks to enforce their intent. This objective is closely related to the concept that the law seeks to protect the individual's freedom of action. For example, if a person provides by will for the distribution of property at death, the law will generally allow the property to pass to the persons intended by the deceased owner. The law will likewise seek to carry out the intention of the parties to a business transaction.

The extent to which the intent of one person or of several persons will be carried out has certain limitations. Sometimes the intent is not effective unless it is manifested by a particular written formality. For example, a deceased person may have intended to leave property to a friend, but in most states that intent must be shown by a written will signed by the deceased owner. Likewise, in some cases the intent of the parties may not be carried out because the law regards the intent as illegal.

(i) PROTECTION FROM EXPLOITATION, FRAUD, AND OPPRESSION. Many rules of law have developed in the courts, and many statutes have been enacted, to protect certain groups or individuals from exploitation or oppression by others. Thus, to protect **minors** (persons under legal age), the law developed that minors could set aside their contracts, subject to certain exceptions.

Persons buying food that is packed in cans are given certain rights against the seller and the manufacturer. Since the contents of the cans are not visible, buyers of such products need special protection from unscrupulous canners. The consumer is also protected by laws against adulteration and poisons in food, drugs, and household products. Laws prohibiting unfair competition and discrimination, both economic and social, are designed to protect from oppression as well.

(j) FURTHERANCE OF TRADE. Society seeks to further trade in a variety of ways, such as establishing a currency as a medium of payment. Other examples include recognizing and giving legal effect to installment sales and adopting special rules for checks, notes, and similar instruments so that they can be widely used as credit devices and substitutes for money. Society has also sought to further trade

---

[10] Re Guardianship of Browning (Fla) 568 So 2d 4, (1990).
[11] Guinn v Church of Christ (Okla) 775 P2d 766 (1989).

by enacting laws to mitigate the harmful effects of alternating periods of depression and inflation.

Laws that have been considered in connection with other objectives may also serve to further trade. For example, laws protecting against unfair competition have the objective of furthering trade, as well as the objective of protecting certain classes from oppression by others.

(k) PROTECTION OF CREDITORS. Society seeks to protect the rights of creditors and to protect them from dishonest or fraudulent acts of debtors. Initially, creditors are protected by the law that makes contracts binding and that provides machinery for the enforcement of contracts. The provision of the federal Constitution that prohibits states from impairing the obligation of contracts also provides protection. Further, creditors may compel a debtor to go into bankruptcy. If the debtor has concealed property or transfers it to a friend to hide it from creditors, the law permits the creditors to claim the property for the payment of the debts due them.

(l) REHABILITATION OF DEBTORS. Society has come to regard it as unacceptable that debtors should be ruined forever by the burden of their debts. Imprisonment for debt has been abolished. Bankruptcy laws have been adopted to provide the debtor with a means of starting a new economic life. In times of widespread depression, the same objective has been served by special laws prohibiting the foreclosure of mortgages.

(m) STABILITY. Stability is particularly important in all business transactions. When you buy a house, for example, you not only want to know the exact meaning of the transaction under today's law, but you also want the transaction to have the same meaning in the future.

Because of the desire for stability, courts will ordinarily follow former decisions unless there is a strong reason to depart from them. Similarly, when no former case directly bears on the point involved, a court will try to reach a decision that is a logical extension of some former decision or that follows a former decision by analogy, rather than to strike out on a fresh path to reach a decision unrelated to the past.

(n) FLEXIBILITY. If stability were always required, the cause of justice would often be defeated. The reason that originally gave rise to a rule of law may have ceased to exist.[12] Also, a rule may later appear unjust because it reflects a concept of justice that is outmoded or obsolete. For example, capital punishment, which one age believed just, has been seriously questioned by another age. We must not lose sight of the fact that the rule of law under question was created to further the sense of social justice existing at that time and that our concepts of justice change.

(1) Means of Attaining Flexibility. Changes by legislative action are relatively easy to make. Furthermore, some statutes recognize the impossibility of laying down in advance a hard-and-fast rule that will do justice in all cases. The typical modern statute, particularly in the field of regulation of business, often contains an escape clause by which a person can escape from the operation of the statute under certain circumstances. Thus, a rent control law may impose a rent ceiling—that is, a maximum above which landlords cannot charge. The same law may also authorize a greater charge when special circumstances make it just to allow such exception. For example, the landlord may have made expensive repairs to the property or taxes may have increased substantially.

---

12 "It is revolting to have no better reason for a rule of law than that it was laid down in the time of Henry IV. It is still more revolting if the grounds upon which it was laid down have vanished long since, and the rule simply persists from blind imitation of the past." Holmes, Collected Papers 187 (1920).

"The law must be stable, but it must not stand still." Roscoe Pound, *Introduction to the Philosophy of Law* (New Haven, Conn.: Yale University Press, 1922).

The rule of law may be stated in terms of what a reasonable or prudent person would do. Thus, whether you are negligent in driving your automobile is determined in court by whether you exercised the degree of care that a prudent person would have exercised in the same situation. This is a vague and variable standard as to how you must drive your car, but it is the only standard that is practical. The alternative would be a detailed motor code specifying how you should drive your car under every situation that might arise. A code obviously could not foresee every possibility, and it certainly would be too long for any driver to remember. Even constitutions are flexible to the extent that they can be changed by amendment or judicial construction. Constitutions state the procedures for their amendment. Making changes in constitutions is purposely made difficult, so as to attain the objective of stability, but change can be made when the need for change is generally recognized by the people of the state or nation.

(2) Protection of the Person and Stability. The social force of protecting the person is frequently the controlling factor in determining whether a court should adhere to the common law, thereby furthering stability; or whether it should change the law, thereby furthering flexibility. Thus, it will be seen that many times the courts retain the common law when that will further the protection of the person. In other instances, the courts change the common law because a change will give the person greater protection. One court retained the common law definition of *person* with the result that a reckless driver injuring a mother and killing her unborn child was not guilty of manslaughter with respect to the death of the unborn child. Such a child was not a person under the common law of crimes.[13] By this decision, the person of the defendant was protected because the common law definition of person required him to be acquitted of the crime of manslaughter. However, in so doing, the court turned its back on protecting the person of the unborn child. Which person should the law protect? The social force of stability tipped the scales in favor of protecting the defendant.

(3) Evolution of Servant to Employee. At common law, the parties to an employment contract were called *master* and *servant*. The servant was in fact regarded as a chattel or thing owned by the master rather than as a human being or a person. With the growth in this century of the rights of the person, the common law servant has been replaced by the modern employee who is a person and has all the rights of a person.

In the *Morton* case, the employer sought to recover for loss caused by the defendant's injuring the plaintiff's employee.

(o) PRACTICAL EXPEDIENCY. Frequently the law is influenced by what is practical or

MORTON v MERRILLVILLE TOYOTA, INC.

(Ind App) 562 NE2d 781 (1990)

Marino was an employee of Merrillville Toyota, Inc. He was struck by a trailer driven by Morton as employee of the Steel & Machinery Transport, Inc. Because of Marino's injuries he could not return to work. Merrillville Toyota sued Morton and Steel on the ground that Morton's negligence had deprived Merrillville of the services of Marino. The defendants asserted that

---

[13] Meadows v Arkansas, 291 Ark 105, 722 SW2d 584 (1987).

Marino's employer could not sue for the loss of Marino's services. The lower court rejected this defense. Marino's employer appealed.

STATON, J. . . . Although the United States became politically emancipated from Great Britain in the late eighteenth century, it did not divorce itself culturally from the mother country. Among the cultural baggage retained by our infant nation was the English common law system. The basis of our present system of jurisprudence, the Anglo-Saxon common law consisted of principles and rules of law which arose and were perpetuated in the judgments and decrees of the English courts, and which were founded upon usages and customs of antiquity. One such rule of law gave rise to an action *per quod servitium amisit*. Literally, "whereby he lost the service," Blackstone described the cause of action as follows:

A master also may bring an action against any man for beating or maiming his servant: but in such a case he must assign, as a special reason for so doing, his own damage by the loss of his service; and the loss must be proved upon the trial. . . .

The action *per quod servitium amisit* was borrowed by the English from the early Roman law. The Roman *actio iniuriarum* seeking recovery for injury to members of a household could only be brought by the head of the household—the *paterfamilias*. The Roman view of the household was broad, and included relatives, dependents, and slaves, all of which were closely identified with the *paterfamilias*. In incorporating this notion into the common law, the English allowed both a direct action for injury to a servant or another under the master's power, as well as an indirect action for the consequential loss of his services. . . . Thus, the action gained acceptance in the time when the master had a proprietary interest in the servant, acquired through the hiring of the servant and purchased through the payment of his wages. . . .

Over time, the makeup of society changed, and the English courts found that the rationale underlying the action *per quod servitium amisit* was no longer viable. The modern employment relation in England, as in the United States, does not depend upon status but arises out of a contract between the "master" and the "servant." . . .

Courts in this country began to note that the rationale for the action for negligent injury to a servant or employee no longer rang true on today's society. The number of states which recognize the action has been gradually decreasing, with many courts noting the trend toward nonrecognition of the action and the repudiation of the action in the country of its origin. . . .

Merrillville Toyota argues that Indiana has adopted the English common law as part of the hierarchy of laws in the State of Indiana, which we must follow. . . . We agree that decisions should be governed by precedent, but when the reasons for a rule of law cease to exist, the rule should be discontinued. . . . It is the duty of the court to investigate the wisdom of precedents established many years ago. . . .

Permitting employers to recover for loss of profits for negligent injury to their employees would result in a multiplicity of actions out of the same tortious act. The overwhelming majority of people in today's society are employed, and thus for nearly every injury another possible claim and another possible party would become a factor in the average lawsuit. . . .

Thus, already overloaded court dockets and burgeoning litigation costs would be augmented by the recognition of the action. . . .

We conclude that the trial court should have granted Morton's motion to dismiss Merrillville Toyota's claim for loss of Marino's services due to the negligence of a third party. Accordingly, we reverse, and remand to the trial court with instructions that the motion to dismiss be granted.

[Judgment reversed and action remanded]

QUESTIONS

1. How would the court have decided the case if Marino had been a cook in a private home?
2. What social forces are advanced by the *Morton* case?
3. Assume that a defendant intentionally injures the key research employee in order to damage the employer of that employee. Would the *Morton* court allow the employer to sue the defendant for damages?

expedient in the situation. Often the law will strive to make its rules fit the business practices of society. For example, a signature is frequently regarded by the law as including a stamping, printing, or typewriting of a name, in recognition of the business practice of signing letters and other instruments by mechanical means. A requirement of a handwritten signature would impose a burden on business that would not be practically expedient.

With the advent of the computer, the law of evidence has changed to allow a computer printout to be admitted in evidence. The old law was that records could not be produced in court unless the person who prepared them was present as a witness.

5. Conflicting Objectives

The specific objectives of the law sometimes conflict with each other. When this is true, the problem is one of social policy. This means social, economic, and moral forces are weighed to determine which objective should be furthered.

At times, a conflict develops between the objective of the state in seeking protection from the conduct of individuals or groups and the objective of freedom of action of those individuals and groups. For example, although protection of the freedom of the individual seeks the utmost freedom of religious belief, society will impose limitations on religious freedom where it believes such freedom will cause harm to the public welfare. Hence, state laws requiring vaccination against smallpox were enforced despite the contention that this violated religious principles. A court may order a necessary blood transfusion for an immature child who opposes it on religious grounds.[14] Similarly, parents failing to provide medical care for a sick child will be held guilty of manslaughter if the child dies, even though the parents sincerely believed as a matter of religious principle that medical care was improper. In contrast, when the harm contemplated is not direct or acute, religious freedom will prevail. For example, a compulsory child education law will not be enforced against Amish parents who as a matter of religion are opposed to state education.[15] A statute may constitutionally authorize owners of mobile parks to adopt a rule limiting residence within

---

[14] Re Long Island Jewish Medical Center, 557 NYS2d 239 (1990).
[15] Wisconsin v Yoder, 406 US 205 (1972) (high school student).

the park to adults, even though this limits the freedom of action of nonadults.[16]

As another example of conflicting objectives, that of protecting title may conflict with the objective of furthering trade. Consider again the example of the stolen property that was sold by the thief to a person who purchased it for value and in good faith, without reason to know that the goods had been stolen. If we are to further the objective of protecting the title to the property, we will conclude that the owner can recover the property from the innocent purchaser. This rule, however, will discourage trade, for people will be less willing to buy goods if they run the risk that the goods were stolen and may have to be surrendered. If we instead think only of taking steps to encourage buying and selling, we will hold that the buyer takes a good title because the buyer acted in good faith and paid value. If we do this, we then destroy the title of the original owner and obviously abandon our objective of protecting title to property. As a general rule, American society has followed the objective of protecting title. In some instances, however, the objective of furthering trade is adopted by statute and the buyer is given good title, as in certain cases of commercial paper (notes, drafts, and checks) or of the purchaser from a regular dealer in other people's goods.

6. Law as an Evolutionary Process

Law changes as society changes. Let us consider an example of this type of change. When the economy was patterned on a local community unit in which everyone knew each other and each other's product, the concept of "let the buyer beware" expressed a proper basis on which to conduct business. Much of the early law of the sale of goods was based on this view. In today's economy, however, with its interstate, national, and even international character, the buyer has little or no direct contact with the manufacturer or seller, and the

packaging of articles makes their presale examination impossible. Under these circumstances, the consumer must rely on the integrity of others. Gradually, practices that were tolerated and even approved in an earlier era have been condemned, and the law has changed to protect the buyer.

Moreover, new principles of law are being developed to meet new situations that arise. Every new invention and every new business practice introduces a number of situations for which there may be no existing rule of law. For example, how could there have been a law relating to stocks and bonds before those instruments came into existence? How could there have been a law with respect to the liability of radio and television broadcasters before such methods of communication were developed?

New inventions and new techniques for investigation have changed or produced new rules of law because it has become possible to prove facts that could not have been proven before. Thus, fingerprint identification, ballistics, and advanced chemical analysis techniques have made identification a certainty. The use of radar to determine speed is now commonplace. Within the last decade, the DNA or genetic fingerprint test for identity of blood cells has become generally recognized as a highly reliable means of proving identity.[17]

7. The Courts and the Making of the Law

In the early days of our country, courts were thought to merely declare the law. That is, they were to apply existing law to existing facts. They had no power to make new law.

Since the 1930s, it has been recognized and accepted that courts do make the law. Changing technology and cultural patterns produce new situations for which there is no law. A strict court will wait until the lawmaker passes

---

[16] Schmidt v Superior Court, 48 Cal 3d 438, 256 Cal Rptr 766, 769 P2d 948 (1989).

[17] Andrews v Florida (Fla App) 533 So 2d 841 (1988). (Expert testified that the chance that two persons would show the same on the DNA test was 1 out of 839,914,540.)

a law. The liberal court will create a new rule to fill the gap. Similarly, the rule of law followed by a former court may appear outmoded in the light of the new technology and cultural pattern. Here the strict court will follow the former decision until the lawmaker makes a change. The liberal court will take charge and make the change by revising the earlier decision. During the last three decades, more and more courts adopted the liberal approach, and their opinions openly recognized that they were making law to advance one or more of the social forces discussed in Section 4 of this chapter.

The extent to which courts can make the law is, of course, limited by existing statutes and constitutions. These cannot be ignored by the courts. In many instances, however, the courts may reinterpret the statute or constitution so that the net result is the same as if they were amended.

8. Law as a Synthesis

Many rules of law do not further one objective alone. Some rules advance a combination of two or more objectives, with each objective working toward the same result. In other instances, the objectives oppose each other, and the rule of law that emerges is a combination or synthesis of the different objectives.

Law as a synthesis may be illustrated by the law as it relates to a contract for the sale of a house. Originally, such a contract could be oral, that is, merely spoken words with nothing in writing to prove that there was such a contract. Of course, there was the practical question of proof—the question of whether the jury would believe that there was such a contract—but no rule of law said that the contract had to be evidenced by a writing. This situation made it possible for a witness in court to swear falsely that Jones had agreed to sell Jones's house for a specified sum. Even though Jones had not made such an agreement, the jury might believe the false witness, and Jones would be required to give up the house on terms to which Jones had never agreed. To prevent such a miscarriage of justice, a statute was passed declaring that con-

tracts for the sale of houses had to be evidenced by a writing.

This law ended the evil of persons lying that there was an oral agreement for the sale of a house, but was justice achieved? Not always, since cases arose in which Jones did in fact make an oral agreement to sell land to Smith. Smith would take possession of the land and would make valuable improvements at great expense and effort, and then Jones would have Smith thrown off the land. Smith would defend on the ground that Jones had orally agreed to sell the land. Jones would then say, "Where is the writing that the statute requires?" To this, Smith could only reply there was no writing. No writing meant no binding legal agreement, and therefore Smith lost the land, leaving Jones with the land and all the improvements that Smith had made. That certainly was not just.

Gradually, the courts developed the rule that even though the statute required a writing, the courts would enforce an oral contract for the sale of land under the following circumstances. When the buyer had gone into possession and made valuable improvements of such a nature that it would be difficult to determine what amount of money would make up the loss to the buyer if the buyer were to be put off the land, the oral contract was enforceable.

Thus, the law passed through three stages, as illustrated in Figure 2-3. The original concept held that all land contracts could be oral and did not require any written evidence. Because the perjury evil arose under that rule, the law swung to the opposite rule that no such contract could be oral without any written evidence. This rule gave rise to the hardship case of the honest buyer under an oral contract who made extensive improvements. The law then swung back, not to the original rule, but to a middle position. This middle position combined the writing requirement as to the ordinary transaction, but allowed oral contracts in special cases to prevent hardship.

This example is also interesting because it shows the way that the courts amend the law by decision. The flat requirement of the statute was eroded by an exception created by the courts in the interest of furthering justice.

SUMMARY

A society's ethical code constitutes the foundation on which its laws are built. In contrast to ethics, however, the law must be more definite and stable to be enforceable. Nevertheless, a society's evolving ethical code can serve as a blueprint for the future pattern of its laws.

Some of the underlying principles that society regards as important in making its ethical decisions and formulating its laws include: protection of the state; protection of the person; protection of public health, safety, and morals; protection of property and title; freedom of personal action; freedom of use of property; enforcement of intent; protection from exploitation, fraud, and oppression; furtherance of trade; creditor protection; debtor rehabilitation; stability; flexibility; and practical expediency. These concerns sometimes conflict with one another and so, as laws are created and evolve, society is continually seeking a proper balance or synthesis of its ultimate objectives.

LAW IN PRACTICE

1. In your dealings recognize the social forces involved, as these determine what society and the law think is right and what is wrong.
2. Analyze facts objectively. Avoid the pitfall of regarding what benefits you as "right" and what benefits the other party as "wrong."
3. In making long-term contracts, try to anticipate changes in the importance the future will assign to the social forces involved. This may suggest the inclusion in your contract of escape clauses or flexible clauses to meet changes.
4. Recognize that the courts to a very large extent make the law; therefore, seek the selection of qualified persons as judges.
5. Recognize that the best protection you have is the integrity of the person with whom you deal.

Figure 2-3   Synthesis and the Law—the Oral Contract for the Sale of Land

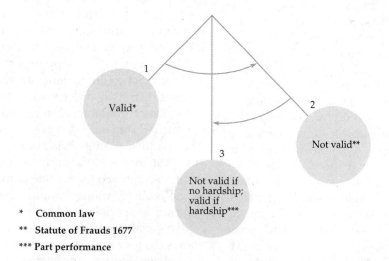

    *   **Common law**

  **   **Statute of Frauds 1677**

*** **Part performance**

QUESTIONS AND CASE PROBLEMS

1. What social force is involved in the rule that a professional association cannot arbitrarily exclude a person from membership?

2. The social force in favor of freedom of personal action permits you to say anything you wish. Appraise the statement.

3. A 13-year-old girl went to a party at the home of her friend. She lied to her parents about where she had been. When they learned the truth, the father beat her severely with a belt while the mother stood by. The State Department of Social Services began a proceeding against the parents for violation of the state's child abuse law. The parents raised the defense that they were guided by the Bible (Proverbs 23:13-14), and the state law was therefore a violation of their religious liberty. Was this defense valid? Why or why not? *[South Carolina Department of Social Services v Father and Mother (App) 294 SC 518, 366 SE2d 40]*

4. Of the specific objectives of the law, which do you consider to be the most important? Why?

5. McCarthy owned a motor scooter. He obtained an insurance policy from the Foundation Reserve Insurance Company. This policy covered medical expenses when the insured was "struck by an automobile." McCarthy rode his scooter into an automobile. The insurance company refused to pay his medical expenses on the ground that he had struck the automobile and had not been struck by an automobile. What social forces are involved in deciding the case?

6. The Reader's Digest Association published an article on truck hijacking. In the article it stated that John Doe, giving his actual name, had taken part in a truck hijacking 11 years before and had thereafter reformed. John Doe sued the Reader's Digest Association for damages. Reader's Digest Association raised the defense that it was not liable because the information was true. What was the theory on which John Doe sued? What social forces are involved? Is John Doe's claim valid?

7. Lopez wrote bad checks on the United Bank of Pueblo and on the Colorado National Bank. He was prosecuted for the crime of issuing bad checks. The prosecution offered in evidence bank statements obtained from the two banks showing the condition of the accounts of Lopez. He objected to this evidence, which would show that his checks were bad, on the ground that his right of privacy was violated when the banks furnished the statements. Decide. *[Colorado v Lopez (Colo) 776 P2d 390]*

8. Every rule of law is designed to further the attainment of justice. Appraise this statement.

9. The New York Social Services Law authorized the Social Services officials to replace necessary furniture and clothing of welfare recipients who lost such items by fire, flood, or other like catastrophe. Howard was on state welfare. Her clothing was stolen from her apartment by a burglar. She claimed that this was a catastrophe and that the Social Service official was required to replace the stolen clothing. Was she correct? Why or why not? *[Re Howard, 28 NY2d 434, 271 NE2d 528]*

10. The U.S. Congress has passed several laws aimed at preventing the sale of narcotics and harmful drugs. One of these laws makes it illegal for an unauthorized person to sell or supply marijuana or LSD. Judith Kuch was prosecuted for violating this act. She admitted that she had transferred the substances covered by the act and that she did not have a license as required by the act. She claimed, however, that she was protected by religious freedom. She was, in fact, an ordained minister of the Neo-American Church, and the substances were used by her only as part of the religious services in her church. Decide.

11. As you read the explanation of how modern scientific tests work, you will become impressed with the fact that only people working in science can understand the way the tests work. [See, for example, the explanation of the DNA (genetic fingerprint) test in *Andrews v Florida* (Fla App) 533 So 2d 841 (1988).] The result is that the typical jury will accept the conclusion of the expert. In a case that turns on the identity of a wrongdoer, the net result is that it is the expert and not the jury that determines that the defendant is the person who is guilty or who is at fault. Discuss the ethical implications.

12. The Federal Railroad Administration adopted regulations requiring railroads to make drug and alcohol tests of railroad employees involved in major train accidents and authorizing railroads to require such tests of employees violating certain safety rules. Several railroad unions brought an action against Skinner, the Secretary of Transportation, to prohibit such tests. The grounds for the objections were that no search warrant would have been obtained and there was no requirement that there be reason to suspect that the employee tested was under the influence of drugs or alcohol. Were the drug and alcohol tests lawful? Why or why not? *[Skinner v Railway Labor Executives' Ass'n. 489 US 602]*

13. A 31-year-old quadriplegic was kept alive by the use of a respirator. He was competent but was afraid of what would happen if his only surviving parent should die. He petitioned the court to order the discontinuance of the respirator to permit him to die. Do you think the court should grant permission? What social force is involved? *[Mckay v Bergstedt, ___ Nev ___, 801 P2d 617]*

14. Robertson was an adult. He drove to Todd's Tavern where he became drunk. On driving away, he was involved in a one-car accident in which he alone was injured. His insurance company, the Ohio Casualty Insurance Company, brought an action against Todd to enforce Robertson's claim against Todd. Was Todd liable for Robertson's injury? What social force would be furthered by a finding that the tavern was not liable? *[Ohio Cas. Ins. Co. v Todd (Okla) 813 P2d 508]*

15. In Illinois, a prostitute, Jane Doe, was charged with the felony of transmitting HIV (human immunodeficiency virus) that leads into AIDS. The television station KSDK wanted to telecast her name and the result of the HIV test that she had taken. To do this, court permission had to be obtained because the Illinois AIDS Confidentiality Act prohibited making known the result of an HIV test unless there was a compelling need to make such disclosure. The application for permission was opposed on the ground that it would invade the privacy of Jane Doe and was barred by the AIDS Confidentiality Act. The criminal proceedings brought against Jane Doe had been brought against her in her actual name. Should the court permit the television station to disclose her actual name and HIV status? What social forces would be furthered by disclosure? by nondisclosure? *[Application of Multimedia KSDK, Inc., ___ Ill ___, ___ Ill Dec ___, 581 NE2d 911]*

CHAPTER 3

THE CONSTITUTION AS THE FOUNDATION OF THE LEGAL ENVIRONMENT

LEARNING OBJECTIVES

After studying this chapter, you will be able to:
1. *Describe the governmental system created by the U.S. Constitution.*
2. *List the branches and levels of government and describe their relationship to each other.*
3. *Explain how the U.S. Constitution adapts to change.*
4. *List and describe three significant federal powers.*
5. *List and describe two significant constitutional limitations on governmental power.*

This chapter introduces you to the powers of government and to the protection that you have for your rights. The Constitution of the United States sets forth not only the structure and powers of government but also limitations on those powers. This Constitution, together with the constitutions of each of the states, forms the foundation of our legal environment.

A. THE FEDERAL SYSTEM

By creating a central government to coexist with the governments of the individual states, the U.S. Constitution created a federal system. In a **federal system**, a central government is given power to administer to national concerns, while the individual states retain the power to administer to local concerns.

1. What a Constitution Is

The term **constitution** refers to either the structure of the government and its relation to the people within its sphere of power or the written document setting forth that structure. When capitalized, the word refers to the written document that specifies the structure and powers of the U.S. national government and its relation to the people within the territory of the United States.

In speaking of the Constitution, it is often necessary to distinguish between the written Constitution and the living Constitution. This is required because the Constitution has grown and changed, as described in Section 7 of this chapter.

2. The Branches of Government

The written Constitution establishes a **tripartite** (three-part) division of government. That is, there is a **legislative branch** (Congress) to make the laws, an **executive branch** (the president) to execute the laws, and a **judicial branch** (courts) to interpret the laws. The national legislature or Congress is a **bicameral** (two-house) body consisting of a Senate and a House of Representatives. Members of the

Senate are popularly elected for a term of six years. Members of the House of Representatives are popularly elected for a term of two years. The president is elected by an Electoral College whose membership is popularly elected. The president serves for a term of four years and is eligible for reelection for a second term. Judges of the United States are appointed by the president with the approval of the Senate and serve for life, subject to removal only by impeachment because of misconduct.

B. THE STATES AND THE CONSTITUTION

The effect of the adoption of the Constitution was to take certain powers away from the states and to give them to the national government.

3. Delegated and Shared Powers

The national government possesses only the powers given by the states. These powers are set forth in the U.S. Constitution.

(a) DELEGATED POWERS. The powers given by the states to the national government are described as **delegated powers**. Some of these delegated powers are given exclusively to the national government. Thus, the national government alone may declare war or establish a currency.

(b) SHARED POWERS. Some of the powers delegated to the national government may still be exercised by the states. For example, the grant of power to the national government to impose taxes did not destroy the state power to tax. Some of the shared powers may only be exercised by the states as long as there is no federal exercise. Thus, a state safety appliance law may apply until a federal law on the subject is adopted by Congress. In other cases, a state may provide regulation along with, but subject to the supremacy of, federal law. Regulation of navigation on navigable waterways within a state is an example.

Figure 3-1   Governments of the United States

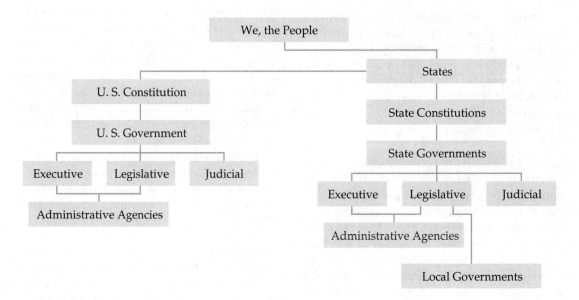

(c) STATE POLICE POWER. The states possess the power to adopt laws to protect the general welfare, health, safety, and morals of the people. This is called the **police power**. Thus, a state may require that an out-of-state business make a security deposit with a state official in order to protect persons dealing with the business from loss.[1] The exercise of the police power is subject to the limitation that it may not unreasonably interfere with the federal powers.

(d) PROHIBITED POWERS. The Constitution prohibits states from doing certain acts, even though the federal government is also similarly prohibited. Thus, neither states nor the national government may adopt ex post facto laws. **Ex post facto** laws make criminal an act already committed that was not criminal when committed. Laws that increase the penalty for an act already committed above the penalty in force at the time the act was committed are also ex post facto laws.

4. Federal Supremacy

Federal law will bar conflicting state action when there is a federal law regulating the particular subject. Federal law will also bar state action when the silence of Congress is seen as showing the congressional intent that there should be no regulation by anyone.

(a) EXPRESS FEDERAL REGULATION. The Constitution and statutes properly adopted by Congress are the supreme law of the land. They cancel out any conflicting state law.

This federal supremacy is expressly declared by the Constitution.[2] When there is a direct conflict between federal and state statutes, the

---

[1] American Network, Inc. v Washington Utilities and Transportation Commission, 113 Wash 2d 59, 776 P2d 950 (1989).

[2] US Const, Art VI, Cl 2. Michigan Canners and Freezers Assn., Inc. v Agricultural Marketing and Bargaining Board, 467 US 461 (1984)

decision as to which prevails is thus easy to make.

In some cases, there is no obvious conflict because the federal statute covers only part of the subject matter. In such cases, the question arises whether a state law can regulate the areas not regulated by Congress or whether the partial regulation made by Congress preempts, or takes over, the field so as to prohibit state legislation.

(b) SILENCE OF CONGRESS. In some situations, the silence of Congress in failing to cover a particular phase of the subject, or in failing to have any law on the subject at all, is held to indicate that Congress does not want any law on the matter. Therefore, no state law will be allowed to regulate the matter. When national uniformity is essential, it is generally held that the silence of Congress means that the subject has been preempted by Congress and that no state law on the subject may be adopted.

C. INTERPRETING AND AMENDING THE CONSTITUTION

The Constitution as it is interpreted today has changed greatly from the Constitution as originally written. The change has been brought about by interpretation, amendment, and practice.

5. Conflicting Theories

Shortly after the Constitution was adopted, conflict arose over whether the Constitution was to be interpreted strictly, so as to give the federal government the least power possible, or broadly, so as to give the federal government the greatest power that the words would permit. These two views may be given the names of the bedrock view and the living document view, respectively.

By the *bedrock view*, the purpose of a constitution is to state certain fundamental principles for all time. By the *living document view*, a constitution is merely a statement of goals and objectives and is intended to grow and change with time.

Whether the Constitution is to be liberally interpreted, under the living document view, or narrowly interpreted, under the bedrock view, has a direct effect on the Constitution. For the last century, the Supreme Court has followed the living document view. This has resulted in strengthening the power of the federal government, permitting the rise of administrative agencies, and expanding the protection of human rights. The living document view has given us the living Constitution described in Section 7 of this chapter. The living document view was first stated by the United States Supreme Court in the *McCulloch* case.

McCULLOCH v MARYLAND
4 Wheat 316 (1819)

The first bank of the United States was chartered in 1791 and again in 1816. Hostile state legislation attempted to drive it out of existence. In 1818, Maryland adopted a law imposing a tax on bank notes issued by any bank not chartered by the state legislature. McCulloch, the cashier of the Baltimore branch of the National Bank, issued bank notes on which this tax had not been paid. Suit was brought by the state of Maryland against him to recover the statutory penalties imposed for violation of the statute.

MARSHALL, C. J. . . . The first question . . . is, has Congress power to incorporate a bank? . . .

This government of the Union . . . is acknowledged by all to be one of enumerated powers. . . .

Among the enumerated powers, we do not find that of establishing a bank or creating a corporation. . . . A constitution, to contain an accurate detail of all the subdivisions of which its great powers will admit, and of all the means by which they may be carried into execution, would partake of the prolixity of a legal code, and could scarcely be embraced by the human mind. It would probably never be understood by the public. Its nature, therefore, requires, that only its great outlines should be marked, its important objects designated, and the minor ingredients which compose those objects be deduced from the nature of the objects themselves. . . .

Although, among the enumerated powers of government, we do not find the word "bank" or "incorporation," we find the great powers to lay and collect taxes; to borrow money; to regulate commerce; to declare and conduct a war; and to raise and support armies and navies. The sword and the purse, all the external relations, and no inconsiderable portion of the industry of the nation, are intrusted to its government. . . . A government, intrusted with such ample powers, on the due execution of which the happiness and prosperity of the nation so vitally depends, must also be intrusted with ample means for their execution. The power being given, it is the interest of the nation to facilitate its execution. . . . Can we adopt that construction [of the Constitution] (unless the words imperiously require it) which would impute to the framers of that instrument, when granting these powers for the public good, the intention of impeding their exercise by withholding a choice of means? If, indeed, such be the mandate of the Constitution, we have only to obey; but that instrument does not profess to enumerate the means by which the powers it confers may be executed; nor does it prohibit the creation of a corporation, if the existence of such a being be essential to the beneficial exercise of those powers. It is, then, the subject of fair inquiry, how far such means may be employed. . . .

The government which has a right to do an act, and has imposed on it the duty of performing that act, must, according to the dictates of reason, be allowed to select the means; and those who contend that it may not select any appropriate means, that one particular mode of effecting the object is excepted, take upon themselves the burden of establishing that exception. . . .

But the Constitution of the United States has not left the right of Congress to employ the necessary means, for the execution of the powers conferred on the government, to general reasoning. To its enumeration of powers is added that of making "all laws which shall be necessary and proper, for carrying into execution the foregoing powers, and all other powers vested by this Constitution, in the government of the United States, or in any department thereof."

. . . This provision is made in a constitution intended to endure for ages to come, and, consequently, to be adapted to the various crises of human affairs. To have prescribed the means by which government should, in all future time, execute its powers, would have been to change, entirely, the character of the instrument, and give it the properties of a legal code. It would have been an unwise attempt to provide, by immutable rules, for exigencies which, if foreseen at all, must have been seen dimly, and which can be best provided for as they occur. [The Court rejected the contention that "necessary" means "absolutely necessary."] . . . Sound construction of the Constitution must allow to the national legislature that discretion, with respect to the means by which the powers it confers are to be carried into execution, which will enable that body to perform the high duties assigned to it, in the manner most beneficial to the people. Let the end be legitimate, let it be within the scope of the Constitution, and all means which are appropriate, which are plainly adapted to that end, which are not prohibited, but consist with the letter and spirit of the Constitution, are constitutional.

. . . It can scarcely be necessary to say, that the existence of state banks can have no possible influence on the question. No trace is to be found in the Constitution of an intention to create a dependence of the government of the Union on those of the states, for the execution of the great powers assigned to it. . . . The choice of means implies a right to choose a national bank in preference to state banks, and Congress alone can make the election.

[Judgment against Maryland on the basis that, as Congress had authority to create a bank, a state law designed to harm that bank was unconstitutional. Therefore Maryland could not recover the penalty authorized by that state statute]

QUESTIONS

1. What section of the Constitution authorizes Congress to create a national bank?
2. Does the Court say that the creation of a national bank system is the best way to do the job?

Can we decide that we should adopt the bedrock view or the living document view? We cannot select one view to the exclusion of the other for the simple reason that we want both. Contradictory as this sounds, it is obvious that we want our Constitution to be durable. We do not want a set of New Year's resolutions that will soon be forgotten. At the same time, we know that the world changes, and therefore we do not want a constitution that will hold us tied in a straitjacket of the past.

In terms of social forces that make the law, we are torn between our desire for stability and our desire for flexibility. We want a constitution that is stable. At the same time, we want one that is flexible. That is why we have conflict.

If we do not see the conflict, we do not see the Constitution as it really is today. Even more important, we lack the understanding needed to meet the problems of tomorrow.

6. Amending the Constitution

The U.S. Constitution has been amended in three ways: (a) expressly, (b) by interpretation, and (c) by practice.

(a) CONSTITUTIONAL METHOD OF AMENDING. Article V of the Constitution sets forth the procedure to be followed for amending the Constitution. Relatively few changes have been made to the Constitution by this formal process, although thousands of proposals have been made.

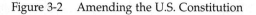

Figure 3-2   Amending the U.S. Constitution

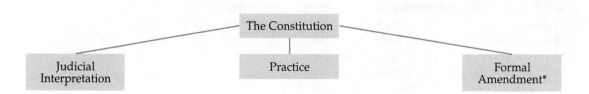

*** Article V of the U.S. Constitution specifies the procedure
for adopting amendments.**

(b) AMENDMENT BY JUDICIAL INTER-PRETATION. The greatest change to the written Constitution has been made by the Supreme Court in "interpreting" the Constitution. Generally, interpretation is used to apply the Constitution to a new situation that could not have been foreseen when the written Constitution was adopted.

(c) AMENDMENT BY PRACTICE. In practice, the letter of the Constitution is not always followed. Departure from the written Constitution began as early as 1793, when Washington refused to make treaties, as required by the Constitution, "by and with the consent of the Senate." Washington began the practice of the president's negotiating the treaty with the foreign country and then submitting it to the Senate for approval. This practice has been followed since that time. Similarly, the Electoral College was originally intended to exercise independent judgment in selecting the president. It now automatically elects the official candidate of the party that elected the members of the Electoral College.

Other aspects of practice have added to the Constitution things that are not there. As written, the Constitution contemplates that Congress will originate and adopt laws. With the rise of the party system, which was not anticipated by the framers of the Constitution, the president has become the leader of the legisla-tive program. This position of leadership has been strengthened greatly by the modern media, beginning with Roosevelt's radio "fire-side chats" of the 1930s and broadening into presidential television appearances in later years.

7. The Living Constitution

The Constitution that has developed in the manner described in the preceding section is radically different from the Constitution that was written on paper. The living Constitution has the following characteristics:

(a) STRONG GOVERNMENT. One of the characteristics of the new Constitution is strong government. Business enterprises can now be regulated and the economy controlled.

(b) STRONG PRESIDENT. Instead of being merely an officer who carries out the laws, the president has become the political leader of a party, exerting a strong influence on the lawmaking process. If the president's political party is in control of both houses of Congress, the president acts as the leader of the lawmaking process.

(c) ECLIPSE OF THE STATES. Under the new Constitution, all governments have powers that they never possessed before, but the center of gravity has shifted from the states to the nation. When the Constitution was adopted in 1789, the federal government was to have only the very limited powers specified in Article I, Section 8 of the Constitution. Whatever regulation of business was permissible was to be imposed by the states. Today, the great bulk of the regulation of business is adopted by the federal government through Congress or its administrative agencies. As the American economy moved from the local community stage to the nationwide stage, the individual states were unable to provide effective regulation of business. It was inevitable that regulation would be drawn to the central government. Consequently, when we speak of government regulation of business, we ordinarily mean the national government, not the state or local governments.

(d) ADMINISTRATIVE AGENCIES. These were virtually unheard of in 1789, and no mention is made of them in the Constitution of 1789. The vast powers of the new Constitution are exercised to a very large degree by administrative agencies. They are in effect a fourth branch of the government, not provided for in the written Constitution. More important, it is the administrative agencies that come in contact with the majority of businesspersons and citizens. The agencies are the "government" for most people.

In other words, the vast power of government to regulate business is not exercised directly by the legislatures, the courts, or the executive officers. Rather, this power is exercised by agencies. The members of the agencies—or the boards, commissions, or persons heading the agencies—are not elected by the voters. The decisions of agencies are to a large degree not subject to effective review or reversal by the courts.

(e) HUMAN RIGHTS. The scope of human rights protected from governments has dramatically broadened. These rights are protected from invasion by not merely the federal government but by any government. Most significant of all, unwritten rights are protected, although they are not guaranteed by any express constitutional provision.

D. FEDERAL POWERS

The federal government possesses powers necessary to administer matters of national concern.

8. Power to Regulate Commerce

The desire to protect commerce from restrictions and barriers set up by the individual states was a prime factor leading to the adoption of the Constitution of 1789. To protect commerce, Congress was given, by Article I, Section 8, Clause 3, the power "to regulate commerce with foreign nations, and among the several states, and with the Indian tribes."

Until 1937, the Supreme Court held that this provision gave Congress the power to control or regulate only that which crossed a state line, such as an interstate railway train or an interstate telegraph message.

(a) THE COMMERCE POWER BECOMES A GENERAL WELFARE POWER. In 1937, the Supreme Court began expanding the concept of interstate commerce. By 1946, the power to regulate interstate commerce had become very broad. By that year, the power had expanded to the point that it gave authority to Congress to adopt regulatory laws that were "as broad as the economic needs of the nation."[3] By virtue of this broad interpretation, Congress can regulate manufacturing, agriculture, mining, stock exchanges, insurance, loan sharking, monopolies, and conspiracies

---

[3] American Power & Light Co. v Securities and Exchange Commission, 329 US 90 (1946). The wide scope of this view is seen in such statutes as the Food, Agriculture, Conservation, and Trade Act of 1990. Act of November 28, 1990, PL 101-624, 104 Stat 3359. The provisions of this statute are allocated to numerous sections of Titles 7 and 16 of USC.

in restraint of trade. If desired, Congress can set standards, quotas, and priorities for industries.

The case that was the starting point in this transition of the commerce clause was the *Jones & Laughlin Steel Corporation* case.

NLRB v JONES & LAUGHLIN STEEL CORP.
301 US 1 (1937)

> The National Labor Relations Board found that Jones & Laughlin Steel Corporation had discharged ten employees to discourage membership in a union. The Board ordered these employees reinstated with full back pay and ordered that the employer cease and desist from such conduct. When the employer failed to comply with the order, the Board petitioned the court of appeals to enforce the order. The court of appeals denied the petition, holding that the Board's order exceeded federal power. The Supreme Court granted certiorari.

HUGHES, C. J. . . . The scheme of the National Labor Relations Act . . . may be briefly stated. The first section sets forth findings with respect to the injury to commerce resulting from the denial by employers of the right of employees to organize and from the refusal of employers to accept the procedure of collective bargaining. There follows a declaration that it is the policy of the United States to eliminate these causes of obstruction to the free flow of commerce. The Act then defines the terms it uses, including the terms "commerce" and "affecting commerce." Section 2. It creates the National Labor Relations Board and prescribes its organization. Sections 3-6. It sets forth the right of employees to self-organization and to bargain collectively through representatives of their own choosing. Section 7. It defines "unfair labor practices." Section 8. It lays down rules as to the representation of employees for the purpose of collective bargaining. Section 9. The Board is empowered to prevent the described unfair labor practices affecting commerce and the Act prescribes the procedure to that end. . . .

. . . The respondent [Jones & Laughlin Steel Corp.] argues (1) that the Act is in reality a regulation of labor relations and not of interstate commerce; . . .

The facts as to the nature and scope of the business of the Jones & Laughlin Steel Corporation have been found by the Labor Board.

[The Court discussed in detail the interstate organization of the employer with various plants in different states.]

Summarizing these operations, the Labor Board concluded that the works in Pittsburgh and Aliquippa "might be likened to the heart of a self-contained, highly integrated body. They draw in the raw materials from Michigan, Minnesota, West Virginia, Pennsylvania in part through arteries and by means controlled by the respondent; they transform the materials and then pump them out to all parts of the nation through the vast mechanism which the respondent has elaborated."

. . . The Scope of the Act.—The Act is challenged in its entirety as an attempt to regulate all industry, thus invading the reserved powers of the States over their local concerns. . . .

. . . The grant of authority to the Board does not purport to extend to the relationship between all industrial employees and employers. Its terms do not impose collective bargaining upon all industry regardless of effects upon interstate or foreign commerce. It purports to reach only what may be deemed to burden or obstruct that commerce and, thus qualified, it must be construed as contemplating the exercise of control within constitutional bounds. It is a familiar principle that acts which directly burden or obstruct interstate or foreign commerce, or its free flow, are within the reach of the congressional power. Acts having that effect are not rendered immune because they grow out of labor disputes. . . . It is the effect upon commerce, not the source of the injury, which is the criterion. Whether or not particular action does affect commerce in such a close and intimate fashion as to be subject to federal control, and hence to lie within the authority conferred upon the Board, is left by the statute to be determined as individual cases arise. . . .

. . . Although activities may be intrastate in character when separately considered, if they have such a close and substantial relation to interstate commerce that their control is essential or appropriate to protect that commerce from burdens and obstructions, Congress cannot be denied the power to exercise that control.

. . . The stoppage of [respondent's] operations by industrial strife would have a most serious effect upon interstate commerce. In view of respondent's far-flung activities, it is idle to say that the effect would be indirect or remote. It is obvious that it would be immediate and might be catastrophic. We are asked to shut our eyes to the plainest facts of our national life and to deal with the question of direct and indirect effects in an intellectual vacuum. Because there may be but indirect and remote effects upon interstate commerce in connection with a host of local enterprises throughout the country, it does not follow that other industrial activities do not have such a close and intimate relation to interstate commerce as to make the presence of industrial strife a matter of the most urgent national concern. When industries organize themselves on a national scale, making their relation to interstate commerce the dominant factor in their activities, how can it be maintained that their industrial labor relations constitute a forbidden field into which Congress may not enter when it is necessary to protect interstate commerce from the paralyzing consequences of industrial war? We have often said that interstate commerce itself is a practical conception. It is equally true that interferences with that commerce must be appraised by a judgment that does not ignore actual experience.

Experience has abundantly demonstrated that the recognition of the right of employees to self-organization and to have representatives of their own choosing for the purpose of collective bargaining is often an essential condition of industrial peace. Refusal to confer and negotiate has been one of the most prolific causes of strife. . . . And of what avail is it to protect the facility of transportation, if interstate commerce is throttled with respect to the commodities to be transported!

. . . It is not necessary again to detail the facts as to respondent's enterprise. . . . It presents in a most striking way the close and intimate relation which [an] industry may have to interstate commerce, and we have no doubt that Congress had constitutional authority. . . .

> *[The National Labor Relations Act was constitutional as applied to the respondent steel company and was within the scope of the power of Congress over interstate commerce]*
>
> QUESTIONS
>
> 1. What statute was involved in the *Jones & Laughlin Steel Corp.* case?
> 2. Was the decision of the Court inevitable?
> 3. Why was it important to hold that the labor relations affected interstate commerce?

(b) THE COMMERCE POWER AS A LIMITATION ON STATES. The federal power to regulate commerce not only gives Congress the power to act but also prevents states from acting in any way that interferes with federal regulation or burdens interstate commerce. For example, if the federal government establishes safety device regulations for interstate carriers, a state cannot require different devices.

Because modern commerce is typically interstate in character, the fact that Congress does not impose any regulation is generally interpreted as excluding state action with respect to interstate commerce.

States may not use their tax power for the purpose of discriminating against interstate commerce, since such commerce is within the protection of the national government. For example, a state cannot impose a higher tax on goods imported from another state than it imposes on the same kind of goods produced in its own territory.

The fact that a local law may have some effect on out-of-state markets does not mean that the local law is unconstitutional as a burden on interstate commerce.

State regulations designed to advance local interests may come into conflict with the interstate commerce clause. In that case, they are invalid.

9. The Financial Powers

The financial powers of the federal government include the powers to tax, borrow, spend, and coin money.

(a) THE TAXING POWER. The federal Constitution provides that "Congress shall have power to lay and collect taxes, duties, imposts and excises, to pay the debts and provide for the common defense and general welfare of the United States. . . ."[4] Subject to the express and implied limitations arising from the Constitution, the states may impose such taxes as they desire and as their own individual constitutions and statutes permit. In addition to express constitutional limitations, both national and local taxes are subject to the unwritten limitation that they be imposed for a public purpose.

The federal government is subject to certain limitations on the form of the taxes it imposes. Capitation or poll taxes and all direct taxes must be apportioned among the states according to their census-determined population.[5] Direct taxes include taxes on real estate or personal property and taxes imposed on persons because of their ownership of property. Income taxes, to the extent that they tax the income from property, are direct, although because of the Sixteenth Amendment, their apportionment is no longer required.

All other taxes imposed by the federal government are regarded as indirect taxes. These include customs duties, taxes on consumption

---

4 US Const, Art 1, Section 8, Cl 1.

5 US Const, Art 1, Section 8, Cl 4.

(such as gasoline and cigarette taxes), taxes on the exercise of a privilege (such as an amusement tax), taxes on the transmission of property at death (such as estate taxes), taxes on the privilege of making a gift, or taxes on the privilege of employing workers (such as the employer's social security tax). In the case of a federal tax on the exercise of a privilege, it is immaterial whether the privilege arises by virtue of a state or a federal law.

The only restriction on the form of indirect federal taxes is that they be uniform throughout the continental United States and the incorporated territories. This requirement of uniformity does not prohibit a progressively graduated tax, in which the greater the monetary value of the tax base, the greater the rate of tax. The requirement of uniformity also is not violated by a provision allowing credits against the federal tax for taxes paid to a state, even though the amount of the federal tax paid will vary from state to state, depending on the existence of a state tax for which credit is allowable.

The federal taxing power is subject to the implied limitation that state and municipal governments may not be directly taxed. In earlier years, this concept was interpreted to exempt from federal income tax any money received from state or local governments by private persons. This immunity of private persons has been destroyed by decisions of the Supreme Court. Now the federal income tax reaches income received by private persons working for or dealing with state and municipal governments. If Congress wishes, it may subject income from state and municipal bonds to the general federal income tax.[6]

(b) THE BORROWING POWER. Congress is authorized "to borrow money on the credit of the United States."[7] No limitation is prescribed to the purposes for which the United States can borrow.

Obligations of the United States issued to those lending money to the United States are binding. Congress cannot attempt to repudiate these obligations or to make them repayable in a less valuable currency than called for by the obligations without violating the legal rights of the holders.

The states have an inherent power to borrow money. State constitutions and statutes may impose a limit on the amount that can be borrowed. Frequently, these limitations can be evaded by the creation of independent authorities or districts that borrow money by issuing bonds. The bonded indebtedness of such independent authorities and districts is not regarded as a debt of the state and therefore is not subject to the limitations applicable to state borrowing.

(c) THE SPENDING POWER. The federal government may use tax money and borrowed money ". . . to pay the debts and provide for the common defense and general welfare of the United States."[8]

Congress may reduce federal funds that would otherwise be distributed to a state if that state has a drinking age lower than 21. The object of Congress in so doing is to eliminate the hazard of persons under 21 driving to the lower-age states, becoming drunk, and then becoming involved in highway accidents.[9]

(d) THE CURRENCY POWER. The Constitution authorizes Congress "to coin money, regulate the value thereof" and "provide for the punishment of counterfeiting the securities and . . . coin of the United States."[10] This federal power is made exclusive by prohibiting the states from coining money, emitting bills of credit, or making anything but gold

---

6 South Carolina v Baker, 485 US 505 (1988).

7 US Const, Art 1, Section 8, Cl 2.

8 US Const, Art 1, Section 8, Cl 1.

9 South Dakota v Dole, 483 US 203 (1987).

10 US Const, Art 1, Section 8, Cls 5, 6.

and silver coins legal tender in payment of debts.[11]

The national government can determine what shall be legal tender and is not restricted to the use of metallic money but may issue paper money.[12] Congress can establish whatever base it desires for paper currency and may change the base of existing currency.

10.   The Power to Own Businesses

In a sense, government ownership of what would ordinarily be deemed private business represents the ultimate in the regulation of private business.

(a) CONSTITUTIONALITY OF GOVERNMENT OWNERSHIP. Speaking generally, there is no constitutional barrier against state or federal government ownership and operation of businesses. It had formerly been assumed that there were certain purposes that were not public or for the general welfare. These purposes were distinguished from those that were public or for the general welfare. It is impossible today to draw such a line between public and private and to prohibit a government from entering into any particular business on the ground that to do so is not in furtherance of a public purpose or does not advance the general welfare.

(b) SALE AND DISTRIBUTION OF GOVERNMENT PRODUCTION. A government may sell or otherwise dispose of the products that the government-owned business manufactures. The power of a government to dispose of its property permits the government to compete with a private enterprise and to dispose of its products at any price it chooses, without regard to whether the price is below cost. No constitutional privilege of the private business is violated by being underpriced by the national, a state, or local government.[13]

E. CONSTITUTIONAL LIMITATIONS ON GOVERNMENT

The limitations discussed in the following sections are the limitations that are most important to the person and to business.

11. Due Process

The most important limitation on the power of government is that found in the Fifth and Fourteenth Amendments to the Constitution. Those amendments prohibit the national government and the state governments, respectively, from depriving any person of life, liberty, or property without due process of law.

(a) EXPANSION OF DUE PROCESS. As a result of liberal interpretation of the Constitution, the **due process clause** is now held to be a guarantee of protection from unreasonable procedures and unreasonable laws. It is also held to be a guarantee of equal protection of the law, and a guarantee of protection of significant interests. The Supreme Court has extended the due process clause to protect the record or standing of a student.

Through judicial construction, due process of law affords the individual a wide protection. However, the guarantee affords no protection when the matter is reasonably debatable. Therefore, due process of law does not bar the regulation of business, because any regulation that would have sufficient support to pass a legislature or the Congress would have sufficient claim to validity as to be debatable. The fact that many persons would deem the law unsound, unwise, hazardous, or un-American does not in itself make the law invalid under the due process clause.

Since the due process concept is a limitation on governmental action, it does not apply to transactions between private persons or to

---

[11] US Const, Art 1, Section 10.

[12] Julliard v Greenman, 110 US 421 (1884). Baird v County Assessors of Salt Lake and Utah Counties (Utah) 779 P2d 676 (1989).

[13] Puget Sound Power & Light Co. v Seattle, 291 US 619 (1934).

private employment or other nonpublic situations. In some cases, however, statutes, such as the federal Civil Rights Act and consumer protection laws, apply due process concepts to private transactions.

(b) SHORTCUT PROCEDURES. The delays of the law have often been a source of criticism. Shortcut procedures are inspired by the legitimate desire to speed up litigation and to give everyone easy access to a day in court. However, procedures must not be so streamlined that they deprive defendants of reasonable notice and an opportunity to be heard. In an era in which a defendant may be a resident or a business of a foreign state, statutes have generally been adopted to allow the plaintiff to sue a foreign defendant in the state where the plaintiff lives. These state statutes are subject to the limitation that they can be applied only when the defendant has such a relationship—for example, as by carrying on business—within the state of the plaintiff that it is reasonable to require the defendant to defend an action in the courts of the plaintiff's state. Conversely, if the defendant does not have such a reasonable relation to the plaintiff's state, it is a denial of due process to require the defendant to go to the plaintiff's state.

12. Equal Protection of the Law

The Constitution prohibits both the state and national governments from denying any person the equal protection of the law.[14] This guarantee prohibits a government from treating one person differently from another when there is no reasonable ground for classifying them differently.

In harmony with this concept of equality, it has been held that a wife may be held responsible for necessaries furnished to her husband.[15] This parallels the common law liability of the husband for necessaries furnished to the wife.

(a) REASONABLE CLASSIFICATION. The equal protection clause does not require that all persons be protected or treated equally, and a law is valid even though it does not apply to everyone or everything. Whether a classification is reasonable depends on whether the nature of the classification bears a reasonable relation to the evil to be remedied or to the object to be attained by the law. In determining this, the courts have been guided generally by considerations of historical treatment and by the logic of the situation. The trend is to permit the classification to stand as long as there is a rational basis for the distinction made.[16] This means that a statute will be sustained unless it is clear that the lawmaking body has been arbitrary or capricious.

(b) IMPROPER CLASSIFICATION. Laws that make distinctions in the regulation of business, the right to work, and the right to use or enjoy property on the basis of race, alienage, or religion are invalid. Also invalid are laws that impose restrictions on some but not all persons without any justification for the distinction.[17] A law prohibiting the ownership of land by aliens has been traditionally regarded as an exception to this rule. Large alien holdings of land is considered such a social evil that it justifies legislation directly prohibiting this. However, it appears that in the course of time, this discrimination may be declared invalid.[18] A state statute taxing out-of-state in-

---

[14] US Const, Fourteenth Amendment as to the states; modern interpretation of due process clause of Fifth Amendment as to national government. Congress has adopted the Civil Rights Act to implement the concept of equal protection. Newport News Shipbuilding and Dry Dock Co. v EEOC, 462 US 669 (1983).

[15] Webb v Hillsborough County Hospital Authority (Fla App) 521 So 2d 199 (1988).

[16] Urton v Hudson, 101 Or App 147, 790 P2d 12 (1990).

[17] Carey v Brown, 447 US 445 (1980).

[18] The alien land laws have been declared unconstitutional by the supreme courts of California, Montana, and Oregon, as being in violation of the Fourteenth Amendment of the U.S. Constitution.

surance companies at a higher rate than in-state insurance companies violates the equal protection clause.[19]

The lawmaker may not discriminate on the basis of moral standards and cultural patterns. People cannot be deprived of the same treatment given to other persons just because they do not have the same moral standards or cul-tural patterns as the lawmaker. Lawmakers cannot penalize people because they do not live, think, and dress the same as the law-makers. In the *Moreno* case, the validity of an entitlement plan was challenged by those who did not receive the benefits.

UNITED STATES DEPARTMENT OF AGRICULTURE v MORENO
413 US 528 (1973)

> The Federal Food Stamp Act provided for the distribution of food stamps to needy "households." In 1971, Section 3(e) of the statute was amended to define households as groups whose members were all related to each other. This was done because of congressional dislike for the life-styles of unrelated "hippies" who were living together in "hippie communes." Moreno and others applied for food stamps but were refused them because the relation-ship requirement was not satisfied. An action was brought to have the rela-tionship requirement declared unconstitutional. The lower court held the statute unconstitutional and the Department of Agriculture appealed.

BRENNAN, J. . . . Appellees [the applicants for the food stamps] . . . consist of sev-eral groups of individuals who allege that, although they satisfy the income eligibil-ity requirements for federal food assistance, they have nevertheless been excluded from the program solely because the persons in each group are not "all related to each other." Appellee Jacinta Moreno, for example, is a 56-year-old diabetic who lives with Ermina Sanchez and the latter's three children. They share common living expenses, and Mrs. Sanchez helps to care for appellee. Appellee's monthly income, derived from public assistance, is $75; Mrs. Sanchez receives $133 per month from public assistance. The household pays $135 per month for rent, gas, and electricity, of which appellee pays $50. Appellee spends $10 per month for transportation to a hospital for regular visits, and $5 per month for laundry. That leaves her $10 per month for food and other necessities. Despite her poverty, appellee has been denied federal food assistance solely because she is unrelated to the other members of her household. Moreover, although Mrs. Sanchez and her three children were permitted to purchase $108 worth of food stamps per month for $18, their participation in the program will be terminated if appellee Moreno continues to live with them.

Appellee Sheilah Hejny is married and has three children. Although the Hejnys are indigent, they took in a 20-year-old girl, who is unrelated to them, because "we felt she had emotional problems." The Hejnys receive $144 worth of food stamps

---

[19] Metropolitan Life Ins. Co. v Ward, 470 US 869 (1985).

each month for $14. If they allow the 20-year-old girl to continue to live with them, they will be denied food stamps by reason of Section 3(e).

Appellee Victoria Keppler has a daughter with an acute hearing deficiency. The daughter requires special instruction in a school for the deaf. The school is located in an area in which the appellee could not ordinarily afford to live. Thus, in order to make the most of her limited resources, appellee agreed to share an apartment near the school with a woman who, like appellee, is on public assistance. Since appellee is not related to the woman, appellee's food stamps will be cut off if they continue to live together. . . .

In essence, appellees contend, and the District Court held, that the "unrelated person" provision of Section 3(e) creates an irrational classification in violation of the equal protection component of the Due Process Clause of the Fifth Amendment. We agree.

Under traditional equal protection analysis, a legislative classification must be sustained if the classification itself is rationally related to a legitimate governmental interest. . . . The purposes of the Food Stamp Act were expressly set forth in the congressional "declaration of policy":

It is hereby declared to be the policy of Congress . . . to safeguard the health and well-being of the Nation's population and raise levels of nutrition among low-income households. The Congress hereby finds that the limited food purchasing power of low-income households contributes to hunger and malnutrition among members of such households. The Congress further finds that increased utilization of food in establishing and maintaining adequate national levels of nutrition will promote the distribution in a beneficial manner of our agricultural abundances and will strengthen our agricultural economy, as well as result in more orderly marketing and distribution of food. To alleviate such hunger and malnutrition, a food stamp program is herein authorized which will permit low-income households to purchase a nutritionally adequate diet through normal channels of trade.

The challenged statutory classification (households of related persons versus households containing one or more unrelated persons) is clearly irrelevant to the stated purposes of the Act. As the District Court recognized, "the relationships among persons constituting one economic unit and sharing cooking facilities have nothing to do with their ability to stimulate the agricultural economy by purchasing farm surpluses, or with their personal nutritional requirements." . . .

If it is to be sustained, the challenged classification must rationally further some legitimate governmental interest other than those specifically stated in the congressional "declaration of policy." . . . The legislative history indicates . . . that that amendment was intended to prevent so-called "hippies" and "hippie communes" from participating in the food stamp program. . . . The challenged classification clearly cannot be sustained by reference to this congressional purpose. For if the constitutional conception of "equal protection of the laws" means anything, it must at the very least mean that a bare congressional desire to harm a politically unpopular group cannot constitute a legitimate governmental interest. As a result, "a purpose to discriminate against hippies cannot, in and of itself and without reference to [some independent] considerations in the public interest, justify the 1971 amendment." . . .

Traditional equal protection analysis does not require that every classification be drawn with precise "mathematical nicety." *Dandridge v Williams*, 397 US 471 (1970). But the classification here in issue is not only "imprecise," it is wholly without any rational basis. The judgment of the District Court holding the "unrelated person" provision invalid under the Due Process Clause of the Fifth Amendment is therefore affirmed.

[Judgment affirmed]

QUESTIONS

1. Is there a constitutional right to receive food stamps?
2. Is it lawful for you to give presents to three of your four nephews and not give the fourth anything because you do not like the way he lives?
3. How would the *Moreno* case have been decided if there had been reason to believe that the excluded claimants were agitating to overthrow the U.S. government?

13. Privileges and Immunities

The federal Constitution declares that "the citizens of each state shall be entitled to all privileges and immunities of citizens in the several states."[20] This means that a person going into another state is entitled to make contracts, own property, and engage in business to the same extent as the citizens of that state. Thus, a state cannot bar a traveler from another state from engaging in local business or from obtaining a hunting or fishing license merely because the traveler is not a resident. Likewise, a law that requires an attorney to be a resident of the state in order to practice is unconstitutional as a violation of this provision.[21]

14. Protection of the Person

The Constitution does not contain any express provision protecting "persons" from governmental action. Persons are expressly protected by the Constitution with respect to particular matters, such as freedom of speech, ownership of property, right to a jury trial, and so on. There is, however, no general provision declaring that the government shall not impair "rights of persons." There is not a word in the Constitution about the inalienable rights that were so important on July 4, 1776.[22]

(a) RISE OF CONSTITUTIONAL PROTECTION OF THE PERSON. During the last four decades, the Supreme Court has been finding constitutional protection for a wide array of rights of the person that are not expressly protected by the Constitution. Examples are the right of privacy, the right to marry

---

[20] US Const, Art IV, Section 2, Cl 1.

[21] Barnard v Thorstenn, 489 US 546 (1989).

[22] The term *inalienable right* is employed in preference to natural right, fundamental right, or basic right. Apart from the question of scope of coverage, the adjective inalienable emphasizes the fact that the people still possess the right, rather than having surrendered or subordinated it to the will of society. The word alien is the term of the old common law for transferring title or ownership. Today we would say transfer and, instead of saying inalienable rights, would say nontransferable rights. Inalienable rights of the people were therefore rights that the people not only possessed, but that they could not give up, even if they wanted to. Thus, these rights are still owned by everyone.

the person one chooses,[23] protection from unreasonable zoning, protection of parental control, protection from durational residency requirements, protection from discrimination because of poverty, and protection from gender discrimination.[24]

(b) WHO IS A LIVING PERSON? Only living persons are protected by the Constitution. But when is a person living? When is a person dead? At common law, the test of being alive was as simple as being whether the person was breathing and had a heartbeat. This is known as the cardiopulmonary test. With the modern advances in medicine it is possible in many cases to keep a person breathing and the heart beating by drugs or mechanical equipment, such as respirators. Is a person alive whose breath and heart beat depend upon external assistance? The question becomes important in determining cases involving organ donations, abortions, and the mercy killing of hopelessly handicapped infants or old or sick persons. In some states the problem has been met by statutes declaring persons dead when the brain ceases to function—the human vegetable case.[25] In a number of states, statutes authorize competent persons to adopt a living will that directs that they be permitted to die if terminally ill.

In the case of *T.A.C.P.* the definition of "death" arose in the context of whether a newly born child could be treated as dead at birth in order to carry out a donation of organs of the child.

RE T.A.C.P.
(Fla) 609 So 2d 588 (1992)

In the eighth month of a woman's pregnancy, she and her husband petitioned the court to declare that their unborn child, T.A.C.P., was legally dead. This was requested because the mother was informed that the child would be born anencephalic. This meant that the child would have much of the brain and part of the skull missing and that the child would die shortly after birth. The parents filed the petition to enable taking the child's organs for transplant immediately upon the child's birth. Speed of removal was essential to the value of the organs, and the parents hoped that others could find life in those organs. The lower court certified the question to the supreme court of the state. While the appeal was pending, the child was

---

[23] Akron v Akron Center for Reproductive Health, Inc. 462 US 416 (1983).

[24] In some cases, the courts have given the due process and equal protection clauses a liberal interpretation in order to find a protection of the person, thereby making up for the fact that there is no express constitutional guarantee of protection of the person. Davis v Passman, 442 US 228 (1979) (due process); Orr v Orr 440 US268 (1979) (equal protection)

[25] A Uniform Determination of Death Act has been adopted in Arkansas, California, Colorado, Delaware, Georgia, Idaho, Indiana, Kansas, Maine, Maryland, Michigan, Minnesota, Mississippi, Missouri, Montana, Nebraska, Nevada, New Hampshire, North Dakota, Ohio, Oklahoma, Oregon, Pennsylvania, Rhode Island, South Carolina, South Dakota, Utah, Vermont, West Virginina, and Wyoming. It has also been adopted for the District of Columbia. The Uniform Act adds brain death to the common law test of death.

born and died four days later. Because of the importance of the question, the state's supreme court proceeded to decide the case.

KOGAN, J. . . . The parties have cited to no authorities directly dealing with the question of whether anencephalics are "alive" or "dead." . . . In the absence of applicable legal authority, this Court must weigh and consider the public policy considerations at stake here.

We agree that a cardiopulmonary definition of death must be accepted in Florida as a matter of our common law. . . . Thus, if cardiopulmonary function is not being maintained artificially, a person is dead who has sustained irreversible cessation of circulatory and respiratory functions. . . .

The question remaining is whether there is good reason in public policy for this Court to create an additional common law standard applicable to anencephalics. Alterations of the common law, while rarely entertained or allowed, are within this Court's prerogative. . . . However, the rule we follow is that the common law will not be altered or expanded unless demanded by public necessity . . . or where required to vindicate fundamental rights. . . .

Such is not the case with petitioners' request. Our review of the medical, ethical, and legal literature on anencephaly discloses absolutely no consensus that public necessity or fundamental rights will be better served by granting this request.

We are not persuaded that a public necessity exists to justify this action, in light of the other factors in this case—although we acknowledge much ambivalence about this particular question. We have been deeply touched by the altruism and unquestioned motives of the parents of T.A.C.P. The parents have shown great humanity, compassion, and concern for others. The problem we as a Court must face, however, is that the medical literature shows unresolved controversy over the extent to which anencephalic organs can or should be used in transplants.

. . . Others note that prenatal screening now is substantially reducing the number of anencephalics born each year in the United States and that, consequently, anencephalics are unlikely to be a significant source of organs as time passes. . . . And still others have frankly acknowledged that there is no consensus and that redefinition of death in this context should await the emergence of a consensus. . . .

We express no opinion today about who is right and who is wrong on these issues—if any "right" or "wrong" can be found here. The salient point is that no consensus exists as to: (a) the utility of organ transplants of the type at issue here; (b) the ethical issues involved; or (c) the legal and constitutional problems implicated.

Accordingly, we find no basis to expand the common law to equate anencephaly with death. We acknowledge the possiblity that some infants' lives might be saved by using organs from anencephalics who do not meet the traditional definition of "death." . . . But weighed against this is the utter lack of consensus, and the questions about the overall utility of such organ donations. The scales clearly tip in favor of not extending the common law in this instance. . . .

Because no Florida statute applies to the present case, the determination of death in this instance must be judged against the common law cardiopulmonary standard. The evidence shows that T.A.C.P.'s heart was beating and she was breathing at the times in question. Accordingly, she was not dead under Florida law, and no donation of her organs would have been legal.

[Petition denied]

QUESTIONS

1. In view of the fact that the child had died, the case was moot and therefore the court should not have decided the case. Appraise this statement.
2. Is the decision of the court based upon a rule of law?
3. The adoption of the Bill of Rights of the federal Constitution shows concern with the protection of persons. Why was no provision made defining when a person is living and when a person is dead?

15. Democracy and Protection of the Person

Since the goal of a democracy is to promote the well-being and development of each individual, the concept of protecting a person and the goal of democracy would appear to be moving toward the same objective. This is ordinarily true, but there may be a conflict between the democratic system of government and the protection of the person. We think of a democratic society as one in which the majority of the people govern. But is being governed by the majority sufficient for those who cherish the American ideal?

If we look closely at our individual and national desires, we see that the American way of life is not a society run by the will of the majority. Instead we find that the American way divides life into two zones. In one zone, the democratic concept is that the majority rules. In the other zone—that of the "person"—not even the majority can interfere. To illustrate, the majority can declare by statute that before you marry, you must have a health certificate. This is perfectly reasonable for the protection of the general health and welfare. But no one, not the majority, nor even the unanimous action of everyone in the United States, can command you to marry or not marry or choose your mate for you.

Most amazing is the fact that a relatively short time ago, the second zone was unheard of, and everything was thought to be in the zone that was controlled by the majority—unless there was an express prohibition of such action by the Constitution. Even more startling, the emergence of the second zone has taken place for the most part within the lifetime of your parents and your lifetime. The expansion of the second zone will have a profound effect on the rest of your life.

SUMMARY

The U.S. Constitution created the structure of our national government and gave it certain powers. It also placed limitations on those powers. It created a federal system, with a tripartite division of government and a bicameral national legislature.

Some governmental powers are possessed exclusively by the national government, while other powers are shared by both the states and the federal government. In areas of conflict, federal law is supreme.

The U.S. Constitution is not a detailed document. It takes its meaning from the way it is interpreted. In recent years, liberal interpretation has expanded the powers of the federal government.

Among the powers of the federal government that directly affect business are the power to regulate commerce; the power to tax, borrow, spend, and coin money; and the power to own and operate businesses. Among the limitations on government that are most important to business are the requirement of due process and the requirement of equal protection of the law.

The due process requirement stipulates that no person shall be deprived of life, liberty, or property without due process of law. The due process requirement applies to both the state and federal governments but does not apply to private transactions.

The equal protection concept of the U.S. Constitution prohibits both the state and federal governments from treating one person differently from another, unless there is a legitimate reason for doing so and unless the basis of classification is reasonable.

LAW IN PRACTICE

1. Recognize that the Constitution may impose limitations on what you or the government can do.
2. Appreciate that, for practical purposes, no major business transaction is beyond the reach of the federal commerce power.
3. Bear in mind that the federal Constitutuion is a constant limitation on statutory reforms adopted by the states.
4. Appreciate the broad sweep of the power of the U.S. Supreme Court in amending the Constitution; therefore, seek the appointment of qualified persons as Justices of that Court.

QUESTIONS AND CASE PROBLEMS

1. What are the characteristics of the Constitution as it is today?
2. Would a constitutional amendment that deleted the present Article V and in its place provided that an amendment could be adopted by a majority of those voting at a presidential election be valid?
3. Does equal protection prevent classification? If not, when is classification proper?
4. The federal interstate commerce power goes no further than to give the federal government power to regulate goods and vehicles crossing state lines. Appraise the statement.
5. The Crafts' home was supplied with gas by the city gas company. Because of some misunderstanding, the gas company believed that the Crafts were delinquent in paying their gas bill. The gas company had an informal complaint procedure for discussing such matters, but the Crafts had never been informed that such a procedure was available. The gas company notified the Crafts that they were delinquent and that the company was shutting off the gas. The Crafts brought an action to enjoin the gas company from doing so, on the theory that a termination without any hearing was a denial of due process. The lower courts held that the interest of the Crafts in receiving gas was not a property interest protected by the due process clause and that the procedures that the gas company followed satisfied the requirements of due process. The Crafts appealed. Were they correct in contending that they had been denied due process of law? Why or why not? [*Memphis Light, Gas and Water Division v Craft, 436 US 1*]
6. The New York Civil Service law provided that only U.S. citizens could hold permanent civil service positions. Dougall was an alien who had lawfully entered and was lawfully residing in the United States. He held a job with the City of New York but was fired because of the state statute. He claimed that the statute was unconstitutional. Was he correct? Why or why not?
7. Montana imposed a severance tax on every ton of coal mined within the state. The tax varied depending on the value of the coal and the cost of production. It could be as high as 30 percent of the price at which the coal was sold. Montana mine operators and some of the out-of-state customers claimed that this tax was unconstitutional as an improper burden on interstate commerce. Decide. [*Commonwealth Edison Co. v Montana, 452 US 609*]
8. What social force guided the court in deciding the *Commonwealth Edison* case in Case Problem 7?
9. Heald was the executor of the estate of a deceased person who had lived in Washington, D.C. Heald refused to pay federal tax owed by

the estate on the ground that the tax had been imposed by an act of Congress, but that, since residents of the District of Columbia had no vote in Congress, the tax law was necessarily adopted without their representation. Not only did District residents have no voice in the adoption of the tax laws, but the proceeds from taxes collected in the District were paid into the general treasury of the United States and were not maintained as a separate District of Columbia fund. Heald objected that the tax law was void as contrary to the Constitution because it amounted to taxation without representation. Decide. [Heald v District of Columbia, 259 US 114]

10. Ellis was employed by the City of Lakewood. By the terms of his contract, he could only be discharged for cause. After working for six years, he was told that he was going to be discharged because of his inability to generate safety and self-insurance programs, because he failed to win the confidence of employees, and because of poor attendance. He was not informed of the facts in support of these conclusions and was given the option to resign. He claimed that he was entitled to a hearing. Decide. [Ellis v City of Lakewood (Colo App) 789 P2d 449]

11. Because of misconduct, Lopez and other public high school students were suspended for periods of up to ten days. A state statute authorized the principal of a public school to suspend a student for periods of up to ten days without any hearing. A suit was brought by Lopez and others. They claimed that the statute was unconstitutional because it deprived them of due process by not giving them notice and a hearing to determine whether a suspension was justified. Was the state statute constitutional? Why or why not? [Gross v Lopez, 419 US 565]

12. New Hampshire adopted a tax law that in effect only taxed the income of nonresidents working in New Hampshire. Austin was a nonresident who worked in New Hampshire. He claimed that the tax law was invalid. Was he correct? Explain. [Austin v New Hampshire, 420 US 656]

13. Arkansas is primarily a rural state and in many areas it is not feasible to employ cable television. Arkansas imposes a tax on sales and services. Cable television service was added to the list of taxed enterprises. No tax was imposed on satellite television service. The cable companies claimed that there was a denial of equal protection by taxing them but not taxing satellite transmission of television. Decide. [Medlock v Leathers, ___ Ark ___ , 842 SW2d 428]

14. In view of the fact that written constitutions constantly change, it can be said that there is no value in having a written constitution. Appraise this statement.

15. The Michigan Constitution provides a special procedure for amending the Constitution. In addition, it gives the voters the right to adopt laws by public vote. Under this plan, called the "initiative" a specified percentage of the voters may require that a particular law be placed on the ballot of the next state general election. If the proposal is then approved by a majority of the voters, it is a law just as though it had been adopted by the state legislature. A public welfare law was adopted by such initiative procedure. The law was challenged as violating the Michigan Constitution. The defense of the law was made that as the law had been adopted by the people it was not subject to the limitations of the state constitution. Was this correct? [Doe v Director of Department of Social Services, ___ Mich App ___ , 468 NW2d 862]

CHAPTER 4

GOVERNMENT REGULATION OF COMPETITION AND PRICES

LEARNING OBJECTIVES

After studying this chapter, you will be able to:
1. *State the extent to which government can regulate business.*
2. *State what Congress has done to protect free enterprise from unfair competition and from unfair restraints.*
3. *State when price discrimination is prohibited and when it is allowed.*
4. *List statutory and judicial exceptions to the Sherman Antitrust Act.*
5. *Describe the constitutional limitations on state regulation of business.*

Constitutionally, the government *can* regulate business and much of our lives. Whether government *should* exercise this power comes down to a question of policy—whether we, the people, want government to do so. Although there is some movement toward deregulation, the overwhelming pattern continues to be regulation of business by government. It may come as a shock that in a country that believes in free enterprise, so much is in fact regulated by government.

A. POWER TO REGULATE BUSINESS

By virtue of their police power, states may regulate all aspects of business, so long as they do not impose an unreasonable burden on interstate commerce or any activity of the federal government. Local governments may also exercise this power to the extent each state permits. The federal government may impose on any phase of business any regulation that is required by the economic needs of the nation.[1]

1. Regulation, Free Enterprise, and Deregulation

The regulation of business is flatly opposed to the concept of free enterprise. Under a true free enterprise system, there would not be any regulation of airline safety, safety of food and drugs for human consumption, prices, and so on.

In recent years, there has been some movement toward deregulation of industry. For many years the banking and savings industry was heavily regulated. Beginning in 1978, various acts were adopted to deregulate this industry. This did not produce the desired

results, and Congress adopted several bank-regulating laws toward the end of the 1980s. The broadest regulation was made by the Financial Institutions Reform, Recovery, and Enforcement Act of 1989 (FIRREA).[2] This act regulates savings and loan associations and similar organizations to ensure their financial stability.

The regulation of rates of plane and truck transport has been removed. It seems unlikely that the move to deregulate will go much beyond removing restrictions on rates.[3]

2. Regulation of Production, Distribution, and Financing

To protect the public from harm, government may prohibit false advertising and labeling, and government may establish health and purity standards for cosmetics, foods, and drugs. Licenses may be required of persons dealing in certain goods, and these licenses may be revoked for improper dealings.[4] Without regard to the nature of the product, government may regulate business with respect to what materials may be used, the quantity of a product that may be produced or grown, and the price at which the finished product may be sold. Government may also engage in competition with private enterprises or own and operate an industry.

Regulation of production may take the form of providing encouragement or assistance for enterprises that would not prove attractive to private investors.[5]

Under its commerce power, the federal government may regulate all methods of interstate transportation. A similar power is exercised by each state over its intrastate traffic.

The financing of business is directly affected by the national government, which

---

[1]   American Power & Light Co. v SEC, 329 US 90 (1946).

[2]   Act of October 9, 1989, PL 101-73, 103 Stat 183, Codified to various sections of Titles 12 and 15 of USC.

[3]   Airline Deregulation Act of Oct. 24, 1978, PL 95-504, 92 Stat 1705, 49 USC §§ 1301 et seq.; Bus Regulatory Reform Act of Sept. 20, 1982, PL 97-261, 96 Stat 1102, 49 USC §§ 10101 et seq.

[4]   Evans Packing Co. v Department of Agriculture and Consumer Services (Fla App) 550 So 2d 112.

[5]   Orphan Drug Act of January 4, 1983, PL 97-44, 96 Stat 2049, 21 USC §§ 301, 306 (encouraging development of drugs to fight diseases that are so rare that there is no commercial interest in developing drugs to prevent or treat them).

Figure 4-1   Government Regulation of American Life

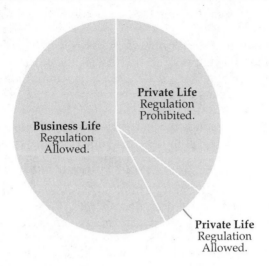

creates a national currency and maintains a federal reserve bank system. State and other national laws may also affect financing by regulating financing contracts and documents, such as bills of lading and commercial paper.

The federal power to regulate interstate commerce gives the national government the power to regulate interstate communication without regard to the manner of communicating. In the *Turner Broadcasting System* case, a regulation of interstate communication by cable television was challenged as a violation of the free speech guarantee of the First Amendment.

TURNER BROADCASTING SYSTEM, INC. v FCC
(DC Dist Col) 819 F Supp 32 (1993)

The federal Cable Television Consumer Protection and Competition Act regulates cable telecasting. Among other things, cable television system operators are required to carry the TV signals of certain commercial and certain noncommercial educational stations. These "must-carry" provisions were challenged as impairing the freedom of speech of the stations that were required to carry the signals of the other stations.

JACKSON, J. . . . In 1989, Congress began the first in a series of several hearings to assess the video programming distribution landscape in light of the 1984 Cable Act. After an exhaustive fact-finding process including hearings held over three years, the 1992 Act was passed. Congress' principal finding was that, for a variety of reasons, concentration of economic power in the cable industry was preventing non-cable programmers from effectively competing for the attention of a television audience. . . .

Congress specifically found that cable had become the "dominant nationwide video medium." . . .

Congress also found that despite the dominance of cable, there is insufficient competition within the cable industry. First, there is little competition between cable operators. For many reasons "including local franchising requirements and the extraordinary expense of constructing more than one cable television system to serve a particular geographic area," most regions of the country are served by one cable operator only. . . . Second, the industry has become horizontally concentrated—many operators share common ownership. Third, the industry is becoming vertically integrated. Many large entities that operate cable franchises also own and operate programming enterprises. . . .

Congress determined that geographic monopolization, horizontal concentration and vertical integration have created barriers to entry for non-cable programmers, primarily broadcasters, attempting to obtain carriage on cable. Vertical integration contributes to this cable "bottleneck" by providing cable operators with economic incentive to grant affiliated programmers access to their systems while denying it to others. . . . Similarly, horizontal concentration and the absence of effective competition among operators have obstructed broadcaster access by creating a climate conducive to another anti-competitive operator practice. Cable operators compete with broadcasters for advertising revenue. . . . Consequently, operators have an economic incentive to refuse carriage of broadcasters' signals to reduce broadcast viewership, thus attracting advertising dollars that otherwise would go to broadcasters. . . .

In summary, Congress concluded that the economic forces at work and the market conditions they had already produced had placed free local broadcast television in serious jeopardy. . . . It determined that mandatory carriage was necessary to remedy unfair trade practices, to preserve local broadcasting for those who do not receive cable television . . . as well as those who do . . . and to ensure that the public will continue to have access to a wide diversity of sources of video programming. . . .

This Court is of the opinion that, in enacting the 1992 Cable Act, Congress employed its regulatory powers over the economy to impose order upon a market in dysfunction, but a market in a commercial commodity nevertheless; not a market in "speech." The commodity Congress undertook to regulate is the means of delivery of video signals to individual receivers. It is not the information the video signals may be used to impart. That the video signals can only be used to convey a message is of no particular significance. The same is true of printing presses, or broadcast transmitters; loudspeakers, or movie projectors. Yet no one doubts that Congress could regulate a market in those commodities in danger of chaos or capture without being accused of attempting to infringe the First Amendment freedoms of those by whom they will be used to express protected "speech." The Cable Act of 1992 is simply industry-specific antitrust and fair trade practice regulatory legislation: to the extent First Amendment speech is affected at all, it is simply a by-product of the fact that video signals have no other function than to convey information. . . .

["Must-carry" provisions held constitutional]

The federal government may establish standards for weights and measures. The Metric Conversion Act of 1975 declares that it is the policy of the United States to convert to the metric system. Various agencies have adopted regulations to carry out this policy.

3. Regulation of Competition

The federal government, and the states in varying degrees, prohibit unfair methods of competition. Frequently, a commission is established to determine whether a given practice comes within the general class of unfair methods of competition. In other instances, the statutes specifically define the practices condemned.

Congress has enacted the Federal Trade Commission Act, which declared unlawful all unfair methods of competition and created a Federal Trade Commission (FTC) to administer the act. The FTC has condemned harassing tactics, coercing by refusing to sell, boycotting, discriminating, disparaging of a competitors products, and enforcing payment wrongfully. The FTC has also condemned cutting off or restricting the market, securing and using confidential information, spying on competitors, and inducing breach of customer contracts. The law prohibits misrepresentation by appropriating business names, simulating trade or corporate names, appropriating trademarks, simulating the appearance of a competitor's goods, simulating a competitor's advertising, using deceptive brands or labels, and using false and misleading advertising. When packaged foods are sold with false statements on the package as to the nutritional content of the food, the seller is guilty of an unfair method of competition.[6]

A shift of emphasis is taking place in appraising methods of doing business. Instead of harm to competitors being the sole consideration, the effect on the consumer is being given increasing recognition. Many practices that were condemned earlier only because they would harm a competitor by diverting customers are now condemned because these practices prevent the customer from getting full value for the money spent.

4. Regulation of Prices

Governments, both national and state, may regulate prices. This may be done directly by the lawmaker (the Congress or the state legislature), or the power to do so may be delegated to an administrative officer or agency. This power extends to prices in any form. It includes not only what a buyer pays for goods purchased from a store but also what a borrower pays as interest on a loan and what a tenant pays for rent.

---

[6] Kraft, Inc. v FTC (CA7 FTC) 970 F2d 311 (1992). In many states, such a seller would also be guilty of a deceptive trade practice or consumer protection statute.

(a) PROHIBITED PRICE DISCRIMINA-TION. The Clayton Act of 1914 applies to interstate and foreign commerce. This act prohibits price discrimination between different buyers of like commodities where the effect of this discrimination may be to substantially lessen competition or to create a monopoly in any line of commerce.[7]

The federal law prohibits the furnishing of advertising or other services that, when rendered to one purchaser but not another, will have the effect of granting the former a price discrimination or lower rate. It is illegal for a seller to accept any fee or commission in connection with a sale except for services actually rendered and unless the services are equally available to all on the same terms. The Clayton Act makes both the giving and the receiving of any illegal price discrimination a crime.

A state may prohibit selling below cost for the purpose of harming competitors.[8]

(b) PERMITTED PRICE DISCRIMINA-TION. Price discrimination is expressly permitted when it can be justified on the basis of: (1) difference in grade, quality, or quantity involved; (2) the cost of the transportation involved in performing the contract; (3) a good-faith effort to meet competition; (4) differences in methods or quantities; (5) deterioration of goods; or (6) a close-out sale of a particular line of goods. The Robinson-Patman Act of 1936 reaffirms the right of a seller to select customers and to refuse to deal with anyone. The refusal, however, must be in good faith and not for the purpose of restraining trade.

When a supplier offers to sell to anyone at a reduced price if certain conditions are met, the fact that every buyer cannot meet the conditions does not condemn the suppliers pricing plan as discriminatory.

5. Prevention of Monopolies and Combinations

To protect competitors and the public from monopolies and combinations in restraint of trade, the federal government and almost all of the states have enacted antitrust statutes.

(a) THE FEDERAL ANTITRUST ACT. The federal antitrust act, known as the Sherman Antitrust Act, is applicable to both sellers and buyers.[9] It provides that "[§ 1] Every contract, combination in the form of trust or otherwise, or conspiracy, in restraint of trade or commerce among the several states, or with foreign nations, is declared to be illegal. [§ 2] Every person who shall monopolize or attempt to monopolize, or combine or conspire with any other person or persons to monopolize any part of the trade or commerce among the several states, or with foreign nations, shall be deemed guilty of a felony."[10]

(b) PROHIBITED CONDUCT. Section 1 of the Sherman Act applies only when two or more persons agree or conspire to restrain trade. There is no violation when there is only an agreement between a corporation and its own employees or officers.

Under Section 2, one person or corporation may violate the law by monopolizing or attempting to monopolize interstate commerce.

As discussed in the *Mandeville* case, the Sherman Act applies not only to buying and selling activities generally associated with trade and commerce, but also to manufacturing and production activities, without regard to whether consumers, brokers, or manufacturers are involved.

The Sherman Act also prohibits professional persons, such as doctors, from using a peer review proceeding to put pressure on

---

[7] Texaco Inc. v Hasbrouck, 496 US ___ , 110 L Ed 2d 492 (1990).

[8] Turnbull & Turnbull v ARA Transportation, Inc. 219 Cal App 3d 811, 268 Cal Rptr 856 (1988).

[9] This act has been amended by the Clayton Act, the Federal Trade Commission Act, the Shipping Act, and other legislation.

[10] 15 USC, Ch. 1, §§ 1,2. Free competition has been advanced by the Omnibus Trade and Competitiveness Act of August 23, 1988, as amended, PL 106-418, 102 Stat 1107, 19 USC §§ 2901 et seq. Gray v Marshall County Board of Education (W Va App) 367 SE2d 751 (1988).

MANDEVILLE ISLAND FARMS v AMERICAN CRYSTAL SUGAR CO.

334 US 219 (1948)

The raising of sugar beets is an important industry in California. Sugar refineries buy the beet crop of the farmers and make sugar from the beets. This sugar is then shipped out of California and sold in many states. In order to hold down the prices paid to the sugar beet farmers, the American Crystal Sugar Company and two other refiners agreed among themselves on the price that they would pay the farmers for sugar beets. Sugar beets were grown on Mandeville Island Farms. Mandeville claimed that the price-fixing agreement between the sugar refiners violated the Sherman Antitrust Act. Mandeville sued American Crystal for treble (triple) damages as authorized by the federal statute. Judgment was entered for Mandeville, and American Crystal appealed.

RUTLEDGE, J. . . . The refiners controlled the seed supply and the only practical market for beets grown in northern California. When the new contracts were offered to the farmers, they had the choice of either signing or abandoning sugar-beet farming. . . .

[American Crystal] claimed that the growing, purchasing, and refining of sugar beets were local activities and not within the reach of the Sherman Act, which applied only to transactions in interstate commerce, and that no illegal practice occurred in the subsequent interstate distribution of the refined sugar.

. . . The broad form of [American Crystal]'s argument cannot be accepted. It is a reversion to conceptions formerly held but no longer effective to restrict either Congress' power . . . or the scope of the Sherman Act's coverage. The artificial and mechanical separation of "production" and "manufacturing" from "commerce," without regard to their economic continuity, the effects of the former two upon the latter, and the varying methods by which the several processes are organized, related, and carried on in different industries, or indeed within a single industry, no longer suffices to put either production or manufacturing and refining processes beyond reach of Congress' authority or of the statute. . . .

. . . The inquiry whether the restraint occurs in one phase or another, interstate or intrastate, of the total economic process is now merely a preliminary step. . . . The vital question becomes whether the effect is sufficiently substantial and adverse to Congress' paramount policy . . . to constitute a forbidden consequence. If so, the restraint must fall; and the injuries it inflicts upon others become remediable under the act's prescribed methods, including the treble damage provision.

. . . It is clear that the [sugar refiners'] agreement is the sort of combination condemned by the act, even though the price fixing was by purchasers and the persons specially injured under the treble damage claim are sellers, not customers or consumers. . . .

. . . The statute does not confine its protection to consumers, or to purchasers, or to competitors, or to sellers. Nor does it immunize the outlawed acts because they are done by any of these. . . . The act is comprehensive in its terms and coverage, protecting all who are made victims of the forbidden practices by whomever they may be perpetrated. . . .

Nor is the amount of the nation's sugar industry which the California refiners control relevant, so long as control is exercised effectively in the area concerned. . . .

. . . Under the facts characterizing this industry's operation and the tightening of controls in this producing area by the new agreements and understandings, there can be no question that their restrictive consequences were projected substantially into the interstate distribution of the sugar. . . .

[Judgment affirmed]

QUESTIONS

1. Is the Sherman Antitrust Act limited to agreements between sellers that restrain trade?
2. Did American Crystal and other refiners intend to affect the price at which sugar was sold in the markets in other states?
3. Does the Sherman Antitrust Act apply to a combination of five manufacturers that agree to the price at which they will sell their furniture throughout the United States?

another professional who competes with them in private practice and refuses to become a member of a clinic formed by them.[11]

The Sherman Act does not deprive a city of the power to impose rent ceilings, since such a regulation does not involve concerted action.

The fact that a manufacturer sells only through a particular distributor and refuses to sell through anyone else does not in itself constitute an illegal restraint of trade.[12]

(c) BIGNESS. The Sherman Antitrust Act does not prohibit bigness. However, § 7 of the Clayton Act, as amended in 1950, provides that "no corporation . . . shall acquire the whole or any part of the assets of another corporation . . . where in any line of commerce in any section of the country, the effect of such acquisition may be substantially to lessen competition, or to tend to create a monopoly."

If the Clayton Act is violated by acquiring the ownership or control of competing enterprises, the court may order the defendant to dispose of such interests.[13] Such a decree is called a **divestiture order**.

(1) Premerger Notification. When large-size enterprises plan to merge, they must give written notice to the Federal Trade Commission and to the attorney in charge of the Antitrust Division of the Department of Justice. This gives the Department the opportunity to block the merger and thus avoid the loss that would occur if the enterprises merged and were then required to separate.[14]

(2) Takeover Laws. Antitrust laws are usually concerned with whether the combination or agreement is fair to society or to a particular class, such as consumers. Some legislation is aimed at protecting the various parties directly involved in the combining of different enterprises. There is concern that one

---

[11] Patrick v Burget, 486 US 83 (1988).

[12] Oakridge Investment, Inc. v Southern Energy Homes, Inc. (Okla App) 719 P2d 848 (1986).

[13] California v American Stores Co. 495 US ___ , 109 L Ed 2d 240 (1990).

[14] Antitrust Improvement Act of 1976, PL 94-435, § 201, PL 94-435, 90 Stat 1383, 15 USC §§ 1311 et seq.

enterprise may in effect be raiding another enterprise. **Takeover laws**, which seek to protect from unfairness in such situations, have been adopted by Congress and four-fifths of the states. State laws are limited in effect because they can only operate within the area over which a state has control. In the *Edgar* case it was claimed that a state takeover law was unconstitutional because it went too far.

EDGAR v MITE CORP.
457 US 624 (1982)

An Illinois statute required a corporation seeking to buy out another corporation to file papers disclosing certain information. MITE Corporation, a Delaware corporation, offered to buy all the stock of the Chicago Rivet Company, an Illinois corporation. Edgar, the Illinois Secretary of State, sought an injunction to block MITE because it had not complied with the requirements of the Illinois statute. MITE claimed that the Illinois statute was unconstitutional because (1) it was in conflict with the federal Williams Act that amended the Securities and Exchange Act of 1934, and (2) it placed an unreasonable burden on interstate commerce. From a decision in favor of MITE, Edgar appealed.

WHITE, J. . . . The Williams Act, passed in 1968, was the congressional response to the increased use of cash tender offers in corporate acquisitions. . . . The Act imposes several requirements. First, it requires that upon the commencement of the tender offer, the offeror file with the SEC, publish or send to the shareholders of the target company, and furnish to the target company detailed information about the offer. The offeror must disclose information about its background and identity; the source of the funds to be used in making the purchase; the purpose of the purchase, including any plans to liquidate the company or make major changes in its corporate structure; and the extent of the offeror's holdings in the target company. . . .

There is no question that in imposing these requirements, Congress intended to protect investors. . . . But it is also crystal clear that a major aspect of the effort to protect the investor was to avoid favoring either management or the takeover bidder. . . . Congress disclaimed any "intention to provide a weapon for management to discourage takeover bids. . ." and expressly embraced a policy of neutrality. . . .

The Illinois Act requires a tender offeror to notify the Secretary of State and the target company of its intent to make a tender offer and the material terms of the offer 20 business days before the offer becomes effective.

. . . By providing the target company with additional time within which to take steps to combat the offer, the precommencement notification provisions furnish incumbent management with a powerful tool to combat tender offers, perhaps to the detriment of the stockholders who will not have an offer before them during this period. These consequences are precisely what Congress determined should be avoided, and for this reason, the precommencement notification provision frustrates the objectives of the Williams Act.

. . . The Commerce Clause permits only *incidental* regulation of interstate commerce by the states; direct regulation is prohibited. . . . The Illinois Act violates these principles for two reasons. First, it directly regulates and prevents, unless its terms are satisfied, interstate tender offers which in turn would generate interstate transactions. Second, the burden the Act imposes on interstate commerce is excessive in light of the local interests the Act purports to further.

The Illinois Act . . . directly regulates transactions which take place across state lines, even if wholly outside the State of Illinois. A tender offer for securities of a publicly-held corporation is ordinarily communicated by the use of the mails or other means of interstate commerce to shareholders across the country and abroad. Securities are tendered and transactions closed by similar means. Thus, in this case, MITE Corporation, the tender offeror, is a Delaware corporation with principal offices in Connecticut. Chicago Rivet is a publicly-held Illinois corporation with shareholders scattered around the country, 27 percent of whom live in Illinois. MITE's offer to Chicago Rivet's shareholders, including those in Illinois, necessarily employed interstate facilities in communicating its offer, which, if accepted, would result in transactions occurring across state lines. These transactions would themselves be interstate commerce. Yet the Illinois law, unless complied with, sought to prevent MITE from making its offer and concluding interstate transactions not only with Chicago Rivet's stockholders living in Illinois, but also with those living in other states and having no connection with Illinois. Indeed, the Illinois law on its face would apply even if not a single one of Chicago Rivet's shareholders were a resident of Illinois, since the Act applies to every tender offer for a corporation meeting two of the following conditions: the corporation has its principal executive office in Illinois, is organized under Illinois laws, or has at least 10% of its stated capital and paid-in surplus represented in Illinois. . . . Thus the Act could be applied to regulate a tender offer which would not affect a single Illinois shareholder.

It is therefore apparent that the Illinois statute is a direct restraint on interstate commerce and that it has a sweeping extraterritorial effect. Furthermore, if Illinois may impose such regulations, so may other states; and interstate commerce in securities transactions generated by tender offers would be thoroughly stifled. . . .

Because the Illinois Act purports to regulate directly and to interdict interstate commerce, including commerce wholly outside the state, it must be held invalid.

. . . When a state statute regulates interstate commerce indirectly, the burden imposed on that commerce must not be excessive in relation to the local interests served by the statute. The most obvious burden the Illinois Act imposes on interstate commerce arises from the statute's previously-described nationwide reach which purports to give Illinois the power to determine whether a tender offer may proceed anywhere.

The effects of allowing the Illinois Secretary of State to block a nationwide tender offer are substantial. Shareholders are deprived of the opportunity to sell their shares at a premium. The reallocation of economic resources to their highest-valued use, a process which can improve efficiency and competition, is hindered. . . .

Appellant [Edgar] . . . contends that Illinois has an interest in regulating the internal affairs of a corporation incorporated under its laws. The internal affairs doctrine is a conflict of laws principle which recognizes that only one state should have the authority to regulate a corporation's internal affairs—matters peculiar to the relationships among or between the corporation and its current officers, directors, and shareholders—because otherwise a corporation could be faced with conflicting demands. See Restatement (Second) of Conflict of Laws, 302, Comment b at 307-308 (1971). That doctrine is of little use to the state in this context. Tender offers contemplate transfers of stock by stockholders to a third party and do not themselves implicate the internal affairs of the target company. . . . Furthermore, the proposed justification is somewhat incredible since the Illinois Act applies to tender offers for any corporation for which 10% of the outstanding shares are held by Illinois residents. . . . The Act thus applies to corporations that are not incorporated in Illinois and have their principal place of business in other states. Illinois has no interest in regulating the internal affairs of foreign corporations.

We conclude with the Court of Appeals that the Illinois Act imposes a substantial burden on interstate commerce which outweighs its putative local benefits. It is accordingly invalid under the Commerce Clause.

[Judgment affirmed]

QUESTIONS

1. Was the Illinois Act intended to regulate commerce?
2. What is the attitude of the court to corporate takeovers?
3. The Illinois Act was valid as a regulation of internal affairs of Illinois corporations. Appraise this statement.

(d) PRICE FIXING. Agreements fixing prices, whether horizontally or vertically, violate the federal antitrust law. Thus, manufacturers cannot agree among themselves on the price at which they will sell (**horizontal price fixing**). Likewise, a wholesaler cannot require a dealer to agree not to resell below a stated price (**vertical price fixing**).[15]

(e) EXCEPTIONS TO THE ANTITRUST LAW. By statute or decision, associations of exporters, marine insurance associations, farmers cooperatives, and labor unions are exempt from the Sherman Antitrust Act with respect to agreements between their members. Certain pooling and revenue-dividing agreements between carriers are exempt from the antitrust law when approved by the appropriate federal agency. The Newspaper Preservation Act of 1970 grants an antitrust exemption to operating agreements entered into by newspapers to prevent financial collapse. The Soft Drink Interbrand Competition Act[16] grants the soft drink industry an exemption when it is shown that, in fact, there is substantial competition in spite of the agreements.

The general approach of the Supreme Court of the United States to the trust problem has been that an agreement should not be automatically or per se condemned as a restraint of interstate commerce merely because it creates a power or a potential to monopolize

---

[15] Vertical price-maintenance agreements were authorized by statutes in varying degrees from 1931 to 1975, but the Consumer Goods Pricing Act of 1975, PL 94-145, 89 Stat 801, abolished the immunity from the federal antitrust law that had been given to such agreements. Although the states may permit such agreements as long as interstate commerce is not involved, the area of intrastate commerce is so slight that for all practical purposes, such agreements are now illegal.

[16] Act of July 9, 1980, PL 96-308, 94 Stat 939, 15 USC §§ 3501 et seq.

interstate commerce. It is only when the restraint imposed is unreasonable that the practice is unlawful.

(f) PUNISHMENT AND CIVIL REMEDY. A violation of either of the Sherman Act provisions stated in Section 5(a) of this chapter is punishable by fine or imprisonment or both, at the discretion of the court. The maximum fine for a corporation is $1 million. A natural person can be fined a maximum of $100,000 or imprisoned for a maximum term of three years or both. In addition to this criminal penalty, the law provides for an injunction to stop the unlawful practices and permits suing the wrongdoers for damages.

(1) Individual Damage Suit. Any person or enterprise harmed may bring a separate action for **treble damages** (three times the damages actually sustained).

(2) Class Action Damage Suit by State Attorney General. When the effect of an antitrust violation is to raise prices, the attorney general of a state may bring a class action to recover damages on behalf of those who have paid the higher prices. This action is called a **parens patriae action**, on the theory that the state is suing as the parent of its people.

B. LIMITATIONS ON STATE POWER TO REGULATE

By virtue of their police power, the states may regulate business to prevent the sale of harmful products, to protect from fraud, and so on. The power of the states is subject to important limitations.

6. Constitutional Limitations

A state law, although made under the police power, cannot impose an unreasonable burden on or discriminate against interstate commerce, or invade a right that is protected by the federal Constitution.

The fact that a city deprives the plaintiffs of their constitutional rights does not give the plaintiffs the right to recover damages for the violation, unless such right is authorized by statute.[17]

7. Federal Supremacy

A state law cannot conflict with a federal law or regulation on the same subject matter. Moreover, when the federal government regulates a particular activity, state regulation is generally excluded even regarding matters not covered by the federal regulation. That is, the federal government occupies or preempts the entire field even though every detail is not regulated.

The federal authority that overrides state action may be a federal administrative agency regulation, as contrasted with an act of Congress. Thus, the Federal Communications Commission (FCC) may prohibit states and cities from imposing stricter standards on cable television companies than those imposed by the FCC.[18]

8. State and Local Governments as Market Participants

When a state or local government, such as a city or county, enters the marketplace to buy or sell goods, whether produced by itself or others, it is not acting as a government. It is a market participant, as contrasted with a government regulating the conduct of others. When a state or local government is a market participant, it is not subject to the limitations imposed on state governments by the U.S. Constitution.

When a state or local government is a market participant, it is subject to all laws applicable to ordinary persons. For example, when a city owns and operates a mass transit system, it is in the position of a private employer and therefore is subject to the federal minimum wage law.

---

[17] Hunter v City of Eugene, 309 Or 298, 787 P2d 881 (1990).
[18] City of New York v FCC, 486 US 57 (1988).

SUMMARY

Regulation by government has occurred primarily to protect one group from the improper conduct of another group. Until the middle third of this century, regulation of business was primarily directed at protecting competitors from misconduct of other competitors. Beginning with the middle third of this century, regulation expanded in the interest of protecting consumers.

In the last 100 years, the federal government has regulated advertising and food, drugs, and cosmetics. This protects consumers from false claims and from untested and possibly unsafe drugs. Unfair methods of competition are prohibited.

Prices have been regulated both by the setting of the exact price or a maximum price and by prohibiting discrimination as to prices. Price discrimination between buyers is prohibited when the effect of such discrimination could tend to create a monopoly or lessen competition. Certain exceptions are made where the circumstances are such that the price discrimination does not have the purpose or result of harming someone else.

The Sherman Antitrust Act prohibits conspiracies in restraint of trade and the monopolization of trade. The Clayton Act prohibits mergers or the acquisition of the assets of another corporation when this conduct would tend to lessen competition or give rise to a monopoly. Violation of these statutes subjects the wrongdoer to criminal prosecution and suit, by persons harmed, for treble damages. The application of these laws is modified to some extent by express exceptions and by the approach of the Supreme Court to antitrust cases.

Many of the regulations imposed by the federal government are paralleled or duplicated by state laws making a similar regulation as to local matters. The action of the states is restricted by the limitations arising from the Constitution and by the doctrine of the supremacy of federal law.

LAW IN PRACTICE

1. Before you enter into a transaction of significance, learn what restrictions are imposed by federal, state, or local regulations of business.
2. Consider whether your contract should contain an escape clause or a modification clause to operate in the event of future governmental regulation or deregulation of the subject matter of the contract.
3. Recognize that government regulation of business has destroyed any concept of absolute freedom of contract or absolute freedom of use of property.
4. Strive for sound regulation of business and seek the selection of qualified persons to the bodies that make the regulations.
5. Remember that government regulations, whether made by a lawmaker or an agency, are the law that must be followed. Do not be misled by abstract concepts of what you think is right and wrong.

QUESTIONS AND CASE PROBLEMS

1. What social forces are involved in each of the following rules of law? (a) Horizontal price fixing is illegal under the federal law without regard to whether the price fixed is fair and reasonable. (b) Farmers' and dairy farmers' cooperatives are exempt by statute from the operation of the Sherman Antitrust Act.
2. What government can regulate business? Why?
3. Cressler owns a factory. She refuses to obey the state safety laws on the ground that there is no constitutional provision that grants the state the power to make such laws. Does this justify Cressler's refusal to obey the state law? Explain.
4. The mayor of Boston issued an executive order that on all construction work done by the city of Boston, at least one-half of the workforce had to be bona fide residents of Boston. An

employer organization claimed that this requirement was a violation of the commerce clause of the U.S. Constitution. Decide. [*White v Massachusetts Council of Construction Employers, Inc. 460 US 204*]

5. The Hines Cosmetic Company sold beauty preparations nationally to beauty shops at a standard or fixed-price schedule. Some of the shops were also supplied with a free demonstrator and with free advertising materials. The shops that were not supplied with these claimed that the giving of the free services and materials constituted unlawful price discrimination. Hines replied that there was no price discrimination because it charged everyone the same. What it was giving free was merely a promotional campaign that was not intended to discriminate against those who were not given anything free. Was Hines guilty of unlawful price discrimination? Explain.

6. Moore ran a bakery in Santa Rosa, New Mexico. His business was wholly intrastate. Meads Fine Bread Company, his competitor, engaged in an interstate business. Mead cut the price of bread in half in Santa Rosa but made no price cut in any other place in New Mexico or in any other state. As a result of this price cutting, Moore was driven out of business. Moore then sued Mead for damages for violation of the Clayton and Robinson-Patman Acts. Mead claimed that the price cutting was purely intrastate and therefore did not constitute a violation of federal statutes. Was Mead correct? Why or why not? [*Moore v Meads Fine Bread Co. 348 US 115*]

7. What statutory limitations are imposed on the purchasing of the assets of an existing business?

8. Copperweld Corp. purchased Regal Tube Co. Some time later the Independence Tube Corp. sued Copperweld and Regal for damages for conspiring in violation of the Sherman Antitrust Act. They denied liability for conspiring because Regal was the wholly owned subsidiary of Copperweld. Were they liable? Explain. [*Copperweld Corp. v Independence Tube Corp. 467 US 752*]

9. What is a decree of divestiture?

10. John Kircos purchased raw pork from the Holiday Food Center. He failed to cook it sufficiently and became infected from the trichinae that were in the pork. He sued Holiday Food for damages on the ground that it had failed to place a warning label on the pork packages instructing the public to cook it to 140 Fahrenheit to destroy trichinae. The Federal Meat Inspection Act specified that any statement required by state law to be in a label that went beyond the statements required by the federal law was void. The federal law did not require any warning as to cooking to be in the labels on raw pork. Kircos claimed that the failure to include such a warning on the label was negligence and that he could therefore sue for damages for the harm he sustained. Was he entitled to recover? [*Kircos v Holiday Food Center, Inc. ____ Mich App ___ , 477 NW2d 130 (1991)*]

11. The Favorite Foods Corporation sold its food to stores and distributors. It established a quantity discount scale that was publicly published and made available to all buyers. The top gave the greatest discount to buyers purchasing more than 100-freight-cars of food in a calendar year. Only two buyers, both national food chains, purchased in such quantities and therefore they alone received the greatest discount. Favorite Foods was prosecuted for making price discrimination in violation of the Clayton Act. Was it guilty?

ADMINISTRATIVE AGENCIES

LEARNING OBJECTIVES

After studying this chapter, you will be able to:
1. *List and illustrate the functions that may be exercised by an administrative agency.*
2. *State the constitutional limitations on the power of an administrative agency to require the production of papers.*
3. *Describe the typical pattern of administrative procedure.*
4. *State the extent to which an administrative agency's decision may be reviewed and reversed by a court.*
5. *Define and state the purpose of the* Federal Register.

Late in the last century, a new type of governmental structure began to develop to meet the highly specialized needs of government regulation of business—the administrative agency. The administrative agency is now typically the way in which government makes and carries out its regulation of your life.

A. NATURE OF THE ADMINISTRATIVE AGENCY

An **administrative agency** is a governmental body charged with administering and implementing legislation. An agency may be a department, independent establishment, commission, administration, authority, board, or bureau. Agencies exist on the federal and state levels. One example of a federal agency is the Federal Trade Commission, the structure of which is shown in Figure 5-1.

1. Importance of the Administrative Agency

Large areas of the American economy are governed by federal administrative agencies created to carry out the general policies specified by Congress. The law governing these agencies is known as **administrative law**.

State administrative agencies may also affect business and the citizen. State agencies may have jurisdiction over fair employment practices, workers' compensation claims, and the renting of homes and apartments.

2. Uniqueness of Administrative Agencies

Federal and state governments alike are divided into three branches—executive, legislative, and judicial. Many of the offices in these branches are filled by persons who are elected. In contrast, members of administrative agencies are ordinarily appointed (in the case of federal agencies, by the President of the United States with the consent of the Senate).

In the tripartite structure, the judicial branch acts as a superguardian to prevent the executive and legislative branches from exceeding the proper spheres of their power. However, the major agencies combine legislative, executive, and judicial powers. These agencies may make the rules, police the community to see that the rules are obeyed, and sit in judgment to determine whether there have been violations of their rules.

In the *Withrow* case, the challenge was made that it was unfair to have the same body both investigate and decide the case.

To meet the objection that the exercise of executive, legislative, and judicial powers by the same body is a potential threat to impartiality, steps have been taken toward decentralizing

Figure 5-1   Federal Trade Commission

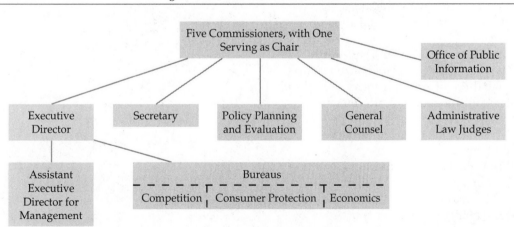

Figure 5-2   The Administrative Chain of Command

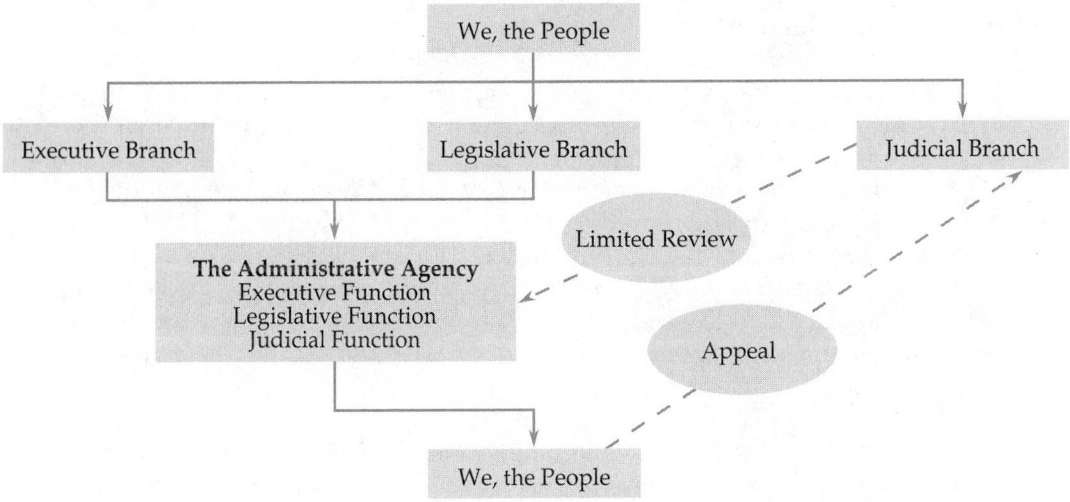

We, the People

Executive Branch   Legislative Branch   Judicial Branch

Limited Review

The Administrative Agency
Executive Function
Legislative Function
Judicial Function

Appeal

We, the People

WITHROW v LARKIN
421 US 35 (1975)

Doctors must obtain a license from the state in which they practice. These licenses are ordinarily issued by a licensing board that reviews the qualifications of each applicant. In addition, the statutes creating these licensing boards ordinarily give them the power to revoke a license when there is good reason to do so. A Wisconsin statute authorized the medical licensing board to investigate any case to see if there was cause for revoking a license. If the board thought that the circumstances appeared sufficiently bad, the same board could then hold a hearing to see what should be done.

Duane Larkin was a doctor licensed under the laws of Wisconsin. The state medical licensing board conducted an investigation of Larkin. The board concluded that it should hold a hearing to determine whether Larkin's license should be suspended. Larkin claimed that his constitutional rights would be violated if the same body that had investigated the case against him were also to act as judge to determine whether his license should be suspended. He brought a lawsuit against Harold Withrow and the other members of the licensing board to enjoin them from holding the hearing. An injunction was granted, and Withrow and the other members of the board appealed.

WHITE, J. . . . Concededly, a "fair trial in a fair tribunal is a basic requirement of due process." . . .

The contention that the combination of investigative and adjudicative functions necessarily creates an unconstitutional risk of bias in administrative adjudication has a . . . difficult burden of persuasion to carry. It must overcome a presumption of honesty and integrity in those serving as adjudicators: and it must convince that, under a realistic appraisal of psychological tendencies and human weakness, conferring investigative and adjudicative powers on the same individuals poses such a risk of actual bias or prejudgment that the practice must be forbidden if the guarantee of due process is to be adequately implemented.

Very similar claims have been squarely rejected in prior decisions of this Court. . . .

More recently we have sustained against due process objection a system in which a social security examiner has responsibility for developing the facts and making a decision as to disability claims, and observed that the challenge to this combination of functions "assumes too much and would bring down too many procedures designed, and working well, for a government structure of great and growing complexity." . . .

That is not to say that there is nothing to the argument that those who have investigated should not then adjudicate. The issue is substantial, it is not new, and legislators and others concerned with the operations of administrative agencies have given much attention to whether and to what extent distinctive administrative functions should be performed by the same persons. No single answer has been reached. Indeed, the growth, variety, and complexity of the administrative processes have made any one solution highly unlikely. Within the Federal Government itself, Congress has addressed the issue in several different ways, providing for varying degrees of separation from complete separation of functions to virtually none at all. For the generality of agencies, Congress has been content with 5 of the Administrative Procedure Act, 5 USC 554(d), which provides that no employee engaged in investigating or prosecuting may also participate or advise in the adjudicating function, but which also expressly exempts from this prohibition "the agency or a member or members of the body comprising the agency."

. . . The case law, both federal and state, generally rejects the idea that the combination [of] judging [and] investigating functions is a denial of due process. . . ." Similarly, our cases . . . offer no support for the bald proposition applied in this case by the District Court that agency members who participate in an investigation are disqualified from adjudicating. . . .

When the Board instituted its investigative procedures, it stated only that it would investigate whether proscribed conduct had occurred. Later in noticing the adversary hearing, it asserted only that it would determine if violations had been committed which would warrant suspension of appellee's license. Without doubt, the Board then anticipated that the proceeding would eventuate in an adjudication of the issue; but there was no more evidence of bias or the risk of bias or prejudgment than inhered in the very fact that the Board had investigated and would now adjudicate. Of course, we should be alert to the possibilities of bias that may lurk in the way particular procedures actually work in practice. The processes utilized by the Board, however, do not in themselves contain an unacceptable risk of bias. The investigative proceeding had been closed to the public, but appellee and his counsel were permitted to be present throughout; counsel actually attended the hearings and knew the facts presented to the Board. No specific foundation has been presented for suspecting that the Board had been prejudiced by its investigation or would be disabled from hearing and deciding on the basis of the evidence to be presented at the contested hearing. The mere exposure to evidence presented in nonadversary investigative procedures is insufficient in itself to impugn the fairness of the board members at a later adversary hearing. Without a showing to the contrary, state administrators, "are assumed to be men of conscience and intellectual discipline, capable of judging a particular controversy fairly on the basis of its own circumstances."

We are of the view, therefore, that the District Court was in error when it entered the restraining order against the Board's contested hearing and when it granted the preliminary injunction based on the untenable view that it would be unconstitutional for the Board to suspend appellee's license "at its own contested hearing on charges evolving from its own investigation. . . ."

[Judgment reversed]

QUESTIONS

1. Who objected to the combining of the functions of investigating and adjudicating?
2. What is the practical basis for this objection?
3. How does the decision in the *Withrow* case compare with the theory of American government?

the administrative functions of some agencies. Thus, the prosecution power of the National Labor Relations Board was withdrawn from the board and entrusted to an independent general counsel by the Labor-Management Relations Act of 1947. In a number of agencies, such as the Federal Trade Commission, the judicial function is assigned to administrative law judges.

3. Right to Know

To avoid the evils of secret government, provision is made for public knowledge of the activity of administrative agencies. This is done through (a) open records, (b) open meetings, and (c) public announcement of agency guidelines. The more recently adopted statutes creating new agencies usually contain provisions regulating these matters. For most federal agencies not otherwise regulated, these matters are controlled by the Administrative Procedure Act (APA). Many states have adopted statutes that copy the provisions of the APA. By definition, these statutes relate only to government records. They do not allow a business to examine the records of a competitor.[1]

(a) OPEN RECORDS. The Freedom of Information Act[2] provides that information contained in records of federal administrative agencies shall be made available upon proper request. Numerous exceptions to this right are made to prevent persons from obtaining information that is not necessary to their legitimate interests. The state statutes typically exempt from disclosure information that would constitute

---

[1] KMEG Television, Inc. v Iowa State Board of Regents (Iowa) 440 NW2d 382 (1989).

[2] Added to the APA by Act of December 31, 1974, PL 93-579, 88 Stat 1897, as amended, 5 USC §§ 552 et seq.

an invasion of the privacy of others. However, freedom of information acts are broadly construed, and unless an exemption of particular papers is clearly given, the papers in question are subject to public inspection. Moreover, the person claiming that there is an exemption that prohibits disclosure has the burden of proving that there is an exemption and that the facts of the case come within the scope of the exemption. Commercial or financial information that is of such nature that it is not ordinarily made public by the person supplying the information is generally exempt from disclosure under a freedom of information act.[3]

In the *Baudin* case, the court had to fix the procedure for considering a claim of exemption under a freedom of information statute.

BAUDIN v CITY OF CRYSTAL LAKE
192 Ill App 3d 530, 139 Ill Dec 554, 548 NE2d 1110 (1989)

Baudin asked the City of Crystal Lake to tell him the policies and procedures followed by its police force in the handling of information and the follow-up as to hit-and-run cases. The city refused to disclose this information. Baudin requested the court to examine the relevant documents *in camera* (in the judge's chambers). This was refused. Baudin appealed.

DUNN, J. . . . Plaintiff originally sought information concerning the policies and procedures of the police department with respect to: (a) handling and receiving information from telephone callers regarding automobile accidents (hit-and-run); (b) receiving information in person concerning an accident; (c) follow-up on information received concerning automobile accidents; and (d) investigation guidelines with respect to automobile accidents, including hit-and-run accidents. Plaintiff also sought excerpts of radio tapes of the City's police department for June 17, 1988, for the period between 8 P.M. and 8:30 P.M., and for June 18, 1988, from 9:15 A.M. to 9:45 A.M.

In response to plaintiff's request, defendant . . . sent a letter to plaintiff on June 23, 1988, denying plaintiff's request and claiming that items (a) through (d) were exempt from disclosure under section 7(w) of the Information Act, which exempts information "related solely to the internal personnel rules and practices of the public body." [The] letter also stated that the radio tapes were exempt from disclosure under section 7(e) of the Act, which exempts records of "State and local law enforcement agencies and correctional agencies that are related to the detection and investigation of crime." . . .

The central issue to be determined is whether the procedures . . . were sufficient to provide plaintiff an adequate . . . determination of whether the requested information was discloseable under the Act; as a corollary, it must be determined whether the City met its burden of showing that the materials requested were exempted under the Act.

_____

[3] Critical Mass Energy Project v Nuclear Regulatory Commission (CA Dist Col) 975 F2d 871 (1992).

The purpose of the Information Act is to open governmental records to the light of public scrutiny. . . . In order to foster governmental accountability and an informed citizenry, the public policy of this State encourages a free flow and disclosure of information between the government and the people; the Information Act is to be liberally construed to achieve this goal, and there is a presumption that public records are open and accessible, subject only to exemptions that are to be read narrowly. . . .

The restraints on access to information are to be regarded as limited exceptions to the general rule that the people have a right to know the decisions, policies, procedures, rules, standards, and other aspects of governmental activity that affect the conduct of government and the lives of people. . . . If any public record is exempt from disclosure under section 7 of the Act . . . and it contains material which is not exempt, the public body shall delete the exempted material and make the remaining information available for inspection and copying. . . .

Under the Information Act, the burden of proof is on the City to establish that the material in question is exempt from disclosure; however, governmental agencies cannot clothe material regarding the affairs of government with an exemption from public disclosure by . . . statements that the material is exempt. . . . Reliance upon self-determination by public officials and employees as to what should or should not be disclosed to the public would frustrate the purposes of the Information Act. . . .

Section 11(f) of the Act requires the . . . court to consider the matter *de novo* and requires the court to conduct whatever *in camera* inspection of the requested records it finds appropriate to determine whether the records or any part of them may be withheld under the Act. . . . Whether the material is exempt under the Act is necessarily a factual determination to be made by the court based on its examination of the affidavits and, if required, based on an examination of the documents themselves *in camera*. . . .

In determining whether matter is exempt under the Act, a case-by-case approach is clearly warranted. . . . An agency such as a police department cannot simply take the position that, since it is involved in investigatory work and some of its records are exempt from disclosure under the Act, every document in its possession somehow comes to share in that exemption. . . . The classification of information as "law enforcement" or "investigatory" does not necessarily foreclose access unless it can be shown, in a particular case, that disclosure would interfere with law enforcement and would, therefore, not be in the public interest. . . .

We find from our examination of the City's affidavits that they were entirely conclusory and merely recite or paraphrase the language of the statute without giving any clue as to the discloseability of the requested documents. As such, they provided an insufficient factual basis to permit the trial court to grant . . . judgment to the City, particularly in the absence of an *in camera* inspection of the disputed material. The burden is on the governmental agency to prove that specific documents fit within one of the statutory exemptions. To meet this burden and to assist the court in making its determination, the agency must provide a *detailed* justification for its claim of exemption, addressing the requested documents specifically. . . .

When an agency meets its burden by means of affidavits, *in camera* review is not necessary. . . . However, the affidavits will not suffice if the agency's claims are conclusory, merely reciting statutory standards, or if they are too vague or sweeping. . . .

If the disclosure significantly risks circumvention of the agency's regulations or of statutes, the material is exempt from mandatory disclosure.

Upon remand, the trial court must make a *de novo* review of the agency's classification decision, and the burden is on the agency to justify nondisclosure. The trial court shall require the agency to create as full a public record as possible concerning the nature of the documents and the justification for nondisclosure without compromising the secret nature of the information. If the affidavits show with reasonable specificity why the documents fall within the claimed exemption under the test announced here, then . . . judgment [against disclosure] is appropriate without *in camera* review. . . . If the agency fails to make a sufficient showing by affidavit to permit a responsible *de novo* review, the trial court may order *in camera* review of the documents. . . .

[Judgment reversed and action remanded]

McLAREN, J., concurring. . . . I concur in the majority opinion. However, I believe one aspect of the opinion needs greater emphasis. The placement of detailed information in an affidavit is necessary if the trial court is to be sufficiently apprised of the nature and extent of the information contained in the contested documentation. Disclosure of such information in an affidavit may foreseeably result in disclosure of the information sought by the plaintiff. The defendant, in attempting to keep such information from the plaintiff, will find it extremely difficult to prepare affidavits that give the court sufficient information to determine that a privilege exists while simultaneously constricting the information to safeguard nondisclosure via the affidavit.

The trial court should be hesitant in determining a privilege exists based solely on the affidavits submitted by the defendant, for without an *in camera* review there is no external means to verify the truthfulness of the affidavits submitted by the defendant. I therefore believe that trial courts, except in rare instances, should not determine that a privilege exists without an *in camera* review of the contested documentation. . . .

QUESTIONS

1. When a citizen seeks the disclosure of public records, how important is it that the government officials in charge of the records say that the records are exempt?
2. How are exemptions in a freedom of information statute interpreted?
3. Compare the decision of the majority of the court with the concurring opinion of Justice McLaren.

(b) OPEN MEETINGS. By means of the Sunshine Act of 1976, the federal government requires most meetings of the major administrative agencies to be open to the public. The object of this statute is to enable the public to know what is being done and to prevent administrative misconduct by making an agency aware that the public is watching. Many states have also enacted sunshine laws.

(c) PUBLIC ANNOUNCEMENT OF AGENCY GUIDELINES. To inform the public of the way administrative agencies operate, the APA, with certain exceptions, requires that each federal agency publish the rules, principles, and procedures followed by the agency.[4]

B. LEGISLATIVE POWER OF AN AGENCY

An administrative agency has power to make laws that regulate a particular segment of life or industry.

4. An Agency's Regulations as Law

An agency may adopt regulations within the scope of its authority. If the regulation is not authorized by the law creating the agency, the regulation is invalid. However, until proven invalid, a rule adopted by an administrative agency is deemed valid.

In the early days of administrative regulation, the legislative character of the administrative rules was not clearly perceived. An agency's sphere of power was so narrow that the agency was, in effect, merely a thermostat. That is, the lawmaker told the agency when to do what, and all the agency did was to act in the manner specified by such direction. For example, the cattle inspector was told to take certain steps when it was determined that cattle had hoof-and-mouth disease. Here it was clear that the lawmaker had set the standard, and the agency authority merely swung into action when the specified situation existed.

The next step in the growth of the administrative power was to authorize the cattle inspector to act on the discovery of a contagious cattle disease. Thus, the inspector had to formulate a rule or guide as to which diseases

were contagious. Here again, the discretionary and the legislative aspects of the agency's conduct were obscured by the belief that the field of science would define *contagious*, leaving no area of discretionary decision to the agency.

Today's health commission, an agency, is authorized to make such rules and regulations for the protection or improvement of the common health as it deems desirable. Its rules thus make up the health law.

Gradually, many courts have come to recognize the authority of an agency, even though the lawmaker creating the agency did nothing more than state the goal or objective to be attained by the agency. The modern approach is to regard the administrative agency as possessing all powers necessary to effectively perform the duties entrusted to it. This liberal approach tends to be taken in particular when the work of the agency involves the protection of the public health and welfare.

It has been sufficient for a legislature to authorize an agency to grant licenses "as public interest, convenience, or necessity requires"; "to prohibit unfair methods of competition"; to regulate prices so that they, "in [the agency's] judgment, will be generally fair and equitable"; to prevent "profiteering"; "to prevent the existence of intercorporate holdings, which unduly or unnecessarily complicate the structure [or] unfairly or inequitably distribute voting power among security holders"; and to renegotiate government contracts to prevent "excessive profits."

In the state courts, greater emphasis is placed on establishing "standards" to prevent the administrative agency from being arbitrary or capricious. In any case, an administrative regulation that goes beyond the power granted the agency is invalid. For example, an insurance commissioner is authorized to regulate the forms of insurance policies and to prevent discrimination. However, this authority does not give the commissioner power to adopt a regulation prohibiting insurers from considering whether an applicant for health

---

[4] APA codified to 5 USC 552, Act of September 13, 1976, PL 94-409, 90 stat 1247. See Section 7 of this chapter for a description of the *Federal Register,* the publication in which these agency rules, principles, and procedures are printed.

insurance has human immunodeficiency virus (HIV). Such a condition clearly affects the health of an applicant and is properly considered by an insurer in deciding whether to accept an application.[5]

An administrative agency cannot act beyond the scope of the statute that created it.[6] However, the authority of an agency is not limited to the technology existing when the agency was created. On the contrary, the sphere in which an agency may act expands with new scientific developments.[7]

When the matter is a question of policy not specifically addressed by statute, the agency given the discretion to administer the statute may establish new policies covering such issues. This power is granted whether the lawmaker had intentionally left such matters to the discretion of the agency or had merely never foreseen the problem. In either case, the matter is one to be determined within the discretion of the agency, and a court will not review an agency's policy decision.[8]

5. Public Participation in Adoption of Regulations

In some instances, nongovernmental bodies or persons play a part in furnishing information or opinions that may ultimately affect the adoption of a rule by an agency. This pattern of public participation can be illustrated by the Federal Trade Commission practice, begun in 1919, of calling together members of each significant industry so that the members can discuss which trade practices are fair and which are not. The conclusions of these conferences are not automatically binding on the Federal Trade Commission. They do, however, serve as a valuable means of bringing to the commission detailed information regarding the conduct of the particular industry or business in question. Under the Federal Trade Commission practice, the rules of fair practice agreed to at a trade conference may be approved or disapproved by the commission. When the rules are approved, a further distinction is made between those rules that are "affirmatively approved" by the commission and those that are merely "accepted as expressions of the trade." In the case of the former, the commission will enforce compliance by the members of the industry. In the case of the latter, the commission will accept the practices as fair trade practices but will not enforce compliance by persons not willing to comply. This technique of industry participation has recently been followed by several other major federal administrative agencies. In addition, the APA, with certain exceptions, requires that a federal agency planning to adopt a new regulation must give public notice of such intent. The agency must then hold a public hearing.[9]

6. Public Knowledge of Regulations

When an agency adopts a regulation, a practical problem arises as to how to inform the public of its existence. Some regulations will have already attracted enough public attention that the news media will provide the desired publicity. The great mass of regulations, however, do not attract such attention. To provide publicity for all regulations, the Federal Register Act provides that an administrative regulation is not binding until it is printed in the *Federal Register*. This is a

---

[5] Health Insurance Assn. v Corcoran, 154 App Div 2d 61, 551 NYS2d 615 (1990).

[6] Benton v Board of Supervisors of Napa County, ___ Cal App 3d ___ , 277 Cal Rptr 481 (1991).

[7] United States v Midwest Video Corp. 406 US 649 (1972) (sustaining a commission regulation that provided that "no CATV system having 3,500 or more subscribers shall carry the signal of any television broadcast station unless the system also operates to a significant extent as a local outlet by cablecasting and has available facilities for local production and presentation of programs other than automated services").

[8] Chevron, U.S.A., Inc. v National Resources Defense Council, Inc. 467 US 837 (1984).

[9] APA codified to 5 USC §§ 553, 556, by Act of September 6, 1966, PL 89-554, 80 Stat 383, as amended. The Negotiated Rulemaking Act of 1990, Act of November 15, 1990, PL 101-552, 104 Stat 2736, ___ USC § ___ , encourages federal agencies to formulate their regulations with the cooperation of those affected thereby.

government publication, published five days a week, that lists all administrative regulations, all presidential proclamations and executive orders, and such other documents and classes of documents as the President or Congress may direct.

The Federal Register Act provides that the printing of an administrative regulation in the *Federal Register* is sufficient to give notice of the contents of the regulation to any person subject thereto or affected thereby. This means that no one can claim as an excuse ignorance of the published regulation. This is so even though the person in fact did not know that the regulation had been published in the *Register*. A regulation is effective 30 days after publication.

C. EXECUTIVE POWER OF THE AGENCY

The modern administrative agency has the power to execute the law and to bring proceedings against violators.

7. Execution of the Law

The power of an agency to execute the law is, of course, confined to matters within an agency's jurisdiction. Within that sphere, an agency typically has the power to investigate, to require persons to appear as witnesses, to require witnesses to produce relevant papers and records, and to bring proceedings against violators of the law. In this connection, the phrase *the law* embraces regulations adopted by an agency as well as statutes and court decisions. Increasingly, agencies are required to file opinions and reports or to give explanations for their actions.

An agency may investigate to see if there is any violation of the law or of its rules generally. An agency may also investigate to determine whether additional rules need to be adopted, to ascertain the facts with respect to a particular suspected or alleged violation, and to see if the defendant in a proceeding before it is complying with its final order.

The federal Antitrust Civil Process Act is an example of the extent to which administrative investigation is authorized. The act authorizes the attorney general or the assistant attorney general in charge of the Antitrust Division of the Department of Justice to make a civil investigative demand (CID) on any person believed to have knowledge relevant to any civil antitrust investigation. This might be in connection with an investigation before bringing a suit to enjoin a monopolistic practice or an investigation made on receiving a premerger notification. The person so notified can be compelled to produce relevant documents, furnish written answers to written questions, or appear in person and give oral testimony.[10] Similar power to require the production of papers is possessed by the Federal Trade Commission, the Federal Maritime Commission, the National Science Foundation, the Treasury Department, the Department of Agriculture, the Department of the Army, the Department of Labor, and the Veterans Administration.

8. Constitutional Limitations on Administrative Investigation

The Constitution does not impose any significant limitations on the power of an agency to conduct an investigation.

(a) INSPECTION OF PREMISES. In general, a person has the same protection against unreasonable search and seizure by an administrative officer as that person has against unreasonable search and seizure by a police officer.

In contrast, when the danger of concealment is great, a warrantless search can be made of the premises of a highly regulated business, such as one selling liquor or firearms. Likewise, when violation of the law is

---

[10] Antitrust Civil Process Act of 1962, as amended by the Antitrust Improvement Act of 1976, §§ 101, 102, PL 94-435, 90 Stat 1383, 15 USC § 1311 et seq.

dangerous to health and safety, the law may authorize inspection of the workplace without advance notice or a search warrant when such a requirement could defeat the purpose of the inspection.

(b) AERIAL INSPECTION. A search warrant is never required when the subject matter can be seen from a public place. For example, when a police officer walking on the public pavement can look through an open window and see illegal weapons, a search warrant is not required to enter the premises and seize the weapons. Using airplanes and helicopters, law enforcement officers can see from the air. Can an agency gather information in this manner? It has been held that a police officer may do so,[11] and there is no reason to believe an agency does not possess the same power.

(c) PRODUCTION OF PAPERS. For the most part, the constitutional guarantee against unreasonable search and seizure does not afford much protection with regard to papers and records being investigated by an agency. That guarantee does not apply if there is not an actual seizure. For example, a subpoena to testify or to produce records cannot be opposed on the ground that it is a search and seizure. The constitutional protection is limited to cases of actual physical search and seizure rather than the obtaining of information by compulsion.

The protection afforded by the guarantee against self-incrimination is likewise narrow. It cannot be invoked when a corporate employee or officer in control of corporate records is compelled to produce the records, even though that person would be incriminated by them.[12] It cannot be invoked if records that by law must be kept by the person subject to the administrative investigation are involved.

(d) FAIR RETURN ON REGULATED BUSINESS. When governments regulate the rates of a public utility or insurance company, the business regulated is constitutionally entitled to a rate that will produce a fair return on the assets used in the business.[13]

D. JUDICIAL POWER OF THE AGENCY

The modern administrative agency possesses judicial powers.

9. The Agency as a Specialized Court

An agency may be given power to sit as a court and to determine whether there have been any violations of the law or of the agency regulations. Thus, the National Labor Relations Board determines whether a prohibited labor practice has been committed. The Federal Trade Commission acts as a court to determine whether unfair competition exists.

Although an administrative agency may be given judicial power, it is not a court.[14]

At first glance, the conferring of any judicial power on an administrative agency seems contrary to American tradition. When an administrative agency sits as judge to determine whether one of its regulations has been violated, there is some question whether the agency is impartial. The agency is trying the accused for violating agency law rather than "the law." There is also the objection that an agency is determining important rights but does so without a jury. This seems inconsistent with the long-established emphasis of our history on the sanctity of trial by jury. In spite of these objections to an agency's exercise of judicial power, such exercise is now firmly established.

---

[11] California v Ciraolo, 476 US 207 (1986)

[12] Braswell v United States, 487 US 99 (1988).

[13] California Automobile Assigned Risk Plan v Gillespie, ___Cal App 3d___ , 280 Cal Rptr 217 (1991).

[14] Beyer v Employees Retirement System of Texas (Tex App) 808 SW2d 622 (1991).

An agency cannot make a decision without first deciding that the matter comes within its scope of authority.

10. Pattern of Administrative Procedure

At the beginning of the era of modern regulation of business, the power of agencies to adjudicate rested, to a large extent, on minor executives or police officers charged with the responsibility of enforcing laws applicable to limited fact situations. The example of the health officer empowered to condemn and destroy diseased cattle was typical. In view of the need for prompt action, and because of the relative simplicity of the fact determination to be made, it was customary for such a person to exercise summary powers. On finding cattle believed to be diseased, the officer would destroy the animals immediately. There would be no delays to find their true owner or to hold a formal hearing to determine whether the animals were in fact diseased.

Today, the exercise of summary powers is the exceptional case. Concepts of due process generally require that some notice be given those who will be adversely affected and that some form of hearing be held at which they may present their case.

(a) PRELIMINARY STEPS. It is commonly provided that either a private individual aggrieved by the conduct of another or an agency may file a written complaint. This complaint is then served on the alleged wrongdoer, who is given the opportunity to file an answer. There may be other phases of pleading between the parties and the agency, but eventually the matter comes before the agency to be heard. After a hearing, the agency makes a decision and enters an order either dismissing the complaint or directing the adverse party to carry out or refrain from certain acts.

The complaint filing and prehearing stage of the procedure may be more detailed. In many of the modern administrative statutes, provision is made for an examination of the informal complaint by some branch of the agency to determine whether the case comes within the scope of the agency's authority. It is also commonly provided that an investigation be made by the agency to determine whether the facts are such as to warrant a hearing of the complaint. If it is decided that the complaint is within the jurisdiction of the agency and that the facts appear to justify it, a formal complaint is issued and served on the adverse party. An answer is then filed as stated above.

With the increasing complexity of the subjects regulated by administrative agencies, the trend is to require greater preliminary examination on the basis of an informal complaint.

(b) THE ADMINISTRATIVE HEARING. To satisfy the requirements of due process, it is generally necessary for an agency to give notice and to hold a hearing at which all persons affected may be present. A person indirectly affected by administrative action cannot take part in the administrative hearing. An existing enterprise has no standing to challenge the granting of a license to a new business that will be a competitor.[15]

A significant difference between an agency's hearing and a court hearing is that there is no right of trial by jury before an agency. For example, a workers' compensation board may decide a claim without any jury. Similarly, there is no right to a jury trial in an action for violation of the Age Discrimination in Employment Act. The absence of a jury does not constitute a denial of due process. A jury trial was demanded in the *Atlas Roofing* case.

An agency is ordinarily not subject to the rules of evidence. Another significant difference between an administrative hearing and a judicial determination is that an agency may be authorized to make an initial determination without holding a hearing. If an agency's conclusion is challenged, the agency will then hold a hearing. A court, on the other hand, must have a trial before it makes a judgment.

---

[15] Pie Mut. Ins. Co. v Kentucky Medical Ins. Co. (Ky App) 782 SW2d 51 (1990).

ATLAS ROOFING COMPANY, INC. v OCCUPATIONAL SAFETY AND HEALTH REVIEW COMMISSION
430 US 442 (1977)

In order to protect factory and industrial workers from unnecessary hazards and unsafe working conditions, Congress adopted the Occupational Safety and Health Act of 1970 (OSHA). The Act is administered by the Occupational Safety and Health Administration (also known as OSHA). If an OSHA examiner finds a dangerous condition in a place of employment, the employer is ordered to eliminate the bad condition. If the employer does not do so, OSHA can impose a fine or civil penalty on the employer. In the *Atlas Roofing* case, the OSHA examiner decided that a condition in the Atlas Roofing Company was hazardous and ordered its correction. Atlas Roofing refused to do so. OSHA imposed a fine on Atlas. Atlas claimed that it was entitled to a jury trial on the question of whether there was a hazardous working condition and whether the company had violated the law. Atlas claimed that this right to trial by jury was guaranteed by the Seventh Amendment of the federal Constitution. That amendment declares: "In suits at common law, where the value in controversy shall exceed twenty dollars, the right of trial by jury shall be preserved. . . ." The lower court decided against Atlas, and it appealed.

WHITE, J. . . . The issue in this case is whether, consistent with the Seventh Amendment, Congress may create a new cause of action in the Government for civil penalties enforceable in an administrative agency where there is no jury trial. After extensive investigation, Congress concluded, in 1970, that work-related deaths and injuries had become a "drastic" national problem.

. . . Congress enacted the Occupational Safety and Health Act of 1970. . . . The Act created a new statutory duty to avoid maintaining unsafe or unhealthy working conditions, and empowers the Secretary of Labor to promulgate health and safety standards. Two new remedies were provided—permitting the Federal Government, proceeding before an administrative agency, (1) to obtain abatement orders requiring employers to correct unsafe working conditions and (2) to impose civil penalties on any employer maintaining any unsafe working condition. Each remedy exists whether or not an employee is actually injured or killed as a result of the condition, and existing state statutory and common law remedies for actual injury and death remain unaffected.

Under the Act, inspectors, representing the Secretary of Labor, are authorized to conduct reasonable safety and health inspections. . . . If a violation is discovered, the inspector, on behalf of the Secretary, issues a citation to the employer fixing a reasonable time for its abatement and, in his discretion, proposing a civil penalty. . . . Such proposed penalties may range from nothing for de minimis and nonserious violations, to not more than $1,000 for serious violations, to a maximum of $10,000 for willful or repeated violations. . . .

If the employer wishes to contest the penalty or the abatement order, he may do so by notifying the Secretary of Labor within 15 days, in which event the abatement order is automatically stayed. . . . An evidentiary hearing is then held before an administrative law judge of the Occupational Safety and Health Review Commission. The Commission consists of three members, appointed for six-year terms, each of whom is qualified to adjudicate contested citations and assess penalties "by reason of training, education or experience." . . . At this hearing the burden is on the Secretary to establish the elements of the alleged violation and the propriety of his proposed abatement order and proposed penalty; and the judge is empowered to affirm, modify, or vacate any or all of these items, giving due consideration in his penalty assessment to "the size of the business of the employer . . . , the gravity of the violation, the good faith of the employer, and the history of previous violations." . . . The judge's decision becomes the Commission's final and appealable order unless within 30 days a Commissioner directs that it be reviewed by the full Commission. . . .

If review is granted, the Commission's subsequent order directing abatement and the payment of any assessed penalty becomes final unless the employer timely petitions for judicial review in the appropriate court of appeals. . . . The Secretary similarly may seek review of Commission orders, . . . but, in either case, "the findings of the Commission with respect to questions of fact, if supported by substantial evidence on the record considered as a whole, shall be conclusive." . . . If the employer fails to pay the assessed penalty, the Secretary may commence a collection action in a federal district court in which neither the fact of the violation nor the propriety of the penalty assessed may be retried. . . . Thus, the penalty may be collected without the employer ever being entitled to a jury determination of the facts constituting the violation.

Congress has often created new statutory obligations, provided for civil penalties for their violation, and committed exclusively to an administrative agency the function of deciding whether a violation has in fact occurred. These statutory schemes have been sustained by this Court. . . .

. . . It is apparent from the history of jury trial in civil matters that factfinding, which is the essential function of the jury in civil cases . . . was never the exclusive province of the jury under either the English or American legal systems at the time of the adoption of the Seventh Amendment; and the question whether a fact would be found by a jury turned to a considerable degree on the nature of the forum in which a litigant found himself. Critical factfinding was performed without juries in suits in equity, and there were no juries in admiralty . . . neither was there in the military justice system. The jury was the factfinding mode in most suits in the common law courts, but it was not exclusively so: condemnation was a suit at common law but constitutionally could be tried without a jury. . . .

The Seventh Amendment was declaratory of the existing law, for it required only that jury trial in suits at common law was to be "preserved." It thus did not purport to require a jury trial where none was required before. . . .

The point is that the Seventh Amendment was never intended to establish the jury as the exclusive mechanism for factfinding in civil cases. It took the existing legal order as it found it, and there is little or no basis for concluding that the

Amendment should now be interpreted to provide an impenetrable barrier to administrative factfinding under otherwise valid federal regulatory statutes. We cannot conclude that the Amendment rendered Congress powerless—when it concluded that remedies available in courts of law were inadequate to cope with a problem within Congress' power to regulate—to create new public rights and remedies by statute and commit their enforcement, if it chose, to a tribunal other than a court of law—such as an administrative agency—in which facts are not found by juries. . . .

Congress found the common law and other existing remedies for work injuries resulting from unsafe working conditions to be inadequate to protect the Nation's working men and women. It created a new cause of action, and remedies therefor, unknown to the common law, and placed their enforcement in a tribunal supplying speedy and expert resolutions of the issues involved. The Seventh Amendment is no bar to the creation of new rights or to their enforcement outside the regular courts of law.

[Judgment affirmed]

QUESTIONS

1. Who was the plaintiff in this case?
2. Who was the defendant in this case?
3. The right to trial by jury exists in all important cases. Appraise this statement.

This has important practical consequences in that when a hearing is sought after an agency has acted, the objecting party has the burden of proof and the cost of going forward. The result is that fewer persons go to the trouble of seeking such a hearing. This, in turn, reduces the number of hearings and the amount of litigation in which an agency becomes involved. Thus, from the government's standpoint, money and time are saved.

It is held that when the administrative action concerns only the individuals directly affected, rather than a class of persons or the community in general, it is necessary to have some form of hearing before an agency may make a judicial decision. Thus, it has been held that, since a civil service employee may only be removed for cause, it is a denial of due process for a statute to authorize an agency to remove the employee without a hearing. It is not sufficient that the employee is given the right to appeal such action. Because the employee has a significant interest in continued employment, there must be some preremoval hearing to determine that there is no basic error in the administrative action.[16]

(c) STREAMLINED PROCEDURE. Informal settlement and consent decrees are practical devices to cut across the procedures outlined above. In many instances, the alleged wrongdoer is willing to change when informally notified that a complaint has been made. It is, therefore, sound public relations, as well as expeditious handling of the matter, for an agency to inform the alleged wrongdoer

---

[16] Cleveland Board of Education v Loudermill, 470 US 532 (1985).

of the charge made prior to the filing of any formal complaint. A matter that has already gone into the formal hearing stage may also be terminated by agreement, and a stipulation or consent decree may be filed setting forth the terms of the agreement.

Streamlining of procedure is encouraged by the Administrative Dispute Resolution Act of 1990, which authorizes federal agencies to use alternative means of dispute resolution.

(d) REHEARING AND CORRECTION OF ADMINISTRATIVE ACTION. Under some statutes, an agency is given power to rehear or correct a decision within a certain time.

11. Punishment and Enforcement Powers of Agencies

Originally, agencies could not impose punishment or enforce decisions. If the person regulated did not voluntarily comply with an agency's decision, the agency could only petition a court to order that person to obey.

Within the last few decades, agencies have been increasingly given the power to impose a penalty and to issue orders that are binding on the regulated person unless an appeal is taken to a court and the administrative decision reversed. As an illustration of the power to impose penalties, the Occupational Safety and Health Act of 1970 provides for the assessment of civil penalties against employers failing to put an end to dangerous working conditions when ordered to do so by the administrative agency created by that statute. Likewise, environmental protection statutes adopted by states commonly give the state agency the power to assess a penalty for a violation of the environmental protection regulations. As an illustration of the issuance of binding orders, the Federal Trade Commission can issue a **cease and desist order** to stop a practice that it

decides is improper. This order to stop is binding unless reversed on an appeal.

(a) COMPLIANCE VERIFICATION. To assure itself that a particular person is obeying the law, including the agency's regulations and orders, an administrative agency may require proof of compliance. At times, the question of compliance may be directly determined by an agency investigation, either of a building or plant or by an examination of witnesses and documents. An agency may require the regulated person or enterprise to file reports in a specified form.[17] An agency may also hold a hearing or audit on the question of compliance and may require the filing of a detailed statement or plan of operation showing that the regulated person or enterprise is acting properly.

(b) COMPLAINANT INDEMNIFICATION. When the administrative decision is that the defendant has caused a loss to or harmed a particular person, can the administrative agency compensate or indemnify the harmed person for the loss? Until the 1930s, the answer to this question was that the administrative agency could stop further wrong but could not undo or compensate for past wrong. Beginning with the New Deal legislation of the 1930s, administrative agencies have been given the power in some cases to provide indemnity to the party harmed by the defendant's wrong. Such power is not unlimited. Its boundaries are defined by the statute creating the agency.

12. Exhaustion of Administrative Remedy

When the law creates an agency, all parties must follow the procedure specified by the law. An appeal may be taken to a court, but it cannot be taken until the agency has acted. The principle is that, as a matter of policy,

---

[17] United States v Morton Salt Co. 338 US 632 (1950).

parties are required to exhaust the administrative remedy before they may go into court or take an appeal.[18]

As long as an agency is acting within the scope of its authority or jurisdiction, a party cannot appeal before the agency has made a final decision. The fact that the complaining party does not want the agency to decide the matter, or is afraid that the agency will reach a wrong decision, is not grounds for bypassing the agency by going to court before the agency has acted.

13. Appeal from Administrative Action

The statute creating the modern administrative agency generally provides for the taking of an appeal from the administrative decision to a particular court. The statute may state that a party in interest or any person aggrieved by the administrative action may appeal. This requires the appellant to have a legally recognized right or interest that is harmed by the administrative action. The fact that a person or persons do not like the action of the agency does not entitle them to appeal.

14. Finality of Administrative Determination

Basic to the Anglo-American legal theory is the belief that no one, not even a branch of the government, is above the law. Thus, the growth of powers of the administrative agency was frequently accepted or tolerated on the theory that if the administrative agency went too far, the courts would review the administrative action. The typical modern statute provides that an appeal may be taken from the administrative action.

When the question that an agency decides is a question of law, the court on appeal will reverse the agency if the court disagrees with the decision.[19] This concept is being eroded to some extent by modern technology. Thus, it is held that the court will accept the agency's interpretation of the statute when the statute relates to a technical matter. Here the court will tend to accept the agency's interpretation as long as it is reasonable, even though it is not the only interpretation that could have been made.[20]

In contrast with an agency's decision on matters of law, the controversy may turn on a question of fact or a mixed question of law and fact. In such cases, a court will accept the conclusion of an agency if it is supported by substantial evidence. This means that the court must examine the entire record of the proceedings before the administrative agency to see if there was substantial evidence to support the administrative findings. A court will not reverse an agency's decision merely because the court would have made a different decision on the same facts.[21] Since most disputes before an agency are based on questions of fact, the net result is that the decision of the agency will be final in most cases.

When the question is whether the administrative action is in harmony with the policy of the statute creating the agency, the appellate court will sustain the administrative action when it is supported by substantial evidence.[22]

The greatest limitation on court review of the administrative action is the rule that a decision involving discretion will not be reversed in the absence of an error of law or a clear abuse of, or the arbitrary or capricious exercise of, discretion. The courts reason that since the members of the agencies were

---

[18] Gezendorf v Washburn, 207 Ill App 3d 397, 152 Ill Dec 372, 565 NE2d 1054 (1991).

[19] Re Minnesota Joint Underwriting Assn. (Minn App) 408 NW2d 599 (1987).

[20] Chemical Mfrs. Assn. v Natural Resources Defense Council, Inc. 470 US 116 (1985).

[21] Gust v Pomeroy (ND) 466 NW2d 137 (1991). The appellate court cannot review the evidence to determine the credibility of the witnesses who testified before the administrative agency. Hammann v City of Omaha, 227 Neb 285, 417 NW2d 323 (1987).

[22] 27 AFL-CIO v OSHA (CA11 OSHA) 965 F2d 962 (1992).

appointed because of expert ability, it would be absurd for the court, which is unqualified technically to make a decision in the matter, to step in and determine whether the agency made the proper choice. Courts will not do so unless the agency has clearly acted wrongly, arbitrarily, or capriciously. As a practical matter, the action of an agency is rarely found to be arbitrary or capricious. As long as an agency has followed the proper procedure, the fact that the court disagrees with the conclusion reached by the agency does not make that conclusion arbitrary or capricious. In areas in which economic or technical matters are involved, it is generally sufficient that the agency had a reasonable basis for the decision made. A court will not attempt to second-guess the agency as to complex criteria with which an administrative agency is intimately familiar. The judicial attitude is that, for protection from laws and regulations that are unwise, improvident, or out of harmony with a particular school of thought, the people must resort to the ballot box, not to the court.

Because of limited funding and staff, an agency must exercise discretion as to which cases should be handled. Ordinarily, the decision of an agency to do nothing about a particular complaint will not be reversed by a court.[23] That is, the courts will not override an agency's decision to do nothing. Exceptions are made, however, when it is obvious that the agency is refusing to act for an improper reason. If it is obvious that the agency wrongly believed that there was no authority to act, that the agency had taken a bribe to keep out, or that, on the basis of the facts, there was no logical explanation for the agency's refusal to act, then the court may override the decision.

The *Consumer Federation* case raised the question of whether the agency's decision to do nothing should be reversed.

CONSUMER FEDERATION OF AMERICA v CONSUMER PRODUCT SAFETY COMMISSION
(CA Dist Col) 990 F2d 1298 (1993)

All-terrain vehicles (ATVs) have a high center of gravity. This requires the rider making a turn to lean to the inside of the turn. Failure to do so may cause the vehicle to topple outward and injure the rider. The federal Consumer Product Safety Commission (CPSC) brought a lawsuit seeking to have a court declare that ATVs were "imminently dangerous." Such a determination would trigger the statutory powers of the Commission to take additional steps to eliminate the danger. The court did not make any decision because the parties ended the lawsuit with a consent decree by which the Commission and the distributor defendants agreed that specified training would be given to buyers of ATVs and that warning labels would be attached to ATVs. The Consumer Federation then filed a petition to compel the Commission to prohibit the sale of adult-size ATVs to buyers under 16 years of age. The frequency of accidents to such buyers was higher because

---

[23] Heckler v Chaney, 470 US 821 (1985).

they did not have sufficient weight or experience to balance the adult-size vehicle.

GINSBURG, J. . . . The consent decrees require that distributors use their best efforts to assure that adult-sized ATVs are not purchased for use by children. The distributors have assured CPSC that they are monitoring the dealers' conformance with the age recommendations. While serious concerns have been raised in the past about the level of conformance, the distributors have declared their intention to monitor and enforce this requirement through their franchise agreements. Therefore, it can be expected that future buyers will be better advised that children should not ride adult-size ATVs.

. . . The Commission added that it would monitor the distributors' efforts to ensure dealer adherence to the age specifications and "could consider whether a [youth] ban . . . is warranted if the distributors' age recommendations prove to be ineffective." . . .

. . . Petitioners . . . urge only that the CPSC acted arbitrarily in failing to ban the sale of adult-size ATVs for use by children. See 5 U.S.C. 706(2)(A) (Administrative Procedure Act instruction that court may set aside agency action that is "arbitrary, capricious, an abuse of discretion, or otherwise not in accordance with law"). Because of the high price of ATVs (in 1989, the average price of a new ATV was $3,000 . . .), a ban on sales for child riders would be directed, in the main, to adult purchasers. The Consent Decree already in place requires multiple notices that adult-size ATVs should *never* be operated by children under 16. . . .

After six years of study, the Commission had before it an extensive record on ATV safety hazards. . . . By instituting the "imminent hazard" action, negotiating the comprehensive Consent Decree, and securing the dealer monitoring agreements, the Commission has taken meaningful action against ATV dangers generally, with harm to children a concern particularly addressed.

We accord due respect, moreover, to an agency's selection of means for pursuing policy goals. Such choices implicate the allocation of scarce administrative resources; they involve forecasts about the consequences of proposed regulatory actions and other matters the agency ordinarily is best equipped to judge. . . .

We leave undisturbed the Commission's . . . decision against a youth ban. . . . Experience under the Consent Decree was not yet adequate to enable the Commission to judge the impact of the decree on ATV casualty rates. . . . The Commission opted, for the time being, to concentrate on monitoring and enforcing the Consent Decree without simultaneously imposing a partial product ban. That choice was rational. . . .

The Commission . . . agrees with petitioners that adult-size ATVs should *never* be sold for use by persons under age 16, and it has taken action we cannot now say will prove ineffective. . . .

We have no cause to doubt the genuineness of the Commission's representation that it "remains especially concerned about the number of children under age 16 who are injured or killed in ATV accidents," . . . and its readiness to revisit the youth ban if current monitoring reveals a need for that measure.

Nothing in the CPSA prevented the Commission from . . . instituting a youth ban. We are not persuaded, however, that the Commission was "arbitrary" or "capricious" in preferring to test and evaluate the efficacy of the Consent Decree before considering additional regulation. In view of the Commission's representations that it "will continue to monitor the effectiveness of [the Consent Decree] program,". . . and "consider whether a ban of ATVs for use by children is warranted if the distributors' [efforts under the Consent Decree] prove ineffective" . . . we deny the instant petition for review.

[Review refused]

QUESTIONS

1. By what authority could the Commission agree to terminate the action before it came to a final conclusion?
2. Why did the parties agree to the consent decree?

15. Liability of the Agency

The decision of an agency may cause substantial loss to a business by increasing its operating costs or by making a decision that later is shown to be harmful to the economy. An agency is not liable for such loss when it has acted in good faith in the exercise of discretionary powers. An administrator who wrongly denies a person the benefit of a government program is not personally liable to that person even though that person's constitutional rights have been violated.[24]

SUMMARY

The administrative agency is unique because it combines the three functions that are kept separate under our traditional governmental system: legislative, executive, and judicial. By virtue of legislative power, an agency adopts regulations that have the force of law, although the members of the agency were not elected by those who are subject to the regulations. By virtue of the executive power, an agency carries out and enforces the regulations, makes investigations, and requires the production of documents. By virtue of the judicial power, an agency acts as a court to determine whether there has been a violation of any regulation. To some extent, an agency is restricted by constitutional limitations in making inspection of premises and in requiring the production of papers. These limitations, however, have a very narrow application. The protection against unreasonable search and seizure and the protection against self-incrimination are so narrowed by judicial construction as to have little protective value. When an agency acts as a judge, it is not required that there be a jury trial or that the ordinary courtroom procedures be followed. Typically, an agency will give notice to the person claimed to be acting improperly, and a hearing will then be held

---

[24] Schweiker v Chilicky, 487 US 412 (1988).

before the agency. When the agency has determined that there has been a violation, the stopping of the violation may be ordered. Under some statutes, the agency may go further and impose a penalty on the violator.

An appeal to a court may be taken from any decision of the agency by a person harmed thereby. Only a person with a legally recognized interest can appeal from the agency ruling. No appeal can be taken until every step available before the agency has been taken; that is, the administrative remedy must first be exhausted.

As a practical matter, an appeal from the administrative action will ordinarily have little value. When the controversy turns on a determination of facts, a court will not reverse the decision of an agency because it disagrees with the conclusion that the agency drew from those facts. When an agency is given discretion to act, a court will never reverse the agency just because it disagrees with the choice the agency made. In contrast, if an agency made a wrong decision as to a question of law, a court will generally reverse the agency when the court disagrees with the decision. In the absence of an error of law, an agency's decision will be reversed only if the court decides that the administrative action was arbitrary and capricious.

Protection from secret government is provided by the right to know what most administrative agency records contain, by the requirement that most agency meetings be open to the public, by the invitation to the public to take part in rule making, and by publicity given, through publication in the *Federal Register*, to the guidelines followed by the agency and to regulations that have been adopted.

LAW IN PRACTICE

1. Understand the role of the administrative agency as a feature of the unwritten constitution.
2. Participate in the rule-making process of the administrative agency affecting your business when such opportunity is available to you.

3. Seek the appointment of qualified persons to administrative agencies, because for most purposes they are the government.

QUESTIONS AND CASE PROBLEMS

1. What social forces are affected by the principle that the same administrative agency may conduct an investigation to determine if there is reason to believe that there has been a violation, and then hold a hearing to determine whether in fact there was a violation?
2. The U.S. Congress adopted a law to provide insurance to protect wheat farmers. The agency in charge of the program adopted regulations to govern applications for this insurance. These regulations were published in the *Federal Register*. Merrill applied for insurance, but his application did not comply with the regulations. He claimed that he was not bound by the regulations because he never knew they had been adopted. Is he bound by the regulations? [*Federal Crop Insurance Corp. v Merrill, 332 US 380*]
3. The federal Department of Housing and Urban Development (HUD) decides to hold a conference of leading building contractors for the purpose of deciding patterns of urban development that should be encouraged by HUD. Culpepper wants to attend the meeting. She is denied admission because she is neither a government official nor a building contractor. Is she entitled to attend the meeting?
4. Adams is appointed the state price control administrator. By virtue of this position, he requires all sellers of goods and suppliers of services to keep records of the prices they charge. He

suspects that the Ace Overhead Garage Door Corporation is charging more than the prices permitted by law. To determine this, he notifies the company to produce the records that it was required to keep. It refuses to do so on the ground that Adams does not have the authority to require the production of papers. Is this a valid defense?

5. Bell was employed by the Sinclair Radio Corporation. She was fired from her job and made a complaint to the National Labor Relations Board that she was fired because she belonged to a union. The examiner of the board held a hearing, at which Bell produced evidence of an antiunion attitude of the employer. The employer produced evidence that Bell had been fired because she was chronically late and did poor work. The examiner and the Labor Relations Board concluded that Bell was fired because of her union membership. Sinclair appealed. The court reached the conclusion that, if the court had been the board, it would have held that the discharge of Bell was justified because it would not have believed the testimony of Bell's witnesses. Will the court reverse the decision of the National Labor Relations Board?

6. Santa Monica adopted a rent control ordinance authorizing the Rent Control Board to set the amount of rents that could be charged. At a hearing before the board, the board determined that McHugh was charging his tenant a rent greater than the maximum rent allowed. McHugh claimed that the action of the board was improper because there was no jury trial. Decide. *[McHugh v Santa Monica Rent Control Board, 49 Cal 3d 348, 261 Cal Rptr 318, 777 P2d 91]*

7. The New York City charter authorizes the New York City Board of Health to adopt a health code and declares that it shall have the force and effect of law. The board adopted a code that provided for the fluoridation of the public water supply. A suit was brought to enjoin the carrying out of this program on the grounds that it was unconstitutional and that money could not be spent to carry out such a program in the absence of a statute authorizing such expenditure. It was also claimed that the fluoridation program was unconstitutional because there were other means of reducing tooth decay; fluoridation was discriminatory in that it benefited only children; it unlawfully imposed medication on the children without their consent; and fluoridation is or may be dangerous to health. Was the code provision valid? *[Paduano v City of New York, 257 NYS2d 531]*

8. The Federal Trade Commission directs the Essex Manufacturing Company to install safety devices in its factory. Essex claims that the order of the commission can be ignored because the members of the commission were not elected by the voters, and therefore the commission cannot make an order that has the force of law. Is this defense valid?

9. By training and work experience, Templeton was a plumbing and heating maintenance worker. Templeton sustained an injury, which made him unable to use his right arm. Because of this, he left his regular employment and took a half-time job with Black Hills State College to run a program of preventive maintenance of equipment. The job required a knowledge of computer programming and data processing. Templeton resigned after a while because he could not live on the half-time pay. He filed a claim for disability benefits under the State Retirement System. The retirement statute defined disability as "any medically determinable physical or mental impairment which prevents a member from performing his usual duties for his employer, or the duties of a position of comparable level for which he is qualified by education, training, and experience . . . ." The Retirement Board denied his application because he could work for the state college. Templeton took an appeal. Decide. *[Re Templeton (SD) 403 NW2d 398]*

10. The Occupational Safety and Health Act of 1970 authorizes the secretary of labor to adopt job safety standards to protect workers from harmful substances. The secretary is directed by the statute to adopt that standard which most adequately assures, to the extent feasible, on the basis of the best available evidence that no employee will suffer material impairment of health. Acting under this authorization, the secretary adopted a Cotton Dust Standard to protect workers exposed to cotton dust. This dust causes serious lung disease that disables about one out of twelve cotton factory workers. The cotton industry attacked the validity of the Cotton Dust Standard on the ground that the secretary, in adopting the standard, had not considered the cost to the cotton industry of complying with the standard (a cost of $656.5 million). Was the Cotton Dust Standard valid? *[American Textile Manufacturers Institute, Inc. v Donovan, 452 US 490]*

11. The Macon County Landfill Corporation (MCL) applied for permission to expand the boundaries of its landfill. This was opposed by Tate and others. After a number of hearings, the appropriate agency granted the requested permission to expand. Tate appealed and claimed that the agency had made a wrong decision on the basis of the evidence presented. Will the court determine if the correct decision was made? *[Tate v Illinois Pollution Control Board, 188 Ill App 3d 994, 136 Ill Dec 401, 544 NE2d 1176]*

12. The planning commissioner and a real estate developer planned to meet to discuss the rezoning of certain land in order to permit the real estate developer to construct certain buildings that were not allowed under the then-existing zoning law. A homeowners' association claimed that it had the right to be present at the meeting. This claim was objected to on the theory that the state's Open Meetings Act applied only to meetings of the specified governmental units and did not extend to a meeting between one of them and an outsider. Was this objection valid?

13. The Michigan Freedom of Information Act declares that it is the state policy to give all persons full information as to the actions of the government and that "the people shall be informed so that they may participate in the democratic process." The union of clerical workers in Michigan State University requested the trustees of the University to give them the names and addresses of persons making money donations to the University. The objection was made that the disclosure of addresses could not be required and was a violation of the right of privacy. Decide. *[Clerical-Technical Union of Michigan State University v Board of Trustees of Michigan State University, ___Mich App___, 475 NW2d 373]*

14. The Jones Corporation wanted to build an additional plant. By state law, it was required to obtain the approval of the state environmental protection agency. Jones made an application for such approval. Nothing happened. Jones Corporation complained about the delay. The state agency explained that it was studying the environmental pollution problems of similar factories in other states and this was taking time. Jones was afraid that the delay would cause it to lose investors. Jones filed a petition in court to obtain approval of its expansion plan. What decision should the court make?

15. A state law authorized the state Insurance Commissioner to impose a fine and suspend the license of any insurance agent selling "unnecessary or excessive" insurance. Eloise was a licensed agent. The Insurance Commissioner fined her $600 and suspended her license for three months for selling "unnecessary and excessive" insurance. She objected to this action on the ground that the statute under which the Insurance Commissioner had acted was unconstitutional in that "unnecessary" and "excessive" were too vague and indefinite to have any meaning and therefore it was unconstitutional to penalize her for violating such a standard. Decide.

CHAPTER 6

THE LEGAL ENVIRONMENT OF INTERNATIONAL TRADE

LEARNING OBJECTIVES

After studying this chapter, you will be able to:
1. *Identify seven major international organizations, conferences, and treaties.*
2. *Describe the forms of business organizations that exist for doing business abroad.*
3. *Identify conduct outside of the United States to which the U.S. antitrust laws will apply.*
4. *Differentiate between secrecy laws and blocking laws in regard to SEC enforcement of U.S. securities laws.*
5. *List and explain the laws that provide protection against unfair competition from foreign goods.*
6. *List and explain the laws that provide economic relief for those adversely affected by import competition.*
7. *List and explain the laws enacted to increase the foreign sales of U.S. firms.*

The success or failure of the American firms doing business in foreign countries may well depend on accurate information about the laws and customs of the host countries. In their domestic operations, American business firms compete against imports from other nations. Such imported goods include Japanese automobiles, German steel, French wine, Taiwanese textiles, and Chilean copper. American business firms should be well aware of the business practices of foreign business firms in order to compete effectively, and also to ascertain if foreign firms are using unfair methods of competition in violation of American antitrust laws, antidumping laws, or international trade agreements.

Individuals from all over the world participate in the U.S. securities markets. Special problems exist in the regulation and enforcement of American securities laws involving financial institutions of countries with secrecy laws.

A. GENERAL PRINCIPLES

Nations enter into treaties and conferences to further international trade. The business world has developed certain forms of organizations for conducting that trade.

1. The Legal Background

Because of the complexity and ever-changing character of the legal environment of international trade, this section will focus on certain underlying elements.

(a) WHAT LAW APPLIES. When there is a sale of goods within the United States, there is typically one law that applies to the transaction. Some variation may be introduced when the transaction is between parties in different states, but for the most part, the law governing the transaction is the American law of contracts and the Uniform Commercial Code. In contrast, when an international sale is made, it is necessary to determine whether it is the law of the exporter's state or the law of the importer's state that will govern. The parties

to an international contract often resolve that question themselves as part of their contract, setting forth which state's law will govern should a dispute arise. Such a provision is called a **choice of law clause**.

A number of treaties have been entered into by the major trading countries of the world. When their citizens deal with each other, and their respective rights are not controlled in their contract, their rights and liabilities are determined by looking at the treaty. These treaties are discussed in Section 2 of this chapter.

(b) THE ARBITRATION ALTERNATIVE. Traditional litigation may be considered too time consuming, expensive, and divisive to the relationships of the parties to an international venture. The parties may therefore agree to arbitrate any contractual disputes that may arise, according to dispute resolution procedures set forth in the contract.

Pitfalls exist for U.S. companies arbitrating disputes in foreign lands. For example, were an American company to agree to arbitrate a contractual dispute with a Chinese organization in China, it would find that the arbitrator must be Chinese. Also, under Chinese law only Chinese lawyers can present an arbitration case, even if one party is an American company. Because of situations like this, it is common for parties to international ventures to agree to arbitrate their disputes in neutral countries.

An arbitration agreement gives the parties greater control over the decision-making process. The parties can require that the arbitrator have the technical, language, and legal qualifications to best understand their dispute. While procedures exist for the prearbitration exchange of documents, full "discovery" is ordinarily not allowed. The decision of the arbitrator is final and binding on the parties, with very limited judicial review possible.

(c) CONFLICTING IDEOLOGIES. Law, for all people and at all times, is the result of the desire of the lawmaker to achieve certain goals. These are the social forces that make the law. In the eyes of the lawmaker, the attainment of these goals is proper and therefore ethical. This does not mean that we all can agree on what the international law should be, because different people have different ideas as to what is right. This affects our views as to ownership, trade, and dealings with foreign merchants. For example, a very large part of the world does not share the American dislike for trusts. Other countries do not have our antitrust laws; therefore, their merchants can form a trust to create greater bargaining power in dealing with American and other foreign merchants.

(d) FINANCING INTERNATIONAL TRADE. There is no international currency. This creates problems as to what currency to use and how to make payment in international transactions. Centuries ago, buyers used precious metals, jewels, or furs in payment. Today the parties to an international transaction agree in their sales contract on the currency to be used to pay for the goods. They commonly require that the buyer furnish a **letter of credit**. By this, an issuer, typically a bank, agrees to pay the amount of drafts drawn against the buyer for the purchase price. In trading with merchants in some countries, the foreign country itself will promise that the seller will be paid.

2. International Trade Organizations, Conferences, and Treaties

A large number of organizations exist that affect the multinational markets for goods, services, and investments. A survey of major international organizations, conferences, and treaties follows.

(a) GATT. The **General Agreement on Tariffs and Trade** (GATT) is a multilateral treaty,

subscribed to by 96 governments, including the United States. Together, these countries account for more than four-fifths of world trade. The basic aim of the GATT is to liberalize world trade and place it on a secure basis, thereby contributing to economic growth and development of the world's peoples.

The GATT is based on the fundamental principles of trade without discrimination and protection through tariffs. The principle of trade without discrimination is embodied in its **most favored nation** clause. In the application and administration of import and export duties and charges, all contracting parties are bound to grant to each other treatment as favorable as they give to any country. Thus, no country is to give special trading advantages to another. All countries that are parties to GATT are to be on an equal basis and share the benefits of any moves toward lower trade barriers. Exceptions to this basic rule are allowed in certain special circumstances involving regional trading arrangements, such as the European Economic Community (the Common Market). Special preferences are also granted to developing countries. The second basic principle is that where protection is given for domestic industry, it should be extended essentially through a tariff, not through other commercial measures. The aim of this rule is to make the extent of protection clear and to make competition possible.

(b) CISG. The **United Nations Convention on Contracts for the International Sale of Goods** (CISG)[1] sets forth uniform rules to govern international sales contracts. The CISG became effective on January 1, 1988, between the United States and the other nations that had approved it.[2] The provisions of the CISG have been strongly influenced by Article 2 of the Uniform Commercial Code.

---

[1] 52 Fed. Reg. 6262 (1987).

[2] As of October 1993, the contracting nations were Argentina, Australia, Austria, Bulgaria, Byelorussia, Canada, Chile, China, Czechoslovakia, Denmark, Ecuador, Egypt, Finland, France, Germany, Guinea, Hungary, Iraq, Italy, Lesotho, Mexico, the Netherlands, Norway, Romania, Russia, Spain, Sweden, Switzerland, Syria, Uganda, the Ukraine, the United States, Yugoslavia, and Zambia. Ratification proceedings are presently under way in other countries.

(c) UNCTAD. The **United Nations Conference on Trade and Development** (UNCTAD) represents the interests of the less developed countries. Its prime objective is the achievement of an international redistribution of income through trade. Through UNCTAD pressure, the developed countries agreed to a system of preferences, with quota limits, for manufactured imports from the developing countries.

(d) EU. The **European Economic Community** (EEC) was established in 1958 to remove trade and economic barriers between member countries and to unify their economic policies. It changed its name and became the **European Union** after the Treaty of Maastricht was ratified on November 1, 1993. The Treaty of Rome contained the governing principles of this regional trading group. The treaty was signed by the original six nations of Belgium, France, West Germany, Italy, Luxembourg, and the Netherlands. Membership expanded by the entry of Denmark, Ireland, Great Britain, Greece, Spain, and Portugal.

There are four main institutions making up the formal structure of the EU. The first, the European Council, consists of the heads of state of the member countries. The council's decisions set broad policy guidelines for the EU. The second, the European Commission, implements decisions of the council and initiates actions against individuals, companies, or member states that violate community law. The third, the European Parliament, has an advisory legislative role with limited veto powers. The fourth, the European Court of Justice (ECJ), is the judicial arm of the EU. The courts of member states may refer cases involving questions on the EU Treaty to the European Court of Justice.

The Single European Act eliminated internal barriers to the free movement of goods, persons, services, and capital between EU countries. The Treaty on European Union signed in Maastricht, Belgium (the Maastricht Treaty) amended the Treaty of Rome, with a focus on monetary and political union. It sets goals for the EU of (1) single monetary and fiscal policies; (2) common foreign and security policies; and (3) cooperation in justice and home affairs.

(e) U.S.–CANADA FTA. Canada and the United States share the world's largest trading relationship between two countries. Under the United States-Canada Free Trade Agreement (FTA),[3] which took effect on January 1, 1989, it is hoped that two-way trade between these countries will be significantly increased. The key feature of the FTA is the progressive elimination of all duties and most nontariff barriers on virtually all trade in goods between the two countries over a ten-year period.[4] Also, the FTA ensures nondiscriminatory and open markets for a wide range of services. These include advertising, public relations, computer and telecommunication services, and management services.[5] A very important provision of the FTA is the lowering of Canadian barriers to U.S. investments. To accommodate the movement of people as well as the exchange of goods and services, the FTA provides for workable immigration provisions for "business persons."[6]

(f) NAFTA. The **North American Free Trade Agreement** (NAFTA) is an agreement between Mexico, Canada, and the United States, which basically includes Mexico in the arrangements initiated under the U.S.–Canada FTA. NAFTA's goal is to eliminate all tariffs between the three countries over a 15-year span. Side agreements exist to prevent the exploitation of Mexico's lower environmental and labor standards.

---

[3] Act of September 19, 1988, PL 100-449, 102 Stat 1815, 19 USC § 2112, 27 ILM 281.

[4] FTA Art. 401.

[5] FTA Art. 1402.

[6] FTA Art. 1502.

(g) REGIONAL TRADING GROUPS OF DEVELOPING COUNTRIES. In recent years, numerous trading arrangements between groups of developing countries have been established.

(h) IMF-WORLD BANK. The **International Monetary Fund (**IMF) was created after World War II by a group of nations meeting in Bretton Woods, New Hampshire. The Articles of Agreement of the IMF state that the purpose is "to facilitate the expansion and balanced growth of international trade" and to "shorten the duration and lessen the disequilibrium in the international balance of payments of members." The IMF helps to achieve such purposes by administering a complex lending system. A country can borrow money from other IMF members or from the IMF by means of **Special Drawing Rights (**SDR) sufficient to permit that country to maintain the stability of its currency's relationship to other world currencies. The Bretton Woods conference also set up the **International Bank for Reconstruction and Development (World Bank)** to facilitate the lending of money by capital surplus countries—such as the United States—to countries needing economic help and wanting foreign investments after World War II.

(i) OPEC. The Organization of Petroleum Exporting Countries (OPEC) is a producer cartel or combination. One of its main goals was to raise the taxes and royalties earned from crude oil production. Another major goal was to take control from the major oil companies over production and exploration. Its early success in attaining these goals led other nations that export raw materials to form similar cartels. For example, copper- and bauxite-producing nations have formed cartels.

3. Forms of Business Organizations

The decision to participate in international business transactions and the extent of that participation depends on the financial position of the individual firm, production and marketing factors, and tax and legal consid-erations. There are a number of forms of business organizations for doing business abroad.

(a) EXPORT SALES. A direct sale to customers in a foreign country is an **export sale**. An American firm engaged in export selling is not present in the foreign country in such an arrangement. The export is subject to a tariff by the foreign country, but the exporting firm is not subject to local taxation by the importing country.

(b) AGENCY ARRANGEMENTS. A U.S. manufacturer may decide to make a limited entry into international business by appointing an agent to represent it in a foreign market. An **agent** is a person or firm with authority to make contracts on behalf of another—the **principal**. The agent will receive commission income for sales made on behalf of the U.S. principal. The appointment of a foreign agent commonly constitutes "doing business" in that country and subjects the U.S. firm to local taxation.

(c) FOREIGN DISTRIBUTORSHIPS. A **distributor** takes title to goods and bears the financial and commercial risks for the subsequent sale of the goods. To avoid making a major financial investment, a U.S. firm may decide to appoint a foreign distributor. A U.S. firm may also appoint a foreign distributor to avoid managing a foreign operation, with its complicated local business, legal, and labor conditions. Care is required in designing an exclusive distributorship for an EEC country, lest it be in violation of EEC antitrust laws.

(d) LICENSING. American firms may select licensing as a means of doing business in other countries. **Licensing** involves the transfer of technology rights in a product so that it may be produced by a different business organization in a foreign country in exchange for royalties and other payments as agreed. The technology being licensed may fall within the internationally recognized categories of patents, trademarks, and "know-how" (trade secrets and unpatented manufacturing processes outside the public domain). These intellectual property rights, which are legally protectable, may be licensed separately or incorporated into a single, comprehensive licensing contract. **Franchising**, which involves granting permission to use a trademark, trade name, or copyright under specified conditions, is a form of licensing that is now very common in international business.

(e) WHOLLY OWNED SUBSIDIARIES. A firm seeking to maintain control over its own operations, including the protection of its own technological expertise, may choose to do business abroad through a wholly owned subsidiary. In Europe the most common choice of foreign business organization, similar to the U.S. corporate form of business organization, is called the **société anonyme (S.A.).** In German-speaking countries, this form is called **Aktiengesellschaft (A.G.).**

Corporations doing business in more than one country pose many taxation problems for the governments in the countries in which the firm does business. The United States has established tax treaties with many countries. These treaties grant corporations relief from double taxation. Credit is normally given by the United States to U.S. corporations for taxes paid to foreign governments.

There is a potential for tax evasion by U.S. corporations by their selling goods to their overseas subsidiaries. Corporations could sell goods at less than the fair market value to avoid a U.S. tax on the full profit for such sales. By allowing the foreign subsidiaries located in countries with lower tax rates to make higher profits, the company as a whole would minimize its taxes. Section 482 of the Internal Revenue Code, however, allows the IRS to reallocate the income between the parent and its foreign subsidiary. The parent corporation is insulated from such a reallocation if it can show, based on independent transactions with unrelated parties, that its charges were at arm's length.[7]

(f) JOINT VENTURES. A U.S. manufacturer and a foreign entity may form a joint venture whereby the two firms agree to perform different functions for a common result. The responsibilities and liabilities of such operations are governed by contract. For example, Hughes Aircraft Co. formed a joint venture with two Japanese firms, C. Itoh & Co. and Mitsui, and successfully bid on a telecommunications space satellite system for the Japanese government.

B. GOVERNMENTAL REGULATION

Nations regulate trade to protect the economic interests of their citizens or to protect themselves in international relations and transactions.

4. Export Regulations

The Export Administration Act[8] (EAA) is the principal statute imposing export controls on goods and technical data from the United States. The Bureau of Export Administration issues the Export Administration Regulations[9] to enforce export controls. Violations of the Export Administration Regulations carry both civil and criminal penalties.

Export licensing is an integral part of exporting. For reasons of national security, foreign policy, or short supply of certain domestic products, the United States controls the export

---

[7] Bausch & Lomb Inc. v Commissioner (CA2 NY) 933 F2d 1084 (1991).

[8] Export Administration Act of 1979, PL 96-72, 93 Stat 503, 50 USC §§ 2401-20; the Export Administration Amendments Act of 1985, Act of July 12, 1985, PL 99-64, 99 Stat 120, 50 USC § 2401.

[9] The Export Administration Regulations are available from the Superintendent of Documents, U.S. Government Printing Office, Washington, D.C. 20230.

of all goods and technology. There are two types of export licenses: general and validated.

A **general license** is a broad grant of authority to all exporters for certain categories of products to all or most destinations. Most U.S. exports are shipped abroad under general licenses. No application process is required for U.S. exporters to use general licenses.

A **validated license** is a specific grant of authority from the government to a particular exporter to export a particular product to a certain destination. These licenses are granted on a case-by-case basis for a single transaction and generally have a two-year validity period. An exporter must apply to the U.S. Commerce Department's Office of Export Licensing for a validated export license.

(a) DETERMINING THE TYPE OF LICENSE NEEDED. In order to determine whether a product requires a general or validated license, a three-step procedure is followed.

(1) Destination of the Product. The exporter must check the schedule of "Country Groups" contained in the Export Administration Regulations to see under which category the export destination falls. The countries making up Country Group 2 (North Korea, and Cuba) are subject to a virtual trade embargo, and no goods may be licensed for export there.

(2) The Product Being Exported. The exporter must check the "Commodity Control List" contained in the Export Administration Regulations to see whether the product requires a validated license for shipment to the "Country Groups" identified in the preceding step.

(3) Special Restrictions. The exporter must determine whether any "special restrictions" apply to the export transaction. An exporter probably will have to apply for a validated export license if exporting the following: (a) a "strategic" commodity to any destination—or in a few cases, only to a destination where exports are restricted for national security purposes; (b) a "short supply" commodity to any destination; (c) any other commodity to a destination where there are

foreign policy concerns; or (d) "unpublished" technical data to certain destinations. This refers to technical information, generally related to the design, production, or use of a product, that is not available to the public.

If after following the above procedures it is determined that a validated license is not required, the exporter may ship its product under a general license.

(b) SHIPPER EXPORT DECLARATION. If the shipment is valued at $500 or more or requires a validated export license, the exporter must complete a Shipper's Export Declaration (SED). The SED is used by the U.S. Customs Service to indicate the type of export license being used and to keep track of what products are exported. SEDs are also used by the Bureau of Census to compile statistics on U.S. trade patterns.

(c) CRIMINAL SANCTIONS. Validated export licenses are required for the export of certain high-technology and military products. For example, a company intending to ship "maraging 350 steel" to a user in Pakistan would find by checking the Commodity Control List that such steel is used in making high-technology products and also has nuclear applications. Thus, a validated export license would be required. Since Pakistan is a nonsignatory nation of the Nuclear Non-Proliferation Treaty, the Department of Commerce would be expected to deny an application for a validated license for the use of this steel in a nuclear plant. However, a license to export this steel for use in the manufacture of high-speed turbines or compressors might be approved. The prospective purchaser must complete a "Statement of Ultimate Consignee and Purchaser" form with the application for a validated license. The prospective purchaser must identify the "end use" for the steel and indicate where the purchaser is located and the location in Pakistan where a U.S. Embassy official can make an on-site inspection of the product's use. Falsification of the information in the license application process is a criminal offense. Thus, if the exporter of maraging 350 steel asserted that it was to be used in manufacturing high-speed turbines when in fact the exporter knew it was being purchased for use in a nuclear facility, the exporter would be guilty of a criminal offense.[10]

In the *Mechanic* case, the defendants claimed that an attempt to violate U.S. export controls could not subject them to criminal sanctions.

UNITED STATES v MECHANIC
(CA5 Tex) 809 F2d 1111 (1987)

Barry and Mary Mechanic attempted to export a "sweep generator." This device is used in laboratories to develop radar and military communication systems, such as guided missile tracking systems. The Mechanics were caught trying to ship the device to Europe without a validated federal license, and they were charged with criminal violation of the Export Administration Regulations. They claimed that a mere *attempt* to violate export controls could not subject them to criminal sanctions. They were convicted, and they appealed.

GEE, C. J. . . . The facts relevant to this appeal are undisputed. Bahram (Barry) Mechanic and his ex-sister-in-law, Mary Akers Mechanic, constituted the entire personnel roster for Faratel, Inc., an operation located in a small office in Houston, Texas. In December 1984, Mary called Hughes Aircraft to obtain a quote for a plug-in sweep generator, stating Faratel had a West German client who wanted one shipped to Switzerland. Hughes gave a foreign price quotation, adding that the item was subject to United States export control regulations and that delivery was contingent upon receipt of a validated export license. In February 1985, Mary called Hughes again, but requested a domestic price quotation, stating that Faratel had a foreign client who intended to use the device in a Houston-based beeper-pager operation. This use is not compatible with the requested equipment, which is primarily used in laboratories to develop radar and military communication systems, such as guided missile tracking.

Hughes shipped the equipment in late March 1985. Executing a search warrant, the U.S. Customs Service intercepted the crate at a Houston airport and installed a tracking device. While maintaining surveillance, Customs Service personnel observed Barry and Mary repack the generator in a footlocker. They later observed one Eugene Krug check the footlocker as baggage on his flight to Zurich. Krug was detained at the airport and Barry and Mary were later arrested. The first trial resulted in a hung jury; the jury at the second trial acquitted Krug, but convicted Barry and Mary. . . .

A regulation, and not the EAA itself, denounced an *attempt* to violate export controls as a criminal offense, as follows:

---

[10] See U.S. v Pervez (CA3 Pa) 871 F2d 310 (1989), on the criminal application of the Export Administration Regulations to an individual who stated a false end use for "maraging 350 steel" on his export application to ship this steel to Pakistan. *See also* U.S. v Bozarov (CA9 Cal) 974 F2d 1037 (1992).

Solicitation and attempt. No person may do any act that solicits the commission of, or that constitutes an attempt to bring about, a violation of the Export Administration Act or any regulation, order, or license issued under the Act.

The EAA of 1979 imposed criminal sanctions on those who knowingly violate any provision of the Act or any regulation issued under it. . . . The EAA goes on to establish that, in order to further these policies, the President may "prohibit or curtail" the exportation of any goods, technology, or other information subject to the jurisdiction of the United States. . . .

[Judgment affirmed]

QUESTIONS

1. Did Mary Mechanic know that a validated export license was required for the sweep generator?
2. How was the U.S. Customs Service alerted to the possible violation of export controls?
3. Were the Mechanics' actions contrary to any of the "Selected Ethical Principles" set forth in the "Analysis of Court Opinions" in the introductory pages of this textbook?

(d) EXPERT ASSISTANCE. The Department of Commerce's Exporter Assistance Staff provides assistance to exporters needing help in determining the proper export license.[11] Licensed foreign freight forwarders are in the business of handling the exporting of goods to foreign destinations. They are experts on U.S. Department of Commerce export license requirements. Licensed foreign freight forwarders can attend to all of the essential arrangements required to transport a shipment of goods from the exporter's warehouse to the overseas buyer's specified port and inland destination. They are well versed in all aspects of ocean, air, and inland transportation as well as banking, marine insurance, and other services relating to exporting.

5. Protection of Intellectual Property Rights

U.S. laws protect **intellectual property rights**, which consist of trademarks, copyrights, and patents.

(a) COUNTERFEIT GOODS. The importation into the United States of counterfeit compact discs, tapes, computer software, and movies violates U.S. copyright laws. Importing goods such as athletic shoes, jeans, or watches bearing counterfeits of U.S. companies' registered trademarks violates the Lanham Trademark Act. Importing machines or devices which infringe on U.S. patents violates U.S. patent laws. A full range of remedies is available to the American firms under U.S. laws. Possible remedies include injunctive relief, seizure and destruction of counterfeit goods that are found in the United States, damages, and attorneys' fees. American firms injured by counterfeit trademarks may recover triple damages from the counterfeiters.[12]

Intellectual property rights are also protected by international treaties such as the Berne Convention, which protects copyrights; the Patent Cooperation Treaty; and the Vienna Trademark Registration Treaty.

---

[11] Exporter Assistance Staff, U.S. Department of Commerce, Washington D.C. 20230.

[12] 15 USC § 1117(b); Nintendo of America v NTDEC (D Ariz) 822 F Supp 1462 (1993).

(b) GREY MARKET GOODS. A U.S. trademark holder may license a foreign business to use its trademark overseas. If a third party imports these foreign-made goods into the United States to compete against the U.S. manufacturer's goods, the foreign-made goods are called **"grey market" goods**. The Tariff Act of 1930 prevents importation of foreign-made goods bearing U.S. registered trademarks owned by U.S. firms, unless the U.S. trademark owner gives written consent.[13]

The Lanham Trademark Act may also be used to exclude grey market goods.

A grey market situation also arises where foreign products made by affiliates of U.S. companies have trademarks identical to U.S. trademarks, but the foreign products are physically different from the U.S. products. In the *Lever Brothers* case, the U.S. trademark holder sought to exclude the importation of the foreign made goods by third parties.

LEVER BROTHERS CO. v U.S.
(Dist Col) 796 F Supp 1 (1992)

Lever Brothers (Lever U.S.) manufactures a soap under the trademark "Shield" and a dishwashing liquid under the trademark "Sunlight" for sale in the United States. A British affiliate, Lever U.K., also makes products using the marks "Shield" and "Sunlight." Due to different preferences of American and British consumers, the products have physical differences. Third parties imported these British products into the United States. Lever U.S. sought an injunction against the U.S. Customs Service, contending that Section 42 of the Lanham Act requires the Customs Service to bar these foreign products. The U.S. Customs Service contended that the products should be allowed to enter the United States under its affiliate exception.

GREENE, D. J. . . . Plaintiff, Lever U.S., is a wholly-owned subsidiary of Unilever U.S., Inc., which in turn is wholly owned by Unilever N.V. A British company, Lever U.K., manufactures "Shield" and "Sunlight," and holds the trademark for those words in the United Kingdom. Lever U.K. is a subsidiary of Unilever PLC. The two corporate parents, Unilever N.V. and Unilever PLC, are not under common ownership but are affiliated with one another and are under common control. . . .

The "Shield" logos on the American and the British versions of the soap are virtually identical. The American product, however, is designed to produce more lather and contains an anti-bacteria agent absent from the British version. The two soaps are also perfumed and colored differently.

The two versions of "Sunlight" dishwashing detergent have similar lettering but the packaging is different. The detergents themselves are also quite different. The British product is designed for water with a mineral content higher than is generally found in the United States. It therefore does not perform as well as the American "Sunlight" in the "soft-water" typical of this country. Thus the trademarks of the American and British versions of the two products are identical but the products are physically different.

---

[13] 19 USC § 1526(a).

Third parties have imported the British versions of the products into the United States without the consent of Lever U.S. or Lever U.K. The outward similarities and substantive differences of the American and British products created confusion and dissatisfaction on the part of American consumers who purchased the British products in the belief that they were purchasing the American version or not realizing that there were two different products under the same name.

This case focuses on interpretation of section 42 of the Lanham Act which states that:

no article of imported merchandise which shall copy or simulate the name of . . . any domestic manufacturer, . . . or which shall copy or simulate a trademark registered in accordance with the provisions of this chapter or shall bear a name or mark calculated to induce the public to believe that the article is manufactured in the United States, . . . shall be admitted to entry at any customhouse of the United States. . . .

15 U.S.C. § 1124 (1982) (emphasis added).

Lever U.S. argues that where a foreign company produces goods that bear the same trademark as a U.S. markholder but that are materially, physically different, the foreign product copies or simulates the domestic trademark within the meaning of section 42 even where the foreign manufacturer is affiliated with the domestic markholder. Defendants argue that a markholder cannot infringe, i.e., "copy or simulate," its own trademark, and that therefore the affiliation of Lever U.S. with Lever U.K. makes all the difference, placing this case outside the scope of section 42.

The Customs Service has permitted the British versions of the two products to enter the United States under its affiliate exception. Under the Customs Service regulation, foreign goods that bear a trademark identical to one owned and recorded by a United States corporation will not be seized by Customs, notwithstanding section 42 of the statute, if "the foreign and domestic trademark or trade name owners are parent and subsidiary companies or are otherwise subject to common ownership or control." 19 C.F.R. 133.(c)(2) (1988).

The Court of Appeals has come to the tentative conclusion that the Lanham Act bars "foreign goods bearing a trademark identical to a valid U.S. trademark but which are physically different, regardless of the trademarks' genuine character abroad or affiliation between the producing firms." *Lever Bros. Co. v United States . . .* 877 F2d at 111. However, as indicated, the appellate court remanded the case for consideration of the legislative history and the administrative practice.

Legislative History

The Court of Appeals regarded its reading of the language of section 42 as being "the natural, virtually inevitable" interpretation. . . . It is well established that where the statute is clear on its face and the legislative intent is expressed in "reasonably plain terms" by the text, the statutory language controls. . . .

Representative Fritz G. Lanham, the sponsor of the Act, explained that one purpose of the statute was "to protect the public so that it may be confident that, in purchasing a product bearing a particular trademark, which it favorably knows, it will get the product which it asks for and wants to get." H R Rep No 219 at 2, 79th Cong, 1st Sess (February 26, 1945) US Code Cong Serv 1946, p. 1274. In this case, the outward similarities and physical differences between the British and American versions of "Shield" and "Sunlight" have already created consumer confusion and dissatisfaction, and they would be likely to do so again in the future. As the House Report on the Lanham Act stated, "Trademarks encourage the maintenance of quality by securing to the producer the benefit of the good reputation which excellence creates." H R No 219 at 3, 1946 US Code Cong Serv at 1274, 1275. Thus, the legislative goals of trademark law generally and of the Lanham Act specifically are served by the barring of goods such as those of the British company. . . .

Neither the legislative history of the statute nor the administrative practice of the Customs Service clearly contradicts the plain meaning of section 42. The Court therefore concludes that section 42 of the Lanham Act prohibits the importation of foreign goods that bear a trademark identical to a valid United States trademark but which are physically different, regardless of the validity of the foreign trademark or the existence of an affiliation between the U.S. and foreign markholders.

Plaintiff's motion for summary judgment will be granted and defendants' motion will be denied. . . .

[Judgment for Lever U.S.]

QUESTIONS

1. Why did Lever U.S. want to exclude the two British products?
2. What was the contention of the U.S. Customs Service?
3. Are the legislative goals of the Lanham Act, as expressed by Representative Lanham, served by barring the British soap products?

6. Antitrust

Antitrust laws exist in the United States to protect the American consumer by assuring the benefits of competitive products from foreign competitors as well as domestic competitors. Competitors' agreements designed to raise the price of imports or to exclude imports from our domestic markets in exchange for not competing in other countries are restraints of trade in violation of our antitrust laws. The antitrust laws also exist to protect American export and investment opportunities against privately imposed restrictions, whereby a group of competitors seeks to exclude another competitor from a particular foreign market. Antitrust laws exist in other countries where American firms compete. These laws are usually not directed at breaking up cartels to further competition, but rather at regulating the cartels in the national interest.

(a) JURISDICTION. In U.S. courts, the U.S. antitrust laws have a broad extraterritorial reach. Our antitrust laws must be reconciled with the rights of other interested countries as embodied in international law.

(1) The Effects Doctrine. Judge Learned Hand's decision in *United States v Alcoa*[14] established the effects doctrine. Under this doctrine, U.S. courts will assume jurisdiction and will apply the antitrust laws to conduct outside of the United States where the activity of the business firms outside the United States has a direct and substantial effect on U.S. commerce. This basic rule has been modified to require that the effect on U.S. commerce also be foreseeable.

---

[14] (CA2 NY) 148 F2d 416 (1945).

(2) The Jurisdictional Rule of Reason. The jurisdictional rule of reason applies when conduct taking place outside of the United States affects U.S. commerce, but a foreign state also has a significant interest in regulating the conduct in question. The **jurisdictional rule of reason** balances the vital interests, including laws and policies, of the United States with those of the foreign country involved. This rule of reason is based on the principle of comity. **Comity** is a principle of international law that the laws of all nations deserve the respect legitimately demanded by equal participants in international affairs.

(b) DEFENSES. Three defenses are commonly raised to the extraterritorial application of the U.S. antitrust laws. These defenses are also commonly raised to attack jurisdiction in other legal actions involving international law.

(1) Act of State Doctrine. By the **act of state doctrine**:

Every sovereign state is bound to respect the independence of every other sovereign state, and the courts of one country will not sit in judgment of another government's acts done within its own territory.[15]

The act of state doctrine is based on the judiciary's concern over its possible interference with the conduct of foreign relations.

Such matters are considered to be political, not judicial, questions.

(2) The Sovereign Compliance Doctrine. The sovereign compliance doctrine allows a defendant to raise as an affirmative defense to an antitrust action the fact that the defendant's actions were compelled by a foreign state. To establish this defense, compulsion by the foreign government is required. The Japanese government uses informal and formal contacts within an industry to establish a consensus on a desired course of action. Such governmental action is not a defense for a U.S. firm, however, because the activity in question is not compulsory.

(3) The Sovereign Immunity Doctrine. This doctrine states that a foreign sovereign generally cannot be sued unless an exception to the Foreign Sovereign Immunities Act of 1976 applies.[16] The most important exception covers the commercial conduct of a foreign state.

The *Timberlane* decision discusses the factors considered by a U.S. court in deciding whether or not to take jurisdiction of a case concerning transactions that occurred outside U.S. borders. This case is an example of the "jurisdictional rule of reason" test.

(c) LEGISLATION. In response to business uncertainty as to when the antitrust laws

TIMBERLANE LUMBER CO. v BANK OF AMERICA
(CA9 Cal) 549 F2d 597 (1976)

The Timberlane Lumber Company, an Oregon partnership, brought an antitrust suit against the Bank of America, several employees of the Bank who worked for the Bank in Honduras, and others. Timberlane alleged that the defendants conspired to prevent Timberlane, through Honduran subsidiar-

---

[15] Underhill v Hernandez, 108 US 250, 252 (1897).
[16] See Verlinden B.V. v Central Bank of Nigeria, 461 US 574 (1983).

ies, from milling lumber in Honduras and exporting it to the United States. Timberlane alleged that the defendants were trying to keep control of the Honduran lumber business in the hands of individuals financed and controlled by the bank. The defendants contended that the action must be dismissed because of the act of state doctrine since a Honduran court approved certain of the challenged activities. Defendants also contended that the court lacked jurisdiction because these activities occurred in Honduras, and the court lacked subject matter jurisdiction under the effects doctrine. A dismissal was granted, and Timberlane appealed.

CHOY, C. J. . . . The defendants argue—as the district court apparently held—that the injuries allegedly suffered by Timberlane resulted from acts of the Honduran government, principally in connection with the enforcement of the security interests in the Maya plant, which American courts cannot review. Such an application of the act of state doctrine seems to us to be erroneous. Even if the *coup de grace* to Timberlane's enterprise in Honduras was applied by official authorities, we do not agree that the doctrine necessarily shelters these defendants or requires dismissal of the Timberlane action.

The leading modern statement of the act of state doctrine appears in *Banco Nacional de Cuba v Sabbatino*, 376 U.S. 398 (1964). The [U.S. Supreme] Court concluded that the doctrine was not compelled by the nature of sovereignty, by international law, or by the text of the Constitution. Rather, it derives from the judiciary's concern for its possible interference with the conduct of foreign affairs by the political branches of the government:

The doctrine as formulated in past decisions expresses the strong sense of the Judicial Branch that its engagement in the task of passing on the validity of foreign acts of state may hinder rather than further this country's pursuit of goals both for itself and for the community of nations as a whole in the international sphere.

. . . A corollary to the act of state doctrine in the foreign trade antitrust field is the often-recognized principle that corporate conduct which is compelled by a foreign sovereign is also protected from antitrust liability, as if it were an act of the state itself. Thus, in *Interamerican Refining Corp. v Texaco Maracaibo, Inc.*, 307 F. Supp. 1291 (D.Del. 1970), a refusal by defendants to sell Venezuelan crude oil to plaintiff was held not to be an illegal restraint of trade because it was a complete defense that the Venezuelan government had imposed a boycott forbidding such sales. The court there observed that "when a nation compels a trade practice, firms there have no choice but to obey. Acts of business become effectively acts of the sovereign." . . .

On the basis of the foregoing analysis, we conclude that the court below erred in dismissing the instant suit. . . . Timberlane does not seek to name Honduras or any Honduran officer as a defendant or co-conspirator, nor does it challenge Honduran policy or sovereignty in any fashion that appears on its face to hold any threat to relations between Honduras and the United States. . . .

Under these circumstances, it is clear that the "act of state" doctrine does not require dismissal of the Timberlane action.

Extraterritorial Reach of the United States Antitrust Laws

There is no doubt that American antitrust laws extend over some conduct in other nations. . . .

That American law covers some conduct beyond this nation's borders does not mean that it embraces all, however. Extraterritorial application is understandably a matter of concern for the other countries involved. Those nations have sometimes resented and protested, as excessive intrusions into their own spheres, broad assertions of authority by American courts. . . .

It is the effect on American foreign commerce which is usually cited to support extraterritorial jurisdiction. *Alcoa* [*United States v Alcoa*, 148 F2d 416 (1945)] set the course, when Judge Hand declared,

It is settled law . . . that any state may impose liabilities, even upon persons not within its allegiance, for conduct outside its borders that has consequences within its borders which the state reprehends; and these liabilities other states will ordinarily recognize.

Despite its description as "settled law," *Alcoa*'s assertion has been roundly disputed by many foreign commentators as being in conflict with international law, comity, and good judgment. Nonetheless, American courts have firmly concluded that there is some extraterritorial jurisdiction under the Sherman Act.

Even among American courts and commentators, however, there is no consensus on how far the jurisdiction should extend. The district court here concluded that a "direct and substantial effect" on United States foreign commerce was a prerequisite, without stating whether other factors were relevant or considered. . . .

[But] an effect on United States commerce, although necessary to the exercise of jurisdiction under the antitrust laws, is alone not a sufficient basis on which to determine whether American authority should be asserted in a given case as a matter of international comity and fairness.

What we prefer is an evaluation and balancing of the relevant considerations in each case— . . . a "jurisdictional rule of reason." . . .

The elements to be weighed include the degree of conflict with foreign law or policy, the nationality or allegiance of the parties and the locations or principal places of business or corporations, the extent to which enforcement by either state can be expected to achieve compliance, the relative significance of effects on the United States as compared with those elsewhere, the extent to which there is explicit purpose to harm or affect American commerce, the foreseeability of such effect, and the relative importance to the violations charged of conduct within the United States as compared with conduct abroad. . . .

We conclude, then, that the problem should be approached in three parts: Does the alleged restraint affect, or was it intended to affect, the foreign commerce of the United States? Is it of such a type and magnitude so as to be cognizable as a violation of the Sherman Act? As a matter of international comity and fairness, should the extraterritorial jurisdiction of the United States be asserted to cover it? The district court's judgment found only that the restraint involved in the instant suit did not produce a direct and substantial effect on American foreign commerce. That holding does not satisfy any of these inquiries. . . .

[Dismissal vacated and action remanded]

apply to international transactions, Congress passed the Foreign Trade Antitrust Improvements Act of 1982. This act, in essence, codified the effects doctrine. The act requires a direct, substantial, and reasonably foreseeable effect on U.S. domestic commerce or exports by U.S. residents before business conduct abroad may come within the purview of the U.S. antitrust laws.[17]

(d) FOREIGN ANTITRUST LAWS.

Attitudes in different countries vary toward cartels and business combinations. Because of this, antitrust laws vary in content and application. Japan, for example, has stressed consumer protection against such practices as price fixing and false advertising. However, with regard to mergers, stock ownership, and agreements among companies to control production, Japanese law is much less restrictive than American law.

Europe is a major market for American products, services, and investments. American firms doing business in Europe are subject to the competition laws of the EEC. The Treaty of Rome uses the term *competition* rather than *antitrust*. Articles 85 and 86 of the Treaty of Rome set forth the basic regulation on business behavior in the EEC.[18]

Article 85 (1) expressly prohibits agreements and concerted practices that:

1. Even indirectly fix prices of purchases or sales, or fix any other trading conditions.

2. Limit or control production, markets, technical development, or investment.
3. Share markets or sources of supply.
4. Apply unequal terms to parties furnishing equivalent considerations, thereby placing one at a competitive disadvantage.
5. Make a contract's formation depend on the acceptance of certain additional obligations that, according to commercial usage, have no connection with the subject of such contracts.

Article 85(3) allows for an individual exemption if the agreement meets certain conditions, such as improving the production or distribution of goods or promoting technical or economic progress, and reserving to consumers a fair share of the resulting economic benefits.

Article 86 provides that it is unlawful for one or more enterprises, having a dominant market position within at least a substantial part of the Common Market, to take improper advantage of such a position if trade between the member states may be affected.

7. Securities Regulation in an International Environment

Illegal conduct in the U.S. securities markets, whether this conduct is initiated in the United States or abroad, threatens the vital economic interests of the United States. Investigation and litigation concerning possible violations of the U.S. securities laws often have an

---

[17] PL 97-290, 96 Stat 1233, 15 USC § 6(a).

[18] See Osakeyhtio v EEC Commission, 1988 CCH Com Mkt Rptr ¶ 14,491 for discussion of the extraterritorial reach of the European Commission.

extraterritorial effect. Conflicts with the laws of foreign countries may occur.

(a) JURISDICTION. U.S. district courts have jurisdiction over violations of the antifraud provisions of the Securities Exchange Act where losses occur from sales to Americans living in the United States. This is true whether or not the actions occurred in this country. U.S. district courts also have jurisdiction where losses occur to Americans living abroad if the acts occurred in the United States. The antifraud provisions do not apply, however, to losses from sales of securities to foreigners outside the United States unless acts within the United States caused the losses.

(b) IMPACT OF FOREIGN SECRECY LAWS IN SEC ENFORCEMENT. **Secrecy laws** are confidentiality laws applied to home-country banks. These laws prohibit the disclosure of business records or the identity of bank customers. **Blocking laws** prohibit the disclosure, copying, inspection, or removal of documents located in the enacting country in compliance with orders from foreign authorities. These laws impede, and sometimes foreclose, the SEC's ability to police its securities markets properly.

The *Banca Della Suizzera* case demonstrates how the SEC, in certain circumstances, can obtain discovery from foreign financial institutions in spite of secrecy laws.

The SEC is not limited to litigation when a securities law enforcement investigation runs

SEC v BANCA DELLA SUIZZERA ITALIANA
92 FRD 111 (DC NY 1981)

Banca Della Suizzera Italiana (BSI) is a Swiss bank with an office in the United States. BSI purchased certain call options and common stock of St. Joe Minerals Corporation (St. Joe), a New York corporation. This purchase was made immediately prior to the announcement on March 11, 1981 of a cash tender offer by Joseph Seagram & Sons Inc. for all St. Joe common stock at $45 per share. On March 10, 1981, when BSI acted, the stock traded at approximately $30 per share. On March 11, 1981 the stock moved sharply higher in price. BSI instructed its broker to close out the purchases of the options and sell most of the shares of stock, resulting in an overnight profit of $2 million. The SEC noticed the undue activity in the options market, initiated suit against BSI, and obtained a temporary restraining order. The restraining order froze the proceeds in BSI's bank account at a New York bank. The SEC, through the Departments of State and Justice, and the Swiss government sought without success to learn the identity of BSI's customers involved in the transactions. The SEC believed that the customers had used inside information in violation of the Securities Exchange Act of 1934. The SEC filed a motion to compel disclosure. BSI, a Swiss bank, contended that it might be subject to criminal liability under Swiss penal and banking laws if it disclosed the requested information.

POLLACK, D. J. . . . BSI claims that it may be subject to criminal liability under Swiss penal and banking law if it discloses the requested information. However, this Court finds the factors in § 40 of the Restatement of Foreign Relations* to tip decisively in favor of the SEC. Moreover, it holds BSI to be "in the position of one who deliberately courted legal impediments . . . and who thus cannot now be heard to assert its good faith after this expectation was realized." BSI acted in bad faith. It made deliberate use of Swiss nondisclosure law to evade in a commercial transaction for profit to it, the strictures of American securities law against insider trading. . . .

The first of the § 40 factors is the vital national interest of each of the States. The strength of the United States' interest in enforcing its securities laws to ensure the integrity of its financial markets cannot seriously be doubted. That interest is being continually thwarted by the use of foreign bank accounts. Congress, in enacting legislation on bank record-keeping, expressed its concern over the problem over a decade ago. . . .

The Swiss government, on the other hand, though made expressly aware of the litigation, has expressed no opposition. In response to BSI's lawyers' inquiries, the incumbent Swiss Federal Attorney General . . . said only that a foreign court could not change the rule that disclosure required the consent of the one who imparted the secret and that BSI might thus be subject to prosecution. The Swiss government did not "confiscate" the Bank records to prevent violations of its law. . . . NEITHER THE UNITED STATES NOR THE SWISS GOVERNMENT has suggested that discovery be halted. . . . The Court of Appeals in *United States v National City Bank*, 396 F2d 897 (2d cir. 1968), found the fact that the governments concerned had not intervened of great importance. It observed that "when foreign governments, including Germany, have considered their vital national interests threatened, they have not hesitated to make known their objections . . . to the issuing court." It is true that BSI may be subject to fines and its officers to imprisonment under Swiss law. However, this Court notes that there is some flexibility in the application of that law. Not only may the particular bank involved obtain waivers from its customers to avoid prosecution, but Article 34 of the Swiss Penal Code contains a "State of Necessity" exception that relieves a person of criminal liability for acts committed to protect one's own good, including one's fortune, from an immediate danger if one is not responsible for the danger and one cannot be expected to give up one's good.

Of course, given BSI's active part in the insider trading transactions alleged here, the Swiss government might well conclude—as this Court has—that BSI is responsible for the conflict it is in and that therefore the "State of Necessity" exception should not apply. However, that is certainly no cause for this Court to withhold its sanctions since the dilemma would be a result of BSI's bad faith. A party's good or bad faith is an important factor to consider, and this court finds that BSI, which deposited the proceeds of these transactions in an American bank account in its name and which certainly profited in some measure from the challenged activity, undertook such transactions fully expecting to use foreign law to shield it from the reach of our laws. Such "deliberate courting" of foreign legal impediments will not be countenanced. . . .

It would be a travesty of justice to permit a foreign company to invade American markets, violate American laws if they were indeed violated, withdraw profits and resist accountability for itself and its principals for the illegality by claiming their anonymity under foreign law. . . .

. . . BSI is directed to complete its answers to all of the demands in the SEC's First Interrogatories, pertaining to St. Joe.

[So ordered]

[*Authors' Note*: Faced with the judge's opinion and the possibility of substantial fines, BSI obtained a waiver of the secrecy laws from its customer and produced the requested information.]

* § 40 reads as follows:

> *§40.   Limitations on Exercise of Enforcement Jurisdiction. Where two states have jurisdiction to prescribe and enforce rules of law and the rules they may prescribe require inconsistent conduct upon the part of a person, each state is required by international law to consider, in good faith, moderating the exercise of its enforcement jurisdiction, in the light of such factors as*
> *(a) vital national interests of each of the states,*
> *(b) the extent and the nature of the hardship that inconsistent enforcement actions would impose upon the person,*
> *(c) the extent to which the required conduct is to take place in the territory of the other state,*
> *(d) the nationality of the person, and*
> *(e) the extent to which enforcement by action of either state can reasonably be expected to achieve compliance with the rule prescribed by that state.*

QUESTIONS

1. What are the dominant factors considered by a court when deciding on whether or not to issue a subpoena or discovery order to a foreign bank in a secrecy jurisdiction?
2. Did the court find that the Swiss interest in bank secrecy outweighed the U.S. interest?
3. Did BSI act in good faith?
4. Did the court give significant weight to BSI's potential liability under Swiss law?

into secrecy or blocking laws. For example, the SEC may rely on the 1977 Treaty of Mutual Assistance in Criminal Matters between the United States and Switzerland.[19] Although this treaty has served to deter the use of Swiss secrecy laws to conceal fraud in the United States, its benefits for securities enforcement have been limited. It applies only where there is a dual criminality—that is, the conduct involved constitutes a criminal offense under the laws of both the United States and Switzerland.

8. Barriers to Trade

The most common barrier to the free movement of goods across borders is a tariff. A wide range of nontariff barriers also restricts the free movement of goods, services, and investments.

Governmental export controls used as elements of foreign policy have proven to be a major barrier to trade with certain countries.

(a) TARIFF BARRIERS. A **tariff** is an import or export duty or tax placed on goods as they move into or out of a country. It is the most common method used by countries to restrict foreign imports. The tariff raises the

---

[19] 27 UST 2021.

total cost and thus the price of the imported product in the domestic market. Thus, the price of a domestically produced product, not subject to the tariff, is more advantageous.

(b) NONTARIFF BARRIERS. Nontariff barriers consist of a wide range of restrictions that inhibit the free movement of goods between countries. An import quota, such as a limitation on the number of automobiles that can be imported into one country from another, is such a barrier. More subtle nontariff barriers exist in all countries. For example, Japan's complex customs procedures resulted in the restriction of the sale of U.S.-made aluminum baseball bats in Japan. The customs procedures required the individual uncrating and "destruction testing" of bats at the ports of entry. Government subsidies are also nontariff barriers to trade.

(c) EXPORT CONTROLS AS INSTRUMENTS OF FOREIGN POLICY. U.S. export controls have been used as instruments of foreign policy in recent years. For example, the United States has sought to deny goods and technology of strategic or military importance to unfriendly nations. The United States has also denied goods such as grain, technology, or machine parts to certain countries to protest or to punish activities considered violative of human rights or world peace.

9. Relief Mechanisms for Economic Injury Caused by Foreign Trade

Certain U.S. industries may suffer severe economic injury because of foreign competition. American law provides protection against unfair competition from foreigners' goods and provides economic relief for U.S. industries, communities, firms, and workers adversely affected by import competition. American law also provides certain indirect relief for American exporters and producers who encounter unfair foreign import restrictions.

(a) ANTIDUMPING LAWS AND EXPORT SUBSIDIES. Selling goods in another country at less than their fair value is called **dumping**. The dumping of foreign goods in the United States is prohibited under the Trade Agreement Act of 1979.[20] Proceedings in antidumping cases are conducted by two federal agencies, which separately examine two distinct components. The International Trade Administration (ITA) of the Department of Commerce investigates the matter of whether specified foreign goods are being sold in the United States at less than fair value (LTFV). The International Trade Commission (ITC) conducts proceedings to determine if there is an injury to a domestic industry as a result of such sales. Findings of both LTFV sales and injury must be present before remedial action is taken. Remedial action might include the addition of duties to reflect the difference between the fair value of the goods and the price being charged in the United States. ITA and ITC decisions may be appealed to the Court of International Trade. Figure 6-1 illustrates an antidumping proceeding.

A settlement of the matter may be reached through a suspension agreement, whereby prices are revised to eliminate any LTFV sales and other corrective measures are taken.

The 1979 act also applies to subsidy practices by foreign countries. If subsidized goods are sold in the United States at less than their fair value, the goods may be subject to a countervailing duty.

(b) RELIEF FROM IMPORT INJURIES. Title II of the Trade Act of 1974[21] provides relief for U.S. industries, communities, firms, and workers when any one or more of them are substantially adversely affected by import competition. The Department of Commerce, the Secretary of Labor, and the President have roles in determining eligibility. The relief provided may be temporary import relief through the imposition of a duty or quota on the foreign goods. Workers, if eligible, may obtain

---

[20] PL 96-39, 106, 93 Stat 193, 19 USC § 160.
[21] PL 93-618, 88 Stat 1978, 19 USC §§ 2251 2298.

Figure 6-1 Antidumping Proceedings

Phase 1: International Trade Administration	
Date	**Event**
December 28, 1992	Complaint by U.S. manufacturers to the International Trade Administration (ITA) alleging dumping of small business telephones on the U.S. market by named Asian manufacturers.
January–July, 1993	ITA investigates whether these foreign-made goods are being sold in the U.S. at less than fair value (LTFV). Investigation includes questionnaires on costs and pricing from all parties.
July 27, 1993	Preliminary finding by the ITA that Japanese and Taiwanese firms are dumping business phones on the U.S. market.
October 11, 1993	Final determination by ITA that the named firms are dumping phones on the U.S. market.
October 11, 1993	U.S. Customs Service commences requirement of cash deposit or bond on imports equal to the difference between the fair value of the goods as determined by the ITA and the prices being charged for the goods in the U.S.

Phase 2: International Trade Commission	
Date	**Event**
October 31, 1993	Hearing before the ITC to determine whether there is an injury to the domestic phone manufacturing industry as a result of the LTFV sales by the named Asian firms.
November 20, 1993	Decision of ITC that U.S. manufacturers of small business telephone systems are suffering injury because of the dumped exports.
November 20, 1993	U.S. Customs Service commences the actual collection of anti-dumping duties.

readjustment allowances, job training, job search allowances, or unemployment compensation.

(c) RETALIATION AND RELIEF AGAINST FOREIGN UNFAIR TRADE RESTRICTIONS. American exporters of agricultural or manufactured goods or of services may encounter unreasonable, unjustifiable, or discriminatory foreign import restrictions. At the same time, producers from the foreign country involved may be benefiting from trade agreement concessions that allow producers from that country access to U.S. markets. Prior trade acts and the Omnibus Trade and Competitiveness Act of 1988[22] contain broad authority to retaliate against "unreasonable," "unjustifiable," or "discriminatory" acts by a foreign country. The authority to retaliate is commonly referred to as "Section 301 authority." The fear or actuality of the economic sting of Section 301

---

[22] PL 100-418.

retaliation often leads offending foreign countries to open their markets to imports. Thus, indirect relief is provided to domestic producers and exporters adversely affected by foreign unfair trade practices.

Enforcement of the act is entrusted to the U.S. trade representative (USTR). The USTR is appointed by the President. Under the 1988 act, mandatory retaliatory action is required if the USTR determines that: (1) rights of the United States under a trade agreement are being denied; or (2) actions or policies of a foreign country are unjustifiable and burden or restrict U.S. commerce. The overall thrust of the trade provisions of the 1988 act is to open markets and liberalize trade.

10. Expropriation

A major concern of U.S. businesses that do business abroad is the risk of expropriation of assets by a host government. Firms involved in the extraction of natural resources, banking, communications, or defense-related industries are particularly susceptible to nationalization. Multinational corporations commonly have a staff of full-time political scientists and former Foreign Service officers studying the countries relevant to their operations to monitor and calculate risks of expropriation. Takeovers of American-owned businesses by foreign countries may be motivated by a short-term domestic political advantage or by the desire to demonstrate political clout in world politics. Takeovers may also be motivated by long-term considerations associated with planned development of the country's economy.

Treaty commitments, or provisions in other international agreements between the United States and the host country, may serve to narrow expropriation uncertainties. Treaties commonly contain provisions whereby property will not be expropriated except for public benefit and with the prompt payment of just compensation.

One practical way to mitigate the risk of investment loss due to foreign expropriation is

to purchase insurance through private companies such as Lloyds of London. Commercial insurance is also available against such risks as host governments' arbitrary recall of letters of credit and commercial losses due to embargoes.

The Overseas Private Investment Corporation (OPIC) is a U.S. agency under the policy control of the Secretary of State. OPIC supports private investments in less developed, friendly countries. OPIC offers asset protection insurance against risk of loss to plant and equipment as well as losses of deposits in overseas bank accounts to companies that qualify on the basis of a "substantial U.S. interest" being involved.

11. Government-Assisted Export Programs

The U.S. government has taken legislative action to increase the foreign sales of U.S. firms.

(a) EXPORT TRADING COMPANY ACT. The Export Trading Company Act of 1982 (ETCA)[23] is designed to stimulate and promote additional U.S. exports. The ETCA promotes the formation of U.S.-based export trading companies and allows banks to invest in these export trading companies. The ETCA also clarifies applicable antitrust restrictions and provides a limited exception from antitrust liability.

Trading companies exist in many European and East Asian countries. They are primary competitors of U.S. exporters. Japan's export trading companies, or *sogo shosha*, provide comprehensive export services and may serve as models for U.S. trading companies created under the 1982 Act. For example, a sogo shosha may participate in the purchase transaction of goods for export. It may then handle the paperwork and documents related to the export transaction. It may obtain insurance coverage and provide warehousing and transportation services. Through access to or ownership of banks, the sogo shosha may extend

---

[23] PL 97-290, 96 Stat 1233.

credit or make loans or loan guarantees to buyers, sellers, and suppliers. It has expertise in marketing research relative to target export markets and expertise in foreign exchange and tariff requirements. By encouraging exporters to form trading companies with banking institutions (banks have been prohibited by law from engaging in commercial as opposed to banking activities) and specifically allowing and encouraging the bank-related firms to perform comprehensive export services, Congress believes that increased export activity will be generated.

(b) FOREIGN SALES CORPORATIONS. The Foreign Sales Corporation Act of 1984[24] provides export incentives for U.S. firms that form Foreign Sales Corporations (FSC). To qualify for the tax incentives provided under the 1984 act, an FSC subsidiary of an American firm must be organized under the laws of a U.S. possession (such as the Virgin Islands or Guam, but not Puerto Rico), or under the laws of a foreign country with an income tax treaty with the United States containing an exchange-of-information program. The FSC must satisfy certain other organizational requirements in order to be eligible for the tax incentives provided by the law.

(c) UNITED STATES EXPORT-IMPORT BANK (EXIMBANK). **Eximbank** is wholly owned by the U.S. government. Its primary purpose is to facilitate U.S. exports by making direct loans in the form of dollar credits to foreign importers for the purchase of U.S. goods and services. Payments are then made directly to the U.S. exporter of goods and services. Such loans are made where private financial sources are unwilling to assume the political and economic risks that exist in the country in question. Loans are also made by Eximbank to enable U.S. suppliers of goods and services to compete for major foreign contracts with foreign firms that have government-subsidized export financing.

(d) OTHER PROGRAMS. As stated previously, OPIC provides expropriation insurance for U.S. private investments in friendly, less developed countries. The Commodity Credit Corporation (CCC) provides financing for agricultural exports. Also, the Small Business Administration has an export loan program.

12. The Foreign Corrupt Practices Act

There are restrictions on U.S. firms doing business abroad, in connection with payments made to foreign government officials in getting business from foreign governments. The Foreign Corrupt Practices Act of 1977[25] requires strict accounting standards and internal control procedures to prevent the hiding of improper payments to foreign officials. The act prohibits any offers, payments, or gifts to foreign officials, or third parties who might have influence with foreign officials, to influence a decision on behalf of the firm making the payment. It provides for sanctions of up to $1 million against the company, and for fines and imprisonment for the employees involved. Moreover, the individuals involved may be responsible for damages as a result of civil actions brought by competitors under federal and state antiracketeering acts.[26]

The Act does not apply to payments to low-level officials to expedite performance of routine government services.

---

[24] Title VIII of the Tax Reform Act of 1984, PL 98-369, 98 Stat 678. See IRC§§ 921 through 927.

[25] Kirkpatrick v ETC International, 493 US 400, 110 SCT 701 (1990).

[26] PL 95-213, 94 Stat 1494.

SUMMARY

The General Agreement on Tariffs and Trade, a multilateral treaty subscribed to by the United States and most of the industrialized countries of the world, is based on the principle of trade without discrimination. The United Nations Convention on Contracts for the International Sale of Goods provides uniform rules for international sales contracts between parties in contracting nations. The European Economic Community is a regional trading group that includes most of Western Europe. The U.S.-Canada FTA eliminates duties on goods traded between the countries, opens markets for a wide range of services, lowers barriers to U.S. investments, and contains immigration provisions for business persons.

American firms may choose to do business abroad by making export sales or contracting with a foreign distributor to take title to their goods and sell them abroad. American firms may also license their technology or trademarks for foreign use. An agency arrangement, or the organization of a foreign subsidiary, may be required to participate effectively in foreign markets. This results in subjecting the U.S. firm to taxation in the host country. However, tax treaties commonly eliminate double taxation.

The Export Administration Act is the principal statute imposing export controls on goods and technical data. The need for a validated license from the U.S. Department of Commerce (as opposed to a general license) is determined by a three-step process. This process involves determinations about the destination of the product, the product being exported, and whether special restrictions apply to the product. Falsification of information on a license application is a criminal offense.

In choosing the form for doing business abroad, U.S. firms must be careful not to violate the antitrust laws of host countries. Anticompetitive foreign transactions may have an adverse impact on competition in U.S. domestic markets. U.S. antitrust laws have a broad extraterritorial reach. The U.S. courts apply a "jurisdictional rule of reason" weighing the interests of the United States with the interests of the foreign country involved in making a decision on whether or not to hear the case. Illegal conduct may occur in the U.S. securities markets. U.S. enforcement efforts sometimes run into foreign countries' secrecy and blocking laws that hinder effective enforcement.

Antidumping laws offer relief for domestic firms threatened by unfair foreign competition. In addition, economic programs exist to assist industries, communities, and workers injured by import competition. Programs also exist to increase the foreign sales of U.S. firms.

LAW IN PRACTICE

1. If your business is hurt by foreign imports being sold in the United States at less than fair value, there is a legal recourse. The practice may be stopped through the antidumping procedures of the Trade Agreement Act of 1979.
2. If you lose your job because of import competition, you may be entitled to job training and job search allowances under the Trade Act of 1974.

3. Be extremely careful in dealing with securities dealers from other countries. While U.S. securities laws have extraterritorial effect, foreign "blocking laws" and "secrecy laws" may impede the SEC in investigatory efforts on your behalf.
4. Make clear to your officers and employees that they may not give any payments or gifts to foreign officials to obtain contracts with their governments.

QUESTIONS AND CASE PROBLEMS

1. What social forces are affected by the extraterritorial application of U.S. antitrust laws?

2. How does the most favored nation clause of the GATT work to foster the principle of trade without discrimination?

3. How does the selling of subsidized foreign goods in the United States adversely affect free trade?

4. Ronald Sadler, a California resident, owned a helicopter distribution company in West Germany, called Delta Avia. This company distributed American-made Hughes civilian helicopters in Western Europe. Sadler's West German firm purchased 85 helicopters from Hughes Aircraft Co. After validated export licenses were obtained in reliance on the purchaser's written assurance that the goods would not be disposed of contrary to the export license, the helicopters were exported to West Germany for resale in Western Europe. Thereafter, Delta Avia exported them to North Korea, which was a country subject to a trade embargo by the United States. The helicopters were converted to military use. Sadler was charged with violating Export Administration regulations. In Sadler's defense, it was contended that the U.S. regulations have no effect as to what occurs in the resale of civilian helicopters in another sovereign country. Decide.

5. Mirage Investments Corporation (MIC) planned a tender offer for the shares of Gulf States International Corp. (GSIC). Archer, an officer of MIC, placed purchase orders for GSIC stock through the New York office of the Bahamian Bank (BB) prior to the announcement of the tender offer, making a $300,000 profit when the tender offer was made public. The Bahamas is a secrecy jurisdiction. The bank informed the SEC that under its law it could not disclose the name of the person for whom it purchased the stock. What, if anything, may the SEC do to discover whether or not the federal securities laws have been violated?

6. National Dynamics Corp. (ND), a large defense contractor, has been selected by the oil-rich African nation of Nirombia to build and deliver 20 ND-21 jet fighter planes at an average price of $16 million per plane. NDs back orders are small, and it needs the contract to avoid layoffs of many hundreds of workers. At a meeting held in Nirombia to finalize the contract, the Prime Minister made it very clear to NDs senior representative that a "finder's fee" of 0.025 percent of the contract price would have to be deposited in his brother-in-law's account in Switzerland in order to finalize the contract. He pointed out that the contract was being made in Nirombia, where American law did not apply. He stated that such a payment was an ordinary business custom in his country and on the African continent and that such payment was offered by ND's European competitor if the contract were awarded to it. The Prime Minister laughed, saying that "the percentage is so small you can consider it an entertainment expense if you want to." Advise National Dynamics of the ethics and legality of making the payment.

7. "Reebok" manufactures and sells fashionable athletic shoes both in America and abroad. It owns the federally registered REEBOK trademark, and has registered this trademark in Mexico as well. Nathan Betech is a Mexican citizen, residing in San Diego, California and has business offices located there. Reebok believed that Betech is in the business of selling counterfeit Reebok shoes in Mexican border towns such as Tijuana, Mexico. It seeks an injunction in a federal district court in California ordering Betech to cease his counterfeiting activity and to refrain from destroying certain documents. It also asks the court to freeze Betech's assets pending the outcome of a Lanham Act lawsuit. Betech contends that a U.S. district court has no jurisdiction nor authority to enter the injunction for the activities allegedly occurring in Mexico. Decide. [*Reebok International, Ltd v Marnatech Enterprises, Inc. (CA 9 Cal) 970 F2d 552*]

8. Assume that prior to the formation of the European Economic Community the lowest-cost source of supply for a certain product consumed in France was producers from the United States. Explain the basis by which, after the EEC was formed, higher-cost German producers could have replaced the U.S. producers as the source of supply.

9. A complaint was filed with the U.S. Commerce Department's International Trade Administration (ITA) by U.S. telephone manufacturers AT&T, Comidial Corp., and Eagle Telephones, Inc. alleging that 12 Asian manufacturers of small business telephones, including the Japanese firms Hitachi, NEC, and Toshiba and the Taiwanese firm Sun Moon Star Corp., were dumping their small-business phones in the U.S. market at prices that were from 6 to 283 percent less than in their home markets. The U.S. manufacturers showed that the domestic industry's market share had dropped from 54 percent in 1985 to 33 percent in 1989. They asserted that it was doubtful if the domestic industry could survive the dumping. Later in a hearing before the International Trade Commission (ITC), the Japanese and Taiwanese respondents contended that the domestic industry was basically sound, and that the U.S. firms simply had to become more efficient to meet world-wide competition. They contended that the U.S. was using the procedures before the ITA and ITC as a nontariff barrier to imports. How should the ITC decide the case? [*American Telephone and Telegraph Co. v Hitachi, 6 ITC 1511*]

10. Timken Roller Bearing Co. of Ohio (American Timken) owns 30 percent of the outstanding shares of British Timken, a foreign competitor. In 1928 American Timken and British Timken organized French Timken, and since that time they have together owned all the stock of the French company. Since 1928 American Timken, British Timken, and French Timken have continuously kept operative "business agreements" regulating the manufacture and sale of antifriction bearings by the three companies and providing for the use by the British and French corporations of the trademark "Timken." Under these agreements the contracting parties have (1) allocated trade territories among themselves, (2) fixed prices on products of one of the parties sold in the territory of the others, and (3) cooperated to protect each other's markets and to eliminate outside competition. The United States Department of Justice contends that American Timken has violated the Sherman Act. American Timken contends that its actions were legal, since it was entitled to enter a joint venture with British Timken to form French Timken, and was legally entitled to license the trademark "Timken" to the British and French companies. Decide. [*Timken Roller Bearing Co. v United States, 341 US 593*]

11. Roland Staemphfli was employed as the chief financial officer of Honeywell Bull S.A. (HB), a Swiss computer company operating exclusively in Switzerland. Staemphfli purportedly arranged financing for HB in Switzerland through the issuance of promissory notes. He had the assistance of Fidenas, a Bahamian company dealing in commercial paper. Unknown to Fidenas, the HB notes were fraudulent. The notes were prepared and forged by Staemphfli, who lost all of the proceeds in a speculative investment. Staemphfli was convicted of criminal fraud. HB denied responsibility for the fraudulently issued notes when they came due. Fidenas' business deteriorated because of its involvement with the HB notes. It sued HB and others in the United States for violations of the U.S. securities laws. HB defended that the U.S. court did not have jurisdiction over the transactions in question. Decide. [*Fidenas v Honeywell Bull, S.A. (CA2 NY) 606 F2d 5*]

12. Marc Rich & Co., A.G., a Swiss commodities trading corporation, refused to comply with a grand jury subpoena requesting certain business records maintained in Switzerland relating to crude oil transactions and possible violations of U.S. income tax laws. Marc Rich contended that a U.S. court has no authority to require a foreign corporation to deliver to a U.S. court documents located abroad. The court disagreed and imposed fines, froze assets, and threatened to close a Marc Rich wholly owned subsidiary that did business in the state of New York. The fines amounted to $50,000 for each day the company failed to comply with the court's order. Marc Rich appealed. Decide. [*Marc Rich v United States (CA2 NY) 707 F2d 633*]

13. The United States Steel Corporation formed Orinoco Mining Company, a wholly owned corporation, to mine large deposits of iron ore that U.S. Steel had discovered in Venezuela. Orinoco, which was incorporated in Delaware, was subject to Venezuela's maximum tax of 50 percent on net income. Orinoco was also subject to U.S. income tax, but the U.S. foreign tax credit offset this amount. U.S. Steel Corp. purchased the ore from Orinoco in Venezuela. U.S. Steel formed Navios, Inc., a wholly owned subsidiary, to transport the ore for it. Navios, a Liberian corporation, was subject to a 2.5 percent Venezuelan excise tax and was exempt from U.S. income taxes. Although U.S. Steel was Navios' primary customer, it charged other customers the same price it charged U.S. Steel. U.S. Steel's investment in Navios was $50,000. In seven years Navios accumulated nearly $80 million in cash, but had not paid any dividends to U.S. Steel. The IRS used Internal Revenue Code Section 482 to allocate $52 million of Navios' income to U.S. Steel. U.S. Steel challenged this action, contending its charges to U.S. Steel were at arm's length and the same it charged other customers. Decide. [*United States Steel Corp. v Commissioner (CA2 NY) 617 F2d 942*]

14. National Computers, Inc., a U.S. firm, entered into a joint venture with a Chinese computer manufacturing organization, TEC. A dispute arose over payments due the U.S. firm under the joint venture agreement with TEC. The agreement called for the dispute to be arbitrated in China with the arbitrator being chosen from a panel of arbitrators maintained by the Beijing arbitration institution, "Cietac." What advantages and disadvantages exist for the U.S. firm under this arbitration arrangement? Advise the American firm on negotiating future arbitration agreements with Chinese businesses.

15. Sensor, a Netherlands business organization wholly owned by Geosource, Inc. of Houston, Texas, made a contract with C.E.P. to deliver 2,400 strings of geophones to Rotterdam by September 20, 1982. The ultimate destination was identified as the U.S.S.R. Thereafter, in June 1982, the President of the United States prohibited the shipment to the U.S.S.R. of equipment manufactured in foreign countries under license from U.S. firms. The president had a foreign policy objective of retaliating for the imposition of martial law in Poland. He was acting under regulations issued under the Export Administration Act of 1979. Sensor, in July and August of 1982, notified C.E.P. that as a subsidiary of an American corporation it had to respect the President's embargo. C.E.P. filed suit in district court of the Netherlands, asking that Sensor be ordered to deliver the geophones. Decide. *[Compagnie Europ_enne des P_troles v Sensor Nederland, 22 ILM 66]*

C H A P T E R 7

CRIMES

A. GENERAL PRINCIPLES
   1. Classification of Crimes
   2. Basis of Criminal Liability
   3. Parties to a Crime
   4. Responsibility for Criminal Acts
   5. Attempts and Conspiracies
   6. Criminal Fines and Administrative Penalties Compared
   7. Indemnification of Crime Victims
   8. Sentencing

B. WHITE COLLAR CRIMES
   9. Crimes Related to Production, Competition, and Marketing
   10. Racketeering
   11. Bribery
   12. Extortion and Blackmail
   13. Corrupt Influence
   14. Counterfeiting
   15. Forgery
   16. Perjury
   17. False Claims and Pretenses
   18. Bad Checks
   19. Cheats and Swindles
   20. Credit Card Crimes
   21. Use of Mails to Defraud
   22. Criminal Libel
   23. Lotteries and Gambling
   24. Embezzlement
   25. Receiving Stolen Goods

C. CRIMES OF FORCE AND CRIMES AGAINST PROPERTY
   26. Larceny
   27. Robbery
   28. Burglary
   29. Arson
   30. Riots and Civil Disorders

LEARNING OBJECTIVES

After studying this chapter, you will be able to:
1. *Define crime.*
2. *Describe three ways of classifying crimes.*
3. *Identify persons who are not held responsible for criminal acts.*
4. *Define white collar crimes.*
5. *Distinguish one criminal offense from another on the basis of the elements of each offense.*

Society sets certain standards of conduct and punishes a breach of those standards as a crime. This chapter introduces how government protects people and businesses from prohibited conduct.

A. GENERAL PRINCIPLES

Crimes are defined and their punishment specified by detailed criminal codes and statutes. These vary from state to state but still show the imprint of a common law background. For this reason, the subject is dealt with in this chapter primarily in terms of the common law.

1. Nature and Classification of Crimes

A **crime** is conduct that is prohibited and punished by a government.

(a) SOURCE OF CRIMINAL LAW. Crimes are classified, in terms of their origin, as common law and statutory crimes. Some offenses that are defined by statute are merely declaratory of the common law. Each state has its own criminal law, although a common pattern among the states may be observed.

(b) SERIOUSNESS OF OFFENSE. Crimes are classified in terms of their seriousness as treason, felonies, and misdemeanors. **Treason** is defined by the Constitution of the United States, which states that Treason against the United States, shall consist only in levying war against them, or in adhering to their enemies, giving them aid and comfort.[1] **Felonies** include the other more serious crimes, such as arson, murder, and robbery, which are punishable by confinement in prison or by death. Crimes not classified as treason or felonies are **misdemeanors**. Reckless driving, weighing goods with uninspected scales, and disturbing the peace by illegal picketing are generally classified as misdemeanors. An act may be a felony in one state and a misdemeanor in another.[2]

(c) NATURE OF CRIMES. Crimes are also classified in terms of the nature of the misconduct. **Crimes mala in se** are crimes that are inherently vicious or, in other words, that are naturally evil as measured by the standards of a civilized community. **Crimes mala prohibita** are acts that are only wrong because they are declared wrong by some statute.

2. Basis of Criminal Liability

A crime generally consists of two elements: (a) a mental state, and (b) an act or omission. Harm may occur as a result of a crime, but harm is not an essential element of a crime.

(a) MENTAL STATE. Mental state does not require an awareness or knowledge of guilt. In most crimes, it is sufficient that the defendant voluntarily did the act that is criminal, regardless of motive or intent. The lawmaker may make an act a crime even though the actor has no knowledge that a law is being broken. In some instances, a particular mental state is required, such as the necessity that a homicide be with **malice aforethought** in order to constitute murder. In some cases, it is the existence of a specific intent that differentiates one crime from other offenses. An assault with intent to kill is distinguished by that intent from an ordinary assault or from an assault with intent to rob.

Actions that are in themselves crimes are not made innocent by the claim that the defendant was exercising a constitutional right. Thus, freedom of speech does not give the right to send threatening letters.

---

[1] US Const, Art 3, § 3, Cl 1.

[2] Some states make a further subdivision in terms of seriousness by defining different degrees of a crime, as first degree murder, second degree murder, and so on. Misdemeanors may be divided, calling minor misdemeanors by special names.

(b) HARM. Causing harm is typical of some crimes, such as murder or arson. Other crimes, however, are committed without harm to others. For example, a person may be guilty of speeding or reckless driving on the highway, although no one is hurt. In such case, it is the social judgment that the act condemned as a crime has such a potential for harm that the act should be prohibited before it does cause harm to others.

3. Parties to a Crime

Two or more parties may directly or indirectly commit or contribute to the commission of a crime. At common law, participants in the commission of a felony may be principals or accessories. The statutory trend is to simplify or abolish these distinctions and to treat everyone taking part in a crime as being guilty of the crime.

4. Responsibility for Criminal Acts

In some cases, particular persons are not held responsible for their criminal acts. In other cases, persons are held criminally responsible for acts committed by others.

(a) EMPLOYERS. An employer is liable for the crime committed by the employee when the employer directs or requires the commission of the crime. The fact that the employee is also guilty of a crime does not shield the employer; both the employer and the employee carrying out the wrongful plan are guilty of crimes. Thus, an employer is guilty of a crime when the employer gives the employee money to bribe a building inspector to overlook violations of the fire code. The employee is also guilty of the crime of bribery when the employee pays the money to the inspector.

Figure 7-1   The Law of Crimes

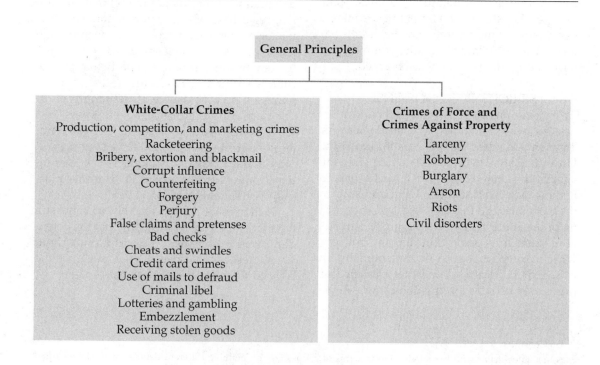

General Principles

White-Collar Crimes

Production, competition, and marketing crimes
Racketeering
Bribery, extortion and blackmail
Corrupt influence
Counterfeiting
Forgery
Perjury
False claims and pretenses
Bad checks
Cheats and swindles
Credit card crimes
Use of mails to defraud
Criminal libel
Lotteries and gambling
Embezzlement
Receiving stolen goods

**Crimes of Force and
Crimes Against Property**

Larceny
Robbery
Burglary
Arson
Riots
Civil disorders

(b) CORPORATIONS. The modern tendency is to hold corporations criminally responsible for their acts. A corporation may also be held liable for crimes based on the failure to act. Thus, a corporation may be held criminally responsible when an employee is killed because of the corporation's failure to install safety devices required by law.

(c) PERSONS UNDER INCAPACITY. Minors below a certain age, insane persons, and, to a limited extent, intoxicated persons are not responsible for their crimes. Intoxication generally does not relieve a person from criminal responsibility unless a crime requires specific intent that cannot be formed because of intoxication. Generally the law applicable to persons under incapacity comes from the common law, although there is an increasing trend toward statutory regulation.[3]

5. Attempts and Conspiracies

Prior to the commission of an intended crime, there may be conduct that is itself a crime, such as an attempt or a conspiracy.

(a) ATTEMPTS. When the criminal fails to commit the crime intended, it may be that what has been done constitutes an **attempt**. Attempts are punished as distinct crimes. However, it is difficult to determine just what constitutes an attempt. Obviously, it is something less than committing the intended crime, but it must be more than merely preparing to commit that crime. Thus, the purchasing of a gun with which to kill the victim is not regarded as an attempt but as preparation. However, when the criminal points the gun at the door through which the victim is expected to leave the building, an attempt has been committed. The modern trend is to condemn as an attempt any conduct that has reached such a point that the potential for harm to others is unreasonably great. Thus, a person attempting to shoot a victim is guilty of an attempt even though the gun may malfunction. Likewise, a robber pointing a gun at the victim and demanding money is guilty of an attempt even though the robber changes his mind and does not take any money.

Courts differ as to how far the defendant must go beyond preparation before an attempt is committed.[4]

(b) CONSPIRACIES. A **conspiracy** is an agreement between two or more persons to commit an unlawful act or to use unlawful means to achieve an otherwise lawful result. The crime is the agreement, and generally it is immaterial that nothing is done to carry out the agreement. Some statutes, however, require that there be some act done to carry out the agreement before the crime of conspiracy is committed.

(c) NUMBER OF OFFENSES. If the criminal actually commits the intended crime, there is no criminal attempt. There can only be an attempt when the intended crime is not committed.

In contrast with the concept of an attempt, a conspiracy is a separate crime. Consequently, the fact that the intended crime is actually committed does not erase the conspiracy. Defendants may thus be prosecuted both for having conspired to commit the crime and for having committed the crime intended. They may be prosecuted for the conspiracy, even though the contemplated crime, in fact, is not committed.

---

[3] See, for example, Insanity Reform Act of 1984, § 401, PL 98-473, 98 Stat 2057, 18 USC § 402.

[4] New York v Acosta, 172 App Div 2d 103, 578 NYS2d 525 (1991).

6. Criminal Fines and Administrative Penalties Compared

The differences between a monetary penalty imposed by an administrative agency and a fine imposed by a court are very slight and largely theoretical. In both the administrative proceeding and the criminal court prosecution, the monetary penalty represents dollars paid by the defending party to the government. Both the fine and the penalty are imposed because the defending party failed to follow a standard of conduct required by the government.

In many instances, the administrative penalty will be significantly larger than fines imposed by a court. The reason is partly historical. The statute defining a particular crime and specifying the maximum fine ordinarily follows the pattern of an earlier statute that may be from the last century. What was then a large fine is today insignificant. Thus, a maximum fine inherited from the past may specify that the fine that can be imposed for armed robbery may not exceed $1,000. In contrast, the agency with power to impose a penalty is a creation of our time; therefore, any penalties are stated in terms of the modern purchasing power of the dollar. Thus, it is not unusual to authorize an agency to impose a penalty not to exceed $10,000.

This difference in the maximum penalty may also be justified theoretically. For instance, in the case of armed robbery there is one victim of the crime, whereas in the case of a violation judged by an administrative agency there may be many victims of the crime (an example would be a factory's pollution of the environment).

7. Indemnification of Crime Victims

Typically, the victim of a crime does not benefit from the criminal prosecution and conviction of the wrongdoer. Any fine that is imposed on the defendant is paid to the government and is not received in any way by the victim.

(a) STATUTORY ASSISTANCE. Several states have adopted statutes to provide a limited degree of indemnification to victims of crime in order to compensate them for the harm or loss sustained.[5] Under some criminal victim indemnification statutes, dependents of a deceased victim are entitled to recover the amount of the support that they were deprived of by the victim's death. The Victims of Crime Act of 1984 creates a federal Crime Victims Fund. This fund receives the fines paid into the federal courts and other moneys. From this fund, grants are made to the states to assist them in financing programs to provide indemnity to and assistance for victims of crime.[6] The Victim and Witness Protection Act of 1982 authorizes the sentencing judge in a federal district court to order, in certain cases, that the defendant make **restitution** (restoration) to the victim or pay the victim the amount of medical expenses or loss of income caused by the crime.[7] When a court enters a restitution order against the defendant, it becomes a lien on all property owned by the defendant at that time.[8]

Mob violence statutes frequently impose liability for property damage on the local government. The term *property* in such a statute generally applies to tangible property and does not authorize recovery for loss of profits or goodwill resulting from business interruption. The fact that the government was unable to prevent the harm or damage is not a defense to liability under such statutes.

---

[5] A Uniform Crime Victims Reparations Act has been adopted in Kansas, Louisiana, Montana, North Dakota, Ohio, and Texas.

[6] Act of October 12, 1984, PL 98-473, 98 Stat 2170, 18 USC §§ 1401 et seq.

[7] Act of October 12, 1982, PL 97-291, 96 Stat 1253, 18 USC § 3579, amended by Act of November 15, 1990, PL 101-581, 104 Stat 2865, 18 USC § ___. USC § 3579; Hughey v United States, 495 US 411 (1990). Some states likewise provide for payment into a special fund. Ex parte Lewis (Ala) 556 So 2d 370 (1989).

[8] United States v Mills (CA9 Cal) 991 F2d 609 (1993).

(b) ACTION FOR DAMAGES. Although the criminal prosecution of a wrongdoer does not financially benefit the victim of the crime, the victim is typically entitled to bring a civil action for damages against the wrongdoer for the harm sustained. The modern pattern of statutes creating business crimes is to give the victim the right to sue for damages. Thus, the wrongdoer violating the federal antitrust act or the Racketeer Influenced and Corrupt Organizations Act (RICO) is liable to the victim for three times the damages actually sustained. A damage suit may be brought under the federal act without proof of a racketeering injury or the prior conviction of the defendant.[9]

A number of states have adopted statutes following the pattern of RICO. State statutes define racketeering broadly and cover both white collar and violent crimes.

In the *Banderas* case, the question was whether the Florida RICO authorized a civil action for damages when (1) the misconduct was making a false claim for payment and (2) there was no proof that the defendant was related to organized crime.

BANDERAS v BANCO CENTRAL DEL ECUADOR
(Fla App) 461 So 2d 265 (1985)

The Banco Central administered a humanitarian plan for the government of Ecuador. Fernando Banderas and his wife presented false claims that were paid by the bank. After the fraud was discovered, the bank sued Banderas and his wife for damages for fraud and treble damages under the Florida version of RICO. Defendants asserted that they were not liable for RICO damages because there was no proof that they were related to organized crime and because the wrong committed by them was merely ordinary fraud. They had not used any racketeering methods. From a judgment in favor of the bank, the defendants appealed.

HENDRY, J. . . . Appellants raise . . . on appeal: (1) whether the civil damages provisions of RICO were improperly applied to these defendants because there was no showing that they were connected to organized crime; (2) whether the civil damages provisions were improperly applied to a mere "garden variety" fraud case.

The Florida RICO Act, promulgated in 1977, is nearly identical to the federal RICO statute, 18 U.S.C. §§ 1961-1968 (1970), passed as Title IX of the Organized Crime Control Act of 1970. Thus, we can also look to a wealth of material on the federal RICO statute for guidance on this issue. The legislative history shows that Congress was clearly concerned, during the drafting of this bill, with the constitutional problems associated with trying to limit the statute's target to "organized crime" only; that is, that the statute would not survive attacks on the grounds that it was unconstitutionally overbroad or that it created status crimes. Status crimes, related as they are to the old English bills of attainder, are especially disfavored. *Cf. Robinson v California*, 370 US 660 (1962) (state cannot make drug addiction a crime); *Lanzetta v New Jersey*, 306 US 451 (1939) (state cannot make being a "gangster" a crime). Secondly, Congress deliberately made the scope of the statute as broad as possible "to avoid opening loopholes through which the minions of organized crime might crawl to freedom." Congress chose the only course available to it which would effectuate the broad purpose of the statute without creating serious constitutional issues. It imposed enhanced sanctions for the types of activities which were characteristic of "organized crime." Thus, all persons who engage, over a period of time, in activities which Congress has defined as being "racketeering activities" are subject to criminal prosecution or civil litigation under RICO.

Against this background, it is now well established in the federal courts that it is not necessary to prove a nexus to organized crime in order to obtain damages in a private civil RICO suit.

Appellants' second argument, that the trial court permitted Central Bank to turn a "garden variety" fraud case into a treble damage civil RICO action is, paraphrasing Mr. Justice Cardozo, to spread the study of horticulture to unaccustomed fields. *United States v Constantine*, 296 US 287, 299 (1935) (Cardozo, J., dissenting). We cannot accept appellants' argument. The statute makes no distinction between levels or degrees of fraudulent activity. *See* § 895.02(1)(a)16. Thus, courts are not in a position to decide whether certain frauds are "garden variety" subject only to simple compensatory and possible punitive damages, and whether other frauds are "exotic arrangements" meriting the full range of enhanced penalties available under RICO. Fraud is not so easily parsed.

Section 895.02(4) defines "pattern of racketeering activity" as:

Engaging in at least two incidents of racketeering conduct that have the same or similar intents, results, accomplices, victims, or methods of commission or that otherwise are interrelated by distinguishing characteristics and are not isolated incidents, provided at least one of such incidents occurred within 5 years after a prior incident of racketeering conduct.

This case fits precisely within the parameters of the statute. This was not a technical securities or business fraud. This was a well-organized, ongoing, systematic, criminal scheme devised by appellants to defraud the government of Ecuador—their own government.

At some time prior to June, 1981, appellants and Florida Aviation Corp. [FAVCO] and Banla formed a conspiracy for the express purpose of carrying out this scheme. In furtherance of this scheme, these appellants created four fictitious "hospitals" in three different states [Florida, Texas and Missouri]. Appellants sent "statements," in medical terminology, on invoices which they caused to be printed in the names of these non-existent hospitals. They sent seventy of these statements over the course of thirteen months, which the Central Bank paid in good faith. The bank didn't realize there was a problem with the medical assistance program until the spring of 1982 when an employee at Southeast Bank noticed that the address listed for St. John's Hospital corresponded to a vacant lot. Appellants earned over $851,000.00 on a few dollars invested in printing and a medical dictionary. Innocent banks were drawn into the scheme. As a result, there were also violations of the federal mail and wire fraud statutes. . . . This case presents one version of precisely the sort of activity that should, without controversy, fall within the statute's application.

[Judgment affirmed]

Under some RICO statutes, it must be shown that the defendant engaged in a pattern of racketeering and that this was done through an enterprise or organization.

(c) INDEMNIFICATION OF UNJUSTLY CONVICTED. If an innocent person is convicted of a crime, the state legislature typically pays the person indemnity to compensate for the wrong that has been done. In some states, this right to indemnity is expressly established by statute, as in the case of the New York Unjust Conviction and Imprisonment Act.[10]

8. Sentencing

Various reform movements are underway to secure more uniform sentencing of criminals.[11]

(a) THE INDIGENT DEFENDANT. When a court imposes sentence, it cannot impose imprisonment as an alterntive to a fine if the defendant does not have the money to pay the fine. For example, it is unconstitutional to sentence a defendant to "$30 or 30 days."[12] This conclusion is reached on the ground that such a sentence in the alternative discriminates on the basis of poverty. It makes a poor person, who cannot pay the fine, go to jail, while a rich person pays the fine and walks out of the court.

(b) WHITE COLLAR CRIMES. There is much criticism about the sentencing of white collar criminals on the ground that the penalties are not sufficiently large to serve the purpose of punishing the defendant or of deterring others from committing similar crimes.

(c) FORFEITURE OF CRIME-RELATED PROPERTY. When a defendant is convicted of a crime, the court may also declare that the defendant's rights in any instrument of that crime are forfeited. When the forfeited property can be used only for a criminal purpose, as in the case of engraved plates used for making counterfeit money, there is no question of the right of the government to confiscate the property. This confiscation is allowable even though this, in effect, increases the penalty imposed on the defendant.

Forfeiture is not limited to property that can be used only for crime. Thus, an automobile that is used to carry illegal merchandise may itself be seized by the government, even though it is obvious that the automobile could also be put to a lawful use.

As we move into the area of white collar crime, this problem of defining crime-related property becomes increasingly difficult because the property involved is not by itself criminal, or even potentially criminal, in character. Legislation in this area has been directed at depriving the wrongdoer of the gains obtained

---

[10] Carter v New York (Court of Claims) 528 NYS2d 292 (1988).

[11] The Sentencing Reform Act of October 12, 1984, Chapter 227, PL 98-473, 98 Stat 1987, 18 USC §§ 3551 et seq. contains provisions designed to produce greater uniformity in sentencing. Mistretta v United States, 488 US 361 (1989). The Commissioners on Uniform Laws have proposed a Model Sentencing and Corrections Act.

[12] Tate v Short, 401 US 395 (1971).

by the crime or at taking away the power to benefit from the crime. An example of the first type of legislation is the Sherman Antitrust Act, under which a defendant guilty of unlawfully acquiring the stock of competing corporations may be ordered by the court to sell or otherwise dispose of such shares. This is called a **divestiture order**. Illustrative of both the first and the second types of legislation is the federal RICO Act. Under this act, the court is required to enter an order against the defendant to for-feit any property acquired or used in exercising unlawful racketeering influence. Under RICO, the fruits of the racketeering activity and related property may be forfeited regardless of their nature.

In the *Kravitz* case, the defendant attacked the validity and application of the RICO forfeiture provisions.

UNITED STATES v KRAVITZ
(CA3 Pa) 738 F2d 102 (1984)

> Kravitz owned 100 percent of the stock of American Health Programs, Inc. (AHP). In order to obtain the Philadelphia Fraternal Order of Police as a customer for AHP, Kravitz paid money bribes to persons whom he thought were officers of that organization, but who, in fact, were federal undercover agents. He was prosecuted for violating RICO. He was convicted, and the court ordered the forfeiture of all of the shares of stock of AHP owned by Kravitz. He claimed that the court was not required to order the forfeiture and that the statute was unconstitutional as interpreted. From a decision against Kravitz, he appealed.

GIBBONS, C. J. . . . Charles Kravitz appeals from a judgment of sentence imposed following his conviction for violations of the Racketeer Influenced and Corrupt Organizations Act, 18 U.S.C. § 1961 et seq. (1982) ("RICO"). He contends that his conviction should be set aside, and that in any event the court erred in ordering forfeiture of his interest as a stockholder in American Health Programs, Inc. (AHP). We hold that his objections to the RICO convictions are without merit, and that the forfeiture order was proper.

A primary question presented by this appeal is whether forfeiture under section 1963 is mandatory upon a finding that the appellant's property was used to promote racketeering. We conclude, as have all other courts to decide the question, that forfeiture is mandatory.

Several factors compel that conclusion. The first is the plain meaning of the language employed in section 1963(a), stating that "whoever violates any provision of section 1962 . . . shall forfeit to the United States" the illegally used interest. As the Fifth Circuit pointed out in *United States v L'Noste*, 609 F2d 796 (CA5, 1980), although there are occasions where "shall" has been interpreted to vest discretionary, rather than mandatory, authority to act, the wording of the statute is the most persuasive evidence of Congressional intent. Nor does the legislative history ever discuss forfeiture in discretionary terms. The wording of the remaining penalties established under section 1963(a) also supports a mandatory interpretation of forfeiture: section 1963(a) states that a defendant "shall be fined not more than $25,000 or imprisoned not more than twenty years, or *both*". (Emphasis added.) Thus, where Congress intended for the penalty to be optional, as in the choice between fine or imprisonment, they specified that there was such a choice. The section's wording provides no choice regarding the imposition of forfeiture.

Moreover, a literal reading of section 1963(a) is consistent with RICO purposes. The criminal forfeiture provision was viewed as an innovative means of addressing the spread of organized crime that has infiltrated so many aspects of American society. Of foremost concern during Congressional hearings on RICO was the weakness of current efforts at curtailing the spread of organized crime to legitimate business endeavors. For instance, the Senate Judiciary Committee's report quoted the Attorney General's testimony that:

While the prosecutions of organized crime leaders can seriously curtail the operations of the Cosa Nostra, as long as the flow of money continues, such prosecutions will only result in a compulsory retirement and promotion system as new people step forward to take the place of those convicted.

S Rep No 91-617 91st Cong 1st Sess 78 (1969). The report stated that forfeiture as a penalty for the criminal offense—although disfavored throughout American history—was an innovative approach which could provide the linchpin in the renewed effort against organized crime:

Title IX recognizes that present efforts to dislodge the forces of organized crime from legitimate fields of endeavor have proven unsuccessful. To remedy this failure, the proposed statute adopts the most direct route open to accomplish the desired objective. Where an organization is acquired or run by defined racketeering methods, then the persons involved can be legally separated from the organization, either by the criminal law approach of fine, imprisonment and forfeiture, or through a civil law approach of equitable relief broad enough to do all that is necessary to free the channels of commerce from all illicit activity.

In light of RICO's central goal of inhibiting organized crime's infiltration of legitimate business, it is certainly not likely that forfeiture was viewed by its drafters as an optional penalty. At the least, a mandatory interpretation of section 1963(a)'s forfeiture would promote, rather than discourage, RICO's intended purpose. Indeed, it is consistent with RICO's own construction clause, Pub.L. No. 91-452, § 904(a), 84 Stat 922, 947 (1970), which states that the statute "shall be liberally construed to effectuate its remedial purposes."

When Congress has opted to provide for discretionary forfeiture, it has done so expressly. Thus, under the Internal Revenue Laws there is district court discretion to remit or mitigate the forfeiture. 18 U.S.C. § 3617 (1982). The Organized Crime Control Act itself elsewhere contains a permissive, rather than mandatory, forfeiture provision. In establishing penalties for illegal gambling, Congress provided that "any property . . . used in violation of the provisions of this section may be seized and forfeited to the United States." 18 U.S.C. § 1955(d) (1982).

Finally, we note that where Congress did provide for the remission or mitigation of the forfeiture order, it vested that decisionmaking authority with the Attorney General, not the federal courts. . . .

Kravitz also challenges the forfeiture on eighth amendment grounds. He argues that forfeiture constitutes a disproportionate penalty because AHP's contract with the FOP expired prior to indictment. Since AHP was no longer providing services pursuant to the illegally secured contract, Kravitz would have us accept that the taint upon the property had dissipated, and thus that the order of forfeiture was cruel and unusual punishment, in violation of the eighth amendment.

Kravitz's eighth amendment argument completely ignores the nature of RICO's forfeiture provision. Forfeiture under RICO is . . . designed as part of the punishment for the criminal offense committed. It is simply incorrect that the termination of the criminal conduct bars the imposition of punishment. Although . . . forfeiture is not commonly used in our system of jurisprudence, it is nonetheless a legitimate weapon in the enforcement of our criminal laws and, as with any punishment for criminal conduct, may be imposed despite the cessation of the criminal conduct charged in the indictment.

[Judgment affirmed]

QUESTIONS

1. What kind of property was ordered forfeited?
2. Would you classify the property forfeited as an instrument of crime?
3. Is it material whether the forfeited property is acquired by means of crime?

B. WHITE COLLAR CRIMES

Those crimes that do not use, or threaten to use, force or violence or do not cause injury to persons or physical damage to property are called **white collar crimes**. A particular defendant may be guilty of both a white collar crime and a traditional crime of the kind described in Part C of this chapter.

9. Crimes Related to Production, Competition, and Marketing

A person or enterprise in business may be guilty of various crimes relating to labor and employment practices, conspiracies, and combinations in restraint of trade, price discrimination, and environmental pollution.

(a) IMPROPER USE OF INTERSTATE COMMERCE. The shipment of improper goods or the transmission of improper information in interstate commerce constitutes a crime under various federal statutes. Thus, it is a federal crime to send in interstate commerce a statement as part of a scheme to defraud; to send a blackmail or extortion threat; to ship adulterated or mislabeled foods, drugs, or cosmetics; or to ship into a state child-labor-made or convict-labor-made goods or intoxicating liquor when the sale of such goods is prohibited by the destination state.

The Communications Act of 1934, as amended,[13] makes it a crime to manufacture or sell devices knowing their primary use is to unscramble satellite telecasts without having paid for the right to do so.[14]

(b) SECURITIES CRIMES. To protect the investing public, both state and federal laws have regulated the issuance and public sale of stocks and bonds. Between 1933 and 1940, seven such regulatory statutes were adopted by Congress. As a practical matter, these fed-

---

[13] Section 705(d)(1), (e)(4), 47 USC § 605(d)(1), (e)(4).

[14] United States v Harrell (CA5 Miss) 983 F2d 36 (1993).

eral statutes have largely displaced state statutes by virtue of the principle of federal preemption. Violation of these statutes is typically made a crime.

10. Racketeering

The United States Congress and many states have adopted laws aimed at racketeering. The victim indemnification provision of the federal RICO statute has been discussed in Section 7 of this chapter. In addition, the federal government has adopted a Money Laundering Control Act.[15] The Act prohibits the knowing and willful participation in any type of financial transaction involving unlawful proceeds when the transaction is designed to conceal or disguise the source of the funds.

11. Bribery

Bribery is the act of giving money, property, or any benefit to a particular person to influence that person's judgment in favor of the giver of the bribe. At common law, the crime was limited to doing such acts to influence a public official. In this century, the common law concept has expanded to include commercial bribery. Thus, it is now a crime to pay a competitor's employee money in order to obtain secret information about the competitor.

The giving and the receiving of a bribe each constitutes a crime. In addition, the act of trying to obtain a bribe may be a crime of solicitation of bribery. In some states, bribery is broadly defined to include solicitation of bribes.

12. Extortion and Blackmail

Extortion and blackmail are crimes by which the wrongdoer seeks to force the victim to do some act—typically paying money—that the victim would not otherwise desire to do.

(a) EXTORTION. When a public officer, acting under the apparent authority of the office, makes an illegal demand, the officer has committed the crime of **extortion**. For example, if a health inspector threatens to close down a restaurant on a false charge of violation of the sanitation laws unless the restaurant pays the inspector a sum of money, the inspector has committed extortion. (If the restaurant voluntarily offers the inspector the money to prevent the restaurant from being shut down because of actual violations of the sanitation laws, the crime committed would be bribery.)

Modern statutes tend to ignore the public officer aspect of the common law and expand extortion to include obtaining anything of value by threat. This might be in connection with loansharking or labor racketeering. In a number of states, statutes extend the extortion concept to include the making of terroristic threats.[16]

(b) BLACKMAIL. In jurisdictions where extortion is limited to conduct of public officials, a nonofficial commits **blackmail** by making demands that would be extortion if made by a public official. Ordinarily, the concept of blackmail is used in the context of a threat to give publicity to some matter that would damage the victim's personal or business reputation.

13. Corrupt Influence

In harmony with changing concepts of right and wrong, society has increasingly outlawed practices on the ground that they exerted a corrupting influence on business transactions. To some extent, this objective of the law was attained by applying the criminal law of extortion, blackmail, and bribery to business situations. In time, the definitions of these crimes were expanded to include practices similar to the old crimes but not within the technical definition of such crimes. Thus,

---

[15] Act of 1986, as amended, 18 USC § 1956. U.S. v Awan (CA11 Fla) 966 F2d 1415 (1992).

[16] Pennsylvania v Bunting, 284 Pa Super 444, 426 A2d 130 (1981).

the crime of bribery was extended to include commercial bribery.

(a) IMPROPER POLITICAL INFLUENCE.

To protect from the improper influencing of political or governmental action, various acts have been classified as crimes. For instance, it is a crime for the holder of a government office to be financially interested in or to receive money from an enterprise that is seeking to do business with the government. Such conflict of interests is likely to produce a result that is harmful to the public. Likewise, lobbyists and foreign agents must register in Washington, D.C.,[17] and must adhere to statutes regulating the giving and receiving of contributions for political campaigns. Violation of these regulatory statutes is a crime.

(b) IMPROPER COMMERCIAL INFLUENCE.

The protection from improper influence is extended to the commercial world by statutes making it a crime to engage in commercial bribery, to engage in loansharking, to use gangster methods to influence legitimate business, or to run a legitimate business for the purpose of laundering gangster money.

Under federal statutes, it is a crime to obtain a benefit by means of a threat of economic or physical loss or harm. Federal statutes also make it a crime to use racketeering methods or money obtained from racketeering to acquire an interest in a legitimate business, or to travel in interstate commerce for the purpose of engaging in racketeering activities. A person convicted of such crimes is subject to punishment by fine, imprisonment, and the forfeiture of money obtained by the criminal conduct. The convicted defendant is also subject to civil liability to the victims of the crime.[18]

14. Counterfeiting

Counterfeiting is the making, with fraudulent intent, of a document or coin that appears to be genuine but is not because the person making it did not have the authority to make it. It is a federal crime to make, to possess with intent to pass, or to pass counterfeit coins, bank notes, or obligations or other securities of the United States. Legislation has also been adopted against the passing of counterfeit foreign securities or notes of foreign banks.

The various states also have statutes prohibiting the making and passing of counterfeit coins and bank notes. These statutes often provide, as does the federal statute, a punishment for the mutilation of bank notes or the lightening (of the weight) or mutilation of coins.

15. Forgery

Forgery consists of the fraudulent making or material altering of an instrument, such as a check, that apparently creates or changes a legal liability of another person. The instrument must have some apparent legal efficacy in order to constitute forgery.

Ordinarily, forgery consists of signing another's name with intent to defraud.[19] It may also consist of making an entire instrument or altering an existing one. It may result from signing a fictitious name or the offender's own name with the intent to defraud. When the nonowner of a credit card signs the owner's name on a credit card invoice without the owner's permission, such act is a forgery.

The issuing or delivery of a forged instrument to another person constitutes the crime of uttering a forged instrument. Any sending of a forged check through the channels of commerce or of bank collection constitutes an uttering of a forged instrument. Thus, the act of

---

[17] Foreign Agents Registration Act, Act of June 8, 1938, 52 Stat 631, 22 USC §§ 611 et seq., as amended.

[18] Act of June 25, 1948, 62 Stat 793, 18 USC § 1951; Travel Act of September 13, 1961, PL 87-228, 75 Stat 498, 18 USC § 1952; Racketeer Influenced and Corrupt Organizations Act of October 15, 1970, PL 91-452, 84 Stat 941, 18 USC §§ 1961 et seq., Criminal Control Act of 1990, Act of November 29, 1990, PL 101-647, 104 Stat 4789, 18 USC § 13001 et seq. A RICO statute is constitutional even though it imposes a heavier penalty than a cumulative sentence for the various unlawful acts that formed the racketeering pattern. Vickery v Florida (Fla App) 539 So 2d 499 (1989).

[19] Missouri v Hudson (Mo App) 793 SW2d 872 (1990).

depositing a forged check into the forger's bank account by depositing it in an automatic teller machine constitutes uttering within the meaning of a forgery statute.[20]

16. Perjury

Perjury consists of knowingly giving false testimony in a judicial proceeding after having been sworn or having affirmed to tell the truth. By statute, knowingly making false answers on any form filed with a government is typically made perjury or is subjected to the same punishment as perjury. In some jurisdictions, the out-of-court offense is called *false swearing*.

17. False Claims and Pretenses

Many statutes declare it a crime to make false claims or to obtain goods by false pretenses.

(a) FALSE CLAIMS. A statute may expressly declare that the making of a false claim to an insurance company, a government office, or a relief agency is a crime. The federal False Statement statute makes it a crime to knowingly and willfully make a false, material statement as to any matter within the jurisdiction of any department or agency of the United States. Thus, it is a crime for a contractor to make a false claim against the United States for payment for work that was never performed by the contractor. Other statutes indirectly regulate the matter by declaring that the signing of a false written claim constitutes perjury or is subject to the same punishment as perjury.

(b) OBTAINING GOODS BY FALSE PRETENSES. In almost all of the states, statutes are directed against obtaining money or goods by means of false pretenses.[21] These statutes vary in detail and scope. Sometimes the statutes are directed against a particular form of deception, such as using a bad check. In some states, the false pretense crime has been expanded to include obtaining any thing or services of value by false pretenses. In any case, an intent to defraud is an essential element of obtaining property by false pretenses.

The Trademark Counterfeiting Act of 1984[22] makes it a federal crime to deal in goods and services under a counterfeit mark.

A false pretense statute is violated when a person delivers a check and assures the person to whom it is delivered that there is sufficient money in the bank to cover the check but in fact there is not and this is known to the speaker.[23]

False representations as to future profits or the identity of the defendant are other common forms of false pretenses.

(c) FALSE INFORMATION SUBMITTED TO GOVERNMENT. Within recent decades, the concept of false claims and pretenses has been expanded to protect governmental agencies reorganizing or liquidating failed banks and savings institutions. In the *Haddock* case, the problem turned on whether the defendant had made a false statement to the FDIC.

18. Bad Checks

The use of a bad check is commonly made a crime by a statute directly aimed at the use of bad checks. In the absence of a bad check statute, the use of a bad check could generally be prosecuted under a false pretenses statute.

Under a bad check statute, it is a crime to use or pass a check with intent to defraud with knowledge that there will not be sufficient funds in the bank to pay the check when it is presented for payment.[24] Knowledge that the bad check will not be paid when presented to the bank is an essential element of the crime.

---

[20] Wisconsin v Tolliver (Wis App) 440 NW2d 571 (1989).

[21] North Carolina v Lang (NC App) 417 SE2d 808 (1992).

[22] Act of October 12, 1984, § 1502, PL 98-473, 98 Stat 2178, 18 USC § 113.

[23] Utah v LeFevre (Utah App) 825 P2d 681 (1992).

[24] Bray v Virginia, ___ Va App ___, 388 SE2d 837 (1990).

UNITED STATES v HADDOCK
(CA10 Kan) 956 F2d 1534 (1992)

> Haddock was the president and sole shareholder of First Finance, Inc. In 1988, during an examination of First Finance by the FDIC, Haddock altered the checkbook of First Finance to change the names of payees, dates of deposits, and to eliminate a substantial overdraft. He was prosecuted for the federal offense of making false "statements" to the FDIC. He raised the defense that what he had done was not the making of a "statement." He was convicted and appealed to the circuit court.

TACHA, C. J. . . . The indictment clearly states that Haddock acted knowingly and with the purpose of influencing actions of the FDIC during the FDIC's investigation of charges related to this case. The only remaining question is whether Haddock's alleged conduct constitutes a "statement."

. . . Citing *Williams v United States*, 458 U.S. 279 . . . (1982), Haddock argues that the alleged alterations do not constitute a "statement." In *Williams*, the Supreme Court—reviewing . . . a check kiting scheme—held that the writing of a check does "not involve the making of a 'false statement'" because a check does not "make any representation as to the state of [the customer's] bank balance." . . . We cannot extend the reasoning of *Williams* to support Haddock's assertion that alterations made to selected check stubs in First Finance's checkbook do not constitute "statements." These alterations were made during an FDIC investigation of which appellant was fully aware. The indictment alleges that they were made in order to hide the truth about payees, account balances, and deposit dates. The alterations . . . clearly represent an attempt to communicate something different to the FDIC than what the FDIC might have found had it reviewed the checkbook without the alterations. Therefore, we conclude that [Haddock's] conduct does include a "statement."

[Conviction sustained as to point discussed. Action remanded for resentencing]

QUESTIONS

1. What was the false statement made by Haddock to the FDIC?
2. What effect did the Financial Institutions Reform, Recovery and Enforcement Act of 1989 have on the *Haddock* decision?
3. What defense could Haddock have made on the basis of the later act?

The bad check statutes typically provide that if the check is not made good within a specified number of days after payment by the bank is refused, it is presumed that the defendant had acted with the intent to defraud.

A statute making the issuing of a bad check a crime punishable by imprisonment does not violate a constitutional prohibition against imprisonment for debt.

19. Cheats and Swindles

Various statutes are designed to protect the public from being deceived.

(a) FALSE WEIGHTS, MEASURES, AND LABELS. Cheating, defrauding, or misleading the public by use of false, improper, or inadequate weights, measures, and labels is a crime. Both the federal and state governments have adopted many statutes on this subject.

(b) SWINDLES AND CONFIDENCE GAMES. The act of a person who, intending to cheat and defraud, obtains money or property by trick, deception, or fraud, is an act known as a **swindle** or **confidence game**. Bad stock and spurious works of art are frequently employed in swindling operations.

The essential elements of the crime of confidence game are (1) an intent to defraud, (2) the creation of confidence of the victim in the defendant, (3) intentional false statements as to past or existing facts, and (4) in some states, the sustaining by the victim of a loss of more than a stated amount, such as $50.

Under one name or another, federal and state statutes prohibit the act of obtaining money by any chain letter or pyramid plan. Under the prohibited plans, persons solicited are persuaded that they can get their money back or win a prize by inducing others to write similar letters.[25]

20. Credit Card Crimes

It is a crime to steal a credit card and, in some states, to possess the credit card of another person without the consent of that person. The use of a credit card without the permission of the rightful cardholder constitutes the crime of obtaining goods or services by false pretenses or with the intent to defraud. Likewise, a person continuing to use a credit card with knowledge that it has been canceled is guilty of the crime of obtaining goods by false pretenses.

When, without permission, the wrongdoer signs the name of the rightful cardholder on the slip for the credit card transaction, the wrongdoer commits the crime of forgery. The district attorney has the discretion to choose the particular crime for which to prosecute the wrongdoer.

The Credit Card Fraud Act of 1984[26] makes it a federal crime to obtain anything of value in excess of $1,000 in a year by means of a counterfeit credit card, to make or traffic in such cards, or to possess more than 15 counterfeit cards at one time.

21. Use of Mails to Defraud

Congress has made it a crime to use the mails to further any scheme or artifice to defraud. To constitute this offense, there must be (a) a contemplated or organized scheme to defraud or to obtain money or property by false pretenses, and (b) the mailing or the causing of another to mail a letter, writing, or pamphlet for the purpose of executing or attempting to execute such scheme or artifice. Illustrations of schemes that come within the statute are false statements to secure credit, circulars announcing false cures, false statements to induce the sale of stock of a corporation, and false statements as to the origin of a fire and the value of destroyed goods for the purpose of securing indemnity from an insurance company. Federal law also makes it a crime to use a telegram or a telephone to defraud.

22. Criminal Libel

A person who falsely defames another without legal excuse or justification may be subject to criminal liability as well as civil liability. Criminal libel is made a crime because of its tendency to cause a breach of the peace. Under some statutes, however, the offense appears to be based on the tendency to injure another.

No publication or communication to third persons is required in the case of criminal libel. The offense is committed when the defendant communicates the libel directly to the person libeled as well as when it is made known to third persons.

---

[25] Sheehan v Bowden (Ala) 572 So 2d 1211 (1990).

[26] Act of October 12, 1984, § 1029, PL 98-473, 98 Stat 2183, 18 USC § 1029.

The truth of the statement is a defense in civil libel. For criminal libel, however, the prevailing view is that a valid defense must include the showing of a proper motive on the part of the accused, as well as proof that the statement was true.

In a number of states, **slander** (oral defamation) or particular kinds of slander have also been made criminal offenses by statutes.

23. Lotteries and Gambling

Running lotteries and gambling are common statutory crimes.

(a) LOTTERIES. There are three elements to a **lottery**: (1) there must be a payment of money or something of value for an opportunity to win, (2) a prize must be available, and (3) it must be offered by lot or by chance. If these elements are present, it is immaterial that the transaction appears to be a legitimate form of business or advertising, or that the transaction is called by some name other than a lottery, such as a raffle. The sending of a chain letter through the mail is generally a federal offense, as a mail fraud, swindle, or an illegal lottery, when the letter solicits contributions or payments.

In many states, government lotteries are legal.

The question has frequently been raised, as in the *St. Augustine* case, whether bingo is a lottery.

SECRETARY OF STATE v ST. AUGUSTINE CHURCH
(Tenn) 766 SW2d 499 (1989)

The Tennessee constitution declares that "the legislatures shall have no power to authorize lotteries for any purpose." The Tennessee legislature adopted several statutes legalizing bingo when conducted for a charitable purpose. St. Augustine Church conducted bingo games for charitable purposes. The Secretary of State brought an action against the church for conducting a "lottery." The church raised the defense that it was protected by the charitable bingo statutes. The court held that the statutes were unconstitutional and that bingo was an illegal lottery. St. Augustine Church appealed. Several organizations intervened in the appeal to assert that bingo was not a lottery.

HARBISON, J. . . . [The constitution's] terms are sweeping and absolute. It simply removes from the General Assembly the authority to authorize lotteries for any purpose—charitable, public, private, or any other. . . .

We recognize, of course, that the constitutional provision did not prohibit all types of gambling. Except for lotteries, there is nothing in the constitution of the State prohibiting gambling, and the regulation of all other types of gambling, except lotteries, is a matter for determination by the General Assembly. The latter may prohibit all types of gambling, or it may legalize some and regulate others. Any form of gambling which consists of a lottery, however, may not be authorized or sanctioned by the General Assembly.

The statutes . . . in this case . . . purported to exempt the game of bingo from the general statutes against gambling and to regulate its conduct by a licensing system.

Implicitly, of course, the General Assembly must have concluded that bingo was not a "lottery" but simply a form of gambling which it could authorize and regulate. In our opinion this conclusion was erroneous. . . . The more recent statutes proceeded on the theory that when cards for bingo play were sold by charitable, religious and similar organizations, the payment made by the customer constituted a charitable contribution rather than a wager, so long as the other terms and provisions of the regulatory statutes were observed.

It is the insistence of the appellants . . . that the provisions of the state constitution . . . were designed to abolish and outlaw only the older forms of "ticket lotteries" which were prevalent in the early nineteenth century and which have again become enormously popular in some states. . . .

The state constitution does not define the term "lottery," but the word is one of general usage. . . .

1: a scheme for the distribution of prizes by lot or chance; esp: a scheme by which prizes are distributed to the winners among those persons who have paid for a chance to win them usu. as determined by the numbers on tickets as drawn at random (as from a lottery wheel) . . . 2: the occasion of selection of prizes by lot 3: an event or affair whose outcome is or seems to be determined by chance . . . (Webster's Third New International Dictionary *338 (1981)).*

. . . The first definition contained in *Black's Law Dictionary* 853 (5th ed. 1979) is as follows:

A chance for a prize for a price. Essential elements of a lottery are consideration, prize and chance and any scheme or device by which a person for a consideration is permitted to receive a prize or nothing as may be determined predominantly by chance.

. . . In the statutes . . . under consideration . . ., the General Assembly undertook to remove the game of bingo from the definition of a lottery by terming the consideration paid by a customer as a charitable contribution rather than a wager. This, in our opinion, is an ineffective means to circumvent the constitutional prohibition, so long as the other elements of prize and chance are present.

Of course, the game "bingo" was not known in 1835 when the original Tennessee constitutional provision became effective. According to the briefs of the parties, the game was first introduced into the United States about 1928. It, of course, like many other games, may be played as a simple parlor game purely for the amusement of the participants. In this respect it is no different from dominoes, parcheesi, or any number of other perfectly innocent parlor games, although it demands less skill on the part of the player and turns almost wholly on the random drawing of numbers.

When conducted on a commercial scale,* however, for profit, and when chances, or tickets, are sold for a consideration, it is agreed by all parties that bingo becomes a form of gambling. In our opinion, "bingo" clearly constitutes a lottery within the meaning of the Tennessee Constitution. . . .

In several states, earlier constitutional prohibitions against lotteries have been amended or modified so that the playing of bingo, either through charitable organizations or under other regulatory schemes, could be legalized by the state legislature. See *e.g.,* Cal Const art IV, 19(c) (1966, amended 1976).

The intervening appellants have relied primarily upon two decisions which held that constitutional prohibitions against lotteries were confined to the earlier form of ticket lotteries and did not include bingo. . . . We decline to follow these decisions.

This Court expresses no opinion, of course, as to the desirability of the legalization of bingo or any other form of gambling. . . . Under the present constitutional provisions, however, the General Assembly may not authorize any form of lottery. . . . . The game of bingo . . . simply falls within the generally accepted definition of the term "lottery."

. . . In our opinion no legislative definition of "bingo" could remove the game as traditionally played from that form of gambling known as a lottery.

*The record in this action shows that receipts from "bingo" operations in Tennessee totalled thirty-one million dollars in 1987.

[Judgment affirmed]

QUESTIONS

1. What did the court hold and why?
2. The decision of the court was in harmony with the will of the people of Tennessee. Appraise this statement.
3. Could the state legislature reverse the decision of the *St. Augustine* case by adopting a statute declaring that bingo was not a lottery?

(b) GAMBLING. Gambling is a crime under modern statutes. It is similar to a lottery in that there are the three elements of payment, prize, and chance. Equipment used in gambling is generally declared by law to be contraband and may be confiscated by the government. If the winner of an electronic video card game receives something of value as a prize, the game is an illegal gambling device. Statutes commonly make it a crime to use a device as a means of aiding a gambler.

(c) CHARITABLE PURPOSE. Gambling conducted by a charity is unlawful gambling even though the purpose is to raise funds for a charitable cause. However, some states expressly exempt fundraising activities of charities from the local gambling statutes.[27]

24. Embezzlement

Embezzlement is the fraudulent conversion of another's property or money by a person to whom it has been entrusted.[28] An example would be an employee's taking of the employer's money for the employee's own use. Embezzlement is a statutory crime designed to cover the case of unlawful takings that are not larceny because the wrongdoer did not take the property from the possession of another, and not robbery because there is neither a taking from the possession of another nor the use of force or fear.

It is immaterial whether the defendant received the money or property from the victim or from a third person to deliver to the victim. Thus, an agent commits embezzlement when the agent receives and keeps payments from third persons—payments the agent should

---

[27] Earnhart v Director of Illinois Department of Revenue, 191 Ill App 3d 613, 138 Ill Dec 851, 548 NE2d 81 (1989).
[28] North Carolina v Speckman (NC) 391 SE2d 165 (1990).

have turned over to the principal. Likewise, when an insured gives money to an insurance agent to pay the insurance company but the insurance agent uses the money to pay premiums on the policies of other persons, the agent is guilty of embezzlement.

Generally, the fact that the defendant intends to return the property or money embezzled, or does in fact do so, is no defense.

Today, every jurisdiction not only has a general embezzlement statute but also various statutes applicable to particular situations. For example, statutes cover embezzlement by trustees, employees, and government officials.

25. Receiving Stolen Goods

The crime of **receiving stolen goods** is the receiving of goods that have been taken with the intent to deprive the owner of them. To be guilty of the crime of receiving stolen goods, a person must know or have reasonable cause to believe that the property was stolen.[29] It is immaterial that the receiver does not know the identity of the owner or of the thief.

C. CRIMES OF FORCE AND CRIMES AGAINST PROPERTY

Crimes that involve the use of force or the threat of force or that cause injury to persons or damage to property contrast with white collar crimes. Crimes of force and crimes against property that affect businesses are discussed in the following sections.

26. Larceny

Larceny is the wrongful or fraudulent taking and carrying away of the personal property of another by any person with a fraudulent intent to deprive the owner of such property. The place from which the property is taken is generally immaterial, although by statute the offense is sometimes subjected to a greater penalty when property is taken from a particular kind of building, such as a warehouse. Shoplifting is a common form of larceny. In many states, shoplifting is made a separate crime.

Although the term is broadly used in everyday speech, not every unlawful taking is a larceny. At common law, a defendant who took property of another with the intent to return it was not guilty of larceny. This has been changed in some states so that a person who borrows a car for a joyride is guilty of larceny, theft, or some other statutory offense.

Statutes in many states penalize as **larceny by trick** the use of any device or fraud by which the wrongdoer obtains the possession of, or title to, personal property from the true owner. In some states, all forms of larceny and robbery are consolidated into a statutory crime of theft. At common law, there was no crime known as "theft."

27. Robbery

Robbery is the taking of personal property from the presence of the victim by use of force or fear. In most states, there are aggravated forms of robbery, such as robbery with a deadly weapon. Snatching a necklace from the neck of the victim involves sufficient force to constitute robbery. When the unlawful taking is not by force or fear, as when the victim does not know that the property is being taken, the offense is larceny, but it cannot be robbery. In contrast, when the property is taken from the victim by use of force or fear, there is both robbery and larceny. In this case, the prosecuting attorney will determine for which crime the defendant is to be prosecuted.

28. Burglary

At common law, **burglary** was the breaking and entering, in the nighttime, of the dwelling house of another, with the intent to commit a felony therein. Making criminal the act of burglary illustrates the social force of protection of the person—in this case, the persons living in

---

[29] Hunt v Indiana (Ind App) 600 NE2d 979 (1992).

the building. When the wrongdoer inserts an automatic teller card in an automatic teller machine set in the wall of the bank, that insertion of the card constitutes an entry into the bank for the purpose of constituting burglary.[30]

Modern statutes have eliminated many of the elements of the common law definition, so that under some statutes it is immaterial when or whether there is an entry to commit a felony. The elements of breaking and entering are frequently omitted. Under some statutes, the offense is aggravated and the penalty is increased in terms of the place where the offense is committed, such as a bank building, freight car, or warehouse. Related statutory offenses have been created, such as the crime of possessing burglar's tools.

29. Arson

At common law, **arson** was the willful and malicious burning of the dwelling house of another. Thus, it was designed to protect human life, although the defendant was guilty if there was a burning of the building even though no one was actually hurt. In most states arson is a felony, so that if someone is killed in the resulting fire, the offense is murder by application of the felony-murder rule. Under the **felony-murder rule**, homicide, however unintended, occurring in the commission of a felony is automatically classified as murder. Statutes may expand the kind of property involved in arson. Thus, a statute may make it arson to burn a structure of such a nature that persons are commonly present.

In virtually every state, a special offense of **burning to defraud** an insurer has been created by statute. Such burning is not arson when the defendant burns the defendant's own house to collect the insurance money.

30. Riots and Civil Disorders

Damage to property in the course of a riot or civil disorder is ordinarily the same type of crime as though only one wrongdoer were involved. That is, there is a crime of larceny or arson and so on, depending on the nature of the circumstances, without regard to whether one person or many are involved. In addition, the act of assembling as a riotous mob and engaging in civil disorders is generally some form of crime in itself, without regard to the destruction or theft of property, whether under common law concepts of disturbing the peace or under modern antiriot statutes.

A statute may make it a crime to riot or to incite to riot. However, a statute relating to inciting must be carefully drawn, to avoid infringing on constitutionally protected free speech.

SUMMARY

When a person does not live up to the standards set by the law, society may regard the conduct of the defendant as so dangerous to the government, to people, or to property that society will prosecute the defendant for such misconduct. This punishable conduct, called *crime*, may be common law or statutory in origin. Crimes are classified as treason, felony, and misdemeanor. A felony is a crime that is punishable by imprisonment or death.

In terms of the parties taking part in a crime, at common law there are principals and accessories. The statutory trend is to abolish distinctions and to treat everyone taking part in a crime as being guilty of the crime.

Employers and corporations may be criminally responsible for their acts and the acts of their employees. Minors, the insane, and the intoxicated are held criminally responsible to a limited extent. This means that in some cases they will not be held responsible for a crime

---

[30] California v Ravenscroft, 198 Cal App 3d 642, 243 Cal Rptr 827 (1988).

when a normal, adult person would be held responsible.

Crimes are often classified in terms of whether force or violence is involved. The phrase *white collar crime* is frequently used in reference to crimes that do not involve force or violence. White collar crimes include those relating to illegal methods of production, competition, and marketing, such as the illegal use of interstate transportation and communication. Other white collar crimes include crimes relating to securities, such as stocks and bonds; computer crimes; bribery; extortion; blackmail; and crimes relating to the exercise of improper influence in politics and in business. Also included as white collar crimes are counterfeiting, forgery, perjury, the making of false claims against the government, and the obtaining of goods or money by false pretenses. The use of bad checks; the use of false weights, measures, and labels; swindles and confidence games; dealing in counterfeit credit cards and possessing more than 15 such cards at one time; using the mails to defraud; making defamatory statements about another; engaging in lotteries and gambling; embezzlement; and receiving stolen goods are other white collar crimes.

In contrast with the foregoing crimes are the crimes of force and violence. The most common examples relating to property are larceny, robbery, burglary, arson, and burning to defraud an insurer. Taking part in a riot or civil disorder may be a crime in itself, in addition to the traditional forms of crime that may be committed in the course of the riot or disorder.

There is no uniform law of crimes. Each state and the federal government defines and punishes crimes as it chooses. Although there is a tendency to follow a common pattern, there are many specific variations between the law of different states and the federal law.

LAW IN PRACTICE

1. Learn whether there is anything about your way of doing business that is illegal and review this information annually. Because of the many trade and environmental regulations, you can no longer rely on a sense of right and wrong to guide you.
2. Protect yourself from being the victim of a crime by security devices for your home, office, or plant; a careful check of personnel; and insurance against loss when insurance is available.
3. Consult your accountant and attorney to see what in-house checking against loss can be established.
4. Keep careful records of employees' history and of any misconduct.

QUESTIONS AND CASE PROBLEMS

1. What are the social forces advanced by the rule of law that a person buying a gun with the intent to kill a neighbor is not guilty of attempted murder?
2. Hunter was employed by the Watson Corporation. He was killed at work by an explosion caused by the gross negligence of the corporation. The corporation was prosecuted for manslaughter. It raised the defense that only people could commit manslaughter and that it was therefore not guilty. Was this defense valid?
3. Johnny took a radio from the Englehart Music Store without the knowledge of any clerk that he was removing it. He was then prosecuted for larceny. He claimed that he could only be prosecuted for shoplifting because larceny was a serious felony, and all that he had done was to take merchandise from a store. Was this defense valid?
4. Garrison purchased goods that she knew had been stolen. When the police traced some stolen articles and discovered Garrison's activities, Garrison was prosecuted for embezzlement. Was she guilty?
5. Compare larceny, robbery, and embezzlement.
6. Gail drove her automobile after having had dinner and several drinks. She fell asleep at the wheel and ran over and killed a pedestrian. She was prosecuted for manslaughter and raised the defense that she did not intend to hurt anyone and

because of the drinks did not know what she was doing. Was this a valid defense?

7. A state law made it a crime to use "a device to assist . . . in analyzing the probability of the occurrence of an event relating to the game." The defendant took part in a card game played for money. Unknown to the other players, he had a microcomputer that he used to show the probabilities of cards appearing in the game. This was discovered, and he was prosecuted under the law quoted above. He raised the defense that a microcomputer was not a device. Was he guilty of violating the statute? Why did the statute state "device" rather than listing the specific devices that were to be outlawed? [*Sheriff, Clark County, Nevada v Anderson, 103 Nev Adv 119, 746 P2d 643*]

8. Buckley took a credit card from the coat of its owner with the intent never to return it. He then purchased some goods at a department store and paid for them by presenting the credit card to the sales clerk and signing the credit card slip with the name of the owner of the credit card. What crimes, if any, did Buckley commit? [*Buckley v Indiana, 163 Ind App 113, 322 NE2d 113*]

9. Berman organized Greatway Travel, Ltd. Greatway sold travel consultant franchises and promised that the franchisees would receive various discounts and assistance. None of these promises were ever kept because Greatway lost all its money through mismanagement. Berman was prosecuted for obtaining money by false pretenses. Was he guilty? [*Berman v Maryland, 35 Md App 193, 370 A2d 580*]

10. Jacobs was a tenant in New Martinsville Towers, a government-financed housing project. The rent of tenants was determined by their ability to pay. Barnes was in charge of the management of the Towers. He borrowed $7,800 from Jacobs on the basis that he was going to buy Easter clothes and other items for his family, and he would see to it that the rent of Jacobs was not raised and that she would be given a particular job. He did not have any authority to prevent an increase in the rent nor to obtain the job, and he knew he had no such authority. The rent of Jacobs was thereafter increased, and she did not get the job. Barnes was prosecuted for obtaining property by false pretenses. He raised the defense that he had spent the

money for the purpose that he had stated and therefore was not guilty of a crime. Was he correct? [*West Virginia v Barnes (W Va) 354 SE2d 606*]

11. Skelton attempted to rob a general store. He used a small wooden toy pistol. The attempt failed, and he was arrested. He was prosecuted for attempted armed robbery. Was he guilty? [*Illinois v Skelton, 83 Ill 2d 58, 46 Ill Dec 571, 414 NE2d 455*]

12. Jennings operated a courier service to collect and deliver money. The contract with his customers gave Jennings a day or so to deliver the money that had been collected. Instead of holding collections until delivered, Jennings made short-term investments with the money. He always made deliveries to the customers on time but kept the profit from the investments for himself. He was prosecuted for larceny. Was he guilty? [*New York v Jennings, 69 NY2d 103, 512 NYS2d 652, 504 NE2d 1079*]

13. Powell was arrested for having possession of 20 unauthorized credit cards and using them to purchase over $1,000 worth of airline tickets which he resold to other persons. He raised the defense that the airlines suffered a loss of less than $1,000 because all of his customers for the tickets had not used them. Was this defense valid?

14. Chaussee sold franchises to a number of persons authorizing them to sell a product that did not exist. He was prosecuted under the Colorado Organized Crime Control Act on the ground that he was guilty of a "pattern" of racketeering. He raised the defense that there was no pattern because there was only one scheme. Was he guilty?

15. Awan was prosecuted for money laundering. He raised the defense that the federal Money Laundering Control Act was unconstitutional because it was too vague. As a matter of constitutional law, if a criminal law statute is too vague to be reasonably understood, it violates the due process clause and cannot be enforced. The Money Laundering Control Act condemns money laundering "knowing that the property involved in a financial transaction represents the proceeds of some form of unlawful activity." Was the Act unconstitutionally vague? [*United States v Awan (CA11 Fla) 966 F2d 1415*]

CHAPTER 8
TORTS

LEARNING OBJECTIVES

After studying this chapter, you will be able to:
1. *Define* torts *and distinguish them from contracts and from crimes.*
2. *Explain the basis of tort liability.*
3. *Define* absolute liability *and describe circumstances where the law imposes it.*
4. *Define* negligence *and explain its application.*
5. *Give examples of both negligent and intentional torts.*

In contrast with the law of crimes, tort law, when applicable, permits you to sue the wrongdoer and recover money for the wrong done. Conversely, if you are the wrongdoer, the victim may sue you and recover money damages.

In some circumstances the law of torts and crimes will protect your rights. In other circumstances, you can obtain better protection by carefully drafting contracts.

A. GENERAL PRINCIPLES

Civil (noncriminal) wrongs other than the breaking of contracts are governed by tort law. In this chapter, you will see many points at which there is a gradual expansion of the law of torts. This expansion is being made in response to what society thinks is right as it strives to promote the social forces.

1. Tort and Crime Distinguished

A crime is a wrong arising from a violation of a public duty, whereas a **tort** is a wrong arising from a violation of a private duty. More practically stated, a crime is a wrong of such a serious nature that the state steps in to prosecute and punish the wrongdoer and to deter others from committing the same wrong. Whenever the act that is punished as a crime causes harm to an identifiable person, that person may sue the wrongdoer for monetary damages to compensate for the harm. As to the person harmed, the wrongful act is called a tort; as to the government, that same wrongful act is a crime. If, however, a crime does not hurt an identifiable person, it is not a tort. For example, bribing a public official is a crime, but no individual person is harmed, so no tort is committed.

When the same act is both a crime and a tort, the government may prosecute the wrongdoer for the crime and the victim may sue for damages. For example, when an automobile is stolen, the government may prosecute the thief for the crime of larceny and the owner may sue the thief for the value of the automobile.

2. Tort and Breach of Contract Distinguished

The wrongs or injuries caused by a breach of contract arise from the violation of an obligation or duty created by the agreement of the parties. In contrast, a tort arises from the violation of an obligation or duty created by law. The same act may be both a breach of contract and a tort. For example, if a contract is negligently performed, there is a breach of the contract and also the tort of improper performance or malpractice.

3. Basis of Tort Liability

The mere fact that a person is hurt or harmed in some way does not mean that such a person can sue and recover damages from the person causing the harm. There must exist a recognized basis for liability.

(a) DUTY. In most cases, the plaintiff is not allowed to recover from the defendant if the defendant did not break a duty that was owed to the plaintiff. However, there is a strong modern trend to ignore whether there is a duty. By this view, the court looks directly at the facts and considers whether there are interests involved that should be protected from harm. If the defendant has harmed such an interest, the defendant is required to pay for the damages.

In the *Hegyes* case, the plaintiff urged the court to adopt the modern view.

(b) VOLUNTARY ACT. For tort liability to exist, the defendant must be guilty of a voluntary act or omission. Acts committed or omitted by one who is confronted with a sudden peril caused by another are considered involuntary acts.

(c) INTENT. Whether intent to do an unlawful act or intent to cause harm is required as a basis for tort liability depends on the nature of the tort involved. Liability is imposed for some torts even though the person committing the tort acted without any intent to do wrong. Thus, a person going on neighboring

HEGYES v UNJIAN ENTERPRISES, INC.
234 Cal App 3d 1103, 286 Cal Rptr 85 (1991)

> Mrs. Hegyes was driving her car when it was negligently struck by a truck of Unjian Enterprises. She was injured and an implant was placed in her body to counteract the injuries. She sued Unjian and the case was settled. Two years later, Mrs. Hegyes became pregnant. The growing fetus pressed against the implant, making it necessary to deliver the child 51 days prematurely by means of a Caesarean birth. Because of this premature birth, the child, named Cassondra, had a breathing handicap. Suit was brought against Unjian Enterprises for the harm sustained by Cassondra. The trial court dismissed the case, and an appeal was taken on behalf of Cassondra.

WOODS, A. J. . . . The trial court correctly held that no legal duty of care existed. Plaintiff urges this court to recognize a novel approach to the tort of negligence, which abandons the concept of duty and works backwards from causation. . . .

California precedent absolutely requires a preliminary finding of duty. . . . "Duty" encompasses the question of whether a defendant is under any obligation to the plaintiff to avoid negligent conduct. Here, there was no relationship between this defendant and this plaintiff which gave rise to any legal obligation on defendant's part for the benefit of plaintiff. . . .

. . . The law does not countenance recovery for all injuries caused by allegedly negligent conduct. . . . On occasion, the law cannot provide a remedy. The courts must draw requisite boundaries. . . .

No legal duty is violated where the plaintiff's injury is not reasonably foreseeable. . . . Every case is governed by the rule of general application that persons are required to use ordinary case for the protection of those to whom harm can be reasonably foreseen. . . . This rule not only establishes, but limits, the principle of negligence liability. The court's task in determining duty is to evaluate "whether the category of negligent conduct at issue is sufficiently likely to result in the kind of harm experienced" such that liability may appropriately be imposed upon the negligent party. . . .

Defendant's conduct was not "likely to result" in plaintiff's conception or birth, let alone her alleged injuries nearly three years after the car accident. . . . Such conception or birth is not a reasonably foreseeable result of the operation of a car. . . .

In determining to whom a legal duty is owed, foreseeability is the prime element by which courts are guided. However, the existence of a legal duty is not to be bottomed on the factor of foreseeability alone. The [California] Supreme Court in *Rowland v Christian*, 69 Cal 2d 108, 112, 70 Cal Rptr 97, 443 P2d 561, advanced the following considerations in evaluating whether a duty of care was owed: "The foreseeability of harm to the plaintiff, the degree of certainty that the plaintiff suffered injury, the closeness of the connection between the defendant's conduct and the injury suffered, the moral blame attached to the defendant's conduct, the policy of preventing future harm, the extent of the burden to the defendant and consequences to the community of imposing a duty to exercise care with resulting liability for breach, and the availability, cost, and prevalence of insurance for the risk involved."

The Supreme Court, however, to ensure recognition that the law does not champion legal redress for *all* foreseeable harm, stated in *Dillon v Legg* (1968) 68 Cal 2d

728, 729, 69 Cal Rptr 72, 441 P2d 912: "In order to limit the otherwise potentially infinite liability which would follow every negligent act, the law of torts holds defendant amenable only for injuries to others which to defendant *at the time were reasonably* foreseeable.". . .

The court in *Dillon* sought to confine the potential reach of foreseeability by limiting it to "those risks or hazards whose likelihood made the conduct unreasonably dangerous" and, then, by evaluating the nature of the injury and its causal relation to the conduct which caused it. . . .

. . . Not every loss can be made compensable in money damages, and legal causation must terminate somewhere. In delineating the extent of a tortfeasor's responsibility for damages under the general rule of tort liability. . . courts must locate the line between liability and nonliability at some point, a decision which is essentially political. . . .

. . . The courts and legislature of this state have decided that not all injuries are compensable at law. . . .

Judicial discretion is an integral part of the duty concept in evaluating foreseeability of harm. That sentiment is best evidenced by the following comment by Dean Prosser: "In the end the court will decide whether there is a duty on the basis of the mores of the community, 'always keeping in mind the fact that we endeavor to make a rule in each case that will be practical and in keeping with the general understanding of mankind.'" (Prosser, Palsgraf Revisited (1953) 52 Mich L Rev 1, 15).

Thus, the concept of legal duty necessarily includes and expresses considerations of social policy. . . .

. . . The law requires more than a mere failure to exercise care and resulting injury. There must be a legal duty owed to the person injured. It is the breach of that duty that must be the proximate cause of the resulting injury. The determination that a duty of care exists is an essential prerequisite to liability founded on negligence. . . . In fact, since it is the breach of that duty which must be the causal factor in the injury alleged, duty must be found before causation or injury can even be considered.

. . . Plaintiff's position is that actual causation substitutes for duty, and the existence of damage obviates the necessity of a finding that duty was violated. In other words, causation and damage would become the sole elements of a cause of action for negligence, jettisoning the traditionally included elements of duty and violation of duty.

. . . In *Renslow v Mennonite Hospital* . . . 67 Ill 2d 348, 10 Ill Dec 484, 367 NE2d 1250 . . . the court *refused* to focus on the aspect of causation in rendering its opinion. Indeed, the court discounted the value of causation analysis in determining whether a child who sustains injury as a result of preconception conduct should be afforded a cause of action. The court instructed: "It has been aptly observed, however, that 'causation cannot be the answer, since in a very real sense the consequences of an act go forward to eternity. . . . Any attempt to impose responsibility on such a basis would result in infinite liability for all wrongful acts, which would "set society on edge and fill the courts with endless litigation."' Thus, policy lines, to some extent arbitrary, must be drawn to narrow an area of actionable causation. We see no inherent advantage to discarding the policy lines, defined traditionally as 'duty,' in favor of new policy lines which would be necessary to circumscribe actionable causation.

We reaffirm the utility of the concept of duty as a means by which to direct and control the course of common law." . . .

The *Renslow* court correctly resolved that causation alone does not impute liability in a negligence context absent a preliminary finding of duty and reasonable foreseeability. California courts agree that in order to establish liabilities, there must be more than a mere failure to exercise care for a resulting injury. . . . There must be a legal duty owed to the person injured to exercise care under the circumstances, and a breach of that duty must be the proximate cause of the resulting injury. . . . The determination that a duty exists is therefore an essential precondition to liability founded on negligence.

We refuse to be persuaded by appellant's notion that causation and injury are the sole determinants of liability. . . .

[Judgment affirmed]

QUESTIONS

1. What does the first paragraph of the opinion printed here mean when the court says that it will not "work backwards from causation"?
2. Does the forseeability test require that the harm be probable?
3. In the 9th paragraph of the portion of the majority opinion printed here, it is stated that the "courts must locate the line between liability and nonliability at some point, a decision which is essentially political." Does this mean that the people vote on the matter?

---

land without consent of the landowner is liable for the tort of trespass. The person intended to go on that land, even though there was an honest mistake as to the location of the boundary line.

(d) MOTIVE. As a general rule, motive is immaterial except as evidence to show the existence of intent. In most instances, a legal right may be exercised even with bad motives, and an act that is unlawful is not made lawful by good motives.

(e) CAUSAL RELATIONSHIP. As a matter of elementary justice, liability for harm should not be imposed unless the defendant's conduct was in some way the cause of the harm. But should a defendant be held liable for every consequence that flows from the defendant's act? Assume that the defendant has negligently run over and killed the key employee of a large industrial enterprise. Assume

further that because of that death, the enterprise goes out of business. This harms its other employees, stockholders, creditors, and the families of all of these, and also the stores where all of these people would buy goods. Should the defendant be held liable for every penny of harm suffered by all of these people because of the negligently caused death of the key employee?

The social force of protecting from hardship causes the law to draw the line at some point and say that no money can be recovered for harm sustained beyond that line. Courts are agreed as to this general objective, but there is conflict as to how and where to draw the dividing line between liability and nonliability.

(1) Proximate Cause. Some courts hold that the defendant's misconduct must be the **proximate cause** of the harm, using *proximate* to mean the cause that was immediately next to the harm. Some courts define *proximate* as

conduct of such a nature that, but for that conduct, the harm would not have been sustained. The modern trend is to regard a cause as sufficient to impose liability when it was a substantial factor in producing the harm, as contrasted with being the sole cause of the harm.[1]

(2) Foreseeability. In many instances, the courts define a causal relationship in terms of foreseeability. That is, if it was reasonably foreseeable that the conduct of the defendant could cause harm to the plaintiff, there is a sufficient causal relationship between the defendant's conduct and the plaintiff's harm to impose liability. In the absence of suchforeseeability, liability is not imposed. Thus, there was no liability for damage caused by a fire that was started when rays of the sun were magnified by crystal glassware on a shelf and set nearby paper on fire.[2] To impose liability, it is not necessary that the exact manner in which the harm was caused could have been foreseen.[3]

(3) Act of Third Person. A wrongful act of a third person may take effect between the time that the defendant acted or failed to act and the time the plaintiff is injured. This occurrence does not establish that the causative chain between the defendant's conduct and the plaintiff's harm has been broken. The action of a third person, therefore, does not insulate the defendant from liability for the plaintiff's harm. If the conduct of the third person was foreseeable, it does not relieve the defendant from liability to the plaintiff. On the contrary, both the defendant and the third person are liable to the plaintiff. The question of division of liability, discussed in Section 7 of this chapter, then arises.

The fact that the plaintiff is harmed by a criminal act of a third person does not break the chain of liability when the defendant was under a duty to protect the plaintiff from the class of harm that was sustained.

(f) LIABILITY FOR TORT OF EMPLOYEE OR CHILD. Ordinarily, a person is not liable for the wrong committed by another nor under any duty to prevent the commission of such wrong.[4] However, the tort of an employee or agent may, in some cases, impose liability on the employer or principal.

A parent is ordinarily not liable for the tort committed by a child. That is, the mere fact that the person sued is the parent of the child committing the wrong does not in itself impose liability on the parent.

There are several instances, however, in which a parent will be held liable. If the parent knows that the child has a dangerous characteristic, such as a disposition to set houses on fire, and does not take reasonable steps to prevent this, the parent will be held liable for the harm caused by the child. If the child is a reckless driver and the parent allows the child to use the parent's car, the parent is liable on the theory that the parent was negligent in entrusting the car to the child. In about half of the states, a parent supplying a family car is liable for any harm negligently caused by any member of the family while driving the car.

In some states, any person lending an automobile is liable for the harm caused by the negligence of the person borrowing or renting the car. In some states, statutes make a parent liable for willful or malicious property damage caused by minor children. Such statutes generally specify a maximum limitation on such liability and are constitutional. Some statutes impose parental liability for personal injury caused by a minor child.[5]

---

[1] Mitchell v Gonzales, ___ Cal ___, 1 Cal Rptr 2d 913, 819 P2d 872 (1991).

[2] Savannah Bank & Trust Co. v Weiner, 193 Ga App 616, 388 SE2d 725 (1989).

[3] Webb v Jarvis (Ind App) 553 NE2d 151 (1990).

[4] McGee v Chalfant, 248 Kan 434, 806 P2d 980 (1991).

[5] Labadie v Semler, 66 Ohio App 3d 540, 585 NE2d 862 (1990).

4. Liability-Imposing Conduct

Generally, American law imposes tort liability only when there is some fault on the part of the defendant. Thus, it is required either that the defendant intended to cause the harm of the plaintiff or that the defendant was negligent. In a number of instances, the law of this century has made exceptions to the concept that liability can only be based on fault and has imposed liability solely because the plaintiff has been harmed by the act of the defendant.

5. Absolute Liability

In some areas of the law, tort liability for harm is imposed without regard to whether there was any fault on the part of the defendant. That is, liability is imposed without regard to whether there was any negligence or intention to cause harm. For example, in most states when a contractor blasts with dynamite and debris is hurled onto the land of another, the landowner may recover damages from the contractor even though the contractor was not negligent and did not intentionally cause the harm.

By this concept of absolute liability, society is saying that the activity is so dangerous to the public that liability must be imposed even though no fault is present. Yet society will not go so far as to outlaw the activity. Instead, a compromise is made. The activity is allowed to continue, but the one who stands to benefit from the activity must pay its injured victims regardless of the circumstances under which the injuries occur.

(a) INDUSTRIAL ACTIVITY. Generally, there is absolute liability for harm caused by the storage of inflammable gas and explosives in the middle of a populated city; crop dusting when the chemical used is dangerous to life and the dusting is likely to be spread by the wind; and for factories emitting dangerous fumes, smoke, and soot in populated areas. However, the mere fact that activity is industrial in nature does not mean that absolute liability is to be applied. Thus, drilling and operating a natural gas well is not an activity that results in absolute liability.

(b) CONSUMER PROTECTION. Pure food statutes may impose absolute liability on the seller of foods in favor of the ultimate consumer who is harmed by them. Decisions and statutes governing product liability impose liability although the defendant is not negligent and intends no harm.

(c) NO-FAULT LIABILITY. **No-fault liability** is another name for absolute liability. Whatever it is called, the defendant is liable for harm caused the plaintiff by virtue of the fact that such harm was caused the plaintiff. Liability is imposed without regard to whether there is fault or intention to harm on the part of the defendant.

No-fault liability is based on statutes. Usually, recovery on no-fault liability is less than the liability that would exist if fault of the defendant could be established. Generally, the plaintiff is allowed to prove such fault and recover a greater amount when serious injury or death has been caused.

Today, no-fault liability is associated with automobiles. A half century before the no-fault concept was applied to automobile liability, it became the basis for workers' compensation. Under such statutes, the worker is compensated when employment-related harm is sustained. No question is raised as to the presence or absence of fault on the part of the employer. The amount recovered by a worker is smaller than could be recovered if a common law action could be prosecuted. The injured worker who is covered by workers' compensation is restricted to the recovery permitted by such law and does not have the choice of bringing a lawsuit to seek a larger recovery.

6. Negligence

The widest range of tort liability today arises in the field of negligence. **Negligence** exists whenever the defendant has acted with less care than would be exercised by a reasonable person under the circumstances. Such negligence must be causally related to the harm sustained by the plaintiff.

(a) THE REASONABLE PERSON. The reasonable person whose behavior is made the standard is an imaginary person. In a given case that is tried before a jury, "reasonable" is what appears to the composite, or combined, minds of the jurors to be sensible or suitable under the circumstances.

This reasonable person does not represent any one of the jurors or an average of the jurors. The law is not concerned with what the jurors would do in a like situation, for it is possible that they may be more careful or less careful than the abstract reasonable person.

(b) VARIABLE CHARACTER OF THE STANDARD. By definition, the standard is a variable standard, for it does not tell you in advance what should be done. This is confusing to everyone, in the sense that the exact answer in any borderline case is unknown until the lawsuit is over. From the standpoint of society, however, this flexibility is desirable because it is obviously impossible to foresee every possible variation in the facts that might arise and even more impossible to keep such a code of conduct up-to-date. Imagine how differently the reasonable person must act while driving today's automobile on today's superhighways than when driving a Model T on dirt roads three-quarters of a century ago.[6]

(c) DEGREE OF CARE. The degree of care required of a person is that which an ordinarily prudent person would exercise under similar circumstances. It does not mean such a degree of care as would have prevented the harm from occurring, nor is it enough that it is just as much care as everyone else exercises. It is not sufficient that one has exercised the degree of care that is customary for persons in the same kind of work or business, or that one has employed the methods customarily used. If one is engaged in services requiring skill, the care must measure up to a higher standard. In any case, the degree of care exercised must be commensurate with the danger that would probably result if such care were lacking. In all cases, it is the diligence, care, and skill that can be reasonably expected under the circumstances. Whether one has exercised the degree of care that is required under the circumstances is a question that is determined by the jury.

(d) CONTRIBUTORY NEGLIGENCE. At common law, a plaintiff could not recover for injuries caused by another's negligence if the plaintiff's own negligence had contributed to the injury. The plaintiff guilty of contributory negligence was denied recovery without regard to whether the defendant was more negligent. The common law did not recognize comparative degrees of negligence, nor did it try to apportion the injury to the two parties in terms of the degree of their respective fault. Some states still follow this contributory negligence rule.

(e) COMPARATIVE NEGLIGENCE. In most states, the common law rule as to contributory negligence has been rejected. States rejecting the common law rule regard it as unjust that the plaintiff who has been contributorily negligent should forfeit all rights even when the plaintiff's negligence was slight in comparison to the defendant's negligence. These states provide that there should be a comparing of the negligence of the plaintiff and the defendant. The negligence of the plaintiff does not bar recovery but only reduces the plaintiff's recovery to the extent that the harm was caused by the plaintiff's fault. For example, if the jury decides that the plaintiff had sustained damages of $100,000 but that the plaintiff's own negligence was one-fourth

---

6 Since the law is stated in terms of reasonableness, it is necessary to make a value judgment in which the extent of harm is measured against the cost and burden of taking precaution to prevent the harm. That is, when the product of the possibility of harm multiplied times the gravity of the harm, if it happens, exceeds the burden of precautions, the failure to take those precautions is negligence. Levi v Southwest Louisiana Electric Membership Cooperative (La) 542 So 2d 1081 (1989).

the cause of the damage, the plaintiff would be allowed to recover $75,000. At common law, the plaintiff in such case would have recovered nothing.

In some states, the comparative negligence concept is modified by ignoring the negligence of the plaintiff if it is slight and the negligence of the defendant is great or gross. At the other extreme, some states refuse to allow the plaintiff to recover anything if the negligence of the plaintiff was more than 50 percent of the cause of the harm.[7]

In the *Langley* case, the argument was made that the court should abolish the defense of contributory negligence and substitute the concept of comparative negligence.

LANGLEY v BOYTER
(App) 284 SC 162, 325 SE2d 550 (1984)

Robin Langley and James Boyter were driving automobiles in opposite directions on a two-lane highway. At a curve in the road the two cars collided. Each driver claimed that the other had crossed into the wrong lane. Langley sued Boyter for the damages sustained. Langley requested the judge to instruct the jury that any negligence on her part would merely reduce the amount that she could recover. The judge refused to do so and instructed the jury that any negligence on Langley's part barred her from recovering anything. The jury returned a verdict against Langley. A judgment was entered in favor of Boyter, and Langley appealed.

SANDERS, C. J. . . . To paraphrase John Locke, there is nothing less powerful than an idea whose time is gone. In our opinion, the doctrine of contributory negligence is an idea whose time is gone in South Carolina. It is extinct almost everywhere it once existed. It no longer exists in England, the country of its birth. It survives only in parts of this country, where it is threatened and endangered. Indeed, the doctrine of contributory negligence exists today as the Ivory-Billed Woodpecker of the common law.

The continued existence of the doctrine of contributory negligence as presently applied in South Carolina cannot be justified on any logical basis. It is contrary to the basic premise of our fault system to allow a defendant, who is at fault in causing an accident, to escape bearing any of its cost, while requiring a plaintiff, who is no more than equally at fault or even less at fault, to bear all of its cost. . . .

While we agree that juries may often ignore the law because of its harshness, we view this proclivity as a compelling reason to abrogate the doctrine rather than retain it. There is something fundamentally wrong with a rule of law which is so contrary to the convictions of ordinary citizens that, when serving as jurors, they often refuse to enforce it in violation of their oaths. The disrespect for the law engendered by perpetuating such a rule is obvious. . . .

We are of the opinion that the common law doctrine of contributory negligence should no longer be applied in South Carolina, and the doctrine of comparative negligence

---

7 Johnson v Grazadzielewski (Wis App) 465 NW2d 503 (1990).

should be adopted in its place. There remains the question of which form of the doctrine of comparative negligence should be adopted.

The four leading versions of the doctrine are the slight-gross version, two modified versions, and the pure version.

Under the slight-gross version, if the defendant's negligence is gross and the plaintiff's negligence is slight, then the plaintiff may recover, with his damages reduced in proportion to his own negligence. This version has been adopted by statute in only two states and has not been looked on with favor by the commentators and courts. . . .

The two modified versions of the doctrine of comparative negligence are similar to each other. One allows recovery by the plaintiff if his negligence was *not as great as* the negligence of the defendant. The other modified version allows the plaintiff to recover if his negligence is *not greater than* the defendant's negligence. In both versions, recovery is reduced by the amount of the plaintiff's negligence. The majority of the states have adopted one of these two versions. The recent trend in the states has been toward the latter version.

Under the pure version of comparative negligence, the plaintiff may recover even if his negligence is greater than that of the defendant, with his recovery diminished by the amount of his negligence. This version is recognized in a minority of the states. . . .

We choose the not-greater-than version of the doctrine for essentially two reasons. Unlike the pure version, it does not allow a plaintiff to recover when he has been the most at fault in causing an accident. But, unlike the not-as-great-as version, it does not allow a defendant to escape all responsibility for an accident which he was equally at fault in causing. Instead, the not-greater-than version of the doctrine strikes the reasonable balance of providing that parties equally at fault in causing an accident share equally in its cost.

In choosing this modified version of the doctrine over the pure version, we are also influenced by the conservative approach taken by our Supreme Court in abrogating doctrines of common law. . . .

[Reversed and remanded]

QUESTIONS

1. Assume that two cars collide at an intersection. The driver of car No. 1 sues the driver of car No. 2. The jury decides that driver No. 1 was 60 percent at fault and that driver No. 2 was 40 percent at fault. The total damages to car No. 1 amounted to $10,000. How much does car owner No. 1 recover in the action?
2. What social forces underlie the concept of comparative negligence?
3. What kind of comparative negligence doctrine is preferable?

(f) PROOF OF NEGLIGENCE. The plaintiff ordinarily has the burden of proving that the defendant did not exercise reasonable care. In some instances, however, it is sufficient for the plaintiff to prove that the injury was caused by something that was within the control of the defendant. If injury ordinarily results from a particular object only when there is negligence, the proof of the fact that injury resulted is held sufficient proof that the defendant was negligent. This is expressed by the maxim *res ipsa loquitur* (the occurrence or the thing speaks for itself).

This concept does not establish that the defendant was negligent but merely allows the jury to conclude or infer that the defendant was negligent. The defendant is not barred from proving lack of negligence or from explaining that the harm was caused by some act for which the defendant was not responsible. The jury, if it believes the defendant's evidence, can refuse to infer negligence from the mere happening of the event and can conclude that the defendant was not negligent.

The burden of proving that the plaintiff was contributorily negligent is on the defendant, both under common law and under the comparative negligence concept.[8]

(g) VIOLATION OF STATUTE. By the general rule, if harm is sustained while the defendant is violating a statute, the defendant is deemed negligent and is liable for the harm. Many courts narrow this concept so that the defendant is liable only if the statute is intended to protect against the kind of harm that was sustained because of the violation of the statute and if the plaintiff was a member of the class that the statute was designed to protect. For example, in a suit over a collision of the automobiles of the plaintiff and defendant, the fact that the defendant was driving without proper tags in violation of an automobile registration law will be ignored. This is because the purpose of the registration statute was not to proscribe negligent driving or to protect other drivers from being negligently harmed.

(h) ASSUMPTION OF RISK. The plaintiff may have taken chances with a known danger. For example, the plaintiff may drive an automobile although its brakes are known to be bad. In such case, there is an assumption of risk by the plaintiff that harm may be sustained because of the defective brakes. Likewise, a farm employee attempting to hammer a metal bolt into shape without wearing any protective goggles assumes the risk that the bolt may splinter and that a flying splinter may cause an eye injury. Consequently, the employee injured in that manner is barred from suing the employer for negligence in failing to supply protective goggles to workers.[9]

At common law, the plaintiff who had assumed risk was barred from recovering from the defendant for the harm sustained. Early in this century, workers' compensation legislation abolished the defense of assumption of risk with respect to workers' compensation claims.

In many situations, there is little or no difference between contributory negligence and assumption of risk. In situations in which that is true, a comparative negligence or comparative fault statute has the effect of abolishing the common law effect of assumption of risk and requires a comparison of the fault of the respective parties, with a reduction of the plaintiff's recovery to the extent directed by the statute.

7. Division of Liability

In some instances, when two or more defendants have caused harm to the plaintiff, it is difficult or impossible to determine what damage was done by each of such wrongdoers or tortfeasors. For example, suppose automobile *A* strikes automobile *B*, which is then struck by automobile *C*. Ordinarily, it is impossible to determine how much damage to automobile *B* was caused by each of the cars. Similarly, a tract of farmland downriver may be harmed because two or more factories have dumped industrial wastes into the river. It is not possible to determine how much damage each of the factories has caused the farmland.

By the older view, a plaintiff was denied the right to recover from any of the wrongdoers in these situations. The courts followed the theory that a plaintiff is not entitled to recover from a defendant unless the plaintiff can prove

---

8   ITT Rayonier, Inc v Puget Sound Freight Lines, 44 Wash App 368, 722 P2d 1310 (1986).

9   Benjamin v Benjamin (ND) 439 NW2d 527 (1989).

what harm was caused by that defendant. The modern trend of the cases is to hold all the defendants jointly and severally (collectively and individually) liable for the total harm sustained by the plaintiff.

8. Who May Sue

Ordinarily, the person who brings suit for a tort is the person whose property has been damaged or who has sustained personal injury. In some torts, not only the immediate victim has the right to sue but also persons standing in certain relationships to the victim. Thus, under certain circumstances, one spouse can sue for an injury to the other spouse, or a parent can sue for an injury to the child. In a wrongful death action, members of the surviving group (typically the spouse, child, and parents of the person who has been killed) have a right to sue the wrongdoer for such death.

9. Immunity from Liability

Basically, every person committing a tort is liable for damages for the harm caused thereby. However, certain persons and entities are not subject to tort liability. This is called **immunity** from liability.

Governments are generally immune from tort liability. This rule has been eroded by decision and in some instances by statutes, such as the Federal Tort Claims Act. Subject to certain exceptions, this act permits the recovery of damages from the United States for property damage, personal injury, or death action claims arising from the negligent act or omission of any employee of the United States under such circumstances that the United States, if a private person, would be liable to the claimant in accordance with the law of the place where the act or omission occurred. A fast-growing number of states have abolished governmental immunity, although many still recognize it.

Figure 8-1　Tort Law

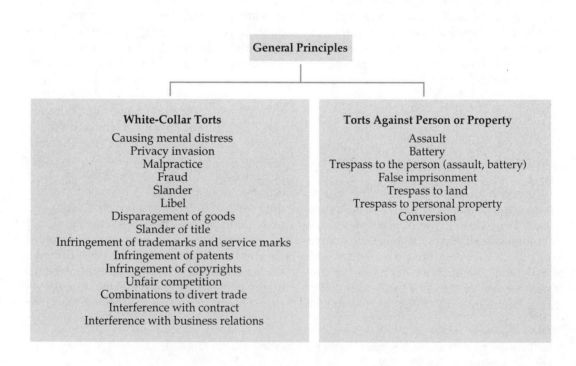

At the beginning of this century, charities were immune from tort liability, and child and parent and spouses could not sue each other. These immunities are fast disappearing. Thus, when the father's negligent driving of the automobile injured his minor child passenger, the child could sue the father for such damages.[10] The disappearance of intrafamily immunity has largely been the result of insurance policies that only cover claims of third persons when such third persons have sued the insured policyholder.

Very young children are immune from tort liability to anyone.

B. WHITE COLLAR TORTS

A classification of torts may be made, similar to that made in the law of crimes, between white collar torts and torts of force. White collar torts are discussed in Part B and torts involving force are discussed in Sections 24 and 26 of this chapter.

10. Causing of Mental Distress

When the defendant commits an act that by itself is a tort, there is ordinarily recovery for the mental distress that is caused thereby. At common law, if no tort was committed, the plaintiff could not recover for mental distress.

(a) INTENTIONALLY CAUSED MENTAL DISTRESS. Since the turn of the century, and particularly in the last four decades, recovery has been allowed in a number of cases in which no ordinary or traditional form of tort was committed. The common element in these cases was that the defendant had willfully subjected the plaintiff to unnecessary emotional disturbance. This result was reached when an outrageous practical joke was played on the plaintiff; the corpse of a close relative was concealed or mistreated, or interference was made with the burial; or statements were made to humiliate the plaintiff because of race, creed, or national origin.

The concept of liability for intentionally caused distress is applicable in a commercial setting, as when a collection agency uses harassing techniques to collect the debt owed by a consumer. Another example is when a manufacturer engages in a continuing campaign, including illegal electronic eavesdropping, to intimidate a critic of the defendant's product. In either case the tort may be called the tort of outrageous conduct, or the tort of outrage.

When there is liability for intentionally caused distress, there is also liability for any physical harm that is caused by the distress.

The *Miller* case turned on how bad the conduct had to be in order to impose liability for emotional stress caused thereby.

MILLER v EQUITABLE LIFE ASSURANCE SOCIETY
181 Ill App 3d 954, 130 Ill Dec 558, 537 NE2d 887 (1989)

Sharon Graziani was employed by the Equitable Life Assurance Society. Because of the way she was treated by supervisors and fellow workers she suffered great emotional distress, to such an extent that a trustee, Miller, had to be appointed to manage her affairs. Miller sued Equitable and a number of its employees to recover damages on behalf of Sharon for the emotional

---

[10] Cates v Cates, ___ Ill App 3d ___, ___ Ill Dec ___, 588 NE2d 330 (1992).

distress that she had suffered. Judgment was entered against Miller and he appealed.

JIGANTI, J. . . . In order to state a cause of action for intentional infliction of emotional distress, the plaintiff must allege facts which establish: (1) the defendant's conduct was extreme and outrageous; (2) the emotional distress suffered by the plaintiff was severe; and (3) the defendant knew that severe emotional distress was certain or substantially certain to result from such conduct. . . .

With respect to the first requirement, the defendant's conduct must be " 'so outrageous in character, and so extreme in degree, as to go beyond all possible bounds of decency. . . .' " (*Public Finance Corp.*, 66 Ill 2d at 90, 4 Ill Dec at 654, 360 NE2d at 767, quoting Restatement (Second) of Torts 46, comment d (1965).) Recovery under this theory does not extend to conduct which merely involves insults, indignities, threats, annoyances, petty oppressions, or other trivialities. . . . With respect to the severity of the plaintiff's distress, " 'the law intervenes only where the distress inflicted is so severe that no reasonable man could be expected to endure it.' " . . .

Determining whether a complaint states a cause of action essentially involves drawing a line "between the slight hurts which are the price of a complex society and the severe mental disturbances inflicted by intentional actions wholly lacking in social utility." . . . We recognize that our decision as to where that line should be drawn is based in large part on common sense and intuition more "subtle than any articulate major premise." . . .

The complaint essentially alleges that for approximately three and one-half years Graziani was surrounded by supervisors and co-workers who were inconsiderate, rude, vulgar, uncooperative, unprofessional and unfair. While we do not condone such behavior, we do not believe that the conduct alleged is so outrageous in character and so extreme in degree as to go beyond all bounds of human decency. Nor do we believe that the distress is so severe that no reasonable person could be expected to endure it. The fact that Graziani alleges that she was a victim of sexual harassment, battery, and retaliatory discharge does not necessarily mean that she has a cause of action for intentional infliction of emotional distress.

In employment situations, personality conflicts, job performance evaluations, or job transfers are unavoidable and often result in stress. However, if such stress formed the basis for the tort of intentional infliction of emotional distress, virtually every employee would have a cause of action. . . .

Because the complaint fails to allege extreme and outrageous conduct . . . we hold that Graziani has failed to allege a cause of action for intentional infliction of emotional distress. . . .

[Judgment affirmed]

QUESTIONS

1. In the *Miller* case was the emotional distress intentionally or negligently caused?
2. How does your answer to Question 1 affect the decision that you would make in the case?
3. Did the court have a precise definition for "extreme and outrageous" conduct?

(b) NEGLIGENTLY CAUSED MENTAL DISTRESS. In many jurisdictions, the concept of liability for distress has been expanded to impose liability for negligently caused mental distress. For example, when an undertaker through negligence buried the decedent the day before the burial was scheduled, the survivors could recover damages for the mental distress they sustained.[11] There is some indication that courts will impose wider liability for emotional distress when the circumstances are such as to exclude false claims, even though the defendant did not intentionally cause the distress. Thus, it has been held that when a mining company removed coal by burrowing under a graveyard, the company was liable for the subsidence and cracking of the graveyard caused by the failure to leave sufficient supporting pillars of coal and earth underneath the graveyard.[12]

In the *Schultz* case, the plaintiff suffered a great emotional shock because of the negligence of the defendant. He claimed that he was entitled to damages for such emotional stress.

SCHULTZ v BARBERTON GLASS CO.
4 Ohio 3d 131, 447 NE2d 109 (1983)

> A truck of the Barberton Glass Co. was transporting large sheets of glass down the highway. Elliot Schultz was driving his automobile some distance behind the truck. Because of the negligent way that the sheets of glass were fastened in the truck, a large sheet fell off the truck, shattered upon hitting the highway, and then bounced up and broke the windshield of Schultz's car. He was not injured but suffered great emotional shock. He sued Barberton to recover damages for such shock. Barberton denied liability on the ground that Schultz had not sustained any physical injury at the time or as the result of the shock. From a decision in favor of Barberton, Schultz appealed.

CELEBREZZE, C. J. . . . The issue raised in this appeal is whether a contemporaneous physical injury is a necessary condition precedent to liability for the negligent infliction of serious emotional distress. For the reasons which follow, we conclude that a contemporaneous physical injury is unnecessary.

In 1908, Ohio adopted the [impact] rule which requires the finding of contemporaneous physical injury before any recovery can be obtained for fright, shock, emotional distress, or mental suffering. *Miller v Baltimore & Ohio S.W. R.R. Co.*, 78 Ohio St. 309, 85 NE 499 (1908). The court reasoned that ". . . 'if the right of recovery in this class of cases should be once established, it would naturally result in a flood of litigation in cases where the injury complained of may be easily feigned without detection, and where the damages must rest upon mere conjecture or speculation. The difficulty which often exists in cases of alleged physical injury, in determining whether they exist, and if so, whether they were caused by the negligent act of the defendant, would not only be greatly increased, but a wide field would be opened for fictitious or speculative claims. To establish such a doctrine would be contrary to principles of public policy.'"

---

[11] Holsen v Heritage Mut. Ins. Co. (Wis App) 478 NW2d 59 (1991).

[12] Bennett v 3 C Coal Co. (W Va App) 379 SE2d 388 (1989).

We find that the reasons set forth in *Miller* are no longer valid. The first concern that a flood of litigation would result if recovery were permitted has not materialized. Commentators and courts in other jurisdictions have concluded that this argument lacks merit. As stated in *Falzone v Busch* (1965), 45 NJ 559, 567, 214 A2d 12, "there is no indication of an excessive number of actions of this type in other states which do not require an impact as a basis for recovery." . . .

Even if there may be a possibility of increased litigation, it is not a valid reason for denying a judicial forum. The Supreme Court of Pennsylvania, quoting Prosser, Intentional Infliction of Mental Suffering: A New Tort (1939), 37 Mich L Rev 874, stated: "'It is the business of the law to remedy wrongs that deserve it, even at the expense of a "flood of litigation"; and it is a pitiful confession of incompetence on the part of any court of justice to deny relief upon the ground that it will give the courts too much work to do.'" *Niederman v Brodsky* (1970), 436 Pa. 401, 412, 261 A2d 84. Even if the caseload increases, the "proper remedy" is an expansion of the judicial machinery, not a decrease in the availability of justice.

Therefore, we are not convinced that the problem of increased litigation is real or inevitable. Moreover, even if the caseload increases, we believe it is an unacceptable reason for denying justice.

A second reason for the physical injury requirement is the fear of fictitious injuries and fraudulent claims. . . .

The danger of illusory claims for mental distress is no greater than in cases of physical injury, especially when the injury is slight. The opportunity for fraud is as likely in such a case as one absent any physical injury. "The problem is one of adequate proof, and it is not necessary to deny a remedy in all cases because some claims may be false." Prosser, Law of Torts (4 Ed 1971) 327-328, Section 54.

. . . The last argument urged by appellee for retaining the physical injury rule is that problems regarding the proof of emotional distress are insurmountable because damages must be based upon conjecture or speculation. . .

Judges and juries will consider the credibility of witnesses and the genuineness of the proof as they do in other cases. In most instances, expert medical testimony will help establish the validity of the claim of serious emotional distress. Three medical doctors and a doctor of psychology testified, in the case *sub judice*, to the effect that appellant suffers from traumatic neurosis which was directly caused by the collision. Appellee did not offer expert testimony to the contrary.

Having carefully examined the arguments in support of the contemporaneous physical injury rule, it is clear that continued adherence to the rule makes little sense. Legal scholars who have considered the rule denying recovery in the absence of contemporaneous physical injury or impact are unanimous in condemning it as unjust and contrary to experience. The justifications for the doctrine are no longer valid and the reasons for abrogating it are strong. Consequently, the earlier cases upholding the doctrine are overruled. . . .

For these reasons, we hold that a cause of action may be stated for the negligent infliction of serious emotional distress without a contemporaneous physical injury. . . . We conclude that appellant has such a cause of action . . . .

[Judgment reversed and action remanded]

(c) BYSTANDER RECOVERY. When a bystander is a spectator to the negligent conduct of the defendant, and the witnessing of such conduct causes serious and reasonably foreseeable emotional distress, some courts hold that the bystander may recover damages for such harm from the wrongdoer. Most of these courts limit this liability to spectators who are closely related to the person directly endangered by the defendant's conduct.

A few courts have eliminated the requirement that the bystander actually see the event that causes shock. Thus, the relative arriving shortly after the actual occurrence may recover damages for the emotional distress caused by the negligence of the defendant.[13]

11. Invasion of Privacy

As an aspect of protecting the person from unreasonable interference, the law has come to recognize a right of privacy. This right is most commonly invaded in one of the following ways: (a) invasion of physical privacy, as by planting a microphone in a person's home; (b) giving unnecessary publicity to personal matters of the plaintiff's life, such as financial status or past careers; (c) false public association of the plaintiff with some product or principle, such as indicating that the plaintiff endorses a product or is in favor of a particular law, when such is not the case; or (d) commercially exploiting the plaintiff's name or picture, as in using them in advertising without permission.

When a party has a legitimate business interest in making information known, such conduct is generally not regarded as an invasion of privacy. The conduct is protected by a privilege as long as good faith is exercised by the disclosing party.

12. Malpractice

Malpractice liability is a tort liability imposed for a poor or bad performance of a duty imposed by contract or by law. Usually, it will be a poor performance because of negligence, as distinguished from harm that is intentionally caused.

13. Fraud

A person is entitled to be protected from fraud and may recover damages for harm caused by fraud. This protects the plaintiff from false statements made with knowledge of their falsity or with reckless indifference as to whether or not they were true.

In some instances, antifraud provisions have been adopted by consumer protection statutes. To illustrate, when the seller of a used car turns the odometer back with the intent to defraud, the seller is liable under the federal Motor Vehicle Information and Cost Savings Act to whomever purchases the automobile. Liability exists without regard to whether the purchaser bought directly from that dealer or from an intermediate dealer. Similarly, specific statutes are aimed at fraudulent practices in the sale of securities.[14]

---

[13] Thing v La Chusa, 48 Cal 3d 664, 257 Cal Rptr 865, 771 P2d 814 (1989).
[14] Naranjo v Paull (App) 111 NM 165, 803 P2d 254 (1990).

14. Defamation by Slander

A person is liable for defamation of another. Reputation is injured by **defamation**, which is a publication tending to cause one to lose the esteem of the community.[15] **Slander** is a form of defamation consisting of the publication or communication to another of false, spoken words. Thus, a false statement by the manager of a business that the former manager had been fired for stealing is slander. The fact that language is offensive or derogatory does not in itself constitute slander.

(a) PRIVILEGE. Under certain circumstances no liability arises when false statements are made, even though they cause damage. This absolute privilege exists in the case of publication by a public officer when the publication is within the officer's line of duty. The rule is deemed necessary to encourage public officers in the performance of their public duties.

Other circumstances may afford a qualified or conditional privilege. A communication made in good faith, on a subject in which the party communicating has an interest or right, is privileged if made to a person with a corresponding interest or right.[16] Thus, the owner of a watch may in good faith charge another person with the theft of the watch. A mercantile agency's credit report is conditionally privileged when made to an interested subscriber in good faith in the regular course of the agency's business.

A Better Business Bureau that has carefully maintained its records has a qualified privilege to state to a consumer that a particular enterprise had a history of failing to remedy complaints.[17] Also, when a client tells an attorney that a customer of the client owes money, such statement does not impose liability for defamation, even though it is wrong. The former employer of a job applicant has a qualified privilege to tell the prospective employer of the applicant why the former employer discharged the applicant.

If a consumer makes false statements about a seller, such as that a particular automobile dealer sold the consumer a lemon, the consumer is liable for defamation. The fact that a person is a consumer does not give rise to any privilege to make false statements.

Statements made in pleadings filed in court are protected by a privilege. In the *Defend* case, the controversy turned on whether this protection was an absolute or a qualified privilege.

DEFEND v LASCELLES
149 Ill App 3d 630, 102 Ill Dec 819, 500 NE2d 712 (1986)

Lascelles and his wife were real estate developers. Defend and Johnson purchased homes constructed by them and later sued the Lascelles. Defend and Johnson claimed that in promoting the development, the defendants had committed mail and wire fraud and were guilty of violating the Racketeer

---

[15] Shannon v Taylor AMC/Jeep, Inc. 168 Mich App 415, 425 NW2d 165 (1988). A person harmed by false advertising statements of a competitor may recover damages for commercial defamation under the Trademark Law Revision Act of 1988, Act of November 16, 1988, PL 100-667, 102 Stat 3935, 15 USC §§ 1051-1127.

[16] Martin v Lincoln General Hospital (La App) 588 So 2d 1329 (1991).

[17] Patio World v Better Business Bureau, Inc. 43 Ohio App 3d 6, 583 NE2d 1098 (1989).

Influenced and Corrupt Organizations Act (RICO). The defendants counterclaimed that the plaintiffs' claim was made maliciously and that the defendants were entitled to damages for defamation. The plaintiffs replied that the statements in their complaint, although defamatory, were absolutely privileged. The court refused to dismiss the counterclaim, and the plaintiffs appealed.

MORTHLAND, J. . . . We begin our analysis by recognizing the oft-stated principle in Illinois that anything said or written in a legal proceeding, including pleadings, is protected by an absolute privilege against defamation actions, subject only to the qualification that the words be relevant or pertinent to the matters in controversy. . .

The privilege itself is steeped in public policy: it is uniformly recognized that the judicial system would best be served if persons with knowledge of relevant facts could report those facts to the court without fear of civil liability.

Plaintiffs call our attention to another view in this area which substitutes a different yardstick for the "relevant and pertinent" inquiry relied upon by many courts. That analysis provides for an absolute privilege when otherwise defamatory material is published in a judicial proceeding if the statements have "some relation" to the litigation. Specifically, section 587 of the Restatement (Second) of Torts states the following:

A party to a private litigation or a private prosecutor or defendant in a criminal prosecution is absolutely privileged to publish defamatory matter concerning another in communications preliminary to a proposed judicial proceeding, or in the institution of or during the course and as a part of, a judicial proceeding in which he participates, if the matter has some relation to the proceeding. (Emphasis added.) Restatement (Second) of Torts § 587, at 248 (1977).

The Restatement standard has gained wide acceptance, becoming the majority rule today. At least two appellate courts in Illinois have heretofore embraced versions of the Restatement rule.

Clearly, then, depending upon the analysis employed, the threshold inquiry concerns whether the complained-of allegations are "relevant and pertinent" or bear "some relation" to the litigation. If so, pleadings in a judicial proceeding are absolutely privileged and cannot ordinarily form the basis of a defamation action. Defendants steadfastly maintain, though, that any pleading filed maliciously should not be granted an absolute privilege.

As a general principle, certain types of statements are deemed so privileged that the person making the statement should not be deterred from speaking by the threat of civil liability. In such a case an absolute privilege is granted, and no cause of action for defamation will lie against the person making the statement even if it is made with malice. This immunity afforded *absolutely* privileged matter is complete. It is not conditioned upon an honest or reasonable belief that the defamatory matter is true, or upon the absence of ill will on the part of the speaker. On the other hand, where only a *qualified* privilege is granted based upon a lesser concern for the freedom of the speaker, the person making the statement is immune from liability unless the privilege is abused or some element such as malice is present. When a qualified privilege is shown, the plaintiff has the burden of alleging and proving actual malice.

. . . The prevailing rule in the United States today is that libelous material contained in a pleading is absolutely privileged so long as it is pertinent, relevant, or bears some reasonable relation to the judicial proceeding, irrespective of whether it is false and malicious. . . .

The weight of authority in Illinois clearly favors recognition of an absolute privilege for statements made in a judicial proceeding based upon public policy. The defense of privilege or immunity in defamation cases rests upon the idea that "conduct which otherwise would be actionable is to escape liability because the defendant is acting in furtherance of some interest of social importance," an interest to be protected "even at the expense of uncompensated harm to the plaintiff's reputation." (Prosser, Torts § 114, at 776 (4th ed. 1971).) Further, comment *a* to section 587 of the Restatement explains:

The privilege stated in this Section is based upon the public interest in according to all men the utmost freedom of access to the courts of justice for the settlement of their private disputes. . . . It protects a party to a private litigation . . . from liability for defamation irrespective of his purpose in publishing the defamatory matter, of his belief in its truth or even his knowledge of its falsity. (Emphasis added.) Restatement (Second) of Torts § 587, comment a, at 249 (1977); see also Bond v Pecaut (N.D. Ill 1983), 561 F Supp. 1037.

. . . We hold that otherwise defamatory statements made in a pleading filed in a judicial proceeding enjoy an absolute privilege if they are relevant, pertinent, or bear some relation to the subject in controversy. Whether or not the occasion gives rise to the privilege is solely a question of law for the court. If the complained-of statements are found not to reasonably relate to the issues, then the absolute privilege is no longer available, and a charge of malice will enter into consideration as if a qualified privilege were involved instead.

Under the precise question certified, then, we find that pleading a civil cause of action for violation of the applicable RICO provision is absolutely privileged from any counterclaim based on defamation so long as it has some relation to the matter in controversy. If such is the case, malicious intent in filing the pleading is irrelevant.

. . . Persons defamed in pleadings or trial testimony may be left without legal redress, even if their reputations are damaged, because of the public policy favoring free and open administration of justice.

[Judgment reversed and action remanded]

QUESTIONS

1. What tests did the court consider using to determine whether statements in a pleading in court are privileged?
2. What is the difference between the tests given in your answer to Question 1?
3. Is it ever important whether statements in a pleading in court were made maliciously?

15. Defamation by Libel

The reputation of a person or a business may be defamed by written statements. This is known as **libel**. Although the defaming statement is described as a writing, it may also be in print, picture, or in any other permanent, visual form. For example, to construct a gallows in front of another's residence is a libel. A written report incorrectly stating that an employee has falsified time work records is libelous.

16. Disparagement of Goods and Slander of Title

In the transaction of business, one is entitled to be free from the interference of malicious, false statements made by others as to the title or the quality of goods or land sold. Actual damage must be proved by the plaintiff to have resulted from the false communications by the defendant to a third person. The plaintiff must show that as a consequence of the statement, the third person refrained from dealing with the plaintiff.[18]

17. Infringement of Trademarks and Service Marks

A **trademark** or **service mark** is a word, name, device, symbol, or any combination of these, used by a manufacturer or seller of goods or a provider of services to distinguish those goods and services from those of other persons. When the mark of a particular person is used or substantially copied by another, it is said that the mark is **infringed**. The owner of the mark may sue for damages and enjoin its wrongful use.

18. Infringement of Patents

A grant of a **patent** entitles the patentee to prevent others from making, using, or selling a particular invention for a period of 17 years. Anyone so doing without the patentee's permission is guilty of a patent infringement. If the inventor does not have a patent or if the patent is invalid, anyone may copy the invention without liability.

An infringement occurs even though all parts or features of an invention are not copied if there is a substantial identity of names, operations, and result between the original and the new device. In the case of a process, however, all successive steps or their equivalent must be copied. In the case of a combination of an ingredient, the use of the same ingredient with others constitutes an infringement, except when the result is a compound essentially different in nature.

19. Infringement of Copyrights

A wrong similar to the infringement of a patent is the infringement of a copyright. A copyright is the right given by statute to prevent others for a limited time from printing, copying, or publishing a production resulting from intellectual labor. The right exists for the life of the author and for 50 years thereafter.[19]

Infringement of a copyright in general consists of copying the form of expression of ideas or conceptions. There is no copyright in the idea or conception itself, but only in the particular way in which it is expressed. In order to constitute an infringement, the production need not be reproduced entirely or be exactly the same as the original. Reproduction of a substantial part of the original constitutes an infringement, but appropriation of only a word or single line does not.

One guilty of infringement of copyright is liable to the owner for damages, which are to be determined by the court. The owner is also entitled to an injunction to restrain further infringement.

20. Unfair Competition

Unfair competition is unlawful. The person injured thereby may sue for damages and an injunction to stop the practice, or may report the matter to the Federal Trade Commission or to an appropriate state agency.

It is unfair competition to imitate signs, storefronts, advertisements, and the packaging of goods of a competitor. Thus, when one adopts a box of distinctive size, shape, and color in which to market a product, and the package is imitated by a competitor, the latter is liable for unfair competition.

Not every similarity to a competitor is necessarily unfair competition. For example, the

---

[18] Kennedy v Kennedy (Mo App) 819 SW2d 406 (1991).

[19] Copyright Act of 1976, Act of October 19, 1976, § 302, PL 94-553, 90 Stat 2541, 2572, 17 USC § 302.

term *downtown* is merely descriptive, so the Downtown Motel cannot obtain an injunction against the use of the name Downtown Motor Inn. A name that is merely descriptive cannot be exclusively appropriated or adopted. As an exception, if the descriptive word has been used by a given business for such a long time as to be identified with that business in the public mind, a competitor cannot use that name.

The goodwill that is related to a trade name is an important business asset. There is a judicial trend in favor of protecting a trade name from a competitor's use of a similar name.

Historically, the law as to unfair competition was concerned only with protecting competitors from unfair competition by their rivals. Under consumer protection statutes, most states now give protection to the consumer who is harmed by unfair competitive practices.

21. Combinations to Divert Trade

Business relations may be harmed by a combination to keep third persons from dealing with one another. Such a combination, resulting in injury, constitutes an actionable wrong known as **conspiracy** if the object is unlawful or if a lawful object is sought by unlawful means.

If the object of a combination is to further a lawful interest of the combination, no actionable wrong exists so long as lawful means are employed. For example, when employees are united in a strike, they may peacefully persuade others to withhold their patronage from the employer. On the other hand, all combinations to drive or keep away customers or prospective employees by violence, force, threats, or intimidation are actionable wrongs.

Labor laws prohibit some combinations as unfair labor practices, and other combinations to divert trade are condemned as illegal trusts.

22. Malicious Interference with Contract

The extent of tort law relating to interference with contracts and other economic relationships has increased greatly in recent years. This increase is a result of society's seeking to impose on the marketplace higher ethical standards to prevent the oppression of victims by improper practices. In general terms, when the defendant interferes with and brings about the breach of the contract between a third person and the plaintiff, the circumstances may be such that the plaintiff has an action in tort against the defendant for interfering with contractual relations.[20]

Since the tort in question is the malicious interfering with contract, it follows that there is no tort when the interference is not malicious but is done to safeguard or protect one's own financial or economic interest.[21] However, the fact that the defendant is a competitor of the plaintiff does not constitute justification for the defendant's causing third persons to break their contracts with the plaintiff.

The fact that a contract is terminable at will does not deprive it of protection from interference.[22] Likewise, it is immaterial that the contract could be ignored because it is not evidenced by a writing that satisfies the statute of frauds.

In addition to protecting existing contracts from deliberate interference, tort liability is imposed for acts intentionally committed to prevent the making of a contract.

---

[20] Idaho First National Bank v Bliss Valley Foods, Inc. (Idaho) 824 P2d 841 (1991).

[21] Wood v Herndon and Herndon Investigations, Inc. 186 Mich App 495, 465 NW2d 5 (1991).

[22] Sterner v Marathon Oil Co. (Tex) 767 SW2d 686 (1989).

23. Wrongful Interference with Business Relations

One of the fundamental rights of an individual is to earn a living by working or by engaging in trade or business. Any wrongful interference with this liberty is a tort. The right to conduct one's business is, nevertheless, subject to the rights of others. Hence, the injuries suffered by one in business through legitimate competition give no right to redress.

C. TORTS AGAINST PERSON OR PROPERTY

In contrast with the white collar torts, some torts involve the use of force or threats of force or the unlawful use of tangible property.

24. Trespass to the Person

Trespass to the person consists of any contact with the victim's person for which consent was not given.

(a) BATTERY AND ASSAULT. Trespass to the person includes what is technically described as a battery. A battery is an intentional, wrongful physical contact with a person, without the consent of the victim, that results in injury or offensive touching. Battery includes an assault in which the victim apprehends the commission of a battery but is in fact not touched. In some instances, as in cases of self-defense, a person has a right to use force that would otherwise constitute an unlawful battery.

(b) FALSE IMPRISONMENT. False imprisonment is the intentional, unprivileged detaining of a person without that person's consent.[23] It may take the extreme form of kidnapping. At the other extreme, a shopper who is detained in a store manager's office and questioned about shoplifting is the victim of false imprisonment where there is no reasonable ground for believing that the shopper is a thief. Similarly, a merchant is liable for false imprisonment when a person detained under suspicion of shoplifting is detained after it is determined that the person was innocent and the original suspicion was a mistake. False imprisonment also includes detention under an official arrest when there is no legal justification for the arrest.

(1) Detention. Any detention at any place by any means for any duration of time is sufficient to satisfy the detention element of false imprisonment. If a robber holds a bank teller at gunpoint for the purpose of preventing the teller from attacking the other robbers or from escaping, there is a sufficient detention.

(2) Consent and Privilege. By definition, no false imprisonment occurs when the person detained consents to it. For example, when a merchant without any justification detains a person on the suspicion of shoplifting, such detention is not a false imprisonment if the victim consents to it without any protest. If the merchant had reasonable grounds for believing that the victim was guilty of shoplifting, the action of the merchant was not false imprisonment, even though the victim was detained under protest and did not consent to it. Statutes frequently give merchants a privilege to detain persons reasonably suspected of shoplifting.[24] Likewise, there is a privilege and it is not false imprisonment to confine a hospital patient in an emergency room in order to prevent harm to the patient and to others.

25. Trespass to Land

A trespass to land consists of any unpermitted entry below, on, across, or above land. This rule is modified to permit the proper flight of aircraft above the land so long as it does not interfere with a proper use of the land.

---

[23] Roddell v Town of Flora (Ind App) 580 NE2d 255 (1991).
[24] Caldwell v K-Mart Corp. (SC App) 410 SE2d 21 (1991).

26. Trespass to Personal Property

An illegal invasion of property rights with respect to property other than land constitutes a **trespass to personal property**, whether done intentionally or negligently. When done in good faith and without negligence, there is no liability. This is in contrast with the case of trespass to land, where good faith and absence of negligence is not a defense.

Negligent damage to personal property imposes liability for harm done. Intentional damage to personal property will impose liability for the damage done and also may justify exemplary or punitive damages.

27. Conversion

In contrast with a trespass to personal property, a **conversion** occurs when personal property is taken by a person not entitled to it and the property is kept from its true owner or prior possessor. For example, a bank clerk commits conversion by unlawfully taking money from the bank. Conversion is the civil side of the crimes relating to stealing. The good faith of the converter, however, is not a defense to civil liability.[25] Thus, even if a buyer of goods did not know they were stolen, the buyer is liable for damages for converting them.

SUMMARY

Conduct that harms other people or their property is generally called a tort. The injured person may sue the wrongdoer to recover damages to compensate for the harm or loss caused. The conduct that is a tort may also be a crime and may sometimes be a breach of contract. Tort liability is generally imposed because of the fault of the wrongdoer; in some cases it is imposed when there is no fault. In any case, the harm-causing conduct of the defendant must be voluntary and must have a causal relationship to the harm sustained. Liability is imposed without fault in connection with certain industrial activity, consumer protection, and certain areas of liability to workers or to victims of automobile collisions.

Negligence is the failure to follow the degree of care that would be followed by a reasonably prudent person in order to avoid foreseeable harm. If the negligence of the plaintiff contributes to the plaintiff's harm, the recovery obtained by the plaintiff may be reduced proportionately or barred, depending on the type of comparative negligence rule that is in force. In a minority of states, the common law contributory negligence rule is still followed. Under this law, any negligence of the plaintiff bars all recovery. Negligence must be proven as a fact, although the plaintiff may be aided by the doctrine of res ipsa loquitur. In most states, the violation of a statute is proof that the defendant was negligent, provided the statute is designed to protect from the kind of harm that has been sustained and the plaintiff is a member of the class that the statute sought to protect.

In general, any person aggrieved or harmed by a tort can sue the defendant. In some instances, a relative of the injured person will have a right to sue the defendant because of the harm caused. When there are two or more persons causing harm in such a way that it is not possible to determine how much harm was caused by each person, all the persons causing the harm are jointly and severally liable to the plaintiff by the modern trend.

Ordinarily, any wrongdoer may be sued, but some wrongdoers have a limited immunity, while others may be liable for the tortious acts of third persons. Governments may be

---

[25] Car Transportation v Garden Spot Distributors, 305 Ark 82, 805 SW2d 532 (1991).

immune from suit. To some extent minors, parents of the aggrieved person, and the spouse of that person may be immune from

suit. The trend of the law is to treat charities the same as other defendants and impose tort liability on them.

LAW IN PRACTICE

1. If you are in business, consult with your attorney whether there is the potential of tort liability in the way that you operate, and review this information annually.

2. Protect yourself from being a victim of a tort by dealing with persons you know or persons of established reputations; carefully check all personnel; and insure against loss when insurance is available.

3. Consult your accountant and attorney to see what in-house and external checking against loss can be established.

4. Keep careful records of prior history of employees and of any misconduct.

5. Consult your attorney whenever you sustain any loss that might be a tort or have committed any act that is claimed to be a tort.

QUESTIONS AND CASE PROBLEMS

1. What are the social forces advanced by each of the following rules of law? (a) In some areas of law, liability for harm exists without regard to whether there was any negligence or intention to cause harm. (b) Geographic and descriptive names cannot ordinarily be adopted as trademarks.

2. The Coleman Construction Company was constructing a highway. It was necessary to blast rock with dynamite. The corporation's employees did this with the greatest of care. In spite of their precautions, some flying fragments of rock damaged a neighboring house. The owner of the house sued the corporation for the damages. The corporation raised the defense that the owner was suing for tort damages and that such damages could not be imposed because the corporation had been free from fault. Was this defense valid?

3. Burnstein drove a car on a country road at 35 miles an hour. The maximum speed limit was 45 miles an hour. He struck and killed a cow that was crossing the road. The owner of the cow sued Burnstein for the value of the cow. Burnstein raised the defense that since he was not driving above the speed limit, there could be no liability for negligence. Was this defense valid?

4. The Brunswick Corporation manufactured and sold raincoats that it advertised to consumers as waterproof when in fact they were merely water resistant. The Brunswick Corporation was sued for engaging in unfair competition. It raised the defense that it was not guilty because it was understood in the trade that waterproof meant only water resistant, so no unfair advantage was taken of any competitor. Was this defense valid?

5. Jessica Sorensen was a minor. She was riding in an automobile driven by her father, Paul. The car collided with another car. Jessica was injured. She sued her father for her injuries. He raised the defense that a father could not be sued by his child for negligence. Was he correct? [*Sorensen v Sorensen, 369 Mass 350, 339 NE2d 907*]

6. Henry Neiderman was walking with his small son. An automobile driven by Brodsky went out of control, ran up on the sidewalk, and struck a fire hydrant, a litter pole and basket, a newsstand, and Neiderman's son. The car did not touch Neiderman, but the shock and fright caused damage to his heart. He sued Brodsky for the harm that he sustained as the result of Brodsky's negligence. Brodsky defended on the ground that he was not liable because he had not touched Neiderman. Was this a valid defense? [*Neiderman v Brodsky, 436 Pa 401, 261 A2d 84*]

7. Carrigan, a district manager of Simples Time Recorder Company, was investigating complaints of mismanagement of the Jackson office of the company. He called at the home of Hooks, the secretary of that office. She expressed the opinion that part of the trouble was caused by stealing of parts and equipment by McCall, another employee. McCall was later discharged and sued Hooks for slander. Was she liable? [*Hooks v McCall (Miss) 272 So 2d 925*]

8. Defendant no. 1 parked his truck in the street near the bottom of a ditch on a dark, foggy night. Iron pipes carried in the truck projected beyond the truck nine feet in back. Neither the truck nor the pipes carried any warning light or flag, thus violating both city ordinance and state statute. Defendant no. 2 was a taxicab owner whose taxicab was negligently driven at an excessive speed. Defendant no. 2 ran into the pipes, thereby killing the passenger in the taxicab. The plaintiff brought an action for the passenger's death against both defendants. Defendant no. 1 claimed he was not liable because it was the negligent act of defendant no. 2 that had caused the harm. Was this defense valid? [Bumbardner v Allison, 238 NC 621, 78 SE2d 752]

9. A statute required that air vent shafts on hotel roofs have parapets at least 30 inches high. Edgar Hotel had parapets only 27 inches high. Nunneley was visiting a registered guest at the Edgar Hotel. She placed a mattress on top of a parapet. When she sat on the mattress, the parapet collapsed and she fell into the air shaft and was injured. She sued the hotel, claiming that its breach of the statute as to the height of the parapets constituted negligence. Decide. [Nunneley v Edgar Hotel, 36 Cal 2d 493, 225 P2d 497]

10. A customer was shopping at the handbag counter of the defendant's store. She did not make any purchase and left the store. When she was a few feet away from the store, an employee of the store tapped her lightly on the shoulder to attract her attention and asked her if she had made any purchase. When she inquired why, he asked, "What about that bag in your hand?" The customer said that it belonged to her and she opened it to show by its contents that it was not a new bag. The employee gave the customer a real dirty look and went back into the store without saying a word. The customer then sued the store for false imprisonment. Was the store liable? [Abner v W. T. Grant Co. 110 Ga App 592, 139 SE2d 408]

11. Collete Bass worked in a building owned by Nooney Company. As part of her job, she was going from one floor to another when the elevator stopped moving. She was alone in the elevator for about an hour before she was rescued. The emergency phone in the elevator was dead. She sued the Nooney Company for the mental distress to which she was subjected. The Nooney Company claimed that it was not liable because there was no proof that it had been negligent. Bass claimed Nooney had the burden of proving that it was not negligent. Was she correct? [Bass v Nooney Co. (Mo) 646 SW2d 765]

12. A farmer sued five factories that were located several miles from his farm. He proved that industrial fumes from the factories had seriously damaged his crops. The defendants did not deny that damage had been done, but each defendant claimed that the farmer could not recover from that defendant without proving how much of the total damage had been caused by that defendant. Since this was not possible, the defendants claimed that judgment should be entered against the farmer. Were they correct? What are the ethics of the problem?

13. Kendra Knight took part in a friendly game of touch football. She had played before and was familiar with football. Michael Jewett was on her team. In the course of play, Michael bumped into Kendra and knocked her to the ground. He stepped on her hand, causing injury to a little finger that later required its amputation. She sued Michael for damages. He defended on the ground that she had assumed the risk. Kendra claimed that assumption of risk could not be raised as a defense because the state legislature had adopted the standard of comparative negligence. Decide.

14. An eight-year old boy with curable cancer was receiving x-ray treatment at a hospital. He was negligently given overdoses of x-ray. This produced deadly radiation poisoning, which produced a "grotesque alteration" of his appearance which the parents of the child could see, and they could see his pain and suffering up to the time of his death within the following year. They sued the hospital for the emotional distress they suffered because of the negligence of the hospital. The hospital raised the defense that the parents had not seen the negligent acts that caused harm and therefore could not recover as a bystander. Decide. [Golstein v San Francisco Superior Court, ___ Cal App 3d___, 273 Cal Rptr 270 (1990)]

15. Blaylock was a voluntary psychiatric outpatient treated by Dr. Burglass. Dr. Burglass became aware that Blaylock was violence-prone. Blaylock told Burglass that he intended to do serious harm to Wayne Boynton, Jr. Shortly thereafter he killed Wayne. The parents of Wayne then sued Dr. Burglass on the theory that he was liable for the death of their son because he failed to give warning or to notify the police of Blaylock's threat and nature. Decide. [Boynton v Burglass (Fla App) 590 So 2d 446]

PART 2

Contracts

CHAPTER 9

NATURE AND CLASSES OF CONTRACTS

LEARNING OBJECTIVES

After studying this chapter, you will be able to:
1. *List the essential elements of a contract.*
2. *Describe the way in which a contract arises.*
3. *State how contracts are classified.*
4. *Differentiate contracts from agreements that are not contracts.*
5. *Differentiate formal contracts from simple contracts.*
6. *Differentiate express contracts from implied contracts.*
7. *Differentiate contractual liability from quasi-contractual liability.*

Practically every business transaction affecting anyone involves a contract.

A. NATURE OF CONTRACTS

This introductory chapter will familiarize you with the terminology needed to work with contract law. In addition, this chapter introduces something called **quasi contracts**. Quasi-contracts are not true contracts but obligations imposed by law.

1. Definition of a Contract

A **contract** is a legally binding agreement.[1] By one definition, "a contract is a promise or a set of promises for the breach of which the law gives a remedy, or the performance of which the law in some way recognizes as a duty."[2] Contracts arise out of agreements, so a contract may be defined as an agreement creating an obligation.

The substance of the definition of a contract is that by mutual agreement or assent, the parties create enforceable duties or obligations. That is, each party is legally bound to do or to refrain from doing certain acts.

2. Elements of a Contract

The elements of a contract are: (a) an agreement, (b) between competent parties, (c) based on the genuine assent of the parties, (d) supported by consideration, (e) made for a lawful objective, and (f) in the form required by law, if any. These elements will be considered in the chapters that follow.

3. Subject Matter of Contracts

The subject matter of a contract may relate to the performance of personal services, such as contracts of employment to work on an assembly line, to work as a secretary, to sing on television, or to build a house. The contract may provide for the transfer of ownership of property, such as a house (real property) or an automobile (personal property), from one person to another. A contract may also call for a combination of these things. For example, a builder may contract to supply materials and do the work involved in installing the materials, or a person may contract to build a house and then transfer the house and the land to the buyer.

4. Parties to a Contract

A person who makes a promise is the **promisor**, and the person to whom the promise is made is called the **promisee**. If the promise is binding, it imposes on the promisor a duty or obligation, and the promisor may be called the **obligor**. The promisee who can claim the benefit of the obligation is called the **obligee**. The parties to a contract are said to stand in privity with each other, and the relationship between them is termed **privity of contract**.

In written contracts, parties may be referred to by name. More often, however, they are given special names that serve to better identify each party. For example, consider a contract by which one person agrees that another may occupy a house upon the payment of money. The parties to this contract are called landlord and tenant, or lessor and lessee, and the contract between them is known as a lease. Parties to other types of contracts also have distinctive names, such as vendor and vendee for the parties to a sales contract, shipper and carrier for the parties to a transportation contract, and insurer and insured for the parties to an insurance policy.

A party to a contract may be an individual, a partnership, a corporation, or a government. A party to a contract may be an agent acting on behalf of another person.

There may be one or more persons on each side of the contract. In some cases there are

---

[1] The Uniform Commercial Code defines *contract* as "the total legal obligation which results from the parties' agreement as affected by [the UCC] and any other applicable rules of law," UCC § 1-201(11).

[2] Restatement, Contracts, 2d § 1.

three-sided contracts, as in the case of a credit card transaction. A credit card transaction involves the company issuing the card, the holder of the card, and the business furnishing goods and services on the basis of the credit card.

If a contract is written, the persons who are the parties and who are bound by it will ordinarily be determined by reading what the paper says and seeing how it is signed.

Ordinarily, only a party to a contract has any rights against another party to the contract.[3] In some cases, third persons have rights on a contract as third-party beneficiaries or assignees.

5.   How a Contract Arises

A contract is based on an agreement. An agreement arises when one person, the **offeror**, makes an offer and the person to whom the offer is made, the **offeree**, accepts. There must be both an offer and an acceptance. If either is lacking, there is no contract.[4]

6.   Intent to Make a Binding Agreement

Because a contract is based on the consent of the parties and is a legally binding agreement, it follows that the parties must have an intent to enter into an agreement that is binding. Sometimes the parties are in agreement, but their agreement does not produce a contract. Sometimes there is merely a preliminary agreement, but the parties never actually make a contract. It may be merely an agreement as to future plans or intentions without any contractual obligation to carry out those plans or intentions. In the *Bowman* case there was a dispute as to whether an agreement was a contract.

BOWMAN v HILL
45 NC App 116, 262 SE2d 376 (1980)

William Hill and the Terrells owned two tracts of land in the town of Dayton. They sold one tract to Dr. Terry O. Bowman and made an agreement with him as to the second lot, which they kept. The agreement stated in part:

. . . whereas the parties of the second part [William Hill and the Terrells] desire to construct a building adjacent to the building of the party of the first part [Dr. Bowman] at some future time; and WHEREAS, all of the parties are desirous of having one large inter-connecting parking lot located in front of the buildings and sidewalks connecting to said parking lots;

WITNESSETH:

That for the mutual considerations expressed hereinabove, the parties do contract as follows: . . . [emphasis added]

The agreement went on to provide that when the Hill-Terrell lot was paved for a parking lot, Bowman would pave a similar parking area on his

---

[3]   National Survival Game of New York, Inc. v NSG of LI Corp. 69 App Div 760, 565 NYS2d 127 (1991).

[4]   Orcutt v S & L Paint Contractors, Ltd (NM App) 791 P2d 71 (1990).

tract. The Hill-Terrell lot was thereafter sold, and the buyer constructed a building where the parking lot would have been. Bowman sued Hill and Terrell for having broken their contract. The lower court held the defendants liable for breach of contract, and they appealed.

HILL, J. . . . One of the elements of a valid contract is a promise, which has been defined as an assurance that a thing will or will not be done. "The mere expression of an intention or desire is not a promise. . . ."

An apparent promise which, according to its terms, makes performance optional with the promisor no matter what may happen, or no matter what course of conduct in other respects he may pursue, is in fact no promise. Such an expression is often called an illusory promise. Williston, Contracts § 1A (3d ed 1957).

When we give the ordinary and usual meaning to the words of the contract—desire and desirous—it is apparent that they express a wish or request. Certainly, they do not carry the thrust of a promise to do or refrain from doing anything with regard to the remaining property. There is no expressed obligation to develop the property at anytime.

In the case of *Jones v Realty Co.*, 226 NC 303, 37 SE2d 906 (1946), the plaintiff sued to recover a sales commission for procuring a purchaser who was ready, willing, and able to buy land on terms set out in an agreement. The trial court interpreted the agreement between the parties to mean that the commission was to be paid "when"—and only when—"the deal is closed up." The deal never closed, and the Court said . . . that,

It can make no difference whether the event be called a contingency or the time of perform-ance. Certainly, under either construction, the result would be the same; since, if the event does not befall, or a time coincident with the happening of the event does not arrive, in nei-ther case may performance be exacted. Nor will it do to say that a promise to pay "when the deal is closed up" is a promise to pay when it ought to be closed up according to the terms of the contract. Such is not the meaning of the words used. It is the event itself, and not the date of its expected or contemplated happening, that makes the promise to pay performable.

By the conveyance of the property . . . the defendants served notice to the plain-tiff, and to all the world, that they would never develop the property, and such con-veyance and notice terminated the agreement, if any there was. . .

[Judgment reversed]

QUESTIONS

1. Who were the defendants in this case?
2. Why didn't the plaintiff sue the purchaser of the second Hill-Terrell tract?
3. Did the purchaser of the second tract know of the agreement as to the parking lot?

B. CLASSES OF CONTRACTS

Contracts are classified with respect to their form, the way in which they were created, their binding character, and the extent to which they have been performed.

Figure 9-1 Contractual Liability

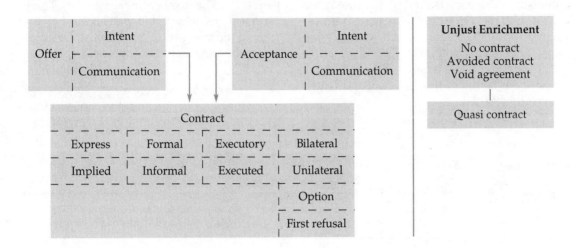

7. Formal and Informal Contracts

Contracts can be classified as formal or informal contracts.

(a) FORMAL CONTRACTS. **Formal contracts** are enforced because the formality with which they are executed is considered sufficient to signify that the parties intend to be bound by their terms. Formal contracts include (1) contracts under seal, (2) contracts of record, and (3) negotiable instruments.

(1) Contracts Under Seal. A **contract under seal** is executed by affixing a seal or making an impression on the paper or on some adhering substance, such as wax, attached to the document. Although at common law an impression was necessary, the courts now treat various signs or marks to be the equivalent of a seal. Most states hold that there is a seal if a person's signature or a corporation's name is followed by a scroll or scrawl, the word *seal*, or the letters *L.S.*[5] *In some jurisdictions, the body of the contract must recite that*

the parties are sealing the contract, in addition to their making a seal following their signatures.[6]

A contract under seal was binding at common law solely because of its formality. In many states, this has been changed by statute. The Uniform Commercial Code makes the law of seals inapplicable to the sale of goods. In some states the law of seals has been abolished generally, without regard to the nature of the transaction involved.

Unless expressly required by statute or administrative regulation, a seal is not needed in order to make a binding contract. The parties have the freedom of choice to use or do without a seal.

(2) Contracts of Record. A **contract of record** is an agreement or obligation that has been recorded by a court. One form of contract of record arises when one acknowledges before a proper court the obligation to pay a certain sum unless a specified condition is met. For example, a party who has been arrested may be released on a promise to appear in court and may agree to pay a certain sum on

---

[5] Some authorities explain *L.S.* as an abbreviation for *Locus Sigilium* (place for the seal).

[6] Johns v First Alabama Bank (Ala Civ App) 612 So 2d 1235 (1992).

failing to do so. An obligation of this kind is known as a **recognizance**.

Similarly, an agreement made with an administrative agency is binding because it has been so made. For example, when a business agrees with the Federal Trade Commission that the enterprise will stop a particular practice that the commission regards as unlawful, the business is bound by its agreement and cannot thereafter reject it.

(b) INFORMAL CONTRACTS. All contracts other than formal contracts are called **informal** (or **simple**) **contracts**, without regard to whether they are oral or written. These contracts are enforceable, not because of the form of the transaction, but because they represent the agreement of the parties.

Figure 9-2 Contract

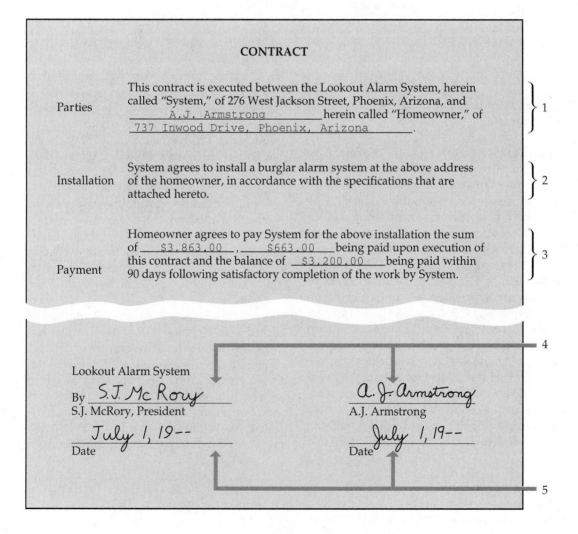

8. Express and Implied Contracts

Simple contracts may be classified in terms of the way they are created, as express contracts or implied contracts.

(a) EXPRESS CONTRACTS. An **express contract** is one in which the agreement of the parties is manifested by their words, whether spoken or written.

(b) IMPLIED CONTRACTS. An **implied contract** (or, as sometimes stated, a contract implied in fact) is one in which the agreement is not shown by words, written or spoken, but by the acts and conduct of the parties. Such a contract arises, for example, when one person renders services under circumstances indicating that payment for them is expected, and the other person, knowing such circumstances, accepts the benefit of those services.[7] Similarly, when an owner requests a professional roofer to make repairs to the roof of a building, an obligation arises to pay the reasonable value of such services, although no agreement has been made as to compensation.

In terms of effect, there is no difference between an implied contract and an express contract. The difference relates solely to the manner of proving the existence of the contract. However, in the case of the implied contract, the plaintiff has the burden of proving the value of the services performed or property sold.[8]

An implied contract cannot arise when there is an existing express contract on the same subject.

No contract is implied when the relationship of the parties is such that by a reasonable interpretation, the performance of services or the supplying of goods was intended as a gift.[9]

In *Novak's Estate*, the mother died, and her daughter claimed compensation for services she had rendered to her mother.

NOVAK'S ESTATE
(Minn App) 398 NW2d 653 (1987)

While Clara Novak was sick, her daughter Janie helped her in many ways. Clara died, and Janie then claimed that she was entitled to be paid for the services that she had rendered to her mother. The court dismissed her claim, and she appealed.

SEDGWICK, J. . . . Clara Novak suffered kidney failure in 1971. Dialysis treatment was required since November 1977. She died on June 23, 1984, just before her 71st birthday.

Clara Novak's will provided $2,000 to her church and the residue of her estate to be divided equally among her children. One daughter, Janie Novak, claims she is entitled to a greater share because she was the primary caretaker for her mother for at least six years. Janie's claim against the estate for $26,105.50 for her services was denied. Her siblings claim Janie was simply doing her part and that three other children also helped their mother.

Janie Novak claims she averaged two hours a day helping her mother. Janie became a licensed practical nurse at her mother's suggestion. She worked nights in order

---

[7] Vortt Exploration Co., Inc. v Chevron U.S.A., Inc. (Tex) 787 SW2d 942 (1990).
[8] Gioffre v Simakis, 72 Ohio App 3d 424, 594 NE2d 1013 (1991).
[9] Re Wilson's Estate, 178 App 2d 996, 579 NYS2d 779 (1991).

to help her mother during the day. She drove her mother to the Little Falls hospital 96 times for dialysis and made seven trips to the Hennepin County Medical Center. Janie also reports the loss of 16 days, 5 hours of vacation time on her mother's behalf. She incurred phone expense because of her mother's condition. She lived a quarter mile distance from her mother and was a frequent visitor. Appellant argued:

Janie . . . provided nursing services on a daily basis in Clara's home. Janie would also check her mother's blood pressure and other vital signs, bathe her, do her hair, clip her toe and fingernails, massage her scalp, and attended to other hygiene needs. Janie would do her mother's shopping for her, pay her bills, provide her with transport to and from various business establishments, and otherwise attend to her mother's needs. After one of her mother's many hospitalizations, Janie kept her mother in her own home for a period of some three months, and personally attended to her mother's various medical ailments at the time. In short, Janie provided nursing services for her mother's well-being for a period in excess of thirteen years.

The family responded that Janie merely did her share; three other siblings also helped out. The trips for dialysis were thrice weekly and since other family members gave Clara rides, 96 trips over 6 years was not an unreasonable figure. The siblings state that Janie's son Jeffrey often made the dialysis trips rather than Janie. In 1978, Clara purchased a new car for the trips and paid for travel expenses. The family offered as evidence a number of checks, mostly for small amounts, payable to Janie Novak. From September 1983 to March 1984, another daughter took Clara in and cared for her. The family also points out that Clara's medical needs were satisfied by the Little Falls hospital, and that the medical services, such as blood pressure checks, temperature, etc., supplied by Janie were solely for her own peace of mind. She did not maintain records as a nurse would when providing professional services. . . .

The courts proceed on the premise that services provided between family/household members are gratuitous.

The presumption of gratuity is dependent on the existence of a family relation and only arises when it is shown that the services rendered were of the type which members of a family usually and ordinarily render to each other by reason of family relation. The authorities stress the fact that the presence of those reciprocal duties within the family is essential to the creation of this presumption.

In re Estate of Tilghman, 240 Minn 494, 495, 61 NW2d 743, 745 (1953). The presumption operates if the family relation exists. . . .

Appellant argues that "family" does not include a blood relation who lives independently from the person to whom the services were rendered, *i.e.*, a non-household member should not be saddled with the presumption. We believe the presumption properly applies to immediate family regardless of their residence. "Household" is simply a more inclusive term since it may include individuals residing with a family and participating in the exchange of services, but absent a blood tie. Whether or not family members reside in the same household, the question is the extent to which care furnished exceeds "reciprocal duties and mutual benefits." *Id.* at 499, 61 NW2d at 747. . . .

The evidentiary presumption arises where there is a family relationship, as evidenced by a close blood relation and/or a membership in a family's household. Once the "close" relationship is established where individuals are presumed to commonly share duties and provide services to other family members, the analysis shifts to an examination of whether the exchange of services was actually mutual and reciprocal. If one party rendered or received an obviously disproportionate share of services, the absence of mutuality may obviate the presumption.

The more distant the kinship or relationship, the easier it is to overcome the presumption since reciprocal benefits are more limited. A daughter-in-law . . . or a daughter with no parental contact for fifty years (*Tilghman*) will be able to avoid the presumption, while a child who has always been close to her parents will have a difficult task overcoming the presumption absent significant inequities. It must be remembered the presumption is an evidentiary device, and it is not an absolute bar to recovery.

In the present case, Janie Novak lived nearby and provided a number of services to her elderly, sick mother. Her care and assistance does not rise to the level in *Tilghman* . . . and does not appear to be disproportionate to the aid provided by her siblings. She also received one-sixth of the estate. Even if she provided more services, while others did less (and perhaps other siblings did nothing), the balancing of the equities does not justify an interference with the testamentary plan of the deceased.

[Judgment affirmed]

QUESTIONS

1. What is the basis for the presumption applied by the court?
2. What is the distinction between family and household?
3. Did the facts of the case confirm or rebut the presumption of gratuity?

9. Valid and Voidable Contracts and Void Agreements

Contracts may be classified in terms of enforceability or validity.

(a) VALID CONTRACTS. A **valid contract** is an agreement that is binding and enforceable.

(b) VOIDABLE CONTRACTS. A **voidable contract** is an agreement that is otherwise binding and enforceable, but because of the circumstances surrounding its execution or the lack of capacity of one of the parties, it may be rejected at the option of one of the parties.

For example, a person who has been forced to sign an agreement that that person would not have voluntarily signed may, in some instances, avoid the contract.

(c) VOID AGREEMENTS. A **void agreement** is without legal effect. An agreement that contemplates the performance of an act prohibited by law is usually incapable of enforcement; hence it is void. Likewise, it cannot be made binding by later approval or ratification.[10]

---

[10] Although the distinction between a void agreement and a voidable contract is clear in theory, there is frequently confusion. Some courts describe a given transaction as void, while others regard it as merely voidable.

10. Executed and Executory Contracts

Contracts may be classified, in terms of the extent to which they have been performed, as executed contracts and executory contracts.

(a) EXECUTED CONTRACTS. An **executed contract** is one that has been completely performed. In other words, an executed contract is one under which nothing remains to be done by either party. A contract may be executed at once, as in the case of a cash sale, or it may be executed or performed in the future.

(b) EXECUTORY CONTRACTS. In an **executory contract**, something remains to be done by one or both parties. For example, if a utility company agrees to furnish electricity to a customer for a specified period of time at a stipulated price, the contract is executory. If the entire price is paid in advance, the contract is still deemed executory, although, strictly speaking, it is executed on one side and executory on the other.

11. Bilateral and Unilateral Contracts

In making an offer, the offeror is in effect extending a promise to do something, such as to pay a sum of money, if the offeree will do what the offeror requests. Contracts are classified as bilateral or unilateral. Some bilateral contracts look ahead to the making of a later contract. Depending on their terms, these are called option contracts or first-refusal contracts.

(a) BILATERAL CONTRACT. If the offeror extends a promise and asks for a promise in return and if the offeree accepts the offer by making the promise, the contract is called a **bilateral contract**. One promise is given in exchange for another, and each party is bound by the obligation. For example, when the house painter offers to paint the owner's house for $1,000, and the owner promises to pay $1,000 for the job, there is an exchange of promises, and the agreement gives rise to a bilateral contract.

(b) UNILATERAL CONTRACT. In contrast, the offeror may offer to do something only when something is done by the offeree.[11] Because only one party is obligated to perform after the contract has been made, this kind of contract is called a **unilateral contract**. This is illustrated by the case of the reward for the return of lost property. The offeror does not wish to have promises by members of the public that they will try to return the property. The offeror wants the property and promises to pay anyone who returns the property. The offer of a unilateral contract calls for an act; a promise to do the act does not give rise to a contract.

(c) OPTION AND FIRST-REFUSAL CONTRACTS. The parties may make a contract that gives a right to one of the parties to enter into a second contract at a later date. If one party has an absolute right to enter into the later contract, the initial contract is called an **option contract**. Thus, a bilateral contract may be made today giving one of the parties the right to buy the other party's house for a specified amount. This is an option contract, since the party with the privilege has the freedom of choice, or option, to buy or not buy. If the option is exercised, the other party to the contract must follow the terms of the option and enter into the second contract. If the option is never exercised, no second contract ever arises, and the offer protected by the option contract merely expires.

In contrast with an option contract, a contract may merely give a **right of first refusal**. This only imposes the duty to make the first offer to the party having the right of first refusal. For example, the homeowner could make a contract providing that, should the owner desire to sell at some future time, the other party to the contract could buy either at a fixed price or at a price matching a good-faith bid by a third person. Here the home-

---

[11] Multicare Medical Center v Washington, 114 Wash 2d 572, 790 P2d 124 (1990).

owner cannot be required to sell, but if the owner attempts to sell, an option immediately comes into existence by which the other party can buy or not buy.

The situation can arise in which there is a question as to whether there is a contract to sell, an option to buy, or a right of first refusal. In all cases, the answer is determined by the intent of the parties. In any case, the non-party seeking to obtain the benefit of the contract must show that there has been compliance with a time limitation or other restrictions specified by the contract.[12]

12. Quasi Contracts

In some cases, the courts will impose an obligation even though there is no contract. Such an obligation is called a **quasi contract**. It is not a contract but merely an obligation imposed

by law in order to do justice.[13] A quasi contract is a contract that is implied in law, as distinguished from a contract implied in fact (discussed in Section 9 (b) of this chapter).

(a) PREVENTION OF UNJUST ENRICHMENT. Quasi contracts are recognized in a limited number of situations to attain an equitable or just result. Recovery in these cases is not based on any fault of the defendant but merely on the fact that the defendant has been unjustly enriched by having received a benefit to which the defendant was not entitled.[14]

In the *Petrie* case, the defendant claimed that he was entitled to keep the insurance money paid to him under his insurance policy.

(1) No Contract. In some cases, the hoped-for contract is never formed. The parties expect that there will be a contract, but something happens that prevents their reach-

PETRIE v LeVAN
(Mo App) 799 SW2d 632 (1990)

LeVan made a contract to sell a house to Petrie. Two days before the actual transfer of title was to be made both parties inspected the property and certified that it was in good condition. On the night before the day on which the title was to be transferred there was a severe storm. It damaged the house, but neither party knew of this damage on the next day when the title to the house was transferred to Petrie. He paid the full purchase price called for by the contract of sale. Some time later, an insurance company paid LeVan for the damage sustained to the house while it was still owned by him. Petrie claimed this money and sued LeVan for it. Judgment was entered for Petrie and LeVan appealed.

SHANGLER, J. . . . . LeVan concludes that since there was no evidence of fraud or other wrongful conduct by him that worked disadvantage to the [buyer] and since in any event the rights and obligations of the parties were defined in the contract, there was no basis for any right of unjust enrichment nor for any remedy of restitution.

---

[12] Schaefer v Spence (Mo App) 813 SW2d 92 (1991).

[13] Re Zents Estate (ND) 459 NW2d 795 (1990).

[14] Ramsey v Ellis (Wis App) 471 NW2d 289 (1991).

A person who has been unjustly enriched at the expense of another is required to make restitution to the other. . . .

The right to restitution for unjust enrichment presupposes: (1) that the defendant was enriched by the receipt of a benefit; (2) that the enrichment was at the expense of the plaintiff; (3) that it would be unjust to allow the defendant to retain the benefits. . . . Thus, a person who has received money from another by mistake, money that in equity and good conscience the person ought not to keep, may be compelled to make restitution—even though the mistake was an honest one. . . .

There is no doubt that the first postulate of this formulation is actual: LeVan was enriched by the receipt of both the full purchase price for the residence property and the insurance proceeds that represented a part of that property. Nor is there doubt that the purchase price was paid by the [buyer]—and received by LeVan—under the mistake that the property was then intact. It is also a fact that LeVan freely accepted the insurance proceeds, and retained them, even after knowledge of the circumstances that attended the payment for the property. . . .

In this case, it is the equitable principle against double recovery that disallows LeVan from retention of both the insurance proceeds and the full purchase price of the property and that good conscience requires that LeVan pay over to the [buyer]. If LeVan may keep the proceeds of the insurance and also the full purchase price, he has a windfall. LeVan is compensated for that which he did not lose and the [buyer pays] for that which [he] did not receive.

Nor does the neglect by the [buyer] to reinspect the property on the very day of the closing render it inequitable to require payment of the insurance proceeds to [him] or justify the windfall to LeVan. . . .

The trial court properly entered judgment for the [buyer] for $2,176.22, the sum of money received by LeVan from the insurance policy, and a sum less than the damage done by the insured event. To prevent an unjust enrichment. . . at the expense of LeVan, nevertheless, the trial court should have reduced the judgment by the cost to LeVan of the insurance premiums. . . .

The case is remanded for entry of a new judgment. The trial court is directed to determine the cost to LeVan of the insurance premium and to subtract, pro rata, the unused premium as of the date of the loss from the $2,176.22 benefit for the entry of the new judgment.

[Action remanded for recomputation of recovery]

QUESTIONS

1. In the second paragraph of the portion of the court's opinion printed herein, it is stated that "A person who has been unjustly enriched at the expense of another is required to make restitution to the other." Did LeVan receive a benefit at the expense of Petrie?
2. How could Petrie have protected himself from the risk and expense involved in this case?
3. Assume that *A* purchases *B*'s house and then two days later sells it to *C* for 50% more than he paid *B*. *B* demands one half of this profit on the ground that *A* is unjustly enriched by the windfall he has received. How does the *Petrie* case affect your answer to this question?

ing a final agreement. Meanwhile, one or more of the parties may have acted prematurely and begun performing as though there were a contract. When it is finally clear that there is no contract, a party who had rendered some performance will seek to be paid for what was done. The claim will be made that if payment is not made, the other party will be unjustly enriched.

The no-contract case may arise in a situation where there is a mistake regarding the subject matter of the contract. For example, a painter may begin painting Adam's house because of a mistake as to the address of the building. Adam sees the work going on and realizes the painter is making a mistake. Nevertheless, Adam does not stop the painter. When the painter finishes the work and presents a bill for painting, Adam refuses to pay because there never was a contract. This is true because Adam never expressly agreed to the painting. Likewise, the conduct of Adam never caused the painter as a reasonable person to believe that Adam was entering into a contract. (There was no contract implied in fact.) The painter just assumed that everything was all right. In such a case, however, the law deems it inequitable that Adam should have remained silent and then reaped the benefits of the painter's mistake. Adam will therefore be required to pay the painter the reasonable value of the painting. This liability is described as quasi-contractual.

The mistake that benefits the defendant may be the mistake of a third person.

When there is no contract because essential terms are missing, but the plaintiff performs the services called for by the contemplated contract, the defendant receiving those services must pay the reasonable value thereof to avoid the unjust enrichment of getting the services without paying for them.[15]

(2) The Avoided Contract. In some situations, one party to the contract may be able to avoid it or set it aside. For example, the contract of a minor can be avoided. If the con-

tract was for something necessary received by the minor, the minor must pay the reasonable value of what was received. The minor is not required to pay the contract price, but only the reasonable value of the benefit received. As the liability enforced against the minor is not based on the contract, it is called quasi-contractual.

Likewise, when the parties rescind or set aside their contract, a party who has already conferred a benefit on the other party before the contract was rescinded may recover in quasi contract for the value of such benefit. Thus, a contractor may recover for the value of an irrigation system installed on the defendant's land before the construction contract was set aside.[16]

(3) The Void Agreement. In some instances, the parties make a contract, one party receives the benefit of the contract, and then the benefited party seeks to avoid paying on the ground that the contract was void because of illegality. For example, governmental units, such as cities, must generally advertise for the lowest responsible bidder when a contract is to be made to obtain supplies or to construct buildings. In some instances, the city officials might improperly skip the advertising. This could be done either because of a corrupt purpose or because the officials honestly, but wrongly, believed that the particular contract came within an exception to the requirement of advertising. Whatever the reason, the city officials enter into a contract with a contractor without following the statutory procedures. The contractor fully performs the contract. When the contractor requests to be paid, the city officials refuse to live up to the contract on the ground that the contract violated the statutory requirements and therefore was illegal and void. In such cases it will be held that although the contract is void, the city must pay the reasonable value of what has been done. In this way, the contractor gets paid for what the contractor really did. The city is not required to pay for any more than it has actually re-

---

[15] Professional Recruiters, Inc. v Oliver, 235 Neb 508, 456 NW2d 1-3 (1990).

[16] Murdock-Bryant Construction Inc. v Pearson, 146 Ariz 48, 703 P2d 1197 (1985).

ceived. The danger of the city's paying inflated prices, which was the evil that the advertising statute sought to avoid, does not arise, because the court does not require the city to pay the contract price but only the reasonable value of the benefit conferred upon the city.

(b) WHEN QUASI-CONTRACTUAL LIABILITY DOES NOT EXIST. While the objective of the quasi contract is to do justice, one must not jump to the conclusion that a quasi contract arises every time there is an injustice. The mere fact that someone has benefited someone else and has not been paid will not necessarily give rise to a quasi contract.[17]

(1) Unexpected Cost. The fact that performance of a contract proves more difficult or more expensive than had been expected does not entitle a party to extra compensation when there was no misrepresentation as to the conditions that would be encountered or the events that would occur. Courts are particularly unwilling to allow extra compensation when the complaining party is experienced with the particular type of contract and the problems that are likely to be encountered. That is, the contractor is not entitled to quasi-contractual recovery for extra expense on the theory that the extra work had conferred a greater benefit than had been contemplated.

(2) Existing Contract. A plaintiff cannot sue in **quantum meruit**, or for reasonable value, when there is an express contract fixing the amount due. In other words, a person cannot recover for the reasonable value of goods or services when there is an existing contract that obligates the obligor of that contract to pay a set price for the goods or services rendered.[18]

A subcontractor doing work that benefits the homeowner can only sue the contractor on the contract between the subcontractor and the contractor. The subcontractor cannot sue the owner merely because the owner was benefited by the work done by the subcontractor. Likewise, when a distributor of tires is not paid by a dealer, the distributor cannot sue the customer who bought the tires from the dealer for the bill that the dealer should have paid the distributor.

In the *Niggel Associates* case it was claimed that a stranger to the transaction had been unjustly enriched by the performance of a contract between two other persons.

(3) No Unjust Enrichment. To recover in quasi contract, the plaintiff must prove that the defendant was enriched, the extent or dollar value of such enrichment, and that such enrichment was unjust. If the plaintiff cannot prove all these elements, there can be no recov-

NIGGEL ASSOCIATES, INC. v POLO'S OF NORTH MYRTLE BEACH, INC.
(App) 296 SC 530, 374 SE2d 507 (1988)

Windy Hill held a long-term lease of a large tract of land from the local airport commission. Beach Investments leased part of this land from Windy Hill. Beach contracted with Niggel Associates and Mechanical Industrial to do tiling, heating, and cooling work in two buildings located on the part of the land rented by Beach. They were not paid and sued everyone related to the property. The lower court held that Windy Hill was unjustly enriched and required it to make restitution to the contractors. Windy Hill appealed.

---

[17] Kaprals Tire Service, Inc. v Aztek Tread Corp. 124 App Div 2d 1011, 508 NYS2d 777 (1986).
[18] Duckworth v Poland, ___ Ark App ___, 785 SW2d 472 (1990).

BELL, J. . . . . The plaintiff must show: (1) that he conferred a non gratuitous benefit on the defendant; (2) that the defendant realized some value from the benefit; and (3) that it would be inequitable for the defendant to retain the benefit without paying the plaintiff its value. . . .

The plaintiff must confer the benefit non gratuitously: that is, it must either be (1) at the defendant's request or (2) in circumstances where the plaintiff reasonably relies on the defendant to pay for the benefit and the defendant understands or ought to understand that the plaintiff expects compensation and looks to him for payment. . . .

In this case, the Contractors did the work under contracts with Beach. They expected to be paid by Beach. They had no dealings whatever with Windy Hill. Indeed, they did not know Windy Hill had an interest in the property when they agreed to perform the work. Windy Hill did not request the work. It did nothing to cause the Contractors to rely on it for payment. It had no reason to suppose the Contractors looked to it for payment. The Contractors were not induced to furnish their labor and materials by any expectation that Windy Hill would pay for them. In these circumstances, Windy Hill had no duty to make restitution to the Contractors. Any benefit it received was an incidental result of dealings between others in which it did not participate and over which it assumed no control.

Additionally, the Contractors failed to prove the value of any benefit Windy Hill may have received from their work. In a case involving improvements to realty, the measure of recovery in restitution is the difference in the fair market value of the property before and after the improvements. . . . The Contractors introduced no evidence to show their work increased the value of Windy Hill's leasehold interest. They neglected to prove the value of the leasehold before and after the work. Accordingly, there was no proof that the defendant realized value from the benefit conferred.

Because Niggel and Mechanical Industrial failed to prove essential elements of their case, the [lower] court erred in granting restitution.

[Judgment reversed]

QUESTIONS

1. What was the basis for the court's decision in the *Niggel Associates* case?
2. Could the contractors have recovered from Beach for unjust enrichment if the facts otherwise remained the same?

ery in quasi contract. A creditor receiving the money that is owed is not unjustly enriched thereby.[19]

(4) Gift Benefit. There can be no recovery for unjust enrichment when the circumstances are such that it is reasonable to conclude that goods or services were fur-

---

[19] Lynch v Deaconess Medical Center, 113 Wash 2d 162, 776 P2d 681 (1989).

nished to the benefited party with the intent to make a gift and not in the expectation of being compensated.[20]

(c) EXTENT OF RECOVERY. When recovery is allowed in quasi contract, the plaintiff recovers the reasonable value of the benefit conferred on the defendant.[21] The fact that the plaintiff may have sustained greater damages, or have been put to greater expense, is ignored. Thus, the plaintiff cannot recover lost profits or other kinds of damages that would be recovered in a suit for breach of a contract.

SUMMARY

A contract is a binding agreement between two or more parties. A contract arises when an offer is accepted with contractual intent (the intent to make a binding agreement).

Contracts may be classified in a number of ways: as to form, the way in which they were created, validity, and obligations. With respect to form, a contract may be either informal or formal, such as those under seal or those appearing on the records of courts or administrative agencies. Contracts may be classified by the way they were created as those that are expressed by words—written or oral—and those that are implied or deduced from conduct. The question of validity requires distinguishing between contracts that are valid; those that are voidable; and those that are not contracts at all, but are merely void agreements. Contracts can be distinguished on the basis of the obligations created, as executed contracts, in which everything has been performed, and executory contracts, in which something remains to be done. The bilateral contract is formed by exchanging a promise for a promise, so each party has the obligation of thereafter rendering the promised performance. In the unilateral contract, which is the doing of an act in exchange for a promise, no further performance is required of the offeree who performed the act. The only obligation is that of the promisor.

In certain situations, the law regards it as unjust that a person should receive a benefit and not pay for it. In such case, the law of quasi contracts allows the performing person to recover the reasonable value of the benefit conferred on the benefited person, even though there is no contract between them requiring any payment. The unjust enrichment, which a quasi contract is designed to prevent, sometimes arises when there never was any contract between the persons involved or when there was a contract, but for some reason it was avoided or held to be merely a void agreement. Quasi-contractual recovery is not allowed merely because someone loses money.

LAW IN PRACTICE

1. When you want to make a contract, be sure that the parties have expressed an intent to make a binding agreement. Just because all of you are friendly and amiable does not mean that the agreement you make is binding. A contractual intent must be manifested.

2. Make a sealed contract when the seal has significance. Check with your attorney to see what effect the seal will have in any of the jurisdictions that will be involved.

3. Avoid unilateral contracts when possible because of the uncertainty as to whether you have or will have a contract. (You do not know if the required performance will ever be rendered.) Make a bilateral contract if that is possible.

---

[20] Lewis Estate v Mordy, 168 Mich App 70, 423 NW2d 600 (1988). As noted in Section 9(b) of this chapter, no implied contract arises in this situation.

[21] Ramsey v Ellis (Wis) 484 NW2d 331 (1992).

4. Keep in mind that you have the possibility of being saved by a quasi contract if for some reason you do not have a binding agreement.

QUESTIONS AND CASE PROBLEMS

1. What social forces that shape the law (from the list in Chapter 2, Section 4) are illustrated by the following quotation: "A person shall not be allowed to enrich himself unjustly at the expense of another?"

Note: As you study the various rules of law in this chapter and the chapters that follow, consider each rule in relationship to its social, economic, and ethical background. Try to determine the particular objective(s) of each important rule. To the extent that you are able to analyze law as the product of society's striving for justice, you will have greater insight into the law itself, the world in which you live, the field of business, and the human mind.

2. What is a contract?

3. Karl went to the phone book and sent letters to randomly selected names. The letter to each stated: "It is agreed that we will paint your house for a price based on the cost of our labor and paint plus an additional 10 percent for profit." Maria received such a letter. Is there a contract between Karl and Maria?

4. Henry made a written contract to paint Betty's house for $500. The reasonable value of such work was $1,000. Henry made the price low in the hope that Betty's neighbors would have him paint their houses. He painted Betty's house. He did not get work from the neighbors. He then sent Betty a bill for $1,000 on the ground that an implied contract existed to pay him the reasonable value of his services. Was he entitled to recover $1,000?

5. Stephen said to Hilda, "I want to buy your old car." She replied, "It's yours for $400." Stephen replied, "I'll take it." Later Stephen changed his mind and refused to take or pay for the car. When Hilda sued him for damages, he raised the defense that he had never made a contract with her because they had never expressly stated, "We hereby make a contract for the sale of the car." Stephen claimed that in the absence of such an express declaration showing that they intended to make a contract, there could not be a binding agreement to purchase the car. Was he correct?

6. Compare an implied contract and a quasi contract.

7. A made a contract to construct a house for B. Subsequently, B sued A for breach of contract. A raised the defense that the contract was not binding because it was not sealed. Is this a valid defense? [*Cooper v G. E. Construction Co.* 116 Ga App 690, 158 SE2d 305]

8. Carlos Estaban was nine years old when his parents were killed in an auto crash. Maria Pedrillo, a friend of the family, took Carlos into her home and raised him. Carlos was never adopted by Maria, but all the neighbors thought he was related to Maria. About 20 years later Maria became very sick and, after a long period, died. During this time she was dependent on Carlos, who ran the house, prepared her meals, and did whatever had to be done. Carlos kept an itemized list of what he had done. He gave a copy of this list to the executor of Maria's estate and demanded that he be paid the reasonable value of his services. Was he entitled to compensation for such services?

9. Dozier and his wife, daughter, and grandson lived in the house Dozier owned. At the request of the daughter and grandson, Paschall made some improvements to the house. Dozier did not authorize these, but he knew that the improvements were being made and did not object to them. Paschall sued Dozier for the reasonable value of the improvements. Dozier defended on the ground that he had not made any contract for such improvements. Was he obligated to pay for such improvements?

10. Harriet went away for the summer. In her absence Landry, a house painter, painted her house. Landry had a contract to paint a neighbor's house, but painted Harriet's house by mistake. The painting of Harriet's house was worth $1,200. When she returned from her vacation, Landry billed her for $1,200. She refused to pay. He claimed that she had a quasi-contractual liability for that amount. Was he correct?

11. Margrethe and Charles Pyeatte were married. They agreed that she would work so that he could go to law school and that when he finished law school, she would go back to school for her masters degree. After Charles was admitted to the Bar and before Margrethe went back to school, the two were divorced. She sued Charles for breaking their contract. The court held that there was no contract because the agreement between them was too vague to be enforced. Margrethe then claimed that she was entitled to quasi-contractual recovery of the money that she had paid for Charles's support and law school tuition. He denied liability. Was she entitled to recover for the money she spent for Charles's maintenance and law school tuition? *[Pyeatte v Pyeatte (App) 135 Ariz 346, 661 P2d 196]*

12. Carriage Way was a real estate development of approximately 80 houses and 132 apartments. The property owners were members of the Carriage Way Property Owners Association. Each year, the association would take care of certain open neighboring areas that were used by the property owners, including a nearby lake. The board of directors of the association would make an assessment or charge against the property owners to cover the cost of this work. The property owners paid these assessments for a number of years and then refused to pay any more. In spite of this refusal, the association continued to take care of the areas in question. The association then sued the property owners and claimed that they were liable for the benefit that had been conferred on them. Were the owners liable? *[Board of Directors of Carriage Way Property Owners Assn v Western National Bank, 139 Ill App 3d 542, 94 Ill Dec 97, 487 NE2d 974]*

13. Lombard insured his car. When it was damaged, the insurer took the car to General Auto Service for repairs. The insurance company did not pay the repair bill. General Auto Service then sued Lombard for the repair bill because he had benefited by the repair work. Was he liable?

14. A student in a junior college course complained about a particular course. The vice president of the college requested the teacher to prepare a detailed report of the course in question. The teacher did so and then demanded additional compensation for the time spent in preparing the report. He claimed that the college was liable on an implied contract to make compensation. Was he correct? *[Zadrozny v City Colleges of Chicago, ____Ill App 3d____, ____Ill Dec____, 581 NE2d 44 (1991)]*

15. Smith made a contract to sell automatic rifles to a foreign country. The sale of such weapons to that country was made illegal by an Act of Congress. Smith was prosecuted by the United States government for making the contract. He raised the defense that because the contract was illegal, it was void, and that when a contract is void there is no binding obligation, and therefore there was no contract in existence for which he could be prosecuted. Was he correct?

CHAPTER 10
THE
AGREEMENT

LEARNING OBJECTIVES

After studying this chapter, you will be able to:
1. *Tell whether a statement is an offer or an invitation to negotiate.*
2. *Tell whether an agreement is too indefinite to be enforced.*
3. *Describe the exceptions that the law makes to the requirement of definiteness.*
4. *List the ways an offer is terminated.*
5. *Compare offers, firm offers, and option contracts.*
6. *Define what constitutes the acceptance of an offer.*

A contract consists of enforceable obligations that have been voluntarily assumed. Thus, one of the essential elements of a contract is an agreement. This chapter explains how the ba-

tion. This intent may be shown by conduct. For example, when one party signs a written contract and sends it to the other party, such action is an offer to enter into a contract on the

Figure 10-1   Offer and Acceptance

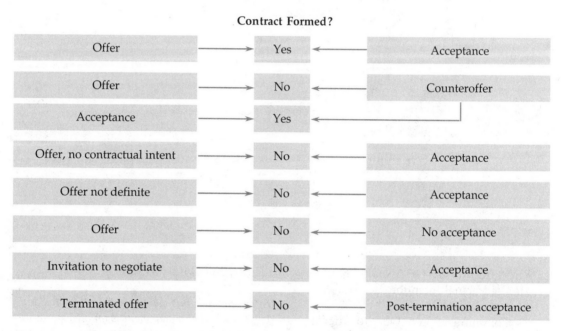

Contract Formed?

Offer	→ Yes ←	Acceptance
Offer	→ No ←	Counteroffer
Acceptance	→ Yes ←	
Offer, no contractual intent	→ No ←	Acceptance
Offer not definite	→ No ←	Acceptance
Offer	→ No ←	No acceptance
Invitation to negotiate	→ No ←	Acceptance
Terminated offer	→ No ←	Post-termination acceptance

sic agreement arises, when there is a contract, and how there can be merely unsuccessful negotiations without any contract resulting.

A. REQUIREMENTS OF AN OFFER

An **offer** expresses the willingness of the offeror to enter into a contractual agreement regarding a particular subject. It is a promise that is conditional upon an act, a forbearance, (a refraining from doing something one has a legal right to do), or a return promise.

1. Contractual Intention

To make an offer, the offeror must intend to or must appear to intend to create a legal obliga-

terms of the writing.[1]

There is no contract when a social invitation is made or when an offer is made in jest or excitement. A reasonable person would not regard such an offer as indicating a willingness to enter into a binding agreement.

(a) INVITATION TO NEGOTIATE. The first statement made by one of two persons is not necessarily an offer. In many instances, there may be a preliminary discussion or an invitation by one party to the other to negotiate or to make an offer. Thus, an inquiry by a school as to whether a teacher wished to continue the following year was merely a survey or invitation to negotiate and was not an offer that could be accepted. Therefore, the

---

[1] Arga Co. v Limbach, 36 Ohio 3d 220, 522 NE2d 1074 (1988).

teacher's affirmative response did not create a contract.[2]

Ordinarily, a seller sending out circulars or catalogs listing prices is not regarded as making an offer to sell at those prices. The seller is merely indicating a willingness to consider an offer made by a buyer on those terms. The reason for this rule is, in part, the practical consideration that since a seller does not have an unlimited supply of any commodity, the seller cannot possibly intend to make a contract with everyone who sees the circular. The same principle is applied to merchandise that is displayed with price tags in stores or store windows and to most advertisements. A "For Sale" advertisement in a newspaper is merely an invitation to negotiate and is not an offer that can be accepted by a reader of the paper.

Quotations of prices, even when sent on request, are likewise not offers unless there have been previous dealings between the parties or unless a trade custom exists that would give the recipient of the quotation reason to believe that an offer was being made. Whether a price quotation is to be treated as an offer or merely an invitation to negotiate is a question of the intent of the party giving the quotation. Although sellers are not bound by quotations and price tags, they will, as a matter of goodwill, ordinarily make every effort to deliver the merchandise at those prices.[3]

In some instances, it is apparent that an invitation to negotiate rather than an offer has been made. When construction work is done for the national government, for a state government, or for a political subdivision, statutes require that a printed statement of the work to be done be published and circulated. Contractors are invited to submit bids on the work, and the statute generally requires that the bid of the lowest responsible bidder be accepted. Such an invitation for bids is clearly an invitation to negotiate, both from its nature and from the fact that it does not specify the price to be paid for the work. The bid of each contractor is an offer, and there is no contract until the government accepts one of these bids.[4] This procedure of advertising for bids is also commonly employed by private persons when a large construction project is involved.

In some cases, the fact that important terms are missing indicates that the parties are merely negotiating and that an oral contract has not been made. When a letter or printed promotional matter of a party leaves many significant details to be worked out later, the letter or printed matter is merely an invitation to negotiate. It is not an offer that may be accepted and a contract thereby formed.

(b) STATEMENT OF INTENTION. In some instances, a person may make a statement of intention but not intend to be bound by a contract. For example, a certain lease does not expressly allow the tenant to terminate the lease in the case of a job transfer. The landlord states that should the tenant be required to leave for that reason, the landlord would try to find a new tenant to take over the lease. This declaration of intention does not give rise to a binding contract. The landlord cannot be held liable for breach of contract if the landlord should fail to obtain a new tenant or not even attempt to obtain a new tenant.

(c) AGREEMENT TO MAKE A CONTRACT AT A FUTURE DATE. No contract arises when the parties merely agree that at a future date they will consider making a contract or will make a contract on terms to be agreed on at that time. In such a case, neither party is under any obligation until the future contract is made. Similarly, there is no contract between the parties if essential terms are left open for future negotiation.[5] Thus, a promise to pay a bonus or compensation to be decided on after three months of business operation is not binding. Likewise, no binding contract to

---

[2] Knipmeyer v Diocese of Alexandria (La App) 492 So 2d 550 (1986).

[3] Statutes prohibiting false or misleading advertising may also require adherence to advertised prices.

[4] Peerless Food Products, Inc. v Washington, 119 Wash 2d 584, P2d 1012 (1992).

[5] Hansen v Phillips Beverage Co. (Minn App) 487 NW2d 925 (1992).

renew a contract when it expires was created by a provision in the original contract that when it expires the parties intend to "negotiate in good faith to renew this agreement for an additional year upon terms and conditions to be negotiated."[6] When the parties have prepared a draft agreement but it is clear that such agreement is not regarded by them as final, the draft is merely a step in negotiations and is not a contract.[7]

The *Beck* case raised the question of whether the parties had entered into a binding agreement.

BECK v AMERICAN HEALTH GROUP INTERNATIONAL

211 Cal App 3d 1555, 260 Cal Rptr 237 (1989)

Beck sued the American Health Group for breach of an alleged contract to employ him as psychiatrist for the Palmdale Hospital Medical Center. He placed in evidence a letter written to him by the executive director of the defendant. The letter stated the terms that were being considered and concluded: "If this is a general understanding of the agreement, I ask that you sign a copy of this letter, so that I might forward to Corporate Counsel for the drafting of a contract. When we have a draft, we will discuss it, and hopefully shall have a completed contract and operating unit in the very near future." Beck claimed that there was a binding contract when he signed and mailed this letter as requested. The defendant denied that there was a contract. Judgment was entered for the defendant, and Beck appealed.

LILLIE, J. . . . "Whether a writing constitutes a final agreement or merely an agreement to make an agreement depends primarily upon the intention of the parties. In the absence of ambiguity this must be determined by a construction of the instrument taken as a whole." . . . "Preliminary negotiations or an agreement for future negotiations are not the functional equivalent of a valid, subsisting agreement. 'A manifestation of willingness to enter into a bargain is not an offer if the person to whom it is addressed knows or has reason to know that the person making it does not intend to conclude a bargain until he has made a further manifestation of assent.' " . . . The words of a written instrument are generally to be understood in their ordinary and popular sense. . . . The objective intent as evidenced by the words of the instrument, not the parties' subjective intent, governs our interpretation. "The outward manifestation or expression of assent is controlling . . . and . . . what the language of an [instrument] means is a 'matter of interpretation for the courts and not controlled in any sense by what either of the parties intended or thought its meaning to be. . . .' "

The letter under consideration begins: "It is a pleasure to draft the *outline of our future agreement.* . . ." (Emphasis added.) After outlining the terms of the proposed agreement the writer of the letter asks plaintiff to sign it "if this is a general understanding

6 Yans Video, Inc. v Hong Kong TV Video Programs, Inc. 133 App Div 2d 575, 520 NYS2d 143 (1987).

7 Spigler v Southeastern Public Service Co. (Fla App) 610 So 2d 521 (1992).

of the agreement," in order that the Hospital may "forward it to Corporate Counsel *for the drafting of a contract.*" (Emphasis added.) The letter concludes: "When we have a draft, we will discuss it, and *hopefully shall have a completed contract* and operating unit in the very near future." (Emphasis added.) Taken in their ordinary sense, the words of the letter manifest an intention of the parties that no binding contract would come into being until the terms of the letter were embodied in a formal contract to be drafted by corporate counsel. Assignment of the drafting to an attorney evidences an expectation that the terms set forth in the letter were subject to his approval. Even after counsel drafted a contract the letter contemplated further negotiations by its statement that "when we have a draft, we will discuss it." By signing the letter plaintiff assented to its terms, i.e., no binding agreement would result until a formal contract was drafted by counsel. That plaintiff may have intended or believed a binding contract came into existence upon his signing the letter is immaterial in the face of its language which plainly indicated otherwise.

We conclude that the letter did not constitute a binding contract, but was merely "an agreement to agree." . . .

[Judgment affirmed]

QUESTIONS

1. How did the court regard the letter relied on by the plaintiff?
2. What was the controlling factor in the decision of the *Beck* case?

2. Definiteness

An offer, and the resulting contract, must be definite and certain.[8] If an offer is indefinite or vague or if an essential provision is lacking,[9] no contract arises from an attempt to accept it. The reason is that the courts cannot tell what the parties are to do. Thus, an offer to conduct a business for as long as it is profitable is too vague to be a valid offer. The acceptance of such an offer does not result in a contract that can be enforced. Likewise, a promise to give an injured employee "suitable" employment that the employee is "able to do" is too vague to be a binding contract. A statement by a landlord to the tenant that "some day it [the rented land] will be your own" is too indefinite to be an offer, and no contract for the sale of the land arises when the tenant agrees to the statement.

The fact that minor details are left for future determination does not make the agreement too vague to be a contract.[10]

The law does not favor the destruction of contracts, because that would go against the social force of carrying out the intent of the parties. Consequently, when it is claimed that a contract is too indefinite to be enforced, a court will do its best to find the intent of the parties and thereby reach the conclusion that the contract is not too indefinite. However, a court may not rewrite the agreement of the parties in order to make it definite.[11]

---

8   Around The World Importing, Inc. v Mercantile Trust Co. (Mo App) 795 SW2d 85 (1990).

9   T.O. Stanley Boot Co., Inc. v Bank of El Paso (Tex) 847 SW2d 218 (1993).

10 Hsu v Vet-A-Mix, Inc. (Iowa App) 479 NW2d 336 (1991).

11 Hamrick v Kelley, 260 Ga 307, 392 SE2d 518 (1990).

(a) DEFINITE BY INCORPORATION. A n offer and the resulting contract that by themselves may appear "too indefinite" may be made definite by reference to another writing. For example, a lease agreement that was too vague by itself was made definite because the parties agreed that the lease should follow the standard form with which both were familiar. An agreement may also be made definite by reference to the prior dealings of the parties and to trade practices.

(b) IMPLIED TERMS. Although an offer must be definite and certain, not all of its terms need to be expressed. Some of the omitted terms may be implied by law. For example, an offer "to pay $50 for a watch" does not state the terms of payment. A court, however, would not condemn this provision as too vague, but would hold that it required that cash be paid and that the payment be made on delivery of the watch. Likewise, terms may be implied from conduct. As an illustration, where the borrowed money was given to the borrower by a check that the word *loan* was written on, the act of the borrower in endorsing the check constituted an agreement to repay the amount of the check.

(c) DIVISIBLE CONTRACTS. When the agreement consists of two or more parts and calls for corresponding performances of each part by the parties, the agreement is a **divisible contract**. Thus, in a promise to buy several separate articles at different prices at the same time, the agreement may be regarded as separate or divisible promises for the articles. When a contract contains a number of provisions or performances to be rendered, the question arises as to whether the parties intended merely a group of separate, divisible contracts or whether it was to be a package deal so that complete performance by each party was essential.

(d) UNIMPORTANT VAGUE DETAILS IGNORED. If a term that is too vague is not important, it may sometimes be ignored. If the balance of the agreement is definite, there can then be a binding contract. For example,

where the parties agreed that one of them would manage a motel that was being constructed for the other, and where it was agreed that the contract would start to run before the completion of the construction, the management contract did not fail because it did not specify any date on which it was to begin. It was apparent that the exact date was not essential and could not be determined at the time when the contract was made.

(e) EXCEPTIONS TO DEFINITENESS. The law has come to recognize certain situations where the practical necessity of doing business makes it desirable to have a contract, yet the situation is such that it is either impossible or undesirable to adopt definite terms in advance. In these cases, the indefinite term is often tied to the concept of good-faith performance or to some independent factor that will be definitely ascertainable at some time in the future. For example, the indefinite term might be tied to market price, cost to complete, or production requirements. Thus, the law recognizes binding contracts in the case of a **requirements contract**, a contract to buy all requirements of the buyer from the seller. The law also recognizes as binding an **output contract**, the contract of a producer to sell the entire production or output to a given buyer. These are binding contracts, although they do not state the exact quantity of goods that are to be bought or sold. Contracts are also binding although they run for an indefinite period of time, require a buyer to pay the costs plus a percentage of costs as profit, or require one person to supply professional services as needed.

3. Communication of Offer to Offeree

The offer must be communicated to the offeree. Otherwise, the offeree cannot accept, even though knowledge of the offer has been indirectly acquired. Internal management communications of an enterprise that are not intended for outsiders or employees do not constitute offers and cannot be accepted by them. Sometimes, particularly in the case of unilateral contracts, the offeree performs the act called for by the offeror without knowing of the offer's existence. Such performance does not constitute an acceptance. Thus, without knowing that a reward is offered for the arrest of a particular criminal, a person may arrest the criminal. In most states, if that person subsequently learns that a reward has been offered for the arrest, the reward cannot be recovered.[12]

Not only must the offer be communicated, but it must be communicated by the offeror or at the offeror's direction.

B. TERMINATION OF OFFER

An offeree cannot accept a terminated offer. Offers may be terminated by revocation, counteroffer, rejection, lapse of time, death or disability of a party, or subsequent illegality.

4. Revocation of Offer by Offeror

Ordinarily, the offeror can revoke the offer before it is accepted. If this is done, the offeree cannot create a contract by accepting the revoked offer. Thus, the bidder at an auction sale may withdraw (revoke) a bid (offer) before it is accepted. The auctioneer cannot later accept that bid.

An ordinary offer may be revoked at any time before it is accepted, even though the offeror has expressly promised that the offer will be good for a stated period and that period has not yet expired. It may also be revoked even though the offeror has expressly promised to the offeree that the offer would not be revoked before a specified later date.

(a) WHAT CONSTITUTES A REVOCATION. No particular form or words are required to constitute a revocation. Any words indicating the offeror's termination of the offer are sufficient. A notice sent to the offeree that the property that is the subject of the offer has been sold to a third person is a revocation of the offer. A customer's order for goods, which is an offer to purchase at certain prices, is revoked by a notice to the seller of the cancellation of the order, provided such notice is communicated before the order is accepted.

(b) COMMUNICATION OF REVOCATION. A revocation of an offer is ordinarily effective only when it is made known to the offeree. Until it is communicated to the offeree, directly or indirectly, the offeree has reason to believe that there is still an offer that may be accepted, and the offeree may rely on this belief.

Except in a few states, a letter or telegram revoking an offer made to a particular offeree is not effective until received by the offeree. It is not a revocation at the time it is written by the offeror or even when it is mailed or dispatched. A written revocation is effective, however, when it is delivered to the offeree's agent, or to the offeree's residence or place of business under such circumstances that the offeree may be reasonably expected to be aware of its receipt.

It is ordinarily held that there is a sufficient communication of the revocation when the offeree learns indirectly of the offeror's revocation. This is particularly true in a land sale, when the seller-offeror, after making an offer to sell the land to the offeree, sells the land to a third person, and the offeree indirectly learns of such sale. The offeree necessarily realizes that the seller cannot perform the original offer and therefore must be considered to have revoked it.[13]

If the offeree accepts an offer before it is effectively revoked, a valid contract is created. Thus, there may be a contract when the offeree mails or telegraphs an acceptance without

---

[12] With respect to the offeror, it should not make any difference, as a practical matter, whether the services were rendered with or without knowledge of the existence of the offer. Only a small number of states have adopted this view, however.

[13] First Development Corp. v Martin Marietta Corp. (CA6 Ky) 959 F2d 617 (1992).

knowing that a letter of revocation has already been mailed.

(c) OPTION CONTRACTS. An **option contract** is a binding promise to keep an offer open for a stated period of time or until a specified date. An option contract requires that the promisor receive consideration—that is, something, such as a sum of money, as the price for the promise to keep the offer open. In other words, the option is a contract to refrain from revoking an offer.

When an option contract recites the giving of a specified consideration, but such consideration in fact was never paid, the option contract is merely an offer. It may be revoked at any time prior to acceptance.

(d) FIRM OFFERS. As another exception to the rule that an offer can be revoked at any time before acceptance, statutes in some states provide that an offeror cannot revoke an offer prior to its expiration when the offeror makes a firm offer. A **firm offer** is an offer that states that it is to be irrevocable, or irrevocable for a stated period of time. Under the Uniform Commercial Code, this doctrine of firm offers applies to a merchant's signed, written offer to buy or sell goods, but with a maximum of three months on its period of irrevocability.[14]

(e) DETRIMENTAL RELIANCE. There is growing authority that when the offeror foresees that the offeree will rely on the offer's remaining open, the offeror is obligated to keep the offer open for a reasonable time. The concept of detrimental reliance can thus prevent the revocation of an offer. This was the issue in the *Arango Construction* case.

ARANGO CONSTRUCTION CO. v SUCCESS ROOFING, INC.

46 Wash App 314, 730 P2d 720 (1986)

Arango Construction Company wanted to do certain construction work for the United States government. In preparing its bid, Arango phoned Success Roofing to see what it would charge for doing the roofing work involved. Success offered to do the work for a specified price. Arango then made a bid to the government. Its bid was accepted. Thereafter Success notified Arango that it was withdrawing its bid to do the roofing work because it had made a significant mistake in its calculation. Arango claimed it could not do this because Arango had used the bid in making its own bid to the United States. Arango sued Success for damages caused by the revocation of its bid. From a judgment for Success, Arango appealed.

COLEMAN, J. . . . In contract law, construction bidding is treated as a unique category. Since construction bidding deadlines make the drafting of written agreements impossible, contractors must rely on oral bids. Therefore, the courts consider the subcontractor's oral bid an irrevocable offer until the general contractor has been awarded the prime contract; then the courts apply promissory estoppel to ensure

---

[14] UCC §2-205.

that the subcontractor does not raise the bid. This concept was explained in J. Feinman, *Promissory Estoppel and Judicial Methods,* 97 Harv L Rev 678, (1984).

A recurrent example of the flexible approach . . . is found in the courts' treatment of construction bidding cases, which have repeatedly generated important promissory estoppel decisions. In the typical case, a general contractor preparing to bid on a construction project receives bids on parts of the job from subcontractors and suppliers. The general then prepares its own bid on the basis of the lowest reliable subcontract bids. Subcontractors occasionally miscalculate, in part because they often compute their bids and telephone them to the general only hours before the general's bid is due. A subcontractor may also intentionally submit a low bid in the hope of receiving the contract and renegotiating the price. Conflict typically arises when, after the general has calculated and submitted its own bid and won the contract, a subcontractor notifies the general that the subcontractor has made an error or an intentionally low bid and refuses to perform.

Under traditional contract analysis, the subcontractor could withdraw with impunity, because its bid was regarded as an offer, revocable until accepted, to enter into a bilateral contract. In the leading case of *Drennan v Star Paving Co.,* [51 Cal 2d 409, 333 P2d 757 (1958)], however, Justice Traynor held that the business context of the bid required that promissory estoppel apply to make the subcontractor's offer irrevocable until the general contractor had an opportunity to accept after being awarded the prime contract. The general's acceptance of the subcontractor's bid then created a traditional bilateral contract, for breach of which the subcontractor was required to pay as damages the difference between its bid and the higher price the general had to pay another subcontractor to perform the work. Cases since *Drennan* have held that promissory estoppel normally binds a subcontractor to the terms of its bid. Although the subcontractor does not make an explicit promise to keep its bid open, the court infers such a promise. . . .

This court has accepted the *Drennan* rationale in *Ferrer v Taft Structural, Inc.,* 21 Wash App 832, 587 P2d 177 (1978).

This concept [of promissory estoppel] applies readily to the unique situation of a subcontractor and a general contractor, as exists here. A subcontractor submits a bid to the general contractor, knowing the general cannot accept the bid as an offer immediately, but must first incorporate it into the general's offer to the prospective employer. The general contractor incorporates the bid in reliance upon the subcontractor to perform as promised, should the prospective employer accept the general's offer. Thus, the elements of predictable and justifiable reliance and change of position are satisfied. Numerous courts and authorities have opined that a subcontractor's bid upon which a general contractor relies should be deemed irrevocable for a reasonable time pursuant to the doctrine of promissory estoppel. . . .

Thus, as a matter of law, a subcontractor's bid is considered an irrevocable offer until the award of the prime contract; then, the general contractor's acceptance of the bid results in a bilateral contract. . . . Thus, if the subcontractor refuses to perform following the award of the contract, the general contractor may recover damages under the doctrine of promissory estoppel. . .

The *Ferrer* court listed the five elements of promissory estoppel:

. . . (1) A promise which (2) the promisor should reasonably expect to cause the promisee to change his position and (3) which does cause the promisee to change his position (4) justifiably

relying upon the promise, in such a manner that (5) injustice can be avoided only by enforcement of the promise.

. . . Success's bid was a promise. Success could reasonably expect that promise to cause Arango to change position by including the Success bid in Arango's prime bid. Success confirmed its bid 2 days after it was given, and Arango informed Success that it would be including that bid in its prime bid to be submitted 13 days later. Arango did include Success's bid in its prime bid, thereby changing its position.

The only element of promissory estoppel in dispute is whether Arango justifiably relied on Success's bid. Success contends that as a prudent and experienced general contractor, Arango should have known that Success's bid was too low for the job involved. . . . Success had to present evidence supporting this assertion. Success, however, has submitted no evidence that Arango should have known. The only other bid found in the record was from Tin Benders. Its bid was for $38,500 . . . as compared to the $34,659 bid by Success. There is nothing in the record to support an inference that Arango knew or should have known that Success had made a mistake.

. . .

The judgment of the trial court is reversed and the cause remanded with instruction to enter judgment in favor of Arango on its complaint for damages.

[Judgment reversed and action remanded]

QUESTIONS

1. Was the decision in the *Arango Construction* case in harmony with general contract law? Explain.
2. What social forces are advanced by the decision? Explain.
3. How could the problem in the *Arango Construction* case have been avoided?

5. Counteroffer by Offeree

If the offeree purports to accept an offer but in so doing makes any change to the terms of the offer, such action is a counteroffer that rejects the original offer.[15]

Ordinarily, if *A* makes an offer, such as to sell a used automobile to *B* for $1,000, and *B* in reply makes an offer to buy at $750, the original offer is terminated. *B* is in effect indicating refusal of the original offer and in its place making a different offer. Such an offer by the offeree is known as a **counteroffer**. No contract arises unless the original offeror accepts the counteroffer.

Counteroffers are not limited to offers that directly contradict the original offers. Any departure from, or addition to, the original offer is a counteroffer, even though the original offer was silent on the point added by the counteroffer. For example, when the offeree stated that the offer was accepted and added that time was of the essence, the acceptance was a counteroffer because the original offer had been silent on that point. A conditional acceptance is a counteroffer.[16]

---

[15] Louisiana Commercial Bank v Georgia International Life Ins. Co. (La App) 618 So 2d 1091 (1993).
[16] Anand v Marple, 167 Ill App 3d 918, 118 Ill Dec 826, 522 NE2d 281 (1988).

6. Rejection of Offer by Offeree

If the offeree rejects the offer and communicates this rejection to the offeror, the offer is terminated. Communication of a rejection terminates an offer even though the period for which the offeror agreed to keep the offer open has not yet expired. It may be that the offeror is willing to renew the offer, but unless this is done, there is no longer any offer for the offeree to accept.

7. Lapse of Time

When the offer states that it is open until a particular date, the offer terminates on that date if it has not yet been accepted. This is particularly so where the offeror declares that the offer shall be void after the expiration of the specified time. Such limitations are strictly construed. When a specified time limitation is imposed on an option, the option cannot be exercised after the expiration of that time, regardless of whether the option was exercised within what would have been held a reasonable time if no time period had been specified.[17] It has been held that the buyer's attempt to exercise an option one day late had no effect.

If the offer does not specify a time, it will terminate after the lapse of a reasonable time. What constitutes a reasonable time depends on the circumstances of each case—that is, on the nature of the subject matter, the nature of the market in which it is sold, the time of year, and other factors of supply and demand. If a commodity is perishable or fluctuates greatly in value, the reasonable time will be much shorter than if the subject matter is a staple article. An offer to sell a harvested crop of tomatoes would expire within a very short time. When a seller purports to accept an offer after it has lapsed by the expiration of time, the seller's acceptance is merely a counteroffer and does not create a contract unless that counteroffer is accepted by the buyer.

8. Death or Disability of Either Party

If either the offeror or the offeree dies or becomes insane before the offer is accepted, the offer is automatically terminated.

9. Subsequent Illegality

If the performance of the contract becomes illegal after the offer is made, the offer is terminated. Thus, if an offer is made to sell alcoholic liquors but a law prohibiting such sales is enacted before the offer is accepted, the offer is terminated.

C. ACCEPTANCE OF OFFER

An **acceptance** is the assent of the offeree to the terms of the offer. No particular form of words or mode of expression is required, but there must be a clear expression that the offeree agrees to be bound by the terms of the offer.

10. Privilege of Offeree

Ordinarily, the offeree may refuse to accept an offer. If there is no acceptance, by definition there is no contract. The fact that there had been a series of contracts between the parties and that one party's offer had always been accepted before by the other does not create any legal obligation to continue to accept subsequent offers.

Certain partial exceptions exist to the privilege of the offeree to refuse to accept an offer.

(a) PLACES OF PUBLIC ACCOMMODATION AND PUBLIC UTILITIES. Places of public accommodation and public utilities are under a duty to serve any fit person. They cannot refuse to serve a person because of a disability.[18] When a person offers to register at a hotel, the hotel has the obligation to accept the offer and to enter into a contract for the renting

---

[17] Watson v Hatch (Utah) 728 P2d 989 (1986).

[18] Americans with Disabilities Act of 1990, Act of July 26, 1990, PL 101-336, 104 Stat 327, 42 USC § 12101.

of the room. However, there is no duty on the part of the hotel to accept unless the person is properly attired, is behaving properly, and the hotel has space available.

(b) ANTIDISCRIMINATION. When offers are solicited from members of the general public, an offer generally may not be rejected because of the race, nationality, religion, or color of the offeror. If the solicitor of the offer is willing to enter into a contract to rent, sell, or employ, antidiscrimination laws compel the solicitor to accept an offer from any otherwise fit person.

(c) CONSUMER PROTECTION. Statutes and regulations designed to protect consumers from false advertising may require a seller to accept an offer from a customer to purchase advertised goods and may impose a penalty for an unjustified refusal.

11. Effect of Acceptance

When an offer has been accepted, a binding agreement or contract is created,[19] assuming that all of the other elements of a contract are present. Neither party can subsequently withdraw from or cancel the contract without the consent of the other party (or the existence of facts that under the law justify such unilateral action). For example, when an enterprise conducts a prize contest, its offer to conduct the contest according to stated rules is accepted when an entrant sends in the entry form. The enterprise must then conduct the contest according to the announced contest rules because it is bound by a contract.

12. Nature of the Acceptance

An acceptance is the offeree's manifestation of intent to enter into a binding agreement on the terms stated in the offer. Whether there is an acceptance depends on whether the offeree

has manifested an intent to accept. It is the objective or outward appearance that is controlling, rather than the subjective or unexpressed intent of the offeree.[20]

In the absence of a contrary requirement in the offer, an acceptance may be indicated by an informal "okay," by a mere affirmative nod of the head, or, in the case of an offer of a unilateral contract, by performing the act called for. However, while the acceptance of an offer may be shown by conduct, it must be very clear that the offeree intended to accept the offer.

The acceptance must be absolute and unconditional. It must accept just what is offered. If the offeree changes any terms of the offer or adds any new term, there is no acceptance, because the offeree does not agree to what was offered.

Where the offeree does not accept the offer exactly as made, the addition of any qualification converts the "acceptance" into a counteroffer, and no contract arises unless such a counteroffer is accepted by the original offeror.[21]

The addition of new terms in the acceptance, however, does not always mean that the attempted acceptance fails. The acceptance is still unqualified if the new terms are merely those that (1) would be implied by law as part of the offer, (2) constitute a mere request, or (3) relate to a mere clerical detail.

In the *Fries* case, the court was faced with the question whether the holder of an option to buy land could elect to buy only a portion of the land.

13. Who May Accept

An offer may be accepted only by the person to whom it is directed. If anyone else attempts to accept it, no agreement or contract with that person arises.

If the offer is directed to a particular class, rather than a specified individual, it may be accepted by anyone within that class. If the

---

[19] Woods v Morgan City Lions Club (La App) 558 So 2d 1196 (1991).
[20] Schwandt Sanitation of Paynesville v City of Paynesville (Minn App) 423 NW2d 59 (1988).
[21] Logan Ranch, Karg Partnership v Farm Credit Bank of Omaha, 238 Neb 814, 472 NW2d 704 (1991).

FRIES v FRIES

(ND) 470 NW2d 232 (1991)

Jake Fries had an option to purchase at $223 an acre a 160-acre farm owned by Mary Fries. He transferred this option to his seven children. He died from cancer a few months later. Six of the seven children then claimed 6/7ths of the land by virtue of the option. Mary refused to recognize a fractional exercise of the option. Some of the children sued her to enforce this option. From a decision enforcing the option, she appealed.

ERICKSTAD, C. J. . . . An optionee must exercise an option within the time and upon the terms and conditions provided in the option agreement. . . . The offer contained in an option agreement must be accepted unequivocally and in accordance with the terms of the option. . . . The acceptance must be unconditional and without modification or imposition of new terms. . . . Because the optionee is free to exercise or not exercise the option, but the optionor is bound to perform if the option is properly exercised, courts strictly hold an optionee to "exact compliance" with the terms of the option. . . .

An option contract is not divisible unless the option agreement expressly provides otherwise. . . .

In the absence of a provision in the option contract authorizing an election to purchase part of the property covered by the option, the optionee is not entitled to elect to purchase less than the whole, which is another way of saying that the election, by the optionee, must conform with the terms of the option.

The attempt . . . to purchase a portion of Mary's quarter section was an ineffective exercise of the option.

[Action remanded with direction to dismiss]

QUESTIONS

1. Why does the court apply the law of acceptance of offers to an option case?
2. What argument could be made in support of the claim of the children that they were not required to buy all or none?
3. What objections are there to the argument that a fractional purchase was not prohibited?
4. What other defense could the defendant have raised in the *Fries* case?

offer is made to the public at large, it may be accepted by any member of the public at large having knowledge of the existence of the offer.

When a person to whom an offer was not made attempts to accept it, the attempted acceptance has the effect of an offer. If the original offeror is willing to accept this offer, a binding contract arises. If the original offeror does not accept the new offer, there is no contract.

14. Manner of Acceptance

The offeror may specify the manner for accepting the offer. When the offeror specifies that there must be a written acceptance, no contract arises when the offeree makes an oral acceptance. If the offeror calls for acceptance by a specified date, a late acceptance has no effect. When an acceptance is required by return mail, it is usually held that the letter of acceptance must be mailed the same day that the offer was received by the offeree. If the offer specifies that the acceptance be made by the performance of an act by the offeree, the latter cannot accept by making a promise to do the act but must actually perform it.

When the offer calls for the performance of an act or of certain conduct, the performance thereof is an acceptance of the offer and creates a unilateral contract.

When a person accepts services offered by another and it reasonably appears that compensation was expected, the acceptance of the services without any protest constitutes an acceptance of the offer. As a result, a contract exists for the payment for the services.

When the offeror has specified a particular manner of acceptance, the offeree cannot accept in any other way.[22] However, acceptance in some other way is effective (a) if the manner of acceptance specified was merely a suggested alternative and was not clearly the exclusive method of acceptance, or (b) if the offeror has proceeded on the basis that there had been an effective acceptance.

(a) SILENCE AS ACCEPTANCE. In most cases, the offeree's silence and failure to act cannot be regarded as an acceptance. Ordinarily, the offeror is not permitted to frame an offer in such a way as to make the silence and inaction of the offeree operate as an acceptance.

In the case of prior dealings between the parties, as in a record or book club, the offeree may have a duty to reject an offer expressly, and the offeree's silence may be regarded as an acceptance.

(b) UNORDERED GOODS AND TICKETS. Sometimes a seller writes to a person with whom the seller has not had any prior dealings stating that, unless notified to the contrary, the seller will send specified merchandise and the recipient is obligated to pay for it at stated prices. There is no acceptance if the recipient of the letter ignores the offer and does nothing. The silence of the person receiving the letter is not an acceptance, and the sender, as a reasonable person, should recognize that none was intended.

This rule applies to all kinds of goods, books, magazines, and tickets sent through the mail when they have not been ordered. The fact that the items are not returned does not mean that they have been accepted; that is, the offeree is neither required to pay for nor return the items. If desired, the recipient of the unordered goods may write "Return to Sender" on the unopened package and put the package back into the mail without any additional postage. The Postal Reorganization Act of 1970 provides that the person who receives unordered mailed merchandise from a commercial (noncharitable) sender has the right "to retain, use, discard, or dispose of it in any manner the recipient sees fit without any obligation whatsoever to the sender."[23] It provides further that any unordered merchandise that is mailed must have attached to it a clear and conspicuous statement of the recipient's right to treat the goods in this manner.

15. Communication of Acceptance

If the offeree accepts the offer, must the offeror be notified? The answer depends on the nature of the offer.

(a) UNILATERAL CONTRACT. If the offeror makes an offer of a unilateral contract, communication of acceptance is ordinarily not necessary. In such a case, the offeror calls for a completed or accomplished act. If that act is performed by the offeree with knowledge of the offer, the offer is accepted without any further action by way of notifying the offeror. As a practical matter, there will eventually be

---

[22] Hreha v Nemecek, 119 Or App 65, 849 P2d 1131 (1993).
[23] Federal Postal Reorganization Act § 3009.

some notice to the offeror, because the offeree who has performed the act will ask the offeror to pay for the performance that has been rendered.

(b) BILATERAL CONTRACT. If the offer pertains to a bilateral contract, an acceptance is not effective unless communicated. The acceptance must be communicated directly to the offeror or the offeror's agent.

16.   Acceptance by Mail

When the offeree sends an acceptance by mail, questions may arise as to the right to use such means of communication and the time the acceptance is effective.

(a) RIGHT TO USE MAIL. Express directions of the offeror, prior dealings between the parties, or custom of the trade may make it clear that only one method of acceptance is proper. For example, in negotiations with respect to property of rapidly fluctuating value, such as wheat or corporation stocks, an acceptance sent by mail may be too slow. When there is no indication that mail is not a proper method, an acceptance may be made by this means regardless of how the offer was made. The trend of the modern decisions supports the following provision of the Uniform Commercial Code relating to sales of personal property: "Unless otherwise unambiguously indicated by the language or circumstances, an offer to make a [sales] contract shall be construed as inviting acceptance in any manner and by any medium reasonable in the circumstances."[24]

(b) WHEN ACCEPTANCE BY MAIL IS EFFECTIVE. If the offeror does not specify otherwise, a mailed acceptance takes effect when the acceptance is properly mailed. This is called the "mailbox rule." If the offeror specifies that an acceptance shall not be effective until received, there is no acceptance until the acceptance is received. Likewise, the "mailbox rule" does not apply when the offeror requires receipt of a payment to accompany an acceptance.

The handing of an acceptance letter by the offeree to the offeree's mail clerk does not constitute mailing within the above mailbox rule.[25]

The letter must be properly addressed to the offeror, and any other precaution that is ordinarily observed to ensure safe transmission must be taken. If it is not mailed in this manner, the acceptance does not take effect when mailed, but only when received by the offeror.

The rule that a properly mailed acceptance takes effect at the time it is mailed is applied strictly. The rule applies even if the acceptance letter never reaches the offeror.

It is probable that the mailbox rule will be applied to an acceptance sent by fax, without regard to whether the transmitting machine is owned by the offeree or by an independent contractor.

(c) PROOF OF ACCEPTANCE BY MAIL. How can the time of mailing be established, or even the fact of mailing in the case of a destroyed or lost letter? The problem is not one of law but one of fact: a question of proving the case to the jury. The offeror may testify in court that an acceptance was never received or that an acceptance was sent after the offer had been revoked. The offeree may then testify that the acceptance letter was mailed at a particular time and place. The offeree's case will be strengthened if postal receipts for the mailing and delivery of a letter sent to the offeror can be produced, although these, of course, do not establish the contents of the letter. Ultimately, the case goes to the jury (or to the judge, if a jury trial has been waived) to determine whether the acceptance was made at a certain time and place as claimed by the offeree.

---

[24] UCC §2-206 (1)(a). DeFeo v Amfarms Associates, 161 App Div 2d 904, 557 NYS2d 469 (1990).

[25] Gibbs v American Savings & Loan Assn. 217 Cal App 3d 1372, 266 Cal Rptr 517 (1990).

17. Acceptance by Telephone

Ordinarily, acceptance of an offer may be made by telephone unless the circumstances are such that, by the intent of the parties or the law of the state, no acceptance can be made or contract arise in the absence of a writing.

A telephoned acceptance is effective when and where the acceptance is spoken into the phone. Consequently, when a person who lived in Kansas applied for a job in Missouri and the employer telephoned from Missouri to Kansas accepting the application, the employment contract was a Missouri contract. Thus, the Kansas Workers' Compensation statute did not apply when the employee was subsequently injured.

18. Auction Sales

At an auction sale, the statements made by the auctioneer to draw forth bids are merely invitations to negotiate. Each bid is an offer, which is not accepted until the auctioneer indicates that a particular offer or bid is accepted. Usually this is done by the fall of the auctioneer's hammer, indicating that the highest bid made has been accepted. Since a bid is merely an offer, the bidder may withdraw the bid at any time before it is accepted by the auctioneer.

Ordinarily, the auctioneer may withdraw any article or all of the property from the sale if not satisfied with the amounts of the bids that are being made. Once a bid is accepted, however, the auctioneer cannot cancel the sale. In addition, if it had been announced that the sale was to be made "without reserve," the property must be sold to the person making the highest bid, regardless of how low that bid may be.

SUMMARY

Because a contract arises when an offer is accepted, it is necessary to find that there was an offer and that it was accepted. If either element is missing, there is no contract.

An offer does not exist unless the offeror has contractual intent. This intent is lacking if the statement of the person is merely an invitation to negotiate, a statement of intention, or an agreement to agree at a later date. Newspaper ads, price quotations, and catalog prices are ordinarily merely invitations to negotiate and cannot be accepted.

An offer must be definite. If an offer is indefinite, its acceptance will not create a contract, because it will be held that the resulting agreement is too vague to enforce. In some cases, an offer that is by itself too indefinite is made definite because some writing or standard is incorporated by reference and made part of the offer. In some cases, the offer is made definite by implying terms that were not stated. In other cases, the indefinite part of the offer is ignored when that part can be divided or separated from the balance of the offer. In other cases, the requirement of definiteness is ignored, either because the matter that is not definite is unimportant or because there is an exception to the rule requiring definiteness.

Assuming that there is in fact an offer that is made with contractual intent and that it is sufficiently definite, it still does not have the legal effect of an offer unless it is communicated to the offeree by or at the direction of the offeror.

In some cases, no contract arises because there is no offer that satisfies the requirements just stated. In other cases there was an offer, but it was terminated before it was accepted. By definition, an attempted acceptance made after the offer has been terminated has no effect. The ordinary offer may be revoked at any time by the offeror. All that is required is the showing of intent to revoke and the communication of that intent to the offeree. The offeror's power to revoke is barred by the existence of an option contract under common law, a firm offer under the Uniform Commercial Code or local non-Code statute, and by the application of the doctrine of detrimental reliance by the offeree. An offer is also terminated by the express rejection of the offer or by the making of a counteroffer; by the lapse of the time stated in the offer, or of a reasonable time when none is stated; by the death or disability of either party; or by a change of law that makes illegal a contract based on the particular offer.

When the offer is accepted, a contract arises. Only the offeree can accept an offer, and the acceptance must be of the offer exactly as made without any qualification or change. Ordinarily, the offeree may accept or reject as the offeree chooses. Limitations on this freedom of action have been imposed by antidiscrimination and consumer protection laws.

The acceptance is any manifestation of intent to agree to the terms of the offer. Ordinarily, silence or failure to act does not constitute acceptance. The recipient of unordered goods and tickets may dispose of the goods or use the goods without such action constituting an acceptance. An acceptance does not exist until the words or conduct demonstrating assent to the offer are communicated to the offeror. Acceptance by mail takes effect at the time and place when and where the letter is mailed. A telephoned acceptance is effective when and where spoken into the phone.

In an auction sale, the auctioneer asking for bids makes an invitation to negotiate. A person making a bid is making an offer, and the acceptance of the highest bid by the auctioneer is an acceptance of that offer and gives rise to a contract. When the auction sale is without reserve, the auctioneer must accept the highest bid. If the auction is not expressly without reserve, the auctioneer may refuse to accept any of the bids.

LAW IN PRACTICE

1. When you want to make a contract, be sure what you and the other person say shows an intent to make a contract.

2. When you think you are making a contract, double-check to make sure that what has been said is definite enough to be enforced. Be objective in evaluating the wording.

3. Examine offers carefully to see if there is any time limitation imposed on acceptance.

4. When you make an offer, specify whether it may be accepted by anyone or only by the offeree.

5. When you make an offer and the acceptance may be mailed, state that the acceptance is effective only when received if that is what you desire.

QUESTIONS AND CASE PROBLEMS

1. What social force influencing the law (from the list in Chapter 2, Section 4) is illustrated by each of the following statements? (a) Economic life would be most uncertain if we did not have the assurance that contracts, once made, would be binding. (b) An offer is terminated by the lapse of a reasonable time, when no time has been stated.

2. The City Paint Company made an offer to paint the Jones Factory for $50,000. The board of directors of Jones held a meeting and the board unanimously voted that they were accepting the City Paint offer. A secretary of the Jones Company was a friend of a secretary of the Paint Company and relayed the information through her that Jones had accepted the City Paint Company offer. The next day, Jones Company's board of directors decided that they had been too reckless in accepting the offer and voted to reject the Paint Company offer. When Jones sent the Paint Company a rejection of the Paint Company's offer, the Paint Company sued Jones for breach of contract. Decide.

3. The Croft Cement Works agreed to supply Grover with as much cement as Grover would buy at a specified price per unit. Was this a requirements contract?

4. Katherine mailed Paul an offer that stated that it was good for ten days. Two days later she mailed Paul another letter stating that the original offer was revoked. That evening, Paul phoned Katherine to say that he accepted the offer. She said that he could not do so because she had mailed him a letter of revocation and that he would undoubtedly receive the letter of revocation in the next morning's mail. Was the offer revoked by Katherine?

5. Nelson wanted to sell his home. Baker sent him a written offer to purchase the home. Nelson made some changes to Baker's offer and wrote him that he, Nelson, was accepting the offer as amended. Baker notified Nelson that he was dropping out of the transaction. Nelson sued Baker for breach of contract. Decide. What social forces and ethical values are involved? *[Nelson v Baker (Mo App) 776 SW2d 52]*

6. The Lessack Auctioneers advertised an auction sale that was open to the public and was to be conducted with reserve. Gordon attended the auction and bid $100 for a work of art that was worth much more. No higher bid, however, was made. Lessack refused to sell the item for $100 and withdrew the item from the sale. Gordon claimed that, since he was the highest bidder, Lessack was required to sell the item to him. Was he correct?

7. The Willis Music Co. advertised a television set at $22.50 in the Sunday newspaper. Ehrlich ordered a set, but the company refused to deliver it on the ground that the price in the newspaper ad was a mistake. Ehrlich sued the company. Was it liable? Why or why not? *[Ehrlich v Willis Music Co. 93 Ohio App 246, 113 NE2d 252]*

8. A movement was organized to build a Charles City College. Hauser and others signed pledges to contribute to the college. At the time of signing, Hauser inquired what would happen if he should die or be unable to pay. The representative of the college stated that the pledge would not then be binding and that it was merely a statement of intent. The college failed financially, and Pappas was appointed receiver to collect and liquidate the assets of the college corporation. He sued Hauser for the amount due on his pledge. Hauser raised the defense that the pledge was not a binding contract. Decide. What ethical values are involved? *[Pappas v Hauser, 293 Iowa 102, 197 NW2d 607]*

9. A owned land. He signed a contract agreeing to sell the land but reserving the right to take the hay from the land until the following October. He gave the contract form to *B*, a broker. *C*, a prospective buyer, agreed to buy the land and signed the contract but crossed out the provision regarding the hay crop. Was there a binding contract between *A* and *C*?

10. A. H. Zehmer discussed selling a farm to Lucy. After a 40-minute discussion of a first draft of a contract, Zehmer and his wife, Ida, signed a sec-

ond draft stating: "We hereby agree to sell to W. O. Lucy the Ferguson Farm complete for $50,000 title satisfactory to buyer." Lucy agreed to purchase the farm on these terms. Thereafter, the Zehmers refused to transfer title to Lucy and claimed that they had made the contract for sale as a joke. Lucy brought an action to compel performance of the contract. The Zehmers claimed that there was no contract. Were they correct? *[Lucy v Zehmer, 198 Va App 493, 84 SE2d 516]*

11. Wheeler operated an automobile service station, which he leased from W. C. Cornitius, Inc. The lease ran for three years. Although the lease did not contain any provision for renewal, the lease was in fact renewed six times for successive three-year terms. The landlord refused to renew the lease for a seventh time. Wheeler brought suit to compel the landlord to accept his offer to renew the lease. Decide. *[William C. Cornitius, Inc. v Wheeler, 276 Or 747, 556 P2d 666]*

12. Cogdill made an offer to the Bank of Benton. The proper officer stated that he would start the paperwork. Did Cogdill have a contract with the Bank of Benton? *[Bank of Benton v Cogdill, 118 Ill App 3d 280, 73 Ill Dec 871, 454 NE2d 1120]*

13. Jacks Bean Company purchased beans from farmers. It stored them in its warehouse and later resold them. In the warehouse there was posted a list of the prices that were paid by Jacks for different grades of beans. Heiting & Sons left some beans with Jacks. Heiting then claimed that by doing this they accepted an offer by Jacks to purchase the beans at the posted prices. Heiting claimed that when Jacks posted the prices he was making an offer to purchase beans at that price and that Heiting's delivery of beans to Jacks was an acceptance of that offer and that therefore there was a contract between them. Was Heiting correct? *[Joseph Heiting & Sons v Jacks Beans Co. 236 Neb 765, 463 NW2d 817]*

14. An agreement was made between *C* Corporation and *S*, a shareholder of *C*, that *S* would sell his stock to *C*. The agreement did not specify any price but stated that the price should be determined by Lenox, a certified public accountant. The agreement also specified that the computations would be made on the basis of the value of the corporate assets as shown by the corporate books. Lenox determined the value of the stock on that basis. *S* then refused to carry out the terms of the agreement. He claimed that (1) there was no contract because the agreement failed for lack of definiteness as it did not state the price to be paid, and (2) he was not bound by the price determined by *L* because inflation and other factors made the corporate assets worth much more than appeared from the corporate books. *S* also claimed that the formula specified in the agreement was not in accord with good accounting practices. Was *S* required to sell his stock to *C* at the price determined by *L*?

15. Sanchis owned a building. He agreed to rent it to Rosell for commercial purposes for 3 years at $50,000 a year. The agreement provided that at the end of that time Rosell had the option to extend the lease for another 3 years at a rent to be then determined. The first 3 years expired. The parties could not agree to the rent to be paid for the next 3 years. Rosell insisted that Sanchis was required to lease the building for another 3 years at the same rent as for the first 3 years. Was he correct?

CAPACITY AND GENUINE ASSENT

A. CONTRACTUAL CAPACITY
    1. Contractual Capacity Defined
    2. Minors
    3. Incompetents
    4. Intoxicated Persons

B. MISTAKE
    5. Unilateral Mistake
    6. Mutual Mistake

C. DECEPTION
    7. Innocent Misrepresentation
    8. Nondisclosure
    9. Fraud

D. PRESSURE
    10. Undue Influence
    11. Duress
    12. Adhesion Contracts

E. REMEDIES
    13. Rescission
    14. Damages
    15. Reformation of Contract by Court

LEARNING OBJECTIVES

After studying this chapter, you will be able to:
1. *Define contractual capacity.*
2. *State the extent and effect of avoidance of a contract by a minor.*
3. *Classify unilateral and bilateral mistakes.*
4. *Distinguish between innocent misrepresentation, fraud, and nondisclosure.*
5. *List those classes of persons who lack contractual capacity.*
6. *Distinguish between undue influence and duress.*

A contract is a binding agreement. This agreement must be made between parties who have the capacity to do so. They must also truly agree, so that all parties have really consented thereto. This chapter explores the elements of contractual capacity of the parties and the genuineness of their assent.

A. CONTRACTUAL CAPACITY

Some persons lack contractual capacity. This embraces both those who have a status incapacity, such as minors, and those who have a factual incapacity, such as insane persons.

1. Contractual Capacity Defined

Contractual capacity is the ability to understand that a contract is being made and to understand its general meaning. However, the fact that a person does not understand the full legal meaning of a contract does not mean that contractual capacity is lacking. Everyone is presumed to have capacity unless it is proven that capacity is lacking, or unless there is status incapacity.[1]

(a) STATUS INCAPACITY. Over the centuries, the law has declared some classes of persons to lack contractual capacity in order to give them protection by giving them the power to get out of unwise contracts. Of these classes, the most important today is the class identified as minors.

Until recent times, some other classes were held to lack contractual capacity in order to discriminate against them. Examples are married women and aliens. Still other classes, such as persons convicted and sentenced for a felony, were held to lack contractual capacity in order to punish them. Today these discriminatory and punitive incapacities have largely disappeared. Married women generally have the same contractual capacity as unmarried persons.[2]

By virtue of international treaties, the discrimination against aliens has been removed. The destruction of contractual capacity as a punishment for crime still exists in some states, but recent cases regard it as unconstitutional, so it is likely that it will soon disappear.

(b) FACTUAL INCAPACITY. A factual incapacity contrasts with incapacity imposed because of the class or group to which a person belongs. A factual incapacity may exist when, because of mental or physical condition caused by shock, medication, drugs, alcohol, illness, or age, a person does not understand that a contract is being made or understand its general nature. If the factual incapacity later disappears, the party affected can ordinarily avoid the contract. In some extreme cases, the contract made while the incapacity existed is void.

2. Minors

Minors may make contracts.[3] However, to protect minors, the law has always treated them as a class as lacking contractual capacity.

(a) WHO IS A MINOR? At common law any person, male or female, under 21 years of age was a **minor** (or an infant). At common law, minority ended the day before the 21st birthday. The "day before the birthday" rule is still followed, but the age of majority has been reduced from 21 years to 18 years in most states and to 19 in a few.

(b) MINOR'S POWER TO AVOID CONTRACTS. With exceptions that will be noted later, a contract made by a minor is voidable at the election of the minor. The minor may affirm or ratify the contract on attaining majority by performing the contract, by expressly ap-

---

[1] Re Smith's Adoption (La App) 578 So 2d 988 (1991).

[2] In a few states, there is a limitation that a married woman cannot make a binding contract to pay the debt of her husband if he fails to do so.

[3] Buffington v State Automobile Mut. Ins. Co. 192 Ga App 389, 384 SE2d 873 (1989).

proving the contract, or by allowing a reasonable time to lapse without avoiding the contract. Once the contract is affirmed, it can no longer be avoided.

In some states, a statute declares that certain kinds of contracts made by minors are void and not merely voidable. When such a statute is applicable, there is no need for a minor to declare that the contract is not binding, since there is nothing for the minor to avoid.[4]

(1) What Constitutes Avoidance. A minor may avoid or disaffirm a contract by any expression of an intention to repudiate the contract. Any act inconsistent with the continuing validity of the contract is also an avoidance.

Thus, when a minor sold property to Martin and later, on reaching majority, made a sale of the same property to Gomez, the second sale was an avoidance of the first.

(2) Time for Avoidance. The minor can avoid a contract only during minority and for a reasonable time after attaining majority. After the lapse of such reasonable time, the contract is deemed ratified and cannot be avoided by the minor.

(3) Minor's Misrepresentation of Age. Generally, the fact that the minor has misrepresented age does not affect the minor's power to avoid the contract. A few states hold that such fraud of the minor prevents the minor from avoiding the contract. Some states permit the minor to avoid the contract in such a case but require the minor to pay for any damage to the property received under the contract.

In any case, the other party to the contract may avoid it because of the minor's fraud.

(c) RESTITUTION BY MINOR AFTER AVOIDANCE. When a minor avoids a contract, the question arises as to what must be returned by the minor to the other contracting party.

(1) Original Consideration Intact.   When a minor still has what was received from the other party, the minor, on avoiding the contract, must return it to the other party or offer to do so. That is, the minor must put things back to the original position or, as it is called, restore the **status quo ante**.

(2) Original Consideration Damaged or Destroyed. What happens if the minor cannot return what has been received because it has been spent, used, damaged, or destroyed? The minor's right to avoid the contract is not affected. The minor can still avoid the contract and is only required to return what remains. The fact that nothing remains or that what remains is damaged does not bar the right to avoid the contract. In those states that follow the common law rule, the minor can thus refuse to pay for what has been received under the contract or can get back what had been paid or given, even though the minor does not have anything to return or returns any property in a damaged condition. There is, however, a trend that would limit this rule.

In the *Star Chevrolet* case the dealer claimed a credit for the salvage value of the automobile purchased by the minor.

(d) RECOVERY OF PROPERTY BY MINOR ON AVOIDANCE. When a minor avoids a contract, the other contracting party must return the money received from the minor. Any property received from the minor

STAR CHEVROLET CO. v GREEN
(Miss) 473 So 2d 157 (1985)

Kevin Green purchased an automobile from Star Chevrolet Company. He later notified Star that he was a minor and was avoiding the contract. Star

---

[4] Moran v Williston Cooperative Credit Union (ND) 420 NW2d 353 (1988).

refused to take back the car and to refund the purchase price. Kevin continued to use the car. He was involved in a collision. His insurance paid his
claim, and he transferred the car to the insurance company. The company
later sold the car for salvage for $1,500. Kevin sued Star for the price that he
had paid for the car. Star claimed that it was entitled to a setoff of $1,500 for
the salvage value of the car. The lower court refused to allow this setoff, and
Star appealed.

SULLIVAN, J. . . . Before reaching the precise question at hand, some general principles warrant restatement. First, the right of a minor to disaffirm his contract is
based upon sound public policy to protect the minor from his own improvidence
and the overreaching of adults. It is the policy of the law to discourage adults from
contracting with minors and the adult cannot complain if, as a consequence of his
violation of this rule of conduct, he is injured by the minor's exercise of the right of
disaffirmance, since this injury might have been avoided if the adult had declined to
enter into the contract.

Second, if upon disaffirmance the minor has in his possession the specific property or any part of it which he received he must return it. Thus, where a minor repudiates an automobile sales contract while the vehicle is still in his hands, he must
tender the vehicle in order for his purchase price to be refunded. . . . The seller may
not deduct from the refunded purchase price allowances for use and depreciation.

Third, the general rule is that upon disaffirmance of a minor's contract, he is required to return the consideration only if it is still in his possession. The minor who
disaffirms a contract is not obliged to return the consideration received by him or its
equivalent where during his minority he has wasted, squandered, destroyed, used,
or otherwise disposed of the consideration.

Finally, depreciation in the value of the vehicle due to the minor's misuse or neglect, short of [an] intentional or grossly negligent act amounting to an independent
tort, is not allowable by way of recoupment. In other words, the minor is not liable
for damages due to the very improvidence and indiscretion of infancy against which
the law seeks to protect him. On the other hand, a minor may not use infancy, which
is a shield for protection, as a sword for attack; such conduct by the minor amounts
to fraud.

Turning to the facts of this case, the minor clearly had the consideration, i.e. the
vehicle, in his possession when he first notified appellant of the disaffirmance of the
contract. Had appellant offered the minor, as the law required, a full refund of his
purchase price, the minor clearly would have been required to return the vehicle. Instead, the appellant did not, and while suit was pending the minor repaired the vehicle and began to use it. There is no hint in the record that the accident which
destroyed the vehicle was the result of any deliberate design on the minor's part to
fraudulently deprive appellant of that which would have placed him in status quo.
For aught that appears in the record, the accident was caused by the carelessness
and improvidence with which the law expects a minor to deal with his property.
Disaffirmance at this point would have required the appellant to refund the full purchase price and the appellee, in turn, to return the damaged Camaro, since the law
does not condition a minor's right to disaffirm a contract upon placing the other
party in status quo, but only requires the return of whatever consideration remains
in the minor's hands.

This case goes one step further. Prior to trial, the minor transferred title to the
vehicle to the insurance company and used the proceeds to purchase another vehicle.
The insurer obtained $1,500 salvage value for the damaged Camaro. We are urged to

offset the minor's recovery by the $1,500 salvage value of the car on the ground that the minor had the duty to tender this consideration to appellant in order to receive a refund of the full purchase price.

. . . We hold that the minor is liable, and the appellant is entitled to a setoff, for the salvage value of the consideration which he intentionally conveyed away. . . .

[Judgment reversed as to setoff claim]

QUESTIONS

1. What is the justification for the common law rule on avoidance of contracts by minors?
2. What is the common law rule as to the liability of a minor avoiding a contract for property that had been damaged?
3. Does the *Star Chevrolet* case follow the common law rule stated in your answer to Question 2?

must also be returned. If the property has been sold to a third person who did not know of the minority of the original seller, the minor cannot get the property back, but in such cases the minor is entitled to recover the monetary value of the property or the money received by the other contracting party from the third person.

(e) CONTRACTS FOR NECESSARIES. A minor can avoid a contract for necessaries but must pay the reasonable value for furnished necessaries. This duty of the minor is a quasi-contractual liability. It is a duty that the law imposes on the minor, rather than a duty created by contract.

(1) What Constitutes Necessaries. Originally, **necessaries** were limited to those things absolutely necessary for the sustenance and shelter of the minor. Thus limited, the term would extend only to the simplest foods, clothing, and lodging. In the course of time, the rule was relaxed to extend generally to things relating to the health, education, and comfort of the minor. Thus, the rental of a house used by a married minor is a necessary. Services reasonably necessary to obtaining employment by a minor have been held to be necessaries.

The rule has also been relaxed to hold that whether an item is a necessary in a particular case depends on the financial and social status, or station in life, of the minor.

The more recent decisions hold that property used by a minor to earn a living is a necessary. Thus, it has been held that a tractor and farm equipment were necessaries for a married minor who supported a family by farming.

Expansion of the definition of "necessaries" has come about because, in this century, minors have taken a greater part in the business and working world. In many cases, minors have left the parental home to lead independent lives.

(2) Contract with Parent or Guardian. When a third person supplies the parents or guardian of a minor with goods or services that are needed by the minor, the minor is not liable for such necessaries. This is so because the contract of the third person is with the parent or guardian, not with a minor.[5]

---

[5] Hammonds Estate v Aetna Cas Co. 141 Ill App 3d 963, 96 Ill Dec 270, 491 NE2d 84 (1986).

(f) RATIFICATION OF FORMER MINOR'S VOIDABLE CONTRACT. A former minor cannot avoid a contract that has been ratified after reaching majority.

(1) What Constitutes Ratification. Ratification consists of any words or conduct of the former minor manifesting an intent to be bound by the terms of a contract made while a minor.

The making of payments after attaining majority may constitute a ratification. Many courts, however, refuse to recognize payment as ratification in the absence of further evidence of an intent to ratify, an express statement of ratification, or an appreciation that such payment might constitute a ratification.

An acknowledgment that a contract had been made during minority, without an intent to be bound thereby, is not a ratification.

(2) Form of Ratification. Generally, no special form is required for ratification of a minor's voidable contract, although in some states a written ratification or declaration of intention is required.

(3) Time for Ratification. A person can avoid a contract any time during minority and for a reasonable time thereafter but, of necessity, can only ratify a contract after attaining majority. The minor must have attained majority, or the "ratification" would itself be regarded as voidable.

(g) CONTRACTS THAT MINORS CANNOT AVOID. Statutes in many states deprive a minor of the right to avoid an educational loan,[6] a contract for medical care, a contract made while running a business, a contract approved by a court, a contract made in performance of a legal duty, or a contract relating to bank accounts, insurance policies, or corporate stock. In most states, the contract of a veteran, although a minor, is binding, particularly a contract for the purchase of a home. In some states, by court decision, a minor who is nearly an adult, or who appears to be an adult, cannot avoid a contract, particularly when it is made in connection with a business or employment.

Some courts take an intermediate position with respect to employment contracts. These courts allow the minor to avoid the contract, but prohibit the minor from using any secret information obtained in the course of the employment or from competing with the former employer when the avoided contract contained a noncompetition clause. It has also been held that when a minor has settled a claim and received the amount specified in a release, the release is binding on the minor and cannot be set aside when the minor attains majority.

(h) LIABILITY OF THIRD PERSON FOR MINOR'S CONTRACT. The question arises whether parents are bound by the contract of their minor child. The question also arises whether a person cosigning a minor's contract is bound if the contract is avoided.

(1) Liability of Parent. Ordinarily, a parent is not liable on a contract made by a minor child. The parent may be liable, however, if the child is acting as the agent of the parent in making the contract. For example, when a mother sends her daughter to the store to buy a coat for the daughter and have it charged on the mother's account, the daughter is acting as agent for her mother, and the contract is the contract of the mother and not the daughter. Also, the parent is liable to a seller for the reasonable value of necessaries supplied by the seller to the child if the parent had deserted the child.

(2) Liability of Cosigner. When the minor makes a contract, another person, such as a parent or a friend, may sign along with the minor to make the contract more attractive to the third person.

---

[6] A Model Student Capacity to Borrow Act makes educational loans binding on minors in Arizona, Mississippi, North Dakota, Oklahoma, and Washington. This act was reclassified from a uniform act to a model act by the Commissioners on Uniform Laws, indicating that it was recognized that uniformity was not important and that the matter was primarily local in character.

With respect to the other contracting party, the cosigner is bound independently of the minor. Consequently, if the minor avoids the contract, the cosigner remains bound by the contract. If the debt to the creditor is actually paid, the obligation of the cosigner is discharged.

If the minor avoids a sales contract but does not return the goods, the cosigner remains liable for the purchase price.

3. Incompetents

A person who is mentally deficient is generally called an **incompetent** and lacks capacity to make a contract. The cause of the incapacity is immaterial. It may be the result of insanity, senile dementia, imbecility, excessive use of drugs or alcohol, or a stroke. If the person is so mentally incompetent as to be unable to understand that a contract is being made or the general nature of the contract, the person lacks contractual capacity. The fact that a person is mentally retarded does not in itself constitute incapacity if the person understands the nature of the transaction and that a contract is being made.[7]

An incompetent may have lucid intervals. If a contract is made during such an interval and is not affected by any delusion, the contract is valid and binding.

(a) EFFECT OF INCOMPETENCY. An incompetent person may ordinarily avoid a contract in the same manner as a minor. Upon the removal of the disability (that is, upon becoming competent), the formerly incompetent person can either ratify or disaffirm the contract.

There is a trend in the law to treat the incompetent's contract as fully binding when its terms and the surrounding circumstances are reasonable and the incompetent person is unable to restore the other contracting party to the status quo ante.

As in the case of minors, the other party to the contract has no right to disaffirm the contract merely because the incompetent has the right to do so.

(b) APPOINTMENT OF GUARDIAN. If a court appoints a guardian for the incompetent person, a contract made by the incompetent before that appointment may be ratified or, in some cases, disaffirmed by the guardian. If the incompetent person makes a contract after a guardian has been appointed, the contract is void and not merely voidable.

4. Intoxicated Persons

The capacity of a party to contract and the validity of the contract are not affected by the party's being drunk at the time of making the contract, as long as the party knew that a contract was being made.

If the degree of intoxication is such that a person does not know that a contract is being made, the contract is voidable by that person. The situation is the same as though the person were insane at the time and did not know what was being done. Upon becoming sober, the person may avoid or rescind the contract. However, an unreasonable delay in taking steps to set aside a known contract entered into while intoxicated may bar the intoxicated person from asserting this right.[8]

B. MISTAKE

The validity of a contract may be affected by the fact that one or both of the parties made a mistake. In some cases the mistake may be caused by the misconduct of one of the parties.

5. Unilateral Mistake

A **unilateral mistake**—that is, a mistake by only one of the parties—as to a fact does not affect the contract. When a contract is made on the basis of a quoted price, the validity of the contract is not affected by the fact that the

---

[7] Wagner v Wagner, 156 App Div 2d 963, 549 NYS2d 256 (1989).

[8] Diedrich v Diedrich (Minn App) 424 NW2d 580 (1988).

Figure 11-1 Avoidance of Contract

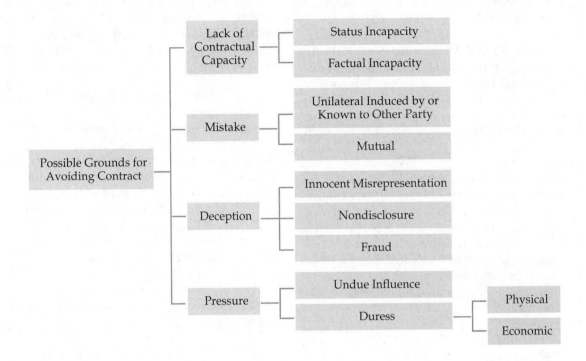

C
P
A
party furnishing the quotation had made a mathematical mistake in computing the price if there was no reason for the other party to recognize that there was a mistake.[9]

As exceptions to the statement that a unilateral mistake of fact does not affect the contract, the agreement has no effect if it states that it shall be void if the fact is not as believed. The party making the mistake may also avoid the contract if the mistake is known, or should be known or recognized, by the other contracting party.

A unilateral mistake as to expectations or the law does not have any effect on the contract. Thus, the fact that a signer of a contract would not have signed if the signer had understood the legal effect of the contract is not a defense.

A minority of states recognize unilateral mistake as a defense unless (1) the mistake is the result of inexcusable lack of due care, or (2) the other party has so changed position in reliance on the contract that rescission would be unconscionable.

(a) MISTAKE AS TO NATURE OF PAPER. When a party makes a negligent mistake as to the nature of a paper, the party is bound according to its terms. For example, when the printed form for a corporation's loan application contained a guaranty by the president of the corporation of the corporate debt, the president signing the application without reading it was bound by this guaranty. This is true even though the president did not know that it was in the application and the application was headed merely "Application for Credit."

9 Procan Construction Co., Inc. v Oceanside Development Corp. 148 App Div 2d 689, 539 NYS2d 437 (1989).

The educated person who signs a promissory note without reading it is bound thereby even though the lender had falsely stated to the signer that the note was merely a character reference.[10]

(b) MISTAKE AS TO TERMS OF PAPER. A person who has the ability and the opportunity to read a paper before signing is bound by its terms even though the person signed without reading.[11] Such a signer cannot avoid liability on the ground that there had not been any explanation given of the terms of the writing.

In contrast to a person who is mistaken as to the terms of a paper because of carelessness in reading it, a person may be unable to read or to understand the terms of a paper. Such a person is bound by signing the paper without obtaining an explanation of it, unless the other contracting party knows, or has reason to know, of the signer's disability or educational limitation.

(c) MISTAKE AS TO RELEASE. An insurance claimant is bound by a release given to the insurance company when there is a unilateral mistake as to its meaning resulting from carelessness in reading the release. When a release is given and accepted in good faith, it is immaterial that the releasor or both of the parties were mistaken as to the seriousness or possible future consequences of a known injury or condition. If the release covers all claims known or unknown, the courts following the common law view hold the releasor bound even though there were other injuries of which the releasor was unaware because the effects of the unknown injuries had not yet appeared. Some courts depart from this and hold the release effective only with respect to the conditions or consequences that were known at the time the release was given.[12]

6. Mutual Mistake

When both parties make the same mistake of fact, the agreement is void. Thus, the agreement is not binding when both contracting parties bargained on the basis that certain property was junk when in fact it was valuable art.[13]

(a) MISTAKE AS TO EXPECTATIONS. A mutual mistake with respect to expectations ordinarily has no effect on the contract unless the realization of those expectations is made an express condition of the contract. For example, certain parties bought and sold a little country highway store in the belief that the United States would build an army base about a mile away. The contract remained binding and was not affected by the fact that the Army did not build the base with the result that the expectations of a thriving business at the store were never realized. This means that the mistake has no effect unless the contract says that it shall be void if the matter is not as believed.

(b) MISTAKE OF LAW. When the mutual or bilateral mistake is one of law, the contract generally is binding. Thus, even if both parties to a lease mistakenly believe that the leased premises can be used for boarding animals because they are unaware of a zoning regulation that prohibits such a use of the property, the tenant does not have a right to rescind the lease for mutual mistake of law. In the eyes of the law, the parties should have known what the zoning regulations allowed. A few courts have refused to follow this rule. In several states, statutes provide that a mutual mistake of law shall have the same effect as a mutual mistake of fact.

---

[10] DeHart v Dodge City of Spartanburg, Inc. (SC App) 427 SE2d 720 (1993).

[11] Hicks v Bridges (Miss) 580 So 2d 743 (1991).

[12] Williams v Glash (Tex) 789 SW2d 261 (1990).

[13] Wilkin v 1st Source Bank (Ind App) 548 NE2d 170 (1990).

C. DECEPTION

One of the parties to a contract may have been misled by an innocent misrepresentation, a failure to disclose information, or a fraudulent statement.

7. Innocent Misrepresentation

Suppose one party to a contract makes a statement of fact that is false but that is innocently made without intending to deceive the other party. Can the other party set aside the contract on the ground of being misled by the statement?

Equity will permit the rescission of the contract when the innocent misstatement of a material fact induces another to make the contract. If the deceived person is a defendant in an action at law for breach of contract, it is generally held that such innocent deception by the plaintiff cannot be asserted as a defense. There is a tendency, however, for the law courts to adopt the rule of equity. For example, it may be possible for an insurance company to avoid its policy because of an innocent misstatement of a material fact by the applicant. Contracts between persons standing in confidential relationships, such as guardian and ward, or parent and child, can be set aside for the same reason. Some courts go beyond this and permit the recovery of damages sustained because of the misrepresentation.

Modern law is increasingly concerned with the plight of the plaintiff and less concerned with whether the defendant was at fault. Courts that take this approach see no difference between an intentional fraudulent statement and innocent misrepresentation—the plaintiff is misled and harmed in either case.

In some states, statutes have defined fraud so as to include innocent misrepresentation. Under such a statute, a wrong statement of the model year of an automobile imposes liability on the seller even though the misrepresentation was a mistake and no common law fraud or bad faith was present.[14]

8. Nondisclosure

Under certain circumstances, nondisclosure will serve to make a contract voidable, especially when the nondisclosure consists of active concealment.

(a) GENERAL RULE OF NONLIABILITY. Ordinarily, there is no duty on a party to a contract to volunteer information to the other. For example, if Fox does not ask Tehan any questions, Tehan is not under any duty to make a full statement of material facts. Consequently, the nondisclosure of information that is not asked for does not impose fraud liability or impair the validity of a contract. A number of states have adopted laws to protect the seller of a house from liability for failing to volunteer that there had been a murder or suicide in the house or that an occupant had certain diseases.[15]

(b) EXCEPTIONS. Some statutes require the seller of a house to volunteer prior murders committed therein. Other exceptions have been created by ther courts. In all such cases, the failure to disclose information that was not requested is regarded as fraudulent. In those cases, the party to whom the information was not disclosed has the same remedies as if a known false statement were intentionally made.

(1) Unknown Defect or Condition. There is developing in the law a duty for one party who knows of a defect or condition to disclose that information to the other party where the defect or condition is obviously unknown to the other person and is of such a nature that it is unlikely that the other person would discover the truth or inquire about it.

Manufacturers and distributors of asbestos were guilty of fraud when they sold asbestos

---

[14] Myers v Liberty Lincoln-Mercury, Inc. 89 NC App 335, 365 SE2d 663 (1988).

[15] See, for example, South Carolina, Act of May 14, 1990, Act No. 481.

products without disclosing the information they possessed showing a relationship between cancer and asbestos products.[16] An automobile dealer who sells a used car without informing the buyer that the odometer had been set back is liable for fraud.[17]

(2) Confidential Relationship. If parties stand in a confidential relationship, failure to disclose information may be regarded as fraudulent. For example, in an attorney-client relationship,[18] the attorney has a duty to reveal anything that is material to the client's interest when dealing with the client. The attorney's silence has the same legal consequence as a knowingly-made false statement that there was no material fact to be told to the client.

The relationship between the buyer of a house and a financial institution lending the money to finance the purchase is not a confidential relationship. Therefore, the lender is not under any duty to disclose information possessed by it.

(3) Fine Print. An intent to conceal may be present when a printed contract or document contains certain clauses in such fine print that it is reasonable to believe that the other contracting party will neither take the time nor even be able to read such provisions.

In some instances, legislatures have outlawed certain fine print contracts. Statutes commonly declare that insurance policies may not be printed in type of smaller size than designated by statute. Consumer protection statutes frequently require that particular clauses be set in large type. When a merchant selling goods under a written contract disclaims the obligation that goods be fit for their normal use, the Uniform Commercial Code requires the waiver to be set forth in "conspicuous" writing. *Conspicuous* is defined as "a term or clause . . . so written that a reasonable person against whom it is to operate ought to

have noticed it. A printed heading in capitals . . . is conspicuous. Language in the body of a form is 'conspicuous' if it is in larger or other contrasting type or color. . . ."[19]

There is a growing trend to treat a fine print clause as not binding on the party who would be harmed by it without considering whether fraud was involved. A provision freeing the other contracting party from liability is not binding when it is printed in type that is so small that a person with normal vision would have difficulty reading it.

(4) Active Concealment.   Nondisclosure may be more than the passive failure to volunteer information. It may consist of a positive act of hiding information from the other party by physical concealment, or it may consist of knowingly or recklessly furnishing the wrong information. Such conduct constitutes fraud.

9. Fraud

Fraud is (1) the making of a false statement of fact, (2) with knowledge of its falsity or with reckless indifference as to its truth, (3) with the intent that the listener rely thereon, (4) with the result that the listener does so rely, and (5) with the consequence that the listener is harmed.[20]

A seller committed fraud when selling a car as a new demonstrator when in fact the car had been damaged and repaired three times.

(a) RELIANCE ON STATEMENT. The fact that a fraudulent statement has been made has no importance unless the other party relies on the statement's truth. Consequently, fraud is not present when the victim has the same knowledge of the true facts as the alleged wrongdoer or when the victim should have known such facts. When the false statements have been made after a contract has been

---

[16] Board of Education of City of Chicago v A, C, and S, Inc. 171 Ill App 3d 737, 121 Ill Dec 643, 525 NE2d 950 (1988).

[17] Pelster v Ray (CA8 Mo) 987 F2d 514 (1993).

[18] Re Boss Trust (Minn App) 487 NW2d 256 (1992).

[19] UCC § 1-201 (10)

[20] Rocky Mountain Helicopters, Inc. v Air Freight, Inc. (Wyo) 773 P2d 911 (1989).

signed, it is obvious that the making of the contract was not induced by the statements and that the other party to the contract had not relied on them.

If the alleged victim of the fraud knew that the statements were false because the truth was commonly known, the victim cannot rely on the false statements.

If the victim of the false statement could have easily determined that it was false, a court will hold that there is no fraud liability.[21] However, the fraud victim is not barred from relief because every possible step was not taken to determine whether statements were true. The modern American economy depends on a fast turnover of goods, and this is possible only when there is reliance by buyers on statements of sellers. Thus, the buyer of a used car is entitled to rely on the statement of the seller that the car had never been in a wreck and that it had nothing wrong with it. This is true even though, if the buyer had the car raised on a lift, the buyer could have seen the wreck-caused damage to the car and thus learned that the statements of the seller were false.

(b) STATEMENT OF INTENTION OR PROMISE. A statement of intention or promise can constitute fraud when made by a person who does not intend to keep it. To illustrate, a customer purchases goods from a merchant on credit and agrees to pay for them in 60 days. If the customer does not intend to pay for the goods and does not do so, the customer is guilty of fraud by misrepresenting intention.

The mere fact that the defendant has not performed a promise does not in itself establish that the defendant was guilty of fraud. It must be shown that the person made the promise with the intention of not keeping it.[22]

(c) STATEMENT OF OPINION OR VALUE. Ordinarily, a misstatement of opinion or value is not regarded as fraudulent.[23] The theory is that the person hearing the statement recognizes or should recognize that it is merely the speaker's personal view and not a statement of fact. A statement that is mere sales talk cannot be the basis of fraud liability.

However, if the defendant, in making a statement as to future expectations, had knowledge not available to the plaintiff that showed that such expectations could not be realized, the statement can be held fraudulent. Thus, a statement that a business would make a stated profit in the future is actionable when the speaker knew that, on the basis of past events, such a prediction was false. Likewise, a statement of opinion may be fraudulent when the speaker knows of past or present facts that make the opinion false.

In the *Master Abrasives* case a franchisee claimed that the sales pitch made by the franchisor was fraudulent. This was denied by the franchisor.

MASTER ABRASIVES CORP. v WILLIAMS
(Ind App) 469 NE2d 1196 (1984)

Master Abrasives Corp. sold a dealership to Williams giving him the exclusive right to sell its products in 22 counties. Williams purchased the dealership because Robert F. Oldham, the vice president and national sales manager of Master, told him that there was the potential for earning $30,000 to $40,000 a

---

[21] Burman v Richmond Homes (Colo App) 821 P2d 913 (1991).

[22] Loula v Snap-On Tools Corp. (Wis App) 498 NW2d 866 (1993).

[23] Tarmann v State Farm Mut. Automobile Ins. Co. ___Cal App 3d___, 2 Cal Rptr 2d 861 (1991).

year, and that the company had distributors who were currently earning that amount. Williams gave Master a down payment. Williams did not pay the balance. When Master sued him, he raised the defense of fraud. From a decision in favor of Williams, Master appealed.

CONOVER, J. . . . On September 18, 1982, Master and Williams entered into a sale and distribution agreement whereby Williams paid Master $1,000 and executed a 90-day note in favor of Master for $2,000. Master was to grant Williams exclusive selling rights to its trademarked product for two territories containing a total of 22 counties, provide product education, and sales assistance. At the time of the agreement, Master Abrasive's product line included grinding wheels and grinding points, in various grits, used in metal fabrication applications.

Prior to signing the agreement, Robert F. Oldham (Oldham), controller, vice president, and national sales manager of Master, represented to Williams there was a potential for earning $30,000 to $40,000 annually from a distributorship, and Master had distributors who were currently earning that amount. . . .

Williams argues Oldham's statements concerning profit potential and ease of earning back the investment are sufficient to support a finding of fraud. We disagree. These statements are mere opinion. Williams had no right to rely thereon. The essential elements of actual fraud are a material representation of past or existing *facts*, which representations are false, made with a knowledge or reckless ignorance of this falsity, which causes a reliance upon these representations, to the detriment of the person so relying.

While Oldham's statements as to the profit potential of the franchise are not sufficient for a finding of fraud, his statements about existing distributorships and their profitability will support such a finding. Testimony by Williams showed he relied on Oldham's representation Master had distributors earning $30,000 per year from the distributorships. Testimony by Johnson, however, shows there were only two distributors at the time, one of them being Oldham, and the *total sales* by these distributors during 1982 was only $10,000 to $15,000. Using Oldham's estimated cost of sales percentage of 40%, this shows earnings of only $6,000 to $9,000 for all the distributorships combined. Such a discrepancy is a clear misrepresentation by Oldham of an existing material fact.

A purchaser may rely on statements of fact made by the seller which are not obviously false and where the buyer lacks facilities for ascertaining the truth, as where facts are peculiarly within the knowledge of the seller. Here, the profitability of existing distributorships could have been known only by the principals of Master or the distributors themselves. Thus Williams reasonably could have relied upon such representations. That they were false statements renders them fraudulent. . . .

[Judgment affirmed]

QUESTIONS

1. What distinction did the court make between statements as to the potential earnings of Williams and the actual earnings of other dealers?
2. How would the case have been decided if nothing had been said as to the earnings of the other dealers?
3. Was Williams entitled to rely on the statements made to him as to the earnings of other dealers? Explain.

(d) STATEMENT OF LAW. A misstatement of law is treated in the same manner as a misstatement of opinion or value. Ordinarily, the listener is regarded as having an opportunity equal to that of the speaker of knowing what the law is, so that the listener is not entitled to rely on what the speaker says. Thus, a claim of fraud cannot be based on the assurance by a landlord that the tenant "should have no trouble" in obtaining a license desired by the tenant.[24] When the speaker has expert knowledge of the law or claims to have such knowledge, however, the misstatement of law can be the basis for fraud liability.

(e) UNCONSCIONABILITY AND CONSUMER PROTECTION. In many states, greater protection than is allowed under the common law doctrine of fraud is given by applying the concept of unconscionability or the specific provisions of a consumer protection statute. That is, relief is at times given the victim in deception and hardship cases, even though some of the elements required to impose fraud liability are not present.

D. PRESSURE

What appears to be an agreement may not in fact be voluntary because one of the parties entered into it because of undue influence or physical or economic duress.

10. Undue Influence

An aged parent may entrust all business affairs to a trusted child; an invalid may rely on a nurse; a client may follow implicitly whatever an attorney recommends. The relationship may be such that for practical purposes, the one person is helpless in the hands of the other. When such a confidential relationship exists, it is apparent that the parent, the invalid, or the client is not exercising free will in making a contract suggested by the child, nurse, or attorney, but is merely following the will of the other person. Because of the great possibility of unfair advantage, the law presumes that the dominating person exerts **undue influence** on the other person whenever the dominating person obtains any benefit from a contract made with the dominated person. The contract is then voidable. It may be set aside by the dominated person unless the dominating person can prove that, at the time the contract was made, no unfair advantage had been taken.

The class of confidential relationships is not well defined. It ordinarily includes the relationships of parent and child, guardian and ward, physician and patient, attorney and client, and any other relationship of trust and confidence in which one party exercises a control or influence over another.

Whether undue influence exists is a difficult question for the court (ordinarily the jury) to determine. The law does not regard every influence as undue. Thus, nagging may drive a person to make a contract, but that is not ordinarily regarded as undue influence. Persuasion and argument are not in themselves undue influence.

An essential element of undue influence is that the person making the contract does not exercise free will. In the absence of a recognized type of confidential relationship, such as that between parent and child, the courts are likely to take the attitude that the person who claims to have been dominated was merely persuaded and there was therefore no undue influence.

11. Duress

A party may enter into a contract to avoid a threatened danger. The danger threatened may be a physical harm to person or property, called **physical duress**; or it may be a threat of financial loss, called **economic duress**.

(a) PHYSICAL DURESS. A person makes a contract under **duress** when there is such violence or threat of violence that the person is

---

[24] Watkins v Gross (Mo App) 772 SW2d 22 (1989).

deprived of free will and makes the contract to avoid harm. The threatened harm may be directed at a near relative of the contracting party as well as against the contracting party. A contract is executed under duress when it is executed by parents under threat that their child will be prosecuted for a crime if they do not make the contract. If a contract is made under duress, the resulting agreement is voidable at the victim's election.

Agreements made to bring an end to mass disorder or violence are ordinarily not binding contracts because they were obtained by duress.

(b) ECONOMIC DURESS. The economic pressure on a contracting party may be so great that it will be held to constitute duress.

Economic duress occurs when the victim is threatened with irreparable loss for which adequate recovery could not be obtained by suing the wrongdoer.

Generally, a threat of economic loss or pressure caused by economic conditions does not constitute duress that makes a contract voidable. The fact that the plaintiff drove a hard bargain does not give rise to the defense of economic duress. When money is in fact owed a creditor, a threat by the creditor to sue the debtor to collect the amount owed does not constitute unlawful duress. It is merely a statement of what the law entitles the creditor to do.[25]

The *Blubaugh* case raised the question of what constitutes economic duress that will make a contract voidable.

BLUBAUGH v TURNER
(Wyo) 842 P2d 1072 (1992)

> Blubaugh was a district manager of Schlumberger Well Services. Turner was an executive employee of Schlumberger. Blubaugh was told that he would be fired unless he chose to resign. He was also told that if he would resign and release the company and its employees from all claims for wrongful discharge he would receive about $5,000 in addition to his regular severance pay of approximately $35,000 and would be given job relocation counselling. He resigned, signed the release, and received about $40,000 and job counselling. Some time thereafter he brought an action to set aside the release and impose liability on his former employer and Turnner for wrongful discharge. From a decision in the employer's favor, the plaintiff appealed.

MACY, C. J. . . . We . . . embrace the three-prong test employed by many courts to determine whether economic duress exists. Under this text, economic duress occurs when (1) a party involuntarily accepts the terms of another, (2) circumstances permit no other alternative, and (3) such circumstances are the result of coercive acts of the other party. . . . Economic duress does not exist, however, unless a person has been the victim of a wrongful act and has no reasonable alternative but to agree with the terms of another or be faced with serious financial hardship. . . . What constitutes a coercive act or reasonable alternative is a question of fact depending upon the circumstances of each case. . . . A person may not have a reasonable alternative or remedy when the delay in pursuing the remedy would cause immediate or irreparable serious loss or

[25] Bank Leumi Trust Co. v D'Evori International, Inc. 163 App Div 2d 26, 558 NYS2d 909 (1990).

financial ruin. . . . In an effort to avoid the effect of the release, Mr. Blubaugh stated . . . that (1) the only alternative he had to signing the release was to be fired and lose the $4,560.78 additional separation pay and the opportunity to have outplacement counseling, (2) he did not have the opportunity to negotiate the terms of his release, (3) he was in shock and distraught. . . .

Economic duress does not exist, however, merely because a person has been the victim of a wrongful act; in addition, the victim must have no choice but to agree to the other party's terms or face serious financial hardship. Thus, in order to avoid a contract, a party must also show that he had no reasonable alternative to agreeing to the other party's terms, or, as it is often stated, that he had no adequate remedy if the threat were to be carried out. . . .

What we apparently have here is someone who was initially satisfied with his settlement, but who, upon subsequent reflection, concludes that he could have gotten more out of the deal and therefore attempts to renege on it. However, it is well settled that the mere fact of an improvident or bad bargain or a feeling of latent discontent is not a sufficient basis to avoid the effect of an otherwise valid release.

[Judgment affirmed]

QUESTIONS

1. In the *Blubaugh* case the court states that one of the elements of economic duress is that the plaintiff "involuntarily accepts the terms of another." Appraise this statement.
2. The court also states that the plaintiff must be in a desperate situation which the court describes as the "circumstances permit no other alternative." Appraise this statement.
3. In the *Blubaugh* case, the court shows a definite desire to restrict the availability of the doctrine of economic pressure. How do you explain this attitude?

12. Adhesion Contracts

Pressure on a contracting party may not be as extreme as physical duress or economic duress. It may still be sufficient to justify the conclusion that there was no genuine assent freely given, and that, accordingly, the basic element of a voluntary agreement was lacking. Because of this, what appears to be a contract is merely a voidable transaction. Such a situation may involve a contract of adhesion. A contract of adhesion is one that is offered by a dominant party to a party with inferior bargaining power on a take-it-or-leave-it basis. The weaker person cannot go elsewhere to obtain the goods or services desired and therefore must deal on the terms dictated by the superior party or do without.

With the rise of the concept of unconscionability and the adoption of consumer protection laws, the need to apply the concept of the adhesion contract has diminished greatly. In most cases, it is held that the concept is not applicable either because there is not a gross inequality of bargaining power or because the goods or services could be obtained elsewhere. And in any case, the fact that the contract places a risk of loss on one party does not in itself establish that there was any improper pressure.[26] It is an essential aspect of freedom of contract that the parties can place any risk of loss where they choose.

---

[26] Hilb, Rogal & Hamilton Agency v Reynolds, 81 Ohio App 3d 330, 610 NE2d 1102 (1992).

The modern view of the concept of the contract of adhesion is seen in the *Hartland Computer* case.

E. REMEDIES

When there is not a genuine agreement of the parties, the remedy may be a rescission of the

HARTLAND COMPUTER LEASING CORP., INC. v INSURANCE MAN, INC.

(Mo App) 770 SW2d 525 (1989)

> In accordance with their prior agreement, Insurance Man selected a computer from Multitask, Inc., and Hartland Computer Leasing then purchased and leased the computer to Insurance Man. The lease between Hartland Computer and Insurance Man stated that Hartland Computer made no warranties. The lease stated that if the computer did not work, Insurance Man had to continue to pay rent and could not sue anyone except Multitask. The leased computer failed to work properly, and Insurance Man stopped making rental payments. Hartland Computer then sued Insurance Man for breach of the lease. Insurance Man raised the defense that the computer did not work properly. Hartland Computer claimed that Insurance Man could not raise that defense because of the provisions of the lease. Insurance Man replied that those terms were not binding because the lease was a contract of adhesion. Judgment was entered for Insurance Man, and Hartland Computer appealed.

GAERTNER, J. . . . An adhesion contract, as opposed to a negotiated contract, has been described as a form contract created and imposed by a stronger party upon a weaker party on a "take this or nothing basis," the terms of which unexpectedly or unconscionably limit the obligations of the drafting party. . . . Some writers view any pre-printed standardized form with filled-in blank spaces to be a contract of adhesion insofar as the pre-printed provisions are concerned. Thus, in *Corbin On Contracts*, § 559A at 660 (Supp. 1989), it is said "the bulk of contracts signed in this country, if not every major Western nation, are adhesion contracts. . . ." . . . Such form contracts are a natural concomitant of our mass production-mass consumer society. . . . Therefore, a rule automatically invalidating adhesion contracts would be completely unworkable. . . . Accordingly, courts do not view adhesion contracts as inherently sinister and automatically unenforceable. Rather, as with all contracts, the courts seek to enforce the reasonable expectations of the parties garnered not only from the words of a standardized form imposed by its proponent, but from the totality of the circumstances surrounding the transaction. . . . Only such provisions of the standardized form which fail to comport with such reasonable expectations and which are unexpected and unconscionably unfair are held to be unenforceable. . . . Because standardized contracts address the mass of users, the test for "reasonable expectations" is objective, addressed to the average member of the public who accepts such a contract, not the subjective expectations of an individual adherent. . . .

We look then to all the evidence surrounding this transaction to determine the objectively reasonable expectations of the parties and to the question of unconscionable unfairness imposed . . . under the terms of the form contract. [The court reviewed the facts and decided that the lease could not be condemned as unconscionable.]

[Judgment reversed and action remanded]

QUESTIONS

1. Was the provision excluding liability of Hartland Computer unreasonably unfair?
2. What insight does the *Hartland Computer* case give into the legal environment of business?
3. What is the significance of "contract of adhesion"?

contract, an action for damages, or an action for reformation of the contract.

Mistake, fraud, undue influence, and duress may make the agreement voidable or, in some instances, void. The following remedies are available.

13. Rescission

If the contract is voidable, it can be **rescinded** or set aside by the party who has been injured or of whom advantage has been taken. In no case can the wrongdoer set aside the contract. The object of rescission is to restore the status quo ante.

If not avoided, the contract that had been voidable is valid and binding. If the agreement is void, neither party can enforce it and no act of avoidance is required by either party to set the contract aside. The power to avoid a contract because of mistake or misrepresentation is lost if, with knowledge or reason to know of the mistake or misrepresentation, the aggrieved party delays an unreasonable time, affirms the transaction, or does any act inconsistent with avoiding the transaction.[27]

14. Damages

Some states allow the person harmed by an innocent misrepresentation to recover compensatory damages. Since such a misrepresentation is, by definition, neither intentional nor reckless, punitive damages cannot be recovered.[28] If the other party was guilty of a wrong, such as fraud, the injured party may sue for damages caused by such a wrong. In the case of the sale of goods, the aggrieved party may both rescind the contract and recover damages, but in other contracts, the victim must choose one of these two remedies.[29]

15. Reformation of Contract by Court

At times, a written contract does not correctly state the agreement already made by the parties. When this occurs, either party can have the court reform or correct the writing to state the agreement actually made. A court action for reformation may be necessary, because a change of circumstances or the occurrence of certain events may cause the other party to refuse to change the written contract voluntarily. For example, suppose Lauer obtains a collision insurance policy on an automobile, but through a mistake the policy describes the wrong car. Lauer can obtain a decree of court

---

[27] Thorstenson v Arco Alaska, Inc. (Alaska) 780 P2d 371 (1989).

[28] Christopher v Heimlich (Ala Civ App) 523 So 2d 466 (1988).

[29] Eklund v Koenig & Associates, Inc. (Wis App) 451 NW2d 150 (1989).

declaring that the policy covers the car that Lauer and the insurance company intended to insure rather than the car wrongly identified in the policy. The insurance company would gladly have made the correction prior to any loss being sustained, but if the car Lauer intended to insure has been damaged, court reformation would probably be necessary.

In the *Phil Bramsen* case the parties contracted in terms of a cost of living index that did not exist.

A party seeking reformation of a contract must clearly prove both the grounds for reformation and what the agreement actually was.[30]

PHIL BRAMSEN DISTRIBUTOR, INC. v MASTRONI AND KUHSE
(App) 151 Ariz 194, 726 P2d 610 (1986)

> Mastroni and Kuhse leased land to Phil Bramsen Distributor. The lease specified the amount of the rent and provided that such amount would be reset every five years according to the cost of living index prepared by the United States Department of Labor for the city of Phoenix. A dispute arose, and the lessee brought a suit to rescind the lease on the ground that there was no such cost of living index. The lessor counterclaimed, seeking a reformation of the lease. The lower court reformed the lease to refer to the Phoenix cost of living index prepared by the Bureau of Business and Economic Research at Arizona State University. The lessee appealed.

HATHAWAY, J. . . . Neither the Bureau of Labor Statistics (BLS) nor any other subdivision of the United States Government prepares a consumer price index (CPI) for Phoenix. . . .

After a trial to the court, judgment was entered . . . reforming the rent escalation clause by replacing the "consumer price index prepared by the United States Bureau of Labor Statistics" with the "consumer price index for Phoenix, Arizona." The court went on to hold that the metropolitan Phoenix consumer price index prepared by the Bureau of Business and Economic Research, Arizona State University, would be used in the reformed escalation clause. . . .

Before reformation can be granted, a court must be presented with clear and convincing evidence that (1) a mutual mistake was made by the parties in drafting the instrument, and (2) that the minds of the parties had met on a definite intention before the instrument was drafted. . . .

In the present case, the parties agreed to an escalation clause based on the rate of inflation. It was a mistake of fact that caused the clause to fail. The draftsman, Mastroni's attorney, inserted the term "cost of living index for the City of Phoenix prepared by the Bureau of Labor Statistics." There is no evidence that either appellees or appellants Bramsen had any independent knowledge of such an index or relied on anyone's word but the attorney's. Therefore, by mutual mistake the parties believed they had a workable formula. Appellants argue that because the attorney was

---

[30] Re Brazelton, ___ Ill App 3d ___, ___ Ill Dec ___, 604 NE2d 376 (1992).

Mastroni's agent, the mistake is still unilateral. Even if we were to agree that the drafter was Mastroni's agent, this argument fails. If a mutual mistake of the parties results from the mistake of the draftsman, it is immaterial, so far as reformation is concerned, which party employed him.

The parties clearly intended to have an escalation clause based on inflation. It was only the error of the scrivener that caused this escalation clause to be unenforceable and the trial court could have found that there was a mutual mistake.

Appellants also argue that there was no agreement by the parties to the lease concerning the escalation clause prior to the drafting of the lease. The parties did, however, agree that there would be an escalation clause based upon inflation. . . . No equitable reason appears for refusing to reform the lease agreement. On the contrary, equity favors the reformation, otherwise appellant would receive an unconscionable windfall if allowed to enforce his lease at the current rental price. . . .

We see no equitable, legal or factual reasons for precluding the trial court from reforming this contract.

[Judgment as to reformation affirmed]

QUESTIONS

1. Why was reformation granted in the *Bramsen* case?
2. What was the significance of the fact that the improper description of the cost of living index was added to the written lease by the attorney for one of the lessors? Explain.
3. Did the court regard the lease provision relating to the cost of living index as ambiguous?

SUMMARY

An agreement that otherwise appears to be a contract may not be binding because a party thereto lacks contractual capacity. In such a case, the contract is ordinarily voidable at the election of that party who lacks contractual capacity. In some cases, the contract is void. Ordinarily, contractual incapacity is the inability, for mental or physical reasons, to understand that a contract is being made and to understand its general terms and nature. This is typically the case when it is claimed that incapacity exists because of insanity or intoxication. The incapacity of minors arises because society is discriminating in favor of that class to protect them from unwise contracts.

In most states today, the age of majority is 18 years. Minors can avoid most contracts. If the minor received anything from the other party, the minor, on avoiding the contract,

must return what had been received from the other party, if the minor still has it.

When a minor avoids a contract for a necessary, the minor must pay the reasonable value of any benefit received. The concept of a necessary has expanded.

Only a minor is liable for the minor's contract. Parents of the minor are not liable on the contracts of the minor merely because they are the parents. Frequently, an adult will enter into the contract as a coparty of the minor. Such an adult is liable on the contract made by such person and the minor without regard to whether the minor has avoided the contract.

The contract of an insane person is voidable to much the same extent as the contract of a minor. An important distinction is that if a guardian has been appointed for the insane person, a contract made by the insane person is void and not merely voidable.

An intoxicated person lacks contractual capacity to make a contract if the intoxication is such that the person does not understand that a contract is being made.

The consent of a party to an agreement is not genuine or voluntary in certain cases of mistake, deception, or pressure. When this is so, what appears to be a contract can be avoided by the victim of such circumstances or conduct.

As to mistake, it is necessary to distinguish between unilateral mistakes that are unknown to the other contracting party and those that are known. Mistakes that are unknown to the other party usually do not affect the binding character of the agreement. A unilateral mistake of which the other contracting party has knowledge or has reason to know makes the contract avoidable by the victim of the mistake.

The deception situation may be one of innocent misrepresentation, nondisclosure, or fraud. The innocent misrepresentation generally has no effect on the binding quality of an agreement, although there is a trend to recognize it as a ground for avoiding the contract. A few courts allow the recovery of damages. When one party to the contract knows of a fact that has a bearing on the transaction, the failure to volunteer information as to that fact to the other contracting party is called nondisclosure. The law ordinarily does not attach any significance to nondisclosure. Contrary to this rule, there is a duty to volunteer information when a confidential relationship exists between the possessor of the knowledge and the other contracting party. A strong modern trend in the law imposes a duty to disclose or volunteer information relating to matters that are not likely to be inquired about by the other contracting party.

When concealment goes beyond mere silence and consists of actively taking steps to hide the truth, the conduct may be classified as fraud rather than nondisclosure. There is a growing trend to hold fine print clauses not binding, on the theory that they are designed to hide the truth from the other contracting party. Consumer protection statutes often outlaw fine print clauses by requiring particular contracts or particular clauses in contracts to be printed in type of a specified size. A statement of opinion, value, or law cannot ordinarily be the basis for fraud liability, although it can be when the maker of the false statement claims to be an expert as to the particular subject matter and is making the statement as an expert.

The free will of a person, essential to the voluntary character of a contract, may be lacking because the agreement had been obtained by pressure. This may range from undue influence, through the array of threats of extreme economic loss (called economic duress), to the threat of physical force that would cause serious personal injury or damage to property (called physical duress). The mere fact that one party to the contract has great bargaining power and offers the other party a printed contract on a take-it-or-leave-it basis (an adhesion contract) does not prove that the agreement was not voluntary. However, some courts have held that in such cases, the agreement is not voluntary if the weaker party cannot obtain the desired goods or services elsewhere.

When the voluntary character of an agreement has been destroyed by mistake, deception, or pressure, the victim may avoid or rescind the contract or may ratify the contract and obtain money damages from the wrongdoer. When the mistake consists of an error in putting an oral contract in writing, either party may ask the court to reform the writing so that it states the actual agreement of the parties.

LAW IN PRACTICE

1. When you make a contract, check that the other contracting parties have the capacity to make a contract. If there is any question on this point, require a cosigner with capacity.

2. Check that the facts are as you believe them to be. Do not be deceived by your own wishful thinking or by false statements of the other party.

3. When dealing in a field of expert knowledge, get an expert to assist you.

4. When facts are known only to the other party, write that party asking specific questions and instruct that party to reply by letter. This way you have the express statements of the other party and written proof of them.

5. If you learn that you entered into a contract by being deceived or pressured, seek judicial relief promptly.

QUESTIONS AND CASE PROBLEMS

1. What social forces influence each of the following rules of law: (a) One party generally cannot set aside a contract because the other party failed to volunteer information that the complaining party would desire to know; (b) In certain close relationships that are regarded as confidential, it is presumed that a contract that benefits the dominating person was obtained by undue influence, and the dominating person has the burden of proving the contrary.

2. Lester purchased a used automobile from MacKintosh Motors. He asked the seller if the car had ever been in a wreck. The MacKintosh salesperson had never seen the car before that morning and knew nothing of its history, but quickly answered Lester's question by stating: "No. It has never been in a wreck." In fact, the auto had been seriously damaged in a wreck and, although repaired, was worth much less than the value it would have had if there had not been any wreck. When Lester learned the truth, he sued MacKintosh Motors and the salesperson for damages for fraud. They raised the defense that the salesperson did not know that the statement was false and had not intended to deceive Lester. Did the conduct of the salesperson constitute fraud?

3. Helen, age 17, wanted to buy a motorcycle. She did not have the money to pay cash but persuaded the dealer to sell a cycle to her on credit. The dealer did so partly because Helen said that she was 22 and showed the dealer an identification card that falsely stated her age as 22. Helen drove the motorcycle away. A few days later, she damaged it and then returned it to the dealer and stated that she avoided the contract because she was a minor. The dealer said that she could not do so because (a) she had misrepresented her age and (b) the motorcycle was damaged. Can she avoid the contract?

4. Yang and Richard make a contract for the sale of an automobile. They orally agree that the price Richard is to pay is $2,000, but when the written contract is typed, the amount is wrongly stated as $3,000. This contract is signed before anyone notices the mistake. Yang then claims that the written contract is binding and that Richard is required to pay $3,000. Richard claims that he is only required to pay the originally agreed-on amount of $2,000. Is he correct?

5. Thompson bought an automobile on credit from Central Motor Co. The contract required him to pay 35 monthly installments of $125 and a final installment of $5,265. Thompson claimed that he agreed to buy because the sales manager falsely assured him that when the last payment was due it could be refinanced by signing another note for that amount at 8 percent interest. Thereafter, Central Motor refused to finance the final payment unless Thompson promised to pay 12 percent interest. He refused to do so and returned the car. Central sold the car and then sued Thompson for the balance remaining due. Is Thompson liable? What are the ethical values involved? *[Central Motor Co. v Thompson (Tex Civ App) 465 SW2d 405]*

6. Thomas Bell, a minor, went to work in the Pittsburgh beauty parlor of Sam Pankas and agreed that when he left the employment, he would not work in or run a beauty parlor business within a ten-mile radius of downtown Pittsburgh for a period of two years. Contrary to this provision, Bell and another employee of Pankas opened up a beauty shop three blocks from Pankas's shop and advertised themselves as former employees of Pankas. Pankas sued Bell to stop the breach of the noncompetition or restrictive covenant. Bell claimed that he was not bound because he was a minor when he had agreed to the covenant. Was he bound by the covenant? *[Pankas v Bell, 413 Pa 494, 198 A2d 312]*

7. Aldrich and Company sold goods to Donovan on credit. The amount owed grew steadily, and finally Aldrich refused to sell any more to Donovan unless Donovan signed a promissory note for the amount due. Donovan did not want to do so but signed the note because he had no money and needed more goods. When Aldrich brought an action to enforce the note, Donovan claimed that the note was not binding because it had been obtained by means of economic duress. Was he correct? [*Aldrich & Co. v Donovan, 238 Mont 431, 778 P2d 397*]

8. Adams claimed that Boyd owed him money. Adams was under the impression that Boyd did not have much money. On the basis of this impression, Adams made a settlement agreement with Boyd for a nominal amount. When Adams later learned that Boyd was in fact reasonably wealthy, Adams sought to set the agreement aside. Was Adams entitled to do so?

9. An agent of Thor Food Service Corp. was seeking to sell Makofske a combination refrigerator-freezer and food purchase plan. Makofske was married and had three children. After being informed of the eating habits of Makofske and his family, the agent stated that the cost of the freezer and food would be about $95 to $100 a month. Makofske carefully examined the agent's itemized estimate and made some changes to it. Makofske then signed the contract and purchased the refrigerator-freezer. The cost proved to be greater than the estimated $95 to $100 a month, and Makofske claimed that the contract had been obtained by fraud. Decide. [*Thor Food Service Corp. v Makofske, 28 Misc 2d 872, 218 NYS2d 93*]

10. In 1622, a fleet of Spanish treasure ships sank 40 nautical miles off the Florida coast. In 1971, Treasure Salvors, Inc. located one of the wrecked ships, the Atocha. Treasure Salvors and the State of Florida believed that the wreck was located on the Florida coastal strip. On this basis, the State of Florida and Treasure Salvors made successive annual contracts giving Treasure Salvors the right to search for sunken treasure in the wreck in return for its giving Florida 25 percent of everything that was found. In a subsequent lawsuit, it was determined that the wreck was not on Florida land. Treasure Salvors claimed that it was not bound by its contract with Florida. Was it correct? [*Florida v Treasure Salvors, Inc. (CA5 Fla) 621 F2d 1340*]

11. Sippy was thinking of buying the house of Christich. He noticed watermarks on the ceiling, but the agent showing the house stated that the roof had been repaired and was in good condition. Sippy was not told that the roof still leaked and that the repairs had not been able to stop the leak-ing. Sippy bought the house. Some time later, heavy rains caused water to leak into the house. Sippy claimed that Christich was guilty of fraud. Was he correct? [*Sippy v Christich, 4 Kan App 2d 511, 609 P2d 204*]

12. Pileggi owed money to Young. Young threatened to bring suit against Pileggi for the amount due. Pileggi feared the embarrassment of being sued and the possibility that he might be thrown into bankruptcy because of the suit. To avoid being sued, Pileggi executed a promissory note promising to pay to Young the amount due. He later asserted that the note was not binding because he had executed it under duress. Is this defense valid? [*Young v Pileggi, 309 Pa Super 565, 455 A2d 1228*]

13. Scott was employed by Litigation Reprographics and Support Services, Inc. The contract of employment was "at will" which gave the employer the right to fire Scott at any time for any reason or for no reason. Reprographics told Scott that if he wanted to keep his job he would have to sign a contract stating that he would not compete with Reprographics when he was no longer employed by Reprographics. He signed the contract but later claimed that he was not bound by it because it had been obtained by economic duress because he had to have the job. Decide.

14. The C & J Publishing Company told the seller of computers that it wanted a computer system that would operate its printing presses. C & J specified that it wanted only new equipment and that no used equipment would be acceptable. The seller delivered to C & J a system that was a combination of new and secondhand parts because it did not have sufficient new parts to fill the order. When the buyer later learned what had happened it sued the seller for fraud. The seller raised the defense that no statement or warranty had been made that all parts of the system were new and that it would not therefore be liable for fraud. Decide.

15. The City of Salinas entered into a contract with Souza & McCue Construction Company to construct a sewer. The city officials knew that unusual subsoil conditions (including extensive quicksand) existed that would make performance of the contract unusually difficult. That information was not disclosed when city officials advertised for bids. The advertisement for bids directed bidders to "examine carefully the site of the work" and declared that the submission of a bid would constitute "evidence that the bidder had made such examination." Souza & McCue was awarded the contract, but because of the subsoil conditions it could not complete on time and was sued by Salinas for breach of contract. Souza & McCue counterclaimed on the basis that the city had not revealed its information of the subsoil conditions and was liable for the loss caused thereby. Was the city liable? [*City of Salinas v Souza & McCue Construction Co. 66 Cal App 2d 217, 57 Cal Rptr 337, 424 P2d 921*]

CHAPTER 12

CONSIDERATION

LEARNING OBJECTIVES

After studying this chapter, you will be able to:
1. *Define what constitutes consideration.*
2. *State the effect of the absence of considera-tion.*
3. *Identify promises that can serve as considera-tion.*
4. *Distinguish between present consideration and past consideration.*
5. *State when forbearance can be consideration.*
6. *Recognize situations in which adequacy of consideration has significance.*
7. *List the exceptions to the requirement of con-sideration.*

Will the law enforce every promise? Generally, a promise will not be enforced unless something is given or received for the promise.

A. GENERAL PRINCIPLES

As a general rule, one of the elements needed to make an agreement binding is consideration.

1. Definition

Consideration is what a promisor demands and receives as the price for the promise.[1] Consideration is something to which the promisor is not otherwise entitled, which the promisor specifies as the price for the promise.

It is not necessary that the promisor expressly use the word *consideration.*

Since consideration is the price paid for the promise, it is unimportant who pays that price, as long as it has been agreed that it should be paid in that way. For example, consideration may be the extending of credit to a third person, such as extending credit to the corporation of which the promisor is a stockholder. Likewise, when a bank lends money to a third person, such lending is consideration for the promise of its customer to repay the loan to the bank if it will loan the money to the third person.

(a) NATURE OF CONTRACT. In a unilateral contract, the consideration for the promise is the doing of the act called for. The doing of the act in such case is also the acceptance of the offer of the promisor.

In a bilateral contract, which is an exchange of promises, each promise is the consideration for the other promise. When a lawsuit is brought for breaking a promise, it is the consideration for the broken promise to which attention is directed.

(b) AGREED EXCHANGE. Consideration is what is agreed to in return for the promise. In most cases, this will directly benefit the promisor and will be some burden or detriment to the promisee. For example, an employer who promises to pay wages sustains detriment by promising to pay the wages in exchange for the benefit of receiving the employee's promise to work. The important thing, however, is that what is received is what was asked for as the price of the promise.

As long as someone gives what was asked for by the promisor, the promisor's obligation is supported by consideration, even though the economic benefit of the promise is not received by the person giving the consideration. Thus, when a third person comes to the financial aid of a debtor by making some promise to the creditor in exchange for some promise from the creditor, consideration exists. The contract is binding, even though the creditor's promise benefits the debtor rather than the third person. A promise guaranteeing repayment of a loan to a corporation is binding although the money loaned was all received by the corporation and nothing was received by the promisor, even though the promisor is not a shareholder of the corporation.[2]

2. Effect of Absence of Consideration

The absence of consideration makes a promise not binding.[3] Thus, a person sued for breaking a promise will not be held liable when no consideration was received for the promise. For example, an employee may promise to refrain from competing with the employer when the employment relationship ends. If the promise is not supported by consideration, the promise is not binding, and the former employee may compete with the former employer.

(a) MORAL OBLIGATION. The fact that the promisor feels morally obligated to make

---

[1] Roark v Stallworth Oil and Gas, Inc. (Tex) 813 SW2d 492 (1991).

[2] Dunkin Donuts of America, Inc. v Liberatore, 138 App Div 2d 559, 526 NYS2d 141 (1988).

[3] Rothell v Continental Cas. Co. ___ Ga App ___, 402 SE2d 283 (1991).

the promise does not make the promise binding when there is no consideration for it.[4]

(b) LEGALITY DISTINGUISHED. While the absence of consideration ordinarily prevents enforcing a promise, the absence of consideration has no greater effect. That is, the agreement is not illegal because there was no consideration. Consequently, when a person keeps the promise, the performance rendered cannot later be revoked on the ground that there was no consideration. To illustrate, a promise to make a gift cannot be enforced because there is no consideration for the promise. However, once the gift is made, the donor cannot take the gift back because there was no consideration.

3. Legality of Consideration

The law will not permit persons to make contracts that violate the law. Accordingly, a promise to do something that the law prohibits or a promise to refrain from doing something that the law requires is not valid consideration, and the contract is illegal.

4. Failure of Consideration

When a promise is given as consideration, the question arises as to whether the promisor will perform the promise.

(a) NONPERFORMANCE OF PROMISE. If the promise is not performed, the law describes the default as a **failure of consideration**. This is a breach of the contract because what was required by the contract has not been performed.[5]

(b) BAD BARGAIN DISTINGUISHED. When the promisor performs the promise, there is never a failure of consideration. The fact that it turns out that the consideration is disappointing does not mean that there has been a failure of consideration. That is, the fact that the contract proves to be a bad bargain for the promisor does not constitute a failure of consideration, nor does it affect the binding character of the contract. Thus, the fact that a business purchased by the buyers does not prove profitable does not constitute a failure of consideration that releases them from their obligation to the seller.[6]

B. WHAT CONSTITUTES CONSIDERATION

The sections that follow analyze certain common situations in which a lawsuit turned on whether the promisor received consideration for the promise sued upon.

5. A Promise as Consideration

In a bilateral contract, each party makes a promise to the other. The promise that one party makes is consideration for the promise made by the other.

The fact that parties appear to be in agreement does not mean that there is a promise. Thus, a statement that a proposed loan would be no problem does not constitute a promise to make a loan.

(a) BINDING CHARACTER OF PROMISE. To constitute consideration, a promise must be binding; that is, it must impose a liability or create a duty. An unenforceable promise cannot be consideration. Suppose

---

[4] Production Credit Ass'n of Mandan v Rub (ND) 475 NW2d 532 (1991). As to the Louisiana rule of moral consideration, see Thomas v Bryant (La App) 596 So 2d 1065 (1992).

[5] Check Control, Inc. v Shepherd (ND) 462 NW2d 644 (1990).

[6] Commerce Bank of Joplin v Shallenburger (Mo App) 766 SW2d 764 (1989).

that a coal company promises to sell to a factory at a specific price all the coal that it orders, and that the factory agrees to pay that price for any coal that it orders from the coal company. The promise of the factory is not consideration because it does not obligate the factory to buy any coal from the coal company.

A promise that in fact does not impose any obligation on the promisor is often called an **illusory promise** because, although it looks like a binding promise, it is not. The *Rosenberg* case turned on whether promises were binding or illusory.

ROSENBERG v LAWRENCE
(Fla App) 541 So 2d 1204 (1988)

Charles Rosenberg and Cynthia Lawrence had married and then divorced. They made a 1978 agreement to share equally in the education, maintenance, support, and health care of their four sons. The agreement stated that the parents "shall consult one another before incurring a material expense." Disputes arose with respect to the consulting, and a 1982 amendment was made stating that the consulting provision meant that neither of them "will be obligated to pay for any material, unusual, or extraordinary expense to which he or she does not consent." At the time of this agreement, one of the sons, Howard, was a student at college. He left to go to work but later enrolled in another college. Cynthia paid all his expenses from September 1984 to November 1985, totaling $43,616.38. She demanded that Charles pay her half of this amount. He refused to pay her, on the ground that he had not been consulted and had not consented to the expense. Cynthia sued Charles for one-half of the expenses. Judgment was entered in favor of Cynthia. Charles appealed.

NESBITT, J. . . . Where one party retains to itself the option of fulfilling or declining to fulfill its obligations under the contract, there is no valid contract and neither side may be bound. . . ."One who in words promises to render a future performance, if he so wills and desires when the future time arrives, has made no real promise at all." 1 *Corbin on Contracts* § 149 (1963). *See also Port Largo Club, Inc. v Warren*, 476 So 2d 1330 (Fla 3d DCA 1985) (vendor's contract obligation wholly illusory where he could breach contract with impunity); *Young v Johnston*, 475 So 2d 1309 (Fla 1st DCA 1985) and cases cited therein (where one party retains to itself the option of fulfilling or declining to fulfill its obligations under the contract, there is no valid contract and neither side may be bound); *Spooner v Reserve Life Ins. Co.*, 47 Wash 2d 454, 287 P2d 735 (1955) (statement by insurance company that sales bonus was voluntary and could be withheld with or without notice rendered promise illusory and unenforceable). "An illusory promise is no promise at all as that term has been . . . defined. If the expression appears to have the form of a promise, this appearance is 'an illusion.'" 1 *Corbin on Contracts* § 16 (1963). "As a matter of course, no action will lie against the party making the illusory promise. Having made no promise, it is not possible for him to be guilty of a breach." 1 *Corbin on Contracts* § 145 (1963).

   Under the 1982 modification, the parties were not "obligated for any material, unusual or extraordinary expense to which he or she does not consent." Because payment was contingent upon each parent's consent to undertake an obligation, Charles and Cynthia's "promise" represented no more than an illusion which did not obligate either party to act. The illusory nature of each parent's promise made that promise void and the mother has no right to seek reimbursement based on that illusory commitment, either by way of direct action for breach or under an estoppel theory.

See 1A Corbin on Contracts § 201 (1963) (action in reliance on a supposed promise creates no obligation on a man whose only promise is wholly illusory). Their "obligation" meant nothing more than, "I will if I want to.". . . .

[Judgment reversed and action remanded]

QUESTIONS

1. What was the basis of the court's decision?
2. Could the court have decided the case on any other grounds?
3. Why does the law hold that an illusory promise is not binding?

(b) CONDITIONAL PROMISE. Can a conditional promise be consideration? Assume that an agreement states buyer promises to buy, provided buyer can obtain financing. Is such a promise consideration for the sellers promise to sell, or is the buyers promise not consideration because it does not impose any obligation on the buyer at the time that the promise is made?

The fact that a promise is conditional does not prevent it from being consideration, even when, as a practical matter, it is unlikely that the condition would ever be satisfied.[7] Thus, the promise of a fire insurance company to pay the homeowner in case of fire is consideration for the payment of premiums by the homeowner, even though it is probable that there will never be a fire.

(c) CANCELLATION PROVISION. Although a promise must impose a binding obligation, it may authorize one or either party to terminate or cancel the agreement under certain circumstances or on giving notice to the other party. The fact that the contract may be terminated in this manner does not make the contract any less binding prior to such termination.

6. Promise to Perform Existing Obligation

Ordinarily, doing or promising to do what one is already under a legal obligation to do is not consideration.[8] Similarly, a promise to refrain from doing what one has no legal right to do is not consideration. This preexisting duty or legal obligation can be based on statute, on general principles of law, on responsibilities of an office held by the promisor, or on a preexisting contract.

(a) COMPLETION OF CONTRACT. Suppose a contractor refuses to complete a building unless the owner promises a payment or bonus in addition to the sum specified in the original contract, and the owner promises to make that payment. The question then arises as to whether the owner's promise is binding. Most courts hold that the second promise of the owner is without consideration.

---

7 Charles Hester Enterprises, Inc. v Illinois Founders Ins. Co. 114 Ill 2d 278, 102 Ill Dec 306, 499 NE2d 1319 (1986).

8 Waide v Tractor and Equipment Co. (Ala) 545 So 2d 1327 (1989).

If the promise of the contractor is to do something that is neither expressed nor implied as part of the first contract, then the promise of the other party is binding. For example, if a bonus of $1,000 is promised in return for the promise of a contractor to complete the building at a date earlier than that specified in the original agreement, the promise to pay the bonus is binding.

(1) Good-Faith Adjustment. There is a trend to enforce a second promise to pay a contractor a greater amount for the performance of the original contract when there are extraordinary circumstances caused by unforeseeable difficulties and when the additional amount promised the contractor is reasonable under the circumstances.

When parties to a contract, in a good-faith effort to meet the business realities of a situation, agree to a reduction of contract terms, there is some authority that the promise of the one party to accept the lesser performance of the other is binding. These cases have held that the promise is binding, even though technically the promise to render the lesser performance is not consideration because the obligor was already obligated to render the greater performance. Thus, a landlord's promise to reduce the rent was binding when the tenant could not pay the original rent and the landlord preferred to have the building occupied even though receiving a smaller rental. A similar good faith adjustment to economic realities was made in the *Angel* case.

ANGEL v MURRAY
113 RI 482, 322 A2d 630 (1974)

John Murray was director of finance for the city of Newport. A contract was made with Alfred Maher to remove trash. Later, Maher requested that the city council increase his compensation. Maher's costs were greater than had been anticipated because four hundred new dwelling units had been put into operation. The city council voted to pay Maher an additional $10,000 a year. After two such annual payments had been made, Angel and other citizens of the city sued Murray and Maher for a return of the $20,000. They said that Maher was already obligated by his contract to perform the work for the contract sum, and there was, accordingly, no consideration for the payment of the increased compensation. From a decision in favor of the plaintiffs, the city and Maher appealed.

ROBERTS, C. J. . . . It is generally held that a modification of a contract is itself a contract, which is unenforceable unless supported by consideration. . . .

The preexisting duty rule is followed by most jurisdictions. . . .

The primary purpose of the preexisting duty rule is to prevent what has been referred to as the "hold-up game". . . . . A classic example of the "hold-up game" is found in *Alaska Packers' Ass'n v Domenico*, 117 F 99 (9th Cir 1902). There 21 seamen entered into a written contract with Domenico to sail from San Francisco to Pyramid Harbor, Alaska. They were to work as sailors and fishermen out of Pyramid Harbor during the fishing season of 1900. The contract specified that each man would be paid $50 plus two cents for each red salmon he caught. Subsequent to their arrival at Pyramid Harbor, the men stopped work and demanded an additional $50. They threatened to return to San Francisco if Domenico did not agree to their demand.

Since it was impossible for Domenico to find other men, he agreed to pay the men an additional $50. After they returned to San Francisco, Domenico refused to pay the men an additional $50. The court found that the subsequent agreement to pay the men an additional $50 was not supported by consideration because the men had a preexisting duty to work on the ship under the original contract, and thus the subsequent agreement was unenforceable.

Another example of the "hold-up game" is found in the area of construction contracts. Frequently, a contractor will refuse to complete work under an unprofitable contract unless he is awarded additional compensation. The courts have generally held that a subsequent agreement to award additional compensation is unenforceable if the contractor is only performing work which would have been required of him under the original contract. . . .

These examples clearly illustrate that the courts will not enforce an agreement that has been procured by coercion or duress and will hold the parties to their original contract regardless of whether it is profitable or unprofitable. However, the courts have been reluctant to apply the preexisting duty rule when a party to a contract encounters unanticipated difficulties and the other party, not influenced by coercion or duress, voluntarily agrees to pay additional compensation for work already required to be performed under the contract. For example, the courts have found that the original contract was rescinded, . . . abandoned, . . . or waived.

Although the preexisting duty rule has served a useful purpose insofar as it deters parties from using coercion and duress to obtain additional compensation, it has been widely criticized as a general rule of law. . . . The modern trend appears to recognize the necessity that courts should enforce agreements modifying contracts when unexpected or unanticipated difficulties arise during the course of the performance of a contract, even though there is no consideration for the modification, as long as the parties agree voluntarily.

Under the Uniform Commercial Code, § 2-209(1), . . . "an agreement modifying a contract [for the sale of goods] needs no consideration to be binding." . . . Although at first blush this section appears to validate modifications obtained by coercion and duress, the comments to this section indicate that a modification under this section must meet the test of good faith imposed by the Code, and a modification obtained by extortion without a legitimate commercial reason is unenforceable.

The modern trend away from a rigid application of the preexisting duty rule is reflected by § 89D(a) of the American Law Institute's Restatement Second of the Law of Contracts, which provides: "A promise modifying a duty under a contract not fully performed on either side is binding (a) if the modification is fair and equitable in view of circumstances not anticipated by the parties when the contract was made. . . ."

We believe that § 89D(a) is the proper rule of law and find it applicable to the facts of this case. It not only prohibits modifications obtained by coercion, duress, or extortion but also fulfills society's expectation that agreements entered into voluntarily will be enforced by the courts. . . .

Section 89D(a), of course, does not compel a modification of an unprofitable or unfair contract; it only enforces a modification if the parties voluntarily agree and if (1) the promise modifying the original contract was made before the contract was fully performed on either side, (2) the underlying circumstances which prompted the modification were unanticipated by the parties, and (3) the modification is fair and equitable.

The evidence, which is uncontradicted, reveals that in June of 1968 Maher requested the city council to pay him an additional $10,000 for the year beginning on July 1, 1968, and ending on June 30, 1969. This request was made at a public meeting of the city council, where Maher explained in detail his reasons for making the request. Thereafter, the city council voted to authorize the Mayor to sign an amendment to the 1964 contract which provided that Maher would receive an additional $10,000 per year for the duration of the contract. Under such circumstances we have no doubt that the city voluntarily agreed to modify the 1964 contract.

Having determined the voluntariness of this agreement, we turn our attention to the three criteria delineated above. First, the modification was made in June of 1968 at a time when the five-year contract which was made in 1964 had not been fully performed by either party. Second, although the 1964 contract provided that Maher collect all refuse generated within the city, it appears this contract was premised on Maher's past experience that the number of refuse-generating units would increase at a rate of 20 to 25 per year. Furthermore, the evidence is uncontradicted that the 1967-1968 increase of 400 units "went beyond any previous expectation." Clearly, the circumstances which prompted the city council to modify the 1964 contract were unanticipated. Third, although the evidence does not indicate what proportion of the total this increase comprised, the evidence does indicate that it was a "substantial" increase. In light of this, we cannot say that the council's agreement to pay Maher the $10,000 increase was not fair and equitable in the circumstances.

[Judgment reversed and action remanded]

QUESTIONS

1. What was the basis for the plaintiff's suit?
2. How would the *Angel* case have been decided under the common law rule as to consideration?
3. Could the contract have been written in a way that would have avoided the problem involved in the *Angel* case?

(2) Contract for Sale of Goods. When the contract is for the sale of goods, any modification made in good faith by the parties to the contract is binding, without regard to the existence of consideration for the modification.

(b) COMPROMISE AND RELEASE OF CLAIMS. The rule that doing or promising to do what one is bound to do is not consideration applies to a part payment made in satisfaction of an admitted debt. Thus, a promise to pay part of an amount that is admittedly owed is not consideration for a promise to discharge the balance. It will not prevent the creditor from demanding the remainder later.

If the debtor pays before the debt is due, there is consideration, since on the day when the payment was made, the creditor was not entitled to demand any payment. Likewise, if the creditor accepts some article (even of slight value) in addition to the part payment, consideration exists, and the agreement is held to be binding.

A debtor and creditor may have a bona fide dispute as to the amount owed or as to whether any amount is owed. In such a case, payment by the debtor of less than the amount claimed by the creditor is consideration for the latter's agreement to release or settle the claim. It is generally regarded as sufficient if the claimant believes in the merit of the claim. Conversely, if the claimant knows that the claim does not have any merit and is merely pressing the claim to force the other party to make some payment to buy peace from the annoyance of a lawsuit, the settlement agreement based on the part payment is not binding.

(c) PART-PAYMENT CHECKS. The acceptance and cashing of a check for part of a debt releases the entire debt when the check bears a notation that it is intended as final or full payment and the total amount due is disputed or unliquidated. It probably has this same effect even though the debt is not disputed or is liquidated.[9] In some jurisdictions, this principle is applied without regard to the form of payment or whether the claim is disputed. The California Civil Code, § 1541, provides: "An obligation is extinguished by a release therefrom given to the debtor by the creditor upon a new consideration, or in writing, with or without new consideration."

(d) COMPOSITION OF CREDITORS. In a **composition of creditors**, the various creditors of one debtor mutually agree to accept a fractional part of their claims in full satisfaction thereof. Such agreements are binding and are supported by consideration. When creditors agree to extend the due date of their debts, the promise of each creditor to forbear is likewise consideration for the promise of other creditors to forbear.

7. Present Consideration Versus Past Benefits

Consideration is what the promisor states must be received in return for the promise. Therefore, consideration must be given when or after the promisor states what is demanded.

(a) PAST CONSIDERATION. Past benefits already received by the promisor cannot be consideration for a later promise.[10] The *Kelsoe* case turned on the effect of past consideration.

C
P
A
C
P
A

KELSOE v INTERNATIONAL WOOD PRODUCTS, INC.

(Ala) 588 So 2d 877 (1991)

Kelsoe worked for International Wood Products, Inc., for a number of years. One day Mr. Hernandez, a director and major stockholder of the company, promised her that the corporation would give her 5% of the stock of the company. This promise was never kept and she sued International for breach of contract. The lower court entered judgment in favor of International and Kelsoe appealed.

HOUSTON, J. . . . International Wood, one of the corporation's directors and its major stockholder, promised Kelsoe that it would issue five percent of the corporation's stock (500 shares) to her at par value ($.10 per share). Kelsoe's undisputed trial testimony reflects the nature of that promise:

> "*Q. Ms. Kelsoe, you were compensated for your work at International Wood, weren't you?*
>
> "*A. Yes, sir, I received a check.*

---

[9] Hearst Corp. v Lauerer, Martin & Gibbs, Inc. 37 Ohio App 3d 87, 524 NE2d 193 (1987).

[10] Sager v Basham, ___ Va ___, 401 SE2d 676 (1991).

"Q. *Were you pleased with your compensation?*

"A. *Yes, sir.*

"Q. *Did you think you were compensated well enough for the work you did?*

"A. *Yes, sir.*

"Q. *Ms. Kelsoe, you never entered an agreement with Mr. Hernandez; 'Mr. Hernandez, if I work long and hard and do this' and then he said, 'I'll give you five percent of the corporation,' did you?*

"A. *No, sir.*

"Q. *You never had that kind of a bargain, did you?*

"A. *No, sir.*

"Q. *And all the time, all the work you did was part of your normal job?*

"A. *Yes, sir."*

. . . It is a well-settled general rule that consideration is an essential element of, and is necessary to the enforceability or validity of, a contract. . . . It is generally stated that in order to constitute consideration for a promise, there must have been an act, a forbearance, a detriment, or a destruction of a legal right, or a return promise, bargained for and given in exchange for the promise. . . .The undisputed evidence here shows that International Wood's promise to issue the stock to Kelsoe was gratuitous in nature and was prompted only by Kelsoe's past favorable job performance. As such, International Wood's promise was without consideration and created no legally enforceable contract right.

[Judgment affirmed]

QUESTIONS

1. Appraise the rule applied by the court.
2. What could Kelsoe have done to protect herself from the breaking of the promise?
3. International was under an obligation of good faith to issue the stock as promised. Appraise this statement.

(b) COMPLEX TRANSACTIONS. In applying the rule that past benefits cannot be consideration, care must be taken to distinguish between the situation in which the consideration is in fact past and the situation in which the earlier consideration and subsequent promises were all part of one complex transaction. In such cases, the earlier consideration is not regarded as past and supports the later promises.[11]

In the *Medley* case a father guaranteed payment of his son's debts but later claimed that the guaranty was not binding because no consideration had been received by him.

8. Forbearance as Consideration

In most cases, consideration consists of the performance of an act or the making of a promise to act. Consideration may also consist

---

[11] Such a complex transaction is called "contemporaneous" in some states. Soukop v Snyder (Hawaii App) 709 P2d 109 (1985).

MEDLEY v SOUTHTRUST
BANK OF QUAD CITIES

(Ala) 500 So 2d 1075 (1986)

> Roy Medley borrowed money from the bank. His father, Oscar, gave the
> bank a guaranty that he would pay his son's existing and future bank loans
> if his son did not repay them. Roy Medley did not repay the loans, and the
> bank sued Oscar Medley on the guaranty. Oscar Medley raised the defense
> that the guaranty was not binding because he had not received any consid-
> eration for it. This defense was overruled and judgment was entered against
> Oscar Medley. He appealed.

JONES, J. . . . Medley contends that there is no consideration because the guaranty
sued upon (1) included pre-existing debts, (2) was not made contemporaneously
with any loan, and (3) contained no expression of new valuable consideration.
SouthTrust, on the other hand, argues that its promise of future advances constitutes
sufficient consideration.

That portion of the guaranty agreement here contested contains the following
language:

*WHEREAS, the undersigned (if more than one, the undersigned jointly and severally) have
requested . . . the Bank to extend credit from time to time to*

*Roy D. Medley . . . (hereinafter referred to as the debtor), and have agreed to guarantee the
payment when due of all such credits, and also of all other indebtedness of every kind and
character now or at any time hereafter (before revocation hereof) owing by the debtor to the
Bank; and*

*WHEREAS, the Bank is willing to extend such credit to the debtor from time to time as, in
the Bank's discretion, is prudent and wise, provided this instrument of guaranty is executed
to the Bank.*

*NOW, THEREFORE, in consideration of the promises, and in order to induce the Bank to ex-
tend to the debtor from time to time in the future as requested by the debtor, such loans, extensions of loans and forbearances as to the Bank may seem prudent and wise, the
undersigned (if more than one, the undersigned jointly and severally) guarantee(s) the
prompt payment on demand of the principal of and interest on any indebtedness of the debtor
now, or at any time hereafter, outstanding, and any and all renewals thereof, together with
all costs of collection, including a reasonable attorney's fee, as may be provided for in the face
of any and all notes heretofore taken, or hereafter executed by the debtor, evidencing any such
indebtedness, or any part thereof.*

It is true that when someone not a party to the original transaction signs an instrument as guarantor after the original contract has been duly executed and delivered, without agreement at the time of the execution of the original contract that
additional security would be furnished, he is entering a new and independent contract;
and, to be binding, this agreement must be supported by consideration, independent
of the original contract.

When dealing with a guarantee of a pre-existing debt, consideration is essential
to sustain the obligation. In the instant case, however, the guaranty agreement is not

limited solely to pre-existing debts. Rather, it covers the "indebtedness of debtor now, or at any time hereafter, . . . and any and all renewals thereof . . . ." In other words, Medley agreed to guarantee all of his son's past and future indebtedness to SouthTrust.

This Court has repeatedly held that the promise of extension of credit in the future to the principal debtor is good consideration in a guaranty contract. . . .

[Judgment affirmed]

QUESTIONS

1. What was the consideration for the father's guaranty?
2. What is your opinion of the reasoning of the court?
3. Was any other analysis available to the court?

of forbearance, which is refraining from doing an act, or a promise of forbearance. In other words, the promisor may desire to buy the inaction or a promise of inaction of the other party.

The waiving or giving up of any right can be consideration for the promise of another. Thus, the relinquishment of a right in property or of a right to sue for damages will support a promise given in return for it.

The promise of a creditor to forbear collecting the debt is consideration for a promise by the debtor to modify the terms of the transaction.

The right that is surrendered in return for a promise may be a right against a third person, as well as against the promisor.

As under the rule governing compromises, forbearance to assert a claim is consideration when the claim has been asserted in good faith, even though it is without merit.[12] In the absence of a good-faith belief, forbearance with respect to a worthless claim is not consideration.

(a) WHAT CONSTITUTES CONSIDERATION. The consideration for forbearance is anything that constitutes consideration under the general rules discussed in this chapter. Usually, it is a payment of money to the promisor or a third person to guarantee the debt of another. The extending of the date for payment of a debt is consideration for the promise of a third person that the debt will be paid.[13]

(b) CONSIDERATION IN EMPLOYMENT CONTRACTS. In employment contracts, an employee may promise not to compete with the employer after leaving the employment. What is the consideration for this promise? When the promise is made at the time of the making of the contract of employment, the promise of the employer to employ and to pay compensation is consideration for the employee's promise to refrain from competing after leaving the employment. If the employee's promise is made after the contract of employment has been made, it is necessary to see whether the contract (1) is for an indefinite duration with no job security provision, or (2) is for a definite period of time, such as five years, or contains job security provisions that prevent the employer from discharging the employee at will. If the employment contract is for a definite period or is covered by job security provisions, the employee's promise

---

[12] Stueber v Picard (NM) 816 P2d 1111 (1991).

[13] Hope Petty Motors of Columbia, Inc. v Hyatt (SC App) 425 SE2d 786 (1992).

not to compete when made after the contract of employment has been made is not binding on the employee unless the employer gives some consideration for the promise not to compete. In the case of the indefinite-duration contract that has no job security provision, the employer can ordinarily terminate the contract at will. Therefore, according to some courts, the employer's continuing to employ the person after the employee's making of the promise not to compete is consideration for that promise, even though the parties did not express these thoughts in words. Other courts, however, do not make a distinction based on the type of employment contract. These courts follow the common law rule that a restrictive covenant agreed to by an employee already under contract of employment is not binding because it is not supported by consideration.

9. Adequacy of Consideration

Ordinarily, courts do not consider the adequacy of the consideration given for a promise.[14] The fact that the consideration supplied by one party is slight when compared with the burden undertaken by the other party is immaterial. It is a matter for the parties to decide when they make their contract whether each is getting a fair return. In the absence of fraud or other misconduct, courts usually will not interfere to make sure that each side is getting a fair return.

C. EXCEPTIONS TO THE LAW OF CONSIDERATION

The ever-changing character of law clearly appears in the area of consideration, since the

Figure 12-1 Consideration and Promises

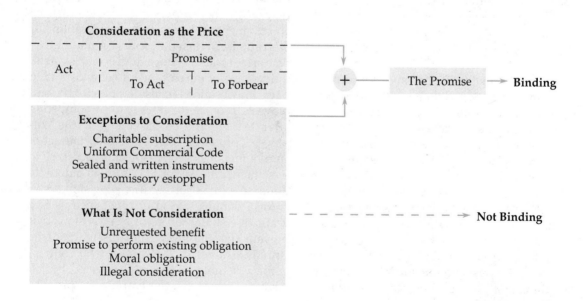

---

[14] Sun World Corp. v City of Phoenix (App) ___ Ariz ___, 800 P2d 26 (1990).

rules stated earlier in this chapter are seen slowly eroding.

10. Exceptions to Adequacy of Consideration Rule

The insufficiency or inadequacy of the consideration may lead a court to the conclusion that a contract is not binding because it is unconscionable. Inadequate consideration may also indicate that fraud was practiced on the promisor.

The inadequacy of the consideration may be evidence of the exercise of undue influence or the taking advantage of the condition of the other contracting party. Several factors may combine to challenge the validity of the contract.

11. Exceptions to Requirement of Consideration

By statute or decision, consideration is no longer required in a number of situations.

(a) CHARITABLE SUBSCRIPTIONS. When charitable enterprises are financed by voluntary subscriptions of a number of persons, the promise of each is generally enforceable. For example, when a number of people make pledges or subscriptions for the construction of a church, for a charitable institution, or for a college, the subscriptions are binding.

The theories for sustaining such promises vary. Consideration is lacking according to the technical standards applied in ordinary contract cases. Nevertheless, the courts enforce such promises as a matter of public policy.

(b) UNIFORM COMMERCIAL CODE. I n a number of situations, the Uniform Commercial Code abolishes the requirement of consideration. For example, under the Code, consideration is not required for (1) a merchant's written, firm offer as to goods, stated to be irrevocable; (2) a written discharge of a claim for an alleged breach of a commercial contract; or (3) an agreement to modify a contract for the sale of goods.[15]

(c) SEALED AND WRITTEN INSTRUMENTS. At common law, consideration was not necessary to support a promise under seal. In a state that gives the seal its original common law effect, the gratuitous promise or a promise to make a gift is enforceable when it is set forth in a sealed instrument.[16]

In some states, a promise under seal must be supported by consideration, just as though it did not have a seal. Other states take a middle position and hold that the presence of a seal is prima facie proof that there is consideration to support the promise. This means that if nothing more than the existence of the sealed promise is shown, it is deemed supported by consideration. The party making the promise, however, may prove that there was no consideration. In that case, the promise is not binding.

In some states a rebuttable presumption arises, whenever a contract is in writing, that the promises of the parties are supported by consideration.

12. Promissory Estoppel

A promise that is not supported by consideration may still be binding if the doctrine of promissory estoppel can be applied. A person may make a promise to another under such circumstances that the promisor should reasonably foresee that the promisee will be induced to rely on it and that the promisee will sustain substantial loss if the promise is not kept. Under the doctrine of **promissory estoppel**, such a promise is binding, even though there is no consideration for it.[17] In applying the doctrine of promissory estoppel, courts are ignoring the requirement of consideration in order to attain a just result.

---

[15] UCC § 2-209(1).

[16] Hopkins v Griffin, ___ Va ___, 402 SE2d 11 (1991).

[17] Hill v Mayers, 104 Or App 629, 802 P2d 694 (1990)

Legal difficulties often arise because parties take certain things for granted. Frequently they will be sure that they have agreed to everything and that they have a valid contract. However, sometimes they do not. The courts are then faced with the problem of leaving them with their broken dreams or coming to their rescue, as in the *Hoffman* case.

HOFFMAN v RED OWL STORES, INC.
26 Wis 2d 683, 133 NW2d 267 (1965)

Red Owl was a corporation that maintained a system of chain stores. Joseph H. Hoffman wanted to acquire a franchise for a Red Owl Grocery Store. The agent of Red Owl informed Hoffman and his wife that if they would sell their bakery in Wautoma, acquire a certain tract of land in Chilton (another city) and put up a specified amount of money, they would be given a franchise as desired. Hoffman sold his business and acquired the land in Chilton, but was never granted a franchise. He and his wife sued Red Owl, which raised the defense that there had only been an assurance that Hoffman would receive a franchise, but no promise supported by consideration. Thus, there was no binding contract to give him a franchise. From a judgment in the Hoffmans' favor, Red Owl appealed.

CURRIE, C. J. . . . The development of the law of promissory estoppel "is an attempt by the court to keep remedies abreast of increased moral consciousness of honesty and fair representations in all business dealings." *Peoples National Bank of Little Rock v Lineberger Constr. Co.*, 219 Ark. 11, 240 SW2d 12, (1951). . . .

The Restatement avoids use of the term "promissory estoppel," and there has been criticism of it as an inaccurate term. . . . Use of the word "estoppel" to describe a doctrine upon which a party to a lawsuit may obtain affirmative relief offends the traditional concept that estoppel merely serves as a shield and cannot serve as a sword to create a cause of action. . . .

Because we deem the doctrine of promissory estoppel, as stated in Sec 90 of Restatement, 1 Contracts, as one which supplies a needed weapon which courts may employ in a proper cause to prevent injustice, we endorse and adopt it.

The record here discloses a number of promises and assurances given to Hoffman by Lukowitz in behalf of Red Owl upon which plaintiffs relied and acted upon to their detriment. . . .

Originally the doctrine of promissory estoppel was invoked as a substitute for consideration rendering a gratuitous promise enforceable as a contract. . . . In other words, the acts of reliance by the promisee to his detriment provided a substitute for consideration. . . . [Under] Sec 90 of Restatement, 1 Contracts, . . . the conditions imposed are:

(1) Was the promise one which the promisor should reasonably expect to induce action or forbearance of a definite and substantial character on the part of the promisee?

(2) Did the promise induce such action or forbearance?

(3) Can injustice be avoided only by enforcement of the promise? . . .

> We conclude that injustice would result here if plaintiffs were not granted some relief because of the failure of defendants to keep their promises which induced plaintiffs to act to their detriment. . . .

[Judgment affirmed on this phase of the case]

QUESTIONS

1. Could the court in the *Hoffman* case have reached the same conclusion by applying the common law rule as to consideration?
2. Compare the concept of firm offer with promissory estoppel.
3. How could Hoffman have avoided the problem that arose in his case?

(a) PROMISSORY ESTOPPEL DISTINGUISHED FROM CONSIDERATION.

Promissory estoppel differs from consideration in that, with promissory estoppel, the reliance of the promisee is not the bargained-for price or response sought by the promisor. Under promissory estoppel it is sufficient that the promisor foresees that there will be such reliance. The doctrine of promissory estoppel applies only when (1) the promisor has reason to foresee the detrimental reliance by the promisee, and (2) the promisee in fact would sustain a substantial loss because of such reliance if the promise were not performed.

Promissory estoppel cannot be applied unless the promise is sufficiently definite for the court to determine what the promisor is required to do.[18]

(b) DETRIMENTAL RELIANCE ESSENTIAL.

Promissory estoppel cannot be applied merely because the promisor has not performed the promise. In the absence of the promisee's detrimental reliance on the promise, the doctrine of promissory estoppel is not applicable. Thus, a promise made to the debtor by the creditor that the creditor would collect only $20 a month on the debt of approximately $12,000 was not binding, because there was no proof that the debtor relied in any manner on such promise.[19]

What constitutes detrimental reliance sufficient to satisfy the promissory estoppel rule has been diluted in recent years. In the early promissory estoppel cases, it was necessary to show that if the defendant did not perform the promise, the plaintiff would suffer a substantial loss—of a nature that could not be compensated for by the payment of money. Many courts are now willing to accept any financial loss as sufficient to show detrimental reliance. Thus, it has been held that when the plaintiff quit a job in reliance on the defendant's promise to employ the plaintiff, there was sufficient detrimental reliance to make the defendant's promise binding.[20]

---

[18] Black Canyon Racquetball Club, Inc. v Idaho First National Bank (Idaho) 804 P2d 900 (1987).

[19] Lawrence v Board of Education, 152 Ill App 3d 187, 105 Ill Dec 195, 503 NE2d 1201 (1987). Some courts hold the promisor liable for tort damages when the promisee has sustained harm because the promisee relied on the promise, but the promise was never kept. ITT Terryphone Corp. v Tri-State Steel Drum, Inc. 178 Ga App 694, 344 SE2d 686 (1986). The explanation for these differing views is that those courts do not believe it is just for the promisor to break a promise on which the promisee had detrimentally relied, but at the same time they do not feel that they can flatly state that consideration is not required to make the broken promise binding on the defendant.

[20] Roberts v Geosource Drilling Services, Inc. (Tex App) 757 SW2d 48 (1988).

SUMMARY

A promise is not binding if there is no consideration for the promise. Consideration is what the promisor requires as the price for the promise. That price may be the doing of an act, refraining from the doing of an act, or merely a promise to do or to refrain. In a bilateral contract, it is necessary to find that the promise of each party is supported by consideration. If either promise is not so supported, it is not binding, and the agreement of the parties is not a contract. Consequently, the agreement cannot be enforced. When a promise is the consideration, it must be a binding promise. The binding character of a promise is not affected by the circumstance that there is a condition precedent to the performance promised. Likewise, the binding character of the promise and of the contract is not affected by a provision in the contract for its cancellation by either one or both of the parties. A promise to do what one is already obligated to do is not consideration, although some exceptions are made. Such exceptions include when the rendering of a partial performance or a modified performance is accepted as a good-faith adjustment to a changed situation, a compromise and release of claims, a part-payment check, or a compromise of creditors. Because consideration is the price that is given to obtain the promise, past benefits conferred on the promisor cannot be consideration. In the case of a complex transaction, however, the past benefit and the subsequent transaction relating to the promise may in fact have been intended by the parties as one transaction. In such a case, the earlier benefit is not past consideration but is the consideration contemplated by the promisor as the price for the promise subsequently made.

A promise to refrain from doing an act can be consideration. A promise to refrain from suing or asserting a particular claim can be consideration. Generally, the promise to forbear must be for a specified time, as distinguished from agreeing to forbear at will. When consideration is forbearance to assert a claim, it is immaterial whether the claim is valid, as long as the claim has been asserted in good faith in the belief that it was valid.

When the promisor obtains the consideration specified for the promise, the law is not ordinarily concerned with the value or adequacy of that consideration. Exceptions are sometimes made in the case of fraud or unconscionability and under consumer protection statutes.

There is a trend to abandon the requirement of consideration. Promissory estoppel is the most extensive repudiation of the requirement of consideration.

All transactions must be lawful; therefore, consideration for a promise must be legal. If it is not, there is no consideration, and the promise is not binding.

When the promisor does not actually receive the price promised for the promise, it is said that there is a failure of consideration. Such failure constitutes a breach of the contract.

Although consideration is required to make a promise binding, the promise that is not supported by consideration is not unlawful or illegal. If the promisor voluntarily performs the promise, the promisor cannot undo the performance and restore matters to their position prior to the making of the agreement. The parties are free to perform their agreement, but the courts will not help either of them, because there is no contract.

LAW IN PRACTICE

1. Be sure that a contract is supported by consideration as defined by the law that will apply to the contract.

2. When a collateral contract, such as guaranty, or a modification is made, be sure that such collateral contract or modification is supported by consideration, except in the case of a modification to a contract for the sale of goods.

3. State specifically in the contract, preferably a written contract, what is the consideration for each promise so that there is clear evidence of what is the price for each promise.

4. When the value of the consideration is small, state specifically in the contract, preferably a writ-ten contract, why the consideration is small, in order to block a later challenge to the contract on the ground of inadequacy of consideration as evidence of fraud.

5. Remember that promissory estoppel may perhaps save your contract that would otherwise fail for want of consideration.

QUESTIONS AND CASE PROBLEMS

1. What social force is advanced by each of the following rules of law? (a) An executed gift or a performance that has been rendered without consideration cannot be rescinded for lack of consideration. (b) In the absence of fraud, the adequacy of consideration is usually immaterial.

2. Sarah's house caught on fire. Through the prompt assistance of her neighbor, Odessa, the fire was quickly extinguished. In gratitude, Sarah promised to pay Odessa $1,000. Can Odessa enforce this promise if Sarah does not pay the money?

3. Clifton agreed to work for Acrylics Incorporated for $400 a month. Clifton later claimed that there was no contract because the consideration for the services to be rendered was inadequate. Is there a binding contract?

4. Ravitts was employed by Richards of Rockford under a contract prohibiting him from competing with Richards for one year after termination of his employment. Thereafter, the parties terminated the employment by mutual agreement and signed a release of all obligations under the contract. The business and all the contract rights of Richards were later sold to Aqua-Aerobic Systems. Meanwhile, Ravitts had begun to compete with the business of Richards and was now competing with Aqua-Aerobic. Aqua-Aerobic sued Ravitts to stop him from such competing. Ravitts raised the defense that he had been released from the contract that imposed the restriction against competing. Aqua-Aerobic claimed that the release was not binding because there had not been any consideration for the release. Was the release binding? What social force is involved? [*Aqua-Aerobic Systems, Inc. v Ravitts, 166 Ill App 3d 168, 117 Ill Dec 77, 520 NE2d 67*]

5. Galloway induced Marian to sell Marian's house to Galloway by false statements that a factory was going to be built on the vacant lot adjoining Marian's house. No factory was ever built, and Marian then sued Galloway for damages for fraud. Marian offered to prove that Galloway had paid Marian only a fraction of the true value of Marian's house. Galloway claimed that this evidence as to value could not be admitted because it was immaterial whether the consideration paid Marian was adequate. Is Galloway correct?

6. Koedding hired West Roofers to put a roof on her house. She later claimed that the roofing job was defective, and she threatened to sue West. Both parties discussed the matter in good faith. Finally, West guaranteed that the roof would be free from leaks for 20 years in return for the guarantee by Koedding not to sue West for damages. The roof leaked the next year. Koedding sued West on the guarantee. West claimed that the guarantee was not binding because there was no consideration for it. According to West, Koedding's promise not to sue had no value because Koedding in fact did not have any valid claim against West; therefore, she was not entitled to sue. Was this defense valid?

7. Fedun rented a building to Gomer, who did business under the name of Mike's Cafe. Later, Gomer was about to sell out the business to Brown and requested Fedun to release him from his liability under the lease. Fedun agreed to do so. Brown sold out shortly thereafter. The balance of the rent due by Gomer under the original lease agreement was not paid, and Fedun sued Gomer on the rent claim. Could he collect after having released Gomer? [*Fedun v Mike's Cafe, 204 Pa Super 356, 204 A2d 776*]

8. Alexander Proudfoot Company was in the business of devising efficiency systems for industry. It told the Sanitary Linen Service Company that it could provide an improved system for Sanitary Linen that would save it money. It made a contract with Sanitary Linen to provide a money-saving system. The system was put into operation, and Proudfoot was paid the amount due under the contract. The system failed to work and did not save money. Sanitary Linen sued to get the money back. Was it entitled to do so? *[Sanitary Linen Service Co. v Alexander Proudfoot Co. (CA5 Fla) 435 F2d 292]*

9. Sears, Roebuck and Co. promised to give Forrer permanent employment. Forrer sold his farm at a loss to take the job. Shortly after beginning work, he was discharged by Sears, which claimed that the contract could be terminated at will. Forrer claimed that promissory estoppel prevented Sears from terminating the contract. Was he correct? *[Forrer v Sears, Roebuck and Co. 36 Wis 2d 388, 153 NW2d 587]*

10. Kemp leased a gas filling station from Baehr. Kemp, who was heavily indebted to the Penn-O-Tex Oil Corporation, transferred to it his right to receive payments on all claims. When Baehr complained that the rent was not paid, he was assured by the corporation that the rent would be paid to him. Baehr did not sue Kemp for the overdue rent but later sued the corporation. The defense was raised that there was no consideration for the promise of the corporation. Decide. *[Baehr v Penn-O-Tex Corporation, 258 Minn 533, 104 NW2d 661]*

11. Bogart owed several debts to the Security Bank & Trust Company. He applied to the bank for a loan to pay the various debts. The bank's employee stated that he would take the application for the loan to the loan committee and "within two or three days, we ought to have something here, ready for you to go with." The loan was not made. The bank sued Bogart for his debts. He filed a counterclaim on the theory that the bank had broken its contract to make a loan to him, and that promissory estoppel prevented the bank from going back on what the employee had said. Was this counterclaim valid? *[Security Bank & Trust Co. v Bogart (Ind App) 494 NE2d 965]*

12. Through a mistake, Midwest Recovery Bureau wrongfully took Cobb's truck. In so doing, the truck was damaged. Later Cobb gave Midwest a release, by which he released Midwest from liability for wrongfully taking his truck. The release was given in consideration of the repairing and the returning of the truck. After the truck was repaired and returned, Cobb sued Midwest for damages. It raised the defense that Cobb had released it from liability. Was Midwest correct? *[Cobb v Midwest Recovery Bureau Co. (Minn) 295 NW2d 232]*

13. Norma Elmore was in a Wal-Mart store. She slipped and fell on an open package of mints that was on the floor. She asked the store representative who came to her aid if the store would pay her medical expenses. The representative assured her that the store would pay the medical expenses. The store failed to do so and Norma sued for medical expenses. Was the store liable?

14. Upon the death of their mother, the children of Jane Smith gave their interests in their mother's estate to their father in consideration of his payment of $1 to each of them and of his promise to leave them the property on his death. The father died without leaving them the property. The children sued their father's second wife to obtain the property in accordance with the agreement. The second wife claimed that the agreement was not a binding contract because the amount of $1 and future gifts given for the children's interests were so trivial and uncertain. Decide.

15. Radio Station KSCS broadcast a popular music program. It announced that it would pay $25,000 to any listener who detected that it did not play three consecutive songs. Steve Jennings listened to and heard a program in which two songs were followed by a commercial program. He claimed the $25,000. The station refused to pay on the ground that there was no consideration for its promise to pay that amount. Was the station liable? *[Jennings v Radio Station KSCS (Tex App) 708 SW2d 60]*

CHAPTER 13

LEGALITY AND PUBLIC POLICY

LEARNING OBJECTIVES

After studying this chapter, you will be able to:
1. *State the effect of illegality on a contract.*
2. *Compare illegality and unconscionability.*
3. *Distinguish between illegality in performing a legal contract and the illegality of a contract.*
4. *Recognize when a contract is invalid because it obstructs legal processes.*
5. *State the elements of a lottery.*
6. *State the extent to which agreements not to compete are lawful.*

A court will not enforce a contract if it is illegal, contrary to public policy, or unconscionable.

A. GENERAL PRINCIPLES

An agreement is illegal when either its formation or performance is a crime or a tort, or it is contrary to public policy or unconscionable.

1. Effect of Illegality

Ordinarily, an illegal agreement is void. When an agreement is illegal, the parties are usually not entitled to the aid of the courts. If the illegal agreement has not been performed, neither party can sue the other to obtain performance or damages.[1] Likewise the party who relied on the validity of the illegal contract cannot obtain its enforcement on the theory of promissory estoppel.[2] If the agreement has been performed, neither party can sue the other for damages or to set the agreement aside.

2. Exceptions to Effect of Illegality

To avoid hardship, exceptions are made to the rules stated in Section 1.

(a) PROTECTION OF ONE PARTY. When the law that the agreement violates is intended for the protection of one of the parties, that party may seek relief. For example, when, in order to protect the public, the law forbids the issuance of securities by certain classes of corporations, a person who has purchased them may recover the money paid.

(b) UNEQUAL GUILT. When the parties are not *in pari delicto*—not equally guilty—the least guilty party is granted relief when public interest is advanced by so doing. For example, when a statute is adopted to protect one of the parties to a transaction, such as a

usury law adopted to protect borrowers, the person to be protected will not be deemed to be in pari delicto with the wrongdoer when entering into a transaction that is prohibited by the statute.

(c) KNOWLEDGE OF ILLEGAL PURPOSE OF OTHER CONTRACTING PARTY. A contract that is in itself lawful is not made unlawful by the fact that one of the parties intends to make unlawful use of the subject matter of the contract, even though this intention is known to the other contracting party.

3. Partial Illegality

An agreement may involve the performance of several promises, some of which are illegal and some legal. The legal parts of the agreement may be enforced, provided that they can be separated from the parts that are illegal.[3]

If a contract is susceptible to two interpretations, one legal and the other illegal, the court will assume that the legal meaning was intended unless the contrary is clearly indicated.

4. Crimes and Civil Wrongs

An agreement is illegal, and therefore void, when it calls for the commission of any act that constitutes a crime. To illustrate, one cannot enforce an agreement by which the other party is to commit an assault, steal property, burn a house, or kill a person.

An agreement that calls for the commission of a civil wrong is also illegal and void. Examples are agreements to slander a third person; defraud another; infringe another's patent, trademark, or copyright; or fix prices.

5. Good Faith and Fairness

The law is evolving toward requiring that contracts be fair and made in good faith. The law

---

[1] Braun's Estate, ___ Ill App 3d ___, ___ Ill Dec ___, 583 NE2d 633 (1991).

[2] Weese v Davis County Commission (Utah) 834 P2d 1 (1992).

[3] Donnel v Stogel, 161 App Div 2d 93, 560 NYS2d 200 (1990).

is becoming increasingly concerned with whether one party has utilized a superior bargaining power or superior knowledge to obtain better terms from the other party than would otherwise have been obtained.

In the case of goods, the seller must act in good faith. In regard to merchant sellers, good faith is defined as "honesty in fact and the observance of reasonable commercial standards of fair dealing in the trade."[4]

6. Unconscionable and Oppressive Contracts

Ordinarily, a court will not consider whether a contract is fair or unfair, is wise or foolish, or operates unequally between the parties. However, in a number of instances the law holds that contracts or contract clauses will not be enforced because they are too harsh or oppressive to one of the parties. This principle is most commonly applied to invalidate a clause providing for the payment by one party of a large penalty upon breaking the contract or a provision declaring that a party shall not be liable for the consequences of negligence. This principle is extended in connection with the sale of goods to provide that "if the court . . . finds the contract or any clause of the contract to have been unconscionable at the time it was made, the court may refuse to enforce the contract, or it may enforce the remainder of the contract without the unconscionable clause, or it may so limit the application of any unconscionable clause as to avoid any unconscionable result."[5]

(a) WHAT CONSTITUTES UNCONSCIONABILITY? A provision that gives what the court believes is too much of an advantage over a buyer is likely to be held void as unconscionable. To bring the unconscionability provision into operation, it is not necessary to prove that fraud was practiced. When there is a grossly disproportionate bargaining power between the parties, so that the weaker or inexperienced party cannot afford to risk confrontation with the stronger party but just signs on the dotted line, courts will hold that grossly unfair terms obtained by the stronger party are void as unconscionable.

Under the Uniform Consumer Credit Code, a particular clause or an entire agreement relating to a consumer credit sale, a consumer lease, or a consumer loan is void when such provision or agreement is unconscionable.[6]

The fact that a contract is a bad bargain does not make it unconscionable.

(b) DETERMINATION OF UNCONSCIONABILITY. Unconscionability is to be determined in the light of the circumstances existing at the time when the contract was made. The fact that later events make the contract unwise or undesirable does not make the contract unconscionable. Hence, the fact that there is a sharp rise in the market price of goods after the contract has been made does not make the contract unconscionable. The decision that a provision or a contract is unconscionable can only be made by a court after holding a hearing to determine the real effect of the contract when viewed in its commercial setting. In a particular state, the concept of unconscionability may be based on the

---

[4] UCC § 2-103(1)(b). Higher standards than those imposed on sellers in general are imposed on merchant sellers by other provisions of the UCC. See § 2-314, as to warranties, and § 2-509(3), as to the transfer of risk of loss. The provisions of the UCC noted above do not apply to contracts generally. However, there is a growing trend of courts to extend Article 2 of the UCC, which relates only to the sale of goods, to contract situations generally. This extension is based on the theory that the UCC represents the latest restatement of the law of contracts made by expert scholars and the legislators of the land. In other articles of the UCC, *good faith* means merely honesty in fact in the conduct or transaction concerned. UCC § 1-201(19). With respect to checks and other commercial paper, this definition has been expanded by the 1990 Revision of Article 3 to honesty in fact and the observance of reasonable commercial standards of fair dealing. UCC § 3-103(a)(4)[1990 Revision].

[5] UCC § 2-302(1).

[6] UCC § 5.108.

Uniform Commercial Code, the Uniform Consumer Credit Code, local nonuniform code statutes, or general principles of equity absorbed by the common law. The concept of unconscionability is given the same interpretation by the courts regardless of the source of the concept. This is seen in the *Williams* case.

WILLIAMS v WALKER-THOMAS FURNITURE CO.
(CA Dist Col) 350 F2d 445 (1965)

> The Walker-Thomas Furniture Co. sold furniture on credit under contracts that contained a provision that a customer did not own the purchase as long as any balance on any purchase remained due. It sold goods to Ora Lee Williams. At the time when the balance of her account was $164, Walker-Thomas Furniture Co. sold her a $514 stereo set with knowledge that she was supporting herself and seven children on a government relief check of $218 a month. From 1957 to 1962, Williams had purchased $1,800 worth of goods and made payments of $1,400. When she stopped making payments in 1962, Walker-Thomas sought to take back everything she had purchased since 1957. From a judgment in favor of Walker-Thomas, Williams appealed.

WRIGHT, J. . . . The notion that an unconscionable bargain should not be given full enforcement is by no means novel. In *Scott v United States*, 79 U.S. (12 Wall) 443, 445 (1870), the Supreme Court stated: "If a contract be unreasonable and unconscionable, but not void for fraud, a court of law will give to the party who sues for its breach damages, not according to its letter, but only such as he is equitably entitled to." . . .

Congress has recently enacted the Uniform Commercial Code, which specifically provides that the court may refuse to enforce a contract which it finds to be unconscionable at the time it was made. . . . The enactment of this section, which occurred subsequent to the contracts here in suit, does not mean that the common law of the District of Columbia was otherwise at the time of enactment, nor does it preclude the court from adopting a similar rule in the exercise of its powers to develop the common law for the District of Columbia. In fact, in view of the absence of prior authority on the point, we consider the congressional adoption of UCC § 2-302 persuasive authority for following the rationale of the cases from which the section is explicitly derived. Accordingly, we hold that where the element of unconscionability is present at the time a contract is made, the contract should not be enforced.

Unconscionability has generally been recognized to include an absence of meaningful choice on the part of one of the parties together with contract terms which are unreasonably favorable to the other party. Whether a meaningful choice is present in a particular case can only be determined by consideration of all the circumstances surrounding the transaction. In many cases the meaningfulness of the choice is negated by a gross inequality of bargaining power. *Henningsen v Bloomfield Motors, Inc. [32 NJ 358 (1960)]* The manner in which the contract was entered is also relevant to this consideration. Did each party to the contract, considering his obvious education or lack of it, have a reasonable opportunity to understand the terms of the contract, or were the important terms hidden in a maze of fine print and minimized by deceptive sales practices? Ordinarily, one who signs an agreement without full knowledge of its terms might be held to assume the risk that he has entered a one-sided bargain. But when a party of little bargaining power, and hence little real choice, signs a commercially unreasonable contract with little or no knowledge of its terms, it is hardly likely that his consent, or even an objective manifestation of his consent, was ever given to all the terms. In such a case the usual rule that the terms of the agreement are not to be questioned should be abandoned and the court should consider whether the terms of the contract are so unfair that enforcement should be withheld. . . .

Because the trial court and the appellate court did not feel that enforcement could be refused, no findings were made on the possible unconscionability of the contracts in [this case]. Since the record is not sufficient for our deciding the issue as a matter of law, the [case is] remanded to the trial court for further proceedings.

[So ordered.]

QUESTIONS

1. Did the court hold that the contract in the *Williams* case was illegal?
2. What is the difference between holding that a contract is unconscionable and holding that the contract is illegal?
3. Why did the court not say that the contract was or was not unconscionable?

7. Social Consequences of Contracts

The social consequences of a contract are an important element today in determining the contract's validity and the power of government to regulate it.

(a) THE PRIVATE CONTRACT IN SOCIETY. The law of contracts was originally oriented to private relations between private individuals. Now it is moving from the field of bilateral private law to multiparty societal considerations. The Supreme Court has held that private contracts lose their private, do-not-touch character when they become such a common part of our way of life that society deems it necessary to regulate them.

(b) THE N FACTOR. The number of times (*n*) that the given contract is used in the modern business world becomes increasingly significant in determining the validity of the contract as between the parties. Courts are considering a contract as a legal relationship only between *A* and *B* less and less often. The modern court is increasingly influenced in its decision by the recognition of the fact that the contract before the court is not one in a million but is one of a million. For example, an insurer makes a contract with Kelley that is of the same nature as one that the insurer makes with Fanta. Also, these contracts are the same as the one that a different insurance company makes with Vidas, and so on. A similar industry-wide pattern is seen in the case of the bank loan made by one bank to a borrower, by a second bank to a different borrower, and so on.

B. AGREEMENTS AFFECTING PUBLIC WELFARE

Agreements that may harm the public welfare are condemned as contrary to public policy and are not binding. Agreements that interfere with public service or the duties of public officials, obstruct legal process, or discriminate against members of minority groups are considered detrimental to public welfare and, as such, are not enforceable.

Figure 13-1 Illegal Agreements Affecting Public Welfare

> Agreements contrary to public policy
> Agreements evading statutes
> Agreements injuring public service
> Agreements involving conflicts of interest
> Agreements obstructing legal process
> Agreements involving illegal discrimination
> Wagers and private lotteries

8. Agreements Contrary to Public Policy

A given agreement may not violate any statute but may still be so offensive to society that the courts feel that enforcing the contract would be contrary to public policy.

(a) THE CONCEPT OF PUBLIC POLICY.

Public policy cannot be defined precisely but is loosely described as protecting from that which tends to be injurious to the public or contrary to the public good, or which violates any established interest of society.[7] Contracts condemned as contrary to public policy frequently relate to the protection of the public welfare, health, or safety; to the protection of the person; and to the protection of recognized social institutions. For example, a contract that prohibits marriage under all circumstances or that encourages divorce is generally held invalid as contrary to public policy. Courts are slow and cautious in invalidating a contract on the ground that it is contrary to public policy. This is so because the courts recognize that, on the one hand, they are applying a very vague standard, and on the other hand, they are restricting the freedom of the contracting parties to contract freely as they choose.[8]

When a statute makes conduct illegal, how far will that statute reach to affect contracts? That was the question underlying the *Bovard* case.

BOVARD v AMERICAN HORSE ENTERPRISES, INC.
201 Cal App 3d 832, 247 Cal Rptr 340 (1988)

American Horse Enterprises was predominantly engaged in manufacturing devices for smoking marijuana and to a minor degree in making jewelry. A state law made it illegal to possess, use, or transfer marijuana. There was no statute prohibiting manufacturing equipment for smoking marijuana. Bovard owned the stock of American Horse Enterprises and contracted to sell the corporation to Ralph. Ralph did not make the payments required by the contract. Bovard then brought suit to enforce the contract. The trial judge

---

7   O'Hara v Ahlgreen, Blumenfeld and Kempster, 127 Ill 2d 333, 130 Ill Dec 401, 537 NE2d 730 (1989).

8   United Steelworkers of America v Quadna Mountain Corp. (Minn App) 435 NW2d 120 (1989).

raised the question whether the contract sued upon was void for illegality. The trial judge held the contract void as contrary to public policy. Bovard appealed.

BUGLIA, J. . . . The trial court concluded the consideration for the contract was contrary to the policy of the law as expressed in the statute prohibiting the possession, use and transfer of marijuana. Whether a contract is contrary to public policy is a question of law to be determined from the circumstances of the particular case. . . . Whenever a court becomes aware that a contract is illegal, it has a duty to refrain from entertaining an action to enforce the contract. . . .

The question whether a contract violates public policy necessarily involves a degree of subjectivity. Therefore, ". . . courts have been cautious in blithely applying public policy reasons to nullify otherwise enforceable contracts. This concern has been graphically articulated by the California Supreme Court as follows: 'It has been well said that public policy is an unruly horse, astride of which you are carried into unknown and uncertain paths.' . . ." While contracts opposed to morality or law should not be allowed to show themselves in courts of justice, yet public policy requires and encourages the making of contracts by competent parties upon all valid and lawful considerations, and courts so recognizing have allowed parties the widest latitude in this regard; and, unless it is entirely plain that a contract is violative of sound public policy, a court will never so declare. "The power of the courts to declare a contract void for being in contravention of sound public policy is a very delicate and undefined power, and . . . should be exercised only in cases free from doubt.". . .

Before labeling a contract as being contrary to public policy, courts must carefully inquire into the nature of the conduct, the extent of public harm which may be involved, and the moral quality of the conduct of the parties in light of the prevailing standards of the community. . . .

These factors are more comprehensively set out in the Restatement Second of Contracts section 178:

(1) *A promise or other term of an agreement is unenforceable on grounds of public policy if legislation provides that it is unenforceable or the interest in its enforcement is clearly outweighed in the circumstances by a public policy against the enforcement of such terms.*

(2) *In weighing the interest in the enforcement of a term, account is taken of*
   (a) *the parties' justified expectations,*
   (b) *any forfeiture that would result if enforcement were denied, and*
   (c) *any special public interest in the enforcement of the particular term.*

(3) *In weighing a public policy against enforcement of a term, account is taken of*
   (a) *the strength of that policy as manifested by legislation or judicial decisions,*
   (b) *the likelihood that a refusal to enforce the term will further that policy,*
   (c) *the seriousness of any misconduct involved and the extent to which it was deliberate, and*
   (d) *the directness of the connection between that misconduct and the term.*

Applying the Restatement test to the present circumstances, we conclude the interest in enforcing this contract is very tenuous. Neither party was reasonably justified in expecting the government would not eventually act to geld American Horse Enterprises, a business harnessed to the production of paraphernalia used to facilitate the use of an illegal drug. Moreover, although avoidance of the contract imposed a forfeiture on Bovard, he did recover the corporate machinery, the only assets of the business which could be used for lawful purposes, i.e., to manufacture jewelry. Thus, the forfeiture was significantly mitigated if not negligible. Finally, there is no special public interest in the enforcement of this contract, only the general interest in preventing a party to a contract from avoiding a debt.

On the other hand, the Restatement factors favoring a public policy against enforcement of this contract are very strong. . . . The public policy against manufacturing paraphernalia to facilitate the use of marijuana is strongly implied in the statutory prohibition against the possession, use, etc., of marijuana, a prohibition which dates back at least to 1929. . . . Obviously, refusal to enforce the instant contract will further that public policy not only in the present circumstances but by serving notice on manufacturers of drug paraphernalia that they may not resort to the judicial system to protect or advance their business interests. Moreover, it is immaterial that the business conducted by American Horse Enterprises was not expressly prohibited by law when Bovard and Ralph made their agreement since both parties knew that the corporation's products would be used primarily for purposes which were expressly illegal. We conclude the trial court correctly declared the contract contrary to the policy of express law and therefore illegal and void. . . .

[Judgment affirmed]

QUESTIONS

1. Who raised the winning argument in the *Bovard* case? What was it?
2. What provision of the contract in the *Bovard* case was illegal?
3. Did the court in Bovard overstep its bounds and infringe on the role of the legislature?

(b) AGREEMENTS EVADING STATUTORY PROTECTION. Statutes frequently confer benefits or provide protection. If an agreement is made that deprives a person of such a statutory benefit, it is generally held that the agreement is invalid because it is contrary to the public policy declared by the statute. For example, a state law provides that automobile insurance policies should cover certain persons. A policy provision that would exclude certain persons who would be covered by the statutory provision is not valid, because it is contrary to the public policy declared in the statute.

The waiver of statutory provisions designed to protect debtors, creditors, or consumers may be held void as contrary to public policy.[9]

9. Agreements Injuring Public Service

An agreement that tends to interfere with the proper performance of the duties of a public officer—whether legislative, administrative, or judicial—is contrary to public policy and void. Thus, an agreement to procure the award of a public contract by corrupt means is not

---

[9] Coastal Caisson Drill Co., Inc. v American Cas. Co. of Reading (Fla App) 523 So 2d 791 (1988).

enforceable. Other examples are agreements to sell public offices, to procure pardons by corrupt means, or to pay a public officer more or less than legal fees or salary. Campaign promises to give a job to a particular person are contrary to public policy and cannot be enforced.[10]

One of the most common agreements within the class is the **illegal lobbying agreement**. This term is used to describe an agreement to use unlawful means to procure or prevent the adoption of legislation by a lawmaking body, such as Congress or a state legislature. Such agreements are clearly contrary to the public interest, since they interfere with the workings of the democratic process. They are accordingly illegal and void.

Some courts hold illegal all agreements to influence legislation, regardless of the means contemplated or employed. Other courts adopt the rule that such agreements are valid in the absence of the use of improper influence or the contemplation of using such influence.

10. Agreements Involving Conflicts of Interest

Various statutes prohibit government officials from being personally interested, directly or indirectly, in any transaction entered into by such officials on behalf of the government. When there is a prohibited conflict of interest, a contract is invalid, without regard to whether its terms are fair or advantageous to the public.

11. Agreements Obstructing Legal Processes

Any agreement intended to obstruct or pervert legal processes is contrary to public interest and therefore void. Agreements that promise to pay money in return for the abandonment of the prosecution of a criminal case,

for the suppression of evidence in any legal proceeding, for initiating litigation, or for the perpetration of any fraud on the court are therefore void.

An agreement to pay an ordinary witness more than the regular witness fee allowed by law, or a promise to pay a greater amount if the promisor wins the lawsuit, is void. The danger here is that the witness will lie in order to help win the case.

12. Illegal Discrimination Contracts

A contract specifying that a homeowner will not sell to a member of a particular race cannot be enforced, because it violates the Fourteenth Amendment of the Constitution.[11] Hotels and restaurants may not deal with their customers on terms that discriminate because of race, religion, color, or national origin.[12]

13. Gambling, Wagers, and Lotteries

Gambling contracts are illegal.[13] Largely as a result of the adoption of antigambling statutes, wagers or bets are generally illegal. Private lotteries involving the three elements of prize, chance, and consideration (or similar affairs of chance) are also generally held illegal. In many states, public lotteries (lotteries run by a state government) have been legalized by statute. Raffles are usually regarded as lotteries. In some states, bingo games, lotteries, and raffles are legalized by statute when the funds raised are used for a charitable purpose.

Sales promotion schemes calling for the distribution of property according to chance among the purchasers of goods are held illegal as lotteries, without regard to whether the scheme is called a guessing contest, a raffle, or a gift.

Giveaway plans and games are lawful as long as it is not necessary to buy anything or

---

[10] Harris v Johnson, ___ Ill App 2d ___, ___ Ill Dec ___, 578 NE2d 1326 (1991).

[11] Shelley v Kraemer, 334 US 1 (1948).

[12] Federal Civil Rights Act of 1964, 42 USC §§ 2000a et seq.

[13] Hertz Commercial Leasing Division v Morrison (Miss) 567 So 2d 832 (1990).

to give anything of value in order to participate. If participation is free, the element of consideration is lacking, and there is no lottery.

An activity is not gambling when the result is solely or predominantly a matter of skill. In contrast, it is gambling when the result is solely a matter of luck. Rarely is any activity 100 percent skill or 100 percent luck. In the *Seattle Times* case the court was faced with the problem of how to classify a contest that involved both skill and chance.

SEATTLE TIMES COMPANY v TIELSCH
80 Wash App 2d 502, 495 P2d 1366 (1972)

The *Seattle Times* ran a football game forecasting contest, called "Guest-Guesser." George Tielsch, the Seattle Chief of Police, claimed that this was illegal as a lottery. The *Times* brought a declaratory judgment action to determine the legality of the contest. The court held that the contest was a lottery, and the *Seattle Times* appealed.

ROSELLINI, J. . . . The result of a football game may depend upon weather, the physical condition of the players and the psychological attitude of the players. It may also be affected by sociological problems between and among the members of a football team. The element of chance is an integral part of the game of football as well as the skill of the players.

The lure of the "Guest-Guesser" contest is partially the participant's love of football, partially the challenge of competition and partially the hope enticingly held out, which is often false or disappointing, that the participant will get something for nothing or a great deal for a very little outlay. . . .

The elements of a lottery are prize, consideration and chance.

. . . Where a contest is multiple or serial, and requires the solution of a number of problems to win the prize, the fact that skill alone will bring contestants to a correct solution of a greater part of the problems does not make the contest any the less a lottery if chance enters into the solution of another lesser part of the problems and thereby proximately influences the final result. . . .

Our research has revealed only one case involving a football forecasting game and the game there was a "pool," that is, a gambling game wherein wagers were placed. The Superior Court of Pennsylvania held that it was a lottery. What is most relevant in the case for our consideration here is the court's discussion of the element of chance in forecasting the result of football games. That court said: It is true that for an avid student of the sport of football the chance taken is not so great as for those who have little interest in the game. However, it is common knowledge that the predictions even among these so-called "experts" are far from infallible. Any attempt to forecast the result of a single athletic contest, be it football, baseball, or whatever, is fraught with chance. This hazard is multiplied directly by the number of predictions made. The operators of the scheme involved in this case were all cognizant of this fact for the odds against a correct number of selections were increased from 5 to 1 for three teams picked up to 900 to 1 for fifteen teams. *Commonwealth v Laniewski*, 173 Pa Super 245, 98 A2d 215 (1953).

The trial court in the instant case recognized the same basic realities attendant upon the enterprise of football game-result forecasting. We are convinced that it correctly held that chance, rather than skill, is the dominant factor in the Times' "Guest-Guesser" contest. The very name of the contest conveys quite accurately the promoter's as well as the participants' true concept of the nature of the contest.

We conclude that the contest, however harmless it may be in the opinion of the participants and the promoters, is a lottery. . . .

[Judgment against Seattle Times]

QUESTIONS

1. Were unilateral or bilateral contracts involved in the *Seattle Times* case?
2. Does the court classify the mixed skill-luck transaction according to which element predominates?
3. In order to be condemned as a lottery, a plan must be shown to have harmful effects upon some members of society. Appraise this statement.

Figure 13-2   Illegal Agreements Affecting Business

> Contracts with unlicensed persons in licensed callings or dealings
>
> Fraudulent sales
>
> Agreements restraining trade
>
> Agreements not to compete
>
> Usurious agreements

C. REGULATION OF BUSINESS

Local, state, and national laws regulate a wide variety of business activities and practices.

14. Effect of Violation

Whether an agreement made in connection with business conducted in violation of the law is binding or void depends on how strongly opposed the public policy is to the prohibited act. Some courts take the view that the agreement is not void unless the statute expressly specifies this. In some instances, the statute expressly preserves the validity of the contract. For example, if someone fails to register a fictitious name under which the business is done, the violator, after registering the name as required by the statute, is permitted to sue on a contract made while illegally conducting business.

15. Statutory Regulation of Contracts

To establish uniformity or to protect one of the parties to a contract, statutes frequently provide that contracts of a given class must follow a statutory model or must contain specified provisions. For example, statutes commonly specify that particular clauses must be included in insurance policies to protect the persons insured and their beneficiaries. Other statutes require that contracts executed in connection with credit buying and loans contain particular provisions designed to protect the debtor.

Consumer protection legislation gives the consumer the right to rescind the contract in certain situations. Laws relating to truth in lending, installment sales, and home improvement contracts commonly require that an installment-sale contract specify the cash price, the down payment, the trade-in value (if any), the cash balance, the insurance costs, and the interest and finance charges.

When the statute imposes a fine or imprisonment for violation, the court should not hold that the contract is void, since that would increase the penalty that the legislature had imposed. If a statute prohibits the making of certain kinds of contracts or imposes limitations on contracts that can be made, the attorney general or other government official may generally be able to obtain an **injunction**, or court order, to stop the parties from entering into a prohibited contract.

16. Licensed Callings or Dealings

Statutes frequently require that a person obtain a license, certificate, or diploma before practicing certain professions, such as law or medicine. A license may also be required before carrying on a particular business or trade, such as that of a real estate broker, peddler, stockbroker, hotel keeper, or pawnbroker.

(a) PROTECTIVE LICENSE. If a license is required to protect the public from unqualified persons, a contract made by an unlicensed person is void.[14] For example, it has been held that when a statute required that contractors be licensed, and an unlicensed contractor made a contract to make repairs, the contractor could not recover from the owner either the price agreed to in their contract or the reasonable value of the services actually performed. A corporation that does not hold a required real estate broker's license cannot sue to recover fees for services as a broker.

Likewise, an agreement with an unlicensed physician for services cannot be enforced by the physician. The patient of the unlicensed physician, however, may sue for damages if the contract is not properly performed.

The illegality of contracts often comes into the picture when parties seek to set up some arrangement to evade government regulations or prohibitions of the criminal law, or to avoid paying taxes.

(b) REVENUE-RAISING LICENSE. In contrast with the protective license, a license may be required solely as a revenue measure by requiring the payment of a fee for the license. In that event, an agreement made in violation of the statute by one not licensed is generally held valid. The contract may also sometimes be held valid when it is shown that no harm has resulted from the failure to obtain a permit to do the work contemplated by the particular contract.

17. Fraudulent Sales

Statutes commonly regulate the sale of certain commodities. Scales and measures of grocers and other vendors must be checked periodically, and they must be approved and sealed by the proper official. Certain articles must be inspected before they are sold. Other articles must be labeled in a particular way to show their contents and to warn the public of the presence of any dangerous or poisonous substance. Since these laws regulating sales are generally designed for the protection of the public, transactions in violation of such laws are void.

18. Administrative Agency Regulation

Large segments of the American economy are governed by federal administrative agencies created to carry out the general policies specified by Congress. A contract must be in harmony with public policy, not only as declared by Congress and the courts, but also as applied by the appropriate administrative agency. For

---

[14] Portable Embryonics, Inc. v J. P. Genetics, Inc. ___ Mont ___, 810 P2d 1197 (1991).

example, a particular contract to market goods might not be prohibited by any statute or court decision but may still be condemned by the Federal Trade Commission as an unfair method of competition. When the proper commission has made its determination, a contract not in harmony with the determination, such as a contract of a railroad charging a higher or a lower rate than that approved by the Interstate Commerce Commission, is illegal.

19. Contracts in Restraint of Trade

An agreement that unreasonably restrains trade is illegal and void on the ground that it is contrary to public policy. Such agreements take many forms, such as a combination to create a monopoly or to obtain a corner on the market, or an association of merchants to increase prices. In addition to the illegality of the agreement based on general principles of law, statutes frequently declare monopolies illegal and subject the parties to various civil and criminal penalties.[15]

20. Agreements Not to Compete

In the absence of a valid restrictive covenant, the seller of a business may compete with the buyer, or an ex-employee may solicit customers of the former employer.[16] If there is no sale of a business nor the making of an employment contract, an agreement not to compete is illegal as a restraint of trade and a violation of the antitrust law. The agreement is therefore void.

(a) SALE OF BUSINESS. When a going business is sold, it is commonly stated in the contract that the seller shall not go into the same or a similar business again within a certain geographic area, or for a certain period of time, or both. In early times, such agreements were held void because they deprived the public of the service of the person who agreed not to compete, impaired the latter's means of earning a livelihood, reduced competition, and exposed the public to monopoly. To the modern courts the question is whether, under the circumstances, the restriction imposed on one party is reasonably necessary to protect the other party. If the restriction is reasonable, it is valid.

(b) EMPLOYMENT CONTRACT. Restrictions to prevent competition by a former employee are held valid when reasonable and necessary to protect the interest of the former employer.[17] For example, the following provision is reasonable and will be enforced. A doctor employed by a medical clinic would not practice medicine within a 50-mile radius of the city in which the clinic was located for one year after leaving the employ of the clinic. Likewise, a provision is valid that prohibited an employee for two years from calling on any customer of the employer called on by the employee during the last six months of employment.

A restrictive covenant is not binding when it places a restriction on the employee that is broader than reasonably necessary to protect the employer. The employer cannot prohibit competition by a former employee for all time or for the entire world merely because some customer might follow the former employee. In determining the validity of a restrictive covenant binding an employee, the court balances the aim of protecting the legitimate interests of the employer with the right of the employee to follow gainful employment and provide services required by the public and other employers.[18]

---

[15] Sherman Antitrust Act, 15 USC §§ 1-7; Clayton Act, 15 USC §§ 12-27; Federal Trade Commission Act, 15 USC §§ 41-58.

[16] Hart v McCormack (Tex App) 746 SW2d 330 (1988).

[17] Hapney v Central Garage, Inc. (Fla App) 579 So2d 127 (1991).

[18] Chambers-Dobson, Inc. v Squier, 238 Neb 748, 472 NW2d 391 (1991).

(c) SALE OF STOCK BY NON-EMPLOYEE SHAREHOLDER. Agreements by one party to a contract not to compete with the other are commonly found when (1) an employee agrees not to compete with the employer after leaving the employment, or (2) the seller of a business agrees not to compete with the buyer of the business. The *Central Water Works Supply* case raised the question of how to classify the situation when a shareholder who was not an employee sold the stock and then competed with the corporation.

CENTRAL WATER WORKS SUPPLY, INC. v FISHER
___Ill App 3d ___, ___ Ill Dec ___, 608 NE2d 618 (1993)

> The Central Water Works Supply, Inc., a corporation, had a contract with its shareholders that they would not compete with it. There were only four shareholders. William Fisher was one of these. He was not an employee of the corporation. He sold his shares in the corporation and began to compete with it. The corporation went to court to obtain an injunction to stop such competition. The court enjoined Fisher from competing. Fisher appealed.

McCULLOUGH, J. . . . Restrictive covenants often appear in employment contracts and contracts for the sale of a business. Courts evaluate these restrictive covenants differently because of the difference in the nature of the interests sought to be protected. Courts impose a more stringent test of reasonableness on restrictive covenants in employment contracts than they do under restrictive covenants ancillary to the sale of a business. The basis for the distinction rests upon the fact that a purchaser in the sale of a business context holds more bargaining power than an ordinary employee in an employment context. . . .

If the covenant is ancillary to the sale of a business by the covenator to the covenantee, then all the covenantee must show is that the restriction is reasonable as to time, geographical area and scope of prohibited business activity. If, however, the covenant is ancillary only to an employment agreement, the covenantee must show additional special circumstances, such as a near-permanent relationship with his employee's customers and that, but for his association with the employer, the former employee would not have had contact with the customers, or the existence of customer lists, trade secrets or other confidential information. . . . A covenant ancillary to an employment contract shields the employer from the possibility of losing his clientele to an employee who appropriates proprietary customer information for his own benefit, and also shields him from the possibility of losing customers with whom he enjoys a near-permanent relationship. A covenant ancillary to the sale of a business ensures the buyer that the former owner will not walk away from the sale with the company's customers and good will, leaving the buyer with an acquisition that turns out to be only chimerical. . . .

We must determine whether the covenant not to compete contained in the shareholder's agreement is more like a covenant ancillary to the sale of a business or a covenant contained in an employment contract. Defendant contends this covenant is more like that of one in an employment contract. Defendant further contends that plaintiff has no protectable interest because he cannot show defendant acquired confidential information through his employment with plaintiff and subsequently attempted to use that information for his own benefit or that the customer relationship is near permanent and that, but for his relationship with plaintiff, defendant would not have had contact with the customers in question. . . .

On the other hand, plaintiff alleges the covenant in question here is more like one ancillary to the sale of a business. Plaintiff contends the covenant was part and parcel of the business transaction forming the company and that the parties all intended it to be evidence of good faith or goodwill to attempt to make the company successful. Plaintiff argues that there was no unequal bargaining power between the parties.

. . . We conclude this covenant is more analogous to a covenant not to compete which is ancillary to the sale of a business. To enforce such a covenant, the purchaser must first show a protectable business interest which has been injured by his former employee's unfair competition. If the purchaser establishes the interest, then the purchaser need only show that the restriction is reasonable as to time, geographical area and scope of prohibitive business activities. . . .

[The court held that this was done.]

[Judgment affirmed]

QUESTIONS

1. State whether the court treats covenants not to compete the same whether they are found in a contract for the sale of a business or a contract of employment.
2. Why did not the court in the *Central Water Works Supply* case follow the prior law?
3. Of what importance was the fact that there were only four stockholders in the corporation?

(d) EFFECT OF INVALIDITY. When a restriction of competition agreed to by the parties is invalid because its scope as to time or geographic area is too great, how does this affect the contract? Some courts trim the restrictive covenant down to a scope that the court deems reasonable and require the parties to abide by that revision. This rule is nicknamed the "blue pencil rule." Other courts refuse to apply the blue pencil rule and hold that the restrictive covenant is void[19] or that the entire contract is void. There is also authority that a court should refuse to apply the blue pencil rule when the restrictive covenant was manifestly unfair and would virtually keep the employee from earning a living.[20]

21. Usurious Agreements

Usury is committed when money is loaned at a greater rate of interest than is allowed by law. Most states prohibit by statute the taking of more than a stated amount of interest. These statutes provide a maximum contract rate of interest that is the highest annual rate that can be exacted or demanded under the law of a given state. This maximum is often stated as a flat percentage rate, although there is a trend to tie the usury ceilings to current market rates. Intentionally charging greater interest on a loan than allowed by law constitutes usury. It is not necessary to prove that the

---

[19] A.L. Williams & Associates v Stelk (CA11 Ga) 960 F2d 942 (1992).
[20] North American Paper Co. v Unterberger, 172 Ill App 3d 410, 122 Ill Dec 362, 526 NE2d 621 (1988).

defendant knew that there was a violation of the usury law.

In many states, the usury law does not apply to loans made to corporations.[21]

When a lender incurs expenses in the making of a loan, such as the cost of appraising property or making a credit investigation of the borrower, the lender will require the borrower to pay the amount of such expenses. Lenders may attempt to obtain more than the expenses from the borrowers. Any fee charged by a lender that goes beyond the reasonable expense of making the loan constitutes "interest" for the purpose of determining whether the transaction is usurious.[22]

22. Credit Sale Contracts

Sales of goods and services on credit are not technically within the scope of the usury laws, since the seller does not make an express "loan" to the buyer. When the sale is made on credit, the price that the seller charges is ordinarily not controlled by the usury law.

(a) CREDIT SALE PRICE. A seller may charge one price for cash sales and a higher price for credit or installment sales. The difference between these two prices is called the **time-price differential**. Since the usury law is not applicable, the time-price differential may be greater than the maximum amount of interest that could be charged on a loan equal to the cash price.[23]

A few states, however, hold that the time-price differential is subject to the usury law, or have amended their usury laws or have adopted statutes to regulate the differential between cash and time prices charged by the seller. Such statutes are sometimes limited to sales by retailers to consumers or apply only to sales under a stated dollar maximum.

Many states have adopted retail and installment-sale laws that apply whenever the sale price is to be paid in installments and the seller retains a security interest in the goods. These laws frequently fix a maximum for the time-price differential, thereby remedying the situation created by the fact that the differential is not subject to the usury laws.

In the *Midland Guardian Company* case the buyer defended an action brought by the finance company on the ground that any liability to the plaintiff could not be enforced because it was usurious. The buyer asserted that she was entitled to statutory damages.

MIDLAND GUARDIAN CO. v THACKER
280 SC App 584, 314 SE2d 26 (1984)

> Sarah Thacker purchased a mobile home from a dealer, Colonial. Thacker paid for it with the money borrowed from a finance company, Midland Guardian Co. When she stopped making payments on the loan, Midland sued to get the home. Thacker asserted that the transaction was usurious and counterclaimed against Midland to recover the statutory damages authorized in cases of usury. From a decision in favor of Midland, Thacker appealed.

---

[21] Computer Sales Corp. v Rousonelos Farms, Inc. 100 Ill App 3d 388, 137 Ill Dec 816, 546 NE2d 761 (1989).

[22] First American Bank & Trust v Windjammer Time Sharing Resort, Inc. (Fla App) 483 So 2d 732 (1986).

[23] O'Connor v Televideo System, Inc. 218 Cal App 3d 709, 267 Cal Rptr 237 (1990).

GOOLSBY, J. . . . [The counterclaim for usury damages raises the question] whether a transaction involving the sale of a mobile home on deferred payments constitutes a sale at a time price or a loan and cloak for usury. . . .

We recognize . . . that a bona fide sale of property on credit at a price which exceeds the cash price by more than the legal rate of interest does not constitute usury. But the sale will be considered usurious when the sale is in fact at an agreed cash price and the form of a sale on credit is employed for the purpose of evading the usury statute. . . .

A close relationship between the seller of personal property and the financing institution can trigger an application of the usury statute despite language in the contract appearing to invoke the time price exception. Indeed, the time price exception has no application to a lending company that purchases the loan instrument from the merchant for the actual cash price when it is privy to the terms of the original transaction.

Here, the evidence shows that Colonial, the seller, and Midland Guardian, the finance company, were so closely allied that the original transaction was, in substance, a direct loan from Midland Guardian to the Thackers. As the record discloses, the finance company furnished the seller with security agreement forms and rate charts. And while the seller undertook to obtain credit information from the buyer, the seller did nothing with the data except transmit it to the finance company. Further, the finance company conducted the credit check and indicated approval of the credit application before any contract was made. Also, the security agreement was assigned to the finance company on the same day of its execution. . . .

Moreover, there are other indicia that the purported time price sale involved a usurious loan. The time price, here referred to as the "deferred payment price," was determined by adding amounts for insurance and a "finance charge" to the "cash price." Additionally, Colonial received from Midland Guardian in exchange for the security agreement its cash price and nothing else. Finally, and in many ways the most revealing, Colonial never contemplated that it would extend credit to the Thackers. This fact is made clear by the following exchange between the buyer's attorney and the mobile home salesman:

Q: *You stated that if the finance company turned you down on a customer's application for credit, you would go to another finance company?*

A: *Yes, M'am.*

Q: *If all the finance companies that you normally dealt with turned you down, would you indeed make a credit sale to that customer?*

A: *No, m'am.*

Thus, the correct conclusion to be drawn from the undisputed facts is "that the real transaction was a sale at a cash price accompanied by a loan or extension of credit to which the [finance company] was privy throughout." When so viewed, the finance charge of Six Thousand One Hundred Sixty-six Dollars ($6,166) on a mobile home costing, exclusive of insurance, Six Thousand Four Hundred Forty-two and 80/100 Dollars ($6,442.80) clearly emerges as usurious interest on a loan and not as an additional price paid for credit. The trial judge, therefore, erred as a matter of law in not holding that the time price rule was inapplicable. . . .

Because we have concluded that the transaction involved here did not constitute, under the particular facts shown, a valid time price sale, the judgment appealed from is reversed and the case is remanded to the Court of Common Pleas for a determination of the amount to which the appellant is entitled on her counterclaim as statutory damages.

[Judgment reversed and action remanded]

QUESTIONS

1. What was the basis for Thacker's claim that the transaction was usurious?
2. Would it affect the decision of the court if Colonial had sold the mobile home to Thacker on credit?
3. The parties agreed to a transaction in the form of a sale. Why doesn't the court accept the agreement and treat the transaction as a sale?

(b) REVOLVING CHARGE ACCOUNTS. When a merchant sells on credit, puts the bill on a charge account, and then adds a charge to the unpaid balance due by the customer, most courts hold that the amount of such a charge is not controlled by the usury law.

SUMMARY

When an agreement is illegal, it is ordinarily void, and no contract arises from it. Courts will not allow one party to an illegal agreement to bring suit against the other party. There are some exceptions to this, such as when the parties are not equally guilty or when the law's purpose in making the agreement illegal is to protect the person who is bringing suit. When possible, an agreement will be interpreted as being lawful. Even when a particular provision is held unlawful, the balance of the agreement will generally be saved, so that the net result is that there is a contract minus the clause that was held illegal.

The term *illegality* embraces situations in which a statute declares that certain conduct is unlawful or a crime; contracts requiring the commission of a tort; contracts that are contrary to public policy; contracts that are unconscionable; and, to some extent, contracts that are oppressive, unfair, or made in bad faith. The question of the legality of an agreement is not considered in the abstract, but the effect of the decision on the rest of society is considered. Increasingly, a given contract is not considered to be in a class by itself but is the same as thousands and even millions of other contracts.

Whether a contract is contrary to public policy may be difficult to determine, because public policy is not precisely defined. That which is harmful to the public welfare or general good is contrary to public policy. Contracts condemned as contrary to public policy include those designed to deprive the weaker party of a benefit that the lawmaker desired to provide; agreements injuring public service, such as an agreement to buy a government job for an applicant; agreements involving conflicts of interests, such as when the purchasing officer of a government buys from a company that the officer privately owns; agreements obstructing legal process, such as an agreement with a witness to disappear; illegal discrimination contracts; and wagers and private lotteries. Statutes commonly make the wager illegal, as a form of gambling. The lottery is any plan under which, for a consideration, a person has a chance to win a prize.

Illegality may consist of the violation of a statute or administrative regulation adopted to regulate business. Statutes may make it illegal to do business unless a particular form of contract is used or unless the party promoting the transaction is licensed. The protection of buyers from fraud of sellers may make it unlawful to sell under certain circumstances or without making certain disclosures. Contracts in restraint of trade are generally illegal as violating federal or state antitrust laws. An agreement not to compete is illegal as a restraint of trade, except when reasonable in its terms and when it is incidental to the sale of a business or to a contract of employment.

The charging by a lender of a higher rate of interest than allowed by law is usury. Courts must examine transactions carefully to see if there is a usurious loan disguised as a legitimate transaction.

When sellers of goods offer their buyers one price for a cash sale and another, higher price for a credit sale, the higher price is lawful. The credit price is not usurious, even though the difference between the cash price and the credit price is greater than the amount that could be charged as interest on a loan equal to the cash price. This concept is called the time-price differential. A minority of states reject or abolish it or limit the increase of the credit price over the cash price to a specified percentage or to the maximum amount that could be charged on a loan equal to the cash price. Most states do not apply the usury law to a revolving charge account. A minority do so, with the result that the charges imposed on the account must not exceed the amount that could be charged as interest on a loan of the amount due on the account.

LAW IN PRACTICE

1. Be on the alert that what looks like a good bargain to you may not be a valid contract because it is illegal, violates public policy, or is unconscionable.

2. Check the past performance and litigation record of the other party to a proposed contract to determine whether you are asking for trouble by contracting with that person.

3. Explore with your attorney whether there is any way of protecting yourself from loss caused by invalidity of a proposed contract, as by requiring the other party to furnish a surety bond or a standby letter of credit.

QUESTIONS AND CASE PROBLEMS

1. What social forces are affected by the rule that a credit sale price is not usurious, although the difference between the credit price and the cash price is greater than the interest that could be charged on a loan in the amount of the cash price?

2. When are the parties to an illegal agreement *in pari delicto*?

3. Alman made a contract to purchase an automobile from Crockett Motors on credit. Alman failed to make payments on time. When Crockett sued to enforce the contract, Alman raised the defense that the price of the car had been increased because she was buying on credit and that this increase was unconscionable. Crockett proved that the automobile was exactly what it was represented to be and that no fraud had been committed in selling the car to Alman. Does Crockett's evidence constitute a defense to Alman's claim of unconscionability?

4. The Civic Association of Plaineville raffled an automobile to raise funds to build a hospital. Lyons won the automobile, but the association refused to deliver it to her. She sued the association for the automobile. Can Lyons enforce the contract?

5. Ewing was employed by Presto-X-Company, a pest exterminator. His contract of employment specified that he would not solicit or attempt to solicit customers of Presto-X for two years after the termination of his employment. After working several years, his employment was terminated. Ewing then sent a letter to customers of Presto-X stating that he no longer worked for Presto-X and that he was still certified by the state. Ewing then set forth his home address and phone number, which the customers did not previously have. The letter then ended with the statement "I thank you for your business throughout the past years."

Presto-X brought an action to enjoin Ewing from sending such letters. He raised the defense that he was only prohibited from soliciting and that there was nothing in the letters that constituted a seeking of customers. Decide. What ethical values are involved? [Presto-X-Company v Ewing (Iowa) 442 NW2d 85]

6. The Minnesota Adoption Statute requires that any agency placing a child for adoption must make a thorough investigation and cannot give a child to an applicant unless such placement is in the best interests of the child. Tibbetts applied to Crossroads, Inc., a private adoption agency, for a child to adopt. He later sued the agency for breach of contract, claiming that the agency was obligated by contract to supply a child for adoption. The agency claimed that it was only required to use best efforts to locate a child and was not required to supply a child to Tibbetts unless it found him to be a suitable parent. Decide. [Tibbetts v Crossroads, Inc. (Minn App) 411 NW2d 535]

7. Florida law prohibits discrimination in a wide range of business transactions. The Florida Human Rights Act prohibits discrimination because of religion. The Florida Fair Housing Act states that it is the "policy" of Florida to provide "fair housing throughout the state." Skolnick and his wife wanted to buy land in the residential section of Bal Harbour. They were told that they could not buy the land unless they were members of the Bal Harbour Club. They applied for membership in the club but were rejected because of their religion. They then sued the club, claiming that it had improperly discriminated against them and that the requirement of membership in the club in order to buy the land was merely a device to evade the prohibition of discrimination in the sale of land. The club settled the suit by paying Skolnick $25,000. The club then demanded that the Ranger Insurance Company pay that amount to the club on the theory that the club's policy from that company covered all claims that could be made against the club by third persons. The insurance company refused to pay on the ground that such payment would be compensating the club for its unlawful discrimination. Was the insurance company liable? [Ranger Ins. Co. v Bal Harbour Club, Inc. (Fla) 549 So 2d 1005]

8. Onderdonk entered a retirement home operated by Presbyterian Homes. The contract between Onderdonk and the home required Onderdonk to make a specified monthly payment that could be increased by the home as the cost of operations increased. The contract and the payment plan were thoroughly explained to Onderdonk. As the cost of operations rose, the monthly payments were continually raised by the home to cover these costs. Onderdonk objected to the increases on the ground that the increases were far more than had been anticipated and that the contract was therefore unconscionable. Was his objection valid? [Onderdonk v Presbyterian Homes, 171 NJ Super 529, 410 A2d 252]

9. Smith was employed as a salesman for Borden, Inc., which sold food products in 63 counties in Arkansas, 2 counties in Missouri, 2 counties in Oklahoma, and 1 county in Texas. Smith's employment contract prohibited him from competing with Borden after leaving its employ. Smith left Borden and went to work for a competitor, Lady Baltimore Foods. Working for this second employer, Smith sold in three counties of Arkansas. He had sold in two of these counties while he worked for Borden. Borden brought an injunction action against Smith and Lady Baltimore to enforce the anticompetitive covenant in Smith's former contract. Was Borden entitled to the injunction? [Borden, Inc. v Smith, 252 Ark 295, 478 SW2d 744]

10. Doherty ran a lounge and bar, known as the Orchid Room, in California, where betting is illegal. Bradley, a patron in the Orchid Room, made bets with Doherty on the scores he could attain on the pinball machine. Bradley lost $70,000 on such bets. He later sued Doherty to recover the money. Doherty raised the defense that Bradley was in pari delicto and therefore could not recover. Bradley claimed that this defense did not apply because the pinball machines were fixed by electronic devices, and also because he, Bradley, was a compulsive gambler. Was Bradley correct? [Bradley v Doherty, 30 Cal App 3d 991, 106 Cal Rptr 725]

11. Vodra was employed as a salesperson and contracting agent for American Security Services. As part of his contract of employment, Vodra signed an agreement that for three years after leaving this employment, he would not solicit any customer of American. Vodra had no experience in the security field when he went to work for American. To the extent that he became known to American's customers, it was by virtue of being the representative of American rather than because of his own reputation in the security field. After some years, Vodra left American and organized a competing company that solicited American's customers. American sued him to enforce the restrictive convenant. Vodra claimed that the restrictive convenant was illegal and not binding.

Was he correct? [*American Securities Services, Inc. v Vodra, 222 Neb 480, 385 NW2d 73*]

12. The Potomac Leasing Company leased an automatic telephone system to Vitality Centers. Claudene Cato signed the lease as guarantor of payments. When the rental was not paid, Potomac Leasing brought suit against Vitality and Cato. They raised the defense that the rented equipment was to be used for an illegal purpose—namely, the random sales solicitation by means of an automatic telephone in violation of state statute; that this purpose was known to Potomac Leasing; and that Potomac Leasing could therefore not enforce the lease. Was this defense valid? [*Potomac Leasing Co. v Vitality Centers, Inc. 290 Ark 265, 718 SW2d 928*]

13. The English publisher of a book called *Cambridge* gave a New York publisher permission to sell that book any place in the world except in England. The New York publisher made several bulk sales of the book to buyers who sold the book throughout the world including England. The English publisher sued the New York publisher and its customers for breach of the restriction prohibiting sales in England. Decide. [*Pevensey Press, Ltd. v Prentice-Hall, Inc. ___App Div 2d ___, 555 NYS2d 769*]

14. A state law required builders of homes to be licensed and declared that an unlicensed contractor could not recover compensation under a contract made for the construction of a residence. Annex Construction, Inc. did not have a license. It built a home for French. When he failed to pay what was owed, Annex Construction Company sued him. He raised the defense that the unlicensed contractor could not recover for the contract price. Annex claimed that the lack of a license was not a bar because the president of the corporation was a licensed builder, he was the only shareholder of the corporation, and the construction had in fact been properly performed. Was Annex entitled to recover?

15. Carlos was campaigning to be elected the next governor of the state. Helena was a rival candidate. He promised Helena that if she would withdraw as a candidate and support him for governor he would appoint her the next attorney general for the state. She did so and her support gave Carlos the necessary additional votes that he needed to be elected. Carlos however appointed Rodrigo as the attorney general. Helena sued Carlos for breach of contract. At the trial it was conceded that Helena was highly qualified for the position and no one even suggested that she was not the best possible candidate for attorney general. Was Carlos liable for breach of contract?

CHAPTER 14

FORM OF CONTRACT

A. STATUTE OF FRAUDS
1. Validity of Oral Contracts
2. Contracts that must be Evidenced by a Writing
3. Note or Memorandum
4. Effect of Noncompliance
5. Judicial Relief from Statute of Frauds

B. PAROL EVIDENCE RULE
6. Exclusion of Parol Evidence Rule
7. Liberalization of Parol Evidence
8. Exclusion of Parol Evidence

LEARNING OBJECTIVES

After studying this chapter, you will be able to:
1. *State when a contract must be evidenced by a writing.*
2. *List the requirements of a writing that evidences a contract.*
3. *State the effects of the absence of a sufficient writing when a contract must be evidenced by a writing.*
4. *List the exceptions that have been made by the courts to the laws requiring written evidence of contracts.*
5. *Compare statute of frauds requirements with the parol evidence rule.*
6. *List exceptions to the parol evidence rule.*

When must a contract be written? What is the effect of a written contract? These questions lead to the statute of frauds and the parol evidence rule.

A. STATUTE OF FRAUDS

A contract is a legally binding agreement. Must the agreement be evidenced by a writing?

1. Validity of Oral Contracts

Generally, a contract is valid whether it is written or oral. By statute, however, some contracts must be evidenced by a writing.[1] Statutes requiring a writing do not apply when an oral agreement has been voluntarily performed by both parties.

The failure to sign and return a written contract does not establish that there is no contract, because there may have been an earlier oral contract. Whether such a prior oral contract exists is to be determined from all the circumstances. The test is what intent was manifested by the parties.

Although oral agreements are ordinarily binding and are therefore contracts, an exception will arise when it is the intent of the parties that there is no binding agreement until a written contract is prepared and signed. If, in fact, the parties intend not to be bound until a written contract is executed, their preliminary oral agreement does not constitute a contract. Such a preliminary agreement cannot be enforced when a written contract is not thereafter executed.

2. Contracts That Must Be Evidenced by a Writing

Ordinarily, a contract, whether oral or written, is binding if the existence and terms of the contract can be established to the satisfaction of the trier of fact—usually the jury. In some instances a statute, commonly called a **statute of frauds**,[2] requires that certain kinds of contracts be evidenced by a writing, or else they cannot be enforced. This means that either the contract itself must be in writing and signed by both parties, or there must be a sufficient written memorandum of the oral contract signed by the person being sued for breach of contract.

(a) AGREEMENT THAT CANNOT BE PERFORMED WITHIN ONE YEAR AFTER THE CONTRACT IS MADE. A writing is required when the contract, by its terms or subject matter, cannot be performed within one year after the date of the agreement.[3] Thus, a joint venture agreement to construct a condominium complex was subject to the one-year provision of the statute of frauds where the contract could not reasonably have been performed within one year. This was due to the complex nature of the project. The plans of the parties projected a development over the course of three years.

The year runs from the time the oral contract was made rather than from the date when performance is to begin. In computing the year, the day on which the contract was made is excluded. The year begins with the following day and ends at the close of the first anniversary of the day on which the agreement was made.

---

[1]   Putt v City of Corinth (Miss) 579 So 2d 534 (1991).

[2]   The name is derived from the original English Statute of Frauds and Perjuries, which was adopted in 1677 and became the pattern for similar legislation in America. The 17th section of that statute governed the sale of goods, and its modern counterpart is § 2-201 of the UCC. The fourth section of the English statute provided the pattern for American legislation with respect to contracts, other than for the sale of goods, described in this section of the chapter. The English statute was repealed in 1954, except as to land sale and guaranty contracts. The American statutes remain in force, but the liberalization by UCC 2-201 of the pre-Code requirements with respect to contracts for the sale of goods may be regarded as a step in the direction of the abandonment of the statute of frauds concept.

[3]   Trovese v O'Meara (SD) 493 NW2d 221 (1992).

Figure 14-1 Hurdles in the Path of a Contact

Writing Required	
Statute of Frauds	**Exceptions**
More than one year to perform Sale of land Answer for another's debt or default Personal representative to pay debt of decedent Promise in consideration of marriage Sale of goods for $500 or more Miscellaneous	Part performance Promisor benefit Detrimental reliance
Parol Evidence Rule	**Exceptions**
Every complete, final written contract	Incomplete contract Ambiguous terms Fraud, accident, or mistake To prove existence or nonbinding character of contract Modification of contract Illegality

The statute of frauds does not apply if it is possible under the terms of the agreement to perform the contract within one year.[4] Thus, a writing is not required when no time for performance is specified and the performance will not necessarily take more than a year. In this case, the statute is inapplicable without regard to the time when performance is actually begun or completed.

When a contract may be terminated at will by either party, the statute of frauds is not applicable, because the contract may be terminated within a year. In the *Boening* case it was claimed that there was no binding contract. There was an oral agreement to continue the plaintiff's franchise for so long as performance thereunder was satisfactory.

D & N BOENING, INC. v KIRSCH BEVERAGES, INC.
63 NY2d 449, 483 NYS2d 164, 472 NE2d 992 (1984)

D & N Boening, Inc. was franchised by the American Beverage Corporation to sell the "Yoo-Hoo" beverage in a certain portion of New York state. The franchise was to continue as long as the franchisee rendered satisfactory

---

4   Kelley v Galina-Bouquet, Inc. 155 App Div 2d 96, 552 NYS2d 305 (1990).

performance. This agreement was oral, and several requests by Boening to put it in writing were refused. Thereafter Kirsch Beverages bought out American Beverage Corporation and notified Boening that its franchise was terminated. No cause for termination was given. Boening then sued Kirsch and American for breach of the franchise. From a judgment for the defendants, the plaintiff appealed.

JASEN, J. . . . The ancient Statute of Frauds . . . was intended to prevent fraud in the proving of certain legal transactions particularly susceptible to deception, mistake and perjury and, with regard specifically to the requirement for a signed writing for a contract not to be performed within one year, "the design of the statute was, not to trust to the memory of witnesses for a longer time than one year."

Unfortunately, the Statute does not in many cases provide an effective means of serving that purpose. There is no necessary relationship between the time of the making of a contract, the time within which its performance is required, and the time when it might come to court to be proven. Accordingly, the courts have generally been reluctant to give too broad an interpretation to this provision of the Statute and instead have limited it to those contracts only which by their very terms have absolutely no possibility in fact and law of full performance within one year.

The parties may well have expected that the contract would continue in force for more than one year; it may well have been very improbable that it would not do so; and it did in fact continue in force for a much longer time. But they made no stipulation which in terms, or by reasonable inference, required that result. The question is not what the probable, or expected, or actual performance of the contract was; but whether the contract, according to the reasonable interpretation of its terms, required that it should not be performed within the year. . . .

. . . Moreover, consistent with that narrow interpretation, this court has continued to analyze oral agreements to determine if, according to the parties' terms, there might be any possible means of performance within one year. Wherever an agreement has been found to be susceptible of fulfillment within that time, in whatever manner and however impractical, this court has held the one-year provision of the Statute to be inapplicable, a writing unnecessary, and the agreement not barred. . . .

On the other hand, while the foregoing oral agreements and similar ones which are performable within one year are saved from the writing requirement of the Statute of Frauds, clearly there are others which simply are impossible of completion within that time by their own terms and are, therefore, void if unwritten. Prominent among these latter agreements falling within the Statute are those which are terminable within one year only upon a breach by one of the parties. A breach can in no way be equated with an option to discontinue or cancel, the exercise of which would constitute an alternative performance of the agreement. . . .

As this court early explained, "termination is not performance, but rather the destruction of the contract . . . where there is no provision authorizing either of the parties to terminate as a matter of right." And, more recently, in deciding that the contract then under review fell within the Statute because not truly performable within one year, this court held that "the contract was not, then, one which might be *performed* within a year, but rather one which could only be *terminated* within that period by a breach of one or the other party to it [emphasis in original]. *The possibility of such wrongful termination is not, of course, the same as the possibility of performance* within the statutory period."

Here, as the Appellate Division correctly held, the oral agreement between the parties called for performance of an indefinite duration and could only be terminated within one year by its breach during that period. . . .

According to its terms, the agreement required defendants to continue plaintiff's subdistributorship indefinitely. It provided for no expiration and there was no contemplation of any completion or final discharge. The sole limitation on the agreement's duration was its explicit requirement—especially crucial to an exclusive agency—that plaintiff conduct its subdistributorship satisfactorily, exerting its best efforts and acting in good faith. Only upon plaintiff's failure to do so within the first year could the agreement have been terminated during that period.

Such a failure would not have constituted a permitted manner of performance or exercise of an option, but rather, a breach of the agreement. And other than such a breach, there was no provision under the terms of the agreement for it to come to an end. Neither party had an option to cancel, and there was no specified time or event which automatically would cause the agreement to terminate. Instead, under a reasonable interpretation of its own terms, the agreement would extend beyond the first year and, indeed, would continue in perpetuity unless plaintiff failed to perform its part of the bargain.

Being terminable only by plaintiff's breach, the agreement alleged in the complaint was not one which by its terms could be *performed* within one year. As such, it came within the gambit of the Statute of Frauds and is void for being unwritten. . . .

[Judgment affirmed]

QUESTIONS

1. What was the evil against which the statute of frauds was intended to guard in connection with the provision involved in the *Boening* case?
2. What has been the attitude of the courts to the one-year provision of the statute of frauds?
3. Why didn't the court sustain the oral contract in view of the fact that it could have ended in less than a year if Boening's performance was not satisfactory to Kirsch?

(b) AGREEMENT TO SELL OR A SALE OF ANY INTEREST IN REAL PROPERTY. All contracts to sell—as well as sales of—land, buildings, or interests in land, such as mortgages, must be evidenced by a writing. The statute applies only to the agreement between the owner and purchaser or between their agents. It does not apply to agreements to pay for an examination or search of the title of the property or to agreements between the buyer and an attorney. The statute ordinarily does not apply to a contract between a real estate agent and one of the parties to the sales contract employing the agent.

An agreement to cancel or set aside a contract for the sale of land must also satisfy the statute of frauds by being evidenced by a writing.

(c) PROMISE TO ANSWER FOR THE DEBT OR DEFAULT OF ANOTHER. If you promise C to pay D's debt to C if D does not do so, you are promising to answer for the debt of another. Such a promise must usually be evidenced by a writing to be enforceable.[5]

If your promise is made directly to the debtor that you will pay the creditor of the debtor what is owed, the statute of frauds is not applicable.[6] In contrast, if you make the promise to the creditor, it comes within the category of a promise made for the benefit of another. It must therefore be evidenced by a writing that satisfies the statute of frauds.

(d) PROMISE BY THE EXECUTOR OR ADMINISTRATOR OF A DECEDENT'S ESTATE TO PAY A CLAIM AGAINST THE ESTATE FROM PERSONAL FUNDS.

The personal representative (executor or administrator) has the duty of handling the affairs of a deceased person, paying the debts from the proceeds of the estate, and distributing any balance remaining. The executor or administrator is not personally liable for the claims against the estate of the decedent. If the personal representative promises to pay the decedent's debts with the representative's own money, the promise cannot be enforced unless it is evidenced by a writing.

If the personal representative makes a contract on behalf of the estate in the course of administering the estate, a writing is not required. The representative is then contracting on behalf of the estate. Thus, if the personal representative employs an attorney to settle the estate or makes a burial contract with an undertaker, no writing is required.

(e) PROMISE MADE IN CONSIDERATION OF MARRIAGE.

If a person makes a promise to pay a sum of money or to give property to another in consideration of marriage or a promise to marry, the agreement must be evidenced by a writing in order to be enforceable. This provision of the statute of frauds is not applicable to ordinary mutual promises to marry. It is not affected by the statutes in some states that prohibit the bringing of any action for breach of promise of marriage.

(f) SALE OF GOODS.

When the contract price for goods is $500 or more, the contract must ordinarily be evidenced by a writing.

(g) MISCELLANEOUS STATUTES OF FRAUDS.

In a number of states, special statutes require other agreements to be in writing or evidenced by a writing. Thus, a statute may provide that an agreement to name a person as beneficiary in an insurance policy must be evidenced by a writing.

The Uniform Commercial Code contains three statutes of frauds relating to sales of personal property. These deal with: (1) goods; (2) securities, such as stocks and bonds; and (3) personal property other than goods and securities.

In some states, contracts with brokers relating to the sale of land are also subject to the statute of frauds. Some statutes require that a contract for medical care comply with the statute of frauds.[7]

3. Note or Memorandum

The statute of frauds requires a writing to evidence those contracts that come within its scope. This writing may be a note or memorandum, as distinguished from a contract.[8] It may be in any form, because its only purpose is to serve as evidence of the contract. The statutory requirement is, of course, satisfied if there is a complete written contract signed by both parties.

(a) SIGNING.

The note or memorandum must be signed by the party sought to be bound by the contract or that person's agent.[9] A letter from an employer setting forth the details of an oral contract of employment satisfies the statute of frauds in a suit brought by the employee against the employer. The writing was signed by the party "sought to be

---

5 Lichtman v Grossbard, 129 App Div 2d 437, 514 NYS2d 9 (1987).

6 Allen v Rosen (Fla App) 526 So 2d 1050 (1988).

7 Powers v Peoples Community Hospital Authority, ___ Mich App ___, 455 NW2d 371 (1990).

8 Busler v D & H Manufacturing, Inc. 81 Ohio App 3d 385, 611 NE2d 352 (1992).

9 Sales Service, Inc. v Daewood Int'l (America) Corp. (Mo App) 770 SW2d 453 (1989).

charged." If the employer had sued the employee in such case, the employer's letter would not satisfy the statute of frauds, since it would not be signed by the employee.

Some states require that the authorization of an agent to execute a contract coming within the statute of frauds must also be in writing. In the case of an auction, it is the usual practice for the auctioneer to be the agent of both parties for the purpose of signing the memorandum.

Ordinarily, the signature may be made at any place on the writing. In some states, it is expressly required that the signature appear at the end of the writing. The signature may be an ordinary one or any symbol that is adopted by the party as a signature. It may consist of initials, figures, or a mark. When a signature consists of a mark made by a person who is illiterate or physically incapacitated, it is commonly required that the name of the person be placed on the writing by someone else, who may be required to sign the instrument as a witness. A person signing a trade or assumed name is liable to the same extent as though the contract had been signed with the signer's name. In the absence of a local statute that provides otherwise, a signature may be made by pencil, pen, typewriter, print, or stamp.

In the *Parma Tile Mosaic* case, the court was faced with the problem of whether a party's printed name at the top of a page sent by facsimile transmission was that party's "signature" so as to satisfy the statute of frauds.

PARMA TILE MOSAIC & MARBLE CO., INC. v SHORT'S ESTATE

590 NYS2d 1019 (1992)

The MRLS Construction Company was the construction manager for a building project. In order to persuade a supplier of tile to continue making deliveries to Simes, the tile contractor, MRLS sent a writing by facsimile transmission to the tile supplier guaranteeing payment for the tile. At the top of the page sent by fax the printed name MRLS appeared, but the writing was not signed in any manner. In litigation between the various parties, it was claimed that the fax guaranty was not binding because it was not signed by the person purporting to guarantee the debt.

LeVINE, J. . . . Plaintiff's position is that the fax constitutes an enforceable guarantee since the name of MRLS appearing across the top of the fax satisfies the subscription required by the Statute of Frauds. . . . Defendants maintain that the subscription required to satisfy the Statute of Frauds is a written signature at the end of the writing.

. . . Subscription is required since it constitutes proof of assent to the terms of the guarantee, is associated with seriousness and deliberation, and confirms the guarantee's existence and the intent of the guarantor to be bound. . . . The signature required does not necessarily have to be written in ink at the bottom of the purported guarantee but may include any symbol or signature; whether written, printed or stamped; on any part of the document so long as the as the intent to be bound is demonstrated. . . .

Applying these legal principles to the matter herein the court determines that the facsimile transmission constitutes an enforceable guarantee of Sime's debt by MRLS . . . despite the fact that the name of MRLS appears only across the top of the fax.

There is no question but that MRLS intended to guarantee Sime's debt to plaintiff and that plaintiff shipped the tile in reliance on that guarantee. MRLS should not be permitted to evade its obligation because of the current and extensive use of electronic transmissions in modern business transactions. . . .

[Judgment for plaintiff]

QUESTIONS

1. Why does the statute of frauds involved in this case require "subscription" of the signature of the obligated party?
2. Does the court hold that there was a subscription of the guarantee?
3. Does the decision of the court prevent fraud?

(b) CONTENT. Except in the case of a sale of goods, the note or memorandum must contain all the material terms of the contract so that the court can determine just what was agreed. If any material term is missing, the writing is not sufficient. The missing term cannot be supplied by parol evidence.[10] A writing evidencing a sale of land that does not describe the land or identify the buyer does not satisfy the statute of frauds. Likewise, a writing is insufficient if the contract is partly oral and partly written. The subject matter must be identified either within the writing itself or in other writings to which it refers. A writing is not sufficient if it does not identify the subject of the contract. A deposit check given by the buyer to the seller does not take an oral land sales contract out of the statute of frauds. This is because the check does not set forth the terms of the sale.

The note or memorandum may consist of one writing or of separate papers, such as letters or telegrams, or of a combination of such papers.[11] The writing that satisfies the statute of frauds may be a letter written by a party's attorney.

Separate writings cannot be considered together unless they are linked. Linkage may be by express reference in each writing to the other or by the fact that each writing clearly deals with the same subject matter.

(c) TIME OF WRITING. The memorandum may be made at the time of the original transaction or at a later date. It must, however, ordinarily exist at the time a court action is brought upon the agreement.

4. Effect of Noncompliance

The majority of states hold that a contract that does not comply with the statute of frauds is voidable.[12] A small minority of states hold that such an agreement is void. Under either view, if an action is brought to enforce the contract, the defendant can raise the objection that it is not evidenced by a writing. However, when it is held that the oral contract is not void but merely voidable, it can be enforced if the defendant does not raise the statute of frauds defense. That is, the court will not refuse to enforce the contract when it notices that it is oral unless the opposing party objects thereto.

---

[10] Hoffius v Maestri, ___ Ark App ___, 786 SW2d 846 (1990).

[11] Machan Hampshire Properties, Inc. v Western Real Estate & Development Co. (Utah App) 779 P2d 230 (1989).

[12] The UCC creates several statutes of frauds of limited applicability in which it uses the phrase "not enforceable"— 1-206 (sale of intangible personal property); § 2-201 (sale of goods); and § 8-319 (sale of securities). The Official Code Comment, point 4, to § 2-201 describes "not enforceable" as meaning what would ordinarily be called "voidable."

No one other than the defendant can make the objection.

(a) RECOVERY OF VALUE CONFERRED. In most instances, a person who is prevented from enforcing a contract because of the statute of frauds is nevertheless entitled to recover from the other party the value of any services or property furnished or money given under the oral contract. Recovery is not based on the terms of the contract but on a quasi-contractual obligation. The other party is to restore to the plaintiff what was received in order to prevent unjust enrichment at the plaintiff's expense. For example, when an oral contract for services cannot be enforced because of the statute of frauds, the person performing the work may recover the reasonable value of the services rendered.

(b) PROOF OF FRAUD. The statute of frauds does not bar proof that the promisor had no intention to pay the debt of the third person but had made such promise fraudulently to induce the promisee to supply goods.

5. Judicial Relief from Statute of Frauds

To prevent hardship, the courts have created certain exceptions to the statute of frauds.

(a) PART PERFORMANCE OF CONTRACT. In spite of the statute of frauds, an oral contract for the sale of an interest in land will be enforced if the buyer has taken possession of the land, has made substantial valuable improvements to the land, and the value of such improvements cannot be easily measured in dollars.

In some states, the concept of part performance has been expanded to bar the defense of the statute of frauds when the plaintiff has fully performed the obligations under the oral contract.[13] To illustrate, the president of a corporation orally promised the insurer to pay the premiums on insurance to be furnished by the corporation. The insurer, after having furnished the corporation with the specified insurance in reliance on the promise of the president, could enforce that promise. Enforcement could be obtained even though there was no writing to satisfy the statute of frauds.

(b) PROMISOR BENEFITED BY PROMISE TO PAY DEBT OF ANOTHER. If a person orally promises a creditor to pay the debt owed to that creditor by a debtor, the promise is ordinarily not binding because of the statute of frauds. If the promise is made primarily to benefit the promisor, however, the courts refuse to apply the statute of frauds.[14] In this case, the promise to pay the debt of the third person is binding even though it is oral and benefits the debtor by discharging the debt that was due. For example, when the purpose of a majority stockholder's promise to pay the debt of the corporation is to benefit that stockholder, the statute of frauds is not applicable to that promise.

(c) DETRIMENTAL RELIANCE ON ORAL CONTRACT. The extent to which judicial relief from the statute of frauds will be granted in cases other than land sales and debt guaranties is not clear. The same forces that gave rise to the doctrine of promissory estoppel in connection with the law of consideration are to some extent causing courts to recognize detrimental reliance as excusing noncompliance with the statute of frauds. However, the mere fact that an employee changed employers in reliance on an oral promise of employment until retirement does not make the oral promise binding on the second employer.[15]

There is a conflict of authority as to whether detrimental reliance excuses noncompliance with the statute of frauds. Some courts refuse to apply the doctrine of detrimental

---

[13] Noesges v Servicemaster Co. ___ Ill App 3d ___, ___ Ill Dec ___, 598 NE2d 437 (1992).

[14] Smith, Seckman, Reid, Inc. v Metro National Corp. (Tex App) 836 SW2d 817 (1992).

[15] Baxley Veneer and Clete Co. v Maddox, ___ Ga ___, 404 SE2d 554 (1991).

reliance to avoid the defense of the statute of frauds because that would defeat the purpose of the statute.[16]

The mere fact that the promisee relies on the oral promise is generally not sufficient to entitle the promisee to enforce the oral promise. The promisee must show that (1) because of the reliance on the promise, substantial or unconscionable injury would be sustained by the promisee, or (2) the promisor would be unjustly enriched if the oral promise were not enforced.

(d) PROMISE TO EXECUTE WRITING. Some courts enforce an oral contract in spite of the statute of frauds when the defendant promised to execute a writing that would satisfy the statute but failed to do so.[17]

B. PAROL EVIDENCE RULE

When the contract is evidenced by a writing, may the contract terms be changed by the testimony of witnesses?

6. Exclusion of Parol Evidence

The general rule is that spoken words, that is, **parol evidence**, will not be allowed to modify or contradict the terms of a written contract that is complete on its face. This rule is not followed if there is clear proof that because of fraud, accident, or a mistake, the writing is not in fact the contract or the complete or true contract. This is called the **parol evidence rule**. It excludes words spoken before or at the time the contract was made.

The parol evidence rule prevents a party from avoiding liability on a written contract by providing evidence that the writing does not mean what it says. For example, when a lender sues to recover the loan set forth in a written contract, the defendant cannot claim that before the contract was signed, the creditor had agreed to extend the time for repayment of the loan. The parol evidence rule also excludes proof of a prior oral agreement that is inconsistent with the later written agreement.[18] In the *Gerlund* case, evidence was offered that contradicted the express provision of an employment contract.

GERLUND v ELECTRONIC DISPENSERS INTERNATIONAL
190 Cal App 3d 263, 235 Cal Rptr 279 (1987)

Leroy and Susan Gerlund were sales representatives of Electronic Dispensers International (EDI). They worked under a contract that specified that the employment could be terminated for any reason. The Gerlunds were the best sales representatives of EDI. After some years, EDI wanted to change the rate of commissions paid to sales representatives. When the Gerlunds did not agree to the changes, EDI discharged them. They sued EDI and offered evidence

---

[16] Meinhold v Huang (Mo App) 687 SW2d 596 (1985). Courts commonly refer to this doctrine as "promissory estoppel." The term *detrimental reliance* is used in the text because the promissory estoppel applied in connection with the question of consideration requires greater detriment than is required by those courts recognizing reliance as avoiding the statute of frauds.

[17] Magcobar North American v Grasso Oilfield Services, Inc. (Tex App) 736 SW2d 787 (1987).

[18] Valley Bank v Christensen (Idaho) 808 P2d 415 (1991).

that EDI had stated they would be employed as long as they did a good job. From a judgment in the Gerlunds' favor, EDI appealed.

BRAUER, J. . . . We quote here the pertinent portions of the agreement:

11. EFFECTIVE PERIOD: TERMINATION

This agreement shall be effective until thirty (30) days after notice of termination given by either party. Notice of termination may be given at any time and for any reason, and the date of any such notice shall be the postmark date if mailed, or the transmission date if wired. . . .

13. THE AGREEMENT COMPLETE.

This agreement contains the entire agreement between the Company and the Representative. There are no oral or collateral agreements of any kind. . . .

. . . The parol evidence rule generally prohibits the introduction of any extrinsic evidence to vary or contradict the terms of an integrated written instrument. It is based upon the premise that the written instrument *is* the agreement of the parties. Its application involves a two part analysis: (1) was the writing intended to be an integration, i.e. a complete and final expression of the parties' agreement, precluding any evidence of collateral agreements, and (2) is the agreement susceptible of the meaning contended for by the party offering the evidence? . . .

In regard to the question of integration, the written agreement of the parties contained an expression of their intent that it supersede any and all other agreements between them and that it constitute their entire agreement. It specifically recited that "there are no oral or collateral agreements of any kind." Our Supreme Court held in *Masterson v Sine*, 68 Cal 2d 222 . . . that such a clause, while it certainly helps to resolve the issue, does not of itself establish an integration; the collateral agreement itself must be examined in order to determine whether the parties intended it to be a part of their bargain. *Masterson*, however, does not go so far as to permit proof of a collateral agreement which contradicts an express provision of the written agreement. The reason for this is clear: it cannot reasonably be presumed that the parties intended to integrate two directly contradictory terms in the same agreement. Under *Masterson* then, parol evidence can be admitted only "'to prove the existence of a separate oral agreement as to any matter on which the document is silent and which is not inconsistent with its terms. . . .'"

The contract provides that either party can give written notice of termination *for any reason*. Thus there is no room for a separate collateral agreement regarding reasons for termination; the precise subject is already covered in the writing.

. . . We find that the alleged oral agreement is completely inconsistent with the language of the written contract. Thus the proffered parol understanding as to grounds for termination would be inadmissible to vary the contractual terms even if the contract were *not* an integration.

We now move on to the second part of our analysis: whether the offered evidence is nonetheless admissible to explain the meaning of the contractual language.

We do not find that the language of the contract lends itself to the proposed meaning. The term "any reason" is plainly all-inclusive, encompassing all reasons "*of whatever kind,*" good, bad, or indifferent. (quoting Webster's Dictionary definition of "any"). Adding the modifier "good" has a delimiting effect which changes the meaning entirely. As written the contract is one which is terminable at will; the interpretation sought by the Gerlunds is that the contract is terminable only for good cause. The two are totally inconsistent. The trial court admitted the evidence on the ground that "both parties have testified as to what they interpreted the contract to mean." Testimony of intention which is contrary to a contract's express terms, however, does not give meaning to the contract: rather it seeks to substitute a different meaning. It follows . . . that such evidence must be excluded.

[Judgment reversed]

QUESTIONS

1. What does the court mean when it speaks of the contract as being an "integration"?
2. How would the *Gerlund* case have been decided if Paragraph 13, stating that it was the complete contract, had not been included?
3. Could the parol evidence in the *Gerlund* case have been admitted to explain the meaning of the terms used in the written contract?

(a) REASON FOR THE PAROL EVIDENCE RULE. The parol evidence rule is based on the theory that either there never was an oral agreement, or if there was, the parties purposely abandoned it when they executed their written contract. The social objective of the parol evidence rule is to give stability to contracts and to prevent the fraudulent assertion of oral terms that never actually existed. Some courts apply the parol evidence rule strictly.

To illustrate the parol evidence rule, assume that L, the landlord who is the owner of several new stores in the same vicinity, discusses leasing one of them to T (tenant). L agrees to give to T the exclusive right to sell soft drinks. L agrees to stipulate in the leases with the tenants of other stores that they cannot do so. L and T then execute a detailed written lease for the store. The lease with T makes no provision with respect to an exclusive right of T to sell soft drinks. Thereafter, L leases the other stores to three other tenants, without restricting them as to the sale of soft drinks. They begin to sell soft drinks, causing T to lose money. T sues L, claiming that the latter has broken the contract by which T was to have the exclusive right to sell soft drinks. L defends on the ground that there was no prior oral agreement to that effect. Will the court permit T to prove that there was such an oral agreement?

On the facts as stated, if nothing more is shown, the court will not permit such parol evidence to be presented. The operation of this principle can be understood more easily if the actual courtroom procedure is followed. When T sues L, the first step will be to prove that there is a lease between them. Accordingly, T will offer in evidence the written lease between T and L. T will then take the witness stand and begin to testify about an oral agreement giving an exclusive right. At this point, L's attorney will object to the admission of the oral testimony by T because it would modify the terms of the written lease. The court will then examine the lease to see if it appears to be complete. If the court decides that it is, the court will refuse to allow T to offer evidence of an oral agreement. The only evidence before the court then will be the written lease. T will lose because nothing is in the written lease about an exclusive right to sell soft drinks.

If a written contract appears to be complete, the parol evidence rule prohibits its alteration not only by oral testimony but also by proof of other writings or memorandums made before or at the time the written contract was executed. An exception is made when the written contract refers to and identifies other writings or memorandums and states that they are to be regarded as part of the written contract. In such a case, it is said that the other writings are integrated or incorporated by reference.

(b) CONFLICT BETWEEN ORAL AND WRITTEN CONTRACTS. Initially, when there is a conflict between the prior oral contract and the later written contract, the variation is to be regarded as (1) a mistake, which can be corrected by reformation, or (2) an additional term which is not binding because it was not part of the written agreement.

7.   Liberalization of Parol Evidence Rule

The strictness of the parol evidence rule has been relaxed in a number of jurisdictions. A trend is beginning to appear that permits the use of parol evidence as to the intention of the parties when the claimed intention is plausible from the face of the contract, even though there is no ambiguity.

There is likewise authority that parol evidence is admissible as to matters occurring before the execution of the contract, in order to give a better understanding of what the parties meant by their written contract.[19]

The liberalization approach is not followed by all courts; some apply the **four corners rule**. Under this rule, the court must look for the contract within the four corners of the writing. The court may not look beyond the paper, in the absence of an exception to the parol evidence rule.

8.   When the Parol Evidence Rule Does Not Apply

The parol evidence rule may not apply in certain cases. The most common of these are discussed in the following paragraphs.

(a) INCOMPLETE CONTRACT. The parol evidence rule necessarily requires that the written contract sum up or integrate the entire contract. If the written contract is on its face or is admittedly not a complete summation, the parties naturally did not intend to abandon the points on which they agreed but that were not noted in the contract, and parol evidence is admissible to show the actual agreement of the parties.

A contract may appear on its face to be complete and yet not include everything the parties agreed on. It must be remembered that there is no official standard by which to determine when a contract is complete. All that the court can do is to consider whether all essential terms of the contract are present. That is, the court can determine whether the contract is sufficiently definite to be enforceable and whether it contains all provisions that would ordinarily be included in a contract of that nature.

The fact that a contract is silent as to a particular matter does not mean that it is incomplete, for the law may attach a particular legal result (called *implying a term*) when the contract is silent. In such a case, parol evidence that is inconsistent with the term that would be implied cannot be shown. For example, when the contract is silent as to the time of payment, the obligation of making payment concurrently with performance by the other party is implied, and parol evidence is not admissible to show that there was an oral agreement to make a payment at a different time.

(b) AMBIGUITY. If a written contract may have two different meanings, parol evidence may generally be admitted to clarify the meaning.[20]

It has also been held that UCC § 1-205 permits proof of trade usage and course of performance with respect to non-Code contracts

---

[19] Plateau Mining Co. v Utah Division of State Lands and Forestry (Utah) 802 P2d 720 (1990).

[20] Berg v Hudesman, ___ Wash ___, 801 P2d 222 (1990). This is also the view followed by UCC § 2-202 (a), which permits terms in a contract for the sale of goods to be "explained or supplemented by a course of dealing or usage of trade . . . or by course of performance." Such evidence is admissible not because there is an ambiguity, but "in order

even though there is no ambiguity. Chase Manhattan Bank v First Marion Bank (CA5 Fla) 437 F2d 1040 (1971). This is particularly true when the contract contains contradictory measurements or descriptions, or when the contract uses symbols or abbreviations that have no general meaning known to the court.

Parol evidence may also be admitted to show that a word used in a contract has a special trade meaning or a meaning in the particular locality that differs from the common meaning of that word.

The fact that the parties disagree as to the meaning of the contract does not mean that it is ambiguous.

(c) FRAUD, ACCIDENT, OR MISTAKE. A contract apparently complete on its face may have omitted a provision that should have been included. Parol evidence may be admitted to show that a provision was omitted as the result of fraud, accident, or mistake, and to further show what that provision stated.[21]

When one party claims to have been fraudulently induced by the other to enter into the contract, the parol evidence rule does not bar proof that there was fraud. For example, the parol evidence rule does not bar proof that the seller of land negligently misrepresented that the land was zoned to permit use as an industrial park.

In the *Touche Ross* case the claim was made that both the terms of the contract and the parol evidence rule barred proof that the underlying transaction had been induced by fraud.

TOUCHE ROSS LIMITED v FILIPEK

(Hawaii App) 778 P2d 721 (1989)

Holdings and Thriftway borrowed money from the Northland Bank. Filipek and others guaranteed that the loans would be paid back. The bank stopped doing business because of financial problems. Touche Ross was appointed to liquidate the assets of the bank. The loan to Holdings and Thriftway was not repaid when due. Touche Ross sued Filipek and the other guarantors on their obligation to repay the loan. They raised the defense that they were not bound by their guarantees because they and the borrowers had been induced to enter into the transactions because of the fraudulent statements and promises of the bank. Touche Ross claimed that the parol evidence rule barred any evidence that the parties had been induced by fraud. Judgment was entered in favor of Touche Ross. Filipek and the others appealed.

TANAKA, J. . . . The Loan Agreement included an integration clause which read as follows:

This Agreement constitutes the entire agreement between the parties hereto relating to the subject matter hereof and supersedes all prior and contemporaneous agreements, understandings, negotiations and discussions, whether oral or written, of the parties and there are

---

that the true understanding of the parties as to the agreement may be reached." Official Code Comment to § 2-202.
[21] Ramsay Health Care, Inc. v Follmer (Ala) 560 So 2d 746 (1990) (fraud).

no warranties, representations or other agreements among the parties in connection with the subject matter hereof except as specifically set forth herein.

. . . Appellants assert that since the Bank fraudulently induced Holdings and Thriftway to execute the First and Second Notes, those Notes are invalid and voidable and, consequently, their personal guarantees of those Notes are also invalid and unenforceable. . . .

Touche Ross argues, however, that since the loan documents are unambiguous in their terms and contain integration clauses, the parol evidence rule precludes all prior or contemporaneous representations and agreements from varying the terms therein. We disagree.

The general rule is that the parol evidence rule is inapplicable "where the issue is whether the contract was procured by fraud." 37 Am Jur 2d *Fraud and Deceit* § 451 at 620 (1968) (footnote omitted). . . . Professor Sweet explains the inapplicability of the parol evidence rule where fraud is involved as follows:

It is clear that a contract can be attacked if there are formation defects of a serious nature. If consent is not freely given, then no contract is formed, and consent is not freely given if it is induced by fraud. It follows that evidence establishing such a defect cannot be excluded by the parol evidence rule. The rule presupposes a contract, since it is grounded on the intention of the parties that the writing is to contain their complete agreement.

Sweet, *Promissory Fraud and the Parol Evidence Rule*, 49 Calif L Rev 877, 887 (1961).

. .

The courts are divided, however, where promissory fraud is involved. Some courts preclude the introduction of parol or extrinsic evidence when the alleged fraud involves a promise which varies the terms of an integrated written instrument. . . . But the majority rule admits the parol or extrinsic evidence even though it conflicts with the terms of the integrated written instrument. . . .

We choose to follow the majority rule because as an Oregon appellate court stated:

Oral promises made without the promisor's intention that they will be performed could be an effective means of deception if evidence of those fraudulent promises were never admissible merely because they were at variance with a subsequent written agreement.

[*Judgment reversed and action remanded to permit proof of alleged fraud*]

QUESTIONS

1. What is the purpose of an integration clause in a contract?
2. What effect does the decision have on the integration clause?
3. How can a party to a contract be protected from a fraudulent claim that the contract was induced by fraud?

(d) EXISTENCE OF CONTRACT. Parol evidence is admissible to identify the writing of the parties. When several documents are executed as part of one transaction, parol evidence is admissible to show the relationship of the documents as forming one transaction.

When it is claimed that there is in fact no contract because of a mutual mistake, parol evidence is admissible to show the existence of such a mistake.

The parol evidence rule does not bar proof that the written contract is in fact not a binding agreement. Thus, it can be shown that there was no consideration for the contract, that the contract was void because it was illegal, or that the contract was voidable because of the incapacity of a party or because of fraud. Likewise, parol evidence may be used to show in a lawsuit between the original parties that a promissory note signed by the defendant was never to be enforced, and that it was merely a dummy note intended to create a paper loss for tax purposes.

(e) MODIFICATION OF CONTRACT. The parol evidence rule prohibits only the contradiction of a complete written contract. It does not prohibit proof that the contract was thereafter modified or terminated.[22]

Written contracts commonly declare that they can be modified only by a writing. In the case of construction contracts, there is ordinarily a statement that no payment will be made for extra work unless there is a written order from the owner or architect calling for such extra work. If the parties proceed in disregard of a clause requiring written modification, it may be shown by parol evidence that they have done so, and the contract will be modified accordingly.[23]

(f) ILLEGALITY. The parol evidence rule does not bar proof of conduct that violates the law. It does not bar the defense that the defendant's signature was a forgery.[24]

In the *Honeywell* case, evidence of precontract statements was offered to show that the defendant had violated the state Deceptive Trade Practices Act.

HONEYWELL, INC. v IMPERIAL CONDOMINIUM ASS'N

(Tex App) 716 SW2d 75 (1986)

Honeywell made a contract with the Imperial Condominium Association to install and service a heating and cooling system. The system did not function properly, and Imperial Condominium sued Honeywell for treble damages under the Texas Deceptive Trade Practices Act (DTPA). Imperial offered in evidence the promotional literature of Honeywell to show that false statements had been made to induce the making of the contract and that this constituted deceptive trade practices. The trial court admitted this evidence, and the jury returned a verdict in favor of Imperial. From the judgment against it, Honeywell appealed.

HOWELL, J. . . .

I. *Extrinsic Evidence of Misrepresentation*

Honeywell first complains that the trial court violated the parol evidence rule by admitting extrinsic evidence of Honeywell's pre-contractual representations. Over

---

[22] Quitta v Fossati (Tex App) 808 SW2d 636 (1991).

[23] DeMean v Ledl (Mo App) 796 SW2d 415 (1990).

[24] Pathway Financial v Miami International Realty Co. (Fla App) 588 So 2d 1000 (1991).

Honeywell's objection, the court allowed the consumer to introduce Honeywell's promotional literature for the limited purpose of proving that Honeywell's representations concerning the quality and benefits of its services did not accurately depict those actually received. We find no merit in Honeywell's complaint.

The [Texas] supreme court recently decided that the parol evidence rule does not prevent a consumer from introducing statements made before the formation of a contract to show that the provider of goods or services engaged in a deceptive trade practice. . . . This holding was based upon the differences between the nature of an action for a breach of contract and that of an action for a deceptive trade practice.

The Supreme Court reasoned that the justifications for the parol evidence rule do not apply in deceptive trade practices cases where the consumer sues on the basis of pre-contractual representations because the consumer's recovery is not dependent upon the alteration or contradiction of a contract but rather upon conduct which was itself actionable under the DTPA without regard to the obligations imposed on the parties by the contract.

In other words, the supreme court recognized that contractual liability and liability under the DTPA derive from two different sources. Contractual liability turns solely on the agreement of the parties whereas liability under the DTPA springs from the statute. As a general proposition, liability under the DTPA is neither increased nor diminished by the presence of a formal written contract covering the identical subject matter.

Unlike contractual liability, resulting from the voluntary agreement of the parties, liability for false, misleading and deceptive acts is provided by the legislature for the breach of a duty imposed by it. These duties cannot be altered by the agreement of the parties. To apply the parol evidence rule in DTPA cases would frustrate the legislature's purpose in passing the statute without furthering the objectives of the parol evidence rule. As the [Texas] supreme court succinctly announced . . . "traditional contractual notions do not apply" when the consumer seeks recovery for the breach of duty imposed by the DTPA. . . . We hold that trial court did not err when it allowed the consumer to introduce Honeywell's promotional literature for the purpose of proving that Honeywell violated the DTPA.

II. Misrepresentation Under the DTPA

Honeywell next contends that as a matter of law the consumer could not recover under the DTPA because a mere breach of contract, without more, is not a false, misleading or deceptive act. Honeywell argues that this case involves a mere breach of contract because all of the representations in its promotional literature were incorporated into the terms of the contract and, therefore, the consumer can show no failure to comply with a pre-contractual representation that was not also a breach of contract. This proposition is untenable in light of the [Texas] supreme court's decision in *Smith v Baldwin*, 611 SW2d at 615-16.

The consumer there counterclaimed against his builder alleging that the builder failed to build a home which, as promised both in the contract and in discussions with the consumer, would qualify for financing by the Veteran's Administration. The consumer sought to recover on the grounds that the builder both breached the construction contract and misrepresented his services in violation of section 17.46 (b)(7) of the DTPA. . . . The supreme court reversed and . . . held that the consumer was entitled to his DTPA remedies. The court ruled that "representing that goods or services are of a particular standard, quality or grade . . . if they are of another" applies to goods and services to be provided in the future, and concluded that the builder committed a deceptive act by representing that the house when built would qualify for V.A. financing.

. . . Honeywell by its literature and by the formal contract represented that it would provide proper water treatment to extend equipment life. These representations later proved to be false. . . . We reject Honeywell's argument that intentional, reckless or negligent conduct must be proved in order to invoke the act. . . .

[Judgment affirmed]

QUESTIONS

1. Does the parol evidence rule bar proof of statements that constitute a violation of a consumer protection statute? Explain.
2. Were the precontract statements oral or written?
3. What significance is there to the fact that precontract statements are or are not included in the written contract?

SUMMARY

An oral agreement can be a contract unless it is the intention of the parties that they should not be bound by the agreement unless a writing is executed by them. If the parties intend to be bound by the oral agreement, it is a contract. As an exception to this statement, certain contracts must be evidenced by a writing, or else they cannot be enforced. The statutes that declare this exception are called statutes of frauds. Statutes of frauds commonly require that a contract be evidenced by writing in the case of (1) an agreement that cannot be performed within one year after the contract is made, (2) an agreement to sell or a sale of any interest in real property, (3) a promise to answer for the debt or default of another, (4) a promise by the executor or administrator of a decedent's estate to pay a claim against the estate from personal funds, (5) a promise made in consideration of marriage, and (6) a contract for the sale of goods for a purchase price of $500 or more. Local statutes may expand the above list to include other types of contracts, such as a contract between a landowner and a real estate agent employed to sell the land.

In order to evidence a contract so as to satisfy a statute of frauds, there must be a writing of all material terms. This must be signed by the defendant against whom suit is brought for enforcement of the contract or damages for its breach. The signing may be made by printing, stamping, typewriting, or any other means that is intended to identify the particular party. Two or more writings can be combined to form a writing sufficient to satisfy the statute of frauds, provided there is an express internal reference in the writings that ties them together.

If the applicable statute of frauds is not satisfied, the oral contract cannot be enforced. To avoid unjust enrichment, a plaintiff barred from enforcing an oral contract may recover from the other contracting party the reasonable value of the benefits conferred by the plaintiff on the defendant. To prevent the statute of frauds from being used to defraud a party to an oral contract, the courts by decision have made certain exceptions to the statute of frauds.

When there is a written contract, the question arises as to whether that writing is the exclusive statement of the agreement of the parties. If the writing is the complete and final statement of the contract, parol evidence as to matters agreed to before or at the time the writing was signed is not admissible to contradict the writing. This is called the parol evidence rule. Some courts have liberalized the rule so that parol evidence is admitted when it will aid in interpreting the writing. In any case, the parol evidence rule does not bar parol evidence when (1) the writing is incomplete; (2) the writing is ambiguous; (3) the writing is not

a true statement of the agreement of the parties because of fraud, accident, or mistake; or (4) the existence, modification, or illegality of a contract is in controversy. The fact that the parties disagree as to the meaning of a contract or that a court decision is required to settle the point does not make the writing ambiguous. Parol evidence may be used to prove that there is in fact no contract because there is a mutual mistake or that the writing that has been executed does not correctly set forth the terms of the contract.

LAW IN PRACTICE

1. Put your important contracts in writing in order to have clear proof as to the exact terms of the transactions.

2. Put in writing or evidence by a writing any contract that must be so evidenced because of a statute of frauds.

3. Make sure that the other party has signed a necessary writing when you have made an oral contract that is subject to a statute of frauds.

4. Read your contract carefully before signing it to avoid including any provision that is ambiguous or that cannot be understood.

QUESTIONS AND CASE PROBLEMS

1. What social forces are affected by the following rule of law? "Parol evidence is not admissible for the purpose of modifying a written contract when that evidence relates to an agreement made before or at the time that the written contract was executed."

2. In a telephone conversation, Roderick agreed to buy Dexter's house. All the details of the transaction were agreed to in the conversation. The next day Dexter wrote Roderick a letter stating: "This confirms the agreement we made last night that I should sell you my home." Later, Dexter refused to go through with the transaction. Roderick sued Dexter. Will Roderick recover?

3. Kelly made a written contract to sell certain land to Brown. Kelly gave Brown a deed to the land. Thereafter, Kelly sued Brown to get back a 20-foot strip of land. Kelly claimed that before making the written contract it was agreed that Kelly would sell all of his land to Brown in order to make it easier for Brown to get a building permit, but that after that was done, the 20-foot strip would be reconveyed to Kelly. Was Kelly entitled to the 20-foot strip? What ethical values are involved? *[Brown v Kelly (Fla App) 545 So 2d 518]*

4. Martin made an oral contract with Cresheim Garage to work as its manager for two years. Cresheim wrote Martin a letter stating that the oral contract had been made and setting forth all its terms. Cresheim later refused to recognize the contract. Martin sued Cresheim for breach of the contract and offered Cresheim's letter in evidence as proof of the contract. Cresheim claimed that the oral contract was not binding because the contract was not in writing and the letter referring to the contract was not a contract but only a letter. Was the contract binding?

5. Lawrence loaned money to Moore. Moore died without repaying the loan. Lawrence claimed that when he mentioned the matter to Moore's widow, she promised to pay the debt. She did not do so, and Lawrence sued her on her promise. Does she have any defense? *[Moore v Lawrence, 252 Ark 759, 480 S W2d 941]*

6. Investors Premium Corporation purchased computer equipment from Burroughs Corporation. It made the purchase because of various statements made by the Burroughs sales representative. A written contract was executed for the purchase of the system. The contract stated that there were no warranties that were not stated in the contract and that the written contract was the complete statement of the obligation of Burroughs. The system did not work properly, and Investors claimed that Burroughs was liable because the system did not perform as the salesman had warranted. Is Burroughs liable for breach of the agent's warranty? *[Investors Premium Corp. v Burroughs Corp. (DC SC) 389 F Supp 39]*

7. Boeing Airplane Co. contracted with Pittsburgh-Des Moines Steel Co. for the latter to construct a supersonic wind tunnel. R. H. Freitag Mfg. Co. sold materials to York-Gillespie Co., which subcontracted to do part of the work. To persuade Freitag to keep supplying materials on credit, Boeing and the principal contractor both assured Freitag that he would be paid. When Freitag was not paid by the subcontractor, Freitag sued Boeing and the contractor. They defended on the ground that the assurances given Freitag were not written. Decide. What ethical values are involved? *[R. H. Freitag Mfg. Co. v Boeing Airplane Co. 55 Wash 2d 334, 347 P2d 1074]*

8. An accounting firm sold out its business to a new firm. The sales contract stated that it was the intention of the parties that the new firm should provide service for clients of the old firm. The new firm agreed to pay the old firm 15 percent of the gross billings for assignments performed by the new firm for a period of 84 months. Later a dispute arose as to whether the 15 percent of gross billings was limited to the billings of those who were originally clients of the old firm or whether it also included billings of new clients of the new firm. In a lawsuit over this point, parol evidence was offered to show what the contract covered. Was this evidence admissible? *[Rullman v LaFrance, Walker, Jackley & Saville, 206 Neb 180, 292 NW2d 19]*

9. With respect to the applicability of the statute of frauds, compare (a) a promise made by an aunt to her niece to pay the niece's bill owed to a department store; (b) a promise made by the aunt to the department store to pay the amount the aunt owes the store for a television set the aunt purchased as a present for her niece; and (c) a promise made by the aunt to the department store that she would pay her niece's bill if the niece did not do so.

10. Louise Pulsifer owned a farm. She desired to sell the farm and ran an ad in the local newspaper. Russell Gillespie agreed to purchase the farm. Pulsifer then wrote him a letter stating that she would not sell the farm. He sued her in order to enforce the contract. Pulsifer raised the defense of the statute of frauds. The letter signed by her did not contain any of the terms of the sale. Gillespie, however, claimed that the newspaper ad could be combined with her letter to satisfy the statute of frauds. Was he correct? *[Gillespie v Pulsifer (Mo App) 655 SW2d 123]*

11. McLarty claimed that he and Wright made an oral contract to start a business under the name of DeKalb Textile Mill, Inc., to incorporate the business, and to divide the stock equally. The alleged contract was not performed. McLarty sued Wright for breach of contract. Wright raised the defense of the statute of frauds, asserting that it was not specified that the contract should be performed within one year of making. Was this defense valid? *[McLarty v Wright (Ala Civ App) 321 So 2d 687]*

12. In February or March, Corning Glass Works orally agreed to retain Hanan as management consultant from May 1 of that year to April 30 of the next year for a total fee of $25,000. Was this agreement binding? Is this decision ethical? *[Hanan v Corning Glass Works, 63 Misc 2d 863, 314 NYS2d 804]*

13. Levina made a contract with Thompson. She later claimed that she could enforce the terms of an earlier agreement that they had made a week before. Thompson claimed that proof of that agreement was barred by the parol evidence rule. Levina claimed that this was not so because (1) she never intended that the written contract should wipe out the earlier oral agreement, and (2) the written contract did not state it was the entire agreement of the parties and displaced all prior agreements. Were her objections valid?

14. Heinrich agreed over the telephone to sell a tract of land to Isabel for $50,000 and to lease to her another tract of land for 8 months beginning the first day of the following week for a rental of $500. The telephone agreement was never put in writing. Heinrich refused to go through with the agreement. Isabel then sued him for breach of the contract to sell the land and to lease the neighboring tract. He raised the defense that the statute of frauds barred enforcement of the agreement because it could not be enforced as to the sale of the land and therefore the entire transaction was barred. Decide.

15. While Celeste was in New York, the manager of the Kendall Corporation of Galveston, Texas interviewed her for the position of head of the corporate accounting department. The manager told her to send her application to Galveston and that he believed that she would be given a 5-year contract for the job. Within a few days after the manager left New York, Celeste sold her New York home, quit her New York job, and went to Texas. When she arrived she was told that the vacancy had been filled by someone else. She sued Kendall Corporation for breach of contract. It raised the defense that there was no writing to evidence the existence of the contract. Celeste raised the counter-defense of promissory estoppel. Decide.

C H A P T E R 1 5

INTERPRETATION OF CONTRACTS

LEARNING OBJECTIVES

After studying this chapter, you will be able to:
1. *Compare the effect of objective and subjective intent of the parties to a contract.*
2. *Distinguish between conditions precedent and conditions subsequent.*
3. *State the rules for interpreting ambiguous terms in a contract.*
4. *State the effect of contradictory terms.*
5. *Define and illustrate implied terms.*
6. *State what controls the choice of la*

When it has been decided that there is a contract between the parties, the next step is to determine what the contract means.

A. RULES OF CONSTRUCTION AND INTERPRETATION

In interpreting contracts, courts are aided by certain rules.

1. Function of Judge and Jury

When there is no dispute as to what a contract stated, the determination of its meaning is a question for the judge. If, however, there is disagreement as to what terms were stated or if the terms are ambiguous, there is a question of fact. Just what the contract provided then needs to be determined and, ordinarily, such disputes will be determined by the jury.[1]

2. Intention of the Parties

When persons enter into an agreement, it is to be presumed that they intend that their agreement should have some effect. A court will strive to determine the intent of the parties and to give effect to it.[2] A contract is therefore to be enforced according to its terms. A court cannot remake or rewrite the contract of the parties under the pretense of interpreting it. If there is a dispute as to the meaning of a contract, the court examines the contract to determine what the parties intended. It will then give effect to what the parties intended, as long as it is lawful.

No particular form of words is required, and any words manifesting the intent of the parties are sufficient. In the absence of proof that a word has a peculiar meaning or that it was employed by the parties with a particular meaning, a common word is given its ordinary meaning.

A word will not be given its literal meaning when it is clear that the parties did not intend such a meaning. For example, *and* may be substituted for *or*, *may* for *shall*, and *void* for *voidable*, and vice versa, when it is clear that the parties so intended.

(a) OBJECTIVE INTENT. When it is stated that the law seeks to enforce the intent of the parties, this means the intent that is outwardly manifested. That is, what would a reasonable third person believe the parties intended? It is this **objective intent** that will be enforced. A party cannot effectively claim that something else was secretly intended. Such secret or **subjective intent** cannot be proven.[3]

The use of the objective intent standard means that an unambiguous contract must be interpreted as written.[4] It cannot be given a different meaning that one party thinks it has. In the *Sterling Merchandise* case the court was faced with the question of whether an insurance policy meant just what it said.

STERLING MERCHANDISE CO.
v HARTFORD INS. CO.
30 Ohio App 3d 131, 506 NE2d 1192 (1986)

Sterling Merchandise Company obtained policies of insurance from the Hartford Insurance Company and from Underwriters at Lloyd's of London

---

[1] First City National Bank v Concord Oil Co. (Tex App) 808 SW2d 133 (1991).
[2] Delmar Crawford, Inc. v Russell Oil Co., Inc. 106 Or App 524, 808 P2d 1021 (1991).
[3] Metropolitan Sports Facilities Commission v General Mills, Inc. (Minn) 470 NW2d 118 (1991).
[4] Edgewater Health Care, Inc. v Health Systems Management, Inc. (Mo App) 752 SW2d 860 (1988).

> to protect the contents of the safe in its jewelry store from burglary. The policy stated that there was coverage of theft from the safe provided that there were visible marks on the safe of a forcible entry. The Sterling safe was robbed. The robber set off the electronic alarm system, but there were no visible marks of forcible entry. The insurer refused to pay for the loss. Sterling claimed that it reasonably expected that the contents of the safe would be covered whenever there was an opening of the safe by a robber. Sterling sued the insurers. From a decision in favor of Sterling, the insurers appealed.

GEORGE, P. J. . . . The insurance contracts issued to Sterling by Underwriters define a "safe burglary" as follows:

"SAFE BURGLARY" means the felonious abstraction of the insured property from within a safe or vault in the premises (or after removal therefrom by burglars) by any person or persons making felonious entry into such safe and also into the vault, if any, containing such safe, when all doors of such safe and vault are duly closed and locked by at least one combination, key or time lock thereof; provided that such entry shall be made by actual force or violence of which there shall be visible marks made by tools, explosives, electricity, gas or chemicals, upon the exterior of (1) all of said doors of such safe and vault, if any, containing such safe if entry is made through such doors, or (2) the top, bottom, or walls of such safe and of the vault through which entry is made, if not made through such doors.

. . . The trial court's decision is based entirely on the doctrine of reasonable expectations. . . .

The doctrine of reasonable expectations is a theory of recovery employed in contract actions. It has been articulated in the following passage contained in the Restatement of the Law 2d, Contracts (Tent. Drafts Nos. 1-7 Rev 1973), Section 237 ("Standardized Agreements"), Comment *f*, at 540-541:

Terms excluded. . . . *Although customers typically adhere to standardized agreements and are bound by them without even appearing to know the standard terms in detail, they are not bound to unknown terms which are beyond the range of reasonable expectation. A debtor who delivers a check to his creditor with the amount blank does not authorize the insertion of an infinite figure. Similarly, a party who adheres to the other party's standard terms does not assent to a term if the other party has reason to believe that the adhering party would not have accepted the agreement if he had known that the agreement contained the particular term. Such a belief or assumption may be shown by the prior negotiations or inferred from the circumstances. Reason to believe may be inferred from the fact that the term is bizarre or oppressive, from the fact that it eviscerates the nonstandard terms explicitly agreed to, or from the fact that it eliminates the dominant purpose of the transaction. The inference is reinforced if the adhering party never had an opportunity to read the term, or if it is illegible or otherwise hidden from view. This rule is closely related to the policy against unconscionable terms and the rule of interpretation against the draftsman. . . .*

This doctrine is grounded on several beliefs. First, that most people never read the insurance contracts they sign, but merely adhere to them. Second, that insurers write the terms of the contracts and usually offer the consumer only a standard preprinted form which the latter is ill-equipped to understand. Third, that the insured lacks any real bargaining power in such a situation because the insurer assumes a take-it-or-leave-it attitude. Fourth, that to enforce the terms of the contract in favor of the insurer is somehow unconscionable. . . .

Although Ohio has adopted rules of construction of insurance contracts which favor the insured, it has not implicitly adopted the theory of recovery known as the reasonable expectations doctrine. That doctrine is based on principles which go far beyond the liberal rules of construction employed by Ohio courts. . . .

The reasonable expectation doctrine requires a court to rewrite an insurance contract which does not meet popular expectations. Such rewriting is done regardless of the bargain entered into by the parties to the contract. Such judicial activism has not been adopted in Ohio by its courts and the courts' use of liberal rules of construction. Further, this court declines to do so. . . .

The facts of this case, as evidenced by the stipulations of the parties, do not indicate any misrepresentation, overreaching, or other conduct on behalf of the insurer which would justify abrogating the parties' agreement. Nor was there any evidence that Sterling was beguiled into believing it had more protection than it actually did.

Sterling tacitly refused to read its policies. The provision defining "safe burglary" was written in the same style and size type as the rest of the policy provisions. The definition was not hidden away in fine print in an obscure place, but was plainly set out. The definition was not so complex or esoteric that a competent businessman could not understand it. . . .

The record in the instant case also reveals that there was comprehensive crime coverage available to Sterling, but at an additional cost. This additional coverage was noted in part seven of Sterling's policy. . . .

The trial court did not find the "safe burglary" definition to be ambiguous. Neither does this court. Provisions requiring visible marks of entry by actual force or violence before coverage is allowed are not ambiguous. Because the definition is not ambiguous, it must be given its plain and ordinary meaning. . . .

[Judgment reversed]

QUESTIONS

1. Was the "safe burglary" paragraph of the policy ambiguous?
2. Why does the court mention the fact that Sterling could have obtained comprehensive crime coverage by paying an additional amount?
3. What effect would the adoption of the Restatement rule have on the business world?

(b) MEANING OF WORDS. Ordinary words are to be interpreted according to their ordinary meaning.[5]

In the *Bartlett* case, property owners claimed to be covered by insurance when a breaking dam caused damage to the property. The insurance company claimed there was no liability for "flood damage."

If technical or trade terms are used in a contract, they are to be interpreted according to the area of technical knowledge or trade from which the terms are taken. If there is a common meaning to a term, that meaning will be followed, even though the dictionary may give a different meaning. The fact that the dictionary states several meanings for the same word does not mean that the word is ambiguous when used in a contract. For example, an insurance policy describing a cause of harm as "sudden and accidental" is not to be regarded

---

5   Tomahawk Village Apartments v Farren (Ind App) 571 NE2d 1286 (1991).

BARTLETT v CONTINENTAL DIVIDE INS. CO.

(Colo App) 697 P2d 412 (1984)

> Perry Bartlett and his wife owned and operated a resort. They obtained a policy of insurance from the Continental Divide Insurance Company protecting the resort from damage. A nearby dam broke, and water from the dam and the debris carried by the water damaged the resort. The Bartletts claimed the insurance company was liable for the loss. It denied liability on the ground that the policy expressly excluded flood damage. The Bartletts claimed that what had happened was not a flood and brought suit against the insurance company. The court decided in favor of the insurance company, and the Bartletts appealed.

STERNBERG, J. . . . Continental denied coverage because the policy contained an exclusion for losses "caused by, resulting from, contributed to, or aggravated by . . . flood, surface water [or] . . . overflow of streams or other bodies of water. . . ."

The plaintiffs filed this action for declaratory relief and damages. . . . The court found that the insurance policy expressly excluded damage due to flood, the term "flood" was not vague or ambiguous in this case, and the failure of Lawn Lake Dam did in fact cause a flood resulting in damage to plaintiffs' property. . . .

The term "flood" is not defined within the policy, and it therefore retains its ordinary, customary, meaning. . . . Ordinarily, "flood" means "a body of water (including moving water) . . . overflowing or inundating land not usually covered," . . . and no distinction is made between natural and artificial causes. . . .

Notwithstanding the ordinary meaning of "flood," plaintiffs urge us to distinguish between natural and artificial causes when reading the terms of the insurance policy. However, there is no such distinction in the contract, and the event in question falls well within the ordinary use of the term; therefore, to make such distinction would be to rewrite terms of the policy, and that is beyond our power. Although the use of the term may in some cases result in ambiguity, we agree with the trial court's conclusion that there was no ambiguity here.

. . . The only event alleged as the cause of the loss was the flood caused by the failure of the dam; and loss by flood was specifically excluded from coverage.

[Judgment affirmed]

QUESTIONS

1. Why wasn't the word *flood* defined in the insurance policy?
2. What effect does the decision have on the social force of protecting from hardship?
3. How would it have affected the decision of the court if the dam had failed because of sabotage by discontented workers?

as ambiguous based on the fact that dictionaries contain a number of definitions for "sudden."[6]

The prior relationships of the parties may give meaning to the words used by the parties.[7]

(c) INCORPORATION BY REFERENCE. The contract may not cover all the agreed terms. The missing terms may be found in another document. Frequently the parties executing the contract will state that it embraces or incorporates the other document. Thus, a contract for storage will simply state that a storage contract is entered into and that the contract applies to the goods that are listed in the schedule that is attached to and made part of the contract. Likewise, a contract for the construction of a building may involve plans and specifications on file in a named city office. The contract will simply state that the building is to be constructed according to those plans and specifications that are "incorporated herein and made part of this contract." When there is such an **incorporation by reference**, the contract consists of both the original or skeleton document and the detailed statement that is incorporated therein.

3. Additional Printed Matter

Frequently a contract is mailed or delivered by one party to the other in an envelope that contains additional printed matter. Similarly, when goods are purchased, the buyer often receives with the goods a manufacturer's manual and various pamphlets. What effect do all these papers have on the contract? The same question arises when a worker gets a new job and the employer hands the new employee a handbook or a set of rules. Is this material accompanying the contract a part of the contract?

(a) INCORPORATION OF OTHER STATEMENT. The contract itself may furnish the answer. Sometimes the contract will ex-pressly refer to and incorporate into the contract the terms of the other writing or printed statement. For example, the contract may say that the customer will be charged at the rates set forth in the approved tariff schedule, "a copy of which is attached hereto and made part of this contract."

(b) EXCLUSION OF OTHER STATEMENT. As the opposite of incorporation, the contract may declare that there is no agreement outside of the contract. This means that either there never was anything else or that any prior agreement was merely a preliminary step that has been canceled out or erased. Namely, the contract in its final form is as stated in the writing. For example, the seller of goods may state in the contract that no statements about the goods have been made to the buyer and that the written contract contains all of the terms of the sale.

(c) REDUCTION OF CONTRACT TERMS. The effect of accompanying or subsequently delivered printed matter may be to reduce the terms of the written contract. That is, one party may have had a better bargain under the original contract. In this case, the accompanying matter will generally be ignored by a court if it is not shown that the party who would be harmed had agreed that it be part of the contract. This is so because a contract, once made, cannot be changed by unilateral action—that is, by the action of one party or one side of the contract without the agreement of the other.

(d) EMPLOYEE'S HANDBOOK. It is a common practice for large employers to hand a new employee a manual or handbook that sets forth various matters relating to the employment. The question can then arise whether the statements in the handbook are binding terms of the employment contract or whether they are merely statements of the employer's existing policies or practices. If the

---

[6] Sylvester Brothers Development Co. v Great Central Ins. Co. (Minn App) 480 NW2d 368 (1992).

[7] See Section 6 of this chapter.

handbook constitutes part of the contract, it cannot be changed by the action of the employer alone. If the handbook is merely a statement of policies or practices, the terms of the handbook can be changed by the employer at will. Litigation frequently arises when an employee who is fired or denied pension rights claims that this is a violation of the terms of the handbook.

Whether the handbook is part of the employment contract depends on the intent of the parties. If the handbook has been carefully written, it will specify whether it represents terms of the contract or merely policies. The handbook is clearly not part of the employment contract when the employee signed a card so stating and agreeing that the employer could change the handbook at any time.[8]

An employee's handbook may become part of the contract of employment when the circumstances surrounding the hiring of the employee manifest the intent that the handbook be so regarded. The same conclusion may be reached when a handbook is distributed to existing employees, and they continue to work thereafter without any objection.[9]

4. Whole Contract

The provisions of a contract must be construed as a whole in such a way that every part is given effect.[10] This rule is followed even when the contract is partly written and partly oral. Every word of a contract is to be given effect if reasonably possible.

(a) DIVISIBLE CONTRACT. A contract may contain a number of provisions or performances to be rendered. If so, the question arises as to whether the parties intended merely a group of separate contracts (a divisible contract).[11] Possibly they intended a package deal so that complete performance of every provision of the contract was essential.

A significant indication that the parties intended a divisible contract is the fact that the consideration given by one party can be apportioned among the performances to be rendered by the other, or a separate consideration is stated for each performance. For example, an insurer may provide coverage for a house and garage and charge a premium that is the sum of one amount specified for insuring the house and another amount for insuring the garage. In such a case, it will be held that the insurance contract is divisible into two contracts. One contract covers the house, and the other covers the garage.

(b) WHAT CONSTITUTES THE WHOLE CONTRACT. The question may arise as to whether separate papers or particular parts of a paper constitute part of the contract.

Terms in a printed letterhead or billhead or on the reverse side of the printed contract form are not part of a contract written thereon unless a reasonable person would regard such terms as part of the contract. An employer's manual that is shown to the job applicant after the signing of an employment contract is not part of that contract. Similarly, provisions in a manufacturer's instruction manual, or in invoices, or on labels that are not seen or called to the attention of a buyer until after a contract of sale has been made are not part of the contract. They do not bind the buyer.

5. Conditions

When the occurrence or nonoccurrence of an event affects the existence of a contract or the obligation of a party to a contract, the event is called a **condition**.

Courts do not favor conditions, because they cause a loss of rights. Therefore, courts will interpret a contract provision as not creating a condition when that interpretation is reasonably possible.

---

[8] Hicks v Baylor University Medical Center (Tex App) 789 SW2d 299 (1990).

[9] Duldulao v Saint Mary of Nazareth Hospital Center, 115 Ill 2d 482, 106 Ill Dec 8, 505 NE2d 314 (1987).

[10] Cardon v Cotton Lane Holdings, Inc. _____ Ariz _____, 841 P2d 198 (1992).

[11] Claussen's Estate (Iowa) 482 NW2d 381 (1992).

(a) CONDITION PRECEDENT. An obligation-triggering event may be described as a **condition precedent**. It precedes the existence of the obligation to perform or the existence of any contract. Terms such as *if, provided that, when, after, as soon as, subject to,* and *on condition that* indicate the creation of a condition.[12]

If an obligation to pay money is subject to a condition precedent, there is no duty to pay if the condition is never satisfied.[13]

In a fire insurance policy, there is no obligation on the insurer to make any payment until there is a fire loss. The occurrence of such a loss is thus a condition precedent to the insurer's duty to pay under the policy. Similarly, when an employee is required to give notice to the employer in order to obtain a particular benefit, the giving of notice is a condition precedent to the employer's duty to provide the benefit.

(b) CONDITION SUBSEQUENT. T h e parties may specify that the contract shall terminate when a particular event occurs or does not occur. Such a provision is a **condition subsequent**. If government approval is required, the parties may specify that the contract shall not bind them if the government approval cannot be obtained.

A contract for the purchase of land may contain a condition subsequent that cancels the contract if the buyer is not able to obtain a zoning permit to use a building for a particular purpose.

(c) CONCURRENT CONDITIONS. I n most bilateral contracts, the performances by the parties are **concurrent conditions**. That is, the duty of each party to perform is dependent on the other party's performing. Thus, neither is required to perform until the other performs or tenders performance. Frequently the contract will specify or indicate that one person must perform first. In this case, that performance is a condition precedent and the conditions are not concurrent. For example, in a contract to pay a painter $1,000 for painting a house, the painter must perform the painting work before the owner is required to perform the promise of paying for the work. Performance by the painter is thus a condition precedent to the owner's obligation to pay.

6. Contradictory and Ambiguous Terms

One term in a contract may conflict with another term, or one term may have two different meanings. It is then necessary for the court to determine whether there is a contract and, if so, what the contract really means. When the terms of a contract are contradictory or conflict as to a significant matter, this conflict precludes the existence of any contract.

In some instances, the conflict between the terms of a contract is eliminated by the introduction of parol evidence or by applying an appropriate rule of construction.

(a) NATURE OF WRITING. When a contract is partly a printed form or partly typewritten and partly handwritten, and the written part conflicts with the printed or typewritten part, the written part prevails. When there is a conflict between a printed part and a typewritten part, the latter prevails. Consequently, when a clause typewritten on a printed form conflicts with what is stated by the print, the conflicting print is ignored, and the typewritten clause controls. This rule is based on the belief that the parties had given greater thought to what they typed or wrote for the particular contract, as contrasted with printed words that were already in a form designed to cover many transactions.

When there is a conflict between an amount or quantity expressed both in words and figures, as on a check, the amount or quantity expressed in words prevails. Words control because there is less danger that a word will be wrong than a number.

---

[12] Harmon Cable Communications v Scope Cable Television, Inc. 237 Neb 871, 468 NW2d 350 (1991).

[13] Williams v P.S. Investment Co., Inc. (NC App) 401 SE2d 79 (1991).

(b) AMBIGUITY. A contract is **ambiguous** when the intent of the parties is uncertain and the contract is capable of more than one reasonable interpretation. Disagreement as to the legal effect of the terms used by the parties does not make the contract ambiguous.[14] This is so because the court, by applying the law to their terms, can reach a conclusion as to the intent manifested by the contract. In contrast, if the intent would still be uncertain even after rules of law were applied, the contract is ambiguous.

Whether a contract is ambiguous cannot always be determined merely by looking at it. In some cases, the written contract will look perfectly clear, and the ambiguity does not become apparent until the contract is applied to the facts or the property concerned.[15]

The fact that a particular situation is not provided for by the contract does not make it ambiguous. For example, a summer camp contract is not ambiguous because it does not contain any provision relating to refunds if cancellation occurs.

The background from which the contract and the dispute arose may help in determining the intention of the parties. Thus, when suit was brought in Minnesota on a Canadian insurance policy, the question arose as to whether the dollar limit of the policy referred to Canadian or American dollars. The court concluded that Canadian dollars were intended. Both the insurer and the insured were Canadian corporations; the original policy, endorsements to the policy, and policy renewals were written in Canada; over the years, premiums had been paid in Canadian dollars; and a prior claim on the policy had been settled by the payment of an amount computed on the basis of Canadian dollars.

(c) STRICT CONSTRUCTION AGAINST DRAFTING PARTY. An ambiguous contract is interpreted strictly against the party who drafted it. Thus, printed forms of a contract, such as insurance policies, which are supplied by the insurer, are interpreted against the insurer and in favor of the insured when two interpretations are reasonably possible. If the contract is clear and unambiguous, it will be enforced according to its terms, even though this benefits the party who drafted the contract.

The interpretation of an insurance policy strictly against the insurer will in some cases result in applying words in a manner in which they are not customarily used. This occurred in the *State Farm* case.

STATE FARM FIRE AND CAS. CO. v PINSON
(CA4 SC) 984 F2d 610 (1993)

Rider owned a boat for which he had boat owner's liability insurance issued by State Farm Fire and Casualty Co. The policy covered liability arising while the boat was "in use." Rider was towing the boat over a highway with a truck when he collided with an automobile driven by Pinson. Pinson sued State Farm to recover damages for his injuries. State Farm denied liability on the ground that the policy only covered harm arising while the boat was in use and that the boat was not in use when it was being towed over land. The lower court entered judgment against State Farm. It appealed.

---

[14] Young Dental Manufacturing Co. v Engineered Products, Inc. (Mo App) 838 SW2d 154 (1992).
[15] Sparrow v Tayco Construction Co. (Utah App) 846 P2d 1323 (1993).

K. K. HALL, C. J. . . . As a threshold matter, we must determine whether a towed boat is in "use." For the following reasons, we find that it is.

First and foremost, this Court has already held that a towed vehicle is a "used" vehicle . . . *see generally* cases collected in Annotation, *Automobile liability insurance: what are accidents or injuries "arising out of ownership, maintenance, or use" of insured vehicle.* 89 A.L.R. 2d 150 § 9(f) (1963 & Supp.) Although these cases address towed automobiles rather than boats, the policy language is identical, and, therefore the analysis is the same. Arguably a towed boat presents a stronger case for coverage than a towed vehicle. Usually, a vehicle is towed only when its owner is *unable* to put it to its intended purpose. A boat, on the other hand, *must* be towed in order for a landlocked owner to derive any enjoyment from boat ownership. . . .

In South Carolina, the term "use" has been broadly, not narrowly, construed. For example, in *Hite v Hartford Acc. & Iden. Co.,* 288 SC 616, 344 SE2d 173, 175 (1986), the court stated that the concept of "use" was broader than the "operation" of a motor vehicle. . . .

Because many boats are not permanently moored, an insurance company writing a boat owner's liability policy knows that landlocked policyholders will frequently tow their boats. . . . This is a complex and lengthy policy. If State Farm had wanted to exclude towing from the boat's liability coverage, it could easily have done so.

[Judgment affirmed]

QUESTIONS

1. Was the decision of the court inevitable that the boat was "in use" while it was being towed over land?
2. Appraise the opinion from the standpoint of the person buying insurance.
3. Can you think of a hypothetical situation in which the boat policy would not cover the harm on the ground that the boat was not "in use"?

7. Implied Terms

In some cases, the court will imply a term to cover a situation for which the parties failed to provide or when needed to give the contract a construction or meaning that is reasonable.

A term will not be implied in a contract when the court concludes that the silence of the contract on the particular point was intentional.

(a) DURATION OF CONTRACT. When a contract is to continue over a period of time but no duration is specified in the contract, courts will imply that the contract is to be performed or will continue for a reasonable time. But either party may terminate the contract by giving notice to the other party.

(b) DETAILS OF PERFORMANCE. Details of performance of a contract not expressly stated in the contract will often be implied by the court. Thus, an obligation to pay a specified sum of money is implied to mean payment in legal tender. In a contract to perform work, there is an implied promise to use such skill as is necessary for the proper performance of the work. In a "cost plus" contract, an undertaking is implied that the costs will be reasonable and proper. When payment is made "as a deposit on account," there is an implied term that if the payment is not used for the purpose stated, the payment will be returned to the person who made the deposit. When a contract does not specify where money is to be paid, it will be implied that the payment is to be made to the creditor at the creditor's office or place of business.

A local custom or trade practice, such as that of allowing 30 days' credit to buyers, may form part of the contract. This occurs when it is clear that the parties intended to be governed by this custom or trade practice, or when a reasonable person would believe that they had so intended.

When a contract does not specify the time for performance, a reasonable time is implied.

(c) GOOD FAITH. In every contract, there is an implied obligation that neither party shall do anything that will have the effect of destroying or injuring the right of the other party to receive the fruits of the contract. This means that in every contract there exists an implied covenant of good faith and fair dealing.

When the satisfaction of a condition involves action by a party to the contract, the implied duty to act in good faith requires that such party make an honest, good-faith effort to bring about the satisfaction of the condition. For example, when a contract is made subject to the condition that one of the parties obtain financing, that party must make reasonable, good-faith efforts to obtain financing. The party is not permitted to do nothing and then claim that the contract is not binding because the condition has not been satisfied. When a contract may reasonably be interpreted in different ways, a court should make the interpretation that is in harmony with good faith and fair dealing. The court should avoid an interpretation that imputes bad faith to a party or produces an inequitable result.

The obligation to act in good faith does not require a party to agree to a modification of the contract or to surrender any right.[16] When a contract expressly gives a party the right to cancel the contract, the duty to act in good faith does not bar canceling the contract. Similarly, a franchisor having a right to terminate the franchise without cause is not barred from so doing because of the duty of good faith. When a franchisee has been granted a nonexclusive franchise, good faith does not prevent the franchisor from granting another franchise that competes with the original franchise.

(d) GOVERNMENTAL APPROVAL. In some situations, the ability to perform a contract will depend on obtaining a governmental permit or approval. When this is so, the failure to obtain such approval or permit may be made an express condition subsequent. The contract is then discharged by such failure. An implied term generally arises that one party to the contract will cooperate with the other in obtaining any necessary governmental permit or approval.

(e) STATUTORY TERMS. Statutes commonly require that certain kinds of contracts contain particular clauses. For example, automobile insurance contracts are often required by statute to contain clauses with respect to no-fault liability and uninsured motorists. When a contract is written that does not contain the required statutory terms, the courts will ordinarily imply the statutory terms and interpret the contract as though it complied with the statute. Similarly, a provision in a contract that would be contrary to a required statutory provision will be ignored.[17]

8. Conduct and Custom

The conduct of the parties and the customs and usages of a particular trade may give meaning to the words of the parties and thus aid in the interpretation of their contract.

---

[16] Metro Communications Co. v Ameritech Mobile Communications, Inc. (CA6 Mich) 984 F2d 739 (1993).

[17] Florida Beverage Corp. v Division of Alcoholic Beverages (Fla App) 503 So 2d 396 (1987). See UCC § 2-208(1) as to course of performance in the interpretation of contracts for the sale of goods and UCC § 1-205 as to both Code and non-Code transactions.

(a) CONDUCT OF THE PARTIES. The conduct of the parties in carrying out the terms of a contract is the best guide to determining the intent of the parties.[18] When performance has been repeatedly tendered and accepted without protest, neither party will be permitted to claim that the contract was too indefinite to be binding. For example, a travel agent made a contract with a hotel to arrange for junkets to the hotel. After some 80 junkets had already been arranged and paid for by the hotel at the contract price, without any dispute as to whether the contract obligation was satisfied, any claim that it was not certain what was intended must be ignored. Moreover, when the conduct of the parties is inconsistent with the original written contract, proof of such conduct may justify concluding that the parties had orally modified the original agreement.

(b) CUSTOM AND USAGE OF TRADE. The customs and usages of the trade or commercial activity to which the contract relates may be used to interpret the terms of a contract. For example, when a contract for the construction of a house calls for a "turn-key construction," industry usage is admissible to show what this means. It is a construction in which all the owner needs to do is "turn the key" in the lock to open the building for use, and in which all risks are assumed by the contractor.[19]

Custom and usage, however, cannot override express provisions of a contract that are inconsistent with such customs and usage.

9. Avoidance of Hardship

As a general rule, a party is bound by a contract, even though it proves to be a bad bargain. If possible, a court will interpret a contract to avoid hardship, particularly when the hardship will hurt the weaker of the two

parties to the contract. Courts will if possible interpret a vague contract in such a way as to avoid any forfeiture. Accordingly, a court will avoid holding that a statement or a promise is a condition precedent, which if unsatisfied would mean that no rights would arise under the contract; or a condition subsequent, which if satisfied would mean that all rights under the contract would be terminated.[20]

When there is ambiguity as to the meaning of a contract, a court will avoid the interpretation that gives one contracting party an unreasonable advantage over the other or that causes a forfeiture of a party's interest. When there is an inequality of bargaining power between the contracting parties, courts will sometimes classify the contract as a contract of adhesion. This means that it was offered on a take-it-or-leave-it basis by the stronger party. The court will then interpret the contract as providing what appeared reasonable from the standpoint of the weaker bargaining party.

In some instances, if hardship cannot be avoided in this manner, the court may hold that the contract or a particular provision is not binding because it is unconscionable or contrary to public policy. The extent to which this protection is available is uncertain.

When the hardship arises because the contract makes no provision for the situation that has occurred, the court will sometimes imply a term in order to avoid the hardship.

In the *Perkins* case, the weaker party claimed that the court should imply or read into the contract a protective term that was not there.

10. Joint, Several, and Joint and Several Contracts

The obligation of defendants bound by a contract may be **several** (separate), joint, or joint and several.[21] Defendants are jointly liable when they are indivisibly liable together.

---

[18] Professional Service Industries, Inc. v J.P. Construction, Inc. 241 Neb 862, 491 NW2d 351 (1992).

[19] Blue v R.L. Glossen Contracting, Inc. 173 Ga App 622, 327 SE2d 582 (1985).

[20] Security State Bank v Valley Wide Electric Supply Co., Inc. (Tex App) 752 SW2d 661 (1988).

[21] Chun v Chun, 190 Cal App 3d 589, 235 Cal Rptr 553 (1987).

PERKINS v STANDARD OIL CO.

235 Or 7, 383 P2d 107 (1963)

> Standard Oil made a jobbing or wholesale dealership contract with Clyde Perkins. The contract limited Perkins to selling Standard's products and required him to maintain certain minimum prices. Standard Oil had the right to approve or disapprove of Perkins' customers. In order to be able to perform under this contract, Perkins had to make a substantial monetary investment, and his only income was from the commissions on the sales of Standard's products. Standard Oil made some sales directly to Perkins' customers. When Perkins protested, Standard Oil pointed out that the contract did not contain any provision making his rights exclusive. Perkins sued Standard Oil to compel it to stop dealing with his customers. From a decision in Standard's favor, Perkins appealed.

ROSSMAN, J. . . . The contract authorized the plaintiff [Perkins] to sell without Standard's written consent "on a nonexclusive basis" the products which Standard consigned to him but only to service stations or consuming accounts. Standard's written consent was required before the plaintiff could sell to any other account. The plaintiff promised in the contract to use his "best efforts to promote the sale of products consigned hereunder" and to sell a specified minimum amount during each year. . . . The plaintiff was required to deliver to Standard a complete list of the names and addresses of all his distributors and submit to it the names of any new potential distributors. . . .

The plaintiff claims that the contract by its very nature contains an implied condition that Standard would not solicit business directly from his (plaintiff's) customers. Standard protests that such an implied condition would be contrary to the express terms of the contract since the latter (1) provides that the plaintiff was authorized to sell Standard's products only "on a nonexclusive basis" and (2) reserved to Standard the "right to select its own customers." Plaintiff proposes a more restricted interpretation. . . . He concedes that the contract reserved to Standard the right to sell to any new accounts which it found, and to accept or reject any new accounts which he (the plaintiff) might obtain, but he insists that it does not permit Standard to solicit accounts which it had approved as his customers. . . .

In order to be successful in his business and to comply with the terms of his contract, the plaintiff was obliged to make substantial investments in storage facilities, delivery trucks, and other equipment. He was also obliged to hire employees. He was required to use his "best efforts" to promote the sale of Standard's products. Only if he sold Standard's products exclusively could it be said that he was using his best efforts to promote their sale. It is clear, then, that the contract limited his dealership to Standard products. Plaintiff was also required to sell a minimum quantity of other designated Standard petroleum products. If he at any time failed to sell the minimum quantity, Standard was at liberty to terminate its contract with him. Plaintiff's compensation was based exclusively on the sales he made to customers, which he secured through his own efforts. No compensation was available for the plaintiff if he obtained customers for Standard who bought directly from it. Nor does the contract obligate Standard to compensate him for sales made directly by Standard to plaintiff's customers. . . .

. . . A condition must be implied that Standard would not solicit customers which had been obtained through plaintiff's efforts. The interpretation of the contract for which Standard contends would leave plaintiff and others in a position similar to his completely at the mercy of Standard. . . .

"We cannot accept [Standard's] construction of its meaning. An intention to make so one-sided an agreement is not readily to be inferred. . . .

"In every contract there is an implied covenant that neither party shall do anything that will have the effect of destroying or injuring the right of the other party to receive the fruits of the contract, which means that in every contract there exists a covenant of good faith and fair dealing." . . . 3 *Corbin [on Contracts 278]* 349-352 . . .

The implication of a condition finds support in many circumstances. . . . Plaintiff's only source of return on his substantial investments in the business was the sales he made to his customers. If Standard was at liberty to solicit his direct customers, as it contends, . . . plaintiff was in a state of economic servility; we do not believe that the parties intended such a result at the time the contract was signed. . . .

The contract before us is obviously a form contract prepared by Standard. It is a contract of "adhesion" in the sense that it is a take-it-or-leave-it whole. Such contracts are regarded by some authorities as anachronistic or inconsistent with real freedom of contract. At least they should be construed with an awareness of the inequality of the bargainers. . . .

[Judgment reversed]

QUESTIONS

1. What created the problem in the *Perkins* case?
2. Could the problem in the *Perkins* case have been avoided?

When they are liable severally, they are each liable separately, or individually. When they are jointly and severally liable, each is separately liable for the full amount. Printed forms will commonly specify that liability is joint and several. Thus, the modern contract will provide that when a daughter buys a motorcycle and the contract is cosigned by her mother, the liability of each of the two is joint and several. This means that the seller may sue and collect the full amount from either of them or part of the amount from each of them until payment has been made in full.

B. CONFLICT OF LAWS

When a lawsuit is brought on a contract, the court will seek to apply the law under which the contract was made. That is, a California court in many cases will not apply California law to a foreign (out-of-state) contract. The principles that determine when a court applies the law of its own state—the **law of the forum**—or some foreign law are called **conflict of laws**.

Because there are 50 state court systems and a federal court system, and a high degree of interstate activity, conflict of laws questions arise frequently.

11. State Courts

It is important to distinguish between the state in which the parties are **domiciled** or have their permanent home, the state in which the contract is made, and the state in which the contract is to be performed. The law of the state where the contract is made determines whether it is valid in substance and satisfies requirements as to form. Matters relating to the performance of the contract, excuse or liability for nonperformance, and the measure of damages for nonperformance are generally governed by the law of the state where the contract is to be performed. Similar considerations apply to the interpretation of international contracts. Thus, a California court will apply Swiss law to a contract made in Switzerland that is to be performed in that country.

When a lawsuit is brought on a contract, the law of the forum determines the procedure and the rules of evidence.

(a) PLACE OF CONTRACTING.

The state in which the contract is made is determined by finding the state in which the last act essential to the formation of the contract was performed. Thus, when an acceptance is mailed in one state to an offeror in another state, the state of formation of the contract is the state in which the acceptance is mailed if the acceptance becomes effective at that time.

If acceptance by telephone is otherwise proper, the acceptance takes effect at the place where the acceptance is spoken into the phone. Thus, an employment contract is made in the state in which the job applicant telephones an acceptance. Consequently, the law of that state governs a claim to workers' compensation, even though the injuries were sustained in another state.

If an action on a contract made in one state is brought in a court of another state, an initial question is whether that court will lend its aid to the enforcement of a foreign contract. Ordinarily, suit may be brought on a foreign contract. If there is a strong contrary local policy, however, recovery may be denied, even though the contract was valid in the state where it was made. But there is also authority that when a contract would be valid by the law of one state but invalid by the law of another, a court will apply the law of the state by which the contract is valid.[22]

The capacity of a natural person to make a contract is governed by the place of contracting. A corporation's capacity to make a contract is determined by the law of the state of incorporation.

(b) CENTER OF GRAVITY.

It is common for contracts with interstate aspects to specify that they shall be governed by the law of a particular state. In the absence of a law-selecting provision in the contract, there is a growing acceptance of the rule that a contract should be governed by the law of the state that has the most significant contacts with the transaction. This is the state to which the contract may be said to gravitate.

For example, assume the buyer's place of business and the seller's factory are located in state *A*, and the buyer is purchasing to resell to customers in state *A*. Many courts will hold that this is a contract governed by the law of state *A* in all respects. The fact that it is a state *B* contract by virtue of the chance circumstance that the seller's offer was accepted by the buyer in state *B* would not change this result. In determining which state has the most significant contacts, the court is to consider the place of contracting, negotiating, and performing; the location of the subject matter of the contract; and the domicile (residence) and states of incorporation and principal place of business of the parties.

When all states have the same rule of law, it is not important which state's law is followed. If, however, the law of the states involved is not the same, the choice of the state whose law is to govern will determine how the lawsuit will end. With the increasing interstate character of big business, the question of choice of law becomes increasingly important. Choice of law was at issue in the *Ashland Oil* case.

12. Federal Courts

When the parties to a contract reside in different states and the amount involved is $50,000

---

22 American Home Assurance Co. v Safway Steel Products Co., Inc. (Tex App) 743 SW2d 693 (1987).

ASHLAND OIL, INC. v TUCKER
(Mo App) 768 SW2d 595 (1989)

Tucker was employed by Ashland Oil. Tucker's contract prohibited him from working for a competitor after the termination of his employment. Tucker worked as a district manager of Ashland in Louisiana, Missouri, and Illinois. When his employment ended, he worked for a competitor in Missouri. This would be a breach of the anticompetitive covenant. However, Tucker claimed that the covenant did not bind him. He claimed that it was invalid by the law of Louisiana, where the contract of employment had originally been made. Suit was brought in Missouri to enforce the covenant. Under Missouri law the covenant was valid. Judgment was entered in favor of Ashland. Tucker appealed.

SIMON, J. . . . Tucker contends that the trial court erred in enforcing the non-competition agreement pursuant to Missouri law because Louisiana law should apply. . . .

The service agreement of August 19, 1985 does not indicate the law governing its interpretation and enforcement . . . Under such circumstances, we follow the Restatement (Second) of Conflicts of Law (1971) . . .

Restatement (Second) of Conflicts 6, Choice-of-Law provides:

(1) A court, subject to constitutional restrictions, will follow a statutory directive of its own state on choice of law.

(2) When there is no such directive, the factors relevant to the choice of the applicable rule of law include:

(a) the need of the interstate and international systems,

(b) the relevant policies of the forum,

(c) the relevant policies of other interested states and the relative interests of those states in the determination of the particular issue,

(d) the protection of justified expectations,

(e) the basic policies underlying the particular field of law,

(f) certainty, predictability and uniformity of result, and

(g) ease in determination and application of the law to be applied.

Restatements (Second) of Conflicts 188 provides, in pertinent part:

(1) The rights and duties of the parties with respect to an issue in contract are determined by the local law of the state which, with respect to that issue, has the most significant relationship to the transaction and the parties under the principles stated in 6,

(2) In the absence of an effective choice of law by the parties, the contacts to be taken into account in applying the principle of 6 to determine the law applicable to an issue include:

(a) the place of the contracting;

(b) the place of negotiation of the contract;

(c) the place of performance;

(d) the location of the subject matter of the contract, and

(e) the domicile, residence, nationality, place of incorporation and place of the parties.

These contacts are to be evaluated according to their relative importance with respect to the particular issue.

(3) If the place of negotiating the contract and the place of performance are in the same state, the local law of this state will usually be applied. . . .

Here, the circumstances warrant application of Missouri law. . . . Tucker executed the service agreement in Louisiana and sent it to Ashland in Ohio. Negotiations occurred in Missouri and Ohio and Tucker's performance as District Manager occurred in Louisiana, Missouri and Illinois. Tucker resides in Missouri and Ashland has offices in Missouri. . . . The competition sought to be restrained would take place in Missouri. Thus, it is clear that Missouri has the most significant interest in the enforcement of this agreement. The interest of Louisiana is slight in comparison. . . .

[Judgment affirmed]

QUESTIONS

1. What was the basis for the court's decision in *Ashland Oil*?
2. What other rule of law could have been applied by the court?
3. The court in *Ashland Oil* made the choice of law that it did because of ethics. Appraise this statement.

or more, an action may be brought in a federal court because of the parties' different citizenship. The federal court must apply the same rules of conflict of laws that would be applied by the courts of the state in which the federal court is sitting. Thus, a federal court in Chicago deciding a case involving parties from different states must apply the same rule of conflict of laws as would be applied by the state courts in Illinois. The state law must be followed by the federal court in such a case, whether or not the federal court agrees with the state law.

SUMMARY

Since a contract is based on the agreement of the parties, courts must determine the intent of the parties manifested in the contract. The intent that is to be enforced is the intent as it reasonably appears to a third person. This objective intent is followed, and the subjective or secret intent is ignored because the recognition of secret intention would undermine the stability of contracts and open the door to fraud.

In interpreting a contract, ordinary words are to be given their ordinary meanings. If trade or technical terms have been used, they are interpreted according to their technical meanings. The court must consider the whole contract and not read a particular part out of context. When different writings are executed as part of the same transaction, or one writing refers to or incorporates another, all the writings are to be read together as the contract of the parties. In some cases, the reverse is done, and a contract is held divisible.

When provisions of a contract are contradictory, the court will try to reconcile or eliminate the conflict. If this cannot be done, the conclusion may be reached that there is no contract because the conflict makes the agreement indefinite as to a material matter. In some cases, conflict is solved by considering the form of the conflicting terms. Handwriting prevails over typing and a printed form, and typing prevails over a printed form. Ambiguity will be eliminated in some cases by the admission of parol evidence or by interpreting the provision strictly against the party preparing the contract, particularly when the party has significantly greater bargaining power.

In most cases, the parties are held to their contract exactly as it has been written. In other cases, the courts will imply certain terms to preserve the contract against the objection that essential terms are missing or to prevent hardship. The law will imply that performance be made within a reasonable time and that details of performance be reasonable when the contract fails to be specific on these points. Also, the law will imply an obligation to act in good faith.

When a contract has interstate aspects, it is necessary to determine which state's law governs the contract. The rules that govern that decision are called the law of conflict of laws. The parties may specify the jurisdiction whose law is to govern. If that jurisdiction bears a reasonable relationship to the contract, the choice will be given effect by the court. In the absence of such a provision, some courts will apply the older rule that the law of the state where the contract was made prevails with respect to most matters and the law of the state where performance is to be made prevails as to matters relating to performance. The modern, or center-of-gravity, view is to choose the jurisdiction that has the most significant relationship to the parties, the contract, and its performance. When an action is brought in a federal court because it involves citizens of different states (diversity of citizenship), the federal court must apply the conflict of laws principles that would be applied by the courts of the state in which the federal court is sitting.

LAW IN PRACTICE

1. Read every contract carefully before you sign it to see that it expresses the intention of the parties. Do not read in expectations and desires that are not expressly stated.
2. Avoid loose language that may or may not impose a condition. When a condition is intended, be sure that the contract expressly states that there is the condition. When no condition is intended, state that there is no condition. If a condition is intended, state specifically whether it is a condition precedent or a condition subsequent.

3. When there are more than two parties to a contract, specify whether the contract is several, joint, or joint and several as to any of the parties.
4. If there is any possibility of an interstate operation of the contract, specify the jurisdiction whose law is to be applied to a legal dispute.
5. Remember that, when the contract fails to state what it should, there is a chance that a court might come to the aid of one of the parties by implying terms or reading in conduct of the parties or usage of trade. But use this as a last resort. The court may read in something that you do not want.

QUESTIONS AND CASE PROBLEMS

1. What social forces are affected by the rule that a secret intention has no effect?
2. Harrison Builders made a contract to build a house for Kendall on the basis of cost plus 10 percent profit. The cost of the finished house was approximately $100,000. Kendall had expected that it would be $60,000 and claimed that Harrison was careless and extravagant in incurring costs of $100,000. Harrison asserted that since Kendall did not deny that the costs were $100,000, he could not dispute that they were proper. Is Harrison correct?
3. In letters between the two, Rita Borelli contracted to sell "my car" to Viola Smith for $2,000. It was later shown that Borelli owned two cars. Borelli refused to deliver either car to Smith. Smith sued Borelli for breach of contract. Borelli raised the defense that the contract was too indefinite to be enforced because it could not be determined from the writing which car was the subject matter of the contract. Is the contract too indefinite to be enforced?
4. Quinn of Ohio sues Norman of California in the federal district court for the southern district of New York. Quinn claims that the court should apply the conflicts of laws rules of Ohio because he is from Ohio and the plaintiff should have the choice

of law. Norman claims that the federal court should apply federal law rather than the law of any particular state. Who is correct?

5. The Panasonic Industrial Company (PIC) made a contract making Manchester Equipment Company, Inc. (MECI) a "non-exclusive wholesale distributor" of its products. The contract stated that PIC "reserves the unrestricted right to solicit and make direct sales of the Products to anyone, anywhere." The contract also stated that it contained the entire agreement of the parties and that any prior agreement or statement was superseded by the contract. PIC subsequently began to make direct sales to two of MECI's established customers. MECI claimed that this was a breach of the distribution contract and sued PIC for damages. Decide. What ethical values are involved? *[Manchester Equipment Co., Inc. v Panasonic Industrial Co. 141 App Div 2d 616, 529 NYS2d 532]*

6. McGill and his grandson, Malo, made an agreement. McGill would live with Malo and receive support and maintenance in return for McGill's deeding his house to Malo. After a number of years, McGill left the house because of the threats and physical violence of the grandson. There was no complaint of lack of support and maintenance. Had the grandson broken the contract? *[McGill v Malo, 23 Conn Supp 447, 184 A2d 517]*

7. A contract was made for the sale of a farm. The contract stated that the buyer's deposit would be returned "if for any reason the farm cannot be sold." The seller later stated that she had changed her mind and would not sell, and she offered to return the deposit. The buyer refused to take the deposit back and brought suit to enforce the contract. The seller defended on the ground that the "any reason" provision extended to anything, including the seller's changing her mind. Was the buyer entitled to recover? *[Phillips v Rogers, 157 W Va 194, 200 SE2d 676]*

8. Gerson Realty Co. rented an apartment to Casaly. The lease stated that it could be renewed on giving notice but declared that "such notice . . . shall be given or served and shall not be deemed to have been duly given or served unless in writing and forwarded by registered mail." Casaly sent a renewal notice by certified mail. Two years after receiving the notice, Gerson claimed that it was not effective because it had not been sent by registered mail. Was this notice effective? *[Gerson Realty Inc. v Casaly, 2 Mass App 875, 316 NE2d 767]*

9. The Norwest Bank had been lending money to Tresch to run a dairy farm. The balance due the

bank after several years was $147,000. The loan agreement stated that Tresch would not buy any new equipment in excess of $500 without the express consent of the bank. Some time later, Tresch applied to the bank for a loan of $3,100 to purchase some equipment. The bank refused to make the loan because it did not believe that the new equipment would correct the condition for which it would be bought and would not result in significant additional income. Tresch then sued the bank claiming that its refusal to make the loan was a breach of the implied covenant of good faith and fair dealing. Decide. *[Tresch v Norwest Bank of Lewistown, 238 Mont 511, 778 P2d 874]*

10. Physicians Mutual Insurance Company issued a policy covering the life of Brown. The policy declared that it did not cover any deaths resulting from "mental disorder, alcoholism, or drug addiction." Brown was killed when she fell while intoxicated. The insurance company refused to pay because of the quoted provision. Her executor, Savage, sued the insurance company. Did the insurance company have a defense? *[Physicians Mut. Ins. Co. v Savage, 156 Ind App 283, 296 NE2d 165]*

11. Buice was employed by the Gulf Oil Corporation as a driver. His contract of employment did not state that it was to continue for any specified time. Buice was fired because of excessive drinking. He was treated for alcoholism and was cured. He then applied to Gulf for reinstatement. Gulf refused to reinstate him. Buice then sued Gulf claiming that Gulf had followed the practice of reinstating addiction patients who were cured of their addictions, and it was his understanding that this was an implied term of his employment contract. Was Buice entitled to reinstatement? *[Buice v Gulf Oil Corp. 172 Ga App]*

12. Carol and John were married. They separated and signed an agreement by which John promised to pay Carol $100 a month. A year later they were divorced, and John stopped making payments. Carol sued him for breach of the contract. John offered to testify that it was his intention that the payments would stop when the parties were divorced. Is this testimony admissible? *[Grady v Grady, 29 NC App 402, 224 SE2d 282]*

13. The Suburban Power Piping Corporation was under contract to construct a building for the LTV Steel Corporation. It made a subcontract with the Power & Pollution Services, Inc. to do some of the work. The subcontract provided that the subcontractor would be paid when the owner (LTV) paid the contractor. LTV went into bankruptcy before making full payment to the contractor. The contractor then refused to pay the subcontractor on the ground that the "pay-when-paid" provision of the subcontractor made payment by the owner a condition precedent to the obligation of the contractor to pay the subcontractor. Was the contractor correct? [*Power & Pollution Services, Inc. v Suburban Power Piping Corp. 74 Ohio App 3d 89, 598 NE2d 69*]

14. Buck and Co., a brewery, gave Gianelli Distributing Company a franchise to distribute Beck's Beer. The franchise agreement specified that it would continue "unless and until terminated at any time by 30 days' written notice by either party to the other." Some time thereafter Beck notified Gianelli that the franchise was terminated. Gianelli claimed that the franchise could only be terminated upon proof of reasonable cause for termination.

Gianelli offered evidence of trade usage to show that there was a common practice to require cause for termination, and further claimed that such usage would be read into the franchise agreement with Beck. Is this evidence admissible?

15. Drews Company contracted to renovate a building owned by Ledwith. There were many delays in performing the contract and finally the contractor quit the job. Ledwith sued the contractor for damages for delay and for breach of the contract. The contractor claimed that it was not liable for damages for delay because the contract did not contain any date by which the work was to be completed and did not state that time was of the essence. Did the silence of the contract excuse the delay?

CHAPTER 16

THIRD PERSONS AND CONTRACTS

LEARNING OBJECTIVES

After studying this chapter, you will be able to:
1. *Distinguish between a third party benefici-ary and an incidental beneficiary.*
2. *Define an assignment of contract rights.*
3. *State the limitations on the assignability of a right to performance.*
4. *Describe what constitutes a delegation of du-ties.*
5. *State the liability of the parties after a proper delegation of duties has been made.*
6. *Describe the status of an assignee with re-spect to defenses and setoffs available against the assignor.*
7. *State the significance of a notice of assign-ment.*
8. *State the liability of an assignor to an as-signee.*

In most cases, contracts only involve the parties making the contract. In some cases, third persons may have rights on contracts made by other persons.

A. THIRD PARTY BENEFICIARY CONTRACTS

Generally only the parties to a contract may sue on it. However, in some cases a third person who is not a party to the contract may sue on the contract.

1. Definition

When a contract is intended to benefit a third person, such a person is a **third party beneficiary** and may bring suit on and enforce the contract. In some states, the right of the third party beneficiary to sue on the contract is declared by statute.

Two parties may make a contract by which a promisor promises the other party that the promisor will make a payment of money to a third person. That is, the contracting parties intend to benefit the third person. Because of this intent, if the promisor fails to perform that promise, the third person, who is not the original promisee, may enforce the contract against the promisor.[1] Such an agreement is a **third party beneficiary contract**. A life insurance contract is a third party beneficiary contract, since the insurance company promises the insured to make payment to the beneficiary. Such a contract entitles the beneficiary to sue the insurance company on the insured's death, even though the insurance company never made any agreement directly with the beneficiary.

In the *Thornton* case a health care provider claimed that it was entitled to sue on a contract that might or might not benefit it.

THORNTON v WINDSOR HOUSE, INC.
57 Ohio 3d 158, 566 NE2d 1220 (1991)

The Ohio Department of Public Welfare (ODPW) made a contract with Grant to audit the accounts of health care providers who were receiving funds under the Medicaid program. Windsor House, that operated six nursing homes, claimed that it was a third party beneficiary of that contract and could sue for its breach. The claim of the Windsor House was rejected, sustained, and it appealed.

WRIGHT, J. . . . Only a party to a contract or an intended third party beneficiary of a contract may bring an action on a contract in Ohio. *Visintine & Co. v New York, Chicago, & St. Louis RR. Co. (1959)*, 169 Ohio St. 505, 9 O.O. 2d 4, 160 NE2d 311. Windsor asserts that it was an intended third party beneficiary of the contract and that the parties to the contract—the ODPW and Grant—intended for Windsor to benefit from the contract. However, this is not the case.

Grant's duty under its contract with the ODPW was intended only to benefit the ODPW. The audit of Windsor was intended solely for the ODPW's use in assessing Windsor's dealings under the state's Medicaid plan. While Windsor arguably stood to benefit from a favorable result in the audit, it just as easily could have been, and here was, harmed by a negative result. The purpose of the audit was to search for

---

[1] Vale Dean Canyon Homeowners Assn. v Dean, 100 Or App 158, 785 P2d 772 (1990).

overpayments to care providers. Any potential benefit to Windsor was merely incidental to the contract and therefore insufficient to support a breach of contract cause of action. *Visintine & Co., supra,* at 507, 9 O.O. 2d at 5, 160 NE2d at 313. Accordingly, we hold that a care provider subject to an audit of reimbursable costs under the Medicaid program is not an intended third party beneficiary of the audit contract between the Ohio Department of Public Welfare and the auditor. The trial court thus properly dismissed Windsor's contract claim.

[Judgment affirmed as to contract claim]

QUESTIONS

1. What was the intent of the state and the auditor in making the contract involved in the *Thornton* case?
2. Would the audit benefit the Windsor House?
3. How would you describe the relationship of Windsor House to the auditing contract?

(a) DESCRIPTION OF THIRD PARTY BENEFICIARY. It is not necessary that the third party beneficiary be identified by name. The beneficiary may be identified by class, with the result that any member of that class is a third party beneficiary.[2] For example, a contract between the promoter of an automobile stock car race and the owner of the race track contains a promise to pay specified sums of money to each driver racing a car in certain races. A person driving in one of the designated races is a third party beneficiary and can sue on the contract for the promised compensation.

(b) BURDEN OF PROOF. Parties to a contract are presumed to have contracted to benefit themselves. A stranger to the contract claiming to be a third party beneficiary has the burden of proving that the contracting parties had the intention to benefit the nonparty.[3]

Figure 16-1   Can a Third Person Sue on a Contract?

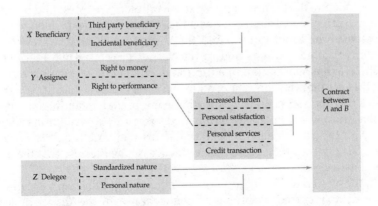

---

[2] J. F. Inc. v S. M. Wilson & Co. 152 Ill App 3d 893, 105 Ill Dec 748, 504 NE2d 1266 (1987).

[3] Brunner v Exxon Co. (Tex App) 752 SW2d 679 (1988).

In *Ron Case Roofing*, the parties to a contract claimed that they never intended that a third person should have the rights of a third party beneficiary.

RON CASE ROOFING & ASPHALT, INC. v BLOMQUIST
(Utah) 773 P2d 1382 (1989)

> Blomquist, Panos, and the Vesper Financial Corporation (known collectively as the Vesper group) were engaged in developing real estate. They used the services of the Brooks Construction Company. Brooks would farm out or subcontract various phases of the work to other persons or subcontractors. Brooks subcontracted the roofing work on the Burton Plaza project to Ron Case Roofing. A dispute arose between Brooks and Ron Case. The dispute was finally settled by agreeing that a judgment be entered for $17,500 in favor of Ron Case and against Brooks. Thereafter a dispute arose between the Vesper and Brooks and others (collectively known as the Brooks group). This was settled by agreement. By this agreement, the Vesper group agreed to pay all claims against Brooks arising in connection with the Vesper projects. Ron Case sued the Vesper group, claiming that it was the third party beneficiary of that promise to pay the debts of Brooks, and that the Vesper group was required to pay to Ron Case the judgment owed to it by Brooks. Judgment was entered in favor of Ron Case. The Vesper group appealed.

ZIMMERMAN, J. . . . The Vesper group argues that it did not intend to assume any of Brooks Construction's liabilities to Ron Case and that the trial court should have permitted Vesper to introduce extrinsic evidence on that point.

The Vesper group's contention about what it really intended and its attempt to rely on extrinsic evidence in support of that contention ignores the settled rule that in interpreting a contract, we first look to the four corners of the agreement to determine the intentions of the parties. . . . The use of extrinsic evidence is permitted only if the document appears to incompletely express the parties' agreement or if it is ambiguous in expressing that agreement. . . . Neither of these tests is met here.

First, the document does not appear to incompletely express the parties' agreement. The settlement agreement . . . deals in a comprehensive fashion with the relationship between the Brooks group and the Vesper group, as it relates both to their various intercorporate dealings and to the Vesper projects. This indicates that the parties' whole agreement is contained in the document. . . . This impression is confirmed by the fact that the contract contains an integration clause in paragraph 19(c) which states that the "agreement sets forth the entire understanding among the parties and shall not be amended or terminated except by a written instrument duly executed by all the parties hereto." The trial court therefore properly precluded the Vesper group from introducing extrinsic evidence on the premise that the instrument is not complete. . . .

Second, the agreement is not ambiguous in expressing the parties' agreement regarding the debts incurred by Brooks in connection with the Vesper projects. Paragraph 4 states in pertinent part:

Panos, Blomquist and Vesper, jointly and severally, agree to pay all indebtedness which is presently outstanding or in the future may arise which claims relate to the furnishing of labor, materials, equipment, tools, fuel, supplies and other items furnished to or incorporated into the Vesper Projects.

. . . The . . . question is whether, under the terms of the settlement agreement, Ron Case had a legal right to proceed against the Vesper group to recover Brooks Construction's unpaid judgment. We begin by reviewing the applicable principles of third-party beneficiary law. Section 302 of the Restatement (Second) of Contracts sets forth the governing principles for determining whether a nonparty is entitled to the rights of a third-party beneficiary under a contract. . . . Section 302 provides:

(1) *Unless otherwise agreed between promisor and promisee, a beneficiary of a promise is an intended beneficiary if recognition of a right to performance in the beneficiary is appropriate to effectuate the intention of the parties and either*

   (a) *the performance of the promise will satisfy an obligation of the promisee to pay money to the beneficiary; or*

   (b) *the circumstances indicate that the promisee intends to give the beneficiary the benefit of the promised performance.*

(2) *An incidental beneficiary is a beneficiary who is not an intended beneficiary.*

For a third party to have enforceable rights under a contract, then, that party must be an "intended beneficiary" of the contract, and the intention of the parties is to be determined from the terms of the contract as well as the surrounding facts and circumstances. . . .

We now consider the terms of paragraph 4 . . . of the settlement agreement under these principles to determine whether Ron Case qualified as a third-party beneficiary. Paragraph 4 states quite clearly that the members of the Vesper group "agree to pay all indebtedness which is presently outstanding or in the future may arise which claims relate to the furnishing of labor, materials, equipment, tools, fuel, supplies and other items furnished to or incorporated into the Vesper Projects." Giving these words their "usual and ordinary meaning," . . . it is plain that the parties intended that the Vesper group would pay all obligations of Brooks due those furnishing labor and materials on any Vesper project, a description that includes Ron Case. Judged by the standards summarized in section 302 of the Restatement and followed by our cases, Ron Case is, therefore, a third-party beneficiary under the settlement agreement. . . .

[Judgment affirmed]

QUESTIONS

1. Did the court allow the Vesper group to testify as to its intention in entering into the settlement agreement with the Brooks group? What was the basis for the court's decision on this point?
2. Did the Vesper group agree to pay judgments entered against Brooks?
3. Of what importance is the Restatement of Contracts to the decision of the case?

2. Modification or Termination of Third Party Beneficiary Contract

Can the parties to the contract modify or terminate it so as to destroy the right of the third party beneficiary? If the contract contains an express provision allowing a change of beneficiaries or cancellation of the contract without the consent of the third party beneficiary, the parties to the contract may destroy the rights of the third party beneficiary by acting in accordance with such a contract provision.[4]

In addition, the rights of a third party beneficiary are destroyed if the contract is discharged or ended by operation of law, for example, through bankruptcy proceedings.

3. Limitations on Third Party Beneficiary

While the third party beneficiary rule gives the third person the right to enforce the contract, it obviously gives no greater rights than the contract provides. Otherwise stated, the third party beneficiary must take the contract as it is. If there is a time limitation or any other restriction in the contract, the third party beneficiary cannot ignore it but is bound by it. Similarly, a third party beneficiary is required to arbitrate a dispute arising under the contract when the original parties to the contract were bound to arbitrate.[5]

4. Incidental Beneficiaries

Not everyone who benefits from the performance of a contract between other persons is entitled to sue as a third party beneficiary. If the benefit was intended, the third person is a third party beneficiary with the rights described in the preceding sections. If the benefit was not intended, the third person is an incidental beneficiary. The fact that the contracting parties know that the performance of their contract will benefit a third person does not in itself make that person a third party beneficiary. In order for the third person to be such a beneficiary, the contract must clearly manifest an intent to confer a direct benefit on the third person.[6]

(a) DIRECT INCIDENTAL BENEFICIARY. When the performance of the contract will confer a direct, although not intended, benefit on the third person, that person is a **direct incidental beneficiary**. For example, when a private employer makes a contract with the U.S. government to employ and train disadvantaged unemployed persons, such persons are merely incidental beneficiaries. They cannot sue for damages if the contract with the government is broken by the employer. Such persons are direct incidental beneficiaries, since the performance of the contract would have directly benefited them.

The fact that a contract requires one of the parties to take steps that will protect or benefit a third person does not make such person a third party beneficiary. For example, when a city hired a contractor to do excavation work, the contract specified that the contractor should be careful about underground facilities. Such care benefited the electric power company that had underground facilities. However, that direct benefit did not make the power company a third party beneficiary to the contract. The power company was merely a direct incidental beneficiary.

A contractor who has not been paid by the owner is not the third party beneficiary of the contract between the owner and the institution lending money to the owner for the construction project.[7]

---

[4] A common form of reservation is the life insurance policy provision by which the insured reserves the right to change the beneficiary. Section 142 of the Restatement of Contracts 2d provides that the promisor and promisee may modify their contract and affect the right of the third party beneficiary thereby unless the agreement expressly prohibits this or the third party beneficiary has changed position in reliance on the promise or has manifested assent to it.

[5] Mayflower Ins. Co. v Pellegrino, 212 Cal App 3d 1326, 261 Cal Rptr 224 (1989).

[6] Baldwin v Leach (Idaho App) 769 P2d 590 (1989).

[7] Fidelity Savings & Loan Assn. v Morrison & Miller, Inc. (Tex App) 764 SW2d 385 (1989).

(b) CONTINGENT INCIDENTAL BENE-FICIARY. In contrast with the incidental beneficiary who is directly benefited by the performance of the contract, the situation may be such that the third party will benefit only if the obligee of the original contract takes some further action that will benefit the third person. For example, a landlord is not a third party beneficiary of the contract by which a bank agreed to lend money to the tenant, even though the tenant intended to use the money to make improvements to the rented premises. In effect, the landlord was an incidental beneficiary once removed. The landlord would benefit only (1) if the bank loaned the money to the tenant, and (2) if the tenant used the money to make the improvements. Thus, the bank could perform its duty by making the loan, but if the tenant never used the money to make the improvements, the landlord would never receive any benefit from that loan. The benefit to the landlord was therefore contingent on the tenant's using proceeds of the loan for making improvements.

(c) CONSEQUENCE OF INCIDENTAL BENEFICIARY STATUS. An incidental beneficiary cannot sue the parties to the contract that gave rise to the benefit or the possible benefit.

The importance in making the distinction between the direct and the contingent incidental beneficiary lies in the value of the distinction as proof of lack of intent to benefit the third person. For example, when the performance of a contract directly benefits the third person, it is necessary to go further and determine whether the parties to the contract had intended to confer that benefit on the third person. In the case of a contingent incidental beneficiary, it is obvious that the parties to the original contract did not intend to confer a benefit on that person who would only benefit if the obligee in turn would choose to confer a benefit. Consequently, once it is established that the third party is, at best, a contingent incidental beneficiary, the lawsuit is ended, and there is no need to make further inquiry as to the intent of the original parties.

B. ASSIGNMENTS

The parties to a contract have both rights and duties. Can rights be transferred or sold to another person? Can duties be transferred to another person?

Figure 16-2   What a Third Party Beneficiary Must Prove

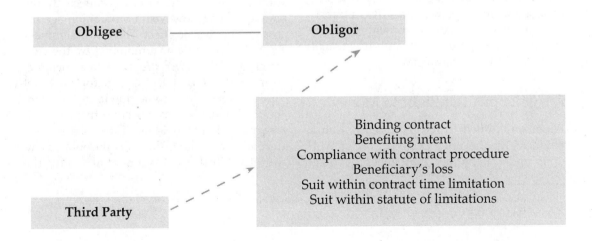

Obligee ———————— Obligor

Binding contract
Benefiting intent
Compliance with contract procedure
Beneficiary's loss
Suit within contract time limitation
Suit within statute of limitations

Third Party

5. Definitions

An **assignment** is a transfer of rights. The party making the assignment is the **assignor**, and the person to whom the assignment is made is the **assignee**. An assignee of a contract may generally sue directly on the contract, rather than suing in the name of the assignor.

6. Form of Assignment

Generally, an assignment may be in any form. Statutes, however, may require that certain kinds of assignments be in writing or be executed in particular form. This requirement is common in statutes limiting the assignment of claims to wages.

Any words, whether written or spoken, that show an intention to transfer or assign will be given the effect of an assignment.[8] It is not necessary to use the word *assign* or *transfer*.

Since no particular words are necessary to create an assignment, an authorization to the obligor (the other party to the original contract) to pay a third person is an assignment to such third person. For example, the printed forms supplied by the health insurer that read, "I hereby authorize payment directly to the below named dentist of the group insurance benefits otherwise payable to me," constitute an assignment to the dentist of such benefits.

Whether or not there is consideration for the assignment does not affect the validity of the assignment. An assignment cannot be challenged by the obligor on the ground that there was no consideration. This is so because an assignment is not a contract. It is a transfer of a property right. An assignment may therefore be made as a gift, although it is usually part of a business transaction.

7. Assignment of Right to Money

A person entitled to receive money, such as payment for the price of goods or for work done under a contract, may generally assign that right to another person. A claim or cause of action against another person may be assigned. A contractor entitled to receive payment from the owner can assign that right to the bank as security for a loan or can assign it to anyone else.

The owner of a right to money may make a partial assignment. Thus, a tenant who is owed $1,000 may wish to assign $600 of this to pay the rent to the landlord. Such a partial assignment is valid. To protect the person owing the original debt of $1,000 from being sued by two claimants, one for $600 and the other for $400, the law requires that both claimants join in a single suit against the obligor in which the recovery is sought of the original $1,000.

(a) FUTURE RIGHTS. By the modern rule, future and expected rights may be assigned.[9] Thus, the contractor may assign money that is not yet due under the contract because the building has not yet been constructed. Similarly, an author may assign royalties that are expected to be received from contracts that the author expects to enter into in the future. The fact that there is nothing in existence now does not prohibit the assignment of what is expected to be existing in the future.

(b) PROHIBITION OF ASSIGNMENT OF RIGHTS. A contract may prohibit the assignment of any rights arising under it. Some courts hold that such a prohibition is binding. This means that an assignment made in violation of the prohibition has no effect. By the modern view, however, a prohibition against assignment has no effect. Thus, an assignment is valid even though prohibited by the contract. By this view, a provision in a construction contract that the contractor may not assign money to become due under the contract without the consent of the other contracting party is not binding. The assignee may recover the amounts due from the obligor. Under the Uniform Commercial Code, the

---

[8]   Lone Mountain Production Co. v Natural Gas Pipeline Co. of America (CA10 Utah) 984 F2d 1551 (1992).

[9]   New Holland, Inc. v Trunk (Fla App) 579 So 2d 215 (1991).

assignment of accounts receivable cannot be prohibited by the parties.[10] A right that is otherwise assignable may be assigned even though the obligor does not consent to the assignment.[11]

8. Assignment of Right to a Performance

When the contractual right of the obligee is that of receiving a performance by the other party, the obligee may ordinarily assign that right. However, if a transfer of a right to a performance would materially affect or alter a duty or the rights of the obligor, an assignment of the right to the performance is not permitted.[12] When an obligee is entitled to assign a right, the assignment may be done by unilateral act. There is no requirement that the obligor consent or agree. Likewise, the act of assigning does not constitute a breach of the contract, unless the contract specifically declares so. The assignee of a service contract is subject to any limitations of liability contained in that contract.[13]

(a) ASSIGNMENT INCREASING BURDEN OF PERFORMANCE. When the assigning of a right would increase the burden of the obligor in performing, an assignment is ordinarily not permitted. To illustrate, if the assignor has the right to buy a certain quantity of a stated article and to take such property from the seller's warehouse, this right can be assigned. However, if the sales contract stipulated that the seller should deliver to the buyer's premises, and the assignee's premises were a substantial distance from the assignor's place of business, the assignment would not be given effect. In this case, the seller would be required to give a different performance, by providing greater transportation, if the assignment were permitted.

(b) PERSONAL SATISFACTION. A similar problem arises when the goods to be furnished must be satisfactory to the personal judgment of the buyer. Since the seller only contracted that the performance would stand or fall according to the buyer's judgment, the buyer may not substitute the personal judgment of an assignee.

(c) PERSONAL SERVICES. An employer cannot assign to another the employer's right to have an employee work.[14] The relationship of employer and employee is so personal that the right cannot be assigned. The performance contracted by the employee was to work for a particular employer at a particular place and at a particular job. To permit an assignee to claim the employee's services would be to change that contract.

(d) CREDIT TRANSACTION. When a transaction is based on extending credit, the person to whom credit is extended cannot assign any rights under the contract to another. For example, when land is sold on credit, the buyer cannot assign the contract unless the seller consents to this. The making of an assignment is prohibited here because the assignee is a different credit risk. Whether the assignee is a better or worse credit risk is not considered.

(e) PERSONAL NATURE. A contract cannot be assigned when there is a personal aspect, such as in the case of a golf club membership.[15]

---

[10] UCC § 9-318(4), although some cases still follow the contrary pre-Code law. See, for example, Cordis Corp. v Sonies International, Inc. (Fla App) 427 So 2d 782 (1983).

[11] Great Southern National Bank v McCullough Environmental Services, Inc. (Miss) 595 So 2d 1282 (1992).

[12] Aslakson v Home Savings Assn. (Minn App) 416 NW2d 786 (1987) (increase of credit risk).

[13] McCrory v Terminix Service Co., Inc. (La App) 609 So 2d 883 (1992).

[14] Mail Concepts, Inc. v Foote & Davies, Inc. ___ Ga App ___, 409 SE2d 567 (1991).

[15] Re Magness (CA6 Ohio) 972 F2d 689 (1992).

9. Rights of Assignee

An assignee stands exactly in the position of the assignor. The assignee's rights are no greater or less than those of the assignor.[16] If the assigned right to payment is subject to a condition precedent, that same condition exists for the assignee. For example, when a contractor is not entitled to receive the balance of money due under the contract until all bills of suppliers of materials have been paid, the assignee to whom the contractor assigns the balance due under the contract is subject to the same condition.

10. Delegation of Duties

A **delegation of duties** is a transfer of duties by a contracting party to another person who is to perform them. Under certain circumstances, a contracting party may obtain someone else to do the work. When the performance is standardized and nonpersonal, so that it is not material who performs, the law will permit the delegation of the performance of the contract. In such cases, however, the contracting party remains liable in the case of default of the person doing the work, just as though no delegation had been made.[17] If performance involves a personal element, delegation is barred unless consented to by the person entitled to the performance.

(a) INTENTION TO DELEGATE DUTIES. An assignment does not in itself delegate the performance of duties to the assignee.[18] In the absence of clear language in the assignment stating that duties are or are not delegated, all circumstances must be examined to determine whether there is a delegation. When the total picture is viewed, it may become clear what was intended. The fact that an assignment is made for security of the assignee is a strong indication that there was no intent to delegate to the assignee the performance of any duty resting on the assignor.[19]

A question of interpretation arises as to whether an assignment of "the contract" is only an assignment of the rights of the assignor or is both an assignment of those rights and a delegation of duties. The trend of authority is to regard such a general assignment as both a transfer of rights and a delegation of duties.

(b) DELEGATION OF DUTIES UNDER THE UCC. With respect to contracts for the sale of goods, "an assignment of 'the contract' or of 'all my rights under the contract' or an assignment in similar general terms is an assignment of rights and, unless the language or the circumstances (as in an assignment for security) indicate the contrary, it is a delegation of performance of the duties of the assignor, and its acceptance by the assignee constitutes a promise . . . to perform those duties. This promise is enforceable by either the assignor or the other party to the original contract."[20]

11. Continuing Liability of Assignor

The making of an assignment does not relieve the assignor of any obligation of the contract. In the absence of a contrary agreement, an assignor continues to be bound by the obligations of the original contract. Thus, the fact that a buyer assigns the right to goods under a contract does not terminate the buyer's liability to make payment to the seller. Similarly, when an independent contractor is hired to perform a party's obligations under a contract, that party is liable if the independent contractor does not properly perform the contract.

---

[16] Properties Investment Group of Mid-America v Applied Communications, Inc. 242 Neb 464, 495 NW2d 483 (1993).

[17] Orange Bowl Corp. v Warren (SC App) 386 SE2d 293 (1989).

[18] Kagan v K-Tel Entertainment, Inc. 172 App Div 2d 375, 568 NYS2d 756 (1991).

[19] City National Bank of Fort Smith v First National Bank and Trust Co. of Rogers, 22 Ark App 5, 732 SW2d 489 (1987).

[20] UCC § 2-210(4).

Figure 16-3   Limitations on Transfer of Rights and Duties

Assignment of Right to Money	Assignment of Right to Performance	Delegation of Duties
Prohibition in government contracts	Increase of burden Personal satisfaction Personal services Credit transaction	Personal or nonstandardized performance

12. Liability of Assignee

It is necessary to distinguish between the question of whether the obligor can assert a particular defense against the assignee and the question of whether any person can sue the assignee for failing to perform the contract. Ordinarily, the assignee is not subject to suit by virtue of the fact that the assignment has been made. In the *Cuchine* case, the buyer of a truck claimed that the dealer's assignee was liable for defects in the truck.

CUCHINE v H.O. BELL, INC.
210 Mont 312, 682 P2d 723 (1984)

Cuchine purchased a pickup truck from H.O. Bell, Inc. The sale was made as a credit installment sale. Bell assigned the contract to the Ford Motor Credit Co. Cuchine brought the truck back to Bell for repairs. When it became apparent that the truck could not be repaired, Cuchine sued Bell and Ford. As to Ford, he claimed that by taking the assignment, Ford guaranteed that the truck would perform properly. Ford asserted that it was not liable for the truck because it was merely an assignee of the right to collect the money from Cuchine and was not a guarantor of the truck. Judgment was entered in favor of Ford, and Cuchine appealed.

SHEEHY, J. . . . Cuchine contends that the credit company assumed full contract liability when the assignment was accepted. Cuchine further contends that the credit company could not avoid this liability during the pendency of the action by reassigning the contract to H.O. Bell. Cuchine predicates the credit company's liability under the contract upon the following language which appears in the contract in bold, capital letters:

NOTICE—ANY HOLDER OF THIS CONSUMER CREDIT CONTRACT IS SUBJECT TO ALL CLAIMS AND DEFENSES WHICH THE DEBTOR COULD ASSERT AGAINST THE SELLER OF GOODS OR SERVICES OBTAINED PURSUANT HERETO OR WITH THE PROCEEDS HEREOF. RECOVERY HEREUNDER BY THE DEBTOR SHALL NOT EXCEED AMOUNTS PAID BY THE DEBTOR HEREUNDER.

This language is consistent with section 9-318 of the Uniform Commercial Code, adopted in Montana as section 30-9-318, MCA. That section reads in pertinent part:

Unless an account debtor has made an enforceable agreement not to assert defenses or claims arising out of a sale as provided in 30-9-206, the rights of an assignee are subject to:

(a) all the terms of the contract between the account debtor and assignor and any defense or claim arising therefrom; . . .

At common law, it is a well established rule that a party to a contract cannot relieve himself of the obligations which the contract imposed upon him merely by assigning the contract to a third person. Therefore, we must determine whether, under the Uniform Commercial Code, the assignment of the contract to the credit company imposed full contract liability on the credit company as assignee.

The case law as to the effect of section 9-318 of the UCC on the liabilities of an assignee of contract rights is scant, but conclusive. In *Michelin Tires v First National Bank of Boston* (1st Cir. 1981), 666 F2d 673, the court examined section 9-318 and determined that:

The key statutory language is ambiguous. That 'the rights of an assignee are subject to . . . (a) all the terms of the contract' connotes only that the assignee's rights to recover are limited by the obligor's rights to assert contractual defenses as a set-off, implying that affirmative recovery against the assignee is not intended.

The court also noted that:

The words 'subject to,' used in their ordinary sense, mean 'subordinate to,' 'subservient to,' or 'limited by.' There is nothing in the use of the words 'subject to,' in their ordinary use, which would even hint at the creation of affirmative rights.

Such a conclusion is buttressed by the official comment to section 9-318. Official Comment 1 provides. . . :

Subsection (1) makes no substantial change in prior law. An assignee has traditionally been subject to defenses or set-offs existing before an account debtor is notified of the assignment.

Under prior law, the assignee of a contract was generally not held liable for the assignor's breach of contract. . . . This rule has been carried into current law as well; where it is not clearly shown that the assignee under a contract expressly or impliedly assumed the assignor's liability under the contract the assignee is not subject to the contract liability imposed by the contract on the assignor.

We believe that the intent of section 9-318 of the Uniform Commercial Code . . . was to allow an account debtor to assert contractual defenses as a set-off; the provisions were not intended, generally, to place the assignee of a contract in the position of being held a guarantor of a product in place of the assignor. . . .

[Judgment affirmed]

QUESTIONS

1. What is the effect of the notice set forth in the first paragraph of the opinion?
2. Why is the assignee of a right not subject to the duties of the assignor?
3. Does the court recognize any exception to the rule of nonliability of the assignee?

(a) CONSUMER PROTECTION LIABIL-ITY OF ASSIGNEE. The assignee of a right to money typically has no relationship to the original debtor, except with respect to receiving payments or collecting. Consumer protection laws, however, may subject the assignee to liability for the misconduct of the assignor. When the circumstances are such that the debtor could recover the money paid to the assignor, the debtor may recover that amount from the assignee by virtue of a Federal Trade Commission Regulation preserving consumer defenses. Some state statutes go beyond this and declare that the assignee must pay the debtor the same penalties that the seller-assignor would have been required to pay under a consumer protection law.[21]

(b) ASSIGNMENT "SUBJECT TO." The assignee of a right that is "subject to" a claim is not personally bound with respect to the payment of the claim. The "subject to" clause merely means that the other claim comes first and has priority over the rights of the assignee.[22]

(c) DEFENSES AND SETOFFS. The assignee's rights are no greater than those of the assignor. If the obligor could successfully defend against a suit brought by the assignor, the obligor will also prevail against the assignee.

The fact that the assignee has given value for the assignment does not give the assignee any immunity from defenses that the other party, the obligor, could have asserted against

the assignor. The rights acquired by the assignee remain subject to any limitations imposed by the contract.

Modern contract forms commonly provide that the debtor waives or will not assert against an assignee of the contract exemptions and defenses that could have been raised against the assignor. Such waivers are generally valid, although consumer protection statutes often prohibit them. Some statutes take a modified position and permit barring a buyer if, when notified of the assignment, the buyer fails to inform the assignee of the defense against the seller.

Assignments of contracts are generally made to raise money. For example, an automobile dealer assigns a customer's credit contract to a finance company and receives cash for it. Sometimes assignments are made when an enterprise closes down and transfers its business to a new owner. The availability of defenses and setoffs is the same for both cases.

13. Notice of Assignment

An assignment, if otherwise valid, takes effect the moment it is made. It is not necessary that the assignee or the assignor give notice to the other party to the contract. As a practical matter, though, the assignee should give prompt notice of the assignment to prevent improper payment of the obligation.[23]

If the obligor is notified in any manner that there has been an assignment and that any money due must be paid to the assignee, the

---

[21] Home Savings Assn. v Guerra (Tex App) 720 SW2d 636 (1986).

[22] Winegar v Froerer Corp. (Utah) 813 P2d 104 (1991).

[23] In some cases, an assignee will give notice of the assignment to the obligor in order to obtain priority over other persons who claim the same right or in order to limit the defenses that the obligor may raise against the assignee. UCC § 9-318.

obligor's obligation can only be discharged by making payment to the assignee. Before the obligor is so notified, any payment made by the obligor to the assignor reduces or cancels the debt, even though, as between the assignor and the assignee, it is the assignee who is entitled to the money. The only remedy of the assignee is to sue the assignor to recover the payments that were made by the obligor.

In the *First Trust and Savings* case, the obligor on the assigned claim continued to make payments to the assignor after learning of the assignment. The assignee claimed that such payments did not discharge the obligor's liability.

FIRST TRUST AND SAVINGS BANK v SKOKIE SAVINGS AND LOAN ASS'N.

126 Ill App 3d 432, 81 Ill Dec 246, 466 NE2d 1048 (1984)

Skokie Federal Savings and Loan Association made an agreement to lend money in installments to Spanish Court II for construction of a condominium. Spanish Court borrowed additional money from First Trust and Savings Bank and assigned to it the right to receive payments from Skokie. The assignment also authorized Skokie to make payments directly to First Trust. Skokie was given a copy of the assignment and authorization but continued to make payments directly to Spanish Court. Two and one-half years later, by which time all the money had been paid by Skokie to Spanish Court, First Trust sued Skokie claiming that it was liable for payments made to Spanish Court after Skokie had notice of the assignment made to First Trust. From a judgment for Skokie, First Trust appealed.

McGLOON, J. . . . In October, 1978, Skokie Federal loaned Spanish Court II, Ltd. (Spanish Court) $2,400,000 to finance the construction of a 32-unit condominium in Highland Park, Illinois. Under the terms of the construction loan agreement, proceeds for the payment of "profit and overhead expenses" were to be disbursed to Spanish Court as various phases of the project were completed. An additional $100,000, needed to purchase labor and materials to commence construction, was obtained from First Trust. This loan was secured by the collateral assignment of the construction loan proceeds that Spanish Court was to receive from Skokie Federal. The language contained in the agreement read as follows:

For value received, I hereby sell, assign, transfer and set unto The First Trust and Savings Bank, Glenview and Robert L. Munzer, their successors and assigns all rights to profit and overhead from a certain construction loan granted to Spanish Court II, Ltd. by Skokie Federal Savings and Loan Association per their Loan Commitment and Construction Loan Agreement dated October 16, 1978.

Said Assignment is made to secure a loan in the amount of $100,000.00 to Spanish Court II, Ltd., which will be used for the start-up costs (labor and materials) prior to the opening of Skokie Federal Savings and Loan Association's Construction Loan.

I hereby authorize Skokie Federal Savings and Loan Association to direct Pioneer National Title Insurance Company as Construction Payout Agent to make all payouts for profit and overhead payable to The First Trust and Savings Bank and Robert L. Munzer.

The assignment was accepted by First Trust and acknowledged by Skokie Federal on October 23, 1978. Between October, 1978 and May, 1981, First Trust did not receive any payments of profit and overhead. Although the owner of Spanish Court, Louis Frappier, occasionally discussed the $100,000 loan with a loan officer at First Trust, Stephen Miles, he never disclosed that Spanish Court was receiving disbursements of construction loan proceeds from Skokie Federal. On May 15, 1981, the final installment of the construction loan proceeds was made to Spanish Court. Thereafter, First Trust made a demand upon Skokie Federal for payment of the construction loan proceeds due under the assignment. Skokie Federal rejected the demand.

First Trust filed an action for declaratory judgment urging the court to determine that Skokie Federal had wrongfully paid funds directly to Spanish Court in derogation of First Trust's rights under the assignment. Thereafter, a motion for summary judgment was filed by Skokie Federal. After a hearing, the trial court granted summary judgment in favor of Skokie Federal based upon its finding that Skokie Federal did not receive an explicit direction to pay First Trust the assigned proceeds.

The sole issue presented for our determination is whether Skokie Federal, as the debtor of an account that had been assigned to First Trust, received sufficient notification that future payments should be made to the assignee to render it liable for continuing to disburse construction loan proceeds directly to Spanish Court.

Section 9-318(3) of the Uniform Commercial Code governs the situation in which a creditor has assigned its right to receive payments to another party. . . . That section provides:

The account debtor is authorized to pay the assignor until the account debtor receives notification that the amount due or to become due has been assigned and that payment is to be made to the assignee. A notification which does not reasonably identify the rights assigned is ineffective. If requested by the account debtor, the assignee must seasonably furnish reasonable proof that the assignment has been made and unless he does so the account debtor may pay the assignor.

Section 9-318(3) has been interpreted as an express authorization for an account debtor to make payments to an assignor until the account debtor receives notification that the right to receive payments has been assigned and that the future payments are to be made to the assignee. Uniform Commercial Code Comment to section 9-318 further indicates that an account debtor may continue to pay the assignor even though the account debtor has knowledge of the assignment. The Illinois cases which rely on section 9-318(3) of the Code hold that enforcement of an assignee's rights under the assignment requires both notification of the assignment and a demand that future payments be made to the assignee. This holding is in accord with the plain language of the statute as clarified by Uniform Commercial Code Comment to section 9-318(3).

In the instant case, the assignment does not contain an explicit demand for Skokie Federal to make future disbursements of its construction loan proceeds to First Trust. The relevant language, which we have quoted above, merely "authorizes" Skokie Federal to direct the payout agent to make the disbursements to First Trust. Our review of the record supports the trial court's conclusion that, although Skokie Federal received notice of the existence of the assignment, it did not receive a demand that payments were to be made to First Trust. The uncontradicted affidavit of Steven Munson, an officer of Skokie Federal, states that Skokie Federal received no notification to pay any amount due under the assignment until after Skokie Federal made its final payment to Spanish Court.

Here . . . the trial court's conclusion that the assignment itself was not intended as a demand for payment directly to First Trust is fortified by the fact that First Trust acquiesced for so long in the payments to the assignor. . . . First Trust's failure in the present case to investigate whether and to whom payments were being made for over a $2^1/2$ year period constituted a lack of common prudence. . . . Accordingly, we hold that First Trust, by its failure to demand direct payments, waived its right to impose liability upon Skokie Federal.

[Judgment affirmed]

QUESTIONS

1. Was it not wrong for Skokie to pay Spanish Court when it knew that the money had been assigned to First Trust?
2. What remedy was available to First Trust?
3. Why was it important for the assignment agreement to authorize Skokie to pay First Trust?
4. What was the basis for the court's decision?

The Uniform Consumer Credit Code (UCCC) restates the protection of the consumer-debtor making payment to the assignor without knowledge of the assignment and imposes a penalty for using a contract term that would destroy this protection of the consumer.

14. Warranties of Assignor

When the assignment is made for a consideration, the assignor is regarded as impliedly warranting that the right assigned is valid. The assignor also warrants that the assignor is the owner of the claim or right assigned and that the assignor will not interfere with the assignee's enforcement of the obligation. The assignor does not warrant that the other party will pay or perform as required by the contract.

SUMMARY

Ordinarily, only the parties to contracts have rights and duties with respect to such contracts. Exceptions are made in the case of third party beneficiary contracts and assignments.

When a contract shows a clear intent to benefit a third person or class of persons, those persons are called third party beneficiaries, and they may sue for breach of the contract. A third party beneficiary is subject to any limitation or restriction found in the contract. A third party beneficiary loses all rights when the original contract is terminated by operation of law or if the contract reserves the right to change beneficiaries and such a change is made.

In contrast, an incidental beneficiary benefits from the performance of a contract, but the conferring of this benefit was not intended by the contracting parties. An incidental beneficiary cannot sue on the contract.

An assignment is a transfer of a right; the assignor transfers a right to the assignee. In the absence of local statute, there are no formal requirements for an assignment. Any words manifesting the intent to transfer are sufficient to constitute an assignment. No consideration is required. Any right to money may be assigned, whether the assignor is entitled to the money at the time of the assignment or will be entitled or expects to be entitled at some time in the future. By the modern view, contract term prohibiting the assignment of a right to money is invalid and does not prevent the making of an assignment.

A right to a performance may also be assigned except when it would increase the burden of performance, when performance under the contract is to be measured by the personal satisfaction of the obligee, or when it involves the performance of personal services or the credit of the person entitled to the performance.

When a valid assignment is made, the assignee has the same rights—and only the same rights—as the assignor. The assignee is also subject to the same defenses and setoffs as the assignor had been.

The performance of duties under a contract may be delegated to another person, except when a personal element of skill or judgment of the original contracting party is involved. The intent to delegate duties may be expressly stated. The intent may also be found in an "assignment" of "the contract," unless the circumstances make it clear that only the right to money was intended to be transferred. The fact that there has been a delegation of duties does not release the assignor from responsibility for performance. The assignor is liable for breach of the contract if the assignee does not properly perform the delegated duties. In the absence of an effective delegation or the formation of a third party beneficiary contract, an assignee of rights is not liable to the obligee of the contract for its performance by the assignor.

Notice is not required to effect an assignment. When notice of the assignment is given to the obligor together with a demand that future payments be made to the assignee, the obligor cannot discharge liability by payment to the assignor.

When an assignment is made for a consideration, the assignor makes implied warranties that the right assigned is valid and that the assignor owns that right and will not interfere with its enforcement by the assignee. The assignor does not warrant that the obligor on the assigned right will perform the obligation of the contract.

LAW IN PRACTICE

1. Consider whether your contract should state that there is no intention to benefit third persons who are not parties to the contract.
2. Know how you can improve your present cash position by assigning your claims against your customers.

3. Consider whether your subsequent transaction should state whether it is a delegation of duties, or an assignment of rights, or both.
4. If you are assigned a right to receive money, notify the obligor (debtor) of the assignment as soon as possible and inform the debtor that payment is to be made to you.

QUESTIONS AND CASE PROBLEMS

1. What social forces are affected by allowing an obligee to assign the right to obtain payment?
2. Give an example of a third party beneficiary contract.
3. A court order required John Baldassari to make specified payments for the support of his wife and child. His wife needed more money and applied for Pennsylvania welfare payments. In accordance with the law, she assigned to Pennsylvania her right to the support payments from her husband. Pennsylvania then made greater payments to her. Pennsylvania obtained a court order directing John, in accordance with the terms of the assignment from his wife, to make the support or-

der payments directly to the Pennsylvania Department of Public Welfare. John refused to pay on the ground that he had not been notified of the assignment or the hearing directing him to make payment to the assignee. Was he correct? [*Pennsylvania v Baldassari, 279 Pa Super 491, 421 A2d 306*]

4. Lee contracts to paint Sally's two-story house for $1,000. Sally realizes that she will not have sufficient money, so she transfers her rights under this agreement to her neighbor Karen, who has a three-story house. Karen notifies Lee that Sally's contract has been assigned to her and demands that Lee paint Karen's house for $1,000. Is Lee required to do so?

5. Assume that Lee agrees to the assignment of the house painting contract to Karen as stated in Question 4. Thereafter, Lee fails to perform the contract to paint Karen's house. Karen sues Sally for damages. Is Sally liable?

6. Jessie borrows $1,000 from Thomas and agrees to repay the money in 30 days. Thomas assigns the right to the $1,000 to the Douglas Finance Company. Douglas sues Jessie. Jessie raises the defense that she had only agreed to pay the money to Thomas and that when she and Thomas had entered into the transaction, there was no intention to benefit the Douglas Finance Company. Are these objections valid?

7. Washington purchased an automobile from Smithville Motors. The contract called for payment of the purchase price in installments and contained the defense preservation notice required by the Federal Trade Commission Regulation. Smithville assigned the contract to the Rustic Finance Company. The car was always in need of repairs, and by the time it was half paid for it would no longer run. Washington canceled the contract. Meanwhile, Smithville had gone out of business. Washington sued Rustic for the amount she had paid Smithville. Rustic refused to pay on the ground that it had not been at fault. Decide.

8. Helen obtained a policy of insurance insuring her life and naming her niece Julie as beneficiary. Helen died, and about a year later the policy was found in her house. When Julie claimed the insurance money, the insurer refused to pay on the ground that the policy required that notice of death be given to it promptly following the death. Julie claimed that she was not bound by the time limitation because she had never agreed to it, since she was not a party to the insurance contract. Is Julie entitled to recover?

9. Lone Star Life Insurance Company agreed to make a long-term loan to Five Forty Three Land,

Inc., whenever requested to do so by that corporation. Five Forty Three wanted this loan in order to pay off its short-term debts. The loan was never made, as it was never requested by Five Forty Three. That corporation owed the Exchange Bank & Trust Company on a short-term debt. Exchange Bank then sued Lone Star for breach of its promise on the theory that the Exchange Bank was a third party beneficiary of the contract to make the loan. Was the Exchange Bank correct? [*Exchange Bank & Trust Co. v Loan Star Life Insurance Co. (Tex Civ App) 546 SW2d 948*]

10. The New Rochelle Humane Society made a contract with the city of New Rochelle to capture and impound all dogs running at large. Spiegler, a minor, was bitten by some dogs while in the school yard. She sued the school district of New Rochelle and the Humane Society. With respect to the Humane Society, she claimed that she was a third party beneficiary of the contract that the Humane Society had made with the city. She claims that she could therefore sue the Humane Society for its failure to capture the dogs that had bitten her. Was she entitled to recover? [*Spiegler v School District of the City of New Rochelle, 39 Misc 2d 946, 242 NYS2d 430*]

11. Townshend purchased an automobile from Falcon Motors. The contract required Falcon to make ordinary wear-and-tear repairs for one year. Several months later Falcon sold out the business to Hawk Motors and assigned its contracts with customers to Hawk. Hawk also purchased the salesroom and repair shop of Falcon and continued to employ the employees of Falcon. A few months later, Townshend came into what had been Falcon Motors for repairs. When he found Hawk instead, he demanded that Hawk make the repairs. Hawk refused to do so on the ground that it had taken only an assignment of the right to money under the Falcon contracts and had not accepted a delegation of duties that had been imposed on Falcon by those contracts. Decide.

12. Henry was owed $10,000 by the Jones Corporation. In consideration of the many odd jobs performed for him over the years by his nephew, Henry assigned the $10,000 claim to his nephew, Charles. Henry died and his widow claimed that the assignment was ineffective, so that the claim was part of Henry's estate. She based her assertion on the ground that the past performance rendered by the nephew was not consideration. Was the assignment effective?

13. The Industrial Construction Company wanted to raise money to construct a canning factory in

Wisconsin. Various persons promised to subscribe the needed amount, which they agreed to pay when the construction was completed. The construction company assigned its rights and delegated its duties under the agreement to Johnson who then built the cannery. Vickers, one of the subscribers, refused to pay the amount that he had subscribed on the ground that the contract could not be assigned. Was he correct?

14. Grand Blanc Landfill, Inc. operated a landfill. The Michigan State Department of Natural Resources began to impose regulations on the landfill operations. Landfill sued to stop the Department from so doing. The court appointed Swanson as an expert to make a study of the environmental impact of the landfill. Landfill did not like his report and brought suit against him for breach of duty, claiming that it (Landfill) was a third party beneficiary of the contract between the court and Swanson. Was Landfill correct? *[Grand Blanc Landfill, Inc. v Swanson Environmental, Inc. ___Mich App___, 463 NW2d 234]*

15. Smith assigned to Roberts his ownership of a condominium apartment house and his contracts with the various condominium unit owners. When Roberts later failed to pay the taxes on the building, the purchasers of the individual apartments sued to compel him to do so. He claimed that he had not assumed any of the obligations of Smith. Decide. *[Radley v Smith and Roberts, 6 Utah 2d 314, 313 P2d 465]*

DISCHARGE OF CONTRACTS

LEARNING OBJECTIVES

After studying this chapter, you will be able to:
1. *List the ways in which a contract can be discharged.*
2. *Distinguish between the effect of a rejected tender of payment and a rejected tender of performance.*
3. *Define when time is of the essence.*
4. *Compare performance to the satisfaction of the other contracting parties, performance to the satisfaction of a reasonable person, and substantial performance.*
5. *State when a consumer contract may be rescinded by the consumer.*
6. *Compare the discharge of a contract by rescission, cancellation, substitution, and novation.*
7. *State the effect on a contract of the death or disability of one of the contracting parties.*
8. *Define the concept of economic frustration.*

In the preceding chapters, you studied how a contract is formed, what it means, and who has rights under a contract. In this chapter, attention is turned to how a contract is ended or discharged. In other words, what puts an end to the rights and duties created by the contract?

A. DISCHARGE BY PERFORMANCE

When it is claimed that a contract is discharged by performance, questions arise as to the nature, time, and sufficiency of the performance.

1. The Normal Discharge of Contracts

A contract is usually discharged by the performance of the terms of the agreement. In most cases, the parties perform their promises and the contract ceases to exist or is thereby discharged. A contract is also discharged by the expiration of the time period specified in the contract.[1]

2. Nature of Performance

Performance may be the doing of an act or the making of payment.

(a) TENDER. An offer to perform is known as a **tender**. If performance of the contract requires the doing of an act, the refusal of a tender will discharge the party offering to perform. If performance requires the payment of a debt, however, a tender that is refused does not discharge the debt. It does stop the running of interest and does prevent the collection of court costs if the party is sued, provided the tender is kept open and the money is produced in court.

A valid **tender of payment** consists of an unconditional offer of the exact amount due on the date when due. A tender of payment is not just an expression of willingness to pay; it must be an actual offer to perform by making payment of the amount owed. The debtor must offer **legal tender** or, in other words, such form of money as the law recognizes as lawful money and declares to be legal tender for the payment of debts. The offer of a check is not a valid tender of payment, since a check is not legal tender (even when it is certified). A tender of part of the debt is not a valid tender. In addition to the amount owed, the debtor must tender all accrued interest and any costs to which the creditor is entitled. If the debtor tenders less than the amount due, the creditor may refuse the offer without affecting the right to collect the amount that is due. If the creditor accepts the smaller amount, the question arises as to whether it has been accepted as payment on account or as full payment of the balance that was due.

(b) PAYMENT. When payment is required by the contract, performance consists of the payment of money or, if accepted by the other party, the delivery of property or the rendering of services.

(1) Application of Payments. If a debtor owes more than one debt to the creditor and pays money, a question may arise as to which debt has been paid. If the debtor specifies the debt to which the payment is to be applied and the creditor accepts the money, the creditor is bound to apply the money as specified.[2] Thus, if the debtor specifies that a payment is to be made for a current purchase, the creditor may not apply the payment to an older balance.

(2) Payment by Check. Payment by commercial paper, such as a check, is ordinarily a conditional payment. A check merely suspends the debt until the check is presented for payment. If payment is then made, the debt is discharged; if not paid, the suspension terminates and suit may be brought on either the

---

[1]   Washington Nat. Ins. Co. v Sherwood Associates (Utah App) 795 P2d 665 (1990).

[2]   Oakes Logging, Inc. v Green Crow, Inc. ___ Wash App ___, 832 P2d 894 (1992).

debt or the check. Frequently, payment must be made by a specified date. It is generally held that the payment is made on time if it is mailed on or before the final date for payment.

3. Time of Performance

When the date or period of time for performance is specified in the contract, performance should be made on that date or within that time period.

(a) NO TIME SPECIFIED. When the time for performance is not specified in the contract, an obligation to perform within a reasonable time will be implied. The fact that no time is stated neither impairs the contract on the ground that it is indefinite, nor allows an endless time in which to perform.

(b) WHEN TIME IS ESSENTIAL. If performance of the contract on or within the exact time specified is vital, it is said that "time is of the essence." Time is of the essence when the contract relates to property that is perishable or that is fluctuating rapidly in value.

An express statement in the contract that time is of the essence may not be controlling. When it is obvious that time is not important, such a statement will be ignored by the courts. It is the nature of the subject matter of the contract and the surrounding circumstances, rather than the declaration of the parties, that control.[3]

(c) WHEN TIME IS NOT ESSENTIAL. Ordinarily, time is not of the essence, and performance within a reasonable time is sufficient. In the case of the sale of property, time will not be regarded as of the essence when there has not been any appreciable change in the market value or condition of the property and when the person who delayed does not appear to have done so for the purpose of speculating on a change in market price.

4. Adequacy of Performance

When a party renders exactly the performance called for by the contract, no question arises as to whether the contract has been performed. In other cases, there may not have been a perfect performance, or a question arises as to whether the performance made satisfies the standard set by the contract.

(a) SUBSTANTIAL PERFORMANCE. Perfect performance of a contract is not always required. A party who in good faith has substantially performed the contract may sue to recover the payment specified in the contract. However, because the performance was not perfect, the performing party is subject to a counterclaim for the damages caused the other party. When a building contractor has substantially performed the contract to construct a building, the measure of damages is the cost of repairing or correcting the defects if that can be done at a reasonable cost.[4] If, however, the cost would be unreasonably disproportionate to the importance of the defect, such as when a virtual rebuilding of the finished building would be required to make a minor correction, the measure of damages is the difference between the value of the building as completed and the value that the building would have had if the contract had been performed perfectly.

This rule of substantial performance applies only when departures from the contract or the defects were not made willfully. A contractor who willfully makes a substantial departure from the contract is in default and cannot recover any payment from the other party to the contract. In large construction contracts, when the total value of the partial performance is large compared to the damages sustained through incomplete or imperfect performance, the courts tend to ignore whether or not the breach was intentional.

---

[3]   O & M Construction, Inc. v Louisiana (La App) 576 So 2d 1030 (1991).

[4]   Salard v Jim Walter Homes, Inc. (La App) 563 So 2d 1327 (1990).

(1) What Constitutes Substantial Performance. There is no exact standard or test by which to determine whether a performance is substantial. A performance cannot be regarded as substantial if what has been done is of no use to the defendant. Thus, when a contractor failed to follow specifications for the construction of a swimming pool and the result was a pool that was so cracked that it would not hold water, the work of the contractor was not of any use to the other party. Therefore, the contractor could not recover on the ground of substantial performance. The performance of a road contractor was not substantial when the deviations from the contract specifications made the road significantly less durable than it would have been had the specifications been followed.[5]

The *Beeson* case raised the question of when is performance substantial.

J.M. BEESON CO. v SARTORI
(Fla App) 553 So 2d 180 (1989)

The Beeson Company made a contract to construct a shopping center for Sartori. Before the work was fully completed, Sartori stopped making the payments to Beeson that were required by the contract. Beeson then stopped working and sued Sartori for the balance due under the contract, just as though it had been fully performed. Sartori defended on the ground that Beeson had not "substantially completed" the work, as that term was defined in the contract. Beeson proved that Sartori had been able to rent most of the stores in the center. Judgment was entered in favor of Sartori, and Beeson appealed.

WARNER, J. . . . Appellant contends that the trial court erred in finding that he did not substantially complete the work. In this case the contract provided that "substantial" completion occurred when "construction is sufficiently complete in accordance with the Contract Documents, so the owner can occupy or utilize the work or designated portion thereof for the use for which it is intended." The "work" under the contract "comprises the completed construction required by the contract documents." Under the contract in this case the work consisted of "construction and completion of a Shopping Center", including all of its component parts such as landscaping and paving. . . .

We agree with appellant's contention that the contractual definition of substantial completion in this case is similar to the well established doctrine of substantial performance, and the terms are interchangeable. . . .

Substantial performance is that performance of a contract which, while not full performance, is so nearly equivalent to what was bargained for that it would be unreasonable to deny the promisee the full contract price subject to the promisor's right to recover whatever damages have been occasioned him by the promisee's failure to render full performance. See 3A *Corbin on Contracts*, Section 702 et seq.

To say that substantial performance is performance which is nearly equivalent to what was bargained for, as the case law defines the term, in essence means that the

---

5 County Asphalt Paving Co., Inc. v 1861 Group, Ltd. (Mo App) 851 SW2d 577 (1993).

owner can use the property for the use for which it is intended. Furthermore, in defining substantial performance, one of the tests as enunciated by Corbin is the "degree of frustration of purpose":

Extremely important factors in solving the present problem [of what is substantial performance] are the character of the performance that the plaintiff promised to render, the purposes and end that it was expected to serve in behalf of the defendant, and the extent to which the nonperformance by the plaintiff has defeated those purposes and ends, or would defeat them if the errors and omissions are corrected.

Corbin on Contracts, 3-A, Section 706. Thus, substantial completion as defined in the contract is the equivalent of substantial performance under the case law and authorities hereinbefore cited.

In the instant case . . . the owner was capable of having tenants occupy the spaces and collecting rents thereon, and he was already collecting substantial rents on many of the tenant spaces. . . .

When the owner was able to occupy . . . the constructed space, the construction was substantially completed. . . . At that point, the appellant was entitled to his full contract price, less the cost to complete.

[Judgment reversed and action remanded]

QUESTIONS

1. How does the court distinguish "substantial completion" from "substantial performance"?
2. What is the characteristic of a performance that is substantial?
3. Assume that a contractor makes a contract to build a house, digs a foundation, and then quits work. Has there been a substantial performance of the contract?

(2) Limitations to Substantial Performance Doctrine. The doctrine of substantial performance will not be applied when the contract makes it clear that a literal and exact compliance is required.[6]

The doctrine of substantial performance does not apply to a condition precedent. Consequently, a lender, obligated to lend a specified amount for the purchase and renovation of an office building, was excused from making such loan when the duty to lend was subject to a condition precedent that a specific number of office space leases had to be signed, but the required number was not obtained. The borrower's claim that the substantial performance rule should be applied to hold that there was a sufficient compliance with the rental condition was rejected.

(b) SATISFACTION OF PROMISEE OR THIRD PERSON. Sometimes an agreement requires that the promisor perform an act to the satisfaction, taste, or judgment of the other party to the contract. The courts are divided as to whether the promisor must so perform the contract as to satisfy the promisee or whether it is sufficient that the performance be such as would satisfy a reasonable person under the circumstances. When personal taste is an important element, the courts generally hold that

---

6   Coastal Seafood Co., Inc. v Alcoa South Carolina, Inc. (SC App) 381 SE2d 502 (1989).

the performance is not sufficient unless the promisee is actually satisfied. In some instances, though, it is insisted on that the dissatisfaction be shown to be in good faith and not merely to avoid paying for the work that has been done. The personal satisfaction of the promisee is generally required under this rule when one promises to make clothes or to paint a portrait to the satisfaction of the other party.

There is a similar division of authority when the subject matter involves the fitness or mechanical utility of property. With respect to things mechanical and to routine performances, however, the courts are more likely to hold that the promisor has satisfactorily performed if a reasonable person should be satisfied with what was done.[7]

When a building contract requires the contractor to perform the contract to the "satisfac-tion" of the owner, the owner generally is required to pay if a reasonable person would be satisfied with the work of the contractor.

When performance is to be approved by a third person, the tendency is to apply the reasonable-person test of satisfaction. This is true especially when the third person has wrongfully withheld approval or has become incapacitated. When work is to be done subject to the approval of an architect, engineer, or other expert, the determination of that expert is ordinarily final and binding on the parties in the absence of fraud.

The *Forman* case raised the question of whether a seller should have been satisfied with the report as to the buyer's credit.

FORMAN v BENSON
112 Ill App 3d 1070, 68 Ill Dec 629, 446 NE2d 535 (1983)

Art Benson owned a tract of land. Eric Forman wanted to buy the land and to pay for it in ten annual installments. Benson was at first unwilling to extend such long credit but agreed to do so if the buyer agreed to include in the contract a provision "subject to the seller's approving buyer's credit report." The buyer agreed to this, and the provision was included in the contract. When the credit report was given to Benson, he stated that it "looked real good" and that he would give it to his attorney to examine. Thereafter Benson tried to get Forman to pay more for the land than stated in the contract. Forman refused to agree to the higher price. Benson then stated that he did not approve the credit report because Forman's liabilities were slightly more than four times his liquid assets. Forman sued to enforce the contract. From a decision in Forman's favor, Benson appealed.

HOPF, J. . . . We have discovered no case dealing with the interpretation of the specific clause in question. However, there is some Illinois case law regarding the interpretation of "satisfaction" clauses in general. In *Reeves & Co. v Chandler* (1903), 113 Ill App 167, 170, the court found that satisfaction clauses generally fall into one of two classes. In one class, the decision as to whether a party is satisfied is completely reserved to the party for whose benefit the clause is inserted, and the reasons for his decision may not be inquired into and overhauled by either the other party or the

---

[7] Cranetex, Inc. v Precision Crane & Rigging of Houston, Inc. (Tex App) 760 SW2d 298 (1988).

courts. Cases falling into this class generally involve matters which are dependent upon the feelings, taste, or judgment of the party making the decision. The second class of cases are those in which the party to be satisfied is to base his determination on grounds which are just and reasonable. These cases generally involve matters which are capable of objective evaluation, or which involve considerations of operative fitness or mechanical utility. Matters of financial concern generally fall into this second category of cases. The adequacy of the grounds of a determination in this class are open to judicial scrutiny and are judged by a reasonable man standard.

However, the *Reeves* case also made it clear that the parties may agree to a reservation in one party of the absolute and unqualified freedom of choice on a matter not involving fancy, taste, or whim. . . .

It is apparent that under *Reeves* the fact that the clause was added as a concession or inducement to one of the parties is significant in determining whether the reasonableness standard should be applied. . . .

It seems clear from [other] cases that a reasonableness standard is favored by the law when the contract concerns matters capable of objective evaluation. However, where the circumstances are such that it is clear the provision was added as a personal concession to one of the contracting parties, the subjective, rather than the objective standard, should be applied.

In the present case, it is uncontroverted that the clause in question was inserted as a concession to the defendant and as an inducement to him to sign the contract, which he subsequently did. Ken Burnell testified that the addition of the provision indeed eased defendant's mind about the plaintiff's credit worthiness. In light of the fact that the relationship between the parties was to endure over a ten-year period of time, we think it is a reasonable construction of the provision that it was intended to allow defendant the freedom of making a personal and subjective evaluation of plaintiff's credit worthiness. . . .

The personal judgment standard, however, does not allow the defendant to exercise unbridled discretion in rejecting plaintiff's credit, but rather is subject to the requirement of good faith. . . . In the instant case the trial court made no specific finding whether defendant Benson rejected plaintiff's credit in good faith. However, the trial court did find that between the time the contract was executed and the time the offer was rejected, defendant attempted to renegotiate the purchase price of the building as well as the interest rate. . . . Both plaintiff and defendant testified that an increased purchase price was discussed. . . . While defendant may have had a basis in his personal judgment for rejecting plaintiff's credit (*i.e.*, outstanding debts and a $2,000 loss reflected in an income tax return), his attempted renegotiation demonstrates that his rejection was based on reasons other than plaintiff's credit rating and was, therefore, in bad faith. . . .

[Judgment affirmed]

QUESTIONS

1. Did the contract specify that the credit report had to be satisfactory to the seller?
2. A satisfaction clause is governed by the objective standard. Comment on this statement and explain your answer.
3. What was the significance of the seller's seeking a higher price?

5. Guarantee of Performance

It is common for an obligor to guarantee the performance. Thus, a builder may guarantee for one year that the work will be satisfactory. The guarantee may be made by a third person. Thus, a surety company may guarantee to the owner that a contractor will perform the contract. In this case, it is clear that the obligation of the surety is in addition to the liability of the contractor and does not take the place of such liability.

6. Discharge by Unilateral Action

Ordinarily, a contract cannot be discharged by the action of either party alone. In some cases, the contract will give one or either party the right to cancel the contract by unilateral action, such as by notice to the other party. If the contract does not specify any duration, or it states a duration in such vague terms as "for life," the contract may be terminated by either party at will.

Figure 17-1   Causes of Contract Discharge

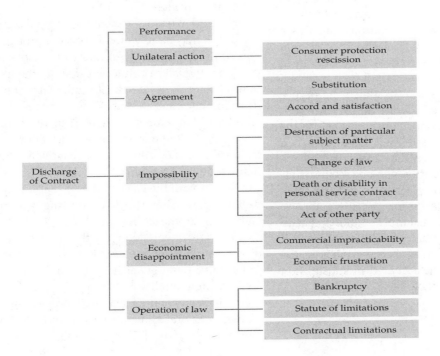

B. DISCHARGE BY ACTION OF PARTIES

Contracts may be discharged by the joint action of both contracting parties or, in some cases, by the action of one party alone.

(a) CONSUMER PROTECTION RESCISSION. A basic principle of contract law is that a contract between competent persons is a binding obligation. Consumer protection legislation is introducing into the law a contrary concept—that of giving the consumer a chance to think things over and to rescind the contract. Thus, the federal Consumer Credit

Protection Act (CCPA) gives the debtor the right to rescind a credit transaction within three business days when the transaction would impose a lien on the debtor's home. A homeowner who mortgages the home to obtain a loan may cancel the transaction for any reason by notifying the lender before midnight of the third full business day after the loan is made.[8]

A Federal Trade Commission regulation gives the buyer three business days in which to cancel a home-solicited sale of goods or services costing more than $25.[9]

7. Discharge by Agreement

A contract may be discharged by the operation of one of its provisions or by a subsequent agreement. Thus, there may be a discharge by (a) terms of the original contract, such as a provision that the contract should end on a specified date; (b) a mutual cancellation, in which the parties agree to end their contract; (c) a mutual **rescission**, in which the parties agree to annul the contract and return both parties to their original positions before the contract had been made;[10] (d) substitution of a new contract between the same parties; (e) a **novation** or substitution of a new contract involving a new party;[11] (f) an accord and satisfaction; (g) a release; or (h) a waiver. To constitute a novation, it must be shown that an obligor to the original contract was released from liability, and that the new party to the second contract was accepted in substitution for the original obligor.[12]

(a) SUBSTITUTION. The parties may decide that their contract is not the one they want. They may then replace it with another contract. If they do so, the original contract is discharged by substitution.[13]

It is not necessary for the parties to state expressly that they are making a substitution. Whenever they make a new contract that is clearly inconsistent with a former contract, the court will conclude that the earlier contract has been superseded by the later. Since the new contract must in itself be a binding agreement, it must be supported by consideration. Any suit brought thereafter must show a breach of the second or subsequent contract.

The fact that a second contract is entered into does not establish that the original contract is canceled. The later contract may merely add to or supplement the original contract, or it may merely modify part of the original contract. For the later contract to displace the first, the later contract must show the intent of the parties to substitute the later contract for the earlier contract. This intent may be shown by an express statement in the later contract that the parties thereby cancel or set aside the earlier contract. Alternatively, the later contract may be so complete and so inconsistent with the earlier writing that the intent is clear that the later writing was a substitute for the earlier one.[14]

The agreement modifying the original contract may be expressed in words or by conduct, but in any event it is essential that an agreement to modify be found.

A written contract may be modified by a subsequent oral agreement, even though the contract itself prohibits oral modification.

---

[8] If the owner is not informed of this right to cancel, the three-day period does not begin until that information is given. In any case, however, the right to cancel is lost if the owner sells the house or three years elapse after the loan transaction. Consumer Credit Protection Act (CCPA) § 125, 15 USC § 1635 (a), (e), (f).

[9] 16 CFR § 429.1. This displaces state laws making similar provision for rescission, such as UCCC § 2.502

[10] Agri Careers, Inc. v Jepsen (Iowa App) 463 NW2d 93 (1990).

[11] Wilson v Midstate Industries, Inc. (Mo App) 777 SW2d 310 (1989). In a few jurisdictions, the term *novation* is used to embrace the substitution of any new contract, whether between the original parties or not.

[12] Oaksmith v Brushich (Alaska) 774 P2d 191 (1989).

[13] Shawnee Hospital Authority v Dow Construction, Inc. (Okla) 812 P2d 1351 (1990).

[14] W. R. Millar Co. v UCM Corp. (Minn App) 419 NW2d 852 (1988).

However, the modification contract must be evidenced by a writing when the modified contract comes within the statute of frauds.

(b) ACCORD AND SATISFACTION. In lieu of the performance of an obligation specified by a contract, the parties may agree to a different performance. Such an agreement is called an **accord**. When the accord is performed or executed, there is an **accord and satisfaction**, which discharges the original obligation. To constitute an accord and satisfaction, there must be a bona fide dispute, an agreement to settle the dispute, and performance of the agreement. To constitute a bona fide dispute, the parties must assert their respective positions in good faith.[15] If one of the parties to the accord and satisfaction owes a fiduciary duty to the other party, such as an attorney to a client, there must be a full disclosure of all material facts by the party under the fiduciary duty.

The accord that is the basis for the accord and satisfaction must be a binding agreement—that is, a contract. It must therefore meet the basic requirements of a simple contract. If it is not a contract (for example, if it is not supported by consideration), there is no binding accord, and the prior contract is not discharged. The making of an accord does not by itself discharge the prior contract. It is not until the terms of the accord are carried out that there is a discharge of the earlier contract.[16]

C. DISCHARGE BY EXTERNAL CAUSES

Circumstances beyond the control of the contracting parties may discharge the contract.

8. Discharge by Impossibility

Impossibility of performance refers to external or extrinsic conditions. This is contrasted with the obligor's personal inability to perform.[17] Thus, the fact that a debtor does not have the money to pay and cannot pay a debt does not present a case of impossibility.

Riots, shortages of materials, and similar factors, even though external, usually do not excuse the promisor from performing a contract. A seller may have contracted to sell goods to a buyer. The fact that the seller cannot obtain these goods from any supplier does not excuse the seller from liability to the buyer, unless the inability to procure the goods was made a condition subsequent to the sales contract. Thus, the fact that the road contractor's contemplated gravel source cannot be used (and it is necessary to transport gravel from a more distant source, making performance more costly) does not discharge the contractor from the obligation to construct a road. If there is nothing in the contract requiring that the gravel be obtained from the unavailable source, no question of impossibility of performance exists. A contract is not discharged merely because performance proves to be more burdensome than was originally contemplated.[18]

The fact that it will prove more costly to perform the contract than originally contemplated, or that the obligor has voluntarily gone out of business, does not constitute impossibility that excuses performance. No distinction is made in this connection between the acts of nature, people, or governments. For example, the adoption of a new government regulation made performance more costly. The contract was not discharged when the regulation was reasonably foreseeable because it was common in many parts of the country.[19]

---

[15] Utah v Robinson (Utah App) 797 P2d 431 (1990).

[16] Chesak v Northern Indiana Bank and Trust Co. (Ind App) 551 NE2d 873 (1990).

[17] Haessly v Safeco Title Ins. Co. (Idaho) 825 P2d 1119 (1992).

[18] Stasyszyn v Sutton East Associates, ___ App Div 2d ___, 555 NYS2d 297 (1990).

[19] Huffines v Swor Sand & Gravel Co., Inc. (Tex App) 750 SW2d 38 (1988).

(a) DESTRUCTION OF PARTICULAR SUBJECT MATTER. When parties contract expressly for or with reference to a particular subject matter, the contract is discharged if the subject matter is destroyed through no fault of either party.

When a contract calls for the sale of a wheat crop growing on a specific parcel of land, the contract is discharged if that crop is destroyed by blight.

On the other hand, if there is merely a contract to sell a given quantity of a specified grade of wheat, the seller is not discharged when the seller's crop is destroyed by blight. The seller had made an unqualified undertaking to deliver wheat of a specified grade. No restrictions or qualifications were imposed as to the source. If the seller does not deliver the goods called for by the contract, the contract is broken, and the seller is liable for damages.

The parties may by their contract allocate the risk of loss. Thus, a contract for the sale of a building and land may specify that any loss from damage to the building should be borne by the seller.

(b) CHANGE OF LAW. A contract is discharged when its performance is made illegal by a subsequent change in the law. Thus, a contract to construct a non fireproof building at a particular place is discharged by the adoption of a zoning law prohibiting such a building within that area. Mere inconvenience or temporary delay caused by the new law, however, does not excuse performance. Similarly, a change of law that merely increases the cost to the promisor is not a "change of law" that discharges the contract. There is authority that the deregulating of an industry is not a change of law that discharges a contract entered into on the assumption of continuing regulation.

In the *N.C. Coastal Motor Line* case a buyer refused to make payments because of the effect of government deregulation of the trucking business.

N.C. COASTAL MOTOR LINE, INC. v EVERETTE TRUCK LINE, INC.

77 NC App 149, 334 SE2d 499 (1985)

N.C. Coastal Motor Line was authorized by the Interstate Commerce Commission (ICC) to engage in interstate trucking operations. Coastal made a contract to sell this authority to Everette Truck Line. Payment was to be made in eight annual installments. At the time of making the contract, it was unlawful to engage in interstate trucking without ICC authority. Everette made four annual payments. The trucking industry was then deregulated, and the authority of the ICC was no longer required to engage in interstate trucking. Everette refused to make any more payments on the ground that what it was paying for was worthless. Coastal sued Everette. Judgment was entered for Everette, and Coastal appealed.

JOHNSON, J. . . . Everette admits the signing of the contract, validity of the contract, and the sale price, which are the essential terms of any instrument. . . . Under section nine (9) entitled, SELLER'S WARRANTIES, it states in subsection (a) "There are *no proceedings pending* which adversely affect the operating rights proposed to be transferred." (Emphasis added.) Everette now argues that government deregulations in 1980, three years after the contract was entered into, rendered plaintiff's operating rights worthless, and thus breaches an "express but implied warranty" of permanent economic value. We find nothing . . . which gives rise to such an implied warranty. . . . Everette's attorney drafted the terms of the agreement whereby Coastal's warranty was expressly limited to no *pending* actions or proceedings which would affect the operating rights purchased by Everette. . . .

Everette . . . raised lack of consideration as an affirmative defense. . . . At the time of purchase Coastal's operating rights were as represented, a valuable set of rights which Everette could not have otherwise acquired. Everette is without a legal defense to Coastal's claim.

[Judgment reversed and action remanded]

QUESTIONS

1. When the trucking industry was deregulated there was a change of law. What effect did that have on the contract of the parties? Explain.
2. What defenses were raised by the defendant?
3. How did the court dispose of the defenses of the defendant?

(c) DEATH OR DISABILITY. When the contract obligates a party to perform an act that requires personal skill or that contemplates a personal relationship with the obligee or some other person, the death or disability of the obligor, obligee, or other person (as the case may be) discharges the contract.[20] For example, the death of a newspaper cartoonist before the expiration of the contract discharges the contract. If the act called for by the contract can be performed by others or by the promisor's personal representative, however, the contract is not discharged.

The death of a person to whom personal services are to be rendered also terminates the contract when the death of that person makes impossible the rendition of the services contemplated. Thus, a contract to employ a person as the musical director for a singer terminates when the singer dies.

When the contract calls for the payment of money, the death of either party does not affect the obligation. If the obligor dies, the obligation is a liability of the obligor's estate. If the obligee dies, the right to collect the debt is an asset of the obligee's estate. The parties to a contract may agree, however, that the death of either the obligee or the obligor shall terminate the debt. In any case, the creditor can obtain insurance on the life of the debtor.

In the *Shutt* case it was claimed by the ex-husband that the agreement with his ex-wife to sell their home was discharged by her death.

SHUTT v BUTNER
62 NC App 701, 303 SE2d 399 (1983)

When Jean and Jerry Butner were divorced, their property settlement and divorce decree specified that when their son no longer needed their home, the

---

[20] Cazares v Saenz, 208 Cal App 3d 279, 256 Cal Rptr 209 (1989).

home would be sold and the proceeds divided equally between Jean and Jerry. Jean died and Marie Shutt, her mother, was appointed her executrix. In a lawsuit between Shutt and Jerry, the court refused to order the sale of the home. Shutt appealed.

PHILLIPS, J. . . . The trial court erred in denying the plaintiff's motion for the sale of the marital homeplace. Though the defendant did become the . . . fee simple owner of the entirety held realty by operation of law upon the death of his wife, . . . he became so subject to his promise and agreement as follows:

(8) It is agreed that the wife shall have complete possession of the homeplace of the parties until the minor child TIMOTHY EUGENE BUTNER attains the age of 18 years or until the child respectively dies, marries, or is otherwise emancipated, at which time the homeplace of the parties will be sold and the proceeds will be divided equally among the parties. It is further agreed that the wife shall make monthly payments on the homeplace . . . and that the husband shall reimburse to the wife the amount by which her monthly mortgage payments have reduced the principal on the mortgage.

. . . The agreement here requires little or no construction, only enforcement. The parties' obligation to sell the property and divide the proceeds was explicit and without ambiguity; nor was it contingent upon either party being alive when the time to sell came . . . . The agreement to sell and divide was absolute and unequivocal; only the time was uncertain and that was clearly ascertainable from the terms used—no later than the boy's eighteenth birthday, then less than two years away, and sooner than that if the boy married, was otherwise emancipated, died, or stopped living there. Though the latter eventuality was not expressly provided for in the agreement as the others were, it is impliable from the obvious fact that the parties delayed the sale as they did only so that the boy could dwell there rent-free until his legally dependent status ended. Therefore, upon his ceasing to live there after his mother died, the reason for delaying the sale vanished, and the parties were obligated to go ahead with the sale if either so requested. . . . The son's eighteenth birthday has passed, and the property must be sold now . . . .

Nor were the defendant's obligations under the contract terminated by the death of the other contracting party. Few contracts are terminated by death in the absence of explicit provisions therein to the contrary. This is because all know that unexpected and untimely death is a constant possibility and are deemed to make their contracts in light thereof, and also because most contracts can be satisfactorily performed by personal representatives. The general rule is that "contracts bind the executor or administrator, though not named therein, and that death does not absolve a man from his engagements.". . . But in this instance it is unnecessary to resort to the general rule, because the parties themselves, leaving nothing to chance or the law's operation, had their agreement to provide that:

. . . this . . . shall be enforceable against the parties, their personal representatives, heirs and assigns.

Having so contracted, the defendant is bound thereby.

It is true, of course, for obvious reasons, that contracts of a personal nature or that require special talent—to marry, to draw a picture, write a book, perform on the stage, be one's companion, etc.—do come to an end upon the death of a party, unless the parties agree otherwise. . . . But selling a house and lot and dividing the proceeds does not depend upon talent or personality and the defendant's obligation with respect thereto still abides. . . .

[Judgment reversed]

QUESTIONS

1. How did the court classify the contract to sell the house?
2. Suppose that a contract is made between a real estate agent and the owner of an apartment house complex for the agent to sell the property. The agent dies before the sale is made. What effect does the death have on the contract?
3. As the ex-wife is no longer alive to receive one half of the proceeds from the sale of the property, the agreement to sell and divide the proceeds had failed; therefore, there was no reason to go through with the transaction. Appraise this statement and argument.

(d) ACT OF OTHER PARTY. Every contract contains "an implied covenant of good faith and fair dealing." As a result of this covenant, a promisee is under an obligation to do nothing that would interfere with performance by the promisor. When the promisee prevents performance or otherwise makes performance impossible, the promisor is discharged from the contract. Thus, a subcontractor is discharged from any obligation when unable to do the work because the principal contractor refuses to deliver the material, equipment, or money required by the subcontract. When the default of the other party consists of failing to supply goods or services, the duty may rest on the party claiming a discharge of the contract to show that substitute goods or services could not be obtained elsewhere.

When the conduct of the other contracting party does not make performance impossible but merely causes delay or renders performance more expensive or difficult, the contract is not discharged. The injured party is, however, entitled to damages for the loss incurred.

A promisor is not excused from performing under the contract when it is the act of the promisor that has made performance impossible. Consequently, when a data service contracted with a bank to process the records of its daily operations, the bank was not excused from its obligation under the contract by the fact that it installed its own computers. The bank could not ignore its contract. It could only terminate the contract with the data service by giving the notice required by the contract.

9. Economic Disappointment

The fact that the contract proves to be a bad bargain does not discharge the contract.[21] Some courts hold that a contract is discharged when, because of a change of circumstances, the performance of the contract has become such an
economic disappointment that it would be unjust and oppressive to insist on performance.

(a) COMMERCIAL IMPRACTICABILITY. At times, the cost of performance rises suddenly and so greatly that performance of the contract will result in a substantial loss. In this case, some courts hold that the contract is discharged because it is **commercially impracticable**

---

[21] Young v Tate, 232 Neb 915, 442 NW2d 865 (1989).

to perform. Although it is possible to perform, it has become such a bad bargain that the courts will not enforce it.

When subsequent developments prove to be different than was assumed by the parties, there is a growing trend to find that there is an impossibility that discharges the contract. This doctrine is described as the doctrine of **supervening impracticability**.

After a contract is made, it may happen that a party's performance is made impracticable by the occurrence of an event, the nonoccurrence of which was the basic assumption on which the contract was made. In such a case, the duty to render that performance is discharged, unless the language or the circumstances indicate the contrary.[22]

(b) ECONOMIC FRUSTRATION. Because of a change of circumstance, the performance of the contract may have no value to the party entitled to receive performance. Some courts sympathize with the disappointed person and hold that the contract is discharged by economic or commercial frustration, or frustration of purpose.

(c) THE MAJORITY RULE COMPARED. The majority or traditional common law rule refuses to recognize commercial impracticability or economic frustration. By the common law rule, the losses and disappointments against which commercial impracticability and economic frustration give protection are merely the risks that one takes in entering into a contract. Moreover, the situations could have been guarded against by including an appropriate condition subsequent in the contract. A condition subsequent declares that the contract will be void if a specified event occurs. Or the contract could have provided for a read-

justment of compensation if there was a basic change of circumstances. The common law approach also rejects these two new concepts because they weaken the stability of a contract. The net result of these new concepts is that a contract ceases to be binding when there is a significant change in circumstances. That is, when a contract is most needed to give stability, the courts by these new concepts hold that there is no contract.

The common law rule is also opposed to the new concepts because they raise questions of measurement of matters that cannot be measured. How much change is needed in order to make a change "significant"?

In spite of the logical and practical objections to the new doctrines, it is likely that they will be given greater recognition by the courts in the future. The expanded recognition of the doctrine of unconscionability is developing a pattern of the judicial monitoring of contracts to prevent injustice. Further indication of a wider recognition of the concept that "extreme" change of circumstances can discharge a contract is found in the Uniform Commercial Code. The UCC provides for the discharge of a contract for the sale of goods when a condition that the parties assumed existed, or would continue, ceases to exist.[23]

If a contract clearly places on one of the parties a particular risk, the contract is not discharged when that risk is realized and loss is sustained. Neither the concept of commercial impracticability nor economic frustration will be applied to cancel out provisions of a contract that allocate risk.

In the *Agosta* case it was claimed that economic frustration discharged a contract for the sale of stock of a corporation when the corporation went out of business.

---

[22] Restatement (2d) of Contracts, § 261.

[23] UCC § 2-615.

RE AGOSTA
122 Misc 2d 1091, 472 NYS2d 538 (1983)

John Agosta and his brother Salvatore each owned one half of the stock of Fontana D'Oro, Inc. The corporate business was the storing and wholesaling of food materials used in the pizza trade. The major asset was the warehouse where the corporation stored the food materials. Because of disputes, an action was brought to end the business. The action was settled by Salvatore's agreeing to sell his stock to John for $505,000. Shortly thereafter, a fire destroyed the warehouse, and the business had to shut down. John refused to go through with the settlement, and Salvatore brought an action for specific performance to compel him to perform his contract.

GOLDBERG, J. . . . This decision presents a novel question in this jurisdiction; whether an agreement for the sale of stock in a business corporation may be set aside when the underlying purpose of the sale is frustrated by unforeseeable circumstances. . . .

Concededly, the value of the stock has declined as a result of the fire. However, John could not be heard to complain on this account because of the well-known commercial policy which prevents one who has contracted to purchase securities from avoiding his obligation by reason of a decline, even a severe one, in the value of what he has agreed to buy. Additionally, the doctrine of impossibility of performance is inapplicable to the case at bar. In general, impossibility of performance may be equated with an inability to perform as promised due to intervening events, such as an act of state or destruction of the subject matter of the contract. When performance depends on the continued existence of a thing, and such continued existence was assumed as the basis of the agreement, the destruction of the thing puts an end to the obligation. Here, the subject matter, the shares of stock in the corporation, were not destroyed. The shares of stock are presently capable of being transferred. . . .

However, to consider the [settlement agreement] as merely a contract for the transfer of corporate stock as it might appear on its face would be to focus on one aspect of the agreement and to ignore the real intent of the parties. It would ignore the very context in which the agreement was entered into. It was contemplated that Fontana D'Oro Foods, Inc. would continue as a going business enterprise, changing merely from a company jointly owned and operated by John and Salvatore to one owned and operated by John alone. Transfer of the securities was a coincidental formality.

Analysis of the [settlement agreement] as a whole clearly demonstrates the accuracy of the foregoing conclusion. . . . It is clear that both parties were treating the underlying corporate assets and liabilities and, indeed, the operation of the corporation itself, as their own personal property and obligations and that the terminology of the [agreement] classifying the transaction as one for the sale of stock was an unfortunate misnomer not representing the true intent of the parties. While transfer of the corporate securities was most certainly contemplated it was but a minor ministerial act when viewed in the overall context of the transaction. . . .

To view this agreement as simply one for the sale of stock and not as one for the sale of a going business would be to exalt form over substance.

The Court now turns to the question of whether a supervening event has occurred of the type necessary to excuse non-performance.

Frustration of purpose is a corollary of the defense of impossibility of performance. . . .

In modern legal parlance, frustration of purpose refers to a situation where an unforeseen event has occurred, which, in the context of the entire transaction, destroys the underlying reasons for performing the contract, even though performance is possible, thus operating to discharge a party's duties of performance. . . .

We are faced with just such a set of circumstances in the instant case. As a result of the fire, performance by Salvatore Agosta would no longer give John Agosta a going business, which is what induced John Agosta to enter into the contract. Although some parts of the business still exist, for all practical purposes that business has been destroyed by the fire. As a result of that fire, the purpose of the contract has been frustrated since there is no longer a functioning business to purchase.

In order to succeed under the doctrine of frustration of purpose, the supervening event must be one which was not foreseeable by the parties. That the parties anticipated the possibility that a fire could destroy their warehouse and inventory is not in doubt. Both must have known, through their involvement in the company's affairs, of insurance coverage on these assets, as well as the existence of a policy covering business interruption. What could not have been foreseen, was the possibility (which has matured into a fact) that the insurance carrier would withhold payment of the corporation's claim based upon its arson investigation. Counsel has advised the Court that the present status of that investigation is not known, but it is not likely that the company will receive compensation for its losses in the foreseeable future, if at all. It is conceivable that the company will recover nothing, and also possible that due to the extended interruption in the company's operations, it may be difficult or impossible for the company ever to resume business, even if the insurance claim is paid in full.

When viewing the stipulation as one for the conveyance of an interest in an operating business it becomes apparent that this purpose has been frustrated by subsequent events that neither side could have reasonably anticipated.

The commercial policy which prevents a contract vendee of corporate stock from escaping his obligation to complete the purchase despite a diminution in value between the time of contract and the time of closing clearly applies when dealing with publicly traded securities or stock purchased primarily for investment purposes. Where, as here, the purpose of the contract to buy or sell corporate stock is to convey control of a functioning business, the Court has the equitable power to set aside the purchase agreement when the purpose has been frustrated by unforeseeable circumstances.

[Motion for specific performance denied]

[The *Agosta* case was appealed several times and was reversed. *Re Fontana D'Oro*, 65 NY2d 886, 493 NY2d 300, 428 NE2d 1216 (1985). The following memorandum opinion was filed by the court of last resort:]

While the Appellate Division properly directed specific performance, both lower courts erroneously disregarded the form of the transaction—which was a stock transfer—and treated the transaction instead as a sale of a business or tangible assets. The well-settled rule is that "ownership of capital stock is by no means identical with or equivalent to ownership of corporate property." We recently reaffirmed this rule in *5303 Realty Corp. v O & Y Equity Corp.*, 64 NY2d 313, 486 NYS2d 877, 476 NE2d 276. . . . We cannot disregard the fact that the parties chose to structure their transaction as one involving stock, or that John agreed to pay $505,000 for Salvatore's stock. Given the form of their transaction, whether the parties might really have intended to transfer control of an ongoing business enterprise, rather than stock, can have no bearing on this conclusion. . . .

Since an agreement to convey stock in a close corporation may be enforced by specific performance, it was within the power of the Appellate Division to award such relief to Salvatore by directing Supreme Court to execute as nominee for John the various documents contemplated by the parties' stipulation.

[Specific performance ordered]

QUESTIONS

1. What social forces are advanced and what defeated by each of the two opinions in the *Agosta* case?
2. Does the appellate court opinion answer the basic question involved?

(d) BAD BARGAIN DISTINGUISHED.

The mere fact that a party to a contract sustained a loss when an expected profit is not realized does not constitute economic frustration. It is immaterial whether the disappointment is caused by the poor way in which the contract was written or by circumstances external to the contract. In the *Rockland* case the plaintiff claimed a discharge from the terms of its obligation because of commercial frustration.

ROCKLAND DEVELOPMENT ASSOCIATES v RICHLOU AUTO BODY, INC
___ App Div 2d ___, 570 NYS2d 343 (1991)

Rockland Development Associates (RDA) rented space to the Richlou Auto Body Shop. Richlou agreed by the lease not to compete with any other tenant in the same building. Shortly thereafter, RDA leased another part of the building to another auto repair shop. The competition of the second shop drove Richlou out of business. Richlou claimed that it was released from its lease contract by virtue of economic frustration. From a decision in favor of RDA, Richlou appealed.

*Authors' Note: This phrase indicates that the entire court felt that the decision was so obvious that it did not think it necessary that any particular judge write a formal opinion and that they all agreed to the "memorandum" or brief statement.

More frequently, such a memorandum opinion will be labeled "per curiam," meaning "by the court."

MEMORANDUM BY THE COURT.* . . . In an action to recover . . . rent, the defendant appeals. . . . The lease provided as follows:

"Tenant agrees not to compete with the services to be offered by other tenants within the two-building complex, to include transmission repairs, muffler installation, tire sales, rust-proofing, fast oil change and lubrication, general engine repairs, tune-up services and related work."

. . . The [lower court] granted the plaintiff's motion. We affirm.

The language of the lease is unmistakably clear. It is the defendant, not the plaintiff, who agreed "not to compete with the services to be offered by the other tenants within the two-building complex." Yet, the defendant seeks to impose a reciprocal obligation on the plaintiff to refrain from leasing any other part of his property to another tenant engaged in the same business. The language of the lease, however, is not reasonably capable of such a construction, and restrictive covenants will not be extended by implication. . . .

The doctrine of frustration of purpose does not apply unless the frustration is substantial. It is not enough that the transaction has become less profitable for the affected party or even that he will sustain a loss. . . . The defendant merely alleges that he has sustained a loss. Thus, the doctrine of frustration of purpose is inapplicable.

[Judgment affirmed]

QUESTIONS

1. Did Richlou sustain a substantial loss?
2. How can you justify the conclusion of the court if you recognize that Richlou's loss was substantial?
3. How could Richlou have protected itself?

10. Temporary Impossibility

Ordinarily, a temporary impossibility has either no effect on the performance obligation of a party, or at most it suspends the duty to perform. If the obligation to perform is suspended, it is revived on the termination of the impossibility. If, however, performance at that later date would impose a substantially greater burden on the obligor, some courts discharge the obligor from the contract.

(a) WEATHER. Acts of God, such as tornadoes, lightning, and floods, usually do not terminate a contract, even though they make performance difficult or impossible. Thus, weather conditions constitute a risk that is assumed by a contracting party in the absence of a contrary agreement. Consequently, extra expense sustained by a contractor because of weather conditions is a risk that the contractor assumes in the absence of an express provision for additional compensation in such a case.

(b) WEATHER CLAUSES. Modern contracts commonly contain a "weather clause." This clause either expressly grants an extension for delays caused by weather conditions or expressly denies the right to any extension of time or additional compensation because of weather condition difficulties. Some courts hold that abnormal weather conditions excuse what would otherwise be a breach of contract. Thus, nondelivery of equipment has been excused when the early melting of a frozen river made it impossible to deliver.

11. Discharge by Operation of Law

A contract is discharged by operation of law by (a) alteration or a material change made by a party, (b) destruction of the written contract with intent to discharge it, (c) bankruptcy, (d) the operation of a statute of limitations, or (e) a contractual limitation.

(a) BANKRUPTCY. Most insolvent debtors may voluntarily enter into a federal court of bankruptcy or be compelled to do so by creditors. The trustee in bankruptcy then takes possession of the debtor's property and distributes it as far as it will go among the creditors. After this is done, the court grants the debtor a discharge in bankruptcy if it concludes that the debtor has acted honestly and has not attempted to defraud creditors. Even though all creditors have not been paid in full, the discharge in bankruptcy discharges ordinary contract claims against the debtor.

(b) STATUTES OF LIMITATIONS. Statutes provide that after a certain number of years have passed, a contract claim is barred. The time limitation provided by state statutes of limitations varies widely. The period usually differs with the type of contract—ranging from a relatively short time for open accounts (ordinary customers' charge accounts) and other sales of goods (4 years),[24] to a somewhat longer period for written contracts (usually 5 to 10 years), to a maximum period for judgments of record (usually 10 to 20 years).

(c) CONTRACTUAL LIMITATIONS. Some contracts, particularly insurance contracts, contain a time limitation within which suit must be brought. This is in effect a private statute of limitations created by the agreement of the parties. A 12-month limitation in an insurance policy for the time for suit is not unconscionable, even though a person obtaining the insurance has virtually no chance of successfully negotiating for a change of the provision.[25]

A contract may also require that notice of any claim be given within a specified time. A party who fails to give notice within the time specified by the contract is barred from suing thereon.

SUMMARY

Most contracts are discharged by performance. An offer to perform is called a tender of performance. If a tender of performance is wrongfully refused, the duty of the tenderer to perform is terminated. If the performance required was the payment of money, the refusal of a proper tender does not discharge the debt. It does, however, prevent the creditor from recovering interest or costs if suit is thereafter brought against the tenderer to recover the amount owed. When the performance called for by the contract is the payment of money, it must be legal tender that is offered. In actual practice it is common to pay and to accept payment by checks or other commercial paper.

When the debtor owes the creditor on several accounts and makes a payment, the debtor may specify which account is to be credited with the payment. If the debtor fails to specify, the creditor may choose which account to credit.

When a contract does not state when it is to be performed, it must be performed within a reasonable time. If time for performance is

[24] UCC § 2-725(1).
[25] Thomas v United Fire and Cas. Co. (Iowa) 426 NW2d 396 (1988).

stated in the contract, the contract must be performed at the time specified if such time is essential (is of the essence). Performance within a reasonable time is sufficient if the specified time is not essential.

Ordinarily, a contract must be performed exactly in the manner specified by the contract. A less than perfect performance is allowed if it is a substantial performance and if damages are allowed the other party. The other contracting party or a third person may guarantee a perfect performance. Such a guarantor is then liable if the performance is less than perfect.

A contract cannot be discharged by unilateral action unless authorized by the contract itself or by statute, as in the case of consumer protection rescission.

As a contract arises from an agreement, it may also be terminated by an agreement. This may be a provision in the original contract or a subsequent agreement to rescind the contract. A contract may also be discharged by substitution of a new contract for the original contract; by a novation, or making a new contract with a new party; by accord and satisfaction; by release; or by waiver.

A contract is discharged when it is impossible to perform. Impossibility may result from the destruction of the subject matter of the contract, the adoption of a new law that prohibits performance, the death or disability of a party whose personal action was required for performance of the contract, or the act of the other party to the contract. Some courts will also hold that a contract is discharged when its performance is commercially impracticable or there is economic frustration. Although increased cost of performance ordinarily has no effect on a contract, if that increase is grossly disproportionate to the original performance cost, some courts will classify the situation as one of commercial impracticability and hold that the contract is discharged. In the case of economic frustration, the contract can be performed, but the performance has ceased to have any significant value to the party who originally contracted to obtain that performance. Temporary impossibility, such as a labor strike or bad weather, has no effect on a contract. It is common, though, to include protective clauses that excuse delay caused by temporary impossibility.

A contract may be discharged by operation of law. This occurs when (1) the liability arising from the contract is discharged by bankruptcy, (2) suit on the contract is barred by the applicable statute of limitations, or (3) a time limitation stated in the contract is exceeded.

LAW IN PRACTICE

1. Know when a contract is ended and how to terminate a contract. Consider whether your contracts should define "termination".

2. Avoid the pitfall of making a wrongful rejection of a proper tender.

3. Consider whether the contract you make should specify a standard for performance. That is, consider whether your contract should state whether exact performance is required and whether compliance with the contract is to be subjectively or objectively determined or determined by a named third person.

4. To protect against damage for failure to fulfill a contract because of the effect of weather and other external matters, include a contract clause to that effect.

5. Consider whether your contract should state or define the effect of frustration, disappointment, or similar unforeseen events.

QUESTIONS AND CASE PROBLEMS

1. What social forces are affected by the doctrine of economic frustration?

2. McMullen Contractors made a contract with Richardson to build an apartment house for a specific price. A number of serious apartment house fires broke out in the city, and an ordinance was adopted by the city council increasing the fire precautions that had to be taken in the construction of a new building. Compliance with these new requirements would make the construction of the apartment house for Richardson more expensive than McMullen had originally contemplated. Is McMullen discharged from the contract to build the apartment house?

3. Grattan contracted to build a house and garage for Boris for $50,000. The job was completed according to the specifications in all respects except that Grattan forgot to put a tool shed next to the garage, as was required by the contract specifications. Boris refused to pay Grattan. Grattan sued Boris. Boris raised the defense that Grattan was not entitled to any money until the contract was completely performed and that the performance was incomplete because the tool shed had not been constructed. Was Boris correct?

4. Cotten was a real estate broker. Deasey owned property. He gave Cotten an exclusive right to sell the property for one year ending on January 30, 1986. The exclusive right provision meant that if Deasey or a broker other than Cotten were to sell the property, Cotten would still get his commission as though he had sold the property. On January 10, 1986, Deasey extended the contract with Cotten through April 30, 1986. The extension did not say anything as to whether the agency was exclusive. Unknown to Cotten, Deasey on February 3, 1986, made a contract to sell the property to Standley. The closing or settlement of the transaction was made on May 1, 1986, the day following the expiration of the extension date of the agreement with Cotten. Cotten sued Deasey to recover the commission on the sale to Standley. Deasey defended on the ground that the contract that had given Cotten an exclusive right had expired and that it had been superseded by the extension agreement that did not give Cotten any exclusive right. Decide. [Cotten v Deasey (Tex App) 766 SW2d 874]

5. Metalcrafters made a contract to design a new earth-moving vehicle for Lamar Highway Construction Company. Metalcrafters was depending on the genius of Samet, the head of its research department, to design a new product. Shortly after the contract was made between Metalcrafters and Lamar, Samet was killed in an automobile accident. Metalcrafters was not able to design the product without Samet. Lamar sued Metalcrafters for damages for breach of the contract. Metalcrafters claimed that the contract was discharged by Samet's death. Is it correct?

6. The Tinchers signed a contract to sell land to Creasy. The contract specified that the sales trans-

action was to be completed in 90 days. At the end of the 90 days Creasy requested an extension of time. The Tinchers refused to grant an extension and stated that the contract was terminated. Creasy claimed that the 90-day clause was not binding because the contract did not state that time was of the essence. Was the contract terminated? [Creasy v Tincher, 154 W Va 18, 173 SE2d 332]

7. Kel Kim Corporation leased a vacant supermarket building from Central Markets. The lease ran for ten years, with the option to extend it for two five-year periods. The parties understood that Kel Kim would be using the building for a public roller skating rink, although the lease did not specify what use was to be made of the building. The lease required Kel Kim to maintain public liability insurance in the amount of one million dollars to protect Central Markets from any liability. Kel Kim obtained a policy for one-half million dollars. The lessor notified Kel Kim that the lease was terminated if proper insurance was not obtained in 30 days. Kel Kim claimed that it was not bound by the requirement of maintaining million-dollar insurance because it was impossible to obtain that much insurance on a roller skating rink. Was Kel Kim released from the million-dollar insurance clause? [Kel Kim Corp. v Central Markets, Inc. 70 NY2d 900, 524 NYS2d 384, 519 NE2d 295]

8. Dickson contracted to build a house for Moran. When it was approximately 25 to 40 percent completed, Moran would not let Dickson work any further because he was not following the building plans and specifications, and there were many defects. Moran hired another contractor to correct the defects and finish the building. Dickson sued Moran for breach of contract, claiming that he had substantially performed the contract up to the point where he had been discharged. Was Dickson correct? [Dickson v Moran (La App) 344 So 2d 102]

9. A lessor leased a trailer park to a tenant. At the time, sewage was disposed of by a septic tank system that was not connected with the public sewage system. The tenant knew this, and the lease declared that the tenant had examined the premises and that the landlord made no representation or guarantee as to the condition of the premises. Some time thereafter, the septic tank system stopped working properly, and the county health department notified the tenant that he was required to connect the sewage system with the public sewage system or else close the trailer park. The tenant did not want to pay the additional cost

involved in connecting with the public system. The tenant claimed that he was released from the lease and was entitled to a refund of the deposit that he had made. Was he correct? [*Glen R. Sewell Sheet Metal v Loverde, 70 Cal 2d 666, 75 Cal Rptr 889, 451 P2d 721*]

10. Oneal was a teacher employed by the Colton Consolidated School District. Because of a diabetic condition, his eyesight deteriorated so much that he offered to resign if he would be given pay for a specified number of "sick leave" days. The school district refused to do this and discharged Oneal for nonperformance of his contract. He appealed to remove the discharge from his record. Decide. What ethical values are involved? [*Oneal v Colton Consolidated School District, 16 Wash App 2d 488, 557 P2d 11*]

11. Northwest Construction, Inc. made a contract with the State of Washington for highway construction. Part of the work was turned over under a subcontract to the Yakima Asphalt Paving Company. The contract required that any claim be asserted within 180 days. Yakima brought an action for damages after the expiration of 180 days. The defense was raised that the claim was too late. Yakima replied that the action was brought within the time allowed by the statute of limitations and that the contractual limitation of 180 days was therefore not binding. Was Yakima correct?

12. The Metropolitan Park District of Tacoma gave Griffith a concession to run the District's park. The agreement gave the right to occupy the parks and use any improvements found therein. The district later wished to set this agreement aside because it was not making sufficient money from the transaction. While it was seeking to set the agreement aside, a boathouse and gift shop in one of the parks were destroyed by fire. The district then claimed that the concession contract with Griffith was discharged by impossibility of performance. Was it correct? [*Metropolitan Park District of Tacoma v Griffith, 106 Wash 2d 5, 723 P2d 1093*]

13. Hutton, as a prospective franchisee, and Mograde, Inc., as a prospective franchisor, entered into a franchise agreement. The agreement stated that it would be cancelled and the deposit refunded if Hutton could not obtain satisfactory financing for the balance of the money due the franchisor. A few days later Hutton notified the franchisor that he could not obtain satisfactory financing, that he was therefore cancelling the contract, and demanded his deposit back. Decide.

14. Ellen borrowed money from the Farmer's Bank. As evidence of the loan she signed a promissory note by which she promised to pay to the bank in installments the amount of the loan, together with interest and administrative costs. She was unable to make the payments on the scheduled dates. She and the bank then executed a new agreement which gave her a longer period of time for making the payments. However, after two months she was unable to pay on this new schedule. The bank then brought suit against her under the terms of the original agreement. She then raised the defense that the oral agreement had been discharged by the execution of the second agreement and could not be sued upon. Decide.

15. The Acme Hydraulic Press Company manufactured large presses and sold them throughout the United States. The agreement of sale contract that Acme would execute with its customers specified that they could make no claim for breach of contract unless notice of the breach had been given within 10 days after the delivery of a press in question to the buyer and that no lawsuit could thereafter be brought if such notice had not been given. Was this time limitation valid?

CHAPTER 18

BREACH OF CONTRACT AND REMEDIES

LEARNING OBJECTIVES

After studying this chapter, you will be able to:
1. *List and define the kinds of damages that may be recovered when a contract is broken.*
2. *Describe the requirement of mitigation of damages.*
3. *State when liquidated damages clauses are valid.*
4. *State when liability-limiting clauses are valid.*
5. *State when a breach of contract is waived.*
6. *List the steps that may be used to prevent a waiver of breach of contract.*

What can be done when a contract is broken?

A. WHAT CONSTITUTES A BREACH OF CONTRACT

The question of remedies does not become important until it is first determined that the contract has been broken, that is, that there has been a breach.

1. Definition of Breach

A **breach** is the failure to act or perform in the manner called for by the contract. When the contract calls for performance, such as the painting of the owner's house, the failure to paint or to paint properly is a breach of contract. If the contract calls for a creditor's forbearance, the action of the creditor in bringing a lawsuit is a breach of the contract.

2. Anticipatory Breach

When the contract calls for performance, a party may make it clear before the time for performance arrives that the contract will not be performed.

(a) ANTICIPATORY REPUDIATION. When a party expressly declares that performance will not be made when required, such declaration is called an **anticipatory repudiation** of the contract. To constitute such a repudiation, there must be a clear, absolute, unequivocal refusal to perform the contract according to its terms.[1]

A party making an anticipatory repudiation may retract or take back the repudiation if the other party has not changed position in reliance on the repudiation. However, if the other party has changed position, the party making the anticipatory repudiation cannot retract it. For example, if the buyer makes another purchase when the seller declares that

the seller will not perform the contract, the buyer has acted in reliance on the seller's repudiation. The seller will therefore not be allowed to retract the repudiation.

(b) ANTICIPATORY REPUDIATION BY CONDUCT. The anticipatory repudiation may be expressed by conduct that makes it impossible for the repudiating party to perform subsequently. To illustrate, there is a repudiation by conduct if a farmer makes a contract to sell an identified mass of potatoes, then sells and delivers them to another buyer before the date specified for the delivery to the first buyer.

B. WAIVER OF BREACH

The breach of a contract may have no importance because the other party to the contract waives the breach.

3. Cure of Breach by Waiver

The fact that one party has broken a contract does not necessarily mean that there will be a lawsuit or a forfeiture of the contract. For practical business reasons, one party may be willing to ignore or **waive** the breach. When it is established that there has been a waiver of a breach, the party waiving the breach cannot take any action on the theory that the contract was broken. The waiver, in effect, erases the past breach. The contract continues as though the breach had not existed.[2]

A tender of performance will often be defective in some respect. There may be delays, or the product tendered may not be exactly what was ordered. The obligee will frequently accept the performance, although defective, without making any complaint as to the defect. Performance may be accepted because the obligee is not really troubled by the defect or because the obligee is in such a position that

---

[1] Thermo Electron Corp. v Schiavone Construction Co. (CA1 Mass) 958 F2d 1158 (1992).

[2] Wheat Belt Public Power District v Batterman, 234 Neb 589, 452 NW2d 49 (1990).

Figure 18-1 What Follows the Breach?

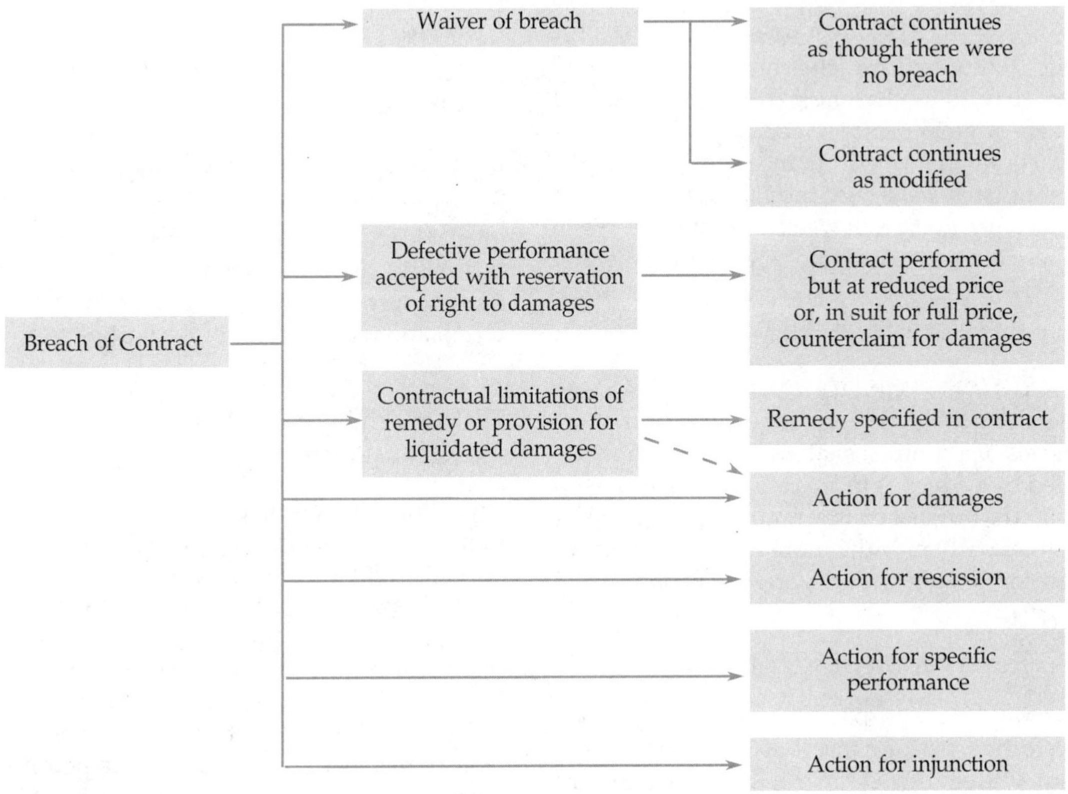

the defective performance must be accepted as better than none.

The waiver may be express, or it may be implied from the continued recognition of the existence of the contract by the aggrieved party.

4. Existence and Scope of Waiver

It is a question of fact whether there has been a waiver.

(a) EXISTENCE OF WAIVER. A party may express or declare that the breach of the contract is waived. A waiver of breach is more often the result of silence or failure to object in timely fashion than the result of an express forgiving of a breach. Thus, a party allowing

the other party to continue performance without objecting that the performance is not satisfactory waives the right to raise that objection when sued for payment by the performing party.

(b) SCOPE OF WAIVER. The waiver of a breach of contract extends only to the matter waived. It does not show any intent to ignore other provisions of the contract.

5. Waiver of Breach as Modification of Contract

When the contract calls for a continuing performance, such as making delivery of goods or paying an installment on the first of each month, the acceptance of a late delivery or a late payment may have more significance than merely waiving a claim for damages because of the lateness.

(a) REPEATED BREACHES AND WAIV-ERS. Repeated breaches and repeated waivers may show that the parties have modified their original contract. For example, the contract calling for performance on the first of the month may have been modified to permit performance in the first week of the month. When there is a modification of the contract, neither party can go back to the original contract without the consent of the other.

(b) ANTIMODIFICATION CLAUSE. Modern contracts commonly specify that the terms of a contract shall not be deemed modified by waiver as to any breaches. This means that the original contract remains as agreed to. Either party may therefore return to and insist on compliance with the original contract.

6. Reservation of Right

It may be that a party is willing to accept a defective performance but does not wish to surrender any claim for damages for the breach. For example, the buyer of coal may need a shipment of coal so badly as to be forced to accept it although it is defective. At the same time, the buyer does not wish to be required to pay the full purchase price for the defective shipment. The buyer wants to claim a deduction for damages because the shipment was defective. In such a case, the buyer should accept the tendered performance with a **reservation of rights**. In the above illustration, the buyer would state that the defective coal was accepted but that the right to damages for nonconformity to the contract was reserved.[3] Frequently the buyer will express the same thought by stating that the coal is accepted "without prejudice" to a claim for damages for nonconformity, or that the shipment is accepted "under protest."

C. REMEDIES FOR BREACH OF CONTRACT

When a party has broken a contract, there are several remedies, one or more of which may be available to the injured party. There is also the possibility that arbitration or a streamlined, out-of-court procedure is available for the determination of the rights of the parties.

7. Remedies upon Anticipatory Repudiation

When there has been an anticipatory repudiation of a contract, the aggrieved person has several options.[4] The aggrieved party may (a) do nothing beyond stating that the performance at the proper time will be required, (b) regard the contract as having been definitively broken and bring a lawsuit against the repudiating party, without waiting to see if there will be a proper performance when the performance date arrives,[5] or (c) regard the repudiation as an offer to cancel the contract. This offer can be accepted or rejected. If accepted, there is a discharge of the original contract by the subsequent cancellation agreement of the parties.

8. Action for Damages

When a breach of contract occurs, the injured party is entitled to bring an action for damages. The amount is the sum of money that will place the injured party in the same position that would have been attained if the contract had been performed.[6]

---

[3] UCC § 1-207.

[4] Jitner v Gersch Development Co. 101 Or App 220, 789 P2d 704 (1990).

[5] If the aggrieved party follows alternative (b), the duty to mitigate damages may arise. This duty is described in Section 8(a) of this chapter.

[6] Leingang v City of Mandan Weed Board (ND) 468 NW2d 397 (1991).

If the defendant has been negligent in performing the contract, the plaintiff may sue for the damages caused by the negligence. Thus, a person contracting to drill a well for drinking water can be sued for the damage caused by negligently drilling the well so as to cause the water to become contaminated. However, damages representing annoyance ordinarily may not be recovered for breach of contract. Similarly, the mere fact that the breaking of the contract causes the injured party to be emotionally upset does not ordinarily entitle that person to recover damages for such emotional distress.[7]

(a) MEASURE OF DAMAGES. A plaintiff who has sustained actual loss is entitled to a sum of money that will, so far as possible, compensate for that loss. Such damages are called **compensatory damages**. An injured party who does not sustain an actual loss from the breach of a contract is entitled to a judgment of a small sum, such as $1, known as **nominal damages**. A party seeking to recover damages for breach of contract must produce evidence that affords a basis for determining the monetary value of the damages with reasonable certainty. If the proof is uncertain, conjectural, or speculative, the plaintiff cannot recover compensatory damages.[8]

The fact that damages cannot be established with mathematical certainty is not a bar to their recovery. All that is required is reasonable certainty. The trier of fact is given a large degree of discretion in determining the damages.

The *Orchid Software* case raised the question of how a new business could prove a loss of profits caused by a breach of contract.

ORCHID SOFTWARE, INC.
v PRENTICE-HALL, INC.
(Tex App) 804 SW2d 208 (1991)

Orchid Software made a contract with Prentice-Hall to develop a line of accounting and business machine computer programs. Prentice-Hall would then market these programs and share the profits with Orchid. Production lagged. Prentice-Hall was not satisfied with the rate of production and two years later canceled its contract with Orchid. Orchid sued Prentice-Hall to recover the loss of the profits it had anticipated. The lower court entered judgment in favor of Prentice-Hall because Orchid did not have any history of making profits and therefore there was nothing to show that there were any profits that were lost. Orchid appealed.

JONES, J. . . . . The general rule is that an injured party may recover damages for lost profits by showing that the loss is a natural and probable result of the act or omission complained of and that the amount of profits that the party would have earned is reasonably certain. . . . The certainty requirement has often been held to prevent a new business enterprise from recovering any lost profits. . . . This prohibition effectively prevents speculative recovery when there is no evidence from which profits could be intelligently estimated. Estimating future profits intelligently has been said

---

7 Hancock v Northcutt (Alaska) 808 P2d 251 (1991).

8 Colorado National Bank of Denver v Friedman (Colo) 846 P2d 159 (1993).

to be difficult, if not impossible, when the business involved depends on uncertain and changing conditions, such as market fluctuations. . . .

Although the general rule has thus correctly prohibited recovery of speculative and uncertain anticipated profits, more recent cases have held that a new business may use other data besides past profit history to show anticipated profits to a reasonable certainty. *See, e.g., White v Southwestern Bell Telephone Co.,* 651 SW2d 260 (Tex 1983) (business records showing past developments and existing conditions sufficient to show loss of normal increase in business); *Pace Corp. v Jackson,* 155 Tex. 179, 284 SW2d 340 (1955) (opinion of business owner based on prior similar business's profit history); *Pena v Ludwig,* 766 SW2d 298 (Tex App 1989, no writ) (opinion of business owner based on prior similar business's profit history); *Anbeck Co. v Zapata Corp.,* 641 SW2d 608 (Tex App 1982), writ ref'd n.r.e.) (contractually agreed upon consideration for sale of assets); *cf. Arabesque Studios, Inc. v Academy of Fine Arts Int'l, Inc.,* 529 SW2d 564 (Tex Civ App 1975, no writ) (employer showed loss of particular clients and their continued business dealings with employee who terminated employment relationship and subsequently breached covenant not to compete). A vast majority of jurisdictions appear to have rejected the so-called "new business rule" as a per se rule of exclusion. *See* Annotation, *Recovery of Anticipated Lost Profits of New Business: Post-1965 Cases,* 55 A.L.R. 4th 507 (1987).

. . . Whether data exists to show the anticipated profits of a new business to a reasonable certainty will depend on the facts and circumstances of each case. . . . We hold that the absence of a history of profits does not, by itself, preclude a new business from recovering lost future profits.

[Judgment reversed and action remanded]

QUESTIONS

1. What was the basic problem involved in the *Orchid* case? Why did it arise?
2. In the opinion, the court comments on a change that has taken place in the applicable rule of law. What has that change been and how do you account for it?
3. Did the *Orchid* case hold that Orchid was entitled to recover for lost profits?

(b) PUNITIVE DAMAGES. Damages in excess of actual loss, imposed for the purpose of punishing or making an example of the defendant, are known as **punitive damages** or **exemplary damages**. In contract actions, punitive damages are not ordinarily awarded. Punitive damages are not awarded for mere negligent breach of contract.[9]

In some consumer situations, the recovery of punitive damages is allowed in order to discourage the defendant from breaking the law with other consumers. For example, in cases in which the plaintiff is a consumer and the seller has acted wrongfully and stubbornly, there is an increasing trend to award punitive damages to prevent a repetition of such conduct.

The fact that the breaching party made prompt efforts to correct the situation when notified of the breach is strong evidence of the lack of the mental state justifying the imposition of punitive damages.

---

[9] Art's Flower Shop, Inc. v Chesapeake and Potomac Telephone Co. (W Va) 413 SW2d 670 (1991).

(c) DIRECT AND CONSEQUENTIAL DAMAGES. The breach of a contract may cause the other party direct and consequential loss.

(1) Direct and Consequential Loss Distinguished. A **direct loss** is one that necessarily is caused by the breach of contract. A **consequential loss** is one that does not necessarily follow the breach of the contract but happens to do so in a particular case, because of the circumstances of the injured party. For example, if the seller breaks the contract to deliver a truck that operates properly, the buyer sustains the damages of receiving a truck that cannot be used. This is the direct loss. If the buyer of the truck needed the truck to take a harvest of ripe tomatoes to the cannery, the loss of the crop that could not be transported would be the consequential loss sustained by the farmer-buyer.

(2) Limitation on Consequential Damages. Consequential damages may be recovered if they were within the contemplation of the parties at the time they entered into their contract. This does not mean that the parties must have actually thought of the consequential damage that would follow from a breach of the contract. It is sufficient that a reasonable person in the same position would have foreseen the probability of such damage.

To recover damages for a particular consequential loss, the plaintiff must show that it was within the defendant's contemplation—that is, it was reasonably foreseeable that the kind of loss in question could be sustained by the plaintiff if the contract was broken.

(d) MITIGATION OF DAMAGES. The injured party is under the duty to **mitigate the damages** if reasonably possible.[10] That is, damages must not be permitted to increase if this can be prevented by reasonable efforts. This means that the injured party must generally stop any performance under the contract to avoid running up a larger bill. It may re-

quire the injured party to buy or rent elsewhere the goods that the wrongdoer was obligated to deliver under the contract. In the case of the breach of an employment contract by the employer, the employee is required to seek other similar employment. The wages earned from other employment must be deducted from the damages claimed. The discharged employee, however, is not required to take employment of an unreasonably inferior nature to the prior work.[11]

(1) Effect of Failure to Mitigate Damages. The effect of the requirement of mitigating damages is to limit the recovery by the injured party to the damages that would have been sustained had the injured party mitigated the damages. That is, recovery is limited to the direct loss, and damages for consequential loss are excluded. For example, assume that a commercial hauler makes a contract to buy a truck. Because the seller fails to deliver the truck, the buyer loses a hauling job on which a profit of $500 would have been made. Assume that the hauler could have rented a truck for $150 in time to do the hauling job. The hauler would then be under a duty to rent the truck so that the $500 profit would not be lost. By failing to do this, the hauler permitted the damages to grow from a rental cost of $150 to a loss of profit of $500. When the hauler sues the seller for breach of the sales contract, the rule of mitigation of damages will limit the hauler to recovering only $150, because the additional $350 loss was unnecessarily sustained. If in fact the hauler had rented a truck, the rental of $150 would be recoverable as damages from the seller. Thus, the hauler will only receive $150 damages, whether or not a truck is rented in order to mitigate the damages.

(2) Excuse for Failure to Mitigate Damages. If there is nothing that the injured party can reasonably do to reduce damages, there is, by definition, no duty to mitigate damages. For example, a leasing company

---

[10] West Pinal Family Health Center, Inc. v McBride (App) 162 Ariz 546, 785 P2d 66 (1989).

[11] Arneson v Board of Trustees, McKendree College (Ill App) 569 NE2d 252 (1991).

broke its contract to supply a specified computer and auxiliary equipment by delivering a less desirable computer. The specified computer and equipment could not be obtained elsewhere by the customer. Therefore, the customer was entitled to recover full damages.

When the cost of mitigating, for example, by purchasing elsewhere the goods that the seller failed to deliver, is unreasonably great, there is no duty to mitigate damages.

(e) CONVERSION OF FOREIGN CURRENCY. Judgments entered in state and U.S. federal courts must be stated in terms of U.S. currency—that is, American dollars. This raises a problem when an international contract is involved, and the plaintiff's damages are measured in terms of a foreign currency. The earlier American rule was to award the plaintiff the number of American dollars that the amount of the foreign currency would buy as of the rate of exchange on the day of the defendant's breach. In view of the present fluctuations in world currencies, the modern trend is to award the foreign plaintiff the number of American dollars determined by the rate of exchange on the date of the judgment when the use of that date will produce a more equitable result.

9. Rescission

When there has been a material breach of the contract, the aggrieved party may rescind the contract. If the wrongdoing party objects, the aggrieved party may bring an action for rescission.

(a) RIGHT TO RESCIND. When one party commits a material breach of the contract, the other party may rescind the contract because of such breach. In some situations, the right to rescind may be governed or controlled by civil service statutes or similar regulations, or by an obligation to submit the matter to arbitration or to a grievance procedure.

An injured party who rescinds after having performed or paid money under the contract may recover the reasonable value of the performance rendered or the money paid. This recovery is not based on the contract that has been rescinded but on a quasi contract that the law implies to prevent the defaulter from keeping the benefit received and thus being unjustly enriched. When a contract for the sale of land is rescinded, the buyer is entitled to the return of the purchase price and to compensation for any improvements made to the land. A deduction will be made from such sums for the reasonable rental value of the property during the time that the buyer was in possession.

Rescission is the undoing of the contract.[12] The rescinding party must restore the other party to that party's original position. If the rescinding party's own acts make this impossible, the contract cannot be rescinded. Thus, a buyer who has placed a mortgage on property purchased cannot rescind the sales contract because the property cannot be returned to the seller in its original unmortgaged condition.

Care must be exercised in deciding to rescind a contract. If proper ground for rescission does not exist, the party who rescinds is guilty of repudiating the contract and is liable for damages for its breach.[13] Rescission and recovery of monetary damages are alternative remedies, except in a contract for the sale of goods, in which case both remedies are available.

(b) JUDICIAL RESCISSION. If the party breaking the contract does not recognize the right of the aggrieved party to rescind the contract, the aggrieved party may bring an action in which the court will declare that the contract has been rescinded. In that action, the court will also specify what payments or exchanges of property are to be made by the

---

[12] Johnny's, Inc. v Njaka (Minn App) 450 NW2d 166 (1990).
[13] Joshua v McBride, 19 Ark App 31, 716 SW2d 215 (1986).

parties in order to return matters to the conditions existing before the contract was made.

10. Action for Specific Performance

C
P
A

Under special circumstances, the injured party may obtain the equitable remedy of specific performance that compels the other party to carry out the terms of a contract. Specific performance is ordinarily granted only if the subject matter of the contract is unique, thereby making a monetary award of damages an inadequate remedy. Monetary damages may be inadequate because it is not possible to make a reasonable determination of the damages the plaintiff will sustain by the breach of the contract. Monetary damages may be inadequate because a replacement or substitute performance cannot be obtained in the marketplace. Contracts for the purchase of land will be specifically enforced, as will contracts for the sale of a business and the franchise held by the business.

Specific performance of a contract to sell personal property can generally be obtained only if the article is of unusual age, beauty, unique history, or other distinction. In the case of heirlooms, original paintings, old editions of books, or relics, identical articles could not be obtained in the market. Specific performance is also allowed a buyer in the case of a contract to buy shares of stock essential for control of a close corporation when those shares have no fixed or market value and are not quoted in the commercial reports or sold on a stock exchange.

The granting of specific performance is discretionary with the court and will be refused when it would impose an unreasonable hardship on the defendant. Specific performance will also be refused when the plaintiff has acted inequitably.[14]

The *Van Wagner Advertising* case turned on what constituted being "unique."

VAN WAGNER ADVERTISING CORP. v S & M ENTERPRISES

67 NY2d 177, 501 NYS2d 628, 492 NE2d 756 (1986)

Michaels owned a building. She made a lease with Van Wagner Advertising Corporation, giving it the right to erect a sign on the walls of the building facing automobile traffic entering Manhattan through the Midtown Tunnel. The lease ran for three years with options to renew up to ten years. Van Wagner erected an illuminated billboard and then leased it to Asch Advertising. Michaels later sold the building to S & M Enterprises. S & M was buying up the property on the block in order to construct a residential-commercial complex. S & M notified Van Wagner that it was terminating the lease. Van Wagner sued S & M for specific performance to make it adhere to the terms of the lease. The court held that the lease was improperly broken but refused to grant specific performance to compel obedience to the lease terms. Van Wagner appealed.

---

[14] Hawthorne's, Inc. v Warrenton Realty, Inc. 414 Mass 200, 606 NE2d 908 (1993).

KAYE, J. . . . Whether or not to award specific performance is a decision that rests in the sound discretion of the trial court, and here that discretion was not abused. Considering first the nature of the transaction, specific performance has been imposed as the remedy for breach of contracts for the sale of real property . . . , but the contract here is to lease rather than sell an interest in real property. While specific performance is available, in appropriate circumstances, for breach of a commercial or residential lease, specific performance of real property leases is not in this State awarded as a matter of course. . . .

Van Wagner argues that specific performance must be granted in light of the trial court's finding that the "demised space is unique as to location for the particular advertising purpose intended." The word "uniqueness" is not, however, a magic door to specific performance. . . . Putting aside contracts for the sale of real property, where specific performance has traditionally been the remedy for breach, uniqueness in the sense of physical difference does not itself dictate the propriety of equitable relief. . . .

The point at which breach of a contract will be redressable by specific performance . . . must lie . . . in the uncertainty of valuing it: "What matters, in measuring money damages, is the volume, refinement, and reliability of the available information about substitutes for the subject matter of the breached contract. When the relevant information is thin and unreliable, there is a substantial risk that an award of money damages will either exceed or fall short of the promisee's actual loss. Of course this risk can always be reduced—but only at great cost when reliable information is difficult to obtain. Conversely, when there is a great deal of consumer behavior generating abundant and highly dependable information about substitutes, the risk of error in measuring the promisee's loss may be reduced at much smaller cost. In asserting that the subject matter of a particular contract is unique and has no established market value, a court is really saying that it cannot obtain, at reasonable cost, enough information about substitutes to permit it to calculate an award of money damages without imposing an unacceptably high risk of undercompensation on the injured promisee. Conceived in this way, the uniqueness test seems economically sound." (45 U Chi L Rev, at 362.) This principle is reflected in the case law . . . , and is essentially the position of the Restatement (Second) of Contracts, which lists "the difficulty of proving damages with reasonable certainty" as the first factor affecting adequacy of damages (Restatement [Second] of Contracts § 360[a]).

Thus, the fact that the subject of the contract may be "unique as to location for the particular advertising purpose intended" by the parties does not entitle a plaintiff to the remedy of specific performance.

Here, the trial court correctly concluded that the value of the "unique qualities" of the demised space could be fixed with reasonable certainty and without imposing an unacceptably high risk of undercompensating the injured tenant. Both parties complain: Van Wagner asserts that while lost revenues on the Asch contract may be adequate compensation, that contract expired February 28, 1985, its lease with S & M continues until 1992, and the value of the demised space cannot reasonably be fixed for the balance of the term. S & M urges that future rents and continuing damages are necessarily conjectural, both during and after the Asch contract, and that Van Wagner's damages must be limited to 60 days—the period during which Van Wagner could cancel Asch's contract without consequence in the event Van Wagner lost the demised space. S & M points out that Van Wagner's lease could remain in effect for the full 10-year term, or it could legitimately be extinguished immediately, either in conjunction with a bona fide sale of the property by S & M, or by a reletting of the building if the new tenant required use of the billboard space for its own purposes. Both parties' contentions were properly rejected.

First, it is hardly novel in the law for damages to be projected into the future. Particularly where the value of commercial billboard space can be readily determined by comparisons with similar uses—Van Wagner itself has more than 400 leases—the value of this property between 1985 and 1992 cannot be regarded as speculative. Second, S & M having successfully resisted specific performance on the ground that there is an adequate remedy at law, cannot at the same time be heard to contend that damages beyond 60 days must be denied because they are conjectural. If damages for breach of this lease are indeed conjectural, and cannot be calculated with reasonable certainty, then S & M should be compelled to perform its contractual obligation by restoring Van Wagner to the premises. Moreover, the contingencies to which S & M points do not, as a practical matter, render the calculation of damages speculative. While S & M could terminate the Van Wagner lease in the event of a sale of the building, this building has been sold only once in 40 years; S & M paid several million dollars, and purchased the building in connection with its plan for major development of the block. The theoretical termination right of a future tenant of the existing building also must be viewed in light of these circumstances. If any uncertainty is generated by the two contingencies, then the benefit of that doubt must go to Van Wagner and not the contract violator. Neither contingency allegedly affecting Van Wagner's continued contractual right to the space for the balance of the lease term is within its own control; on the contrary, both are in the interest of S & M. Thus, neither the need to project into the future nor the contingencies allegedly affecting the length of Van Wagner's term render inadequate the remedy of damages for S & M's breach of its lease with Van Wagner.

The trial court, additionally, correctly concluded that specific performance should be denied on the ground that such relief "would be inequitable in that its effect would be disproportionate in its harm to defendant and its assistance to plaintiff." It is well settled that the imposition of an equitable remedy must not itself work an inequity, and that specific performance should not be an undue hardship. . . .

[Judgment affirmed as to denial of specific performance]

QUESTIONS

1. What did the court hold and why?
2. How would the case have been decided if the action for specific performance had been brought by Asch Advertising?
3. Could the damages in the Van Wagner case be proven with mathematical certainty?

Ordinarily, contracts for the performance of personal services will not be specifically ordered. This is because of the difficulty of supervision by the court and because of the restriction of the Thirteenth Amendment of the federal Constitution prohibiting involuntary servitude except as criminal punishment.

To do complete justice, the court in awarding specific performance can also award damages to compensate for the direct and consequential loss caused by the defendant's refusal to perform the contract.

11. Action for an Injunction

When the breach of contract consists of doing an act prohibited by the contract, a possible remedy is an injunction against the doing of this act. For example, when the obligation in the employee's contract is to refrain from competing and the obligation is broken by competing, a court may order or enjoin the employee to stop competing. Similarly, when a singer breaks a contract to record exclusively for a particular company, the singer may be enjoined from recording for any other company. This may indirectly have the effect of compelling the singer to record for the plaintiff.

D. CONTRACT PROVISIONS AFFECTING REMEDIES AND DAMAGES

The contract of the parties may contain provisions that affect the remedies available or the recovery of damages.

12. Limitation of Remedies

The contract of the parties may limit the remedies of the aggrieved parties. For example, the contract may give one party the right to repair or replace a defective item sold or to refund the contract price. The contract may require both parties to submit any dispute to arbitration or other streamlined out-of-court procedure.

13. Liquidated Damages

The parties may stipulate in their contract that a certain amount should be paid in case of a breach. This amount is known as **liquidated damages**. Liquidated damages may be variously measured by the parties. When delay is in mind, liquidated damages may be a fixed sum, such as $100 for each day of delay. When there is a total default, damages may be a percentage of the contract price or may be the amount of the down payment.

(a) EFFECT. When a liquidated damages clause is held valid, the injured party cannot collect more than the amount specified by the clause. The defaulting party is bound to pay such damages once the fact is established that there has been a default.[15] The injured party is not required to make any proof as to damages sustained, and the defendant is not permitted to show that the damages were not as great as the liquidated sum.

(b) VALIDITY. To be valid, a liquidated damages clause must satisfy two requirements: (1) the situation must be one in which it is difficult or impossible to determine the actual damages, and (2) the amount specified must not be excessive when compared with the probable damages that would be sustained.[16] To illustrate, the owner of land made a contract to sell it for $100,000. The buyer made a down payment of $50,000. The contract stated that if the buyer defaulted, the seller could keep the buyer's down payment as liquidated damages. The buyer subsequently refused to go through with the sale. The seller claimed the right to keep the $50,000. The seller could not do this because the liquidated damages clause was void. While land does not have any fixed value, it is clear that the seller could not sustain damages of $50,000. That amount was a penalty, the liquidated damages clause was void, and the seller would be required to prove the actual

---

[15] Burst v R. W. Beal & Co., Inc. (Mo App) 771 SW2d 87 (1989).

[16] Southeast Alaska Construction Co., Inc. v Alaska (Alaska) 791 P2d 339 (1990).

damages that were sustained and to return the excess of the down payment to the buyer.

The validity of a liquidated damage clause is determined on the basis of the facts existing when the clause was agreed to. Excessive damages that are subsequently sustained are ignored.[17]

A contract provision that purports to be a liquidated damages clause is not binding when the actual damages can be readily determined—for example, by comparing the contract price and the market price of the subject matter of the contract.[18]

If the liquidated damages clause calls for the payment of a sum that is clearly unreasonably large and unrelated to the possible actual damages that might be sustained, the clause will be held to be void as a **penalty**. A liquidated damages provision tries to measure the compensation for a breach of the contract. In contrast, a penalty provision punishes the breach. When a liquidated damages clause is held invalid, the effect is merely to erase the clause from the contract. A party injured by breach of the contract may proceed to recover damages for its breach. Instead of recovering the liquidated damages amount, the injured party will recover such damages as are established by the evidence.

In the *Walter Implement* case, the validity of a liquidated damage clause was challenged.

WALTER IMPLEMENT, INC. v FOCHT
107 Wash 2d 533, 730 P2d 1340 (1987)

Walter Implement, Inc. was a dealer in farm equipment. It leased five pieces of farm equipment to Focht and his wife for five years. The lease provided that if annual rental payments were not made, Walter could take back the equipment, resell it, and then sue Focht for any unpaid balance. The lease also required Focht to pay Walter liquidated damages in such case. These damages were to be "20 percent of the aggregate minimum rental charges for the unexpired portion of the term [of the lease]." Focht could not make the second annual payment and returned the equipment to Walter. It sold the equipment and then sued Focht for the liquidated damages. The court entered judgment for Walter for the liquidated damages, computing them by the formula contained in the lease. Focht appealed. The court of appeals held the liquidated damage clause void. Walter then appealed to the state supreme court.

GOODLOE, J. . . . The . . . issue we must decide is whether the liquidated damages clause in the resell remedy provision is enforceable. The clause provides for "an amount equal to twenty (20) percent of the aggregate minimum rental charges for the unexpired portion of the term of this agreement, not as a penalty, but as and for liquidated damages." . . . The trial court enforced this clause. The court calculated that Focht, having made only one of the five annual payments, had an unexpired portion of $43,255.28 (four payments at $10,806.32) which was multiplied by 20 percent

---

[17] Kendrick v Alexander (Tenn App) 844 SW2d 187 (1992).
[18] Hickox v Hickox, 195 Ill App 3d 976, 142 Ill Dec 392, 552 NE2d 1133 (1990).

to get the liquidated damages figure of $8,645.06. The Court of Appeals reversed. It held the clause was unenforceable because it was not a product of the parties' negotiations, was inherently unfair, and bore no relation to the anticipated actual damages.

True liquidated damages clauses, those that are not penalties, are favored and will be upheld. This court follows the United States Supreme Court view that liquidated damages agreements fairly and understandingly entered into by experienced, equal parties with a view to just compensation for the anticipated loss should be enforced. The fact that the contracting parties designate a sum as liquidated damages is a circumstance given serious consideration, but it is not necessarily controlling or conclusive. The designation in this contract that the additional amount is not a penalty but is liquidated damages, therefore, does not decide the issue. Courts will look to the intention of the parties to make an accurate assessment of the clause's purpose. "A provision in a contract which bears no reasonable relation to actual damages will be construed as a penalty." *Enders*, 74 Wash 2d at 594, 446 P2d 200.

This court has adopted and applied a 2-part test to determine whether a liquidated damages clause is enforceable. First, the amount fixed must be a reasonable forecast of just compensation for the harm that is caused by the breach. Second, the harm must be such that it is incapable or very difficult of ascertainment. Reasonableness of the forecast will be judged as of the time the contract was entered. Determination of whether the test is met depends upon the facts and circumstances of each case. . . .

First, we look at the amount fixed to see if it is a reasonable forecast of just compensation for the harm caused by the breach. The involved liquidated damages clause which does not require a fixed amount but instead requires 20 percent of the outstanding rental payments does not appear to have any relation, reasonable or not, to an estimation of damages. A fixed amount of 20 percent of the full lease figure may be a reasonable forecast. In fact, the parties orally agreed that if Focht wished to buy the equipment at the end of the lease term, the cost would be 20 percent of the entire lease figure. This liquidated damages clause by containing a variable makes the amount of liquidated damages depend upon when the default occurs. Even this could be acceptable if . . . the variable was reasonably related to the damages. Here, the liquidated damages could vary from $2161.26 (default in the 4th year) to $8645.06 (default in the first year). No reasoning has been offered explaining how the variation reflects a reasonable forecast of the harm that is caused by the breach. For example, using this formula, the earlier the default the greater the penalty although the equipment is returned sooner resulting in less depreciation of the equipment.

Besides the formula not appearing to have any relation to the anticipated actual damages, such damages are not difficult to ascertain. *American Fin. Leasing & Servs. Co. v Miller*, 41 Ohio App 2d 69, 322 NE2d 149 (1974), which uses the same 2-part test to evaluate liquidated damages clauses, involved a similar equipment lease provision. The *Miller* lease contained several optional remedies, one of which included a recovery of 10 percent of the actual cost to lessor of equipment sold in the event of a default. The court held that actual damages could be easily ascertained. Because of recoupment of the actual damages, the court determined the 10 percent figure

neither bears a reasonable relationship to such damage, nor is in a reasonable proportion thereto.

Such amount is patently in excess of the actual damage which could be suffered by the lessor, and therefore must be considered as a "penalty" rather than a stipulated "liquidated damage."

Miller, at 75, 322 NE2d 149. Using the same reasoning, the liquidated damages clause in this case fails. . . .

The consequence of the preceding analysis is that Walter Implement is entitled to a deficiency judgment. The deficiency judgment is based on actual damages. . . . In a true lease situation, the lessor has a right not only to the contract price but also to the return of the leased goods. The lessor is thus entitled at breach to the value the goods would have had at the expiration of the lease term in addition to the unpaid portion of the contract price. . . .

Evidence presented at trial suggested that the equipment was expected to be worth about 20 percent of the total lease price at the end of the lease, or about $10,000. If that forecast was reasonable, then Walter Implement's damages are the unpaid rents ($43,225.28) plus about $10,000, both reduced to present value, minus the value of the recovered equipment (about $35,000). We affirm the Court of Appeals and find the liquidated damages clause is a penalty and unenforceable. We remand to the trial court to determine how much the equipment reasonably could have been expected to be worth at the end of the lease term. That value should be included in the Fochts' debt and the deficiency adjusted accordingly.

[Judgment affirmed and action remanded]

QUESTIONS

1. Did the court hold that the lease arrangement for damages was illegal?
2. In view of the fact that the Washington supreme court affirmed the judgment of the court of appeals, why did it remand the action?
3. What was the basis for the court's decision?

14. Limitation of Liability Clauses

A contract may contain a provision stating that one of the parties shall not be liable for damages in case of breach. Such a provision is called an **exculpatory clause** or a **limitation-of-liability clause**. As an example of such a provision, a construction contract may state that the contractor shall not be liable for damages from delay caused by third persons.

(a) CONTENT AND CONSTRUCTION. An exculpatory clause, as in the case of any other contract provision, is to be given the scope intended by the parties. An exculpatory clause must be clear and unambiguous. Moreover, such a clause is strictly construed. For example, a limitation of liability for negligence does not bar liability for violation of a consumer protection statute. Likewise a limitation is not binding when the party breaking the contract showed reckless indifference to the rights of others in so doing.[19]

---

[19] Sommer v Federal Signal Corp. 79 NY2d 540, 583 NYS2d 957, ___ NE2d ___, (1992).

(b) VALIDITY. Exculpatory clauses are generally valid, particularly between experienced business persons. Thus, a telephone company may limit its liability to a nominal amount for the omission of a customer's name and number from the yellow page directory where the limitation is conspicuous, the customer is experienced in business, and the omission was merely the result of simple negligence.[20] Release forms signed by participants in athletic and sporting events declaring that the sponsor, proprietor, or operator of the event shall not be liable for injuries sustained by the participants because of negligence are binding. Such forms are invalid, though, when the harm was caused by willful or wanton conduct.[21]

There is a growing trend to hold exculpatory provisions invalid when it is felt that they are oppressive or unconscionable because of the superior bargaining power of the party they protect. This is particularly likely to be the result when the party in question is a public utility. Such an enterprise is under the duty to provide the service to the public in a nonnegligent way.

In recent years, the concept has developed that a limitation of liability is invalid when persons in an inferior bargaining position are involved. In any case, a limitation of liability is not binding if obtained by misconduct or deception.

In the *Madison* case it was claimed that a release did not bar suit for breach of a teaching contract that resulted in the death of a student.

MADISON v SUPERIOR COURT

203 Cal App 3d 589, 250 Cal Rptr 299 (1988)

Ken Sulejmanagic, aged 19, signed up for a course in scuba diving taught by Madison at the local YMCA. Before the instruction began, Ken was required to sign a form releasing Madison and the YMCA from liability for any harm that might occur. At the end of the course, Madison, Ken, and another student went out into deep water. Ken made the final dive required by the course program. Madison left Ken alone in the water while he took the other student for a dive. When Madison returned, Ken could not be found. It was later determined that he had drowned. The parents of Ken sued Madison and the YMCA for negligence in the performance of the teaching contract. The defendants raised the defense that the release signed by Ken shielded them from liability. The court held that the release was void. The defendants then filed a petition in the higher court requesting it to order the lower court to give effect to the release and to enter summary judgment in their favor.

CROSKEY, J. . . . The relevant portions of the agreement provide as follows:

"For and in consideration of permitting (1) Ken Salejmanagie [sic] to enroll in and participate in diving activities and class instruction of skin and/or scuba diving given by (2) Norman Madison/Westchester YMCA . . . the Undersigned hereby voluntarily releases,

---

[20] Southwestern Bell Tel. Co. v FDP Corp. (Tex) 811 SW2d 572 (1991).

[21] Barnes v Birmingham International Raceway (Ala) 551 So 2d 929 (1989).

discharges, waives and relinquishes any and all actions or causes of action for personal injury, property damage or wrongful death occurring to him/herself arising as a result of engaging or receiving instructions in said activity or any activities incidental thereto wherever or however the same may occur and for whatever period said activities or instructions may continue, and the Undersigned does for him/herself, his/her heirs, executors, administrators and assigns hereby release, waive, discharge and relinquish any action or causes of action, aforesaid, which may hereafter arise for him/herself and for his/her estate, and agrees that under no circumstances will he/she or his/her heirs, executors, administrators and assigns prosecute, present any claim for personal injury, property damage or wrongful death against (2) Norman Madison/Westchester YMCA or any of its officers, agents, servants or employees for any of said causes of action, whether the same shall arise by the negligence of any of said persons, or otherwise. **IT IS [MY] INTENTION TO EXEMPT AND RELIEVE <u>Norman Madison/Westchester YMCA</u> FROM LIABILITY FOR PERSONAL INJURY, PROPERTY DAMAGE OR WRONGFUL DEATH CAUSED BY NEGLIGENCE."**

The agreement concludes with the following acknowledgment:

The Undersigned acknowledges that he/she has read the foregoing two paragraphs, has been fully and completely advised of the potential dangers incidental to engaging in the activity and instructing of skin and/or scuba diving, and is fully aware of the legal consequences of signing the within instrument.

. . . The record does not disclose precisely how or why Ken lost his life. . . . The critical question, however, is whether the agreement absolves defendants, in spite of their actions, from any liability to the plaintiffs. . . .

A plaintiff in a wrongful death action is subject to any defenses which could have been asserted against the decedent, including an express agreement by the decedent to waive the defendant's negligence and assume all risks. . . .

Although the words "assumption of the risk" are not specifically used [in Ken's release], it is clear that Ken expressly acknowledged his intent to do just that. In heavy bold type the release expressly states that it was Ken's intent to exempt and relieve the defendants from any liability for their *negligence*. By this language Ken expressly manifested his intent to relieve the defendants of any duty to him and to assume the entire risk of any injury. . . . The result is that the [defendants are] relieved of legal duty to the plaintiff; and being under no duty, [they] cannot be charged with negligence. . . .

Our examination of the agreement compels the conclusion that it was clear and free from ambiguity. It would be difficult to imagine language more clearly designed to put a lay person on notice of the significance and legal effect of subscribing to it. The emphasized references to the exemption and relief from "liability for personal injury, property damage or wrongful death caused by negligence" could not be more explicit.

Moreover, we perceive of no reason why Ken could not validly execute such a broad agreement. "No public policy opposes private, voluntary transactions in which one party, for a consideration, agrees to shoulder a risk which the law would otherwise have placed upon the other party. . . ."

. . . The court in *Kurashige v Indian Dunes, Inc.* (1988) 200 Cal App 3d 606, 246 Cal Rptr 310, concluded that a release signed by motorcycle dirtbike riders did not involve a public interest. The court, in language equally applicable here, stated that the release ". . . agreement used here was printed legibly, contained adequate, clear and explicit exculpatory language and indicated defendants were to be absolved from the consequences of their own negligence. . . . Furthermore, it did not involve the public interest: defendants' business was not generally thought to be suitable for public regulation; defendants did not perform a service of great importance to the public, and the business was not a matter of practical necessity for members of the public; and defendants' customers did not place their persons under defendants' control. . . .

Here, Ken certainly had the option of not taking the class. There was no practical necessity that he do so. In view of the dangerous nature of this particular activity defendants could reasonably require the execution of the release as a condition of enrollment. Ken entered into a private and voluntary transaction in which, in exchange for an enrollment in a class which he desired to take, he freely agreed to waive any claim against the defendants for a negligent act by them. This case involves no more a question of public interest than does motorcross racing . . . sky diving . . . or motorcycle dirtbike riding. . . .

Therefore, we conclude that the agreement is enforceable and, as against any action brought by Ken, would have served as *"a complete defense."* It had the obviously intended legal effect of shifting the responsibility for any negligence by the defendants from the defendants to Ken. By this agreement, Ken effectively assumed all of the risks of any injury he might suffer as a result of defendants' negligence during the training course. . . .

We therefore determine that the legal effect of the release and waiver provisions of the agreement is to provide to defendants "a complete defense" to plaintiffs' action. . . .

[Judgment reversed]

QUESTIONS

1. Was it important whether Ken's release expressly declared that he "assumed the risk" of scuba diving?
2. What social force is furthered by the decision of the court?
3. Should the court in the *Madison* case have decided specifically whether the defendants were or were not negligent?

Some courts refuse to recognize provisions releasing a party from liability for negligence when the provisions are so inconspicuous as to raise a question of whether the party knowingly agreed.[22]

15. Invalid Provision Relating to Remedies or Damages

When a contract contains a valid provision governing remedies or damages, the parties are bound by it. That means that they must follow the procedures specified, or the aggrieved person is bound by the provision as to damages. What happens if the provision in

---

[22] Conradt v Four Star Promotions, Inc. 45 Wash App 847, 728 P2d 617 (1986).

question is invalid? The provision is merely ignored. The balance of the contract remains valid. This means that if the limitation of remedies is not valid, an aggrieved person may follow any remedy that would otherwise be available. If a liquidated damages or a limitation-of-damages clause is invalid, the aggrieved person may sue for the damages sustained, but must actually prove what those damages were.

SUMMARY

When a party fails to perform a contract or performs improperly, the other contracting party may sue for damages caused by the breach. What may be recovered by the aggrieved person is stated in terms of being direct or consequential damages. Direct damages are those that ordinarily will result from the breach. Consequential damages are those that are in fact caused by the breach but do not ordinarily or necessarily result from every breach of the particular kind of contract. Direct damages may be recovered on proof of causation and amount. Consequential damages can only be recovered if, in addition to proving causation and amount, it is shown that they were reasonably within the contemplation of the contracting parties as a probable result of a breach of the contract. The right to recover consequential damages is lost if the aggrieved party could reasonably have taken steps to avoid such damages. That is, the aggrieved person has a duty to mitigate or reduce damages by reasonable means.

In any case, the damages recoverable for breach of contract may be limited to a specific amount by a liquidated damages clause. Damages may be canceled out completely by a limitation-of-liability clause.

In a limited number of situations, the aggrieved party may bring an action for specific performance to compel the other contracting party to perform the acts called for by the contract. Specific performance is always obtainable by the seller for a breach of a contract to sell land or real estate, on the theory that such property has a unique value. With respect to other contracts, specific performance will not be ordered unless it is shown that there was some unique element present, so that the aggrieved person would suffer a damage that could not be compensated for by the payment of money damages.

The aggrieved person also has the option of rescinding the contract if (1) the breach has been made concerning a material term and (2) the aggrieved party returns everything to the way that it was before the contract was made. Rescission and recovery of monetary damages are alternative remedies, except when the contract relates to the sale of goods. In the latter case, the aggrieved party may both rescind and obtain money damages.

Although there has been a breach of the contract, the effect of this breach is nullified if the aggrieved person by word or conduct waives the right to object to the breach. Conversely, an aggrieved party may accept a defective performance without thereby waiving a claim for breach if the party makes a reservation of rights. A reservation of rights can be made by stating that the defective performance is accepted "without prejudice," "under protest," or "with reservation of rights."

The continued waiver of a breach of a particular clause may indicate that the parties have modified their contract by abandoning the clause to which the waiver relates. To guard against the unintended modification of a contract by waiver, the contract may contain a clause stating that nothing shall constitute a modification of the contract unless stated in writing.

LAW IN PRACTICE

If you think that the other party has breached the contract:

1. Get all the facts and analyze them objectively and without emotion.
2. Examine what remedies are available, both in court and out of court.

3. Mitigate your damages when reasonably possible.
4. Make a realistic assessment of your damages.
5. Avoid losing your right by delay or unintended waiver.

QUESTIONS AND CASE PROBLEMS

1. What social forces are affected by the rule governing the mitigation of damages?

2. Anthony makes a contract to sell a rare painting to Laura for $100,000. The written contract specifies that if Anthony should fail to perform the contract, he will pay Laura $5,000 as liquidated damages. Anthony fails to deliver the painting and is sued by Laura for $5,000. Can she recover this amount?

3. Rogers owned land. He made a contract with Salisbury Brick Corporation that allowed it to remove earth and sand from his land. The contract ran for four years, with provision to renew it for additional four-year terms up to a total of 96 years. The contract provided for compensation to Rogers based on the amount of earth and sand removed. By an unintentional mistake, Salisbury underpaid Rogers the amount of $863 for the months of November and December of 1986. Salisbury offered this amount to Rogers, but he refused to accept it and claimed that he had been underpaid in other months. Rogers claimed that he was entitled to rescind the contract. Was he correct? [Rogers v Salisbury Brick Corp. (SC) 382 SE2d 915]

4. A contractor departed at a number of points from the specifications in a contract to build a house. The cost to put the house in the condition called for by the contract was approximately $1,000. The contractor was sued for $5,000 for breach of contract and emotional disturbance caused by the breach. Decide.

5. Protein Blenders, Inc. made a contract with Gingerich to buy from him the shares of stock of a small corporation. When the buyer refused to take and pay for the stock, Gingerich sued for specific performance of the contract on the ground that the value of the stock was unknown and could not be readily ascertained because it was not sold on the general market. Was he entitled to specific performance? [Gingerich v Protein Blenders, Inc. 250 Iowa 646, 95 NW2d 522]

6. The buyer of real estate made a down payment. In the contract, it was stated that the buyer would be liable for damages in an amount equal to the down payment if the buyer broke the contract. The buyer refused to go through with the contract and demanded his down payment back. The seller refused to return it and claimed that he was entitled to additional damages from the buyer because the damages that he had suffered were greater than the amount of the down payment. Decide. [Waters v Key Colony East, Inc. (Fla App) 345 So 2d 367]

7. Kuznicki made a contract for the installation of a fire detection system by Security Safety Corp. for $498. The contract was made one night and canceled at 9:00 the next morning. Security then claimed one-third of the purchase price from Kuznicki by virtue of a provision in the contract that "in the event of cancellation of this agreement . . . the owner agrees to pay 33 1/3 percent of the contract price, as liquidated damages." Was Security Safety entitled to recover the amount claimed? [Security Safety Corp. v Kuznicki, 350 Mass 157, 213 NE2d 866]

8. Stabler was under contract to play professional football for Alabama Football, Inc. The corporation was not able to pay Stabler the amount due him under the contract. He sued for rescission. The club defended on the theory that nonpayment was not a sufficiently substantial breach of the contract to justify rescission. Was the club correct? [Alabama Football, Inc. v Stabler, 294 Ala 551, 319 So 2d 678]

9. Melodee Lane Lingerie Co. was a tenant in a building that was protected against fire by a sprinkler and alarm system maintained by the American District Telegraph Co. Because of the latter's fault, the controls on the system were defective and allowed the discharge of water into the building, which damaged Melodee's property. When Melodee sued A.D.T., it raised the defense that its service contract limited its liability to 10 percent of

the annual service charge made to the customer. Was this limitation valid? [*Melodee Lane Lingerie Co. v American District Telegraph Co. 18 NY2d 57, 271 NYS2d 937, 218 NE2d 661*]

10. In May, a homeowner made a contract with a roofer to make repairs to her house by July 1. The roofer never came to repair the roof, and heavy rains in the fall damaged the interior of the house. The homeowner sued the roofer for breach of contract and claimed damages for the harm done to the interior of the house. Is the homeowner entitled to recover such damages?

11. Hembree, a contractor, wanted to borrow $40,000. He discussed borrowing that amount from Bradley. They agreed that vacant land owned by Hembree would be used as collateral. The parties then executed a contract by which Hembree contracted to sell the vacant land to Bradley for $40,000 and agreed to repurchase the land after one year for $50,000. The contract also required Hembree to pay a penalty of $1,000 a month if he failed to repurchase the land. If this transaction constituted a loan of $40,000, it was usurious. Under the applicable law, that would result only in the forfeiting of the right to any interest. It would not affect the right to collect the $40,000. Hembree did not transfer the title to Bradley as required by the contract. Bradley brought an action to obtain specific performance of the contract. Decide. [*Hembree v Bradley (Fla App) 528 So 2d 116*]

12. Wassenaar worked for Panos under a three-year contract that stated that if the contract was terminated wrongfully by Panos before the end of the three years, he would pay as damages the salary for the remaining time that the contract had to run. After three months, Panos terminated the contract, and Wassenaar sued him for pay for the balance of the contract term. Panos claimed that this amount could not be recovered because the contract provision for the payment of such amount was a void penalty. Was this provision valid? [*Wassenaar v Panos, 111 Wis 2d 518, 331 NW2d 357*]

13. Soden was a contractor, he made a contract to build a house for Clevert. The sales contract stated that "if either party defaults in the performance of this contract" that party would be liable to other for attorney's fees incurred in suing the defaulter. Soden was 61 days late in completing the contract and some of the work was defective. In a suit by the buyer against the contractor, the contractor claimed that he was not liable for the attorney's fees of the buyer because he had only made a defective performance; and that "default" in the phrase quoted above meant "nonperformance of the contract." Was the contractor liable for the attorney's fees? [*Clevert v Soden, ___ Va ___, 400 SE2d 181*]

14. The Protection Alarm Company made a contract to provide burglar alarm security for the home of Fretwell. The contract stated that the maximum liability of the alarm company was the actual loss sustained or $50, whichever was the lesser and that this provision was agreed to "as liquidated damages, and not as a penalty." Fretwell's home was burglarized. He sued for the loss of approximately $91,000 claiming that the alarm company had been negligent. The alarm company asserted that its maximum liability was $50. Fretwell claimed that this was invalid because it bore no relationship to the loss that could have been foreseen when the contract was made or that in fact "had been sustained." Decide.

15. Shepherd-Will made a contract to sell Emma Cousar "5 acres land adjoining property owned by the purchaser and this being formerly land of Shepherd-Will, Inc. located on north side of Highway 223. This 5 acres to be surveyed at earliest time possible at which time plat will be attached and serve as further description on property." Shepherd-Will owned only one 100-acre tract of land that adjoined the property of Emma. This tract had a common boundary with her property of 1,140 feet. Shepherd-Will failed to perform this contract. Emma sued it for specific performance of the contract. Decide. [*Cousar v Shepherd-Will, Inc. (SC App) 387 SE2d 723*]

C H A P T E R   1 9

ACCOUNTANTS' LIABILITY AND MALPRACTICE

LEARNING OBJECTIVES

After studying this chapter, you will be able to:
1. *Define malpractice.*
2. *Distinguish malpractice liability from breach of contract liability.*
3. *State the relationship between malpractice liability of accountants and other professionals.*
4. *State the effect of contributory negligence of a plaintiff suing to impose malpractice liability.*
5. *State the extent to which third persons may enforce the malpractice liability of accountants.*
6. *State the extent to which statutes have regulated the malpractice liability of accountants.*

When is a professional, such as an accountant, an attorney, or a physician, liable for harm caused by improper performance?

A. GENERAL PRINCIPLES

The liability of a contracting party for malpractice raises questions of what constitutes malpractice, what remedies are available to enforce liability for malpractice, and the effect of conduct of the plaintiff and of limitations of liability.

1. What Constitutes Malpractice

When an accountant, a physician, or an attorney makes a contract to perform services, there is a duty to exercise the skill and care that are common within the community for persons performing similar services. If the services are not properly rendered in accordance with those standards, there is an improper practicing of the particular profession or, as it is commonly called, **malpractice**.

2. Choice of Remedy

Because in cases of malpractice performance falls below the proper standard, malpractice is classified as negligence and constitutes a tort. In addition, because the services called for by the contract have not been rendered, malpractice is also a breach of the contract.

(a) BREACH OF CONTRACT OR TORT ACTION. Since malpractice is both a breach of the contract and an independent tort, the client or patient who is harmed has the choice of suing for breach of contract or for the particular tort that is involved. Generally, the client or patient will bring a tort action when justified by the facts. This is so because the tort claimant may recover greater damages than the breach-of-contract plaintiff. Moreover, the tort claimant may have a longer period of time in which to sue. The statute of limitations runs on the tort claim from the date when the harm was discovered. In a contract action, the statute of limitations runs from the date when the

contract was broken. This may be very important, because in some cases the plaintiff does not realize that any harm has been sustained until a substantially long period of time after there was a breach of the contract.

(b) ACTION BY THIRD PERSON. When the malpractice claim is brought by a third person rather than a client or patient of the defendant, the malpractice action will be brought on the tort theory. Suit cannot be brought by the third person on the original contract. The third person is not a party to that contract and ordinarily cannot be classified as a third party beneficiary of that contract.

3. The Environment of Accountants' Malpractice Liability

In the course of this century, there have been several changes that have influenced the law of malpractice liability as it relates to accountants.

First, the accountant has in many cases moved from being a clerical employee to being an essential participant in the planning of business strategies. In addition, the accountant in many instances has moved from being an employee of one employer to being an independent contractor performing accounting services for many clients. Also, the accountant is now employed in many cases for the purpose of producing data on which third persons will rely. For example, the accountant will prepare statements that will be submitted to banks to induce them to lend to the accountant's client. Similarly, such information may be supplied to prospective purchasers of stock of the client corporation.

As these changes took place, it became natural for courts to allow third persons relying on the work product of the accountant to sue the accountant when malpractice caused loss to the third person.

At the same time that the changes noted above were taking place in the economy and in the legal status of the accountant, changes were taking place in other areas of the law. Manufacturers and remote sellers became liable to the ultimate users for damages caused by defective products. Technicians became liable to third persons harmed by their negligence. Thus, this century brings a rising tide of liability to third persons. This background of liability to third persons in other areas has naturally influenced the law with respect to accountants.[1]

4. Limitation of Liability

Can accountants protect themselves from liability for malpractice with respect to their clients and third persons? Since the law generally permits any contracting party to limit or disclaim liability for negligence, an accountant may exclude liability for malpractice based on the theory of negligence. Influenced by the consumer protection movement and by the law as to product liability, courts will require such disclaimers to be (a) clear and unambiguous and (b) conspicuous. If these requirements are not met, the disclaimers will not be held effective.

(a) SCOPE OF LIMITATION. Disclaimers are valid when the circumstances are such that it is not reasonable to expect the accountant to stand behind particular data. For example, when the client owns land in a foreign country, it is reasonable for the accountant to accept the valuation placed on the land by someone in that foreign country. If the accountant includes in the financial statement prepared for the client a statement that the valuation of that land was obtained from an identified person in the foreign country and that the accountant assumes no responsibility for the accuracy of that valuation, the accountant is protected from the falsity of that information. Similarly, if the accountant's examination has been re-

stricted, the accountant is protected from claims of third persons when the accountant makes a certification or statement that certain assets were not examined and that the figures relating to them had not been verified. For example, when the accountant was restricted from examining accounts receivable and the accountant's certificate stated that no opinion was expressed as to accounts receivable, the accountant could not be held liable because the information relating to accounts receivable was not accurate.[2]

(b) LIMITATIONS ON EXCULPATORY PROVISIONS. A disclaimer based on lack of knowledge does not protect the accountant from liability if the accountant had knowledge or reason to know that the statements made were in fact false. In such a case, a court would hold that the disclaimer was not binding. The theory would be misrepresentation—when the accountant stated that personal knowledge was lacking, the accountant impliedly represented that the accountant did not have any knowledge or reason to know that the statements were not correct.

In some states, a limitation of liability or exculpatory clause will only protect the accountant from a malpractice suit brought by the client, not from a suit brought by a third person. In such cases, the court applies the general rule of contract law that only a party to a contract is bound by an exculpatory or limitation-of-liability clause of the contract.

When the malpractice liability of the accountant is based on intentional falsification of data, a limitation of liability will not be binding. This follows from the general rule of law that it is against public policy to permit a limi-

---

[1] The interplay between the various areas of malpractice liability and that of accountants is further seen in the fact that the Restatement of Torts, 2d, does not contain a separate provision applicable only to accountants, but deals with the subject of malpractice liability of accountants to third persons in a general section, § 552. Section 552 declares that "one who in the course of his business, profession or employment, or in any other transaction in which he has a pecuniary interest, supplies false information for the guidance of others in their business transactions, is subject to liability for pecuniary loss caused to them by their justifiable reliance on the information, if he fails to exercise reasonable care or competence in obtaining or communicating the information." The section then continues to define what persons can enforce this liability.

[2] Stephans Industries Inc. v Haskins & Sells (CA10 Colo) 438 F2d 357 (1971).

tation of liability to immunize an intentional tort.

5. Contributory Negligence of Plaintiff

When the suit for malpractice is brought against the accountant by the client, the comparative negligence of the client may reduce the liability of the accountant. To do this, it is necessary that the negligence of the client contributed to the accountant's failure or that the client ignored instructions of the accountant.

When suit is brought by a third person for malpractice, the defendant accountant may raise the defense of the contributory negligence of the plaintiff. If the plaintiff acted negligently in relying on a financial statement, the plaintiff cannot sue the accountant for negligently preparing the statement. For example, when the statement recites that it is merely a working examination and is not certified by the accountant, the third person is negligent if reliance is placed on the statement. In harmony with general principles of negligence law, the plaintiff is then barred by such contributory negligence.

In some cases, it may be apparent on the face of the financial statement that the business it represents is in poor financial condition. When a prudent person would see danger in the financial statement, the plaintiff not perceiving such danger cannot sue the accountant on the ground that the statement was negligently prepared.

B. MALPRACTICE LIABILITY OF NONACCOUNTANTS

The law governing the accountant's liability for malpractice has developed against the background of general principles governing the liability for improper performance of contract by technicians, surveyors, inspectors, and professionals other than accountants.

6. Standard of Care

When is a contracting party guilty of such poor performance that the conduct may be called malpractice? Historically, the term *malpractice* was applied only to persons engaged in the practice of medicine or law. In the last half century, the concepts of liability for poor performance of a professional have been extended to technicians, surveyors, and safety inspectors. All of these, as well as doctors and lawyers, must exercise the degree of skill and care commonly exercised by others following the same calling within the same community.

The standard just described is a variable standard, affected by time and place. As new knowledge develops and is accepted within the community, it is malpractice to fail to keep in step with the changing times. With respect to place, the community standards of one geographic area may differ from those of another. The geographic differential has become less significant as modern methods of transportation and communication have led to a greater exchange of knowledge and skills between different parts of the country.

7. Persons Entitled to Damages

Once it is shown that a contracting party is guilty of malpractice, the next step is to determine who may recover damages for this improper conduct.

(a) OTHER CONTRACTING PARTY. When a party is guilty of malpractice, there is a breach of contract, and the other contracting party can sue for the damages caused by the breach.

(b) THIRD PERSONS. Prior to this century, there was no malpractice liability to third persons. In this century, liability to third persons is recognized to some extent.

(1) Privity of Contract Rule. The rule of law that bars a third person from suing for malpractice is called the **privity of contract rule**. According to this rule, a third person could not sue for breach of a contract, because there was no privity of contract between the third person and the defendant. This is the

same concept that for several centuries barred a third person from claiming the right to sue on a contract as a third party beneficiary. The privity of contract rule also barred the stranger to the contract from suing one of the contracting parties for malpractice.

Some courts continue to follow this rule today. They fear that by abandoning the requirement of privity, they may be subjecting the defendant to an endless number of lawsuits that, in effect, would cause the defendant's economic death. In some states, the nonprivity plaintiff is barred from suing a remote defendant for malpractice negligence when the only damage sustained by the plaintiff is economic, as distinguished from personal injury or damage to other property.[3]

(2) Abandonment of Privity of Contract Rule.   In this century, a number of courts have abandoned the privity of contract rule. In some cases, the court felt that no evil would follow the abandonment of the rule. The number of persons who might be affected would be small, so there was no danger of a flood of litigation. The defendant would not be economically destroyed, because insurance was available or the burden of liability could be passed on to other customers and clients by the defendant's raising fees and charges.

In one case in which the privity of contract rule was rejected, an insurance company was negligent in making a safety examination of the boiler in the insured building. Because of that negligence, an employee was scalded from a bursting boiler. The court held that suit could be brought against the insurance company by the widow of the employee who died from his burns.[4] Similarly, the repairer of an automobile who negligently repairs the brakes is liable to a pedestrian injured when the brakes fail. A surveyor making a negligent survey for a real estate developer is liable to a subsequent purchaser of the land for loss caused by a mistake in the survey. Architects designing buildings may be sued for malpractice by the purchasers of such buildings for loss caused by the negligence of the architects in designing the buildings.[5] An owner, seeking to sell a building, may have an architect make an inspection and prepare a report on its condition. The architect may be careless and report that the building condition was good, when in fact it was poor. When a buyer buys the building in reliance on the false report, the buyer may sue the architect for the damages sustained. The negligence of an attorney in preparing a will may result in the exclusion of an intended beneficiary. Courts differ as to whether the intended beneficiary may sue the attorney. Some courts refuse to allow recovery because there was no privity of contract between the intended beneficiary and the attorney.[6] Others allow recovery on the theory that negligence malpractice liability may be imposed without privity of contract or on the theory that the intended beneficiary of the will was a third party beneficiary of the contract between the attorney and the client.[7] In some states the requirement of privity of contract has been abolished by statute.[8]

In the *A. E. Investment Corporation* case the third person sued the architect for economic loss.

(3) Relaxation of Privity of Contract Rule.   Some courts have been unwilling to follow the privity rule and yet have been faced with a case in which they were reluctant to abandon that rule. At times, such a court has escaped from this dilemma by concluding that the facts presented a situation that could be described as being the equivalent of privity or substantially the same as privity of contract.

---

[3]   Sensenbrenner v Rust, Orling & Neale, Architects, Inc., 236 Va 419, 374 SE2d 55 (1988) (plaintiff denied right to sue remote architect and installer of swimming pool when negligence caused leaking of pool that damaged house).

[4]   Seay v Travelers Indemnity Co. (Tex App) 730 SW2d 774 (1987).

[5]   Beachwalk Villas Condominium Ass'n, Inc. v Martin (SC) 406 SE2d 382 (1991).

[6]   Thomas v Pryor (Tex App) 847 SW2d 303 (1992).

[7]   Hale v Groce, 304 Or 281, 744 P2d 1289 (1987).

[8]   Hosford v McKissack (Miss) 589 So 2d 108 (1991).

A. E. INVESTMENT CORP.
v LINK BUILDERS, INC.

62 Wis 2d 479, 214 NW2d 764 (1974)

> The More-Way Development Company contracted with Link to construct a building. DeQuardo, Robinson, Crouch & Associates, Inc., were the architects who designed the building. After the building was constructed, A. E. Investment Corporation rented a part of the building. Because of the negligence of the architects, the building settled. A. E. Investment Corporation was forced to leave the building because of this condition. It then sued the architects for the economic loss sustained thereby. The architects filed a demurrer to the complaint. The lower court overruled the demurrer. The defendant architects appealed.

HEFFERNAN, J. . . . It was alleged that the architect was negligent in its failure to adequately supervise the construction, in that it failed to determine the nature and condition of the subsoil prior to and during construction. It was also alleged that, in view of the subsoil conditions, the plans were negligently drawn because they did not provide for the construction of a floor that was necessary to accommodate the plaintiff's business enterprise.

It was alleged that the defendant knew that the building would be used as a commercial store and the plaintiff would therein operate a supermarket. It was alleged that, as the direct and proximate result of the negligence, the floor space leased to the plaintiff began to settle, damage was caused to the walls, the floor became uneven, and eventually the premises became untenantable. . . .

The defendant defines the question . . . as being whether the defendant had a "duty to protect the subtenant plaintiff's future economic interests from loss allegedly resulting from a condition of the building." It responds to that question only by attempting to show that an architect owes no duty to a person with whom he is not in privity of contract. As a consequence, the defendant relies on the narrow argument that it has no responsibility for any economic loss to the plaintiff because it has no duty to the plaintiff at all and no responsibility to be answerable for any damages, irrespective of the nature of the loss. . . .

We believe that the narrow concept of duty relied on by the defendant architect has long been discarded in Wisconsin law. The duty of any person is the obligation of due care to refrain from any act which will cause foreseeable harm to others even though the nature of that harm and the identity of the harmed person or harmed interest is unknown at the time of the act. . . . ". . . Once an act has been found to be negligent, we no longer look to see if there was a duty to the one who was in fact injured." . . .

In the instant case . . . the defendant's alleged failure to properly take into account the condition of the subsoil when designing and supervising the construction of the building was an act or omission that would foreseeably cause some harm to someone. The duty was to refrain from such act or omission. Where, as here, it is alleged that the architect knew the purpose for which the building was being constructed, it was clearly foreseeable that a future tenant of the building was within the ambit of the harm. Hence, the harm to the particular plaintiff was foreseeable, although under the methodology of this court, it is not necessary that either the person harmed or the type of harm that would result be foreseeable. The act or omission in the face of foreseeable harm was negligence. . . .

Under Wisconsin negligence law, architects may be liable to third parties with whom they are not in privity of contract. The lack of privity does not constitute a policy reason for not imposing liability where negligence is shown to be a substantial factor in occasioning the harm.

The defendant also argues that, since an architect is a professional, his paramount duty is to his client, and that, if no duty is breached in connection with the architect-client relationship, there is no responsibility to third parties. We disagree with the argument that a professional can exonerate himself from liability for a negligent act which will foreseeably cause harm to third parties, merely because his client does not object. The very essence of a profession is that the services are rendered with the understanding that the duties of the profession cannot be undertaken on behalf of a client without an awareness and a responsibility to the public welfare. The entire ambit of state regulations as they apply to the profession of architecture is intended, not solely for the protection of the person with whom the architect deals, but for the protection of the world at large. Professionalism is the very antithesis to irresponsibility to all interests other than those of an immediate employer.

In the instant case, however, if, as it is alleged, the defendant architect negligently designed or permitted the erection of an unsuitable or unstable structure, it was hardly acting in the interests of its client, whether that client has seen fit to complain or not. . . .

[Judgment affirmed]

QUESTIONS

1. Was there a contract between the architect and the tenants of the building?
2. Were the tenants third party beneficiaries of the contract between the building owner and the architect?
3. Only a party to a contract or a third party beneficiary of a contract can sue for harm caused by the improper performance of a contract. Appraise this statement.

Such a court will allow the recovery of malpractice damages by a stranger to the contract when there is a sufficiently close connection of the stranger to the transaction or sufficient contact with the defendant that it appears proper to allow suit by the stranger.

As protection against imposing unlimited liability for negligent misrepresentation, some courts require both that the person harmed relied on the misrepresentations and that such reliance was foreseeable by the provider of that information.[9]

C. ACCOUNTANTS' MALPRACTICE LIABILITY

Most of the accountants' malpractice litigation involves the question of whether third persons

---

[9] John Martin Co., Inc. v Morse/Diesel, Inc. (Tenn App) 819 SW2d 428 (1991).

may sue rather than what standards of conduct accountants should observe.

8. Standards of Conduct for Accountants

Accountants are liable to their clients when loss is caused the clients because the accountants failed to observe the standards of sound accounting practices. Accountants are also liable if their failure to call attention to a condition causes a client to fail to take preventive steps and to thereby sustain a loss.

"Certified public accountants are liable for damages proximately caused by their negligence just like other skilled professions. . . . Accordingly they owe their clients a duty to exercise the degree of care, skill, and competence that reasonably competent members of their profession would exercise under similar circumstances."[10] Basically, the concept is the same as the one applied to doctors and attorneys.

An accountant is liable to the client when the accountant negligently fails to detect or fraudulently conceals signs that an employee of the client is embezzling from the client, or that the internal audit controls of the client's business are not being observed. An accountant who prepares tax returns and acts as tax manager for the client will be liable when additional taxes or penalties are assessed against the client as a result of negligently given advice. Similarly, a client may recover damages from the client's accountant when the latter negligently failed to inform the client of the tax consequences of the sale of the business.[11]

9. Liability of Accountant for Client's Liability

In some cases, the accountant's malpractice is followed almost immediately by a loss to the client. In other cases, such as those involving taxes, the misconduct of the accountant causes a tax liability to attach to the client but there is an interval before the client is required to pay those taxes. That is, there is liability for taxes before there is a loss by the payment of the taxes. The *Thomas* case turned on whether the client could sue because of the accountant's fault as soon as the client became liable for greater taxes.

THOMAS v CLEARY
(Alaska) 768 P2d 1090 (1989)

Cleary and the other owners of Cleary Diving Service, Inc. wanted to sell the business. They hired the accounting firm of Thomas, Head, & Greisen (THG) to advise them on how to proceed in order to reduce federal income tax liability. They were advised to sell the assets of the company. This was wrong advice, since the tax liability would have been less if all the stock of the company had been sold. Notice was given to the Internal Revenue Service (IRS) that the company was being liquidated. Liquidation should have been completed within 12 months, but the owners were not informed that there would be greater tax liability if liquidation took longer. The liquidation took more than a year. In addition, THG failed to file a corporate tax return for the following year. Eighteen months after the sale of the assets, THG notified the

---

[10] Greenstein, Logan & Co. v Burgess Marketing, Inc. (Tex App) 744 SW2d 170 (1987).

[11] Deloitte, Haskins & Sells v Green, ___ Ga App ___, 403 SE2d 818 (1991).

Clearys that they owed an additional $100,000 in taxes. The Clearys then sued Thomas individually and THG for malpractice in failing to advise them to make the sale by selling the stock, in failing to tell them to complete liquidation within one year, and for failing to file a tax return and pay taxes for the year following the liquidation. The defendants raised the defense that they could not be liable because the IRS had not made any claim for additional taxes against the Clearys. Judgment was entered against THG, and it appealed.

BURKE, J. . . . The thrust of Thomas' and THG's argument on appeal concerns the amount of damages awarded. They argue first that the verdict improperly includes potential tax liability which has not yet been paid to, or assessed by, the IRS, and is therefore speculative damage. . . . We agree with Thomas and THG that the damages awarded to the Clearys were improper.

The elements of a cause of action for professional negligence are: (1) a duty, (2) a breach of that duty, (3) a proximate causal connection between the negligent conduct and the resulting injury, and (4) *actual loss or damage resulting from the professional's negligence.* . . . Injury or damage, then, is an essential element of a cause of action for professional malpractice. As we stated in *Austin v Fulton Insurance*, 444 P2d 536, 539 (Alaska 1968):

A tort is ordinarily not complete until there has been an invasion of a legally protected interest of the plaintiff. . . . There must be an injury or harm to appellant as a consequence of appellees' negligence to serve as a basis for recovery of damages before the tort [becomes] actionable. . .

. . . Thus, in discussing a client's claim against an attorney for malpractice, the California Supreme Court has said:

The mere breach of a professional duty, causing only nominal damages, speculative harm, or the threat of future harm—not yet realized—does not suffice to create a cause of action for negligence. Hence, until the client suffers appreciable harm as a consequence of [the professional's] negligence, the client cannot establish a cause of action for malpractice. Budd, 98 Cal Rptr at 852, 491 P2d at 436. . .

We hold that the Clearys have not suffered the required injury or harm as a result of the defendant's negligence. The record establishes that the IRS has never sent the Cleary's a deficiency notice nor imposed any tax assessment as a result of the failure to file . . . corporate tax returns.

An analogous situation arose in *Philips v Giles*, 620 SW2d 750 (Tex Civ App 1981), where a party in a divorce proceeding sued her attorney for malpractice, alleging he negligently advised her that the settlement she entered into would involve no tax implications. [She] was subsequently told by her accountant that there were tax consequences. She filed returns, but the IRS never assessed taxes on the money [she] reported and never determined that the money in question was taxable. . . . The court held that her malpractice action had been properly abated because her suit was "prematurely instituted." . . . The court concluded that [her] cause of action has not accrued because no tax liability has been established by the Internal Revenue Service. Thus, [she] had yet to be injured.

. . . Although [she] believes the taxes are due, she may be mistaken, and, indeed, no tax liability, insofar as we know, may exist.

. . . Similarly, we conclude that since it has not yet been determined whether the Clearys are liable for the taxes in question, they have "not been harmed and, therefore, [their] cause of action has not accrued.". . .

We find further support for our conclusion in those cases which discuss the accrual of causes of action in the context of statutes of limitations. In *Atkins v Crosland*, 417 SW2d 150, 153 (Tex 1967), the court found that:

plaintiff's cause of action [for accountant malpractice] did not arise until the tax deficiency was assessed by the Commissioner of Internal Revenue. Prior to assessment the plaintiff had not been injured. . . . If a deficiency had never been assessed, the plaintiff would not have been harmed and therefore would have had no cause of action. (Emphasis added.)

Similarly, in *Streib v Veigel*, 109 Idaho 174, 178, 706 P2d 63, 67 (1985), the court held that "no damages accrued to the plaintiffs until the time of the Internal Revenue Service's assessment of penalties and interest." . . . *See also Leonhart v Atkinson*, 265 Md. 219, 289 A2d 1, 4 (1972) (the date the notice of tax deficiency assessment was received is date statute of limitations begins to run, since legal harm was sustained at that time); *Chisholm v Scott*, 86 NM 707, 526 P2d 1300, 1302 (App 1974) (liability imposed by the IRS' notice becomes the injury which forms the plaintiff's cause of action); *Wall v Lewis*, 366 NW2d 471, 473 (ND 1985) (actual damage has been incurred when the IRS imposes a tax assessment, thereby creating an enforceable obligation against the client); . . .

The IRS has not yet assessed a tax deficiency against the Clearys. Therefore, they have incurred no damage, and consequently, no tort has occurred. Only when the tax deficiency is assessed will the tort of which the Clearys complain ripen. Until then, the Clearys have not been harmed and are not entitled to recover. *See Greater Area Inc. v Bookman*, 657 P2d 828, 829 n. 3 (Alaska 1982) (even if client discovers attorney's negligent acts before he suffers damages, the cause of action for malpractice is not complete until actual damages are suffered).

We hold that the Cleary's action for accounting malpractice is not yet ripe. The case is [thus] REMANDED to the superior court with instructions to VACATE the judgment without prejudice.

QUESTIONS

1. What element did the plaintiffs fail to prove?
2. What was the significance of the fact that the IRS had not sent the Clearys a notice of tax deficiency?
3. Did the Court hold that the plaintiffs could never recover from the accountants?

10. Nonliability to the Interloper

No court imposes liability on the accountant to a total stranger who gets possession of the accountant's work and then sustains a loss because of a false statement in the work. This applies regardless of whether the statement was negligent or intentional. For example, assume that a negligently prepared financial statement of a corporation is thrown in the wastepaper basket. It is then retrieved by a security guard. If the guard thinks that the statement is a "hot tip" and invests in the stock of the corporation on the basis of the statement, the guard cannot sue the accountant for negligence in preparing the statement. The courts have struggled to form a rule that will exclude what the court regards as interlopers but permit suits by those the courts regard as proper plaintiffs.

11. Nonliability to Person Affected by the Decision of Accountant's Client

On the basis of information furnished by the accountant to the client, the client may make a decision that affects a third person. For example, the report of the independent auditor may indicate that a fiscal officer of the client has not handled funds properly. The report may indicate that it is economically unsound to enter into a contract with a third person. Assume that the client relies on the accountant's report and fires the employee or refuses to make a contract with the third person. If the report of the accountant was negligently made, and the true facts would not have justified the action taken by the client, the question arises as to whether the third person or the discharged employee may sue the negligent accountant. It has been held that such a suit may not be brought.[12]

12. Accountants' Negligence Malpractice Liability to Third Persons

In the last century, the negligence of the accountant would impose liability only to the client of the accountant. Today, many states permit third persons to recover damages from the accountant.

(a) STATUS OF ACCOUNTANT. The accountant sued by the third person for malpractice may be an in-house accountant working full time for the particular employer. The accountant may be an independent contractor who regularly does accounting-related work, such as preparing financial statements and tax returns for different clients. The accountant may be an independent auditor.

What constitutes negligence is the same for all three types of accountants. As a practical matter, a third person would not ordinarily sue the employee-accountant, because the claim would probably be much more than the employee could pay. In such a case, it would be more practical to sue the employer. The latter would be liable for the negligent performance of the employee.

(b) CONFLICTING THEORIES. A number of theories have been developed in this century to determine whether a third person sustaining a loss because of the accountant's negligence can sue the accountant for loss or whether such a person is an interloper who cannot sue. These views may be identified as (1) the privity rule, (2) the contact rule, (3) the known user rule, and (4) the foreseeable user rule. In addition, some courts follow (5) a flexible rule, deciding each case as it arises.

Each of these views represents an attempt to draw a boundary line between the interloper and the "proper" plaintiff. Each view is supported by honest judges seeking to do justice. They have the same goal and are all guided by ethics, but the resultant rules of law are different.

(1) The Privity Rule. The privity rule excludes a negligence malpractice suit by a third person. This rule holds that only the person in privity with the accountant—that is, the client of the accountant—may sue the accountant.[13]

---

[12] Harper v Inkster Public Schools and Arthur Andersen & Co. 158 Mich App 456, 404 NW2d 776 (1987).

[13] This rule was originally known as the New York rule, Ultramares Corp. v Touche, 255 NY 170, 174 NE 441 (1931). Although it has been replaced in New York by the contact rule, the privity rule is still the law in many jurisdictions.

When the privity rule is applied, a bank lending money to the client of the accountant cannot sue the accountant for malpractice.

(2) The Contact Rule. As a relaxation of the privity requirement, New York now holds that a third person may sue a negligent accountant when there was some contact between the third person and the accountant. For example, an accountant may go to a bank to see what information the bank requires in order for the accountant's client to obtain a loan. In this case, there is a sufficient "link" or "contact" between the bank and the accountant to allow the bank to sue the accountant if it sustains loss because of the accountant's negligence.[14] It appears that the New York contact rule requires that the accountant meet or communicate with the nonprivity plaintiff to establish a relationship equivalent to privity. It also appears that the accountant must know of the purpose of the accounting work and foresee the nonprivity plaintiffs reliance on that work.[15]

Thus, there must be enough contact with or dealings between the plaintiff and the accountant to give the accountant reason to know that the plaintiff was relying for a particular purpose on the financial statements prepared by the accountant.

The contact rule applies to malpractice defendants generally. It is not limited to suits against accountants.[16]

(3) The Known User Rule. By this rule, the accountant is liable for a third person's negligently caused loss when the accountant knew that the third person would be using the accountant's work product. The fact that the nonprivity plaintiff's reliance on a financial statement was foreseeable does not entitle the plaintiff to sue the accountant for negligent preparation of the statement. It must be shown that the accountant knew that the statement would be furnished to that plaintiff. Under the known user rule the plaintiff's reliance must thus be actually foreseen and not merely reasonably foreseeable.[17]

In the *First Florida Bank* case, the accountant claimed that the bank that had loaned money to the accountant's client was barred from suing the accountant because of lack of privity.

Under the known user rule, it is sufficient if the user is a member of a known class even though the identity of the particular user is not

---

[14] Credit Alliance Corp. v Arthur Andersen & Co. 65 NY2d 536, 483 NE2d 110 (1985). Some courts are reluctant to turn their backs on the requirement of privity and describe the contact rule not as a different rule but as requiring "a relationship sufficiently intimate to be equated with privity." Empire of America v Arthur Andersen & Co. 129 App Div 2d 990, 514 NYS2d 578 (1987). A further attempt to define the New York rule was made in William Iselin & Co., Inc. v Landau, 71 NY2d 420, 527 NYS2d 176, 522 NE2d 21 (1988) (involving a review report), in which the court declared that it was necessary for a nonprivity plaintiff suing an accountant for negligent misrepresentation to establish "a nexus between them sufficiently approaching privity (Credit Alliance Corp. . . . .)." The contact rule has been adopted by a minority of states. Idaho Bank & Trust Co v First Bankcorp of Idaho (Idaho) 772 P2d 720 (1989).

[15] Security Pacific Business Credit, Inc. v Peat Marwick Main & Co., 79 NY2d 695, 586 NYS2d 87, 597 NE2d 1080 (1992). In Franko v Mitchell (App) 158 Ariz 391, 762 P2d 1345 (1988), the court held that when the borrower's attorney met and discussed the proposed loan details with both the lender and the borrower, it could be found that there was an implied contract of employment between the borrower's attorney and the creditor so as to permit the creditor to bring a malpractice action against the attorney. This would have been classified as "equivalent to privity" if the court had followed the New York terminology.

[16] Ossining Union Free School District v Anderson, 73 NY2d 417, 539 NE2d 91 (1989) ("The long-standing rule is that recovery may be had for pecuniary loss arising from negligent representations where there is actual privity of contract between the parties or a relationship so close as to approach that of privity. Nor does the rule apply only to accountants. We have never drawn that categorical distinction, and see no basis for establishing such an arbitrary limitation now.") Board of Managers of the Astor Terrace Condominium v Shuman, Lichtenstein, Claman & Efron, ___ App Div 2d ___, 583 NYS2d 398 (1992).

[17] Lindner Fund v Abney (Mo App) 770 SW2d 437 (1989). The rule that the nonprivity plaintiff may recover from the accountant for malpractice negligence only if the accountant's statement was furnished to that plaintiff or the accountant knew that the client who was given the statement would in turn give the statement to the plaintiff, is often identified as "the Restatement rule." This rule is based on Restatement (Second) Torts (1977) § 522(2). There is, however, some uncertainty as to the exact boundaries of the Restatement rule. See Selden v Burnett (Alaska) 754 P2d 256 (1988), Raritan River Steel Co. v Cherry, Bekaert & Holland, 322 NC 200, 367 SE2d 609 (1988).

FIRST FLORIDA BANK v MAX MITCHELL & CO.
(Fla) 558 So 2d (1990)

Maxwell was a CPA and president of the accounting firm of Max Mitchell & Co. He went to the first Florida Bank to negotiate a loan on behalf of a client, C.M. Systems. The bank was induced to make the requested loan because the audit statements for several years showed that the client was in good financial condition. In reply to questions of the bank official, Maxwell stated that there was no change in the financial condition of the client from that shown in the audit statements and that the client did not owe any money to any bank. First Florida Bank loaned the money to the client. The money was never repaid. It was then discovered that the audit statements were seriously inaccurate and that the client owed a substantial sum to another bank. First Florida sued Max Mitchell & Co., claiming that the accounting firm had been negligent in the preparation of the financial statements. The defendant raised the defense that it could not be sued because it was not in privity with the bank. Judgment was entered for the accounting firm. The bank appealed.

GRIMES, J. . . . The doctrine of privity has undergone substantial erosion in Florida. Indeed, in cases involving injuries caused by neligently manufactured products the requirement that there be privity between the plaintiff and the manufacturer has been abolished. . . . Further, this Court . . . held that a general contractor could sue an architect or engineer for damages proximately caused by their negligence on a building project despite the absence of privity of contract between the parties. The liability of a lawyer in the absence of privity has been limited to cases where the legal service neligently performed was apparently initiated by the lawyer's client to benefit a third party, such as in the drafting of a will. . . .

Most significant, however, to the instant case is this Court's decision in *First American Title Insurance Co. v First Title Service Co.*, 457 So 2d 467 (Fla 1984). . . .

Where the abstracter knows, or should know, that his customer wants the abstract for the use of a prospective purchaser, and the prospect purchases the land relying on the abstract, the abstracter's duty of care runs . . . not only to his customer but to the purchaser. Moreover, others involved in the transaction through their relationship to the purchaser—such as lender-mortgagees, tenants and title insurers—will also be protected where the purchaser's reliance was known or should have been known to the abstracter. But a party into whose hands the abstract falls in connection with a subsequent transaction is not among those to whom the abstracter owes a duty of care.

. . . The opinion in *First American Title Insurance* is also important for the arguments which this Court rejected. We declined to approve the principle that an abstracter is liable in negligence to all persons who might foreseeably use and rely on the abstract. . . .

Some of the competing interests involved in selecting the proper standard for accountants' liability to third parties are set forth in Annotation, *Liability of Public Accountant to Third Parties*, 46 A.L.R. 3d 979, 984 (1972):

It is contended by those favoring such liability that accountants, due to their professional status and the respect they command, invite reliance on their work by the business community, and that investors and creditors do, in fact, rely upon their accuracy and integrity; on the other hand, it is pointed out that unlike members of other professions, accountants have no control over the identity or number of those who rely on their work, and that imposition of liability, in negligence, to third parties would place an enormous potential burden on the profession. Those in favor of expanding liability argue that the accounting profession no longer needs the protection of nonliability in this area, due to its wealth, and contend that the cost of insurance protection could be passed on to the client, stating that the innocent relier should not be damaged because of the error of the negligent accountant. In reply, it is observed that the cost of such insurance protection is prohibitive and, in many cases, that such coverage is not available at any price; furthermore, it is said, such higher costs would tend to lead dominance of the profession by the large national accounting firms and to a curtailment of the availability of accountancy services to small businesses. Nor, it is contended, does the argument for extended liability take into consideration the ever more acute shortage of qualified public accountants in private practice. Those in favor of expanding liability argue that liability could easily be limited by the increased use of disclaimers and limited certifications, pointing to the success of the British experience in this area. Opponents, however, observe that the use of such devices is a commercial impossibility unless all accountants follow this practice, since it tends to dissatisfy the client, who will then turn to the use of other accountants not following this practice. . . .

Because of the heavy reliance upon audited financial statements in the contemporary financial world, we believe permitting recovery only from those in privity or near privity is unduly restrictive. On the other hand, we are persuaded by the wisdom of the rule which limits liability to those persons or classes of persons whom an accountant "knows" will rely on his opinion rather than those he "should have known" would do so because it takes into account the fact that an accountant controls neither his client's accounting records nor the distribution of his reports. . . .

There remains the need to apply this rule to the facts at hand. At the time Mitchell prepared the audits for C.M. Systems, it was unknown that they would be used to induce the reliance of First Florida Bank to approve a line of credit for C.M. Systems. Therefore, except for the unusual facts of this case, Mitchell could not be held liable to the bank for any negligence in preparing the audit. However, Mitchell actually negotiated the loan on behalf of his client. He personally delivered the financial statements to the bank with the knowledge that it would rely upon them in considering whether or not to make the loan. Under this unique set of facts, we believe that Mitchell vouched for the integrity of the audits and that his conduct in dealing with the bank sufficed to meet the requirements of the rule which we have adopted in this opinion.

[Judgment vacated and action remanded]

QUESTIONS

1. Did the availability of malpractice insurance affect the decision in the *First Florida Bank* case?
2. How would the court have decided the *First Florida Bank* case if the client, C.M. Systems, had taken the audit statements to the bank and negotiated directly with the bank to obtain the loan?
3. How can a bank protect itself when the applicant for a loan submits financial statements prepared by an accountant?

known to the accountant. However, there is authority that when the identity of the intended user is known to the accountant, another person coming within the same class as the known user cannot sue the accountant.[18] For example, an accountant prepares a financial statement for the client with the knowledge that the client will take it to the First National Bank to obtain a loan. The First National Bank may sue the accountant for negligent loss, even though the bank never had any direct contact or dealings with the accountant and was not in privity with the accountant. However, no one other than First National may sue the accountant for negligence. The fact that the plaintiff was a foreseeable user does not give the right to sue in a "known user" state. Accordingly, when the accountant prepared a financial statement for the client and nothing was said about what further use of the statement would be made, creditors of the client could not sue the accountant for negligent preparation of the statement. It was the client who was the known user.

If the court follows the privity rule or the contact rule described in the two preceding sections, the known user cannot sue the accountant for negligent malpractice. Moreover, some courts that follow the known user rule apply it so strictly that a substitute foreseeable user is not allowed to sue. To illustrate, assume that in the example just given the client was refused the loan by the First National Bank. The client might then make an application for a loan to the Second National Bank. It has been held that the Second National Bank could not sue the accountant, because the Second National Bank was not a known user. However, the Second National Bank would be allowed to sue under the rules discussed in the sections that follow.

(4) The Foreseeable User Rule. The accountant may foresee that a particular class of unknown persons will rely on the accountant's work. For example, when the accountant prepares a financial statement knowing that the client is going to use it to borrow money from some bank or finance company, the accountant foresees that there is a class of lenders. Similarly, the accountant may know that the financial statement will be used to sell the stock of the client corporation. Here again, there is a foreseeable class consisting of unknown persons.

When it is reasonable to foresee that there will be persons who will rely on the statement of the accountant, the foreseeable user rule imposes liability on the accountant for negligent malpractice. The foreseeable user rule allows such third persons to sue for their loss without regard to the lack of privity of contract between the third persons and the accountants.[19]

In the *Spherex* case, the lawsuit turned on whether the plaintiff could recover from the accountant hired by the plaintiff's customer.

(5) The Intended User Rule. The fear that the foreseeability rule does not sufficiently restrict the number of potential plaintiffs has led some courts to limit suit to those nonprivity plaintiffs who were not merely foreseeable but who were expected or intended to rely on the work of the accountant in a particular transaction or another similar transaction.[20] By this view the accountant must have furnished the information directly to the nonprivity plaintiff or to the client with knowledge that the client

---

[18] Blue Bell, Inc. v Peat, Marwich, Mitchell & Co. (Tex App) 715 SW2d 408 (1986) ("If under current business practice and the circumstances of that case, an accountant preparing audited financial statements knows or should know that such statements will be relied upon by a limited class of persons, the accountant may be liable for injuries to members of that class relying on his certification of the audited reports.") Note that to the extent that a court speaks in terms of should know, there is the inference that the court is embracing "foreseeability" and is thus moving from the known user rule to the foreseeable user rule.

[19] Bily v Arthur Young & Co. 230 Cal App 3d 835, 271 Cal Rptr 470 (1990). This rule is regarded by some courts as representing the majority view. The foreseeable user rule brings the law with respect to accountants into harmony with the tort law relating to other persons and activities.

[20] Bily v Arthur Young & Co. 3 Cal 4th 370, 11 Cal Rptr 2d 51, 834 P2d 745 (1992).

SPHEREX, INC. v ALEXANDER GRANT & CO.

122 NH 898, 451 A2d 1308 (1982)

General Home Products (GHP) hired the accounting firm of Alexander Grant & Company to prepare an unaudited financial statement of GHP. The statement was to be based on financial information provided by GHP. GHP submitted the financial statement to Spherex so that GHP could buy on credit. The financial statement had been negligently prepared, and Spherex lost money by selling to GHP on credit. Spherex sued Alexander Grant on the ground that it knew that the financial statement prepared by it would be submitted to Spherex to obtain credit, but Grant was negligent in preparing it. Grant raised the defense that its potential liability did not extend to a party with whom it was not in privity. Grant also asserted that it is unreasonable, as a matter of law, for a third party to rely on an unaudited financial statement.

DOUGLAS, J. . . . It should be noted at the outset that the question before this court is not Alexander Grant's liability to Spherex for intentional misrepresentation, or fraud. *Ultramares Corp. v Touche*, 255 NY 170, 174 NE 441 (1931), the seminal case on an accountant's liability to third parties, from which Alexander Grant's privity defense stems, distinguished intentional from negligent misrepresentation, and held that an accountant could be liable to a non-client whom he intentionally deceived. Justice Cardozo, writing for the New York Court of Appeals, took note of the defendant accountant's liability in that case to a plaintiff who detrimentally relied on *intentional* material misstatements:

The defendants owed to their employer a duty imposed by law to make their certificate without fraud, and a duty growing out of contract to make it with the care and caution proper to their calling. Fraud includes the pretense of knowledge when knowledge there is none. To creditors and investors to whom the employer exhibited the certificate, the defendants owed a like duty to make it without fraud, since there was notice in the circumstances of its making that the employer did not intend to keep it to himself.

In other words, where an accountant or other supplier of information knows that a materially false statement is to be conveyed to some party other than to whom it is made, public policy is served by holding the intentional wrongdoer accountable to the one who relies to his detriment on the misstatement of fact.

The considerations are different when the misrepresentation is *negligently* made. "If liability for negligence exists, a thoughtless slip or blunder, the failure to detect a theft or forgery beneath the cover of deceptive entries, may expose accountants to a liability in an indeterminate amount for an indeterminate time to an indeterminate class." Courts have read this language in *Ultramares* as requiring privity between a defendant-accountant and a plaintiff before liability for negligent misrepresentation can attach. . . .

Counsel for both parties agree, and our research has revealed no cases to the contrary, that this question is unsettled in New Hampshire. Yet, we have expressed our disfavor for the privity doctrine in personal injury cases. Our reluctance to apply the privity rule has extended to allowing a proper plaintiff to recover for mere financial loss resulting from the negligent performance of services. The duty that Spherex alleges it was owed by Alexander Grant is not entirely dissimilar to the duty we have held a promisor owes to an intended third-party beneficiary. In *Tamposi Associates v Star Mkt. Co.*, 119 NH 630, 406 A2d 132 (1979), we said "[a] third-party beneficiary relationship exists if . . . the contract is so expressed as to give the promisor reason to know that a benefit to a third party is contemplated by the promisee as one of the motivating causes of his making the contract." In the instant case, Spherex claims Alexander Grant's duty to produce an unaudited financial statement in a non-negligent manner grew out of Alexander Grant's engagement contract with GHP. Spherex's status as a third-party user of the financial statement prepared by Alexander Grant, if proved at trial, would be akin to an intended third-party beneficiary to whom Alexander Grant owed a duty of due care.

The *Ultramares* holding, and its apparent privity requirement, has been distinguished primarily on two bases. First, courts have sought to link the privity doctrine with Justice Cardozo's "social utility" rationale of protecting professionals from the specter of unlimited liability to a virtually limitless class of plaintiffs. Thus, judges have not hesitated to permit recovery where the plaintiff's identity was specifically known to the negligent defendant. . . . Beyond that, courts have been less willing to expand the frontier of liability. The question is "whether the defendant has some special reason to anticipate the reliance of the plaintiff."

Second, *Ultramares* has been distinguished as a relic of a bygone economic era. Both the sophistication of modern accounting procedures and the accountant's central role in the financing and investment industry are a far cry from the fledgling profession in need of judicial protection that existed at the time of *Ultramares*. One commentator has stated:

The accountant today has a role of central responsibility in the business community. . . . This new circumstance, not present when Ultramares was decided, makes it clear that 'between the innocent reliant party and the negligent public accountant, the accountant should bear the burden of his negligence.' The accountant then must accept the burdens of legal responsibility that go along with the benefits derived from his important role in the modern business community.

The Restatement (Second) of Torts § 552 has sought to harmonize the accountant's contemporary role and his potential liability by holding him accountable to a "person or one of a limited group of persons for whose benefit and guidance he intends to supply the information or knows that the recipient intends to supply it. . . . " In effect, an accountant who negligently misrepresents information is held liable not only to known third parties but to an actually foreseeable class of third persons. As comment *a* to section 552 explains, extending an accountant's liability to an intended recipient of information "promotes the important social policy of encouraging the flow of commercial information upon which the operation of the economy rests." Furthermore, an accountant, like the manufacturer under products liability law, is in the best position to regulate the effects of his conduct by controlling the degree of care exercised during the performance of his professional duties. The accountant, through the fee structure, can pass along to his clients the cost of insuring against financial loss sustained by them through reliance upon his negligent misstatement of fact.

We believe section 552 of the Restatement represents a reasoned approach to the issue of professional liability for negligent misrepresentation. . . .

Nevertheless, we acknowledge that an accountant's potential liability is not boundless. "It is not enough that the maker merely knows of the ever-present possibility of repetition [of information supplied by him] to anyone, and the possibility of action in reliance upon it, on the part of anyone to whom it may be repeated." Restatement (Second) of Torts § 552 comment *h*, at 133. The plaintiff's relationship to the accountant becomes crucial because

the risk of liability to which the supplier subjects himself by undertaking to give the information, while it may not be affected by the identity of the person for whose guidance the information is given, is vitally affected by the number and character of the persons, and particularly the nature and extent of the proposed transaction.

Therefore, while an accountant is to employ a sufficient degree of care in the performance of professional activities in order to protect himself from liability, the law must not arbitrarily extend that liability beyond his reasonable expectations as to whom the information will reach. "The risk reasonably to be perceived defines the duty to be obeyed. . . ." *Palsgraf v Long Island R. Co.*, 248 NY 339, 162 NE 99 (1928). We believe section 552 of the Restatement preserves such reasonable boundaries of liability.

We are unable, as a matter of law, to consider it unreasonable for a third party to rely upon information presented in an unaudited financial statement prepared by the defendant accountant, or to rely upon an accountant to verify the substantive accuracy of the information presented in an unaudited financial statement. It is for Spherex at trial to adduce evidence as to any duty undertaken by the accounting firm in its engagement contract with the client, irrespective of the unaudited nature of the financial statement it prepared.

[Action remanded]

QUESTIONS

1. Why does the court begin the discussion of the case with the statement that the case did not involve liability for intentional misrepresentation or fraud?
2. Was the court influenced by a change in the role of accountants? Explain your answer.
3. What standard is adopted by the Restatement of Torts for determining the negligence liability of accountants to third persons?

would transmit the information to the non-privity plaintiff.

(6) The Flexible Rule. Some courts have rejected the requirement of privity in malpractice suits against accountants but have not adopted any one of the rules discussed in the preceding sections. These courts prefer to keep the question open and to decide each case as it arises.

When the malpractice claim relates to advice given to a client, there are strong arguments for retaining the privity rule. Thus, it has been held that when the accountant orally recommended to the client the making of an investment as a tax shelter, third persons to whom the client repeated the advice cannot sue the accountant for malpractice.[21]

---

[21] *Selden v Burnett* (Alaska) 754 P2d 256 (1988).

13. Accountants' Fraud Malpractice Liability to Third Persons

Society in general condemns fraud more strongly than it does negligence. This is seen in the greater liability of accountants for fraudulent malpractice.

(a) WHAT CONSTITUTES FRAUD WITH RESPECT TO ACCOUNTANTS.

Fraud is defined as a false statement made with knowledge that it was false or with reckless indifference as to whether or not it was true. This statement was made with the intent that the listener rely on it, and the listener did rely on it and sustained loss. In the field of accounting, the false statement will typically be one of accounting in such a way as to make the client appear to be in a better financial position than is actually the case. For example, the client may own assets that are worthless, but the accountant retains them in the financial statement at cost or some other unreasonable value.

At times, the falsification of the financial statement may be designed to downgrade the financial condition of the corporation. This has been done when the object was to induce shareholders to sell their stock to a dominant group of shareholders. The false financial statement purposely undervalued the assets of the corporation to make the stockholders believe that their stock had little value and that, therefore, they should sell at the low price offered by the dominant group.

(b) FRAUD LIABILITY OF ACCOUNTANT TO INTENDED VICTIMS.

When an accountant commits fraud, it is typically intended to mislead a third person whose identity is known to the accountant or a class of persons whose identity is known to the accountant. Any such victim, whether an identified person or the member of a contemplated class of potential victims, may sue the accountant for loss caused by fraud. The problem of privity (relating to liability for negligence) is ignored when the basis of the malpractice suit is fraud. The social force of preventing fraud overrides the concern for creating a hardship on the accountant by allowing third persons to bring suit.

An accountant might make a false financial statement for a corporate client, with knowledge that it will be used in selling securities of the corporation to third persons. If so, the third persons may sue the accountant for the damages sustained. Thus, the accountant has been held liable for disguising the true character of a hoped-for profit from the sale and resale of real estate. The accountant described it as "deferred income," although there was little reason to believe that the transaction could ever be completed. In this case, the buyer, who was obligated to pay $5 million for the property, had assets of only $100,000. The financial statement would have shown a loss instead of a substantial profit if the true character of the transaction had been disclosed.

14. Accountants' Malpractice Liability Under Statutes

Statutes, particularly those relating to the sale of securities, may impose liability on accountants to third persons not in privity.

(a) FEDERAL SECURITIES STATUTES.

Federal statutes regulate the sale of stocks and bonds. Accountants involved in the issuance and sale of securities may be liable to investors under a number of provisions of the Securities Act of 1933 and the Securities Exchange Act of 1934.

(1) Securities Act of 1933.

The Securities Act of 1933 deals with original distribution of securities. The act requires disclosure of specific financial information in a **registration statement** filed with the Securities and Exchange Commission. Under Section 11 of the act, accountants, lawyers, engineers, and appraisers who consent to being named in the registration statement as preparing any part of that statement are liable to purchasers of the securities for any untrue statement or omission of material fact made in the registration statement. "Due diligence" is a defense for these professionals.

Section 12 of the 1933 act applies to those who "offer or sell" securities and employ any device or scheme to defraud and obtain money by means of any untrue statement of material fact. Liability may be imposed on accountants whose conduct is a substantial factor in bringing about the fraudulent sale of a security. The more extensive the involvement or control of an accountant over a sale, the more likely the accountant is to be considered a seller under Section 12. Accountants who, in conjunction with clients, prepare fraudulent registration statements may be subject to civil liability as "aiders and abettors" under Section 12(2) of the 1933 act. They may also be subject to criminal liability under Section 17(a) of the 1933 act.

(2) Securities Exchange Act of 1934. The Securities Exchange Act of 1934 regulates secondary distribution of securities. Section 10(b) of the 1934 act and SEC Rule 10b-5 impose liability on any person who employs any device, scheme, or artifice to defraud in connection with the purchase or sale of any security.[22] Section 10(b) and Rule 10b-5 are the most effective federal security law provisions against accountants who participate in a fraudulent securities transaction. Under Section 10(b) and Rule 10b-5, a civil action for damages may be brought by any injured party who purchased or sold securities because of false, misleading, or undisclosed information. However, proof of *scienter*—proof that the accountant acted with guilty knowledge or intent to deceive—is required. Liability cannot be based on negligence. Because fraudulent intent is required, an accountant is not liable to the purchaser of corporate securities when the accountant was negligent in failing to use appropriate auditing procedures and so failed to discover internal accounting practices of the corporate client that prevented the making of an effective audit.[23] However, a showing of shady accounting practices amounting to a "pretended audit" has supported a finding of liability. A showing of grounds supporting a representation so flimsy as to lead to the conclusion that there was no genuine belief behind it has also supported a finding of liability.[24]

(b) LIABILITY OF ACCOUNTANTS UNDER ANTIRACKETEERING STATUTES. The federal Racketeer Influenced and Corrupt Organizations Act (RICO) authorizes the victim of a pattern of racketeering practices to sue for treble damages. Many states have similar laws. When an accountant's conduct that constitutes malpractice aids or furthers a pattern of racketeering practices, the person injured may bring suit under RICO.[25]

SUMMARY

When a contract requires a party to perform services, the party must perform with the care exercised by persons performing similar services within the same community. If the party negligently fails to observe those standards, there is both a breach of contract and a tort. This tort of negligent breach of contract constitutes malpractice, and the other party to the contract can sue the wrongdoer either for breach of contract or for the negligence involved.

---

[22] Akin v Q-L Investments, Inc. (CA5 Tex) 959 F2d 521 (1992).

[23] Ernst & Ernst v Hochfelder, 425 US 185 (1976).

[24] McLean v Alexander (CA3) 599 F2d 1190, 1198 (1979).

[25] Bank of America v Touche Ross & Co. (CA11 Ga) 782 F2d 966 (1986); Equitable Life Assur. Soc. v Alexander Grant & Co. (DC NY) 627 F Supp 1023 (1985); First Fed. S. & L. Assn. v Oppenheim, Appel, Dixon & Co. (DC NY) 629 F Supp 427 (1986). Criminal liability is also imposed by the antiracketeering statutes. If the accountant has the intent to defraud, there may be federal criminal liability for using the mail, a wire, or radio or television with intent to defraud, or for defrauding a bank, 18 USC §§ 1341 et seq. Most states have similar anti-fraud laws.

By the modern view, third persons may also sue the wrongdoer for malpractice. In states that follow the older law, the third person is barred from suing because of lack of privity. The rules governing the right of the third person to sue are applied in suits against technicians, architects, attorneys, and physicians.

When the malpractice suit is brought against an accountant for negligence, courts differ as to when a third person may sue. Some courts refuse to let the third person sue; these courts require privity between the parties. Most courts allow suit by the third person against the wrongdoer but differ as to what the plaintiff must show in order to bring such a suit. In New York, the plaintiff must show as a minimum that there was a "contact" with the accountant. In some states, it is sufficient that the third person was a known user of the accountant's information. Other courts go further and allow the third person to sue if it was reasonable to foresee that the third person would make use of the accountant's information. Some courts limit suit to those nonprivity plaintiffs who were intended to rely on the accounting work.

When the accountant is guilty of fraud, the intended victim of the fraud may sue the accountant, even though privity of contract is lacking.

In a suit brought under federal securities statutes, lack of privity is not a defense for an accountant.

To a limited degree, an accountant is protected from malpractice liability by a disclaimer of liability or by the contributory negligence of the plaintiff.

When the malpractice of the accountant involves or promotes racketeering activity or fraud, the accountant is subject to civil and criminal liability under RICO and similar state laws.

LAW IN PRACTICE

1. Be sure that you exercise the degree of care required of your calling. If you are an accountant, put all your opinions and statements in writing. When a writing recites any fact that you have not been able to verify personally, be sure to add a notice stating that such recital is not based on your personal observation, explain why that is so, and state what basis there is for such recital. Set forth in the writing the purpose for which it has been prepared, that it was prepared only for the use of your named client, that no third person is entitled or intended to rely thereon and that the client agrees that you are not to be liable for any negligent error.

2. If you have been harmed because your accountant has failed to exercise the required degree of care, determine whether you have the choice of suing for malpractice or breach of contract. Determine whether there is more than a mere nonperformance, with the breach constituting negligent or fraudulent conduct.

3. Recognize that by suing for malpractice in tort you may be able to sue the defendant, as against the defense that privity of contract did not exist. The damages recovered may be greater than for breach of contract, as there is the potential of recovering punitive damages.

4. Do not obstruct the accountant in making necessary investigations (as by concealing information, documents, and so on) or give the accountant information that you know is or may be false.

QUESTIONS AND CASE PROBLEMS

1. What social forces are affected by allowing a stranger to a contract to sue for the harm caused by the negligent performance of the contract?

2. The president of Jones Corporation was concerned about whether it would be necessary to borrow money to pay taxes. The corporation employed Roanne to prepare a financial statement of the corporation. When the president saw this statement, he decided that money should be borrowed. The lending bank required that the corporation submit a financial statement. The statement prepared by Roanne was submitted. It contained a number of negligent mistakes that misled the bank into lending the money to Jones. Jones went into bankruptcy shortly thereafter, and the bank recovered only a small percentage of the loan. The bank sued Roanne for the amount it could not collect. Was she liable in a state that followed the known user rule?

3. Thomas & Sons, certified public accountants, prepared a financial statement of the Continental Land Development Company. Much of the assets of the company consisted of land in foreign countries. Some of the land had been confiscated by the local governments. The financial statement prepared by Thomas said that, based on the best information available, the land described therein was owned by Continental and had not been confiscated. The financial statement further recited that Thomas was entirely dependent on foreign sources for the information relating to the foreign land and had no knowledge of its accuracy. On the strength of this financial statement, the Fifth National Bank loaned money to Continental. The recitals as to the land owned by Continental and its value proved false, and the bank could not get back its loan. The bank sued Thomas. Was Thomas liable?

4. Samari Brothers built an office building for the Pierce Corporation. Pierce rented one of the first-floor stores of the building to Byron. Because of defective construction work, there were water leaks into Byron's store. Byron sued Samari for the damage caused to his inventory by the leaks. Samari denied liability, on the ground that the building had been approved by the architect and accepted by the Pierce Corporation, so a third person, such as Byron, could not bring suit against Samari. Samari claimed Byron was merely an incidental beneficiary of the contract between Samari and Pierce. Is this a valid defense?

5. Air-Speed, Inc. retained Hansman to obtain insurance to cover workers' compensation payments for its employees. Hansman notified Air-Speed that the insurance had been obtained. In fact it had not been, because Hansman negligently failed to forward the premiums to the insurance company to pay for the insurance. Thomas Rae was an employee of Air-Speed. He was killed in the course of his employment. His wife Christine was appointed as administratrix of his estate. She sued Air-Speed and Hansman for the payments that would have been received under a workers' compensation insurance policy if one had been obtained. Hansman denied liability on the ground that he had not made any contract with Christine

Rae to obtain insurance. Was this defense valid? *[Rae v Air-Speed, Inc. 386 Mass 167, 435 NE2d 628]*

6. Johnson was a notary public. Albin, pretending to be Werner, showed Johnson a deed signed with the name of Werner. Johnson did not do anything to determine the true identity of Albin, as required by law. Instead, he assumed that the signature was genuine and filled in the acknowledgment form on the deed, falsely reciting that Werner had appeared before him and that Werner had acknowledged the deed as being his deed. Actually, the deed was a forgery. Suit was brought by a member of the Werner family who sustained damage when the true owner reclaimed the land. Decide. *[Werner v Johnson, 84 Wash 2d 360, 526 P2d 370]*

7. The certified public accounting partnership of James, Guinn and Head prepared a certified audit report of four corporations, known as the Paschal Enterprises, with knowledge that their report would be used to induce Shatterproof Glass Corporation to lend money to those corporations. The report showed the corporations to be solvent when in fact they were insolvent. Shatterproof relied on the audit report, loaned approximately $500,000 to the four corporations, and lost almost all of it because the liabilities of the companies were in excess of their assets. Shatterproof claimed that James and other accountants had been negligent in preparing the report and sued them to recover the loss on the loan. The accountants raised the defense that they had not been retained by the plaintiff but rather by Paschal. Was this defense valid? *[Shatterproof Glass Corporation v James (Tex Civ App) 466 SW2d 873]*

8. The Milwaukee Sanitary Drain Commission made a contract with Nagel Construction, Inc. to construct drains according to the plans prepared by Progressive Engineering, Inc. Nagel made a subcontract with National Sand to perform part of the work. Because of the negligence of Progressive Engineering, a poor site was selected for the work of National Sand, and National Sand was subjected to additional costs. National Sand sued all parties involved. Progressive Engineering raised the defense that it could not be sued by National Sand because there was no privity of contract between them. Was this defense valid? *[National Sand, Inc. v Nagel Construction, Inc., 132 Mich App 327, 451 NW2d 618]*

9. Copenhaver made a will. It was prepared by his attorney, Rogers. The will attempted to create a trust that would benefit the grandchildren of Copenhaver. Because of the negligence of Rogers, the trust was void. The grandchildren sued him for malpractice. Was he liable? The court followed the common law. [*Copenhaver v Rogers, 238 Va 361, 384 SE2d 593*]

10. Suits Galore, Inc. was a clothing manufacturer. Landau made an audit and a financial report of Suits Galore. The statement prepared by Landau was not certified. It stated that it was a review report only and that no opinion was expressly stated by the accountant. On the basis of this report, William Iselin & Co., Inc. extended credit to Suits Galore. Shortly thereafter, Suits Galore went into bankruptcy. Iselin was not repaid the money it had loaned. Iselin sued Landau on the ground that the financial report had been negligently prepared and that Iselin could sue Landau for the loss sustained. Was it correct? [*William Iselin & Co., Inc. v Landau, 128 App Div 2d 453, 513 NYS2d 3*]

11. Alton Packaging owned an airplane that was serviced by Garrett. Garrett found corrosion in the fuel tanks and replaced some of the tanks. Garrett did not enter the making of the repairs or the existence of the corrosion problem into the logbook of the plane. Alton sold the plane to B. L. Jet Sales, Inc. Difficulties developed because of the corrosion problem. B. L. sued Alton and Garrett. The claim against Garrett was the negligent failure to make the proper repair entry in the logbook of the plane so that subsequent purchasers would be aware of the problem. Garrett raised the defense that there was no privity of contract between him and the plaintiff and that the plaintiff was seeking to recover only for economic loss. Was this defense valid? [*B. L. Jet Sales, Inc. v Alton Packaging Corp. (Mo App) 724 SW2d 669*]

12. The U.S.F.& G. Co. issued policies of fire and public liability insurance to the Roosevelt Hotel and agreed to make periodic inspections of the premises for fire hazards and conditions dangerous to guests. Marie Hill and her husband were guests at the hotel. The insurer negligently failed to find a hazard that resulted in a fire that injured Hill and killed her husband. She sued the insurer for damages for her injuries and for the wrongful death of her husband. The insurer denied liability because there was no privity of contract between the plaintiff and the insurer. Was this defense valid? [*Hill v U.S.F.& G. Co. (CA5 Fla) 428 F2d 112*]

13. For almost 13 years, Touche Ross had prepared the annual audit of Buttes Gas and Oil Co. Butte wanted to obtain a loan from Dimensional Credit Corp. (DDC). It showed DDC its most recent annual audit. DDC made the loan on the basis of what it learned from the audit. The loan was not repaid and DDC then realized that it had been misled by negligent statements as to the financial condition of Butte that appeared in the annual statement prepared by Touche Ross. Suit was brought against Touche Ross for its negligence in preparing this report. Was it liable?

14. Wright owned a home. He contracted with Orkin Exterminating Co. to exterminate termites in a house. Two years later Wright sold the house to Teunissen. Thereafter she found that the house was infested with termites. She then found out that there had been a termite extermination two years before. She sued Orkin claiming that the prior inspection had been negligently performed and that Orkin was liable to her for the damage she sustained. Was she correct?

15. Ernst & Whinney made an audit report for W.L. Jackson Mfg. Co. On the basis of this report, Bethlehem Steel sold on credit to Jackson Mfg. Co. The report had been negligently prepared and Jackson went broke shortly thereafter. Bethlehem Steel did not get paid and then sued Ernst & Whinney for negligent malpractice. It raised the defense that it was not liable because it was not in privity with Bethlehem and did not know the name of Bethlehem in connection with its audit statements. Was this a valid defense? [*Bethlehem Steel Corp. v Ernst & Whinney (Tenn) 822 SW2d 592*]

PART 3

Personal Property and Bailments

CHAPTER 20

PERSONAL PROPERTY

LEARNING OBJECTIVES

After studying this chapter, you will be able to:
1. *Write a definition of personal property.*
2. *Differentiate between patents, copyrights, trademarks, and trade secrets.*
3. *List and explain the various types of gifts.*
4. *Identify the four forms of multiple ownership of personal property.*
5. *Set forth the remedies for violations of property rights.*

What is personal property? Who owns it? How is it acquired?

A. GENERAL PRINCIPLES

In common usage, the term *property* refers to a piece of land or a thing or an object. As a legal concept, however, property also refers to the rights that an individual may possess in that piece of land or that thing or that object.[1] Property includes the rights of any person to possess, use, enjoy, and dispose of a thing or object of value. A right in a thing is property, without regard to whether this right is absolute or conditional, perfect or imperfect, legal or equitable.

Real property means land and things embedded in the land, such as oil tanks. It also includes things attached to the earth, such as buildings or trees, and rights in any of these things. **Personal property** is property that is movable or intangible, as described in the next section of this book, or rights in such things.

1. Personal Property

Personal property consists of: (a) whole or fractional rights in things that are tangible and movable, such as furniture and books; (b) claims and debts, which are called **choses in action**; and (c) intangible proprietary rights, such as trademarks, copyrights, and patents.

The modern techniques of sound and image recording have led to the necessity of giving protection against copying. Federal law provides for the copyright protection of compositions, and federal and state laws create crimes of record and tape piracy.[2]

The concept of personal property is expanding. For example, courts now generally include gas and water within the definition of property. Thus, persons who tap water mains and gas pipes to obtain water and gas without paying are guilty of taking property.

2. Limitations on Ownership

A person who has all possible rights in and over a thing is said to have **absolute ownership** of it. The term *absolute*, however, is somewhat misleading, for one's rights with respect to the use, enjoyment, and disposal of things are subject to certain restrictions. An owner's property is subject to the government's powers to tax, to regulate under the police power, and to take by eminent domain. Property is subject to the creditors of the owner. Above all, the owner may not use property in a way that will unreasonably infringe on the rights of others.

B. ACQUISITION OF TITLE TO PERSONAL PROPERTY

Title to personal property may be acquired in different ways. For example, property is commonly purchased. The purchase and sale of goods is governed by the law of sales. In this chapter, the following methods of acquiring personal property will be discussed: gift, the finding of lost property, transfer by a nonowner, occupation, and escheat.

3. Gifts

Title to personal property may be transferred by the voluntary act of the owner without receiving anything in exchange—that is, by **gift**. The person making the gift, the **donor**, may do so because of things that the recipient of the gift, the **donee**, had done in the past or is expected to do in the future. However, such things are not deemed consideration and thus do not alter the "free" character of the gift. Five types of gifts are discussed below.

(a) INTER VIVOS GIFTS. The ordinary gift that is made between two living persons is an **inter vivos gift**. For practical purposes, such a gift takes effect when the donor (1)

---

[1] Presley Memorial Foundation v Crowell (Tenn App) 733 SW2d 89 (1987).

[2] PL 92-140, 85 Stat 391, 17 USC §§ 1, 5, 20, 101; Wyo Stat Ann § 40-13-205 (1989).

expresses an intent to transfer title and (2) makes delivery, subject to the right of the donee to disclaim the gift within a reasonable time after learning that it has been made.[3] Since there is no consideration for a gift, there is no enforceable contract, and an intended donee cannot sue for breach of contract if the donor fails to complete the gift.

essential to or closely associated with the ownership of the property, such as documents of title or a ship's papers. A signed blank check is capable of being delivered, and may be a gift when the donee fills out the check in the amount designated by the donor and cashes the check.[4] The delivery of a symbol is effective as a gift if the intent to make a gift is established. This is in contrast to merely giv-

Figure 20-1   Inter Vivos Gift

Inter Vivos Gift			
Law:	Donor	1. Intent and 2. Delivery	Unless the gift is disclaimed, title passes to Donee.
Application:	Smith owns the Van Gogh painting "The Irises"	1. He states, "This is for you, Michael," and 2. personally presents the painting to his son Michael	Michael becomes the owner.

(1) Intent. The intent to make a gift requires an intent to transfer title at that time. In contrast, an intent to confer a benefit at a future date is not a sufficient intent to create any right in the intended donee.

A delivery of property without the intent to make a gift does not transfer title. For example, there is no gift when the owner lends a VCR to another person.

(2) Delivery. Ordinarily, the delivery required to make a gift will be an actual handing over to the donee of the thing that is given.

The delivery of a gift may also be made by a **symbolic** or **constructive delivery**, such as by the delivery of means of control of property. Such means of control might be keys to a lock or keys to a garden tractor, or papers that are

ing the recipient of the token temporary access to the property—for example, until the deliverer comes back from the hospital.

(3) Donor's Death. If the donor dies before doing what is needed to make an effective gift, the gift fails. An agent or the executor or administrator of the estate cannot thereafter perform the missing step on behalf of the decedent. For example, in a state where a transfer of title to a motor vehicle could not be made without a transfer of the title certificate, that transfer must be made while the donor is living and cannot be made after the donor's death by the executor of the estate.

(b) GIFTS CAUSA MORTIS. A **gift causa mortis** is made when the donor, contemplating

---

[3] Owen v Owen (SD) 351 NW2d 139 (1984).

[4] Dial v Dial (Ala) 603 So 2d 1020 (1992).

imminent and impending death, delivers personal property to the donee with the intent that the donee shall own it if the donor dies.[5] This is a conditional gift, and the donor is entitled to take the property back if (1) the donor does not die, (2) the donor revokes the gift before dying, or (3) the donee dies before the donor.

(c) GIFTS AND TRANSFERS TO MINORS. Uniform Acts provide for transferring property to a custodian to hold for the benefit of a minor.[6]

The Uniform Transfers to Minors Act, which expands the type of property that can be made the subject of a gift, was originally proposed in 1983. It has been adopted, often with minor variations, in the following states: Alabama, Alaska, Arizona, Arkansas, California, Colorado, Florida, Hawaii, Idaho, Illinois, Indiana, Iowa, Kansas, Kentucky, Louisiana, Maine, Massachusetts, Maryland, Minnesota, Missouri, Montana, New Jersey, Nevada, New Hampshire, Nebraska, North Carolina, North Dakota, Oklahoma, Oregon, Rhode Island, South Dakota, Tennessee, Utah, Virginia, West Virginia, Washington, Wisconsin, and Wyoming. It has also been adopted by the District of Columbia. When property is held by a custodian for the benefit of a minor under one of the Uniform Acts, the custodian has discretionary power to use the property "for the support, maintenance, education, and benefit" of the minor, but the custodian may not use the custodial property for the custodian's own personal benefit. The gift is final and irrevocable for tax and all other purposes on complying with the procedure of the acts. Under the Uniform Acts, custodianships terminate and the property is distributed when the minor reaches age 21.

(d) CONDITIONAL GIFTS. A gift may be made subject to a condition, such as "This car is yours when you graduate," or "This car is yours unless you drop out of school." In the first example, the gift is subject to a condition precedent—graduation. A condition precedent must be satisfied before any gift or transfer takes place. In the second example, the gift is subject to a condition subsequent—dropping out of school. A condition subsequent operates to destroy or divest a title that had already been transferred.

Ordinarily no condition is recognized unless it is expressly stated. However, most courts regard an engagement ring as a conditional gift subject to the condition subsequent of a failure to marry. The inherent symbolism of the gift itself is deemed to foreclose the need to establish an express condition that there be a marriage. Most jurisdictions allow recovery of conditional engagement gifts only if the party seeking recovery has not unjustifiably broken off the engagement. The *Harris* case illustrates the application of this rule. However, a few states reject considerations of "fault" as to the breaking of an engagement and always require the return of the ring to the donor where there is a broken engagement. This viewpoint is based on the theory that in most cases there is no real fault as such, but rather a change of mind.[7]

(e) ANATOMICAL GIFTS. Persons may make gifts of parts of their bodies, as in the case of kidney transplants. Persons may also make postdeath gifts. The Uniform Anatomical Gift Act[8] permits persons 18 years or older to make gifts of their bodies or any parts thereof. The gift takes effect on the death of the donor. The gift may be made to a school, a hospital, an organ bank, or to a named patient. Such a gift may also be made, subject to certain

---

5 Pina v Flaglore (SD) 443 NW2d 627 (1989).

6 The Uniform Gifts to Minors Act (UGMA) was originally proposed in 1956. It was revised in 1965 and again in 1966. One of these versions is in effect in the following states: Connecticut, Delaware, Georgia, Mississippi, New York, Ohio, Pennsylvania, South Carolina, Texas, and Vermont. It has been adopted for the U.S. Virgin Islands.

7 McIntire v Raukhorst, 65 Ohio App 3d 728, 585 NE2d 456 (1989).

8 This act has been adopted in every state.

HARRIS v DAVIS
139 Ill App 3d 1046, 94 Ill Dec 326, 487 NE2d 1204 (1986)

Chip Harris gave Rebecca Davis a diamond ring upon their engagement to be married. Some time later Davis informed Harris that she no longer wanted to see him and that she had thrown the ring into a drainage ditch near her mother's home. Harris rented a metal detector and searched the area to no avail. He sued Davis for the value of the ring. From a judgment for Davis, Harris appealed.

JONES, J. . . . On appeal, the plaintiff argues that under Illinois law, the party failing to comply with an engagement or a contract to be married has no right to property acquired in contemplation of the marriage. . . . Plaintiff further argues that where an engagement is terminated because of the fault of the woman, the man is ordinarily entitled to the return of gifts made in contemplation of the marriage. . . . We agree.

The law in Illinois appears established that a gift given in contemplation of marriage is deemed to be conditional on the subsequent marriage of the parties, and the party who fails to perform on the condition of the gift has no right to property acquired under such pretenses.

A Pennsylvania court said: "A gift given by a man to a woman on condition that she embark on the sea of matrimony with him is no different from a gift based on the condition that the donee sail on any other sea", and "if, after receiving the provisional gift, the donee refuses to leave the harbor,—if the anchor of contractual performance sticks in the sands of irresolution and procrastination—the gift must be restored to the donor." *Pavlicic v Vogtsberger* (1957), 390 Pa. 502, 507-09, 136 A2d 127, 130.

There can be no question that the ring in the instant case was given by the plaintiff to the defendant in contemplation of marriage. Neither party disputes that fact. Neither is there any question that it was the defendant fiancee who broke the engagement. There is no allegation that plaintiff's acts caused the defendant to break the engagement. The record does not reveal the cause of the break-up. At any rate, the defendant failed to perform on the condition of the gift and, therefore, had no right either to retain the ring or to dispose of it. We, therefore, reverse the judgment of the trial court and hold that the defendant is liable to the plaintiff for the $1,390 value of the engagement ring.

[Judgment reversed]

QUESTIONS

1. State the rule of law set forth in this decision.
2. If Chip Harris had broken off the engagement, would he have been entitled to the return of the ring?

restrictions, by the spouse, adult child, parent, adult brother or sister, or guardian of a deceased person.

4. Finding of Lost Property

Personal property is lost when the owner does not know where it is located but intends to retain title to or ownership of it. The person finding lost property does not acquire title but only possession. Ordinarily, the finder of lost property is required to surrender the property to the true owner when the latter establishes ownership. Meanwhile, the finder is entitled to retain possession as against everyone else.

Without a contract with the owner or a statute so providing, the finder of lost property usually is not entitled to a reward or to compensation for finding or caring for the property.

(a) FINDING IN PUBLIC PLACE. If the lost property is found in a public place, such as a hotel, under such circumstances that to a reasonable person it would appear that the property had been intentionally placed there by the owner and that the owner would be likely to recall where the property had been left and to return for it, the finder is not entitled to possession of the property. The finder must give it to the proprietor or manager of the public place to keep it for the owner. This exception does not apply if it appears that the property was not intentionally placed where it was found. In that case, it is not likely that the owner will recall having left it there.

(b) STATUTORY CHANGE. In some states, statutes have been adopted permitting the finder to sell the property or keep it if the owner does not appear within a stated period of time. In this case, the finder is required to give notice—for example, by newspaper publication—to attempt to reach the owner.

5. Transfer by Nonowner

Ordinarily, a sale or other transfer by one who does not own the property will pass no title. No title is acquired by theft. The thief acquires possession only; and if the thief makes a sale or gift of the property to another, the latter acquires only possession of the property. The true owner may reclaim the property from the thief or from the thief's transferee.

(a) AUTOMOBILES. In some states, the general rule stated above is fortified by statutes that declare that the title to an automobile cannot be transferred, even by the true owner, without a delivery of a properly endorsed title certificate. The states that follow the common law do not make the holding of a title certificate essential to the ownership of an automobile, although as a matter of police regulation, the owner must obtain such a certificate.

(b) EXCEPTIONS. As an exception to the rule that a nonowner cannot transfer title, an agent, who does not own the property but who is authorized to sell it, may transfer the title of the agent's principal. Likewise, certain relationships, such as a pledge or an entrustment, create a power to sell and to transfer title. Moreover, an owner of property may be barred or estopped from claiming ownership when the owner has acted in a way that deceives an innocent buyer into believing that someone else was the owner or had authority to sell.

6. Occupation of Personal Property

In some cases, title to personal property may be acquired by occupation—that is, by taking and retaining possession of the property.

(a) WILD ANIMALS. Wild animals, living in a state of nature, are not owned by any individual. In the absence of restrictions imposed by game laws, the person who acquires dominion or control over a wild animal becomes its owner. What constitutes sufficient dominion or control varies with the nature of the animal and the surrounding circumstances. If the animal is killed, tied, imprisoned, or otherwise prevented from going at its will, the hunter exercises sufficient dominion or control over the animal and becomes its owner. If the wild animal, subsequent to its capture, should escape and return to its natural state, it resumes the status of a wild animal.

As a qualification to the ordinary rule, the following exception developed. If an animal is killed or captured on the land of another while the hunter is on the land without permission of the landowner, the animal, when killed or captured, does not belong to the hunter but to the landowner.

(b) ABANDONED PERSONAL PROPERTY. Personal property is deemed abandoned when the owner relinquishes possession of it with the intention to disclaim title to it. Yesterday's newspaper that is thrown out in the trash is abandoned personal property. Title to abandoned property may be acquired by the first person who obtains possession and control of it. A person becomes the owner at the moment of taking possession of the abandoned personal property. If, however, the owner of property flees in the face of an approaching peril, property left behind is not abandoned. An abandonment occurs only when the owner voluntarily leaves the property.

7. Escheat

Who owns unclaimed property? In the case of personal property, the practical answer is that the property will probably "disappear" after a period of time, or, if in the possession of a carrier, hotel, or warehouse, it may be sold for unpaid charges. A growing problem arises with respect to unclaimed corporate dividends, bank deposits, insurance payments, and refunds. Most states have a statute providing for the transfer of such unclaimed property to the state government. This transfer to the government is often called by its feudal name of **escheat**. Funds held by stores for layaway items for customers, who fail to complete the layaway purchases, are subject to escheat to the state.[9] To provide for unclaimed property, many states have adopted the Uniform Disposition of Unclaimed Property Act (UDUPA).[10]

In the case below, both Elvis Presley's estate and the state of Tennessee claimed the unrefunded ticket proceeds of a concert canceled because of the singer's death.

PRESLEY v CITY OF MEMPHIS
(Tenn App) 769 SW2d 221 (1988)

Elvis Presley contracted with Mid-South Coliseum Board (City of Memphis) for the rental of the Coliseum and for personnel to sell tickets for concerts on August 27 and 28, 1977. $325,000 worth of tickets were sold. On August 16, 1977 Elvis Presley died. Refunds were given to those who returned their tickets to the Coliseum Board. Ten years after his death, however, $152,279 worth of ticket proceeds remained unclaimed in the custody of the Board. This fund had earned $223,760 in interest. Priscilla Presley and the co-executors of the estate of Elvis Presley brought an action, claiming the unrefunded

---

[9] Rose's Stores Inc. v Boyles (NC App) 416 SE2d 200 (1992).

[10] The 1954 version of the act has been adopted in Arkansas. A 1966 version of the act has been adopted in Alabama, Georgia, Indiana, Mississippi, Missouri, Nebraska, Oklahoma, South Dakota, and the District of Columbia. A 1981 version of the act has been adopted in Alaska, Arizona, Colorado, Florida, Hawaii, Idaho, Illinois, Louisiana, Maine, Montana, Nevada, New Hampshire, New Jersey, New Mexico, North Dakota, Oregon, Rhode Island, South Carolina, Utah, Virginia, Washington, Wisconsin, and the Virgin Islands. Several states have adopted a composite of an earlier version of the act and the 1981 version: Iowa, Maryland, Minnesota, Tennessee, and Vermont.

ticket proceeds for the canceled concerts. The state of Tennessee claimed that it was entitled to the proceeds under the Uniform Disposition of Unclaimed Property Act. From a judgment for the co-executors, the state appealed.

HIGHERS, J. . . . Although the ticket may have some value as memorabilia apart from its intended function, such value was not the essence of the contract, had no bearing on the original proceeds, and has none now.

When Presley died, performance of the concert became impossible, and the contract was void. . . . The ticketholder was vested with a right to a refund of contract proceeds from the Coliseum as Presley's agent. . . .

Tennessee's version of the UDUPA is codified at T.C.A. § 66-29-101 et seq. . . . § 66-29-113 requires that the holder of the [abandoned] property report that property to the state treasurer. After notice is given . . . the property is to be delivered to the treasurer. . . .

The owner may recover at any time no matter how remote. . . .

The state has asserted that the definition in T.C.A. § 66-29-111 is applicable to the case at bar. That statute provides in pertinent part as follows:

66-29-111. Miscellaneous property held for another person.—All property, not otherwise covered by this chapter, including any income or increment thereon and deducting any lawful charges, that is held or owing in this state in the ordinary course of the holder's business and has remained unclaimed by the owner for more than seven (7) years after it became payable or distributable is presumed abandoned.

We agree with the state's assertion. The refunds in question have remained unclaimed in the more than seven years they have been held by the Coliseum in the ordinary course of its business. The ticketholder's right to a refund vested when the contract was voided. That right arose and the seven-year statutory period began when Elvis Presley died on August 16, 1977. Therefore, a presumption of abandonment as to unclaimed refunds matured on August 16, 1984. The present action . . . does not qualify as a claim under the statute because the plaintiffs have no legal right to the funds. Any right they might have had was lost when the contract was voided.

The presumption of abandonment under the UDUPA is statutory and therefore independent of common law principles of abandonment. . . . Intentional and voluntary relinquishment is not required under the statute. Statutory abandonment occurs when the conditions set out in the UDUPA exist. . . . Only statutorily abandoned property is disposed of under the UDUPA. . . .

We are well aware that this fund would not exist were it not for Elvis Presley's unique skills and talents while living and the legendary status he continues to hold in the years after his death. . . . These considerations might in the absence of the Tennessee statute merit granting the windfall to Presley's estate. But Presley's death voided the contract represented by each ticket sold . . . and Presley's estate [has] no legal claim to the ticket proceeds. Granting the proceeds to either of them or to the Coliseum constitutes the type of windfall the drafters of UDUPA sought to address. . . . We believe the drafters of the UDUPA and our legislature intended such windfalls to benefit the public rather than individuals in precisely the manner we hold here. . . .

In summary, pursuant to the Tennessee UDUPA, we hold that the Coliseum must deliver all of the unclaimed ticket refunds and all of the accumulated interest thereon to the treasurer. Further, the treasurer shall publish the existence of the unclaimed funds and hold those amounts until such time as they are claimed by the rightful owners, the ticketholders.

[Judgment reversed and action remanded]

QUESTIONS

1. On what basis did the Estate of Elvis Presley claim the unrefunded ticket proceeds and interest?
2. Present the state's legal position before the court.
3. Did the court think the intent of the drafters of the UDUPA would support the "windfall" in this case benefiting the estate of the individual whose legendary status generated the unclaimed funds? Explain.

C. PROTECTION OF INTANGIBLE PROPRIETARY RIGHTS

Property rights in trademarks, copyrights, and patents are acquired as provided by federal statutes. The nature and extent of their legal protection will be covered in this part.

8. Trademarks and Service Marks

A **mark** is any word, name, symbol, or design, or a combination of these, used to identify a product or service.[11] If the mark identifies a product, such as an automobile or soap, it is called a **trademark**. If it identifies a service, such as a restaurant or dry cleaners, it is called a **service mark**.

The owner of a mark may obtain protection from others using it by registering the mark in accordance with federal law.[12] To be registered, a mark must distinguish the goods or service of the applicant from those of others. Under the federal statute, a register, called the *Principal Register*, is maintained for the recording of such marks. Inclusion on the Principal Register grants the registrant the exclusive right to use the mark. Challenges may be made to the registrant's right within five years of registration, but after five years the right of the registrant is incontestable.

An advance registration of a mark may be made not more than three years before its actual use by filing an application certifying a bona fide "intent-to-use." Fees must be paid at six-month intervals from the filing of the application until actual use begins.[13]

(a) REGISTRABLE MARKS. Marks that are coined, completely fanciful, or arbitrary are capable of registration on the Principal Register. The mark *Exxon*, for example, was coined by the owners. The name *Kodak* is also a creation of the owners of this trademark, has no other meaning in English, but serves to distinguish the goods of its owners from all others.

A suggestive term may also be registered. Such a term suggests rather than describes some characteristics of the goods to which it applies and requires the consumer to exercise

---

[11] 15 USC § 1127. See also Trademark Clarification Act of 1984, PL 98-620, 98 Stat 333.

[12] Lanham Act, 15 USC §§ 1050-1127.

[13] PL 100-667, 15 USC § 1051 (1988); effective November 16, 1989.

some imagination to reach a conclusion about the nature of the goods. For example, as a trademark for refrigerators, the term *Penguin* would be suggestive. As a trademark for paperback books, the term *Penguin* is arbitrary and fanciful.

Ordinarily, descriptive terms, surnames, and geographic terms are not registrable on the Principal Register.[14] A descriptive term identifies a characteristic or quality of an article or service, such as color, odor, function, or use. Thus, *Arthriticare* was held not to be registrable on the Principal Register because it was merely descriptive of a product used to treat symptoms of arthritis.[15] However, an exception is made when a descriptive or geographic term or a surname has acquired a secondary meaning; such a mark is registrable. A term or terms that have a primary meaning of their own acquire a **secondary meaning** when, through long use in connection with a particular product, they have come to be known by the public at large as identifying the particular product and its origin. For example, the geographic term *Philadelphia* has acquired a secondary meaning as applied to cream cheese. It is widely accepted by the public as denoting a particular brand rather than any cream cheese made in Philadelphia. Factors considered by a court in determining whether a trademark has acquired secondary meaning are the amount and manner of advertising, volume of sales,

length and manner of use, direct consumer testimony, and consumer surveys.

Generic terms—that is, terms that designate a kind or class of goods, such as *cola* or *rosé wine*—are never registrable.

(b) INJUNCTION AGAINST IMPROPER USE OF MARK. A person who has the right to use a mark may obtain a court order prohibiting a competitor from imitating or duplicating the mark. The basic question in such litigation is whether the general public is likely to be confused by the mark of the defendant and to believe wrongly that it identifies the plaintiff. If there is this danger of confusion, the court will enjoin the defendant from using the particular mark.

In some cases, the fact that the products of the plaintiff and the defendant did not compete in the same market was held to entitle the defendant to use a mark that would have been prohibited as confusingly similar if the defendant manufactured the same product as the plaintiff. For example, it has been held that *Cadillac* as applied to boats is not confusingly similar to *Cadillac* as applied to automobiles; therefore, its use cannot be enjoined.[16]

In the *University of Georgia Athletic Association* case, the court was faced with the question of whether there was likelihood of confusion between the UGAA's service mark and athletic symbol *Bulldogs* and a company's trademark *Battlin' Bulldog Beer*.

UNIVERSITY OF GEORGIA ATHLETIC ASS'N v LAITE
(CA11 Ga) 756 F2d 1535 (1985)

The University of Georgia Athletic Association (UGAA) brought suit against beer wholesaler Bill Laite for marketing Battlin' Bulldog Beer. The UGAA

---

[14] A Supplemental Register exists for recording such marks. This recording does not give the registrant any protection, but it provides a source to which other persons designing a mark can go to make sure they are not duplicating an existing mark. See Cushman v Mutton Hollow Land, Inc. (Mo App) 782 SW2d 150 (1990).

[15] Bernard v Commerce Drug Co. (CA2 NY) 964 F2d 1338 (1992).

[16] General Motors Corporation v Cadillac Marine and Boat Co. 140 USPQ 447 (1964). See also Amstar Corp. v Dominos Pizza Inc. (CA5 Ga) 615 F2d 252 (1980), where the mark *Domino* as applied to pizza was held not be confusingly similar to *Domino* as applied to sugar.

claimed that the cans infringed on its symbol for its athletic teams, which it had registered as a service mark and which depicted an English Bulldog wearing a sweater with a *G* and the word *BULLDOGS* on it. Soon after the beer appeared on the market, the university received telephone calls from friends of the university. They were concerned that Battlin' Bulldog Beer was not the sort of product that should in any way be related to the University of Georgia. The university's suit was based on the theory of false designation of origin in violation of the Lanham Act. Laite contended that the University of Georgia Bulldog was not a valid service mark; that his bulldog was different from the university's; and that his cans bore the disclaimer "Not associated with the University of Georgia." The district court permanently enjoined Laite from marketing the beer under the challenged label design. Laite appealed.

KRAVITCH, C. J. . . . Laite's first argument on appeal is that the "University of Georgia Bulldog" is not a valid trade or service mark worthy of protection. Laite cites *Universal City Studios, Inc. v Nintendo Co.*, 578 F. Supp. 911 (S.D.N.Y. 1983), for the proposition that "[t]o make a successful claim of false designation of origin in violation of § 43(a) of the Lanham Act, 15 U.S.C. § 1125(a), [plaintiff] must demonstrate that its trademark possesses 'secondary meaning'—'the power of a name or other configuration to symbolize a particular business, product or company. . . .'" Laite contends that the record does not contain sufficient proof of secondary meaning, and that the vagueness of UGAA's mark, coupled with extensive third-party uses of the same or similar marks, demonstrates the absence of secondary meaning. . . . The general rule in this circuit is that proof of secondary meaning is required *only* when protection is sought for descriptive marks, as opposed to arbitrary or suggestive marks. We have long recognized that:

Service marks fall into four categories. A strong mark is usually fictitious, arbitrary or fanciful and is generally inherently distinctive. It is afforded the widest ambit of protection. . . . A descriptive mark tells something about the product; it is protected only when secondary meaning is shown. . . . In contrast to the above is the suggestive mark, which subtly connotes something about the service or product. Although less distinctive than a fictitious, arbitrary or fanciful mark . . . a suggestive mark will be protected without proof of secondary meaning. . . . Lastly, there are generic terms, which communicate 'information about the nature or class of an article or service,' and therefore can never become a service or trademark.

Thus, secondary meaning is best characterized not as a general prerequisite for trade or service mark protection, but as a means by which otherwise unprotectable descriptive marks may obtain protection. As one commentator has explained:

Secondary meaning converts a word originally incapable of serving as a mark into a full fledged trademark. . . . An arbitrary, fanciful, or otherwise distinctive word qualifies as a trademark immediately, because in the particular industry it has no primary meaning to overcome. Therefore it is initially registrable, and also protectable at common law. In the case of words with primary meaning, the reverse is true. Such words, be they descriptive or geographical, are initially nonregistrable and unprotectable unless and until they have attained secondary meaning as trademarks.

We therefore hold that . . . proof of secondary meaning is required in an action under section 43(a) only when protection is sought for a descriptive mark, as opposed to an arbitrary or suggestive mark. Turning to the mark at issue in the instant case, we are convinced beyond a shadow of a doubt that the "University of Georgia Bulldog" is not a descriptive mark. In our view, the portrayal of an English bulldog chosen by the university as a symbol for its athletic teams is, at best, "suggestive," if not downright "arbitrary." Thus, contrary to Laite's assertion, UGAA was not required to prove secondary meaning in order to prevail on its Lanham Act claim, and the district court did not err in granting injunctive relief to UGAA under section 43(a) despite the absence of proof of secondary meaning.

Laite's next argument is that the district court used the wrong factors in comparing the "Battlin' Bulldog" with the "University of Georgia Bulldog." Laite correctly points out that this circuit has recognized seven factors as relevant to the determination of a "likelihood of confusion" between two trade or service marks: (1) the type of mark at issue, (2) the similarity of design between the two marks, (3) the similarity of product, (4) the identity of retail outlets and purchasers, (5) the identity of advertising media utilized, (6) the defendant's intent, and (7) actual confusion between the two marks. . . .

As the district court pointed out, it is the combination of similar design elements, rather than any individual element, that compels the conclusion that the two bulldogs are similar. Had the cans of "Battlin' Bulldog Beer" been printed in different colors, or had the "Battlin' Bulldog" worn a different monogram on its sweater, we might have a different case. Instead, the cans are red and black, the colors of the University of Georgia, and the "Battlin' Bulldog" wears the letter "G." To be sure, the "Battlin' Bulldog" is not an exact reproduction of the "University of Georgia Bulldog." Nevertheless, we find the differences between the two so minor as to be legally, if not factually, nonexistent.

. . . Laite candidly admitted in the court below, and at oral argument in this court, that "Battlin' Bulldog Beer" was intended to capitalize on the popularity of the University of Georgia football program. In short, there can be no doubt that Laite hoped to sell "Battlin' Bulldog Beer" not because the beer tastes great, but because the cans would catch the attention of University of Georgia football fans.

Although we find the defendant's intent and the similarity of design between the two marks sufficient to support the district court's finding of a "likelihood of confusion," we also note that the remaining five factors either support the same conclusion or, at least, do not undermine it. For example, as we previously noted, the type of mark at issue in this case is at best "suggestive," if not downright "arbitrary." Such marks traditionally have been characterized as "strong." The fact that many other colleges, junior colleges, and high schools use an English bulldog as a symbol does not significantly diminish the strength of UGAA's mark, since almost all of the other schools (1) are geographically remote, (2) use a different color scheme, or (3) have names that begin with a letter other than "G." . . .

The "Battlin' Bulldog's" football career thus comes to an abrupt end. Laite devised a clever entrepreneurial "game plan," but failed to take into account the strength of UGAA's mark and the tenacity with which UGAA was willing to defend that mark. Like the University of Georgia's famed "Junkyard Dog" defense, UGAA was able to hold its opponent to little or no gain. . . . [W]e find that the district court did not err, in fact or in law, when it granted permanent injunctive relief to UGAA. . . .

[Judgment affirmed]

QUESTIONS

1. When is proof of secondary meaning required in a trademark or service mark infringement lawsuit?
2. In what category of service mark is the University of Georgia Bulldog?
3. What are the seven factors considered by this circuit court in determining whether "likelihood of confusion" exists between two marks?

(c) ABANDONMENT OF EXCLUSIVE RIGHT TO MARK.   An owner who has an exclusive right to use a mark may lose that right. If other persons are permitted to use the mark, it loses its exclusive character and is said to pass into the English language and become generic. Examples of formerly enforceable marks that have made this transition into the general language are *aspirin, thermos, cellophane,* and *shredded wheat.*

9. Copyrights

A **copyright** is the exclusive right given by federal statute to the creator of a literary or artistic work to use, reproduce, or display the work. By international treaties, copyrights given under the laws of one nation are generally recognized in another.[17]

A copyright does not prevent the copying of an idea, but only the copying of the way the idea is expressed.[18] That is, the copyright is violated when there is a duplicating of the words or the pictures of the creator, but not when there is merely a copying of the idea those words or pictures express.

(a) WHAT IS COPYRIGHTABLE.   Copyrights protect literary, musical, dramatic, and artistic work. Protected are books and periodicals; musical and dramatic compositions; choreographic works; maps; works of art such as paintings, sculptures, and photographs; motion pictures and other audiovisual works; sound recordings; and computer programs.

(b) UNPUBLISHED WORK.   As long as a work is not made public, it has the same protection as though it had been copyrighted.

(c) SECURING A COPYRIGHT.   A copyright registration is obtained from the Copyright Office in Washington, D.C. A registration application must be accompanied by two copies of the work for deposit in the Library of Congress. Each copy of the published work must contain (1) a copyright notice, such as *copyright* or "©," (2) the date of first publication, and (3) the name of the copyright owner.

(d) DURATION OF COPYRIGHT.   For works created after January 1, 1978, a copyright in the creator's name lasts for the creator's lifetime plus 50 years.[19] If a work is a "work made for

---

[17] Under the international treaty called the Berne Convention, copyright in the works of all U.S. authors are protected automatically in all Berne Convention nations. Berne Convention nations agreed in the treaty to treat nationals of other member countries like their own nationals.

[18] Under the Berne Convention Implementation Act of 1988 PL 100-568, 102 Stat 2854, 17 USC §§ 101 et seq., a law that adjusts U.S. copyright law to conform to the Berne Convention, it is no longer mandatory that works published after March 1, 1989 contain a notice of copyright. However, placing a notice of copyright on published works is strongly recommended. This notice prevents an infringer from claiming innocent infringement of the work, which would reduce the amount of damages owed. In order to bring a copyright infringement suit for a work of U.S. origin, the owner must have submitted two copies of the work to the Copyright Office for registration.

[19] Copyright Act of 1976, § 302(a), 17 USC § 302(a).

hire," the business employing the creator registers the copyright. This copyright runs for 100 years from creation or 75 years from publication of the work, whichever period is shorter. After a copyright has expired, the work is in the public domain and may be used by anyone without cost.

(e) LIMITATIONS ON EXCLUSIVE CHARACTER OF COPYRIGHT. A limitation on the exclusive rights of copyright owners exists under the principle of "fair use," which allows a limited use of copyrighted material in connection with criticism, news reporting, teaching, and research. Two important factors in judging if the use is fair are: (1) the amount of text used in relation to the copyrighted work as a whole and (2) the effect of the use on the value of the original copyrighted work.[20]

10. Patents

A **patent** is the exclusive right that the inventor of a device can obtain under federal law. The patent gives the inventor an exclusive 17-year right to make, use, and sell the thing invented. At the end of 17 years the patent expires and cannot be renewed. If a patent is not obtained, or if the patent has expired, anyone may make, use, or sell the invention without permission of the inventor and without making any payment for it.

Patents cannot be defeated by combining components outside the United States for sale in global markets. U.S. suppliers of components of a patented invention who actively induce the combination of components outside the United States in a manner that would infringe the patent if the activity occurred in the United States are liable as infringers under the Patent Law Amendments Act of 1984.[21]

(a) WHAT IS PATENTABLE. To be patentable, the invention must be something that is new and useful and must be something that would not have been obvious to a person of ordinary skill or knowledge in the art or technology to which the invention is related.[22]

The invention is the thing that is patented, whether it be a machine, a process, or a particular chemical composition of matter. The idea or inspiration, ways of doing business, and scientific principles cannot be patented unless there is some physical thing on which they are based. Patent law has been interpreted to permit the patenting of human-made life forms.

(b) CONTRACTUAL PROTECTION OF INVENTIONS. Frequently, an employee will invent a patentable device during working hours or use the employer's equipment and materials. To protect the employer in such situations, employment contracts commonly provide that any invention relating to the employer's business that is discovered by the employee while still an employee or during the first one or two years after leaving the employment shall be assigned to the employer. Such provisions are generally held valid, although a provision requiring the assignment of all inventions, whether or not related to the employer's business, has been held contrary to public policy and therefore invalid.

11. Secret Business Information

A business may have developed information that is not generally known but that cannot be protected under federal law. As long as such information is kept secret, it will be protected under state law relating to trade secrets.[23] The protection of trade secrets is necessary to

---

[20] Copyright Act of 1976, § 107, 17 USC § 107. Acuff-Rose Music Inc. v Campbell (CA6 Tenn) 972 F2d (1992).

[21] PL 98-622, 98 Stat 3383, 35 USC § 361.

[22] 35 USC §§ 101, 102, 103; Nitto Boseki Co. Ltd. v Owens Corning Corp. (DC Del) 597 F Supp 248 (1984).

[23] The Uniform Trade Secrets Act was officially amended in 1985. In either its original or amended form it is now in force in Arkansas, Alabama, Alaska, Arizona, California, Colorado, Connecticut, Delaware, Florida, Hawaii, Idaho, Iowa, Illinois, Iowa, Indiana, Kansas, Kentucky, Louisiana, Maine, Minnesota, Montana, Mississippi, Nebraska, Nevada, New Hampshire, New Mexico, North Dakota, Oklahoma, Oregon, Rhode Island, South Carolina, South

encourage and protect invention and commercial enterprise, and to provide for standards of commercial ethics in the marketplace.

(a) TRADE SECRETS. A trade secret may consist of any formula, device, or compilation of information that is used in one's business and that is of such a nature that it gives an advantage over competitors who do not have such information. It may be a formula for a chemical compound; a process of manufacturing, treating, or preserving materials; and, to a limited extent, certain confidential customer lists.[24]

The courts will not protect customer lists where customer identities are readily ascertainable from industry or public sources or where products or services are sold to a wide group of purchasers based on their individual needs.[25]

(b) LOSS OF PROTECTION. When secret business information is made public, it loses the protection it had while secret. Such loss of protection occurs when the information is made known without any restrictions. In contrast, there is no loss of protection when secret information is shared or communicated for a special purpose and the person receiving the information knows that it is not to be made known to others.

When an article is unprotected by a patent or a copyright and is sold in significant numbers to the public who are free to resell to whomever they choose, competitors are free to "reverse engineer" (start with the known product and work backwards to discover the process) or copy the article. To illustrate, boatbuilder *A* develops a hull design which is not patented. Boatbuilder *B* purchases one of *A*'s boats and copies *A*'s hull by creating a mold from the boat it purchased. Boatbuilder *B* is free to build and sell boats utilizing the copied hull.[26]

(c) DEFENSIVE MEASURES. Employers seek to avoid the expense of trade secret litigation by limiting disclosure of trade secrets only to employees with a "need to know." Employers also have employees sign nondisclosure agreements and conduct exit interviews when employees with confidential information terminate employment with the business, reminding the employees of the employer's intent to enforce the nondisclosure agreement. In addition, employers have adopted industrial security plans to protect their unique knowledge from "outsiders," who may engage in theft, trespass, wiretapping, or other forms of commercial espionage.

One of the broad policies behind trade secrecy law is the maintenance of standards of commercial ethics. In the *Campbell Soup Co.* decision the court demonstrated its concern about promoting an atmosphere of commercial morality and fairness between competitors.

12. Remedies for Violation of Property Rights

The remedy most commonly used by the owner of personal property for violations of property rights is an action for monetary damages when the property is negligently or willfully harmed, taken, or destroyed by the act of another. When the owner's property is taken under circumstances that would constitute larceny, the owner may sue for the wrong, called *conversion*. The remedy is recovery of the monetary value of the property at the time of the unlawful taking, or the owner may recover the property itself by an action at law.

Dakota, Utah, Virginia, Washington, West Virginia, and Wisconsin. Trade secrets are protected in all states either under the Uniform Act or the common law and under both criminal and civil statutes.

[24] Restatement of Torts § 757, Comment b. See also Schiller and Schmidt Inc. v Nordisco Corp. (CA7 Ill) 969 F2d 410 (1992).

[25] Xpert Automation Systems, Corp. v Vibromatic Co. (Ind App) 569 NE2d 351 (1990).

[26] Bonito Boats, Inc. v Thunder Craft Boats, Inc. 103 L Ed 2d 118 (1989).

CAMPBELL SOUP CO. v CONAGRA, INC.
(DC NJ) 801 F Supp 1298 (1991)

> Sallie O'Brien Rosenthal worked for Campbell Soup Company as a Product Development Technologist for Campbell's "Never Fried Chicken" project. Research on that project had been underway at Campbell for over five years before Rosenthal's employment with Campbell. Rosenthal had signed a Patent-Trade Secret Agreement as a condition of her employment. This agreement prevented her from using any trade secrets which she conceived or to which she was exposed while working for Campbell. After a year ConAgra, through an executive recruiter, recruited Rosenthal to work for them. She became a researcher on Project Nova—a new line of chicken products. Within two months after her arrival, Rosenthal developed a process which allowed ConAgra to eliminate all frying from its Project Nova chicken products. ConAgra and Rosenthal obtained a patent for this process. Campbell sued to enjoin ConAgra and Rosenthal from using and disclosing Campbell's trade secrets relating to its "Never Fried Chicken" project. Campbell also sought to enjoin ConAgra and Rosenthal from exploiting the patent, which it claimed was based on Campbell's trade secrets.

BROTMAN, D. J. . . . In order to prove a claim for misappropriation of trade secrets, the plaintiff has the burden of proving:

(1) the existence of a trade secret; (2) communicated in confidence by the plaintiff to the employee; (3) disclosed by the employee in breach of that confidence; (4) acquired by the competitor with knowledge of the breach of confidence; and (5) used by the competitor to the detriment of the plaintiff.

. . . The New Jersey Supreme Court has adopted the definition of a trade secret from comment b to § 757 of the *First Restatement of Torts:*

A trade secret may consist of any formula, pattern, device or compilation of information which is used in one's business, and which gives him an opportunity to obtain an advantage over competitors who do not know or use it.

. . . When Rosenthal informed Campbell that she would be leaving for work for a competitor, Campbell excluded Rosenthal from its research facilities. Campbell also put ConAgra on notice of Rosenthal's confidentiality obligations vis-a-vis the Patent-Trade Secret Agreement and informed ConAgra that Rosenthal had worked on Campbell's non-fried chicken product. ConAgra never questioned Rosenthal about the trade secrets she learned at Campbell. Despite its failure to make any inquiry into the subject, ConAgra responded to Campbell's notification letter that it was not interested in acquiring any trade secrets of Campbell. To promote an atmosphere of commercial morality and fairness, the court believes that ConAgra, with the knowledge it possessed with respect to Rosenthal's background and duties at Campbell, should have questioned Rosenthal regarding the notice letter sent by Campbell. . . .

The amount of effort or money expended in developing the information also leads the court to hold that Campbell's trade secret claim has merit. Rosenthal was hired to work on the design, development and testing of the "Never Fried Chicken" product. She began working on the process soon after she arrived. Moreover, Campbell conducted an extensive series of tests on the formula and procedure involved with the "Never Fried Chicken" product including five scale-up runs in its Farmington research facility.

. . . The ease or difficulty with which the process could be acquired or duplicated by others, also favors Campbell. Prior to Rosenthal's arrival, ConAgra had not used a humidified oven, a bread crumb mixture which included encapsulated or beaded shortening or sprayed or misted vegetable oil as part of the "Never Fried Chicken" process. Once Rosenthal arrived at ConAgra, ConAgra used these steps to create a non-fried chicken product. There is no proof that ConAgra was able to eliminate frying from its "Project Nova" chicken before Rosenthal started working for them.

In addition to proving the existence of its trade secrets, Campbell has produced evidence demonstrating every other element of its misappropriation of trade secrets claim. Campbell's trade secrets were communicated in confidence by Campbell to Rosenthal and Rosenthal disclosed Campbell's trade secrets to ConAgra in breach of that confidence. The various measures taken by Campbell to protect its proprietary information and the explicit language of the Patent-Trade Secret Agreement requiring Rosenthal to keep all of Campbell's trade secrets strictly confidential are proof of this.

Although, there is no direct evidence indicating that trade secrets were acquired by ConAgra with knowledge of Rosenthal's breach of confidence, Campbell has produced sufficient evidence to convince the court that ConAgra did know or should have known of Rosenthal's breach of confidence. ConAgra knew that Rosenthal was working on frozen poultry products for Campbell. She was immediately assigned to work on ConAgra's frozen poultry products. After receiving Campbell's April 23, 1985 notification letter, ConAgra did not question Rosenthal concerning her non-fried chicken work for Campbell. Moreover, Rosenthal was not asked review ConAgra's June 3, 1985 response to Campbell's notification letter.

ConAgra also used Campbell's process to the detriment of Campbell. ConAgra, a direct competitor of Campbell's, and Rosenthal patented a process for making a nonfried chicken product, a process which was developed at Campbell and which also belonged to Campbell.

For these reasons, the court holds that Campbell has met its burden in proving likelihood of prevailing on the merits on its claim that its process for making a nonfried food product is a trade secret and that ConAgra and Rosenthal misappropriated it. . . .

Campbell contends that it will suffer irreparable harm if ConAgra and Rosenthal are not preliminarily enjoined from using and disclosing Campbell's trade secrets and other confidential and proprietary information relating to Campbell's frozen food technology. The court agrees. In the . . . patent, ConAgra and Rosenthal have already disclosed to the public Campbell's trade secrets and proprietary information. ConAgra's and Rosenthal's further use of Campbell's proprietary frozen poultry technology will lead to more irreparable harm. A clear showing of immediate irreparable harm is met since the . . . patent gives ConAgra the exclusive rights to utilize the process developed at Campbell to Campbell's detriment.

[Request for preliminary injunction granted]

QUESTIONS

1. Is it unethical for a business to utilize an executive recruiter (sometimes referred to by business persons as "headhunter") to recruit an experienced researcher away from a competitor?
2. In a trade secrets case, are courts properly concerned about promoting an atmosphere of commercial morality and fairness?
3. Did ConAgra act with prudence regarding Rosenthal and her Patent-Trade Secret Agreement with Campbell?

The owner's right to recover damages for conversion may also be asserted against an innocent wrongdoer—that is, a person who in good faith has exercised dominion over the plaintiff's property. For example, a buyer of a stolen television set gives value and acts in good faith in the belief that the seller is the owner of the set. The conduct of the innocent buyer in taking possession of the set and exercising control over it is a conversion for which the innocent buyer is liable to the true owner.

If the defendant has infringed copyrights, patents, or marks of the plaintiff, the plaintiff may obtain an injunction ordering the defendant to stop such practices. If the infringement was intentional, the plaintiff may also recover from the defendant any profits obtained by the defendant from such infringement. If the infringement conduct constitutes an unfair trade practice, the plaintiff may obtain a cease-and-desist order against the defendant from the Federal Trade Commission.

D. MULTIPLE OWNERSHIP OF PERSONAL PROPERTY

When all rights in a particular object of property are held by one person, that property is held in **severalty**. However, two or more persons may hold concurrent rights and interests in the same property. In that case, the property is said to be held in **cotenancy**. The various forms of cotenancy include (1) tenancy in common, (2) joint tenancy, (3) tenancy by entirety, and (4) community property.

13. Tenancy in Common

A tenancy in common is a form of ownership by two or more persons. The interest of a tenant in common may be transferred or inherited, in which case the taker becomes a tenant in common with the others. This tenancy is terminated only when there is a partition or division of the property, giving each a specific portion, or when one person acquires all of the interests of the co-owners.

14. Joint Tenancy

A joint tenancy is another form of ownership by two or more persons, but a joint tenancy has a right of survivorship. On the death of a joint tenant, the remaining tenants take the share of the deceased tenant. The last surviving joint tenant takes the property as a holder in severalty.

A joint tenant's interest may be transferred to a third person, but this destroys the joint tenancy. If the interest of one of two joint tenants is transferred to a third person, the remaining joint tenant becomes a tenant in common with the third person.

Statutes in many states have modified the common law by adding a formal requirement to the creation of a joint tenancy with survivorship. At common law, such an estate would be created by a transfer of property to "A and B as joint tenants." Under these statutes, however, it is necessary to add the words "with right of survivorship," or other similar words, if it is desired to create a right of survivorship. If no words of survivorship are used, the transfer of property to two or more persons will be construed as creating a tenancy in common. Under such a statute, a certificate of deposit issued only in the name of "A or B" does not create a joint tenancy, because it does not contain words of survivorship.

The effect of creating a joint tenancy in a bank deposit in statutory form can be seen in the *Auffert* case.

AUFFERT v AUFFERT

(Mo App) 829 SW2d 95 (1992)

Rachel Auffert purchased a $10,000 certificate of deposit on January 7, 1981 creating a joint tenancy in this bank deposit payable to herself or either of two children, Mary Ellen or Leo, "either or the survivor." When Rachel died, a note dated January 7, 1981 written in Rachel's handwriting and signed by her was found with the certificate of deposit. The note stated:

Leo:
If I die this goes to Sr. Mary Ellen,
Wanted another name on it.
s/ Rachel Auffert
Jan 7 1991

Mary Ellen cashed the certificate of deposit and retained the proceeds. Leo sued to recover one half the value of the certificate. From a judgment for Mary Ellen, Leo appealed.

PER CURIAM. . . . Compliance with § 362.470.1, [Revised Statutes of Missouri] 1986, creates a conclusive presumption of joint tenancy in a bank deposit. . . . Such joint tenancy results, and the right to survivorship ensues when a would-be joint depositor either (1) makes the deposit payable to the depositors as joint tenants or (2) makes the account payable to one or more of the depositors or the survivor or survivors of them. . . . Maintenance of an account or deposit in the statutory form is conclusive evidence, absent proof of fraud or undue influence, that the deposit is the property of the joint tenants and that title passes to the survivors. . . As between two surviving joint tenants following the death of the third, evidence of the intent of the parties when the deposit was established is irrelevant and cannot be used to divest one of the survivors of the ownership. . . .

The undisputed facts show statutory compliance: Rachel deposited her money in the bank in the names of and payable to herself or Mary Ellen or Leo, "either or the survivor"; Leo and Mary Ellen survived Rachel's death. By virtue of § 362.470, Leo and Mary Ellen conclusively succeeded to ownership of the certificate of deposit as joint tenants. . .

Once the existence of a joint bank deposit is established, the inquiry shifts to the proportionate ownership interests of the surviving joint tenants. The law presumes equal ownership. The creation of a joint bank account in the statutory form raises a rebuttable presumption that the co-owners share equally in the ownership of the funds on deposit. . . .

Rachel's note found with the certificate of deposit directing unequal division after her death failed to defeat the survivors' status as joint tenants and the presumption of equal ownership. During one's lifetime, an individual who has deposited all the funds in a joint account has the power to divest the interests of a non-contributing joint tenant by transferring those funds to a new account. . . . Creation of such new account requires compliance with § 362.470.1 by listing the names of the new joint owners with the appropriate language of survivorship. . . . Consequently, after the creation of a statutory joint tenancy, the only means available to alter the joint tenants' proportionate interests is to change the names on the account. Because Rachel failed to comply with the statutory formalities during her lifetime, the law presumes that Leo and Mary Ellen equally owned the certificate of deposit.

The trial court misapplied the law, and improvidently granted summary judgment in favor of Mary Ellen Auffert. . . .

[Reversed and remanded]

QUESTIONS

1. Give your opinion why maintenance of an account in statutory form is conclusive evidence, absent fraud or undue influence, that the deposit is the property of the joint tenants?
2. What effect did Rachel Auffert's handwritten note have on the outcome of this case?
3. Was it ethical for Leo to seek to obtain a share of the certificate of deposit by bringing a lawsuit, when his mother had expressed the clear intention to give the entire deposit to Mary Ellen?

15. Tenancy by Entirety

At common law, a **tenancy by entirety** or **tenancy by the entireties** was created when property was transferred to both husband and wife. It differs from joint tenancy in that it exists only when the transfer is to husband and wife. Also, the right of survivorship cannot be extinguished, and one spouse's interest cannot be transferred to a third person. However, in some jurisdictions, a spouse's right to share the possession and the profits may be transferred. This form of property holding is popular in common law jurisdictions because creditors of only one of the spouses cannot reach the property while both are living. Only a creditor of both the husband and wife under the same obligation can obtain execution against the property. Moreover, the tenancy by entirety is, in effect, a substitute for a will, since the surviving spouse acquires the complete property interest on the death of the other. There are usually other reasons, however, why each spouse should make a will.

In many states, the granting of an absolute divorce converts a tenancy by the entireties into a tenancy in common.

16. Community Property

In some states, property acquired during the period of marriage is the community property of the husband and wife. Some statutes provide for the right of survivorship; others provide that half of the property of the deceased husband or wife shall go to the heirs of that spouse or permit such half to be disposed of by will. It is commonly provided that property acquired by either spouse during the marriage is prima facie community property, even though title is taken in the spouse's individual name, unless it can be shown that it was obtained with property possessed by the spouse prior to the marriage.

SUMMARY

Personal property consists of whole or fractional ownership rights in things that are tangible and movable, as well as rights in things that are intangible.

Personal property may be acquired by purchase. Personal property may also be acquired by gift where the donor has present intent to make a gift and delivers possession to the donee or makes a constructive delivery. Personal property may be acquired by occupation and under some statutes may also be acquired by finding. The state may acquire property by escheat.

Property rights in trademarks, copyrights, and patents are acquired as provided in federal statutes. A trademark or service mark is any word, symbol, or design, or a combination of these used to identify a product (in the case of a trademark) or a service (in the case of service mark). Terms will fall into one of four categories: (1) generic, (2) descriptive, (3) suggestive, or (4) arbitrary or fanciful. Generic terms are never registrable. Ordinarily, descriptive terms are not registrable. However, if a descriptive term has acquired a "secondary meaning," it is registrable. Suggestive and arbitrary marks are registrable. If there is likelihood of confusion, a court will enjoin the second user from using a particular registered mark.

A copyright is the exclusive right given by federal statute to the creator of a literary or artistic work to use, reproduce, or display the work for the life of the creator and 50 years after the creator's death. A patent gives the inventor an exclusive right for 17 years to make, use, and sell an invention that is new and useful and not obvious to those in the business to which the invention is related. Trade secrets that give an owner an advantage over competitors are protected under state law for an unlimited period so long as they are not made public.

All rights in a particular object of property can be held by one individual, in which case it is said to be held in severalty. Ownership rights may be held concurrently by two or more individuals, in which case it is said to be held in cotenancy. The major forms of cotenancy are (1) tenancy in common, (2) joint tenancy, (3) tenancy by entirety, and (4) community property.

LAW IN PRACTICE

1. Advance registration of trademarks is now possible, allowing start-up business persons to fully disclose their business plans to potential investors without fear that their trademark might be duplicated.

2. A copyright will not protect your innovative ideas, only the way they are expressed.

3. Employees with access to company trade secrets or those working in research and development should, as a condition of their employment, be required to sign Patent-Trade Secret Agreements prohibiting disclosure or use of company secrets.

4. Understanding the difference between tenancy in common, joint tenancy and tenancy by the entirety is of great importance when a husband and wife buy a house, open bank accounts, and purchase securities. Know your rights as a joint owner of property.

QUESTIONS AND CASE PROBLEMS

1. What social forces give rise to the rule of law requiring that there be an actual or symbolic delivery in order to make a gift?

2. What qualities must an invention possess to be patentable?

3. Compare the protection afforded by a patent and the protection afforded by a trademark registration.

4. How does capturing a wild animal on unrestricted land during the hunting season compare with finding lost property?

5. Sullivan sold T-shirts with the name *Boston Marathon* and the year of the race imprinted on them. The Boston Athletic Association (BAA) sponsors and administers the Boston Marathon and has used the name *Boston Marathon* since 1917. The BAA registered the name *Boston Marathon* on the Principal Register. In 1986, the BAA entered into an exclusive license with Image, Inc. to use its service mark on shirts and other apparel. Thereafter when Sullivan continued to sell shirts imprinted with the name *Boston Marathon*, the BAA sought an injunction. Sullivan's defense was that the general public was not being misled into thinking that his shirts were officially sponsored by the BAA. Without this confusion of source, he contended, no injunction should be issued. Decide. [*Boston Athletic Ass'n. v Sullivan (CA1 Mass) 867 F2d 22*]

6. The New York Banking Law provides that a presumption arises that a joint tenancy has been created when a bank account is opened in the names of two persons "payable to either or the survivor." While he was still single, Richard Coddington opened a savings account with his mother, Amelia. The signature card they signed stated that the account was owned by them as joint tenants with the right of survivorship. No statement as to survivorship was made on the passbook. Richard later married Margaret. On Richard's death, Margaret claimed a share of the account on the ground that it was not held in joint tenancy, because the passbook did not contain words of survivorship and because the statutory presumption of a joint tenancy was overcome by the fact that Richard had withdrawn substantial sums from the account during his life. Decide. [*Coddington v Coddington, 56 App Div 2d 697, 391 NYS2d 760*]

7. Twentieth Century Fox (Fox) owned and distributed the successful motion picture "The Commitments." The film tells the story of a group of young Irishmen and women who form a soul music band. In the film the leader of the band, Jimmy, tries to teach the band members what it takes to be successful soul music performers. Toward that end, Jimmy shows the band members a videotape of James Brown's energetic performance of the song "Please, Please, Please." This performance came from Brown's appearance in 1965 on a program called the "TAMI Show." Portions of the 1965 performance are shown in "The Commitments" in seven separate "cuts" for a total of 27 seconds. Sometimes the cuts are in the background of a scene and sometimes they occupy the entire screen. Brown's name is not mentioned at all during these relatively brief cuts. His name is mentioned only once later in the film, when Jimmy urges the band members to abandon their current musical interests and tune into the great soul performers, including James Brown:

"Listen, from now on I don't want you listening to Guns & Roses and The Soup Dragons. I want you on a strict diet of soul. James Brown for the growls, Otis Redding for the moans, Smokey Robinson for the whines, and Aretha for the whole lot put together."

Would it be "fair use" under U.S. copyright law for Fox to use just twenty-seven seconds of James Brown cuts in the film without formally obtaining permission to use the cuts? Advise Fox as to what if anything would be necessary to protect it from a Copyright Act lawsuit. [*See Brown v Twentieth Century Fox Film Corp. (DC) 799 F Supp 166*]

8. Acuson Corporation manufactures ultrasonic imaging equipment in California and has sold hundreds of these machines. Aloka Co. Ltd., a Japanese company, also manufactures ultrasonic equipment. Aloka asked its American distributor, Johnson & Johnson Ultrasound, to purchase an "Acuson 128" machine. Johnson & Johnson did so through a distributor without identifying Aloka as the ultimate purchaser. After the machine was delivered to Aloka's Tokyo plant, nine of its engineers spent eleven days reverse engineering the Acuson machine. Acuson later discovered that Aloka had indirectly purchased the machine, and it brought suit against Aloka, alleging exploitation of its trade secrets. Aloka defended that it was free to examine and even copy the machine, since it was in the public domain. Decide. [*Acuson v Aloka Co. Ltd. 209 App 3d 425, 257 Cal Rptr 368*]

9. Mona found a wallet on the floor of an elevator in the office building in which she worked. She posted in the building several notices informing of the finding of the wallet, but no one appeared to claim it. She waited for six months and then spent the money in the wallet in the belief that she owned it. Jason, the person who lost the wallet, subsequently brought suit to recover the money. Mona's defense was that the money was hers, since Jason did not claim it within a reasonable time after she posted the notices. Is she correct? (Assume that the common law applies.)

10. In 1971, Harry Gordon turned over $40,000 to his son, Murray Gordon. Murray opened two $20,000 custodian bank accounts under the Uniform Gifts to Minors Acts for his minor children, Eden and Alexander. Murray was listed as the custodian of both accounts. On January 9, 1976, both accounts were closed, and a single bank check representing the principal of the accounts was drawn to the order of Harry Gordon. In April 1976, Murray and his wife, Joan, entered into a separation agreement and were later divorced. Thereafter, Joan, on behalf of her children Eden and Alexander, brought suit against Murray to recover the funds withdrawn in January 1976, contending that the deposits in both accounts were irrevocable gifts. Murray contended that the money was his father's and that it was never intended as a gift but was merely a means of avoiding taxes. Decide. [*Gordon v Gordon, 419 NYS2d 684, 70 App Div 2d 86*]

11. Carol and Robert, both over 21, became engaged. Robert gave Carol an engagement ring. He was killed in an automobile crash before they were married. His estate demanded that Carol return the ring. Was she entitled to keep it? [*Cohen v Bayside Federal Savings and Loan Assn. 62 Misc 2d 738, 309 NYS2d 980*]

12. The plaintiff, Herbert Rosenthal Jewelry Corporation, and the defendant, Kalpakian, manufactured jewelry. The plaintiff obtained a copyright registration of a jeweled pin in the shape of a bee. Kalpakian made a similar pin. Rosenthal sued Kalpakian for infringement of copyright registration. Kalpakian raised the defense that he was only copying the idea, not the way the idea was expressed. Was he liable for infringement of the plaintiff's copyright? [*Herbert Rosenthal Jewelry Corp. v Kalpakian (CA9 Cal) 446 F2d 738*]

13. Mineral Deposits Ltd. (MD Ltd.), an Australian company, manufactures the Reichert Spiral, a device used for recovering gold particles from sand and gravel. The spiral was patented in Australia, and MD Ltd. had applied for a patent in the United States. Theodore Zigan contacted MD Ltd., stating he was interested in purchasing up to 200 devices for use in his gravel pit. MD Ltd. agreed to lend Zigan a spiral for the purpose of testing its efficiency. Zigan made molds of the spiral's components and proceeded to manufacture 170 copies of the device. When MD Ltd. found out that copies were being made, it demanded the return of the spiral. MD Ltd. also sought lost profits for the 170 spirals manufactured by Zigan. Recovery was sought on a theory of misappropriation of trade secrets. Zigan offered to pay for the spiral lent him by MD Ltd. He argued that trade secrecy protection was lost by the public sale of the spiral. What ethical values are involved? Was Zigan's conduct a violation of trade secrecy law? [*Mineral Deposits Ltd. v Zigan (Colo App) 773 P2d 609*]

14. From October 1965 through July 1967, Union Carbide Corporation sold certain bulbs for high-intensity reading lamps under its EVEREADY trademark. Carbide's sales of electrical products under the EVEREADY mark exceeded $100 million for every year after 1963; from 1963 to 1967, Carbide spent $50 million in advertising these products. In 1969, the defendant, Ever-Ready, Inc., imported miniature lamp bulbs for high-intensity lamps with *Ever-Ready* stamped on their base. In two surveys conducted by Carbide, 50 percent of those interviewed associated Carbide products with the marks used by Ever-Ready, Inc. Carbide sought an injunction against Ever-Ready's use of the name Ever-Ready on or in connection with the sale of electrical products. No monetary damages were sought. Ever-Ready, Inc. defended that Carbide's trademark EVEREADY was descriptive, and therefore the registration of the mark was improper and invalid. Carbide raised the defense that its mark had acquired secondary meaning. Decide. [*Union Carbide Corp. v Ever-Ready, Inc. (CA7 Ill) 531 F2d 366*]

15. Anheuser-Busch had been interested in producing a low-alcohol beer. Anheuser-Busch made an application for registration of the trademark LA and began marketing its low-alcohol product under the LA label. Following Anheuser-Busch's introduction of its product, the Stroh Brewery Company introduced *Schaefer LA*, also a low-alcohol beer. An action to enjoin Strohs use of *LA* followed. Anheuser-Busch contended that the term

LA was suggestive in that it required some imagination to connect it with the product and, accordingly, was a protectable trademark. Stroh argued that LA was generic or descriptive in nature, since the term is comprised of the initials of the phrase "low alcohol." Decide. *[Anheuser-Busch Inc. v The Stroh Brewery Company (CA8 Mo) 750 F2d 631]*

CHAPTER 21

COMPUTERS
AND THE LAW

LEARNING OBJECTIVES

After studying this chapter, you will be able to:
1. *Tell how the changing technology of the business environment has led to changes in the law.*
2. *List and describe several computer crimes.*
3. *List and describe several computer torts.*
4. *State the extent to which the law does and does not protect hardware and software from harm and misuse.*
5. *Specify how a computer is a threat to the person.*
6. *State the relation of computers to the law of nuisance.*

Traditional rules of law drawn from contract law, tort law, and criminal law may be applied to computers. Also, in the last few years, many statutes that apply specifically to computers have been adopted.

A. GENERAL PRINCIPLES

The modern electronic computer has been in use for little over one-third of a century. In that time, changes in the design, size, and capacity of computers have resulted in their widespread use.

judges and lawmakers have been making new law to govern the new computer situations. While waiting for new laws to be adopted, courts have tried to cover the new computer situations with the prior law.

In the *Wilkens* case the court was faced with whether a pre-computer era statute requiring a "signature" was satisfied when the signature was made mechanically by a computer-controlled device.

In this chapter, the word *computer*, unless otherwise indicated, is used to refer collectively to hardware, software, and data. *Hardware* refers to the tangible objects, including

Figure 21-1   Law and the Computer

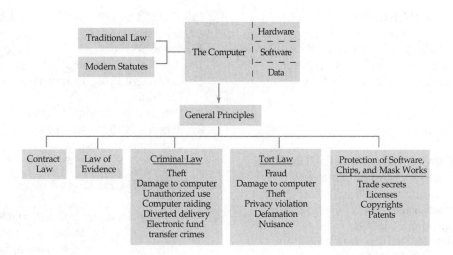

1. Computers and the Environment of the Law

Computers are now part of the business environment. They have created new situations for which no prior law exists, or for which prior law is inadequate. In the last three decades,

the piece of equipment commonly known as the computer and all auxiliary attachments, such as disk and tape drives, monitors, printers, and terminals. *Software* describes the programs or instructions that control the operation of the hardware. *Data* refers to information, other than operating software, that is

WILKENS v IOWA INSURANCE COMMISSIONER
(Iowa) 457 NW2d 1 (1990)

> A 1939 Iowa statute requires that insurance policies written for residents of Iowa must be signed by a resident agent. Wilkens and other agents of the Allstate Insurance Company brought suit claiming that the statute had been violated by Allstate's signing policies with the names of the agents by means of a typewriter that was controlled by a computer. From a decision of the Insurance Commission sustaining this method of signing, Wilkens and other agents appealed.

SACKETT, J. . . . The commissioner determined the computer-generated signatures were permissible to meet the requirements of a signature for purposes of the applicable statute. Appellants contend that they were not. Iowa Code section 4.1(17) . . . provides:

Written—in writing—signature. The words "written" and "in writing" may include any mode of representing words or letters in general use. A signature, when required by law, must be made by the writing or markings of the person whose signature is required. If a person is unable due to a physical handicap to make a written signature or mark, that person may [make substitutions] in lieu of a signature required by law. . . .

In *Cummings v Landes*, 140 Iowa 80, 82-83, 117 NW 22, 23 (1908), the Iowa court addressed the meaning of the word "signature" in the context of a statute requiring that notice of service be signed by a plaintiff or his or her attorney. The court discussed how the word "signature" is generally considered to be nearly synonymous with autograph, but allowed the name to be attached by any known method of impressing a name. . . .

We find the fact that the signature is computer-generated rather than handsigned does not defeat the purpose of the act. The issue is not how the name is placed on a sheet of paper; rather, the issue is whether the person whose name is affixed intends to be bound. No one argues that the agent whose name was affixed did not intend to be bound. We find the signature requirements of the statute were met.

. . . The primary purpose of the section is to assure the Iowa consumer an acceptable product and to require that agents licensed in Iowa have input in the writing of policies sold in Iowa. The legislature has provided for the consumer purchasing insurance in Iowa to have the benefit of the expertise of a resident agent who has passed the required tests showing knowledge of local law and who knows the policy, the coverage, the risk, and the premiums. . . .

Appellants next contend Allstate's record-keeping does not comply with the statute. Iowa Code section 515.57 . . . provides:

It shall be the duty of every resident countersigning agent for business originating without this state but covering property or business transactions within this state, and the insurance companies issuing such policies, to keep a written record of each such transaction which shall contain [specific information], and such records shall be subject to the inspection of the commissioner of insurance for the purpose of verifying the amount of premium tax payable by such company. . .

Allstate maintains the required information in its computer system and all countersigning agents have access to the information. The Commissioner [found that] this procedure complies with Section 515.57. . . .

Section 515.57 originated in 1939. We recognize, as the commissioner argues, that methods of doing business have changed considerably since the time of the enactment of the statute. The advent of the computer age has resulted in businesses making substantial changes in record keeping procedures. The insurance commissioner determined the records as kept were sufficient for his purposes. . . .

[Judgment affirmed]

QUESTIONS

1. What was the purpose of requiring a signature of a resident agent on the policy?
2. The decision in the *Wilkens* case turns on the meaning of the word "signature." What do you mean when you use the word "signature"?
3. Do you think the decision in the *Wilkens* case was correct? Why or why not?

contained within the memory of the computer during processing or stored on some magnetic medium.

2. Management and the Computer

The law of computers relating to management is merely an extension of prior principles to new situations.

(a) NEGLIGENT USE OF THE COMPUTER. Management may be liable under ordinary negligence principles because of careless use of the computer. If management knows that its computer is not working properly but continues to use it without attempting to correct it, management may be held liable to third persons who are harmed by computer error.[1] Here the rules of law are the same as when management knowingly uses any other defective equipment. For example, a store making deliveries in a truck that is known to have bad brakes would be liable for negligence if the bad brakes led to a collision causing harm.

(b) PROTECTION OF THE COMPUTER. If the enterprise has a computer, management must take reasonable steps to maintain, protect, and ensure the accuracy of the computer. The duty to maintain is the same as the duty to maintain the building or any other equipment of the enterprise. Management must exercise care in the selection of personnel operating the computer, for the purpose of protecting against computer crimes and torts and protecting customers of the enterprise from inaccuracy.

Under general principles of law, a breach of the preceding duties can cause a court to impose liability on management. Again, there is the limitation that management has discretion to make choices. Liability will not be imposed if the choice made by management with respect to the computer personnel or computer protection appeared reasonable under the circumstances.

---

[1] Swiss Air Transportation Co. v Benn, 467 NYS2d 341 (1983).

3. Non-Computer Law and the Computer

When the computer is treated as a thing without any distinction as to its special nature, it is subject to the general principles of pre-computer non-computer law that applies to things.

(a) CONTRACT LAW. Contract law has not been affected by the computer, although contracts have been developed to govern computer-related transactions. Thus, the law for the sale of a computer is the same as the law governing the sale of a television set. Computer software constitutes "goods," and its sale is governed by Article 2 of the Uniform Commercial Code.[2] When the customer asks the dealer for computer equipment that is compatible with an existing system, the law is the same as in any other case in which the buyer asks the seller to provide goods that will meet the particular needs of the buyer. If the seller of hardware or software makes false statements, the contract is avoidable as in any other case. Similarly, the seller may be subject to penalties under consumer protection and deceptive trade practices statutes.[3]

Contracts may relate to the sale or lease of computers, the sale or lease of software, the development of customized software, and the providing of services for maintenance and repair. There may be a contract for an outside organization to provide the computer services needed by the enterprise. In connection with software, there will probably be special contract provisions imposing restrictions as to matters that are trade secrets or otherwise protected.

There is some indication that when experienced business enterprises make a computer-related contract, the contract will be interpreted very strictly. In such a case, it has been held that the customer was bound by fine print provisions of the contract on the theory that the customer knew from experience that such clauses would probably be in the contract.[4] Because of the consumer protection movement, it is unlikely that a court will take this approach with a small business purchasing its first computer or a person purchasing a computer for home use.

(b) TORT LAW. The computer has not altered existing principles of tort law, such as the law governing fraud.[5]

(c) TAXATION. Transactions in computers are subject to taxation whenever similar transactions in other personal property would be so subject.

(d) ANTITRUST AND MARKETING LAWS. Transactions involving computers, both hardware and software, and supplementary servicing of systems, are subject to the existing market regulatory laws and antitrust laws.[6]

(e) PUBLIC RECORDS. Under Freedom of Information Acts, much information held by the government is open to disclosure to the public. The fact that such information is stored in a computer does not make it immune from an otherwise proper request for disclosure. In such case, the person seeking the information should pay the government office the cost of producing a copy of the computer tape or of the other material on which the information is stored.[7]

---

[2]   Systems Design and Management Information, Inc. v Kansas City Post Office Employees Credit Union, 14 Kan App 2d 266, 788 P2d 878 (1990).

[3]   Integrated Title Data Systems v Dulaney (Tex App) 800 SW2d 336 (1990).

[4]   AMF, Inc. v Computer Automation (SD Ohio) 573 F Supp 924 (1983).

[5]   Comfax Corp. v North American Van Lines, Inc. (Ind App) 587 NE2d 118 (1992).

[6]   Virtual Maintenance, Inc. v Prime Computer, Inc. (CA6 Mich) 995 F2d 1324 (1993).

[7]   Ohio v City of Cleveland, 62 Ohio 3d 456, 584 NE2d 665 (1992).

4. The Computer and the Law of Evidence

The law of evidence has changed drastically to make it possible to admit evidence produced by the computer.

Computer printouts of "business records stored on electronic computing equipment are admissible in evidence if relevant and material, without the necessity of identifying, locating, and producing as witnesses the individuals who made the entries in the regular course of business if it is shown that (1) the electronic computing equipment is recognized as standard equipment, (2) the entries are made in the regular course of business at or reasonably near the time of the happening of the event recorded, and (3) the foundation testimony satisfies the court that the sources of information, method, and time of preparation were such as to indicate its trustworthiness and justify its admission."[8]

(a) COMPUTER EVIDENCE FROM A PARTY TO LITIGATION. When a store sues its customer, can it prove what the customer owed by what the store's computer says? This question can arise in any contract setting, such as a suit for wages, commissions, or refunds.

In the *Victory Memorial Hospital* case the defendant objected to the admission of the hospital computer's printout on the ground that the information that had been supplied to the computer as input was wrong.

VICTORY MEMORIAL HOSPITAL v RICE
143 Ill App 3d 621, 97 Ill Dec 635, 493 NE2d 117 (1986)

Michael Rice was treated for gunshot wounds at the Victory Memorial Hospital. He refused to pay the hospital bill because he claimed it was not correct. As proof of the amount owed to it, the hospital offered in evidence a computer printout of the services rendered the defendant and the amounts owed for them. The court refused to admit the printout on the ground that there was no proof that the printout represented what the defendant owed. Judgment was entered against the hospital, and the hospital appealed.

LINDBERG, J. . . . Plaintiff . . . argues that the trial court erred when it refused to admit the computerized bills into evidence as business records. In Illinois, business records supplied by a computer are admissible in evidence without testimony of the persons who made the entries in the regular course of business if it is shown that (1) the electronic computing equipment is recognized as standard; (2) the entries are made in the regular course of business at or reasonably near the time of the happening of the event recorded; and (3) the foundation testimony satisfies the court that the sources of information, method and time of preparation were such as to indicate its trustworthiness and justify its admission.

In the present case the court stated that there was insufficient proof that the items listed on the bills represented services actually performed on defendant. In

---

[8] Prudential Ins. Co. v Kinney Plantation, Inc. (La App) 496 So 2d 1211 (1986); Federal Rules of Evidence, Rule 1001(1); (3); 803(5); 804(b)(5); 901(b)(9).

other words, the court questioned the reliability and trustworthiness of the data before its entrance into the computer. The only method of verifying such information would have been to match the computerized bill against the original entry data. There was testimony that in order for the hospital to have produced all of the documents of original entry in the present case it would have been forced to inaugurate an extremely involved and time consuming retrieval process, especially since defendant had been hospitalized on several occasions and had been treated on an outpatient basis also. The record indicates that a hospital witness produced approximately 30 slips indicating certain laboratory tests that were done on defendant and the results of those tests. She matched them to the corresponding date and charge on the bill. The original slips in question were in five parts, the last part of which went to the data processing department to be entered into the computer by code number. In contrast to the other four portions of the slip, the part which went to the billing department contained only numbers which were fed into the computer by trained personnel. The trial court questioned the verification testimony because the slips produced by the witness were not the actual number coded slips which were used to enter the data. Since the five slips in each packet contained the same information, however, and since the slips produced could be matched to the corresponding date and charge on the bill, as to those tests, the supporting documentation verifying the trustworthiness of the input information was sufficient in our opinion to show that defendant had been given the service for which he was charged.

In view of the rationale supporting prior decisions in Illinois regarding the admissibility of computerized evidence, we also conclude that the proper foundation was presented to establish that the source of information and method of preparation indicated trustworthiness and supported admission of the entire computerized bill. In *People v Gauer* (1972), 7 Ill App 3d 512, 514, 288 NE2d 24 this court stated that considering the general use of electronic computing and recording equipment in the business world and the business world's reliance on the equipment, the scientific reliability of such machines can scarcely be questioned. The Illinois Supreme Court held in *Grand Liquor Co., Inc. v Department of Revenue* (1977), 67 Ill 2d 195, 10 Ill Dec 472, 367 NE2d 1238 that computer printouts are admissible pursuant to Supreme Court Rule 238 (87 Ill 2d R 238) as long as the foundational tests . . . were met. Although . . . the trial court must be satisfied from the foundation testimony that the sources of information, method, and time of preparation were such as to indicate trustworthiness and justify admission, we are of the opinion that in the present case the trial court erred in not admitting the computerized bill into evidence as a business record based on the foundational evidence offered. The jury would still be free to accord the bills as much weight as in their opinion they deserved.

[Judgment reversed and action remanded]

QUESTIONS

1. Before the printout of a computer will be admitted in evidence, what must be shown?
2. What had been done by the hospital to support the admission of the computer printout into evidence?
3. Does the computer printout establish that the defendant owed the amount claimed by the plaintiff?

(b) COMPUTER EVIDENCE FROM A THIRD PERSON. Can the computer evidence generated by a third person be used to establish such facts as are shown thereby? This arises most frequently in a criminal prosecution in which a link in the chain of evidence against the defendant is the fact that a phone call was made from one particular place to another at a particular time. The computer-generated records of the telephone company have been admitted in evidence in such case to prove the making of the phone call.

(c) WEIGHT OF COMPUTER EVIDENCE. In all matters relating to evidence, there are basically two steps: (1) Can the particular evidence be admitted in court and considered in deciding the case? (2) Assuming that the evidence can be admitted and considered, what weight is to be given to it? Must it be believed, or can it be contradicted?

Computer evidence must meet these two challenges. Thus, the proper foundation must be established before the computer printout is admissible in court. After that, it is for the trier of fact to decide if the computer printout should be regarded as conclusive or inconclusive, or if it should be ignored.

(d) LIMITATIONS ON COMPUTER EVIDENCE. In some cases, computer evidence was excluded because the court believed the circumstances were such as to require greater proof of the reliability of the evidence. In other cases, the evidence was excluded because the court did not believe that the computer could do what was required to make the evidence reliable.

The mere fact that a computer states a conclusion does not make the conclusion admissible in evidence.

B. CRIMINAL LAW AND THE COMPUTER

In some situations, the ordinary law of crimes fits the computer crime situation. In other situations, new law is required.

5. What Is a Computer Crime?

The term *computer crime* is frequently used. It has no established definition. Generally, the phrase is used to refer to a crime that can only be committed by a person having some knowledge of the operation of a computer. Just as stealing an automobile requires knowledge of how to operate and drive a car, so the typical computer crime requires knowledge of how the computer works. This concept of a computer crime is satisfactory for the purpose of setting the stage, but it fails to tell us what law will be applied: the law of crimes or a new law relating to computers.

Some crimes may involve a computer without making direct use of one. In this case, the ordinary law of crimes will apply. For example, a person using the mail to falsely advertise a service as computerized is guilty of committing the federal crime of using the mails to defraud.

The more serious and costly wrongs relating to computers do not fit into the ordinary definitions of crime. There is a definite trend of adopting statutes to declare new computer crimes. These statutes are strictly construed. Only that conduct that is covered by the statute in question can be punished as the crime.

A criminal law statute must be sufficiently clear to be understood by ordinary persons of ordinary intelligence. In some cases, computer crimes statutes have been held unconstitutional as being too vague.

6. The Computer as "the Victim"

A traditional crime may be committed by stealing or intentionally damaging the computer.

(a) THEFT OF HARDWARE. When the computer itself is stolen, the ordinary law relating to theft crimes should apply. No reason can be found why a theft of a computer should not be subject to the same law as the theft of a typewriter or a desk. Whatever the crime would be by statute in the case of these other objects, the same crime is committed when a computer is the subject matter of the theft.

(b) THEFT OF SOFTWARE. When a thief takes software, whether in the form of a program written on paper or a program on a disk or tape, a situation arises that does not fit into the common law definition of larceny. This is so because larceny at common law was confined to the taking of tangible property. At common law, the value of stolen software would be determined by the value of the tangible substance on which the program was recorded. Thus, under a traditional concept of property, which would ignore the value of the intangible program, the theft would only be petty larceny. Now, however, virtually every state has amended its definition of larceny or theft so that the stealing of software is a crime. In some states, the unauthorized taking of information may constitute a crime under a trade secrets protection statute.

(c) INTENTIONAL DAMAGE. The computer may be the "victim" of a crime when the computer is intentionally destroyed or harmed. In the most elementary form of damage, the computer could be harmed if smashed with an ax or destroyed in an explosion or a fire. In such cases, the wrongdoer may be seeking to do more than merely destroy or harm the computer. The intent may be to cause the computer's owner the financial loss of the computer and the destruction of the information that is stored in it.

When the wrongdoer has the purpose of destroying software or the stored information, it is more likely that a more subtle way of committing the crime will be employed. In this case, the wrongdoer might gain access to the computer and then erase or alter the data in question. The wrongdoer might also achieve the desired purpose by interfering with the air-conditioning required by the computer, thus causing it to malfunction. Or the wrongdoer may intentionally plant a "bug" or "vi-rus" in software, causing the program to malfunction or to give incorrect output. Such damage may be the work of an angry employee or ex-employee, or it may be the work of a competitor. In the area of criminal law, it might be a person destroying the record of prior convictions.

In earlier years, the criminal was probably only guilty of the crime of malicious destruction of or damage to property.[9] Again, the lawmakers have filled the gap between the technological environment and the law. Statutes adopted in many states now make it a crime to damage software or computer-stored information.

7. Unauthorized Use of Computer

In contrast with conduct intended to harm the computer or its rightful user or to acquire secret information, the least serious of computer crimes is the unlawful use of someone else's computer. In some states, the unlawful use of a computer is not a crime. Although the user is stealing the time of the computer, the wrongdoer is not regarded as committing the crime of larceny because the wrongdoer has no intent to deprive the owner permanently of the computer.

In some states, the borrowing of another's automobile without the owner's permission is not a crime where there is no intention to deprive the owner of the automobile permanently. If following the common law, states would undoubtedly use the same approach in the case of the unauthorized use of a computer.[10] The unauthorized taking of information from a computer is more serious, however. This computer crime has been widely regulated by recent statutes, noted in Section 8 of this chapter. Instead of making an unauthorized use of a computer, the wrongdoer may make an unlawful use of informa-

---

[9] The crime of maliciously damaging or destroying property is ordinarily a misdemeanor and, as such, is subject only to a relatively small fine or short imprisonment.

[10] The court in Indiana v McGraw (Ind) 480 NE2d 552 (1985) followed this approach.

tion contained in a properly acquired printout. Is this a criminal taking of property?

In the *Evans* case a statute creating crimes of larceny, embezzlement, and false pretenses in connection with computer time, services, or stored information was applied.

EVANS v VIRGINIA
226 Va 292, 308 SE2d 126 (1983)

The Central Fidelity Bank had a department that sold stocks and bonds, primarily to large institutions. Evans and Smith worked in this department as salesmen. At intervals the bank would make computer printouts of the names and addresses of its customers and maturity dates of their investments. Smith asked that an extra copy of this printout be made for him. Smith was given two extra copies. He gave one to Evans. Thereafter Evans and Smith resigned from the bank and went to work for a competing bank. Smith gave the computer printout of customers to the new employer. Evans and Smith were then prosecuted for and convicted of petit (petty) larceny by embezzlement. They appealed.

GORDON, J. . . . According to an officer of Central Fidelity, a customer security list would be useful for many years to come, an invaluable sales tool to produce profits. Another officer testified that if a competitor obtained the information on a list, the competitor would be given an edge in the business.

Central Fidelity brought a civil suit under Code § 18.2-500 for injury to its trade or business, resulting in a favorable decree. The indictments involved in this appeal followed.

In *Lund v Commonwealth*, 217 Va. 688, 232 SE2d 745 (1977), this Court held that the taking of computer time and services in the form of printouts could not constitute larceny because the subject matter of larceny must be goods and chattels. Computer time and services, reasoned the Court, were not goods or chattels.

In 1978 the General Assembly enacted Code § 18.2-98.1:

Computer time or services or data processing services or information or data stored in connection therewith is hereby defined to be property which may be the subject of larceny under §§ 18.2-95 or 18.2-96, or embezzlement under § 18.2-111, or false pretenses under § 18.2-178.

Code § 18.2-111, under which Evans and Smith were prosecuted, makes a person guilty of larceny if he [does] "wrongfully and fraudulently use, dispose of, conceal or embezzle any . . . personal property, tangible or intangible, which he shall have received . . . by virtue of his . . . employment. . . ."

The indictments charged that Evans and Smith "unlawfully and feloniously did steal computer information or data stored in connection therewith, to-wit: a customer securities list."*. . .

*The trial did not proceed on the theory that the defendants embezzled a piece of paper. As observed by the trial judge, "there was never any indication, any observation, any allegation that this was a case involving the theft of paper."

The trial court instructed the jury that to convict it must find that the customer security list "was of some value." Code § 18.2-96 makes "simple larceny not from the person of another of goods and chattels of the value of less than $200" punishable as a misdemeanor.

The Commonwealth adduced no proof, says counsel, of the value of the list. Counsel therefore concludes that the evidence does not support the giving of the instruction. . . .

The petit larceny statute, Code § 18.2-96, does not require proof of any minimum value.

"At the common law, an article to be the subject of larceny must be of some value. It is sufficient, however, it is said, if it be worth less than the smallest coin known to the law." *Wolverton v Commonwealth*, 75 Va. 909, 913 (1881). Under settled Virginia law, no proof need be adduced to show that the subject of petit larceny has a specific value.

The evidence respecting the nature and use of the customer security list supplied proof that the list had value. The proof was augmented by testimony that the list was an invaluable sales tool, giving a competitor a valuable edge if the list fell into the competitor's hands. . . .

This Court in a recent case . . . described the elements of embezzlement:

A person entrusted with possession of another's personalty who converts such property to his own use or benefit is guilty of the statutory offense of embezzlement. Code § 18.2-111.

C. D. Smith v Commonwealth, 222 Va. 646, 649, 283 SE2d 209, 210 (1981). And Black's Law Dictionary 300 (5th ed. 1979), . . . gives this definition of the noun form of *to convert*:

Unauthorized and wrongful exercise of dominion and control over another's personal property, to exclusion of or inconsistent with rights of the owner.

Proof was adduced that Evans and Smith converted the customer security list by exercising dominion and control inconsistent with the rights of Central Fidelity, the owner. The proof therefore justified the conviction of statutory embezzlement. . . .

[Conviction affirmed]

QUESTIONS

1. Is the decision in the *Evans* case in harmony with the common law?
2. Why was the prosecution for embezzlement?
3. Which of the two statutes quoted in the *Evans* case was the more essential to the prosecution?

8. Computer Raiding

A serious computer crime involves taking information from a computer without the consent of the owner of the information. Whether this is done by having the computer make a print-out of stored information or by tapping into the data bank of the computer by some electronic means is not important. In many instances, the taking of information from the computer constitutes a crime of stealing trade secrets. In some states it is known as the crime of "computer trespass."[11]

Both Congress and state legislatures have adopted statutes that declare it a crime to make any unauthorized use of a computer or to gain unauthorized access to a computer or the information stored in its database in order to cause harm to the computer or its rightful user.[12]

9. Diverted Delivery by Computer

In many industries, deliveries are controlled by a computer. The person in charge of that computer or a criminal unlawfully gaining access to the computer may cause the computer to direct delivery to an improper place. That is, instead of shipping goods to the customers to whom they should go, the wrongdoer diverts the goods to a different place, where they will be received by the wrongdoer or by a confederate.

In pre-computer days, written orders were sent from the sales department to the shipping department. The shipping department would then send the ordered goods to the proper places. If the person in the sales department or the person in the shipping department were dishonest, either one of them could divert the goods from the proper destination. Today, this fraudulent diversion of goods may be effected by causing the computer to give false directions. Basically, the crime has not changed. The computer is merely the new instrument by which the old crime is committed. This old crime has taken on a new social significance because of the amazingly large dollar value of the theft accomplished by means of it. In one case, several hundred loaded freight cars were made to disappear. In another case, a loaded oil tanker was diverted to unload into a fleet of tank trucks operated by an accomplice of the computer operator.

The crime of diverted delivery is not limited to goods. It has embraced transferring money from a proper account to a wrong account. Here millions of dollars have been involved in a single crime.

The case of diverted delivery by computer does not require any new law, because the appropriation of goods or money improperly delivered comes within the larceny-theft-embezzlement spectrum of crime. However, when a diverted delivery crime is effected by means of a computer, future statutes may classify the crime as aggravated larceny or the like, in order to impose the more severe penalty that society feels is called for by the huge dollar values involved. This feeling of society has led to the Electronic Fund Transfers Act described in the following section.

10. Electronic Fund Transfer Crimes

The Electronic Fund Transfers Act (EFTA)[13] makes it a crime to use any counterfeit, stolen, or fraudulently obtained card, code, or other device to obtain money or goods in excess of a specified amount through an electronic fund transfer system. The EFTA also makes it a crime to ship such devices or goods so obtained in interstate commerce, or knowingly to receive goods that have been obtained by means of the fraudulent use of the transfer system.

C. TORT LAW AND THE COMPUTER

Tort law applies to the computer with respect to damage to the computer, fraud, theft, the

---

[11] Washington v Riley, ___ Wash ___, 846 P2d 1365 (1993).

[12] The Counterfeit Access Device and Computer Fraud Act of October 12, 1984, § 2102, PL 98-473, 98 Stat 2190, 18 USC §§ 1030 et seq.; Computer Fraud and Abuse Act of 1986, Act of October 16, 1986, PL 99-474, 100 Stat 1213, 18 USC § 1001, as amended; Electronic Communications Privacy Act of 1986, Act of October 21, 1986, PL 99-508, 100 Stat 1848, 18 USC § 2510; Computer Fraud Act of 1987, Act of January 8, 1988, PL 100-235, 101 Stat 1724, 15 USC § 272, 278, 40 USC § 759. Provision is made for training small businesses in the use and security of computers by the Small Business and Computer Security and Education Act of July 16, 1984, PL 98-362, 98 Stat 431, 15 USC §§ 633 et seq.

[13] Act of November 10, 1978, § 916(n), PL 95-630, 92 Stat 3738, 15 USC § 1693n.

11. Fraud

The basic principles of tort law for fraud are applicable in computer situations. For example, if false statements are knowingly made to induce the sale of a computer, the seller is liable for fraud damages to the same extent as though any other kind of goods were the subject of the sale. If the wrongdoer feeds false information to the computer and then uses the printout to deceive the victim, the wrongdoer is subject to the ordinary tort law governing fraud.

12. Damage to the Computer

Tort liability for damage to the computer arises in connection with damage to hardware and software.

(a) DAMAGE TO HARDWARE. Damage to hardware, including its destruction, will impose tort liability under the same principles of law that would apply if a typewriter, a car, a desk, or any other tangible property were damaged or destroyed. The fact that the dam-

protection of privacy, defamation, and nuisance.

age to the computer may cause a shutdown of the activities of the computer owner is significant in determining whether the defendant's act was done with such wantonness or reckless indifference to consequences as to authorize imposing punitive or exemplary damages on the wrongdoer. Punitive or exemplary damages are those in excess of the amount needed to compensate the plaintiff for loss. Such damages are imposed to punish or make an example of the defendant.

(b) DAMAGE TO SOFTWARE. The defendant may have damaged the software, for example, by erasing a part of the computer's memory. Here the tort law aspect of liability and of recovery of punitive damages is the same as for any other kind of property. In addition, many recently adopted statutes expressly impose tort liability for such misconduct.

(c) INSURANCE. When an insurance policy does not expressly state that it covers computer property, a question may arise as to whether hardware, software, and a database are protected by such a policy. The *Magnetic Data* case, which follows, raised this question.

MAGNETIC DATA, INC. v
ST. PAUL FIRE AND MARINE INS. CO.
(Minn App) 430 NW2d 483 (1988)

Magnetic Data, Inc. (MDI) is in the business of inspecting and repairing computer cartridges. A cartridge may be inspected by visual examination, a gauge measurement, or an electronic inspection. When an electronic inspection is made, all data that is stored in the cartridge is erased. The Sanger Corporation sent 22 cartridges to MDI for examination. Twelve of these were not to be inspected electronically because the cartridges were the only copy of the stored information. Through a mistake of MDI employees, all 22 cartridges were erased. Sanger sued MDI for the loss caused by such erasing. MDI claimed that the loss was covered by its comprehensive general liability policy (CGL) issued by the St. Paul Fire and Marine Insurance Company. MDI sued on the policy. Judgment was entered in its favor, and the insurance company appealed.

NIERENGARTEN, J. . . . [The inspection] of the twelve critical cartridges was an "accidental event" within the meaning of MDI's CGL policy because the loss of

Sanger's data on the critical cartridges was "an unexpected, unforeseen, or unde-signed happening or consequence." . . . The record does not indicate MDI's employees realized the erasure would result in loss of unduplicated information. While the technical task of erasing the data from the disks was performed intentionally, the electronic process itself was accidentally or mistakenly employed, and the loss of the computer data was the type of accidental loss intended to be covered by MDI's CGL policy. . . .

We conclude the erasure of the data on the critical cartridges was an "accidental event" within the meaning of the CGL policy. . . .

The parties dispute whether the erasure of the magnetically encoded data re-sulted in damage to "tangible" property. MDI states "it is the information stored on the disk cartridges which is of value to MDI's customers" and contends erasure of the information caused rearrangement of the subatomic particles on the cartridge disks. MDI submitted affidavits from two computer experts who suggest the sub-atomic particles on the surface of a magnetic disk are tangible property. St. Paul Fire claims erasure did not result in damage to tangible property and asserts the CGL policy does not cover any loss unless some damage to "tangible" property occurs.

. . . The policy does not limit coverage to claims arising from damage to tangible property. So long as an accidental event occurred which resulted in unexpected or unintended "property damage," including "loss of use of others' property that hasn't been physically damaged," the property damage is covered. . . . Even if mag-netically encoded computer data is not tangible property, the computer information encoded on the critical cartridge disks was property of Sanger and its clients. . . . Since the computer information encoded on the critical cartridge disks was property and was unexpectedly or unintentionally destroyed during the [electronic] process, Sanger's loss of use of that property constitutes "property damage" within the meaning of MDI's CGL policy because the erasure was "caused by an accidental event.". . . The CGL policy . . . excludes coverage of damage to "property on MDI's premises . . . for the purposes of being worked on by MDI's behalf." . . . We distin-guish between the physical components of the disk cartridges and the information encoded on the cartridge disks. Even though . . . the disk cartridges were "located at the business premises of MDI" and the "disk cartridges were . . . in the care, custody and control of MDI," we do not believe coverage necessarily is precluded . . . be-cause the damaged property—Sanger's computer information—was not on MDI's premises "for the purposes of being worked on." Sanger suspected certain computer disk cartridges were defective and that the cartridges may have caused Sanger's computer system to malfunction. However, there is no evidence in the record indi-cating the information encoded on the magnetic disks was the source of the sus-pected defects; nor is there any indication in the record that MDI was authorized or expected to perform any inspection processes that would affect Sanger's computer information.

Our distinction between the physical computer disk cartridges and the magneti-cally encoded information stored on the disks may be technical because the com-puter disks and the magnetically encoded information contained on those disks are intimately related. However, we do not believe the distinction is artificial given the unique characteristics of the property involved. Sanger's information apparently was readily transferable and could have existed independent of the specific disks upon which it was encoded, and its existence on the critical cartridge disks apparently was fortuitous. Sanger's expectations about the type of work which would be performed on the critical cartridges also supports our conclusion that the disk cartridges and the information encoded on the disks were separate property. Sanger authorized only visual inspection and gauge testing of the critical cartridges and did not authorize electronic inspection because that process necessarily would erase unduplicated information stored in the critical cartridges. We only can conclude therefore that while the critical cartridges were on MDI's premises for the purposes of being worked on, the information encoded on the critical cartridge disks was separate property and not on MDI's premises for the purposes of being worked on. . . .

[Judgment affirmed]

QUESTIONS

1. What kind of property was involved in the *Magnetic Data* case?
2. Was the court in the *Magnetic Data* case concerned about damage to Sanger's program, by which Sanger stored information on the disks?
3. How would the case have been decided if MDI had been retained to verify the information on the disks, and that information was accidentally erased in the process of verification?

Another case has held that a computer tape and the data stored on the tape are protected by an insurance policy covering damage to tangible property.[14]

13. Theft of the Computer

The civil or tort liability for the theft of a computer parallels the criminal law with respect to such theft. Thus, an actual taking away of the hardware constitutes the tort of conversion.

14. The Computer and the Protection of Privacy

The law relating to the protection of privacy applies whether or not a computer is involved. That is, there is no change made or needed in the law of privacy because a computer had

been used to invade the privacy in question. Statutes have been adopted to protect against such invasion as to computer-stored data.[15]

(a) WHY IS THERE CONCERN OVER PROTECTION OF PRIVACY? There is much public concern over protection of privacy because of the efficiency of the computer. Consider the number of places that have some information about you. Every school you ever attended has some of your personal history. If you have applied for any kind of license, purchased goods on credit, obtained insurance, applied for a job, been treated by a doctor, or been admitted to a hospital, more of your life story is on paper. But this has never bothered you because, assuming that you had thought about it, you would have recognized that it would be practically impossible for anyone to

---

[14] Retail Systems, Inc. v CNA Insurance Companies (Minn App) 469 NW2d 735 (1991).

[15] The federal Electronic Communications Privacy Act of October 21, 1986, PL 99-508, 100 Stat 1848, 18 USC § 2510 note. Protection from the invasion of privacy by the improper release of data stored in the federal government computers is made by the Computer Security Act of 1987, Act of January 8, 1988, PL 100-235, 101 Stat 899, 15 USC §§ 272, 278, 40 USC 159, and the Computer Matching and Privacy Protection Act of October 18, 1988, PL 100-503, 102 Stat 2507, 5 USC § 552a note.

assemble all the information about you from all the places where it is kept. Even assuming that the prying stranger would know where to inquire, the cost of going back into old files to dig up information would be prohibitive.

In the computer age, by connecting separate computers into a network, it is possible to print out the story of your life within a matter of seconds. Thus, nothing that you did lies hidden away in dusty filing cabinets. Everything can be brought into the light within seconds.

To this danger of efficiency, we add the ability of an outsider to invade a computer by computer raiding and acquire its information, even without anyone knowing that this has been done. We then have a terrifying product of: *A* [efficiency of the computer] times *B* [availability of information to unauthorized outsiders].

(b) WHO IS LIABLE FOR COMPUTER INVASION OF PRIVACY? The person making public the information stored in the computer may be an authorized user of the computer. The person may be an outsider without authority, who invades the computer and then makes public the private information obtained from the computer. In either case, there is no problem in applying ordinary tort law to hold such a person liable for tort damages for invasion of privacy.

Can management be held liable for the invasion of privacy? If the wrongdoer is an employee, it is possible that management will be liable for the employee's misconduct, on the theory that management had not properly screened job applicants, or was negligent in supervising employees, or is liable for employee misconduct under the circumstances. If the wrongdoer is an outsider, can management be held liable for the invasion of privacy? It may be argued that management could have prevented the invasion of privacy by maintaining a better security system over the com-

puter. It can be claimed that because of the negligence of management, it was possible for the outsider to raid the computer and obtain the information that was later made public.

As an analogy, in some states, if the owner of an automobile leaves it parked on the street with the ignition key in the car and a thief steals the car and runs into a third person, the third person may sue the car owner for the injury caused by the thief who drove the car. Other courts refuse to impose liability in such a case. A court that would impose liability on the negligent car owner could impose liability on the negligent protector of the computer. This liability would be for the harm caused by the thief who raided the computer and then injured the plaintiff by making public information that had been private up to that point. The area is one in which statutory regulation can be expected.

15. Defamation by Computer

A person's credit standing or reputation may be damaged because a computer contains erroneous information that is supplied to third persons. Will the data bank operator or service company be held liable to the person who is harmed? If the operator or the company had exercised reasonable care to prevent errors and to correct errors, it is probable that there will not be liability on either the employee operating the equipment or the management providing the computer service.

The supplier of the wrong information is liable for the damages caused thereby when the error was caused by its negligence. Since the supplier is furnishing information to a limited group of subscribers, it is not protected by the guarantee of free speech.[16]

When negligence or an intent to harm is shown, the wrongdoer could be held liable for what may be called *defamation by computer*. It is likely that liability could be avoided by supplying the person to whom the information

---

[16] Dunn & Bradstreet, Inc. v Greenmoss Builders, 472 US 749 (1985).

relates with a copy of any printout of information that the data bank supplies the third person. This would tend to show good faith and due care on the part of the management of the data bank operation and a reasonable effort to keep the information accurate.

Liability for defamation by computer may arise under the federal Fair Credit Reporting Act of 1970 when the person affected is a consumer. The federal Credit Card Act of 1970 further protects from defamation by computer.

16. The Computer as a Nuisance

The modern world generally looks on the computer as a blessing. At times, it may be a nuisance. This was the claim made in the *Page County Appliance* case.

PAGE COUNTY APPLIANCE CENTER, INC. v HONEYWELL, INC.

(Iowa) 347 NW2d 171 (1984)

ITT Electronic Services, Inc. (ITT), a subsidiary of Honeywell, Inc., leased a Honeywell computer to the Central Travel Service. A nearby enterprise, the Page County Appliance Center, Inc. claimed that there was radiation leakage from the computer that interfered with the reception of the display televisions in the store and that this caused a loss of sales. Appliance Center sued the travel agency, Honeywell, and ITT. The defendants moved the trial court to enter a verdict in their favor. The court refused to do so. They appealed.

REYNOLDSON, C. J. . . . Appliance Center has owned and operated an appliance store in Shenandoah, Iowa, since 1953. In 1975 the store was acquired from his father by John Pearson, who sold televisions, stereos, and a variety of appliances. Before 1980 Pearson had no reception trouble with his display televisions. In early January 1980, however, ITT placed one of its computers with Central Travel Service in Shenandoah as part of a nationwide plan to lease computers to retail travel agents. Central Travel was separated by only one other business from the Appliance Center. [The] ITT computer was manufactured, installed, and maintained by Honeywell.

Thereafter many of Pearson's customers told him his display television pictures were bad; on two of the three channels available in Shenandoah he had a difficult time "getting a picture that was fit to watch." After unsuccessfully attempting several remedial measures, in late January 1980, he finally traced the interference to the operations of Central Travel's computer. Both defendants concede Pearson's problems were caused by radiation leaking from the Honeywell computer.

Appliance Center is alleging a "private nuisance," that is, an actionable interference with a person's interest in the private use and enjoyment of his or her property. . . .

Principles governing our consideration of nuisance claims are well established. One's use of property should not unreasonably interfere with or disturb a neighbor's comfortable and reasonable use and enjoyment of his or her estate. A fair test of whether the operation of a lawful trade or industry constitutes a nuisance is the reasonableness of conducting it in the manner, at the place, and under the circumstances shown by the evidence. Each case turns on its own facts. . . . The existence of a nuisance is not affected by the intention of its creator not to injure anyone. . . .

When the alleged nuisance is claimed to be offensive to the person, courts apply the standard of "normal persons in a particular locality" to measure the existence of a nuisance. This normalcy standard also is applied where the use of property is claimed to be affected. "The plaintiff cannot, by devoting his own land to an unusually sensitive use, . . . make a nuisance out of conduct of the adjoining defendant which would otherwise be harmless." W. Prosser, *The Law of Torts* § 87, at 579 (4th ed. 1971).

In the case before us, ITT asserts the Appliance Center's display televisions constituted a hypersensitive use of its premises. . . .

Clearly, the presence of televisions on any premises is not such an abnormal condition that we can say, as a matter of law, that the owner has engaged in a *peculiarly* sensitive use of the property.

ITT's second contention asserts [that the] trial court should have directed a verdict in its favor because it did not participate in the creation or maintenance of the alleged nuisance. We have noted ITT was engaged in a multimillion dollar, national program to lease computers to travel agencies. It owned this computer and leased it to Central Travel. It was to ITT that the agency first turned when the effect of the computer radiation became apparent. ITT continued to collect its lease payments; the computer did not operate for the benefit of Crowell [owner of Central Travel Service] alone. The jury could have found ITT evidenced some measure of its responsibility, as owner of the computer, in contacting Honeywell and making belated inquiries regarding Appliance Center's problems both to Pearson and Crowell.

It is no ground for directed verdict that the computer was leased to Central Travel. "One is subject to liability for a nuisance caused by an activity, not only when he carries on the activity but also when he participates to a substantial extent in carrying it on." Restatement (Second) of Torts § 834 (1979). Even one who contracts out nuisance-causing work to independent contractors may have the duty, upon notice, "to take reasonably prompt and efficient means to suppress the nuisance." . . . A failure to act under circumstances in which one is under a duty to take positive action to prevent or abate the invasion of the private interest may make one liable, Restatement (Second) of Torts § 824, and this may include a lessor or licensor. *Id.* comment *d*.

An action for damages for nuisance need not be predicated on negligence. Nuisance ordinarily is considered as a condition, and not as an act or failure to act on the part of the responsible party. A person responsible for a harmful condition found to be a nuisance may be liable even though that person has used the highest possible degree of care to prevent or minimize the effect.

Where there is reasonable doubt whether one of several persons is substantially participating in carrying on an activity, the question is for the trier of fact. . . . We hold such reasonable doubt existed on the record made in this case, and trial court did not err in refusing to direct a verdict on this ground.

[Judgment affirmed as to the matters set forth in the above excerpt from the opinion]

QUESTIONS

1. In the *Page County Appliance* case, who was negligent?

2. How does your answer to Question 1 affect the decision in the case?
3. Did the fact that the computer was leased have any significance?

D. PROTECTION OF PROGRAMS, CHIPS, AND MASK WORKS

Computer programs, chip designs, and mask works are protected from piracy, with varying degrees of success, by secrecy, restrictive licensing, or federal statutes.

17. Trade Secrets

Whenever practical, industry will employ trade secrecy to protect computer programs. This gives complete protection to the program owner. When computer tapes containing trade secrets are unlawfully taken away by an employee, the employee is guilty of the crime of theft of trade secrets.[17]

18. Restrictive Licensing

To retain greater control over software, it is common for the creator of software to license its use to others rather than to sell it to them. Such licensing agreements typically include restrictions on the use of the software by the licensee and give the licensor greater protection than given by the copyright law. These restrictions will commonly prohibit the licensee from renting copies of the software to third persons or from subjecting the software to reverse engineering.[18]

(a) ANTI-REVERSE ENGINEERING. A license will commonly prohibit the licensee from engaging in reverse engineering to discover the details of the structure of the licensed program. Existing statutes do not give this protection.

(b) ANTIRENTING. A license to use a computer program will commonly prohibit the licensee from renting or relicensing the program to third persons. This is done to protect the program owner from the loss of such third persons as customers. Of greater importance, it removes the danger that such third persons will make copies of the program and then compete with the original program owner.

(c) VALIDITY. The validity of the restrictions noted above is uncertain.[19] It may be held that such license terms are displaced by federal law. An additional problem arises with respect to anti-reverse engineering provisions in those states that have adopted the Uniform Trade Secrets Act.[20] Although the act does not contain any provision as to reverse engineering, the Official Comment of the Commissioners on Uniform Laws to Section 1 of the act expressly approves "reverse engineering" as a proper means of breaking a trade secret. While the comments of the commissioners are not adopted by the states, a court could hold that such comments manifested a local public policy

---

[17] Leonard v Texas (Tex App) 267 SW2d 171 (1988).

[18] Such provisions in a licensing agreement are not to be confused with the anticompetitive provisions in the employment contracts between the owner and its employees, by which they agree that after their employment is ended, they will not compete with the owner or work for a competitor of the owner for a stated period of time or within a stated geographic area.

[19] Vault Corp. v Quaid Software (DC Cal) 655 F Supp 750 (1987).

[20] This act has been adopted in Alabama, Alaska, Florida, California, Colorado, Connecticut, Delaware, Illinois, Indiana, Kansas, Louisiana, Maine, Minnesota, Montana, Nevada, North Dakota, Oklahoma, Oregon, Rhode Island, South Dakota, Virginia, Washington, West Virginia, and Wisconsin.

that was violated by an anti-reverse engineering provision in a software license.

19. Copyright Protection of Written Programs

Under the Computer Software Copyright Act of 1980,[21] a written program is given the same protection as any other copyrighted material. This is so whether the program is written in source code (ordinary language) or object code (machine language). In determining whether there is a copyright violation under this statute, courts will examine the two programs in question to compare their structure, flow sequence, and organization. Moreover, the courts in their infringement analysis look to see if the most significant steps of the program are similar, rather than whether most of the programs steps are similar. To illustrate a copyright violation, substantial similarity in structure of two computer programs for record keeping was found, even though the programs were dissimilar in a number of respects, where five particularly important subroutines within both programs performed almost identically.[22]

The protection afforded software by the copyright law is not entirely satisfactory because of the distinction made by the copyright law of protecting expressions but not ideas.[23] Because of this limitation, a person using the algorithm, the equivalent of the idea, underlying a program could recreate the program without violating the copyright of the manner in which the program had been originally expressed. Because of this, there is a sound move underway to make a clean break from the copyright law of the past and adopt a distinctive software protection statute that would protect both the idea and the expression.

A computer program is copied for the purpose of the copyright law when the program is transferred from permanent storage to the computer's random access memory.[24]

20. Patent Protection of Written Programs

Patents have been granted for computer programs. In fact, the extent to which computer programs can be patented is expanding rapidly. For example, a method of using a computer to carry out translations from one language to another was held to be patentable.

The patenting of a program has the disadvantage that the program is placed in the public records. It may be examined by anyone. This has the potential danger that the program will be copied. To detect patent violators and bring legal action is difficult and costly.

21. Copyright Protection of Chip Design and Mask Works

The operations of a computer are controlled by electric current passing through its circuitry and activating transistors that work as switches. These transistors and connecting metallic tape are mounted on a small laminated base. The base is generally 1/4" square or smaller. Because of this small size, the base is called a **chip**. The chip is made of substances that are medium conductors of electricity—medium as contrasted with substances that are good conductors, such as copper, or with substances that are insulators, such as glass. Hence, the chip is called a **semiconductor chip**. In making the finished chip, some of the chip is eaten or etched away, and up to thousands of transistors are attached to the chip. This process is guided and controlled by a set of stencils or **masks**.[25] The making of the mask

---

[21] Act of December 12, 1980, PL 96-517, 17 USC §§ 101, 117, 94 Stat 3015.

[22] Whelan Associates v Jaslow Dental Laboratory (CA3 Pa) 797 F2d 1222 (1986).

[23] Autoskill Inc. v National Education Support Systems, Inc. (CA10 NM) 994 F2d 1476 (1993).

[24] Mai Systems Corp. v Peak Computer, Inc. (CA9 Cal) 991 F2d 511 (1993).

[25] This process is not to be confused with the printing of circuits, in which there is merely the pressing of a conducting wire or circuit on a nonconductor base.

changes to a chip takes the program from the drawing board and incorporates it into the chip, which, when added to the computer as a component part, can make the computer perform according to the program. It is relatively easy for anyone with a set of masks (mask work) to mass produce the chip. Mask works piracy is very profitable; huge sums, even up to millions of dollars, may have been spent in designing and manufacturing a mask work.

(a) THE SEMICONDUCTOR CHIP PROTECTION ACT. This act (SCPA) gives copyright protection to mask works.[26] The act gives the mask work owner the exclusive right to use and exploit the work for ten years. Such privilege cannot be obtained if the mask work deals with matter that is ordinarily generally known in the computer chip industry. When the privilege is granted, the mask work is marked with the symbol *M* or Ⓜ. This gives the public notice that the exclusive right under the act has been obtained. The act is violated when any part of a protected chip is copied.[27]

The act does not protect from reverse engineering, provided the alleged infringer can show that substantial time and money were devoted to reverse engineering, as against the contention that the infringer merely copied the original.

(b) APPLICATION FOR PROTECTION. To obtain protection under SCPA, application must be made to the Register of Copyrights within two years after the first commercial exploitation of the mask work.

(c) PENALTY FOR VIOLATION OF SCPA. A person knowingly infringing the copyright created by SCPA is liable to the mask work owner for damages sustained by the owner. The wrongdoer can be required to forfeit to the owner any profits made by the infringement. As an alternative, the owner may elect to receive statutory damages of up to $250,000, as determined by the court.[28] The court may also order destruction or other disposition of the products and the equipment used to make the products. SCPA remedies include temporary restraining orders and injunctions against infringement.

SUMMARY

The law applicable to computers may be traditional rules of law, or it may be new rules that apply only to computers. The law of contracts has not been changed by the computer. In contrast, the law of evidence has changed to allow computer printouts to be admitted in evidence when the proper foundation is laid. That is, before printouts may be admitted in evidence, it is necessary to establish that they were properly made, by standard procedures, using a standard computer. The law of torts has remained unchanged with respect to fraud, property damage, theft, defamation, privacy, and nuisance. Statutes have expanded the area of criminal law to meet situations in which computers are involved. The unauthorized taking of information from a computer is made a crime under federal and state statutes. Criminal conduct of diverting deliveries of goods and the transfer of funds, the theft of software, and computer raiding are made crimes to some extent by the federal Computer Access Device and Computer Fraud and Abuse Act of 1984 and the Electronic Fund Transfers Act of 1978. Protection of computer programs and the design of computer chips and mask works is commonly obtained, subject to certain limitations, under the law of trade secrets, by restrictive licensing agreements, and by complying with federal statutes.

---

[26] Act of November 8, 1984, as amended, PL 98-620, 98 Stat 3347, 17 USC §§ 901 et seq.

[27] Brooktree Corp. v Advanced Micro Devices, Inc. (CA Fed) 977 F2d 1555 (1992).

[28] 17 USC § 911(c).

LAW IN PRACTICE

1. Maintain and use your computer system properly so that persons will not be harmed by computer error and so that its printouts will be admissible in court as evidence.

2. Avoid and protect yourself from computer crimes by screening employees and maintaining plant security.

3. Learn the limitations on copyright and licensing agreement protection of software by checking with your attorney as to the state of the law.

4. Recognize the importance of industry and government cooperation in solving computer protection problems.

QUESTIONS AND CASE PROBLEMS

1. What social forces are affected by allowing computer printouts to be introduced as evidence?

2. The Johnsville Warehouse negotiated with the Hercules Computer Company for the purchase of a computer. Johnsville purchased a particular computer from Hercules on the basis of the statement of its vice president that the computer was the best on the market for controlling warehouse operations. The computer failed to work properly. Can Johnsville avoid the contract on the basis of fraud?

3. Employers in East Berwick formed an association to exchange information on job applicants. In a computer, the association stored information received from members about the grounds for discharging employees. Maria had been employed as a bank teller. She was later fired because she was arrested for embezzlement of the bank funds. Maria was never able to obtain other work in the community because of the computer printout of the association showing her arrest. She sued the association for defamation. It raised the defense that the computer did not lie—she had been arrested for embezzlement. She replied that it was publicly known that shortly after she was arrested, she was released because it was established that the embezzlement had been committed by a cashier in the bank and that the cashier was arrested and convicted for the crime. Is the association protected by the fact that the computer printout was correct in what it stated?

4. Eastman needed public aid. The Department of Public Aid claimed that she had received more food stamps than she was entitled to. A hearing was held to determine whether this was true. On the basis of the computer printout showing distribution of food stamps, it was held that Eastman had received more than she should have. There was no other evidence on this point. Were these proceedings proper? *[Eastman v Department of Pub-*

lic Aid, 178 Ill App 3d 993, 128 Ill Dec 276, 534 NE2d 458]

5. In a common law state, Hinkin steals a computer chip on which is stored information having commercial value of a million dollars. He is prosecuted for grand larceny. He raises the defense that he only committed petty larceny because the chip only costs $10, and by statute a larceny under $100 is petty larceny. Is he correct?

6. The Clayton factory controls a series of manufacturing operations by computer. The large number of computers, concentrated in a small area, set up an electromagnetic field that interfered with the fine instruments used by the Scientific Testing Laboratories, housed in a neighboring building. Scientific sues Clayton, claiming that the operation of Clayton's computers constitutes a nuisance. Clayton replies that it cannot be responsible for any side effects, because it was not negligent. Clayton states that, therefore, there cannot be a nuisance. Is Clayton correct?

7. Taylor was employed by Hopkins Company. After he was fired, he sought revenge against his former employer. He turned off the air-conditioning in the computer room. It was midsummer, and the heat during the night ruined the memory bank of the computer. Hopkins asked the district attorney to prosecute Taylor. For what crimes could Taylor be prosecuted?

8. Lund was a graduate student at a university. In working on his doctoral dissertation, he made use of the university computer and was assisted by the personnel of the computer facility. The value of the information he thus obtained was about $30,000. Lund had not been authorized to use the computer, and he was prosecuted for common law grand larceny. Was he guilty? *[Lund v Virginia, 217 Va 688, 232 SE2d 745]*

9. Banion manufactures semiconductor chips. She wants to obtain complete protection from reverse engineering. She states that she will register under the federal statute that gives copyright protection to mask works. Is this what she should do?

10. Schlicht had a bank account. The bank's computer made a mistake and showed that he had a balance of $9,000 more than he really had in his account. He withdrew the $9,000. When the bank learned of the mistake, he was prosecuted for the crime of theft. Was he guilty? *[Colorado v Schlicht (Colo App) 709 P2d 94]*

11. Electric Supply Co. (ESCO) supplied Kitchens Construction, Inc. with materials that Kitchens used in constructing a building for the state of New Mexico. When ESCO was not paid, it brought suit for its unpaid bill. In support of its claim, it offered in evidence a computer printout of the invoices for goods for which payment had not been made. Two ESCO employees testified how the original invoices had been prepared and that the database from which the computer printout was made was a compilation of the original records. Were the computer printouts admissible in evidence? *[New Mexico for the use of Electric Supply Co., Inc. v Kitchens Construction, Inc. 106 NM 753, 750 P2d 114]*

12. The El Paso Oil Company controlled its delivery to tankers by means of computer-controlled pipelines. Carlson was employed by El Paso as the operator of the computer that controlled the deliveries. Carlson made a plan with the owner of a fleet of tank trucks by which the El Paso oil would be diverted from the proper tanker depot to a different depot, where the oil would be delivered into the tank trucks of Carlson's accomplice. The tank trucks would then disappear, and the oil would later be sold by Carlson and the accomplice and the money kept by them. When the security guards discovered this plan, Carlson was prosecuted for theft. He raised the defense that there was no statute punishing the diversion of deliveries by computer. Is this defense valid?

13. In a lawsuit by a third person against an automobile insurance company, the question arose whether the insurer had sent a particular notice to the insured. The insurer presented as evidence the computer record that the notice had been prepared on a certain date. The insured denied that the notice was ever received. Was the computer record sufficient to show that notice was sent and received? *[Cole v Lavine (La App) 595 So 2d 398]*

14. Aguimatang brought suit against the California State Lottery. The state introduced into evidence the printout from the lottery computer. Aguimatang claimed that the printout was not admissible because the printout was not made contemporaneously with the events to which they related, and (2) the printout was not the best evidence of the information shown because the slips given to the person feeding the computer constituted the best evidence. Should the computer printout be admitted in evidence? *[Aguimatang v California State Lottery, ___ Cal App 3d ___, 286 Cal Rptr 57]*

15. The Lindheim Software Company designed and sold software programs to its customers. In one of the states in which it sold them, the state tax collector claimed that the software programs were subject to the tangible property state tax on sales over $50. Lindheim claimed that the only tangible property that it sold were the pieces of paper and that, as these were worth less than $50, the pieces of paper were not subject to tax. Was Lindheim correct?

CHAPTER 22
BAILMENTS

LEARNING OBJECTIVES

After studying this chapter, you will be able to:
1. *Describe how a bailment is created.*
2. *List and distinguish the various classifications of bailments.*
3. *Contrast the renting of space with the creation of a bailment.*
4. *Explain the standard of care a bailee is required to exercise over bailed property.*
5. *State the burden of proof when a bailor sues a bailee for damages to bailed property.*
6. *Define a bailor's implied warranty concerning goods furnished by the bailor.*

Many instances arise in which the owner of personal property entrusts it to another—a person checks a coat at a restaurant, delivers a watch to a jeweler for repairs, or loans hedge clippers to a neighbor; or a company rents a car to a tourist for a weekend. The delivery of property to another under such circumstances is a bailment.

A. GENERAL PRINCIPLES

A bailment is based on an agreement regarding personal property.

1. Definition

A **bailment** is the relationship that arises when one person delivers possession of personal property to another under an agreement by which the latter is under a duty to return the identical property to the former or to deliver it or dispose of it as agreed. The person who turns over the possession of the property is the **bailor**. The person who accepts possession is the **bailee**.

2. Elements of Bailment

A bailment is created when the following elements are present.

(a) AGREEMENT. The bailment is based on an agreement. This agreement may be express or implied. Generally, it will contain all the elements of a contract. The bailment transaction in fact consists of (1) a contract to bail and (2) the actual bailing of the property. Ordinarily, there is no requirement that the contract of bailment be in writing.[1]

The subject of a bailment may be any personal property of which possession may be given. Real property cannot be bailed.

(b) DELIVERY AND ACCEPTANCE. The bailment arises when, pursuant to the agreement of the parties, the property is delivered to the bailee and accepted by the bailee as subject to the bailment agreement.[2]

Delivery may be **actual**, as when the bailor physically hands a book to the bailee, or it may be **constructive**, as when the bailor points out a package to the bailee, who then takes possession of it. In the absence of a prior agreement

Figure 22-1 Bailment of Personal Property

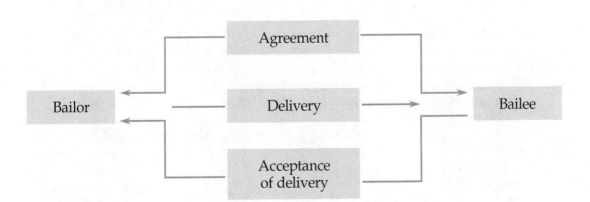

---

[1] Commercial bailments or leases are regulated by the Uniform Commercial Code, Article 2A, in the states listed in the footnote in Appendix 3, of this text.

[2] Merrit v Nationwide Warehouse Co., Ltd. (Tenn App) 605 SW2d 250 (1980).

to the contrary, a valid delivery and acceptance generally require that the bailee be aware that goods have been placed within the bailee's exclusive possession or control.

In the *Berglund* case the bailee was unaware that goods had been placed within its exclusive possession or control.

BERGLUND v ROOSEVELT UNIVERSITY
18 Ill App 3d 842, 310 NE2d 773 (1974)

Richard Berglund, the plaintiff, was a full-time student at Roosevelt University. He was also the editor and photographer of the student newspaper. The university was unaware that Richard kept his own photographic equipment in the rooms it had assigned to the newspaper. One night this equipment was stolen from the newspaper office. Richard sued the university, on the theory that it had breached its duty as a bailee. He showed that former editors had also left their equipment in the university rooms. The university denied that it was a bailee. The trial court awarded $1,789.15 to Richard on the theory of an implied bailment, and the university appealed.

McNAMARA, J. . . . The characteristics common to every bailment are the intent to create a bailment, delivery of possession of the bailed items, and the acceptance of the items by the bailee. . . . A bailment can be established by express contract or by implication. . . . In determining the existence of an implied-in-fact bailment, one must analyze the facts surrounding the transaction, such as the benefits to be received by the parties, their intentions, the kind of property involved, and the opportunity of each to exercise control over the property. . . .

In the present case, plaintiff attempted to show that an implied-in-fact bailment had arisen between the parties. It is clear, however, that the failure of the plaintiff to prove any knowledge on the part of the defendant of the storage of the items doomed this attempt.

Knowledge on the part of the bailee is essential to prove proper delivery and acceptance. Physical control over the property allegedly bailed and an intention to exercise that control are needed to show that one is in possession of the bailed item. . . . And before acceptance can be inferred on the part of the alleged bailee of the goods purportedly bailed, there must be evidence to show notice or knowledge on the part of the bailee that the goods are in fact in his possession. . . . Yet in the present case defendant's consistent denial of having any knowledge that plaintiff had stored his camera equipment on the premises is supported by plaintiff's own testimony. Although normal procedure required plaintiff to seek permission of certain agents of defendant to store his property on the premises, plaintiff never bothered to do so. . . . Nor does the fact that prior student paper photographers may have similarly stored their equipment in the darkroom, without more, prove knowledge on the part of defendant. The record also reveals that defendant's security officers never exercised any degree of intentional control over plaintiff's goods. We conclude that plaintiff's failure to prove knowledge on the part of defendant of the goods stored resulted in his inability to prove a valid delivery of the camera equipment and a true acceptance of the goods by defendant. . . . Our holding on this issue obviates the necessity of considering whether defendant was negligent in its capacity as bailee.

[Judgment reversed]

QUESTIONS

1. What did the plaintiff claim?
2. Was it essential for the plaintiff to prove that the defendant had knowledge of the storage of the items in order to prove proper delivery and acceptance in this case?
3. Did the court find that there was a bailment?

3. Nature of the Parties' Interests

The bailor and bailee have different legal interests in the bailed property.

(a) BAILOR'S INTEREST. The bailor is usually the owner, but ownership by the bailor is not required. It is sufficient that the bailor have physical possession.[3]

In the *Magee* case the defendant contended that it was not liable for a fur jacket it lost during summer storage because the customer did not prove that she owned the fur jacket in question.

MAGEE v WALBRO, INC.

171 Ill App 3d 774, 121 Ill Dec 668, 525 NE2d 975 (1988)

Crella Magee delivered a blue fox jacket for summer storage to Walbro, Inc. (dba Mysel's Furs). When it was not returned, she sued Walbro for the fur's replacement cost of $3,400. Magee testified that she bought the jacket from Evans' Furs. Evans' Furs, however, showed no record of having made the sale. Walbro contended that since Magee had not proven that she owned the jacket, Walbro could not be held liable. Moreover, it contended that its liability was limited to $100, the amount on the receipt it sent Magee six weeks after the jacket was received for storage.

O'CONNOR, J. . . . In the instant case, the trial court ruled that the evidence established a bailment between Magee and defendants Walbro and Mysel. . . . Walbro and Mysel produced no evidence, however, to rebut the presumption of [their] negligence. Instead, they attacked Magee's assertion of ownership, a fact irrelevant to bailment, and maintained that Mysel's never received the fur jacket.

The evidence shows that a fur jacket was delivered to Mysel's. . . .

We now address whether the liability of defendants Walbro and Mysel may be limited to $100.00, as stated on the receipt that Magee received in July, 1982. . . .

---

3 Williams v Boswell (Minn App) 444 NW2d 887 (1989).

In the instant case, Magee testified that she was not told of the limitation until after the fur was lost. . . . Magee should have known of the limitation after she received the receipt in July, but by that time her furs had been at Mysel's for six weeks.

Although the liability of Walbro and Mysel appears to be limited to $100, the limitation does not apply in the instant case because Magee had no knowledge of the limitation before agreeing to store her furs. . . . In the instant case, it would be unjust to permit Mysel and Walbro to assert a limitation that was not made clear at the time that the bailment contract was made because the coat was lost. We therefore hold that the $100 limitation of liability is inapplicable in this case.

For the foregoing reasons, judgment in favor of the defendants is reversed, and this case is remanded to the trial court to enter a judgment against defendants Walbro, Inc. and Mysel Furs and in favor of plaintiff Crella Magee in the amount of $3,400.00.

[Reversed and remanded]

QUESTIONS

1. Was it necessary for the bailor, Magee, to prove that she owned the fur in order to recover for its loss?
2. Did Walbro effectively limit its liability for the loss of the item to $100?
3. Did Walbro rebut the presumption of its negligence in this case?

(b) BAILEE'S INTEREST. The bailee has only possession of the property. Title to the property does not pass to the bailee, and the bailee cannot sell the property to a third person. If the bailee attempts to sell the property, such sale transfers only possession, and the owner may recover the property from the buyer.

There are some exceptions to the rule that a bailee cannot transfer title. A bailee who is an agent authorized to sell the property may transfer title. As another exception, the bailor may cause third persons to believe that the bailee is the owner of the bailed property. If the bailor does so, the bailor is estopped from denying that the bailee is the owner as against persons who have relied on the bailor's representations. As a further exception, if the bailee is a dealer in goods of the kind entrusted to the bailee by the bailor, a sale by the bailee to a buyer in the ordinary course of business will pass the bailor's title to the buyer.

4. Classification of Bailments

Bailments are classified as ordinary and extraordinary (or special). **Extraordinary bailments** are those in which the law imposes unusual duties and liabilities on the bailee, as in the case of bailments in which a motel or a common carrier is involved. **Ordinary bailments** include all other bailments.

Bailments may or may not provide for compensation to the bailee. On the basis of compensation bailments may be classified as (1) **contract bailments**, or **bailments for hire**, and (2) **gratuitous bailments**. The fact that no charge is made by the bailor does not necessarily make the transaction a gratuitous bailment. If the bailment is made to further a business interest of the bailor, as when something is loaned free to a customer, the bailment is not gratuitous.

Bailments may also be classified in terms of benefit. A bailment may be for the sole benefit of the bailor, as when one farmer gratuitously transports another farmer's produce to the city. A bailment may be for the sole benefit of the bailee, as when a person borrows a friend's automobile. A bailment may be for the benefit of both parties (mutual benefit bailment), as when someone rents a power tool. A mutual benefit bailment also arises when a prospective buyer of an automobile leaves the automobile that is to be traded in with the dealer so that the latter may test it and appraise it.

5. Constructive Bailments

When one person comes into possession of personal property of another without the owner's consent, the law treats the possessor as a bailee and calls the relationship a **constructive bailment**. It is thus held that the finder of lost property is a bailee of that property. When a city or state impounds an automobile or water craft, a constructive bailment arises as to such object and its contents. A seller who has not yet delivered the goods to the buyer is treated as bailee of the goods if title has passed to the buyer.

6. Renting of Space Distinguished

When a person rents space in a locker or building under an agreement that gives the renter the exclusive right to use that space, the placing of goods by the renter in that space does not create a bailment.[4] In such a case, putting property into the space does not constitute a delivery of goods into the possession of the owner of the space. An example of a nonbailment space rental is the use of a coin-activated package or luggage locker in an airport.

7. Bailment of Contents of Container

It is a question of the intention of the parties, as that appears to a reasonable person, whether a bailment of a container also constitutes a bailment of articles contained in it—for example, whether a bailment of a coat is a bailment of articles in the coat. When the contained articles are of a class that is reasonably or normally to be found in the container, they may be regarded as bailed in the absence of an express disclaimer. If the articles are not of such a nature and their presence in the container is unknown to the bailee, there is no bailment of such articles. Consequently, although the circumstances may be such that the parking of a car constitutes a bailment, there is no bailment of valuable drawings and sporting equipment that are on the back seat but not visible from the outside of the car. However, there is ordinarily a bailment of whatever is locked in the trunk.

B. RIGHTS AND DUTIES OF THE PARTIES

A bailment creates certain rights and imposes certain duties on each party. These may be increased or modified by statute, by custom, or by the express agreement of the parties.

8. Duties of the Bailee

The bailee has certain duties concerning performance, care, maintenance, and return of the bailed property. A bailee's lien gives the bailee the right to keep possession of the bailed property until charges are paid. Unauthorized use of the bailed property is forbidden.

(a) PERFORMANCE. If the bailment is based on a contract, the bailee must perform the bailee's part of the contract and is liable to the bailor for ordinary contract damages arising out of the failure to perform the contract.[5] Thus, if the bailment is for repair, the bailee is under the duty to make the repairs properly. The fact that the bailee used due care in attempting to perform the contract does not excuse

---

4 Magliocco v American Locker Co. 239 Cal Rptr 497 (1987).
5 Computer Systems v Western Reserve Life, 19 Mass App 430, 475 NE2d 745 (1985).

the bailee from liability for failing to perform the contract.

(b) CARE OF PROPERTY. The bailee is under a duty to care for the bailed property. If the property is damaged or destroyed, the bailee is liable for the loss (1) if the harm was caused in whole or in part by the bailee's failure to use reasonable care under the circumstances, or (2) if the harm was sustained during unauthorized use of the property by the bailee. Otherwise, the bailor bears the loss. Thus, if the bailee was exercising due care and was making an authorized use of the property, the bailor must bear the loss of or damage to the property caused by an act of a third person, whether willful or negligent; by an accident or occurrence for which no one was at fault; or by an act of God. In this connection, the phrase "act of God" means a natural phenomenon that is not reasonably foreseeable, such as a sudden flood or lightning.

(1) Standard of Care. The standard for ordinary bailments is reasonable care under the circumstances—that is, the degree of care that a reasonable person would exercise in the situation to prevent reasonably foreseeable harm. The significant factors in determining what constitutes reasonable care in a bailment are the time and place of making the bailment, the facilities for taking care of the bailed property, the nature of the bailed property, the bailee's knowledge of its nature, and the extent of the bailee's skills and experience in taking care of goods of that kind.

Some courts state the standard of care in terms of the benefit characteristic of the bailment. Thus, when the bailment is for the sole benefit of the bailee, the bailee is held liable for the slightest negligence. When the bailment is for the mutual benefit of the parties, the bailee is held liable for ordinary negligence. In contrast, if the bailment is for the sole benefit of the bailor, the bailee is only required to exercise slight care and will only be liable for gross negligence.[6]

(2) Contract Modification of Liability. A bailee's liability may be expanded by contract. A provision that the bailee assumes absolute liability for the property is binding.

An ordinary bailee may limit liability, except for willful misconduct, by agreement or contract.[7] However, in some states statutes prohibit certain kinds of paid bailees, such as automobile parking garages, from limiting their liability for negligence.

Also, statutes in some states declare that a party cannot bar liability for negligent violations of common law standards of care where a public interest is involved. In the *Gardner* case the court was faced with the problem of whether an automobile repair business could exempt itself from liability for ordinary negligence by a clause in its service order contract where the service it performed affected the public interest.

GARDNER v DOWNTOWN PORSCHE AUDI
180 Cal App 3d 713, 225 Cal Rptr 757 (1986)

In June, 1978, Bruce Gardner took his 1976 Porsche 911 automobile to be repaired at Downtown Porsche Audi (Downtown). Gardner signed a repair order bearing the disclaimer "not responsible for loss (of) cars . . . in case of . . . theft." While Gardner's car was parked in the repair garage, the car was stolen because of Downtown's negligence. Gardner sued Downtown for failing

---

[6] Strang v Hollowell (NC App) 387 SE2d 655 (1990); Benz v Benz (Fla App) 557 So 2d 124 (1990).
[7] State Farm Fire and Casualty Co. v B&F Marine Inc. (Fla App) 520 So 2d 649 (1988).

to redeliver his car. Downtown defended that the disclaimer barred liability for its negligence. From a judgment in favor of Gardner for $16,000, Downtown appealed.

JOHNSON, J. . . . Downtown concedes negligence but argues the disclaimer absolves it of liability for this failure to exercise due care. Assuming the truth of Downtown's contention Gardner signed a repair slip containing this exculpatory language, and even assuming he read and understood it, we find the attempted exemption from liability to be against public policy and thus ineffective to excuse Downtown's negligence.

In the absence of a disclaimer the duties and liabilities of a bailee for hire—such as Downtown—are clear. Unless it can redeliver the subject of the bailment—in this instance, the 1976 Porsche—the bailee must prove it exercised due care in its care and custody of this property. If it fails to establish the absence of negligence the bailee is liable to the bailor for any damages suffered due to the failure to redeliver the bailed property. . . .

Traditionally the law has looked carefully and with some skepticism at those who attempt to contract away their legal liabilities for the commission of torts. . . . This general policy of the common law found legislative expression early in California's history with the enactment of Civil Code section 1668. This 1872 statute reads:

CERTAIN CONTRACTS UNLAWFUL. All contracts which have for their object, directly or indirectly, to exempt any one from responsibility for his own fraud, or willful injury to the person or property of another, or violation of law, whether willful or negligent, *are against the policy of the law.*

Civ Code § 1668 (emphasis added).

This section made it clear a party could not contract away liability for his fraudulent or intentional acts or for his negligent violations of *statutory* law. Less clear was the status of negligent violations of *common law* standards of care. While acknowledging some conflict in the cases, Witkin concludes California now follows the modern view of the Restatement of Contracts—"a contract exempting from liability for *ordinary* negligence is valid where *no public interest* is involved . . . and no statute expressly prohibits it. . . ."

The converse is also true, however. Under Civil Code section 1668 an automobile repair garage cannot exempt itself from liability even for ordinary negligence if the service it provides implicates the public interest. In a leading case striking down exculpatory clauses in hospital admission forms, *Tunkl v Regents of University of California* (1963) 60 Cal 2d 92, the Supreme Court set forth six characteristics typical of contracts affecting the public interest.

(1) It concerns a business of a type generally thought suitable for public regulation. (2) The party seeking exculpation is engaged in performing a service of great importance to the public, which is often a matter of practical necessity for some members of the public. (3) The party holds himself out as willing to perform this service for any member of the public who seeks it, or at least any member coming within certain established standards. (4) As a result of the essential nature of the service, in the economic setting of the transaction, the party invoking exculpation possesses a decisive advantage of bargaining strength against any member of the public who seeks his services. (5) In exercising a superior bargaining power the party confronts the public with a standardized adhesion contract of exculpation, and makes

no provision whereby a purchaser may pay additional fees and obtain protection against negligence. (6) Finally, as a result of the transaction, the person or property of the purchaser is placed under the control of the seller, subject to the risk of carelessness by the seller or his agents. . . .

To begin with, automobile repair shops are in a "business of a type . . . thought suitable for public regulation" in the state of California. They are licensed by the state and their performance is regulated by the Bureau of Automotive Repair of the State Department of Consumer Affairs.

Secondly, these repair shops are most definitely engaged in "performing a service of great importance to the public . . ." and, moreover, one which is a "matter of practical *necessity*" for nearly *all* not just "*some* members of the public." . . .

The modern citizen lives—and all too frequently dies—by the automobile. Members of the general public need cars not merely for discretionary recreational purposes but to get to and from their places of employment, to reach the stores where they can purchase the necessities—as well as the frivolities—of life, and the like. An out of repair automobile is an unreliable means of transportation. Moreover, it is a dangerous one as well—to pedestrians and other drivers not just the owner. What is true of modern society in general is doubly true in Southern California, the capital of the motor vehicle. Indeed it is virtually impossible to exist in the Los Angeles area without a fully operational automobile. Thus, except for the few who can afford to buy a new car every time the ash trays fill up, people in this area find the automobile repair business a "service of great importance" and a "practical necessity."

Thirdly, Downtown held itself "out as willing to perform" this important service "for any member of the public" or at least for any member of the public who fell within the "established standard" of owning an automobile of the type it was equipped to repair, in this case a Porsche.

Fourthly, Downtown indisputably "possesses a decisive advantage of bargaining strength against" Gardner or almost "any member of the public who seeks [its] services." Like the hospital in *Tunkl* it is one of a relatively small number of entities dispensing a service which is a "practical necessity" to a large number of consumers.

Fifthly, it is apparent Downtown "confronts the public with a standardized adhesion contract of exculpation." The exculpatory language is incorporated in the printed form "repair order" all customers are expected to sign before Downtown will begin work on the car.

Finally, Gardner's Porsche was "placed under the control of" Downtown, "subject to the risk of carelessness by" Downtown and its employees. In order to make the repairs on Gardner's vehicle, Downtown took possession of the car and keys to the car. During this period, the security of the automobile was entirely in Downtown's hands. If this dealer were careless in storing the vehicle or the keys, the Porsche would become an easy target for theft and there would be little the owner could do about it.

Based on application of the *Tunkl* criteria, we therefore conclude automobile repair contracts "affect the public interest." It follows that clauses which exculpate repair firms for ordinary negligence in handling and securing vehicles under repair run afoul of Civil Code section 1668 and are "invalid as contrary to public policy."

Downtown concedes it was negligent. We hold its attempt to avoid legal responsibility for this negligence is unavailing. It follows Downtown is liable for non-delivery of the subject of the bailment, Gardner's Porsche.

[Judgment affirmed]

QUESTIONS

1. Was Gardner bound by the clear language of the repair order that he signed that said that Downtown was "not responsible for loss (of) cars . . . in case of . . . theft"?
2. Did Downtown admit it was negligent in taking care of the automobile during the bailment?
3. What characteristics are typical of contracts affecting the public interest?

By definition, a limitation of liability must be a term of the bailment contract before any question arises as to whether it is binding. Thus, a bailor is not bound by a limitation of liability that was not known at the time the bailment was made. For example, a limitation contained in a receipt mailed by a bailee after receiving a coat for storage is not effective to alter the terms of the bailment as originally made.

(3) Insurance. In the absence of a statute or contract provision, a bailee is not under any duty to insure for the benefit of the bailor the property entrusted to the bailee.

One of the most common bailments occurs when an automobile is rented. The car rental agencies alter the common law rule that bailees are not responsible for damages unattributable to their fault, by setting forth in their standard rental contracts that bailees (lessees) are responsible for any damages however caused. The rental agencies then offer bailees protection against damages, even those caused by the bailees' fault, through the purchase of collision damage waiver (CDW) insurance. In the fine print of the rental contracts, exclusions commonly exist voiding coverage if, for example, the bailee operates the vehicle while intoxicated. Some courts have refused to enforce these standardized form exclusions because they are unreasonable, in that the lessee would not reasonably expect the coverage would be subject to any exclusion.[8] Other courts have found exclusions related to alcohol use to be invalid as against public policy because the exclusions punish innocent victims of drunk drivers. The *Hertz* case deals with an explicit exclusion of liability coverage by the rental agency where the driver was intoxicated.

HERTZ CORP. v GARROTT

238 Ill App 3d 231, 179 Ill Dec 387, 606 NE2d 219 (1992)

Angelique Garrott rented an automobile from Hertz Rent-a-Car in Chicago on October 4, 1986. In small print on the reverse side of the rental contract, it provided that if the customer permitted the use of the vehicle in a prohibited manner, all liability protection and other insurance coverage would be voided. The provision went on to say that the customer "may" then be responsible for all losses and damages to the vehicle. One of the prohibited

---

8   Lauvetz v Alaska Sales and Service Co. (Alaska) 828 P2d 162 (1991).

uses was operating the vehicle while under the influence of alcohol. Angelique permitted her husband Rodney to operate the vehicle. At 3:00 A.M., while under the influence of alcohol, Rodney was involved in a collision with a taxi, in which the occupants Ferraro and Whitehead were injured. The trial court determined that Hertz's contractual obligation to provide liability coverage was voided by the intoxication of the driver. The Garrotts, Ferraro and Whitehead appealed.

MURRAY, J. . . . Now on appeal, defendants Ferraro and Whitehead argue that the trial court erred when it held that Hertz's contractual obligation to provide liability coverage was voided by the intoxication of the driver. . . . They contend that the ruling offends public policy concerns because it punishes the innocent victims of drunk drivers, and not the drunk drivers, by nullifying coverage which would compensate the victims, who are third-party beneficiaries to the insurance contract. . . .

Hertz, on the other hand, argues that the trial court correctly enforced the exclusionary clause within the rental contract, thereby nullifying liability coverage upon the showing of a prohibited use of the rental vehicle, *i.e.*, the intoxication of the driver. . . . Nowhere on the front of the form did it state what the ramifications would be for failing to comply with the various restrictions. Nor did it indicate on the front of the form that liability protection would be withdrawn if the vehicle was operated in any one of a number of prohibited ways. That information was only contained on the reverse side of the form, in "paragraphs 4 and 5," written in small print.

. . . There are no cases in this State which have dealt with the circumstance presented in this case. However, *Standard Mutual Insurance Co. v General Casualty Cos.* (1988), 11 Ill App 3d 758, 761, 121 Ill Dec 658, 525 NE2d 965, is an Illinois case wherein the insurer of the car rental company contended that its obligation to provide liability insurance became null and void when an authorized user of the rental vehicle violated the rental agreement by driving the vehicle outside the State (in Canada) without the written permission of the rental agency. The court found that "the conditions precedent to coverage in the rental agreement drastically reduce the amount of coverage provided to the renter under the Policy (the auto insurance policy issued by General Casualty to the rental agency). This not only contravenes public policy, it also directly contradicts [the renter's] reasonable expectations that when he paid [the rental agency] for liability coverage, he would be relieved from liability in the event of collision."

. . . There have been a number of cases in other jurisdictions where the courts have considered the issue and ruled that such exculpatory clauses are void as against public policy. These cases include *Bass. v Horizon Assurance Co.* (Del Supr 1989), 562 A2d 1194. . . .

As stated in *Bass*, a situation very close to the one at bar,

"the fixing of penalties for antisocial conduct is, in the first instance, a governmental responsibility through legislative response. The Delaware General Assembly has expressly determined the consequences which result from a conviction of driving under the influence. These sanctions include the criminal penalties of fine and/or imprisonment, 21 Del C § 4177(d) and license revocation through administrative action, 21 Del C § 4177A. We do not believe that the General Assembly, in addition to the imposition of these substantial penalties, also

intended, by implication, to work a forfeiture of insurance protection purchased in conformity with State law."

So, too, in this case, we believe that Hertz, a private entity, does not have the ability to separately impose sanctions upon private citizens for driving while intoxicated, in the name of the public policy, when such sanctions work a hardship upon the general public and, at the same time, benefit the rental agency and/or its insurer.

. . . We believe that invalidating the exculpatory provision as against public policy requires only that we strike the offending provision. The contract, which set the contractual obligation for liability protection, remains in force. . . .

[Judgment reversed]

QUESTIONS

1. This was a case of first impression (a case without precedent) for Illinois. Analyze the "critical thinking" process the court followed in making its decision.
2. Respond to the argument which could be made on behalf of Hertz, that if lessees know they will lose their liability coverage by driving while intoxicated, they will not expose themselves to this immense risk, and will therefore not drink and drive. Thus, the exclusion actually serves the public policy of preventing driving while intoxicated.
3. Explain the court's conclusion that Hertz's sanctions "work a hardship upon the general public and, at the same time, benefit the rental agency."
4. Would it be ethical for a car rental agency to continue to apply the exclusion to small claim cases where no attorneys are likely to be involved?

(c) MAINTENANCE OF PROPERTY. In a bailment for hire, such as when a business rents an office copier from a leasing firm, the bailee, in the absence of a contrary contract provision, must bear the expense of repairs that are ordinary and incidental to the use of the machine. If, however, the repairs required are of an unusual nature or if the bailment is for a short period of time, the bailor is required to make the repairs unless the need for the repairs arose from the fault of the bailee.

(d) UNAUTHORIZED USE. The bailee is liable for conversion, just as though the bailee stole the property, if the bailee uses the property without authority or uses it in any manner to which the bailor had not agreed. Ordinarily, the bailee will be required to pay compensatory damages, although punitive damages may be imposed when the improper use was deliberate and when the bailee was recklessly indifferent to the effect of the use on the property.

(e) RETURN OF PROPERTY. The bailee is under a duty to return the identical property that is the subject of the bailment or to deliver it as directed by the bailment agreement. An exception exists for **fungible goods**, which are those goods of a homogeneous nature of which any unit is the equivalent of any other like unit. Examples of fungible goods are grain, potatoes (within the same grade), and petroleum (within the same grade). In the case of fungible goods, if the bailee contracts to return an equal amount of the same kind and quality, the transaction is a bailment. If the bailee has the option of paying an amount of money or returning property other than that which was delivered by the bailor, there is generally no bailment, but rather a sale. Thus, when a farmer delivers wheat to a grain elevator that gives the farmer a receipt that promises to return either a similar amount of wheat or a certain sum of money on presentment of the receipt, the relationship is generally not a bailment.

The redelivery to the bailor or delivery to a third person must be made in accordance with the terms of the bailment contract as to time, place, and manner. When the agreement between the parties does not control these matters, the customs of the community govern.

(f) BAILEE'S LIEN. By common law or statute, a bailee is given a **lien** or the right to retain possession of the bailed property until the bailee has been paid by the bailor for any charges due for storage or repairs.[9] The lien is lost if the property is voluntarily returned to the bailor. If the bailor is guilty of any misconduct in regaining possession of the property, there is no loss of lien, and the bailee may retain possession if possession can be reacquired.

A bailee who is authorized by statute to sell the bailed property to enforce a charge or claim against the bailor must give such notice as is required by the statute. A bailee who sells without giving the required notice is liable for conversion of the property.

In some states, a bailee's lien may be extinguished where the bailee intentionally claims an amount greater than that to which the bailee is entitled. Thus, a car stereo seller's lien was extinguished when he knowingly demanded in his lien statement an additional charge of $50 per day for storage of the bailor's truck.[10] This charge was clearly excessive and an intentional demand for an amount greater than that due the bailee.

9. Burden of Proof

When the bailor sues the bailee for damages to the bailed property, the bailor has the burden of proving that the bailee was at fault and that such fault was the proximate cause of the loss.[11] A prima facie right of the bailor to recover is established, however, by proof that the property was delivered by the bailor to the bailee and subsequently could not be returned or was returned in a damaged condition. When this is done, the bailee has the burden of proving that the loss or damage was not caused by the bailee's failure to exercise the care required by law or by an unauthorized use of the property.

10. Rights of the Bailor

A commercial bailment is a mutual benefit bailment. Under such a bailment the bailor has the right to compensation, commonly called rent, for the bailee's use of the property. If the bailor is obligated to render a service to the bailee, such as maintenance of the rented property, the bailor's failure to do so will ordinarily bar the bailor from recovering compensation from the bailee.[12]

(a) RIGHTS AGAINST THE BAILEE. The bailor may sue the bailee for breach of contract if the goods are not redelivered to the bailor or delivered to a third person, as specified by the bailment agreement. The bailor may also maintain an action against a bailee for negligence, willful destruction, and unlawful retention or conversion of the goods.

(b) RIGHTS AGAINST THIRD PERSONS. The bailor may sue third persons who damage or take the bailed property from the bailee's possession, even though the bailment is for a fixed period that has not yet expired. In such a case the bailor is said to recover damages for injury to the bailor's **reversionary interest**— that is, the right that the bailor has to regain the

---

[9] Boyd v Panama City Boatyard Inc. (Fla App) 522 So 2d 1058 (1988).

[10] First Bank Southdale v Kinney (Minn App) 392 NW2d 740 (1986).

[11] Puissegur v Delchamps (La App) 595 So 2d 691 (1992).

[12] See the footnote in Appendix 3, as to what states have adopted UCC, Article 2A, which applies to leases of personal property.

property on the expiration of the period of the bailment.

11.   Duties of the Bailor

The bailor has certain duties concerning the bailed property. Sometimes the duty concerning goods furnished by the bailor is described as an implied warranty.

(a) CONDITION OF THE PROPERTY. In a mutual benefit bailment, such as a bailment for hire, the bailor is under a duty to furnish goods reasonably fit for the purpose contemplated by the parties. If the bailee is injured or the bailee's property is damaged because of the defective condition of the bailed property, the bailor may be held liable. If the bailment is for the sole benefit of the bailee, the bailor is under a duty to inform the bailee of known defects.[13] If the bailee is harmed by a defect that was known by the bailor and not communicated to the bailee, the bailor is liable for damages.[14] If the bailor receives a benefit from the bailment, the bailor must not only inform the bailee of known defects, but must also make a reasonable investigation to discover defects. The bailor is liable for the harm resulting from the defects that would have been disclosed if the bailor had made such an examination, in addition to the harm stemming from the defects that were known to the bailor. If the defect would not have been revealed by a reasonable examination, the bailor, regardless of classification of the bailment, is not liable for the harm that results.

In any case, a bailee who is aware of a defective condition of the bailed property but makes use of the property and sustains injury because of its condition is barred from collecting damages from the bailor. This bar may be based on either contributory negligence or assumption of risk.

(b) BAILOR'S IMPLIED WARRANTY. In many cases, the duty of the bailor is described as an implied warranty that the goods will be reasonably fit for their intended use. Apart from an implied warranty, the bailor may make an express warranty as to the condition of the property.

With the increase in car and equipment leasing, a new trend in the cases is beginning to appear. This trend extends to the bailee and third persons the benefit of an implied warranty by the bailor that the article is fit for its intended use and will remain so. This is distinguished from the warranty that the article was merely reasonably fit, or that it was fit at the beginning of the bailment, or that the property was free from defects known to the bailor or that a reasonable investigation would disclose. The significance of an analysis on the basis of warranty lies in the fact that warranty liability may exist even though the bailor was not negligent.[15]

12.   Liability to Third Persons

When injuries resulting from the use of bailed property are sustained by third persons, liability may, under certain circumstances, be imposed on the bailee or the bailor.

(a) LIABILITY OF BAILEE. When the bailee injures a third person with the bailed property—for example, when the bailee runs into a third person while driving a rented automobile—the bailee is liable to the third person to the same extent as though the bailee were the owner of the property. When the bailee repairs bailed property, the bailee is liable to a third person who is injured as a result of the negligent way in which the repairs were made.

(b) LIABILITY OF BAILOR. The bailor is ordinarily not liable to a third person injured

---

[13] McMaster v Swicker, 194 Ill App 3d 923, 141 Ill Dec 467, 551 NE2d 654 (1990).
[14] Acampora v Acampora, 599 NYS2d 615 (1993).
[15] Kemp v Miller (Wis) 453 NW2d 872 (1990).

by the bailee while using the bailed property. In states that follow the common law, a person lending an automobile to another is not liable to a third person injured by the bailee when the lender did not know or have reason to know that the bailee was not a fit driver.

The bailor is liable, however, to the injured third person: (1) if the bailor has entrusted a dangerous instrumentality to one known to the bailor to be ignorant of its dangerous character; (2) if the bailor has entrusted an instrumentality, such as an automobile, to one known to the bailor to be so incompetent or reckless that injury of third persons is a foreseeable consequence; (3) if the bailor has entrusted property with a defect that causes harm to the third person when the circumstances are such that the bailor would be liable to the bailee if the bailee were injured by the defect; or (4) if the bailee is using the bailed article, such as driving an automobile, as the bailor's employee in the course of employment.

(c) TEST DRIVES. When a prospective purchaser takes an automobile for a test drive unaccompanied by the dealer, the law of bailments applies and the bailee must exercise due care. In such case, the customer would not be liable for harm not caused by his or her fault. However, a prospective purchaser (bailee) who promises to return the car in good condition after a test drive is responsible for damage to the car during the test drive.[16] Such a bailee assumes the liability of an insurer for the condition of the car, and it is no defense that the bailee exercised due care. Third persons injured by the negligence of a prospective purchaser during a test drive unaccompanied by the dealer ordinarily have no recourse against the dealer.

In the *Blackburn* case, the plaintiff claimed that the dealer should be held responsible for the negligence of a prospective purchaser during a test drive.

(d) FAMILY PURPOSE DOCTRINE. Under what is called the **family purpose doctrine**,

BLACKBURN v EVERGREEN CHRYSLER PLYMOUTH

53 Wash App 146, 765 P2d 922 (1989)

Donald Lougee was considering the purchase of a used Chrysler "Lazer" from Evergreen Chrysler Plymouth. After a brief test drive Donald was undecided about buying the car. The salesman suggested that he take it home overnight for an extended test drive. Later that night Donald asked his best friend Bret Blackburn, a mechanic, to accompany him on a test drive. During that drive, Lougee struck a power pole. Blackburn was seriously injured. Blackburn sued Lougee and Evergreen for damages. Evergreen denied liability for the damage caused during the test drive. The court directed a verdict in favor of Evergreen, and Blackburn appealed.

REED, C. J. . . . The sole issue is whether the owner of a car can be held vicariously liable for its negligent operation by a prospective purchaser during a test drive. The Washington Supreme Court twice has considered this issue, in *Hamp v Universal Auto Co.* . . . and *Robbins v Greene* . . . The rule set forth in those cases, and followed

16 Universal Ins. Co. v Vallejo, 179 Mich App 637, 446 NW2d 510 (1989).

in the overwhelming majority of jurisdictions, is that the owner of a car is not liable for a prospective purchaser's negligence, because the purchaser usually is regarded as a bailee, and not as an agent of the owner. The exception to this rule applies only when the prospective purchaser is accompanied by the owner or his agent, *who retains the right to direct the operation of the car*; the question is not decided by the owner's mere presence in the car, but is a function of the degree of control exercised, and is a question for the jury. . . .

It was undisputed that no Evergreen representative was present at the time of the accident. When the owner does not accompany the prospective purchaser on the test drive, he loses any right he had to control physical actions of the prospective purchaser. He has wholly surrendered the operation and control of the car to the test driver. . . . We find no meaningful factual distinctions between this case and *Hamp*.

We note that the majority of those courts that have considered this issue have concluded that an agency relationship is not present in situations such as that presented by this case. . . .

In conclusion, we hold that the evidence presented in this case could support only the conclusion that Lougee was a bailee as a matter of law. As such, Evergreen has no liability for Lougee's actions, and Evergreen was entitled to [a] directed verdict.

[Judgment affirmed]

QUESTIONS

1. State the issue before the court.
2. What was the legal relationship between Lougee, the driver, and Evergreen, the dealer?
3. On what basis did the court decide the case?

many courts hold that when the bailor supplies a car for the use of members of his or her family, the bailor is liable for harm caused by a family member while negligently driving the car. Other jurisdictions reject this doctrine and refuse to impose liability on the bailor of the automobile unless there is an agency relationship between the bailor and the driver.

SUMMARY

A bailment is the relationship that exists when tangible personal property is delivered by the bailor into the possession of the bailee under an agreement, express or implied, that the identical property will be returned or delivered in accordance with the agreement. No title is transferred by a bailment. The bailee has the right of possession. When a person comes into the possession of the personal property of another without the owner's consent, the law classifies the relationship as a constructive bailment.

Bailments may be classified in terms of benefit—that is, for the (1) sole benefit of the bailor, (2) sole benefit of the bailee, or (3) benefit of both parties (mutual benefit bailment). Some courts state the standard of care required of a bailee in terms of the class of bailment. Thus, if the bailment is for the sole benefit of the bailor, the bailee is required to exercise only slight care and is liable for gross negligence only. When the bailment is for the sole benefit of the bailee, the bailee is liable for the slightest negligence. When the bailment is for the mutual benefit of the parties, as in a commercial bailment, the bailee is liable for ordinary negligence. In other states, the courts do not make the above distinctions based on the class of bailment but apply a "reasonable care under the circumstances" standard. An ordinary bailee may limit liability, except for willful misconduct or where prohibited by law.

A bailee (1) must perform the bailee's part of the contract; (2) unless otherwise agreed, must bear the repair expenses incidental to the use of property in a bailment for hire situation; and (3) must return the identical property. The bailee has a lien on the bailed property until paid for storage or repair charges.

In a mutual benefit bailment, the bailor is under a duty to furnish goods reasonably fit for the purposes contemplated by the parties. The bailor may be held liable for damages or injury caused by the defective condition of the bailed property. If a bailee injures a third person while driving a rented motor vehicle, the bailee is liable to the third person as though the bailee were the owner of the vehicle.

LAW IN PRACTICE

1. Recognize that a bailee is not an insurer of goods and cannot be held liable for the loss of the bailed property unless the bailee is at fault.
2. If your company is regularly involved in the bailment of goods as a bailee, audit the company's security and handling procedures to make sure that its practices are reasonable under the circumstances.

3. Consider adding a limitation of liability clause in your bailment contracts to limit your businesses' liability for negligence.
4. Recognize that limitation of liability language found on a claim check is ineffective unless called to the attention of the bailor by a sign or other means at the time the bailment is made.
5. Know that a bailee has a lien on the bailed property until the bailee is paid for the storage or repairs.

QUESTIONS AND CASE PROBLEMS

1. What social forces are affected by the recognition of a bailment relationship?
2. Martin Acampora purchased a shotgun at a garage sale in the 1960s and never used the weapon and did not know of any defects in the weapon. His 31-year-old son Marty borrowed the shotgun to go duck hunting. As Marty attempted to engage the safety mechanism, the shotgun fired. The force of the shotgun's firing caused it to fall to the ground and to discharge another shot, which struck Marty in the hand. Classify the bailment in this case. What duty of care was owed by the bailor in this case? Is Martin liable to his son for the injury?
3. What is a bailee's lien?
4. Compare a gift with a bailment.
5. Schroeder parked his car in a parking lot operated by Allright, Inc. The parking stub given him had printed in large, heavy type that the lot closed at 6:00 P.M. Under this information, printed in smaller, lighter type, was a provision limiting the liability of Allright for theft or loss. A large sign at the lot stated that after 6:00 P.M. patrons could obtain their car keys at another location. Schroeder's car was stolen from the lot some time after the 6:00 P.M. closing, and he sued Allright for damages. Allright defended on the basis of the limitation of liability provision contained in the parking stub and the notice given Schroeder that the lot closed at 6:00 P.M. Decide. *[Allright, Inc. v Schroeder (Tex Civ App) 551 SW2d 745]*
6. Compare a bailment with a constructive bailment.
7. John Hayes and Lynn Magosian, auditors for a public accounting firm, went to lunch at the Bay View Restaurant in San Francisco. John left his raincoat with a coatroom attendant, while Lynn took her new raincoat with her to the dining room, where she hung it on a coat hook near her booth. When leaving the restaurant, Lynn discovered that someone had taken her raincoat. When John sought to claim his raincoat at the coatroom, it

could not be found. The attendant advised that it might have been taken while he was on his break. John and Lynn sue the restaurant, claiming that the restaurant was a bailee of the raincoats and had a duty to return them. Are both John and Lynn correct?

8. Before Todd returned to college in late August, he left his Boston Whaler motorboat at Terry's High Tide Marina for land storage during the fall and winter months. On a number of occasions when all of his rental boats were in use, Terry rented the Whaler to customer. Todd discovered this and he sued Terry for conversion. Terry stated that he did no harm to anybody in renting the boat. Moreover, he contended that he had the legal status of bailee, had proper possession of the boat, and that accordingly, he could not have committed conversion. Were Terry's actions ethical? Is Terry liable for conversion?

9. Rhodes parked his car in the self-service, park-and-lock lot of Pioneer Parking Lot, Inc. The ticket that he received from the ticket meter stated the following, "NOTICE. THIS CONTRACT LIMITS OUR LIABILITY—READ IT. WE RENT SPACE ONLY. NO BAILMENT IS CREATED. . . ." Rhodes parked the car himself and kept the keys. There was no attendant at the lot. The car was stolen from the lot. Rhodes sued the parking lot on the theory that it had breached its duty as a bailee. Was there a bailment? *[Rhodes v Pioneer Parking Lot, Inc. (Tenn) 501 SW2d 569]*

10. Lewis put a paper bag containing $3,000 in cash in a railroad station coin-operated locker. After the period of the coin rental expired, a locker company employee opened the locker, removed the money, and because of the amount, surrendered it to police authorities, as was required by the local law. When Lewis demanded the return of the money from Aderholdt, the police property clerk, the latter required Lewis to prove his ownership of the funds because there were circumstances leading to the belief that Lewis had stolen the money. Lewis sued the police property clerk and the locker company. Was the locker company liable for breach of duty as a bailee? *[Lewis v Aderholdt (Dist Col App) 203 A2d 919]*

11. Newman underwent physical therapy at PTAR Inc. in Rome, Georgia for injuries sustained in an auto accident. At a therapy session on February 6, it was necessary for Newman to take off two necklaces. Newman placed one of the necklaces on a peg on the wall in the therapy room, and the therapist placed the other necklace on the peg. After the session, Newman forgot to retrieve her jew-

elry from the wall pegs. When she called the next day for the forgotten jewelry, it could not be found. She sued PTAR Inc. for the value of the jewelry on a bailment theory. PTAR Inc. raised the defense that there was no bailment, since Newman retained the right to remove the jewelry from the wall pegs. Decide. *[Newman v Physical Therapy Associates of Rome, Inc. 89 Ga App 211, 375 SE2d 253]*

12. Contract Packers rented a truck from Hertz Truck Leasing. The brakes of the truck did not function properly. This resulted in the injuring of Packers' employee, Cintrone, while he was riding in the truck as it was driven by his helper. Cintrone sued Hertz for breach of the implied warranty that the truck was fit for normal use on public highways. Hertz defended that implied warranties apply only to sales and not to bailments for hire. Decide. *[Cintrone v Hertz Truck Leasing & Rental Service, 45 NJ 434, 212 A2d 769]*

13. Herbert Pellegrini and Hardie Maloney traveled together to the Georgia Numismatic Association coin show in Atlanta. After the show, Pellegrini suggested that Maloney get the car, while Pellegrini checked out of the Waverly Hotel. Maloney agreed to do so, after being assured by Pellegrini that he would watch Maloney's briefcase containing $31,000 in coins. Pellegrini watched as Maloney set the briefcase down beside Pellegrini's three bags. When Maloney returned with the car, Pellegrini was carrying all three pieces of his luggage as he walked up to the vehicle, but he had left Maloney's briefcase in front of the hotel. When they returned for the briefcase, it was gone. Maloney sued Pellegrini, who defended that he was not liable for the criminal acts of some unknown person. Decide. *[Simon v Maloney (La App) 579 So 2d 925]*

14. June Southard was employed in the Sporting Goods Department of K-Mart. While at work, she was struck by a mounted fish that fell from the wall. The fish was owned by taxidermist Marty Hansen. The fish had been delivered to K-Mart as a sample of Hansen's work in case the public wanted to contact him directly. Southard sued Hansen for her injuries, on the basis that Hansen was vicariously liable for the negligence of his agent, K-Mart, in improperly hanging the fish. Hansen contended that his legal relationship with K-Mart was that of bailor and bailee respectively, and that as the bailor he was not liable to Southard. Decide. *[Southard v Hansen (SD) 376 NW2d 56]*

15. Baena Brothers agreed to reupholster and reduce the size of the arms of Welge's sofa and chair.

The work was not done according to the contract, and the furniture when finished had no value to Welge and was not accepted by him. Baena sued him for the contract price. Welge counterclaimed for the value of the furniture. Decide. *[Baena Brothers v Welge, 3 Conn Cir 67, 207 A2d 749]*

CHAPTER 23

SPECIAL BAILMENTS AND DOCUMENTS OF TITLE

LEARNING OBJECTIVES

After studying this chapter, you will be able to:
1. *Differentiate between negotiable and nonnegotiable warehouse receipts.*
2. *List the three types of carriers of goods.*
3. *State the common carrier's liability for loss or damage to goods.*
4. *Explain the effect of a sale on consignment.*
5. *Describe a hotelkeeper's liability for loss of a guest's property.*

All bailments are not created equal. Because of the circumstances under which possession of that property is transferred, the law imposes special duties in some cases. The storage of goods in a warehouse as well as the transportation of goods by a common carrier are **special bailments**.

A. WAREHOUSERS

The storage of goods with a warehouser is a special bailment.

1. Definitions

A **warehouser** is a person engaged in the business of storing the goods of others for compensation. **Public warehousers** hold themselves out to serve the public generally, without discrimination.

A building is not essential to warehousing. Thus, an enterprise that stores boats outdoors on land is engaged in warehousing, since it is engaged in the business of storing goods for hire.

2. Rights and Duties of Warehousers

The rights and duties of a warehouser are for the most part the same as those of a bailee under a mutual benefit bailment.[1] A warehouser is not an insurer of goods. A warehouser is liable for loss or damage to goods stored in its warehouse where the warehouser was negligent.

(a) STATUTORY REGULATION. The rights and duties of warehousers are regulated by the Uniform Commercial Code, Article 7. In addition, most states have passed warehouse acts defining the rights and duties of warehousers and imposing regulations. Regulations govern charges and liens, bonds for the protection of patrons, maintenance of storage facilities in a suitable and safe condition, inspections, and general methods of transacting business.

(b) LIEN OF WAREHOUSER. The public warehouser has a lien against the goods for reasonable storage charges.[2] It is a **specific lien** in that it attaches only to the property on which the charges arose and cannot be asserted against any other property of the same owner in the possession of the warehouser. However, the warehouser may make a lien carry over to other goods by noting on the receipt for one lot of goods that a lien is also claimed thereon for charges as to the other goods. The warehouser's lien for storage charges may be enforced by sale after due notice has been given to all persons who claim any interest in the property stored.

In the *Tate* case the warehouser contended that the sale of the stored property to pay for storage and other charges was proper under Article 7.

TATE v ACTION MOVING & STORAGE, INC.
95 NC App 541, 383 SE2d 229 (1989)

> On March 24, 1984, Joseph Tate requested Action-Mayflower Moving & Storage Co. (Action) to ship his household belongings from Charlotte, North Carolina to Monrovia, Liberia. On March 26, 1984, Action prepared a detailed

---

[1] UCC § 7-204.

[2] UCC § 7-209 (1). The warehouser's lien provision of the UCC is constitutional as a continuation of the common law lien.

inventory of Tate's belongings, loaded them on its truck, and received the belongings at its warehouse. It was paid $1,000 down, with the balance to be paid prior to shipping. On September 26, 1984, Tate sent a check for $3,800 and requested that his goods be shipped to Monrovia. A dispute arose over the total cost to be paid. On October 24, 1984, Tate advised Action to deduct $2,708.20 from the $4,800 already paid to cover Action's charges, and to allow Tate to have a different carrier pick up the goods. Action did not accept this offer. Thereafter, Action sought payment for its charges. Fifteen months later, after due notice to Tate and after publishing a notice of public sale in the newspaper, Action sold Tate's goods at a public sale. Tate brought suit for conversion. Action defended that it was entitled to sell the goods to satisfy what was owed for storage and other charges.

BECTON, J. . . . It is well settled that "[a] warehouseman has a lien against the bailor on the goods covered by a warehouse receipt." [UCC §] 7-209(1). . . .

A warehouse receipt is defined by the U.C.C. as simply "a receipt issued by a person engaged in the business of storing goods for hire." [UCC §] 1-201(45). Further, "[a] warehouse receipt need not be in any particular form." [UCC §] 7-201. Action's admission in its answer that it agreed to store plaintiff's goods for up to six months supports the contention that the "Household Goods Descriptive Inventory" which was given to plaintiff when his goods were loaded was intended by Action to serve as a warehouse receipt. We also believe it was sufficient to constitute a warehouse receipt for purposes of holding Action responsible under Article Seven for its actions as a warehouseman. This document issued by Action listed each item picked up, its condition, the owner's name, the origin loading address, and was signed and dated by Action's authorized agent and driver. . . .

In enforcing any lien against plaintiff, defendant had the duty to comply with [UCC §] 7-210, "Enforcement of warehouseman's lien." [UCC §] 7-210(3) provides the following:

Before any sale pursuant to this section any person claiming a right in the goods may pay the amount necessary to satisfy the lien and the reasonable expenses incurred under this section. In that event the goods must not be sold, but must be retained by the warehouseman subject to the terms of the receipt and this article.

The record shows, as quoted above, that on 24 October 1984 plaintiff wrote a letter to defendant instructing defendant to deduct from the $4800.00 which defendant was holding, $2708.20 to cover defendant's charges to date, and that plaintiff would arrange to have a different carrier pick up his goods from defendant. Defendant admitted receiving this letter. In its letter of 29 October 1984, defendant stated that the charges incurred thus far for storage and origin charges amounted to $2010.70 ($709.80 storage plus $1300.90 origin charges). Therefore, plaintiff's offer of $2708.20 was far more than adequate to cover the amount owed to defendant.

Defendant's president, Jack Taylor, was questioned in his deposition about plaintiff's letter of 24 October 1984:

Q. But you remember getting this letter? And I'll represent to you that I've been furnished with a copy from your attorney, so it was in your file.

A. I don't remember when I got it. I remember reading it, but, yes, I remember reading it. I don't remember when I got it.

Q. And it contains the language that I just read to you?

A. Yes.

Q. And you still refused to do that at that time?

A. We didn't ship his goods.

Q. You didn't deduct the amount that he said you could and release his goods so he could make other arrangements for shipment, did you?

A. Huh-uh (no), I did not. We returned the entire amount of money to him.

Q. Months later?

A. (Witness nods head affirmatively.)

Defendant's admission by Jack Taylor that he refused to accept payment by plaintiff, but instead continued to hold the goods, mounting up storage fees, was a clear violation of [UCC §] 7-210(3). Plaintiff effectively satisfied the lien on his goods by giving defendant $4800.00 and instructing him to take out of that amount even more than defendant needed to satisfy the debt. After this payment, defendant then had no right to sell the goods.

[UCC §] 7-210(9) states that "the warehouseman is liable for damages caused by failure to comply with the requirements for sale under this section and in case of willful violation is liable for conversion." We believe defendant's failure to comply with the requirements of [UCC §] 7-210(3) as stated above, constituted a willful violation of the requirements for sale and that the defendant was properly held liable for conversion of plaintiff's goods. . . .

[Judgment affirmed]

QUESTIONS

1. Did Action issue a warehouse receipt to Tate?
2. What is the significance of the warehouser's issuing a warehouse receipt?
3. In this case did Action have the right to sell the goods to cover its storage and other charges?

3. Warehouse Receipts

A **warehouse receipt** is a written acknowledgment by a warehouser (bailee) that certain property has been received for storage from a named person called a **depositor** (bailor). The warehouse receipt is a memorandum of the contract between the **issuer**, the warehouser that prepares the receipt, and the depositor. It sets forth the terms of the contract for storage. No particular form is required, but usually the receipt will provide (a) the location of the warehouse where the goods are stored, (b) the date of issuance of the receipt, (c) the number of the receipt, (d) information on negotiability or nonnegotiability of the receipt, (e) the rate of storage and handling charges, (f) a description of the goods or the packages containing them, and (g) a statement of any liabilities incurred for which the warehouser claims a lien or security interest.[3]

---

[3] UCC § 7-202(2). The Act of October 28,1992, PLA 102-553, 106 Stat 4140, 7 USC § 259, authorizes the Secretary of Agriculture to adopt regulations authorizing warehouses to use electronic instead of paper receipts for stored cotton.

The warehouse receipt is a **document of title**—that is, a document that in the regular course of business or financing is treated as evidencing that a person is entitled to receive, hold, and dispose of the document and the goods it covers.[4] The person holding this receipt or the person specified in the receipt is entitled to the goods represented by the receipt. A warehouse receipt as a document of title can be bought or sold and can be used as security for a loan.

4. Rights of Holders of Warehouse Receipts

The rights of the holders of warehouse receipts differ, depending on whether the receipts are nonnegotiable or negotiable.

(a) NONNEGOTIABLE WAREHOUSE RECEIPTS. A warehouse receipt in which it is stated that the goods received will be delivered to a specified person is a **nonnegotiable warehouse receipt**. A transferee of a nonnegotiable receipt acquires only the title and rights that the transferor had actual authority to transfer. Therefore, the transferee's rights may be defeated by a good faith purchaser of the goods from the transferor of the receipt.

(b) NEGOTIABLE WAREHOUSE RECEIPTS. A warehouse receipt stating that the goods will be delivered "to the bearer" or "to the order of" any named person is a **negotiable warehouse receipt**.

(1) Negotiation. If the receipt provides for the delivery of the goods "to the bearer," the receipt may be negotiated by transfer of the document. If the receipt provides for delivery of the goods "to the order of" a named individual, the document must be indorsed[5] and delivered by that person in order for the document to be negotiated.

(2) Due Negotiation. If a receipt is duly negotiated, the person to whom it is negotiated may acquire rights superior to those of the transferor. A warehouse receipt is "duly negotiated" when the holder purchases the document in good faith, without notice of any defense to it, for value, in an ordinary transaction in which nothing appears improper or irregular.[6] The holder of a duly negotiated document acquires title to the document and title to the goods.[7] The holder also acquires the direct obligation of the issuer to hold or deliver the goods according to the terms of the warehouse receipt. The rights of a holder of a duly negotiated document cannot be defeated by the surrender of the goods by the warehouser to the depositor.

It is the duty of the warehouser to deliver the goods only to the holder of the negotiable receipt and to cancel such receipt on surrendering the goods.[8]

The rights of a purchaser of a warehouse receipt by due negotiation are not cut off by the fact that (a) an original owner was deprived of the receipt in "bearer" form by misrepresentation, fraud, mistake, loss, theft, or conversion; or (b) a bona fide purchaser bought the goods from the warehouser.

A purchaser of a warehouse receipt who takes by due negotiation does not cut off all prior rights. If the person who deposited the goods with the warehouser did not own the goods or did not have power to transfer title to them, the purchaser of the receipt is subject to the title of the true owner. Accordingly, when goods are stolen and delivered to a warehouse, and a warehouse receipt is issued for them, the owner of the goods prevails over the due-negotiation purchaser of the warehouse receipt.

---

4 UCC § 1-201(15).

5 The spelling *endorse* is commonly used in business. The spelling *indorse* is used in the UCC.

6 UCC § 7-501(4).

7 UCC § 7-502(1).

8 UCC § 7-403(3).

Figure 23-1 Negotiable Warehouse Receipt

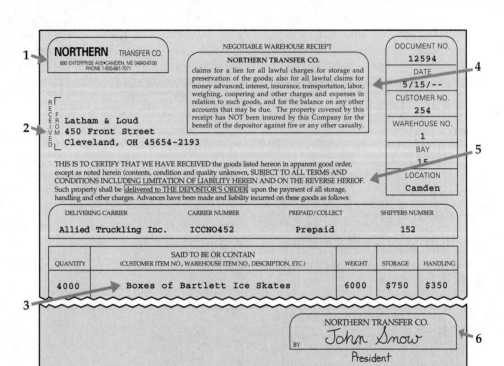

Front of receipt

Reverse side

(c) WARRANTIES. The transferor of a negotiable or nonnegotiable warehouse receipt makes certain implied warranties for the protection of the transferee. These warranties are that (1) the receipt is genuine, (2) its transfer is rightful and effective, and (3) the transferor has no knowledge of any facts that impair the validity or worth of the receipt.[9]

5. Field Warehousing

Ordinarily, stored goods are placed in a warehouse belonging to the warehouser. In other instances, the owner of goods, such as a manufacturer, keeps the goods in the owner's own storage room or building. The warehouser may then take exclusive control over the room or the area in which the goods are stored and issue a receipt for the goods, just as though they were in the warehouse. Such a transaction

---

[9] UCC § 7-507. These warranties are in addition to any that may arise between the parties by virtue of the fact that the transferor is selling the goods represented by the receipt to the transferee. See Chapter 27 with respect to seller's warranties.

has the same legal effect with respect to other persons and purchasers of the warehouse receipts as though the property were in fact in the warehouse of the warehouser. This practice is called **field warehousing**, since the goods are not taken to the warehouse but remain "in the field."

The purpose of field warehousing is to create warehouse receipts that the owner of the goods may pledge as security for loans. The owner could, of course, have done this by actually placing the goods in a warehouse, but this would have involved the expense of transportation and storage.

6. Limitation of Liability of Warehouser

A warehouser may limit liability by a provision in the warehouse receipt specifying the maximum amount for which the warehouser can be held liable. This privilege is subject to two qualifications. First, the customer must be given the choice of storing the goods without such limitation if the customer pays a higher storage rate, and second, the limitation must be stated as to each item or as to each unit of weight. A limitation is proper when it states that the maximum liability for a piano is $1,000 or that the maximum liability per bushel of wheat is a stated amount. Conversely, there cannot be a blanket limitation of liability, such as "maximum liability $50," when the receipt covers more than one item.

General contract law determines whether a limitation clause is a part of the contract between the warehouser and the customer. A limitation in a warehouse receipt is not part of the contract when the receipt is delivered to the customer a substantial period of time after the goods have been left for storage.

B. COMMON CARRIERS

The purpose of a bailment may be transportation. In this case, the bailee may be a common carrier.

7. Definitions

A **carrier** of goods is an individual or organization undertaking the transportation of goods, regardless of the method of transportation or the distance covered. The **consignor** or shipper is the person who delivers goods to the carrier for shipment. The **consignee** is the person to whom the goods are shipped and to whom the carrier should deliver the goods.

A carrier may be classified as a common carrier, a contract carrier, or a private carrier. A **common carrier** holds itself out as willing to furnish transportation for compensation without discrimination to all members of the public who apply, assuming that the goods to be carried are proper and facilities of the carrier are available. A **contract carrier** transports goods under individual contracts, and a **private carrier** is owned and operated by the shipper. For example, a truck fleet owned and operated by an industrial firm is a private carrier. The common carrier law or special bailment law applies to common carriers, ordinary bailment law to contract carriers, and the law of employment to private carriers.

In the *Harms* case, the court considered whether the issuance of a common carrier permit was proper.

APPLICATION OF HARMS
(SD) 491 NW2d 760 (1992)

The Public Utilities Commission (PUC) granted Doyle Harms a Class B permit authorizing performance as a common carrier. The circuit court considered challenges made by other common carriers in the area and reversed the PUC's decision. Harms appealed to the state Supreme Court.

TIMM, C. J. . . . The PUC's findings of fact state . . . :

Applicant does not intend to haul for everyone who requests transportation within his authority. Applicant will primarily haul cattle he has purchased, cattle he has purchased for others, and partial loads which he does not own or has not purchased.

This finding is drawn from Harms' testimony. Asked if it was his intention to haul in a different direction than he was already going, Harms stated:

No way, that's not what I'm asking for. I've got enough business of my own, it's just the times when you get done with a sale at the end of the day and you've got a half load and somebody else has a half a load, then you'd be able to help each other out. It's kind of the name of the game in my mind.

He also testified that the application was so he could haul cattle for his own customers. . .

With certain exceptions . . . any person or entity that desires to engage in intrastate transporation of persons or property, for hire, must apply for authorization from the PUC. . . . The PUC may authorize one of two types of operation: (1) it may grant a permit (Class A or Class B) authorizing performance as a common carrier; or, (2) it may register an applicant (Class C) authorizing it to operate as a contract carrier.

It is clear from certain provisions of SDCL 49-28 that common and contract carriers are distinct types of carriers and that a carrier cannot be both. . . . SDCL 49-28-1(15) defines a common carrier as "a motor carrier which holds itself out to the general public as engaged in the business of transporting persons or property in intrastate commerce which it is accustomed to and is capable of transporting from place to place in this state, for hire." Its property is "devoted to the public service." SDCL 49-28-9.1(2)(e). It may not "make or give any preference or advantage to any person, company, partnership, corporation or locality, or any description of traffic nor subject any person, company, partnership, corporation or locality, or any description of traffic, to any prejudice or disadvantage." SDCL 49-28-30. In contrast, a contract carrier "does not engage in or hold itself out to furnish service to the general public." SDCL 49-28-4.1. Its property is not devoted to the public service. SDCL 49-28-9.1(3). It is not prohibited from granting preference or advantage. SDCL 49-28-30.

Based on these statutes it is obvious that the service Harms proposed falls outside the realm of common carriage. Harms' dedication of his equipment to first serve his own needs and those of his customers is in contravention of a common carrier's duty to devote itself to public service without discrimination. Failure to recognize this led the PUC to issue a common carrier permit to a motor carrier that is not a common carrier. There is no statutory authority to do so. We therefore agree with the circuit court that the PUC exceeded its statutory authority in granting the Class B permit to Harms.

[Judgment affirmed]

8. Bills of Lading

When the carrier accepts goods for shipment or forwarding, the carrier ordinarily issues to the shipper a **bill of lading** in the case of land or water transportation or an **airbill** for air transportation.[10] This instrument is a document of title and provides rights similar to those provided by a warehouse receipt. A bill of lading is both a receipt for the goods and a memorandum of a contract stating the terms of carriage. Title to the goods may be transferred by transfer of the bill of lading made with that intention.

With respect to intrastate shipments, bills of lading are governed by the Uniform Commercial Code. With regard to interstate shipments, bills of lading are regulated by the Federal Bills of Lading Act.[11]

(a) CONTENTS OF BILL OF LADING. The form of the bill of lading is regulated in varying degrees by administrative agencies.[12] For example, the Interstate Commerce Commission requires that negotiable bills of lading be printed on yellow paper, and nonnegotiable or straight bills of lading be printed on white paper.[13]

As against the good faith transferee of the bill of lading, a carrier is bound by the recitals in the bill as to the contents, quantity, or weight of goods.[14] This means that the carrier must produce the goods that are described or pay damages for failing to do so. This rule is not applied if facts appear on the face of the bill that should keep the transferee from relying on the recital.

(b) NEGOTIATION. A bill of lading is a **negotiable bill of lading** when by its terms the goods are to be delivered "to the bearer" or "to the order of" a named person.[15] Any other bill of lading, such as one that consigns the goods to a named person, is a **nonnegotiable** or **straight bill of lading**. Like transferees of warehouse receipts who take by due negotiation, holders of bills of lading who take by due negotiation ordinarily also acquire the title to the bills and title to the goods represented by them.

Rights of a transferee are defeated by the true owner, however, when a thief delivers the goods to the carrier and then negotiates the bill of lading. The thief had no title to the goods at any time.

(c) WARRANTIES. By transferring for value a bill of lading, whether negotiable or nonnegotiable, the transferor makes certain implied warranties to the transferee. The transferor impliedly warrants that (1) the bill of lading is genuine, (2) its transfer is rightful

---

[10] Imitiaz v Emery Airfreight, Inc. (Tex Civ App) 728 SW2d 897 (1987).

[11] Title 49, USC § 81 et seq.

[12] The UCC contains no provision regulating the form of the bill of lading.

[13] Bill of Lading, 55 ICC 671.

[14] UCC § 7-301(1).

[15] UCC § 7-104(1)(a).

and is effective to transfer the goods represented thereby, and (3) the transferor has no knowledge of facts that would impair the validity or worth of the bill of lading.[16]

9.   Rights of Common Carrier

A common carrier of goods has the right to make reasonable and necessary rules for the conduct of its business. It has the right to charge such rates for its services as yield it a fair return on the property devoted to the business of transportation. However, the exact rates charged are regulated by the Interstate Commerce Commission in the case of interstate carriers and by state commissions in the case of intrastate carriers. As an incident of the right to charge for its services, a carrier may charge **demurrage**—a charge for the detention of its cars or equipment for an unreasonable length of time by either the consignor or consignee.[17]

As security for unpaid transportation and service charges, a common carrier has a lien on goods that it transports. The carrier's lien also secures demurrage, the costs of preservation of the goods, and the costs of sale to enforce the lien.[18] The lien of a carrier is a specific lien. It attaches only to goods shipped under the particular contract, but includes all of the shipment even if it is sent in installments. When part of the shipment is delivered to the consignee, the lien continues on the portion remaining in possession of the carrier.

10.   Duties of Common Carrier

A common carrier is required (a) to receive and carry proper and lawful goods of all persons who offer them for shipment as long as the carrier has space; (b) to furnish facilities that are adequate for the transportation of freight in the usual course of business, and to furnish proper storage facilities for goods awaiting shipment or awaiting delivery after shipment; (c) to follow the directions given by the shipper; (d) to load and unload goods delivered to it for shipment (in less-than-carload lots in the case of railroads), but the shipper or consignee may assume this duty by contract or custom; and (e) to deliver the goods in accordance with the shipment contract.

Goods must be delivered at the usual place of delivery at the specified destination. When goods are shipped under a negotiable bill of lading, the carrier must not deliver the goods without obtaining possession of the bill, properly indorsed. When goods are shipped under a straight bill of lading, the carrier may deliver the goods to the consignee or the consignee's agent without receiving the bill of lading, unless notified by the shipper to deliver the goods to someone else. If the carrier delivers the goods to the wrong person, the carrier is liable for breach of contract and for the tort of conversion.

11.   Liabilities of Common Carrier

When goods are delivered to a common carrier for immediate shipment and while they are in transit, the carrier is absolutely liable for any loss or damage to the goods unless it can prove that the loss or damage was due solely to one or more of the following excepted causes: (a) act of God, meaning a natural phenomenon that is not reasonably foreseeable;[19] (b) act of public enemy, such as the military forces of an opposing government, as distinguished from ordinary robbers; (c) act of public authority, such as a health officer removing goods from the carrier; (d) act of the shipper, such as fraudulent labeling or defective packing;

---

[16] UCC § 7-507; Federal Bills of Lading Act (FBLA), 49 USC § 114, 116. When the transfer of the bill of lading is part of a transaction by which the transferor sells the goods represented thereby to the transferee, there will also arise the warranties that are found in other sales of goods.

[17] Betsy Ross Foods v A, C & Y Railway Co. 17 Ohio App 3d 145, 468 NE2d 338 (1983).

[18] UCC § 7-307(1); FBLA, 49 USC § 105.

[19] Utilities Pipeline Co. v American Petrofina (Tex Civ App) 760 SW2d 719 (1988).

or (e) inherent nature of the goods, such as those naturally tending to spoil or deteriorate.

(a) CARRIER'S LIABILITY FOR DELAY. A carrier is liable for losses caused by its failure to deliver goods within a reasonable time. Thus, the carrier is liable for losses arising from a fall in price or a deterioration of the goods caused by the carrier's unreasonable delay. The carrier, however, is not liable for every delay. The risk of ordinary delays incidental to transporting goods is assumed by the shipper.

(b) LIMITATION OF LIABILITY OF CARRIER. In the absence of a constitutional or statutory prohibition, a carrier generally has the right to limit its liability by contract.[20]

Nonrail common carriers operating interstate may limit their liability for the negligent loss of consigned items to a stated dollar amount, such as $100 per package. Such limitations must be filed with and approved by the Interstate Commerce Commission (ICC) as part of the carriers' tariffs (rate schedules). Additionally, shippers must be allowed the option of selecting a higher value for the shipment, with payment of higher freight charges. The ICC is barred from approving tariffs limiting the common law liability of rail common carriers for losses to property transported by rail in interstate commerce.[21]

(c) NOTICE OF CLAIM. The bill of lading and applicable government regulations may require that a carrier be given notice of any claim for damages or loss of goods within a specified time, generally within nine months.

(d) C.O.D. SHIPMENT. A common carrier transporting goods under a C.O.D. (cash on delivery) shipment may not make delivery of the goods without first receiving payment. If it does so, it is liable to the shipper for any loss resulting therefrom. If the carrier accepts a check from the consignee without the shipper's approval and the check is not honored by the bank on which it is drawn, the carrier is liable to the shipper for the amount thereof.

(e) REJECTED SHIPMENTS. When a common carrier tenders delivery of consigned goods to a consignee that refuses to accept the delivery, the carrier is no longer a common carrier, but becomes a warehouser. When the carrier-turned-warehouser receives new shipping instructions from the owner, its status again changes to that of a common carrier.

In the *Fisher* case the status of the trucking firm, and therefore its liability, was in question.

FISHER CORPORATION v CONSOLIDATED FREIGHTWAYS, INC.

230 Neb 832, 434 NW2d 17 (1989)

In June Fisher Corporation delivered 132 VCRs (recorders) to Consolidated Freightways, Inc. at its California warehouse for shipment to World Radio, Inc. at Council Bluffs, Iowa. On July 6, World Radio rejected the shipment as

---

20 Hughes Aircraft Co. v North American Van Lines Inc. (CA9 Cal) 970 F2d 609 (1992).

21 49 USC § 20 (11).

duplicative of earlier shipments. On July 7, Consolidated loaded all of the VCRs onto a trailer, sealed it, and placed the trailer at the south end of its terminal. Also on July 7, it sent a letter to Fisher notifying it of World Radio's rejection and seeking disposition instructions. Consolidated's security measures were reasonable and equal to those of other trucking companies in the area. On July 17, Consolidated discovered that a 5-foot hole had been cut in the chain link fence and that fifty-four VCRs were missing. After the theft had occurred, but before Consolidated had discovered the theft, Fisher notified Consolidated to return the VCRs to its California warehouse. When Consolidated did not return the stolen VCRs, Fisher sued Consolidated for their value. The district court dismissed the suit, and Fisher appealed.

CAPORALE, J. . . . In its original petition, Fisher pled that it was entitled to recover on the theory that at the time of the theft, Consolidated was serving as a warehouser, or alternatively, on the theory that at the relevant time, Consolidated was serving as a common carrier. A warehouser, that is, one "engaged in the business of storing goods for hire," U.C.C. § 7-102(1)(h), is, in the absence of a contrary agreement, liable for goods lost while in its possession only if . . . the loss occurred through its negligence. See U.C.C. § 7-204. A common carrier, on the other hand, is an insurer against loss from whatever cause, [unless the carrier can show that the loss was due to one or more of the following causes: (a) act of God, (b) act of public enemy, (c) act of public authority, (d) act of shipper, or (e) inherent nature of the goods.]. . .

Once a common carrier tenders delivery of the consigned goods to a consignee which refuses delivery, the carrier loses its status as a common carrier and becomes a warehouser. . . . Where a common carrier turned warehouser, acting as a bailee, accepts instructions from the bailor to ship goods to a specified location, its status as a warehouser again changes to that of common carrier. . . .

The evidence is sufficient to sustain the jury's special finding that Consolidated did not receive Fisher's return authorization until after the theft had taken place, thereby making Consolidated a warehouser at the time of the loss rather than a common carrier. Moreover, the evidence concerning the manner in which Consolidated stored the recorders . . . support[s] the finding implicit in the general verdict that Consolidated had not been negligent. . . .

[Judgment affirmed]

QUESTIONS

1. When does a common carrier's warehouse status change back to that of a common carrier with respect to a shipment rejected by the consignee?
2. Was Consolidated a common carrier at the time the recorders were stolen from the trailer?
3. Was Consolidated negligent in the manner in which it stored the recorders? Why is this significant?

C. FACTORS

A **factor** is a special type of bailee who sells consigned goods as though the factor were the owner of those goods.

12. Definitions

Entrusting a person with the possession of property for the purpose of sale is commonly called **selling on consignment**.[22] The owner who consigns the goods for sale is the **consignor**. The person or agent to whom they are consigned is the factor or **consignee**; this individual may also be known as a commission merchant. A consignee's compensation is known as a **commission** or **factorage**.

13. Effect of Factor Transaction

In a sale on consignment, the property remains the property of the owner or consignor, and the consignee acts as the agent of the owner to pass the owner's title to the buyer. Since a factor is by definition authorized by the consignor to sell the goods entrusted to the factor, such a sale will pass the title of the consignor to the purchaser. Before the factor makes the sale, the goods belong to the consignor, but in some instances creditors of the factor may ignore the consignor and treat the goods as though they belonged to the factor.[23] If the consignor is not the owner, as when a thief delivers stolen goods to the factor, a sale by the factor passes no title and is an unlawful conversion. It is constitutional, however, to provide by statute that the factor who sells in good faith in ignorance of the rights of other persons in the goods is protected from liability.

D. HOTELKEEPERS

A hotelkeeper has a bailee's liability with respect to property specifically entrusted to the hotelkeeper's care. In addition, the hotelkeeper has special duties with respect to a guest's property brought into the hotel. The rules governing the special relationship between a hotelkeeper and guest arose because of the special needs of travelers.

14. Definitions

The definitions of *hotelkeeper* and *guest* exclude lodging of a more permanent character, such as that provided by boardinghouse keepers to boarders.

(a) HOTELKEEPER. A **hotelkeeper** is an operator of a hotel, motel, or tourist home, or anyone who is regularly engaged in the business of offering living accommodations to transient persons. In the early law, the hotelkeeper was called an innkeeper or a tavernkeeper.

(b) GUEST. A **guest** is a transient. The guest need not be a traveler or come from a distance. A person living within a short distance of a hotel who engages a room at the hotel and remains there overnight is a guest.

In contrast, a person who enters a hotel at the invitation of a guest or attends a dance or a banquet given at the hotel is not a guest. Similarly, the guest of a registered occupant of a motel room who shares the room with the occupant without the knowledge or consent of the management is not a guest of the motel, since there is no relationship between that person and the motel.

15. Duration of Guest Relationship

The relationship of guest and hotelkeeper does not begin until a person is received as a guest by the hotelkeeper. The guest-hotelkeeper relationship does not automatically end when the hotel bill is paid.

---

[22] Amoco Oil Co. v DZ Enterprises Inc. (DC NY) 607 F Supp 595 (1985).
[23] UCC § 2-326.

The relationship terminates when the guest leaves or ceases to be a transient, as when the guest arranges for a more or less permanent residence at the hotel. The transition from the status of guest to the status of boarder or lodger must be clearly indicated. It is not established by the mere fact that one remains at the hotel for a long period, even though it runs into months.

16. Hotelkeeper's Liability for Guest's Property

With respect to property expressly entrusted to the hotelkeeper's care, the hotelkeeper has a bailee's liability. At common law, the hotelkeeper was absolutely liable for damage to or loss of a guest's property unless the hotelkeeper could show that the damage or loss was caused solely by an act of God, public enemy, act of public authority, the inherent nature of the property, or the fault of the guest.[24]

In most states, statutes limit or provide a method of limiting the common law liability of a hotelkeeper. The statutes may limit the extent of liability, reduce the liability of a hotelkeeper to that of an ordinary bailee, or permit the hotelkeeper to limit liability by contract or by posting a notice of the limitation. Some statutes relieve the hotelkeeper from liability when the guest has not complied with directions for depositing valuables with the hotelkeeper.[25] When a statute permits a hotel receiving valuables for deposit in its safe deposit box to limit its liability to the amount specified in the agreement signed by the guest, this limitation binds the guest even though the loss was caused by negligence on the part of the hotel. A hotelkeeper must substantially comply with such a statute in order to obtain its protection.

In the *Hicks* case, the court considered the question of whether a statute limiting a hotelkeeper's liability for the loss of a guest's property applies when the hotel's negligence caused the loss.

HICKS v DAYS INNS OF AMERICA INC.
183 Ga App 4, 357 SE2d 847 (1987)

The Hicks family, thinking that their room at the Days Inn was secure against theft, left several hundred dollars and a valuable antique pistol in the room. When they returned, they discovered that the money and pistol had been stolen. They sued the hotelkeeper, contending that it was responsible for the loss of the money and the pistol because of its negligence in not providing better security for the room. They further asserted that the limitation of liability under state law did not apply to limit a hotelkeeper's liability for its own negligence. The court held that under state law the hotelkeeper's liability for negligence in the loss of a guest's property was limited to $100. The Hicks family appealed.

CARLEY, J. . . . Appellee [Days Inn] had posted, on the inside of the door to appellants' motel room, a notice which required guests to store their valuables in the motel's safe and which otherwise limited appellee's liability for the loss of a guest's

[24] Cook v Columbia Sussex Corp. (Tenn App) 807 SW2d 567 (1991)
[25] Numismatic Enterprise v Hyatt Corp. (D Ind) 797 F Supp 687 (1992).

property to $100 unless the guest had made prior written notification that the value of his property exceeded that amount. See OCGA § 43-21-10; former OCGA § 43-21-12. This was a sufficient disclosure of the security measures that were made available by appellee for its guests' property and of the limitation on its liability as provided by the applicable statutes. . . .

In support of its motion for summary judgment as to appellants' negligence claim, appellee did not rely upon its publication of the notice authorized by OCGA § 43-21-10, pursuant to which it would "be relieved from responsibility" for appellants' "valuable articles" which were not placed in appellee's safe. Instead, appellee relied only upon its publication of the notice that is authorized by OCGA § 43-21-12 and which applies to the loss of property "other than valuable articles." The evidence is undisputed that appellee had posted, on the inside of the door to appellants' room, the notice authorized by OCGA § 43-21-12. Appellants assert only that they did not read the entire notice. They did not notify appellee in writing that their property's value was in excess of $100. Under these circumstances and OCGA § 43-21-12 as it existed at the time of appellants' loss, appellee's liability for their property damage was limited to $100. Accordingly, the trial court was correct in granting summary judgment limiting appellee's liability for its alleged negligence to a recovery of this amount. "The General Assembly by [enacting OCGA § 43-21-12] authorizing a limitation of liability has pre-empted the field on that subject." *Ellerman v Atlanta American Hotel Corp.*, 126 Ga App 194, 196 (2), 191 SE2d 295 (1972).

[Judgment affirmed]

QUESTIONS

1. Did Days Inns comply with the state law limiting the common law liability of hotelkeepers?
2. Does the statutory limitation of liability for loss of a guest's property to $100 apply to situations where it is proven that the hotel's negligence caused the loss?

17. Hotelkeeper's Lien

The hotelkeeper has a lien on the baggage of guests for the agreed charges or, if no express agreement was made, for the reasonable value of the accommodations furnished. Statutes permit the hotelkeeper to enforce this lien by selling the goods of the guests at a public sale. The lien of the hotelkeeper is terminated by (a) the guest's payment of the hotel charges, (b) any conversion of the guest's goods by the hotelkeeper, or (c) final return of the goods to the guest.

18. Boarders or Lodgers

The hotelkeeper owes only the duty of an ordinary bailee of personal property under a mutual benefit bailment to those persons who are permanent boarders or lodgers rather than transient guests.

A hotelkeeper has no lien on property of boarders or lodgers, as distinguished from guests, in the absence of an express agreement creating such a lien. In a number of states, however, legislation giving a lien to a boardinghouse or a lodging house keeper has been adopted.

SUMMARY

A warehouser stores the goods of others for compensation and has the rights and duties of a bailee in an ordinary mutual benefit bailment. A warehouser issues a warehouse receipt to the depositor of the goods. This receipt is a document of title that ordinarily entitles the person in possession of the receipt to receive the goods. The warehouse receipt can be bought, sold, or used as security to obtain a loan. A nonnegotiable warehouse receipt states that the goods received will be delivered to a specified person. A negotiable warehouse receipt states that the goods will be delivered "to the bearer" or "to the order of" a named person. If a negotiable warehouse receipt is duly negotiated, the transferee may acquire rights superior to those of the transferor. A warehouser may limit its liability for loss or damage to goods due to its own negligence to an agreed valuation of the property stated in the warehouse receipt, provided the depositor is given the right to store the goods without the limitation, at a higher storage rate.

A common carrier of goods is in the business of transporting goods received from the general public. It issues to the shipper a bill of lading or an airbill. Both of these are documents of title and provide rights similar to those provided by a warehouse receipt. A common carrier is absolutely liable for any loss or damage to the goods unless the carrier can show that the loss was caused solely by an act of God, an act of a public enemy, an act of a public authority, an act of the shipper, or the inherent nature of the goods. The carrier may limit its liability in the same manner as a warehouse.

A factor is a special type of bailee, who has possession of the owner's property for the purpose of sale. The factor, or consignee, receives a commission on the sale.

A hotelkeeper is in the business of providing living accommodations to transient persons called guests. Subject to exceptions, at common law hotelkeepers were absolutely liable for loss or damage to their guests' property. Most states, however, provide a method of limiting this liability. A hotelkeeper has a lien on the property of the guest for the agreed charges.

LAW IN PRACTICE

1. Remember, general contract law determines whether a limitation of liability clause is part of the contract between a warehouser and customer.
2. Recognize that a common carrier's lien not only secures unpaid transportation charges, but also secures other charges such as demurrage and the costs of preserving the goods. Plan on paying for goods when delivered and on not detaining the cars or equipment of common carriers.
3. Where a buyer's financial status is uncertain, the C.O.D. shipment may be used to protect the seller because common carriers may not make delivery without receiving payment.
4. Where a reputable agent is available, the consignment sale may be a very simple method of selling goods.
5. Employees traveling on company business with valuable company property should be instructed to utilize the safe deposit boxes provided by hotels, rather than leaving the company property in their rooms.

QUESTIONS AND CASE PROBLEMS

1. What social forces are involved in the rule of law governing the liability of a common carrier for loss of freight?
2. American Cyanamid shipped 7000 vials of DPT, a vaccine for immunization of infants and children against diphtheria and tetanus from its Pearl River, N.Y. facility to the U.S. Defense Department Depot in Mechanicsburg, Pennsylvania by New Penn Express Co., a common carrier. Cyanamid's bill of lading included a "release value," which stated the value of the property was declared as not exceeding $1.65 per pound.

Cyanamid's shipment weighed 1260 pounds. The bill of lading accepted by New Penn upon picking up the DPT vaccine on February 6 also clearly stated that the shipment contained drugs and to "protect from freezing." The bill further recited "rush . . . must be delivered by February 8, 1989." New Penn permitted the vaccine to sit in an unheated uninsulated trailer while it gathered enough other merchandise to justify sending a truck to Mechanicsburg. The DPT vaccine was delivered on February 10, in worthless condition, having been destroyed by the cold. New Penn admitted it owes $2079 in damages pursuant to the bill of lading. ($1.65 x 1260 lbs.) Cyanamid claimed that the actual loss was much greater, $53,936.75. It stated that since New Penn breached its contract with Cyanamid it cannot invoke the benefits of that same contract, namely the release value clause. Was it ethical for New Penn to hold the vaccine while waiting for enough merchandise to justify the trip? How would you decide the case? [American Cyanamid Co. v New Penn Motor Express Inc. (CA3 Pa) 979 F2d 301]

3. Compare the liens of carriers, warehousers, and hotels in terms of being specific.

4. Compare the limitation of the liability of a warehouser and of a hotel.

5. Compare warehouse receipts and bills of lading as to negotiability.

6. Latham and Loud, sporting goods manufacturers' representatives in Cleveland, Ohio, hijacked a truckload of ice skates from the Bartlett Shoe and Skate Company of Bangor, Maine. Latham and Loud warehoused the skates at the Northern Transfer Company's warehouse and received a negotiable warehouse receipt. Preston, a lender who had previous business dealings with Latham and Loud and believed them to be honest individuals, made a good-faith purchase of the receipt. Bartlett discovered that the skates were at Northern's Warehouse and informed Northern of the hijacking. Northern delivered the skates to Bartlett. Preston, claiming that he was entitled to delivery of the skates, brought an action against Northern, since he acquired the negotiable receipt by due negotiation. Was Preston entitled to the skates?

7. Welch Brothers Trucking, Inc., a common carrier, made an agreement with B & L Export and Import Co. of San Francisco to transport a shipment of freshly harvested bluefin tuna from Calais, Maine to the Japan Air Lines freight terminal at New York's Kennedy Airport. The bluefin had been packed in ice and were to be shipped by Ja-

pan Air to Tokyo. Fresh bluefin are used in the traditional Japanese raw fish dish sashimi and command very high prices. When transportation charges were not paid by B & L's representative in New York, Welch Brothers refused to release the shipment to Japan Air Lines. B & L's representative in New York explained that he had no check-writing authority, but assured Welch that it would be paid and pleaded for the release of the cargo because of its perishable nature. Transportation charges were not paid in the next 12-hour period because the principals of B & L were on a business trip to the Far East and could not be contacted. After waiting the 12-hour period, Welch sent a telegram to B & L's offices in San Francisco stating the amount due and that it intended to auction the cargo in 24 hours if transportation charges were not paid. Welch also sent telegrams, seeking bidders, to all fish wholesalers listed in the New York City yellow pages. In the telegrams, Welch advised that the cargo would be sold at auction in 24 hours if the charges were not paid. Welch sold the shipment to the highest bidder at the appointed time for an amount just in excess of the transportation charges plus a demurrage charge for the 36-hour waiting period. When the principals of B & L were later informed of what happened, they sued Welch for the profits they would have earned if the cargo had been shipped and sold in Japan. Decide.

8. Richard Schewe and others placed personal property in a building occupied by the Winnebago County Fair Association, Inc. Prior to placing their property in the building they signed a "Storage Rental Agreement" prepared by the County Fair Association, which stated that "No liability exists for damage or loss to the stored equipment from the perils of fire. . . ." The property was destroyed by fire. Suit was brought against the County Fair Association to recover damages for the losses on the theory of negligence of a warehouser. The County Fair Association defended that the language in the storage agreement relieved it of all liability. [Allstate Ins. Co. v Winnebago County Fair Association, Inc. 131 Ill App 3d 225, 86 Ill Dec 233, 475 NE2d 230]

9. Buffett sent a violin to Strotokowsky by International Parcel Service (IPS), a common carrier. Buffett declared the value of the parcel at $500 on the pick-up receipt given him by the IPS driver. The receipt also stated: "Unless a greater value is declared in writing on this receipt, the shipper hereby declares and agrees that the released value of each package covered by this receipt is $100.00,

which is a reasonable value under the circumstance surrounding the transportation." When the parcel was not received by Strotokowsky, he sued IPS for the full retail value of the violin—$2,000. IPS raised the defense that it was liable for just $100. Decide.

10. Glen Smith contracted with Dave Watson, a common carrier, to transport 720 hives of live bees along with associated equipment from Idabel, Oklahoma to Mandan, North Dakota. At 9:00 A.M. on May 24, 1984, while en route, Watson's truck skidded off the road and tipped over, severely damaging the cargo. Watson notified Smith of what had happened, and Smith immediately set out for the scene of the accident. He arrived at 6:00 P.M. with two bee experts and a Bobcat loader. They were hindered by the turned-over truck on top of the cargo, and they determined that they could not safely salvage the cargo that evening. The next day an insurance adjuster determined that the cargo was a total loss. The adjuster directed a bee expert, Dr. Moffat, to conduct the cleanup; and Moffat was allowed to keep the salvageable cargo, valued at $12,326 as compensation. Smith sued Watson for damages. Watson denied liability and further contended that Smith failed to mitigate damages. Decide. [*Smith v Watson (ND) 406 NW2d 685*]

11. A guest in a motel opened the bedroom window at night and went to sleep. During the night, a prowler pried open the screen, entered the room, and stole property of the guest. The guest sued the motel. The motel asserted that it was not responsible for property in the possession of the guest and that the guest had been contributorily negligent in opening the window. Could the guest recover damages? [*Buck v Hankin, 217 Pa Super 262, 269 A2d 344*]

12. On March 30, Emery Air Freight Corp. picked up a shipment of furs from Hopper Furs, Inc. Hopper's chief of security filled in certain items in the airbill. In the box entitled ZIP Code, he mistakenly placed the figure "61,045," which was the value of the furs. The ZIP Code box is immediately above the "declared value" box. The airbill contained a clause limiting liability to $10 per pound of cargo lost or damaged, unless the shipper makes a declaration of value in excess of the amount and pays a higher fee. A higher fee was not charged in this case, and Gerald Doane signed the airbill for the carrier and took possession of the furs. The furs were lost in transit by Emery, and Hopper sued for the value of the furs, $61,045. Emery's offer to pay $2,150, the $10-per-pound

rate set forth in the airbill, was rejected. Hopper claims that the amount $61,045, which was mistakenly placed in the ZIP Code box, was in fact part of the contract set forth in the airbill and that Emery, on reviewing the contract, must have realized a mistake was made. Decide. [*Hopper Furs, Inc. v Emery Air Freight Corp. (CA8 Mo) 749 F2d 1261*]

13. De Lema, a Brazilian resident, arrived in New York City. His luggage consisted of three suitcases, an attaché case, and a cylindrical bag. The attaché case and the cylindrical bag contained jewels, valued at $300,000. De Lema went from JFK Airport to the Waldorf Astoria Hotel, where he gave the three suitcases to hotel staff in the garage, and then he went to the lobby to register. The assistant manager, Baez, summoned room clerk Tamburino to assist him. De Lema stated, "The room clerk asked me if I had a reservation. I said, 'Yes. The name is José Berga de Lema.' And I said, 'I want a safety deposit box.' He said, 'Please fill out your registration.'" While de Lema was filling out the registration form, paying $300 in cash as an advance, and Tamburino was filling out a receipt for that amount, de Lema had placed the attaché case and the cylindrical bag on the floor. A woman jostled de Lema, apparently creating a diversion, and when he next looked down, he discovered that the attaché case was gone. De Lema brought suit against the hotel for the value of the jewels stolen in the hotel's lobby. The hotel maintained a safe for valuables and posted notices in the lobby, garage, and rooms, as required by the New York law that modifies a hotelkeeper's common law liability. The notices stated in part that the hotel was not liable for the loss of valuables that a guest neglected to deliver to the hotel for safekeeping. The hotel defended that de Lema neglected to inform it of the presence of the jewels and to deliver the jewels to the hotel. Is the hotel liable for the value of the stolen jewels? [*De Lema v Waldorf Astoria Hotel, Inc. (DC NY) 588 F Supp 19*]

14. Frosty Land Foods shipped a load of beef from its plant in Montgomery, Alabama to Scott Meat Company in Los Angeles via the Refrigerated Transport Co. (RTC), a common carrier. Early Wednesday morning, December 7, at 12:55 A.M., two of RTC's drivers left the Frosty Land plant with the load of beef. The bill of lading called for delivery at Scott Meat Company on Friday, December 9, at 6:00 A.M. The RTC drivers arrived in Los Angeles at approximately 3:30 P.M. on Friday, December 9. Scott notified the drivers that it could not process the meat at that time. The drivers checked into a motel for the weekend, and the load was delivered to Scott on Monday, December 12. After inspecting 65 of the 308 carcasses, Scott determined that the meat was in "off condition" and refused the shipment. On Tuesday, December 13, Frosty Land sold the meat, after extensive trimming, at a loss of $13,529. Frosty Land brought suit against RTC for its loss. Decide. [*Frosty Land Foods v Refrigerated Transport Co. (CA5 Ala) 613 F2d 1344*]

15. The Singer Corporation had been storing air conditioners in Stoda warehouses for several years. In May 1974, Singer's transportation manager, Guy Bataglia, went to Stoda's "Hoffman Plant" warehouse, accompanied by Stoda's president, Larry Ellis. While looking over the building, Bataglia noticed the sprinkler system and inquired about it. Ellis, who knew the system had been turned off, said the system was active. Singer stored 133 cartons of air-conditioning units at the Hoffman Plant as of that day. On July 7, 1974, a fire broke out in the Hoffman Plant, totally destroying Singer's goods. Singer claimed that it was entitled to recover the value of the destroyed air conditioners from Stoda, since it made out a prima facie case of negligence, which was not rebutted. Stoda defended that it was not an insurer of the goods. Decide. [*Singer Co. v Stoda, 79 App Div 2d 227, 435 NYS2d 508*]

PART 4

Sales
and
Leases
of
Personal
Property

C H A P T E R 2 4

NATURE AND FORM OF SALES

LEARNING OBJECTIVES

After studying this chapter, you will be able to:
1. *Distinguish between a sale of goods and
   other transactions relating to goods.*
2. *List points of difference between general contract law and the law of sales.*
3. *State when a contract for the sale of goods
   must be evidenced by a writing.*
4. *List and explain the exceptions to the requirement that certain contracts be evidenced by a writing.*
5. *Define and state the purpose of the United
   Nations Convention on Contracts for the International Sale of Goods.*
6. *State the distinguishing features of a consumer lease and a finance lease.*

The sale of goods is a very common transaction, ranging from the sale of a newspaper to the purchase of a multimillion-dollar electrical generator. The law of sales is a special branch of the law of contracts. It is derived from the law merchant, the common law of England, and former statutes as codified and modified by Article 2 of the Uniform Commercial Code.

A. NATURE AND LEGALITY

A **sale of goods** is a present transfer of title to movable property for a price. This price may be a payment of money, an exchange of other property, or the performance of services. When a free item is given with the purchase of other goods, it is the purchasing of the other goods that is the price for the "free" goods; hence, the transaction as to the free goods is a sale.

The parties to a sale are the person who owns the goods and the person to whom the title is transferred. The transferor is the seller or vendor, and the transferee is the buyer or vendee.

1. Subject Matter of Sales

Goods, the subject matter of a sale under Article 2 of the Uniform Commercial Code, means anything movable at the time it is identified as the subject of the transaction.[1] The subject matter may not be (a) investment securities, such as stocks and bonds, the sale of which is regulated by Article 8 of the UCC; (b) choses in action, such as insurance policies and promissory notes, because they are assigned or negotiated rather than sold, or which, because of their personal nature, are not transferable in any case; or (c) real estate, such as a house, factory, or farm.

(a) NATURE OF GOODS. Most goods are tangible and solid, such as an automobile or a chair. But goods may also be fluid, such as oil or gasoline. Goods may also be intangible, such as natural gas and electricity.

The UCC is applicable to both new and used goods.

(b) EXISTING AND FUTURE GOODS. Goods that are physically existing and owned by the seller at the time of the transaction are called **existing goods**. All other goods are called **future goods**. Future goods include both goods that are physically existing but not owned by the seller and goods that have not yet been produced.

A person can make a contract to sell goods at a future date. However, no sale can be made of future goods. Because the "seller" does not have any title to future goods, there can be no transfer of that title now, and hence no sale. For example, an agreement made today that all fish caught on a fishing trip tomorrow shall belong to a particular person does not make that person the owner of any fish today.

When the parties attempt to effect a present sale of future goods, the agreement operates only as a *contract to sell* rather than a *sale* of the goods. Thus, a farmer purporting to transfer the title today to a future crop would be held subject to a contract duty to transfer the crop when it came into existence. The contract itself does not pass the title to the crop.

2. Sale Distinguished from Other Transactions

A sale is an actual present transfer of title. If there is a transfer of a lesser interest than title, the transaction is not a sale.

(a) BAILMENT. A bailment is not a sale, because only possession is transferred to a bailee. Title to the property is not transferred. A lease of goods, such as a lease of an automobile, is a bailment and is regulated by Article 2A of the UCC.[2]

---

[1] It may also include things that are attached to the land, such as (a) minerals or buildings or materials forming part of buildings if they are to be removed or severed by the seller, and (b) other things attached to the land to be removed by either party.

(b) GIFT. There can be no sale without a price. A **gift** is a gratuitous or free transfer of the title to property.

(c) CONTRACT TO SELL. When the parties intend that title to goods will pass at a future time and they make a contract so providing, a **contract to sell** is created.

(d) OPTION TO PURCHASE. A sale—a present transfer of title—differs from an **option to purchase**. The latter is neither a transfer of title nor a contract to transfer title, but a power to make a contract to sell.

(f) CONTRACT FOR SERVICES. A contract for services is an ordinary contract and is not a sale of goods.

(g) CONTRACT FOR GOODS AND SERVICES. If a contract calls for both the rendering of services and the supplying of materials to be used in performing the services, the contract is classified according to its dominant element. If the sale of goods is dominant, it is a sales contract covered by Article 2 of the UCC. If the service element is dominant, it is a service contract and not covered by the UCC. For example, the contract of a repairer is a

Figure 24-1 Comparison of Sales with Other Transactions

Transaction	Essential Characteristic
Sale	Present transfer of title for a price
Bailment	Transfer of possession of goods while retaining title
Gift	Gratuitous transfer of title
Contract to sell	Transfer of title at a future date
Option to purchase	Power to make a contract to sell
Conditional sale	Title passes to purchaser when condition is satisfied

(e) CONDITIONAL SALE. A **conditional sale** customarily refers to a "condition precedent" transaction, by which title does not vest in the purchaser until payment in full has been made for the property purchased. This was formerly a common type of sale, used when the purchase was made on credit and payment was to be made in installments. The conditional sale has been replaced by a secured transaction under Article 9 of the UCC.

contract for services, even though parts are supplied to perform the task. The supplying of such parts is not regarded as a sale but is merely incidental to the primary contract of making repairs. In contrast, the purchase of a television set, with incidental service of installation, is a sale of goods because the purchase of the set is the dominant element. In the *Insul-Mark* case the court was faced with deciding whether a mixed transaction involving both goods and services is subject to the Uniform Commercial Code.

---

2 Article 2A of the UCC codifies the law of leases. Article 2A applies to any transaction, regardless of form, that creates a lease of personal property or fixtures. Many of the provisions of the law of sales were carried over and changed to reflect differences in style, leasing terminology, or leasing practices. These include, among others, statute of frauds provisions, rules relating to offer and acceptance, and warranties.

INSUL-MARK MIDWEST v MODERN MATERIALS

(Ind App) 612 NE2d 550 (1993)

Kor-It is a business principally engaged in the sale of roofing fasteners. Insul-Mark is the marketing arm of Kor-It, and it distributes Kor-It's roofing applications nationwide. Kor-It sent roofing fasteners to Modern Materials for application of a fluorocarbon coating to increase rust resistance. Kor-It and Insul-Mark filed suit against Modern Materials, alleging that rust defects in some of the screws were caused by Modern Materials' deficient applications. They also claimed a breach of warranty under the UCC Modern Materials claimed that the UCC was inapplicable because the contract with Kor-It and Insul-Mark was predominantly for services. From a judgment for Modern Materials, Kor-It and Insul-Mark appealed.

SHEPARD, J. . . . The Sales chapter of the Indiana U.C.C. . . . "applies to transactions in goods," unless the context otherwise requires. [UCC § 2-102] The code defines goods as "all things (including specially manufactured goods) which are movable at the time of identification to the contract for sale." [UCC § 2-105 (1)] An agreement solely for the performance of services is not subject to the sales provisions of the U.C.C. . . .

Many modern commercial transactions cannot be classified as transactions purely for goods or for services, but are "mixed," involving both goods and services. . . . The coating transactions in this case between Kor-It and Modern Materials are indeed "mixed," involving both goods (the coating material) and services (the application of coating). Kor-It did not purchase the coating material directly from Modern Materials, but provided Modern Materials its screws for application of coating (a service).

Given that the transaction is "mixed," we must determine whether it falls within the U.C.C., or falls outside of the code and is thus governed by the common law. The Indiana Court of Appeals has formulated and applied tests for determining the applicability of the U.C.C. to mixed transactions. In *Baker v Compton* (1983), Ind App, 455 NE2d 382, the Second District adopted the "predominant thrust" test. . . .

Under the predominant thrust test, the applicability of the U.C.C. to a mixed transaction is determined by considering whether the transaction's "predominant factor, [its] thrust, [its] purpose, reasonably stated, is the rendition of service, with goods incidentally involved (e.g., contract with artist for painting) or is a transaction of sale, with labor incidentally involved (e.g., installation of a water heater in a bathroom)." . . .

We conclude that the predominant thrust test is the best and most workable approach for determining the applicability of the U.C.C. to mixed transactions. Under the predominant thrust test, courts look to the agreement between the parties to determine their understanding about the predominant purpose of the contract. In focusing on the goals of the contracting parties, the predominant thrust approach preserves parties' expectations regarding their agreement. . . .

Kor-It and Insul-Mark contend that the undisputed facts establish . . . that provision of the coating material, a good, was the predominant thrust of the contract. They argue that this goods aspect predominates over the services aspect, which was only a necessary part of the procurement of coating.

Modern Materials argues that the Sales article of the U.C.C. does not apply in this case because its contract with Kor-It and Insul-Mark was predominantly for services. . . . Modern Materials contends that it was the complicated coating process that was purchased, and not the coating material used to coat the screws. . . .

We hold that the thrust of the agreement between Kor-It and Modern Materials was predominantly for performance of a service. Kor-It's main purpose in entering into the coating transaction was to improve the rust-resistance of its screws. Its specifications regarding rust-resistance related to the quality of its screws after application of a fluorocarbon coating material, and not to the quality of the coating material by itself. Kor-It bargained for a service which would improve the durability of its screws. . . .

Based upon the facts of this case as well as the well-reasoned conclusions of other courts, we hold as a matter of law that the thrust of the coating agreement between Kor-It and Modern Materials was predominantly for the performance of services. The U.C.C. does not apply to the transaction, and the parties' dispute is therefore governed by our common law.

[Judgment affirmed]

QUESTIONS

1. What was the importance of determining whether there was a sale of services or a sale of goods?
2. How did the court use the predominant thrust test to make its decision?
3. How were the rights of the parties determined?

3. Law of Contracts Applicable

To make the law harmonize with business practices, a sales contract is not required to meet the same standards as ordinary contracts. For a sales contract, it is sufficient that the parties by their conduct recognize the existence of a contract, even though it cannot be determined when the contract was made, and (generally) even though one or more terms are left open.[3]

In most instances, the UCC treats all buyers and sellers alike. In some cases, it treats merchants differently than it does the occasional or casual buyer or seller. In this way, the UCC recognizes that the merchant is experienced and has a special knowledge of the relevant commercial practices.

(a) OFFER. Contract law as to offers is applicable to a sales contract, with the following exception. A **firm offer** by a merchant cannot be revoked if the offer (1) expresses an intention that it will not be revoked, (2) is in a writing, and (3) is signed by the merchant. For example, on May 15, Smith, a dealer, offered in a signed writing to sell a stereo set to Bart for $500. By the terms of the offer, Bart was given until June 25 to accept the offer. On June 15, Bart received a writing from Smith revoking the offer. On June 20, Bart wrote Smith, "I hereby accept your offer of May 15." Smith's

CPA
CPA
CPA
CPA
CPA
CPA
CPA

---

[3] UCC § 2-204. This provision is limited by requiring that there be "a reasonably certain basis for giving an appropriate remedy."

offer was a firm offer, which could not be revoked before June 25. There was a contract.

An express period of irrevocability in the offer cannot exceed three months. If nothing is said as to the duration of the offer, irrevocability continues only for a reasonable time. A firm offer is effective regardless of whether the merchant received any consideration to keep the offer open.

(b) ACCEPTANCE. An offer to buy or sell goods may be accepted in any manner and by any medium that is reasonable under the circumstances.[4] However, if a specific manner or medium is clearly required by the terms of the offer or the circumstances of the case, the offer can only be accepted in that manner. An order or other offer to buy goods that are to be sent promptly or currently can be accepted by the seller's actually shipping the goods.

(1) Additional Term in Offer. Unless it is expressly specified that an offer to buy or sell goods must be accepted just as made, the offeree may accept an offer and at the same time propose an additional term. Contrary to the general contract law rule, the new term does not reject the original offer. A contract arises on the terms of the original offer, and the new term is a counteroffer. If, however, the offer states that it must be accepted exactly as made, the ordinary contract law rules apply. If the additional term is treated as a counteroffer, that term does not become binding until accepted by the original offeror.

In a transaction between merchants, the additional term becomes part of the contract if that term does not materially alter the offer and no objection is made to it. However, if such an additional term in the seller's form of acknowledgment operates solely to the seller's advantage, it is a material term and must be accepted to be effective.

In the *Herzog Oil* case the seller sued the buyer for a late payment charge and attorney's fees, pursuant to terms contained in a written confirmation of an oral contract between the parties. The confirmation was sent after delivery of the goods.

HERZOG OIL FIELD SERVICE v OTTO TORPEDO COMPANY

391 Pa Super 133, 570 A2d 549 (1990)

Herzog delivered 2,000 feet of pipe-drilling equipment to Otto. The delivery of the materials was accompanied by the delivery of a "pipe tally report," a type of invoice used in the business, which stated that a finance charge of 1.5 percent per month of the unpaid balance would be added after 30 days. On the same day, a written invoice was sent, listing the materials delivered, the price, the terms (net 30 days) and indicating that balances over 30 days would carry a 1.5 percent monthly finance charge. It also stated that if an account were turned over for collection, attorney's fees in the amount of 25 percent of the balance would be added. No objection to the terms of the invoice was made by Otto to Herzog. Subsequently, Otto refused to pay on the invoice. The trial court held that there was a breach of contract but refused to grant any late payment charge or attorney's fees. Herzog appealed.

---

[4] UCC § 2-206(1).

BRODSKY, J. . . . There seems to be little dispute that the invoice sent by Herzog on the day of delivery is a written confirmation within the meaning of UCC § 2-207. The question appears to be whether a confirmation sent *after delivery* of the goods falls within the scope of § 2-207. We conclude that it does.

. . . The "general rule" portion of § 2-207 states "a written confirmation which is sent within a reasonable time operates as an acceptance even though it states terms additional to or different from those offered or agreed upon. . . ." Subsection (b) indicates that these additional terms are to be construed as proposals for addition which, between merchants, become part of the contract if they are not objected to and if they do not materially alter the agreement. No objection to the terms in question was lodged and, at least as to the late payment charge, the court indicated that they did not constitute a material alteration of the contract. Thus, initially it would seem that there is no requirement that the written documents be sent prior to a delivery of the goods.

. . . The first official comment to UCC § 2-207 states "this section is intended to deal with two typical situations. The one is the written confirmation, where *an agreement has been reached* either orally or by informal correspondence between the parties *and is followed* by one or both of the parties sending formal memoranda embodying the terms so far as agreed upon and adding terms not discussed." (Emphasis added.) The second comment adds: "Under this Article a proposed deal which in commercial understanding has in fact been closed is recognized as a contract. Therefore, any additional matter contained in the confirmation or in the acceptance falls within subsection (2) and must be regarded as a proposal for an added term. . . ." Comment three states: "[w]hether or not additional or different terms will become part of the agreement depends upon the provision of subsection (2). If they are such as materially to alter the original bargain, they will not be included unless expressly agreed to by the other party. If, however, they are terms which would not so change the bargain they will be incorporated unless notice of objection to them has already been given or is given within a reasonable time." . . .

The above material conclusively establishes that confirming memoranda of a previously reached agreement are subject to § 2-207. The only possible distinguishing feature of the present case is that the confirmation was sent after delivery, rather than before. However, from a standpoint of legal principle, this would seem to be an immaterial distinction. All of the above references indicate that the confirming memoranda can effectuate terms in the agreement even when submitted after a commercially acceptable and legally binding contract has been formed. The point of importance is the recognition that a contract can be formed even if many of the particulars or specifics have not been discussed or agreed upon.

Under the Code, there are many ways in which parties can enter into a legal contractual relationship. . . . And certainly upon shipment or acceptance of the goods at the drilling site. . . .

We have little difficulty in determining that the late payment charge term is not one that materially alters the agreement. The trial court reached that conclusion, and comment 5 to § 2-207 states, as an example of a term that does not materially alter the contract, "a clause providing for interest on overdue invoices . . . where they are within the range of trade practice. . . ." Furthermore, it is common in commercial circles, including transactions with nonmerchants, for balances to be subjected to late payment charges. As such, and since no objection to the term was lodged, we find that the trial court erred in not allowing appellant late payment charges as provided in the written confirmation. Under operation of § 2-207 the term must be considered as part of the agreement. . . .

In contrast, however, we find that the provision calling for the addition of an attorney's fee of 25% of the balance due is a material alteration and, therefore, did not become part of the agreement. We come to this conclusion for a few reasons. First, in common experience an attorney's fee provision is considerably less common than a late payment charge provision; thus, it would not be as readily expected or anticipated.

Secondly, when found, such clauses are usually less than 25% of the balance, often 10 or 15%, thus bringing the reasonableness of this particular clause into question. Thirdly, a lump sum addition of 25% changes the obligor's financial obligation under the contract to, what must be considered, a material degree. Fourthly, we choose to follow the precedent of *Johnson Tire Service, Inc. v Thorn, Inc.*, 613 P2d 521, 529 (Utah, 1980), where this conclusion was also reached. There, the Utah court disallowed a clause, purportedly added under operation of § 2-207, which called for the buyer to pay costs of collection including "reasonable attorney's fees," because it found that such a clause constituted a material alteration. Thus, we conclude that the attorney's fee provision constitutes a material alteration of the agreement under § 2-207 and that the trial court correctly refused to enforce it. . . .

[Reversed as to late payment charge, affirmed as to attorney's fee]

QUESTIONS

1. When will additional or different terms to a paper described by UCC § 2-207 become part of an agreement?
2. Did the provision for a late payment charge and the provision for attorney's fees materially alter the agreement?
3. State the decision of the court and the basis for the decision.

A buyer may expressly or by conduct agree to a term added by the seller to the acceptance of the buyer's offer. The buyer may agree orally or in writing to the additional term. There is an acceptance by conduct if the buyer accepts the goods with knowledge that the term has been added by the seller.

(2) Conflicting Term in Offer. When a term of an acceptance conflicts with a term of an offer, but it is clear that the parties intended to be bound by a contract, the UCC recognizes the formation of a contract. The terms that are conflicting cancel out and are ignored. The contract then consists of the terms of the offer and acceptance that agree, together with those terms that the UCC or contract law implies into a contract.

(c) DETERMINATION OF PRICE. The price for goods may be expressly fixed by the contract. If not fixed by the contract, the price may be an open term, whereby the parties merely indicate how the price should be determined at a later time or make no provision whatever as to the price.

When persons experienced in a particular industry make a contract for goods without specifying the price to be paid, the price will be determined by the manner that is customary in the industry. Ordinarily, if nothing is said as to price, the buyer is required to pay the reasonable value of the goods, which is generally the market price.

In recent years, there has been an increase in the use of the "cost plus" formula for determining price. Under this formula, the buyer pays the seller a sum equal to the cost to the seller of obtaining the goods plus a specified percentage of that cost. The percentage represents the seller's profit.

The contract may expressly provide that one of the parties may determine the price. In such a case, that party must act in good faith.[5] The contract may specify that the price shall be determined by some standard or by a third person. For example, Lauf agreed to sell Glynn 1,000 yards of woolens at a price to be fixed by White, a woolen expert. If White fixes the price at $7 a yard, that price is as binding on the buyer and the seller as though it had been fixed by agreement between them. If White refuses to fix a price through no fault of the parties, the price will be a reasonable price, probably the current market price.

(d) OUTPUT AND REQUIREMENTS CONTRACTS.

Somewhat related to the open-term concept concerning price is the concept involved in the output and requirements contracts that the quantity to be sold or purchased is not a specific quantity. Instead, it is the amount that the seller should produce or the buyer should require. Although this introduces an element of uncertainty, such sales contracts are valid. To prevent oppression, they are subject to two limitations: (1) the parties must act in good faith, and (2) the quantity offered or demanded must not be unreasonably disproportionate to prior output or requirements or to a stated estimate.

(e) INDEFINITE DURATION CONTRACT.

When the sales contract is a continuing contract, such as one calling for periodic delivery of fuel, but no time is set for the life of the contract, the contract runs for a reasonable time. It may be terminated on notice by either party.

(f) MODIFICATION OF CONTRACT.

An agreement to modify a contract for the sale of goods is binding even though the modification is not supported by consideration.[6]

(g) PAROL EVIDENCE RULE.

The parol evidence rule applies to the sale of goods, with the slight modification that a writing is not presumed to represent the entire contract of the parties unless the court specifically decides that it does. If the court so decides, parol evidence is not admissible to add to or contradict the terms of the writing. However, such evidence may be admitted to show what the parties meant by their words.

If the court decides that the writing was not intended to represent the entire contract, the writing may be supplemented by parol proof of additional terms, as long as these terms are not inconsistent with the written terms.

(h) USAGE OF TRADE AND COURSE OF DEALING.

The patterns of doing business as shown by the prior dealings of the parties and the usages of the trade enter into and form part of their contract. These patterns may be looked to in order to find what was intended by the express provisions and to supply otherwise missing terms.

(i) FRAUD AND OTHER DEFENSES.

The defenses that may be raised in a suit on a sales contract are, in general, the same as those that may be raised in a suit on any other contract. A defrauded party may cancel the transaction and recover what was paid or the goods that were delivered, together with damages for any loss sustained. If the buyer obtained title by means of fraud, the title is voidable by an innocent seller.

---

[5] Good faith requires that the party act honestly and, in the case of a merchant, also requires the party to follow reasonable commercial standards of fair dealing that are recognized in the trade. UCC §§ 1-201(19), 2-103(1)(b).

[6] UCC § 2-209(1).

If the sales contract or any clause in it was unconscionable when made, a court may refuse to enforce the contract or the unconscionable clause.

4. Illegal Sales

At common law, a sale was illegal if the subject matter itself was illegal. A transaction may also be illegal even though the subject matter of the sale is unobjectionable, if the agreement provides that the goods sold shall be employed for some unlawful purpose or if the seller assists the buyer in an unlawful act.

(a) ILLEGALITY UNDER STATUTES. Every state has legislation prohibiting certain sales when they are not conducted according to the requirements of the statutes. Statutes commonly regulate sales by establishing standards as to grading, size, weight, and measure, and by prohibiting adulteration.

Statutes may regulate the sale of "secondhand" goods. Such a statute does not apply to a casual seller, but only to one whose regular business consists of selling goods of the kind covered by the statute.

States may prohibit the making of sales on Sunday. This may apply either to sales generally or to particular classes of commodities or stores.

The federal Food, Drug, and Cosmetic Act prohibits the interstate shipment of misbranded or adulterated foods, drugs, cosmetics, and therapeutic devices. Such a product that does not carry adequate use instructions and warnings is deemed "misbranded."

(b) EFFECT OF ILLEGAL SALE. An illegal sale or contract to sell cannot be enforced. As a general rule, courts will not aid either party in recovering money or property transferred pursuant to an illegal agreement. Here, the ordinary contract law rule as to illegality is applied. However, if a sale is made illegal by statute, a seller who violates the law may be held liable for the damage caused.

5. Bulk Transfers

Bulk transfer law, Article 6 of the UCC, was created to deal with situations in which sellers of businesses fail to pay creditors but instead use the proceeds of the sale for their own use.

Under Article 6 of the Uniform Commercial Code, when merchants are about to transfer a major part of their materials, supplies, merchandise, or other inventory, not in the ordinary course of business, advance notice of the transfer should be given to creditors. This notice should be given by the transferee.[7] The essential characteristic of businesses subject to Article 6 is that they sell from inventory or a stock of goods, as contrasted with businesses that render services. Thus, a beauty salon is ordinarily a service enterprise and is not subject to the bulk transfer article. This is contrasted with a store selling cosmetics, which is subject to Article 6.

(a) EFFECT OF NONCOMPLIANCE WITH ARTICLE 6. If the notice required by Article 6 is not given, the creditors of the seller may reach the sold property in the hands of the buyer. Creditors may also reach the property in the hands of any subsequent transferee who knew that there had not been compliance with the UCC or who did not pay value. This provision is designed to protect the creditors of a merchant from the merchant's selling all the inventory, pocketing the money, and then disappearing, leaving the creditors unpaid. The protection given to creditors by the bulk transfer legislation is in addition to the protection that they have against their debtor for fraudulent transfers or conveyances, and the

---

[7] In 1989, the National Conference of Commissioners on Uniform State Laws recommended that UCC Article 6 be repealed on the ground that it was obsolete and had little value in the modern business world. At the same time, the commissioners adopted a revised version of Article 6 (Alternative B) for adoption by those states that desired to retain the concept with respect to bulk sales. The states that have adopted each version are listed in the first footnote in Appendix 3. Rather than relying on the bulk sales law, the trend is for suppliers to use UCC, Article 9, "Secured Transactions," for protection.

remedies that can be employed in bankruptcy proceedings.

The fact that there has been noncompliance with Article 6 of the UCC regulating bulk transfers, however, does not affect the validity of a bulk sale of goods between the immediate parties to the transfer. Article 6 governs only the rights of creditors of the transferor.

(b) LIABILITY OF BULK PURCHASER.

Ordinarily, the bulk purchaser who receives the goods does not become liable for the debts of the bulk seller merely because the requirements of Article 6 have not been satisfied. In contrast, if the buyer mixes the transferred goods with other goods so that it is not possible for the creditor to identify the transferred goods that are subject to the creditor's claim, the bulk buyer is personally liable for the debts of the bulk seller, up to the value of the transferred goods.

B. FORM OF SALES CONTRACT

A contract for the sale of goods may be oral or written. In some cases, it must be evidenced by a writing or it cannot be enforced in court.

6. Amount

Whenever the sales price of goods is $500 or more, the sales contract must be evidenced by a writing to be enforceable.[8] The section of the UCC setting forth this requirement is known as the *statute of frauds*.

7. Nature of the Writing Required

The writing evidencing the sales contract may be either (a) a complete written contract signed by both parties or (b) a memorandum signed by the defendant.

(a) TERMS.

The writing must indicate that there has been a completed transaction as to certain goods. Specifically, it need only (1) indicate that a sale or contract to sell has been made[9] and (2) state the quantity of goods involved. Any other missing terms may be shown by parol evidence.

(b) SIGNATURE.

The writing must be signed by the person who is being sued or by the authorized agent of that person. The signature must be placed on the paper with the intention of authenticating the writing. The signature may consist of initials or may be printed, stamped, or typewritten, as long as it is made with the necessary intent.

When the transaction is between merchants, an exception is made to the requirement of signing. The failure of a merchant to repudiate a confirming letter sent by another merchant within ten days of receiving such a letter binds the nonsigner, just as if the receiving merchant had signed the letter. This makes it necessary for a merchant seller to watch the mail and to act within ten days of receiving a mailed confirmation. For example, Allen and Stevens, both merchants, entered into an oral agreement for the sale of chairs to Allen for $1,000. Allen immediately sent Stevens a letter confirming the agreement. Stevens did not make a written objection to the contents of Allen's letter within ten days, but Stevens refuses to deliver the chairs. Stevens is bound by the agreement.

The question of whether the statute of frauds had been satisfied arose in the *Thomson Printing* case.

(c) PURPOSE OF EXECUTION.

A writing can satisfy a statute of frauds, even though it was not made for that purpose. Accordingly, when the buyer writes to the seller 45 days after delivery and merely criticizes the quality of the goods, the letter satisfies the statute,

---

8   UCC § 2-201.
9   Beehive Brick Co. v Robinson Brick Co. (Utah App) 780 P2d 827 (1989).

THOMSON PRINTING MACHINERY CO. v B. F. GOODRICH CO.
(CA7 Ill) 714 F2d 744 (1983)

Thomson Printing buys and sells used printing machinery. Thomson brought suit on an oral contract for the purchase from B.F. Goodrich Company of printing machinery. Goodrich defended on the basis that the Statute of Frauds required a writing. Thomson argued that the statute had been satisfied when Goodrich failed to object to a memorandum of the sale that had been sent within four days after the oral agreement had been made. Goodrich alleged that Thomson had not sufficiently addressed the envelope containing the memorandum and that, consequently, it had never been received by anyone who had reason to know what it concerned. The court sustained these objections and held that the "between merchants" provision had not been satisfied and that accordingly any oral contract between the parties could not be enforced. From a judgment in favor of the defendant, Thomson appealed.

CUDAHY, C. J. . . . A modern exception to the usual writing requirement is the "merchants" exception of the Uniform Commercial Code, § 2-201(2), which provides:

Between merchants if within a reasonable time a writing in confirmation of the contract and sufficient against the sender is received and the party receiving it has reason to know its contents, it satisfies the [writing requirement] against such party unless written notice of objection to its contents is given within 10 days after it is received.

We must emphasize that the only effect of this exception is to take away from a merchant who receives a writing in confirmation of a contract the Statute of Frauds defense if the merchant does not object. The sender must still persuade the trier of fact that a contract was in fact made orally, to which the written confirmation applies.

In the instant case, James Thomson sent a "writing in confirmation" to Goodrich four days after his meeting with Ingram Meyers, a Goodrich employee and agent. The purchase order contained Thomson Printing's name, address, telephone number and certain information about the machinery purchase. The check James Thomson sent to Goodrich with the purchase order also had on it Thomson Printing's name and address, and the check carried notations that connected the check with the purchase order.

Goodrich argues, however, that Thomson's writing in confirmation cannot qualify for the 2-201(2) exception because it was not received by anyone at Goodrich who had reason to know its contents. Goodrich claims that Thomson erred in not specifically designating on the envelope, check or purchase order that the items were intended for Ingram Meyers or the surplus equipment department. Consequently, Goodrich contends, it was unable to "find a home" for the check and purchase order despite attempts to do so, in accordance with its regular procedures, by sending copies of the documents to several of its various divisions. Ingram Meyers testified that he never learned of the purchase order until weeks later when James Thomson called to arrange for removal of the machines. By then, however, the machines had long been sold to someone else.

We think Goodrich misreads the requirements of 2-201(2). First, the literal requirements of 2-201(2), as they apply here, are that a writing "is received" and that Goodrich "has reason to know its contents." There is no dispute that the purchase order and check were received by Goodrich, and there is at least no specific or express requirement that the "receipt" referred to in 2-201(2) be by any Goodrich agent in particular.

These issues are not resolved by [2-201(2)], but it is probably a reasonable projection that a delivery at either the recipient's principal place of business, a place of business from which negotiations were conducted, or to which the sender may have transmitted previous communications, will be an adequate receipt.

As for the "reason to know its contents" requirement, this element "is best understood to mean that the confirmation was an instrument which should have been anticipated and therefore should have received the attention of appropriate parties. The receipt of a spurious document would not burden the recipient with a risk of losing the [Statute of Frauds] defense. . . ." In the case before us there is no doubt that the confirmatory writings were based on actual negotiations (although the legal effect of the negotiations was disputed), and therefore the documents were not "spurious" but could have been anticipated and appropriately handled.

. . . Section 1-201, the definitional section of the U.C.C., provides that notice received by an organization

is effective for a particular transaction . . . from the time when it would have been brought to [the attention of the individual conducting that transaction] if the organization had exercised due diligence.

The Official Comment states:

reason to know, knowledge, or a notification, although "received" for instance by a clerk in Department A of an organization, is effective for a transaction conducted in Department B only from the time when it was or should have been communicated to the individual conducting that transaction.

Thus, the question comes down to whether Goodrich's mailroom, given the information it had, should have notified the surplus equipment manager, Ingram Meyers, of Thomson's confirmatory writing. At whatever point Meyers should have been so notified, then at that point Thomson's writing was effective even though Meyers did not see it.

The definitional section of the U.C.C. also sets the general standard for what mailrooms "should do":

An organization exercises due diligence if it maintains reasonable routines for communicating significant information to the person conducting the transaction and there is reasonable compliance with the routines.

One cannot say that Goodrich's mailroom procedures were reasonable as a matter of law: if Goodrich had exercised due diligence in handling Thomson Printing's purchase order and check, these items would have reasonably promptly come to Ingram Meyers' attention. First, the purchase order on its face should have alerted the mailroom that the documents referred to a purchase of used printing equipment. Since Goodrich had only one surplus machinery department, the documents' "home" should not have been difficult to find. Second, even if the mailroom would have had difficulty in immediately identifying the kind of transaction involved, the purchase order had Thomson Printing's phone number printed on it and we think a "reasonable routine" in these particular circumstances would have involved at some point in the process a simple phone call to Thomson Printing. Thus, we think Goodrich's mailroom mishandled the confirmatory writings. This failure should not permit Goodrich to escape liability by pleading nonreceipt.

We note that the jury verdict for Thomson Printing indicates that the jury found as a fact that the contract had in fact been made and that the Statute of Frauds had been satisfied. Also, Goodrich acknowledges those facts about the handling of the purchase order which we regard as determinative of the "merchants" exception question. We think that there is ample evidence to support the jury findings both of the existence of the contract and of the satisfaction of the Statute.

The district court, in holding as a matter of law that the circumstances failed to satisfy the Statute of Frauds, was impressed by James Thomson's dereliction in failing to specifically direct the purchase order and check to the attention of Ingram Meyers or the surplus equipment department. We agree that Thomson erred in this respect, but, for the reasons we have suggested, Goodrich was at least equally derelict in failing to find a "home" for the well-identified documents. Goodrich argues that in the "vast majority" of cases it can identify checks within a week without contacting an outside party; in the instant case, therefore, if Goodrich correctly states its experience under its procedures, it should presumably have checked with Thomson Printing promptly after the time it normally identified checks by other means—in this case, by its own calculation, a week at most. Under the particular circumstances of this case, we therefore think it inappropriate to set aside a jury verdict on Statute of Frauds grounds. . . .

[Reversed and remanded]

QUESTIONS

1. What does the UCC provide when a merchant sends to another merchant a signed, written confirmation of their oral contract?
2. Does a signed confirmation have to be actually received at the seller's principal place of business?
3. How did the court decide the contention of Goodrich that the confirmation was not received by anyone who had reason to know its contents?

since it indicates that there was a sale of those goods.

(d) PARTICULAR WRITINGS. Formal contracts, bills of sale, letters, and telegrams are common forms of writings that satisfy the requirement. Purchase orders, cash register receipts, sales tickets, invoices, and similar papers generally do not satisfy the requirement as to a signature, and sometimes they do not specify any quantity or commodity.

Two or more writings may constitute the "writing" that satisfies the statute of frauds.[10]

---

[10] Nebraska Building Prod. Co. v The Indus. Erectors, Inc., 239 NEB 744, 478 NW2d 257 (1992).

8. Effect of Noncompliance

A sales agreement that does not satisfy the statute of frauds cannot be enforced. However, the oral contract itself is not unlawful and may be voluntarily performed by the parties.

9. Exceptions to Requirement of a Writing

The absence of a writing does not always bar proof of a sales contract.

(a) NONRESELLABLE GOODS. N o writing is required when the goods are specially made for the buyer and are of such an unusual nature that they are not suitable for sale in the ordinary course of the seller's business. For example, 14 steel doors were tailor-made by the seller for the buyer's building. The doors were not suitable for sale to anyone else in the ordinary course of the seller's business, and they could only be sold as scrap. In this case, the oral contract of sale could be enforced.

In order for the nonresellable goods exception to apply, the seller must have made a substantial beginning in manufacturing the goods or, if a distributor, in procuring them, before notice of repudiation by the buyer is received.

(b) RECEIPT AND ACCEPTANCE. A n oral sales contract may be enforced if it can be shown that the goods were delivered by the seller and were both received and accepted by the buyer. Thus, if the buyer receives and accepts goods on credit, the seller may sue for the purchase price, even if it is over $500 and there is no writing. The receipt and acceptance of the goods by the buyer took the contract out of the statute of frauds. Both a receipt and an acceptance by the buyer must be shown. If only part of the goods had been received and accepted, the contract may be enforced only insofar as it relates to those goods received and

accepted.[11] For example, a seller orally agreed to sell to a buyer 12,000 fountain pens at $12 a dozen. The buyer actually received and accepted from the seller only 1,200 pens. The acceptance and receipt of these pens by the buyer satisfies the statute and enables the parties to enforce against each other the oral contract to the extent of the goods accepted and received. The balance of the contract is unenforceable.

(c) PAYMENT. An oral contract may be enforced if the buyer has made full payment. In the case of part payment for divisible units of goods, a contract may be enforced only with respect to the goods for which payment has been made and accepted. If part payment is made for indivisible goods, such as an automobile, a part payment avoids the statute of frauds and permits proof of the entire oral contract.

(d) ADMISSION. An oral contract may be enforced if the party against whom enforcement is sought admits in pleadings, testimony, or otherwise in court that a contract for sale was made. The contract, however, is not enforceable beyond the quantity of goods admitted.[12]

10. Non-Code Requirements

In addition to the UCC requirement as to a writing, other statutes may impose requirements. For example, state consumer protection legislation commonly requires the execution of a detailed contract and the giving of a copy of it to the consumer.

11. Bill of Sale

Regardless of the requirement of the statute of frauds, the parties may wish to execute a writing as evidence or proof of the sale. Through custom, this writing has become known as a

---

[11] Allied Grape Growers v Bronco Wine Co. 203 Cal App 3d 432, 249 Cal Rptr 872 (1988).
[12] Harvey v McKinney, 221 Ill App 3d 140, 581 NE2d 786 (1991).

520 Part 4 Sales and Leases of Personal Property

bill of sale, but it is neither a bill nor a contract. It is merely a receipt or writing signed by the seller reciting the transfer to the buyer of the title to the described property. The only effect of the bill of sale is to bar the seller from later denying the making of the sale.

C. UNIFORM LAW FOR INTERNATIONAL SALES

The United Nations Convention on Contracts for the International Sale of Goods (CISG) applies to contracts between parties in the United States and parties in the other nations that have ratified the convention.[13] The provisions of this convention or international agreement have been strongly influenced by Article 2 of the Uniform Commercial Code. The international rules of the convention automatically apply to contracts for the sale of goods if the buyer and seller have places of business in different countries that have ratified the convention. The parties may, however, choose to exclude the convention provisions in their sales contract.

12. Scope of the CISG

The CISG does not govern all contracts between parties in the countries that have ratified it. The CISG does not apply to goods bought for personal, family, or household use. The CISG does not apply to contracts in which the preponderant part of the obligations of the party who furnishes the goods consists of the supply of labor or other services. In addition, it does not apply to the liability of the seller to any person for death or personal injury caused by the goods.

The CISG governs the formation of the contract of sale and the rights and obligations of the seller and the buyer arising from such a contract. The CISG provides a basis for an-

swering questions and settling issues the parties failed to deal with in their contracts.

13. Irrevocable Offers

An offer under the CISG is irrevocable if it states that it is irrevocable or if the offeree reasonably relies on it as being irrevocable. Such an offer is irrevocable even if there is no writing and no consideration. In contrast, the UCC requires that an irrevocable offer without consideration must be in writing.

14. Statute of Frauds

Under the CISG, a contract for the sale of goods need not be in any particular form and can be proven by any means. The convention, by this provision, has abolished the statute of frauds requirement of a writing. Countries may, however, retain the UCC requirements of the statute of frauds by requiring certain contracts to be evidenced by a writing.

D. LEASES OF GOODS

Article 2A of the UCC covers leases of tangible movable goods. Any such goods can be sold or leased. As a practical matter leases will be of durable goods, such as equipment and vehicles of any kind, computers, boats, airplanes, and household goods and appliances. A **lease** is "a transfer of the right to possession and use of goods for a term in return for consideration."[14]

15. Types of Leases

Article 2A regulates consumer leases, commercial leases, finance leases, nonfinance leases, and subleases. These categories may overlap in some cases, such as when there is a commercial finance lease.

---

[13] 52 Fed Reg 6262 (1987).
[14] UCC § 2A-103(1)(j).

(a) CONSUMER LEASE. A consumer lease is made by a merchant—a lessor regularly engaged in the business of leasing or selling the kind of goods involved. A consumer lease is made to a natural person (not a corporation) who takes possession of the goods primarily for personal, family, or household use. Total rental payments under a consumer lease cannot exceed $25,000.[15]

(b) COMMERCIAL LEASE. When a lease does not satisfy the definition of a consumer lease, it may be called a nonconsumer or commercial lease. For example, a contractor's rental of a truck for a year to haul building materials is a commercial lease.

(c) FINANCE LEASE. A finance lease is a three-party transaction involving a lessor, a lessee, and a supplier. Instead of going directly to a supplier for goods, the customer goes to a financer and tells the financer where to obtain the goods and what to obtain. The financer then acquires the goods and either leases or subleases the goods to its customer. The financer/lessor is in effect a paper channel, or conduit, between the supplier and the customer/lessee. The customer/lessee must approve of the terms of the transaction between the supplier and the financer/lessor.[16]

16.   Form of the Lease Contract

The lease must be in writing if the total of the payments under the lease will be $1,000 or more. The writing must be signed by the party against whom enforcement is sought. The writing must describe the leased goods, state the term of the lease, and indicate that a lease contract has been made between the parties.[17]

17.   Warranties

Under Article 2A the lessor, except in the case of finance leases, makes all the usual warranties that are made by a seller in a sale of goods. In a finance lease, however, the real parties in interest are the supplier who supplies the lessor with the goods, and the lessee who leases the goods. The supplier and the lessee stand in a position similar to that of seller and buyer. The lessee looks to the supplier of the goods for warranties. Any warranties express or implied made by the supplier to the lessor are passed on to the lessee, who has a direct cause of action on them against the supplier regardless of the lack of privity.[18] The finance lessor does not make any implied warranty; any warranty liability of a financer/lessor must rest upon the lessor's express warranty.

18.   Irrevocable Promises: Commercial Finance Leases

Under the ordinary rule of contract law, the obligations of the lessee and lessor are mutually dependent. In contrast, upon a commercial finance lessee's acceptance of the goods, the lessee's promises to the lessor become irrevocable and independent from the obligations of the lessor. This irrevocability and independence require the lessee to perform even if the lessor's performance after the lessee's acceptance is not in accordance with the lease contract. The lessee must make payment to the lessor no matter how badly the leased goods perform. This is known as a "hell or high water" clause. It does not apply to consumer leases.[19]

In a finance lease the only remedy of the lessee for nonconformity of the goods is to sue the supplier. That is, the lessee can only sue the lessor if it is not a finance lease or if the lessor has made an express warranty or promise.

---

[15] UCC § 2A-103(1)(e).

[16] UCC § 2A-103(1)(g).

[17] UCC § 2A-201(b).

[18] UCC § 2A-209.

[19] UCC § 2A-407.

19. Default

The lease agreement and provisions of Article 2A determine whether the lessor or lessee is in default. If either the lessor or the lessee is in default under the lease contract, the party seeking enforcement may obtain a judgment, or otherwise enforce the lease contract by any available judicial or nonjudicial procedure.

Neither the lessor nor the lessee is entitled to notice of default or notice of enforcement from the other party. Both the lessor and the lessee have rights and remedies similar to those given to a seller in a sales contract.[20] If the lessee defaults, the lessor is entitled to recover any rent due, future rent, and incidental damages.[21]

SUMMARY

A sale of goods is a present transfer of title to movable property for a price. **Goods** means anything movable at the time it is identified as the subject of the transaction. Goods physically existing and owned by the seller at the time of the transaction are existing goods. Goods that are not existing goods are known as future goods. There can be no present sale of future goods, and any agreement to sell such goods operates as a contract to sell.

A bailment is not a sale because no title is transferred. A gift is not a sale since there is no price paid for the gift. A contract for services is an ordinary contract and is not governed by the UCC. If a contract calls for both the rendering of services and the supplying of goods, the contract is classified according to its dominant element.

The law of contracts is applicable to a sale of goods. Contract law as to offers is applicable to a sale of goods, except for rules concerning a firm offer and an acceptance with new terms. In sales contracts, a contract arises on the terms of the original offer and the new terms are considered counteroffers. If the transaction is between merchants, the additional terms become part of the contract if those terms do not materially alter the offer and no objection is made to them.

The price term may be expressly fixed by the parties. The parties may make no provision as to price, or they may indicate how the price should be determined later. In output or requirements contracts, the quantity that is to be sold or purchased is not specified, but such contracts are nevertheless valid. A contract relating to a sale of goods may be modified even though the modification is not supported by consideration. The parol evidence rule applies to a sale of goods in much the same manner as to ordinary contracts that are not for sale of goods. There is the slight modification that a writing is not presumed to represent the entire contract of the parties unless the court specifically decides that it does. Most contract defenses may be raised in a suit on a sales contract. An illegal sale or an illegal contract to sell cannot be enforced.

In many states, if a merchant transfers a major part of the merchants merchandise or inventory not in the ordinary course of business, there must be compliance with the bulk transfer provisions of the UCC.

A sales contract for $500 or more must be evidenced by a writing. Several exceptions exist: the goods are specially made or procured for the buyer and are nonresellable in the seller's ordinary market; the buyer received and accepted the goods; the buyer has made either full or part payment; or the party against whom enforcement is sought admits in court pleadings or testimony that a contract for sale was made.

Uniform rules for international sales are applicable to contracts for sales among parties in countries that have ratified the CISG. Under

---

[20] UCC § 2A-501, 503.

[21] UCC § 2A-529.

the CISG, a contract for the sale of goods need not be in any particular form and can be proven by any means.

Article 2A of the UCC regulates consumer leases, commercial leases, finance leases, non- finance leases, and subleases of tangible mov- able goods. A lease subject to Article 2A must be in writing if the total of the lease payments will be $1,000 or more.

LAW IN PRACTICE

1. Remember that the rules of offer and accep- tance with regard to a sale of goods are different than with ordinary contracts.
2. Contracts for the sale of goods under $500 do not require a writing to be enforceable. However, it is a good practice to have all important contracts evidenced by a writing.
3. If you are a merchant and you receive a confir- mation letter from another merchant concerning your oral agreement, you will become liable even

without your signature if you fail to repudiate the letter within ten days.
4. If your sales contract is with a party in a for- eign country, you should be familiar with the CISG and with which countries have ratified it.
5. Remember, if you are a lessee under a com- mercial finance lease, you are liable to the lessor for payment even if the goods are defective. Your remedy for nonconforming goods is to sue the supplier.

QUESTIONS AND CASE PROBLEMS

1. What social forces are affected by the rule that consideration is not required for a modification of a contract for the sale of goods?
2. Smith-Scharff had sold paper bags to P.N. Hirsch for 36 years. These bags were imprinted with the P.N. logo. A supply of these bags was kept in stock so that when a purchase order was received from Hirsch, Smith-Scharff could fill it promptly. Smith-Scharff ordered these bags from the manufacturer based on its own historical re- cord of sales to Hirsch. Hirsch was aware of the ar- rangement and would provide a generalized profile of its business forecasts to Smith-Scharff. Hirsch was liquidated and its retail outlets sold. The president of Hirsch refused to pay for the bal- ance of the bags remaining in stock with Smith- Scharff on the ground that any oral contract for the bags could not be enforced because there was no writing as required by the statute of frauds. What result? [Smith-Scharff Paper Co. v P.N. Hirsch & Co. (Mo) 754 SW2d 928]
3. Smythe wrote to Lasco Dealers, inquiring as to the price of a certain freezer. Lasco wrote her a let- ter signed by its credit manager stating that Smythe could purchase the freezer in question during the next 30 days at the price of $400. Smythe wrote back the next day ordering a freezer at that price. Smythe's letter was received by Lasco the following day, but Lasco wrote an answering

letter stating that it had changed the price to $450. Smythe claims that Lasco could not change its price. Is she correct?
4. Kucera purchases a refrigerator-freezer from the Elton Appliance Shop for $600. The purchase is made over the phone. Thereafter, Elton sends Kucera a letter thanking her for the purchase of the refrigerator-freezer. Before the refrigerator- freezer is delivered to her, Kucera telephones Elton and cancels the purchase. Elton then sues her for damages. She raises the defense of the statute of frauds. Elton produces a copy of the letter that it sent to Kucera. Does this letter avoid the defense of the statute of frauds?
5. Danfie Company of New York owns leather hides stored in a warehouse in the south of France. Danfie sells some of these hides to the Haldane Company of Chicago. Danfie and Haldane agree that the price shall be determined by Rumfort, who lives in the south of France and is recognized in the trade as an expert in leather. Haldane be- comes dissatisfied with the contract and claims that it is not binding because it is too indefinite in that it does not state the price to be paid for the leather. Is Haldane correct?
6. Valley Trout Farms ordered fish food from Rangen. Both parties were merchants. The invoice that was sent with the order stated that a specified charge would be added to any unpaid bills. This

was a percentage that was common in the industry. Valley Farms did not pay for the food and did not make any objection to the late charge stated in the invoice. When sued by Rangen, Valley Trout claimed that it had never agreed to the late charge and therefore was not required to pay it. Is Valley Farms correct? [Rangen, Inc. v Valley Trout Farms, Inc. 104 Idaho 284, 658 P2d 955]

7. The Tober Foreign Motors, Inc. sold an airplane to Skinner on installments. Later, it was agreed that the amount of the monthly installments should be reduced by one-half. Thereafter, Tober claimed that the reduction agreement was not binding because it was not supported by consideration. Was this claim correct? [Skinner v Tober Foreign Motors, Inc. 345 Mass 429, 187 NE2d 669]

8. The LTV Aerospace Corporation manufactured all-terrain vehicles for use in Southeast Asia. LTV made an oral contract with Bateman under which Bateman would supply the packing cases needed for their overseas shipment. Bateman made substantial beginnings in the production of packing cases following LTV's specifications. LTV thereafter stopped production of its vehicles and refused to take delivery of any cases. When sued by Bateman for breach of contract, LTV raised the defense that the contract could not be enforced because there was no writing that satisfied the statute of frauds. Was this a valid defense? [LTV Aerospace Corp. v Bateman (Tex Civ App) 492 SW2d 703]

9. Syrovy and Alpine Resources, Inc. entered into a "Timber Purchase Agreement." The terms of the agreement were for two years. Syrovy agreed to sell and Alpine agreed to buy all the timber produced during the two years. The timber to be sold, purchased, and delivered was to be produced by Alpine from timber on seller's land. Alpine continued harvesting for one year and then stopped after making an initial payment. Syrovy sued Alpine. Alpine alleged that there was no contract since the writing to satisfy the statute of frauds must contain a quantity term. Decide. [Syrovy v Alpine Resources, Inc. 68 Wash App 35, 841 P2d 1279]

10. Members of the Colonial Club purchased beer from outside the state and ordered it sent to the Colonial Club. The club then kept it in the club refrigerator and served the beer to its respective owners on demand. The club received no compensation or profit from the transaction. The club was indicted for selling liquor. Was it guilty? [North Carolina v Colonial Club, 154 NC 177, 69 SE 771]

11. Fastener Corporation sent a letter to Renzo Box Company. The letter, signed by Ronald Lee, Fasteners sales manager, read as follows: "We hereby offer you 200 type #14 Fastener bolts at $5 per bolt. This offer will be irrevocable for 10 days." On the fifth day, Fastener informed Renzo it was revoking the offer, alleging that there was no consideration for the offer. Could Fastener revoke? Explain.

12. Baker and Smith entered into an oral contract for the purchase and sale of certain goods for the amount of $5,000. Smith admitted in his testimony that he entered into a contract, but he contended that the amount was only $4,500 and that the oral contract was unenforceable because of the statute of frauds. Do you agree with this contention? Why?

13. REMC furnished electricity to Helvey's home. The voltage furnished was in excess of 135 volts causing extensive damage to his 110 volt household appliances. Helvey sued REMC for breach of warranty. Helvey argued that the providing of electrical energy is not a transaction in goods but a furnishing of services so that he had six years to sue REMC rather than the UCC statute of limitations of four years which had expired. Was it a sale of goods or a sale of services? Identify the ethical principles involved in this case. [Helvey v Wabash County REMC (Ind App) 278 NE2d 608]

14. Lawrence Fashions, a retail dress merchant, placed a telephone order with Bentley Company for 240 dresses for a total price of $5,000. The next week, Lawrence Fashions received, inspected, and accepted 120 dresses. Lawrence Fashions refused to accept the balance when tendered and sought to return the other 120 dresses, claiming it was not obligated to keep and pay for them. Decide.

15. Compare a sale, a bailment, and a gift.

16. A is a lessee under two leases. One is a consumer lease, the other is a finance lease. Assume there is a breach of an implied warranty in both situations. Can A prevail in a suit against the supplier for breach of warranty under both types of leases? Why or why not?

CHAPTER 25

RISK AND PROPERTY RIGHTS

LEARNING OBJECTIVES

After studying this chapter, you will be able to:
1. *State when title and risk of loss pass with respect to goods.*
2. *State who bears the risk of loss when goods are damaged or destroyed.*
3. *Classify transactions in which the person dealing with the seller may return the goods.*
4. *Describe contrasting views of courts as to when a sale occurs in a self-service store.*

In most sales, the buyer receives the proper goods and makes payment, and the transaction is thus completed. However, problems may arise. If the parties can foresee potential problems, they can state in their contract what results they desire if such problems do in fact occur. If the parties do not provide in their contract for potential problems, the rules in this chapter apply.

A. TYPES OF TRANSACTIONS AND POTENTIAL PROBLEMS

The solution to problems of risk and property rights depends on the kind and terms of the transaction between the seller and the buyer.

1. Types of Problems

Problems involving risk and property rights in sales transactions often relate to damage to the goods, the claims of creditors of the parties to the sales contract, or the obtaining of insurance by those parties.

(a) DAMAGE TO GOODS. One potential problem occurs if the goods are damaged or totally destroyed without any fault of either the buyer or the seller. Must the seller bear the loss and supply new goods to the buyer? Or is it the buyer's loss, so that the buyer must pay the seller the purchase price even though the goods are damaged or destroyed?[1] The fact that there may be insurance does not avoid this question, because the answer to it determines whose insurer is liable and the extent of that insurer's liability.

(b) CREDITORS' CLAIMS. Another potential problem is that creditors of a seller may seize the goods as belonging to the seller. The buyer's creditors may seize them on the theory that they belong to the buyer. In such cases, the question arises as to whether the creditors are correct about who owns the goods. The question of ownership is also important in connection with the consequence of a resale by the buyer, or the liability for or the computation of certain kinds of taxes, and the liability under certain registration and criminal law statutes.[2]

(c) INSURANCE. Until the buyer has received the goods and the seller has been paid, both the seller and buyer have an economic interest in the sales transaction.[3] The question arises as to whether either or both have enough interest to entitle them to insure the property involved; that is, whether they have an insurable interest.[4]

2. Nature of the Transaction

The answer to each of the questions noted in the preceding section depends on the nature of the transaction between the seller and the buyer. Transactions in goods may be classified according to the nature of the goods and the terms of the transaction.

(a) EXISTING AND IDENTIFIED GOODS. Existing goods are physically in existence and owned by the seller. When particular goods have been selected by either the buyer or the seller, or both, as being the goods called for by the sales contract, the goods are called **identified goods**. Thus, when you go into a store, point at a particular item, and tell the clerk, "I'll take that one," the sales transaction relates to existing and identified goods.

---

[1] The subject is regulated by UCC § 2-509.

[2] UCC § 2-401.

[3] See UCC § 2-501(1),(2).

[4] To insure property, a person must have such a right or interest in the property that its damage or destruction would cause financial loss. This is called an *insurable interest* in the property. The ownership of goods that are the subject of a sales transaction is determined by the UCC for the purpose of insurance.

(b) FUTURE AND UNIDENTIFIED GOODS. Goods are future goods when they are not yet owned by the seller, or when they are not yet in existence. For example, a wholesaler learns from a woolen mill that certain goods have been manufactured and are available for purchase. Before purchasing any of the woolens, the wholesaler makes a contract with Burns, a buyer, to sell a quantity of the merchandise to Burns. These goods are future goods because they are not yet owned by the wholesaler-seller. Before goods have been identified to the contract, they are unidentified. Consequently, when you tell the clerk in the store you want one of the items advertised in the paper, the transaction relates to unidentified goods. Your reference to the newspaper ad describes the thing you want, but it does not identify any particular item as the one the seller is to deliver. Future goods are involved if a store tells you that it is out of the advertised item but can order it from the factory or that the factory is going to make a new run of the item and that it will arrive next month.

(c) TERMS OF THE TRANSACTION. The transaction may involve a transfer of goods or of documents.

(1) Transfer of Goods. Ordinarily, the seller is only required to make the goods available to the buyer. If transportation is provided, the seller is normally only required to make shipment, and the seller's part of the contract is performed by handing the goods over to a carrier for shipment to the buyer. However, the terms of the contract may obligate the seller to deliver the goods at a particular place—for example, to make delivery at the buyer's warehouse. The seller's part of the contract is then not completed until the goods are brought to the destination point and there tendered to the buyer. If the transaction calls for sending the goods to the buyer, it is ordinarily required that the seller deliver the goods to a carrier under a proper contract for shipment to the buyer. Actual physical delivery at destination is required only when the contract expressly so states.

(2) Transfer of Documents. Instead of calling for the actual delivery of goods, the sales transaction may relate to a transfer of the document of title representing the goods. For example, the goods may be stored in a warehouse and the seller and the buyer may have no intention of moving the goods. The parties intend that there shall be a sale and a delivery of the warehouse receipt that stands for the goods. Here the obligation of the seller is to produce the proper paper, as distinguished from the goods themselves. The same is true when the goods are represented by any other document of title, such as a bill of lading issued by a carrier.

3. Existing Goods Identified at Time of Contracting

In a transaction relating to existing and identified goods, where there is no document of title, such as a warehouse receipt or a bill of lading, the title to the goods passes to the buyer at the time the parties agree to the transaction. If there is a document of title, then title to the goods will pass when the buyer receives the document. The parties may always agree in the contract that title to the goods shall not pass to the buyer until the full purchase price has been paid.

When existing goods are identified at the time of contracting, the buyer has an insurable interest in the goods even before title passes to the buyer. The seller also has an insurable interest in the goods before title passes to the buyer. The insurable interest of the seller terminates when title passes to the buyer, unless the seller has a lien or a security interest to protect any balance due on the purchase price.

Regarding risk of loss, a distinction must be made between a merchant seller and a nonmerchant seller. If the seller is a merchant, the risk of loss passes to the buyer on receiving the goods from the merchant. If the seller is a nonmerchant, the risk of loss passes when the seller makes the goods available to the buyer. The risk thus remains longer on the merchant seller. Receiving the goods from a merchant means that the buyer takes actual physical possession of the goods.[5]

When the buyer leaves the purchased goods with the seller, who bears the risk of loss if the goods are destroyed? In the *Schock* case the buyer claimed that the seller bore the risk of loss.

SCHOCK v RONDEROS
(ND) 394 NW2d 697 (1986)

Schock negotiated to purchase a mobile home that was owned by and located on the sellers' property. On April 15, buyer appeared at sellers' home and paid them the agreed-upon purchase price of $3,900. Schock received a bill of sale and an assurance from sellers that the title certificate to the mobile home would be delivered soon. On that date, with the permission of sellers, Schock prepared the mobile home for removal. His preparations included the removal of skirting around the mobile home's foundation, removal of the tie-downs, and removal of the foundation blocks, causing the mobile home to rest on the wheels of its chassis. Schock intended to remove the mobile home from the sellers' property a week later, and sellers had no objection to having the mobile home remain on their premises until that time. Sellers also promised to have the electricity and natural gas disconnected by that time. Two days later, the mobile home was destroyed by high winds as it sat on sellers' property. Schock received in the mail a clear certificate of title to the mobile home. Thereafter, Schock sued the sellers for return of his money on the ground that when the mobile home was destroyed, the risk of loss was on the sellers. From a judgment in favor of the sellers, Schock appealed.

ERICKSTAD, J. . . . The issue of which party in this case must bear the loss of the mobile home is determined by the risk of loss provisions under [UCC § 2-509], which provide in relevant part:

3. In any case not within subsection 1 or 2, the risk of loss passes to the buyer on his receipt of the goods if the seller is a merchant; otherwise the risk passes to the buyer on tender of delivery.

It is undisputed that the Sellers are not merchants; therefore, the risk of loss was on them until they made a "tender of delivery" of the mobile home at which time the risk of loss passed to Buyer. The location or status of the title is not a relevant consideration in determining which party must bear the loss of the mobile home. *Martin v Melland's Inc.*, 283 NW2d 76 (ND 1979).

Pursuant to [UCC § 2-503], tender of delivery requires that the seller "put and hold conforming goods at the buyer's disposition. . . ." The trial court determined that there had been payment for and acceptance of the mobile home by Buyer. Within that conclusion is an implicit determination that there was a completed tender of delivery by Sellers.

---

[5] Spikes v Baier, 6 Kan App 2d 45, 626 P2d 816 (1981).

The Sellers disconnected the electricity and natural gas to the mobile home prior to its destruction, and nothing remained for them to do as a prerequisite to Buyer's taking possession of the home. . . . The Sellers testified that following Buyer's payment for the home on April 15, 1985, Buyer could have removed the home from their premises at any time. . . . The Sellers, consistent with a completed tender of delivery, acquiesced in Buyer's decision to prepare, on April 15, 1985, the mobile home for removal. As part of those preparations Buyer removed the skirting, the tie downs, and the blocks. He also removed and took with him a set of steps to the mobile home. We believe those actions by Buyer constituted an exercise of possession which is consistent with our conclusion that Sellers had tendered delivery of the mobile home to him on that date. Thus, we hold that on April 15, 1985, the Sellers tendered delivery of the mobile home and the risk of loss passed to Buyer. Accordingly, we further hold that the trial court did not err in denying Buyer's claim for return of the $3,900 purchase money. . . .

[Judgment affirmed]

QUESTIONS

1. Did the title certificate have any bearing on who had risk of loss?
2. Was there a tender of delivery of the mobile home?
3. Would the result have been different if the sellers had been merchants?

4. Goods Represented by Negotiable Document of Title

Merchants dealing in large quantities of goods often prefer to deal with negotiable documents of title to the goods rather than to make a physical delivery of the goods. In such a transaction, the buyer acquires an insurable interest in the goods at the time and place of contracting. Unless otherwise provided in the contract, however, the buyer does not become subject to the risk of loss or acquire the title until delivery of the document is made.[6]

5. Future and Unidentified Goods

If the goods either are future goods or have not been identified by the time the transaction is agreed to, the rules stated in Sections 3 and 4 of this chapter do not apply. Instead, the following rules govern the transaction if the parties do not state otherwise.

(a) MARKING FOR BUYER. A buyer may send an order for goods to be manufactured by the seller or to be filled from inventory or by purchases from third persons. If so, one step in the process of filling the order is the seller's act of marking, tagging, labeling, or in some way indicating to the shipping department that certain goods are the ones to be sent or delivered to the buyer under the order. This act of unilateral identification of the goods is enough to give the buyer a property interest in the goods, and it entitles the buyer to insure them. Neither risk of loss nor title passes to the buyer at that time, however. Risk of loss and title remain with the seller, who, as the continuing owner, also has an insurable interest in the goods. Identification takes place and title

---

[6] Express provision is made for the case of a nonnegotiable document and other factual variations. UCC § 2-509(2)(c), § 2-503(4).

will pass when the seller completes performance with respect to the physical delivery of the goods or there is a contract for shipment to the buyer or a contract for delivery at a destination and the seller has tendered the goods to the buyer at that point.

(b) CONTRACT FOR SHIPMENT TO BUYER. In a contract for shipment of future goods to a buyer, the contract is performed by the seller by delivering the goods to a carrier for shipment to the buyer. Under such a contract, the risk of loss and the title pass to the buyer when the goods are delivered to the carrier—that is, at the time and place of shipment. After the goods are delivered to the carrier, the seller has no insurable interest unless the seller has reserved a security interest in the goods.

The fact that a shipment of goods is represented by a bill of lading or an airbill issued by the carrier, and that in order to complete the transaction it will be necessary to transfer that bill to the buyer, does not affect these rules or bring the transaction within Section 4 of this chapter.

(c) CONTRACT FOR DELIVERY AT DESTINATION. When the contract requires the seller to make delivery of future goods at a particular destination, the buyer acquires a property right and an insurable interest in the goods at the time and place they are marked or shipped. However, the risk of loss and the title do not pass until the carrier tenders or makes the goods available at the destination. The seller retains an insurable interest until that time.

Figure 25-1 Risk and Property Rights in Sales Contract

Nature of Goods	Terms of Transaction	Transfer of Risk of Loss to Buyer	Transfer of Title to Buyer	Acquisition of Insurable Interest by Buyer
Existing Goods Identified at Time of Contracting	1. Without document of title	Buyer's receipt of goods from merchant seller, tender of delivery by nonmerchant seller §2–509(3)	Time and place of contracting §2–401(3)(b)	Time and place of contracting §2–501(1)(a)
	2. Delivery of document of title only	Buyer's receipt of negotiable document of title §2–509(2)(a)	Time and place of delivery of documents by seller §2–401(3)(a)	Time and place of contracting §2–501(1)(a)
Future Goods	3. Marking for buyer	No transfer until a later event	No transfer until a later event	At time of marking §2–501(1)(b)
	4. Contract for shipment to buyer	Delivery of goods to carrier §2–509(1)(a)	Delivery of goods to carrier §2–401(2)(a)	Delivery to carrier or marking for buyer §2–501(1)(b)
	5. Contract for delivery at destination	Tender of goods at destination §2–509(1)(b)	Tender of goods at destination §2–401(2)(b)	Delivery to carrier or marking for buyer §2–501(1)(b)

A provision in the contract directing the seller to "ship to" the buyer does not convert the contract into a destination contract.

6. Damage to or Destruction of Goods

In the absence of a contrary agreement, damage to or destruction of the goods affects the transaction as follows.

(a) DAMAGE TO IDENTIFIED GOODS BEFORE RISK OF LOSS PASSES. Goods that were identified at the time the contract was made may be damaged or destroyed without the fault of either party before the risk of loss has passed. If so, the contract is avoided if the loss is total. The loss may be partial or the goods may have so deteriorated that they do not conform to the contract. In this case, the buyer has the option, after inspecting the goods, to either avoid the contract or accept the goods subject to an allowance or deduction from the contract price. In either case, the buyer cannot assert any claim against the seller for breach of contract.

(b) DAMAGE TO IDENTIFIED GOODS AFTER RISK OF LOSS PASSES. If partial damage or total destruction occurs after the risk of loss has passed to the buyer, it is the buyer's loss. The buyer may be able to recover the amount of the damages from the person in possession of the goods or from a third person causing the loss.

(c) DAMAGE TO UNIDENTIFIED GOODS. As long as the goods are unidentified, no risk of loss passes to the buyer. If any goods are damaged or destroyed during this period, the loss is the seller's. The buyer is still entitled to receive the goods described by the contract. The seller is therefore liable for breach of contract if the proper goods are not delivered.

The only exceptions arise when the parties have expressly provided in the contract that the destruction of the seller's supply shall release the seller from liability, or when it is clear that the parties contracted for the purchase and sale of part of the seller's supply to the exclusion of any other possible source of such goods. In this case, the destruction of or damage to the seller's supply is a condition subsequent that discharges the contract.

(d) RESERVATION OF TITLE OR POSSESSION. When the seller reserves title or possession solely as security to make certain that the buyer will pay the purchase price, the risk of loss is borne by the buyer if the circumstances are such that the loss would be on the buyer in the absence of such a reservation.

7. Effect of Seller's Breach

When the seller breaches the contract by sending the buyer goods that do not conform to the contract and the buyer rejects the goods, the risk of loss does not pass to the buyer. This means that the risk of loss remains on the seller, even though the risk would ordinarily have passed to the buyer.[7]

In the *Graybar* case the seller claimed that the buyer should bear the loss of rejected goods when the loss occurred before the seller took the goods back.

8. Returnable Goods Transactions

The parties may agree that conforming goods can be returned to the seller. This may be (a) a sale on approval, (b) a sale or return, or (c) a consignment sale. In the first two types of transactions, the buyer is allowed to return the goods as an added inducement to purchase. The consignment sale is used when the seller is actually the owner's agent for the purpose of selling goods.

Classifying the transaction is the first step in determining the rights of the parties when

---

[7] If, because of the nature of the transaction, the risk of loss had already passed to the buyer before there was the opportunity to inspect the goods, the buyer's rejection of the goods returns the risk of loss to the seller.

GRAYBAR ELECTRIC CO. v SHOOK

283 NC 213, 195 SE2d 514 (1973)

Harold Shook ordered three reels of burial cable from Graybar Company for use in construction work. By mistake, two of the three reels that were sent were aerial cable, although each carton was marked "burial cable." Shook accepted the one reel of proper cable and rejected the two nonconforming reels. Because of their size they were left on the ground at the construction site, Six Run Grocery Store, in a rural community. Graybar was notified of the rejection. Graybar did not collect the cable. Shook attempted to return the cable but could not do so because there was a strike of truck drivers. About four months later the two reels of cable were stolen by unidentified persons. Graybar sued Shook for the purchase price. From a judgment for Shook, Graybar appealed.

HIGGINS, J. . . . The plaintiff contends the defendant contracted to [return the nonconforming cable.] The defendant contends he agreed to contact a trucking company and request that it pick up and return the nonconforming reels. The defendant's request was turned down by three different trucking concerns on account of a strike in the trucking industry.

As the defendant's underground cable work progressed beyond the Six Run Grocery Store, the defendant left the nonconforming cable at the store and so notified the plaintiff. The evidence discloses that the cable was stored directly beside the grocery store building near the owner's dwelling in a space which the defendant rented for storage purposes. "The area where the cable was stored was well lighted at all times."

On July 20, 1970, the defendant discovered that one of the reels had been stolen and the following day notified the plaintiff. On that day, also, the defendant contacted a garage operator who promised to pick up the remaining reel and store it in his garage some distance from Six Run. However, before the transfer, the second reel was stolen. The defendant so notified the plaintiff.

The court, upon the disputed facts, found the defendant had not entered into a contract to return the nonconforming cable. . . .

The plaintiff, having made the error of delivering the nonconforming goods on a moving job in the country, was entitled to notice of the nonconformity sufficient to enable it to repossess the nonconforming goods. The plaintiff was given prompt notice but delayed action for more than three months. The cable was stolen from the defendant's regular storage space where the plaintiff had delivered it. Evidence is lacking that a safer storage space was available. The defendant's workmen moved on, leaving the cable and the responsibility for its safety on the owner.

The plaintiff, failing in its efforts to establish a contract on the part of the defendant to return the shipment, however, contends in the alternative that [UCC §] 2-602(2)(b) . . . required the defendant to exercise reasonable care in holding the rejected goods pending the plaintiff's repossession and removal and that the defendant failed to exercise the required care in storage.

Actually, the plaintiff made an on the spot delivery at a store and dwelling in the country. The defendant's work force was stringing underground cable along the highway and the crew was in continual movement. Obviously the crew could not be expected to carry with it two thousand pounds of useless cable and was within its rights placing the cable in its regular storage space and notifying the plaintiff of the place of storage. Both parties realized that cable weighing almost a ton would require men and a truck to remove it. Also both parties assumed that the danger of theft from a well lighted store area was a minimal risk. The property itself was a poor candidate for larceny. The cable was permitted to remain where the plaintiff knew it was located for more than three months. The plaintiff, therefore, had ample opportunity to repossess its property.

The Uniform Commercial Code emphasizes promptness and good faith. The prospective purchaser may exercise a valid right to reject and even if he takes possession, responsibility expires after a reasonable time in which the owner has opportunity to repossess. "Where a tender or delivery of goods so fails to conform to the contract as to give a right of rejection, the risk of their loss remains on the seller until cure or acceptance." [UCC §] 2-510(1). The defendant did not accept the aerial cable. According to the evidence and the court's findings, the defendant acted in accordance with the request of the owner in attempting to facilitate the return of that which the defendant rejected. The plaintiff with full notice of the place of storage which was at the place of delivery did nothing but sleep on its rights for more than three months.

The superior court was fully justified in the findings of fact, conclusions of law, and in the judgment dismissing the action. The judgment of the Court of Appeals affirming the superior court was correct. . . .

[Judgment affirmed]

QUESTIONS

1. What was the theory of the plaintiff seller?
2. Did the court agree with the seller's theory? Explain.
3. What decision would the court have made if the cable had been stolen within twenty-four hours after the seller was notified of the buyer's rejection?

the buyer may return the goods to the seller. A consignment sale is easily recognized because of its agency characteristics. The agreement of the parties may expressly state that the transaction is a sale on approval or a sale or return. If the agreement of the parties is not clear on this point, and the transaction is not an agency or consignment, classification of the transaction is controlled by the use the buyer will make of the goods. It is a **sale on approval** if the goods are purchased for use by a consumer. It is a **sale or return** if purchased for resale—that is, by a merchant.[8]

If the transaction does not give the buyer the right to return the goods, the buyer cannot return goods that conform to the contract if the seller refuses to take them back.

(a) SALE ON APPROVAL. In a sale on approval, no sale takes place (meaning there is no transfer of title) until the buyer approves. Title and risk of loss remain with the seller

---

[8] Minor v Stevenson, 227 Cal App 3d 1613, 278 Cal Rptr 558 (1991).

until there is an approval. Since the buyer is not the "owner" of the goods before approval, the buyer's creditors cannot reach the goods before the buyer's approval of the goods.

The buyer's approval may be shown by (1) express words, (2) conduct, or (3) the lapse of time. Use of the goods that is merely a trying out or testing does not constitute approval. Any use that goes beyond trying out or testing, such as repairing or giving away as a present, is inconsistent with the continued ownership of the seller. Therefore, such use shows approval by the buyer. The contract may give the buyer a fixed number of days for approval. The expiration of that period of time, without any action by the buyer, constitutes an approval. If no time is stated in the contract, the lapse of a reasonable time without action by the buyer constitutes an approval. If the buyer gives the seller notice of disapproval, the lapse of time thereafter has no effect. For example, Roger sells a motorboat to Bott on two months' trial. At the end of the first month, Bott has the boat repainted. Ownership of the boat passes to Bott at that time, since he has done an act indicating assumption of ownership. If Bott had not repainted the boat but had kept it for two months and a day, ownership in the boat would have been vested likewise in Bott, since he retained possession beyond the agreed trial period. If the boat had been damaged or destroyed during the trial period through no fault of Bott, Roger would bear the loss and would have no action against Bott for the value of the boat.

If the goods are returned by the buyer, the seller bears the risk and expense of the return.[9]

(b) SALE OR RETURN. A sale or return is a completed sale with an option for the buyer to return the goods. The buyer thereby sells or transfers back to the seller the title that had already passed to the buyer. The option to return must be exercised within the time speci-

fied by the contract, or within a reasonable time if none is specified.

As to the original sale, title and risk of loss pass to the buyer, as in the case of the ordinary or absolute sale. Until the actual return of the goods is made, the title and risk of loss remain with the buyer. The expense and risk of return are on the buyer. As long as the goods remain in the buyer's possession, the buyer's creditors may treat the goods as belonging to the buyer.

(c) SALE ON CONSIGNMENT. By a consignment, the owner of goods sends them to a dealer to sell. The seller is the consignor and the dealer is the consignee. The consignee is paid a fee after selling the goods on behalf of the consignor. A consignment sale is treated as a sale or return under the Code. For this reason, creditors of the consignee may obtain possession of the goods and prevail over the consignor. If, however, the consignor complies with the filing provisions of Article 9 (Secured Transactions) to give public notice of the consignment, the goods will then be subject to the claims of the seller's creditors.[10] The goods will not be subject to claims of the consignee's creditors.

9.   Reservation of a Security Interest

The seller may fear that the buyer will not pay for the goods. The seller could protect against this danger by insisting that the buyer pay cash immediately. This may not be practical, for geographic or business reasons. The seller may then give credit to the buyer but obtain protection by retaining a security interest in the goods. When goods are shipped to the buyer, the creditor may create a temporary security interest so that the buyer must make payment before obtaining the goods from the carrier. Between merchants this is done by various ways of handling the bill of lading issued by the carrier. In the case of a consumer

---

[9] UCC § 2-327(1).

[10] Belmont International, Inc. v American International Shoe Co. 313 Or 112, 831 P2d 15 (1992); UCC §2-326(3).

buyer, it is customary for the seller to make the shipment C.O.D. In a C.O.D. shipment, the consumer must pay for the goods before taking possession from the carrier. Under the bill of lading or the C.O.D. shipment, the security interest of the seller ends when the goods are delivered to the buyer. If a seller desires a security interest that will continue as long as the purchase price remains unpaid, a secured transaction under Article 9 of the Uniform Commercial Code could be created.

The fact that a seller has a security interest in the goods, by virtue of a C.O.D. provision or any other device, has no effect on the question of whether title or risk of loss has passed to the buyer. These questions are answered just as though there were no security interest. For example, under a shipment contract of future goods from a distant seller, the risk of loss and the title pass to the buyer on delivery to the carrier. The result is the same even though such shipment is made C.O.D.

10.   Effect of Sale on Title

As a general rule, a seller can sell only what the seller owns. If a person in possession of goods is not the owner, as in the case of a finder, thief, or a bailee, a sale by such possessor passes only possession. It is immaterial that the buyer from the possessor had purchased in good faith and had given value. The attempted sale does not pass any title. Consequently, the buyer of stolen goods must surrender them to the true owner and can be sued by the true owner for damages for conversion of the goods. The fact that the negligence of the owner made the theft possible or contributed to the losing of the goods does not bar the owner from recovering the goods or money damages from the thief, the finder, or the purchaser from either the thief or finder.

In some instances, however, either because of the conduct of the owner or the desire of society to protect the good faith purchaser for value, the law permits a greater title to be transferred than the seller possessed, as in the following situations.

(a) ESTOPPEL.   Because of acting in a way that misleads others, the owner of personal property may be estopped from asserting ownership. The owner would thus be barred from denying the right of another person to sell the property. For example, a minor son buys a car and puts it in his father's name so he can obtain lower insurance rates. If the father then sells the car to a good faith purchaser, the son would be estopped from claiming ownership.

(b) POWERS.   In certain circumstances, persons in possession of someone else's property may sell the property. This is true in the case of pledgees, lienholders, and some finders who, by statute, may have authority to sell the property, either to enforce their claim or when the owner cannot be found.

(c) NEGOTIABLE DOCUMENTS OF TITLE.   By statute, documents of title—bills of lading and warehouse receipts—are negotiable when executed in proper form. By virtue of such provisions the holder of a negotiable document of title may transfer to a good faith purchaser for value such title as was possessed by the person leaving the property with the issuer of the document. In cases of this nature, it is immaterial that the holder had not acquired the document in a lawful manner.

(d) VOIDABLE TITLE.   If the buyer has a voidable title—for example, when the goods were obtained by fraud—the seller can rescind the sale. However, if the buyer resells the property to a good faith purchaser before the seller has rescinded the transaction, the subsequent purchaser acquires valid title. It is immaterial whether the buyer having the voidable title had obtained title by fraud as to identity or by larceny by trick, or had paid for the goods with a bad check, or that the transaction was a cash sale and the purchase price had not been paid.[11]

If the transferee from the holder of the voidable title is not a good faith purchaser, the title remains voidable. The true owner may reclaim the goods.

(e) SALE BY ENTRUSTEE. If the owner entrusts goods to a merchant who deals in goods of that kind, the latter has the power to transfer the entruster's title to anyone who buys from the entrustee in the ordinary course of business.

It is immaterial why the goods were entrusted to the merchant. Hence, the leaving of a watch for repair with a jeweler who sells new and secondhand watches gives the jeweler the power to pass the title of the repair customer to a buyer in the ordinary course of business. Goods in inventory thus have a degree of "negotiability." The ordinary buyer, whether a consumer or another merchant, buys the goods free of the ownership interest of the person entrusting the goods to the seller. The entrustee is, of course, liable to the owner for damages caused by the entrustee's sale of the goods. The entrustee is also guilty of some form of statutory offense of embezzlement.

In the case of an entrustee who is not a merchant, such as a prospective customer trying out an automobile, there is no transfer of title to the buyer from the entrustee. Similarly, there is no transfer of title when a mere bailee, such as a repairer, who is not a seller of goods of that kind, sells the property of a customer.

In the *Alamo* case there was a question of whether an entrustment occurred.

ALAMO RENT-A-CAR, INC. v WILLIAMSON CADILLAC CO.

(Fla App) 613 A2d 517 (1993)

Frank Verdi rented a Cadillac from Alamo for a week for his individual use. Two days later, Verdi incorporated Verdi Fleet Systems, Inc., listing himself as sole director and registered agent. Verdi then forged an application for and received a duplicate title to the car. Three days after he received the duplicate title, and two days after he was to return the car to Alamo, Verdi had the corporation sell the car to Williamson. Two other Cadillacs had also been sold to Williamson. Those cars had apparently been simlarly obtained and titled. Alamo appealed from a judgment giving Williamson superior rights to the cars.

SCHWARTZ, C. J. . . . It is of course the general rule that a thief such as Verdi cannot pass good title. . . . Williamson's invocation of the exception to that rule contained in [UCC § 2-]403(2) is to no avail. That provision states:

(2) Any entrusting of possession of goods to a merchant who deals in goods of that kind gives him power to transfer all rights of the entruster to a buyer in ordinary course of business.

This section does not apply because Alamo did not "entrust" the Cadillac to "a merchant who deals in goods of that kind." At the time he leased the car, Verdi was plainly not such a person; he, or rather his corporation, only became one two days later. Moreover . . . the vehicle could not have been "entrusted"—a term which itself connotes knowledge and volition—in the admitted absence of any indication that Alamo was aware of Verdi's unlawful business or intent. The very basis of [UCC §2-]403(2) is to place on the owner the burden of losing his property if he knowingly

---

[11] Florida East Coast Properties, Inc. v Best Contract Furnishings, Inc. (Fla App) 593 So 2d 560 (1992).

takes the chance of delivering it to a person in the business of dealing with goods of that kind. . . .

The point is made by the distinction between these facts and those in the case on which Williamson most heavily relies, *Carlsen v Rivera*, 382 So 2d 825 [29 UCC Rep Serv 500] (Fla 4th DCA 1980). That decision, in which the purchaser from the embezzler of a leased vehicle indeed prevailed over the owner, rested entirely upon the fact that the lessor rented the car to

"one James McEnroe who he knew to be the owner of an automobile dealership."

Carlsen, 382 So 2d at 825. The principles applicable when this is *not* the case are well stated . . . [and] we are content to follow and adopt [them].

[Judgment reversed]

QUESTIONS

1. What is meant by an entrustment under the UCC?
2. Was there an entrustment by Alamo?
3. What was the basis for the court's decision?
4. Were Verdi's actions ethical?

B. SPECIAL SITUATIONS

Risk and property rights in the case of goods in self-service stores and goods sold at auction will be discussed in the following sections.

11. Self-Service Stores

In the case of goods in a self-service store, the reasonable interpretation of the circumstances is that the store, by its act of putting the goods on display on the shelves, makes an offer to sell such goods for cash and confers on a prospective customer a license to carry the goods to the cashier in order to make payment. Most courts hold that there is no transfer of title until the buyer makes payment to the cashier. On this rationale, no warranty liability of the store arises before the buyer pays.

A contrary rule adopts the view that "a contract to sell" is formed when the customer "accepts" the seller's offer by taking the item from the shelf.

By another contrary view, a sale actually occurs when the buyer takes the item from the shelf. That is, title passes at that moment to the buyer, even though the goods have not yet been paid for. Under this view, if the buyer places the item back on the shelf, this is merely a "return" by the buyer. By this return, the buyer transfers back to the seller the title that had already passed to the buyer when the item was removed from the shelf.

12. Auction Sales

When goods are sold at an auction in separate lots, each lot is a separate transaction, and title to each passes independently of the other lots. Title to each lot passes when the auctioneer announces by the fall of the hammer or in any other customary manner that the lot in question has been sold to the bidder.

SUMMARY

Problems relating to risk and property rights in sales transactions often involve damage to the goods, the claims of creditors, and insurance. The solution to these problems often depends on the nature of the transaction between the seller and the buyer. Sales transactions may be classified according to the nature of the goods and the terms of the transactions.

Existing goods are physically in existence and owned by the seller. Future goods are not yet owned by the seller or are not yet in existence. The title to existing goods that are identified at the time of the contract passes to the buyer at the time the parties agree to the transaction. Once the goods are identified, both the buyer and the seller have an insurable interest in the goods. If the goods are damaged after the sales agreement has been made, a merchant seller bears the loss occurring until the time the buyer receives the goods. If the seller is not a merchant, the risk of loss passes to the buyer when the goods are tendered or made available to the buyer. In a shipment contract, title and risk of loss pass at the time and place of shipment; in a destination contract, title and risk pass when the goods are made available at the destination. As long as the goods are unidentified, neither title nor risk of loss passes to the buyer.

In cases where the risk of loss would ordinarily pass to the buyer, the risk remains with the seller if the goods do not conform to the contract. Even when the goods do conform to the contract, the buyer and seller could have agreed in their contract that the goods may be returned. The nature of their agreement, such as a sale on approval, sale or return, or consignment sale, determines who has title and who bears the risk of loss.

The reservation of a security interest in goods does not affect the question of whether title or risk of loss has passed to the buyer.

Ordinarily, sellers cannot pass any better title than they possess. In some cases, however, the law permits a greater title to be transferred.

In an auction sale, title passes when the auctioneer accepts the bidder's offer.

LAW IN PRACTICE

1. Important written sales contracts should state when title and risk of loss are to pass.
2. If you transfer goods on consignment, be sure to comply with the filing provisions of the UCC to obtain protection from the consignee's creditors.

3. If a consumer buyer's credit is in doubt, sell goods on a COD basis or by a secured transaction under UCC Article 9.

QUESTIONS AND CASE PROBLEMS

1. What social forces are affected by the rule that the buyer has an insurable interest when future goods are marked for shipment to the buyer?
2. Stanley borrowed a lawn mower from Rita, his neighbor. He immediately sold it to Jones. Jones purchased the lawn mower without knowledge that Rita was the true owner. Does Rita have the right to recover the lawn mower from Jones? Explain.
3. Kirk buys a television set from the Janess Television Store. At the time of the sale, Kirk gives Janess a check for the purchase price and obtains a receipt marked "paid in full." The check is a bad check, since it is drawn on an account in which the balance is insufficient to cover the amount of the check. Kirk knows this but hopes to leave town with the television set before Janess learns that the check is bad. Is Kirk the owner of the television set?
4. Lotus Corporation sold and delivered a photocopier to Smith, for use in Smith's business. According to their agreement, Smith may return the copier within 30 days. During the 30-day period, Smith's place of business burns to the ground. Who had title to the photocopier at the time it was destroyed? Who had risk of loss? Explain.

5. Jamison wants to buy a new truck. Kenton, a dealer, tries to sell him a particular truck. Jamison is not certain that this is the truck he wants. To encourage him to buy, Kenton sells the truck to him on "30-day approval." Jamison owes the First National Bank on an overdue debt, and 25 days later the bank has the sheriff seize the truck in order to sell it to pay off the debt owed by Jamison. Both Kenton and Jamison object that the bank cannot do this. Are they correct?

6. A thief stole a television set and sold it to a good faith purchaser for value. This person resold the set to another buyer, who also purchased in good faith and for value. The original owner of the set sued the second purchaser for the set. The defendant argued that he had purchased it in good faith from a seller who had sold in good faith. Was this defense valid? *[Johnny Dell, Inc. v New York State Police, 84 Misc 2d 360, 375 NYS2d 545]*

7. Using a bad check, *B* purchased a used automobile from a dealer. *B* then took the automobile to an auction, at which the automobile was sold to a party who had no knowledge of its history. When *B's* check was dishonored, the dealer brought suit against the party who purchased the automobile at the auction. Was the dealer entitled to reclaim the automobile? *[Greater Louisville Auto Auction, Inc. v Ogle Buick, Inc. (Ky) 387 SW2d 17]*

8. Coppola collected coins. He joined a coin club, First Coinvestors, Inc. The club would send coins to its members, who were to pay for them or return them within ten days. What was the nature of the transaction? *[First Coinvestors, Inc. v Coppola, 88 Misc 2d 495, 388 NYS2d 833]*

9. Sandford signed an agreement to purchase a used calculator from Roberts, a dealer in such equipment. Sandford agreed to pick it up the next day. The Roberts salesperson marked the calculator "sold," placed Sandford's name on it, and moved it to the storeroom. That night thieves broke into the storeroom and took everything, including the calculator. This was in no way caused by the negligence of Roberts. Sandford refuses to pay unless he receives his calculator. Who bears the risk of loss? Why?

10. A manufacturer of knitwear loaded a trailer with goods ordered by the buyer. The loaded trailer was to be hauled away by a carrier. After the trailer was loaded but before it was taken away, it was damaged by fire. The manufacturer claimed that the buyer must bear the risk of loss because the goods were future goods covered by a shipment contract. Was the manufacturer correct?

[A. M. Knitwear Corp. v All America Export-Import Corp. 50 App Div 2d 558, 375 NYS2d 23]

11. Larsen Jewelers sold a necklace to Conway on a layaway plan. Conway paid a portion of the price and made additional payments from time to time. The necklace was to remain in the possession of Larsen until payment was fully made. The Larsen jewelry store was burglarized. Conway's necklace and other items were taken in the burglary. Larsen argues that Conway must bear the risk of loss. Conway seeks recovery of the full value of the necklace. Decide. *[Conway v Larsen Jewelers, 429 NYS2d 378, 104 Misc 2d 872]*

12. The Leton Wholesale Company sold and delivered ten executive desks on consignment to Frelow, the owner and manager of the Handy Office Supply Company. Frelow had severe financial problems, and her creditors petitioned the court to allow attachment of her inventory. A marshal seized the entire inventory of the Handy Office Supply Company, including the ten executive desks. Explain how the Leton Wholesale Company could have prevented the desks from becoming subject to the claim of Frelow's creditors.

13. Smith operated a marina and sold and repaired boats. Gallagher rented a stall at the marina, where he kept his vessel, the River Queen. Without any authorization, Smith sold the vessel to Courtesy Ford. Gallagher sued Courtesy Ford for the vessel. What was the result? *[Gallagher v Unenrolled Motor Vessel River Queen (CA5 Tex) 475 F2d 117]*

14. Without permission, Grissom entered onto land owned by another. He then proceeded to cut and sell the timber from the land. On learning that the timber had been sold, the owner of the land brought an action to recover the timber from the purchaser. The purchaser argued that he was a good faith purchaser who had paid value and therefore was entitled to keep the timber. Decide. *[Baysprings Forest Products, Inc. v Wade (Miss) 435 So 2d 690]*

15. Brown Sales ordered goods from Everhard Manufacturing Company. The contract contained no agreement as to who would bear the risk of loss. There were no shipping terms. The seller placed the goods on board a common carrier with instructions to deliver the goods to Brown. While in transit, the goods were lost. Which party will bear the loss? Explain. *[Eberhard Manufacturing Co. v Brown, 61 Mich App 268, 232 NW2d 378]*

CHAPTER 26

OBLIGATIONS AND PERFORMANCE

LEARNING OBJECTIVES

After studying this chapter, you will be able to:
1. *Define the obligation of good faith as applied to merchants and nonmerchants.*
2. *State what steps can be taken by a party to a sales contract who feels insecure.*
3. *State the obligations of the seller and the buyer in a sales contract.*
4. *Identify conduct that constitutes an acceptance of goods.*

Contracts for the sale of goods impose certain obligations on the parties.

A. GENERAL PRINCIPLES

Each party to a sales contract is bound to perform according to the terms of the contract. Each is likewise under the duty to exercise good faith in the contract's performance and to do nothing that would impair the other party's expectation that the contract will be performed.

1. Obligation of Good Faith

"Every contract or duty within [the UCC] imposes an obligation of good faith in its performance or enforcement."[1] The UCC defines good faith as meaning "honesty in fact in the conduct or transaction concerned."[2] In the case of a merchant seller or buyer of goods, the UCC carries the concept of good faith further. The UCC imposes the additional requirement that the merchant observe "reasonable commercial standards of fair dealing in the trade."[3]

In the *Umlas* case, the owner of a car wanted to trade it in on the purchase of a new car. He claimed that the dealer did not observe good faith in making a reappraisal of the used car.

UMLAS v ACEY OLDSMOBILE, INC.

(NY Civil Court) 62 Misc 2d 819, 310 NYS2d 147 (1970)

Harry Umlas made a contract to buy a new automobile from Acey Oldsmobile. He was allowed to keep his old car until the new car was delivered. The sales contract gave him a trade-in value of $650 on the old car, but specified that it would be reappraised when it was actually brought in to the dealer. When Umlas brought the trade-in to the dealer, an employee of Acey took it for a test drive and told Acey that it was worth from $300 to $400. Acey stated to Umlas that the trade-in would be appraised at $50. Umlas refused to buy from Acey and purchased from another dealer who appraised the trade-in at $400. Umlas sued Acey for breach of contract. Acey defended on the ground that its conduct was authorized by the reappraisal clause.

SANDLER, J. . . . Underlying plaintiff's lawsuit is the charge . . . that the reappraisal was not done in good faith.

The defendant interposed a counterclaim for an amount just in excess of $300.00 that is totally without any semblance of merit, and that was obviously designed to harass the plaintiff by removing the case from the Small Claims Part of this Court.

I find as a fact that defendant's employee did state to plaintiff that he had reappraised plaintiff's car in the amount of $50.00 . . . and that this valuation was not made in good faith.

---

[1] UCC § 1-203.
[2] UCC § 1-201(19); Chemical Bank of Rochester v Haskell, 51 NY2d 85, 432 NYS2d 478, 411 NE2d 1339 (1980).
[3] UCC § 2-103(1)(b).

The critical legal question thus becomes whether the provision of the form order, under which defendant reserved the right to reappraise the used car allowance at the time of delivery where delivery is deferred, implies that the right of reappraisal is to be exercised in good faith. I conclude as a matter of law that good faith is an essential implied condition for the exercise of the right of reappraisal. See Uniform Commercial Code, 1-201, 2-103; c.f. 2-305.

To hold otherwise would mean that the order agreement, and the promises exchanged therein, was intended to be wholly illusory until delivery had been completed. Such a construction would make a travesty of an agreement that evoked from the plaintiff, as it was intended to, the following substantial reliance: a down payment, suspension for a period of his right to acquire a car elsewhere, and the securing of a bank loan. . . .

In reaching the above conclusion, I do not wish to be understood as doubting the legitimate considerations prompting the provision in question when the delivery of the car is to be deferred. Obviously, the buyer's car may suffer some deterioration during the intervening period. . . .

But the fact that the clause represents a reasonable response to a practical problem does not obscure the reality that it is open to, and indeed lends itself to, serious and recurrent abuse. In the presence of a potential buyer, searching for the optimum price for his used car, a dealer may well be disposed to place a generous value on the used car, realizing that he could later renegotiate the figure when his bargaining position was immensely strengthened.

For it is surely clear that when a buyer has signed an order for a particular car of a certain color and with special accessories, has made a cash down payment, has secured a bank loan, and has arrived in his somewhat worn old car ready to receive a resplendent new vehicle, his ability to resist a new less-favorable deal is at a very low ebb indeed.

Surely, it is no surprise that defendant's witness acknowledged that used car allowances are often lowered at the delivery date. And although no testimony was presented directly, it is surely a fair surmise that instances in which used cars are found to have a higher value at the delivery date would represent extraordinary phenomena in the annals of any car dealer.

. . . The plaintiff, like any purchaser under the circumstances, was entitled to a good faith valuation of his car on the delivery date.

In the absence of any good faith reappraisal by the defendant, the only valuation by the defendant is that fixed at the time of the original order, and I find that to be controlling.

Accordingly, I find for the plaintiff. . . .

QUESTIONS

1. What part of the contract between Umlas and Acey was violated?
2. What could Umlas have done for his protection?
3. Compare the *Umlas* decision and the common law concept of "let the buyer beware."

2. Time Requirements of Obligations

In the case of a cash sale not requiring the physical moving of the goods, the duties of the seller and buyer are concurrent. Each one has the right to demand that the other perform at the same time. That is, as the seller hands over the goods, the buyer theoretically must hand over the purchase money. If either party refuses to act, the other party has the right to withhold performance.

3. Repudiation of the Contract

The seller or the buyer may refuse to perform the contract when the time for performance arises. This is a **repudiation** of the contract. Similarly, before the time for performance arrives, one party may inform the other that the contract will never be performed. This repudiation made in advance of the time for performance is called an **anticipatory repudiation**.[4]

4. Adequate Assurance of Performance

A party to a sales contract may think that the other party will not perform the contract. For example, the seller's warehouse is destroyed by fire. The buyer could fear that the seller will not be able to make a delivery scheduled for the following month. Whenever a party to a sales contract has reasonable grounds for being concerned about the future performance of the other party, a written demand may be made on such other party for assurance that the contract will be performed.[5]

(a) FORM OF ASSURANCE. The person on whom demand for assurance is made must give "such assurance of due performance as is adequate under the circumstances of the particular case." The exact form of assurance is not specified by the UCC. If the party on whom demand is made has an established reputation, a reaffirmation of the contract obligation and a statement that it will be performed may be sufficient to assure a reasonable person that it will be performed. In contrast, the person's reputation or economic position at the time may be such that mere words and promises would not give any real assurance. In this case, it may be necessary to have a third person (or an insurance company) guarantee performance or to put up property as security for performance.

(b) FAILURE TO GIVE ASSURANCE. If adequate assurance is not given within 30 days, the demanding party may treat the contract as repudiated. The demanding party may then sue for damages for breach of contract. In addition, a demanding buyer may make a substitute contract with a third person to obtain goods covered by a broken contract.

In the *Ward Transformer* case, the buyer objected to a demand for adequate assurance of performance.

WARD TRANSFORMER CO. v DISTRIGAS OF MASSACHUSETTS CORP.
(ED NC) 18 UCCRS 2d 29 (1992)

Ward Transformer and Distrigas of Massachusetts Corp. (DOMAC) entered into a contract for the sale of a reconditioned transformer. The date of delivery was left open. DOMAC, the buyer, inquired as to the seller's charges for cancelling

---

[4] SS, Inc. v Meyer (Iowa App) 478 NW2d 587 (1991).
[5] Scott v Crown Co. (Colo App) 765 P2d 1043 (1988).

the contract. Ward then sent an invoice to the buyer demanding payment in full within thirty days, even though payment was not due under the contract until after delivery. The buyer declined to pay the full purchase price but offered to make a progress payment of 15 percent. Ward demanded 50 percent immediately and the other 50 percent within thirty days after delivery. DOMAC refused and cancelled the contract. DOMAC subsequently purchased a transformer from another company for substantially the same price. Ward filed an action for breach of contract. Ward argued that it had reasonable grounds for insecurity and that its invoice was a demand for adequate assurance and that the buyer's response was not adequate. DOMAC contended that it never gave Ward reasonable grounds to believe that it would not perform and that even if it did, Ward never made a written demand for adequate assurance in proper form. DOMAC further contends that if demand was proper, the demand called for assurances that were commercially unreasonable.

DUPREE, J. . . . In arguing that DOMAC repudiated the contract, Ward relies on UCC § 2-609 to support its position. Section 2-609 provides, in part, as follows:

"(1) A contract for sale imposes an obligation on each party that the other's expectation of receiving due performance will not be impaired. When reasonable grounds for insecurity arise with respect to the performance of either party the other may in writing demand adequate assurance of due performance and until he receives such assurance may if commercially reasonable suspend any performance for which he has not already received the agreed return.
. . .
"(4) After receipt of a justified demand failure to provide within a reasonable time not exceeding thirty days such assurance of due performance as is adequate under the circumstances of the particular case is a repudiation of the contract."

[UCC § 2-609.

. . . Before a party to a contract can properly demand adequate assurances of performance, he must first have reasonable grounds to believe that the other party will not duly perform its obligations under the contract, UCC § 2-609(1), and a subsequent determination of whether reasonable grounds existed is a question of fact. . . . In this regard, the court first notes that Ward claims the invoice it sent to DOMAC . . . constituted its demand for adequate assurances of performance. Although the court challenges the correctness of this assertion, accepting it as true would mean that DOMAC would have to have done or omitted to do something which gave rise to reasonable grounds for insecurity on the part of Ward. . . .

Assuming . . . that Ward did have reasonable grounds for insecurity, and that it made a demand for adequate assurances of performance which was proper in form, the court is nonetheless drawn to the conclusion that Ward unreasonably suspended its performance.

Section 2-609(1) provides a party having reasonable grounds for insecurity may suspend its performance if it is commercially reasonable to do so, and then, only until such time as he receives adequate assurances of performance. Ward's suspension of its performance was commercially unreasonable. . . .

Ward demanded payment of the entire purchase price . . . even though the contract terms expressly made payment due thirty days after satisfactory delivery.

. . . DOMAC, in a good faith effort to avoid a dispute, offered Ward a progress payment of fifteen percent of the purchase price, even though such a payment was not required under the terms of the contract. Although Ward subsequently reduced its demand to a payment of fifty percent of the purchase price . . . the fact remains that it was actually entitled to nothing prior to shipment of the transformer. If Ward had truly had reasonable grounds for insecurity, then DOMAC's offer to pay fifteen percent of the purchase price ought to have adequately assured Ward that DOMAC intended to honor the contract.

. . . DOMAC authorized the "immediate shipment" of the transformer, but Ward continued to refuse delivery without a fifty percent payment. . .

Ward's stance on the delivery issue was especially unreasonable in light of the fact that it knew at the time it contracted that the date of delivery was uncertain, and in light of the fact that it had indicated that it would be flexible with DOMAC in determining a delivery date.

. . . In the absence of any evidence that DOMAC was not ready, willing and able to comply fully with its . . . request for immediate delivery of the transformer and pay the full purchase price within thirty days following delivery such request constituted adequate assurance of performance and terminated any right which Ward may have had under its own theory to suspend performance on its part.

In sum, the court concludes that Ward's suspension of its performance pending the payment of fifty percent of the purchase price constituted a violation of the contract of purchase and was commercially unreasonable. . . .

[Judgment for DOMAC]

QUESTIONS

1. What is meant by "adequate assurance of performance"?
2. Were there grounds for insecurity?
3. Could a buyer's request for cancellation be a basis for grounds for demanding adequate assurance of performance?
4. What was the basis for the court's decision?

B. DUTIES OF THE PARTIES

The obligations of the parties to a sales contract include (1) the seller's duty to deliver the goods, (2) the buyer's duty to accept the goods, and (3) the buyer's duty to pay for the goods. In addition, special terms may give rise to other duties of the parties.

5. Seller's Duty to Deliver

The seller has the duty to deliver the goods in accordance with the terms of the contract. This duty to make "delivery" does not require physical transportation but merely means that the seller must permit the transfer of possession of the goods to the buyer. That is, the seller makes the goods available to the buyer. The delivery is sufficient if it is made in accordance with the terms of the sale or contract to sell.

(a) PLACE, TIME, AND MANNER OF DELIVERY. The terms of the contract determine whether the seller is to send the goods or the buyer is to call for them, whether the goods must be transported by the seller to the buyer, or whether the transaction is to be completed by the delivery of documents without the movement of the goods. In the absence of a provision in the contract or a contrary course of performance or usage of trade, the place of delivery is the seller's place of business, if the seller has one; otherwise, it is the seller's residence. However, if the subject matter of the contract consists of identified goods that are known by the parties to be in some other place, that place is the place of delivery. If no time for shipment or delivery is stated, delivery or shipment is required within a reasonable time.

When a method of transportation called for by the contract becomes unavailable or commercially unreasonable, the seller must make delivery by means of a commercially reasonable substitute, if available.

(b) QUANTITY DELIVERED. The buyer has the right to insist that all the goods be delivered at one time. If the seller delivers a smaller or larger quantity than what is stipulated in the contract, the buyer may refuse to accept the goods.

(c) CURE OF DEFECTIVE TENDER OR DELIVERY. If the seller tenders or delivers nonconforming goods, the buyer may reject them. This does not end the transaction. The seller is given a second chance to make a proper or **curative tender** of conforming goods.[6]

This right is restricted in terms of whether the second tender can be made within the time called for by the contract. If the time for making delivery under the contract has not expired, the seller need only give the buyer **seasonable** (timely) notice of the intention to make a proper delivery within the time allowed by the contract. The seller may then do so. However, if the time for making the delivery has expired, the seller may be given an additional reasonable time in which to make a substitute conforming tender. Additional time is allowed if (1) the seller so notifies the buyer, and (2) the seller had acted reasonably in making the original tender, believing that it would be acceptable to the buyer.

The *Worldwide* case deals with the right of the seller to cure a tender of goods that did not conform to the contract specifications.

WORLDWIDE RV SALES & SERVICE, INC. v BROOKS
(Ind App) 534 NE2d 1132 (1989)

Brooks agreed to buy from Worldwide a motor home with dual air conditioners. Brooks discovered that the motor home had only one air conditioner. Brooks rejected the motor home. Worldwide offered to put in the two air conditioners originally requested and remove the other one, leaving a hole in the roof. Brooks refused the offer. Worldwide refused to refund his down payment. From a judgment in favor of Brooks, Worldwide appealed.

STATION, J. . . . This matter falls under the Uniform Commercial Code Sales, [Section] 2-101 et seq. Worldwide argues that [UCC §] 2-508 entitled it to cure the problem and prevent cancellation of the contract. That section states that:

---

6 UCC § 2-508. Stephenson v Frazier (Ind App) 399 NE2d 794 (1980).

(1) Where any tender or delivery by the seller is rejected because non-conforming and the time for performance has not yet expired, the seller may seasonably notify the buyer of his intention to cure and may then within the contract time make a conforming delivery.

(2) Where the buyer rejects a non-conforming tender which the seller had reasonable grounds to believe would be acceptable with or without money allowance the seller may if he seasonably notifies the buyer have a further reasonable time to substitute a conforming tender.

Worldwide claims that on the same day Brooks rejected the motorhome Worldwide offered to install a second roof air conditioner at no extra charge. Our examination of the record reveals that Worldwide's representative asked if the deal could be saved if they installed a second roof air conditioner. This "offer to cure" was accompanied with the warning that this alteration would result in a hole in the center of the motorhome. To benefit from the remedial effect of [UCC §] 2-508 the seller must "make a conforming delivery" or "substitute a conforming tender." Worldwide did not fulfill this statutory requirement.

Worldwide's brief states that Worldwide tendered conforming goods on the same day Brooks rejected them. The facts do not substantiate this claim. [UCC §] 2-503 states in pertinent part that "tender of delivery requires that the seller put and hold conforming goods at the buyer's disposition and give the buyer any notification reasonably necessary to enable him to take delivery." We have already determined that Brooks rejected the goods because they were non-conforming and that Worldwide's offer to cure was inadequate.

[Judgment affirmed]

QUESTIONS

1. Was the buyer's rejection proper?
2. What are the requirements for the seller's right to cure?
3. Did the seller act properly in exercising the right to cure?

6. Buyer's Duty to Accept Goods

The buyer must accept goods that conform to the contract. Refusal to do so is a breach of the contract.

(a) RIGHT TO EXAMINE GOODS. To see if the goods in fact conform to the contract, the buyer has the right to examine the goods when tendered by the seller. As an exception to this rule, when goods are sent C.O.D. the buyer has no right to examine them until payment is made.

(b) WHAT CONSTITUTES ACCEPTANCE OF GOODS. Acceptance of goods means that the buyer, pursuant to a contract, takes goods as the buyer's own. This may be done by an express statement of approval. A buyer is also deemed to have accepted goods if the buyer fails to reject the goods after having a reasonable opportunity to inspect them, or if a reasonable time has elapsed after the buyer inspected the goods. A third way of accepting goods is by conduct inconsistent with rejection.[7]

---

7 UCC §§ 2-602(1) and § 2-606(1). Tonka Tours, Inc. v Chadima (Minn) 372 NW2d 723 (1985).

A buyer accepts goods by making continued use of them and by not attempting to return the goods. A buyer, of course, accepts goods by modifying them, because such action is inconsistent with a rejection or with the continued ownership of the goods by the seller. Consequently, when the purchaser of a truck installs a hoist and a dump bed on it, such action constitutes an acceptance by conduct. The buyer therefore becomes liable for the contract price of the truck.

7. Buyer's Duty to Pay

The buyer must pay for goods accepted and must pay the amount stated in the sales contract.

(a) TIME OF PAYMENT. The sales contract may require payment in advance or may give the buyer credit by postponing the time for payment.

(b) FORM OF PAYMENT. Unless otherwise agreed, payment by the buyer requires payment in cash.

The seller may accept a check or a promissory note from the buyer. If the check is not paid by the bank, the purchase price remains unpaid. A promissory note payable at a future date gives the buyer credit by postponing the time for payment.

The seller may refuse to accept a check or promissory note. When the seller does so, the seller must give the buyer reasonable time in which to obtain legal tender with which to make payment.

8. Duties Under Particular Terms

A sale may be as simple as a face-to-face exchange of money and goods. It frequently involves a more complicated pattern, however, with some element of transportation, generally by a common carrier. This, in turn, generally results in the addition of certain special terms to the sales transaction.

(a) C.I.F., C&F. Under a **C.I.F.** (cost, insurance, and freight) contract, the buyer pays the seller a lump sum covering the cost (selling price) of the goods, insurance on the goods, and freight to the specified destination. **C&F** (cost-and-freight) contracts are similar, except that under such contracts, the seller is not obligated to insure the goods for the buyer's benefit. Under both these terms, the risk of loss and title to the goods pass to the buyer after the goods have been delivered to the carrier.

(b) F.O.B. The term *F.O.B.* (free on board) is a condensed way of saying that the seller has the obligation of (1) putting the goods on board a named vessel, truck, or other carrier, or (2) making tender at a named geographic point. When used to specify a geographic point, it may be F.O.B. the seller's city, the buyer's city, or an intermediate point. For example, the F.O.B. point may be the Port of New York for goods that are to be sent by land to New York and by water to a foreign country. Under the F.O.B. term, risk of loss and title pass to the buyer at the F.O.B. point. This is so even though such transfer would have occurred at a different point if the shipment had not been F.O.B. The seller pays the cost of transporting the goods to the F.O.B. point. The buyer pays transportation costs beyond that point.

(c) F.A.S., EX-SHIP. The term *F.A.S.* means free alongside the named vessel. The seller, at the seller's own expense and risk, must deliver the goods alongside a named vessel. Risk of loss and title pass to the buyer at that point.

The term *ex-ship* obligates the seller to deliver or unload the goods from a ship that has reached a place at the named port of destination where goods of the kind are usually discharged. Risk of loss and title pass to the buyer when the goods leave the ship's tackle or are otherwise properly unloaded.

Figure 26-1 Obligations and Performance

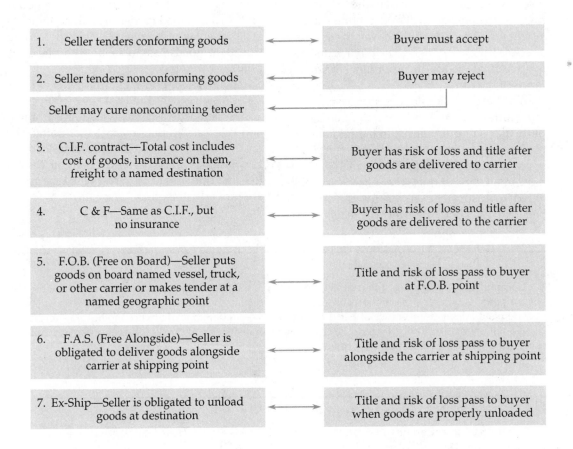

1. Seller tenders conforming goods	Buyer must accept
2. Seller tenders nonconforming goods	Buyer may reject
Seller may cure nonconforming tender	
3. C.I.F. contract—Total cost includes cost of goods, insurance on them, freight to a named destination	Buyer has risk of loss and title after goods are delivered to carrier
4. C & F—Same as C.I.F., but no insurance	Buyer has risk of loss and title after goods are delivered to the carrier
5. F.O.B. (Free on Board)—Seller puts goods on board named vessel, truck, or other carrier or makes tender at a named geographic point	Title and risk of loss pass to buyer at F.O.B. point
6. F.A.S. (Free Alongside)—Seller is obligated to deliver goods alongside carrier at shipping point	Title and risk of loss pass to buyer alongside the carrier at shipping point
7. Ex-Ship—Seller is obligated to unload goods at destination	Title and risk of loss pass to buyer when goods are properly unloaded

SUMMARY

Every sales contract imposes an obligation of good faith in its performance. Good faith means honesty in fact in the conduct or transaction concerned. For merchants, the UCC imposes the additional requirement of observing "reasonable commercial standards of fair dealing in the trade."

In the case of a cash sale where no transportation of the goods is required, both the buyer and the seller may demand concurrent performance.

A buyer's or seller's refusal to perform a contract is called a repudiation. A repudiation made in advance of the time for performance is called an anticipatory repudiation and is a breach of the contract. If either party to a contract feels insecure about the performance of the other, that party may demand in writing adequate assurance of performance. If that assurance is not given, the demanding party may treat the contract as repudiated.

The seller has the duty to deliver the goods in accordance with the terms of the contract. This duty does not require physical transportation; it requires that the seller permit the transfer of possession of the goods to the buyer. If the seller tenders nonconforming goods, the buyer may reject them. Subject to certain limitations, the seller may then make a curative tender.

The buyer has a duty to accept goods that conform to the contract. Refusal to do so is a breach of contract. The buyer is deemed to have accepted goods when the buyer expresses acceptance or does something inconsistent with rejection. A third way of accepting goods is by lapse of time. The buyer must pay for accepted goods in accordance with the terms of the contract.

The parties to a sales contract assume certain duties where goods are shipped under particular shipping terms. In a C.I.F. contract, the buyer pays the seller the price of the goods, insurance, and freight to the specified destination. In a C&F contract, the seller is not obligated to insure the goods for the buyer's benefit. Under both these terms, the risk of loss and title to the goods pass to the buyer after the goods have been delivered to the carrier.

In an F.O.B. (free-on-board) contract, the seller has the obligation of putting the goods on board a named carrier or making delivery at a particular destination. The risk of loss and title to the goods pass to the buyer at the F.O.B. point.

In an F.A.S. contract, the seller, at the seller's own expense and risk, must deliver the goods alongside a named vessel. Risk of loss and title pass to the buyer at that point. The term *ex-ship* obligates the seller to unload the goods at the named port of destination. Risk of loss and title pass to the buyer when the goods are properly unloaded.

LAW IN PRACTICE

1. Comply with the terms of the contract; otherwise, a party may have a basis for insecurity and may demand adequate assurance of performance.
2. Do not ship a smaller or larger quantity than called for by the contract or the buyer can refuse to accept the goods.

3. Remember, if you use delivered goods as if they are your own, acceptance will be presumed.
4. Understand that certain shipping terms can transfer title and risk of loss at different points.

QUESTIONS AND CASE PROBLEMS

1. What social forces are involved in the rule of law governing the substitution of a different method of transportation to replace the method specified in the contract of sale?
2. Elkins Appliance Store makes a contract to purchase 100 electric toasters from the Greystone Electric Company, with delivery to be made on November 1. A week later, Greystone informs Elkins that its factory has been severely damaged by fire and that Greystone is not sure whether it will be able to deliver the toasters by November 1 or at any time. Elkins claims that this statement is an anticipatory repudiation of the contract. Is Elkins correct?
3. Custom Built Homes purchased unassembled prefabricated houses from Page-Hill in Minnesota to be delivered by the seller "F.O.B. building site Kansas." The seller brought the houses to the building site by tractor-trailer, where he would unhitch the trailer and unload the shipment. Kansas taxed Custom Built on the sale. Custom-Built denied liability. Decide. [*Custom Built Homes Co. v Kansas State Commission of Revenue, 184 Kan 31, 334 P2d 808*]
4. Washington orders a computer by mail from Grant Company in Seattle. It is sent C.O.D. to her. To be sure that there has been no mistake, Washington wants to examine the computer before she pays the carrier. Can she do so?
5. The Melvin Electric Motor Corporation makes a contract with the Raskob Gear Company for Raskob to supply 10,000 sets of reduction gears according to specifications supplied by Melvin. The president of Melvin reads in the newspaper that there is a strike at the Raskob plant. The president of Melvin telephones the president of Raskob to express concern over whether Raskob will be able to perform the contract. The conversation does not lessen the fears of the president of Melvin, and the conversation concludes with Melvin's president demanding assurance from Raskob that performance will be made. The president of Melvin does not hear anything further from Raskob during the next 30 days. What are Melvin's rights?

6. International Minerals and Metals Corporation contracted to sell Weinstein scrap metal, to be delivered within 30 days. Later, the seller informed the buyer that it could not make delivery within that time. The buyer agreed to an extension of time, but no limiting date was set. Within what time must the seller perform? [*International Minerals and Metals Corp. v Weinstein, 236 NC 558, 73 SE2d 472*]

7. Carlson ordered equipment from the Ventresca Foundry in St. Louis, Missouri, to be sent "F.O.B. Chicago, Illinois." The equipment was placed on a motor freight truck under a proper shipment contract. The truck was wrecked before it reached Chicago. Ventresca demanded payment of the purchase price from Carlson on the theory that the risk of loss passed to Carlson when the equipment was delivered to the carrier in St. Louis. Was Ventresca correct?

8. The Spaulding & Kimball Co. ordered from the Aetna Chemical Co. 75 cartons of window washers. The buyer received them and sold about a third to its customers. The buyer later refused to pay for them, claiming that the quality was poor. The seller sued for the price. Decide. [*Aetna Chemical Co. v Spaulding & Kimball Co. 98 Vt 51, 126 A 582*]

9. A computer manufacturer promoted the sale of a digital computer as a "revolutionary breakthrough." The manufacturer made a contract to deliver one of these computers to a buyer. The seller failed to deliver the computer and explained that its failure was caused by unanticipated technological difficulties. Was this an excuse for nonperformance by the seller? [*United States v Wegematic Corp. (CA2 NY) 360 F2d 674*]

10. Economy Farms Corp. sold concrete-forming equipment to Kandy. Kandy notified Economy that the equipment was inadequate after using the equipment for over six months. Economy Farms alleged that Kandy had accepted the goods. Kandy denied liability. Was there an acceptance? Why? [*Economy Forms Corp. v Kandy, Inc. (ND Ga) 391 F. Supp 944*]

11. Teeman made a contract to purchase lumber from the Oakhill Mill. The contract called for payment to be made on delivery to Teeman. When the truck from the mill arrived to deliver the lumber, Teeman gave the driver a check for the purchase price. The driver refused to take the check or leave the lumber. The driver returned to the mill, and the mill then notified Teeman that the contract was canceled. Was the mill entitled to cancel the contract?

12. Lury has a contract to sell with Burns, with whom he has not previously dealt, to make four quarterly deliveries of a product on 30 days' credit. Two months after the first delivery under the contract, Burns has not yet paid. May Lury demand adequate assurance of performance?

13. Matsuda was in the process of furnishing her apartment. She purchased a leather sofa and three leather chairs from Davenport Furniture, Inc. These items were to be delivered in 20 days. She paid part of the purchase price on executing the order and agreed to pay the balance on delivery. Davenport delivered the sofa and the chairs a week later, but the leather chairs did not match the sofa. Matsuda thereupon rejected the sofa and the chairs. She also demanded the return of her money. What rights, if any, does Davenport have?

14. Phillips ordered naphtha from Tradax Petroleum. The contract provided that the naphtha was to be shipped from Algeria to Puerto Rico. The contract specified a shipping date and stated that the sale was C&F. The vessel selected by the parties began its journey within the contract time, but was detained at Gibraltar after a sister ship sank and defects were discovered in the vessel selected by Phillips and Tradax. Tradax presented its documents to Phillips and demanded payment. Payment was refused. Phillips argued that the vessel defects, which prevented delivery, excused performance of the contract. Tradax argued that risk of loss had passed to Phillips. Did the risk of loss pass? If so, when? [*Phillips Puerto Rico Core, Inc. v Tradax Petroleum Ltd. (CA2 NY) 782 F2d 314*]

15. Compare an F.O.B. shipping term with an F.O.B. destination term with respect to when the risk of loss and title pass to the buyer.

CHAPTER 27

WARRANTIES AND OTHER PRODUCT LIABILITY THEORIES

LEARNING OBJECTIVES

After studying this chapter, you will be able to:
1. *List the theories of product liability.*
2. *Say who may sue and who may be sued when a defective product causes harm.*
3. *List and define the implied warranties and distinguish them from express warranties.*
4. *Explain and distinguish between full warranties and limited warranties under federal law.*
5. *State what constitutes a breach of warranty.*
6. *Describe the extent and manner in which implied warranties may be disclaimed under the UCC and the CISG.*

What happens when goods do not work? Who can sue for injury caused by defective goods? What can you do when you are sent the wrong goods?

A. GENERAL PRINCIPLES

The remedy in such cases may be governed by the common law, by the UCC, or by the newly emerging case law.

1. Theories of Liability

Two centuries ago, a buyer was limited to suing a seller for breach of an express guarantee or for negligence or fraud. After the onset of mass production and distribution, however, these remedies had little value. A guarantee was good, but in the ordinary sales transaction no one stopped to get a guarantee. One never asked the manager of the supermarket to give a guarantee that the loaf of bread purchased was fit to eat. Further, negligence and fraud have become generally impossible to prove in a mass production world. How can one prove how a can of soup was prepared months earlier? The making of fraudulent statements by the seller is rare.

To give protection from economic loss and personal injuries, the law developed the concept of warranty liability. Warranties are either express or implied and are governed by the UCC. More recently, many courts have decided that still broader protection was required and have created an additional concept of strict tort liability.

Accordingly, there are six theories in the law to protect economic loss and personal injuries: guarantee, express warranty, implied warranty, negligence, fraud, and strict tort liability. If the plaintiff is a consumer or an employee, there might also be consumer protection liability or employee protection liability. In every case, the plaintiff does not have a choice of all theories. The facts of the case will ordinarily exclude some theories. In some situations, the plaintiff will have the choice of two or more theories.

2. Nature of Harm

When a product is defective, harm may be caused to (a) a person, (b) property, or (c) economic or commercial interests. The buyer of a truck may be injured when it goes out of control and plunges down the side of a hill. Third persons, such as passengers in the truck, bystanders, or the driver of a car hit by the truck, may also be injured. The defective truck may cause injury to a total stranger who seeks to rescue one of the victims. Property damage is sustained when the buyer's truck is damaged when it plunges down the slope. The car of another driver may be damaged, or a building into which the runaway truck careens may be damaged. Commercial and economic interests of the buyer are affected by the fact that the truck is defective. Even if no physical harm is sustained, the fact remains that the truck is not as valuable as it would have been. The buyer who has paid for the truck on the basis of the value it should have had has sustained an economic loss. If the buyer is required to rent a truck from someone else or loses an opportunity to haul freight for compensation, the fact that the truck was defective also causes economic or commercial loss.

The harm sustained may be a breach of contract because the buyer was sent the wrong goods. The harm sustained may be the failure of the goods to meet the particular needs of the buyer, even though there was no defect in the goods.

3. Who May Sue and Be Sued

Until the early part of this century, only the parties to the sales contract could sue each other. Thus, a seller could be sued by the buyer, but other persons could not sue, because they were not in privity of contract.

This requirement of privity of contract has now been widely rejected. The law is moving toward the conclusion that persons harmed because of an "improper" product may sue anyone who is in any way responsible.

(a) THE PLAINTIFF. By the modern view, not only the buyer, but also customers and employees of the buyer and even third persons or bystanders, may sue because of harm caused by an improper product. Most states have abolished the requirement of privity when the plaintiff is a member of the buyer's family or household or is a guest of the buyer and has sustained personal injury because of the product.[1] Some states require privity of contract, particularly when the plaintiff does not sustain personal injury or property damage and seeks to recover only economic loss.

(b) THE DEFENDANT. The plaintiff who is entitled to sue may sue the seller, a remote seller, a manufacturer, and generally even the manufacturer of the component part of the product that caused the harm.[2] For example, when a person is struck by an automobile because of its defective brakes, the victim may sue the seller and the manufacturer of the car. The maker of the brake assembly or system that the car manufacturer installed in the car may also be sued.

(c) DIRECT SALES CONTACT. In many instances, recovery is allowed by a buyer against a manufacturer because there have been direct dealings between them. These dealings justify the conclusion that the buyer and the manufacturer are in privity, as against the contention that the buyer was only in privity with the local dealer from whom the product was bought.[3] When the manufacturer enters into direct negotiations with the ultimate buyer with respect to any phase of the manufacturing or financing of the transaction, the sale will probably be treated as though it were made directly by the manufacturer to the ultimate purchaser. This is so even though, for the purpose of record keeping, the transaction is treated as a sale by the manufacturer to the dealer and by that dealer to the ultimate purchaser. Likewise, recovery may be allowed when the consumer mails to the manufacturer a warranty registration card that the manufacturer packed with the manufactured article.

In the *Nobility Homes* case the purchaser of a mobile home sued the manufacturer for breach of warranty. The manufacturer claimed that the purchaser could sue only the dealer from whom the home had been purchased.

NOBILITY HOMES OF TEXAS v SHIVERS
(Tex Civ App) 539 SW2d 190 (1976)

John Shivers and his wife purchased a mobile home from Marvin Hurley. Because of many defects, the home had a market value of approximately $9,000 less than the contract price. The buyers sued the manufacturer, Nobility Homes of Texas, for this amount. From a judgment in favor of the plaintiffs, Nobility Homes appealed.

DIES, C. J. . . . Hurley had previously purchased this unit from the defendant, the manufacturer thereof. Hurley was not an agent for the defendant. . . .

Defendant . . . asserts that it could not be liable for any damages to plaintiffs because there was no privity of contract between them, and plaintiffs are only seeking

---

[1] UCC § 2-318, Alternative A. The Code gives the states the option to adopt the provision summarized in this chapter or to make a wide abolition of the requirement of privity by adopting Alternative B or C of § 2-318. As of January 1, 1994, most states had adopted Alternative A.

[2] Mendelson v General Motors Corp. 432 NYS2d 132 (1980).

[3] Richards v Goerg Boat & Motors, Inc. (Ind App) 384 NE2d 1084 (1979).

economic loss. . . . The generally recognized landmark case for support of the principle that privity is not required in pure economic loss cases is *Santor v A & M Karagheusian, Inc.* 44 NJ 52, 207 A2d 305 (1965). There, Santor brought suit against the manufacturer of a carpet which he had purchased from one of its distributors. The only contract was between Santor and the distributor, which had subsequently gone out of business. Santor sought recovery only for the loss of value of the carpeting.

After a thorough discussion of the positions of the various states and the concomitant rationale of the divergent views, the New Jersey Supreme Court held that privity was not necessary to maintain an action by a consumer against the manufacturer for redress of an economic loss. The Court restated the holdings which do not require privity for recovery in instances of personal injury and said:

But we see no just cause for recognition of the existence of an implied warranty of merchantability and a right to recovery for breach thereof regardless of lack of privity of the claimant in the one case and the exclusion of recovery in the other simply because loss of value of the article sold is the only damage resulting from the breach. . . .

From the standpoint of principle, we perceive no sound reason why the implication of reasonable fitness should be attached to the transaction and be actionable against the manufacturer where the defectively made product has caused personal injury, and not actionable when inadequate manufacture has put a worthless article in the hands of an innocent purchaser who has paid the required price for it. In such situations considerations of justice require a court to interest itself in originating causes and to apply the principle of implied warranty on that basis, rather than to test its application by whether personal injury or simply loss of bargain resulted from the breach of the warranty. True, the rule of implied warranty had its gestative stirrings because of the greater appeal of personal injury claim. But, once in existence, the field of operation of the remedy should not be fenced in by such a factor.

The court accepted these logical principles of equity and incorporated with them the substantive law of strict liability in tort. It again refused to accept the personal injury/economic loss dichotomy and held that only through tort liability would the burden of the injury be placed where it should be—on the maker of the product. This is because, though the breach arose initially from the sales contract, it was a "'tortuous wrong suable by a noncontracting party . . .'"

It is our opinion that the interests of equity and justice will best be served by accepting the view that privity in cases now under consideration should not be required. Matters of public policy dictate that no different treatment should be accorded in instances where a consumer suffers personal injury or damage to other property, and situations where the harm is the diminution of value of the product itself and the resulting economic loss. In both circumstances there is an "injury" to the public sector, whose only action in the commercial transaction is to purchase goods placed in the stream of commerce by the manufacturer. To insulate the maker of the goods under these conditions can result only by resort to reasoning which is no longer viable in our current economic practices and present sense of justice. . . .

A practical consideration also supports the position advanced by this Court today; the problem of wasteful litigation. In quoting from *Randy Knitwear, Inc. v American Cyanamid Company* (226 NYS2d 363, 181 NE2d 399) the Court in *Santor* restated:

It is true that in many cases the manufacturer will ultimately be held accountable for the falsity of his representations, but only after an unduly wasteful process of litigation. Thus, if the consumer or ultimate business user sues and recovers, for breach of warranty, from his immediate seller and if the latter, in turn, sues and recovers against his supplier in recoupment of his damages and costs, eventually, after several separate actions by those in the chain of distribution, the manufacturer may finally be obliged to shoulder the responsibility which should have been his in the first instance.

. . . The pursuit of such wasteful litigation which is often inadequate should not be required in this State.

This jurisdiction should refrain from the "narrow legalistic view" that privity is necessary before the public may recover for damages suffered when the product diminishes in value and/or becomes worthless because of the defective workmanship of the manufacturer. . . .

[Judgment affirmed]

QUESTIONS

1. What was the theory on which the plaintiff sued the defendant?
2. What kind of loss was sustained by the plaintiff?
3. Was the court in the *Nobility Homes* case influenced by the nature of the plaintiff's loss?

B. EXPRESS WARRANTIES

A warranty may be express or implied. Both have the same effect and operate as though the defendant had made an express guarantee. An express guarantee is governed by the common law of contracts. Warranties are governed primarily by the UCC.

4. Definition of Express Warranty

An **express warranty** is a statement by the defendant relating to the goods, which statement is part of the basis of the bargain.[4] This means that the buyer has purchased the goods on the reasonable assumption that they were as stated by the seller. Thus, a statement by the seller with respect to the quality, capacity, or other characteristic of the goods is an express warranty. To illustrate, the seller may say: "This cloth is all wool," "This paint is for household woodwork," or "This engine can produce 50 horsepower."

A representation that an airplane is a 1992 model is an express warranty. A statement that a product was particularly developed for a special purpose is an express warranty that it will achieve that purpose.

5. Form of Express Warranty

No particular form of words is necessary to constitute an express warranty. A seller need not state that a warranty is being made or that one is intended. It is sufficient that the seller assert a fact that becomes a part or term of the bargain or transaction between the parties.

It is not necessary that the seller make an express statement, because the express warranty may be found in conduct. Accordingly, if the buyer asks for a can of outside house paint and the seller hands over a can of paint, the

---

[4] Daughtrey v Ashe, 243 Va 73, 413 SE2d 336 (1992).

seller's conduct expresses a warranty that the can contains outside house paint.

The seller's statement may be written or printed as well as oral. The words on the label of a can and in a newspaper ad for "boned chicken" constitute an express warranty that the can contains chicken that is free of bones.

The illustrations in a seller's catalog are descriptions of the goods. An express warranty arises that the goods will conform to a catalog illustration.

6. Time of Making Express Warranty

It is immaterial whether the express warranty is made at the time of or after the sale. No separate consideration is required for the warranty when it is a part of a sale. If a warranty is made after the sale, no consideration is required, since it is regarded as a modification of the sales contract.

In the *Werner* case the buyer claimed that oral statements made by the seller before the sale were express warranties as to the future performance of the goods.

WERNER v MONTANA
117 NH 721, 378 A2d 1130 (1977)

> Peter Werner purchased the White Eagle, a wooden sailing sloop, from Robert Montana. The sloop leaked, and Werner brought an action to cancel the sale on the ground that there had been an express oral warranty that it would not leak. Montana contended that no warranty was stated in any of the writings involved in the transaction, that the parol evidence rule prevented proof of statements made in the course of negotiations, and that accordingly there was no express warranty. The case was heard by a master, who recommended that judgment be entered for Werner. Montana appealed.

LAMPRON, J. . . . Plaintiff put the White Eagle into the water. After allowing ordinarily sufficient time for the planking to swell, or "make up," to form a watertight hull, plaintiff found that the White Eagle still leaked and could not be sailed. Plaintiff then discovered that there was extensive dry rot in the hull and that the cost of repairs would be substantial. After some discussions with defendant in the course of the summer concerning the problem, on September 8, 1972, plaintiff wrote defendant a letter complaining about the dry rot and unseaworthiness of the White Eagle and demanding that defendant take back the White Eagle and refund the purchase price. Defendant refused and plaintiff brought this action.

The basis for plaintiff's action is that there was a breach of an express warranty. [UCC §] 2-313. Plaintiff alleged that defendant, in the course of negotiations prior to sale, made certain statements to the effect that the White Eagle would "make up" when placed in the water and become watertight and that such statements amounted to an express warranty as to the sloop's condition. Defendant argues that any statements made by the defendant prior to sale could not be admitted or considered as constituting an express warranty by virtue of [UCC §] 2-202 (Parol or Extrinsic Evidence Rule). . . .

Under the Uniform Commercial Code an express warranty may be created by a seller who makes "any affirmation of fact or promise . . . to the buyer which relates to the goods and becomes part of the basis of the bargain." [UCC §] 2-313(1)(a). In addition, "any description of the goods which is made part of the basis of the bargain creates an express warranty that the goods shall conform to the description." [UCC §] 2-313(1)(b).

In general, affirmations of fact made by a seller about the goods being sold are considered a part of the description of the goods and are regarded as forming a part of the sales agreement. Uniform Laws Comment 3 to [UCC §] 2-313; 1 R. Anderson, Uniform Commercial Code § 2-313:45 (2d ed 1970). There was evidence that during the course of negotiations the parties had discussed the ship's watertightness and that defendant had told plaintiff that the White Eagle would become watertight once placed in water and allowed sufficient time to "make up." Considering the negotiations of the parties as a whole, particularly plaintiff's concern with whether the White Eagle was watertight, and considering the importance of watertightness for a ship, these assurances by defendant regarding the condition of the White Eagle could properly be considered as making part of the basis of the bargain. *See* 1 R. Anderson, *supra* § 2-313:7. Therefore, . . . the master did not err in ruling that these affirmations or descriptions of the White Eagle by the defendant created an express warranty under both [UCC §] 2-313(1)(a) and (b).

[UCC §] 2-202 excludes evidence of any additional oral agreement or terms when a written agreement is intended by the parties to be a final expression of their agreement. However, unless the writing was intended as a complete and exclusive statement of the terms of the agreement, evidence of consistent additional terms are admissible. [UCC §] 2-202(b). There was no evidence that the writings in this case, the notice of intent to purchase, the bill of sale, and the advertisement incorporated therein by reference, were intended by the parties as constituting a complete and exclusive statement of the terms of their agreement. The master therefore could properly find defendant's statements regarding the White Eagle's watertightness as being an express warranty which was a consistent additional term of the agreement . . . 1 R. Anderson, Uniform Commercial Code § 2-313:22; R. Nordstrom, Sales § 53 (1970). . . .

Defendant argues that plaintiff failed to prove a breach of warranty because the evidence did not establish that the leaking of the White Eagle was caused by the dry rot, or by any other cause, and therefore did not establish that the leaking constituted a breach of the alleged warranty. It is true that the master found there was no evidence to connect the leaking with the dry rot in the hull. However, the master did not find that defendant had made any warranty that the White Eagle was free from dry rot. Rather, the master found that defendant had told plaintiff that the White Eagle was suitable for sailing, and that defendant's statements which created the warranty were to the effect that the White Eagle had not leaked and would not leak after a sufficient swelling period was allowed. The master found that the White Eagle's "inability to 'make up'" created a breach of this warranty. While it is true that there was no evidence to establish the cause of the leaking, such evidence was not necessary. The plaintiff was required only to establish the existence of an express warranty and to establish that the White Eagle was defective in that its condition did not comply with the condition warranted by defendant. . . . The evidence was undisputed that the White Eagle continued to leak and was not seaworthy despite being allowed to soak for over six weeks. Plaintiff therefore met his burden establishing the boat's defective condition.

Defendant also argues that any warranty made related only to the condition of the White Eagle at the time of sale and that plaintiff failed to prove that the White

Eagle was not as warranted at that time. While an express warranty generally relates only to the condition of the goods at the time of sale, a warranty may relate to another point in time if so specified. 1 R. Anderson, supra § 2-313:12. The warranty found by the master to have been made by defendant was that the White Eagle would not leak; that it would be tight after a two-week swelling period. The discussions between the parties prior to sale occurred after September 1, 1971, and the bill of sale was dated January 1, 1972. It would not be until the following spring or summer that plaintiff would have the first occasion to put the White Eagle in the water and allow for the swelling defendant indicated would occur. The warranty as to tightness therefore did not relate simply to the condition of the White Eagle as of the date of sale, but necessarily related to the time when the boat would be put in the water and prepared for sailing. Under these circumstances defendant's statement amounted to an express warranty.

Although reliance on the part of the buyer is not necessary for the creation of an express warranty, the master properly found that plaintiff did in fact rely on defendant's affirmation that the boat would not leak and it became part of the bargain. . .

[Judgment affirmed]

QUESTIONS

1. Why did the plaintiff sue the defendant?
2. Did the seller guarantee that the sloop would not leak?
3. Did the seller say that he warranted that the sloop would not leak after being placed in the water?

7. Seller's Opinion or Statement of Value

"An affirmation merely of the value of goods or a statement purporting to be merely the seller's opinion or commendation of the goods does not create a warranty."[5] A purchaser, as a reasonable person, should not believe such statements implicitly. Therefore, the buyer cannot hold the seller to them should they prove false. Thus, "sales talk" or "puffery" by a seller that "this is the best piece of cloth in the market" or that glassware is "as good as anyone else's" is merely an opinion that the buyer cannot ordinarily treat as a warranty.

Statements made by the seller of cosmetics that its products were "the future of beauty" and that they were "just the product for you [the plaintiff]" were "sales talk" arising "in the ordinary course of merchandising." They did not constitute warranties.

It is probable, however, that the UCC will permit an exception to be made, as under the prior law, when the circumstances are such that a reasonable person would rely on such a statement. If the buyer has reason to believe that the seller has expert knowledge of the conditions of the market and the buyer requests the seller's opinion as an expert, the buyer would be entitled to accept as a fact the seller's statement as to whether a given article was the best obtainable. The statement could be reasonably regarded as forming part of the basis of the bargain. Thus, a statement by a florist that bulbs are of first-grade quality may be a warranty.

---

5 UCC § 2-313(2); Pell City Wood, Inc. v Forke Bros, Auctioneers, Inc. (Ala) 474 So 2d 694 (1985).

8. Warranty of Conformity to Description, Sample, or Model

When the contract is based in part on the understanding that the seller will supply goods according to a particular description or that the goods will be the same as the sample or a model, the seller is bound by an express warranty that the goods shall conform to the description, sample, or model.[6] Ordinarily, a **sample** is a portion of the whole mass that is the subject of the transaction. A **model** is a replica of the article in question.

9. Federal Regulation of Express Warranties

A seller who makes an express warranty for a consumer product costing more than $15 must conform to certain standards imposed by federal statute[7] and by regulations of the Federal Trade Commission.[8] The seller is not required to make any express warranty. However, if the supplier makes an express warranty, it must be stated in ordinary, understandable language and must be made available for inspection before purchasing so that the consumer may comparison shop.

(a) FULL WARRANTIES. If the seller or the label states that a **full warranty** is made, the seller is obligated to fix or replace a defective product within a reasonable time, without cost to the buyer. If the product cannot be fixed or if a reasonable number of repair attempts are unsuccessful, the buyer has the choice of a cash refund or a free replacement. No unreasonable burden may be placed on a buyer seeking to obtain warranty service. For example, a warrantor making a full warranty cannot require that the buyer pay the cost of sending the product to or from a warranty service point. A warrantor making a full warranty cannot require the buyer to return the product to a warranty service point if the product weighs over 35 pounds, to return a part for service unless it can be easily removed, or to fill out and return a warranty registration card shortly after purchase in order to make the warranty effective. If the warrantor imposes any of these burdens, the warranty must be called a limited warranty. A full warranty runs for its specified life without regard to who owns the product.

(b) LIMITED WARRANTIES. Any warranty that does not provide the complete protection of a full warranty is a **limited warranty**. For instance, a warranty is limited if the buyer must pay any cost for repair or replacement of a defective product, if only the first buyer is covered by the warranty, or if the warranty covers only part of the product. A limited warranty must be conspicuously described as such by the seller.

10. Effect of Breach of Express Warranty

If the express warranty is false, there is a breach of the warranty. The warrantor is then liable just as though the truth of the warranty had been guaranteed. It is no defense that the defendant honestly believed that the warranty was true, had exercised due care in manufacturing or handling the product, or had no reason to believe that the warranty was false.

C. IMPLIED WARRANTIES

Whenever a sale of goods is made, certain warranties are implied unless they are expressly excluded. Implied warranties differ depending on whether the seller is a merchant or a casual seller.

---

[6] Curry Motor Co. v Hasty (Ala) 505 So 2d 347 (1987).

[7] PL 93-637, 15 USC §§ 2301 et seq.

[8] 16 CFR § 700.1 et seq.

11. Definition of Implied Warranty

An **implied warranty** is one that was not made by the seller but is implied by law. In certain instances, the law implies or reads a warranty into a sale, although the seller did not make it. That is, the implied warranty arises automatically from the fact that a sale has been made.

Express warranties arise because they form part of the basis on which the sale has been made. The fact that express warranties are made does not exclude implied warranties. When both express and implied warranties exist, they should be construed as being consistent with each other and cumulative if such construction is reasonable. In case it is unreasonable to construe them as consistent and cumulative, an express warranty prevails over an implied warranty as to the subject matter, except in the case of an implied warranty of fitness for a particular purpose. When there is an express warranty as to a particular matter, it is unnecessary to find an implied warranty relating thereto.

12. Implied Warranties of All Sellers

A distinction is made between a merchant seller and the casual seller. There is a greater range of warranties in the case of the merchant seller.

(a) WARRANTY OF TITLE. Every seller, by the mere act of selling, makes a warranty that the seller's title is good and that the transfer is rightful.

A warranty of title may be specifically excluded, or the circumstances may be such as to prevent the warranty from arising. The latter situation is found when the buyer has reason to know that the seller does not claim to hold the title or that the seller is purporting to sell only such right or title as the seller or a third person may have. For example, no warranty of title arises when the seller makes the sale in a representative capacity, such as a sheriff, an auctioneer, or an administrator of a decedent's estate. Similarly, no warranty arises when the seller makes the sale as a pledgee or mortgagee.

(b) WARRANTY AGAINST ENCUMBRANCES. Every seller, by the mere act of selling, makes a warranty that the goods shall be delivered free from any security interest or any other lien or encumbrance of which the buyer at the time of the sales transaction had no knowledge. Thus, there is a breach of warranty if the automobile sold to the buyer is delivered subject to an outstanding encumbrance placed on it by the original owner and unknown to the buyer at the time of the sale.

This warranty refers to the goods only at the time they are delivered to the buyer. The warranty is not concerned with an encumbrance that existed before or at the time the sale was made. For example, a seller may not have paid in full for the goods, and the original supplier may have a lien on them. The seller may resell the goods while that lien is still on them, but the seller has the duty to pay off the lien before delivering the goods to the buyer.

(c) WARRANTY OF FITNESS FOR A PARTICULAR PURPOSE. A buyer may intend to use the goods for a particular or unusual purpose, as contrasted with the ordinary use for which they are customarily sold. If so, the seller makes an implied warranty that the goods will be fit for that purpose when the buyer relies on the seller's skill or judgment to select or furnish suitable goods, and when the seller at the time of contracting knows or has reason to know the buyer's particular purpose and of the buyer's reliance on the seller's judgment.[9] When the seller knows that the buyer is purchasing an accounting machine in order to produce a payroll on time and with reduced work hours, an implied warranty arises that the machine will perform as desired by the buyer.

---

9 UCC § 2-315. This warranty applies to every seller, but as a matter of fact it will ordinarily be a merchant seller who has such skill and judgment that the UCC provision would be applicable.

When the buyer makes the purchase without relying on the seller's skill and judgment, no warranty of fitness for a particular purpose arises.[10]

13. Additional Implied Warranties of Merchant Seller

A seller who deals in goods of the kind in question is classified as a **merchant** by the UCC and is held to a higher degree of responsibility for the product than one who is merely making a casual sale.

(a) WARRANTY AGAINST INFRINGEMENT. Unless otherwise agreed, every merchant seller warrants that the goods will be delivered free of the rightful claim of any third person by way of patent or trademark infringement or the like.

(b) WARRANTY OF MERCHANTABILITY OR FITNESS FOR NORMAL USE. A merchant seller makes an implied warranty of the merchantability of the goods sold.[11] This warranty is in fact a group of warranties, the most important of which is that the goods are fit for the ordinary purposes for which they are sold.

(c) EFFECT OF A WARRANTY. Warranty liability is not merely an assurance that the defendant has exercised due care but is an undertaking or guarantee that the product is as warranted. A merchant is not protected from warranty liability by the fact that every possible step was taken to make the product safe. Similarly, it is no defense that the defendant could not have known of or discovered the defective character of the product.

14. Warranties in Particular Sales

Particular types of sales may involve special considerations.

(a) SALE ON BUYER'S SPECIFICATIONS. When the buyer furnishes the seller with exact specifications for the preparation or manufacture of goods, the same warranties arise as in the case of any other sale of such goods by the particular seller. No warranty of fitness for a particular purpose can arise, however. It is clear that the buyer is purchasing on the basis of the buyer's own decision and is not relying on the seller's skill and judgment. Similarly, the manufacturer is not liable for loss caused by a design defect.

(b) SALE OF SECONDHAND OR USED GOODS. As far as the UCC is concerned, there is no difference between the warranties arising in the sale of used goods and those arising in the sale of new goods. With respect to ordinary goods, what is "fit for normal use" will be a lower standard for used than for new goods. Some courts still follow their pre-Code law, under which no warranties of fitness arose in the sale of used goods.

(c) SALE OF FOOD OR DRINK. The sale of food or drink, whether to be consumed on or off the seller's premises, is a sale. When made by a merchant, a sale of food or drink carries the implied warranty that the food is fit for its ordinary purpose—human consumption.[12] Thus, the seller of canned crabmeat has broken this warranty when the can contains a nail. Does it make any difference if the thing which harms the buyer is a crabshell?

Some courts refuse to impose warranty liability if the thing in the food that causes the harm was naturally present, such as the crabshell in crabmeat, prune stones in stewed prunes, or bones in canned fish. Other courts reject this "natural substance" exception. They

---

[10] Lorfano v Dura Stone Steps, Inc. (Me) 569 A2d 195 (1990).

[11] Miller v Badgley, 51 Wash App 285, 753 P2d 530 (1988).

[12] Fernandes v Union Bookbinding Co. Inc. 400 Mass 27, 507 NE2d 728 (1987).

hold that there is liability if the seller does not deliver to the buyer goods of the character that the buyer reasonably expected. Under this view there is a breach of the implied warranty of fitness for normal use if the buyer reason-ably expected the food to be free of harm-causing natural things, such as shells and bones.

This was the situation in the *Phillips* case.

PHILLIPS v WEST SPRINGFIELD
405 Mass 411, 540 NE2d 1331 (1989)

Phillips, a high school senior, was eating in the high school cafeteria. He bit into a cube of turkey, which contained a bone that injured him. He sued the city for breach of warranty. From a judgment in favor of the city, Phillips appealed.

WILKINS, J. . . . Twenty-five years ago Justice Reardon wrote for this court a much cited opinion holding that a restaurant was not liable for breach of warranty under [UCC] § 2-314(2)(c), for injuries caused by a fish bone in fish chowder. *Webster v Blue Ship Tea Room, Inc.*, 347 Mass. 421, 198 NE2d (1964). In this appeal, which we trans-ferred here on our own motion, we decide a somewhat similar case. This one in-volves not a fish bone in fish chowder served in a quaint restaurant on a wharf overlooking Boston Harbor, but rather a turkey bone in a bite-sized cube of white turkey meat ladled, along with gravy and peas, onto a mount of mashed potatoes in a high school cafeteria in West Springfield. The plaintiff, a high school senior, bit into one of the turkey cubes, felt something in his throat, and after some effort expelled "a small, $1^1/2$ inch hooked bone." He sustained injury to his esophagus and was hospitalized for four days.

The plaintiff argues that the judge, who heard the case without a jury, erred in deciding the breach of warranty claim against him because she applied the "foreign substance–natural substance" test rather than the consumer's "reasonable expecta-tions" test. When the foreign substance–natural substance test is applied, there is no liability as a matter of law for breach of warranty if the injury-causing substance is natural to the food, and liability is automatic if the offending item is foreign to the food. . . . 3 R. A. Anderson, Uniform Commercial Code 2-314:183- 2-314:185 (1983 & Supp. 1988). The reasonable expectations test, on the other hand, considers whether the consumer reasonably should have expected to find the injury-causing substance in the food. . . .

The reasonable expectations test has been generally recognized as preferable to the foreign substance–natural substance test. The foreign substance–natural sub-stance test exonerates a seller of food from liability for the lack of fitness of the food for ordinary purposes simply because the injury causing substance was natural to the food. It fails to focus the seller's attention on the consumer's reasonable beliefs and to recognize that sellers may fairly be held responsible in some instances for natural substances in food that cause injury. This court's discussion in its *Webster* opinion focused on the reasonable expectations of a consumer of fish chowder and concluded, as a matter of law, that bones in fish chowder should reasonably be ex-pected. *Webster v Blue Ship Tea Room, Inc.*, supra, 347 Mass. at 426, 198 NE2d 309. In our view, the reasonable expectations test is the appropriate one to apply in determining liability for breach of warranty of merchantability under [UCC] § 2-314(2)(c), by reason of a bone or other substance in food that caused harm to a consumer.

We turn to the judge's findings and rulings. The judge found that "[t]he plaintiff reasonably expected that the turkey meat was boneless based on its being white meat, the fact that it was cut into bite size pieces and the manner in which it was served, i.e., ladled with gravy onto potatoes." She ruled as a matter of law, however, that the plaintiff had failed to prove that the defendant breached its warranty of merchantability. She noted that "[t]he bone in the turkey was not a foreign substance and did not render the meal unwholesome," citing the *Webster* case. She ruled further that "[t]he plaintiff as an ordinary consumer of the turkey meal should have reasonably expected the likelihood of a bone in the turkey meat.". . .

We disagree with the plaintiff's claim that the judge decided the case against him solely on the ground that a turkey bone in a piece of turkey is not a foreign substance. Her discussion of reasonable expectations would have been unnecessary if she had decided the case by applying the foreign substance–natural substance test.

The trial judge's finding of fact that the plaintiff reasonably expected that the turkey meat was boneless contrasts with her ruling of law that an ordinary consumer of the turkey meal should have reasonably expected the likelihood of a bone in the turkey meat. The plaintiff's subjective expectations may not have been those of an ordinary objective consumer of the meal, and thus the judge's findings and rulings are not necessarily inconsistent. . . . On the other hand, the reasons she provided for the reasonableness of the plaintiff's expectation that there would be no bones (the bite size pieces of only white meat served on top of mashed potatoes) seem to be objective, and not subjective, criteria.

The plaintiff is entitled to a clarification of the judge's findings of fact and rulings of law. Although we recognize that in particular circumstances no consumer could reasonably expect not to find the injury-causing object and thus a directed verdict for a defendant would be proper, on the facts found in this case, the defendant was not entitled to prevail as a matter of law. The answer depends on what the reasonable expectations of an ordinary high school student would be concerning the likely presence of a bone in this meal. As the trier of fact, the judge has not made and should make a finding on that dispositive question.

[Judgment vacated and case remanded to the Superior Court for further consideration]

QUESTIONS

1. What did the plaintiff argue?
2. What is the difference in result if the foreign substance test is applied as opposed to the reasonable expectation test?
3. Why was this case sent back to the lower court for further action?

15. Necessity of Defect

To impose liability for breach of the implied warranty of merchantability, it is ordinarily necessary to show that there was a defect in the product and that this defect made the product not fit for its normal use and that this caused the plaintiff's harm. A product may be defective because there is (a) a manufacturing defect, (b) a design defect, (c) inadequate instruction on how to use the product, or (d) inadequate warning against dangers involved in using the product.

If the manufacturer's blueprint shows that there should be two bolts at a particular place and the factory puts in only one bolt, there is a manufacturing defect. If the two bolts are put in but the product breaks because four bolts are required to provide sufficient strength, there is no manufacturing defect, but there is a design defect. A product that is properly designed and properly manufactured may be dangerous because the user is not given sufficient instructions on how to use the product. Also, a product is defective if there is a danger that is not obvious and there is no warning at all or a warning that does not describe the full danger. For example, a can of adhesive used to cement tiles to a floor is defective when the label on the can merely states that the cement should not be used near an open flame, but does not state that a newly cemented floor would throw off vapor that would stay in the room for several hours and would explode if any spark or flame were present.

Many courts are relaxing the requirement of proving the existence of a specific defect. These courts impose liability when the goods are in fact not fit for their normal purpose. These courts allow the buyer to prove goods are not fit for their normal purpose by evidence that the goods do not function properly, even though the buyer does not establish the specific defect.

In contrast with the suit for breach of the implied warranty of merchantability, when the plaintiff sues for breach of the implied warranty of fitness for a particular purpose or of an express warranty or a guarantee, it is not necessary to show that there was a defect that caused the breach. It is sufficient to show that the goods did not perform to meet the particular purpose or did not conform to the guarantee or to the express warranty. Why they did not is immaterial.

16. Warranties in the International Sale of Goods

The warranties of both merchantability and fitness for a particular purpose exist under the Convention on Contracts for the International Sale of Goods (CISG). In most cases, the provisions are identical to those of the UCC. Sellers, however, can expressly disclaim the convention's warranties without mentioning merchantability or making the disclaimer conspicuous.

D. DISCLAIMER OF WARRANTIES

The seller and the buyer may ordinarily agree that there shall be no warranties. In some states, disclaimers of warranties are prohibited for reasons of public policy or consumer protection.

17. Validity of Disclaimer

Warranties may be disclaimed by agreement of the parties, subject to the limitation that such a provision must not be unconscionable.

When there is a written disclaimer of warranties, the disclaimer must be conspicuous. If the implied warranty of merchantability is disclaimed, the disclaimer must also expressly mention the word "merchantability."

(a) CONSPICUOUSNESS. A disclaimer provision is made conspicuous by printing it under a conspicuous heading that indicates that there is an exclusion or modification of warranties. A heading cannot be relied on to make such a provision "conspicuous" when the heading is misleading and wrongfully gives the impression that there is a warranty. For example, the heading "Vehicle Warranty" is misleading if the provision that follows contains a limitation of warranties. A disclaimer that is hidden in a mass of printed material handed to the buyer is not conspicuous and is not effective to exclude warranties. Similarly, an inconspicuous disclaimer of warranties under a heading of "Notice to Retail Buyers" has no effect.

When a disclaimer of warranties fails to be effective because it is not conspicuous, the implied warranties that would arise in the absence of any disclaimer are operative.

(b) UNCONSCIONABILITY AND PUBLIC POLICY. An exclusion of warranties made in the manner specified by the UCC is not unconscionable. In some states, warranty disclaimers are invalid as contrary to public policy or because they are prohibited by consumer protection laws.

There is authority that when a breach of warranty is the result of negligence of the seller, the disclaimer of warranty liability and a limitation of remedies to refunding the purchase price is not binding. Such a limitation is unreasonable, unconscionable, and against public policy.

If a seller makes any written warranty of a consumer product costing more than $15, the seller is barred from excluding any warranty that would be implied under the UCC.[13]

18. Particular Provisions

A statement such as "There are no warranties that extend beyond the description on the face hereof" excludes all implied warranties of fitness. Implied warranties (other than the warranty of title and the warranty against encumbrances) are excluded by the statement "as is," "with all faults," or other language that in normal, common speech calls attention to the warranty exclusion and makes it clear that there is no implied warranty.

In order for a disclaimer of warranties to be a binding part of an oral sales contract, the disclaimer must be called to the attention of the buyer.

In a sales contract, provisions excluding warranties have only that effect. They do not bar the buyer from recovering damages for fraud, negligence, or strict tort liability.

19. Exclusion of Warranties by Examination of Goods

There is no implied warranty with respect to defects in goods that an examination should have revealed when the buyer, before making the final contract, has examined the goods, or model or sample, or has refused to make such examination. For example, Jones purchased a secondhand automobile for $9,000. He refused to inspect the car before the sale, although the seller offered it to him for that purpose. Later, after using the car, Jones found it necessary to reline the brakes and to repair other defects that would have been obvious if he had made a reasonable examination of the car. Jones cannot recover in an action for breach of warranty against the seller, since he had the opportunity to examine the car but had failed to do so.

The examination of the goods by the buyer does not ordinarily exclude the existence of an express warranty. It may, however, if it can be concluded that the buyer, by the examination, learned of the falsity of the statement claimed to be a warranty. As a result, such statement did not in fact form part of the basis of the bargain.

20. Postsale Disclaimer

Frequently, a statement purporting to exclude or modify warranties appears for the first time in a written contract sent to confirm or memorialize the oral contract made earlier. The exclusion or modification may likewise appear in an invoice, a bill, or an instruction manual delivered to the buyer at or after the time the goods are received. Such postsale disclaimers have no effect on warranties that arose at the time of the sale.

An exclusion of warranties in a manufacturer's manual given to the buyer after the sale

---

[13] Ismael v Goodman, 106 NC App 421, 417 SE2d 290 (1992).

is not binding on a buyer, because it is not a term of the sales contract.

If the buyer assents to the postsale disclaimer, however, it is effective as a modification of the sales contract.

E. OTHER THEORIES OF PRODUCT LIABILITY

In addition to suit for breach of an express guarantee, an express warranty, or an implied warranty, a plaintiff in a given product liability case may be able to sue for negligence, fraud, or strict tort liability.

21. Negligence

A person injured because of the defective condition of a product may be entitled to sue the seller or manufacturer for the damages for negligence. The injured person must be able to show that the defendant was negligent in the preparation or manufacture of the article or failed to provide proper instructions and warnings as to dangers. An action for negligence rests on common law tort principles. It does not require privity of contract.

22. Fraud

The UCC expressly preserves the pre-Code law as to fraud. Thus, a person defrauded by a distributor's or manufacturer's false statements about a product will generally be able to recover damages for the harm sustained because of such misrepresentations. False state-ments are fraudulent if made with knowledge that they are false or with reckless indifference as to whether they are true.

23. Strict Tort Liability

Independently of the UCC, a manufacturer or distributor of a defective product is liable under strict tort liability to a person who is injured by the product. This liability exists without regard to whether the person injured is a purchaser, a consumer, or a third person, such as a bystander. It is no defense that privity of contract does not exist between the injured party and the defendant. Likewise, it is no defense that the defect was found in a component part purchased from another manufacturer.[14] This concept is not one of absolute liability; that is, it must first be shown that there was a defect in the product at the time it left the control of the defendant.[15] The defendant is liable if the product is defective and unreasonably dangerous and has caused harm. It is immaterial whether or not the defendant was negligent or whether the user was guilty of contributory negligence. Assumption of risk by the injured party, on the other hand, is a defense available to the defendant.[16]

24. Cumulative Theories of Liability

The theories of product liability are not mutually exclusive. Thus, a given set of facts may give rise to two or more theories of liability, as in the *Shaw* case.

---

[14] The concept of strict tort liability was judicially declared in Greenman v Yuba Power Products, 59 Cal 2d 57, 27 Cal Rptr 697, 377 P2d 897 (1963). This concept has been incorporated in the Restatement of Torts 2d as § 402A.

[15] McLaughlin v Michelin Tire Corp. (Wyo) 778 P2d 59 (1989).

[16] Monsanto Co. v Logisticon, Inc. (Mo App) 736 SW2d 371 (1989).

SHAW v GENERAL MOTORS
(Colo App) 727 P2d 387 (1986)

General Motors (GM) manufactured the cab and chassis of a truck that was sold unchanged by Daniels Motors (DM) to the city of Colorado Springs. Fontaine Truck Equipment Co.(FTE) manufactured a dump bed and hoist that was sold by another equipment company to the City of Colorado Springs. Fontaine installed the dump bed and hoist on the General Motors truck and made further modifications as specified by the city, so that the truck would be usable as a pothole repair truck by the city. Shaw, while in the city's employ, was injured when his co-worker backed the pothole repair truck over him. Shaw brought suit against GM, DM, and FTE. Shaw argued that the truck was defective and unreasonably dangerous to its user because of defendants' failure to warn of the necessity of installing a back-up alarm, and because of defendants' alleged failure to fulfill their duty in installing such a back-up alarm. He claimed liability because of (1) strict tort liability, (2) negligence, (3) breach of implied warranties of fitness and merchantability, and (4) breach of express warranties. From a judgment in favor of defendants, Shaw appealed.

PIERCE, J. . . .

I. Strict [Tort] Liability

General Motors

A manufacturer of component parts, such as GM here, may be held strictly liable for injuries as a result of design defects in the component when it is expected to and does reach the consumer without substantial change in condition. While it may be arguable whether GM's cab and chassis underwent "substantial change in condition" because of the modifications made by the City, other issues regarding strict [tort] liability must be considered as to GM.

The critical questions as concerns GM are whether the condition of the truck at the time of its delivery to DM was defective and unreasonably dangerous without a back-up alarm or unreasonably dangerous as a result of a failure to warn.

Based on the pleadings and other materials submitted, the truck was not in such a defective condition so as to impose strict [tort] liability upon GM.

The record here shows that the GM cab and chassis could be equipped for numerous different uses; that, at the time of assembly by GM, there was no restriction of rear vision; and that it was assembled by GM with two rear-view mirrors for visibility around most body installations. In rebuttal, plaintiff points to deposition testimony by a GM engineer who admitted that a back-up alarm system would be "desirable" given the City's use of the truck as a pothole repair truck. This testimony, however, does not show that a defective condition existed at the time of the truck's delivery to DM.

As a result, at the time that the truck left GM's control, it had no "inherent dangers" such as would expose GM to liability for failure to warn of an unreasonably dangerous condition. Based on the record, the likelihood of an accident resulting from the GM truck in the condition in which it was delivered was not such as to require warnings.

Plaintiff argues that GM should have foreseen that its truck would be transformed into a pothole filling truck which had visual impairment. Under the circumstances of this case, to require such foreseeability would be tantamount to making GM an insurer against all accidents. The principle of strict [tort] liability does not impose such absolute liability.

Thus, plaintiff could not have prevailed against GM on a theory of strict [tort] liability. Accordingly, judgment was proper.

. . .

Fontaine

The critical questions as to FTE are whether the dump bed and hoist were in such a condition at the time of their delivery to the equipment company as to be defective and unreasonably dangerous without a back-up alarm or unreasonably dangerous as a result of a failure to warn. . . .

The fundamental bases for plaintiff's allegations that the dump bed and hoist are defective are that: (1) it lacked a back-up alarm and (2) FTE failed to warn that lack of a back-up alarm constituted an inherent danger. The lack of a back-up alarm cannot be considered an unreasonably dangerous or defective condition until final assembly of all components, because, until assembled, there can be no need for the back-up device.

. . . With respect to plaintiff's allegation that FTE failed to warn, considering the unlikelihood of the dump bed and hoist backing up by themselves, we conclude there is no reasonable likelihood of an accident as a result of FTE's failure to warn. The condition of FTE's product was not, therefore, defective and unreasonably dangerous without a warning. Thus, liability could not attach to FTE. Strict [tort] liability does not equate to absolute liability.

Therefore, plaintiff's allegations did not provide a valid basis for relief, and judgment was proper in favor of FTE.

II. Negligence

Before liability can be found in a negligence action, the existence of a duty of care must be determined. This is a question of law. Whether the law should impose a duty requires consideration of the risk involved, the foreseeability and likelihood of injury as weighed against the social utility of the actor's conduct, the magnitude of the burden of guarding against injury or harm, and the consequences of placing the burden upon the actor.

Based on these considerations, there may be a duty to install an alarm system, but it does not lie with the defendants here.

We rule that defendants here owed no duty to the class to which plaintiff belongs. GM, DM, and FTE, as manufacturers and sellers of component parts that were assembled by the City, could not properly evaluate, or likely foresee, the risks arising from not installing a specific safety feature such as a back-up alarm. The burden of guarding against the injury suffered here should appropriately be placed upon the entity that designed the final product, arranged for acquisition of all the component parts, and directed their assembly. We find little social utility in placing this burden upon the manufacturers and sellers of the component parts, who did not partake in the designing or assembling of the final product.

Thus, absent a duty of care, plaintiff's claims of negligence were properly dismissed against GM, DM, and FTE.

III. Implied Warranties

Implied warranty liability can extend to the manufacturer of component parts. Such liability can also extend to sellers of component parts. However, the lack of fitness for ordinary purposes as well as for particular purposes must be found in the component parts before they leave the component parts manufacturers or sellers.

Plaintiff claims that the GM cab and chassis were not safe and fit for this use and application. However, as was discussed in Part I herein, the record does not show that a defective condition existed at the time that the truck left GM and DM. The documentation presented here unrebuttably shows that the GM truck was safe and fit for ordinary use and for its particular purpose, as that particular purpose was identifiable prior to assembly by the City. Therefore, based on the record, plaintiff could not prevail on his claims of breach of implied warranties against GM and DM.

Moreover, the record shows that DM sold to the City a truck which met the specifications set forth in the City's bidding form. DM, having substantially complied with the specifications will not be held to have extended a warranty of fitness.

The record also supports FTE's substantial compliance with the City's specifications. Therefore, it too cannot be held liable on implied warranties of fitness for particular or ordinary purposes.

IV. Express Warranties

In their pleadings, plaintiff alleges that GM, DM, and FTE breached express warranties of safety and fitness, and other express warranties set forth in their publications. On appeal, plaintiff specifically argues that deposition testimony stating that "Chevy's business is providing the right truck for your business" represents an express warranty to which the GM truck did not conform. This language does not constitute an affirmation of fact or a promise; it is "merely the sellers' opinion or commendation of the goods." See [UCC §] 2-313(2). . . . Thus, no warranty was created. . . .

[Judgments affirmed]

QUESTIONS

1. How did the court decide the question of strict tort liability against the defendants?
2. How did the court decide the issue of negligence?
3. Was there a breach of either express or implied warranties?

SUMMARY

There are six theories to protect from loss caused by nonconforming goods. They are (1) guarantee, (2) express warranty, (3) implied warranty, (4) negligence, (5) fraud, and (6) strict tort liability.

Theories of product liability are not mutually exclusive. A given set of facts may give rise to liability under two or more theories.

The requirement of privity of contract (that is, that only the parties to the sales contract could sue each other) has been widely rejected. The law is moving toward the conclusion that persons harmed because of an improper product may sue anyone who is in any way responsible. The requirement of privity has been abolished by most states in cases where the plaintiff is a member of the buyer's family or household or a guest in the buyer's home and has sustained personal injury because of the product.

Warranties may be express or implied. Both have the same effect and operate as though the defendant had made an express guarantee.

A warranty made after a sale does not require consideration. It is regarded as a modification of the sales contract.

Express warranties are regulated by federal statute and the FTC. These warranties must be labeled as full or limited warranties and must conform to certain standards.

A distinction is made between a merchant seller and the casual seller. A merchant seller is responsible for a greater range of warranties.

A seller makes a warranty of good title unless such warranty is excluded. Any description, sample, or model made part of the basis of the bargain creates an express warranty that the goods shall conform to the description, sample, or model. Warranties of fitness for a particular purpose and merchantability are implied warranties.

Warranties may be disclaimed by agreement of the parties, provided the disclaimer is not unconscionable. A written disclaimer to exclude warranties must be conspicuous. To disclaim the implied warranty of merchantability, the term *merchantability* must be used. Postsale disclaimers have no effect on warranties that arose at the time of the sale.

The warranties of merchantability and fitness exist under the CISG. However, disclaimers under CISG need not mention merchantability, nor must the disclaimer be conspicuous.

The strict tort liability plaintiff must show that there was a defect in the product at the time it left the control of the defendant. No negligence need be established on the part of the defendant, nor is contributory negligence of the plaintiff a defense. The defendant may show that the injured party assumed the risk.

LAW IN PRACTICE

1. When you are buying, be aware that every assurance of quality is not a warranty. Some statements may be "sales talk," and such statements will not be the basis for a breach of warranty action.
2. When you buy goods "as is" or "with all faults," there are no implied warranties of fitness or merchantability.

3. Watch for postsale disclaimers of warranties. If you agree to them, they are treated as modifications of the contract and will be binding.
4. When you are selling, remember that the words "I warrant" need not be used in order for the courts to conclude that a warranty has been made.

QUESTIONS AND CASE PROBLEMS

1. What social forces are affected by the abolition of the requirement of privity in product liability suits?
2. Mrs. Jackson purchased a sealed can of Katydids, chocolate-covered, pecan caramel candies manufactured by Nestle. Shortly thereafter, Jackson bit into one of the candies and allegedly broke a tooth on a pecan shell embedded in the candy. Jackson filed a complaint asserting breach of implied warranty. How would you argue on behalf of the company? How would you argue on behalf of Mrs. Jackson? In your answer discuss both the reasonable expectation test and the foreign–natural test. [*Jackson v Nestle-Beich, Inc. (Ill App) 589 NE2d 547*]
3. Webster purchased a used automobile from an automobile dealer, and the contract of sale provided: "This automobile is sold 'AS IS.'" Have the warranties (a) of title, or (b) against encumbrances been disclaimed?
4. Steve purchases an electric kitchen range from the Shermack Electric Appliance Company. In the instruction manual that is enclosed in the crate in which the range is delivered to Steve's home, there is a statement that Shermack makes no warranty, express or implied, with respect to the range. The

range works properly for two weeks and then ceases to function. When Steve demands his money back from Shermack, it raises the defense that all warranties, including that of fitness for normal use, were excluded by the statement in the manual. Is Shermack correct?

5. Edgmore has a class reunion at his house. There is a substantial amount of food left over. He sells the surplus food to his neighbor Hartranft for a fraction of its price. In eating this food, Hartranft is injured from a piece of glass that was contained in a can of salmon. Hartranft sues Edgmore for the injuries sustained. Is Edgmore liable?

6. A buyer purchased a new drive-through car wash machine from a dealer. It washed the cars effectively, but it would knock off external accessories such as mirrors and radio antennas. When the buyer complained, the seller stated that the contract made no provision with respect to such matters. Was this a valid defense?

7. Avery purchased a refrigerator from a retail store. The written contract stated that the refrigerator was sold "as is" and that the warranty of merchantability and all warranties of fitness were excluded. This was stated in large capital letters printed just above the line on which Avery signed her name. The refrigerator worked properly for a few weeks and then stopped. The store refused to do anything about it because of the exclusion of the warranties made by the contract. Avery claimed that this exclusion was not binding because it was unconscionable. Was Avery correct? [*Avery v Aladdin Products Div., Natl. Service Industries, Inc. 128 Ga App 266, 196 SE2d 357*]

8. A manufacturer advertised its product in national magazines. The advertisement induced a buyer to purchase the product. The product did not live up to the statements in the advertisement. The buyer claimed that there was a breach of warranty. The manufacturer contended that the statements in the advertisement were obviously sales talk and therefore could not constitute a warranty. Was this a valid defense? [*Westrie Battery Co. v Standard Electric Co. (CA10 Colo) 482 F2d 1307*]

9. Clark suffered an injury due to a defect in a chain saw he had purchased from Grey Hardware. The saw was manufactured by Lee Tool Corp. Clark commences an action against Lee Tool Corp., based on strict tort liability. Lee Tool Corp. argues that absent privity, the suit should be dismissed. Is Lee Tool Corp. correct? Why?

10. The defendant, Zogarts, manufactured and sold a practice device for beginning golfers. The statements on the package stated that the device was completely safe and that a player could never be struck by the golf ball of the device. Hauter was hit by the ball when practicing with the device. He sued Zogarts. Zogarts denied liability on the ground that the statements were merely matters of opinion, so liability could not be based on them. Was this a valid defense? [*Hauter v Zogarts, 14 Cal 104, 120 Cal Rptr 681, 534 P2d 377*]

11. A buyer purchased an engine to operate an irrigation pump. The buyer selected the engine from a large number that were standing on the floor of the seller's stockroom. A label on the engine stated that it would produce 100 horsepower. The buyer needed an engine that would generate at least 80 horsepower. In actual use in the buyer's irrigation system, the engine generated only 60 horsepower. The buyer sued the seller for damages. The seller raised the defense that no warranty of fitness for the buyer's particular purpose of operating an irrigation pump had arisen because the seller did not know of the use to which the buyer intended to put the engine. Also, the buyer had not relied on the seller's skill and judgment in selecting the particular engine. Did the seller have any liability based on warranties? [*Potter v Ryndall, 22 NC App 129, 205 SE2d 808, cert. den. 285 NC 661, 207 SE2d 762*]

12. The Old Fort Trading Post sold an antique pistol to McCoy. Some time later the police took the gun from McCoy when they learned it was stolen property. The gun was turned over to its rightful owner. McCoy notified Old Fort and demanded his money back. The refund was denied. What remedy, if any, does McCoy have. Explain. [*Trial v McCoy (Tex App) 553 SW2d 199*]

13. A lawyer sold his yacht to a buyer who, upon discovering defects in the yacht, sued the lawyer for breach of the implied warranty of merchantability. Will he recover? Why?

14. A strict tort liability defendant may raise the defense that there was no negligence involved and that, even if there was negligence, the plaintiff cannot recover because the plaintiff was guilty of contributory negligence. Appraise this statement.

15. Mark went to the Happy Hour Cafe to eat breakfast. While drinking milk, his throat was cut because the milk contained a piece of glass. Mark thereupon brought an action against Happy Hour to recover damages for personal injuries resulting from breach of an implied warranty. Will he be successful?

C H A P T E R   2 8

REMEDIES FOR BREACH OF SALES CONTRACTS

LEARNING OBJECTIVES

After studying this chapter, you will be able to:
1. *List the remedies of the seller when the buyer breaches a sales contract.*
2. *List the remedies of the buyer when the seller breaches a sales contract.*
3. *Distinguish between rejection of nonconforming goods and revocation of acceptance.*
4. *Determine the validity of clauses limiting damages.*
5. *Discuss the waiver of and preservation of defenses of a buyer.*

If one of the parties to a sale fails to perform the contract, the law makes several remedies available to the other party. In addition, the parties may have included provisions pertaining to remedies in their contract.

A. STATUTE OF LIMITATIONS

Judicial remedies are ordinarily subject to a time limitation that bars resort to the courts after the expiration of a particular period of time. The UCC supplies the statute of limitations for sales of goods except when suit is brought on a tort theory, such as negligence, fraud, or strict tort.

1. Code Claim

An action for a breach of a sales contract must be commenced within four years after the cause of action arises. This time limit applies regardless of when the aggrieved party learned that there was a cause of action. Thus the breach of a warranty occurs when tender of delivery is made to the buyer, even though no defect then appears and no harm is sustained until a later date.[1] The time limit may be reduced to one year by agreement of the parties but may not be extended.

(a) FUTURE PERFORMANCE WARRANTY. When an express warranty is made as to future performance, the statute of limitations does not run from the time of the tender but from the date when the future performance begins.[2]

(b) NOTICE OF BREACH. The buyer who sues the seller for damages claimed because of a breach of the sales contract must give the seller notice of the breach within a reasonable time after the buyer discovers or should have discovered it.[3]

2. Non-Code Claim

When the plaintiff sues on a non-Code theory, even though it relates to goods, the UCC statute of limitations does not apply. Thus, when the plaintiff sues on the basis of strict tort, fraud, or negligence, the action is subject to the tort statutes of limitations. When the plaintiff sues on the basis of an express guarantee, the action is governed by the contract statute of limitations. Contract and tort statutes of limitations are based on state laws, and the time limitations vary by state.

B. REMEDIES OF THE SELLER

When a sales contract is broken by the buyer, the seller has a number of remedies.

3. Seller's Lien

In the absence of an agreement for the extension of credit to the purchaser, the seller has a lien on the goods. That is, the seller has the right to retain possession of the goods until the buyer pays for them.

The seller's lien may be lost by (a) waiver, such as by a later extension of credit, (b) delivery of the goods to a carrier or other bailee, without a reservation of title or possession, for the purpose of delivery to the buyer, (c) acquisition of the property by the buyer or the buyer's agent by lawful means, or (d) payment or tender of the price by the buyer.

4. Resale by Seller

When the buyer has broken the contract, the seller may resell any of the goods in the seller's possession. After the resale, the seller is not liable to the original buyer on the contract or for any profit obtained on the resale. On the other hand, if the proceeds are less than the

---

[1]　American Ally Steel, Inc. v Armco, Inc. (Tex Civ App) 777 SW2d 173 (1989).

[2]　Safeway Stores, Inc. v Certain-Teed Corp. (Tex App) 710 SW2d 544 (1986).

[3]　UCC § 2-607(3)(a).

contract price, the seller may recover the loss from the original buyer.[4]

Reasonable notice must be given to the original buyer of the intention to make a private sale. Such notice must also be given of a public sale, unless the goods are perishable in nature or threaten to decline rapidly in value. Notice of a public sale must be given to the general public in such a way that is commercially reasonable under the circumstances.

5. Cancellation by Seller

When the buyer makes a material breach of the contract, other than failing to pay the purchase price, the seller may cancel the contract. Such action puts an end to the contract, discharging all obligations on both sides that are still unperformed. The seller retains any remedy with respect to the breach by the buyer. Cancellation revests the seller with title to the goods.

6. Seller's Action for Purchase Price or Damages

When the buyer fails to pay for accepted goods, the seller may bring an ordinary contract action to recover the purchase price. If the buyer breaches the contract in any other way, the seller may sue the buyer for damages.

Ordinarily, the amount of damages is to be measured by the difference between the market price at the time and place of the tender of the goods and the contract price. If this measure of damages does not place the seller in the position in which the seller would have been placed by the buyer's performance, the seller may be permitted to recover lost profits. The seller may also receive an allowance for overhead. The seller may in any case recover, as incidental damages, any commercially reasonable charges, expenses, or commissions incurred in enforcing that remedy. For example, the seller may recover expenses for the transportation, care, and custody of the goods after the buyer's breach and may recover costs incurred in the return or resale of the goods. Such damages are recovered in addition to any other damages that may be recovered by the seller.

If goods are specially manufactured and the buyer refuses to take them, can the seller recover as damages the full purchase price and keep the goods?[5] This was the issue in the *Royal Jones* case.

ROYAL JONES & ASSOC. v FIRST THERMAL
(Fla App) 566 So 2d 853 (1990)

Royal Jones ordered three steel rendering tanks from First Thermal for use in its business of constructing rendering plants. Under the terms of the contract, First Thermal would manufacture the tanks according to Royal Jones's specifications for a price of $64,350. When the work was done, Royal Jones refused to accept them and refused to pay the contract price. First Thermal brought an action for the contract price of the tanks. From a judgment in favor of First Thermal, Royal Jones appealed.

---

4 UCC § 2-706(1), (6). Eades Commodities v Hoeper (Mo App) 825 SW2d 34 (1992).

5 Hapag-Lloyd, A.G. v Marine Indemnity Ins. Co. of America (Fla App) 576 So 2d 1330 (1991).

ZEHMER, J. . . . [UCC § 2-]709(1)(b) provides that when the buyer fails to pay the price for goods as it becomes due, the seller may recover, together with incidental damages, the price "of goods identified to the contract if the seller is unable after reasonable effort to resell them at a reasonable price or the circumstances reasonably indicate that such effort will be unavailing." Royal Jones contends that the lower court erred in awarding First Thermal the full contract price as damages for the tanks pursuant to section [2-709], because there was no evidence presented at trial that either First Thermal was unable to resell the tanks after making a reasonable effort to do so, or that the circumstances reasonably indicated that such effort would be unavailing. In reply, First Thermal contends that there was uncontroverted testimony at trial that the tanks were specially manufactured for Royal Jones and that any efforts at resale would have been unavailing. . . .

The trial court did not err in awarding First Thermal the full contract price as damages, because the evidence presented at trial by First Thermal was sufficient to meet its burden of proving that the circumstances reasonably indicated that any effort to resell the tanks would have been unavailing. . . . First Thermal proved that any effort at resale would have been unavailing because these were the only rendering tanks First Thermal ever made, the tanks were manufactured according to Royal Jones's specifications, First Thermal had no other customers to which it could resell the tanks, and it was unaware how the tanks could have been marketed for resale. Also, the tanks were built without needed internal components and to a special size in accordance with Royal Jones's specifications and could not be used as rendering tanks without special engineering to which First Thermal had no access. Finally, there was testimony that the tanks had only scrap value to First Thermal of about $700 if they were processed for a scrap dealer. This evidence was sufficient to shift the burden to Royal Jones to show that any effort at resale would not have been unavailing, or that the tanks had some potential market value beyond the salvage value claimed by First Thermal. . . . However, Royal Jones presented no evidence to the contrary at trial, and the lower court did not err in awarding First Thermal the full contract price pursuant to section [2-]709.

Royal Jones next contends that allowing First Thermal to recover the contract price, while allowing it to keep the rendering tanks, amounts to an impermissible double recovery on the part of First Thermal. . . .

First Thermal contends that section [2-709(2)] permits it to hold the tanks prior to collecting on the judgment. Section [2-709(2)] provides that:

where the seller sues for the price he must hold for the buyer any goods which have been identified to the contract and are still in his control except that if resale becomes possible he may resell them at any time prior to collection of the judgment. The net proceeds of any such resale must be credited to the buyer and payment of the judgment entitles him to any goods not resold.

Section [2-709(2)] permits First Thermal to hold the tanks for Royal Jones's credit prior to collection of the judgment and requires First Thermal to credit Royal Jones with the net proceeds of any resale of the tanks made prior to collection on the judgment or to turn over any tanks not resold upon Royal Jones's payment of the judgment. First Thermal has reaffirmed its willingness to turn the tanks over to Royal Jones upon payment. Consequently, there is no impermissible double recovery. . . .

[Judgment affirmed]

QUESTIONS

1. Why was it important that the goods were specially manufactured?
2. What was the argument of Royal Jones?
3. What was the basis for the court's decision?

---

7. Seller's Nonsale Remedies

In addition to possessing the above stated remedies as a seller, the modern seller enters into other transactions that protect against breach by a buyer. Such a transaction may be a secured transaction under UCC Article 9. **Secured transactions** include credit sales that enable the seller to take possession of the goods if the buyer fails to pay the amount owed. Either in addition to or in place of a secured transaction, the buyer may have been required to deposit a sum of money with a neutral party, such as a bank, to make payment to the seller upon the buyer's default. Instead of such an **escrow deposit**, the buyer may have furnished the seller with a standby letter of credit or a surety bond to protect the seller from default by the buyer. A **letter of credit** is a written agreement by which the issuer, usually a bank, agrees to honor the drafts drawn on it by the person named in the letter.

C. REMEDIES OF THE BUYER

When a sales contract is broken by the seller, the buyer has a number of remedies provided by Article 2 of the UCC. Additional remedies based on contract or tort theories of liability may also be available.

8. Rejection of Improper Tender

If the seller's tender or the goods do not conform to the contract in any respect, the buyer may reject the goods. For example, the buyer may reject a mobile home when it does not contain an air conditioner with the capacity specified by the contract. The buyer may reject a tender that is not perfect, as against the contention that a substantial performance is sufficient.

Goods tendered may consist of different units, some of which conform to the contract and some of which do not. In such a case, the buyer has the choice of (a) rejecting the entire quantity tendered, (b) accepting the entire tender, or (c) accepting any one or more commercial units and rejecting the rest.

The rejection must be made within a reasonable time after the delivery or tender, and the buyer must notify the seller of the choice made.[6]

After rejecting the goods, the buyer may not exercise any right of ownership as to the goods. The buyer must hold the goods, awaiting instructions from the seller. If the buyer disposes of the goods before the seller has had a reasonable time in which to give instructions, the buyer is liable for any loss.

9. Revocation of Acceptance

The buyer may revoke acceptance of the goods when they do not conform to the contract and the defect substantially impairs the value of the contract to the buyer. For example, a buyer purchased an emergency electric power plant. The plant produced only about 65 percent of the power called for by the contract. This was not sufficient to operate the buyer's equipment. Repeated attempts to improve the system failed. The nonconformity was so great that it substantially impaired the value of the

---

[6] UCC § 2-602(1).

contract to the buyer, and the buyer was entitled to revoke acceptance.

Proof of substantial impairment is required to justify revocation of acceptance. The mere fact that the goods do not conform to the contract does not entitle the buyer to revoke acceptance. On the other hand, it is not necessary that the buyer show that the goods are worthless.

A revocation of acceptance does no more than revoke the acceptance. In itself, it does not cancel the contract with the seller. After revoking acceptance, the buyer has the choice of canceling that contract or insisting that the seller deliver conforming goods in place of the goods originally delivered.

10. Procedure for Revoking Acceptance

To revoke acceptance of the goods, the buyer must take certain steps.

(a) NOTICE OF REVOCATION. The buyer must give the seller notice of revocation. The revocation of acceptance is effective when the buyer notifies the seller. It is not necessary that the buyer make an actual return of the goods to make the revocation effective.

(b) TIME FOR REVOCATION. The notice of revocation must be given within a reasonable time after the buyer discovers that the goods do not conform or after the buyer should have discovered such nonconformity. A buyer is not required to notify the seller of the revocation of acceptance until the buyer is reasonably certain that the nonconformity of the goods substantially impairs the value of the contract. Thus, the mere fact that the buyer suspects that the goods do not conform and that such nonconformity may substantially impair the value of the contract does not itself require that the buyer immediately give notice to the seller.

In the *Cato* case the buyer claimed that he had revoked his acceptance within a reasonable time.

A buyer is not barred from revoking acceptance of the goods because the buyer has de-

CATO EQUIPMENT CO. INC. v MATTHEWS
91 NC App 546, 372 SE2d 872 (1988)

Matthews purchased a crankshaft for installation in a rebuilt engine. He returned the first crankshaft, in the belief that it was too small. Cato assured Matthews that it would stand behind its product. Relying on this assurance, Matthews requested and installed a second crankshaft. It was used for several months, during which time it was discovered that the second crankshaft had cracks that caused damage to other engine parts. Matthews promptly notified Cato of the defect, requesting a further replacement. Cato sued for the purchase price when Matthews refused to pay for the second crankshaft. Matthews counterclaimed on the ground of breach of implied warranty and revoked his acceptance. From a judgment in favor of Matthews, Cato appealed.

ARNOLD, J. . . . Under UCC § 2-608, a buyer

may revoke his acceptance of a lot or commercial unit whose nonconformity substantially impairs its value to him if he has accepted it . . . without discovery of such nonconformity if his acceptance was reasonably induced either by the difficulty of discovery before acceptance or by the seller's assurances. [UCC§] 2-608(1)(b).

. . . In order for a buyer to show that his revocation was justifiable, the following four elements must be proved: (1) that the goods contained a nonconformity that substantially impaired their value to him; (2) that he either accepted the goods knowing of the nonconformity but reasonably assuming that it would be cured, or that he accepted the goods not knowing of the nonconformity due to the difficulty of the discovery or reasonable assurances from the seller that the goods were conforming; (3) that revocation occurred within a reasonable time after he discovered or should have discovered the defect; and (4) that he has notified the seller of his revocation. . . .

The trial court determined that the crankshaft was cracked when defendant installed it in the engine. It also found that the crack caused damage to the rod bearing. Obviously a crankshaft which was cracked and caused damage to other parts of the engine substantially impaired its value to defendant.

From the record and the trial court's findings of fact, it is apparent that the cracks were impossible to discover prior to their use in the engine. Only when the crankshaft was removed from the engine and cleaned up did defendant discover the cracks.

What is a reasonable time for a buyer to revoke his acceptance is ordinarily a question of fact for the jury. . . . In determining what is a reasonable time, it is proper to consider all the surrounding circumstances, including the nature of the defect, the complexity of the goods involved, the sophistication of the buyer, and the difficulty of the discovery.

Defendant was not able to discover the hairline cracks in the crankshaft until after its use in the engine when they became more severe and apparent. . . . There was no reasonable delay in defendant's revocation.

Defendant notified plaintiff of his revocation as soon as he learned of the damage to the crankshaft and bearings. . . .

Under [UCC §] 2-608(3), a buyer who revoked his acceptance has the same rights and duties with regard to the goods involved as if he had rejected them. The measure of damages for breach of warranty is the difference at the time of acceptance between the value of the goods accepted and the value they would have had if they had been warranted. [UCC §] 2-714(2). The crankshaft had no value as delivered and the damages were the purchase price. We find error neither in the trial court's implicit determination of revocation and damages, nor in its setoff of defendant's damages against the purchase price owed to plaintiff. . . .

[Judgment affirmed]

QUESTIONS

1. When must revocation of acceptance occur?
2. Did Matthews make a timely revocation? Explain.
3. Could Matthews have sued for breach of warranty?

layed until attempts of the seller to correct the defects proved unsuccessful. For example, the lapse of even a year does not bar revocation of acceptance where the goods are of a complex nature, such as a computer, and the seller was continuously experimenting and assuring the buyer that the goods would be made to work.

(c) DISPOSITION OF GOODS AFTER REVOCATION. After making a revocation of acceptance, the buyer must hold the goods, awaiting instructions from the seller. If the buyer has paid the seller in advance, the buyer may retain possession of the goods after revoking acceptance as security for the refund of the money that has been paid.

11. Buyer's Action for Damages for Nondelivery

If the seller fails to deliver as required by the contract or repudiates the contract, the buyer is entitled to sue the seller for damages for breach of contract. The buyer is entitled to recover the difference between the market price at the time the buyer learned of the breach and the contract price.

Within a reasonable time after the seller's breach, the buyer may cover—that is, procure the same or similar goods elsewhere.[7] If the buyer acts in good faith, the measure of damages for the seller's nondelivery or repudiation is then the difference between the cost of cover and the contract price.

12. Action for Breach of Warranty

One remedy that may be available to a buyer is an action for breach of warranty.

(a) NOTICE OF BREACH. If the buyer has accepted goods that do not conform to the contract or as to which there is a breach of warranty, the buyer must notify the seller of the breach within a reasonable time after the breach is discovered or should have been discovered. Otherwise the buyer is not entitled to complain.[8]

(b) MEASURE OF DAMAGES. If the buyer has given the necessary notice of breach, the buyer may recover damages measured by the loss resulting in the normal course of events from the breach. If suit is brought for breach of warranty, the measure of damages is the difference between the value of the goods as they were when accepted and the value that they would have had if they had been as warranted.

In other cases, the buyer may recover the difference between the contract price and the actual value of the goods.

Where the condition that breaches the warranty induces fright that causes illness, the warranty liability includes damages for such illness.

A buyer who is entitled to recover damages from the seller may deduct the amount of such damages from any balance remaining due on the purchase price, provided the seller is notified of the buyer's intention to do so.

(c) NOTICE OF THIRD-PARTY ACTION AGAINST BUYER. The buyer may be sued in consequence of the seller's breach of warranty. For example, the buyer's customers may sue because of the condition of the goods that the buyer has resold to them. In such a case, it is optional with the buyer whether or not to give the seller notice of the action and to request the seller to defend that action.

The buyer may also be sued by a third person because of patent infringement. In this case, however, the buyer must give notice of the action to the seller. Moreover, the seller can demand control over the defense of that action.[9]

---

[7] Erie Casein Co. Inc. v Anric Corp. 217 Ill App 3d 602, 577 NE2d 892 (1991).

[8] Hapag-Lloyd, A.G. v Marine Indemnity Ins. Co. of America (Fla App) 576 So 2d 1330 (1991).

[9] UCC § 2-607(5).

13. Cancellation by Buyer

The buyer may cancel or rescind the contract if the seller fails to deliver the goods or repudiates the contract or if the buyer has rightfully rejected tender of the goods or rightfully revoked acceptance of them. A buyer who cancels the contract is entitled to recover as much of the purchase price as has been paid, including the value of any property given as a trade-in as part of the purchase price. The fact that the buyer cancels the contract does not destroy the buyer's cause of action against the seller for breach of that contract. The buyer may therefore recover from the seller not only any payment made on the purchase price, but also damages for the breach of the contract. The damages represent the difference between the contract price and the cost of cover.[10]

The right of the buyer to cancel or rescind the sales contract may be lost by a delay in exercising the right. A buyer who, with full knowledge of the defects in the goods, makes partial payments or performs acts of dominion inconsistent with any intent to cancel cannot thereafter cancel the contract.

14. Buyer's Resale of Goods

When the buyer has possession of the goods after rightfully rejecting them or after rightfully revoking acceptance, the buyer is treated the same as a seller in possession of goods after the default of a buyer. That is, the aggrieved buyer has a security interest in the goods to protect the claim against the seller and may resell the goods. From the proceeds of the sale, the aggrieved buyer is entitled to deduct any payments made on the price and any expenses reasonably incurred in the inspection, receipt, transportation, care and custody, and resale of the goods.[11]

15. Action for Conversion or Recovery of Goods

When, as a result of the sales agreement, ownership passes to the buyer and the seller wrongfully refuses or neglects to deliver the goods, the buyer may maintain any action allowed by law to the owner of goods wrongfully converted or withheld. The obligation of the seller to deliver proper goods may be enforced by an order for specific performance in certain circumstances, such as when the goods are unique. Distributors have been granted specific performance against suppliers to deliver the goods covered by supply contracts. Specific performance will not be granted, however, merely because the price of the goods purchased from the seller has gone up. In such a case, the buyer can still purchase the goods in the open market. The fact that it will cost more to cover can be compensated for by allowing the buyer to recover greater damages from the seller.

16. Nonsale Remedies of the Buyer

In addition to the remedies given the buyer by UCC Article 2, the buyer may have remedies based on contract or on tort theories of liability.

(a) CONTRACT REMEDIES. The sales transaction may give the buyer the protection of an escrow account deposit or a standby letter of credit.

(b) TORT REMEDIES. The pre-Code law as to torts continues under the Code. The seller may therefore be held liable to the buyer for negligence, fraud, or strict tort.

In contrast with the pre-Code law of contracts, a defrauded buyer is not required to elect between avoiding the contract and suing

---

[10] UCC § 2-712(1), (2).
[11] UCC § 2-715(1).

for damages. A defrauded buyer may both avoid the contract and recover damages. The buyer also has the choice of retaining the contract and recovering damages for the fraud-caused loss.

D. CONTRACT PROVISIONS ON REMEDIES

The parties to a sales contract may modify or limit their remedies.

17. Limitation of Damages

The parties to the sales contract may limit or exclude the recovery of damages in case of breach.

(a) LIQUIDATION OF DAMAGES. The parties may specify the exact amount of damages that may be recovered in case of breach. Such a **liquidation of damages clause** is valid if the amount so specified is reasonable in the light of the actual harm that would be caused by the breach, the difficulty of proving the amount of such loss, and the inconvenience and impracticality of suing for damages or enforcing other remedies for breach.

(b) EXCLUSION OF DAMAGES. The sales contract may provide that in case of breach no damages may be recovered, or that no consequential damages may be recovered. When goods are sold for consumer use and personal injuries are sustained, such total exclusions are prima facie unconscionable and therefore prima facie not binding. Thus, a defendant in such a case cannot rely on the contract limitation unless the defendant is able to prove that the limitation of liability was commercially reasonable and fair, rather than oppressive and surprising. Moreover, when the seller would be liable to the buyer for damages, the seller cannot exclude liability for personal injuries to members of the buyer's family or household or to guests of the buyer.

If neither consumer goods nor personal injuries are involved, the exclusion of damages is binding unless the plaintiff proves that it is unconscionable. When the seller knows that the failure of the product, such as a harvester, to perform will cause serious economic loss, a limitation of damages to the return of the purchase price is void as unconscionable.

18. Down Payments and Deposits

The buyer may have made a deposit with the seller or an initial or down payment at the time of making the contract. If the contract contains a valid provision for liquidation of damages and the buyer defaults, the seller must return any part of the down payment or deposit in excess of the amount specified by the liquidated damages clause. In the absence of such a clause and in the absence of proof of greater damages sustained, according to UCC § 2-718, the seller's damages are computed as 20 percent of the purchase price or $500, whichever is smaller. The extent to which the down payment exceeds this amount must be returned to the buyer. For example, if in a contract for sale where the purchase price is $10,000, the buyer has paid $2,000 and then breaches the contract, the buyer would forfeit $500 of the amount paid and would be entitled to return of the balance of the payments made under the contract, namely, $1,500.

19. Limitation of Remedies

The parties may validly limit the remedies that are provided by the Code in the case of breach of contract. Thus, a seller may specify that the only remedy of the buyer for breach of warranty shall be the repair or replacement of the goods, or that the buyer shall be limited to returning the goods and obtaining a refund of the purchase price. A limitation of remedies need not be conspicuous.

If the parties agree to limit the seller's obligation to repair of goods or replacement of defective parts and the seller is unable or unwilling to make the goods function properly within a reasonable time, the agreed limitation is not binding. The buyer may then use any remedy authorized by the Code, just as though the contract had not contained any limitation on remedies.

In the *Osburn* case the dealer and the manufacturer of a mobile home claimed that their only obligation was to make repairs and that it did not matter if the repairs were unsuccessful.

OSBURN v BENDIX HOME SYSTEMS, INC.
(Okla) 613 P2d 445 (1980)

> Vernon and Phyllis Osburn purchased a mobile home from Bendix Home Systems, Inc. The "warranty" of the dealer and of the manufacturer stated that the liability for breach of warranty was limited to repairing any defects. The Osburns' home had numerous defects. After repeated repairs the home was still defective. The Osburns sued the dealer and the manufacturer for breach of warranty. The defendants asserted that their only obligation was to make repairs. From a judgment for the Osburns, the defendants appealed.

OPALA, J. . . . . Was the evidence with respect to the existence of defects sufficient to sustain a legal claim for breach of warranty? Did the limitation-of-remedy clause in [the] manufacturer's warranty "fail of its essential purpose" so as to make expanded UCC remedies available to the buyer under [UCC §] 2-719(2)? . . .

The proof here amply shows that, in addition to the substantial water leakage, numerous other defects and deficiencies existed. These consisted of (a) leaking water faucets, (b) buckled wall paneling, (c) missing interior trim, (d) insecurely fastened kitchen cabinets, (e) torn carpet and (f) a roof that made rumbling noises. All of these defects came to be discovered by the buyer shortly after he had moved into the home and all were promptly reported to the dealer pursuant to the warranty requirements. . . .

The warranty here in suit restricts the buyer's right of recovery for its breach to "repair or replacement of defective parts." The limitation so imposed is not, on its face, unconscionable. In fact, § 2-719(1)(a) expressly sanctions its employment. Limiting the buyer to the remedy of repair or replacement does not appear unfair because the warranty clause amply assures him of receiving the goods which either do or will conform to the contract. The purpose of the clause, as applied to this case, was hence to provide the buyer with a mobile home substantially free of defects. Implicit in the warranty-imposed obligation to repair or replace is the duty of providing conformable goods within a reasonable time after a defect in the original delivery is discovered.* Where the seller is afforded a reasonable opportunity to correct the defect and fails timely to respond or is repeatedly unsuccessful in the efforts to meet the warranty-imposed obligation, the limitation of remedy is deemed to have failed of its essential purpose *eo instante* and without the necessity of a prior judicial declaration.** The buyer is then free to invoke any of the broader remedies available under the Code.

Neither the seller nor the manufacturer was successful in the effort of rectifying the faulty conditions before the home was severely damaged by water leakage. When the home was not made to conform to the warranty within a reasonable time, the buyer—then left without the substantial value of his bargain—was relieved by the Code of the warranty-imposed limitation and hence able to seek broader recovery.

Manufacturer next complains that the trial court gave improper instructions upon the measure of damages for the breach in suit. The charge given called upon the jury to apply the difference—at the time and place of acceptance—between the actual value of the goods accepted and the value they would have had if they had been as warranted. This measure is, of course, proper when the evidence shows, as it did here, that the warranty-imposed limited-recovery clause "failed of its essential purpose."

*What is a "reasonable time" for taking any action under the UCC depends on the nature, purpose, and circumstances of such action . . . The terms of § 2-719(1) permit parties to tailor the outer limit of allowable recovery to their particular requirements, giving effect to reasonable agreements limiting or modifying existing remedies. They are designed to facilitate a fair recompense for breach of the contractual obligations. UCC § 2-719, Official Comment No. 1 *Conte v Dwan Lincoln-Mercury*, 172 Conn 112, 374 A2d 144 [1976]; . . . "The purpose of an exclusive remedy of replacement or repair of defective parts, whose presence constitute a breach of an express warranty, is to give the seller an opportunity to make the goods conforming while limiting the risks to which he is subject by excluding direct and consequential damages that might otherwise arise." *Beal v General Motors Corp.* 354 F Supp 423, 426 [D Del 1973].

**When a manufacturer limits its obligation to repair and replacement of defective parts, and repeatedly fails to correct the defect as promised within a reasonable time, it is liable for the breach of that promise as a breach of warranty. *Matthews v Ford Motor Co.*, 479 F2d 399 [4th Cir 1973]. . . . The fact that a manufacturer in good faith attempts to repair the defect whenever requested to do so is not a fulfillment of the warranty; he must demonstrate that the defect is permanently remedied as promised in the express warranty . . . . He can be liable for failure to fulfill the warranty obligation even if his failure to repair is neither willful nor negligent. *Soo Line R. Co. v Fruehauf Corp.*, 547 F2d 1365 [8th Cir 1977].

[Judgment affirmed]

QUESTIONS

1. What defense did the defendants raise?
2. How did the plaintiffs meet this argument?
3. Is there any relationship between the implied warranty provisions of the Code and the Code's provision as to the failure of a limited remedy?

20. Waiver of Defenses

A buyer may be barred from objecting to a breach of the contract by the seller because the sales contract expressly states that the buyer will not assert any defenses against the seller. As a matter of general contract law, a buyer may lose a defense by waiver even though nothing relating thereto was stated in the sales contract.

21. Preservation of Defenses

Consumer protection law protects consumers by preserving defenses. In such cases, there is no waiver of defenses. If the basis for the defense to a home-solicited sale becomes apparent within time to cancel the sale, it is possible that the consumer may assert the defense by exercising the right of cancellation.

(a) PRESERVATION NOTICE. Consumer defenses are preserved by a Federal Trade Commission regulation. This regulation requires that the papers signed by a consumer contain a provision that expressly states that the consumer is reserving any defense arising from the transaction.[12] A defense of the consumer arising from the original transaction may therefore be asserted against a third person acquiring such papers.

(b) PROHIBITION OF WAIVER. When the Federal Trade Commission preservation notice is included in the paper that is received by the third person, it is unnecessary to consider whether a waiver of defenses could be validly made. If the preservation notice is not included, the seller has committed an unfair trade practice. The question then arises as to whether the buyer may assert against an assignee a defense that could have been asserted against the seller. The answer to this question depends on state law. In many states, consumer protection statutes nullify a waiver of defenses by expressly providing that the buyer may assert against the seller's transferee any defense that might have been raised against the seller. Under some statutes, the buyer must give notice of any defense within a specified number of days after being notified of the assignment. Some courts extend consumer protection beyond the scope of the statute by ignoring a time limitation on the giving of notice of defenses and allow consumers to give late notice of defenses.

E. REMEDIES IN THE INTERNATIONAL SALE OF GOODS

The United Nations Convention on Contracts for the International Sale of Goods (CISG) provides remedies for breach of a sales contract between parties from nations that have approved the CISG.

22. Remedies of the Seller

Under the CISG, if the buyer fails to perform any obligations under the contract, the seller is given various remedies. The seller may require the buyer to pay the price, take delivery, and perform other obligations under the contract. The seller may also declare the contract void if the failure of the buyer to perform obligations under the contract amounts to a fundamental breach of contract.

23. Remedies of the Buyer

Under the CISG, a buyer may reject goods only if the tender is a fundamental breach of the contract. This is in contrast to the UCC requirement of perfect tender. Under the CISG, a buyer may also reduce the price when nonconforming goods are delivered, even though no notice of nonconformity is given. The buyer in this case must have a reasonable excuse for failure to give notice.

SUMMARY

The law provides a number of remedies for the breach of a sales contract. Remedies based on UCC theories are subject to a four-year statute of limitations. If the remedy sought is based on a non-UCC theory, a tort or contract statute of limitations established by state statute will apply.

Remedies of the seller may include (1) a lien on the goods until the seller is paid, (2) the right to resell goods, (3) the right to cancel the sales contract, and (4) the right to bring an action for damages or, in some cases, for the purchase price. A seller may also have remedies because of secured transactions, escrow

---

12 16 CFR § 433.1. It is an unfair or deceptive trade practice to take or receive a consumer credit contract that fails to contain such a preservation notice.

deposits, standby letters of credit, or surety bonds.

Remedies of the buyer may include (1) rejection of nonconforming goods, (2) revocation of acceptance, (3) an action for damages for nondelivery of conforming goods, (4) an action for breach of warranty, (5) cancellation of the sales contract, (6) the right to resell the goods, (7) the right to bring an action for conversion, recovery of goods, or specific performance, and (8) the right to sue for damages and cancel if the seller has made a material breach of the contract. The buyer may also have the protection of an escrow deposit or a standby letter of credit.

The parties may modify their remedies by contractual provision for liquidated damages, limitations on statutory remedies, or waiver of defenses. When consumers are involved, this freedom of contract is to some extent limited for their protection.

Under the CISG, the seller may require the buyer to pay the price, take delivery, and perform obligations under the contract, or may avoid the contract if there is a fundamental breach.

Under the CISG, a buyer may reject goods only if there is a fundamental breach of contract. The buyer may also reduce the price of goods if nonconforming.

LAW IN PRACTICE

1. Remember that warranties as to future performance run from the date when the future performance is to begin, not from the time of tender.

2. Be aware that when you revoke acceptance of goods, you must show that a nonconformity substantially impairs the value of the goods accepted.

QUESTIONS AND CASE PROBLEMS

1. What social forces are involved in the rule of law allowing the buyer to cover on the seller's breach?

2. Donna purchased a snowmobile from the Park Manufacturing Company. Three years later, it rolled over and injured her. She sued Park two years after her accident, alleging that Park had breached its implied warranty of merchantability. The suit was based on the theory that the snowmobile had rolled over because of a design defect and that this defect showed that the snowmobile was not fit for its normal use. Is Park liable for Donna's injuries?

3. Formetal Engineering submitted to Presto a sample and specification for precut polyurethane pads to be used in making air conditioning units. The goods were paid for as soon as they were delivered. Defendant subsequently discovered that the pads did not conform to the sample and specifications in that there were incomplete cuts, color variances, and faulty adherence to the pad's paper backing. Plaintiff was then informed of the defects. Formetal notified Presto that the pads would be rejected and returned to Presto. The goods were not returned for some five months. Presto argued

that it was denied the right to cure in that the goods were not returned until some 125 days after defendant promised to do so. Was the rejection proper? Explain. [*Presto Mfg. Co. v Formetal Engineering Co. (Ill App) 360 NE2d 510*]

4. Leeper purchased a can of starch from Banks Wonder Market. She was injured by it on January 30. On April 4 she notified the manufacturer, Colgate-Palmolive Company. She did not notify Banks until she commenced a lawsuit against him on January 29 of the next year on the theory that there was a defect which breached a warranty of the seller. Banks denied liability. Decide. [*Leeper v Banks (Ky) 487 So 2d 58*]

5. The Best Card Company shipped 50 decks of playing cards to the Winner Club in Reno, Nevada. After inspecting the cards, Winner discovered that some of the decks contained five kings instead of four and three aces instead of four. What remedy, if any, does Winner have? Explain.

6. The goods purchased by the buyer were defective. The seller made repeated attempts to correct the defect. It became apparent that it was impossible to correct the defect. The buyer notified the seller that the buyer was revoking acceptance of the goods. The seller offered to try again to repair the goods. The buyer rejected this offer and repeated that acceptance of the goods was being revoked. The seller claimed that the buyer could not revoke acceptance as long as the seller offered to repair the goods. Was the seller correct? [*Fenton v Contemporary Development Co. 12 Wash App 345, 529 P2d 883*]

7. McAuliffe & Burke Co. sold plumbing fixtures to Levine but refused to deliver them unless immediate payment was made in cash. The buyer gave the sellers a worthless check that he assured the sellers was "as good as gold." On the basis of this statement, the sellers surrendered the goods to the buyer. Thereafter, a creditor of Levine brought an action against him, and the sheriff, Gallagher, seized the goods that were delivered to Levine. The sellers, learning that the check was worthless, claimed that they had a lien on the goods. The sellers sued Gallagher for their return. Can they recover the goods?

8. Sam wants to buy a car on credit from Henry Motors. He is afraid, however, that Henry will assign his contract to a finance company and that the finance company will be able to collect the balance due on the car even if the car does not run properly. Sam wants to be able to defend against the finance company by showing that there are defects in the car. Is this possible?

9. Wolosin purchased a vegetable and dairy refrigerator case from the Evans Manufacturing Corp. Evans sued Wolosin for the purchase price. Wolosin raised as a defense a claim for damages for breach of warranty. The sales contract provided that Evans would replace defective parts free of charge for one year and that "This warranty is in lieu of any and all other warranties stated or inferred, and of all other obligations on the part of the manufacturer, which neither assumes nor authorizes anyone to assume for it any other obligations or liability in connection with the sale of its products." Evans claimed that it was only liable for replacement of parts. Wolosin claimed that the quoted clause was not sufficiently specific to satisfy the limitation of remedies requirement of UCC § 2-719. Decide. [*Evans Mfg. Corp. v Wolosin (Pa) 47 Luzerne County Leg Reg 238*]

10. McInnis purchased a tractor and scraper as new equipment of current model from the Western Tractor & Equipment Co. The written contract stated that the seller disclaimed all warranties and that no warranties existed except as were stated in the contract. Actually, the equipment was not the current model but that of the prior year. The equipment was not new but had been used for 68 hours as a demonstrator model, after which the hour meter had been reset to zero. The buyer sued the seller for damages. The latter defended on the ground that all liability for warranties had been disclaimed. Was this defense valid? [*McInnis v Western Tractor & Equipment Co. 63 Wash 2d 652, 388 P2d 562*]

11. Compare or contrast the statute of limitations for a breach of warranty on tender of delivery of goods with the statute of limitations for breach of an express warranty as to future performance.

12. Keenan rejected nonconforming goods delivered to him by Ross. After the rejection, but before Ross had been allowed a reasonable time to give instructions for the disposition of the goods, Keenan arranged a sale of the goods at a substantially reduced price. In the meantime, Ross had sold the goods to another of his customers. What rights, if any, does Ross have against Keenan?

13. Peters, the buyer, received merchandise from Hadley, the seller. On looking over the goods, Peters noticed that some of the goods did not conform to the contract. He therefore called Hadley, who stated, "We always take care of our customers." Peters then accepted the goods. Since the nonconformity was not remedied within a reasonable time, Peters informed Hadley that he revoked his acceptance. Hadley refused to take back the goods. Who will prevail?

14. A buyer purchased goods and later telephoned the seller that he revoked his acceptance of the goods. The seller claimed that the revocation of acceptance was not effective because it was not accompanied by a return or offer to return the goods. Was the seller correct?

15. Stephan's Machine & Tool Inc., purchased a boring mill from D & H Machinery Consultants. The mill was a specialized type of equipment and was essential to the operation of Stephan's plant. The purchase price was $96,000 and Stephan had to borrow this amount from a bank in order to finance the sale. This loan exhausted Stephan's borrowing capacity. The mill was unfit and D & H agreed to replace it with another one. D & H did not keep its promise and Stephans sued D & H for specific performance of the contract as modified by the replacement agreement. Decide. [*Stephan's Machine & Tool, Inc. v D & H Machinery Consultants, Inc. 65 Ohio App 2d 197, 417 NE2d 579 (1979)*]

CHAPTER 29
CONSUMER PROTECTION

LEARNING OBJECTIVES

After studying this chapter, you will be able to:
1. *State the purpose of truth in advertising legislation.*
2. *Explain and apply the more-than-four-installments rule.*
3. *Explain the effect of the Federal Warranty Disclosure Act of 1974.*
4. *State the extent to which the holder of a credit card is liable for purchases made by a person finding or stealing the card.*
5. *Explain the Federal Trade Commission regulation for the preservation of consumer defenses.*
6. *Explain what the Fair Credit Reporting Act provides for the protection of consumers' credit standing and reputation.*
7. *List the remedies available for a breach of a consumer protection law.*

In the last few decades, the consumer protection movement has made a substantial number of changes to traditional law.

A. GENERAL PRINCIPLES

Consumer protection began with the aim of protecting persons of limited means and limited knowledge.

1. Expansion of Protection

The social forces of protecting the person and protecting from fraud, exploitation, and oppression have expanded the category of protected consumers. Many consumer protection statutes now define *consumer* as any person, partnership, corporation, bank, or government that uses goods or services. Thus, it has been held that the word *consumer* includes a collector paying nearly $100,000 for jade art objects, a glass manufacturer purchasing 3 million gallons of diesel oil fuel, or the City of Boston purchasing insurance. In addition, the protected consumer may be a firm of attorneys.[1] In Texas, the protected group of buyers of goods and services includes the State of Texas, its governmental agencies, and businesses with assets under $25 million. In contrast with the foregoing expansive definition of *consumer*, some statutes are so worded as to apply only to natural persons.[2]

A person violating the provisions of a consumer protection statute is liable even though there was no intention to violate the law. Liability also exists even though the breach was a single occurrence rather than a pattern of repeated conduct.[3]

2. Proof of Consumer Status

A consumer claiming that there has been a violation of the consumer protection statute has the burden of proving that the statutory definition of *consumer* has been satisfied. However, the consumer is not required to prove that none of the statutory exceptions or defenses are available to the defendant.

3. Who Is a Defendant in a Consumer Protection Suit?

The defendant in consumer protection situations is a person or an enterprise that regularly enters into the kind of transaction in which the injured consumer was involved. For example, it is the merchant seller, the finance company, the bank, the leasing company, the home repairer, and any others who enter regularly into a particular kind of transaction.

Under the consumer protection statutes, it is immaterial that there is no privity of contract between the consumer and the defendant.[4]

4. Fault of Defendant

Consumer protection laws typically require some fault on the part of the defendant. This ordinarily means that there must be some act or omission that is condemned by general principles of law or by the particular consumer protection statute in question. The status of the "innocent" defendant was raised in the *Hughes* case.

---

1 Catallo Associates, Inc. v MacDonald & Goren, 186 Mich App 571, 465 NW2d 28 (1990). Statutes that broaden the protected group to protect buyers of goods and services are often called *deceptive trade practices statutes*, instead of the earlier name of *consumer protection statutes*.

2 Classic Car Centre, Inc. v Haire Machine Corp. (Ind App) 580 NE2d 722 (1991).

3 Ashlock v Sunwest Bank of Roswell, 107 NM 100, 753 P2d 346 (1988).

4 Luker v Arnold (Tex App) 843 SW2d 108 (1992).

HUGHES v MILLER
72 Ohio App 3d 633, 595 NE2d 960 (1991)

Miller was a used car dealer. He purchased a car from an owner without knowledge that the owner had turned back the odometer. Miller believed that the odometer reading was accurate and resold the car to Hughes on that basis. When Hughes learned that the odometer had been rolled back, she sued Miller under the state Odometer Rollback and Disclosure Act. From a judgment in her favor, Miller appealed.

HADLEY, J. . . . Both parties agree that the original version of R.C. 4549.46 applies to this action. That section reads:

"No transferor shall fail to provide the true odometer disclosures required by section 4505.06 of the Revised Code. The transferor of a motor vehicle is not in violation of this section's provisions requiring a true odometer reading if the odometer reading is incorrect due to a previous owner's violation of any of the provisions contained in sections 4549.42 to 4549.46 of the Revised Code, *unless the transferor knows of the violation.*" (Emphasis added.)

. . . It was undisputed at oral argument that had defendant been responsible for the tampering with the odometer of the vehicle sold to plaintiff, he would be strictly liable under R.C. 4549.46. Rather, the crux of defendant's appeal focuses on the impact of the exception to liability given in the second sentence of the section.

Plaintiff asserts that the entire paragraph imposes strict liability on the transferor without regard to culpability for the odometer tampering, while defendant claims that the exception given in the second sentence only attaches liability to the transferor who has actual knowledge of the tampering. After reviewing case law, we conclude that the defendant was within the exception stated in the second sentence of R.C. 4549.46, and as such, he must have had actual knowledge of the odometer tampering in order to be liable.

The leading case interpreting the provisions of R.C. 4549.46 is *Flint v Ohio Bell Tel. Co.* (1982), 2 Ohio App 3d 136, 2 OBR 150, 440 NE2d 1244. *Flint* involved the sale of a company van by the defendant telephone company to plaintiff. The telephone company failed to disclose that the odometer had rolled over so that the van actually had 100,000 more miles on it than was registered on the odometer. Plaintiff sued under the Act. The defendant denied liability on the basis that recklessness on its part had to be proven by the plaintiff. The court disagreed and concluded:

"That the legislature intended to hold transferors who fail to disclose the true mileage of the vehicle strictly liable to the transferees for their conduct.

"* * *

"Indeed, motor vehicle laws are one of eight areas of the law listed by the United States Supreme Court as amenable to imposition of strict liability [citations omitted]. Further, because of the difficulties inherent in determining the accused's subjective intent under R.C. 4549.46, requiring the transferee to prove recklessness in a lawsuit pursuant to R.C. 4549.49 would make the statute virtually unenforceable." . . .

The second case on point is *Prickett v The Foreign Exchange* (1990), 68 Ohio App 3d 236, 587 NE2d 972. . . . The court held that the defendant car dealer was not strictly liable under R.C. 4549.46, because the defendant fell under the exception provided for in the second sentence. The court, in reaching this conclusion, reasoned:

"The plain meaning of the word 'knows' in this context is that the transferor must have actual knowledge of odometer discrepancies caused by previous owners before he can be held liable for them. This construction is supported by the fact that the General Assembly saw fit to amend R.C. 4549.46(A) to read that a transferor is not culpable for a previous owner's having rolled back the odometer 'unless the transferor knows of or recklessly disregards facts indicating the violation.' If the previous statute had encompassed more than actual knowledge, this amendment would have been unnecessary." Id. at 239, 587 NE2d at 974. . . .

Strict liability under R.C. 4549.46 applies to a transferor when a discrepancy in the odometer reading occurs during their ownership of the vehicle, unless the transferor properly discloses the discrepancy upon transfer. This holding logically follows the *Flint* decision, where that court stated the premise of strict liability on the basis that "[transferor] had the means of knowing the true odometer reading. In fact, [transferor] was the only person with access to such knowledge." *Id.*, 2 Ohio App 3d at 137, 2 OBR at 151, 440 NE2d at 1246. The second sentence of R.C. 4549.46 places liability only on the transferor of a vehicle which has not had its odometer tampered with during his ownership, but the transferor nevertheless has actual knowledge of tampering with, or discrepancy in, the odometer reading. . . .

[Judgment reversed]

QUESTIONS

1. What was prohibited by the state statute?
2. Could Miller have found out the truth about the car he sold to Hughes?
3. What is the difference between the statute on which the *Hughes* decision is based and the amendment that was made to the statute?

5. Consumer Negligence

Consumer protection law is directed at protecting the consumer from the misconduct of others. Disclosure provisions are frequently imposed. These provisions give the consumer the information that the consumer would lack and would not have enough experience or bargaining power to demand. In a limited number of situations, the consumer is given the power to rescind a transaction if hindsight makes the consumer unhappy with the deal that had been made.

Consumer protection, however, does not protect a consumer from the consumer's own negligence. Thus, if a consumer signs a contract without reading or understanding what it means, the consumer is bound. Moreover, when the contract signed by the consumer clearly states one thing, the consumer cannot prove that the other contracting party had made statements contradicting what was stated in the signed contract. Consumers should exercise reasonable care and not blindly trust consumer protection law to rescue them from their own blunders.

6. Consumer Remedies

The theoretical right of the consumer to sue or to assert a defense is often of little practical value to the consumer. The amount involved may be small compared with the cost of litigation.

Consumer protection legislation provides special remedies.

(a) GOVERNMENT AGENCY ACTION. The Uniform Consumer Credit Code (UCCC) provides for an administrator who will, in a sense, police business practices to ensure conformity with the law.

(b) ACTION BY ATTORNEY GENERAL. A number of states provide that the state attorney general may bring an action on behalf of a particular group of consumers. In these actions, the attorney general sues to obtain cancellation of the consumers' contracts and restitution of whatever they had paid.

Many states permit the attorney general to bring an action to enjoin violation of the consumer protection statute. Consumer protection statutes commonly give the attorney general the authority to seek a voluntary stopping of improper practices before seeking an injunction from a court.

When proof of a consumer law violation is made before an agency or commission, proof of guilt is only required by a preponderance of the evidence. The proceeding is not criminal in nature requiring proof beyond a reasonable doubt just because the agency could impose a penalty for a violation.[5]

(c) ACTION BY CONSUMER. Some consumer protection statutes provide that a consumer who is harmed by a violation of the statutes may sue the enterprise that acted improperly. The consumer may sue to recover a specified penalty or may bring an action on behalf of consumers as a class. Consumer protection statutes are often designed to rely on private litigation as an aid to enforcement of the statutory provisions. The Consumer Product Safety Act of 1972 authorizes "any interested person" to bring a civil action to enforce a consumer product safety rule and certain orders of the Consumer Product Safety Commission. In other cases, however, the individual consumer cannot bring any action, and enforcement of the law is entrusted exclusively to an administrative agency. Likewise a consumer may have lost the right to a statutory remedy by waiver or delay.[6]

In any case, a consumer who shows only that the defendant had broken a contract is not entitled to recover under a fair business practices or deceptive trade practices act. In addition, the plaintiff must show misconduct of the kind prohibited by the statutes.[7]

The *Varady* case illustrates the use of a statutory penalty in the Uniform Consumer Credit Code to induce private litigation as an enforcement aid.

VARADY v WHITE
42 Colo App 389, 661 P2d 284 (1982)

Robert White was an electronic technician. His wife Marilyn was a homemaker. The Whites owned a 90-acre tract of land, which they subdivided and sold as unimproved lots. The sixth lot was sold to Kenneth Varady. All sales were made partly on credit, with an unpaid balance being secured by some form of collateral agreement. The Whites failed to inform Varady of certain matters that the UCCC required them to disclose. Within three days after the

---

5 Minnesota v Alpine Air Products, Inc. (Minn) 500 NW2d 788 (1993).
6 Frey v Vin Devers, Inc. 80 Ohio App 3d 1, 608 NE2d 796 (1992).
7 Fidelity & Casualty Co. v Underwood (Tex App) 791 SW2d 635 (1990).

transfer of ownership of the land to Varady, Varady notified the Whites that he was rescinding the transaction. The Whites refused to return Varady's money to him or to take back the land. Varady brought an action against the Whites. From a judgment in their favor, he appealed.

KELLY, J. . . . [UCCC] Section 5-2-104(1)(a) provides that a "consumer credit sale" is a sale of an interest in land in which "credit is granted . . . by a person who *regularly* engages as a seller in *credit transactions of the same kind . . .*". (Emphasis added.) Thus, in order to determine whether the disputed transaction is subject to the disclosure requirements of the UCCC, we must consider whether, as a matter of law, the prior transactions constituted "regular" credit transactions and whether they were of "the same kind" as the subject transaction.

Colorado's UCCC is based on the Federal Consumer Credit Protection Act (CCPA), 15 U.S.C.A. § 1601, et seq., and the intent of the CCPA "seems to have been to except from the Act only those lenders whose extensions of credit are an occasional, isolated, and incidental portion of their business." *Eby v Reb Realty, Inc.*, 495 F2d 646 (9th Cir. 1974). Thus, private homeowners who take back second mortgages upon selling their homes would normally not be required to comply with the disclosure requirements of the Act.

Although the Whites sold their own home and took a second mortgage, they had subdivided their 90-acre property and sold five unimproved lots in their subdivision prior to the sale to plaintiffs. Neither defendant had a real estate license or worked full time in the real estate business: Robert White was an electronic technician and Marilyn White was a housewife. However, the subdivision and the sale of lots is itself a business venture. After five separate sales of lots from a 90-acre tract, the Whites cannot claim ignorance of real estate transactions. Moreover, they sold more unimproved lots after the sale to plaintiffs. In *Eby, supra*, the realty firm was held to have engaged in "regular" credit transactions although it had sold only three parcels on credit within a time span of nineteen months. The Whites sold lots in September and October of 1974, and April, June, and July of 1976 before the sale to the Varadys. This constitutes "regular" credit transactions for purposes of § 5-2-104(1)(a), C.R.S. 1973.

Since the phrase "credit transactions of the same kind" is not included in the definition of a credit transaction under the CCPA, we must interpret this phrase without the aid of federal guidelines. While the Whites sold the Varadys improved land and the prior sales conveyed unimproved lots, the presence or absence of improvements is not a critical factor in determining whether transactions are of the same kind. All the sales consisted of an "interest in land" purchased primarily for a personal, family, or household use under § 5-2-104(1)(c), C.R.S. 1973.

The two sales in 1974 and the sale to the Varadys in 1976 involved second deeds of trust, while the other three sales in 1976 involved first deeds of trust. However, the Whites were the creditors in each of the transactions, so the form of the security interest is not determinative of this issue. Although these six transactions were not identical in each minute detail, we conclude, as a matter of law, that they were "credit transactions of the same kind." Therefore, since the Whites regularly engaged in credit transactions of the same kind, their sale to the Varadys was a "consumer credit sale" under § 5-2-104(1)(a), C.R.S. 1973.

Since the Varady-White transaction was a consumer credit sale of an interest in land, the debtors have rescission rights under § 5-5-204, C.R.S. 1973. This section permits the debtor to rescind the transaction "until midnight of the third business day following the consummation of the transaction or the delivery of the disclosures required under this section . . . whichever is later. . . ." When a debtor rescinds, § 5-5-204(2), C.R.S. 1973, affords him a number of rights. First, he is not liable for any credit service charge, and any security interest given by the debtor becomes void upon the rescission. Second, within ten days after receipt of a notice of rescission, the creditor must return to the debtor "the money or property given as earnest money, down payment, or otherwise," and must terminate any security interest created under the transaction. And third, upon the performance of the creditor's obligations, the debtor must tender the property to the creditor, and unless the creditor takes possession of the property within ten days after the tender by the debtor, the debtor may keep the property without paying for it.

Where, as here, the creditors have not made the disclosures required by the UCCC, the debtors are at liberty to rescind the contract at their pleasure. . . . Since the Varadys gave the Whites notice of their intent to rescind within three days of closing, and the Whites did not return the Varadys' payments and terminate their security interest within ten days of the notice of rescission, the Whites must return all money paid to them by the Varadys, and ownership of the property vests in the Varadys without their obligation to pay for it.

The Whites were subject to a statutory duty to inform the Varadys of their right to rescind the transaction. . . . Although the Whites did not act purposefully to deprive the Varadys of their rights, it is up to the creditor to avoid forfeiture by complying with the UCCC. . . .

[Judgment reversed]

QUESTIONS

1. Why did the court hold that the UCCC was applicable?
2. Was the answer to the first question inevitable?
3. What social forces are affected by this decision?

7. Civil and Criminal Penalties

The seller or lender engaging in improper consumer practices may be subject to civil penalties and criminal punishment. In some instances, the laws in question are the general laws applicable to improper conduct, while in other cases, the laws are specifically aimed at the particular consumer practices. An example of a violation of the general law is a contractor who falsely stated to a homeowner that certain repairs needed on the roof cost, with labor and materials, $650, when in fact they cost only $200. The contractor was guilty of the crime of obtaining money by false pretenses. As an example of a specific consumer protection statute, the Truth in Lending Act subjects the creditor to a separate claim for damages for each periodic statement that violates the disclosure requirements. Furthermore, consumer protection statutes of the disclosure type generally provide that the creditor cannot enforce the obligation of the debtor if the required information is not set forth in the contract.

B. AREAS OF CONSUMER PROTECTION

The following sections discuss the more important areas of consumer protection.

8. Advertising

Statutes commonly prohibit fraudulent advertising. Most advertising regulations are entrusted to an administrative agency, such as the Federal Trade Commission (FTC). The FTC is authorized to issue orders to stop false or misleading advertising. Statutes prohibiting false advertising are liberally interpreted.

A store is liable for false advertising when it advertises a reduced price sale of a particular item but that item is out of stock even at the time the sale begins. It is no defense to the store that the presale demand was greater than usual.[8]

(a) DECEPTION. Under consumer protection statutes, *deception* rather than *fraud*, is the significant element.[9] There is a breach of such statutes even though there is no proof that the wrongdoer intended to defraud or deceive anyone.

This is a shift of social point of view. That is, instead of basing the law in terms of fault of the actor, the law is concerned with the problem of the buyer who is likely to be misled. The good faith of an advertiser or the absence of intent to deceive is immaterial. The purpose of false advertising legislation is to protect the consumer rather than to examine the advertiser's motives.

Figure 29-1 The Legal Environment of the Consumer

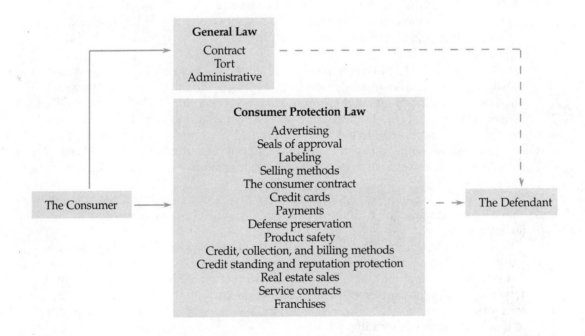

---

8 De Santis v Sears, Roebuck and Co. 148 App Div 2d 36, 543 NYS2d 228 (1989).

9 Rucker v Huffman (NC App) 392 SE2d 419 (1990).

The FTC requires that an advertiser maintain a file containing the data claimed to support an advertising statement as to safety, performance, efficacy, quality, or comparative price of an advertised product. The FTC can require the advertiser to produce this material.

If it is in the interest of the consumer, the FTC can make this information public, except to the extent that it contains trade secrets or material that is privileged.

In the *Colgate-Palmolive* case, advertising that was attacked as deceptive was defended on the ground that it was not fraudulent.

FTC v COLGATE-PALMOLIVE CO.
380 US 374 (1965)

The Colgate-Palmolive Co. sells a shaving cream, Rapid Shave. To test the effectiveness of the cream, the company put it on sandpaper and then shaved the sandpaper. The company then wanted to run a commercial on television showing this test as proof that the product could soften even the toughness of sandpaper. When the actual test was telecast, the sandpaper looked like ordinary colored paper. In order to have something that really looked like sandpaper, the advertiser used a sheet of Plexiglass on which sand had been sprinkled. The Federal Trade Commission prohibited this commercial on the ground that it deceived the viewer. The advertiser claimed that there was no deception because the viewer was merely being given an accurate visual representation of the test that had actually been made. The FTC issued an order to stop the commercial. The court of appeals reversed this order. The case was then appealed to the U.S. Supreme Court.

WARREN, C. J. . . . The Commission found that the undisclosed use of a plexiglass substitute for sandpaper was [a] material misrepresentation that was a deceptive act separate and distinct from [any] misrepresentation concerning Rapid Shave's underlying qualities. Even if the sandpaper could be shaved just as depicted in the commercials, the Commission found that viewers had been misled into believing they had seen it done with their own eyes. As a result of these findings the Commission entered a cease-and-desist order against the respondents [Colgate and the advertiser]. . . .

. . . The Commission expressed the view that without this visible proof of Rapid Shave's moisturizing ability some viewers might not have been persuaded to buy the product. . . .

. . . When the Commission was created by Congress in 1914, it was directed by § 5 to prevent "unfair methods of competition in commerce." Congress amended the Act in 1938 to extend the Commission's jurisdiction to include "unfair or deceptive acts or practices in commerce"—a significant amendment showing Congress' concern for consumers as well as for competitors. It is important to note the generality of these standards of illegality. . . .

This statutory scheme necessarily gives the Commission an influential role in interpreting § 5 and in applying it to the facts of particular cases arising out of unprecedented situations. Moreover, as an administrative agency which deals continually with cases in the area, the Commission is often in a better position than are courts to determine when a practice is "deceptive" within the meaning of the Act. . . .

We accept the Commission's determination that the commercials involved in this case contained three representations to the public: (1) that sandpaper could be shaved by Rapid Shave; (2) that an experiment had been conducted which verified this claim; and (3) that the viewer was seeing this experiment. . . . For the purposes of our review, we can assume that the first two representations were true; the focus of our consideration is on the third, which was clearly false. The parties agree that § 5 prohibits the intentional misrepresentation of any fact which would constitute a material factor in a purchaser's decision whether to buy. They differ, however, in their conception of what "facts" constitute a "material factor" in a purchaser's decision to buy. Respondents submit, in effect, that the only material facts are those which deal with the substantive qualities of a product. The Commission, on the other hand, submits that the misrepresentation of *any* fact so long as it materially induces a purchaser's decision to buy is a deception prohibited by § 5.

The Commission's interpretation of what is a deceptive practice seems more in line with the decided cases than that of respondents. . . .

We agree with the Commission . . . that the undisclosed use of plexiglass in the present commercials was a material deceptive practice. . . . Respondents claim that it will be impractical to inform the viewing public that it is not seeing an actual test, experiment or demonstration, but we think it inconceivable that the ingenious advertising world will be unable, if it so desires, to conform to the Commission's insistence that the public be not misinformed. If, however, it becomes impossible or impractical to show simulated demonstrations on television in a truthful manner, this indicates that television is not a medium that lends itself to this type of commercial, not that the commercial must survive at all costs. . . .

[Judgment reversed]

QUESTIONS

1. Was Colgate-Palmolive being sued for damages for fraud?
2. Who was harmed by the commercial for Rapid Shave?
3. Was Colgate-Palmolive guilty of fraudulent selling practices?

(b) CORRECTIVE ADVERTISING.

When an enterprise has made false and deceptive statements in advertising, the Federal Trade Commission may require that new advertising be made in which the former statements are contradicted and the truth stated. This corrective advertising required by the Federal Trade Commission is also called **retractive advertising**.

9. Seals of Approval

Many commodities are sold or advertised with a sticker or tag stating that the article has been approved or is guaranteed by some association or organization. Ordinarily, when a product is sold in such a way, it will in fact have been approved by some testing laboratory and will probably have proven adequate to meet ordinary consumer needs. Selling with a seal of approval of a third person makes, in effect, a guarantee that the product has been so approved. Such a seller is liable if the product was, in fact, not approved. In addition, the seller is ordinarily liable for fraud if the statement is not true.

10. Labeling

Closely related to the regulation of advertising is the regulation of labeling and marking of products. Various federal statutes are designed to give the consumer accurate information about the product, while others require warnings about dangers of use or misuse. Consumer protection regulations prohibit the use in the labeling or marking of products of such terms as *jumbo*, *giant*, or *full*, which tend to exaggerate and mislead.

11. Selling Methods

Consumer protection statutes prohibit the use of improper and deceptive selling methods.[10] These statutes are liberally construed to protect consumers from improper practices.

(a) DECEPTIVE PRACTICES. Consumer protection statutes and deceptive trade practice acts are violated when the statements or the business methods of the defendant are deceptive. It is not necessary to prove that the defendant was guilty of fraud. Hence it is immaterial that the defendant who misrepresented the facts did not intentionally do so.

(b) DISCLOSURE OF TRANSACTION TERMS. The federal law requires the disclosure of all interest charges, points or fees for granting loans, and similar charges. These charges must be set forth as an annual percentage rate (APR) so that the consumer can see just how much the transaction costs a year and can compare alternatives.[11]

The obligation of disclosure has been further extended by the Fair Credit and Charge Card Disclosure Act of 1988. Act of November 3, 1988, PL 100-583, 102 Stat 2960, 15 USC § § 1601 note, et seq. and by the Home Equity Loan Consumer Protection Act of November 23, 1988, PL 100-709, 102 Stat 4729, 15 USC § § 1601 note, et seq.

If sellers advertise that they will sell or lease on credit, they cannot state merely the monthly installments that will be due. They must give the consumer additional information: (1) the total cash price; (2) the amount of the down payment required; (3) the number, amounts, and due dates of payments; and (4) the annual percentage rate of the credit charges.[12]

In various ways, consumer protection statutes seek to protect the consumer from surprise or unbargained-for terms and from unwanted contracts. Under consumer protection statutes, it is commonly a deceptive trade practice to fail to disclose to a consumer information that would have prevented the consumer from entering into the transaction if the disclosure had been made.

(1) More-Than-Four-Installments Rule. Whenever a consumer sale or contract provides for payment in more than four installments, it is subject to the Truth in Lending Act. This is so even though no service or finance charge is expressly added because of the installment pattern of paying.

---

[10] Regarding states adopting the UCCC, see Chapter 1, footnote 5. The Uniform Consumer Sales Practices Act has been adopted in Kansas, Ohio, and Utah; a Uniform Deceptive Trade Practices Act (1966 revision) has been adopted in Colorado, Georgia, Hawaii, Minnesota, Nebraska, New Mexico, Ohio, and Oregon; the 1964 version of the Uniform Deceptive Trade Practices Act was adopted in Delaware, Illinois, Maine, and Oklahoma; and a Model Land Sales Practice Act has been adopted in Alaska, Connecticut, Florida, Hawaii, Idaho, Kansas, Minnesota, Montana, South Dakota, and Utah. The federal government has expanded the protection of the consumers food supply by the Nutrition Labeling and Education Act of 1990, Act of November 8, 1990, PL 101-535, 104 Stat 2353, ___ USC § ___; and the Sanitary Food Transportation Act of 1990, Act of November 3, 1990, PL 101-500, 104 Stat 1213, ___ USC § ___.

[11] Consumer Credit Protection Act (CCPA), 15 USC § § 1605, 1606, 1636; Regulation Z adopted by the Federal Reserve Board of Governors, § 226.5.

[12] Regulation Z, § 1210, Consumer Leasing Act of 1976, 15 USC § 1667.

When consumer credit is advertised as repayable in more than four installments and no finance charge is expressly imposed, the advertisement must "clearly and conspicuously" state that "the cost of credit is included in the price" quoted for the goods and services.

(2) Contract on Two Sides. To be sure that the consumer sees disclosures required by federal law, special provision is made for the case when the terms of the transaction are printed on both the front and back of a sheet or contract. In this case, (a) both sides of the sheet must carry the warning: "NOTICE: see other side for important information," and (b) the page must be signed at the end of the second side. Conversely, the requirements of the federal law are not satisfied when there is no warning of "see other side" and the parties sign the contract only on the face, or the first side, of the paper.

(3) Particular Sales and Leases. The Motor Vehicle Information and Cost Savings Act requires a dealer to disclose to the buyer various elements in the cost of an automobile. The act prohibits selling an automobile without informing the buyer that the odometer has been reset below the true mileage. A buyer who is caused actual loss by odometer fraud may recover from the seller three times the actual loss or $1,500, whichever is greater.[13] There is a breach of the federal statute when the seller has knowledge that the odometer has turned itself at 100,000 miles but the seller then states that the mileage is 20,073 miles instead of 120,073. The Consumer Leasing Act of 1976 requires that persons leasing automobiles and other durable goods to consumers make a full disclosure to the consumer of the details of the transaction.

Although the federal statute imposes liability only when the seller "knowingly" violates the statute, it is not necessary to prove actual knowledge. An experienced auto dealer cannot claim lack of knowledge that the odometer was false when that conclusion was reasonably apparent from the condition of the car.[14]

(c) HOME-SOLICITED SALES. A sale of goods or services for $25 or more made to a buyer at home may be set aside within three business days. This right may be exercised merely because the buyer does not want to go through with the contract. There is no requirement of proving any misconduct of the seller or any defect in the goods or services.[15]

When the buyer has made an oral agreement to purchase and the seller comes to the buyer's home to work out the details, the transaction is not a home-solicited sale and cannot be avoided under the Federal Regulation.[16]

(d) REFERRAL SALES. The technique of giving the buyer a price reduction for customers referred to the seller is theoretically lawful. In effect, it is merely paying the buyer a commission for the promotion of other sales. In actual practice, however, the referral sales technique is often accompanied by fraud or by exorbitant pricing, so that consumer protection laws variously condemn referral selling. As a result, the referral system of selling has been condemned as unconscionable under the UCC and is expressly prohibited by the UCCC.

12. The Consumer Contract

There are several ways in which consumer contracts are affected by consumer protection legislation.

(a) FORM OF CONTRACT. Consumer protection laws commonly regulate the form of the contract, requiring that certain items be specifically listed, that payments under the

---

[13] Act of October 20, 1972, § § 403, 409, PL 92-513, 86 Stat 947, 15 USC § 1901 et seq., as amended.

[14] Denmon v Nicks Auto Sales (La App) 537 So 2d 796 (1989).

[15] Federal Trade Commission Regulation, 16 CFR § 429.1.

[16] Cooper v Crow (La App) 574 So 2d 438 (1991).

contract be itemized, and that the allocation to such items as principal, interest, and insurance be indicated. Generally, certain portions of the contract or all of the contract must be printed in type of a certain size, and a copy must be furnished to the buyer. Such statutory requirements are more demanding than the statute of frauds section of the UCC. It is frequently provided that the copy furnished the consumer must be completely filled in. Back-page disclaimers are void if the front page of the contract does not call attention to the presence of such terms.

(b) CONTRACT TERMS. Consumer protection legislation does not ordinarily affect the right of the parties to make a contract on whatever terms they choose. It is customary, however, to prohibit the use of certain clauses that are believed to bear too harshly on the debtor or that have too great a potential for exploitive abuse by a creditor. For example, the UCCC prohibits provisions permitting a creditor to enter a judgment against a debtor without giving the debtor any chance to make a defense.[17]

The federal Warranty Disclosure Act of 1974 establishes disclosure standards for consumer goods warranties, to help the consumer understand them.[18]

The parties to a credit transaction may agree that payment should be made in installments but that if there is a default with respect to any installment, the creditor may declare the entire balance due at once. This cancels or destroys the schedule for payments by making the entire balance immediately due. Such acceleration of the debt can cause the debtor great hardship. Because of this, some statutes limit or prohibit the use of acceleration clauses.

(c) LIMITATION OF CREDIT. Various laws may limit the ability to borrow money or purchase on credit. Some states prohibit **open-end mortgages**, by which the mortgage secures a specified debt and additional loans that may later be made. Consumer protection is also afforded in some states by placing a time limit on smaller loans.

A Federal Trade Commission regulation declares it an unfair trade practice to require a consumer borrowing or buying on credit to give the lender or seller as collateral a security interest in all of the consumer's household goods.[19]

(d) UNCONSCIONABILITY. To some extent, consumer protection has been provided under the UCC by those courts that hold that the "unconscionability" provision protects from "excessive" or "exorbitant" prices when goods are sold on credit.[20]

Some statutes are aimed at preventing price gouging with respect to goods or services for which the demand is abnormally greater than the supply. The New York statute provides: "During any abnormal disruption of the market for consumer goods and services vital and necessary for the health, safety, and welfare of consumers, resulting from stress of weather, convulsion of nature, failure or shortage of electric power or other source of energy . . . no merchant shall sell or offer to sell any such consumer goods or services for an amount which represents an unconscionably excessive price." Consumer goods and services are defined as "those used, bought, or rendered primarily for personal, family, or household purposes." Such a statute protects, for example, purchasers of electric generators for home use during a hurricane-caused blackout.

---

[17] UCCC § § 2.415, 3.407.

[18] Act of January 4, 1975, PL 93-637, 88 Stat 2183, 15 USC § 2301.

[19] 16 CFR § 444.2(4)(1988).

[20] UCC § 2-302(1).

13. Credit Cards

The credit card permits the cardholder to buy on the credit or reputation of the issuer of the card.

(a) UNSOLICITED CREDIT CARDS. The unsolicited distribution of credit cards to persons who have not applied for them is prohibited.

(b) SURCHARGE PROHIBITED. By some statutes, a seller cannot add any charge to the purchase price because the buyer uses a credit card instead of paying with cash or a check.[21]

(c) UNAUTHORIZED USE. A cardholder is not liable for more than $50 for the unauthorized use of a credit card. To impose liability up to that amount, the issuer must show that (1) the credit card was an accepted card,[22] (2) the issuer had given the holder adequate notice of possible liability in such case, (3) the issuer had furnished the holder with a self-addressed, prestamped notification form to be mailed by the holder in the event of the loss or theft of the credit card, (4) the issuer had provided a method by which the user of the card could be identified as the person authorized to use it,[23] and (5) unauthorized use of the card had occurred or might occur as a result of loss, theft, or some other event.

(d) UNAUTHORIZED PURPOSE DISTINGUISHED. There is an unauthorized use of a credit card only when it is used without the permission or approval of the cardholder. In contrast, the holder may authorize another person to use the card but to use it for a particular purpose, such as to buy a particular item. If the person uses the card for a purpose other than the one specified by the holder, there is still an authorized use of the card, even though it is for an unauthorized purpose.[24] In such a case, the cardholder is liable for all charges made on the card, even though they were not intended by the cardholder when the card was loaned. The same rule is applied when an employer has cards issued to employees for making employment-related purchases, but an employee uses the card for personal purposes.

14. Payments

Consumer legislation may provide that when a consumer makes a payment on an open charge account, the payment must be applied toward payment of the earliest charges. The result is that, should there be a default at a later date, any right of repossession of the creditor is limited to the later, unpaid items. This outlaws a contract provision by which, on the default of the buyer, the seller could repossess all purchases that had been made at any prior time. Such a provision is outlawed by the UCCC and probably would be found unconscionable under the UCC.

15. Preservation of Consumer Defenses

Consumer protection laws generally prohibit a consumer from waiving or giving up any defense provided by law.

In the ordinary contract situation, when goods or services purchased or leased by a consumer are not proper or are defective, the consumer is not required to pay the seller or lessor or is only required to pay a reduced amount. With the modern expansion of credit

---

[21] In contrast, the Truth in Lending Act Amendment of 1976, 15 USC § 1666f, permits a merchant to offer a discount to cash-paying customers but not customers using a credit card.

[22] A credit card is accepted when the cardholder has requested and received or has signed or has used, or authorized another to use, for the purpose of obtaining money, property, labor, or services on credit. CCPA § 103(l).

[23] Regulation Z of the Board of Governors of the Federal Reserve, § 226.13(d), as amended, provides that the identification may be signature, photograph, or fingerprint on the credit card or by electronic or mechanical confirmation.

[24] American Express Travel Related Services Co., Inc. v Web, Inc. ___ Ga ___, 405 SE2d 652 (1991).

transactions, sellers and lessors have used several techniques for getting paid without regard to whether the consumer had any complaint against them. To prevent this, the Federal Trade Commission has adopted a regulation that requires that in every sale or lease of goods or services to a consumer, the contract of the consumer contain a clause giving the consumer the right to assert defenses. These defenses may be asserted not only against the seller or lessor but also against a third person, such as a bank or finance company, to which the seller or lessor transfers the collection rights. The FTC regulation requires that the following notice be included in boldface type at least ten points in size:

NOTICE

Any holder of this consumer credit contract is subject to all claims and defenses which the debtor could assert against the seller of goods or services obtained pursuant hereto or with the proceeds hereof. Recovery hereunder by the debtor shall not exceed amounts paid by the debtor hereunder.

16. Product Safety

The health and well-being of consumers is protected by a variety of statutes and rules of law, some of which antedate the modern consumer protection era.

Most states have laws governing the manufacture of various products and establishing product safety standards. The federal Consumer Product Safety Act provides for research and the setting of uniform standards for products in order to reduce health hazards. This act also establishes civil and criminal penalties for the distribution of unsafe products, recognizes the right of an aggrieved person to sue for money damages and to obtain an injunction against the distribution of unsafe

products, and creates a Consumer Product Safety Commission to administer the act.[25]

A consumer, as well as various nonconsumers, may hold a seller or manufacturer liable for damages when a product causes harm. Liability may be based on guarantees, warranties, negligence, fraud, or strict tort liability.

The federal Anti-Tampering Act[26] makes it a federal crime to tamper with consumer products.

17. Credit, Collection, and Billing Methods

Various provisions have been made to protect consumers from discriminatory and improper credit and collection practices.

(a) CREDIT DISCRIMINATION. It is unlawful to discriminate against an applicant for credit on the basis of race, color, religion, national origin, sex, marital status, or age; because all or part of the applicant's income is obtained from a public assistance program; or because the applicant has in good faith exercised any right under the Consumer Credit Protection Act (CCPA). When a credit application is refused, the applicant must be furnished with a written explanation of why the application was rejected.

(b) CORRECTION OF ERRORS. When the consumer believes that an error has been made in billing by the issuer of a credit card, the consumer should send the creditor a written statement and explanation of the error. The creditor or card issuer must investigate and make a prompt written reply to the consumer.[27]

---

[25] Act of October 27, 1972, PL 92-573, 86 Stat 1207, 15 USC § 2051-2081; as amended by the Consumer Product Safety Improvements Act of 1990, Act of November 16, 1990, PL 101-608, 104 Stat 3110, ___ USC § ___.

[26] Act of October 13, 1983, PL 98-127, 97 Stat 831, 13 USC § 1365.

[27] Fair Credit Billing Act, Act of October 18, 1974, PL 93-495, 15 USC § 1601.

(c) IMPROPER COLLECTION METH-ODS. Unreasonable methods of debt collection are often expressly prohibited by statute or are held by courts to constitute an unreasonable invasion of privacy.[28] Statutes generally prohibit sending bills in such a form that they give the impression that a lawsuit has been begun against the consumer and that the bill is legal process or a warrant issued by the court. The CCPA prohibits the use of extortionate methods of loan collection. A creditor may be prohibited from informing the employer of the debtor that the latter owes money.

A creditor is liable for unreasonably attempting to collect a bill that in fact has been paid. This liability can arise under general principles of tort law, as distinguished from special consumer protection legislation.

(1) Fault of Agent or Employee. When improper collection methods are used, it is no defense to the creditor that the improper acts were performed by an agent, employee, or any other person acting on behalf of the creditor.

(2) Fair Debt Collection Practices Act (FDCPA). The FDCPA prohibits improper practices in the collection of debts incurred primarily for personal, family, or household purposes.[29]

A debt collection letter sent to the debtor's place of employment was found to be a violation of the FDCPA. The words "final demand for payment" could be read through the envelope. The fact that it was likely that the debtor would be embarrassed by the delivery of such a letter to the employer's address affected the outcome of the case. In another case, a bank's threat to prosecute the depositors if they did not return to the bank money that had been paid to them by mistake violated a state debt collection law. No criminal statute prohibited the depositors' conduct.

When a collection agency violates the FDCPA, it is liable to the debtor for damages. It is no defense that the debtor in fact owed the money that the agency was seeking to collect.

In the *Johnson* case the consumer sued the collection agency for trying to collect a debt that was admittedly owed.

The Fair Debt Collection Practices Act applies only to those who regularly engage in the

JOHNSON v STATEWIDE COLLECTIONS, INC.
(Wyo) 778 P2d 93 (1989)

Johnson purchased a shotgun and paid with a check. He returned the gun the next day. He could not get his money back from the store, so he stopped payment on his check. The store claimed that it was not required to make a refund of the purchase price and gave its claim for the purchase price to the Statewide Collection Agency (also doing business as CheckRite). CheckRite sent a demand for payment to Johnson. This was answered by Johnson's attorney by a letter sent to CheckRite by certified mail. CheckRite ignored the attorney and made another demand on Johnson for payment. Johnson sued Statewide for damages, claiming that it violated the Fair Debt Collection Practices Act (FDCPA) because it had not obtained a verification of the debt

---

[28] Fair Debt Collection Practices Act, Act of September 20, 1977, PL 95-109, 91 Stat 874, 15 USC § § 1692 et seq.; Federal Trade Commission Regulation, 16 CFR Part 237.

[29] Bloom v I.C. System, Inc. (CA9 Or) 972 F2d 1067 (1992).

from the creditor nor sent such a verification to Johnson, that it demanded from the debtor more money than was due, and that it ignored the debtor's attorney. Judgment was entered in favor of Johnson, and Statewide appealed.

THOMAS, J. . . . We . . . consider the merits of the several asserted grounds for recovery under the FDCPA. Congress adopted this legislation in 1977 to protect consumers from abusive, deceptive, and unfair debt collection activities by eliminating certain offensive and unethical practices in vogue with many third-party debt collectors. . . . The objectionable practices, still prevalent even after the adoption of the FDCPA, often are exacerbated because independent collectors generally are unconcerned with the consumer's opinion of them, or their own reputations in the eyes of the public, and they proceed accordingly. This attitude is different from that of the direct creditor who often wishes to maintain some good will as well as some prospect of salvaging future business from their effort. . . . Some of the objectionable practices, more blatant and egregious than others, that transgress the FDCPA include obscene and profane language, direct threats of violence, harassing phone calls made at any and all hours of the day or night, disclosure of the debtor's personal affairs to friends and employers, attempts to collect more than is owed, intentional misrepresentation of legal rights and obligations, and impersonation of public officials and attorneys. . . .

Because the goal of the FDCPA is to eliminate abusive collection practices, it is applicable whether or not a valid debt exists. . . . A violation of the FDCPA cannot be defended even by establishing that the debt was long overdue and difficult to collect. Standing is afforded an aggrieved consumer to proceed under the act as long as the collector was purporting to attempt to collect an alleged debt. In a report from the subcommittee, its chairman said, "every individual, *whether or not he owes the debt,* has the right to be treated in a reasonable and civil manner." . . .

Administrative enforcement of the FDCPA is assigned to the Federal Trade Commission, 15 U.S.C. § 1692*l*, but the primary enforcement, in order to eliminate the objectionable practices, is self enforcement by the aggrieved debtor acting as a "private attorney general" through a civil action like that initiated by Johnson. . . . The incentive provided by the FDCPA for private enforcement is the recovery of attorney fees and costs, plus a civil penalty of up to $1000, in addition to actual damages when the debtor is successful in the civil action. . . .

Against this general background, we address the several claimed violations of the FDCPA that Johnson contends support the judgment awarded by the county court. The first of those arises under 15 U.S.C. § 1692g(b) which provides:

(b) Disputed debts. If the consumer notifies the debt collector in writing within the thirty-day period described in subsection (a) of this section that the debt, or any portion thereof, is disputed, or that the consumer requests the name and address of the original creditor, the debt collector shall cease collection of the debt, or any disputed portion thereof, until the debt collector obtains verification of the debt or a copy of a judgment, or the name and address of the original creditor, and a copy of such verification or judgment, or name and address of the original creditor, is mailed to the consumer by the debt collector.

This provision of the FDCPA requires the verification, or validation, of the alleged debt in order to prevent collection activities from being directed against the wrong person or against a debtor who has paid. . . .

CheckRite did not send verification of the debt to either Johnson or Johnson's attorney. The manager testified that he had communicated with the retail store on several other occasions on each of which the debt was verified to him.

It was CheckRite's duty, under the statute, to cease collection activities on the date it received the letter from Johnson's counsel until it sent Johnson, through his counsel, verification of the alleged debt. . . .

. . . CheckRite had failed to comply with 15 U.S.C. § 1692g because it had not received a verification or validation from the retail store that it could mail to Johnson. . . . . CheckRite made no attempt to comply with the mailing requirement. The burden is upon the debt collector to demand adequate verification so that it can comply with the mailing requirement of the statute. The failure to do so by CheckRite, in this instance, subjects it to the sanctions provided under 15 U.S.C. § 1692k.

The next basis for liability raises the issue of whether CheckRite violated the provisions of 15 U.S.C. § 1692f(1) by attempting to collect more from Johnson than was permitted either by agreement or by law. . . . CheckRite agrees that this is true, but defends its conduct as not a violation of the FDCPA by contending that the improper claim was the product of an inadvertent clerical error. . . .

The . . . FDCPA provides:

A debt collector may not use unfair or unconscionable means to collect or attempt to collect any debt. Without limiting the general application of the foregoing, the following conduct is in violation of this section:

(1) The collection of any amount (including any interest, fee, charge, or expense incidental to the principal obligation) unless such amount is expressly authorized by the agreement creating the debt or permitted by law. 15 U.S.C. § 1692f.

The concession by CheckRite that the demand encompassed an overcharge manifests a prima facie violation of the FDCPA. . . . In submitting its argument that the overcharge was the result of an inadvertent clerical error, CheckRite invokes . . . 15 U.S.C. § 1692k(c) that provides:

(c) Intent. A debt collector may not be held liable in any action brought under this subchapter if the debt collector shows by a preponderance of evidence that the violation was not intentional and resulted from a bona fide error notwithstanding the maintenance of procedures reasonably adapted to avoid any such error.

. . . While CheckRite's explanation is plausible . . . the record is silent with respect to any procedures reasonably adopted by CheckRite to preclude just such an error. . . . The collector is liable under the act without regard to whether the overcharge was intentional or not unless proper procedures to preclude the error are maintained. . . .

CheckRite also violated the FDCPA by sending a demand letter directly to him after it had been advised that he was represented by counsel. The pertinent provision is 15 U.S.C. § 1692c(a)(2) that provides:

(a) Communication with the consumer generally—Without the prior consent of the consumer given directly to the debt collector or the express permission of a court of competent jurisdiction, a debt collector may not communicate with a consumer in connection with the collection of any debt— . . .

(2) if the debt collector knows the consumer is represented by an attorney with respect to such debt and has knowledge of, or can readily ascertain, such attorney's name and address, unless the attorney fails to respond within a reasonable period of time to a communication from the debt collector or unless the attorney consents to direct communication with the consumer. . . .

CheckRite admits that it sent an additional communication to Johnson after receiving the advice that he was represented by counsel. . . . The communication directly with Johnson . . . was an additional violation of the FDCPA. . . .

[Judgment affirmed]

QUESTIONS

1. Can a debt collection agency defend against the claim for violating the FDCPA by proving that the debt in fact was owed and that the debtor knew that it was owed?
2. What must a collection agency do when a consumer notifies it in writing within a 30-day period that a debt assigned to it for collection is disputed?
3. Assume that a collection agency knows that the debtor's affairs are frequently handled by the attorney John Jones, Esq. To whom should the agency send the verification of the debt?

business of collecting debts for others—primarily to collection agencies. The act does not apply when a bank attempts to collect debts owed to it by directly contacting the debtors.

18. Protection of Credit Standing and Reputation

In many instances, one party to a transaction wishes to know certain things about the other party. This situation arises when a person purchases on credit or applies for a loan, a job, or an insurance policy. Between 2,000 and 3,000 private credit bureaus gather such information on borrowers, buyers, and applicants and sell the information to interested persons.

The Fair Credit Reporting Act (FCRA) of 1970[30] seeks to protect consumers from various abuses that may arise.

FCRA applies only to **consumer credit**, which is defined as credit for "personal, family, and household" use; it does not apply to business or commercial transactions. The act does not apply to the investigation report made by an insurance company of a policy claim.[31]

(a) PRIVACY. A report on a person based on personal investigation and interviews is called an **investigative consumer report**. It may not be made without informing the person investigated of the right to discover the results of the investigation. Bureaus are not permitted to disclose information to persons not having a legitimate use for it. It is a federal crime to obtain or to furnish a bureau report for an improper purpose.

On request, a bureau must tell a consumer the names and addresses of persons to whom it has made a credit report during the previous six months. It must also tell, when requested,

---

[30] Act of October 26, 1970, PL 91-508, 84 Stat 1128, 15 USC § § 1681 et seq.
[31] Kemp v County of Orange, 211 Cal App 3d 1422, 260 Cal Rptr 131 (1989).

which employers were given such a report during the previous two years.

A store may not publicly display a list of named customers from whom it will not accept checks; such action is an invasion of the privacy of those persons.

(b) PROTECTION FROM FALSE INFORMATION.

Much of the information obtained by credit bureaus is based on statements made by persons, such as neighbors, when interviewed by the bureau's investigator. Sometimes the statements are incorrect. Quite often they are hearsay evidence and would not be admissible in a legal proceeding. Nevertheless, such statements may go on the records of the bureau without further verification and be furnished to a client of the bureau, who will tend to regard them as accurate and true.

A person has a limited right to request that a credit bureau disclose the nature and substance of the information it possesses. The right to know does not extend to medical information. It is not required that the bureau identify the persons giving information to its investigators. The bureau is not required to give the applicant a copy of, or to permit the applicant to see, any file.

When a person claims that the information of the bureau is erroneous, the bureau must take steps within a reasonable time to determine the accuracy of the disputed item.

Adverse information obtained by investigation cannot be given to a client after three months unless verified to determine that it is still valid. Most legal proceedings cannot be reported by a bureau after seven years. A bankruptcy proceeding cannot be reported after ten years.

In the *Thompson* case a person who was denied credit because of the mistake of a credit reporting agency brought suit against the agency. Was it liable? The court was faced with determining what standard of care should be required of a credit reporting agency.

THOMPSON v SAN ANTONIO RETAIL MERCHANTS ASS'N

(CA5 Tex) 682 F2d 509 (1982)

The San Antonio Retail Merchants Association (SARMA) was a credit reporting agency. It was asked by one of its members to furnish information on William Douglas Thompson, III. It supplied information from a file that contained data on William III and also on William Daniel Thompson, Jr. The agency had jumbled information related to William Jr. into the file relating to William III, so that all information appeared to relate to William III. William Jr. had a bad credit standing, and SARMA gave a bad report on William III. Because of this report, he was denied credit by several enterprises. He then sued SARMA for its negligence in confusing him with William Jr. From a judgment in Williams's favor, SARMA appealed.

PER CURIAM. . . SARMA provides a computerized credit reporting service to local business subscribers. This service depends heavily upon credit history information fed into SARMA's files by subscribers. A key mechanism used by SARMA to update its files is a computerized "automatic capturing" feature. A subscriber must feed certain identifying information from its own computer terminal into SARMA's central computer in order to gain access to the credit history of a particular consumer. When presented with this identifying information, SARMA's computer searches its records and displays on the subscriber's terminal the credit history file that most nearly matches the consumer. The decision whether to accept a given file as being that of a particular consumer is left completely to the terminal operator. When a subscriber does accept a given file as pertaining to a particular consumer, however, the computer automatically captures into the file any information input from the subscriber's terminal that the central file did not already have.

A disadvantage of an automatic capturing feature is that it may accept erroneous information fed in by subscribers, unless special auditing procedures are built into the system. In the instant case, SARMA failed to check the accuracy of a social security number obtained by its automatic capturing feature. The social security number is the single most important identifying factor for credit-reference purposes. As a result, the computer erroneously began to report the bad credit history of "William Daniel Thompson, Jr.," to subscribers inquiring about "William Douglas Thompson, III."

Under 15 U.S.C. § 1681o of the Fair Credit Reporting Act (Act), a "consumer reporting agency" is liable to "any consumer" for negligent failure to comply with "any requirement imposed" by the Act. In the instant case, the district court determined that SARMA was liable under section 1681o for negligent failure to comply with section 1681e(b) of the Act, which provides:

When a consumer reporting agency prepares a consumer report, it shall follow reasonable procedures to assure maximum possible accuracy of information concerning the individual about whom the report relates.

15 U.S.C. § 1681e(b) (emphasis added).

Section 1681e(b) does not impose strict liability for any inaccurate credit report, but only a duty of reasonable care in preparation of the report. That duty extends to updating procedures, because "preparation" of a consumer report should be viewed as a continuing process and the obligation to insure accuracy arises with every addition of information. The standard of conduct by which the trier of fact must judge the adequacy of agency procedures is what a reasonably prudent person would do under the circumstances.

Applying the reasonable-person standard, the district court found two acts of negligence in SARMA's updating procedures. First, SARMA failed to exercise reasonable care in programming its computer to automatically capture information into a file without requiring any minimum number of "points of correspondence" between the consumer and the file or having an adequate auditing procedure to foster accuracy. Second, SARMA failed to employ reasonable procedures designed to learn the disparity in social security numbers for the two Thompsons. . . .

With respect to the first act of negligence, George Zepeda, SARMA's manager, testified that SARMA's computer had no minimum number of points of correspondence to be satisfied before an inquiring subscriber could accept credit information. Moreover, SARMA had no way of knowing if the information supplied by the subscriber was correct. Although SARMA did conduct spot audits to verify social security numbers, it did not audit all subscribers. With respect to the second act of negligence, SARMA's verification process failed to uncover the erroneous social security number even though. . . . a specific request [had been made] for a "revision" to check the adverse credit history ascribed to the plaintiff. SARMA's manager, Mr. Zepeda, testified that what should have been done upon the request for a revision, was to pick up the phone and . . . learn, among other things, the social security number for William Daniel Thompson, Jr. It was the manager's further testimony that the social security number is the single most important information in a consumer's credit file. In light of this evidence, this Court cannot conclude that the district court was clearly erroneous in finding negligent violation of section 1681e(b). . . .

The district court's award of $10,000 in actual damages was based on humiliation and mental distress to the plaintiff. Even when there are no out-of-pocket expenses, humiliation and mental distress do constitute recoverable elements of damage under the Act. In the instant case, the amount of damages is a question of fact which may be reversed by this Court only if the district court's findings are clearly erroneous. . . .

[Judgment affirmed]

QUESTIONS

1. What justification was there for the improper reporting by SARMA?
2. What was the significance of the social security numbers?
3. Was the question of liability of SARMA affected by the fact that the report had been supplied by a computer?

On general principles of agency law, a creditor hiring someone or a collection agency to collect a debt is liable to the debtor for damages for unlawful conduct of the collector. It is no defense that the creditor did not intend or have any knowledge of this conduct.

19. Expansion of Consumer Protection

Various state laws aimed at preventing fraudulent sales of corporate securities, commonly called **blue sky laws**, have been adopted. Other statutes have been adopted to protect purchasers of real estate, buyers of services, and prospective franchisees.

(a) REAL ESTATE DEVELOPMENT SALES. Anyone promoting the sale of a real estate development that is divided into 50 or more parcels of less than five acres each must file with the secretary of Housing and Urban Development (HUD) a **development state-ment**. This statement must set forth significant details of the development, as required by the federal Land Sales Act.[32]

Anyone buying or renting one of the parcels in the subdivision must be given a **property report**. This is a condensed version of the development statement filed with the secretary of HUD. This report must be given to the prospective customer more than 48 hours before the signing of the contract to buy or lease.

If the development statement is not filed with the secretary, the sale or rental of the real estate development may not be promoted through the channels of interstate commerce or by the use of the mail.

If the property report is given to the prospective buyer or tenant less than 48 hours before the signing of a contract to buy or lease, or after it has been signed, the contract may be avoided within 48 hours. If the property report is never received, the contract may be avoided, and there is no statutory limitation on the time in which this may be done.

---

[32] Act of August 1, 1968, as amended, PL 90-448, 82 Stat 590, 15 USC § § 1701-1720.

The federal statute prohibits imposing or receiving unauthorized payments in connection with a real estate settlement.

State statutes frequently require that particular enterprises selling property tell or disclose certain information to prospective buyers.

(b) SERVICE CONTRACTS. The UCCC treats a consumer service contract the same as a consumer sale of goods if (1) payment is made in installments or a credit charge is made, and (2) the amount financed does not exceed $25,000. It defines services broadly as embracing work, specified privileges, and insurance provided by a noninsurer. The inclusion of privileges makes the UCCC apply to contracts calling for payment on the installment plan or including a financing charge for transportation, hotel and restaurant accommodations, education, entertainment, recreation, physical culture (such as athletic clubs or bodybuilding schools), hospital accommodations, funerals, and cemetery accommodations.

In some states, it is unlawful for a repair shop to make unauthorized repairs to an automobile and then to refuse to return the automobile to the customer until paid for such repairs.

(c) FRANCHISES. A franchisee is a consumer entitled to sue the franchisor for violation of a state deceptive practices act. To protect a prospective franchisee from deception, a Federal Trade Commission regulation requires that the franchisor give a prospective franchisee a disclosure statement ten days before the franchisee signs a contract or pays any money for a franchise. The disclosure statement provides detailed information relating to the franchisor's finances, experience, size of operation, and involvement in litigation. The statement must set forth any restrictions imposed on the franchisee; any costs that must be paid initially or in the future; and the provisions for termination, cancellation, and renewal of the franchise. False statements

MORRIS v INTERNATIONAL YOGURT CO.
107 Wash 2d 314, 729 P2d 33 (1986)

The International Yogurt Company (IYC) had developed a unique mix for making frozen yogurt and related products. Morris and his wife purchased a franchise from the company. They were not told that a franchise was not required to obtain the mix—that the company would sell its yogurt mix to anyone. The franchise business of the Morrises was a failure, and they sold it at a loss after three years. They then sued the company for fraud and for violation of the state Franchise Investment Protection Act (FIPA) and the state Consumer Protection Act. From a decision against them, they appealed.

DURHAM, J. . . . The next issue we must consider is if IYC violated FIPA by failing to disclose to the Morrises that the yogurt mix was available to nonfranchisees. [The statute] provides in part:

It is unlawful for any person in connection with the offer, sale, or purchase of any franchise directly or indirectly: (2) To sell or offer to sell a franchise in this state by means of any written or oral communication which includes an untrue statement of a material fact or omits to state a material fact necessary in order to make the statements made in light of the circumstances under which they were made not misleading.

. . . Initially, we must determine when a fact is under [the FIPA]. This provision is essentially the same as the antifraud provision in the Securities Act of Washington. . . . For purposes of the latter provision, a "material fact" is "a fact to which a reasonable man would attach importance in determining his choice of action in the transaction in question." . . .

The next question is if IYC's failure to disclose to the Morrises that the yogurt mix was available to nonfranchisees was an omission of a material fact. In order to determine if a reasonable person would consider this fact important in purchasing the franchise, it is necessary to consider initially the importance of the yogurt mix itself to the potential franchisee.

The evidence in the record indicates that the yogurt mix was an essential element of the franchise. First, the franchise agreement placed particular emphasis on the fact that, in exchange for purchasing an IYC franchise, the franchisee would obtain the right to purchase and use a special yogurt mix. The agreement goes to considerable length in discussing the yogurt mix. Section 9 of the agreement states in part:

The yogurt mix to be used in the preparation of all frozen yogurt sold at the Franchised Location is unique, and its formula and process for manufacture may be regarded as a trade secret. The right to purchase and use the mix is granted to Franchisee pursuant to this Agreement.

Thus, the agreement clearly indicates that the right to purchase this one-of-a-kind yogurt mix is a key feature of the franchise.

Section 9 of the agreement further provides that the franchisor will make the formula for the manufacture of the mix available to certain dairy manufacturers, which shall be regarded as approved sources from which the franchisee will purchase the mix. If the franchisee wishes to purchase the mix from a different manufacturer, he must request in writing that the franchisor disclose the formula and process for manufacture to that manufacturer. The agreement further states:

Franchisor shall exercise its reasonable good business judgment in determining whether the formula and process should be disclosed to that manufacturer, taking into consideration such factors as that manufacturer's ability to produce a mix of satisfactory quality, and that manufacturer's ability to adequately protect the formula and process from disclosure to unauthorized persons.

(Emphasis ours.) By suggesting that IYC will limit access to the formula for the yogurt mix, this provision reinforces the fact that the mix is significant to IYC's product.

. . . In summary, the evidence as a whole indicates that the yogurt mix as well as the flavoring contributed to the distinctiveness of IYC's final product. . . . This yogurt mix was a major, essential element of IYC yogurt.

. . . IYC's failure to disclose to the Morrises the availability of the yogurt mix to nonfranchisees was an omission of a material fact. In deciding whether to purchase the franchise, a reasonable person reading the franchise agreement would have considered it important that the same yogurt mix was available to persons not purchasing the franchise. The fact that an essential component of the franchise's major product is unique and considered a trade secret is a far less value to the potential franchisee if that ingredient is generally available to all persons whether or not they have purchased the franchise. A person might not consider it worthwhile to invest in the franchise if he knew he could obtain the mix without paying the franchise fee. For these reasons, we conclude that IYC's failure to disclose to the Morrises the availability of the yogurt mix to nonfranchisees was an omission of a material fact necessary to make the statements IYC made not misleading, and therefore, was a violation of [the FIPA].

. . . FIPA's provision on damages states that a person who sells a franchise in violation of the statute "shall be liable to the franchisee . . . who may sue at law or in equity for damages caused thereby."

We hold . . . that in an action alleging the omission of a material fact in violation of [FIPA], proof of nondisclosure of a material fact establishes a presumption of reliance which the defendant may rebut by proving that the plaintiff would still have purchased the franchise even if the material fact had been disclosed. This case is remanded to the trial court to determine, in a manner consistent with this opinion, if IYC's failure to disclose to the Morrises the availability of the mix to nonfranchisees caused the Morrises to suffer damages.

. . . We reverse the Court of Appeals decision that IYC did not omit a material fact in violation of [FIPA] when it failed to disclose to the Morrises the availability of the yogurt mix to nonfranchisees. We remand the case to the trial court to decide if the Morrises may recover damages for IYC's violation . . . , according to the principles in this opinion.

[Reversed on the issue of the effect of the omission and action remanded to determine damages]

QUESTIONS

1. Did the company expressly state that its unique yogurt mix would be sold only to franchisees?
2. Why does the court describe the availability of the yogurt mix to nonfranchisees as a material fact?
3. Why is the court concerned with "reliance" by the prospective franchise buyer?

regarding sales, income, or profits are prohibited. Violation of the regulation is subject to a fine of $10,000.

In the *Morris* case the franchisees claimed that they were misled by the concealment of a material fact by the franchisor.

(d) AUTOMOBILE LEMON LAWS. All of the states have adopted special laws for the protection of consumers buying automobiles that develop numerous defects or defects that cannot be corrected. These statutes protect only persons buying for personal, family, or household use. They generally classify an automobile as a lemon if it cannot be put in proper or warranted condition within a specified period of time or after a specified number of repair attempts. In general, they give the buyer greater protection than is given to other buyers by the Uniform Commercial Code or the other consumer protection statutes. In some states, the seller of the lemon car is required to give the buyer a brand new replacement car. In some states, a government official may also bring an action to collect civil penalties from the seller of a lemon car.[33]

SUMMARY

With the modern era of consumer protection, society has accepted the premise that equality before the law is not appropriate to the marketplace, where modern methods of marketing, packaging, and financing have reduced the ordinary consumer to a subordinate position. To protect the consumer from the hardship, fraud, and oppression that could result from being in such an inferior position, the law has, at many points, limited the freedom of action of the enterprise with which the consumer deals.

Consumer protection laws are directed at false and misleading advertising; misleading or false use of seals of approval and labels; and the methods of selling—requiring the disclosure of terms, permitting consumer cancellation of home-solicited sales, and, in some states, prohibiting referral sales. The consumer is protected in a contract agreement by regulation of its form, prohibition of unconscionable

terms, and limitation of the credit that can be extended to a consumer. Credit card protections include the prohibition of the unauthorized distribution of such cards and limited liability of the cardholder for the unauthorized use of a credit card. The application of payments; the preservation of consumer defenses as against a transferee of the consumer's contract; product safety; the protection of credit standing and reputation; and (to some extent) real estate development sales, franchises, and service contracts are all included in consumer protection laws. Lemon laws provide special protection to buyers of automobiles for personal, household, or family use.

When a consumer protection statute is violated, an action may sometimes be brought by the consumer against the wrongdoer. More commonly, such action is brought by an administrative agency or by the attorney general of the state.

LAW IN PRACTICE

1. Learn whether you and the other contracting party are "consumers" within the scope of applicable state and federal law.

2. Protect yourself from credit card abuses by rejecting unsolicited cards and notifying the issuer if your card is lost or stolen.

3. Protect your credit standing and reputation by demanding that any collection agency verify a debt you dispute and drop old items from your record.

4. If you are a merchant, learn what disclosures you must make to credit buyers.

QUESTIONS AND CASE PROBLEMS

1. What is the object of each of the following rules of law? (a) Back-page disclaimers are void if the front page of the contract does not call attention to the presence of such terms. (b) A consumer's waiver of a statute designed for consumer protection is void, but the transaction otherwise binds the consumer.

2. Cora telephoned from her home to the Nowlin Music Supply Company and ordered an electric guitar. The employee of Nowlin answering the phone stated that Cora's order was accepted and that the guitar would be sent to her within a few

days. That night Cora saw an ad in the newspaper for the same guitar for $100 less than the Nowlin price. She wrote and mailed a letter the next day to the Nowlin Company stating that she canceled her order. May she do so?

3. Ward purchased an ice-making machine from Kold-Serve Corp. The machine had been sold by Kold-Serve to another buyer but was returned to Kold-Serve. The president of Kold-Serve sold this machine as a "demonstrator model." He did not inform Ward of its prior sale and return. Later Ward sued Kold-Serve, claiming that it had

---

[33] Adams v Nissan Motor Corp. in U.S.A. (W Va App) 387 SE2d 288 (1989).

Kold-Serve. The president of Kold-Serve sold this machine as a "demonstrator model." He did not inform Ward of its prior sale and return. Later Ward sued Kold-Serve, claiming that it had "knowingly" committed an unfair trade practice in the sale of the machine to him. Was Ward correct? [Kold-Serve Corp. v Ward (Tex App) 736 SW2d 750]

4. The California consumer protection statute prohibits the use of false or misleading representations in the sale of goods or services. Mayne borrowed money from the Bank of America National Trust and Savings Association. He later sued the bank, claiming that it had violated the statute. The bank asserted that Mayne was required to prove that he had been deceived by the information furnished by the bank. Was the bank correct? [Mayne v Bank of America National Trust and Savings Assn. (Cal App) 242 Cal Rptr 357]

5. The Merit Breakfast Food Company sold its breakfast cereal in ordinary-sized packages, but the packages were labeled *jumbo size*. Merit was ordered by the Federal Trade Commission to stop using this term. Merit raised the defense that the term *jumbo* was not used with any intent to defraud, so its use was not improper. Was this a valid defense?

6. Thomas was sent a credit card through the mail by a company that had taken his name and address from the telephone book. Because he never requested the card, Thomas left the card lying on his desk. A thief stole the card and used it to purchase merchandise in several stores in the name of Thomas. The issuer of the credit card claimed that Thomas was liable for the total amount of the purchases made by the thief. Thomas claimed that he was not liable for any amount. The court decided that Thomas was liable for $50. Who is correct?

7. A federal statute prohibits the interstate shipment of deceptively or fraudulently labeled goods. Acting under the authority of this statute, federal officers seized a shipment of 95 barrels that were labeled apple cider vinegar. This vinegar had been made from dried apples that had been soaked in water. The government claimed that the label was false, because apple cider vinegar meant to the average person that the vinegar had been made from fresh apples. The shipper claimed that since the barrels in fact contained vinegar that had been made from cider produced from apples, the labels were truthful in calling the contents by the name of apple cider vinegar. Was the shipper correct?

[United States v 95 Barrels of Alleged Apple Cider Vinegar, 265 US 438]

8. Wilke was contemplating retiring. In response to an advertisement, he purchased from Coinway 30 coin-operated testing machines. He purchased these because Coinway's representative stated that by placing these machines at different public places, Wilke could obtain supplemental income. This statement was made by the representative although he had no experience as to the cost of servicing such machines or their income-producing potential. The operational costs of the machines by Wilke exceeded the income. Wilke sued Coinway to rescind the contract, alleging that it was fraudulent. Coinway defended on the ground that the statements made were merely matters of opinion and did not constitute fraud. Was Wilke entitled to rescission? [Wilke v Coinway, Inc., 257 Cal App 2d 126, 64 Cal Rptr 845]

9. Greif obtained credit cards from Socony Mobil Oil Co. for himself and his wife. The card specified, "This card is valid unless expired or revoked. Named holder's approval of all purchases is presumed unless written notice of loss or theft is received." Later Greif returned his card to the company, stating that he was canceling it, but that he could not return the card in his wife's possession because they had separated. Subsequently, Socony sued Greif for purchases made by the wife on the credit card in her possession. He defended on the ground that he had canceled the credit card contract. Decide. [Socony Mobil Oil Co. v Greif, 10 App Div 2d 119, 197 NYS2d 522]

10. The Southwestern Bell Telephone Company held a judgment against Wilson for $9,500. It instructed two attorneys and some of its employees to collect the judgment. In their attempts to do so, they allegedly committed various torts and harassed Wilson. He sued Southwestern. It denied liability for the conduct of the attorneys and the employees because it had not authorized any improper collection practices. Was this defense valid? [Southwestern Bell Tele. Co. v Wilson (Tex App) 768 SW2d 755]

11. A suit was brought against General Foods on the ground that it was violating the state law prohibiting false and deceptive advertising. It raised the defense that the plaintiffs had failed to show that the public had been deceived by the advertising, that the public in fact had not relied on the advertising, and that there was no proof that anyone had sustained any damage because of the advertising. Were these valid defenses? [Committee on

Childrens Television, Inc. v General Foods Corp. 35 Cal 3d 197, 197 Cal Rptr 783, 673 P2d 660]

12. The town of Newport obtained a corporate MasterCard. The card was given to the town clerk to use in purchasing fuel for the town hall. The town clerk used the card for personal restaurant, hotel, and gift shop debts. The town refused to pay the card charges on the ground that they were unauthorized. Was the town correct? *[MasterCard v Town of Newport, 133 Wis App 2d 328, 396 NW2d 345]*

13. How do you explain the rise of consumer protectionism?

14. Stevens purchased a pair of softball shoes manufactured by Hyde Athletic Industries. Because of a defect in the shoes, she fell and broke an ankle. She sued Hyde under the state consumer protection act which provided "any person who is injured in . . . business or property . . . could sue for damages sustained." Hyde claimed that the Act did not cover personal injuries. Stevens claimed that she was injured in her "property" because of the money that she had to spend for medical treatment and subsequent care. Decide. *[Stevens v Hyde Athletic Industries, Inc. ___ Wash App ___, 773 P2d 871]*

15. How do you justify a large city, a state government, and a millionaire being given the protection of consumer protection statutes?

Negotiable Commercial Paper

CHAPTER 30

KINDS OF PAPER, PARTIES, AND NEGOTIABILITY

LEARNING OBJECTIVES

After studying this chapter, you will be able to:
1. *Explain the importance and function of commercial paper.*
2. *Name the parties to commercial paper.*
3. *Describe the concept of negotiability and distinguish it from assignability.*
4. *List the essential elements of a negotiable instrument.*

Over the course of centuries, the business community and then the law came to accept certain kinds of paper as substitutes for money or as a means of giving credit. The 1952 version of UCC Article 3 calls them *commercial paper*. The 1990 version uses the name *negotiable instruments.*

A. KINDS OF COMMERCIAL PAPER AND PARTIES

The UCC defines negotiable commercial paper and the parties to such paper.

1. Definition

Commercial paper or a **negotiable instrument** is a transferable written, signed promise or order to pay a specified sum of money. Instruments are negotiable when they contain the terms required by the UCC. These terms are listed and explained in Section 6 of this chapter.

1952 UCC

2. Kinds of Commercial Paper

Commercial paper falls into four categories: (1) promissory notes, (2) drafts or bills of exchange, (3) checks, and (4) certificates of deposit.[1]

1990 UCC

There are two categories of negotiable instruments: (1) promissory notes and (2) drafts.[2] A certificate of deposit is classified as a promissory note. Drafts may also be called bills of exchange. A check is a particular kind of draft.

(a) PROMISSORY NOTES. A **negotiable promissory note** is an unconditional promise in writing made by one person to another, signed by the maker, engaging to pay on demand or at a definite time a sum certain in money to order or to bearer. (See Figure 30-1.)

(b) DRAFTS. A **negotiable draft** or **bill of exchange** is an unconditional order in writing addressed by one person to another, signed by

Figure 30-1 Promissory Note

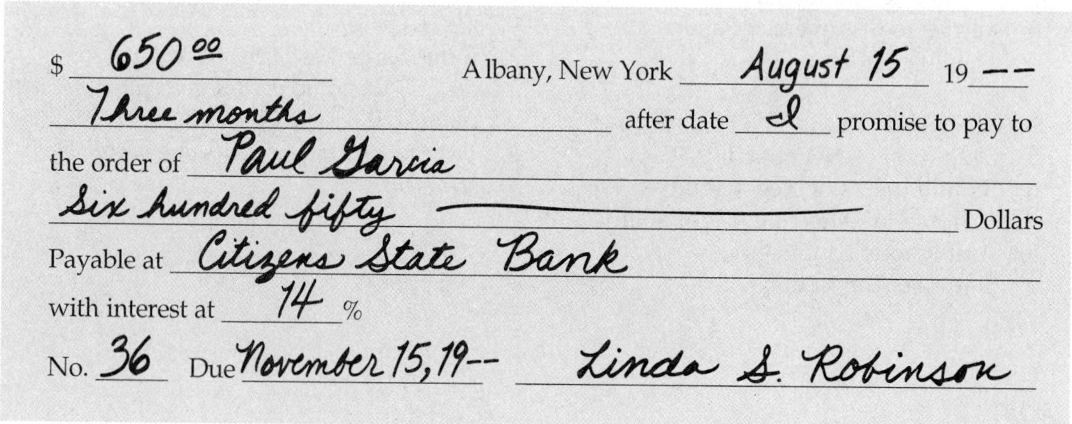
$ 650.00 Albany, New York August 15 19--

Three months after date I promise to pay to

the order of Paul Garcia

Six hundred fifty Dollars

Payable at Citizens State Bank

with interest at 14 %

No. 36 Due November 15, 19-- Linda S. Robinson

1 UCC § 3-104(e) [1990]. The year in brackets following the citation of a UCC section is the date of the version cited.

2 UCC § 3-104(2) [1952]. The year in brackets following the citation of a UCC section is the date of the version cited.

(b) DRAFTS. A **negotiable draft** or **bill of exchange** is an unconditional order in writing addressed by one person to another, signed by the person giving it, requiring the person to whom it is addressed to pay on demand, or at a definite time, a sum certain in money to order or to bearer. (See Figure 30-2.) In effect, it is an order by one person on a second person to pay a sum of money. The person who gives the order is called the *drawer* and is said to draw the bill. The person on whom the order to pay is drawn is the *drawee*. The person to whom payment is to be made is the *payee*. The drawer may also be named as the drawee.

The drawee who is ordered to pay the paper is not bound to do so. However, the drawee may agree to pay the paper, in which case the drawee is called an *acceptor*.

Figure 30-2 Draft (Bill of Exchange)

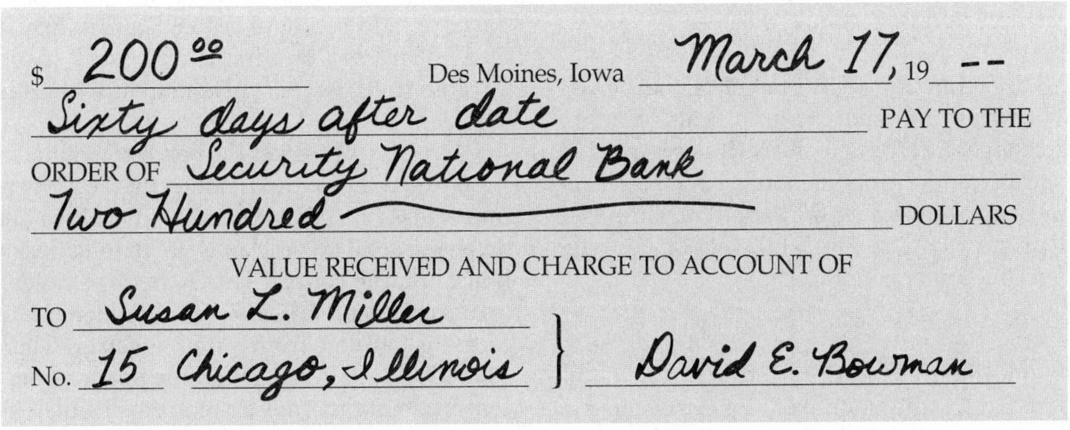
$ 200 00 Des Moines, Iowa March 17, 19 --
Sixty days after date PAY TO THE
ORDER OF Security National Bank
Two Hundred DOLLARS
VALUE RECEIVED AND CHARGE TO ACCOUNT OF
TO Susan L. Miller
No. 15 Chicago, Illinois } David E. Bowman

(c) CHECKS. A **check** is a draft drawn on a bank and is payable on demand.[3] It is an order by a depositor (the drawer) on a bank (the drawee) to pay a sum of money to the order of another person (the payee). A check is always drawn on a bank as drawee and is always payable on demand.

1952 UCC

*****

1990 UCC

In addition to the ordinary check described above, there are also the cashier's check, the teller's check, the traveler's check, and the bank money order. A **cashier's check** is a draft drawn by a bank on itself. A **teller's check** is a draft drawn by a bank on another bank in which it has an account. A **traveler's check** is a check that is payable on demand, provided it is countersigned by the person whose specimen signature appears on the check. A **bank money order** is a check, even though it bears the words *money order*.[4]

(d) CERTIFICATES OF DEPOSIT. A **certificate of deposit** (CD) is an instrument issued by a bank. A CD acknowledges the

3 UCC § 3-104(2)(b)[1952];.§ 3-104(f)[1990)].

4 UCC § 3-104(f) to (i) [1990].

deposit of a specific sum of money and promises to pay the holder of the certificate that amount, usually with interest, when the certificate is surrendered.

3.   Parties to Commercial Paper

A note has two original parties—the maker and the payee. A draft or a check has three original parties—the drawer, the drawee, and the payee. In addition to these original parties, a commercial paper may have one or more of the parties described under (e) through (k) of this section.

The term *party* may refer to a natural person, or to an artificial person, such as a corporation. It may also mean an unincorporated enterprise, a government, or a bank account number.

(a) MAKER. The **maker** is the person who writes out and creates a promissory note thereby promising to pay the amount specified in the note. If the paper is not a promissory note, the creator has a different name, for example "drawer" for a check.

(b) DRAWER. The **drawer** is the person who writes out and creates a draft or bill of exchange, including a check. It is essential to bear in mind the distinction between a maker and a drawer because the liability of the maker is primary or absolute, while that of a drawer is secondary or conditional.

(c) DRAWEE. The **drawee** is the person to whom the draft is addressed and who is ordered to pay the amount of money specified in the draft.

(d) PAYEE. The **payee** is the person named on the face of the paper to receive payment. In a check stating "pay to the order of John Jones," the named person, John Jones, is the payee.

A payee has no rights in the paper until it has been delivered by the drawer or the maker. Likewise, the payee is not liable on the paper in any way until the payee transfers the paper to someone else.

(e) ACCEPTOR. When the drawee has signified in writing on the draft the willingness to make the specified payment, the drawee is called the **acceptor**.

(f) INDORSER. The owner of commercial paper who signs on the back of the paper is an **indorser**. Thus, if a check is made payable to the order of Dawn Mullin, she may indorse it to Juanita Alford to pay a debt that Dawn owes Juanita. In such a case, Dawn, who is the payee of the check, is now also an indorser.

(g) INDORSEE. The person to whom an indorsement is made payable is called an **indorsee**. The indorsee may in turn indorse the instrument and then is also an indorser.

(h) BEARER. The person in physical possession of a commercial paper that is payable to bearer is called a **bearer**.

(i) HOLDER. A **holder** is a person in possession of commercial paper that is payable at that time either to the order of such person, as payee or indorsee, or to bearer. For example, if Dan Hillard has possession of a check made payable "to the order of Dan Hillard," Dan is a holder.

A person who takes the paper for value, in good faith, and without notice that it is overdue or has been dishonored or that there are defenses against or claims to it is called a **holder in due course**. The law gives a holder in due course preferred status. A holder in due course is immune from certain defenses when such a holder brings suit on the paper. A person becoming the holder of an instrument at any time after it was once held by a holder in due course is described as a **holder through a holder in due course**. Ordinarily, a holder through a holder in due course is given the same special rights as a holder in due course.

(j) ACCOMMODATION PARTY. A person who becomes a party to a commercial paper in order to add strength to the paper for the benefit of another party to the paper is called an **accommodation party**.
1952 UCC

1990 UCC

When a person who does not own the negotiable instrument indorses it to accommodate a party to the instrument, such indorsement is called an **anomalous indorsement**.

(k) GUARANTOR. A **guarantor** is a person who signs a commercial paper and adds a promise to pay the instrument under certain circumstances. Ordinarily, this is done by merely adding "payment guaranteed" or "collection guaranteed" to the signature of the guarantor on the paper.

C P A (1) Nature of Guaranty. The addition of "payment guaranteed" or similar words means that the guarantor will pay the instrument when due. The liability of a guarantor of payment is as extensive as that of the original debtor. "Collection guaranteed" or similar words means that the guarantor will not pay the paper until after the holder has sought to collect payment from the maker or acceptor and has been unable to do so.

1952 UCC

(2) Construction of Guaranty. If the meaning of the guaranty is not clear, it is construed as a guaranty of payment. For example, when an indorser adds a statement that the paper is guaranteed or adds the word *guarantor* to the indorsement, without specifying whether it is payment or collection that is guaranteed, the indorser is deemed to be a guarantor of payment.[5]

1990 UCC

(2) Construction of Guaranty.

4. Liability of Parties

A person who by the terms of the instrument is absolutely required to pay is **primarily liable**. On a note, the maker is primarily liable.

On a draft, the acceptor (the drawee who has accepted) is primarily liable. A guarantor of payment is primarily liable in any case. Other parties are either secondarily or conditionally liable, as in the case of an indorser, or they are not liable in any capacity. A person who transfers the paper but does not sign it is not liable for its payment.[6]

(a) ACCOMMODATION PARTIES. An accommodation party is liable on the paper regardless of whether the paper is signed merely as a matter of friendship or in return for payment.

The accommodation party is not liable to the party accommodated. If the accommodation party is required to pay the paper, that party has a right to recover the payment from the person accommodated. Parol evidence may be admitted to show that a party to the paper had signed to accommodate another party.[7]

(b) GUARANTORS. A **guarantor of payment** has primary liability. The guarantor of payment is liable for payment of the paper even though the holder has not sought to obtain payment from any other party. It is immaterial that payment was not demanded from the original primary party or that such party had sufficient assets to pay the paper.

The **guarantor of collection** is not required to pay the paper until collection has been attempted and has failed, or unless an attempt to collect would obviously be useless.

B. NEGOTIABILITY

Negotiability is the characteristic that distinguishes commercial paper and instruments from ordinary contracts.

---

5 UCC § 3-416 [1952].

6 Pike Burden Printing, Inc. v Pike Burden, Inc. (La App) 396 So 2d 361 (1981).

7 Citizens Savings Bank and Trust Co. v Hardaway (Tenn App) 724 SW2d 352 (1986).

5. Definition of Negotiability

Negotiability is a quality that the law gives to certain commercial paper. By virtue of this quality, the paper may be transferred by negotiation. This makes the transferee the holder of the instrument. More important, in the hands of certain holders, the paper is not subject to certain claims and defenses that could be raised against an assignee of a contract. When paper is transferred by negotiation, the transferee can acquire rights greater than those of the transferor.

6. Requirements of Negotiability

To be negotiable, an instrument must be (a) in writing and (b) signed by the maker or drawer; it must contain (c) a promise or order (d) of an unconditional character (e) to pay in money (f) a sum certain[8] (g) it must be payable on demand or at a definite time; and (h) it must contain no other promise, order, obligation, or power given by the maker or drawer except as authorized by UCC Article 3.

1952 UCC

The instrument must also be payable to order or bearer.

1990 UCC

The instrument must also be payable to order or bearer. However, a check is negotiable even though not payable to order or bearer. Thus, a bank money order that reads "Pay to Jones" is negotiable. In contrast, a note that reads "I promise to pay Jones" is not negotiable.[9]

In addition to these formal requirements, the instrument must be delivered or issued by the maker or drawer to the payee or the latter's agent with the intent that it be effective to create a legal obligation.

If an instrument is not negotiable, the rights of the parties are governed by contract law rather than by Article 3 of the UCC.

Sometimes, as in the *Frank* case, what appears to be a negotiable instrument may contain a provision that impairs its negotiability and converts it to a simple contract.

FRANK v HERSHEY NATIONAL BANK
269 Md App 138, 306 A2d 207 (1973)

East Penn Broadcasting Company borrowed money from the Hershey National Bank. The promissory note representing the loan was made payable "to the Hershey National Bank." It also contained a provision authorizing confession of judgment against the borrower at any time. This provision allowed a judgment to be entered against East Penn without giving the defendant the opportunity to make a defense or to oppose the entry of such judgment. The note was signed with the typewritten name of the borrowing corporation and the handwritten signature of three individuals including the defendant, Frank. The loan was not paid. The bank sued Frank and the others on the note. Frank and the other individuals raised defenses under the UCC. The bank claimed that the UCC was not applicable. From a judgment in favor of the bank, Frank and the others appealed.

---

[8] Amberbox v Societe de Banque Privee (Tex App) 831 SW2d 793 (1992).

[9] UCC §3-104(c) [1990].

DIGGES, J. . . . We find the notes to be nonnegotiable and the UCC to be inapplicable. Therefore, the liability of the parties is determined as a matter of simple contract law. . . .

To be negotiable, an instrument must, among other requirements, "be payable to order or to bearer." (§ 3-104(1)(d)) The absence of these magic words renders a note nonnegotiable. Here, the notes in question contain just a "promise to pay to the Hershey National Bank" the amount due. However, § 3-805 entitled "instruments not payable to order or to bearer" specifies that: "This subtitle *applies* to any instrument whose terms do not preclude transfer and *which is otherwise negotiable within this subtitle* but which is not payable to order or to bearer, except that there can be no holder in due course of such an instrument." . . . The official comments to this section indicate that: "This section covers the 'nonnegotiable instrument.' As it has been used by most courts, this term has been a technical one of art. It does not refer to a writing, such as a note containing an express condition, which is not negotiable and is entirely outside of the scope of this Subtitle and to be treated as a simple contract. It refers to a particular type of instrument which meets all requirements as to form of a negotiable instrument except that it is not payable to order or to bearer."

Thus, while these notes could still be governed by the Code even though they lack words of negotiability, they must meet all other "requirements as to form of a negotiable instrument" except for that. The notes here do not conform to this standard. The UCC § 3-112(1)(d) provides that the negotiability of an instrument is not affected by "a term authorizing confession of judgment on the instrument if it is not paid when due." We held in *Stankovich v Lehman*, 230 Md 426, 187 A2d 309 (1963), a case decided under the Negotiable Instruments Act, that the authorization to confess judgment "as of any term" permitted entry of judgment at any time prior to the maturity of the note and therefore destroyed negotiability. . . . "It would seem logical that if the statute, as it does, preserves negotiability only if the confession of judgment is at or after maturity, the warrant to confess must expressly, or by necessary implication, restrict its exercise to that time if the note is to be negotiable, and that if the warrant is silent as to the time when it can be exercised, the reasonable implication must be that it can be done at any time. Most of the cases involving this general area of the law have arisen in Pennsylvania, and the Courts of that State have held that notes containing stipulations for confession of judgment without specification or limitation as to time are, like those expressly authorizing judgment prior to maturity, nonnegotiable." . . .

Since these nonnegotiable notes are not governed by the UCC, their effect is, as already noted, determined under principles of simple contract law.

[Judgment affirmed]

QUESTIONS

1. What made the instrument nonnegotiable? Explain.
2. Why was the issue of negotiability important?

C
P
A   (a) WRITING. A commercial paper must be in writing. *Writing* includes handwriting, typing, printing, and any other method of setting words down in a permanent form. The   C
P
A

use of a pencil is not wise, because such writing is not as durable as ink, and the instrument may be more easily altered. A commercial paper may be partly printed and partly typewritten.

Since the commercial paper is a writing, the parol evidence rule applies. This rule prohibits modifying the instrument by proving the existence of a conflicting oral agreement alleged to have been made before or at the time of the execution of the commercial paper.

(b) SIGNATURE. The instrument must be signed by the maker or drawer. This signature usually appears at the lower right-hand corner of the face of the instrument, but it is immaterial whether the signature is so placed.

The signature may consist of the full name or of any symbol adopted for that purpose. It may consist of initials, figures, or a mark. A person signing a trade or an assumed name is liable to the same extent as though the signer's own name had been used.

(1) Agent. A signature may be made by the drawer or maker or by an authorized agent. No particular form of authorization to an agent to execute or sign a commercial paper is required.

An agent signing commercial paper should disclose on the paper (a) the identity of the principal and (b) the fact that the signing is made in a representative capacity. When both are done, an authorized agent is not liable on the paper. The representative capacity of an officer of an organization is sufficiently shown by the signature of the officer preceded or followed by the title of the office and the organization's name.

(2) Nondisclosure of Agency or Principal. If a person who signs a commercial paper in a representative capacity, such as an agent or an officer of a corporation, executes the paper without disclosing both the identity of the principal and the existence of the representative capacity, the agent appears to be signing the paper as a personal obligation. Under these circumstances, the agent is personally bound by the paper.[10]

In the *First National Bank* case the question was whether corporate officers were personally liable on the notes of the corporation where there was no indication of signing in a representative capacity.

FIRST NATIONAL BANK v BLACKHURST

(W Va) 345 SE2d 567 (1986)

Long, Blackhurst, and Sheets formed a corporation to own and operate a ski apparel shop. They served as president, vice president, and secretary-treasurer, respectively, of the corporation, Josh, Inc. Before opening the store the three officers established a line of credit with the First National Bank. This line of credit was to be used to finance the purchase of inventory. On different dates they executed eight notes of varying amounts, totaling $94,190. The shop failed and filed for bankruptcy. It was unable to pay its debt to the bank. The bank sued the officers, claiming that the notes were personal obligations of the defendants. The defendants argued that at all times they were acting in a representative capacity as officers of Josh, Inc., that the loans were made to the corporation, and that they were not personally liable. From a judgment in favor of the bank, the officers appealed.

NEELY, J. . . . In this case we decide whether the defendants, Jo Debra Long, A. A. Blackhurst, and Robert A. Sheets, are personally liable on notes they executed in favor of the plaintiff, First National Bank. . . .

Commercial paper's value lies largely in its negotiability. Accordingly, Article Three of the *Uniform Commercial Code*, which governs commercial paper, was designed to avoid situations where it would be unclear whether a representative signing a negotiable instrument obligated his principal or himself. [UCC §] 3-403 . . . establishes rules to enable subsequent holders to determine, by reference solely to the instrument itself, which party is liable on the instrument. In general, representative capacity must be shown on the face of the instrument if a representative signs his own name to an instrument but wishes to avoid personal liability. On each of the notes in this case the three defendants' signatures are affixed in the bottom right hand corner under a typewritten legend stating "Josh, Inc." The defendants argue that the legend indicates that they were signing in their corporate capacity rather than as individuals. The legend alone is not enough to free the defendants of personal liability. . . .

[Judgment affirmed]

QUESTIONS

1. Did the notes show the name of the principal?
2. How should officers of a corporation sign notes of the corporation to avoid personal liability?
3. What was the basis for the court's decision?

1952 UCC

(3) Agent's Avoidance of Liability. When the agent is liable in the case just noted, the liability may be avoided when sued by the party with whom the agent dealt.[11] That is, the agent can prove that it was the intention of the original parties that the agent should not be personally liable. Such proof is not admissible when the agent is sued by anyone else.

(4) Principal's Bank Account.

*****

1990 UCC

(3) Agent's Avoidance of Liability. When the agent is liable in the case just noted, the agent may avoid this liability by proving that it was the intent of the agent and the other party with whom the agent dealt that the agent should not be personally liable. This cannot be done if the suit is brought by a holder in due course who had no notice that the intent of the original parties was that the agent should not be personally liable.

(4) Principal's Bank Account. Contrary to the general rule stated in subsection (2) above, an agent is not personally liable on a check that is drawn on the bank account of the principal even though no representative capacity is disclosed. Thus, a check that is already imprinted with the employer's name is not the check of an employee, regardless of whether the employee signs only the employee's name or also adds a title such as "payroll clerk" or "Treasurer."[12]

(c) PROMISE OR ORDER TO PAY. A promissory note must contain a promise to pay money. No particular form of promise is required; the intention as gathered from the

---

[10] Avery v Whitworth, 202 GA App 508, 414 SE2d 725 (1992).

[11] UCC § 3-403(2)(b) [1952].

[12] UCC § 3-402(c) [1990].

face of the instrument controls.[13] A mere acknowledgment of a debt, such as a writing stating "I.O.U.," is not a promise.

A draft or check must contain an order or command to pay money. As in the case of a promise in a note, no particular form of order is required.

(d) UNCONDITIONAL PROMISE OR ORDER. For an instrument to be negotiable, the promise or order to pay must be unconditional. For example, when an instrument makes the duty to pay dependent on the completion of the construction of a building, the promise is conditional, and the instrument is nonnegotiable. Also, the promise or order is conditional, and the instrument is nonnegotiable, if the instrument states that it is subject to another agreement. In such a case, the paper is not negotiable because the obligation of the paper is dependent on the performance of the other agreement.

1952 UCC

(1) Source of Payment. An order for the payment of money out of a particular fund, such as $10 from next week's salary, is conditional. If, however, the instrument is based on the general credit of the drawer and the reference to a particular fund is merely to indicate a source of reimbursement for the drawee, such as "charge my expense account," the order is considered unconditional. As exceptions to the above, a paper is not made conditional because payment is only to be made from an identified fund if the issuer is a government, or governmental unit or agency, or when payment is to be made from the assets of a partnership, unincorporated association, trust, or estate.[14]

(e) PAYMENT IN MONEY. A commercial paper must call for payment in *money*—

that is, any circulating medium of exchange that is legal tender at the place of payment.

1990 UCC

(1) Source of payment. The payment called for by a negotiable instrument may be payment from a designated fund or source. It is not required that the issuer of the instrument be personally obligated to pay.[15]

(e) PAYMENT IN MONEY. A negotiable instrument must call for the payment of money. This may be any medium of exchange adopted or authorized by the United States, a foreign government, or an intergovernmental organization.

If the order or promise is not for money, the instrument is not negotiable. For example, an instrument that requires the holder to take stock or goods in place of money is nonnegotiable.

(f) SUM CERTAIN. This means an exact amount. Unless the instrument is definite on its face as to how much is to be paid, there is no way of determining how much the instrument is worth.

Minor variations from the above rule are allowed in certain cases. Thus, commercial paper is not made nonnegotiable because the interest rate changes at maturity or because certain costs and attorney's fees may be recovered by the holder.[16]

1952 UCC

(1) Variable Interest. There is a conflict of authority as to whether paper providing for floating or variable interest is negotiable.[17]

1990 UCC

(1) Variable Interest. The sum payable under an instrument is certain although it calls for the payment of a floating or variable interest rate. Thus, an instrument is negotiable

---

[13] Fejta v Werner Enterprises (La App) 412 So 2d 155 (1982).

[14] UCC § 3-106(b) [1990].

[15] UCC § 3-105 [1952].

[16] Means v Clardy (Mo App) 735 SW2d 6 (1987).

[17] Goss v Trinity Savings & Loan Assn. (Okla) 813 P2d 492 (1991) (holding paper negotiable).

although it requires the payment of 1 percent above the prime rate of a named bank. It is immaterial that the exact amount of interest that will be paid cannot be determined at the time the paper is issued because the rate may later change. It is also immaterial that the amount due on the instrument cannot be de-termined without looking at records outside of the face of the instrument.[18]

Is a state treasury warrant a negotiable instrument? This was the issue in the *National Bank* case.

NATIONAL BANK v UNIVENTURES 1231
(Alaska) 824 P2d 1381 (1992)

The State of Alaska was a tenant in a large office building owned by Univentures, a partnership. The state made a lease payment of $28,143.47 to Univentures with state treasury warrant No. 21045102. Charles LeViege, the managing partner of Univentures, assigned the warrant to Lee Garcia. After a dispute arose between the partners of Univentures, the state was notified that it should no longer pay Charles LeViege the monthly rent due the partnership. The state treasury placed a stop payment order on the warrant. Garcia presented the warrant to National Bank of Alaska (NBA), which paid Garcia on the warrant. NBA sued the State of Alaska, Charles LeViege, and Lee Garcia to recover the sum of money paid to Garcia. NBA alleged that it was a holder in due course and took the warrant free from the defenses presented by Univentures and the state. The state and Univentures claimed that NBA was not a holder in due course because the warrant was not a negotiable instrument and because NBA had notice of the stop payment order when it paid Garcia on the warrant. A judgment was entered against the bank, and it appealed.

MOORE, J. . . . Article III of the Uniform Commercial Code provides that the holder in due course of an instrument takes the instrument free of all but a very limited class of defenses that the original payor might have against the original payee. [UCC § 3-302(1)]. If a holder of an instrument is not a holder in due course, the holder takes the instrument subject to all valid claims to the instrument, as well as subject to several classes of defenses. [UCC § 3-]306.

The superior court held that NBA was not a holder in due course because the state treasury warrant involved is not a negotiable instrument to which the Uniform Commercial Code applies. As a result, the superior court concluded that NBA took the warrant subject to the state's defense that it had issued a valid stop payment order pursuant to [UCC § 4-]403(a). NBA argues that the warrant is a negotiable instrument, and that NBA is therefore a holder in due course. . . .

[UCC § 3-104(1)] provides that for a writing to be a negotiable instrument it must:

_____

[18] UCC § 3-112 [1990].

(1) be signed by the maker or drawer;

(2) contain an unconditional promise or order to pay a sum certain in money and no other promise, order, obligation, or power given by the maker or drawer except as authorized by this chapter;

(3) be payable on demand or at a definite time, and

(4) be payable to order or to bearer.

[UCC § 1-102(1)] provides that the Code is to be "liberally construed and applied to promote the underlying purposes and policies." The underlying purposes and policies of the Uniform Commercial Code are:

(1) to simplify, clarify, and modernize the law governing commercial transactions;

(2) to permit the continued expansion of commercial practices through custom, usage, and agreement of the parties;

(3) to make uniform the law among the various jurisdictions.

[UCC § 1-102(2)].

Warrant No. 21045102 satisfies all four elements of the definition of a negotiable instrument. First, the warrant is signed by the maker, Governor Steve Cowper. Second, the warrant contains an unconditional promise or order to pay a sum certain of $28,143.47. . . . Third, the warrant is payable at a definite time. Although the warrant states that it "will be deemed paid unless redeemed within two years after the date of issue," [UCC § 3-]109 provides that an instrument is payable at a definite time if by its terms it is payable on or before a stated date. [UCC § 3-]109(a)(1). Finally, the warrant clearly indicates that it is payable to the order of Univentures. An "instrument is payable to order if by its terms it is payable to the order or assigns of a person specified in the instrument with reasonable certainty." [UCC § 3-]110(a). Because the warrant meets the statutory definition in [UCC § 3-]104, we hold that the warrant is a negotiable instrument.

The purposes for which the Uniform Commercial Code was enacted support the conclusion that warrants which satisfy the statutory definition of negotiability must be deemed negotiable. Univentures claims that state warrants should be deemed nonnegotiable because the state must retain its rights to assert the defenses of a maker in order to maintain and protect its fiscal policies, practices, and procedures. This argument is directly contrary to the Code's policy of promoting commercial transactions by allowing a party to ascertain the negotiability of an instrument from its face. 5 R. Anderson, *Uniform Commercial Code*, § 3-104:4 (1984) ("The whole idea of the facilitation of easy transfer of notes and instruments requires that a transferee be able to trust what the instrument says, and be able to determine the validity of the note and its negotiability from the language in the note itself.") To carve out an exception to the statutory definition of negotiability would jeopardize Article III's purposes of clarifying and modernizing commercial transactions by allowing reliance on written instruments. The transferee of an instrument must be able to rely on the negotiability of the instrument as evidenced by the instrument's terms, so that the transaction is not stalled while the transferee verifies its rights on the instrument.

No Alaska case law addresses the issue of whether a state treasury warrant constitutes a negotiable instrument. Prior to the enactment of the Uniform Commercial Code, warrants issued by states, local governments, and municipalities were almost universally deemed nonnegotiable. . . . The drafters of the Uniform Commercial

Code apparently intended to change this body of law, however, as evidenced by the Official Code Comment to § 3-105. 5 R. Anderson, *Uniform Commercial Code*, § 3-105:1, at 228 (1984) ("[Section 3-105(1)(g)] will permit some municipal warrants to be negotiable if they are in proper form.")

Those courts which have considered the negotiability of government warrants have generally found those warrants to be negotiable so long as they satisfy the Code's requirements. . .

[Judgment reversed]

QUESTIONS

1. Why did the National Bank of Alaska want to prove that it was a holder in due course?
2. Was the warrant a negotiable instrument?
3. If the warrant had been nonnegotiable, would the National Bank still qualify as a holder in due course?
4. Why is it important to determine from the face of the instrument whether or not it is negotiable?

Although this case was decided under the 1952 version of Article 3, the same . . . *the 1990 version.*

occurrence of a specified contingency. Thus, a promissory note is payable at a definite date when it is payable one year from date subject to a six months' automatic extension in case there is a national transportation strike.[20]

(3) Missing Date. Paper that is not dated is deemed dated on the day it is issued to the payee. Any holder may add the correct date to the paper.

1952 UCC

(4) Effect of Date on Demand Paper.
*****

(h) ORDER OR BEARER. A commercial paper must be payable to order or bearer.[21]

1990 UCC

(4) Effect of Date on Demand Paper. The date on demand paper controls the time of payment, and the paper is not due before its date. Consequently, a check that is postdated ceases to be demand paper and is not properly payable before the date on the check. A bank making earlier payment does not incur any liability unless the drawer has given the bank a postdated check notice.

(h) ORDER OR BEARER. An instrument that is not a check must be payable to order or bearer.

This requirement is met by such expressions as "Pay to the order of John Jones," "Pay to John Jones or order," "Pay to bearer," and "Pay to John Jones or bearer." The use of the phrase "to the order of John Jones" or "to John Jones or order" shows that the person executing the instrument had no intention to restrict payment of the instrument to John Jones only. These phrases indicate that there is no objection to paying anyone to whom John Jones orders the paper to be paid. Similarly, if the person executing the instrument originally states that it will be paid "to bearer" or "to John Jones or bearer," there is no restricting of payment of the paper to the original payee.

1952 UCC

If the instrument is payable on its face "to John Jones," however, the instrument is not negotiable.

1990 UCC

However, if the instrument is not a check and it is payable on its face "to John Jones," the instrument is not negotiable.[22]

(1) Order Paper. An instrument is **payable to order** when by its terms it is payable to the order of any person described therein ("pay to the order of K. Read"), or to a person or order ("pay to K. Read or order").

(2) Bearer Paper. An instrument is **payable to bearer** when by its terms it is payable (a) to bearer or the order of bearer, (b) to a specified person or bearer, (c) to "cash," or "the order of cash," or any other designation that does not purport to identify a person, or (d) if the last or only indorsement is a bla[nk] indorsement (an indorsement that doe[s] name the person to whom the paper is [indic]ated).

1952 UCC

An instrument that does no[t] payee is not negotiable and ca[n] until completed.[23]

1990 UCC

An instrument tha[t] payee is payable to b[earer]

7. Factors N

The word[s]
statem[ent]
give[n]

---

[20] UCC § 3-108 [1990].

[21] Beyer v First National Bank (Mont) 612 P2d 1285

[22] UCC § 3-104(a)(1) [1990].

[23] UCC § 3-115(1) [1952].

[24] UCC § 3-109(a)(2) [1990].

C P A
C P A
C P A
C P A
C P A
C P A
C P A
C P A
C P A
C P A
C P A
C P A
C P A

The omission of a date of execution or antedating or postdating an instrument has no effect on negotiability.

Provisions relating to collateral, such as specifying the collateral as security for the debt, or a promise to maintain, protect, or give additional collateral, do not affect negotiability.

8. Ambiguous Language

The following rules are applied when ambiguous language exists in words or descriptions:

(a) Words control figures where conflict exists.

(b) Handwriting supersedes conflicting typewritten and printed terms.

(c) Typewritten terms supersede preprinted terms.

(d) In the case of failure to provide for the payment of interest, or if there is a provision for the payment of interest but no rate is mentioned, the judgment rate at

C P A

the place of payment applies from the date of the instrument.
1952 UCC

9. Statute of Limitations

The 1952 version of the UCC does not contain any statute of limitations governing actions with respect to commercial paper. The courts have variously applied local non-Code statutes governing contract actions, tort actions, or actions based on a writing.
1990 UCC

9. Statute of Limitations

The 1990 version of the UCC establishes a three-year statute of limitations for most actions as to negotiable instruments. This also applies to actions for the conversion of such instruments and for breach of warranty. A six-year statute is imposed for suits on certificates of deposit and accepted drafts.

SUMMARY

Commercial paper or a negotiable instrument is a transferable, written, signed promise or order to pay a specified sum of money. Commercial paper is negotiable when it contains the terms required by the UCC.
1952 UCC

There are four categories of commercial paper: (1) promissory notes, (2) drafts or bills of exchange, (3) checks, and (4) certificates of deposit.
1990 UCC

There are two categories of negotiable instruments: (1) promissory notes and (2) drafts. A certificate of deposit is classified as a promissory note. In addition to ordinary checks, there are also cashier's checks and teller's checks. A bank money order is a check, even though it bears the words *money order*.

The original parties to a note are the maker and payee. The original parties to a draft are the drawer, the drawee, and the payee. The term *party* may refer to a natural person or to an artificial person such as a corporation. It

may also mean an unincorporated enterprise, a government, or a bank account. One who signs on the back of the paper is called an indorser. The person to whom an indorsement is made payable is called an indorsee. A person in physical possession of a commercial paper that is payable to bearer is called a bearer and a holder.

A holder in due course is a favored holder of commercial paper and is immune from certain defenses when such holder brings suit on commercial paper. A person taking commercial paper through a holder in due course is a holder through a holder in due course and is likewise immune from certain defenses as a holder in due course.
1952 UCC

The requirements of negotiability are that the instrument (1) be in writing, (2) be signed by the maker or drawer, (3) contain an unconditional promise or order, (4) to pay a sum certain in money, (5) on demand or at a definite time, (6) to order or to bearer. If an instrument is not negotiable, it is governed by contract law.

1990 UCC

The requirements of negotiability are that the instrument (1) be in writing, (2) be signed by the maker or drawer, (3) contain an uncon-ditional promise or order, (4) to pay a sum certain in money, (5) on demand or at a defi-nite time, (6) to order or to bearer. A check may be negotiable without being payable to order or bearer. If an instrument is not negotiable, it is governed by contract law.

LAW IN PRACTICE

1. If you become a guarantor of payment, you are primarily liable without resort to any other party on the paper.

2. Do not lend your name to commercial paper unless you are prepared to pay the full amount of the instrument.

3. Even though an I.O.U. is not a negotiable in-strument, you are still liable on your debt unless you have some valid defense.

4. If you are signing commercial paper in a rep-resentative capacity, state the name of your princi-pal and your representative capacity on the paper. Otherwise you may be personally liable on the pa-per.

5. Be sure that the words and figures are the same when you issue paper; if not, the words will prevail.

QUESTIONS AND CASE PROBLEMS

1. What social forces are affected by the rule of law governing what constitutes a signature on commercial paper?

2. Name the kinds of commercial paper.

3. The Charter Bank of Gainsville had in its pos-session a note containing the following provision: "This note with interest is secured by a mortgage on real estate, of even date herewith, made by the maker hereof in favor of said payee. . . . The terms of said mortgage are by this reference made a part hereof." When the bank sued on the note, the de-fendant raised the defense that the payee was guilty of fraud in obtaining the mortgage. The bank claimed to be a holder in due course. Is the bank precluded from being a holder in due course by the above provision? Why or why not? *[Holly Hill Acres, Ltd. v Charter Bk. of Gainsville, (Fla App) 314 So 2d 209]*

4. Hampton purchased cloth from Regal Fibres, Inc., on behalf of Twentieth Century Clothing Company, by whom Hampton was employed. Hampton informed Regal that she was acting for Twentieth Century and signed a promissory note for the purchase price of the cloth. The note stated, "I promise to pay . . ." and was signed "Gertrude Hampton." Regal sold the note to the Commercial Finance Company. Commercial sued Hampton on the note. Hampton claimed that she was not liable, because she had acted as agent for Twentieth Cen-tury and had so informed Regal Fibres. Is this a valid defense?

5. A Republican delivered his promissory note to a friend, a Democrat, promising to pay a thousand dollars "30 days after the Republican candidate for Governor shall be defeated in the November elec-tion." Give your opinion as to whether or not the expression of time of payment is proper for a ne-gotiable instrument.

6. Nation-Wide Check Corp. sold money orders through local agents. A customer would purchase a money order by paying an agent the amount of the desired money order plus a fee. The customer would then sign the money order as the remitter or sender and would fill in the name of the person who was to receive the money following the printed words "Payable to" In a lawsuit between Nation-Wide and Banks, a payee on some of these orders, the question was raised whether these money orders were checks and could be nego-tiable even though not payable to order or to bearer. Decide. *[Nation-Wide Check Corp. v Banks (Dist Col App) 260 A2d 367]* Would your answer be the same in a jurisdiction not adopting the 1990 UCC?

7. Nelson gave Buchert the following instru-ment, dated July 6, 1988:

One year after date I promise to pay to the order of Dale Buchert one thousand dollars in United States Savings Bonds payable at Last Mortgage Bank. (signed) Ronald K. Nelson

Does this instrument qualify as a negotiable instrument?

8. Compare the liability of the acceptor of a draft with the liability of the maker of a note.

9. Money was borrowed from a bank by a corporation. The president of the corporation negotiated the loan and signed the promissory note. On the first line, he wrote the name of the corporation. On the second line, he signed his own name. The note was negotiated by the lending bank to the Federal Reserve Bank. The note was not paid when due, and the Federal Reserve Bank sued the corporation and the president. The president raised the defense that he was not bound on the note because he did not intend to bind himself and because the money obtained by the loan was used by the corporation. Is the president liable on the note? *[Talley v Blake (La App) 322 So 2d 877 (non-Code); Geer v Farquhar, 270 Or 642, 528 P2d 1335]*

10. Rinehart issues a check that satisfies all the requirements of negotiability. It is payable to the order of cash. Is the instrument payable to order or to bearer?

11. Is the following instrument negotiable?

I, Richard Bell, hereby promise to pay to the order of Lorry Motors Ten Thousand Dollars ($10,000) upon the receipt of the final distribution from the estate of my deceased aunt, Rita Dorn. This negotiable instrument is given by me as the down payment on my purchase of a 1986 Buick to be delivered in three weeks.

Richard Bell (signature)

12. Smith has in his possession the following instrument.

September 1, 1986

I, Selma Ray, hereby promise to pay Helen Savit One Thousand Dollars ($1,000) one year after date. This instrument was given for the purchase of Two Hundred (200) shares of Redding Mining Corporation, Interest 6%.

Selma Ray (signature)

Smith purchased the instrument from Helen Savit at a substantial discount. Savit specializes in the sale of counterfeit stock. Selma Ray was one of her innocent victims. Smith is seeking to collect on the instrument. What are the rights of Smith against Ray on the instrument?

13. Master Homecraft Company received a promissory note with a stated face value from Mr. and Mrs. Zimmerman. The note was payment for remodeling their home. The note contained unused blanks for installment payments. There was no maturity date. Master Homecraft sued the Zimmermans on the note. They argue that they should not be liable on the note because it is impossible to determine from its face the amount due or the date of maturity. Decide. *[Master Homecraft Co. v Zimmerman, 208 Pa 401, 22 A2d 440]*

14. Ruth Laudati obtained a student loan from Brown University and signed a promissory note for the repayment of the loan. Her mother, Josephine, guaranteed payment of the note. When the note was not paid, Brown University sued Josephine. She raised the defense that Brown had not sued Ruth. Decide. *[Brown University v Laudati, 113 RI 926, 320 A2d 609]*

15. Indicate whether a promissory note is payable (1) to order, (2) to bearer, or (3) neither to order nor bearer if the instrument states: (a) Pay to cash. (b) Pay to the order of bearer. (c) Pay to the order of John Jones. (d) Pay to John Jones. (e) Pay to bills payable.

C H A P T E R   3 1

TRANSFER OF COMMERCIAL PAPER

LEARNING OBJECTIVES

After studying this chapter, you will be able to:
1. *List the types of indorsements and describe their respective uses.*
2. *Distinguish the effect of a transfer by assignment from that of a negotiation.*
3. *Explain the difference between negotiation of order paper and negotiation of bearer paper.*
4. *Determine the legal effect of forged and unauthorized indorsements.*
5. *Be familiar with the forged payee impostor exceptions.*
6. *List the indorser's warranties and describe their significance.*
7. *Solve problems involving the transfer of commercial paper.*

Much of the commercial importance of negotiable instruments or commercial paper is in the ease with which it may be transferred and the effect of a negotiation.

A. TRANSFER OF NEGOTIABLE COMMERCIAL PAPER

Commercial paper is typically transferred by negotiation.

1. Effect of Transfer

The effect of the transfer of commercial paper depends on whether the transfer is an assignment or a negotiation.

(a) TRANSFER BY ASSIGNMENT. When a negotiable commercial paper is assigned, the transferee has the rights of the transferor. This means that the transferee is entitled to enforce the paper. But the assignee has no greater rights than the assignor.[1]

In a suit to enforce the paper, the assignee is subject to any defense that could be raised in a suit on an assigned contract.[2]

(b) TRANSFER BY NEGOTIATION. When a negotiable commercial paper is transferred by negotiation, the transferee becomes the holder of the paper. In addition, the holder may be a holder in due course. This status will give immunity from certain defenses which might have been asserted against the transferor.

(c) DEFINITION OF NEGOTIATION. The word *negotiation* is defined in terms of its primary effect. It is the transferring of negotiable commercial paper in such a way as to make the transferee the holder. It is not sufficient that the transferee be a possessor or an assignee of the paper. The transferee must be the holder.

2. Time for Determining Order or Bearer Character of Paper

The order or bearer character of the paper determines how it may be negotiated. This character is determined as of the time when the negotiation is about to take place, without regard to the character of the paper originally or at any intermediate time. Accordingly, when the last indorsement specifies the person to whom the indorser makes the instrument payable, the paper is order paper, without regard to whether it was bearer paper originally or at any intermediate time. The holder cannot treat the paper as bearer paper merely because it had once been bearer paper.

3. Negotiation of Order Paper

An instrument payable to order may be negotiated only by indorsement and delivery of the paper.[3] Indorsement and delivery may be made by the person to whom the paper is then payable or by an authorized agent of that person.

(a) MULTIPLE PAYEES AND INDORSEES. Ordinarily, one person is named as the payee in the instrument, but two or more payees may be named. In that case, the instrument may specify that it is payable to any one or more of them or that it is payable to all jointly. For example, if the instrument is made payable "to the order of Ferns and Piercy," the two persons named are joint payees. The indorsements of both Ferns and Piercy are required to negotiate the instrument.

If the instrument is payable to **alternate payees** or if it has been negotiated to alternate indorsees, as "Stahl or Glass," or as

---

[1] Ballengee v New Mexico Federal S. & L. Assn. 109 NM 423, 786 P2d 37 (1990).

[2] An exception may arise with respect to defenses. If the transferor had the rights of a holder in due course, those rights are transferred to the assignee unless the assignee was a party to fraud or illegality affecting the instrument.

[3] UCC § 3-202(1) [1952]; § 3-201(b) [1990].

"Stahl/Glass," it may be indorsed and delivered by either of them.

1952 UCC

(1) Construction of Instrument. If multiple payees or indorsees are named in the paper but nothing is stated about whether they are joint or alternative, the instrument is payable to all jointly.[4]

1990 UCC

(1) Construction of Instrument. If it is not clearly stated in the paper that multiple payees or indorsees are joint, they are declared to be alternative. If the paper is ambiguous, the payees or indorsees are entitled in the alternative.[5]

(b) AGENT OR OFFICER AS PAYEE. The instrument may be made payable to the order of an officeholder. For example, a check may read "Pay to the order of Receiver of Taxes." Such a check may be received and negotiated by the person who at the time is the Receiver of Taxes. This is a matter of convenience, since the person writing the check is not required to find out the actual name of the Receiver of Taxes at that time.

1952 UCC

If the instrument is drawn in favor of a person as "Cashier" or some other officer of a bank or corporation, it is payable to the bank or corporation of which such person is an officer. However, the instrument may be negotiated by the indorsement of either the bank or the corporation, or of the specified officer. If drawn in favor of an agent, it is similarly payable to the principal and may be negotiated by the agent or the principal.[6]

1990 UCC

If an instrument is drawn in favor of an officer of a named corporation, the instrument is payable to the corporation, the officer, or any

successor to such officer. Whichever of these is in possession of the instrument is the holder and may negotiate the instrument.[7]

(c) MISSING INDORSEMENT. When the parties intend to make a negotiation of order paper but for some reason the holder fails to indorse the paper, there is no negotiation. The transaction has only the effect of an assignment of the paper. If the transferee gave value for the paper, the transferee has the right to require that the transferor indorse the instrument unqualifiedly and thereby effect a negotiation of the instrument.

4. Negotiation of Bearer Paper

Any commercial paper payable to bearer may be negotiated by a mere transfer of possession. Thus, bearer paper is negotiated to a person taking possession of it, without regard to whether such taking of possession was done with the consent of the owner of the paper.

The paper may be negotiated by a mere transfer of possession not only when the instrument expressly states that it is payable to bearer, but also when the law interprets it as being payable to bearer. For example, a check payable to the order of "Cash" is declared to be bearer paper and may be negotiated by a transfer of possession.

Although bearer paper may be negotiated by a mere transfer of possession, the one to whom it is delivered may insist that the bearer indorse the paper. This situation most commonly arises when a check payable to "Cash" is presented to a bank for payment. The reason a transferee of bearer paper might require an indorsement is to obtain the protection of an indorser's warranties.

---

[4] UCC § 3-116(b) [1952].

[5] UCC § 3-110(d) [1990].

[6] UCC § 3-110(c)(2)(ii) [1990].

[7] UCC § 3-117 [1952].

5. Forged and Unauthorized Indorsements

A forged or unauthorized indorsement is by definition no indorsement of the person by whom it appears to have been made.[8] Accordingly, the possessor of the paper is not the holder when the indorsement of the person whose signature was forged was necessary for effective negotiation of the paper to the possessor.

If payment of commercial paper is made to one claiming under or through a forged indorsement, the payor is ordinarily liable to the person who is the rightful owner of the paper. An exception exists if this person is estopped or barred by negligence or other conduct from asserting any claim against the payor.

A forged or unauthorized indorsement may be ratified.[9] In that case, it is effective as though it had been genuine and authorized.

The *Mott* case deals with the question of whether a bank should be held liable for allowing the manager of a corporation to deposit in his own account checks that were payable to the corporation.

MOTT GRAIN CO. v FIRST NATIONAL BANK & TRUST CO.
(ND) 259 NW2d 667 (1977)

Baszler was a manager of the grain elevator of the Mott Company and an officer of the company. A corporate resolution that the Mott Company executed with the bank authorized officers to indorse or deposit in the corporate account checks payable to the corporation. Baszler took seventeen checks payable to the company and, instead of depositing them in the company account, indorsed and deposited them in his own account with the bank. The Mott Company claimed that the bank was liable for the amount of these checks that were improperly deposited. From a judgment in favor of the Mott Company, the bank appealed.

VOGEL, J. . . . The bank is liable to the payee of checks which are negotiated upon indorsements which are forged or unauthorized.

Under UCC § 3-404, a payee of a check may recover from a bank which cashes a check on which the payee's signature is unauthorized.

An unauthorized signature is one which is either forged or made without actual, apparent, or implied authority. [UCC § 1-201 (43)].

Forged indorsements are inoperative as signatures of the payee, whether they are indorsements for deposit UCC § 3-205 or in blank UCC § 3-204, unless ratified or unless the owner is precluded from denying authority. [UCC § 3-404].

A bank which negotiates checks bearing forged or unauthorized indorsements is therefore liable in conversion to the true owner of the checks.

The bank asserts that the general law stated above does not apply because of the terms of the "Corporate Authorization Resolution." It points in particular to the language [of the resolution] authorizing any of the three owner-officers of the grain

8 UCC § 3-404(b) [1952]; UCC § 53-403(a) [1990].
9 Bank of Hoven v Rausch (SD) 382 NW2d 39 (1986).

company to sign "checks, drafts and other withdrawal orders and any and all other directions and instructions of any character with respect to funds of this corporation now or hereafter with said Bank" and that the bank is authorized to "pay and charge to such account or accounts any checks, drafts and other withdrawal orders so signed, and to honor any directions or instructions so signed, whether or not payable to the individual order of or deposited to the individual account of or inuring to the individual benefit of any of the foregoing officers or persons."

Since the meaning of this terminology is unclear, we could simply hold that it is ambiguous and construe it against the party which drew it and submitted it to the grain company.

However, we believe that accepted methods of construing contractual language require us to hold that the language in question does not authorize the bank to negotiate checks payable to the grain company but indorsed by one of the officers and either cashed or deposited to his own account. The quoted language authorizes the bank to honor checks, drafts, and other withdrawal orders and directions and instructions of any character "with respect to funds of this corporation now or hereafter with said Bank. . . ." While the use of the word "with" is unfortunate and less than clear, we understand the language to mean that money of the corporation on deposit with the bank is subject to being withdrawn by checks, drafts, or other withdrawal orders, or transferred as directed or instructed by any one of the officers. However, the language does not cover money which is not deposited with the bank or in its hands. When the improperly indorsed checks involved in this appeal were presented to the bank, they were not presented as funds of the corporation, but as funds of the individual officer indorsing them. The bank did not treat them as funds of the corporation, but treated them as funds of the individual. The checks therefore were not "funds of this corporation now or hereafter with said Bank" and were not within the description of the language quoted above in the "Corporate Authorization Resolution."

[Judgment affirmed]

QUESTIONS

1. What is the liability of a bank that negotiates a check bearing a forged or unauthorized indorsement?
2. What was the argument of the bank?
3. Was the bank correct?

6. Impostor Rule

The impostor rule makes three exceptions to the rule that a forged indorsement has no effect.

(a) WHEN IMPOSTOR RULE APPLICABLE. The impostor rule applies in the case of the impersonating payee and two cases of a dummy payee.[10]

(1) Impersonating Payee. The rule makes one exception when an impostor has

---

[10] UCC § 3-405 [1952]; UCC § 3-404 [1990]. Shearson Lehman Brothers, Inc. v Wasatch Bank (Utah) 7888 F Supp 1184 (1992).

induced the maker or drawer to issue the instrument to a payee whose identity has been assumed by the impostor, or to a confederate, in the name of that payee. For example, a person impersonates the holder of a savings account and, by presenting a forged withdrawal slip to the savings bank, gets the bank to issue a check payable to the bank's customer. The bank then hands the check to the impersonator in the belief that the impersonator is the customer.

1952 UCC

*****

1990 UCC

The impersonation exception includes impersonation of the agent of the person who is named as payee. Thus, if Jones pretends to be the agent of Brown Corporation and thereby induces the preparation of a check payable to the order of the corporation, the impostor exception applies.

(2) Dummy Payee. The preparer of the instrument may have had the intent that the payee should never benefit from the instrument. Such a nominal or dummy payee may be an actual or a fictitious person. The impostor rule applies when the person signing as, or on behalf of, the drawer or maker intends the named payee to have no interest in the paper. This situation arises when the owner of a checking account wishes to conceal the true purpose of taking money from the bank. The account owner makes out a check purportedly in payment of a debt that in fact does not exist.

(3) Dummy Payee Supplied by Employee. The third exception applies when an agent or employee of the maker or drawer has supplied the name to be used for the payee, intending that that payee should not have any interest in the paper. This last situation is illustrated by the case of an employee who fraudulently causes an employer to sign a check made to a customer or another person, whether existing or not. The employee does not intend to send it to that person but rather intends to forge the latter's indorsement, to cash the check, and to keep the money.

(b) EFFECT OF IMPOSTOR RULE. When the impostor rule is applicable, any person may indorse the name of the payee. This indorsement is treated as a genuine indorsement by the payee and cannot be attacked on the ground that it is a forgery. This is so even though the dummy payee of the paper is a fictitious person.[11]

1952 UCC

*****

1990 UCC

The fact that the indorsement is not an exact copy of the name of the payee is not important. It is sufficient that the indorsed name be substantially similar to the name of the payee as it appears in the instrument. Before dummy payee paper is specially indorsed specifying the person to whom the indorser makes the instrument payable, it is treated as bearer paper. Anyone in possession of the paper is the holder. This quality of the paper ends as soon as it is specially indorsed.

(c) LIMITATIONS ON IMPOSTOR RULE. The impostor rule does not apply when there is a valid check to an actual creditor for a correct amount owed by the drawer, and someone later forges the payee's name. The impostor rule does not apply in this situation even if the forger is an employee of the drawer.

Even when the unauthorized indorsement of the payee's name is effective by virtue of the impostor rule, a person forging the payee's name is subject to civil and criminal liability for making such an indorsement.

1952 UCC

*****

1990 UCC

To claim the protection of the impostor rule, the taker of the instrument must show that it had been taken (1) in good faith (2) for payment or collection.

---

[11] UCC § 3-405(1) [1952]; UCC § 3-404(b) [1990].

(d) NEGLIGENCE OF DRAWEE NOT REQUIRED. The impostor rule applies without regard to whether or not the drawee bank acted with reasonable care.

The *Stone Manufacturing* case deals with negligence of a drawee bank in accepting fraudently drawn payroll checks.

STONE MFG. CO. v NCNB OF SOUTH CAROLINA

(SC App) 417 SE2d 628 (1992)

Burke was an employee of Stone. She controlled the preparation of checks issued by Stone. For several years she directed that checks be drawn to payees who in fact were dummy payees: either former employees or employees who were out on leave. Burke would then take these checks, indorse them with the names of their payees, and cash them at NCNB, the drawee bank. Stone was a good customer of that bank and Burke was known at the bank as an employee of Stone. The bank did not know that Burke was doing anything wrong and apparently believed that she was cashing the checks as favors for employees who did not want to come down to the bank. After several years, Stone discovered what had happened and sued the bank for the $176,000 obtained by Burke. From a judgment in favor of the bank, Stone appealed.

SHAW, J. . . . [UCC §] 3-405(1)(c) provides:

An indorsement by any person in the name of a named payee is effective if. . . an agent or employee of the maker or drawer has supplied him with the name of the payee intending the latter to have no such interest.

Official Comment 4 to this section states:

Paragraph (c) is new. It extends the rule of the original Subsection 9(3) to include the padded payroll cases, where the drawer's agent or employee prepares the check for signatures or otherwise furnishes the signing officer with the name of the payee. The principle followed is that the loss should fall upon the employer as a risk to his business enterprise rather than upon the subsequent holder or drawee. The reasons are that the employer is normally in a better position to prevent such forgeries by reasonable care in the selection or supervision of his employees, or, if he is not, is at least in a better position to cover the loss by fidelity insurance; and that the cost of such insurance is properly an expense of his business rather than of the business of the holder or drawee.

The provision applies only to the agent or employee of the drawer, and only to the agent or employee who supplies him with the name of the payee. The following situations illustrate its application.

a. *An employee of a corporation prepares a padded payroll for its treasurer, which includes the name of P. P does not exist, and the employee knows it, but the treasurer does not. The treasurer draws the corporation's check payable to P.*

b.   The same facts as a, except that P exists and the employee knows it but intends him to have no interest in the check. In both cases an indorsement by any person in the name of P is effective and the loss falls on the corporation.

Another pattern of the fraudulent employee is illustrated by the payroll clerk who, not having authority to draw checks, submits a list of names or fills out checks which are signed by the employer or some other official of the company. The fraudulent payroll clerk then takes the checks and indorses them in the name of the payee. The drawee bank, recognizing the drawer's signature, pays them. When the fraud is discovered the employer demands a recrediting of his account. The indorsement by the employer is effective, thus placing the loss on the drawer-employer and not the payee bank.

A majority of jurisdictions confronted with the issue of a bank's negligence in the application of the padded payroll defense have "recognized the import of the code section to be that any loss arising from situations provided for therein should fall upon the employer and negligence on the part of the bank is irrelevant." *Northbrook Property & Casualty Insurance Company v Citizens & Southern National Bank*, 184 Ga App 326, 361 SE2d 531 (1987). Strong support for this position is found in the fact that [UCC §] 3-405 makes no reference to the bank's negligence as an exception to its application while Official Comment 4 clearly indicates the loss should fall upon the employer of an unfaithful employee as a risk of business. If the drafters had intended to make the bank's negligence an exception to the padded payroll defense, they could have easily so provided, just as they delineated a standard of care for banks. . . . Accordingly, we hold a bank's negligence is immaterial to the application of [UCC §] 3-405(1)(c).

However, Stone also argues lack of good faith on the part of the bank is a defense to [UCC §] 3-405(1)(c). . . .

[UCC §] 3-102 . . . entitled "Definitions and index of definitions" provides under subsection (4) as follows:

In addition [Article 1] contains general definitions and principles of construction and interpretation applicable throughout this [Article].

Under [Article 1, UCC §] 1-203 . . . provides "Every contract or duty within this act imposes an obligation of good faith in its performance or enforcement." [UCC §] 1-201(19) . . . defines "good faith" as "honesty in fact in the conduct or transaction concerned." At the most, the evidence of the bank's conduct in this matter demonstrated mere negligence. We agree with the trial judge that, even if lack of good faith is an exception to the padded payroll defense, there is no evidence the bank's actions lacked "honesty in fact."

[Judgment affirmed]

QUESTIONS

1.   Did Burke act ethically?
2.   Did the forgery pass title?
3.   Did the bank meet its obligation of good faith?

7. Effect of Incapacity or Misconduct on Negotiation

A negotiation is effective even though (a) it was made by a minor or any other person lacking capacity; (b) it was an act beyond the powers of a corporation; (c) it was obtained by fraud, duress, or a mistake of any kind; or (d) the negotiation was part of an illegal transaction or was made in breach of duty. Under general principles of law apart from the UCC, the transferor in such cases may be able to set aside the negotiation or to obtain some other form of legal relief.

1952 UCC

However, the negotiation cannot be set aside if the paper is held by a person having the rights of a holder in due course.[12]

1990 UCC

However, the negotiation cannot be set aside if the paper is held by a person having the rights of a holder in due course or a person paying the instrument in good faith and without knowledge of the facts on which the rescission claim is based.[13]

8. Lost Paper

The effect of losing commercial paper depends on who is suing or demanding payment from whom. It also depends on whether the paper was order paper or bearer paper when it was lost.

(a) ORDER PAPER. If the paper is order paper, the finder does not become the holder, because the paper has not been indorsed and delivered by the person to whom it was then payable. The former holder who lost it is still the rightful owner of the paper, although technically not the holder because not in possession of the paper.

(b) BEARER PAPER. If the paper is in bearer form when it is lost, the finder, as the possessor of bearer paper, is the holder and is entitled to enforce payment.

B. KINDS OF INDORSEMENTS

Indorsements are classified in terms of whether the indorser has added any words to the indorsement and what those words are.

9. Blank Indorsement

When the indorser merely signs the paper, the indorsement is called a **blank indorsement**. (See Figure 31-1.) A blank indorsement does not indicate the person to whom the instrument is to be paid—that is, the transferee. A person who is in possession of paper on which the last indorsement is blank is the holder.

CPA
CPA
CPA
CPA
CPA

Figure 31-1 Blank Endorsement

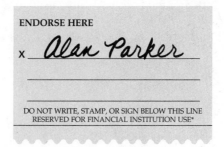

ENDORSE HERE

x *Alan Parker*

DO NOT WRITE, STAMP, OR SIGN BELOW THIS LINE
RESERVED FOR FINANCIAL INSTITUTION USE*

---

[12] UCC § 3-207 [1952].

[13] UCC § 3-202(b) [1990].

(a) EFFECT OF BLANK INDORSEMENT. Negotiation by a blank indorsement does four things: (1) it passes the ownership of the instrument; (2) it gives rise to certain implied warranties; (3) it imposes on the indorser secondary liability for payment of the paper; and (4) it changes the paper to bearer paper, which may be negotiated by transfer of possession alone.

(b) CONVERTING THE BLANK INDORSEMENT. The holder of an instrument on which the last indorsement is blank may write above the blank indorsement a statement that the instrument is payable to that particular holder.[14] This is called completing the indorsement or converting the blank indorsement to a special indorsement by specifying the identity of the indorsee. It protects the holder, because the paper cannot be negotiated without the indorsement and delivery of the holder.

10. Special Indorsement

A **special indorsement** consists of the signature of the indorser and words specifying the person to whom the indorser makes the instrument payable—that is, the indorsee. (See Figure 31-2.)

It is not necessary that the indorsement contain the word *order* or *bearer*.

Consequently, the paper indorsed as shown in Figure 31-2 continues to be negotiable and may be negotiated further.

1952 UCC

However, a paper that reads on its face "Pay to E. S. Flynn" is not negotiable.

1990 UCC

However, a noncheck instrument that reads on its face "Pay to E. S. Flynn" is nonnegotiable. In contrast, a check that on its face is so payable is negotiable.

An indorsement of "pay to account [number]" is a special indorsement. In contrast, the inclusion of a notation indicating the debt to be paid is not a special indorsement.

A special indorsement has the same effect as a blank indorsement.[15] As in the case of the blank indorsement, a special indorsement transfers title to the instrument. It also means the indorser makes certain warranties about the instrument, and it imposes on the indorser a secondary liability to pay the amount of the instrument when certain requirements are satisfied. When a special indorsement is made, the paper becomes order paper and may only be negotiated by an indorsement and delivery.

11. Qualified Indorsement

A **qualified indorsement** is one that qualifies the effect of a blank or a special indorsement by disclaiming or destroying the liability of the

Figure 31-2   Special Endorsement

ENDORSE HERE

Pay to Tom Houlton

X Marcia L. Diaz

DO NOT WRITE, STAMP, OR SIGN BELOW THIS LINE
RESERVED FOR FINANCIAL INSTITUTION USE*

---

[14] UCC § 3-204(3) [1952]; UCC § 3-205(c) [1990].

[15] See Section 9(a) of this chapter.

indorser to answer for dishonor by the maker or drawee. This may be done by including the phrase "without recourse" in the body of the indorsement. Any other words that indicate an intention to destroy the indorser's secondary liability for dishonor by the maker or drawee can also be used.[16] (See Figure 31-3.)

made payable to the agent or attorney might make a qualified indorsement. Here the transferee recognizes that the transferor is not a party to the transaction and therefore should not be asked to vouch for the payment of the paper.

Figure 31-3   Qualified Endorsement

The qualification of an indorsement does not affect the passage of title or the negotiable character of the paper. It merely disclaims the indorser's secondary liability for payment of the paper.

This form of indorsement is most commonly used when the qualified indorser is known to be a person who has no personal interest in the transaction. For example, an agent or an attorney who is merely indorsing to a principal or client a check of a third person

12. Restrictive Indorsements

A **restrictive indorsement** specifies the purpose of the indorsement or the use to be made of the paper. (See Figure 31-4.) An indorsement is restrictive when it includes words showing that the paper is to be deposited (such as "for deposit only") or is negotiated for collection or to an agent or trustee, or when the negotiation is conditional.[17]

Figure 31-4 Restricted Endorsement

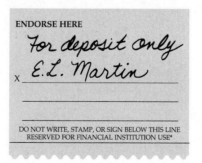

---

[16] Florida Coast Bank v Monarch Dodge (Fla App) 430 So 2d 607 (1983).
[17] UCC § 3-205.

A restrictive indorsement does not prevent transfer or negotiation of the paper, even when it expressly states that transfer or negotiation is prohibited.

With the exception of the indorsement "for deposit," modern business makes little use of the restrictive indorsements.

The distinction between a blank, special, and restrictive indorsement is illustrated by the *Walcott* case.

1952 UCC

WALCOTT v MANUFACTURERS HANOVER TRUST

133 Misc 2d 725, 507 NYS2d 961 (1986)

Walcott sent his October paycheck, together with a money order, to Midatlantic Mortgage Company in payment of his November mortgage installment payment. Walcott alleged that he signed his name to the back of the check and placed his mortgage number and the Midatlantic mailing sticker on the back of the check. He then placed the check and money order in an envelope addressed to Midatlantic Mortgage Company and dropped the envelope into a United States Postal box. Some time later Walcott was notified that he was late with the November payment. Walcott learned that his check had been cashed by Bilko Check Cashing and deposited in Bilko's account with Manufacturers Hanover. The check was finally cleared through Citibank and charged to the account of the original payor, the New York City Transit Authority. Walcott claimed that the check was stolen and Manufacturer's Hanover had wrongfully credited it to Bilko's account. Walcott sued Manufacturers and Bilko for the amount of the check. Walcott claimed that his indorsement was either a special or restrictive indorsement, which should have prevented a thief from cashing the check.

HARKAVY, J. . . .

SPECIAL INDORSEMENT

Uniform Commercial Code § 3-204 subdivision (1) defines a special indorsement as being one that ". . . specifies the person to whom or to whose order it makes the instrument payable. Any instrument specially indorsed becomes payable to the order of the special indorsee and may be further negotiated only by his indorsement."

Examination of the back of the check, reveals that Mr. Walcott did not specify any particular indorsee. In order for the alleged attached sticker to have served that purpose it must have also complied with UCC § 3-202 subdivision (2): "An indorsement must be written by or on behalf of the holder and on the instrument or a paper so firmly affixed thereto as to become a part thereof." The back of the check shows no sticker attached at all. Even if it had originally been affixed thereto, as plaintiff claims, it obviously became detached easily, thus failing to meet the indorsement requirements under the UCC to constitute a special indorsement.

RESTRICTIVE INDORSEMENT

As to the numbers written underneath plaintiff's signature, they did not have the effect of restricting plaintiff's indorsement. "An indorsement is restrictive which either

(a) is conditional; or

(b) purports to prohibit further transfer of the instrument; or

(c) includes the words 'for collection,' 'for deposit,' 'pay any bank,' or like terms signifying a purpose of deposit or collection; or

(d) otherwise states that it is for the benefit or use of the indorser or of another person." UCC § 3-205.

This section of the Uniform Commercial Code is very specific. The series of numbers representing plaintiff's mortgage account was insufficient to restrict negotiation of plaintiff's check.

BLANK INDORSEMENT

Plaintiff's indorsement had the effect of converting the check into a bearer instrument. The series of numbers having no restrictive effect, Mr. Walcott indorsed the check in blank, or otherwise stated, he simply signed his name. A blank indorsement under UCC § 3-204 subdivision (2) ". . . specifies no particular indorsee and may consist of a mere signature." Additionally, "An instrument payable to order and indorsed in blank becomes payable to bearer and may be negotiated by delivery alone. . . ." Consequently, since plaintiff failed to limit his blank indorsement, the check was properly negotiated by delivery to third party defendant Bilko and properly cashed.

[Judgment for defendants]

QUESTIONS

1. Was Walcott's indorsement either special or restrictive?
2. What was the nature and effect of Walcott's indorsement?
3. What was the basis for the decision of the court?

13. Anomalous Indorsement

*****

1990 UCC

13. Anomalous Indorsement

The person indorsing a negotiable instrument will ordinarily be the holder or the holder's authorized agent. If an indorsement is made by a person who is not the holder or the authorized agent, the indorsement is called an **anomalous indorsement**. Typically, the object of making such an indorsement is to accommodate a party to the instrument. The anomalous indorser has the status of an ordinary indorser. But the anomalous indorsement has no effect on the character of the paper as being order or bearer paper. Consequently, order paper remains such even though the anomalous indorsement is blank.

14. Correction of Name by Indorsement

Sometimes the name of the payee or indorsee of a commercial paper is improperly spelled. Thus, H. A. Price may receive a paycheck that improperly is payable to the order of "H. O. Price." If this was a clerical error and the check is intended for H. A. Price, the employee may ask the employer to write a new check payable to the proper name. Instead of doing this, the payee or indorsee whose name is misspelled may indorse the wrong name, the correct name, or both.

1952 UCC

A person giving or paying value for the instrument may require both.[18]

1990 UCC

A person paying or taking the instrument for value or collection may require both.

This correction of name by indorsement may be used only when it was intended that the instrument should be payable to the person making the corrective indorsement. If there were in fact two employees, one named H. A. Price and the other H. O. Price, it would be illegal as a forgery for one to take the check intended for the other and, by indorsing it, obtain the benefit of the proceeds of the check.

1952 UCC

*****

1990 UCC

A fictitious, assumed, or trade name is treated the same as a wrong name. The law regarding correction of a wrong name by indorsement applies to such names.[19]

15. Bank Indorsement

To simplify the transfer of commercial paper from one bank to another in the process of collecting items, "any agreed method which identifies the transferor bank is sufficient for the item's further transfer to another bank." Thus, a bank may indorse with its Federal Reserve System number instead of using its name.

Likewise, when a customer has deposited an instrument with a bank but has failed to indorse it, the bank may make an indorsement for the customer unless the instrument expressly requires the payee's personal indorsement. Furthermore, the mere stamping or marking on the item of any notation showing that it was deposited by the customer or credited to the customer's account is declared to be effective as an indorsement by the customer.

C. NEGOTIATION WARRANTIES

When a negotiable instrument is transferred by negotiation, certain warranties binding the transferor are implied.

16. Warranties of Unqualified Indorser

When the transferor receives consideration for the indorsement and makes an unqualified indorsement, the warranties stated in this section are implied. No distinction is made between an unqualified blank indorsement and an unqualified special indorsement.

(a) SCOPE OF WARRANTIES. The warranties of the unqualified indorser are:

1952 UCC

1. The transferor has good title. The warranty of good title includes the warranty that all indorsements necessary to title to the instrument are genuine or that the indorser has or is authorized to act for one who has good title.

2. The act of transferring the instrument is rightful, independent of the question of title or authority to act. For example, if a payee of a note breaches a contract with the maker to hold the note until certain goods are shipped by transferring the note before the goods are shipped, the transfer is not rightful. This payee becomes liable to the transferee for any loss occasioned by the early transfer of the note.

3. The signatures on the instrument are genuine or executed by authorized agents.

4. The instrument has not been materially altered.

---

[18] UCC § 3-416 [1990].

[19] UCC § 3-204(d) [1990].

5. The indorser has no knowledge of the existence or commencement of any insolvency proceeding against the maker or acceptor of the instrument, or against the drawer of an unaccepted draft or bill of exchange.

6. No defense of any party is good against the indorser.[20]
   1990 UCC

1. The transferor is entitled to enforce the instrument.

2. All signatures on the instrument are genuine and authorized.

3. The instrument has not been altered.

4. The instrument is not subject to any defense or claim of any party that could be asserted against the transferor.

5. The transferor had no knowledge of any insolvency proceedings against a maker, an acceptor, or the drawer of an unaccepted draft.[21]

(b) WHAT IS NOT WARRANTED. The implied warranties stated here do not guarantee that payment of the paper will be made. Similarly, the holder's indorsement of a check does not give rise to any warranty that the account of the drawer in the drawee bank contains funds sufficient to cover the check.
   1952 UCC

(c) BENEFICIARY OF IMPLIED WARRANTIES. The implied warranties of the unqualified indorser pass to the transferee of the paper and any subsequent holder who acquires the instrument in good faith.
   1990 UCC

(c) BENEFICIARY OF IMPLIED WARRANTIES. The implied warranties of the unqualified indorser pass to the transferee and any subsequent transferee. There is no requirement of good faith as to the subsequent transferee. Likewise, it is not required that the transferee be a holder.

1952 UCC

(d) DISCLAIMER OF WARRANTIES.
The implied warranties of the unqualified indorser may be disclaimed.
   1990 UCC

(d) DISCLAIMER OF WARRANTIES.
The unqualified indorser cannot disclaim any warranty when the instrument is a check. Warranties may be disclaimed when the instrument is not a check.

A disclaimer of warranties is ordinarily made by adding "Without warranties" to the indorsement.
   1952 UCC

(e) NOTICE OF BREACH OF WARRANTY.
   *****
   1990 UCC

(e) NOTICE OF BREACH OF WARRANTY. To enforce an implied warranty of an indorser, the claimant must give the indorser notice of the breach of warranty. This must be given within 30 days after the claimant learns or has reason to know of the breach and the identity of the indorser. If proper notice is not given, the warranty claim is reduced by the amount of the loss that could have been avoided had timely notice been given.

17. Warranties of Other Parties

Warranties are also made by the indorser who indorses "without recourse" and by one who transfers by delivery only.
   1952 UCC

(a) QUALIFIED INDORSER. The warranty liability of the indorser who indorses "without recourse" is the same as that of the unqualified indorser, with one difference. The warranty as to "no defenses" is limited to a

---

[20] UCC § 3-417 [1952].
[21] UCC § 3-416 [1990].

warranty that the indorser does not have knowledge of any defense, rather than that no defense exists. The warranties of a qualified indorser run to the same persons as those of an unqualified indorser.[22]

1990 UCC

(a) QUALIFIED INDORSER. The warranty liability of a qualified indorser is the same as that of an unqualified indorser.[23]

1952 UCC

(b) TRANSFEROR BY DELIVERY. The warranties made by one who transfers a commercial paper by delivery are the same as those made by an unqualified indorser, with one exception. The warranties run only to the immediate transferee, and then only if consideration has been given for the transfer. Subsequent holders cannot enforce such warranties against this prior transferor by delivery, regardless of the character of such holders.

1990 UCC

(b) TRANSFEROR BY DELIVERY. When the negotiable instrument is negotiated by delivery without indorsement, the warranty liability of the transferor runs only to the immediate transferee. In all other respects, the warranty liability is the same as in the case of the unqualified indorser.

For example, Thomas, a minor, gives Craig his note payable to bearer. Craig transfers the note for value and by delivery only to Walsh, who negotiates it to Hall. Payment was refused by Thomas on the ground of minority. Hall cannot hold Craig liable. Craig, having negotiated the instrument by delivery only, is liable on his implied warranties only to his immediate transferee, Walsh. Likewise, since Craig did not indorse the note, he is not secondarily liable for payment of the note.

D. ASSIGNMENT OF COMMERCIAL PAPER

Commercial paper may be assigned by the act of the parties or by operation of law.

18. Assignment by Act of the Parties

If commercial paper is transferred by the express act of the holder in such a way that it has not been negotiated, the transfer is an assignment.

When a necessary indorsement is missing, the transferee has only the rights of an assignee. If the transferee acquires the paper for value, the transferee is entitled, however, to require that the transferor indorse the instrument. If the indorsement is obtained, then the transferee is deemed a holder, but only from the time when the indorsement is made.

In the *Duxbury* case the court dealt with a promissory note that was transferred without indorsement.

DUXBURY v ROBERTS
338 Mass 385, 446 NE2d 401 (1983)

Roberts issued a promissory note payable to the order of Baines. Baines handed this note over to Duxbury without indorsing it. Baines also gave him a separate paper, in which Baines stated that the note was being transferred

---

[22] UCC § 3-417(3) [1952].
[23] UCC § 3-416(a) [1990].

to Duxbury. When Duxbury sued Roberts on the note, Roberts contended that he was not liable, because Duxbury was not a holder in due course of the paper. From a judgment in favor of Duxbury, Roberts appealed.

HENNESSEY, C. J. . . . One does not become a holder of a negotiable instrument unless there is a negotiation of that instrument as required under the Uniform Commercial Code, 3-202(1). To have a negotiation of an instrument payable to order, the instrument must be delivered with any necessary indorsement. "An indorsement must be written by or on behalf of the holder and on the instrument or on a paper so firmly affixed thereto as to become a part thereof." In this case Baines did not sign the note when he transferred it to Duxbury. Rather, he signed only the document entitled, "Partial Assignment of Note and Mortgage." His signing of this document does not constitute an indorsement of the note because it was not "so firmly affixed thereto as to become a part thereof." Therefore, Duxbury did not become a holder or a holder in due course. However, [we] reject the . . . contention that the assignment to Duxbury was not valid. Under [UCC] § 3-201(1), even though the instrument was not negotiated, Duxbury acquired the rights of his transferor, Baines, subject to all defenses available against Baines. . . .

[Judgment affirmed]

QUESTIONS

1. How is order paper negotiated?
2. Was there a negotiation by Baines to Duxbury?
3. What rights did Duxbury have on the note?

19. Assignment by Operation of Law

An assignment by operation of law occurs when, by virtue of the law, one person's title to commercial paper is vested in another. For example, if the holder of a commercial paper becomes a debtor under the Bankruptcy Code, the title to the instrument vests automatically in the trustee in bankruptcy. If the holder of a commercial paper dies, title to the paper vests in the personal representative of the decedent's estate.

SUMMARY

Negotiable commercial paper can be transferred by assignment or negotiation. It is typically transferred by negotiation. The legal effect depends on whether the transfer is an assignment or a negotiation. When a negotiable instrument is assigned, the transferee has the rights of the transferor. This means that the transferee is entitled to enforce the paper, but the assignee-transferee has no greater rights than the assignor-transferor. If sued, the assignee is subject to any defense that could be raised in a suit on an assigned contract. When a negotiable instrument is transferred by negotiation, the transferee becomes the holder of the paper. If such a holder is a holder in due course, the holder will be immune to certain defenses. Negotiation is the transferring of a negotiable instrument in such a way as to make the transferee the holder.

Order paper is negotiated by an indorsement and a delivery by the person to whom it is then payable. Bearer paper is negotiated by a change of possession alone. The order or bearer character of paper is determined by the face of the paper, as long as the paper is not indorsed. If the paper has been indorsed, the character is determined by the last genuine indorsement.

A forged or unauthorized indorsement is no indorsement, and the possessor of the paper cannot be a holder. The impostor rule makes three exceptions to this rule.

A negotiation is effective even though (1) it is made by a minor, (2) it is an act beyond the powers of a corporation, (3) it is obtained by fraud, or (4) the negotiation is part of an illegal transaction. However, the transferor may be able to set aside the negotiation under general legal principles apart from the UCC. The negotiation may not be set aside if the paper is held by a person having the rights of a holder in due course.

1952 UCC
*****

1990 UCC
The negotiation cannot be set aside if the paper is held by a person paying the instrument in good faith and without knowledge of the facts on which the rescission claim is based.

There are a number of different kinds of indorsements that can be made on commercial paper. When an indorser merely signs the paper, the indorsement is called a blank indorsement. If the last indorsement is a blank indorsement, the paper is bearer paper, which may be negotiated by change of possession alone. A special indorsement consists of the signature of the indorser and words specifying the person to whom the indorser makes the instrument payable. If the last indorsement is a special indorsement, the paper is order paper and may be negotiated only by an indorsement and delivery. A qualified indorsement destroys the liability of the indorser to answer for dishonor of the paper by the maker or drawee. A restrictive indorsement specifies the purpose of the indorsement or the use to be made of the paper.

1952 UCC
An indorser who negotiates by an unqualified indorsement and receives consideration makes the following warranties: (1) title is good, (2) all the signatures are genuine, (3) the instrument has not been materially altered, (4) the indorser has no knowledge of any insolvency proceeding against the maker or drawer, and (5) no defense of any party is good against the indorser. A transferor indorsing with a qualified indorsement warrants only that the transferor has no knowledge of any defense, rather than that no defense exists. Otherwise the qualified indorser makes the same warranties as an unqualified indorser. A transferor who does not indorse the instrument makes these warranties to the immediate transferee only.

1990 UCC
An indorsement by someone not the holder or the holder's authorized agent is known as an "anomalous indorsement." Such an indorser has the status of an ordinary indorser. However, the anomalous indorsement has no effect on whether the paper is order or bearer paper.

The warranties of the unqualified indorser who receives consideration are: (1) the transferor is entitled to enforce the instrument, (2) all signatures on the instrument are genuine and authorized, (3) the instrument has not been altered, (4) the instrument is not subject to any defense or claim of any party that could be asserted, against the transferor, and (5) the transferor had no knowledge of any insolvency proceedings against a maker, an acceptor, or the drawer of an unaccepted draft.

LAW IN PRACTICE

1. Do not issue bearer paper unless you expect to receive payment for it immediately. An unauthorized person may obtain it and misuse it.
2. Be sure that the named payee is not an impostor; otherwise as an issuer you will bear the ultimate loss.

3. If you receive paper indorsed "without recourse" you have no cause of action against the indorser if the issuer dishonors the instrument.
4. When you indorse commercial paper and receive consideration you warrant that all the prior signatures on the instrument are genuine.

QUESTIONS AND CASE PROBLEMS

1. What social forces are affected by the law as to qualified indorsements?

2. As soon as Carol Kamiya gets her weekly paycheck, she carefully writes her name on the back so that everyone will know that it is her check. Is Kamiya protected by doing this?

3. Allan pays Bestor $100, which Allan owes Bestor, with a check stating "pay to the order of Dale Bestor $100." How can Bestor transfer this check to Wickard in such a way as to make Wickard the holder of the check?

4. Higgins owes the Packard Appliance store $100. He mails a check to Packard. The check is drawn on the First National Bank and states "pay to the order of cash $100." This check is stapled to a letter stating that the $100 is in payment of the debt owed by Higgins. Edwards is employed by Packard in the mailroom. Edwards removes the letter from its envelope, detaches the check, and disappears. No one knows what becomes of the check until it is presented at the First National Bank by a person identifying himself as Gene Howard. The bank pays this person $100 and debits that amount against the account of Higgins. Higgins protests that this cannot be done because the check was lost and never belonged to Howard. Is Higgins correct?

5. A thief steals a blank promissory note from Roger, makes it payable to Dodd, and forges Roger's name to it as maker. Dodd gives value for the note and indorses it to Nell, who in turn indorses it to Robert, a holder in due course. Robert attempts to collect against Roger, who proves that his signature was a forgery. Does Robert have any rights against Dodd or Nell? Why?

6. The Gasts owned a building which they contracted to sell to the Hannas. The building was insured against fire with the American Casualty Co. Thereafter, when the building was damaged by fire, a settlement was reached with the insurance company through Sidney Rosenbaum, a public fire adjuster. In order to make payment for the loss, the insurance company drew a draft on itself payable to the Hannas, the Gasts, and to Sidney Rosenbaum. Apparently the Hannas indorsed the draft, forged the names of the other payees as indorsers, cashed the draft by presenting it to the American Casualty Company, and disappeared. Thereafter the Gasts sued the American Casualty Company. Decide. [Gast v American Casualty Co. 99 NJ Super 538, 240 A2d 682]

7. The Snug Harbor Realty Co, had a checking account in the First National Bank. When construction work was obtained by Snug Harbor, its superintendent, Magee, would examine the bills submitted for labor and materials. He would instruct the bookkeeper as to what bills were approved, and checks were then prepared by the bookkeeper in accordance with such instructions. After the checks were signed by the proper official of Snug Harbor, they were picked up by Magee for delivery. Instead of delivering certain checks, he forged the signatures of the respective payees as indorsers and cashed the checks. The drawee bank then debited the Snug Harbor account with the amount of the checks. Snug Harbor claimed this was improper and sued the bank for the amount of such checks. The bank claimed they were protected by the impostor rule. Will the bank be successful? Explain. [Snug Harbor Realty Co. v First National Bank, 105 NJ Super 572, 253 A2d 581]

8. Benton, as agent for Savidge, received an insurance settlement check from the Metropolitan Life Insurance Co. He indorsed it "For deposit" and deposited it in the Bryn Mawr Trust Company in the account of Savidge. What was the nature and effect of this indorsement? [Savidge v Metropolitan Life Insurance Co. 380 Pa 205, 110 A2d 730]

9. Humphrey drew a check for $100. It was stolen, and the thief forged the payee's indorsement. The check was then negotiated to Miller, who had no knowledge of these facts. Miller indorsed the check to the Citizens Bank. Payment of the check was voided on the ground of the forgery. The Citizens Bank then sued Miller as indorser. Decide. [*Citizens Bank of Hattiesburg v Miller, 194 Miss 557, 11 So 2d 457*]

10. When claims filed with the insurance company were approved for payment, they were given to the claims clerk, who would prepare checks to pay those claims and then give the checks to the treasurer to sign. The claims clerk of the insurance company made a number of checks payable to persons who did not have any claims and gave them to the treasurer together with the checks for valid claims, and the treasurer signed all the checks. The claims clerk then removed the false checks, indorsed them with the names of their respective payees, and cashed them at the bank where the insurance company had its account. The bank debited the account of the insurance company with the amount of these checks. The insurance company claimed that the bank could not do this because the indorsements on the checks were forgeries. Is the insurance company correct? [*General Acci. Fire & Life Assur. Corp. v Citizens Fidelity Bank & Trust Co. (Ky) 519 SW2d 817*]

11. Eutsler forged his brother Richard's indorsement on certified checks and cashed them at the First National bank. Richard sought to recover the funds from the bank. The bank stated that it would press criminal charges against Eutsler. Richard asked the bank to delay prosecution of his brother to give him time to collect directly from his brother. His brother promised to repay him the money but vanished some six months later without having paid any money. Richards sued the bank. What result? [*Eutsler v First National Bank, Pawhuska (Okla) 639 P2d 1245*]

12. Charles made an instrument payable to Larry, a minor. Larry indorsed and delivered the instrument to Quest, a holder in due course. When Quest sued Charles on the instrument, he claimed that he was not liable, since the instrument was negotiated by a minor. Decide.

13. A negotiable instrument is payable to bearer. A person to whom the bearer wishes to negotiate the instrument, however, refuses to take the instrument without the indorsement of the bearer. What reason can you give for insistence on such indorsement?

14. A note was indorsed "without recourse" to the Hudson Bank by Starlit Equipment. When the bank tried to collect on the note, the maker of the note alleged that his signature was forged. The bank then sued Starlit. Starlit defended the action on the basis that the instrument was signed "without recourse." Decide.

15. Two employees of the State of New Mexico fraudulently procured and indorsed a warrant (a draft drawn against funds of the state) made out to the Greater Mesilla Valley Sanitation District. There was no such sanitation district. The employees obtained payment from the Citizens Bank. Western Casualty, the state's insurer, reimbursed the state for its loss and then brought suit against the bank for negligently paying the warrant. Decide. [*Western Casualty & Surety Co. v Citizens Bank of Las Cruces (CA10 NM) 676 F2d 1344*]

CHAPTER 32

RIGHTS OF HOLDERS AND DEFENSES

LEARNING OBJECTIVES

After studying this chapter, you will be able to:
1. *Distinguish between an ordinary holder and a favored holder.*
2. *List the requirements for becoming a holder in due course.*
3. *Explain the rights of a holder through a holder in due course.*
4. *List and explain the limited defenses not available against a holder in due course.*
5. *List and explain the universal defenses available against all holders.*
6. *Describe how the rights of a holder in due course have been limited by the Federal Trade Commission.*

What rights do the parties to commercial paper have? What defenses do they have?

A. KINDS OF CLAIMANTS

The rights and defenses of the parties to commercial paper are determined by the kind of parties involved.

1. Kinds of Parties

The person claiming to have rights on commercial paper may be an assignee or a holder. A holder may be an ordinary holder or a favored holder: meaning a holder in due course or a holder through a holder in due course.

2. Ordinary Holders and Assignees

You will recall that a holder is a person to whom commercial paper has been negotiated. Any holder has all the rights relating to the paper. The holder, although an ordinary holder, is the only person who may demand payment or bring suit for the collection of the paper. A holder is also the only person who may give a discharge or release from liability on the paper, or who may cancel the liability of another party to the paper.

When the holder sues on the paper, the holder is required only to produce the paper in court and show that the signature of the defendant is genuine or admitted. If that is done and there is no evidence of a defense, the holder is entitled to a judgment for the full face amount of the paper. The fact that the holder is merely an ordinary holder has no significance if the defendant does not have a defense.

The holder may sue any one or more prior parties liable on the paper without regard to the order in which such persons signed the paper.

The assignee of a commercial paper is in the same position and has the same rights as an ordinary holder. It is immaterial whether the person is an assignee by express assignment, by operation of law, or in consequence of the omission of an essential indorsement.

3. Favored Holders

The law gives certain holders of commercial paper a preferred standing by protecting them from certain defenses when they sue to collect payment. This protection is given to make commercial paper more attractive. Favored holders have an immunity not possessed by ordinary holders or assignees. The favored holders are known as the holder in due course and the holder through a holder in due course.

(a) HOLDER IN DUE COURSE. To have the preferred status of a holder in due course, a person must first be a holder. That is, the person in question must be the possessor of bearer paper or must be the possessor of order paper payable to that person as the payee or indorsee.[1] It is easier to understand the concept of due course if you substitute modern terminology and think of "due course" as meaning an ordinary transaction.

In addition to being a holder, the holder in due course must (1) give value, (2) act good faith, (3) be ignorant of the paper's being overdue or dishonored, and (4) be ignorant of defenses and adverse claims.

(1) Value. Since the law of commercial paper is fundamentally a merchant's or businessperson's law, it favors only the holders who have give value for the paper. For example, since a person receiving property under a will does not give value, a person receiving bonds in that way is not a holder in due course.

A person takes an instrument for value (a) by performing the act for which the instrument was given, such as delivering the goods for which the check was sent in payment, (b) by acquiring a security interest in the paper— for example, when it has been pledged as security for another obligation, or (c) by taking the instrument in payment of, or as security

---

[1] Although it is an uncommon occurrence, the original payee may also be a holder in due course, provided the necessary elements are satisfied. First National Bank v Creston Livestock Auction, Inc. (Iowa) 447 NW2d 132 (1989).

for, a prior or current debt. When value is given, the courts do not measure or appraise the value given.

A promise not yet performed, although sufficient as consideration for a contract, does not constitute value to satisfy this requirement for a holder in due course.[2]

A bank does not give value for a deposited check when it credits the depositor's account with the amount of the deposit. The bank gives value to the extent that the depositor withdraws money against that credit.

In the *Trail Leasing* case a bank alleged it paid value, thus making it a holder in due course.

TRAIL LEASING, INC. v DROVERS FIRST AMERICAN BANK

(Minn) 447 NW2d 190 (1989)

Over a period of about two years, Pamela Haas, employed as assistant book-keeper by Trail Leasing, embezzled funds from her employer. Haas got corporate officers to sign checks payable to Drovers Bank that she would then cash for herself. Trail Leasing alleged that the bank should not have allowed Haas, who was not authorized to write checks, to obtain funds in this manner. The bank claimed that it was a holder in due course, protected from liability. Trail Leasing agreed that the bank took the checks in good faith and without notice of the embezzlement scheme, but contended that the bank never gave value. From a judgment in favor of Trail Leasing, the bank appealed.

SIMONETT, J. . . . . Under [UCC §]3-302, a holder in due course is anyone who takes the instrument "(a) for value; and (b) in good faith; and (c) without notice that it is overdue or has been dishonored or of any defense against or claim to it on the part of any person." Here it has been stipulated that Drovers took the Haas checks in good faith and without notice of any claims. The issue then becomes, as it did for the appeals panel, whether Drovers meets the third requirement of taking the checks "for value." This, too, is the issue raised in the petition for further review by Drovers.

We conclude that Drovers took the Haas checks "for value" and, therefore, was a holder in due course.

"A holder takes the instrument for value," says [UCC §]3-303(a), "to the extent that the agreed consideration has been performed or that he acquires a security interest in or lien on the instrument otherwise than by legal process." This provision eliminated a conflict in prior law by making clear that merely a promise to the transferor is not value until the promise has been performed. Here Drovers performed; it paid cash for the checks. Trail Leasing argues that at best Drovers gave only "conditional value" because it retained and exercised the right to debit Trail Leasing's commercial account. But even so, the bank first had to pay out its money before debiting Trail Leasing's account. As the comment to [UCC §]3-303 says, "Where an agreed sum of

---

[2] Sea Air Support, Inc. v Herrmann, 96 Nev 574, 613 P2d 413 (1980).

money is actually paid for an instrument . . . as the purchase price for it . . . the instrument is clearly taken 'for value' . . . ." *Roland v Republic Nat'l Bank of Dallas*, 463 SW2d 747, 749 (Tex Civ App 1971) (bank becomes a holder in due course when bank paid face value for checks presented by payee and drawn on an account at bank and thus had right to reimburse itself from customer's account.) Cases cited by Trail Leasing where a bank takes a check, credits the depositor's account, but never issues cash against the check, are not on point. This is not a case, either, where Haas withdrew money from Trail Leasing's account with a simple withdrawal slip. Here she used a valid negotiable instrument.

[Judgment reversed]

QUESTIONS

1. When does a person take an instrument for value?
2. What was the argument of Trail Leasing?
3. Did Drovers take the Haas checks for value? Explain.

1952 UCC

In a few special cases, a purchaser of commercial paper is not considered a holder in due course even though all the elements have been satisfied. This is true when the sales are not of an ordinary commercial nature, such as when paper is acquired by judicial sale, sale of the assets of an estate, or a bulk sale not in the regular course of business of the transferor.[3]

1990 UCC

In a few special cases, a purchaser of commercial paper is not considered a holder in due course even though all these elements have been satisfied. This is true when the paper is acquired by legal process or by purchase in an execution, bankruptcy, or creditor's sale or similar proceeding. It is also true when the paper is acquired as part of a bulk transaction not in the ordinary course of the transferor's business or as the successor in interest to an estate or other organization.[4]

1952 UCC

(2) Good Faith. The element of good faith requires that the taker of commercial paper act with honesty in acquiring the paper.[5]

1990 UCC

(2) Good Faith. The element of good faith requires that the taker of the negotiable instrument acted honestly in acquiring the instrument. In addition, the taker must have observed reasonable standards of fair dealing.[6]

Bad faith may sometimes be indicated by the small value given. This does not mean that the transferee must give value equal to the face of the paper. However, a gross inadequacy of value may be evidence of bad faith. Bad faith is established by proof that the transferee had knowledge of facts that made it improper to acquire the instrument under the circumstances.

The fact that a transferee acted carelessly does not establish bad faith.[7] If the transferee takes the instrument in good faith, it is

---

[3] UCC § 3-302(3) [1952].

[4] UCC § 3-302(c) [1990].

[5] UCC § 1-201(19) [1952].

[6] UCC § 3-103(a)(4) [1990].

[7] Carnegie Bank v Shallegl, 256 NJ Super 23, 606 A2d 389 (1992).

immaterial whether the transferor acted in good faith.

(3) Ignorance of the Paper's Being Overdue or Dishonored. Commercial paper may be negotiated even though (a) it has been dishonored, whether by nonacceptance or nonpayment; (b) the paper is overdue, whether because of lapse of time or the acceleration of the due date; or (c) it is demand paper that has been outstanding more than a reasonable time. Ownership of the paper may still be transferred. Nevertheless, the fact that the paper is circulating at a late date or after it has been dishonored is a suspicious circumstance that should alert the person acquiring the paper that there is some adverse claim or defense. A person who acquires title to the paper under such circumstances cannot be a holder in due course.

(4) Ignorance of Defenses and Adverse Claims. Prior parties on the paper may have defenses that they could raise if sued by the person who transferred the instrument to them. For example, the drawer of a check, if sued by the payee, might have the defense that the merchandise delivered by the payee was defective. In addition, third persons, whether prior parties or not, may be able to assert that the instrument belongs to them and not to the possessor. A person who acquires the commercial paper with notice or knowledge that any person might have a defense or that there is any adverse claim of ownership of the instru-

ment cannot be a holder in due course. Thus, the holder of commercial paper cannot be a holder in due course when the holder acquired the paper with knowledge that there had been a failure of consideration with respect to the contract for which the paper had been given. In general, takers who are aware of facts that would make a reasonable person ask questions are deemed to know what they would have learned if they had asked questions.

1952 UCC

*****

1990 UCC

The fact that there are documents of record filed in a public office does not give notice of any defense or claim that would bar a taker from being a holder in due course. Knowledge that a party to the paper has been discharged from the obligation bars suit against that party, but it does not bar the taker from being a holder in due course.[8]

Knowledge acquired by the taker after acquiring the paper does not prevent the taker from being a holder in due course. Consequently, the fact that the taker, after acquiring the paper, learns of a defense does not operate retroactively to destroy the taker's character as a holder in due course.

In the *Money Mart* case the drawer of a payroll check argued that the purchaser of that check should have inquired as to whether the check would be honored before cashing it.

MONEY MART CHECK CASHING CENTER INC. v EPICYCLE CORPORATION

(Colo) 667 P2d 1372 (1983)

An employee of Epicycle cashed his final paycheck at Money Mart Check Cashing Center. Epicycle had issued a stop payment order on the check. Money Mart deposited the check through normal banking channels. The check was returned to Money Mart marked "Payment Stopped." Money Mart brought an action against Epicycle claiming that, as a holder in due

---

[8]   UCC § 3-302(b) [1990]. An exception exists if the discharge occurred in insolvency proceedings.

course, it was entitled to recover against Epicycle. Epicycle argued that Money Mart could not be a holder in due course because it failed to verify the check as good prior to cashing it. From a judgment in favor of Epicycle, Money Mart appealed.

ROVIRA, J. . . . The question before us is whether Money Mart is a holder in due course. If it is, it takes the check free of any of Epicycle's claims to the check or defenses against [its employee. UCC § 3-302(1)] provides:

(1) A holder in due course is a holder who takes the instrument:

(a) For value; and

(b) In good faith; and

(c) Without notice that it is overdue or has been dishonored or of any defense against or claim to it on the part of any person.

That Money Mart took the check for value is undisputed, leaving the questions of "good faith" and "notice."

"Good faith" is defined as "honesty in fact in the conduct or transaction concerned." The drafters of the Uniform Commercial Code intended that this standard be a subjective one. Thus, the question is: "Was this alleged holder in due course acting in good faith, however stupid and negligent his behavior might have been?"

The only testimony on the question of good faith is that Money Mart cashed the check without knowing that a stop payment order had been issued on it. The Superior Court concluded that Money Mart was not a holder in due course because it "did not inquire as to the check itself and had no knowledge as to whether the check was stolen, incomplete, or secured by fraud." Under a subjective standard, an absence of knowledge is not equivalent to a lack of good faith.

We now consider whether Money Mart had "notice" of the fact that payment had been stopped on the check or that Cronin had obtained the check improperly. A person has "notice" of a fact when:

(a) He has actual knowledge of it; or

(b) He has received a notice or notification of it; or

(c) From all the facts and circumstances known to him at the time in question he has reason to know that it exists.

As can be seen, tests other than "actual knowledge" may be used in determining whether a person is a holder in due course. There is no allegation that Money Mart had received notification of the defenses, so we must now determine whether Money Mart had "reason to know" of them. . . .

The Superior Court held that Money Mart's failure to inquire about the validity of the check constituted negligence. However, there is nothing in the Uniform Commercial Code and nothing in the record to support such a conclusion.

A determination of whether a holder has "reason to know" is based upon "all the facts and circumstances known to him." A person "knows" of a fact when he has "actual knowledge" of it. The question therefore is whether Money Mart had actual knowledge of facts giving it reason to know that a defense existed. There is nothing to distinguish the facts of this case from any other of the thousands of checks that Money Mart and others cash each year: A man came to Money Mart to cash his paycheck;

Money Mart is in the business of cashing paychecks; the face of the check disclosed nothing to raise even a suspicion that there was something wrong with it.

It has often been held that where an instrument is regular on its face there is no duty to inquire as to possible defenses unless the circumstances of which the holder has knowledge are of such a nature that failure to inquire reveals a deliberate desire to evade knowledge because of a fear that investigation would disclose the existence of a defense. There is nothing in using a check-cashing service instead of a bank that would lead to a rule imposing different standards on the two kinds of institutions.

Accordingly, we hold that Money Mart is a holder in due course and, as such, is not subject to the defenses Epicycle may have against Cronin.

[Judgment reversed]

QUESTIONS

1. Did Money Mart take the check for value?
2. Did Money Mart take the check in good faith and without notice that payment had been stopped or that Cronin had obtained the check improperly?
3. What was the basis for the court's decision?

(b) HOLDER THROUGH A HOLDER IN DUE COURSE. Those persons who become holders of the instrument after a holder in due course are given the same protection as the holder in due course, provided they are not parties to fraud or illegality that affects the instrument. This is so even if the transferee from a holder in due course does not satisfy one or more of the elements required for holder in due course status. This is often referred to as the "shelter rule". It allows a person who is not a holder in due course to hide under the "umbrella" with a holder in due course and be sheltered from claims and defenses enjoyed by a holder in due course.

This means that if an instrument is negotiated from Arens to Bell to Cook to Day, and Bell is a holder in due course, both Cook and Day will enjoy the same rights as Bell. If Cook received the instrument as a gift or with knowledge of failure of consideration or other defense, or if Day took the instrument after maturity, they could not themselves be holders in due course. Nevertheless, they are given the same protection as the prior holder in due course because they took the instrument through such a holder, namely Bell. It is not only Cook, the person taking directly from Bell, but also Day, who is given this extra protection.

1952 UCC

*****

1990 UCC

A plaintiff is not required to prove holder in due course status until the defendant asserts a defense that cannot be raised against a person with such rights.

B. DEFENSES

Whether a defense may be raised against a plaintiff suing on a negotiable instrument depends on the status of the plaintiff (i.e., the holder or holder in due course) and the nature of the defense.

4. Classification of Defenses

The importance of being a holder in due course or a holder through a holder in due course is that such holders are not subject to certain defenses when those holders demand payment or bring suit on a commercial paper.

These defenses are called **limited defenses**. Another class of defenses, **universal defenses**, may be asserted against any plaintiff, whether the party is an assignee, an ordinary holder, a holder in due course, or a holder through a holder in due course.[9]

1952 UCC

*****

1990 UCC

The 1990 version of Article 3 preserves the distinction between universal and limited defenses, although it speaks in terms of "defenses and claims in recoupment" and "claims to an instrument."[10]

At common law, a claim in recoupment was a claim for damages caused by the plaintiff's breach of the contract on which suit was brought. The recoupment claim could only reduce or cancel the amount to which the plaintiff was entitled because of the plaintiff's breach. Recoupment procedure has been replaced in this century by counterclaim procedure that entitles the defendant to recover damages from the plaintiff if the counterclaim is sustained for an amount greater than the plaintiff's damages.

5. Defenses Against Assignee or Ordinary Holder

An assignee suing on commercial paper is subject to every defense held by the defendant. Similarly, a holder who is neither a holder in due course nor a holder through a holder in due course is subject to every defense, just as though the instrument were not negotiable. Thus, an ordinary holder suing on the promissory note of a buyer is subject to the buyer's defense of breach of warranty.[11]

6. Limited Defenses Not Available Against a Holder in Due Course

Neither a holder in due course nor one having the rights of such a holder is subject to any of the following defenses.

(a) ORDINARY CONTRACT DEFENSES. In general terms, the defenses that could be raised against a suit on an ordinary contract cannot be raised against a holder in due course. Accordingly, the defendant cannot assert against the holder in due course the defense of lack, failure, or illegality of consideration with respect to the transaction between the defendant and the person with whom the defendant dealt.

(b) INCAPACITY OF DEFENDANT. Ordinarily, the incapacity of the defendant, other than that of minority, may not be raised against a holder in due course. Such incapacity is a defense, however, if by general principles of law that incapacity makes the instrument a nullity.[12] For example, a promissory note made by an insane person for whom a court had appointed a guardian is a nullity. In the case of a lawsuit on the note by a holder in due course, the incapacity of the maker would be a defense.

(c) FRAUD IN THE INDUCEMENT. A person may knowingly execute commercial paper and know its essential terms. If, however, the person was persuaded or induced to execute the paper because of fraudulent statements, such fraud cannot be raised against a holder in due course or a holder through a holder in due course. As an illustration, Mills is persuaded to purchase an automobile

---

[9] Under the pre-Code law, the universal defense was called a real defense and the limited defense was called a personal defense. The terms *real* and *personal* are now obsolete, since they have been abandoned by both the 1952 and 1990 versions of Article 3. Some licensing and CPA examinations may continue to use these pre-Code terms.

[10] UCC § § 3-305, 3-306 [1990].

[11] Pascal v Tardera, 123 App Div 2d 752, 507 NYS2d 225 (1986).

[12] UCC § 3-305(2) [1952].

because of Pagan's statements concerning its condition. Mills gives Pagan a note, which is negotiated until it reaches Han, who is a holder in due course. Mills meanwhile learns that the car is not as represented and that Pagan's statements were fraudulent. When Han demands payment of the note, Mills cannot refuse to pay on the ground of Pagan's fraud. Mills must pay the note. Mills may then sue Pagan for damages for fraud.

(d) MISCELLANEOUS DEFENSES. T h e limited defenses listed in the preceding three

subsections are those most commonly raised in lawsuits. The following limited defenses may also be asserted: (1) prior payment or cancellation of the instrument, (2) nondelivery, (3) conditional or special purpose delivery, (4) duress consisting of threats, (5) unauthorized completion, and (6) theft of paper.

Can an issuer be liable for an unauthorized completion? This was the issue in the *National Loan* case.

NATIONAL LOAN INVESTORS, L.P. v MARTIN
(Iowa App) 488 NW2d 163 (1992)

William Martin was a business customer of Pisgah Saving Bank from 1975 until he quit farming in March 1984. He would sign blank notes when he purchased cattle and rely on the banker to fill in the correct amount later when the bank learned the purchase price. In 1988 the bank became insolvent. In April 1989, the FDIC sold some of the bank's assets including two promissory notes signed by Martin to the plaintiff. The notes show the signature of William L. Martin as maker. The amount of the two notes was close to $100,000. The notes were dated after 1984. Both the notes contained erasures and suspicious-looking type. The FDIC sued Martin on the notes. The trial court concluded that the notes were forgeries even though the notes had been signed by Martin. From a judgment in favor of Martin, the plaintiff appealed.

SCHULTZ, J. . . . We agree with the trial court that someone without authority filled in the dates and amounts on the two notes. We find that the two notes were signed by William with the loan amounts left blank prior to the time he discontinued doing business with the Bank. William did not do business with the Bank after March 1984. We also find the amounts were completed in the years 1986 and 1987. . . .

These findings do not aid William. Since we find William signed the notes, his signatures are not "'unauthorized' signature[s] or endorsement[s]" which could constitute forgery under our commercial code. . . . Notwithstanding our finding that the loan amounts on the notes were inappropriately filled in later, a holder in due course "may enforce [the notes] as completed." . . .

William was a farmer and businessman. He was obviously literate and had signed many notes previously. In a similar case, a maker who signed a blank note was not allowed to assert a fraud in factum defense. FDIC v Culver, 640 F.Supp. 725, 730 [1 UCC Rep Serv 2d 1585] (D.Kan.1986). The court emphasized that the note maker was literate and rejected his argument that he had no opportunity to learn of the essential terms which were left blank at the time he signed the note.

Based on the foregoing, we conclude that plaintiff has a right to enforce the two promissory notes as completed. . . .

[Judgment reversed]

QUESTIONS

1. What is the importance of the distinction between a limited and a universal defense?
2. How did the court decide?

7. Universal Defenses Available Against All Holders

Certain defenses are regarded as so basic that the social interest in preserving them outweighs the social interest of giving commercial paper the free-passing qualities of money. Accordingly, such defenses are given universal effect and may be raised against all holders, whether ordinary holders, holders in due course, or holders through a holder in due course. Such defenses are therefore appropriately called *universal defenses.*

(a) FRAUD AS TO THE NATURE OR ESSENTIAL TERMS OF THE PAPER. The fact that a person signs a commercial paper because the person is fraudulently deceived as to its nature or essential terms is a defense available against all holders.[13]

This is the situation when one person induces another to sign a note by falsely representing that, for example, it is a contract for repairs or that it is a character reference. This defense, however, cannot be raised when the defending party was negligent in learning the true nature and terms of the instrument.

(b) FORGERY OR LACK OF AUTHORITY. The defense that a signature was forged or signed without authority may be raised against any holder, unless the person whose name was signed has ratified it or is estopped by conduct or negligence from denying it.[14] The fact that the negligence of the drawer helped the wrongdoer does not prevent the drawer from raising the defense of forgery.

(c) DURESS DEPRIVING CONTROL. A person may execute or indorse a commercial paper in response to a force of such a nature that, under general principles of law, there is duress that makes the transaction a nullity rather than merely voidable. If so, such duress may be raised as a defense against any holder.

(d) INCAPACITY. The fact that the defendant is a minor, who under general principles of contract law may avoid the obligation, is a matter that may be raised against any kind of holder. Other kinds of incapacity may only be raised as a defense if the effect of the incapacity is to make the instrument a nullity.[15]

(e) ILLEGALITY. If the law declares that an instrument is void when executed in connection with certain conduct, such as gambling or usury, that defense may be raised against any holder. Similarly, when contracts of a corporate seller are a nullity because its charter has been forfeited, a promissory note given to it by a buyer is void. That defense

---

[13] UCC § 3-305(2)(c) [1952]; UCC § 3-305(a)(1)(iii) [1990].
[14] Bank of Hoven v Rausch (SD) 382 NW2d 39 (1986).
[15] UCC § 3-305(2)(a)(b) [1952]; UCC § 3-305(a)(1)(ii) [1990].

may be raised as against a holder in due course. If the law merely makes the transaction illegal but does not make the instrument void, the defense cannot be asserted against a holder in due course or a holder through a holder in due course.

1952 UCC

(f) ALTERATION. An **alteration** is a change to an instrument that is both material and fraudulently made by a party to the instrument. An alteration is material when it changes the contract of any party, such as by changing the date, place of payment, rate of interest, or any other important term. Material alterations also include any modification that changes the number or the relationship of the parties to the paper, by adding new terms or by cutting off a part of the paper itself.

An alteration must be made to the instrument itself. An oral or a collateral written agreement between the holder and one of the parties that modifies the obligation of the party is not an "alteration" within the sense just discussed. This is true even though the obligation of a party is changed as a result.

1990 UCC

(f) ALTERATION. An alteration is an unauthorized change or completion of a negotiable instrument designed to modify the obligation of a party to the instrument.[16]

(1) Person Making Alteration. B y definition an alteration is a change made by a party to the instrument. A change of the instrument made by a nonparty has no effect. Recovery may be had on the instrument as though the change had not been made, provided it can be proven what the instrument had been in its original form.

1952 UCC

(2) Effect of Alteration. The fact that an instrument has been altered may be raised against any holder. Unlike other defenses, however, it is only a partial defense against a favored holder. That is, a holder in due course or a holder through a holder in due course may enforce the instrument according to its original terms prior to its alteration.

1990 UCC

(2) Effect of Alteration. If the alteration was fraudulently made, the person whose obligation is affected by it is discharged from liability on the instrument. The instrument, however, may be enforced according to its original terms or its terms as completed. The persons who are given this right are those taking the instrument for value in good faith and without notice of the change or improper completion, or a payor bank or drawee.[17] It is not required that such a person have the rights of a holder in due course, although such a person would come within the protected class.

For example, Ryan signed a negotiable demand note for $100, made payable to Long. A subsequent holder changed the amount from $100 to $700. A later holder in due course presented the note to Ryan for payment. Ryan would still be liable for the original amount, $100.

8. Adverse Claims to the Paper

Distinct from a defense that a defendant may raise against the plaintiff as a reason against paying the instrument is a claim of a third person to be the owner of the paper. Assume that a check was made payable to the order of Brian Fry; that blank indorsements are subsequently made by Fry, Roland, and Dorgan; and that Ruoff—in possession of the check—appears to be the holder. Fry might then claim and show, if this is the case, that Roland had fraudulently deceived Fry into indorsing the check; that Fry therefore avoids the indorsement because of this fraud; and that, accordingly, the check still belongs to Fry. Fry in such a case is making an adverse claim to the instrument. A holder in due course holds commercial

---

[16] UCC § 3-407(a) [1990].
[17] UCC § 3-407(b),(c) [1990].

paper free and clear from all adverse claims of any other person to the paper.

9. Avoidance of Holder in Due Course Protection

In certain situations, the taker of a commercial paper is denied the status of a holder in due course or is denied the protection of a holder in due course.

(a) PARTICIPATING TRANSFEREE. The seller of goods on credit frequently assigns the sales contract and buyer's promissory note to the manufacturer who made the goods, to a finance company, or to a bank. In such a case, the assignee of the seller will be a holder in due course of the buyer's commercial paper if the paper is properly negotiated and the transferee satisfies all the elements of being a holder in due course. The transferee, however, may take such an active part in the sale to the seller's customer or may be so related to the seller that it is proper to conclude that the transferee was in fact a party to the original transaction. When this conclusion is reached, the transferee is held to have had notice or knowledge of any defense of the buyer against the seller. This bars holding that the transferee is a holder in due course.

(b) THE FEDERAL TRADE COMMISSION RULE. In 1976, the FTC adopted a rule that limits the rights of a holder in due course in a **consumer credit transaction**. The rule protects consumers who purchase goods or services for personal, family, or household use.[18] When the buyer is sued by a transferee of the note given to the seller, the buyer may raise any defense that could have been raised against the seller if the consumer's contract contains the notice required by the FTC regulation. The FTC regulation requires that the following notice be included in boldface type at least ten points in size:

Notice
Any holder of this consumer credit contract is subject to all claims and defenses which the debtor could assert against the seller of goods or services obtained with the proceeds hereof. Recovery hereunder by the debtor shall not exceed amounts paid by the debtor hereunder.

1952 UCC
*****
1990 UCC
When a notice preserving consumer defenses is stated in a negotiable instrument, no subsequent person can be a holder in due course of the instrument.[19]

SUMMARY

A holder of commercial paper can be either an ordinary holder or a favored holder. The ordinary holder has the same rights that an assignee would have. Favored holders are protected from certain defenses. Favored holders are (1) holders in due course and (2) holders through a holder in due course. To be a holder in due course, a person must first be a holder; that is, the person must have acquired the paper by a proper negotiation. The holder must meet certain requirements to be a holder in due course. The holder must take for value, in good faith, without notice that the paper is overdue or dishonored, and without notice of defenses and adverse claims. Those persons who become holders of the instrument

---

[18] The regulation does not cover purchases of real estate, securities, or consumer goods or services for which the purchase price is more than $25,000. Roosevelt Federal Sav. & Loan Assn. v Crider (Mo App) 722 SW2d 325 (1986).

[19] UCC § 3-106(d) [1990]. This goes beyond the scope of the Federal Trade Commission regulation. The latter merely preserves the defenses of the consumer but does not bar holder in due course protection with respect to other parties, such as the accommodation party to a consumer's note.

after a holder in due course are given the same protection as the holder in due course, provided they are not parties to any fraud or illegality affecting the instrument.

The importance of being a holder in due course or a holder through a holder in due course is that those holders are not subject to certain defenses when they demand payment or bring suit on commercial paper. These defenses are limited defenses and include ordinary contract defenses, incapacity unless it makes the instrument a nullity, fraud in the inducement, prior payment or cancellation, nondelivery of an instrument, conditional delivery, duress consisting of threats, unauthorized completion, and theft of the paper. Universal defenses may be asserted against any plaintiff, whether that party is an assignee, an ordinary holder, a holder in due course, or a holder through a holder in due course. Universal defenses include fraud as to the nature

or essential terms of the paper, forgery or lack of authority, duress depriving control, infancy, illegality that makes the instrument void, and alteration. Alteration is only a partial defense; the favored holder may enforce the instrument according to its original terms.

The Federal Trade Commission provides for limiting the immunity of a holder in due course from defenses of consumer buyers against their sellers. Immunity is limited in consumer credit transactions if the notice specified by the FTC regulation is included in a sales contract.

1952 UCC

*****

1990 UCC

When a notice preserving consumer defenses is stated in a negotiable instrument, no subsequent person can be a holder in due course.

LAW IN PRACTICE

1. It is better to be a holder in due course than an ordinary holder because in many cases you can overcome most defenses that an issuer can raise against you.
2. Knowledge acquired after the taking of commercial paper will not bar holder in due course status.

3. Read a negotiable instrument carefully before you sign it, as you will probably be bound by its terms although you did not intend that. Not reading a document may create liability to a holder in due course.
4. You cannot have the protection of a holder in due course if you take a negotiable instrument that preserves consumer defenses.

QUESTIONS AND CASE PROBLEMS

1. What social forces are affected by the holder in due course rule?
2. Holton owes Zeigler $100. Holton draws a check on her bank payable to the order of Zeigler for $100 and delivers the check to Zeigler. Holton argues that Zeigler did not give anything in return for the check and therefore has not given value. Is this argument correct?
3. Halleck executed a promissory note payable to the order of Leopold. Halleck did not pay the note when due and Leopold brought suit on the note. Leopold produced the note in court. Halleck admitted that he had signed the note but claimed

that the plaintiff was required to prove that the note had been issued for consideration, and that the plaintiff was in fact the holder. Decide. [*Leopold v Halleck, 106 Ill App 3d, 386, 62 Ill Dec 447, 436 NE2d 29*]
4. Johnson issued an order promissory note to James. However, Johnson did not fill in James's name. Henry knew this but still took the note from James for value, after James inserted his name and indorsed the note. Johnson did not pay on the due date, alleging lack of consideration, which was a fact. Henry brings suit. Will he recover? Why?

5. What is the reasoning behind making universal defenses available against all holders?

6. Compare the rights of (a) an assignee, (b) a holder, (c) a holder in due course, and (d) a holder through a holder in due course, when the defendant is 17 years of age.

7. Jones, wishing to retire from a business enterprise which he had been conducting for a number of years, sold all of the assets of the business to Jackson Corporation. Included among such assets were a number of promissory notes payable to the order of Jones which he had taken from his customers. On the maturity of one of the notes, the maker refused to pay, because there was a failure of consideration. Jackson Corporation sues the maker of the note. Who should succeed? Explain.

8. Elliot, an officer of Impact Marketing, drew six postdated checks on Impact's account. The checks were payable to Bell for legal services to be subsequently performed for Impact. Financial Associates purchased them from Bell. Financial collected on four of the checks. Payment was stopped on the last two when Bell's services were terminated. Financial argues that it was a holder in due course and had the right to collect on the checks. Impact claims that since the checks were postdated and issued for an executory promise, Financial could not be a holder in due course. Who is correct? Why? *[Financial Associates v Impact Marketing, 90 Misc 2d 545, 394 NYS2d 814]*

9. D drew a check to the order of P. It was later claimed that P was not a holder in due course, because the check was postdated and because P knew that D was having financial difficulties and that the particular checking account on which this check was drawn had been frequently overdrawn. Do these circumstances prevent P from being a holder in due course? *[Citizens Bank, Booneville v National Bank of Commerce (CA10 Okla) 334 F2d 257; Franklin National Bank v Sidney Gotowner (NY Sup Ct) 4 UCCRS 953]*

10. H acquired a check by indorsement. At the time that H acquired the check, he knew of all the circumstances surrounding the original issue of the check. If H had known the legal significance of those circumstances, he would have realized that the drawer of the check had a valid defense. Because H did not know the law, he did not realize that the drawer had a defense. He took the check in good faith, believing that everything was proper. In a subsequent lawsuit on the check, the question arose as to whether H was a holder in due course. The defendant claimed that H was not, because H knew of the defense based on the surrounding circumstances, and H's ignorance of the law did not excuse him from the consequence of that knowledge, because ignorance of the law is no excuse. Was H a holder in due course? *[Hartford Life Ins. Co. v Title Guarantee Co., 172 App DC 156, 520 F2d 1170]*

11. A customer of a bank purchased a bank money order and paid for it with a forged check. The money order was negotiable and was acquired by N, who was a holder in due course. When N sued the bank on the money order, the bank raised the defense that its customer had paid with a bad check. Could this defense be raised against N? *[Bank of Niles v American State Bank, 14 Ill App 3d 729, 303 NE2d 186]*

12. Clary received a check from Sanders that was incomplete as to the amount. The check was given as advance payment on the purchase of 100 LT speakers. The amount was left blank, because Clary had the right to substitute other LT speakers if they became available. This substitution would change the price. It was agreed that in no event would the purchase price exceed $5,000. Desperate for cash, Clary wrongfully substituted much more expensive LT speakers, thereby increasing the price to $5,700. Clary then negotiated the check to Lawrence, one of his suppliers. Clary filled in the $5,700 in Lawrence's presence, showing him the shipping order and the invoice applicable to the sale to Sanders. Lawrence accepted the check in payment of $5,000 overdue debts and $700 in cash. Can Lawrence recover the full amount? Why or why not?

13. France fraudulently obtained a negotiable promissory note from Frey by misrepresentation of a material fact. France subsequently negotiated the note to Smith, a holder in due course. David, a business associate of France, was aware of the fraud perpetrated by France. David purchased the note for value from Smith. Upon presentment, Frey defaulted on the note. What are the rights of David? Why?

14. Shade asked Dow to give him a check for $100 in return for Shade's delivery the next day of a television set. Dow gave the check, but Shade never delivered the television set. Does Dow have a defense if sued on the instrument: (a) by Shade; (b) by Shade's brother, to whom Shade gave the unindorsed check as a gift; (c) by a grocer to whom Shade's brother gave the instrument for value in the ordinary course of business the next day (the grocer took the check without knowledge of the defense and while acting in good faith)? Explain your answer.

15. Dorsey was negligent in not determining that the paper he was signing was actually a promissory note. The note was negotiated by proper indorsement and delivery to the New Jersey Mortgage and Investment Co. New Jersey Mortgage and Investment was a holder in due course. Dorsey refused to pay, alleging fraud as to the nature of essential terms. Decide. [*New Jersey Mortgage and Investment Co. v Dorsey, 33 NJ 448, 165 A2d 297*]

CHAPTER 33

LIABILITY AND DISCHARGE OF PARTIES

LEARNING OBJECTIVES

After studying this chapter, you will be able to:

1. *Distinguish between primary parties and secondary parties.*
2. *Explain why presentment for payment and presentment for acceptance are important.*
3. *Explain the importance of giving notice of dishonor and when such notice is excused.*
4. *List and explain the various methods of discharge.*
5. *Distinguish the discharge of individual parties from the discharge of all parties.*

What puts an end to liability on commercial paper?

A. PARTIES TO AN INSTRUMENT

The character of a party determines how the liability of that party is discharged.

1. Primary Parties

Primary parties are the parties required to pay the instruments when they are due. The maker of a promissory note and the drawee-acceptor of a draft are primary parties. An **acceptance** is the drawee's written and signed promise to pay the draft. An acceptance must be written on the draft. It may consist of only the word *accepted* or *certified* and the signature of the acceptor.

The liability of a primary party on an instrument continues for the period of the statute of limitations. The holder does not need to give the primary party any advance notice or demand.

2. Secondary Parties

Secondary parties have conditional liability that may be enforced only if the primary party fails to pay. The drawer of a draft and the unqualified indorser of a draft or a note are secondary parties.

The conditional liability of secondary parties does not arise until three conditions are met—presentment of the instrument for payment or acceptance, dishonor, and notice of dishonor.[1]

3. Parties with No Liability for Payment

Certain parties have no liability for payment of the paper. The holder of the paper cannot obtain payment from such persons, regardless of whether payment is demanded or suit brought on the paper.

(a) QUALIFIED PARTIES. A signer of paper who signs with a qualification of liability is not liable for payment of the paper. Ordinarily, this will be the indorser who signs "without recourse."

(b) NONSIGNING NAMED PARTY. Certain persons will be named in a paper but are not liable for its payment before they have signed it in some manner. Such nonsigners are the drawee who has not accepted a draft or check, the payee who has not indorsed the paper, and an indorsee who has not made a further indorsement of the paper.

(c) NONSIGNING BEARER. A bearer of a negotiable instrument who does not indorse it is not liable for its payment. Assume that a tenant merely signs his paycheck with his name and delivers it to the landlord, who without indorsing it delivers it to the finance company. The landlord was a bearer of the paper but did not indorse the paper and therefore has no personal liability for payment of the paper.

B. PRESENTMENT, DISHONOR, AND NOTICE OF DISHONOR

Presentment, dishonor, and notice of dishonor are conditions precedent to the liability of secondary parties.

4. Presentment

Presentment is a demand on a drawee for acceptance or a demand on a maker, acceptor, or indorser for payment.[2] Failure to make presentment when the paper is due will discharge all secondary parties, but not primary parties.

---

[1] Binford v Lichtenberger Estate, 62 Or App 439, 660 P2d 1077 (1983).

[2] UCC § 3-504(1) [1952]; UCC § 3-501(a) [1990].

Figure 33-1 Liabilities of Parties for Payment

Party	Primary Liability	Secondary Liability	No Liability
Acceptor	X		
Drawee			X
Drawer		X	
Guarantor of payment	X		
Maker of note	X		
Unqualified indorser		X	
Qualified signer			X
Non-signing party			X
Non-signing bearer			X

(a) HOW PRESENTMENT IS MADE. Presentment must be made by or on behalf of the holder to the party who is primarily liable. Presentment must occur at the place specified in the instrument. The presentment must be made at a reasonable time and, if made at a bank, must be made during its banking day. It is not necessary that there be actual physical presentation of the paper, although the person to whom presentment is made usually will ask that the instrument be shown. Once the paper is paid, the holder must surrender the instrument.

1952 UCC

*****

1990 UCC

It may be agreed that an electronic presentment must be made on a bank. This may be either an electronic transmission of an image of the instrument or of information relating to the terms of the instrument. When there is an agreement that presentment may be made in this manner, an instrument is deemed presented when the electronic communication is received by the bank.[3]

(b) WHEN PRESENTMENT IS EXCUSED OR UNNECESSARY. Presentment for payment may not be made for various reasons. It will be excused or unnecessary (1) if presentment has been waived by the party being charged, (2) if presentment cannot be made in spite of due diligence, (3) if the primary party has died, or (4) if the secondary party has no reason to expect that the instrument will be paid.

5. Dishonor

Dishonor occurs when an instrument has been duly presented for acceptance or payment, but acceptance or payment cannot be obtained or is refused.

---

3 UCC § 4-110 [1990].

6. Notice of Dishonor

If commercial paper is dishonored, any secondary party who is not given proper notice of the dishonor is released from liability, unless the giving of notice is excused.

It was a failure to give proper notice of dishonor that caused problems for the holder in the *Hane* case.

HANE v EXTEN
255 Md 668, 259 A2d 290 (1969)

> Theta Electronic Laboratories executed a promissory note payable to Thomson and his wife. The note was indorsed by Gerald Exten, Emil O'Neil, and James Hane, and their wives. The Thomsons assigned the note to John Hane. The note was not paid when due. John Hane took judgment by confession against the maker and the Extens. Upon learning of the judgment, the Extens moved that the judgment be vacated as to them, and their motion was granted. John Hane appealed.

SINGLEY, J. . . . John B. Hane is the assignee of the note of Theta Electronic Laboratories, Inc. (Theta) in the stated amount of $15,377.07. . . . [The note provided] that "In the event of the failure to pay the interest or principal, as the same becomes due on this Note, the entire debt represented hereby shall at the end of thirty (30) days become due and demandable. . . ." The note was assigned without recourse to Hane by George B. and Marguerite F. Thomson, the original payees, on 26 November 1965. A default having occurred in the making of the monthly payments, Hane took judgments by confession in the Circuit Court for Montgomery County on 7 June 1967 against Theta and three individuals, Gerald M. Exten, Emil L. O'Neil, and James W. Hane, and their wives, who had indorsed Theta's note. On motion of the Extens, the judgment was vacated as to them. . . . From a judgment for the Extens, Hane has appealed.

This case raises the familiar question: Must Hane show that the Extens were given notice of presentment and dishonor before he can hold them on their indorsement?

The court below, in finding for the Extens, relied on the provisions of Uniform Commercial Code. . . . Section 3-414(1) provides:

Unless the indorsement otherwise specifies (as by such words as "without recourse") every indorser engages that upon dishonor and any necessary notice of dishonor and protest he will pay the instrument according to its tenor at the time of his indorsement to the holder or to any subsequent indorser who takes it up, even though the indorser who takes it up was not obligated to do so.

Section 3-501(1)(b) provides that "Presentment for payment is necessary to charge any indorser" and § 3-501(2)(a) that "Notice of any dishonor is necessary to charge any indorser," in each case subject, however, to the provisions of § 3-511 which recite the circumstances under which notice of dishonor may be waived or excused, none of which is here present. Section 3-502(1)(a) makes it clear that unless presentment or notice of dishonor is waived or excused, unreasonable delay will discharge an indorser.

There was testimony from which the trier of facts could find as he did that presentment and notice of dishonor were unduly delayed.

It is clear that Hane held the note from November 1965, until some time in April, 1967, before he made demand for payment. UCC § 3-503(1)(d) provides that "Where an instrument is accelerated, presentment for payment is due within a reasonable time after the acceleration." "Reasonable time" is not defined in § 3-503, except that § 3-503(2) provides, "A reasonable time for presentment is determined by the nature of the instrument, any usage of banking or trade, and the facts of the particular case." But § 1-204(2) characterizes it: "What is a reasonable time for taking any action depends on the nature, purpose, and circumstances of such action."

Reasonableness is primarily a question for the fact finder . . . 1 Anderson's Uniform Commercial Code, Commentary, § 1-204:3. . . . We see no reason to disturb the lower court's finding that Hane's delay of almost 18 months in presenting the note "was unreasonable from any viewpoint." . . .

As regards notice of dishonor, § 3-508(2) requires that notice be given by persons other than banks "before midnight of the third business day after dishonor or receipt of notice of dishonor." Exten, called as an adverse witness by Hane, testified that his first notice that the note had not been paid was the entry of the confessed judgment on 7 June 1967. Hane's brother testified that demand had been made about 15 April 1967. He was uncertain as to when he had given Exten notice of dishonor, but finally conceded that it was "within a week." The lower court found that the ambiguity of this testimony, coupled with Exten's denial that he had received *any* notice before 7 June fell short of meeting the three-day notice requirement of the UCC. The date of giving notice of dishonor is a question of fact, solely for determination by the trier of facts. . . . We cannot say that the court erred in its finding.

In the absence of evidence that presentment and notice of dishonor were waived or excused, Hane's unreasonable delay discharged the Extens, § 3-502(1)(a). . . .

[Judgment affirmed]

QUESTIONS

1. Within what time must notice of dishonor be given?
2. Within what time must a holder in due course give notice of dishonor?

(a) HOW NOTICE IS GIVEN. Notice is ordinarily given by the holder who has been refused payment. Notice may be given in any reasonable manner, oral or written. It may have any terms, as long as it identifies the instrument and states that it has been dishonored. Any necessary notice must be given by a bank before midnight of the next banking day following the banking day on which the bank receives the instrument or notice. By a non-bank, notice must be given before midnight of the third full business day following the dishonor or receipt of notice of dishonor. Written notice is effective when sent, even if it is not received.

In the *Greer* case a bank claimed that it had acted promptly in giving notice.

Written notice is effective when sent. It makes no difference when it is received. It is still effective although not received.

GREER v WHITE OAK STATE BANK
(Tex App) 673 SW2d 326 (1984)

Jack Greer and Donald Biesel owned a bowling alley. George Ford and Bowling and Billiard Supply of Dallas (B & B) had outstanding liens on the alley. Greer, Biesel, Ford, and B & B were named as beneficiaries of an insurance policy on the bowling alley. The bowling complex burned, and a check from the insurance company was issued to Greer, Biesel, Ford, and B & B. All the parties indorsed the check. The insurance check was deposited in Greer's account at the White Oak State Bank. Greer then issued checks drawn on that account to Ford and B & B in payment of their claims. The insurance company was insolvent; therefore, the drawee bank dishonored the insurance check on August 3, 1981, and notified the White Oak Bank that same day by telephone. The oral notification was followed by written notice of dishonor, which was received by the White Oak Bank ten days later, on August 13, 1981. White Oak then notified the indorsers of the dishonor on August 14, 1981. White Oak brought suit against the indorsers on the dishonored check. They denied liability because of White Oak's failure to notify them promptly of the dishonor. From a judgment in favor of White Oak, the indorsers appealed.

CORNELIUS, C. J. . . . [UCC §§ 3-501, 3-503, and 3-502], respectively, provide that unless excused, notice of dishonor is necessary to charge any indorser of an item; notice must be given by a bank before its midnight deadline (the next banking day after the banking day it received the item); and that any unexcused delay in giving notice of dishonor discharges any indorser. The bank argues that these code provisions do not apply to Greer, Ford and B & B because (1) oral notice of dishonor is not effective and the indorsers were promptly notified after the bank received written notice of the check's dishonor on August 14, 1981, and (2) the telephone notice from the bank in Dallas did not specify that Ford and B & B were indorsers, so in any event it did not receive notice of dishonor *as to them* until August 13, 1981. We cannot agree with either of these propositions.

Section 3-508 expressly provides that notice of dishonor may be oral. The bank contends that Section 4-202(1)(b) supersedes Section 3-508 with respect to notice from a collecting bank, and because that section refers to "sending" notice of dishonor, only a written notice is contemplated. We disagree. The adequacy of oral notice is confirmed by Section 4-104(3) which specifically makes the notice of dishonor provisions of Section 3-508 applicable to transactions under Article 4. Moreover, the jury found upon sufficient evidence that White Oak State Bank and the First National Bank in Dallas had agreed prior to August 3, 1981, that notice of returned items could be sent by telephone. The requirements of Article 4 may be modified by agreement.

The failure of the telephone notice to name Ford and B & B as indorsers did not render the notice ineffective as to them. Section 3-502(1)(a) provides that if notice of dishonor is not given when due, *any* indorser is discharged. Delay in giving notice may be excused when a party does not know it is due or when the delay is caused by circumstances beyond his control. But there was no jury finding here that any circumstance existed which would excuse the Bank from notifying Ford and B & B.

In fact, the employee who received the telephone notice testified that the information she received was sufficient to enable her to identify the check and all parties to it.

As indicated, Greer, Ford and B & B were all discharged, *as indorsers*, from any obligation on the check. . . .

[Judgment reversed]

QUESTIONS

1. What was the argument of White Oak Bank?
2. Why is it important for indorsers to receive timely notice of dishonor?
3. State the decision of the court and the basis for the decision.

(b) EXCUSE FOR DELAY OR ABSENCE OF NOTICE OF DISHONOR. Delay in giving notice of dishonor is excused under the same circumstances as those that excuse presentment for payment. These include (1) waiver, (2) inability to give notice in spite of due diligence, and (3) the fact that the party to be notified did not have any reason to believe that the instrument would be paid.
1952 UCC

(c) EXCUSE FOR DELAY OF BANK.
*****
1990 UCC

(c) EXCUSE FOR DELAY OF BANK. T h e delay of a bank is excused when caused by computer or equipment failure.

A payor bank is excused in making a delayed return of an item if there has been a breach of a presentment warranty or if fraud has been practiced on the payor bank.

A branch or separate office of a bank is a "separate bank" for the purpose of time limitations established by the 1990 version of Article 4, without regard to whether deposit ledgers are maintained there.[4]

C. DISCHARGE FROM LIABILITY

A party may be discharged individually or by some act that discharges all parties to the paper at one time.

7. Discharge of Individual Parties

A party to a commercial paper is discharged from liability when payment is made to the proper person. The discharge from liability may also be effected in a number of other ways.

(a) THE LAW OF CONTRACTS. Commercial paper may be discharged in the same manner as an ordinary contract for the payment of money. Accordingly, there may be a discharge by accord and satisfaction, by a novation, or by operation of law, such as a discharge in bankruptcy and the operation of the statute of limitations.[5]

(b) PAYMENT. The obligation of a particular party on commercial paper is discharged by payment of the amount of the instrument to the holder or to the holder's authorized agent.[6]

---

[4] UCC § 4-107 [1990].
[5] Duke v Young (Ala) 496 So 2d 37 (1986).
[6] UCC § 3-603(1) [1952]; UCC § 3-602(a),(b) [1990].

(c) CANCELLATION AND RENUNCIATION. The party entitled to enforce the instrument discharges any party to it by a writing stating that the party will not be sued or that all rights against that party are renounced. No consideration is required for this agreement. A party is also discharged if the person entitled to enforce the instrument surrenders it to that party. A person entitled to enforce an instrument may cancel the instrument or a party's liability on the instrument by intentionally crossing out words or signatures on the instrument. In such a case, it is immaterial that the original signatures or terms can still be seen.

There is no discharge if the cancellation was the result of fraud, accident, or mistake.

Does a bank's clerical error discharge a note? This was the problem in the *FirsTier* case.

FIRSTIER BANK, N.A. v TRIPLETT

242 Neb 614, 497 NW2d 339 (1993)

> The Tripletts were indebted on two promissory notes to FirsTier bank. The notes were secured by cars owned by the Tripletts. Upon selling one of the cars they tendered a check to FirsTier for a payment on the notes. At the time of tender, substantial payments were owed on both notes. Subsequently, the Tripletts received a letter from FirsTier containing an original Note and Security agreement stamped PAID. The stamp was signed by a clerk and hand dated. Some time thereafter, the other note was returned to the Tripletts. It was also stamped PAID but was signed by another clerk. More than a year after receiving the last note, FirsTier notified the Tripletts they still owed money on one of the notes and demanded payment. The Tripletts claimed the loan was paidup. FirsTier claimed that a clerk pulled the wrong file and marked the first note paid and had no authority to release a note which had not been paid in full. It was only the bank's collection department that could authorize the release of an unpaid note and it had never received authorization to release the note. The Tripletts did not dispute that money was still owed on the note but claimed that the bank had intentionally canceled the note and that such a cancellation is irrevocable. From a judgment in favor of the bank, the Tripletts appealed.

FAHRNBRUCH, J. . . . Discharge by cancellation or renunciation is governed by Neb. UCC § 3-604 . . . Section 3-604(a) provides that "[a] person entitled to enforce an instrument . . . may discharge the obligation of a party to pay the instrument (i) by an *intentional* voluntary act, such as *surrender* of the instrument to the party . . . or *cancellation* of the instrument. . . ." (Emphasis supplied.) This language requires that discharge be intentional, whether by cancellation or surrender.

All jurisdictions that have considered the issue have concluded that clerical error does not have the legal effect of canceling an existing debt or discharging an instrument. . . . This is simply an application of the general rule that cancellation or surrender of an instrument has no effect when done by a person without authority from the holder of the instrument. . . . A bank may recover even when its agents or officers have acted negligently, to prevent the maker of a note from retaining a gratuitous benefit to which he or she is not entitled. . . .

Therefore, the issue before the court is whether FirsTier possessed the requisite intent to discharge the Tripletts' indebtedness . . . by either cancellation or surrender of the note. Intent is a question of fact. . . .

Two of FirsTier's vice presidents testified that FirsTier had no intention to discharge . . . without payment in full, that no one with authority to discharge . . . had done so, and that the cancellation and surrender of the note was done through clerical error. The Tripletts offered no evidence to refute this testimony.

. . . We hold that the unintentional cancellation and surrender of a promissory note through clerical error do not discharge the maker of the note. . . .

[Judgment affirmed]

QUESTIONS

1. Was there an intentional cancellation of the note?
2. Did the Tripletts act ethically in claiming that the note was canceled?
3. Should banks prevail in cases like this?

(d) IMPAIRMENT OF RIGHT OF RECOURSE OR OF COLLATERAL. A holder may, in some cases, extend the time of payment, release the principal debtor, or impair collateral security furnished as security for the payment of the instrument. Such actions discharge any party whose rights are affected by such impairment and who did not consent to those actions.[7]

1952 UCC

*****

1990 UCC

Impairment of collateral may consist of a failure to file or record an interest in the collateral. Impairment of collateral may also include a release of, a failure to preserve the value of, or an improper disposition of the collateral.

(e) ALTERATION. When an instrument is altered, any party whose obligation is changed thereby is discharged. Exceptions exist if such a party has assented to the alteration or is barred by conduct from asserting a discharge.

8. Discharge of All Parties

The primary party on an instrument—that is, the maker of a note or the acceptor of a draft—has no right of recourse against any party to the paper. Conversely, every other party who may be liable on the paper has a right of recourse against the party primarily liable. If the holder discharges a party who is primarily liable, all parties to the instrument are discharged.[8]

No discharge is effective against a holder in due course, unless such a holder has notice of the discharge when taking the instrument.[9]

---

[7] Valley Bank & Trust v Rite Way Concrete (Utah App) 742 P2d 105 (1987).

[8] Heintz v Woodson (Mo App) 714 SW2d 782 (1986).

[9] UCC § 3-602. [1952]; UCC § 3-601(b) [1990].

SUMMARY

The maker of a promissory note and the acceptor of a draft are primarily liable for paying the face of the instrument. Payment may be demanded from the maker or acceptor as soon as the paper is due.

Secondary parties are required to pay the paper if the primary party failed to do so after proper presentment and if proper notice of default was given to the secondary party.

Presentment and notice of dishonor may be excused under certain circumstances.

Dishonor occurs when an instrument has been properly presented for acceptance or payment but such acceptance or payment cannot be obtained or is refused. After giving proper notice to the secondary parties of such refusal or inability to obtain acceptance or payment, the holder has an immediate right of recourse against them. Any secondary party not given proper notice will be discharged from liability on the instrument. Notice of dishonor is excused under the same circum-

stances as those that excuse presentment for payment. Notice may be given in any reasonable manner. Notice may be oral or written, and it must be given (if the holder is not a bank) before midnight of the third full business day after dishonor.

A party may be discharged individually or by some act that has discharged all parties to the paper at one time. There may be a discharge by accord and satisfaction, novation, or operation of law. There may be a discharge by payment of the instrument to the holder or the holder's authorized agent, by cancellation, renunciation, impairment of right of recourse or of collateral, or by an alteration.

A discharge of the party primarily liable discharges all persons who had a right of recourse against the primary party. No discharge is effective against a holder in due course, unless such holder has notice of the discharge when taking the instrument.

LAW IN PRACTICE

1. Make presentment to the primary party on the due date, or you will release secondary parties.
2. Always give proper notice of dishonor to secondary parties, because any such party not properly notified will be released from liability unless notice is excused.

3. If an instrument is canceled because of fraud, accident, or mistake, the paper is not discharged.
4. Remember that a holder in due course may not be subject to a discharge of the paper, unless he or she was aware of the discharge when taking the paper.

QUESTIONS AND CASE PROBLEMS

1. What social forces are affected by the rule that giving notice of dishonor to a secondary party before midnight of the third business day following dishonor is sufficient?
2. Ragno borrows money from the Main Street Bank and gives a promissory note for the amount of the loan. The note is due in 60 days. Main Street indorses and delivers the note to the Third National Bank. Ragno fails to pay the note when it is due. A month after it is due, the Third National Bank sues the Main Street Bank for the amount of the note. Is it liable?
3. Henri draws a draft on Marchamp, directing Marchamp to pay $1,000 on demand to the order

of Jacqueline. Marchamp is indebted to Henri for $10,000. When Jacqueline presents the draft of Henri, Marchamp refuses to make any payments to Jacqueline. She sues Marchamp. Can she recover?
4. Discuss the need for presentment of the instrument for payment with respect to (a) the maker of a note payable at a definite time, (b) an acceptor of a draft payable at a definite time, and (c) an unqualified indorser of such a note or draft.
5. Lionel executed a negotiable promissory note for $5,000 to the order of Danielle. Prior to the due date, Danielle gave Lionel a signed writing whereby she renounced all her rights against

Lionel on the note. Danielle subsequently negotiated the note before maturity to Richards, a holder in due course. When the note became due, Richards presented the note to Lionel for payment. Lionel contended that he had been discharged by a renunciation. Decide.

6.   Four promissory notes were executed by Continental Diamond Mines, Inc., payable to the order of M. Kopp. The notes were thereafter indorsed to M. Kopp, Inc., and then to Rafkin. Rafkin was the holder on the due date. Was it necessary for him to make a presentment of the notes to Continental Diamond Mines in order to hold it liable on the notes? [*Rafkin v Continental Diamond Mines, Inc. 33 Misc 2d 156, 228 NYS2d 317*]

7.   *A* indorsed a promissory note on the back. At the top of the back, above all indorsements, the words "Notice of protest waived" were printed. The note was not paid when due. The holder sent *A* notice that the note was not paid, but *A* did not receive the notice because it was sent to a former address at which he no longer lived. *A* denied liability since he had not been properly notified. Decide. [*Lizza Asphalt Construction Co. v Greenvale Construction Co. (NY Sup Ct) 4 UCCRS 954*]

8.   Mellen-Wright Lumber Co., the holder of a note, sued McNett, as maker, and Kendall, as indorser. The latter claimed that he had not received notice of the dishonor of the note by the maker. The holder proved that he had sent the following letter, dated June 10, to Kendall.

Dear Sir: We hold note for $2,000 with interest at 7 percent signed by Earl P. McNett and Anna J. McNett, his wife, on which you indorsed guaranteeing payment.

This note will be due June 12 and we are going to ask that you arrange to pay same promptly. We would appreciate this being paid by not later than Friday, June 18.

Kindly advise if you wish to make payment at our office or at one of our local banks.

We are enclosing a stamped self-addressed envelope for reply.

Was Kendall liable? [*Mellen-Wright Lumber Co. v McNett, 242 Mich 369, 218 NW 709*]

9.   An examination of Hugh's books shows a past due note of $100,000 made by Warner an indorsed by Carey. Warner is bankrupt, but Carey is very wealthy. How much is the note worth? Explain.

10.   As part of a business plan, Schwald executed and delivered a note to Montgomery. The parties then made a new business arrangement, and Montgomery intentionally tore up the note and threw it into the wastebasket. It was subsequently contended that this note had been canceled. Do you agree? [*Montgomery v Schwald, 117 Mo App 75, 166 SW 831*]

11.   Gorman executed and delivered to the First National Bank a negotiable promissory note payable to its order. The note was stolen from the bank. Some time later, Richardson, a former employee of the bank, delivered the note to Gorman in return for Gorman's payment of the balance then due. The note was returned to Gorman, marked "paid." First National Bank sued Gorman for the balance of the loan. He raised the defense that the note had been discharged by payment. Decide. [*First National Bank v Gorman, 45 Wyo 519, 21 P2d 549*]

12.   Paul Heyman indorsed a note executed by his son as maker. His son defaulted on the note. When Heyman was sued as indorser, he claimed that he was discharged, since the note had not been properly presented for payment to his son. The holder replied that the son had disappeared and, after reasonable diligence, such a presentment could not be made and was therefore excused. Decide. [*Gaffin v Heyman (RI) 428 A2d 1066*]

13.   The Citizens State Bank issued a cashier's check payable to the order of Donovan. He indorsed it to Denny, who did business as the Houston Aircraft Co., and included in the indorsement a recital that it was "in full satisfaction of any and all claims of any character whatever." Denny crossed out this quoted phrase and wrote Donovan and the bank that he had done so. The Houston Aircraft Co. sued the Citizens National Bank on the check. Was the bank liable? [*Houston Aircraft v Citizens State Bank (Tex Civ App) 184 SW2d 335*]

14.   The holder of a note failed to present it to the maker for payment. The maker proves that he had the money ready for payment on the due date. Since that time, however, he has had some disastrous business losses. He now contends that he need not pay. Is the maker liable? Why?

15.   First Properties, Inc. issued a promissory note to the order of Fletcher. Fletcher indorsed the note to Dannon, who in turn took the note to his bank for collection. The teller at the bank mistakenly stamped the note "paid," although payment had not yet been received. Dannon had no knowledge that the note was so stamped. The creditors of First Properties, Inc. argued that the note had been canceled. Decide.

CHAPTER 34

CHECKS AND FUNDS TRANSFERS

LEARNING OBJECTIVES

After studying this chapter, you will be able to:
1. *Discuss the significance of certification.*
2. *List and explain the duties of the drawee bank.*
3. *Set forth the methods for and legal effect of stopping payment.*
4. *State when a check must be presented for payment in order to charge secondary parties.*
5. *Describe the liability of a bank for improper payment and collection.*
6. *Discuss the legal effect of forgeries and material alterations.*
7. *Specify the time limitations for reporting forgeries and alterations.*
8. *Describe the wire transfer of funds.*

What do banks have to do with commercial paper? With the transfer of funds?

A. CHECKS

Checks are used to transmit money and pay debts.

1. Nature of a Check

A check is a particular kind of draft. The first three of the following features of a check distinguish it from other drafts or bills of exchange.[1]

(a) DRAWEE. The drawee of a check is always a bank.

(b) SUFFICIENT FUNDS ON DEPOSIT. As a practical matter, the check is drawn on the assumption that the bank has on deposit in the drawer's account an amount sufficient to pay the check. In the case of other drafts, there is no assumption that the drawee has any of the drawer's money with which to pay the instrument.

If a draft is dishonored, the drawer is civilly liable. If a check is drawn with intent to defraud the person to whom it is delivered, the drawer is also subject to criminal prosecution in most states. The laws under which such drawers are prosecuted are known as bad check laws. Most states provide that if the check is not made good within a stated period, such as ten days, it will be presumed that the drawer originally issued the check with the intent to defraud.

(c) DEMAND PAPER. A check is demand paper. A draft may be payable either on demand or at a future date. The standard form of check does not specify when it is payable, and it is therefore automatically payable on demand.

One exception arises when a check is postdated—that is, when the check shows a date later than the actual date of execution. Here the check is not payable until the date arrives.[2] This, in effect, changes the check from demand paper to time paper without expressly stating so.

A check may be any writing.[3] A card, given to a computer terminal located away from a bank for the purpose of withdrawing money from the bank or making a repayment on a loan, is also a check.[4]

(d) DELIVERY NOT ASSIGNMENT. The delivery of a check is not an assignment of the money on deposit. Therefore, it does not automatically transfer the rights of the depositor against the bank to the holder of the check. There is no duty on the part of the drawee bank to the holder to pay the holder the amount of the check.[5]

1952 UCC
*****
1990 UCC

A check may be either the ordinary check, a cashier's check, or a teller's check. The name on the paper is not controlling. A bank "money order" payable to John Jones is a check and is negotiable.[6] A cashier's check is a check or draft drawn by a bank upon itself. If drawn on

---

[1] Checks are governed by both Article 3 of the UCC relating to commercial paper and Article 4 governing bank deposits and collections.

[2] Howells, Inc. v Nelson (Utah) 565 P2d 1147 (1977).

[3] The printed bank check is preferable, because it generally carries magnetic ink figures that facilitate sorting and posting.

[4] Illinois v Continental Illinois National Bank (CA7 Ill) 536 F2d 176 (1976).

[5] Galaxy Boat Mfg. Co. v East End State Bank (Tex App) 641 SW2d 594 (1982).

[6] UCC § 3-104(f) [1990].

Figure 34-1   Differences Between a Check and a Draft

Check	Draft
1. Drawee is always a bank	1. Drawee is not necessarily a bank
2. Check is drawn on assumption money in bank to cover check	2. No assumption drawee has any of drawer's money to pay instrument
3. Check is payable on demand (unless postdated)	3. Draft may be payable on demand or at future date

another bank in which the drawer bank has an account, it is a teller's check. Although the drawer and drawee are the same on a cashier's check, the holder must treat it as a check, not a note. Unless otherwise agreed, the delivery of a certified check, a cashier's check, or a teller's check discharges the debt for which it is given up to the amount of the check.

2. Certified Checks

The drawee bank may certify or accept a check drawn on it. The certification must be written on the check and signed by an authorized representative of the bank.

    When a bank certifies a check, the bank will set aside in a special account maintained by the bank as much of the depositor's account as is needed to pay the certified check. With respect to the holder of the check, the certification is an undertaking by the bank that when the check is presented for payment, the bank will make payment according to the terms of the check. Payment is without regard to the status of the depositor's account at that time.

    A holder or drawer may request that check be certified by a bank. When certification is at the request of the holder, all prior indorsers and the drawer are released from liability. When certification is at the request of the drawer, secondary parties are not released.

3. Liability of Drawer

If the check is presented to the drawee bank for payment and paid, the drawer has no liability.

    (a) DISHONOR. If the bank refuses to make payment, the drawer is then subject to the same liability as in the case of the nonpayment of an ordinary draft. If proper notice of dishonor is not given the drawer of the check, the drawer will be discharged from liability to the same extent as the drawer of an ordinary draft.[7]

    (b) OVERDRAFT. If the bank pays the check but the account is not sufficient to cover the amount, the excess of the payment over the amount on deposit is an overdraft. This is treated as a loan from the bank to the customer, and the customer must repay that amount to the bank.

1952 UCC

    (1) Nonsigning Account Owner.

*****

1990 UCC

    (1) Nonsigning Account Owner. If the account is the account of two or more persons, a person who does not sign the check that creates an overdraft is not liable for the amount of the overdraft if such person did not receive benefit from the proceeds of that check.[8]

---

[7] Under Federal Reserve regulations, notice of dishonor may be given by telephone. Security Bank and Trust Co. v Federal Nat. Bank (Okla App) 554 P2d 119 (1976).

[8] UCC § 4-401(b) [1990].

4. The Depositor-Bank Relationship

The depositor-bank relationship imposes duties on the bank.

(a) PRIVACY. The bank owes the depositor the duty of maintaining secrecy concerning information that the bank acquires in connection with the depositor-bank relationship. Law enforcement officers and administrative agencies cannot require the disclosure of information relating to a depositor's account without obtaining the depositor's consent or a search warrant, or following the statutory procedures designed to protect depositors from unreasonable invasions of privacy.[9]

(b) PAYMENT. A bank is under a general contractual duty to its depositor to pay on demand all checks to the extent of the funds in the depositor's account.

(1) Stale Checks. A bank acting in good faith may pay a check presented more than six months after its date (commonly known as a stale check), but unless the check is certified, the bank is not required to do so. The fact that a bank may refuse to pay a check that is more than six months old does not mean that it must pay a check that is less than six months old or that it is not required to exercise reasonable care in making payment of any check.

(2) Payment After Depositor's Death. Subject to certain exceptions, the authority of a bank to act with respect to its depositor's check terminates with the death of the depositor. As an exception to this general rule, the drawee bank's power continues for some time after the death of the depositor. For the first ten days after the depositor's death, the bank may continue to pay or certify checks of the depositor even though it knows of the depositor's death, unless ordered to stop payment by a person claiming an interest in the account.[10] If the bank does not initially know of the death of the drawer, its power to pay and certify checks of the depositor continues for ten days after it has actually been notified of the death.

5. Stopping Payment of Check

The drawer may stop payment of a check by notifying the drawee bank not to pay it when it is presented for payment. This procedure is useful when a check is lost or mislaid. A duplicate check can be written, and, to make sure that the payee does not receive payment twice or that an improper person does not receive payment on the first check, payment on the first check can be stopped. Likewise, if payment is made by check and then the payee defaults on the contract, so that the drawer would have a claim for breach of contract, payment on the check can be stopped, provided the check has not been paid.

The drawer cannot stop payment of a certified check. A bank customer cannot stop payment of a cashier's check.

The *First Financial* case involved the question of whether payment could be stopped on a cashier's check.

FIRST FINANCIAL BANK v FIRST AMERICAN BANK
(La App) 489 So 2d 388 (1986)

First Financial filed suit against First American Bank, seeking payment of a cashier's check issued by First American to First Financial in the amount of

---

9 Right to Financial Privacy Act of 1978, PL 95-630, 92 Stat 3697, 12 USC § 3401 et seq.

10 UCC § 4-405 [1952], 4-405 [1990], Hieber v Uptown Nat'l Bank of Chicago, 199 Ill App 3d 542, 557 NE2d 408 (1990).

eighteen hundred dollars ($1,800). First American had issued its cashier's check in exchange for a personal check on which a stop payment order had been issued. From a judgment in favor of First Financial, First American appealed.

WICKER, J. . . . On Friday, May 3, 1985, Mrs. Tommy Marzoni, a customer of First American, deposited a personal check in the amount of Eighteen Hundred Dollars ($1,800.00) into First Financial. The check was drawn on her account at First American. On that same date, she spoke to Cindy Pilgram, an employee at First American, and informed her that she wished to stop payment on her personal check. She was informed, however, that she would have to place her request in writing. Consequently, she appeared at First American on Monday, May 6, 1985 at 9:00 A.M. to institute the stop payment order. On that same date, subsequent to her written request, but prior to the time at which all window tellers could be informed of the order, one of First Financial's employees appeared at First American and presented the personal check to Gloria Detillier, a cashier at First American, and requested a cashier's check in exchange. Such a check in the amount of Eighteen Hundred Dollars ($1,800.00) was issued by First American in exchange for Mrs. Marzoni's personal check.

Shortly thereafter, the employees of First American learned of the stop payment order on the personal check and immediately notified First Financial that the bank would not honor the cashier's check. On Tuesday, May 7, 1985, First American issued a stop payment order on its cashier's check. Prior to that order reaching First Financial, it credited the amount to pay off a loan in the name of Mr. Tommy Marzoni and to credit the account of Mrs. Marzoni with the remaining funds. The amount so credited to the account was subsequently withdrawn prior to the stop payment order on the cashier's check reaching First Financial. . . .

This appeal presents questions of . . . whether a bank can stop payment on its cashier's check and whether it can assert a defense of failure of consideration in that payment on the personal check accepted in exchange for the cashier's check had been stopped. . . .

Louisiana's version of Articles 1, 3, 4 and 5 of the Uniform Commercial Code (U.C.C.) and Articles 7 and 8 is contained in L.S.A..S. 10:1-101 et seq. Our version is similar to that of the U.C.C. in that it also has only one reference to cashier's checks. L.S.A.-R.S. 10:4-211 provides . . . :

(1) A collecting bank may take in settlement of an item . . .

(b) a cashier's check or similar primary obligation of a remitting bank which is a member of or clears through a member of the same clearing house or group as the collecting bank. . . .

The majority of jurisdictions define a cashier's check as a substitute for cash.

Most of the courts which follow the majority view disallow defenses on the part of the issuing bank.

New York courts in particular have favored a rule which opposes the stopping of payment of a cashier's check. In *Kaufman [v Chase Manhattan Bank*, 370 F Supp 276 (SDNY 1973)] the court summarized New York law as having accorded a special status to a cashier's check as follows:

An ordinary check is an order by one party (drawer) directing a second party (drawee) to pay, on demand, a fixed sum of money to a third party (payee). The drawer is primarily liable to the payee for the amount of the check until that check has been accepted by the drawee. Payment on the check may be stopped by the drawer only if the drawee receives notice prior to acceptance. . . .

A cashier's check, however, is a check drawn by the bank upon itself, payable to another person, and issued by an authorized officer of the bank. The bank, therefore, becomes both the drawer and drawee; and the check becomes a promise by the bank to draw the amount of the check from its own resources and to pay the check upon demand. Thus, the issuance of the cashier's check constitutes an acceptance by the issuing bank; and the cashier's check becomes the primary obligation of the bank. . . .

. . . The *Kaufman* court looked to the public policy regarding the nature and usage of cashier's checks in the commercial world and the fact that such a policy would favor a rule which prohibits the stop payment of a cashier's check.

The rationale behind an approach which treats cashier's checks as cash equivalents is explained in the leading case of *National Newark & Essex Bank [v Giordano*, III NJ Super 347, 268 A2d 327 (1970)] as follows:

a cashier's check circulates in the commercial world as the equivalent of cash. . . . People accept a cashier's check as a substitute for cash because the bank stands behind it, rather than an individual. In effect the bank becomes a guarantor of the value of the check and pledges its resources to the payment of the amount represented upon presentation. To allow the bank to stop payment on such an instrument would be inconsistent with the representation it makes in issuing the check. Such a rule would undermine the public confidence in the bank and its checks and thereby deprive the cashier's check of the essential incident which makes it useful. People would no longer be willing to accept it as a substitute for cash if they could not be sure that there would be no difficulty in converting it into cash. . . .

In contrast, a minority of the jurisdictions look to the status of the instrument and view the cashier's check as a negotiable instrument. Of this minority, most of these courts view it as a bank draft, the others view it as a negotiable promissory note.

These courts, however, do recognize the validity of certain defenses to payment. In the instant case, appellant raises the defense of lack of consideration. It contends that since it issued a cashier's check for a personal check which it subsequently learned had a stop payment order, it received no consideration and thus can assert this defense. It relies on the legal analysis which treats the cashier's check as a negotiable instrument subject to the defenses relative to a holder or a holder in due course.

We adhere to the majority view that a cashier's check is a substitute for cash or a cash equivalent. Moreover, we adopt the analysis used by several courts of applying U.C.C. Section 4-303(1)(a) to prohibit a bank from asserting a defense to payment of a cashier's check.

In *Kaufman, supra*, the court held that:

Since a cashier's check is a bank's primary obligation, a cashier's check is presumed to have been issued for value. This presumption cannot be overcome by evidence that the bank did not receive consideration for the cashier's check from the payee. Such proof is irrelevant and provides no defense.

By its act of issuing the cashier's check, the bank undertakes a primary obligation to pay the amount when presented. In particular, it undertakes the obligation to pay the amount from its own resources.

The applicable section in our statute is L.S.A.-R.S. 10:4-303(1)(a) which provides that:

(1) Any knowledge, notice or stop order received by, legal process served upon or setoff exercised by a payor bank, whether or not effective under other rules of law to terminate, suspend or modify the bank's right or duty to pay an item or to charge its customer's account for the item, comes too late to so terminate, suspend or modify such right or duty if the knowledge, notice, stop order or legal process is received or served and a reasonable time for the bank to act thereon expires or the setoff is exercised after the bank has done any of the following:

(a) accepted or certified the item. . . .

Accordingly, since L.S.A.-R.S. 10:4-303(1)(a) disallows stop payment orders on accepted items, the bank cannot issue a stop payment order on its cashier's check. . . . We hold that a cashier's check is a cash equivalent and therefore a bank is prohibited from issuing a stop payment order on its own cashier's check for failure of consideration.

[Judgment affirmed]

QUESTIONS

1. What is a cashier's check?
2. What was the argument of the appellant, First American?
3. What reason did the court give for its decision?

(a) FORM OF STOP PAYMENT ORDER. The stop payment order may be either oral or written. If oral, however, it is only binding on the bank for 14 calendar days unless confirmed in writing within that time. A written stop payment order or confirmation is effective for six months.

(b) LIABILITY TO HOLDER FOR STOPPING PAYMENT. The act of stopping payment may in some cases make the drawer liable to the holder of the check. If the drawer has no proper ground for stopping payment, the drawer is liable to the holder of the check. In any case, the drawer is liable for stopping payment with respect to any holder in due course or any other party having the rights of a holder in due course, unless payment was stopped for a reason that may be asserted against such a holder as a defense. The fact that payment of a check has been stopped does not affect its negotiable character.[11]

1952 UCC

6. Time of Presentment of Check for Payment

To charge a secondary party to demand paper, presentment for payment must generally be

---

[11] Perini Corp. v First Nat. Bank (CA5 Ga) 553 F2d 398 (1977).

made on the primary party to the instrument within a reasonable time after that secondary party has signed it. Reasonable time is determined by the nature of the instrument, by commercial usage, and by the facts of the particular case.

Failure to make timely presentment discharges all prior indorsers of the instrument. It also discharges the drawer, to the extent that the drawer has lost, through the bank's failure, money that was on deposit at the bank to meet the payment of the instrument.[12]

The UCC establishes two presumptions as to what is a reasonable time in which to present a check for payment. If the check is not certified and is both drawn and payable within the United States, it is presumed as to the drawer that 30 days after the date of the check or the date of its issuance, whichever is later, is the reasonable period in which to make presentment for payment. With respect to the liability of an indorser, seven days after indorsing is presumed to be a reasonable time.

1990 UCC

If the check is dated with the date of issue, it may be presented immediately for payment. If it is postdated, it may ordinarily not be presented until that date arrives. If the holder delays in making presentment, the delay discharges the drawer if the bank fails during such delay to the extent that the drawer has lost, through the banks failure, money that was on deposit at the bank to meet the payment of the instrument.[13]

A check is overdue the day after the demand for payment has been made or 90 days after the date of the check if no demand has been made, whichever date is the earlier.

If the holder of the check does not present it for payment or collection within 30 days after an indorsement was made, the indorser is discharged from liability.

7. Dishonor of Check

A check is wrongfully dishonored by the drawee bank if it refuses to pay the amount of the check although it is (a) properly payable and (b) the account on which it is drawn is sufficient to pay the item.

1952 UCC

*****

1990 UCC

Dishonor for lack of funds is also wrongful if the customer has an agreement with the bank that it will pay overdraft items.

(a) BANK'S LIABILITY TO DRAWER OF CHECK. The contract between the depositor (drawer) and the bank (drawee) obligates the latter to pay in accordance with the orders of its depositor as long as there is sufficient money on deposit to make such payment. If the bank improperly refuses to make payment, it is liable to the drawer for damages sustained by the drawer as a consequence of such dishonor.

(b) BANK'S LIABILITY TO HOLDER. If the check has not been certified, the holder has no claim against the bank for the dishonor of the check, regardless of the fact that the bank acted in breach of its contract with its depositor. A bank that certified the check is liable to the holder when it dishonors the check. The certification imposes on the bank a primary liability to pay the face amount of the check.

(c) HOLDER' NOTICE OF DISHONOR OF CHECK. When a check is dishonored by nonpayment, the holder must follow the same procedure of notice to the secondary parties as in the case of other drafts to hold the secondary parties liable for payment. As in the case of any drawer of a draft who countermands

---

[12] Act of November 10, 1978, PL 95-630, 92 Stat 3728, 15 USC § 1693 et seq.
[13] Act of November 10, 1978, PL 95-630, 92 Stat 3728, 15 USC § 1693 et seq.

payment, notice of dishonor need not be given to the drawer who has stopped payment on a check. Notice is also excused under any circumstances that would excuse notice in the case of a promissory note. For example, no notice need be given a drawer or an indorser who knows that insufficient funds to cover the check are on deposit. Such party has no reason to expect that the check will be paid by the bank.

8. Agency Status of Collecting Bank

When a person deposits a commercial paper in a bank, the bank is ordinarily thereby made an agent to collect or obtain the payment of the paper. Unless the contrary intent clearly appears, a bank receiving an item is deemed to take it as agent for the depositor rather than as purchaser of the paper. This presumption is not affected by the form of the indorsement or by the absence of any indorsement. The bank is also regarded as being merely an agent even though the depositor has the right to make immediate withdrawals against the deposited item.

In consequence of the agency status, the depositor remains the owner of the item and is therefore subject to the risks of ownership involved in its collection, in the absence of fault on the part of any collecting bank.

When a bank cashes a check deposited by its customer or cashes a check drawn by its customer on the strength of a deposited check, it is a holder of the check deposited by its customer ~   bank may sue the parties
ther-   ugh as between the customer
              ınk is an agent for collection
              charge back the amount of
              if it cannot be collected.
              ?s final settlement for an
              'on, the agency status
              ıerely a debtor of its
              ı the customer had
              ɔosit in the bank.

9. Duty of Bank

A bank is required to exercise ordinary care in the handling of items. The liability of a bank is determined by the law of the state where the bank, branch, or separate office involved is located.

(a) MODIFICATION OF BANK DUTIES. The parties in the bank collection process may modify their rights and duties by agreement. However, a bank cannot disclaim liability for lack of good faith or failure to exercise ordinary care, nor can it limit the measure of damages for such lack of care.
1952 UCC
*****
1990 UCC
When a bank handles checks by automated processes, the standard of ordinary care does not require the bank to make a physical examination of each item unless the bank's own procedures require such examination or general banking usage regards the absence of physical examination of the items as a lack of ordinary care.

(b) ENCODING WARRANTY AND ELECTRONIC PRESENTMENT. In addition to transfer and presentment warranties, an encoding warranty arises. By this warranty, anyone placing information on an item or transmitting the information electronically warrants that the information is correct. When there is an agreement for electronic presentment, the maker of such a presentment warrants that it is made and that the item is retained in accordance with the terms of the agreement for such transmissions.[14]

B. LIABILITY OF BANK

A bank may be liable for improperly collecting, paying, or refusing to pay a check.
1952 UCC

10. Premature Payment of Postdated Check

In most states, a postdated check is not payable until the stated date. If a bank pays a check before that time, it is making an improper payment and it is liable to its customer.

1990 UCC

A check may be postdated but the bank is not liable for making payment on the check before the date stated unless the drawer had given the bank prior notice. This notice must inform the bank that postdated checks would thereafter be presented and that the bank should not make payment thereof until the stated date.[15]

11. Payment Over a Stop Payment Order

A bank must be given a reasonable time to put a stop payment order into effect. However, if the bank makes payment of a check after it has been properly notified to stop payment, it is liable to the depositor for the loss the depositor sustains, in the absence of a valid limitation of the bank's liability.[16] The burden of establishing the loss resulting in such a case rests on the depositor.

12. Payment on Forged Signature of Drawer

A forgery of the signature occurs when the name of the depositor has been signed by another person without authority to do so and with the intent to defraud by making it appear that the check was signed by the depositor. The bank is liable to the depositor (drawer) if it pays a check on which the drawer's signature has been forged, since a forgery ordinarily has no effect as a signature. The risk of loss caused by the forged signature of the drawer is thus placed on the bank, without regard to whether the bank could have detected the forgery.[17]

The bank's customer whose signature was forged may be barred from holding the bank liable. If the negligence of the customer substantially contributed to the making of the forgery, the customer is precluded (prevented) from making a forgery claim against the bank. This is known as the "preclusion rule."

1952 UCC

*****

1990 UCC

The 1990 version of Article 4 extends the above pattern to alterations and to unauthorized signings (those made with no fraudulent intent).

If the principal is an organization and has a requirement that two or more designated persons sign negotiable instruments on its behalf, a signing by fewer than the specified number is classified as "unauthorized."

If the bank was negligent in failing to detect the forgery or the alteration, the bank must have cashed the check in good faith or taken it for value or collection; or it is not protected by the preclusion rule.[18]

13. Payment on Forged or Missing Indorsement

A drawee bank that honors a depositor's check bearing a forged indorsement must recredit the drawer's account upon the drawer's discovery of the forgery and notification to the bank.

A drawee bank is liable for the loss when it pays a check that lacks an essential indorsement. In such a case, the instrument is not properly payable. By definition, the person presenting the check for payment is not the holder of the instrument and is not entitled to demand or receive payment.

---

[15] UCC § 4-401, 402 [1990]. Noncheck that are postdated may not be presented until the specified date has arrived.

[16] UCC § 4-403 (2) [1952], § 4-403(c) [1990].

[17] Perini Corp. v First Nat. Bank (CA5 Ga) 553 F2d 398 (1977).

[18] UCC § 3-406 [1952], § 4-406(e) [1990].

When a person deposits a check but does not indorse it, the depositor's bank may make an indorsement on behalf of the depositor unless the check expressly requires the customer's indorsement. A bank cannot add the missing indorsement of a person who is not its customer depositing the item in the customer's account in the bank.[19]

14. Alteration of Check

If the face of the check has been altered so that the amount to be paid has been increased, the bank is liable to the drawer for the amount of the increase when it makes payment of the greater amount.

The drawer may be barred from claiming that there was an alteration because of conduct with respect to writing the check or conduct after receiving the canceled check from the bank. As to the former, the drawer is barred if the check was carelessly written, the negligence substantially contributed to the making of the material alteration, and the bank honored the check in good faith and observed reasonable commercial standards in so doing. For example, the drawer is barred when the check was written with blank spaces so that it was readily possible to change "four" to "four hundred," and the drawee bank paid out the latter sum without any cause to know that there was an alteration. Therefore, a careful person will write figures and words close together and run a line through or cross out any blank spaces.

15. Unauthorized Collection of Check

Although a bank acts as agent for its customer in obtaining payment of a check deposited with it by its customer, the bank may be liable to a third person when the act of its customer is unauthorized or unlawful with respect to the third person. That is, if the customer has no authority to deposit the check, the bank, in obtaining payment from the drawee of the check and later depositing the proceeds of the check in the account of its customer, may be liable for conversion of the check to the person lawfully entitled to the check and its proceeds.

1952 UCC

*****

1990 UCC

A collecting bank is protected from liability when it follows the instructions of its depositor. It is not required to inquire or verify that the depositor had the authority to give such instructions. In contrast, instructions do not protect a payor bank. It has an absolute duty to make proper payment. If it does not, it is liable unless it is protected by estoppel or by the preclusion rule. The person giving wrongful instructions is liable for the loss caused thereby.

16. Time Limitations

The liability of the bank to its depositor is subject to certain time limitations.

(a) NON-CODE STATUTE OF LIMITATIONS. To the extent not provided by the UCC, a local non-Code statute of limitations will fix the maximum time for asserting a claim against a bank for the breach of the customer-bank deposit contract. Non-Code statutes of limitations will also set the maximum time for bringing an action against any bank for conversion of an item of commercial paper, or an action by one bank against another bank or party to paper to obtain indemnity or contribution.

1952 UCC

(b) FORGERY AND ALTERATION REPORTING TIME. A depositor must examine with reasonable care and promptness a bank statement and relevant checks that are paid in good faith and sent to the depositor by the bank, and must try to discover any unauthorized signature or alteration on the checks. The depositor must notify the bank promptly after

---

[19] Krump Constr. Co., Inc. v First Nat. Bank, 98 Nev 570, 655 P2d 524 (1982).

C
P
A
C
P
A
C
P
A
C
P
A
C
P
A

discovering either of the foregoing. If the bank exercises ordinary care in paying a forged or altered check and suffers a loss because the depositor fails to discover and notify the bank of the forgery or alteration, the depositor cannot assert the unauthorized signature or the alteration against the bank.[20]

Regardless of the care or lack of care of either the depositor or the bank, the depositor is precluded from asserting the depositor's unauthorized signature or any alteration if the depositor does not report it within one year from the time the bank statement is received. A forged indorsement must be reported within three years.

In the *Southern Guaranty Insurance* case a customer claimed that the drawee bank failed to exercise reasonable care by honoring checks with forged signatures and indorsements.

1990 UCC

SOUTHERN GUARANTY INSURANCE COMPANY v FIRST ALABAMA BANK

(Ala) 540 So 2d 732 (1989)

Southern issued an insurance policy to Bay Paper, insuring it against losses from employee dishonesty. Bay Paper's president hired Sue Russell as Paper's bookkeeper. Russell was solely responsible for Paper's payroll and check procedures, and she was solely responsible for reviewing the company's bank statements and canceled checks. She was also the only Paper employee responsible for reconciling the company's bank statements with the checking and payroll records. Paper maintained a payroll checking account at First Alabama Bank (FAB). Soon after being hired, Russell began writing duplicate payroll checks drawn on Bay Paper's payroll account at FAB and made payable to existing Bay Paper employees. She forged the signature of the president of Bay Paper on these checks and then forged the indorsements of the payees. She then deposited the checks into her personal checking account. Only one of the 25 checks that FAB tellers accepted for deposit into Russell's account bore her indorsement. Some of the checks bore restrictive indorsements restricting the checks to deposit for credit of the named payee; nevertheless, FAB accepted these checks for deposit into Russell's account. Southern sued FAB, claiming that they were negligent in failing to follow established banking practices, failing to act in a commercially reasonable manner, failing to detect the forged signatures on Bay Paper's checks, and failing to detect forged indorsements. Southern also claimed that the bank's negligence had proximately caused Southern to sustain damages. From a judgment in favor of the bank, Southern appealed.

SHORES, J. . . . Under [the UCC], a bank may charge a customer's account only when an item is deemed "properly payable." [UCC §] 4-401. Thus, by negative implication, 4-401 imposes liability on a drawee bank that charges a customer's account for items not properly payable. . . . The crux of the plaintiff's claim is that FAB

---

[20] Vending Chattanooga v American Nat. Bank and Trust (Tenn) 730 SW2d 624 (1987).

improperly paid those items forged by Ms. Russell, and, therefore, that Southern is entitled to recover from FAB the funds that it reimbursed Bay Paper.

[The UCC] however, imposes certain duties not only upon the bank, but upon the bank customer as well. Section 4-406(1) provides:

When a bank sends to its customer a statement of account accompanied by items paid in good faith in support of the debit entries or holds the statement and items pursuant to a request or instructions of its customer or otherwise in a reasonable manner makes the statement and items available to the customer, the customer must exercise reasonable care and promptness to examine the statement and items to discover his unauthorized signature or any alteration on an item and must notify the bank promptly after discovery thereof.

The record [shows] that Bay Paper's bookkeeper, Ms. Russell, worked on Bay Paper's payroll account, kept the general ledger, and maintained Bay Paper's payables checkbook. She was solely responsible for Bay Paper's payroll and checking procedures, and she was solely responsible for reviewing the company's bank statements and canceled checks. Moreover, she was the only Bay Paper employee responsible for reconciling the company's bank statements with the checking and payroll records. This evidence is sufficient to warrant the conclusion that Bay Paper failed to exercise reasonable care as required under § 4-406(1). . . .

A customer's failure to comply with [UCC §] 4-406(1) is dealt with by § 4-406(2):

If the bank establishes that the customer failed with respect to an item to comply with the duties imposed on the customer by subsection (1) the customer is precluded from asserting against the bank:

(a) His unauthorized signature or any alteration on the item if the bank also establishes that it suffered a loss by reason of such failure. . . .

A third subsection, however, also bears upon the issue in this case. Section 4-406(3) states that "the preclusion under subsection (2) does not apply if the customer establishes lack of ordinary care on the part of the bank in paying the item(s)." Our Court of Civil Appeals has held that under this section the bank is not required to establish that it exercised ordinary care, but that the plaintiff has the burden of establishing the bank's lack of ordinary care. . . . We agree. Thus, we now look to determine whether the plaintiff adduced any evidence that would permit a finding that the bank failed to exercise ordinary care when it deposited forged checks into Ms. Russell's account.

FAB's failure to require Ms. Russell to indorse the checks she presented for deposit, and FAB's acceptance of checks for deposit into Ms. Russell's account despite the presence of restrictive indorsements constitutes some evidence from which the jury could find that FAB failed to exercise ordinary care in paying forged Bay Paper checks.

FAB argues, however, that checks involving "double forgeries," that is, cases where both the drawer's signature and the indorsement are forged, are regarded as forged checks only, and that, therefore, any negligence of the drawee bank with regard to indorsements is irrelevant. See *Perini Corp. v First Nat'l Bank*, 553 F2d 398 (5th Cir 1977).

We do not believe the "double forgery" issue as addressed in *Perini* is implicated under the present facts, and, therefore, we neither adopt nor reject the view represented by that case. The *Perini* court dealt with the question of where to allocate loss as between a drawee bank and a depository bank; the question before this Court addresses where to allocate loss as between the drawee bank and the customer. We further note that, under the present facts, FAB acted as both the drawee bank and the depository bank; thus, there can be no question as to where the loss will be allocated as between the drawee bank and the depository bank.

It is true that other courts have held that, where a "double forgery" exists, the customer's cause of action against the drawee bank is based upon the forged drawer's signature, and not upon the forged indorsement. *Id.* However, the fact that the customer does not have a cause of action based upon the forged indorsement when there is a "double forgery" does not mean that the drawee bank's failure to exercise ordinary care with regard to indorsements is irrelevant for purposes of imposing liability on the drawee bank based upon its payment of a check with a forged drawer's signature. Section 4-406(3) requires the bank to exercise ordinary care in paying items. The language of § 4-406(3) is unqualified. The statute does not distinguish between items bearing forged drawer's signatures and items bearing forged indorsements, but requires the exercise of ordinary care as to all items. Therefore, one can not, as FAB suggests, selectively exercise ordinary care with regard to the drawer's signature and remain true to the clear mandate of the statute; rather, the statute requires the exercise of ordinary care with regard to the item as a whole. To rule otherwise, we believe, would narrow the scope of the provision beyond what we think the drafters intended.

We are impressed with the reasoning of the Supreme Court of North Dakota in a case involving the exact issue before us. There, the plaintiff customer brought suit against the drawee bank for payment of checks drawn on the customer's account which bore forged drawer's signatures. The drawee bank asserted that the customer was precluded from recovering on these checks under § 4-406(2) of the UCC. The customer contended that the preclusion of § 4-406(2) did not apply because the drawee bank, in paying the checks, had failed to exercise "ordinary care" within the meaning of § 4-406(3) because the indorsements of the checks were defective. The issue before the court was whether the drawee bank, in making payment on the forged checks, had failed to exercise ordinary care within the meaning of § 4-406(3) of the UCC. The Supreme Court of North Dakota stated:

Each of the nine forged checks at issue on this appeal has Wayne Anderson's signature forged as drawer of the check by Averill Anderson. All nine checks are payable to the order of Wayne Anderson as payee; however, none of the checks is indorsed with Wayne Anderson's signature, either genuine or forged. In our determination of whether or not the trial court erred in finding that Citizens failed to exercise ordinary care in making payment on the forged checks we must scrutinize Citizens' payment of each check with respect to:

(1) the drawer's signature on the check, and

(2) the indorsement(s) on the check.

Thoreson v Citizens State Bank, 294 NW2d 397, 400 (ND 1980).

We hold, therefore, that the drawee bank's negligence with regard to the indorsements on checks is relevant for purposes of § 4-406(3).

Because material evidence exists supporting the position of the non-moving party, we must reverse FAB's summary judgment.

[Reversed and remanded]

QUESTIONS

1. What was the argument of Southern?
2. Did Bay Paper exercise reasonable care?
3. What did the court decide?

(b) FORGERY AND ALTERATION REPORTING TIME. Instead of returning canceled checks and a bank statement to its customer, a customer and the bank may agree that the bank should retain canceled checks and merely provide the customer with a list of paid items, identifying them by number, amount, and date of payment. The bank may then destroy paid items after making copies of them. In such a case, it must be able for seven years thereafter to furnish legible copies of paid items to the customer. On receiving either canceled checks or a statement of the items paid, the customer must with reasonable promptness make an examination to see if any of the items were improperly paid because of an alteration or because the customer's signature was a forgery or was unauthorized. The customer must then report any unauthorized payment that is discovered or that should have been discovered by a reasonable examination.

The customer has one year from the date of receiving the disputed item or relevant information in which to notify the bank that the item was improperly paid. After that year, no claim for recrediting the improper payment can be made, without regard to whether the bank had failed to exercise ordinary care.

If the bank's customer fails to make the examination for unauthorized payments or fails to report any alteration or unauthorized or forged signature of the customer, the customer is barred from requiring the bank to recredit the account with the amount of the unauthorized payment. The customer is not so barred if only one item is involved and the bank cannot show that it sustained loss because of the breach of duty by the customer.
1952 UCC

(c) UNAUTHORIZED SIGNATURE OR ALTERATION BY SAME WRONGDOER. Often the same wrongdoer perpetrates a series of forgeries or alterations. The depositor must warn the bank as soon as possible of the first forgery or altered item so that the bank can protect itself from a repetition of the misconduct. If the depositor fails to notify the bank within 14 days after a statement of account with the paid items is sent, the depositor cannot hold the bank liable for the loss on additional checks forged or altered by the same wrongdoer and later paid in good faith by the bank.
1990 UCC

(c) UNAUTHORIZED SIGNATURE OR ALTERATION BY SAME WRONGDOER. I f there is a series of improperly paid items and the same wrongdoer is involved, the customer is precluded only as to those items that were paid by the bank before it received notification from the customer and the customer had a reasonable amount of time in which to examine items or statements and to notify the bank. The time limit on the customer's duty to examine the bank statement and report forgeries is 30 days. If the customer failed to exercise reasonable promptness and failed to notify the bank, but the customer can show the bank failed to exercise ordinary care in paying the item, the loss will be allocated between the customer and the bank.[21]
1952 UCC

---

[21] UCC § 4-406 [1990].

(d) STATUTE OF LIMITATIONS.

*****

1990 UCC

(d) STATUTE OF LIMITATIONS. An action to enforce a liability imposed by Article 4 must be commenced within three years after the cause of action accrued.

C. CONSUMER FUNDS TRANSFERS

Federal statute protects consumers making electronic funds transfers.

17. Electronic Fund Transfers Act

Congress adopted the Electronic Fund Transfers Act (EFTA) to protect consumers making electronic transfers of funds.[22]

The term **electronic fund transfer** means any transfer of funds (other than a transaction originated by check, draft, or similar paper instrument) that is initiated through an electronic terminal, telephone, computer, or magnetic tape so as to authorize a financial institution to debit or credit an account. The service available from an automated teller machine is a common form of EFT.

18. Kinds of Electronic Fund Transfer Systems

There are currently four common kinds of EFT systems in use. In some of these systems, the consumer has a card to access the machine. The consumer usually has a private code that prevents others, who wrongfully obtain the card, from using it.

(a) AUTOMATED TELLER MACHINE. The automated teller machine (ATM) performs many of the tasks of human bank tellers. Once an individual activates the ATM, the user can deposit and withdraw funds from his or her account, transfer funds between accounts, make payment on loan accounts, and obtain cash advances from bank credit cards.[23]

(b) PAY-BY-PHONE SYSTEM. This system facilitates the paying of telephone and utility bills without writing checks. The consumer calls the bank and directs the transfer of funds to a designated third party.

(c) DIRECT DEPOSIT AND WITHDRAWAL. An employee may authorize an employer to deposit the former's wages directly to the employee's account. A consumer who has just purchased an automobile on credit may elect to have monthly payments withdrawn from the consumer's bank account and paid directly to the seller.

(d) POINT-OF-SALE TERMINAL. This device allows a business with such a terminal to transfer funds from the consumer's account to the store account.

The consumer must be furnished in advance with the terms and conditions of all EFT services and must be given periodic statements covering account activity. Any automatic EFT from an individual's account must be authorized in writing in advance.

The financial institution is liable to a consumer for all damages proximately caused by its failure to make an EFT in accordance with the terms and conditions of an account. Exceptions exist if the consumer's account has insufficient funds, the funds are subject to legal process, the transfer would exceed an established credit limit, or insufficient cash is available in an ATM.

19. Consumer Liability

A consumer who notifies the issuer of the EFT card within two days after learning of a loss or theft of the card is limited to a maximum liability of $50 for unauthorized use of the card.

---

[22] Act of November 10, 1978, PL 95-630, 92 Stat 3728, 15 USC § § 1693 et seq.

[23] Curde v Tri-City Bank & Trust Company, (Tenn App) 826 SW2d 911 (1992).

Failure to notify within this time will increase the consumer's liability for losses to a maximum of $500.

The consumer has a responsibility to examine periodic statements provided by the financial institution. If it is established that a loss would not have occurred but for the failure of the consumer to report within 60 days of the transmittal of the statement any unauthorized transfer, then the loss is borne by the consumer.

In the *Kruser* case, customers of the bank brought an action to recover for an unauthorized electronic transfer of funds.

KRUSER v BANK OF AMERICA

230 Cal App 3d 741, 281 Cal Rptr 463 (1991)

> The Krusers had a checking account with the Bank of America. They received a Versatel plastic card that enabled them to obtain cash from an automatic teller machine. They believed that the husband's card was destroyed. Apparently it had been lost. The account statement for December showed that an unauthorized $20 withdrawal had been made with the use of the husband's card. However, the Krusers did not notice this until August or September of the following year. The bank statements for July and August showed 47 unauthorized withdrawals totaling over $9,000. The Krusers promptly notified the bank and demanded that their account be recredited with the amount of the withdrawals. From a judgment in favor of the bank, the Krusers appealed.

STONE, J. . . . The ultimate issue we address is whether, as a matter of law, the failure to report the unauthorized $20 withdrawal which appeared on the December . . . . statement barred appellants from recovery for the losses incurred in July and August. . . . Resolution of the issue requires the interpretation of section 909 of the EFTA (15 U.S.C. § 1693g) and section 205.6 of Regulation E (12 C.F.R. § 205.6), one of the regulations prescribed by the Board of Governors of the Federal Reserve System in order to carry out the purposes of the EFTA. . . . Regulation E provides:

"(b) Limitations on amount of liability. *The amount of a consumer's liability for an unauthorized eletronic fund transfer or a series of related unauthorized transfers shall not exceed $50 or the amount of unauthorized transfers that occur before notice to the financial institution under paragraph (c) of this section, whichever is less, unless one or both of the following exceptions apply:*

"...

"(2) If the consumer fails to report within 60 days of transmittal of the periodic statement any unauthorized electronic fund transfer that appears on the statement, the consumer's liability shall not exceed the sum of

"(i) The lesser of $50 or the amount of unauthorized electronic fund transfers that appear on the periodic statement or that occur during the 60-day period, and

"(ii) The amount of unauthorized electronic fund transfers that occur after the close of the 60 days and before notice to the financial institution and that the financial

institution establishes would not have occurred but for the failure of the consumer to notify the financial institution within that time.

"(3) Paragraphs (b)(1) and (2) of this section may both apply in some circumstances. Paragraph (b)(1) shall determine the consumer's liability for any unauthorized transfers that appear on the periodic statement and occur before the close of the 60-day period, and paragraph (b)(2)(ii) shall determine liability for transfers that occur after the close of the 60-day period.

. . .

The trial court concluded the Bank was entitled to judgment as a matter of law because the unauthorized withdrawals of July and August occurred more than 60 days after appellants received a statement which reflected an unauthorized transfer in December. The court relied upon section 205.6(b)(2) of Regulation E.

Appellants contend the December withdrawal of $20 was so isolated in time and minimal in amount that it cannot be considered in connection with the July and August withdrawals. They assert the court's interpretation of section 205.6(b)(2) of Regulation E would have absurd results which would be inconsistent with the primary objective of the EFTA—to protect the consumer. (See 15 U.S.C. § 1693.) They argue that if a consumer receives a bank statement which reflects an unauthorized minimal electronic transfer and fails to report the transaction to the bank within 60 days of transmission of the bank statement, unauthorized transfers many years later, perhaps totaling thousands of dollars, would remain the responsibility of the consumer.

The result appellants fear is avoided by the requirement that the bank establish the subsequent unauthorized transfers could have been prevented had the consumer notified the bank of the first unauthorized transfer. . . . Here, although the unauthorized transfer of $20 occurred approximately seven months before the unauthorized transfers totaling $9,020, it is undisputed that all transfers were made by someone using Mr. Kruser's card which the Krusers believed had been destroyed prior to December. . . . According to the declaration of Yvonne Maloon, the Bank's Versatel risk manager, the Bank could have and would have canceled Mr. Kruser's card had it been timely notified of the December unauthorized transfer. In that event, Mr. Kruser's card could not have been used to accomplish the unauthorized transactions in July and August. Although appellants characterize this assertion as speculation, they offer no evidence to the contrary. . . .

Appellants contend evidence of mailing the December bank statement was insufficient to establish "transmittal" as that word is used in section 205.6(b)(2) of Regulation E. They contend actual knowledge is required and rely on the Federal Reserve Board's official staff interpretation of Regulation E relating to the loss or theft provision of section 205.6(b)(1). (See official staff interpretation, 12 C.F.R. part 205, supp II (Jan. 1, 1987 ed.) p. 125.)

Section 205.6(b)(1) requires the consumer to notify the bank "within 2 business days after learning of the loss or theft of the access device. . . ." (Emphasis added.) The question addressed by the staff comment is whether the consumer's receipt of a periodic statement that reflects unauthorized transfers is sufficient to establish knowledge of loss or theft of an access device. The comment provides:

"Receipt of the periodic statement reflecting unauthorized transfers may be considered a factor in determining whether the consumer had knowledge of the loss or theft, but cannot be

deemed to represent conclusive evidence that the consumer had such knowledge." (Official staff interpretation, 12 C.F.R. part 205, supp. II, (Jan. 1, 1987 ed.) § 205.6(b), p. 125.)

Here we are not concerned with the loss or theft of an access device. Rather, our question is whether the bank has established the loss of $9,020 in July and August would not have occurred but for the failure of appellants to report timely the $20 unauthorized transfer which appeared on the December . . . statement. (15 U.S.C. § 1693g(a)(2).)

Appellants cite no authority which supports their claim the consumer must not only receive the statement provided by the bank, but must acquire actual knowledge of an unauthorized transfer from the statement. Such a construction of the law would reward consumers who choose to remain ignorant of the nature of transactions on their account by purposely failing to review periodic statements. Consumers must play an active and responsible role in protecting against losses which might result from unauthorized transfers. A banking institution cannot know of an unauthorized electronic transfer unless the consumer reports it.

The Bank has established that the losses incurred in July and August . . . as a result of the unauthorized electronic transfers by someone using Mr. Kruser's Versatel card could have been prevented had appellants reported the unauthorized use of Mr. Kruser's card as reflected on the December . . . statement. The Bank is entitled to judgment as a matter of law.

[Judgment affirmed]

QUESTIONS

1. What was the argument of the Krusers?
2. How did the bank answer this argument?
3. Do you think the decision is fair?

D. FUNDS TRANSFERS

The funds transfers made by big business are governed by UCC and Federal Reserve Regulation.

20. What Law Governs

In states that have adopted Article 4A of the Uniform Commercial Code, such transfers are governed by that article. In addition, whenever a Federal Reserve Bank is involved, the provisions of Article 4A apply by virtue of Federal Reserve Regulation.

21. Characteristics of Funds Transfers

The transfers regulated by Article 4A have the characteristics of being made between highly sophisticated parties who are dealing with large sums of money. Speed of transfer is often an essential characteristic. An individual transfer may involve many millions of dollars, and the national total of such transfers on a business day can amount to trillions of dollars.

22. Pattern of Funds Transfers

In the simplest form of funds transfer, both the debtor and the creditor have a separate account in the same bank.[24] In such a situation, the debtor can instruct the bank to pay the creditor a specified sum of money by subtracting that amount from the debtor's account and adding it to the creditor's account. As a practical matter, the debtor will merely instruct the bank to make the transfer and the bank on making the transfer will debit the debtor's account.

A more complex situation is involved if each party has an account in a different bank. In such a case, the funds transfer could involve only these two banks and no clearing house. Thus, the buyer could instruct the buyer's bank to direct the seller's bank to make payment to the seller. Here there would be direct communication between the two banks. In a more complex situation, the buyer's bank may relay the payment order to another bank, called an intermediary bank, and that bank in turn would transmit it to the seller's bank.

Further complexity is found when there are two or more intermediary banks, or a clearing house is involved.

23. Scope of UCC Article 4A

Article 4A applies to all funds transfers except as expressly excluded by its own terms, by federal preemption, or by agreement of the parties or clearing house rules.

Some funds transfers are excluded from Article 4A because of their nature or because of the parties involved.

(a) EFTA AND CONSUMER TRANSACTIONS. By the express provision of Article 4A, it does not apply to consumer transactions payments to which the EFTA applies. If any part of the fund transfer is subject to the EFTA, the entire transfer is expressly excluded from the scope of UCC Article 4A.[25]

(b) DEBIT TRANSFERS. When the person making payment, such as the buyer, makes the request that payment be made to

the beneficiary's bank, the transaction is called a **credit transfer**. If the beneficiary entitled to money goes to the bank, pursuant to prior agreement, and requests payment to it, the transaction is called a **debit transfer**. The latter kind of transfer is not regulated by Article 4A. Article 4A applies only to transfers begun by the person desiring to make payment to the beneficiary.

(c) NONBANK TRANSFERS. In order for Article 4A to apply to a money transfer, it is necessary that once the transfer is begun, all communication is between banks. Thus, sending money by Western Union does not come under 4A, because there is no bank-to-bank communication. Payment by check is also not covered, because the drawer of the check sends the check directly to the payee. There is no involvement of banks until the payee deposits the check or presents it to cash it. Likewise excluded from Article 4A by the bank-to-bank requirement is payment by use of a credit card even when the transaction would not come within the scope of the EFTA.

24. Definitions

Article 4A employs a number of terms that are peculiar to Article 4A or that are used in that article in a particular context.

(a) FUNDS TRANSFER. A **funds transfer** is more accurately described as a communication of instructions or requests to pay a specific sum of money to or to the credit of a specified account or person. There is no actual physical transfer or passing of money or precious metal.

(b) ORIGINATOR. The person starting the funds transfer is called the **originator** of the funds transfer.[26]

---

[24] The text refers to debtor and creditor in the interest of simplicity and because that situation is the most common in the business world. However, a gift may be made by a funds transfer. Likewise, a person having separate accounts in two different banks may transfer funds from one bank to another.

[25] UCC § 4A-108. This exclusion applies when any part is subject to Regulation E adopted under the authority of that statute.

(c) BENEFICIARY. The **beneficiary** is the ultimate recipient of the benefit of the funds transfer. Whether it is the beneficiary personally, an account owned by the beneficiary, or a third person to whom the beneficiary owes money is determined by the payment order.

(d) BENEFICIARY'S BANK. The **beneficiary's bank** is the final bank in the chain of transfer, which carries out the transfer by making payment or application as directed by the payment order.

(e) PAYMENT ORDER. The **payment order** is the direction given by the originator to the originator's bank or by any bank to a subsequent bank to make the specified funds transfer. Although called an order, it is in fact a request. No bank is required or obligated to accept a payment order unless it is so bound by a contract or clearing house rule that operates outside of Article 4A.

(f) ACCEPTANCE OF PAYMENT ORDER. When a receiving bank other than the beneficiary's bank receives a payment order, it accepts or executes that order by issuing a payment order to the next bank in the transfer chain. When the beneficiary's bank agrees to or actually makes the application of funds as directed by the payment order, the order is termed accepted by that bank.

25. Form of Payment Order

There is no regulation of any kind of the form of the payment order. There is no requirement that there be any writing as to any matter relating to a funds transfer. As a practical matter, it is probable that there will be a written contract between an originator and the originator's bank. There may be agreements between parties and banks, and also clearing house and funds transfer system rules that require a writing.

26. Manner of Transmitting Payment Order

Article 4A makes no regulation of the manner of transmitting a payment order. As a practical matter, most funds transfers coming under Article 4A are controlled by computers, and payment orders will be electronically transmitted. Article 4A, however, applies to any funds transfer payment order, even though made orally, such as by telephone, or in a writing— for example, by a letter.

Again, the agreement of the parties or clearing house and funds transfer system rules may impose some restrictions as to the method of communicating orders.

27. Security Procedure

Because there is no writing and no face-to-face dealing in the typical funds transfer, Article 4A contemplates that the banks in the transfer chain will agree on a commercially reasonable security procedure. Under such a procedure, a bank receiving a payment order should be able to verify that the payment order was authorized by the purported sender and that it is free from error.[27]

A bank that receives a payment order that passes the security procedure may act on the basis of the order. It is immaterial that in fact the order was not authorized or was fraudulent.

28. Regulation by Agreement and Funds Transfer System Rule

Article 4A, with minor limitations, permits the parties to make agreements that modify or change the provisions of Article 4A that would otherwise govern. Likewise, the rules of a clearing house or a funds transfer system through which the banks operate may change the provisions of the Code.

---

[26] UCC § 4A-201.
[27] UCC § 4A-201.

(a) CHOICE OF LAW. When the parties enter into an agreement governing a funds transfer, they may designate the jurisdiction whose law is to apply in interpreting the agreement. The parties are given a free hand to select any jurisdiction they choose. Contrary to the rule applicable in other Code transactions, there is no requirement that the jurisdiction selected bear any relationship to the transaction.

(b) CLEARING HOUSE RULES. The banks involved in a particular funds transfer may be members of the same clearing house. In such a case, they will be bound by the lawful rules and regulations of the house. Thus, the rights of the parties may be determined by the rules of FedWire, a clearing house system operated by the Federal Reserve System, or by CHIPS, which is a similar system operated by the New York clearing house.

29. Acceptance of Payment Order

A bank receiving a payment order accepts the order when the bank complies with its terms. What this means depends on whether the receiving bank is an intermediary bank or is the beneficiary's bank.

(a) INTERMEDIARY BANK. An intermediary bank accepts a payment order when it carries out or executes the order by transmitting a similar payment order to the next bank in the transfer chain. Unlike a check that is sent through bank collection channels, the original payment order is not transferred, but a new payment order by the intermediary bank is dispatched.

(b) BENEFICIARY'S BANK. The beneficiary's bank accepts a payment order when it notifies the beneficiary that the beneficiary's bank holds the amount of the payment order at the disposal of the beneficiary. The payment order may require the beneficiary's bank to credit the amount to an account or to a named person. The person so named may be the beneficiary, as when a buyer uses a funds transfer to pay the purchase price to the seller. It may also be a designated third person. This would be the case when the buyer directs the crediting of the bank account of a manufacturer in order to discharge or reduce the debt of the seller to the manufacturer. The transfer to the manufacturer would of course also reduce or discharge the debt of the buyer to the seller.

When the beneficiary's bank acts as directed by the payment order, it accepts the order. When it does so, it takes the place of the originator as the debtor owing the beneficiary. In such a case, the originator no longer owes the beneficiary, and the debt to the beneficiary is discharged or reduced by the amount of the payment order.[28]

30. Reimbursement of Bank

After the beneficiary's bank accepts the payment order, it, and every bank ahead of it in the funds transfer chain, is entitled to reimbursement of the amount paid to or for the beneficiary. This reimbursement is due from the preceding bank. By going back along the funds transfer chain, the originator's bank, and ultimately the originator, makes payment of this reimbursement amount.

31. Refund on Noncompletion of Transfer

If the funds transfer is not completed for any reason, the sender or originator is entitled to a refund of any payment that has been made in advance to the originator's bank. The sender or originator is not required to reimburse any bank for payment made by it.

---

[28] UCC § 4A-406.

32. Error in Funds Transfer

There may be an error in a payment order. The effect of an error depends on its nature.

(a) KIND OF ERROR. The error in a payment order may consist of a wrong identification or a wrong amount.

(1) Wrong Beneficiary or Account Number. The payment order received by the beneficiary's bank may contain an error in the designation of the beneficiary or in the account number. This error may result in payment being made to or for the wrong person or account.

(2) Excessive Amount. The payment order may call for the payment of an amount that is greater than it should be. For example, the order may wrongly add an additional zero to the specified amount.

(3) Duplicating Amount. The payment order may be issued overlooking the fact that a similar payment order has already been transferred, so that the second order duplicates the first. This duplication would result in double the proper amount's being paid by the beneficiary's bank.

(4) Underpayment. The payment order may call for the payment of a smaller sum than was ordered. For example, the order may drop off one of the zeros from the amount ordered by the originator.

(b) EFFECT OF ERROR. When the error is one of the first three classes noted above, the bank committing the error will bear the loss because it will not be allowed reimbursement for any amount that it caused to be wrongfully paid. In contrast, when the error is merely underpayment, the bank making the mistake can cure the fault by making a supplementary order for the amount of the underpayment. If verification by agreed security procedure would disclose an error in the payment order, a bank is liable for any loss caused by the error if it failed to verify the payment order by such a procedure. In contrast, if the security procedure was followed but did not reveal any error, there is no liability for accepting the payment order.

When an error of any kind is made, there is also the possibility that there may be liability arising by virtue of a collateral agreement of the parties, a clearing house or funds transfer system rule, or general principles of contract law. However, the right of the originator to complain that there is an error may be lost in certain cases by failing to notify the involved bank that the mistake had been made.

33. Liability for Loss

Unless otherwise regulated by agreement or clearing house rule, there is very slight liability imposed on a bank in the funds transfer chain that follows the agreed security procedure.

(a) UNAUTHORIZED ORDER. If a bank executes or accepts an unauthorized payment order, it is liable to any prior party in the transfer chain for the loss caused. However, as a practical matter, such loss will rarely be imposed, because the transfer is typically made under an agreement establishing a security procedure. If a bank acts on the basis of an unauthorized order that nevertheless is verified by the security procedure, the bank is not liable for the loss caused thereby.

The customer, however, can avoid this effect of verification by a security procedure by proving that the security procedure was not commercially reasonable or that the payment order was initiated by a total stranger. The latter requires that the customer show that the initiator was not an employee or agent of the customer having access to confidential security information or a person who obtained that information from a source controlled by the customer. However, it is immaterial whether the customer was at fault.

(b) FAILURE TO ACT. A bank that fails to carry out a payment order is usually liable at the most for interest loss and expenses. There is no liability for the loss sustained by the originator or for consequential damages suffered because payment was not made to satisfy the originator's obligation to the beneficiary. Thus, a person seeking to exercise an option by forwarding money to the optionor cannot recover for the loss of the option when the failure of a bank to act results in the optionor's not receiving the money in time.

SUMMARY

A check is a particular kind of draft; it is drawn on a bank and payable on demand. A delivery of a check is not an assignment of money on deposit with the bank on which it is drawn. Therefore, it does not automatically transfer the rights of the depositor against the bank to the holder of the check, and there is no duty on the part of the drawee bank to the holder to pay the holder the amount of the check.

1952 UCC

*****

1990 UCC

A check may be either an ordinary check, a cashier's check, or a teller's check. The name on the paper is not controlling. Unless otherwise agreed, the delivery of a certified check, a cashier's check, or a teller's check discharges the debt for which it is given, up to the amount of the check.

Certification of a check by the bank is the acceptance of the check—the bank becomes the primary party. Certification may be at the request of the drawee or the holder. On certification by the holder all prior indorsers and the drawer are released from liability.

Notice of nonpayment of a check must be given to the drawer of a check. If no notice is given, the drawer is discharged from liability to the same extent as the drawer of an ordinary draft. The drawee bank owes the depositor certain duties.

A depositor may stop payment on a check. However, the depositor is liable to a holder in due course unless such stopping of payment was for a reason that may be raised against a holder in due course. The stop payment order may be oral (binding for 14 calendar days) or written (effective for six months).

Liability of a secondary party cannot be enforced unless that party was given proper notice of the dishonor.

The depositary bank is the agent of the depositor for the purpose of collecting a deposited item. The bank may become liable for paying a check contrary to a stop payment order or when there has been a forgery or alteration. The bank is not liable, however, if the drawer's negligence has substantially contributed to the forgery. A bank that pays on a forged instrument must recredit the drawer's account. A depositor is subject to certain time limitations in order to enforce liability of the bank.

1952 UCC

A depositor must examine with reasonable care and promptness bank statements and returned checks to discover unauthorized signatures or alterations.

1990 UCC

A customer and a bank may agree that the bank should retain canceled checks and simply provide the customer with a list of paid items. The customer must examine canceled checks or paid items to see if any were improperly paid.

An electronic fund transfer is a transfer of funds (other than a transaction originated by check, draft, or other commercial paper) that is initiated through an electronic terminal, telephone, computer, or magnetic tape so as to authorize a financial institution to debit or credit an account. The Electronic Fund Transfers Act requires that a financial institution furnish consumers with specific information containing all the terms and conditions of all EFT services. Under certain conditions, the financial institution will bear the loss for unauthorized transfers. Under other circumstances, the loss will be borne by the consumer.

Funds transfers regulated by UCC, Article 4A, are those made between highly sophisticated parties who deal with large sums of money. If any part of the funds transfer is subject to the EFTA, such as consumer transactions, the entire transfer is expressly excluded from the scope of UCC Article 4A. A funds transfer is simply a communicating of instructions or requests to pay a specific sum of money to or to the credit of a specified person. The person starting the funds transfer is called the originator of the funds transfer. The beneficiary is the ultimate recipient of the funds transfer.

LAW IN PRACTICE

1. Remember that once you have a check certified, you cannot stop payment on that check.

2. Always examine your bank statements. If you fail to notify the bank of your forged signature, you may be precluded from having the bank recredit your account if you fail to act within one year from receiving your statements.

3. Always inform your bank of a loss of an EFT card, otherwise you may be liable for its unauthorized use.

QUESTIONS AND CASE PROBLEMS

1. What social forces are involved in the common statutory provision that it will be presumed that a check was issued with intent to defraud if the drawer does not pay the amount of the check within ten days after its dishonor?

2. A thief stole Helen's debit card. Helen was a very forgetful person, so she had placed her bank code (PIN number) on the back of her card. The thief was able to take $100 from an automatic teller machine the day of the theft. That same day, Helen realized that the card was gone and phoned her bank. The following morning, the same person withdrew another $100. For how much, if anything, is Helen responsible? Why?

3. Shirley drew a check on her account in the First Central Bank. She later telephoned the bank to stop payment on the check. The bank agreed to do so. Sixteen days thereafter, the check was presented to the bank for payment and was paid by the bank. Shirley sued the bank for violating the stop payment order. The bank claimed it was not liable. Is Shirley entitled to recover?

4. Tom had a checking account with the Farmers National Bank. A check was written by an unknown person, who forged the signature of Tom as a drawer of the check and then presented the check to the Farmers National Bank for payment. The bank paid the check and debited Toms account for the amount of the check. When Tom received the monthly statement from the bank, he demanded that the bank restore the amount of this debit. Could he recover?

5. Shipper was ill for 14 months. His wife did not take care of his affairs carefully, nor did she examine his bank statements as they arrived each month. One of Shipper's acquaintances had forged his name to a check in favor of himself for $10,000. The drawee bank paid the check and charged Shipper's account. Shipper did not notify the bank for 13 months after he received the statement and the forged check. Can he compel the bank to reverse the charge? Why?

6. Gloria maintains a checking account at the First Bank. On the third day of January, the bank sent Gloria a statement of her account for December, accompanied by the checks that the bank had paid. One of the checks had her forged signature, which Gloria discovered on the 25th of the month, when she prepared a bank reconciliation. On discovering this, Gloria immediately notified the bank. On January 21, the bank paid another check forged by the same party who had forged the December item. Who must bear the loss on the forged January check?

7. Dean bought a car from Cannon. In payment, Dean gave him a check drawn on the South Dorchester Bank of the Eastern Shore Trust Company. The payee, Cannon, cashed the check at the Cambridge Bank of the Eastern Shore Trust Company. The drawee bank refused payment when the check was presented on the ground that Dean had stopped payment because of certain misrepresentations made by Cannon. Will the Eastern Shore Trust Company succeed in an action against Dean for payment? [*Dean v Eastern Shore Trust Co.* 159 Md 213, 150 A 797]

8. A depositor drew a check and delivered it to the payee. Fourteen months later, the check was presented to the drawee bank for payment. The bank did not have any knowledge that anything was wrong and paid the check. The depositor then sued the person receiving the money and the bank. The depositor claimed that the bank could not pay a stale check without asking the depositor whether payment should be made. Was the depositor correct? [*Advanced Alloys, Inc. v Sergeant Steel Corp. 340 NYS2d 266*]

9. Siniscalchi drew a check on his account in the Valley Bank of New York. About a week later, the holder cashed the check at the bank on a Saturday morning. The following Monday morning, Siniscalchi gave the bank a stop payment order on the check. The Saturday morning transactions had not yet been recorded, and neither the bank nor Siniscalchi knew that the check had been cashed. When that fact was learned, the bank debited Siniscalchi's account for the amount of the check. He claimed that the bank was liable because the stop payment order had been violated. Was the bank liable? [*Siniscalchi v Valley Bank of New York, 359 NYS2d 173*]

10. Bogash drew a check on the National Safety Bank and Trust Co., payable to the order of the Fiss Corp. At the request of the Fiss Corp., the bank certified the check. The bank later refused to make payment on the check because there was a dispute between Bogash and the corporation as to the amount due to the corporation. The corporation sued the bank on the check. Decide. [*Fiss Corp. v National Safety Bank and Trust Co. 191 Misc 397, 77 NYS2d 293*]

11. Compare the differences between certification of a check by a bank at the request of the depositor and at the request of a holder.

12. Norris was ill in the hospital. His sister visited him during his last days. Norris was very fond of his sister. He wrote out a check to her and she deposited it in her bank account. Before the check cleared, Norris died. May the sister collect on the check even though the bank knew of the death of the depositor? Explain. [*In re Estate of Norris (Colo) 532 P2d 981*]

13. Paradine drew a check on the Citizen's National Bank and gave it to Davis in payment of a debt. Davis asked an assistant teller at the bank whether Paradine had sufficient funds on deposit to cover the check. He was informed that he had. Instead of presenting the check for payment at the bank, Davis deposited the check at his own bank, which then began the collection process. Before collection was completed, Paradine had withdrawn his entire balance from Citizen's National Bank. Davis sued the Citizen's National Bank for the amount of the check. Will he recover? Why?

14. Hixson owed money to Galyen Petroleum Company. He paid with three checks. The bank refused to cash the three checks because there was not sufficient money in the Hixson account to pay all three. Galyen sued the bank. What result? Why? [*Galyen Petroleum Co. v Hixson (Neb) 331 NW2d 1*]

15. Stanley Salton delivered a $50 check to Doris Dean. Dean wrongfully raised the amount to $250, using spaces that Salton negligently had left blank. Dean then indorsed and delivered the check to Watkins, who took it for value, in good faith, and without notice of the alteration. In due course, the check was presented for payment to Salton's bank, which paid it in good faith and in accordance with reasonable commercial standards. Salton protested when the bank charged his account for $250. What is the argument of the bank?

PART 6

Debtor-Creditor Relations and Risk Management

SECURED TRANSACTIONS IN PERSONAL PROPERTY

LEARNING OBJECTIVES

After studying this chapter, you will be able to:
1. *Describe a secured transaction in personal property.*
2. *Explain the requirements for creating a valid security interest.*
3. *List the four major types of collateral.*
4. *Distinguish between secured credit sales of consumer goods and secured credit sales of inventory.*
5. *State the rights of the parties upon the debtor's default.*

Money is loaned and sales are made on credit. What can the creditor do to be sure that the debt is paid?

A. GENERAL PRINCIPLES

A secured transaction in personal property may be the answer to this question.

1. Definitions

A **secured transaction** in personal property is created by giving the creditor a security interest in that property.[1] A security interest is a property right that enables the creditor to take possession of the property if the debtor does not pay the amount owed. For example, if you borrow money from a bank to buy a car, the bank will take a security interest in the car. If you do not repay the loan, the bank can take possession of the car and resell it to recover the money the bank had loaned to you.

The property that is subject to the security interest is called **collateral**. In the preceding example, the car was the collateral for the loan.

(a) PARTIES. The person owed the money, whether as a seller or a lender, is called **creditor** or **secured party**. The buyer on credit or the borrower is called the **debtor**.

(b) PURCHASE MONEY SECURITY. When a seller sells on credit and is given a security interest in the goods, that interest is called a **purchase money security interest**. If the buyer borrows money from a third person so that the purchase can be made for cash, a security interest given the lender in the goods is also called a **purchase money security interest**.[2]

(c) NATURE OF CREDITOR'S INTEREST. The creditor does not own the collateral, but the security interest is a property right. Having a security interest gives the creditor standing to sue a third person who damages, destroys, or improperly repossesses the collateral.

If the creditor has possession of the collateral, the UCC imposes a duty of care on the creditor. The UCC provides that reasonable care must be exercised in preserving the property. The creditor is liable for damage that results from failing to do so.

(d) NATURE OF DEBTOR'S INTEREST. A debtor who is a borrower will ordinarily own the collateral.[3] As such, the debtor has all the rights of any property owner to recover damages for the loss or improper seizure of or damage to the collateral. A buyer or lessee also has such rights.

When the debtor is a buyer or a lessee, it is not material that the debtor is not the owner of the collateral. The debtor still has certain property rights in the collateral.

2. Creation of a Security Interest

A security interest is created, or **attaches**, when the following three conditions are satisfied: there is a security agreement; value has been given; and the debtor has rights in the collateral. These three conditions can occur in any order. Thus, the interest will attach when the last of these conditions has been met. When the security interest attaches, it is then enforceable against the debtor.

(a) AGREEMENT. There must be an agreement of the creditor and the debtor that the creditor will have a security interest.

(b) VALUE. The creditor either lends money to the debtor or delivers goods on credit.

---

[1] UCC § 1-201 (37).

[2] Borg Warner Acceptance v Tascosa Nat. Bank (Tex Civ App) 784 SW2d 129 (1990).

[3] The collateral may be owned by a third person.

C
P
A

(c) RIGHTS IN THE COLLATERAL. The debtor has rights in the collateral. These rights may be ownership or the right to possession.

Whether a security interest attached was the question in the *Ford Motor Credit Company* case.

C
P
A

FORD MOTOR CREDIT COMPANY v STATE BANK & TRUST COMPANY

(Miss App) 571 So 2d 937 (1990)

Buffington Ford, Inc., was an auto dealer, dealing in used and new vehicles. It owed money to Ford Motor Credit Company (FMCC). In order to obtain an extension of time on this debt, Buffington executed a security agreement giving FMCC "a security interest in the following types of property located at the undersigned's place(s) of business . . . now owned or hereby acquired by the undersigned (a) all furniture, fixtures, machinery, supplies, and other equipment, (b) all motor vehicles, tractors, trailers, and other inventory of every kind. . . ." Buffington removed some of its used cars from its regular place of business. When Buffington failed to pay its debt to FMCC, FMCC attempted repossess the used cars that were not on Buffington's premises. This was opposed by State Bank, a rival creditor, on the ground that there was no security agreement creating an interest in vehicles that were not at the debtor's place of business and on the theory that Ford had not given any value for the security interest. Judgment was entered for State Bank, and FMCC appealed.

PITTMAN, J. . . . . A security interest attaches when: (1) there is an agreement; (2) value is given; and (3) the debtor has rights in the collateral. [UCC §] 9-203(1)(a), (b) and (c). As noted, the lower court held that FMCC gave no value for the security interest [in the used vehicles]. While it is undisputed that FMCC did not provide Buffington with money to purchase the used cars, this does not mean that FMCC did not give value.

[UCC §] 1-201(44) defines value as: "security for or in total or partial satisfaction of a pre-existing claim" or "any consideration sufficient to support a simple contract." Furthermore Mississippi case law has recognized that a security interest may be given for a pre-existing debt. *Peoples Bank & Trust Co. v Comfort Eng. Co., Inc.*, 408 So 2d 1190 (Miss. 1982). In that case, this Court noted that, "several parties have argued that a creditor does not give value if he takes a security interest to secure a pre-existing claim against the debtor. The courts have tossed these parties out on their ears, as well they ought. This section does not invalidate a security interest in after acquired property where a pre-existing claim is the value given. . . ."

In this case, FMCC entered into the security agreement with Buffington when it discovered that he had sold vehicles [without paying FMCC]. The parties entered into the agreement so that Buffington might remain in business and repay the money that he already owed FMCC. This forbearance by FMCC falls squarely within the broad definition of value provided in [UCC §] 1-201(44).

The existence of a signed writing describing the collateral is also a prerequisite to attachment. [UCC §] 9-203(1)(a). The lower court held that there was no evidence in the record establishing an agreement between FMCC and Buffington for a security interest to attach to the used vehicles. [J. White & R. Summers, in *Handbook of the Law Under the Uniform Commercial Code*] break this requirement into three parts, "the writing must: (1) contain sufficient language to embody a 'security agreement,' (2) include an adequate 'description of the collateral,' and (3) be 'signed by the debtor.'"

In this case there can be no doubt that the document contained sufficient language to serve as a security agreement or that the document was signed by the debtor. The lower court then must have decided that Buffington did not know or did not intend for the description of the collateral to include the used vehicles not [financed] by FMCC. There is no evidence in the record to support this belief. The parties entered into a security agreement. Among the items listed as collateral are, "[a]ll motor vehicles . . . and other inventory of every kind." *See, Boudreau v Borg-Warner Acceptance Corp.*, 616 F2d 1077 (9th Cir 1980) (a factually similar case that holds that "all inventory" is broad enough to cover vehicles not subject to a floor plan agreement.). . . .

[Judgment reversed]

QUESTIONS

1. What is the importance of attachment?
2. Value is one of the prerequisites for a security interest to attach. Did the court determine that value had been given? Explain?

3. The Security Agreement

The security agreement is the agreement of the creditor and the debtor that the creditor have a security interest. The agreement must identify the parties, contain a reasonable description of the collateral, manifest the intention that the creditor have a security interest in it, and describe the debt or the performance that is secured thereby.

If the creditor has possession of the collateral, the security agreement may be oral regardless of the amount involved.[4] If the creditor does not have possesion of the collateral, as in the case of the credit sale and of most secured loans, the security agreement must be written and signed by the debtor.

4. Future Transactions

The security agreement may contemplate the making of additional loans or future advances or the extension of the creditor's security interest to property that may later be acquired by the debtor.

(a) ATTACHMENT IN FUTURE TRANSACTIONS. When the security interest is intended to cover future loans or advances, the interest already existing expands to cover the future advance when a future advance is received by the debtor. If the security agreement so provides, the security interest attaches to after-acquired goods. Such attachment occurs as soon as the debtor acquires rights in those goods.

---

[4]   UCC § 9-203.

(b) PROTECTION OF CONSUMERS. A n after-acquired property clause in a security agreement cannot bind all consumer goods that the debtor may ever acquire. It can only bind such goods as are acquired by the debtor within ten days after the creditor gave value to the debtor.

(c) PROCEEDS. The debtor may receive payments for selling or leasing the collateral to a third person. If the collateral has been insured and is damaged or destroyed, the debtor will receive money from the insurance company. All of these payments are called **proceeds** of the collateral and are automatically subject to the creditor's security interest unless the contrary was stated in the security agreement. The proceeds may be in any form, such as cash, checks, or other property.

5. Classification of Tangible Collateral

The UCC divides tangible personal property or goods into four different classes: consumer goods, equipment, inventory, and farm products.[5] Goods are classified by the debtor's use.

(a) CONSUMER GOODS. Goods are **consumer goods** if they are used or bought primarily for personal, family, or household use, for example, home appliances.

(b) EQUIPMENT. Goods are **equipment** if they are used or bought primarily for use in a business, for example, a fax machine used in a lawyer's office.

(c) INVENTORY. Goods are **inventory** if they are held primarily for sale or lease to others or if they are raw materials, work in process, or materials consumed in a business. Examples of inventory include a retailer's goods and also keyboards and processing units used by a computer manufacturer in assembling its final product.

(d) FARM PRODUCTS. Goods are **farm products** if they are crops, livestock, or supplies used or produced in farming operations.

6. Perfection of Security Interest

Attachment of the security interest makes it enforceable against the debtor. Attachment allows the secured party to resort to the collateral to enforce the debt on default. The creditor holding a security interest in collateral may face competing claims of other creditors of the debtor or persons to whom the debtor has sold the collateral. If the security interest of the original creditor is held superior to all such other claims it is called a **perfected security interest**. If it is not superior, it is not perfected or is unperfected. If there is no competing claim as just described, it is immaterial whether a security interest is perfected. A security interest is valid against the debtor whether or not it is perfected.

7. How Perfection Is Obtained

The nature of the goods or the transaction determines what must be done to obtain perfection.

(a) CREDITOR'S POSSESSION. If the collateral is in the possession of the creditor, the security interest therein is perfected. It remains such until that possession is surrendered.

(b) CONSUMER GOODS PURCHASE. A purchase money security interest in consumer goods is perfected from the moment it attaches. No other action is required although the interest may be destroyed by the consumer's resale of the goods to a consumer who does not know of the security interest.

(c) MOTOR VEHICLES. In most states, a non-Code statute provides that a security interest in a noninventory motor vehicle must be

---

5   UCC § 9-109.

noted on the vehicle title registration. When so noted, the interest is perfected. In states that do not provide for this, there must be a filing of a financing statement, as described in the next section.[6]

8. The Financing Statement

The financing statement is a brief statement that gives sufficient information to alert third persons that a particular creditor may have a security interest in the collateral described. (See Figure 35-1.)

Figure 35-1   Financing Statement

Uniform Commercial Code – FINANCING STATEMENT

This FINANCING STATEMENT is presented to a Filing Officer for filing pursuant to the Uniform Commercial Code	No. of Additional Sheets Presented:	3. ☐ The Debtor is a transmitting utility.
1. Debtor(s) (Last Name First) and Address(es): 2. Secured Party(ies) Name(s) and Address(es):		4. For Filing Officer: Date, Time, No. Filing Office:
5. This Financing Statement covers the following types (or items) of property:		6. Assignee(s) of Secured Party and Address(es):

☐ Products of the Collateral are also covered.

		7. ☐ The described crops are growing or to be grown on:* ☐ The described goods are or are to be affixed to:* ☐ The lumber to be cut or minerals or the like (including oil and gas) is on:* *(Describe Real Estate Below)
8. Describe Real Estate Here:	☐ This statement is to be indexed in the Real Estate Records:	9. Name of a Record Owner

No. & Street	Town or City	County	Section	Block	Lot

10. This statement is filed without the debtor's signature to perfect a security interest in collateral (check appropriate box)
    ☐ under a security agreement signed by debtor authorizing secured party to file this statement, or
    ☐ which is proceeds of the original collateral described above in which a security interest was perfected, or
    ☐ acquired after a change of name, identity or corporate structure of the debtor, or ☐ as to which the filing has lapsed, or
    already subject to a security interest in another jurisdiction:
    ☐ when the collateral was brought into the state, or ☐ when the debtor's location was changed to this state.

By _____
       Signature(s) of Debtor(s)

By _____
       Signature(s) of Secured Party(ies)

---

[6] The place of filing depends on whether the goods are consumer goods, equipment, inventory, or farm products.

The **financing statement** must be signed by the debtor. It must give an address of the secured party from which information concerning the security interest may be obtained. The financing statement must give a mailing address of the debtor, and it must contain a statement indicating the kind, or describing the items, of collateral.[7]

The financing statement does not set forth the terms of the agreement between the parties. This is done in the security agreement.

(a) ERRORS IN FINANCING STATEMENT. Errors in the financing statement have no effect unless they are seriously misleading. If they are seriously misleading, the filing has no effect and does not perfect the security interest.

(b) DEFECTIVE FILING. When the filing of the statement is defective, either because the statement is so erroneous that it is seriously misleading or the filing is made in a wrong county or office, the filing fails to perfect the security interest.

9. Loss of Perfection

The perfection of the security interest is lost depending on how the perfection was obtained.

(a) POSSESSED COLLATERAL. When perfection was obtained by the creditor's taking possession of the collateral, that perfection is lost if the creditor voluntarily surrenders the collateral to the debtor without any restrictions.[8]

(b) CONSUMER GOODS. The perfection is lost in some cases by removal of the goods to another state. The security interest may also be destroyed by resale of the goods to a consumer.

(c) LAPSE OF TIME. The perfection obtained by filing a financing statement lasts five years. The perfection may be continued for successive five-year periods by filing a continuation statement within six months before the end of each five-year period.

(d) REMOVAL FROM STATE. In most cases, the perfection of a security interest lapses when the collateral is taken by the debtor to another state, unless the creditor makes a filing in that second state within four months thereafter.

(e) MOTOR VEHICLES. If the security interest is governed by a non-Code statute creating perfection by title certificate notation, the interest if so noted remains perfected without regard to lapse of time or removal to another state. This perfection is lost only when a new title certificate is issued by a proper state but the interest is omitted from the new certificate. In states that require the interest in the motor vehicle to be perfected under the Code, the perfection of this interest is lost as described in the preceding subsection.

B. SECURED CREDIT SALES

Secured credit sales are classified in terms of the nature of the collateral involved.

10. Credit Sale of Consumer Goods

When the parties to a credit sale of consumer goods agree that the seller should retain a security interest in the goods, that agreement must be in writing. As soon as the security interest attaches, it is perfected without the seller's taking any further step.[9] However, the seller must file a financing statement to protect the security interest from destruction by resale. If no such filing is made and the buyer resells the collateral to another consumer who

---

[7] UCC § 9-402.

[8] If there is no written security agreement, the interest is destroyed when the collateral is surrendered.

[9] Howell State Bank v Jericho Boats, Inc. 533 NYS2d 363 (1988).

pays value and has no knowledge of the seller's security interest, that interest is destroyed or discharged by the resale.

The *Balon* case illustrates the rights of sub-purchasers of consumer goods who purchased the goods from a consumer-purchaser.

BALON v CADILLAC AUTOMOBILE CO.
113 NH 108, 303 A2d 194 (1973)

Balon and Gibert each purchased a Cadillac for personal use from Russell Saia, a private owner. They did not know that each car was subject to an unfiled security interest in favor of the original seller, the Cadillac Automobile Company of Boston. Balon and Gibert claimed that they owned their cars free of the security interest of Cadillac. Cadillac contended that Balon and Gibert did not believe that they were purchasing a clear title and that they were subject to its unfiled security interests. Cadillac repossessed the cars. Balon and Gibert sued Cadillac. From a judgment in favor of Balon and Gibert, Cadillac appealed.

LAMPRON, J. . . . The issue to be decided is whether the trial court properly found and ruled that Balon and Gibert each had clear title to his automobile by virtue of § 9-307 of the [UCC]. . . .

On September 28, 1965, Charles Pernokas was a salesman for Cadillac Automobile in Boston, Massachusetts. He had previously worked for another employer as a car salesman with Russell Saia. On that day Saia came to Cadillac Automobile looking for a convertible for a customer. Pernokas showed him two cars and Saia said he would hear from him shortly. He telephoned soon thereafter saying that his customer, Peter J. Russell, would take one of the Cadillac convertibles and gave the required credit information and references. On the next day, Saia telephoned Pernokas again and told him another customer, Joseph P. DeLuca, would take the other convertible and gave credit information on him.

Pernokas testified that in each instance he delivered the car to Saia's place and that Saia and another person, supposedly Russell in one instance and DeLuca in the other, identified himself and signed the security agreements. The selling price, $5300 for each car, was paid by a $1000 cash down payment on each and the balance financed on a conditional sale agreement.

At about that time, an individual named Arthur Freije told Balon in Manchester that "somebody" had "a friend" who could get a good deal on Cadillacs. "Somebody" was Fred Sarno who had accompanied Saia on his visit to the Cadillac garage after which the two cars in question were bought. The "friend" was Russell Saia. Balon passed the information along to his stepfather, Gibert, and eventually both Balon and Gibert purchased a Cadillac convertible through Freije for $4300 each.

The October and November payments on these Cadillacs were not made to Cadillac Automobile. As a result of these defaults, Simons, its credit manager, made an investigation and concluded that Peter J. Russell and Joseph P. DeLuca, the apparent purchasers, did not exist and decided that "both of these were two straw deals." The trial court properly found on the evidence that the two Cadillac automobiles in question were purchased by Russell Saia and that he was the principal in their sale to Balon and Gibert.

[UCC §] 9-307 . . . reads as follows:

(1) A buyer in the ordinary course of business . . . takes free of a security interest created by his seller even though the security interest is perfected and even though the buyer knows of its existence.

(2) In the case of consumer goods . . . a buyer takes free of a security interest even though perfected if he buys without knowledge of the security interest, for value and for his own personal, family or household purposes . . . unless prior to the purchase the secured party has filed a financing statement covering such goods.

The secured interest of Cadillac Automobile was perfected when the agreement of the parties was executed. . . . However the security agreements covering these two automobiles were never filed. . . .

The buyer protected by § 9-307(1) is one who purchases in the ordinary course of business from a person in the business of selling goods of the kind involved. § 1-201(9). Hence § 9-307(1) applies primarily to purchases from the inventory of a dealer in the type of goods sold. 4 Anderson, Uniform Commercial Code 323:24 (2d ed. 1971); *see National Shawmut Bank v Jones*, 108 NH 386, 236 A2d 484 (1967). The buyer protected under § 9-307(2) is one who purchases goods for consumer use, that is, for personal, family or household purposes, from a consumer seller. In order to fall within the protection of this section the goods must be consumer goods in the hands of both the buyer and the seller. . . .

The categorization of these automobiles at the time of the execution of the security agreement with Cadillac Automobile is an important factor in determining whether they were inventory or consumer goods in the hands of Saia when he sold them. . . . This classification of the goods remains unchanged in the controversy between Balon, Gibert, and Cadillac Automobile when it seeks to enforce its security agreement. Simon, Cadillac's credit manager, testified that it is company policy to record security agreements except when the buyer is an individual consumer as determined by the contract. Their security agreement provides that if the car is purchased for business purposes the address of the buyer's place of business must appear as the address on the front of the contract. There was evidence that the address on the front of the Peter Russell contract was listed in the Boston directory as the residence of Mrs. Jean Saia. Simon also testified that as far as the seller was concerned these sales were made to two private consumers for their personal, family and household use. Accordingly, following its policy with respect to consumer purchasers, the security agreements were not filed.

We hold that the trial court properly found and ruled that Russell Saia was a dishonest consumer purchaser of these automobiles. We further hold that these cars remained consumer goods in his hands at the time of the sales to Balon and Gibert who are protected by [UCC §] 9-307(2) if they were good faith consumer buyers for value without knowledge of Cadillac's security interest.

The company maintains, however, that the only conclusion which can be reached on the evidence is that Balon and Gibert "could not have conceivably held honest convictions that these transactions were legitimate." In support it cites § 1-201(19) which provides: "'Good faith' means honesty in fact in the conduct or transaction concerned." By its terms this is a subjective standard of good faith, that is, whether the particular purchaser believed he was in good faith, not whether anyone else would have held the same belief. The test is what the particular person did or thought in the given situation and whether or not he was honest in what he did. . .

There was evidence that Gibert had known Freije, who made the approaches which culminated in these sales, in a social way for about fifteen years. His wife had known him all her life. Balon knew him also and had purchased a 1963 Cadillac from him without any untoward incidents. Balon and Gibert learned from inquiries made to dealers known to them that the asking price of $4300 was consistent with prices at which such cars could be bought. The explanation advanced that these convertibles sold in September, when the new models were due, could be found by them plausible reasons for the price quoted. Simon testified that when Balon and Gibert came to Boston after their cars were taken they seemed genuinely concerned [in] trying to figure out what happened. There was no evidence that they had actual knowledge of the status of the title to these cars. The fact that others might have acted differently, made more inquiries, or been more suspicious does not require a conclusion that they lacked good faith when they purchased these cars. . . . The evidence is clear that they paid value and bought for personal, family, or household purposes.

We hold that the trial court properly found and ruled that Balon and Gibert were good faith consumer buyers for value from a consumer seller without knowledge of Cadillac Automobile's security interest which had not been filed. . . . Consequently they were entitled to the protection of UCC §] 9-307(2). . . .

[Judgment affirmed]

QUESTIONS

1. Classify the collateral in the hands of Russell Saia.
2. What did Cadillac Automobile need to do to perfect its security interest against most third parties?
3. Did Balon and Gibert acquire title clear of any prior security interest?

11. Credit Sale of Inventory

In contrast with one who buys goods for personal use, the buyer may be a merchant or dealer who intends to resell the goods. The goods that such a merchant or dealer buys are classified as inventory. The financing of the purchase of inventory may involve a third person, rather than the seller, as creditor. For example, a third person, such as a bank or finance company, may lend the dealer the money with which to make the purchase and to pay the seller in full. In such a case the security interest in the goods may be given by the buyer to the third person rather than to the seller. Accordingly, the terms **creditor** and **secured party** may refer to a seller who sells on credit or to a third person who finances the purchase of goods.

In general, the provisions regulating a secured transaction in inventory follow the same pattern that is applicable to the secured credit sale of consumer goods. Variations recognize the differences in the commercial settings of the two transactions.

Initially there must be possession of the goods or there must be a written security agreement. If perfection of the interest is desired, there must be a filing of a financing statement, or the creditor must hold possession of the collateral.

(a) USE OF GOODS. A secured transaction relating to inventory generally gives the buyer full freedom to deal with the collateral as though such goods were not subject to a security interest. Thus, the buyer-dealer may mingle the goods with existing inventory, resell the goods, take goods back and make exchanges, and so on, without being required to keep any records of just what became of the goods covered by the security agreement, or to replace the goods sold with other goods, or to account for the proceeds from the sale of the original goods.

(b) AFTER-ACQUIRED GOODS. The security agreement may expressly provide that the security interest of the creditor shall bind after-acquired property. The combination of the buyer's freedom to use and dispose of the collateral and the subjecting of after-acquired goods to the interest of the secured creditor permits the latter to have a floating lien. A **floating lien** is a claim in a changing or shifting stock of goods of the buyer. The UCC rejects the common law concept that the security interest was lost if the collateral was not maintained and accounted for separately.

12. Credit Sale of Equipment

In general, secured credit sales of equipment are treated the same as secured sales of inventory. However, the various provisions relating to resale by the buyer and the creditor's rights in proceeds have no practical application. The buyer does not resell the property but makes the purchase with the intention of keeping and using it. Filing is required to perfect a security interest in equipment.

C. SECURED LOANS

A secured transaction in personal property may be used to protect the lender of money.

13. Possessory Transaction

If a purchaser buys on credit, tangible things or documents may be delivered into the possession of the creditor to hold until the debtor pays the debt. This is commonly called a **pledge**, the creditor is a **pledgee**, and the debtor is a **pledgor**. A pledge is illustrated by a borrower obtaining a loan from a pawnshop and leaving personal property with the pawnbroker as security or collateral.

(a) KIND OF COLLATERAL. The collateral in a pledge may be a tangible object or thing. Collateral may be a document, such as a document of title (warehouse receipt or bill of lading) or a certificate of stock.

(b) ATTACHMENT AND PERFECTION. Since the pledge is by definition a possessory transaction (the creditor having possession of the collateral), the security agreement need not be written. When the creditor makes the loan and receives possession of the collateral under the agreement with the debtor, the security interest attaches and is perfected. No filing of a financing statement is required.

14. Nonpossessory Transaction

A secured transaction may allow the debtor to keep possession of the collateral as long as the debtor does not default in performing the secured obligation. Since the creditor does not have possession of the collateral, the transaction is called nonpossessory. In a nonpossessory transaction, the security agreement must be in writing.[10]

(a) KIND OF COLLATERAL. The tangible thing that is the collateral for a nonpossessory secured transaction may be an automobile, household goods, goods in the process of being manufactured, inventory, crops, farm products, minerals, equipment, fixtures, or negotiable documents. The collateral may also be accounts receivable and other claims of the debtor against third persons.

(b) ATTACHMENT AND PERFECTION. The creditor's security interest in the nonpossessory transaction attaches when the three elements for attachment described in Section 2 of this chapter have been satisfied. Generally, perfection is obtained by filing a financing statement. In the case of crops, timber, and minerals, the security agreement and the financing statement must describe the land involved and be filed in the county in which that land is located.

D. RIGHTS OF PARTIES BEFORE DEFAULT

The rights of parties to a secured transaction change when there is a default.

15. Status of Creditor Before Default

The status of a creditor who loaned money to the debtor is determined by ordinary principles of contract law. A creditor who is a seller of goods has the rights granted by Article 2, "Sales," of the Uniform Commercial Code. If the creditor is the lessor of goods, that status is determined by Article 2A, "Leases," of the Uniform Commercial Code.

16. Status of Debtor Before Default

The status of the debtor before default depends on whether there is a loan, a sale, or a lease.

The status of a debtor who borrowed money from the creditor is determined by ordinary principles of contract law. If the debtor is a buyer or lessee of goods, the debtor's status is determined by Article 9, "Secured

---
10 UCC § 9-302(1).

Transactions," and by either Article 2 or 2A of the Uniform Commercial Code.

17. Statement of Account

To keep the record straight, the debtor may send the creditor a written statement of the amount the debtor thinks is due and an itemization of the collateral, together with the request that the creditor approve the statement as submitted or correct and return the statement. Within two weeks after receiving the debtor's statement, the creditor must send the debtor a written approval or correction. If the secured creditor has assigned the secured claim, the creditor's reply must state the name and address of the assignee.

18. Termination Statement

A debtor who has paid the debt in full may make a written demand on the secured creditor, or the latter's assignee if the security interest has been assigned, to send the debtor a termination statement. A **termination statement** states that a security interest is no longer claimed under the specified financing statement. The debtor may present this statement to the filing officer, who marks the record "terminated" and returns to the secured party the various papers that had been filed. The termination statement clears the debtor's record so subsequent buyers or lenders will not find the prior filing standing against him or her.

E. PRIORITIES

Two or more parties may have conflicting interests in the same collateral.

19. Conflicting Interests

When there are two secured parties and neither party perfected the security interest, the interest first attaching prevails.

If one party has an unperfected interest and the other party has a perfected interest, the party with the perfected interest prevails.

If both parties have perfected interests, the general rule is that the first to attach, file, or perfect prevails.[11]

20. Purchase Money Security Interest

The priority of a purchase money security interest depends on the type of collateral involved.

(a) INVENTORY COLLATERAL. If the collateral is inventory, the purchase money secured creditor must do two things to prevail. The creditor must perfect before the debtor receives possession of the goods. The creditor must also give written notice to any other secured party who has previously filed a financing statement with respect to that inventory. The other secured parties must receive this notice before the debtor receives possession of the goods covered by the purchase money security interest.

(b) NONINVENTORY COLLATERAL. If the collateral is noninventory collateral, such as equipment, the purchase money secured creditor will prevail over all others as to the same collateral if a financing statement is filed within ten days after the giving of possession to the debtor. For example, First Bank gives value to debtor Kwik Copy and properly files a financing statement covering all of Kwik Copy's present and after-acquired copying equipment. Second Bank gives value to Kwik Copy to enable Kwik Copy to purchase a new copier. Second Bank's interest in the copier will be superior to First Bank's interest if Second Bank perfects its interest by filing either before the debtor receives the copier or within ten days thereafter.

21. Status of Repair or Storage Lien

What happens when the debtor does not pay for the repair or storage of the collateral? In most states, a person repairing or storing goods has a lien or right to keep possession of the goods until paid for such services. The repairer or storer also has the right to sell the goods to obtain payment if the customer fails to pay and if proper notice is given.

The Code declares that the lien for repairs or storage is superior to the perfected security interest in the collateral. The only exception to this rule makes the perfected security interest superior if the lien was created by statute, rather than by common law, and that statute expressly states that the lien is subordinate to a perfected security interest in the collateral.

22. Status of Buyer of Collateral from Debtor

The debtor may sell the collateral to a third person. What effect does this have against the secured creditor?

(a) UNPERFECTED SECURITY INTEREST. Such a security interest has no effect against a buyer who gives value and buys in ignorance of the security interest. A buyer who does not satisfy these conditions is subject to the security interest.

(b) PERFECTED SECURITY INTEREST. If the security interest was perfected, the buyer of the collateral is ordinarily subject to the security interest unless the creditor had consented to the sale.

(c) DEBTOR BUYING FROM INVENTORY. The consent of the secured creditor to a sale by the debtor is not required if the debtor had originally purchased the collateral from a dealer's inventory in the ordinary course of business. In this case, a resale by the debtor to another buyer destroys the security interest regarding such goods that was held by the

---

[11] UCC § 9-312.

dealer's creditor in the dealer's inventory, even though that final buyer knew of the security interest and that interest was perfected.[12]

(d) RESALE OF CONSUMER GOODS. When the collateral constitutes consumer goods in the hands of the debtor, a resale of the goods to another consumer destroys the security interest of the debtor's creditor, provided that it had not been perfected by filing and was unknown to the ultimate buyer.

F. RIGHTS OF PARTIES AFTER DEFAULT

When a debtor defaults on an obligation in a secured transaction, the secured creditor has the option of suing the debtor to enforce the debt or of proceeding against the collateral.

23. Creditor's Possession and Disposition of Collateral

On the debtor's default, the secured party is entitled to take the collateral from the debtor. Self-help repossession is allowed if this can be done without causing a breach of the peace. If a breach of the peace might occur, the seller must use court action to obtain the collateral.

In the *Ragde* case the debtor alleged a breach of the peace by a repossession at 5 A.M.

The secured creditor may sell, lease, or otherwise dispose of the collateral to pay the defaulted debt. A sale may be private or public, at any time and place, and on any terms, provided that the sale is done in a manner that is commercially reasonable. The creditor's sale destroys all interest of the debtor in the collateral.

RAGDE v PEOPLES BANK
53 Wash App 173, 767 P2d 949 (1989)

Ragde executed a note in favor of Peoples Bank. His 1974 Mercedes automobiles were collateral for the note. When Ragde defaulted on the note, Peoples hired a towing company to repossess the cars in which it held a security interest. At 5 A.M. two tow trucks under contract with the bank took the cars from Ragde's driveway. The repossession was uneventful, and no confrontation or verbal exchange took place. Ragde alleged that the repossession caused a tremendous ruckus, awakening him and causing him to leap out of bed, fall onto some furniture, and hurt his back. He also alleged that the noise caused him severe emotional and mental shock. Ragde filed a complaint against the bank and the towing company, alleging breach of the peace. From summary judgment in favor of the bank and the towing company, Ragde appealed.

WINSOR, J. . . . [UCC §] 9-503 empowers a secured creditor to take possession of collateral upon default by the debtor, provided the creditor can do so without a "breach of the peace." When a repossession results in a "breach of the peace," the creditor is liable for resultant damages, including damages for personal injuries sustained by the debtor in resisting the repossession. . . .

---

[12] Central Finance Loan v Bank of Illinois, 149 Ill App 3d 724, 102 Ill Dec 965, 500 NE2d 1066 (1986).

Ragde contends that because the repossession at issue here was conducted at night, in his driveway, in a remote and private area, it breached the peace. He argues that a breach of the peace need not involve a physical confrontation, but includes acts likely to provoke disturbance. According to Ragde, a "night raid" that causes a "tremendous ruckus" in a secluded residential neighborhood has potential for provoking a disturbance, and therefore it should be a jury question as to whether such a repossession is in fact a breach of the peace.

We agree that a breach of the peace does not necessarily require a physical confrontation. In *Stone Mach. Co. v Kessler*, 1 Wash App 750, 463 P2d 651 (1970), the court quoted with approval the following definitions of breach of the peace:

A breach of the peace is a public offense done by violence, or one causing or likely to cause an immediate disturbance of public order.

To constitute a "breach of the peace" it is not necessary that the peace be actually broken, and if what is done is unjustifiable and unlawful, tending with sufficient directness to break the peace, no more is required, nor is actual personal violence an essential element of the offense.

. . . We do not agree, however, that the repossession here breached the peace. First, Ragde offers no support for his conclusory statement that the repossession caused a "tremendous ruckus." . . . Ragde offers no legal authority for his position that noise alone can be a breach of the peace for purposes of [UCC §] 9-503. Without such authority, we are unwilling to hold that making noise is an act likely to break the peace. . . .

Second, Ragde's argument that a "night raid" is a breach of the peace is without legal basis. Although there is little case law on the "night raid" issue, the Arkansas Supreme Court recently held that a 4 A.M. repossession from the debtor's driveway was not a breach of the peace, reasoning:

There is no evidence that McClendon entered any gates, doors, or other barricades to reach the truck. He just attached the truck to his wrecker in the dead of the night and drove away. There was no confrontation with Baldwin. He was asleep when the truck was repossessed. The repossession was accomplished without breaching the peace according to our cases.

. . . So long as the law permits automobiles to be repossessed from residential property, it is reasonable to allow the repossession to occur in the early morning hours. At that hour, a confrontation with the debtor is likely avoided, and the debtor is not subjected to the humiliation of having his or her automobile repossessed from a public place. Moreover,

the business community must be given some latitude to pursue reasonable methods of collecting debts even though such methods often might result in some inconvenience or embarrassment to the debtor.

. . . We hold that the circumstances of the Radge repossession did not amount to a breach of the peace.

[Judgment affirmed]

24. Creditor's Retention of Collateral

Instead of selling the collateral, the creditor may wish to keep it and cancel the debt owed.

(a) NOTICE OF INTENTION. To retain the collateral in satisfaction of the debt, the creditor must send the debtor written notice of this intent.

(b) COMPULSORY DISPOSITION OF COLLATERAL. In two situations, the creditor must proceed to dispose of the collateral. A creditor must do so if the person receiving the notice of intention to retain makes a written objection to retention within 21 days after the retention notice was sent.

The creditor must also dispose of the collateral if it consists of consumer goods and the debtor has paid 60 percent or more of the cash price or of the loan secured by the security interest. However, the debtor, after default, may sign a writing surrendering the right to require the resale.

A creditor failing to dispose of the collateral when required to do so is liable to the debtor for conversion of the collateral or for the penalty imposed by the Code for violation of Article 9.[13]

25. Debtor's Right of Redemption

The debtor may redeem the collateral at any time prior to the time the secured party has disposed of the collateral or entered into a binding contract for resale. To redeem, the debtor must tender the entire obligation that is owed, plus any legal costs and expenses incurred by the secured party.

26. Disposition of Collateral

On the debtor's default, the creditor may sell the collateral at public or private sale or may lease it to a third party. The creditor must give any required notice and act in a commercially reasonable manner.[14]

(a) NOTICE OF DISPOSITION OF COLLATERAL. Ordinarily, notice must be given of the disposition of the collateral. The UCC does not specify the form of notice, and any form of notice that is reasonable is sufficient. A letter to the debtor can satisfy this requirement. If a public sale is made, the notice must give the time and place of the sale. If a private sale is made, it is sufficient to give notice of the after which the private sale will be made.

(b) WHEN NOTICE IS NOT REQUIRED. No notice is required when the collateral is perishable, is threatening to decline rapidly in value, or is sold on a recognized market or exchange.

27. Postdisposition Accounting

When the creditor disposes of the collateral, the proceeds are applied in the following order. Proceeds are first used to pay the expenses of disposing of the collateral. Next, proceeds are applied to the debt owed the secured creditor

---

[13] UCC § 9-507.
[14] UCC § 9-504. John Deere Leasing Co. v Franken (Iowa) 395 NW2d 885 (1986).

making the disposition. Remaining proceeds are applied to any debts owed other creditors holding security interests in the same collateral that are subordinate to the interest of the disposing creditor.

(a) DISTRIBUTION OF SURPLUS. I f there is any money remaining, the surplus is paid to the debtor.

(b) LIABILITY FOR DEFICIT. If the proceeds of the disposition are not sufficient to pay the costs and the debt of the disposing creditor, the debtor is liable for the deficit.

However, the disposition of the collateral must have been conducted in the manner required by the Code. This means that proper notice was given, if required, and that the disposition was made in a commercially reasonable manner.[15]

If either of these requirements was not satisfied, some states refuse to allow the creditor to recover any deficiency. Other states allow a deficiency recovery limited in such a case to the difference between the amount owed to the creditor and the fair market value of the collateral at the time of the disposition plus the costs.

SUMMARY

A security interest is an interest in personal property or fixtures that secures payment or performance of an obligation. The property that is subject to the interest is called the collateral, and the party holding the interest is called the secured party. Attachment is the creation of a security interest. To secure protection against third parties' claims to the collateral, the secured party must perfect the security interest.

Tangible collateral is divided into four classes: consumer goods, equipment, inventory, and farm products. These classifications are based on the debtor's intended use, not on the physical characteristics of the goods.

In the ordinary credit sale of consumer goods, no filing in any state or government office is required in order to perfect the secured party's interest. The secured party who does not file will still have priority over other creditors of the buyer. The secured party will not have priority over a subpurchaser of the debtor who buys for personal, family, or household use without knowledge of the security interest. If the secured party wants to be protected against the subpurchaser, a financing statement must be filed.

In the case of goods classified as inventory, unless the secured party holds possession of

the collateral, the secured party must file a financing statement to perfect the interest. A financing statement must be signed by the debtor, must have the names and addresses of the parties, and must describe the collateral. A security interest covers proceeds from the sale of the collateral unless such interest is expressly excluded. Any customer of the dealer selling from inventory will take the goods free from the security interest of the dealer's supplier, even though the customer knows that the goods are subject to a perfected security interest. The filing, however, will protect the secured creditor from other creditors.

A secured credit sale of equipment is treated the same as a secured credit sale of inventory, except that the provisions relating to resale by the buyer have no practical application.

A secured transaction may be created to secure a debt owed by the debtor to the secured creditor. If the creditor has possession of the collateral, the transaction is possessory, the security agreement may be oral, and perfection exists without filing. If the debtor has possession of the collateral, the transaction is nonpossessory, the security agreement must

---

[15] UCC § 9-504. General Electric Capital Corp. v Vashi (Iowa App) 480 NW2d 880 (1992).

be written, and perfection requires a filing or a motor vehicle title certificate notation.

On default, a secured party may repossess the collateral from the buyer if this can be done without a breach of the peace. If a breach of the peace might occur, the secured party must use court action to regain the collateral. If the buyer has paid 60 percent or more of the cash price of the consumer goods, the seller must resell them within 90 days after repossession unless the buyer, after default, has waived this right in writing. Notice to the debtor of the sale of the collateral is usually required. A debtor may redeem the collateral prior to the time the secured party disposes of it or contracts to resell it.

If two or more parties have conflicting interests in the same collateral, priorities are determined according to UCC Article 9.

LAW IN PRACTICE

1. Be sure that the prerequisites for attachment have taken place; otherwise, as a creditor you will not have an enforceable security interest against the debtor.
2. If you are a secured creditor, perfect your security interest so that you will not lose your rights as against some third parties.
3. Be sure that the financing statement offered for filing has no serious errors; if it does, your security interest will not be perfected.

4. If you are the debtor in a secured transaction and the obligation has been paid in full, be sure that a termination statement is filed.
5. If you are a secured creditor and you sell the debtor's property after default, act in a commercially reasonable manner and give proper notice of the sale.

QUESTIONS AND CASE PROBLEMS

1. What social forces are affected by the destruction of a security interest in consumer goods when a consumer debtor resells the goods to another consumer who does not know of the security interest?
2. Name the two ways a creditor can perfect a security interest.
3. Wayne Smith purchased a computer from Lee Sounds, Inc., for personal use. Smith signed an installment purchase note and a security agreement. Under the terms of the note, Smith was to pay $100 down and $50 a month for 20 months. The security agreement included a description of the computer. However, Lee did not file a financing statement. Did Lee fulfill the requirements necessary for the attachment and perfection of its security interest in the computer? Why?
4. Thompson Home Appliance Store purchased refrigerator-freezers from the Henson Manufacturing Company and financed the purchase by obtaining a loan from the First National Bank. Thompson signed an agreement which gave the bank a security interest in its inventory of refrigerator-freezers. Erhart purchased a refrigerator-freezer from Thompson on credit. The bank claimed that its security interest extended to the down payment that Erhart had made and to the unpaid balance that she owed Thompson. Was the bank correct?
5. Murray purchased an air conditioner from the Electric Company, to be used in his residence. Classify the air conditioner as collateral when in the possession of (a) the Electric Company and (b) Murray.
6. Compare or contrast attachment of a security interest with perfection of a security interest.
7. Rawlings purchased a typewriter from the Kroll Typewriter Co. for $600. At the time of the purchase, he made an initial payment of $75 and agreed to pay the balance in monthly installments. A security agreement was prepared that complied with the UCC. No financing statement was ever filed for the transaction. Rawlings, at a time when he still owed a balance on the typewriter and without the consent of Kroll, sold the typewriter to a neighbor. The neighbor, who had no knowledge of the security interest, used the typewriter in her home. Can Kroll repossess the typewriter from the neighbor?

8. Kim purchased on credit a $1,000 freezer from the Silas Household Appliance Store. After she had paid approximately $700, Kim missed the next monthly installment payment. Silas repossessed the freezer and billed Kim for the balance of the purchase price of $300. Kim claimed that the freezer, now in the possession of Silas, was worth much more than the balance due, and requested Silas to sell the freezer in order to wipe out the balance of the debt and to leave something over for Kim. Silas claimed that as Kim had broken her contract to pay the purchase price, she had no right to say what should be done with the freezer. Was Silas correct? Explain.

9. Benson purchased a new Ford Thunderbird automobile. She traded in her old car and used the Magnavox Employees Credit Union to finance the balance. The credit union took a security interest in the Ford. Subsequently, the Ford was involved in a number of accidents. It was taken to a dealer for repairs. Benson was unable to pay for the work done. The dealer claimed a lien on the car for services and materials furnished. The Magnavox Employees Credit Union claimed priority. Which claim has priority? [Magnavox Employees Credit Union v Benson, 165 Ind App 155, 331 NE2d 46]

10. Lockovich borrowed money from a bank to purchase a motorboat. The bank took a security interest in the boat but never filed a financing statement. A subsequent default on the loan took place and the debtor was declared bankrupt. The bank claimed priority to the boat alleging that no financing statement had to be filed. Do you agree? Why? [In re Lockovich, (WD Pa) 124 Bankr. 660]

11. Hull-Dobbs sold an automobile to Mallicoat and then assigned the sales contract to the Volunteer Finance & Loan Corp. Later Volunteer repossessed the automobile and sold it. When Volunteer sued Mallicoat for the deficiency between the contract price and the proceeds on resale, Mallicoat raised the defense that he had not been properly notified of the resale. The loan manager of the finance company testified that Mallicoat had been sent a registered letter stating that the car would be sold. He did not state whether the letter merely declared in general terms that the car would be sold or specified a date for its resale. He admitted that the letter never was delivered to Mallicoat and was returned to the finance company "unclaimed." The loan manager also testified that the sale was advertised by posters, but on cross examination, he admitted that he was not able to state when or where it was advertised. It was shown that Volunteer knew where Mallicoat and

his father lived and where Mallicoat was employed. Mallicoat claimed that he had not been properly notified. Volunteer asserted that sufficient notice had been given. Was the notice of the resale sufficient? [Mallicoat v Volunteer Finance & Loan Corp. 57 Tenn App 106, 415 SW2d 347]

12. A borrowed money from B. He orally agreed that B had a security interest in certain equipment that was standing in A's yard. There was nothing in writing, and no filing of any kind was made. Nine days later, B took possession of the equipment. What kind of interest did B have in the equipment after taking possession of it? [Transport Equipment Co. v Guaranty State Bank (CA10 Kan) 518 F2d 377]

13. Cook sold Martin a new tractor truck for approximately $13,000, with a down payment of approximately $3,000 and the balance to be paid in 30 monthly installments. The sales agreement provided that "on default in any payment, Cook could take immediate possession of the property... without notice or demand. For this purpose vendor may enter upon any premises the property may be." Martin failed to pay the installments when due, and Cook notified him that the truck would be repossessed. Martin left the tractor truck, attached to a loaded trailer, locked on the premises of a company in Memphis. Martin intended to drive to the West Coast with the trailer. When Cook located the tractor truck, no one was around. To disconnect the trailer from the truck (since Cook had no right to the trailer), Cook removed the wire screen over a ventilator hole by unscrewing it from the outside with his penknife. He next reached through the ventilator hole with a stick and unlocked the door of the tractor truck. He then disconnected the trailer and had the truck towed away. Martin sued Cook for unlawfully repossessing the truck by committing a breach of the peace. Decide. [Martin v Cook, 237 Miss 267, 114 So 2d 669]

14. Muska borrowed money from the Bank of California. He secured the loan by giving the bank a security interest in equipment and machinery that he had at his place of business. The bank filed a financing statement to perfect the interest. The statement contained all the information required by the Code, except that it failed to state the residence address of the debtor. Muska filed for bankruptcy. The trustee in bankruptcy claimed that the security interest of the bank was not perfected on the theory that the omission of the residence address from the financing statement made it defective.

Decide. *[Lines v Bank of California (CA9 Cal) 467 F2d 1274]*

15. Kimbrell's Furniture Company sold a new television set and tape player to Charlie O'Neil and his wife. Each purchase was on credit and in each instance there was executed a security agreement. Later, on the same day of purchase, O'Neil carried the items to Bonded Loan, a pawnbroker, and pledged the television and tape deck as security for a loan. Bonded Loan holds possession of the television set and tape player as security for its loan and contends that its lien is prior to the unrecorded security interest of Kimbrell. Decide. *[Kimbrell's Furniture Company, Inc. v Sig Friedman, d/b/a Bonded Loan (SC) 198 SE2d 803]*

CHAPTER 36

OTHER SECURITY DEVICES

LEARNING OBJECTIVES

After studying this chapter, you will be able to:
1. *Distinguish a contract of suretyship from a contract of guaranty.*
2. *Define the parties to a contract of suretyship and a contract of guaranty.*
3. *List and explain the rights of sureties to protect themselves from loss.*
4. *Explain the defenses available to a surety.*
5. *Explain the nature of a letter of credit and the liabilities of the various parties to a letter of credit.*

Subject to certain exceptions, Article 9 of the UCC regulates all secured transactions dealing with personal property. The secured credit sales of consumer goods, inventory, and equipment were discussed in Chapter 35. This chapter considers other common forms of security devices.

A. SURETYSHIP AND GUARANTY

Parties may make a contract by which one party agrees to pay if another party does not pay or defaults in the performance of an obligation. The relationship by which one person becomes responsible for the debt or undertaking of another person is used most commonly to ensure that a debt will be paid or that a contractor will perform the work called for by a contract.

1. Definitions

One kind of agreement to answer for the debt or default of another is called a contract or undertaking of **suretyship**. The obligor is called a **surety**. The other kind of agreement is called a contract or undertaking of **guaranty**, and the obligor is called a **guarantor**. In both cases, the person who owes the money or is under the original obligation to pay or perform is called the **principal**, the principal debtor, or debtor.[1] The person to whom the debt or obligation is owed is the **obligee** or **creditor**.

Suretyship and guaranty undertakings have the common feature of a promise to answer for the debt or default of another, but they have a basic difference. The surety is primarily liable for the debt or obligation of the principal. Ordinarily, the guarantor is only secondarily liable. This means that the moment the principal is in default, the obligee may demand performance or payment from the surety. The obligee generally cannot do so in the case of the guarantor and must first attempt to collect from the principal. An exception is an **absolute guaranty**, which creates the same obligation as a suretyship. A guaranty of payment creates an absolute guaranty.

The *General Motors Acceptance* case illustrates the difference between a surety and a guarantor.

GENERAL MOTORS ACCEPTANCE CORP. v DANIELS

303 Md 254, 492 A2d 1306 (1985)

In June, 1981, John Daniels agreed to purchase a used automobile from Lindsay Cadillac Company. Because John had a poor credit rating, his brother Seymoure agreed to cosign the installment sales contract. On June 23, 1981, Seymoure accompanied John to Lindsay Cadillac and signed the contract on the line designated *Buyer*. John signed the contract on the line designated *Co-Buyer*. Lindsay Cadillac then assigned the contract to General Motors Acceptance Corporation (GMAC), a company engaged in the business of financing automobiles. Installment payments were not made, and GMAC then sued Seymoure to collect the amount due. No suit was brought against John because he was not served with process. Seymoure claimed that he was simply a guarantor, not a surety, and therefore could not be sued until GMAC had

---

[1] Unless otherwise stated, *surety* as used in the text includes guarantor as well as surety, and *guaranty* is limited to a conditional guaranty. The word *principal* is also used by the law to identify the person who employs an agent. The principal in suretyship must be distinguished from the agent's principal.

brought suit against John. From a judgment in favor of Seymoure, GMAC appealed.

COLE, J. . . . GMAC marshals several alternative arguments in support of its position that the District Court was clearly erroneous in finding that Seymoure was a guarantor of the contract between John and itself. In particular, GMAC argues that Seymoure was a surety for his brother in this transaction. We agree.

Maryland law has consistently maintained a distinction between a contract of suretyship and a contract of guaranty. A review of the distinguishing characteristics of each of these contracts, together with a summary of the relevant principles governing the interpretation and construction of contracts, provides a useful, if not necessary, predicate to the resolution of the issue presented in this case.

A contract of suretyship is a tripartite agreement among a principal obligor, his obligee, and a surety. This contract is a direct and original undertaking under which the surety is primarily or jointly liable with the principal obligor, and therefore is responsible at once if the principal obligor fails to perform. A surety is usually bound with his principal by the same instrument, executed at the same time, and on the same consideration. . . .

Ultimate liability rests upon the principal obligor rather than the surety, but the obligee has remedy against both. The surety, however, becomes subrogated to the rights of the obligee when the surety pays the debt for the principal obligor. . . .

A contract of guaranty . . . is collateral to and independent of the principal contract that is guaranteed and, as a result, the guarantor is not a party to the principal obligation. A guarantor is therefore secondarily liable to the creditor on his contract and his promise to answer for the debt, default, or miscarriage of another becomes absolute upon default of the principal debtor and the satisfaction of the conditions precedent to liability. Second, the original contract of the principal is not the guarantor's contract. . . . Rather, the guarantor agrees that the principal is able to and will perform a contract that he has made or is about to make, and that if he defaults the guarantor will pay the resulting damages provided the guarantor is notified of the principal's default. As such, the guarantor insures the ability or solvency of the principal. Third, the contract of guaranty is often founded upon a separate consideration from that supporting the contract of the principal and, consequently, the consideration for the guarantor's promise moves wholly or in part to him. . . .

Our review of the evidence in this case convinces us that the District Court erred in finding that Seymoure was a guarantor rather than a surety with respect to the installment sales contract. In our judgment the indicia for determining whether a contract is one for suretyship or one for guaranty all point to the existence of a suretyship agreement.

Initially, we note that because the contractual language is clear and unambiguous on its face, we confine our review to the contract itself. Seymoure agreed to purchase the subject automobile by affixing his signature to the installment sales contract on the line designated "Buyer."

The contract clearly stated that all buyers agreed to be jointly and severally liable for the purchase of that vehicle. Therefore, under the objective law of contracts, a reasonable person knew or should have known that he was subjecting himself to primary liability for the purchase of the automobile. . . .

Seymoure executed the same contract as his brother, thereby making himself a party to the original contract. There is no evidence that Seymoure executed an agreement collateral to and independent of this contract. This fact, standing alone, ordinarily negates the existence of a guaranty. As one court observed, "it is certain that in most cases 'the joint execution of a contract by the principal and another operates to exclude the idea of a guaranty and that in all cases such fact is an index pointing to suretyship.'"*Phoenix Insurance Co. v Lester Bros.*, 203 Va. 802, 807, 127 SE2d 432, 436 (1962).

Both Seymoure and John signed the contract at the same time. Although not dispositive, this fact tends to establish the existence of a contract of suretyship rather than a contract of guaranty. Furthermore, there are no competent facts indicating that Seymoure expressly agreed to pay for the automobile only upon the default of John. Seymoure also did not qualify his signature in any manner. Thus, by the terms of the contract Seymoure agreed to be primarily and jointly liable with John for the purchase of the automobile. GMAC was therefore not required to proceed against John in the first instance, and the failure of GMAC promptly to notify Seymoure of the default in payments and of the lapse in physical damage insurance coverage does not constitute a discharge.

Finally, on the facts of this case it is immaterial that the contract did not expressly designate Seymoure as a "surety." Whether a party has entered into a contract of suretyship or guaranty is to be determined by the substance of the agreement and not by its nomenclature.

[Judgment reversed]

QUESTIONS

1. What is the principal difference between a surety and a guarantor?
2. Was Seymoure a surety or a guarantor?
3. What was the basis for the court's decision?

2. Indemnity Contract Distinguished

Both suretyship and guaranty differ from an indemnity contract. An **indemnity contract** is an undertaking by one person, for a consideration, to pay another person a sum of money in the event that the other person sustains a specified loss. A fire insurance policy is an example of an indemnity contract.

3. Creation of the Relation

The suretyship, guaranty, and indemnity relationships are based on contract. The principles relating to capacity, formation, validity, and interpretation of contracts are applicable. Generally, the ordinary rules of offer and accep-

tance apply. Notice of acceptance must usually be given by the obligee to the guarantor.

In most states, the statute of frauds requires that contracts of guaranty be in writing to be enforceable. No writing is required when the promise is made primarily for the promisor's benefit.

In the absence of a special statute, no writing is required for contracts of suretyship or indemnity because they impose primary liability and not a secondary liability to answer for the debt or default of another. Special statutes or sound business practice, however, commonly require the use of written contracts for both suretyship and indemnity.

When the contract of guaranty is made at the same time as the original transaction, the consideration for the original promise that is covered by the guaranty is also consideration for the promise of the guarantor. When the guaranty contract is entered into subsequent to and separate from the original transaction, there must be new consideration for the promise of the guarantor.

4. Rights of Sureties

Sureties have a number of rights to protect them from loss, to obtain their discharge because of the conduct of others that would be harmful to them, or to recover money that they were required to pay because of the debtor's breach.

(a) EXONERATION. If the position of the surety becomes endangered, such as when the debtor is about to leave the state, the surety may call on the creditor to take action against the debtor. If at that time the creditor could proceed against the debtor and fails to do so, the surety is released or exonerated from liability to the extent that the surety has been harmed by such failure.

(b) SUBROGATION. When a surety pays a claim that it is obligated to pay, it automatically acquires the claim and the rights of the creditor. This is known as **subrogation**. That is, once the claimant is paid in full, the surety stands in the same position as the claimant and may sue the debtor or enforce any security that was available to the claimant in order to recover the amount it has paid. The effect is the same as if the claimant, on being paid, made an express assignment of all rights to the surety.

(c) INDEMNITY. A surety that has made payment of a claim for which it was liable as surety is entitled to indemnity from the principal; that is, it is entitled to demand from the principal reimbursement of the amount that it has paid.

(d) CONTRIBUTION. If there are two or more sureties, each is liable to the claimant for the full amount of the debt, until the claimant has been paid in full. Between themselves, however, each is liable only for a proportionate share of the debt. Accordingly, if a surety has paid more than its share of the debt, it is entitled to demand that its co-sureties contribute to it. In the absence of a contrary agreement, co-sureties must share the burden equally.

In the *Collins* case a person paying a debt claimed that he was entitled to contribution.

COLLINS v THROCKMORTON
(Del App) 425 A2d 146 (1981)

Throckmorton and Collins were the sole stockholders as well as officers and directors in Central Ceilings Inc. Central borrowed money from the Wilmington Trust Co. A demand note was executed by the corporate officers. Throckmorton, and his wife, and Collins, and his wife, signed as unconditional guarantors of the note on behalf of Central. Central eventually went out of business. Throckmorton and his wife took out a bank loan to satisfy the demand note. The bank then assigned the original demand note with all its rights to Throckmorton. He claimed contribution from the Collinses for half of the amounts paid by him. From a judgment in favor of the plaintiff, the defendants appealed.

McNEILLY, J. . . . . The right of a surety or guarantor, upon being compelled to pay more than his just proportion of the principal's debt, to be reimbursed by his fellow guarantors for the excess is grounded on equitable principles. . . .

The Restatement of the Law of Security provides in pertinent part:

(1) A surety who has discharged more than his proportionate share of the principal's duty is entitled to contribution from a co-surety.

(a) who has consented to the surety's becoming bound, in the proportionate amount of the net outlay properly expended. . . .

The undisputed facts show that the 1973 note was guaranteed by four persons. Consequently, each was potentially liable for one-quarter of Central's default on the note. Although the complaint alleged the plaintiff [Throckmorton] personally satisfied Central's default by paying the entirety of the principal and interest owed on the note in May, 1975, the defendants argue that the trial proofs show that the plaintiff's wife, the fourth co-guarantor, contributed equally with the plaintiff to this satisfaction. Thus, of the $9,668.73 paid to satisfy the 1973 note, the defendants claim the plaintiff contributed only half ($4,834.36). Of that amount the plaintiff was personally liable for half, which constituted one-quarter of Central's total default ($2,417.18). Thus argue the defendants, the maximum amount of contribution which the plaintiff could recover from the two defendants was $2,417.18, *i.e.*, the amount in excess of his share of Central's default which the plaintiff personally paid to satisfy the 1973 note. Therefore, the defendants argue that the Trial Court's decision, which was premised on the assumption that the plaintiff satisfied the entire default by Central (or at least three-quarters thereof), erroneously awarded judgment against each defendant in the amount of $2,417.18, double the excess amount which the plaintiff allegedly paid in satisfaction of the note and, thus, double the total amount of contribution which he was entitled to recover from the defendants collectively. . .

Although there was no direct testimony concerning the respective amounts which the plaintiff and his wife contributed to satisfaction of the 1973 note, the bank's assignment of the note to the plaintiff, individually, gives rise to a reasonable inference that, as between the plaintiff and his wife, the plaintiff alone was entitled to seek contribution from the defendants. While it would obviously be desired to have a more detailed and explicit factual record on this point, the failure to so develop the record must be laid at the defendants' doorstep. Therefore, we will not disturb that portion of the Trial Court's judgment which requires each defendant to pay the plaintiff $2,417.18 for their contributive shares on the demand note as satisfied. . . .

[Judgment affirmed]

QUESTIONS

1. What was the basis for the court's decision?
2. When there is more than one surety, can the creditor hold one surety liable for the full amount of the debt?

5. Defenses of Sureties

The surety's defenses include those that may be raised by a party to any contract and also special defenses that are peculiar to the suretyship relation.

(a) ORDINARY CONTRACT DEFENSES. Since the relationship of suretyship is based on a contract, the surety may raise any defense that a party to an ordinary contract may raise. For example, a surety may raise the defense of lack of capacity of parties, absence of consideration, fraud, or mistake.

Fraud and concealment are common defenses. Fraud on the part of the principal that is unknown to the creditor and in which the creditor has not taken part does not ordinarily release the surety.

Since the risk of the principal's default is thrown on the surety, it is unfair for the claimant to conceal from the surety facts that are material to the surety's risk. By common law, the claimant was not required to volunteer information to the surety and was not required to disclose that the principal was insolvent. There is a growing modern view that the claimant should be required to inform the surety of matters material to the risk when the claimant has reason to believe that the surety does not possess such information.

(b) SURETYSHIP DEFENSES. In addition to the ordinary defenses that can be raised against any contract, the following defenses are peculiar to the suretyship relation.

1. The original obligation was invalid.
2. The principal was discharged by payment or some other means.
3. The original contract was modified without the surety's consent.

B. LETTERS OF CREDIT

A letter of credit is an agreement that the issuer of the letter will pay drafts drawn by the beneficiary of the letter. It is thus a form of advance arrangement for financing, in that it is known in advance how much money may be obtained from the issuer of the letter. It may also be used by a creditor as a security device, because the creditor knows that the drafts that the creditor draws will be accepted or paid by the issuer of the letter.

The use of letters of credit arose in international trade. While this continues to be the primary area of use, there is a growing use of letters in domestic sales and in transactions in which the letter of credit takes the place of a surety bond. Thus, a letter of credit has been used to ensure that a borrower would repay a loan, that a tenant would pay the rent due under a lease, and that a contractor would properly perform a construction contract. This kind of letter of credit is known as a **standby letter**.

There are few formal requirements for creating a letter of credit. Although banks often use a standardized form for convenience, they may draw up individualized letters of credit for particular situations. (See Figure 36-1.)

6. Definition

A **letter of credit** is an engagement by its issuer that it will pay or accept drafts when the conditions specified in the letter are satisfied. The issuer is usually a bank.

Three contracts are involved in letter-of-credit transactions: (1) the contract between the issuer and the customer of the issuer; (2) the letter of credit itself; and (3) the underlying agreement, often a contract of sale, between the beneficiary and the customer of the issuer of the letter of credit. (See Figure 36-2.) The letter of credit is completely independent from the other two contracts. Consideration is not required to establish or modify a letter of credit.

The issuer of the letter of credit is in effect the obligor on a third party beneficiary contract made for the benefit of the beneficiary of the letter.

In the *Comdata Network* case, the issuer of a letter of credit refused to pay the beneficiary the amount of cash advances that the beneficiary had made.

Figure 36-1 Letter of Credit

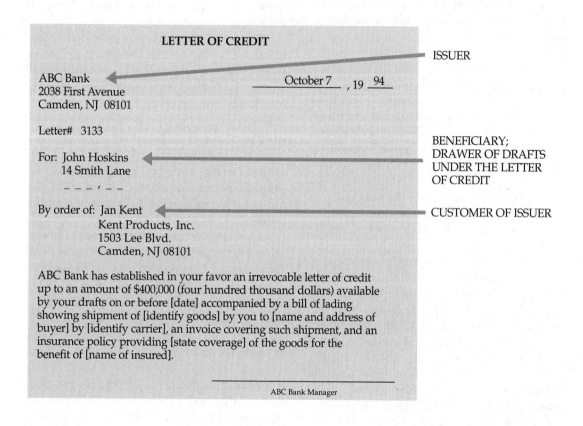

LETTER OF CREDIT

ABC Bank
2038 First Avenue
Camden, NJ 08101

Letter#   3133

For: John Hoskins
      14 Smith Lane
      _ _ _ , _ _

By order of: Jan Kent
              Kent Products, Inc.
              1503 Lee Blvd.
              Camden, NJ 08101

ABC Bank has established in your favor an irrevocable letter of credit
up to an amount of $400,000 (four hundred thousand dollars) available
by your drafts on or before [date] accompanied by a bill of lading
showing shipment of [identify goods] by you to [name and address of
buyer] by [identify carrier], an invoice covering such shipment, and an
insurance policy providing [state coverage] of the goods for the
benefit of [name of insured].

ABC Bank Manager

October 7 , 19 94

ISSUER

BENEFICIARY;
DRAWER OF DRAFTS
UNDER THE LETTER
OF CREDIT

CUSTOMER OF ISSUER

Figure 36-2 Three Contracts Involved in Letter of Credit Transactions

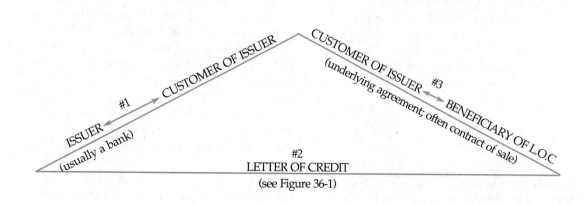

COMDATA NETWORK, INC. v FIRST INTERSTATE BANK OF FORT DODGE
(Iowa App) 497 NW2d 807 (1993)

First Interstate Bank issued a letter of credit in favor of Comdata Network, Inc. Comdata is engaged in money transfer services. It provides money to truckers on the road by way of cash advances through form checks written by truckers. When Comdata enters into a business relationship with a trucking company, it requires a letter of credit. This requirement is to secure advances made on behalf of the trucking company. One of the trucking companies defrauded the bank which issued the letter of credit. Comdata demanded that the bank make payment to it under the letter of credit for cash advances which the trucking company had not repaid. The bank, alleging fraud by the trucking company, refused. From a judgment in favor of Comdata, the bank appealed.

HARRIS, J. . . . A letter of credit is defined as "an engagement by a bank . . . made at the request of a customer . . . that the issuer will honor drafts or other demands for payment upon compliance with the conditions specified in the credit." . . . Stated otherwise:

A letter of credit . . . constitutes an enforceable obligation . . . in the nature of a contract by the issuer . . . in favor of the beneficiary . . . The duty created in the letter of credit is wholly independent of the underlying contract between the issuer's customer . . . and the beneficiary.

. . .

The key to the commercial vitality and function of a letter of credit is that the issuing bank's promise is independent of the underlying contracts, and the bank should not resort to them in interpreting a letter of credit. The respective parties are protected by careful description of the documents which will trigger payment. . .

The strict compliance doctrine . . . refers to the face of the documents, judged by the terms of credit, not to their efficacy or continued viability. . . .

The principle that the letter of credit is an independent promise . . . has been uniformly applied and enforced. . . .

. . . . Misconduct . . . is not relevant to this dispute which is between Comdata and the bank. The rule is settled that

the claim of a beneficiary of a letter of credit is not subject to [defenses normally applicable to third-party contracts]. The insurer must honor his drafts even if the insurer's customer has failed to pay agreed fees, has defrauded the insurer, has unequivocally repudiated, and so on. . . .

[Judgment affirmed]

QUESTIONS

1. Identify the three contracts involved in this letter of credit transaction.
2. Why should Comdata be allowed to recover on the letter of credit?
3. What is the rule of strict compliance?

7. Parties

The parties to a letter of credit are (a) the issuer, (b) the customer who makes the arrangements with the issuer, and (c) the beneficiary who will be the drawer of the drafts that will be drawn under the letter of credit. There may also be (d) an advising bank,[2] if the local issuer of the letter of credit requests its correspondent bank where the beneficiary is located to notify or advise the beneficiary that the letter has been issued.

As an illustration of the above, an American merchant may buy goods from a Spanish merchant. There may be a prior course of dealings between the parties, so that the seller is willing to take the buyer's commercial paper as payment or to take trade acceptances drawn on the buyer. If the foreign seller is not willing to do this, the American buyer, as customer, may go to a bank, the issuer, and obtain a letter of credit naming the Spanish seller as beneficiary. The American bank's correspondent or advising bank in Spain notifies the Spanish seller that this has been done. The Spanish seller will then draw drafts on the American buyer. By the letter of credit, the issuer is required to accept or pay these drafts.

8. Duration

A letter of credit continues for any length of time it specifies. Generally, a maximum money amount is stated in the letter, so that the letter is exhausted or used up when drafts aggregating that maximum have been accepted or paid by the issuer. A letter of credit may be used in installments as the beneficiary chooses. A letter of credit cannot be revoked or modified by the issuer or the customer without the consent of the beneficiary unless that right is expressly reserved in the letter.

9. Form

A letter of credit must be in writing and signed by the issuer. If the credit is issued by a bank and requires a documentary draft or a documentary demand for payment,[3] or if the credit is issued by a nonbank and requires that the draft or demand for payment be accompanied by a document of title, the instrument is presumed to be a letter of credit (rather than a contract of guaranty). Otherwise, the instrument must conspicuously state that it is a letter of credit.[4]

10. Duty of Issuer

The issuer is obligated to honor drafts drawn under the letter of credit if the conditions specified in the letter have been satisfied. The issuer takes the risk that the papers submitted are the ones required by the letter. If they are not, the issuer cannot obtain reimbursement for payment made in reliance on such documents. The issuer has no duty to verify that the papers are properly supported by facts or that the underlying transaction has been performed.

---

[2] Artoc Bank & Trust v Sun Marine Terminals (Tex App) 760 SW2d 311 (1988).

[3] A *documentary draft* or a *documentary demand for payment* is one for which honor is conditioned on the presentation of one or more documents. A document could be a document of title, security, invoice, certificate, notice of default, or other similar paper. UCC § 5-103(1)(b).

[4] Hendry Const. Co., Inc. v Bank of Hattiesburg (Miss) 562 So 2d 100 (1990).

It is thus immaterial that the goods sold by the seller in fact do not conform to the contract, as long as the seller tenders the documents specified by the letter of credit. If the issuer dishonors a draft without justification, it is liable to its customer for breach of contract.[5]

11. Reimbursement of Issuer

When the issuer of a letter of credit makes proper payment of drafts drawn under the letter of credit, it may obtain reimbursement from its customer for such payments. No reimbursement can be obtained if the payment was not proper. This will be the case when payment is made after the letter has expired or if the payment is in an amount greater than authorized by the letter. Reimbursement cannot be obtained if payment is made without the proper presentation of proper documents or it payment has been made in violation of a court injunction against payment.

SUMMARY

Suretyship and guaranty undertakings have the common feature of a promise to answer for the debt or default of another. A surety is primarily liable for the debt or obligation of the principal debtor. The guarantor is ordinarily only secondarily liable, unless the guarantor has made an absolute guaranty. The surety and guaranty relationships are based on contract. Sureties have a number of rights to protect them. They are exoneration, subrogation, indemnity, and contribution. In addition to those rights, sureties also have certain defenses. They include ordinary contract defenses, as well as some defenses peculiar to the suretyship relationship.

A letter of credit is an agreement that the issuer of the letter will pay drafts drawn on the issuer by the beneficiary of the letter. The issuer of the letter of credit is usually a bank.

There are three contracts involved in letter of credit transactions: (1) the contract between the issuer and the customer of the issuer, (2) the letter of credit itself, and (3) the underlying agreement between the beneficiary and the customer of the issuer of the letter of credit. The parties to a letter of credit are the issuer, the customer who makes the arrangement with the issuer, and the beneficiary who will be the drawer of the drafts to be drawn under the letter of credit. The letter of credit continues for any time it specifies. The letter of credit must be in writing and signed by the issuer. Consideration is not required to establish or modify a letter of credit. If the conditions in the letter of credit have been complied with, the issuer is obligated to honor drafts drawn under the letter of credit.

LAW IN PRACTICE

1. Remember if you are a guarantor of payment, you are liable at once on default of the principal debtor.
2. If a guaranty is made subsequent to and separate from the original transaction, there must be new consideration for the promise of the guarantor.
3. If you are a surety, fraud by the principal debtor which is unknown to the creditor and in which the creditor has not taken part will not release you.

---

[5] New Braunfels Nat. Bank v Odiorne, (Tex App) 780 SW2d 313 (1989).

QUESTIONS AND CASE PROBLEMS

1. What social forces are affected by the use of a letter of credit?

2. Kiernan Construction Company makes a contract with Jackson to build a house for her. The Century Surety Company executes a bond to protect Jackson from loss if Kiernan should fail to construct the house or pay labor and material bills. Kiernan fails to build the house. Jackson sues the Century Surety Company. It raises the defense that Jackson must first sue Kiernan. Is it correct?

3. Identify the parties to a letter of credit.

4. Fern Schimke's husband, Norbert was obligated on two promissory notes in favor of the Union Bank. Some time prior to his death, the Union Bank prepared a guaranty contract which was given to Norbert to be signed by his wife. She signed the guaranty at the request of her husband without any discussion with him at to the provisions for the document she was signing. Upon the death of Norbert, the bank brought suit against Fern on the basis of the guaranty. Fern argued that since there was no consideration for the guaranty, she could not be liable. Decide. [*Union National Bank v Fern Schmike (ND) 210 NW2d 176*]

5. The surety right of subrogation arises as soon as the surety pays any part of the debt that the surety is obligated to pay. Appraise this statement.

6. Eberstadt owed Terence $500. He gave his note for that amount to Terence. At the same time, an agreement signed by Reid and given to Terence was as follows: "I agree to be surety for the payment of Eberstadt's note for $500." On maturity of the note, Eberstadt paid $200 on account and gave a new note for $300 due in three months. Reid was not informed of this transaction. The new note was not paid at maturity. Terence sues Reid. Does Reid have any defense?

7. Gilbert signed a guaranty for the benefit of his son with the Cobb Exchange Bank. The guaranty included all extensions and renewals of the son's obligation. Subsequently, a renewal of the note added an additional $600 to the original obligation. Upon the son's default, the Cobb Bank brought suit on the guaranty. Who should win? Why? [*Gilbert v Cobb Exchange Bank, 140 Ga App 514, 231 SE2d 508*]

8. Keller made a contract to purchase goods from Conti Co. To assure Conti that it would be paid, Keller obtained a letter of credit from Enterprise Bank. The letter was irrevocable and provided that Enterprise would honor drafts for the purchase price of goods shipped to Keller on presentment to the bank of the drafts, the bill of lading showing shipment to Keller, and the invoice showing the nature and price of the goods shipped. Because of financial difficulties, Keller did not want to receive the goods under the contract and made an agreement with Enterprise that no drafts would be honored pursuant to the letter of credit. Conti shipped goods to Keller under the contract and presented drafts, the proper bills of lading, and invoices to Enterprise. Enterprise refused to honor the drafts. Conti sued Enterprise. It claimed that it was not liable because the letter of credit that had obligated it to accept the drafts had been terminated by the agreement of its customer. Was this a valid defense?

9. The Kitsap County Credit Bureau held against Alderman a claim, the payment of which had been guaranteed by Richards. When Richards was sued on his guaranty, he proved that the claim against Alderman had been settled by compromise upon Aldermans paying $100 to the creditor. What was the result? [*Kitsap County Credit Bureau v Richards, 52 Wash 381, 325 P2d 292*]

10. Hugill agreed to deliver shingles to the W. I. Carpenter Lumber Co. He furnished a surety bond to secure the faithful performance of the contract on his part. After a breach of the contract by Hugill, the lumber company brought an action to recover its loss from the surety, the Fidelity & Deposit Co. of Maryland. The surety denied liability, on the grounds that there was concealment of (a) the price to be paid for the shingles and (b) the fact that a material advance had been made to the contractor equal to the amount of the profit that he would make by performing the contract. Decide. [*W. I. Carpenter Lumber Co. v Hugill, 149 Wash 45, 270 P 94*]

11. Donaldson sold plumbing supplies. The St. Paul-Mercury Indemnity Co., as surety for him, executed and delivered a bond to the State of California for the payment of all sales taxes. Donaldson failed to pay, and the surety paid the taxes that he owed. The surety then sued him for the taxes. What was the result? [*St. Paul-Mercury Indemnity Co. v Donaldson, 225 SC 476, 83 SE2d 159*]

12. Paul owed Charles a $1,000 debt, due September 1. On August 15, George, for consideration, orally promised Charles to pay the debt if Paul did not. On September 1, Paul did not pay, so Charles demanded $1,000 from George. Is George liable? Why?

13. First National Bank hired Longdon as a secretary and obtained a surety bond from Belton covering the bank against losses up to $100,000 resulting from Longdon's improper conduct in the performance of his duties. Both Longdon and the bank signed the application for the bond. After one year of service, Longdon was promoted to the position of teller in the bank, and the original bond remained in effect. Shortly after Longdon's promotion, examination showed that after his promotion Longdon had taken advantage of his new position and had stolen $50,000 from the bank. He was arrested and charged with embezzlement. Longdon had only $5,000 in assets at the time of his arrest. (a) If the bank demands a payment of $50,000 from Belton, what defense, if any, might Belton raise to deny any obligation to the bank? (b) If Belton fully reimburses the bank for its loss, under what theory or theories, if any, may Belton attempt to recover from Longdon?

14. List and explain the rights of a surety.

15. Partridge lends $1,000 to Fazio, who agrees to repay the amount in three months. A month after the loan, Partridge requests security. Shank, without asking for or receiving payment for so doing, gives Partridge a written promise to answer in the event of default by Fazio. Fazio defaults. Partridge sues Fazio and obtains judgment; execution is issued and returned unsatisfied. Partridge then sues Shank, who claims there is no consideration for her promise. Is this defense valid? Explain.

BANKRUPTCY

LEARNING OBJECTIVES

After studying this chapter, you will be able to:
1. *List the requirements for the commencement of a voluntary bankruptcy case and an involuntary bankruptcy case.*
2. *Describe the rights of the trustee in bankruptcy.*
3. *Explain the procedure for the administration of the debtor's estate.*
4. *List the debtor's duties and exemptions.*
5. *Explain the significance of a discharge in bankruptcy.*
6. *Explain when a business reorganization and an extended time payment plan might be used.*

What can a person or business do when crushed by debts? Bankruptcy proceedings will often provide the solution.

A. BANKRUPTCY LAW

Bankruptcy is a statutory proceeding.

1. The Federal Law

Bankruptcy law is based on the Bankruptcy Reform Act of 1974, as amended, and by the Bankruptcy Rules adopted by the U.S. Supreme Court. Jurisdiction over bankruptcy proceedings is vested in the federal district courts. The district courts have the authority to transfer such matters to subordinate bankruptcy courts.

2. Kinds of Bankruptcy Proceedings

Three kinds of bankruptcy proceedings are available to individuals and businesses:
1. Liquidation, sometimes called a "Chapter 7" bankruptcy
2. Reorganization, sometimes called a "Chapter 11" bankruptcy
3. Extended time payment, sometimes called a "Chapter 13" bankruptcy

B. LIQUIDATION UNDER CHAPTER 7

In liquidation proceedings, the debtor's nonexempt assets are collected by the trustee, who represents the creditors. The trustee liquidates the assets and distributes the proceeds to the creditors. The debtor is then discharged from most debts.

3. Commencement of the Case

A bankruptcy case refers to the proceeding in the bankruptcy court. A liquidation can be voluntary or involuntary.

(a) VOLUNTARY. A **voluntary case** is begun by the debtor's filing a petition with the bankruptcy court. A joint petition may be filed by a husband and wife. When a voluntary case is begun, a debtor must file a schedule of current income and current expenditures, unless the court excuses the filing of this schedule. When a voluntary petition is filed, the debtor automatically obtains an order for relief. This happens without the court's filing any decree so stating.[1]

Individuals, partnerships, and corporations—except railroads, banks, insurance companies, savings and loan associations, and credit unions—may file a voluntary petition.[2]

(b) INVOLUNTARY. An **involuntary case** is begun by creditors' filing a petition with the bankruptcy court. An involuntary case may be commenced against any individual, partnership, or corporation, except those excluded from filing voluntary petitions. Farmers and nonprofit corporations are also exempt from involuntary proceedings.[3]

4. Number and Claims of Petitioning Creditors

If there are 12 or more creditors, at least three, whose unsecured claims total $5,000 or more, must sign the involuntary petition. If there are fewer than 12 creditors, excluding employees or **insiders** (that is, the debtor's relatives, partners, directors, and controlling persons), any creditor whose unsecured claim is at least $5,000 may sign the petition.

If the creditor holds security for the claim, only the amount of the claim in excess of the value of the security is counted. The holder of

---

[1] 11 USC § 301.

[2] 11 USC § 109(b).

[3] 11 USC § 303(a).

a claim that is the subject of a bona fide dispute may not be counted as a petitioning creditor.[4]

5. Grounds for Relief for Involuntary Case

The mere filing of an involuntary case petition does not constitute an order for relief. The debtor may contest the bankruptcy petition. If the debtor does not contest the petition, the court will enter an order for relief if at least one of the following grounds exists: (a) the debtor is generally not paying debts as they become due, or (b) within 120 days before the filing of the petition, a custodian has been appointed for the debtor's property. No act of misconduct on the part of the debtor needs to be shown.[5]

In the *Arker* case the court was faced with the problem of whether a failure to pay a debt to a single creditor should be grounds for relief in an involuntary case.

IN RE SOL ARKER
6 BR 632 (ED NY 1980)

Bank Leumi Trust Company commenced an involuntary case in bankruptcy against Sol Arker. The bank claimed that Arker was generally not paying his debts, since the bank had been unable to collect on a $190,000 judgment that it held against Arker. Arker denied that he was generally not paying his debts and asserted further that he had no assets that could be used to satisfy the bank's claim.

PARENTE, B. J. . . . Should the Court grant an order for relief where the petitioning creditor contends that the alleged debtor has failed to pay one creditor and where the alleged debtor has no assets for the Bankruptcy Court to administer[?]

. . . An involuntary case may be commenced under Chapter 7 or Chapter 11 of the Bankruptcy Code against any person that may be a debtor under those chapters. In cases such as the case at bar, where the debtor has fewer than twelve creditors, . . . a petition may be brought by a single entity which is a holder of a claim against the alleged debtor that is not contingent as to liability. . . .

Subsection (h) of § 303 [of the Bankruptcy Code] enunciates the standard for an order for relief on an involuntary petition.

[It] provides . . . :

(h) If the petition is not timely controverted, the court shall order relief against the debtor in an involuntary case under the chapter under which the petition was filed. Otherwise, after trial, the court shall order relief against the debtor in an involuntary case under the chapter which the petition was filed, only if

(1) The debtor is generally not paying such debtor's debts as such debts become due: or . . .

The phrase "the debtor is generally not paying such debtor's debts as such debts become due" is not defined in the Bankruptcy Code.

---

[4]   11 USC § 303(b)(1).

[5]   11 USC § 303(h)(1) and (2).

However, when faced with this issue, the bankruptcy courts have consistently held that in order to determine whether the alleged debtor is generally paying his debts as they become due, the amount of the debts not being paid and the number of creditors not being paid are significant factors. . . .

Specifically, in the *Matter of 7H Land & Cattle Co.*, 2 CBC 2d 554 (D Nev. 1980), the bankruptcy court was faced with the following issue:

Does an allegation that the alleged debtors have failed to pay one creditor constitute "generally not paying such debtors' debts as they become due"?

The Court stated that as a general rule:

It may be assumed that in the ordinary case there can be no order for relief with no more proof than mere failure to meet liability to a single creditor.

However, the Court further states that there should be two exceptions to this general rule:

First: An order for relief should be granted in the exceptional case of an alleged debtor with a sole creditor who would otherwise be without an adequate remedy under non-bankruptcy law.

Second: If the petitioning creditor makes a showing of special circumstances amounting to fraud, trick, artifice, or scam, then an order for relief should be granted.

This Court agrees with the principle of law enunciated in the *Matter of 7H Land and Cattle Co.* Thus, given the facts of the case at bar, unless one of the exceptions to the general rule stated in said case applies, the petitioning creditor's request for an order for relief should be denied.

The petitioning creditor did not put before this Court a claim that there were circumstances surrounding the petitioning creditor which bear closely upon trick, artifice, scam or fraud by the alleged debtor. Therefore, the second exception to the general rule does not apply to the case at bar.

With respect to the first exception, i.e., an alleged debtor with a sole creditor who would otherwise be without an adequate remedy under non-bankruptcy law, although there is ample evidence in the record to support the Court's finding that the petitioning creditor has exhausted all possible nonbankruptcy remedies, there is an additional factor in this case which was not present in the *Matter of 7H Land and Cattle Co.*

The Court in the case at bar is faced with the following situation: an involuntary petition has been filed against an alleged debtor who has no free assets which could be liquidated for the benefit of his creditors and who has only one creditor which has yet to be paid. It is manifest that the alleged debtor has no free assets to be liquidated which is decisive to this Court's conclusion that an order for relief should not be granted in the case at bar. This conclusion is predicated on the purpose of an involuntary proceeding which is to secure an equitable distribution of the assets of the alleged debtor among all his creditors. . . . To grant an order for relief in a case where there are no assets to be liquidated for the benefit of creditors would not be in comport with this long standing policy underlying involuntary proceedings.

Further support for this precept is found in the *Matter of Oak Winds*, 2 CBC 2d 417 (ND Fla 1980). In that case . . . the court stated in relevant part:

In sum, it is evident and this Court is satisfied that there would not be any useful purpose to retain jurisdiction of this case either as a reorganization case under Chapter 11 of the Code since there is obviously no desire by the debtor to effectuate any involuntary reorganization nor would it serve any useful purpose to consider a conversion of this case into a liquidating case under Chapter 7 simply because there are no free assets which could be liquidated for the benefit of the general unsecured creditors or, the only one in this instance. *(Emphasis added.)*

Just as the court in the *Matter of Oak Winds* refused to convert the involuntary Chapter 11 case to a Chapter 7 case on the ground that there were no free assets to liquidate, this Court is constrained to deny the granting of an order for relief in the case at bar. To grant an order for relief in the case at bar would serve no purpose since there are no assets for this Court to administer.

[Petition denied]

QUESTIONS

1. What are the requirements for the commencement of an involuntary case?
2. How many creditors signed the petition in this case?
3. Did the court grant the relief requested?

6. Automatic Stay

The filing of either a voluntary or an involuntary petition operates as an **automatic stay**. An **automatic stay** prevents creditors from taking action, such as filing suits or foreclosure actions, against the debtor.[6] The stay freezes all creditors in their filing date position, so that no one creditor gets an advantage over the others. This automatic stay ends when the bankruptcy case is closed or dismissed or when the debtor is granted a discharge.

7. Rights of Debtor in Involuntary Case

If an involuntary petition is dismissed other than by consent of all petitioning creditors and the debtor, the court may award costs, reasonable attorney's fees, or damages to the debtor. The damages are those that were caused by the taking of possession of the debtor's property. The debtor may also recover damages against any creditor who filed the petition in bad faith.[7]

8. Trustee in Bankruptcy

The trustee in bankruptcy is elected by the creditors. An interim trustee will be appointed by the court or by the United States Trustee if a trustee is not elected by the creditors.

(a) STATUS OF THE TRUSTEE. The trustee is the successor to the property rights of the debtor. By operation of law, the trustee automatically becomes the owner of all the property of the debtor in excess of the property to which the debtor is entitled under exemption laws. Property inherited by the debtor within six months after the filing of the petition also passes to the trustee.

---

[6] 11 USC § 362.

[7] Arizona Public Service v Apache County (Ariz Tax) 847 P2d 1339 (1993).

Everyone is charged with notice of the fact that the trustee is the owner of rights formerly owned by the debtor.

(b) RIGHTS OF THE TRUSTEE. The bankruptcy trustee possesses the rights and the powers of the most favored creditor of the debtor. This means that the trustee can avoid (1) transfers by the debtor that a creditor holding a valid claim under state law could have avoided at the commencement of the bankruptcy case; (2) **preferences**, that is, transfers of property by the debtor to a creditor, the effect of which enables the creditor to obtain payment of a greater percentage of the creditor's claim than the creditor would have received if the debtor's assets had been liquidated in bankruptcy; and (3) statutory liens that became effective against the debtor at the commencement of the bankruptcy.

9. Voidable Transfers

A debtor may not transfer property to prevent creditors from satisfying their legal claims. The trustee may avoid any such transfer made or obligation incurred by the debtor within one year of bankruptcy when the debtor's actual intent was to hinder, delay, or defraud creditors by so doing.

The trustee may also avoid certain transfers of property made by a debtor merely because their effect is to make the debtor insolvent or to reduce the debtor's assets to an unreasonably low amount.[8]

(a) THE INSOLVENT DEBTOR. A debtor is insolvent when the total fair value of all the debtor's assets does not exceed the debts owed by the debtor. This is commonly called the **balance sheet test**, because it is merely a comparison of assets to liabilities, without considering whether the debtor will be able to meet future obligations as they become due.

(b) PREFERENTIAL TRANSFERS. A transfer of property by the debtor to a creditor may be set aside and the property recovered by the debtor's trustee in bankruptcy if (1) the transfer was to pay a debt incurred at some earlier time, (2) the transfer was made when the debtor was insolvent and within 90 days before the filing of the bankruptcy petition, and (3) by the transfer the creditor received more than the creditor would have received in a liquidation of the debtor's estate. A debtor is presumed to be insolvent on and during the 90 days immediately preceding the date of the filing of the bankruptcy petition.[9]

Transfers made to insiders within the 12 months prior to the filing of the petition may be set aside.[10]

Certain transfers by a debtor may not be attacked by the trustee as preferences. A transaction for a present consideration, such as a cash sale, is not subject to attack.[11] A payment by a debtor in the ordinary course of business, such as the payment of a utility bill, is not subject to attack. A payment by an individual debtor whose debts are primarily consumer debts is not subject to attack if the aggregate value of the transfer is less than $600.

In the *Jaggers* case a trustee objected to a debtor's payments on a promissory note on the grounds that these payments were preferences.

C. ADMINISTRATION OF DEBTOR'S ESTATE

Bankruptcy law regulates the manner in which creditors present their claims and how the assets of the debtor are to be distributed in payment of such claims.

---

[8] 11 USC § 548.

[9] 11 USC § 547(f).

[10] 11 USC § 547(b)(4)(B).

[11] Matter of Tolona Pizza Product Corp. (CA7 Ill) 3 F3d 1029 (1993).

IN RE JAGGERS
48 BR 33 (WD Tex 1985)

On May 7, 1981, Joseph Jaggers filed a petition under Chapter 7 of the Bankruptcy Code. At the time the petition was filed, he was indebted to the Cove State Bank on a promissory note. The principal amount of the note had originally been in excess of $68,000. Two payments had been made on the note. One payment was made on February 23, 1981, in the form of a check drawn on the account of T-Vest Corporation and signed by Dorothea M. Kerr, an authorized signatory on the T-Vest account. Another payment was made on March 23, 1981, in the form of a check drawn on the account of J. & D. Finance and signed by Jaggers, an authorized signatory on the J. & D. account. The trustee in bankruptcy claimed that these payments were preferential transfers.

THOMPSON, C. J. . . . The T-Vest Corporation is a Texas Corporation. The Debtor and his wife were directors of the corporation. The Debtor was the Chairman of the Board of Directors and his wife was the secretary of the corporation. One Hundred percent of the stock of T-Vest Corporation was owned by the Debtor and his wife. The Debtor controlled and directed the disbursement of the funds from the T-Vest Corporation account. At the direction of the Debtor, payments of both personal and business expenses were made as well as payments to the Debtor and his associates for consulting fees.

[The account] maintained by the T-Vest Corporation and controlled by the Debtor was a "conduit" or depository account for funds received by the T-Vest Corporation from Astroglass Boat Company, Star Custom Trailers, and other entities with which the Debtor was associated. Funds belonging to the various entities and funds belonging to the Debtor were commingled in the T-Vest account. At the time of the payments in question the Debtor exercised effective control over Astroglass Boat Company and Star Custom Trailers. The T-Vest account was also used for the receipt of consulting fees earned by the Debtor, Monty Tounsend, and other associates of the Debtor. . . .

J. & D. Finance Co. was not a corporation. The account in the name of J. & D. Finance was used for both personal and business purposes of the Debtor. All disbursements from this account were controlled by the Debtor. Funds from Astroglass Boat Company and Maiden-Craft, a Tennessee Corporation wholly owned and controlled by the Debtor and his wife, were funneled through the J. & D. Finance Co. account for payment of various operating and business expenses. The J. & D. Finance Co. account was used as a depository account for funds from Astroglass Boat Co., Maiden-Craft and the T-Vest Corporation. Funds belonging to these entities and the Debtor were commingled in the account. . . .

The payments to Cove State Bank from the T-Vest and J. & D. Finance Co. accounts directly benefited the Debtor because Joseph N. Jaggers was personally liable on the debt to Cove State Bank. The disbursements from these funds were credited on the general ledgers of Joseph Jaggers as salary fulfillments.

The threshold question before the Court is whether the payments . . . by the Debtor to Cove State Bank constituted a preferential transfer in violation of 11 U.S.C. Section 547(b).

In order to avoid a transfer, the trustee must establish by a fair preponderance of the evidence each controverted element of a voidable preference. The six elements which must be present for this Court to find that a preference exists under 11 U.S.C. Section 547(b) are:

(1) *The property transferred was the property of the Debtor;*
(2) *The transfer was "to or for the benefit of a creditor;"*
(3) *The payment was made "for or on account of an antecedent debt owed by the debtor before such transfer was made;"*
(4) *The transfer was made while the Debtor was insolvent;*
(5) *The transfer was made on or within 90 days before the date of the filing of the petitions; and*
(6) *The transfer enabled the creditor to receive more than such creditor would have received if the transfer had not been made, and the creditor received payment of the debt to the extent provided under the bankruptcy code.*

The parties have stipulated that the payments . . . were for the benefit of Cove State Bank, that they were made on or before 90 days before the date of the filing of the Debtor's petition, that the payments were made while the debtor was insolvent, and that these payments enabled Cove State Bank to receive more than it would otherwise have received in the Debtor's Chapter 7 case. The only issue then before the Court is whether the funds transferred constituted "property of the estate" within the meaning of 11 U.S.C. Section 547(b).

In order to ascertain whether certain monies constitute property of the debtor the Court must determine whether the debtor had an interest in the funds such that a transfer thereof would result in a diminution of the estate.

In the case at bar, though the Debtor did have ownership rights in the accounts from which the payments to Cove State Bank were made, it is apparent that he did not own the funds in their entirety. The Debtor shared ownership interests in the accounts in question with Astroglass Boat Co., Star Custom Trailers and Mr. Monty Tounsend. It is clear, therefore, that the funds which the debtor used to pay Cove State Bank were, in part, the property of a third party.

When a debtor uses the funds of a third party to pay an obligation of the debtor the Court must look to the source of the control over the disposition of the funds in order to determine whether a preference exists. If the debtor controls the disposition of the funds and designates the creditor to whom the monies will be paid independent of the third party whose funds are being used in partial payment of the debt, then the payments made by the debtor to the creditor constitute a preferential transfer. Hence, if the funds are available for payment to the creditors of the debtor generally the funds are an asset of the estate and payment thereof constitutes a diminution of the estate.

The question the Court must ask is whether the funds of the third party were available for use by the debtor generally or were the funds solely available for the purpose of discharging a particular debt to a particular creditor. . . .

In the case at bar, the Debtor made two payments to Cove State Bank in check form in the amounts of $7,900.43 and $5,000.00 respectively. The $5,000.00 check on the account of J. & D. Finance Company was signed by the Debtor and the Debtor directed that payment be made to Cove State Bank. This transfer, on its face, was directed solely by the Debtor. By virtue of the Debtor's exclusive control over the disposition of the funds in payment of a personal obligation of the Debtor, the funds were available for payment to creditors of the Debtor generally and constituted an asset of the estate. The $7,900.43 check on the T-Vest Corporation account was tendered to Cove State Bank for the purpose of reducing the balance on the promissory note owed by the Debtor to Cove State Bank. Though the check was not signed by the Debtor, there is no evidence that the use of the funds in the T-Vest account by the Debtor was conditioned upon payment of those funds to Cove State Bank. It is apparent that the Debtor controlled the distribution of funds from the T-Vest Corporation account. As a result of that control, the funds used by the Debtor for the payment of Cove State Bank were available to the creditors of the Debtor generally and constituted assets of the estate. The payments to Cove State Bank, therefore, were made with property of the estate. The payments resulted in a diminution of the estate and thereby constituted a preferential transfer of the property of the estate. . . .

[Judgment for the trustee]

QUESTIONS

1. When does payment to a creditor constitute a voidable preference?
2. Did Jaggers intend to prefer Cove State Bank over other creditors?
3. Did the court agree with the trustee?

10. Proof of Claim

In a bankruptcy case, the debtor will file a list of creditors. The court will then send a notice of the case to listed creditors. The creditors that wish to participate in distribution of the proceeds of the liquidation of the debtor's estate must file a proof of claim. A **claim** is a right to payment, whether liquidated (certain and not disputed), unliquidated, contingent, unmatured, disputed, legal, or equitable. A **proof of claim** is a written statement, signed by the creditor or an authorized representative, setting forth any claim made against the debtor and the basis for it. It must ordinarily be filed within 90 days after the first meeting of creditors.[12] A creditor must file within that time, even though the trustee in bankruptcy in fact knows of the existence of the creditor's claim.

11. Priority of Claims

Creditors who hold security for payment, such as a lien or a mortgage on the debtor's property, are not affected by the debtor's bankruptcy. Secured creditors may enforce their security to obtain payment of their claims. The unsecured creditors share in the remaining assets of the debtor. Some have priority over others. Any balance remaining after all creditors have been paid is paid to the debtor.

The unsecured debts that have priority and the order of priority are:[13]

a. Costs and expenses of administration of the bankruptcy case, including fees to trustees, attorneys, and accountants, and the reasonable expenses of creditors in recovering property transferred or concealed by the debtor.

[12] Bankruptcy Rule 3002(c).
[13] 11 USC § 507(1) to (6).

b. Claims arising in the ordinary course of a debtor's business or financial affairs after the commencement of the case and before the appointment of a trustee.

c. Claims for wages, salaries, or commissions, including vacation, severance, or sick leave pay earned within 90 days before the filing of the petition or the date of cessation of the debtor's business, whichever occurred first. The amount of such claims is limited, however, to $2,000 for each person.

d. Claims arising for contributions to employee benefit plans based on services rendered within 180 days before the filing of the petition or when the debtor ceased doing business, whichever occurred first.

e. Claims by consumer creditors, not to exceed $900 for each claimant, arising from the purchase of consumer goods or services, when such property or services were not delivered or provided.

f. Certain taxes, such as income taxes and property taxes. Each class must be paid in full before any lower class is paid anything. If a class of claims cannot be paid in full, the claims in that class are paid on a pro rata basis.

D. DEBTOR'S DUTIES AND EXEMPTIONS

Bankruptcy law imposes certain duties on the debtor and provides for specific exemptions of some of the debtor's estate from the claims of creditors.

12. Debtor's Duties

The debtor must file with the court a list of creditors, a schedule of assets and liabilities, and a statement of the debtor's financial affairs. The debtor must also appear for examination under oath at the first meeting of creditors.

13. Debtor's Exemptions

The debtor is permitted to claim certain property of the estate in the trustee's possession and keep it free from claims of creditors. The debtor may choose either the exemptions permitted by the law of the debtor's state of domicile or those permitted by the Bankruptcy Code.[14] The principal exemptions provided by the Bankruptcy Code are: the debtor's interest in real or personal property used as a residence to the extent of $7,500; the debtor's interest in a motor vehicle to the extent of $1,200; household furnishings of the debtor or the debtor's dependents, not to exceed $200 per item, or $4,000 in aggregate value; payments under a life insurance contract; alimony and child support payments; and awards from personal injury causes of action.[15]

E. DISCHARGE IN BANKRUPTCY

The main objectives of a bankruptcy proceeding are the collection and distribution of the debtor's assets and the discharge of the debtor from obligations. The decree terminating the bankruptcy proceeding is generally a **discharge** that releases the debtor from most debts.

14. Denial of Discharge

The court will refuse to grant a discharge if the debtor has (a) within one year of the filing of the petition fraudulently transferred or concealed property with intent to hinder, delay, or defraud creditors, (b) failed to keep proper financial records, (c) made a false oath or account, (d) failed to explain satisfactorily any loss of assets, (e) refused to obey any lawful order of the court or refused to testify after

---

[14] The law of the state of the debtor's domicile may prohibit making such an election and limit the debtor to the exemptions allowed by state law.

[15] 11 USC § 522.

C P A C P A C P A C P A C P A C P A C P A

having been granted immunity, (f) obtained a discharge within the last six years, or (g) filed a written waiver of discharge that is approved by the court.[16]

15. Effect of Discharge

A discharge releases the debtor from the unpaid balance of most debts. However, a discharge does not release a person from all debts. A tax,

customs duty, or tax penalty is not discharged by bankruptcy. Likewise, release is not obtained for student loans, unless the loan first became due more than five years before bankruptcy or unless excepting the loan from discharge would impose undue hardship on the debtor.

In the *Reilly* case a student requested a discharge of her student loan, based upon undue hardship.

C P A C P A C P A C P A C P A C P A

IN RE REILLY
118 BR 38 (D Md 1990)

> Reilly is a divorced mother of three young children. Her former husband is incurably ill and is unable to contribute significantly to their support. The family house was sold at foreclosure, and Reilly and her children were forced to move in with her parents, where she pays rent of $250 per month. Reilly works, sometimes full-time and sometimes part-time. Her monthly income cannot meet the necessary family expenses. Reilly's monthly income is only slightly above poverty guidelines for a family of four. There is a monthly deficit because expenses are greater than income. Reilly requires 24 credits in order to obtain her college degree. Until it is completed, she is not in a position to advance in her employment. Reilly's student loan is $2,762. Reilly filed a complaint to discharge her student loan because paying it would impose an inordinate burden upon her.

SCHNEIDER, B. J. . . . Paragraph (B) of Bankruptcy Code Section 523(a)(8) permits an exception to the nondischargeability of student loans. The exception exists when repayment of the student loan would impose an undue hardship on the debtor. The "hardship" provision of § 523(a)(8)(B) is

discretionary with the bankruptcy judge who will have to determine whether payment of the debt will cause undue hardship on the debtor and his dependents thus defeating the "fresh start" concept of the bankruptcy laws. There may well be circumstances that justify failure to repay a student loan such as illness, incapacity or other extenuating circumstances. When the court finds that such circumstances exist, it may order the debt discharged. . . .

Courts have developed a number of tests to determine if a debtor's student loan should be discharged under § 523(a)(8)(B). In *Andrews v South Dakota Student Loan Assistance Corporation*, 661 F2d 702 (8th Cir 1981), the court considered whether the debtor's present and anticipated future income was sufficient to cover the debtor's reasonable living expenses. The court held that if the debtor's income is adequate to

---

[16] 11 USC § 727.

support the debtor and the debtor's dependents at a "minimal standard of living," as well as to repay the student loan, the debt cannot be discharged.

In *Andrews*, even though debtor was a 36 year old with Hodgkins disease, divorced, and receiving no alimony, the court vacated and remanded the bankruptcy court's discharge of the debtor's student loan debts on the grounds that the determination of undue hardship required the bankruptcy court to examine the debtor's "necessary living expenses." Thus, the court required a subjective evaluation of the debtor's reasonable living expenses and then a determination as to whether the debtor could repay her loan out of the balance of her estimated income less reasonable living expenses.

In denying a discharge based on undue hardship, the court in *Brunner v New York State Higher Education Services Corporation*, 46 B.R. 752 (S.D.N.Y. 1985) held that

obtaining a discharge of student loans in bankruptcy prior to five years after they first come due requires a three-part showing: (1) that the debtor cannot, based on current income and expenses, maintain a "minimal" standard of living for himself or herself and his or her dependents if forced to repay the loans, (2) that this state of affairs is likely to persist for a significant portion of the repayment period of the student loan, and (3) that the debtor has made good faith efforts to repay the loans.

In *Brunner*, the court did not allow discharge because the debtor's master's degree in social work made it quite possible that she would get a higher paying job in the near future, enabling her to pay off her student loan while still maintaining a "minimal" standard of living for herself and because by filing for discharge within a month of when her first loan payment was due, she did not adequately demonstrate good faith in attempting to pay off her student loans.

In *Conner v Illinois State Scholarship Commission*, 89 B.R. 744 (Bankr N.D. Ill 1988) the court applied a test which considered (1) whether the debtor had the ability to pay off the student debt and still maintain a minimal standard of living, (2) whether the debtor had made a good faith effort to pay off the loan by minimizing expenses, renegotiating the terms of the loan or finding a better job and (3) whether discharge would frustrate the legislative intent to prevent abuse of student loans under § 523(a)(8)(B).

The court suggested that discharge of student loans should be denied if the debtor's motivation in filing bankruptcy was solely to discharge student loan obligations. Such motivation is to be discovered by determining the percentage of debt attributable to the student loan.

Finally, in *Bryant v Pennsylvania Higher Education Assistance Agency*, 72 B.R. 913 (Bankr E.D. Pa 1987), the court developed its own test by studying the purpose of Section 523(a)(8)(B) as indicated in the Report of the Commission on the Bankruptcy Laws of the United States:

In order to determine . . . "undue hardship" . . . the rate and amount of [the debtor's] future resources should be estimated reasonably in terms of ability to obtain, retain, and continue employment and the rate of pay that can be expected. Any unearned income or other wealth which the debtor can be expected to receive should also be taken into account. The total amount of income, its reliability, and the periodicity of its receipt should be adequate to maintain the debtor and his dependents at a minimal standard of living within their management capacity as well as to pay the education debt.

. . . Unusual responsibilities arising from the needs of dependents can be a circumstance supporting discharge. If the debtor's net annual income is near the poverty line, then discharge may be in order. Further, if the debtor's net annual income is below the federal poverty level, then the creditor must show that some "unique" or "extraordinary" circumstance exists to exclude the debt from discharge. Without this showing of a special circumstance, the loan should be discharged because repayment would likely cause the debtor an undue hardship.

The *Bryant* court discharged student loans in two Chapter 7 cases based on undue hardship, while denying a discharge in a third case. In applying its objective test, the court held that the obligation of a debtor whose annual *gross* income was beneath the federal poverty guideline should be discharged because the debtor could not afford to repay her debt and still maintain a minimal standard of living; the obligation of a debtor whose income was "significantly more" than the poverty income guideline should not be discharged because the debtor had no "unique" or "extraordinary" circumstances that would support a determination of undue hardship, and the obligation of a debtor whose net annual income was approximately at federal poverty guidelines should be discharged because the likelihood of a higher income and better circumstances was not so clear as to constitute "unique" or "extraordinary" circumstances.

Applying any one of the foregoing tests in the instant case, there is no question that the repayment of the student loans will impose an undue hardship upon this debtor. . . .

The Court is satisfied that this debtor would have made all such payments if she were financially able to do so, which clearly she is not. Therefore, the student loans in this case will be discharged.

[Discharge granted]

QUESTIONS

1. What is the purpose of a discharge in bankruptcy from the standpoint of a debtor?
2. When will the court deny a discharge of student loans?
3. What tests are used by the courts to determine if a debtor's student loan should be discharged?

In addition to those mentioned above, the following debts are not discharged by bankruptcy: (a) loans obtained by use of a false financial statement, made with intent to deceive, and on which the creditor reasonably relied; (b) debts not scheduled or listed with the court in time for allowance; (c) liability for fraud while acting in a fiduciary capacity or by reason of embezzlement or larceny; (d) liability for alimony and child support; (e) liability for willful and malicious injury to property; (f) judgments against the debtor for liability for driving while intoxicated; (g) a consumer debt to a single creditor totalling more than $500 for luxury goods or services; and (h) cash advances exceeding $1,000 based on consumer open end credit such as credit card.[17] To be nondischargeable, the debt for luxury goods

---

[17] 11 USC § 523.

C
P
A

must be incurred within 40 days of the order for relief; the cash advances must be incurred within 20 days of the order for relief.

In the *Cunningham* case, a passenger injured as a result of the debtor's driving while intoxicated sought to have the passenger's

C
P
A

Figure 37-1 Debts from Which a Debtor is Not Discharged

Nondischargeable Debts

1. Tax penalty
2. Student loans received within five years of bankruptcy unless undue hardship will result
3. Loans obtained by use of false financial statement
4. Unscheduled debts
5. Liability for fraud while acting as fiduciary; embezzlement; larceny
6. Alimony and child support
7. Liability for willful and malicious injury to property
8. Judgments based on driving while intoxicated
9. Consumer debts for luxury goods
10. Cash advances exceeding $1,000 within 20 days of order for relief

IN RE CUNNINGHAM
48 BR 641 (WD Tenn 1985)

Cunningham pleaded guilty to driving while intoxicated after having an accident. Brunswick, a passenger in the car brought a civil action against the debtor and recovered a judgment of $800,000. Cunningham had $10,000 worth of insurance. This amount was paid to Brunswick, leaving Cunningham liable for the remaining portion of the judgment. In Cunningham's subsequent bankruptcy proceeding, Brunswick sought to have his judgment declared nondischarged.

LEFFLER, W. B. . . . On Sunday, October 3, 1982 the Debtor and a friend purchased three six-packs of beer and proceeded to drive around Obion County and drink. The friend drove and the Debtor was a passenger. Between the hours of two o'clock and ten o'clock P.M. the Debtor and his drinking partner consumed all eighteen beers, sharing the beer equally. After the young men finished the beer they continued to drive around town and talk. At about eleven-thirty P.M. the Debtor and his friend parked the friend's car and got into the Debtor's new Trans-Am automobile. Shortly thereafter the Debtor and his friend encountered the Plaintiff and his fiancée. The Plaintiff and his fiancée got in the back seat of Debtor's automobile and the Debtor drove; they traveled out a rural road in Obion County, Tennessee. Some time near midnight Debtor turned south on Pleasant Hill Road and traveled for about one mile at which point he turned around and proceeded to travel in a northern direction from whence he just came. For some unknown reason the Debtor increased the speed of his automobile to about sixty miles per hour, an unsafe speed considering that it was a foggy night and they were traveling on a dark rural road. Debtor did not stop at the intersection, nor did he reduce the speed of his automobile as he approached the intersection. Debtor drove his automobile through the intersection, across the road, and into a dirt embankment. The accident caused serious and permanent injuries to the Plaintiff and less serious injuries to the other passengers. By virtue of the accident, the Plaintiff is permanently paralyzed from the waist down and he is confined to a wheelchair.

After the Debtor drove through the intersection and crashed into the dirt embankment the investigating police officers charged the Debtor with the criminal offense of driving while intoxicated ("DWI") . . . . The Debtor pled guilty to DWI in the General Sessions Court, . . . was fined and sentenced [and] the Debtor's driving privileges [were suspended] one (1) Year.

On August 24, 1983 the Plaintiff instituted the civil action against the Debtor. The Complaint in the state court action alleged that the Debtor operated his motor vehicle in violation of Tenn Code Ann § 55-10-401, which makes it unlawful for any person to drive an automobile while under the influence of an intoxicant. The Complaint additionally set forth that the accident was a direct result of the Debtor's operation of his automobile recklessly and negligently and that he intentionally drove his automobile while under the influence of alcohol.

In the civil proceeding in state court the Debtor never denied that he was intoxicated at the time of the accident. His defense was based upon contributory negligence and assumption of the risk on the part of the Plaintiff. The essence of the defense was that the Plaintiff knew that the Debtor was drunk when he got in the car with him.

On November 7, 1984 the Debtor filed a Chapter 7 Petition in Bankruptcy. The Plaintiff has been listed as an unsecured creditor in the amount of $790,000.

In the instant proceeding the Debtor takes the position that he was not intoxicated at the time of the accident and that the accident was merely a result of Debtor's negligence, therefore, neither section 523(a)(9), nor section 523(a)(6) is applicable and a debt based on mere negligence is dischargeable pursuant to 11 U.S.C. § 727.

The Debtor put into evidence a copy of the hospital report showing that debtor's blood alcohol level was .05 when Debtor was treated at the hospital after the accident. In rebuttal, the Plaintiff pointed out that the accident occurred after midnight on a Sunday on an isolated rural road and that it is not noted on the hospital record that time the blood test was performed. . . .

Conclusions of Law

Section 523(a)(6) [as amended] states as follows:

(a) A discharge under section 727, 1141, or 1328(b) of this title does not discharge an individual debtor from any debt—

(9) to any entity, to the extent that such debt arises from a judgment or consent decree entered in a court of record against the debtor wherein liability was incurred by such debtor as a result of the debtor's operation of a motor vehicle while legally intoxicated under the laws or regulations of any jurisdiction within the United States or its territories wherein such motor vehicles was operated and within which such liability was incurred; . . .

. . . Section (a)(9) allows the court to rely on state laws or regulations in determining whether a debtor was legally intoxicated at the time of the accident.

It seems obvious from the plain language of the statute that Section 523 (a)(9) was meant to apply to situations exactly like the one that is now before this Court. . . .

In the case at bar, all the requirements to except a debt from discharge under Section 523(a)(9) are present. The Plaintiff has a valid judgment against the Debtor, the liability was incurred by the Debtor as a result of the Debtor driving his automobile while legally intoxicated under Tennessee law, as evidenced by the guilty plea entered by the Debtor in the state court. Therefore, this Court holds that the $790,000 debt in question is nondischargeable pursuant to 11 U.S.C. § 523(a)(9).

[Judgment for plaintiff]

QUESTIONS

1. What was the argument of the debtor in the bankruptcy court?
2. Did the bankruptcy court agree with the debtor?
3. Was the judgment nondischargeable?

judgment declared nondischarged by the debtor's bankruptcy.

F. REORGANIZATIONS AND PAYMENT PLANS UNDER CHAPTERS 11 AND 13

In addition to liquidation under Chapter 7, the Bankruptcy Code permits the debtors to restructure the organization and finances of their businesses so that they may continue to operate. In these rehabilitation plans, the debtor keeps all the assets (exempt and nonexempt), remains in business, and makes a settlement that is acceptable to the majority of the creditors. This settlement is binding on the minority creditors. Reorganizations are covered by Chapter 11 of the Bankruptcy Code and are discussed in Section 16 below.

The Bankruptcy Code also provides for the adoption of extended time payment plans for individual debtors who have regular income. These debtors must owe unsecured debts of less than $100,000 and secured debts of less than $350,000. These "Chapter 13" plans are discussed in Section 17 below.

16. Business Reorganizations Under Chapter 11

Individuals, partnerships, and corporations in business may be reorganized under the Bankruptcy Code. The first step is to file a plan for the reorganization of the debtor. This plan may be filed by the debtor or by any party in interest or by a committee of creditors.

(a) CONTENTS OF PLAN. The plan divides ownership interests and debts into those that will be affected by the adoption of the plan and those that will not. It then specifies what will be done to those interests and claims that are affected. For example, where mortgage payments are too high for the income of a corporation, a possible plan would be to reduce the mortgage payments and give the mortgage holder preferred stock to compensate for the loss sustained.

All persons within a particular class must be treated the same way. For example, the holders of first mortgage bonds must all be treated similarly.

A plan may also provide for the assumption, rejection, or assignment of executory contracts. Thus, the trustee or debtor may under certain circumstances suspend performance of a contract not yet fully performed. Collective bargaining agreements may be rejected, with the approval of the bankruptcy court.[18]

(b) CONFIRMATION OF PLAN. After the plan is prepared, it must be approved or **confirmed** by the court. A plan will be confirmed if it has been submitted in good faith and if its provisions are reasonable.[19] After the plan is confirmed, the owners and creditors of the enterprise have only the rights that are specified in the plan. They cannot go back to their original positions.

17. Extended Time Payment Plans Under Chapter 13

An individual debtor who has a regular income may submit a plan for the installment payment of outstanding debts. If approved by the court, the debtor may then pay the debts in the installments specified by the plan, even if the creditors had not originally agreed to such installment payments.

(a) CONTENTS OF PLAN. The individual debtor plan is, in effect, a budget of the debtor's future income with respect to outstanding debts. The plan must provide for the eventual payment in full of all claims entitled to priority under the Bankruptcy Code. All creditors holding the same kind or class of claim must be treated the same way.

(b) CONFIRMATION OF PLAN. The plan has no effect until it is approved or confirmed by the court. A plan will be confirmed if it was submitted in good faith and is in the best interests of the creditors.[20] When the plan is confirmed, debts are payable in the manner specified in the plan.

(c) DISCHARGE OF DEBTOR. After all the payments called for by the plan have been made, the debtor is given a discharge. The discharge releases the debtor from liability for all debts except those that would not be discharged by an ordinary bankruptcy discharge.[21]

18. Protection Against Discrimination

Federal, state, or local law may not discriminate against anyone on the basis of a discharge in bankruptcy.[22]

This principle is illustrated in the *Young* case.

IN RE YOUNG, DEBTOR
10 BR 17 (SD Cal 1980)

Marion Young, the debtor, filed her extended time payment plan with the court. Prior to the filing of the petition, she was issued a citation for a traffic

[18] 11 USC § 1113.
[19] 11 USC § 1129.
[20] 11 USC § 1325.
[21] 11 USC § 1328.
[22] 11 USC § 525.

violation. In her confirmed plan, she proposed to pay 100 percent of her debts. Her application for renewal of her driver's license was denied because of her failure to pay the traffic ticket. She moved to have the bankruptcy court order the state to renew her license.

KATZ, B. J. . . .

1. Section 525 of the [bankruptcy] Code provides . . . that "A governmental unit may not deny, revoke, suspend, or refuse to renew a license . . . solely because the bankrupt or debtor . . . has not paid a debt that is dischargeable in the case under this Title or that was discharged under the Bankruptcy Act." *11 USC § 525.*

2. Plaintiff's obligation on account of the traffic citation is a criminal fine that is not dischargeable [in Chapter 7 cases] under section 523(a)(7) of the Code. *11 USC § 523(a)(7). . . .*

3. . . . After completion by the debtor of all payments under [a Chapter 13] plan, the court shall grant the debtor a discharge of all debts provided for by the plan or disallowed under section 502 except for certain debts and obligations on account of support excepted from discharge. Other obligations, including fines excepted from discharge [in Chapter 7 cases] under section 523(a)(7) of the Code, are dischargeable in a Chapter 13 case. *11 USC § 1328(a).*

4. A criminal fine dischargeable in a Chapter 13 case is a dischargeable debt within the provisions of section 525 of the Code, and defendant Department of Motor Vehicles is a governmental unit subject to the provisions of that section. *11 USC §§ 1328(a)(2), 525.*

5. Defendant's action in denying plaintiff's application for a renewal license is in violation of the anti-discrimination provisions of the Bankruptcy Code. *11 USC § 525.*

6. Plaintiff is entitled to a renewal license during the pendency of her Chapter 13 case, and discharge of her obligations upon completion of the payments provided for in her Chapter 13 plan. Should plaintiff convert to a liquidation case . . . the obligation for the traffic fine would not be dischargeable, and the Department of Motor Vehicles would be justified in revoking plaintiff's license. . . .

. . . Counsel for plaintiff shall prepare an order directing the Department of Motor Vehicles to issue plaintiff a renewal California driver's license.

QUESTIONS

1. Was the Department of Motor Vehicles required to issue a license to Young? Why or why not?
2. Would there have been a different result if Young's case had been a Chapter 7 rather than a Chapter 13 case? Why would the Bankruptcy Code so provide?

SUMMARY

Jurisdiction over bankruptcy cases is in the U.S. District Courts, which may refer all cases and related proceedings to adjunct bankruptcy courts.

Three bankruptcy proceedings are available. They are liquidation, reorganization, and extended time payment.

A liquidation proceeding under Chapter 7 may be either voluntary or involuntary. A voluntary case is commenced by the debtor by filing a petition with the bankruptcy court. An involuntary case is commenced by the creditors by filing a petition with the bankruptcy court. If there are 12 or more creditors, at least three, whose unsecured claims total $5,000 or more, must sign the involuntary petition. If there are fewer than 12 such creditors, any creditor whose unsecured claim is at least $5,000 may sign the petition. If the debtor contests the bankruptcy petition, it must be shown that the debtor is not paying debts as they become due, or that within 120 days before the date of the filing of the petition a custodian had been appointed for the debtor's property.

An automatic stay prevents creditors from taking legal action against the debtor after a bankruptcy petition is filed.

The trustee in bankruptcy is elected by the creditors and is the successor to and acquires the rights of the debtor. In certain cases the trustee can avoid transfers of property to prevent creditors from satisfying their claims. Preferential transfers may be set aside. A transfer for a present consideration, such as a cash sale, is not a preference.

Bankruptcy law regulates the way creditors present their claims and how the assets of the debtor are to be distributed in payment of the claims.

Secured claims are not affected by the bankruptcy of the debtor. Unsecured claims are paid in the following order of priority: (1) administrative expenses, (2) claims arising in the ordinary course of the debtor's business, (3) wage claims limited to $2,000 for each claimant and to wages earned within 90 days before the filing of the petition, (4) claims for contributions to employee benefit plans, (5) claims by consumer creditors, (6) certain taxes, and (7) general creditors. Certain property of the debtor is exempt from the claims of creditors.

The decree terminating the bankruptcy proceedings is generally a discharge that releases the debtor from most debts. Certain debts, such as income taxes, student loans, loans obtained by use of a false financial statement, alimony, and debts not duly scheduled, are not discharged.

Individuals, partnerships, and corporations in business may be reorganized so that a business may continue to operate. A plan for reorganization must be approved by the court.

Individual debtors with a regular income may adopt extended time payment plans for the payment of debts. A plan for extended time payment must also be confirmed by the court.

Federal, state, or local law may not discriminate against anyone on the basis of a discharge in bankruptcy.

LAW IN PRACTICE

1. Bankruptcy can be either voluntary or involuntary. Your creditors may file against you if sufficient claims exist.

2. If you file, or your creditors file a bankruptcy petition against you, creditors are prevented from taking action against you.

3. If you try to prefer certain creditors over others, the trustee in bankruptcy may prevent such creditors from satisfying their legal claims.

4. If you are not an honest debtor, you may be barred from obtaining a discharge in bankruptcy.

5. If you have a regular income, you may submit an extended time payment plan for paying off outstanding debts.

QUESTIONS AND CASE PROBLEMS

1. What social forces are affected by permitting a debtor to avoid paying debts by going into bankruptcy?

2. What is meant by the term *insider*, as used in preferential transfers?

3. Barron sold goods on credit to Charles by relying on a false financial statement issued by Charles. Charles later filed for voluntary bankruptcy, still owing this debt to Barron. Barron claimed that Charles was not entitled to a discharge from this particular debt because of the fraud. Was Barron correct?

4. Ruth commenced a voluntary case in bankruptcy. After her assets subject to the claims of creditors were liquidated, her trustee had possession of $2,000 in cash. Various creditors had filed claims for $20,000. Ruth's trustee claimed that the $2,000 should be used to pay the fee of the trustee, the fee of Ruth's accountant, and other administrative expenses of the bankruptcy case. The other creditors claimed that they were entitled to a portion of the $2,000. Who was correct?

5. Anita knows Jean is insolvent. She sells Jean her car for $500 and receives cash in payment. Some time later, an involuntary bankruptcy case is commenced against Jean by the creditors. The trustee in bankruptcy attempts to recover the $500 on the ground that it was a preferential transfer. Will the trustee be successful?

6. Okamoto owed money to Hornblower and Weeks-Hemphill, Noyes. Hornblower filed an involuntary bankruptcy petition against Okamoto. Okamoto moved to dismiss the petition on the ground that he had more than twelve creditors and that the petition could not be filed by only one. Hornblower replied that the claims of the other creditors were too small to count and therefore, the petition could be filed by one creditor. Decide. *[In re Okamoto (CA9 Cal) 491 F2d 496]*

7. Which of the following, if any, survive Rogers's discharge in bankruptcy? (a) Wages amounting to $400 owed to three employees, earned within 60 days of the bankruptcy. (b) A judgment against Rogers for injuries received because of Rogers' negligent operation of an automobile. (c) A judgment against Rogers by Landers for breach of contract. (d) Rogers obligation for alimony and child support.

8. Kentile sold goods over an extended period of time to Winham. The credit relationship began without Winham's being required to furnish any financial statement. After some time, payments were not made regularly. Kentile requested a financial statement. Winham submitted a statement for the year that had just ended. Thereafter, Kentile requested a second statement. The second statement was false. Kentile objected to Winham's discharge in bankruptcy because of the false financial statement. Should the discharge be granted? Why or why not?

9. Essex is in serious financial difficulty and is unable to meet current unsecured obligations of $40,000 to some 20 creditors, who are demanding immediate payment. Essex owes Stevens $5,000, and Stevens has decided to file an involuntary petition against Essex. Can Stevens file the petition?

10. Sonia, a retailer, has the following assets: a factory worth $1,000,000; accounts receivable amounting to $750,000, which fall due in from four to six months; and $20,000 cash in the bank. Sonia's sole liability is a $200,000 note falling due today, which Sonia is unable to pay. May Sonia be forced into involuntary bankruptcy under the Bankruptcy Code?

11. Samson Industries, Inc. ceased doing business and is in bankruptcy proceedings. Among the claimants are five employees seeking unpaid wages. Three of the employees are owed $3,500 each, and two are owed $1,500 each. These amounts became due within 90 days preceding the filing of the petition. Where, in the priority of claims, will the employees' wage claims fall?

12. The Vega Baja Lumber Yard owed money to the First City National Bank. The bank sued the lumber yard and attached some of its property. Thereafter bankruptcy proceedings were begun and the lumber yard was adjudicated a bankrupt. The bank filed a claim in bankruptcy. The referee rejected the bank's claim because it had been filed more than 90 days after the debtor had been adjudicated a bankrupt. The bank claimed that the 90 day limitation did not bar it because the trustee knew of the claim. What result? Why? *[In re Baja Lumber Yard, Inc. (DC Puerto Rico) 285 F Supp 143]*

13. Carol Cott, doing business as Carol Cott Fashions, is worried about an involuntary bankruptcy proceeding being filed by her creditors. Her net worth using a balance sheet approach is $8,000 ($108,000 assets minus $100,000 liabilities). However, her cash flow is negative, and she has been hard pressed to meet current obligations as they mature. She is, in fact, some $12,500 in arrears in payments to her creditors on bills submitted during the past two months. Will the fact that Cott is solvent in the balance sheet sense result in the court's dismissing the creditors' petition if Cott objects to the petition? Explain.

14. The Guaranteed Student Loan Program provides funds for students attending college. A student borrowed money under the program to attend school. Some time thereafter, she filed a petition in bankruptcy and listed the student loans on her list of obligations. Is she entitled to a discharge from the loan. Under, what conditions, if any, can such an obligation be discharged? Explain. [*Massachusetts Higher Education Assistance Corporation v Taylor, (Mass) 459 NE2d 807*]

15. On July 1, Roger Walsh, a sole proprietor operating a grocery, was involuntarily petitioned into bankruptcy by his creditors. At that time, and for at least 90 days prior to that time, Walsh was unable to pay current obligations. On June 16, Walsh paid the May electric bill that was incurred in his business. The trustee in bankruptcy claims that this payment was a voidable preference. Is the trustee correct? Explain.

CHAPTER 38

INSURANCE

LEARNING OBJECTIVES

After studying this chapter, you will be able to:
1. *Define insurable interest.*
2. *Compare contracts of insurance with ordinary contracts.*
3. *Explain the purpose of business liability insurance, marine insurance, fire and homeowners insurance, automobile insurance, and life insurance.*
4. *Explain the effect of an incontestability clause.*

By means of insurance, protection from loss and liability may be obtained.

A. THE INSURANCE CONTRACT

Insurance is a contract by which one party for a stipulated consideration promises to pay another party a sum of money on the destruction of, loss of, or injury to something in which the other party has an interest or to indemnify that party for any loss or liability to which that party is subjected.

1. The Parties

The promisor in an insurance contract is called the **insurer** or **underwriter**. The person to whom the promise is made is the **insured**, the assured, or the policyholder. The promise of the insurer is generally set forth in a written contract called a **policy**.

Insurance contracts are ordinarily made through an agent or broker. The **insurance agent** is an agent of the insurance company, generally working exclusively for one company. For the most part, the ordinary rules of agency law govern the dealings between this agent and the applicant for insurance.[1]

An **insurance broker** is generally an independent contractor who is not employed by any one insurance company. When a broker obtains a policy for a customer, the broker is the agent of the customer for the purpose of that transaction. Under some statutes, the broker is made an agent of the insurer with respect to transmitting the applicant's payments to the insurer.

2. Insurable Interest

A person obtaining insurance must have an insurable interest in the subject matter insured. If not, the insurance contract cannot be enforced.

(a) INSURABLE INTEREST IN PROPERTY. A person has an insurable interest in property whenever the destruction of the property will cause a direct pecuniary loss to that person.

It is immaterial whether the insured is the owner of the legal or equitable title, a lien holder, or merely a person in possession of the property.[2] Thus, a contractor remodeling a building has an insurable interest in the building to the extent of the money that will be paid under the contract, because the contractor would not be able to receive that money if the building were destroyed by fire.

To collect on property insurance, the insured must have an insurable interest at the time the loss occurs.

(b) INSURABLE INTEREST IN LIFE. A person who obtains life insurance can name anyone as beneficiary, regardless of whether that beneficiary has an insurable interest in the life of the insured. A beneficiary who obtains a policy, however, must have an insurable interest in the life of the insured. Such an interest exists if the beneficiary can reasonably expect to receive pecuniary gain from the continued life of the other person and, conversely, would suffer financial loss from the latter's death. Thus, a creditor has an insurable interest in the life of the debtor, since the death of the debtor may mean that the creditor will not be paid the amount owed.

A partner or partnership has an insurable interest in the life of each of the partners, because the death of any one of them will dissolve the firm and cause some degree of loss to the partnership. A business enterprise has an insurable interest in the life of an executive or a key employee, because that person's death would inflict a financial loss on the business to the extent that a replacement might not be readily available or could not be found.

In the case of life insurance, the insurable interest must exist at the time the policy is

---

[1] Tidelands Life Insurance Co. v France (Tex Civ App) 711 So 2d 728 (1986).

[2] Hunter v State Farm Fire & Casualty Co. (Ala) 543 So 2d 679 (1989).

obtained. It is immaterial that the interest no longer exists when the loss is actually sustained. Thus, the fact that a husband (insured) and wife (beneficiary) are divorced after the life insurance policy was procured does not affect the validity of the policy. Also, the fact that a partnership is terminated after a life insurance policy is obtained by one partner on another does not invalidate the policy.

In the *Graves* case the court was faced with two questions: (1) Does a partner have an insurable interest in the life of another partner? (2) Was the surviving partner required to remit the insurance proceeds to the estate of the deceased partner?

GRAVES v NORRED

(Ala) 510 So 2d 816 (1987)

Jewell Norred's husband, James Norred, was the business partner of Clyde Graves for about ten years. On May 7, 1979, Graves and Norred took out term life insurance policies, with Graves being the beneficiary of Norred's policy and Norred being the beneficiary of Graves' policy. Premiums were paid out of partnership funds. On February 28, 1983, Graves and Norred divided the partnership assets but did not perform the customary steps of dissolving the partnership. Graves became the sole owner of the business and continued to pay the premiums on both insurance policies until James Norred died on December 5, 1983. Jewell Norred sued Graves seeking the proceeds of the insurance policy for herself, alleging that Graves had no insurable interest in the life of James Norred at the time of his death. She also contended that the proceeds should go to the estate as a payment for Norred's interest in the partnership. From a judgment on behalf of the estate, Graves appealed.

ADAMS, J. . . . Jewell Norred argues that she should receive the benefits of the insurance policy because she alone had an insurable interest in the insurance contract. . . . The prevailing rule among the states is that a partner or partnership has an insurable interest in the life of one of the partners. . . . It is not the mere existence of the partnership which provides the basis for the insurable interest. It is the insuring partner's "reasonable expectation of pecuniary benefit from the continuance of the insured's life." . . . This interest continues even if the partnership is discontinued prior to death of one of the partners, . . .

In the instant case each partner took out a life insurance policy on the other. Both sides testified that the purpose was to provide for one partner at the other partner's death. . . . There is not legal uncertainty that both partners had an insurable interest in the life of the other partner.

We next turn our analysis to the designation of the beneficiary in order to determine who should be entitled to the proceeds of the life insurance policy. In the case of *Williams v Williams*, 438 So 2d 735 (Ala. 1983), a partner designated the other partners (his brothers), as the beneficiaries of his life insurance policy. Pursuant to the partnership's dissolution agreement, the surviving partners were to receive the insurance proceeds and then use those proceeds to purchase the deceased partner's interest. . . . Unlike the present case, in *Williams* a written partnership agreement and a dissolution agreement existed. However, both agreements involved the designation of the partners as beneficiaries instead of the spouse or estate. As stated by Chief Justice Torbert, "The fact that the decedent selected his partners, as opposed to his spouse or estate, as beneficiaries of the life insurance . . . is unquestionably permissible. Partners continue to be free to select whomever they wish to benefit from insurance on their lives." *Williams*, 438 So 2d at 739. In this case, the plaintiff's evidence that the decedent intended for the proceeds to go to his estate consisted solely of oral testimony from the plaintiff's brother (the insurance agent), and an ambiguous statement from a mutual friend of both partners. No ambiguity existed in the designation of the beneficiary. There was no written agreement like the dissolution agreement in *Williams*, supra, which provided that the surviving partners were to use the proceeds to purchase the deceased partner's interest. We require more than oral testimony, like the testimony presented here, in order to show that it was not the intention of the decedent that the designated beneficiary retain the proceeds. Therefore, we reverse the trial court's judgment designating Norred's estate as the rightful recipient of the proceeds instead of the designated beneficiary.

[Reversed and remanded]

QUESTIONS

1. Did Graves have an insurable interest in the life of Norred following the discontinuance of the partnership?
2. Was Graves required to remit the proceeds of the insurance to Norred's estate?
3. Can a partner select his or her partner, as opposed to his or her spouse or estate, as beneficiary under a life insurance policy?

3. The Contract

The formation of a contract of insurance is governed by the general principles applicable to contracts. By statute, it is now commonly provided that an insurance policy must be written. To avoid deception, many statutes also specify the content of certain policies, in whole or in part. Some statutes specify the size and style of type to be used in printing the policies. Provisions in a policy that conflict with statutory requirements are generally void. Frequently, a question arises as to whether advertising material, estimates, and statistical projections constitute a part of the contract.

(a) THE APPLICATION AS PART OF THE CONTRACT. The application for insurance is generally attached to the policy when issued and is made part of the contract of insurance by express stipulation of the policy.

The insured is bound by all statements in the attached application, if the policy and the attached application are retained without objection to such statement.[3]

(b) STATUTORY PROVISIONS AS PART OF THE CONTRACT. When a statute requires that insurance contracts contain certain provisions or cover certain specified losses, a contract of insurance that does not comply with the statute will be interpreted as though it contained all the provisions required by the

---

3 Old Line Life Insurance Co. v Superior Court, 229 Cal App 3d 1600, 281 Cal Rptr 15 (1991).

statute. When a statute requires that all terms of the insurance contract be included in the written contract, the insurer cannot claim that a provision not stated in the written contract was binding on the insured.

4. Antilapse and Cancellation Statutes and Provisions

If the premiums are not paid on time, the policy under ordinary contract law would lapse because of nonpayment. However, with life insurance policies, either by policy provision or statute, the insured is allowed a grace period of 30 or 31 days in which to make payment of the premium due.[4] When there is a default in the payment of a premium by the insured, the insurer may be required by statute to (a) issue a paid-up policy in a smaller amount, (b) provide extended insurance for a period of time, or (c) pay the cash surrender value of the policy.

The contract of insurance may expressly declare that it may or may not be canceled by the insurer's unilateral act. By statute or policy provision, the insurer is commonly required to give a specific number of days' written notice of cancellation.

5. Modification of Contract

As is the case with most contracts, a contract of insurance can be modified if both insurer and insured agree to the change. The insurer cannot modify the contract without the consent of the insured when the right to do so is not reserved in the insurance contract.

To make changes or corrections to the policy, it is not necessary to issue a new policy. An endorsement on the policy or the execution of a separate rider is effective for the purpose of changing the policy. When a provision of an endorsement conflicts with a provision of the policy, the endorsement controls, because it is the later document.

6. Interpretation of Contract

A contract of insurance is interpreted by the same rules that govern the interpretation of ordinary contracts. Words are to be given their ordinary meaning and interpreted in light of the nature of the coverage intended. Thus, an employee who has been killed is not regarded as disabled within the meaning of a group policy covering employees.

The courts are increasingly recognizing the fact that most persons obtaining insurance are not specially trained. Therefore, the contract of insurance is to be read as it would be understood by the average person or by the average person in business, rather than by one with technical knowledge of the law or of insurance.[5]

If there is an ambiguity in the policy, the provision is interpreted against the insurer.

7. Burden of Proof

When an insurance claim is disputed by the insurer, the person bringing suit has the burden of proving that there was a loss, that it occurred while the policy was in force, and that the loss was of a kind that was within the coverage or scope of the policy.

A policy will contain exceptions to the coverage. This means that the policy is not applicable when an exception applies to the situation.[6] Exceptions to coverage are generally strictly interpreted against the insurer. The insurer has the burden of proving that the facts were such that there was no coverage because an exception applied. Although an exception is literally applicable, it will be ignored by some courts and coverage sustained if there is no cause-and-effect relationship between the

---

4 Flowers v Provident Life and Acc. Ins. Co. (Tenn) 713 SW2d 69 (1986).

5 Farm Bureau Mutual Insurance Co. v Winters (Kan) 806 P2d 993 (1991).

6 Fireman's Fund Ins. v Fibreboard Corp. 182 Cal App 3d 462, 227 Cal Rptr 203 (1986).

loss and the conduct that was the violation of the exception.

8. Insurer Bad Faith

As is required in the case of all contracts, an insurer must act in good faith in processing and paying claims under its policy. In some states, laws have been enacted making an insurer liable for a statutory penalty and attorneys' fees in case of a bad faith failure or delay, to pay a valid claim within a specified period of time. A bad faith refusal is generally considered to be any frivolous or unfounded refusal to comply with the demand of a policyholder to pay according to the policy.[7]

When it is a liability insurer's duty to defend the insured and the insurer wrongfully refuses to do so, the insurer is guilty of breach of contract and is liable for all consequential damages resulting from the breach. In some jurisdictions, an insured can recover for an excess judgment rendered against the insured when it is proven that the insurer was guilty of negligence or bad faith in failing to defend the action or settle the matter within policy limits.

In the *South Park* case the court was faced with the question of whether the insured was

SOUTH PARK AGGREGATES INC. v NORTHWESTERN NATIONAL INSURANCE CO.
(Colo App) 847 P2d 218 (1993)

South Park Aggregates Inc. was engaged in gravel production in Fairplay, Colorado. As part of its operation, South Park employed a frontend loader that was insured by Northwestern National Insurance Co. under an "all risk" policy, which provided coverage against "all risk of direct physical loss or damage from any external cause except as hereafter provided." Among the losses excluded from coverage was loss resulting from "mechanical breakdown." On July 2, 1987, the oil plug on the frontend loader appeared to be tampered with, causing the engine to seize up from loss of oil. Northwestern refused to pay the insurance claim on the grounds that the loader was damaged due to "mechanical difficulties." South Park was unable to pay for the repair or the rental of a loader. This forced South Park to go out of business. From a judgment entered on behalf of South Park for $915,000 plus $457,000 in exemplary damages, Northwestern appealed.

PIERCE, J. . . . Northwestern contends that it is entitled to a new trial because the jury's damage award was so unconscionably excessive as to indicate that it was influenced by bias, prejudice, or passion. . . . We disagree.

The amount of damages to be awarded is within the sole province of the jury, and its award will not be disturbed unless it is completely unsupported by the record. . . . A jury verdict may not be set aside on grounds of passion, prejudice, or corruption unless damages are "'so outrageous as to strike everyone with the enormity or injustice of them.'" . . .

Here, South Park presented evidence that the damaged loader was valued at $60,000 and other equipment owned by South Park was valued at $286,500. In addition,

---

[7] Automobile Insurance Co. of Hartford v Davila (Tex Civ App) 805 SW2d 897 (1991).

South Park presented evidence that its processed inventory was worth between $357,000 to $640,500. Finally, South Park presented evidence that the cost of repairing the loader and renting a replacement was approximately $20,000. Deducting from this amount the $66,000 South Park owed creditors on its equipment, South Park's total damages from the loss of its business, based on this evidence, ranged from approximately $675,000 to $941,000.

Thus, there is support in the record for the award of damages, and it is binding on appeal. . . .

Initially, Northwestern contends that South Park presented no evidence of willful or wanton conduct or "evil intent" on the part of Northwestern. Thus, it concludes, as a matter of law, the jury could not have found beyond a reasonable doubt that Northwestern acted with a wrongful motive which would justify an award of exemplary damages. We disagree.

Exemplary damages may be recovered only as provided by statute. . . . To support an award of exemplary damages, a party must establish its claim by proof beyond a reasonable doubt. . . .

Exemplary damages may be recovered on a claim of bad faith breach of an insurance contract if the breach is accompanied by circumstances of fraud, malice, or willful and wanton conduct. . . . Malice or wanton conduct may be established by evidence that the defendant knew or should have known that injury would result from its actions. . . .

Here, South Park presented evidence that Northwestern was aware that the damage to the loader was a probable result of vandalism. The independent adjuster's report submitted to Northwestern, which was admitted into evidence at trial, concluded that the "mechanical breakdown" of the loader occurred as a result of the vandalism. In addition, notes from the claim file of Northwestern's own insurance adjuster . . . indicated that there "appears to be tampering with the [oil] plug, not by insured," and "we can't prove insured is the one." In another note, which referred to the Park County sheriff's report, Northwestern's adjuster wrote, "I said it looks like cop is going out of his way to not show vandalism—[independent adjuster] agreed."

Moreover, South Park presented evidence that Northwestern was aware of the consequences of its denial of its claim. A person who leased a replacement loader to South Park testified that he had contacted Northwestern's adjuster and informed him that he could not lease the loader to South Park if Northwestern did not pay the rental and that South Park would likely be driven out of business without the loader.

Thus, there is substantial evidence . . . that would support a jury finding of willful and wanton conduct beyond a reasonable doubt. Consequently, the trial court did not err in denying the motion for judgment notwithstanding the verdict. . . .

[Judgment affirmed]

QUESTIONS

1. What was the amount of the claim and what was the total amount of the judgment against the insured?
2. What must an insured prove in order to be entitled to recover exemplary damages in an action claiming bad faith breach of an insurance contract?
3. Was the ethical principle of "doing no harm" applicable to this case?

entitled to compensatory and exemplary damages for bad faith breach of the insurance contract.

If there is a reasonable basis for the insurer's belief that a claim is not covered by its policy, its refusal to pay the claim does not subject it to liability for a breach of good faith or for a statutory penalty.[8] This is so, even though the court holds that the insurer is liable for the claim.

9. Time Limitations on Insured

The insured must comply with a number of time limitations in making a claim. For example, the insured must promptly notify the insurer of any claim that may arise, submit a proof-of-loss statement within the time set forth in the policy, and bring any court action based on the policy within a specified time period.

10. Subrogation of Insurer

In some instances, the insured has a claim against a third person for the harm covered by the insurance policy. For example, the insured (who has an automobile collision insurance policy) who is in a collision may have a claim against the other driver. If the insurer pays the insured the full amount of the insured's claim, the insurer is then subrogated to the insured's claim against the third person who caused the harm. This means that the insurer acquires the claim of the insured against the third person, just as though the insured had assigned the claim to the insurer. When the insurer is subrogated to the insured's claim, the insurer may enforce that claim against the third person.[9] From the money recovered from the third person, the insurer is entitled to keep an amount equal to the payment made by the insurer to the insured, together with interest and costs.

Figure 38-1   Subrogration

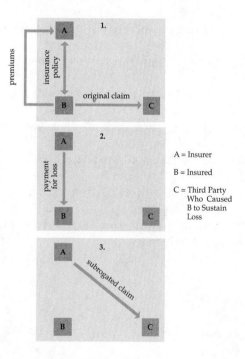

A = Insurer

B = Insured

C = Third Party Who Caused B to Sustain Loss

---

[8] Shipes v Hanover Ins. Co. (CA11 Ga) 884 F2d 1357 (1989).

[9] Patton v Jenkins (Okla App) 847 P2d 831 (1993).

B. KINDS OF INSURANCE

Businesses today have specialized risk managers who identify the risks to which individual businesses are exposed, measure those risks, and purchase insurance to cover those risks (or decide to self-insure in whole or in part).

Insurance policies can be grouped into certain categories. Five major categories of insurance are considered below: (1) business liability insurance, (2) marine and inland marine insurance, (3) fire and homeowners insurance, (4) automobile insurance, and (5) life insurance.

11. Business Liability Insurance

Businesses may purchase "Comprehensive General Liability" (CGL) policies. This insurance is a broad, "all-risk" form of insurance providing coverage for all sums that the insured may become legally obligated to pay as damages because of "bodily injury" or "property damage" caused by an "occurrence." The insurer is obligated to defend the insured business and pay damages under CGL policies for product liability cases, actions for wrongful termination of employees, and damages caused by the business's advertising.[10] The insurer may also be obligated to pay for damages in the form of cleanup costs imposed for contamination of land, water, and air under environmental statutes.[11]

Businesses may purchase policies providing liability insurance for their directors and officers. Manufacturers and sellers may purchase product liability insurance. Professional persons, such as accountants, physicians, lawyers, architects, and engineers, may obtain liability insurance protection against malpractice suits.

12. Marine Insurance

Marine insurance policies cover perils relating to the transportation of goods. **Ocean marine** insurance policies cover the transportation of goods in vessels in international and coastal trade. **Inland marine** insurance principally covers domestic shipments of goods over land and inland waterways.

(a) OCEAN MARINE. Ocean marine insurance is a form of insurance that covers ships and their cargoes against "perils of the sea." Four classes of ocean marine insurance are generally available: (1) hull, (2) cargo, (3) liability, and (4) freight. **Hull insurance** covers physical damage to the vessel. **Cargo insurance** protects the cargo owner against financial loss if the goods being shipped are lost or damaged at sea. This insurance does not cover risks prior to the loading of the insured cargo on board the vessel.[12] An additional warehouse coverage endorsement is needed to insure merchandise held in warehouse prior to import or export voyages.

Liability insurance covers the shipowner's liability if the ship causes damage to another ship or its cargo. **Freight insurance** insures that the shipowner will receive payment for the transportation charges.

In the *Commodities Reserve Co.* case a cargo owner sued the insurer for breach of an ocean marine cargo policy.

(b) INLAND MARINE. Inland marine insurance evolved from marine insurance. It protects goods in transit over land, by air, or on rivers, lakes, and coastal waters. Inland marine insurance can be used to insure property held by a bailee. Moreover, it is common for institutions financing automobile dealers' new car inventories to purchase inland marine insurance policies to insure against damage to the automobiles while in inventory.[13]

---

[10] US Fire Insurance Co. v Good Humor Corp. (Wis App) 496 NW2d 730 (1993).

[11] Chemical Leaman Tank Lines Inc. v Aetna Casualty Co. (DC NJ) 788 F Supp 846 (1992); US v Pepper's Steel Inc. (SD Fla) 823 F Supp 1574 (1993). *But see* Borg-Warner v INA, 577 NYS2d 953 (1992).

[12] S.P. Duggal Corp. v Aetna Casualty Co. 580 NYS2d 767 (1992).

COMMODITIES RESERVE CO. v
ST. PAUL FIRE & MARINE INS. CO.
(CA9 Cal) 879 F2d 640 (1989)

Commodities Reserve Co. (CRC) contracted to sell 1,008 tons of beans and 50 tons of seeds to purchasers in Venezuela. CRC purchased the beans and seeds in Turkey and chartered space on the ship MV West Lion. The cargo was insured under an ocean marine policy issued by St. Paul Fire & Marine Insurance Co. (St. Paul). While the ship was sailing through Greek waters, Greek authorities seized the vessel for carrying munitions. CRC had to go to the expense of obtaining an order from a court in Crete to release the cargo. When St. Paul refused to pay the costs of the Cretan litigation to release the cargo, CRC brought suit against St. Paul. Judgment was entered for St. Paul. CRC appealed.

FARRIS, C. J. . . . Commodities Reserve primarily seeks recovery under the Sue & Labor Clause of its insurance contract with St. Paul, which provides:

In case of any loss or misfortune, it shall be lawful and necessary to and for the Assured . . . to sue, labor and travel for, in and about the defense, safeguard and recovery of the said goods and merchandise . . . to the charges whereof, the [insurer] will contribute according to the rate and quantity of the sum hereby insured.

This standard provision requires the insurer to reimburse the assured for expenses incurred in preventing a loss for which, if it had occurred, the insurer would be liable. . . .

The Average Clause is the general basis for liability. It provides that the policy covers "all risks of physical loss or damage from any external cause excepting those risks excluded by the F.C. & S. [Free of Capture & Seizure] and S.R. & C.C. [Strikes, Riots & Civil Commotions] Clauses. . . ."

The F.C. & S. Clause, one of the Paramount Warranties, declares that:

Notwithstanding anything herein contained to the contrary, this insurance is warranted free from: (a) capture, seizure, arrest, restraint, detainment, confiscation, preemption, requisition or nationalization, and the consequences thereof or any attempt thereat, whether in time of peace or war and whether lawful or otherwise. . . .

St. Paul argues that the F.C. & S. Clause . . . excuses it from liability. . . .

When the Greek authorities detained the ship, they did not claim jurisdiction over Commodities Reserve's cargo. . . . Instead, the captain refused to release the cargo. Due to the captain's conduct, Commodities Reserve had to secure a court order compelling the release of its cargo. The litigation expenses incurred to release the cargo are recoverable under the Average Clause, which covers "all risks of physical loss or damage from any external cause." *See Champion Int'l Corp. v Arkwright-Boston Mfr. Mutual Ins. Co.*, 1982 AMC 2496 (S.D.N.Y.), aff'd, 714 F2d 112 (2d Cir 1982) (insured entitled to recover for expenses, including litigation, incurred to recover cargo after carrier converted it under policy insuring plaintiff against "all risk of physical loss or damage to its cargo from an external source"). The Sue and Labor Clause required Commodities Reserve to "sue . . . for . . . recovery of said goods and merchandise" in case of loss or misfortune, and mandates payment of the charges by the insurer.

The detention by Greek authorities was not the proximate cause of the litigation expenses. The detention did not necessitate the suit in Crete. The litigation expenses were incurred solely because of the captain's refusal to release the cargo. Consequently, the Free of Capture and Seizure Clause does not preclude recovery of these expenses.

The district court erred in granting St. Paul summary judgment on this issue. Summary judgment for the litigation expenses should be awarded to Commodities Reserve on its cross-motion for summary judgment.

[Reversed and remanded]

QUESTIONS

1. What defense did the insurer raise?
2. Were the litigation expenses incurred because of the seizure of the vessel by Greek authorities?
3. Under the ocean marine policy in effect, was the insurer held liable for the litigation expenses?

13. Fire and Homeowners Insurance

A **fire insurance** policy is a contract to indemnify the insured for property destruction or damage caused by fire. In almost every state, the New York standard fire insurance form is the standard policy. A **homeowners insurance** policy is a combination of the standard fire insurance policy and comprehensive personal liability insurance. It thus provides fire, theft, and certain liability protection in a single insurance contract.

(a) FIRE INSURANCE. In order for fire loss to be covered by fire insurance, there must be an actual, hostile fire that is the immediate cause of the loss. A **hostile fire** is one that becomes uncontrollable, burns with excessive heat, or escapes from the place where it is intended to be.[14] To illustrate, when soot is ignited and causes a fire in the chimney, the fire is hostile. On the other hand, if a loss is caused by the smoke or heat of a fire that has not broken out of its ordinary container or become uncontrollable, it results from a friendly fire. Damage from a friendly fire is not covered by the policy.

By policy endorsement, the coverage may be extended to include loss by a friendly fire.

(1) Coinsurance. The insurer is liable for the actual amount of the loss sustained, up to the maximum amount stated in the policy. An exception exists when the policy contains a coinsurance clause. A **coinsurance clause** requires the insured to maintain insurance on the covered property up to a certain amount or a certain percent of the value (generally 80 percent). Under such a provision, if the policyholder insures the property for less than the required amount, the insurer is liable only for the proportionate share of the amount of insurance required to be carried. To illustrate, suppose the owner of a building with a value of $200,000 insures it against loss to the extent of $120,000. The policy contains a coinsurance clause requiring that insurance of 80 percent of the value of the property be carried (in this case, $160,000). Assume that an $80,000 loss is

13 Boyd Motors Inc. v Employers Insurance of Wausau (CA10 Okla) 880 F2d 270 (1989).

14 American Star Insurance Co. v Grice (Wash) 854 P2d 622 (1993).

then sustained. The insured would not receive $80,000 from the insurer. The insured would receive only three-fourths of that amount, which is $60,000, because the amount of the insurance carried ($120,000) is only three-fourths of the amount required ($160,000).

In some states, use of a coinsurance clause is prohibited.

(2) Assignment. Fire insurance is a personal contract, and in the absence of statute or contractual authorization it cannot be assigned without the consent of the insurer.

(3) Occupancy. Provisions in a policy of fire insurance relating to the use and occupancy of the property are generally strictly construed, because they relate to the hazards involved.

(b) HOMEOWNERS INSURANCE. In addition to providing protection against losses resulting from fire, the homeowners policy provides liability coverage for accidents or injuries that occur on the premises of the insured. Moreover, the liability provisions provide coverage for unintentional injuries to others away from home for which the insured or any member of the resident family is held responsible, such as injuries caused others by golfing, hunting, or fishing accidents.[15] Generally, motor vehicles, including mopeds and recreation vehicles, are excluded from such personal liability coverage.

A homeowners policy also provides protection from losses caused by theft.

A homeowners policy provides protection for all permanent residents of the household, including all family members living with the insured. Thus, a child of the insured who lives at home is protected under the homeowner's policy for the value of personal property lost when the home is destroyed by fire.[16]

14. Automobile Insurance

Associations of insurers, such as the National Bureau of Casualty Underwriters and the National Automobile Underwriters Association, have proposed standard forms of automobile insurance policies. These forms have been approved by the association members in virtually all states. The form used today by most insurers is the Personal Auto Policy (PAP).

(a) PERILS COVERED. Part A of the policy provides liability coverage that protects the insured driver or owner from the claims of others for bodily injuries or damage to their property. Part B of the policy provides the coverage for medical expenses sustained by a covered person or persons in an accident. Part C of the PAP provides coverage for damages the insured is entitled to recover from an **uninsured motorist**. Part D provides coverage for loss or damage to the covered automobile. Coverage under Part D includes collision coverage and coverage of "other than collision" losses, such as fire and theft.

(b) COVERED PERSONS. Covered persons include the named insured or any family member (a person related by blood, marriage, or adoption or a ward or foster child who is a resident of the household). If an individual is driving with the permission of the insured, that individual is also covered.

(c) USE AND OPERATION. The coverage of the PAP policy is limited to claims arising from the "use and operation" of an automobile. The term *use and operation* does not require that the automobile be in motion. Thus, the term embraces loading and unloading as well as actual travel.[17]

---

[15] American Concept Insurance Co. v Lloyds of London (SD) 467 NW2d 480 (1991).

[16] Gulf Insurance Co. v Mathis, 183 Ga App 323, 358 SE2d 307 (1987).

[17] State Farm Ins. v Whithead (Mo App) 711 SW2d 198 (1986).

(d) NOTICE AND COOPERATION. The insured is under a duty to give notice of claims, to inform, and to cooperate with the insurer. Notice and cooperation are conditions precedent to the liability of the insurer.

(e) NO-FAULT INSURANCE. Traditional tort law (negligence law) placed the economic losses resulting from an automobile accident on the one at fault. The purpose of automobile liability insurance is to relieve the wrongdoer from the consequences of a negligent act by paying defense costs and the damages assessed. Under no-fault laws, injured persons are barred from suing the party at fault for ordinary claims. When the insured is injured while using the insured automobile, the insurer will make a payment without regard to whose fault caused the harm. However, if the automobile collision results in a permanent serious disablement or disfigurement, or death, or if the medical bills and lost wages of the plaintiff exceed a specified amount, suit may be brought against the party who was at fault.

15. Life Insurance

There are three basic types of life insurance: term insurance, whole life insurance, and endowment insurance.

Term insurance is written for a specified number of years and terminates at the end of that period. If the insured dies within the time period covered by the policy, the face amount is paid to the beneficiary. If the insured is still alive at the end of the time period, the contract expires and the insurer has no further obligation. Term policies have little or no cash surrender value.

Whole life insurance (or ordinary life insurance) provides lifetime insurance protection. It also has an investment element. Part of every premium covers the cost of insurance, and the remainder of the premium builds up a **cash surrender value** of the policy.

An **endowment insurance** policy is one that pays the face amount of the policy if the insured dies within the policy period. If the insured lives to the end of the policy period, the face amount is paid to the insured at the end of the period.

Many life insurance companies pay double the amount of the policy, called **double indemnity**, if death is caused by an accident and death occurs within 90 days after the accident. A comparatively small additional premium is charged for this special protection.

In consideration of an additional premium, many life insurance companies also provide insurance against total permanent disability of the insured. **Disability** is usually defined in a life insurance policy as any "incapacity resulting from bodily injury or disease to engage in any occupation for remuneration or profit."

(a) EXCLUSIONS. Life insurance policies frequently provide that death is not within the protection of the policy and that a double indemnity provision is not applicable when death is caused by (1) suicide,[18] (2) narcotics, (3) the intentional act of another, (4) execution for a crime, (5) war activities, or (6) operation of aircraft.

(b) THE BENEFICIARY. The recipient of life insurance policy proceeds that are payable on the death of the insured is called the **beneficiary**. The beneficiary may be a third person or the estate of the insured. There may be more than one beneficiary.

The beneficiary named in the policy may be barred from claiming the proceeds of the policy. It is generally provided by statute or stated by court decision that a beneficiary who has feloniously killed the insured is not entitled to receive the proceeds of the policy.

The customary policy provides that the insured reserves the right to change the beneficiary without the latter's consent. When the policy contains such a provision, the beneficiary

---

[18] Mirza v Maccabees Life and Annuity Co. 187 Mich App 76, 466 NW2d 340 (1991).

cannot object to a change that destroys all of that beneficiary's rights under the policy and that names another person as beneficiary.

The insurance policy will ordinarily state that to change the beneficiary, the insurer must be so instructed in writing by the insured, and the policy must then be endorsed by the company with the change of the beneficiary. These provisions are construed liberally. If the insured has notified the insurer but dies before the endorsement of the change by the company, the change of beneficiary is effective. However, if the insured has not taken any steps to comply with the policy requirements, a change of beneficiary is not effective, even though a change was intended.

(c) INCONTESTABILITY CLAUSE.

Statutes commonly require the inclusion of an **incontestability clause** in life insurance poli-cies. Ordinarily, this clause states that after the lapse of two years the policy cannot be contested by the insurance company. The insurer is free to contest the validity of the policy at any time during the contestability period. Once the period has expired, the insurer must pay the stipulated sum on the death of the insured and cannot claim that in obtaining the policy, the insured had been guilty of misrepresentation, fraud, or any other conduct that would entitle it to avoid the contract of insurance.[19]

In the *Kane* case the insurer believed that there should be an exception to the incontestability period. The criminal history of the insured was not discoverable in a background check because the insured was given a new identity under the federal witness protection program.

BANKERS SECURITY LIFE INSURANCE SOCIETY v KANE

(CA11 Fla) 885 F2d 820 (1989)

In 1976 Arthur Katz testified for the U.S. government in a stock manipulation case. He also pled guilty and testified against three of his law partners in an insurance fraud case. He received a six-month sentence in a halfway house and a $5,000 fine. Katz was placed in the Federal Witness Protection Program. Katz and his wife changed their names to Kane and moved to Florida under the program. Both he and his wife obtained new driver's licenses and social security numbers. Using his new identity, "Kane" obtained two life insurance policies totaling $1.5 million and named his wife beneficiary. A routine criminal background check on Kane found no criminal history. From 1984 to 1987 Kane invested heavily in the stock market. On October 17, 1987, the day the stock market crashed, Kane shot and wounded his stockbroker, shot and killed the office manager, and then committed suicide. The insurers refused to pay on the policies, claiming that they never insure persons with criminal records. Mrs. Kane contended that the policies were incontestable after they had been in effect for two years. From a judgment for Mrs. Kane, the insurers appealed.

SHOOB, D. J. . . . Essentially, appellants seek a court-created exception to the Florida rule that insurance policies are incontestable after they have been in effect for

---

[19] Rapak v Companion Life Insurance Co. (SC) 424 SE2d 486 (1992).

two years. Fla Stat § 627.455 (1984). Appellants correctly argue that the purpose of this statute is to create a reasonable time period during which insurance companies can investigate applicants and void policies issued in error, while protecting consumers from untimely efforts to void policies. . . . Appellants maintain that this purpose is not served, however, by enforcing the incontestability clauses at issue here.

Appellants urge the Court to adopt the reasoning of several Pennsylvania cases that have created an "imposter" exception where the insurance company, through reasonable investigation, could not have discovered fraud in the issuance of a policy. . . . See Unity Mutual Life Insurance Co. v Moses, 621 F. Supp. 13 (E.D.Pa. 1985). Appellants maintain that in such cases no contract exists (and no incontestability clause) because there is no meeting of the minds as to the identity of the insured.

Although appellants present a novel argument, it must fail based on the strict construction of the incontestability clauses under Florida law. . . .

We will not create exceptions to Florida law or void insurance policies ab initio in a manner that would undermine the intent of the Florida legislature and the practice in the Florida courts.

We also reject appellants' argument that the district court should not have dismissed their complaints without leave to amend. Any amendments to the complaints would have been futile. There is no set of facts upon which appellants could succeed because the district court correctly held that appellants are not entitled to an exception to Florida's incontestability statute.

. . . Finally, appellants cannot bring a separate tort suit for fraud. . . .

In this case a fraud suit would merely provide a different means to challenge the validity of the insurance contract. The district court properly rebuffed appellants' efforts to evade the Florida incontestability statute in this manner. . . .

[Judgment affirmed]

QUESTIONS

1. What is the purpose of the statute requiring the inclusion of incontestability clauses in life insurance policies?
2. How are incontestability clauses construed?
3. Did the court leave the insurer other legal means to challenge the enforceability of the policy?

SUMMARY

Insurance is a contract, called a policy. By an insurance policy, provision is made by the insurer, in consideration of premium payments to pay the insured or beneficiary a sum of money if the insured sustains a specified loss or is subjected to a specified liability. These contracts are made through an insurance agent, who is an agent for the insurance company, or through an insurance broker. An insurance broker is the agent of the insured when obtaining a policy for the latter.

The person purchasing an insurance contract must have an insurable interest in the insured life or property. An insurable interest in property exists when the damage or destruction of the property will cause a direct monetary loss to the insured. In the case of property insurance, the insured must have an insurable interest at the time of loss. An insurable interest in the life of the insured exists if the purchaser would suffer a financial loss from the insured's death. This interest must exist as of the time the policy is obtained.

Ocean marine policies insure ships and their cargoes against the perils of the sea. Inland marine policies insure goods being transported by land, air, or on inland and coastal waterways.

In order for a fire loss to be covered by fire insurance, there must be an actual, hostile fire that is the immediate cause of the loss. The insurer is liable for the actual amount of the loss sustained up to the maximum amount stated in the policy. An exception exists when the policy contains a coinsurance clause requiring the insured to maintain insurance up to a certain percentage of the value of the property. To the extent this is not done, the insured is deemed a coinsurer with the insurer, and the insurer is liable for only its proportional share of the amount of insurance required to be carried. A homeowners insurance policy provides fire, theft, and liability protection in a single contract.

Automobile insurance may provide protection for collision damage to the insured's property and injury to persons. It may also cover liability to third persons for injury and property damage, and loss by fire or theft.

A life insurance policy requires the insurer to pay a stated sum of money to a named beneficiary on the death of the insured. It may be a term insurance policy, a whole life policy, or an endowment policy. State law commonly requires the inclusion of an incontestability clause, whereby at the conclusion of the incontestable period the insurer cannot contest the validity of the policy.

LAW IN PRACTICE

1. Recognize that to get insurance you must have an insurable interest in the life or property being insured.

2. If your property is underinsured, the application of a fire policy's coinsurance clause result in the insurer's paying only a proportionate share of a loss due to fire.

3. You should video tape the contents of your home and business and keep the tape in a safe deposit box so that you can document your losses should your property be destroyed.

4. Remember, with life insurance policies, that the insured has a thirty day grace period during which the insurer is obligated to continue coverage and the insured has the opportunity to make the past due payment.

5. Recognize that insurance applications must be filled out with care and accuracy, and that the life insurer may contest the validity of a policy at any time during the contestability period.

QUESTIONS AND CASE PROBLEMS

1. What social forces are affected by requiring an insurable interest?

2. Compare (a) a contract of insurance and (b) an ordinary contract.

3. What time limits may bar an insured from recovering on an insurance policy?

4. On April 6, 1988 Luis Serrano purchased for $75,000 a 26′ 8″ long Carrera speed boat named "Hot Shot". First Federal Savings Bank provided $65,000 financing for this purchase. Serrano obtained a marine yacht policy for hull insurance on the boat for $75,000 from El Fenix, with First Federal being named as payee under the policy. On May 2, 1988 Serrano sold the boat to Reinaldo Polito, and Serrano furnished First Federal with documents evidencing the sale. Polito assumed the obligation to pay off the balance due First Federal. On October 6, 1989 Serrano again applied to El Fenix for a new yacht policy covering the period from October 6, 1989 through October 6, 1990; and the coverage extended to peril of confiscation by a governmental agency. Serrano did not have ownership or possession of the boat on October 6, 1989. First Federal, the named payee, had not perfected or recorded a mortgage on "Hot Shot" until July 5, 1990. On November 13, 1989, in the waters off Cooper Island in the British Virgin Islands (BVI) "Hot Shot" was found abandoned after a chase by governmental officials. A large shipment of cocaine was recovered, although no one was arrested. When Serrano and First Federal were informed that Hot Shot was subject to mandatory forfeiture under BVI law, they both filed claims under the October 6, 1989 insurance policy. What defenses would you raise on behalf of the insurer in this case? Decide. [*El Fenix v Serrana Gutierrez (DC PR) 786 F Supp 1065*]

5. From the United Insurance Co., Rebecca Foster obtained a policy insuring the life of Lucille McClurkin and naming herself as beneficiary. McClurkin did not live with Foster, and Foster did not inform McClurkin of the existence of the policy. Foster paid the premiums on the policy and, on the death of McClurkin, sued the United Insurance Co. for the amount of the insurance. At the trial, Foster testified vaguely that her father had told her that McClurkin was her second cousin on his side of the family. Was Foster entitled to recover on the policy? [*Foster v United Insurance Co. 250 SC 423, 158 SE2d 201*]

6. Dr. George Allard and his brother-in-law, Tom Rowland, did not get along after family land which was once used solely by Rowland was partitioned among family members after the death of Rowland's father. Rowland had a reputation in the community for being a bully and a violent person. On December 17, Allard was moving cattle down a dirt road by "trolling" (leading the cattle with a bucket of feed, causing them to follow him). When he saw a forestry truck coming along the road, he led the cattle off the road onto Rowland's land in order to prevent frightening the cattle. When Rowland saw Allard, Rowland ran towards him screaming at him for being on his land. Allard, a small older man retreated to his truck and obtained a 12-gauge shotgun. He pointed the gun toward the ground about an inch above the ground in front of Rowland's left foot, and fired it. He stated he fired the shot in this fashion to bring Rowland to his senses, and that Rowland stepped forward into the line of fire. Allard claimed that if Rowland had not stepped forward, he would not have been hit and injured. Allard was insured by Farm Bureau homeowners and general liability policies, which did not cover liability resulting from intentional acts by the insured. Applying the policy exclusion to the facts of this case, was Farm Bureau obligated to pay the $100,000 judgment against Allard? [*Southern Farm Bureau Casualty Co. v Allard (Miss) 611 So 2d 966*]

7. Assistant manager trainee R. G. Smith suspected Bowen of shoplifting at Broad & Marshall Department Store. After getting permission from the store manager to follow her, he observed Bowen driving out of the store's parking lot. Smith followed her in his car and forced her into a ditch, where her car overturned and was destroyed. Bowen received the fair market value for her car from her insurance company, General National Mutual (GNM), and executed a subrogation agreement in connection with this payment. GNM brings suit against Smith and the store to obtain reimbursement for the amount paid by it for the damage to the car. They defend that GNM is not the proper party plaintiff. Decide.

8. Linda Filasky held policies issued by the Preferred Risk Mutual Insurance Co. Following an injury in an automobile accident and storm damage to the roof of her home, Filasky sustained loss of income, theft of property, and water damage to her home. These three kinds of loss were covered by the policies with Preferred, but the insurer delayed unreasonably in processing her claims and raised numerous groundless objections to them. Finally, the insurer paid the claims in full. Filasky then sued the insurer for the emotional distress caused by the bad faith delay and obstructive tactics of the insurer. [*Filasky v Preferred Risk Mut. Ins. Co. 152 Ariz 591, 734 P2d 76*]

9. Collins owned a Piper Colt airplane. He obtained from the South Carolina Insurance Company a liability policy covering the plane. The policy provided that it did not cover loss sustained while the plane was being piloted by a person who did not have a valid pilot's certificate and a valid medical examination certificate. Collins held a valid pilot's certificate, but his medical examination certificate had expired three months before. Collins was piloting the plane when it crashed, and he was killed. The insurer denied liability because Collins did not have a valid medical certificate. It was stipulated by both parties that the crash was in no way caused by the absence of the medical certificate. Decide. [*South Carolina Ins. Co. v Collins (SC) 237 SE2d 358*]

10. Marshall Produce Co. insured its milk and egg processing plant against fire. Smoke from a fire near its plant was absorbed by its egg powder. Cans of the powder delivered to the U.S. government were rejected as contaminated. Marshall Produce sued the insurance company for a total loss. The insurer contended that there had been no fire involving the insured property and no total loss.

Decide. [*Marshall Produce Co. v St. Paul Fire & Marine Ins. Co. 256 Minn 404, 98 NW2d 280*]

11. Amador Pena had three insurance policies on his life. He wrote a will in which he specified that the proceeds from the insurance policies should go to his children instead of to Leticia Pena Salinas and other beneficiaries named in the policies. He died the next day. The insurance companies paid the proceeds of the policies to the named beneficiaries. The executor of Penas estate sued Salinas and the other beneficiaries for the insurance money. Decide. [*Pena v Salinas (Tex Civ App) 536 SW2d 671*]

12. Spector owned a small automobile repair garage in rural Kansas, valued at $40,000. He purchased fire insurance coverage against loss to the extent of $24,000. The policy contained an 80 percent coinsurance clause. A fire destroyed a portion of his parts room, causing a loss of $16,000. Spector believes he is entitled to be fully compensated for this loss, since it is less than the $24,000 of fire protection that he purchased and paid for. Is Spector correct?

13. Carman Tool & Abrasives, Inc. (Carman) purchased two milling machines, F.O.B. Taiwan, from the Dah Lih Machinery Co. Carman obtained ocean marine cargo insurance on the machines from St. Paul Fire and Marine Insurance Co. Carman authorized Dah Lih to arrange for the shipment of the two machines to Los Angeles, using the services of Evergreen Lines. Dah Lih booked the machinery for shipment on board Evergreen's container ship, the M/V Ever Giant, arranged for the delivery of the cargo to the ship, provided all the shipping information for the bill of lading, and was the party to whom the bill was issued. Dah Lih then delivered the bill of lading to its bank, which in turn negotiated it to Carman's bank to authorize payment to Dah Lih. After the cargo was removed from the vessel in Los Angeles but before it was delivered to Carman, the milling machines

were damaged to the extent of $115,000. Is the insurer liable to Carman? Can the insurer recover from Evergreen? [*Carman Tool & Abrasives, Inc. v Evergreen Lines (CA9 Cal) 871 F2d 897*]

14. Vallot was driving his farm tractor on the highway. It was struck from the rear by a truck, overturned, exploded, and burned. Vallot was killed, and a death claim was made against All American Insurance Company. The death of Vallot was covered by the company's policy if Vallot had died from "being struck or run over by" the truck. The insurance company claimed that the policy was not applicable because Vallot had not been struck, in that the farm tractor had been struck and Vallot's death occurred when the overturned tractor exploded and burned. The insurance company also claimed that it was necessary that the insured be both struck and run over by another vehicle. Decide. [*Vallot v All American Insurance Co. (La App) 302 So 2d 625*]

15. When Jorge de Guerrero applied for a $200,000 life insurance policy with John Hancock Insurance Co., he stated on the insurance application that he had not seen a physician within the past five years. In fact, he had several consultations with his physician, who three weeks prior to the application had diagnosed him as overweight and suffering from goiter. His response to the question on drug and alcohol use was that he was not an alcoholic or user of drugs. In fact he had been an active alcoholic since age 16 and was a marijuana user. De Guerrero died within the two-year contestability period included in the policy, and John Hancock refused to pay. The beneficiary contended that all premiums were fully paid on the policy, and any misstatements in the application were unintentional. John Hancock contended that if the deceased had given the true facts, the policy would not have been issued. Decide. [*de Guerrero v John Hancock Mutual Life Insurance Co. (Fla App) 522 So 2d 1032*]

PART 7

Agency and Employment

CHAPTER 39

AGENCY— CREATION AND TERMINATION

LEARNING OBJECTIVES

After studying this chapter, you will be able to:
1. *Differentiate between an agent and an independent contractor.*
2. *Explain and illustrate who may be a principal and who may be an agent.*
3. *State the three classifications of agents.*
4. *List the four ways an agency relationship may be created.*
5. *List six ways an agency may be terminated by an act of one or both of the parties to the agency agreement.*
6. *List five ways an agency may be terminated by operation of law.*

One of the most common business relationships is that of agency. By virtue of the agency device, one person can make contracts at numerous places with many different parties at the same time.

A. NATURE OF THE AGENCY RELATIONSHIP

Agency is ordinarily based on the consent of the parties and for that reason is called a *consensual relationship*. However, the law sometimes imposes an agency relationship. If consideration is present, the agency relationship is contractual.

1. Definitions and Distinctions

Agency is a relationship based on an express or implied agreement by which one person, the **agent**, is authorized to act under the control of and for another, the **principal**, in negotiating and making contracts with third persons.[1] The acts of the agent obligate the principal to third persons and give the principal rights against third persons.

The term *agency* is frequently used with other meanings. It is sometimes used to denote the fact that one has the right to sell certain products, such as when a dealer is said to possess an automobile agency. In other instances, the term is used to mean an exclusive right to sell certain articles within a given

Figure 39-1   Agency Relationship

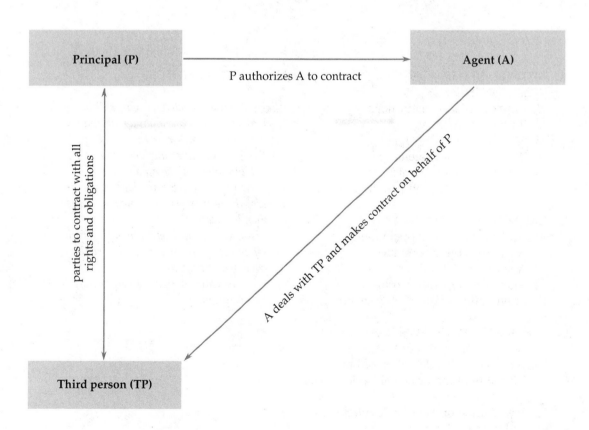

---

[1] Restatement, Agency, 2d §1; Union Miniere, S.A. v Parday Corp. (Ind App) 521 NE2d 200 (1988).

territory. In these cases, however, the dealer is not an agent in the sense of representing the manufacturer.[2] Courts are sometimes called on to determine if an agency relationship existed although the term *agent* had not been used.

It is important to be able to distinguish agencies from other relationships, because there are certain rights and duties in agencies that are not present in other relationships.

(a) EMPLOYEES AND INDEPENDENT CONTRACTORS.
Control and authority are characteristics that distinguish ordinary employees and independent contractors from agents.

(1) Employees. An agent is distinguished from an ordinary employee, who is not hired to represent the employer in making contracts with third persons. It is possible, however, for the same person to be both an agent and an employee. For example, the driver of a milk delivery truck is an agent, as well as an employee, in making contracts between the milk company and its customers but is only an employee with respect to the work of delivering milk.

(2) Independent Contractors. An independent contractor is bound by a contract to produce a certain result—for example, to build a house. The actual doing of the work is controlled by the contractor and is independent of control by the other contracting party. An agent or employee differs from an independent contractor in that the principal or employer has control over and can direct the agent or an employee but does not have control over the performance of work by an independent contractor.

In the *Yelverton* case the "right to control" test determined whether an individual was an agent, an employee, or an independent contractor.

YELVERTON v LAMM
(NC App) 380 SE2d 621 (1989)

Patricia Yelverton died as a result of injuries sustained when an automobile owned and driven by Joseph Lamm crossed the center line of a roadway and struck the automobile driven by Yelverton. Yelverton's executor brought suit against Lamm and Lamm's alleged employer Premier Industrial Products Inc. The executor contended that Premier was liable for the negligence of Lamm. Premier defended that Lamm was not its agent or employee, but was an independent contractor. From a judgment for Premier, Yelverton appealed.

COZORT, J. . . . An independent contractor, as distinguished from an employee, is "one who exercises an independent employment and contracts to do certain work according to his own judgment and method, without being subject to his employer except as to the result of his work." *Cooper v Asheville-Citizen Times Publishing Co.,* 258 NC 578, 587, 129 SE2d 107, 113 (1963). . . . The test in determining a worker's status is whether the employer has the right to control the worker with respect to the manner or methods of doing the work or the agents to be employed in it. . . . If the requisite right to control is found to exist, then an employer is held liable. . . for the

2 Professional Lens Plan, Inc. v Polaris Leasing Corp. 238 Kan 384, 710 P2d 1297 (1985).

negligent acts of its agents, servants, or employees which cause injuries to third persons; but an employer is not liable to third parties for the negligence of an independent contractor. . . .

. . . The evidence before the trial court was that, since 1963, Lamm had represented Premier as a sales agent who took orders from customers for a certain line of Premier's products. The relationship between Lamm and Premier was governed by a written contract entitled "Independent Agent Agreement" wherein Lamm, as "Independent Agent," was given a nonexclusive right to sell Premier's products in a designated territory. The Agreement provided that all orders were subject to acceptance by Premier and were not binding upon Premier until so accepted.

Pursuant to the contract, Lamm was paid by commission only and did not receive a commission for any order which was rejected by Premier. All expenses incurred by Lamm in his business as sales agent for Premier were to be borne by Lamm. Lamm was allowed to work on a self-determined schedule, retain assistants at his own expense, and render services to or sell the products of other companies not in competition with Premier. In addition, the Agreement contained the following provision:

Independent Agent and the Company recognize that the Company has no right to control Independent Agent in the manner in which he or she performs his or her obligations under this Agreement and that Independent Agent is free to perform such obligations in the manner he or she sees fit.

Uncontradicted testimony confirms that the parties conducted their relationship as delineated in the Independent Agent Agreement. Plaintiff does not appear to dispute testimony that Lamm worked when, in his judgment, he felt he needed to, was paid solely on a commission basis, was not reimbursed for his expenses, and operated his business as he saw fit. Premier's sales manager stated in his affidavit that Lamm was "among the most independent of independent contractors taking orders for Premier"; that he "did not want, or accept, any guidance or suggestions as to how he should operate his business"; and that he "was not required to, and generally did not, follow any suggestions I made but instead adopted his own methods, and he was perfectly entitled to do this." Affiant also stated that from time to time he had gone with Lamm to make calls and on one occasion had seen in the trunk of Lamm's car "hundreds of pairs" of men's socks which Lamm said he was selling to customers, as he was entitled to do under the terms of the parties' Agreement.

In addition, Premier deducted no income taxes from Lamm's commissions and made no deductions or payments for social security for Lamm. Premier filed Forms 1099 rather than W-2 forms with the Internal Revenue Service; payments to Lamm were designated "nonemployee compensation." . . .

It is true that "a mere contractual declaration is not determinative of the relationship and the rights of the parties." *Watkins v Murrow*, 253 NC 652, 657, 118 SE2d 5, 8 (1961). But this is simply to say that the court will not ignore the true relationship existing between the parties, and that an employer who exercises control in spite of a contractual declaration to the contrary may be held vicariously liable. . . . The undisputed evidence in the case before us, however, establishes more than a "mere contractual declaration"; it clearly shows that the parties intended Lamm's status to be that of an independent contractor and in fact conducted their dealings according to those express intentions. . . .

> We therefore affirm the trial court's ruling that Premier was entitled to judgment in its favor as a matter of law.
>
> *[Judgment affirmed]*
>
> ## QUESTIONS
>
> 1. Was Lamm Premier's agent?
> 2. Was Lamm an employee of Premier?
> 3. Was Lamm an independent contractor?
> 4. Can an employer avoid liability for the acts of employees under its control by having the workers sign contracts stating that they are independent contractors?

A person who appears to be an independent contractor may in fact be so controlled by the other party that the contractor is regarded as an agent of, or employee of, the controlling person.

The separate identity of an independent contractor may be concealed so that the public believes that it is dealing with the principal. When this situation occurs, the principal is liable as though the contractor were an agent or employee.

A person may be an independent contractor generally but an agent with respect to a particular transaction.[3] Thus, an "agency" or a "broker" rendering personal services to customers is ordinarily an independent contractor but will be the agent of a customer when the rendering of a service involves making a contract on behalf of the customer with a third person.

(b) REAL ESTATE BROKERS. A real estate broker is generally not an agent with authority to make a contract with a third person that will bind the broker's client. Typically, the broker's authority is limited to locating a seller or buyer and bringing the parties together. Even when the third person and the broker sign a "contract," it is generally only an offer by the third person, and it does not become a binding contract until accepted by the client of the broker.

(c) BAILEES. When personal property is delivered to another under an agreement that the property will be returned to the deliverer or transferred to a third person, a bailment arises. The person to whom the property is delivered, the bailee, is not an agent, because the bailee has no authority to act for or make any contract on behalf of the bailor.

Situations commonly arise, however, in which the same person is both an agent and a bailee. A salesperson who is lent a company car is a bailee with respect to the car, but with respect to making sales contracts, the same person is an agent.

(d) REQUIRED ACT. The mere fact that one person requires another person to perform an act does not make the latter person the agent of the former. For example, when a bank directs a borrower to obtain the signature of another person to secure a bank loan, the borrower is not the agent of the bank in making contact with the other person and procuring the required signature.

2. Purpose of Agency

An agency may be created to perform almost any act that the principal could lawfully do. The object of the agency must not be criminal, nor may it be contrary to public policy. Some acts must be performed in person and cannot

---

[3] Kight v Sheppard Building Supply Co. (Miss) 537 So 2d 1355 (1989).

be entrusted or delegated to an agent. Voting, swearing to the truth of documents, testifying in court, and making a will are instances when personal action is required. In the preparation of a document, however, it is proper to employ someone else to prepare the paper that is then signed or sworn to by the employing party. Various forms that are required by statute, such as applications for licenses and tax returns, in some instances expressly authorize the execution of such forms by an agent, as long as the identities of both principal and agent and the latter's representative capacity are clearly shown.

3. Who May Be a Principal

Any person who is competent to act may act through an agent. The appointment of an agent by a person lacking capacity is generally void or voidable to the same extent that a contract made by such a person would be. Thus, a minor acting through an agent will effect a contract that will be voidable to the same extent as though made by the minor.

4. Who May Be an Agent

Since a contract made by an agent is, in law, the contract of the principal, it is immaterial whether the agent has legal capacity to make a contract. Therefore, it is permissible to employ as agents persons who are minors and others who are under a natural or legal disability.

Ordinarily, an agent is one person acting for another, but an agent may be a partnership or a corporation.

5. Classification of Agents

A **special agent** is authorized by the principal to handle a definite business transaction or to do a specific act. One who is authorized by another to purchase a particular house is a special agent.

A **general agent** is authorized by the principal to transact all affairs in connection with a particular kind of business or trade, or to transact all business at a certain place. To illus-

trate, a person who is appointed as manager by the owner of a store is a general agent.

A **universal agent** is authorized by the principal to do all acts that can be delegated lawfully to a representative. This form of agency arises when a person absent because of being in the military service gives another person a blanket power of attorney to do anything that must be done during such absence.

6. Agency Coupled with an Interest

An agent has an **interest in the authority** when consideration has been given or paid for the right to exercise the authority. To illustrate, when a lender, in return for making a loan of money, is given, as security, authority to collect rents due to the borrower and to apply those rents to the payment of the debt, the lender becomes the borrower's agent with an interest in the authority given to collect the rents.

An agent has an **interest in the subject matter** when, for a consideration, the agent is given an interest in the property with which the agent is dealing. Hence, when the agent is authorized to sell property of the principal and is given a lien on such property as security for a debt owed to the agent by the principal, the agent has an interest in the subject matter.

B. CREATING THE AGENCY

An agency may arise by appointment, conduct, ratification, or operation of law.

7. Authorization by Appointment

The usual method of creating an agency is by express authorization; that is, a person is appointed to act for or on behalf of another.

In most instances, the authorization of the agent may be oral. However, some appointments must be made in a particular way. A majority of the states, by statute, require the appointment of an agent to be in writing when the agency is created to acquire or dispose of any interest in land. A written authorization of agency is called a **power of attorney**. An agent acting under a power of attorney is referred to as an **attorney in fact**.[4]

Ordinarily, no agency arises from the fact that two people are married to each other or that they are co-owners of property. Consequently, when a check is made payable to the order of husband and wife, it is necessary for each to indorse the check. The fact that both names are on the check does not create an agency by which the husband can indorse the wife's name and deposit the money into the husband's own bank account.

8. Authorization by Conduct

Conduct consistent with the existence of an agency relationship may be sufficient to show authorization.

(a) PRINCIPAL'S CONDUCT AS TO AGENT. An agency is created by the consent of the parties. Therefore, any conduct of the principal, including words, that gives a person reason to believe that the principal consents to that person's acting as agent is sufficient to create an agency. Likewise, if one person, knowingly and without objection, permits another to act as agent, the law will find in such conduct an expression of authorization to the agent. The principal will then not be permitted to deny that the agent was in fact authorized. Thus, if the owner of a hotel allows another person to assume the duties of hotel clerk, that person may infer the authority to act as the hotel clerk from the owner's conduct.

(b) PRINCIPAL'S CONDUCT AS TO THIRD PERSONS. The principal may have such dealing with third persons as to cause them to believe that the "agent" has authority. Thus, if the owner of a store places another person in charge, third persons may assume that the person in charge is the agent for the owner in that respect. The "agent" then appears to be authorized and is said to have **apparent authority**, and the principal is estopped from contradicting the appearance that has been created.[5]

The term *apparent authority* is used when there is only the appearance of authority, but no actual authority, and that appearance of authority was created by the principal.[6] The test for the existence of apparent authority is an objective test determined by the principal's outward manifestations through words or conduct that lead a third person reasonably to believe that the "agent" has authority. A principal's express restriction on authority not made known to a third person is no defense.

Apparent authority extends to all acts that a person of ordinary prudence, familiar with business usages and the particular business, would be justified in believing that the agent has authority to perform. It is essential to the concept of apparent authority that the third person reasonably believe that the agent has authority. The mere placing of property in the possession of another does not give that person either actual or apparent authority to sell the property.

In the *Lundberg* case, the court was faced with deciding whether a third party was justified in believing that a breeding farm manager had authority to contract on behalf of the owner of the farm.

(c) ACQUIESCENCE BY PRINCIPAL. The principal's conduct that gives rise to the agent's authority may be acquiescence in or failure to object to acts done by the purported or apparent agent over a period of time. For example, a person collecting payments on a note and remitting the proper amounts to the holder of the note will be regarded as the latter's agent for collection when this conduct has been followed over a period of years without objection.

---

[4] DeBueno v Castro (Fla App) 543 So 2d 393 (1989).

[5] Intersparex Leddin KG v Al-Haddad (Tenn App) 852 SW2d 245 (1992).

[6] Foley v Allard (Minn App) 405 NW2d 503 (1987).

LUNDBERG v CHURCH FARMS, INC.

151 Ill App 3d 452, 104 Ill Dec 309, 502 NE2d 806 (1986)

Gilbert Church owned Church Farms, Inc. in Manteno, Illinois, and he advertised its well-bred stallion Imperial Guard for breeding rights at $50,000, directing all inquiries to "Herb Bagley, Manager." Herb Bagley lived at Church Farms and was the only person available to visitors. Vern Lundberg answered the advertisement. After discussions with Bagley, wherein Bagley stated that Imperial Guard would remain in Illinois for at least a two-year period, Lundberg and Bagley executed a two-year breeding rights agreement, which was signed by Lundberg and by Bagley as "Church Farms Inc., H. Bagley, Mgr." When Gil Church moved Imperial Guard to Oklahoma prior to the second year of the contract, Lundberg brought suit for breach of contract. Church testified that Bagley had no authority to sign contracts for Church Farms or to change or add terms. From a judgment for Lundberg, Church appealed.

UNVERZAGI, J. . . . . Defendant contends that plaintiffs have failed to establish that Bagley had apparent authority to negotiate and sign the Lundberg contract for Church Farm. . . .

The party asserting an agency has the burden of proving its existence, but may do so by inference and circumstantial evidence. Additionally, an agent may bind his principal by acts which the principal has not given him *actual* authority to perform, but which he *appears* authorized to perform. An agent's apparent authority is that authority which "the principal knowingly permits the agent to assume or which he holds his agent out as possessing. It is the authority that a reasonably prudent man, exercising diligence and discretion, in view of the principal's conduct, would naturally suppose the agent to possess." The agent's authority must be derived from some act or statement of the *principal*. Defendant argues that plaintiffs' proof is based on Bagley's own assertions of authority rather than the acts or statements of Church Farm or Gil Church. We disagree.

Plaintiffs produced evidence at trial that Gil Church approved the Imperial Guard advertisement listing Herb Bagley as Church Farm's manager, and directing all inquiries to him. Church also permitted Bagley to live on the farm and to handle its daily operations. Bagley was the only person available to visitors to the farm. Bagley answered Church Farm's phone calls, and there was a preprinted signature line for him on the breeding rights package.

The conclusion is inescapable that Gil Church affirmatively placed Bagley in a managerial position giving him complete control of Church Farm and its dealings with the public. We believe that this is just the sort of "holding out" of an agent by a principal that justifies a third person's reliance on the agent's authority. See *Scholenberger v Chicago Transit Authority* (1980), 84 Ill App 3d 1132, 1138 (noting that apparent authority exists when principal allows public to deal exclusively with agent).

We cannot accept defendant's contention that the Lundbergs were affirmatively obligated to seek out Church to ascertain the actual extent of Bagley's authority. Where an agent has apparent authority to act, the principal will be liable in spite of any undisclosed limitations the principal has placed on that authority.

[Judgment affirmed]

QUESTIONS

1. Did the court find that Bagley had authority to bind Church Farms, Inc.? Explain.
2. What could Gil Church have done to prevent the dispute in this case?

9. Agency by Ratification

An agent may attempt, on behalf of the principal, to do an act that was not authorized, or a person who is not the agent of another may attempt to act as such an agent. Generally, in such cases, the principal for whom the agent claimed to act has the choice of ignoring the transaction or of ratifying it. Ordinarily, any unauthorized act may be ratified.

(a) INTENTION TO RATIFY. Initially, ratification is a question of intention. Just as in the case of authorization, when there is a question of whether or not the principal authorized the agent, so there is a question of whether or not the principal intended to approve or ratify the action of the unauthorized agent.

The intention to ratify may be expressed in words, or it may be found in conduct indicating an intention to ratify.[7]

In the *Werlein* case it was asserted that the defendant's conduct manifested the intent to ratify another person's unauthorized act of signing defendant's name.

PHILIP WERLEIN, LTD. v DANIELS
(La App) 538 So 2d 722 (1989)

Vera Daniels and Fredrine Julian were employed by the Marriott Hotel in New Orleans and were close personal friends. One day after work Daniels and Julian went to Werlein's music store to open up a credit account. Julian, with Daniels' authorization and in her presence, applied for credit using Daniels' name and credit history. Later, Julian went to Werlien's without Daniels and charged the purchase of a television set to Daniels' account, executing a retail installment contract by signing Daniels' name. When the payments were not made, Werlien's sued Daniels for the unpaid balance. Daniels denied that she authorized or ratified the purchase of the television. From a judgment for Werlein's, Daniels appealed.

WARD, J. . . . Julian testified that Daniels saw the television at her home on the day it was delivered [in late December 1986], and that when she told Daniels she charged the television to the Werlein's account, Daniels merely told her to continue making payments on the account. After Werlein's presented [Julian's] check [in payment of the account] to the bank, the bank returned the check with the notation that the checking account was closed.

---

7 Richardson Greenshield Securities Inc v Lau (SD NY) 819 F Supp 1246 (1993).

Werlein's managers testified that Daniels expressed no surprise or concern when first contacted about the delinquency of the account. Instead, she responded to the first call by claiming that a money order for the television deposit was in the mail. When contacted a second time, she asked for a "payout balance" on the account. Not until April 1987 did Daniels make any effort to object to the account or inform Werlein's that she would not pay for the purchases. This evidence shows that Daniels, rather than repudiating the purchases, remained silent and essentially acknowledged the debt when confronted by Werlein's. . . .

A person is bound by her signature being executed by another person when done in her presence and under her authority. *Nationwide Finance Co. of Gretna, Inc. v Pitre*, 243 So 2d 326 (La App 4th Cir 1971). The Trial Judge found, and the evidence clearly shows, that Daniels accompanied Julian to Werlein's to open the account. . . .

The evidence, however, neither indicates that Daniels accompanied Julian to Werlein's for the purchase of the television nor that Daniels authorized or even knew about Julian's plan to purchase the television. When a person's signature is executed by another person outside of her presence or without her knowledge or authority, the person must be proven to have ratified the unauthorized act to be bound by her signature. . . . The facts must indicate a clear and absolute intent to ratify the act. . . . In this case, Daniels's conduct displays her clear intent to ratify Julian's unauthorized act of signing her name to the contract for the purchase of the television. Applying principles of agency law in this case, we find that the Trial Judge did not err in finding Daniels liable to Werlein's. . . .

[Judgment affirmed]

QUESTIONS

1. Did Daniels authorize Julian to purchase the television set?
2. State the applicable rule of law regarding responsibility for unauthorized signatures.
3. What actions of Daniels show that Daniels ratified the unauthorized signing of her name to the contract for the purchase of the television by Julian?

If the conditions of ratification are satisfied, a principal ratifies an agent's act when, with knowledge of the act, the principal accepts or retains the benefit of the act.[8] A principal also ratifies an act when the principal brings an action to enforce legal rights based on the agent's act, defends an action by asserting the existence of a right based on the unauthorized transaction, or fails to repudiate the agent's act within a reasonable time. The receipt, acceptance, and deposit of a check by the principal with knowledge that it arises from an unauthorized transaction is a common illustration of ratification of the unauthorized transaction by conduct.

(b) CONDITIONS FOR RATIFICATION. In addition to the intent to ratify, expressed in some instances with certain formality, the following conditions must be satisfied for the intention to take effect as a ratification:

1. The agent must have purported to act on behalf of or as agent for the identified principal.

___
[8] MSP Industries Inc. v Diversified Mortgage Services Inc. (Colo App) 777 P2d 237 (1989).

2. The principal must have been capable of authorizing the act both at the time of the act and at the time it was ratified.

3. The principal must ratify the act before the third person withdraws.

4. The act to be ratified must generally be legal.

5. The principal must have full knowledge of all material facts. If the agent conceals a material fact, the ratification of the principal that is made in ignorance of such fact is not binding. Of course, there can be no ratification when the principal does not know of the making of the contract by the alleged agent. Consequently, when the owner's agent and a contractor make unauthorized major changes to an installation contract without knowledge of the owner, the fact that the owner had no knowledge of the matter bars any claim of ratification of the agents act.

It is not always necessary, however, to show that the principal had actual knowledge. Knowledge will be imputed if a principal knows of other facts that would lead a prudent person to make inquiries, or if that knowledge can be inferred from the knowledge of other facts or from a course of business. Knowledge is likewise not an essential factor when the principal does not care to know the details and is willing to ratify the contract regardless of this lack of knowledge.

(c) FORM OF RATIFICATION. An agreement that is binding although oral may be ratified orally or by conduct. If a contract cannot be enforced unless evidenced by a writing, it is generally held that a ratification of the contract must be in writing.

(d) EFFECT OF RATIFICATION. When an unauthorized act is ratified, the effect is the same as though the act had been originally authorized. Ordinarily, this means that the principal and the third party are bound by the contract made by the agent.[9] When the principal ratifies the act of the unauthorized person, such ratification releases that person from the liability that would otherwise be imposed for having acted without authority.

10. Agency by Operation of Law

In certain instances, the courts—influenced by necessity or social desirability—create or find an agency when there is none. For example, a minor may purchase necessaries on the parent's credit when the latter fails to supply them.

An emergency power of an agent to act under unusual circumstances not covered by the agent's authority is recognized when the agent is unable to communicate with the principal and when failure to act would cause the principal substantial loss.

11. Proving the Agency Relationship

The burden of proving the existence of an agency relationship rests on the person who seeks to benefit by such proof. The third person who desires to bind the principal because of the act of an alleged agent has the burden of proving that the latter person was in fact the authorized agent of the principal and possessed the authority to do the act in question.[10] For example, when the buyer asserts that there has been a breach of an express warranty made by the seller's agent, the buyer must establish that there was an actual or apparent authority to make the warranty. In the absence of sufficient proof, the jury must find that there was no authority.

C. TERMINATION OF AGENCY

An agency may be terminated by the act of one or both of the parties to the agency agreement or by operation of law. When the authority of

---

[9] Bill McCurley Chevrolet v Rutz (Wash App) 808 P2d 1167 (1991).

[10] Fleck v Jaques Seed Co. (ND) 445 NW2d 649 (1989).

an agent is terminated, the agent loses all right to act for the principal.

12. Termination by Act of Parties

In most cases, either party to an agency relationship has the power to terminate that relationship at any time. In some cases, however, the terminating party may be liable to the other party for damages.

(a) EXPIRATION OF AGENCY CONTRACT. The ordinary agency may expire by the terms of the contract creating it. Thus, the contract may provide that it shall last for a stated period, such as five years; or until a particular date arrives; or until the happening of a particular event, such as the sale of certain property. In such a case, the agency is automatically terminated when the specified date arrives or the event at which it is to end occurs.

When it is provided that the agency shall last for a stated period of time, it terminates on the expiration of that period, without regard to whether the acts contemplated by the creation of the agency have been performed. If no period is stated, the agency continues for a reasonable time, but it may be terminated at the will of either party.

(b) AGREEMENT. Since the agency relationship is based on consent, it can be terminated by the consent of the principal and agent.

(c) OPTION OF A PARTY. An agency agreement may provide that upon the giving of notice or the payment of a specified sum of money, one party may terminate the relationship.

(d) REVOCATION BY PRINCIPAL. The relationship between principal and agent is terminated whenever the principal discharges the agent, even if the agency was stated to be "irrevocable." If the agency was not created

for a specified time but was to exist at will, or if the agent has been guilty of misconduct, the principal may discharge the agent without liability. The intent to revoke must be clearly and unequivocally expressed.

Any conduct that shows an intent to revoke the authority is sufficient. For example, a principal may take back from the agent the property that had been entrusted to the agent for the purpose of the agency, or the principal may retain another agent to do what the original agent had been authorized to do. When the agency is based on a contract to employ the agent for a specified period of time, the principal is liable for damages if the principal wrongfully discharges the agent. The fact that the principal is liable for damages does not, however, prevent the principal from terminating the agency by discharging the agent.[11] In such a case, it is said that the principal has the power to terminate the agency by discharging the agent but does not have the right to do so.

(e) RENUNCIATION BY AGENT. The agency relationship is terminated if the agent refuses to continue to act as agent.

If the relationship is an agency at will, the agent has the right, as well as the power, to renounce or abandon the agency at any time. The agent has the right to renounce the relationship in any case if the principal is guilty of making wrongful demands or of other misconduct.

If, however, the agency is based on a contract calling for the continuation of the relationship for a specified or determinable period (that is, until a particular date arrives or a certain event occurs), the agent has no right to abandon or renounce the relationship if the principal is not guilty of wrongdoing.

When the renunciation by the agent is wrongful, the agent is liable to the principal for the damages that the principal sustains.

(f) RESCISSION. The agency contract may be terminated by rescission to the same

---

[11] Airline Reporting Corp. v Incentive Internationale Travel, Inc. (Fla App) 566 So 2d 1377 (1990).

extent that any other contract may be so terminated.

13. Termination by Operation of Law

The agency relationship is a personal one, and anything that renders one of the parties incapable of performing will result in the termination of the relationship by operation of law.

(a) DEATH. The death of either the principal or agent ordinarily terminates the authority of an agent automatically, even if the death is unknown to the other.[12]

(b) INSANITY. The insanity of either the principal or the agent ordinarily terminates the agent's authority. If the incapacity of the principal is only temporary, the agent's authority may be merely suspended rather than terminated.

(c) BANKRUPTCY. Bankruptcy of the principal or agent usually terminates the relationship. It is generally held, however, that the bankruptcy of an agent does not terminate the agent's power to deal with goods of the principal held by the agent.

Insolvency, as distinguished from a formal adjudication of bankruptcy, usually does not terminate the agency. In most states, accordingly, the authority of an agent is not terminated by the appointment of a receiver for the principal.

(d) IMPOSSIBILITY. The authority of an agent is terminated when it is impossible to perform the agency for any reason. Examples are the destruction of the subject matter of the agency, the death or loss of capacity of the third person with whom the agent is to con-tract, or a change in law that makes it impossible to perform the agency lawfully.

(e) WAR. When the country of the principal is at war with that of the agent, the authority of the agent is usually terminated or at least suspended until peace is restored. When the war has the effect of making performance impossible, the agency is, of course, terminated. For example, the authority of an agent who is a nonresident enemy alien to sue is terminated, because such an alien is not permitted to sue.

14. Disability of the Principal Under the UDPAA

The Uniform Durable Power of Attorney Act (UDPAA) permits the creation of an agency by a writing that specifies that "this power of attorney shall not be affected by subsequent disability or incapacity of the principal." Alternatively, the UDPAA permits the agency to come into existence upon the "disability or incapacity of the principal." For this to be effective, the principal must designate the attorney in fact in writing. The writing must contain words showing the intent of the principal that the authority conferred shall continue notwithstanding the disability or incapacity of the principal. The UDPAA, which has been adopted by most states,[13] changes the common law and the general rule that insanity of the principal terminates the agent's authority to act for the principal. Society today recognizes that it may be in the best interest of a principal and good for the business environment for a principal to designate another as an attorney in fact to act for the principal when the principal becomes incapacitated.[14]

---

[12] New York Life Ins. Co. v Estate of Haelen, 521 NYS2d 970 (1987).

[13] The Uniform Durable Power of Attorney Act has been adopted in some fashion in all states except Georgia, Louisiana, and Illinois.

[14] The Uniform Probate Code and the Uniform Durable Power of Attorney Act provide for the coexistence of durable powers and guardians or conservators. These acts allow the attorney in fact to continue to manage the principal's financial affairs, while the court-appointed fiduciary would take the place of the principal in overseeing the actions of

BANK IV, OLATHE v CAPITOL FEDERAL SAVINGS AND LOAN ASS'N.

(Kan) 828 P2d 355 (1992)

Tillie Flinn executed a durable power of attorney designating her nephew James C. Flanders and/or Martha E. Flanders, his wife, as her attorney in fact. Seven months later Martha Flanders went to the Capital Federal Savings and Loan Association office. She had the durable power of attorney instrument, five certificates of deposit and a hand-printed letter identifying Martha as an attorney in fact and stating that Tillie wished to cash her five CD's that Martha had with her. At approximately 10:31 A.M., five checks were given to Martha in the aggregate amount of $135,791.34, representing the funds in the five CD's less penalties for early withdrawal. Some of the checks were drawn to the order of Martha individually, and some to the order of James and Martha, as individuals. Tillie was found dead of heart disease later that day. The time of death stated on her death certificate was 11:30 A.M. The Flanders spent the money for themselves. Bank IV as administrator of Tillie's estate sued Capitol Federal to recover the amount of the funds paid to the Flanders. It contends that Capitol Federal breached its duty to investigate before issuing the checks. Capitol Federal contends it did all that it had a duty to do. From a judgment for Capitol Federal, Bank IV appeals.

McFARLAND, J. . . . The estate contends that Capitol Federal should have: (1) determined whether or not Tillie's "true wishes" were being carried out; and (2) checked to see whether Tillie was still alive. Capitol Federal argues that its duty only requires a favorable comparison of the signatures of the depositor with that on the power of attorney, proper identification of the attorney in fact, and a determination that the transaction is within the scope of the power of attorney. Capitol Federal further contends any requirement for additional investigation would be unduly burdensome on lending institutions.

The first aspect of this issue concerns Tillie's competency. It is unclear whether the estate is contending that Capitol Federal should have made inquiry into Tillie's competency as of the time of the execution of the power of attorney or as of the time of the request for the transfer of funds, or both.

As far as the question relates to competency at the time of the transfer of funds is concerned, the matter is resolved by statute. Kansas has adopted the Uniform Durable Power of Attorney Act (K.S.A. 58-610 et seq.) . . . which provides:

"All acts done by an attorney in fact pursuant to a durable power of attorney during any period of disability or incapacity of the principal have the same effect and inure to the benefit of and bind the principal and the principal's successors in interest as if the principal were competent and not disabled."

Additionally, the instrument itself expressly provides: "This power of attorney is durable and shall not be affected by the subsequent disability or incompetence of the principal."

Thus, incapacity of Tillie at the time of the withdrawal of funds is not a factor in the determination by the lending institution on whether or not to honor the request by an attorney in fact for withdrawal of funds. If it were otherwise, the very purpose of many powers of attorney, which is to allow the orderly transaction of a person's business during contemplated disability or incompetency without expensive and time-consuming probate proceedings, would be defeated.

Did Capitol Federal have a duty, under the facts herein, to investigate into the capacity of Tillie at the time of the execution of the instrument in determining whether or not to honor the request for the withdrawal of funds? We believe not. The circumstances involved herein demonstrate the impracticality of imposing such a requirement. . . . The test for capacity to execute a power of attorney would presumably be comparable to that for capacity to execute a will. An individual who is incompetent most of the time may have lucid intervals in which he or she has the capacity to contract to make a will. Determination of a person's capacity to contract or make a will involves determination of capacity at the particular point in time the instrument was executed. Frequently, there is conflicting testimony among lay persons and health care professionals and the judicial hearings thereon are lengthy and involved. As a practical matter, how could the Capitol Federal employee, responding to the attorney in fact's request for withdrawal of funds, make such a determination? Capitol Federal notes in its brief that every working day it has over 500 transactions involving an agency or power of attorney relationship. The practical effect of requiring such a determination would, again, be to eliminate the power of attorney as a useful tool in the transaction of the business of any elderly, disabled, absent, or otherwise incapacitated individual.

As noted by the district court . . . :

"The duty of Capitol Federal to Tillie Flinn, its depositor, focuses on an issue which has drastic and far reaching implications. The final decision of our Appellate Courts will impact upon the management of the assets of our elderly, disabled and also upon the management of our financial institutions. The Durable Power of Attorney provides an inexpensive vehicle for family members to manage the finances of the impaired relative without incurring the substantial expenses of creating a conservatorship. The start-up for a conservatorship is in the range of $10,000.00. Annual accounting fees are much less than the start up costs, but are incurred annually.

"The Power of Attorney eliminates the necessity of opening and maintaining a conservatorship. In order to function the powers of the Attorney-in-Fact must be recognized by financial institutions.

This brings us to the claim that Capitol Federal should have ascertained whether or not Tillie was alive when the request for transfer was made.

K.S.A. 58-613 provides:

"(a) The death of a principal who has executed a written power of attorney, durable or otherwise, does not revoke or terminate the agency as to the attorney in fact or other person, who, without actual knowledge of the death of the principal, acts in good faith, under the power. Any action so taken, unless otherwise invalid or unenforceable, binds the principal's successors in interest."

Here again, the estate cites no authority for the proposition Capitol Federal was under some duty to determine that Tillie was alive before transferring the funds. There is no claim made that Capitol Federal had actual knowledge that Tillie was deceased when the transfer was requested. In fact, based upon the death certificate's stated time of death, Tillie was alive when the transfer was made. We find no merit in this point. . . .

We conclude that when confronted with the request for withdrawal of funds herein, Capitol Federal had a duty to:

1. compare the signature on the power of attorney with Tillie's signature on file as a depositor as to the authenticity thereof;

2. obtain proper identification of the person seeking withdrawal as the person designated attorney in fact;

3. determine whether or not the requested transaction was within the scope of the durable power of attorney presented.

In the case before us, Capitol Federal was presented with a power of attorney which it is agreed was signed by Tillie, its depositor. Martha Flanders was properly identified as being the Martha Flanders designated as attorney in fact. We conclude the request to cash the CD's and the issuance of checks in the individual name(s) of the attorney(s) in fact was within the scope of the power of attorney. Capitol Federal had the right to assume the attorney in fact was acting lawfully in the performance of her agency duties and to honor the agent's request that the checks be drawn in her name and that of her husband, also an attorney in fact for Tillie. Capitol Federal had no knowledge the funds would be subsequently misappropriated by Flanders, nor did it participate in such misappropriation. Absent an act and acts amounting to participation in the wrongdoing, Capitol Federal's issuance of the checks in the name(s) of the attorney(s) in fact imposes no liability on Capitol Federal. . . .

[Judgment affirmed]

ABBOTT, J., concurring and dissenting. . . . I would adopt an additional requirement: If a transaction dependent upon a durable power of attorney is more than a routine transaction and if an officer of the bank is involved directly and has actual or constructive knowledge leading a reasonable person to suspect funds are about to be misappropriated, then the bank has a duty either to inquire into the circumstances before it pays out the money or to pay the funds out in such a manner that will protect the depositor. . . .

My proposed standard raises a fact question of whether a reasonable person would find that Capitol Federal had actual or constructive knowledge funds were about to be misappropriated. . . .

[Bank officer] Morley testified by deposition that the use of a power of attorney is "an unusual occurrence at most banks. You don't see it that often. You want to pay attention to what you are doing." In its brief and at oral argument, Capitol Federal stated that it averages 500 transactions involving agency or the power of attorney relationship each day. Capitol Federal's statement, which is noted in the majority opinion, seems at odds with the deposition testimony of Morley, an assistant vice president of Capitol Federal. . . .

In summary, a complete stranger entered a financial institution and a bank officer, who had never seen that person before and who did not know the depositor, accepted a durable power of attorney that clearly shows on its face that it was clipped out of a magazine usually sold at a supermarket checkout stand. The bank then paid out a large sum of money to the holders of the power of attorney. . . . The transaction was based on signatures that clearly showed a deteriorating depositor. To me, the above presents a question of fact whether a reasonable person would be put on notice that funds were about to be misappropriated. . . .

I would reverse and remand for trial.

opinion, seems at odds with the deposition testimony of Morley, an assistant vice president of Capitol Federal. . . .

In summary, a complete stranger entered a financial institution and a bank officer, who had never seen that person before and who did not know the depositor, accepted a durable power of attorney that clearly shows on its face that it was clipped out of a magazine usually sold at a supermarket checkout stand. The bank then paid out a large sum of money to the holders of the power of attorney. . . . The transaction was based on signatures that clearly showed a deteriorating depositor. To me, the above presents a question of fact whether a reasonable person would be put on notice that funds were about to be misappropriated. . . .

I would reverse and remand for trial.

QUESTIONS

1. If it could be shown that Tillie was incompetent at the time of the request to transfer funds, would this prevent the exercise of the durable power of attorney?
2. What practical purpose is served in society by durable powers of attorney?
3. What are the obligations of a banking institution when requested by an attorney in fact to withdraw funds belonging to the principal?
4. What additional obligation would the dissent add when an attorney in fact seeks to withdraw the principal's funds?

15. Termination of Agency Coupled with an Interest

An agency coupled with an interest is an exception to the general rule as to the termination of an agency. Such an agency cannot be revoked by the principal before the expiration of the interest. It is not terminated by the death or insanity of either the principal or the agent.

16. Protection of Agent from Termination of Authority

The modern world of business has developed several methods of protecting an agent from the termination of authority for any reason.[15]

(a) EXCLUSIVE AGENCY. An agency to sell may specify that the agent shall have the exclusive right to sell. Such a provision gives the agent the right to collect commissions on the sale of the property involved regardless of who makes the sale. Even if the principal revokes the authority and makes the sale in person or by another agent, the principal must pay the original agent the commission.

(b) SECURED TRANSACTION UNDER UCC ARTICLE 9. The principal may give the agent a security interest to cover the commissions or any other debt owed the agent.

(c) PAYMENT FROM A FUND OR THIRD PERSON. These are separate agreements that are executed that call for the payment to the agent of the amounts specified if there is a termination of authority. The agreement may call for the payment of the total fund involved or only the damages sustained by the agent because of the termination. Payment may be required when there is a termination of authority for any reason or only for

---

[15] These methods generally replace the concept of an agency coupled with an interest because of the greater protection given to the agent. Typically, the rights of the agent under these modern devices cannot be defeated by the principal, by operation of law, or by claims of other creditors.

specified reasons. The agreements involved here may be an escrow deposit agreement under which a sum of money is held by a neutral party, such as a bank, until payment is required. It may be a standby letter of credit under Article 5 of the Code, obliging the issuer of the letter to make the specified payments upon the specified termination of authority. The agreement may also be a guaranty agreement executed by the principal, a third person, or an insurance company imposing the obligation to make payments on specified conditions.

17. Effect of Termination of Authority

If the agency is revoked by the principal, the authority to act for the principal is not termi-

nated until the agent receives notice of revocation. As between the principal and the agent, the *right* of the agent to bind the principal to third persons generally ends immediately on the termination of the agent's authority. This termination is effective without the giving of notice to third persons.

When the agency is terminated by the act of the principal, notice must be given to third persons. If this notice is not given, the agent may have the *power* to make contracts that will bind the principal and third persons. This rule is predicated on the theory that a known agent will have the appearance of still being the agent unless notice to the contrary is given to third persons. This situation arose in the *Record* case.

RECORD v WAGNER
100 NH 419, 128 A2d 921 (1957)

Donald Record owned a farm that was operated by his agent, David Berry, who lived on the property. The latter hired Fred Wagner to bale the hay in 1953 and told him to bill Record for this work. He did so and was paid by Record. By the summer of 1954 the agency had been terminated by Record, but Berry remained in possession as tenant of the farm, and nothing appeared changed. Later in the same year Berry asked Wagner to bale the hay the same as in the prior year and bill Record for the work. Wagner did so, but Record refused to pay on the ground that Berry was not then his agent. When Wagner sued Record and recovered a judgment against him, Record appealed.

DUNCAN, J. . . . "It is a familiar principle of law that the authority of the agent to bind his principal continues, even after an actual revocation, until notice of the revocation is given." *Claflin v Lenheim*, 66 NY 301.

By paying the 1953 bill, the defendant recognized Berry's authority to hire the plaintiff on the former's credit. Berry then resided on the defendant's farm, and was properly found the defendant's agent at that time. In 1954, Berry continued to reside on the main farm, and to all appearances was operating it in the same manner and in the same capacity. If in fact he had ceased to occupy the farm as agent, but did so as a tenant, the defendant made no effort to notify the plaintiff of the change in Berry's status.

It could be found that in the exercise of reasonable diligence the plaintiff was justified as a result of the defendant's conduct in believing that Berry had authority to pledge the defendant's credit in 1954 for the same services which the defendant recognized as a proper charge against himself in 1953. . . . The important fact is that the defendant permitted the outward appearances of Berry's authority to remain unchanged in 1954 from what they were in 1953, and by not notifying the plaintiff of the termination of the agency permitted the plaintiff to be misled. Having done so, he rather than the plaintiff should bear the loss. . . . We do not consider the circumstance that Berry had previously pledged the defendant's credit upon only one occasion . . . to be of controlling importance. . . . The evidence that no question of the agent's authority was raised on the occasion, coupled with the evidence of the misleading circumstances of his continued occupancy and management of the farms and the cattle in the defendant's continued absence, was sufficient to warrant the verdict.

[Judgment for Wagner]

QUESTIONS

1. Was Berry the agent of Record in 1954 when Berry asked Wagner to bale hay and bill Record for the work?
2. After termination of the agency by Record, did Berry continue to have the power to bind Record?
3. Of what significance was the fact that Berry had pledged Record's credit in only one prior transaction?

When the law requires the giving of notice in order to end the power of the agent to bind the principal, individual notice must be given or mailed to all persons who had prior dealings with the agent. In addition, notice to the general public can be given by publishing in a newspaper of general circulation in the affected geographic area a statement that the agency has been terminated.

If a notice is actually received, the power of the agent is terminated, without regard to whether the method of giving notice was proper. Conversely, if proper notice is given, it is immaterial that it does not actually come to the attention of the party notified. Thus, a member of the general public cannot claim that the principal is bound on the ground that the third person did not see the newspaper notice stating that the agent's authority had been terminated.

SUMMARY

An agency relationship is created by an express or implied agreement whereby one person, the agent, is authorized to make contracts with third persons on behalf of and subject to the control of another person, the principal. An agent differs from an independent contractor in that the principal, who controls the acts of an agent, does not have control over the details of performance of work by the independent contractor. Likewise, an independent contractor does not have authority to act on behalf of the other contracting party.

A special agent is authorized by the principal to handle a specific business transaction. A general agent is authorized by the principal to transact all business affairs of the principal at a certain place. A universal agent is authorized to perform all acts that can be lawfully delegated to a representative.

The usual method of creating an agency is by express authorization. However, an agency relationship may be found to exist when the principal causes or permits a third person to reasonably believe that an agency relationship exists. In such a case, the "agent" appears to be authorized and is said to have apparent authority.

An unauthorized transaction by an agent for a principal may be ratified by the principal.

The duration of the agency relationship is commonly stated in the contract creating the relationship. In most cases, either party has the power to terminate the agency relationship at any time. However, the terminating party may be liable for damages to the other if the termination is in violation of the agency contract. When a principal terminates an agent's authority, it is not effective until the notice is received by the agent. Since a known agent will have the appearance of still being an agent, notice must be given to third persons of the termination, and the agent may have the

power to bind the principal and third persons until this notice is given. An agency is terminated by operation of law on (1) the death of the principal or agent; (2) insanity of the principal or agent; (3) bankruptcy of the principal or agent; (4) impossibility of performance, such as the destruction of the subject matter; or (5) war. An agent may be protected from loss caused by termination of authority by means of an exclusive agency contract, a secured transaction, an escrow deposit, a standby letter of credit, or a guaranty agreement.

In states that have adopted the Uniform Durable Power of Attorney Act (UDPAA), an agency may be created that is not affected by subsequent disability or incapacity of the principal. In UDPAA states the agency may also come into existence on the "disability or incapacity of the principal." The designation of an attorney in fact under the UDPAA must be in writing.

LAW IN PRACTICE

1. Even though you are not legally required to do so in all cases, it is prudent to set forth the agent's powers and duties in writing. The writing, called a "power of attorney," should attempt to resolve all questions concerning the agent's authority to act for the principal.

2. Remember that apparent authority cannot come solely from the representations of the agent. If you, as a third person, have questions about the extent of an agent's authority, talk to the principal.

3. If, after disclosure of all material facts, you accept the benefits of the unauthorized act of your

agent, you must also accept the fact that you will be fully bound by the contract made by the agent.

4. Recognize that an agent may continue to appear to have authority to bind a principal after the agency is terminated. Notify third persons who have dealt with your former agent when you terminate the agency.

5. Execute a durable power of attorney to protect yourself, your family, and your business should you become incapacitated or disabled.

QUESTIONS AND CASE PROBLEMS

1. What social forces are affected by allowing an agent to make a contract that will bind the agent's principal and a third person?

2. How does an agent differ from an independent contractor?

3. Compare authorization of an agent by (a) appointment and (b) ratification.

4. Bryan Bruno, while a loan officer of Anchor Equities Ltd., a mortgage banking firm, deposited funds into the bank accounts of certain loan applicants. He then received bank verification statements that the applicants had the required 20 percent cash down payments in their accounts. The funds were withdrawn from each bank account once the statement was received. On the basis of these verification statements, Anchor approved the loan applications. Tristan Joya was part owner of the corporation that built the homes for which the mortgage loan applications were submitted. Bruno received commissions on all loans approved. Bruno told Joya that there was nothing wrong with facilitating the applications as he had been doing. Joya's corporation received the loan proceeds. The loans went into default. Anchor sued Joya and others for fraud. Joya contends that Anchor clothed its loan officer Bruno with apparent authority to complete the applications as he did, and Anchor therefore cannot recover from Joya. Decide. [*Anchor Equities Ltd. v Joya (App) 160 Ariz 463, 773 P2d 1022*]

5. Ernest A. Kotsch executed a durable power of attorney when he was 85 years old, giving his son Ernie the power to manage and sell his real estate and personal property "and to do all acts necessary for maintaining and caring for [the father] during his lifetime." Thereafter Mr. Kotsch began "keeping company" with a widow, Margaret Gradl. Ernie believed that she was attempting to alienate his father from him; and he observed that she was exerting a great deal of influence over him. Acting under the durable power of attorney, and without informing his father, Ernie created the "Kotsch Family Irrevocable Trust" to which he transferred $700,000, the bulk of his father's liquid assets, with the father being the grantor and initial beneficiary, and Ernie's three children being additional beneficiaries. He named himself trustee. The father sued to avoid the trust. Ernie defended that he had authority to create the trust under the durable power of attorney. Decide. [*Kotsch v Kotsch (Fla App) 608 So 2d 879*]

6. Compare (a) the termination of an agency with (b) the discharge of a contract.

7. Ken Jones, the number-one-ranked prizefighter in his weight class, signed a two-year contract with Howard Stayword. The contract obligated Stayword to represent and promote Jones in all business and professional matters, including the arrangement of fights. For these services, Jones was to pay Stayword 10 percent of gross earnings. After a year, when Stayword proved unsuccessful in arranging a title match with the champion, Jones fired Stayword. During the following year, Jones earned $4 million. Stayword sued Jones for $400,000. Jones defended himself on the basis that a principal has the absolute power at any time to terminate an agency relationship by discharging the agent, so he was not liable to Stayword. Was Jones correct?

8. Paul Strich did business as an optician in Duluth, Minnesota. Paul used only the products of the Plymouth Optical Company, a national manufacturer of optical products and supplies with numerous retail outlets and some franchise arrangements in areas other than Duluth. To increase business, Paul renovated his office and changed the sign on his office to read "Plymouth Optical Co." Paul did business this way for more than three years—advertised under that name, paid bills with checks bearing the name of Plymouth Optical Co., and listed himself in the telephone and city directories by that name. Plymouth immediately became aware of what Paul was doing. However, since Paul used only Plymouth products, it saw no advantage at that time in prohibiting Paul from using the name and losing him as a customer, since Plymouth did not have a franchisee in Duluth. Paul contracted with the *Duluth Tribune* for advertising, making the contract in the name of Plymouth Optical Co. When the advertising bill was not paid, the *Duluth Tribune* sued Plymouth Optical Company for payment. Plymouth defended that it had never authorized Paul to do business under the name, nor had it authorized him to make a contract with the newspaper. Decide.

9. Phyllis Thropp opened a margin trading account with Bache broker R. Gregory, placing in his care securities valued at $40,000. Subsequently, her husband, a friend of the broker, forged his wife's signature on a blank power of attorney form and sent it to the broker. Mr. Thropp then ordered Gregory to sell his wife's securities for cash and ordered Bache to issue seven checks in his wife's name. Mr. Thropp later forged and cashed the checks. Mrs. Thropp and her husband saw the broker socially, and her frequent questions about her account brought vague answers about the condition of the market, but he never mentioned the numerous sales for cash. In December 1972, Mr. Thropp confessed that he had stolen the money to pay gambling debts and assured her that the broker was not involved in depleting her account. Mrs. Thropp, being seven months pregnant at the time, took no action. In 1975 she filed for a divorce, and in a deposition from the broker relating to the divorce she learned that he might have mishandled her account. An assistant manager of the firm testified that a broker would not be authorized to take directions to trade in an account from one who held a power of attorney similar to the document forged by Mr. Thropp. Mrs. Thropp brought suit against Bache. Bache contended that Mrs. Thropp ratified the actions of Mr. Thropp and Bache. Decide. [*Thropp v Bache Halsey Stuart Shields, Inc. (CA6 Ohio) 650 F2d 817 (1981)*]

10. Beck, president of Anita Beck Cards & Such Inc., and Hutton, a national sales director for Mary Kay Cosmetics, agreed that Beck would manufacture calendars and stationery to be sold at Mary

Kay conventions. To finance the project, Hutton gave $20,000 to Beck. They prepared and signed a document to reflect the quantity and prices of goods shipped from Beck to the Dallas convention for sale under Huttons supervision. The document stated, "Commission is 15% on all but calendars." The unsold goods were shipped back to Beck's business at Beck's expense. The undertaking proved to be a substantial failure. Hutton sued Beck for the return of the $20,000, claiming that she was Beck's agent and that the money had been a loan. Beck claimed that the money was the down payment on the actual purchase of the goods by Hutton. Decide. [*Hutton v Anita Beck Cards and Such, Inc. (Minn App) 366 NW2d 358 (1985)*]

11. Walker owned a trailer that he wished to sell. He took it to the business premises of Pacific Mobile Homes. The only person on the premises at that time, and several other times when Walker was there, was Stewart. Stewart identified himself as a salesman of Pacific and agreed to take possession of Walker's trailer and to attempt to sell it for him. Stewart filled out some forms of Pacific Mobile Homes and thereafter wrote some letters to Walker on the letterhead of Pacific. Walker's trailer was sold, but the salesman disappeared with most of the money. Walker sued Pacific for the proceeds of the sale. It denied liability, on the ground that Stewart lacked authority to make any sales agreement and that all of Pacific's salespeople were expressly forbidden to take used trailers to sell for their owners. Is this defense valid? [*Walker v Pacific Mobile Homes, 68 Wash 2d 347, 413 P2d 3*]

12. Hill purchased furniture from Grant Furniture. When she complained that it was damaged, she was told that they would send someone to repair the damage. An independent contractor, Newman, was sent to mend the furniture. He identified himself as the man from Grant's. The lacquer he put on the furniture exploded and caused serious injury to Hill. She sued both Newman and Grant. Grant claimed that Newman was an independent contractor and that it was therefore not liable for his conduct. Was Grant correct? [*Hill v Newman, 126 NJ Super 557, 316 A2d 8*]

13. Mrs. Bird, although a woman of means, was living in deplorable conditions. Neighbors got in contact with her cousin, Logan Ledbetter, who in turn had Mrs. Bird examined by Dr. Phillips, a psychiatrist. Dr. Phillips determined that Mrs. Bird was suffering from "an organic brain syndrome, chronic," that "her mental function was very impaired," and that in his opinion, Mrs. Bird was "mentally incompetent at the time of the examina-

tion." Ledbetter planned to deal with the situation by selling off a number of valuable real estate holdings owned by Mrs. Bird and using the proceeds to pay for proper care for Mrs. Bird. Soon thereafter, Mrs. Bird executed a power of attorney designating Logan Ledbetter as her attorney in fact, and Ledbetter entered into a contract to sell a large parcel of her land to Andleman Associates. Mrs. Bird's niece, Barbara, who disliked Ledbetter, filed a petition to have Mrs. Bird declared incompetent and herself named guardian of her estate. The court appointed Barbara as guardian, and she refused to allow the sale of the land to Andleman. In the lawsuit that resulted, Ledbetter and Andleman contended that Ledbetter acted in good faith and had a properly executed power of attorney, and therefore, his signing the sales contract with Andleman was binding on Mrs. Bird (the principal). Atkins (the real estate agent who produced the ready, willing, and able buyer) sought his 10 percent commission under the listing agreement signed by Ledbetter as agent for Mrs. Bird. Barbara contended that the power of attorney was void and that Ledbetter owed the real estate commission since he breached his implied warranty that he had a principal with capacity. Decide.

14. Jane Byrne, while a candidate for reelection as mayor of the city of Chicago, told Stanley Gapshis, president of Progress Printing Corp., "you will have my campaign. . . . Mr. Griffin will get in touch with you." Shortly thereafter, Griffin called Gapshis and said "you have the Byrne campaign" and "you will get your copy from [Mary] Pitz." One week later, Gapshis went to Pitz's office at her request. There, Pitz told him she would be "handling all the artwork and copy for the campaign." Shortly after completion of each printing job, Progress prepared an invoice, which described the items printed and the quantity; these invoices were sent to Griffin on Pitz's instructions. Griffin testified that he never reviewed these invoices. According to Gapshis, the candidate called him in November 1983, nine months after her unsuccessful reelection bid to say that she was sending a check for $10,000 and would have more later. When the full printing bill was not paid, Progress sued the candidate for $91,000. Byrne defended that she could not be held personally liable for the campaign committee's debts because she was not a party to the transactions. Progress responded that she had ratified the actions of her agents Griffin and Pitz. Decide. [*Progress Printing v Jane Byrne Political Committee (Ill App) 601 NE2d 1055*]

15. Lew owns a store on Canal Street in New Orleans. He paid a person named Mike and other individuals commissions for customers brought into the store. Lew testified that he had known Mike for less than a week. Boulos and Durso, partners in a wholesale jewelry business, were visiting New Orleans on a business trip when Mike brought them into the store to buy a stereo. While Durso finalized the stereo transaction with the stores manager, Boulos and Mike negotiated to buy two cameras, three videos, and twenty gold Dupont lighters. Unknown to the store's manager, Mike was given $8,250 cash and was to deliver the merchandise later that evening to the Marriott Hotel where Boulos and Durso were staying. Mike gave a receipt for the cash, but it showed no sales tax or indication that the goods were to be delivered. Boulos testified that he believed Mike was the store owner. Mike never delivered the merchandise and disappeared. Boulos and Durso contend that Lew is liable for the acts of his agent, Mike. Lew denied that Mike was his agent, and the testimony showed that Mike had no actual authority to make a sale, to use a cash register, or even to go behind a sales counter. What ethical principle applies to the conduct of Boulos and Durso? Decide. [Boulos v Morrison (La) 503 So 2d 1]

CHAPTER 40

PRINCIPAL AND AGENT

LEARNING OBJECTIVES

After studying this chapter, you will be able to:
1. *Differentiate between express authority, incidental authority, customary authority, and apparent authority.*
2. *Explain the effect of the proper exercise of authority by an agent.*
3. *Describe the duty of a third person to determine the extent of an agent's authority.*
4. *State and illustrate when an agent may and may not delegate authority to another.*
5. *Explain the duties and liabilities of an agent to the principal during and after the agency.*
6. *Explain the duties and liabilities of a principal to the agent during and after the agency.*

What duties do the principal and agent owe each other?

A. AGENT'S AUTHORITY

When there is an agent, it is necessary to determine the scope of the agent's authority.

1. Scope of Agent's Authority

The scope of an agent's authority may be determined from the express words of the principal to the agent, or it may be implied from the principal's words or conduct or from the customs of the trade or business.

(a) EXPRESS AUTHORITY. If the principal tells the agent to perform a certain act, the agent has **express authority** to do so. Express authority can be given orally or in writing.

(b) INCIDENTAL AUTHORITY. An agent has implied **incidental authority** to perform any act reasonably necessary to execute the express authority given to the agent. To illustrate, if the principal authorizes the agent to purchase goods without furnishing funds to the agent to pay for them, the agent has the implied incidental authority to purchase the goods on credit.[1]

(c) CUSTOMARY AUTHORITY. An agent has implied **customary authority** to do any act that, according to the custom of the community, usually accompanies the transaction for which the agent is authorized to act. For example, an agent who has express authority to receive payments from third persons has the implied authority to issue receipts.

(d) APPARENT AUTHORITY. A person has apparent authority as an agent when the principal's words or conduct leads a third person to reasonably believe that the person has that authority and the third person relies on that appearance.[2]

2. Effect of Proper Exercise of Authority

When an agent with authority properly makes a contract with a third person that purports to bind the principal, there is by definition a binding contract between the principal and the third person. The agent is not a party to this contract. Consequently, when the owner of goods is the principal, the owner's agent is not liable for breach of warranty with respect to the goods "sold" by the agent. The owner-principal, not the agent, was the "seller" in the sales transaction.[3]

3. Duty to Ascertain Extent of Agent's Authority

A third person who deals with a person claiming to be an agent cannot rely on the statements made by the agent concerning the extent of authority. If the agent is not authorized to perform the act or is not even the agent of the principal, the transaction between the alleged agent and the third person will have no legal effect between the principal and the third person.

Third persons who deal with an agent whose authority is limited to a special purpose are bound at their peril to find out the extent of the agent's authority. An attorney is such an agent. Unless the client holds the attorney out as having greater authority than usual, the attorney has no authority to settle a claim without approval from a client.

The extent of an attorney's authority to settle a claim was disputed in the *Miotk* case.

---

[1] Badger v Paulson Investment Co. 311 Or 14, 803 P2d 1178 (1991).

[2] Draemel v Rufenacht, Dromagen & Hertz, Inc. 223 Neb 645, 392 NW2d 759 (1986).

[3] Wright Waterproofing Co. v Allied Polymers (Tex Civ App) 602 SW2d 67 (1980).

MIOTK v RUDY
227 Kan 296, 605 P2d 587 (1980)

Irene Miotk was a passenger in a car when it was struck by another car driven by Vernon Rudy. Miotk retained attorney John D. Logsdon to represent her in a personal injury action against Rudy. Logsdon filed suit on behalf of Miotk and later entered negotiations with Rudy's attorney to settle the case. As an offer of settlement, Rudy's attorney sent Logsdon a check made out to "Irene Miotk and John D. Logsdon, her attorney" along with a release for Ms. Miotk to sign. Logsdon failed to return the signed release by the day the case was set for trial, but he advised Rudy's attorney that the settlement was agreed to; the court approved the settlement and dismissed the case. Unknown to all parties and the court, Logsdon had apparently forged Irene Miotk's indorsement to the check and had kept the proceeds. Miotk hired new counsel, who filed a motion to set aside the dismissal of her action. In an accompanying affidavit, Miotk stated that she at no time authorized the settlement of the case, nor was she ever offered any sum of money by Logsdon. The trial court denied the motion to set aside the dismissal, and Miotk appealed.

SWINEHART, J. . . . It has been recognized generally that a client is bound by the appearance, admissions, and actions of counsel acting on behalf of his client. The client has control over the subject matter of litigation. An attorney has no authority to compromise or settle his client's claim without his client's approval. . . .

Defendant . . . points out that he clearly relied on the representations of plaintiff's attorney and that the dismissal was entered pursuant to the express representation of plaintiff's attorney to the court and defense counsel that the settlement was authorized. Defendant urges as matter of public policy that the dismissal should not be set aside.

Defendant's argument is essentially that an attorney should be held to have apparent authority to settle an action. This appears to be the rationale of the trial court's denial of the plaintiff's motion. This argument is at first glance appealing. It is clear that the relation of attorney and client is one of agency and the general rules of law that apply to agency apply to that relation. . . . The law recognizes two distinct types of agency, actual and . . . apparent. . . . The evidence is uncontradicted that Logsdon lacked actual authority to settle plaintiff's case and there is no issue in that regard. However, the liability of the principal for the acts and contracts of his agent is not limited to such acts and contracts of the agent as are expressly authorized, necessarily implied from express authority, or otherwise actually conferred by implication from the acts and conduct of the principal. . . .

The difficulty in the present case is that there is no evidence of apparent authority on the part of Logsdon to settle plaintiff's case other than his retention as her attorney. . . .

Kansas law is in accord on the general agency principle that those who deal with an agent whose authority is limited to special purposes are bound at their peril to know the extent of his authority. . . . An attorney as agent for his client, is limited to control over procedural matters incident to litigation. . . . An attorney ordinarily has no apparent authority to settle his client's action without the client's consent.

There being no evidence other than Logsdon's employment as plaintiff's attorney of Logsdon's apparent authority to settle plaintiff's action, we hold that the trial court abused its discretion in denying plaintiff's motion pursuant . . . to set aside the judgment of dismissal. The case is remanded with directions to grant plaintiff's motion and proceed with trial of the issues on the merits.

[Judgment reversed and action remanded]

QUESTIONS

1. What did the defendant contend?
2. Did the court sustain the defendant's contention?
3. Was Irene Miotk bound by the representation of attorney Logsdon to the court that she had authorized the settlement of the case?

(a) AGENT'S ACTS ADVERSE TO PRINCIPAL. The third person who deals with an agent is required to take notice of any acts that are clearly adverse to the interest of the principal. Thus, if the agent is obviously making use of funds of the principal for the agent's personal benefit, persons dealing with the agent should recognize that the agent may be acting without authority and that they are dealing with the agent at their peril.

The only certain way that third persons can protect themselves is to inquire of the principal whether the agent is in fact the agent of the principal and has the necessary authority. If the principal states that the agent has the authority, the principal cannot later deny this authorization unless the subject matter is such that an authorization must be in writing to be binding.

(b) DEATH OF THIRD PERSON. The extent of the agent's authority becomes particularly significant when the third person dies after the transaction with the agent but before the principal has taken any action. If the agent had authority to contract on behalf of the principal, the agent's agreement with the third person would give rise immediately to a binding contract. The third person's subsequent death would ordinarily not affect that contract. In contrast, if the agent did not have authority to contract but only to transmit an offer from the third person, the death of the third person

before the principal had accepted the offer would work a revocation of the offer. The principal could not create a contract by purporting to accept after the death of the third person.

4. Limitations on Agent's Authority

A person who has knowledge of a limitation on the agent's authority cannot ignore that limitation. When the third person knows that the authority of the agent depends on whether financing has been obtained, the principal is not bound by the act of the agent if the financing in fact was not obtained. If the authority of the agent is based on a writing, and the third person knows that there is such a writing, the third person is charged with knowledge of limitations contained in it.

(a) OBVIOUS LIMITATIONS. In some situations, it will be obvious to third persons that they are dealing with an agent whose authority is limited. When third persons know that they are dealing with an officer of a private corporation or a representative of a government agency, they should recognize that such a person will ordinarily have limited authority. Third persons should recognize that a contract made with such an officer or representative may not be binding unless ratified by the principal.

(b) SECRET LIMITATIONS. If the principal has clothed an agent with authority to perform certain acts but the principal gives secret instructions that limit the agent's authority, the third person is allowed to take the authority of the agent at its face value. The third person is not bound by the secret limitations of which the third person has no knowledge.

5. Delegation of Authority by Agent

As a general rule, an agent cannot delegate to another person the authority given by the principal. In other words, unless the principal expressly or in an implied manner consents, an agent cannot appoint subagents to carry out the agent's duties. The reason for this rule is that since an agent is usually selected because of some personal qualifications, it would be unfair and possibly injurious to the principal if the authority to act could be shifted by the agent to another person. Subagents cannot be used without the principal's consent, particularly when the agent was originally appointed for the performance of a task requiring discretion or judgment.

Agents, however, may authorize others to perform their work for them in the following instances:

1. When the acts to be done involve only mechanical or ministerial duties. Thus, an agent to make application for hail insurance on wheat may delegate to someone else the clerical act of writing the application. Also, it may be shown that there is customary authority for a clerk in the office of the insurance agent to sign the agent's name so as to have the effect of a signing by the agent and be binding on the insurance company, the agent's principal.
2. When a well-known custom recognizes such appointment. To illustrate, if one is authorized to buy from or sell to a grain elevator, one may do so through a broker as that is the customary method.
3. When the appointment is justified by necessity or sudden emergency and it is impractical to communicate with the principal, and the appointment of a subagent is reasonably necessary for the protection of the interests of the principal entrusted to the agent.
4. When it is contemplated by the parties that subagents would be employed. For example, a bank may now generally use subagents to receive payments of notes that have been left for collection, since the parties contemplate that this will be done. Also, the authority to appoint subagents can be inferred where the principal knows or has reason to know that the agent employs subagents. Thus, an agent may grant subagents power to bind a principal fire insurance company when the agent had a long-standing practice of appointing subagents and this was known to the principal.[4]

B. DUTIES AND LIABILITIES OF PRINCIPAL AND AGENT

The creation of the principal-agent relationship gives rise to duties and liabilities.

6. Duties and Liabilities of Agent During Agency

While the agency relationship exists, the agent owes certain duties to the principal.

(a) LOYALTY. An agent must be loyal or faithful to the principal. The agent must not obtain any secret benefit from the agency. If the principal is seeking to buy or rent property, the agent cannot secretly obtain the property and then sell or lease it to the principal at a profit.

An agent who owns property cannot sell it to the principal without disclosing that ownership

---

[4] Nguyen v Scott, 206 Cal App 3d 725, 253 Cal Rptr 800 (1988).

to the principal. If disclosure is not made, the principal may avoid the contract, even if the agent's conduct did not cause the principal any financial loss. Alternatively, the principal can approve the transaction and sue the agent for any secret profit obtained by the agent.

A contract is voidable by the principal if the agent who was employed to sell the property purchases the property, either directly or indirectly, without full disclosure to the principal.

An agent cannot act as agent for both parties to a transaction unless both know of the dual capacity and agree to it. If the agent does act in this capacity without the consent of both parties, any principal who did not know of the agent's double status can avoid the transaction.

An agent must not accept secret gifts or commissions from third persons in connection with the agency. If the agent does so, the principal may sue the agent for those gifts or commissions. Such practices are condemned because the judgment of the agent may be influenced by the receipt of gifts or commissions.

It is a violation of an agent's duty of loyalty to make and retain secret profits.

In the *Ellison* case the agent took additional secret compensation for himself.

An agent is, of course, prohibited from aiding the competitors of a principal or disclosing

ELLISON v ALLEY
(Tenn) 842 SW2d 605 (1992)

Real estate broker Donald Alley Sr. had a listing contract which gave him the exclusive right to sell Wayman Ellison's farm for at least $200,000. Ellison was told that a buyer was found. The buyer, Cora Myers, who had been paid $585,000 for her small farm because the land was needed for a commercial development, agreed to pay $380,000 for the large Ellison farm. Alley told Ellison that the sale price was $200,000. The buyer paid $380,000 and Alley kept the difference. When Ellison later learned of these details, he sued Alley for the $180,000. From a judgment for Ellison, Alley appealed, seeking at least his commission on the sale.

O'BRIEN, J. . . . We are in agreement with the finding of breach of fiduciary duty and the award to the plaintiff of the defendant's profits. But, on the narrow issue upon which this appeal was granted, we find that the defendant [is] not entitled to a commission on the sale of the Ellison property. It is apparent that the defendant manipulated [the] transactions in such a manner as to willfully, and wrongfully, conceal [his] true role and [his] intention to reap a $180,000 ill-gained profit from the sale of the property.

It is well settled that the real estate agent acts as a fiduciary to the client. In any transaction or dealing related to such relationship, "the agent can in no way and under no circumstances act for himself or for any other than the principal without first making full and complete disclosure of the facts to the principal. He cannot profit by his failure to make such disclosure." . . . When a broker procures legal title to property, in violation of a fiduciary duty owed to the owner, equity constructs a trust out of the transaction. In such a case, the property owner is entitled to the profits wrongfully received by the broker in the transaction. . . . The construction of such a trust is without regard to whether the principal received a fair price for the conveyance of the property. . . .

Likewise, "where a broker's actions in a sale transaction amounts to bad faith or misconduct, the broker is not entitled to a commission on the sale." . . . It is undeniable that the defendant acted in these transactions with bad faith and beyond the bounds of ethical conduct. To permit the defendant credit for a reasonable commission on the sale of the Ellison property would be no more than offering an undeserved reward for avarice. . . .

[Judgment affirmed]

QUESTIONS

1. Isn't the seller's right to a remedy defeated by the fact that the seller received the net price he sought?
2. May an agent ever buy a principal's property?
3. Did Alley act contrary to any of the ethical principles set forth in Figure 1 of the Preface.
4. Since Alley did find a ready, willing, and able buyer, isn't he at least entitled to his commission?

---

to them information relating to the business of the principal. It is also a breach of duty for the agent to knowingly deceive a principal.[5]

(b) OBEDIENCE AND PERFORMANCE.

An agent is under a duty to obey all lawful instructions.[6] The agent is required to perform the services specified for the period and in the way specified. An agent who does not is liable to the principal for any harm caused. For example, if an agent is instructed to take cash payments only but accepts a check in payment, the agent is liable for the loss caused the principal if a check is dishonored by nonpayment. Similarly, when an insurance broker undertakes to obtain an insurance policy for a principal to provide a specified coverage but fails to obtain a policy with the proper coverage, the broker, as agent of the principal, is liable to the principal for any loss caused.

If the agent violates instructions, it is immaterial that the agent acted in good faith or intended to benefit the principal. It is the fact that the agent violated the instructions and thereby caused the principal a loss that im-

poses a liability on the agent. In determining whether the agent has obeyed instructions, they must be interpreted in a way that a reasonable person would interpret them.

(c) REASONABLE CARE.

It is the duty of an agent to act with the care that a reasonable person would exercise under the circumstances. In addition, if the agent possesses a special skill, as in the case of a broker or an attorney, the agent must exercise that skill.

(d) ACCOUNTING.

An agent must account to the principal for all property or money belonging to the principal that comes into the agent's possession. The agent must, within a reasonable time, give notice of collections made and render an accurate account of all receipts and expenditures. The agency agreement may state at what intervals or on what dates such accountings are to be made.

An agent must keep the principal's property and money separate and distinct from that of the agent. If property of the agent is mingled with property of the principal so that

---

[5] Koontz v Rosener (Colo App) 787 P2d 192 (1990).

[6] Stanford v Neiderer, 178 Ga 56, 341 SE2d 892 (1986).

the two cannot be identified or separated, the principal may claim all of the commingled mass. Furthermore, when funds of the principal and the agent are mixed, any loss that occurs must be borne by the agent.

(e) INFORMATION. It is the duty of an agent to keep the principal informed of all facts relating to the agency that are relevant to protecting the principal's interests.[7]

The *Allen Industries* case raised questions of an agent's duty of disclosure.

ALLEN INDUSTRIES INC. v SHELDON GOOD CO.
153 Ill App 3d 120, 106 Ill Dec 313, 505 NE2d 1104 (1987)

Joan Kulwin owned Allen Industries Inc., which owned a commercial building in Evanston, Illinois. She granted the Sheldon Co. the exclusive right to sell the building and agreed to pay a commission to Sheldon upon the sale. This commission was to be divided in half between Sheldon and a cooperating broker, should a cooperating broker secure the purchaser. On August 21, 1985, Sheldon Co. presented Kulwin a written offer in final contract form from J.W. Collier. She rejected this offer of $335,000 and made a counteroffer of $350,000. On August 22 Collier accepted the counteroffer. The contract called for the seller to take back a mortgage for $249,000. At the closing Sheldon Co. received a $18,000 commission. Kulwin later found out that Maurice Leviton, President of TLC, on his third inspection of the property on August 16, 1985, advised Sheldon Co. that he was preparing an all-cash offer on the property. He made this offer to Sheldon Co. on August 22, 1985, and it was rejected by Sheldon Co. because Kulwin had accepted Collier's offer at that point. Kulwin sued Sheldon Co. for breach of the fiduciary duty in failing to inform her of all facts material to the sale. She asserted that Sheldon Co. failed to do so to avoid sharing half the commission with the cooperating broker who showed TLC the property. Sheldon Co. denied that it had a duty to report conversations of a speculative nature to the seller. From a judgment for Sheldon Co., Kulwin appealed.

STAMOS, J. . . . The relationship between principal and agent for the purchase or sale of property is a fiduciary one, and the agent in the exercise of good faith must make known to his principal all material facts within his knowledge which in any way affect the transaction and the subject matter of his agency. Material facts are those facts which the agent should realize have or are likely to have a bearing upon the desirability of the transaction from the viewpoint of the principal.

If a party employs an agent to make a sale of land he is entitled to all the skill, ability and industry of such agent to make the sale on the best terms that can be had.

---

[7] Restatement, Agency 2d § 381; Cole v Jennings (Colo App) 847 P2d 200 (1991).

An agent cannot deal for his own advantage with things to be sold because of his confidential relationship with his principal and because of his duty to disclose to his principal every fact, circumstance or advantage in relation to a sale, which may come to his knowledge. . . .

A purchaser's expressions of interest in property to be sold and his statements that he is preparing an offer for said property are material facts which a real estate broker has a duty to convey to his client. It is evident that plaintiffs would have been in an improved position to gain a better price or more favorable terms had they known that there was more than one purchaser interested in their property. Plaintiffs would have benefited from the heightened demand for their property by allowing each prospective purchaser to compete against the other for plaintiffs' property. In fact, TLC's offer included more favorable terms than the contract made with the ultimate purchaser, J.W. Collier. . . . It is possible that plaintiffs would have found TLC's cash offer to have been more favorable than Collier's. In any event, defendants had a duty to inform the seller of all facts that might influence him in accepting or rejecting the offer. It cannot be said that plaintiffs would not have been influenced by TLC's offer in accepting or rejecting Collier's offer. Therefore, we hold that [there was a] breach of a fiduciary duty to plaintiffs by failing to disclose material facts to them regarding the sale of their property.

Plaintiffs allege, additionally, that defendants' failure to inform plaintiffs of TLC's offer was an attempt to make personal gain by receiving a higher commission. Such conduct, if proven, is strictly prohibited in this state because it violates an agent's duty of honesty and loyalty toward his principal. This obligation toward a principal prohibits an agent from dealing independently of the interests of his principal to his personal gain in the subject matter of the agency, on the grounds that such activities will necessarily tempt that agent to abandon the interests of his principal in favor of his own interests. In fact, an agent who deals independently of the interests of his principal breaches his fiduciary duty and is therefore barred from any recovery for his services. (When a broker breaches his duties toward his employer he will, in almost every case, lose his commission.) In this instance, defendants allegedly received an $18,000 commission from the sale of plaintiffs' property to J.W. Collier, a client brought in by defendants. Under the listing agreement, defendants would have received only 1/2 of that commission or $9,000 and advertising expenses up to $5,000 if the property was sold to TLC, a prospective purchaser not brought in by defendants.

[Reversed and remanded with directions]

QUESTIONS

1. Did Sheldon Co. have an obligation to report each conversation of a speculative nature that the agent had with a prospective purchaser concerning offers that might be made in the indeterminate future?
2. Did Sheldon Co. have a right to protect its full commission by preserving the sale for its purchaser, as opposed to the purchaser produced by another broker?
3. Is a real estate agent who breaches a duty owed the seller entitled to the full commission when the property is sold?

7. Duties and Liabilities of Agent After Termination of Agency

When the agency relationship ends, the duties of the agent continue only to the extent necessary to perform prior obligations. For example, the agent must return to the former principal any property that had been entrusted to the agent for the purpose of the agency. With the exception of such "winding-up" duties, the agency relationship is terminated, and the former agent can deal with the principal as freely as with a stranger.[8]

8. Enforcement of Liability of Agent

When the agent's breach of duty causes harm to the principal, the amount of the loss may be deducted from any compensation due the agent or may be recovered in an ordinary lawsuit.

When the agent handles money for the principal, the contract of employment may provide that the amount of any shortages in the agent's account may be deducted from the compensation to which the agent would otherwise be entitled.

If the agent has made a secret profit, the principal may recover that profit from the agent. In addition, the agent may forfeit the right to all compensation, without regard to whether the principal benefited from some of the actions of the agent and without regard to whether the principal had actually been harmed.

9. Duties and Liabilities of Principal to Agent

The principal must perform the contract, compensate the agent for services, make reimbursement for proper expenditures, and under certain circumstances must indemnify the agent for loss.

(a) EMPLOYMENT ACCORDING TO TERMS OF CONTRACT. When the contract is for a specified time, the principal is under the obligation to permit the agent to act as such for the term of the contract. Exceptions are made for just cause or contract provisions that permit the principal to terminate the agency sooner. If the principal gives the agent an exclusive right to act as such, the principal cannot give anyone else the authority to act as agent, nor may the principal do the act to which the exclusive agent's authority relates. If the principal or another agent does so, the exclusive agent is entitled to full compensation, just as though the act had been performed by the exclusive agent.

(b) COMPENSATION. The principal must pay the agent the agreed compensation.[9] If the parties have not fixed the amount of the compensation by their agreement but intended that the agent should be paid, the agent may recover the customary compensation for such services. If there is no established compensation, the agent may recover the reasonable value of the services rendered.[10]

(1) Repeating Transactions. In certain industries, third persons make repeated transactions with the principal. In these cases, the agent who made the original contract with the third person commonly receives a certain compensation or percentage of commissions on all subsequent renewal or additional contracts. In the insurance business, for example, the insurance agent obtaining the policyholder for the insurer receives a substantial portion of the first year's premium and then receives a smaller percentage of the premiums paid by the policyholder in subsequent years.

(2) Postagency Transactions. An agent is not ordinarily entitled to compensation in connection with transactions, such as sales or renewals of insurance policies, occurring after the termination of the agency, even if the

---

8   Corron & Black of Illinois, Inc. v Magner, 145 Ill App 3d 151, 98 Ill Dec 663, 494 NE2d 785 (1986).

9   American Chocolates Inc. v Mascot Pecan Co. Inc. (Miss) 592 So 2d 93 (1992).

10 Lone Star Steel Co. v Scott (Tex Civ App) 759 SW2d 144 (1988).

postagency transactions are the result of the agent's former activities. However, some contracts between a principal and an agent expressly state whether the agent has the right to posttermination compensation.[11]

(c) REIMBURSEMENT. The principal is under a duty to reimburse the agent for all disbursements made at the request of the principal and for all expenses necessarily incurred in the lawful discharge of the agency for the benefit of the principal. The agent cannot recover, however, for expenses caused by the agent's own misconduct or negligence. For example, if the agent transfers title to the wrong person, the agent cannot recover from the principal the expense incurred in correcting the error.

(d) INDEMNITY. It is the duty of the principal to indemnify the agent for any losses or damages suffered on account of the agency that were not caused by the agent's fault.

When the loss sustained was caused by the agent's misconduct or illegal act, the principal is not liable for indemnification.

SUMMARY

An agent acting with authority has the power to bind the principal. The scope of an agent's authority may be determined from the express words of the principal to the agent; this is called express authority. An agent has incidental authority to perform any act reasonably necessary to execute the authority given the agent. An agent's authority may be implied so as to enable the agent to perform any act in accordance with the general customs or usages in the business or industry. This authority is often referred to as customary authority. An individual is clothed with apparent authority when the principal, by words or conduct, leads a third person reasonably to believe that the individual has the authority of an agent.

The effect of a proper exercise of authority by an agent is to bind the principal and third person to a contract. The agent, not being a party to the contract, is not liable in any respect under the contract. A third person dealing with a person claiming to be an agent has a duty to ascertain the extent of the agent's authority and has a duty to take notice of any acts that are clearly adverse to the principal's interests. The third person cannot claim that apparent authority existed when the person has notice that the agent's conduct is adverse to the interests of the principal. A third person who has knowledge of limitations on an agent's authority is bound by those limitations. A third person is not bound by secret limitations.

An agent cannot appoint subagents to do the agent's duties unless (1) the duties are ministerial, (2) to do so is a custom in the industry in question, (3) to do so is justified by emergency conditions, or (4) it was contemplated by the parties that subagents would be employed.

While the agency relationship exists, the agent owes the principal the duties of (1) being loyal, (2) obeying all lawful instructions, (3) exercising reasonable care, (4) accounting for all property or money belonging to the principal, and (5) informing the principal of all facts relating to the agency that are relevant to the principal's interests. The duties of an agent continue after termination of the agency only to the extent necessary to perform prior obligations, such as return of the former principal's property. After termination of the agency, the agent may deal with the principal as freely as with a stranger.

The principal owes certain duties to the agent, including (1) fulfilling all terms of their contract, (2) paying the agreed compensation for services of the agent, (3) reimbursing the

---

[11] Friction Materials Co. v Stinson (Ky App) 833 SW2d 388 (1992).

agent for proper expenditures, and (4) indemnifying the agent for losses suffered on account of the agency through no fault of the agent.

LAW IN PRACTICE

1. Recognize that as a principal your conduct and words may reasonably create the impression that an individual is authorized to act as your agent, even though the individual has no such authority. You may be bound by a contract made by this individual on the apparent authority theory.

2. Sellers contracting with an agent representing a buyer should realize that the contract is with the principal/buyer, not the agent. Investigate the reputation and credit standing of the buyer. The agent is not liable for any breach of the contract.

3. In either formal or informal training sessions with your agents, make clear their fiduciary responsibilities of loyalty, obedience, performance, reasonable care, accounting, and information.

4. If you discover that your agent has made a secret profit, you may not only recover the profit, but you may withhold any compensation owed for the period during which the secret profit was made.

5. Anticipate problems that commonly occur in agency relationships. Resolve these issues in writing in the agency agreement.

QUESTIONS AND CASE PROBLEMS

1. What social forces are affected by the rule that a third person must determine the extent of an agent's authority?

2. Harvey Marks was agent for the Trojian Sportswear Co., covering the company's Midwest territory. He contracted on behalf of Trojian to provide the Lynnfield High School football team with 60 "game" football jerseys. The jerseys delivered to the school were of such poor quality that they were clearly not fit for the intended purpose of serving as "game" jerseys. The Lynnfield School Department sued Marks, the person who sold them the jerseys, for breach of warranty. Decide.

3. Can a person act as agent for both parties to a transaction?

4. Compare (a) secret limitations on authority of an agent with (b) apparent authority of an agent.

5. After an agency has been terminated, the agent is not entitled to further compensation. Appraise this statement.

6. Martha Christiansen owns women's apparel stores bearing her name in New Seabury, Massachusetts; Lake Placid, New York; Palm Beach, Florida; and Palm Springs, California. At a meeting with her four store managers, she discussed styles she thought appropriate for the forthcoming season, advised them as always to use their best judgment in the goods they purchased for each of their respective stores, and cautioned, "but no blue jeans." Later, Jane Farley, the manager of the Lake Placid store, purchased a line of high-quality blue denim outfits (designer jeans with jacket and vest options) from Women's Wear, Inc. for the summer season. The outfits did not sell. Martha refused to pay for them, contending that she told all of her managers "no blue jeans," and that if it came to a lawsuit, she would fly in three managers to testify that Jane Farley had absolutely no authority to purchase denim outfits and was, in fact, expressly forbidden to do so. Women's Wear sued Martha, and the three managers testified for Martha. Is the fact that Martha had explicitly forbidden Farley to purchase the outfits in question sufficient to protect her from liability for the purchases made by Farley?

7. The Taylors were depositors of the Equitable Trust Company of Maryland. Equitable issued them a treasurer's check for $20,000. Mr. Vittetoe, a loan officer of the bank, received a long-distance telephone call from a person who identified himself as Mr. Taylor and requested that the $20,000 represented by the treasurer's check be transferred to the account of Jody Associates at Irving Trust Company in New York. Mr. Vittetoe did not know Mr. Taylor personally and replied that written instructions from Taylor would be required. Some time later, Frank Terranova appeared at the bank and stated that he was Taylor's agent, surrendered the treasurer's check, which had not been indorsed, and requested that the money represented thereby be transferred to the account of Jody Associates in the Irving Trust Company. Terranova also presented a letter that he had signed in his own name that repeated the request to transfer the $20,000. Equitable verified Mr. Terranova's signature by checking his driver's license and a major credit card and then made the transfer as requested. Taylor denied that Terranova had the authority to request the transfer and sued Equitable for damages. The bank contends that it was entitled to rely on the written instructions submitted to the bank by Terranova. Decide.

8. Fred Schilling, the president and administrator of Florence General Hospital made a contract, dated August 16, 1989 on behalf of the hospital with CMK Associates to transfer the capacity to utilize 25 beds from the hospital to the Faith Nursing Home. Schilling on behalf of the hospital had previously made a contract with CMK Associates on May 4, 1987. Schilling had been specifically authorized by the hospital board to make the 1987 contract. The hospital refused to honor the 1989 contract because the board had not authorized it. CMK contends that Schilling had apparent authority to bind the hospital because he was president and administrator of the hospital and he had been the person who negotiated and signed a contract with CMK in 1987. Thus, according to CMK, the hospital had held out Schilling as having apparent authority to make the contract. The hospital disagrees. Decide. *[Pee Dee Nursing Home v Florence General Hospital (SC App) 419 SE2d 843]*

9. Barbara Fox was the agent of Burt Hollander, a well-known athlete. She discovered that Tom Lanceford owned a '57 Chevrolet convertible, which had been stored in a garage for the past fifteen years. After demonstrating to Lanceford that she was the authorized agent of Hollander, she made a contract with Lanceford on behalf of Hollander to purchase the Chevrolet. Lanceford later discovered that the car was much more valuable than he originally believed, and he refused to deliver the car to Fox. Fox sued Lanceford for breach of contract. Can she recover?

10. Michael Johnson was employed as a real estate agent. He inquired of Byron Hand whether he wished to sell certain property. Hand responded that he would be willing to sell the property for a specified net price. Johnson returned with a sales contract, which he presented for Hand's acceptance. The sale price was sufficient to net Hand the amount that he had specified. Johnson did not disclose, however, that the purchaser who was named in the sales contract was his own father-in-law. Hand signed the contract. Shortly after title to the property had been transferred to his father-in-

law, Johnson sold the property to a third party for a price that was much greater than the price Hand had been paid. A large part, if not all, of the profit from the resale went to Michael Johnson and not to his father-in-law. When Hand learned that the property had been resold for a price greater than he had been paid, he brought an action against Johnson, claiming that Johnson had breached his duty to Hand. *[Johnson v Hand, 189 Ga App 706, 377 SE2d 176]*

11. An attorney received a check made payable to the order of his client. The attorney indorsed the client's name and cashed the check at the bank on which it was drawn. The client then sued the bank for the amount that had been paid the attorney. The bank raised the defense that the attorney had authority to sign for the client and to receive payment on the client's behalf. Was this a valid defense? *[Aetna Casualty & Surety Co. v Traders Natl. Bank & Trust Co. (Mo App) 514 SW2d 860]*

12. Kribbs owned real estate that had been leased through his agent, Jackson, at a monthly rental of $275. When this lease ended, Jackson and a third person, Solomon, made an agreement that if Solomon obtained a new tenant for a rental of $500 a month, Jackson would pay Solomon $100 a month. The latter obtained a new tenant, who paid a monthly rental of $550. Jackson continued to send Kribbs $275 a month, less his commissions and janitor and utility costs; paid Solomon $100 a month; and kept the balance of the rental for himself. When Kribbs learned of these facts three years later, he sued Jackson for the money he had kept for himself and the money he had paid Solomon. Jackson defended that Kribbs accepted and was satisfied with the $275 per month, that the additional funds were the sole result of Jackson's own entrepreneurship, and that the funds should accrue solely to Jackson's benefit. Was he correct? *[Kribbs v Jackson, 387 Pa 611, 129 A2d 490]*

13. DSG is in the government food service contracting business. Fredrick Anderson was employed by DSG to survey contracts in preparation for bids. Edward Mitura served as manager of DSG's Fort Riley, Kansas, contract. In early November, 1982, the food service contract at Fort Campbell, Kentucky, became available for bidding. On November 8, Anderson and Mitura toured the Fort Campbell facility with other prospective bidders, and Mitura informed Anderson of his intention to bid personally on the contract. Anderson hired an accountant, Larry Golden, concerning the cost per hour to be used in a bid, and it was determined to be $7.78. Anderson provided

Mitura with this figure, and Mitura paid Golden's bill. On November 16, DSG submitted a bid. DSG was not notified by Anderson that Mitura was going to submit a bid. On November 22, Mitura, through his wife, submitted a bid. On November 23, Mitura notified DSG that he had submitted a bid on the Fort Campbell contract and quit his job. On November 24, the bids were opened, and Mitura's bid turned out to be the lowest. On December 12, Anderson resigned from DSG to work with Mitura, and the Fort Campbell contract was subsequently awarded to Mitura. DSG sued Mitura and Anderson for breach of their fiduciary duty to DSG by competing with it while employed by DSG. Mitura and Anderson contend that they were free to compete with their former employer once their employment relationship was terminated. They point out that their contract at Fort Campbell did not begin until well after both had terminated their work for DSG. Decide. [*DSG Corp v Anderson (CA6 Ky) 754 F2d 678*]

14. Cristallina S.A., a Panamanian corporation engaged in the purchase and sale of works of art, employed Christie's International to sell eight paintings at a May 19 auction. Based on the assessment of its experts, Christie's notified the press on May 12 that it expected to receive between $5 million and $9 million for the paintings. On the day before the auction, Christie's president David Bathurst recommended that the "reserves"—the private agreement between the seller and auctioneer on the prices below which an item may not be sold—be set at $9,250,000. The auction was a failure, with just one of the eight paintings being sold. Cristallina sued Christie's, contending that as its agent, Christie's failed to inform it of the information released to the press on May 12 and the un-

derlying information on which the press estimates were made, and that the released estimates made it virtually impossible to sell the paintings unless the reserves were lowered. Christie's contended that as an auctioneer, it could not guarantee the results of a sale. Decide. [*Cristallina S.A. v Christie, Manson & Woods, 117 App Div 2d 284, 502 NYS2d 165*]

15. Bankerd and his wife Virginia owned a home in Maryland, as tenants by the entirety. They lived there until 1966, when Mrs. Bankerd moved out as a result of marital problems. Mr. Bankerd continued to live in the house until July 1968, when he "left for the west." Mrs. Bankerd then resumed residency and paid all expenses for the home. Before Mr. Bankerd's departure, he executed a power of attorney to King. The power of attorney was later changed to authorize King to sell the property "on such terms as to him seem best." In 1977, Mrs. Bankerd asked King to exercise the power of attorney and to transfer Mr. Bankerd's interest in the property to her so that she could sell the property and retire. King wrote to Mr. Bankerd on three occasions at various addresses, but was unsuccessful in reaching him. King believed that Mr. Bankerd did not care about the property and that he had abandoned his interest in it. King therefore conveyed Mr. Bankerd's interest in the property to Mrs. Bankerd. Mrs. Bankerd paid no consideration for the transfer, and King received no compensation. Later, Mr. Bankerd sued King, claiming that King had breached his duty of loyalty in connection with the conveyance of the property. King defended that under the broad language of the power of attorney, he had acted within his authority. Decide. [*King v Bankerd, 303 Md 98 492 A2d 608*]

CHAPTER 41

THIRD PERSONS IN AGENCY

LEARNING OBJECTIVES

After studying this chapter, you will be able to:
1. *Describe how to execute a contract as an agent on behalf of a principal.*
2. *Identify when an agent is liable to a third person on a contract.*
3. *State the effect of a payment made by a third person to an authorized agent.*
4. *Explain and illustrate the doctrine of respondeat superior.*
5. *Contrast the liability of an owner for a tort committed by an independent contractor with the liability of an employer for a tort committed by an employee.*
6. *Distinguish between the authority of a soliciting agent and a contracting agent.*

The rights and liabilities of the principal, the agent, and the third person with whom the agent deals are generally determined by contract law. In some cases, tort or criminal law may be applicable.

A. LIABILITY OF AGENT TO THIRD PERSON

The liability of the agent to the third person depends on the existence of authority and the manner of executing the contract.

1. Action of Authorized Agent of Disclosed Principal

If an agent makes a contract with a third person on behalf of a disclosed principal and has proper authority to do so, and if the contract is executed properly, the agent has no personal liability on the contract. Whether the principal performs the contract or not, the agent cannot be held liable by the third party.

In speaking of an agent's action as authorized or unauthorized, it must be remembered that *authorized* includes action that, though originally unauthorized, was subsequently ratified by the principal. Once there is an effective ratification, the original action of the agent is no longer treated as unauthorized.

2. Unauthorized Action

If a person makes a contract as agent for another but lacks authority to do so, the contract does not bind the principal. When a person purports to act as agent for a principal, an implied warranty arises that that person has authority to do so.[1] If the agent lacks authority, there is a breach of this warranty. If the agent's act causes loss to the third person, that third person may generally hold the agent liable for the loss.

It is no defense for the agent in such a case that the agent acted in good faith or misunderstood the scope of authority. The purported agent is not liable for conduct in excess of authority when the third person knows that the agent is acting beyond the authority given by the principal.

An agent with a written authorization may avoid liability on the implied warranty of authority by showing the written authorization to the third person and permitting the third person to determine the scope of the agent's authority.

3. No Principal with Capacity

A person purporting to act as agent warrants by implication that there is an existing principal and that the principal has legal capacity. If there is no principal, or if the principal lacks capacity, the person acting as an agent is liable for any loss caused the third person.

The agent can avoid liability on the implied warranty of the existence of a principal with capacity by making known to the third person all material facts or by obtaining the agreement of the third person that the agent shall not be liable.

4. Disclosure of Principal

There are three degrees to which the existence and identity of the principal may be disclosed or not disclosed. An agent's liability as a party to a contract with a third person is affected by the degree of disclosure.

(a) DISCLOSED PRINCIPAL. When the agent makes known the identity of the principal and the fact that the agent is acting on behalf of that principal, the principal is called a **disclosed principal**. The third person dealing with an agent of a disclosed principal ordinarily intends to make a contract with the principal, not with the agent. Consequently, the agent is not a party to and is not bound by the contract that is made.[2]

---

[1] Walz v Todd & Honeywell Inc. 599 NYS2d 638 (1993).

(b) PARTIALLY DISCLOSED PRINCIPAL. When the agent makes known the existence of a principal but not the principal's identity, the principal is a **partially disclosed principal**. Since the third party does not know the identity of the principal, the third person is making the contract with the agent, and the agent is therefore a party to the contract.

(c) UNDISCLOSED PRINCIPAL. When the third person is not told or does not know

that the agent is acting as an agent for anyone else, the unknown principal is called an **undisclosed principal**.[3] In this case, the third person is making the contract with the agent, and the agent is a party to that contract.

In the *Rothschild* case the court was faced with deciding whether an agent was liable under contracts made on behalf of a principal.

ROTHSCHILD SUNSYSTEMS INC. v PAWLUS
514 NYS2d 572 (1987)

Richard Pawlus was an owner of Dutch City Wood Products Inc., which did business as "Dutch City Marketing." Pawlus believed he was acting on behalf of the corporation and purchased merchandise from Rothschild Sunsystems Inc. from April 24, 1985 to June 24, 1985, using the designation "Richard Pawlus Dutch Marketing" on orders and correspondence. In October, when a balance of $9,882.34 was owed Rothschild, the seller was notified by Pawlus' attorney that Pawlus was acting on behalf of the corporation when the merchandise was purchased. Rothschild sued Pawlus for payment for the merchandise. Pawlus contended that he was an agent of the corporation and therefore not personally liable. Judgment was entered in favor of Rothschild. Pawlus appealed.

MURPHY, J. . . . . Plaintiff's complaint alleges that it shipped goods to Pawlus at his request, that Pawlus accepted the goods without objection and that the balance due on the account had not been paid despite reasonable demand having been made. . . . Plaintiff also alleged that Pawlus never stated that he was acting on behalf of a corporation. . . . Pawlus . . . did not deny that he placed the orders or received the merchandise. Nor did he dispute any of the items in the account. He simply alleged that he acted on behalf of the corporation, Dutch City Wood Products, Inc., which was doing business as Dutch City Marketing. Further, he stated that plaintiff was made aware of this fact on October 17, 1985. However, this was well after the orders were placed and filled. The record also includes a letter from Pawlus dated September 12, 1985 which he signed "Richard Pawlus Dutch City Marketing" and which bears a letterhead "Dutch City Marketing." No mention of a corporation is made.

An agent will be liable as a principal if the fact of the agency relationship is not known by the person with whom the agent deals. Such disclosure must be made at

---

2　New York Times v Glynn-Palmer Inc. 525 NYS2d 565 (1988).

3　Crown Controls Inc. v Smiley, 47 Wash App 832, 737 P2d 709 (1987).

the time of the contract. Here, Pawlus has failed to even allege that the existence of an agency was made known to plaintiff. . . .

[Judgment affirmed]

QUESTIONS

1. Was Dutch City Wood Products Inc. a partially disclosed principal?
2. Did the fact that Rothschild was notified that Pawlus was acting as an agent prior to the lawsuit relieve Pawlus from liability?
3. State the rule of the case.

5. Wrongful Receipt of Money

If an agent obtains a payment of money from a third person by use of illegal methods, the agent is liable to the third person.

If the third person makes an overpayment to the agent or a payment when none is due, the agent is also usually liable to the third person for the amount of such overpayment or payment. If the agent has acted in good faith and does not know that the payment was improperly made, however, the agent is liable to the third person only so long as the agent has possession or control of the overpayment. If the agent has remitted the overpayment to the principal before its return is demanded by the third person, the agent is not liable to the third person. In the latter case, the third person's right of action, if one exists, is only against the principal. But payment to the principal does not relieve the agent of liability when the agent knows that the payment was not proper.

6. Assumption of Liability

Agents may intentionally make themselves liable on contracts with third persons.[4] This situation frequently occurs when the agent is a well-established local brokerage house or other agency and when the principal is located out of town and is not known locally.

In some situations, the agent will make a contract that will be personally binding. If the principal is not disclosed, the agent is necessarily the other contracting party and is bound by the contract. Even when the principal is disclosed, the agent may be personally bound if it was the intention of the parties that the agent assume a personal obligation, even though this was done to further the business of the principal. To illustrate, if an attorney hires an expert witness to testify on behalf of a client, the attorney is an agent acting on behalf of a disclosed principal and is not personally liable for an expert witness fee. However, where an expert witness asks the attorney about payment and the attorney states, "Don't worry, I will take care of it," the attorney (agent) has assumed a personal obligation and is liable for the fee.[5]

7. Execution of Contract

A simple contract that would appear to be the contract of the agent can be shown by other evidence, if believed, to have been intended as a contract between the principal and the third party.

The *Memorial Hospital* case raised the question of whether a daughter had signed a payment guarantee as an agent for her mother.

---

[4] Fairchild Publications v Rosston, 584 NYS2d 389 (1992).
[5] Boros v Carter (Fla App) 537 So 2d 1134 (1989).

MEMORIAL HOSPITAL v BAUMANN
475 NYS2d 636 (1984)

During the early morning hours of January 10, 1981, Beverly Baumann accompanied her mother to Memorial Hospital, where her mother was placed in intensive care for symptoms of heart ailment. Baumann signed various documents, including one that authorized the hospital to release medical information and to receive directly the mother's insurance benefits. This form stated, "I understand I am financially responsible to the hospital for charges not covered by this authorization." Baumann's mother died during the course of her hospitalization. Thereafter, the hospital sued Baumen to recover $19,013.42 in unpaid hospital charges based upon the form, signed by Baumann, that the hospital called a "guarantee of payment." Baumann contended that she signed the document as an agent for a disclosed principal and was thus not personally liable. From a judgment for Baumann, the hospital appealed.

MEMORANDUM DECISION. . . . Defendant's affidavit clearly states that she "signed [the] documents understanding that it was on behalf of [her] mother", thereby giving notice of an agency claim in this case. Plaintiff made no attempt to refute this assertion and does not claim on this appeal that it was surprised or prejudiced by defendant's reliance on the agency defense. . . .

We recognize as well settled the proposition that an agent assumes no personal liability in executing a contract for a disclosed principal, unless it is clear that the agent intends to be bound personally. Defendant's unrefuted [evidence] establishes that she did not intend to be bound personally because she signed the forms on behalf of her incapacitated mother who was clearly, as the patient to whom services were to be rendered in an emergency situation, the principal. Thus, [the] conclusions that defendant was acting as an agent for a disclosed principal and could not be personally liable to the hospital were correct.

[Judgment affirmed]

QUESTIONS

1. On what basis did the hospital believe Baumann was responsible for the unpaid bills?
2. What was Baumann's defense?
3. What could Baumann have done that would have avoided any question as to her responsibility for unpaid charges?

To avoid any question of interpretation, an agent should execute an instrument by signing the principal's name and either *by* or *per* and the agent's name. For example, if Jane R. Craig is an agent for B. G. Gray, Craig should execute instruments by signing either "B. G. Gray, by Jane R. Craig" or "B. G. Gray, per Jane R. Craig." Such a signing is in law a signing by Gray, and the agent is therefore not a party to the contract. The signing of the principal's name by an authorized agent without indicating the agent's name or identity is likewise in law the signature of the principal.

If the instrument is ambiguous as to whether the agent has signed in a representative or an individual capacity, parol evidence is admissible as between the original parties to the transaction, in order to establish the character in which the agent was acting. If the body of the contract states an obligation that clearly refers only to the principal, then the agent is not bound by the contract even though it is signed in the agent's individual name without indicating any agency.

8. Failure to Obtain Commitment of Principal

In some situations, the agent is in effect an intermediary, or go-between, who has the duty to the third person to see to it that the principal is bound to the third person. For example, an agent of a fire insurance company has authority to write policies of insurance. The agent tells a policyholder whose fire policy has been canceled that the agent will look into the matter and that the insured should forget about it unless notified by the agent. In such a case, the insurance agent is under an obligation to make reasonable efforts to obtain the reinstatement of the policy or to notify the insured that it is not possible to do so. The agent is liable to the insured for the latter's fire loss if the agent does not obtain the reinstatement of the policy and fails to inform the insured of this.

9. Torts and Crimes

Agents are liable for harm caused third persons by the agents' fraudulent, intentional, or negligent acts.[6] The fact that persons were acting as agents at the time or that they acted in good faith under the directions of a principal does not relieve them of liability if their conduct would impose liability on them were they acting for themselves.

If an agent commits a crime, such as stealing from a third person or shooting the third person, the agent is liable for the crime, without regard to the fact of acting as an agent. The agent is liable, without regard to whether the agent acted in self-interest or sought to advance the interest of the principal.

B. LIABILITY OF THIRD PERSON TO AGENT

A third party may be liable to an agent because of the way the transaction was conducted or because of acts causing harm to the agent.

10. Action of Authorized Agent of Disclosed Principal

Ordinarily, the third person is not liable to the agent for a breach of contract that the agent has made with the third person on behalf of a disclosed principal.

11. Undisclosed and Partially Disclosed Principal

If the agent executed the contract without the third party's knowing both of the existence of the agency and the identity of the principal, and the third party breaches the contract, the agent may sue the third party for the breach.

In such instances, if the contract is a simple contract, the principal may also sue the third person even though the third person thought the contract was only with the agent.

If the contract is a commercial paper, the undisclosed principal not appearing on the instrument as a party may not bring an action to enforce the contract.

12. Agent Intending to Be Bound

If the third person knew that the agent was acting as an agent but the parties still intended that the agent should be personally bound by

---

[6] Mannish v Lacayo (Fla App) 496 So 2d 242 (1986).

the contract, the agent may sue the third person for breach of contract.

13. Execution of Contract

The principles that determine when an agent is liable to the third person because of the way in which a written contract was executed apply equally in determining when the third person is liable to the agent because of the way the contract is executed. If the agent could be sued by the third person, the third person can be sued by the agent.

14. Agent as Transferee

The agent may sue the third person for breach of the latter's obligation to the principal when the principal has assigned or otherwise transferred a claim or right to the agent. This is true whether the transfer was for the agent's own benefit or for the purpose of collecting the money and remitting it to the principal.

C. LIABILITY OF PRINCIPAL TO THIRD PERSON

The principal is liable to the third person for the properly authorized and executed contracts of the agent and, in certain circumstances, for the agent's unauthorized contracts.

15. Agent's Contracts

The liability of a principal to a third person on a contract made by an agent depends on the extent of disclosure of the principal and the form of the contract that is executed.

(a) SIMPLE CONTRACT WITH PRINCIPAL DISCLOSED. When a disclosed principal with contractual capacity authorizes or ratifies an agent's transaction with a third per-

son, and when the agent properly executes a contract with the third person, a binding contract exists between the principal and the third person. The principal and the third person may each sue the other in the event of a breach of the contract. The agent is not a party to the contract, is not liable for its performance, and cannot sue for its breach.[7]

The liability of a disclosed principal to a third person is not discharged by the fact that the principal gives the agent money with which to pay the third person. Consequently, the liability of a buyer for the purchase price of goods is not terminated by the fact that the buyer gave the buyer's agent the purchase price to remit to the seller.

(b) SIMPLE CONTRACT WITH PRINCIPAL PARTIALLY DISCLOSED. A partially disclosed principal is liable for a simple contract made by an authorized agent. The third person may recover from either the agent or the principal.

(c) SIMPLE CONTRACT WITH PRINCIPAL UNDISCLOSED. An undisclosed principal is liable for a simple contract made by an authorized agent. Although the third person initially contracted with the agent alone, the third person—on learning of the existence of the undisclosed principal—may sue that principal. In some states, the third person must elect whether to hold the agent or the previously undisclosed principal liable for the debt. Under this "election of remedies rule," if the third person elects to hold the principal liable, and the principal turns out to be insolvent, the third person may not collect from the agent.[8] The trend in the law is to reject this rule. The modern rule allows judgments to be entered simultaneously against the agent and the undisclosed principal. It allows a third person to collect from the agent, the principal, or both until the judgment is fully satisfied (joint and several liability).[9]

---

7 Levy v Gold & Co. Inc. 141 App Div 2d 511, 529 NYS2d 133 (1988).

8 Orruck v Crouse Realtors Inc. (Mo App) 823 SW2d 40 (1991).

(d) COMMERCIAL PAPER WITH PRINCIPAL UNDISCLOSED. An undisclosed principal whose name or description does not appear on commercial paper is not liable as a party thereto.[10] Thus, an undisclosed principal is not liable on commercial paper executed by an agent in the agent's own name.

16. Payment to Agent

When the third person makes payment to an authorized agent, the payment is deemed made to the principal. The principal must give the third person full credit for the payment made to the agent, even if the agent never remits or delivers the payment to the principal, as long as the third person made the payment in good faith and had no reason to know that the agent would be guilty of misconduct.[11]

Since apparent authority has the same legal effect as actual authority, a payment made to a person with apparent authority to receive the payment is deemed a payment to the apparent principal.

When payment by a debtor is made to a person who is not the actual or apparent agent of the creditor, such a payment does not discharge the debt unless that person in fact pays the money over to the creditor.

17. Agent's Statements

A principal is bound by a statement made by an agent while transacting business within the scope of authority.[12] This means that the principal cannot later contradict the statement of the agent and show that it is not true. Statements or declarations of an agent, in order to bind the principal, must be made at the time of performing the act to which they relate, or shortly thereafter.

18. Agent's Knowledge

The principal is bound by knowledge or notice of any fact that is acquired by an agent while acting within the scope of actual or apparent authority.

When a commercial paper is indorsed to the principal, and the agent acting for the principal has knowledge of a matter that would be a defense to the paper, such knowledge of the agent is imputed to the principal and bars the principal from being a holder in due course. When a fact is known to the agent of the seller, the sale is deemed made by the seller with knowledge of that fact. When an employee knows that there has been water pollution contrary to law, such knowledge is imputed to the corporate employer, even if no officer or director in fact had any knowledge of it.

The rule that the agents knowledge is imputed to the principal is extended in some cases to knowledge gained prior to the creation of the agency relationship. The notice and knowledge in any case must be based on reliable information. Thus, when the agent hears only rumors, the principal is not charged with notice.

(a) EXCEPTIONS. If the subject matter is outside the scope of the agent's authority, the agent is under no duty to inform the principal of the knowledge, and the principal is not bound by it.

The principal is not charged with knowledge of an agent: (1) when the agent is under a duty to another person to conceal such knowledge; (2) when the agent is acting adversely to

---

9 Crown Controls Inc. v Smiley, 110 Wash 2d 695, 756 P26 717 (1988).

10 UCC § § 3-401, 3-403 of the 1952 version and § § 3-401, 3-402 of the 1990 version. The 1990 version changes prior law when an agent or employee authorized to sign checks signs with only the agent's or employee's name. In such a case, if the check shows on its face that it is drawn on the account of the employer or principal, the employee or agent is not liable for the payment of the check. § 3-402(c) [1990].

11 This general rule of law is restated in some states by § 2 of the Uniform Fiduciaries Act, which is expressly extended by § 1 thereof to agents, partners, and corporate officers. Similar statutory provisions are found in a number of other states.

12 Potomac Leasing Co. v Bulger (Ala) 531 So 2d 307 (1988).

the principal's interest; or (3) when the third party acts in collusion with the agent for the purpose of cheating the principal. In such cases, it is not likely that the agent would communicate knowledge to the principal. The principal is therefore not bound by the knowledge of the agent.

(b) COMMUNICATION TO PRINCIPAL. As a consequence of regarding the principal as possessing the knowledge of the agent, when the law requires that a third person communicate with the principal, that duty may be satisfied by communicating with the agent. Thus, an offeree effectively communicates the acceptance of an offer to the offeror when the offeree makes such communication to the offeror's agent. An offeror effectively communicates the revocation of an offer to the offeree by communicating the revocation to the offeree's agent.

D. LIABILITY OF PRINCIPAL FOR TORTS AND CRIMES OF AGENT

Under certain circumstances, the principal may be liable for the torts or crimes of the agent or employee.

19. Vicarious Liability for Torts and Crimes

Assume that an agent or an employee causes harm to a third person. Is the principal or employer liable for this conduct? If the conduct constitutes a crime, can the principal or employer be criminally prosecuted? The answer is that in many instances, the principal or employer is liable civilly and may also be prosecuted criminally. That is, the principal or employer is liable although personally free from fault and not guilty of any wrong. This concept of imposing liability for the fault of another is known as **vicarious liability**.

The situation arises both when an employer has an employee and a principal has an agent who commits the wrong. The rules of law governing the vicarious liability of the principal and the employer are the same. In the interest of simplicity, this section will be stated in terms of employees acting in the course of employment. Remember that these rules are equally applicable to agents acting within the scope of their authority. As a practical matter, some situations will arise only with agents. For example, the vicarious liability of a seller for the misrepresentations made by a salesperson will arise only when the seller appointed an agent to sell. In contrast, both the employee hired to drive a truck and the agent being sent to visit a customer could negligently run over a third person. In many situations, a person employed by another is both an employee and an agent, and the tort is committed within the phase of "employee" work.

The rule of law imposing vicarious liability on an innocent employer for the wrong of an employee is also known as the doctrine of **respondeat superior**. In modern times, this doctrine can be justified on the grounds that the business should pay for the harm caused in the doing of the business, that the employer will be more careful in the selection of employees if made responsible for their actions, and that the employer may obtain liability insurance to protect against claims of third persons.

(a) NATURE OF ACT. The wrongful act committed by the employee may be a negligent act, an intentional act, a fraudulent act, or a violation of a government regulation. It may give rise only to civil liability of the employer, or it may also subject the employer to prosecution for crime.

(1) Negligent Act. Historically, the act for which liability would be imposed under the doctrine of respondeat superior was a negligent act committed within the scope of employment.

(2) Intentional Act. Under the common law, a master was not liable for an intentional tort committed by a servant. The modern law holds that an employer is liable for an intentional tort committed by an employee for the purpose of furthering the employer's business. In contrast, an employer is not liable for an intentional, unprovoked assault committed by an employee on a third person or customer of the employer because of

a personal grudge or for no reason. However, the employer will be held liable by the modern view when the employee's assault was committed in the belief that the employee was advancing the employer's interest.[13] For example, an employee may be hired to retake property, as in the case of an employee of a finance company hired to repossess automobiles on which installment payments have not been made. In such a case, the employer is generally liable for any unlawful force used by the employee in retaking the property or in committing an assault on a debtor.

(3) Fraud. The modern decisions hold

principal is not liable for the agent's fraud when the principal did not authorize or know of the fraud of the agent.

(4) Governmental Regulation. T h e employer may be liable because of the employee's violation of a governmental regulation. These regulations are most common in the areas of business and of protection of the environment. In such a case, the employer may be held liable for a penalty imposed by the government. In some cases, the breach of the regulation will impose liability on the employer in favor of a third person who is injured in consequence of the violation.

Figure 41-1 Liability for Torts of Agent or Employee

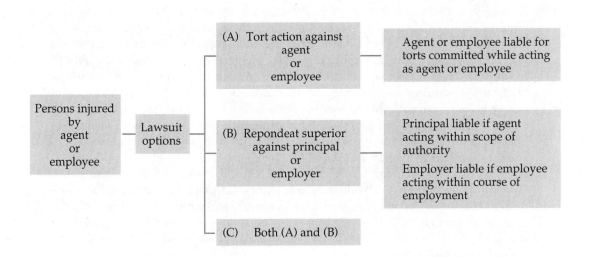

the employer liable for fraudulent acts or misrepresentations. The rule is commonly applied to a principal-agent relationship. To illustrate, when an agent makes fraudulent statements in selling stock, the principal is liable for the buyer's loss. In states that follow the common law rule of no liability for intentional torts, the

(b) COURSE OF EMPLOYMENT. T h e mere fact that a tort or crime is committed by an employee does not necessarily impose vicarious liability on the employer. It must also be shown that the employee was acting within the scope of authority if an agent, or in the course of employment if an employee.[14] If an

---

[13] Restatement, 2d Agency § 231; Carrero v NYC Housing Authority (DC NY) 668 F Supp 196 (1987).
[14] Rubin v Yellow Cab Co. 154 Ill App 3d 336, 107 Ill Dec 450, 507 NE2d 114 (1987).

employee was not acting within the scope of employment, there is no vicarious liability.

The *Studebaker* case raised questions of whether the tortfeasor was an employee of the

STUDEBAKER v NETTIE'S FLOWER GARDEN
(Mo App) 842 SW2d 227 (1992)

Judith Studebaker was injured when a van driven by James Ferry collided with her vehicle. She brought an action against Nettie's Flower Garden, Inc. (Nettie's) on a *respondeat superior* theory on the belief that Ferry was Nettie's employee at the time of the accident. Nettie's defended that Ferry was an independent contractor not an employee. From a judgment in favor of Studebaker for $125,000, Nettie's appealed.

CRANDALL, P. J. . . . Ferry delivered flowers for Nettie's from its main shop on Grand Avenue in the City of St. Louis. Ferry was paid, not by the hour, but at a rate of $2.50 to $3.00 per delivery. If there were no deliveries, he was not paid. He delivered only in an area of St. Louis which Nettie's designated as his territory. Nettie's required him to make two runs each day: one in the morning at 9:30 A.M.; one in the afternoon at 1:30 P.M. When he arrived at the shop, he set up his own route based upon the location of the deliveries in his area. He generally got to work at 8:00 A.M. to prepare for the morning run and at 12:00 P.M. to prepare for the afternoon run. Nettie's also required Ferry to stop by its shop in downtown St. Louis at St. Louis Centre before noon each day to pick up items which needed to be transported to the Grand Avenue shop. After this stop, Ferry proceeded to the Grand Avenue shop for his afternoon run. Nettie's paid Ferry $5.00 for this stop, whether or not there was anything for him to take to the Grand Avenue shop.

Ferry used his own van for the deliveries; Nettie's required that it be heated and air-conditioned to protect the flowers and plants. Although he did not wear a uniform, Nettie's directed that Ferry be neat in appearance and that he conduct himself in a certain manner when on the job. If his behavior or appearance fell below its standards, Nettie's reprimanded Ferry. Ferry paid his own expenses and received no fringe benefits from Nettie's.

On August 9, 1989, the date of the accident in question, Ferry made his morning run and then his mid-day stop at the downtown shop at about 11:00 A.M. There was nothing for him to transport to the Grand Avenue shop. After Ferry left the downtown shop, he stopped at a pawn shop to conduct personal business. He then proceeded to the Grand Avenue shop to prepare for his afternoon run. On the way to the Grand Avenue shop, at approximately 11:45 A.M., Ferry's van collided with plaintiff's automobile. . . .

Under the doctrine of respondeat superior an employer is liable for those negligent acts or omissions of his employee which are committed within the scope of his employment. . . Liability based on respondeat superior requires some evidence that a master-servant relationship existed between the parties. . . . The test to determine if respondeat superior applies to a tort is whether the person sought to be charged as master had the right or power to control and direct the physical conduct of the other in the performance of the act. . . . If there was no right to control there is no liability; for those rendering services but retaining control over their own movements are not servants. . . . The master-servant relationship arises when the person charged as master has the right to direct the method by which the master's service is performed. . . . . An additional inquiry is whether the person sought to be charged as the servant was engaged in the prosecution of his master's business and not simply whether the accident occurred during the time of employment. . . . Whether a party is liable under the doctrine of respondeat superior depends on the facts and circumstances in evidence in each particular case and no single test is conclusive of the issue of the party's interest in the activity and his right of control . . .

Nettie's first asserts that, when the accident in question occurred, Ferry was not driving his vehicle to serve Nettie's business interests. It argues that Ferry was on his own time, conducting his own business. . . .

Ferry's slight detour prior to the accident to conduct personal business did not mean that he was using his van exclusively for his independent purposes. . . . The object of Ferry's trip was not just to go to the pawn shop. At the time of the accident, Ferry was doing Nettie's business because he was returning to the Grand Avenue shop after making his routine mid-day stop at the downtown shop. This stop was so encompassed within his daily routine that it would be difficult to segregate it from his morning and afternoon runs.

There was sufficient evidence for the jury to determine that at the time of the accident, Ferry was engaged primarily in advancing the business interests of Nettie's and thus was acting within the scope of his employment. Nettie's first point is denied.

Nettie's further contends that there was no substantial evidence that Nettie's controlled or had the right to control Ferry at the time of the collision. Whether or not the right of control existed in a particular case is ordinarily a question of fact for the jury. . . .

In the instant action, Ferry furnished his own means of transportation; but it was mandatory that he have a vehicle to carry out his job responsibilities. Nettie's required that his vehicle be equipped with heating and air-conditioning systems. Nettie's also set standards for Ferry's dress and conduct while he was on the job, and monitored his compliance with these standards. In addition, although Ferry mapped out his own route to deliver the flowers, Nettie's gave him the list of customers and determined his territory. Nettie's directed Ferry to make the mid-day stop at its downtown shop on a daily basis and paid him for that stop. Ferry incorporated that stop into his route. The stop usually occurred after his morning run and prior to his return trip to the Grand Avenue shop for his afternoon run. In addition, Nettie's always paid him for this stop, whether or not he transported anything. There was substantial evidence from which a jury reasonably could have found that, at the time of the accident in question, Nettie's either controlled or had the right to control the manner in which Ferry performed the duties for which he was employed. Nettie's second point is denied.

[Judgment affirmed]

QUESTIONS

1. Did Nettie's control or have the right to control Ferry at the time of the collision?

2. Is not the fact that Ferry, just prior to the accident, had gone to a pawn shop compelling evidence he was using his van exclusively for his independent purposes and was not acting within the course of his employer's business?

3. Review the ethical principles set forth in the Preface and give your opinion on the ethics of businesses converting employees to independent contractors to reduce or eliminate costs, such as health and retirement benefits, overtime, and maintenance and proper insurance of motor vehicles.

defendant and had acted in furthering the employer's business.

(c) EMPLOYEE OF THE UNITED STATES. The Federal Tort Claims Act declares that the United States shall be liable vicariously whenever a federal employee driving a motor vehicle in the course of employment causes harm under such circumstances that a private employer would be liable. Contrary to the general rule, the statute exempts the employee driver from liability.

20. Negligent Hiring and Retention of Employees

In addition to a complaint against the employer based on the doctrine of *respondeat superior*, a lawsuit may often raise a second theory, that of negligent hiring or retention of an employee.[15] Unlike the *respondeat superior* theory by which the employer may be vicariously liable for the tort of an employee, the negligent hiring theory is based upon the negligence of the employer in the hiring process. Under the *respondeat superior* rule the employer is only liable for those torts committed within the scope of employment or in the furtherance of the employer's interests. The negligent hiring theory has been used to impose liability in cases where an employee commits an intentional tort, almost invariably outside the scope of employment, against a customer or the general public, where the employer knew or should have known that the employee was incompetent, violent, dangerous, or criminal.

(a) NEED FOR DUE CARE IN HIRING. An employer may be liable on a theory of negligent hiring when it is shown that the employer knew, or in the exercise of ordinary care should have known, that the job applicant would create an undue risk of harm to others in carrying out job responsibilities. Moreover, it must also be shown that the employer could have reasonably foreseen injury to the third party. Thus, an employer who knows of an employee's preemployment drinking problems and violent behavior may be liable to customers assaulted by that employee.[16]

Employers might protect themselves from liability in a negligent hiring case by having each prospective employee fill out an employment application form and then checking into the applicant's work experience, background, character, and qualifications. This would be evidence of due care in hiring. Generally, the scope of pre-employment investigation should correlate to the degree of opportunity the prospective employee would have to do harm to third persons. A minimum investigation consisting of the filling out of an application form and a personal interview would be satisfactory for the hiring of an outside maintenance person, but a full background inquiry would be necessary for the hiring of a security guard. However, such inquiry does not bar respondeat superior liability.

---

[15] Medina v Graham's Cowboy's Inc. (NM App) 827 P2d 859 (1992).

[16] Vadez v Warner 106 NM 305, 308, 742 P2d 517, 520 (1987).

(b) EMPLOYEES WITH CRIMINAL RE-
CORDS. The hiring of an individual with a
criminal record does not by itself establish the
tort of negligent hiring.[17] An employer who
knows that an applicant has a criminal record
has a duty to investigate to determine if the
nature of the conviction in relationship to the
job to be performed creates an unacceptable
risk to third persons. The *Island City Flying
Service v General Electric* case deals with the

ISLAND CITY FLYING SERVICE v GENERAL ELECTRIC

(Fla) 585 So 2d 274 (1991)

Steve Diezel, an employee of Island City Flying Service in Key West, Florida,
stole a General Electric Credit Corporation (GECC) aircraft and crashed the
plane while attempting to take off. GECC brought suit against Island City on
the theory that it had negligently hired Diezel as an employee, and it was
therefore legally responsible for Diezel's act of theft. Diezel had a military
prison record as a result of a drug offense and had been fired by Island City
twice previously but was immediately reinstated. Island City claimed that
the evidence was insufficient to establish that Island City had been negligent
in employing Diezel.

OVERTON, J. . . . The first question we must resolve is whether Island City is liable
for its negligent hiring or retention of Diezel under the facts established in this record. The Second District Court of Appeal, in its decision in *Williams v Feather Sound,
Inc.* 386 So 2d 1238 (Fla 2d DCA 1980), *review denied*, 392 So 2d 1374 (Fla 1981), articulated the legal principles for this type of action as follows:

*Most jurisdictions, including Florida, recognize that independent of the doctrine of respon-
deat superior, an employer is liable for the willful tort of his employee committed against a
third person if he knew or should have known that the employee was a threat to others. Many
of these cases involve situations in which the employer was aware of the employee's propen-
sity for violence prior to the time that he committed the tortious assault. The more difficult
question, which this case presents, is what, if any, responsibility does the employer have to
try to learn pertinent facts concerning his employee's character. . . .*

. . . To say that an employer can never hire a person with a criminal record at the risk
of being held liable for his tortious assault flies in the face of the premise that society
must make a reasonable effort to rehabilitate those who have gone astray. . . .

Id. *at 1241 (emphasis added).*

It is clear in the instant case that the district court relied almost entirely on
Diezel's military criminal record. We are concerned . . . that an employer who hires
a person with a criminal record will be at substantial risk of liability for any intentional tort of that employee because of that past criminal record, irrespective of its
connection to the conduct in issue. In *Feather Sound*, the type of criminal offense for

---

[17] Connes v Molalla Transportation Systems (Colo) 831 P2d 1316 (1992).

which the employee was previously convicted [breaking and entering and assault with intent to murder] was the same as the offense that he committed against the owner of the condominium unit after his employer placed him in a position to commit that act by giving him a passkey. That type of connection and foreseeability is not present in the instant case. Island City had reprimanded Diezel for failing to ground airplanes when he refueled them, for being late, and for taking off from work without authority. While Diezel had a military criminal record of imprisonment for a drug offense, there is no showing that there was any imprisonment for theft. Further, we do not believe that this record establishes that it was foreseeable that this employee would take a joy ride in an easily identified commercial commuter plane that he had never flown before. . . . Based on this record, Island City could not have foreseen Diezel's theft of this airplane. . .

[Judgment for Island City]

QUESTIONS

1. Did the court determine that an employer who hires a person with a criminal record must run the risk of liability for any subsequent intentional tort of that employee?
2. When will an employer be liable for negligently hiring and retaining an employee with a criminal record?
3. Was Island Flying Service liable for negligently hiring and retaining Diezel because of his prior criminal record? Why or why not?

question of whether an employer was liable for negligent hiring of an employee because of his past criminal record.

(c) NEGLIGENT RETENTION. Courts assign liability under negligent retention on a basis similar to negligent hiring.

A hospital is liable for negligent retention when it continues the staff privileges of a physician that it knew or should have known had sexually assaulted a female patient in the past.[18]

21. Agent's Crimes

The principal is liable for the crimes of the agent committed at the principal's direction. When not authorized, however, the principal is ordinarily not liable for an agent's crime merely because it was committed while the agent was otherwise acting within the scope of the latter's authority or employment.

As an exception to the rule of nonliability just stated, courts now hold an employer criminally liable when the employee has in the course of employment violated environmental protection laws, liquor sales laws, pure food laws, or laws regulating prices or prohibiting false weights. Thus, an employer may be held criminally responsible for an employee's sale of liquor to a minor in violation of the liquor law, even though the sale was not known to the employer and violated instructions given to the employee.

22. Owner's Liability for Acts of an Independent Contractor

If the work is done by an independent contractor rather than by an employee, the owner is not liable for harm caused by the contractor to

---

[18] Capithorne v Framingham Union Hospital, 401 Mass 860, 520 NE2d 139 (1988).

third persons or their property. Likewise, the owner is not bound by the contracts made by the independent contractor. The owner is ordinarily not liable for harm caused to third persons by the negligence of the employees of the independent contractor.

(a) EXCEPTIONS TO OWNER'S IMMUNITY. There is a trend toward imposing liability on the owner when the work undertaken by the independent contractor is inherently dangerous.[19] That is, the law is taking the position that if the owner wishes to engage in a particular activity, the owner must be responsible for the harm it causes. The owner cannot be insulated from such liability by the device of hiring an independent contractor to do the work.

Regardless of the nature of the activity, the owner may be liable for the torts and contracts of the independent contractor when the owner controls the conduct of the independent contractor.[20] For example, when the franchisor exercises a high degree of control over the franchisee, the relationship will be recognized as an agency relationship, and the franchisor is bound by the action of the franchisee.

In certain circumstances, such as providing security for a business, bill collecting, and repossessing collateral, there is an increased risk that torts may be committed by the individuals performing such duties. The trend of the law is to refuse to allow the use of an independent contractor for such work to insulate the employer.[21]

When the immunity based on the use of an independent contractor would make it possible for an enterprise using the contractor to avoid liability under copyright laws or to defraud others, the immunity will be ignored.

(b) UNDISCLOSED INDEPENDENT CONTRACTOR. In some situations, the owner appears to be doing the act in question because the existence of the independent contractor is not disclosed or apparent. This situation occurs most commonly when a franchisee does business under the name of the franchisor; when a concessionaire, such as a restaurant in a hotel, appears to be the hotel restaurant, although in fact it is operated by an independent concessionaire; or when the buyer of a business continues to run the business in the name of the seller. In such cases of an undisclosed independent contractor, it is generally held that the apparent owner (that is, the franchisor, the grantor of the concession, or the seller) is liable for the torts and contracts of the undisclosed independent contractor.

23. Enforcement of Claim by Third Person

A lawsuit by a third person may be brought against the agent or the principal if each is liable. In most states and in the federal courts, the plaintiff may sue either or both in one action when both are liable. If both are sued, the plaintiff may obtain a judgment against both, although the plaintiff is allowed to collect the full amount of the judgment only once.

E. TRANSACTIONS WITH SALES PERSONNEL

Many transactions with sales personnel do not result in a contract with the third person with whom the salesperson deals.

24. Soliciting and Contracting Agents

The giving of an order to a salesperson often does not give rise to a contract. Ordinarily, a salesperson is a **soliciting agent** whose authority is limited to soliciting offers from third persons and transmitting them to the principal for acceptance or rejection. Such an agent does not have authority to make a con-

---

[19] Christie v Ranieri and Sons 599 NYS2d 271 (1993).

[20] Parish v Omaha Public Power District, 242 Neb 783, 496 NW2d 902 (1993).

[21] General Finance Corp. v Smith (Ala) 505 So 2d 1045 (1987).

tract that will bind the principal to the third person. The employer of the salesperson is not bound by a contract until the employer accepts the order. And the third person (customer) may withdraw the offer at any time prior to acceptance.

In contrast, if the person with whom the buyer deals is a **contracting agent**, with authority to make contracts, there is by definition a binding contract between the principal and the customer from the moment that the agent agrees with the customer. That is, the contract arises when the agent accepts the customer's order.

SUMMARY

An agent of a disclosed principal who makes a contract within the scope of authority with a third person has no personal liability on the contract. It is the principal and third person who may each sue the other in the event of a breach. A person purporting to act as an agent for a principal warrants by implication that there is an existing principal with legal capacity and that the principal has authorized the agent to act. The person acting as an agent is liable for any loss caused the third person for breach of these warranties. An agent of a partially disclosed or an undisclosed principal is a party to the contract with the third person. The agent may enforce the contract against the third person and is liable for its breach. To avoid problems of interpretation, an agent should execute a contract "Principal, by Agent." Agents are liable for harm caused third persons by their fraudulent, malicious, or negligent acts.

An undisclosed or partially disclosed principal is liable to a third person on a simple contract made by an authorized agent. When a third person makes payment to an authorized agent, it is deemed paid to the principal.

A principal or employer is vicariously liable under the doctrine of respondeat superior for the torts of an agent or employee committed within the scope of authority or course of employment. The principal or employer may also be liable for some crimes committed in the course of employment. An owner is not liable for torts caused by an independent contractor to third persons or their property, unless the work given to the independent contractor is inherently hazardous.

A salesperson is ordinarily an agent whose authority is limited to soliciting offers (orders) from third persons and transmitting them to the principal. The principal is not bound until the principal accepts the order. The customer may withdraw an offer at any time prior to acceptance.

LAW IN PRACTICE

1. Know that if an agent fails to make known that he or she is acting as an agent of a principal, then the agent will be personally liable on the contracts made.

2. To avoid controversy as to whether or not an individual was acting as an agent rather than as a principal, an agent should execute instruments by signing the principal's name followed by "per" or "by" followed by the agent's name.

3. When you do not know the principal or its credit or performance standards, but you do know the agent, it may be prudent to insist that the agent assume personal obligations under the contract.

4. Since employers may be vicariously liable for the torts of their employees, it is prudent for employers to identify areas where there is a risk of liability, and then train their employees on how to avoid these risks. Employers should follow up training with supervision and, if needed, discipline to make sure that the risks are reduced.

5. Consider whether work should be performed by an independent contractor rather than your employees.

QUESTIONS AND CASE PROBLEMS

1. What social forces are affected by the rule that an agent receiving an overpayment is not liable for that amount when the payment was received in ignorance of the mistake and was remitted to the principal?

2. Myles Murphy was appointed by Cy Sinden, a famous developer, to purchase land for a shopping center near the intersection of I-95 and Route 1. Mary Mason, the property owner, contracted with Murphy for the sale of the property. Due to an economic downturn, Sinden was unable to provide the planned behind-the-scenes financing for the venture, and the contract was not performed. Mason's real estate experts determined that she lost $2 million because of the breach of contract. Mason also discovered that Sinden was "behind the deal." If Mason elects to sue Sinden, who turns out to be unable to pay the judgment because of the collapse of his business "empire," can she later bring suit against Murphy?

3. Compare a third party beneficiary contract with a contract made by an agent on behalf of an undisclosed principal.

4. What is the justification for the doctrine of respondeat superior?

5. Compare the liability of an agent's undisclosed principal to a third person on (a) a promissory note and (b) an oral contract.

6. Mills Electric Company signed a contract with S&S Horticulture Architects, a two-person landscaping partnership operated by Sullivan and Smyth, to maintain the grounds and flowers at the Mills Electric Company plant in Jacksonville, Florida. Mills checked references of S&S and found the company to be highly reputable. The contract set forth that S&S would select the flowers for each season and would determine when to maintain the lawns, so long as the lawns were properly maintained. The contract called for payments to be made to S&S on the first workday of each month, and the contract stipulated that "nothing herein shall make S&S an agent of the company." The contract also required that S&S personnel wear uniforms identifying them as employees of S&S. S&S had other accounts, but the large Mills Electric plant took up most of their time. While working on a terraced area near the visitors' entrance to the plant, Sullivan lost control of his large commercial mower, and the mower struck Gillespie, a plant visitor, causing serious injury to her. A witness heard Sullivan apologizing to Gillespie, saying "running that mower on the terrace is a two-person job." Gillespie brought suit against Mills Electric Company, contending Mills should be held vicariously liable? Decide.

7. A. D. McLeod contacted Thompson's agent and it was agreed that certain property would be leased for a period of two years at a rental of $700 per month for the first year and $800 per month for the second year. The first month's rent was paid with McLeod's personal check. McLeod and his associates manufactured mattresses on the premises under the trademark "Sleep" and the business was incorporated as Sleep System Inc. After some six months of operation during which the rent was paid by the corporation, McLeod informed Thompson that he had been "kicked out" of the company. When the subsequent rent was not paid, Thompson sued McLeod for the back rent. McLeod alleged that Thompson knew or should have known that McLeod was acting as an agent of Sleep Inc., and that after he was "kicked out" of the company it should have been very clear that he would no longer be responsible for rent. Thompson responded that if McLeod was an agent, he had an obligation to disclose that he was acting in a representative capacity when the lease was made, not six months later. Decide. *[McLeod v Thompson (Ala Civ App) 615 So 2d 90]*

8. On July 11, 1984, Jose Padilla was working as a vacation-relief route salesperson for Frito-Lay. He testified that he made a route stop at Sal's Beverage Shop. He was told by Mrs. Ramos that she was dissatisfied with Frito-Lay service and no longer wanted their products in the store. He asked if there was anything he could do to change her mind. She said no and told him to pick up his merchandise. He took one company-owned merchandise rack to his van and was about to pick up another rack when Mr. Ramos said that the rack had been given to him by the regular route salesperson. Padilla said the route salesperson had no authority to give away Frito-Lay racks. A confrontation occurred over the rack, and Padilla pushed Mr. Ramos against the cash register, injuring Ramos' back. Frito-Lay has a company policy, clearly communicated to all employees, that prohibits them from getting involved in any type of physical confrontation with a customer. Frito-Lay contended that Padilla was not acting within the course and scope of his employment when the pushing incident took place, and that the company was therefore not liable to Ramos. Ramos contended that Frito-Lay was responsible for the acts of its employee Padilla. *[Frito-Lay Inc. v Ramos (Tex Civ App) 770 SW2d 887]*

9. Jason Lasseigne, a Little League baseball player, was seriously injured at a practice session when he was struck on the head by a poorly thrown baseball from a team member, Todd Landry. The league was organized by American Legion Post 38. Claude Cassel and Billy Johnson were the volunteer coaches of the practice session. The Lasseignes brought suit on behalf of Jason against Post 38, claiming that the coaching was negligent and that Post 38 was vicariously liable for the harm caused by such negligence. Post 38 contends that it had no right to control the work of the volunteer coaches or the manner in which practices were conducted, and as a result should not be held vicariously liable for the actions of the coaches. Decide. *[Lasseigne v American Legion Post 38 (La App) 543 So 2d 1111]*

10. Moritz was a guest at the Pines Hotel. While she was sitting in the lobby, Brown, a hotel employee, dropped a heavy vacuum cleaner on her knee. When she complained, he insulted her and hit her with his fist, knocking her unconscious. She sued the hotel for damages. Was the hotel liable? *[Moritz v Pines Hotel, Inc. 53 App Div 2d 1020, 383 NYS2d 704]*

11. Allan and Joan Butler purchased a television set from Rex Radio and Television, Inc. (Rex) on October 24, 1988 by a consumer credit contract with Rex. The contract provided that payment in full was required within 90 days and that no interest would be charged if the balance owed was paid within this period. The Butlers had asked Rex's salesperson what would happen if they did not pay off the account within 90 days, and they were informed that ITT Financial Services would set up a payment plan and that forms were available at the store. They asked what interest ITT charged. The salesperson responded, "I'm not sure, but it is somewhere between 10 and 15 percent." When the Butlers did not pay within 90 days, ITT informed the Butlers that if they wished to finance the balance owed on the contract with ITT, the annual interest rate would be 27 percent. The Butlers refinanced the debt with ITT and later sued ITT for fraud, claiming that Rex's salesperson was the agent of ITT when the salesperson made the statement on interest rates. *[Butler v Aetna Finance Co. (Ala) 587 So 2d 308]*

12. The Bay State Harness Horse Racing and Breeding Association conducted horse races. Music was supplied for the patrons by an independent contractor hired by the association. Some of the music played was subject to a copyright held by Famous Music Corporation. The playing of that music was a violation of the copyright unless royalties were paid to Famous Music. None were paid, and Famous Music sued the association. It raised the defense that the violation had been committed by an independent contractor that was specifically instructed not to play Famous Music's copyrighted material. Decide. *[Famous Music Corporation v Bay State Harness Horse Racing and Breeding Association, Inc. (CA1 Mass) 554 F2d 1213]*

13. Steven Trujillo was told by the assistant door manager of Cowboys Bar "to show up to work tonight in case we need you as a doorman." He came to the bar that evening, wearing a jacket with the bar logo on it. Trujillo "attacked" Rocky Medina in the parking lot of the bar causing him serious injury. Prior to working for Cowboys, Trujillo was involved in several fights at that bar and in their parking lot; and Cowboys knew of these matters. Medina sued Cowboys on two theories of liability (1) respondeat superior and (2) negligent hiring of Trujillo. Cowboys defends that the respondeat superior theory should be dismissed because the assault was clearly not within the course of his employment. Concerning the negligent hiring theory, Cowboys asserts that Trujillo was not on duty that night as a doorman. Decide. *[Medina v Graham's Cowboys Inc. (NM App) 827 P2d 859]*

14. Neal Rubin, while driving his car in Chicago, inadvertently blocked the path of a Yellow Cab Co. taxi driven by Robert Ball, causing the taxi to swerve and hit Rubin's car. Angered by Rubin's driving, Ball got out of his cab and hit Rubin over the head and shoulders with a metal pipe. Rubin sued the Yellow Cab Co. for the damages caused by this beating, contending that the employer was vicariously liable for the beating under the doctrine of respondeat superior, since the beating occurred in furtherance of the employer's business, which was to obtain fares without delay. The company defended that Ball's beating of Rubin was not an act undertaken to further the employer's business. Is the employer liable under respondeat superior? *[Rubin v Yellow Cab Co. 154 Ill App 3d 336, 107 Ill Dec 450, 507 NE2d 114]*

15. Brazilian & Columbian Co. (B&C), a food broker, ordered 40 barrels of olives from Mawer-Gulden-Annis, Inc. (MGA). MGA's shipping clerk was later told to make out the bill of lading to B&C's customer, Pantry Queen; the olives were shipped directly to Pantry Queen. Eight days after the delivery, the president of B&C wrote MGA to give it the name of its principal, Pantry Queen, and advised MGA to bill the principal directly. Pantry Queen was unable to pay for the olives, and MGA sued B&C for payment. B&C defended that it was well known to MGA that B&C was a food broker (agent), and the olives were shipped directly to the principal by MGA. It stated that as an agent it was not a party to the contract and was thus not liable. Decide. [*Mawer-Gulden-Annis, Inc. v Brazilian & Columbian Coffee Co.* 49 Ill App 2d 400, 199 NE2d 222]

CHAPTER 42

REGULATION OF EMPLOYMENT

LEARNING OBJECTIVES

After studying this chapter, you will be able to:
1. *Explain the contractual nature of the employment relationship.*
2. *Identify the five employer unfair labor practices.*
3. *Identify the nine union unfair labor practices.*
4. *State the four ways in which ERISA provides protection for the pension interests of employees.*
5. *Set forth the eligibility requirements for unemployment compensation.*
6. *Explain how the Occupational Safety and Health Act is designed to reach the goal of ensuring safe and healthful working conditions.*
7. *List the three types of benefits provided by workers' compensation statutes.*

Employment law involves the law of contracts and the law established by lawmakers, courts, and administrative agencies.

A. THE EMPLOYMENT RELATIONSHIP

The relationship of an employer and an employee exists when, pursuant to an express or implied agreement of the parties, one person, the **employee**, undertakes to perform services or to do work under the direction and control of another, the **employer**, for compensation. In the older cases, this relationship was called the master-servant relationship.

1. Characteristics of Relationship

An employee is hired to work under the control of the employer. An employee differs from an agent, who is to negotiate or make contracts with third persons on behalf of and under the control of a principal. However, a person may be both an employee and an agent for the other party. An employee also differs from an independent contractor, who is to perform a contract independent of, or free from, control by the other party.[1]

2. Creation of Employment Relationship

The relationship of employer and employee can be created only with the consent of both parties. Generally, the agreement of the parties is a contract. It is therefore subject to all of the principles applicable to contracts. The contract will ordinarily be express. It may be implied, such as when the employer accepts the rendering of services that a reasonable person would recognize as being rendered with the expectation of receiving compensation.

(a) INDIVIDUAL EMPLOYMENT CONTRACTS. As in contracts generally, both parties must assent to the terms of the employment contract. Subject to statutory restrictions, the parties are free to make a contract on any terms they wish.

(b) COLLECTIVE BARGAINING CONTRACTS. Collective bargaining contracts govern the rights and obligations of employers and employees in many private and public areas of employment. Under collective bargaining, representatives of the employees bargain with a single employer or a group of employers for an agreement on wages, hours, and working conditions for the employees. The agreement worked out by the representatives of the employees, usually union officials, is generally subject to a ratification vote by the employees. Terms usually found in collective bargaining contracts are: (1) identification of the work belonging exclusively to designated classes of employees; (2) wage and benefits clauses; (3) promotion and layoff clauses, which are generally tied in part to seniority; (4) a management's rights clause; and (5) a grievance procedure. A grievance procedure provides a means by which persons claiming that the contract was violated or that they were disciplined or discharged without just cause may have their cases decided by impartial labor arbitrators.

3. Duration and Termination of Employment Contract

In many instances, the employment contract does not state any time or duration. In such a case, it may be terminated at any time by either party. In contrast, the employment contract may expressly state that it shall last for a specified period of time; an example would be a contract to work as general manager for five years. In some instances, a definite duration may be implied by the circumstances.

---

[1] Bill Rivers Trailers Inc. v Miller (Fla App) 489 So 2d 1139 (1986).

(a) EMPLOYMENT-AT-WILL DOC-
TRINE AND DEVELOPING EXCEPTIONS.
Ordinarily, a contract of employment may be
terminated in the same manner as any other
contract. If it is to run for a definite period of
time, the employer cannot terminate the contract at an earlier date without justification. If
the employment contract does not have a definite duration, it is terminable at will. Under
the **employment-at-will doctrine**, the employer has historically been allowed to terminate the employment contract at any time for
any reason or for no reason.[2] Recent court decisions—and in some instances, statutes—
have changed the rule in some states by
limiting the power of the employer to dis-

charge the employee. Some courts have
carved out exceptions to the employment-at-
will doctrine when the discharge violates an
established public policy.

Public policy exceptions are often made to
the employment-at-will doctrine when an employee is discharged in retaliation for insisting
that the employer comply with the state's food
and drug act[3] or for filing a workers' compensation claim.[4]

The *Winters* case deals with the issue of
whether or not a whistleblower is protected
from retaliatory discharge by an employer under the public policy exception to the employment-at-will doctrine.

WINTERS v HOUSTON CHRONICLE PUBLISHING CO.

795 SW2d 723 (Tex 1990)

In April 1977, Richard Winters was hired by the Houston Chronicle Publishing Co. as an at-will employee for a lower-level management position. In
January 1986, he told upper-level management that *The Chronicle* was falsely
reporting an inflated number of paid subscriptions, that several employees
were involved in inventory theft, and that his supervisor offered him an opportunity to participate in a kickback scheme with the manufacturers of
plastic bags. Winters did not report his charges to law enforcement agencies.
He was terminated some six months after his report to upper management.
Winters sued *The Chronicle*, alleging that the sole cause of his termination
was his report of the illegal activities of his fellow employees. The employer
contended that there is no rule of law that gives relief for private employees
who are discharged for reporting illegal activities to their employers. The
district court dismissed the action; the court of appeals affirmed; and the
matter was appealed to the state supreme court.

GONZALEZ, J. . . . The long-standing rule in Texas is that employment for an indefinite term may be terminated at will and without cause. . . . To date, this court has
created only two exceptions. In *Sabine Pilot Service, Inc. v Hauck*, 687 SW2d 733, 735
(Tex. 1985), we recognized a narrow exception for an employee discharged "for the
sole reason that the employee refused to perform an illegal act." Winters does not fit

---

[2] Brown v Hammond (Ed Pa) 810 F Supp 644 (1993).

[3] Sheets v Teddys Frosted Foods, 179 Conn 471, 427 A2d 385 (1980).

[4] Hartlein v Illinois Power Co. 209 Ill App 3d 948, 154 Ill Dec 520, 568 NE2d 520 (1991).

within the *Sabine Pilot* exception because he was not unacceptably forced to choose between risking criminal liability or being discharged from his livelihood. We have also recognized another exception for an employee who demonstrates that the principal reason for discharge was the employer's desire to avoid contributing or paying benefits under the employer's pension fund. . . .

The legislature has also placed restrictions upon the at will employment doctrine. In protecting employees who report illegal activities in the workplace, the legislature has enacted protection for a limited class of employees. Public employees are protected from retaliation for reporting, in good faith, violations of law to an appropriate law enforcement agency. Certain private sector employees are also protected. A nursing home employee has a cause of action against the institution or its owner if he or she is terminated for reporting abuse or neglect of a resident of the institution. An employer who uses hazardous chemicals may not discharge an employee who reports a violation of the Hazard Communication Act. Finally, an employer cannot retaliate against an employee for reporting violations of the Commission on Human Rights Act.

Winters admits that he does not come within any of the statutory or common law exceptions to the at will doctrine. He is asking this court to recognize a cause of action for private employees who are discharged for reporting illegal activities.

We decline to do so at this time on these facts. . . .

[Judgment affirmed]

DOGGETT, J., concurring opinion.* . . . By stating that it declines to recognize such a cause of action "at this time on these facts," the court leaves the clear implication that it will do so at a future time on other facts. This conclusion is strengthened by the court's reference to the many states that "protect private sector employees who report illegal activity in the workplace."** I very reluctantly concur with the court that this may not be the most appropriate case in which to announce an important new rule of law.

To offer guidance to both employers and employees, I write to define the elements of a cause of action for employees who suffer employer retaliation for exposing from within activities in the workplace that have a probable adverse effect upon the public. . . .

In creating such a cause of action, the judiciary must be mindful of our long adherence to the employment-at-will doctrine in Texas, recognizing the right of an employer to fire employees at any time with or without cause. *East Line & R.R.R. Co. v Scott*, 72 Tex. 71, 10 SW 99 (1888). We must respect the need for employers to make difficult managerial decisions vital to the effective operation of business organizations without unnecessary judicial intrusion. This court has nonetheless been willing to carve out narrow exceptions when the employer's primary motivation for termination of employment directly contradicted important social interests. Thus, in *Sabine Pilot* we refused to condone the firing of an employee if grounded upon a refusal to perform an illegal act even though such conduct might have produced a financial benefit to the employer.

We have been urged to demonstrate judicial restraint by deferring employee protection exclusively to the legislature. Yet the absence of safeguards stems largely from this court's recognition of the at-will employment doctrine in *East Line* over a century ago. In carving out narrow exceptions to this rule, the court balances precariously between the need for stability and continuity in the law and the need to preserve the law's vitality and applicability in a changing society. Here, no societal interest can be advanced that would support an employer's retaliation against an employee who reported activities harmful to the public. In this situation, judicial failure to modify the law constitutes neither restraint nor neutrality, but rather an active participation in perpetuating injustice. This is particularly true when the judiciary can craft a narrow exception that protects the interests of responsible, law-abiding employers while holding accountable those whose activities threaten the public interest.

The very case that Respondent urges as dispositive, *Maus v National Living Centers, Inc.*, 633 SW2d 674 (Tex App—Austin 1982, writ ref'd n.r.e.), demonstrates the shocking result of a judicial refusal to protect workers who report injurious activities. A person described by that court as "a dedicated worker who often worked double shifts and took an active interest in the patients" was discharged, allegedly for complaining to her employer concerning the neglect and poor quality of care provided nursing homes residents. *Id*. at 675. One of her complaints concerned the death of a patient for whom her employer allegedly refused to call a doctor. Moreover, she claimed her firing violated a "substantial, stated public policy" embodied in a statute providing criminal penalties for failure to report cases of abuse and neglect. *Id*. Not finding a specific legislative remedy for the dismissal, the court apparently viewed itself as incapable of altering a rule laid down a century before. Seven years and unknown numbers of dismissed employees or unreported observations of nursing home patient neglect later, the legislature finally adopted protection for such employees.

The judiciary should not ignore those unscrupulous employers who wield the powerful weapon of the pink slip to intimidate workers into silence in order to conceal and perpetuate activities in the workplace that endanger the public. Fortunately, this court has recognized that waiting for the legislature is not the only alternative available, as it is highly appropriate "to judicially amend a judicially created doctrine." *Sabine Pilot*, 687 SW2d at 735. Mindful of this responsibility, our courts must refine and modify this judicially created employment-at-will doctrine to prevent dismissal of those who seek, by internal or external report, to bring to a halt activities in the workplace that have a probable adverse effect upon the public. . . .

This court has been asked to recognize a cause of action for "whisteblowers." The term is derived from the act of an English bobby blowing his whistle upon becoming aware of the commission of a crime to alert other law enforcement officers and the public within the zone of danger. . . .

While many contemporary definitions of the term have been advanced, no one definition captures the essence of a "whistle-blower"—the public need and benefit, the conflict of loyalties to the employer and to the public good, and the corresponding personal anguish involved. One definition states that whistleblowing is "the act of a man or woman who, believing that the public interest overrides the interest of the organization he serves, publicly 'blows the whistle' if the organization is involved in corrupt, illegal, fraudulent, or harmful activity."

. . . Some business leaders acknowledge that the free enterprise system itself is a beneficiary of whistleblowing; a former president of the National Association of Manufacturers, Alexander B. Trowbridge, has stated that:

The modern corporation must encourage the honest and concerned employee to blow the whistle on illegalities and actual malpractices. It must give the whistle blower access to the people who can change things. And it must protect him against recrimination. . . . It must create an atmosphere in which the individual, when confronted with something clearly illegal, unethical or unjust, can feel free to speak up—and to bring the problem to the attention of those high enough up in the corporation to solve it. . .

Among the more highly publicized events where whistleblowing was a factor are Watergate, Love Canal, Three Mile Island and the *Challenger* shuttle disaster. Whistleblower Ernest Fitzgerald achieved national attention in his almost single-handed effort to expose waste and intentional cost overruns by defense contractors. *See generally* [M. Glazer and P. Glazer,] *The Whistleblowers, [Exposing Corruption in Government and Industry* (1989)] at 21-24; *Report on Professional Responsibility*, [(R. Nader, P. Petkas, & K. Blackwell eds. 1972)] at 39-54. Prominent engineers have similarly warned management at major corporations of alleged product defects only to see their warnings ignored, accidents and deaths occur and costly litigation begin.

In a democratic, free enterprise system, a commitment to whistleblowing represents a fundamental confidence in the ability of individuals to make a difference. Society can never eradicate wrongdoing, but it can shield from retaliation those citizens who, urged on by their integrity and social responsibility, speak out to protect its well-being. . .

The elements of this new cause of action must be carefully crafted to accomplish a dual objective—noninterference with the legitimate interest of responsible, law-abiding employers in making ordinary managerial decisions and protection for those employees who are willing to put their jobs on the line to avoid harm to the public. Recognizing the broad discretion accorded employers to make independent, good faith judgments about employees, trial courts should effectively exercise their power to render summary judgment when appropriate so that all internal management disputes are not inflated into lengthy jury trials.

To establish a prima facie cause of action, an individual must prove by a preponderance of the evidence that the principal motivation for employer retaliation was that employee's report, either internally or publicly, of activities within the workplace that would have a probable adverse effect upon the public. Additionally, there must be a two-part showing of good faith: (1) that the employee undertook to report the activities in the workplace in good faith rather than as a result of some less admirable motive such a malice, spite, jealousy or personal gain and (2) the employee had reasonable cause to believe that the activities would have a probable adverse effect upon the public. . .

. . . The employer may refute the causation element by proving dismissal for reasons other than the act of whistleblowing. Employers remain free under present Texas law to terminate employment relationships for no reasons, or for cause, but not for a very limited class of unconscionable reasons, as determined by judicial decision and statute.

The object of the employee's report should not be limited to some outside official, as Respondent recommends. Rather, internal reporting of wrongdoing should be encouraged, so that an employer may have an opportunity to investigate and remedy problems before involving outside authorities. Defining the cause of action in this manner reflects our confidence that most employers are eager to avoid conduct that is potentially injurious to the public. To impose an outside reporting requirement would deprive them of an opportunity to correct, internally and without unnecessary publicity, harmful conduct which may be the result of inadvertence or a lack of communication. The underlying policy goals to avert harm to the public may be just as effectively served by communication within an organization to achieve prompt compliance as they are by public disclosure.

With confidence in the power of a few courageous individuals to make a lasting contribution to improving our public and private institutions, I have outlined appropriate elements for other courts throughout Texas to employ in affording the shield from retaliation that employees need now. By applying this cause of action, the trial courts can both provide whistleblowers with vital protection and assist this court in meeting its responsibilities. It can only be hoped that the availability of legal recourse for employer retaliation will give a few employees, agonizing in silence as to whether to alert the public to danger, "the courage to take the final extra step."

*A concurring opinion reaches the same result as the majority opinion, but for different reasons.

**Other jurisdictions, through legislative or judicial action, protect private sector employees who report illegal activity in the workplace. [Here the court lists court decisions from 14 states and statutes from 12 other states that protect from retaliation private sector employees who report illegal activities in the workplace.]

QUESTIONS

1. Does the *Winters* decision create a new cause of action for whistleblowers?
2. Must a court wait for the legislature to carve out an exception to the employment-at-will doctrine to protect private employees who are discharged for reporting illegal activities from retaliatory discharge by their employer?
3. Why should the law protect private sector whistleblowers from retaliation by their employers?
4. Review the guidelines to "Business Ethics" in the Preface of this book, especially the ethical principles of "loyalty," "doing no harm," and "whistleblowing." Does an employee have an ethical obligation to inform a responsible corporate official of wrongdoing before going public?

The obligation to act in good faith and deal fairly has been held by some courts to bar the employers from terminating an at-will contract when this is done to benefit the employer financially at the expense of the employee. Thus, an employer may not discharge an at-will employee to avoid paying commissions or pension benefits to the employee.[5]

The contract of employment may be construed to bar a discharge of the employee except for cause. If so, good cause would then be required for the discharge of an at-will employee. Also, written personnel policies used as guidelines for the employer's supervisors have been interpreted as being part of the employment contract. These policies have thus been held to restrict the employer's right to discharge at-will employees without proof of good or just cause. Moreover, employee handbooks that provide for "proper notice and investigation" before termination may bar employers from terminating employees without providing such notice and an investigation.[6]

Other courts still follow the common law at-will rule because they believe that a court should not rewrite the contract of the parties to provide employee protection that was never

---

[5] Metcalf v Intermountain Gas Co. (Idaho) 778 P2d 744 (1989).

[6] Duldulao v St. Mary Nazareth Hospital Center, 115 Ill 2d 482, 106 Ill Dec 8, 505 NE2d 314 (1987). But see Bankey v Storer Broadcasting Co. 149 Mich 401, 443 NW2d 112 (1989).

intended. Some courts favor the view limiting the employer from making an at-will discharge but will not adopt such a rule by decision, since it is felt that such a significant change should be made (if at all) by the legislature.[7]

If an employment contract provides that an employee can be fired only for "good cause" or "just cause," an at-will discharge will not be allowed.

(b) JUSTIFIABLE DISCHARGE. An employer may be justified in discharging an employee because of the employee's (1) nonperformance of duties, (2) misrepresentation or fraud in obtaining the employment, (3) disobedience to proper directions, (4) disloyalty, (5) theft or other dishonesty, (6) possession or use of drugs or intoxicants, (7) misconduct, or (8) incompetence.

Employers generally have the right to lay off employees because of economic conditions, including a lack of work. Such actions are sometimes referred to as reductions in force or RIFs. However, employers must be very careful not to make layoffs based on age, for that is a violation of the Age Discrimination in Employment Act.

In some states, a "service letter" statute requires an employer on request to furnish to a discharged employee a letter stating the reason for the discharge.

4. Duties of the Employee

The duties of an employee are determined primarily by the contract of employment with the employer. The law also implies certain obligations.

(a) SERVICES. Employees are under the duty to perform such services as may be required by the contract of employment.

(b) TRADE SECRETS. An employee may be given confidential trade secrets by the em-

ployer. The employee must not disclose this knowledge to others. An agreement by the employee to refrain from disclosing trade secrets is binding. Even in the absence of such an agreement, an employee is prohibited from disclosing the trade secrets of the employer. If the employee violates this obligation, the employer may enjoin the use of the information by the employee and by any person to whom it has been disclosed by the employee.

Former employees who are competing with their former employer may be enjoined from using information about suppliers and customers that they obtained while employees, when this information is of vital importance to the employer's business. This relief is denied if the information is not important or not secret.

(c) INVENTIONS. Employment contracts commonly provide that the employer will own any invention or discovery made by the employee, whether during work hours, after work hours, or for a period of one or two years after leaving the employment. In the absence of an express or implied agreement to the contrary, the inventions of an employee belong to the employee. This is true even though the employee used the time and property of the employer in the discovery. However, in this case the employer has the "shop right" to use the invention without cost in its operations.

5. Rights of the Employee

The rights of an employee are determined by the contract of employment and the law, as declared by courts, lawmakers, and administrative agencies.

(a) COMPENSATION. The rights of an employee with respect to compensation are governed in general by the same principles that apply to the compensation of an agent. In the absence of an agreement to the contrary, when an employee is discharged, whether for

---

[7] D'Avino v Trachtenburg, 149 App Div 2d 401, 539 NYS2d 755 (1989). Fiammetta v St. Francis Hospital, 168 App Div 2d 556, 562 NYS2d 777 (1990).

cause or not, the employer must pay wages down to the expiration of the last pay period.[8] State statutes commonly authorize employees to sue employers for wages improperly withheld and to recover penalties and attorneys' fees. In addition to hourly wages, payments due for vacations and certain bonuses are considered "wages" under the state statutes.[9]

(b) FEDERAL WAGE AND HOUR LAW.

Workers at enterprises engaged in interstate commerce are covered by the Fair Labor Standards Act (FLSA)[10], popularly known as the Wage and Hour Act. These workers cannot be paid less than a specified minimum wage. The FLSA has been amended to cover domestic service workers, including housekeepers, cooks, and full-time baby-sitters. Executive, administrative, and professional employees, and outside salespersons are exempt from both the minimum wage and overtime provisions of the law.

(1) Subminimum Wage Provisions. The FLSA allows for the employment of full-time students at institutions of higher education at wage rates below the statutory minimum. Also, individuals whose productive capacity is impaired by age, physical or mental deficiency, or injury may also be employed at less than the minimum wage in order to prevent the curtailment of work opportunities for these individuals. However, a special certificate is needed by the employer from the Department of Labor's Wage and Hour Division, which has offices throughout the United States.

(2) Wage issues. Deductions made from wages due to cash or merchandise shortages, or for tools of the trade are not legal if they reduce wages below the minimum wage. Or, should an employer require employees to provide uniforms or tools of their own, to the extent that the expenses for these items reduce wages below the minimum wage, such is a violation of the law.

(3) Overtime pay. Overtime must be paid at a rate of $1^1/_2$ times the employee's regular rate of pay for each hour worked in excess of forty hours in a work week.

(4) Child labor provisions. The FLSA child labor provisions are designed to protect the educational opportunities of minors and prohibit their employment in occupations detrimental to their health and well-being. The FLSA restricts hours of work for minors under 16 and lists hazardous occupations too dangerous for minors to perform.

B. LABOR RELATIONS LAWS

Even if employers are not presently unionized, they are subject to certain obligations under federal labor relations law. It is important to both unionized and non-unionized employers to know their rights and obligations under the National Labor Relations Act.[11] Employee rights and obligations are also set forth in this act. The Labor Management Reporting and Disclosure Act regulates internal union affairs.

6. The National Labor Relations Act

The National Labor Relations Act (NLRA), passed in 1935, was based on the federal government's power to regulate interstate commerce granted in Article 1, Section 8 of the Constitution. Congress, in enacting this law, explained that its purpose was to remove obstructions to commerce caused by some employers who denied their employees the right to join unions and refused to accept the procedure of collective bargaining.[12] Congress stated that these obstructions resulted in

---

[8] Lorentz v Coblentz (La App) 600 So 2d 1376 (1992).

[9] Knutson v Snyder Industries, Inc. 221 Neb 374, 436 NW2d 496 (1989).

[10] Fair Labor Standards Act. PL 75-718, 52 Stat 1060, 29 USC §201 et seq.

[11] Note that in the *Lechmere* and *Transportation Management* cases, presented in this section, the employers were not unionized.

[12] Section 1 of the NLRA, 29 USC §141 et seq.

depression of wages, poor working conditions, and diminution of purchasing power.

Section 7 of the amended NLRA is the heart of the act, and states in part that: "Employees shall have the right to self organization . . . to bargain collectively through representatives of their own choosing and to engage in other concerted activities for the purpose of collective bargaining or other mutual aid or protection. . . and shall have the right to refrain from such activities. . ."

Section 8 of the NLRA sets contains employer and union unfair labor practices, set forth in Figure 42-1, and authorizes the National Labor Relations Board to conduct proceedings to stop such practices.

The act applies to private sector employers with gross income of $500,000 or more. The Railway Labor Act applies to employees of railroad and air carriers.

Figure 42-1 Employer and Union Unfair Labor Practices

Unfair Labor Practices Charges Against Employers	Section of the NLRA
1. Restrain or coerce employees in the exercise of their rights under Section 7; threat of reprisals or promise of benefits	8 (a) (1); 8 (c)
2. Dominate or interfere with the formation or administration of a labor organization or contribute financial or other support to it.	8 (a) (2) 8 (a) (2)
3. Discriminate in regard to hire or tenure of employment or any term or condition of employment in order to encourage or discourage membership in any labor organization.	8 (a) (3)
4. Discharge or otherwise discriminate against employees because they have given testimony under the Act.	8 (a) (4)
5. Refuse to bargain collectively with representatives of its employees.	8 (a) (5)

Unfair Labor Practices Charges Against Employees	Section of the NLRA
1. Restrain or coerce employees in exercise of their rights under Section 7.	8 (b) (1) (A)
2. Restrain or coerce an employer in the selection of its representatives.	8 (b) (1) (B)
3. Cause or attempt to cause an employer to discriminate against an employee.	8 (b) (2)
4. Refuse to bargain collectively with the employer.	8 (b) (3)
5. Require employees to pay excessive fees for membership.	8 (b) (5)
6. Engage in "featherbed practices" of seeking pay for services not performed.	8 (b) (6)
7. Secondary boycotts (banned, except for publicity proviso).	8 (b) (4)
8. Recognitional and organizational picketing by an uncertified union.	8 (b) (7)
9. Hot cargo agreements, except for construction and garment industries	8 (e)

7. National Labor Relations Board

Administration of the NLRA is entrusted to the five-member National Labor Relations Board (NLRB or Board) and the General Counsel of the Board. The General Counsel is responsible for investigating and prosecuting all unfair labor practice cases. The five member Board's major function is to decide the unfair labor practice cases brought before it by the General Counsel.

The Board is also responsible for conducting representation and decertification elections. This responsibility is delegated to regional directors in the 32 regional offices located throughout the United States, who make determinations on (1) the appropriateness of each proposed bargaining unit for the purpose of collective bargaining, (2) investigate petitions for the certification or decertification of unions, and (3) conduct elections to determine the choice of the majority of those employees voting in the election. Should a majority of the employees voting select a union, the NLRB will certify that union as the exclusive representative of all employees within the unit for the purpose of bargaining with the employer to obtain a contract with respect to wages, hours, and other conditions of employment.

8. Election Conduct

The Board has promulgated preelection rules restricting electioneering activities so that the election will express the true desire of employees. The National Labor Relations Act prohibits employer interference or coercion during the preelection period. The act also prohibits employer statements during this period that contain threats of reprisal or promises of benefits.

The Board prohibits all electioneering activities at polling places, and has formulated a "24-hour rule," which prohibits both unions and employers from making speeches to captive audiences within 24 hours of an election. The rationale is to preserve free elections and prevent any party from obtaining undue advantage.

9. Union Activity on Private Property

While Section 7 of the NLRA gives employees the statutory right to self-organization, employers have the undisputed right to make rules to maintain discipline in their establishments. Generally speaking, employers may prohibit union solicitation by employees during work periods. During nonworking time employers may prohibit activity and communications only if legitimate efficiency and safety reasons exist and if the prohibitions are not manifestly intended to impede employees' exercise of their rights under the law.

An employer may validly post its property against all nonemployee solicitations, including distribution of union literature, if reasonable efforts by the union through other available channels of communication would enable it to reach the employees with its message. Nonemployee union organizers have lesser rights than employees on company property, as stated in the *Lechmere Inc.* case.

LECHMERE INC. v NLRB
112 S Ct 841 (1992)

Petitioner Lechmere, Inc. owns and operates a retail store located in a shopping plaza in Newington, a suburb of Hartford, Connecticut. Lechmere is also part owner of the plaza's parking lot, which is separated from a public highway by a 46-foot wide grassy strip. Almost all of the strip is public property. In a campaign to organize Lechmere employees, nonemployee union organizers from Local 919 of the UFCW union placed handbills on the windshields of cars parked in the employees' part of the parking lot. After Lechmere denied the organizers access to the lot, they picketed from the grassy strip. In addition, they were able to contact directly some 20 percent of the employees. The union filed an unfair labor practice charge with the Board, alleging that Lechmere had violated the NLRA by barring the organizers from its property. An administrative law judge ruled in the union's favor. The Board affirmed, and the Court of Appeals enforced the Board's order.

THOMAS, J. . . . Section 7 of the NLRA provides in relevant part that "employees shall have the right to self-organization, to form, join, or assist labor organizations." 29 U.S.C. § 157. Section 8 (a) (1) of the Act, in turn, makes it an unfair labor practice for an employer "to interfere with, restrain, or coerce employees in the exercise of rights guaranteed in [§7]." 29 U.S.C. §158 (a) (1). By its plain terms, thus, the NLRA confers rights only on *employees*, not on unions or their nonemployee organizers. In *NLRB v Babcock & Wilcox Co.*, 351 U.S. 105 (1956), however, we recognized that insofar as the employees' "right of self-organization depends in some measure on [their] ability. . . to learn the advantages of self-organization from others," . . . , §7 of the NLRA may, in certain limited circumstances, restrict an employer's right to exclude nonemployee union organizers from his property. It is the nature of those circumstances that we explore today. . .

[In *Babcock* the Board ordered the Company to allow the nonemployee organizers to distribute literature on its parking lot and walkways; the Court of Appeals refused to enforce the order; and the Supreme Court decided to hear the case and held] that the Board had erred by failing to make the critical distinction between the organizing activities of employees (to whom §7 guarantees the right of self-organization) and nonemployees (to whom §7 applies only derivatively). Thus, while "no restriction may be placed on the employees' right to discuss self-organization *among themselves*, unless the employer can demonstrate that a restriction is necessary to maintain production or discipline," . . . "no such obligation is owed non-employee organizers." . . . As a rule, then, an employer cannot be compelled to allow distribution of union literature by nonemployee organizers on his property. As with many other rules, however, we recognized an exception. Where "the location of a plant and the living quarters of the employees place the employees beyond the reach of reasonable union efforts to communicate with them," . . . employers' property rights may be "required to yield to the extent needed to permit communication of information on the right to organize," . . .

The threshold inquiry in this case, then, is whether the facts here justify application of *Babcock's* inaccessibility exception. . . . The exception to *Babcock's* rule is a narrow one. It does not apply wherever nontrespassory access to employees may be cumbersome or less-than-ideally effective, but only where "the *location of a plant and the living quarters of the employees* place the employees *beyond the reach* of reasonable union efforts to communicate with them," . . . Classic examples include logging camps . . . and mountain resort hotels. . . . *Babcock's* exception was crafted precisely to protect the §7 rights of those employees who, by virtue of their environment, are isolated from the ordinary flow of information that characterizes our society. The union's burden of establishing such isolation is, as we have explained, "a heavy one," and one not satisfied by mere conjecture or the expression of doubts concerning the effectiveness of nontrespassory means of communication.

The Board's conclusion in this case that the union had no reasonable means short of trespass to make Lechmere's employees aware of its organizational efforts is based on a misunderstanding of the limited scope of this exception. Because the employees do not reside on Lechmere's property, they are presumptively not "beyond the reach," . . . of the union's message. Although the employees live in a large metropolitan area (Greater Hartford), that fact does not in itself render them "inaccessible" in the sense contemplated by *Babcock*. Their accessibility is suggested by the union's success in contacting a substantial percentage of them directly, via mailings, phone calls, and home visits. Such direct contact, of course, is not a necessary element of "reasonably effective" communication; signings or advertising also may suffice. In this case, the union tried advertising in local newspapers; the Board said that this was not reasonably effective because it was expensive and might not reach the employees. . . . Whatever the merits of that conclusion, other alternative means of communication were readily available. Thus, signs (displayed, for example, the public grassy strip adjoining Lechmere's parking lot) would have informed the employees about the union's organizational efforts. (Indeed, union organizers picketed the shopping center's main entrance for months as employees came and went every day.) *Access* to employees, not *success* in winning them over, is the critical issue—although success, or lack thereof, may be relevant in determining whether reasonable access exists. Because the union in this case failed to establish the existence of any "unique obstacles," that frustrated access to Lechmere's employees, the Board erred in concluding that Lechmere committed an unfair labor practice by barring the nonemployee organizers from its property.

[Judgment reversed]

WHITE, J., dissenting. . . . In the case before us, the Court holds that *Babcock* itself stated the correct accommodation between property and organizational rights; it interprets that case as construing §§7 and 8(a)(1) of the National Labor Relations Act to contain a general rule forbidding third-party access, subject only to a limited exception where the union demonstrates that the location of the employer's place of business and the living quarters of the employees place the employees beyond the reach of reasonable efforts to communicate with them. The Court refuses to enforce the Board's order in this case, which rested on its prior decision in *Jean Country*, 291 N.L.R.B. 11 (1988), because, in the Court's view, *Jean Country* revealed that the Board misunderstood the basic holding in *Babcock*, as well as the narrowness of the exception to the general rule announced in that case.

. . . The Court errs in this case. . .

. . . The Court in *Babcock* recognized that actual communication with nonemployee organizers, not mere notice that an organizing campaign exists, is necessary to vindicate §7 rights. . . . If employees are entitled to learn from others the advantages of self-organization, . . . it is singularly unpersuasive to suggest that the union has sufficient access for this purpose by being able to hold up signs from a public grassy strip adjacent to the highway leading to the parking lot. . . .

QUESTIONS

1. State the *Babcock* rule as set forth in the majority opinion. Is the exception to the rule a broad one?

2. State the two-stage test set forth in *Lechmere* to determine if the proper accommodation between employees' and the employer's rights have taken place.
3. Did the nonemployee union organizers have reasonable access to Lechmere employees outside of the employer's property?
4. Did the dissent agree with the majority about whether there was sufficient access given the union organizers?

10. Firing Employees For Union Activity

Employers and supervisors often feel betrayed by individual employees who take leadership roles in forming organizations. The NLRA prohibits discrimination against such employees because of their union activity.

The NLRB has found evidence of discrimination against active union supporters where the employer:

(1) discharges on the strength of past misdeeds that were condoned;

(2) neglects to give customary warnings prior to discharge;

(3) discharges for a rule generally unenforced;

(4) applies disproportionately severe punishment to union supporters; or

(5) effects layoffs in violation of seniority status with disproportionate impact on union supporters.

The NLRA preserves the right of the employer to maintain control over the workforce in the interest of discipline, efficiency, and pleasant and safe customer relations. Employees, on the other hand, have the right to be free from coercive discrimination resulting from union activity.

At times these two rights may collide. For example, an employee may be discharged for apparently two reasons: (1) violation of a valid company rule, and (2) union activity. The former is given by the employer as the reason for termination; the latter remains unstated on the employer's part, causing the filing of a Section 8(a)(3) unfair labor practice charge against the employer. These are known as *dual-motive cases*. The General Counsel must present on behalf of the dismissed employee, a prima facie case that protected conduct such as union activity was a motivating factor in the dismissal. After this showing the burden shifts to the employer, who must prove that the employee would have been dismissed for legitimate business reasons even absent the protected conduct. The *Transportation Management* case is a dual motive case.

NLRB v TRANSPORTATION MANAGEMENT CORP.

462 US 393 (1983)

Prior to his discharge, Sam Santillo was a bus driver for Transportation Management Corp. On March 19, 1979, Santillo talked to officials of the Teamster's Union about organizing the drivers who worked with him. Over the next four days Santillo discussed with his fellow drivers the possibility of joining the Teamsters and distributed authorization cards. On the night of March 23, George Patterson, who supervised Santillo and the other drivers, told one of the drivers that he had heard of Santillo's activities. Patterson referred to Santillo as two-faced, and promised to get even with him. Later that evening Patterson talked to Ed West, who was also a bus driver for respondent. Patterson asked, "What's with Sam and the Union?" Patterson said that he took Santillo's actions personally, recounted several favors he had done for Santillo, and added that he would remember Santillo's activities when Santillo again asked for a favor. On Monday, March 26, Santillo was discharged. Patterson told Santillo that he was being fired for leaving his keys in the bus and taking unauthorized breaks. Santillo filed charges with the Board, and the General Counsel issued a complaint alleging that Santillo was discharged because of his union activities in distributing authorization cards to fellow employees. The administrative law judge (ALJ) determined that Patterson's disapproval of Santillo's practice of leaving his keys in the bus was clearly a pretext as the practice of leaving keys in buses was commonplace among company employees. The company identified two types of unauthorized breaks: coffee breaks and stops at home. With respect to both coffee breaks and stopping at home, the ALJ found that Santillo was never cautioned or admonished about such behavior, and that the employer had not followed its customary practice of issuing three written warnings before discharging a driver. The ALJ also found that the taking of coffee breaks during work hours was normal practice, and that the company tolerated the practice unless the breaks interfered with the driver's performance of his duties. The ALJ found that the company had never taken any adverse personnel action against an employee because of such behavior. The Board adopted the ALJ's findings. The First Circuit Court of Appeals refused to enforce the Board's order. An appeal was taken to the Supreme Court.

WHITE, J. . . . The Court of Appeals erred in holding that §10 (c) forbids placing the burden on the employer to prove that absent the improper motivation he would have acted in the same manner for wholly legitimate reasons. . . .

The employer is a wrongdoer; he has acted out of a motive that is declared illegitimate by the statute. It is fair that he bear the risk that the influence of legal and illegal motives cannot be separated, because he knowingly created the risk and because the risk was created not by innocent activity but by his own wrongdoing. . . .

The Board was justified in this case in concluding that Santillo would not have been discharged had the employer not considered his efforts to establish a union. At least two of the transgressions that purportedly would have in any event prompted Santillo's discharge were commonplace, and yet no transgressor had ever before received any kind of discipline. Moreover, the employer departed from its usual practice in dealing with rules infractions; indeed, not only did the employer not warn Santillo that his actions would result in being subjected to discipline, it never even expressed its disapproval of his conduct. In addition, Patterson, the person who made the initial decision to discharge Santillo, was obviously upset with Santillo for engaging in such protected activity. It is thus clear that the Board's finding that Santillo would not have been fired if the employer had not had an anti-union animus was "supported by substantial evidence on the record considered as a whole," . . . .

[Judgment reversed]

QUESTIONS

1. According to the General Counsel, why was Santillo fired by his employer?
2. According to the company, why was Mr. Santillo fired ?
3. Did the Supreme Court find that the Board was justified in concluding that Santillo would not have been discharged had the employer not considered his efforts to establish a union?

11. Duty of Employer to Bargain Collectively

Once a union wins a representative election, the Board certifies the union as the exclusive bargaining representative of the employees. The employer then has the obligation under the NLRA to bargain with the union in good faith over wages, hours, and working conditions. These matters are **mandatory subjects of bargaining**, and include seniority provisions, promotions, layoff and recall provisions, no-strike no-lockout clauses, and grievance procedures. Employers also have an obligation to bargain about the "effects" of the shut down of a part of a business;[13] and may have an obligation to bargain over the decision to relocate bargaining unit work to other plants.[14]

Permissive subjects of bargaining are those subjects where an employer's refusal to bargain over them is not a Section 8(a)(5) unfair labor practice. Examples are the required use of union labels, internal union affairs, union recognition clauses, and benefits for already retired workers.

12. Right to Work

The NLRA allows states to enact **right to work laws**. These laws restrict unions and employers from negotiating clauses in their collective bargaining agreements that make union membership compulsory.[15]

Advocates of such laws contend that compulsory union membership is contrary to the First Amendment right of freedom of association. Unions have attacked these laws as unfair because unions must represent all employees, and, in right to work states where a majority of employees vote for union representation, nonunion employees receive all the benefits of collective bargaining contracts without paying union dues.

13. Strike and Picketing Activities

If the parties reach an impasse in the negotiation process for a collective bargaining agreement, a union may call a strike and undertake picketing activity to enforce its bargaining demands. Strikers in such a situation are called **economic strikers**. Although the strike activity is legal, the employers may respond by hiring temporary or permanent replacement workers.

(a) RIGHTS OF STRIKERS. Economic strikers who unconditionally apply for reinstatement at a time when their positions are filled by permanent replacements are not entitled to return to work at the end of the economic strike. They are entitled to full reinstatement

---

[13] *First National Maintenance v NLRB*, 452 US 666 (1981).

[14] Dubuque Packing Co. and UFCWIU, Local 150A, 303 NLRB No. 66 (1991).

[15] Right to work statutes declare unlawful any agreement which denies persons the right to work because of nonmembership in a union or the failure to pay dues to a union as a condition of employment. These laws have been adopted in Alabama, Arizona, Arkansas, Florida, Georgia, Idaho, Iowa, Kansas, Louisiana, Mississippi, Nebraska, Nevada, North Carolina, North Dakota, South Carolina, South Dakota, Tennessee, Texas, Utah, Virginia, and Wyoming.

when positions become available. Strikers responsible for misconduct while out on strike may be refused reemployment by the employer.

When employees go out on strike to protest an unfair labor practice of an employer, such as the firing of an employee for union organizing activity, these **unfair labor practice strikers** have a right to return to their jobs immediately at the end of the strike. This right exists even if the employer has hired permanent replacements.

(b) PICKETING. Placing persons outside of a business at the site of a labor dispute so that they may by signs or banners inform the public of the existence of a labor dispute is called **primary picketing**. Such picketing is legal. Should the picketing employees mass together in great numbers in front of the gates of the employer's facility to effectively shut down the entrances, such coercion is called **mass picketing** and is illegal. **Secondary picketing** is picketing an employer with whom a union has no dispute to persuade the employer to stop doing business with a party to the dispute. Secondary picketing is generally illegal under the NLRA. An exception exists for certain product picketing at supermarkets or other multi-product retail stores, provided it is limited to asking customers not to purchase the struck product at the neutral employer's store.[16]

14. Regulation of Internal Union Affairs

To ensure the honest and democratic administration of unions, Congress passed the Labor-Management Reporting and Disclosure Act (LMRDA).[17] Title IV of the LMRDA establishes democratic standards for all elections for union offices including the following:

(1) secret ballots in local union elections;
(2) opportunity for members to nominate candidates;
(3) advance notice of elections;
(4) observers at polling and at ballot-counting stations for all candidates;
(5) publication of results and preservation of records for one year;
(6) prohibition of any income from dues or assessments being used to support candidates for union office; and
(7) advance opportunity of each candidate to inspect the membership name and address lists.

C. PENSION PLANS AND FEDERAL REGULATION

The Employees Retirement Income Security Act (ERISA)[18] was adopted in 1974 to provide protection for the pension plan interests of employees.

15. ERISA

The act sets forth fiduciary standards and requirements for vesting, funding, and termination insurance.

(a) FIDUCIARY STANDARDS AND REPORTING. Persons administering a pension fund must handle it so as to protect the interest of the employees.[19] The fact that an employer contributed all or part of the money does not entitle the employer to use the fund as though it were still owned by the employer. Persons administering pension plans must make detailed reports to the secretary of labor.

(b) VESTING. Vesting means the right of an employee to pension benefits paid into a pension plan in the employee's name by the

---

[16] *NLRB v Fruit and Vegetable Packers, Local 760 (Tree Fruits Inc.)*, 377 US 58 (1964); *but see NLRB v Retail Clerks, Local 1001, (Safeco Title Insurance Co.)*, 477 US 607 (1980).

[17] 29 USC Sections 401-531.

[18] PL 93-406, 88 Stat 829, 29 USC §§ 1001-1381.

[19] John Hancock Mutual Life Insurance Co. v Harris Trust 114 S Ct 517 (1993).

C
P
A
employer. Prior to ERISA, many pension plans did not vest accrued benefits until an employee had 20 to 25 years of service. Thus, an employee who was forced to terminate service after 18 years would not receive any pension rights or benefits at all. Under ERISA, employees' rights must be fully vested within five or seven years in accordance with the two vesting options available under the law.

In the past, it was common for pension plans to contain break-in-service clauses, whereby employees who left their employment for a period longer than one year for any reason other than an on-the-job injury, lost pension eligibility rights. Under the Retirement Equity Act of 1984,[20] an individual can leave the workforce for up to five consecutive years and still retain eligibility for pension benefits.

(c) FUNDING. ERISA requires that employers make contributions to their pension funds on a basis that is actuarially determined so that the pension fund will be large enough to make the payments that will be required of it.

(d) TERMINATION INSURANCE. ERISA establishes an insurance plan to protect employees when the employer goes out of business. To provide this protection, the statute creates a Pension Benefit Guaranty Corporation (PBGC). In effect, this corporation guarantees that the employee will receive benefits, in much the same way as the Federal Deposit Insurance Corporation protects bank depositors. The PBGC is financed by small payments made by employers for every employee covered by a pension plan.

(e) ENFORCEMENT. ERISA authorizes the secretary of labor and employees to bring court actions to compel the observance of the statutory requirements.

D. EMPLOYMENT BENEFITS, FAMILY LEAVES, AND SOCIAL SECURITY

Generally, when employees are without work through no fault of their own, they are eligible for unemployment compensation benefits. Twelve-week maternity, paternity, or adoption leaves and family and medical leaves are available for qualifying employees. Social Security provides certain benefits, including retirement and disability benefits.

16. Unemployment Compensation

Unemployment compensation today is provided primarily through a federal-state system under the unemployment insurance provisions of the Social Security Act of 1935. All of the states have laws that provide similar benefits, and the state agencies are loosely coordinated under the federal act. Agricultural employees, domestic employees, and state and local government employees are not covered by this federal-state system. Federal programs of unemployment compensation exist for federal civilian workers and former military service personnel. A separate federal unemployment program applies to railroad workers.

(a) ELIGIBILITY. In most states, the unemployed person must be available for placement in a similar job and be willing to take such employment at a comparable rate of pay. Full-time students generally have difficulty proving that they are "available" for work while they are still going to school.

If an employee quits a job without cause or is fired for misconduct, the employee is ordinarily disqualified from receiving unemployment compensation benefits.

An employee's stealing property from an employer constitutes misconduct for which

---

[20] PL 98-397, 29 USC § 1001.

benefits will be denied. Moreover, an employee's refusal to complete the aftercare portion of an alcohol treatment program has been found to be misconduct connected with work, disqualifying the employee from benefits.[21]

(b) FUNDING. Employers are taxed for unemployment benefits based on each employer's "experience rating" account. Thus employers with a stable workforce with no layoffs, who therefore do not draw upon the state unemployment insurance fund, pay lower tax rates. Employers whose experience ratings are higher pay higher rates. Motivated by the desire to avoid higher unemployment taxes, employers commonly challenge the state's payment of unemployment benefits to individuals whom they believe are not properly entitled to benefits.

17. Family and Medical Leaves of Absence

The Family and Medical Leave Act of 1993 (FMLA) entitles an eligible employee, whether male or female, to a total of 12 workweeks of unpaid leave during any 12-month period: (1) due to the birth or adoption of the employee's son or daughter; (2) in order to care for the employee's spouse, son, daughter, or parent with a serious health condition; or (3) because of a serious health condition that makes the employee unable to perform the functions of the employee's position. In the case of an employee's serious health condition or that of a covered family member, an employer may require that the employee use any accrued paid vacation, personal, medical, or sick leave toward any part of the 12-week leave provided by the act. When an employee requests leave due to the birth or adoption of a child, the employer may require that the employee use all available paid personal, vacation, and fam-

ily leave, but not sick leave, toward any FMLA leave.

To be eligible for FMLA leave, an employee must have been employed by a covered employer for at least 12 months and worked at least 1250 hours during the 12-month period preceding the leave. Upon return from FMLA, the employee is entitled to be restored to the same or an equivalent position, with equivalent pay and benefits.

18. Social Security

Employees and employers are required to pay social security taxes. These taxes provide employees with four types of insurance protection—retirement benefits, disability benefits, life insurance benefits, and health insurance (Medicare).

The federal Social Security Act established a federal program of aid for the aged, the blind, and the disabled. This is called the Supplemental Security Income program (SSI). Payments are administered directly by the Department of Health and Human Services.

E. EMPLOYEES' HEALTH AND SAFETY

The Occupational Safety and Health Act of 1970 (OSHA) was passed to assure every worker, so far as possible, safe and healthful working conditions and to preserve the country's human resources.[22] OSHA provides for (1) establishing safety and health standards and (2) effective enforcement of these standards and the other employer duties required by OSHA.

19. Standards

The secretary of labor has broad authority under OSHA to promulgate occupational safety and health standards.[23] Except in emergency

---

[21] Henson v Employment Security Department, 113 Wash 2d 374, 779 P2d 715 (1989).

[22] 29 USC §§ 651 et seq.

[23] Martin v OSHRC, 111 S.Ct. 1171 (1991).

situations, public hearings and publication in the *Federal Register* are required before the secretary can issue a new standard. Any person adversely affected may then challenge the validity of the standard in a U.S. court of appeals. The secretary's standards will be upheld if they are reasonable and supported by substantial evidence. The secretary must demonstrate a need for a new standard by showing that it is reasonably necessary to protect employees against a "significant risk" of material health impairment. The cost of compliance with new standards may run into billions of dollars. The secretary is not required to do a cost-benefit analysis for a new standard. However, the secretary must show that the standard is economically feasible.

20. Employer Duties

Employers have a "general duty" to furnish to each employee a place of employment that is free from hazards that are likely to cause death or serious physical injuries.

Employers are required by OSHA to maintain records of occupational illness and injuries if they result in death, loss of consciousness, or one or more lost workdays, or if they require medical treatment other than first aid. Such records have proven to be a valuable aid in recognizing areas of risk. They have been especially helpful in identifying the presence of occupational illnesses.

21. Enforcement

The Occupational Safety and Health Administration (also identified as OSHA) is the agency within the Department of Labor that administers the act. OSHA has authority to conduct inspections and to seek enforcement action where there has been noncompliance. Worksite inspections are conducted when employer records indicate incidents involving fatalities or serious injuries. These inspections may also result from employee complaints. The act protects employees making complaints from employer retaliation. Employers have the right to require that an OSHA inspector secure a warrant before inspecting the employer's plant.

If OSHA issues a citation for a violation of workplace health or safety standards, the employer may challenge the citation before the Occupational Safety and Health Review Commission. Judicial review of a commission ruling is obtained before a U.S. court of appeals.

The Occupational Safety and Health Act provides that no employer shall discharge or in any manner discriminate against employees because the employees filed a complaint with OSHA, testified in any OSHA proceeding, or exercised any right afforded by the act. A regulation issued by the secretary of labor under the act provides that if employees with no reasonable alternative refuse in good faith to expose themselves to a dangerous condition, they will be protected against subsequent discrimination. The secretary of labor may obtain injunctive and other appropriate relief in a U.S. district court against an employer who discriminates against employees for testifying or exercising "any right" under the act. In the *Whirlpool* case the court was faced with the problems of whether two employees were exercising any right under the Act when they refused to perform work that they considered dangerous and whether the employer's disciplinary action against the employees was discriminatory.

WHIRLPOOL CORPORATION v MARSHALL

445 US 1 (1980)

At the Whirlpool Corporation's plant in Marion, Ohio, mesh guard screens were located about 20 feet above the plant floor. A maintenance employee fell to his death through the screen in an area where newer, stronger mesh had not yet been installed. Following this incident, Whirlpool made some repairs and forbade maintenance employees from stepping on either the screens or the angle-iron supporting structure. Twelve days after the employee fell to his death two of Whirlpool's maintenance employees, Virgil Deemer and Thomas Cornwell, met with the plant maintenance superintendent to express concern about the safety of the screen. The superintendent disagreed with their view, but permitted the two men to inspect the screen with their foreman and to point out dangerous areas needing repair. Unsatisfied with Whirlpool's response to the results of this inspection, Deemer and Cornwell met with the plant safety director. At that meeting, they requested the name, address, and telephone number of a representative of the local office of the Occupational Safety and Health Administration (OSHA). Although the safety director told the men that they "had better stop and think about what they were doing," he furnished the men with the information they requested. Later that same day, Deemer contacted an official of the regional OSHA office and discussed the guard screen. The next day, Deemer and Cornwell reported for the night shift. Their foreman, after himself walking on some of the angle-iron frames, directed the two men to perform their usual maintenance duties on a section of the old screen. Claiming that the screen was unsafe, they refused to carry out this directive. The men were ordered to punch out and leave the plant. They were not paid for the remaining six hours of their shift. Written reprimands for insubordination were placed in their employment files.

The Occupational Safety and Health Act provides that no employer shall discharge or in any manner discriminate against an employee because the employee filed a complaint with OSHA, or testified in any OSHA proceeding, or exercised any right afforded by the Act. A regulation issued by the Secretary of Labor under the Act provides that an employee who, with no reasonable alternative, refuses in good faith to be exposed to a dangerous condition will be protected against subsequent discrimination. The Secretary of Labor filed suit in U.S. district court against Whirlpool, contending that Whirlpool's actions against Deemer and Cornwell constituted "discrimination" under the Secretary's regulation and the Act. Whirlpool contended that the regulation encouraged workers to engage in "self-help" and unlawfully permitted a "strike with pay." The court held that the Secretary's regulation was inconsistent with the Act and denied relief. The U.S. court of appeals reversed this decision, and Whirlpool appealed.

STEWART, J. . . . Circumstances may sometimes exist in which the employee justifiably believes that the express statutory arrangement [OSHA] does not sufficiently protect him from death or serious injury. Such circumstances will probably not often occur, but such a situation may arise when (1) the employee is ordered by his employer to work under conditions that the employee reasonably believes pose an imminent risk of death or serious bodily injury, and (2) the employee has reason to believe that there is not sufficient time or opportunity either to seek effective redress from his employer or to apprise OSHA of the danger.

Nothing in the Act suggests that those few employees who have to face this dilemma must rely exclusively on the remedies expressly set forth in the Act at the risk of their own safety. But nothing in the Act explicitly provides otherwise. Against this background of legislative silence, the Secretary has exercised his rulemaking power . . . and has determined that, when an employee in good faith finds himself in such a predicament, he may refuse to expose himself to the dangerous condition, without being subjected to "subsequent discrimination" by the employer. . . .

The regulation clearly conforms to the fundamental objective of the Act—to prevent occupational deaths and serious injuries. The Act, in its preamble, declares that its purpose and policy is "to assure so far as possible every working man and woman in the Nation safe and healthful working conditions and to preserve our human resources." . . .

To accomplish this basic purpose, the legislation's remedial orientation is prophylactic in nature. The Act does not wait for an employee to die or become injured. It authorizes the promulgation of health and safety standards and the issuance of citations in the hope that these will act to prevent deaths or injuries from ever occurring. It would seem anomalous to construe an Act so directed and constructed as prohibiting an employee, with no other reasonable alternative, the freedom to withdraw from a workplace environment that he reasonably believes is highly dangerous.

Moreover, the Secretary's regulation can be viewed as an appropriate aid to the full effectuation of the Act's "general duty" clause. That clause provides that "each employer . . . shall furnish to each of his employees employment and a place of employment which are free from recognized hazards that are causing or are likely to cause death or serious physical harm to his employees." . . . As the legislative history of this provision reflects, it was intended itself to deter the occurrence of occupational deaths and serious injuries by placing on employers a mandatory obligation independent of the specific health and safety standards to be promulgated by the Secretary. Since OSHA inspectors cannot be present around the clock in every workplace, the Secretary's regulation ensures that employees will in all circumstances enjoy the rights afforded them by the "general duty" clause.

[The Court next considered and rejected Whirlpool's contention that the legislative history is contrary to the Secretary's regulation. The Court explained its view as follows:]

When it rejected the "strike with pay" concept, therefore, Congress very clearly meant to reject a law unconditionally imposing upon employers an obligation to continue to pay their employees their regular pay checks when they absented themselves from work for reasons of safety. But the regulation at issue here does not require employers to pay workers who refuse to perform their assigned tasks in the face of imminent danger. It simply provides that in such cases the employer may not "discriminate" against the employees involved. An employer "discriminates" against an employee only when he treats that employee less favorably than he treats others similarly situated.

[In a footnote to the decision, the Court applied the above principles to the situation of Deemer and Cornwell. The Court stated that the placing of reprimands in their personnel files clearly represents discrimination. The Court stated that whether the denial of work and pay for the six-hour period also represented discrimination was a question not before the Court.]

[Judgment of Court of Appeals affirmed]

22. State "Right-to-Know" Legislation

Laws that guarantee individual workers the "right to know" if there are hazardous substances in their workplaces have been enacted by many states in recent years. These laws commonly require an employer to make known to an employee's physician the chemical composition of certain substances in the workplace, in connection with the diagnosis and treatment of an employee by the physician. Further, local fire and public health officials, as well as local neighborhood residents, are given the right to know if local employers are working with hazardous substances that could pose health or safety problems.

F. COMPENSATION FOR EMPLOYEE'S INJURIES

For most kinds of employment, workers' compensation statutes govern compensation for injuries. These statutes provide that the injured employee is entitled to compensation for accidents occurring in the course of employment from a risk involved in that employment.

23. Common Law Status of Employer

In some employment situations, the common law principles apply. Workers' compensation statutes commonly do not apply to employers with fewer than a prescribed minimum number of employees or to agricultural, domestic, or casual employment. When an exempted area of employment is involved, it is necessary to consider the duties and defenses of employ-

ers apart from workers' compensation statutes.

(a) DUTIES. The employer is under the common law duty to furnish an employee with a reasonably safe place in which to work, reasonably safe tools and appliances, and a sufficient number of competent fellow employees for the work involved. The employer is also under the common law duty to warn the employee of any unusual dangers particular to the employer's business.

(b) DEFENSES. At common law, the employer is not liable to an injured employee if the employee is harmed by the act of a fellow employee. Similarly, an employer is not liable at common law to an employee harmed by an ordinary hazard of the work, because the employee assumed such risks. If the employee is guilty of contributory negligence, regardless of the employer's negligence, the employer is not liable at common law to an injured employee.

24. Statutory Changes

The rising incidence of industrial accidents resulting from the increasing use of more powerful machinery and the growth of the industrial labor population led to a demand for statutory modification of common law rules relating to liability of employers for industrial accidents.

(a) MODIFICATION OF EMPLOYER'S COMMON LAW DEFENSES. One kind of change by statute was to modify the defenses that an employer could assert when sued by an employee for damages. For example, under the Federal Employer's Liability Act (FELA), which covers railroad workers, the injured employee must still bring an action in court and prove the negligence of the employer or other employees. However, the burden of proving the case is made lighter by limitations on employers' defenses. Under FELA, contributory negligence is a defense only in mitigation of damages; assumption of the risk is not a defense.[24]

(b) WORKERS' COMPENSATION. A more sweeping development was made by the adoption of workers' compensation statutes in every state. In addition, civil employees of the U.S. government are covered by the Federal Employees' Compensation Act. When an employee is covered by a workers' compensation statute, and when the injury is job connected, the employee's remedy is limited to that provided in the workers' compensation statute.[25]

Workers' compensation proceedings are brought before a special administrative agency or workers' compensation board. In contrast, a common law action for damages or an action for damages under an employer's liability statute is brought in a court of law.

The *Wal-Mart Stores Inc.* case illustrates the exclusivity of the Workers' Compensation Act.

For injuries arising within the course of the employee's work from a risk involved in that work, the workers' compensation statutes

BRYANT v WAL-MART STORES INC.

(Ga App) 417 SE2d 688 (1992)

Bryant is the administrator of the estate of the deceased and the guardian of the deceased's minor child. Bryant sued Wal-Mart for damages following the death of the deceased based on the theory of unlawful false imprisonment. While working on the night restocking crew, the deceased suffered a stroke. Medical personnel arrived six minutes later but could not enter the store because management had locked all doors of the store, and no manager was present to open a door. By the time the medical crew entered the store to assist her, they were unable to revive her and she died 15 minutes later. Bryant contends that false imprisonment occurred between the time the deceased became ill until the time the medical team was able to enter the store. Wal-Mart claimed that Bryant's exclusive remedy was under the Workers' Compensation Act. From a judgment for Wal-Mart, Bryant appealed.

COOPER, J. . . . Even if appellant established a claim of false imprisonment, "it is well settled in this state that a claim under the workers' compensation act is the employee's sole and exclusive remedy for injury or occupational disease incurred *in the course of employment*. This edict is statutory . . . as well as judicial, and its policy reasons are well understood. . . . The Act precludes recovery "for willful or intentional acts of the employer so long as the injury arises out of and in the course of employment. . . . It is undisputed that the deceased was locked in the store for business purposes, that she was engaged in the performance of her work duties at the time she suffered

---

[24] Federal Employer's Liability Act, 45 USC §§ 1 et seq.
[25] Arrow Uniform Rental, Inc. v Suter (Ind App) 545 NE2d 832 (1989).

the stroke and that the emergency medical crew was unable to render immediate assistance to the deceased due to the delay in gaining entrance to the store. Therefore, insofar as appellant seeks to recover for the death of the deceased, that claim is barred by the exclusivity provisions of the Act.

Appellant contends however, that in certain counts of his complaint, he seeks to recover for injuries to the deceased's peace, happiness, and feelings and that these "nonphysical" injuries are not included within the definition of injury found in the Act. . . . "That an injury is not *compensable* under the act does not necessarily mean it is not within the *purview* of the act. . . . 'In exchange for the right to recover scheduled compensation without proof of negligence on the part of the employer in those cases in which a right of recovery is granted, the employee forgoes other rights and remedies which he might otherwise have had, but if he accepts the terms of the Act he as well as the employer is limited to those things for which the Act makes provision.' ". . . Appellant argues that the deceased's nonphysical injuries and subsequent death occurred due to the inability of the emergency medical personnel to render prompt medical attention. That injuries to the deceased's peace, happiness, and feelings may not be compensable under the Act does not take those injuries out of the purview of the Act. . . . Accordingly, we hold that under the facts of this case, the Workers' Compensation Act provides the exclusive remedy and precludes appellant's common law tort action.

[Judgment affirmed]

QUESTIONS

1. State the issue before the court.
2. Why did Bryant bring an action for damages in a court of law when the deceased was covered by the Workers' Compensation law?
3. When nonphysical injuries are not compensable under the Workers' Compensation Act, may the victim sue under a common law tort theory such as false imprisonment?

usually provide: (1) immediate medical benefits; (2) prompt periodic wage replacement, often computed as a percentage of weekly wages (ranging from 50 to 80 percent of the injured employee's wage) for a specified number of weeks; and (3) a death benefit of a limited amount. In such cases, compensation is paid without regard to whether the employer or the employee was negligent. However, no compensation is generally allowed for a willful, self-inflicted injury or one sustained while intoxicated.

There has been a gradual widening of the workers' compensation statutes, so compensation today is generally recoverable for both accident-inflicted injuries and occupational diseases. In some states, compensation for occupational diseases is limited to those named in the statute. These diseases may include silicosis, lead poisoning, or injury to health from radioactivity. In other states, any disease arising from an occupation is compensable.

G. EMPLOYER-RELATED IMMIGRATION LAWS

The Immigration and Naturalization Act (INA), the Immigration Reform and Control Act of 1986 (IRCA), and the Immigration Act of 1990[26] are the principal employer-related immigration laws.

25. Employer Liability

The IRCA sets forth criminal and civil penalties against employers who knowingly hire aliens who have illegally entered the United States. The IRCA was designed to stop illegal immigration through the elimination of job opportunities for these aliens.

26. Employer Verification

On hiring a new employee, an employer must verify that the employee is legally entitled to work in the United States. Both the employer and the employee must fill out portions of Form I-9. Verification documents include a U.S. passport, a certificate of U.S. citizenship, or an Alien Registration Card ("green card"). In lieu of these documents, a state driver's license and a social security card are sufficient to prove eligibility to work. The 1990 act prohibits employers from demanding other documentation. Thus, if a prospective employee with a "foreign accent" offers a driver's license and social security card and the employer seeks a certificate of U.S. citizenship or a green card, the employer has committed an unfair immigration practice. The employer will be ordered to hire the individual and provide back pay.

SUMMARY

The relationship of employer and employee is created by the agreement of the parties and is subject to the principles applicable to contracts. If the employment contract sets forth a specific duration, the employer cannot terminate the contract at an earlier date unless just cause exists. If no definite time period is set forth, the individual is an at-will employee. Under the employment-at-will doctrine, an employer can terminate the contract of an at-will employee at any time, for any reason or for no reason. Courts in many jurisdictions, however, have carved out exceptions to this doctrine when the discharge violates public policy or is contrary to good faith and fair dealing in the employment relationship. The Fair Labor Standards Act regulates minimum wages, overtime hours, and child labor.

Under the National Labor Relations Act, employees have the right to form a union to obtain a collective bargaining contract or to refrain from organizational activities. The National Labor Relations Board conducts elections to determine whether employees in an appropriate bargaining unit desire to be represented by a union. The NLRA prohibits employers' and unions' unfair labor practices and authorizes the NLRB to conduct proceedings to stop such practices. Economic strikes have limited reinstatement rights. Federal law sets forth democratic standards for the election of union offices.

The Employees Retirement Income Security Act (ERISA) protects employees' pensions by requiring (1) high standards of those administering the funds, (2) reasonable vesting of benefits, (3) adequate funding, and (4) an insurance program to guarantee payments of earned benefits.

Unemployment compensation benefits are paid to persons for a limited period of time if they are out of work through no fault of their own. Persons receiving unemployment compensation must be available for placement in a job similar in duties and comparable in rate of pay to the job they lost. Twelve-week maternity, paternity, and adoption leaves are available under the Family and Medical Leave Act. Employers and employees pay social security taxes to provide retirement benefits, disability benefits, life insurance benefits, and Medicare.

The Occupational Safety and Health Act provides for (1) the establishment of safety and health standards and (2) the effective en-

---

[26] PL 101-649, 8 USC § 1101.

forcement of these standards. Many states have enacted "right-to-know" laws. These laws require employers to inform their employees of any hazardous substances present in the workplace.

Workers' compensation laws provide for the prompt payment of compensation and medical benefits to persons injured in the course of employment, without regard to fault. The injured employee's remedy is generally limited to the remedy provided by the workers' compensation statute. Most states provide compensation to workers for occupational diseases.

The immigration laws prohibit the employment of aliens who have illegally entered the United States.

LAW IN PRACTICE

As an employer:

1. If you allow the Salvation Army or local athletic teams to solicit employees for contributions or allow political candidates to solicit support on your business property, you will lose your right to prohibit nonemployee union organizers from soliciting on your property. "No Solicitation" rules must be consistently enforced in order to be used against union organizers.

2. Realize that the firing of a union activist during an organizational campaign will be strictly scrutinized. Be certain the firing is for just cause.

3. To avoid lawsuits by permanent replacements if replaced at the end of a strike, condition all offers to such individuals as "permanent subject to settlement with the union."

4. Remember, you have a right to challenge the payment of unemployment compensation to individuals who are fired for misconduct.

5. Know that you have a right to require that an OSHA inspector secure a warrant before inspecting plant.

QUESTIONS AND CASE PROBLEMS

1. What social forces are affected by the "shop right" rule applicable to inventions of an employee?

2. Compare the protection of trade secrets and the protection given an unpublished literary or artistic work (common law copyright).

3. What remedies does an employee who has been wrongfully discharged have against an employer?

4. Michael Hauck claims that he was discharged by his employer, Sabine Pilot Service, Inc., because he refused his employer's direction to perform the illegal act of pumping the bilges of his employer's vessel into the waterways. Hauck was an employee at will, and Sabine contends that it therefore had the right to discharge him without having to show cause. Hauck brought a wrongful discharge action against Sabine. Decide. *[Sabine Pilot Service Inc v Hauck (Tex) 687 SW2d 733]*

5. Jeanne Eenkhoorn worked as a supervisor at a business office for the New York Telephone Co. While at work, she invented a process for terminating the telephone services of delinquent subscribers. The telephone company used the process and refused to compensate her for it. The company claimed a "shop right." Eenkhoorn then sued for damages on a quasi contract theory. Decide. *[Eenkhoorn v New York Telephone Co. 568 NYS2d 677]*

6. One Monday a labor organization affiliated with the International Ladies Garment Workers Union began an organization drive among the employees of Whittal & Son, Inc. On the following Monday six of the employees who were participating in the union drive were discharged. Immediately after the firings the head of the company gave a speech to the remaining workers in which he made a variety of antiunion statements and threats. The union filed a complaint with the NLRB. The complaint alleged that the six employees were fired because they were engaging in organizational activity and that they were thus discharged in violation of the NLRA. The employer defended, arguing that it had a business to run and that it was barely able to survive in the global economy against cheap labor from third world countries. It asserted that the last thing it needed was "union baloney." Was the NLRA violated?

7. David Stark submitted an application to the maintenance department of Wyman-Gordon Company. Stark was a journeyman millwright with nine years experience at a neighboring company at the time of his application to Wyman-Gordon. Stark was vice president of the local industrial workers' union. In his preliminary interview with the company, Ms. Peevler asked if Stark was involved in union activity, and Stark detailed his involvement to her. She informed Stark that Wyman-Gordon was a nonunion shop and asked how he felt about this. Peevler's notes from the interview characterize Stark's response to this question as "seems to lean toward third party intervention." Company officials testified that Stark's qualifications were "exactly what we were looking for." Stark was not employed by the company. Stark claimed that he was discriminated against. Wyman-Gordon denied that any discrimination had occurred. Is a job applicant (as opposed to an employee) entitled to protection from antiunion discrimination? On the facts of this case, has any discrimination taken place? *[(Wyman-Gordon Company v NLRB, 108 LRRM 2085 (1st Cir.)]*

8. Juan Ortiz was regularly employed by Donegan Productions Co. as an actor on an afternoon television series. A dispute arose as to how much Donegan owed Juan. Donegan claimed that the dispute must be resolved solely on the basis of the written individual employment contract that Juan and Donegan had signed. Donegan claimed that past practice, usages of the profession, and an existing collective bargaining contract with AFTRA (American Federation of Television and Radio Artists) were not relevant. Was Donegan correct?

9. Jane Richards was employed as the sole crane operator of the Gale Corporation. She also held the part-time union position of shop steward for the plant. On May 15, Richards complained to OSHA concerning what she contended were seven existing violations of the Occupational Safety and Health Act. These violations were brought to her attention by members of the bargaining unit. On May 21, she stated to the company's general manager at a negotiating session: "If we don't have a new contract by the time the present one expires on June 15, we will strike." On May 22, an OSHA inspector arrived at the plant, and Richards told her supervisor that "I blew the whistle." On May 23, the company rented and later purchased two large electric forklifts that were used to do the

work previously performed by the crane, and the crane operator's job was abolished. Under the existing collective bargaining contract, the company had the right to lay off for lack of work. The contract also provided for arbitration, and it prohibited discipline or discharge without "just cause." On May 23, Richards was notified that she was being laid off "for lack of work" within her classification of crane operator. She was also advised that the company was not planning on using the crane in the future and that, if she were smart, she would get another job. Richards claims that her layoff was in violation of the National Labor Relations Act, the Occupational Safety and Health Act, and the collective bargaining agreement. Is she correct?

10. Samuel Sullivan, president of the Truck Drivers and Helpers International Union, also holds the position of president of the union's pension fund. The fund consists of both employer and employee contributions, which are forwarded quarterly to the fund's offices in New York City. Sullivan ordered Mark Gilbert, the treasurer of the fund, not to give out any information to anyone at any time concerning the fund, because it is union money and because the union is entitled to take care of its own internal affairs. Is Sullivan correct?

11. In May, the nurses' union at Waterbury Hospital went out on strike, and the hospital was shut down. In mid-June the hospital began hiring replacements, and gradually opened many units. In order to induce nurses to take employment during the strike, the hospital guaranteed replacement nurses their choice of positions and shifts. If a preferred position was in a unit that was not open at that time, the hospital guaranteed that the individual would be placed in that position at the end of the strike. The strike ended in October; and as the striking workers returned to work, the hospital began opening units that had been closed during the strike. It staffed many of these positions with replacement nurses. The nurses who had the positions prior to the strike, and who were waiting to return to work, believed that they should have been called to fill these positions rather than the junior replacements who had held other positions during the strike. Decide. *[The Waterbury Hospital v NLRB. (CA2 Conn) 950 F2d 849]*

12. Buffo was employed by the Baltimore & Ohio Railroad Co. Along with a number of other workers, he was removing old brakes from railroad cars and replacing them with new brakes. In the course of the work, rivet heads and scrap from the brakes accumulated on the tracks under the cars. This debris was removed only occasionally, when the workers had time. Buffo, while holding an air hammer in both arms, was crawling under a car when his foot slipped on scrap on the ground. This incident caused him to strike and injure his knee. He sued the railroad for damages under the Federal Employers Liability Act. Decide. *[Buffo v Baltimore & Ohio Railroad Co. 364 Pa 437, 72 A2d 593]*

13. Mark Phipps was employed as a cashier at a Clark gas station. A customer drove into the station and asked him to pump leaded gasoline into her 1976 Chevrolet—an automobile equipped to receive only unleaded gasoline. The station manager told Phipps to comply with the request, but he refused, believing that his dispensing leaded gasoline into the gas tank was a violation of law. Phipps stated that he was willing to pump unleaded gas into the tank, but the manager immediately fired him. Phipps sued Clark for wrongful termination. Clark contended that it was free to terminate Phipps, an employee at will, for any reason or no reason. Decide. *[Phipps v Clark Oil & Refining Corp (Minn App) 396 NW2d 588]*

14. Cream was an officer and employee of Leo Silfen, Inc. He was discharged and then went into business for himself, conducting a business similar to that of his former employer. He obtained lists of users of his products from enterprises publishing mailing and commercial lists. Out of the persons he solicited from these lists, 47 were customers of Silfen. Silfen brought an action to enjoin Cream from soliciting its customers. Cream showed that Silfen had approximately 1,100 customers. Decide. *[Leo Silfen, Inc. v Cream, 29 NY2d 387, 328 NYS2d 423, 278 NE2d 636]*

15. Michael Kittell was employed at Vermont Weatherboard Company. While operating a saw at the plant, Kittell was seriously injured when a splinter flew into his eye and penetrated his head. Kittell sued Vermont Weatherboard, seeking damages on a common law theory. His complaint alleged that he suffered severe injuries solely because of the employer's wanton and willful acts and omissions. The complaint stated that he was an inexperienced worker, put to work without instructions or warning on a saw from which the employer had stripped away all safety devices. Vermont Weatherboard made a motion to dismiss the complaint on the ground that the Workers' Compensation Act provided the exclusive remedy for his injury. Decide. *[Kittell v Vermont Weatherboard, Inc. 138 Vt 439, 417 A2d 926]*

CHAPTER 43

EQUAL EMPLOYMENT OPPORTUNITY LAW

LEARNING OBJECTIVES

After studying this chapter you will be able to:
1. *Explain and illustrate the difference between disparate treatment employment discrimination and disparate impact employment discrimination.*
2. *Recognize and remedy sexual harassment problems in the workplace.*
3. *Evaluate the legality of voluntary affirmative action programs by applying five court-approved principles.*
4. *State the consequences of discriminating against employees and job applicants because of their age.*
5. *State and illustrate an employer's legal obligation to make reasonable accommodations for disabled individuals to work.*

Our laws reflect our society's interest that all American's including minorities, women, and the disabled have equal employment opportunities, and that the workplace be free from discrimination and harassment. Title VII of the Civil Rights Act of 1964, as amended in 1972, 1978, and 1991 is the principal law regulating equal employment opportunities in the United States. Other federal laws require equal pay for men and women doing substantially the same work and forbid discrimination because of age or disability.

A. TITLE VII OF THE CIVIL RIGHTS ACT OF 1964, AS AMENDED

Title VII of the Civil Rights Act of 1964[1] seeks to eliminate employer and union practices that discriminate against employees and job applicants on the basis of race, color, religion, sex, or national origin. The law applies to the hiring process, to discipline, discharge, promotion, and benefits.

1. Theories of Discrimination

The Supreme Court has created, and the Civil Rights Act of 1991 has codified, two principal legal theories under which a plaintiff may prove a case of unlawful employment discrimination: disparate treatment and disparate impact (see Figure 43-1).

A **disparate treatment** claim exists where an employer treats some individuals less favorably than others because of their race, color, religion, sex, or national origin. Proof of the employer's discriminatory motive is essential in a disparate treatment case.

Disparate impact exists when an employer's facially neutral employment practices, such as hiring or promotion examinations, though neutrally applied and making no adverse reference to race, color, religion, sex, or national origin, have a significantly adverse or disparate impact on a protected group. In addition, the employment practice in question is not shown to be job related and consistent with business necessity by the employer. Under the disparate impact theory, it is not a defense for an employer to demonstrate that the employer did not intend to discriminate. The *Griggs v Duke Power Co.* case is a disparate impact case.

GRIGGS v DUKE POWER COMPANY
401 US 424 (1971)

Griggs and other black employees at the Duke Power Company's Dan River Station challenged Duke Power's high school diploma requirement and the passing of standardized general intelligence tests in order to transfer to more desirable "inside" jobs. The district court and court of appeals found no violation of Title VII because the employer did not adopt the diploma and test requirements with the purpose of intentionally discriminating against black employees. The case was appealed to the Supreme Court.

---

[1]   42 USC 2000(e) et seq.

BURGER, C. J. . . . The objective to Congress in the enactment of Title VII is plain from the language of the statute. It was to achieve equality of employment opportunities and remove barriers that have operated in the past to favor an identifiable group of white employees over other employees. Under the Act, practices, procedures, or tests neutral on their face, and even neutral in terms of intent, cannot be maintained if they operate to "freeze" the status quo of prior discriminatory employment practices.

. . . In short, the Act does not command that any person be hired simply because he was formerly the subject of discrimination, or because he is a member of a minority group. Discriminatory preference for any group, minority or majority, is precisely and only what Congress has proscribed. What is required by Congress is the removal of artificial, arbitrary, and unnecessary barriers to employment when the barriers operate invidiously to discriminate on the basis of racial or other impermissible classification.

Congress has now provided that tests or criteria for employment or promotion may not provide equality of opportunity merely in the sense of the fabled offer of milk to the stork and the fox. On the contrary, Congress has now required that the posture and condition of the job-seeker be taken into account. It has—to resort again to the fable—provided that the vessel in which the milk is proffered be one all seekers can use. The Act proscribes not only overt discrimination but also practices that are fair in form, but discriminatory in operation. The touch-stone is business necessity. If an employment practice which operates to exclude Negroes cannot be shown to be related to job performance, the practice is prohibited.

On the record before us, neither the high school completion requirement nor the general intelligence test is shown to bear a demonstrable relationship to successful performance of the jobs for which it was used. Both were adopted, as the Court of Appeals noted, without meaningful study of their relationship to job-performance ability. Rather, a vice president of the Company testified, the requirements were instituted on the Company's judgment that they generally would improve the overall quality of the work force.

The evidence, however, shows that employees who have not completed high school or taken the tests have continued to perform satisfactorily and make progress in departments for which the high school and test criteria are now used. . . .

The Court of Appeals held that the Company had adopted the diploma and test requirements without any "intention to discriminate against Negro employees." We do not suggest that either the District Court or the Court of Appeals erred in examining the employer's intent; but good intent or absence of discriminatory intent does not redeem employment procedures or testing mechanisms that operate as "built-in headwinds" for minority groups and are unrelated to measuring job capability.

The Company's lack of discriminatory intent is suggested by special efforts to help the undereducated employees through Company financing of two-thirds the cost of tuition for high school training. But Congress directed the thrust of the Act to the *consequences* of employment practices, not simply the motivation. More than that, Congress has placed on the employer the burden of showing that any given requirement must have a manifest relationship to the employer in question.

The facts of this case demonstrate the inadequacy of broad and general testing devices as well as the infirmity of using diplomas or degrees as fixed measures of capability. History is filled with examples of men and women who rendered highly effective performance without the conventional badges of accomplishment in terms of certificates, diplomas, or degrees. Diplomas and tests are useful servants, but Congress has mandated the common sense proposition that they are not to become masters of reality.

The Company contends that its general intelligence tests are specifically permitted by Section 703(h) of the Act. That section authorizes the use of "any professionally developed ability test" that is not "designed, intended or *used* to discriminate because of race. . ." (Emphasis added.)

The Equal Employment Opportunity Commission, having enforcement responsibility, has issued guidelines interpreting Section 703(h) to permit only the use of job-related tests. The administrative interpretation of the Act by the enforcing agency is entitled to great deference. . . . Since the Act and its legislative history support the Commission's construction, this affords good reason to treat the guidelines as expressing the will of Congress. . .

Nothing in the Act precludes the use of testing or measuring procedures, obviously they are useful. What Congress has forbidden is giving these devices and mechanisms controlling force unless they are demonstrably a reasonable measure of job performance. Congress has not commanded that the less qualified be preferred over the better qualified simply because of minority origins. Far from disparaging job qualifications as such, Congress has made such qualifications the controlling factor, so that race, religion, nationality, and sex become irrelevant. What Congress has commanded is that any tests used must measure the person for the job and not the person in the abstract. . . .

[Judgment reversed]

QUESTIONS

1. What is the question before the Supreme Court?
2. What was the objective of Congress in the enactment of Title VII?
3. Would the Court order the case against the employer to be dismissed if it found that the employer had adopted the diploma and test requirements without any intention to discriminate against minority employees?
4. As a result of the *Griggs* decision, may employers insist that both minority and white job applicants meet the applicable job qualifications as determined through the use of testing or measuring procedures?

2. The Equal Employment Opportunity Commission

The Equal Employment Opportunity Commission (EEOC) is a five-member commission appointed by the president to establish equal employment opportunity policy under the laws it administers. The EEOC supervises the conciliation and enforcement efforts of the agency.

The EEOC administers Title VII of the Civil Rights Act, the Equal Pay Act (EPA), the Age Discrimination in Employment Act (ADEA), Section 501 of the Rehabilitation Act (which prohibits federal sector discrimination against the handicapped), and Title I, the employment provisions of the Americans with Disabilities Act (ADA).

(a) PROCEDURE. Where there is a state or local EEO agency with the power to act on claims of discriminatory practices, the charging party must file a complaint with that agency. The charging party must wait 60 days

Figure 43-1

Discriminatory treatment in employment decisions on the basis of: Race Color Religion Sex National Origin	
Disparate Treatment Theory	**Disparate Impact Theory**
Nonneutral practice or Nonneutral application	Facially neutral practice and Neutral application
Requires proof of discriminatory intent	Does not require proof of discriminatory intent Requires proof of adverse effect on protected group and Employer is unable to show that the challenged practice is job related for the position in question and is consistent with business necessity
Either party has a right to require a jury trial when seeking compensatory or punitive damages	No right to a jury trial
Remedy: Reinstatement, hiring, or promotion Back pay less interim earnings Retroactive seniority Attorneys' and expert witness fees **plus** Compensatory* and punitive damages. Damages capped for cases of sex and religious discrimination depending on size of employer:	**Remedy:** Reinstatement, hiring, or promotion Back pay less interim earnings Retroactive seniority Attorneys' and expert witness fees

Number of employees	Damages cap
100 or fewer	$50,000
101 to 200	100,000
201 to 500	200,000
over 500	300,000

No cap on damages for race cases.

* Compensatory damages include future pecuniary losses and nonpecuniary losses such as emotional pain and suffering.

or until the termination of the state proceedings, whichever occurs first, before filing a charge with the EEOC. If no state or local agency exists, charges may be filed directly with the EEOC. The Commission conducts an investigation to determine whether reasonable cause exists to believe that the charge is true. If such cause is found to exist, the EEOC attempts to remedy the unlawful practice through conciliation. If the EEOC does not resolve the matter to the satisfaction of the parties, it may decide to litigate the case where unusual circumstances exist, including a "pattern or practice of discrimination." In most instances, however, the EEOC will issue the charging party a *right to sue* letter. Thereafter, the individual claiming a violation of EEO law, has ninety days to file a lawsuit in a federal district court.[2]

(b) DAMAGES. Damages available to victims of discrimination under Title VII are as set forth in Figure 43-1. Compensatory damages, including back pay, received by victims of disparate treatment (intentional) discrimination are excludable from gross income for federal income tax purposes.[3]

B. PROTECTED CLASSES AND EXCEPTIONS

In order to successfully pursue a Title VII lawsuit, the individual must belong to a protected class and meet the appropriate burden of proof. Exceptions exist for certain employment practices.

3. Race and Color

The legislative history of Title VII of the Civil Rights Act demonstrates that a primary purpose of the act is to provide fair employment opportunities for black Americans. The protections of the act are applied to blacks based on race or color. The word *race* as used in the act applies to all members of the four major racial groupings: white, black, native American, and Asian-Pacific. Native Americans can file charges and receive the protection of the act on the basis of national origin, race, or in some instances color. Individuals of Asian-Pacific origin may file discrimination charges based on race, color, or in some instances national origin. Whites are also protected against discrimination because of race and color. For example, two white professors at a predominately black university were successful in discrimination suits against the university where it was held that the university discriminated against them based on race and color in tenure decisions.[4]

4. Religion

Title VII requires employers to accommodate their employees' or prospective employees' religious practices. Most cases involving allegations of religious discrimination revolve around the determination of whether an employer has made reasonable efforts to accommodate religious beliefs. For example, if an employee's religious beliefs prohibit working on Saturday, an employer's obligation under Title VII is to try to find a volunteer to cover for the employee on Saturdays. The employer would not have an obligation to violate a seniority provision of a collective bargaining agreement, or call in a substitute worker if such accommodation would require more than a *de minimis* or very small cost.

Title VII permits religious societies to grant hiring preferences in favor of members of their religion. It also provides an exemption for educational institutions to hire employees of a particular religion if the institution is owned,

---

[2] Where an individual misses the filing deadline of Title VII, the individual may be able to bring a race discrimination case under the two-year time limit allowed under Section 1981 of the Civil Rights Act of 1866, codified as 42 USC § 1981 and sometimes called a Section 1981 lawsuit.

[3] IRS Bulletin No. 1993-41, December 20, 1993.

[4] Turgeon v Howard University (DC DC) 571 F Supp 679 (1983).

controlled, or managed by a particular religious society. The exemption is a broad one and is not restricted to the religious activities of the institution.

5. Sex

Employers who discriminate against female or male employees because of their sex are held to be in violation of Title VII. The EEOC and the courts have determined that the word *sex* as used in Title VII means a person's gender and not the person's sexual orientation. State and local legislation, however, may provide specific protection against discrimination based on sexual orientation.

(a) HEIGHT, WEIGHT, AND PHYSICAL ABILITY REQUIREMENTS. Under the *Griggs v Duke Power* precedent, an employer must be able to show that criteria used to make an employment decision that has a disparate impact on women, such as minimum height and weight requirements, are in fact job-related. All candidates for a position requiring physical strength must be given an opportunity to demonstrate their capability to perform the work. Women cannot be precluded from consideration just because they have not traditionally performed such work.

(b) PREGNANCY-RELATED BENEFITS. Title VII was amended by the Pregnancy Discrimination Act (PDA) in 1978. The amendment prevents employers from treating pregnancy, childbirth, and related medical conditions in a manner different than the treatment of other disabilities. Thus, women disabled due to pregnancy, childbirth, or other related medical conditions must be provided with the same benefits as other disabled workers. This includes temporary and long-term disability insurance, sick leave, and other forms of employee benefit programs. An employer who does not provide disability benefits or paid sick leave to other employees is not required to provide them for pregnant workers.

6. Sexual Harassment

Quid pro quo sexual harassment involves supervisors' seeking sexual favors from their subordinates in return for job benefits such as continued employment, promotion, a raise, or a favorable performance evaluation.[5] In such a case, where a supervisor's actions affect job benefits, Title VII's prohibition against sex discrimination has been violated. The employer is then liable to the employee for the loss of benefits plus punitive damages because of the supervisor's misconduct.

A second form of sexual harassment is **hostile working environment harassment**. With this type of harassment, an employee's economic benefits have not been affected by the supervisor's conduct, but the supervisor's sexually harassing conduct has nevertheless caused anxiety and "poisoned" the work environment. Such conduct may include unwelcome sexual flirtation, propositions, or other abuse of a sexual nature including the use of degrading words or the display of sexually explicit or suggestive pictures. An injunction against such conduct can be obtained and attorney's fees awarded. Moreover, if such conduct drives the employee to quit the job, the employer may be responsible for all of the economic losses caused the employee plus punitive damages.[6] In the *Harris v Forklift Systems Inc.* case an individual sued her former employer alleging a constructive discharge because of the abusive work environment.

---

[5]   According to EEOC Guidelines § 1604.11(f), "Unwelcome sexual advances, requests for sexual favors, and other verbal or physical conduct of a sexual nature constitute sexual harassment when (1) submission to such conduct is made either explicitly or implicitly a term or condition of an individual's employment, [and] (2) submission to or rejection of such conduct has the purpose or effect of unreasonably interfering with an individual's work performance or creating an intimidating, hostile, or offensive working environment."

[6]   Meritor Savings Bank v Vinson, 477 US 57 (1968).

HARRIS v FORKLIFT SYSTEMS INC.
114 S Ct 367 (1993)

Teresa Harris sued her former employer Forklift Systems Inc. under Title VII of the Civil Rights Act of 1964 claiming that the company's president, Charles Hardy, created "an abusive work environment" with a constant stream of sexually offensive jokes and remarks. When Hardy's conduct continued after Harris complained to him, she quit her job. A federal district court denied Harris' case because she had not shown severe psychological injury. The Sixth Circuit affirmed and the case was appealed to the U.S. Supreme Court.

O'CONNOR, J. . . . Title VII of the Civil Rights Act of 1964 makes it "an unlawful employment practice for an employer. . . to discriminate against any individual with respect to his compensation, terms, conditions, or privileges of employment, because of such individual's race, color, religion, sex, or national origin." 42 U.S.C. § 2000e-2(a)(1). As we made clear in *Meritor Savings Bank v Vinson*, 477 U.S. 57 (1986), this language "is not limited to 'economic' or 'tangible discrimination. The phrase 'terms, conditions, or privileges of employment' evinces a congressional intent 'to strike at the entire spectrum of disparate treatment of men and women' in employment," which includes requiring people to work in a discriminatorily hostile or abusive environment. . . . When the workplace is permeated with "discriminatory intimidation, ridicule, and insult," . . . that is "sufficiently severe or pervasive to alter the conditions of the victim's employment and create an abusive working environment," . . . Title VII is violated.

This standard, which we reaffirm today, takes a middle path between making actionable any conduct that is merely offensive and requiring the conduct to cause a tangible psychological injury. As we pointed out in *Meritor*, "mere utterance of an . . . epithet which engenders offensive feelings in a employee," . . . does not sufficiently affect the conditions of employment to [violate] Title VII. Conduct that is not severe or pervasive enough to create an objectively hostile or abusive work environment—an environment that a reasonable person would find hostile or abusive—is beyond Title VII purview. Likewise, if the victim does not subjectively perceive the environment to be abusive, the conduct has not actually altered the conditions of the victim's employment, and there is no Title VII violation.

But Title VII comes into play before the harassing conduct leads to a nervous breakdown. A discriminatorily abusive work environment, even one that does not seriously affect employees' psychological well-being, can and often will detract from employees' job performance, discourage employees from remaining on the job, or keep them from advancing in their careers. . . .

We . . . believe the District Court erred in relying on whether the conduct "seriously affect[ed] plaintiff's psychological well-being" or led her to "suffe[r] injury." Such an inquiry may needlessly focus the factfinder's attention on concrete psychological harm, an element Title VII does not require. Certainly Title VII bars conduct that would seriously affect a reasonable person's psychological well-being, but the statute is not limited to such control. So long as the environment would reasonably be perceived, and is perceived, as hostile or abusive, . . . there is no need for it also to be psychologically injurious.

This is not, and by its nature cannot be, a mathematically precise test. We need not answer today all the potential questions it raises. . . . But we can say that whether an environment is "hostile" or "abusive" can be determined only by looking at all the circumstances. These may include the frequency of the discriminatory conduct; its severity; whether it is physically threatening or humiliating, or a mere offensive utterance; and whether it unreasonably interferes with an employee's work performance. The effect on the employee's psychological well-being is, of course, relevant to determining whether the plaintiff actually found the environment abusive. But while psychological harm, like any other relevant factor, may be taken into account, no single factor is required.

[Judgment reversed and action remanded]

QUESTIONS

1. Classify the form of sexual harassment claimed in this case.
2. Did the Court indicate that a "reasonable woman standard" should be applied in determining whether or not conduct was severe enough to create a hostile work environment?
3. List the factors that a factfinder may consider in determining whether or not a hostile work environment existed in a specific case.

An employer is liable for the sexual harassment caused its employees by co-workers or its customers only when it fails to take remedial action after being informed of the misconduct. Employers may avoid liability for "hostile environment" sexual harassment by affirmatively raising the subject with all of the employees, expressing strong disapproval of such conduct, advising employees how to inform the employer of instances of sexual harassment, and taking disciplinary action against wrongdoers. (See Figure 43-2.)

Figure 43-2 Employer Procedure

A. Develop and implement an equal employment policy that specifically prohibits sexual harassment and imposes discipline up to and including discharge. Set forth specific examples of conduct that will not be tolerated.

B. Establish ongoing educational programs, including role playing and films, to demonstrate unacceptable behavior.

C. Designate a responsible senior official to whom complaints of sexual harassment can be made. Avoid any procedure that requires an employee to first complain to the employee's supervisor, since that individual may be the offending person.

D. Investigate all complaints promptly and thoroughly.

E. If a complaint has merit, the employer should impose appropriate and consistent discipline.

880   Part 7 Agency and Employment

7. National Origin

Title VII protects members of all nationalities from discrimination. The judicial principles that have emerged from cases involving race, color, and gender employment discrimination are generally applicable to cases involving allegations of national origin discrimination. Thus, physical standards such as minimum height requirements, which tend to exclude persons of a particular national origin because of the physical stature of the group, have been unlawful when these standards cannot be justified by business necessity.

Adverse employment based on an individual's lack of English language skills violate Title VII when the language requirement bears no demonstrable relationship to the successful performance of the job to which it is applied. In the *Fragante* case the court considered whether there was unlawful national origin discrimination when a job applicant with a heavy Filipino accent was not selected for employment.

FRAGANTE v CITY AND COUNTY OF HONOLULU
(CA9 Hawaii) 888 F2d 591 (1989)

Manuel Fragante applied for a clerk's job with the City and County of Honolulu. Although he placed high enough on a civil service eligibility list to be chosen for the position, he was not selected because of a deficiency in oral communication skill caused by his "heavy Filipino accent." Fragante brought suit, alleging that the defendants discriminated against him on the basis of his national origin, in violation of Title VII of the Civil Rights Act. The district court held that the ability to communicate orally and clearly was a legitimate occupational qualification for the job in question. There was no proof of a discriminatory intent or motive of the defendant. The court dismissed Fragante's complaint. Fragrante appealed to the court of appeals.

TROTT, C. J. . . . Preliminarily, we do well to remember that this country was founded and has been built in large measure by people from other lands, many of whom came here—especially after our early beginnings—with a limited knowledge of English. This flow of immigrants has continued and has been encouraged over the years. From its inception, the United States of America has been a dream to many around the world. We hold out promises of freedom, equality, and economic opportunity to many who only know these words as concepts. It would be more than ironic if we followed up our invitation to people such as Manuel Fragante with a closed economic door based on national origin discrimination. It is no surprise that Title VII speaks to this issue and clearly articulates the policy of our nation: unlawful discrimination based on national origin shall not be permitted to exist in the workplace. But, it is also true that there is another important aspect of Title VII: the "preservation of an employer's remaining freedom of choice." . . .

Accent and national origin are obviously inextricably intertwined in many cases. It would therefore be an easy refuge in this context for an employer unlawfully discriminating against someone based on national origin to state falsely that it was not the person's national origin that caused the employment or promotion problem, but the candidate's inability to measure up to the communication skills demanded by the job. We encourage a very searching look by the district courts at such a claim.

An adverse employment decision may be predicated upon an individual's accent when—but only when—it interferes materially with job performance. There is nothing improper about an employer making an *honest* assessment of the oral communication skills of a candidate for a job when such skills are reasonably related to job performance. EEOC Compliance Manual (CCH) 4035 at 3877-78 (1986); *see also Mejia v New York Sheraton Hotel*, 459 F. Supp. 375, 377 (S.D.N.Y. 1978) (Dominican chambermaid properly denied promotion to front desk because of her "inability to articulate clearly or coherently and to make herself adequately understood in . . English"); *Carino v University of Oklahoma Board of Regents*, 750 F2d 815, 819 (10th Cir. 1984) (plaintiff with a "noticeable" Filipino accent was improperly denied a position as supervisor of a dental laboratory where his accent did not interfere with his ability to perform supervisory tasks); *Berke*, 628 F2d at 981 (employee with "pronounced" Polish accent whose command of English was "well above that of the average adult American" was improperly denied two positions because of her accent). . .

. . . In a letter, dated June 28, 1982, the reasons why [Fragante] was not selected were [stated] as follows:

As to the reason for your non-selection we felt the two selected applicants were both superior in their verbal communication ability. As we indicated in your interview, our clerks are constantly dealing with the public and the ability to speak clearly is one of the most important skills required for the position. Therefore, while we were impressed with your educational and employment history, we felt the applicants selected would be better able to work in our office because of their communication skills.

The interviewers' record discloses Fragante's third place ranking was based on his "pronounced accent which is difficult to understand." Indeed, Fragante can point to no facts which indicate that his ranking was based on factors other than his inability to communicate effectively with the public. This view was shared by the district court. . . .

Fragante argues the district court erred in considering "listener prejudice" as a legitimate, nondiscriminatory reason for failure to hire. We find, however, that the district court did not determine defendants refused to hire Fragante on the basis that some listeners would "turn off" a Filipino accent. The district court after trial noted that: "Fragante, in fact, has a difficult manner of pronunciation and the Court further finds as a fact from his general testimony that he would often not respond directly to the questions as propounded. . .

In sum, the record conclusively shows that Fragante was passed over because of the deleterious *effect* of his Filipino accent on his ability to communicate orally, not merely because he had such an accent.

[Judgment affirmed]

QUESTIONS

1. Why do courts take a very careful look at non-selection decisions based on foreign accents?
2. Why was Fragante not selected for the clerk's position, when he had higher test scores than the two successful candidates?
3. Is it ethical for employers to hire "Americans" over individuals with heavy foreign accents who have the legal credentials to work in the United States?

8. Title VII Exceptions

Section 703 of Title VII defines which employment activities are unlawful. This same section, however, also exempts several key practices from the scope of Title VII enforcement. The most important are the bona fide occupational qualification exception, the testing and educational requirement exception, and the seniority system exception.

(a) BONA FIDE OCCUPATIONAL QUALIFICATION EXCEPTION. It is not an unlawful employment practice for an employer to hire employees on the basis of religion, sex, or national origin in those certain instances where religion, sex, or national origin is a bona fide occupational qualification (BFOQ) reasonably necessary to the normal operation of a particular enterprise. An example of a valid BFOQ is a men's clothing store's policy of hiring only males to do measurements for suit alterations. An airline's policy of hiring only female flight attendants is not a valid BFOQ, because such a policy is not reasonably necessary to safely operate an airline. Note that there is no BFOQ for race or color.

The court in the *Johnson Controls* case considered the employer's BFOQ defense to its "fetal-protection policy" which discriminated against women.

UAW v JOHNSON CONTROLS
499 US 187 (1991)

Johnson Controls, Inc. (JCI) manufactures batteries. A primary ingredient in the battery manufacturing process is lead. Occupational exposure to lead entails health risks, including the risk of harm to any fetus carried by a female employee.

After eight of its employees became pregnant while maintaining blood lead levels exceeding levels set by the Center for Disease Control (CDC) as dangerous for a worker planning to have a family, respondent JCI announced a new personnel policy. This policy barred all women, except those whose infertility was medically documented, from jobs involving actual or potential lead exposure exceeding the OSHA standards. Petitioners brought a class action in the district court, claiming that the policy constituted sex discrimination violative of Title VII of the Civil Rights Act of 1964, as amended. The court granted summary judgment for JCI, and the court of appeals affirmed. The case was appealed to Supreme Court.

BLACKMUN, J. . . . The bias in Johnson Controls' policy is obvious. Fertile men, but not fertile women, are given a choice as to whether they wish to risk their reproductive health for a particular job. Section 703(a) of the Civil Rights Act of 1964, 78 Stat 255, as amended, 42 U.S.C. § 2000e-2(a), prohibits sex-biased classifications in terms and conditions of employment, in hiring and discharging decisions, and in other employment decisions that adversely affect an employee's status. Respondent's fetal-protection policy explicitly discriminates against women on the basis of their sex. The policy excludes women with childbearing capacity from lead-exposed jobs and so creates a facial classification based on gender. . . .

First, Johnson Controls' policy classifies on the basis of gender and childbearing capacity, rather than fertility alone. Respondent does not seek to protect the unconceived children of all its employees. Despite evidence in the record about the debilitating effect of lead exposure on the male reproductive system, Johnson Controls is concerned only with the harms that may befall the unborn offspring of its female employees. . . .

. . . We hold that Johnson Controls' fetal-protection policy is sex discrimination forbidden under Title VII unless respondent can establish that sex is a "bona fide occupational qualification."

Under § 703(e)(1) of Title VII, an employer may discriminate on the basis of "religion, sex, or national origin in those certain instances where religion, sex, or national origin is a bona fide occupational qualification reasonably necessary to the normal operation of that particular business or enterprise." We therefore turn to the question whether Johnson Controls' fetal-protection policy is one of those "certain instances" that come within the BFOQ exception.

The BFOQ defense is written narrowly, and this Court has read it narrowly. . . . Our emphasis on the restrictive scope of the BFOQ defense is grounded on both the language and the legislative history of § 703.

The wording of the BFOQ defense contains several terms of restriction that indicate that the exception reaches only special situations. The statute thus limits the situations in which discrimination is permissible to "certain instances" where sex discrimination is "reasonably necessary" to the "normal operation" of the "particular" business. Each one of these terms—certain, normal, particular—prevents the use of general subjective standards and favors an objective, verifiable requirement. But the most telling term is "occupational"; this indicates that these objective, verifiable requirements must concern job-related skills and aptitudes.

Johnson Controls argues that its fetal-protection policy falls within the so-called safety exception to the BFOQ. Our cases have stressed that discrimination on the basis of sex because of safety concerns is allowed only in narrow circumstances. In *Dothard v Rawlinson*, this Court indicated that danger to a women herself does not justify discrimination. 433 U.S., at 335, 97 S. Ct. at 2729-2730. We there allowed the employer to hire only male guards in contact areas of maximum-security male penitentiaries only because more was at stake than the "individual woman's decision to weigh and accept the risks of employment." *Ibid*. We found sex to be a BFOQ inasmuch as the employment of a female guard would create real risks of safety to others if violence broke out because the guard was a woman. Sex discrimination was tolerated because sex was related to the guard's ability to do the job—maintaining prison security. We also required in *Dothard* a high correlation between sex and ability to perform job functions and refused to allow employers to use sex as a proxy for strength although it might be a fairly accurate one. . . .

Our case law, therefore, makes clear that the safety exception is limited to instances in which sex or pregnancy actually interferes with the employee's ability to perform the job. This approach is consistent with the language of the BFOQ provision itself, for it suggests that permissible distinctions based on sex must relate to ability to perform the duties of the job. Johnson Controls suggests, however, that we expand the exception to allow fetal-protection policies that mandate particular standards for pregnant or fertile women. We decline to do so. Such an expansion contradicts not only the language of the BFOQ and the narrowness of its exception but the plain language and history of the Pregnancy Discrimination Act. . . .

We have no difficulty concluding that Johnson Controls cannot establish a BFOQ. Fertile women, as far as appears in the record, participate in the manufacture of batteries as efficiently as anyone else. Johnson Controls' professed moral and ethical concern about the welfare of the next generation do not suffice to establish a BFOQ of female sterility. Decisions about the welfare of future children must be left to the parents who conceive, bear, support, and raise them rather than to the employers who hire those parents. . . .

A word about tort liability and the increased cost of fertile women in the workplace is perhaps necessary. . . .

More than 40 states currently recognize a right to recover for a prenatal injury based either on negligence or on wrongful death. According to Johnson Controls, however, the company complies with the lead standard developed by OSHA and warns its female employees about the damaging effects of lead. It is worth nothing that OSHA gave the problem of lead lengthy consideration and concluded that "there is no basis whatsoever for the claim that women of childbearing age should be excluded from the workplace in order to protect the fetus or the course of pregnancy." Instead, OSHA established a series of mandatory protections which, taken together, "should effectively minimize any risk to the fetus and newborn child." . . . Without negligence, it would be difficult for a court to find liability on the part of the employer. If, under general tort principles, Title VII bans sex-specific fetal-protection policies, the employer fully informs the woman of the risk, and the employer has not acted negligently, the basis for holding an employer liable seems remote at best. . . .

[Judgment reversed and action remanded]

QUESTIONS

1. Did Johnson Controls' "fetal-protection policy" discriminate against women?
2. JCI's fetal-protection policy was adopted only after 8 employees became pregnant, while maintaining blood lead levels exceeding the level set by the CDC as critical. Considering JCI's moral and ethical obligations to the unborn fetuses and its possible extensive liability in future lawsuits, should not the BFOQ defense be available to it?
3. Was JCI's policy within the so-called safety exception to the BFOQ?

(b) TESTING AND EDUCATIONAL RE-QUIREMENTS. Section 703(h) of the act authorizes the use of "any professionally developed ability test [that is not] designed, intended, or used to discriminate." Employment testing and educational requirements must be "job related"; that is, the employers must prove that the tests and educational requirements bear a relationship to job performance.

Courts will accept prior court-approved validation studies developed for a different employer in a different state or region so long as it is demonstrated that the job for which the test was initially validated is essentially the same job function for which the test is cur-rently being used. Thus, a firefighters test that had been validated in a study in California will be accepted as valid when later used in Virginia. Such application is called **validity generalization**.

The Civil Rights Act of 1991 makes it an unlawful employment practice for an employer to adjust scores or use different cut-off scores or otherwise alter the results of employment tests in order to favor any race, color, religion, sex, or national origin. This provision addresses the so-called "race norming" issue, whereby the results of hiring and promotion tests were adjusted to assure that a minimum number of minorities were included in application pools.

(c) SENIORITY SYSTEM. Section 703(h) provides that differences in employment terms based on a bona fide seniority system are sanctioned as long as the differences do not stem from an intention to discriminate. The term *seniority system* is generally understood to mean a set of rules that ensures that workers with longer years of continuous service for an employer will have a priority claim to a job over others with fewer years of service. Because such rules provide workers with considerable job security, organized labor has continually and successfully fought to secure seniority provisions in collective bargaining agreements.

9. Affirmative Action and Reverse Discrimination

Employers have an interest in affirmative action because it is fundamentally fair to have a diverse and representative workforce. Employers, under affirmative action plans (AAPs), may undertake special recruiting and other efforts to hire and train minorities and women and help them advance within the company. The plan may also provide job preferences for minorities and women. Such aspects of affirmative action plans have resulted in numerous lawsuits contending that Title VII, the Fourteenth Amendment, or collective bargaining contracts have been violated.

(a) PERMISSIBLE AAP'S. A permissible AAP should conform to the following criteria:
1. The affirmative action must be in connection with a "plan."
2. There must be a showing that affirmative action is justified as a remedial measure. The plan then must be remedial to open opportunities in occupations closed to protected classes under Title VII or de-

signed to break down old patterns of racial segregation and hierarchy.
3. The plan must be voluntary.
4. The plan must not unnecessarily trammel the interests of whites.
5. The plan must be temporary.[7]

(b) REVERSE DISCRIMINATION. When an employer's AAP is not shown to be justified, or "unnecessarily trammels" the interests of nonminority employees, it is often called "reverse discrimination." For example, a city's decision to rescore police promotional tests in order to achieve specific racial and gender percentages unnecessarily trammeled the interests of nonminority police officers.[8]

(c) EXECUTIVE ORDER. Presidential Executive Order 11246, regulates contractors and subcontractors doing business with the federal government. This order forbids discrimination against minorities and women, and in certain situations requires affirmative action to be taken to offer better employment opportunities to minorities and women. The Secretary of Labor has established the Office of Federal Contract Compliance Programs (OFCCP) to administer the order.

C. OTHER EEO LAWS

Major federal laws require equal pay for men and women doing equal work and forbid discrimination against older people and those with disabilities.

10. Equal Pay

The Equal Pay Act prohibits employers from paying employees of one gender lower wages than the rate paid employees of the other gender for equal work or substantially equal work in the same establishment, on jobs that require substantially equal skill, effort, and responsibility

---

[7] Steelworkers v Weber, 443 US 193 (1979); Johnson v Santa Clara County Transportation Agency 480 US 616 (1987).

[8] San Francisco Police Officers Association v San Francisco (CA9 Cal) 812 F2d 1125 (1987).

and that are performed under similar working conditions.[9] The Equal Pay Act does not prohibit all variations in wage rates paid men and women, but only those variations based solely on gender. The act sets forth four exceptions. Variances in wages are allowed pursuant to (1) a seniority system, (2) a merit system, (3) a system that measures earnings by quantity or quality of production, or (4) a differential based on any factor other than gender.

11. Age Discrimination

The Age Discrimination in Employment Act (ADEA) forbids discrimination by employers, unions, and employment agencies against persons over 40 years of age.[10]

Section 4(a) of the ADEA sets forth the employment practices that are unlawful under the act, including the failure to hire because of age and the discharge of employees because of age. Section 7(b) of the ADEA allows for the doubling of damages in cases of "willful violations of the act. Consequently, an employer who willfully violates the ADEA is liable not only for back wages and benefits but also for "an additional amount as liquidated damages."

The Older Workers Benefit Protection Act (OWBPA) of 1990[11] amends the ADEA by prohibiting age discrimination in employee benefits and establishing minimum standards for determining the validity of waivers of age claims. The OWBPA amends the ADEA by adopting an "equal benefit or equal cost" standard which provides that older workers must be given benefits which are at least equal to those provided for younger workers unless the employer can prove that the cost of providing an equal benefit would be more for an older worker than for a younger one.

Employers commonly require that employees electing to take "early retirement" packages waive all claims against their employers, including their rights or claims under the ADEA. The OWBPA requires that employees be given a specific period of time to evaluate a proposed package. Moreover, employers are obligated to pay for eight hours of an attorney's time to aid each employee in this evaluation.

Enforcement of the ADEA is the responsibility of the EEOC. Procedures and time limitations for filing and processing ADEA charges are the same as those under Title VII.

12. Discrimination Against Persons with Disabilities

The right of disabled persons to enjoy equal employment opportunities was established on the federal level with the enactment of the Rehabilitation Act of 1973.[12] Although not designed specifically as an employment discrimination measure but rather as a comprehensive plan to meet many of the needs of the disabled, the act contains three sections that provide guarantees against discrimination in employment. Section 501 is applicable to the federal government itself, Section 503 applies to federal contractors, and Section 504 applies to the recipients of federal funds.

The Americans With Disabilities Act[13] extends protection beyond the federal level. It prohibits all private employers with 15 or more employees from discriminating against disabled individuals, who, with or without reasonable accommodations are qualified to perform the essential functions of the job. Enforcement of the ADA is the responsibility of the EEOC.

---

[9] 29 USC § 206 (d)(1).

[10] 29 USC § 623.

[11] PL 101-422 October 16, 1990. This law reverses the Supreme Court's 1989 ruling in *Public Employees Retirement System of Ohio v Betts*, 492 US 158 (1989), which had the effect of exempting employee benefit programs from the ADEA.

[12] 29 USC §§ 701-794.

[13] 42 USC §§ 12101-12117.

An employer may make preemployment inquiries into the ability of a job applicant to perform job-related functions. However, an employer is prohibited from making inquiries as to whether the applicant has a disability.

(a) REASONABLE ACCOMMODATIONS UNDER THE ADA. Section 101(9) of the ADA defines an employer's obligation to make "reasonable accommodations" for individuals with disabilities to include (1) making existing facilities accessible to and usable by individuals with disabilities, and (2) job restructuring, modified work schedules, and acquisition or modification of equipment or devices. Employers are not obligated under the ADA to make accommodations that would be an "undue hardship" on the employer.

Prior to the ADA a supermarket meatcutter unable to carry meat from a refrigerator to a processing area may have been refused clearance to return to work after a back injury until the individual was able to perform all job functions. Today under the ADA it would be the employer's obligation to provide that disabled worker with a cart to assist the individual to perform the job, even if the cart cost $500. However, if the disabled meatcutter was employed by a small business with limited financial resources, an "accommodation" costing $500 may be an undue hardship which the employer could lawfully refuse to make.

(b) CONTAGIOUS DISEASES. A person with a contagious disease many be protected under the Rehabilitation Act and the Americans With Disabilities Act. The courts determine if the employee can work based on individualized medical judgments. Considerations include: (a) how the disease is transmitted, (b) the duration of the risk, (c) the severity of the risk, (d) the probability that the disease will be transmitted, and (e) whether the individual is otherwise qualified.

Persons with AIDS are within the protection of both the Rehabilitation Act and the Americans with Disabilities Act. Such persons must be treated like anyone else with a disability.[14]

(c) EXCLUSIONS FROM COVERAGE OF THE ADA. The act excludes from its coverage employees or applicants who are "currently engaging in the illegal use of drugs." The exclusion does not include an individual who has been successfully rehabilitated from such use or is participating in or has completed supervised drug rehabilitation and is no longer engaging in the illegal use of drugs.

Title V of the act states that behaviors such as transvestitism, transsexualism, pedophilia, exhibitionism, compulsive gambling, kleptomania, pyromania, or psychoactive substance use disorders resulting from current illegal use of drugs are not in and or themselves considered disabilities.

D. EXTRATERRITORIAL EMPLOYMENT

The Civil Rights Act of 1991 amended both Title VII and the ADA to provide protection for U.S. citizens employed in a foreign country by American-owned or controlled companies from discrimination based on race, color, religion, national origin, sex or disability.[15] The 1991 act contains an exemption if compliance with Title VII or the ADA would cause the company to violate the law of the foreign country in which it is located.

---

[14] Chalk v U.S. District Court (CA9 Cal) 840 F2d 701 (1988).

[15] Section 109 of the CRA of 1991, 102-166.

SUMMARY

Title VII of the Civil Rights Act of 1964, as amended, forbids discrimination on the basis of race, color, religion, sex, or national origin. The EEOC administers the act. Intentional discrimination is unlawful where there is disparate treatment of individuals because of their race, color, religion, gender, or national origin. Also, employment practices that make no reference to race, color, religion, sex or national origin, but that nevertheless have an adverse or disparate impact on the protected group are unlawful. In disparate impact cases the fact that the employer did not intend to discriminate is no defense. The employer must show that there is a job-related business necessity for the disparate impact practice in question. Employers have several defenses they may raise in a Title VII case to explain differences in employment conditions. They are: (1) bona fide occupational qualifications reasonably necessary to the normal operation of the business, (2) job-related professionally developed ability tests, and (3) bona fide seniority systems. If a state EEO agency or the EEOC is not able to bring about the resolution of the case, the EEOC issues a right-to-sue letter which enables the person claiming a Title VII violation to sue in a federal district court.

Affirmative action plans are legal under Title VII provided there is a voluntary "plan" which is justified as a remedial measure, and provided it does not unnecessarily trammel the interests of whites.

Under the Equal Pay Act (EPA) employers must not pay employees of one gender lower wages than the rate paid to employees of the other gender for substantially equal work. Workers over forty years of age are protected from discrimination by the Age Discrimination in Employment Act (ADEA). Employment discrimination against the disabled is prohibited by the Americans with Disabilities Act (ADA). Under the ADA employers must make reasonable accommodations, without undue hardship, to enable disabled individuals to work.

LAW IN PRACTICE

As an employer:

1. Make certain that the degree of discipline imposed on minorities and women "fits" the workplace problem or misconduct in question. Also research your records to make sure the discipline is consistent with the discipline imposed on nonminority employees for similar offenses.

2. Conduct ongoing educational programs on your company's sexual harassment policy. Effective programs will not only cut down the incidents of harassment, but may serve as a defense should a "hostile work environment" case go to court.

3. Occasionally audit your business payroll records in conjunction with employee job classifications and job descriptions to make sure that women are being paid the same wages as men when performing substantially the same work.

4. If your business is reducing the size of its workforce, make certain that older workers are not discriminated against. An early retirement program may be best for the morale of all workers, and less costly to your business, because ADEA damages for intentional discrimination allow for the doubling of damages.

As an employee:

5. If you have a Title VII complaint that is not resolved by the EEOC through conciliation, the EEOC will generally not litigate the matter on your behalf but will send you a "right-to-sue letter", and you will have to retain an attorney to bring a lawsuit. Hire an attorney with EEO expertise. If you are successful in your lawsuit, you will be reimbursed for reasonable attorneys' fees.

QUESTIONS AND CASE PROBLEMS

1. What social forces give rise to laws requiring equal employment opportunity for all individuals entitled to work in the United States?

2. List the major federal statutes dealing with the regulation of equal rights in employment

3. State the general purpose of Title VII of the Civil Rights Act of 1964.

4. Continental Photo, Inc. is a portrait photography company. Alex Riley, a black man, applied for a position as a photographer with Continental. Riley submitted an application and was interviewed. In response to a question on a written application, Riley indicated that he had been convicted for forgery (a felony) six years prior to the interview, had received a suspended sentence, and was placed on five-year probation. He also stated that he would discuss the matter with his interviewer if necessary. The subject of the forgery conviction was subsequently not mentioned by Continental's personnel director in his interview with Riley. Riley's application for employment was eventually rejected. Riley inquired as to the reason for his rejection by Continental. The personnel director, Geuther, explained to him that the prior felony conviction on his application was a reason for his rejection. Riley contended that the refusal to hire him because of his conviction record was actually discrimination against him because of his race in violation of Title VII. Riley felt that his successful completion of a five-year probation without incident and his steady work over the years qualified him for the job. Continental maintained that since its photographers handle approximately $10,000 in cash per year, its policy of not hiring applicants whose honesty was questionable was justified. Continental's policy excluded all applicants with felony convictions. Decide. Would the result be different if Riley had been a convicted murderer? *[Continental Photo, Inc., 26 FEP 1799 (EEOC)]*

5. What are the guidelines to be used in determining whether or not an affirmative action plan is permissible under Title VII?

6. Mohen is a member of the Sikh religion. The practice of Sikhism forbids the cutting or shaving of facial hair and also requires the wearing of a turban that covers the head. In accordance with the dictates of his religion, Mohen wore a long beard. He applied for a position as breakfast cook at the Island Manor restaurant. He was told that the restaurant's policy was to forbid cooks to wear facial hair for sanitary and good grooming reasons

and that he would have to shave his beard or be denied a position. Mohen contended that the restaurant had an obligation to make a reasonable accommodation to his religious beliefs, and let him keep his beard. Is he correct?

7. Sylvia Hayes worked as a staff technician in the radiology department of Shelby Memorial Hospital. On October 1 Hayes was told by her physician that she was pregnant. When Hayes informed the doctor of her occupation as an X-ray technician, the doctor advised Hayes that she could continue working until the end of April as long as she followed standard safety precautions. On October 8 Hayes told Gail Nell, the director of radiology at Shelby, that she had discovered that she was two months pregnant. On October 14 Hayes was discharged by the hospital. The hospital's reason for terminating Hayes was its concern for the safety of her fetus given the X-ray exposure that occurs during employment as an X-ray technician. Hayes brought an action under Title VII claiming that her discharge was unlawfully based on her condition of pregnancy. She cited scientific evidence and the practice of other hospitals where pregnant women were allowed to remain in their jobs as X-ray technicians. The hospital claimed that Hayes' discharge was based on business necessity. Moreover, the hospital claimed that the potential for future liability existed if an employee's fetus was damaged by radiation encountered at the workplace. Decide. *[Hayes v Shelby Memorial Hospital, (ND Ala) 546 F Supp 259]*

8. Overton suffered from depression and was made sleepy at work by medication taken for this condition. Also, because of his medical condition Overton needed a work area away from public access and needed substantial supervision to complete his tasks. The employer terminated him because of his routinely sleeping on the job, his inability to maintain contact with the public, and his need for supervision. Overton defended that he is a disabled person under the ADA and Rehabilitation Acts, fully qualified to perform the essential functions of the job, and that the employer had an obligation to make reasonable accommodations, such as allowing some catnaps as needed and providing some extra supervision. Decide. *[Overton v Reilly, (CA7 Ill) 977 F2d 1190]*

9. A teenage, female, high school student named Salazar was employed part-time at Church's Fried Chicken restaurant. Salazar was hired and supervised by Simon Garza, the assistant manager of the restaurant. Garza had complete supervisory powers when the restaurant's manager, Garza's roommate, was absent. Salazar claimed that while she worked at the restaurant, Garza would refer to her and all other females by a Spanish term that she found objectionable. According to Salazar, Garza once made an offensive comment about her body and repeatedly asked her about her personal life. On another occasion, Garza allegedly physically removed eye shadow from Salazar's face because he claimed it was unattractive. Salazar also claimed that one night she was restrained in a back room of the restaurant while Garza and another employee fondled her. Later that night, when Salazar told a customer what had happened, she was fired. Salazar brought suit under Title VII against Garza and Church's Fried Chicken, Inc., alleging sexual harassment. Church's, the corporate defendant, maintains that it should not be held liable under Title VII for Garza's harassment. Church's bases its argument on the existence of a published "fair treatment policy." Decide. [Salazar v Church's Fried Chicken, Inc. 44 FEP 472 (SD Tex)]

10. John Chadbourne was hired by Raytheon on February 4, 1980. His job performance reviews were uniformly high. In December 1983, Chadbourne was hospitalized and diagnosed as having AIDS. In January 1984, his physician informed Raytheon that Chadbourne was able to return to work. On January 20, 1984, Chadbourne took a return-to-work physical examination required by Raytheon. The company's doctor wrote that County Communicable Disease Control Director, Dr. Juels, seeking a determination on the appropriateness of Chadbourne's returning to work. Dr. Juels informed the company that ". . .contact of employees to an AIDS patient appears to pose no risk from all evidence accumulated to date." Dr. Juels also visited the plant and advised the company doctor that there was no medical risk to other employees at the plant if Chadbourne returned to work. Ratheon refused to reinstate Chadbourne to his position until July 19, 1984. Its basis for denying reinstatement was that co-workers might be at risk of contracting AIDS. Was Raytheon entitled to bar Chadbourne from work during the six-month period of January through July? [Raytheon v Fair Employment and Housing Commission, 212 Cal App 3d 1242, 261 Cal Rptr 197]

11. Connie Cunico, a white woman, was employed by the Pueblo, Colorado School District as a social worker. She and other social workers were laid off in seniority order because of the district's poor financial situation. However, the school board thereafter decided to retain Wayne Hunter, a black social worker with less seniority than Cunico, because he was the only black on the administrative staff. No racial imbalance existed in the relevant workforce. Black persons constituted 2 percent of the workforce. Cunico, who was rehired over two years later, claimed that she was the victim of reverse discrimination. She stated that she lost $110,361 in back wages, plus $76,000 in attorneys' fees and costs. The school district replied that it was correct in protecting with special consideration the only black administrator in the district under the general principles it set forth in its AAP. Did the employer show that its affirmative action in retaining Hunter was justified as a remedial measure? Decide. [Cunico v Pueblo School District No. 6 (CA 10 Colo) 917 F2d 431]

12. Della Janich was employed as a matron at the Yellowstone County Jail in Montana. The duties of the position of matron resemble those of a parallel male position-jailer. Both employees have the responsibility for booking prisoners, showering and dressing them, and placing them in the appropriate section of the jail depending on the sex of the offender. Because 95 percent of the prisoners at the jail were men and 5 percent were women, the matron was assigned more bookkeeping duties than the jailer. At all times during Della's employment at the jail, her male counterparts received $125 more per month as jailers. Della brought an action under the Equal Pay Act alleging discrimination against her in her wages because of her sex. The county sheriff denied the charge. Decide. [Janich v Sheriff (DC Mont) 29 FEP 1195]

13. Carlyle Cline, age 42, was employed for ten years by Roadway Express Company, most recently as a loading dock supervisor at a Roadway terminal in North Carolina. Cline had received periodic merit pay raises, and his personnel file contained an even amount of both complimentary and unfavorable evaluations by supervisors. When R.W. Hass became vice-president for Roadway's southern division, he decided that the division needed to "upgrade" the quality of its personnel. Hass directed terminal managers to "look at" employees who had been with the company for five years without being promoted and decide whether they should be replaced with higher quality employees, preferably college graduates. Thus the ultimate decision regarding "promotability" was left to the terminal managers. They were not told they were not to consider age when determining promotability. After the announcement of the new policy, Cline was discharged and classified "unpromotable." The terminal manager compiled a list of negative comments from Cline's file as evidence that Cline was discharged for "poor work performance." Roadway immediately replaced Cline with a man in his early thirties. Cline brought an action against Roadway under the Age Discrimination in Employment Act, claiming he was discharged "because of his age in violation of the Act." Roadway maintained that Cline was discharged because of poor work performance. Decide. [Cline v Roadway Express (CA4 NC) 689 F2d 48]

14. Mazir Coleman had driven a school bus for the Casey County, Kentucky, Board of Education for four years. After that time, Coleman's left leg had to be amputated. Coleman was fitted with an artificial leg and underwent extensive rehabilitation to relearn driving skills. When his driving skills had been sufficiently relearned over the course of four years, Coleman applied to the county board of education for a job as a school bus driver. The county refused to accept Coleman's application. The county board said that it had no alternative but to deny Coleman a bus-driving job because of a Kentucky administrative regulation. That regulation stated in part: "No person shall drive a school bus who does not possess both of these natural bodily parts: feet, legs, hands, arms, eyes, and ears. The driver shall have normal use of the above named body parts." Coleman brought an action under the Rehabilitation Act claiming discrimination based on his physical handicap.

The county board of education denied this charge claiming that the reason they rejected Coleman was because of the requirement of the state regulation. May Coleman maintain an action of employment discrimination in light of the state regulation on natural body parts? Decide. [Coleman v Casey County Board of Education (ND Ky) 510 F Supp 301]

15. Marcia Sexton worked for Jerry Richardson, a supervisor at AT&T's International Division. Richardson made advances to Saxton on two occasions over a three-week period. Each time Saxton told him she did not appreciate his advances. No further advances were made. Thereafter, Saxton felt that Richardson treated her condescendingly and stopped speaking to her on a social basis at work. Four months later Saxton filed a formal internal complaint, asserting sexual harassment, and went on "paid leave." AT&T found inconclusive evidence of sexual harassment, but determined that the two employees should be separated. Saxton declined a transfer to another department, so AT&T transferred Richardson instead. Saxton still refused to return to work. Thereafter, AT&T terminated Saxton for refusal to return to work. Saxton contends she is a victim of a hostile working environment sexual harassment. AT&T defends that while the supervisor's conduct was inappropriate and unprofessional, it falls short of the type of action necessary for sexual harassment under federal law (the *Harris* case). Decide. [Saxton v AT&T Co. (CA7 Ill) 10 F3d 526]

PART 8

Business Organizations

FORMS OF BUSINESS ORGANIZATIONS

LEARNING OBJECTIVES

After studying this chapter, you will be able to:
1. *List the advantages and disadvantages of the three principal forms of business.*
2. *Determine if a business arrangement is a franchise.*
3. *State the reasons for the FTC disclosure requirements.*
4. *Distinguish a joint venture from a partnership.*
5. *Compare an unincorporated association with a cooperative.*

What form of legal organization should you have for your business? The answer will be found in your needs for money, personnel, control, tax and estate planning, and protection from liability.

A. PRINCIPAL FORMS OF BUSINESS ORGANIZATIONS

The law of business organizations may be better understood if advantages and disadvantages of proprietorships, partnerships, and corporations are first considered.

1. Individual Proprietorships

A **sole** or **individual proprietorship** is a form of business ownership in which one individual owns the business. The owner may be the sole worker of the business or may employ as many others as needed to run the concern. Individual proprietorships are commonly used in retail stores, service businesses, and agriculture.

(a) ADVANTAGES. The proprietor or owner is not required to expend resources on organizational fees. The proprietor, as the sole owner, controls all of the decisions and receives all of the profits. The business' net earnings are not subject to the corporate income tax, but are taxed only as personal income.

(b) DISADVANTAGES. The proprietor is subject to unlimited personal liability for the debts of the business and cannot limit this risk. The investment capital in the business is limited by the resources of the sole proprietor. Since all contracts of the business are made by the owner or in the owner's name by agents of the owner, the authority to make contracts terminates on the death of the owner, and the business is subject to disintegration.

2. Partnerships

A **partnership** involves the pooling of capital resources and the business or professional talents of two or more individuals with the goal of making a profit. Law firms, medical associations, and architectural and engineering firms may operate under the partnership form, although normally they will form professional corporations or limited liability companies. A wide range of retail and service businesses operate as partnerships.

(a) ADVANTAGES. The partnership form of business organization allows individuals to pool resources and then initiate and conduct their business without the requirement of a formal organizational structure.

(b) DISADVANTAGES. Major disadvantages of a partnership are the unlimited personal liability of each partner and the uncertain duration of the business because the partnership is dissolved by the death of a partner.

3. Corporations

Business corporations exist to make a profit. They are created by government grant. The statute regulating the creation of corporations requires a corporate structure consisting of shareholders, directors, and officers. The shareholders, as the owners of the business, elect a board of directors, who are responsible for the management of the business. The directors employ officers, who serve as the agents of the business and who run the day-to-day operations. Corporations range in size from incorporated one-owner enterprises to large multinational concerns.

(a) ADVANTAGES. The major advantage to the shareholder, or investor, is that the shareholder's risk of loss from the business is limited to the amount of capital that the shareholder invested in the business or paid for shares. This factor, coupled with the free transferability of corporate shares, makes the corporate form of business organization attractive to investors. By purchasing shares, a large number of investors may contribute the capital assets needed to finance large business enterprises. As the capital needs of a business expand, the corporate form becomes more attractive.

A corporation is a separate legal entity capable of owning property, contracting, suing, and being sued in its own name. It has perpetual life. In other words, a corporation is not affected by the death of any of its shareholders nor the transfer of their shares. In contrast to the case of a partnership or proprietorship, the death of an owner has no legal effect on the corporate entity.

(b) DISADVANTAGES. A corporation is required to pay corporate income taxes. Shareholders, when they receive a distribution of profits for the corporation, are required to pay personal income taxes on the amount received. This is a form of double taxation, which may be significant if the corporation is owned by a small group.

Incorporation involves the expenditure of funds for organizational expenses. Documents necessary for the formation of a corporation, which are required by state law, must be prepared, and certain filing fees must be paid. State corporation laws may also require the filing of an annual report and other reports.

B. SPECIAL FORMS OF ORGANIZATIONS

Special forms of business organizations have developed to meet special needs.

4. Franchises

The franchise serves as a franchisor's method of controlling and financing operations and as a franchisee's method of investment and participation.

(a) DEFINITIONS. The Federal Trade Commission has defined a **franchise** as "an arrangement in which the owner of a trade-mark, trade name, or copyright licenses others, under specified conditions or limitations, to use the trademark, trade name, or copyright in purveying goods or services." The **franchisor** is the party granting the franchise, and the **franchisee** is the person to whom the franchise is granted.

A common issue in litigation under state laws protecting franchises is whether or not the business arrangement of the parties to the dispute is a franchise under the applicable state law. A factor in determining whether a "franchise" exists is whether the purported franchise agreement conveys authority or license to the franchisee to use the trademark, logo, or trade name of the franchiser.

The fact that the parties to a franchise do not use the word *franchise* does not prevent their relationship from being so classified. If the realities of the business arrangement fit within the definition of the term *franchise*, the franchising law will apply regardless of the terms used in the parties contract.

(b) NATURE OF RELATIONSHIP. The relationship between the franchisor and the franchisee is an arm's-length relationship between two independent contractors. Their respective rights are determined by the contract existing between them. A franchise is a business relationship between distinct business organizations, which is governed by the franchise contract.

(1) Duration and Termination. The franchise may last for as long as the parties agree. The laws in some states may require advance written notice of cancellation.[1] Franchise contracts generally specify the causes for which the franchisor may terminate the franchise, such as the franchisee's death, bankruptcy, failure to make payments, or failure to meet sales quotas. Implied obligations of good faith and fair dealing apply to these contracts.[2]

The *McDonald's Corp.* case is an example of the basic contractual nature of franchising.

---

[1] See, for example, Mo Rev Stat § 407.405; Ridings v Thoele (Mo) 739 SW2d 547 (1987).

[2] Dunkin Donuts of America v Minerva Inc. (CA11 Fla) 956 F2d 1566 (1992).

MCDONALD'S CORP. v ROBERT A. MAKIN, INC.
(DC NY) 653 F Supp 401 (1986)

McDonald's Corporation leased one of its restaurants to Makin and gave it a franchise to run the restaurant. The franchise agreement required Makin to make monthly payments of license and lease fees to McDonald's, and the agreement provided for the termination of the franchise if Makin should fail to make all payments under the agreement. Makin failed to make monthly payments from October 1985 through February 10, 1986. McDonald's gave notice that it had terminated the franchise. Makin refused to terminate operations and surrender the premises. McDonald's brought suit for the amount due for the period and sought a court order granting it the right to enter and take possession of the restaurant. Makin's defense was that McDonald's engaged in a coercive pricing policy in violation of the Sherman Antitrust Act.

CURTIN, D. J. . . . The franchise agreement obligates the defendant to pay monthly fees to plaintiff for the franchise. Nowhere [does] the defendant deny [its] failure to pay these fees since October, 1985. Yet, defendant [has] maintained possession and operation of the franchise property. At oral argument, counsel for defendant contended that McDonald's conduct . . . caused defendant's inability to make the payments. Defendant's counterclaims do not allege that McDonald's conduct caused the non-payment; moreover, defendant contends that most of McDonald's alleged illegal conduct began 7-14 years ago, over which time defendant regularly made the monthly fee payments. In any event, it should be clear to all concerned that

it is against the law as well as sound morals to permit a party to a contract to repudiate the contract or his obligation under it, and at the same time retain the consideration that he has received. . . .

Defendant's counterclaims will, of course, be adjudicated in their own right; however, the alleged wrongs of plaintiff do not constitute affirmative defenses to defendant's non-payment of franchise fees. The defendant may not use [its] counterclaims to avoid judgment for the amounts already due under the franchise agreement. The failure of defendant to pay the monthly franchise fees is a breach of contract as to which there exists no genuine factual issue. . . .

The franchise contract, consisting of the license and lease documents referenced herein, has been lawfully terminated as of February 10, 1986. In accordance with the provisions of the agreement, McDonald's has an immediate right to enter and take possession of the North Transit Road McDonald's and to require defendant to forthwith return all material containing McDonald's trade secrets, operating instructions, or business practices and to discontinue the use of the McDonald's System. . . .

[So ordered]

QUESTION

On what basis did McDonald's contend that it had a right to receive monthly payments and, when the payments were not made, the right to terminate the franchise and take possession of the restaurant?

Franchise contracts frequently contain an arbitration provision under which a neutral party is to make a final and binding determination as to whether there has been a breach of the contract sufficient to justify cancellation of the franchise. The arbitration provision may provide that the franchisor can appoint a trustee to run the business of the franchisee while the arbitration proceedings are pending.

(2) Regulation. Holders of automobile dealership franchises are protected from bad-faith termination of their dealerships by the federal Automobile Dealers' Franchise Act.[3] When an automobile manufacturer makes arbitrary and unreasonable demands and then terminates the dealer's franchise for failure to comply with the demands, the manufacturer is liable for the damages caused. However, a manufacturer is justified in terminating an automobile dealership if the dealership fails to maintain the required sales quota when the manufacturer has given the dealer repeated warnings, when the quota is reasonable, and when the quota has been reduced to reflect local economic conditions.

The Petroleum Marketing Practices Act (PMPA) gives a gasoline franchisee the opportunity to continue in business by purchasing the entire premises used in selling motor fuel when the franchisor determines to sell the property and not to renew a lease.[4]

When the relationship between the franchisor and the franchisee is created primarily for the sale of products manufactured by the franchisor, the rights of the parties are governed by the law of sales of Article 2 the UCC.

Also, vertical price-fixing agreements between a franchisor-manufacturer and its franchisee-distributor are a violation of the federal antitrust laws. Thus, when a manufacturer of winches terminated one of the distributorships for discounting prices contrary to the manufacturer's resale price maintenance policy, the manufacturer was in violation of Section 1 of the Sherman Antitrust Act. The manufacturer was required to pay three times the actual damages caused by the termination.[5]

There continue to be statutory reform movements, both at the federal and state levels, to provide general protection for the franchise holder. Protective regulation of franchisees generally relates to problems of fraud in the sale of the franchise and to the protection of the franchisee from unreasonable demands and termination by the franchisor.

The *Crone* case illustrates the application of a state retail franchising law to a case alleging the unlawful cancellation of a franchise without reasonable cause.

To protect a prospective franchisee from deception, the Federal Trade Commission adopted a rule that requires the franchisor to give a prospective franchisee a full disclosure statement. The statement sets forth the franchisee's financial and legal obligations. The statement must include: (1) the material terms of the franchise agreement, (2) initial and recurring payments, (3) restrictions on territories, and (4) grounds for termination of the franchise. The statement must be given to the prospective franchisee ten days before the

---

[3] 15 USC § 1222. A number of states have similar statutes.

[4] Baker v Amaco Oil Co. (CA7 Wis) 956 F2d 639 (1992).

[5] Pierce v Ramsey Winch Co. (CA5 Tex) CCH Bus Fran Rptr, Paragraph 8318 (1985).

CRONE v RICHMOND NEWSPAPERS, INC.
238 Va 262, 384 SE2d 77 (1989)

James Crone and other newspaper distributors brought actions against Richmond Newspapers, Inc. (RNI), under a state retail franchising act. The plaintiffs sought damages for the cancellation of their contracts to distribute newspapers for RNI. The distributors used racks in the sale of the newspaper and were required under their contract with RNI to paint and maintain the racks and display the RNI logo on each rack. In March of 1986, RNI canceled the franchises. The distributors contended that the cancellations were without reasonable cause as defined in the state retail franchising act. RNI contended that its contracts were not franchises within the meaning of the act. From a judgment ruling that the contracts were not franchises within the meaning of the act, Crone and the other distributors appealed.

COMPTON, J. . . . The policy of the Commonwealth, as declared in the Act, is "to regulate commerce partly or wholly within the Commonwealth of Virginia" in order to correct "such inequities as may exist in the franchise system so as to establish a more even balance of power between franchisors and franchisees; to require franchisors to deal fairly with their franchisees . . . and to provide franchisees more direct, simple, and complete judicial relief against franchisors who fail to deal in a lawful manner with them." Code § 13.1-558.

The Act further provides . . . that a franchise is "a written contract or agreement . . . between two or more persons" in which a franchisee "is granted the right to engage in the business of offering, selling or distributing goods or services at retail under a marketing plan or system prescribed in substantial part by a franchisor," and the "operation of the franchisee's business pursuant to such plan or system is substantially associated with the franchisor's trademark, service mark, trade name, logotype, advertising or other commercial symbol designating the franchisor or its affiliate." § 13.1-559(b)(1) and (2).

The present dispute stems from the following sentence in § 13.1-559: "This chapter shall apply only to a franchise the performance of which contemplates or requires the franchisee to establish or maintain a place of business within the Commonwealth of Virginia."

The Act further provides: "It shall be unlawful for a franchisor to cancel a franchise without reasonable cause. . . ."

. . . The Act applies only to an agreement "the performance of which contemplates or requires the franchisee to establish or maintain a place of business within the Commonwealth of Virginia." A plain reading of that provision, in the context of the whole Act, demonstrates to us that it simply requires the business transacted under the franchise agreement to have a nexus to the Commonwealth. The proviso merely records the intention of the General Assembly to legislate constitutionally by regulating business within the State in a field which often involves transactions in interstate commerce.

In our view, the provision is not so restrictive, as RNI contends, as to place the burden upon a party seeking protection of the Act to show that a fixed physical site where business is transacted, such as a shop, office or warehouse, has been established. The franchisee need not prove, for example, that a freestanding, coin-operated newspaper rack, resting at a street corner unattended by any salesperson, meets some technical definition of "place of business." Rather, the party seeking coverage of the Act must show only a business connection or link with this State. The distributor in this case has alleged such a connection.

Here, a Virginia resident has agreed to distribute a product from a specified location within a designated Virginia [rack account] territory. In other words, the obligations of the contract require the distributor to perform business from "places" within the State. As we interpret the Act, the focus is not on whether a single vending machine, a [rack account] territory, or the distributor's residence qualify independently as a "place of business." So long as the places where the distributor operates under the contract, disseminating RNI's product, are within the State, the required nexus exists. . . .

[Reversed and remanded]

QUESTIONS

1. Why did the state pass the retail franchising act?
2. Can a business avoid the application of the state franchising act by carefully avoiding all reference to the words "franchise," "franchising," "franchisor," and "franchisee" in its contract with each distributor?
3. Assess the validity of the following statement: "Because an unattended, coin-operated newspaper rack is not a 'place of business' within the state, the retail franchising law did not apply to the distributors."

franchisee signs a contract or pays any money for a franchise. Under the FTC disclosure rule, a franchisor must pay a civil penalty of as much as $10,000 for each violation when it is shown that a "sale" relating to a franchise subject to the FTC rule was made, the franchisor "knew or should have known" of the disclosure rule, and no disclosure statement was given to the "buyer."[6]

(c) THE FRANCHISOR AND THIRD PERSONS. In theory, the franchisor is not liable to a third person dealing with or affected by the franchise holder. This freedom from liability is one of the reasons franchisors use franchises. If the negligence of the franchisee causes harm to a third person, the franchisor is not liable, because the franchisee is an independent contractor.[7]

The *Henry v Taco Tio Inc.* case involved the apparent authority of a franchisee.

HENRY v TACO TIO INC.
(La App) 606 So 2d 1376 (1992)

For a five-year period, Laurie Henry worked for James Doull, the owner of four Taco Bell franchises. During that time she had an affair with Doull. He

---

[6] US v TCI Inc. CCH Trade Cases, Paragraph 62,058 (1987).

[7] Cislaw v 7-Eleven, Inc. 6 Cal Rptr 2d 386 (1992).

was the father of her two illegitimate children. Enraged over a domestic matter, Doull physically assaulted Henry, then fired her and ordered her off the premises. Later, on Doull's recommendation, Henry was hired by a "company store" in an adjoining state. Henry brought a tort suit against Doull, his corporate entity Taco Tio, Inc., and the Taco Bell Corporation (TBC). She did not characterize her suit as one for sexual harassment. Rather, she contended that TBC was responsible for Doull's actions because he was TBC's agent. She sought damages for the loss of romantic and material satisfactions a person might expect from a traditional courtship and wedding. TBC denied that Doull was an employee or agent of TBC. The evidence showed that Henry knew that Doull's stores were not owned by TBC and that his stores differed from TBC "company" stores. The trial court dismissed all claims against TBC, and Henry appealed.

LINDSAY, J. . . . The plaintiff was fully aware that she was employed by a franchise owned by Mr. Doull through his corporation. As a franchise owner, Mr. Doull was her employer with the sole right to hire or fire her without any interference or input from TBC. Accordingly, TBC cannot he held liable to the plaintiff as her employer.

Nor can TBC be held vicariously liable as Mr. Doull's employer. The record fails to show an employment relationship between them . . .

The plaintiff asserts the applicability of the doctrine of apparent authority. However, "apparent authority results from a manifestation by the principal to a third person that another is his agent. But apparent authority exists only to the extent that it is reasonable for the third person dealing with the agent to believe that the agent is authorized." . . . Furthermore, the third person must actually believe that the agent is authorized. . . .

. . . The plaintiff, who eventually achieved the status of a store manager, had actual knowledge soon after her employment by Mr. Doull that she was working at a franchise, not a company store.

Additionally, the record fails to support the plaintiff's allegations of some sort of conspiracy concerning the plaintiff's transfer from the Doull's restaurants to a company store in Mississippi. The testimony is consistent that the plaintiff's transfer was represented to TBC as a simple relocation by an employee who was moving to be closer to a family member (the plaintiff's sister).

Based on the foregoing, we find that there are no disputed issues of material fact and that TBC is entitled to summary judgment as a matter of law . . .

[Judgment affirmed]

QUESTIONS

1. Who was Henry's employer, Doull or TBC?
2. Was Taco Bell Corporation found responsible for the torts of its franchisee on an apparent authority theory?
3. Why do you think Henry included TBC as a party to this lawsuit?

When the franchisee makes a contract with a third person, the franchisor is not liable on the contract. The franchisee is not the agent of the franchisor and does not have any authority to bind the franchisor by contract.

In some cases, the franchisor has exercised such control over the franchisee that the latter has lost the status of an independent contractor and is treated as an employee or agent. When this happens, the franchisor may be liable to third persons as though the franchisee were in fact an agent or employee. In other cases, liability is imposed on the franchisor because the franchisee appeared to have the authority to impose such liability.

To insulate themselves from liability, franchisors often require that individual franchisees take steps to publicly maintain their own individual identity as a business. Thus, a gasoline service station may post a sign stating that it is "dealer owned and operated," or a real estate franchisee may list on its business sign the franchise name and the name of the local owner, such as "Century 21, L & K Realty Co."

(1) Actual Control. A franchisor is liable to third persons when the franchisor exercises such actual control over the operations of the franchisee that the latter is not to be regarded as an independent contractor but rather as an employee or agent of the franchisor.[8] Moreover, a franchisor is liable for its own negligence in inspecting and recommending fixtures and equipment to be used by its franchisees.

(2) Product Liability. Sometimes a franchise involves the resale of goods manufactured or obtained by the franchisor and supplied to the franchisee. If such a product causes harm to the franchisee's customer, the franchisor may be liable to the customer on a theory of product liability.

(d) THE FRANCHISEE AND THIRD PERSONS. When the franchise holder has any contract relationship or contact with a third person, the contract or tort liability of the franchisee is the same as though there were no franchise. The fact that there is a franchise does not add to or subtract from the liability that the franchisee would have in the same situation if there had been no franchise. For example, if the franchise is to operate a restaurant, the franchise holder is liable to a customer for breach of an implied warranty of the fitness of the food for human consumption to the same extent as though the franchise holder were running an independent restaurant. If the franchise holder negligently causes harm to a third person—for example, by running over that person with a truck used in the enterprise—the tort liability of the franchise holder is determined by the principles that would be applicable if no franchise existed. The franchise holder is liable on a contract made in the franchise holder's own name.

5. Joint Ventures

A **joint venture**, or joint adventure, is a relationship in which two or more persons combine their labor or property for a single business undertaking and share profits and losses equally, or as otherwise agreed.[9] When several contractors pool all their assets in order to construct one tunnel, the relationship is a joint venture.

A joint venture is similar in many respects to a partnership. It differs primarily in that the joint venture typically relates to the pursuit of a single enterprise or transaction, although its accomplishment may require several years. A partnership is generally a continuing business or activity. A partnership may, however, be expressly created for a single transaction. Because the distinction is so insubstantial, most courts hold that joint ventures are subject to the same principles of law as partnerships.[10] Thus, the duties owed by the joint venturers to each other are the same as those that partners owe to each other.

---

8 Martin v McDonald's Corp. 213 Ill App 3d 487, 157 Ill Dec 609, 572 NE2d 1073 (1991).
9 See Latiolais v BFI of Louisiana Inc. (La App) 567 So 2d 1159 (1990).

It is essential that the venturers have a common purpose and that each has an equal right to control the operations or activities of the undertaking.[11] The actual control of the operations may be entrusted to one of the joint venturers. Thus, the fact that one joint venturer is placed in control of the farming and livestock operations of the undertaking and appears to be the owner of the land does not destroy the joint venture relationship.

(a) DURATION OF JOINT VENTURE.   A joint venture continues for the time specified in the agreement of the parties. In the absence of a fixed-duration provision, a joint venture is ordinarily terminable at the will of any participant. When the joint venture clearly relates to a particular transaction, such as the construction of a specified bridge, the joint venture ordinarily lasts until the particular transaction or project is completed or becomes impossible to complete.

(b) LIABILITY TO THIRD PERSONS.   The conclusion that persons are joint venturers is important when a suit is brought by or against a third person for personal injuries or property damage. If there is a joint venture, the fault or negligence of one venturer will be imputed to the other venturers.[12]

6.   Unincorporated Associations

An **unincorporated association** is a combination of two or more persons for the furtherance of a common purpose.[13] No particular form of organization is required. Any conduct or agreement indicating an attempt to associate or work together for a common purpose is sufficient.

The authority of an unincorporated association over its members is governed by ordi-nary contract law. An association cannot expel a member for a ground that is not expressly authorized by the contract between the association and the member.

Except when otherwise provided by statute, an unincorporated association does not have any legal existence apart from its members. Thus, an unincorporated association cannot sue or be sued in its own name.

Generally, the members of an unincorporated association are not liable for the debts or liabilities of the association by the mere fact that they are members. It must usually be shown that they authorized or ratified the act in question. If either authorization or ratification by a particular member can be shown, that member has unlimited liability for the act.

7.   Cooperatives

A **cooperative** consists of a group of two or more independent persons or enterprises that cooperate with respect to a common objective or function. Thus, farmers may pool their farm products and sell them. Consumers may likewise pool their orders and purchase goods in bulk.

(a) INCORPORATED COOPERATIVES. Statutes commonly provide for the special incorporation of cooperative enterprises. Such statutes often provide that any excess of payments over cost of operation shall be refunded to each participant member in direct proportion to the volume of business that the member has done with the cooperative. This contrasts with the payment of a dividend by an ordinary business corporation, in which the payment of dividends is proportional to the number of shares held by the shareholder and is unrelated to the extent of the shareholder's business activities with the enterprise.

---

[10] Pardco v Spinks (Tex Civ App) 836 SW2d 649 (1992).

[11] Dunbar v RKG Engineering, Inc. (Tex Civ App) 746 SW2d 314 (1988).

[12] Kim v Chamberlain (Ala App) 504 So 2d 1213 (1987).

[13] The Commissioners on Uniform State Laws have adopted a Uniform Unincorporated Nonprofit Association Act. In addition, community associations are being widely formed primarily for the purpose of community planning and environmental protection.

(b) ANTITRUST LAW EXEMPTION. The agreement by the members of sellers' cooperatives that all products shall be sold at a common price is an agreement to fix prices. Therefore, the sellers' cooperative is basically an agreement in restraint of trade and a violation of antitrust laws. The Capper-Volstead Act of 1922 expressly exempts normal selling activities of farmers' and dairy farmers' cooperatives from the operation of the federal Sherman Antitrust Act, as long as the cooperatives do not conspire with outsiders to fix prices.

SUMMARY

The three principal forms of business organizations are sole proprietorships, partnerships, and corporations. A sole proprietorship is a form of business organization in which one person owns the business, controls all decisions, receives all profits, and has unlimited liability for all obligations and liabilities. A partnership involves the pooling of capital resources and talents of two or more persons with the goal of making a profit; the partners are subject to unlimited personal liability. A business corporation exists to make a profit. It is created by government grant, and its shareholders elect a board of directors, who are responsible for managing the business. A shareholder's liability is limited to the capital the shareholder invested in the business or paid for shares. The corporate existence continues without regard to the death of shareholders or the transfer of stock by them.

The selection of the form of organization is determined by the nature of the business, tax considerations, the financial risk involved and the importance of limited liability, and the extent of control of management desired.

By a franchise, the owner of a trademark, trade name, or copyright licenses others to use the mark or copyright in the selling of goods or services. To protect against fraud, the FTC requires that franchisors provide prospective franchisees with a disclosure statement ten days prior to any transaction. The Automobile Dealers' Franchise Act and the Petroleum Marketing Practices Act are federal laws that provide covered franchisees with protection from bad faith terminations. State laws also provide protection to franchisees in a wide range of businesses. The franchisor is not liable to third persons dealing with the franchisee. Liability of the franchisor may, however, be imposed on the ground of the apparent authority of the franchisee or the latter's control by the franchisor. Liability of the franchisor may also arise with respect to product liability.

A joint venture exists when two or more persons combine their labor or property for a single business undertaking and share profits and losses as agreed. An unincorporated association is a combination of two or more persons for the pursuit of a common purpose.

A cooperative consists of two or more persons or enterprises, such as farmers, who cooperate with respect to a common objective, such as the distribution of farm products.

LAW IN PRACTICE

1. The selection of the most appropriate form of business organization can only be accomplished after all of your particular circumstances have been reviewed. It will serve your best interests to consult with a qualified lawyer and a tax accountant on this matter.

2. Recognize that you may be protected under a state franchise protection law even though the arrangement under which you are operating does not use the word "franchise."

3. If you are a franchisor, make certain that your franchisees clearly inform the public that their businesses are "independently owned and operated" in order to insulate you from liability for the franchisees' actions.

4. Recognize that if you form a joint venture, the fault or negligence of another venturer will be imputed to you.

5. Know that members of an unincorporated association are not liable for the debts of the association unless it is shown that those members authorized or ratified the actions in question.

QUESTIONS AND CASE PROBLEMS

1. What social forces are affected by the federal Automobile Dealers' Franchise Act?

2. When is a franchisor held liable to a third person dealing with or affected by the franchisee?

3. Elizabeth, Josephine, and Mark entered into an agreement to purchase a tract of land, build houses on it, sell the houses, and then divide the net profit. What kind of business organization was intended?

4. Jerome, Sheila, Gary, and Ella agreed to purchase a tract of land and make it available for use as a free playground for neighborhood children. They called the enterprise the Meadowbrook Playground. One of the playground swings was improperly hung by Jerome and Gary, and a child was injured. Suit was brought against the Meadowbrook Playground. Can damages be recovered?

5. Katherine Apostoleres owned the rights to Dunkin Donuts franchises in Brandon and Temple Terrace, Florida. In early 1982 the franchisor offered all its franchisees the right to renew their existing franchise agreements if they agreed to abide by advertising decisions favored by two-thirds of the local franchise owners in a given television market. Apostoleres refused the offer because she did not want to be bound by the two-thirds clause. Soon thereafter Dunkin Donuts audited the two stores, and using a "yield and usage" analysis, it concluded that gross sales were being underreported. Based on these audits and a subsequent audit Dunkin Donuts gave notice of immediate termination of the franchises, contending that the franchise agreement had been violated. Apostoleres stated that an implied obligation of good faith exists by operation of law in every contract and she asserted that the 1982 audits were in retaliation for her refusal to accept the renewal agreement. The "yield and usage" test used in the audit was not specified in the franchise agreement as a measure to be used to enforce the franchisor's rights, and certain accounting experts testified as to the unreliability of this test. Was Dunkin Donuts liable for breach of its implied obligation of good faith in this case? [*Dunkin Donuts of America v Minerva Inc. (CA 11 Fla) 956 F2d 1566*]

6. If a group of farmers agree among themselves to pool their products and set a common price for the sale of these products, would this be price fixing in violation of the federal antitrust laws?

7. Compare and contrast a franchise and a contract.

8. The Armory Committee was composed of officers from various National Guard units. They organized a New Year's Eve dance, at a charge of $2 per person to defray costs. Perry, along with others, was a member of the Armory Committee. Libby was a paying guest at the dance and was injured by slipping on frozen ruts in the immediate approaches of the steps leading to the armory building where the dance was held. He sued Perry, Turner, and the other committee members. The evidence showed that every member of the committee had taken some part in planning or running the dance, with the exception of Turner. Was the Armory Committee an unincorporated association or a joint venture? Decide. [*Libby v Perry (Me) 311 A2d 527*]

9. The Kawasaki Shop of Aurora, Illinois (dealer) advised the Kawasaki Motor Corp. (manufacturer) that it intended to move its Kawasaki franchise from New York Street to Hill Avenue, which was in the same market area. The Hill Avenue location was also the site of a Honda franchise. The manufacturer's sales manager advised the dealer that he did not want the dealer to move in with Honda at the Hill Avenue site. In February 1982, the dealer moved to the Hill Avenue location. Effective May 1, 1982, the manufacturer terminated the dealer's franchise. The dealer brought suit against the manufacturer under the state motor vehicle franchise act, which made it unlawful to terminate franchises for site control (requiring that the dealer's site be used exclusively as a Kawasaki dealership). The manufacturer defended that it had a right to have its products sold by a dealer who was not affiliated with a competitor. Decide. [*Kawasaki Shop v Kawasaki Motors Corp. 188 Ill App 3d 664, 136 Ill Dec 4, 544 NE2d 457*]

10. Goodward, a newly hired newspaper reporter for the Cape Cod News, learned that the local cranberry growers had made an agreement under which they pooled their cranberry crops each year and sold the crops at what they determined to be a fair price. Goodward believes that such an agreement is in restraint of trade and a violation of the antitrust laws. Is he correct?

11. Food Caterers, Inc., of East Hartford, Connecticut, obtained a franchise from Chicken Delight, Inc., to use that name at its store. Food Caterers agreed to the product standards and controls specified by the franchisor. The franchise contract required the franchisee to maintain a free delivery service in order to deliver hot, freshly prepared food to customers. The franchisee used a delivery truck that bore no sign or name. Its employee, Carfiro, drove the truck in making a delivery of food. He negligently struck and killed McLaughlin. The victim's estate sued Chicken Delight on the theory that Carfiro was its agent because he was doing work that Chicken Delight required to be done and that benefited Chicken Delight. Was Carfiro the agent of Chicken Delight? [McLaughlins Estate v Chicken Delight, Inc. 164 Conn 317, 321 A2d 456]

12. Groseth had the International Harvester (IH) truck franchise in Yankton, North Dakota. The franchise agreement Groseth signed required dealers to "cooperate with the Company by placing orders for goods in accordance with advance ordering programs announced by the Company." IH wanted to terminate Groseth's franchise because Groseth refused to comply with IH's requirement that a computerized "dealer communication network" (DCN) be set up. Under the DCN, each dealer was required to obtain a computer terminal, display screen, and software. The DCN was initially used for ordering parts. The DCN allowed IH to reduce the number of employees needed for manual processing of "parts" orders. Groseth refused to set up the DCN because of the expense of the system. Moreover, it contended that the task of ordering parts was easily accomplished by telephone or written orders. Did IH have good cause to terminate Groseth's franchise? [Matter of Groseth International Harvester Inc. v International Harvester (SD) 442 NW2d 229]

13. Brenner was in the scrap iron business. Almost daily, Plitt lent Brenner money with which to purchase scrap iron. The agreement of the parties was that when the scrap was sold, Plitt would be repaid and would receive an additional sum as compensation for making the loans. The loans were to be repaid in any case, without regard to whether Brenner made a profit. A dispute arose as to the nature of the relationship between the two men. Plitt claimed that it was a joint venture. Decide. [Brenner v Plitt, 182 Md 348, 34 A2d 853]

14. Donald Salisbury, William Roberts, and others purchased property from Laurel Chapman, a partner of Chapman Realty, a franchisee of Realty World, Inc. The purchasers made payments directly to Laurel Chapman at the Realty World office, and Chapman was to make payments on the property's mortgage. However, Chapman did not make the payments and absconded with the funds. Salisbury and Roberts sued the franchisor, Realty World, claiming that Realty World was liable for the wrongful acts of the apparent agent, Chapman. Realty World and Chapman Realty are parties to a franchise agreement that states that the parties are franchisor and franchisee. The agreement contains a clause that required Chapman to prominently display a certificate in the office setting forth Chapman's status as an independent franchisee. Chapman displayed such a sign, but the plaintiffs do not recall seeing it. Chapman Realty hires, supervises, and sets the compensation for all of its employees. The plaintiffs point out that Chapman Realty used the service mark *Realty World* on its signs, both outside and inside its offices. They point out that a Realty World manual sets forth the general standards by which franchisees must run their businesses and that this represents clear control over the franchise. They contend that, all things considered, Realty World held out Chapman Realty as having authority to bind Realty World. Realty World disagrees, stating that both are independent businesses. Decide. [Salisbury v Chapman and Realty World, Inc. 124 Ill App 3d 1057, 65 NE2d 127]

15. H. C. Blackwell Co. held a franchise from the Kenworth Truck Co. to sell its trucks. After 12 years, the franchise was nearing expiration. Kenworth notified Blackwell that the franchise would not be renewed unless Blackwell sold more trucks and improved its building and bookkeeping systems within the next 90 days. Blackwell spent $90,000 in attempting to meet the demands of Kenworth but could not do so because a year was required to make the specified changes. Kenworth refused to renew the franchise. Blackwell sued Kenworth for damages under the Federal Automobile Dealers' Franchise Act. Blackwell claimed that Kenworth had refused to renew in bad faith. Decide. [Blackwell v Kenworth Truck Co. (CA5 Ala) 620 F2d 104]

CHAPTER 45

CREATION AND TERMINATION OF PARTNERSHIPS

A. NATURE AND CREATION
  1. Definition
  2. Characteristics of a Partnership
  3. Rights of Partners
  4. Purposes of a Partnership
  5. Classification of Partnerships
  6. Firm Name
  7. Classification of Partners
  8. Who May Be Partners
  9. Creation of Partnership
  10. Partnership Agreement
  11. Determining Existence of Partnership
  12. Partners as to Third Persons
  13. Partnership Property
  14. Tenancy in Partnership
  15. Assignment of Partner's Interest

B. DISSOLUTION AND TERMINATION
  16. Effect of Dissolution
  17. Dissolution by Act of Parties
  18. Dissolution by Operation of Law
  19. Dissolution by Decree of Court
  20. Notice of Dissolution
  21. Winding up Partnership Affairs
  22. Distribution of Assets
  23. Continuation of Partnership Business

LEARNING OBJECTIVES

After studying this chapter, you will be able to:
1. *Describe the characteristics of a partnership.*
2. *Distinguish between general and special partnerships and trading and nontrading partnerships.*
3. *List the seven rules that aid in determining whether the parties have created a partnership.*
4. *Explain the effect of a dissolution of a partnership.*
5. *Describe how a partnership may be dissolved by the acts of the partners, by operation of law, and by order of a court.*
6. *Describe the extent of a partner's authority during the winding up of a partnerships business.*

What can you do if a sole proprietorship does not meet your business needs? You might form a partnership.

A. NATURE AND CREATION

Partnerships are created by agreement. Modern partnership law shows traces of Roman law, the law merchant, and the common law of England. A codification of partnership law is found in the Uniform Partnership Act (UPA), which has been adopted by 49 states.[1]

1. Definition

A **partnership** is a relationship created by the voluntary "association of two or more persons to carry on as co-owners a business for profit."[2] The persons so associated are called **partners**. A partner is the agent of the partnership and of each partner with respect to partnership matters. A partner is not an employee of the partnership, even when doing work that would ordinarily be done by an employee.

2. Characteristics of a Partnership

A partnership has distinguishing characteristics.
a. A partnership is a voluntary, consensual relationship.
b. A partnership involves partners' contributions of capital, services, or a combination of these.
c. The partners are associated as co-owners to transact the business of the firm for profit.
  If profit is not the object, the group will commonly be an unincorporated association.
  The UPA does not make the partnership a separate entity, and therefore, suit cannot be brought by the firm in its name in the absence of a special statute or procedural rule so providing.[3] Some courts regard a partnership as distinct from the individual partners, so a partnership cannot claim the benefit of a personal immunity possessed by an individual partner. For the purposes of the Uniform Commercial Code, a partnership is regarded as a commercial entity.

3. Rights of Partners

The rights of partners are determined by the partnership agreement. If written, this agreement is interpreted by the same rules that govern the interpretation of any other written document. Any matter not covered by the partnership agreement, may be covered by a provision of the applicable Uniform Partnership Act.

4. Purposes of a Partnership

A partnership may be formed for any lawful purpose. A partnership cannot be formed to commit immoral or illegal acts, or acts that are contrary to public policy.

5. Classification of Partnerships

Partnerships may be classified by the scope and nature of their activity.

(a) GENERAL AND SPECIAL PARTNERSHIPS. A **general partnership** is created for the general conduct of a particular kind of business, such as a hardware business or a manufacturing business. A **special partnership** is formed for a single transaction, such as the purchase and resale of a certain building.

---

[1] The UPA has been adopted in all states except Louisiana, and it is in force in the District of Columbia, Guam, and the Virgin Islands. A new UPA was approved in 1992 and amended in 1993. Sections 901 and 902 of the revised UPA allow general partnerships to convert to limited partnerships and *vice versa*. Section 904 of the new act also allows general partnerships to merge with other general partnerships and with limited partnerships.

[2] Uniform Partnership Act, § 6(1).

[3] Telamarketing Communications Inc v Liberty Partners (Ky) 798 SW2d 462 (1990).

(b) TRADING AND NONTRADING PARTNERSHIPS. A **trading partnership** is organized for the purpose of buying and selling, such as a firm engaged in the retail grocery business. A **nontrading partnership** is one organized for a purpose other than engaging in commerce—for example, the practice of law or medicine. The distinction between trading and nontrading partnerships was utilized in the *Patel* case.

PATEL v PATEL
212 Cal App 3d 6, 260 Cal Rptr 255 (1989)

> L.G. and S.L. Patel, husband and wife, along with their son Rajeshkumar, ("R") formed a partnership in 1986 to own and operate the City Center Motel in Eureka, California. L.G. and S.L. decided to sell the motel and contracted with P.V. and Kirit Patel for its sale. Neither the broker nor the purchasers knew of "R"'s interest in the hotel. When L.G. and S.L. notified "R" of their plans, he refused to sell his 35 percent interest in the motel. L.G. and S.L. therefore notified P.V. and Kirit that they wished to withdraw from the deal. P.V. and Kirit sued for specific performance. From a judgment for the hotel owners, P.V. and Kirit appealed.

CHANNELL, J. . . . Generally, every partner is an agent of the partnership for the purpose of its business, and the act of every partner to carry on the business of the partnership binds the partnership. [UPA § 9(1)] However, partners acting without the approval of the remaining partners may not do any act which would make it impossible to carry on the ordinary business of the partnership. [UPA § 9(3)(c)] These provisions distinguish between acts of a partner which bind the partnership without the express authority of the remaining partners and acts binding on the partnership only after express authorization by all partners. A contract executed by less than all of the partners to sell partnership real estate binds the other partners if the partnership *is in the business of buying or selling real estate* and the property covered by the contract is *part* of the stock held for sale. . . . Enforcement of the contract for sale of the motel, executed by L.G. and S.L. without the approval of their partner Rajeshkumar, would result in the sale of *all* of the partnership assets, making it impossible for the partnership to continue, in violation of subdivision (3)(c) of section [9].

Historically, partnerships were divided into two types: commercial or trading partnerships and noncommercial or nontrading partnerships. Although this distinction has been rejected in California, it remains a valuable tool in considering whether L.G. and S.L. exceeded their statutory authority by entering into the real estate sale contract, thus making it impossible to carry on the ordinary business of the partnership. . . . In the case of a commercial or trading partnership in which the usual partnership business is to hold and sell real property, a contract such as that involved in this case—to sell the sole partnership asset—would be enforceable. . . . By contrast, when—as in the present case—the usual partnership business is to run a business, rather than to hold it in anticipation of its eventual sale, the partnership is not bound by a contract selling that business without the approval of all partners. . . . Under these circumstances, the trial court properly denied specific performance of the unauthorized contract in order to prevent destruction of the partnership, in compliance with subdivision (3)(c) of section [9]. . . .

. . . To enforce the contract of sale without Rajeshkumar's approval would frustrate the purpose of subdivision (3)(c) of section [9] by making it impossible for the partnership to continue. As the purpose of the partnership is to operate a motel, rather than to hold it for eventual sale, we believe that the better result would be to preserve the partnership and hold the contract unenforceable. . . .

[Judgment affirmed]

QUESTIONS

1. Does a contract for the sale of partnership real estate executed by fewer than all of the partners of a "trading partnership" that holds and sells real estate bind the other partners?
2. Was the City Center Motel partnership a real estate "trading partnership"?
3. Apply UPA § 9(3)(c) to the facts of this case.

6. Firm Name

In the absence of a statutory requirement, a partnership need not have a firm name, although it is customary to have one. The partners may, as a general rule, adopt any firm name they desire, including a fictitious name. There are, however, certain limitations on the adoption of a firm name:

a. The name cannot be the same as, or deceptively similar to, the name of another enterprise for the purpose of attracting its patrons.
b. Some states prohibit the use of the words "and company" unless they indicate an additional partner.
c. Most states provide for the registration of a fictitious partnership name. For example, Ken and Steve Swain transact business under a partnership name: The Berkshire Dairy Farm. Since such a name does not reveal the names of the partners, a certificate stating the names and addresses of the partners can be filed at the public office designated by state law, usually a city or town clerk's office.

7. Classification of Partners

Partners are classified according to their activity.

a. **General partners** are those who publicly and actively engage in the transaction of firm business.
b. **Nominal partners** hold themselves out as partners or permit others to hold them out as such. They are not in fact partners.
c. **Silent partners** are those who, although they may be known to the public as partners, take no active part in the business.
d. **Secret partners** are those who take an active part in the management of the firm but who are not known to the public as partners.
e. **Dormant partners** are ones who take no active part in transacting the business and who remain unknown to the public.

8. Who May Be Partners

In the absence of statutory provisions to the contrary, persons who are competent to contract may form a partnership. A minor may be a partner but may avoid the contract of partnership and withdraw.

In general, the capacity of a mentally incompetent person to be a partner is similar to that of a minor, except that an adjudication of incompetence makes subsequent agreements void rather than merely voidable. An enemy alien may not be a partner, but other aliens may enter into partnerships. At common law, a corporation could not be a partner. However, statutes for certificates of incorporation now typically permit corporations to become partners.

9. Creation of Partnership

If the parties agree that the legal relationship between them shall be such that they in fact operate a business for profit as co-owners, a partnership is created, even though the parties may not have labeled their new relationship a partnership.[4] The law is concerned with the substance of what is done rather than the name. Conversely, a partnership does not arise if the parties do not agree to the elements of a partnership, even though they call it a partnership.

Figure 45-1 Partnership Agreement

PARTNERSHIP AGREEMENT

This is a partnership agreement executed at Cincinnati, Ohio, this 9th day of September, 1994 by and among Louis K. Hall, Sharon B. Young, and C. Lynn Mueller, individuals residing in Cincinnati, Ohio, hereinafter sometimes referred to individually as "Partner" and collectively as "Partners."

RECITALS

The Partners to this agreement desire to acquire a certain parcel of real estate and to develop such real estate for lease or sale, all for investment purposes. This agreement is being executed to delineate the basis of their relationship.

PROVISIONS

1. Name; and Principal Offices. The name of the partnership shall be: Hall, Young and Mueller, Associates. Its principal place of business shall be at: 201 River Road, Cincinnati, Ohio 45238.

2. Purpose. The purpose of the partnership shall be to purchase and own for investment purposes, a certain parcel of real estate located at 602 Sixth Street, Cincinnati, Ohio, and to engage in any other type of investment activities that the partnership may from time to time hereinafter unanimously agree upon.

3. Capital Contributions. The capital of the partnership shall be the aggregate amount of cash and property contributed by the Partners. A capital account shall be maintained for each Partner.

A. Capital Contributions. Any additional capital which may be required by the partnership shall be contributed to the partnership by the Partners in the same ratio as that Partner's original contribution to capital as to the total of all original capital contributions to the partnership unless otherwise agreed by the Partners.

---

[4] Halbersbery v Berry (SC App) 394 SE2d 7 (1990).

The way in which an enterprise is described in a tax return or an application for a license is significant in determining whether it is a partnership as against a person making the return or the application.[5] The mere fact that the enterprise is described as a partnership is not controlling or binding, however, with regard to a person named as a partner in the return or in the application if that person did not know of its preparation, did not sign it, and did not know what it said. When the parties are in fact employer and employee, there is no partnership, even though the employer files a partnership form of income tax return.

10. Partnership Agreement

Because of the complexity of the problems involved, partnership agreements are typically written. However, there is no requirement that they be in writing,[6] unless compliance with a statute of frauds is required, such as when a duration of more than one year is specified by the agreement. The formal document that is prepared to evidence the contract of the parties is termed a **partnership agreement**, articles of partnership, or **articles of co-partnership**. The partnership agreement will govern the partnership during its existence and may also contain provisions relating to dissolution.

The *Smith* case illustrates the importance of having a written partnership agreement. The case sets forth factors considered by courts in determining whether a partnership exists.

SMITH v REDD
(Miss) 593 So 2d 989 (1991)

Thomas Smith and Jackie Lea were partners in the logging business. In 1981 they joined Gordon Redd and went into business running a sawmill, calling the business Industrial Hardwood Products (IHP). Smith and Lea used their logging equipment at the mill site. Smith hauled 400 loads of gravel, worth some $26,000, from his father's land for the mill yard in the process of getting the mill operational. Smith and Lea received $300 a week compensation, which was reported on federal W-2 forms. They worked up to 65 hours per week and were not paid overtime. All three discussed business decisions. Smith and Lea had check-writing authority and the authority to hire and fire employees. Lea left the business in 1983 and was paid $20,000. The testimony indicated that the three individuals agreed in January of 1981 that as soon as the bank loan was paid off and Redd was paid his investment, Lea and Smith would be given an interest in the mill. No written agreement existed. Redd invested $410,452 in the business and had withdrawn $500,575 from the business. As of December 31, 1986 IHP had sufficient retained earnings to pay off the bank loan. In April of 1987 Smith petitioned the Chancery Court for the dissolution of the "partnership" and an accounting. Redd denied that any partnership was formed and asserted that Smith was an employee. The Chancery Court awarded Smith $50,000 for the gravel and use of equipment, but held that no partnership existed. Smith appealed.

5 Shinn v Vaughn, 83 Or App 251, 730 P2d 1290 (1986).
6 Beck v Clarkson (SC App) 387 SE2d 681 (1989).

PRATHER, J. . . . Smith asserts that the trial court erred in finding that no partnership existed between himself and Redd. A partnership as defined by statute is "an association of two (2) or more persons to carry on as co-owners a business for profit." [UPA § 6(1). The determination of whether a partnership exists is governed by statute. . . .

These statutes codified the common-law rules of partnership. . . . However, the common law is still used to supplement the statute in determining when a partnership exists. Generally, a partnership exists when two or more persons join together with their money, goods, labor, or skill for purposes of carrying on a trade, profession or business with a community interest in the profits and losses. . . . The three main questions that are considered in partnership determination are (1) the intent of the parties, (2) the control question, and (3) profit sharing. . . .

A. Intent

Intent of the parties to form a partnership must be established by the proof. In this case this Court does not have to look to circumstances to infer such an intent. The parties—Lea, Smith, and Redd—all agree that there was an express intent to form a partnership. Additionally, the surrounding circumstances bear out that express intent; Lea and Smith brought assets of L & S Logging into the IHP business, prepared the plant site without remuneration, and ran the sawmill business.

The issue here, then, is not whether the parties intended to become partners. The issue is whether the condition precedent occurred to seal that partnership contract. Those expressed conditions precedent to the partnership's formation were two: (1) the payment of the bank debt; and (2) the repayment of Redd of his initial investment. . . .

B. Control

The undisputed arrangement for operating IHP was for Redd to handle the financial matters, being his expertise, and for Lea and Smith to direct the sawmill operations, being their expertise. All parties made business decisions; all parties hired and fired employees and supervised them. All three entered into management decisions, such as building an office building and constructing a mill to build pallets. The facts shown support the conclusion that control over the business was exercised by Smith, not just as a manager or supervisor, but as one with ownership interest.

C. Profit Sharing

Admittedly, there was no profit-sharing evidenced by the testimony except as to splitting cash on occasions. But that division evidences the position of Smith. Additionally, Lea received $20,000 from Redd at his departure from the business evidencing more than an ordinary employer-employee relationship.

Lea and Smith were paid as employees with withholdings of income tax and social security tax. Benefits from workers' compensation were claimed by Smith. On the other hand, Smith and Lea worked approximately sixty-five (65) hours a week in 1981 without overtime pay.

Recognizing that Smith was working toward the retirement of debts of IHP to Redd and the bank so that the partnership could come to fruition, the receipt of wages during this preliminary period does not per se defeat the existence of a partnership. Smith was working long hours for little remuneration to establish the business and to pay off the debts. It was for this reason that the chancellor awarded Smith the amount of $50,000 to be equitable for his labor.

D. Chancellor's Finding

The chancellor found that Smith and Lea were employees drawing a regular salary and that there was an agreement to enter into a partnership as soon as the bank and Redd were repaid. Since the bank, not Redd, had not been paid, the chancellor found there was no partnership and Smith was owed nothing. These findings overlook important testimony. Redd admitted to Smith in a tape-recorded statement that a partnership existed:

SMITH: O.K. Gordon, I want to ask you, do you remember what all you told me when ever we went to logging?

. . . .

REDD: I called ya'll to come up here and we went right in there and sit down, and I asked ya'll if you want to do it? Said yes. Alright, I said when we get the debt paid down, when we get me paid, that's the words I said, I said you get a percentage in it, you can get a third, a half, a quarter or all of whatever you want. Ya'll spoke up and said no we want you to have controlling interest. I said well whatever, we'll do it.

SMITH: Right, right.

REDD: That's the words I said.

SMITH: Well, I don't remember about when we get the debt paid and paying you, I mean that part.

REDD: I said that at least a dozen times.

SMITH: Well, I'm being honest now with what I said, I don't remember you saying that part. O.K. Me and you set over there in the office before Christmas and talked about it and what all you told me, I mean how come you never did do nothing about it.

REDD: Because I got tied up on some more business and I just hadn't had a chance. I've had my nose to the grind stone.

. . . .

SMITH: Well, I mean what I'm talking about its been going on 6 years, I mean. Alright, now, after Jackie got out of it, what did you feel like Gordon, I mean when Jackie got out of it, being honest between me and you?

. . . .

SMITH: Well, do you remember telling me that when Jackie got out of it that it would mean more to me and you?

REDD: That's right, that's exactly right.

SMITH: That maybe, the way it sounded to me that I would have a little bit more in it and you would have a little bit more in it.

. . . .

REDD: . . . that's what I said, it just mean more to you.

SMITH: Well as of last week, if you were going to draw it up and everything what percentage would you base your figures on over there?

REDD: I'd base the figures on about a third for you and two-thirds for me.

SMITH: On it?

REDD: That's what I base it on.

SMITH: In other words if Jackie had stayed on, it a been a third for him, say and a third, you know, for me, and then, you know, a third for you?

REDD: No, if Jackie had stayed in, it been about 20/20 and 60. Cause the words ya'll said, no, I said, I said a quarter, a third, a half or all of whatever and that, you know, that even. . . .

SMITH: a third, or a quarter or half or whatever we wanted?

REDD: . . . that's right. And then ya'll both spoke up and said naugh we wanted you to have control of the thing, naugh and that's the same words that you told me over there when we sit. . . .

. . . .

SMITH: In other words, what you saying you figure my percentage is a, is a third. . . .

REDD: Yes, sir.

SMITH: a third? In other words, whatever the sawmill is worth and whatever its all valued at and the cash and what on the books add up I should get a third?

REDD: And whatever, and less whatevers owed.

SMITH: Ya, and what's ever less is owed, I should get a third of it?

REDD: In other words, the net that's what I feel like.

    . . . In sum, the partnership should have come into existence according to Redd and Smith's agreement no later than December 31, 1986. This Court reverses the chancellor on these two findings and renders judgment on the issue of whether a partnership existed between Smith and Redd as of December 31, 1986. That is, this Court holds that a partnership did indeed exist.

    . . . The cause is remanded for a determination by the chancellor of the partnership interests of Redd and Smith. . . . Upon that determination, the chancery court will be in a position to determine the value of Smith's interest as of December 31, 1986, for dissolution of the partnership.

[Reversed in part and remanded]

QUESTIONS

1. Does the fact that Smith received wages defeat his claim that he was a partner?
2. What were Smith's contributions to the partnership?
3. Assess the ethics of the parties, applying the ethical principles set forth in the Preface. Should persons form a partnership without setting forth their underlying agreement in writing concerning such matters as contributions, control, and profits and losses?

11. Determining Existence of Partnership

A partnership is shown to exist when it is established that the parties have agreed to the formation of a business organization that has the characteristics of a partnership.

The burden of proving the existence of a partnership is on the person who claims that one exists.[7]

When the nature of the relationship is not clear, the following rules aid in determining whether the parties have created a partnership.

(a) CONTROL. The presence or absence of control of a business enterprise is significant in determining whether there is a partnership and whether a particular person is a partner.

(b) SHARING PROFITS AND LOSSES. The fact that the parties share profits and losses is strong evidence of a partnership.

(c) SHARING PROFITS. An agreement that does not provide for sharing losses but does provide for sharing profits is evidence that the parties are partners. If the partners share profits, it is assumed that they will also share losses. Sharing profits is prima facie evidence of a partnership. However, a partnership is not to be inferred when profits are received in payment of (1) a debt, (2) wages, (3) an annuity to a deceased partner's surviving spouse or representative, (4) interest, or (5) payment for the goodwill of the business.[8] The fact that one doctor receives one-half of the net income does not establish that doctor as a partner of another doctor when the former was guaranteed a minimum annual amount. Also, federal income tax and social security contributions were deducted from the payments to the doctor, thus indicating that the relationship was employer and employee. If there is no evidence of the reason for receiving the profits, a partnership of the parties involved exists.

(d) GROSS RETURNS. The sharing of gross returns is itself very slight, if any, evidence of partnership. To illustrate, in a case in which one party owned a show that was exhibited on land owned by another under an agreement to divide the gross proceeds, no partnership was proven. There was no co-ownership or community of interest in the business. Similarly, it was not established that there was a partnership when it was shown that a farmer rented an airplane to a pilot to do aerial chemical spraying under an agreement by which the pilot would pay the farmer, as compensation for the use of the plane, a share of the fees that the pilot received.

(e) CO-OWNERSHIP. Neither the co-ownership of property nor the sharing of profits or rents from property that two or more persons own creates a partnership. Thus, the fact that a person acquires a 49 percent interest in a trailer park does not establish that such person is a partner. This in itself does not establish that the co-owners are together conducting the trailer park business for profit. Conversely, the mere fact that there is a sharing of the income from property by joint owners does not establish that they are partners.

(f) CONTRIBUTION OF PROPERTY. The fact that all persons have not contributed capital to the enterprise does not establish that the enterprise is not a partnership. A partnership may be formed even though some of its members furnish only skill or labor.

(g) FIXED PAYMENT. When a person who performs continuing services for another receives a fixed payment for such services, not dependent on the existence of profit and not affected by losses, that person is not a partner.

---

[7] Maasen v Lucier (CA8 Mo) 961 F2d 717 (1992).

[8] UPA § 7(4).

12. Partners as to Third Persons

In some instances, persons who are in fact not partners may be held liable to third persons as though they were partners. This liability arises when they conduct themselves in such a manner that others are reasonably led to believe that they are partners and to act in reliance on that belief, to their injury.[9] A person who is held liable as a partner under such circumstances is termed a *nominal partner*, a *partner by estoppel*, or an *ostensible partner*.

Partnership liability may arise by estoppel when a person who in fact is not a partner is described as a partner in a document filed with the government, provided the person so described has in some way participated in the filing of the document and the person claiming the benefit of the estoppel had knowledge of that document and relied on the statement. For example, suppose that the partnership of Holt and Schwark, in registering its fictitious name, specifies Holt, Schwark, and Collins as partners and that the registration certificate is signed by all of them. If a creditor who sees this registration statement extends credit to the firm in reliance in part on the fact that Collins is a partner, Collins is estopped from denying that she is a partner. She has a partner's liability insofar as that creditor is concerned.

Conversely, no estoppel arises when the creditor does not know of the existence of the registration certificate and consequently does not rely on it in extending credit to the partnership. Likewise, such liability does not arise when the nonpartner whose name is used does not know of the certificate.

13. Partnership Property

In general, partnership property consists of all the property contributed by the partners or acquired for the firm or with its funds.[10]

There is usually no limitation on the kind and amount of property that a partnership may acquire. The firm may own real as well as personal property, unless it is prohibited from doing so by statute or by the partnership agreement.

The parties may agree that real estate owned by one of the partners should become partnership property. When this intent exists, the particular property constitutes partnership property even if it is still in the name of the original owner.

In the *Mehl* case a dispute arose as to whether or not a bar purchased by one partner with checks written on the partnership bank account was a partnership asset.

M E H L v M E H L
(Mont) 786 P2d 1173 (1990)

Eugene and Marlowe Mehl are brothers. Since 1950 they have operated the family farm as a partnership known as "Mehl Brothers" or "Mehl Farms." The partnership operated without a written partnership agreement, and it had no definite term. Property held by the partnership consisted primarily of farming equipment and machinery. All proceeds were deposited in a checking account at a local bank, and expenses were paid from that account. The brothers had agreed to split all profits on a fifty-fifty basis. Whenever money

---

[9] UPA § 16(1); Johnson v Slusser, 33 Wash App 439, 655 P2d 261 (1982); Royal Bank and Trust Co. v Weintraub, Gold & Alper, 68 NY2d 124, 506 NYS2d 151 (1986).

[10] UPA § 8. King v Evans (Tex Civ App) 791 SW2d 531 (1990).

was needed by either partner, the practice was that he would tell the other and withdraw such money. In 1973, Eugene Mehl withdrew $7,200 from the partnership account and bought the Dagmar Bar located in Dagmar, Montana. The warranty deed and the liquor license to the bar were held in the names of Eugene Mehl and his wife, Bonnie. In 1980, Eugene and Bonnie were divorced, and Bonnie received the bar and liquor license as part of the property settlement. The partnership was dissolved by written notice from Marlowe to Eugene in 1983. A complaint was filed in court over whether the Dagmar Bar was a partnership asset. From a decision that the bar was a partnership asset, Eugene appealed.

McDONOUGH, J. . . . Eugene Mehl contends it was reversible error for the District Court to treat the Dagmar Bar as a partnership asset, and it was reversible error to assign a $50,000 value to the bar. We disagree. [UPA § 8(2)] states: "Unless a contrary intention appears, property acquired with partnership funds is partnership property."

The record shows that Eugene purchased the Dagmar Bar with two checks written on the partnership account. Therefore, the burden is on him to show that the bar did not belong to the partnership.

Documentation of ownership of the bar was submitted by both parties. Eugene Mehl submitted the warranty deed and liquor license to the bar which were in his and his wife's name. He also entered into evidence bank statements, employment registrations and other financial records which tended to indicate that he was the owner of the bar.

Marlowe Mehl submitted tax records and the property settlement between Eugene and his ex-wife Bonnie, which stated that the bar was partnership property. The lower court reviewed the evidence submitted by both parties and determined that the evidence submitted by Eugene did not overcome the presumption contained in [UPA § 8(2)].

. . . In light of the presumption created by UPA § 8(2), and in light of the evidence of ownership contained within the tax records and property settlement, we find there is substantial evidence for the court's findings and there is no abuse of discretion. Accordingly, the District Court's findings must be affirmed. . . .

[Judgment affirmed]

QUESTIONS

1. State the basic dispute in this case.
2. What rule of law was applied to resolve the dispute over the ownership of the bar?
3. How did the court decide the case?

14. Tenancy in Partnership

Partners hold title to firm property by **tenancy in partnership**.[11] The characteristics of such a tenancy are:

a. Each partner has an equal right to use firm property for partnership purposes in the absence of a contrary agreement.

b. A partner possesses no divisible interest in any specific item of partnership property that can be voluntarily sold, assigned, or mortgaged by a partner.[12]

c. A creditor of a partner cannot proceed against any specific items of partnership property.[13] The creditor can proceed only against the partner's interest in the partnership. This is done by applying to a court for a **charging order**. By this procedure, the share of any profits that would be paid to the debtor-partner is paid to a receiver on behalf of the creditor, or the court may direct the sale of the interest of the debtor-partner in the partnership.

d. On the death of a partner, the partnership property vests in the surviving partners for partnership purposes and is not subject to the rights of the surviving spouse of the deceased partner.

15. Assignment of Partner's Interest

Although a partner cannot transfer specific items of partnership property in the absence of authority to so act on behalf of the partnership, a partner's interest in the partnership may be voluntarily assigned by the partner.[14] The assignee does not become a partner without the consent of the other partners. Without this consent, the assignee is entitled to receive only the assignor's share of the profits during the continuance of the partnership and the assignor's interest on the dissolution of the firm. The assignee has no right to participate in the management of the partnership, nor does the assignee have a right to inspect the books of the partnership.

B. DISSOLUTION AND TERMINATION

The end of partnership existence is marked by dissolution and termination.

16. Effect of Dissolution

Dissolution ends the right of the partnership to exist as a going concern, but it does not end the existence of the partnership.[15] Dissolution is followed by a winding-up period, at the conclusion of which the partnership's legal existence terminates.

Dissolution reduces the authority of the partners. From the moment of dissolution, the partners lose authority to act for the firm, "except so far as may be necessary to wind up partnership affairs or to complete transactions begun but not then finished."[16] The vested rights of the partners are not extinguished by dissolving the firm, and the existing liabilities remain. Thus, when the partnership is dissolved by the death of a partner, the estate of the deceased partner is liable to the same extent as the deceased partner.

17. Dissolution by Act of Parties

A partnership may be dissolved by action of the parties. Certain other acts of the parties do not cause a dissolution.

(a) AGREEMENT. A partnership may be dissolved in accordance with the terms of the original agreement of the parties. This may be by the expiration of the period for which the relationship was to continue or by the performance of the object for which the partnership was organized.[17] The relationship may

---

[11] UPA § 25(1); Krause v Vollmar 83 Ohio App 3d 378, 614 NE2d 1136 (1992).

[12] Putnam v Shoaf (Tenn App) 620 SW2d 510 (1981).

[13] UPA § 25(2) (c).

[14] Farmers State Bank v Mikesell, 51 Ohio App 3d 69, 554 NE2d 900 (1988).

[15] Sheppard v Griffin (Tenn App) 776 SW2d 119 (1989).

[16] UPA § 33.

[17] UPA § 31(1) (a).

also be dissolved by subsequent agreement. The partners may agree to dissolve the firm before the lapse of the time specified in the articles of partnership or before the attainment of the object for which the firm was created.

(b) EXPULSION. A partnership is dissolved by the expulsion of any partner from the business, whether or not authorized by the partnership agreement.[18]

(c) ALIENATION OF INTEREST. Neither a voluntary sale of a partner's interest nor an involuntary sale for the benefit of creditors works a dissolution of the partnership.

(d) WITHDRAWAL. A partner has the power to withdraw from the partnership at any time. However, if the withdrawal violates the partnership agreement, the withdrawing partner becomes liable to the co-partners for damages for breach of contract.[19] When the relationship is for no definite purpose or time, a partner may withdraw without liability at any time. Restrictive provisions on later employment are commonly found in professional and marketing partnership agreements.

18. Dissolution by Operation of Law

A partnership is dissolved by operation of law in the following instances.

(a) DEATH. A partnership is dissolved immediately on the death of any partner. Thus, when the executor of a deceased partner carries on the business with the remaining partner, there is legally a new firm.

(b) BANKRUPTCY. Bankruptcy of the firm or of one of the partners causes the dissolution of the firm; insolvency alone does not.

(c) ILLEGALITY. A partnership is dissolved "by an event which makes it unlawful for the business of the partnership to be carried on or for the members to carry it on in partnership." To illustrate, when it is made unlawful by statute for judges to engage in the practice of law, a law firm is dissolved when one of its members becomes a judge.

19. Dissolution by Decree of Court

A court may decree the dissolution of a partnership for proper cause. A court will not order the dissolution for trifling causes or temporary grievances that do not involve a permanent harm or injury to the partnership.

The filing of a complaint seeking a judicial dissolution does not in itself cause a dissolution of the partnership; it is the decree of the court that has that effect.

A partner may obtain a decree of dissolution for any of the following reasons.

(a) INSANITY. A partner has been judicially declared insane or of unsound mind.

(b) INCAPACITY. One of the partners has become incapable of performing the terms of the partnership agreement.

(c) MISCONDUCT. One of the partners has been guilty of conduct that substantially prejudices the continuance of the business. The habitual drunkenness of a partner is a sufficient cause for judicial dissolution.

(d) IMPRACTICABILITY. One of the partners persistently or willfully acts in such a way that it is not reasonably practicable to carry on the partnership business. Dissolution will be granted when dissensions are so serious and persistent that continuance is impracticable, or when all confidence and cooperation between the partners have been destroyed.

---

[18] Susman v Cypress Venture, 187 Ill App 3d 312, 134 Ill Dec 901, 543 NE2d 184 (1989).

[19] Tabco Exploration Inc. v Tadlock Pipe Co. (La App) 617 So 2d 606 (1993).

(e) LACK OF SUCCESS. The partnership cannot continue in business except at a loss.

(f) EQUITABLE CIRCUMSTANCES. A decree of dissolution will be granted under any other circumstances that equitably call for a dissolution. Such a situation exists when one partner had been induced by fraud to enter into the partnership.

20. Notice of Dissolution

Under some circumstances, one partner may continue to possess the power to make a contract binding the partnership even though the partnership has been dissolved.

(a) NOTICE TO PARTNERS. When the firm is dissolved by the act of a partner, notice must be given to the other partners, unless that partner's act clearly shows an intent to withdraw from or to dissolve the firm. If the withdrawing partner acts without notice to the other partners, that partner is bound by contracts created for the firm.

Where the dissolution is caused by the act, death, or bankruptcy of a partner, each partner is liable to the co-partners for a share of any liability created by any other partner acting for the partnership without knowledge or notice of the act, death, or bankruptcy of the partner who caused the dissolution.

(b) NOTICE TO THIRD PERSONS. When dissolution is caused by the act of a partner or of the partners, notice must be given to third parties. A notice should expressly state that the partnership has been dissolved. Circumstances from which a termination may be inferred are generally not sufficient notice. Thus, the fact that the partnership checks added *Inc.* after the partnership name was not sufficient notice that the partnership did not exist and that the business had been incorporated.

Actual notice of dissolution must be given to persons who have dealt with the firm.

To persons who have had no dealings with the firm, a publication of the fact of dissolution is sufficient. Such notice may be by newspaper publication, by posting a placard in a public place, or by any similar method. Failure to give proper notice continues the power of each partner to bind the others with respect to third persons on contracts within the scope of the business.

When dissolution has been caused by operation of law, notice to third persons is not required. As between the partners, however, the UPA requires knowledge or notice of dissolution by death and bankruptcy.

21. Winding Up Partnership Affairs

In the absence of an express agreement permitting the surviving partners to continue the business, they must wind up the business and account for the share of any partner who had withdrawn, been expelled, or died.[20] If the remaining partners continue the business and use the partner's distributive share, that partner is entitled to that share, together with interest or the profit earned on it.

Partners have no authority after dissolution to create new obligations. They have authority only to do acts necessary to wind up the business. The *King* decision illustrates the distinction between the winding up of the partnership business and the continuation of the partnership business as usual.

When dissolution is obtained by court decree, the court may appoint a receiver to conduct the winding up of the partnership business. This may be done in the usual manner, or the receiver may sell the business as a going concern to those partners who wish to continue its operation.

With a few exceptions, all partners have the right to participate in the winding up of the business.[21]

---

[20] Ross v Walsh (Tex Civ App) 629 SW2d 823 (1982).

[21] UPA § 37.

KING v STODDARD
28 Cal App 3d 708, 104 Cal Rptr 903 (1972)

The Stoddard family—father, mother, and son—formed a partnership that published a newspaper, the *Walnut Kernel*. The parents died, and the son continued to run the paper. King performed accounting services for the paper. When he was not paid, King sued the son and the executors of the estates of the deceased partners, claiming that his bill was a partnership liability for which each was liable. The executors defended on the ground that the son, as surviving partner, did not have authority to employ an accountant but was only authorized to wind up the partnership business. To this defense King answered that the newspaper was continued in order to preserve its asset value as a going concern, so that it could be sold. The running of the paper was therefore part of the winding-up process. If true, this would give the surviving partner the authority to employ the accountant. From a judgment in favor of the accountant, the executors appealed.

BROWN, J. . . . The estate's liability was predicated upon the court's finding that the services were rendered during the process of winding up the partnership operation of the Walnut Kernel newspaper. We have concluded that the trial court erred and that the continuation of the business was not a winding up of the affairs of the partnership.

The partnership was dissolved by operation of law upon the deaths of Alda and Lyman E. Stoddard, Sr. . . . "In general a dissolution operates only with respect to future transactions; as to everything past the partnership continues until all pre-existing matters are terminated.". . .

[UPA § 35] provides that "after dissolution a partner can bind the partnership. . . (a) By any act appropriate for winding up partnership affairs. . . ."

It is this latter provision upon which the court based its decision that the estates of the deceased partners were liable for the accounting services performed after dissolution. The court found that "LYMAN STODDARD, JR.'S continuation of the WALNUT KERNEL business was an appropriate act for winding up the partnership, since the assets of the business would have substantial value only if it was a going business. . . .

We disagree with this finding. It is probably true that there might have been advantages to the partnership to sell the business as a going business, but the indefinite continuation of the partnership business is contrary to the requirement for winding up of the affairs upon dissolution. In *Harvey v Harvey,* 90 Cal App 2d 549, 203 P2d 112, the court disapproved a finding that the business and assets of a partnership were of such character as to render its liquidation impracticable and inadvisable until a purchaser could be found. The court stated: "In effect it [the finding] authorizes the indefinite continuation of the partnership after the death of a partner, a procedure not in accordance with section 571 of the Probate Code. Respondents counter with the argument that the business is such that it cannot be wound up profitably, and the estate given its share. But this argument overlooks the distinction between winding up a business and winding up the partnership interest in that business.". . .

Even if we assume that a situation might exist where continuation of the business for a period would be appropriate to winding up the partnership interest, such a situation did not exist here. The record reflects the fact that the surviving partner was not taking action to wind up the partnership as was his duty . . . nor did the estates consent in any way to a delay. Rather, their insistence on winding up took the form of an effort to sell the business and a suit to require an accounting. There is nothing in the record upon which to base the argument made by respondent that appellants consented to his continued employment. The fact that they did not object is of no relevance. They had no right to direct and did not participate in the operation of the business. Therefore, the determination that the acts of the accountants were rendered during a winding up process is not based upon substantial evidence. . . .

We conclude that the services of respondents were rendered after the dissolution resulting from the deaths of the partners, Lyman, Sr., and Alda Stoddard, and do not constitute services during the "winding up" processes of the partnership. . . .

[Judgment reversed]

QUESTIONS

1. What did King contend?
2. Did the court agree with King?
3. Based upon the first sentence of Section 20 of this chapter, when would it be possible for a surviving partner to temporarily continue a business during the winding-up process?

When the firm is dissolved by the death of one partner, the partnership property vests in the surviving partners for the purpose of administration. They must collect and preserve the assets, pay the debts, and make an accounting to the representative of the deceased partner's estate. A partner cannot purchase any of the partnership property without the consent of the other partners.

22. Distribution of Assets

Creditors of the firm have first claim on the assets of the partnership.[22] Difficulty arises when there is a contest between the creditors of the firm and the creditors of the individual partners. The general rule is that firm creditors have first claim on assets of the firm. The individual creditors share in the remaining assets, if any.

After the firm's liabilities to nonpartners have been paid, the assets of the partnership are distributed as follows: (a) each partner is entitled to a refund of advances made to or for the firm; (b) contributions to the capital of the firm are then returned; (c) the remaining assets, if any, are divided equally as profits among the partners unless there is some other agreement. A partner who contributes only services to the partnership is not considered to have made a capital contribution. If the partnership has sustained a loss, the partners bear it equally in the absence of a contrary agreement.

Distribution of partnership assets must be made on the basis of actual value when it is clear that the book values are merely nominal or arbitrary amounts.

A provision in a partnership agreement that on the death of a partner the interest of the

---

[22] Holmes v Holmes, 119 Or App 36, 849 P2d 1140 (1993).

partner shall pass to that partner's surviving spouse is valid. Such a provision takes effect as against the contention that it is not valid because it does not satisfy the requirements applicable to wills.

23. Continuation of Partnership Business

As a practical matter, the business of the partnership is commonly continued after dissolution and winding up. In all cases, however, there is a technical dissolution, winding up,

and termination of the life of the original partnership.

If the business continues, either with the surviving partners or with them and additional partners, it is a new partnership. Again, as a practical matter, the liquidation of the old partnership may in effect be merely a matter of bookkeeping entries, with all partners contributing again or relending to the new business any payment to which they would be entitled from the liquidation of the original partnership.

SUMMARY

A partnership is a relationship created by the voluntary association of two or more persons to carry on as co-owners a business for profit.

A partnership agreement governs the partnership during its existence and may also contain provisions relating to dissolution. The partnership agreement will generally be in writing, and this may be required by the statute of frauds. The existence of a partnership may be found from the existence of shared control in the running of the business and the fact that the parties share profits and losses. The sharing of gross returns, as opposed to profits, is very slight evidence of a partnership.

Partners hold title to firm property by tenancy in partnership. A creditor of a partner cannot proceed against any specific item of partnership property, but must obtain a charging order to seize the debtor-partner's share of the profits. An assignee of a partner's interest does not become a partner without the consent of the other partners, and is entitled only to a share of the profits and the assignor's interest upon dissolution.

Dissolution ends the right of the partnership to exist as a going concern. Dissolution is

followed by a winding-up period and the distribution of assets. A partnership may be dissolved by the parties themselves in accordance with the terms of the partnership agreement, by expulsion of a partner, by withdrawal of a partner, or by the bankruptcy of the firm or one of the partners. A court may order dissolution of a partnership, on the petition of a partner, because of the insanity, incapacity, or major misconduct of a partner. Dissolution may be decreed because of lack of success, impracticability, or other circumstances that equitably call for dissolution. Notice of dissolution, except dissolution by operation of law, must be given. Actual notice must be given to those who have dealt with the firm as a partnership.

All partners generally have a right to participate in the winding up of the business. After the firm's liabilities to nonpartners have been paid, the assets are distributed among the partners as follows: (1) refund of advances, (2) return of contributions to capital, and (3) division of remaining assets in accordance with the partnership agreement or, if no agreement is stated, division of net assets equally among the partners.

LAW IN PRACTICE

1. When the partnership business is conducted under a fictitious name, the partners must comply

with state filing requirements for revealing the names and addresses of the partners.

2. While no requirement may exist that there be a written partnership agreement for a particular firm, memories fade. It is therefore best for partners to set forth their agreement in writing.

3. When partners utilize personal items for firm business over a long period of time, partners may misperceive whether the items were intended to remain personal property or were intended to be partnership assets. Make sure that a written statement, made at the time the personal item was brought to the firm, is on file to resolve such a situation.

4. If a partner assigns his or her interest in a firm, the other partners are not "stuck" with the assignee as a partner. The assignee is entitled to the appropriate share of profits, but does not have a right to participate in management or inspect the books.

5. Remember, when dissolution of a partnership is caused by the act of a partner, actual notice must be given to persons who have dealt with the firm. A simple announcement card will suffice.

QUESTIONS AND CASE PROBLEMS

1. What social forces are affected by the rule that distribution of partnership assets must be made on the basis of actual value when it is clear that the book values are merely nominal or arbitrary amounts?

2. What is the effect of dissolution on a partnership?

3. In proving that Powell and Castillo are partners, compare the effect of proof that they (a) share gross returns, (b) are co-owners of property used in or by a business, or (c) share profits of a business.

4. Ray, Linda, and Nancy form a partnership. Ray and Linda contribute property and cash. Nancy contributes only services. Linda dies, and the partnership is liquidated. After all debts are paid, there is not sufficient surplus to pay back Linda's estate and Ray for the property and cash originally contributed by Linda and Ray. Nancy claims that the balance should be divided equally between Ray, Linda's estate, and Nancy. Is she correct?

5. Compare the requirement of notice to third persons when (a) an agency is terminated and (b) a partnership is dissolved.

6. Baxter, Bigelow, Owens, and Dailey were partners in a New York City advertising agency. Owens, who was in poor health and wanted to retire, advised the partners that she had assigned her full and complete interest in the partnership to her son, Bartholomew, a highly qualified person with ten years of experience in the advertising business. Baxter, Bigelow, and Dailey refused to allow Bartholomew to attend management meetings and refused his request to inspect the books. Bartholomew pointed out that his mother had invested as much in the firm as any other partner. He believed, as assignee of his mother's full and complete partnership interest, that he is entitled to (a) inspect the books as he sees fit and (b) participate fully in the management of the firm. Is Bartholomew correct?

7. Amy Gargulo and Paula Frisken operated as a partnership "Kiddies Korner," an infants' and children's clothing store. They operated the business very successfully for three years, with both Paula and Amy doing the buying and Paula keeping the books and paying the bills. Amy and Paula decided to expand the business when an adjoining store became vacant. At the same time, they incorporated the business. Children's Apparel, Inc. was a major supplier to the business before the expansion. After the expansion, business did not increase as anticipated, and when a nationally known manufacturer of children's apparel opened a factory outlet nearby, the business could no longer pay its bills. Children's Apparel, Inc., which had supplied most of the store's stock after expansion, sued Amy and Paula as partners for bills due for expansion stock. Children's Apparel, Inc. did not know that Amy and Paula had incorporated. Amy and Paula defended that the business was incorporated and that they therefore were not liable for business debts occurring after incorporation. Are Amy and Paula correct?

8. Calvin Johnson and Rudi Basecke did business as the Stockton Cheese Co., a partnership. The partnership owned a building and equipment. The partners agreed to dissolve the partnership but never got around to completing the winding-up process. Calvin continued to use the building. He continued to pay insurance on the building but removed Rudi's name as an insured on the policy. When the building was later destroyed by fire, Calvin claimed the proceeds of the fire insurance policy as he and his wife were the named insureds on the policy and they had paid the premiums. Rudi claimed that although the partnership was dissolved before the fire, the winding up of the partnership was not completed at the time of the fire. He therefore claimed that he was entitled to half of the net proceeds of the policy. Decide. [*State Casualty v Johnson (Mo App) 766 SW2d 113*]

9. Samuel Shaw purchased a ticket through Delta Airlines to fly a "Delta Connection" flight on SkyWest Airlines to Elko, Nevada. He was seriously injured when the SkyWest plane crashed near Elko, Nevada. SkyWest's relationship with Delta is a contractual business referral arrangement whereby Delta benefits through its charges for issuing tickets to connecting passengers to and from smaller communities, and SkyWest benefits from revenue generated by passengers sent to it by Delta. Both firms make a profit from this arrangement. SkyWest and Delta are often mentioned together by Delta in national print advertisements. Shaw believes that regardless of how the airlines characterize themselves these airlines are in fact partners because they share profits from their combined efforts. Delta contends that it has no control over SkyWest's airplane operations, and it contends that sharing profits as compensation for services does not create a partnership. Decide. [*Shaw v Delta Airlines, Inc. (DC Nev) 798 F Supp 1453*]

10. Larson entered into a Special Manager Incentive Agreement (SMIA) with Tandy Corporation. Larson agreed to manage a Radio Shack store for compensation equal to one-half of the adjusted gross profit of the store, as computed by a specific formula, and to provide the company with a $20,000 "security deposit" on equipment used to set up the store. The agreement was for a period of two years, automatically renewable annually until either party gave notice of termination 30 days prior to the end of a fiscal year. After some eight and one-half years of operating under renewed agreements, Tandy gave Larson notice of his termination. Larson sued Tandy, claiming that the SMIA was a partnership agreement, since there were shared risks, expenses, profits, and losses. He sought an accounting for his reasonable share in the value of the store. Tandy defended that under the SMIA Larson was an employee-manager, not a partner, and that the ultimate decision making on all matters was Tandy's. Decide. [*Larson v Tandy Corp. 187 Ga App 893, 371 SE2d 663*]

11. In 1974, Weeks joined an accounting firm as a partner. In 1980, a new partner was admitted and a new partnership agreement was executed by all the partners. In early 1983, two partners retired and the partners agreed to admit two other persons as partners, but no new partnership agreement was executed. Later, on July 31, 1984, Weeks gave notice of his election to dissolve the partnership. The remaining partners denied Weeks access to the firm's records, and Weeks sued for confirmation of the dissolution and for an accounting. The partners counterclaimed for enforcement of the 1980 partnership agreement, which would preclude a dissolution. The partners also claimed that Weeks violated a noncompetition clause in the 1980 agreement. Decide whether the 1980 partnership agreement should be controlling. [*Weeks v McMillan (SC App) 353 SE2d 289*]

12. Bowen owned and operated the Havana Club in a rented building. He owned all the physical assets of the business. He made an agreement with Cutler, the bartender, that she would operate the club, purchase supplies, pay bills, keep the books, and hire and fire employees. Cutler and Bowen were each to receive $100 a week and to divide the net profits. A partnership form of income tax return was filed for the business. At a later date, the Redevelopment Agency took the building in which the Havana Club was operated. The club went out of business because it could not find a new location. The Redevelopment Agency paid the club $10,000 damages for disruption of business. Cutler sued Bowen for one-half of the sum paid by the Redevelopment Agency on the theory that they had been a partnership. Bowen claimed that he was the sole owner of the business because he was the owner of the physical assets. Decide. [*Cutler v Bowen (Utah) 543 P2d 1349*]

13. Chaiken and two others ran a barber shop. The Delaware Employment Security Commission claimed that the other two persons were employees of Chaiken and that Chaiken had failed to pay the unemployment compensation tax assessed against employers. He defended on the ground that he had not "employed" the other two and that all three were partners. The evidence showed that Chaiken owned the barber shop; he continued to do business in the same trade name as he had before he was joined by the two additional barbers; and he had a separate contract with each of the two, which specified the days for work and the days off. It was also shown that Chaiken had registered the partnership name and the names of the three partners and that federal tax returns used for partnerships had been filed. Decide. [*Chaiken v Employment Security Commission (Del Super) 274 A2d 707*]

14. Gus Jebeles and his brother-in-law Gus Costellos entered into an oral partnership agreement on September 2, 1977, to conduct a business under the name of "Dino's Hot Dogs" at a location on the Montgomery Highway. Jebeles, who had expertise in this kind of business, arranged for the lease and furnished the logo used by the partnership. From the beginning, Costellos devoted himself to the business full time, and Jebeles devoted relatively little time to the business. Marital difficulties developed between Jebeles and his wife, who was Costellos's sister. Divorce proceedings began in January 1979. At that time, Costellos ceased to pay any money to Jebeles and changed the locks on the doors of the premises. Jebeles filed suit seeking a dissolution of the partnership and an accounting of all profits. As judge, you believe that it would be ill-advised to dissolve the partnership and lose the valuable lease to the business premises and the future profits of the business. Instead, you are considering ordering that the partnership continue, with Costellos as the sole active partner and Jebeles as a silent partner. You plan on ordering an accounting. Would your decision be upheld on appeal? *[Jebeles v Costellos (Ala) 391 So 2d 1024]*

15. Friedman, the "O" Street Carpet Shop, Inc., and Langness formed a partnership known as NFL Associates. "O" Street Carpet's net contribution to capital was $5,004. Langness contributed $14,000 in cash. Friedman contributed his legal services, on which no value was placed by the articles of partnership. The articles stated that Friedman was entitled to 10 percent of the profits. The articles provided that Langness was to receive payments of $116.66 per month. The partnership's accountant treated the payments to Langness as a return to Langness of her capital. Years later, the partnership sold the rental property owned by the partnership, and the partnership was wound up. Friedman claimed that he was entitled to 10 percent of the partnership capital upon dissolution. Langness claimed that Friedman was not entitled to a capital distribution and that the monthly payments to her should not have been treated as a return of capital. Decide. *[Langness v "O" Street Carpet, Inc. 217 Neb 569, 353 NW2d 709]*

CHAPTER 46

PARTNERSHIPS, LIMITED PARTNERSHIPS, AND LIMITED LIABILITY COMPANIES

LEARNING OBJECTIVES

After studying this chapter, you will be able to:
1. *Distinguish between express authority and customary authority of a partner to act for the partnership.*
2. *Identify the situations that indicate the existence of limitations on a partner's authority.*
3. *Name six transactions that a partner cannot undertake unless expressly authorized to do so.*
4. *List the duties of partners to one another.*
5. *State the rights of partners as owners of the business.*
6. *Explain the nature and extent of a partner's liability for the debts of the firm.*
7. *Recognize what actions of a limited partner will cause the loss of protection from limited liability.*
8. *Explain the advantages of a limited liability company.*

What is the authority of a partner? What are the duties of partners?

A. AUTHORITY OF PARTNERS

The scope of a partner's authority is determined by the partnership agreement and by the nature of the partnership.

1. Authority of Majority of Partners

When there are more than two partners in a firm, the decision of the majority prevails in matters involving how the ordinary functions of the business will be conducted. To illustrate, a majority of the partners of a firm decide to increase the firm's advertising. They subsequently enter into a contract for that purpose. The transaction is valid and binds the firm and all of the partners.

Majority action is not binding if it contravenes the partnership agreement. For such matters, unanimous action is required.[1] Thus, the majority of the members cannot change the nature of the business against the protests of the minority.

When there is an even number of partners, there is the possibility of an even division on a matter that requires majority approval. In such a case, the partnership is deadlocked. When the partners are evenly divided on any question, one partner has no authority to act.

If the division is over a basic issue and the partners persist in the deadlock, so that it is impossible to continue the business, any one of the partners may petition the court to order the dissolution of the firm.

2. Express Authority of Individual Partners

An individual partner may have express authority to perform certain acts, either because the partnership agreement provides for this or because a sufficient number of partners have agreed to it.

A partner's authority to act for the firm is similar to that of an agent to act for a principal. Thus, in addition to express authority, a partner has the authority to do those acts that are customary for a member of a partnership conducting the particular business of that partnership.[2] As in the case of an agent, the acts of a partner in excess of authority do not ordinarily bind the partnership.

3. Customary Authority of Individual Partners

A partner, by virtue of being a co-manager of the business, customarily has certain powers necessary and proper for carrying out that business. The scope of such powers varies with the nature of the partnership and also with the business customs and usages of the area in which the partnership operates.

The following are the more common of the customary or implied powers of individual partners.

(a) CONTRACTS. A partner may make any contract necessary to the transaction of the firm business.[3] When a plaintiff sues on a promissory note or other contract executed by a partner who does not possess express authority to enter into such a transaction, the plaintiff has the burden of proving that the making of the contract or the giving of commercial paper was "usual" for a business like the partnership.

(b) SALES. A partner may sell the firm's goods in the regular course of business and make the usual warranties incidental to such sales. However, this authority is limited to the goods held for sale by the partnership.

---

[1] Uniform Partnership Act, § 18(h).

[2] Ball v Carlson (Colo App) 641 P2d 303 (1981).

[3] Barnes v Campbell Chain Co., Inc. 47 NC App 488, 267 SE2d 388 (1980).

(c) PURCHASES. A partner may purchase any kind of property within the scope of the business and for this purpose may pledge the credit of the firm. This authority is not affected by the fact that the partner subsequently misuses or keeps the property instead of turning it over to the firm.

(d) LOANS. A partner in a trading firm may borrow money for partnership purposes. In doing so, the partner may execute commercial paper in the firm name or give security, such as a mortgage or a pledge of the personal property of the firm. If the third person acts in good faith, the transaction is binding even if the partner thereafter misappropriates the money. A partner in a nontrading partnership does not ordinarily possess the power to borrow in the name of the firm.

(e) INSURANCE. A partner may insure the firm property, cancel an insurance policy, or make proof of loss and accept a settlement for the loss.

(f) EMPLOYMENT. A partner may hire any employees and agents that are necessary to carry out the purpose of the enterprise.

(g) CLAIMS AGAINST FIRM. A partner has the authority to compromise, adjust, and pay bona fide claims against the partnership. A partner may pay debts out of the firm funds or by transferring firm property.

(h) CLAIMS OF FIRM. A partner may adjust, receive payment of, and release debts and other claims of the firm. In doing this, a partner may take money or commercial paper in payment. One who makes a proper payment is protected even if the partner to whom the payment is made embezzles the money.

(i) ADMISSIONS. A partnership is bound by admissions or statements that are adverse to the interests of the partnership if they are made in regard to firm affairs and in pursuance of firm business. For example, when a buyer takes a purchase back to the partnership's store, the admission by the partner then in the store that the product is defective binds the firm.

(j) NOTICE. Notice given to a partner of a matter affecting the partnership business is effective as notice to the partnership.[4]

4. Limitations on Authority

The partners may agree to limit the powers of each partner. When a partner, contrary to such an agreement, executes a contract on behalf of the firm with a third person, the firm is bound if the third person was unaware of the limitation. In this case, the partner violating the agreement is liable to the other partners for any loss caused by the breach of the limitation. If the third person knew of the limitation, the firm would not be bound.[5]

In the *Schnucks Markets* case the court was faced with deciding whether a partner whose authority was limited could bind the partnership contrary to the limitation.

SCHNUCKS MARKETS INC. v CASSILLY

(Mo App) 724 SW2d 664 (1987)

David Cassilly and Joseph Mason, doing business as Glen Park Properties, were partners in the real estate development business. Schnucks Markets

---

[4] Grayson v Wolfsey, Rosen, Kweskin & Kuriansky, 40 Conn Supp 1, 478 A2d 629 (1984).

[5] UPA § 9(4). First National Bank & Trust Co. v Scherr (ND) 467 NW2d 427 (1991).

brought an action against the partners for breach of contract. Schnucks testified that Cassilly and Schnucks agreed that Glen Park and the Market would split the cost of extending a sewer line to the market and that Glen Park did not pay its share of the $25,263.36 cost. Glen Park denied that Cassilly had authority to contract for Glen Park. Schnucks sued the partners and the partnership for the share of the costs. Judgment was entered for Schnucks The partnership appealed.

PUDLOWSKI, P. J. . . . Glen Park . . . contends [that] the court erred in not directing a verdict for them as the evidence conclusively established that Cassilly did not have the authority to bind the partnership and that the trial court failed to include an instruction on the issues of Cassilly's authority . . . Glen Park rests its defense on a statement made by Cassilly in a deposition that he did not have such authority. As it was "uncontradicted," Glen Park reasons that Schnuck's failed its burden of proving authority.

[UPA § 9(1)] states:

1. Every partner is an agent of the partnership for the purpose of its business, and the act of every partner, . . . for apparently carrying on in the usual way the business of the partnership of which he is a member binds the partnership, unless the partner so acting has in fact no authority to act for the partnership in the particular matter, and the person with whom he is dealing has knowledge of the fact that he has no such authority.

Cassilly and Mason conceded that Glen Park was a partnership, thus they are both agents of the partnership and of each other. As the statute notes, there are exceptions to this rule. First, the act of the partner must be "for the purpose of its business" and in "carrying on in the usual way the business of the partnership." Negotiating . . . an oral contract to divide the costs of sewer installation necessary for development of property certainly fits these requirements. . . . Glen Park . . . contends that negotiating the installation of sewer lines is a one-time deal and thus not in the course of partnership business. This is clearly refuted by the record. . . .

Glen Park urges error in the failure to include an instruction . . . on whether Cassilly served as Glen Park's agent. Glen Park argues that since Cassilly denied agency, there arose a disputed issue of material fact which required the court to give an instruction. . . . Cassilly's denial of agency did not elevate this to a legally material issue for even if Cassilly did not possess authority, Glen Park would still be bound. [UPA § 9(1)] requires that if the partner in fact has no authority, "the person with whom he is dealing must have knowledge that he has no such authority." Glen Park presented no evidence that Schnucks had knowledge of Cassilly's supposedly limited status. It thus became unnecessary for the trial court to submit on this issue. . . .

[Judgment affirmed]

QUESTIONS

1. Did Glen Park believe that the partnership was not liable because the plaintiff failed to prove that Cassilly had authority to bind the partnership?
2. How did the court dispose of Glen Park's contentions on the authority of Cassilly?
3. Can a partner whose authority is limited nevertheless bind the partnership contrary to the limitation?

A third person must not assume that a partner has all the authority that the partner purports to have. If there is anything that would put a reasonable person on notice that the partner's powers are limited, the third person is bound by that limitation.

The third person must be on the alert for the following situations in particular, since they warn that the partner with whom the third person deals either has restricted authority or no authority at all.

(a) NATURE OF BUSINESS. A third person must take notice of limitations arising out of the nature of the business. A partnership may be organized for a particular kind of business, trade, or profession. Third persons are presumed to know the limitations commonly imposed on partners in such enterprises. An act of a partner that would ordinarily bind a commercial firm, such as the issuance of a note, would not bind a partnership engaged in a profession. A partner in a trading partnership has greater powers than one in a nontrading firm.

(b) SCOPE OF BUSINESS. A third person must recognize and is bound by limitations that arise from the scope of the business. A partner cannot bind the firm to a third person in a transaction not within the scope of the firm's business unless the partner had express authority to do so. Thus, when a partner in a dental firm speculates in land or when a partner in a firm dealing in automobiles buys television sets for resale, the third person, in the absence of estoppel or express authority, cannot hold the partnership or the other partners liable on such a contract. The scope of the business is a question of fact to be determined by the jury from the circumstances of each case. In general, the scope comprises the activities commonly recognized as a part of a given business at a given place and time.

However, the usual scope may be enlarged by agreement or by conduct.

(c) TERMINATION OF PARTNERSHIP. A third person should watch for the termination of the partnership, either when the partnership is terminated under conditions requiring no notice or when notice of the termination has been properly given.

(d) ADVERSE INTEREST. A third person must take notice of an act of a partner that is obviously against the interest of the firm. To illustrate, if a partner issues a promissory note in the firm name and delivers it to a creditor in payment of a personal obligation, the creditor risks nonpayment. Such an act may be a fraud upon the firm.

5. Prohibited Transactions

There are certain transactions into which a partner cannot enter on behalf of the partnership unless the partner is expressly authorized to do so. A third person entering into such a transaction does so at the risk that the partner has not been authorized.

The following are prohibited transactions.

(a) CESSATION OF BUSINESS. A partner cannot bind the firm by a contract that would make it impossible for the firm to conduct its usual business.[6]

(b) SURETYSHIP. A partner has no implied authority to bind the firm by contracts of surety, guaranty, or indemnity for purposes other than the firm business.[7]

(c) ARBITRATION. A partner cannot submit controversies of the firm to arbitration "unless authorized by the other partners or unless they have abandoned the business."[8]

---

[6] Wales v Roll (Wyo) 769 P2d 899 (1989).

[7] First Interstate Bank of Oregon v Bergendahl, 80 Or App 479, 723 P2d 1005 (1986).

[8] UPA § 9(3) (e).

(d) CONFESSION OF JUDGMENT. All partners should have an opportunity to defend in court. Because of this, a partner cannot confess judgment against the firm on one of its obligations. Exceptions exist when the other partners consent or when they have abandoned the business.

(e) ASSIGNMENT FOR CREDITORS. A partner cannot make a general assignment of firm property for the benefit of creditors, unless authorized by the other partners or unless they have abandoned the business.

(f) PERSONAL OBLIGATIONS. A partner cannot discharge personal obligations or claims of the firm by interchanging them in any way.

B. DUTIES, RIGHTS, REMEDIES, AND LIABILITIES OF PARTNERS

The rights and duties of partners are based on their dual capacity of agent and co-owner.

6. Duties of Partners

In many respects, the duties of a partner are the same as those of an agent.

(a) LOYALTY AND GOOD FAITH. Each partner must act in good faith toward the partnership. One partner must not take any advantage over the other(s) by the slightest misrepresentation or concealment. Each partner owes a duty of loyalty to the firm. This duty requires a partner's devotion to the firm's business and bars the making of any

Figure 46-1   Limitations on Authority of Individual Partner to Bind Partnership

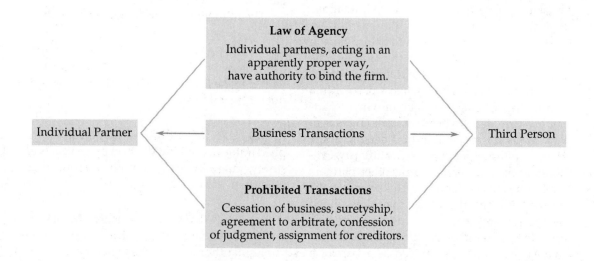

secret profit at the expense of the firm, the use of the firm's property for personal benefit, or the exploitation for personal gain of a business opportunity of the partnership.[9] To illustrate, when one partner renewed a lease of the building occupied by the firm but the lease was renewed in the name of that partner alone, that partner was compelled to hold the lease for the firm. The failure to renew the lease in the name of the firm was a breach of the duties of good faith and loyalty owed to the firm.

A partner cannot promote a competing business. If the partner does so, the partner is liable for damages sustained by the partnership.

Each partner also owes a fiduciary duty of good faith to all other partners. This duty extends to any transaction connected with the formation, conduct, or liquidation of the partnership. In the *Steeby* case the court had to decide whether a partner violated his fiduciary duty to the other partner.

STEEBY v FIAL
(Colo App) 765 P2d 1081 (1988)

Roger Steeby and Charles Fial formed a partnership at will in January 1977 to perform auditing services. The partnership hired individuals on a contract basis to perform the actual auditing work. Steeby and Fial spent their time supervising the auditors' work and finding new business. Fial brought in 80 percent of the new business but was receiving 50 percent of the profits. He decided to dissolve the partnership and did so by notice to Steeby dated July 11, 1984. During the winding up of the partnership's affairs, Fial terminated contracts with partnership clients and negotiated new contracts with them on behalf of his new firm. From September 1984 through February 1985 he signed up the auditors to work for his new firm. The partnership was formally terminated on May 23, 1985. Steeby brought suit against Fial for damages caused by his competition and his breach of fiduciary duty. Fial contended that once the partnership was dissolved it was proper business judgment to start setting up his new business by making new contracts with clients and signing up the auditors to perform work for the new firms. From a judgment for Steeby, Fial appealed.

PLANK, J. . . . Partners in a business enterprise owe to one another the highest duty of loyalty; they stand in a relationship of trust and confidence to each other and are bound by standards of good conduct and square dealing. . . . This principle is codified in [UPA § 21(1)] which provides that:

Every partner must account to the partnership for any benefit and hold as trustee for it any profits derived by him without the consent of the other partners from any transaction connected with the formation, conduct, or liquidation of the partnership or from any use by him of his property.

---

[9] Gilroy v Conway, 151 Mich App 628, 391 NW2d 419 (1986); Hooper v Yoder (Colo) 737 P2d 852 (1987).

Furthermore, each partner has the right to demand and expect from the other a full, fair, open, and honest disclosure of everything affecting the relationship. . . *See* [UPA § 20].

Generally, a partnership proceeds through a three-step dismantling: dissolution, winding up, and termination. . . . The parties' relationship changes and their partnership dissolves when a partner ceases to be associated in the carrying on, as distinguished from the winding up, of the business. . . . That dissolution, however, does not terminate the partnership. Rather, the partnership continues until the winding up of partnership affairs is completed. Upon the completion of winding up, the partnership is thereby terminated.

Here, during the winding up period, Steeby and Fial agreed that the auditors would be told that the partnership was being dissolved but that they were to continue their work on partnership accounts. Thereafter, Fial unilaterally contracted with the auditors to do auditing for clients which had been clients of the partnership. Fial dealt individually with existing partnership clients and established new contractual relationships with them but on the behalf of his new firm. The trial court determined correctly that Fial had breached his fiduciary duty to Steeby by concealing the termination of the contracts with the auditors and partnership clients and subsequently renegotiating these contracts for his own personal gain.

Even after dissolution of a partnership, both partners continue to have a fiduciary duty to the other partner that continues until the partnership assets have been divided and the liabilities have been satisfied. . . . A partner is not entitled to take any action with respect to unfinished partnership business which leads to purely personal gain. . . . Further, a partner completing unfinished partnership business cannot cut off the rights of the other partners in the dissolved partnership by the tactic of entering into a "new" contract to complete such business. . . .

When a breach of fiduciary duty has been established, the injured party may recover his share of the partnership profits and property through the imposition of a constructive trust. . . . "Constructive trusts are raised by equity in respect of property which has been acquired by fraud, or where, though acquired originally without fraud, it is against equity that it should be retained by him who holds it." *Page v Clark*, 197 Colo. 306, 592 P2d 792 (1979).

Here, the trial court imposed a constructive trust on behalf of Steeby for one-half of all profits received by Fial as an equitable remedy for Fial's breach of duty. We conclude that, in doing so, the trial court properly exercised its equitable power. . . .

[Judgment affirmed]

QUESTIONS

1. When was the partnership dissolved?
2. Once the partnership was dissolved, was Fial free to set up a new business with clients and auditors from the partnership, without the consent of Steeby?
3. What was the measure of damages?
4. After reviewing the ethical principles set forth in the Preface, identify the ethical principles that apply to this case.

The obligation of a partner to refrain from competing with the partnership continues after the termination of the partnership if the partnership agreement contains a valid anti-competitive covenant. In the absence of any such restriction, or if the restriction agreed on is held invalid, a partner is free to compete with the remaining partners, even though they continue the partnership business.

(b) OBEDIENCE. Each partner is obligated to perform all duties and to obey all restrictions imposed by the partnership agreement or by the vote of the required number of partners.[10] Consequently, each partner must observe any limitation imposed by a majority of the partners with respect to the ordinary details of the partnership business. If a majority of the partners operating a retail store decide that no sales shall be made on credit, a partner who is placed in charge of the store must obey this limitation. If a third person does not know of the limitation, the managing partner has the power to make a binding sale on credit to that person. If the third person does not pay the bill and the firm suffers a loss as a result, the partner who violated the no-credit limitation is liable to the firm for the loss caused by such disobedience.

(c) REASONABLE CARE. A partner must use reasonable care in transacting the business of the firm and is liable for any loss resulting from a failure to do so. A partner is not liable, however, for honest mistakes or errors of judgment.

(d) INFORMATION. A partner has the duty to inform the partnership of matters relating to the partnership. A partner must "render on demand true and full information of all things affecting the partnership to any partner or the legal representative of any deceased partner or partner under legal disability."[11]

The obligation to inform embraces matters relating to the purchase by one partner of the interest of another and to matters relating to the liquidation of the partnership.

(e) ACCOUNTING. A partner transacting any business for the firm must make and keep, or turn over to the proper person, correct records. If the partners have delegated to one of the partners the task of keeping the books and accounts for all the business of the firm, that partner must keep proper records. If they are disputed, the recordkeeper has the burden of proving their accuracy.[12] If it is not shown that the records are correct, the recordkeeper is held liable.

When an action is brought to compel a partner to account, the court may require the making of an audit by a disinterested third person.

When a partnership is organized for an illegal purpose or for conducting a lawful business in an unlawful manner, a wrongdoing partner cannot obtain an accounting by the partnership. For example, when the members of an engineering partnership did not have the license required for engineering work, one of the partners, an unlicensed engineer, could not require the other partners to account.

7. Rights of Partners as Owners

Each partner, in the absence of a contrary agreement, has the following rights. These rights stem from the fact that the partner is a co-owner of the partnership business.

(a) MANAGEMENT. Each partner has a right to take an equal part in transacting the business of the firm. It is immaterial that one partner contributed more than another or that one contributed only services.

Incidental to the right to manage the partnership, each partner has the right to posses-

---

[10] Cobin v Rice (Ind) 823 FSupp 1419 (1993).

[11] UPA § 20.

[12] Laurence v Floshner Medical Partnership, 206 Ill App 3d 777, 151 Ill Dec 875, 565 NE2d 146 (1990).

sion of the partnership property for the purposes of the partnership.

(b) INSPECTION OF BOOKS. All partners are equally entitled to inspect the books of the firm. "The partnership books shall be kept, subject to any agreement between the partners, at the principal place of business of the partnership, and every partner shall at all times have access to and may inspect and copy any of them."[13]

(c) SHARE OF PROFITS. Each partner is entitled to a share of the profits. The partners may provide, if they so wish, that profits shall be shared in unequal proportions. In the absence of such a provision in the partnership agreement, each partner is entitled to an equal share of the profits, without regard to the amount of capital contributed or services performed for the partnership.

The right to profits is personal property, regardless of the nature of the partnership assets. On the death of a partner, the right to a share of the profits and an accounting passes to the deceased partner's executor or administrator.

(d) COMPENSATION. In the absence of a contrary agreement, a partner is not entitled to compensation for services performed for the partnership. There is no right to compensation even if the services are unusual or more extensive than the services rendered by other partners. Consequently, when one partner becomes seriously ill and the other partners transact all of the firm's business, they are not entitled to compensation for those services. The sickness of a partner is considered a risk assumed in the relationship. No agreement can be inferred that the active partners are to be compensated, even though the services rendered by them are such that they would ordinarily be rendered in the expectation of receiving compensation. As an exception, "a surviving partner is entitled to reasonable compensation for services performed in winding up the partnership affairs."[14]

Contrary to the above, the partners may agree that one of the partners shall devote full time as manager of the business and receive for such services a salary in addition to the managing partner's share of the profits.

(e) REPAYMENT OF LOANS. A partner is entitled to the return of any money advanced to or for the firm. Such amounts must be separate and distinct from original or additional contributions to the capital of the firm.

(f) PAYMENT OF INTEREST. In the absence of an agreement to the contrary, contributions to capital do not draw interest. The theory is that the profits constitute sufficient compensation. Advances by a partner in the form of loans are treated as if they were made by a stranger and bear interest from the date the advance is made.

(g) CONTRIBUTION AND INDEMNITY. A partner who pays more than a proportionate share of the debts of the firm has a right to contribution from the other partners. Under this principle, if an employee of a partnership negligently injures a third person while acting within the scope of employment, and if the injured party collects damages from one partner, the latter may enforce contribution from the other partners in order to divide the loss equally between them.

The partnership must indemnify every partner for payments made and personal liabilities reasonably incurred in the ordinary and proper conduct of its business or for the preservation of its business or property. A partner has no right, however, to indemnity or reimbursement if the partner has (1) acted in bad faith, (2) negligently caused the necessity for payment, or (3) previously agreed to bear the expense alone.[15]

---

[13] UPA § 19.

[14] UPA § 18(f).

(h) DISTRIBUTION OF CAPITAL. After the payment of all creditors and the repayment of loans made to the firm by partners, every partner is entitled to receive a share of the firm property upon dissolution. Unless otherwise stated in the partnership agreement, all partners are entitled to the return of their capital contributions.

After such distribution is made, each partner is the sole owner of the fractional part distributed to that partner, rather than a co-owner of all the property as during the existence of the partnership.

8. Liability of Partners and Partnership

The liability of a partnership and of the partners for the acts of individual partners and of employees is governed by the same principles that apply to the liability of an employer or a principal for the acts of an employee or agent.

(a) NATURE AND EXTENT OF PARTNER'S LIABILITY. Partners are jointly liable on all firm contracts. They are jointly and severally liable for all torts committed by an employee or one of the partners in the scope of the partnership business. When partners are liable for the wrongful injury caused a third person, the latter may sue all or any of the members of the firm.

Partners who have satisfied a claim against the partnership have the right to contribution from the other partners, whereby the liability is apportioned among all the partners.[16]

(b) LIABILITY FOR BREACH OF DUTY. When a partner violates a duty owed to the partnership, the partner's liability is determined by the general principles of contract, tort, or agency law that may be applicable to such conduct. When one partner breaches a duty owed to another partner, the injured partner may recover damages.[17]

(c) LIABILITY OF NEW PARTNERS. A person admitted as a partner into an existing partnership has limited liability for all the obligations of the partnership arising before such admission. This is a limited liability, in that the preadmission claim may be satisfied only out of partnership property and does not extend to the individual property of the newly admitted partner.[18] The incoming partner does not become personally liable for preadmission claims unless the incoming partner expressly promises to pay such claims.

(d) EFFECT OF DISSOLUTION ON PARTNER'S LIABILITY. A partner remains liable after dissolution of the partnership unless expressly released by the creditors or unless all claims against the partnership have been satisfied.[19] The dissolution of the partnership does not of itself discharge the existing liability of any partner. The individual property of a deceased partner is liable for the obligations of the partnership that were incurred while the deceased partner was alive. However, the individual creditors of the deceased partner have priority over the partnership creditors with respect to such property.[20]

---

[15] Gramacy Equities Corp. v DuMont, 72 NY2d 560, 531 NE2d 629 (1988).

[16] U.S. Trust Co. v Bamco18, 585 NYS2d 186 (1992).

[17] Walsh v Chestnut Hill Bank and Trust Co. 414 Man 283, 607 NE2d 737 (1993).

[18] UPA § 17; see also UPA § 41(1), (7).

[19] Gjovik v Strope (Minn) 401 NW2d 664 (1987).

[20] UPA § 36.

9. Enforcement and Satisfaction of Creditor's Claims

The firm may have been sued in the name of all the individual partners doing business as the partnership, as in the case of "Plaintiff v *A, B, C*, doing business as the Ajax Warehouse." The partners named are bound by the judgment against the firm if they have been properly served in the suit.

If a debt is contractual in origin, the common law requires that the partnership's assets be resorted to and exhausted before partnership creditors can reach a partner's individual assets.[21]

In the *Smith Construction* case the partners claimed that a creditor could not reach their personal assets to satisfy a judgment against the partnership for a debt.

SMITH CONSTRUCTION CO. v WOLMAN DUBERSTEIN & THOMPSON

65 Ohio St 3d 383, 604 NE2d 157 (1992)

> Smith Construction Co. Inc. obtained a judgment in South Carolina for breach of contract by an Ohio general partnership Wolman, Duberstein and Thompson (the partnership). The suit arose because of the partnership's failure to fulfill its contractual commitments concerning the building of two homes in South Carolina. Smith then brought suit in Ohio seeking judgment against the partnership and the individual partners to recover the $105,549 South Carolina judgment. The partnership admitted the debt, and stated that the partnership's assets were insufficient to satisfy the South Carolina judgment. However, the partners denied their personal liability. From a judgment in favor of Smith, the partnership appealed.

HOLMES, J. . . . We must determine the nature of the liability of a partner for partnership debts, and then determine whether a judgment creditor must first exhaust all partnership assets before resorting to the partner's personal assets in satisfaction of the judgment.

The applicable general law is relatively clear. Ohio's R.C. 1775.14, like Section 15 of the Uniform Partnership Act ("UPA"), distinguishes the nature of a partner's liability for contractual obligations of the partnership from the nature of his or her liability for tortious claims against the firm. . . .

At common law, partnership contracts were the joint obligations of all of the partners. . . . Unlike contractual liability, the liability of partners for torts committed in the course of firm business is joint and several. R.C. 1775.14(A).

These early rules have, in the main, been adopted within the UPA, and within the applicable Ohio law . . . adopting the UPA. . . .

As in sole proprietorships, one of the legal realities of the general partnership form of business, and often the deciding factor in choosing the corporate rather than the partnership form of business organization, concerns the personal liability of the partners. Whether the third-party creditor can reach the general partner's personal

---

[21] McCune v Mountain Bell (Utah) 758 P2d 914 (1988); Midwood Development Corp. v K 12th Associates, 146 App Div 2d 754, 537 NYS2d 237 (1989).

assets on principles of *joint liability* or on those of *joint and several liability*, the burden of responding to a partnership obligation remains.

Joint liability apportions responsibility for a contractual debt equally, in the absence of a partnership agreement to the contrary, among the partners and thereby limits the creditor's execution on one individual partner's personal property to a pro rata share of the debt. Joint and several liability, on the other hand, allows for disproportionate satisfaction of the partnership obligation by rendering each general partner responsible for the entire amount of the partnership debt. The partner's right to indemnification or contribution from the other partners mitigates this burden such that responsibility for the partnership's wrongful act or breach of trust is, at a later date, spread fairly among the individual partners.

At common law, as well as pursuant to R.C. 1775.14(B), general partners are jointly liable, rather than jointly and severally liable, for partnership contractual debts in the absence of an agreement among themselves to the contrary.

A number of jurisdictions, like Ohio, which have adopted both joint and joint and several liability provisions in their partnership acts have not allowed third-party creditors immediate access to the personal assets of individual partners when the partnership debt arose out of contractual obligations. . .

Statutes in other jurisdictions have not codified the common-law rule which treats the nature of a partner's liability for contractual obligations of the partnership differently from that for tort claims against the firm. For example, Arizona's statute, Ariz Rev Stat Ann Section 29-215, deviates from the UPA by providing that partners are liable jointly and severally not only for tort claims against the partnership but also for all the firm's other debts and obligations. . . . In these jurisdictions, the courts hold that partnership creditors are not required to establish the insufficiency of partnership assets before they pursue the personal assets of the individual partners for payment of the unsatisfied contractual debt. The Supreme Court of Alabama, in *Head v Henry Tyler Constr. Corp., supra*, recognized the legal impact of its statute's departure from the common law:

"The major impact of making partners not merely jointly liable but also severally liable is that if a creditor chooses to bring an action against one of the partners, that partner is liable for all of the partnership debts, regardless of whether the creditor first attempted to recover the debt from the partnership or prove that the partnership had no assets. Several liability is "liability separate and distinct from liability of another to the extent that an independent action may be brought without joinder of others.' . . .

Accordingly, the partners who are jointly liable have the right to demand payment of the third party's claim from their joint assets (i.e., partnership assets) before their personal property can be called upon to satisfy that contractual debt. . . .

As it can be seen, the common law applicable to partnerships has been that while the partnership is primarily responsible for judgments obtained against it, partnership judgment creditors were not foreclosed from further recourse should the partnership assets be inadequate, or the partnership itself insolvent.

That the partnership assets be the primary source for satisfaction of such a judgment has been specifically provided by R.C. 2329.09, which in pertinent part states: "An execution on a judgment rendered against a partnership firm by its firm name shall operate only on the partnership property." In accord with R.C. 2329.09, we hold that partners are not primarily liable for the contractual obligations incurred by their firm. A partnership creditor in proceedings in execution of a judgment against the partnership must first exhaust partnership property before resorting to the personal assets of partners under R.C. 1775.14(B).

Appellants argue that execution may not be carried out against their individual property to satisfy a judgment against the partnership. . . . Ohio law pertaining to execution provides in R.C. 2329.09 that "an execution on a judgment rendered against a partnership firm by its firm name shall operate only on the partnership property."

We reject the appellants' arguments upon the following reasoning:

First, we conclude that it was not the intent of the General Assembly to overturn the long-standing common law rule that partners are jointly liable for partnership contractual obligations. We also conclude that it was the intent of the General Assembly to adopt the common law rule that in order to levy upon the individual property of a partner in satisfaction of a judgment against the partnership, the creditor must first show that partnership assets have proven insufficient.

As we have previously concluded . . . the opinion of the South Carolina Court of Appeals, although resulting in a judgment against the partnership only, did not preclude an action against the partners and their individual assets to be held jointly liable for the partnership debt. This judgment against the partnership is a valid judgment that has been certified to Ohio for execution purposes and our courts will give it the appropriate full faith and credit. In aid of execution of this judgment in Ohio, all of the property of the partnership has been levied upon. . . .

After a creditor pursues proceedings in aid of execution to satisfy a judgment against the partnership, and demonstrates that the judgment remains unsatisfied due to insufficient partnership property, the creditor may, by appropriate action, subject the partners and their individual property to such unsatisfied partnership judgment. The judgment creditor may bring an action seeking to have the partners made parties to the judgment against the partnership. In such actions between the plaintiff judgment creditor and the partners, the plaintiff must offer proof that the judgment has not been satisfied due to insufficient partnership assets. If the court finds that the judgment against the partnership has been unsatisfied due to insufficiency of partnership assets, the court may enter an order making the partners parties to the partnership judgment, finding the partners jointly liable for such unsatisfied judgment against the partnership, and setting forth the individual amounts due from each partner to satisfy his individual joint partnership obligation. . . .

[Judgment affirmed]

QUESTIONS

1. Review Clause 1, Section 1, Article IV of the United States Constitution (see Appendix 2 of this book). On what basis did the Ohio courts consider and enforce the South Carolina judgment?
2. Distinguish between "joint and several liability" and "joint liability."
3. Under what circumstances is a judgment creditor entitled to reach the assets of individual partners to satisfy a judgment against the partnership for contractual debts?

Personal creditors of a partner must first pursue the assets of that partner for satisfaction of their claims. After a partner's personal assets are exhausted, the creditor may enforce the unpaid portion of a judgment by obtaining a **charging order** against the partner's interest in the partnership. Under such an order, a court requires that the partner's share of the profits be paid to the creditor until the debt is discharged.

C. LIMITED PARTNERSHIPS

A limited partnership is a special kind of partnership.

10. Formation of Limited Partnerships

A limited partnership can be created only by complying with the appropriate local statute. Some states have adopted the Uniform Limited Partnership Act (ULPA).[22] Others have adopted the Revised Uniform Limited Partnership Act (RULPA) or the RULPA as amended in 1985.[23]

(a) MEMBERS OF A LIMITED PARTNERSHIP. In a limited partnership, certain members contribute capital but have limited liability for firm debts. The most these members can lose is their investment. These members are known as **limited partners**. The partners who manage the business and are personally liable for the firm debts are **general partners**.[24] A limited partnership can be formed by "one or more general partners and one or more limited partners."[25]

(b) CERTIFICATE OF LIMITED PARTNERSHIP. Unlike a general partnership, a limited partnership can be created only by executing a certificate of limited partnership. Under the ULPA, the certificate must set forth the name and business address of each partner, specifying which partners are general partners and which are limited partners. The essential details of the partnership and the relative rights of the partners must also be specified. The certificate, when executed, must be recorded locally in the office of the official in charge of public records. Ordinarily, this will be the office of the county clerk or recorder of deeds of the county in which the principal place of business of the partnership is located.

Under the 1985 amendments to the RULPA, the certificate need only include (1) the limited partnership's name, (2) the address of the partnership's registered office and the name and business address of its agent for service of process, (3) the name and business address of each general partner, (4) its mailing address, and (5) the latest date on which the limited partnership is to dissolve. The names of the limited partners (the investors) are not required. This allows for the preservation of the confidentiality of the investors' names from competitors. Moreover, new investors may be admitted as limited partners without the significant administrative burden involved in amending the certificate as is required under the ULPA. The RULPA provides for filing of the certificate with the office of the secretary of state, as opposed to the local filing required under the ULPA.

When there is no filing of the limited partnership certificate, all participants have the status and liability of general partners in a general partnership. However, technical de-

---

[22] The ULPA governs limited partnerships in Vermont. Louisiana has not enacted either the ULPA or the RULPA.

[23] The 1976 RULPA has been adopted by California, Delaware, District of Columbia, Georgia, Hawaii, Illinois, Indiana, Maine, Maryland, Nebraska, New Jersey, New York, Ohio, Pennsylvania, Tennessee, Texas, Utah, Virginia. The RULPA with the 1985 amendments has been adopted by Alabama, Arizona, Arkansas, Colorado, Connecticut, Florida, Idaho, Iowa, Kansas, Kentucky, Massachusetts, Mississippi, Missouri, Montana, Newark, New Hampshire, New Mexico, North Carolina, North Dakota, Oklahoma, Oregon, Rhode Island, South Carolina, South Dakota, Washington, West Virginia, Wisconsin, Wyoming.

[24] Brooke v Mt. Hood Meadows Ltd. 81 Or App 387, 725 P2d 925 (1986).

[25] ULPA § 1; RULPA § 101(7).

fects in the certificate do not prevent formation of a limited partnership if there has been substantial, good faith compliance with the filing requirements.[26]

In the *Brookwood Fund* case it was argued that since the newly admitted investors to a limited partnership were not noted on the certificate of limited partnership, as then required by the ULPA, they were liable as general partners.

8 BROOKWOOD FUND v BEAR STEARNS & CO., INC.

148 App Div 2d 661, 539 NYS2d 411 (1989)

8 Brookwood Fund was formed as a limited partnership on April 24, 1987. The certificate of limited partnership was filed with the Westchester County Clerk in April 1987. Between May and August of 1987 additional investors joined Brookwood as limited partners. On October 17, 1987, the stock market crashed. On October 19, 1987, Bear Stearns liquidated Brookwood's margin accounts. On October 23, 1987, a certificate amending the original certificate of limited partnership to state the newly admitted limited partners was filed with the Westchester County Clerk. In late October, Bear Stearns started arbitration proceeds against Brookwood, seeking to recover $1,849,183, that was owed after the liquidation of the margin account. Brookwood sought an injunction against any arbitration proceedings against the limited partners of Brookwood. From a judgment for the limited partners, Bear Stearns appealed.

PER CURIAM. . . The record indicates that Brookwood was originally formed as a limited partnership. The original certificate of limited partnership, filed with the Westchester County Clerk on April 24, 1987, listed Kenneth Stein as the "General Partner" and Barbara Stein as the "Original Limited Partner." Between May and August 1987, additional investors joined Brookwood as limited partners pursuant to Article 10 of the Agreement of Limited Partnership. . . .

Each of the additional investors signed a document entitled "Supplement to Agreement of Limited Partnership of 8 Brookwood Fund" and, pursuant thereto, each of the additional investors agreed to become an "Additional Limited Partner" in accordance with the terms of the original Agreement of Limited Partnership. In this regard, Article 8 of the Agreement of Limited Partnership provides as follows:

Article 8. Limitation on Liability of Limited Partners.

No Limited Partner . . . shall be liable for any debts, obligations or loss of the Partnership in excess of the amount of such Limited Partner's capital in the Partnership. The General Partner shall have unlimited liability for the debts of the Partnership.

Thereafter, these additional investors conducted themselves, at all times, as limited partners, *i.e.*, they did not participate in the management of the partnership.

---

[26] ULPA § 2(2); RULPA § 201(b); Fabry Partnership v Christensan (Nev) 794 P2d 719 (1990).

Finally, the record indicates that a certificate amending the original certificate of limited partnership, so as to reflect the newly added limited partners, was not filed with the Westchester County Clerk until October 23, 1987, six days after the October 19th 1987 liquidation of Brookwood's margin account.

On the instant appeal, the defendants argue that (1) pursuant to statutory mandate, (*see*, [ULPA § 8 and 25]) the certificate amending the original certificate of limited partnership, so as to reflect the newly added limited partners, had to be filed with the Westchester County Clerk, and (2) until October 23, 1987, when Brookwood complied with that statutory mandate, those investors who joined Brookwood after the filing of the original certificate of limited partnership were not limited partners, as they mistakenly believed, but rather were general partners, and therefore obligated to arbitrate any controversy arising out of the liquidation of Brookwood's margin account on October 19, 1987. However, even if we were to assume, arguendo, that there is merit to this argument . . . an affirmance would still be warranted. The record supports the finding of the Supreme Court that the additional investors and purported limited partners in Brookwood, upon receiving a notice of intention to arbitrate from Bear Stearns and Sloate Weisman dated October 26, 1987, concerning the "debit balance . . . in the amount of $1,849,183.00," "promptly renounced" their interests in the profits of the limited partnership, pursuant to [ULPA § 11]. Partnership Law [§ 11] provides as follows:

Status of person erroneously believing himself a limited partner.

"A person who has contributed to the capital of a business conducted by a person or partnership erroneously believing that he has become a limited partner in a limited partnership is not, by reason of his exercise of the rights of a limited partner, a general partner with the person or in the partnership carrying on the business, or bound by the obligations of such person or partnership; provided that on ascertaining the mistake he promptly renounces his interest in the profits of the business, or other compensation by way of income. . . .

Accordingly, the Supreme Court properly enjoined the [brokerage firm] from commencing "any action, proceeding or arbitration claim against Brookwood's limited partners." . . .

[Judgment affirmed]

QUESTIONS

1. Was the certificate amending the original certificate of limited partnership filed in time to protect the newly admitted "limited partners" from liability beyond their investments?
2. Did ULPA § 11 provide an escape from personal liability beyond their investment for the newly admitted "limited partners"?
3. Would the newly admitted "limited partners" have been subject to the same legal problems if the limited partnership had been formed in a RULPA state?

11. Characteristics of Limited Partnerships

A limited partnership has the following characteristics.

(a) CAPITAL CONTRIBUTIONS. Under the ULPA, the limited partner contributes cash or property but not services. Under the RULPA, however, the limited partner may contribute services.

(b) FIRM NAME. With certain exceptions, the limited partner's name cannot appear in the firm name. If the name of a limited partner is used in the firm name so as to give the impression that the limited partner is an active partner, the limited partner loses the protection of limited liability and becomes liable without limit as a general partner. Under the RULPA, the words *limited partnership* must appear without abbreviation in the firm name.

(c) MANAGEMENT AND CONTROL OF THE FIRM. The general partners manage the business and are personally liable for firm debts. Limited partners (the investors) have the right to a share of the profits and a return of capital upon dissolution and have limited liability. The limitation of liability is lost, however, if they participate in the control of the business.[27]

The RULPA lists a number of "safe harbor" activities in which limited partners may engage without losing their protection from liability. These activities include:

1. Being a contractor for or an agent or employee of the limited partnership or of a general partner
2. Consulting with and advising a general partner regarding the partnership business
3. Acting as a surety for the limited partnership

Figure 46-2 Comparison of Limited Partnership and General Partnership

	Limited Partnership	**General Partnership**
Creation	Filing a certificate of limited partnership with appropriate state office	No formality required
Liability	General partners: unlimited liability for firm debts Limited partners: no liability beyond loss of investment	Unlimited liability of each partner for firm debts
Management	General partners according to their partnership agreement or Uniform Partnership Act (UPA) Limited partners excluded	All partners according to their partnership agreement or Uniform Partnership Act (UPA)
Dissolution	As set forth in the partnership agreement or the ULPA or RULPA	All set forth in partnership agreement or the UPA

---

[27] Gonzalez v Chalpin, 77 NY2d 74, 565 NE2d 1253 (1990).

4. Voting on partnership matters such as dissolution and winding up the limited partnership or the removal of a general partner

(d) RIGHT TO SUE. A limited partner may bring an action on behalf of the limited partnership against outsiders for economic injury to the firm when the general partners refuse to do so. Also, the limited partners may sue the general partners to protect the limited partners' interests.

(e) DISSOLUTION. The dissolution and winding up of limited partnerships is governed by the same principles applicable to general partnerships.

D. LIMITED LIABILITY COMPANIES

Limited liability company (LLC) acts are rapidly being adopted by state legislatures throughout the country, following a favorable tax ruling on this form of organization by the Internal Revenue Service.[28]

12. Characteristics of LLCs

The IRS has determined that an LLC may qualify for partnership federal tax treatment. That is, unlike a corporation, the LLC pays no federal taxes on its income as an entity. Instead, the income (or losses, deductions and credits) flows through to the LLCs' owners (called members) based on their proportionate interests in the company. The members report the income on their personal tax returns. The LLC combines this tax advantage with the limited liability feature of the corporate form of business organization. The owners and managers are not personally liable for the debts and obligations of the entity.

(a) FORMATION. An LLC is formed by filing articles of organization with the secretary of state in a manner similar to the filing of articles of incorporation by a corporation. The articles must contain the name, purpose, duration, registered agent, and principal office of the LLC. An LLC must use the words "limited liability company" or "LLC" in the company's name. The LLC is a legal entity with authority to conduct business in its own name.

(b) CAPITAL CONTRIBUTIONS. An ownership interest in an LLC may be issued for cash, property or services. The owners of the entity are known as members.

(c) MANAGEMENT. Management of a LLC is vested in its members. An *operating agreement*, equivalent to the bylaws of a corporation or a partnership agreement, sets forth the specific management authority of members and managers. Commonly members delegate authority to run the entity to managers who may or may not be required to be members of the LLC. Managers have the same fiduciary duties to the entity as corporate officers have to a corporation.

(d) DISTRIBUTIONS. Profits and losses are shared according to the terms of the operating agreement.

(e) ASSIGNMENT. An interest in an LLC is personal property and is generally assignable. However, LLC members cannot transfer the right to participate in management without the consent of the other members of the LLC.

---

[28] IRS Rev Rul 88-76. As of March 1, 1994 legislation allowing for the use of the LLC form of business organization has been enacted in the following states: Alabama, Arizona, Arkansas, Colorado, Connecticut, Delaware, Florida, Georgia, Idaho, Illinois, Indiana, Iowa, Kansas, Louisiana, Maryland, Michigan, Minnesota, Missouri, Montana, Nebraska, Nevada, New Hampshire, New Jersey, New Mexico, North Carolina, North Dakota, Oklahoma, Oregon, Rhode Island, South Dakota, Texas, Utah, Virginia, West Virginia, Wisconsin, and Wyoming. LLC legislation is pending before other state legislatures.

(f) DISSOLUTION. Statutes creating LLCs commonly limit the existence of the entity to no more than thirty years. And most statutes provide that an LLC will dissolve by the consent of the members, or upon the death, retirement, resignation, expulsion or bankruptcy of a member. Statutes also provide, however, that the business of the LLC may be continued with the consent of all of the remaining members.

Upon the winding up of an LLC, the assets are distributed according to the operating agreement. Should the agreement fail to provide for this event, then the assets will be distributed according to the state's LLC statute.

13. LLCs and Other Entities

LLCs are distinguishable from Subchapter S corporations and limited partnerships.

(a) LLC DISTINGUISHED FROM A SUBCHAPTER S CORPORATION. Under a Subchapter S Corporation shareholders of a close corporation may be treated as partners for tax purposes and retain the benefit of limited liability under the corporate form. An "S Corporation" is limited to 35 shareholders, who must be U.S. citizens or resident aliens, none of whom may be a partnership or a corporation.

In contrast, an LLC has no limit on the number of owners nor is there any restriction on the types of entities or persons that may own an LLC. Thus, partnerships, corporations and foreign investors may be owners of an LLC.

(b) LLC DISTINGUISHED FROM A LIMITED PARTNERSHIP. Limited partners in a limited partnership have the advantage of limited liability. However, every limited partnership must have a general partner who manages the business, and this partner is subject to unlimited liability. This structural feature is a major disadvantage to the limited partnership form, which does not exist in a limited liability company (LLC). Also, limited partners may lose their limited liability if they participate in the control of the business. Under the LLC, the members may actively participate in the control of the business and still receive limited liability protection.

(c) USAGE. It is expected that the LLC will in many instances replace general and limited partnerships as well as close corporations and S corporations. The LLC will not replace the publicly traded corporation, however, since publicly traded partnerships may be classified as corporations for tax purposes.[29]

SUMMARY

When there are more than two partners in a firm, the decisions of the majority prevail on ordinary matters relating to the firm's business, unless the decisions are contrary to the partnership agreement. A partner's authority to act for the firm is similar to that of an agent to act for a principal. A partner may have express authority to act as set forth in the partnership agreement or as agreed to by a sufficient number of partners. A partner has the customary or implied power to make contracts to transact the firm's business; to sell the

firm's goods in the regular course of business; to make purchases within the scope of the business; and to borrow money for firm purposes. Further, a partner may purchase insurance, hire employees, and adjust claims for and against the firm. A partner may not bind the firm by a contract that makes it impossible for the firm to conduct its business. In the absence of express authority from the firm, an individual partner cannot enter into a suretyship contract or an agreement to submit a partnership dispute to arbitration. Nor can a partner

---

[29] See IRS Notice 88-75, 1988, 1988-2 CB 386.

confess judgment against the firm, make an assignment of the firm's assets for the benefit of its creditors, or discharge personal obligations of the partner by paying them with obligations of the firm.

A partner's duties are the same as those of an agent. These duties include loyalty and good faith, obedience, reasonable care, providing full information on all matters affecting the firm, and keeping proper and correct records. If there is no contrary agreement, each partner has the right to take an equal part in the management of the business, to inspect the books, to share in the profits, and after payment of all of the firm's debts and the return of capital, to share in the firm's property or surplus upon dissolution.

Partners have unlimited personal liability for partnership liabilities. Partners are jointly liable on all firm contracts. They are jointly and severally liable for all torts committed by one of the partners or by a firm employee within the scope of the partnership's business. A partner remains liable after dissolution, unless expressly released by creditors. An incoming partner is not liable for the existing debts of the partnership unless the new partner expressly assumes those debts.

A limited partnership consists of one or more limited partners, who contribute cash, property, or services without liability for losses beyond their investment, and one or more general partners, who manage the business and have unlimited personal liability. A certificate must be properly executed and filed when limited partnership is formed.

A limited liability company is a hybrid form of business organization that combines the tax advantages of a partnership with the limited liability feature of the corporation.

LAW IN PRACTICE

1. A partner who advances money to a firm should have a written statement signed by all partners identifying that the money is a loan and not a capital contribution.

2. Remember that a partner cannot promote a competing business, for such is a violation of the partner's duty of loyalty.

3. Recognize in dealing with a partner that a partner cannot bind a firm by making a contract to sell an asset essential to the operation of the partnership's business.

4. Remember that a limited partnership can only be created by complying with the appropriate state statute.

QUESTIONS AND CASE PROBLEMS

1. What social forces are affected by the rule giving the majority of partners authority to bind the firm as to routine business matters?

2. Compare the right of a partner to engage in a business that competes with the firm (a) while still a partner and (b) after leaving the partnership.

3. Ross, Marcos, and Albert are partners. Ross and Marcos each contributed $60,000 to the partnership. Albert contributed $30,000. At the end of the fiscal year, there are distributable profits totaling $150,000. Ross claims $60,000 as his share of the profits. Is he entitled to this sum?

4. What is the effect of dissolution on a partner's liability?

5. Leland McElmurry was one of three partners of MHS Enterprises, a Michigan partnership.

Commonwealth Capital Investment Corporation sued the partnership and obtained a judgment of $1,137,285 against it. The partnership could not pay the judgment. Commonwealth then sued McElmurry for the entire debt, on the theory that as a partner of MHS, he was liable for its debts. What, if any, is McElmurry's liability? [*Commonwealth Capital Investment Corporation v McElmurry, 102 Mich App 536, 302 NW2d 222*]

6. Daniel Zuckerman, a minor, and Elaine Zuckerman, his mother, brought a medical malpractice action against Dr. Joseph Antenucci and Dr. Jose Pena. Although the summons did not state that the two defendants were partners, the undisputed evidence at the trial established that relationship. The evidence also established that the alleged acts of malpractice were done in the course of partnership business. The jury returned a verdict finding that Pena was guilty of malpractice but that Antenucci was not guilty of malpractice. The amount of the verdict was $4 million. Antenucci contended that he should not be held liable on a partnership theory for the act of his partner when the plaintiffs had not named the partnership entity on the summons and when the summons did not designate him as a partner. Decide. [*Zuckerman v Antenucci, 124 Misc 2d 971, 478 NYS2d 578*]

7. Charles and Sonny Monin are brothers. They formed a partnership in 1967 for hauling milk for Dairymen Incorporated (DI), an organization of milk producers. The brothers had a falling out in 1984, and Sonny notified Charles that he was dissolving the partnership in July 1984. The partnership's contract with DI expired on October 16, 1984. On September 24, 1984, the brothers executed an agreement to conclude their business arrangement, whereby they would hold a private auction between themselves for all the assets of the partnership, "including equipment and milk routes." The agreement contained a covenant not to compete. Charles was the successful bidder at $86,000. The value of the milk-hauling equipment was $22,000 and the milk routes $64,000. Sonny notified DI that he wanted to apply for the right to haul milk after the expiration of the partnership's contract. Charles was the only other applicant for the milk routes. Sonny was selected over Charles for the new DI contract. Charles sued Sonny for breach of his fiduciary duty because Sonny failed to withdraw his application with DI for the milk routes after agreeing to allow Charles to buy his interest in those milk routes. Sonny contended that the partnership had no interest in the milk routes after the contract expired on October 16, 1984, and that he was therefore free to pursue the contract. Decide. [*Monin v Monin (Ky App) 785 SW2d 499*]

8. Compare the effect of a secret limitation on the authority of (a) an agent and (b) a partner.

9. George and James McCune did business as McCune & McCune, a general law partnership. Mountain Bell provided telephone service to McCune & McCune through November 1983, when the partnership dissolved and its telephone service was discontinued. Mountain Bell transferred the unpaid balance of the partnership's account to the individual business account of George McCune. George brought suit against Mountain Bell to enjoin it from suspending his service when this transferred bill was not paid. He contended that partnership law requires that partnership assets be marshaled and exhausted before a partnership creditor can reach a partner's individual assets. Mountain Bell contended that it had the right to cross-bill customers' accounts for unpaid bills, and if the bill remained unpaid, it had a right to suspend service on the account to which the debt has been transferred. Decide. [*McCune & McCune v Mountain Bell Tel. Co. (Utah) 758 P2d 914*]

10. Mason and Phyllis Ledbetter operated a business in Northbrook, Illinois, as a partnership. This partnership, called Ledbetters' Nurseries, specialized in the sale of garden lilies. The grounds of the nurseries were planted with numerous species of garden lilies, and hundreds of people toured the Ledbetters' gardens every day. After a tour, Sheila Clark offered to buy the facilities at a "top-notch price." Mason felt he could not refuse the high offer, and he signed a contract to sell the entire facilities, including all flowers and the business name. When Phyllis refused to go along with the contract, Clark sued the Ledbetters' Nurseries partnership, seeking to obtain specific performance of the sales contract. Decide.

11. Holmes and Clay are partners in a medical partnership. Each had invested $25,000 in the practice; the total market value of all firm assets was $50,000. Marsh, a former patient of Holmes, sued Holmes and Clay for malpractice involved in surgery performed by Holmes. Marsh's suit was successful, and a judgment was entered for $150,000 against the two partners. Holmes had suffered a prior financial setback, and he did not have funds or property other than partnership assets to pay the judgment. Arrangements were made by Holmes and Clay to pay $50,000 using the firm assets. Marsh now seeks to collect $100,000 from Clay. Clay objects that it is absurd to seek payment from her out of her own personal assets when she was not at fault. Is Clay liable to Marsh for the unpaid balance of the judgment?

12. Hacienda Farms, Limited, was organized as a limited partnership, with Ricardo de Escamilla as the general partner and James L. Russell and H. W. Andrews as limited partners. The partnership raised vegetables and truck crops that were marketed principally through a produce concern controlled by Andrews. All three individuals decided which crops were to be planted. The general partner had no power to withdraw money from the partnership's two bank accounts without the signature of one of the limited partners. After operating for some seven and one-half months under these procedures, the limited partners demanded that the general partner resign as farm manager, which he did. Six weeks later, the partnership went into bankruptcy. Laurance Holzman, as trustee in bankruptcy, brought an action against Russell and Andrews, claiming that they had become liable to the creditors of the partnership as general partners because they had taken part in the control of the partnership business. How would you decide the case under the ULPA? Would the outcome be different under the RULPA? [Holzman v de Escamilla, 86 Cal App 2d 858, 195 P2d 833]

13. The St. John Transportation Co., a corporation, made a contract with the partnership of Bilyeu & Herstel, contractors, by which the latter was to construct a ferryboat. Herstel, a member of the firm of contractors, executed a contract in the firm name with Benbow for certain materials and labor in connection with the construction of the ferryboat. In an action brought by Benbow to enforce a lien against the ferryboat, the James Johns, it was contended that all members of the firm were bound by the contract made by Herstel. Do you agree? [Benbow v the James Johns, 56 Or 554, 108 P 634]

14. Jerome Micco was a major shareholder and corporate officer of "Micco and Company, Inc." Micco and Company Inc. was a limited partner in "Harbor Creek Limited," a limited partnership formed to build a condominium complex. Hommel, an electrical contractor, was the successful bidder on certain electrical work for the project. For several months Hommel worked under the direction of the construction supervisor and he was paid by the limited partnership for his work. Be-

cause of financial difficulties the supervisor was released. Thereafter, Jerome Micco played a major role in the building of the project, directing what work was to be performed. Hommel submitted payment invoices directly to Micco. When Hommel was not paid, he sued Micco, contending that Micco was a limited partner who ran the operation personally and was personally responsible for the debt. Micco defended that he was an employee or agent of a corporation (Micco and Co., Inc.), and thus could not be held liable for the debt. The evidence reveals that Micco had no occasion to tell Hommel that he was acting as a corporate officer. Is it ethical for a corporate officer and shareholder to seek to avoid individual liability in this case. How would you decide the case? [Hommel v Micco (Ohio App) 602 NE2d 1259]

15. Zemelman and others did business as a partnership under the name of Art Seating Company. The partnership obtained a fire insurance policy from the Boston Insurance Company. There was a fire loss, and a claim was filed under the policy. The claim was prepared by one of the partners, Irving Zemelman. The insurance company asserted that false statements were made by Zemelman and that the insurer was therefore not liable on the policy. The policy contained an express provision stating that it was void if a false claim were made. The partnership replied that it was not bound by any fraudulent statement of Zemelman, since the making of fraudulent statements was not within the scope of his authority. Is the partnership correct? [Zemelman v Boston Insurance Co. 4 Cal App 3d 15, 84 Cal Rptr 206]

CHAPTER 47

INTRODUCTION TO CORPORATION LAW

LEARNING OBJECTIVES

After studying this chapter, you will be able to:
1. *Classify corporations according to nature, state of incorporation, and functions performed.*
2. *State why when the corporate entity will be ignored.*
3. *List the steps to be taken in forming a corporation.*
4. *Compare corporations de jure, de facto, and by estoppel.*
5. *List and describe the ways in which corporate existence may be terminated.*
6. *Compare consolidations, mergers, and conglomerates.*

The corporation is one of the most important forms of business organization.

A. NATURE AND CLASSES

A corporation is an artificial person that is created by governmental action.

1. The Corporation as a Person

A **corporation** is an artificial person, created by government action and given with certain powers. The corporation exists in the eyes of the law as a person, separate and distinct from the persons who own the corporation.

The concept that the corporation is a distinct legal person means that property of the corporation is not owned by the persons who own shares in the corporation, but by the corporation. Debts of the corporation are debts of this artificial person, not of the persons running the corporation or owning shares of stock in it.[1] The corporation can sue and be sued in its own name. Shareholders cannot be sued as to corporate liabilities.

A corporation is formed by obtaining approval of a **certificate of incorporation**, **articles of incorporation**, or a **charter** from the state or national government.[2]

2. Classifications of Corporations

Corporations may be classified in terms of their relationship to the public, the source of their authority, and the nature of their activities.

(a) PUBLIC, PRIVATE, AND QUASI-PUBLIC CORPORATIONS. A **public corporation** is one established for governmental purposes and for the administration of public affairs. A city is a public or municipal corporation acting under authority granted to it by the state.

A **private corporation** is one organized for charitable and benevolent purposes or for purposes of finance, industry, and commerce. Private corporations are often called "public" in business circles when their stock is sold to the public.

A **quasi-public corporation**, sometimes known as a public-service corporation or a public utility, is a private corporation furnishing services on which the public is particularly dependent. An example of a quasi-public corporation is a gas and electric company.

(b) PUBLIC AUTHORITIES. The public increasingly demands that government perform services. Some of these are performed directly by government. Others are performed by separate corporations or **authorities** that are created by government. For example, a city parking facility may be organized as a separate municipal parking authority. A public low-cost housing project may be operated as an independent housing authority.

(c) DOMESTIC AND FOREIGN CORPORATIONS. A corporation is called a **domestic corporation** with respect to the state under whose law it has been incorporated. Any other corporation going into that state is called a **foreign corporation**. Thus, a corporation holding a Texas charter is a domestic corporation in Texas but a foreign corporation in all other states.

(d) SPECIAL SERVICE CORPORATIONS. Corporations formed for transportation, banking, insurance, savings and loan operations, and similar specialized functions are subject to separate codes or statutes with regard to their

---

[1] American Truck Lines, Inc. v Albino (Ga App) 424 SE2d 367 (1992).

[2] *Charter, certificate of incorporation,* and *articles of incorporation* are all terms used to refer to the documents that serve as evidence of a government's grant of corporate existence and powers. Most state incorporation statutes now provide for a certificate of incorporation issued by the secretary of state, but a Revised Model Business Corporation Act has done away with the certificate of incorporation. Under the RMBCA, corporate existence begins when articles of incorporation are filed with the secretary of state. An endorsed copy of the articles together with a fee, receipt, or acknowledgment replace the certificate of incorporation. See RMBCA §§ 1.25 and 2.03 and footnote 5 in this chapter.

organization. In addition, federal and state laws and administrative agencies regulate in detail the way these businesses are conducted.

(e) CLOSE CORPORATIONS. A corporation whose shares are held by a single shareholder or a small group of shareholders is known as a **close corporation**. The shares are not traded publicly. Many such corporations are small firms that in the past would have operated as proprietorships or partnerships but are incorporated to obtain either the advantage of limited liability or a tax benefit, or both.

In many states, statutes have liberalized the corporation law as it applies to close corporations. For example, some statutes permit incorporation by a smaller number of persons, allow a one-person board of directors, and eliminate the requirement of formal meetings.[3]

(f) "SUBCHAPTER S CORPORATIONS." Subchapter S is a subdivision of the Internal Revenue Code. If corporate shareholders meet the requirements of this subdivision they may elect Subchapter S status. This status allows the shareholders to be treated as partners for tax purposes and retain the benefit of limited liability under the corporate form. A Subchapter S corporation is limited to 35 shareholders, none of which may be partnerships or corporations.

(g) PROFESSIONAL CORPORATIONS. A corporation may be organized for the purpose of conducting a profession.

(h) NONPROFIT CORPORATIONS. A **nonprofit corporation** (or an eleemosynary corporation) is one that is organized for charitable or benevolent purposes. Nonprofit corporations include hospitals, homes, and universities.[4] Special procedures for incorporation are prescribed, with provision for a detailed examination and hearing with regard to the purpose, function, and methods of raising money for the enterprise.

3. Corporations and Governments

Problems arise with respect to the power of governments to create and regulate corporations.

(a) POWER TO CREATE. Since by definition a corporation is created by government, the right to be a corporation must be obtained from the proper government. The federal government may create corporations whenever appropriate to carry out the powers granted to it.

Generally, a state by virtue of its police power may create any kind of corporation for any purpose. Most states have a **general corporation code** that lists certain requirements, and anyone who satisfies the requirements and files the necessary papers with the government may automatically become a corporation. In 1950, the American Bar Association published a Model Business Corporation Act (ABA MBCA) to assist legislative bodies in the modernization of state corporation laws. An updated version was published in 1969. Statutory language similar to the language contained in the 1969 version of the MBCA has been adopted in whole or in part by 35 states. The 1984 revision of the Model Act (RMBCA) represents the first complete revision in more than 30 years.[5] Jurisdictions following the

---

[3] This distinction between large and small corporations is part of the same current of legal development that in the Uniform Commercial Code has given rise to the distinction between the merchant seller or buyer on the one hand and the casual seller or buyer on the other. It is also part of the movement that has given rise to LLCs, see Chapter 46.

[4] The Committee on Corporate Laws of the American Bar Association has prepared a Model Nonprofit Corporation Act. The Nonprofit Corporation Act has formed the basis for nonprofit corporation statutes in Alabama, Iowa, Nebraska, North Carolina, North Dakota, Ohio, Oregon, Texas, Virginia, Washington, Wisconsin, and the District of Columbia. A revised Model Nonprofit Corporation Act was approved in 1986.

[5] The Revised Model Business Corporation Act (1984) was approved by the Committee on Corporate Laws of the Section of Corporation, Banking and Business Law of the American Bar Association. The committee approved revisions

Model Act have made numerous modifications to reflect their differing views in the balancing of interests of public corporations, shareholders, and management. Caution must therefore be exercised in making generalizations about Model Act jurisdictions. There is no *uniform* corporation act.

(b) POWER TO REGULATE. Subject to constitutional limitations, corporations may be regulated by statutes.

(1) Protection of the Corporation as a Person. The Constitution of the United States prohibits the national government and the state governments from depriving any "person" of life, liberty, or property without due process of law. Many state constitutions contain a similar limitation on their respective state governments. A corporation is regarded as a "person" within the meaning of such provisions.

The federal Constitution prohibits a state from denying to any "person" within its jurisdiction the equal protection of the laws. No such express limitation is placed on the federal government, although the due process clause binding the federal government is liberally interpreted so that it prohibits substantial inequality of treatment.

(2) Protection of the Corporation as a Citizen. For certain purposes, such as determining the right to bring a lawsuit in a federal court, a corporation is a citizen of any state in which it has been incorporated and of the state where it has its principal place of business. The actual citizenship of the individual persons owning the stock of the corporation is ignored. Thus, the corporation incorporated in New York is citizen of a New York even though its shareholders are citizens of many other states. Likewise, a Delaware corporation having its principal place of business in New York is deemed a citizen of New York as well as of

Delaware.[6] An environmental protection law authorizing any citizen to bring suit to prevent pollution permits a corporation to bring such a suit.

The federal Constitution prohibits states from abridging "the privileges or immunities of citizens of the United States." A corporation, however, is not regarded as a citizen within this clause. Thus, with one exception, a foreign corporation has no constitutional right to do business in another state if that other state wishes to exclude it. For example, Pennsylvania can deny a New York corporation the right to come into Pennsylvania to do business. As a practical matter, most states do not exclude foreign corporations but seize on this power as justifying special regulation or taxation. On this basis it is commonly provided that a foreign corporation must register or even take out a domestic charter, file copies of its charter, pay certain taxes, or appoint a resident agent before it can do business within the state. As an exception to the power of states, a state cannot require a license or registration of a foreign interstate commerce corporation or impose a tax on the right to engage in such a business.

4. Ignoring the Corporate Entity

Ordinarily, a corporation will be regarded and treated as a separate legal person, and the law will not look behind a corporation to see who owns or controls it.

The fact that two corporations have identical shareholders does not justify a court in regarding the two corporations as being one. Similarly, the fact that there is a close working relationship between two corporations does not in itself constitute any basis for ignoring their separate corporate entities when they in fact are separately run enterprises.[7]

---

to Sections 6.40 and 8.33 on March 27, 1987. Excerpts of the 1984 act, as revised, are found in Appendix 6 to this book. Model Act citations are to the 1984 Revised Model Business Corporation Act (RMBCA) unless designated otherwise.

[6] 28 USC § 1332(c).

[7] Extra Energy Coal Co. v Diamond (Ind) 467 NE2d 439 (1984).

(a) "PIERCING THE CORPORATE VEIL." A court may disregard the corporate entity, or figuratively "pierce the corporate veil," when exceptional circumstances warrant. The decision whether to disregard the corporate entity is made on a case-by-case basis, weighing all factors before the court. Factors that may lead to piercing the corporate veil and imposing liability on its owners (the shareholders) are (1) failure to maintain adequate corporate records and the commingling of corporate and other funds, (2) grossly inadequate capitalization, (3) diversion by shareholders of corporate funds or assets, (4) the formation of the corporation to evade an existing obligation, (5) the formation of the corporation to perpetrate a fraud or conceal illegality,[8] and (6) a determination that injustice and inequitable consequences would result if the corporate entity were recognized.

In the *K.C. Roofing Center* case, creditors claimed that the corporate entity should be ignored.

K.C. ROOFING CENTER v ON TOP ROOFING, INC.

(Mo App) 807 SW2d 545 (1991)

Russell Nugent ran a roofing business as a corporation named Russell Nugent Roofing, Inc. In 1985, the name was changed to On Top Roofing, Incorporated. On August 27, 1987, On Top, Inc. ceased to exist and RNR, Inc. was incorporated. RNR, Inc. went out of business in 1988 and RLN Construction, Inc. was incorporated. In 1989, the business was organized as Russell Nugent, Inc. Nugent and his wife were the sole shareholders, officers, and directors of each corporation. When one roofing company was incorporated, the prior roofing company ceased doing business. All of the companies were located at the same business address and used the same telephone number. Nugent paid himself and his wife over $100,000 in salaries in 1986. In 1986, the corporation paid $99,290 in rent for property that was owned by the Nugents. Nugent testified that he changed to a new corporation every time he needed to get a "fresh start." The evidence showed that he used the "On Top Roofing" logo on his trucks and Yellow Page advertisements throughout the period of the successive corporations. Suppliers who were not paid for materials in 1986 and 1987 by the insolvent corporations sought to pierce the corporate veils and hold Nugent personally liable. Nugent defended that as a shareholder he had no personal liability. From a judgment for the creditors, Nugent appealed.

KENNEDY, J. . . . Shareholder insulation from liability for corporate debts or obligations has been a cornerstone of corporate law in the United States since the 19th century. . . . Although courts will look through corporate organizations to individuals when necessary to prevent injustice, doing so is the exception rather than the rule, and, ordinarily, a corporation will be regarded as a separate legal entity even though there is but a single stockholder. . . .

---

8 Brock Builders Inc. v Dahlbeck, 223 Neb 493, 391 NW2d 110 (1986).

Courts will pierce the corporate veil or disregard the corporate entity once a plaintiff shows:

(1) Control, no mere majority or complete stock control, but complete domination, not only of finances, but of policy and business practice in respect to the transaction attacked so that the corporate entity as to this transaction had at the time no separate mind, will or existence of its own; and

(2) Such control must have been used by the defendant to commit fraud or wrong, to perpetrate the violation of a statutory or other positive legal duty, or dishonest and unjust act in contravention of plaintiff's legal rights; and

(3) The aforesaid control and breach of duty must proximately cause the injury or unjust loss complained of.

. . . "Where a corporation is used for an improper purpose and to perpetrate injustice by which it avoids its legal obligations, 'equity will step in, pierce the corporate veil and grant appropriate relief.'" . . .

There was substantial evidence to support the trial court's finding that the three-part test for piercing the corporate veil was satisfied in this case. Russell Nugent was clearly in control of On Top Roofing, Inc. He and his wife were the sole shareholders of the corporation and he was the president and chief operating officer and clearly made all the decisions.

There also was substantial evidence to support the second and third prongs of the test. A court may pierce the corporate veil or disregard the separate legal entity of the corporation and the individual where the separateness is used as a subterfuge to defraud a creditor. . . . But actual fraud is not necessarily a predicate for piercing the corporate veil; it may also be pierced to prevent injustice or inequitable consequences. . . . From the evidence it appears that Russell Nugent was operating an intricate corporate shell game in which he would cease doing business as one corporate entity when he was unable to pay the corporation's creditors and he then would form another corporation in place of the prior one in order to get a "fresh start." After On Top supposedly went out of business in the summer of 1987, for at least two years Nugent continued to run an On Top Roofing Yellow Pages ad, kept the On Top Roofing name on the sign on the building at 614 Main, kept the On Top Roofing name on the side of his roofing trucks, continued to use bid estimate sheets with the On Top Roofing name on them, and continued to represent to callers over the telephone that he was still operating as On Top Roofing. Although Nugent was only paying secured creditors of On Top, he went ahead and ordered the supplies from the plaintiffs—both of which were unsecured—at a time when On Top was insolvent and had outstanding debt of approximately $100,000 to other roofing suppliers.

Through his domination and control over On Top, Russell Nugent was using it for the unfair or inequitable purpose of avoiding their debts to plaintiffs. Nugent continued to hold On Top out to the public as though it was still operating after it supposedly went out of business, yet he refused to honor On Top's obligations to its creditors. The actions of Nugent worked at least an injustice if not to defraud the plaintiffs. It would be unfair, unjust or inequitable to allow Nugent to hide behind the corporate shield and avoid his legal obligations to plaintiffs. We hold that the trial court did not err in piercing the corporate veil and holding Russell Nugent personally liable for the debts owed plaintiffs. . . .

[Judgment affirmed]

QUESTIONS

1. Will the courts ordinarily pierce the corporate veil in situations where there is only a single stockholder or family running the business?
2. Must actual fraud be shown in order for the court to pierce the corporate veil?
3. Review the ethical principles set forth in the Preface and assess the ethics of Nugent's business practices.

When a person uses a corporation as a mask behind which to hide from a person being defrauded, the court will hold the wrongdoer liable for the acts of the corporation. The court may state that the corporation is the alter ego of the wrongdoer.[9]

(b) FUNCTIONAL REALITY. When a corporation is in effect merely a department of a large enterprise—for example, when a large manufacturer incorporates its marketing department while continuing to hold itself out to the public as a single enterprise—it is likely that the separate corporate character of the incorporated department will be ignored.

(c) OBTAINING ADVANTAGES OF CORPORATE EXISTENCE. The court will not go behind the corporate identity merely because the corporation has been formed to obtain tax savings or to obtain limited liability for its shareholders. Similarly, the corporate entity will not be ignored merely because the corporation does not have sufficient assets to pay the claims against it.

One-person, family, and other closely held corporations are permissible and entitled to all of the advantages of corporate existence. The fact that the principal shareholder runs or oversees the day-to-day operations does not justify ignoring the corporate entity.

B. CREATION AND TERMINATION OF THE CORPORATION

All states have general laws governing the creation of corporations.

5. Promoters

Corporations come into existence as the result of the activities of one or more persons known as promoters. The **promoter** brings together persons interested in the enterprise, aids in obtaining subscriptions to stock, and sets in motion the machinery that leads to the formation of the corporation itself.

A corporation is not liable on a contract made by its promoter for its benefit unless the corporation takes some affirmative action to adopt such a contract. This action may be express words of adoption or by acceptance of the benefits of the contract. A corporation may also become bound by such contracts by assignment or by novation.

The promoter is personally liable for all contracts made on behalf of the corporation before its existence unless the promoter is exempted by the terms of the agreement or by the circumstances surrounding it.[10]

---

[9] El Paso Development Co. v Berryman (Tex Civ App) 769 SW2d 584 (1989).

[10] Tin Cup Pass Ltd. v Daniels, 195 Ill App 3d 847, 142 Ill Dec 732, 553 NE2d 82 (1990).

In the *Clinton Investors* case a person executing a pre-incorporation lease in the name of a proposed corporation did not believe himself to be a promoter, nor did he think that he could be personally liable for obligations incurred under the lease.

CLINTON INVESTORS CO. v WATKINS
146 App Div 2d 861, 536 NYS2d 270 (1989)

Clinton Investors Co. (Clinton), as landlord, entered into a three-year lease with "The Clifton Park Learning Center" (learning center) as tenant. The lease was signed by Berne Watkins, as treasurer of the learning center. On May 31, 1984, the day before the lease term commenced, Watkins signed a rider to the lease. He again signed as treasurer of the tenant, but identified the tenant as "the Clifton Park Learning Center, Inc." Watkins had not consulted an attorney regarding the formation of the corporation. He mistook the reservation of the business name with the Secretary of State for the filing of a certificate of incorporation. On February 11, 1985, a certificate of incorporation was filed. By March 1986 the learning center had become delinquent in rental payments and other fees in the amount of $18,103. Clinton sued Watkins and the learning center for the amounts due. The court dismissed the complaint, and Clinton appealed.

VESAWICH, J. . . . Because no corporation existed when Watkins signed the lease with plaintiff, his legal status was that of a promoter of the learning center. . . . Generally, a promoter who executes a preincorporation contract in the name of a proposed corporation is himself personally liable on the contract unless the parties have otherwise agreed. Watkins asserts that because the learning center corporation subsequently adopted the lease he is therefore no longer liable on the lease. However, corporate adoption of a contract "gives rise to corporate liability in addition to any individual liability" (*Universal Inds. Corp. v Lindstrom*, 92 A.D. 2d 150, 152, 459, NYS2d 492) so that the promoter nevertheless remains obligated unless there has been a novation between the corporation and the plaintiff, which is not the situation here. Nor does the record disclose any explicit or implicit agreement by plaintiff not to hold Watkins personally liable on the lease. . . .

[Judgment reversed and summary judgment entered against Watkins]

QUESTIONS

1. What was Watkins' status when he signed the lease?
2. Is it true that because the learning center corporation subsequently adopted the lease, Watkins was no longer liable on the lease?

A promoter is liable for all torts committed in connection with the promoter's activities. The corporation is not ordinarily liable for the torts of the promoter, but it may become liable by its conduct after incorporation. If a promoter induces the making of a contract by fraud, the corporation is liable for the fraud if with knowledge or notice of such fraud it assumes or ratifies the contract.

A promoter stands in a fiduciary relation to the corporation and to stock subscribers. The promoter cannot make secret profits at their expense. Accordingly, if a promoter makes a secret profit on a sale of land to the corporation, the promoter must surrender the profit to the corporation.

The corporation is not liable in most states for the expenses and services of the promoter unless it subsequently promises to pay for them or unless the corporation's charter or a statute imposes such liability on it.

6. Incorporation

One or more natural persons or corporations may act as **incorporators** of a corporation by signing and filing appropriate forms with a designated government official.[11] These papers are filed in duplicate, and a filing fee must be paid. The designated official (usually the secretary of state), after being satisfied that the forms conform to the statutory requirements, stamps *filed* and the date on each copy. The official then retains one copy and returns the other copy, along with a filing fee receipt, to the corporation.[12]

Statutes may require the incorporators to give some form of public notice, such as by advertising in a newspaper, of the intention to form the corporation, stating its name, address, and general purpose.

7. Application for Incorporation

In most states, the process of forming a corporation is begun by filing an application for a certificate of incorporation. This application will contain or be accompanied by the articles of incorporation. The instrument is filed with

the secretary of state and sets forth certain information about the new corporation. The articles of incorporation must contain (a) the name of the corporation, (b) the number of shares of stock the corporation is authorized to issue, (c) the street address of the corporations initial registered office and the name of its initial registered agent, and (d) the name and address of each incorporator.[13] The articles of incorporation may also state the purpose or purposes for which the corporation is organized. If there is no "purpose clause," the corporation will automatically have the purpose of engaging in any lawful business.[14] Also, if no reference is made to the duration of the corporation in the articles of incorporation, it will automatically have perpetual duration.[15]

8. The Certificate of Incorporation

Most state incorporation statutes now provide for a certificate of incorporation to be issued by the secretary of state after articles of incorporation that conform to state requirements have been filed. The Revised Model Business Corporation Act has eliminated the certificate of incorporation in an effort to reduce the volume of paperwork handled by the secretary of state. Under the RMBCA, corporate existence begins when the articles are filed with the secretary of state.[16] In some states, corporate existence begins when the proper government official issues a certificate of incorporation. In other states, it does not begin until an organization meeting is held by the new corporation.

---

[11] RMBCA § 2.01.
[12] RMBCA § 1.25.
[13] RMBCA § 2.02.
[14] RMBCA § 3.01.
[15] RMBCA § 3.02.
[16] RMBCA § 2.03(a).

9. Proper and Defective Incorporation

If the procedure for incorporation has been followed, the corporation has a legal right to exist. It is then called a **corporation de jure**, meaning that it is a corporation by virtue of law.

Assume that there is some defect in the corporation that is formed. If the defect is not a material one, the law usually will overlook the defect and hold that the corporation is a corporation de jure.

The RMBCA abolishes objections to irregularities and defects in incorporating. It provides that the "secretary of state's filing of the articles of incorporation is conclusive proof that the incorporators satisfied all conditions precedent to incorporation. . . ."[17] Many state statutes follow this pattern. Such an approach is based on the practical consideration that when countless persons are purchasing shares of stock and entering into business transactions with thousands of corporations, it becomes an absurdity to expect that anyone is going to make the detailed search that would be required to determine whether a given corporation is a de jure corporation.[18]

(a) DE FACTO CORPORATION. The defect in the incorporation may be so substantial that the law cannot ignore it and will not accept the corporation as a de jure corporation. Yet there may be sufficient compliance so that the law will recognize that there is a corporation. When this occurs, the association is called a **de facto corporation**.

Although there is conflict among the authorities, the traditional elements of a de facto corporation are that (1) a valid law exists under which the corporation could have been properly incorporated, (2) an attempt to organize the corporation has been made in good faith, (3) a genuine attempt to organize in compliance with the requirements of the statute has been made, and (4) there has been a use of the corporate powers.

(b) PARTNERSHIP VERSUS CORPORATION BY ESTOPPEL. The defect in incorporation may be so great that the law will not accept the association as a de facto corporation. In such a case, in the absence of a contrary statute, there is no corporation. If the individuals proceed to run the business in spite of such irregularity, they may be held liable as partners.[19]

The partnership liability rule is sometimes not applied when the third person dealt with the business as though it were a corporation. In such instances, the third person is estopped from denying that the "corporation" had legal existence. In effect, there is a corporation by estoppel with respect to that person.

Several jurisdictions that follow the 1969 MBCA have expressly retained the doctrines of corporation by estoppel and de facto corporations.[20] However, some courts interpreting the language of the 1969 MBCA have held that the de facto corporation doctrine and the corporation by estoppel doctrine no longer exist. The court in the *Thompson & Green* case dealt with these doctrines.

With respect to preincorporation debts the 1984 act imposes liability only on persons who act as or on behalf of a corporation knowing that no corporation exists.[21]

---

[17] RMBCA § 2.03(b).

[18] This trend and the reasons for it may be compared to those involved in the concept of the negotiability of commercial paper. Note the similar protection from defenses given to the person purchasing shares of stock for value and without notice. UCC § 8-202.

[19] In a minority of states, the court will not hold the individuals liable as partners but will hold liable the person who committed the act on behalf of the business, on the theory that that person was an agent who acted without authority and is therefore liable for breach of the implied warranties of the existence of a principal possessing capacity and of proper authorization.

[20] See Ga. Bus. Corp. Code § 22-5103; Minn. Bus. Corp. Act § 301:08. See also H. Rich Corp. v Feinberg (Fla App) 518 So 2d 377 (1987).

[21] RMBCA § 2.04.

THOMPSON & GREEN MACHINERY CO.
v MUSIC CITY LUMBER CO.

(Tenn App) 683 SW2d 340 (1984)

On January 27, 1982, Joe Walker purchased a wheel loader machine from the Thompson & Green Machinery Co. (T-G). Walker signed a promissory note for $37,886.30 on behalf of "Music City Sawmill, Inc. by Joe Walker, President." When Sawmill was unable to make payments on the loader, the machine was returned to T-G and later resold for $17,925. T-G brought suit against Sawmill for the unpaid balance on May 5, 1983 and thereafter discovered that Sawmill had not been incorporated on January 27, 1982, when the machine was sold, but rather had been incorporated on January 28, 1982. T-G then sued Walker individually. The lawsuit was Walker's first notice that Sawmill was not incorporated on the date of the sale. Walker insisted that T-G dealt with Sawmill as a corporation and did not intend to bind him personally on the note and that T-G was therefore estopped from denying Sawmill's corporate existence. T-G replied that the doctrines of *de facto* corporations and corporation by estoppel no longer existed in the state, and Walker was personally liable. From a judgment for Walker, T-G appealed.

LEWIS, J. . . . It is conceded that Sawmill did not have a corporate existence on January 27th. It therefore follows that Mr. Walker could not and did not have authority to act for Sawmill on January 27th when he executed the promissory note to plaintiff.

It is a general rule that one who deals with an apparent corporation as such and in such manner as to recognize its corporate existence de jure or de facto is thereby estopped to deny the fact thus admitted. . . . The estoppel extends as well to the privies as to the parties to such transactions. The general rule is applied in actions brought by either of the contracting parties against the other, and in actions by the persons dealing with the corporation, wherein the existence of the corporation is assailed for the purpose of establishing individual partnership liability on the part of its members.

Tennessee has long recognized the foregoing rule. Our Supreme Court, in *Ingle System Co. v Norris & Hall*, 134 Tenn 472, 178 SW 1113 (1915), stated:

When a private person enters into a contract with a body purporting to be a corporation, in which that body is described by the corporate name which it has assumed, such private person thereby admits the existence of the corporation for the purpose of the suit brought to enforce the obligations, and will not be permitted to deny the corporate existence of the plaintiff.

However, in 1968 the Tennessee General Assembly enacted the "Tennessee General Corporations Act," Chapter 523, Pub. Acts of 1968.

Our research reveals no Tennessee decision which has addressed either de facto corporation or corporation by estoppel since the passage of the act in 1968.

Courts in other jurisdictions which have considered the question of de facto corporations under statutes similar to Tenn Code Ann §§ 48-1-204 and 48-1-1405 have held that under the act, de facto corporations no longer exist. . . .

Corporate existence does not begin until such time as "the charter is filed by the secretary of state." [See 1969 MBCA § 56]. . . .

[1969 MBCA § 146] mandates that "all persons who assume to act as a corporation without authority so to do shall be jointly and severally liable for all debts and liabilities incurred or arising as a result thereof."

The General Assembly, in enacting [MBCA § 146] saw fit to place statutory liability upon those who assume to act as a corporation without authority. [Section 146] does not contain an exception that one who assumes to act as a corporation without authority shall be jointly and severally liable for debts and liabilities except when the plaintiff thereafter dealt with the corporation as a corporation or when the plaintiff did not intend to bind one who assumed to act personally. No exceptions are contained in [§ 146]. For this Court to hold that under the circumstances here Mr. Walker is not liable, it would be necessary that this Court rewrite the Tennessee General Corporations Act and hold that the Act does not mean what it says. We are not at liberty to do so. We find nothing ambiguous in [§ 146]. It is clear that "all persons who assume to act as a corporation without authority so to do shall be jointly and severally liable for all debts and liabilities incurred or arising as a result thereof." We find no good faith exception in the act. To allow an estoppel would be to nullify [§ 146].

We are of the opinion that the doctrine of corporation by estoppel met its demise by the enactment of the Tennessee General Corporations Act of 1968.

[Judgment reversed and action remanded]

QUESTIONS

1. Did Walker make the contract on behalf of Sawmill, Inc., in the good faith belief that it was a corporation?
2. Did T-G intend to hold Walker individually liable on the promissory note when it was signed?
3. State the rule of the case.

10. Insolvency, Bankruptcy, and Reorganization

When a corporation has financial troubles that are so serious that it is insolvent, the best thing may be to go through bankruptcy or reorganization proceedings. The law with respect to bankruptcy and reorganizations is discussed in Chapter 37.

11. Forfeiture of Charter

In states that have adopted the RMBCA, the secretary of state may commence proceedings to administratively dissolve a corporation if (a) the corporation does not pay franchise taxes within 60 days after they are due, (b) the corporation does not file its annual report within 60 days after it is due, or (c) the corporation is without a registered agent or registered office for 60 days or more.[22] In other states, judicial proceedings may be brought to forfeit a corporate charter when the corporation repeatedly acts beyond the powers granted it or engages in illegal activity. After a corporate charter has been forfeited, the owners and officers of the dissolved corporation

---

[22] RMBCA § 14.20.

are not shielded from personal liability by using the corporate name when making contracts.[23]

12. Judicial Dissolution

Judicial dissolution of a corporation may be decreased when its management is deadlocked and the deadlock cannot be broken by the shareholders.[24] In some states, a "custodian" may be appointed for a corporation when the shareholders are unable to break a deadlock in the board of directors and irreparable harm is threatened or sustained by the corporation because of the deadlock.

C. CORPORATE POWERS

All corporations do not have the same powers. For example, those that operate banks, insurance companies, and railroads generally have special powers and are subject to special restrictions.

Except for limitations in the federal Constitution or the state's own constitution, a state legislature may give corporations any lawful powers. The RMBCA contains a general provision on corporate powers granting the corporation "the same powers as an individual to do all things necessary or convenient to carry out its business and affairs."[25] State statutes generally contain similar broad catchall grants of powers.

13. Particular Powers

Modern corporation codes give corporations a wide range of powers.

(a) PERPETUAL LIFE. One of the distinctive features of a corporation is its perpetual or continuous life—the power to continue as an entity forever or for a stated period of time, regardless of changes in stock ownership or the death of any shareholders.

(b) CORPORATE NAME. A corporation must have a name to identify it. As a general rule, it may select any name for this purpose.

Most states require that the corporate name contain some word indicating the corporate character[26] and that the name shall not be the same as or deceptively similar to the name of any other corporation. Some statutes prohibit the use of a name that is likely to mislead the public.

(c) CORPORATE SEAL. A corporation may have a distinctive seal. However, a corporation need not use a seal in the transaction of business unless this is required by statute or unless a natural person in transacting that business would be required to use a seal.

(d) BYLAWS. **Bylaws** are the rules and regulations enacted by a corporation to govern the affairs of the corporation and its shareholders, directors, and officers.

Bylaws are adopted by shareholders, although in some states, they may be adopted by the directors of the corporation. Approval by the state or an amendment of the corporate charter is not required to make the bylaws effective.

The bylaws are subordinate to the general law of the state, the statute under which the corporation is formed, and the charter of the corporation.[27] Bylaws that conflict with such superior authority or that are in themselves unreasonable are invalid. Bylaws that are valid are binding on all shareholders, regardless of whether they know of the existence of those bylaws or were among the majority that

---

[23] Priceco, Inc. v Youngstrom (Idaho App) 786 P2d 606 (1990).

[24] RMBCA § 14.30 (2)(I).

[25] RMBCA § 3.02.

[26] RMBCA § 4.01(a) declares that the corporate name must contain the word *corporation, company, incorporated, limited,* or an abbreviation of one of these words.

[27] Roach v Bynum (Ala) 403 So 2d 187 (1981).

consented to their adoption. Bylaws are not binding on third persons, however, unless they have notice or knowledge of them.

(e) STOCK. A corporation may issue certificates representing corporate stock. Under the RMBCA, authorized but unissued shares may be issued at the price set by the board of directors. Under UCC, Article 8, 1977 Version, securities may be "uncertificated," or not represented by an instrument.

(f) MAKING CONTRACTS. Corporation codes give corporations the power to make contracts.

(g) BORROWING MONEY. Corporations have the implied power to borrow money in carrying out their authorized business purposes.

(h) EXECUTING COMMERCIAL PAPER. Corporations have the power to issue or indorse commercial paper and to accept drafts.

(i) ISSUING BONDS. A corporation may exercise its power to borrow money by issuing bonds.

(j) TRANSFERRING PROPERTY. The corporate property may be leased, assigned for the benefit of creditors, or sold. In many states, however, a solvent corporation may not transfer all of its property without the consent of all or a substantial majority of its shareholders.

A corporation, having power to incur debts, may mortgage or pledge its property as security for those debts. This rule does not apply to public service companies, such as street transit systems and gas and electric companies.

(k) ACQUIRING PROPERTY. A corporation has the power to acquire and hold such property as is reasonably necessary for carrying out its express powers.

(l) BUYING BACK STOCK. Generally, a corporation may purchase its own stock if it is solvent at the time and the purchase does not impair capital. Stock that is reacquired by the corporation that issued it is commonly called **treasury stock**.

Although treasury stock retains the character of outstanding stock, it has an inactive status while it is held by the corporation.[28] Thus, the treasury shares cannot be voted, nor can dividends be declared on them.

(m) DOING BUSINESS IN ANOTHER STATE. A corporation has the power to engage in business in other states. However, this does not exempt the corporation from satisfying valid restrictions imposed by the foreign state in which it seeks to do business.

(n) PARTICIPATING IN ENTERPRISE. Corporations may generally participate in an enterprise to the same extent as individuals. They may enter into joint ventures. The modern statutory trend is to permit a corporation to be a member of a partnership. A corporation may be a limited partner. The RMBCA authorizes a corporation "to be a promoter, partner, member, associate, or manager of any partnership, joint venture, trust, or other entity."[29]

(o) PAYING EMPLOYEE BENEFITS. The RMBCA empowers a corporation "to pay pensions and establish pension plans, pension trusts, profit-sharing plans, share bonus plans, share option plans, and benefit or incentive plans for any or all of its current or former directors, officers, employees, and agents."[30]

---

[28] When a corporation reacquires its own shares, it has the choice of retiring them and thus restoring them to the status of authorized but unissued shares or of treating them as still issued and available for transfer. It is the latter that are described as treasury shares.

[29] RMBCA § 3.02(9).

[30] RMBCA § 3.02(12).

(p) CHARITABLE CONTRIBUTIONS. The RMBCA authorizes a corporation, without any limitation, "to make donations for the public welfare or for charitable scientific, or educational purposes."[31] In some states, a limitation is imposed on the amount that can be donated for charitable purposes.

14. Ultra Vires Acts

When a corporation acts in excess of or beyond the scope of its powers, the corporation's act is described as *ultra vires*. Such an action is improper in the same way that it is improper for an agent to act beyond the scope of the authority given by the principal. It is also improper with respect to shareholders and creditors of the corporation, because corporate funds have been diverted to unauthorized uses.

The modern corporation statute will state that every corporation formed under the statute will have certain powers unless the articles of incorporation expressly exclude some of the listed powers, and then the statute will list every possible power that is needed to run a business. In some states, the legislature makes a blanket grant of all the power that a natural person running the business would possess.[32] The net result is that the modern corporation possesses such a broad scope of powers that it is difficult to find an action that is ultra vires. If a mining corporation should begin to manufacture television sets, there might be an ultra vires transaction, but such an extreme departure rarely happens.

Nonprofit corporations have a more restricted range of powers than business corporations. Actions not authorized by the charters of nonprofit corporations may be found to be ultra vires.[33]

D. CONSOLIDATIONS, MERGERS, AND CONGLOMERATES

Two or more corporations may be combined to form a new structure or enterprise.

15. Definitions

Enterprises may be combined by a consolidation or merger of corporations or the formation of a conglomerate.

(a) CONSOLIDATION. In a **consolidation** of two or more corporations, their separate existences cease, and a new corporation with the property and the assets of the old corporations comes into being.

When a consolidation occurs, the new corporation ordinarily succeeds to the rights, powers, and immunities of its component parts. However, limitations may be imposed by constitution, statute, or certificate of incorporation.

(b) MERGER. When two corporations merge, one absorbs the other. One corporation retains its original charter and identity and continues to exist; the other disappears, and its corporate existence terminates.

(1) Objection of Shareholder. A stockholder who objects to a proposed consolidation or merger, or who fails to convert existing shares into stock of the new or continuing corporation, may apply to a court to appraise the value of the stock held. Should either party act arbitrarily, vexatiously, or not in good faith in the appraisal process, the courts have the right to assess court costs and attorneys' fees.[34] The new or continuing corporation is then required to pay the value of the stock to the stockholder, and the stockholder is required to transfer the stock to the new or continuing

---

[31] RMBCA § 3.02(13).

[32] Note the broad powers granted under the RMBCA § 3.02; see also Cal Corp Code §§ 202(b), 207, 208 for an all-purpose clause granting all of the powers of a natural person in carrying out business activities.

[33] Lovering v Seabrook Island Property Owners Association 289 SC App 77, 344 SE2d 862 (1986). But see St. Louis v Institute of Med. Ed. & Res. (Mo App) 786 SW2d 885 (1990).

[34] RMBCA §13:31; see Santa's Workshop v A.B. Hirschfeld Press Inc. (Colo App) 851 P2d 264 (1993).

Figure 47-1   Consolidation

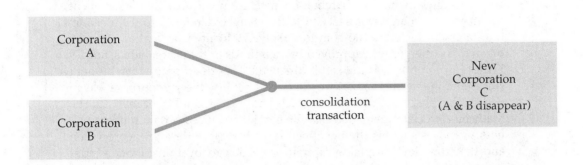

corporation. In effect, the court orders the new or continuing corporation to buy the stock from the dissenting stockholder.

(2) Origin of Plan. In some cases, the plan to merge or consolidate will originate within the corporations involved. In other cases, it will originate with an outside investor. In that situation, the transaction is frequently called a *two-step merger*. First, an outside inves-

tor purchases control of the majority shares of the target corporation. Then this newly acquired control is used to arrange for the target and a second corporation controlled by the outside investor to merge.

The *Alpert* case involved the question of the extent to which a court would review a two-step merger.

ALPERT v 28 WILLIAMS STREET CORPORATION
63 NY2d 557, 473 NE2d 19 (1984)

Since 1955, a valuable 17-story office building located at 79 Madison Avenue in New York City had been owned by 79 Realty Corporation, which had no other substantial assets. About two-thirds of 79 Realty Corporation's outstanding shares were held by two couples, the Kimmelmans and the Zauderers, who were also the company's sole directors and officers. Jack Alpert and three others (the Alpert group) owned 26 percent of the outstanding shares. A consortium of investors formed a limited partnership known as Madison 28 Associates for the purpose of purchasing the building. In March of 1980, Madison Associates began negotiations with the Kimmelmans and Zauderers to purchase the controlling block of stock at a price equal to its proportion of the building's value—agreed in June 1980 to be $6,500,000. In addition, Madison Associates promised that it would offer to purchase the Alpert group's stock under the same terms within four months of the closing of the stock purchase agreement in September, 1980.

Upon selling their shares, the Kimmelmans and the Zauderers resigned their positions with the 79 Realty Corporation and were replaced by four partners of Madison Associates. Acting as the controlling directors of 79 Realty Corporation on October 17, 1980, they approved a plan to merge the 79 Realty Corporation with Williams Street Realty Corporation, which Madison Associates owned. A shareholders meeting was called, and a statement of intention to merge was sent out to the shareholders prior to the meeting; the statement included the plan to dissolve 79 Realty Corporation after the merger. The merger was approved by two-thirds of the shareholders, and 79 Realty Corporation was thereafter dissolved. The Alpert group then brought suit claiming that the merger was unlawful because the sole purpose was to benefit the Madison Associates, which had a clear conflict of interest. The Madison Associates defended that the merger advanced certain proper business purposes such as the beneficial tax advantages through depreciation and the attraction of outside capital for needed renovations. From a judgment for the Madison Associates, the Alpert group appealed.

COOKE, C. J. . . . On this appeal, the principal task facing this court is to prescribe a standard for evaluating the validity of a corporate transaction that forcibly eliminates minority shareholders by means of a two-step merger. It is concluded that the analysis employed by the courts below was correct: the majority shareholders' exclusion of minority interests through a two-step merger does not violate the former's fiduciary obligations so long as the transaction viewed as a whole is fair to the minority shareholders and is justified by an independent corporate business purpose. Accordingly, this court now affirms.

In New York, two or more domestic corporations are authorized to "merge into a single corporation which shall be one of the constituent corporations," known as the "surviving corporation" (see Business Corporation Law, § 901). The statute does not delineate substantive justifications for mergers, but only requires compliance with certain procedures: the adoption by the boards of each corporation of a plan of merger setting forth, among other things, the terms and conditions of the merger, a statement of any changes in the certificate of incorporation of the surviving corporation; the submission of the plan to a vote of shareholders pursuant to notice to all shareholders; and adoption of the plan by a vote of two thirds of the shareholders entitled to vote on it.

Generally, the remedy of a shareholder dissenting from a merger and the offered "cash-out" price is to obtain the fair value of his or her stock through an appraisal proceeding. This protects the minority shareholder from being forced to sell at unfair prices imposed by those dominating the corporation while allowing the majority to proceed with its desired merger. . . . The pursuit of an appraisal proceeding generally constitutes the dissenting stockholder's exclusive remedy. An exception exists, however, when the merger is unlawful or fraudulent as to that shareholder, in which event an action for equitable relief is authorized. . . . Thus, technical compliance with the Business Corporation Law's requirements alone will not necessarily exempt a merger from further judicial review.

Because the power to manage the affairs of a corporation is vested in the directors and majority shareholders, they are cast in the fiduciary role of "guardians of the corporate welfare." . . . In this position of trust, they have an obligation to all shareholders to adhere to fiduciary standards of conduct and to exercise their responsibilities in good faith when undertaking any corporate action, including a merger. . . .

It has long been recognized in this State that, under certain circumstances, "the particular interest of the few must give way to the general interest of the many." . . . Thus, departure from precisely uniform treatment of stockholders may be justified, of course, where a bona fide business purpose indicates that the best interests of the corporation would be served by such departure.". . .

In the context of a freeze-out merger, variant treatment of the minority share-holders—i.e., causing their removal—will be justified when related to the advancement of a general corporate interest. The benefit need not be great, but it must be for the corporation. For example, if the sole purpose of the merger is reduction of the number of profit sharers—in contrast to increasing the corporation's capital or profits, or improving its management structure—there will exist no "independent corporate interest" of the remaining shareholders. What distinguishes a proper corporate purpose from an improper one is that, with the former, removal of the minority shareholders furthers the objective of conferring some general gain upon the corporation. Only then will the fiduciary duty of good and prudent management of the corporation serve to override the concurrent duty to treat all shareholders fairly. . . .

In sum, in entertaining an equitable action to review a freeze-out merger, a court should view the transaction as a whole to determine whether it was tainted with fraud, illegality, or self-dealing, and whether the minority shareholders were dealt with fairly, and whether there exists any independent corporate purpose for the merger.

Noting that defendants had not employed any neutral committees in negotiating the merger, [the lower court] conducted its own objective review of the transaction. There is evidence in the record to support its conclusion that, viewed as a whole, the transaction was fair. Full disclosure of material information was made in the statement of intent mailed to plaintiffs who also had access to Realty Corporation's books. The stock price was tied to the fair market value of the office building, the corporation's only substantial asset, which was determined in arm's length negotiations.

Without passing on all of the business purposes cited . . . as underlying the merger, it is sufficient to note that at least one justified the exclusion of plaintiffs' interests: attracting additional capital to effect needed repairs of the building. There is proof that there was a good-faith belief that additional, outside capital was required. Moreover, this record supports the conclusion that this capital would not have been available through the merger had not plaintiffs' interest in the corporation been eliminated. Thus, the approval of the merger, which would extinguish plaintiffs' stock, was supported by a bona fide business purpose to advance this general corporate interest of obtaining increased capital.

[Judgment affirmed]

QUESTIONS

1. What is a freeze-out merger?
2. Did the defendants follow the statutory procedures for the merger of the two domestic corporations?
3. What protection does state law provide shareholders dissenting from a merger?

Figure 47-2   Merger

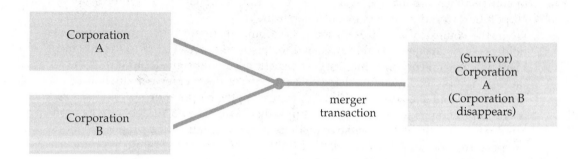

Statutes commonly regulate mergers and consolidations by requiring disclosure of the details a stated number of days before any action can be taken. The purpose of these statutes is not to prohibit or restrain mergers and consolidations but only to make certain that all stockholders are fully informed about the nature and effect of the proposed action.

(c) CONGLOMERATE. **Conglomerate** describes the relationship of a parent corporation to subsidiary corporations engaged in diversified fields of activity unrelated to the field of activity of the parent corporation. For example, a wire manufacturing corporation that owns all the stock of a newspaper corporation and of a drug manufacturing corporation would be described as a conglomerate. In contrast, if the wire manufacturing company owned a mill to produce the metal used in making the wire and owned a mine that produced the ore that was used by the mill, the relationship would probably be described as an integrated industry rather than as a conglomerate. This term is merely a matter of usage rather than of legal definition. Likewise, when the parent company is not engaged in production or the rendering of services, it is customary to call it a holding company.

Without regard to whether the enterprise is a holding company or whether the group of corporations constitutes a conglomerate or an integrated industry, each part is a distinct corporation to which the ordinary corporation law applies. In some instances, additional principles apply because of the nature of the relationship existing between the several corporations involved.

16. Legality

Consolidations, mergers, and asset acquisitions between enterprises are prohibited by federal antitrust legislation when the effect is to lessen competition in interstate commerce. A business corporation may not merge with a charitable corporation, because this combination would divert the assets of the respective corporations to purposes not intended by their shareholders.

17. Liability of Successor Corporations

When corporations are combined in any way, the question arises of who is liable for the debts and obligations of the predecessor corporations.

(a) MERGERS AND CONSOLIDATIONS. Generally, the enterprise engaging in or continuing the business after a merger or consolidation succeeds to all of the rights and property of the predecessor, or disappearing, corporations. The enterprise continuing the

C
P
A

C
P
A

C
P
A

C
P
A

business is also subject to all of the debts and liabilities of the predecessor corporations. Thus, a successor corporation is liable for the contracts of a predecessor corporation. When the successor corporation is sued on such an inherited liability, it cannot raise the defense that the plaintiff did not have a contract with it.

(b) ASSET SALES. In contrast with a merger or consolidation, a corporation may merely purchase the assets of another business. In that case, the purchaser does not become liable for the obligations of the predecessor business.[35]

Corporations may seek to avoid liability for the obligations of a predecessor corporation by attempting to disguise a consolidation or merger as being merely a sale of assets. Courts will not recognize such a sham and will impose a successor's liability on the successor corporation.

In the *Marks* case the court was faced with deciding whether the transactions were asset sales, which insulated the purchaser from liability, or *de facto* mergers, which made the purchaser liable for the obligations of the predecessor corporations.

MARKS v MINNESOTA MINING
AND MANUFACTURING CO.
187 Cal App 3d 1429, 232 Cal Rptr 594 (1986)

In April 1977 Mary Marks had breast augmentation surgery; two implants manufactured by McGhan/Cal. Inc. were used. Because of defects in the McGhan implants, Marks underwent three additional operations, eventually having the McGhan products replaced with implants manufactured by another company. Beginning in 1976 McGhan/Cal. received numerous complaints about its implants and received inquiries from the FDA. In June of 1977 McGhan/Cal. Inc., was acquired by a wholly owned Delaware subsidiary of 3M, called McGhan/Del. Inc. McGhan/Del. continued to receive complaints about the implants and removed the product from the market in April of 1979. On January 1, 1981, 3M's wholly owned subsidiary McGhan/Del. Inc. was reorganized as a division of 3M and dissolved. In January 1982, following her fourth surgery, Marks brought a product liability suit against 3M. 3M contended that it was not liable for the actions of the predecessor corporation. The jury returned a verdict of $25,850 in compensatory damages and $75,000 in punitive damages. The trial judge deleted the punitive damages, and both parties appealed.

NEWSOM, J. . . . While it is the general rule that a purchaser of assets for cash does not assume the seller's liabilities, there are several exceptions to that rule, one of which—where a de facto merger has occurred—we find applicable here. This exception applies where the assets of one corporation are transferred without consideration which can be made available to satisfy claims or "where the consideration

---

[35] Hamaker v Kenwel-Jackson Machine, Inc. (SD) 387 NW2d 515 (1986).

consists wholly of shares of the purchaser's stock which are promptly distributed to the seller's shareholders in conjunction with the seller's liquidation. (*Shannon v Samuel Langston Company* (W.D. Mich. 1974) 379 F.Supp 797, 801)."

Our analysis of the McGhan/Cal. to McGhan/Del. transfer reveals that the first transaction was carried out pursuant to an agreement, dated May 11, 1977, between 3M and McGhan/Cal. entitled "Agreement and Plan of Reorganization." Pursuant to its terms, McGhan/Cal. was to receive shares of 3M stock in exchange for all of its business, assets and goodwill, including the corporate name and the shares of stock of its foreign subsidiary. McGhan/Cal. was required by the agreement to change its name, distribute the 3M stock to its shareholders and dissolve as soon as practicable. All McGhan/Cal. employees, including the seven shareholders, were requested to sign employment agreements with 3M. All five founders of McGhan/Cal. continued to work for McGhan/Del. in substantially the same capacity after the reorganization. Thus, as described by Donald McGhan, the "operating board" (if not the formal board of directors) remained the same. All McGhan/Cal. shareholders became shareholders of 3M.

The agreement also provided for the assumption by 3M of specified liabilities shown on the balance sheets. . . .

We find *Shannon, supra,* particularly persuasive. There, Harris Intertype Corporation entered into an agreement with Samuel M. Langston Company to purchase assets in exchange for Harris stock. . . . Langston was required to change its name. It was subsequently dissolved and the Harris stock distributed to its shareholders. Harris assumed all obligations which were "necessary for the uninterrupted continuation of normal business operations. . . ." A Harris subsidiary took over and continued the operations of Langston under the name The Langston Company. The subsidiary was merged into Harris the year after the plaintiff was injured by a product manufactured by the first Langston corporation. The court characterized this transaction as a de facto merger, and on that basis found Harris liable for the damages due to the defective product. Reasoning from the premise that "a purchaser of corporate assets will be liable for the debts and liabilities of the transferor when the transaction amounts to a consolidation or merger of the seller and purchaser", the court concluded: "Public policy requires that Harris Intertype, having received the benefits of a going concern, should also assume the costs which all other going concerns must ordinarily bear." The court added that "solvent corporations, going concerns, should not be permitted to discharge their liabilities to injured persons simply by shuffling paper and manipulating corporate entities."

Here, as in *Shannon, supra,* the result of the transaction was exactly that which would have occurred had a statutory merger taken place, and we are accordingly convinced of the necessity and the fairness of transferring liability from McGhan/Cal. to McGhan/Del. . . .

With respect to the second reorganization, McGhan/Del., the wholly owned subsidiary of 3M which manufactured the defective product at issue, was "reorganized" into its parent company 11 months before plaintiff's injury. Evidence of the nature of these transactions is sparse, consisting of the declaration of a 3M officer that effective January 1, 1981, McGhan/Del. was reorganized as a division of 3M and then dissolved. Counsel for 3M refers to the transaction as a "merger."

. . . McGhan/Del. continued doing business after the reorganization as "McGhan/3M," a component of its corporate parent. And since 3M was the sole shareholder, it is highly unlikely that cash was paid for the business of

McGhan/Del. We therefore find that the reorganization amounted to a continuation of a de facto merger. Thus, when McGhan/Del. became a part of its parent, as a matter of corporate law it carried with it all of its liabilities.

... While there was more than one merger or reorganization, an analysis of each transaction discloses to us that its intrinsic structure and nature, unlike a sale of assets for cash, was of a type in which the corporate entity was continued and all liability was transferred. All the indicia of a merger are present. We accordingly conclude that the second reorganization, like the first, transferred all liabilities to the surviving corporation. 3M is therefore liable for all liabilities of its subsidiary, including the punitive damages awarded to plaintiff.

[Judgment affirmed as to compensatory damages and reversed as to punitive damages]

QUESTIONS

1. Why did the court find that the result of the transaction between McGhan/Cal. and McGhan/Del. was exactly what would have occurred had a statutory merger taken place?
2. What is the basis for holding a successor corporation liable for the debts of a predecessor corporation when there is a *de facto* merger?
3. If 3M had purchased all of the assets of McGhan/Cal. for cash and used the former McGhan/Cal. plant and equipment to make tapes, would it have been held liable to Marks?

SUMMARY

A corporation is an artificial person, created by government action. It exists as a separate and distinct entity possessing certain powers. In most states, the corporation comes into existence when the secretary of state issues a certificate of incorporation. The most common forms of corporations are private business corporations whose stock is sold to the public (publicly held) and close corporations, which are business firms whose shares are not traded publicly. Corporations may be formed for purposes other than conducting a business. For example, there are nonprofit corporations, municipal corporations, and public authorities for governmental purposes.

Ordinarily, each corporation will be treated as a separate person, and the law will not look beyond the corporate identity merely because the corporation had been formed to obtain tax savings or limited liability. The fact that two corporations have the same shareholders does not justify disregarding the separate corporate entities. However, when a corporation is formed to perpetrate a fraud, a court will ignore the corporate form, or "pierce the corporate veil." The corporate form will also be ignored to prevent injustice or because of the functional reality that the two corporations in question are one.

A promoter is a person who brings together the persons interested in the enterprise and sets in motion all that must be done to form a corporation. A corporation is not liable on contracts made by its promoter for the corporation unless it adopts the contracts. The promoter is personally liable for contracts made for the corporation before its existence. A promoter stands in a fiduciary relation to the corporation and stockholders.

The procedures for incorporation are set forth in the statutes of each state. In most states, the corporation comes into existence upon issuance of the certificate of incorporation. When all requirements have been satisfied, the corporation is a corporation de jure. When there has not been full compliance with all requirements for incorporation, a de facto corporation may be found to exist. Or, when sufficient compliance for a de facto corporation does not exist, in some jurisdictions a third person may be estopped from denying the legal existence of the "corporation" with which it did business (corporation by estoppel).

A corporation has the power to continue as an entity forever or for a stated period of time, regardless of changes in the ownership of the stock or the death of a shareholder. It may make contracts, issue stocks and bonds, borrow money, execute commercial paper, transfer and acquire property, acquire its own stock if it is solvent and the purchase does not impair capital, and make charitable contributions. Subject to limitations, a corporation has the power to do business in other states. A corporation also may participate in a business enterprise to the same extent as an individual. That is, it may be a partner in a partnership, or it may enter a joint venture or other enterprise. Special service corporations such as banks, insurance companies, and railroads are subject to separate statutes with regard to their organization and powers.

An ultra vires act occurs when a corporation acts beyond the scope of the powers given it. Because states now grant broad powers to corporations, it is unlikely that a modern corporation would act beyond the scope of its powers.

Two or more corporations may be combined to form a new enterprise. This combination may be a consolidation—with a new corporation coming into existence—or a merger, in which one corporation absorbs the other.

LAW IN PRACTICE

1. Recognize that lending institutions may refuse loan money to small corporations unless some of its shareholders agree to be personally liable for the debt should the corporation default.
2. Be aware that unusual situations occur where courts will pierce the corporate veil.
3. Remember that after a corporate charter has been forfeited, owners and officers of the dissolved corporation are not shielded from personal liability even if they use the corporate name when making contracts.
4. Recognize that courts will see through a sham transaction, such as when a successor corporation seeks to disguise a consolidation or merger by calling it a "sale of assets."

QUESTIONS AND CASE PROBLEMS

1. What social forces are affected by the recognition of a corporation as a distinct legal entity?
2. Susan sued the Mobile Construction Company. Philip was the only shareholder of the corporation. Susan obtained a judgment against the corporation. Philip then dissolved the corporation and took over all its assets. He agreed to pay all outstanding debts of the corporation except the judgment in favor of Susan. She sued Philip on the ground that he was liable for the judgment against the corporation. He claimed that the judgment was only the liability of the corporation and that he was not liable because he was merely a shareholder and had not assumed the liability for the judgment. Is Philip liable on the judgment?
3. Edwin Edwards and Karen Davis owned EEE, Inc., which owned three convenience stores, all of which sold gasoline. Reid Ellis delivered to the three convenience stores $26,675.02 worth of gasoline, for which he was not paid. Ellis proved that Edwards and Davis owned the business, ran it, and in fact personally ordered the gasoline. He claims that they are personally liable for the debt owed him by EEE, Inc. Decide. [*Ellis v Edwards, 180 Ga App 301, 348 SE2d 764*]
4. What are common grounds for forfeiture of the corporate charter?
5. Compare and contrast consolidations, mergers, and conglomerates.

6. North Pole Inc. approved a plan to merge with its subsidiary Santa's Workshop Inc. The merger plan provided that certain of Workshop's shareholders would receive $3.50 per share. The highest independent appraisal of the stock was $4.04 per share. Hirschfeld Inc., a shareholder, claimed the fair value was $16.80 per share. Workshop offered to make its corporate books and records available to Hirschfeld in order to assess the validity of the $16.80 demand. This offer was declined. Hirschfeld did not attempt to base the $16.80 demand on any recognizable method of stock valuation. Hirschfeld contends it has a right to get the asking price. Refer to RMBCA §§13.02, 13.28 and 13:31. Can Hirschfeld block the merger until Workshop pays the $16.80? Decide. *[Santa's Workshop v Hirschfeld Inc. (Colo App) 851 P2d 264]*

7. Norman was organizing a new corporation: the Collins Home Construction Company. Fairchild knew that the corporation was not yet formed but made a contract by which he agreed to sell certain goods to Collins. The corporation was later organized and ratified the contract that Norman had made with Fairchild. Fairchild, however, did not perform the contract and was sued by Collins. Fairchild raised the defense that he had never made any contract with Collins and that a corporation that did not exist could not have made a contract. Were these defenses valid?

8. In 1977, Morris Gray leased waterfront property on the Ross Barnett Reservoir to a restaurant, Edgewater Landing Inc., for a ten-year term. After a year and a half, Edgewater's original shareholder, Billy Stegall, sold all of his shares in the corporation to Tom Bradley. As of 1986, Tom Bradley and Bradley's bookkeeper, Sandra Martin, owned all the shares in the restaurant. Sandra's husband Randy acted as its manager. Gray visited the property in September 1986 and found many problems with the condition of the property. He claimed that the lease required the tenant to make necessary repairs. Gray sued Edgewater Landing Inc. and Tom Bradley and Sandra Martin individually for breach of the lease. Bradley and Martin replied that they were not liable for the debt of the corporation. Decide. *[Gray v Edgewater Landing, Inc. (Miss) 541 So 2d 1044]*

9. Emmick was a director and shareholder of Colonial Manors, Inc. (CM). He organized another corporation named Oahe Enterprises, Inc. To obtain shares of the Oahe stock, Emmick transferred CM shares arbitrarily valued by him at $19 per share to Oahe Corporation. The CM shares had a book value of $.47 per share, but Emmick believed that the stock would increase to a value of $19. The directors of Oahe approved Emmick's payment with the valuation of $19 per share. Golden sued Emmick on the ground that he had fraudulently deceived the Oahe Corporation about the value of the CM shares and thus had made a secret profit when he received the Oahe shares that had a much greater value than the CM shares he gave in exchange. Emmick defended that it was his firm opinion that the future potential value of CM shares would surely reach $19 per share. Decide. *[Golden v Oahe Enterprises, Inc. (SD) 295 NW2d 160]*

10. The Branmar Theatre Co., a family corporation, leased a theater from Branmar, Inc. The lease prohibited it from assigning the lease. The holders of the stock of Branmar Theatre Co. sold their stock to the Schwartzes. The lessor, Branmar, Inc., claimed that this sale of stock was a prohibited assignment and threatened to cancel the lease. Branmar Theatre Co. subsequently brought an action for a declaratory judgment to enjoin the cancellation of the lease. Should the court enjoin the cancellation of the lease? *[Branmar Theatre Co. v Branmar, Inc. (Del Ch) 264 A2d 526]*

11. In May 1985, Ed Klein was the sole shareholder, director, and chief executive officer of The Gun Exchange, Inc., a retail firearms dealership. The inventory of The Gun Exchange had been pledged as security for a $622,500 debt owed to InterFirst Bank. It also owed $231,484.60 to Sporting Goods, Inc.; this debt was unsecured. On May 20, 1985, InterFirst Bank notified Klein of its intention to foreclose on the inventory and sell it at public auction. InterFirst Bank further advised Klein that, pursuant to his personal guarantee, he would be responsible for any deficiency following the sale. Klein immediately incorporated "The Gun Store Inc." for the purpose of purchasing the assets of The Gun Exchange at the foreclosure sale. Before the foreclosure sale, Klein obtained a $650,000 line of credit from CharterBank on behalf of the Gun Store. At the sale Klein purchased the assets of The Gun Exchange for $650,000, even though the highest prior bid was $175,000. (Had the $175,000 bid been accepted, Klein would have been personally liable for the deficiency to InterFirst Bank). After the foreclosure sale no funds existed to pay the unsecured creditors of The Gun Exchange. Following the sale, The Gun Store began operating as a retail firearms dealer with the inventory purchased from the foreclosure sale. It operated in the same location and with the same personnel as The Gun Exchange. Sporting Goods Inc. sued Klein individually for the $231,484.60. Klein defended that the corporate form under which he did business insulated him as a shareholder from liability for corporate obligations. Decide. Is it ethical to seek limited liability under the corporate form as was done by Klein in this case? [*Klein v Sporting Goods, Inc. (Tex Civ App) 772 SW2d 173*]

12. The Seabrook Island Property Owners Association, Inc. (the association) is a nonprofit corporation organized under state law to maintain streets and open spaces owned by property owners of Seabrook Island. The Seabrook Island Company is the developer of Seabrook Island and has majority control of the board of directors of the association. The association's bylaws empower the board of directors to levy an annual maintenance charge. Neither the association's charter nor its bylaws authorize the board to assess any other charges. When the board levied, in addition to the annual maintenance charge, an "emergency budget assessment" on all members to rebuild certain bridges and to revitalize the beach, the Loverings and other property owners challenged in court the association's power to impose the assessment. Decide. [*Lovering v Seabrook Island Property Owners Association, 289 SC App 77, 344 SE2d 862*]

13. Adams and two other persons were promoters for a new corporation, the Aldrehn Theaters Co. The promoters retained Kridelbaugh to perform legal services in connection with the incorporation of the new business and promised to pay him $1,500. Aldrehn was incorporated through Kridelbaugh's services, and the promoters became its only directors. Kridelbaugh attended a meeting of the board of directors at which he was told that he should obtain a permit for the corporation to sell stock, because the directors wished to pay him for his prior services. The promoters failed to pay Kridelbaugh, and he sued the corporation. Was the corporation liable? [*Kridelbaugh v Aldrehn Theaters Co. 195 Iowa 147, 191 NW 803*]

14. On August 19, 1980, the plaintiff, Joan Ioviero, injured her hand when she slipped and fell while leaving the dining room at the Hotel Excelsior in Venice, Italy. This hotel was owned by the Italian corporation "Cigahotels, S.p.A." (The designation *S.p.A.* stands for Societa per Azionean, the Italian term for corporation.) In 1973, a firm called "Ciga Hotels, Inc." was incorporated in New York. Its certificate of incorporation was amended in 1979, changing the name of the firm to "Landia International Sevices, Inc." This New York corporation was employed by the Italian corporation, Cigahotels, S.p.A., to provide sales and promotional services in the United States and Canada. Ioviero sought to hold the New York corporation liable for her hand injury at the Venice hotel. She pointed to the similarity of the first corporate name used by the New York firm to the name Cigahotels, S.p.A., and the fact that the New York firm represented the interests of the Italian firm in the United States, as clear evidence that the two firms were the same, single legal entity. She asked that the court disregard the separate corporate entities. The New York corporation moved that the case be dismissed, because it was duly incorporated in New York and did not own the Excelsior Hotel in which Ioviero was injured. Decide. [*Ioviero v CigaHotel, Inc. aka Landia I.S. Inc. 101 App Div 2d 852, 475 NYS2d 880*]

15. William Sullivan was ousted from the presidency of the New England Patriots Football Club, Inc. Later, he borrowed $5,348,000 to buy 100 percent control of the voting shares of the corporation. A condition of the loan was that he reorganize the Patriots so that the income from the corporation could be devoted to repayment of the personal loan and the team's assets could be used as collateral. Sullivan therefore arranged for a cash freeze-out merger of the holders of the 120,000 shares of nonvoting stock. David Coggins, who owned 10 shares of nonvoting stock and took special pride in the fact that he was an owner of the team, refused the $15-a-share buyout and challenged the merger in court. He contended that the merger was not for a legitimate corporate purpose but rather to enable Sullivan to satisfy his personal loan. Sullivan contended that legitimate business purposes were given in the merger proxy statement, such as the NFL policy of discouraging public ownership of teams. Coggins responded that before the merger Sullivan had 100 percent control of the voting stock and thus control of the franchise, and that no legal basis existed to eliminate public ownership. Decide. [*Coggins v New England Patriots Football Club, 397 Mass 525, 492 NE2d 1112*]

CHAPTER 48

CORPORATE STOCK AND BONDS

LEARNING OBJECTIVES

After studying this chapter, you will be able to:
1. *Distinguish between subscriptions for stock and transfers of stock.*
2. *Describe the mechanics of transferring stock.*
3. *Describe the rights of shareholders.*
4. *State the exceptions to the limited liability of shareholders.*
5. *Distinguish between stocks and bonds.*

The two most common instruments used to provide funds for a corporation are stocks and bonds.

A. CORPORATE STOCK

Ownership of a corporation is represented by stock.

1. Nature of Stock

Membership in a corporation is based on ownership of one or more shares of stock of the corporation. Each share represents a fractional interest in the total property of the corporation. The shareholder does not own or have an interest in any specific property of the corporation; the corporation is the owner of all of its property. The terms *share*, *stock*, and *share of stock* mean the same thing.

(a) CAPITAL AND CAPITAL STOCK. **Capital** refers to the net assets of the corporation. Shares that have been issued to holders are said to be **outstanding**. **Capital stock** refers to the value received by the corporation for its outstanding stock.

(b) VALUATION OF STOCK. Corporate stock may have a specified **par value**. This means that the person subscribing to the stock and acquiring it from the corporation must pay that amount. When stock is issued by the corporation for a price greater than the par value, some statutes provide that only the par value amount is to be treated as stated capital, the excess being allocated to surplus.

Shares may be issued with no par value. In that case, no amount is stated in the certificate, and the amount that the subscriber pays the corporation is determined by the board of directors. The Revised Model Business Corporation Act eliminates the concept of par value, so stock issued by corporations in states following the RMBCA is always no par.

The value found by dividing the value of the corporate assets by the number of shares outstanding is the **book value** of the shares. The **market value** of a share of stock is the price at which that stock can be voluntarily bought or sold in the open market.

2. Certificates of Stock and Uncertificated Shares

The corporation ordinarily issues a **certificate of stock** or **share certificate** as evidence of the shareholder's ownership of stock. The issuance of such certificates is not essential either to the existence of a corporation or to the ownership of its stock.

In states that have adopted the 1977 amendments to Article 8 of the Uniform Commercial Code, uncertificated shares may be issued. Uncertificated shares are not represented by instruments. Their ownership and transfer are registered on the books maintained by or on behalf of the issuer corporation.[1]

3. Kinds of Stock

The stock of a corporation may be divided into two or more classes.

(a) CLASSIFICATION BY PREFERENCES. **Common stock** is ordinary stock that has no preferences. Each share usually entitles the holder to have one vote, to receive a share of the profits in the form of dividends when declared, and to

participate in the distribution of capital on dissolution of the corporation. **Preferred stock** has a priority over common stock. The priority may be with respect to either dividends or the distribution of capital on dissolution of the corporation or both. Preferred stock is ordinarily nonvoting.

(1) Cumulative Preferred Stock. The right to receive dividends is dependent on the declaration of dividends by the board of directors

---

[1] UCC § 8-102(1)(b). The 1977 Amendments to Article 8 of the UCC have been adopted in all of the states except Alabama.

for that particular period of time. If there is no fund from which the dividends may be declared or if the directors do not declare them from an available fund, the shareholder has no right to dividends. The fact that a shareholder has not received dividends for the current year does not in itself give the right to accumulate or carry over into the next year a claim for those dividends. However, in the absence of a statement that the right to dividends is noncumulative, it is frequently held that preferred stock has the right to accumulate dividends for each year in which there was a surplus available for dividend payment but dividends were not declared.

(2) Participating Preferred Stock. Sometimes the preferred stock is given the right of participation. If so, after the common shares receive dividends or a capital distribution equal to that first received by the preferred stock, both kinds participate or share equally in the balance.

(b) DURATION OF SHARES. Ordinarily, shares continue to exist for the life of the corporation. However, any kind of shares, whether common or preferred, may be made terminable at an earlier date.

Convertible shares entitle the shareholder to exchange owned shares for a different kind of share or for bonds of the corporation.

(c) FRACTIONAL SHARES. A corporation may issue fractional shares or scrip or certificates representing fractional shares. These can be sold or combined for the acquisition of whole shares.

B. ACQUISITION OF SHARES

Shares may be acquired from the corporation or from an existing shareholder.

4. Nature of Acquisition

Shares of stock may be acquired (1) from the corporation by subscription, either before or after the corporation is organized, or (2) by transfer of existing shares from a shareholder or from the corporation. The transfer may be voluntary, as by sale, gift, or bequest by will; or involuntary, as by an execution sale to pay the judgment of a creditor. The transfer may also take place by operation of law as when the stock of a shareholder passes to the shareholder's trustee in bankruptcy.

5. Statute of Frauds

A contract for the sale of corporate shares must be evidenced by a writing or it cannot be enforced.[2] The writing must show that there has been a contract for the sale of a stated quantity of described securities at a defined or stated price. The writing must be signed in the manner required by the statute of frauds for the sale of goods.

No writing is required for a contract by which a broker agrees with a customer to buy or sell securities for the customer. That is an agency agreement and not a sale made between the customer and the broker.

6. Subscription

A **stock subscription** is a contract or agreement to buy a specific number and kind of shares when they are issued by the corporation. As in the case of any other contract, the agreement to subscribe to shares of a corporation may be avoided for fraud.

(a) SUBSCRIPTION BEFORE INCORPORATION. In many states, a preincorporation subscription of shares is an offer to the corporation. According to this view, it is necessary for the corporation to accept the subscription offer either expressly or by conduct. A few states hold that subscriptions automatically become binding contracts when the organization

---

[2]   UCC § 8-319(a). Goldfinger v Brown, 169 App Div 2d 703, 564 NYS2d 461 (1991).

of the corporation has been completed. In some states, the preincorporation subscription is irrevocable for a stated period.[3] The RMBCA provides that "a subscription for shares entered into before incorporation is irrevocable for six months unless the subscription agreement provides a longer or shorter period or all the subscribers agree to revocation."[4]

(b) SUBSCRIPTION AFTER INCORPORATION. Subscriptions may be made after incorporation. In that event, the transaction is like any other contract with the corporation. The offer of the subscription may come from the subscriber or from the corporation. In either case, there must be an acceptance. On acceptance, the subscriber immediately becomes a shareholder with all the rights, privileges, and liabilities of a shareholder, even though the subscriber has not paid any of the purchase price. Moreover, the subscriber is a shareholder even though no share certificate has been issued. In contrast with a contract for immediate subscription to shares, the contract may be one for the future issue of shares. In that case, the contracting party has only a contract and is not a shareholder as of the formation of the contract.

7. Transfer of Shares

In the absence of a valid restriction, a shareholder may transfer shares to anyone.

(a) RESTRICTIONS ON TRANSFER. Restrictions on the transfer of stock are valid if they are not unreasonable. It is lawful to require that the corporation or other stockholders be given the first right to purchase stock before a shareholder may sell it to an outsider.[5]

A provision giving a corporation the right to purchase a shareholder's shares on the death of the shareholder is valid.

A restriction on the right to transfer is not valid as against the purchaser of the certificate unless the restriction is conspicuously noted on the certificate or unless the transferee had actual knowledge of the restriction. A restriction on the transfer of stock is strictly interpreted. For example, a restriction on the sale of stock is not applicable to a gift of stock.

In the *Fought* case the court considered whether shares of stock were sold in violation of a restriction on transfer.

FOUGHT v MORRIS
(Miss) 543 So 2d 167 (1989)

In 1974 Billy Fought, Brady Morris, Clayton Strong, and John Peyton organized Vicksburg Mold and Die, Inc., for the purpose of designing and manufacturing plastic and metal products. Each individual was issued twenty-five shares of stock. The shareholders entered into an agreement requiring a stockholder wishing to sell his stock to offer proportionate shares to each of the other stockholders. Morris was elected president and Fought vice president, and all four individuals worked at the plant. Strong retired in 1979 and sold his shares in accordance with the agreement. In 1983 Peyton decided to sell his shares and agreed to sell them all to Morris, thus giving Morris control of the corporation. Fought sued Morris for breach of his fiduciary duty

---

[3] Prejean v Commonwealth for Community Change, Inc. (La App) 503 So 2d 661 (1987).

[4] RMBCA § 6.20(a).

[5] Hardy v South Bend Sash & Door Co. (Ind App) 603 NE2d 895 (1992).

to Fought and for the value of Fought's *pro rata* share of Peyton's stock. From a judgment for Morris, Fought appealed.

ANDERSON, J. . . . The evidence indicates that Morris' intent in offering to purchase all Peyton's shares was to "freeze out" Fought.

As we discussed above, directors and officers of a corporation stand in a fiduciary relationship to the corporation and its stockholders. These duties include exercising the utmost good faith and loyalty in discharge of the corporate office. . . .

The chancellor found that Morris won in the scramble between Fought and Morris for Peyton's stock. However, at the inception of the corporation the four stockholders entered into [an] Agreement to prevent such a scramble. Section 2 of the agreement provided in pertinent part that:

In the event that any stockholder should desire to dispose of any of his stock in the Company during his lifetime, he shall first offer to sell all of this stock to the Company. . . . Any share not purchased by the Company within thirty days after receipt of such offer shall be offered to the other stockholders, each of whom shall have the right to purchase such portion of the stock offered for sale as the number of shares owned by him at such date shall bear to the total number of shares owned by all the other stockholders *provided, however, that if any stockholder does not purchase his full proportionate share of the stock, the unaccepted stock may be purchased by the other stockholders. . . . (Emphasis added.)*

This agreement insured that stock in the corporation always would be offered to the corporation, or in the alternative, each shareholder would have a right to purchase a pro-rata share.

[An] agreement . . . may restrain the transferability of stock. Shareholders in a close corporation have an interest in maintaining a balance of power that frequently is protected by such agreements. . . .

Generally, a director violates no duty by dealing in his own stock on his own account. This rule is not applicable, however, when there is an . . . stock redemption agreement, in order to maintain proportionate control of the corporation. . . .

In [this case] the stockholders had entered into an agreement which constituted corporate policy. This policy was adhered to when Strong sold his stock. However, the record reveals that Morris was unhappy with Fought. When Peyton decided to sell his stock, Morris saw a way to take control, as evidenced by his statement that he would undertake to relieve Peyton from liability on the bank note only if he could purchase all of Peyton's stock.

The court below failed to perceive Morris' fiduciary duty, as an officer and director of Vicksburg Mold and Die, Inc., to conduct his office with prudence and all good fidelity. Morris' intended exclusion of Fought from the purchase of Peyton's shares was a breach of the . . . Agreement and bylaws, and, therefore, a breach of his fiduciary duty as an officer, a director and a stockholder under the good faith standard we adopt today. . . . We hold, therefore, that Morris breached his fiduciary duty in purchasing all of Peyton's stock, contrary to the Stock Redemption Agreement. . .

We find: (1) Morris breached his fiduciary duty as director, an officer and stockholder by purchasing Peyton's total shares of stock in violation of the . . . agreement, (2) the Foughts are entitled to the fair market value of the stock in accordance with paragraph 6 of the stock redemption agreement.

QUESTIONS

1. What was Section 2 of the stock redemption agreement devised to achieve?
2. What did Morris expect to achieve by purchasing all of Peyton's stock?
3. Did Morris breach any fiduciary duty to Fought?

(b) INTEREST TRANSFERRED. The transfer of shares may be absolute; that is, it may divest all ownership and make the transferee the full owner. The transfer may be of only a partial interest in the stock, or the transfer may be for security, such as when stock is pledged to secure the repayment of a loan.

8. Mechanics of Transfer

When stock is represented by a certificate, the ownership of shares is transferred by the delivery of the certificate of stock, indorsed by its owner in blank or to a specified person. Ownership may also be transferred by the delivery of the certificate accompanied by a separate assignment or power of attorney executed by the owner.[6]

A delivery from the owner of the shares directly to the transferee is not required. It can be made to an intermediary.[7] When there is no delivery of the share certificate to anyone, however, there is no transfer of ownership of the shares.

A physical transfer of the certificate without a necessary indorsement is effective as between the parties. Thus, a gift of shares is binding even though no indorsement has been made. An indorsement is required to make the transferee a bona fide purchaser.

9. Effect of Transfer

The transfer of existing shares of stock may raise questions as between the parties to the transfer and between them and the corporation.

(a) VALIDITY OF TRANSFER. Since a transfer of shares is a transfer of ownership, the transfer must satisfy the requirements governing any other transfer of property or agreement to transfer property. As between the parties, a transfer may be set aside for any ground that would warrant similar relief under property law. If the transfer has been obtained by duress, the transferor may obtain a rescission of the transfer.

(b) NEGOTIABILITY. Under the common law, the transferee of shares of stock had no greater right than the transferor because the certificate and the shares represented by the certificate were nonnegotiable. By statute, the common law rule has been changed by imparting negotiability to the certificated. Just as various defenses cannot be asserted against the holder in due course of a commercial paper, it is provided that similar defenses cannot be raised against the person acquiring the certificate in good faith and for value. As against such a person, the defenses cannot be raised that the transferor did not own the shares or did not have authority to deliver the certificate,

[6] UCC § 8-309. The second alternative of a delivery of an unindorsed certificate is designed to keep the certificate "clean"—for example, when the transfer is for a temporary or special purpose, as in the case of a pledge of the certificate as security for a loan.

[7] Broadcourt Capital Corp. v Summa Medical Corp (CA10 Utah) F2d 1183 (1992).

or that the transfer was made in violation of a restriction on transfer not known to the person and not noted conspicuously on the certificate.

Statements sent by the issuer identifying the ownership of uncertificated securities are neither certificated securities nor negotiable instruments. Although certificated securities have the quality of negotiability, they are not commercial paper within Article 3 of the UCC.

(c) SECURED TRANSACTION. Corporate stock is frequently delivered to a creditor as security for a debt owed by the shareholder. Thus, a debtor borrowing money from a bank may deliver shares of stock to the bank as collateral security for the repayment of the loan. A broker's customer purchasing stock on margin may leave the stock in the possession of the broker as security for the payment of any balance due. The delivery of the security to the creditor is a pledge. This gives rise to a perfected security interest without any filing by the creditor. In itself, the pledge does not make the pledgee of the corporate stock the owner of the stock.

(d) EFFECT OF TRANSFER ON CORPORATION. The corporation is entitled to treat as the owner of shares the person whose name is on the corporation's books as the owner. Therefore, until there is a transfer on its books, the corporation may still treat a transferor of shares as the owner. The corporation may properly refuse to recognize a transferee when the corporation is given notice or has knowledge that the transfer is void or in breach of trust. In such a case, the corporation properly refuses to register a transfer until the rights of the parties have been determined. The corporation may also refuse to register the transfer of shares when the outstanding certificate is not surrendered to it, in the absence of satisfactory proof that it has been lost, destroyed, or stolen.

10. Lost, Destroyed, and Stolen Share Certificates

The owner of a lost, destroyed, or stolen share certificate is entitled to a replacement if the owner files a sufficient indemnity bond and requests the new certificate within a reasonable time before the issuer has notice that the original certificate has been acquired by a bona fide purchaser. If, after the new security is issued, a bona fide purchaser appears with the original certificate, the corporation must register a transfer of the security to that person and accept that person as the owner of the shares.

C. RIGHTS OF SHAREHOLDERS

The rights of shareholders stem from their status as owners.

11. Ownership Rights

The control of the shareholders over the corporation is indirect. Periodically (ordinarily, once a year) the shareholders elect directors and by this means control the corporation. At other times, however, the shareholders have no right or power to control the corporate activity so long as it is conducted within lawful channels.

(a) CERTIFICATES OF STOCK. A shareholder has the right to have a properly executed certificate as evidence of ownership of shares. An exception is made when the corporation is authorized to issue uncertificated securities.

(b) TRANSFER OF SHARES. Unless limited by a valid restriction,[8] a shareholder has the right to transfer the shares. The shareholder may sell the shares at any price or transfer them as a gift. The fact that the seller sells at a price higher than the market price is not unlawful, even though seller is a director or an officer.

---

[8]   See Section 7(a) of this chapter. Draper v Hay (Fla App) 555 So 2d 1306 (1990).

In the *Shoaf* case the court considered whether a shareholder who controlled a majority of the corporation's shares had a duty to refrain from making a profit by selling his controlling stock above the market price.

SHOAF v WARLICK
(SC App) 380 SE2d 865 (1989)

Paul Warlick, Jr. was the president and chief executive officer and a stockholder of Coca-Cola Bottling Co. of Anderson S.C. (Coke-Anderson). He controlled 273.5 shares of stock of the total of 480 shares of stock outstanding, including the stock of his mother, uncle, and aunt. Warlick agreed to sell this controlling interest in Coke-Anderson to Coke-Ashville for $4 million, which included a premium (difference between market and sale price) to be paid him for his controlling interest. Wayne Shoaf, a minority shareholder, brought suit against Warlick, contending that Warlick had violated his fiduciary duty to the corporation and had received an unlawful premium for the sale of the majority interest in Coke-Anderson. From a judgment for Warlick, Shoaf appealed.

SHAW, J. . . . The issues we are asked to consider are whether Mr. Warlick had a fidiciary duty owed to the other stockholders and whether he breached this duty, and, whether Mr. Warlick has a basis to claim appellants are equitably estopped from attacking his premium received for his stock.

South Carolina has long followed the general rule that corporate stock is personal property which the owner may "dispose of . . . as he sees fit." . . . Concomitantly, when selling stock, stockholders must "necessarily act for themselves, and not as trustees for other stockholders." . . . This general rule applies as well to majority shareholders:

A dominant or majority shareholder is generally under no duty to the minority stockholders to refrain from receiving a premium upon the sale of his controlling stock.

The law of the marketplace dictates that a shareholder who has a controlling interest in a corporation will likely be able to receive a higher price per share than a minority shareholder. *As a general rule, nothing in the law of the courthouse prevents a majority shareholder from retaining this "control premium." . . . This is so even if, as is so frequently the case, the controlling shareholder is an officer or director of the corporation. . . . A shareholder, irrespective of whether he is also a director, officer, or both, may sell his shares, just as he may sell other kinds of personal property, for whatever price he can obtain, even if his shares constitute a controlling block and the price per share is enhanced by that fact.* Further, the courts generally hold that neither the selling shareholder nor his purchaser is under an obligation to see that other shareholders are provided opportunities to sell their shares on the same favorable terms as the controlling shareholder or even to inform minority shareholders of the price and other terms of the sale of the controlling interest."
Martin v Martin, 529 So 2d 1174 (Fla 3d Dist Ct App 1988)

[Judgment affirmed]

12. Right to Vote

The right to vote means the right to vote at shareholders' meetings for the election of directors and on other special matters that the shareholders must vote on. For example, a proposal to change the capital structure of the corporation or a proposal to sell all or substantially all the assets of the corporation must be approved by the shareholders.

(a) WHO MAY VOTE. Ordinarily, only **shareholders of record**—those common shareholders in whose name the stock appears on the books of the corporation—are entitled to vote. The board of directors may fix a date for closing the corporate books for this purpose.[9]

(b) NUMBER OF VOTES. Unless there is a provision to the contrary, for each share owned each shareholder is entitled to one vote on each matter to be voted. This procedure is called **straight voting**, and it is the normal method for shareholder voting on corporate matters. However, in the case of voting to elect directors only, cumulative voting is mandatory in nearly half of the states. This requirement is imposed either by state constitution or by statute. Cumulative voting is permitted by law in other states when provided for in the articles of incorporation or bylaws.

Cumulative voting is a form of voting that is designed to give proportional representation on the board of directors to minority shareholders. Under a cumulative voting plan, each shareholder has as many votes as the number of shares owned multiplied by the number of directors to be elected. A shareholder may cast all of these votes for one candidate or may divide the votes between two or more candidates. This system enables minority shareholders to cast all of their votes for a candidate who will represent their interests on the board of directors. Under straight voting, minority shareholders would always be outvoted. For example, assume that minority shareholder Susan Jones owned 400 shares of stock and majority shareholder C. J. Katz controlled the remaining 600 shares. Also assume that five directors are to be elected to the board. If straight voting were used for the election of directors, C. J. with 600 shares would always outvote Susan's 400 shares. However, under cumulative voting, Susan would be allowed 2,000 votes (400 shares times five directors) and C. J. would be allowed 3,000 votes (600 shares times five directors). The five candidates with the highest number of votes will be elected. If Susan casts 1,000 votes for each of two directors, and C. J. casts 1,000 votes for each of three directors, Susan, who owns 40 percent of the stock, is able to elect two-fifths of the board to represent her interests.

(c) VOTING BY PROXY. A shareholder has the right to authorize another to vote the shares owned by the shareholder. This procedure is known as **voting by proxy**. In the absence of restrictions to the contrary, any person, even someone who is not a shareholder, may act as a proxy. The authorization from the shareholder may be made by any

---

[9] RMBCA § 7.07.

writing.[10] The authorization is also commonly called a *proxy*.

(d) VOTING AGREEMENTS AND TRUSTS.

Shareholders, as a general rule, are allowed to enter into an agreement by which they concentrate their voting strength for the purpose of electing directors or voting on any other matter.

A **voting trust** is created when by agreement a group of shareholders, or all of the shareholders, transfer their shares in trust to one or more persons as trustees. The trustees are authorized to vote the stock during the life of the trust agreement.[11] In general, such agreements are upheld if their object is lawful. In some jurisdictions, such trusts cannot run beyond a stated number of years. There are some signs of a relaxation as to time. Several states have abandoned all time limitations, several have extended the time limitation, and many provide for an extension or renewal of the agreement.

13. Preemptive Offer of Shares

If the capital stock of a corporation is increased, shareholders ordinarily have the **preemptive right** to subscribe to the same percentage of the new shares that their old shares represented of the former total of capital stock. This right is given to enable shareholders to maintain their relative interests in the corporation.

The existence of a preemptive right may make it impossible to conclude a transaction in which the corporation is to transfer a block of stock as consideration. Moreover, practical difficulties arise as to how stock should be allocated among shareholders of different classes.

The RMBCA provides that shareholders do not have preemptive rights unless the articles of incorporation provide for them.

14. Inspection of Books

A shareholder has the right to inspect the books of the shareholder's corporation. In some states, there are no limitations on this right. In most states, the inspection must be made in good faith, for proper motives, and at a reasonable time and place.[12] In many states, a shareholder must own a certain percentage of the outstanding stock of a corporation (commonly 5 percent) or must own at least one share of stock for a minimum amount of time (commonly six months) in order to have the right to inspect the books.

The purpose of inspection must be reasonably related to the shareholder's interest as a shareholder. A shareholder is entitled to inspect the records to determine the financial condition of the corporation, the quality of its management, and any matters relating to rights or interests in the corporate business, such as the value of stock.[13]

A shareholder is entitled to inspect the books to obtain information needed for a lawsuit against the corporation or its directors or officers, to organize the other shareholders into an "opposition" party to remove the board of directors at the next election, or to buy the shares of other shareholders.

Inspection has frequently been refused when it was sought merely from idle curiosity or for "speculative purposes." Inspection has sometimes been denied on the ground that it was merely sought to obtain a mailing list of persons who would be solicited to buy products of another enterprise. Inspection has also been refused when the object of the shareholder was to advance political or social beliefs without regard to the welfare of the corporation. Cases that deny the right of inspection do so when it would be harmful to the corporation or is sought only for the purpose of annoying, harassing, or causing vexation,

---

[10] RMBCA § 7.07.

[11] Bettner Trust v Bettner (Ind App) 495 NE2d 194 (1986).

[12] RMBCA § 16.02(c).

[13] State v Continental Boiler Works, Inc. (Mo App) 807 SW2d 164 (1991).

C P A

or for the purpose of aiding competitors of the corporation.

Whether a stockholder who became part owner and employee of a competing business could inspect the books was the issue in the *Carter* case.

CARTER v WILSON CONSTRUCTION CO., INC.

(NC App) 348 SE2d 830 (1986)

William Carter, a former officer and employee of Wilson Construction Co. Inc., owned 317 shares of stock in the corporation. He left the Wilson corporation to become part owner and employee of C & L Contracting Co., which was a direct competitor of the Wilson corporation. Carter asked to inspect the Wilson corporate books in order to determine the value of his shares. The corporation refused, not wanting to divulge its business practices to a direct competitor. From a decision for Carter, which also assessed a $500 penalty against both the corporation's president and the corporation, the Wilson corporation and its president appealed.

JOHNSON, J. . . . Defendants contend . . . that the court erred in finding that plaintiff had a proper purpose for obtaining access to the corporate information he requested. Defendants further contend that plaintiff's stated purpose was "a mask for more illegitimate purposes that would damage [defendant corporation's] ability to compete." Defendants characterize plaintiff as a "disgruntled minority shareholder" who "left his position without notice," leaving [the Wilson corporation] "in pretty bad shape" in order to start his own competing business. . . .

[North Carolina statutes,] G. S. § 55-38 provides as follows:

(b) A qualified shareholder, upon written demand stating the purpose thereof, shall have the right, in person, or by attorney, accountant or other agent, at any reasonable time or times, for any proper purpose, to examine at the place where they are kept and make extracts from, the books and records of account, minutes and record of shareholders of a domestic corporation or those of a foreign corporation actually or customarily kept by it within this State. . . . A shareholder's rights under this subsection may be enforced by an action. . . . (Emphasis added.)

It is undisputed by the parties that plaintiff is a qualified shareholder. The issue is whether plaintiff's request to examine the corporate records was for "any proper purpose." Absent a statutory restriction, a shareholder has a common law right to inspect and examine the books and records of the corporation, given to him for the protection of his interests. G.S. § 55-38(b) does not give a qualified shareholder an absolute right of inspection and examination for a mere fishing expedition, or for a purpose not germane to the protection of his economic interest as a shareholder in the corporation. For a shareholder to have the right to actually visit a corporation's office and possibly disrupt its normal operation in order to inspect corporate books and records of account, our legislature has correctly decided that his motives must be "proper." Purposes which previously have been deemed proper are the shareholder's good faith desire to (1) determine the value of his stock; (2) investigate the conduct of the management; and (3) determine the financial condition of the corporation.

The burden of proof rests upon the defendants, if they wish to defeat the shareholder's demand, to allege and show by facts, if they can, that the shareholder is motivated by some improper purpose. . . .

Here, plaintiff stated a proper purpose in his complaint. Defendants must overcome the presumption of good faith in plaintiff's favor by showing that plaintiff's purpose is improper. The evidence adduced at trial by plaintiff tended to show: that plaintiff tried to sell his stock in defendant corporation to defendant corporation, who declined plaintiff's offer to sell; . . . and that the net worth of defendant corporation decreased from August 1983 to August 1984. This evidence supports plaintiff's allegation of a proper purpose.

The evidence adduced at trial by defendants showed that plaintiff is currently part owner and employee of a business, C & L Contracting. According to the testimony of defendant Wilson, "We are in direct competition on all work in the Piedmont, North Carolina, that is bridge work" and that to allow plaintiff access to the books and records of accounts of defendant corporation "would put us at a disadvantage."

This evidence is insufficient to override the presumption that plaintiff is acting in good faith. . . . The mere possibility that a shareholder may abuse his right to gain access to corporate information will not be held to justify a [refusal to allow the inspection requested]. . . .

[Judgment affirmed]

QUESTIONS

1. Is the state statute applicable in this case similar to the RMBCA provision authorizing inspection of corporate records?
2. Did the court agree with the Wilson corporation that its refusal was justified because Carter, now a direct competitor for bridge work in the state, would gain an unfair competitive advantage?
3. Who has the burden of proving that a shareholder's purpose in inspecting a corporation's books is "proper"?

(a) FORM OF BOOKS. There are generally no requirements regarding the form of corporate books and records. The RMBCA recognizes that corporate books and records may be stored in modern data storage systems. "A corporation shall maintain its records in written form or in any other form capable of conversion into written form within a reasonable time."[14]

(b) FINANCIAL STATEMENTS. The RMBCA requires a corporation to furnish annual financial statements. These statements include a balance sheet as of the end of the fiscal year, an income statement for that year, and a statement of changes in shareholders' equity for that year.[15] A number of state statutes contain similar provisions.

---

[14] RMBCA § 16.01(d).

[15] RMBCA § 16.20.

In the *Cousins* case the court was faced with the question of whether the president of a close corporation was subject to a statutory penalty for failing to provide requested financial statements.

COUSINS v BROWNFIELD
83 Ohio App 3d 782, 615 NE2d 1064 (1992)

Joseph Cousins was a shareholder of Marv VI Pipeline Co. On September 18, 1985 Cousins, made a written request to Lyman Brownfield, the president and sole director of Marv VI, for the financial statements of the company. Cousins made a subsequent written request for this information. The financial statements were not furnished to him until February 22, 1990. Cousins filed a lawsuit against Brownfield and contended that Brownfield should be assessed a statutory penalty for failing to provide the financial statements. Brownfield defended that no financial statement existed. The jury awarded $15,420 as the statutory damages for failure to provide the financial statements, and the trial court reduced this award to $2000. Both parties appealed.

WHITESIDE, J. . . . [This appeal involves Ohio Statutes] R.C. 1701.94, which provides . . .:

"(A) Every corporation which fails to:

" * **

"(4) Mail to any shareholder making written request there for, within the period provided for in division (C) of section 1701.38 of the Revised Code, a copy of the financial statement referred to in that section;

" * **

*"(6) * * * shall be subject to a forfeiture of one hundred dollars and * * * to a further forfeiture of ten dollars for every day that such failure continues * * *.*

*"(B) If any officer charged with one of the duties specified in division (A) of this section fails to perform such duty after written request by any shareholder, he shall be subject to a forfeiture of one hundred dollars, and to the further forfeiture of ten dollars for every day that such default continues * * *."*

There is no question but that plaintiff made a request for some type of financial statement at various times, but did not receive any from defendant until after the commencement of this action when the financial information was furnished on February 22, 1990, plaintiff contending that the request should date back to September 18, 1985.

. . . R.C. 1701.38 requires that every corporation prepare a financial statement and lay it before the shareholders at the annual meeting or a meeting held in lieu thereof and shall make a coy available to any shareholder upon written request made within sixty days after notice of the meeting . . .

Defendant . . . contends that there were no financial statements in existence which could be the subject of a request pursuant to R.C. 1701.38. However, defendant's exhibits G, H and I constitute balance sheets and statements of operations for fiscal years ending June 30, 1984 and June 30, 1985, even though they are unaudited. Defendant contends that since the accuracy of the statements could not be verified because of the state of the records, these statements do not constitute financial statements within the contemplation of R.C. 1701.38. First, the statements indicate they are "unaudited" and defendant could have, in submitting them to plaintiff, advised him that the statements were the best available even though their accuracy could not be verified. In other words, compliance with the statutory requirement was not prevented nor excused because of the questionable nature of the financial statements . .

. . . A financial statement was in existence and defendant should have made a copy available to plaintiff upon his request even if a disclaimer as to the accuracy of the statement were necessary. . . .

The jury awarded $15,420 as the statutory damages for failure of defendant to provide financial statements to plaintiff. The trial court reduced this award to $2,000. Plaintiff contends that this was prejudicial error. Although R.C. 1701.94(B) provides for the penalty that the jury awarded, R.C. 1701.49(C) provides that:

"The court in which an action is brought to enforce any forfeiture under this section may reduce, remit, or suspend such forfeiture on such terms as it deems reasonable when it appears that the failure was excusable or that the imposition of the full forfeiture would be unreasonable or unjust."

The trial court found that the imposition of the full forfeiture would be unreasonable or unjust. It is within the discretion of the trial court to reduce the statutory award. . . . There was discretion in the trial court to reduce the penalty, and we find no abuse of discretion. . . .

[Judgment affirmed]

QUESTIONS

1. Was Brownfield excused from the statutory obligation to provide financial statements because the corporation's statements were unaudited?
2. On what basis was Brownfield held personally liable for the failure to provide the financial statements?
3. Does RMBCA §16:20 require audited financial statements and assess statutory penalties for failure to comply with written requests for financial statements?

15. Dividends

A shareholder has the right to receive a proportion of dividends as they are declared, subject to the relative rights of other shareholders to preferences, accumulation of dividends, and participation. There is no absolute right that dividends be declared, but dividends, when declared, must be paid in the manner indicated.

(a) FUNDS AVAILABLE FOR DECLARATION OF DIVIDENDS.

Statutes commonly provide that no dividends may be declared unless there is an "earned surplus" for their payment. Earned surplus, also known as "retained earnings," consists of the accumulated profits earned by the corporation since its formation less prior dividend distributions. Dividend payments are prohibited if the corporation is insolvent or would be rendered insolvent by the payment of the dividend.

As an exception to these rules, a wasting assets corporation may pay dividends out of current net profits without regard to the preservation of the corporate assets. **Wasting assets corporations** are those designed to exhaust or use up the assets of the corporation (for example, by extracting oil, coal, iron, and other ores), as compared with manufacturing plants, where the object is to preserve the plant as well as to continue to manufacture. A wasting assets corporation may also be formed for the purpose of buying and liquidating a stock of merchandise from a company that has received a discharge in bankruptcy court.

In some states, statutes provide that dividends may be declared from earned surplus or from current net profits, without regard to the existence of a deficit from former years.

(b) DISCRETION OF DIRECTORS.

Assuming that a fund is available for the declaration of dividends, it is then a matter primarily within the discretion of the board of directors whether a dividend shall be declared. The fact that there is an earned surplus that could be used for dividends does not mean that they must be declared. This rule is not affected by the nature of the shares. Thus, the fact that the shareholders hold cumulative preferred shares does not give them any right to demand a declaration of dividends or to interfere with an honest exercise of discretion by the directors.

Maintaining an adequate cash and working capital position is an important practical consideration in determining whether or not to declare a cash dividend. In general, a court will refuse to substitute its judgment for the judgment of the directors of the corporation and will interfere with their decision on dividend declaration only when it is shown that their conduct is harmful to the welfare of the corporation or its shareholders.[16]

(c) FORM OF DIVIDENDS.

Customarily, a dividend is paid in money. However, it may be paid in property, such as a product manufactured by the corporation, in shares of other corporations held by the corporation, or in shares of the corporation itself.

(d) EFFECT OF TRANSFER OF SHARES.

When a corporation declares a cash or property dividend, the usual practice is for the board of directors to declare a dividend as of a certain date—the *declaration date*; payable to shareholders of record on a stated future date—the *record date*; with a *payment date* following the record date, usually by some thirty days. The person who is the owner of the shares on the record date is entitled to the dividend, even if the shares are transferred prior to the payment date.

If the dividend consists of shares in the corporation declaring the dividend, ownership of the dividend is determined by the date of distribution. Whoever is the owner of the shares when the stock dividend is distributed is entitled to the stock dividend. The reason for this variation from the cash dividend rule is that the declaration of a stock dividend has the effect of diluting the existing corporate assets among a larger number of shares. The value of the holding represented by each share is diminished as the result. Unless the person who owns the stock on the distribution date receives a proportionate share of the stock

---

[16] Gabelli & Co. v Liggett Group, Inc. (Del Sup) 479 A2d 276 (1984).

dividend, the net effect will be to lessen that person's holding.

16. Capital Distribution

On the dissolution of the corporation, the shareholders are entitled to receive any balance of the corporate assets that remains after the payment of all creditors. Certain classes of stock may have a preference or priority in this distribution.

17. Shareholders' Actions

When the corporation has the right to sue its directors or officers or third persons for damages caused by them to the corporation or for breach of contract, one or more shareholders may bring such action if the corporation refuses to do so. This is a **derivative** (secondary) **action**, in that the shareholder enforces only the cause of action of the corporation, and any money recovery is paid into the corporate treasury.[17]

In a derivative action, when a corporation has failed to enforce a right, a shareholder bringing such a suit must show that a demand was made on the directors to enforce the right in question. The shareholder must show that the directors refused to enforce the right,[18] or that it would obviously have been useless to demand that they enforce the right. The Investment Company Act of 1940 (ICA) authorizes shareholders to sue investment advisors to recover excessive fees paid the advisors by the corporation. The shareholders may bring such action without any prior demand on the directors of the corporation.

Shareholders may also intervene or join in an action brought against the corporation when the corporation refuses to defend the action against it or is not doing so in good faith. Otherwise, the shareholders may take no part in an action by or against the corporation.

Lawsuits may be brought by minority shareholders against majority shareholders who are oppressive toward minority shareholders. Oppressive conduct may include payment of grossly excessive salaries and fringe benefits to the majority stockholders who are also officers of the corporation.[19] Shareholders may bring a derivative action to obtain a dissolution of the corporation by judicial decree.

D. LIABILITY OF SHAREHOLDERS

The shareholder is ordinarily protected from the liabilities of the corporation. Some exceptions are made by statute.

18. Limited Liability

The liability of a shareholder is generally limited. This means that the shareholder is not personally liable for the debts and liabilities of the corporation. The capital contributed by the shareholders may be exhausted by the claims of creditors, but there is no personal liability for any unpaid balance.[20]

19. Exceptions to Limited Liability

Liability may be imposed on a shareholder as though there were no corporation when the court ignores the corporate entity, either because of the particular circumstances of the case or because the corporation is so defectively organized that it is deemed not to exist.

(a) WAGE CLAIMS. Statutes sometimes provide that the shareholders shall have unlimited liability for the wage claims of corporate employees. This exception has been abandoned in some states in recent years or

---

[17] Brown v Tenny, 125 Ill App 3d 348, 532 NE2d 230 (1988).

[18] Greenfield v Hamilton Oil Corp (Colo App) 760 P2d 664 (1988).

[19] Maschmeier v Southside Press Ltd. (Iowa App) 435 NW2d 377 (1988).

[20] Salem Tent & Awning Co. v Schmidt, 79 Or App 475, 719 P2d 899 (1986).

has been confined to the major shareholders of corporations of which the stock is not sold publicly.

(b) UNPAID SUBSCRIPTIONS. Most states prohibit the issuance of par value shares for less than par or except for "money, labor done, or property actually received." Whenever shares issued by a corporation are not fully paid for, the original subscriber receiving the shares, or any transferee who does not give value or who knows that the shares were not fully paid, is liable for the unpaid balance if the corporation is insolvent and the money is required to pay its creditors.[21]

If the corporation has issued the shares as fully paid, or has given them as a bonus, or has agreed to release the subscriber for the unpaid balance, the corporation cannot recover that balance. The fact that the corporation is thus barred does not prevent the creditors of the corporation from bringing an action to compel payment of the balance. The same rules are applied when stock is issued as fully paid in return for property or services that were overvalued, so that the stock is not actually paid for in full. There is a conflict of authority, however, as to whether the shareholder is liable from the mere fact that the property or service given for the shares was in fact overvalued by the directors or whether it must also be shown that the directors had acted in bad faith in making the erroneous valuation. The trend of modern statutes is, in the absence of proof of fraud, to prohibit disputing the valuation placed by the corporation on services or property.

(c) UNAUTHORIZED DIVIDENDS. I f dividends are improperly paid out of capital, the shareholders are generally liable to creditors to the extent of such depletion of capital. In some states, the liability of the shareholder depends on whether the corporation was insolvent at the time and whether debts were existing at the time.

20. The Professional Corporation

The extent to which incorporation limits the liability of shareholders of a professional corporation depends on the interpretation of the statute under which the corporation was formed.

(a) ACT OF SHAREHOLDER IN CREATING LIABILITY. The statutes that authorize the formation of professional corporations usually require that share ownership be limited to duly licensed professionals. If a shareholder in a professional corporation, such as a corporation of physicians, negligently drives the professional corporation's automobile in going to attend a patient, or is personally obligated on a contract made for the corporation, or is guilty of malpractice, the physician-shareholder is liable without limit for the liability that has been created. This is the same rule of law that applies in the case of the ordinary business corporation.

Professional corporation statutes generally repeat the rule with respect to malpractice liability by stating that the liability of a shareholder for malpractice is not affected by the fact of incorporation.

(b) MALPRACTICE LIABILITY OF AN ASSOCIATE. The liability of a shareholder in a professional corporation for the malpractice of an associate varies from state to state, depending on the language of the professional corporation statute in effect and on the court decisions under the statute.[22]

If the statute provides for limited liability, as in a business corporation, then where doctors

---

[21] Frasier v Trans-western Land Corp. 210 Neb 681, 316 NW2d 612 (1982). But see Brunfield v Horn (Ala) 547 So 2d 415 (1989).

[22] ABA Model Professional Corporation Amendments (1984) § 34 offers three alternative positions regarding the liability of shareholders: (1) limited liability, as in a business corporation; (2) vicarious personal liability, as in a partnership; and (3) personal liability limited in amount conditioned on financial responsibility in the form of insurance or a surety bond.

A, *B*, and *C* are a professional corporation, *B* will not be liable for the malpractice of *C*. If the statute provides for vicarious personal liability, as in a partnership, and doctors *A*, *B*, and *C* are a professional corporation, each will have unlimited liability for any malpractice liability incurred by the other. Often the statutory reference to malpractice liability is not very clear and the courts are called on to resolve the question of the liability of a shareholder-professional for the malpractice of an associate.

E. BONDS

Bonds are instruments issued by a corporation to persons lending money to it.

21. Characteristics of Bonds

A **bond** is an instrument promising to repay a loan of money to a corporation. Typically, the loan is for a relatively long period of time, generally five years or longer. A bond obligates the corporation to pay the bondholder the amount of the loan, called the **principal**, at a stated time, called the **maturity date**; and to pay a fixed amount of interest at regular intervals, commonly every six months. The relationship between the bondholder and the issuing corporation is that of creditor and debtor. And, unlike dividends, which are discretionary, bond interest must be paid.

A bond may be secured by a mortgage or lien on corporate property. A **debenture** is an unsecured bond of the corporation, with no specific corporate assets pledged as security for payment.

Bonds are negotiable securities.[23] Bonds held by owners whose names and addresses are registered on the books of the corporation are called **registered bonds**.

22. Terms and Control

The contractual terms of a particular bond issue are set forth in an agreement called a **bond indenture** or deed. An **indenture trustee**, usually a commercial banking institution, represents the interests of the bondholders in making sure that the terms and covenants of the bond issue are met by the corporation.[24] For example, the terms of the bond indenture may require a **sinking fund**, by which the borrowing corporation is required to set aside a fixed amount of money each year toward the ultimate payment of the bonds. The indenture trustee makes certain that such terms are complied with in accordance with its responsibilities set forth in the bond indenture.

Bondholders do not vote for directors or have the right to vote on matters on which shareholders vote. However, where the debt is risky, it is highly likely that there will be significant restraints on the corporations freedom of action, imposed by the terms of the indenture.

SUMMARY

The ownership of a corporation is evidenced by a holders shares of stock that have been issued by the corporation. Common stock is ordinary stock that has no preferences but entitles the holder to (1) participate in the control of the corporation by exercising one vote per share of record, (2) share in the profits in the form of dividends, and (3) participate, on dissolution, in the distribution of net assets, after the satisfaction of all creditors (including bondholders). Other classes of stock exist, such as preferred stock, which has priority over common stock with regard to distribution of dividends and/or assets on liquidation. Shares may be acquired by subscription of an original issue or by transfer of existing shares.

---

[23] UCC § 8-105.
[24] Lorenc v CSX Corp. (DC Pa) CCH Sec L Rpts 95298 (1990).

Shareholders control the corporation, but this control is indirect. Through their voting rights they elect directors, and by this means they can control the corporation. Preemptive rights, if they exist, allow shareholders to maintain their voting percentage when the corporation issues additional shares of stock. Shareholders have the right to inspect the books of the corporation, unless it would be harmful to the corporation. Shareholders also have the right to receive dividends when declared at the discretion of the directors. Share-holders may bring a derivative action on behalf of the corporation for damages to the corporation. Shareholders are ordinarily protected from liability for the acts of the corporation.

Bonds are debt securities, and a bondholder is a creditor rather than an owner of the corporation. Bondholders' interests are represented by an indenture trustee, who is responsible for ensuring that the corporation complies with the terms of the bond indenture.

LAW IN PRACTICE

1. As an employer, have employees who have access to confidential financial information sign an "integrity policy statement" prohibiting the use or disclosure of material inside information for personal gain.
2. In organizing your corporation make certain that you protect your standing relative to other shareholders by adopting a stock transfer restriction requiring that a shareholder wishing to sell stock must offer proportionate shares to each shareholder.
3. Avoid the pitfall of wrongfully refusing a shareholder the right to inspect the books.
4. Comply with state corporation laws which require that shareholders be furnished annual financial statements.
5. Before bringing a shareholder action on behalf of the corporation, make a demand on the directors to enforce the rights in question.

QUESTIONS AND CASE PROBLEMS

1. What social forces are affected by the rule requiring that a transfer restriction be known to the transferee or conspicuously noted on the share certificate?
2. What is the distinction between capital and capital stock?
3. Barbara, Joel, and Edna each own less than 5 percent of the stock of the Enrico Storm Door Corporation. Individually, their holdings are too small to be significant in any stockholder's election. Barbara suggests that they and other small shareholders combine their votes by transferring their shares to trustees who will vote the aggregate of their shares as a block. Joel agrees with the idea but says he is afraid that this is an illegal conspiracy. Is he correct?
4. Compare the effect of an oral contract (a) by Stone to sell 100 shares of Liberty Corporation stock to Coffey and (b) by stockbroker Mendez to sell Stones stock in the Liberty Corporation when the market price reaches $10 a share.
5. The stock of the West End Development Company was subject to a transfer restriction. This restriction required that any shareholder selling shares must first offer every other shareholder the right to purchase a proportion of the shares being sold. The proportion was to be the same as the percentage of the outstanding shares that the other shareholders already owned. This restriction was stated in the articles of incorporation but was not stated on the stock certificate of the corporation. The Taylors owned stock in the company. They sold their stock to Vroom, an officer of the corporation, without first offering any stock to the other shareholders, as required by the restriction. The other shareholders brought an action against Vroom to recover from him the percentages of the shares they would have been entitled to if the Taylors had followed the transfer restriction. Decide. [*Irwin v West End Development Co. (CA10 Colo) 481 F2d 34*]
6. Siebrecht organized a corporation called the Siebrecht Realty Co. and then transferred his building to the corporation in exchange for its stock. The corporation rented different parts of the building to different tenants. Elenkrieg, an employee of one of the tenants, fell and was injured

because of the defective condition of a stairway. She sued Siebrecht individually on the ground that the corporation had been formed by him for the purpose of securing limited liability. Decide. [Elenkrieg v Siebrecht, 238 NY 254, 144 NE 519]

7. Dixon requests an inspection of the books of G. S. & M. Company. The objection was raised that he did not own 5 percent or more of the corporate stock. If this is true, is Dixon barred from inspecting the books?

8. Ken and Charlotte Maschmeier were the majority shareholders of the Southside Press. Ken and Charlotte each owned 1,300 shares. Marty and Larry Maschmeier each owned 1,200 shares of the corporation. Marty and Larry had a falling out with Ken and Charlotte and were terminated as employees of the business in the summer of 1985. Ken and Charlotte started a new corporation, which employed most of the employees of the old corporation and which took most of the former customers of the old corporation. Gross receipts of the Southside Press went from $613,258 in 1985 to $18,172 in 1987. The $18,172 figure was from the lease of equipment. Ken and Charlotte continued to draw from Southside annual salaries of $20,000, which were in excess of the gross receipts of the business. Marty and Larry brought suit against Ken and Charlotte alleging "oppressive" conduct. Ken and Charlotte stated that they paid Marty and Larry excellent salaries when they were employed by the corporation. Ken and Charlotte contended they had a right to start a new corporation as they saw fit. Decide. [Maschmeier v Southside Press Inc. (Iowa App) 435 NW2d 377]

9. Harper owned corporate stock. He told O'Brien that he was going to give the stock to O'Brien and handed the stock certificate to O'Brien. O'Brien requested that Harper indorse the certificate. Harper refused to do so. Who was the owner of the stock? [Smith v Augustine, 82 Misc 2d 326, 368 NYS2d 675]

10. Shares of stock represent debts owed by the corporation to the shareholders. Is this statement correct?

11. Ibanez owned shares of stock in the Farmers Underwriters. He left the shares of stock lying on top of his desk in his office. Many persons continually passed through the office, and one day Ibanez realized that someone had taken the shares of stock from the top of his desk. Ibanez applied to Farmers Underwriters for the issuance of a duplicate stock certificate. The corporation refused to issue a duplicate, on the ground that it was Ibanez's own fault that the original certificate had been sto-

len. Ibanez claimed that he was entitled to a new certificate even though he had been at fault. Was he correct? [Ibanez v Farmers Underwriters Assn. 14 Cal 3d 390, 121 Cal Rptr 256, 534 P2d 1336]

12. On March 3, 1995, pursuant to a public offering, the First All State Trucking Corporation (FAST) issued securities to investors in denominations of $1,000. The interest rate was 11 percent per year, payable semiannually, and the maturity date was March 3, 2005. The rights and obligations of the issuer, FAST, and the holders of the securities were set forth in an indenture agreement. Since the securities were not secured by a mortgage or lien on corporate property, Alec believes that they are shares of preferred stock. Is Alec correct? Fully explain the type of security involved, and discuss the extent of the holders' voting rights.

13. Linhart owned shares of stock in the First National Bank. She borrowed money from the bank and pledged the stock as security. She later decided to transfer 70 head of cattle and the shares of stock to her son. She could not deliver the share certificate to him because it was held by the bank. She therefore executed a bill of sale reciting the transfer of the cattle and the stock to the son. She gave him the bill of sale, and he had the bill recorded. After her death, the son brought an action to determine the ownership of the stock. Was the son the owner of the shares?

14. Birt was a patient in the hospital. The doctor who treated him was a shareholder of a professional corporation organized under the Indiana Medical Professional Corporation Act. Birt claimed that the doctor who treated him was guilty of malpractice and sued the doctor. He also sued the professional corporation and all of the officers, directors, and shareholders of the professional corporation. These other defendants asserted that they were not liable because the corporate entity shielded them. The plaintiff claimed that the corporation was not a shield, because in fact all the persons were rendering medical services and should therefore be held liable as in a partnership. The statute did not expressly regulate the matter beyond declaring that it did not change the law between a person supplying medical services and the patient. Decide. [Birt v St. Mary Mercy Hospital, 175 Ind App 32, 370 NE2d 379]

15. Ronald Naquin, an employee of Air Engineered Systems & Services, Inc., owned one-third of its outstanding shares. After six years he was fired, and an offer was made to buy out his interest in Air Engineered at a price that Naquin

thought inadequate. He then formed a competing business and made a written request to examine the corporate records of Air Engineered. This request was denied. Naquin filed suit to require Air Engineered to allow him to examine the books. Air Engineered raised the defense that he was a competitor seeking to gain unfair competitive advantage. Decide. [*Naquin v Air Engineered Systems & Services, Inc. (La App) 463 So 2d 992*]

C H A P T E R   4 9

SECURITIES REGULATION

LEARNING OBJECTIVES

After studying this chapter, you will be able to:
1. *Determine whether state or federal securities laws apply to a transaction.*
2. *Define a security.*
3. *Compare and distinguish between the Securities Act of 1933 and the Securities Exchange Act of 1934.*
4. *Discuss the factors that subject an individual to liability for insider trading.*
5. *List the reasons for the regulation of cash tender offers.*
6. *Identify the sections of the federal securities laws under which accountants may be subject to liability.*

Is there anything that protects you when you buy corporate securities?

regulations, which can be adopted by states with different regulatory philosophies.

A. STATE REGULATION

To protect the public from the sale of fraudulent securities, many states have adopted statutes regulating the intrastate sale of securities.

1. State Blue Sky Laws

State laws regulating securities are called **blue sky laws**. The term *blue sky* is derived from the purpose of such laws, which is to prevent the sale of speculative schemes that have no more value than the blue sky. The state statutes vary in detail. They commonly contain (1) an antifraud provision prohibiting fraudulent practices and imposing criminal penalties for violations;[1] (2) broker-dealer licensing provisions regulating the persons engaged in the securities business;[2] and (3) provisions for the registration of securities, including disclosure requirements, with a designated governmental official.

State blue sky laws are subject to the very important limitation that they can apply only to intrastate transactions. They cannot apply to sales made in interstate commerce.

2. Uniform Securities Act

A Uniform Securities Act,[3] covering the foregoing three categories of regulations, exists to provide guidance to states in updating their securities laws. This Act contains alternative

B. FEDERAL REGULATION

The stock market crash of 1929 and the Great Depression that followed led to the enactment of federal legislation to regulate the securities industry.

3. Federal Laws Regulating the Securities Industry

Six federal securities regulation laws were passed between 1933 and 1940. The two principal laws that provide the basic framework for the federal regulation of the sale of securities in interstate commerce are the Securities Act of 1933 and the Securities Exchange Act of 1934. The 1933 act deals with the original distribution of securities by the issuing corporations. The 1934 act is concerned with the secondary distribution of securities in the national securities markets and in the over-the-counter markets. That is, the 1933 act regulates the issuance of securities by a corporation to the first owner. The 1934 act regulates the sale of securities from one owner to another. Four other federal laws deal with specific aspects of the securities industry.[4] These aspects include holding companies in utility businesses, trustees for debt securities, mutual funds, and investment advisors.

The Securities Enforcement Remedies and Penny Stock Reform Act of 1990[5] (Remedies Act) expands the enforcement remedies of the

---

[1] Bridwell v Texas (Tex App) 804 SW2d 900 (1991).

[2] Probst v State (Okla) 807 P2d 279 (1991).

[3] 7B Uniform Laws Annotated 515.

[4] The Public Utility Holding Company Act of 1935 (15 USC §§ 79-792-6) provides comprehensive regulation of holding companies and their subsidiaries in the interstate gas and electric utilities businesses. The Trust Indenture Act of 1939 (15 USC §§ 77aaa to 77bbb) was enacted to protect the interests of the holders of bonds and other debt securities offered to the public in interstate commerce, by requiring the appointment of independent institutional trustees. The Investment Company Act of 1940 (15 USC §§ 80a-1 to 80a-52) provides for the registration and comprehensive regulation of mutual funds and all other investment companies. The Investment Advisors Act of 1940 (15 USC §§ 80b-1 to 80b-21) requires registration with the SEC of all persons engaged in the business of providing investment advice in interstate commerce. In 1970 the Securities Investors Protection Act was enacted to protect investors from the business failures of brokers and dealers.

[5] PL 101-429, 104 Stat 931, 15 USC § 77g.

SEC to reduce fraudulent financial reporting and financial fraud. Under the 1990 Remedies Act, the SEC may start administrative proceedings against any person or entity, whether regulated by the SEC or not. In these proceedings, the SEC compels the person or entity to cease and desist from committing or causing a violation of federal securities law. Sometimes the SEC determines the delay of a notice and hearing would be contrary to the public interest because of the likelihood of dissipation of assets or significant harm to investors. In such a case, the SEC may issue a temporary cease and desist order prior to notice and a hearing. The SEC may also order an accounting and disgorgement of ill-gotten gains. And, it may seek in federal court an injunction and a money penalty. This penalty can be up to the amount of the gross financial gain or up to $100,000 for an individual and $500,000 for an entity. The Remedies Act also authorizes courts to bar individuals who have engaged in fraudulent activities from serving as officers and directors of public corporations.

The Securities Acts Amendments of 1990[6] authorize sanctions against SEC-regulated persons for violation of foreign laws. The Amendments facilitate the ability of the SEC and foreign regulators to exchange information and cooperate in international securities law enforcement.

The Market Reform Act of 1990[7] was enacted to provide the SEC with powers to deal with market volatility. Under the law, the SEC has the power to suspend all trading when markets are excessively volatile. Also, the SEC may require "large traders" to identify themselves and provide information concerning their trading.

4. Definition of *Security*

In order for the Securities Acts to apply, the transaction must involve a "security" within the meaning of the acts.[8] Congress adopted a definition of *security* sufficiently broad to encompass virtually any instrument that might be sold as an investment.

The definition of *security* includes not only investment instruments such as stocks and bonds but also "investment contracts." The definition of an *investment contract* developed by the Supreme Court is sufficiently broad to allow the Securities Acts to apply to a wide range of investment transactions or schemes, including the sale of bottled whiskey, the sale of cattle breeding programs, and limited partnerships for oil and gas exploration. Under the Supreme Court's definition, an investment contract exists if the following elements are present: (1) an investment of money, (2) a common enterprise, (3) an expectation of future profits, (4) from the efforts of others.[9] Thus, the sale of citrus groves to investors, coupled with the execution of service contracts to plant, harvest, sell the fruit, and distribute the profits of the venture to the investors, is an investment contract.

In the *Reves* case the Supreme Court had to decide whether a note issued by an agricultural cooperative was a "security" within the meaning of the 1934 Act.

5. Securities Act of 1933

The 1933 act deals with the original issue of securities. It prohibits the offer or sale of securities to the public in interstate commerce before a registration statement is filed with the SEC. A **registration statement** is a document disclosing specific financial information regarding

---

[6] PL 101-550, 104 Stat 2713, 15 USC § 78a.

[7] PL 101-432, 104 Stat 963, 15 USC § 78a.

[8] The Supreme Court has consistently held that the definition of a security set forth in § 3(a)(10) of the 1934 act is identical to the definition set forth in § 2(1) of the 1933 act. The definition of "security" under these acts is not to be confused with the narrower definition made by Article 8 of the Uniform Commercial Code.

[9] SEC v W. J. Howey Co. 328 US 293 (1946), as restated by United Housing Foundation Inc. v Forman, 421 US 837 (1975).

REVES v ERNST & YOUNG

494 US ___, 108 L Ed 2d 47 (1990)

In order to raise money to support its general business operations, the Farmer's Cooperative of Arkansas and Oklahoma (Co-Op) sold uncollateralized and uninsured promissory notes, payable on demand by the holder. Offered to both Co-Op members and nonmembers and marketed as an "Investment Program," the notes paid a variable interest rate higher than that of local financial institutions. After the Co-Op filed for bankruptcy, Bob Reves and the other holders of the notes filed suit in the U.S. district court against the Co-Op's auditor, Arthur Young Co., the predecessor firm to Ernst & Young. They alleged that it had violated the antifraud provisions of the Securities Exchange Act of 1934—which regulates certain specified instruments, including "any note[s]"—by intentionally failing to follow generally accepted accounting principles that would have made the Co-Op's insolvency apparent to potential note purchasers. Ernst & Young defended that the notes were not "securities" under the 1934 Act. Judgment was entered for the noteholders, but the Court of Appeals reversed. The noteholders appealed to the U.S. Supreme Court.

MARSHALL, J. . . . This case requires us to decide whether the note issued by the Co-Op is a "security" within the meaning of the 1934 Act. Section 3(a)(10) of that Act is our starting point:

"The term "security" means any note, stock, treasury stock, bond, debenture, certificate of interest or participation in any profit-sharing agreement or in any oil, gas, or other mineral royalty or lease, any collateral-trust certificate, preorganization certificate or subscription, transferable share, investment contract, voting-trust certificate, certificate of deposit . . . or in general, any instrument commonly known as a "security"; or any certificate of interest or participation in, temporary or interim certificate for, receipt for, or warrant or right to subscribe to or purchase, any of the foregoing; but shall not include currency or any note, draft, bill of exchange, or banker's acceptance which has a maturity at the time of issuance of not exceeding nine months, exclusive of days of grace, or any renewal thereof the maturity of which is likewise limited. 48 Stat 884, as amended, 15 U.S.C. § 78c(a)(10).

. . . Congress' purpose in enacting the securities laws was to regulate *investments*, in whatever form they are made and by whatever name they are called. . . . Some instruments are obviously within the class Congress intended to regulate because they are by their nature investments. In *Landreth Timber Co. v Landreth*, 471 US 681, 105 S Ct 2297, 85 L Ed 2d 692 (1985), we held that an instrument bearing the name "stock" that, among other things, is negotiable, offers the possibility of capital appreciation, and carries the right to dividends contingent on the profits of a business enterprise is plainly within the class of instruments Congress intended the securities laws to cover. *Landreth Timber* does not signify a lack of concern with economic reality; rather, it signals a recognition that stock is, as a practical matter, always an investment if it has the economic characteristics traditionally associated with stock. Even if sparse exceptions to this generalization can be found, the public perception of common stock as the paradigm of a security suggests that stock, in whatever context it is sold, should be treated as within the ambit of the Acts. . . .

We made clear in *Landreth Timber* that stock was a special case, explicitly limiting our holding to that sort of instrument. . . . Although we refused finally to rule out a similar *per se* rule for notes, we intimated that such a rule would be unjustified. Unlike "stock," we said, "'note' may now be viewed as a relatively broad term that encompasses instruments with widely varying characteristics, depending on whether issued in a consumer context, as commercial paper, or in some other investment context.". . .

The Second Circuit's "family resemblance" approach begins with a presumption that *any* note with a term of more than nine months is a "security." See, *e.g., Exchange Nat'l Bank of Chicago v Touche Ross & Co.*, 544 F2d 1126, 1137 (CA2 1976). Recognizing that not all notes are securities, however, the Second Circuit has also devised a list of notes that it has decided are obviously not securities. Accordingly, the "family resemblance" test permits an issuer to rebut the presumption that a note is a security if it can show that the note in question "bear[s] a strong family resemblance" to an item on the judicially crafted list of exceptions or convinces the court to add a new instrument to the list. . . .

In contrast, the Eighth and District of Columbia Circuits apply the test we created in *SEC v W.J. Howey Co.*, 328 US 293, 66 S Ct 1100, 90 L Ed 1244 (1946), to determine whether an instrument is an "investment contract" to the determination whether an instrument is a "note." Under this test, a note is a security only if it evidences "(1) an investment; (2) in a common enterprise; (3) with a reasonable expectation of profits; (4) to be derived from the entrepreneurial or managerial efforts of others.". . .

The . . . two contenders—the "family resemblance" and "investment versus commercial" tests—are really two ways of formulating the same general approach. Because we think the "family resemblance" test provides a more promising framework for analysis, however, we adopt it. The test begins with the language of the statute; because the Securities Acts define "security" to include "any note," we begin with a presumption that every note is a security. We nonetheless recognize that this presumption cannot be irrebuttable. . . . Congress was concerned with regulating the investment market, not with creating a general federal cause of action for fraud. In an attempt to give more content to that dividing line, the Second Circuit has identified a list of instruments commonly denominated "notes" that nonetheless fall without the "security" category. See *Exchange Nat. Bank, supra,* at 1138 (types of notes that are not "securities" include "the note delivered in consumer financing, the note secured by a mortgage on a home, the short-term note secured by a lien on a small business or some of its assets, the note evidencing a 'character' loan to a bank customer, short-term notes secured by an assignment of accounts receivable, or a note which simply formalizes an open-account debt incurred in the ordinary course of business (particularly if, as in the case of the customer of a broker, it is collateralized)"); . . . (adding to list "notes evidencing loans by commercial banks for current operations"). . . .

We conclude, then, that in determining whether an instrument denominated a "note" is a "security," courts are to apply the version of the "family resemblance" test that we have articulated here: a note is presumed to be a "security," and that presumption may be rebutted only by a showing that the note bears a strong resemblance (in terms of the four factors we have identified) to one of the enumerated categories of instrument. If an instrument is not sufficiently similar to an item on the list, the decision whether another category should be added is to be made by examining the same factors.

Applying the family resemblance approach to this case, we have little difficulty in concluding that the notes at issue here are "securities." Ernst & Young admits that "a demand note does not closely resemble any of the Second Circuit's family resemblance examples." . . . Nor does an examination of the four factors we have identified as being relevant to our inquiry suggest that the demand notes here are not "securities" despite their lack of similarity to any of the enumerated categories. The Co-Op sold the notes in an effort to raise capital for its general business operations, and purchasers bought them in order to earn a profit in the form of interest. Indeed, one of the primary inducements offered purchasers was an interest rate constantly revised to keep it slightly above the rate paid by local banks and savings and loans. From both sides, then, the transaction is most naturally conceived as an investment in a business enterprise rather than as a purely commercial or consumer transaction.

As to the plan of distribution, the Co-Op offered the notes over an extended period to its 23,000 members, as well as to nonmembers, and more than 1,600 people held notes when the Co-Op filed for bankruptcy. To be sure, the notes were not traded on an exchange. They were, however, offered and sold to a broad segment of the public, and that is all we have held to be necessary to establish the requisite "common trading" in an instrument. . . .

The third factor—the public's reasonable perceptions—also supports a finding that the notes in this case are "securities." We have consistently identified the fundamental essence of a "security" to be its character as an "investment." . . . The advertisements for the notes here characterized them as "investments," and there were no countervailing factors that would have led a reasonable person to question this characterization. In these circumstances, it would be reasonable for a prospective purchaser to take the Co-Op at its word.

Finally, we find no risk-reducing factor to suggest that these instruments are not in fact securities. The notes are uncollateralized and uninsured. . . . The notes here would escape federal regulation entirely if the Acts were held not to apply. . . .

We therefore hold that the notes at issue here are within the term "note" in § 3(a)(10).

. . . . In light of Congress' broader purpose in the Acts of ensuring that investments of all descriptions be regulated to prevent fraud and abuse, we interpret the exception not to cover the demand notes at issue here. Although the result might be different if the design of the transaction suggested that both parties contemplated that demand would be made within the statutory period, that is not the case before us.

For the foregoing reasons, we conclude that the demand notes at issue here fall under the "note" category of instruments that are "securities" under the 1933 and 1934 Acts. . . .

[Judgment reversed and action remanded]

QUESTIONS

1. What was Congress' purpose in enacting the securities laws?
2. List the types of notes that are not "securities."
3. What factors did the Supreme Court consider in deciding whether a transaction involved a security?
4. Apply the factors identified in the answer to Question 3 to the facts of the Reves case.

the security, the issuer, and the underwriter. The seller must also provide a prospectus to each potential purchaser of the securities. The **prospectus** sets forth the key information contained in the registration statement. The object is to provide the interested investor with detailed information about the security and the enterprise. The SEC does not approve or disapprove the securities as being good or bad investments but only reviews the form and content of the registration statement and the prospectus to ensure full disclosure. The requirements of advance disclosure to the public through the filing of the registration statement with the SEC and the sending of a prospectus to each potential purchaser are commonly referred to as the **registration requirements** of the 1933 act.

(a) APPLICABILITY. The 1933 act applies to (1) stocks, (2) corporate bonds, and (3) any conceivable kind of corporate interest or instrument that has the characteristics of an investment security, including convertible securities and variable annuities. The act applies to all such instruments that have investment characteristics.

(b) THE REGISTRATION PROCESS. Section 5 of the 1933 act provides for the division of the registration process into three time periods: (1) the prefiling period; (2) the waiting period, from the date of filing with the SEC to the date the registration statement becomes effective (a minimum of 20 days, but commonly extended for additional 20-day periods after each amendment by the issuer in compliance with SEC requirements for additional information); and (3) the posteffective period. The time divisions allow the public an opportunity to study the information disclosed in the registration process before a sale can be made. Permissible, required, and prohibited activities during the time periods are set forth in Figure 49-1.

Figure 49-1 Registration Periods

	Prohibited or Required Activities	Permitted Activities
Prefiling Period	Issuer must not sell or offer for sale a security before registration statement is filed.	Issuer may plan with underwriters the distribution of the security.
Waiting Period	No final sale of a security permitted during this period.	Preliminary prospectus* containing information from the registration statement being reviewed by the SEC may be distributed to investors, who may make offers. Advertisements may be placed in financial publications, identifying particulars of the security, from whom a prospectus can be obtained, and by whom orders will be executed.**
Posteffective Period	Must provide a copy of final prospectus with every written offer, confirmation of sale, or delivery of security. Must update prospectus whenever important new developments occur, or after nine months.	Sales of the security may be completed.

* The preliminary prospectus is commonly called the "red herring" prospectus because of the red ink caption required by the SEC, informing the public that a registration statement has been filed but is not yet effective, and that no final sale can be made until after the effective date.

** These advertisements are sometimes called "tombstone ads" because they are commonly framed by a black ink border.

(c) REGULATION A OFFERINGS. Regulation A provides a simplified registration process for small issues of securities by small businesses. Although technically exempt from the 1933 act registration requirements, a Regulation A offering involves a "mini-registration" with the SEC. Under the SEC's Small Business Initiative which became effective in August of 1992, the SEC expanded Regulation A to facilitate the offerings of securities from the previous $1.5 million in a 12-month period to $5 million in a 12-month period.[10] Under the new procedures, disclosure requirements are simplified by the use of the small corporate offerings registration (SCOR) forms, with its question and answers "fill-in-the-blank" format. Also, the financial statements required in a Regulation A offering are less extensive than those required for a registered public offering.

Issuers may broadly solicit indications of interest from prospective investors before filing an *offering statement* with the SEC. This allows the issuer to "test the waters" and explore investor interest before incurring the expenses associated with a Regulation A offering. Solicitation of interest documents must be factual and comply with the antifraud provisions of the securities acts. No sales may be made until the SEC qualifies the offering statement and the seller delivers the final offering circular including the offering price to the investor.

(d) REGISTRATION EXEMPTIONS. Certain private and limited offerings of securities are exempt from the registration requirements of the act. Under SEC Regulation D, offerings of any amount made solely to accredited investors, such as banks, insurance companies, investment companies, or directors and executive officers of the issuing corporation, are exempt from the registration requirements of the act. These accredited investors generally have access to the kinds of information disclosed in a registration statement and prospectus.

Offerings of securities restricted to residents of the state in which the issuing corporation is organized and doing business are exempt from federal regulation. This intrastate offering exemption is applied very narrowly by the SEC and the courts, and such offerings are subject to state laws.

(1) Rule 505 Exemption. SEC Rule 505 of Regulation D exempts from registration offerings of less than $5 million to fewer than 35 nonaccredited purchasers (not offerees) over a 12-month period. No limit exists on the number of accredited investors who may participate. No general solicitation or general advertising is permitted under Rule 505. If any prospective investors are nonaccredited, the issuer must furnish all investors with specific information on the issuer, its business, and the securities offered for sale.

(2) Rule 506 Exemption. SEC Rule 506, the so-called private placement exemption, has no limitation on the amount that may be raised by the offering. As in Rule 505, specific information must be provided to all buyers if any buyers are nonaccredited investors, and the number of nonaccredited investors is limited to fewer than 35. Further, the rule requires that the issuer shall reasonably believe that each nonaccredited investor has enough experience in investments to be capable of evaluating the merits and risks of the investment.

(3) Restrictions. Securities acquired under Rules 505 and 506 exemptions from registration are considered **restricted securities**. Their resale may require registration. Rules requiring registration of these Regulation D securities prior to resale ensure that investors purchase these securities as an investment rather than for public distribution. When there is no attempt to make public distributions, investors ordinarily fit within one of several exemptions to registration upon resale.

---

[10] CFR § 230.251 et seq.

(4) Rule 504 Exemption. Under SEC Rule 504 of Regulation D, as amended in 1992, an issuer may offer and sell securities up to $1 million within a 12-month period without registration and without the restrictions contained in Rules 505 and 506.[11] No limitations exist concerning the number of investors being solicited or the method of soliciting investors. And no restrictions exist on the resale of the securities. The Rule 504 exemption is commonly used by small business issuers in raising seed money to start or expand a business.

Rule 504 differs from a Regulation A offering in that no registration whatsoever is required when the Rule 504 exemption is used, while a "mini-registration" with the SEC is required under a Regulation A offering. The SEC's anti-fraud provisions apply to both.

(e) LIABILITY. Issuers, sellers, and "aiders and abettors" may be subject to civil and criminal liability under the 1933 act.

(1) Issuer's Civil Liability for False or Misleading Statements. The Securities Act of 1933 imposes civil liability under Section 11 for making materially false or misleading statements in a registration statement and for the omission of any required material fact. Any investor who sustains a loss because of the false statements or omissions of the registration statement may sue to recover damages under Section 11. An issuing company has virtually no defense in such an action if there has been a false statement and a loss. However, individual defendants, such as accountants who helped prepare portions of the registration statement, may defend by proving they acted in good faith and with due diligence.[12]

(2) Civil Liability of Sellers of Securities. Section 12 of the 1933 act applies to those who "offer or sell" securities and employ any device or scheme to defraud or obtain money by means of untrue statements of material facts. This section makes such persons or firms liable to purchasers for damages sustained.

Where there are untrue statements of material facts, purchasers may recover under § 12(2), unless they have actual knowledge of the untruth or omission.[13] The fact that the plaintiff could have acquired knowledge by exercising ordinary care (such as reading documents supplied by the seller), but failed to do so, does not bar the plaintiff from recovering.[14]

(3) Criminal Liability. Section 24 of the 1933 act imposes criminal penalties on anyone who willfully makes untrue statements of material facts or omits required material facts from a registration statement. Section 17 of the act makes it unlawful for any person to employ any device, scheme, or artifice to defraud in the offer or sale of securities. Law firms and public accounting firms that prepare fraudulent registration statements in conjunction with clients may be subject not only to civil liability as "aiders and abettors" under Section 12(2) of the act but may also be subject to criminal liability under Section 17(a) of the act. Even if a security is exempt from registration, the civil and criminal liabilities just discussed apply if interstate commerce or the mail is involved in the offer or sale of the security.

(4) Persons Who Are Liable. Prior to the passing of the 1990 Remedies Act, the SEC could proceed against individuals only if they

---

[11] 17 CFR § 230.504 et seq.

[12] ACC/Lincoln S & L Litigation (D.Ariz) 794 F Supp 142 (1992).

[13] As codified, § 12(2) provides: Any person who . . . (2) offers or sells a security . . . by means of a prospectus or oral communication, which includes an untrue statement of a material fact or omits to state a material fact necessary in order to make the statements, in the light of circumstances under which they were made, not misleading (the purchaser not knowing of such untruth or omission), and who shall not sustain the burden of proof that he did not know, and in the exercise of reasonable care could not have known, of such untruth or omissions, shall be liable to the person purchasing such security from him, who may sue either at law or in equity in any court of competent jurisdiction, to recover the consideration paid for such security with interest thereon, less the amount of any income received thereon, upon the tender of such security, or for damages if he no longer owns the security. 15 USC § 77l(2).

[14] Caselz v Weff (CA9 Cal) 883 F2d 805 (1989).

directly violated or aided and abetted a violation of securities law. Under the 1990 Remedies Act, all persons are liable who "knew or should have known" that their acts or omissions "would contribute" to a violation of the law.

6. Securities Exchange Act of 1934

The 1934 act deals with the secondary distribution of securities. It was designed to prevent fraudulent and manipulative practices on the security exchanges and in over-the-counter markets. The act requires the disclosure of information to buyers and sellers of the securities. Furthermore, the act controls credit in these markets.

(a) REGISTRATION REQUIREMENTS. Exchanges, brokers, and dealers who deal in securities traded in interstate commerce or on any national security exchange must register with the SEC unless exempted by it.

Companies whose securities are listed on a national securities exchange, and unlisted companies that have assets in excess of $3 million and have 500 or more shareholders, are subject to the reporting requirements of the act.[15]

Form 10-K is the principal annual report form used by commercial and industrial companies required to file under the 1934 act. The reports require nonfinancial information about the registrant's activities during the year, such as the nature of the firm's business, the property or businesses it owns, and a statement concerning legal proceedings by or against the company. The report requires the submission of financial statements, with management's analysis of the financial condition of the company, and a report and analysis of the performance of corporate shares. It requires a listing of all directors and executive officers and disclosure of executive compensation information.

Registrants who are required to file 10-K reports must also file quarterly reports, called 10-Q reports. The 10-Q reports are principally concerned with financial information relevant to the quarterly period.

The SEC requires that annual shareholder reports be submitted to shareholders in any proxy solicitation on behalf of management. These reports contain essentially the same information provided in the 10-K.

(b) ANTIFRAUD PROVISION. Section 10(b) of the 1934 act makes it unlawful for any person to use any manipulative or deceptive device in contravention of SEC rules.[16] Under the authority of Section 10(b) of the 1934 act, the SEC has promulgated Rule 10b-5. This rule is the principal antifraud rule relating to the secondary distribution of securities. The rule states:

It shall be unlawful for any person, directly or indirectly, by use of any means or instrumentality of interstate commerce, or of the mails or of any facility of any national securities exchange,

(a) To employ any device, scheme, or artifice to defraud.

(b) To make any untrue statement of a material fact or to omit to state a material fact necessary in order to make the statements made, in the light of the circumstances under which they were made, not misleading, or

(c) To engage in any act, practice, or course of business that operates or would operate as a fraud or deceit upon any person, in connection with the purchase or sale of any security.[17]

(1) Scope of Application. Rule 10b-5 applies to all securities, whether registered or not, as long as use is made of the mail, interstate commerce, or a national stock exchange.

---

[15] SEC Release No. 34-18647 (April 15, 1982).

[16] 15 USC § 78j(b).

[17] 17 CFR § 240, 10b-5 (1982).

Under this rule, a civil action for damages may be brought by any injured party who purchased or sold securities because of false, misleading, or undisclosed information. Criminal penalties may also be imposed for willful violation of the act or SEC regulations promulgated under the act.

(2) Overlap Between the Acts. In some instances, there is an overlap between the provisions of the 1933 act and the 1934 act. Thus, purchasers of registered securities who allege they were defrauded by misrepresentations in a registration statement filed under the 1933 act may bring an action under the catchall antifraud provision of Section 10(b) of the 1934 act and SEC Rule 10b-5. This action may be brought regardless of the express remedy for misstatements in registration statements provided by Section 11 of the 1933 act.[18]

(3) Liability for "Material Misstatements or Omissions of Fact." Rule 10b-5 prohibits the making of any untrue statement of a "material" fact or the omission of a material fact necessary to render statements made not misleading. In every Rule 10b-5 case, the plaintiff must show "reliance" on the misrepresentation and resulting injury.

In a merger context, "materiality" depends on the probability that the transaction will be consummated and on the significance to the issuer of the securities. That is, "materiality" depends on the facts and must be determined on a case-by-case basis. Assume that corporation A was involved in merger discussions with corporation B. During this time, corporation A made public statements denying that any merger negotiations were taking place or that it knew of any corporate developments that would account for heavy trading activity in its stock. Corporation A may be held liable for damages to its shareholders who sold their stock after the public denial of merger activity and before a later merger announcement.

In *Basic Inc. v Levinson* the Supreme Court dealt with the question of what should be the standard of "materiality" in merger cases.

BASIC INC. v LEVINSON
485 US 224 (1988)

In December of 1978, Combustion Engineering Inc. and Basic Inc. agreed to merge. During the preceding two years, representatives of the two companies had meetings regarding the possibility of a merger. During this time, Basic made three public statements denying that any merger negotiations were taking place or that it knew of any corporate developments that would account for the heavy trading activity in its stock. Some time later it was publicly announced that there would be a merger. Certain former shareholders who sold this stock between Basic's first public denial of merger activity and the public announcement of the merger brought a Section 10(b) and Rule 10b-5 action against Basic and some of its directors, contending that material misrepresentation had been made by Basic in its public statements denying merger activity. Basic raised the defense that the alleged misrepresentations were not material and that there was no showing of reliance by the shareholders on Basic's statements. The Court of Appeals reversed the district court's summary judgment for Basic that preliminary merger discussions are not material information. Basic appealed to the U.S. Supreme Court.

---

[18] Herman & MacLean v Huddleston, 459 US 375 (1983).

BLACKMUN, J. . . . The 1934 Act was designed to protect investors against manipulation of stock prices. . . . Underlying the adoption of extensive disclosure requirements was a legislative philosophy: "There cannot be honest markets without honest publicity. Manipulation and dishonest practices of the market place thrive upon mystery and secrecy." H R Rep No 1383, 73d Cong 2d Sess, 11 (1934). This Court "repeatedly has described the 'fundamental purpose' of the Act as implementing a 'philosophy of full disclosure.'". . .

Pursuant to its authority under § 10(b) of the 1934 Act, 15 U.S.C. § 78j, the Securities and Exchange Commission promulgated Rule 10b-5. Judicial interpretation and application, legislative acquiescence, and the passage of time have removed any doubt that a private cause of action exists for a violation of § 10(b) and Rule 10b-5, and constitutes an essential tool for enforcement of the 1934 Act's requirements. . . .

The Court previously has addressed various positive and common-law requirements for a violation of § 10(b) or of Rule 10b-5. . . . The Court also explicitly has defined a standard of materiality under the securities laws, see *TSC Industries, Inc. v Northway, Inc.*, 426 US 438, 96 S Ct 2126, 48 L Ed 2d 757 (1976), concluding in the proxy-solicitation context that "an omitted fact is material if there is a substantial likelihood that a reasonable shareholder would consider it important in deciding how to vote." . . . Acknowledging that certain information concerning corporate developments could well be of "dubious significance," . . . the Court was careful not to set too low a standard of materiality; it was concerned that a minimal standard might bring an overabundance of information within its reach, and lead management "simply to bury the shareholders in an avalanche of trivial information—a result that is hardly conducive to informed decision making." . . . It further explained that to fulfill the materiality requirement "there must be a substantial likelihood that the disclosure of the omitted fact would have been viewed by the reasonable investor as having significantly altered the 'total mix' of information made available." . . . We now expressly adopt the *TSC Industries* standard of materiality for the § 10(b) and Rule 10b-5 context. . . .

Even before this Court's decision in *TSC Industries*, the Second Circuit had explained the role of the materiality requirement of Rule 10b-5, with respect to contingent or speculative information or events, in a manner that gave the term meaning that is independent of the other provisions of the Rule. Under such circumstances, materiality "will depend at any given time upon a balancing of both the indicated probability that the event will occur and the anticipated magnitude of the event in light of the totality of the company activity." *SEC v Texas Gulf Sulphur Co.*, 401 F2d, at 849. . . .

In a subsequent decision, the late Judge Friendly, writing for a Second Circuit panel, applied the *Texas Gulf Sulphur* probability/magnitude approach in the specific context of preliminary merger negotiations. . . .

Whether merger discussions in any particular case are material therefore depends on the facts. Generally, in order to assess the probability that the event will occur, a factfinder will need to look to indicia of interest in the transaction at the highest corporate levels. Without attempting to catalog all such possible factors, we note by way of example that board resolutions, instructions to investment bankers, and actual negotiations between principals or their intermediaries may serve as indicia of interest. To assess the magnitude of the transaction to the issuer of the securities allegedly manipulated, a factfinder will need to consider such facts as the size of the two corporate entities and of the potential premiums over market value. No particular event or factor short of closing the transaction need be either necessary or sufficient by itself to render merger discussions material.

As we clarify today, materiality depends on the significance the reasonable investor would place on the withheld or misrepresented information. . . . Because the standard of materiality we have adopted differs from that used by both courts below, we remand the case for reconsideration of the question whether a grant of summary judgment is appropriate on this record.

We turn to the question of reliance and the fraud-on-the-market theory. Succinctly put:

The fraud on the market theory is based on the hypothesis that, in an open and developed securities market, the price of a company's stock is determined by the available material information regarding the company and its business. . . . Misleading statements will therefore defraud purchasers of stock even if the purchasers do not directly rely on the misstatements. . . . The causal connection between the defendants' fraud and the plaintiffs' purchase of stock in such a case is no less significant than in a case of direct reliance on misrepresentations. Peil v Speiser, 806 F2d 1154, 160-1161 (CA3 1986). . . .

Requiring proof of individualized reliance from each member of the proposed plaintiff class effectively would have prevented respondents from proceeding with a class action, since individual issues then would have overwhelmed the common ones. The District Court found that the presumption of reliance created by the fraud-on-the-market theory provided "a practical resolution to the problem of balancing the substantive requirement of proof of reliance in securities cases against the procedural requisites of [Fed Rule Civ Proc] 23." The District Court thus concluded that with reference to each public statement and its impact upon the open market for Basic shares, common questions are predominated over individual questions, as required by Fed Rule Civ Proc 23(a)(2) and (b)(3). . .the fraud-on-the-market theory effectively eliminates the requirement that a plaintiff asserting a claim under Rule 10b-5 prove reliance.

We agree that reliance is an element of a Rule 10b-5 cause of action. . . . Reliance provides the requisite causal connection between a defendant's misrepresentation and a plaintiff's injury. . . . Commentators generally have applauded the adoption of one variation or another of the fraud-on-the-market theory. An investor who buys or sells stock at the price set by the market does so in reliance on the integrity of that price. Because most publicly available information is reflected in market price, an investor's reliance on any public material misrepresentations, therefore, may be presumed for purposes of a Rule 10b-5 action. . . .

Any showing that severs the link between the alleged misrepresentation and either the price received (or paid) by the plaintiff, or his decision to trade at a fair market price, will be sufficient to rebut the presumption of reliance. For example, if petitioners could show that the "market makers" were privy to the truth about the merger discussions here with Combustion, and thus that the market price would not have been affected by their misrepresentations, the causal connection could be broken: the basis for finding that the fraud had been transmitted through market price would be gone. Similarly, if, despite petitioners' allegedly fraudulent attempt to manipulate market price, news of the merger discussions credibly entered the market and dissipated the effects of the misstatements, those who traded Basic shares after the corrective statements would have no direct or indirect connection with the fraud. Petitioners also could rebut the presumption of reliance as to plaintiffs who would have divested themselves of their Basic shares without relying on the integrity of the market. For example, a plaintiff who believed that Basic's statements were false and that Basic was indeed engaged in merger discussions, and who consequently believed that Basic stock was artificially underpriced, but sold his shares nevertheless because of other unrelated concerns, *e.g.*, potential antitrust problems, or political pressures to divest from shares of certain businesses, could not be said to have relied on the integrity of a price he knew had been manipulated.

In summary:

We specifically adopt, for the § 10(b) and Rule 10b-5 context, the standard of materiality set forth in *TSC Industries, Inc. v Northway, Inc.*, 426 US, at 449. . . .

Materiality in the merger context depends on the probability that the transaction will be consummated, and its significance to the issuer of the securities. Materiality depends on the facts and thus is to be determined on a case-by-case basis.

It is not inappropriate to apply a presumption of reliance supported by the fraud-on-the-market theory.

That presumption, however, is rebuttable.

[Judgment vacated and action remanded]

QUESTIONS

1. What was the legislative philosophy underlying the adoption of the extensive disclosure requirements of the 1934 Act?
2. What is the standard of materiality to be applied in a merger-related context?
3. What is the "fraud-on-the-market theory"?

7. Trading on Insider Information

Section 10(b) and Rule 10b-5 form a basis for imposing sanctions for trading on **insider information**. The Insider Trading Sanctions Act of 1984, which amended the 1934 act, gave the SEC authority to bring an action against an individual purchasing or selling a security while in possession of material, inside information. The court may impose a civil penalty of up to three times the profit gained or loss avoided as a result of the unlawful sale.[19] Persons who "aid or abet" in the violation may also be held liable under the act.

Under the 1988 Insider Trading Act "controlling persons," including employers whose lax supervision may allow employees to commit insider trading violations, are subject to civil penalties.[20] The SEC must prove "knowing" or "reckless" behavior by the controlling person. The 1988 law establishes bounty programs that allow the SEC to reward informants giving information on insider trading activity. The reward is up to 10 percent of any penalty imposed.

(a) TRADING BY INSIDERS AND TIPPEES. An **insider** may be a director or corporate employee. A **temporary insider** is someone retained by the corporation for professional services, such as an attorney, accountant, or investment banker. Insiders or temporary insiders are liable for inside trading when they fail to disclose material, nonpublic

---

[19] PL 98-376, 58 Stat 1264, 15 USC § 780.

[20] PL 100-704, 102 Stat 4677, 15 USC § 78 u A (b)(2).

information before trading on it and thus make a secret profit. A **tippee** is an individual who receives information from an insider or temporary insider. A tippee is subject to the insider's fiduciary duty to shareholders when the insider has breached the fiduciary duty to shareholders by improperly disclosing the information to the tippee and when the tippee knows or should know there has been a breach.[21] Such a breach occurs when an insider benefits personally from his or her disclosure. Where the insider does not breach a fiduciary duty, a tippee does not violate the securities laws.

In the *Dirks* case the Supreme Court discussed the factors that subject a tippee to liability.

DIRKS v SECURITIES AND EXCHANGE COMMISSION
463 US 646 (1983)

On March 6, 1973, Raymond Dirks, an investment analyst, received information from Ronald Secrist, a former officer of Equity Funding of America, alleging that the assets of Equity Funding were vastly overstated as the result of fraudulent corporate practices. Upon investigation Dirks received only denials from senior management, but certain corporation employees corroborated the charges of fraud. Neither Dirks nor his firm owned or traded any Equity Funding stock, but throughout his investigation he openly discussed the information he had obtained with a number of clients and investors, causing liquidation of Equity Fund stock in excess of $16 million. Dirks urged *The Wall Street Journal* to publish a story on the fraud allegations. However, it declined because it feared that publishing damaging hearsay might be libelous. Dirks continued his investigation and spread word of Secrist's charges during the next two weeks. During this time, Equity Funding stock fell from $26 per share to less than $15 per share. On March 27, the NYSE halted trading of Equity Funding stock, and a subsequent investigation revealed the vast fraud that had taken place. The SEC, investigating Dirks' role in the exposure of the fraud, found that Dirks had aided and abetted violations of the Securities Act of 1933, the Securities Exchange Act of 1934, and SEC Rule 10b-5 by publicly repeating the allegations of fraud. Upon appeal by Dirks, the decision of the lower court was upheld by the U.S. Court of Appeals. An appeal was taken to the Supreme Court.

POWELL, J. . . . In the seminal case of *In re Cady, Roberts & Co.*, 40 S.E.C. 907 (1961), the SEC recognized that the common law in some jurisdictions imposes on "corporate 'insiders', particularly officers, directors, or controlling stockholders" an "affirmative duty of disclosure . . . when dealing in securities." The SEC found that not only did breach of this common-law duty also establish the elements of a Rule 10b-5 violation, but that individuals other than corporate insiders could be obligated either to disclose material nonpublic information before trading or to abstain from trading

---

[21] U.S. v Chestman (CA2 NY) 974 F2d 564 (1991).

altogether. In *Chiarella* [445 U.S. 222 (1980)], we accepted the two elements set out in *Cady, Roberts* for establishing a Rule 10b-5 violation: "(i) the existence of a relationship affording access to inside information intended to be available only for a corporate purpose, and (ii) the unfairness of allowing a corporate insider to take advantage of that information by trading without disclosure." In examining whether Chiarella had an obligation to disclose or abstain, the Court found that there is no general duty to disclose before trading on material nonpublic information, and held that "a duty to disclose under § 10(b) does not arise from the mere possession of nonpublic market information." Such a duty arises rather from the existence of a fiduciary relationship.

Not "all breaches of fiduciary duty in connection with a securities transaction," however, come within the ambit of Rule 10b-5. There must also be "manipulation or deception." In an inside-trading case this fraud derives from the "inherent unfairness involved where one takes advantage" of "information intended to be available only for a corporate purpose and not for the personal benefit of anyone." Thus, an insider will be liable under Rule 10b-5 for inside trading only where he fails to disclose material nonpublic information before trading on it and thus makes "secret profits."

We were explicit in *Chiarella* in saying that there can be no duty to disclose where the person who has traded on inside information "was not [the corporation's] agent, . . . was not a fiduciary, [or] was not a person in whom the sellers [of the securities] had placed their trust and confidence." Not to require such a fiduciary relationship, we recognized, would "depart radically from the established doctrine that duty arises from a specific relationship between two parties" and would amount to "recognizing a general duty between all participants in market transactions to forgo actions based on material, nonpublic information." This requirement of a specific relationship between the shareholders and the individual trading on inside information has created analytical difficulties for the SEC and courts in policing tippees who trade on inside information. Unlike insiders who have independent fiduciary duties to both the corporation and its shareholders, the typical tippee has no such relationships.* In view of this absence, it has been unclear how a tippee acquires the *Cady, Roberts* duty to refrain from trading on inside information.

The SEC's position, as stated in its opinion in this case, is that a tippee "inherits" the *Cady, Roberts* obligation to shareholders whenever he receives inside information from an insider. . . .

In effect, the SEC's theory of tippee liability . . . appears rooted in the idea that the antifraud provisions required equal information among all traders. This conflicts with the principle set forth in *Chiarella* that only some persons, under some circumstances, will be barred from trading while in possession of material nonpublic information. . . .

Imposing a duty to disclose or abstain solely because a person knowingly receives material nonpublic information from an insider and trades on it could have an inhibiting influence on the role of market analysts, which the SEC itself recognizes is necessary to the preservation of a healthy market. It is commonplace for analysts to "ferret out and analyze information," and this often is done by meeting with and questioning corporate officers and others who are insiders. And information that the analysts obtain normally may be the basis for judgments as to the market worth of a corporation's securities. The analyst's judgment in this respect is made available in market letters or otherwise to clients of the firm. It is the nature of this type of information, and indeed of the markets themselves, that such information cannot be made simultaneously available to all of the corporation's stockholders or the public generally.

The conclusion that recipients of inside information do not invariably acquire a duty to disclose or abstain does not mean that such tippees always are free to trade on the information. The need for a ban on some tippee trading is clear. Not only are insiders forbidden by their fiduciary relationship from personally using undisclosed corporate information to their advantage, but they may not give such information to an outsider for the same improper purpose of exploiting the information for their personal gain. See 15 U.S.C. § 78t(b) (making it unlawful to do indirectly "by means of any other person" any act made unlawful by the federal securities laws). Similarly, the transactions of those who knowingly participate with the fiduciary in such a breach are "as forbidden" as transactions "on behalf of the trustee himself.". . .

*Under certain circumstances, such as where corporate information is revealed legitimately to an underwriter, accountant, lawyer, or consultant working for the corporation, these outsiders may become fiduciaries of the shareholders. The basis for recognizing this fiduciary duty is not simply that such persons acquired nonpublic corporate information, but rather that they have entered into a special confidential relationship in the conduct of the business of the enterprise and are given access to information solely for corporate purposes. . . . When such a person breaches his fiduciary relationship, he may be treated more properly as a tipper than a tippee. . . For such a duty to be imposed, however, the corporation must expect the outsider to keep the disclosed nonpublic information confidential, and the relationship at least must imply such a duty.

Thus, some tippees must assume an insider's duty to the shareholders not because they receive inside information, but rather because it has been made available to them *improperly*. And for Rule 10b-5 purposes, the insider's disclosure is improper only where it would violate his *Cady, Roberts* duty. Thus, a tippee assumes a fiduciary duty to the shareholders of a corporation not to trade on material nonpublic information only when the insider has breached his fiduciary duty to the shareholders by disclosing the information to the tippee and the tippee knows or should know that there has been a breach.

In determining whether a tippee is under an obligation to disclose or abstain, it thus is necessary to determine whether the insider's "tip" constituted a breach of the insider's fiduciary duty. All disclosures of confidential corporate information are not inconsistent with the duty insiders owe to shareholders. . . . Thus, the test is whether the insider personally will benefit, directly or indirectly, from his disclosure. Absent some personal gain, there has been no breach of duty to stockholders. And absent a breach by the insider, there is no derivative breach. . . .

Under the inside-trading and tipping rules set forth above, we find that there was no actionable violation by Dirks. It is undisputed that Dirks himself was a stranger to Equity Funding, with no pre-existing fiduciary duty to its shareholders. He took no action, directly or indirectly, that induced the shareholders or officers of Equity Funding to repose trust or confidence in him. There was no expectation by Dirks' sources that he would keep their information in confidence. Nor did Dirks misappropriate or illegally obtain the information about Equity Funding. Unless the insiders breached their *Cady, Roberts* duty to shareholders in disclosing the nonpublic information to Dirks, he breached no duty when he passed it on to investors as well as to *The Wall Street Journal*.

It is clear that neither Secrist nor the other Equity Funding employees violated their *Cady, Roberts* duty to the corporation's shareholders by providing information to Dirks. The tippers received no monetary or personal benefit for revealing Equity Funding's secrets, nor was their purpose to make a gift of valuable information to Dirks. As the facts of this case clearly indicate, the tippers were motivated by a desire to expose the fraud.

[Judgment reversed]

BLACKMUN, J., dissenting. . . . The Court today takes still another step to limit the protections provided investors by § 10(b) of the Securities Exchange Act of 1934. . . . The device employed in this case engrafts a special motivational requirement on the fiduciary duty doctrine. This innovation excuses a knowing and intentional violation of an insider's duty to shareholders if the insider does not act from a motive of personal gain. Even on the extraordinary facts of this case, such an innovation is not justified. . . .

In my view, Secrist violated his duty to Equity Funding shareholders by transmitting material nonpublic information to Dirks with the intention that Dirks would cause his clients to trade on that information. Dirks, therefore, was under a duty to make the information publicly available or to refrain from actions that he knew would lead to trading. Because Dirks caused his clients to trade, he violated § 10(b) and Rule 10b-5. Any other result is a disservice to this country's attempt to provide fair and efficient capital markets.

QUESTIONS

1. State the SEC's theory of tippee liability. Would such a theory have an inhibiting influence on the role of market analysts?
2. When is a tippee subject to a fiduciary duty to the shareholders not to trade on material nonpublic information?
3. Does the court establish a "constructive insider" rule in its footnote?

(b) MISAPPROPRIATORS. Individuals who misappropriate or steal valuable nonpublic information in breach of a fiduciary duty to their employer and trade in securities on that information are guilty of insider trading as "misappropriators."[22] Thus, an employee working for a financial printing firm was found guilty of insider trading under Section 10(b) and Rule 10b-5 under the following circumstances.[23] While proofreading a financial document being prepared for a client firm, he figured out the identity of tender offer targets.

Soon after that, he traded on this valuable nonpublic information to his advantage.

It is no defense to a Section 10(b) and Rule 10b-5 criminal charge of participating in a "scheme to defraud" that the victim of the fraud had no economic interest in the securities traded. The convictions of a stockbroker and a columnist for the *Wall Street Journal* were upheld under Section 10(b) of the 1934 act. The columnist violated his fiduciary duty to his employer by revealing prepublication information about his column to the stockbroker. The stockbroker then used the information to

---

[22] U.S. v Willis (SD NY) 737 F Supp 269 (1990).
[23] SEC v Materia (CA2 NY) 745 F2d 197 (1984).

trade in the securities identified in the column.[24]

(c) REMEDY FOR INVESTORS. Investors who lacked the inside information possessed by the insider and sold their stock during the relevant time period may recover damages from any insider who had made use of the undisclosed information. Recovery is by a civil action based on Rule 10b-5.

8. Disclosure of Ownership and Short-Swing Profit

Corporate directors and officers owning equity securities in their corporation and any shareholder owning more than 10 percent of any class of the corporation's equity securities must file with the SEC a disclosure statement regarding such ownership. This is required under § 16(a) of the 1934 act.

Section 16 is designed to prevent the unfair use of information available to these corporate insiders. This section prevents insiders from participating in short-term trading in their corporation's securities.

If such a person sells at a profit any of such securities in less than six months after their purchase, the profit is called a **short-swing profit**. Under Section 16(b), the corporation may sue the director, officer, or major stockholder for the short-swing profit. The corporation may recover that profit even though there was no fraudulent intent in acquiring and selling the securities.[25]

9. Tender Offers

A corporation or group of investors may seek to acquire control of another corporation by making a general offer to all shareholders of the target corporation to purchase their shares for cash at a specified price. This is called a **cash tender offer**. The offer to purchase is usually contingent on the tender of a fixed number of shares sufficient to ensure takeover. The bid price is ordinarily higher than the prevailing market price. Should more shares be tendered than the offeror is willing to purchase, the tender offeror must purchase shares from each shareholder on a pro rata basis.

The Williams Act, which amended the 1934 act,[26] was passed to ensure that public shareholders who are confronted with a cash tender offer will not be required to act without adequate information. Under Section 14(d) of the Williams Act, a person making a tender offer must file appropriate SEC forms. These forms provide information about the background and identity of the person filing, the source of funds used to make purchases of stock, the amount of stock beneficially owned, the purpose of the purchases, any plan the purchaser proposes to follow if it gains control over the target corporation, and any contracts or understandings that it has with other persons concerning the target corporation.[27]

Section 14(e) of the Williams Act is the antifraud section. It prohibits fraudulent, deceptive, or manipulative practices. SEC Rule 14e-1 requires any tender offer to remain open for a minimum of 20 business days from the date it is first published or given to security holders. Federal and state legislation, as well as administrative regulation, is aimed at requiring disclosure of information and allowance of a reasonable length of time for consideration of the facts. These requirements are designed to make agreement to takeovers

---

[24] Carpenter v U.S. 484 US 19 (1987).

[25] Synalloy Corp. v Gray (D Del) 816 F Supp 963 (1993).

[26] PL 90-439, 82 Stat 454, 15 USC §§ 78m(d), (e).

[27] Section 14(d) requires a filing by any person making a tender offer that, if successful, would result in the acquisition of 5 percent of any class of an equity security required to be registered under the 1934 act. Section 13(d) of the act requires disclosure to the issuer, the SEC, and the appropriate stock exchange when a person acquires 5 percent of a class of equity security through stock purchases on exchanges or through private purchases. The person may have acquired the stock for investment purpose and not for control, but must still file disclosure forms under Section 13(d). *See* SEC v Bilzerian (DDC) 814 F Supp 116 (1993). Section 14(d) applies only to shares to be acquired by tender offer.

the result of voluntary action based on full knowledge of material facts.

As far as the courts are concerned, take-overs must be regarded with a neutral eye. If there is misrepresentation or other misconduct, the law will interfere. Otherwise, freedom of contract requires that courts not interfere with the judgment of the contracting parties.

10. Regulation of Accountants by the SEC

Accountants play a vital role in financial reporting under the federal securities laws administered by the SEC. Sections 1, 12, 17, and 24 of the 1933 act and Section 10(b) of the 1934 act are the sections under which accountants may be subject to liability. An accountant who prepares any statement, opinion, or other legal paper filed with the SEC with the preparer's consent is deemed to be practicing before the SEC.[28] Because the SEC relies so heavily on accountants, the SEC has promulgated Rule 2(e). This rule regulates and provides the basis for discipline of accountants, attorneys, and consultants who practice before the SEC. Under Rule 2(e), the SEC may suspend or disbar from practice before it those who are unqualified or unethical or who have violated federal securities laws or SEC rules.[29]

The authority of the SEC to promulgate the rule was upheld in Touche Ross v SEC (CA2 NY) 609 F2d 570 (1979).

C. INDUSTRY SELF-REGULATION

To protect the public from unprofessional or negligent conduct of securities salespersons, the securities industry itself has provided means to resolve controversies relating to the sales of securities.

11. Arbitration of Securities Disputes

Member firms of the self-regulatory organization, the National Association of Securities Dealers (NASD), have adopted a code of arbitration which allows customers of NASD members to submit disputes to arbitration. The arbitration rights are contractual and are set forth in writing on opening an account with a dealer. Securities firms with seats on the New York Stock Exchange have a similar arbitration code. Parties who have agreed to arbitrate their securities disputes can be compelled to arbitrate rather than sue in courts.[30] Courts are very reluctant to vacate an arbitration award.

In the *FSC Securities Corp.* decision, a securities dealer sought to set aside an arbitration award in favor of a customer.

FSC SECURITIES CORP v FREEL
811 F Supp 439 (1993)

Judy and Mirle Freel filed an arbitration claim against FSC Securities (FSC), a NASD member, alleging that FSC's agent, Marlis Gilbert, had recom-

---

[28] 17 CFR § 201.2e (1979).

[29] Rule 2(e) provides: Suspension and disbarment. (1) The Commission may deny, temporarily or permanently, the privilege of appearing or practicing before it in any way to any person who is found by the Commission after notice of an opportunity for hearing in the matter (i) not to possess the requisite qualifications to represent others, or (ii) to be lacking in character or integrity or to have engaged in unethical or improper professional conduct, or (iii) to have willfully violated, or willfully aided and abetted the violation of any provision of the federal securities laws (15 U.S.C. 77a to 80B-20), or the rules and regulations thereunder. 17 CFR § 201.2(e) (1979).

[30] 99 Commercial Street, Inc. v Goldberg (SD NY) 811 F Supp 900 (1992).

mended unsuitable investments for them. The arbitration panel issued an award for the Freels of damages and interest, and FSC sued to vacate the award.

MacLAUGHLIN, D. J. . . . This action arises out of investment advice given to defendants Judy Freel and Mirle Freel by plaintiff Marlis Gilbert, a financial planner. The Freels sought Gilbert's advice on investing $94,000 they had received from Judy Freel's parents. The money was intended, among other things, to help care for Judy Freel's developmentally disabled twin sister. One of the Freels' stated objectives was to protect the principal of their investments. Gilbert advised the Freels to invest in a variety of limited partnerships involved in commercial and residential property, equipment leasing, oil reserves, and medical stock. Gilbert also advised the Freels to take out a mortgage on their debt-free home and place the money into an investment. As a result of Gilbert's advice, the Freels lost approximately $81,000.

. . . The Freels filed an arbitration claim against Gilbert and plaintiffs FSC Securities Corp., Integrated Financial Services, and Richard E. Connolly, alleging that Gilbert, as agent for the other named parties, recommended unsuitable investments for them. The Freels sought $81,000 in loss of principal, $56,000 in interest, and punitive damages.

. . . After a two-day hearing on the merits of the claim, respondents reiterated their motion to dismiss. Approximately one month after the hearing, the panel issued an award in favor of the Freels. The panel denied respondents' motion to dismiss, and awarded the Freels $122,421 plus costs.

The respondents—plaintiffs in this action—commenced this suit under the Federal Arbitration Act (FAA), 9 U.S.C. § 1 et seq. They seek to vacate the award, arguing that the arbitrators exceeded their powers. . . .

Judicial review of an arbitration award is extremely limited. A court may disturb an arbitration award only on grounds set forth in the FAA. The United States Court of Appeals for the Eighth Circuit has held that by its express terms, the FAA allows a reviewing court to alter or vacate an award only if the arbitrators exceeded their power, or the arbitrators made a simple formal, descriptive, or mathematical error. *Stroh Container Co. v Delphi Industries, Inc.*, 783 F2d 743 (8th Cir.) *cert. denied*, 476 US 1141. . .

. . . Plaintiffs argue that the award should be vacated because it was made in manifest disregard of the law. . . . Plaintiffs have pointed to nothing in the record to support their manifest disregard claim, other than the result obtained. Because there is no showing in the record that the arbitrators knew the law and expressly disregarded it, the arbitration award could not be vacated even if the Court were to adopt the manifest disregard standard. . . .

[Arbitration award affirmed]

QUESTIONS

1. Did the Freels obtain the right to arbitrate this dispute under federal securities law?
2. On what basis will courts vacate an arbitration award?
3. Review Figure 1 of the Preface. Do financial planners have ethical obligations to their customers?

SUMMARY

State blue sky laws, which apply only to intrastate transactions, protect the public from the sale of fraudulent securities. The term *security* is defined sufficiently broadly to encompass not only stocks and bonds, but any conceivable kind of corporate interest that has investment characteristics. There are two principal laws providing the basic framework for federal regulation of the sale of securities in interstate commerce. The Securities Act of 1933 deals with the issue or original distribution of securities by the issuing corporations. The Securities Exchange Act of 1934 regulates the secondary distribution or sale of securities on exchanges. These acts are administered by the Securities and Exchange Commission. Except for certain private and limited offerings, the 1933 act requires that a registration statement be filed with the SEC and that a prospectus be provided to each potential purchaser. Criminal and civil penalties exist for fraudulent statements made in this process. The 1934 act provides reporting requirements for companies whose securities are listed on a national exchange and unlisted companies that have assets in excess of $3 million and 500 or more shareholders. Rule 10b-5 is the principal antifraud rule under the 1934 act. Trading on "inside information" is unlawful and may subject those involved to a civil penalty of three times the profit made on the improperly disclosed information. Cash tender offers are regulated by the SEC under authority of the Williams Act. The securities industry provides arbitration procedures to resolve disputes between customers and firms.

LAW IN PRACTICE

1. With very limited resources available when starting a business, an entrepreneur does not have to spend resources fulfilling SEC registration requirements in order to raise money from investors. Seed money of up to $1 million over a 12-month period may be raised without any registration under Rule 504.

2. Know that offerings of securities up to $5 million in a 12-month period can be made to investors under the mini-registration procedures of SEC Regulation A.

3. Be aware that the definition of a "security" under the securities acts is so broad as to encompass virtually any instrument that you might sell as an investment. You simply cannot get around it.

4. Recognize that Rule 10b-5, the SEC's principal antifraud rule, applies to all interstate securities whether registered or not.

5. Be aware that you may be obligated to arbitrate any disputes with your brokerage firm under arbitration obligations created with the firm when you opened your brokerage account.

QUESTIONS AND CASE PROBLEMS

1. What social forces are affected by the rule of law that prohibits corporate insiders from making short-term sale of their company's stock?

2. What is the major distinction between the Securities Act of 1933 and the Securities Exchange Act of 1934?

3. On what rationale does the SEC allow for the private placement of securities with accredited investors, without any limitation on the amount that may be raised?

4. Mark Magnison, a state lottery game $1 million winner, reviewed the registration statement and prospectus of the Northern Sprinkler Supply Co., which had been filed on time with the SEC. He tells you that he cannot make much sense of these documents, but that he is going to invest in the company, because "the SEC approved the securities, and the federal government would not knowingly approve a bad investment." Is Mark correct?

5. The following transactions in Heritage Cosmetics Co., Inc. stock took place: On January 21, Jones, the corporation's vice president of marketing, purchased 1,000 shares of stock at $25 per share. On January 24, Sylvan, a local banker and director of Heritage, purchased 500 shares of stock at $26 per share. On January 30, McCarthy, a secretary at Heritage, purchased 300 shares of stock at $26 1/2. On February 12, Winfried, a rich investor from New England, purchased 25,000 shares at an average price of $26 per share. At that time, Heritage had a total of 200,000 shares of stock outstanding. On June 14, Winfried sold his entire holding in Heritage at an average price of $35 per share. In a local newspaper interview, Winfried was quoted regarding his reasons for selling the stock: "I have not had the pleasure of meeting any person from Heritage, but I have the highest regard for the Heritage Company. . . . I sold my stock simply because the market has gone too high and in my view is due for a correction." After independently reading Winfried's prediction on the stock market, Jones, Sylvan, and McCarthy sold their shares on June 15 for $33 per share. On June 20, Heritage Co. demanded that Jones, Sylvan, McCarthy, and Winfried pay the corporation the profits made on the sale of the stock. Was the corporation correct in making such a demand on each of these people?

6. The Canadian Express Club solicited buyers to purchase shares in a group comprised of shareholders whose money is pooled to purchase lottery tickets in Canada. Total winnings from tickets are split among shareholders, with Canadian Express administering the purchasing, record keeping, and disbursements. The state securities commission claimed that Canadian Express was selling securities, on the theory that the lottery ticket purchase agreement was an investment contract. Canadian Express contended that playing the lottery was not an "investment" of money. Decide. [*Ontario, Inc. v Mays, 14 Kan App 1, 780 P2d 1126*]

7. Mary Dale worked in the law office of Emory Stone, an attorney practicing securities law. In proofreading Mary's keying of a document relating to the merger of two computer software companies, Emory joked to her, "If I weren't so ethical, I could make a few bucks on this info. Nomac Software stock prices are going to take off when this news hits 'The Street.'" That evening, Mary told her friend Rick Needleworth, a stockbroker, what her boss had said. Needleworth bought 500 shares of Nomac Software stock the next day and sold it three days later when the news of the merger was made public. He made a profit of $3,500. Did Dale, Stone, or Needleworth violate

any securities law(s) or ethical principles with respect to the profit made by Needleworth?

8. International Advertising Inc. (IA) would like to raise $10 million in new capital in order to open new offices in Eastern Europe. It believes it could raise the capital by selling shares of stock to its directors and executive officers, as well to its bank and a large insurance company whose home office is located near IA's headquarters. Opposition to the financing plan exists because of the trouble, time, and cost involved with registering with the SEC. Advise IA how best to proceed with the registration of the new issue of stock.

9. Dubois sold Hocking a condominium that included an option to participate in a rental pool arrangement. Hocking elected to participate in the arrangement. Under it, the rental pools agent rented condominiums, pooled the income, and after deducting a management fee, distributed the income to the owners on a pro rata basis. Hocking brought a Rule 10b-5 fraud action against Dubois. Dubois contended that the sale of the condominium was not a "security under the Securities Acts," so Hocking could not bring a securities suit against her. Was Dubois correct? [*Hocking v Dubois (CA9 Hawaii) 839 F2d 560*]

10. William Rubin, president of Tri-State Mining Co., sought a loan from Bankers Trust Co. To secure the loan, he pledged worthless stock in six companies and represented that the stock was worth $1.7 million. He also arranged for fictitious quotations to appear in an investment reporting service used by the bank to value the pledged securities. The bank loaned Rubin $475,000 and took the securities as pledged collateral. In a criminal action against Rubin under § 17(a) of the 1933 act, Rubin defended that pledging of securities did not constitute an "offer or sale" of securities under the act. Was Rubin correct? [*Rubin v U.S. 449 US 424*]

11. J. C. Cowdin, a director of the Curtis-Wright Co., phoned Robert Gintel, a partner of Cady, Roberts & Co., a stock brokerage house, and advised him that Curtis Wright's quarterly dividend had been cut. Gintel immediately entered orders selling Curtis-Wright shares for his customers' accounts. The stock was selling at over $40 a share when the orders were executed but fell to $30 soon after the dividend cut was announced to the public. The SEC contended that the firm, Cady, Roberts & Co., and Gintel violated § 10(b) of the 1934 act, Rule 10b-5, and § 17(a) of the 1933 act. Gintel and Cady, Roberts & Co. disagreed. Decide. [*Re Cady, Roberts & Co. 40 SEC 907*]

12. The Baileys bought shares in a real estate limited partnership from Blarney Castle, Ltd., in reliance on false representations by Joan Casey that "Blarney Castle is qualified by the IRS as an IRS-approved tax shelter" and that "Blarney Castle will return your investment plus a profit in a reasonable period of time . . . it is a secure investment, a sure thing." The offering memorandum Casey provided to the Baileys stated that Blarney Castle limited partnership interests were a risky investment, the IRS had not approved and would probably challenge some of the deductions, and buyers should not rely on oral descriptions of this security. The Baileys did not read this document before investing. The limited partnership went into bankruptcy, and the Baileys sued Casey for making material misrepresentations in violation of § 12(2) of the 1933 act. Casey defended that her statements were innocuous "puffery" or mere statements of opinion and were not actionable. Casey asserted that the Baileys are bound by the offering memorandum, which fully informed the Baileys of all relevant facts. Decide.

13. Douglas Hansen, Leo Borrell, and Bobby Lawrence were three psychiatrists who recognized the need for an inpatient treatment facility for adolescents and children in their community. They became limited partners in the building of a for-profit psychiatric facility. Each had a 6.25 percent interest in the partnership. Healthcare International Inc., the general partner with a 75 percent interest, had expertise in hospital construction, management, and operation. Hansen, Borrell, and Lawrence assert that the managerial control of the partnership was undertaken and operated by the general partner to the exclusion of the limited partners. The doctors claimed that their interest was a security—"investment contracts"—so as to give them status to file a securities suit against the general partner under the 1934 act. The general partner disagreed. Decide. [*L & B Hospital Ventures Inc. v Healthcare International Inc. (CA5 Tex) 894 F2d 150*]

14. Texas International Speedway, Inc. (TIS) filed a registration statement and prospectus with the Securities and Exchange Commission, offering a total of $4,398,900 in securities to the public. The proceeds of the sale were to be used to finance the construction of an automobile speedway. The entire issue was sold on the offering date. TIS did not meet with success, and the corporation filed a petition for bankruptcy. Huddleston and Bradley instituted a class action in the U.S. district court on behalf of themselves and other purchasers of TIS securities. Their complaint alleged violations of § 10(b) of the 1934 act. The plaintiffs sued most of the participants in the offering, including the accounting firm, Herman & MacLean. Herman & MacLean had issued an opinion concerning certain financial statements and a pro forma balance sheet that were contained in the registration statement and prospectus. The plaintiffs claimed that the defendants had engaged in a fraudulent scheme to misrepresent or conceal material facts regarding the financial condition of TIS, including the costs incurred in building the speedway. Herman & MacLean defended that the case should be dismissed because § 11 of the 1933 act provides an express remedy for a misrepresentation in a registration statement, so an action under § 10(b) of the 1934 act is precluded. Decide. [*Herman & MacLean v Huddleston, 459 US 375*]

15. Melvin J. Ford, President of International Loan Network, Inc. (ILN) promoted ILN's financial enrichment programs to ILN members and prospective members with evangelical fervor at revival-style "President's Night" gatherings. His basic philosophy was:

The movement of money creates wealth. What we believe is that if you organize people and get money moving, it can actually create wealth.

One ILN program was the Maximum Consideration Program which, somewhat like a chain letter, provided for $5,000 awards to members who sold $3,000 worth of new "PRA" members, and made a deposit on the purchases of non-residential real estate. According to Ford, an individual purchasing $16,000 worth of PRAs could receive an award of up to $80,000 because "all of a sudden the velocity of money increases to such a point, the ability to create wealth expands to such a degree, that we could come back and give somebody an award for up to $80,000." The SEC contends that ILA is selling unregistered investment contracts in violation of the 1933 act. ILA disagrees, contending that the program never guaranteed a return and is thus not an investment contract. Decide. Could ILN provide full disclosure to investors concerning the program in a prospectus if required by the 1933 Act? [*SEC v ILN, Inc. (CA DC) 968 F2d 1304*]

MANAGEMENT OF CORPORATIONS

LEARNING OBJECTIVES

After studying this chapter, you will be able to:

1. *Identify the persons entitled to manage a corporation and describe their powers.*
2. *State the requirements with respect to meetings of shareholders and directors.*
3. *Define and illustrate the liability of corporate officers and directors to the corporation.*
4. *Define and illustrate the liability of corporate officers and directors to third persons.*
5. *State the criminal liability of officers and directors of a corporation.*
6. *State when an officer, director, or employee of a corporation may obtain indemnification from the corporation.*

A corporation is managed, directly or indirectly, by its shareholders, board of directors, and officers.

A. SHAREHOLDERS

As owners, the shareholders have the right to control the corporation.

1. Extent of Management Control by Shareholders

As a practical matter, the control of the shareholders is generally limited to voting at shareholders' meetings to elect directors. In this sense, shareholders indirectly determine the management policies of the business. Also, they may vote at shareholders' meetings to amend bylaws, approve shareholder resolutions, or vote on so-called extraordinary corporate matters. Extraordinary matters include the sale of corporate assets outside the regular course of the corporation's business or the merger or dissolution of the corporation.

2. Meetings of Shareholders

To have legal effect, action by the shareholders must ordinarily be taken at a regular or special meeting.

(a) REGULAR MEETINGS. The time and place of regular or stated meetings are usually prescribed by the articles of incorporation or bylaws. Notice to shareholders of such meetings is ordinarily not required, but it is usually given as a matter of good business practice. Some statutes require that notice be given of all meetings.

(b) SPECIAL MEETINGS. Generally, notice must be given specifying the subject matter of special meetings. Unless otherwise prescribed, special meetings are called by the directors. It is sometimes provided that a special meeting may be called by a certain percentage of shareholders.[1] Notice of the day, hour, and place of a special meeting must be given to all shareholders. The notice must include a statement of the nature of the business to be transacted. No other business may be transacted at such a meeting.

(c) QUORUM. A valid meeting requires the presence of a quorum of the voting shareholders. A **quorum** is the minimum number of persons (shareholders or persons authorized to vote a stated proportion of the voting stock) required to transact business. If a quorum is present, a majority of those present may act with respect to any matter, unless there is an express requirement of a greater affirmative vote.

When a meeting opens with a quorum, the quorum is generally not broken if shareholders leave the meeting and those remaining are not sufficient to constitute a quorum.

3. Action Without Meeting

A number of statutes provide for corporate action by shareholders without holding a meeting. The RMBCA provides that "action required or permitted by this Act to be taken at a shareholders' meeting may be taken without a meeting if the action is taken by all shareholders entitled to vote on the action."[2] The action must be evidenced by a written consent describing the action taken, signed by all the shareholders entitled to vote on the action, and delivered to the corporation for inclusion in the minutes.

B. DIRECTORS

The management of a corporation is usually under the control of a board of directors elected by the shareholders. Most states now

---

[1] NY Bus. Corp. Law § 603.

[2] RMBCA § 7.04 (a).

permit the number of directors to be fixed by the bylaws. Many specify that the board of directors shall consist of not less than three directors. A few authorize one or more directors.[3] Professional corporation legislation often authorizes or is interpreted as authorizing a one- or two-person board of directors.

4. Qualifications

Eligibility for membership on a board of directors is determined by statute, articles of incorporation, or bylaws. In the absence of a contrary provision, any person (including a nonresident, a minor, or a person who is not a shareholder) is eligible for membership. Bylaws may require that a director own stock in the corporation, although this requirement is not ordinarily imposed.

5. Powers of Directors

The board of directors has authority to manage the corporation. The court will not interfere with the board's discretion in the absence of (a) illegal conduct or (b) fraud harming the rights of creditors, shareholders, or the corporation.

The board of directors may enter into any contract or transaction necessary to carry out the business for which the corporation was formed. The board may appoint officers and other agents to act for the company, or it may appoint several of its own members as an executive committee to act for the board between board meetings.

Broad delegation of authority may, however, run the risk of being treated as an unlawful abdication of the board's management power.

In the *Boston Athletic Association* case the court considered whether the board improperly delegated authority to an officer.

Figure 50-1　Powers of Directors

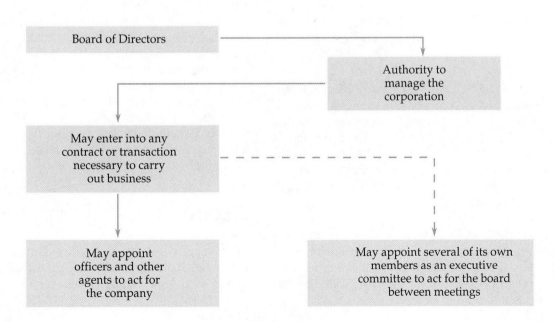

3 Del. Code § 141 (b). See Also ABA MBCA § 36.

BOSTON ATHLETIC ASSOCIATION v INTERNATIONAL MARATHON, INC.

292 Mass 356, 467 NE2d 58 (1984)

On April 27, 1981, the board of the Boston Athletic Association (BAA), a non-profit corporation whose principal activity is the presentation of an annual road race (the Boston Marathon), approved the following proposal:

That William T. Cloney, as President of the Association, be and hereby is authorized and directed to negotiate and to execute in the name of and in behalf of this Association such agreements as he deems in the best interest of the Association for the perpetuation, sponsorship, or underwriting of the Boston A.A. Marathon.

There was no mention at this meeting of hiring an exclusive promoter. In the past all sponsorship and broadcast coverage contracts were negotiated between Cloney and individual sponsors. On September 23, 1981, Cloney executed an agreement on behalf of the BAA with Marshall Medoff, an attorney and president of IMI (a business corporation headed by Medoff). The agreement designated Medoff as the exclusive promoter of the Marathon, with the BAA transferring all right to the use of the Boston Marathon name and logos to IMI. The agreement's financial terms were extremely favorable to IMI. The agreement was automatically renewable year to year, at the option of IMI, with no way for the BAA to end the relationship. A majority of the Board members learned of the existence of the agreement in late February, 1982. By a vote taken on September 9, 1982, the board declared the agreement to be beyond the authorization vested in Cloney on April 27, 1981. The board brought an action to have the agreement set aside. IMI defended that Cloney had been given authority to make the contract with IMI, so the contract bound the corporation. From a judgment for the BAA, IMI (Medoff) appealed.

LYNCH, J. . . . Whether the board intended by its vote of April 27, 1981, to confer upon Cloney the authority to enter into the sponsorship agreement with IMI, that contract is void. The board of directors of a corporation cannot delegate total control of the corporation to an individual officer. . . . Neither can it delegate authority which is so broad that it enables the officer to bind the corporation to extraordinary commitments or significantly to encumber the principal asset or function of the corporation.

The contract seriously encumbers the manner in which the BAA may conduct the Marathon. The BAA is obliged to produce the race in its traditional form and to pay the entire bill. But it is not entitled to "present" the race. That right, as well as the right to use the name and logo of the BAA, belongs to IMI or its assignee. The BAA may not use its own logo in any way "inconsistent" with IMI's rights pursuant to the contract. The right to enter into sponsorship agreements belongs exclusively to IMI, although the BAA can reasonably withhold its approval. The BAA may not make independent agreements without written permission from IMI. Finally, the contract between IMI and the BAA is automatically renewable at the option of IMI.

Under the plain language of the agreement, there is no way for the BAA to end the relationship.

In return for carrying out its obligations under the contract, the BAA is to be paid a $400,000 fee. Any revenues in excess of $400,000 are directly payable to IMI, and there is no limit to the number of sponsors who may be solicited or to the amount of money which may be raised. The annual fee is to be paid prior to the actual running of the race, but if the Marathon should not be run for some reason, the fee is to be returned to IMI.

According to the traditional principles of corporate governance, the board of governors of the BAA does not have the power to delegate to an individual officer authority to enter into a contract which so totally encumbers the most significant purpose of the BAA, the presentation of the Marathon. The by-laws of the BAA indicate that its organization and operation are, in all material respects, the same as those of a Massachusetts business corporation. Principles of corporate governance with respect to the power of the board of governors to delegate authority to individual officers are applicable to profit and nonprofit corporations alike. . . .

Corporate officers are generally empowered, by delegation of authority of the board of directors, with general managerial functions. They are responsible for the day to day operation of the corporation. Courts are usually flexible and accommodating in allowing boards to delegate authority as necessary or expedient. But certain powers cannot be delegated generally. Certain transactions require specific authorization by the board in order to be valid. For example, in *Stoneman v Fox Film Corp.*, 295 Mass. 419, 4 NE2d 63 (1936), the court found that the president, although authorized to act as a general manager on behalf of a film company, was not authorized to commit the company to the purchase of a theatre, an extraordinary transaction which involved a large financial commitment. The court indicated that delegation of authority to conduct such business was a "course of conduct manifestly . . . unusual and extraordinary in the management of a corporation." It was an abdication of "the entire control" of the corporation and "the functions of directors may not be abdicated." . . .

In light of these principles, it is clear that if the delegation to Cloney was so broad as to enable him to commit the BAA to an extraordinary contract which encumbered substantially all its assets, the board would have delegated away control of the very essence of the BAA's corporate existence. . . . It is the obligation of the board of governors to oversee the presentation of the Marathon, not to surrender virtually complete control of the event to another organization. The fact that the agreement is automatically renewable and thus potentially perpetual demonstrates the pervasive nature of the limitation on the main purpose of the BAA. Authority to make such a contract was beyond the power of the board to delegate to Cloney.

Furthermore, the contract between IMI and the BAA is especially vulnerable because it is antithetical to the BAA's nature as a nonprofit corporation inasmuch as this agreement turns the solicitation of sponsors from a way to support the Marathon to a way for IMI to make a profit. It is entirely inconsistent with the nonprofit nature of the organization to permit such a substantial segment of the revenue earning capacity of the Marathon to be used as a vehicle for personal gain. . . .

Although the promotion contract between IMI and the BAA is unenforceable, nevertheless as the BAA concedes IMI is entitled to recover the fair value of its services. . . .

[Judgment affirmed]

QUESTIONS

1. May a board of directors delegate control of a corporation to one officer?
2. Was the September 23, 1981, contract negotiated by Cloney and Medoff fair or unfair? Explain.

6. Conflict of Interests

A director is disqualified from taking part in corporate action with respect to a matter in which the director has an undisclosed conflicting interest. Since it cannot be known how the other directors would have acted if they had known of the conflict of interests, the corporation generally may avoid any transaction because of the director's secret disqualification.

A number of states provide by statute that the conflict of interests of a director does not impair the transaction or contract entered into or authorized by the board of directors if the disqualified director disclosed the interest and if the contract or transaction is fair and reasonable with respect to the corporation. Thus, a director may lend money to a corporation if the board of directors is informed of the transaction and the terms approximate the market rate for businesses with similar credit ratings.

The *Dunbar* case involved a conflict of interest.

DUNBAR v WILLIAMS
(La App) 554 So 2d 56 (1989)

Childs E. Dunbar, Jr. was a minority shareholder of Algiers Ironworks and Dry Dock Co., Inc. (AIW). He brought a shareholder's derivative action against the majority shareholders to recover damages on behalf of the corporation, AIW. Thomas S. Williams was the president and director of AIW. His wife served as a director of AIW. Mr. and Mrs. Williams also owned Tower Crane Co. Tower used AIW's phones, address, land for storage of cranes, and some personnel but Tower did not pay for them. Tower sold two cranes to AIW, and AIW's board did not consider or approve these transactions. Williams personally bought the yacht PATTY JEAN. He testified that work valued at $43,303 was expended on the vessel by AIW and that over $50,000 worth of business entertaining on behalf of AIW was conducted on the vessel. Mr. and Mrs. Williams charged $17,583 on an AIW credit card. Williams admitted that $4,571.45 was not business-related. Williams also admitted that $4,590.56 in gasoline charges to AIW were not business-related. The trial court issued a judgment against Williams for $9,162, reflecting these two admissions, and the minority shareholders appealed.

BARRY, J. . . . [A Louisiana statute provides that]

No contract or transaction between a corporation and one or more of its directors or officers, or between a corporation and any other business . . . in which one or more of its directors or officers are directors or officers or have a financial interest, shall be void or voidable solely for this reason . . . or solely because his or their votes were counted for such purpose, if:

1. The material facts as to his interest and as to the contract or transaction were disclosed or known to the board of directors or the committee, and the board or committee in good faith authorized the contract or transaction by a vote sufficient for such purpose without counting the vote of the interested director or directors; or

2. The material facts as to his interest and as to the contract or transaction were disclosed or known to the shareholders entitled to vote thereon, and the contract or transaction was approved in good faith by vote of the shareholders; or

3. The contract or transaction was fair as to the corporation as of the time it was authorized, approved or ratified by the board of directors, committee, or shareholders.

The questioned officer or director has the burden to establish that the transaction was fair and in good faith, essentially that it was at arms length. . . . *Noe v Roussel*, 310 So 2d 806, 818-19 (La 1975). The Noe court explained: "[T]he agent or fiduciary may not take even the slightest advantage, but must zealously, diligently and honestly guard and champion the rights of his principal. . . ."

. . . The two crane purchases by Williams (as president of AIW) from his company (Tower) were not authorized by AIW's Board, hence, both purchases fail the test of [the statute]. . . . [On rehearing, May 9, 1989, on the issue of the Tower crane transactions, the district court was reversed. On second rehearing on the crane transactions held on November 16, 1989, the amount owed AIW was set at $15,000, which represented the profit gained by Tower from the sale to AIW.]

The use of AIW's premises, services, and personnel by Tower was clearly improper. AIW received no payment or discernible benefit and Williams' actions on behalf of Tower violated his fiduciary duty to AIW. . . .

We therefore remand for the trial court to conduct a hearing to determine the value of the various benefits and to enter a judgment in favor of AIW and against Williams. . . .

Williams personally bought the PATTY JEAN for $5,000 in August or September, 1977, apparently in very poor condition. Williams testified that he informally told [members of the board of directors] Dr. and Mrs. Grundmeyer and Edgar Williams that he intended to use the yacht to entertain customers and they approved. Williams did not discuss the matter with Dunbar, the other Board member. . . .

The trial court adjusted all of Williams' estimates amounts spent to refurbish, repair, and maintain the yacht] to reflect the costs of a regular customer and concluded the work should be valued at $43,303. We have no basis to find manifest error in that valuation.

As for the alleged benefits AIW received from the PATTY JEAN, twenty-one fishing trips were made entertaining approximately 152 people. Plaintiffs complain that not all of those trips were business related. Dunbar acknowledged the necessity for AIW to entertain, but maintained it would have been cheaper to charter a boat.

Jack Faulkner, an expert on overnight charters in the Gulf Coast area, testified that the standard charter fee for a vessel similar to the PATTY JEAN for a three-day fishing trip would be $125 per person per day with a four person minimum (not including alcohol) or $1,500. According to Williams, a trip cost approximately $600 to $800 and he computed the value of all the trips at over $50,000.

We disagree that a promotional trip is not business related, or that a guest unrelated to the shipping industry constitutes nonbusiness usage. It appears that the value of the trips fairly approximates the expense incurred by AIW to repair the vessel.

We conclude there was no fiduciary breach by Williams or manifest error in the trial court's finding that use of the PATTY JEAN by AIW in exchange for repairs, maintenance and refurbishing was reasonable and carried out in good faith. . . .

Plaintiffs claim the defendants breached their fiduciary duties by giving themselves unearned compensation in the form of . . . fringe benefits. . . .

The questioned benefits are (a) American Express charges (b) gas charges (c) charges at service stations, restaurants and food stores (d) company cars (e) home phone bills (f) Grundmeyer's country club bills and Williams' carnival club dues.

Plaintiffs contend those personal expenses were paid by AIW and are not business related, and the failure to keep records as to the business purpose constitutes a fiduciary breach. There is no question that AIW paid the expenses and the defendants must show their connection to AIW's business.

Mr. and Mrs. Williams, according to two ledger sheets in evidence, charged $17,583.97 on an AIW American Express account from February 1980 through August 1985. Of that amount Williams admitted $4,571.45 was not business related. As to gasoline charges from 1980 to 1984, Williams admitted that he or his family charged $4,590.56 which was not business related. The trial court judgment against Williams for $9,162.01, [the total of these] two sums, was not appealed and is final.

As for Williams' carnival club dues, . . . a local businessman testified for the defense that he considered them to be legitimate business expenses. . . .

Carnival dues are not, ipso facto, business related. Nor is there proof that Williams' membership in a carnival organization produced any revenue to AIW. The record and briefs are unclear as to which organizations Williams belonged to and at what costs to AIW.

We remand to the trial court to determine the amounts paid by AIW for carnival club dues and to enter the appropriate judgment in favor of AIW and against Williams.

[Judgment affirmed in part; reversed and action remanded in part]

QUESTIONS

1. Did a state law set guidelines to validate a corporate transaction in which an officer or director had a personal interest?
2. Was the board of directors required to approve the crane purchases in order to satisfy the state conflict of interest law?
3. Review the ethical principles set forth in Figure 1 of the preliminary pages of this book and express an opinion on the ethics of the following conduct: (1) sale of the cranes to AIW; (2) use of AIW facilities and personnel by Tower Crane Co.; (3) AIW's payment to refurbish the yacht PATTY JEAN; and (4) AIW's payment of fringe benefits, including carnival club dues.

7. Meetings of Directors

Action by directors is ordinarily taken at a meeting of the board of directors. Bylaws sometimes require the meeting to be held at a particular place. Most states expressly provide that the directors may meet either in or out of the state of incorporation. Directors who participate without objection in a meeting irregularly held as to place or time other than as specified in the bylaws cannot object later. Generally, a director is not allowed to vote by proxy.

Most states permit action to be taken by the board of directors without the holding of an actual meeting. It is required when such action is taken that it be set forth in writing and signed by all the directors.

8. Liability of Directors

In dealing with the corporation, the directors act in a fiduciary capacity. It is to their care that the stockholders have entrusted the control of the corporate property and the management of the business.

(a) THE BUSINESS JUDGMENT RULE. Courts recognize that the decisions of corporate directors often involve the weighing and balancing of legal, ethical, commercial, promotional, public relations, and other factors. Accordingly, courts will not sit in judgment on the wisdom of decisions made by directors. If the directors have acted in good faith on the basis of adequate information, courts will not enjoin the course of action taken by the directors. Moreover, even though such action causes loss to the corporation, the directors will not be held personally liable for it. This principle is called the **business judgment rule**.

(1) The Traditional Rule. Courts apply the business judgment rule as a presumption that in making a business decision the directors acted (a) on an informed basis, (b) in good faith, and (c) in the honest belief that the action taken was in the best interest of the corporation.[4] The party challenging the directors' actions has the burden of proving that the directors did not act on an informed basis or in good faith or that the directors acted in self-interest rather than in the interest of the corporation.[5]

(2) Application in Corporate Control Transactions. When a corporation receives a takeover bid, the target board of directors may tend to take actions that are in their own interest and not in the interests of the shareholders. Courts have recognized the potential for director self-interest in this situation.

In the *Smith v Van Gorkom* case the directors relied upon the business judgment rule to shield themselves from individual liability in a lawsuit charging that the directors did not act on an "informed basis" in accepting and recommending a merger.

SMITH v VAN GORKOM
(Del) 488 A2d 858 (1985)

On September 13, Jerome Van Gorkom as chairman and chief executive officer of Trans Union Inc., a holding company in the railcar leasing business, arranged a meeting with Jay Pritzker, a well-known takeover specialist and a social acquaintance, to determine his interest in acquiring Trans Union. On Thursday, September 18, Pritzker made an offer of $55 per share (a price suggested by Van Gorkom) with a decision to be made by the Board no later than Sunday, September 21. On Friday, Van Gorkom called a special meeting of the board of directors for noon the following day; no agenda was

---

4 Alford v Shaw, 318 NC 289, 349 SE2d 41 (1986).
5 Gaillard v Natmos Co. 208 Cal App 3d 1250, 256 Cal Rptr 702 (1989).

announced. At the directors' meeting Van Gorkom made a 20-minute oral analysis of the merger transaction, showed that the company was having difficulty generating sufficient income, and discussed his meeting with Pritzker and the reasons for the meeting. Copies of the proposed merger agreement were delivered too late to be studied before or during the meeting. No consultants or investment advisers were called upon to support the merger price of $55 per share. The merger was approved at the end of the two-hour meeting. Certain shareholders brought a class action suit against the directors, contending that the board's decision was not the product of informed business judgment. The directors replied that their good faith decision was shielded by the business judgment rule. From a decision for the directors, the shareholders appealed.

HORSEY, J. . . . Under Delaware law, the business judgment rule is the offspring of the fundamental principle, codified in 8 *Del. C.* § 141(a), that the business and affairs of a Delaware corporation are managed by or under its board of directors. In carrying out their managerial roles, directors are charged with an unyielding fiduciary duty to the corporation and its shareholders. The business judgment rule exists to protect and promote the full and free exercise of the managerial power granted to Delaware directors. The rule itself "is a presumption that in making a business decision, the directors of a corporation acted on an informed basis, in good faith and in the honest belief that the action taken was in the best interests of the company." *Aronson [v. Lewis*, Del. Supr., 473 A2d 805,] 812. Thus, the party attacking a board decision as uninformed must rebut the presumption that its business judgment was an informed one.

The determination of whether a business judgment is an informed one turns on whether the directors have informed themselves "prior to making a business decision, of all material information reasonably available to them.". . . .

A director's duty to exercise an informed business judgment is in the nature of a duty of care, as distinguished from a duty of loyalty. . . .

The standard of care applicable to a director's duty of care has also been recently restated by this Court. In *Aronson, supra*, we stated:

While the Delaware cases use a variety of terms to describe the applicable standard of care, our analysis satisfies us that under the business judgment rule director liability is predicated upon concepts of gross negligence.

473 A2d at 812.

We again confirm that view. We think the concept of gross negligence is also the proper standard for determining whether a business judgment reached by a board of directors was an informed one.

In the specific context of a proposed merger of domestic corporations, a director has a duty under 8 *Del. C.* 251(b), along with his fellow directors, to act in an informed and deliberate manner in determining whether to approve an agreement of merger before submitting the proposal to the stockholders. Certainly in the merger context, a director may not abdicate that duty by leaving to the shareholders alone the decision to approve or disapprove the agreement. . . .

It is against those standards that the conduct of the directors of Trans Union must be tested. . . regarding their exercise of an informed business judgment in voting to approve the Pritzker merger proposal.

. . . The issue of whether the directors reached an informed decision to "sell" the Company on September 20, 1980 must be determined only upon the basis of the information then reasonably available to the directors and relevant to their decision to accept the Pritzker merger proposal. . . .

On the record before us, we must conclude that the Board of Directors did not reach an informed business judgment on September 20, 1980 in voting to "sell" the Company for $55 per share pursuant to the Pritzker cash-out merger proposal. Our reasons, in summary, are as follows:

The directors (1) did not adequately inform themselves as to Van Gorkom's role in forcing the "sale" of the Company and in establishing the per share purchase price; (2) were uninformed as to the intrinsic value of the Company; and (3) given these circumstances, at a minimum, were grossly negligent in approving the "sale" of the Company upon two hours' consideration, without prior notice, and without the exigency of a crisis or emergency.

As has been noted, the Board based its September 20 decision to approve the cash-out merger primarily on Van Gorkom's representations. None of the directors, other than Van Gorkom and Chelberg, had any prior knowledge that the purpose of the meeting was to propose a cash-out merger of Trans Union. No members of Senior Management were present, other than Chelberg, Romans and Peterson; and the latter two had only learned of the proposed sale an hour earlier. Both general counsel Moore and former general counsel Browder attended the meeting, but were equally uninformed as to the purpose of the meeting and the documents to be acted upon.

Without any documents before them concerning the proposed transaction, the members of the Board were required to rely entirely upon Van Gorkom's 20-minute oral presentation of the proposal. No written summary of the terms of the merger was presented; the directors were given no documentation to support the adequacy of $55 price per share for sale of the Company; and the Board had before it nothing more than Van Gorkom's statement of his understanding of the substance of an agreement which he admittedly had never read, nor which any member of the Board had ever seen. . . .

We hold, therefore, that the Trial Court committed reversible error in applying the business judgment rule in favor of the director defendants in this case.

On remand, the Court of Chancery shall conduct an evidentiary hearing to determine the fair value of the shares represented by the plaintiffs' class, based on the intrinsic value of Trans Union on September 20, 1980. . . . Thereafter, an award of damages may be entered to the extent that the fair value of Trans Union exceeds $55 per share.

[Judgment reversed and action remanded]

QUESTIONS

1. Did the court hold that the business judgment rule shielded the directors from personal liability in this case?
2. Upon what facts did the court rely in reaching its decision in this case?
3. State the applicable standard of care for determining whether a board of directors' decision was an informed one?

(3) Protection of Directors. In the wake of court decisions holding directors personally liable for damages for gross negligence and in the wake of the resulting general reluctance of individuals to serve as directors, states have passed statutes to protect directors. The aim of the various state laws is essentially the same: to reduce the risk of personal liability for directors who act in good faith when their decisions are challenged. The laws permit a corporation, by a stockholder-approved amendment to its charter or certificate of incorporation, to protect its directors from monetary liability for duty of care violations (gross negligence), provided they have not acted in bad faith, breached their duty of loyalty, or gained an improper personal benefit.[6] The laws provide for indemnification and advancement of expenses.

(b) ACTION AGAINST DIRECTOR. Actions against directors should be brought by the corporation. If the corporation fails to act, as is the case when the directors alleged to be liable control the corporation, shareholders may bring the action in a representative capacity for the corporation.[7]

(c) REMOVAL OF DIRECTOR. Ordinarily, directors are removed by the vote of the shareholders. In some states, the board of directors may remove a director and elect a successor on the ground that the director removed (1) did not accept office; (2) failed to satisfy the qualifications for office; (3) was continually absent from the state without a leave of absence granted by the board, generally for a period of six months or more; (4) was discharged in bankruptcy; (5) was convicted of a felony; (6) was unable to perform the duties of director because of any illness or disability, generally for a period of six months or more; or (7) has been judicially declared of unsound mind.[8]

The RMBCA provides for removal of directors "with or without cause" by a majority vote of the shareholders, unless the articles of incorporation provide that directors may be removed only for cause.[9] Directors may always be voted out of office at a regular meeting of shareholders held for the election of directors.

C. OFFICERS, AGENTS, AND EMPLOYEES

Corporations generally have a president, at least one vice president, a secretary, a treasurer, and frequently a chief executive officer (CEO). The duties of these officers are generally set forth in the corporation's bylaws. The duty of the secretary to keep minutes of the proceedings of shareholders and directors is commonly included. Corporation codes generally expressly permit the same person to be both secretary and treasurer. In larger corporations, there is often a recording secretary and a corresponding secretary.

Sometimes the officers are elected by the shareholders, but usually they are appointed by the board of directors. The RMBCA follows the general pattern of providing for the appointment of officers by the board of directors.[10] Ordinarily, no particular formality is required to make such appointments. Unless prohibited, a director may hold an executive office.

Officers ordinarily hire the employees and agents of the corporation.

---

[6] See Del. Code § 102(b)(7) (1987); NY Bus. Corp. Law § 721-723 (1987); Ohio Gen. Corp. Law § 1701.59 (1986); Ind. Bus. Corp. Law, Ch 35, § 1 (e) (1986); and Mo. Gen. Bus. Corp. Law 351.355 § 2, 7.

[7] John v John (Wis App) 450 NW2d 795 (1989).

[8] See California Corporations Code § 807, recognizing grounds (1), (2), (5), and (7).

[9] RMBCA § 8.08 (a).

[10] RMBCA § 8.40 (a).

9. Powers of Officers

The officers of a corporation are its agents. Consequently, their powers are controlled by the laws of agency.[11] As in the case of any other agency, the third person has the burden of proving that a particular officer had the authority that such officer purported to have.

The fact that the officer or employee acting on behalf of the corporation is a major shareholder does not give the officer or employee any greater agency powers. Moreover, the person dealing with the officer or employee is charged with knowledge of any limitation on authority contained in the recorded corporate charter or articles of incorporation.

When the nature of the transaction is unusual, that unusual nature should alert a third person to the necessity of specific authorization from the corporation.

(a) PRESIDENT. It is sometimes held that, in the absence of some limitation on authority, the president of a corporation has by virtue of that office the authority to act as agent on behalf of the corporation within the scope of the business in which the corporation is empowered to engage. It has also been held, however, that the president has such broad powers only when the president is the general manager of the corporation. In some instances a corporation may have a president and chief executive officer (CEO). This officer has authority to exercise personal judgment and discretion in the administrative and executive functions of the corporation as endowed by the corporation's bylaws and the resolutions of the board of directors. Where a corporation utilizes both a CEO and a president, the CEO is ordinarily the officer entrusted with the broader decisional powers, while the president is the executing officer. The president does not have authority by virtue of that office to make a contract that, because of its unusual character, would require action by the board of directors or shareholders.

The president cannot make a contract to fix long-term or unusual contracts of employment, to release a claim of the corporation, to promise that the corporation will later repurchase shares issued to a subscriber, or to mortgage a corporate property.[12]

It is ordinarily held that the president of a business corporation is not authorized to execute commercial paper in the name of the corporation. However, the president may do so when authorized by the board of directors to borrow money for the corporation.

(b) OTHER OFFICERS AND EMPLOYEES. The authority of corporate employees and other officers, such as secretary or treasurer, is generally limited to the duties of their offices. However, the authority may be extended by the conduct of the corporation, in accordance with the general principles governing apparent authority based on the conduct of the principal. An unauthorized act may, of course, be ratified. The authority of the general manager of the corporation is determined by principles of ordinary agency law.

10. Liability Relating to Fiduciary Duties

The relationship of officers to the corporation, like that of directors, is a fiduciary one. Because corporate officers devote all or most of their time to a corporation's business and receive a salary as officers, the fiduciary duties are more extensive than those of directors who do not work for the corporation on a daily basis and also receive little or no salary.[13] Officers, because of their accessibility to corporate information developed in the pursuit of their daily duties on behalf of the corporation, have an obligation to inform the directors of material information relating to the business.

---

[11] IFC Credit Corp v Nuova Pasta Co. Inc. (ND Ill) 815 F Supp 268 (1993).

[12] Schmidt v Farm Credit Services (CA10 Kas) 977 F2d 511 (1992).

[13] Fletcher Cyc. Corp. §991 (perm ed 1986).

Officers have an obligation to not make any secret financial gain at the expense of the corporation. Because of their level of knowledge of the business, officer-directors have a high fiduciary duty to the corporation.

(a) CORPORATE OPPORTUNITIES.

If an officer diverts a corporate opportunity, the corporation may recover from the officer the profits of which the corporation has been deprived.[14] An opportunity that would be advantageous to the corporation must first be offered to the corporation before an officer or director, who owes a fiduciary duty to the corporation, can take advantage of the opportunity. Full disclosure is required. Only if the opportunity is rejected by a majority of disinterested directors may the officer then take advantage of the opportunity. Thus, when two officers, unknown to the board of directors, purchased in their own names a building which their corporation was negotiating to purchase, they were held liable for usurping of this corporate opportunity.[15]

Officers may avail themselves of all opportunities lying outside the field of their duties as officers, when business opportunities come to them in an individual capacity.[16]

(b) SECRET PROFITS.

Officers are liable to the corporation for secret profits made in connection with or at the expense of the business of the corporation.

In the *Enstar Group Inc.* case, the court was faced with determining whether or not secret profits were made, and, if so, what measure of damages should be applied.

ENSTAR GROUP INC. v GRASSGREEN
(MD Ala) 812 F Supp 1562 (1993)

Richard Grassgreen was Executive Vice President and later President and Chief Operating Officer of Kinder-Care Inc., the largest proprietary provider of child care in the country. The company was restructured in 1989 and changed its name to the Enstar Group Inc. Between 1985 and 1990, while Grassgreen was the corporation's investment manager, he retained certain fees for himself. When the corporation discovered this, it sued him to recover any compensation paid him over the five-year period during which the secret payments were made, and it sought punitive damages. Greengrass defended that his conduct caused little if any damage to the corporation since the corporation did not lose any money on any of the investments for which he received personal fees.

ALBRITTON, D. J. . . . Michael Milken worked for Drexel Burnham Lambert, Inc. ("Drexel"), in the 1980s. Milken was an expert at raising large sums of money. Milken's primary method of raising cash was through the issuance of "junk bonds."* Much of this money was raised to facilitate a series of corporate takeovers that occurred in the 1980's. When an individual or corporation sought to take over another corporation, financing was normally needed to fund that deal. Investment bankers,

---

[14] Bankers Trust Co. v Bernstein, 169 App Div 400, 563 NYS2d 821 (1991).

[15] Case v Murdock (SD) 488 NW2d 885 (1992).

[16] Hill v Southeastern Floor Covering (Miss) 596 So 2d 874 (1992).

such as Milken, would then arrange for the financing for the takeover. Because so many takeover deals never went through, Milken developed a procedure whereby money wasn't actually raised, initially. Rather, Milken would merely make sure that there were individuals or entities lined up who agreed to finance the takeover if the deal actually [took place]. These agreements to fund the deals were called commitments. In return for committing to the investments, both for the deals that went through and for the deals that did not go through, Milken would pay a fee to those individuals or entities that had made the commitments. These payments were called commitment fees. These fees were normally 0.75% of the amount committed. . .

* The bonds were called "junk" because they were considered too risky to be investment quality bonds. While the risk associated with these bonds was significantly higher than other types of investments, the returns were also significantly higher. . . .

Grassgreen was an officer and director of Enstar (previously Kinder-Care) at the time the actions complained of took place. The first step, therefore, in determining the issues presented is to consider the nature of that relationship. . . .

Fletcher states that, "The unbending rule is that the director must act in the utmost good faith, and this good faith forbids placing himself in a position where his individual interest clashes with his duty to his corporation." *Fletcher Cyc Corp § 838, P. 181 (Perm Ed).*

These are not obscure rules of law that must be found by lawyers and judges for the purposes of lawsuits. They are basic concepts of our economic system which are known, or instinctively assumed, by all who participate in it. They are there for the protection of all who answer the invitation to invest their money in corporate America. Whether it be a seasoned investor of private funds, a manager of the investment of retirees' pension funds, or an unsophisticated occasional investor of small sums who hopes that the free enterprise system will provide for a better future, the investor assumes that these rules will be followed.

The free enterprise system does not guarantee success in business, and neither does it guarantee that investing one's funds on the stock of a corporation will be risk free. An investment in stock assumes the many risks of the marketplace, from changes in technology, to losing out to competition, to problems resulting from bad business decisions by poor, but honest, management. One risk which the investor should not assume, however, is that the officers and directors who have accepted the responsibility of using that investor's money might put their personal interests ahead of that of the corporation. For this country's economic system to work in the area of corporate investment, the investor must be assured that the corporation's officers and directors will put the interests of the corporation first and that their decisions will not be clouded in any way by competing personal interests. If an officer and director violates that trust which is placed in him, and breaks the rules which govern his position of trust, the law requires that he must answer for that breach.

THE BREACH

Richard Grassgreen breached his duty as an officer and director by placing his personal interests ahead of the interests of his corporation.

In 1985 and 1986, Grassgreen was Kinder-Care's Executive Vice President and then its President and Chief Operating Officer, as well as being a director. He also served as the corporation's investment manager. With millions of dollars of corporate funds available for investment, he was the person who decided where those funds should go. The law required him to make those decisions wholly for the benefit of the corporation, with no thought to personal gain. That rule was part of the bargain which investors made when they bought stock in the corporation, and that is the rule which Grassgreen consciously broke.

On several different occasions, Grassgreen was paid money, and kept it personally, in exchange for investing, or at least committing to invest, the corporation's funds in junk bonds sold to finance corporate takeovers. On other occasions, he was able to take personal advantage of lucrative investment opportunities because of his handling of the corporation's funds.

Investing corporate funds in junk bonds with high interest rates certainly may be a legitimate act by an investment manager. It is the manager's duty, however, to see that his corporation receives the full benefit of the transaction, and this would include fees paid for making a commitment to invest the corporate funds. The president of a corporation has no more right to personally receive hundreds of thousands of dollars for commitments to invest millions of his corporation's dollars than the company's purchasing agent has to take kickbacks from a firm from whom he buys supplies. The principle is the same: the person's duty to the corporation must be exercised without thought of personal gain. . . .

FORFEITURE AND RECOVERY OF COMPENSATION

Enstar claims that Grassgreen should be required to forfeit and repay all compensation which he received from Enstar during the period following his initial misappropriation of commitment fees that rightfully belonged to the corporation, in March, 1985, and up to the time he was forced to resign in October, 1990.

Because of the legal principles discussed above, cases have held that a corporate officer is not entitled to compensation for services during a period in which that officer engages in activities constituting a breach of the officer's duty to loyalty to the corporation. Accordingly, an officer who is found to have engaged in such conduct may be required to forfeit all compensation which he received during such time, including salary and bonuses. . . .

Grassgreen portrays his conduct as having caused very little, if any, actual damage to the corporation. He points out that the corporation did not lose money on any of the investments for which he received personal commitment fees, but, in fact, made money. He also points out that all of these commitment fees have now been paid over to the corporation. Accordingly, he says that it would be grossly inequitable for the corporation to receive his services for the entire period of time in question without paying him any compensation whatsoever for those services.

Grassgreen's argument ignores the basic reasons behind the rules of law involved in this issue. Damage to the corporation is not required to be shown, because it is not relevant to this issue. Who knows what would have happened to this corporation if Grassgreen had honestly fulfilled his duty to put the corporation, rather than himself, first? Could he, perhaps, have found more profitable investments if he had not been personally paid money for making the ones he did? If the commitment fees had been paid to the corporation at the time they were paid to [him], rather than years later, would the corporation have been able to change its economic future? We know that the corporation is now in bankruptcy. Enstar did not attempt to prove at trial that its bankruptcy was caused by these wrongful acts of Grassgreen. This would certainly require speculation. If Grassgreen had been a faithful servant to his corporation, however, such speculation would not even arise. . . .

This court considers it to be of crucial importance to the economic well-being of this country for corporate officers and directors to understand without question that in the discharge of the duties of their offices they must subordinate their personal interests to the interests of the corporation which they serve. This court will not hesitate to enforce that duty as forcefully as is possible. It is not a duty concerning which there should be any equivocation.

Richard Grassgreen breached his duty flagrantly. He elected to profit personally by the way in which he invested the funds of his corporation, which he held in trust. He did so in secret, without advising his Board of Directors and stockholders, who were paying him well and who had the right to assume that he was making all investment decisions wholly in the interest of the corporation and without any thought to personal gain. Grassgreen was in breach of the duties which he owed to his corporation from the time he initially decided to put his personal financial interests first and keep his corporation ignorant of that fact, in 1985, until he was forced to resign in 1990 as a result of his fraudulent activities.

In the exercise of its discretion based on all the circumstances presented by the evidence of this case, the court is of the opinion that Richard Grassgreen should forfeit all salary, bonuses, and other compensation which were paid to him by his corporation while he was in breach of his duties. . . . Therefore, the court will enter judgment against the Defendant on the Plaintiff's claim for forfeiture and recovery in the amount of $5,197,663.30. . . .

[So ordered]

QUESTIONS

1. What are "commitment fees"?
2. Appraise the validity of the following statement: "Since the corporation did not lose money as a result of Grassgreen's actions, Grassgreen did not violate any duty to the corporation, and he certainly should not forfeit all of his earned compensation for the entire five-year period."
3. Did Grassgreen violate any of the ethical principles set forth in Figure 1 in the Preface?

11. Agents and Employees

The authority, rights, and liabilities of an agent or employee of a corporation are governed by the same rules as those applicable when the principal or employer is a natural person. The authority of corporate employees also is governed by general agency principles.

The fact that a person is acting on behalf of a corporation does not act as a shield from the liability that would be imposed for such acts if done on behalf of a natural person.[17]

D. LIABILITY

Limited liability is a major reason for incorporating. However, management is not free from all civil and criminal liability simply because the corporate form is used.

12. Liability of Management to Third Persons

Officers and managers of a corporation are not liable for the economic consequence of their advice on third persons, even if they cause the corporation to refuse to deal with or to break its contract with such third persons, as long as

---

[17] Smith v NiteLife Inc. (Ky) 777 SW2d 912 (1989).

the officers and managers acted in good faith to advance the interests of the corporation.

Ordinarily, the management of a corporation (its directors, officers, and executive employees) is not liable to third persons for the effect of their management or advice on such third persons. The liability of a director or officer for misconduct may usually be enforced only by the corporation or by shareholders bringing a derivative action on behalf of the corporation. Ordinarily, directors or officers are not liable to a third person for loss caused by the negligent performance of their duties as directors or officers, even if, because of such negligence, the corporation is in turn liable to the third person to whom the corporation owed the duty to use care or was under a contract obligation to render a particular service.

13. Criminal Liability

Officers and directors, as well as the corporation itself may be criminally accountable for business regulatory offenses.

(a) ACTIVE PARTICIPATION. Officers and directors, as in the case of agents, are personally responsible for any crimes committed by them, even when they act on behalf of the corporation.[18] At the local level, they may be criminally responsible for violation of ordinances relating to sanitation, safety, and hours of closing.

At the state level, they may be criminally liable for conducting a business without obtaining necessary licenses or after the corporate certificate of incorporation has been forfeited.

At the federal level officers and directors may be criminally liable for tax and securities laws violations as well as egregious environmental protection law and worker safety law violations. International transactions may

lead to potential criminal exposure. Under the Foreign Corrupt Practices Act it is a crime to make payments or gifts to a foreign officer to obtain business for an American firm. Not only is the American corporation subject to a fine, but the officers and individuals involved are subject to fine and imprisonment.

(b) LIABILITY OF CONTROLLING PERSONS. Officers and directors may be criminally liable under a number of federal and state statutes for failure to prevent the commission of a crime if they are found to be the "responsible corporate officer." These statutes include the Food, Drug and Cosmetic Act, the Federal Hazardous Substances Act, the Occupational Safety and Health Act, the Federal Water Pollution Act, and, at the state level, the California Corporate Criminal Liability Act. The president of a national food retail corporation was found to be a controlling person under the "responsible corporate officer" doctrine, and was held criminally liable for a violation of the Food, Drug and Cosmetic Act (FDCA) because of his failure to implement measures to prevent rodent contamination at a warehouse, as required by the FDCA. The California Corporate Criminal Liability Act requires managers in control of corporate operations who have knowledge of "serious concealed dangers" to employees or customers to notify appropriate regulatory authority or be subject to criminal liability.[19]

(c) LIABILITY OF THE CORPORATION ITSELF. A corporation itself may be convicted of a criminal offense if the offense was committed by its agent acting within the scope of the agent's authority.[20] Thus, an incorporated nursing home may be found guilty of criminal recklessness for the neglect of a patient. Moreover, a corporation itself may be convicted of a crime involving specific intent, such as theft by swindle or forgery, when (a)

---

[18] Joy Management Co. v City of Detroit, 183 Mich App 334, 455 NW2d 55 (1990).

[19] Cal Penal Code § 387 (West Publishing 1993).

[20] People v Film Recovery Systems Inc. 194 Ill App 3d 79, 141 Ill Dec 44, 550 NE2d 1090 (1990).

the agent was acting at least in part in furtherance of the corporation's business interests
and (b) corporate management authorized,
tolerated, or ratified the criminal activity.

(d) PUNISHMENT OF CORPORATIONS.
With the enactment of the Organizational
Federal Sentencing Guidelines in 1991, organizations, including corporations, trusts, pension funds, unions and non-profit
organizations are subject to greatly increased
fines for criminal convictions. However, corporations and other covered organizations
that implement an effective compliance program designed to prevent and detect corporate crimes and voluntarily disclose such
crimes to the government will be subject to
much lower fines under the Guidelines.[21]

14. Indemnification of Officers, Directors, Employees, and Agents

While performing what they believe to be their
duty, officers, directors, employees, and
agents of corporations may commit acts for
which they are later sued or criminally prosecuted.
The RMBCA broadly authorizes the corporation to indemnify such persons if they acted in
good faith and in a manner reasonably believed to be in or not opposed to the interests
of the corporation and had no reason to believe that their conduct was unlawful.[22] In
some states, statutory provision is made requiring the corporation to indemnify directors
and officers for reasonable expenses incurred
by them in defending unwarranted suits
brought against them by shareholders.

15. Liability for Corporate Debts

Since the corporation is a separate legal person, debts owed by the corporation are ordinarily the obligations of the corporation only.
Consequently, neither directors nor officers are
individually liable for the corporate debts,
even though it may have been their acts that
gave rise to the debts.

In some states, liability for corporate debts
is imposed on the officers and directors of the
corporation when the corporation improperly
engages in business.

16. Protection of Shareholders

Shareholders may obtain protection from misconduct by management and by the majority
of the shareholders. Shareholders may protect
themselves by voting at the next annual election for new directors and also for new officers, if the latter are elected. Shareholders may
take remedial action at a special meeting
called for that purpose. Objecting shareholders may bring a legal action when the management misconduct complained of constitutes a
legal wrong.[23]

17. Civil Liability of Corporation

A corporation is liable to third persons for the
acts of its officers, employees, and agents to
the same extent that a natural person is liable
for the acts of agents and employees. This
means that the ordinary rules of agency law
determine the extent to which the corporation
is liable to a third person for a contract made
or a tort committed by management personnel, employees, and agents.[24]

[21] United States Sentencing Commission Guidelines Manual, §§ 8C2.5(f) and 8C2.6.
[22] Subchapter 8E, added 1980 and revised in 1994.
[23] Christner v Anderson, Nietzke & Co. 433 Mich 1, 444 NW2d 779 (1989).
[24] Jenson v Alaska Valuation Service, Inc. (Alaska) 688 P2d 161 (1984).

SUMMARY

Ordinarily, stockholder action is taken at a regular or special meeting of the stockholders. The presence of a quorum of the voting shareholders is required.

Management of a corporation is under the control of a board of directors elected by the shareholders. The courts will not interfere with the board's judgment in the absence of unusual conduct such as fraud. A director is disqualified from taking part in corporate action when the director has a conflict of interests. Action by directors is usually taken at a properly called meeting of the board. Directors act in a fiduciary capacity in dealing with the corporation. Directors who act in good faith and have exercised reasonable care are not liable for losses resulting from their management decisions. Ordinarily, directors are removed by shareholders.

Officers of a corporation, including a CEO, president, vice president, secretary, and treasurer, are usually selected and removed by the board of directors. Officers are agents of the corporation, and their powers are governed by the law of agency. Their relations with the corporation are fiduciary in nature, and they are liable for any secret profits and for diverting corporate opportunities to their own advantage.

Directors and officers, as in the case of agents generally, are personally responsible for any torts or crimes they commit, even if they act on behalf of the corporation. The corporation itself may be prosecuted for crimes and is subject to fines if convicted. The ordinary rules of agency law determine the extent to which a corporation is liable for a contract made or tort committed by a director, officer, corporate agent, or employee.

LAW IN PRACTICE

1. If you are invited to serve on a corporate board of directors, make sure that the corporation maintains liability insurance to defend and indemnify you in case of a duty of care violation in fulfilling your duties as director.

2. If you, as an officer or director, wish to pursue a corporate opportunity for your own benefit, fully disclose the situation to the board of directors.

3. Should a corporate officer be found to have made a secret profit at the expense of the corporation, not only should the secret profit be recovered

but the corporation should consider bringing suit against that individual to recover all compensation paid during the period the secret profit was received.

4. A corporate officer is an agent of the corporation and is not personally liable for corporate contracts or debts. If you are an officer, remember to always sign corporate contracts in your corporate capacity, such as "Elizabeth Smith, President," so that there will be no doubt about your status. Also, name the corporation in the contract.

QUESTIONS AND CASE PROBLEMS

1. What social forces are affected by the rule that a person dealing with a corporate officer is charged with knowledge of any limitation on the officers authority contained in the recorded corporate charter?

2. What constitutes a quorum at a meeting of shareholders?

3. Roxanne Washington owns 100 of the 10,000 outstanding shares of Microchip International Inc. She disagrees with the future plans of the board of directors. Should she bring a lawsuit against the directors?

4. Larry Phillips was hired for a two-year period as executive secretary of the Montana Education Association (MEA). Six months later, he was fired. He then sued MEA for breach of contract and sued the directors and some of the other employees of MEA on the theory that they had caused MEA to break the contract with him and were therefore guilty of the tort of maliciously interfering with his contract with MEA. The evidence showed that the individual defendants, without malice, had induced the corporation to break the contract with Phillips but that this had been done in order to further the welfare of the corporation. Was MEA liable for breach of contract? Were the individual defendants shielded from personal liability? *[Phillips v Montana Education Association, 187 Mont 419, 610 P2d 154]*

5. Christy Pontiac, a corporation, was indicted for theft by swindle and forgery involving a GM cash rebate program. Hesli, a middle-management employee of Christy Pontiac, had forged the cash rebate applications for two cars, so that the rebate money was paid to Christy Pontiac instead of to its customers. When confronted by a customer who should have received a rebate, the president of the dealership attempted to negotiate a settlement. The president did not contact GM headquarters until after an investigation was begun by the state attorney general. Christy Pontiac argued that it could not be held responsible for a crime involving specific intent because only "natural" persons, as opposed to corporations, can form such intent. Decide. *[State v Christy Pontiac-GMC, Inc. (Minn) 354 NW2d 17]*

6. Directors must always own stock of the corporation in order to ensure that they will be attentive to their duties. Appraise this statement.

7. Discuss the power of a corporation president to employ a sales manager and to agree that the manager should be paid a stated amount per year plus a percentage of any increase in the dollar volume of sales that might take place.

8. Thywissen owned 60 percent of Flexbin Corp., and Cron owned 40 percent. When they formed the corporation, Thywissen obtained a right of first refusal on a note, which was taken in his own name. He saw this right as a means of protecting Flexbin Corp. and increasing the value of Flexbin's corporate stocks. Due to lack of success, the Flexbin Corp. was liquidated. The "right of first refusal" was worth $92,000. Cron expected to received 40 percent of the proceeds. Thywissen claimed that since the right of first refusal was in his own name, it was a personal right, not a corporate asset. He claimed that he had no legal obligation to Cron, only a "moral obligation" to him. He offered him $7,200. Cron bought suit against Thywissen, claiming that Thywissen had breached his fiduciary duty to him by taking this corporate asset for himself. Decide.

9. Danny Hill was general manager of Southeastern Floor Covering Co. Inc. (SE). He had full authority to run the business. His responsibilities included preparing and submitting bid proposals to general contractors for floor coverings and ceilings on construction projects. Hill worked up a bid

on a job for Chata Construction Co. for asbestos encapsulation, ceramic tile, ceilings, carpets and vinyl tile flooring. However, because SE was not licensed by the EPA, the asbestos work was withdrawn. In the past SE had used Larry Barnes' company, which was EPA licensed, to do asbestos work under a subcontract agreeent. Hill did not pursue a subcontract with Barnes for the Chata job. Rather Hill and Barnes worked up a bid and submitted it to Chata for the asbestos work. The bid was accepted by Chata. Hill made $90,000 from the Chata job. Two years later SE found out about Hill's role in the asbestos work done for Chata and the corporation sued him for the lost profits. Hill defended that SE was not licensed by the EPA to do asbestos work and thus SE cannot claim a lost corporate opportunity, where it was not qualified to do the work. Decide. Are any ethical principles applicable to this case? *[Hill v Southeastern Floor Covering Co. Inc. (Miss) 596 So 2d 874]*

10. A director of a corporation cannot lend money to the corporation, because that would create the danger of a conflict of interests between the director's status as a director and status as a creditor. Appraise this statement.

11. Hamway and other minority shareholders brought an action against majority shareholders of the Libbie Rehabilitation Center, Inc., including Frank Giannotti, CEO-director; Alex Grossman, president-director; Henry Miller, vice president-director; Ernest Dervishian, secretary and corporate attorney; and Lewis Cowardin, treasurer-director. The minority shareholders contended that the corporation paid excessive salaries to these director-officers and was wasting corporate assets. Prior to coming to Libbie, Giannotti had been a carpet and tile retailer, Grossman a pharmacist, Miller a real estate developer, Dervishian a lawyer, and Cowardin a jeweler. The evidence showed that the extent of their work for the corporation was very limited. For example, Cowardin, Libbie's finance officer who was paid $78,121 in 1985 demonstrated no knowledge of the Medicare and Medicaid programs, the principal source of Libbie's income. Although he claimed to have spent 20 to 25 hours per week on corporate duties, he reported on the tax return for his jewelry business that he spent 75 percent of his working time in that business in 1984. One expert witness of the plaintiff testified that the five men were performing the management functions of one individual. The director-officers contended that the business was making a profit and that all salaries were approved by a board of directors that had extensive business experience. Were the directors within their rights to elect themselves officers and set pay for themselves as they saw fit? Did they violate any legal or ethical duty to their shareholders?

12. Anthony Yee was the president of the Waipahu Auto Exchange, a corporation. As part of his corporate duties, he arranged financing for the company. The Federal Services Finance Corporation drew 12 checks payable to the order of the Waipahu Auto Exchange. These were then indorsed by its president, "Waipahu Auto Exchange, Limited, by Anthony Yee, President," and were cashed at two different banks. The Bishop National Bank of Hawaii, on which the checks were drawn, charged its depositor, Federal Services, with the amount of the checks. Federal Services then sued Bishop National Bank to restore to its account the amount of the 12 checks, on the theory that Bishop National Bank had improperly made payment on the checks, because Anthony Yee had no authority to cash them. Did Yee have authority to indorse and cash the checks? *[Federal Services Finance Corp. v Bishop National Bank of Hawaii (CA9 Hawaii) 190 F2d 442]*

13. Klinicki and Lundgren incorporated Berlinair, Inc., a closely held Oregon corporation. Lundgren was president and was responsible for developing business. Klinicki served as vice president and director and was responsible for operations and maintenance. Klinicki owned one-third of the stock, and Lundgren controlled the rest. They both met with BFR about contracting to approve charter flights. After the initial meeting, all contracts with BFR were made by Lundgren. Lundgren learned that there was a good chance that the BFR contract would be available. He incorporated Air Berlin Charter company (ABC) and was its sole owner. He presented BFR with a contract proposal. BFR awarded the contract to Air Berlin. Although Lundgren was using Berlinair working time and facilities, he managed to keep the negotiations a secret from Klinicki. When Klinicki discovered Lundgren's actions he sued him for usurping a corpoate opportunity of Berlinair. Lundgren raised the defense that it was not a usurpation of corporate opportunity because Berlinair did not have the financial ability to undertake the contract with BFR. Decide. Are any ethical principles applicable to this case? Consider the applicability of Chief Justice Cardozo's statement in *Meinhard v Salmon*, 249 NY 458, 164 NE 545 (1928), concerning the

level of conduct for fiduciaries: "A trustee is held to something stricter than the morals of the market place. Not honestly alone, but the punctillo of an honor the most sensitive, is then the standard of behavior. . . ." *[Klinicki v Lundgren 298 Or 662, 695 P2d 906]*

14. Rudolph Redmont was the president of Abbott Thinlite Corporation. He left that corporation to run the Circle Corporation in competition with his former employer. It was claimed that he diverted contracts from his former employer to his new one, having gained the advantage of the specific information of the deals in progress while employed by Abbott. The former employer sued Redmont and Circle Corporation to recover lost profits. Redmont contended that all of the contracts in question were made after he left Abbott, at which time his fiduciary duty to Abbott had ceased. Decide. *[Abbott Thinlite Corp. v Redmont (CA2 NY) 475 F2d 85]*

15. William Gurtler was president and a board member of Unichem Corporation, which produced and sold chemical laundry products. While president of Unichem, he encouraged his plant manager to leave to join a rival business, which Gurtler was going to join in the near future. Moreover, Gurtler sold Unichem products to his son, G. B. Gurtler, in January 1982, at a figure substantially below their normal price and on credit, even though G. B. had no credit history. Gurtler made the sales with full knowledge that G. B. was going to start a rival business. Also at that time, Gurtler was aware that his wife was soliciting Unichem employees to join the new Gurtler Chemical Co., and he helped her design Gurtler's label so that it would look like Unichem's. On February 9, 1982, Gurtler guaranteed a $100,000 loan for Gurtler Chemical Co. with funds to be disbursed after he left Unichem, which occurred on March 12, 1982. On March 15, 1982, he became president of Gurtler Chemical Co. Unichem sued Gurtler for breach of fiduciary duty and for the loss of profits that resulted. Gurtler contended that his sales to G. B. guaranteed needed revenue to Unichem and constituted a sound business decision that should be applauded and that was protected under the business judgment rule. Decide. Are any ethical principles applicable to this case? *[Unichem Corp. v Gurtler, 148 Ill App 3d 284, 101 Ill Dec 400, 498 NE2d 724]*

PART 9

Real
Property
and
Estates

CHAPTER 51
REAL PROPERTY

LEARNING OBJECTIVES

After studying this chapter, you will be able to:
1. *List the kinds of real property.*
2. *Distinguish between liens, licenses, and easements.*
3. *List and illustrate the forms of co-ownership of real property.*
4. *Define a deed and describe its operation.*
5. *Describe and illustrate the warranties of the grantor and the grantee of real estate.*
6. *Describe the characteristics and effect of a mortgage.*

The law of real property is technical and to a large extent uses a vocabulary drawn from the days of feudalism. Much of the earlier law of real property is no longer of practical importance in the modern business world. The following is therefore a simplified presentation of the subject.

A. NATURE OF REAL PROPERTY

Real property has special characteristics of permanence and uniqueness. These characteristics have strongly influenced the rules that society has developed to resolve disputes concerning real property.

1. Definitions

Real property includes (a) land, (b) buildings and fixtures, and (c) rights in the land of another.

(a) LAND. **Land** means more than the surface of the earth. It comprises the soil and all things of a permanent nature affixed to the ground, such as herbs, grass, or trees, and other growing, natural products. The term also includes the waters on the ground and things that are embedded beneath the surface.

For example, coal, oil, and marble embedded beneath the surface are part of the land.

Technically, land is considered to extend downward to the earth's center and upward indefinitely. The Uniform Aeronautics Act states that the owner of the land owns the space above subject to the right of flying aircraft that do not interfere with the use of the land and are not dangerous to persons or property lawfully on the land.[1]

(b) BUILDINGS AND FIXTURES. A **building** includes any structure placed on or beneath the surface of land, without regard to

its purpose or use. A **fixture** is personal property that has been attached to the earth or placed in a building in such a way or under such circumstances that it is considered part of the real property.

(c) RIGHTS IN LAND OF ANOTHER. These rights include easements, such as the right to cross another's land. Rights in another person's land also include profits. **Profits** are the rights to take part of the soil or the produce of the land belonging to another. An example of a profit is the right to remove coal from another's land.

2. Easements

An **easement** is a right to use another person's land for a limited purpose. The right belongs to the land that is benefited. The benefited land is called the **dominant tenement**, and the land that is subject to the easement is called the **servient tenement**.

Since an easement is an interest in land, an oral promise to create an easement is not binding, because of the statute of frauds.

(a) CREATION OF EASEMENT. An easement may be created in several ways:
1. An easement may be created by deed.
2. An easement may be created by implication. This occurs when one conveys part of the land that has been used as a dominant estate in relation to the part retained. To illustrate, if water pipes or drain pipes run from the part conveyed through the part retained, there is an implied right to continue using the pipes. In order for an easement to be implied in such a case, the use must be apparent, continuous, and reasonably necessary.
3. An easement may also be created by implication when the easement is necessary to the use of the land conveyed. This

---

[1] The Uniform Aeronautics Act (UAA) has been adopted in Arizona, Delaware, Georgia, Hawaii, Idaho, Indiana, Maryland, Minnesota, Missouri, Montana, Nevada, New Jersey, North Carolina, North Dakota, Pennsylvania, South Carolina, South Dakota, Tennessee, Utah, Vermont, and Wisconsin, but was withdrawn by the Commissioners on Uniform State Laws in 1943.

ordinarily arises when one subdivides land and sells a portion to which no entry can be made except over the land retained or over the land of a stranger. The grantees right to use the land retained by the grantor for the purpose of going to and from the land conveyed is known as a **way of necessity**.[2]

4. An easement may be created by estoppel, such as when the grantor states that the plot conveyed is bounded by a street. In such a case, if the grantor owns the adjoining land, the public cannot be denied the right to use the area that the owner has described as a street.

5. An easement may be created by prescription. Under **prescription**, a person acquires an easement by adverse use, or use contrary to the landowners use, for a statutory period. No easement is acquired by prescription if the use of the land is with the permission of the owner. The adverse use by which an easement is acquired is similar to the adverse possession by which title is acquired, as discussed in Section 26 of this chapter.

(b) TERMINATION OF EASEMENT. Once an easement has been granted, it cannot be destroyed by the act of the grantor. A "revocation" attempted without the easement owner's consent has no effect.

An easement may be lost by nonuse when there are surrounding circumstances that show an intent to abandon the easement.[3] For example, when a surface transit system had an easement to maintain trolley tracks, it could be found that there was an abandonment of the easement when the tracks were removed and when all surface transportation was discontinued. Likewise, when the owner of the easement planted a flower bed on the land across the end of the path of the easement, the intent to abandon the easement was evident.

3. Licenses

A **license** is a personal, revocable privilege to perform an act or series of acts on the land of another. Unlike an easement, a license is not an interest in land. The person allowed to come into the house to use the telephone has a license. The advertising company that has permission to paint a sign on the side of a building also has a license.

A license may be terminated at the will of the licensor. It continues only as long as the licensor is the owner of the land.

4. Liens

Real property may be subject to liens that arise by the voluntary act of the owner of the land. For example, the lien of a mortgage is created when the owner borrows money and uses the land as security for repayment of the debt.

Liens may also arise involuntarily, as in the case of tax liens, judgment liens, and mechanics' liens. In the case of taxes and judgments, the liens provide a means for enforcing the obligations of the owner of the land to pay the taxes or the judgment. Mechanics' liens give persons furnishing labor and materials in the improvement of real estate the right to proceed against the real estate for the collection of the amounts due them.

5. Duration and Extent of Ownership

A person's interest in real property may be defined in terms of the period of time for which the person will remain the owner, as (a) a fee simple estate or (b) a life estate. These estates are termed **freehold estates**, which are interests of uncertain duration. At the time of creation of a freehold estate, a termination date is not known. Although a person may own property for a specified period of time, this interest is not regarded as a freehold estate; it is a **leasehold estate**, subject to special rules of law.

---

2   Canei v Cullex (W Va) 374 SE2d 523 (1988).

3   Dean v Mod Properties, Ltd. (Fla App) 528 So 2d 432 (1988).

(a) FEE SIMPLE ESTATE. An **estate in fee**, a **fee simple**, or a **fee simple absolute** lasts forever. The owner of such a fee has the absolute and entire interest in the land. The important characteristics of this estate are: (1) it is alienable, or transferable, during life; (2) it is alienable by will; (3) it descends to heirs generally if not devised (transferred by will); (4) it is subject to rights of the owner's surviving spouse; and (5) it is liable for debts of the owner before or after death.

(b) LIFE ESTATE. A **life estate** (or life tenancy), as its name indicates, lasts only during the life of a person (ordinarily, its owner). On the death of the person by whose life the estate was measured, the owner of the life estate has no interest remaining to pass to heirs or by will.

B. FIXTURES

By the concept of fixtures, personal property becomes real property, and third persons and creditors may acquire rights therein.

6. Definition

A **fixture** is personal property that is attached to the earth or placed in a building in such a way or under such circumstances that it is considered part of the real property.

A person buys a refrigerator, an air conditioner, a furnace, or some other item that is used in a building, and then has the item installed. The question of whether the item is a fixture, and therefore part of the building, can arise in a variety of situations. (a) The real estate tax assessor assesses the building and adds in the value of the item, on the theory that it is part of the building. (b) The buyer of the item owns and then sells the building, and the new owner of the building claims that the item stays with the building. (c) The buyer places a mortgage on the building, and the mortgagee claims that the item is bound by the mortgage. (d) The buyer is a tenant in the building in which the item is installed, and the landlord claims that the item must stay in the building when the tenant leaves. (e) The buyer does not pay in full for the item, and the seller of the item has a security interest that the seller asserts against the buyer of the item or against the landlord of the building in which the buyer installs the item. The seller of the item may also be asserting a claim against the mortgagee of the building or against the buyer of the building. The determination of the rights of these parties depends on the common law of fixtures, as occasionally modified by statute.

7. Tests of a Fixture

In the absence of an agreement between the parties, the courts apply three tests to determine whether personal property has become a fixture.

(a) ANNEXATION. Generally, the personal property becomes a fixture if it is so attached to the realty that it cannot be removed without materially damaging the realty or destroying the personal property itself. If the property is so affixed as to lose its specific identity, such as bricks in a wall, it becomes part of the realty. When railroad tracks are so placed as to be immovable, they are fixtures.

(b) ADAPTATION. Personal property especially adapted or suited to the use made of the building may constitute a fixture.

(c) INTENT. The true test is the intention of the person affixing the property.[4] Intent is considered as of the time the property was affixed. In the absence of direct proof of such intent, it is necessary to resort to the nature of the property, the method of its attachment, and all the surrounding circumstances to determine the intent.

---

4 Hubbard v Hardeman County Bank (Tenn) 868 SW2d 656 (1993).

In the *Premonstratensian Fathers* case the court considered all three tests in deciding if refrigeration equipment had become a fixture.

The fact that machinery installed in a plant would be very difficult and expensive to move, or so delicate that the moving would

PREMONSTRATENSIAN FATHERS v BADGER MUTUAL FIRE INS. CO.
46 Wis 2d 362, 175 NW2d 337 (1970)

In 1958, a supermarket was constructed by Jacobs Realty Corporation and was owned by that corporation. The market contained five large walk-in coolers or refrigerators. Title to the market was thereafter transferred to the Premonstratensian Fathers and was insured against fire by Badger Mutual Insurance Company. The building was severely damaged by fire, and the insurer paid approximately $80,000 for the building damage. The Fathers claimed an additional $20,000 for the destruction of the coolers. The insurer refused to pay this amount, asserting that the coolers were not owned by the Fathers. From a judgment for the Fathers, the insurer appealed.

HANSE, J. . . . If the coolers are determined to be common-law fixtures, and were such at the time of the construction of the building and the installation of the coolers, then they would have passed to the Fathers under the warranty deed of March 7, 1960, and they would be insured under the terms of the policy. The issue then is whether these coolers constitute fixtures.

The rule which has developed . . . as to what constitutes a fixture is not really a comprehensive definition, but rather a statement of the factors which are to be applied to the facts and circumstances of a particular case to determine whether or not the property in question does constitute a fixture. . . .

Annexation

. . . An object will not acquire the status of a fixture unless it is in some manner or means . . . attached or affixed, either actually or constructively, to the realty. . . . The trial court ably pointed out the physical facts which led to its conclusion that there is indeed annexation in this case. The more important of these are as follows: (1) The exterior walls of the cooler, in four instances, constituted the interior wall of another room. (2) In the two meat coolers, a meat hanging and tracking system was built into the coolers. These tracks were used to move large cuts of meats from the cooler area into the meat preparation areas, and were suspended from the steel girders of the building structure by means of large steel bolts. These bolts penetrated through the roof of the cooler supporting wooden beams, which, in turn, supported the tracking system. The tracking in the coolers was a part of a system of tracking throughout the rear portion of the supermarket. (3) The coolers were attached to hardwood plank which was, in turn, attached to the concrete floor of the supermarket. The attachment of the plank to the floor was accomplished through the use of a ramsetting gun. The planks were laid on the floor, and the bolts were driven through them into the concrete floor, where they then exploded, firmly fixing the coolers into place. There was a material placed on the planks which served both as an adhesive and as an insulation. (4) The floor of the coolers was specially sloped during the construction of the building so that the slope would carry drainage into a specially constructed drain in the concrete. In addition, four of the coolers were coated with a protective coating to seal the floors. In the freezer, a special concrete buildup was constructed in the nature of a trough, the purpose of which was to carry away moisture as frozen chickens melted. (5) A refrigeration unit was built into each cooler. The unit was suspended from the ceiling of the cooler, and tubing was run through the wall of the cooler to compressors located elsewhere in the store. (6) Electric lights and power receptacles were built into each cooler and were connected by electrical wiring through the walls and the ceiling of the cooler to the store's electrical power supply. (7) The walls of the cooler were interlocked, and set into the splines, the hardwood planks ramset into the concrete floor, in tongue and groove fashion.

These factors adequately support the conclusion that the coolers were indeed physically annexed to the premises. The insurers argue that the coolers were removable without material injury to the premises, which detracts from the annexation. There was a dispute in the evidence introduced at the trial, with the insurers' expert testifying that this type of cooler was easily severable from the building, while one of the members of the Jacobs family testified that when he removed some of the bolts from the floor following the fire, large sections of concrete would crack on the floor. This was a conflict for resolution by the trial court. In any event, the element of removability without material damage to the building no longer enjoys the position of prominence in the law of fixtures which it once held. It is now only one of the factors which is to be considered by the trial court. . . .

Adaptation

Adaptation refers to the relationship between the chattel and the use which is made of the realty to which the chattel is annexed. The use of the realty was that of a retail grocery, commonly known as a supermarket. This was the intent of the parties at the time of the construction of the building, and the intent of the parties throughout the entire history of the business. The fact of operation has borne out this intent. In a business which carries fresh foods, frozen foods, produce, meats and butter, coolers used for storage and handling of these perishables are patently related to the use of the building. In fact, it would be hard to picture any equipment more closely related to the operation of a supermarket, where large quantities of perishables must, of necessity, be purchased for storage and processing.

The insurers raise a number of points to dispute this finding. They state: The coolers were not custom made; the coolers are useful not to the building, but to the use to which the building is put; the coolers could have been used anywhere; other coolers could have been used. There is no requirement that the coolers be custom made, but only that they be adapted to the use to which the building is put. The test here is not the adaptability to the building, but the adaptability to the use to which the building is put. The fact that other coolers could have been used, or that these coolers could have been used elsewhere, does not alter the fact that there was a close connection between these coolers and the retail grocery business conducted on the property. . . .

Intent

This court has repeatedly held that intent is the primary determinant of whether a certain piece of property has become a fixture. . . .

In its decision, the trial court found, as a reasonable and legitimate inference from all the facts and circumstances surrounding the placement of the coolers onto the realty, that there was an intention that the coolers become a permanent accession to the realty; that when Jacobs Realty Corporation conveyed the land together with all buildings and improvements thereon to Jacobs Brothers Stores, Inc., the intention still prevailed that the coolers were a permanent accession to the realty; and that the same intention still prevailed when Jacobs Brothers Stores, Inc., conveyed the building and improvements to the plaintiff, and when the plaintiff leased the premises (the land, with all buildings and improvements thereon) back to the corporation as lessee. . . .

The coolers were fixtures when installed; passed to Jacobs Brothers Stores, Inc., through the warranty deed; subsequently passed to the Fathers through that warranty deed; and are in fact fixtures within the meaning of the coverage clause of the insurance policy in this case. . . .

[Judgment affirmed]

QUESTIONS

1. Which party to the lawsuit had installed the coolers?
2. What difference would it make whether the coolers were or were not fixtures?
3. Does the adaptation test require that the goods be made especially for use in the particular building?

cause damage and unbalancing, is significant in reaching the conclusion that the owner of the plant had installed the equipment as a permanent addition and thus had the intent to make the equipment fixtures. When the floors in a large apartment house are of concrete covered with a thin sheet of plywood to which wall-to-wall carpeting is stapled, the carpeting constitutes a fixture that cannot be removed from the building. Removal would probably destroy the carpeting, since it was cut to size. In addition, the carpeting is necessary to make the building livable as an apartment.

8. Movable Machinery and Equipment

Machinery and equipment that is movable is ordinarily held not to be fixtures, even though, in order to move it, it is necessary to unbolt it from the floor or to disconnect electrical wires or water pipes. It is ordinarily held that refrigerators, freezers, and gas and electric ranges are not fixtures. They do not lose their character as personal property when they are readily removable after disconnecting pipes or unplugging wires. A portable window air conditioner that rests on a rack that is affixed to the window sill by screws and is connected directly to the building only by an electric cord plug is not a fixture.

The mere fact that an item may be unplugged, however, does not establish that it is not a fixture. For example, a computer and its related hardware constituted fixtures when there was such a mass of wires and cables under the floor that the installation gave the impression of permanence.

9. Trade Fixtures

Equipment a tenant attaches to a rented building and uses in a trade or business is ordinarily removable by the tenant when the tenant permanently leaves the premises. Such equipment is commonly called a **trade fixture**.[5]

---

[5]   B. Kreisman & Co. v First Arlington National Bank, 91 Ill App 3d 47, 47 Ill Dec 757, 415 NE2d 1070 (1981).

C. LIABILITY TO THIRD PERSONS FOR CONDITION OF REAL PROPERTY

A person entering the land of another may be injured by the condition of the land. Who is liable for such harm?

10. Status-of-Plaintiff Common Law Rule

Under the common law, liability to a person entering on real estate was controlled by the status of the injured person—that is, whether the person injured was a trespasser, a licensee, or an invitee. A different duty was owed by the occupier of land to persons in each of these three categories.[6]

(a) TRESPASSERS. As to **trespassers**, the occupier ordinarily owes only the duty of refraining from causing intentional harm once the presence of the trespasser is known. The occupier is not under any duty to warn of dangers or to make the premises safe to protect the trespasser from harm. The most significant exception to this rule arises in the case of small children. Even when they are trespassers, they are generally afforded greater protection through the **attractive nuisance doctrine**. For example, the owner of a private residential swimming pool was liable for the drowning of a five-year-old trespasser when the owner did not maintain adequate fencing around the pool. The court reasoned that the placing of such fencing would not have imposed a great burden.

(b) LICENSEES. As to **licensees**, who are on the premises with the permission of the occupier, the latter owes the duty of warning of nonobvious dangers that are known to the occupier. A host must warn a guest of such dangers. For example, when a sliding glass door is "invisible" if the patio lights are on and the house lights are off, the host must warn guests of the presence of the glass. The host is liable if the guest is injured in shattering the glass. However, the occupier owes no duty to the licensee to take any steps to learn of the presence of dangers unknown to the occupier.

(c) INVITEES. **Invitees** are persons who enter another's land by invitation. The entry is connected with the occupier's business or with an activity the occupier conducts on the land. For example, business customers are invitees.

An occupier has a duty to take reasonable steps to discover any danger and a duty to warn the invitee or to correct the danger. For instance, a store must make a reasonable inspection of the premises to determine that there is nothing on the floor that would be dangerous, such as a slippery substance that might cause a patron to fall. The store must correct the condition, appropriately rope off the danger area, or give suitable warning. If the occupier of the premises fails to conform to the degree of care described and if harm results to an invitee on the premises, the occupier is liable for such harm.

In most states, the courts have expanded the concept of invitees beyond the category of those persons whose presence will economically benefit the occupier. Invitees now usually include members of the public who are invited when it is apparent that such persons cannot be reasonably expected to make an inspection of the premises before using them and that they would not be making repairs to correct any dangerous condition. Some courts have also made inroads into the prior law by treating a recurring licensee, such as a letter carrier, as an invitee.

In the *Lucas* case the court was asked to abolish the distinction between an invitee and a licensee.

---

[6] Huyck v Hecla Mining Co. 101 Idaho 299, 612 P2d 142 (1980).

LUCAS v B. JONES FORD LINCOLN MERCURY
(Miss App) 518 So 2d 646 (1988)

Joyce Lucas left her youngest son, Mark, at the Buddy Jones Ford dealership so that her husband, an employee there, could babysit Mark while Joyce kept an appointment with her doctor. After her appointment, Joyce returned for Mark. She parked her automobile and walked across the lot toward the service area of the dealership, where her husband worked. When she reached the freight ramp, she slipped and fell on ice that had accumulated because of a severe winter storm earlier in the day. Joyce injured her arm when she fell. She charged Buddy Jones with the negligent maintenance of the entrances to its business. Jones argued that Joyce was a licensee, not an invitee as she contended. From a judgment in favor of Buddy Jones, Joyce appealed.

ZUCCARO, J. . . . Lucas argues that she was not a licensee, but was instead an invitee. The basis for this contention is the fact that Buddy Jones Ford had on occasion encouraged the relatives of employees to pick up payment checks, so that the employee would not have to leave the job site. Thus, as Lucas had an implied invitation, Buddy Jones Ford owed to her a duty of ordinary care to make the premises safe. . . .

In looking to the facts presented in the case, we must note that on the date in question, Lucas was not going to Buddy Jones Ford to pick up her husband's check. Instead, as she stated in her deposition, she was on her way to a doctor's appointment, and had dropped her son off so that her husband might "babysit." When the accident occurred, Lucas was simply in the process of picking up her son so that they could go home. Further, in her deposition, Lucas admitted that there was no business purpose in her visit to Buddy Jones Ford, and that the business derived no benefit from her visit. The stop was made simply for her personal convenience.

In drawing the long standing, and traditional distinction between a "licensee" and an "invitee" it must be noted that a licensee is a person who enters upon the property of another for his own convenience, pleasure or benefit pursuant to the licenses or implied permission of the owner. . . . On the other hand, an invitee is a person who goes upon the premises of another in answer to an express or implied invitation of the owner or occupier for their *mutual advantage*. . . . From this distinction, and as can be seen from Lucas' own testimony, she clearly falls into the category of a "licensee."

The significance in drawing the above distinction can be found in the duty owed by the landowner, in the present case Buddy Jones Ford, to a licensee. A landowner owes a licensee the bare duty to refrain from willfully or wantonly injuring him. There is one recognized exception, in that ordinary reasonable care is required where the landowner engages in active conduct and the plaintiff's presence is known to him. This exception is not applicable where the licensee is injured as a result of the condition of the premises, or passive negligence. Conversely, a landowner always owes to a business invitee the duty to exercise reasonable care for said invitee's safety. As Lucas was a mere licensee, not falling within the above exception, Buddy Jones Ford owed to her only the duty not to willfully or wantonly harm her. The failure of Buddy Jones Ford to warn her of the open and obvious ice could hardly be said to rise to this level.

In *Graves v Massey*, 227 Miss. 848, 87 So 2d 270 (1956), this Court stated that where the undisputed facts disclose that a plaintiff was a mere licensee, the court should not allow the jury to consider the question of whether or not his status was otherwise. The case presently at bar presents a similar situation, in that Lucas, in her own deposition, admitted that Buddy Jones Ford derived no advantage from her husband being allowed to babysit their son. As such, the lower court was correct in finding Lucas a licensee. Summary judgment was properly granted.

Additionally, we feel compelled to add that the views expressed in this opinion should not be construed as an indication that Buddy Jones Ford would be liable to Lucas if she were an invitee. Were appellant an invitee, (which as previously stated she obviously was not), Buddy Jones Ford would have only owed her the duty of exercising reasonable care to keep the premises safe, or of warning Lucas of *hidden or concealed perils* of which appellee knew or should have known in the exercise of reasonable care. The ice which caused Lucas to fall was in no way hidden or concealed.

Lucas next argues that if this Court cannot find her to be an invitee, that it should abolish the long-held distinction between an invitee and a licensee. In this context it must be noted that this Court has continuously and regularly adhered to the common law distinction between an invitee and a licensee since the world was young. Further, in very recent decisions, we have specifically refused to abandon our long-held recognition of the categories now in question.

Prosser and Keeton note that recently courts considering abandoning the distinction between an invitee and a licensee have refused to do so. *Prosser and Keeton on Torts*, § 62 (5th ed. 1984). As such, this Court will not at this time do away with a legal principle so long held and thoroughly developed. The assignment of error is meritless. . . .

[Judgment affirmed]

QUESTIONS

1. Was Lucas an invitee or a licensee?
2. Upon what basis did she allege she was an invitee?
3. Did the court abolish the distinction between an invitee and a licensee? Explain.

11. Negligence Rule

A number of courts have begun ignoring these common law distinctions between trespassers, licensees, and invitees. These courts hold the occupier liable according to ordinary negligence standards. That is, when the occupier as a reasonable person should foresee from the circumstances that harm would be caused a third person, the occupier has the duty to take reasonable steps to prevent such harm. This duty exists regardless of whether the potential victim would be traditionally classified as a trespasser, a licensee, or an invitee.

12. Intermediate Rule

Some courts have taken an intermediate position. They have merely abolished the distinction between licensees and invitees, so that the occupier owes the same duty of care to all lawful visitors. Whether one is a licensee or an invitee is merely a circumstance to be considered by the jury in applying the ordinary rule of negligence.

In some states, the distinction between licensees and invitees has been retained in name but destroyed in fact. In these states, an occupier is required to warn the licensee of unknown dangers of which the occupier in the exercise of reasonable care should have known. Or a licensee may be classified as an invitee.

13. Recreational Use Statutes

Most states have enacted a statute commonly referred to as a **recreational use** statute. Such statutes provide that a landowner owes to persons using the property for recreational purposes and without charge, no duty to keep the property safe for entry or use. In addition, no duty is imposed on the landowner to give any warning of a dangerous condition or structure on the property.[7]

In the *Monteville* case an action was brought against a parish for injuries sustained as a result of a defect in a boat ramp at a public boat-launching facility.

MONTEVILLE v TERREBONNE PARISH CON. GOV.
(La) 567 So 2d 1097 (1990)

Monteville launched his boat from a trailer at the Cocodrie boat launching and vehicle/trailer parking facility, which is operated by the Terrebonne Parish Consolidated Government. One wheel of the trailer became caught in an underwater hole as he was pulling the trailer out of the water. Monteville tried to pull the trailer out of the hole by rapidly accelerating the truck, but this maneuver caused a sudden jerk of the vehicle as the wheel was pulled from the hole. As a result of this episode, Monteville suffered both property damage to his trailer and injuries to his back. The premises where the injury took place include a fisherman's landing store, a cement ramp, and clam shell driveways and parking areas. Monteville sued the parish government and its insurer, alleging that the parish's negligent maintenance of the boat launch caused his injuries. The parish government moved for summary judgment on the grounds that the Recreational Use Statutes absolve it from any mere negligence in maintaining the facility. From a judgment in favor of the parish, Monteville appealed.

DENNIS, J. . . . The Recreational Use Statutes are in derogation of common or natural right and, therefore, are to be strictly interpreted, and must not be extended beyond their obvious meaning. . . .

The stated goal of the Recreational Use Statutes is "to encourage owners of land to make land and water areas available to the public for recreational purposes by limiting their liability toward persons entering thereon for such purposes". . . . If a

---

7 Rankin v Harding (NY) 594 NYS2d 910 (1993).

suitable tract is properly dedicated to one or more of the specified recreational purposes, the landowner or occupier's exposure to liability to a person who enters or uses the premises for such a recreational purpose is drastically limited. In such cases, the owner owes no duty of care to keep the premises safe or to give warnings of hazards, use, structure or activity on the premises. However, there is no limitation of liability for willful or malicious failure to guard or warn against a dangerous condition, structure, use or activity, or for injury when the premises are used as a commercial recreational development or facility or used primarily for a commercial, recreational enterprise for profit. . . .

The purpose of the Recreational Use Statutes, their legislative history and the state of the law at the time of original enactment indicate that the legislature intended to confer immunity only on owners of private lands. The texts of the statutes are silent on the subjects of sovereign, state, or governmental immunity. Consequently, there being at least a reasonable doubt about the meaning of the Recreational Use Statutes on this issue, the Statutes must be strictly construed as making the least rather than the most change in the preexisting general law. Accordingly, we conclude that the qualified immunity offered by the Recreational Use Statutes must be interpreted strictly as a legislated inducement granted only to the owners of large acreages of private land to open them to the public as outdoor recreational areas.

As other courts and commentators have noted, many aspects of the enactment of the recreational use-immunity legislation strongly indicate that it was intended to benefit only private land owners. The history of the legislative movement indicates that it began as a response to the efforts of individual forest owners, sportsmen and conservationists who wanted to make private lands more available for recreational purposes. The purpose of limiting liability is explicitly stated in the commentary of the model act, from which virtually all states' acts are derived, to be that of encouraging private owners to make their land available for the recreation of the public. . .

Construing the Recreational Use Statute strictly . . . we conclude that the Recreational Use Statutes were not intended to apply to public lands or to grant immunity to the state, its agencies or subdivisions. . . .

Because the purpose of the Recreational Use Statutes was to induce owners of large, remote acreages to dedicate suitable tracts for these particular recreational purposes, and because it was unrealistic to expect owners of farms, forests or other large, remote tracts to undertake the heavy cost of monitoring and maintaining these vast and remote lands for safe public use, it was thought necessary to free the owners of this burden by granting them limited tort immunity in order to persuade them to dedicate large acreages for these recreational purposes. By contrast, smaller readily accessible tracts of land are less apt to be suitable for the specified recreational purposes and are less costly for the owner to have monitored and maintained due to their size and proximity to population and urban services. Consequently, in view of the purpose and underlying policy considerations of the Recreational Use Statutes, and in light of the many cogent reasons for construing them narrowly and in keeping with their purpose, the statutes must be strictly interpreted to limit liability only when the recreational activity takes place on large, remote acreage dedicated to and suitable for one of the specified recreational purposes. . . .

Accordingly, this court [has] held that the legislature did not intend to grant tort immunity to all premises open for swimming, even though "swimming" is included within the statutory definition of "recreational purposes," because the purpose of the statutes is to confer immunity only on "open and undeveloped expanses of property" suitable for the type of recreational activities enumerated.

By the same token, in instances when the activity of the entrant is not one of those enumerated by the statute that can be accommodated only on large expanses of open and undeveloped lands, courts have held that the recreational use acts do not apply. . . .

Moreover, an owner who does not evidence an intent to permit the public to enter without charge for recreational use may not invoke the recreational use statute's protective benefits against liability. *Gibson v Keith*, 492 A2d 241 (Del.1985). This case arose from a swimming accident at a water hole in a gravel pit in an isolated area. The plaintiff, a 17 year old minor, suffered paralytic injuries when he dove into shallow water from a rope swing affixed to a nearby tree. The defendants denied giving him permission to enter and swim in the borrow pit. The Delaware Supreme Court held that the recreational use statute may only be invoked to limit the liability of real property owners who directly or indirectly invite or permit without charge the public at large to use their property for recreational purposes. . . .

Applying the foregoing precepts, we conclude that, even if the boat launching facility had been privately owned, the Recreational Use Statutes would not be applicable to afford qualified immunity in the present case. The premises which the defendant opened to the public was not a large, remote or open and undeveloped expanse of land. It was instead a fully developed 5.21 acre boat launching and vehicle/trailer parking facility containing a fisherman's landing store, a cement ramp and clam shell driveways and parking areas, located strategically between a state highway and a navigable bayou. The premises was small, readily accessible and, thus, much less costly to maintain and monitor than a large, remote tract more difficult in approach, size and arrangement. Construing the Recreational Use Statutes strictly and in conformity with the legislative purpose, it is evident that the parish government's facility is not the type of open and undeveloped expanse of land that the legislature sought to induce owners to dedicate to ultimate recreational purposes.

Although we conclude that the Recreational Use Statutes are not applicable to the parish government or to the particular tract of land involved for the reasons assigned, it should be noted that the summary judgment was incorrectly granted for an additional reason. Even if the Recreational Use Statutes were applicable, the moving party, the parish government, did not carry its burden of showing that the plaintiff entered or used the premises for a recreational purpose. The summary judgment evidence shows only that he launched and retrieved a boat. It does not sustain the mover's burden of proof that the plaintiff entered or used the premises for recreational, as opposed to commercial or work-related, boating activities.

[Judgment reversed and action remanded]

QUESTIONS

1. What is the purpose of limiting liability under recreational use statutes?
2. When will an owner of property not be able to invoke the recreational use statute?
3. What was the basis for the court's decision?

D. CO-OWNERSHIP OF REAL PROPERTY

Real property may be owned by one or several persons.

14. Multiple Ownership

Several persons may have concurrent interests (or interests that exist at the same time) in the same real property. The forms of multiple ownership for real property are the same as those for personal property. When co-owners sell property, they hold the proceeds of sale by the same kind of tenancy as that in which they held the original property.

15. Condominiums

A **condominium** is a combination of co-ownership and individual ownership. For example, persons owning an office building or an apartment house by condominium are co-owners of the land and of the halls, lobby, elevators, stairways, exits, surrounding land, incinerator, laundry rooms, and other areas used in common. Each apartment or office in the building, however, is individually owned by its occupant.

(a) CONTROL AND EXPENSE. In some states, the owners of the various units in the condominium have equal voice in the management and share an equal part of its expenses. In others, control and liability for expenses are shared by a unit owner in the same ratio that the value of the unit bears to the value of the entire condominium project. In all states, the unit owners have an equal right to use the common areas.

The owner of each condominium unit makes the repairs required by the owners deed or contract of ownership. The owner is prohibited from making any major change that would impair or damage the safety or value of an adjoining unit.

(b) COLLECTION OF EXPENSES FROM UNIT OWNER. When a unit owner fails to pay the owner's share of taxes, operating expenses, and repairs, it is commonly provided that a lien may be entered against that owner's unit for the amount due.

(c) TORT LIABILITY. Most condominium projects fail to make provision as to the liability of unit owners for a tort occurring in the common areas. A few states expressly provide that when a third person is injured in a common area, a suit may only be brought against the condominium association. Any judgment recovered is a charge against the association, to be paid off as a common expense. When the condominium association is incorporated, the same result should be obtained by applying ordinary principles of corporation law. Under principles of corporation law, liability for torts occurring on the premises of the corporation would not be the liability of the individual shareholders.

(d) COOPERATIVES DISTINGUISHED. Ownership in a condominium is to be distinguished from ownership in a **cooperative**. An apartment cooperative is typically a corporation renting apartments to persons who are also owners of stock of the corporation. The apartment complex is owned only by the corporation. The only "ownership" interests of the stockholders are as tenants of their respective apartments or offices.

(e) ADVANTAGES OF CONDOMINIUM OWNERSHIP. The owner of a condominium unit has the benefits of limited liability, tax deductions, and the ownership of property that can be transferred or sold.

(1) Freedom from Enterprise Liability. The owner of a unit is not personally liable for an enterprise liability, nor may the unit of the owner be taken to pay for such a liability.

(2) Tax Deductions. A deduction for a share of the mortgage interest and property taxes paid may be claimed by the unit owners on their individual income tax returns. Over a period of time, the unit owner can thus enjoy

a tax savings that in effect will lower the cost of the condominium unit.

(3) Transferability of Unit. The condominium unit is property that the unit owner can transfer as freely as any other kind of property.

E. TRANSFER OF REAL PROPERTY BY DEED

Although many of the technical limitations of the feudal and earlier common law days have disappeared, much of the law relating to the modern deed originated in those days.

16. Definitions

A **deed** is an instrument or writing by which an owner or **grantor** transfers or conveys an interest in land to a new owner. The new owner is called a **grantee** or transferee.

In contrast to the situation with a contract, no consideration is required to make a deed effective. Although consideration is not required to make a deed valid or to transfer title by deed, the absence of consideration may be evidence to show that the transfer is made by the owner in fraud of creditors. The creditors may then be able to set aside the transfer.

Real property may either be sold or given as a gift. However, a deed is necessary to transfer title to land, even if it is a gift.

17. Classification of Deeds

Deeds may be classified in terms of the interest conveyed as quitclaim deeds and warranty deeds. A **quitclaim deed** transfers merely whatever interest, if any, the grantor may have in the property, without specifying that interest in any way. A **warranty deed** transfers a specified interest and warrants or guarantees that such interest is transferred.

A deed may also be classified as a common law deed or a statutory deed. A **common law deed** is a long form that sets forth the details of the transaction. A statutory deed in substance merely recites that a named person is making a certain conveyance to a named grantee.

18. Execution of Deeds

Ordinarily, a deed must be signed, by signature or mark, or sealed by the grantor. In order to have the deed recorded, statutes generally require that two or more witnesses sign the deed and that the grantor then acknowledge the deed before a notary public or other officer. In the interest of legibility, it is frequently required that the signature of the parties be followed by their printed or typewritten names.

In many states, the statute that authorizes a short or simplified form of deed also declares that no seal is required to make effective a writing that purports to convey an interest in land.

A deed must be executed and delivered by a person having capacity. It may be set aside by the grantor on the ground of the fraud of the grantee, provided that innocent third persons have not acquired rights in the land.

The deed remains binding as between the grantor and the grantee even if it has not been acknowledged or recorded.

19. Delivery and Acceptance of Deeds

A deed has no effect, and title does not pass, until the deed has been delivered. Delivery is a matter of intent as shown by words and conduct; no particular form of ceremony is required. The essential intent in delivering a deed is not merely that the grantor intends to hand over physical control and possession of the paper on which the deed is written, but that the grantor intends thereby to transfer the ownership of the property described in the deed. That is, the grantor must deliver the deed with the intent that it should take effect as a deed and convey an interest in the property.

A deed is ordinarily made effective by handing it to the grantee with the intention that the grantee should then be the owner of the property described in the deed. A delivery may also be made by placing the deed, addressed to the grantee, in the mail or by giving it to a third person with directions to hand it to the grantee.

When a deed is delivered to a third person for the purpose of delivery to the grantee upon the happening of some event or contingency, the transaction is called a **delivery in escrow**. No title passes until the fulfillment of the condition or the happening of the event or contingency.

An effective delivery of a deed may be made symbolically, such as by delivering to the grantee the key to a locked box and informing the grantee that the deed to the property is in the box.

In the *Green* case it was claimed that the delivery of a safety deposit box key was a delivery of a deed that was in the box.

GREEN v STANFILL
(Mo App) 612 SW2d 435 (1981)

Charlsie Green and her husband executed a deed of property to their son Frankie Green. She put the deed in a safety deposit box. Attached to the deed was a slip of paper stating that Frankie was not to "bother" with the deed until his parents were dead. Thereafter, the mother rented a new safety deposit box, put the deed and other papers in it, and gave one of the two keys for the box to Frankie. Unknown to the mother, Frankie thereafter removed the deed from the box and recorded it. He then executed a deed transferring the property to himself and his wife. The mother was never told that the deed had been taken from the safety deposit box and recorded. Later Frankie was killed. His wife remarried and was then known as Violet Green Stanfill. The mother sued Violet to set aside the deed to Frankie on the ground that it had never been delivered. From a judgment against the mother, she appealed.

PREWITT, P. J. . . . Whether there is delivery of a deed depends upon the facts of each case and all relevant facts and circumstances should be considered in determining the question. "Whether or not a deed has been delivered is a mixed question of law and fact. The element which controls the resolution of that question is the intention of the parties, especially the intention of the grantor. The vital inquiry is whether the grantor intended a complete transfer—whether the grantor *parted with dominion over the instrument* with the intention of relinquishing *all* dominion over it and of making it presently operative as a conveyance of the title to the land." *Meadows v Brich*, 606 SW2d 258 (Mo App 1980). Intention of the parties may be manifested by words or acts or both. . . .

Defendant Stanfill contends that the trial court's determination of the effect of giving the key to Frankie was correct, citing *McBride v Mercantile-Commerce Bank & Trust Co.* 330 Mo 259, 48 SW2d 922 (banc 1932), and *Foley v Harrison*, 233 Mo 460, 136 SW 354 (1911). However, in those cases there was evidence that the donor intended to make a present gift of the contents of the box. Here there was contrary evidence as to plaintiff's intention. Plaintiff' acts, as described in her testimony, indicated that by giving Frankie the key to the safety deposit box she did not then intend to deliver the deed and make a present conveyance of the property. She had the deed with her and deposited it in the box instead of giving it to her son. A note, apparently still attached to it, said he was not to take it until her death. It is essential to a valid delivery that the grantor part with the deed without reservation, with intention that it take effect at that time as a transfer of title. . . . Placing an executed and acknowledged deed in a place where the grantee has access and from which he can, without hindrance, transfer it to his possession, but with the intent that the grantee not take it and have it recorded until after the grantor's death, does not constitute a delivery. . . .

We hold that the delivery of the key to the safety deposit box did not constitute delivery of the deed as a matter of law and that plaintiff made a prima facie case. The judgment of dismissal is reversed and the cause remanded for a new trial.

[Judgment reversed and action remanded]

QUESTIONS

1. Does this case hold that there can never be a delivery of a deed by making a delivery of a key to a safety deposit box containing the deed?
2. What additional evidence would have changed the result in the *Green* case?
3. What was the significance of the fact that the mother was not told that the deed had been taken from the box and recorded?

Generally, there must be an acceptance by the grantee. In all cases, an acceptance is presumed. However, the grantee may disclaim the transfer if the grantee acts within a reasonable time after learning that the transfer has been made.

20. Recording of Deeds

The owner of land may record the deed in the office of a public official, sometimes called a recorder or commissioner of deeds. The recording is not required to make the deed effective to pass title, but it is done so that the public will know that the grantee is the present owner and thereby prevent the former owner from making any other transaction relating to the property. The recording statutes provide that a person purchasing land from the last holder of record will take title free of any unrecorded claim to the land of which the purchaser does not have notice or knowledge.

The fact that a deed is recorded charges everyone with knowledge of its existence, even if they in fact do not know of it because they have neglected to examine the record.

The recording of a deed, however, is only such notice if the deed was properly executed. Likewise, the grantee of land cannot claim any protection by virtue of the recording of a deed when (a) a claim is made by one whose title is superior to that of the owner of record, (b) the grantee had notice or knowledge of the adverse claim when title was acquired, (c) a person acting under a hostile claim was then in possession of the land, (d) the grantee received the land as a gift, or (e) the transfer to the grantee was fraudulent.

21. Additional Protection of Buyers

Apart from the protection given to buyers and third persons by the recorded title to property, a buyer may generally also be protected by procuring title insurance or an abstract of title. An **abstract of title** is a summarized report of the title to the property as shown by the records, together with a report of all judgments, mortgages, and similar recorded claims against the property.

22. Cancellation of Deeds

A deed, although delivered, acknowledged, and recorded, may be set aside or canceled by the grantor upon proof of circumstances that would warrant the setting aside of a contract. For example, when a conveyance is made in consideration of a promise to support the grantor, the failure of the grantee to perform will ordinarily justify cancellation of the deed.

23. Grantor's Warranties

The warranties of the grantor relate to the title transferred by the grantor and to the fitness of the property for use.

(a) WARRANTIES OF TITLE. In the common law deed, the grantor may expressly warrant or make certain covenants as to the title conveyed. The statutes authorizing a short form of deed provide that unless otherwise stated in the deed, the grantor shall be presumed to have made certain warranties of title.

The more important of the covenants or warranties of title that the grantor may make are (1) **covenant of seisin**, or guarantee that the grantor owns the estate conveyed; (2) **covenant of right to convey**, or guarantee that the grantor—if not the owner, as in the case of an agent—has the right or authority to make the conveyance; (3) **covenant against encumbrances**, or guarantee that the land is not subject to any right or interest of a third person, such as a lien or easement; (4) **covenant of quiet enjoyment**, or covenant by the grantor that the grantee's possession of the land shall not be disturbed either by the grantor, in the case of a limited covenant, or by the grantor or any person claiming title under the grantor, in the case of a general covenant; and (5) **covenant of further assurances**, or promise that the grantor will execute any additional docu-

ments that may be required to perfect the title of the grantee.

(b) FITNESS FOR USE. Courts in most states hold that when a builder or real estate developer sells a new house to a home buyer, an implied warranty that the house and foundation are fit for occupancy or use arises. This warranty arises regardless of whether the house was purchased before, during, or after completion of construction.[8] This warranty will not be implied against the first buyer when the house is resold. However, there is authority that the second buyer may sue the original contractor for breach of the implied warranty, even though there is no privity of contract.

24. Grantee's Covenants

In a deed, the grantee may agree to do or to refrain from doing certain acts. Such an agreement becomes a binding contract between the grantor and the grantee. The grantor may sue the grantee for its breach.

(a) COVENANTS RUNNING WITH THE LAND. When the covenant of the grantee relates directly to the property conveyed, such as an agreement to maintain fences on the property or that the property shall be used only for residential purposes, it is said not only that the covenant is binding between the grantor and the grantee but also that it **runs with the land**. This means that anyone acquiring the land from the grantee is also bound by the covenant of the grantee, even though the subsequent owner has not made any such agreement with anyone.

The right to enforce the covenant also runs with the land owned by the grantor to whom the promise was made. For example, Hensler owns adjoining tracts of land and conveys one of them to Asmus. If Asmus covenants to

---

[8] The buyer of a house should give notice to the seller of any defects within a reasonable time after the buyer learns or should have learned of the defects. Pollard v Saxe & Yolles Development Co. 12 Cal 3d 374, 115 Cal Rptr 648, 525 P2d 88 (1974) (extending the concept of UCC § 2-607(3), although recognizing that it was applicable only to the sale of goods).

Figure 51-1 Form of Warranty Deed

THIS DEED, made the twentieth day of November, nineteen hundred and... between James K. Damron, residing at 132 Spring Street in the Borough of Manhattan, City and State of New York, party of the first part, and Terrence S. Bloemker, residing at 14 Steinway Street in the Borough of Queens, City and State of New York, party of the second part,

WITNESSETH, that the party of the first part, in consideration of the sum of one dollar ($1), lawful money of the United States, and other good and valuable consideration paid by the party of the second part, does hereby grant and release unto the party of the second part, his heirs and assigns forever,

ALL that certain lot, piece, and parcel of land situated in the Borough of Manhattan, City and County of New York, and State of New York, and bounded and described as follows:

Beginning at a point on the northerly side of Spring Street, distant two hundred (200) feet westerly from the corner formed by the intersection of the northerly side of Spring Street with the westerly side of 6th Avenue, running thence northerly parallel with 6th Avenue one hundred (100) feet, thence westerly and parallel with said Spring Street one hundred (100) feet; thence southerly, again parallel with said 6th Avenue one hundred (100) feet to the northerly side of Spring Street, and thence easterly along the said northerly side of Spring Street one hundred (100) feet to the point or place of beginning.

Together with the appurtenances and all the estate and rights of the party of the first part in and to said premises.

TO HAVE AND TO HOLD the premises herein granted unto the party of the second part, his heirs and assigns forever.

AND the party of the first part covenants as follows:

First. That the party of the first part is seised of the said premises in fee simple, and has good right to convey the same;

Second. That the party of the second part shall quietly enjoy the said premises;

Third. That the said premises are free from encumbrances except as expressly stated;

Fourth. That the party of the first part will execute or procure any further necessary assurance of the title to said premises;

IN WITNESS WHEREOF, the party of the first part has hereunto set his hand and seal the day and year first above written.

JAMES K. DAMRON (L.S.)

In presence of:

DIANA L. REILMAN

State of New York   } s.s.:
County of New York

On the twentieth day of November in the year nineteen hundred and ..., before me personally came James K. Damron, to me known and known to me to be the individual described in, and who executed, the foregoing instrument, and he acknowledged that he executed the same.

DIANA L. REILMAN
Notary Public, New York County

[AUTHORS'S NOTE: ACKNOWLEDGMENT BEFORE A NOTARY PUBLIC IS NOT ESSENTIAL TO THE EFFECTIVENESS OF A DEED, BUT IT IS TYPICALLY REQUIRED TO QUALIFY THE DEED FOR RECORDING.]

maintain the surface drainage on the land so that it will not flood Hensler's land, the benefit of this covenant will run with the land retained by Hensler. If Hensler sells the remaining tract of land to Stein, Asmus is bound to perform the covenant so as to benefit the neighboring tract even though it is now owned by Stein.

(b) RESTRICTIVE AND AFFIRMATIVE COVENANTS. A covenant that provides that the grantee shall refrain from certain conduct is termed a **restrictive** (or negative) **covenant**. It runs with the land in the same manner as a covenant that calls for the performance of an act—that is, an **affirmative covenant**.

A restrictive covenant may impose a limitation on the kind of structure that can be erected on the land. A restrictive covenant may also impose a limitation on the use that may be made of the land.

(1) General Building Scheme. When a tract of land is developed and when individual lots or homes are sold to separate purchasers, it is common to use the same restrictive covenants in all deeds. Thus, uniform restrictions and patterns are imposed on the property. Any person acquiring a lot within the tract is bound by the restrictions if they are in the deed or a prior recorded deed, or if the grantee has notice or knowledge of such restrictions. Any person owning one of the lots in the tract may bring suit against another lot owner to enforce the restrictive covenant. The effect is to create a zoning code based on the agreement of the parties in their deeds, as distinguished from one based on government regulation.

(2) Restraints on Alienation. Covenants may restrict the sale or transfer of the property. It is lawful to provide that the grantor shall have the option to repurchase the property, or that if the grantee offers to sell it to anyone, the grantor will be given an opportunity to match the price that a third person is willing to pay. Restrictions on the grantee's right to sell the property are not enforceable when the restriction discriminates against potential buyers because of race, color, creed, or national origin.

F. OTHER METHODS OF TRANSFERRING REAL PROPERTY

Title to real property can also be acquired by eminent domain and by adverse possession.

25. Eminent Domain

By **eminent domain**, property is taken from its private owner and the title is acquired by the taking government or public authority. Two important questions arise: whether there is a taking of property and whether the property is taken for a public use. In respect to the first, it is not necessary that the owner be physically deprived of the property. It is sufficient that the normal use of the property has been impaired or lost. As to the second, it is not necessary that the public at large actually use the property. It is sufficient that it is appropriated for the public benefit.

26. Adverse Possession

Title to land may be acquired by holding it adversely to the true owner for a certain period of time. In such a case, the possessor gains title by **adverse possession**. If such possession is maintained, the possessor automatically becomes the owner of the property, even though the possessor admittedly had no lawful claim to the land.

To acquire title in this manner, possession must be (a) actual, (b) visible and notorious, (c) exclusive, (d) hostile, and (e) continuous for a required period of time.[9]

Commonly the period of time is 21 years, but state statutes may provide 10 to 20 years. Occupation of land in the mistaken belief that one is the owner is a "hostile" possession.

What constitutes "visible" or "open and notorious" use of property? This was the problem in the *Appalachian* case.

---

[9]   Garringer v Wingard (Ala) 585 So 2d 898 (1991).

APPALACHIAN REG. HEALTHCARE v ROYAL CROWN

(Ky) 824 SW2d 878 (1992)

Thirty-five years ago, Royal Crown Bottling Company (RC), leased a small plot of land from Stumbo Supply Company, Inc. RC erected a billboard advertising Royal Crown Cola. The billboard was eight by twenty-four feet in size and twenty feet from the edge of the highway. The plot of land was small but wide enough for the sign. In October 1967, RC purchased the land from Annie Stumbo and recorded the deed. In 1986, Appalachian Regional Healthcare, Inc. (ARH), owner of the adjoining property, approached RC and requested that it permit ARH to place a sign on the property. The permission was granted. Shortly thereafter, ARH asserted legal title to the property and demanded that RC remove its sign. ARH based its claim on a deed dated September 1963. Accordingly, RC stipulated that ARH had superior record title but continued to claim ownership of the property by adverse possession. The parties also stipulated that RC continuously maintained a sign on the land for the statutory period of fifteen years under Kentucky law. From a judgment in favor of ARH, RC appealed.

HOWERTON, J. . . . One may obtain a perfect title to real property by adverse possession for the statutory period of time of fifteen years even when there is no intention by the adverse possessor to claim land not belonging to him. . . . There are, however, five elements, all of which must be satisfied, before adverse possession will bar record title: (1) possession must be hostile and under a claim of right, (2) it must be actual, (3) it must be exclusive, (4) it must be continuous, and (5) it must be open and notorious. . . . The trial court found that RC's possession was not open and notorious and quieted title in ARH, the record title holder.

The "open and notorious" element required that the possessor openly evince a purpose to hold dominion over the property with such hostility that will give the nonpossessory owner notice of the adverse claim. . . . It is the legal owner's knowledge, either actual or imputable, of another's possession of lands that affects the ownership. . . .

An intent to exercise dominion over land may be evidenced by the erection of physical improvements on the property. . . . Further, the character of the property, its physical nature and the use to which it has been put, determine the character of the acts necessary to put the true owner on notice of the hostile claim. . . .

It is clear in this case that RC evidenced its intent to exercise dominion over the plot of land. RC erected a billboard sign on the property approximately thirty-five years before ARH initiated this action. In 1967 RC purchased the property so that it could continue to maintain its sign on the property. The plot of land is small and located on a highway rendering it ideally suitable for the erection of a sign. In fact, ARH wanted title to the property so that it could display its sign. Thus, we find that the physical nature of the property and the past use of the property both indicate that there could be no more practical use for this land.

In addition, we find that RC's use of the land was an "open and notorious" one. The trial court found that the use was not "open and notorious" because billboards are universally placed along highways on property not owned by the sign owners, but with the landowner's permission. However, we do not agree with the trial court as to what satisfies the "open and notorious" requirement. To be "open and notorious" the possession must be conspicuous and not secret, so that the legal title holder has notice of the adverse use. . . .

RC's adverse use consisted of the erection and maintenance of a billboard along Kentucky Highway 15 for greater than the statutory period of time. There could be no more conspicuous use. Further, it is clear that ARH, the record title holder, had actual notice of RC's possession. This is evidenced by the fact that ARH sought permission from RC to place its sign on the property.

The trial court also denied title to RC based on its finding that RC's erection of the billboard did not indicate the extent of RC's claim. We agree that, in order to make an adverse claim definite, the adverse possessor must have either some color of title that will show the extent of the claim or there must be a definite boundary. . . . However, any instrument that purports to convey land and shows the extent of the grantee's claim may afford color of title. . . . Thus even a deed that is defective or invalid is sufficient to afford color of title. One in the actual adverse possession of a portion of land under a deed is in adverse possession of the entire tract described in the deed; while one in adverse possession without color of title must indicate the extent of his claim by well-defined boundaries. . . .

In this case RC had color of title through its 1967 deed. It is immaterial that the deed was junior to ARH's deed. Accordingly, we find that the extent of RC's claim is evidenced by the description contained in its 1967 deed. . . .

[Judgment reversed]

QUESTIONS

1. Did ARH act ethically by trying to eject someone who had possessed the land for fifteen years?
2. What is needed to establish the elements of "open and notorious"?
3. What is meant by color of title?
4. Do you agree with the decision?

G. MORTGAGES

An agreement that creates an interest in real property as security for an obligation, which interest is to cease on the performance of the obligation, is a **mortgage**. The person whose interest in the property is given as security is the **mortgagor**. The person who receives the security is the **mortgagee**.

27. Characteristics of a Mortgage

There are three characteristics of a mortgage: (a) the termination of the mortgagee's interest upon the performance of the obligation secured by the mortgage; (b) the right of the mortgagee to enforce the mortgage by foreclosure upon the mortgagors failure to perform; and (c) the mortgagor's right to redeem or regain the property.

28. Property Subject to Mortgage

In general, any form of property that may be sold or conveyed may be mortgaged. It is immaterial whether the right is a present right or a future interest, or merely a right in the land of another. It is not necessary that the mortgagor have complete or absolute ownership in the property. The mortgagor may mortgage any interest, legal or equitable, divided or undivided.

29. Form of Mortgage

Since a mortgage of real property transfers an interest in the property, it must be in writing by virtue of the statute of frauds.

As a general rule, no particular form of language is required, provided the language used expresses the intent of the parties to create a mortgage. In many states the substance of a mortgage is practically identical to that of a deed, except a mortgage contains a defeasance clause, a description of the obligation secured, and sometimes a covenant to pay or perform the obligation. The **defeasance clause** states that the mortgage shall cease to have any effect when the obligation is performed, such as when the debt of the mortgagor is paid. In many states, statutes provide a standardized form of mortgage that may be used.

30. Recording or Filing of Mortgage

An unrecorded mortgage is valid and binding between the parties to it. The heirs or donees of a mortgagor cannot defend against the mortgage on the ground that it has not been recorded. Recording statutes in most states, however, provide that purchasers or creditors who give value and act in good faith in ignorance of an unrecorded mortgage may enforce their respective rights against the property without regard to the existence of the unrecorded mortgage. Accordingly, the purchaser of the land in good faith for value from the mortgagor holds the land free of the unrecorded mortgage. The mortgagee's only remedy is against the mortgagor on the debt due the mortgagee. The mortgagee can proceed against the transferee only if the mortgagee can prove that the transferee of the land did not purchase it in good faith, for value, and in ignorance of the unrecorded mortgage.

31. Responsibilities of the Parties

The mortgagor and mortgagee have the following duties and liabilities when a mortgage is placed on real estate.

(a) REPAIRS AND IMPROVEMENTS. In the absence of an agreement to the contrary, a mortgagor is under no duty to make improvements or to restore or repair parts of the premises that are destroyed or damaged through no fault of the mortgagor.

A mortgagee, when in possession, must make reasonable and necessary repairs in order to preserve the property. The mortgagee is entitled to reimbursement for such repairs. Ordinarily, however, the mortgagee may not charge to the mortgagor expenditures for valuable or enduring improvements.

(b) TAXES, ASSESSMENTS, AND INSURANCE. The duty to pay taxes and assessments rests with the mortgagor. In the absence of an agreement, neither party is under a duty to insure the mortgaged property. Both parties, however, may insure their respective interests. It is common practice for the mortgagor to obtain a single policy of insurance on the property payable to the mortgagee and the mortgagor as their interests may appear.[10]

(c) IMPAIRMENT OF SECURITY. The mortgagor is liable to the mortgagee for any damage to the property, caused by the mortgagor's fault, that impairs the security of the mortgage by materially reducing the value of the property. Both the mortgagor and mortgagee have a right of action against a third person who wrongfully injures the property.

---

[10] Beneficial Standard Life Insurance Co. v Trinity National Bank (Tex App) 763 SW2d 52 (1988).

32. Transfer of Interest

Questions arise as to transfers by the mortgagor and the mortgagee of their respective interests and of the liability of a transferee of the mortgagor.

(a) TRANSFER BY MORTGAGOR. The mortgagor may ordinarily transfer the property without the consent of the mortgagee. Such a transfer passes only the interest of the mortgagor and does not divest or impair a properly recorded mortgage.

The transfer of the property by the mortgagor does not affect the liability of the mortgagor to the mortgagee. Unless the latter has agreed to substitute the mortgagor's grantee for the mortgagor, the latter remains liable for the mortgage debt as though no transfer had been made.

(b) LIABILITY OF MORTGAGOR'S TRANSFEREE. The purchaser of mortgaged property does not become personally liable for the mortgage debt unless the purchaser expressly assumes that debt. Such an assumption of the debt does not release the mortgagor from liability to the mortgagee unless the mortgagee agrees to such substitution of parties.

(c) TRANSFER BY MORTGAGEE. In most states, a mortgage may be transferred or assigned by the mortgagee.

33. Rights of Mortgagee
After Default

Upon the mortgagor's default, the mortgagee in some states is entitled to obtain possession of the property and collect the rents or to have a receiver appointed for that purpose. In all states, the mortgagee may enforce the mortgage by **foreclosure**, a procedure resulting in sale of the mortgaged property.

Generally, it is provided that upon any default under the terms of the mortgage agreement, the mortgagee has the right to declare that the entire mortgage debt is due. The mortgagee generally has this right even though the default related only to an installment or to the doing of some act, such as maintaining insurance on the property or producing receipts for taxes.

A sale on the foreclosure of the mortgage destroys the mortgage, and the property passes free of the mortgage to the buyer at the sale. However, the extinction of the mortgage by foreclosure does not destroy the debt that was secured by the mortgage. The mortgagor remains liable for any unpaid balance or deficiency. By statute, the mortgagor is generally given credit for the fair value of the property if it was purchased by the mortgagee.

34. Rights of Mortgagor
After Default

After default, the mortgagor may seek to stop or stay foreclosure or to redeem the mortgaged land.

(a) STAY OF FORECLOSURE. In certain cases, authorized by statute, a **stay** (or delay) **of foreclosure** may be obtained by the mortgagor to prevent undue hardship.

(b) REDEMPTION. The **right of redemption** means the right of the mortgagor to free the property of the mortgage lien after default. By statute in many states, the right may be exercised during a certain time following foreclosure and sale of the mortgaged land.

SUMMARY

Real property includes land, buildings and fixtures, and rights in the land of another.

The interest held by a person in real property may be defined in terms of the period of time for which the person will remain the owner. The interest may be a fee simple estate, which lasts forever, or a life estate, which lasts for the life of a person. These estates are known as freehold estates. If the ownership interest exists for a specified number of days, months, or years, the interest is a leasehold estate.

Personal property may be attached to or associated with real property in such a way that it becomes real property. In such a case, it is called a fixture. To determine whether property has in fact become a fixture, the courts look to the method of attachment, to how the property is adapted to the realty, and to the intent of the person originally owning the personal property.

Under common law, the liability of an occupier of land for injury to third persons on the premises is dependent on the status of the third persons as trespassers, licensees, or invitees. Many jurisdictions are ignoring these common law distinctions, however, in favor of an ordinary negligence standard, or giving licensees the same protection as invitees. Recreational use statutes limit or eliminate a landowner's liability for personal injuries to a person using the owner's land for recreational purposes.

Real property may be the subject of multiple ownership. The forms of multiple ownership are the same as for personal property. In addition, there are special forms of co-ownership for real property, such as condominiums and cooperatives.

A deed is an instrument transferring an interest in land by a grantor to a grantee. A deed can be a quitclaim deed, a warranty deed, or a statutory deed. To be effective, a deed must be signed or sealed by the grantor and delivered to the grantee. Recording the deed is not required to make the deed effective to pass title, but recording provides notice to the public that the grantee is the present owner. The warranties of the grantor relate to the title transferred by the grantor and to the fitness of the property for use. In the absence of any express warranty in the deed, no warranty of fitness arises under the common law in the sale or the conveyance of real estate. Most states today hold that when a builder or real estate developer sells a new home to a buyer, an implied warranty of habitability arises. Title to real estate may also be acquired by eminent domain and adverse possession.

An agreement that creates an interest in real property as security for an obligation and that ends upon the performance of the obligation is a mortgage. A mortgage must be in writing under the statute of frauds. If the mortgage is unrecorded, it is valid between the parties. The mortgage should be recorded to put good-faith purchasers on notice of the mortgage. A purchaser of the mortgaged property does not become liable for the mortgaged debt unless such a purchaser assumes the mortgage. The mortgagor still remains liable unless the mortgagee agrees to a substitution of parties. If the mortgagor defaults, the mortgagee may enforce the mortgage by foreclosure. Such foreclosure may be delayed because of undue hardship.

LAW IN PRACTICE

1. Be sure that if personal property is to be attached to realty your intention is clearly indicated as to whether this is or is not to be considered a fixture.

2. Understand that in a cooperative, you are a shareholder in a corporation. In a condominium, however, you are an owner of property that can be sold or transferred.

3. Be sure that any deed to land that you purchase is promptly recorded to prevent a good faith purchaser from defeating your title.

4. Remember that if you do not assume a mortgage, you have no personal liability on the mortgage debt.

QUESTIONS AND CASE PROBLEMS

1. What social forces are affected by recognizing the right of aircraft to fly over land at such a height that the flight does not interfere with the use of the land and is not dangerous to persons or property on the land?

2. Bunn and his wife claimed that they had an easement to enter and use the swimming pool on neighboring land. A contract between the former owners of the Bunns' property and the adjacent apartment complex contained a provision that the use of the apartment complex's swimming pool would be available to the purchaser and family. No reference to the pool was made in the contract between the former owners and the Bunns nor was there any reference thereto in the deed conveying the property to the Bunns. Decide. [*Bunn v Offutt*, 216 Va 681, 222 SE2d 522]

3. Richard sold land to Smith by a warranty deed. Smith did not record the deed. Some time thereafter, Richard sold the same land to Wayne by a warranty deed. Wayne was a good-faith purchaser for value who had no knowledge of the prior unrecorded deed. Wayne recorded his deed. Who owns the land, Smith or Wayne? Why?

4. Joyce, who was the owner of a fee-simple estate in Blackacre, died without leaving a will. Who is now the owner of Blackacre? Explain.

5. Compare the status of an apartment owner in (a) a condominium and (b) a cooperative.

6. What is the most important difference between a license and an easement?

7. Bradham and others, trustees of the Mount Olivet Church, brought an action to cancel a mortgage on the church property. The mortgage had been executed by Davis and others as trustees of the church and given to Robinson as mortgagee. It was found by the court that the church was not indebted to the mortgagee for any amount. Should the mortgage be canceled? [*Bradham v Robinson*, 236 NC 589, 73 SE2d 555]

8. Miller executed a deed to real estate, naming Zieg as grantee. He placed the deed in an envelope on which was written, To be filed at my death, and put the envelope and deed in a safe-deposit box in the National Bank. The box had been rented in the names of Miller and Zieg. After Millers death, Zieg removed the deed from the safe-deposit box. Moseley, as executor under Millers will, brought an action against Zieg to declare the deed void. Decide. [*Moseley v Zieg, 180 Neb 810, 146 NW2d 72*]

9. Henry Lile owned a house. When the land on which it was situated was condemned for a highway, he moved the house to the land of his daughter, Sarah Crick. In the course of construction work, blasting damaged the house. Sarah Crick sued the contractors, Terry & Wright. They claimed that Henry should be joined in the action as a plaintiff and that Sarah could not sue by herself, because it was Henrys house. Were the defendants correct? [*Terry & Wright v Crick (Ky) 418 SW2d 217*]

10. Bradt believed his back yard ran all the way to a fence. Actually there was a strip on Bradt's side of the fence which belonged to his neighbor, Giovannone. Bradt never intended to take land away from anyone. Bradt later brought an action against Giovannone to determine who owned the strip on ,Bradt's side of the fence. Who is the owner? Why? [*Bradt v Giovannone, 35 App Div 2d 322, 315 NYS2d 961*]

11. Larry Wiersema was building a house for himself in the country. He made a contract with Workman Plumbing, Heating & Cooling, Inc., to do most of the plumbing and heating work in the new house. This work included the installation of a septic tank. Workman performed the contract correctly. However, because of the peculiar kind of clay surrounding the house, the drainage from the septic tank system was very poor, and the basement of Larrys house was frequently flooded. He sued Workman for breach of the implied warranty of habitability. Was Workman liable? [*Wiersema v Workman Plumbing, Heating & Cooling, Inc. 87 Ill App 3d 535, 42 Ill Dec 664, 409 NE2d 159*]

12. Davis Store Fixtures sold certain equipment on credit to Head, who installed it in a building that was later owned by the Cadillac Club. When payment was not made, Davis sought to repossess the equipment. If the equipment constituted fixtures, this could not be done. The equipment consisted of a bar for serving drinks, a bench, and a drain board. The first two were attached to the floor or wall with screws, and the drain board .was connected to water and drainage pipes. Did the equipment constitute fixtures?

13. Smikahl sold to Hansen a tract of land on which there were two houses and four trailer lots equipped with concrete patios and necessary connections for utility lines. The tract purchased by Hansen was completely surrounded by the land owned by Smikahl and third persons. To get onto the highway, it was necessary to cross the Smikahl tract. Several years later, Smikahl put a barbed wire fence around his land. Hansen sued to prevent obstruction to travel between his land and the highway over the Smikahl land. Smikahl defended on the ground that no such right of travel had been given to Hansen. Was he correct? *[Hansen v Smikahl, 173 Neb 309, 113 NW2d 210]*

14. Martin Manufacturing decided to raise additional long-term capital by mortgaging an industrial park that it owned. First National Loan Company agreed to lend Martin $1 million and to take a note and first mortgage on the land and building. The mortgage was duly recorded. Martin sold the property to Marshall, who took the property and assumed the mortgage debt. Does Marshall have any personal liability on the mortgage debt? Is Martin still liable on the mortgage debt? Explain.

15. In 1980, Ortleb, Inc., a Delaware corporation, purchased certain land in Montana from the Alberts but neglected to record the deed. In 1988, the Alberts sold the same property to Bently, a resident of Montana, who purchased in good faith and recorded his deed. Ortleb sues Bently to determine who owned the land. Who will win? Explain.

C H A P T E R 5 2

ENVIRONMENTAL LAW AND COMMUNITY PLANNING

A. PREVENTION OF POLLUTION
   1. Statutory Environmental Protection
   2. Waste Control
   3. Environmental Impact Statements
   4. Regulation by Administrative
     Agencies
   5. Litigation
   6. Criminal Liability

B. COMMUNITY PLANNING
   7. Restrictive Covenants in Private
     Contracts
   8. Public Zoning
   9. Eminent Domain

C. NUISANCES
   10. Definition of Nuisance
   11. The Technological Environment of
     the Law of Nuisance

LEARNING OBJECTIVES

After studying this chapter, you will be able to:
1. *List the significant statutes adopted to pro-*
   tect the environment.
2. *List the methods for enforcing environ-*
   mental protection controls.
3. *Distinguish between private and public com-*
   munity planning.
4. *Define and illustrate restrictive covenants as*
   to real estate.
5. *Compare zoning, eminent domain, and the*
   law of nuisance with respect to interference
   with rights of owners of property.

Americans now recognize that resources must be conserved and the environment must be protected from pollution.

A. PREVENTION OF POLLUTION

As America changed from a rural, agricultural society to an urban, industrial one, new laws were needed to prevent the pollution of the environment.

1. Statutory Environmental Protection

Beginning with the National Environmental Policy Act of 1969 (NEPA), Congress has adopted a series of laws designed to prevent the pollution of the air and water and to reduce noise.[1] Congress has adopted other statutes designed to reduce the problem of waste disposal by encouraging recycling or reuse of various products.[2] Many of the federal statutes authorize the Environmental Protection Agency (EPA) to adopt standards and regulations to carry out the provisions of the statutes.[3]

State legislatures have also been active in this area, and many states have laws that are similar to the federal laws. A state law or local ordinance must not (a) conflict with a federal statute or (b) place an unreasonable burden on interstate commerce.

Figure 52-1 The Legal Environment of Resource Protection and Community Planning

	Environmental Issues	
	Resource Protection	Community Planning
Legal Body Exercising Control	International governments U.S. government State governments Local governments	State governments Local governments
Type of Control and Devices Used	Direct control through statutes and ordinances Limited or incidental state governmental control through nuisance law and restrictive covenants	Direct control through statutes, ordinances, and restrictive covenants

---

[1] For example, see the Clean Air Act, 42 USC §§ 1857 et seq.; the National Motor Vehicles Emissions Standards Act, 42 USC §§ 1857f et seq.; the Noise Control Acts of 1970 and 1972, 42 USC § 4901; the Water Pollution Control Act Amendments of 1972, 33 USC §§ 1251 et seq. The pollution of navigable waters had already been prohibited by the River and Harbor Appropriations Act of 1899. See also the Wildfire Disaster Recovery Act of 1989, Act of May 9, 1990, PL 101-286, 104 Stat 171, ___ USC §§ ___ et seq.; the Oil Pollution Act of 1990, Act of August 18, 1990, PL 101-380, 104 Stat 484, 33 USC §§ 2701 et seq., increases the maximum liability of persons causing oil spills, establishes a cleanup fund to pay for cleanup expenses when produced by an unknown person or the person liable has paid the maximum amount of liability, and requires that all oil tankers built hereafter or in use after the year 2015 be constructed with double hulls.

[2] See, for example, the Solid Waste Disposal Act, Act of October 20, 1965, 79 Stat 997, 42 USC §§ 3251 et seq.; the Resource Recovery and Policy Act of 1970, Act of October 26, 1970, PL 91-512, 84 Stat 1227, 42 USC §§ 3251 et seq.; the Resource Conservation and Recovery Act of 1976, Act of October 21, 1976, PL 94-580, 90 Stat 2795, 42 USC §§ 6901 et seq. These statutes have been amended many times.

[3] International Fabricare Institute v U.S. Environmental Protection Agency (CA Dist Col) 972 F2d 384 (1992).

2. Waste Control

Modern industries and lifestyles produce a large quantity of waste materials. Some of the industrial waste can be used to make by-products. Some can be used again or recycled. Some wastes are biodegradable.

In contrast, some waste materials remain. Some are dangerous to life, both human and animal, and to vegetation and water supplies. The state and federal governments have adopted programs for protecting the nation and the public from harmful wastes.[4] A license may be required for the disposal of radioactive wastes. A state law providing for a spill fund to compensate persons for damage from hazardous waste disposal is valid.

The Comprehensive Environmental Response, Compensation and Liability Act of 1980 (CERCLA)[5] provides for the establishment of a national inventory of inactive hazardous waste sites. It also provides for the creation of a multimillion-dollar Hazardous Waste Fund, commonly called Superfund, to pay the cost of eliminating or containing the condemned waste sites.

The Environmental Protection Agency (EPA) is authorized to sue responsible parties to recover the costs of cleanup operations. Under CERCLA, a private enterprise may sue a state to recover the cost of cleanup made necessary by state action.

In many states the approval of a local Board of Health is required to operate a hazardous waste facility.[6]

The *Taylor* case raised questions whether a person disposed of hazardous waste by leaving it where it was formed and whether the

CALIFORNIA v TAYLOR
___ Cal App 3d ___, 9 Cal Rptr 227 (1992)

Taylor operated a small factory in a rented building. In the course of production, hazardous waste materials were generated. These were stored in drums in the factory yard. The business went broke and Taylor left the factory because he could not pay the rent. He left 200 drums of hazardous waste in the factory yard. Criminal proceedings were begun against Taylor for knowingly "disposing" of the waste in an unlicensed area. He raised the defenses that (1) he had merely abandoned the waste but had not disposed of it, and (2) he could not have taken the waste elsewhere because he did not have the money to do so. On the motion of Taylor, the lower court vacated the proceeding and the state appealed.

TIMLIN, A. J. . . . The trial court read a requirement of "movement of waste to some location other than the premises on which it was created" into . . . the word "disposal" in section 25189.5(a). . . . On appeal, defendant argues that the trial court correctly understood the generally accepted meaning of "abandon" to involve the concept of "dumping"—that is, to "drop *elsewhere*." We disagree. The common understanding of "abandonment" is not limited in such fashion. It is commonplace to

---

[4] See, for example, the Nuclear Waste Policy Act of 1982, Act of January 7, 1983, PL 97-425, 42 USC §§ 10101-10226; Minnesota v Gerring (Minn App) 418 NW2d 517 (1988).

[5] Act of December 11, 1980, PL 96-510, 94 Stat 2767, 42 USC §§ 9601 et seq., as amended.

[6] Clean Harbors of Braintree, Inc. v Board of Health of Braintree, 409 Mass 834, 570 NE2d 987 (1991).

speak of abandoning something where it lies—to simply walk away from something which is no longer wanted. . . .

Our understanding of the word "abandonment" . . . is reinforced by the 1989 amendments to section 25113 which were adopted by the Legislature. In 1989, section 25113 was amended to read:

"(a) 'Disposal' means either of the following:

"(1) The discharge, deposit, injection, dumping, *spilling, leaking, or placing of any waste so that the waste or any constituent of the waste is or may be emitted into the air or discharged into or on any land or waters, including groundwaters, or may otherwise enter the environment.*

"(2) The abandonment *of any waste.*

"(b) The amendment *of the section made at the 1989-90 Regular Session of the Legislature does not constitute a change in, but* is declaratory of, the existing law." *(Emphasis added.)*

It is clear, then, that under section 25113 abandonment is something different than dumping and that an abandonment of waste does not require some sort of affirmative relocation of that waste. An abandonment of waste under section 25113 is simply the permanent and intentional surrendering of dominion and control over that waste; such an abandonment connotes a final act of severing or terminating a possessory or controlling interest in hazardous waste—and the connotation applies irrespective of the fact that, prior to the act of abandonment, the possessor of the hazardous waste had properly stored the waste on the premises at which it was eventually abandoned. In this case, defendant is alleged to have committed just such an abandonment with respect to the drums of hazardous waste liquids.

Finally, we note that the interpretation we here give the "abandonment" aspect of the word "disposal" in section 25189.5(a) is consistent with the expressed Legislative intent in enacting the California Hazardous Waste Control Law: "In order to protect the public health and the environment and to conserve natural resources, it is in the public interest to establish regulations and incentives which ensure that the generators of hazardous waste employ technology and management practices for the safe handling, treatment, recycling, and destruction of their hazardous wastes prior to disposal." (§ 25101(a).) Any statutory interpretation of section 25189.5(a) which would countenance a hazardous waste generator simply walking away from almost 200 drums of hazardous liquid waste without providing for their safe disposal would *not* be consistent with the Legislature's intent and purpose in enacting the California Hazardous Waste Control Law. Although hazardous waste might be properly labelled and securely stored at the time of its abandonment, the ever present possibility that, with the passage of time, the containers of waste would be breached by vandals, by the effects of weather or by any one of a number of different sorts of natural disasters, resulting in the waste being discharged into the environment, militates against an interpretation of "disposal by abandonment" which would require that the meaning of "abandonment" include the elements of "discharge into the environment" and "movement from the existing place of storage." Such an interpretation would be clearly contrary to the protective public policy underlying the California Hazardous Waste Control Law.

. . . The trial court [did not] agree with defendant's argument that his financial inability to hire an authorized hazardous waste hauler to remove the hazardous materials from the manufacturing premises was a defense to the criminal charge brought against him. Defendant has renewed his argument before this court—but it is similarly unavailing here.

Defendant has cited no California authority for his position. . .

[Judgment vacated and prosecution remanded]

QUESTIONS

1. Did the defendant deny disposing of the toxic waste?
2. What management lesson is to be learned from the *Taylor* case?
3. How could Taylor be convicted of "knowingly" violating the law when he did not know that what he had done constituted an "abandonment" prohibited by the law?
4. Was there anything unusual about the procedure followed in the Taylor case?

lack of money to take the waste elsewhere was a defense.

3. Environmental Impact Statements

Environmental protection legislation generally requires that any activity that might have a significant effect on the environment be supported by an environmental impact statement (EIS). Whenever a bill is proposed in Congress, and whenever federal action significantly affecting the quality of the human environment is considered, a statement must be prepared as to the environmental impact of the action. A number of states impose the same requirement on government officials, and some require an environmental impact statement for the construction of any large private building.

In the *Chinese Staff* case the underlying question was what was included in the environment.

CHINESE STAFF AND WORKERS ASS'N v NEW YORK
68 NY2d 359, 502 NE2d 176 (1986)

Henry Street Partners wished to build a high-rise luxury condominium on a vacant lot in the Chinatown section of New York City. The appropriate city agencies issued a permit allowing the construction of the building. The issuance of the permit was then attacked by a lawsuit brought by the Chinese Staff and Workers Association and others, protesting on the ground that the proposed building would have a harmful effect on the Chinatown section by driving out the poorer residents and businesses. From a judgment against the objectors, they appealed.

ALEXANDER, J. . . . The regulations promulgated by the City of New York (Executive Order No. 91, Aug. 24, 1977, entitled City Environmental Quality Review [CEQR]) as authorized by and in implementation of the State Environmental Quality Review Act (ECL art. 8 [SEQRA]) require lead agencies to consider both the short- and long-term and primary and secondary effects of a proposed action in determining whether the action may have a significant effect on the environment so as to require the preparation of an Environmental Impact Statement (EIS). . . .

In reviewing administrative proceedings in general and SEQRA determinations in particular, we are limited to considering "whether a determination was made in violation of lawful procedure, was affected by an error of law or was arbitrary and capricious or an abuse of discretion." . . . The limited issue presented for our review is whether the respondents identified the relevant areas of environmental concern, took a "hard look" at them, and made a "reasoned elaboration" of the basis for their determination. . . .

The initial determination to be made under SEQRA and CEQR is whether an EIS is required, which in turn depends on whether an action may or will not have a significant effect on the environment. In making this initial environmental analysis, the lead agencies must study the same areas of environmental impacts as would be contained in an EIS, including both the short-term and long-term effects as well as the primary and secondary effects of an action on the environment. The threshold at which the requirement that an EIS be prepared is triggered is relatively low: it need only be demonstrated that the action may have a significant effect on the environment. . . .

The dispute here concerns the reach of the term "environment", which is defined [in the State Environmental Quality Review Act and the city regulations] as "the *physical conditions* which will be affected by a proposed action, *including* land, air, water, minerals, flora, fauna, noise, objects of historic or aesthetic significance, *existing patterns of population concentration, distribution, or growth, and existing community or neighborhood character*" [emphasis supplied]. Petitioners argue that the displacement of neighborhood residents and businesses caused by a proposed project is an environmental impact within the purview of SEQRA and CEQR, and the failure of respondents to consider these potential effects renders their environmental analysis invalid. Respondents contend that any impacts that are not either directly related to a primary physical impact or will not impinge upon the physical environment in a significant manner are outside the scope of the definition of "environment", and that the lead agencies were therefore not required to investigate the potential effects alleged by petitioners.

. . . It is clear from the express terms of the statute and the regulations that environment is broadly defined . . . and expressly includes as physical conditions such considerations as "existing patterns of population concentration, distribution, or growth, and existing community or neighborhood character". Thus, the impact that a project may have on population patterns or existing community character, with or without a separate impact on the physical environment, is a relevant concern in an environmental analysis since the statute includes these concerns as elements of the environment. That these factors might generally be regarded as social or economic is irrelevant in view of this explicit definition. By their express terms, therefore, both SEQRA and CEQR require a lead agency to consider more than impacts upon the physical environment in determining whether to require the preparation of an EIS. In sum, population patterns and neighborhood character are physical conditions of the environment under SEQRA and CEQR regardless of whether there is any impact on the physical environment. . . .

Turning to the specific allegations in this case, we conclude that under CEQR the potential displacement of local residents and businesses is an effect on population patterns and neighborhood character which must be considered in determining whether the requirement for an EIS is triggered. A significant effect on the environment may be found if a proposed project impairs "the character or quality of . . . existing community or neighborhood character" (CEQR 6[a][5]) or impacts upon "existing patterns of population concentration, distribution, or growth" (ECL 8-0105[6]; *see*, CEQR 6[a][10]). It is not relevant whether the proposed project may effect these concerns primarily or secondarily or in the short term or in the long term since the regulations expressly include all such effects (CEQR 1[g]).

The potential acceleration of the displacement of local residents and businesses is a secondary long-term effect on population patterns, community goals and neighborhood character such that CEQR requires these impacts on the environment to be considered in an environmental analysis. . . .

We do not decide whether these impacts will in fact flow from the construction of Henry Street Tower nor do we express any opinion on the merits of the proposed project. Our holding is limited to a determination that existing patterns of population concentration, distribution or growth and existing community or neighborhood character are physical conditions such that the regulations adopted by the City of New York pursuant to SEQRA require an agency to consider the potential long-term secondary displacement of residents and businesses in determining whether a proposed project may have a significant effect on the environment. Since respondents did not consider these potential effects on the environment in their environmental analysis, their determination does not comply with the statutory mandate and therefore is arbitrary and capricious. . . .

[Judgment reversed]

QUESTIONS

1. What was the basic controversy in the *Chinese Staff* case?
2. Which interpretation was adopted by the court? What reason did the court give for its position?
3. How did the court describe the action of issuing the permit for the construction of the high-rise building?

While an EIS must consider alternative methods, it is not required to discuss every alternative that could be imagined. It is only required to consider alternatives that are practical and feasible.[7]

When the law requires that an EIS be filed before a particular construction or improvement can be made, a court will prohibit the construction or improvement if no statement has been filed. It will also do so if a statement has been filed but is so deficient or poor that, in effect, it is no statement at all.

The duty of a federal agency does not end with its issuance of an EIS. It has a continuing duty to gather relevant information, to evaluate such information, and to issue a revised or supplemental EIS if the new information indicates such course of action.

---

[7] Bowman v City of Petaluma, 185 Cal App 3d 1065, 230 Cal Rptr 413 (1986).

4. Regulation by Administrative Agencies

For the most part, the law against pollution is a matter of the adoption and enforcement of regulations by administrative agencies. One such agency is the federal Environmental Protection Agency (EPA). Administrative agency control is likely to increase in the future because of the technical nature of the problems involved and because of the interrelationship of pollution problems and nonpollution problems.

5. Litigation

A private person may bring a lawsuit to recover damages or obtain an injunction against a polluter if damages peculiar to such a plaintiff can be shown.

This requirement of harm to the plaintiff has to some extent been relaxed, so that a person may sometimes sue without proving any harm different than that sustained by any other member of the general public. For example, federal statutes authorize a private suit by any person in a federal district court to stop a violation of the air, water, and noise pollution standards. Courts have been increasingly willing to recognize the right of organizations to sue on behalf of their members.

A private person does not always have the right to sue for violation of an environmental protection control. In some instances, the right to sue is restricted to a particular government agency or to the attorney general of the United States.

It is reasonable to expect that courts will not take an active part in the solution of pollution problems. It is likely that on these technical problems they will defer to the decisions made or to be made by the appropriate administrative agency.[8] This is true particularly when the matter is merely a small segment of the total pollution problem or when jurisdiction by a court could hamper or disrupt the work of administrative agencies and study groups.[9]

6. Criminal Liability

Knowingly doing an act prohibited by an environmental protection statute is generally a crime. For example, the dumping of hazardous wastes without a federal permit is a crime.

In a prosecution for such a crime, it is no defense that the defendant did not intend to violate the law or was not negligent. It is also no defense that the defendant operated a business in the customary way and did not produce a greater amount of pollution than other, similar enterprises.

The *Arizona Mines* case involved the question of whether good intentions is a defense to a criminal prosecution for air pollution.

ARIZONA v ARIZONA MINES SUPPLY CO.
107 Ariz 199, 484 P2d 619 (1971)

Maricopa County, Arizona adopted an air pollution control regulation. The Arizona Mines Supply Company operated a mine within the county. It installed equipment in its mine in order to meet the standards of the regula-

---

8 Boomer v Atlantic Cement Co. 26 NY2d 219, 309 NYS2d 312, 257 NE2d 870 (1970).

9 Ohio v Wyandotte Chemicals Corp. 401 US 493 (1971) (Ohio sought to enjoin Canada, Michigan, and Delaware corporations from dumping mercury into tributaries of Lake Erie. This dumping allegedly polluted the lake used by parts of Ohio as a water supply. The Supreme Court refused to decide the case).

tion. In spite of these efforts, Arizona Mines polluted the air. It was prosecuted by Arizona for violating the regulation. It raised the defense that it was not guilty because it had not violated the regulation intentionally. To back up this argument, it showed that it had done its best to comply with the regulation by installing the special equipment. The prosecution objected to the admission of this evidence on the ground that it was sufficient to show that the defendant had violated the law. That is, the prosecution claimed that it was not necessary to show that the defendant had intentionally violated the law. The trial court admitted the evidence of the defendant's attempt to comply with the law. The prosecution claimed that this was wrong and filed a petition with the state supreme court to review the decision of the trial judge admitting such evidence.

UDALL, J. . . . [The defendant contends] that the State must prove knowledge or intent as a prerequisite to conviction. [The] Maricopa County Air Pollution Control Regulation . . . provides that:

No person shall cause, suffer, allow or permit the discharge into the atmosphere from any single source of emission whatsoever any air contaminants for a period or periods aggregating more than three minutes in any one hour which is:

a. *As dark as or darker in shade than that designated as No. 2 on the Ringelmann Chart as published by the U.S. Bureau of Mines, or*

b. *Of an opacity equal to or greater than an air contaminant designated as No. 2 on the Ringelmann Chart.*

Nowhere does this regulation (or the Air Pollution Act, for that matter) provide, either expressly or impliedly, that before the state may convict someone of "air pollution" it must first prove that the air contaminant was discharged knowingly or intentionally. Defendant argues that some degree of knowledge or intent is prerequisite to conviction. The State, on the other hand, contends that it need not prove intent or knowledge since this offense is more in the nature of "malum prohibitum."

After having carefully considered the apparent intent of legislature, . . . and the consequences of unabated air pollution to public health; we find that the state need not prove intent or knowledge on the part of the accused as a prerequisite to conviction. That the legislature may make the doing of an act or the neglect to do something a crime without requiring criminal intent is well-settled. *Troutner v State*, 17 Ariz 506, 154 P 1048 (1916). . . .

Whether a criminal intent or guilty knowledge is a necessary element of a statutory offense is a matter of construction to be determined from the language of the statute, in view of its manifest purpose and design. *There are many instances in recent times where the legislature in the exercise of the police power has prohibited, under penalty, the performance of a specific act.* The doing of the inhibited act constitutes the crime, *and the moral turpitude or* purity of the motive *by which it was prompted* and knowledge or ignorance *of its criminal character* are immaterial circumstances *on the question of guilt. The only fact to be determined in these cases is whether the defendant did the act.*

With regard to the introduction by a defendant of evidence of expenditures made in installing pollution control equipment and precautions taken to avoid pollution, such will not constitute a defense to prosecution and conviction, and are, therefore, inadmissible at trial. Evidence of "extenuating circumstances" may, however, be presented to the court *after verdict* in mitigation of the penalty to be imposed. "*. . . Although extenuating circumstances would be no legal bar to conviction, they would certainly be important factors in determining a penalty, and might even warrant granting of probation.*" [Emphasis added.] *Fitzpatrick v Board of Examiners*, 96 Ariz 309 at 315, 394 P2d 423 at 427.

[Admission of evidence sustained for limited purpose of determining the penalty to be imposed after the guilt of the defendant was established]

QUESTIONS

1. Why did Arizona Mines Supply Company claim that it was not guilty of violating the regulation?
2. What is the Ringelmann chart?
3. What was the basis for the defense that knowledge or intent was necessary for conviction?

B. COMMUNITY PLANNING

To provide for the orderly growth of communities, some planning and control is necessary. Community planning may be classified as private (restrictive covenants) and public (zoning).

7. Restrictive Covenants in Private Contracts

In the case of private planning, a real estate developer will take an undeveloped tract or area of land, map out on paper an ideal community, and then construct the buildings shown on the plan. These are then sold to private purchasers. The buyers deeds will contain **restrictive covenants** that obligate the buyers to observe certain limitations in the use of their property, the nature of buildings that will be maintained or constructed on the land, and so on. If a restrictive covenant is valid, it binds anyone becoming the owner of the land if the covenant is stated in a recorded deed or

if the buyer has notice or knowledge of the restriction. Consequently, the owner of any one of the tracts may sue another owner for violating the covenant, even though there is no contract between the property owners. If a restrictive covenant violates a statute, rule of law, or public policy, it is not valid and will not be enforced.

A restrictive covenant is to be construed by the same rules of construction that are applied in interpreting contracts. A restrictive covenant will be given its ordinary meaning.

A restrictive covenant must be clearly stated in order to be effective.[10] If there is any uncertainty, the covenant will be construed strictly in favor of the free use of the land. When there is no uncertainty and no reason to depart from the meaning of the words of the covenant, a court will enforce those words.

The social forces favoring freedom of action and the free use of property cause courts to interpret restrictive covenants narrowly, so as to permit the greatest possible use of the land.[11]

---

[10] Rhodes v Palmetto Pathway Homes, Inc. (SC) 400 SE2d 484 (1991).
[11] Angel v Truitt (NC) 424 SE2d 660 (1993).

8. Public Zoning

By **zoning**, a governmental unit, such as a city, adopts an ordinance imposing restrictions on the use of the land. The object of zoning is to ensure an orderly physical development of the regulated area. In effect, zoning is the same as the restrictive covenants; the difference is in the source of authority. In most cases, zoning is based on an ordinance of a local political subdivision, such as a municipality or a county. Restrictive covenants, on the other hand, are created by agreement of the parties.

The zoning power permits any regulation that is conducive to advancing public health, welfare, and safety. The object of a particular zoning regulation may be to prevent high density of population.

Some zoning ordinances may be conservation-inspired. Thus, the ordinance may prohibit or regulate the extraction of natural resources from any land within the zoned area.[12]

The fact that a house is designed for the landowner by an internationally known architect does not give the landowner the right to build the house when it violates the local zoning ordinance on a number of points.[13]

(a) NONCONFORMING USE. When the use of the land is in conflict with a zoning ordinance at the time the ordinance goes into effect, such use is described as a **nonconforming use**. For example, when a zoning ordinance is adopted that requires a setback of 25 feet from the boundary line, an existing building that has a 10-foot setback is a nonconforming use.

A nonconforming use has a constitutionally protected right to continue. If the nonconforming use is discontinued, however, it cannot be resumed. The right to a nonconforming use may thus be lost by abandonment. If a garage is a nonconforming use and the owner of a garage stops using it as a garage and uses it for storing goods, a return to the use of the property as a garage will be barred by abandonment.

(b) VARIANCE. The administrative agency charged with the enforcement of a zoning ordinance may grant a **variance**. This permits the owner of the land to use it in a specified manner that is inconsistent with the zoning ordinance.

The agency will ordinarily be reluctant to permit a variance when neighboring property owners object, because to the extent that variation is permitted, the basic plan of the zoning ordinance is defeated. Likewise, the allowance of an individual variation, or **spot zoning**, may result in such inequality as to be condemned by the courts.[14] In addition, there is a consideration of practical expediency. If variances are readily granted, every property owner will request a variance and thus flood the agency with such requests.

When the desired use of the land is in harmony with the general nature of the surrounding areas, it is probable that a zoning variance will be granted. A zoning variance will not be granted on the ground of hardship when the landowner created the hardship by purchasing land that was subject to a zoning ordinance later claimed to create the hardship.[15] Hardship may have been created by purchasing a lot that was too small to satisfy the zoning requirements, or by selling portions of a tract and leaving the remaining part undersized. A homeowner will not be allowed to add a dining room to the rear of a home when this would violate the rear-yard setback zoning requirement.[16]

It is unlikely that a variance from the zoning standard will be granted when the only

---

[12] Vinson v Medley (Okla) 737 P2d 932 (1987).

[13] Burroughs v Town of Paradise Valley (App) 150 Ariz 570, 724 P2d 1239 (1986).

[14] Gullickson v Stark County Board (ND) 474 NW2d 890 (1991).

[15] Vernons Tri-State Pawn, Inc. v City of Mobile Board of Adjustment (Ala Civ App) 571 So 2d 309 (1990).

[16] Mizrachi v Siegel, 160 App Div 2d 801, 553 NYS2d 839 (1990).

reason advanced for the variance is that it would enable the owner to make more money. For example, a variance would not be granted to an outdoor advertiser on the basis that it would permit the construction of billboards that would produce more money.

9. Eminent Domain

Eminent domain is the power of government to take private property for a public purpose. The power of eminent domain plays an important role in community planning, because it is the means by which the land required for public housing, redevelopment, and other projects may be acquired. Eminent domain has not become important in the area of environmental protection, although it is always present as a possible alternative. The theory would be that the operators of a government-owned plant would be more concerned than private owners with the protection of the environment.

When property is taken by government through eminent domain, it must be taken for a public purpose and the government must pay the owner the fair value of the property taken. The taking of property for a private purpose is void as a deprivation of property without due process of law.

The fact that a zoning restriction may have the effect of preventing the landowner from making the most profitable use of the land, and may thereby lower the value of the land, does not constitute an eminent domain taking of the land. It does not entitle the landowner to compensation.

C. NUISANCES

The common law, supplemented by statutes, prohibits conduct constituting a nuisance.

10. Definition of Nuisance

Conduct that unreasonably interferes with the enjoyment or use of land is a **nuisance**.[17] This may be smoke from a chemical plant that damages the paint on neighboring houses. It may be noise, dirt, and vibration from the passing of heavy trucks. Some conduct is clearly so great an interference with others that it is easy to conclude that it constitutes a nuisance, but not every interference is a nuisance. Furthermore, it is frequently difficult to determine whether the interference is sufficiently great to be condemned as unreasonable and therefore a nuisance. The fact that the activity or business of the defendant is lawful and is conducted in a lawful manner does not establish that it is not a nuisance. It is the effect on others that determines whether there is a nuisance. Thus, a landfill may be a nuisance even though operated by a city in a nonnegligent manner and in accordance with the states solid waste disposal statutes.[18]

The courts attempt to balance the social utility of the protection of a plaintiff with the social utility of the activity of the defendant. Thus, the mere fact that the plaintiff shows harm does not establish that the defendants conduct is a nuisance. The court may believe that the conduct is socially desirable and therefore should be allowed to continue at the expense of the plaintiffs interest. For example, it has been held that smoke, fumes, and noise from public utilities and power plants were not nuisances, although they harmed the complaining plaintiffs. The courts believed that the interests of the community in the activity of the defendants outweighed the interests of the plaintiffs affected. Similarly, the proper use of land does not constitute a nuisance as to a neighbor, even though the neighbor does not like the use. In any case, to constitute a nuisance, the plaintiff must sustain a harm that goes beyond mere inconvenience or annoyance with the defendants activity.[19] For example,

---

[17] Adkins v Thomas Solvent Co. 440 Mich 293, 487 NW2d 715 (1992).

[18] Wilhelm v Great Falls, 225 Mont 251, 732 P2d 1315 (1987).

[19] Crites v Sho-Me Dragways, Inc. (Mo App) 725 SW2d 90 (1987).

when trees and underbrush on the land-owners land served as a screen to hide the neighbors backyard from public view, the neighbor has no legal ground for objecting to the landowners removing such trees and underbrush, even though the neighbor has lost the privacy that such trees and underbrush had given.

The fact that neighbors do not approve of the aesthetics of a building or fence does not make it a nuisance.[20]

An owners use of land may restrict the freedom of use of neighboring land.

In the *Hendricks* case the court was faced with the claim that digging a water well was a nuisance.

HENDRICKS v STALNAKER
(W Va App) 380 SE2d 198 (1989)

Stalnaker dug a water well on his land. Hendricks, the owner of the neighboring land, applied to the Health Department for a permit to construct a septic system on his land. The permit was refused because it would place the system too near the water well on Stalnaker's land. The Hendrickses brought a suit to have the water well declared a nuisance because it restricted their use of their land. The lower court held that the water well was a nuisance and Stalnaker appealed.

NEELY, J. . . . We define a private nuisance as a substantial and unreasonable interference with the private use and enjoyment of another's land. The definition of private nuisance includes conduct that is intentional and unreasonable, negligent or reckless, or that results in abnormally dangerous conditions or activities in an inappropriate place.

Early West Virginia cases indicate that the existence of a private nuisance was determined primarily by the harm caused. . . . Gradually the focus included an examination of the reasonableness of the property's use. . . .

Any determination of liability for a private nuisance must include an examination of the private use and enjoyment of the land seeking protection and the nature of the interference.

Because the present case concerns conduct that is not a negligent, reckless, or abnormally dangerous activity, our discussion of private nuisance is limited to conduct that is intentional and unreasonable. An interference is intentional when the actor knows or should know that the conduct is causing a substantial and unreasonable interference. Restatement (Second) of Torts § 825 (1979). The unreasonableness of an intentional interference must be determined by a balancing of the landowners' interests. An interference is unreasonable when the gravity of the harm outweighs the social value of the activity alleged to cause the harm.* . . . Restatement (Second) of Torts §§ 827 and 828 (1979) list some of the factors to be considered in determining the gravity of the harm and the social value of the activity alleged to cause the harm.* However, this balancing to determine unreasonableness is not absolute.

---

[20] Indiana State Board of Registration v Norde (Ind App) 600 NE2d 124 (1992).

Additional consideration might include the malicious or indecent conduct of the actor. Restatement (Second) of Torts § 829.

. . . In the case before us, the Hendrickses' inability to operate a septic system on their property is clearly a substantial interference with the use and enjoyment of their land. The record indicates that the installation of the water well was intentional, but there was no evidence that the installation was done so as maliciously to deprive the Hendrickses of a septic system. Mr. Stalnaker wanted to insure himself of an adequate water supply and found no alternative to the well he dug.

The critical question is whether the interference, the installation of a water well, was unreasonable. Unreasonableness is determined by balancing the competing landholders' interests. We note that either use, well or septic system, burdens the adjacent property. Under Health Department regulations, a water well merely requires non-interference within 100 feet of its location. In the case of a septic system, however, the 100 foot safety zone, extending from the edge of the absorption field, may intrude on adjacent property. Thus, the septic system, with its potential for drainage, places a more invasive burden on adjacent property. Clearly both uses present similar considerations of gravity of harm and social value of the activity alleged to cause the harm. Both a water well and a septic system are necessary to use this land for housing; together they constitute the in and out of many water systems. Neither party has an inexpensive and practical alternative. The site of the water well means quality water for Mr. Stalnaker and the Hendrickses have only one location available for their septic system.

In the case before us, we are asked to determine if the water well is a private nuisance. But if the septic system were operational, the same question could be asked about the septic system. Because of the similar competing interests, the balancing of these landowners' interests is at least equal or, perhaps, slightly in favor of the water well. Thus, the Hendrickses have not shown that the balancing of interests favors their septic system. We find that the evidence presented clearly does not demonstrate that the water well is an unreasonable use of land and, therefore, does not constitute a private nuisance.

. . . Because the evidence is not disputed and only one interference is reasonable, the trial court should have held as a matter of law that the water well was not a private nuisance. . . .

[Judgment reversed]

*The Restatement (Second) of Torts § 827 (1979) lists the following "gravity of harm" factors: (a) The extent of the harm involved; (b) the character of the harm involved; (c) the social value that the law attaches to the type or use or enjoyment invaded; (d) the suitability of the particular use or enjoyment invaded to the character of the locality; and (e) the burden on the person harmed of avoiding the harm.

The Restatement (Second) of Torts § 828 lists the following "utility factors: (a) the social value that the law attaches to the primary purpose of the conduct; (b) the suitability of the conduct to the character of the locality; and (c) the impracticability of preventing or avoiding the invasion.

QUESTIONS

1. The *Hendricks* case states a clear rule that makes it easy to determine whether there is a private nuisance. Appraise this statement.

2. Is conduct *A* a nuisance because *A* interferes with the use that *B* makes of neighboring land?
3. What is the significance of whether conduct of the actor that affects the use of neighboring property is intentional?

If conduct is held to constitute a nuisance, the persons affected may be awarded monetary damages for the harm caused and may obtain an injunction or court order to stop the offending conduct.

(a) PRIVATE AND PUBLIC NUISANCES. When a nuisance affects only one or a few persons, it is called a **private nuisance**. When it affects the community or public at large, it is called a **public nuisance**. At this point, the law of nuisance is very close to environmental protection, although there is a difference between the two. Environmental protection law is more concerned with harm to the environment and less concerned with the social utility of the defendants conduct than is the law of nuisance.

The planting of trees or erecting of a fence although otherwise lawful constitutes a public nuisance when it creates a traffic hazard by obscuring an intersection.[21]

The existence of a statutory environmental protection procedure may bar or supersede the prior common law of nuisance.[22]

(b) CRIMINAL NUISANCE. Distinct from the nuisance that is harmful to other persons or to the enjoyment of the use of their land is the nuisance classified as such because it is a place where criminal acts repeatedly occur. Either by virtue of common law principles or express provisions of statute, places conducting illegal gambling or the illegal sale of liquor or narcotics are declared to be nuisances.[23]

The reason for this classification is one of practical expediency. Not only can individuals involved in crime be prosecuted, but the place may be shut down in the same way that any nuisance may be stopped or closed by the police.[24]

(c) PERMANENT AND CONTINUING NUISANCES. A nuisance may be classified as permanent or continuing. A **permanent nuisance** consists of a single act that has caused permanent harm to the plaintiff. A **continuing nuisance** is a series of related acts or a continuation of an activity, such as the emission of smoke from a factory.

(d) NUISANCES PER SE AND NUISANCES IN FACT. Nuisances may also be classified as nuisances per se and nuisances in fact. A **nuisance per se** is an act, occupation, or structure that is a nuisance at all times and under any circumstances. In contrast, a **nuisance in fact** is situational. Whether there is a nuisance in fact depends on the surrounding circumstances viewed objectively that is, by the effect they would have on a normal person of ordinary sensitivity.[25] For example, the raising of pigs in a farming area is not a nuisance. The same activity in a large city would be a nuisance. It is therefore not a nuisance per se and could only be a nuisance in fact.

Noise is not a nuisance per se. It may be of such a character or so excessive as to become one, even though it arises from a lawful activity or business.[26]

---

[21] Indiana State Board of Registration v Norde (Ind App) 600 NE2d 124 (1992).

[22] Crites v Sho-Me Dragways, Inc. (Mo App) 725 SW2d 90 (1987).

[23] Colorado v Garner (Colo) 732 P2d 1194 (1987).

[24] New York v Castro, 542 NYS2d 101 (1989).

[25] Statler v Catalano, 167 Ill App 3d 397, 118 Ill Dec 283, 521 NE2d 565 (1988).

The fact that neighbors are afraid of fire or explosions does not make an activity per se a nuisance. Thus, such fears do not condemn a gasoline filling station with ground fuel storage tanks as a nuisance per se.[27]

11. The Technological Environment of the Law of Nuisance

As technology changes, new ways of manufacturing, new methods of transportation, and new ways of living develop. As the environment changes, corresponding changes are reflected in the law.

In the *Prah* case the ancient law of property rights was tested against the modern need for solar heating.

PRAH v MARETTI
108 Wis 2d 223, 321 NW2d 182 (1982)

Prah bought one of two vacant lots. On his lot he built a house heated by solar energy. Maretti purchased the neighboring vacant lot and made plans to build a house on it. If Maretti built according to his plans, his house would interfere with the solar energy utilized by Prah's house. Prah requested Maretti to build his house a few feet further away from the boundary line. There was no evidence that Maretti would be harmed if he relocated his proposed house as requested. However, Maretti refused. His proposed location satisfied the zoning law and the restrictive covenant in his deed. Prah then sued to enjoin Maretti from building his house in such a way as to interfere with the solar energy of Prah's house. From a decision against Prah, Maretti appealed.

ABRAHAMSON, J. . . . The defendant asserts that he has a right to develop his property in compliance with statutes, ordinances and private covenants without regard to the effect of such development upon the plaintiff's access to sunlight. In essence, the defendant is asking this court to hold that the private nuisance doctrine is not applicable in the instant case and that his right to develop his land is a right which is per se superior to his neighbor's interest in access to sunlight. This position is expressed in the maxim "cujus est solum, ejus est usque ad coelum et ad infernos," that is the owner of land owns up to the sky and down to the center of the earth. The rights of the surface owner are, however, not unlimited.

The defendant is not completely correct in asserting that the common law did not protect a landowner's access to sunlight across adjoining property. At English common law a landowner could acquire a right to receive sunlight across adjoining land by both express agreement and under the judge-made doctrine of "ancient lights." Under the doctrine of ancient lights if the landowner had received sunlight across adjoining property for a specified period of time, the landowner was entitled to continue to receive unobstructed access to sunlight across the adjoining property.

[26] Racine v Glendale Shooting Club, Inc. (Mo App) 755 SW2d 369 (1988).

[27] Milligan v General Oil Co., Inc. 293 Ark 401, 738 SW2d 404 (1987).

Under the doctrine the landowner acquired a negative prescriptive easement and could prevent the adjoining landowner from obstructing access to light.

Although American courts have not been as receptive to protecting a landowner's access to sunlight as the English courts, American courts have afforded some protection to a landowner's interest in access to sunlight. American courts honor express easements to sunlight. American courts initially enforced the English common law doctrine of ancient lights, but later every state which considered the doctrine repudiated it as inconsistent with the needs of a developing country. Indeed, for just that reason this court concluded that an easement to light and air over adjacent property could not be created or acquired by prescription and has been unwilling to recognize such as easement by implication.

Many jurisdictions in this country have protected a landowner from malicious obstruction of access to light (the spite fence cases) under the common law private nuisance doctrine. If an activity is motivated by malice it lacks utility and the harm it causes others outweighs any social values. This court was reluctant to protect a landowner's interest in sunlight even against a spite fence, only to be overruled by the legislature. Shortly after this court upheld a landowner's right to erect a useless and unsightly sixteen-foot spite fence four feet from his neighbor's windows, *Metzger v Hochrein*, 107 Wis. 267, 83 NW 208 (1900), the legislature enacted a law specifically defining a spite fence as an actionable private nuisance. Thus a landowner's interest in sunlight has been protected in this country by common law private nuisance law at least in the narrow context of the modern American rule invalidating spite fences.

This court's reluctance in the nineteenth and early part of the twentieth century to provide broader protection for a landowner's access to sunlight was premised on three policy considerations. First, the right of landowners to use their property as they wished, as long as they did not cause physical damage to a neighbor, was jealously guarded.

Second, sunlight was valued only for aesthetic enjoyment or as illumination. Since artificial light could be used for illumination, loss of sunlight was at most a personal annoyance which was given little, if any, weight by society.

Third, society had a significant interest in not restricting or impeding land development. . . . These three policies are no longer fully accepted or applicable. They reflect factual circumstances and social priorities that are now obsolete.

First, society has increasingly regulated the use of land by the landowner for the general welfare.

Second, access to sunlight has taken on a new significance in recent years. In this case the plaintiff seeks to protect access to sunlight, not for aesthetic reasons or as a source of illumination but as a source of energy. Access to sunlight as an energy source is of significance both to the landowner who invests in solar collectors and to a society which has an interest in developing alternative sources of energy.

Third, the policy of favoring unhindered private development in an expanding economy is no longer in harmony with the realities of our society. The need for easy and rapid development is not as great today as it once was, while our perception of the value of sunlight as a source of energy has increased significantly.

Courts should not implement obsolete policies that have lost their vigor over the course of the years. The law of private nuisance is better suited to resolve landowners' disputes about property development in the 1980's than is a rigid rule which does not recognize a landowner's interest in access to sunlight. As we said in

Ballstadt v Pagel, 202 Wis. 484, 489, 232 NW 862 (1930), "What is regarded in law as constituting a nuisance in modern times would no doubt have been tolerated without question in former times.". . .

Yet the defendant would have us ignore the flexible private nuisance law as a means of resolving the dispute between the landowners in this case and would have us adopt an approach . . . of favoring the unrestricted development of land and of applying a rigid and inflexible rule protecting his right to build on his land and disregarding any interest of the plaintiff in the use and enjoyment of his land. This we refuse to do.

[Judgment reversed and action remanded]

QUESTIONS

1. Was the nuisance involved in the Prah case a public or private nuisance?
2. In its opinion the court states that the American courts have repudiated the doctrine of ancient lights as "inconsistent with the needs of a developing country." What does this statement tell you as to the nature and the development of the law?
3. In its opinion, the court states that, by using private nuisance law, it is departing from the narrow protection of a landowner's access to sunlight because that law is obsolete. What factors does the court give in support of this conclusion?

SUMMARY

America has awakened to the fact that resources are not unlimited and that the misuse of resources can be harmful to life. This realization has led to the adoption of numerous state and federal laws aimed at preventing the pollution of air, water, and earth. With the advent of the nuclear age, the problem of disposing of wastes in such a way as to avoid environmental pollution has become increasingly acute. A person violating an environmental protection law is subject to administrative agency action, civil suit, and criminal prosecution.

Community planning has both governmental and private aspects. With respect to government, community planning ordinarily takes the form of a zoning statute or ordinance that regulates land use. When a zoning ordinance is adopted, there may be some spots in the zoned area that are being used in a manner that violates the zoning plan. Such a nonconforming use cannot be outlawed by the zoning ordinance. As the converse of allowing the nonconforming use to continue, a person wishing to use land in a way not permitted by the zoning ordinance may petition the zoning board or authority for a variance from the general zoning plan. Government may also take part in community planning by taking land by eminent domain for use for a public purpose. At the private level, community planning is accomplished by means of restrictive covenants in deeds.

Traditional equity power authorizes enjoining (stopping) of nuisances. A public nuisance may also be stopped by direct government action.

LAW IN PRACTICE

1. Learn what restrictions are imposed on the use of your property by zoning regulations, restrictive covenants, and environmental protection laws.
2. Learn the same as to neighboring property.
3. Do not rely on the opinion of a seller or a real estate agent as to what you can do with property you buy.

4. If restrictions on the use of your land prove too burdensome, consult your attorney as to whether any exception can be obtained.
5. Understand the possibility of tort liability if other persons or property are harmed by your improper use of your property.

QUESTIONS AND CASE PROBLEMS

1. Smoke, fumes, and noise from public utilities and power plants are not to be condemned as nuisances merely because some harm is sustained from their activity by a particular plaintiff. Which of the objectives of the law listed in Chapter 2 are operative?

2. The Federal Oil Company was loading a tanker with fuel oil. The loading hose snapped for some unknown reason, and about 1,000 gallons of oil poured into the ocean. The Federal Oil Company was prosecuted for water pollution. It raised the defense that it had exercised due care, was not at fault in any way, and had not intended to pollute the water. Was it guilty?

3. Magnolia City wanted to build a thruway from one side of the city to the other in order to facilitate thru traffic. To acquire the land for such a highway, it purchased various parcels of land from private owners. Thompson refused to sell his land. The city tendered to Thompson the fair value of his land and demanded that he surrender the land to the city. Thompson claimed that the city could not require him to sell the land. Was Thompson correct?

4. The McConnells bought a home in the Sherwood Estates. The land was subject to a restrictive covenant that no building, fence, or other structure could be built on the land without the approval of the developer of the property. The McConnells built a dog pen in their yard. It consisted of a cement base with fencing surrounding the base. They claimed that approval was not required, on the theory that the restrictive covenant did not apply because it showed an intent to restrict only major construction, not minor additions to the landscape. A lawsuit was brought to compel the McConnells to remove the dog pen because prior approval had not been obtained. Decide. *[Sherwood Estates Homes Assn., Inc. v McConnell (Mo App) 714 SW2d 848]*

5. Carlotta owns a grocery store. It is located in an area that is later zoned as exclusively residential. Can Carlotta continue to run the grocery store after the adoption of the zoning regulation?

6. Mark divides a large tract of land into small lots. He then sells the lots. In the deed to each buyer is a provision stating that the buyer will not build a house closer than 6 feet to any boundary line of the lot. Madeline buys one of these lots and begins to build 2 feet from the boundary line. Her neighbor, Jason, protests that Madeline cannot do this because of the 6-foot restriction in her deed. Madeline replies that this restriction was made with Mark and has no effect between Jason and Madeline. Is Madeline correct?

7. A zoning ordinance of the city of Dallas, Texas, prohibited the use of property in a residential district for gasoline filling stations. Lombardo brought an action against the city to test the validity of the ordinance. He contended that the ordinance violated the rights of the owners of property in such districts. Do you agree with this contention? *[Lombardo v City of Dallas, 124 Tex 1, 73 SW2d 475]*

8. Taback began building a vacation home on a parcel of wooded land. It was to be a 3-story house, 31 feet high. This violated the local zoning ordinance that limited residential homes to 2 ½ stories, not exceeding 35 feet. When Taback learned of this violation, he applied for a zoning variance. Because of the delay of the zoning board and because winter was approaching, Taback finished the construction of the building as a 3-story house. At the later hearing before the zoning board, he showed that it would be necessary for him to rebuild the third floor in order to convert the house into a $2^1/2$-story house. The zoning board recognized that the violation of Taback could not be seen from neighboring properties. Was Taback entitled to a zoning variance? *[Taback v*

Town of Woodstock Zoning Board of Appeals, 134 App Div 2d 733, 521 NYS2d 838]

9. The Belmar Drive-In Theatre Co. brought an action against the Illinois State Toll Highway Commission because the bright lights of the toll road station interfered with the showing of motion pictures at the drive-in. Decide. *[Belmar Drive-In Theatre Co. v Illinois State Toll Highway Commission, 34 Ill 2d 544, 216 NE2d 788]*

10. The Stallcups lived in a rural section of the state. In front of their house ran a relatively unused, unimproved public county road. Wales Trucking Co. transported concrete pipe from the plant where it was made to a lake where the pipe was used to construct a water line to bring water to a nearby city. In the course of four months Wales made 825 trips over the road, carrying from 58,000 to 72,000 pounds of pipe per trip and making the same number of empty return trips. The heavy use of the road by Wales cut up the dirt and made it like ashes. The Stallcups sued Wales for damages caused by the deposit of dust on their house and for the physical annoyance and discomfort caused by the dust. Wales defended on the ground that it had not been negligent and that its use of the road was not unlawful. Decide. *[Wales Trucking Co. v Stallcup (Tex Civ App) 465 SE2d 44]*

11. Some sections of the city of Manitou Springs have hills of varying degrees of slope. To protect from water drainage and erosion, the city adopted a hillside zoning ordinance that required homes on hillsides to be surrounded by more open land than in the balance of the city. Sellon owned land on a hillside and claimed that the hillside ordinance was unconstitutional because it did not treat all homeowners equally. Was the ordinance valid? *[Sellon v City of Manitou Springs (Colo) 745 P2d 229]*

12. Patrick Bossenberry owned a house in a planned community area. Each lot in the area was limited by a restrictive covenant to use for a single-family dwelling. The covenant defined family so as to require blood or marital relationship between most of the occupants. Bossenberry rented his building to Kay-Jan, Inc. Kay-Jan wanted to use the building as a care home for not more than six adult mentally retarded persons. The neighbors sought to enjoin this use as a breach of the covenant. A number of Michigan statutes had been adopted that advanced the public policy of providing care for mentally retarded persons. Could the neighbors prevent the use of the property as a care home for mentally retarded adults? *[Craig v Bossenberry, 134 Mich App 543, 351 NW2d 596]*

13. The McConnells bought a home in the Sherwood Estates. The land was subject to a restrictive covenant that "no building, fence, or other structure" could be built on the land without the approval of the developer of the property. The McConnells built a dog pen in their yard. They claimed that approval was not required on the theory that the restrictive covenant did not apply because it showed an intent to restrict only major construction and not minor additions to the landscape. A lawsuit was brought to compel the McConnells to remove the dog pen because prior approval had not been obtained. Decide. *[Sherwood Estates Homes Ass'n, Inc. v McConnell (Mo App) 714 SW2d 848]*

14. Kenneth and Mary Norpel purchased a house. He attached a 35' flagpole to it. He did not obtain the permission of the architectural committee of the Stone Hill Community Association. This consent was required by a restrictive covenant to which the Norpel house was subject. The Association objected to the flagpole. Norpel then flew the American flag from the pole. The Association brought an action to compel the removal of the pole. Norpel claimed that as a combat veteran of World War II he had a constitutionally protected right to fly the American flag. Can he be compelled to remove the flagpole?

15. Drabik owned a tract of land. He used the eastern fifth of the land as an automobile junkyard. At just about that time, the county adopted a zoning ordinance which zoned for agricultural use the part of the county in which Drabik's land was located. Drabik expanded his junkyard business so that in a few years it covered almost the entire tract of his land. The county then brought an action to compel him to confine his junkyard business to its former area. He claimed that he could make a nonconforming use of his land. Was he correct?

CHAPTER 53
LEASES

LEARNING OBJECTIVES

After studying this chapter, you will be able to:
1. *Define a lease and list its essential elements.*
2. *List the ways in which a lease may be termi-nated.*
3. *List and explain the rights and duties of the parties to a lease.*
4. *Describe the remedies of a landlord for breach by the tenant.*
5. *Describe a landlord's liability for a tenant's and a third person's injuries sustained on the premises.*
6. *Define and distinguish between a sublease and an assignment of a lease.*

If you cannot buy a house or piece of business property, leasing may be the answer.

A. CREATION AND TERMINATION

Leases are governed by the common law of property as modified by judicial decisions and statutes.[1]

1. Definition and Nature

A **lease** is the relationship by which one person is in lawful possession of real property owned by another. In common speech, the term *lease* also refers to the agreement that creates that relationship.

The person who owns the real property and permits the occupation of the premises is known as the **lessor** or **landlord**. The **lessee**, or **tenant**, is the one who occupies the property. A lease establishes the relationship of landlord and tenant.

Basically, a lease parallels a bailment, in which there is an agreement to make the bailment and a subsequent transfer of possession to carry out that agreement. In the case of a lease, there is the lease contract and the interest thereafter acquired by the tenant when possession is delivered under the lease contract. The common law looked at the transfer of possession and regarded the lease as merely the creation of an interest in land. The modern law looks at the contract and regards the lease as the same as the renting of an automobile. With this new approach, typical contract law concepts of unconscionability, mitigation of damages, and the implication of warranties are brought into the law of leases.

2. Creation of the Lease Relationship

The relationship of landlord and tenant is created by an express or implied contract. An oral lease is valid at common law, but statutes in most states require written leases for certain tenancies. Many states provide that a lease for a term exceeding three years must be in writing. Statutes in other states require written leases when the term exceeds one year.

(a) ANTIDISCRIMINATION. Statutes in many states prohibit an owner who rents property for profit from discriminating against prospective tenants on the basis of race, color, religion, or national origin. Enforcement of such statutes is generally entrusted to an administrative agency.

(b) COVENANTS AND CONDITIONS. Some obligations of the parties in the lease are described as **covenants**. Thus, a promise by the tenant to make repairs is called a covenant to repair. Sometimes it is provided that the lease shall be forfeited or terminated upon a breach of a promise. That provision is then called a **condition** rather than a covenant.

(c) OTHER AGREEMENTS. The lease may be the only agreement between the parties. In contrast, there may also be a separate guaranty or a letter of credit to protect the landlord from breach by the tenant. The tenant, in addition to holding under the lease, may hold a franchise from the lessor.

(d) UNCONSCIONABILITY. At common law, the parties to a lease had relatively uncontrolled freedom to include such terms as they chose. Since the lease is increasingly treated as a contract, some states require that leases conform to the concept of conscionability and follow the pattern of UCC § 2-302.[2] A provision in a residential lease stating that curtailment of services by the landlord will not constitute an eviction unless caused willfully or by gross negligence and that such interruption will not entitle the tenant to any compensation is

---

[1] A uniform act, the Uniform Residential Landlord and Tenant Act (URLTA), has been adopted in Alaska, Arizona, Connecticut, Florida, Hawaii, Iowa, Kansas, Kentucky, Michigan, Montana, Nebraska, New Mexico, Oklahoma, Oregon, Rhode Island, South Carolina, Tennessee, Virginia, and Washington.

[2] Flam v Herrmann, 90 Misc 2d 434, 395 NYS2d 136 (1977); § URLTA 1.303.

unconscionable. It does not bar the tenant from suing for breach of the implied warranty of habitability. Similarly, a provision in a lease declaring that the landlord is not responsible for interruptions in the various services provided tenants will not protect the landlord when the air-conditioning system is out of operation for six weeks in midsummer.

3. Essential Elements

The following elements are the essential elements of a lease:

a. The occupying of the land must be with the express or implied consent of the landlord.

b. The tenant must occupy the premises in subordination to the rights of the landlord.

c. A **reversionary interest** in the land must remain in the landlord. That is, the landlord must be entitled to retake the possession of the land upon the expiration of the lease.

d. The tenant must have an **estate of present possession** in the land. This means a right to be in possession of the land now.

4. Classification of Tenancies

Tenancies are classified by duration as tenancies for years, from year to year, at will, and by sufferance.

(a) TENANCY FOR YEARS. A **tenancy for years** is one under which the tenant has an estate of definite duration. The expression "for years" is used to describe such a tenancy even if the duration of the tenancy is for only one year or for less than a year.

(b) TENANCY FROM YEAR TO YEAR. A **tenancy from year to year** is one under which a tenant, holding an estate in land for an indefinite duration, pays an annual, monthly, or weekly rent. This tenancy does not terminate at the end of a year, month, or week except upon proper notice.

In almost all states, a tenancy from year to year is implied if the tenant, with the consent of the landlord, stays in possession of property after a tenancy for years. Consent may be shown by an express statement or by conduct, such as continuing to accept rent.[3] The lease frequently states that a holding over shall give rise to a tenancy from year to year unless written notice to the contrary is given.

(c) TENANCY AT WILL. When land is held for an indefinite period, which may be terminated at any time by the landlord or the tenant, a **tenancy at will** exists. A person who enters into possession of land for an indefinite period, with the owners permission but without any agreement as to rent, is a tenant at will.

Statutes in some states and decisions in others require advance notice of termination of this kind of tenancy.

(d) TENANCY BY SUFFERANCE. When a tenant remains in possession after the termination of the lease without permission of the landlord, the latter may treat the tenant as either a trespasser or a tenant. Until the landlord elects to do one or the other, a **tenancy by sufferance** exists.

5. Termination of Lease

A lease is generally not terminated by the death, insanity, or bankruptcy of either party, except in the case of a tenancy at will. Leases may be terminated in the following ways.

(a) TERMINATION BY NOTICE. A lease may give the landlord the power to terminate it by giving notice to the tenant. In states that follow the common law, it is immaterial why the landlord terminates the lease by notice. A provision giving the landlord the right to terminate

---

[3] In some jurisdictions, when rent is accepted from a tenant holding over after the expiration of the term of the lease and there is no agreement to the contrary, there results only a periodic tenancy from month to month rather than a tenancy from year to year.

the lease by notice if specified conditions exist is strictly construed against the landlord.

(b) EXPIRATION OF TERM IN A TENANCY FOR YEARS. When a tenancy for years exists, the relation of landlord and tenant ceases upon the expiration of the term. There is no requirement that one party give the other any notice of termination. Express notice to end the term may be required of either or both parties by provisions of the lease, except when a statute prohibits the landlord from imposing such a requirement.

(c) NOTICE IN A TENANCY FROM YEAR TO YEAR. In the absence of an agreement of the parties, notice is now usually governed by statute. It is common practice for the parties to require 30 or 60 days' notice to end a tenancy from year to year. As to tenancies for periods of less than a year, the provisions of the statutes commonly require notice of only one week.

(d) SURRENDER. A surrender or giving up of the tenant's estate to the landlord terminates the tenancy if the surrender is accepted by the landlord.[4] A surrender may be made expressly or may be implied. An express surrender must, under the statute of frauds, be in writing and be signed by the person making the surrender or by an authorized agent.

(e) FORFEITURE. The landlord may terminate the lease by forfeiting the relationship because of the tenant's misconduct or breach of a condition if a term of the lease or a statute so provides. In the absence of such a provision, the landlord may only claim damages for the breach. Terminating the relationship by forfeiture is not favored by the courts.

(f) DESTRUCTION OF PROPERTY. If a lot and a building on it are leased, either an express provision in the lease or a statute generally releases the tenant from liability to pay rent if the building is destroyed. Alternatively, the amount of rent may be reduced in proportion to the loss sustained. Such statutes do not impose on the landlord any duty to repair or restore the property to its former condition.

When the lease covers rooms or an apartment in a building, a destruction of the leased premises terminates the lease.

(g) FRAUD. Since a lease is based on a contract, a lease may be avoided when the circumstances are such that a contract could be avoided for fraud.

(h) TRANSFER OF THE TENANT. Residential leases may contain a provision for termination upon the tenant's being transferred by an employer to another city or upon the tenant's being called into military service. Such provisions are strictly construed against the tenant. Therefore, when entering a lease, the tenant should exercise care to see that the provision is sufficiently broad to cover the situations that may arise.

6. Notice of Termination

When notice of termination is required, no particular words are necessary to constitute a sufficient notice, provided the words used clearly indicate the intention of the party. The notice, whether given by the landlord or the tenant, must be definite. Statutes sometimes require that the notice be in writing. In the absence of such a provision, however, oral notice is generally sufficient.

7. Renewal of Lease

When a lease terminates for any reason, the landlord and the tenant ordinarily enter into a new agreement if they wish to extend or renew the lease. The power to renew the lease may be stated in the original lease by declaring that the lease runs indefinitely, as from year to year, subject to being terminated by either party's

---

4 Roosen v Schaffer, 127 Ariz App 346, 621 P2d 33 (1980).

giving written notice of a specified number of days or months before the termination date. Renewal provisions are strictly construed against the tenant.

The lease may require the tenant to give written notice of the intention to renew the lease. In such a case, there is no renewal if the tenant does not give the required notice but merely remains on the premises after the expiration of the original term.[5]

B. RIGHTS AND DUTIES OF PARTIES

The rights and duties of the landlord and tenant are based on principles of real estate law and contract law. With the rising tide of consumer protectionism, there is an increasing tendency to treat the relationship as merely a contract and to govern the rights and duties of the parties by general principles of contract law.

8. Possession

Possession involves both the right to acquire possession at the beginning of the lease and the right to retain possession until the lease is ended.

(a) TENANT'S RIGHT TO ACQUIRE POSSESSION. By making a lease, the lessor covenants by implication to give possession of the premises to the tenant at the agreed time. If the landlord rents a building that is being constructed, there is an implied covenant that it will be ready for occupancy at the commencement of the term of the lease.

(b) TENANT'S RIGHT TO RETAIN POSSESSION. After the tenant has entered into possession, the tenant has the exclusive possession and control of the premises during the term of the lease. This right exists as long as the

lease continues and so long as there is no default under the lease, unless the lease otherwise provides. Thus, the tenant can refuse to allow the lessor to enter the property

for the purpose of showing it to prospective customers, although today most leases expressly give this right to the landlord.

If the landlord interferes with this possession by evicting the tenant, the landlord commits a wrong for which legal remedies are available. An **eviction** occurs when the tenant is deprived of the possession, use, and enjoyment of the premises by the interference of the lessor or the lessor's agent. If the landlord wrongfully deprives the tenant of the use of one room when the tenant is entitled to use an entire apartment or building, there is a **partial eviction**.

(c) COVENANT OF QUIET ENJOYMENT. Most written leases today contain an express promise by the landlord to respect the possession of the tenant. This promise is called a **covenant of quiet enjoyment**. Such a provision protects the tenant from interference with possession by the landlord or the landlord's agent, but it does not impose liability on the landlord for the unlawful acts of third persons.[6] Thus, such a covenant does not require the landlord to protect a tenant from damages by a rioting mob.

(d) CONSTRUCTIVE EVICTION. An eviction may be actual or constructive. It is a **constructive eviction** when some act or omission of the landlord substantially deprives the tenant of the use and enjoyment of the premises.

It is essential in a constructive eviction that the landlord intended to deprive the tenant of the use and enjoyment of the premises. This intent may, however, be inferred from conduct. There is no constructive eviction unless the tenant leaves the premises. If the tenant continues to occupy the premises for more than a reasonable time after the acts claimed to

---

[5] Ahmed v Scott, 65 Ohio App 2d 271, 418 NE2d 406 (1979).

[6] Rittenbert v Donohoe Construction Co. (Dist Col App) 426 A2d 338 (1981).

C
P
A
C
P
A

constitute a constructive eviction, the tenant waives or loses the right to object to the conduct of the landlord. The tenant cannot thereafter abandon the premises and claim to have been evicted.[7]

The issue in the *JMB Properties* case was whether the tenant waived any constructive eviction.

JMB PROPERTIES URBAN CO. v PAOLUCCI
(Ill App) 604 NE2d 967 (1992)

Defendant Paolucci opened a jewelry store in an Illinois mall in 1978. Barretts Audio and Video Store (Barretts) moved in next door to defendant in November of 1984. Barretts and Paolucci shared a common wall. In December of 1985, defendant began complaining to the landlord, Carlyle, about the high level of noise emanating from Barretts. Defendant and his employees testified that when Barretts' employees conducted demonstrations of their stereo equipment, the wall of their jewelry store literally shook. This caused pictures to rattle on the jewelry store walls. The vibrations caused merchandise in display cases to move or topple over so that the display cases had to be reset almost daily. The stereo store refused to lower the volume, even after many requests. One employee had to resort to wearing ear plugs. Barretts insulated the wall at the landlord's direction, but the problem was not alleviated. Defendant failed to pay rent for July 1990 and vacated the premises in August 1990, some two years prior to the end of the lease it renewed in 1986. The landlord filed an action against the defendant, seeking recovery of past due rent and penalties for violating the lease. Defendant filed a counterclaim claiming he had been constructively evicted as a result of the failure of the landlord to control the noise generated by Barretts. Barretts had moved out in February of 1990. From a judgment in favor of the defendant, the landlord appealed.

SLATER, J. . . . On appeal, Carlyle contends that the trial court erred in finding that the noise emanating from Barretts was sufficient to amount to a constructive eviction. A constructive eviction results from a landlord's failure to keep the premises in a tenantable condition. . . . Untenantability exists when the interference with occupancy is of such a nature that the property cannot be used for the purpose for which it was rented. . . .

We need not address the question of whether the noise was sufficient to render the premises untenantable because we find that defendant waived any claim of constructive eviction by remaining on the premises for an unreasonable length of time after the rise of the untenantable condition. Constructive eviction cannot exist where

---

7 Some states prohibit a landlord of residential property from willfully turning off the utilities of a tenant for the purpose of evicting the tenant. Kinney v Vaccari, 23 Cal 3d 348, 165 Cal Rptr 787, 612 P2d 877 (1980) (imposing civil penalty of $100 a day for every day utilities are shut off). Such conduct is also a violation of URLTA §§ 2.104, 4.105.

the tenant does not surrender the property. . . . Following a constructive eviction, the tenant is not required to vacate the premises immediately, but is entitled to a reasonable time to do so. . . . The tenant bears the burden of proving that he did abandon the premises within a reasonable time after the untenantable condition occurred. . . . If the tenant fails to vacate within a reasonable time, the tenant is considered to have waived the landlord's breach of covenant. . . . The reasonableness of a delay is generally a question of fact. . . .

The untenantable condition in this case first arose in December of 1985. Defendant remained on the leasehold premises until August of 1990, nearly five years after the condition arose and six months after Barretts moved out of the mall. Defendant claims that he remained on the premises for six months after Barretts left because his new store was still under construction. We realize that one factor to be considered in determining the reasonableness of the delay is the time required to find a new location. . . . Even if the last six months of defendant's occupancy could be excused on this basis, defendant fails to explain why he tolerated the alleged untenantable condition for more than four years. Defendant cites no case, and our research reveals none, where a delay of this length was excused. The trial court relied on *American National Bank & Trust Co. v Sound City, U.S.A., Inc.* (1979), 67 Ill App 3d 599, 24 Ill Dec 377, 385 NE2d 144, in finding the delay in this case to be reasonable. However, in that case the constructively evicted tenant remained in possession of the leased premises for only three months.

We also note that defendant entered into a new six year lease with Carlyle in 1986, nearly two years after Barretts moved in. . . . While defendant claims that he received assurances . . . before he signed the new lease that the noise problem would be taken care of, we believe the fact that defendant had an opportunity to leave the mall in 1986 but instead chose to remain and enter into a new six year lease is a factor to be considered in our determination of the reasonableness of the delay in this case. In light of the above facts we find the trial court's determination that defendant did not waive his claim of constructive eviction to be against the manifest weight of the evidence.

[Judgment reversed]

QUESTIONS

1. Did defendant act ethically in claiming a constructive eviction?
2. Was there a constructive eviction?
3. Was the tenant excused from paying rent?
4. Was there a breach of the implied warranty of habitability?

9. Use of Premises

The lease generally specifies the use to which the tenant may put the property. The landlord is often authorized by the lease to adopt regulations with respect to the use of the premises. These regulations are binding on the tenant as long as they are reasonable, lawful, and not in conflict with the terms of the lease. In the absence of express or implied restrictions, a tenant is entitled to use the premises for any lawful purpose for which they are adapted or for which they are ordinarily employed or in a manner contemplated by the parties in executing the lease. A provision specifying the use to be made of the property is strictly construed against the tenant.

(a) CHANGE OF USE. The modern lease will, in substance, make a change of use a condition subsequent. That is, if the tenant uses the property for any purpose other than the one specified, the landlord has the option of declaring the lease terminated.

(b) CONTINUED USE OF PROPERTY. The modern lease will ordinarily require the tenant to give the landlord notice of nonuse or vacancy of the premises. This is because of the increased danger of damage to the premises by vandalism or fire when a building is vacant. Also, there is commonly a provision in the landlord's fire insurance policy making it void if a vacancy continues for a specified time.

(c) RULES. The modern lease generally contains a blanket agreement by the tenant to abide by the provisions of rules and regulations adopted by the landlord. These rules are generally binding on the tenant, whether they exist at the time the lease was made or are adopted thereafter.

(d) PROHIBITION OF PETS. A restriction in a lease prohibiting the keeping of pets is valid.

10.   Rent

The tenant is under a duty to pay rent as compensation to the landlord. The amount of rent agreed to by the parties may be subject to governmental regulation.

(a) TIME OF PAYMENT. The time of payment of rent is ordinarily fixed by the lease. When the lease does not specify, rent generally is not due until the end of the term. However, statutes or custom may require rent to be paid in advance when the agreement of the parties does not regulate the point. Rent that is payable in crops is generally payable at the end of the term.

(b) ASSIGNMENT. If the lease is **assigned** (the tenant's entire interest is transferred to a third person), the assignee is liable to the landlord for the rent. However, the assignment does not in itself discharge the tenant from the duty to pay the rent. The landlord thus may bring an action for the rent against either the original tenant or the assignee, or both, but is entitled to only one satisfaction. A **sublessee** (a person to whom part of a tenant's interest is transferred) ordinarily is not liable to the original lessor for rent unless that liability has been expressly assumed or is imposed by statute.

(c) RENT ESCALATION. When property is rented for a long term, it is common to include some provision for the automatic increase of the rent at periodic intervals. Such a provision is often tied to increases in the cost of living or in the landlords operating costs. Such a provision is called an **escalation clause**.

11.   Repairs and Condition of Premises

In the absence of an agreement to the contrary, the tenant has no duty to make repairs. When the landlord makes repairs, reasonable care must be exercised to make them in a proper manner. The tenant is liable for any damage to the premises caused by willful or negligent acts of the tenant.

(a) INSPECTION OF PREMISES. Most states deny the landlord the right to enter the leased premises except when the right is expressly reserved in the lease.

(b) HOUSING LAWS. Various laws protect tenants, such as by requiring landlords to observe specified safety, health, and fire prevention standards. Some statutes require that a landlord who leases a building for dwelling purposes must keep it in a condition fit for habitation. Leases commonly require the tenant to obey local ordinances and laws relating to the care and use of the premises.

(c) WARRANTY OF HABITABILITY. At common law, a landlord was not bound by any obligation that the premises be fit for use unless the lease contained an express warranty to that effect. Most jurisdictions now reject this view and imply from residential leases of furnished and unfurnished property a warranty that the premises are habitable. If the landlord breaches a warranty of habitability, the tenant is entitled to damages. These damages may be set off against the rent that is due, or if no rent is due, the tenant may bring an independent lawsuit to recover damages from the landlord.[8]

In the *Abram* case a tenant whose personal property was destroyed in a fire sued the landlord for property damage based upon a breach of the implied warranty of habitability.

ABRAM v LITMAN
150 Ill App 3d 174, 103 Ill Dec 349, 501 NE2d 370 (1986)

Abram lived at property owned and operated by Litman. A fire, resulting from faulty wiring, occurred on the premises. The tenant's personal possessions were destroyed. Abram sued Litman, alleging a breach of the implied warranty of habitability. Litman argued that Abram did not show that Litman had notice of the alleged defects or dangerous condition, nor had he received such notice. Litman also argued that the implied warranty of habitability cannot serve as a basis of recovery for property damage. From a judgment in favor of Litman, Abram appealed.

WEBER, J. . . . In *Jack Spring, Inc. v Little* (1972), 50 Ill 2d 351, 280 NE2d 208, the Supreme Court of Illinois held that the implied warranty of habitability applied to leases, both oral and written, of multiple-unit dwellings. In *Jack Spring* the court stated that the warranty was fulfilled by substantial compliance with the pertinent provisions of the applicable building code. Subsequently several districts of the appellate court of Illinois interpreted the court's statement in *Jack Spring* to mean that the implied warranty of habitability is only fulfilled by substantial compliance with a building code. In *Glasoe [v Trinkle* (1985)] our supreme court clarified this confusion by holding "that the implied warranty of habitability applies to all leases of residential real estate regardless of the existence of housing or building codes." . . . The *Glasoe* court continued by examining the scope of the implied warranty of habitability. In so doing, the court stated:

As did the Pennsylvania court, we decline to establish rigid standards for determining habitability and its breach. However, we think the guidelines above stated, which have been enunciated in other jurisdictions, will be helpful to the fact finder in determining the extent of the warranty of habitability and whether there has been a breach thereof in a particular case. In addition to the guidelines stated, there, of course, must be notice of the alleged defects given by the tenant to the landlord and the landlord must have had a reasonable time within which to correct the alleged deficiencies.

---

[8] Lawrence v Triangle Capital Corp. 628 NE2d 74, 90 Ohio App 3d 105 (1993).

The trial court relied on the above-quoted statement in determining that plaintiff was required to plead and prove that she gave notice of the alleged defects to defendants.

Plaintiff argues that the above-quoted statement is mere dicta and that we should follow our holding in *Jarrell v Hartman* (1977), 48 Ill App 3d 985, 6 Ill Dec 812, 363 NE2d 626. In *Jarrell* we rejected the argument that a tenant seeking to establish a breach of the implied warranty of habitability is first required to give the landlord notice of the defect and an opportunity to repair. Our [principal] reason for rejecting defendants' argument was that no such requirement had been discussed in *Jack Spring*. This question was resolved in *Glasoe*.

In our opinion the trial court interpreted the statement of the supreme court in *Glasoe* concerning notice too broadly. *Glasoe* involved patent defects. Even in the case of such defects the court laid down no precise rule as to the nature of the required notice, only that some notice must be given. The court was not called upon to decide the matter of notice in the context of latent defects of the type involved in the instant case. If such defects were not apparent nor discoverable by either the landlord or the tenant until after the damage had occurred, it is at once apparent that notice of them would be logically impossible to give. We find that *Glasoe* is factually distinguishable from the instant case.

A short discussion of how other jurisdictions have treated the question of notice is in order.

. . . Some jurisdictions have stated that a landlord's knowledge may be either actual knowledge or constructive knowledge. . . .

We believe that one of the soundest approaches was that taken in *Old Town Development*. In *Old Town Development* the court held that the notice requirement may be satisfied in various ways depending upon the facts and circumstances of the case. Actual notice of the alleged defect given to the landlord by the tenant would always be sufficient. In addition, actual knowledge of the alleged defect on the part of the landlord would also be sufficient. In some instances the landlord could be charged with constructive knowledge of the alleged defect. For example, where the alleged defect is a latent defect and the landlord was also the builder of the premises, the landlord could properly be charged with constructive knowledge of the alleged defect. (*Old Town.*) However, defendants herein could not be charged with constructive knowledge of the faulty wiring since plaintiff did not allege that defendants were the builders of the premises leased to plaintiff. See *W.C. Haas Realty Management* (noting that liability could not be imposed on a nonbuilder landlord for a breach of the implied warranty of habitability which allegedly resulted from faulty wiring which had caused a fire on the premises).

Because the instant case concerns a latent defect about which the tenant knew nothing and because there is no allegation in the pleadings upon which the landlord could be charged with constructive notice of the defect, we find that the trial court properly dismissed the complaint. While its reliance upon the broad language in *Glasoe* was perhaps misplaced, its result was correct. As we have pointed out, the instant case differs from *Glasoe*, which was concerned with patent defects. An additional reason for the proper dismissal of the complaint is that the warranty of habitability cannot serve as a basis for recovery of property damage. *Auburn v Amoco Oil Co.* (1982), 106 Ill App 3d 60, 61 Ill Dec 939, 435 NE2d 780.

In *Auburn* the plaintiffs' complaint alleged that the defendant landlords breached the implied warranty of habitability by providing in the leased house a furnace which was neither in working order nor reasonably safe for its intended purpose. The complaint alleged further that as a result of the landlord's breach, an explosion occurred destroying the house and causing the plaintiffs to suffer personal injury and property damage. The complaint sought damages. Stating that no cause of action exists for personal injuries resulting from a breach of the implied warranty of habitability, the trial court dismissed the complaint. On appeal we affirmed, holding that the warranty of habitability implied in a lease of a dwelling does not give rise to a cause of action for personal injuries or property damage. We noted that although the implied warranty of habitability may be used as a sword as well as a shield and that an independent action for a landlord's breach of warranty may stand, such claims are "for a deterioration in the benefits from the lease rather than for personal injuries or property damage arising from a catastrophe." . . . Because the complaint herein seeks recovery of damages for property damage, the court below properly dismissed the action. . . .

[Judgment affirmed]

QUESTIONS

1. How may notice of breach of implied warranty of habitability be satisfied?
2. Was proper notice given?
3. Why did the court refuse to give recovery for property damage?

(d) ABATEMENT AND ESCROW PAYMENT OF RENT. To protect tenants from unsound living conditions, statutes sometimes provide that a tenant is not required to pay rent as long as the premises are not fit to live in. As a compromise, some statutes require the tenant to continue to pay the rent but require that it be paid into an escrow or agency account. The money in the escrow account is paid to the landlord only upon proof that the necessary repairs have been made to the premises.

12. Improvements

In the absence of special agreement, neither the tenant nor the landlord is under the duty to make improvements, as contrasted with repairs. Either party may, as a term of the original lease, agree or covenant to make improvements, in which case a failure to perform will result in liability in an action for damages for breach of contract brought by the other party. In the absence of an agreement to the contrary, improvements become part of the realty and belong to the landlord.

13. Taxes and Assessments

In the absence of an agreement to the contrary, the landlord, not the tenant, is usually under a duty to pay taxes or assessments. The lease may provide for an increase in rent if taxes on the rented property are increased.[9]

If taxes or assessments are increased because of improvements made by the tenant, the landlord is liable for such increases if the improvements remain with the property. If the improvements can be removed by the tenant, the amount of the increase must be paid by the tenant.

---

[9] Brazelton v Jackson Drug Co., Inc. (Wyo) 796 P2d 808 (1990).

14. Tenant's Deposit

A landlord may require a tenant to make a deposit to protect the landlord from any default on the part of the tenant. In some states, protection is given the tenant who is required to make a payment to the landlord as a deposit to ensure compliance with the lease. It is sometimes provided that the landlord holds such payment as a trust fund and must inform the tenant of the bank in which the money is deposited. The landlord becomes subject to a penalty if the money is used before the tenant has breached the lease.

15. Protection from Retaliation

There is a modern trend to protect tenants from retaliation by the landlord for the tenants' exercising their lawful rights or reporting the landlord for violating a housing and sanitation code.[10] The retaliation of the lessor may take the form of refusing to renew a lease or evicting the tenant.

16. Remedies of Landlord

If a tenant fails to pay rent, the landlord may bring an ordinary lawsuit to collect the amount due and in some states may seize and hold the property of the tenant.

(a) LANDLORD'S LIEN. In the absence of an agreement or statute so providing, the landlord does not have a lien on the personal property or crops of the tenant for money due for rent. The parties may create by express or implied contract a lien in favor of the landlord for rent and also for advances, taxes, or damages for failure to make repairs.

In the absence of a statutory provision, the lien of the landlord is superior to the claims of all other persons, except prior lienors and good-faith purchasers without notice.

(b) SUIT FOR RENT. Whether or not the landlord has a lien for unpaid rent, the landlord may sue the tenant on the latter's obligation to pay rent as specified in the lease. In some jurisdictions, the landlord is permitted to bring a combined action to recover the possession of the land and the overdue rent at the same time.

(c) DISTRESS. The common law devised a speedy remedy to aid the landlord in collecting rent. It permitted seizure of personal property found on the premises and allowed the landlord to hold such property until the arrears of rent were paid. This right was known as **distress**. It was not an action against the tenant for rent but merely a right to retain the property as security until the rent was paid. Statutes have generally either abolished or greatly modified the remedy of distress.[11]

(d) RECOVERY OF POSSESSION. The lease commonly provides that upon the breach of any of its provisions by the tenant, such as the failure to pay rent, the lease shall terminate or the landlord may exercise the option to declare the lease terminated. When the lease is terminated for any reason, the landlord then has the right to evict the tenant and retake possession of the property. At common law, the landlord, when entitled to possession, could regain it without resorting to legal proceedings. This **right of reentry** is available in many states even when the employment of force is necessary. Other states deny the right to use force.

Modern cases hold that a landlord cannot lock out a tenant for overdue rent. The landlord must employ legal process to regain possession, even if the lease expressly gives the landlord the right to self-help.

The landlord may resort to legal process to evict the tenant in order to enforce the right to possession of the premises. Statutes in many states provide a summary remedy to recover

---

[10] Mobil Oil Corp. v Handly, 76 Cal App 3d 956, 143 Cal Rptr 321 (1978); URLTA § 5.101.

[11] It is abolished by the URLTA § 4.205(b). Callen v Sherman's, Inc. 182 NJ Super 438, 442 A2d 626 (1982).

possession that is much more efficient than the slow common law remedies.

(e) LANDLORD'S DUTY TO MITIGATE DAMAGES.

If the tenant leaves the premises before the expiration of the lease, is the landlord under any duty to rent the premises again in order to reduce the rent or damages for which the departing tenant will be liable? By the common law and majority rule, a tenant owns an estate in land, and if the tenant abandons it, there is no duty upon the landlord to seek to find a new tenant for the premises. A growing minority view places greater emphasis on the contractual aspects of a lease. Thus, when the tenant abandons the property and thereby defaults or breaks the contract, the landlord is under the duty to seek to mitigate the damages caused by the tenant's breach and must make a reasonable effort to rent the abandoned property.

In the *Sommer* case a tenant who abandoned a rented apartment asserted that the landlord was required to make reasonable efforts to rent the apartment to someone else in order to reduce the rent owed by the tenant.

SOMMER v KRIDEL
74 NJ 446, 378 A2d 767 (1977)

Abraham Sommer owned an apartment building. He rented one of the apartments to James Kridel for two years. Kridel intended to marry and move into the apartment with his bride. The engagement was broken. Kridel did not marry and never moved into the apartment. He never received any keys to the apartment. In May of 1972, he wrote to Sommer explaining the situation and requesting to be released from the obligations of the lease. Sommer never replied to this letter. Shortly thereafter, a stranger asked to rent the Kridel apartment. She was admittedly a proper applicant but the Kridel apartment was not rented to her because it was under the lease to Kridel. In October of 1972, Sommer sued Kridel and claimed the rent for the entire two years that the lease would have run. Sommer did not show the Kridel apartment to anyone until the next year, when the apartment was relet to a tenant under a lease beginning September 1, 1973. In the lawsuit brought by Sommer, Kridel claimed that the amount due to Sommer should be reduced because Sommer had failed to mitigate the damages by attempting to relet the apartment. From a judgment against Kridel, he appealed.

PASHMAN, J. . . . The weight of authority in this State supports the rule that a landlord is under no duty to mitigate damages caused by a defaulting tenant. . . . This rule has been followed in a majority of states, and has been tentatively adopted in the American Law Institute's Restatement of Property, *Restatement (Second) of Property*, § 11.1(3) (Tent. Draft No 3, 1975).

Nevertheless, while there is still a split of authority over this question, the trend among recent cases appears to be in favor of a mitigation requirement. . . .

The majority rule is based on principles of property law which equate a lease with a transfer of a property interest in the owner's estate. Under this rationale the lease conveys to a tenant an interest in the property which forecloses any control by the landlord; thus, it would be anomalous to require the landlord to concern himself with the tenant's abandonment of his own property.

For instance, in *Muller v Beck*, [94 NJL 311, 110 A 831 (Sup Ct 1920)] where essentially the same issue was posed, the court clearly treated the lease as governed by property, as opposed to contract, precepts. The court there observed that the "tenant had an estate for years, but it was an estate qualified by this right of the landlord to prevent its transfer," and that "the tenant has an estate with which the landlord may not interfere."

Yet the distinction between a lease for ordinary residential purposes and an ordinary contract can no longer be considered viable. As Professor Powell observed, evolving "social factors have exerted increasing influence on the law of estates for years." 2 *Powell on Real Property* (1977 ed), § 221 [1] at 180-81. The result has been that:

the complexities of city life, and the proliferated problems of modern society in general, have created new problems for lessors and lessees and these have been commonly handled by specific clauses in leases. This growth in the number and detail of specific lease covenants has reintroduced into the law of estates for years a predominantly contractual ingredient.

Thus in 6 *Williston on Contracts* (3 ed 1962), § 890A at 592, it is stated:

There is a clearly discernible tendency on the part of courts to cast aside technicalities in the interpretation of leases and to concentrate their attention, as in the case of other contracts, on the intention of the parties, . . .

Application of the contract rule requiring mitigation of damages to a residential lease may be justified as a matter of basic fairness. Professor McCormick first commented upon the inequity under the majority rule when he predicted in 1925 that eventually:

the logic, inescapable according to the standards of a "jurisprudence of conceptions" which permits the landlord to stand idly by the vacant, abandoned premises and treat them as the property of the tenant and recover full rent, [will] yield to the more realistic notions of social advantage which in other fields of the law have forbidden a recovery for damages which the plaintiff by reasonable efforts could have avoided. [McCormick, "The Rights of the Landlord Upon Abandonment of the Premises by the Tenant," 23 MichLRev 211 (1925)]

Various courts have adopted this position. . . .

We therefore hold that antiquated real property concepts which served as the basis for the pre-existing rule, shall no longer be controlling where there is a claim for damages under a residential lease. Such claims must be governed by more modern notions of fairness and equity. A landlord has a duty to mitigate damages where he seeks to recover rents due from a defaulting tenant.

If the landlord has other vacant apartments besides the one which the tenant has abandoned, the landlord's duty to mitigate consists of making reasonable efforts to re-let the apartment. In such cases he must treat the apartment in question as if it was one of his vacant stock.

As part of his cause of action, the landlord shall be required to carry the burden of proving that he used reasonable diligence in attempting to re-let the premises. . ..

The landlord will be in a better position to demonstrate whether he exercised reasonable diligence in attempting to re-let the premises. . . .

The *Sommer v Kridel* case presents a classic example of the unfairness which occurs when a landlord has no responsibility to minimize damages. Sommer waited 15 months and allowed $4658.50 in damages to accrue before attempting to re-let the apartment. Despite the availability of a tenant who was ready, willing and able to rent the apartment, the landlord needlessly increased the damages by turning her away. . . .

Here there has been no showing that the new tenant would not have been suitable. We therefore find that plaintiff could have avoided the damages which eventually accrued, and that the defendant was relieved of his duty to continue paying rent. Ordinarily we would require the tenant to bear the cost of any reasonable expenses incurred by a landlord in attempting to re-let the premises, but no such expenses were incurred in this case.

In assessing whether the landlord has satisfactorily carried his burden, the trial court shall consider, among other factors, whether the landlord, either personally or through an agency, offered or showed the apartment to any prospective tenants, or advertised it in local newspapers. Additionally, the tenant may attempt to rebut such evidence by showing that he proffered suitable tenants who were rejected. However, there is no standard formula for measuring whether the landlord has utilized satisfactory efforts in attempting to mitigate damages, and each case must be judged upon its own facts.

[Judgment reversed]

QUESTIONS

1. What did the plaintiff claim?
2. Was the landlord entitled to recover the agreed rental specified in the lease for the two-year term of the lease?
3. Did the lessor act in a reasonable manner?

C. LIABILITY FOR INJURY ON PREMISES

When the tenant, a member of the tenant's family, or a third person is injured because of the condition of the premises, the question arises as to who is liable for the damages sustained by the injured person.

17. Landlord's Liability to Tenant

In the absence of a covenant to keep the premises in repair, the landlord is ordinarily not liable to the tenant for the latter's personal injuries caused by the defective condition of the premises that, by the lease, are placed under the control of the tenant. Likewise, the landlord is not liable for the harm caused by an obvious condition that was known to the tenant at the time the lease was made.[12] For example, a landlord is not liable for the fatal burning of a tenant whose clothing was set on fire by an open-faced radiant gas heater.

(a) CRIMES OF THIRD PERSONS. Ordinarily, the landlord is not liable to the tenant for crimes committed on the premises by third persons, such as when a third person

---

[12] English v Kienke (Utah) 848 P2d 153 (1993).

enters the premises and commits larceny or murder.[13] The landlord is not required to establish a security system to protect the tenant from crimes of third persons.

In contrast, when the criminal acts of third persons are reasonably foreseeable, the landlord may be held liable for the harm caused a tenant. Consequently, when a tenant has repeatedly reported that the dead bolt on the apartment door is broken, the landlord is liable for the tenant's loss when a thief enters through the door, because such criminal conduct was foreseeable. Likewise, when the landlord of a large apartment complex does not take reasonable steps to prevent repeated criminal acts, the landlord is liable to the tenant for the harm caused by the foreseeable criminal act of a third person.

In the *Rivera* case the court takes up the issue of a social hall owner's ability to foresee criminal acts occurring on the premises.

RIVERA v UNITED AUTO WORKERS LOCAL 179
(Cal App 2d Dist) 266 Cal Rptr 262 (1990)

Rivera attended a birthday party at a union meeting hall owned by defendant. The hall was leased by a Maria Garcia, a resident of the area. Some members of two rival teenage gangs came to the party. Those from one gang had been invited by the lessee. The members of the rival gang had not been invited. During the course of the evening, a fight between members of the two gangs erupted. Shots were fired. Rivera was struck by one of the bullets. Rivera argued that the incident was foreseeable and that the defendant, by failing to protect him, breached a duty owed to him as an invited guest on defendant's premises. From summary judgment in favor of the defendant, Rivera appealed.

COMPTON, J. . . . Defendant in the past had leased the building to over 100 different individuals and organizations for various functions. Defendant, however, provided nothing more than permission to use the premises. Garcia was in complete control of the party. Defendant did not undertake to control the guest list or to regulate the party in any way. Defendants had no representative on the premises and had no knowledge of who would attend the party. . . .

Plaintiff's position is that the incident was foreseeable and that the defendant, by failing to protect plaintiff, breached a duty owed to him as an invited guest on defendant's premises.

Plaintiff's claim of foreseeability is premised on the assertion that certain members of the . . . Police Department would provide depositions and testify at a trial that the [area in which the party was held] has experienced a high level of teenage gang violence . . . and that the police were aware of a number of instances of "gang violence" in the area where the union hall was located. In the past, some, but not all, of the lessees of the building had hired off-duty policemen to act as security guards.

. . . Plaintiff argues that defendant was chargeable with constructive knowledge of the information possessed by the police.

---

[13] Pamer v Pritchard, 60 Ohio Misc 2d 150, 575 NE2d 903 (1990).

It is undisputed, of course, that plaintiff was completely unknown to defendant and was not invited to the hall by defendant. Similarly, plaintiff's assailant was neither known to nor invited by defendant. . . .

The basic law of property owner's liability is easily stated but its application to a particular set of circumstances is not easily determined: "A possessor of land who holds it open to the public for entry for his business purposes is subject to liability to members of the public while they are upon the land for such a purpose, for physical harm caused by accidental, negligent, or intentionally harmful acts of third persons. . . ." (Rest 2d Torts, § 344, pp. 223-224.) Section 315 of Restatement Second of Torts provides: "There is no duty to control the conduct of a third person as to prevent him from causing physical harm to another unless (a) a special relation exists between the actor and the third person which imposes a duty upon the actor to control the third person's conduct or (b) a special relation exists between the actor and the other which gives to the other a right to protection." . . .

Earlier cases applying these principles involved situations where the conduct of the third person was overt and in the presence of the property owner and the property owner had clear knowledge of the threat and the ability to prevent it. . . .

The zeal with which injured persons have sought a "deep pocket" and the tendency of some courts to socialize losses resulting from criminal conduct has produced some decisions which appear to have expanded the original precepts by creation of a duty of a property owner to somehow deter and prevent crime in general. . . .

As we pointed out in *7735 Hollywood Blvd. Venture v Superior Court*, 116 Cal App 3d 901, 906, 172 Cal Rptr 528, "anyone can foresee that a crime may be committed anywhere at any time. But that foreseeability which the owners of rental property or the proprietors of public premises share with the public at large, does not per se, impose a duty on such property owners or proprietors to [institute security measures]."

Furthermore, since the identity of those youth gangs and their membership is generally not a matter of public knowledge and is learned only through police intelligence channels, the average citizen would be hard pressed to know just when and where conflict between these gangs might erupt.

In *Totten v More Oakland Residential Housing, Inc.* (1976) 63 Cal App 3d 538, 543, 134 Cal Rptr 29, the court observed: "A landlord is not bound to anticipate the criminal activities of third persons, especially where . . . the wrongdoers were complete strangers to both the landlord and the victim, and where the fight and the shooting incident leading to the injury came about precipitously. . . ."

To our mind there is a qualitative difference between the recognized duty to control the conduct of an identifiable person or persons engaged in overt conduct which threatens particular individuals under circumstances where the property owner has the duty to control that conduct and the ability to exercise effective control, and the creation of a duty to take measures aimed at affording protection from an amorphous threat of violent crime by unknown individuals.

This latter concept of crime prevention and deterrence is the primary basis for maintaining a regular police establishment. As we pointed out in [an earlier case]

Government Code section 845 provides that: 'Neither a public entity nor a public employee is liable for failure to establish a police department or otherwise provide police protection service or, if police protection service is provided, for failure to provide sufficient *police protection service' (Emphasis added.) That section is clear recognition of the difficulty, if not impossibility, of assessing the efficacy of a particular policing pattern and is designed to immunize public entities from speculative law suits such as the case at bench. It seems anomalous to us that a public entity which has the primary role in providing police protection is so immunized while persons not generally considered to have that general responsibility are not so immunized.*

In the case at bench, defendant can be said to have known of the potential for gang violence in the . . . area—the knowledge which it shared with the public in general. The question is whether it had any additional knowledge which would create a duty to protect this plaintiff. There is no question that both plaintiff and his assailant were unknown to defendant.

Defendant did nothing more than rent the premises to a young woman] whose avowed purpose was to hold a birthday party and who would presumptively invite her friends and acquaintances. Nothing in that situation could create any special relationship between defendant and plaintiff which would support the establishment of a duty to protect plaintiff.

Plaintiff's case also founders on the issue of causation since plaintiff's injuries did not result from any defective condition of the premises itself nor any affirmative conduct on the part of defendant or its agents. The question is what inaction on the part of defendant caused plaintiff's injury? As noted earlier, the identity and the plans of these gangs to which plaintiff attributes the violence are generally unknown except to certain police specialists and since neither the penal statutes of California nor the efforts of the . . . Police Department in the area have served to deter the numerous violent confrontations that plaintiff alleges have occurred, there is obviously no reasonable action which defendant could have taken that would have prevented the violence that did occur.

Tragic as this case is, it must be remembered that the primary cause of plaintiff's injury was the person who did the shooting and not the defendant.

Based upon the foregoing, the trial court correctly concluded that there was no triable issue of fact which would have supported plaintiff's case.

[Judgment affirmed]

QUESTIONS

1. Did the defendant have knowledge of the potential for violence in his area?
2. Is a landlord bound to anticipate the criminal activities of third persons?
3. Was the landlord guilty of negligence?

(b) LIMITATION OF LIABILITY. A provision in a lease excusing or exonerating the landlord from liability is generally valid, regardless of the cause of the tenant's loss. A number of courts, however, have restricted the landlord's power to limit liability in the case of residential, as distinguished from commercial, leasing. A provision in a residential lease that the landlord shall not be liable for damage caused by water, snow, or ice is void. A modern trend holds that clauses limiting liability of the landlord are void with respect to harm caused by the negligence of the landlord when the tenant is a residential tenant generally or is in a government low-cost housing project.

Third persons on the premises, even with the consent of the tenant, are generally not bound by a clause exonerating the landlord. Such third persons may therefore sue the landlord when they sustain injuries. Thus, it has been held that members of the tenants family, employees, and guests are not bound when they do not sign the lease. However, there is authority to the contrary.

(c) INDEMNIFICATION OF LANDLORD. The modern lease commonly contains a provision declaring that the tenant will indemnify the landlord for any liability (of the landlord to a third person) that arises from the tenants use of the rented premises.

18. Landlord's Liability to Third Persons

The landlord is ordinarily not liable to third persons injured because of the condition of any part of the rented premises that is in the possession of a tenant by virtue of a lease.[14]

If the landlord retains control over a portion of the premises, such as hallways or stairways, however, a landlord's liability exists for injuries to third persons caused by failure to exercise proper care in connection with that part of the premises. The modern trend of cases imposes liability on the landlord when a third person is harmed by a condition that the landlord, under a contract with the tenant, was obligated to correct or when the landlord was obligated, under a contract with the tenant, to keep the premises in repair.

19. Tenant's Liability to Third Persons

A tenant in possession has control of the property and is liable when the tenant's failure to use due care under the circumstances causes harm to (a) licensees, such as a person allowed to use a telephone, and (b) invitees, such as customers entering a store. With respect to

both classes, the liability is the same as that of an owner in possession of property. It is likewise immaterial whether the property is used for residential or business purposes.

The liability of the tenant to third persons is not affected by the fact that the landlord may have contracted in the lease to make repairs, which, if made, would have avoided the injury. The tenant can be protected, however, in the same manner that the landlord can, by procuring liability insurance for indemnity against loss from claims of third persons.

D. TRANSFER OF RIGHTS

Both the landlord and the tenant have property and contract rights with respect to the lease. Can they be transferred or assigned?

20. Transfer of Landlord's Reversionary Interest

The reversionary interest of the landlord may be transferred voluntarily by the landlord, or involuntarily by a judicial or execution sale. The tenant then becomes the tenant of the new owner of the reversionary interest, and the new owner is bound by the terms of the lease.

21. Tenant's Assignment of Lease and Sublease

An assignment of a lease is a transfer by the tenant of the tenant's entire interest in the premises to a third person. A tenancy for years may be assigned by the tenant unless the latter is restricted from so doing by the terms of the lease or by a statute. A sublease is a transfer to a third person, the sublessee, of less than the tenant's entire interest.

(a) LIMITATIONS ON RIGHTS. The lease may contain provisions denying the right to assign or sublet or may contain provisions imposing specified restrictions on the

---

[14] Buente v Van Voorst, 213 Ill App 3d 116, 156 Ill Dec 729, 571 NE2d 513 (1991).

privilege of assigning or subletting. Such restrictions enable the landlord to obtain protection from new tenants who would damage the property or be financially irresponsible.

Restrictions in the lease are construed liberally in favor of the tenant. There is no violation of a provision prohibiting assignment or subleasing when the tenant merely permits someone else to use the premises.

(b) EFFECT OF ASSIGNMENT OR SUBLEASE. An assignee or a sublessee has no greater rights than the original lessee.[15] An assignee becomes bound by the obligations of the lease by the act of taking possession of the premises. In contrast, a sublessee is not obligated to the lessor in the absence of an express contract imposing such liability.

Neither the act of subletting nor the landlord's agreement to it releases the original tenant from liability under the terms of the original lease. When a lease is assigned, the original tenant remains liable for the rent that becomes due thereafter.

It is customary and desirable for the tenant to require the sublessee to covenant or promise to perform all obligations under the original lease and to indemnify the tenant for any loss caused by the default of the sublessee. An express covenant or promise by the sublessee is necessary to impose such liability. The fact that the sublease is made "subject to" the terms of the original lease merely recognizes the superiority of the original lease but does not impose any duty on the sublessee to perform the tenant's obligation under the original lease. If the sublessee promises to assume the obligations of the original lease, the landlord, as a third party beneficiary, may sue the sublessee for breach of the provisions of the original lease.

SUMMARY

The agreement between a lessor and a lessee by which the latter holds possession of real property owned by the former is a lease. Statutes in many states prohibit discrimination by an owner who rents property. Statutes in some states require that the lease not be unconscionable. Tenancies are classified as to duration as tenancies for years, from year to year, at will, and by sufferance. A lease is generally not terminated by the death, insanity, or bankruptcy of either party, except for a tenancy at will. Leases are usually terminated by the expiration of the specified term, notice, surrender, forfeiture, or destruction of the property, or because of fraud. A tenant has the right to acquire possession at the beginning of the lease and has the right to retain possession until the lease is ended. Evictions may be either actual or constructive. The tenant is under a duty to pay rent as compensation for the landlord.

An assignment of a lease by the tenant is a transfer of the tenant's entire interest in the property to a third person; a sublease is a transfer of less than an entire interest—either in space or time. A lease may prohibit both an assignment and a sublease. If the lease is assigned, the assignee is liable to the landlord for the rent. Such an assignment, however, does not discharge the tenant from the duty to pay rent. In a sublease, the sublessee is not liable to the original lessor for rent unless that liability has been assumed or is imposed by statute.

The tenant need not make repairs to the premises, absent agreement to the contrary. A warranty of habitability was not implied at common law. Most states now reject this view and imply in residential leases a warranty that the premises are fit for habitation.

A landlord is usually liable to the tenant only for injuries caused by latent defects, or those that are not apparent, of which the landlord

---

[15] Gulden v Newberry Wrecker Service, Inc. 154 Ga App 130, 267 SE2d 763 (1980).

had knowledge. Some states apply a strict tort liability, holding the landlord liable to a tenant or a child or guest of the tenant when there is a defect that makes the premises dangerously

defective, even if the landlord does not have any knowledge of the defect. The landlord is not liable to the tenant for crimes of third persons unless they are reasonably foreseeable.

LAW IN PRACTICE

1. Always read a lease before you sign it.
2. If you claim a constructive eviction, vacate the premises within a reasonable time or you will still be liable for the payment of rent.

3. If you as a tenant want to transfer your interest to a third person, check to be sure the lease or statutes do not restrict you from doing so.
4. If you as a tenant vacate the leased premises, notify the landlord so that the landlord can protect the property.

QUESTIONS AND CASE PROBLEMS

1. What social forces are affected by the rule governing the duty of a landlord to relet premises wrongfully abandoned by a tenant?

2. King leased a single dwelling to Moorehead. King brought an action against Moorehead to recover the premises because of the nonpayment of rent and in order to collect the unpaid rent. Moorehead raised the defense that the house was not habitable and that it violated the housing code. The defense was established at the trial. What result? Explain. *[King v Moorehead (Mo App) 495 SW2d 65]*

3. Rod had a five-year lease in a building owned by Darwood. Rod agreed to pay $800 a month rent. After two years, Rod assigned his rights under the lease to Kelly. Kelly moved in and paid the rent for a year. Kelly then moved out without Darwood's knowledge or consent, owing two months' rent. Darwood demanded that Rod pay him the past due rent. Must Rod do so? Why or why not?

4. Williams, who had leased a building from Jones for a period of ten years, subleased the building to various tenants with the consent of Jones. Many of the tenants failed to pay the rent as it became due, and Jones brought an action against the sublessees to collect the rent. Will Jones recover? Why or why not?

5. Compare (a) an actual eviction of the tenant, (b) a constructive eviction of the tenant, and (c) a breach of the warranty of habitability.

6. Clay owned a tract of land. Clay permitted Hartney to live in a cabin on the land. Nothing was said as to the length of time that it could be used by Hartney. Nothing was said as to Hartney's paying anything for the use of the cabin. Hartney

died. The next day Clay closed up the cabin and put Hartney's possessions outside the door. Paddock was appointed the executor of Hartney's will. Paddock claimed the right to use the cabin. Was he entitled to do so?

7. Phillips Petroleum, Inc. leased a service station to Prather. McWilliam was a customer at the service station. A rusted window fell from the wall, injuring her. She sued Phillips Petroleum. There was no evidence to show that Phillips knew of the rusted condition of the window. Was Phillips liable? *[McWilliam v Phillips Petroleum, Inc. 269 Or 526, 525 P2d 1011]*

8. Morgan rented an apartment in the Melrose Apartments. Morgan wanted Melrose to hire additional security guards to protect the lessees in the apartment house from possible crimes. Was Melrose required to do so when crimes by third persons were not reasonably foreseeable?

9. The Old Dover Tavern, Inc. rented a building from Amershadian to conduct a "business under the style and trade name of 'Old Dover Tavern, Inc.' engaging in the serving and selling [of] cigars, tobacco and all kinds of drinks and beverages of any name, nature and description." Thereafter, the tenant claimed that it was entitled to sell cold foods, such as sandwiches, on the theory that such sale was "incidental to the sale of beverages." The corporation brought an action to establish that it was so entitled. Was it? *[Old Dover Tavern, Inc. v Amershadian, 2 Mass App 882, 318 NE2d 191]*

10. Cantanese leased a drugstore building from Saputa. Cantanese moved his store from the rented store to another location but continued to pay the rent to Saputa. Saputa, fearing that he was losing his tenant, entered the premises without the permission of Cantanese and made extensive alterations to the premises to suit two physicians who had agreed to rent the premises from Saputa. Cantanese informed Saputa that he regarded the making of the unauthorized repairs as ground for canceling the lease. Saputa then claimed that Cantanese was liable for the difference between the rent that Cantanese had agreed to pay and the rent that the doctors would pay for the remainder of the term of the Cantanese lease. Was Cantanese liable for such rent? *[Saputa v Cantanese (La App) 182 So 2d 826]*

11. Sargent rented a second-floor apartment in an apartment house owned by Ross. Anna, the four-year-old daughter of Sargent, fell from an outdoor stairway and was killed. Suit was brought against Ross for her death. Ross defended on the ground that she did not have control over the stairway and therefore was not liable for its condition. Was this defense valid? *[Sargent v Ross, 113 NH 388, 308 A2d 528]*

12. What is the liability of the landlord to the tenant for crimes committed on the premises by third parties?

13. Green rented an apartment from Stockton Realty. The three-story building had a washroom and clothesline on the roof for use by the tenants. The clothesline ran very near the skylight. There was no guard rail between the clothesline and the skylight. Mrs. Green's friend, who was 14 years old, was helping her remove clothes from the line. Her friend tripped on an object and fell against the skylight. The glass was too weak to support her weight and she fell to the floor below, sustaining serious injuries. Is the landlord responsible for damages for the injury sustained? Decide. *[Reiman v Moore, 42 Cal 2d 130, 180 P2d 452]*

14. What is the distinction between a tenancy for years and a tenancy from year to year? What is the importance of the distinction?

15. Williams rented an apartment in the Parker House. He was an elderly man who was sensitive to heat. His apartment was fully air-conditioned, which enabled him to stand the otherwise unbearable heat of the summer. The landlord was dissatisfied with the current rental and, although the lease had a year to run, insisted that Williams agree to an increase. Williams refused. The landlord attempted to force Williams to pay the increase by turning off the electricity and thereby stopping the apartment's air conditioners. He also sent up heat on the hot days. After one week of such treatment, Williams—claiming that he had been evicted—moved out. Has there been an eviction? Explain.

CHAPTER 54

DECEDENTS' ESTATES AND TRUSTS

LEARNING OBJECTIVES

After studying this chapter, you will be able to:
1. *Define testamentary capacity and testamentary intent.*
2. *Distinguish between signing, attesting, and publishing a will.*
3. *Explain how a will may be modified or revoked.*
4. *Describe briefly the probate and contest of a will.*
5. *Describe the ordinary pattern of distribution by intestacy.*
6. *Explain the nature of a trust.*

What happens to your property after you die?

Public policy dictates that when an individual dies, the cost of proper burial and other expenses that may arise in connection with death be paid. Public policy also dictates that just debts contracted before death be settled, that property owned at the time of death be taken care of and applied to the payment of expenses and the debts mentioned, and that any remainder be distributed among those entitled to receive it.

The law of decedents' estates is governed by state statutes and court decisions. The general principles and the procedures that will be discussed in this chapter may be considered typical, but state variations exist. A step toward national uniformity has been taken by the American Bar Association and the National Conference of Commissioners on Uniform Laws by approving a Uniform Probate Code (UPC) and submitting it to the states for adoption.[1]

A. WILLS

After all of the debts of a decedent are paid, distribution is made of any balance of the estate to those entitled to receive it. If the decedent made a valid will, the will determines which persons are entitled to receive the property. If the decedent did not make a valid will, the distribution is determined by intestate law.

1. Definitions

Testate distribution describes the distribution that is made when the decedent leaves a valid will. A **will** is ordinarily a writing that provides for a distribution of property upon the death of the writer but which confers no rights prior to that time. A man who makes a will is called a **testator**; a woman, a **testatrix**.

The person to whom property is left by a will is a **beneficiary**. A gift of personal property by will is a **legacy** or **bequest**, in which case the beneficiary may also be called a **legatee**. A gift of real property by will is a **devise**, and the beneficiary may be called a **devisee**.

2. Parties to Will

Each state has a right to prescribe the qualifications of persons who wish to make a will. There are some variations among the states, but the following is typical.

(a) TESTATOR. Generally, the right to make a will is limited to persons 18 or older. The testator must have **testamentary capacity**.[2] In order to have testamentary capacity, a person must have sufficient mental capacity to understand that the writing that is being executed is a will—that is, that it disposes of the person's property after death. The testator must also have a reasonable appreciation of the identity of relatives and friends and of the nature and extent of the property that may exist at death.

The excessive and continued use of alcohol, producing mental deterioration, may be sufficient to justify the conclusion that the decedent lacked testamentary capacity.

(b) BENEFICIARY. Generally, there is no restriction with respect to the capacity of the beneficiary. However, when part of a decedent's estate passes to a minor, it is ordinarily necessary to appoint a guardian to administer such interest for the minor. There are two common exceptions. If there is a will that directs that any share payable to a minor be held by a particular person as trustee for the minor, the minor's interest will be so held, and a guardian is not required. Statutes often provide that if the estate or interest of the minor is not large,

---

[1] The Uniform Probate Code has been adopted in Alaska, Arizona, Colorado, Florida, Hawaii, Idaho, Maine, Michigan, Minnesota, Montana, Nebraska, New Mexico, North Dakota, South Carolina, and Utah. A number of minor amendments have since been made. Kentucky has adopted only Article VII, Part I, of the UPC. Alabama has adopted substantial portions of Articles I and II.

[2] Succession of Cahn (La App) 552 So 2d 1160 (1988).

it may be paid directly to the minor or to the parent or person by whom the minor is maintained.

3. Testamentary Intent

There cannot be a will unless the testator manifests an intention to make a provision that will be effective only upon death. This is called a **testamentary intent**.[3] Ordinarily, this is an intention that certain persons shall become the owners of certain property on the death of the testator. However, a writing also manifests a testamentary intent when the testator only designates an executor and does not make any disposition of property.

4. Form

Since the privilege of disposing of property by will is purely statutory, the will must be executed in the manner and with the formalities required by state statutes. Unless statutory requirements are met, the will is invalid, and the testator is considered to have died intestate. In such a case, the decedent's property will be distributed according to the laws of intestacy of the particular state.[4]

(a) WRITING. Ordinarily, a will must be in writing. Some state statutes, however, permit oral wills made by soldiers and sailors.

(b) SIGNATURE. A written will must be signed by the testator. In the absence of a provision of the statute stating that the will must be signed "in writing," a rubber stamp signature has been held sufficient. It is common, however, to require a written signature.

Generally, a will must be signed at the bottom or end. The purpose of this requirement is to prevent unscrupulous persons from taking a will that has been validly signed and writing or typing additional provisions in the space below the signature.

(c) ATTESTATION. **Attestation** is the act of witnessing the execution of a will. Generally, it includes signing the will as a witness, after a clause that recites that the witness has observed either the execution of the will or the testator's acknowledgment of the writing as the testator's will. This clause is commonly called an **attestation clause**. Statutes often require that attestation be made by the witnesses in the presence of the testator and in the presence of each other.

Publication is the act of the testator of informing the attesting witnesses that the document that is signed before them or is shown to them is the testator's will. Some states require publication.

Most states and the UPC require two witnesses. A few states require three. It is usual to have three in the event that one becomes disqualified.

In most jurisdictions, a witness cannot be a beneficiary under the will. Use of a beneficiary as a witness will not affect the will, but the witness's share is limited to whatever would have been received if there had been no will. Under the UPC, a will or any provision therein is not invalid because the will is signed by an interested person.

(d) DATE. There is generally no requirement that a testator must date a will, but it is advisable to do so. When there are several wills, the most recent prevails with respect to conflicting provisions.

5. Modification of Will

A will may be modified by executing a codicil. A **codicil** is a separate writing that amends a will. The will, except as changed by the codicil, remains the same. The result is as though the testator rewrote the will, substituting the provisions of the codicil for those provisions of the will that are inconsistent with the codicil. A codicil must be executed with all the formality

3 Burns v Adamson (Ark) 854 SW2d 723 (1993).
4 Burns v Adamson (Ark) 854 SW2d 723 (1993).

of a will and is treated in all other respects the same as a will.

A will cannot be modified merely by crossing out a clause and writing in what the testator wishes. Such an interlineation is not operative unless it is executed with the same formality required of a will, or in some states unless the will is republished in its interlineated form.

6. Revocation of Will

At any time during the testator's life, the testator may revoke the will made or may make changes in its terms. It may be revoked by act of the testator or by operation of law.

(a) REVOCATION BY ACT OF TESTATOR. A will or a codicil is revoked when the testator destroys, burns, or tears the will, or crosses out the provisions of the will with the intention to revoke it. The revocation may be in whole or in part.

In the *Tolin* case, a testator believed that his codicil was revoked by destruction of a photographic copy of the codicil.

IN RE ESTATE OF TOLIN

(Fla App) 622 So 2d 988 (1993)

In 1984, Tolin executed a will. Under the will, the residue of Tolin's estate was to be devised to his friend, Adair Creaig. The will was prepared by Tolin's attorney and executed in the attorney's office. The original will was retained by the attorney, and a blue-backed photocopy was given to Tolin. In 1989, Tolin executed a codicil to the will which changed the residuary beneficiary from Creaig to Broward Art Guild, Inc. The codicil was also prepared by Tolin's attorney who retained the original and gave Tolin a blue-backed photocopy of the original executed codicil. Tolin died in 1990. Six months prior to his death, he told his neighbor, who was a retired attorney, that he made a mistake and wished to revoke the codicil and reinstate Creaig as the residuary beneficiary. His neighbor said that he could do this by tearing up the original codicil. Tolin handed his neighbor a blue-backed document which Tolin said was the original codicil. The neighbor looked at the document—it appeared to him to be the original—and gave it back to Tolin. Tolin then tore up and destroyed the document with the intent and for the purpose of revocation. Some time after Tolin's death, his neighbor spoke with the original attorney and found out for the first time that the original will and codicil were held by Tolin's attorney. Tolin had torn up the blue-backed copy which had been given to Tolin at the time of execution. The document that Tolin tore up was identical to the original except for the original signatures. Tolin's personal representative petitioned the court to have the will and codicil admitted to probate. Creaig filed a petition to determine if there had been a revocation of the codicil. From a judgment that the testator's destruction of a copy of the codicil was not an effective revocation of the codicil, Creaig appealed.

HARDING, J. . . . The primary rule of construction in construing a will is ascertaining and giving effect to the testator's intent. . . . Additionally, it is well settled that strict compliance with the will statutes is required in order to effectuate a revocation of a will or codicil. . . . Section 732.506 [of the Florida statutes] provides the procedure for revoking a will or codicil by physical act. Section 732.506 provides that

a will or codicil is revoked by the testator, or by some other person in [the testator's] presence and at [the testator's] direction, by burning, tearing, canceling, defacing, obliterating, or destroying it with the intent, and for the purpose, of revocation.

Thus, in order for a testator to effectively revoke a codicil, there must be a "joint operation of act and intention to revoke." . . .

Creaig argues that section 732.506 does not specifically require the destruction of the original codicil, but allows a testator to revoke a will or codicil by intentionally destroying a copy. She focuses on the language of section 732.506 that the testator revokes the will or codicil by "destroying *it* with the intent, and for the purpose, of revocation." (Emphasis added.) Creaig urges that the use of the pronoun "it" does not specifically require the revocation of the original document, and that the Legislature left open the question of whether the destruction of a copy would be adequate to revoke a will or codicil. Thus, she concludes that because the testator in the instant case intentionally revoked the codicil and destroyed a "correct copy," the testator effectively revoked the codicil.

We reject Creaig's argument and find that the plain language of section 732.506 requires the intentional destruction of the original will or codicil in order to effectuate a revocation. Section 732.506, which describes the manner for revoking a will or codicil by a physical act, uses the pronoun "it" in reference to the terms "will or codicil" contained therein. The terms "will or codicil" are specifically defined as instruments "executed by a person in the manner prescribed by this code." Section 731.201(35), Fla Stat (1989). Further, section 732.502, Florida Statutes (1989), prescribes the manner used to properly execute a will or codicil. The use of the terms "will or codicil," which have specific statutory definitions, shows a legislative intent that in order to effectively revoke a will or codicil by a physical act, the document destroyed must be the original document.

Applying the law to the instant case, it is clear that the testator did not effectively revoke the codicil. The parties' stipulation shows that the testator destroyed a document which "was an exact copy of the fully executed original Codicil and was in all respects identical to the original except for the original signatures." Because the testator destroyed a copy of the codicil rather than the original codicil, his attempted revocation was ineffective. . . .

[Judgment affirmed]

QUESTIONS

1. What is a codicil?
2. How must a codicil be executed?
3. Did the will and the codicil in this case qualify for probate?
4. Do you agree with the decision? Why or why not?

A testator must have the same degree of mental capacity to revoke a will as is required to make a will.[5]

(b) REVOCATION BY OPERATION OF LAW.

In certain instances, statutes provide that a change of circumstances has the effect of a revocation. Thus it may be provided that when a person marries after executing a will, the will is revoked or is presumed revoked, unless it was made in contemplation of marriage or unless it provided for the future spouse. In some states, the revocation is not total but only to the extent of allowing the spouse to take such share of the estate as that to which the spouse would have been entitled had there been no will.

It is also commonly provided that the birth or adoption of a child after the execution of a will works a revocation or partial revocation of the will as to that child. In the case of a partial revocation, the child is entitled to receive the same share as if the testator had died intestate.

The divorce of the testator does not in itself work a revocation. However, the majority of courts hold that if a property settlement is carried out on the basis of the divorce, a prior will of the testator is revoked, at least to the extent of the legacy given to the divorced spouse.

7. Probate of Will

Probate is the act by which the proper court or official accepts a will and declares that the instrument satisfies the statutory requirements as the will of the testator. Until a will is probated, it has no legal effect.

When witnesses have signed a will, generally they must appear and state that they saw the testator sign the will. If those witnesses cannot be found, have died, or are outside the jurisdiction, the will may be probated nevertheless. When no witnesses are required, it is customary to require two or more persons to identify the signature of the testator at time of probate.

After the probate witnesses have made their statements under oath, the officer or court will ordinarily admit the will to probate, in the absence of any particular circumstances indicating that the writing should not be probated. A certificate or decree that officially declares that the will is the will of the testator and has been admitted to probate is then issued.

Any qualified person wishing to object to the probate of the will on the ground that it is not a proper will may appear before the official or court prior to the entry of the decree of probate. A person may petition after probate to have the probate of the will set aside.

8. Will Contest

The probate of a will may be refused or set aside on the ground that the will is not the free expression of the intention of the testator. It may be attacked on the ground of (a) lack of mental capacity to execute a will; (b) undue influence, duress, fraud, or mistake existing at the time of the execution of the will that induced or led to its execution; or (c) forgery. With the exception of mental capacity, these terms mean the same as they do in contract law.

If it is found that any one of these elements exists, the probate of the will is refused or set aside. The decedent's estate is then distributed as if there had been no will unless an earlier will can be probated.

The *Bailey* case involved a will contest.

---

[5]   May v Estate of McCormick (Wyo) 769 P2d 395 (1989).

BAILEY v CLARK

203 Ill App 3d 1017, 149 Ill Dec 89, 561 NE2d 367 (1990)

Everett Clark died March 28, 1987. Harold Clark, a nephew of the decedent, filed a petition to have the will declared invalid. Everett Clark had lived with his sister Lola. Everett Clark met with his attorney Wham to discuss preparation of his last will and testament. He was to return the next day and execute the instrument. He was unable to do so because he developed complications from a perforated ulcer and was hospitalized. He underwent surgery. From that time until his death, he was in intensive care and was provided with an endotracheal tube attached to a ventilator to help him breathe. The placement of this tube made it impossible for him to speak. Everett Clark's cousin John Bailey and Vera Horton, John Bailey's sister-in-law, retrieved the will prepared by Wham. They took it to another attorney, Frank Walker, to have him finalize the execution of the will. Everett Clark was asked a few questions at the hospital to determine whether he understood what he was doing. Everett Clark marked "X" on the will with the assistance of Walker but in no way acknowledged that it was his will or that he knew the contents of the instrument. From a decision in favor of Harold Clark, Bailey filed a petition contesting the denial of the will to probate.

CHAPMAN, J. . . . Dr. Martin, the emergency room physician who attended Clark when he was admitted to the hospital, testified that he followed Clark's case and saw him every day while Clark was in the hospital. Dr. Martin testified that in his medical opinion, on March 25 Everett Clark was alert, competent, and capable of executing legal documents. It was revealed during cross-examination that Everett Clark passed into a coma on March 26. Dr. Martin testified, however, that it was possible that the decedent could have been perfectly competent before noon on March 25, and could have passed into a coma on March 26.

Dorothy Smith, an attesting witness to the will, testified that she had known Everett Clark for eight years, and believed him to be of "sound mind and memory and under no undue influence" when she was asked to witness the signing of the will. Immediately prior to signing the will she spoke with Everett Clark. Smith testified that "he couldn't talk verbally, but he could answer in a different way by nodding his head yes and no." She asked Clark "if he knew me and if he knew we were all there and he shook his head yes." Dorothy Smith testified that Mr. Walker then talked with Clark and said, "this is your will and testament, asked if John Bailey was his cousin. He asked if he wanted to leave everything to John Bailey; if he knew everything about this will." When asked by counsel whether Everett Clark indicated to Walker that he knew all about the will, Smith testified that he "didn't indicate that as such. He gave me the impression and I believed the man knew what was going on."

The second attesting witness, Vera Mae Horton, also testified that she had known Clark for eight years, and that at the time the will was executed she believed Everett Clark to be of sound mind and memory. She answered affirmatively when asked whether she believed Clark was capable of understanding ordinary business transactions and competent to make a will at the time he signed the document.

When a person executes a will he must possess sufficient mental capacity to know the natural objects of his bounty, to comprehend the character and extent of his property, to understand the particular business in which he is engaged, and to dispose of said property pursuant to a plan formed in his mind. . . . Lay persons may testify in a will contest concerning the issue of testamentary capacity as long as they testify to sufficient facts and circumstances indicating that their opinion is not a guess, speculation or suspicion. . . . No witness testified that he or she believed Everett Clark was lacking in the elements of testamentary capacity on March 25, 1987. All of the witnesses who testified as to the decedent's mental state declared their belief that Clark was of sound mind and memory at the time he signed the will. We find that there was sufficient evidence from which the jury could conclude that the decedent possessed the requisite testamentary capacity to make a will.

Section 4-3 of the Probate Act of 1975 (Ill Rev Stat 1987, ch. 110 1/2 , par. 4-3) provides that "Every will shall be in writing, signed by the testator or by some person in his presence and by his direction and attested in the presence of the testator by 2 or more credible witnesses." There is no question that the will was in written form. Evidence was presented, however, which raised the question of whether the will was signed as contemplated by section 4-3.

The will consists of two pages. At the bottom of page one is a typed signature line with the name Everett J. Clark typed underneath. Above the signature line is a handwritten "X". Although it is not designated on the instrument that the "X" represents the testator's mark, this is not enough to invalidate the will. A will may be valid where it is signed by mark even though the mark is not accompanied by the testator's name or by the words "his mark." . . .

There was testimony that Everett Clark did not mark the "X" without assistance. It was Dr. Martin's testimony that "from the first night post-operative, Mr. Clark pulled his [endotracheal] tube out, so his arms were restrained throughout the time." Attorney Walker testified that when the will was executed he placed a pencil in Everett Clark's hand because Clark's hand was tied down. Walker testified that he helped Everett Clark "find the line and we guided his hand and he made an "X" and I held the pen in his hand." Dorothy Smith and Vera Mae Horton each confirmed Walker's assisting Everett Clark mark the "X" on the will. Dorothy Smith could not recall whether Clark was asked to make the mark himself, but recalled that he was given a pencil and helped to mark.

If a guided or assisted signature is placed on a will at the request of the person making the will and such person thereafter in the presence of two witnesses acknowledges the instrument to be his will, voluntarily made, the requirements of the statute have been met. There was no testimony presented that Everett Clark requested assistance in marking the "X". There was sufficient evidence presented, however, that Everett Clark's condition necessitated that he be assisted in marking the "X". The greatest dispute in the testimony is whether the testator, in the presence of the attesting witnesses, acknowledged the instrument as his will or was aware of the contents of the document.

William Wham, the attorney who prepared the will, testified that after he prepared the instrument he never had the opportunity to read or review the will with Everett Clark.

Vera Mae Horton testified that prior to March 25, 1987, the will was never read to Everett Clark in her presence. She further testified that she did not know whether the will was read to Everett Clark on March 25. When counsel asked her whether

Clark ever told her by any means on March 25, 1987, that the document was his last will and testament, she testified, "no, not me." Horton did testify, however, "When Mr. Walker asked him if this is what—if this was his will and if this is what he wanted and he shook his head, yes."

Smith, the other attesting witness, testified that just prior to Everett Clark's signing the will, she asked him if he knew that the attorney was there, and he responded by nodding affirmatively. She testified that Walker then spoke with Everett Clark, and explained to him that "he was there at the last will and testament. . . . He said, this is your will and testament, asked if John Bailey was his cousin . . . if he wanted to leave everything to John Bailey; if he knew everything about the will." When counsel asked Smith whether Clark indicated to the attorney that he knew all about the will, Smith testified, "he didn't indicate that as such . . . I believed the man knew what was going on."

The only witness who testified that the will was read to Everett Clark and that Clark was asked if he wanted to sign the will, was attorney Frank Walker. Walker, who represents the proponent in this case, testified that when he asked Clark, after reading the will to him, whether that is what Clark wanted, Clark shook his head yes.

The testimony of the witnesses who attested the execution of the will was not wholly conclusive on the issues of whether Everett Clark acknowledged the instrument as his will or knew the contents of the instrument executed as his will. Although Clark's physical disability alone cannot be considered as evidence that he did not know the contents of the instrument which he executed . . . based on the testimony presented in the instant case, it was entirely reasonable for the jury to find that Everett Clark did not acknowledge that the instrument was his will, and did not know the contents of the instrument.

On the question of the valid execution of a will in a proceeding for its probate, the question of the credibility of the witnesses is for the court hearing the case, and where it has given credit to the testimony of subscribing witnesses, this court will not disturb its judgment. . . . The credibility of witnesses and the weight to be accorded their testimony are matters for the jury to determine, and unless its determination is manifestly against the weight of the evidence, it will not be disturbed on appeal. . . . We conclude that the record does not support the proponent's contention that the verdict was against the manifest weight of the evidence, and therefore the judgment must be affirmed.

[Judgment affirmed]

QUESTIONS

1. Did the decedent possess the requisite testamentary capacity to make a will?
2. Is a will valid where it is signed by a mark?
3. What was the basis for the court's decision?

9. Special Kinds of Wills

In certain situations, special kinds of wills are used.

(a) HOLOGRAPHIC WILLS. A **holographic will** is an unwitnessed will that is written by the testator entirely by hand. In some states, no distinction is made between holographic and other wills. In other states, the general body of the law of wills applies, but certain variations are established. Thus, it may be required that a holographic will be dated.

Under the UPC, a holographic will is valid whether or not witnessed, if the signatures and the material provisions are in the handwriting of the testator.

(b) SELF-PROVED WILLS. **Self-proved wills** are wills that eliminate some formalities of proof by being executed in the way set forth by statute. Self-proved wills are recognized in those states following the Uniform Probate Code. A will may be simultaneously executed, attested, and made self-proved, by acknowledgment by the testator and by affidavits of the witnesses. The acknowledgment and affidavits must each be made before an officer authorized to administer oaths under the laws of the state in which execution occurs. They must be evidenced by the officer's certificate, under official seal.

The self-proving provisions attached to the will are not a part of the will. They concern only the matter of its proof. The only purpose served by self-proving provisions is to admit a will to probate without the testimony of a subscribing witness. It was not the purpose of legislatures, upon enacting the statute permitting self-proving wills, to amend or repeal the requirement that the will itself must meet the requirements of the law. The execution of a valid will is a condition precedent to the use of the self-proving provisions.

(c) LIVING WILLS. **Living wills** are documents by which individuals may indicate that, if they become unable to express their wishes and they are in an irreversible, incurable condition, they do not want life-sustaining medical treatments. (See Figure 54-1.) Living wills are legal in most states. Such personal wishes are entitled to constitutional protection, as long as they are expressed clearly.

B. DISTRIBUTION UNDER THE WILL

If the decedent died leaving a valid will, the last phase of the administration of the estate by the decedent's personal representative is the distribution of property remaining after the payment of all debts and taxes, in accordance with the provisions of the will.

10. Legacies

The testator will ordinarily bequeath to named persons certain sums of money, called **general legacies** because no particular money is specified. The testator may bequeath identified property, called **specific legacies** or **specific devises**. Thus, the testator may say, "$1,000 to A; $1,000 to B; my automobile to C." The first two bequests are general; the third is specific. After such bequests, the testator may make a bequest of everything remaining, called a **residuary bequest**—for example, "the balance of my estate to D."

(a) ABATEMENT OF LEGACIES. Assume in the preceding example that after all debts are paid, there remains only $1,500 and the automobile. What disposition is to be made? Legacies **abate** or bear loss in the following order: (1) residuary, (2) general, (3) specific. The law also holds that legacies of the same class abate proportionately. Accordingly, in the hypothetical case, C, the specific legatee, would receive the automobile; A and B, the general legatees, would each receive $750, and D, the residuary legatee, would receive nothing.

(b) ADEMPTION OF PROPERTY. When specifically bequeathed property is sold or given away by the testator prior to death, the bequest is considered **adeemed**, or canceled.

Figure 54-1 Living Will

Living Will

INSTRUCTIONS:

This is an important legal document. It sets forth your directions regarding medical treatment. You have the right to refuse treatment you do not want. You may make changes in any of these directions, or add to them, to conform them to your personal wishes.

I, _John Jones_ , being of sound mind, make this statement as a directive to be followed if I become permanently unable to participate in decisions regarding my medical care. These instructions reflect by firm and settled commitment to decline medical treatment under the circumstances indicated below:

I direct my attending physician to withhold or withdraw treatment that serves only to prolong the process of my dying, if I should be in an incurable or irreversible mental or physical condition with no reasonable expectation of recovery.

These instructions apply if I am a) in a terminal condition; b) permanently unconscious; or c) if I am conscious but have irreversible brain damage and will never regain the ability to make decisions and express my wishes.

I direct that treatment be limited to measures to keep me comfortable and to relieve pain, including any pain that might occur by withholding or withdrawing treatment.

While I understand that I am not legally required to be specific about future treatments, if I am in the condition(s) described above I feel especially strongly about the following forms of treatment:

I do not want cardiac resuscitation.
I do not want mechanical respiration.
I do not want tube feeding.
I do not want antibiotics.
I do want maximum pain relief.
Other directions (insert personal instructions): _NONE_

These directions express my legal right to refuse treatment, under the law of [name of state]. I intend my instructions to be carried out, unless I have rescinded them in a new writing or by clearly indicating that I have changed my mind.

Signed: _John Jones_

Witness: _Earl Hummel_

Address: _7852 Bailey Avenue_
Buffalo, New York

Witness: _Ramona Valey_

Address: _8921 Clinton Street_
Buffalo, New York

Sign and date here in the presence of two adult witnesses, who should also sign.

Keep the signed original with your personal papers at home. Give copies of the signed original to your doctor, family, lawyer and others who might be involved in your care.

The specific legatee in this instance is not entitled to receive any property or money. Ademption has the same consequence as though the testator had formally canceled the bequest.

(c) ANTILAPSE STATUTES. If the beneficiary named in the testator's will has died before the testator and the testator did not make any alternate provision applicable in such a case, the gift ordinarily does not lapse.

Antilapse statutes commonly provide that the gift to the deceased beneficiary shall not lapse but that the children or heirs of that beneficiary may take the legacy in the place of the deceased beneficiary.[6] An antilapse statute does not apply if the testator specifies a disposition that should be made of the gift if the original legatee has died.

11. Election to Take Against the Will

To protect the husband or wife of a testator, the surviving spouse may generally ignore the provisions of a will and elect to take against the will. In such a case, the surviving spouse receives the share of the estate he or she would have received had the testator died without leaving a will, or a fractional share specified by statute.

The right to take against the will is generally barred by certain kinds of misconduct of the surviving spouse. Thus, if the spouse is guilty of such desertion or nonsupport as would have justified the decedent's obtaining a divorce, the surviving spouse usually cannot elect to take against the will.

12. Disinheritance

With two exceptions,[7] any person may be disinherited or excluded from sharing in the estate of a decedent. A person who would inherit if there were no will is excluded from receiving any part of a decedent's estate if the decedent has left a will giving everything to other persons.

13. Construction of Will

The will of a decedent is to be interpreted according to the ordinary or plain meaning evidenced by its words. The court will strive to give effect to every provision of the will in order to avoid concluding that any part of the

decedent's estate was not disposed of by the will.[8]

C. INTESTACY

If the decedent does not effectively dispose of all property by will or does not have a will, the decedent's property is distributed to certain relatives. Since such persons acquire or succeed to the rights of the decedent and since the circumstances under which they do so is the absence of an effective will, it is said that they acquire title by **intestate succession**.

The right of intestate succession or inheritance is not a basic right of the citizen or an inalienable right. It exists only because the state legislature so provides. It is within the power of the state legislature to modify or destroy the right to inherit property.

14. Plan of Intestate Distribution

Although wide variations exist among the statutory provisions of the states, a common pattern of intestate distribution can be observed.

(a) SPOUSES. The surviving spouse of the decedent, whether husband or wife, shares in the estate. Generally, the amount received is a fraction that varies with the number of children. If no children survive, the spouse is generally entitled to take the entire estate. Otherwise, the surviving spouse ordinarily receives a one-half or one-third share of the estate.

(b) LINEALS. **Lineals** or **lineal descendants** are blood descendants of the decedent. That portion of the estate that is not distributed to the surviving spouse is generally distributed to lineals.

---

6 Malecki's Estate, 79 App Div 2d 799, 435 NYS2d 112 (1980).

7 The exceptions to this rule are based (a) on the election of a spouse to take against the will and (b) in certain cases on the partial revocation of a will by a subsequent marriage, birth, or adoption.

8 Estate of Christensen (Iowa App) 461 NW2d 469 (1990).

(c) PARENTS. If the estate has not been fully distributed by this time, the remainder is commonly distributed to the decedent's parents.

(d) COLLATERAL HEIRS. These are persons who are not descendants of the decedent but who are related through a common ancestor. Generally, brothers and sisters and their descendants share any part of the estate that has not already been distributed.

Statutes vary as to how far distribution will be made to the descendants of brothers and sisters. Under some statutes a degree of relationship is specified, such as first cousins, and no person more remotely related to the decedent is permitted to share in the estate.

when there is no relative of the decedent, however remotely related.

(e) DISTRIBUTION PER CAPITA AND PER STIRPES. The fact that different generations of distributees may be entitled to receive the estate creates a problem of determining the proportions in which distribution is to be made. (See Figure 54-2.) When all the distributees stand in the same degree of relationship to the decedent, **distribution** is made **per capita**, each receiving the same share. Thus, if the decedent is survived by three children, A, B, and C, each of them is entitled to receive one-third of the estate.

If the distributees stand in different degrees of relationship, distribution is made in as

---

Figure 54-2 Distribution Per Capita and Per Stirpes

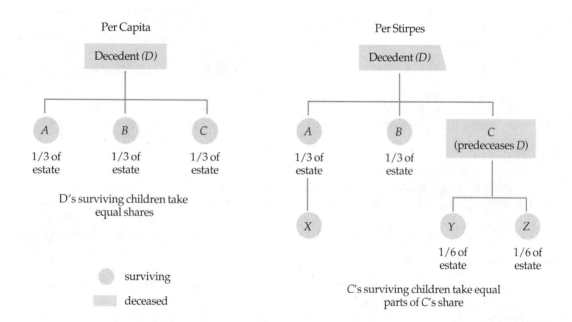

If the entire estate is not distributed within the permitted degree of relationship, the property that has not been distributed is given to the state government. This right of the state to take the property is the **right of escheat**. Under some statutes, the right of escheat arises only

many equal parts as there are family lines, or **stirpes**, represented in the nearest generation. Parents take to the exclusion of their children or subsequent descendants; and when members of the nearest generation have died, their descendants take by way of representation.

This is called **distribution per stirpes** or stipital distribution.

(f) MURDER OF DECEDENT. Statutes generally provide that a person who murders the decedent cannot inherit from the victim by intestacy. In the absence of such a statute, courts are divided as to whether the heir may inherit.

(g) DEATH OF DISTRIBUTEE AFTER DECEDENT. The persons entitled to distribution of a decedent's estate are determined as of the date of death. If a distributee dies thereafter, the rights of the distributee are not lost but pass from the original decedent's estate to the deceased distributee's estate.

(h) SIMULTANEOUS DEATH. The Uniform Simultaneous Death Act[9] provides that when survivorship cannot be established, "the property of each person shall be disposed of as if he had survived the other."[10]

D. ADMINISTRATION OF DECEDENTS' ESTATES

A decedent's estate consists of the assets that a person owns at death. It must be determined who is entitled to receive that property. If the decedent owed debts, those debts must be paid first. After that, any balance is to be distributed according to the terms of the will, or by the intestate law if the decedent did not leave a valid will.

15. Definitions

The decedent has the privilege of naming in the will the person who will administer the estate. A man named in a will to administer the estate of the decedent is an **executor**; a woman, an **executrix**. If the decedent failed to name an executor or did not leave a will, the law permits another person, usually a close relative, to obtain the appointment of someone to wind up the estate. This person is an **administrator** or **administratrix**.

Administrators and executors are often referred to generally as **personal representatives** of the decedents, since they represent the decedents or stand in their place.

16. When Administration Is Not Necessary

No administration is required when the decedent did not own any property at the time of death or when all the property owned was jointly owned with another person who acquired the decedent's interest by right of survivorship. Thus, if all of the property of a husband and wife is held as tenants by the entireties, no administration is required upon the death of either of them. The other automatically acquires the entire estate free of any debts or liabilities of the decedent.

In some states, special statutes provide for a simplified administration when the decedent leaves only a small estate.

17. Appointment of Personal Representative

Both executors and administrators must be appointed to act as such by a court or officer designated by law. The appointment is made by granting to the personal representative **letters testamentary**, in the case of an executor, or **letters of administration**, in the case of an administrator.

18. Proof of Claims Against the Estate

The statutes vary widely with respect to the presentation of claims against a decedent's estate.

---

[9] This act has been adopted for the District of Columbia and the Panama Canal Zone and in every state except Louisiana and Ohio.

[10] Special provision is made in the case of beneficiaries, joint tenants, tenants by entireties, community property, and insurance policies.

In very general terms, the statutes provide for some form of public notice of the grant of letters, as by advertisement. Creditors are then required to give notice of their claims within a period specified either by statute or a court order (for example, within six months). In most states, the failure to present the claim within the specified time bars the claim.

E. TRUSTS

A **trust** is a legal device by which property, real or personal, is held by one person for the benefit of another. Legal problems in the area of trusts invariably require a determination as to the nature of the relationship created by the trust and the rights and obligations of the parties with respect to that relationship.

19. Definitions

The property owner who creates the trust is the **settlor**. (The word *settlor* is taken from the old legal language of "settling the property in trust.") The settlor is sometimes called the donor or trustor. The person to whom the property is transferred in trust is the **trustee**. The person for whose benefit the trustee holds the property is the **beneficiary** (or cestui que trust).

Property held in trust is sometimes called the **trust corpus**, **trust fund**, **trust estate**, or **trust res**. A distinction is made between the **principal**, or the property in trust, and the **income** that is earned by the principal and distributed by the trustee.

Although an express trust is ordinarily created by a transfer of property, the settlor may retain the property as trustee for the beneficiary. The fact that there is a duty to make a payment does not create a trust.

If the trust is created to take effect within the lifetime of the settlor, it is a **living trust** or an **inter vivos trust**. If the trust is provided for in the settlor's will and is to become effective only when the will takes effect after death, the trust is called a **testamentary trust**.

20. Creation of Trusts

The requirements to create a trust are not uniform, but the following are typical.

(a) CONSIDERATION. Since a trust is a transfer of property, consideration is not required, although the absence of consideration may show that the trust is a transfer in fraud of creditors.

(b) LEGALITY. A trust may generally be created for any lawful purpose. A trust is invalid when it is for an unlawful purpose or is in fraud of creditors.

(c) CAPACITY OF BENEFICIARY. The capacity of the beneficiary of the trust to hold property or to contract is immaterial. Many trusts are created because the beneficiary lacks legal or actual capacity to manage the property.

(d) FORMALITY. In creating a trust, it is common practice to execute a writing, called a **trust agreement** or **deed of trust**. No particular form of language is necessary to create a trust, so long as the property, the trust purpose, and the beneficiaries are designated. If an inter vivos trust relates to an interest in land, the statute of frauds requires that the trust be evidenced by a writing setting forth the details of the trust. A writing signed by the trustee and referring to a deed from the trustor can satisfy this requirement. When the trust depends on a transfer of title to land, there must be a valid transfer of the title to the trustee.

A trust in personal property may be declared orally without any writing. If a trust is created by the will of the settlor, there must be a writing that meets the requirements of a will. The same is true when the trust is not intended to come into existence until the death of the settlor.

In the absence of a specific requirement of the statute of frauds as to land or of the statutes setting forth the formal requirements for wills, any conduct or writing that shows an intent to create a trust will be given effect. In the *McCaffrey* case it was alleged that no trust was created.

McCAFFREY v LAURSEN
215 Mont 305, 697 P2d 103 (1985)

> T. K. Laursen executed a deed that purported to convey his Lincoln County property to his son Orville. On the day the deed was executed, Orville Laursen executed an affidavit acknowledging a transfer of property from T. K. Laursen and agreeing that the property would be held in trust for T. K., that T. K. was to receive all rents and profits from the property, and that the property would be reconveyed upon trustor's request or death. Because of the father's mental and physical condition, a conservator was appointed to manage his affairs. McCaffrey, the conservator, sued Orville to recover title to the property. Orville contended that no trust existed. From a judgment in favor of the conservator of the father's estate, Orville appealed.

SHEEHY, J. . . . On July 21, 1981, T. K. executed a deed which purported to convey all title and interest in his Lincoln County property to his son Orville A. Laursen, defendant-appellant herein. On the same day, a separate document, defendant's Exhibit B, was executed and signed by Orville A. Laursen. The document provided:

The undersigned acknowledges that as of this date his father, T. K. LAURSEN, did by written Deed convey certain property to him to be held by him in Trust for the said T. K. Laursen (a copy of said Deed is attached hereto). Undersigned covenants and agrees that all income from such properties shall belong to T. K. Laursen and that he, the affiant will re-convey the property to T. K. Laursen at anytime the said T. K. Laursen requests and that if the said T. K. Laursen should die while the property is still in the name of affiant such property shall be considered as an asset of T. K. Laursen's estate and be disposed of in accordance with T. K. Laursen's Will.

This document was delivered by appellant to Shelton R. Williams, T. K.'s attorney.

Based on these documents and the testimony of defendant, the District Court ruled that defendant holds the properties in trust for his father and by the terms of the trust, defendant is obligated to reconvey the property to T. K. and to account for all income from the properties. Appellant appeals this order and contends that there is no evidence that a trust existed. . . .

The creation of a voluntary trust as to the trustor is governed by § 72-20-107, MCA. Section 72-20-108, MCA, governs as to the trustee. They provide:

72-20-107. Voluntary trust—how created as to trustor. Subject to the provisions of 72-24-102, a voluntary trust is created, as to the trustor and beneficiary, by any words or acts of the trustor indicating with reasonable certainty:

(1) an intention on the part of the trustor to create a trust; and

(2) the subject, purpose, and beneficiary of the trust.

72-20-108. Voluntary trust—how created as to trustee. Subject to the provisions of 72-24-102, a voluntary trust is created, as to the trustee, by any words or acts of his indicating with reasonable certainty:

(1) his acceptance of the trust or his acknowledgment, made upon sufficient consideration, of its existence; and

(2) the subject, purpose, and beneficiary of the trust.

Section 72-24-102, MCA, refers to trusts concerning real property. It provides:

No trust in relation to real property is valid unless created or declared by:

(1) a written instrument subscribed by the trustee or his agent thereto authorized in writing;

(2) the instrument under which the trustee claims the estate affected; or

(3) operation of law.

The status of Orville A. Laursen, the appellant in this action, is that of trustee. He was entrusted with the property of T. K. Laursen. Exhibit B previously set forth herein and signed by appellant acknowledges that T. K. will receive all rents and profits from the properties and that appellant promises to reconvey the property on request. Together with the deed referred to therein, they satisfy the requirements of § 72-24-102, MCA. This instrument on its face conclusively proves that appellant accepted the deed from his father with the intent of holding the property for the benefit of his father. Appellant promised to convey the property to T. K. on request. He also promised to convey the property to T. K.'s estate if T. K. should die without demanding its return. These promises show appellant's intent to act as trustee for his father's property. Appellant's testimony concerning his intent was consistent with the document. He stated that the purpose of the transaction was estate planning. We hold appellant met the requirements of § 72-20-108, MCA.

T. K. Laursen did not sign Exhibit B, the aforementioned document. However, he was not required to sign the document to meet the requirements of § 72-24-102, MCA. Once those requirements are met by the actions of the trustee, the trustor, T. K., must by words or acts indicate with reasonable certainty: (1) an intention to create a trust; and (2) the subject, purpose, and beneficiary of the trust.

The fact that the document was given to T. K.'s now deceased attorney, Shelton Williams, for safekeeping is an act that tends to show T. K. intended a trust to be created. Appellant testified that he believed T. K. deeded the property to appellant because T. K. wanted someone to take care of the property and to take care of him; that T. K. wanted to make it more difficult for his wife to get the property in T. K.'s upcoming divorce action; and that T. K. deeded the property to appellant for estate planning purposes. Appellant's testimony taken with the circumstances of this case show with reasonable certainty that T. K.'s intention was to create a trust when he deeded his property to appellant. We hold the District Court's finding to be factually sound and legally correct.

[Judgment affirmed]

(e) INTENTION. An intention to impose a duty on the trustee with respect to specific property must be expressed. It is not necessary, however, that the word *trust* or *trustee* be used. The settlor will ordinarily name a trustee, but failure to do so is not fatal to the trust, because a trustee will be appointed by the court.

(f) ACTIVE DUTY. A trust does not exist unless an active duty is placed on the trustee to manage the property in some manner or to exercise discretion or judgment. A bare direction to hold the property in trust, without any direction as to its use or distribution, is not sufficient for an active duty. Thus, when a decedent transferred $5,000 to a trustee to be held in trust for *A*, no trust was created. In such a case the intended beneficiary is entitled to receive the property outright as though the decedent had not attempted to create a trust.

(g) IDENTITY OF BENEFICIARY. Every trust must have a beneficiary. In a private trust the beneficiaries must be identified by name, description, or designation of the class to which the beneficiaries belong.[11] In a charitable trust, it is sufficient that the beneficiaries be members of the public at large or a general class of the public.

(h) ACCEPTANCE OF TRUST. Since the performance of a trust imposes duties on the trustee, a trustee may renounce or reject the trust. Acceptance will be presumed in the absence of a disclaimer. A renunciation does not affect the validity of the trust, because a court will appoint a substitute trustee if the settlor does not do so.

21. Nature of Beneficiary's Interest

The effect of a transfer in trust is to divide the property so that the legal title is given to the trustee and the **equitable title**, or beneficial interest, is given to the beneficiary. The beneficiary may ordinarily transfer or assign such interest in the trust. The beneficiary's creditors may reach that interest in satisfaction of their claims. An exception arises when the settlor has restricted the trust in such a way that the beneficiary cannot assign nor creditors reach the interest. This is commonly called a **spendthrift trust**.

22. Powers of Trustee

A trustee can exercise only those powers that are given by law or the trust instrument or those that the court will construe as being given by implication. Modern trusts commonly give the trustee discretion to make decisions on matters that could not be foreseen by the settlor. For example, the trustee may be authorized to expend principal as well as income when, in the trustee's opinion, it is necessary for the education or medical care of a beneficiary. The trustee must exercise discretion in a reasonable manner.

23. Duties of Trustee

The duty of a trustee is to administer the trust. The trustee who accepts the appointment

---

[11] Schroeder v Herbert C. Coe Trust (SD) 437 NW2d 178 (1989).

must take all the necessary steps to carry out the trust in a proper manner.

(a) PERFORMANCE. A trustee is under a duty to carry out the trust according to its terms and is personally liable for any loss sustained from an unjustified failure to perform such duties. A trustee cannot delegate the performance of personal duties.

(b) DUE CARE. The trustee is under a duty to use reasonable skill, prudence, and diligence in the performance of trust duties. More simply stated, the trustee must use the care that would be exercised by a reasonable person under the circumstances.[12]

(c) LOYALTY. A trustee is not permitted to profit personally from the position of trustee, other than to receive the compensation allowed by contract or law.

(d) POSSESSION AND PRESERVATION OF TRUST PROPERTY. The trustee is under a duty to take possession of trust property and to preserve it from loss or damage. If the property includes accounts receivable or outstanding debts, the trustee is under the duty to collect them.

(e) DEFENSE OF TRUST. The trustee must defend the trust when its validity is disputed in court.

(f) PRODUCTION OF INCOME. By either express or implied direction, the trustee is required to invest the money or property in enterprises or transactions that will yield an income to the estate.

A trustee is generally permitted to invest in bonds of the United States or of instrumentalities of the United States; bonds of states, cities, and counties, subject to certain restrictions; first mortgages on real estate when the mortgage does not represent more than a specified percentage of the value of the land; and mortgage bonds of certain kinds of corporations. Most states now permit a trustee to invest in corporate stocks. Court approval is generally required for investments in real estate.

(g) ACCOUNTING AND INFORMATION. A trustee must keep accurate records so that it can be determined whether the trust has been properly administered. Upon request by a beneficiary, the trustee must furnish information with respect to the trust. Periodically, or at certain times, as determined by the law in each state, a trustee must file an account in court. At such time the court examines the stewardship of the trust.

24. Remedies for Breach of Trust

A breach of trust may occur in a variety of ways, which in turn affects the remedies available. These remedies include:

a. Money judgment against trustee for loss caused
b. Injunction or order to compel the trustee to do or refrain from doing an act
c. Criminal prosecution of the trustee for misconduct
d. Tracing and recovery of trust property that has been converted by the trustee, unless the property had been acquired by a bona fide purchaser who gave value and purchased without notice of the breach of trust
e. Judgment against surety on the trustee's bond for loss caused the trust by the trustee's default
f. Removal of the trustee for misconduct
g. Suit against third persons who participated in a breach of trust

25. Termination of Trust

A trust may be terminated (a) in accordance with its terms;[13] (b) because of the impossibil-

---

[12] Matter of Green Charitable Trust, 172 Mich App 298, 431 NW2d 492 (1988).

[13] Schwartzkopf v American Heart Ass'n. (Fla App) 541 So 2d 1348 (1989).

ity of attaining the object of the trust; (c) via revocation by the settlor, when allowed by the terms of the trust; (d) by merger of all interests in the same person; and (e) upon the request of all the beneficiaries when there is no express purpose that requires continuation of the trust.

SUMMARY

A will is a writing that provides for a disposition of property, to take effect upon death. A man who makes a will is called a testator; a woman, a testatrix. The person to whom property is left by will is a beneficiary. A legacy is a gift of personal property by will; a gift of real property by will is a devise.

A testator must have testamentary capacity to make a will and must manifest some intention that the will be effective only upon death. The will must be signed by the testator and be witnessed.

A will may be modified by a codicil or revoked either by the act of the testator or by operation of law.

Probate is the act by which a proper court official accepts a will. Probate may be refused or set aside on grounds that the will is not the free expression of the testator.

A holographic will is an unwitnessed will written entirely in the handwriting of the testator. A self-proved will may be admitted to probate without the testimony of subscribing witnesses. A living will allows a person to make wishes known regarding life-sustaining medical treatment.

If there is a valid will, the last phase of administration of the estate is the distribution of property after the payment of all debts and taxes. General legacies are bequests of money, whereas specific legacies or specific devises are gifts of identified personal or real property. Legacies abate in the following order: residuary, general, and specific. If a beneficiary named in the will has died before the testator and no alternate provision has been made for such beneficiary, antilapse statutes provide that the gift will not lapse. In that event the children or heirs of the beneficiary may take the legacy in the place of the deceased beneficiary.

If the decedent does not dispose of all property by will or does not have a will, the property will be distributed according to state intestacy statutes. A surviving spouse may generally elect to take the statutory allocation instead of that provided in the will.

The estate of the testator will be administered by the person appointed in the will (the executor) or, if there is no will, by a person appointed by the court (an administrator). Creditors who have claims against the estate are required to give notice of their claim to the personal representative; otherwise, the claim will be barred.

A trust is a legal device by which property is held by one person for the benefit of another. The settlor creates the trust, and the person for whose benefit the trustee holds the property is the beneficiary. Property held in trust is called the trust corpus, trust fund, trust estate, or res.

A trust is usually created by a writing called a trust agreement or deed of trust. No particular form or language is required. A trust is not created unless an active duty is placed upon the trustee to manage the property in some manner. A trustee's acceptance of duties is presumed.

Legal title to trust property is given to the trustee, but equitable title is held by the beneficiary. A beneficiary may transfer an interest in the trust, except in the case of a spendthrift trust.

The trustee can exercise only those powers that are given by law or the trust instrument. The trustee must administer the trust and carry out the trust in a proper manner. A trustee may be sued for breach of the terms of the trust agreement. A trust comes to an end when its terms so provide or when it becomes impossible to attain the object of the trust.

LAW IN PRACTICE

1. If you fail to prepare a will in accordance with legal requirements, it will not be admitted to probate and your estate will be distributed by statute.
2. A codicil may be used to change or update your will.
3. If you decide to revoke your will, be sure the revocation follows the procedures required by law.

4. If you do not wish life-sustaining devices or medical treatments to be used if you become incurably ill, you may indicate your wishes by a living will.
5. Through the use of a trust, property can be held by one person for the benefit of another.

QUESTIONS AND CASE PROBLEMS

1. What social forces are affected by allowing a person to give property after death by means of leaving a will?

2. Jean repeatedly told her best friend Diane and their neighbors that Jean would leave her house to Diane when she died. Jean died without having written any will. Diane claimed the house, and the neighbors testified in court that Jean had repeatedly declared that she would leave the house to Diane. Is Diane entitled to the house?

3. Iona wrote her will. The following year she wrote another will that expressly revoked the earlier will. Later, while cleaning house, she came across the second will. She mistakenly thought that it was the first will and tore it up because the first will had been revoked. Iona died shortly thereafter. The beneficiaries named in the second will claimed that the second will should be probated. The beneficiaries named in the first will claimed that the second will had been revoked when it was torn up. Had the second will been revoked?

4. Logsdon, who had three children, disliked one of them without any reason. In his will he left only a small amount to the child he disliked and gave the bulk of his estate to the remaining two. Upon his death, the disliked child claimed that the will was void and had been obtained by undue influence. Do you agree? [Logsdon v Logsdon, 412 Ill 19, 104 NE2d 622]

5. Field executed a will. Upon her death the will was found in her safe-deposit box, but the part of the will containing the fifth bequest was torn from the will. This torn fragment was also found in the box. There was no evidence that anyone other than Field had ever opened the box. A proceeding was brought to determine whether the will was entitled to be probated. Decide. [Flora v Hughes, 312 Ky 478, 228 SW2d 27]

6. Miller wrote a will 11 pages long and enclosed it in an envelope, which she sealed. She then wrote on the envelope, "My last will & testament," and signed her name below this statement. This was the only place where she signed her name on any of the papers. Was this signature sufficient to allow this writing to be admitted to probate as her will? [Millers Executor v Shannon (Ky) 299 SW2d 103]

7. Probate of the will of Lingenfelter was opposed. It was shown that the testatrix was sick, highly nervous, and extremely jealous and that she committed suicide a week after executing the will. In support of the will, it was shown that she understood the will when she discussed it with an attorney, that her husband was seriously ill when she wrote the will, that he died the following day, and that she grieved his death. A proceeding was brought to determine whether the will was entitled to probate. Decide. [Lingenfelters Estate, 38 Cal 2d 571, 241 P2d 990]

8. Copenhaver wrote a will in ink. At her death, it was found with her other papers in her bedroom. Pencil lines had been drawn through every provision of the will and the signature. There was no evidence as to the circumstances under which this had been done. Was the will revoked? Why? [Franklin v Maclean, 192 Va 684, 66 SE2d 504]

9. Dolores states in her will, "I leave $10,000 to the First National Bank in trust for my niece, Clara." After the death of Dolores, the will is probated. Is the trust for Clara valid?

10. What is the difference between an inter vivos trust and a testamentary trust?

11. Smith died without leaving a will. He was survived by his widow, two children, and a brother. How will the estate be distributed in most states?

12. Rachael conveyed certain land to Roland in trust for her daughter, Mary. Roland refused to accept the trust. What effect does this refusal have on the rights of her daughter, Mary?

13. By her will, Hendricks provided: "I give, devise, and bequeath [the balance of my estate] to the City of Brookfield, Missouri, for the sole purpose of building and equipping and maintaining a city hospital. . . ." The city claimed that this was an absolute gift to the city, subject to a condition as to its use. Do you agree? [*Ramsey v City of Brookfield, 361 Mo 857, 237 SW2d 143*]

14. The Pioneer Trust and Savings Bank was trustee of certain land for the benefit of Harmon. Under the terms of the trust, Harmon could require the trustee to sell the land as he directed. Schneider wrote Pioneer Trust, offering to buy the land. Harmon made a written notation on the letter that he accepted the offer and sent it back to Schneider. Schneider withdrew his offer and claimed that there was no contract. Harmon claimed that Schneider was bound by a contract. Decide. [*Schneider v Pioneer Trust and Savings Bank, 26 Ill App 2d 463, 168 NE2d 808*]

15. Jason created a trust for the benefit of the ABC charity. He later changed his mind and decided that he would prefer to create the trust for a private university. Could Jason do this, if no provision for revocation was contained in the trust? Explain.

Appendices..

Appendix 1
How to Find
the Law

In order to determine what the law on a particular question or issue is, it may be necessary to examine (1) compilations of constitutions, treaties, statutes, executive orders, proclamations, and administrative regulations; (2) reports of state and federal court decisions; (3) digests of opinions; (4) treatises on the law; and (5) loose-leaf services.

Compilations

In the consideration of a legal problem in business it is necessary to determine whether the matter is affected or controlled by the Constitution, national or state; by a national treaty; by an Act of Congress or a state legislature, or by a city ordinance; by a decree or proclamation of the President of the United States, a

governor, or a mayor; or by a regulation of a federal, state, or local administrative agency.

Each body or person that makes laws, regulations, or ordinances usually compiles and publish at the end of each year or session all of the matter that it has adopted. In addition to the periodical or annual volumes, it is common to compile all the treaties, statutes, regulations, or ordinances in separate volumes. To illustrate, the federal Anti-Injunction Act may be cited as the Act of March 23, 1932, 47 Stat 70, 29 USC Sections 101 et seq. This means that this law was enacted on March 23, 1932, and that it can be found at page 70 in Volume 47 of the reports that contain all of the statutes adopted by the Congress.

The second part of the citation, 29 USC Sections 101 et seq., means that in the collection of all of the federal statutes, which is known as the United States Code, the full text of the statute can be found in the sections of the 29th title beginning with Section 101.

Court Deisions

For complicated or important legal cases or when an appeal is to be taken, a court will generally write an opinion, which explains why the court made the decision. Appellate courts as a rule write opinions. The great majority of these decisions, particularly in the case of the appellate courts, are collected and printed. In order to avoid confusion, the opinions of each court are ordinarily printed in a separate set of reports, either by official reporters or private publishers.

In the reference "Pennoyer v Neff, 95 US 714, 24 LEd 565," the first part states the names of the parties. It does not necessarily tell who was the plaintiff and who was the defendant. When an action is begun in a lower court, the first name is that of the plaintiff and the second name that of the defendant. When the case is appealed, generally the name of the person taking the appeal appears on the records of the higher court as the first one and that of the adverse party as the second. Sometimes, therefore, the original order of the names of the parties is reversed.

The balance of the reference consists of two citations. The first citation, 95 US 714, means that the opinion which the court filed in the case of Pennoyer and Neff may be found on page 714 of the 95th volume of a series of books in which are printed officially the opinions of the United States Supreme Court. Sometimes the same opinion is printed in two different sets of volumes. In the example, 24 LEd 565 means that in the 24th volume of another set of books, called Lawyer's Edition, of the United States Supreme Court Reports, the same opinion begins on page 565.

In opinions by a state court there are also generally two citations, as in the case of "Morrow v Corbin, 122 Tex 553, 62 SW2d 641." This means that the opinion in the lawsuit between Morrow and Corbin may be found in the 122d volume of the reports of the highest court of Texas, beginning on page 553; and also in Volume 62 of the Southwestern Reporter, Second Series, at page 641.

The West Publishing Company publishes a set of sectional reporters covering the entire United States. They are called "sectional" because each reporter, instead of being limited to a particular court or a particular state, covers the decisions of the courts of a particular section of the country. Thus the decisions of the courts of Arkansas, Kentucky, Missouri, Tennessee, and Texas are printed by the West Publishing company as a group in a sectional reporter called the Southwestern Reporter.[1] Because of the large number of decisions involved, generally only the opinions of the state appellate courts are printed. A number of states[2] have discontinued publication of the opinions of their courts, and those opinions are now found only in the West reporters.

The reason for the "Second Series" in the Southwestern citation is that when there were 300 volumes in the original series, instead of calling the next volume 301, the publisher called it Volume 1, Second Series. Thus 62 SW2d Series really means the 362d volume of the Southwestern Reporter. Six to eight volumes appear in a year for each geographic section.

In addition to these state reporters, the West Publishing Company publishes a Federal Supplement, which primarily reports the opinions of the Federal District Courts; the Federal Reporter, which primarily reports the decisions of the United States Courts of Appeals; and the Supreme Court Reporter, which reports the decisions of the United States Supreme Court. The Supreme Court decisions

---

[1] The sectional reporters are: Atlantic—A. (Connecticut, Delaware, District of Columbia, Maine, Maryland, New Hampshire, New Jersey, Pennsylvania, Rhode Island, Vermont); Northeastern—

[2] See, for example, Alaska, Florida, Iowa, Kentucky, Louisiana, Maine, Mississippi, Missouri, North Dakota, Oklahoma, Texas, and Wyoming.

are also reported in a separate set called the Lawyers' Edition, published by the Lawyers Cooperative Publishing Company.

The reports published by the West Publishing Company and Lawyers Cooperative Publishing Company are unofficial reports, while those bearing the name or abbreviation of the United States or of a state, such as "95 US 714" or "122 Tex 553" are official reports. This means that in the case of the latter, the particular court, such as the United States Supreme Court, has officially authorized that its decisions be printed and that by federal statute such official printing is made. In the case of the unofficial reporters, the publisher prints the decisions of a court on its own initiative. Such opinions are part of the public domain and not subject to any copyright or similar restriction.

Digests Of Opinions

The reports of court decisions are useful only if one has the citation—that is, the name and volume number of the book and the page number of the opinion one is seeking. For this reason, digests of the decisions have been prepared. These digests organize the entire field of law under major headings, which are then arranged in alphabetical order. Under each heading, such as "Contracts," the subject is divided into the different questions that can arise with respect to that field. A master outline is thus created on the subject. This outline includes short paragraphs describing what each case holds and giving its citation.

Treatises And Restatements

Very helpful in finding a case or a statute are the treatises on the law. These may be special books, each written by an author on a particular subject, such as Williston on Contracts, Bogert on Trusts, Fletcher on Corporations, or they may be general encyclopedias, as in the case of American Jurisprudence, American Jurisprudence, Second, and Corpus Juris Secundum.

Another type of treatise is found in the restatements of the law prepared by the American Law Institute. Each restatement consists of one or more volumes devoted to a particular phase of the law, such as the Restatement of the Law of Contracts, Restatement of the Law of Agency, and Restatement of the Law of Property. In each restatement the American Law Institute, acting through special committees of judges, lawyers, and professors of law, has set forth what the law is; and in many areas where there is no law or the present rule is regarded as unsatisfactory, the restatement specifies what the Institute deems to be the desirable rule.

Loose-leaf Services

A number of private publishers, notably Commerce Clearing House and Prentice-Hall, publish loose-leaf books devoted to particular branches of the law. Periodically, the publisher sends to the purchaser a number of pages that set forth any decision, regulation, or statute made or adopted since the prior set of pages was prepared. Such services are unofficial.

Computers And Legal Research

National and local computer services are providing constantly widening assistance for legal research. The database in such a system may be opinions, statutes, or administrative regulations stored word for word; or the later history of a particular case giving its full citation and showing whether the case has been followed by other courts; or the text of forms and documents. By means of a terminal connected to the system, the user can retrieve the above information at a great saving of time and with the assurance that it is up-to-date.

There are two leading national systems for computer aided research. Listed alphabetically, they are LEXIS and WESTLAW.

A specialized service of legal forms for business is provided by Shepard's BUSINESS LAW CASE MANAGEMENT SYSTEM.

The computer field has expanded to such an extent that there is now a Legal Software Review of over 500 pages prepared by Lawyers Library, 12761 New Hall Ferry, Florissant, MO 63033.

Appendix 2
The Constitution Of The United States

We the people of the United States, in order to form a more perfect union, establish justice, insure domestic tranquillity, provide for the common defense, promote the general welfare, and secure the blessings of liberty to ourselves and our posterity, do ordain and establish this Constitution for the United States of America.

Article 1

Section 1. All legislative powers herein granted shall be vested in a Congress of the United States, which shall consist of a Senate and House of Representatives.

Section 2. 1. The House of Representatives shall be composed of members chosen every second year by the people of the several States, and the electors in each State shall have the qualifications requisite for electors of the most numerous branch of the State legislature.

2. No person shall be a representative who shall not have attained to the age of twenty-five years, and been seven years a citizen of the United States, and who shall not, when elected, be an inhabitant of that State in which he shall be chosen.

3. Representatives and direct taxes shall be apportioned among the several States which may be included within this Union, according

to their respective numbers, which shall be determined by adding to the whole number of free persons, including those bound to service for a term of years, and excluding Indians not taxed, three fifths of all other persons.[1] The actual enumeration shall be made within three years after the first meeting of the Congress of the United States, and within every subsequent term of ten years, in such manner as they shall by law direct. The number of representatives shall not exceed one for every thirty thousand, but each State shall have at least one representative; and until such enumeration shall be made, the State of New Hampshire shall be entitled to choose three, Massachusetts eight, Rhode Island and Providence Plantations one, Connecticut five, New York six, New Jersey four, Pennsylvania eight, Delaware one, Maryland six, Virginia ten, North Carolina five, South Carolina five, and Georgia three.

4. When vacancies happen in the representation from any State, the executive authority thereof shall issue writs of election to fill such vacancies.

5. The House of Representatives shall choose their speaker and other officers; and shall have the sole power of impeachment.

Section 3. 1. The Senate of the United States shall be composed of two senators from each State, chosen by the legislature thereof, for six years; and each senator shall have one vote.

2. Immediately after they shall be assembled in consequence of the first election, they shall be divided as equally as may be into three classes. The seats of the senators of the first class shall be vacated at the expiration of the second year, of the second class at the expiration of the fourth year, and of the third class at the expiration of the fourth year, and of the third class at the expiration of the sixth year, so that one third may be chosen every second year; and if vacancies happen by resignation, or otherwise, during the recess of the legislature of any State, the executive thereof may make temporary appointments until the next meeting of the legislature, which shall then fill such vacancies.[2]

3. No person shall be a senator who shall not have attained to the age of thirty years, and been nine years a citizen of the United States, and who shall not, when elected, be an inhabitant of that State for which he shall be chosen.

4. The Vice President of the United States shall be President of the Senate, but shall have no vote, unless they be equally divided.

5. The Senate shall choose their other officers, and also a president pro tempore, in the absence of the Vice President, or when he shall exercise the office of the President of the United States.

6. The Senate shall have the sole power to try all impeachments. When sitting for that purpose, they shall be on oath or affirmation. When the President of the United States is tried, the chief justice shall preside: and no person shall be convicted without the concurrence of two thirds of the members present.

7. Judgment in cases of impeachment shall not extend further than to removal from office, and disqualifications to hold and enjoy any office of honor, trust or profit under the United States: but the party convicted shall nevertheless be liable and subject to indictment, trial, judgment and punishment, according to law.

Section 4. 1. The times, places, and manner of holding elections for senators and representatives, shall be prescribed in each State by the legislature thereof; but the Congress may at any time by law make or alter such regulations, except as to the places of choosing senators.

2. The Congress shall assemble at least once in every year, and such meeting shall be on the first Monday in December, unless they shall by law appoint a different day.

Section 5. 1. Each House shall be the judge of the elections, returns and qualifications of its own members, and a majority of each shall constitute a quorum to do business; but a

---

[1] See the 14th Amendment.

[2] See the 17th Amendment.

smaller number may adjourn from day to day, and may be authorized to compel the attendance of absent members, in such manner, and under such penalties as each House may provide.

2. Each House may determine the rules of its proceedings, punish its members for disorderly behavior, and, with the concurrence of two thirds, expel a member.

3. Each House shall keep a journal of its proceedings, and from time to time publish the same, excepting such parts as may in their judgment require secrecy; and the yeas and nays of the members of either House on any question shall, at the desire of one fifth of those present, be entered on the journal.

4. Neither House, during the session of Congress, shall, without the consent of the other, adjourn for more than three days, nor to any other place than that in which the two Houses shall be sitting.

Section 6. 1. The senators and representatives shall receive a compensation for their services, to be ascertained by law, and paid out of the Treasury of the United States. They shall in all cases, except treason, felony, and breach of the peace, be privileged from arrest during their attendance at the session of their respective Houses, and in going to and returning from the same; and for any speech or debate in either House, they shall not be questioned in any other place.

2. No senator or representative shall, during the time for which he was elected, be appointed to any civil office under the authority of the United States, which shall have been created, or the emoluments whereof shall have been increased during such time; and no person holding any office under the United States shall be a member of either House during his continuance in office.

Section 7. 1. All bills for raising revenue shall originate in the House of Representatives; but the Senate may propose or concur with amendments as on other bills.

2. Every bill which shall have passed the House of Representatives and the Senate, shall, before it becomes a law, be presented to the President of the United States; if he approves he shall sign it, but if not he shall return

it, with his objections to that House in which it shall have originated, who shall enter the objections at large on their journal, and proceed to reconsider it. If after such reconsideration two thirds of that House shall agree to pass the bill, it shall be sent, together with the objections, to the other House, by which it shall likewise be reconsidered, and if approved by two thirds of that House, it shall become a law. But in all such cases the votes of both Houses shall be determined by yeas and nays, and the names of the persons voting for and against the bill shall be entered on the journal of each House respectively. If any bill shall not be returned by the President within ten days (Sundays excepted) after it shall have been presented to him, the same shall be a law, in like manner as if he had signed it, unless the Congress by their adjournment prevent its return, in which case it shall not be a law.

3. Every order, resolution, or vote to which the concurrence of the Senate and the House of Representatives may be necessary (except on a question of adjournment) shall be presented to the President of the United States; and before the same shall take effect, shall be approved by him, or being disapproved by him, shall be repassed by two thirds of the Senate and House of Representatives, according to the rules and limitations prescribed in the case of a bill.

Section 8. The Congress shall have the power

1. To lay and collect taxes, duties, imposts, and excises, to pay the debts and provide for the common defense and general welfare of the United States; but all duties, imposts, and excises shall be uniform throughout the United States;

2. To borrow money on the credit of the United States;

3. To regulate commerce with foreign nations, and among the several States, and with the Indian tribes;

4. To establish a uniform rule of naturalization, and uniform laws on the subject of bankruptcies throughout the United States;

5. To coin money, regulate the value thereof, and of foreign coin, and fix the standard of weights and measures;

6. To provide for the punishment of counterfeiting the securities and current coin of the United States;

7. To establish post offices and post roads;

8. To promote the progress of science and useful arts, by securing for limited times to authors and inventors the exclusive rights to their respective writings and discoveries;

9. To constitute tribunals inferior to the Supreme Court;

10. To define and punish piracies and felonies committed on the high seas, and offenses against the law of nations;

11. To declare war, grant letters of marque and reprisal, and make rules concerning captures on land and water;

12. To raise and support armies, but no appropriation of money to that use shall be for a longer term than two years;

13. To provide and maintain a navy;

14. To make rules for the government and regulation of the land and naval forces;

15. To provide for calling forth the militia to execute the laws of the Union, suppress insurrections and repel invasions;

16. To provide for organizing, arming, and disciplining the militia, and for governing such part of them as may be employed in the service of the United States, reserving to the States respectively, the appointment of the officers, and the authority of training the militia according to the discipline prescribed by Congress.

17. To exercise exclusive legislation in all cases whatsoever, over such distinct (not exceeding ten miles square) as may, by cession of particular States, and the acceptance of Congress, become the seat of the government of the United States, and to exercise like authority over all places purchased by the consent of the legislature of the State in which the same shall be, for the erection of forts, magazines, arsenals, dockyards, and other needful buildings; and

18. To make all laws which shall be necessary and proper for carrying into execution the foregoing powers, and all other powers vested by this Constitution in the government of the United States, or in any department or officer thereof.

Section 9. 1. The migration or importation of such persons as any of the States now existing shall think proper to admit, shall not be prohibited by the Congress prior to the year one thousand eight hundred and eight, but a tax or duty may be imposed on such importation, not exceeding ten dollars for each person.

2. The privilege of the writ of habeas corpus shall not be suspended, unless when in cases of rebellion or invasion the public safety may require it.

3. No bill of attainder or ex post facto law shall be passed.

4. No capitation, or other direct, tax shall be laid, unless in proportion to the census or enumeration hereinbefore directed to be taken.[3]

5. No tax or duty shall be laid on articles exported from any State.

6. No preference shall be given by any regulation of commerce or revenue to the ports of one State over those of another: nor shall vessels bound to, or from, one State be obliged to enter, clear, or pay duties in another.

7. No money shall be drawn from the treasury, but in consequence of appropriations made by law; and a regular statement and account of the receipts and expenditures of all public money shall be published from time to time.

8. No title of nobility shall be granted by the United States: and no person holding any office of profit or trust under them, shall, without the consent of the Congress, accept of any present, emolument, office, or title, of any kind whatever, from any king, prince, or foreign State.

Section 10. 1. No State shall enter into any treaty, alliance, or confederation; grant letters of marque and reprisal; coin money; emit bills of credit; make anything but gold and silver coin a tender in payment of debts; pass any bill

[3] See the 16th Amendment

of attainder, ex post facto law, or law impairing the obligation of contracts, or grant any title of nobility.

2. No State shall, without the consent of the Congress, lay any imposts or duties on imports or exports, except what may be absolutely necessary for executing its inspection laws: and the net produce of all duties and imposts laid by any State on imports or exports, shall be for the use of the treasury of the United States; and all such laws shall be subject to the revision and control of the Congress.

3. No State shall, without the consent of the Congress, lay any duty of tonnage, keep troops, or ships of war in time of peace, enter into any agreement or compact with another State, or with a foreign power, or engage in war, unless actually invaded, or in such imminent danger as will not admit of delay.

Article II

Section 1. 1. The executive power shall be vested in a President of the United States of America. He shall hold his office during the term of four years, and, together with the Vice President, chosen for the same term, be elected as follows:

2. Each State shall appoint, in such manner as the legislature thereof may direct, a number of electors, equal to the whole number of senators and representatives to which the State may be entitled in the Congress: but no senator or representative, or person holding an office of trust or profit under the United States, shall be appointed an elector.

The electors shall meet in their respective States, and vote by ballot for two persons, of whom one at least shall not be an inhabitant of the same State with themselves. And they shall make a list of all the persons voted for, and of the number of votes for each; which list they shall sign and certify, and transmit sealed to the seat of the government of the United States, directed to the president of the Senate.

The president of the Senate shall, in the presence of the Senate and House of Representatives, open all the certificates, and the votes shall then be counted. The person having the greatest number of votes shall be the President, if such number be a majority of the whole number of electors appointed; and if there be more than one who have such majority, and have an equal number of votes, then the House of Representatives shall immediately choose by ballot one of them for President; and if no person have a majority, then from the five highest on the list the said House shall in like manner choose the President. But in choosing the President, the votes shall be taken by States, the representation from each State having one vote; a quorum for this purpose shall consist of a member or members from two thirds of the States, and a majority of all the States shall be necessary to a choice. In every case, after the choice of the President, the person having the greatest number of votes of the electors shall be the Vice President. But if there should remain two or more who have equal votes, the Senate shall choose from them by ballot the Vice President.[4]

3. The Congress may determine the time of choosing the electors, and the day on which they shall give their votes; which day shall be the same throughout the United States.

4. No person except a natural born citizen, or a citizen of the United States, at the time of the adoption of this Constitution, shall be eligible to the office of President; neither shall any person be eligible to that office who shall not have attained to the age of thirty-five years, and been fourteen years a resident within the United States.

5. In the case of removal of the President from office, or of his death, resignation, or inability to discharge the powers and duties of the said office, the same shall devolve on the Vice President, and the Congress may by law provide for the case of removal, death, resignation, or inability, both of the President and Vice President, declaring what officer shall

---

[4] Superseded by the 12th Amendment.

then act as President, and such officer shall act accordingly, until the disability be removed, or a President shall be elected.

6. The President shall, at stated times, receive for his services a compensation, which shall neither be increased nor diminished during the period for which he shall have been elected, and he shall not receive within that period any other emolument from the United States, or any of them.

7. Before he enter on the execution of his office, he shall take the following oath or affirmation:—"I do solemnly swear (or affirm) that I will faithfully execute the office of President of the United States, and will to the best of my ability, preserve, protect and defend the Constitution of the United States."

Section 2. 1. The President shall be commander in chief of the army and navy of the United States, and of the militia of the several States, when called into the actual service of the United States; when called into the actual service of the United States; he may require the opinion, in writing, of the principal officer in each of the executive departments, upon any subject relating to the duties of their respective office, and he shall have power to grant reprieves and pardons for offenses against the United States, except in cases of impeachment.

2. He shall have power, by and with the advice and consent of the Senate, to make treaties, provided two thirds of the senators present concur; and he shall nominate, and by and with the advice and consent of the Senate, shall appoint ambassadors, other public ministers and consuls, judges of the Supreme Court, and all other officers of the United States, whose appointments are not herein otherwise provided for, and which shall be established by law: but the Congress may by law vest the appointment of such inferior officers, as they think proper, in the President alone, in the courts of law, or in the heads of departments.

3. The President shall have power to fill up all vacancies that may happen during the recess of the Senate, by granting commissions which shall expire at the end of their next session.

Section 3. He shall from time to time give to the Congress information of the state of the Union, and recommend to their consideration such measures as he shall judge necessary and expedient; he may, on extraordinary occasions, convene both Houses, or either of them, and in case of disagreement between them with respect to the time of adjournment, he may adjourn them to such time as he shall think proper; he shall receive ambassadors and other public ministers; he shall take care that the laws be faithfully executed, and shall commission all the officers of the United States.

Section 4. The President, Vice President, and all civil officers of the United States, shall be removed from office on impeachment for, and conviction of, treason, bribery, or other high crimes and misdemeanors.

Article III

Section 1. The judicial power of the United States shall be vested in one Supreme Court, and in such inferior courts as the Congress may from time to time ordain and establish. The judges, both of the Supreme and inferior courts, shall hold their offices during good behavior, and shall, at stated times, receive for their services, a compensation, which shall not be diminished during their continuance in office.

Section 2. 1. The judicial power shall extend to all cases, in law and equity, arising under this Constitution, the laws of the United States, and treaties made, or which shall be made, under their authority;—to all cases affecting ambassadors, other public ministers and consuls;—to all cases of admiralty and maritime jurisdiction;—to controversies to which the United States shall be a party;—to controversies between two or more States; between a State and citizens of another State;[5] —between citizens of different States;—between citizens of the same State claiming lands under grants of different States, and between a State, or the citizens thereof, and foreign States citizens or subjects.

2. In all cases affecting ambassadors, other public ministers and consuls, and those in which a State shall be party, the Supreme Court shall have original jurisdiction. In all the other cases before mentioned, the Supreme Court shall have appellate jurisdiction, both as to law and to fact, with such exceptions, and under such regulations as the Congress shall make.

3. The trial of all crimes, except in cases of impeachment, shall be by jury; and such trial shall be held in the State where the said crimes shall have been committed; but when not committed within any State, the trial shall be at such place or places as the Congress may by law have directed.

Section 3. 1. Treason against the United States shall consist only in levying war against them, or in adhering to their enemies, giving them aid and comfort. No person shall be convicted of treason unless on the testimony of two witnesses to the same overt act, or on confession in open court.

2. The Congress shall have power to declare the punishment of treason, but no attainder of treason shall work corruption of blood, or forfeiture except during the life of the person attained.

Article IV

Section 1. Full faith and credit shall be given in each State to the public acts, records, and judicial proceedings of every other State. And the Congress may by general laws prescribe the manner in which such acts, records and proceedings shall be proved, and the effect thereof.

Section 2. 1. The citizens of each State shall be entitled to all privileges and immunities of citizens in the several States.[6]

2. A person charged in any State with treason, felony, or other crime, who shall flee from justice, and be found in another State, shall on demand of the executive authority of the State from which he fled, be delivered up to be removed to the State having jurisdiction of the crime.

3. No person held to service or labor in one State under the laws thereof, escaping into another, shall in consequence of any law or regulation therein, be discharged from such service or labor, but shall be delivered up on claim of the party to whom such service or labor may be due.[7]

Section 3. 1. New States may be admitted by the Congress into this Union; but no new State shall be formed or erected within the jurisdiction of any other State, nor any State be formed by the junction of two or more States, or parts of States, without the consent of the legislatures of the States concerned as well as of the Congress.

2. The Congress shall have power to dispose of and make all needful rules and regulations respecting the territory or other property belonging to the United States; and nothing in this Constitution shall be so construed as to prejudice any claims of the United States, or of any particular State.

Section 4. The United States shall guarantee to every State in this Union a republican form of government, and shall protect each of them against invasion; and on application of the legislature, or of the executive (when the legislature cannot be convened) against domestic violence.

Article V

The Congress, whenever two thirds of both Houses shall deem it necessary, shall propose

---

[5] See the 11th Amendment.

[6] See the 14th Amendment, Sec. 1.

[7] See the 13th Amendment.

amendments to this Constitution, or, on the application of the legislature of two thirds of the several States, shall call a convention for proposing amendments, which in either case, shall be valid to all intents and purposes, as part of this Constitution when ratified by the legislatures of three fourths of the several States, or by conventions in three fourths thereof, as the one or the other mode of ratification may be proposed by the Congress; Provided that no amendment which may be made prior to the year one thousand eight hundred and eight shall in any manner affect the first and fourth clauses in the ninth section of the first article; and that no State, without its consent, shall be deprived of its equal suffrage in the Senate.

Article VI

1. All debts contracted and engagements entered into, before the adoption of this Constitution, shall be as valid against the United States under this Constitution, as under the Confederation.[8]

2. This Constitution, and the laws of the United States which shall be made in pursuance thereof; and all treaties made, or which shall be made, under the authority of the United States, shall be the supreme law of the land; and the Judges in every State shall be bound thereby, anything in the Constitution or laws of any State to the contrary notwithstanding.

3. The senators and representatives before mentioned, and the members of the several State legislatures, and all executive and judicial officers, both of the United States and of the several States, shall be bound by oath or affirmation to support this Constitution; but no religious test shall ever be required as a qualification to any office or public trust under the United States.

Article VII

The ratification of the conventions of nine States shall be sufficient for the establishment of this Constitution between the States so ratifying the same.

Done in Convention by the unanimous consent of the States present the seventeenth day of September in the year of our Lord one thousand seven hundred and eighty-seven, and of the independence of the United States of America the twelfth. In witness whereof we have hereunto subscribed our names.

AMENDMENTS

First Ten Amendments passed by Congress Sept. 25, 1789.

Ratified by three-fourths of the States December 15, 1791.

Amendment I

Congress shall make no law respecting an establishment of religion, or prohibiting the free exercise thereof; or abridging the freedom of speech, or of the press; or the right of the people peaceably to assemble, and to petition the government for a redress of grievances.

Amendment II

A well regulated militia, being necessary to the security of a free State, the right of the people to keep and bear arms, shall not be infringed.

Amendment III

No soldier shall, in time of peace be quartered in any house, without the consent of the owner, nor in time of war, but in a manner to be prescribed by law.

---

[8] See the 14th Amendment, Sec. 4.

Amendment IV

The right of the people to be secure in their persons, houses, papers, and effects, against unreasonable searches and seizures, shall not be violated, and no warrants shall issue, but upon probable cause, supported by oath or affirmation, and particularly describing the place to be searched, and he person or things to be seized.

Amendment V

No person shall be held to answer for a capital, or otherwise infamous crime, unless on a presentment or indictment of a grand jury, except in cases arising in the land or naval forces, or in the militia, when in actual service in time of war or public danger; nor shall any person be subject for the same offense to be twice put in jeopardy of life or limb; nor shall be compelled in any criminal case to be a witness against himself, nor be deprived of life, liberty, or property, without due process of law; nor shall private property be taken for public use without just compensation.

Amendment VI

In all criminal prosecutions, the accused shall enjoy the right to a speedy and public trial, by an impartial jury of the State and district wherein the crime shall have been committed, which district shall have been previously ascertained by law, and to be informed of the nature and cause of the accusation; to be confronted with the witnesses against him; to have compulsory process for obtaining witnesses in his favor, and to have the assistance of counsel for his defense.

Amendment VII

In suits at common law, where the value in controversy shall exceed twenty dollars, the right of trial by jury shall be preserved, and no fact tried by a jury shall be preserved, and no fact tried by a jury shall be otherwise reexamined in any court of the United States, then according to the rules of the common law.

Amendment VIII

Excessive bail shall not be required, nor excessive fines imposed, nor cruel and unusual punishments inflicted.

Amendment IX

The enumeration in the Constitution of certain rights shall not be construed to deny or disparage others retained by the people.

Amendment X

The powers not delegated to the United States by the Constitution, nor prohibited by it to the States, are reserved to the States respectively, or to the people.

Amendment XI

Passed by Congress March 5, 1794. Ratified January 8, 1798.

The judicial power of the United States shall not be construed to extend to any suit in law or equity, commenced or prosecuted against one of the United States by citizens of another State, or by citizens or subjects of any foreign State.

Amendment XII

Passed by Congress December 12, 1803. Ratified September 25, 1804.

The electors shall meet in their respective States, and vote by ballot for President and Vice President, one of whom, at least, shall not be an inhabitant of the same State with themselves; they shall name in their ballots the person voted for as President, and in distinct ballots, the person voted for as Vice President, and they shall make distinct lists of all persons voted for as President and of all persons voted for as Vice President, and of the number of votes for each, which lists they shall sign and certify, and transmit sealed to the seat of the government of the United States, directed to the President of the Senate;—The President of the Senate shall, in the presence of the Senate and House of Representatives, open all the certificates and the votes shall then be counted;—The person having the greatest number of votes for President, shall be the President, if such number be a majority of the whole number of electors appointed; and if no person have such majority, then from the persons having the highest numbers not exceeding three on the list of those voted for as President, the House of Representatives shall choose immediately, by ballot, the President. But in choosing the President, the votes shall be taken by States, the representation from each State having one vote; a quorum for this purpose shall consist of a member or members from two thirds of the States, and a majority of all the States shall be necessary to a choice. And if the House of Representatives shall not choose a President whenever the right of choice shall devolve upon them, before the fourth day of March next following, then the Vice President shall act as President, as in the case of the death or other constitutional disability of the President. The person having the greatest number of votes as Vice President shall be the Vice President, if such number be a majority of the whole number of electors appointed, and if no person have a majority, then from the two highest numbers on the list, the Senate shall choose the Vice President; a quorum for the purpose shall consist of two thirds of the whole number of Senators, and a majority of the whole number shall be necessary to a choice. But no person constitutionally ineligible to the office of President shall be eligible to that of Vice President of the United States.

Amendment XIII

Passed by Congress February 1, 1865. Ratified December 18, 1865.

Section 1. Neither slavery nor involuntary servitude, except as punishment for crime whereof the party shall have been duly convicted, shall exist within the United States, or any place subject to their jurisdiction.

Section 2. Congress shall have power to enforce this article by appropriate legislation.

Amendment XIV

Passed by Congress June 16, 1866. Ratified July 23, 1868.

Section 1. All persons born or naturalized in the United States, and subject to the jurisdiction thereof, are citizens of the United States and of the State wherein they reside. No State shall make or enforce any law which shall abridge the privileges or immunities of citizens of the United States; nor shall any State deprive any person of life, liberty, or property, without due process of law; nor deny to any person within its jurisdiction the equal protection of the laws.

Section 2. Representatives shall be apportioned among the several States according to their respective numbers, counting the whole number of persons in each State, excluding Indians not taxed. But when the right to vote at any election for the choice of electors for President and Vice President of the United States, representatives in Congress, the executive and judicial officers of a State, or the members of the legislature thereof, is denied to any of the male inhabitants of such State, being twenty-one years of age, and citizens of the United States, or in any way abridged, except for participation in rebellion, or other crime, the basis of representation therein shall be reduced in the proportion which the number of such male citizens shall bear to the whole number of male citizens twenty-one years of age in such State.

Section 3. No person shall be a senator or representative in Congress, or elector of President and Vice President, or hold any office, civil or military, under the United States, or under any State, who having previously taken an oath, as a member of Congress, or as an officer of the United States, or as a member of any State legislature, or as an executive or judicial officer of any State, to support the Constitution of the United States, shall have engaged in insurrection or rebellion against the same, or given aid or comfort to the enemies thereof. But Congress may by a vote of two thirds of each House, remove such disability.

Section 4. The validity of the public debt of the United States, authorized by law, including debts incurred for payment of pensions and bounties for services in suppressing insurrection or rebellion, shall not be questioned. But neither the United States nor any State shall assume or pay any debt or obligation incurred in aid of insurrection or rebellion against the United States, or any claim for the loss or emancipation of any slave; but all such debts, obligations, and claims shall be held illegal and void.

Section 5. The Congress shall have power to enforce, by appropriate legislation, the provisions of this article.

Amendment XV

Passed by Congress February 27, 1869. Ratified March 30, 1870.

Section 1. The right of citizens of the United States to vote shall not be denied or abridged by the United States or by any State on account of race, color, or previous condition of servitude.

Section 2. The Congress shall have power to enforce this article by appropriate legislation.

Amendment XVI

Passed by Congress July 12, 1909. Ratified February 25, 1913.

The Congress shall have power to lay and collect taxes on incomes, from whatever source derived, without apportionment among the several States, and without regard to any census or enumeration.

Amendment XVII

Passed by Congress May 16, 1912. Ratified May 31, 1913.

The Senate of the United States shall be composed of two senators from each State, elected by the people thereof, for six years; and each senator shall have one vote. The electors in each State shall have the qualifications requisite for electors of the most numerous branch of the State legislature.

When vacancies happen in the representation of any State in the Senate, the executive authority of such State shall issue writs of election to fill such vacancies: Provided, That the legislature of any State may empower the executive thereof to make temporary appointments until the people fill the vacancies by election as the legislature may direct.

This amendment shall not be so construed as to affect the election or term of any senator chosen before it becomes valid as part of the Constitution.

Amendment XVIII

Passed by Congress December 17, 1917. Ratified January 29, 1919.

After one year from the ratification of this article, the manufacture, sale, or transportation of intoxicating liquors within, the importation thereof into, or the exportation thereof from the United States and all territory subject to the jurisdiction thereof for beverage purposes is hereby prohibited.

The Congress and the several States shall have concurrent power to enforce this article by appropriate legislation.

This article shall be inoperative unless it shall have been ratified as an amendment to the Constitution by the legislatures of the several States, as provided in the Constitution, within seven years from the date of the submission hereof to the States by Congress.

Amendment XIX

Passed by Congress June 5, 1919. Ratified August 26, 1920.

The right of citizens of the United States to vote shall not be denied or abridged by the United States or by any State on account of sex.

The Congress shall have power by appropriate legislation to enforce the provisions of this article.

Amendment XX

Passed by Congress March 3, 1932. Ratified January 23, 1933.

Section 1. The terms of the President and Vice President shall end at noon on the 20th day of January, and the terms of Senators and Representatives at noon on the 3d day of January, of the years in which such terms would have ended if this article had not been ratified; and the terms of their successors shall then begin.

Section 2. The Congress shall assemble at least once in every year, and such meeting shall begin at noon on the 3d day of January, unless they shall by law appoint a different day.

Section 3. If, at the time fixed for the beginning of the term of the President, the President-elect shall have died, the Vice President-elect shall become President. If a President shall not have been chosen before the time fixed for the beginning of his term, or if the President-elect shall have failed to qualify, then the Vice President-elect shall act as President until a President shall have qualified; and the Congress may by law provide for the case wherein neither a President-elect nor a Vice President-elect shall have qualified, declaring who shall then act as President, or the manner in which one who is to act shall be selected, and such person shall act accordingly until a President or Vice President shall have qualified.

Section 4. The Congress may by law provide for the case of the death of any of the persons from whom the House of Representatives may choose a President whenever the right of choice shall have devolved upon them, and for the case of the death of any of the persons from whom the Senate may choose a Vice President whenever the right of choice shall have devolved upon them.

Section 5. Sections 1 and 2 shall take effect on the 15th day of October following the ratification of this article.

Section 6. This article shall be inoperative unless it shall have been ratified as an amendment to the Constitution by the legislatures of three-fourths of the several States within seven years from the date of its submission.

Amendment XXI

Passed by Congress February 20, 1933. Ratified December 5, 1933.

Section 1. The Eighteenth Article of amendment to the Constitution of the United States is hereby repealed.

Section 2. The transportation or importation into any State, Territory, or possession of the United States for delivery or use therein of intoxicating liquors in violation of the laws thereof, is hereby prohibited.

Section 3. This article shall be inoperative unless it shall have been ratified as an amendment to the Constitution by conventions in the several States, as provided in the Constitution, within seven years form the date of the submission thereof to the States by the Congress.

Amendment XXII

Passed by Congress March 24, 1947. Ratified February 26, 1951.

Section 1. No person shall be elected to the office of the President more than twice, and no person who has held the office of President, or acted as President, for more than two years of a term to which some other person was elected President shall be elected to the office of the President more than once. But this article shall not apply to any person holding the office of President when this article was proposed by the Congress, and shall not prevent any person who may be holding the office of President, or acting as President, during the term within which this article becomes operative from holding the office of President or acting as President during the remainder of such term.

Section 2. This article shall be inoperative unless it shall have been ratified as an amendment to the Constitution by the legislatures of three-fourths of the several States within seven years from the date of its submission to the States by the Congress.

Amendment XXIII

Passed by Congress June 16, 1960. Ratified April 3, 1961.

Section 1. The District constituting the seat of Government of the United States shall appoint in such manner as the Congress may direct:

A number of electors of President and Vice President equal to the whole number of Senators and Representatives in Congress to which the District would be entitled if it were a State, but in no event more than the least populous State; they shall be in addition to those appointed by the States, but they shall be considered, for the purposes of the election of President and Vice President, to be electors appointed by a State; and they shall meet in the District and perform such duties as provided by the twelfth article of amendment.

Section 2 .The Congress shall have power to enforce this article by appropriate legislation.

Amendment XXIV

Passed by Congress August 27, 1962. Ratified February 4, 1964.

Section 1. The right of citizens of the United States to vote in any primary or other election for President or Vice President, for electors for President or Vice President, or for Senator or Representative in Congress, shall not be denied or abridged by the United States or any State by reason of failure to pay any poll tax or other tax.

Section 2. The Congress shall have power to enforce this article by appropriate legislation.

Amendment XXV

Passed by Congress July 6, 1965. Ratified February 23, 1967.

Section 1 In case of the removal of the President from office or of his death or resignation, the Vice President shall become President.

Section 2 Whenever there is a vacancy in the office of the Vice President, the President shall nominate a Vice President who shall take office upon confirmation by a majority vote of both Houses of Congress.

Section 3 Whenever the President transmits to the President pro tempore of the Senate and the Speaker of the House of Representatives has written declaration that he is unable to discharge the powers and duties of his office, and until he transmits to them a written declaration to the contrary, such powers and duties shall be discharged by the Vice President as Acting President.

Section 4. Whenever the Vice President and a majority of either the principal officers of the executive departments or of such other body as Congress may by law provide, transmit to the President pro tempore of the Senate and the Speaker of the House of Representatives their written declaration that the President is unable to discharge the powers and duties of his office, the Vice President shall immediately assume the powers and duties of the office as Acting President.

Thereafter, when the President transmits to the President pro tempore of the Senate and the Speaker of the House of Representatives his written declaration that no inability exists, he shall resume the powers and duties of his office unless the Vice President and a majority of either the principal officers of the executive department or of such other body as Congress may by law provide, transmit within four days to the President pro tempore of the Senate and the Speaker of the House of Representatives their written declaration that the President is unable to discharge the powers and duties of his office. Thereupon Congress shall decide the issue, assembling within forty-eight hours for that purpose if not in session. If the Congress, within twenty-one days after receipt of the latter written declaration, or, if Congress is not in session, within twenty-one days after Congress is required to assemble, determines by two-thirds vote of both Houses that the President is unable to discharge the powers and duties of his office, the Vice President shall continue to discharge the same as Acting President; otherwise, the President shall resume the powers and duties of his office.

Amendment XXVI

Passed by Congress March 23, 1971. Ratified July 5, 1971.

Section 1. The right of citizens of the United States, who are eighteen years of age or older, to vote shall not be denied or abridged by the United States or by any State on account of age.

Amendment XXVII

Passed by Congress September 25, 1789. Ratified May 18, 1992.

No law, varying the compensation for the services of the Senators and Representatives, shall take effect, until an election of Representatives shall have intervened.

Appendix 3
Uniform
Commercial
Code*

(Excerpts)

*The Code has been adopted in every state except Louisiana. It has also been adopted for Guam, the Virgin Islands, and the District of Columbia. Louisiana has adopted Articles 1 and 3 and 9, of the Code.

In 1972, a group of Amendments to the Code was recommended. These have now been adopted in all states and for Guam. The changes made by the 1972 Amendments to the UCC are confined mainly to Article 9 on secured transactions.

In 1977, Article 8 of the Code, relating to investment securities, was amended. This amended version has been adopted in all states except Alabama. The Uniform Law Commissioners have adopted a 1994 revision of Capitol A Article 8 in order to regulate the indirect holding system of securities.

Article 2A on leases was completed by the Uniform Law Commissioners in 1987 and amended in 1990. The 1987 act has been adopted by Florida and South Dakota. As of October, 1994, the 1987 act with 1990 amendments has been adopted by Alabama, Alaska, Arizona, Arkansas, California, Colorado, Delaware, District of Columbia, Georgia, Hawaii, Idaho, Illinois, Indiana, Iowa, Kansas, Kentucky, Maine, Maryland, Michigan, Minnesota, Mississippi, Missouri, Montana, Nebraska, Nevada, New Hampshire, New Jersey, New Mexico, New York, North Carolina, North Dakota, Ohio, Oklahoma, Oregon, Pennsylvania, Rhode Island, Tennessee, Texas, Utah, Vermont, Virginia, Washington, Wisconsin, and Wyoming.

Article 4A, Funds Transfers, has been adopted in all states except South Carolina as of October, 1994. Article 4A has also been adopted by the District of Columbia.

The 1989 Article 6, Bulk Sales, Alternative A (repeal) has been adopted in Alaska, Arkansas, Colorado, Connecticut, Florida, Idaho, Illinois, Iowa, Kansas, Kentucky, Louisiana, Maine, Minnesota, Mississippi, Montana, Nebraska, Nevada, New Hampshire, New Jersey, New Mexico, North Dakota, Oregon, Pennsylvania, South Dakota, Texas, Vermont, Washington, West Virginia, and Wyoming. Alternative B (revision) has been adopted in Arizona, California, Hawaii, Oklahoma, and Utah.

The 1990 Article 3, Negotiable Instruments, and the 1990 Article 4, Bank Collections, have been adopted in Alaska, Arizona, Arkansas, California, Colorado, Connecticut, Florida, Hawaii, Idaho, Illinois, Indiana, Iowa, Kansas, Louisiana, Maine, Michigan, Minnesota, Mississippi, Missouri, Montana, Nebraska, Nevada, New Hampshire, New Mexico, North Dakota, Ohio, Oklahoma, Oregon, Pennsylvania, South Dakota, Utah, Vermont, Virginia, Washington, West Virginia, and Wyoming.

Article 1*

General Provisions

Part 1
Short Title, Construction, Application and Subject Matter of the Act

§ 1—102. Purposes; Rules of Construction; Variation by Agreement

(1)This Act shall be liberally construed and applied to promote its underlying purposes and policies.

(2)Underlying purposes and policies of this Act are

(a)to simplify, clarify and modernize the law governing commercial transactions;

(b)to permit the continued expansion of commercial practices through custom, usage and agreement of the parties;

(c)to make uniform the law among the various jurisdictions.

(3)The effect of provisions of this Act may be varied by agreement, except as otherwise provided in this Act and except that the obligations of good faith, diligence, reasonableness and care prescribed by this Act may not be disclaimed by agreement, but the parties may by agreement determine the standards by which the performance of such obligations is to be measured if such standards are not manifestly unreasonable.

. . .

§ 1—103. Supplementary General Principles of Law Applicable

Unless displaced by the particular provisions of this Act, the principles of law and equity, including the law merchant and the law relative to capacity to contract, principal and agent, estoppel, fraud, misrepresentation, duress, coercion, mistake, bankruptcy, or other validating or invalidating cause shall supplement its provisions.

§ 1—106. Remedies to Be Liberally Administered

(1)The remedies provided by this Act shall be liberally administered to the end that the aggrieved party may be put in as good a position as if the other party had fully performed, but neither consequential or special nor penal damages may be had except as specifically provided in this Act or by other rule of law.

(2)Any right or obligation declared by this Act is enforceable by action unless the provision declaring it specifies a different and limited effect.

§ 1—107. Waiver or Renunciation of Claim or Right After Breach

Any claim or right arising out of an alleged breach can be discharged in whole or in part without consideration by a written waiver or renunciation signed and delivered by the aggrieved party.

Part 2
General Definitions and Principles of Interpretation

§ 1—201. General Definitions

Subject to additional definitions contained in the subsequent Articles of this Act which are applicable to specific Articles or Parts thereof, and unless the context otherwise requires, in this Act:

(1)Action in the sense of a judicial proceeding includes recoupment, counterclaim, set-off, suit in equity and any other proceedings in which rights are determined.

(2)Aggrieved party means a party entitled to resort to a remedy.

(3)Agreement means the bargain of the parties in fact as found in their language or by implication from other circumstances including course of dealing or usage of trade or course of performance as provided in this Act (Sections 1—205 and 2—208). Whether an agreement has legal consequences is determined by the provisions of this Act, if applicable; otherwise by the law of contracts (Section 1—103). (Compare Contract.)

. . .

(5)Bearer means the person in possession of an instrument, document of title, or certificated security payable to bearer or indorsed in blank.

(6)Bill of lading means a document evidencing the receipt of goods for shipment issued by a person engaged in the business of transporting or forwarding goods, and includes an airbill. Airbill means a document serving for air transportation as a bill of lading does for marine or rail transportation, and includes an air consignment note or air waybill.

. . .

(8)Burden of establishing a fact means the burden of persuading the triers of fact that the existence of the fact is more probable than its nonexistence.

(9)Buyer in ordinary course of business means a person who in good faith and without knowledge that the sale to him is in violation of the ownership rights or security interest of a third party in the goods buys in ordinary course from a person in the business of selling goods of that kind but does not include a pawnbroker. All persons who sell minerals or the like (including oil and gas)at wellhead or minehead shall be deemed to be persons in the business of selling goods of that kind. Buying may be for cash or by exchange of other property or on secured or unsecured credit and includes receiving goods or documents of title under a preexisting contract for sale but does not include a transfer in bulk or as security for or in total or partial satisfaction of a money debt.

(10)Conspicuous: A term or clause is conspicuous when it is so written that a reasonable person against whom it is to operate ought to have noticed it. A printed heading in capitals (as: NON-NEGOTIABLE BILL OF LADING) is conspicuous. Language in the body of a form is conspicuous if it is in larger or other contrasting type or color. But in a telegram any stated term is conspicuous. Whether a term or clause is conspicuous or not is for decision by the court.

(11)Contract means the total legal obligation which results from the parties agreement as affected by this Act and any other applicable rules of law. (Compare Agreement.)

. . .

(15)Document of title includes bill of lading, dock warrant, dock receipt, warehouse receipt or order for the delivery of goods, and also any other document which in the regular course of business or financing is treated as adequately evidencing that the person in possession of it is entitled to receive, hold and dispose of the document and the goods it covers. To be a document of title a document must purport to be issued by or addressed to a bailee and purport to cover goods in the bailees possession which are either identified or are fungible portions of an identified mass.

. . .

(18)Genuine means free of forgery or counterfeiting.

(19)Good faith means honesty in fact in the conduct or transaction concerned.

(20)Holder means a person who is in possession of a document of title or an instrument or a certificated investment security drawn, issued or indorsed to him or to his order or to bearer or in blank.

. . .

(25)A person has notice of a fact when

(a)he has actual knowledge of it; or

(b)he has received a notice or notification of it; or

(c)from all the facts and circumstances known to him at the time in question he has reason to know that it exists.

A person knows or has knowledge of a fact when he has actual knowledge of it. Discover or learn or a word or phrase of similar import refers to knowledge rather than to reason to know. The time and circumstances under which a notice or notification may cease to be effective are not determined by this Act.

(26)A person notifies or gives a notice or notification to another by taking such steps as may be reasonably required to inform the other in ordinary course whether or not such other actually comes to know of it. A person receives a notice or notification when

(a)it comes to his attention; or

(b)it is duly delivered at the place of business through which the contract was made or at any other place held out by him as the place for receipt of such communications.

(27)Notice, knowledge or a notice or notification received by an organization is effective for a particular transaction from the time when it is brought to the attention of the individual conducting that transaction, and in any event from the time when it would have been brought to his attention if the organization had exercised due diligence. An organization exercises due diligence if it maintains reasonable routines for communicating significant information to the person conducting the transaction and there is reasonable compliance with the routines. Due diligence does not require an individual acting for the organization to communicate information unless such communication is part of his regular duties or unless he has reason to know of the transaction and that the transaction would be materially affected by the information.

(28)Organization includes a corporation, government or governmental subdivision or agency, business trust, estate, trust, partnership or association, two or more persons having a joint or common interest, or any other legal or commercial entity.

. . .

(31)Presumption or presumed means that the trier of fact must find the existence of the fact presumed unless and until evidence is introduced which would support a finding of its nonexistence.

(32)Purchase includes taking by sale, discount, negotiation, mortgage, pledge, hen, issue or re-issue, gift or any other voluntary transaction creating an interest in property.

(33)Purchaser means a person who takes by purchase.

. . .

(37)Security interest means an interest in personal property or fixtures which secures payment or performance of an obligation. The retention or reservation of title by a seller of goods notwithstanding shipment or delivery to the buyer (Section 2—401)is limited in effect to a reservation of a security interest. The term also includes any interest of a buyer of accounts or chattel paper which is subject to Article 9. The special property interest of a buyer of goods on identification of such goods to a contract for sale under Section 2—401 is not a security interest, but a buyer may also acquire a security interest by complying with Article 9. Unless a lease or consignment is intended as security, reservation of title thereunder is not a security interest but a consignment is in any event subject to the provisions on consignment sales (Section 2—326). Whether a lease is intended as security is to be determined by the facts of each case; however, (a) the inclusion of an option to purchase does not of itself make the lease one intended for security, and (b) an agreement that upon compliance with the terms of the lease the lessee shall become or has the option to become the owner of the property for no additional consideration or for a nominal consideration does make the lease one intended for security.

(38)Send in connection with any writing or notice means to deposit in the mail or deliver for transmission by any other usual means of communication with postage or cost of transmission provided for and properly addressed and in the case of an instrument to an address specified thereon or otherwise agreed, or if there be none to any address reasonable under the circumstances. The receipt of any writing or notice within the time at which it would have arrived if properly sent has the effect of a proper sending.

(39)Signed includes any symbol executed or adopted by a party with present intention to authenticate a writing.

. . .

(46)Written or writing includes printing, typewriting or any other intentional reduction to tangible form.

§ 1—203. Obligation of Good Faith

Every contract or duty within this Act imposes an obligation of good faith in its performance or enforcement.

§ 1—204. Time; Reasonable Time; Seasonably

(1)Whenever this Act requires any action to be taken within a reasonable time, any time which is not manifestly unreasonable may be fixed by agreement.

(2)What is a reasonable time for taking any action depends on the nature, purpose and circumstances of such action.

(3)An action is taken seasonably when it is taken at or within the time agreed or, if no time is agreed, at or within a reasonable time.

§ 1—205. Course of Dealing and Usage of Trade

(1)A course of dealing is a sequence of previous conduct between the parties to a particular transaction which is fairly to be regarded as establishing a common basis of understanding for interpreting their expressions and other conduct.

(2)A usage of trade is any practice or method of dealing having such regularity of observance in a place, vocation or trade as to justify an expectation that it will be observed with respect to the transaction in question. The existence and scope of such a usage are to be proved as facts. If it is established that such a usage is embodied in a written trade code or similar writing the interpretation of the writing is for the court.

(3)A course of dealing between parties and any usage of trade in the vocation or trade in which they are engaged or of which they are or should be aware give particular meaning to and supplement or qualify terms of an agreement.

(4)The express terms of an agreement and an applicable course of dealing or usage of trade shall be construed wherever reasonable as consistent with each other; but when such construction is unreasonable, express terms control both course of dealing and usage of trade and course of dealing controls usage of trade.

(5)An applicable usage of trade in the place where any part of performance is to occur shall be used in interpreting the agreement as to that part of the performance.

(6)Evidence of a relevant usage of trade offered by one party is not admissible unless and until he has given the other party such notice as the court finds sufficient to prevent unfair surprise to the latter.

§ 1—206. Statute of Frauds for Kinds of Personal Property Not Otherwise Covered

(1)Except in the cases described in subsection (2) of this section, a contract for the sale of personal property is not enforceable by way of action or defense beyond five thousand dollars in amount or value of remedy unless there is some writing which indicates that a contract for sale has been made between the parties at a defined or stated price, reasonably identifies the subject matter, and is signed by the party against whom enforcement is sought or by his authorized agent.

(2)Subsection (1) of this section does not apply to contracts for the sale of goods (Section 2—201) nor of securities (Section 8—319) nor to security agreements (Section 9—203).

§ 1—207. Performance or Acceptance Under Reservation of Rights

A party who with explicit reservation of rights performs or promises performance or assents to performance in a manner demanded or offered by the other party does not thereby prejudice the rights reserved. Such words as without prejudice, under protest or the like are sufficient.

§ 1—208. Option to Accelerate at Will

A term providing that one party or his successor in interest may accelerate payment or performance or require collateral or additional collateral at will or when he deems himself insecure or in words of similar import shall be construed to mean that he shall have power to do so only if he in good faith believes that the prospect of payment or performance is impaired. The burden of establishing lack of good faith is on the party against whom the power has been exercised.

Article 2

Sales

Part 1
Short Title, General Construction and Subject Matter

§ 2—103. Definitions and Index of Definitions

(1)In this Article, unless the context otherwise requires,

(a)Buyer means a person who buys or contracts to buy goods.

(b)Good faith in the case of a merchant means honesty in fact and the observance of reasonable commercial standards of fair dealing in the trade.

(c)Receipt of goods means taking physical possession of them.

(d)Seller means a person who sells or contracts to sell goods.

§ 2—104. Definitions: Merchant; Between Merchants; Financing Agency

(1)Merchant means a person who deals in goods of the kind or otherwise by his occupation holds himself out as having knowledge or skill peculiar to the practices or goods involved in the transaction or to whom such knowledge or skill may be attributed by his employment of an agent or broker or other intermediary who by his occupation holds himself out as having such knowledge or skill.

. . .

(3)Between merchants means in any transaction with respect to which both parties are chargeable with the knowledge or skill of merchants.

§ 2—105. Definitions: Transferability; Goods; Future Goods; Lot; Commercial Unit

(1)Goods means all things (including specially manufactured goods) which are movable at the time of identification to the contract for sale other than the money in which the price is to be paid, investment securities (Article 8) and things in action. Goods also includes the unborn young of animals and growing crops and other identified things attached to realty as described in the section on goods to be severed from realty (Section 2—107).

(2)Goods must be both existing and identified before any interest in them can pass. Goods which are not both existing and identified are future goods. A purported present sale of future goods or of any interest therein operates as a contract to sell.

. . .

(5)Lot means a parcel or a single article which is the subject matter of a separate sale or delivery, whether or not it is sufficient to perform the contract.

(6)Commercial unit means such a unit of goods as by commercial usage is a single whole for purposes of sale and division of which materially impairs its character or value on the market or in use. A commercial unit may be a single article (as a machine) or a set of articles (as a suite of furniture or an assortment of sizes) or a quantity (as a bale, gross, or carload) or any other unit treated in use or in the relevant market as a single whole.

§ 2—106. Definitions: Contract; Agreement; Contract for Sale; Sale; Present Sale; Conforming to Contract; Termination; Cancellation

(1)In this Article unless the context otherwise requires, contract and agreement are limited to those relating to the present or future sale of goods. Contract for sale includes both a present sale of goods and a contract to sell goods at a future time. A sale consists in the passing of title from the seller to the buyer for a price (Section 2—401). A present sale means a sale which is accomplished by the making of the contract.

(2)Goods or conduct, including any part of a performance, are conforming or conform to the contract when they are in accordance with the obligations under the contract.

...

Part 2
Form, Formation and Readjustment of Contract

§ 2—201. Formal Requirements; Statute of Frauds

(1)Except as otherwise provided in this section, a contract for the sale of goods for the price of $500 or more is not enforceable by way of action or defense unless there is some writing sufficient to indicate that a contract for sale has been made between the parties and signed by the party against whom enforcement is sought or by his authorized agent or broker. A writing is not insufficient because it omits or incorrectly states a term agreed upon but the contract is not enforceable under this paragraph beyond the quantity of goods shown in such writing.

(2)Between merchants, if within a reasonable time a writing in confirmation of the contract and sufficient against the sender is received and the party receiving it has reason to know its contents, it satisfies the requirements of subsection (1) against such party unless written notice of objection to its contents is given within 10 days after it is received.

(3)A contract which does not satisfy the requirements of subsection (1) but which is valid in other respects is enforceable

(a)if the goods are to be specially manufactured for the buyer and are not suitable for sale to others in the ordinary course of the sellers business and the seller, before notice of repudiation is received and under circumstances which reasonably indicate that the goods are for the buyer, has made either a substantial beginning of their manufacture or commitments for their procurement; or

(b)if the party against whom enforcement is sought admits in his pleading, testimony or otherwise in court that a contract for sale was made, but the contract is not enforceable under this provision beyond the quantity of goods admitted; or

(c)with respect to goods for which payment has been made and accepted or which have been received and accepted (Section 2—606).

§ 2—202. Final Written Expression: Parol or Extrinsic Evidence

Terms with respect to which the confirmatory memoranda of the parties agree or which are otherwise set forth in a writing intended by the parties as a final expression of their agreement with respect to such terms as are included therein may not be contradicted by evidence of any prior agreement or of a contemporaneous oral agreement but may be explained or supplemented

(a)by course of dealing or usage of trade (Section 1—205) or by course of performance (Section 2—208); and

(b)by evidence of consistent additional terms unless the court finds the writing to have been intended also as a complete and exclusive statement of the terms of the agreement.

§ 2—204. Formation in General

(1)A contract for sale of goods may be made in any manner sufficient to show agreement, including conduct by both parties which recognizes the existence of such a contract.

(2)An agreement sufficient to constitute a contract for sale may be found even though the moment of its making is undetermined.

(3)Even though one or more terms are left open a contract for sale does not fail for indefiniteness if the parties have intended to make a contract and there is a reasonably certain basis for giving an appropriate remedy.

§ 2—205. Firm Offers

An offer by a merchant to buy or sell goods in a signed writing which by its terms gives assurance that it will be held open is not revocable, for lack of consideration, during the time stated or if no time is stated for a reasonable time, but in no event may such period of irrevocability exceed three months; but any such term of assurance on a form supplied by the offeree must be separately signed by the offeror.

§ 2—206. Offer and Acceptance in Formation of Contract

(1)Unless otherwise unambiguously indicated by the language or circumstances

(a)an offer to make a contract shall be construed as inviting acceptance in any manner and by any medium reasonable in the circumstances;

(b)an order or other offer to buy goods for prompt or current shipment shall be construed as inviting acceptance either by a prompt promise to ship or by the prompt or current shipment of conforming or non-conforming goods, but such a shipment of non-conforming goods does not constitute an acceptance if the seller seasonably notifies the buyer that the shipment is offered only as an accommodation to the buyer.

(2)Where the beginning of a requested performance is a reasonable mode of acceptance, an offeror who is not notified of acceptance within a reasonable time may treat the offer as having lapsed before acceptance.

§ 2—207. Additional Terms in Acceptance or Confirmation

(1)A definite and seasonable expression of acceptance or a written confirmation which is sent within a reasonable time operates as an acceptance even though it states terms additional to or different from those offered or agreed upon, unless acceptance is expressly made conditional on assent to the additional or different terms.

(2)The additional terms are to be construed as proposals for addition to the contract. Between merchants such terms become part of the contract unless:

(a)the offer expressly limits acceptance to the terms of the offer;

(b)they materially alter it; or

(c)notification of objection to them has already been given or is given within a reasonable time after notice of them is received.

(3)Conduct by both parties which recognizes the existence of a contract is sufficient to establish a contract for sale although the writings of the parties do not otherwise establish a contract. In such case the terms of the particular contract consist of those terms on which the writings of the parties agree, together with any supplementary terms incorporated under any other provisions of this Act.

§ 2—208. Course of Performance or Practical Construction

(1)Where the contract for sale involves repeated occasions for performance by either party with knowledge of the nature of the performance and opportunity for objection to it by the other, any course of performance accepted or acquiesced in without objection shall be relevant to determine the meaning of the agreement.

(2)The express terms of the agreement and any such course of performance, as well as any course of dealing and usage of trade, shall be construed whenever reasonable as consistent with each other; but when such construction is unreasonable, express terms shall control course of performance and course of performance shall control both course of dealing and usage of trade (Section 1—205).

(3)Subject to the provisions of the next section on modification and waiver, such course of performance shall be relevant to show a waiver or modification of any term inconsistent with such course of performance.

§ 2—209. Modification, Rescission and Waiver

(1)An agreement modifying a contract within this Article needs no consideration to be binding.

(2)A signed agreement which excludes modification or rescission except by a signed writing cannot be otherwise modified or rescinded, but except as between merchants such a requirement on a form supplied by the merchant must be separately signed by the other party.

(3)The requirements of the statute of frauds section of this Article (Section 2—201) must be satisfied if the contract as modified is within its provisions.

(4)Although an attempt at modification or rescission does not satisfy the requirements of subsection (2) or (3) it can operate as a waiver.

(5)A party who has made a waiver affecting an executory portion of the contract may retract the waiver by reasonable notification received by the other party that strict performance will be required of any term waived, unless the retraction would be unjust in view of a material change of position in reliance on the waiver.

§ 2—210. Delegation of Performance; Assignment of Rights

(1)A party may perform his duty through a delegate unless otherwise agreed or unless the other party has a substantial interest in having his original promisor perform or control the acts required by the contract. No delegation of performance relieves the party delegating of any duty to perform or any liability for breach.

(2)Unless otherwise agreed, all rights of either seller or buyer can be assigned except where the assignment would materially change the duty of the other party, or increase materially the burden or risk imposed on him by his contract, or impair materially his chance of obtaining return performance. A right to damages for breach of the whole contract or a right arising out of the assignors due performance of his entire obligation can be assigned despite agreement otherwise.

(3)Unless the circumstances indicate the contrary, a prohibition of assignment of the contract is to be construed as barring only the delegation to the assignee of the assignors performance.

(4)An assignment of the contract or of all my rights under the contract or an assignment in similar general terms is an assignment of rights and, unless the language or the circumstances (as in an assignment for security) indicate the contrary, it is a delegation of performance of the duties of the assignor, and its acceptance by the assignee constitutes a promise by him to perform those duties. This promise is enforceable by either the assignor or the other party to the original contract.

(5)The other party may treat any assignment which delegates performance as creating reasonable grounds for insecurity and may without prejudice to his rights against the assignor demand assurances from the assignee (Section 2—609).

Part 3
General Obligation and Construction of Contract

§ 2—301. General Obligations of Parties

The obligation of the seller is to transfer and deliver and that of the buyer is to accept and pay in accordance with the contract.

§ 2—302. Unconscionable Contract or Clause

(1)If the court as a matter of law finds the contract or any clause of the contract to have been unconscionable at the time it was made, the court may refuse to enforce the contract, or it may enforce the remainder of the contract without the unconscionable clause, or it may so limit the application of any unconscionable clause as to avoid any unconscionable result.

(2)When it is claimed or appears to the court that the contract or any clause thereof may be unconscionable, the parties shall be afforded a reasonable opportunity to present evidence as to its commercial setting, purpose and effect to aid the court in making the determination.

§ 2—303. Allocation or Division of Risks

Where this Article allocates a risk or a burden as between the parties unless otherwise agreed, the agreement may not only shift the allocation but may also divide the risk or burden.

§ 2—305. Open Price Term

(1)The parties, if they so intend, can conclude a contract for sale even though the price is not settled. In such a case, the price is a reasonable price at the time for delivery if

(a)nothing is said as to price; or

(b)the price is left to be agreed by the parties and they fail to agree; or

(c)the price is to be fixed in terms of some agreed market or other standard as set or recorded by a third person or agency and it is not so set or recorded.

(2)A price to be fixed by the seller or by the buyer means a price for him to fix in good faith.

(3)When a price left to be fixed otherwise than by agreement of the parties fails to be fixed through fault of one party, the other may at his option treat the contract as cancelled or himself fix a reasonable price.

(4)Where, however, the parties intend not to be bound unless the price be fixed or agreed and it is not fixed or agreed, there is no contract. In such a case, the buyer must return any goods already received or if unable so to do must pay their reasonable value at the time of delivery and the seller must return any portion of the price paid on account.

§ 2—306. Output, Requirements and Exclusive Dealings

(1)A term which measures the quantity by the output of the seller or the requirements of the buyer means such actual output or requirements as may occur in good faith, except that no quantity unreasonably disproportionate to any stated estimate or in the absence of a stated estimate to any normal or otherwise comparable prior output or requirements may be tendered or demanded.

(2)A lawful agreement by either the seller or the buyer for exclusive dealing in the kind of goods concerned imposes, unless otherwise agreed, an obligation by the seller to use best efforts to supply the goods and by the buyer to use best efforts to promote their sale.

§ 2—312. Warranty of Title and Against Infringement; Buyers Obligation Against Infringement

(1)Subject to subsection (2), there is in a contract for sale a warranty by the seller that

(a)the title conveyed shall be good, and its transfer rightful; and

(b)the goods shall be delivered free from any security interest or other lien or encumbrance of which the buyer at the time of contracting has no knowledge.

(2) A warranty under subsection (1) will be excluded or modified only by specific language or by circumstances which give the buyer reason to know that the person selling does not claim title in himself or that he is purporting to sell only such right or title as he or a third person may have.

(3) Unless otherwise agreed a seller who is a merchant regularly dealing in goods of the kind warrants that the goods shall be delivered free of the rightful claim of any third person by way of infringement or the like but a buyer who furnishes specifications to the seller must hold the seller harmless against any such claim which arises out of compliance with the specifications.

§ 2—313. Express Warranties by Affirmation, Promise, Description, Sample

(1) Express warranties by the seller are created as follows:

(a) Any affirmation of fact or promise made by the seller to the buyer which relates to the goods and becomes part of the basis of the bargain creates an express warranty that the goods shall conform to the affirmation or promise.

(b) Any description of the goods which is made part of the basis of the bargain creates an express warranty that the goods shall conform to the description.

(c) Any sample or model which is made part of the basis of the bargain creates an express warranty that the whole of the goods shall conform to the sample or model.

(2) It is not necessary to the creation of an express warranty that the seller use formal words such as warrant or guarantee or that he have a specific intention to make a warranty, but an affirmation merely of the value of the goods or a statement purporting to be merely the sellers opinion or commendation of the goods does not create a warranty.

§ 2—314. Implied Warranty; Merchantability; Usage of Trade

(1) Unless excluded or modified (Section 2—316), a warranty that the goods shall be merchantable is implied in a contract for their sale if the seller is a merchant with respect to

goods of that kind. Under this section, the serving for value of food or drink to be consumed either on the premises or elsewhere is a sale.

(2) Goods to be merchantable must be at least such as

(a) pass without objection in the trade under the contract description; and

(b) in the case of fungible goods, are of fair average quality within the description; and

(c) are fit for the ordinary purposes for which such goods are used; and

(d) run, within the variations permitted by the agreement, of even kind, quality and quantity within each unit and among all units involved; and

(e) are adequately contained, packaged, and labeled as the agreement may require; and

(f) conform to the promises or affirmations of fact made on the container or label if any.

(3) Unless excluded or modified (Section 2—316), other implied warranties may arise from course of dealing or usage of trade.

§ 2—315. Implied Warranty: Fitness for Particular Purpose

Where the seller at the time of contracting has reason to know any particular purpose for which the goods are required and that the buyer is relying on the sellers skill or judgment to select or furnish suitable goods, there is unless excluded or modified under the next section an implied warranty that the goods shall be fit for such purpose.

§ 2—326. Sale on Approval and Sale or Return; Consignment Sales and Rights of Creditors

(1) Unless otherwise agreed, if delivered goods may be returned by the buyer even though they conform to the contract, the transaction is

(a) a sale on approval if the goods are delivered primarily for use, and

(b) a sale or return if the goods are delivered primarily for resale.

(2) Except as provided in subsection (3), goods held on approval are not subject to the claims of the buyers creditors until acceptance; goods held on sale or return are subject to such claims while in the buyers possession.

(3)Where goods are delivered to a person for sale and such person maintains a place of business at which he deals in goods of the kind involved, under a name other than the name of the person making delivery, then with respect to claims of creditors of the person conducting the business the goods are deemed to be on sale or return. The provisions of this subsection are applicable even though an agreement purports to reserve title to the person making delivery until payment or resale or uses such words as on consignment or on memorandum. However, this sub-section is not applicable if the person making delivery

(a)complies with an applicable law providing for a consignors interest or the like to be evidenced by a sign, or

(b)establishes that the person conducting the business is generally known by his creditors to be substantially engaged in selling the goods of others, or

(c)complies with the filing provisions of the Article on secured Transactions (Article 9).

(4)Any or return term of a contract for sale is to be treated as a separate contract for sale within the statute of frauds section of this Article (Section 2—201) and as contradicting the sale aspect of the contract within the provisions of this Article on parol or extrinsic evidence (Section 2—202).

§ 2—327. Special Incidents of Sale on Approval and Sale or Return

(1)Under a sale on approval, unless otherwise agreed

(a)although the goods are identified to the contract, the risk of loss and the title do not pass to the buyer until acceptance; and

(b)use of the goods consistent with the purpose of trial is not acceptance but failure seasonably to notify the seller of election to return the goods is acceptance, and if the goods conform to the contract acceptance of any part is acceptance of the whole; and

(c)after due notification of election to return, the return is at the sellers risk and expense but a merchant buyer must follow any reasonable instructions.

(2)Under a sale or return, unless otherwise agreed

(a)the option to return extends to the whole or any commercial unit of the goods while in substantially their original condition, but must be exercised seasonably; and

(b)the return is at the buyers risk and expense.

Part 4
Title, Creditors and Good Faith Purchasers

§ 2—401. Passing of Title; Reservation for Security; Limited Application of This Section

Each provision of this Article with regard to the rights, obligations and remedies of the seller, the buyer, purchasers or other third parties applies irrespective of title to the goods except where the provision refers to such title. Insofar as situations are not covered by the other provisions of this Article and matters concerning title become material the following rules apply:

(1)Title to goods cannot pass under a contract for sale prior to their identification to the contract (Section 2—501), and unless otherwise explicitly agreed the buyer acquires by their identification a special property as limited by this Act. Any retention or reservation by the seller of the title (property) in goods shipped or delivered to the buyer is limited in effect to a reservation of a security interest. Subject to these provisions and to the provisions of the Article on Secured Transactions (Article 9), title to goods passes from the seller to the buyer in any manner and on any conditions explicitly agreed on by the parties.

(2)Unless otherwise explicitly agreed, title passes to the buyer at the time and place at which the seller completes his performance with reference to the physical delivery of the goods, despite any reservation of security interest and even though a document of title is to be delivered at a different time or place; and in particular and despite any reservation of a security interest by the bill of lading

(a)if the contract requires or authorizes the seller to send the goods to the buyer but does not require him to deliver them at destination, title passes to the buyer at the time and place of shipment; but

(b)if the contract requires delivery at destination, title passes on tender there.

(3)Unless otherwise explicitly agreed, where delivery is to be made without moving the goods,

(a)if the seller is to deliver a document of title, title passes at the time when and the place where he delivers such documents; or

(b)if the goods are at the time of contracting already identified and no documents are to be delivered, title passes at the time and place of contracting.

(4)A rejection or other refusal by the buyer to receive or retain the goods, whether or not justified, or a justified revocation of acceptance revests title to the goods in the seller. Such revesting occurs by operation of law and is not a sale.

§ 2—403. Power to Transfer; Good Faith Purchase of Goods; Entrusting

(1)A purchaser of goods acquires all title which his transferor had or had power to transfer except that a purchaser of a limited interest acquires rights only to the extent of the interest purchased. A person with voidable title has power to transfer a good title to a good faith purchaser for value. When goods have been delivered under a transaction of purchase, the purchaser has such power even though

(a)the transferor was deceived as to the identity of the purchaser, or

(b)the delivery was in exchange for a check which is later dishonored, or

(c)it was agreed that the transaction was to be a cash sale or

(d)the delivery was procured through fraud punishable as larcenous under the criminal law.

(2)Any entrusting of possession of goods to a merchant who deals in goods of that kind gives him power to transfer all rights of the entruster to a buyer in ordinary course of business.

(3)Entrusting includes any delivery and any acquiescence in retention of possession regardless of any condition expressed between the parties to the delivery or acquiescence and

regardless of whether the procurement of the entrusting or the possessors disposition of the goods have been such as to be larcenous under the criminal law.

(4)The rights of other purchasers of goods and of lien creditors are governed by the Articles on Secured Transactions (Article 9), Bulk Transfers (Article 6) and Documents of Title (Article 7).

Part 5
Performance

§ 2—501. Insurable Interest in Goods; Manner of Identification of Goods

(1)The buyer obtains a special property and an insurable interest in goods by identification of existing goods as goods to which the contract refers even though the goods so identified are non-conforming and he has an option to return or reject them. . . .

(2)The seller retains an insurable interest in goods so long as title to or any security interest in the goods remains in him; and where the identification is by the seller alone, he may until default or insolvency or notification to the buyer that the identification is final substitute other goods for those identified.

. . .

§ 2—503. Manner of Sellers Tender of Delivery

(1)Tender of delivery requires that the seller put and hold conforming goods at the buyers disposition and give the buyer any notification reasonably necessary to enable him to take delivery. The manner, time and place for tender are determined by the agreement and this Article, and in particular

(a)tender must be at a reasonable hour, and, if it is of goods, they must be kept available for the period reasonably necessary to enable the buyer to take possession; but

(b)unless otherwise agreed, the buyer must furnish facilities reasonably suited to the receipt of the goods.

(2)Where the case is within the next section respecting shipment, tender requires that the seller comply with its provisions.

(3)Where the seller is required to deliver at a particular destination, tender requires that he comply with subsection (1) and also, in any appropriate case, tender documents as described in subsections (4) and (5) of this section.

(4)Where goods are in the possession of a bailee and are to be delivered without being moved

(a)tender requires that the seller either tender a negotiable document of title covering such goods or procure acknowledgment by the bailee of the buyers right to possession of the goods; but

(b)tender to the buyer of a nonnegotiable document of title or of a written direction to the bailee to deliver is sufficient tender unless the buyer seasonably objects, and receipt by the bailee of notification of the buyers rights fixes those rights as against the bailee and all third persons; but risk of loss of the goods and of any failure by the bailee to honor the nonnegotiable document of title or to obey the direction remains on the seller until the buyer has had a reasonable time to present the document or direction, and a refusal by the bailee to honor the document or to obey the direction defeats the tender.

(5)Where the contract requires the seller to deliver documents

(a)he must tender all such documents in correct form, except as provided in this Article with respect to bills of lading in a set (subsection (2) of Section 2—323); and

(b)tender through customary banking channels is sufficient and dishonor of a draft accompanying the documents constitutes nonacceptance or rejection.

§ 2—504. Shipment by Seller

Where the seller is required or authorized to send the goods to the buyer and the contract does not require him to deliver them at a particular destination, then, unless otherwise agreed, he must

(a)put the goods in the possession of such a carrier and make such a contract for their transportation as may be reasonable having regard to the nature of the goods and other circumstances of the case; and

(b)obtain and promptly deliver or tender in due form any document necessary to enable the buyer to obtain possession of the goods or

otherwise required by the agreement or by usage of trade; and

(c)promptly notify the buyer of the shipment.

Failure to notify the buyer under paragraph (c) or to make a proper contract under paragraph (a) is a ground for rejection only if material delay or loss ensues.

§ 2—508. Cure by Seller of Improper Tender or Delivery; Replacement

(1)Where any tender or delivery by the seller is rejected because non-conforming and the time for performance has not yet expired, the seller may seasonably notify the buyer of his intention to cure and may then within the contract time make a conforming delivery.

(2)Where the buyer rejects a non-conforming tender which the seller had reasonable grounds to believe would be acceptable with or without money allowance, the seller may if he seasonably notifies the buyer have a further reasonable time to substitute a conforming tender.

§ 2—509. Risk of Loss in the Absence of Breach

(1)Where the contract requires or authorizes the seller to ship the goods by carrier

(a)if it does not require him to deliver them at a particular destination, the risk of loss passes to the buyer when the goods are duly delivered to the carrier even though the shipment is under reservation (Section 2—505); but

(b)if it does require him to deliver them at a particular destination and the goods are there duly tendered while in the possession of the carrier, the risk of loss passes to the buyer when the goods are there duly so tendered as to enable the buyer to take delivery.

(2)Where the goods are held by a bailee to be delivered without being moved, the risk of loss passes to the buyer

(a)on his receipt of a negotiable document of title covering the goods; or

(b)on acknowledgment by the bailee of the buyers right to possession of the goods; or

(c)after his receipt of a nonnegotiable document of title or other written direction to deliver, as provided in subsection (4)(b) of Section 2—503.

(3)In any case not within subsection (1) or (2), the risk of loss passes to the buyer on his receipt of the goods if the seller is a merchant; otherwise the risk passes to the buyer on tender of delivery.

(4)The provisions of this section are subject to contrary agreement of the parties and to the provisions of this Article on sale on approval (Section 2—327) and on effect of breach on risk of loss (Section 2—510).

§ 2—510. Effect of Breach on Risk of Loss

(1)Where a tender or delivery of goods so fails to conform to the contract as to give a right of rejection, the risk of their loss remains on the seller until cure or acceptance.

(2)Where the buyer rightfully revokes acceptance, he may to the extent of any deficiency in his effective insurance coverage treat the risk of loss as having rested on the seller from the beginning.

(3)Where the buyer, as to conforming goods already identified to the contract for sale, repudiates or is otherwise in breach before risk of their loss has passed to him, the seller may to the extent of any deficiency in his effective insurance coverage treat the risk of loss as resting on the buyer for a commercially reasonable time.

Part 6
Breach, Repudiation and Excuse

§ 2—601. Buyers Rights on Improper Delivery

Subject to the provisions of this Article on breach in installment contracts (Section 2—612) and unless otherwise agreed under the sections on contractual limitations of remedy (Sections 2—718 and 2—719), if the goods or the tender of delivery fail in any respect to conform to the contract, the buyer may

(a)reject the whole; or

(b)accept the whole; or

(c)accept any commercial unit or units and reject the rest.

§ 2—602. Manner and Effect of Rightful Rejection

(1)Rejection of goods must be within a reasonable time after their delivery or tender. It is ineffective unless the buyer seasonably notifies the seller.

(2)Subject to the provisions of the two following sections on rejected goods (Sections 2—603 and 2—604),

(a)after rejection any exercise of ownership by the buyer with respect to any commercial unit is wrongful as against the seller; and

(b)if the buyer has before rejection taken physical possession of goods in which he does not have a security interest under the provisions of this Article (subsection (3) of Section 2—711), he is under a duty after rejection to hold them with reasonable care at the sellers disposition for a time sufficient to permit the seller to remove them; but

(c)the buyer has no further obligations with regard to goods rightfully rejected.

(3)The sellers rights with respect to goods wrongfully rejected are governed by the provisions of this Article on Sellers remedies in general (Section 2—703).

§ 2—605. Waiver of Buyers Objections by Failure to Particularize

(1)The buyers failure to state in connection with rejection a particular defect which is ascertainable by reasonable inspection precludes him from relying on the unstated defect to justify rejection or to establish breach

(a)where the seller could have cured it if stated seasonably; or

(b)between merchants when the seller has after rejection made a request in writing for a full and final written statement of all defects on which the buyer proposes to rely.

(2)Payment against documents made without reservation of rights precludes recovery of the payment for defects apparent on the face of the documents.

§ 2—606. What Constitutes Acceptance of Goods

(1)Acceptance of goods occurs when the buyer

(a)after a reasonable opportunity to inspect the goods signifies to the seller that the goods are conforming or that he will take or retain them in spite of their non-conformity; or

(b)fails to make an effective rejection (subsection (1) of Section 2—602), but such acceptance does not occur until the buyer has had a reasonable opportunity to inspect them; or

(c)does any act inconsistent with the sellers ownership; but if such act is wrongful as against the seller it is an acceptance only if ratified by him.

(2)Acceptance of a part of any commercial unit is acceptance of that entire unit.

§ 2—607. Effect of Acceptance; Notice of Breach; Burden of Establishing Breach After Acceptance; Notice of Claim or Litigation to Person Answerable Over

(1)The buyer must pay at the contract rate for any goods accepted.

(2)Acceptance of goods by the buyer precludes rejection of the goods accepted and if made with knowledge of a non-conformity cannot be revoked because of it unless the acceptance was on the reasonable assumption that the non-conformity would be seasonably cured but acceptance does not of itself impair any other remedy provided by this Article for non-conformity.

(3)Where a tender has been accepted

(a)the buyer must within a reasonable time after he discovers or should have discovered any breach notify the seller of breach or be barred from any remedy; and

(b)if the claim is one for infringement or the like (subsection (3) of Section 2—312) and the buyer is sued as a result of such a breach, he must so notify the seller within a reasonable time after he receives notice of the litigation or be barred from any remedy over for liability established by the litigation.

(4)The burden is on the buyer to establish any breach with respect to the goods accepted.

(5)Where the buyer is sued for breach of a warranty or other obligation for which his seller is answerable over

(a)he may give his seller written notice of the litigation. If the notice states that the seller may come in and defend and that if the seller does not do so he will be bound in any action against him by his buyer by any determination of fact common to the two litigations, then unless the seller after seasonable receipt of the notice does come in and defend he is so bound.

(b)if the claim is one for infringement or the like (subsection (3) of Section 2—312), the original seller may demand in writing that his buyer turn over to him control of the litigation including settlement or else be barred from any remedy over and if he also agrees to bear all expense and to satisfy any adverse judgment, then unless the buyer after seasonable receipt of the demand does turn over control the buyer is so barred.

(6)The provisions of subsections (3), (4) and (5) apply to any obligation of a buyer to hold the seller harmless against infringement or the like (subsection (3) of Section 2—312).

§ 2—608. Revocation of Acceptance in Whole or in Part

(1)The buyer may revoke his acceptance of a lot or commercial unit whose non-conformity substantially impairs its value to him if he has accepted it

(a)on the reasonable assumption that its non-conformity would be cured and it has not been seasonably cured; or

(b)without discovery of such non-conformity if his acceptance was reasonably induced either by the difficulty of discovery before acceptance or by the sellers assurances.

(2)Revocation of acceptance must occur within a reasonable time after the buyer discovers or should have discovered the ground for it and before any substantial change in condition of the goods which is not caused by their own defects. It is not effective until the buyer notifies the seller of it.

(3)A buyer who so revokes has the same rights and duties with regard to the goods involved as if he had rejected them.

§ 2—615. Excuse by Failure of Presupposed Conditions

Except so far as a seller may have assumed a greater obligation and subject to the preceding section on substituted performance:

(a)Delay in delivery or nondelivery in whole or in part by a seller who complies with paragraphs (b) and (c) is not a breach of his duty under a contract for sale if performance as agreed has been made impracticable by the occurrence of a contingency the non-occurrence of which was a basic assumption on which the contract was made or by compliance in good faith with any applicable foreign or domestic governmental regulation or order whether or not it later proves to be invalid.

(b)Where the causes mentioned in paragraph (a) affect only a part of the sellers capacity to perform, he must allocate production and deliveries among his customers but may at his option include regular customers not then under contract as well as his own requirements for further manufacture. He may so allocate in any manner which is fair and reasonable.

(c)The seller must notify the buyer seasonably that there will be delay or non-delivery and, when allocation is required under paragraph (b), of the estimated quota thus made available for the buyer.

Part 7
Remedies

§ 2—701. Remedies for Breach of Collateral Contracts Not Impaired

Remedies for breach of any obligation or promise collateral or ancillary to a contract for sale are not impaired by the provisions of this Article.

§ 2—706. Sellers Resale Including Contract for Resale

. . . The seller may resell the goods concerned or the undelivered balance thereof. Where the resale is made in good faith and in a commercially reasonable manner, the seller may recover the difference between the resale price and the contract price together with any incidental damages allowed under the provisions of this Article (Section 2—710), but less expenses saved in consequence of the buyers breach.

(2)Except as otherwise provided in subsection (3) or unless otherwise agreed, resale may be at public or private sale including sale by way of one or more contracts to sell or of identification to an existing contract of the seller. Sale may be as a unit or in parcels and at any time and place and on any terms but every aspect of the sale including the method, manner, time, place and terms must be commercially reasonable. The resale must be reasonably identified as referring to the broken contract, but it is not necessary that the goods be in existence or that any or all of them have been identified to the contract before the breach.

(3)Where the resale is at private sale, the seller must give the buyer reasonable notification of his intention to resell.

(4)Where the resale is at public sale

(a)only identified goods can be sold except where there is a recognized market for a public sale of futures in goods of the kind; and

(b)it must be made at a usual place or market for public sale if one is reasonably available and except in the case of goods which are perishable or threaten to decline in value speedily the seller must give the buyer reasonable notice of the time and place of the resale; and

(c)if the goods are not to be within the view of those attending the sale, the notification of sale must state the place where the goods are located and provide for their reasonable inspection by prospective bidders; and

(d)the seller may buy.

(5)A purchaser who buys in good faith at a resale takes the goods free of any rights of the original buyer even though the seller fails to comply with one or more of the requirements of this section.

(6)The seller is not accountable to the buyer for any profit made on any resale. . . .

§ 2—711. Buyers Remedies in General; Buyers Security Interest in Rejected Goods

(1)Where the seller fails to make delivery or repudiates or the buyer rightfully rejects or justifiably revokes acceptance, then with respect to any goods involved, and with respect to the whole if the breach goes to the whole contract (Section 2—612), the buyer may cancel and whether or not he has done so may in addition to recovering so much of the price as has been paid

(a)cover and have damages under the next section as to all the goods affected whether or not they have been identified to the contract; or

(b)recover damages for nondelivery as provided in this Article (Section 2—713).

(2)Where the seller fails to deliver or repudiates, the buyer may also (a)if the goods have been identified recover them as provided in this Article (Section 2—502); or

(b)in a proper case obtain specific performance or replevy the goods as provided in this Article (Section 2—716).

(3)On rightful rejection or justifiable revocation of acceptance, a buyer has a security interest in goods in his possession or control for any payments made on their price and any expenses reasonably incurred in their inspection, receipt, transportation, care and custody and may hold such goods and resell them in like manner as an aggrieved seller (Section 2—706).

§ 2—712. Cover; Buyers Procurement of Substitute Goods

(1)After a breach within the preceding section, the buyer may cover by making in good faith and without unreasonable delay any reasonable purchase of or contract to purchase goods in substitution for those due from the seller.

(2)The buyer may recover from the seller as damages the difference between the cost of cover and the contract price together with any incidental or consequential damages as hereinafter defined (Section 2—715), but less expenses saved in consequence of the sellers breach.

(3)Failure of the buyer to effect cover within this section does not bar him from any other remedy.

§ 2—713. Buyers Damages for Nondelivery or Repudiation

(1)Subject to the provisions of this Article with respect to proof of market price (Section 2—723), the measure of damages for nondelivery or repudiation by the seller is the difference between the market price at the time when the buyer learned of the breach and the contract price together with any incidental and consequential damages provided in this Article (Section 2—715), but less expenses saved in consequence of the sellers breach.

(2)Market price is to be determined as of the place for tender or, in cases of rejection after arrival or revocation of acceptance, as of the place of arrival.

§ 2—714. Buyers Damages for Breach in Regard to Accepted Goods

(1)Where the buyer has accepted goods and given notification (subsection (3) of Section 2—607), he may recover as damages for any non-conformity of tender the loss resulting in the ordinary course of events from the sellers breach as determined in any manner which is reasonable.

(2)The measure of damages for breach of warranty is the difference at the time and place of acceptance between the value of the goods accepted and the value they would have had if they had been as warranted, unless special circumstances show proximate damages of a different amount.

(3)In a proper case any incidental and consequential damages under the next section may also be recovered.

§ 2—715. Buyers Incidental and Consequential Damages

(1)Incidental damages resulting from the sellers breach include expenses reasonably incurred in inspection, receipt, transportation and care and custody of goods rightfully rejected, any commercially reasonable charges, expenses or commissions in connection with effecting cover and any other reasonable expense incident to the delay or other breach.

(2)Consequential damages resulting from the sellers breach include

(a)any loss resulting from general or particular requirements and needs of which the seller at the time of contracting had reason to know and which could not reasonably be prevented by cover or otherwise; and

(b)injury to person or property proximately resulting from any breach of warranty.

§ 2—719. Contractual Modification or Limitation of Remedy

(1). . .

(a)the agreement may provide for remedies in addition to or in substitution for those provided in this Article and may limit or alter the measure of damages recoverable under this Article, as by limiting the buyers remedies to return of the goods and repayment of the price or to repair and replacement of nonconforming goods or parts; and (b)resort to a remedy as provided is optional unless the remedy is expressly agreed to be exclusive, in which case it is the sole remedy.

(2)Where circumstances cause an exclusive or limited remedy to fail of its essential purpose, remedy may be had as provided in this Act.

(3)Consequential damages may be limited or excluded unless the limitation or exclusion is unconscionable. Limitation of consequential damages for injury to the person in the case of consumer goods is prima facie unconscionable but limitation of damages where the loss is commercial is not.

§ 2—725. Statute of Limitations in Contracts for Sale

(1)An action for breach of any contract for sale must be commenced within four years after the cause of action has accrued. By the original agreement, the parties may reduce the period of limitation to not less than one year but may not extend it.

(2)A cause of action accrues when the breach occurs, regardless of the aggrieved partys lack of knowledge of the breach. A breach of warranty occurs when tender of delivery is made, except that where a warranty explicitly extends to future performance of the goods and discovery of the breach must await the time of such performance the cause of action accrues when the breach is or should have been discovered.

. . .

Article 2A

Leases

Part 1
General Provisions

§ 2A—103. Definitions and Index of Definitions

(1)In this Article unless the context otherwise requires:

. . .

(e)Consumer lease means a lease that a lessor regularly engaged in the business of leasing or selling makes to a lessee, except an organization, who takes under the lease primarily for a personal, family, or household purpose, if the total payments to be made under the lease contract, excluding payments for options to renew or buy, do not exceed $25,000.

. . .

(g)Finance lease means a lease in which (i) the lessor does not select, manufacture or supply the goods, (ii) the lessor acquires the goods or the right to possession and use of the goods in connection with the lease, and (iii) either the lessee receives a copy of the contract evidencing the lessors purchase of the goods on or before signing the lease contract, or the lessees approval of the contract evidencing the lessors purchase of the goods is a condition to effectiveness of the lease contract.

. . .

(j)Lease means a transfer of the right to possession and use of goods for a term in return for consideration, but a sale, including a sale on approval or a sale or return, or retention or creation of a security interest is not a lease. Unless the context clearly indicates otherwise, the term includes a sublease.

(k)Lease agreement means the bargain, with respect to the lease, of the lessor and the lessee in fact as found in their language or by implication from other circumstances including course of dealing or usage of trade or course of performance as provided in this Article. Unless the context clearly indicates otherwise, the term includes a sublease agreement.

(l)Lease contract means the total legal obligation that results from the lease agreement as affected by this Article and any other applicable rules of law. Unless the context clearly indicates otherwise, the term includes a sublease contract.

. . .

(o)Lessee in ordinary course of business means a person who in good faith and without knowledge that the lease to him [or her] is in violation of the ownership rights or security interest or leasehold interest of a third party in the goods leases in ordinary course from a person in the business of selling or leasing goods of that kind but does not include a pawnbroker. Leasing may be for cash or by exchange of other property or on secured or unsecured credit and includes receiving goods or documents of title under a pre-existing lease contract but does not include a transfer in bulk or as security for or in total or partial satisfaction of a money debt.

. . .

(t)Merchant lessee means a lessee that is a merchant with respect to goods of the kind subject to the lease.

§ 2A—106. Limitation on Power of Parties to Consumer Lease to Choose Applicable Law and Judicial Forum

(1)If the law chosen by the parties to a consumer lease is that of a jurisdiction other than a jurisdiction in which the lessee resides at the time the lease agreement becomes enforceable or within 30 days thereafter or in which the goods are to be used, the choice is not enforceable.

(2)If the judicial forum chosen by the parties to a consumer lease is a forum that would not otherwise have jurisdiction over the lessee, the choice is not enforceable.

Part 2
Formation and Construction of Lease Contract

§ 2A—209. Lessee Under Finance Lease as Beneficiary of Supply Contract

(1)The benefit of the suppliers promises to the lessor under the supply contract and of all warranties, whether express or implied, under the supply contract, extends to the lessee to the extent of the lessees leasehold interest under a finance lease related to the supply contract, but subject to the terms of the supply contract and all of the suppliers defenses or claims arising therefrom.

(2)The extension of the benefit of the suppliers promises and warranties to the lessee (Section 2A—209(1)) does not: (a) modify the rights and obligations of the parties to the supply contract, whether arising therefrom or oth-erwise, or (b) impose any duty or liability under the supply contract on the lessee.

(3)Any modification or rescission of the supply contract by the supplier and the lessor is effective against the lessee unless, prior to the modification or rescission, the supplier has received notice that the lessee has entered into a finance lease related to the supply contract. If the supply contract is modified or rescinded after the lessee enters the finance lease, the lessee has a cause of action against the lessor, and against the supplier if the supplier has notice of the lessees entering the finance lease when the supply contract is modified or re-scinded. The lessees recovery from such action shall put the lessee in as good a position as if the modification or rescission had not oc-curred.

§ 2A—210. Express Warranties

(1)Express warranties by the lessor are cre-ated as follows:

(a)Any affirmation of fact or promise made by the lessor to the lessee which relates to the goods and becomes part of the basis of the bargain creates an express warranty that the goods will conform to the affirmation or promise.

(b)Any description of the goods which is made part of the basis of the bargain creates an express warranty that the goods will conform to the description.

(c)Any sample or model that is made part of the basis of the bargain creates an express warranty that the whole of the goods will con-form to the sample or model.

(2)It is not necessary to the creation of an express warranty that the lessor use formal words, such as warrant or guarantee, or that the lessor have a specific intention to make a warranty, but an affirmation merely of the value of the goods or a statement purporting to be merely the lessors opinion or commenda-tion of the goods does not create a warranty.

§ 2A—219. Risk of Loss

(1)Except in the case of a finance lease, risk of loss is retained by the lessor and does not pass to the lessee. In the case of a finance lease, risk of loss passes to the lessee.

(2)Subject to the provisions of this Article on the effect of default on risk of loss (Section

2A—220), if risk of loss is to pass to the lessee and the time of passage is not stated the following rules apply:

(a)If the lease contract requires or authorizes the goods to be shipped by carrier

(i)and it does not require delivery at a particular destination, the risk of loss passes to the lessee when the goods are duly delivered to the carrier; but

(ii)if it does require delivery at a particular destination and the goods are there duly tendered while in the possession of the carrier, the risk of loss passes to the lessee when the goods are there duly so tendered as to enable the lessee to take delivery.

(b)If the goods are held by a bailee to be delivered without being moved, the risk of loss passes to the lessee on acknowledgment by the bailee of the lessees right to possession of the goods.

(c)In any case not within subsection (a) or (b), the risk of loss passes to the lessee on the lessees receipt of the goods if the lessor, or, in the case of a finance lease, the supplier, is a merchant: otherwise the risk passes to the lessee on tender of delivery.

§ 2A—220. Effect of Default on Risk of Loss

(1)Where risk of loss is to pass to the lessee and the time of passage is not stated:

(a)If a tender or delivery of goods so fails to conform to the lease contract as to give a right of rejection, the risk of their loss remains with the lessor, or, in the case of a finance lease, the supplier, until cure or acceptance.

(b)If the lessee rightfully revokes acceptance, he [or she], to the extent of any deficiency in his [or her] effective insurance coverage, may treat the risk of loss as having remained with the lessor from the beginning.

(2)Whether or not risk of loss is to pass to the lessee, if the lessee as to conforming goods already identified to a lease contract repudiates or is otherwise in default under the lease contract, the lessor, or, in the case of a finance lease, the supplier, to the extent of any deficiency in his [or her] effective insurance coverage may treat the risk of loss as resting on the lessee for a commercially reasonable time.

§ 2A—221. Casualty to Identified Goods

If a lease contract requires goods identified when the lease contract is made, and the goods suffer casualty without fault of the lessee, the lessor or the supplier before delivery, or the goods suffer casualty before risk of loss passes to the lessee pursuant to the lease agreement or Section 2A—219, then:

(a)if the loss is total, the lease contract is avoided; and

(b)if the loss is partial or the goods have so deteriorated as to no longer conform to the lease contract, the lessee may nevertheless demand inspection and at his [or her] option either treat the lease contract as avoided or, except in a finance lease that is not a consumer lease, accept the goods with due allowance from the rent payable for the balance of the lease term for the deterioration or the deficiency in quantity but without further right against the lessor.

Part 3
Effect of Lease Contract

§ 2A—301. Enforceability of Lease Contract

Except as otherwise provided in this Article, a lease contract is effective and enforceable according to its terms between the parties, against purchasers of the goods, and against creditors of the parties.

§ 2A—303. Alienability of Partys Interest Under Lease Contract or of Lessors Residual Interest in Goods; Delegation of Performance; Assignment of Rights

(1)Any interest of a party under a lease contract and the lessors residual interest in the goods may be transferred unless

(a)the transfer is voluntary and the lease contract prohibits the transfer; or

(b)the transfer materially changes the duty of or materially increases the burden or risk imposed on the other party to the lease contract, and within a reasonable time after notice of the transfer the other party demands that the transferee comply with subsection (2) and the transferee fails to comply.

(2)Within a reasonable time after demand pursuant to subsection (1)(b), the transferee shall:

(a)cure or provide adequate assurance that he [or she] will promptly cure any default other than one arising from the transfer;

(b)compensate or provide adequate assurance that he [or she] will promptly compensate the other party to the lease contract and any other person holding an interest in the lease contract, except the party whose interest is being transferred, for any loss to that party resulting from the transfer;

(c)provide adequate assurance of future due performance under the lease contract; and

(d)assume the lease contract.

(3)Demand pursuant to subsection (1)(b) is without prejudice to the other partys rights against the transferee and the party whose interest is transferred.

(4)An assignment of the lease or of all my rights under the lease or an assignment in similar general terms is a transfer of rights, and unless the language or the circumstances, as in an assignment for security, indicate the contrary, the assignment is a delegation of duties by the assignor to the assignee and acceptance by the assignee constitutes a promise by him [or her] to perform those duties. This promise is enforceable by either the assignor or the other party to the lease contract.

(5)Unless otherwise agreed by the lessor and the lessee, no delegation of performance relieves the assignor as against the other party of any duty to perform or any liability for default.

(6)A right to damages for default with respect to the whole lease contract or a right arising out of the assignors due performance of his [or her] entire obligation can be assigned despite agreement otherwise.

(7)To prohibit the transfer of an interest of a party under a lease contract, the language of prohibition must be specific, by a writing, and conspicuous.

§ 2A—304. Subsequent Lease of Goods by Lessor

(1)Subject to the provisions of Section 2A—303, a subsequent lessee from a lessor of goods under an existing lease contract obtains, to the extent of the leasehold interest transferred, the leasehold interest in the goods that the lessor had or had power to transfer, and except as provided in subsection (2) and Section 2A—527(4), takes subject to the existing lease contract. A lessor with voidable title has power to transfer a good leasehold interest to a good faith subsequent lessee for value, but only to the extent set forth in the preceding sentence. When goods have been delivered under a transaction of purchase the lessor has that power even though:

(a)the lessors transferor was deceived as to the identity of the lessor;

(b)the delivery was in exchange for a check which is later dishonored;

(c)it was agreed that the transaction was to be a cash sale; or

(d)the delivery was procured through fraud punishable as larcenous under the criminal law.

(2)A subsequent lessee in the ordinary course of business from a lessor who is a merchant dealing in goods of that kind to whom the goods were entrusted by the existing lessee before the interest of the subsequent lessee became enforceable against the lessor obtains, to the extent of the leasehold interest transferred, all of the lessors and the existing lessees rights to the goods, and takes free of the existing lease contract.

(3)A subsequent lessee from the lessor of goods that are subject to an existing lease contract and are covered by a certificate of title issued under a statute of this State or of another jurisdiction takes no greater rights than those provided both by this section and by the certificate of title statute.

§ 2A—305. Sale or Sublease of Goods by Lessee

(1)Subject to the provisions of Section 2A—303, a buyer or sublessee from the lessee of goods under an existing lease contract obtains, to the extent of the interest transferred, the leasehold interest in the goods that the lessee had or had power to transfer, and except as provided in subsection (2) and Section 2A—511(4), takes subject to the existing lease contract. A lessee with a voidable leasehold interest has power to transfer a good leasehold interest to a good faith buyer for value or a good faith sublessee for value, but only to the extent set forth in the preceding sentence. When goods have been delivered under a transaction of lease the lessee has that power even though:

(a)the lessor was deceived as to the identity of the lessee;

(b)the delivery was in exchange for a check which is later dishonored; or

(c)the delivery was procured through fraud punishable as larcenous under the criminal law.

(2)A buyer in the ordinary course of business or a sublessee in the ordinary course of business from a lessee who is a merchant dealing in goods of that kind to whom the goods were entrusted by the lessor obtains, to the extent of the interest transferred, all of the lessors and lessees rights to the goods, and takes free of the existing lease contract.

(3)A buyer or sublessee from the lessee of goods that are subject to an existing lease contract and are covered by a certificate of title issued under a statute of this State or of another jurisdiction takes no greater rights than those provided both by this section and by the certificate of title statute.

Part 4
Performance of Lease Contract: Repudiated, Substituted and Excused

§ 2A—401. Insecurity: Adequate Assurance of Performance

(1)A lease contract imposes an obligation on each party that the others expectation of receiving due performance will not be impaired.

(2)If reasonable grounds for insecurity arise with respect to the performance of either party, the insecure party may demand in writing adequate assurance of due performance.

. . .

(4)Between merchants, the reasonableness of grounds for insecurity and the adequacy of any assurance offered must be determined according to commercial standards.

(5)Acceptance of any nonconforming delivery or payment does not prejudice the aggrieved partys right to demand adequate assurance of future performance.

§ 2A—407. Irrevocable Promises: Finance Leases

(1)In the case of a finance lease that is not a consumer lease the lessees promises under the lease contract become irrevocable and independent upon the lessees acceptance of the goods.

(2)A promise that has become irrevocable and independent under subsection (1):

(a)is effective and enforceable between the parties, and by or against third parties including assignees of the parties, and

(b)is not subject to cancellation, termination, modification, repudiation, excuse, or substitution without the consent of the party to whom the promise runs.

Part 5
Default

A. In General

§ 2A—501. Default: Procedure

(1)Whether the lessor or the lessee is in default under a lease contract is determined by the lease agreement and this Article.

(2)If the lessor or the lessee is in default under the lease contract, the party seeking enforcement has rights and remedies as provided in this Article and, except as limited by this Article, as provided in the lease agreement.

(3)If the lessor or the lessee is in default under the lease contract, the party seeking enforcement may reduce the partys claim to judgment, or otherwise enforce the lease contract by self-help or any available judicial procedure or nonjudicial procedure, including administrative proceeding, arbitration, or the like, in accordance with this Article.

(4)Except as otherwise provided in this Article or the lease Agreement, the rights and remedies referred to in subsections (2) and (3) are cumulative.

(5)If the lease agreement covers both real property and goods, the party seeking enforcement may proceed under this Part as to the goods, or under other applicable law as to both the real property and the goods in accordance with his [or her] rights and remedies in respect of the real property, in which case this Part does not apply.

§ 2A—502. Notice After Default

Except as otherwise provided in this Article or the lease agreement, the lessor or lessee in default under the lease contract is not entitled to notice of default or notice of enforcement from the other party to the lease agreement.

§ 2A—503. Modification or Impairment of Rights and Remedies

(1)Except as otherwise provided in this Article, the lease agreement may include rights and remedies for default in addition to or in substitution for those provided in this Article and may limit or alter the measure of damages recoverable under this Article.

(2)Resort to a remedy provided under this Article or in the lease agreement is optional unless the remedy is expressly agreed to be exclusive. If circumstances cause an exclusive or limited remedy to fail of its essential purpose, or provision for an exclusive remedy is unconscionable, remedy may be had as provided in this Article.

. . .

§ 2A—506. Statute of Limitations

(1)An action for default under a lease contract, including breach of warranty or indemnity, must be commenced within 4 years after the cause of action accrued. By the original lease contract the parties may reduce the period of limitation to not less that one year.

(2)A cause of action for default accrues when the act or omission on which the default or breach of warranty is based is or should have been discovered by the aggrieved party, or when the default occurs, whichever is later. A cause of action for indemnity accrues when the act or omission on which the claim for indemnity is based is or should have been discovered by the indemnified party, whichever is later.

. . .

B. Default by Lessor

§ 2A—513. Cure by Lessor of Improper Tender or Delivery; Replacement

(1)If any tender or delivery by the lessor or the supplier is rejected because nonconforming and the time for performance has not yet expired, the lessor or the supplier may seasonably notify the lessee of the lessors or the suppliers intention to cure and may then make a conforming delivery within the time provided in the lease contract.

(2)If the lessee rejects a nonconforming tender that the lessor or the supplier had reasonable grounds to believe would be acceptable with or without money allowance, the lessor or the supplier may have a further reasonable time to substitute a conforming tender if he [or she] seasonably notifies the lessee.

§ 2A—514. Waiver of Lessees Objections

(1)In rejecting goods, a lessees failure to state a particular defect that is ascertainable by reasonable inspection precludes the lessee from relying on the defect to justify rejection or to establish default:

(a)if, states seasonably, the lessor or the supplier could have cured it (Section 2A—513); or

(b)between merchants if the lessor or the supplier after rejection has made a request in writing for a full and final written statement of all defects on which the lessee proposes to rely.

(2)A lessees failure to reserve rights when paying rent or other consideration against documents precludes recovery of the payment for defects apparent on the face of the documents.

§ 2A—515. Acceptance of Goods

(1)Acceptance of goods occurs after the lessee has had a reasonable opportunity to inspect the goods and

(a)the lessee signifies or acts with respect to the goods in a manner that signifies to the lessor or the supplier that the goods are conforming or that the lessee will take or retain them in spite of their nonconformity; or

(b)the lessee fails to make an effective rejection of the goods (Section 2A—509(2)).

(2)Acceptance of a part of any commercial unit is acceptance of that entire unit.

§ 2A—518. Cover; Substitute Goods

(1)After default by a lessor under the lease contract of or contract to purchase or lease goods in substitution for those due from the lessor.

. . .

§ 2A—519. Lessees Damages for Nondelivery, Repudiation, Default and Breach of Warranty in Regard to Accepted Goods

(1)Except as otherwise provided with respect to damages liquidated in the lease agreement . . . or determined by agreement of the parties (Section 1—102(3)), if a lessee elects not to cover or a lessee elects to cover and the cover ... is by purchase or otherwise, the measure of damages for non-delivery or repudiation by the lessor or for rejection or revocation of acceptance by the lessee is the present value as of the date of the default of the difference between the then market rent and the original rent, computed for the remaining lease term of the original lease agreement together with incidental and consequential damages, less expenses saved in consequence of the lessors default.

. . .

(4)The measure of damages for breach of warranty is the present value at the time and place of acceptance of the difference between the value of the use of the goods accepted and the value if they had been as warranted for the lease term, unless special circumstances show proximate damages of a different amount, together with incidental and consequential damages, less expenses saved in consequence of the lessors default or breach of warranty.

§ 2A—520. Lessees Incidental and Consequential Damages

(1)Incidental damages resulting from a lessors default include expenses reasonably incurred in inspection, receipt, transportation, and care and custody of goods rightfully rejected or goods the acceptance of which is justifiably revoked, any commercially reasonable charges, expenses or commissions in connection with effecting cover, and any other reasonable expense incident to the default.

(2)Consequential damages resulting from a lessors default include:

(a)any loss resulting from general or particular requirements and needs of which the lessor at the time of contracting had reason to know and which could not reasonably be prevented by cover or otherwise; and

(b)injury to person or property proximately resulting from any breach of warranty.

C. Default by Lessee

§ 2A—525. Lessors Right to Possession of Goods

(1)If a lessor discovers the lessee to be insolvent, the lessor may refuse to deliver the goods.

(2)The lessor has on default by the lessee under the lease contract the right to take possession of the goods. If the lease contract so provides, the lessor may require the lessee to assemble the goods and make them available to the lessor at a place to be designated by the lessor which is reasonably convenient to both parties. Without removal, the lessor may render unusable any goods employed in trade or business, and may dispose of goods on the lessees premises (Section 2A—527).

(3)The lessor may proceed under subsection (2) without judicial process if that can be done without breach of the peace or the lessor may proceed by action.

§ 2A—527. Lessors Rights to Dispose of Goods

(1)After a default by a lessee under the lease contract of goods . . . , the lessor may dispose of the goods concerned or the undelivered balance thereof by lease, sale or otherwise.

(2)Except as otherwise provided with respect to damages liquidated in the lease agreement . . . or determined by agreement of the parties (Section 1—102(3)), if the disposition is by lease agreement substantially similar to the original lease agreement and the lease agreement is made in good faith and in a commercially reasonable manner, the lessor may recover from the lessee as damages (a) accrued and unpaid rent as of the date of default, (b) the present value as of the date of default of the difference between the total rent for the remaining lease term of the original lease agreement and the total rent for the lease term of the new lease agreement, and (c) any incidental damages allowed under Section 2A—530, less expenses saved in consequence of the lessees default.

. . .

(4)A subsequent buyer or lessee who buys or leases from the lessor in good faith for value as a result of a disposition under this section takes the goods free of the original lease contract and any rights of the original lessee even though the lessor fails to comply with one or more of the requirements of this Article.

(5)The lessor is not accountable to the lessee for any profit made on any disposition. . . .

§ 2A—529. Lessors Action for the Rent

(1)After default by the lessee under the lease contract . . . , if the lessor complies with subsection (2), the lessor may recover from the lessee as damages:

(a)for goods accepted by the lessee and for conforming goods lost or damaged within a commercially reasonable time after risk of loss passes to the lessee . . . , (i) accrued and unpaid rent as of the date of default, (ii) the present value as of the date of default of the rent for the remaining lease term of the lease agreement, and (iii) any incidental damages allowed under Section 2A—530, less expenses saved in consequence of the lessees default; and

(b)for goods identified to the lease contract if the lessor is unable after reasonable effort to dispose of them at a reasonable price or the circumstances reasonably indicate that effort will be unavailing, (i) accrued and unpaid rent as of the date of default, (ii) the present value as of the date of default of the rent for the remaining lease term of the lease agreement, and (iii) any incidental damages allowed under Section 2A—530, less expenses saved in consequence of the lessees default.

(2)Except as provided in subsection (3), the lessor shall hold for the lessee for the remaining lease term of the lease agreement any goods that have been identified to the lease contract and are in the lessors control.

(3)The lessor may dispose of the goods at any time before collection of the judgment for damages obtained pursuant to subsection (1).

. . .

(4)Payment of the judgment for damages obtained pursuant to subsection (1) entitles the lessee to use and possession of the goods not then disposed of for the remaining lease term of the lease agreement.

. . .

§ 2A—530. Lessors Incidental Damages

Incidental damages to an aggrieved lessor include any commercially reasonable charges, expenses, or commissions incurred in stopping delivery, in the transportation, care and custody of goods after the lessees default, in connection with return or disposition of the goods, or otherwise resulting from the default.

Article 3 [1952 Version]

Commercial Paper

Part 1
Short Title, Form and Interpretation

§ 3—102. Definitions and Index of Definitions

(1)In this Article unless the context otherwise requires

(a)Issue means the first delivery of an instrument to a holder or a remitter.

(b)An order is a direction to pay and must be more than an authorization or request. It must identify the person to pay with reasonable certainty. It may be addressed to one or more such persons jointly or in the alternative but not in succession.

(c)A promise is an undertaking to pay and must be more than an acknowledgment of an obligation.

(d)Secondary party means a drawer or indorser.

(e)Instrument means a negotiable instrument.

. . .

§ 3—104. Form of Negotiable Instruments; Draft; Check; Certificate of Deposit; Note

(1)Any writing to be a negotiable instrument within this Article must

(a)be signed by the maker or drawer; and

(b)contain an unconditional promise or order to pay a sum certain in money and no other promise, order, obligation or power given by the maker or drawer except as authorized by this Article; and

(c)be payable on demand or at a definite time; and

(d)be payable to order or to bearer.

(2)A writing which complies with the requirements of this section is

(a)a draft (bill of exchange) if it is an order;

(b)a check if it is a draft drawn on a bank and payable on demand;

(c)a certificate of deposit if it is an acknowledgment by a bank of receipt of money with an engagement to repay it;

(d)a note if it is a promise other than a certificate of deposit.

(3)As used in other Articles of this Act, and as the context may require, the terms draft, check, certificate of deposit and note may refer to instruments which are not negotiable within this Article as well as to instruments which are so negotiable.

Part 2
Transfer and Negotiation

§ 3—201. Transfer: Right to Indorsement

(1)Transfer of an instrument vests in the transferee such rights as the transferor has therein, except that a transferee who has himself been a party to any fraud or illegality affecting the instrument or who as a prior holder had notice of a defense or claim against it cannot improve his position by taking from a later holder in due course.

(2)A transfer of a security interest in an instrument vests the foregoing rights in the transferee to the extent of the interest transferred.

(3)Unless otherwise agreed, any transfer for value of an instrument not then payable to bearer gives the transferee the specifically enforceable right to have the unqualified indorsement of the transferor. Negotiation takes effect only when the indorsement is made and until that time there is no presumption that the transferee is the owner.

§ 3—202. Negotiation

(1)Negotiation is the transfer of an instrument in such form that the transferee becomes a holder. If the instrument is payable to order, it is negotiated by delivery with any necessary indorsement; if payable to bearer, it is negotiated by delivery.

(2)An indorsement must be written by or on behalf of the holder and on the instrument or on a paper so firmly affixed thereto as to become a part thereof.

(3)An indorsement is effective for negotiation only when it conveys the entire instrument or any unpaid residue. If it purports to be of less, it operates only as a partial assignment.

(4)Words of assignment, condition, waiver, guaranty, limitation or disclaimer of liability and the like accompanying an indorsement do not affect its character as an indorsement.

Part 3
Rights of a Holder

§ 3—301. Rights of a Holder

The holder of an instrument whether or not he is the owner may transfer or negotiate it and, except as otherwise provided in Section 3—603 on payment or satisfaction, discharge it or enforce payment in his own name.

§ 3—302. Holder in Due Course

(1)A holder in due course is a holder who takes the instrument

(a)for value; and

(b)in good faith; and

(c)without notice that it is overdue or has been dishonored or of any defense against or claim to it on the part of any person.

(2)A payee may be a holder in due course.

(3)A holder does not become a holder in due course of an instrument:

(a)by purchase of it at judicial sale or by taking it under legal process; or

(b)by acquiring it in taking over an estate; or

(c)by purchasing it as part of a bulk transaction not in regular course of business of the transferor.

(4)A purchaser of a limited interest can be a holder in due course only to the extent of the interest purchased.

§ 3—305. Rights of a Holder in Due Course

To the extent that a holder is a holder in due course, he takes the instrument free from

(1)all claims to it on the part of any person; and

(2)all defenses of any party to the instrument with whom the holder has not dealt except

(a)infancy, to the extent that it is a defense to a simple contract; and

(b)such other incapacity, or duress, or illegality of the transaction, as renders the obligation of the party a nullity; and

(c)such misrepresentation as has induced the party to sign the instrument with neither knowledge nor reasonable opportunity to obtain knowledge of its character or its essential terms; and

(d)discharge in insolvency proceedings; and

(e)any other discharge of which the holder has notice when he takes the instrument.

§ 3—306. Rights of One Not Holder in Due Course

Unless he has the rights of a holder in due course, any person takes the instrument subject to

(a)all valid claims to it on the part of any person; and

(b)all defenses of any party which would be available in an action on a simple contract and

(c)the defenses of want or failure of consideration, nonperformance of any condition precedent, nondelivery, or delivery for a special purpose (Section 3—408); and

(d)the defense that he, or a person through whom he holds the instrument, acquired it by theft, or that payment or satisfaction to such holder would be inconsistent with the terms of a restrictive indorsement. The claim of any third person to the instrument is not otherwise available as a defense to any party liable

thereon unless the third person himself defends the action for such party.

§ 3—307. Burden of Establishing Signatures, Defenses and Due Course

(1)Unless specifically denied in the pleadings, each signature on an instrument is admitted. When the effectiveness of a signature is put in issue

(a)the burden of establishing it is on the party claiming under the signature; but

(b)the signature is presumed to be genuine or authorized except where the action is to enforce the obligation of a purported signer who has died or become incompetent before proof is required.

(2)When signatures are admitted or established, production of the instrument entitles a holder to recover on it unless the defendant establishes a defense.

(3)After it is shown that a defense exists, a person claiming the rights of a holder in due course has the burden of establishing that he or some person under whom he claims is in all respects a holder in due course.

Part 4
Liability of Parties

§ 3—401. Signature

(1)No person is liable on an instrument unless his signature appears thereon.

(2)A signature is made by use of any name, including any trade or assumed name, upon an instrument, or by any word or mark used in lieu of a written signature.

§ 3—405. Impostors; Signature in Name of Payee

(1)An indorsement by any person in the name of a named payee is effective if

(a)an impostor by use of the mails or otherwise has induced the maker or drawer to issue the instrument to him or his confederate in the name of the payee; or

(b)a person signing as or on behalf of a maker or drawer intends the payee to have no interest in the instrument; or

(c)an agent or employee of the maker or drawer has supplied him with the name of the payee intending the latter to have no such interest.

(2)Nothing in this section shall affect the criminal or civil liability of the person so indorsing.

§ 3—406. Negligence Contributing to Alteration or Unauthorized Signature

Any person who by his negligence substantially contributes to a material alteration of the instrument or to the making of an unauthorized signature is precluded from asserting the alteration or lack of authority against a holder in due course or against a drawee or other payor who pays the instrument in good faith and in accordance with the reasonable commercial standards of the drawees or payors business.

§ 3—407. Alteration

(1)Any alteration of an instrument is material which changes the contract of any party thereto in any respect, including any such change in

(a)the number or relations of the parties; or

(b)an incomplete instrument, by completing it otherwise than as authorized; or

(c)the writing as signed, by adding to it or by removing any part of it.

(2)As against any person other than a subsequent holder in due course.

(a)alteration by the holder which is both fraudulent and material discharges any party whose contract is thereby changed unless that party assents or is precluded from asserting the defense;

(b)no other alteration discharges any party and the instrument may be enforced according to its original tenor, or as to incomplete instruments, according to the authority given.

(3)A subsequent holder in due course may in all cases enforce the instrument according to its original tenor, and when an incomplete instrument has been completed, he may enforce it as completed.

§ 3—419. Conversion of Instrument; Innocent Representative

(1)An instrument is converted when

(a)a drawee to whom it is delivered for acceptance refuses to return it on demand; or

(b)any person to whom it is delivered for payment refuses on demand either to pay or to return it; or

(c)it is paid on a forged indorsement.

(2)In an action against a drawee under subsection (1), the measure of the drawees liability is the face amount of the instrument. In any other action under subsection (1), the measure of liability is presumed to be the face amount of the instrument.

(3)Subject to the provisions of this Act concerning restrictive indorsements, a representative, including a depositary or collecting bank, who has in good faith and in accordance with the reasonable commercial standards applicable to the business of such representative dealt with an instrument or its proceeds on behalf of one who was not the true owner, is not liable in conversion or otherwise to the true owner beyond the amount of any proceeds remaining in his hands.

(4)An intermediary bank or payor bank which is not a depositary bank is not liable in conversion solely by reason of the fact that proceeds of an item indorsed restrictively (Sections 3—205 and 3—206) are not paid or applied consistently with the restrictive indorsement of an indorser other than its immediate transferor.

Part 5
Presentment, Notice of Dishonor and Protest

§ 3—501. When Presentment, Notice of Dishonor, and Protest Necessary or Permissible

(1)Unless excused (Section—3511), presentment is necessary to charge secondary parties as follows:

(a)presentment for acceptance is necessary to charge the drawer and indorsers of a draft where the draft so provides, or is payable elsewhere than at the residence or place of business of the drawee, or its date of payment depends upon such presentment. The holder may at his option present for acceptance any other draft payable at a stated date;

(b)presentment for payment is necessary to charge any indorser;

(c)in the case of any drawer, the acceptor of a draft payable at a bank or the maker of a note payable at a bank, presentment for payment is necessary, but failure to make presentment discharges such drawer, acceptor, or maker only as stated in Section 3—502(1)(b).

(2)Unless excused (Section—3511)

(a)notice of any dishonor is necessary to charge any indorser;

(b)in the case of any drawer, the acceptor of a draft payable at a bank or the maker of a note payable at a bank, notice of any dishonor is necessary, but failure to give such notice discharges such drawer, acceptor or maker only as stated in Section 3—502(1)(b).

(3)Unless excused (Section 3—511), protest of any dishonor is necessary to charge the drawer and indorsers of any draft which on its face appears to be drawn or payable outside of the states, territories, dependencies and possessions of the United States, the District of Columbia and the Commonwealth of Puerto Rico. The holder may at his option make protest of any dishonor of any other instrument and in the case of a foreign draft may on insolvency of the acceptor before maturity make protest for better security.

(4)Notwithstanding any provision of this section, neither presentment nor notice of dishonor nor protest is necessary to charge an indorser who has indorsed an instrument after maturity.

§ 3—504. How Presentment Made

(1)Presentment is a demand for acceptance or payment made upon the maker, acceptor, drawee or other payor by or on behalf of the holder.

(2)Presentment may be made

(a)by mail, in which event the time of presentment is determined by the time of receipt of the mail; or

(b)through a clearing house; or

(c)at the place of acceptance or payment specified in the instrument or, if there be none, at the place of business or residence of the party to accept or pay. If neither the party to accept or pay nor anyone authorized to act for him is present or accessible at such place, presentment is excused.

(3)It may be made

(a)to any one of two or more makers, acceptors, drawees or other payors; or

(b)to any person who has authority to make or refuse the acceptance or payment.

(4)A draft accepted or a note made payable at a bank in the United States must be presented at such bank.

(5)In the cases described in Section 4—210 presentment may be made in the manner and with the result stated in that section.

§ 3—507. Dishonor; Holders Right of Recourse; Term Allowing Re-Presentment

(1)An instrument is dishonored when

(a)a necessary or optional presentment is duly made and due acceptance or payment is refused or cannot be obtained within the prescribed time or in case of bank collections the instrument is seasonably returned by the midnight deadline (Section 4—301); or

(b)presentment is excused and the instrument is not duly accepted or paid.

(2)Subject to any necessary notice of dishonor and protest, the holder has upon dishonor an immediate right of recourse against the drawers and indorsers.

(3)Return of an instrument for lack of proper indorsement is not dishonor.

(4)A term in a draft or an indorsement thereof allowing a stated time for re-presentment in the event of any dishonor of the draft by nonacceptance if a time draft or by nonpayment if a sight draft gives the holder as against any secondary party bound by the term an option to waive the dishonor without affecting the liability of the secondary party and he may present again up to the end of the stated time.

Part 6
Discharge

§ 3—602. Effect of Discharge Against Holder in Due Course

No discharge of any party provided by this Article is effective against a subsequent holder in due course unless he has notice thereof when he takes the instrument.

§ 3—603. Payment or Satisfaction

(1)The liability of any party is discharged to the extent of his payment or satisfaction to the holder even though it is made with knowledge of a claim of another person to the instrument unless prior to such payment or satisfaction the person making the claim either supplies indemnity deemed adequate by the party seeking the discharge or enjoins payment or satisfaction by order of a court of competent jurisdiction in an action in which the adverse claimant and the holder are parties. This subsection does not, however, result in the discharge of the liability

(a)of a party who in bad faith pays or satisfies a holder who acquired the instrument by theft or who (unless having the rights of a holder in due course) holds through one who so acquired it; or

(b)of a party (other than an intermediary bank or a payor bank which is not a depositary bank) who pays or satisfies the holder of an instrument which has been restrictively indorsed in a manner not consistent with the terms of such restrictive indorsement.

(2)Payment or satisfaction may be made with the consent of the holder by any person including a stranger to the instrument. Surrender of the instrument to such a person gives him the rights of a transferee (Section 3—201).

§ 3—606. Impairment of Recourse or of Collateral

(1)The holder discharges any party to the instrument to the extent that, without such partys consent, the holder

(a)without express reservation of rights releases or agrees not to sue any person against whom the party has to the knowledge of the holder a right of recourse or agrees to suspend the right to enforce against such person the instrument or collateral or otherwise discharges such person, except that failure or delay in effecting any required presentment, protest or notice of dishonor with respect to any such person does not discharge any party as to whom presentment, protest or notice of dishonor is effective or unnecessary; or

(b)unjustifiably impairs any collateral for the instrument given by or on behalf of the party or any person against whom he has a right of recourse.

(2)By express reservation of rights against a party with a right of recourse, the holder preserves

(a)all his rights against such party as of the time when the instrument was originally due; and

(b)the right of the party to pay the instrument as of that time; and

(c)all rights of such party to recourse against others.

Article 3 [1990 Revision]

Negotiable Instruments

Part 1
General Provisions and Definitions

§ 3—102. Subject Matter

(a)This Article applies to negotiable instruments. It does not apply to money, to payment orders governed by Article 4A, or to securities governed by Article 8.

. . .

§ 3—103. Definitions

(a)In this Article:

. . .

(4)Good faith means honesty in fact and the observance of reasonable commercial standards of fair dealing.

. . .

(7)Ordinary care in the case of a person engaged in business means observance of reasonable commercial standards, prevailing in the area in which the person is located, with respect to the business in which the person is engaged. In the case of a bank that takes an instrument for processing for collection or payment by automated means, reasonable commercial standards do not require the bank to examine the instrument if the failure to examine does not violate the banks prescribed procedures and the banks procedures do not vary unreasonably from general banking usage not disapproved by this Article or Article 4.

. . .

(11)Remitter means a person who purchases an instrument from its issuer if the instrument is payable to an identified person other than the purchaser.

. . .

§ 3—104. Negotiable Instrument

(a)Except as provided in subsections (c) and (d), negotiable instrument means an unconditional promise or order to pay a fixed amount of money, with or without interest or other charges described in the promise or order, if it:

(1)is payable to bearer or to order at the time it is issued or first comes into possession of a holder;

(2)is payable on demand or at a definite time; and

(3)does not state any other undertaking or instruction by the person promising or ordering payment to do any act in addition to the payment of money, but the promise or order may contain (i) an undertaking or power to give, maintain, or protect collateral, to secure payment, (ii) an authorization or power to the holder to confess judgment or realize on or dispose of collateral, or (iii) a waiver of the benefit of any law intended for the advantage or protection of an obligor.

(b)Instrument means a negotiable instrument.

(c)An order that meets all of the requirements of subsection (a), except paragraph (1), and otherwise falls within the definition of check in subsection (f) is a negotiable instrument and a check.

(d)A promise or order other than a check is not an instrument if, at the time it is issued or first comes into possession of a holder, it contains a conspicuous statement, however expressed, to the effect that the promise or order is not negotiable or is not an instrument governed by this Article.

(e)An instrument is a note if it is a promise and is a draft if it is an order. If an instrument falls within the definition of both note and draft, a person entitled to enforce the instrument may treat it as either.

(f)Check means (i) a draft, other than a documentary draft, payable on demand and drawn on a bank or (ii) a cashiers check or tellers check. An instrument may be a check even though it is described on its face by another term, such as money order.

(g)Cashiers check means a draft with respect to which the drawer and drawee are the same bank or branches of the same bank.

(h)Tellers check means a draft drawn by a bank (i) on another bank, or (ii) payable at or through a bank.

(i)Travelers check means an instrument that (i) is payable on demand, (ii) is drawn on or payable at or through a bank, (iii) is designated by the term travelers check or by a substantially similar term, and (iv) requires, as a condition to payment, a countersignature by a person whose specimen signature appears on the instrument.

(j)Certificate of deposit means an instrument containing an acknowledgment by a bank that a sum of money has been received by the bank and a promise by the bank to repay the sum of money. A certificate of deposit is a note of the bank.

§ 3—105. Issue of Instrument

(a)Issue means the first delivery of an instrument by the maker or drawer, whether to a holder or nonholder, for the purpose of giving rights on the instrument to any person.

. . .

§ 3—106. Unconditional Promise or Order

(a)Except as provided in this section, for the purposes of Section 3—104(a), a promise or order is unconditional unless it states (i) an express condition to payment, (ii) that the promise or order is subject to or governed by another writing, or (iii) that rights or obligations with respect to the promise or order are stated in another writing. A reference to another writing does not of itself make the promise or order conditional.

(b)A promise or order is not made conditional (i) by a reference to another writing for a statement of rights with respect to collateral, prepayment, or acceleration, or (ii) because payment is limited to resort to a particular fund or source.

(c)If a promise or order requires, as a condition to payment, a countersignature by a person whose specimen signature appears on the promise or order, the condition does not make the promise or order conditional for the purposes of Section 3—104(a).

. . .

(d)If a promise or order at the time it is issued or first comes into possession of a holder contains a statement, required by applicable statutory or administrative law, to the effect that the rights of a holder or transferee are subject to claims or defenses that the issuer could assert against the original payee, the promise or order is not thereby made conditional for the purposes of Section 3—104(a); but if the promise or order is an instrument, there cannot be a holder in due course of the instrument.

§ 3—110. Identification of Person to Whom Instrument Is Payable

(a)The person to whom an instrument is initially payable is determined by the intent of the person, whether or not authorized, signing as, or in the name or behalf of, the issuer of the instrument. The instrument is payable to the person intended by the signer even if that person is identified in the instrument by a name or other identification that is not that of the intended person. If more than one person signs in the name or behalf of the issuer of an instrument and all the signers do not intend the same person as payee, the instrument is payable to any person intended by one or more of the signers.

(b)If the signature of the issuer of an instrument is made by automated means, such as a check-writing machine, the payee of the instrument is determined by the intent of the person who supplied the name or identification of the payee, whether or not authorized to do so.

(c)A person to whom an instrument is payable may be identified in any way, including by name, identifying number, office, or account number. For the purpose of determining the holder of an instrument, the following rules apply:

(1)If an instrument is payable to an account and the account is identified only by number, the instrument is payable to the person to whom the account is payable. If an instrument is payable to an account identified by number and by the name of a person, the instrument is payable to the named person, whether or not that person is the owner of the account identified by number.

. . .

§ 3—118. Statute of Limitations

(a)Except as provided in subsection (e), an action to enforce the obligation of a party to pay a note payable at a definite time must be commenced within six years after the due date or dates stated in the note or, if a due date is accelerated, within six years after the accelerated due date.

(b)Except as provided in subsection (d) or (e), if demand for payment is made to the maker of a note payable on demand, an action to enforce the obligation of a party to pay the note must be commenced within six years after the demand. If no demand for payment is made to the maker, an action to enforce the note is barred if neither principal nor interest on the note has been paid for a continuous period of 10 years.

(c)Except as provided in subsection (d), an action to enforce the obligation of a party to an unaccepted draft to pay the draft must be commenced within three years after dishonor of the draft or 10 years after the date of the draft, whichever period expires first.

(d)An action to enforce the obligation of the acceptor of a certified check or the issuer of a tellers check, cashiers check, or travelers check must be commenced within three years after demand for payment is made to the acceptor or issuer, as the case may be.

(e)An action to enforce the obligation of a party to a certificate of deposit to pay the instrument must be commenced within six years after demand for payment is made to the maker, but if the instrument states a due date and the maker is not required to pay before that date, the six-year period begins when a demand for payment is in effect and the due date has passed.

(f)An action to enforce the obligation of a party to pay an accepted draft, other than a certified check, must be commenced (i) within six years after the due date or dates stated in the draft or acceptance if the obligation of the acceptor is payable at a definite time, or (ii) within six years after the date of the acceptance if the obligation of the acceptor is payable on demand.

(g)Unless governed by other law regarding claims for indemnity or contribution, an action (i) for conversion of an instrument, for money had and received, or like action based on conversion, (ii) for breach of warranty, or (iii) to enforce an obligation, duty, or right arising under this Article and not governed by this section must be commenced within three years after the [cause of action] accrues.

Part 2
Negotiation, Transfer, and Indorsement

§ 3—201. Negotiation

(a)Negotiation means a transfer of possession, whether voluntary or involuntary, of an instrument by a person other than the issuer to a person who thereby becomes its holder.

(b)Except for negotiation by a remitter, if an instrument is payable to an identified person, negotiation requires transfer of possession of the instrument and its indorsement by the holder. If an instrument is payable to bearer, it may be negotiated by transfer of possession alone.

§ 3—203. Transfer of Instrument; Rights Acquired by Transfer

(a)An instrument is transferred when it is delivered by a person other than its issuer for the purpose of giving to the person receiving delivery the right to enforce the instrument.

(b)Transfer of an instrument, whether or not the transfer is a negotiation, vests in the transferee any right of the transferor to enforce the instrument, including any right as a holder in due course, but the transferee cannot acquire rights of a holder in due course by a transfer, directly or indirectly, from a holder in due course if the transferee engaged in fraud or illegality affecting the instrument.

(c)Unless otherwise agreed, if an instrument is transferred for value and the transferee does not become a holder because of lack of indorsement by the transferor, the transferee has a specifically enforceable right to the unqualified indorsement of the transferor, but

negotiation of the instrument does not occur until the indorsement is made.

(d)If a transferor purports to transfer less than the entire instrument, negotiation of the instrument does not occur. The transferee obtains no rights under this Article and has only the rights of a partial assignee.

§ 3—204. Indorsement

(a)Indorsement means a signature, other than that of a signer as maker, drawer, or acceptor, that alone or accompanied by other words is made on an instrument for the purpose of (i) negotiating the instrument, (ii) restricting payment of the instrument, or (iii) incurring indorsers liability on the instrument, but regardless of the intent of the signer, a signature and its accompanying words is an indorsement unless the accompanying words, terms of the instrument, place of the signature, or other circumstances unambiguously indicate that the signature was made for a purpose other than indorsement. For the purpose of determining whether a signature is made on an instrument, a paper affixed to the instrument is a part of the instrument.

. . .

§ 3—205. Special Indorsement; Blank Indorsement; Anomalous Indorsement

(a)If an endorsement is made by the holder of an instrument, whether payable to an identified person or payable to bearer, and the indorsement identifies a person to whom it makes the instrument payable, it is a special indorsement. When specially indorsed, an instrument becomes payable to the identified person and may be negotiated only by the indorsement of that person. The principles stated in Section 3—110 apply to special indorsements.

(b)If an endorsement is made by the holder of an instrument and it is not a special indorsement, it is a blank indorsement. When indorsed in blank, an instrument becomes payable to bearer and may be negotiated by transfer of possession alone until specially indorsed.

(c)The holder may convert a blank indorsement that consists only of a signature into a special indorsement by writing, above the signature of the indorser, words identifying the person to whom the instrument is made payable.

(d)Anomalous indorsement means an indorsement made by a person who is not the holder of the instrument. An anomalous indorsement does not affect the manner in which the instrument may be negotiated.

Part 3
Enforcement of Instruments

§ 3—301. Person Entitled to Enforce Instrument

Person entitled to enforce an instrument means (i) the holder of the instrument, (ii) a nonholder in possession of the instrument who has the rights of a holder, or (iii) a person not in possession of the instrument who is entitled to enforce the instrument pursuant to Section 3—309 or 3—418(d). A person may be a person entitled to enforce the instrument even though the person is not the owner of the instrument or is in wrongful possession of the instrument.

§ 3—302. Holder in Due Course

(a)Subject to subsection (c) and Section 3106(d), holder in due course means the holder of an instrument if:

(1)the instrument when issued or negotiated to the holder does not bear such apparent evidence of forgery or alteration or is not otherwise so irregular or incomplete as to call into question its authenticity; and

(2)the holder took the instrument (i) for value, (ii) in good faith, (iii) without notice that the instrument is overdue or has been dishonored or that there is an uncured default with respect to payment of another instrument issued as part of the same series, (iv) without notice that the instrument contains an unauthorized signature or has been altered, (v) without notice of any claim to the instrument described in Section 3—306, and (vi) without notice that any party has a defense or claim in recoupment described in Section 3—305(a).

(b)Notice of discharge of a party, other than discharge in an insolvency proceeding, is not notice of a defense under subsection (a),

but discharge is effective against a person who became a holder in due course with notice of the discharge. Public filing or recording of a document does not of itself constitute notice of a defense, claim in recoupment, or claim to the instrument.

(c)Except to the extent a transferor or predecessor in interest has rights as a holder in due course, a person does not acquire rights of a holder in due course of an instrument taken (i) by legal process or by purchase in an execution, bankruptcy, or creditors sale or similar proceeding, (ii) by purchase as part of a bulk transaction not in ordinary course of business of the transferor, or (iii) as the successor in interest to an estate or other organization.

(d)If, under Section 3—303(a)(1), the promise of performance that is the consideration for an instrument has been partially performed, the holder may assert rights as a holder in due course of the instrument only to the fraction of the amount payable under the instrument equal to the value of the partial performance divided by the value of the promised performance.

(e)If (i) the person entitled to enforce an instrument has only a security interest in the instrument and (ii) the person obliged to pay the instrument has a defense, claim in recoupment, or claim to the instrument that may be asserted against the person who granted the security interest, the person entitled to enforce the instrument may assert rights as a holder in due course only to an amount payable under the instrument which, at the time of enforcement of the instrument, does not exceed the amount of the unpaid obligation secured.

(f)To be effective, notice must be received at a time and in a manner that gives a reasonable opportunity to act on it.

(g)This section is subject to any law limiting status as a holder in due course in particular classes of transactions.

§ 3—305. Defenses and Claims in Recoupment

(a)Except as stated in subsection (b), the right to enforce the obligation of a party to pay an instrument is subject to the following:

(1)a defense of the obligor based on (i) infancy of the obligor to the extent it is a defense to a simple contract, (ii) duress, lack of legal capacity, or illegality of the transaction which, under other law, nullifies the obligation of the obligor, (iii) fraud that induced the obligor to sign the instrument with neither knowledge nor reasonable opportunity to learn of its character or its essential terms, or (iv) discharge of the obligor in insolvency proceedings;

(2)a defense of the obligor stated in another section of this Article or a defense of the obligor that would be available if the person entitled to enforce the instrument were enforcing a right to payment under a simple contract; and

(3)a claim in recoupment of the obligor against the original payee of the instrument if the claim arose from the transaction that gave rise to the instrument; but the claim of the obligor may be asserted against a transferee of the instrument only to reduce the amount owing on the instrument at the time the action is brought.

(b)The right of a holder in due course to enforce the obligation of a party to pay the instrument is subject to defenses of the obligor stated in subsection (a)(1), but is not subject to defenses of the obligor stated in subsection (a)(2) or claims in recoupment stated in subsection (a)(3) against a person other than the holder.

(c)Except as stated in subsection (d), in an action to enforce the obligation of a party to pay the instrument, the obligor may not assert against the person entitled to enforce the instrument a defense, claim in recoupment, or claim to the instrument (Section 3—306) of another person, but the other persons claim to the instrument may be asserted by the obligor if the other person is joined in the action and personally asserts the claim against the person entitled to enforce the instrument. An obligor is not obliged to pay the instrument if the person seeking enforcement of the instrument does not have rights of a holder in due course and the obligor proves that the instrument is a lost or stolen instrument.

(d)In an action to enforce the obligation of an accommodation party to pay an instrument, the accommodation party may assert against the person entitled to enforce the instrument any defense or claim in recoupment under subsection (a) that the accommodated party could assert against the person entitled to enforce the instrument, except the defenses of discharge in insolvency proceedings, infancy, and lack of legal capacity.

§ 3—306. Claims to an Instrument

A person taking an instrument, other than a person having rights of a holder in due course, is subject to a claim of a property or possessory rights in the instrument or its proceeds, including a claim to rescind a negotiation and to recover the instrument or its proceeds. A person having rights of a holder in due course takes free of the claim to the instrument.

§ 3—310. Effect of Instrument on Obligation for Which Taken

(a)Unless otherwise agreed, if a certified check, cashiers check, or tellers check is taken for an obligation, the obligation is discharged to the same extent discharge would result if an amount of money equal to the amount of the instrument were taken in payment of the obligation. Discharge of the obligation does not affect any liability that the obligor may have as an indorser of the instrument.

(b)Unless otherwise agreed and except as provided in subsection (a), if a note or an uncertified check is taken for an obligation, the obligation is suspended to the same extent the obligation would be discharged if an amount of money equal to the amount of the instrument were taken, and the following rules apply:

(1)In the case of an uncertified check, suspension of the obligation continues until dishonor of the check or until it is paid or certified. Payment or certification of the check results in discharge of the obligation to the extent of the amount of the check.

(2)In the case of a note, suspension of the obligation continues until dishonor of the note or until it is paid. Payment of the note results in discharge of the obligation to the extent of the payment.

(3)Except as provided in paragraph (4), if the check or note is dishonored and the obligee of the obligation for which the instrument was taken is the person entitled to enforce the instrument, the obligee may enforce either the instrument or the obligation. In the case of an instrument of a third person which is negotiated to the obligee by the obligor, discharge of the obligor on the instrument also discharges the obligation.

(4)If the person entitled to enforce the instrument taken for an obligation is a person other than the obligee, the obliges may not enforce the obligation to the extent the obligation is suspended. If the obligee is the person entitled to enforce the instrument but no longer has possession of it because it was lost, stolen, or destroyed, the obligation may not be enforced to the extent of the amount payable on the instrument, and to that extent the obligees rights against the obligor are limited to enforcement of the instrument.

(c)If an instrument other than one described in subsection (a) or (b) is taken for an obligation, the effect is (i) that stated in subsection (a) if the instrument is one on which a bank is liable as maker or acceptor, or (ii) that stated in subsection (b) in any other case.

§ 3—311. Accord and Satisfaction by Use of Instrument

(a)If a person against whom a claim is asserted proves that (i) that person in good faith tendered an instrument to the claimant as full satisfaction of the claim, (ii) the amount of the claim was unliquidated or subject to a bona fide dispute, and (iii) the claimant obtained payment of the instrument, the following subsections apply.

(b)Unless subsection (c) applies, the claim is discharged if the person against whom the claim is asserted proves that the instrument or an accompanying written communication contained a conspicuous statement to the effect that the instrument was tendered as full satisfaction to the claim.

(c)Subject to subsection (d), a claim is not discharged under subsection (b) if either of the following applies:

(1)The claimant, if an organization, proves that (i) within a reasonable time before the tender, the claimant sent a conspicuous statement to the person against whom the claim is asserted that communications concerning disputed debts, including an instrument tendered as full satisfaction of a debt, are to be sent to a designated person, office, or place, and (ii) the instrument or accompanying communication was not received by that designated person, office, or place.

(2)The claimant, whether or not an organization, proves that within 90 days after payment of the instrument, the claimant tendered repayment of the amount of the instrument to the person against whom the claim is asserted. This paragraph does not apply if the claimant is an organization that sent a statement complying with paragraph (1)(i).

(d)A claim is discharged if the person against whom the claim is asserted proves that within a reasonable time before collection of the instrument was initiated, the claimant, or an agent of the claimant having direct responsibility with respect to the disputed obligation, knew that the instrument was tendered in full satisfaction of the claim.

Part 4
Liability of Parties

§ 3—401. Signature

(a)A person is not liable on an instrument unless (i) the person signed the instrument, or (ii) the person is represented by an agent or representative who signed the instrument and the signature is binding on the represented person under Section 3—402.

(b)A signature may be made (i) manually or by means of a device or machine, and (ii) by the use of any name, including a trade or assumed name, or by a word, mark, or symbol executed or adopted by a person with present intention to authenticate a writing.

§ 3—402. Signature by Representative

(a)If a person acting, or purporting to act, as a representative signs an instrument by signing either the name of the represented person or the name of the signer, the represented person is bound by the signature to the same extent the represented person would be bound if the signature were on a simple contract. If the represented person is bound, the signature of the representative is the authorized signature of the represented person and the represented person is liable on the instrument, whether or not identified in the instrument.

(b)If a representative signs the name of the representative to an instrument and the signature is an authorized signature of the represented person, the following rules apply:

(1)If the form of the signature shows unambiguously that the signature is made on behalf of the represented person who is identified in the instrument, the representative is not liable on the instrument.

(2)Subject to subsection (c), if (i) the form of the signature does not show unambiguously that the signature is made in a representative capacity or (ii) the represented person is not identified in the instrument, the representative is liable on the instrument to a holder in due course that took the instrument without notice that the representative was not intended to be liable on the instrument. With respect to any other person, the representative is liable on the instrument unless the representative proves that the original parties did not intend the representative to be liable on the instrument.

(c)If a representative signs the name of the representative as drawer of a check without indication of the representative status and the check is payable from an account of the represented person who is identified on the check, the signer is not liable on the check if the signature is an authorized signature of the represented person.

§ 3—403. Unauthorized Signature

(a)Unless otherwise provided in this Article or Article 4, an unauthorized signature is ineffective except as the signature of the unauthorized signer in favor of a person who in good faith pays the instrument or takes it for value. An unauthorized signature may be ratified for all purposes of this Article.

(b)If the signature of more than one person is required to constitute the authorized signature of an organization, the signature of the organization is unauthorized if one of the required signatures is lacking.

(c)The civil or criminal liability of a person who makes an unauthorized signature is not affected by any provision of this Article which makes the unauthorized signature effective for the purposes of this Article.

§ 3—404. Impostors; Fictitious Payees

(a)If an impostor, by use of the mails or otherwise, induces the issuer of an instrument to issue the instrument to the impostor, or to a person acting in concert with the impostor, by impersonating the payee of the instrument or a person authorized to act for the payee, an indorsement of the instrument by any person in the name of the payee is effective as the indorsement of the payee in favor of a person who, in good faith, pays the instrument or takes it for value or for collection.

(b)If (i) a person whose intent determines to whom an instrument is payable (Section 3—110(a) or (b)) does not intend the person identified as payee to have any interest in the instrument, or (ii) the person identified as payee of an instrument is a fictitious person, the following rules apply until the instrument is negotiated by special indorsement:

(1)Any person in possession of the instrument is its holder.

(2)An indorsement by any person in the name of the payee stated in the instrument is effective as the indorsement of the payee in favor of a person who, in good faith, pays the instrument or takes it for value or for collection.

(c)Under subsection (a) or (b), an indorsement is made in the name of a payee if (i) it is made in a name substantially similar to that of the payee or (ii) the instrument, whether or not indorsed, is deposited in a depositary bank to an account in a name substantially similar to that of the payee.

(d)With respect to an instrument to which subsection (a) or (b) applies, if a person paying the instrument or taking it for value or for collection fails to exercise ordinary care in paying or taking the instrument and that failure substantially contributes to loss resulting from payment of the instrument, the person bearing the loss may recover from the person failing to exercise ordinary care to the extent the failure to exercise ordinary care contributed to the loss.

§ 3—405. Employers Responsibility for Fraudulent Indorsement by Employee

(a)In this section:

(1)Employee includes an independent contractor and employee of an independent contractor retained by the employer.

(2)Fraudulent indorsement means (i) in the case of an instrument payable to the employer, a forged indorsement purporting to be that of the employer, or (ii) in the case of an instrument with respect to which the employer is the issuer, a forged indorsement purporting to be that of the person identified as payee.

(3)Responsibility with respect to instruments means authority (i) to sign or indorse instruments on behalf of the employer, (ii) to process instruments received by the employer for bookkeeping purposes, for deposit to an account, or for other disposition, (iii) to prepare or process instruments for issue in the name of the employer, (iv) to supply information determining the names or addresses of payees of instruments to be issued in the name of the employer, (v) to control the disposition of instruments to be issued in the name of the employer, or (vi) to act otherwise with respect to instruments in a responsible capacity. Responsibility does not include authority that merely allows an employee to have access to instruments or blank or incomplete instrument forms that are being stored or transported or are part of incoming or outgoing mail, or similar access.

(b)For the purpose of determining the rights and liabilities of a person who, in good faith, pays an instrument or takes it for value or for collection, if an employer entrusted an employee with responsibility with respect to the instrument and the employee or a person acting in concert with the employee makes a fraudulent indorsement of the instrument, the indorsement is effective as the indorsement of the person to whom the instrument is payable if it is made in the name of that person. If the person paying the instrument or taking it for value or for collection fails to exercise ordinary care in paying or taking the instrument and that failure substantially contributes to loss resulting from the fraud, the person bearing the loss may recover from the person failing to exercise ordinary care to the extent the failure to exercise ordinary care contributed to the loss.

(c)Under subsection (b), an indorsement is made in the name of the person to whom an instrument is payable if (i) it is made in a name substantially similar to the name of that person or (ii) the instrument, whether or not indorsed, is deposited in a depositary bank to an account in a name substantially similar to the name of that person.

§ 3—406. Negligence Contributing to Forged Signature or Alteration of Instrument

(a)A person whose failure to exercise ordinary care substantially contributes to an alteration of an instrument or to the making of a forged signature on an instrument is precluded from asserting the alteration or the forgery against a person who, in good faith, pays the instrument or takes it for value or for collection.

(b)Under subsection (a), if the person asserting the preclusion fails to exercise ordinary care in paying or taking the instrument and that failure substantially contributes to loss, the loss is allocated between the person precluded and the person asserting the preclusion according to the extent to which the failure of each to exercise ordinary care contributed to the loss.

(c)Under subsection (a), the burden of proving failure to exercise ordinary care is on the person asserting the preclusion. Under subsection (b), the burden of proving failure to exercise ordinary care is on the person precluded.

§ 3—407. Alteration

(a)Alteration means (i) an unauthorized change in an instrument that purports to modify in any respect the obligation of a party, or (ii) an unauthorized addition of words or numbers or other change to an incomplete instrument relating to the obligation of a party.

(b)Except as provided in subsection (c), an alteration fraudulently made discharges a party whose obligation is affected by the alteration unless that party assents or is precluded from asserting the alteration. No other alteration discharges a party, and the instrument may be enforced according to its original terms.

(c)A payor bank or drawee paying a fraudulently altered instrument or a person taking it for value, in good faith and without notice of the alteration, may enforce rights with respect to the instrument (i) according to its original terms, or (ii) in the case of an incomplete instrument altered by unauthorized completion, according to its terms as completed.

§ 3—411. Refusal to Pay Cashiers Checks, Tellers Checks, and Certified Checks

(a)In this section, obligated bank means the acceptor of a certified check or the issuer of a cashiers check or tellers check bought from the issuer.

(b)If the obligated bank wrongfully (i) refuses to pay a cashiers check or certified check, (ii) stops payment of a tellers check, or (iii) refuses to pay a dishonored tellers check, the person asserting the right to enforce the check is entitled to compensation for expenses and loss of interest resulting from the nonpayment and may recover consequential damages if the obligated bank refuses to pay after receiving notice of particular circumstances giving rise to the damages.

(c)Expenses or consequential damages under subsection (b) are not recoverable if the refusal of the obligated bank to pay occurs because (i) the bank suspends payments, (ii) the obligated bank asserts a claim or defense of the bank that it has reasonable grounds to believe is available against the person entitled to enforce the instrument, (iii) the obligated bank has a reasonable doubt whether the person demanding payment is the person entitled to enforce the instrument or (iv) payment is prohibited by law.

§ 3—412. Obligation of Issuer of Note or Cashiers Check

The issuer of a note or cashiers check or other draft drawn on the drawer is obliged to pay the instrument (i) according to its terms at the time it was issued or, if not issued, at the time it first came into the possession of a holder, or (ii) if the issuer signed an incomplete instrument, according to its terms when completed, to the extent stated in Sections 3—115 and 3—407. The obligation is owed to a person entitled to enforce the instrument or to an indorser who paid the instrument under Section 3—415.

§ 3—413. Obligation of Acceptor

(a)The acceptor of a draft is obliged to pay the draft (i) according to its terms at the time it was accepted, even though the acceptance states that the draft is payable as originally drawn or equivalent terms, (ii) if the acceptance varies the terms of the draft, according to the terms of the draft as varied, or (iii) if the acceptance is of a draft that is an incomplete instrument, according to its terms when completed, to the extent stated in Sections 3—115 and 3—407. The obligation is owed to a person entitled to enforce the draft or to the drawer or an indorser who paid the draft under Section 3—414 or 3—415.

(b)If the certification of a check or other acceptance of a draft states the amount certified or accepted, the obligation of the acceptor is that amount. If (i) the certification or acceptance does not state an amount, (ii) the amount of the instrument is subsequently raised, and (iii) the instrument is then negotiated to a holder in due course, the obligation of the acceptor is the amount of the instrument at the time it was taken by the holder in due course.

§ 3—416. Transfer Warranties

(a)A person who transfers an instrument for consideration warrants to the transferee and, if the transfer is by indorsement, to any subsequent transferee that:

(1)the warrantor is a person entitled to enforce the instrument;

(2)all signatures on the instrument are authentic and authorized;

(3)the instrument has not been altered;

(4)the instrument is not subject to a defense or claim in recoupment of any party which can be asserted against the warrantor; and

(5)the warrantor has no knowledge of any insolvency proceeding commenced with respect to the maker or acceptor or, in the case of an unaccepted draft, the drawer.

(b)A person to whom the warranties under subsection (a) are made and who took the instrument in good faith may recover from the warrantor as damages for breach of warranty an amount equal to the loss suffered as a result of the breach, but not more than the amount of the instrument plus expenses and loss of interest incurred as a result of the breach.

(c)The warranties stated in subsection (a) cannot be disclaimed with respect to checks. Unless notice of a claim for breach of warranty is given to the warrantor within 30 days after the claimant has reason to know of the breach and the identity of the warrantor, the liability of the warrantor under subsection (b) is discharged to the extent of any loss caused by the delay in giving notice of the claim.

(d) A [cause of action] for breach of warranty under this section accrues when the claimant has reason to know of the breach.

§ 3—417. Presentment Warranties

(a)If an unaccepted draft is presented to the drawee for payment or acceptance and the drawee pays or accepts the draft, (i) the person obtaining payment or acceptance, at the time of presentment, and (ii) a previous transferor of the draft, at the time of transfer, warrant to the drawee making payment or accepting the draft in good faith that:

(1)the warrantor is, or was, at the time the warrantor transferred the draft, a person entitled to enforce the draft or authorized to obtain payment or acceptance of the draft on behalf of a person entitled to enforce the draft;

(2)the draft has not been altered; and

(3)the warrantor has no knowledge that the signature of the drawer of the draft is unauthorized.

(b)A drawee making payment may recover from any warrantor damages for breach of warranty equal to the amount paid by the drawee less the amount the drawee received or is entitled to receive from the drawer because of the payment. In addition, the drawee is entitled to compensation for expenses and loss of interest resulting from the breach. The

right of the drawee to recover damages under this subsection is not affected by any failure of the drawee to exercise ordinary care in making payment. If the drawee accepts the draft, breach of warranty is a defense to the obligation of the acceptor. If the acceptor makes payment with respect to the draft, the acceptor is entitled to recover from any warrantor for breach of warranty the amounts stated in this subsection.

(c)If a drawee asserts a claim for breach of warranty under subsection (a) based on an unauthorized indorsement of the draft or an alteration of the draft, the warrantor may defend by proving that the indorsement is effective under Section 3—404 or 3—405 or the drawer is precluded under Section 3—406 or 4—406 from asserting against the drawee the unauthorized indorsement or alteration.

(d)If (i) a dishonored draft is presented for payment to the drawer or an indorser or (ii) any other instrument is presented for payment to a party obliged to pay the instrument, and (iii) payment is received, the following rules apply:

(1)The person obtaining payment and a prior transferor of the instrument warrant to the person making payment in good faith that the warrantor is, or was, at the time the warrantor transferred the instrument, a person entitled to enforce the instrument or authorized to obtain payment on behalf of a person entitled to enforce the instrument.

(2)The person making payment may recover from any warrantor for breach of warranty an amount equal to the amount paid plus expenses and loss of interest resulting from the breach.

(e)The warranties stated in subsections (a) and (d) cannot be disclaimed with respect to checks. Unless notice of a claim for breach of warranty is given to the warrantor within 30 days after the claimant has reason to know of the breach and the identity of the warrantor, the liability of the warrantor under subsection (b) or (d) is discharged to the extent of any loss caused by the delay in giving notice of the claim.

(f)A [cause of action] for breach of warranty under this section accrues when the claimant has reason to know of the breach.

§ 3—418. Payment or Acceptance by Mistake

(a)Except as provided in subsection (c), if the drawee of a draft pays or accepts the draft and the drawee acted on the mistaken belief that (i) payment of the draft had not been stopped pursuant to Section 4—403 or (ii) the signature of the drawer of the draft was authorized, the drawee may recover the amount of the draft from the person to whom or for whose benefit payment was made or, in the case of acceptance, may revoke the acceptance. Rights of the drawee under this subsection are not affected by failure of the drawee to exercise ordinary care in paying or accepting the draft.

(b)Except as provided in subsection (c), if an instrument has been paid or accepted by mistake and the case is not covered by subsection (a), the person paying or accepting may, to the extent permitted by the law governing mistake and restitution, (i) recover the payment from the person to whom or for whose benefit payment was made or (ii) in the case of acceptance, may revoke the acceptance.

(c)The remedies provided by subsection (a) or (b) may not be asserted against a person who took the instrument in good faith and for value or who in good faith changed position in reliance on the payment or acceptance. This subsection does not limit remedies provided by Section 3—417 or 4—407.

(d)Notwithstanding Section 4—215, if an instrument is paid or accepted by mistake and the payor or acceptor recovers payment or revokes acceptance under subsection (a) or (b), the instrument is deemed not to have been paid or accepted and is treated as dishonored, and the person from whom payment is recovered has rights as a person entitled to enforce the dishonored instrument.

§ 3—420. Conversion of Instrument

(a)The law applicable to conversion of personal property applies to instruments. An instrument is also converted if it is taken by transfer, other than a negotiation, from a person not entitled to enforce the instrument or a bank makes or obtains payment with respect to the instrument for a person not entitled to enforce the instrument or receive payment. An action for conversion of an instrument may not be brought by (i) the issuer or acceptor of the instrument or (ii) a payee or indorsee who did not receive delivery of the instrument either directly or through delivery to an agent or a co-payee.

(b)In an action under subsection (a), the measure of liability is presumed to be the amount payable on the instrument, but recovery may not exceed the amount of the plaintiffs interest in the instrument.

(c)A representative, other than a depositary bank, who has in good faith dealt with an instrument or its proceeds on behalf of one who was not the person entitled to enforce the instrument is not liable in conversion to that person beyond the amount of any proceeds that it has not paid out.

Part 5
Dishonor

§ 3—501. Presentment

(a)Presentment means a demand made by or on behalf of a person entitled to enforce an instrument (i) to pay the instrument made to the drawee or a party obliged to pay the instrument or, in the case of a note or accepted draft payable at a bank, to the bank, or (ii) to accept a draft made to the drawee.

(b)The following rules are subject to Article 4, agreement of the parties, and clearinghouse rules and the like:

(1)Presentment may be made at the place of payment of the instrument and must be made at the place of payment if the instrument is payable at a bank in the United States; may be made by any commercially reasonable means, including an oral, written, or electronic communication; is effective when the demand for payment or acceptance is received by the person to whom presentment is made; and is effective if made to any one of two or more makers, acceptors, drawees, or other payors.

(2)Upon demand of the person to whom presentment is made, the person making presentment must (i) exhibit the instrument, (ii) give reasonable identification and, if presentment is made on behalf of another person, reasonable evidence of authority to do so, and (iii) sign a receipt on the instrument for any payment made or surrender the instrument if full payment is made.

(3)Without dishonoring the instrument, the party to whom presentment is made may (i) return the instrument for lack of a necessary indorsement, or (ii) refuse payment or acceptance for failure of the presentment to comply with the terms of the instrument, an agreement of the parties, or other applicable law or rule.

(4)The party to whom presentment is made may treat presentment as occurring on the next business day after the day of presentment if the party to whom presentment is made has established a cut-off hour not earlier than 2 p.m. for the receipt and processing of instruments presented for payment or acceptance and presentment is made after the cut-off hour.

§ 3—502. Dishonor

(a)Dishonor of a note is governed by the following rules:

(1)If the note is payable on demand, the note is dishonored if presentment is duly made to the maker and the note is not paid on the day of presentment.

(2)If the note is not payable on demand and is payable at or through a bank or the terms of the note require presentment, the note is dishonored if presentment is duly made and the note is not paid on the day it becomes payable or the day of presentment, whichever is later.

(3)If the note is not payable on demand and paragraph (2) does not apply, the note is dishonored if it is not paid on the day it becomes payable.

(b)Dishonor of an unaccepted draft other than a documentary draft is governed by the following rules:

(1)If a check is duly presented for payment to the payor bank otherwise than for immediate payment over the counter, the check is dishonored if the payor bank makes timely return of the check or sends timely notice of dishonor or nonpayment under Section 4—

301 and 4—302, or becomes accountable for the amount of the check under Section 4—302.

(2)If a draft is payable on demand and paragraph (1) does not apply, the draft is dishonored if presentment for payment is duly made to the drawee and the draft is not paid on the day of presentment.

(3)If a draft is payable on a date stated in the draft, the draft is dishonored if (i) presentment for payment is duly made to the drawee and payment is not made on the day the draft becomes payable or the day of presentment, whichever is later, or (ii) presentment for acceptance is duly made before the day the draft becomes payable and the draft is not accepted on the day of presentment.

(4)If a draft is payable on elapse of a period of time after sight or acceptance, the draft is dishonored if presentment for acceptance is duly made and the draft is not accepted on the day of presentment.

(c)Dishonor of an unaccepted documentary draft occurs according to the rules stated in subsection (b)(2), (3), and (4), except that payment or acceptance may be delayed without dishonor until no later than the close of the third business day of the drawee following the day on which payment or acceptance is required by those paragraphs.

(d)Dishonor of an accepted draft is governed by the following rules:

(1)If the draft is payable on demand, the draft is dishonored if presentment for payment is duly made to the acceptor and the draft is not paid on the day of presentment.

(2)If the draft is not payable on demand, the draft is dishonored if presentment for payment is duly made to the acceptor and payment is not made on the day it becomes payable or the day of presentment, whichever is later.

(e)In any case in which presentment is otherwise required for dishonor under this section and presentment is excused under Section 3—504, dishonor occurs without presentment if the instrument is not duly accepted or paid.

(f)If a draft is dishonored because timely acceptance of the draft was not made and the person entitled to demand acceptance consents to a late acceptance, from the time of acceptance the draft is treated as never having been dishonored.

Part 6
Discharge and Payment

§ 3—601. Discharge and Effect of Discharge

(a)The obligation of a party to pay the instrument is discharged as stated in this Article or by an act or agreement with the party which would discharge an obligation to pay money under a simple contract.

(b)Discharge of the obligation of a party is not effective against a person acquiring rights of a holder in due course of the instrument without notice of the discharge.

§ 3—602. Payment

(a)Subject to subsection (b), an instrument is paid to the extent payment is made (i) by or on behalf of a party obliged to pay the instrument, and (ii) to a person entitled to enforce the instrument. To the extent of the payment, the obligation of the party obliged to pay the instrument is discharged even though payment is made with knowledge of a claim to the instrument under Section 3—306 by another person.

(b)The obligation of a party to pay the instrument is not discharged under subsection (a) if:

(1)a claim to the instrument under Section 3—306 is enforceable against the party receiving payment and (i) payment is made with knowledge by the payor that payment is prohibited by injunction or similar process of a court of competent jurisdiction, or (ii) in the case of an instrument other than a cashiers check, tellers check, or certified check, the party making payment accepted, from the person having a claim to the instrument, indemnity against loss resulting from refusal to pay the person entitled to enforce the instrument; or

(2)the person making payment knows that the instrument is a stolen instrument and pays a person it knows is in wrongful possession of the instrument.

Article 4 [1952 Version]

Bank Deposits and Collections

Part 1
General Provisions and Definitions

§ 4—103. Variation by Agreement; Measure of Damages; Certain Action Constituting Ordinary Care

(1)The effect of the provisions of this Article may be varied by agreement except that no agreement can disclaim a banks responsibility for its own lack of good faith or failure to exercise ordinary care or can limit the measure of damages for such lack or failure; but the parties may by agreement determine the standards by which such responsibility is to be measured if such standards are not manifestly unreasonable.

(2)Federal Reserve regulations and operating letters, clearing house rules, and the like, have the effect of agreements under subsection (1), whether or not specifically assented to by all parties interested in items handled.

(3)Action or nonaction approved by this Article or pursuant to Federal Reserve regulations or operating letters constitutes the exercise of ordinary care and, in the absence of special instructions, action or nonaction consistent with clearing house rules and the like or with a general banking usage not disapproved by this Article, prima facie constitutes the exercise of ordinary care.

(4)The specification or approval of certain procedures by this Article does not constitute disapproval of other procedures which may be reasonable under the circumstances.

(5)The measure of damages for failure to exercise ordinary care in handling an item is the amount of the item reduced by an amount which could not have been realized by the use of ordinary care, and where there is bad faith it includes other damages, if any, suffered by the party as a proximate consequence.

§ 4—108. Delays

(1)Unless otherwise instructed, a collecting bank in a good faith effort to secure payment may, in the case of specific items and with or without the approval of any person involved, waive, modify or extend time limits imposed or permitted by this Act for a period not in excess of an additional banking day without discharge of secondary parties and without liability to its transferor or any prior party.

(2)Delay by a collecting bank or payor bank beyond time limits prescribed or permitted by this Act or by instructions is excused if caused by interruption of communication facilities, suspension of payments by another bank, war, emergency conditions or other circumstances beyond the control of the bank provided it exercises such diligence as the circumstances require.

Part 2
Collection of Items: Depository and Collecting Banks

§ 4—204. Methods of Sending and Presenting; Sending Direct to Payor Bank

(1)A collecting bank must send items by reasonably prompt method taking into consideration any relevant instructions, the nature of the item, the number of such items on hand, and the cost of collection involved and the method generally used by it or others to present such items.

(2)A collecting bank may send

(a)any item direct to the payor bank;

(b)any item to any nonbank payor if authorized by its transferor; and

(c)any item other than documentary drafts to any nonbank payor, if authorized by Federal Reserve regulation or operating letter, clearing house rule or the like.

(3)Presentment may be made by a presenting bank at a place where the payor bank has requested that presentment be made.

§ 4—205. Supplying Missing Indorsement; No Notice from Prior Indorsement

(1)A depositary bank which has taken an item for collection may supply any indorsement of the customer which is necessary to title unless the item contains the words payees indorsement required or the like. In the absence of such a requirement, a statement placed on the item by the depositary bank to the effect that the item was deposited by a customer or credited to his account is effective as the customers indorsement of.

(2)An intermediary bank, or payor bank which is not a depositary bank, is neither given notice nor otherwise affected by a restrictive indorsement of any person except the banks immediate transferor.

§ 4—206. Transfer Between Banks

Any agreed method which identifies the transferor bank is sufficient for the items further transfer to another bank.

§ 4—211. Media of Remittance; Provisional and Final Settlement in Remittance Cases

(1)A collecting bank may take in settlement of an item

(a)a check of the remitting bank or of another bank on any bank except the remitting bank; or

(b)a cashiers check or similar primary obligation of a remitting bank which is a member of or clears through a member of the same clearing house or group as the collecting bank; or

(c)appropriate authority to charge an account of the remitting bank or of another bank with the collecting bank; or

(d)if the item is drawn upon or payable by a person other than a bank, a cashiers check, certified check or other bank check or obligation.

(2)If before its midnight deadline the collecting bank properly dishonors a remittance check or authorization to charge on itself or presents or forwards for collection a remittance instrument of or on another bank which is of a kind approved by subsection (1) or has not been authorized by it, the collecting bank is not liable to prior parties in the event of the dishonor of such check, instrument or authorization.

(3)A settlement for an item by means of a remittance instrument or authorization to charge is or becomes a final settlement as to both the person making and the person receiving the settlement

(a)if the remittance instrument or authorization to charge is of a kind approved by subsection (1) or has not been authorized by the person receiving the settlement and in either case the person receiving the settlement acts seasonably before its midnight deadline in presenting, forwarding for collection or paying the instrument or authorizationat the time the remittance instrument or authorization is finally paid by the payor by which it is payable;

(b)if the person receiving the settlement has authorized remittance by a nonbank check or obligation or by a cashiers check or similar primary obligation of or a check upon the payor or other remitting bank which is not of a kind approved by subsection (1)(b)at the time of the receipt of such remittance check or obligation; or

(c)if in a case not covered by subparagraphs (a) or (b) the person receiving the settlement fails to seasonably present, forward for collection, pay or return remittance instrument or authorization to it to charge before its midnight deadlineat such midnight deadline.

§ 4—213. Final Payment of Item for Payor Bank; When Provisional Debits and Credits Become Final; When Certain Credits Become Available for Withdrawal

(1)An item is finally paid by a payor bank when the bank has done any of the following, whichever happens first:

(a)paid the item in cash; or

(b)settled for the item without reserving a right to revoke the settlement and without having such right under statute, clearing house rule or agreement; or

(c)completed the process of posting the item to the indicated account of the drawer, maker or other person to be charged therewith; or

(d)made a provisional settlement for the item and failed to revoke the settlement in the time and manner permitted by statute, clearing house rule or agreement.

Upon a final payment under subparagraphs (b), (c) or (d), the payor bank shall be accountable for the amount of the item.

(2)If provisional settlement for an item between the presenting and payor banks is made through a clearing house or by debits or credits in an account between them, then to the extent that provisional debits or credits for the item are entered in accounts between the presenting and payor banks or between the presenting and successive prior collecting banks seriatim, they become final upon final payment of the item by the payor bank.

(3)If a collecting bank receives a settlement for an item which is or becomes final (subsection 3) of Section 4—211, subsection (2) of Section 4—213), the bank is accountable to its customer for the amount of the item and any provisional credit given for the item in an account with its customer becomes final.

(4)Subject to any right of the bank to apply the credit to an obligation of the customer, credit given by a bank for an item in an account with its customer becomes available for withdrawal as of right

(a)in any case where the bank has received a provisional settlement for the item,when such settlement becomes final and the bank has had a reasonable time to learn that the settlement is final;

(b)in any case where the bank is both a depositary bank and a payor bank and the item is finally paid,at the opening of the banks second banking day following receipt of the item.

(5)A deposit of money in a bank is final when made but, subject to any right of the bank to apply the deposit to an obligation of the customer, the deposit becomes available for withdrawal as of right at the opening of the banks next banking day following receipt of the deposit.

Part 3
Collection of Items: Payor Banks

§ 4—301. Deferred Posting; Recovery of Payment by Return of Items; Time of Dishonor

(1)Where an authorized settlement for a demand item (other than a documentary draft) received by a payor bank otherwise than for immediate payment over the counter has been made before midnight of the banking day of receipt, the payor bank may revoke the settlement and recover any payment if before it has made final payment (subsection (1) of Section 4—213) and before its midnight deadline it

(a)returns the item; or

(b)sends written notice of dishonor or nonpayment if the item is held for protest or is otherwise unavailable for return.

(2)If a demand item is received by a payor bank for credit on its books, it may return such item or send notice of dishonor and may revoke any credit given or recover the amount thereof withdrawn by its customer, if it acts within the time limit and in the manner specified in the preceding subsection.

(3)Unless previous notice of dishonor has been sent, an item is dishonored at the time when for purposes of dishonor it is returned or notice sent in accordance with this section.

(4)An item is returned:

(a)as to an item received through a clearing house, when it is delivered to the presenting or last collecting bank or to the clearing house or is sent or delivered in accordance with its rules; or

(b)in all other cases, when it is sent or delivered to the banks customer or transferor or pursuant to his instructions.

§ 4—302. Payor Banks Responsibility for Late Return of Item

In the absence of a valid defense such as breach of a presentment warranty (subsection (1) of Section 4—207), settlement effected or the like, if an item is presented on and received by a payor bank the bank is accountable for the amount of

(a)a demand item other than a documentary draft whether properly payable or not if

the bank, in any case where it is not also the depositary bank, retains the item beyond midnight of the banking day of receipt without settling for it or, regardless of whether it is also the depositary bank, does not pay or return the item or send notice of dishonor until after its midnight deadline; or

(b)any other properly payable item unless within the time allowed for acceptance or payment of that item the bank either accepts or pays the item or returns it and accompanying documents.

Part 4
Relationship Between Payor Bank and Its Customer

§ 4—401. When Bank May Charge Customers Account

(1)As against its customer, a bank may charge against his account any item which is otherwise properly payable from that account even though the charge creates an overdraft.

(2)A bank which in good faith makes payment to a holder may charge the indicated account of its customer according to

(a)the original tenor of his altered item; or

(b)the tenor of his completed item, even though the bank knows the item has been completed unless the bank has notice that the completion was improper.

§ 4—407. Payor Banks Right to Subrogation on Improper Payment

If a payor bank has paid an item over the stop payment order of the drawer or maker or otherwise under circumstances giving a basis for objection by the drawer or maker, to prevent unjust enrichment and only to the extent necessary to prevent loss to the bank by reason of its payment of the item, the payor bank shall be subrogated to the rights

(a)of any holder in due course on the item against the drawer or maker, and

(b)of the payee or any other holder of the item against the drawer or maker either on the item or under the transaction out of which the item arose; and

(c)of the drawer or maker against the payee or any other holder of the item with respect to the transaction out of which the item arose.

Part 5
Collection of Documentary Drafts

§ 4—501. Handling of Documentary Drafts; Duty to Send for Presentment and to Notify Customer of Dishonor

A bank which takes a documentary draft for collection must present or send the draft and accompanying documents for presentment and, upon learning that the draft has not been paid or accepted in due course, must seasonably notify its customer of such fact even though it may have discounted or bought the draft or extended credit available for withdrawal as of right.

Article 4 [1990 Revision]

Bank Deposits and Collections

§ 4—102. Applicability

(a)To the extent that items within this Article are also within Articles 3 and 8, they are subject to those Articles. If there is conflict, this Article governs Article 3, but Article 8 governs this Article.

(b)The liability of a bank for action or non-action with respect to an item handled by it for purposes of presentment, payment or collection is governed by the law of the place where the bank is located. In the case of action or non-action by or at a branch or separate office of a bank, its liability is governed by the law of the place where the branch or separate office is located.

§ 4—103. Variation by Agreement; Measure of Damages; Action Constituting Ordinary Care

(a)The effect of the provision of this Article may be varied by agreement, but the parties to the agreement cannot disclaim a banks responsibility for its lack of good faith or failure to exercise ordinary care or limit the measure of damages for the lack or failure. However, the parties may determine by agreement the standards by which the banks responsibility is to be measured if those standards are not manifestly unreasonable.

(b)Federal Reserve regulations and operating circulars, clearing-house rules, and the like have the effect of agreements under subsection (a), whether or not specifically assented to by all parties interested in items handled.

(c)Action or non-action approved by this Article or pursuant to Federal Reserve regulations or operating circulars is the exercise of ordinary care and, in the absence of special instructions, action or non-action consistent with clearing-house rules and the like or with a general banking usage not disapproved by this Article, is prima facie the exercise of ordinary care.

(d)The specification or approval of certain procedures by this Article is not disapproval of other procedures that may be reasonable under the circumstances.

(e)The measure of damages for failure to exercise ordinary care in handling an item is the amount of the item reduced by an amount that could not have been realized by the exercise of ordinary care. If there is also bad faith it includes any other damages the party suffered as a proximate consequence.

§ 4—107. Separate Office of Bank

A branch or separate office of a bank is a separate bank for the purpose of computing the time within which and determining the place at or to which action may be taken or notice or orders must be given under this Article and under Article 3.

§ 4—109. Delays

(a)Unless otherwise instructed, a collecting bank in a good faith effort to secure payment of a specific item drawn on a payor other than a bank, and with or without the approval of any person involved, may waive, modify, or extend time limits imposed or permitted by this Act for a period not exceeding two additional banking days without discharge of drawers or indorsers or liability to its transferor or a prior party.

(b)Delay by a collecting bank or payor bank beyond time limits prescribed or permitted by this Act or by instructions is excused if (i) the delay is caused by interruption of communication or computer facilities, suspension of payments by another bank, war, emergency conditions, failure of equipment, or other circumstances beyond the control of the bank, and (ii) the bank exercises such diligence as the circumstances require.

§ 4—110. Electronic Presentment

(a) Agreement for electronic presentment means an agreement, clearing-house rule, or Federal Reserve regulation or operating circular, providing that presentment of an item may be made by transmission of an image of an item or information describing the item (presentment notice) rather than delivery of the item itself. The agreement may provide for procedures governing retention, presentment, payment, dishonor, and other matters concerning items subject to the agreement.

(b) Presentment of an item pursuant to an agreement for presentment is made when the presentment notice is received.

(c) If presentment is made by presentment notice, a reference to item or check in this Article means the presentment notice unless the context otherwise indicates.

§ 4—111. Statute of Limitations

An action to enforce an obligation, duty, or right arising under this Article must be commenced within three years after the [cause of action] accrues.

§ 4—204. Methods of Sending and Presenting; Sending Directly to Payor Bank

(a) A collecting bank shall send items by a reasonably prompt method, taking into consideration relevant instructions, the nature of the item, the number of those items on hand, the cost of collection involved, and the method generally used by it or others to present those items.

(b) A collecting bank may send:

(1) an item directly to the payor bank;

(2) an item to a nonbank payor if authorized by its transferor; and

(3) an item other than documentary drafts to a nonbank payor, if authorized by Federal Reserve regulation or operating circular, clearing-house rule, or the like.

(c) Presentment may be made by a presenting bank at a place where the payor bank or other payor has requested that presentment be made.

§ 4—205. Depository Bank Holder of Unindorsed Item

If a customer delivers an item to a depositary bank for collection:

(1) the depositary bank becomes a holder of the item at the time it receives the item for collection if the customer at the time of delivery was a holder of the item, whether or not the customer indorses the item, and, if the bank satisfies the other requirements of Section 3—302, it is a holder in due course; and

(2) the depositary bank warrants to collecting banks, the payor bank or other payor, and the drawer that the amount of the item was paid to the customer or deposited to the customers account.

§ 4—207. Transfer Warranties

(a) A Customer or collecting bank that transfers an item and receives a settlement or other consideration warrants to the transferee and to any subsequent collecting bank that:

(1) the warrantor is a person entitled to enforce the item;

(2) all signatures on the item are authentic and authorized;

(3) the item has not been altered;

(4) the item is not subject to a defense or claim in recoupment (Section 3—305(a)) of any party that can be asserted against the warrantor; and

(5) the warrantor has no knowledge of any insolvency proceeding commenced with respect to the maker or acceptor or, in the case of an unaccepted draft, the drawer.

(b) If an item is dishonored, a customer or collecting bank transferring the item and receiving settlement or other consideration is obliged to pay the amount due on the item (i) according to the terms of the item at the time it was transferred, or (ii) if the transfer was of an incomplete item, according to its terms when completed as stated in Sections 3—115 and 3—407. The obligation of a transferor is owed to the transferee and to any subsequent collecting bank that takes the item in good faith. A transferor cannot disclaim its obligation under this subsection by an indorsement stating that it is made without recourse or otherwise disclaiming liability.

(c)A person to whom the warranties under subsection (a) are made and who took the item in good faith may recover from the warrantor as damages for breach of warranty an amount equal to the loss suffered as a result of the breach, but not more than the amount of the item plus expenses and loss of interest incurred as a result of the breach.

(d)The warranties stated in subsection (a) cannot be disclaimed with respect to checks. Unless notice of a claim for breach of warranty is given to the warrantor within 30 days after the claimant has reason to know of the breach and the identity of the warrantor; the warrantor is discharged to the extent of any loss caused by the delay in giving notice of the claim.

(e)A cause of action for breach of warranty under this section accrues when the claimant has reason to know of the breach.

§ 4—208. Presentment Warranties

(a)If an unaccepted draft is presented to the drawee for payment or acceptance and the drawee pays or accepts the draft, (i) the person obtaining payment or acceptance, at the time of presentment, and (ii) a previous transferor of the draft, at the time of transfer, warrant to the drawee that pays or accepts the draft in good faith that:

(1)the warrantor is, or was, at the time the warrantor transferred the draft, a person entitled to enforce the draft or authorized to obtain payment or acceptance of the draft on behalf of a person entitled to enforce the draft or authorized to obtain payment or acceptance of the draft on behalf of a person entitled to enforce the draft;

(2)the draft has not been altered; and

(3)the warrantor has no knowledge that the signature of the purported drawer of the draft is unauthorized.

(b)A drawee making payment may recover from a warrantor damages for breach of warranty equal to the amount paid by the drawee less the amount the drawee received or is entitled to receive from the drawer because of the payment. In addition, the drawee is entitled to compensation for expenses and loss of interest resulting from the breach. The right of the drawee to recover damages under

this subsection is not affected by any failure of the drawee to exercise ordinary care in making payment. If the drawee accepts the draft (i) breach of warranty is a defense to the obligation of the acceptor, and (ii) if the acceptor makes payment with respect to the draft, the acceptor is entitled to recover from a warrantor for breach of warranty the amounts stated in this subsection.

(c)If a drawee asserts a claim for breach of warranty under subsection (a) based on an unauthorized indorsement of the draft or an alteration of the draft, the warrantor may defend by proving that the indorsement is effective under Section 3—404 or 3—405 or the drawer is precluded under Section 3—406 or 4—406 from asserting against the drawee the unauthorized indorsement or alteration.

(d)If (i) a dishonored draft is presented for payment to the drawer or an indorser or (ii) any other item is presented for payment to a party obliged to pay the item, and the item is paid, the person obtaining payment and a prior transferor of the item warrant tot he person making payment in good faith that the warrantor is, or was, at the time the warrantor transferred the item, a person entitled to enforce the item or authorized to obtain payment on behalf of a person entitled to enforce the item. The person making payment may recover from any warrantor for breach of warranty an amount equal to the amount paid plus expenses and loss of interest resulting from the breach.

(e)The warranties stated in subsections (a) and (d) cannot be disclaimed with respect to checks. Unless notice of a claim for breach of warranty is given to the warrantor within 30 days after the claimant has reason to know of the breach and the identity of the warrantor, the warrantor is discharged to the extent of any loss caused by the delay in giving notice of the claim.

(f)A cause of action for breach of warranty under this section accrues when the claimant has reason to know of the breach.

§ 4—209. Encoding and Retention Warranties

(a)A person who encodes information on or with respect to an item after issue warrants to any subsequent collecting bank and to the payor bank or other payor that the information is correctly encoded. If the customer of a depositary bank encodes, that bank also makes the warranty.

(b)A person who undertakes to retain an item pursuant to an agreement for electronic presentment warrants to any subsequent collecting bank and to the payor bank or other payor that retention and presentment of the item comply with the agreement. If a customer of a depositary bank undertakes to retain an item, that bank also makes this warranty.

(c)A person to whom warranties are made under this section and who took the item in good faith may recover from the warrantor as damages for breach of warranty an amount equal to the loss suffered as a result of the breach, plus expenses and loss of interest incurred as a result of the breach.

§ 4—213. Medium and Time of Settlement by Bank

(a)With respect to settlement by a bank, the medium and time of settlement may be prescribed by Federal Reserve regulations or circulars, clearing-house rules, and the like, or agreement. In the absence of such prescription:

(1)the medium of settlement is cash or credit to an account in a Federal Reserve bank of or specified by the person to receive settlement; and

(2)the time of settlement is:

(i)with respect to tender of settlement by cash, a cashiers check, or tellers check, when the cash or check is sent or delivered;

(ii)with respect to tender of settlement by credit in an account in a Federal Reserve Bank, when the credit is made;

(iii)with respect to tender of settlement by a credit or debit to an account in a bank, when the credit or debit is made or, in the case of tender of settlement by authority to charge an account, when the authority is sent or delivered; or

(iv)with respect to tender of settlement by a funds transfer, when payment is made pursuant to Section 4A—406(a) to the person receiving settlement.

(b)If the tender of settlement is not by a medium authorized by subsection (a) or the time of settlement is not fixed by subsection (a), no settlement occurs until the tender of settlement is accepted by the person receiving settlement.

(c)If settlement for an item is made by cashiers check or tellers check and the person receiving settlement, before its midnight deadline:

(1)presents or forwards the check for collection, settlement is final when the check is finally paid; or

(2)fails to present or forward the check for collection, settlement is final at the midnight deadline of the person receiving settlement.

(d)If settlement for an item is made by giving authority to charge the account of the bank giving settlement in the bank receiving settlement, settlement is final when the charge is made by the bank receiving settlement if there are funds available in the account for the amount of the item.

§ 4—214. Right of Charge-Back or Refund; Liability of Collecting Bank; Return of Item

(a)If a collecting bank has made provisional settlement with its customer for an item and fails by reason of dishonor, suspension of payments by a bank, or otherwise to receive a settlement for the item which is or becomes final, the bank may revoke the settlement given by it, charge back the amount of any credit given for the item to its customers account, or obtain refund from its customer, whether or not it is able to return the item, if by its midnight deadline or within a longer reasonable time after it learns the facts it returns the item or sends notification of the facts. If the return or notice is delayed beyond the banks midnight deadline or a longer reasonable time after it learns the facts, the bank may revoke the settlement, charge back the credit, or obtain refund from its customer, but it is liable for any loss resulting from the delay. These rights to revoke, charge back, and obtain refund terminate if and when a settlement for the item received by the bank is or becomes final.

(b)A collecting bank returns an item when it is sent or delivered to the banks customer or transferor or pursuant to its instructions.

(c)A depository bank that is also the payor may charge back the amount of an item to its customers account or obtain refund in accordance with the section governing return of an item received by a payor bank for credit on its books (Section 4—301).

(d)The right to charge back is not affected by:

(1)previous use of a credit given for the item; or

(2)failure by any bank to exercise ordinary care with respect to the item, but a bank so failing remains liable.

(e)A failure to charge back or claim refund does not affect other rights of the bank against the customer or any other party.

(f)If credit is given in dollars as the equivalent of the value of an item payable in foreign money, the dollar amount of any charge-back or refund must be calculated on the basis of the bank-offered spot rate for the foreign money prevailing on the day when the person entitled to the charge-back or refund learns that it will not receive payment in ordinary course.

§ 4—215. Final Payment of Item by Payor Bank; When Provisional Debits and Credits Become Final; When Certain Credits Become Available for Withdrawal

(a)An item is finally paid by a payor bank when the bank has first done any of the following:

(1)paid the item in cash;

(2)settled for the item without having a right to revoke the settlement under statute, clearing-house rule, or agreement; or

(3)made a provisional settlement for the item and failed to revoke the settlement in the time and manner permitted by statute, clearing-house rule, or agreement.

(b)If provisional settlement for an item does not become final, the item is not finally paid.

(c)If provisional settlement for an item between the presenting and payor banks is made through a clearing house or by debits or credits in an accounting between them, then to the extent that provisional debits or credits for the

item are entered in accounts between the presenting and payor banks or between the presenting and successive prior collecting banks seriatim, they become final upon final payment of the items by the payor bank.

(d)If a collecting bank receives a settlement for an item which is or becomes final, the bank is accountable to its customer for the amount of the item and any provisional credit given for the item in an account with its customer becomes final.

(e)Subject to (i) applicable law stating a time for availability of funds and (ii) any right of the bank to apply the credit to an obligation of the customer, credit given by a bank for an item in a customers account becomes available for withdrawal as of right:

(1)if the bank has received a provisional settlement for the item, when the settlement becomes final and the bank has had a reasonable time to receive return of the item and the item has not been received within that time;

(2)if the bank is both the depository bank and the payor bank, and the item is finally paid, at the opening of the banks second banking day following receipt of the item.

(f)Subject to applicable law stating a time for availability of funds and any right of a bank to apply a deposit to an obligation of the depositor, a deposit of money becomes available for withdrawal as of right at the opening of the banks next banking day after receipt of the deposit.

§ 4—302. Payor Banks Responsibility for Late Return of Item

(a)If an item is presented to and received by a payor bank, the bank is accountable for the amount of:

(1)a demand item, other than a documentary draft, whether properly payable or not, if the bank, in any case in which it is not also the depository bank, retains the item beyond midnight of the banking day of receipt without settling for it or, whether or not it is also the depository bank, does not pay or return the item or send notice of dishonor until after its midnight deadline; or

(2)any other properly payable item unless, within the time allowed for acceptance or payment of that item, the bank either accepts or pays the item or return it and accompanying documents.

(b)The liability of a payor bank to pay an item pursuant to subsection (a) is subject to defenses based on breach of a presentment warranty (Section 4—208) or proof that the person seeking enforcement of the liability presented or transferred the item for the purpose of defrauding the payor bank.

§ 4—401. When Bank May Charge Customers Account

(a)A bank may charge against the account of a customer an item that is properly payable from that account even though the charge creates an overdraft. An item is properly payable if it is authorized by the customer and is in accordance with any agreement between the customer and bank.

(b)A customer is not liable for the amount of an overdraft if the customer neither signed the item nor benefited from the proceeds of the item.

(c)A bank may charge against the account of a customer a check that is otherwise properly payable from the account, even though payment was made before the date of the check, unless the customer has given notice to the bank of the postdating describing the check with reasonable certainty. The notice is effective for the period stated in Section 4—403(b) for stop-payment orders, and must be received at such time and in such manner as to afford the bank a reasonable opportunity to act on it before the bank takes any action with respect to the check described in Section 4—303. If a bank charges against the account of a customer a check before the date stated in the notice of postdating, the bank is liable for damages for the loss resulting from its act. The loss may include damages for dishonor of subsequent items under Section 4—402.

(d)A bank that in good faith makes payment to a holder may charge the indicated account of its customer according to:

(1)the original terms of the altered item; or

(2)the terms of the completed item, even though the bank knows the item has been completed unless the bank has notice that the completion was improper.

§ 4—402. Banks Liability to Customer for Wrongful Dishonor; Time of Determining Insufficiency of Account

(a)Except as otherwise provided in this Article, a payor bank wrongfully dishonors an item if it dishonors an item that is properly payable, but a bank may dishonor an item that would create an overdraft unless it has agreed to pay the overdraft.

(b)A payor bank is liable to its customer for damages proximately caused by the wrongful dishonor of an item. Liability is limited to actual damages proved and may include damages for an arrest or prosecution of the customer or other consequential damages. Whether any consequential damages are proximately caused by the wrongful dishonor is a question of fact to be determined in each case.

(c)A payor banks determination of the customers account balance on which a decision to dishonor for insufficiency of available funds is based may be made at any time between the time the item is received by the payor bank and the time that the payor bank returns the item or gives notice in lieu of return, and no more than one determination need be made. If, at the election of the payor bank, a subsequent balance determination is made for the purpose of reevaluating the banks decision to dishonor the item, the account balance at that time is determinative of whether a dishonor for insufficiency of available funds is wrongful.

§ 4—403. Customers Right to Stop Payment; Burden of Proof of Loss

(a)A customer or any person authorized to draw on the account if there is more than one person may stop payment of any item drawn on the customers account or close the account by an order to the bank describing the item or account with reasonable certainty received at a time and in a manner that affords the bank a reasonable opportunity to act on it before any action by the bank with respect to the item described in Section 4—303. If the signature of more than one person is required to draw on an account, any of these persons may stop payment or close the account.

(b)A stop-payment order is effective for six months, but it lapses after 14 calendar days if the original order was oral and was not confirmed in writing within that period. A stop-payment order may be renewed for additional six-month periods by a writing given to the bank within a period during which the stop-payment order is effective.

(c)The burden of establishing the fact and amount of loss resulting from the payment of an item contrary to a stop-payment order or order to close an account is on the customer. The loss from payment of an item contrary to a stop-payment order may include damages for dishonor of subsequent items under Section 4—402.

§ 4—406. Customers Duty to Discover and Report Unauthorized Signature or Alteration

(a)A bank that sends or makes available to a customer a statement of account showing payment of items for the account shall either return or make available to the customer the items paid or provide information in the statement of account sufficient to allow the customer reasonably to identify the items paid. The statement of account provides sufficient information if the item is described by item number, amount, and date of payment.

(b)If the items are not returned to the customer, the person retaining the items shall either retain the items or, if the items are destroyed, maintain the capacity to furnish legible copies of the items until the expiration of seven years after receipt of the items. A customer may request an item from the bank that paid the item, and that bank must provide in a reasonable time either the item or, if the item has been destroyed or is not otherwise obtainable, a legible copy of the item.

(c)If a bank sends or makes available a statement of account or items pursuant to subsection (a), the customer must exercise reasonable promptness in examining the statement or the items to determine whether any payment was not authorized because of an alteration of an item or because a purported signature by or on behalf of the customer was not authorized. If, based on the statement or items provided, the customer should reasonably have discovered the unauthorized payment, the customer must promptly notify the bank of the relevant facts.

(d)If the bank proves that the customer failed, with respect to an item, to comply with the duties imposed on the customer by subsection (c), the customer is precluded from asserting against the bank:

(1)the customers unauthorized signature or any alteration on the item, if the bank also proves that it suffered a loss by reason of the failure; and

(2)the customers unauthorized signature signature or alteration by the same wrongdoer on any other item paid in good faith by the bank if the payment was made before the bank received notice from the customer of the unauthorized signature or alteration and after the customer had been afforded a reasonable period of time, not exceeding 30 days, in which to examine the item or statement of account and notify the bank.

(e)If subsection (d) applies and the customer proves that the bank failed to exercise ordinary care in paying the item and that the failure substantially contributed to loss, the loss is allocated between the customer precluded and the bank asserting the preclusion according to the extent to which the failure of the customer to comply with subsection (c) and the failure of the bank to exercise ordinary care contributed to the loss. If the customer proves that the bank did not pay the item in good faith, the preclusion under subsection (d) does not apply.

(f)Without regard to care or lack of care of either the customer or the bank, a customer who does not within one year after the statement or items are made available to the customer (subsection (a)) discover and report the customers unauthorized signature on or any alteration on the item is precluded from asserting against the bank the unauthorized signature or alteration. If there is a preclusion under this subsection, the payor bank may not recover for breach of warranty under Section 4—208 with respect to the unauthorized signature or alteration to which the preclusion applies.

Article 4A

Funds Transfers

Part 1
Subject Matter and Definitions

§ 4A—103. Payment Order, Definitions

(a)In this Article:

(1)Payment order means an instruction of a sender to a receiving bank, transmitted orally, electronically, or in writing, to pay, or to cause another bank to pay, a fixed or determinable amount of money to a beneficiary if:

(i)the instruction does not state a condition to payment to the beneficiary other than time of payment,

(ii)the receiving bank is to be reimbursed by debiting an account of, or otherwise receiving payment from, the sender, and

(iii)the instruction is transmitted by the sender directly to the receiving bank or to an agent, funds-transfer system, or communication system for transmittal to the receiving bank.

(2)Beneficiary means the person to be paid by the beneficiarys bank.

(3)Beneficiarys bank means the bank identified in a payment order in which an account of the beneficiary is to be credited pursuant to the order or which otherwise is to make payment to the beneficiary if the order does not provide for payment to an account.

(4)Receiving bank means the bank to which the senders instruction is addressed.

(5)Sender means the person giving the instruction to the receiving bank.

(b)If an instruction complying with subsection (a)(1) is to make more than one payment to a beneficiary, the instruction is a separate payment order with respect to each payment.

(c)A payment order is issued when it is sent to the receiving bank.

§ 4A—104. Funds Transfers; Definitions

In this Article:

(a)Funds transfer means the series of transactions, beginning with the originators payment order, made for the purpose of making payment of the beneficiary of the order. The term includes any payment order issued by the originators bank or an intermediary bank intended to carry out the originators payment order. A funds transfer is completed by acceptance by the beneficiarys bank of a payment order for the benefit of the beneficiary of the originators payment order.

(b)Intermediary bank means a receiving bank other than the originators bank or the beneficiarys bank.

(c)Originator means the sender of the first payment order in a funds transfer.

(d)Originators bank means (i) the receiving bank to which the payment order of the originator is issued if the originator is not a bank, or (ii) the originator if the originator is a bank.

§ 4A—105. Other Definitions

(a)In this Article:

(1)Authorized account means a deposit account of a customer in a bank designated by the customer as a source of payment of payment orders issued by the customer to the bank. If a customer does not so designate an account, any account of the customer is an authorized account if payment of a payment order from that account is not inconsistent with a restriction on the use of that account.

(2)Bank means a person engaged in the business of banking and includes a savings bank, savings and loan association, credit union, and trust company. A branch or separate office of a bank is a separate bank for purposes of this Article.

(3)Customer means a person, including a bank, having an account with a bank or from whom a bank has agreed to receive payment orders.

(4)Funds-transfer business day of a receiving bank means the part of a day during which the receiving bank is open for the receipt, processing, and transmittal of payment orders and cancellations and amendments of payment orders.

(5)Funds-transfer system means a wire transfer network, automated clearing house, or other communication system of a clearing house or other association of banks through which a payment order by a bank may be transmitted to the bank to which the order is addressed.

(6)Good faith means honesty in fact and the observance of reasonable commercial standards of fair dealing.

...

§ 4A—108. Exclusion of Consumer Transactions Governed by Federal Law

This Article does not apply to a funds transfer any part of which is governed by the Electronic Fund Transfer Act of 1978 (Title XX, Public Law 95630, 92 Stat. 3728, 15 U.S.C. 1693 et seq.) as amended from time to time.

Part 2
Issue and Acceptance of Payment Orders

§ 4A—201. Security Procedure

Security procedure means a procedure established by agreement of a customer and a receiving bank for the purpose of (i) verifying that a payment order or communication amending or cancelling a payment order is that of the customer, or (ii) detecting error in the transmission or the content of the payment order or communication. A security procedure may require the use of algorithms or other codes, identifying words or numbers, encryption, callback procedures, or similar security devices. Comparisons of a signature on a payment order or communication with an authorized specimen signature of the customer is not by itself a security procedure.

§ 4A—202. Authorized and Verified Payment Orders

(a)A payment order received by the receiving bank is the authorized order of the person identified as sender if that person authorized the order or is otherwise bound by it under the law of agency.

(b)If a bank and its customer have agreed that the authenticity of payment orders issued to the bank in the name of the customer as sender will be verified pursuant to a security procedure, a payment order received by the receiving bank is effective as the order of the customer, whether or not authorized, if (i) the security procedure is a commercially reasonable method of providing security against unauthorized payment orders, and (ii) the bank proves that it accepted the payment order in

good faith and in compliance with the security procedure and any written agreement or instruction of the customer restricting acceptance of payment orders issued in the name of the customer. The bank is not required to follow an instruction that violates a written agreement with the customer or notice of which is not received at a time and in a manner affording the bank a reasonable opportunity to act on it before the payment order is accepted.

(c)Commercial reasonableness of a security procedure is a question of law to be determined by considering the wishes of the customer expressed to the bank, the circumstances of the customer known to the bank, including the size, type, and frequency of payment orders normally issued by the customer to the bank, alternative security procedures offered to the customer, and security procedures in general use by customers and receiving banks similarly situated. A security procedure is deemed to be commercially reasonable if (i) the security procedure was chosen by the customer after the bank offered, and the customer refused, a security procedure that was commercially reasonable for that customer, and (ii) the customer expressly agreed in writing to be bound by any payment order, whether or not authorized, issued in its name and accepted by the bank in compliance with the security procedure chosen by the customer.

(d)The term sender in this Article includes the customer in whose name a payment order is issued if the order is the authorized order of the customer under subsection (a), or it is effective as the order of the customer under subsection (b).

(e)This section applies to amendments and cancellations of payment orders to the same extent it applies to payment orders.

(f)Except as provided in this section and in Section 4A—203(a)(1), rights and obligations arising under this section or Section 4A—203 may not be varied by agreement.

§ 4A—204. Refund of Payment and Duty of Customer to Report With Respect to Unauthorized Payment Orders

(a)If a receiving bank accepts a payment order issued in the name of its customer as sender which is (i) not authorized and most effective as the order of the customer under Section 4A—202, or (ii) not enforceable, in whole or in part, against the customer under Section 4A—203, the bank shall refund any payment of the payment order received from the customer to the extent the bank is not entitled to enforce payment and shall pay interest on the refundable amount calculated from the date the bank received payment to the date of the refund. However, the customer is not entitled to interest from the bank on the amount to be refunded if the customer fails to exercise ordinary care to determine that the order was not authorized by the customer and to notify the bank of the relevant facts within a reasonable time not exceeding 90 days after the date the customer received notification from the bank that the order was accepted or that the customers account was debited with respect to the order. The bank is not entitled to any recovery from the customer on account of a failure by the customer to give notification as stated in this section.

(b)Reasonable time under subsection (a) may be fixed by agreement as stated in Section 1—204(1), but the obligation of a receiving bank to refund payment as stated in subsection (a) may not otherwise be varied by agreement.

§ 4A—205. Erroneous Payment Orders

(a)If an accepted payment order was transmitted pursuant to a security procedure for the detection of error and the payment order (i) erroneously instructed payment to a beneficiary not intended by the sender, (ii) erroneously instructed payment in an amount greater than the amount intended by the sender, or (iii) was an erroneously transmitted duplicate of a payment order previously sent by the sender, the following rules apply:

(1)If the sender proves that the sender or a person acting on behalf of the sender pursuant to Section 4A—206 complied with the security procedure and that the error would have been detected if the receiving bank had also complied, the sender is not obliged to pay the order to the extent stated in paragraphs (2) and (3).

(2)If the funds transfer is completed on the basis of an erroneous payment order described in clause (i) or (iii) of subsection (a), the sender is not obliged to pay the order and the receiving bank is entitled to recover from the beneficiary any amount paid to the beneficiary to the extent allowed by the law governing mistake and restitution.

(3)If the funds transfer is completed on the basis of a payment order described in clause (ii) if subsection (a), the sender is not obliged to pay the order to the extent the amount received by the beneficiary is greater than the amount intended by the sender. In that case, the receiving bank is entitled to recover from the beneficiary the excess amount received to the extent allowed by the law governing mistake and restitution.

(b)If (i) the sender of an erroneous payment order described in subsection (a) is not obliged to pay all or part of the order, and (ii) the sender receives notification from the receiving bank that the order was accepted by the bank or that the senders account was debited with respect to the order, the sender has a duty to exercise ordinary care, on the basis of information available to the sender, to discover the error with respect to the order and to advise the bank of the relevant facts within a reasonable time, not exceeding 90 days, after the banks notification was received by the sender. If the bank proves that the sender failed to perform that duty, the sender is liable to the bank for the loss the bank proves it incurred as a result of the failure, but the liability of the sender may not exceed the amount of the senders order.

(c)This section applies to amendments to payment orders to the same extent it applies to payment orders.

§ 4A—206. Transmission of Payment Order Through Funds-Transfer or Other Communication System

(a)If a payment order addressed to a receiving bank is transmitted to a funds-transfer system or other third-party communication system for transmittal to the bank, the system is deemed to be an agent of the sender for the purpose of transmitting the payment order to the bank. If there is a discrepancy between the terms of the payment order transmitted to the system and the terms of the payment order transmitted by the system to the bank, the terms of the payment order transmitted by the system to the bank, the terms of the payment order of the sender are those transmitted by the system. This section does not apply to a funds-transfer system of the Federal Reserve Banks.

(b)This section applies to cancellations and amendments of payment orders to the same extent it applies to payment orders.

§ 4A—209. Acceptance of Payment Order

(a)Subject to subsection (d), a receiving bank other than the beneficiarys bank accepts a payment order when it executes the order.

(b)Subject to subsections (c) and (d), a beneficiarys bank accepts a payment order at the earliest of the following times:

(1)when the bank (i) pays the beneficiary as stated in Section 4A—405(a) or 4A—405(b), or (ii) notifies the beneficiary of receipt of the order or that the account of the beneficiary has been credited with respect to the order unless the notice indicates that the bank is rejecting the order or that funds with respect to the order or that funds with respect to the order may not be withdrawn or used until receipt of payment from the sender of the order;

(2)when the bank receives payment of the entire amount of the senders order pursuant to Section 4A—403(a)(1) or 4A—403(a)(2); or

(3)the opening of the next funds-transfer business day of the bank following the payment date of the order if, at that time, the amount of the senders order is fully covered by a withdrawable credit balance in an authorized account of the sender or the bank has otherwise received full payment from the sender, unless the order was rejected before that time or is rejected within (i) one hour after that time, or (ii) one hour after the opening of the next business day of the sender following the payment date if that time is later. If notice of rejection is received by the sender after the payment date and the authorized account of the sender does not bear interest, the bank is obliged to pay interest to the sender on the amount of the order for the number of days elapsing after the payment date to the day the sender receives notice or learns that the order was not accepted, counting that day as an elapsed day. If the withdrawable credit balance during that period falls below the amount of the order, the amount of interest payable is reduced accordingly.

(c)Acceptance of a payment order cannot occur before the order is received by the receiving bank. Acceptance does not occur under subsection (b)(2) or (b)(3) if the beneficiary of the payment order does not have an account with the receiving bank, the account has been closed, or the receiving bank is not permitted by law to receive credits for the beneficiarys account.

(d)A payment order issued to the originators bank cannot be accepted until the payment date if the bank is the beneficiarys bank, or the execution date if the bank is not the beneficiarys bank. If the originators bank executes the originators payment order before the execution date or pays the beneficiary of the originators payment order before the payment date and the payment order is subsequently canceled pursuant to Section 4A—211(b), the bank may recover from the beneficiary any payment received to the extent allowed by the law governing mistake and restitution.

Part 3
Execution of Senders Payment Order by Receiving Bank

§ 4A—301. Execution and Execution Date

(a)A payment order is executed by the receiving bank when it issues a payment order intended to carry out the payment order received by the bank. A payment order received by the beneficiarys bank can be accepted but cannot be executed.

(b)Execution date of a payment order means the day on which the receiving bank may properly issue a payment order in execution of the senders order. The execution date may be determined by instruction of the sender but cannot be earlier than the day the order is received and, unless otherwise determined, is the day the order is received. If the senders instruction states a payment date, the execution date is the payment date or an earlier date on which execution is reasonably necessary to allow payment to the beneficiary on the payment date.

§ 4A—302. Obligations of Receiving Bank in Execution of Payment Orders

(a)Except as provided in subsections (b) through (d), if the receiving bank accepts a payment order pursuant to Section 4A—209(a), the bank has the following obligations in executing the order:

(1)The receiving bank is obliged to issue, on the execution date, a payment order complying with the senders order and to follow the senders instructions concerning (i) any intermediary bank or funds-transfer system to be used in carrying out the funds transfer, or (ii) the means by which payment orders are to be transmitted in the funds transfer. If the originators bank issues a payment order to an intermediary bank, the originators bank is obliged to instruct the intermediary bank according to the instruction of the originator. An intermediary bank in the funds transfer is similarly bound by an instruction given to it by the sender of the payment order it accepts.

(2)If the senders instruction states that the funds transfer is to be carried out telephonically or by wire transfer or otherwise indicates that the funds transfer is to be carried out by the most expeditious means, the receiving bank is obliged to transmit its payment order by the most expeditious available means, and to instruct any intermediary bank accordingly. If a senders instruction states a payment date, the receiving bank is obliged to transmit its payment order at a time and by means reasonably necessary to allow payment to the beneficiary on the payment date or as soon thereafter as is feasible.

(b)Unless otherwise instructed, a receiving bank executing a payment order may (i) use any funds-transfer system if use of that system is reasonable in the circumstances, and (ii) issue a payment order to the beneficiarys bank or to an intermediary bank through which a payment order conforming to the senders order can expeditiously be issued to the beneficiarys bank if the receiving bank exercises ordinary care in the selection of the intermediary bank. A receiving bank is not required to follow an instruction of the sender designating a funds-transfer system to be used in carrying out the funds transfer if the receiving bank, in good faith, determines that it is not feasible to follow the instruction or that following the instruction would unduly delay completion of the funds transfer.

(c)Unless subsection (a)(2) applies or the receiving bank is otherwise instructed, the bank may execute a payment order by transmitting its payment order by first class mail or by any means reasonable in the circumstances. If the receiving bank is instructed to execute the senders order by transmitting its payment order by a particular means, the receiving bank may issue its payment order by the means stated or by any means as expeditious as the means stated.

(d)Unless instructed by the sender, (i) the receiving bank may not obtain payment of its charges for services and expenses in connection with the execution of the senders order by issuing a payment order in an amount equal to the amount of the senders order less the amount of the charges, and (ii) may not instruct a subsequent receiving bank to obtain payment of its charges in the same manner.

§ 4A—303. Erroneous Execution of Payment Order

(a)A receiving bank that (i) executes the payment order of the sender by issuing a payment order in an amount greater than the amount of the senders order, or (ii) issues a payment order in execution of the senders order and then issues a duplicate order, is entitled to payment of the amount of the senders order under Section 4A—402(c) if that subsection is otherwise satisfied. The bank is entitled to recover from the beneficiary of the erroneous order the excess payment received to the extent allowed by the law governing mistake and restitution.

(b)A receiving bank that executes the payment order of the sender by issuing a payment order in an amount less than the amount of the senders order is entitled to payment of the amount of the senders order under Section 4A—402(c) if (i) that subsection is otherwise satisfied and (ii) the bank corrects its mistake by issuing an additional payment order for the benefit of the beneficiary of the senders order.

If the error is not corrected, the issuer of the erroneous order is entitled to receive or retain payment from the sender of the order it accepted only to the extent of the amount of the erroneous order. This subsection does not apply if the receiving bank executes the senders payment order by issuing a payment order in an amount less than the amount of the senders order for the purpose of obtaining payment of its charges for services and expenses pursuant to instruction of the sender.

(c)If a receiving bank executes the payment order of the sender by issuing a payment order to a beneficiary different from the beneficiary of the senders order and the funds transfer is completed on the basis of that error, the sender of the payment order that was erroneously executed and all previous senders in the funds transfer are not obliged to pay the payment orders they issued. The issuer of the erroneous order is entitled to recover from the beneficiary of the order the payment received to the extent allowed by the law governing mistake and restitution.

§ 4A—305. Liability for Late or Improper Execution or Failure to Execute Payment Order

(a)If a funds transfer is completed but execution of a payment order by the receiving bank in breach of Section 4A—302 results in delay in payment to the beneficiary, the bank is obliged to pay interest to either the originator or the beneficiary of the funds transfer for the period of delay caused by the improper execution. Except as provided in subsection (c), additional damages are not recoverable.

(b)If execution of a payment order by a receiving bank in breach of Section 4A—302 results in (i) noncompletion of the funds transfer, (ii) failure to use an intermediary bank designated by the originator, or (iii) issuance of a payment order that does not comply with the terms of the payment order of the originator, the bank is liable to the originator for its expenses in the funds transfer and for incidental expenses and interest losses, to the extent not covered by subsection (a), resulting from the improper execution. Except as provided in subsection (c), additional damages are not recoverable.

(c)In addition to the amounts payable under subsections (a) and (b), damages, including consequential damages, are recoverable to the extent provided in an express written agreement of the receiving bank.

(d)If a receiving bank fails to execute a payment order it was obliged by express agreement to execute, the receiving bank is liable to the sender for its expenses in the transaction and for incidental expenses and interest losses resulting from the failure to execute. Additional damages, including consequential damages, are recoverable to the extent provided in an express written agreement of the receiving bank, but are not otherwise recoverable.

(e)Reasonable attorneys fees are recoverable if demand for compensation under subsection (a) or (b) is made and reused before an action is brought on the claim. If a claim is made for breach of an agreement under subsection (d) and the agreement does not provide for damages, reasonable attorneys fees are recoverable if demand for compensation under subsection (d) is made and refused before an action is brought on the claim.

(f)Except as stated in this section, the liability of a receiving bank under subsections (a) and (b) may not be varied by agreement.

Part 4
Payment

§ 4A—401. Payment Date

Payment date of a payment order means the day on which the amount of the order is payable to the beneficiary by the beneficiarys bank. The payment date may be determined by instruction of the sender but cannot be earlier than the day the order is received by the beneficiarys bank and, unless otherwise determined, is the day the order is received by the beneficiarys bank.

§ 4A—405. Payment by Beneficiarys Bank to Beneficiary

(a)If the beneficiarys bank credits an account of the beneficiary of a payment order, payment of the banks obligation under Section 4A—404(a) occurs when and to the extent (i) the beneficiary is notified of the right to withdraw the credit, (ii) the bank lawfully applies the credit to a debt of the beneficiary, or (iii) funds with respect to the order are otherwise made available to the beneficiary by the bank.

(b)If the beneficiarys bank does not credit an account of the beneficiary of a payment order, the time when payment of the banks obligation under Section 4A—404(a) occurs is governed by principles of law that determine when an obligation is satisfied.

(c)Except as stated in subsections (d) and (e), if the beneficiarys bank pays the beneficiary of a payment order under a condition to payment or agreement of the beneficiary giving the bank the right to recover payment from the beneficiary if the bank does not receive payment of the order, the condition to payment or agreement is not enforceable.

(d)A funds-transfer system rule may provide that payments made to beneficiaries of funds transfers made through the system are provisional until receipt of payment by the beneficiarys bank of the payment order it accepted. A beneficiarys bank that makes a payment that is provisional under the rule is entitled to refund from the beneficiary if (i) the rule requires that both the beneficiary and the originator be given notice of the provisional nature of the payment before the funds transfer is initiated, (ii) the beneficiary, the beneficiarys bank and the originators bank agreed to be bound by the rule, and (iii) the beneficiarys bank did not receive payment of the payment order that it accepted. If the beneficiary is obliged to refund payment to the beneficiarys bank, acceptance of the payment order by the beneficiarys bank is nullified and no payment by the originator of the funds transfer to the beneficiary occurs under Section 4A—406.

. . .

§ 4A—406. Payment by Originator to Beneficiary; Discharge of Underlying Obligation

(a)Subject to Sections 4—A211(e), 4A4—05(d), and 4A—405(e), the originator of a funds transfer pays the beneficiary of the originators payment order (i) at the time a payment order for the benefit of the beneficiary is accepted by the beneficiarys bank in the funds transfer and (ii) in an amount equal to the amount of the order accepted by the bene-

ficiarys bank, but not more than the amount of the originators order.

(b)If payment under subsection (a) is made to satisfy an obligation, the obligation is discharged to the same extent discharge would result from payment to the beneficiary of the same amount in money, unless (i) the payment under subsection (a)was made by a means prohibited by the contract of the beneficiary with respect to the obligation, (ii) the beneficiary, within a reasonable time after receiving notice of receipt of the order by the beneficiarys bank, notified the originator of the beneficiarys refusal of the payment, (iii) funds with respect to the order were not withdrawn by the beneficiary or applied to a debt of the beneficiary, and (iv) the beneficiary would suffer a loss that could reasonably have been avoided if payment had been made by a means complying with the contract. If payment by the originator does not result in discharge under this section, the originator is subrogated to the rights of the beneficiary to receive payment from the beneficiarys bank under Section 4A—404(a).

(c)For the purpose of determining whether discharge of an obligation occurs under subsection (b), if the beneficiarys bank accepts a payment order in an amount equal to the amount of the originators payment order less charges of one or more receiving banks in the funds transfer, payment to the beneficiary is deemed to be in the amount of the originators order unless upon demand by the beneficiary the originator does not pay the beneficiary the amount of the deducted charges.

(d)Rights of the originator or of the beneficiary of a funds transfer under this section may be varied only by agreement of the originator and the beneficiary.

Part 5
Miscellaneous Provisions

§ 4A—501. Variation by Agreement and Effect of Funds-Transfer System Rule

(a)Except as otherwise provided in this Article, the rights and obligations of a party to a funds transfer may be varied by agreement of the affected party.

(b)Funds-transfer system rule means a rule of an association of banks (i) governing transmission of payment orders by means of a funds-transfer system of the association or rights and obligations with respect to those orders, or (ii) to the extent the rule governs rights and obligations between banks that are parties to a funds transfer in which a Federal Reserve Bank, acting as an intermediary bank, sends a payment order to the beneficiarys bank. Except as otherwise provided in this Article, a funds-transfer system rule governing rights and obligations between participating banks using the system may be effective even if the rule conflicts with this Article and indirectly affects another party to the funds transfer who does not consent to the rule. A funds-transfer system rule may also govern rights and obligations of parties other than participating banks using the system to the extent stated in Sections 4A—404(c), 4A—405(d), and 4A—507(c).

§ 4A—503. Injunction or Restraining Order With Respect to Funds Transfer

For proper cause and in compliance with applicable law, a court may restrain (i) a person from issuing a payment order to initiate a funds transfer, (ii) an originators bank from executing the payment order of the originator, or (iii) the beneficiarys bank from releasing funds to the beneficiary or the beneficiary from withdrawing the funds. A court may not otherwise restrain a person from issuing a payment order, paying or receiving payment of a payment order, or otherwise acting with respect to a funds transfer.

§ 4A—505. Preclusion of Objection to Debit of Customers Account

If a receiving bank has received payment from its customer with respect to a payment order issued in the name of the customer as sender and accepted by the bank, and the customer received notification reasonably identifying the order, the customer is precluded from asserting that the bank is not entitled to retain the payment unless the customer notifies the bank of the customers objection to the payment within one year after the notification was received by the customer.

Article 5

Letters of Credit

§ 5—102. Scope

(1)This Article applies

(a)to a credit issued by a bank, if the credit requires a documentary draft or a documentary demand for payment; and

(b)to a credit issued by a person other than a bank, if the credit requires that the draft or demand for payment be accompanied by a document of title; and

(c)to a credit issued by a bank or other person, if the credit is not within subparagraphs (a) or (b) but conspicuously states that it is a letter of credit or is conspicuously so entitled.

(2)Unless the engagement meets the requirements of subsection (1), this Article does not apply to engagements to make advances or to honor drafts or demands for payment, to authorities to pay or purchase to guarantees or to general agreements.

(3)This Article deals with some but not all of the rules and concepts of letters of credit as such rules or concepts have developed prior to this act or may hereafter develop. The fact that this Article states a rule does not by itself require, imply or negate application of the same or a converse rule to a situation not provided for or to a person not specified by this Article.

§ 5—103. Definitions

(1)In this Article unless the context otherwise requires

(a)Credit or letter of credit means an engagement by a bank or other person, made at the request of a customer and of a kind within the scope of this Article (Section 5—102), that the issuer will honor drafts or other demands for payment upon compliance with the conditions specified in the credit. A credit may be either revocable or irrevocable. The engagement may be either an agreement to honor or a statement that the bank or other person is authorized to honor.

(b)A documentary draft or a documentary demand for payment is one honor of which is conditioned upon the presentation of a document or documents. Document means any paper including document of title, security, invoice, certificate, notice of default and the like.

(c)An issuer is a bank or other person issuing a credit.

(d)A beneficiary of a credit is a person who is entitled under its terms to draw or demand payment.

(e)An advising bank is a bank which gives notification of the issuance of a credit by another bank.

(f)A confirming bank is a bank which engages either that it will itself honor a credit already issued by another bank or that such a credit will be honored by the issuer or a third bank.

(g)A customer is a buyer or other person who causes an issuer to issue a credit. The term also includes a bank which procures issuance or confirmation on behalf of that banks customer.

. . .

§ 5—104. Formal Requirements; Signing

(1)Except as otherwise required in subsection (1)(c) of Section 5—102 on scope, no particular form of phrasing is required for a credit. A credit must be in writing and signed by the issuer, and a confirmation must be in writing and signed by the confirming bank. A modification of the terms of a credit or confirmation must be signed by the issuer or confirming bank.

(2)A telegram may be a sufficient signed writing if it identifies its sender by an authorized authentication. The authentication may be in code and the authorized naming of the issuer in an advice of credit is a sufficient signing.

§ 5—105. Consideration

No consideration is necessary to establish a credit or to enlarge or otherwise modify its terms.

§ 5—106. Time and Effect of Establishment of Credit

(1)Unless otherwise agreed, a credit is established

(a)as regards the customer, as soon as a letter of credit is sent to him or the letter of credit or an authorized written advice of its issuance is sent to the beneficiary; and

(b)as regards the beneficiary, when he receives a letter of credit or an authorized written advice of its issuance.

(2)Unless otherwise agreed, once an irrevocable credit is established as regards the customer, it can be modified or revoked only with the consent of the customer; and once it is established as regards the beneficiary, it can be modified or revoked only with his consent.

(3)Unless otherwise agreed after a revocable credit is established, it may be modified or revoked by the issuer without notice to or consent from the customer or beneficiary.

(4)Notwithstanding any modification or revocation of a revocable credit, any person authorized to honor or negotiate under the terms of the original credit is entitled to reimbursement for or honor of any draft or demand for payment duly honored or negotiated before receipt of notice of the modification or revocation and the issuer in turn is entitled to reimbursement from its customer.

§ 5109. Issuers Obligation to Its Customer

(1)An issuers obligation to its customer includes good faith and observance of any general banking usage but, unless otherwise agreed, does not include liability or responsibility

(a)for performance of the underlying contract for sale or other transaction between the customer and the beneficiary; or

(b)for any act or omission of any person other than itself or its own branch or for loss or destruction of a draft, demand or document in transit or in the possession of others; or

(c)based on knowledge or lack of knowledge of any usage of any particular trade.

(2)An issuer must examine documents with care so as to ascertain that on their face they appear to comply with the terms of the credit but, unless otherwise agreed, assumes no liability or responsibility for the genuineness, falsification or effect of any document which appears on such examination to be regular on its face.

(3)A nonbank issuer is not bound by any banking usage of which it has no knowledge.

§ 5—114. Issuers Duty and Privilege to Honor; Right to Reimbursement

(1)An issuer must honor a draft or demand for payment which complies with the terms of the relevant credit regardless of whether the goods or documents conform to the underlying contract for sale or other contract between the customer and the beneficiary. The issuer is not excused from honor of such a draft or demand by reason of an additional general term that all documents must be satisfactory to the issuer, but an issuer may require that specified documents must be satisfactory to it.

(2)Unless otherwise agreed, when documents appear on their face to comply with the terms of a credit but a required document does not in fact conform to the warranties made on negotiation or transfer of a document of title (Section 7—507) or of a certificated security (Section 8—306) or is forged or fraudulent or there is fraud in the transaction

(a)the issuer must honor the draft or demand for payment, if honor is demanded by a negotiating bank or other holder of the draft or demand which has taken the draft or demand under the credit and under circumstances which would make it a holder in due course (Section 3—302) and in an appropriate case would make it a person to whom a document of title has been duly negotiated (Section 7—502) or a bona fide purchaser of a certificated security (Section 8—302); and

(b)in all other cases, as against its customer, an issuer acting in good faith may honor the draft or demand for payment despite notification from the customer of fraud, forgery or other defect not apparent on the face of the documents but a court of appropriate jurisdiction may enjoin such honor.

(3)Unless otherwise agreed, an issuer which has duly honored a draft or demand for payment is entitled to immediate reimbursement of any payment made under the credit and to be put in effectively available funds not later than the day before maturity of any acceptance made under the credit.

. . .

Article 6

Bulk Transfers [Revision]

§ 6—101. Short Title

This Article shall be known and may be cited as Uniform Commercial CodeBulk Transfers.

§ 6—102. Bulk Transfers; Transfers of Equipment; Enterprises Subject to This Article; Bulk Transfers Subject to This Article

(1)A bulk transfer is any transfer in bulk and not in the ordinary course of the transferors business of a major part of the materials, supplies, merchandise or other inventory (Section 9—109) of an enterprise subject to this Article.

(2)A transfer of a substantial part of the equipment (Section 9—109) of such an enterprise is a bulk transfer if it is made in connection with a bulk transfer of inventory, but not otherwise.

(3)The enterprises subject to this Article are all those whose principal business is the sale of merchandise from stock, including those who manufacture what they sell.

(4)Except as limited by the following section, all bulk transfers of goods located within this state are subject to this Article.

§ 6—104. Schedule of Property, List of Creditors

(1)Except as provided with respect to auction sales (Section 6—108), a bulk transfer subject to this Article is ineffective against any creditor of the transferor unless:

(a)The transferee requires the transferor to furnish a list of his existing creditors prepared as stated in this section; and

(b)The parties prepare a schedule of the property transferred sufficient to identify it; and (c)The transferee preserves the list and schedule for six months next following the transfer and permits inspection of either or both and copying therefrom at all reasonable hours by any creditor of the transferor, or files the list and schedule in (a public office to be here identified).

(2)The list of creditors must be signed and sworn to or affirmed by the transferor or his agent. It must contain the names and business addresses of all creditors of the transferor, with the amounts when known, and also the names of all persons who are known to the tr ansferor to assert claims against him even though such claims are disputed. If the transferor is the obligor of an outstanding issue of bonds, debentures or the like as to which there is an indenture trustee, the list of creditors need include only the name and address of the indenture trustee and the aggregate out standing principal amount of the issue.

(3)Responsibility for the completeness and accuracy of the list of creditors rests on the transferor, and the transfer is not rendered ineffective by errors or omissions therein unless the transferee is shown to have had knowledge.

§ 6—105. Notice to Creditors

In addition to the requirements of the preceding section, any bulk transfer subject to this Article, except one made by auction sale (Section 6—108), is ineffective against any creditor of the transferor unless at least ten days before he takes possession of the goods or pays for them, whichever happens first, the transferee gives notice of the transfer in the manner and to the persons hereafter provided (Section 6—107).

§ 6—107. The Notice

(1)The notice to creditors (Section—6105) shall state:

(a)that a bulk transfer is about to be made; and

(b)the names and business addresses of the transferor and transferee, and all other business names and addresses used by the transferor within three years last past so far as known to the transferee; and

(c)whether or not all the debts of the transferor are to be paid in full as they fall due as a result of the transaction, and if so, the address to which creditors should send their bills.

(2)If the debts of the transferor are not to be paid in full as they fall due or if the transferee is in doubt on that point, then the notice shall state further:

(a)the location and general description of the property to be transferred and the estimated total of the transferors debts;

(b)the address where the schedule of property and list of creditors (Section 6—104) may be inspected;

(c)whether the transfer is to pay existing debts and if so, the amount of such debts and to whom owing;

(d)whether the transfer is for new consideration and if so, the amount of such consideration and the time and place of payment; [and]

[(e)if for new consideration, the time and place where creditors of the transferor are to file their claims.]

(3)The notice in any case shall be delivered personally or sent by registered or certified mail to all the persons shown on the list of creditors furnished by the transferor (Section 6—104) and to all other persons who are known to the transferee to hold or assert claims against the transferor.

Note: The words in brackets are optional.

§ 6—110. Subsequent Transfers

When the title of a transferee to property is subject to a defect by reason of his noncompliance with the requirements of this Article, then:

(1)a purchaser of any of such property from such transferee who pays no value or who takes with notice of such noncompliance takes subject to such defect, but

(2)a purchaser for value in good faith and without such notice takes free of such defect.

§ 6—111. Limitation of Actions and Levies

No action under this Article shall be brought nor levy made more than six months after the date on which the transferee took possession of the goods unless the transfer has been concealed. If the transfer has been concealed, actions may be brought or levies made within six months after its discovery.

Article 6

Bulk Sales [Revision]

Alternative B

§ 6—102. Definitions and Index of Definitions [Alternative B 1989]

(1)In this Article, unless the context otherwise requires:

(a)Assets means the inventory that is the subject of a bulk sale and any tangible and intangible personal property used or held for use primarily in, or arising from, the sellers business and sold in connection with that inventory, but the term does not include:

(i)fixtures (Section 9—13(1)(a)) other than readily removable factory and office machines;

(ii)the lessees interest in a lease of real property; or

(iii)property to the extent it is generally exempt from creditor process under nonbankruptcy law.

. . .

(c)Bulk sale means:

(i)in the case of a sale by auction or a sale or series of sales conducted by a liquidator on the sellers behalf, a sale or series of sales not in the ordinary course of the sellers business of more than half of the sellers inventory, as measured by value on the date of the bulk-sale agreement, if on that date the auctioneer or liquidator has notice, or after reasonable inquiry would have had notice, that the seller will not continue to operate the same or a similar kind of business after the sale or series of sales; and

(ii)in all other cases, a sale not in the ordinary course of the sellers business of more than half the sellers inventory, as measured by value on the date of the bulk-sale agreement, if on that date the buyer has notice, or after reasonable inquiry would have had notice, that the seller will not continue to operate the same or a similar kind of business after the sale.

(d)Claim means a right to payment from the seller, whether or not the right is reduced to judgment, liquidated, fixed, matured, disputed, secured, legal, or equitable. The term includes costs of collection and attorneys fees only to the extent that the laws of this state permit the holder of the claim to recover them in an action against the obligor.

. . .

§ 6—103. Applicability of Article [Alternative B 1989]

(1)Except as otherwise provided in subsection (3), this Article applies to a bulk sale if:

(a)the sellers principal business is the sale of inventory from stock; and

(b)on the date of the bulk-sale agreement the seller is located in this state or, if the seller is located in a jurisdiction that is not a part of the United States, the sellers major executive office in the United States is in this state.

(2)A seller is deemed to be located at his [or her] place of business. If a seller has more than one place of business, the seller is deemed located at his [or her] chief executive office.

(3)This Article does not apply to:

(a)a transfer made to secure payment or performance of an obligation;

(b)a transfer of collateral to a secured party pursuant to Section 9—503;

(c)a sale of collateral pursuant to Section 9—504;

(d)retention of collateral pursuant to Section 9—505;

(e)a sale of an asset encumbered by a security interest or item if (i) all the proceeds of the sale are applied in partial or total satisfaction of the debt secured by the security interest or lien or (ii) the security interest or lien is enforceable against the asset after it has been sold to the buyer and the net contract price is zero;

(f)a general assignment for the benefit of creditors or to a subsequent transfer by the assignee;

(g)a sale by an executor, administrator, receiver, trustee in bankruptcy, or any public officer under judicial process;

(h)a sale made in the course of judicial or administrative proceedings for the dissolution or reorganization of an organization;

(i)a sale to a buyer whose principal place of business is in the United States and who:

(i)not earlier than 21 days before the date of the bulk sale, (A) obtains from the seller a verified and dated list of claimants of whom the seller has notice three days before the seller sends or delivers the list to the buyer or (B) conducts a reasonable inquiry to discover the claimants;

(ii)assumes in full the debts owed to claimants of whom the buyer has knowledge on the date the buyer receives the list of claimants from the seller or on the date the buyer completes the reasonable inquiry, as the case may be:

(iii)is not insolvent after the assumption; and

(iv)gives written notice of the assumption not later than 30 days after the date of the bulk sale by sending or delivering a notice to the claimants identified in subparagraph (ii) or by filing a notice in the office of the [Secretary of State]:

(j)a sale to a buyer whose principal place of business is in the United States and who:

(i)assumes in full the debts that were incurred in the sellers business before the date of the bulk sale;

(ii)is not insolvent after the assumption; and

(iii)gives written notice of the assumption not later than 30 days after the date of the bulk sale by sending or delivering a notice to each creditor whose debt is assumed or by filing a notice in the office of the [Secretary of State];

(k)a sale to a new organization that is organized to take over and continue the business of the seller and that has its principal place of business in the United States if:

(i)the buyer assumes in full the debts that were incurred in the sellers business before the date of the bulk sale;

(ii)the seller receives nothing from the sale except an interest in the new organization that is subordinate to the claims against the organization arising from the assumption; and

(iii)the buyer gives written notice of the assumption not later than 30 days after the date of the bulk sale by sending or delivering a notice to each creditor whose debt is assumed or by filing a notice in the office of the [Secretary of State];

(l)a sale of assets having:

(i)a value, net of liens and security interests, of less than $10,000. If a debt is secured by assets and other property of the seller, the net value of the assets is determined by subtracting from their value an amount equal to the product of the debt multiplied by a fraction, the numerator of which is the value of the assets on the date of the bulk sale and the denominator of which is the value of all property securing the debt on the date of the bulk sale; or

(ii)a value of more than $25,000,000 on the date of the bulk-sale agreement; or

(m)a sale required by, and made pursuant to statute.

. . .

§ 6—104. Obligations of Buyer [Alternative B 1989]

(1)In a bulk sale as defined in Section 6—102(1)(c)(ii) the buyer shall:

(a)obtain from the seller a list of all business names and addresses used by the seller within three years before the date the list is sent or delivered to the buyer;

(b)unless excused under subsection (2), obtain from the seller a verified and dated list of claimants of whom the seller has notice three days before the seller sends or delivers the list to the buyer and including, to the extent known by the seller, the address of and the amount claimed by each claimant;

(c)obtain from the seller or prepare a schedule of distribution (Section 6—106(1));

(d)give notice of the bulk sale in accordance with Section 6105;

(e)unless excused under Section 6—106(4), distribute the net contract price in accordance with the undertakings of the buyer in the schedule of distribution; and

(f)unless excused under subsection (2), make available the list of claimants (subsection (1)(b)) by:

(i)promptly sending or delivering a copy of the list without charge to any claimant whose written request is received by the buyer no later than six months after the date of the bulk sale;

(ii)permitting any claimant to inspect and copy the list at any reasonable hour upon request received by the buyer no later than six months after the date of the bulk sale; or

(iii)filing a copy of the list in the office of the [Secretary of State] no later than the time for giving a notice of the bulk sale (Section 6—105(5)). A list filed in accordance with this subparagraph must state the individual, partnership, or corporate name and a mailing address of the seller.

. . .

§ 6—105. Notice to Claimants [Alternative B 1989]

(1)Except as otherwise provided in subsection (2), to comply with Section 6—104(1)(d) the buyer shall send or deliver a written notice of the bulk sale to each claimant on the list of claimants (Section 6—104(1)(b)) and to any other claimant of whom the buyer has knowledge at the time the notice of the bulk sale is sent or delivered.

(2)A buyer may comply with Section 6—104(1)(d) by filing a written notice of the bulk sale in the office of the [Secretary of State] if:

(a)on the date of the bulk-sale agreement the seller has 200 or more claimants, exclusive of claimants holding secured or matured claims for employment compensation and benefits, including commissions and vacation, severance, and sick-leave pay; or

(b)the buyer has received a verified statement from the seller stating that, as of the date of the bulk-sale agreement, the number of claimants, exclusive of claimants holding secured or matured claims for employment compensation and benefits, including commissions and vacation, severance, and sick-leave pay, is 200 or more.

(3)The written notice of the bulk sale must be accompanied by a copy of the schedule of distribution (Section 6—106(1)) and state at least:

(a)that the seller and buyer have entered into an agreement for a sale that may constitute a bulk sale under the laws of the State of _____ ;

(b)the date of the agreement;

(c)the date on or after which more than ten percent of the assets were or will be transferred;

(d)the date on or after which more than ten percent of the net contract price was or will be paid, if the date is not stated in the schedule of distribution;

(e)the name and a mailing address of the seller;

(f)any other business name and address listed by the seller pursuant to Section 6—104(1)(a);

(g)the name of the buyer and an address of the buyer from which information concerning the sale can be obtained;

(h)a statement indicating the type of assets or describing the assets item by item;

(i)the manner in which the buyer will make available the list of claimants (Section 6—104(1)(f)), if applicable; and

(j)if the sale is in total or partial satisfaction of an antecedent debt owed by the seller; the amount of the debt to be satisfied and the name of the person to whom it is owed.

(4)For purposes of subsections (3)(e) and (3)(g), the name of a person is the persons individual, partnership, or corporate name.

(5)The buyer shall give notice of the bulk sale not less than 45 days before the date of the bulk sale and, if the buyer gives notice in accordance with subsection (l), not more than 30 days after obtaining the list of claimants.

(6)A written notice substantially complying with the requirements of subsection (3) is effective even though it contains minor errors that are not seriously misleading.

§ 6—106. Schedule of Distribution [Alternative B 1989]

(1)The seller and buyer shall agree on how the net contract price is to be distributed and set forth their agreement in a written schedule of distribution.

(2)The schedule of distribution may provide for distribution to any person at any time, including distribution of the entire net contract price to the seller.

(3)The buyers undertakings in the schedule of distribution run only to the seller. However, a buyer who fails to distribute the net contract price in accordance with the buyers undertakings in the schedule of distribution is liable to a creditor only as provided in Section 6—107(1).

. . .

§ 6—107. Liability for Noncompliance [Alternative B 1989]

(1)Except as provided in subsection (3), and subject to the limitation in subsection (4):

(a)a buyer who fails to comply with the requirements of Section 6—104(1)(e) with respect to a creditor is liable to the creditor for damages in the amount of the claim, reduced by any amount that the creditor would not have realized if the buyer had complied; and

(b)a buyer who fails to comply with the requirements of any other subsection of Section 6—104 with respect to a claimant is liable to the claimant for damages in the amount of the claim, reduced by any amount that the claimant would not have realized if the buyer had complied.

(2)In an action under subsection (1), the creditor has the burden of establishing the validity and amount of the claim, and the buyer has the burden of establishing the amount that the creditor would not have realized if the buyer had complied.

(3)A buyer who:

(a)made a good faith and commercially reasonable effort to comply with the requirements of Section 6—104(1) or to exclude the sale from the application of this Article under Section 6—103(3); or

(b)on or after the date of the bulk sale agreement, but before the date of the bulk sale, held a good faith and commercially reasonable belief that this Article does not apply to the particular sale is not liable to creditors for failure to comply with the requirements of Section 6—104. The buyer has the burden of establishing the good faith and commercial reasonableness of the effort or belief.

(4)In a single bulk sale the cumulative liability of the buyer for failure to comply with the requirements of Section 6—104(1) may not exceed an amount equal to:

(a)if the assets consist only of inventory and equipment, twice the net contract price, less the amount of any part of the net contract price paid to or applied for the benefit of the seller or a creditor; or

(b)if the assets include property other than inventory and equipment, twice the net value of the inventory and equipment less the amount of the portion of any part of the net contract price paid to or applied for the benefit of the seller or a creditor which is allocable to the inventory and equipment.

. . .

§ 6—110. Limitation of Actions [Alternative B 1989]

(1)Except as provided in subsection (2), an action under this Article against a buyer, auctioneer, or liquidator must be commenced within one year after the date of the bulk sale.

(2)If the buyer, auctioneer, or liquidator conceals the fact that the sale has occurred, the limitation is tolled and an action under this Article may be commenced within the earlier of (i) one year after the person bringing the action discovers that the sale has occurred or (ii) one year after the person bringing the action should have discovered that the sale has occurred, but no later than two years after the date of the bulk sale. Complete noncompliance with the requirements of this Article does not of itself constitute concealment.

. . .

Article 7
Warehouse Receipts, Bills of Lading and Other Documents of Title

Part 1
General

§ 7—104. Negotiable and Nonnegotiable Warehouse Receipt, Bill of Lading or Other Document of Title

(1)A warehouse receipt, bill of lading or other document of title is negotiable

(a)if by its terms the goods are to be delivered to bearer or to the order of a named person; or

(b)where recognized in overseas trade, if it runs to a named person or assigns.

(2)Any other document is nonnegotiable. A bill of lading in which it is stated that the goods are consigned to a named person is not made negotiable by a provision that the goods are to be delivered only against a written order signed by the same or another named person.

Part 2
Warehouse Receipts: Special Provisions

§ 7—202. Form of Warehouse Receipt; Essential Terms; Optional Terms

(1)A warehouse receipt need not be in any particular form.

(2)Unless a warehouse receipt embodies within its written or printed terms each of the following, the warehouseman is liable for damages caused by the omission to a person injured thereby:

(a)the location of the warehouse where the goods are stored;

(b)the date of issue of the receipt;

(c)the consecutive number of the receipt;

(d)a statement whether the goods received will be delivered to the bearer, to a specified person, or to a specified person or his order;

(e)the rate of storage and handling charges, except that where goods are stored under a field warehousing arrangement a statement of that fact is sufficient on a non-negotiable receipt;

(f)a description of the goods or of the packages containing them;

(g)the signature of the warehouseman, which may be made by his authorized agent;

(h)if the receipt is issued for goods of which the warehouseman is owner, either solely or jointly or in common with others, the fact of such ownership; and

(i)a statement of the amount of advances made and of liabilities incurred for which the warehouseman claims a lien or security interest (Section 7—209). If the precise amount of such advances made or of such liabilities incurred is, at the time of the issue of the receipt, unknown to the warehouseman or to his agent who issues it, a statement of the fact that advances have been made or liabilities incurred and the purpose thereof is sufficient.

(3)A warehouseman may insert in his receipt any other terms which are not contrary to the provisions of this Act and do not impair his obligation of delivery (Section 7—403) or his duty of care (Section 7—204). Any contrary provisions shall be ineffective.

§ 7—203. Liability for Non-Receipt or Misdescription

A party to or purchaser for value in good faith of a document of title other than a bill of lading relying in either case upon the description therein of the goods may recover from the issuer damages caused by the non-receipt or misdescription of the goods, except to the extent that the document conspicuously indicates that the issuer does not know whether any part or all of the goods in fact were received or conform to the description, as where the description is in terms of marks or labels or kind, quantity or condition, or the receipt or description is qualified by contents, condition and quality unknown, said to contain or the like, if such indication be true, or the party or purchaser otherwise has notice.

§ 7—204. Duty of Care; Contractual Limitation of Warehousemans Liability

(1)A warehouseman is liable for damages for loss of or injury to the goods caused by his failure to exercise such care in regard to them as a reasonably careful man would exercise under like circumstances but, unless otherwise agreed, he is not liable for damages which could not have been avoided by the exercise of such care.

(2)Damages may be limited by a term in the warehouse receipt or storage agreement limiting the amount of liability in case of loss or damage, and setting forth a specific liability per article or item, or value per unit of weight, beyond which the warehouseman shall not be liable; provided, however, that such liability may on written request of the bailor at the time of signing such storage agreement or within a reasonable time after receipt of the warehouse receipt be increased on part or all of the goods thereunder, in which event increased rates may be charged based on such increased valuation, but that no such increase shall be permitted contrary to a lawful limitation of liability contained in the warehousemans tariff, if any. No such limitation is effective with respect to the warehousemans liability for conversion to his own use.

(3)Reasonable provisions as to the time and manner of presenting claims and instituting actions based on the bailment may be included in the warehouse receipt or tariff.

§ 7—205. Title Under Warehouse Receipt Defeated in Certain Cases

A buyer in the ordinary course of business of fungible goods sold and delivered by a warehouseman who is also in the business of buying and selling such goods takes free of any claim under a warehouse receipt even though it has been duly negotiated.

§ 7—209. Lien of Warehouseman

(1)A warehouseman has a lien against the bailor on the goods covered by a warehouse receipt or on the proceeds thereof in his possession for charges for storage or transportation (including demurrage and terminal charges), insurance, labor, or charges present or future in relation to the goods, and for expenses necessary for preservation of the goods or reasonably incurred in their sale pursuant to law. If the person on whose account the goods are held is liable for like charges or expenses in relation to other goods whenever deposited and it is stated in the receipt that a lien is claimed for charges and expenses in relation to other goods, the warehouseman also has a lien against him for such charges and expenses whether or not the other goods have been delivered by the warehouseman. But against a person to whom a negotiable warehouse receipt is duly negotiated, a warehousemans lien is limited to charges in an amount or at a rate specified on the receipt or if no charges are so specified then to a reasonable charge for storage of the goods covered by the receipt subsequent to the date of the receipt.

(2)The warehouseman may also reserve a security interest against the bailor for a maximum amount specified on the receipt for charges other than those specified in subsection (1), such as for money advanced and interest. Such a security interest is governed by the Article on Secured Transactions (Article 9).

(3)(a)A warehousemans lien for charges and expenses under subsection (1) or a security interest under subsection (2) is also effective against any person who so entrusted the bailor with possession of the goods that a pledge of them by him to a good faith purchaser for value would have been valid but is not effective against a person as to whom the document confers no right in the goods covered by it under Section 7—503.

(b)A warehousemans lien on household goods for charges and expenses in relation to the goods under subsection (1) is also effective against all persons if the depositor was the legal possessor of the goods at the time of deposit. Household goods means furniture, furnishings and personal effects used by the depositor in a dwelling.

(4)A warehouseman loses his lien on any goods which he voluntarily delivers or which he unjustifiably refuses to deliver.

Part 3
Bills of Lading: Special Provisions

§ 7—301. Liability for Non-Receipt or Misdescription; Said to Contain; Shippers Load and Count; Improper Handling

(1)A consignee of a nonnegotiable bill who has given value in good faith or a holder to whom a negotiable bill has been duly negotiated relying in either case upon the description therein of the goods, or upon the date therein shown, may recover from the issuer damages caused by the misdating of the bill or the non-receipt or misdescription of the goods, except to the extent that the document indicates that the issuer does not know whether any part or all of the goods in fact were received or conform to the description, as where the description is in terms of marks or labels or kind, quantity, or condition or the receipt or description is qualified by contents or condition of contents of packages unknown, said to contain, shippers weight, load and count or the like, if such indication be true.

(2)When goods are loaded by an issuer who is a common carrier, the issuer must count the packages of goods if package freight and ascertain the kind and quantity if bulk freight. In such cases, shippers weight, load and count or other words indicating that the description was made by the shipper are ineffective except as to freight concealed by packages.

(3)When bulk freight is loaded by a shipper who makes available to the issuer adequate facilities for weighing such freight, an issuer who is a common carrier must ascertain the kind and quantity within a reasonable time after receiving the written request of the shipper to do so. In such cases, shippers weight or other words of like purport are ineffective.

(4)The issuer may by inserting in the bill the words shippers weight, load and count or other words of like purport indicate that the goods were loaded by the shipper, and if such statement be true, the issuer shall not be liable for damages caused by the improper loading. But their omission does not imply liability for such damages.

(5)The shipper shall be deemed to have guaranteed to the issuer the accuracy at the time of shipment of the description, marks, labels, number, kind, quantity, condition and weight, as furnished by him; and the shipper shall indemnify the issuer against damage caused by inaccuracies in such particulars. The right of the issuer to such indemnity shall in no way limit his responsibility and liability under the contract of carriage to any person other than the shipper.

§ 7—307. Lien of Carrier

(1)A carrier has a lien on the goods covered by a bill of lading for charges subsequent to the date of its receipt of the goods for storage or transportation (including demurrage and terminal charges) and for expenses necessary for preservation of the goods incident to their transportation or reasonably incurred in their sale pursuant to law. But against a purchaser for value of a negotiable bill of lading, a carriers lien is limited to charges stated in the bill or the applicable tariffs, or if no charges are stated then to a reasonable charge.

(2)A lien for charges and expenses under subsection (1) on goods which the carrier was required by law to receive for transportation is effective against the consignor or any person entitled to the goods unless the carrier had notice that the consignor lacked authority to subject the goods to such charges and expenses. Any other lien under subsection (1) is effective against the consignor and any person who permitted the bailor to have control or possession of the goods unless the carrier had notice that the bailor lacked such authority.

(3)A carrier loses his lien on any goods which he voluntarily delivers or which he unjustifiably refuses to deliver.

§ 7—309. Duty of Care; Contractual Limitation of Carriers Liability

(1)A carrier who issues a bill of lading, whether negotiable or nonnegotiable, must exercise the degree of care in relation to the goods which a reasonably careful man would exercise under like circumstances. This subsection does not repeal or change any law or rule of law which imposes liability upon a common carrier for damages not caused by its negligence.

(2)Damages may be limited by a provision that the carriers liability shall not exceed a value stated in the document if the carriers rates are dependent upon value and the consignor by the carriers tariff is afforded an opportunity to declare a higher value or a value as lawfully provided in the tariff, or, where no tariff is filed, he is otherwise advised of such opportunity; but no such limitation is effective with respect to the carriers liability for conversion to its own use.

(3)Reasonable provisions as to the time and manner of presenting claims and instituting actions based on the shipment may be included in a bill of lading or tariff.

Part 4
Warehouse Receipts and Bills of Lading: General Obligations

§ 7—401. Irregularities in Issue of Receipt or Bill or Conduct or Issuer

The obligations imposed by this Article on an issuer apply to a document of title regardless of the fact that

(a)the document may not comply with the requirements of this Article or of any other law or regulation regarding its issue, form or content; or (b)the issuer may have violated laws regulating the conduct of his business; or

(c)the goods covered by the document were owned by the bailee at the time the document was issued; or

(d)the person issuing the document does not come within the definition of warehouseman, if it purports to be a warehouse receipt.

§ 7—403. Obligation of Warehouseman or Carrier to Deliver; Excuse

(1)The bailee must deliver the goods to a person entitled under the document who complies with subsections (2) and (3), unless and to the extent that the bailee establishes any of the following:

(a)delivery of the goods to a person whose receipt was rightful as against the claimant;

(b)damage to or delay, loss or destruction of the goods for which the bailee is not liable [, but the burden of establishing negligence in such cases is on the person entitled under the document];

Note: The brackets in (1)(b) indicate that State enactments may differ on this point without serious damage to the principle of uniformity.

(c)previous sale or other disposition of the goods in lawful enforcement of a lien or on warehousemans lawful termination of storage;

(d)the exercise by a seller of his right to stop delivery pursuant to the provisions of the Article on Sales (Section 2—705);

(e)a diversion, reconsignment or other disposition pursuant to the provisions of this Article (Section 7—303) or tariff regulating such right;

(f)release, satisfaction or any other fact affording a personal defense against the claimant;

(g)any other lawful excuse.

(2)A person claiming goods covered by a document of title must satisfy the bailees lien where the bailee so requests or where the bailee is prohibited by law from delivering the goods until the charges are paid.

(3)Unless the person claiming is one against whom the document confers no right

under Sec. 7—503(1), he must surrender for cancellation or notation of partial deliveries any outstanding negotiable document covering the goods, and the bailee must cancel the document or conspicuously note the partial delivery thereon or be liable to any person to whom the document is duly negotiated.

(4)Person entitled under the document means holder in the case of a negotiable document, or the person to whom delivery is to be made by the terms of or pursuant to written instructions under a non-negotiable document.

§ 7—404. No Liability for Good Faith Delivery Pursuant to Receipt or Bill

A bailee who in good faith, including observance of reasonable commercial standards, has received goods and delivered or otherwise disposed of them according to the terms of the document of title or pursuant to this Article is not liable therefor. This rule applies even though the person from whom he received the goods had no authority to procure the document or to dispose of the goods and even though the person to whom he delivered the goods had no authority to receive them.

Part 5
Warehouse Receipts and Bills of Lading: Negotiation and Transfer

§ 7—501. Form of Negotiation and Requirements of Due Negotiation

(1)A negotiable document of title running to the order of a named person is negotiated by his indorsement and delivery. After his indorsement in blank or to bearer, any person can negotiate it by delivery alone.

(2)(a)A negotiable document of title is also negotiated by delivery alone when by its original terms it runs to bearer.

(b)When a document running to the order of a named person is delivered to him, the effect is the same as if the document had been negotiated.

(3)Negotiation of a negotiable document of title after it has been indorsed to a specified person requires indorsement by the special indorsee as well as delivery.

(4)A negotiable document of title is duly negotiated when it is negotiated in the manner stated in this section to a holder who purchases it in good faith without notice of any defense against or claim to it on the part of any person and for value, unless it is established that the negotiation is not in the regular course of business or financing or involves receiving the document in settlement or payment of a money obligation.

(5)Indorsement of a nonnegotiable document neither makes it negotiable nor adds to the transferees rights.

(6)The naming in a negotiable bill of a person to be notified of the arrival of the goods does not limit the negotiability of the bill nor constitute notice to a purchaser thereof of any interest of such person in the goods.

§ 7—502. Rights Acquired by Due Negotiation

(1)Subject to the following section and to the provisions of Section 7—205 on fungible goods, a holder to whom a negotiable document of title has been duly negotiated acquires thereby:

(a)title to the document;

(b)title to the goods;

(c)all rights accruing under the law of agency or estoppel, including rights to goods delivered to the bailee after the document was issued; and

(d)the direct obligation of the issuer to hold or deliver the goods according to the terms of the document free of any defense or claim by him except those arising under the terms of the document or under this Article. In the case of a delivery order, the bailees obligation accrues only upon acceptance and the obligation acquired by the holder is that the issuer and any indorser will procure the acceptance of the bailee.

(2)Subject to the following section, title and rights so acquired are not defeated by any stoppage of the goods represented by the document or by surrender of such goods by the bailee, and are not impaired even though the negotiation or any prior negotiation constituted a breach of duty or even though any person has been deprived of possession of the document by misrepresentation, fraud, accident, mistake, duress, loss, theft or conversion, or even though a previous sale or other transfer of the goods or document has been made to a third person.

§ 7—507. Warranties on Negotiation or Transfer of Receipt or Bill

Where a person negotiates or transfers a document of title for value otherwise than as a mere intermediary under the next following section, then unless otherwise agreed he warrants to his immediate purchaser only, in addition to any warranty made in selling the goods,

(a)that the document is genuine; and

(b)that he has no knowledge of any fact which would impair its validity or worth; and

(c)that his negotiation or transfer is rightful and fully effective with respect to the title to the document and the goods it represents.

§ 7—508. Warranties of Collecting Bank as to Documents

A collecting bank or other intermediary known to be entrusted with documents on behalf of another or with collection of a draft or other claim against delivery of documents warrants by such delivery of the documents only its own good faith and authority. This rule applies even though the intermediary has purchased or made advances against the claim or draft to be collected.

Part 6
Warehouse Receipts and Bills of Lading: Miscellaneous Provisions

§ 7—602. Attachment of Goods Covered by a Negotiable Document

Except where the document was originally issued upon delivery of the goods by a person who had no power to dispose of them, no lien attaches by virtue of any judicial process to goods in the possession of a bailee for which a negotiable document of title is outstanding unless the document be first surrendered to the bailee or its negotiation enjoined, and the bailee shall not be compelled to deliver the goods pursuant to process until the document is surrendered to him or impounded by the court. One who purchases the document for value without notice of the process or injunction takes free of the lien imposed by judicial process.

Article 8

Investment Securities

Part 1
Short Title and General Matters

§ 8—102. Definitions and Index of Definitions

(1)In this Article, unless the context otherwise requires:

(a)A certificated security is a share, participation, or other interest in property of or an enterprise of the issuer or an obligation of the issuer which is

(i)represented by an instrument issued in bearer or registered form;

(ii)of a type commonly dealt in on securities exchanges or markets or commonly recognized in any area in which it is issued or dealt in as a medium for investment; and

(iii)either one of a class or series or by its terms divisible into a class or series of shares, participations, interests, or obligations.

(b)An uncertificated security is a share, participation, or other interest in property or an enterprise of the issuer or an obligation of the issuer which is

(i)not represented by an instrument and the transfer of which is registered upon books maintained for that purpose by or on behalf of the issuer;

(ii)of a type commonly dealt in on securities exchanges or markets; and

(iii)either one of a class or series or by its terms divisible into a class or series of shares, participations, interests, or obligations.

(c)A security is either a certificated or an uncertificated security. If a security is certificated, the terms security and certificated security may mean either the intangible interest, the instrument representing that interest, or both, as the context requires. A writing that is a certificated security is governed by this Article and not by Article 3, even though it also meets the requirements of that Article. This Article does not apply to money. If a certificated security has been retained by or surrendered to the issuer or its transfer agent for reasons other than registration of transfer, other temporary purpose, payment, exchange, or acquisition by the issuer, that security shall be treated as an uncertificated security for purposes of this Article.

(d)A certificated security is in registered form if

(i)it specifies a person entitled to the security of the rights it represents; and

(ii)its transfer may be registered upon books maintained for that purpose by or on behalf of the issuer, or the security so states.

(e)A certified security is in bearer form if it runs to bearer according to its terms and not by reason of any indorsement.

. . .

§ 8—105. Certificated Securities Negotiable; Statements and Institutions Not Negotiable; Presumptions

(1)Certified securities governed by this Article are negotiable instruments.

(2)Statements (Section 8—408), notices, or the like, sent by the issuer of uncertificated securities and instructions (Section 8—308) are neither negotiable instruments nor certificated securities.

. . .

§ 8—107. Securities Transferable; Action for Price

(1)Unless otherwise agreed and subject to any applicable law or regulation respecting short sales, a person obligated to transfer securities may transfer any certificated security of the specified issue in bearer form or registered in the name of the transferee, or indorsed to him or in blank, or he may transfer an equivalent uncertificated security to the transferee or a person designated by the transferee.

(2)If the buyer fails to pay the price as it comes due under a contract of sale, the seller may recover the price of:

(a)certificated securities accepted by the buyer;

(b)uncertificated securities that have been transferred to the buyer or a person designated by the buyer; and

(c)other securities if efforts at their resale would be unduly burdensome or if there is no readily available market for their resale.

Part 2
Issue Issuer

§ 8—202. Issuers Responsibility and Defenses; Notice of Defect or Defense

(1)Even against a purchaser for value and without notice, the terms of a security include:

(a)if the security is certificated, those stated on the security;

(b)if the security is uncertificated, those contained in the initial transaction statement sent to such purchaser or, if his interest is transferred to him other than by registration of transfer, pledge, or release, the initial transaction statement sent to the registered owner or registered pledgee; and

(c)those made part of the security by reference, on the certificated security or in the initial transaction statement, to another instrument, indenture, or document or to a constitution, statute, ordinance, rule, regulation, order or the like, to the extent that the terms referred to do not conflict with the terms stated on the certificated security or contained in the statement. A reference under this paragraph does not of itself charge a purchaser for value with notice of a defect going to the validity of the security, even though the certificated security or statement expressly states that a person accepting it admits notice.

(2)A certificated security in the hands of a purchaser for value or an uncertificated security as to which an initial transaction statement has been sent to a purchaser for value, other than a security issued by a government or governmental agency or unit, even though issued with a defect going to its validity, is valid with respect to the purchaser if he is without notice of the particular defect unless the defect involves a violation of constitutional provisions, in which case the security is valid with respect to a subsequent purchaser for value and without notice of the defect. This subsection applies to an issuer that is a government or governmental agency or unit only if either there has been substantial compliance with the legal requirements governing the issue or the issuer has received a substantial consideration for the issue as a whole or for the particular security and a stated purpose of the issue is one for which the issuer has power to borrow money or issue the security.

(3)Except as provided in the case of certain unauthorized signatures (Section 8—205), lack of genuineness of a certificated security or an initial transaction statement is a complete defense, even against a purchaser for value and without notice.

(4)All other defenses of the issuer of a certificated or uncertificated security, including nondelivery and conditional delivery of a certificated security, are ineffective against a purchaser for value who has taken without notice of the particular defense.

(5)Nothing in this section shall be construed to affect the right of a party to a when, as and if issued or a when distributed contract to cancel the contract in the event of a material change in the character of the security that is the subject of the contract or in the plan or arrangement pursuant to which the security is to be issued or distributed.

§ 8—203. Staleness as Notice of Defects or Defenses

(1)After an act or event creating a right to immediate performance of the principal obligation represented by a certificated security or that sets a date on or after which the security is to be presented or surrendered for redemption or exchange, a purchaser is charged with notice of any defect in its issue or defense of the issuer if:

(a)the act or event is one requiring the payment of money, the delivery of certificated securities, the registration of transfer of uncertificated securities, or any of these on presentation or surrender of the certificated security, the funds or securities are available on the date set for payment or exchange, and he takes the security more than one year after that date; and

(b)the act or event is not covered by paragraph (a) and he takes the security more than 2 years after the date set for surrender or presentation or the date on which performance became due.

(2)A call that has been revoked is not within subsection (1).

§ 8—204. Effect of Issuers Restrictions on Transfer

A restriction on transfer of a security imposed by the issuer, even if otherwise lawful, is ineffective against any person without actual knowledge of it unless:

(a)the security is certificated and the restriction is noted conspicuously thereon; or

(b)the security is uncertificated and a notation of the restriction is contained in the initial transaction statement sent to the person or, if his interest is transferred to him other than by registration of transfer, pledge, or release, the initial transaction statement sent to the registered owner or the registered pledgee.

§ 8—205. Effect of Unauthorized Signature on Certificated Security or Initial Transaction Statement

An unauthorized signature placed on a certificated security prior to or in the course of issue or placed on an initial transaction statement is ineffective, but the signature is effective in favor of a purchaser for value of the certificated security or a purchaser for value of an uncertificated security to whom the initial transaction statement has been sent, if the purchaser is without notice of the lack of authority and the signing has been done by:

(a)an authenticating trustee, registrar, transfer agent, or other person entrusted by the issuer with the signing of the security, or similar securities, or of initial transaction statements or the immediate preparation for signing of any of them; or

(b)an employee of the issuer, or of any of the foregoing, entrusted with responsible handling of the security or initial transaction statement.

§ 8—208. Effect of Signature of Authenticating Trustee, Registrar, or Transfer Agent

(1)A person placing his signature upon a certificated security or an initial transaction statement as authenticating trustee, registrar, transfer agent, or the like, warrants to a purchaser for value of the certificated security or a purchaser for value of an uncertificated security to whom the initial transaction statement has been sent, if the purchaser is without notice of the particular defect, that:

(a)the certificated security or initial transaction statement is genuine;

(b)his own participation in the issue or registration of the transfer, pledge, or release of the security is within his capacity and within the scope of the authority received by him from the issuer; and

(c)he has reasonable grounds to believe the security is in the form and within the amount the issuer is authorized to issue.

(2)Unless otherwise agreed, a person by so placing his signature does not assume responsibility for the validity of the security in other respects.

Part 3
Transfer

§ 8—301. Rights Acquired by Purchaser

(1)Upon transfer of a security to a purchaser (Section 8—313), the purchaser acquires the rights in the security which his transferor had or had actual authority to convey unless the purchasers rights are limited by Section 8—302(4).

. . .

§ 8—302. Bona Fide Purchaser; Adverse Claim; Title Acquired by Bona Fide Purchaser

(1)A bona fide purchaser is a purchaser for value in good faith and without notice of any adverse claim:

(a)who takes delivery of a certificated security in bearer form or in registered form, issued or indorsed to him or in blank;

(b)to whom the transfer, pledge, or release of an uncertificated security is registered on the books of the issuer; or

(c)to whom a security is transferred under the provisions of paragraph (c), (d), (i), or (g) of Section 8—313(1).

(2)Adverse claim includes a claim that a transfer was or would be wrongful or that a particular adverse person is the owner of or has an interest in the security.

(3)A bona fide purchaser in addition to acquiring the rights of a purchaser (Section 8—301) also acquires his interest in the security free of any adverse claim.

(4)Notwithstanding Section 8—301(1), the transferee of a particular certificated security who has been a party to any fraud or illegality affecting the security, or who as a prior holder of that certificated security had notice of an adverse claim, cannot improve his position by taking from a bona fide purchaser.

§ 8—304. Notice to Purchaser of Adverse Claims

(1)A purchaser (including a broker for the seller or buyer, but excluding an intermediary bank) of a certificated security is charged with notice of adverse claims if:

(a)the security, whether in bearer or registered form, has been indorsed for collection or for surrender or for some other purpose not involving transfer; or

(b)the security is in bearer form and has on it an unambiguous statement that it is the property of a person other than the transferor. The mere writing of a name on a security is not such a statement.

(2)A purchaser (including a broker for the seller or buyer, but excluding an intermediary bank) to whom the transfer, pledge, or release of an uncertificated security is registered is charged with notice of adverse claims as to which the issuer has a duty under Section 8—403(4) at the time of registration and which are noted in the initial transaction statement sent to the purchaser or, if his interest is transferred to him other than by registration of transfer, pledge, or release, the initial transaction statement sent to the registered owner or the registered pledgee.

(3)The fact that the purchaser (including a broker for the seller or buyer) of a certificated or uncertificated security has notice that the security is held for a third person or is registered in the name of or indorsed by a fiduciary does not create a duty of inquiry into the rightfulness of the transfer or constitute constructive notice of adverse claims. However, if the purchaser (excluding an intermediary bank) has knowledge that the proceeds are being used or the transaction is for the individual benefit of the fiduciary or otherwise in breach of duty, the purchaser is charged with notice, of adverse claims.

§ 8—305. Staleness as Notice of Adverse Claims

An act or event that creates a right to immediate performance of the principal obligation represented by a certificated security, or sets a date on or after which a certificated security is to be presented or surrendered for redemption or exchange does not itself constitute any notice of adverse claims except in the case of a transfer;

(a)after one year from any date set for presentment or surrender for redemption or exchange; or

(b)after 6 months from any date set for payment of money against presentation or surrender of the security if funds are available for payment on that date.

§ 8—306. Warranties on Presentment and Transfer of Certificated Securities; Warranties of Originators of Instructions

(1)A person who presents a certificated security for registration of transfer or for payment or exchange warrants to the issuer that he is entitled to the registration, payment, or exchange. But, a purchaser for value and without notice of adverse claims who receives a new, reissued, or re-registered certificated security on registration of transfer or receives an initial transaction statement confirming the registration of transfer of an equivalent uncertificated security to him warrants only that he has no knowledge of any unauthorized signature (Section 8—311) in a necessary indorsement.

(2)A person by transferring a certificated security to a purchaser for value warrants only that:

(a)his transfer is effective and rightful;

(b)the security is genuine and has not been materially altered; and

(c)he knows of no fact which might impair the validity of the security.

(3)If a certificated security is delivered by an intermediary known to be entrusted with delivery of the security on behalf of another or with collection of a draft or other claim against delivery, the intermediary by delivery warrants only his own good faith and authority, even though he has purchased or made advances against the claim to be collected against the delivery.

. . .

(5)A person who originates an instruction warrants to the issuer that:

(a)he is an appropriate person to originate the instruction; and

(b)at the time the instruction is presented to the issuer he will be entitled to the registration of transfer, pledge, or release.

(6)A person who originates an instruction warrants to any person specially guaranteeing his signature (subsection 8—312(3)) that:

(a)he is an appropriate person to originate the instruction; and

(b)at the time the instruction is presented to the issuer

(i)he will be entitled to the registration of transfer, pledge, or release; and

(ii)the transfer, pledge, or release requested in the instruction will be registered by the issuer free from all liens, security interests, restrictions, and claims other than those specified in the instruction.

(7)A person who originates an instruction warrants to a purchaser for value and to any person guaranteeing the instruction (Section 8—312(6)) that:

(a)he is an appropriate person to originate the instruction;

(b)the uncertificated security referred to therein is valid; and

(c)at the time the instruction is presented to the issuer

(i)the transferor will be entitled to the registration of transfer, pledge, or release;

(ii)the transfer, pledge, or release requested in the instruction will be registered by

the issuer free from all liens, security interests, restrictions, and claims other than those specified in the instruction; and

(iii)the requested transfer, pledge, or release will be rightful.

. . .

(9)A person who transfers an uncertificated security to a purchaser for value and does not originate an instruction in connection with the transfer warrants only that:

(a)his transfer is effective and rightful; and

(b)the uncertificated security is valid.

(10)A broker gives to his customer and to the issuer and a purchaser the applicable warranties provided in this section and has the rights and privileges of a purchaser under this section. The warranties of and in favor of the broker, acting as an agent are in addition to applicable warranties given by and in favor of his customer.

§ 8—307. Effect of Delivery Without Indorsement; Right to Compel Indorsement

If a certificated security in registered form has been delivered to a purchaser without a necessary indorsement he may become a bona fide purchaser only as of the time the indorsement is supplied; but against the transferor, the transfer is complete upon delivery and the purchaser has a specifically enforceable right to have any necessary indorsement supplied.

§ 8—308. Indorsements; Instructions

(1)An indorsement of a certificated security in registered form is made when an appropriate person signs on it or on a separate document an assignment or transfer of the security or a power to assign or transfer it or his signature is written without more upon the back of the security.

(2)An indorsement may be in blank or special. An indorsement in blank includes an indorsement to bearer. A special indorsement specifies to whom the security is to be transferred, or who has power to transfer it. A holder may convert a blank indorsement into a special indorsement.

(3)An indorsement purporting to be only of part of a certificated security representing units intended by the issuer to be separately transferable is effective to the extent of the indorsement.

(4)An instruction is an order to the issuer of an uncertificated security requesting that the transfer, pledge, or release from pledge of the uncertificated security specified therein be registered.

(5)An instruction originated by an appropriate person is:

(a)a writing signed by an appropriate person; or

(b)a communication to the issuer in any form agreed upon in a writing signed by the issuer and an appropriate person.

If an instruction has been originated by an appropriate person but is incomplete in any other respect, any person may complete it as authorized and the issuer may rely on it as completed even though it has been completed incorrectly.

. . .

§ 8—309. Effect of Indorsement Without Delivery

An indorsement of a certificated security, whether special or in blank, does not constitute a transfer until delivery of the certificated security on which it appears or, if the indorsement is on a separate document, until delivery of both the document and the certificated security.

§ 8—310. Indorsement of Certificated Security in Bearer Form

An indorsement of a certificated security in bearer form may give notice of adverse claims (Section 8—304) but does not otherwise affect any right to registration the holder possesses.

§ 8—311. Effect of Unauthorized Indorsement or Instruction

Unless the owner or pledgee has ratified an unauthorized indorsement or instruction or is otherwise precluded from asserting its effectiveness:

(a)he may assert its ineffectiveness against the issuer or any purchaser, other than a purchaser for value and without notice of adverse claims, who has in good faith received a new, reissued, or re-registered certificated security on registration of transfer or received an initial transaction statement confirming the registration of transfer, pledge, or release of an equivalent uncertificated security to him; and

(b)an issuer who registers the transfer of a certificated security upon the unauthorized indorsement or who registers the transfer, pledge, or release of an uncertificated security upon the unauthorized instruction is subject to liability for improper registration (Section 8—404).

§ 8—313. When Transfer to Purchaser Occurs; Financial Intermediary as Bona Fide Purchaser; Financial Intermediary

(1)Transfer of a security or a limited interest (including a security interest) therein to a purchaser occurs only:

(a)at the time he or a person designated by him acquires possession of a certificated security;

(b)at the time the transfer, pledge, or release of an uncertificated security is registered to him or a person designated by him;

(c)at the time his financial intermediary acquires possession of a certificated security specially indorsed to or issued in the name of the purchaser;

(d)at the time a financial intermediary, not a clearing corporation, sends him confirmation of the purchase and also by book entry or otherwise identifies as belonging to the purchaser

(i)a specific certificated security in the financial intermediarys possession;

(ii)a quantity of securities that constitute or are part of a fungible bulk of certificated securities in the financial intermediarys possession or of uncertificated securities registered in the name of the financial intermediary; or

(iii)a quantity of securities that constitute or are part of a fungible bulk of securities shown on the account of the financial intermediary on the books of another financial intermediary;

(e)with respect to an identified certificated security to be delivered while still in the possession of a third person, not a financial intermediary, at the time that person acknowledges that he holds for the purchaser;

(f)with respect to a specific uncertificated security the pledge or transfer of which has been registered to a third person, not a financial intermediary, at the time that person acknowledges that he holds for the purchaser;

. . .

§ 8—314. Duty to Transfer, When Completed

(1)Unless otherwise agreed, if a sale of a security is made on an exchange or otherwise through brokers:

(a)the selling customer fulfills his duty to transfer at the time he:

(i)places a certificated security in the possession of the selling broker or a person designated by the broker;

(ii)causes an uncertificated security to be registered in the name of the selling broker or a person designated by the broker;

(iii)if requested, causes an acknowledgment to be made to the selling broker that a certificated or uncertificated security is held for the broker; or

(iv)places in the possession of the selling broker or of a person designated by the broker a transfer instruction for an uncertificated security, providing the issuer does not refuse to register the requested transfer if the instruction is presented to the issuer for registration within 30 days thereafter; and

(b)the selling broker, including a correspondent broker acting for a selling customer, fulfills his duty to transfer at the time he:

(i)places a certificated security in the possession of the buying broker or a person designated by the buying broker;

(ii)causes an uncertificated security to be registered in the name of the buying broker or a person designated by the buying broker;

(iii)places in the possession of the buying broker or of a person designated by the buying broker a transfer instruction for an uncertificated security, providing the issuer does not refuse to register the requested transfer if the instruction is presented to the issuer for registration within 30 days thereafter; or

(iv)effects clearance of the sale in accordance with the rules of the exchange on which the transaction took place.

(2)Except as provided in this section or unless otherwise agreed, a transferors duty to transfer a security under a contract of purchase is not fulfilled until he:

(a)places a certificated security in form to be negotiated by the purchaser in the possession of the purchaser or of a person designated by the purchaser;

(b)causes an uncertificated security to be registered in the name of the purchaser or a person designated by the purchaser; or

(c)if the purchaser requests, causes an acknowledgment to be made to the purchaser that a certificated or uncertificated security is held for the purchaser.

(3)Unless made on an exchange, a sale to a broker purchasing for his own account is within subsection (2) and not within subsection (1).

§ 8—315. Action Against Transferee Based Upon Wrongful Transfer

(1)Any person against whom the transfer of a security is wrongful for any reason, including his incapacity, as against anyone except a bona fide purchaser, may:

(a)reclaim possession of the certificated security wrongfully transferred;

(b)obtain possession of any new certificated security representing all or part of the same rights;

(c)compel the origination of an instruction to transfer to him or a person designated by him an uncertificated security constituting all or part of the same rights; or

(d)have damages.

. . .

§ 8—318. No Conversion by Good Faith Conduct

An agent or bailee who in good faith (including observance of reasonable commercial standards if he is in the business of buying, selling, or otherwise dealing with securities) has received certificated securities and sold, pledged, or delivered them or has sold or caused the transfer or pledge of uncertificated securities over which he had control according to the instructions of his principal, is not liable for conversion or for participation in breach of fiduciary duty although the principal had no right so to deal with the securities.

§ 8—319. Statute of Frauds

A contract for the sale of securities is not enforceable by way of action or defense unless:

(a)there is some writing signed by the party against whom enforcement is sought or by his authorized agent or broker, sufficient to indicate that a contract has been made for sale of a stated quantity of described securities at a defined or stated price;

(b)delivery of a certificated security or transfer instruction has been accepted, or transfer of an uncertificated security has been registered and the transferee has failed to send written objection to the issuer within 10 days after receipt of the initial transaction statement confirming the registration, or payment has been made, but the contract is enforceable under this provision only to the extent of the delivery, registration, or payment;

(c)within a reasonable time a writing in confirmation of the sale or purchase and sufficient against the sender under paragraph (a) has been received by the party against whom enforcement is sought and he has failed to send written objection to its contents within 10 days after its receipt; or

(d)the party against whom enforcement is sought admits in his pleading, testimony, or otherwise in court that a contract was made for the sale of a stated quantity of described securities at a defined or stated price.

§ 8—320. Transfer or Pledge Within Central Depositary System

(1)In addition to other methods, a transfer, pledge, or release of a security or any interest therein may be effected by the making of appropriate entries on the books of a clearing corporation reducing the account of the transferor, pledgor, or pledgee and increasing the account of the transferee, pledgee, or pledgor by the amount of the obligation or the number of shares or rights transferred, pledged, or released, if the security is shown on the account of a transferor, pledgor, or pledgee on the books of the cleaning corporation; is subject to the control of the clearing corporation; and

(a)if certificated,

(i)is in the custody of the clearing corporation, another clearing corporation, a custodian bank, or a nominee of any of them; and

(ii)is in bearer form or indorsed in blank by an appropriate person or registered in the name of the cleaning corporation, a custodian bank, or a nominee of any of them; or

(b)if uncertificated, is registered in the name of the clearing corporation, another clearing corporation, a custodian bank, or a nominee of any of them.

. . .

Part 4
Registration

§ 8—401. Duty of Issuer to Register Transfer, Pledge, or Release

(1)If a certificated security in registered form is presented to the issuer with a requent to register transfer or an instruction is presented to the issuer with a request to register transfer, pledge, or release, the issuer shall register the transfer, pledge, or release as requested if:

(a)the security is indorsed or the instruction was originated by the appropriate person or persons (Section 8—308);

(b)reasonable assurance is given that those indorsements or instructions are genuine and effective (Section 8—402);

(c)the issuer has no duty as to adverse claims or has discharged the duty (Section 8—403);

(d)any applicable law relating to the collection of taxes has been complied with; and

(e)the transfer, pledge, or release is in fact rightful or is to a bona fide purchaser.

(2)If an issuer is under a duty to register a transfer pledge, or release of a security, the issuer is also liable to the person presenting a certificated security or an instruction for registration or his principal for loss resulting from any unreasonable delay in registration or from failure or refusal to register the transfer, pledge, or release.

§ 8—403. Issuers Duty as to Adverse Claims

(1)An issuer to whom a certificated security is presented for registration shall inquire into adverse claims if:

(a)a written notification of an adverse claim is received at a time and in a manner affording the issuer a reasonable opportunity to act on it prior to the issuance of a new, reissued, or re-registered certificated security, and the notification identifies the claimant, the registered owner, and the issue of which the security is a part, and provides an address for communications directed to the claimant; or

(b)the issuer is charged with notice of an adverse claim from a controllin g instrument it has elected to require under Section 8—402(4).

(2)The issuer may discharge any duty of inquiry by any reasonable means, including notifying an adverse claimant by registered or certified mail at the address furnished by him or, if there be no such address, at his residence or regular place of business that the certificated security has been presented for registration of transfer by a named person, and that the transfer will be registered unless within 30 days from the date of mailing the notification, either:

(a)an appropriate restraining order, injunction, or other process issues from a court of competent jurisdiction; or

(b)there is filed with the issuer an indemnity bond, sufficient in the issuers judgment to protect the issuer and any transfer agent, registrar, or other agent of the issuer involved from any loss it or they may suffer by complying with the adverse claim.

. . .

§ 8—404. Liability and Non-Liability for Registration

(1)Except as provided in any law relating to the collection of taxes, the issuer is not liable to the owner, pledgee, or any other person suffering loss as a result of the registration of a transfer, pledge, or release of a security if:

(a)there were on or with a certificated security the necessary indorsements or the issuer had received an instruction originated by an appropriate person (Section 8—308); and

(b)the issuer had no duty as to adverse claims or has discharged the duty (Section 8—403).

(2)If an issuer has registered a transfer of a certificated security to a person not entitled to it, the issuer on demand shall deliver a like security to the true owner unless:

(a)the registration was pursuant to subsection (1);

(b)the owner is precluded from asserting any claim for registering the transfer under Section 8—405(1); or

(c)the delivery would result in overissue, in which case the issuers liability is governed by Section 8—104.

(3)If an issuer has improperly registered a transfer, pledge, or release of an uncertificated security, the issuer on demand from the injured party shall restore the records as to the injured party to the condition that would have obtained if the improper registration had not been made unless:

(a)the registration was pursuant to subsection (1); or

(b)the registration would result in overissue, in which case the issuers liability is governed by Section 8—104.

§ 8—408. Statements of Uncertificated Securities

(1)Within 2 business days after the transfer of an uncertificated security has been registered, the issuer shall send to the new registered owner and, if the security has been transferred subject to a registered pledge, to the registered pledgee a written statement containing:

(a)a description of the issue of which the uncertificated security is a part;

(b)the number of shares or units transferred;

(c)the name and address and any taxpayer identification number of the new registered owner and, if the security has been transferred subject to a registered pledge, the name and address and any taxpayer identification number of the registered pledgee;

(d)a notation of any liens and restrictions of the issuer and any adverse claims (as to which the issuer has a duty under Section 8—403(4)) to which the uncertificated security is or may be subject at the time of registration or a statement that there are none of those liens, restrictions, or adverse claims; and

(e)the date the transfer was registered.

. . .

(6)At periodic intervals no less frequent than annually and at any time upon the reasonable written request of the registered owner, the issuer shall send to the registered owner of each uncertificated security a dated written statement containing:

(a)a description of the issue of which the uncertificated security is a part;

(b)the name and address and any taxpayer identification number of the registered owner;

(c)the number of shares or units of the uncertificated security registered in the name of the registered owner on the date of the statement;

(d)the name and address and any taxpayer identification number of any registered pledgee and the number of shares or units subject to the pledge; and

(e)a notation of any liens and restrictions of the issuer and any adverse claims (as to which the issuer has a duty under Section 8—403(4)) to which the uncertificated security is or may be subject or a state ment that there are none of those liens, restrictions, or adverse claims.

. . .

(9)Each statement sent pursuant to this section must bear a conspicuous legend reading substantially as follows: This statement is merely a record of the rights of the addressee as of the time of its issua nce. Delivery of this statement, of itself, confers no rights on the recipient. This statement is neither a negotiable instrument nor a security.

Article 9
Secured Transactions; Sales of Accounts and Chattel Paper

Part 1
Short Title, Applicability and Definitions

§ 9—102. Policy and Subject Matter of Article

(1) Except as otherwise provided in Section 9—104 on excluded transactions, this Article applies

(a) to any transaction (regardless of its form) which is intended to create a security interest in personal property or fixtures including goods, documents, instruments, general intangibles, chattel paper or accounts; and also

(b) to any sale of accounts or chattel paper.

(2) This Article applies to security interests created by contract including pledge, assignment, chattel mortgage, chattel trust, trust deed, factor's lien, equipment trust, conditional sale, trust receipt, other lien or title retention contract and lease or consignment intended as security. This Article does not apply to statutory liens except as provided in Section 9—310.

(3) The application of this Article to a security interest in a secured obligation is not affected by the fact that the obligation is itself secured by a transaction or interest to which this Article does not apply.

§ 9—105. Definitions and Index of Definitions

(1) In this Article unless the context otherwise requires:

(a) "Account debtor" means the person who is obligated on an account, chattel paper or general intangible;

(b) "Chattel paper" means a writing or writings which evidence both a monetary obligation and a security interest in or a lease of specific goods, but a charter or other contract involving the use or hire of a vessel is not chattel paper. When a transaction is evidenced both by such a security agreement or a lease and by an instrument or a series of instruments, the group of writings taken together constitutes chattel paper;

(c) "Collateral" means the property subject to a security interest, and includes accounts and chattel paper which have been sold;

(d) "Debtor" means the person who owes payment or other performance of the obligation secured, whether or not he owns or has rights in the collateral, and includes the seller of accounts or chattel paper. Where the debtor and the owner of the collateral are not the same person, the term "debtor" means the owner of the collateral in any provision of the article dealing with the collateral, the obligor in any provision dealing with the obligation, and may include both where the context so requires;

(f) "Document" means document of title as defined in the general definitions of Article 1 (Section 1—201), and a receipt of the kind described in subsection (2) of Section 7—201;

(i) "Instrument" means a negotiable instrument (defined in Section 3—104), or a certificated security (defined in Section 8—102) or any other writing which evidences a right to the payment of money and is not itself a security agreement or lease and is of a type which is in ordinary course of business transferred by delivery with any necessary indorsement or assignment;

§ 9—106. Definitions: "Account"; "General Intangibles"

"Account" means any right to payment for goods sold or leased or for services rendered which is not evidenced by an instrument or chattel paper, whether or not it has been earned by performance. "General intangibles" means any personal property (including things in action) other than goods, accounts, chattel paper, documents, instruments, and money. All rights to payment earned or unearned under a charter or other contract involving the use or hire of a vessel and all rights incident to the charter or contract are accounts.

§ 9—107. Definitions: "Purchase Money Security Interest"

A security interest is a "purchase money security interest" to the extent that it is

(a) taken or retained by the seller of the collateral to secure all or part of its price; or

(b) taken by a person who, by making advances or incurring an obligation, gives value to enable the debtor to acquire rights in or the use of collateral, if such value is in fact so used.

§ 9—109. Classification of Goods; "Consumer Goods"; "Farm Products"; "Inventory"

Goods are

(1) "consumer goods" if they are used or bought for use primarily for personal, family or household purposes;

(2) "equipment" if they are used or bought for use primarily in business (including farming or a profession) or by a debtor who is a non-profit organization or a governmental

subdivision or agency or if the goods are not included in the definitions of inventory, farm products or consumer goods;

(3) "farm products" if they are crops or livestock or supplies used or produced in farming operations or if they are products of crops or livestock in their unmanufactured states (such as ginned cotton, wool-clip, maple syrup, milk and eggs) and if they are in the possession of a debtor engaged in raising, fattening, grazing or other farming operations. If goods are farm products, they are neither equipment nor inventory;

(4) "inventory" if they are held by a person who holds them for sale or lease or to be furnished under contracts of service or if he has so furnished them, or if they are raw materials, work in process or materials used or consumed in a business. Inventory of a person is not to be classified as his equipment.

§ 9—110. Sufficiency of Description

For the purposes of this Article, any description of personal property or real estate is sufficient whether or not it is specific if it reasonably identifies what is described.

§ 9—113. Security Interests Arising Under Article on Sales

A security interest arising solely under the Article on Sales (Article 2) is subject to the provisions of this Article except that to the extent that and so long as the debtor does not have or does not lawfully obtain possession of the goods

(a) no security agreement is necessary to make the security interest enforceable; and

(b) no filing is required to perfect the security interest; and

(c) the rights of the secured party on default by the debtor are governed by the Article on Sales (Article 2).

Part 2
Validity of Security Agreement and Rights of Parties Thereto

§ 9—201. General Validity of Security Agreement

Except as otherwise provided by this Act, a security agreement is effective according to its terms between the parties, against purchasers of the collateral and against creditors. Nothing in this Article validates any charge or practice illegal under any statute or regulation thereunder governing usury, small loans, retail installment sales, or the like, or extends the application of any such statute or regulation to any transaction not otherwise subject thereto.

§ 9—202. Title to Collateral Immaterial

Each provision of this Article with regard to rights, obligations and remedies applies whether title to collateral is in the secured party or in the debtor.

§ 9—203. Attachment and Enforceability of Security Interest; Proceeds; Formal Requisites

(1) Subject to the provisions of Section 4—208 on the security interest of a collecting bank, Section 8—321 on security interests in securities and Section 9—113 on a security interest arising under the Article of Sales, a security interest is not enforceable against the debtor or third parties with respect to the collateral and does not attach unless

(a) the collateral is in the possession of the secured party pursuant to agreement, or the debtor has signed a security agreement which contains a description of the collateral and in addition, when the security interest covers crops growing or to be grown or timber to be cut, a description of the land concerned; and

(b) value has been given; and

(c) the debtor has rights in the collateral.

(2) A security interest attaches when it becomes enforceable against the debtor with respect to the collateral. Attachment occurs as soon as all of the events specified in subsection (1) have taken place unless explicit agreement postpones the time of attaching.

(3) Unless otherwise agreed, a security agreement gives the secured party the rights to proceeds provided by Section 9—306.

(4) A transaction, although subject to this Article, is also subject to ... | ... | ... | ...*, and in the case of conflict between the provisions of this Article and any such statute, the provisions of such statute control. Failure to comply with any applicable statute has only the effect which is specified therein.

Note: At * in subsection.

(4) insert reference to any local statute regulating small loans, retail installment sales and the like.

§ 9—204. After-Acquired Property; Future Advances

(1) Except as provided in subsection (2), a security agreement may provide that any or all obligations covered by the security agreement are to be secured by after-acquired collateral.

(2) No security interest attaches under an after-acquired property clause to consumer goods other than accessions (Section 9—314) when given as additional security unless the debtor acquires rights in them within ten days after the secured party, gives value.

(3) Obligations covered by a security agreement may include future advances or other value whether or not the advances or value are given pursuant to commitment (subsection (1) of Section 9—105).

§ 9—205. Use or Disposition of Collateral Without Accounting Permissible

A security interest is not invalid or fraudulent against creditors by reason of liberty in the debtor to use, commingle or dispose of all or part of the collateral (including returned or repossessed goods) or to collect or compromise accounts or chattel paper, or to accept the return of goods or make repossessions, or to use, commingle or dispose of proceeds or by reason of the failure of the secured party to require the debtor to account for proceeds or replace collateral. This section does not relax the requirements of possession where perfection of a security interest depends upon possession of the collateral by the secured party, or by a bailee.

§ 9—206. Agreement Not to Assert Defenses Against Assignee; Modification of Sales Warranties Where Security Agreement Exists

(1) Subject to any statute or decision which establishes a different rule for buyers or lessees of consumer goods, an agreement by a buyer or lessee that he will not assert against an assignee any claim or defense which he may have against the seller or lessor is enforceable by an assignee who takes his assignment for value, in good faith and without notice of a claim or defense, except as to defenses of a type which may be asserted against a holder in

due course of a negotiable instrument under the Article on Commercial Paper (Article 3). A buyer who as part of one transaction signs both a negotiable instrument and a security agreement makes such an agreement.

(2) When a seller retains a purchase money security interest in goods, the Article on Sales (Article 2) governs the sale and any disclaimer, limitation or modification of the seller's warranties.

Part 3
Rights of Third Parties; Perfected and Unperfected Security Interests; Rules of Priority

§ 9—301. Persons Who Take Priority Over Unperfected Security Interests; Rights of "Lien Creditor"

(1) Except as otherwise provided in subsection (2), an unperfected security interest is subordinate to the rights of

(a) persons entitled to priority under Section 9—312;

(b) a person who becomes a lien creditor before the security interest is perfected;

(c) in the case of goods, instruments, documents, and chattel paper, a person who is not a secured party and who is a transferee in bulk or other buyer not in ordinary course of business or is a buyer of farm products in ordinary course of business, to the extent that he gives value and receives delivery of the collateral without knowledge of the security interest and before it is perfected;

(d) in the case of accounts and general intangibles, a person who is not a secured party and who is a transferee, to the extent that he gives value without knowledge of the security interest and before it is perfected.

(2) If the secured party files with respect to a purchase money security interest before or within ten days after the debtor receives possession of the collateral, he takes priority over the rights of a transferee in bulk or of a lien creditor which arise between the time the security interest attaches and the time of filing.

(3) A "lien creditor" means a creditor who has acquired a lien on the property involved by attachment, levy or the like and includes an assignee for benefit of creditors from the time of assignment, and a trustee in bankruptcy

from the date of the filing of the petition or a receiver in equity from the time of appointment.

(4) A person who becomes a lien creditor while a security interest is perfected takes subject to the security interest only to the extent that it secures advances made before he becomes a lien creditor or within 45 days thereafter or made without knowledge of the lien or pursuant to a commitment entered into without knowledge of the lien.

§ 9—302. When Filing Is Required to Perfect Security Interest; Security Interests to Which Filing Provisions of This Article Do Not Apply

(1) A financing statement must be filed to perfect all security interests except the following:

(a) a security interest in collateral in possession of the secured party under Section 9—305;

(b) a security interest temporarily perfected in instruments or documents without delivery under Section 9—304 or in proceeds for a 10 day period under Section 9—306;

(c) a security interest created by an assignment of a beneficial interest in a trust or a decedent's estate;

(d) a purchase money security interest in consumer goods; but filing is required for a motor vehicle required to be registered; and fixture filing is required for priority over conflicting interests in fixtures to the extent provided in Section 9—313;

(e) an assignment of accounts which does not alone or in conjunction with other assignments to the same assignee transfer a significant part of the outstanding accounts of the assignor;

(f) a security interest of a collecting bank (Section 4—208) or in securities (Section 8—321) or arising under the Article on Sales (see Section 9—313) or covered in subsection (3) of this section;

(g) an assignment for the benefit of all the creditors of the transferor, and subsequent transfers by the assignee thereunder.

(2) If a secured party assigns a perfected security interest, no filing under this Article is required in order to continue the perfected

status of the security interest against creditors of and transferees from the original debtor.

(3) The filing of a financing statement otherwise required by this Article is not necessary or effective to perfect a security interest in property subject to

(a) a statute or treaty of the United States which provides for a national or international registration or a national or international certificate of title or which specifies a place of filing different from that specified in this Article for filing of the security interest; or

(b) the following statutes of this state; st any certificate of title statute covering automobiles, trailers, mobile homes, boats, farm tractors, or the like, and any central filing statute*.]; but during any period in which collateral is inventory held for sale by a person who is in the business of selling goods of that kind, the filing provisions of this Article (Part 4) apply to a security interest in that collateral created by him as debtor; or

(c) a certificate of title statute of another jurisdiction under the law of which indication of a security interest on the certificate is required as a condition of perfection (subsection (2) of Section 9—103).

(4) Compliance with a statute or treaty described in subsection (3) is equivalent to the filing of a financing statement under this Article, and a security interest in property subject to the statute or treaty can be perfected only by compliance therewith except as provided in Section 9—103 on multiple state transactions. Duration and renewal of perfection of a security interest perfected by compliance with the statute or treaty are governed by the provisions of the statute or treaty; in other respects the security interest is subject to this Article.

Note: It is recommended that the provisions of certificate of title acts for perfection of security interests by notation on the certificates should be amended to exclude coverage of inventory held for sale.

§ 9—303. When Security Interest Is Perfected; Continuity of Perfection

(1) A security interest is perfected when it has attached and when all of the applicable steps required for perfection have been taken. Such steps are specified in Section 9—302, 9—304, 9—305 and 9—306. If such steps are taken before the security interest attaches, it is perfected at the time when it attaches,

(2) If a security interest is originally perfected in any way permitted under this Article and is subsequently perfected in some other way under this Article, without an intermediate period when it was unperfected, the security interest shall be deemed to be perfected continuously for the purposes of this Article.

9—306. "Proceeds"; Secured Party's Rights on Disposition of Collateral

(1) "Proceeds" includes whatever is received upon the sale, exchange, collection or other disposition of collateral or proceeds. Insurance payable by reason of loss or damage to the collateral is proceeds, except to the extent that it is payable to a person other than a party to the security agreement. Money, checks, deposit accounts, and the like are "cash proceeds." All other proceeds are "non-cash proceeds."

(2) Except where this Article otherwise provides, a security interest continues in collateral notwithstanding sale, exchange or other disposition thereof unless the disposition was authorized by the secured party in the security agreement or otherwise, and also continues in any identifiable proceeds including collections received by the debtor.

(3) The security interest in proceeds is a continuously perfected security interest if the interest in the original collateral was perfected, but it ceases to be a perfected security interest and becomes unperfected ten days after receipt of the proceeds by the debtor unless

(a) a filed financing statement covers the original collateral and the proceeds are collateral in which a security interest may be perfected by filing in the office or offices where the financing state ment has been filed and, if the proceeds are acquired with cash proceeds, the description of collateral in the financing statement indicates the types of property constituting the proceeds; or

(b) a filed financing statement covers the original collateral and the proceeds are identifiable cash proceeds; or

(c) the security interest in the proceeds is perfected before the expiration of the ten day period.

Except as provided in this section, a security interest in proceeds can be perfected only by the methods or under the circumstances permitted in this Article for original collateral of the same type.

9—312. Priorities Among Conflicting Security Interests in the Same Collateral

(1) The rules of priority stated in other sections of this Part and in the following sections shall govern when applicable: Section 4—208 with respect to the security interests of collecting banks in items being collected, accompanying documents and proceeds; Section 9—103 on security interests related to other jurisdictions; Section 9—114 on consignments.

(2) A perfected security interest in crops for new value given to enable the debtor to produce the crops during the production season, and given not more than three months before the crops become growing crops by planting or otherwise, takes priority over an earlier perfected security interest to the extent that such earlier interest secures obligations due more than six months before the crops become growing crops by planting or otherwise, even though the person giving new value had knowledge of the earlier security interest.

(3) A perfected purchase money security interest in inventory has priority over a conflicting security interest in the same inventory and also has priority in identifiable cash proceeds received on or before the delivery of the inventory to a buyer if

(a) the purchase money security interest is perfected at the time the debtor receives possession of the inventory; and

(b) the purchase money secured party gives notification in writing to the holder of the conflicting security interest if the holder had filed a financing statement covering the same types of inventory (i) before the date of the filing made by the purchase money secured party, or (ii) before the beginning of the 21 day period where the purchase money security interest is temporarily perfected without filing or possession (subsection (5) of Section 9—304); and

(c) the holder of the conflicting security interest receives the notification within five years before the debtor receives possession of the inventory; and

(d) the notification states that the person giving the notice has or expects to acquire a purchase money security interest in inventory of the debtor, describing such inventory by item or type.

(4) A purchase money security interest in collateral other than inventory has priority over a conflicting security interest in the same collateral or its proceeds if the purchase money security interest is perfected at the time the debtor receives possession of the collateral or within ten days thereafter.

(5) In all cases not governed by other rules stated in this section (including cases of purchase money security interests which do not qualify for the special priorities set forth in subsections (3) and (4) of this section), priority between conflicting security interests in the same collateral shall be determined according to the following rules:

(a) Conflicting security interests rank according to priority in time of filing or perfection. Priority dates from the time a filing is first made covering the collateral or the time the security interest is first perfected, whichever is earlier, provided that there is no period thereafter when there is neither filing nor perfection.

(b) So long as conflicting security interests are unperfected, the first to attach has priority.

(6) For the purposes of subsection (5), a date of filing or perfection as to collateral is also a date of filing or perfection as to proceeds.

(7) If future advances are made while a security interest is perfected by filing or the taking of possession, or under Section 8—321 on securities, the security interest has the same priority for the purposes of subsection (5) with respect to the future advances as it does with respect to the first advance. If a commitment is made before or while the security interest is so perfected, the security interest has the same priority with respect to advances made pursuant thereto. In other cases, a perfected security interest has priority from the date the advance is made.

§ 9—318. Defenses Against Assignee; Modification of Contract After Notification of Assignment; Term Prohibiting Assignment Ineffective; Identification and Proof of Assignment

(1) Unless an account debtor has made an enforceable agreement not to assert defenses or claims arising out of a sale as provided in Section 9—206, the rights of an assignee are subject to

(a) all the terms of the contract between the account debtor and assignor and any defense or claim arising therefrom; and

(b) any other defense or claim of the account debtor against the assignor which accrues before the account debtor receives notification of the assignment.

(2) So far as the right to payment or a part thereof under an assigned contract has not been fully earned by performance, and notwithstanding notification of the assignment, any modification of or substitution for the contract made in good faith and in accordance with reasonable commercial standards is effective against an assignee unless the account debtor has otherwise agreed, but the assignee acquires corresponding rights under the modified or substituted contract. The assignment may provide that such modification or substitution is a breach by the assignor.

(3) The account debtor is authorized to pay the assignor until the account debtor receives notification that the amount due or to become due has been assigned and that payment is to be made to the assignee. A notification which does not reasonably identify the rights assigned is ineffective. If requested by the account debtor, the assignee must seasonably furnish reasonable proof that the assignment has been made; and unless he does so, the account debtor may pay the assignor.

(4) A term in any contract between an account debtor and an assignor is ineffective if it prohibits assignment of an account or prohibits creation of a security interest in a general intangible for money due or to become due or requires the account debtor's consent to such assignment or security interest.

Part 4
Filing

§ 9—401. Place of Filing; Erroneous Filing; Removal of Collateral

(2) A filing which is made in good faith in an improper place or not in all of the places required by this section is nevertheless effective with regard to any collateral as to which the filing complied with the requirements of this Article and is also effective with regard to collateral covered by the financing statement against any person who has knowledge of the contents of such financing statement.

(3) A filing which is made in the proper place in this state continues effective even though the debtor's residence or place of business or the location of the collateral or its use, whichever controlled the original filing, is thereafter changed.

Alternative Subsection (3)

[(3) A filing which is made in the proper county continues effective for four months after a change to another county of the debtor's residence or place of business or the location of the collateral, whichever controlled the original filing. It becomes ineffective thereafter unless a copy of the financing statement signed by the secured party is filed in the new county within said period. The security interest may also be perfected in the new county after the expiration of the four-month period; in such case, perfection dates from the time of perfection in the new county. A change in the use of the collateral does not impair the effectiveness of the original filing.]

§ 9—402. Formal Requisites of Financing Statement; Amendments; Mortgage as Financing Statement

(1) A financing statement is sufficient if it gives the names of the debtor and the secured party, is signed by the debtor, gives an address of the secured party from which information concerning the security interest may be obtained, gives a mailing address of the debtor and contains a statement indicating the types, or describing the items, of collateral. A financing statement may be filed before a security agreement is made or a security interest otherwise attaches. When the financing statement

covers crops growing or to be grown, the statement must also contain a description of the real estate concerned. When the financing statement covers timber to be cut or covers minerals or the like (including oil and gas) or accounts subject to subsection (5) of Section 9—103, or when the financing statement is filed as a fixture filing (Section 9—313) and the collateral is goods which are or are to become fixtures, the statement must also comply with subsection (5). A copy of the security agreement is sufficient as a financing statement if it contains the above information and is signed by the debtor. A carbon, photographic or other reproduction of a security agreement or a financing statement is sufficient as a financing statement if the security agreement so provides or if the original has been filed in this state.

(2) A financing statement which otherwise complies with subsection (1) is sufficient when it is signed by the secured party instead of the debtor if it is filed to perfect a security interest in

(a) collateral already subject to a security interest in another jurisdiction when it is brought into this state, or when the debtor's location is changed to this state. Such a financing statement must state that the collateral was brought into this state or that the debtor's location was changed to this state under such circumstances; or

(b) proceeds under Section 9—306 if the security interest in the original collateral was perfected. Such a financing statement must describe the original collateral; or

(c) collateral as to which the filing has lapsed; or

(d) collateral acquired after a change of name, identity or corporate structure of the debtor (subsection (7)).

(4) A financing statement may be amended by filing a writing signed by both the debtor and the secured party. An amendment does not extend the period of effectiveness of a financing statement. If any amendment adds collateral, it is effective as to the added collateral only from the filing date of the amendment. In this Article, unless the context otherwise requires, the term "financing state-ment" means the original financing statement and any amendments.

(7) A financing statement sufficiently shows the name of the debtor if it gives the individual, partnership or corporate name of the debtor, whether or not it adds other trade names or names of partners. Where the debtor so changes his name or, in the case of an organization, its name, identity or corporate structure that a filed financing statement becomes seriously misleading, the filing is not effective to perfect a security interest in collateral acquired by the debtor more than four months after the change, unless a new appropriate financing statement is filed before the expiration of that time. A filed financing statement remains effective with respect to collateral transferred by the debtor even though the secured party knows of or consents to the transfer.

(8) A financing statement substantially complying with the requirements of this section is effective even though it contains minor errors which are not seriously misleading.

Part 5
Default

§ 9—501. Default; Procedure When Security Agreement Covers Both Real and Personal Property

(1) When a debtor is in default under a security agreement, a secured party has the rights and remedies provided in this Part and, except as limited by subsection (3), those provided in the security agreement. He may reduce his claim to judgment, foreclose or otherwise enforce the security interest by any available judicial procedure. If the collateral is documents, the secured party may proceed either as to the documents or as to the goods covered thereby. A secured party in possession has the rights, remedies and duties provided in Section 9—207. The rights and remedies referred to in this subsection are cumulative.

(2) After default, the debtor has the rights and remedies provided in this Part, those provided in the security agreement and those provided in Section 9—207.

§ 9—502. Collection Rights of Secured Party

(1) When so agreed, and in any event on default, the secured party is entitled to notify an account debtor or the obligor on an instrument to make payment to him whether or not the assignor was theretofore making collections on the collateral, and also to take control of any proceeds to which he is entitled under Section 9—306.

(2) A secured party who by agreement is entitled to charge back uncollected collateral or otherwise to full or limited recourse against the debtor and who undertakes to collect from the account debtors or obligors must proceed in a commercially reasonable manner and may deduct his reasonable expenses of realization from the collections. If the security agreement secures an indebtedness, the secured party must account to the debtor for any surplus, and unless otherwise agreed, the debtor is liable for any deficiency. But, if the underlying transaction was a sale of accounts or chattel paper, the debtor is entitled to any surplus or is liable for any deficiency only if the security agreement so provides.

§ 9—503. Secured Party's Right to Take Possession After Default

Unless otherwise agreed, a secured party has on default the right to take possession of the collateral. In taking possession, a secured party may proceed without judicial process if this can be done without breach of the peace or may proceed by action. If the security agreement so provides, the secured party may require the debtor to assemble the collateral and make it available to the secured party at a place to be designated by the secured party which is reasonably convenient to both parties. Without removal, a secured party may render equipment unusable and may dispose of collateral on the debtor's premises under Section 9—504.

§ 9—504. Secured Party's Right to Dispose of Collateral After Default; Effect of Disposition

(1) A secured party after default may sell, lease or otherwise dispose of any or all of the collateral in its then condition or following any commercially reasonable preparation or proc-

essing, Any sale of goods is subject to the Article on Sales (Article 2)... l.

§ 9—505. Compulsory Disposition of Collateral; Acceptance of the Collateral as Discharge of Obligation

(1) If the debtor has paid sixty percent of the cash price in the case of a purchase money security interest in consumer goods or sixty percent of the loan in the case of another security interest in consumer goods and has not signed after default a statement renouncing or modifying his rights under this Part, a secured party who has taken possession of collateral must dispose of it under Section 9—

504; and if he fails to do so within ninety days after he takes possession, the debtor at his option may recover in conversion or under Section 9—507(1) on secured party's liability.

(2) In any other case involving consumer goods or any other collateral, a secured party in possession may, after default, propose to retain the collateral in satisfaction of the obligation. Written notice of such proposal shall be sent to the debtor if he has not signed after default a statement renouncing or modifying his rights under this subsection. In the case of consumer goods, no other notice need be given. In other cases, notice shall be sent to any other secured party from whom the secured party has received (before sending his notice to the debtor or before the debtor's renunciation of his rights) written notice of a claim of an interest in the collateral. If the secured party receives objection in writing from a person entitled to receive notification within twenty-one days after the notice was sent, the secured party must dispose of the collateral under Section 9—504. In the absence of such written objection, the secured party may retain the collateral in satisfaction of the debtor's obligation.

§ 9—507. Secured Party's Liability for Failure to Comply With This Part

(1) If it is established that the secured party is not proceeding in accordance with the provisions of this Part, disposition may be ordered or restrained on appropriate terms and conditions. If the disposition has occurred, the debtor or any person entitled to notification or whose security interest has been made known

to the secured party prior to the disposition has a right to recover from the secured party any loss caused by a failure to comply with the provisions of this Part. If the collateral is consumer goods, the debtor has a right to recover in any event an amount not less than the credit service charge plus ten percent of the principal amount of the debt or the time price differential plus 10 percent of the cash price.

Appendix 4
United Nations Convention on Contracts for the International Sale of Goods (Excerpts)

The States Parties to this Convention,

Bearing in mind the broad objectives in the resolutions adopted by the sixth special session of the General Assembly of the United Nations on the establishment of a New International Economic Order,

Considering that the development of international trade on the basis of equality and mutual benefit is an important element in promoting friendly relations among States,

Being of the opinion that the adoption of uniform rules which govern contracts for the international sale of goods and take into account the different social, economic and legal systems would contribute to the removal of legal barriers in international trade and promote the development of international trade,

Have agreed as follows:

PART I. SPHERE OF APPLICATION AND GENERAL PROVISIONS

Chapter I. Sphere of Application

ARTICLE 1

(1) This Convention applies to contracts of sale of goods between parties whose places of business are in different States:

(a) when the States are Contracting States; or

(b) when the rules of private international law lead to the application of the law of a Contracting State.

(2) The fact that the parties have their places of business in different States is to be disregarded whenever this fact does not appear either from the contract or from any dealings between, or from information disclosed

by, the parties at any time before or at the conclusion of the contract.

(3) Neither the nationality of the parties nor the civil or commercial character of the parties or of the contract is to be taken into consideration in determining the application of this Convention.

ARTICLE 2

This Convention does not apply to sales:

(a) of goods bought for personal, family or household use, unless the seller, at any time before or at the conclusion of the contract, neither knew nor ought to have known that the goods were bought for any such use;

(b) by auction;

(c) on execution or otherwise by authority of law;

(d) of stocks, shares, investment securities, negotiable instruments or money;

(e) of ships, vessels, hover craft or aircraft;

(f) electricity

ARTICLE 3

(1) Contracts for the supply of goods to be manufactured or produced are to be considered sales unless the party who orders the goods undertakes to supply a substantial part of the materials necessary for such manufacture or production.

(2) This Convention does not apply to contracts in which the preponderant part of the obligations of the party who furnishes the goods consists in the supply of labour or other services.

ARTICLE 4

This Convention governs only the formation of the contract of sale and the rights and obligations of the seller and the buyer arising from such a contract. In particular, except as otherwise expressly provided in this Convention, it is not concerned with:

(a) the validity of the contract or of any of its provisions or of any usage;

(b) the effect which the contract may have on the property in the goods sold.

ARTICLE 5

This Convention does not apply to the liability of the seller for death or personal injury caused by the goods to any person.

ARTICLE 6

The parties may exclude the application of this Convention or, subject to article 12, derogate from or vary the effect of any of its provisions.

Chapter II. General Provisions

ARTICLE 7

(1) In the interpretation of this Convention, regard is to be had to its international character and to the need to promote uniformity in its application and the observance of good faith in international trade.

(2) Questions concerning matters governed by this Convention which are not expressly settled in it are to be settled in conformity with the general principles on which it is based or, in the absence of such principles, in conformity with the law applicable by virtue of the rules of private international law.

ARTICLE 8

(1) For the purposes of this Convention statements made by and other conduct of a party are to be interpreted according to his intent where the other party knew or could not have been unaware what that intent was.

(2) If the preceding paragraph is not applicable, statements made by and other conduct of a party are to be interpreted according to the understanding that a reasonable person of the same kind as the other party would have had in the same circumstances.

(3) In determining the intent of a party or the understanding a reasonable person would have had, due consideration is to be given to all relevant circumstances of the case including the negotiations, any practices which the parties have established between themselves, usages and any subsequent conduct of the parties.

ARTICLE 9

(1) The parties are bound by any usage to which they have agreed and by any practices which they have established between themselves.

(2) The parties are considered, unless otherwise agreed, to have impliedly made applicable to their contract or its formation a usage of which the parties knew or ought to have known and which in international trade is widely known to, and regularly observed by, parties to contracts of the type involved in the particular trade concerned.

ARTICLE 10

For the purposes of this Convention:

(a) if a party has more than one place of business, the place of business is that which has the closest relationship to the contract and its performance, having regard to the circumstances known to or contemplated by the parties at any time before or at the conclusion of the contract;

(b) if a party does not have a place of business, reference is to be made to his habitual residence.

ARTICLE 11

A contract of sale need not be concluded in or evidenced by writing and is not subject to any other requirements as to form. It may be proved by any means, including witnesses.

ARTICLE 12

Any provision of article 11, article 29 or Part II of this Convention that allows a contract of sale or its modification or termination by agreement of any offer, acceptance or other indication of intention to be made in any form other than in writing does not apply where any party has his place of business in a Contracting State which has made a declaration under article 96 of this Convention. The parties may not derogate from or vary the effect of this article.

ARTICLE 13

For the purposes of this Convention "writing" includes telegram and telex.

PART II. FORMATION OF THE CONTRACT

ARTICLE 14

(1) A proposal for concluding a contract addressed to one or more specific persons constitutes an offer if it is sufficiently definite and indicates the intention of the offeror to be bound in case of acceptance. A proposal is sufficiently definite if it indicates the goods and expressly or implicitly fixes or makes provision for determining the quantity and the price.

(2) A proposal other than one addressed to one or more specific persons is to be considered merely as an invitation to make offers, unless the contrary is clearly indicated by the person making the proposal.

ARTICLE 15

(1) An offer becomes effective when it reaches the offeree.

(2) An offer, even if it is irrevocable, may be withdrawn if the withdrawal reaches the offeree before or at the same time as the offer.

ARTICLE 16

(1) Until a contract is concluded an offer may be revoked if the revocation reaches the offeree before he has dispatched an acceptance.

(2) However, an offer cannot be revoked:

(a) if it indicates, whether by stating a fixed time for acceptance or otherwise, that it is irrevocable; or

(b) if it was reasonable for the offeree to rely on the offer as being irrevocable and the offeree has acted in reliance on the offer.

ARTICLE 17

An offer, even if it is irrevocable, is terminated when a rejection reaches the offeror.

ARTICLE 18

(1) A statement made by or other conduct of the offeree indicating assent to an offer is an acceptance. Silence or inactivity does not in itself amount to acceptance.

(2) An acceptance of an offer becomes effective at the moment the indication of assent reaches the offeror. An acceptance is not effective if the indication of assent does not reach the offeror within the time he has fixed or, if no time is fixed, within a reasonable time, due account being taken of the circumstances of the transaction, including the rapidity of the means of communication employed by the offeror. An oral offer must be accepted immediately unless circumstances indicate otherwise.

(3) However, if, by virtue of the offer or as a result of practices which the parties have established between themselves or of usage, the offeree may indicate assent by performing an act, such as one relating to the dispatch of the goods or payment of the price, without notice to the offeror, the acceptance is effective at the moment the act is performed, provided that the act is performed within the period of time laid down in the preceding paragraph.

ARTICLE 19

(1) A reply to an offer which purports to be an acceptance but contains additions, limitations or other modifications is a rejection of the offer and constitutes a counter-offer.

(2) However, a reply to an offer which purports to be an acceptance but contains additional or different terms which do not materially alter the terms of the offer constitutes an acceptance, unless the offeror, without undue delay, objects orally to the discrepancy or dispatches a notice to that effect. If he does not so object, the terms of the contract are the terms of the offer with the modifications contained in the acceptance.

(3) Additional or different terms relating, among other things, to the price, payment, quality and quantity of the goods, place and time of delivery, extent of one party's liability to the other or the settlement of disputes are considered to alter the terms of the offer materially.

ARTICLE 20

(1) A period of time for acceptance fixed by the offeror in a telegram or a letter begins to run from the moment the telegram is handed in for dispatch or from the date shown on the letter or, if no such date is shown, from the date shown on the envelope. A period of time for acceptance fixed by the offeror by telephone, telex or other means of instantaneous communication, begins to run from the moment that the offer reaches the offeree.

(2) Official holidays or non-business days occurring during the period for acceptance are included in calculating the period. However, if a notice of acceptance cannot be delivered at the address of the offeror on the last day of the period because that day falls on an official holiday or a non-business day at the place of business of the offeror, the period is extended until the first business day which follows.

ARTICLE 21

(1) A late acceptance is nevertheless effective as an acceptance if without delay the offeror orally so informs the offeree or dispatches a notice to that effect.

(2) If a letter or other writing containing a late acceptance shows that is has been sent in such circumstances that if its transmission had been normal it would have reached the offeror in due time, the late acceptance is effective as an acceptance unless, without delay, the offeror orally informs the offeree that he considers his offer as having lapsed or dispatches a notice to that effect.

ARTICLE 22

An acceptance may be withdrawn if the withdrawal reaches the offeror before or at the same time as the acceptance would have become effective.

ARTICLE 23

A contract is concluded at the moment when an acceptance of an offer becomes effective in accordance with the provisions of this Convention.

ARTICLE 24

For the purposes of this Part of the Convention, an offer, declaration of acceptance or any other indication of intention "reaches" the addressee when it is made orally to him or delivered by any other means to him personally, to his place of business or mailing address or, if he does not have a place of business or mailing address, to his habitual residence.

PART III. SALE OF GOODS

Chapter I. General Provisions

ARTICLE 25

A breach of contract committed by one of the parties is fundamental if it results in such detriment to the other party as substantially to deprive him of what he is entitled to expect under the contract, unless the party in breach did not foresee and a reasonable person of the same kind in the same circumstances would not have foreseen such a result.

ARTICLE 26

A declaration of avoidance of the contract is effective only if made by notice to the other party.

ARTICLE 27

Unless otherwise expressly provided in this Part of the Convention, if any notice, request or other communication is given or made by a party in accordance with this Part and by means appropriate in the circumstances, a delay or error in the transmission of the communication or its failure to arrive does not deprive that party of the right to rely on the communication.

ARTICLE 28

If, in accordance with the provisions of this Convention, one party is entitled to require performance of any obligation by the other party, a court is not bound to enter a judgment for specific performance unless the court would do so under its own law in respect of similar contracts of sale not governed by this Convention.

ARTICLE 29

(1) A contract may be modified or terminated by the mere agreement of the parties.

(2) A contract in writing which contains a provision requiring any modification or termination by agreement to be in writing may not be otherwise modified or terminated by agreement. However, a party may be precluded by his conduct from asserting such a provision to the extent that the other party has relied on that conduct.

Chapter II. Obligations of the Seller

ARTICLE 35

(1) The seller must deliver goods which are of the quantity, quality and description required by the contract and which are contained or packaged in the manner required by the contract.

(2) Except where the parties have agreed otherwise, the goods do not conform with the contract unless they:

(a) are fit for the purposes for which goods of the same description would ordinarily be used;

(b) are fit for any particular purpose expressly or impliedly made known to the seller at the time of the conclusion of the contract, except where the circumstances show that the buyer did not rely, or that it was unreasonable for him to rely, on the seller's skill and judgment;

(c) possess the qualities of goods which the seller has held out to the buyer as a sample or model;

(d) are contained or packaged in the manner usual for such goods or, where there is no such manner, in a manner adequate to preserve and protect the goods.

(3) The seller is not liable under subparagraphs (a) to (d) of the preceding paragraph for any lack of conformity of the goods if at the time of the conclusion of the contract the buyer knew or could not have been unaware of such lack of conformity.

ARTICLE 36

(1) The seller is liable in accordance with the contract and this Convention for any lack of conformity which exists at the time when the risk passes to the buyer, even though the lack of conformity becomes apparent only after that time.

(2) The seller is also liable for any lack of conformity which occurs after the time indicated in the preceding paragraph and which is due to a breach of any of his obligations, including a breach of any guarantee that for a period of time the goods will remain fit for their ordinary purpose or for some particular purpose or will retain specified qualities or characteristics.

ARTICLE 37

If the seller has delivered goods before the date for delivery, he may, up to that date, deliver any missing part or make up any deficiency in the quantity of the goods delivered, or deliver goods in replacement of any nonconforming goods delivered or remedy any lack of conformity in the goods delivered, provided that the exercise of this right does not cause the buyer unreasonable inconvenience or unreasonable expense. However, the buyer retains any right to claim damages as provided for in this Convention.

Chapter III. Obligations of the Buyer

Chapter IV. Passing of Risk

ARTICLE 66

Loss of or damage to the goods after the risk has passed to the buyer does not discharge him from his obligation to pay the price, unless the loss or damage is due to an act or omission of the seller.

ARTICLE 67

(1) If the contract of sale involves carriage of the goods and the seller is not bound to hand them over at a particular place, the risk passes to the buyer when the goods are handed over to the first carrier for transmission to the buyer in accordance with the contract of sale. If the seller is bound to hand the goods over to a carrier at a particular place, the risk does not pass to the buyer until the goods are handed over to the carrier at that place. The fact that the seller is authorized to retain documents controlling the disposition of the goods does not affect the passage of risk.

(2) Nevertheless, the risk does not pass to the buyer until the goods are clearly identified to the contract, whether by markings on the goods, by shipping documents, by notice given to the buyer or otherwise.

ARTICLE 68

The risk in respect of goods sold in transit passes to the buyer from the time of the conclusion of the contract. However, if the circumstances so indicate, the risk is assumed by the buyer from the time the goods were handed over to the carrier who issued the documents embodying the contract of carriage. Nevertheless, if at the time of the conclusion of the contract of sale the seller knew or ought to have known that the goods had been lost or damaged and did not disclose this to the buyer, the loss or damage is at risk of the seller.

ARTICLE 69

(1) In cases not within articles 67 and 68, the risk passes to the buyer when he takes over the goods or, if he does not do so in due time, from the time when the goods are placed at his disposal and he commits a breach of contract by failing to take delivery.

(2) However, if the buyer is bound to take over the goods at a place other than a place of business of the seller, the risk passes when delivery is due and the buyer is aware of the fact that the goods are placed at his disposal at that place.

(3) If the contract relates to goods not then identified, the goods are considered not to be placed at the disposal of the buyer until they are clearly identified to the contract.

ARTICLE 70

If the seller has committed a fundamental breach of contract, articles 67, 68 and 69 do not impair the remedies available to the buyer on account of the breach.

PART IV. FINAL PROVISIONS

ARTICLE 96

A Contracting State whose legislation requires contracts of sale to be concluded in or evidenced by writing may at any time make a declaration in accordance with article 12 that any provision of article 11, article 29, or Part II of this Convention, that allows a contract of sale or its modification or termination by agreement or any offer, acceptance, or other indication of intention to be made in any form other than writing, does not apply where any party has his place of business in that State.

DONE at Vienna, this day of eleventh day of April, one thousand nine hundred and eighty, in a single original, of which the Arabic, Chinese, English, French, Russian and Spanish texts are equally authentic.

IN WITNESS WHEREOF the undersigned plenipotentiaries, being duly authorized by their respective Governments, have signed this Convention.

Appendix 5
UNIFORM PARTNERSHIP ACT

Part I

Preliminary Provisions

§ 1. Name of Act

This act may be cited as Uniform Partnership Act.

§ 2. Definition of Terms

In this act, "Court" includes every court and judge having jurisdiction in the case.

"Business" includes every trade, occupation, or profession.

"Person" includes individuals, partnerships, corporations, and other associations.

"Bankrupt" includes bankrupt under the Federal Bankruptcy Actor insolvent under any state insolvent act.

"Conveyance" includes every assignment, lease, mortgage, or encumbrance.

"Real property" includes land and any interest or estate inland.

§ 3. Interpretation of Knowledge and Notice

(1) A person has "knowledge" of a fact within the meaning of this act not only when he has actual knowledge thereof, but also when he has knowledge of such other facts as in the circumstances shows bad faith.

(2) A person has "notice" of a fact within the meaning of this act when the person who claims the benefit of the notice

    (a) States the fact to such person, or

    (b) Delivers through the mail, or by other means of communication, a written statement of the fact to such person or to a proper person at his place of business or residence.

§ 4. Rules of Construction

(1) The rule that statutes in derogation of the common law are to be strictly construed shall have no application to this act.

(2) The law of estoppel shall apply under this act.

(3) The law of agency shall apply under this act.

(4) This act shall be so interpreted and construed as to effect its general purpose to make uniform the law of those states which enact it.

(5) This act shall not be construed so as to impair the obligations of any contract existing when the act goes into effect, nor to affect any action or proceedings begun or right accrued before this act takes effect.

§ 5. Rules for Cases Not Provided for in this Act

In any case not provided for in this act the rules of law and equity, including the law merchant, shall govern.

Part II

Nature of Partnership

§ 6. Partnership Defined

(1) A partnership is an association of two or more persons to carry on as co-owners a business for profit.

(2) But any association formed under any other statute of this state, or any statute adopted by authority, other than the authority of this state, is not a partnership under this act, unless such association would have been a partnership in this state prior to the adoption of this act; but this act shall apply to limited partnerships except in so far as the statutes relating to such partnerships are inconsistent herewith.

§ 7. Rules for Determining the Existence of a Partnership

In determining whether a partnership exists, these rules shall apply:

(1) Except as provided by Section 16 persons who are not partners as to each other are not partners as to third persons.

(2) Joint tenancy, tenancy in common, tenancy by the entireties, joint property, common property, or part ownership does not of itself establish a partnership, whether such co-owners do or do not share any profits made by the use of the property.

(3) The sharing of gross returns does not of itself establish a partnership, whether or not the persons sharing them have a joint or common right or interest in any property from which the returns are derived.

(4) The receipt by a person of a share of the profits of a business is prima facie evidence that he is a partner in the business, but no such inference shall be drawn if such profits were received in payment:

  (a) As a debt by installments or otherwise,

  (b) As wages of an employee or rent to a landlord,

  (c) As an annuity to a widow or representative of a deceased partner,

  (d) As interest on a loan, though the amount of payment vary with the profits of the business,

  (e) As the consideration for the sale of a goodwill of a business or other property by installments or otherwise.

§ 8. Partnership Property

(1) All property originally brought into the partnership stock or subsequently acquired by purchase or otherwise, on account of the partnership, is partnership property.

(2) Unless the contrary intention appears, property acquired with partnership funds is partnership property.

(3) Any estate in real property may be acquired in the partnership name. Title so acquired can be conveyed only in the partnership name.

(4) A conveyance to a partnership in the partnership name, though without words of inheritance, passes the entire estate of the grantor unless a contrary intent appears.

Part III

Relations of Partners to Persons Dealing with the Partnership

§ 9. Partner Agent of Partnership as to Partnership Business

(1) Every partner is an agent of the partnership for the purpose of its business, and the act of every partner, including the execution in the partnership name of any instrument, for apparently carrying on in the usual way the business of the partnership of which he is a member binds the partnership, unless the partner so acting has in fact no authority to act for the partnership in the particular matter, and the person with whom he is dealing has knowledge of the fact that he has no such authority.

(2) An act of a partner which is not apparently for the carrying on of the business of the partnership in the usual way does not bind the partnership unless authorized by the other partners.

(3) Unless authorized by the other partners or unless they have abandoned the business, one or more but less than all the partners have no authority to:

    (a) Assign the partnership property in trust for creditors or on the assignee's promise to pay the debts of the partnership,

    (b) Dispose of the goodwill of the business,

    (c) Do any other act which would make it impossible to carry on the ordinary business of a partnership,

    (d) Confess a judgment,

    (e) Submit a partnership claim or liability to arbitration or reference.

(4) No act of a partner in contravention of a restriction on authority shall bind the partnership to persons having knowledge of the restriction.

§ 10. Conveyance of Real Property of the Partnership

(1) Where title to real property is in the partnership name, any partner may convey title to such property by a conveyance executed in the partnership name; but the partnership may recover such property unless the partner's act binds the partnership under the provisions of paragraph (1) of section 9 or unless such property has been conveyed by the grantee or a person claiming through such grantee to a holder for value without knowledge that the partner, in making the conveyance, has exceeded his authority.

(2) Where title to real property is in the name of the partnership, a conveyance executed by a partner, in his own name, passes the equitable interest of the partnership, provided the act is one within the authority of the partner under the provisions of paragraph (1) of Section 9.

(3) Where title to real property is in the name of one or more but not all the partners, and the record does not disclose the right of the partnership, the partners in whose name the title stands may convey title to such property, but the partnership may recover such property if the partners' act does not bind the partnership under the provisions of paragraph (1) of section 9, unless the purchaser or his assignee, is a holder for value, without knowledge.

(4) Where the title to real property is in the name of one or more or all the partners, or in a third person in trust for the partnership, a conveyance executed by a partner in the partnership name, or in his own name, passes the equitable interest of the partnership, provided the act is one within the authority of the partner under the provisions of paragraph (1) of section 9.

(5) Where the title to real property is in the names of all the partners a conveyance executed by all the partners passes all their rights in such property.

§ 11. Partnership Bound by Admission of Partner

An admission or representation made by any partner concerning partnership affairs within the scope of his authority as conferred by this act is evidence against the partnership.

§ 12. Partnership Charged with Knowledge of or Notice to Partner

Notice to any partner of any matter relating to partnership affairs, and the knowledge of the partner acting in the particular matter, acquired while a partner or then present to his mind, and the knowledge of any other partner who reasonably could and should have communicated it to the acting partner, operate as notice to or knowledge of the partnership, except in the case of a fraud on the partnership committed by or with the consent of that partner.

§ 13. Partnership Bound by Partner's Wrongful Act

Where, by any wrongful act or omission of any partner acting in the ordinary course of the business of the partnership or with the authority of his co-partners, loss or injury is caused to any person, not being a partner in the partnership, or any penalty is incurred, the partnership is liable therefor to the same extent as the partner so acting or omitting to act.

§ 14. Partnership Bound by Partner's Breach of Trust

The partnership is bound to make good the loss:

    (a) Where one partner acting within the scope of his apparent authority receives money or property of a third person and misapplies it; and

    (b) Where the partnership in the course of its business receives money or property of a third person and the money or property so received is misapplied by any partner while it is in the custody of the partnership.

§ 15. Nature of Partner's Liability

All partners are liable

    (a) Jointly and severally for everything chargeable to the partnership under sections 13 and 14.

    (b) Jointly for all other debts and obligations of the partnership; but any partner may enter into a separate obligation to perform a partnership contract.

§ 16. Partner by Estoppel

(1) When a person, by words spoken or written or by conduct, represents himself, or consents to another representing him to any one, as a partner in an existing partnership or with one or more persons not actual partners, he is liable to any such person to whom such representation has been made, who has, on the faith of such representation, given credit to the actual or apparent partnership, and if he has made such representation or consented to its being made in a public manner he is liable to such person, whether the representation has or has not been made or communicated to such person so giving credit by or with the knowledge of the apparent partner making the representation or consenting to its being made.

    (a) When a partnership liability results, he is liable as though he were an actual member of the partnership.

    (b) When no partnership liability results, he is liable jointly with the other persons, if any, so consenting to the contract or representation as to incur liability, otherwise separately.

(2) When a person has been thus represented to be a partner in an existing partnership, or with one or more persons not actual partners, he is an agent of the persons consenting to such representation to bind them to the same extent and in the same manner as though he were a partner in fact, with respect to persons who rely upon the representation. Where all the members of the existing partnership consent to the representation, a partnership act or obligation results; but in all other cases it is the joint act or obligation of the person acting and the persons consenting to the representation.

§ 17. Liability of Incoming Partner

A person admitted as a partner into an existing partnership is liable for all the obligations of the partnership arising before his admission as though he had been a partner when such obligations were incurred, except that this liability shall be satisfied only out of partnership property.

Part IV

Relations of Partners to One Another

§ 18. Rules Determining Rights and Duties of Partners

The rights and duties of the partners in relation to the partnership shall be determined, subject to any agreement between them, by the following rules:

(a) Each partner shall be repaid his contributions, whetherby way of capital or advances to the partnership property andshare equally in the profits and surplus remaining after all liabilities, including those to partners, are satisfied; and must contribute toward the losses, whether of capital or otherwise, sustained by the partnership according to his share in the profits.

(b) The partnership must indemnify every partner in respect of payments made and personal liabilities reasonably incurred by him in the ordinary and proper conduct of its business, or for the preservation of its business or property.

(c) A partner, who in aid of the partnership makes any payment or advance beyond the amount of capital which he agreed to contribute, shall be paid interest from the date of the payment or advance.

(d) A partner shall receive interest on the capital contributed by him only from the date when repayment should be made.

(e) All partners have equal rights in the management and conduct of the partnership business.

(f) No partner is entitled to remuneration for acting in the partnership business, except that a surviving partner is entitled to reasonable compensation for his services in winding up the partnership affairs.

(g) No person can become a member of a partnership without the consent of all the partners.

(h) Any difference arising as to ordinary matters connected with the partnership business may be decided by a majority of the partners; but no act in contravention of any agreement between the partners may be done rightfully without the consent of all the partners.

§ 19. Partnership Books

The partnership books shall be kept, subject to any agreement between the partners, at the principal place of business of the partnership, and every partner shall at all times have access to and may inspect and copy any of them.

§ 20. Duty of Partners to Render

Information Partners shall render on demand true and full information of all things affecting the partnership to any partner or the legal representative of any deceased partner or partner under legal disability.

§ 21. Partner Accountable as a Fiduciary

(1) Every partner must account to the partnership for any benefit, and hold as trustee for it any profits derived by him without the consent of the other partners from any transaction connected with the formation, conduct, or liquidation of the partnership or from any use by him of its property.

(2) This section applies also to the representatives of a deceased partner engaged in the liquidation of the affairs of the partnership as the personal representatives of the last surviving partner.

§ 22. Right to an Account

Any partner shall have the right to a formal account as to partnership affairs:

(a) If he is wrongfully excluded from the partnership business or possession of its property by his co-partners,

(b) If the right exists under the terms of any agreement,

(c) As provided by Section 21,

(d) Whenever other circumstances render it just and reasonable.

§ 23. Continuation of Partnership Beyond Fixed Term

(1) When a partnership for a fixed term or particular undertaking is continued after the termination of such term or particular undertaking without any express agreement, the rights and duties of the partners remain the same as they were at such termination, so far as is consistent with a partnership at will.

(2) A continuation of the business by the partners or such of them as habitually acted therein during the term, without any settlement or liquidation of the partnership affairs, is prima facie evidence of a continuation of the partnership.

Part V

Property Rights of a Partner

§ 24. Extent of Property Rights of a Partner

The property rights of a partner are (1) his rights in specific partnership property, (2) his interest in the partnership, and (3) his right to participate in the management.

§ 25. Nature of a Partner's Right in Specific Partnership Property

(1) A partner is co-owner with his partners of specific partnership property holding as a tenant in partnership.

(2) The incidents of this tenancy are such that:

(a) A partner, subject to the provisions of this act and to any agreement between the partners, has an equal right with his partners to possess specific partnership property for partnership purposes; but he has no right to possess such property, for any other purpose without the consent of his partners.

(b) A partner's right in specific partnership property is not assignable except in connection with the assignment of rights of all the partners in the same property.

(c) A partner's right in specific partnership property is not subject to attachment or execution, except on a claim against the partnership. When partnership property is attached for a partnership debt the partners, or any of them, or the representatives of a deceased partner, cannot claim any right under the homestead or exemption laws.

(d) On the death of a partner his right in specific partnership property vests in the surviving partner or partners, except where the deceased was the last surviving partner or partners, or the legal representative of the last surviving partner, has no right to possess the partnership property for any but a partnership purpose.

(e) A partner's right in specific partnership property is not subject to dower, courtesy, or allowances to widows, heirs, or next of kin.

§ 26. Nature of Partner's Interest in the Partnership

A partner's interest in the partnership is his share of the profits and surplus, and the same is personal property.

§ 27. Assignment of Partner's Interest

(1) A conveyance by a partner of his interest in the partnership does not of itself dissolve the partnership, nor, as against the other partners in the absence of agreement, entitle the assignee, during the continuance of the partnership to interfere in the management or administration of the partnership business or affairs, or to require an information or account of partnership transactions, or to inspect the partnership books; but it merely entities the assignee to receive in accordance with his contract the profits to which the assigning partner would otherwise be entitled.

(2) In case of a dissolution of the partnership, the assignee is entitled to receive his assignor's interest and may require an account

from the date only of the last account agreed to by all the partners.

§ 28. Partner's Interest Subject to Charging Order

(1) On due application to a competent court by any judgment creditor of a partner, the court which entered the judgment, order, or decree, or any other court, may charge the interest of the debtor partner with payment of the unsatisfied amount of such judgment debt with interest thereon; and may then or later appoint a receiver of his share of the profits, and of any other money due or to fall due to him in respect of the partnership, and make all other orders, directions, accounts and inquiries which the debtor partner might have made, or which the circumstances of the case may require.

(2) The interest charged may be redeemed at any time before foreclosure, or in case of a sale being directed by the court may be purchased without thereby causing a dissolution:

    (a) With separate property, by any one or more of the partners, or

    (b) With partnership property, by any one or more of the partners with the consent of all the partners whose interests are not so charged or sold.

(3) Nothing in this act shall be held to deprive a partner of his right, if any, under the exemption laws, as regards his interest in the partnership.

Part VI

Dissolution and Winding Up

§ 29. Dissolution Defined

The dissolution of a partnership is the change in the relation of the partners caused by any partner ceasing to be associated in the carrying on as distinguished from the winding up of the business.

§ 30. Partnership Not Terminated by Dissolution

On dissolution the partnership is not terminated, but continues until the winding up of partnership affairs is completed.

§ 31. Causes of Dissolution

Dissolution is caused: (1) Without violation of the agreementbetween the partners,

    (a) By the termination of the definite term or particular undertaking specified in the agreement,

    (b) By the express will of any partner when no definite term or particular undertaking is specified,

    (c) By the express will of all the partners who have not assigned their interests or suffered them to be charged for their separate debts, either before or after the termination of any specified term or particular undertaking,

    (d) By the expulsion of any partner from the business bona fide in accordance with such a power conferred by the agreement between the partners;

(2) In contravention of the agreement between the partners, where the circumstances do not permit a dissolution under any other provision of this section, by the express will of any partner at any time;

(3) By any event which makes it unlawful for the business of the partnership to be carried on or for the members to carry it on in partnership;

(4) By the death of any partner;

(5) By the bankruptcy of any partner or the partnership;

(6) By decree of court under Section 32.

§ 32. Dissolution by Decree of Court

(1) On application by or for a partner the court shall decree a dissolution whenever:

    (a) A partner has been declared a lunatic in any judicial proceedingor is shown to be of unsound mind,

    (b) A partner becomes in any other way incapable of performing his part of the partnership contract,

(c) A partner has been guilty of such conduct as tends to affect prejudicially the carrying on of the business,

(d) A partner willfully or persistently commits a breach of the partnership agreement, or otherwise so conducts himself in matters relating to the partnership business that it is not reasonably practicable to carry on the business in partnership with him,

(e) The business of the partnership can only be carried on at a loss,

(f) Other circumstances render a dissolution equitable.

(2) On the application of the purchaser of a partner's interest under Sections 27 or 28:

(a) After the termination of the specified term or particular undertaking,

(b) At any time if the partnership was a partnership at will when the interest was assigned or when the charging order was issued.

§ 33. General Effect of Dissolution on Authority of Partner

Except so far as may be necessary to wind up partnership affairs or to complete transactions begun but not then finished, dissolution terminates all authority of any partner to act for the partnership,

(1) With respect to the partners,

(a) When the dissolution is not by the act, bankruptcy or death of a partner, or

(b) When the dissolution is by such act, bankruptcy or death of a partner, in cases where Section 34 so requires.

(2) With respect to persons not partners, as declared in Section 35.

§ 34. Right of Partner to Contribution from Copartners After Dissolution

Where the dissolution is caused by the act, death or bankruptcy of a partner, each partner is liable to his copartners for his share of any liability created by any partner acting for the partnership as if the partnership had not been dissolved unless

(a) The dissolution being by act of any partner, the partner acting for the partnership had knowledge of the dissolution, or

(b) The dissolution being by the death or bankruptcy of a partner, the partner acting for the partnership had knowledge or notice of the death or bankruptcy.

§ 35. Power of Partner to Bind Partnership to Third Persons After Dissolution

(1) After dissolution a partner can bind the partnership except as provided in Paragraph (3)

(a) By any act appropriate for winding up partnership affairs or completing transactions unfinished by dissolution;

(b) By any transaction which would bind the partnership if dissolution had not taken place, provided the other party to the transaction

(I) Had extended credit to the partnership prior to dissolution and had no knowledge or notice of the dissolution; or

(II) Though he had not so extended credit, had nevertheless known of the partnership prior to dissolution, and, having no knowledge or notice of dissolution, the fact of dissolution had not been advertised in a newspaper of general circulation in the place (or in each place if more than one) at which the partnership business was regularly carried on.

(2) The liability of a partner under paragraph (1b) shall be satisfied out of partnership assets alone when such partner had been prior to dissolution.

(a) Unknown as a partner to the person with whom the contract is made; and

(b) So far unknown and inactive in partnership affairs that the business reputation of the partnership could not be said to have been in any degree due to his connection with it.

(3) The partnership is in no case bound by any act of a partner after dissolution.

   (a) Where the partnership is dissolved because it is unlawful to carry on the business, unless the act is appropriate for winding up partnership affairs; or

   (b) Where the partner has become bankrupt; or

   (c) Where the partner has no authority to wind up partnership affairs; except by a transaction with one who

       (I) Had extended credit to the partnership prior to dissolution and had no knowledge or notice of his want of authority; or

       (II) Had not extended credit to the partnership prior to dissolution, and, having no knowledge or notice of his want of authority, the fact of his want of authority has not been advertised in the manner provided for advertising the fact of dissolution in paragraph (1bII).

(4) Nothing in this section shall affect the liability under section 16 of any person who after dissolution represents himself or consents to another representing him as a partner in a partnership engaged in carrying on business.

§ 36. Effect of Dissolution on Partner's Existing Liability

(1) The dissolution of the partnership does not of itself discharge the existing liability of any partner.

(2) A partner is discharged from any existing liability upon dissolution of the partnership by an agreement to that effect between himself, the partnership creditor and the person or partnership continuing the business; and such agreement may be inferred from the course of dealing between the creditor having

knowledge of the dissolution and the person or partnership continuing the business.

(3) Where a person agrees to assume the existing obligations of a dissolved partnership, the partners whose obligations have been assumed shall be discharged from any liability to any creditor of the partnership who, knowing of the agreement, consents to a material alteration in the nature or time of payment of such obligations.

(4) The individual property of a deceased partner shall be liable for all obligations of the partnership incurred while he was a partner but subject to the prior payment of his separate debts.

§ 37. Right to Wind Up

Unless otherwise agreed the partners who have not wrongfully dissolved the partnership or the legal representative of the last surviving partner, not bankrupt, has the right to wind up the partnership affairs; provided, however, that any partner, his legal representative or his assignee, upon cause shown, may obtain winding up by the court.

§ 38. Rights of Partners to Application of Partnership Property

(1) When dissolution is caused in any way, except in contravention of the partnership agreement, each partner as against his co-partners and all persons claiming through them in respect of their interests in the partnership, unless otherwise agreed, may have the partnership property applied to discharge its liabilities, and the surplus applied to pay in cash the net amount owing to the respective partners. But if dissolution is caused by expulsion of a partner, bona fide under the partnership agreement and if the expelled partner is discharged from all partnership liabilities, either by payment or agreement under Section 36(2), he shall receive in cash only the net amount due him from the partnership.

(2) When dissolution is caused in contravention of the partnership agreement the rights of the partners shall be as follows:

   (a) Each partner who has not caused dissolution wrongfully shall have,

(I) All the rights specified in paragraph (1) of this section, and

(II) The right, as against each partner who has caused the dissolution wrongfully, to damages for breach of the agreement.

(b) The partners who have not caused the dissolution wrongfully, if they all desire to continue the business in the same name, either by themselves or jointly with others, may do so, during the agreed term for the partnership and for that purpose may possess the partnership property, provided they secure the payment by bond approved by the court, or pay to any partner who has caused the dissolution wrongfully, the value of his interestin the partnership at the dissolution, less any damages recoverable under clause (2aII) of the section, and in like manner indemnify him against all present or future partnership liabilities.

(c) A partner who has caused the dissolution wrongfully shall have:

(I) If the business is not continued under the provisions of paragraph (2b) all the rights of a partner under paragraph (1), subject to clause (2aII), of this section,

(II) If the business is continued under paragraph (2b) of this section the right as against his co-partners and all claiming through them in respect of their interests in the partnership, less any damages caused to his co-partners by the dissolution, ascertained and paid to him in cash, or the payment secured by bond approved by the court, and to be released from all existing liabilities of the partnership; but in ascertaining the value of the partner's interest the value of the goodwill of the business shall not be considered.

§ 39. Rights Where Partnership is Dissolved for Fraud or Misrepresentation

Where a partnership contract is rescinded on the ground of the fraud or misrepresentation of one of the parties thereto, the party entitled to rescind is, without prejudice to any other right, entitled,

(a) To a lien on, or right of retention of, the surplus of the partnership property after satisfying the partnership liabilities to third persons for any sum of money paid by him for the purchase of an interest in the partnership and for any capital or advances contributed by him; and

(b) To stand, after all liabilities to third persons have been satisfied, in the place of the creditors of the partnership for any payments made by him in respect of the partnership liabilities; and

(c) To be indemnified by the person guilty, of the fraud or making the representation against all debts and liabilities of the partnership.

§ 40. Rules for Distribution

In settling accounts between the partners after dissolution, the following rules shall be observed, subject to any agreement to the contrary:

(a) The assets of the partnership are:

(I) The partnership property,

(II) The contributions of the partners necessary for the payment of all the liabilities specified in clause (b) of this paragraph.

(b) The liabilities of the partnership shall rank in order of payment, as follows:

(I) Those owing to creditors other than partners,

(II) Those owing to partners other than for capital and profits,

(III) Those owing to partners in respect of capital,

(IV) Those owing to partners in respect of profits.

(c) The assets shall be applied in the order of their declaration in clause (a) of this paragraph to the satisfaction of the liabilities.

(d) The partners shall contribute, as provided by Section 18(a) the amount necessary to satisfy the liabilities; but if any, but not all, of the partners are insolvent, or, not being subject to process, refuse to contribute, the other parties shall contribute their share of the liabilities, and, in the relative proportions in which they share the profits, the additional amount necessary to pay the liabilities.

(e) An assignee for the benefit of creditors or any person appointed by the court shall have the right to enforce the contributions specified in clause (d) of this paragraph.

(f) Any partner or his legal representative shall have the right to enforce the contributions specified in clause (d) of this paragraph, to the extent of the amount which he has paid in excess of his share of the liability.

(g) The individual property of a deceased partner shall be liable for the contributions specified in clause (d) of this paragraph.

(h) When partnership property and the individual properties of the partners are in possession of a court for distribution, partnership creditors shall have priority on partnership property and separate creditors on individual property, saving the rights of lien or secured creditors as heretofore.

(i) Where a partner has become bankrupt or his estate is insolvent the claims against his separate property shall rank in the following order:

(I) Those owing to separate creditors,

(II) Those owing to partnership creditors,

(III) Those owing to partners by way of contribution.

§ 41. Liability of Persons Continuing the Business in Certain Cases

(1) When any new partner is admitted into an existing partnership, or when any partner retires and assigns (or the representative of the deceased partner assigns) his rights in partnership property to two or more of the partners, or to one or more of the partners and one or more third persons, if the business is continued without liquidation of the partnership affairs, creditors of the first or dissolved partnership are also creditors of the partnership so continuing the business.

(2) When all but one partner retire and assign (or the representative of a deceased partner assigns) their rights in partnership property to the remaining partner, who continues the business without liquidation of partnership affairs, either alone or with others, creditors of the dissolved partnership are also creditors of the person or partnership so continuing the business.

(3) When any partner retires or dies and the business of the dissolved partnership is continued as set forth in paragraphs (1) and (2) of this section, with the consent of the retired partners or the representative of the deceased partner, but without any assignment of his right in partnership property, rights of creditors of the dissolved partnership and of the creditors of the person or partnership continuing the business shall be as if such assignment had been made.

(4) When all the partners or their representatives assign their rights in partnership property to one or more third persons who

promise to pay the debts and who continue the business of the dissolved partnership, creditors of the dissolved partnership are also creditors of the person or partnership continuing the business.

(5) When any partner wrongfully causes a dissolution and theremaining partners continue the business under the provisions of Section 38(2b), either alone or with others, and without liquidation of the partnership affairs, creditors of the dissolved partnership are also creditors of the person or partnership continuing the business.

(6) When a partner is expelled and the remaining partners continue the business either alone or with others, without liquidation of the partnership affairs, creditors of the dissolved partnership are also creditors of the person or partnership continuing the business.

(7) The liability of a third person becoming a partner in the partnership continuing the business, under this section, to the creditors of the dissolved partnership shall be satisfied out of partnership property only.

(8) When the business of a partnership after dissolution is continued under any conditions set forth in this section the creditors of the dissolved partnership, as against the separate creditors of the retiring or deceased partner or the representative of the deceased partner, have a prior right to any claim of the retired partner or the representative of the deceased partner against the person or partnership continuing the business, on account of the retired partner or the representative of the deceased partner against the person or partnership continuing the business, on account of the retired or deceased partner's interest in the dissolved partnership or on account of any consideration promised for such interest or for his right in partnership property.

(9) Nothing in this section shall be held to modify any right of creditors to set aside any assignment on the ground of fraud.

(10) The use by the person or partnership continuing the business of the partnership name, or the name of a deceased partner as part thereof, shall not of itself make the individual property of the deceased partner liable

for any debts contracted by such person or partnership.

§ 42. Rights of Retiring or Estate of Deceased Partner When the Business Is Continued

When any partner retires or dies, and the business is continued under any of the conditions set forth in Section 41 (1, 2, 3, 5, 6), or Section 38(2b), without any settlement of accounts as between him or his estate and the person or partnership continuing the business, unless otherwise agreed, he or his legal representative as against such persons or partnership may have the value of his interest at the date of dissolution ascertained, and shall receive as an ordinary creditor an amount equal to the value of his interest in the dissolved partnership with interest, or, at his option or at the option of his legal representative, in lieu of interest, the profits attributable to the use of his right in the property of the dissolved partnership as against the separate creditors, or the representative of the retired or deceased partner, shall have priority on any claim arising under this section, as provided by Section 41(8) of this act.

§ 43. Accrual of Actions

The right to an account of his interest shall accrue to any partner, or his legal representative, as against the winding up partners or the surviving partners or the person or partnership continuing the business, at the date of dissolution, in the absence of any agreement to the contrary.

Part VII

Miscellaneous Provisions

§ 44. When Act Takes Effect

This act shall take effect on the day of one thousand nine hundred and .

§ 45. Legislation Repealed

All acts or parts of acts inconsistent with this act are hereby repealed.

Appendix 6
REVISED MODEL BUSINESS CORPORATION ACT

As Amended in 1986 and 1987 (EXCERPTS)

§ 1.20. FILING REQUIREMENTS

(a) A document must satisfy the requirements of this section, and of any other section that adds to or varies from these requirements, to be entitled to filing by the secretary of state.

(b) This Act must require or permit filing the document in the office of the secretary of state.

(c) The document must contain the information required by this Act. It may contain other information as well.

(d) The document must be typewritten or printed.

(e) The document must be in the English language. A corporate name need not be in English if written in English letters or Arabic or Roman numerals, and the certificate of existence required of foreign corporations need not be in English if accompanied by a reasonably authenticated English translation.

(f) The document must be executed:
   (1) by the chairman of the board of directors of a domestic or foreign corporation, by its president, or by another of its officers;
   (2) if directors have not been selected or the corporation has not been formed, by an incorporator; or
   (3) if the corporation is in the hands of a receiver, trustee, or other court-appointed fiduciary, by that fiduciary.

(g) The person executing the document shall sign it and state beneath or opposite his signature his name and the capacity in which he signs. The document may but need not contain:
   (1) the corporate seal,

(2) an attestation by the secretary or an assistant secretary,

(3) an acknowledgment, verification, or proof.

(h) If the secretary of state has prescribed a mandatory form for the document under section 1.21, the document must be in or on the prescribed form.

(i) The document must be delivered to the office of the secretary of state for filing and must be accompanied by one exact or conformed copy (except as provided in sections 5.03 and 15.09), the correct filing fee, and any franchise tax, license fee, or penalty required by this Act or other law.

§ 1.21. FORMS

(a) The secretary of state may prescribe and furnish on request forms for:

(1) an application for a certificate of existence,

(2) a foreign corporation's application for a certificate of authority to transact business in this state,

(3) a foreign corporation's application for a certificate of withdrawal, and

(4) the annual report. If the secretary of state so requires, use of these forms is mandatory.

(b) The secretary of state may prescribe and furnish on request forms for other documents required or permitted to be filed by this Act but their use is not mandatory.

§ 1.23. EFFECTIVE TIME AND DATE OF DOCUMENT

(a) Except as provided in subsection (b) and section 1.24(c), a document accepted for filing is effective:

(1) at the time of filing on the date it is filed, as evidenced by the secretary of state's date and time endorsement on the original document; or

(2) at the time specified in the document as its effective time on the date it is filed.

(b) A document may specify a delayed effective time and date, and if it does so the document becomes effective at the time and date specified. If a delayed effective date but no time is specified, the document is effective at the close of business on that date. A delayed effective date for a document may not be later than the 90th day after the date it is filed.

§ 1.25. FILING DUTY OF SECRETARY OF STATE

(a) If a document delivered to the office of the secretary of state for filing satisfies the requirements of section 1.20, the secretary of state shall file it.

(b) The secretary of state files a document by stamping or otherwise endorsing "Filed," together with his name and official title and the date and time of receipt, on both the original and the document copy and on the receipt for the filing fee. After filing a document, except as provided in sections 5.03 and 15.10, the secretary of state shall deliver the document copy, with the filing fee receipt (or acknowledgment of receipt if no fee is required) attached, to the domestic or foreign corporation or its representative.

(c) If the secretary of state refuses to file a document, he shall return it to the domestic or foreign corporation or its representative within five days after the document was delivered, together with a brief, written explanation of the reason for his refusal.

(d) The secretary of state's duty to file documents under this section is ministerial. His filing or refusing to file a document does not:

(1) affect the validity or invalidity of the document in whole or part;

(2) relate to the correctness or incorrectness of information contained in the document;

(3) create a presumption that the document is valid or invalid or that information contained in the document is correct or incorrect.

§ 1.40. ACT DEFINITIONS

In this Act:

(1) "Articles of incorporation" include amended and restated articles of incorporation and the articles of merger.

(2) "Authorized shares" means the shares of all classes a domestic or foreign corporation is authorized to issue.

(3) "Conspicuous" means so written that a reasonable person against whom the writing is to operate should have noticed it. For example, printing in italics or boldface or contrasting color, or typing in capitals or underlined, is conspicuous.

(4) "Corporation" or "domestic corporation" means a corporation for profit, which is not a foreign corporation, incorporated under or subject to the provisions of this Act.

(5) "Deliver" includes mail.

(6) "Distribution" means a direct or indirect transfer of money or other property (except its own shares) or incurrence of indebtedness by a corporation to or for the benefit of its shareholders in respect of any of its shares. A distribution may be in the form of a declaration or payment of a dividend; a purchase, redemption, or other acquisition of shares; a distribution of indebtedness; or otherwise.

(7) "Effective date of notice" is defined in section 1.41.

(8) "Employee" includes an officer but not a director. A director may accept duties that make him also an employee.

(9) "Entity" includes corporation and foreign corporation; not-for-profit corporation; profit and not-for-profit unincorporated association; business trust, estate, partnership, trust, and two or more persons having a joint or common economic interest; and state, United States, and foreign government.

(10) "Foreign corporation" means a corporation for profit incorporated under a law other than the law of this state.

(11) "Governmental subdivision" includes authority, county, district, and municipality.

(12) "Includes" denotes a partial definition.

(13) "Individual" includes the estate of an incompetent or deceased individual.

(14) "Means" denotes an exhaustive definition.

(15) "Notice" is defined in section 1.41.

(16) "Person" includes individual and entity.

(17) "Principal office" means the office (in or out of this state) so designated in the annual report where the principal executive offices of a domestic or foreign corporation are located.

(18) "Proceeding" includes civil suit and criminal, administrative, and investigatory action.

(19) "Record date" means the date established under chapter 6 or 7 on which a corporation determines the identity of its shareholders and their shareholdings for purposes of this Act. The determinations shall be made as of the close of business on the record date unless another time for doing so is specified when the record date is fixed.

(20) "Secretary" means the corporate officer to whom the board of directors has delegated responsibility under section 8.40(c) for custody of the minutes of the meetings of the board of directors and of the shareholders and for authenticating records of the corporation.

(21) "Shares" means the units into which the proprietary interests in a corporation are divided.

(22) "Shareholder" means the person in whose name shares are registered in the records of a corporation or the beneficial owner of shares to the extent of the rights granted by a nominee certificate on file with a corporation.

(23) "State," when referring to a part of the United States, includes a state and commonwealth (and their agencies and governmental subdivisions) and a territory and insular possession (and their agencies and governmental subdivisions) of the United States.

(24) "Subscriber" means a person who subscribes for shares in a corporation, whether before or after incorporation.

(25) "United States" includes district, authority, bureau, commission, department, and any other agency of the United States.

(26) "Voting group" means all shares of one or more classes or series that under the articles of incorporation or this Act are entitled to vote and be counted together collectively on a matter at a meeting of shareholders. All shares entitled by the articles of incorporation of this Act to vote generally on the matter are for that purpose a single voting group.

§ 1.41. NOTICE

(a) Notice under this Act must be in writing unless oral notice is reasonable under the circumstances.

(b) Notice may be communicated in person; by telephone, telegraph, teletype, or other form of wire or wireless communication; or by mail or private carrier. If these forms of personal notice are impracticable, notice may be communicated by a newspaper of general circulation in the area where published; or by radio, television, or other form of public broadcast communication.

(c) Written notice by a domestic or foreign corporation to its shareholder, if in a comprehensible form, is effective when mailed, if mailed postpaid and correctly addressed to the shareholder's address shown in the corporation's current record of shareholders.

(d) Written notice to a domestic or foreign corporation (authorized to transact business in this state) may be addressed to its registered agent at its registered office or to the corporation or its secretary at its principal office shown in its most recent annual report or, in the case of a foreign corporation that has not yet delivered an annual report, in its application for a certificate of authority.

(e) Except as provided in subsection (c), written notice, if in a comprehensible form, is effective at the earliest of the following:

    (1)   when received;

    (2)   five days after its deposit in the United States Mail, as evidenced by the postmark, if mailed postpaid and correctly addressed;

    (3)   on the date shown on the return receipt, if sent by registered or certified mail, return receipt requested, and the receipt is signed by or on behalf of the addressee.

(f) Oral notice is effective when communicated if communicated in a comprehensible manner.

(g) If this Act prescribes notice requirements for particular circumstances, those requirements govern. If articles of incorporation or bylaws prescribe notice requirements, not inconsistent with this section or other provisions of this Act, those requirements govern.

§ 1.42. NUMBER OF SHAREHOLDERS

(a) For purposes of this Act, the following identified as a shareholder in a corporation's current record of shareholders constitutes one shareholder:

    (1)   three or fewer co-owners;

    (2)   a corporation, partnership, trust, estate, or other entity;

    (3)   the trustees, guardians, custodians, or other fiduciaries of a single trust, estate, or account.

(b) For purposes of this Act, shareholdings registered in substantially similar names constitute one shareholder if it is reasonable to believe that the names represent the same person.

§ 2.01. INCORPORATIONS

One or more persons may act as the incorporator or incorporators of a corporation by delivering articles of incorporation to the secretary of state for filing.

§ 2.02. ARTICLES OF INCORPORATION

(a) The articles of incorporation must set forth:

    (1)   a corporate name for the corporation that satisfies the requirements of section 4.01;

    (2)   the number of shares the corporation is authorized to issue;

    (3)   the street address of the corporation's initial registered office and the name of its initial registered agent at that office; and

    (4)   the name and address of each incorporator.

(b) The articles of incorporation may set forth:

    (1)   the names and addresses of the individuals who are to serve as the initial directors;

    (2)   provisions not inconsistent with law regarding:

(i) the purpose or purposes for which the corporation is organized;

(ii) managing the business and regulating the affairs of the corporation;

(iii) defining, limiting, and regulating the powers of the corporation, its board of directors, and shareholders;

(iv) a par value for authorized shares or classes of shares;

(v) the imposition of personal liability on shareholders for the debts of the corporation to a specified extent and upon specified conditions; and

(3) any provision that under this Act is required or permitted to be set forth in the bylaws.

(c) The articles of incorporation need not set forth any of the corporate powers enumerated in this Act.

§ 2.03. INCORPORATION

(a) Unless a delayed effective date is specified, the corporate existence begins when the articles of incorporation are filed.

(b) The secretary of state's filing of the articles of incorporation is conclusive proof that the incorporators satisfied all conditions precedent to incorporation except in a proceeding by the state to cancel or revoke the incorporation or involuntarily dissolve the corporation.

§ 2.04. LIABILITY FOR PREINCORPORATION TRANSACTIONS

All persons purporting to act as or on behalf of a corporation, knowing there was no incorporation under this Act, are jointly and severally liable for all liabilities created while so acting.

§ 2.05. ORGANIZATION OF CORPORATION

(a) After incorporation:

(1) if initial directors are named in the articles of incorporation, the initial directors shall hold an organizational meeting, at the call of a majority of the directors, to complete the organization of the corporation by appointing officers, adopting bylaws, and carrying on any other business brought before the meeting;

(2) if initial directors are not named in the articles, the incorporator or incorporators shall hold an organizational meeting at the call of a majority of the incorporators:

(i) to elect directors and complete the organization of the corporation; or

(ii) to elect a board of directors who shall complete the organization of the corporation.

(b) Action required or permitted by this Act to be taken by incorporators at an organizational meeting may be taken without a meeting if the action taken is evidenced by one or more written consents describing the action taken and signed by each incorporator.

(c) An organizational meeting may be held in or out of this state.

§ 2.06. BYLAWS

(a) The incorporators or board of directors of a corporation shall adopt initial bylaws for the corporation.

(b) The bylaws of a corporation may contain any provision for managing the business and regulating the affairs of the corporation that is not inconsistent with law or the articles of incorporation.

§ 2.07. EMERGENCY BYLAWS

(a) Unless the articles of incorporation provide otherwise, the board of directors of a corporation may adopt bylaws to be effective only in an emergency defined in subsection (d). The emergency bylaws, which are subject to amendment or repeal by the shareholders, may make all provisions necessary for managing the corporation during the emergency, including:

    (1)   procedures for calling a meeting of the board of directors;

    (2)   quorum requirements for the meeting; and

    (3)   designation of additional or substitute directors.

(b) All provisions of the regular bylaws consistent with the emergency bylaws remain effective during the emergency. The emergency bylaws are not effective after the emergency ends.

(c) Corporate action taken in good faith in accordance with the emergency bylaws:

    (1)   binds the corporation; and

    (2)   may not be used to impose liability on a corporate director, officer, employee, or agent.

(d) An emergency exists for purposes of this section if a quorum of the corporation's directors cannot readily be assembled because of some catastrophic event.

§ 3.01. PURPOSES

(a) Every corporation incorporated under this Act has the purpose of engaging in any lawful business unless a more limited purpose is set forth in the articles of incorporation.

(b) A corporation engaging in a business that is subject to regulation under another statute of this state may incorporate under this Act only if permitted by, and subject to all limitations of, the other statute.

§ 3.02. GENERAL POWERS

Unless its articles of incorporation provide otherwise, every corporation has perpetual duration and succession in its corporate name and has the same powers as an individual to do all things necessary or convenient to carry out its business and affairs, including without limitation power:

    (1) to sue and be sued, complain and defend in its corporate name;

    (2) to have a corporate seal, which may be altered at will, and to use it, or a facsimile of it, by impressing or affixing it or in any other manner reproducing it;

    (3) to make and amend bylaws, not inconsistent with its articles of incorporation or with the laws of this state, for managing the business and regulating the affairs of the corporation;

    (4) to purchase, receive, lease, or otherwise acquire, and own, hold, improve, use, and otherwise deal with, real or personal property, or any legal or equitable interest in property, wherever located;

    (5) to sell, convey, mortgage, pledge, lease, exchange, and otherwise dispose of all or any part of its property;

    (6) to purchase, receive, subscribe for, or otherwise acquire; own, hold, vote, use, sell, mortgage, lend, pledge, or otherwise dispose of; and deal in and with shares or other interests in, or obligations of, any other entity;

    (7) to make contracts and guarantees, incur liabilities, borrow money, issue its notes, bonds, and other obligations (which may be convertible into or include the option to purchase other securities of the corporation), and secure any of its obligations by mortgage or pledge of any of its property, franchises, or income;

    (8) to lend money, invest and reinvest its funds, and receive and hold real and personal property as security for repayment;

    (9) to be a promoter, partner, member, associate, or manager of any partnership, joint venture, trust, or other entity;

    (10) to conduct its business, locate offices, and exercise the powers granted by this Act within or without this state;

    (11) to elect directors and appoint officers, employees, and agents of the corporation, define their duties, fix their compensation, and lend them money and credit;

    (12) to pay pensions and establish pension plans, pension trusts, profit sharing plans, share bonus plans, share option plans, and benefit or incentive plans for any or all of its current or former directors, officers, employees, and agents;

    (13) to make donations for the public welfare or for charitable, scientific, or educational purposes;

(14) to transact any lawful business that will aid governmental policy;

(15) to make payments or donations, or do any other act, not inconsistent with law, that furthers the business and affairs of the corporation.

§ 3.03. EMERGENCY POWERS

(a) In anticipation of or during an emergency defined in subsection (d), the board of directors of a corporation may:

    (1)   modify lines of succession to accommodate the incapacity of any director, officer, employee, or agent; and

    (2)   relocate the principal office, designate alternative principal offices or regional offices, or authorize the officers to do so.

(b) During an emergency defined in subsection (d), unless emergency bylaws provide otherwise:

    (1)   notice of a meeting of the board of directors need be given only to those directors whom it is practicable to reach and may be given in any practicable manner, including by publication and radio; and

    (2)   one or more officers of the corporation present at a meeting of the board of directors may be deemed to be directors for the meeting, in order of rank and within the same rank in order of seniority, as necessary to achieve a quorum.

(c) Corporate action taken in good faith during an emergency under this section to further the ordinary business affairs of the corporation:

    (1)   binds the corporation; and

    (2)   may not be used to impose liability on a corporate director, officer, employee, or agent.

(d) An emergency exists for purposes of this section if a quorum of the corporation's directors cannot readily be assembled because of some catastrophic event.

§ 3.04. ULTRA VIRES

(a) Except as provided in subsection (b), the validity of corporate action may not be challenged on the ground that the corporation lacks or lacked power to act.

(b) A corporation's power to act may be challenged:

    (1)   in a proceeding by a shareholder against the corporation to enjoin the act;

    (2)   in a proceeding by the corporation, directly, derivatively, or through a receiver, trustee, or other legal representative, against an incumbent or former director, officer, employee, or agent of the corporation; or

    (3)   in a proceeding by the Attorney General under section 14.30.

(c) In a shareholder's proceeding under subsection (b)(1) to enjoin an unauthorized corporate act, the court may enjoin or set aside the act, if equitable and if all affected persons are parties to the proceeding, and may award damages for loss (other than anticipated profits) suffered by the corporation or another party because of enjoining the unauthorized act.

§ 4.01. CORPORATE NAME

(a) A corporate name:

    (1)   must contain the word "corporation," "incorporated," "company," or "limited," or the abbreviation "corp.," "inc.," "co.," or "ltd.," or words or abbreviations of like import in another language; and

    (2)   may not contain language stating or implying that the corporation is organized for a purpose other than that permitted by section 3.01 and its articles of incorporation.

(b) Except as authorized by subsections (c) and (d), a corporate name must be distinguishable upon the records of the secretary of state from:

    (1)   the corporate name of a corporation incorporated or authorized to transact business in this state;

(2) a corporate name reserved or registered under section 4.02 or 4.03;

(3) the fictitious name adopted by a foreign corporation authorized to transact business in this state because its real name is unavailable; and

(4) the corporate name of a not-for-profit corporation incorporated or authorized to transact business in this state.

(c) A corporation may apply to the secretary of state for authorization to use a name that is not distinguishable upon his records from one or more of the names described in subsection (b). The secretary of state shall authorize use of the name applied for if:

(1) the other corporation consents to the use in writing and submits an undertaking in form satisfactory to the secretary of state to change its name to a name that is distinguishable upon the records of the secretary of state from the name of the applying corporation; or

(2) the applicant delivers to the secretary of state a certified copy of the final judgment of a court of competent jurisdiction establishing the applicant's right to use the name applied for in this state.

(d) A corporation may use the name (including the fictitious name) of another domestic or foreign corporation that is used in this state if the other corporation is incorporated or authorized to transact business in this state and the proposed user corporation:

(1) has merged with the other corporation;

(2) has been formed by reorganization of the other corporation; or

(3) has acquired all or substantially all of the assets, including the corporate name, of the other corporation.

(e) This Act does not control the use of fictitious names.

§ 5.01. REGISTERED OFFICE AND REGISTERED AGENT

Each corporation must continuously maintain in this state:

(1) a registered office that may be the same as any of its places of business; and

(2) a registered agent, who may be:

(i) an individual who resides in this state and whose business office is identical with the registered office;

(ii) a domestic corporation or not-for-profit domestic corporation whose business office is identical with the registered office; or

(iii) a foreign corporation or not-for-profit foreign corporation authorized to transact business in this state whose business office is identical with the registered office.

§ 6.03. ISSUED AND OUTSTANDING SHARES

(a) A corporation may issue the number of shares of each class or series authorized by the articles of incorporation. Shares that are issued are outstanding shares until they are reacquired, redeemed, converted, or canceled.

(b) The reacquisition, redemption, or conversion of outstanding shares is subject to the limitations of subsection (c) of this section and to section 6.40.

(c) At all times that shares of the corporation are outstanding, one or more shares that together have unlimited voting rights and one or more shares that together are entitled to receive the net assets of the corporation upon dissolution must be outstanding.

§ 6.20. SUBSCRIPTION FOR SHARES BEFORE INCORPORATION

(a) A subscription for shares entered into before incorporation is irrevocable for six months unless the subscription agreement provides a longer or shorter period or all the subscribers agree to revocation.

(b) The board of directors may determine the payment terms of subscriptions for shares that were entered into before incorporation, unless the subscription agreement specifies them. A call for payment by the board of directors must be uniform so far as practicable as to all shares of the same class or series, unless the subscription agreement specifies otherwise.

(c) Shares issued pursuant to subscriptions entered into before incorporation are fully paid and nonassessable when the corporation receives the consideration specified in the subscription agreement.

(d) If a subscriber defaults in payment of money or property under a subscription agreement entered into before incorporation, the corporation may collect the amount owed as any other debt. Alternatively, unless the subscription agreement provides otherwise, the corporation may rescind the agreement and may sell the shares if the debt remains unpaid more than 20 days after the corporation sends written demand for payment to the subscriber.

(e) A subscription agreement entered into after incorporation is a contract between the subscriber and the corporation subject to section 6.21.

§ 6.22. LIABILITY OF SHAREHOLDERS

(a) A purchaser from a corporation of its own shares is not liable to the corporation or its creditors with respect to the shares except to pay the consideration for which the shares were authorized to be issued (section 6.21) or specified in the subscription agreement (section 6.20).

(b) Unless otherwise provided in the articles of incorporation, a shareholder of a corporation is not personally liable for the acts or debts of the corporation except that he may become personally liable by reason of his own acts or conduct.

§ 7.01. ANNUAL MEETING

(a) A corporation shall hold a meeting of shareholders annually at a time stated in or fixed in accordance with the bylaws.

(b) Annual shareholders' meetings may be held in or out of this state at the place stated in or fixed in accordance with the bylaws. If no place is stated in or fixed in accordance with the bylaws, annual meetings shall be held at the corporation's principal office.

(c) The failure to hold an annual meeting at the time stated in or fixed in accordance with a corporation's bylaws does not affect the validity of any corporate action.

§ 7.04. ACTION WITHOUT MEETING

(a) Action required or permitted by this Act to be taken at a shareholders' meeting may be taken without a meeting if the action is taken by all the shareholders entitled to vote on the action. The action must be evidenced by one or more written consents describing the action taken, signed by all the shareholders entitled to vote on the action, and delivered to the corporation for inclusion in the minutes or filing with the corporate records.

(b) If not otherwise fixed under section 7.03 or 7.07, the record date for determining shareholders entitled to take action without a meeting is the date the first shareholder signs the consent under subsection (a).

(c) A consent signed under this section has the effect of a meeting vote and may be described as such in any document.

(d) If this Act requires that notice of proposed action be given to nonvoting shareholders and the action is to be taken by unanimous consent of the voting shareholders, the corporation must give its nonvoting shareholders written notice of the proposed action at least 10 days before the action is taken. The notice must contain or be accompanied by the same material that, under this Act, would have been required to be sent to nonvoting shareholders in a notice of meeting at which the proposed action would have been submitted to the shareholders for action.

§ 7.05. NOTICE OF MEETING

(a) A corporation shall notify shareholders of the date, time, and place of each annual and special shareholders' meeting no fewer than 10 nor more than 60 days before the meeting date. Unless this Act or the articles of incorporation require otherwise, the corporation is required to give notice only to shareholders entitled to vote at the meeting.

(b) Unless this Act or the articles of incorporation require otherwise, notice of an annual meeting need not include a description of the purpose or purposes for which the meeting is called.

(c) Notice of a special meeting must include a description of the purpose or purposes for which the meeting is called.

(d) If not otherwise fixed under section 7.03 or 7.07, the record date for determining shareholders entitled to notice of and to vote at an annual or special shareholders' meeting is the day before the first notice is delivered to shareholders.

(e) Unless the bylaws require otherwise, if an annual or special shareholders' meeting is adjourned to a different date, time, or place, notice need not be given of the new date, time, or place if the new date, time, or place is announced at the meeting before adjournment. If a new record date for the adjourned meeting is or must be fixed under section 7.07, however, notice of the adjourned meeting must be given under this section to persons who are shareholders as of the new record date.

§ 7.06. WAIVER OF NOTICE

(a) A shareholder may waive any notice required by this Act, the articles of incorporation, or bylaws before or after the date and time stated in the notice. The waiver must be in writing, be signed by the shareholder entitled to the notice, and be delivered to the corporation for inclusion in the minutes or filing with the corporate records.

(b) A shareholder's attendance at a meeting:

(1) waives objection to lack of notice or defective notice of the meeting, unless the shareholder at the beginning of the meeting objects to holding the meeting or transacting business at the meeting;

(2) waives objection to consideration of a particular matter at the meeting that is not within the purpose or purposes described in the meeting notice, unless the shareholder objects to considering the matter when it is presented.

§ 7.07. RECORD DATE

(a) The bylaws may fix or provide the manner of fixing the record date for one or more voting groups in order to determine the shareholders entitled to notice of a shareholders' meeting, to demand a special meeting, to vote, or to take any other action. If the bylaws do not fix or provide for fixing a record date, the board of directors of the corporation may fix a future date as the record date.

(b) A record date fixed under this section may not be more than 70 days before the meeting or action requiring a determination of shareholders.

(c) A determination of shareholders entitled to notice of or to vote at a shareholders' meeting is effective for any adjournment of the meeting unless the board of directors fixes a new record date, which it must do if the meeting is adjourned to a date more than 120 days after the date fixed for the original meeting.

(d) If a court orders a meeting adjourned to a date more than 120 days after the date fixed for the original meeting, it may provide that the original record date continues in effect or it may fix a new record date.

§ 7.21. VOTING ENTITLEMENT OF SHARES

(a) Except as provided in subsections (b) and (c) or unless the articles of incorporation provide otherwise, each outstanding share, regardless of class, is entitled to one vote on each matter voted on at a shareholders' meeting. Only shares are entitled to vote.

(b) Absent special circumstances, the shares of a corporation are not entitled to vote if they are owned, directly or indirectly, by a second corporation, domestic or foreign, and the first corporation owns, directly or indirectly, a majority of the shares entitled to vote for directors of the second corporation.

(c) Subsection (b) does not limit the power of a corporation to vote any shares, including its own shares, held by it in a fiduciary capacity.

(d) Redeemable shares are not entitled to vote after notice of redemption is mailed to the holders and a sum sufficient to redeem the shares has been deposited with a bank, trust company, or other financial institution under an irrevocable obligation to pay the holders the redemption price on surrender of the shares.

§ 7.22. PROXIES

(a) A shareholder may vote his shares in person or by proxy.

(b) A shareholder may appoint a proxy to vote or otherwise act for him by signing an appointment form, either personally or by his attorney-in-fact.

(c) An appointment of a proxy is effective when received by the secretary or other officer of agent authorized to tabulate votes. An appointment is valid for 11 months unless a longer period is expressly provided in the appointment form.

(d) An appointment of a proxy is revocable by the shareholder unless the appointment form conspicuously states that it is irrevocable and the appointment is coupled with an interest. Appointments coupled with an interest include the appointment of:

(1) a pledgee;

(2) a person who purchased or agreed to purchase the shares;

(3) a creditor of the corporation who extended it credit under terms requiring the appointment;

(4) an employee of the corporation whose employment contract requires the appointment; or

(5) a party to a voting agreement created under section 7.31.

(e) The death or incapacity of the shareholder appointing a proxy does not affect the right of the corporation to accept the proxy's authority unless notice of the death or incapacity is received by the secretary or other officer or agent authorized to tabulate votes before the proxy exercises his authority under the appointment.

(f) An appointment made irrevocable under subsection (d) is revoked when the interest with which it is coupled is extinguished.

(g) A transferee for value of shares subject to an irrevocable appointment may revoke the appointment if he did not know of its existence when he acquired the shares and the existence of the irrevocable appointment was not noted conspicuously on the certificate representing the shares or on the information statement for shares without certificates.

(h) Subject to section 7.24 and to any express limitation on the proxy's authority appearing on the face of the appointment form, a corporation is entitled to accept the proxy's vote or other action as that of the shareholder making the appointment.

§ 8.01. REQUIREMENT FOR AND DUTIES OF BOARD OF DIRECTORS

(a) Except as provided in subsection (c), each corporation must have a board of directors.

(b) All corporate powers shall be exercised by or under the authority of, and the business and affairs of the corporation managed under the direction of, its board of directors, subject to any limitation set forth in the articles of incorporation.

(c) A corporation having 50 or fewer shareholders may dispense with or limit the authority of a board of directors by describing in its articles of incorporation who will perform some or all of the duties of a board of directors.

§ 8.03. NUMBER AND ELECTION OF DIRECTORS

(a) A board of directors must consist of one or more individuals, with the number specified in or fixed in accordance with the articles of incorporation or bylaws.

(b) If a board of directors has power to fix or change the number of directors, the board may increase or decrease by 30 percent or less the number of directors last approved by the shareholders, but only the shareholders may increase or decrease by more than 30 percent the number of directors last approved by the shareholders.

(c) The articles of incorporation or bylaws may establish a variable range for the size of the board of directors by fixing a minimum and maximum number of directors. If a variable range is established, the number of directors may be fixed or changed from time to time, within the minimum and maximum, by the shareholders or the board of directors. After shares are issued, only the shareholders may change the range for the size of the board or change from a fixed to a variable-range size board or vice versa.

(d) Directors are elected at the first annual shareholders' meeting and at each annual meeting thereafter unless their terms are staggered under section 8.06.

§ 8.04. ELECTION OF DIRECTORS BY CERTAIN CLASSES OF SHAREHOLDERS

If the articles of incorporation authorize dividing the shares into classes, the articles may also authorize the election of all or a specified number of directors by the holders of one or more authorized classes of shares. A class (or classes) of shares entitled to elect one or more directors is a separate voting group for purposes of the election of directors.

§ 8.05. TERMS OF DIRECTORS GENERALLY

(a) The terms of the initial directors of a corporation expire at the first shareholders' meeting at which directors are elected.

(b) The terms of all other directors expire at the next annual shareholders' meeting following their election unless their terms are staggered under section 8.06.

(c) A decrease in the number of directors does not shorten an incumbent director's term.

(d) The term of a director elected to fill a vacancy expires at the next shareholders' meeting at which directors are elected.

(e) Despite the expiration of a director's term, he continues to serve until his successor is elected and qualifies or until there is a decrease in the number of directors.

§ 8.06. STAGGERED TERMS FOR DIRECTORS

If there are nine or more directors, the articles of incorporation may provide for staggering their terms by dividing the total number of directors into two or three groups, with each group containing one half or one-third of the total, as near as may be. In that event, the terms of directors in the first group expire at the first annual shareholders' meeting after their election, the terms of the second group expire at the second annual shareholders' meeting after their election, and the terms of the third group, if any, expire at the third annual shareholders' meeting after their election. At each annual shareholders' meeting held thereafter, directors shall be chosen for a term of two years or three years, as the case may be, to succeed those whose terms expire.

§ 8.08. REMOVAL OF DIRECTORS BY SHAREHOLDERS

(a) The shareholders may remove one or more directors with or without cause unless the articles of incorporation provide that directors may be removed only for cause.

(b) If a director is elected by a voting group of shareholders, only the shareholders of that voting group may participate in the vote to remove him.

(c) If cumulative voting is authorized, a director may not be removed if the number of votes sufficient to elect him under cumulative voting is voted against his removal. If cumulative voting is not authorized, a director may be removed only if the number of votes cast to remove him exceeds the number of votes cast not to remove him.

(d) A director may be removed by the shareholders only at a meeting called for the purpose of removing him and the meeting notice must state that the purpose, or one of the purposes, of the meeting is removal of the director.

§ 8.20. MEETINGS

(a) The board of directors may hold regular or special meetings in or out of state.

(b) Unless the articles of incorporation or bylaws provide otherwise, the board of directors may permit any or all directors to participate in a regular or special meeting by, or conduct the meeting through the use of, any means of communication by which all directors participating may simultaneously hear each other during the meeting. A director participating in a meeting by this means is deemed to be present in person at the meeting.

§ 8.30. GENERAL STANDARDS FOR DIRECTORS

(a) A director shall discharge his duties as a director, including his duties as a member on a committee:

    (1)   in good faith;

    (2)   with the care an ordinarily prudent person in a like position would exercise under similar circumstances; and

    (3)   in a manner he reasonably believes to be in the best interests of the corporation.

(b) In discharging his duties a director is entitled to rely on information, opinions, reports, or statements, including financial statements and other financial data, if prepared or presented by:

    (1)   one or more officers or employees of the corporation whom the director reasonably believes to be reliable and competent in the matters presented;

    (2)   legal counsel, public accountants, or other persons as to matters the director reasonably believes are within the person's professional or expert competence; or

    (3)   a committee of the board of directors of which he is not a member if the director reasonably believes the committee merits confidence.

(c) A director is not acting in good faith if he has knowledge concerning the matter in question that makes reliance otherwise permitted by subsection (b) unwarranted.

(d) A director is not liable for any action taken as a director, or any failure to take any action, if he performed the duties of his office in compliance with this section.

§ 8.31. DIRECTOR CONFLICT OF INTEREST

(a) A conflict of interest transaction is a transaction with the corporation in which a director of the corporation has a direct or indirect interest. A conflict of interest transaction is not voidable by the corporation solely because of the director's interest in the transaction if any one of the following is true:

    (1)   the material facts of the transaction and the director's interest were disclosed or known to the board of directors or a committee of the board of directors and the board of directors or committee authorized, approved, or ratified the transaction;

    (2)   the material facts of the transaction and the director's interest were disclosed or known to the shareholders entitled to vote and they authorized,

approved, or ratified the transaction; or

(3) the transaction was fair to the corporation.

(b) For the purposes of this section, a director of the corporation has an indirect interest in a transaction if

(1) another entity in which he has a material financial interest or in which he is a general partner is a party to the transaction or

(2) another entity of which he is a director, officer, or trustee is a party to the transaction and the transaction is or should be considered by the board of directions of the corporation.

(c) For purposes of subsection (a)(1), a conflict of interest transaction is authorized, approved, or ratified if it receives the affirmative vote of a majority of the directors on the board of directors (or on the committee) who have no direct or indirect interest in the transaction, but a transaction may not be authorized, approved, or ratified under this section by a single director. If a majority of the directors who have no direct or indirect interest in the transaction vote to authorize, approve, or ratify the transaction, a quorum is present for the purpose of taking action under this section. The presence of, or a vote cast by, a director with a direct or indirect interest in the transaction does not affect the validity of any action taken under subsection (a)(1) if the transaction is otherwise authorized, approved, or ratified as provided in that subsection.

(d) For purposes of subsection (a)(2), a conflict of interest transaction is authorized, approved, or ratified if it receives the vote of a majority of the shares entitled to be counted under this subsection. Shares owned by or voted under the control of a director who has a direct or indirect interest in the transaction, and shares owned by or voted under the control of an entity described in subsection (b)(1), may not be counted in a vote of shareholders to determine whether to authorize, approve, or ratify a conflict of interest transaction under subsection (a)(2). The vote of those shares, however, is counted in determining whether

the transaction is approved under other sections of this Act. A majority of the shares, whether or not present, that are entitled to be counted in a vote on the transaction under this subsection constituted a quorum for the purpose of taking action under this section.

§ 8.33. LIABILITY FOR UNLAWFUL DISTRIBUTIONS

(a) A director who votes for or assents to a distribution made in violation of section 6.40 or the articles of incorporation is personally liable to the corporation for the amount of the distribution that exceeds what could have been distributed without violating section 6.40 or the articles of incorporation if it is established that he did not perform his duties in compliance with section 8.30. In any proceeding commenced under this section, a director has all of the defenses ordinarily available to a director.

(b) A director held liable under subsection (a) for an unlawful distribution is entitled to contribution:

(1) from every other director who could be held liable under subsection (a) for the unlawful distribution; and

(2) from each shareholder for the amount the shareholder accepted knowing the distribution was made in violation of section 6.40 or the articles of incorporation.

(c) A proceeding under this section is barred unless it is commenced within two years after the date on which the effect of the distribution was measured under section 6.40(e) or (g).

§ 8.40. REQUIRED OFFICERS

(a) A corporation has the officers described in its bylaws or appointed by the board of directors in accordance with the bylaws.

(b) A duly appointed officer may appoint one or more officers or assistant officers if authorized by the bylaws or the board of directors.

(c) The bylaws or the board of directors shall delegate to one of the officers responsibility for preparing minutes of the directors' and shareholders' meetings and for authenticating records of the corporation.

(d) The same individual may simultaneously hold more than one office in a corporation.

§ 8.41. DUTIES OF OFFICERS

Each officer has the authority and shall perform the duties set forth in the bylaws or, to the extent consistent with the bylaws, the duties prescribed by the board of directors or by direction of an officer authorized by the board of directors to prescribe the duties of other officers.

§ 8.42. STANDARDS OF CONDUCT FOR OFFICERS

(a) An officer with discretionary authority shall discharge his duties under that authority:
- (1)   in good faith;
- (2)   with the care an ordinarily prudent person in a like position would exercise under similar circumstances; and
- (3)   in a manner he reasonably believes to be in the best interests of the corporation.

(b) In discharging his duties an officer is entitled to rely on information, opinions, reports, or statements, including financial statements and other financial data, if prepared or presented by:
- (1)   one or more officers or employees of the corporation whom the officer reasonably believes to be reliable and competent in the matters presented; or
- (2)   legal counsel, public accountants, or other persons as to matters the officer reasonably believes are within the person's professional or expert competence.

(c) An officer is not acting in good faith if he has knowledge concerning the matter in question that makes reliance otherwise permitted by subsection (b) unwarranted.

(d) An officer is not liable for an action taken as an officer, or any failure to take any action, if he performed the duties of his office in compliance with this section.

§ 11.01. MERGER

(a) One or more corporations may merge into another corporation if the board of directors of each corporation adopts and its shareholders (if required by section 11.03) approve a plan of merger.

(b) The plan of merger must set forth:
- (1)   the name of each corporation planning to merge and the name of the surviving corporation into which each other corporation plans to merge;
- (2)   the terms and conditions of the merger; and
- (3)   the manner and basis of converting the shares of each corporation into shares, obligations, or other securities of the surviving or any other corporation or into cash or other property in whole or part.

(c) The plan of merger may set forth:
- (1)   amendments to the articles of incorporation of the surviving corporation; and
- (2)   other provisions relating to the merger.

§ 13.02. RIGHT TO DISSENT

(a) A shareholder is entitled to dissent from and obtain payment of the fair value of his shares in the event of, any of the following corporate actions:
- (1)   consummation of a plan of merger to which the corporation is a party (i) if shareholder approval is required for the merger by section 11.03 or the articles of incorporation and the shareholder is entitled to vote on the merger or (ii) if the corporation is a subsidiary that is

merged with its parent under section 11.04;

(2) consummation of a plan of share exchange to which the corporation is a party as the corporation whose shares will be acquired, if the shareholder is entitled to vote on the plan;

(3) consummation of a sale or exchange of all, or substantially all, of the property of the corporation other than in the usual and regular course of business, if the shareholder is entitled to vote on the sale or exchange, including a sale in dissolution, but not including a sale pursuant to court order or a sale for cash pursuant to a plan by which all or substantially all of the net proceeds of the sale will be distributed to the shareholders within one year after the date of sale;

(4) an amendment of the articles of incorporation that materially and adversely affects rights in respect of a dissenter's shares because it:

(i) alters or abolishes a preferential right of the shares;

(ii) creates, alters, or abolishes a right in respect of redemption, including a provision respecting a sinking fund for the redemption or repurchase, of the shares;

(iii) alters or abolishes a preemptive right of the holder of the shares to acquire shares or other securities;

(iv) excludes or limits the right of the shares to vote on any matter, or to cumulate votes, other than a limitation by dilution through issuance of shares or other securities with similar voting rights; or

(v) reduces the number of shares owned by the shareholder to a fraction of a share if the fractional share so created is to be

acquired for cash under section 6.04; or

(5) any corporate action taken pursuant to a shareholder vote to the extent the articles of incorporation, by-laws, or a resolution of the board of directors provides that voting or nonvoting shareholders are entitled to dissent and obtain payment for their shares.

(b) A shareholder entitled to dissent and obtain payment for his shares under this chapter may not challenge the corporate action creating his entitlement unless the action is unlawful or fraudulent with respect to the shareholder or the corporation.

§ 13.28. PROCEDURE IF SHAREHOLDER DISSATISFIED WITH PAYMENT OR OFFER

(a) A dissenter may notify the corporation in writing of his own estimate of the fair value of his shares and amount of interest due, and demand payment of his estimate (less any payment under section 13.25), or reject the corporation's offer under section 13.27 and demand payment of the fair value of his shares and interest due, if:

(1) the dissenter believes that the amount paid under section 13.25 or offered under section 13.27 is less than the fair value of his shares or that the interest due is incorrectly calculated;

(2) the corporation fails to make payment under section 13.25 within 60 days after the date set for demanding payment; or

(3) the corporation, having failed to take the proposed action, does not return the deposited certificates or release the transfer restrictions imposed on uncertified shares within 60 days after the date set for demanding payment.

(b) A dissenter waives his right to demand payment under this section unless he notifies the corporation of his demand in writing under subsection (a) within 30 days after the corporation made or offered payment for his shares.

Subchapter C.   Judicial Appraisal of Shares

§ 13.30 COURT ACTION

(a) If a demand for payment under section 13.28 remains unsettled, the corporation shall commence a proceeding within 60 days after receiving the payment demand and petition the court to determine the fair value of the shares and accrued interest. If the corporation does not commence the proceeding within the 60-day period, it shall pay each dissenter whose demand remains unsettled the amount demanded.

(b) The corporation shall commence the proceeding in the [name or describe] court of the county where a corporation's principal office (or, if none in this state, its registered office) is located. If the corporation is a foreign corporation without a registered office in this state, it shall commence the proceeding in the county in this state where the registered office of the domestic corporation merged with or whose shares were acquired by the foreign corporations was located.

(c) The corporation shall make all dissenters (whether or not residents of this state) whose demands remain unsettled parties to the proceeding as in an action against their shares and all parties must be served with a copy of the petition. Nonresidents may be served by registered or certified mail or by publication as provided by law.

(d) The jurisdiction of the court in which the proceeding is commenced under subsection (b) is plenary and exclusive. The court may appoint one or more persons as appraisers to receive evidence and recommended decision on the question of fair value. The appraisers have the powers described in the order appointing them, or in any amendment to it. The dissenters are entitled to the same discovery rights as parties in other civil proceedings.

(e) Each dissenter made a party to the proceeding is entitled to judgment (1) for the amount, if any, by which the court finds the fair value of his shares, plus interest, exceeds the amount paid by the corporation, or (2) for the fair value, plus accrued interest, of his after-acquired shares for which the corporation elected to withhold payment under section 13.27.

§ 13.31 COURT COSTS AND COUNSEL FEES

(a) The court in an appraisal proceeding commenced under section 13.30 shall determine all costs of the proceeding, including the reasonable compensation and expenses of appraisers appointed by the court. The court shall assess the costs against the corporation, except that the court may assess costs against all or some of the dissenters, in amounts the court finds equitable, to the extent the court finds dissenters acted arbitrarily, vexatiously, or not in good faith in demanding payment under section 13.28.

(b) The court may also assess the fees and expenses of counsel and experts for the respective parties, in amounts the court finds equitable:

(1) against the corporation and in favor of any or all dissenters if the court finds the corporation did not substantially comply with the requirements of sections 13.20 through 13.28; or

(2) against either the corporation or a dissenter, in favor of any other party, if the court finds that the party against whom the fees and expenses are assessed acted arbitrarily, vexatiously, or not in good faith with respect to the rights provided by this chapter.

(c) If the court finds that the services of counsel for any dissenter were of substantial benefit to other dissenters similarly situated, and that the fees for those services should not be assessed against the corporation, the court may award to these counsel reasonable fees to be paid out of the amounts awarded the dissenters who were benefited.

§ 16.01. CORPORATE RECORDS

(a) A corporation shall keep as permanent records minutes of all meetings of its shareholders and board of directors, a record of all actions taken by the shareholders or board of directors without a meeting, and a record of all actions taken by a committee of the board of directors in place of the board of directors on behalf of the corporation.

(b) A corporation shall maintain appropriate accounting records.

(c) A corporation or its agent shall maintain a record of its shareholders, in a form that permits preparation of a list of the names and addresses of all shareholders, in alphabetical order by class of shares showing the number and class of shares held by each.

(d) A corporation shall maintain its records in written form or in another form capable of conversion into written form within a reasonable time.

(e) A corporation shall keep a copy of the following records at its principal office:

   (1)   its articles or restated articles of incorporation and all amendments to them currently in effect;

   (2)   its bylaws or restated bylaws and all amendments to them currently in effect;

   (3)   resolutions adopted by its board of directors creating one or more classes or series of shares, and fixing their relative rights, preferences, and limitations, if shares issued pursuant to those resolutions are outstanding;

   (4)   the minutes of all shareholders' meetings, and records of all action taken by shareholders without a meeting, for the past three years;

   (5)   all written communications to shareholders generally within the past three years, including the financial statements furnished for the past three years under section 16.20;

   (6)   a list of the names and business addresses of its current directors and officers; and

   (7)   its most recent annual report delivered to the secretary of state under section 16.22.

§ 16.02. INSPECTION OF RECORDS BY SHAREHOLDERS

(a) A shareholder of a corporation is entitled to inspect and copy, during regular business hours at the corporation's principal office, any of the records of the corporation described in section 16.01(e) if he gives the corporation written notice of his demand at least five business days before the date on which he wishes to inspect and copy.

(b) A shareholder of a corporation is entitled to inspect and copy, during regular business hours at a reasonable location specified by the corporation, any of the following records of the corporation if the shareholder meets the requirements of subsection (c) and gives the corporation written notice of his demand at least five business days before the date on which he wishes to inspect and copy:

   (1)   excerpts from minutes of any meeting of the board of directors, records of any action of a committee of the board of directors while acting in place of the board of directors on behalf of the corporation, minutes of any meeting of the shareholders, and records of action taken by the shareholders or board of directors without a meeting, to the extent not subject to inspection under section 16.02(a);

   (2)   accounting records of the corporation; and

   (3)   the record of shareholders.

(c) A shareholder may inspect and copy the records described in subsection (b) only if:

   (1)   his demand is made in good faith and for a proper purpose;

   (2)   he describes with reasonable particularity his purpose and the records he desires to inspect; and

(3)   the records are directly connected with his purpose.

(d) The right of inspection granted by this section may not be abolished or limited by a corporation's articles of incorporation or by-laws.

(e) This section does not affect:

(1)   the right of a shareholder to inspect records under section 7.20 or, if the shareholder is in litigation with the corporation, to the same extent as any other litigant;

(2)   the power of a court, independently of this Act, to compel the production of corporate records for examination.

(f) For purposes of this section, "shareholder" includes a beneficial owner whose shares are held in a voting trust or by a nominee on his behalf.

§ 16.20. FINANCIAL STATEMENTS FOR SHAREHOLDERS

(a) a corporation shall furnish its shareholders annual financial statements, which may be consolidated or combined statements of the corporation and one or more of its subsidiaries, as appropriate, that include a balance sheet as of the end of the fiscal year, an income statement for that year, and a statement of changes in shareholders' equity for the year unless that information appears elsewhere in the financial statements. If financial statements are prepared for the corporation on the basis of generally accepted accounting principles, the annual financial statements must also be prepared on that basis.

(b) If the annual financial statements are reported upon by a public accountant, his report must accompany them. If not, the statements must be accompanied by a statement of the president or the person responsible for the corporation's accounting records:

(1)   stating his reasonable belief whether the statements were prepared on the basis of generally accepted accounting principles and, if not, describing the basis of preparation; and

(2)   describing any respects in which the statements were not prepared on a basis of accounting consistent with the statements prepared for the preceding year.

(c) A corporation shall mail the annual financial statements to each shareholder within 120 days after the close of each fiscal year. Thereafter, on written request from a shareholder who was not mailed the statements, the corporation shall mail him the latest financial statements.

Glossary

A

abandon: give up or leave employment; relinquish possession of personal property with intent to disclaim title.

abate: put a stop to a nuisance; reduce or cancel a legacy because the estate of the decedent is insufficient to make payment in full.

ab initio: from the beginning.

abrogate: recall or repeal; make void or inoperative.

absolute liability: liability for an act that causes harm even though the actor was not at fault.

absolute privilege: protection from liability for slander or libel given under certain circumstances regardless of the fact that the statements are false or maliciously made.

abstract of title: history of the transfers of title to a given piece of land, briefly stating the parties to and the effect of all deeds, wills, and judicial proceedings relating to the land.

acceleration clause: provision in a contract or any legal instrument that upon a certain event the time for the performance of specified obligations shall be advanced; for example, a provision making the balance due upon debtor's default.

acceptance: unqualified assent to the act or proposal of another; as the acceptance of a draft (bill of exchange), of an offer to make a contract, of goods delivered by the seller, or of a gift or deed.

accession: acquisition of title to personal property by virtue of the fact that it has been attached to property already owned or was the offspring of an owned animal.

accessory after the fact: one who after the commission of a felony knowingly assists the felon.

accessory before the fact: one who is absent at the commission of the crime but who aided and abetted its commission.

accident: an event that occurs even though a reasonable person would not have foreseen its occurrence, because of which the law holds no one responsible for the harm caused.

accommodation party: a person who signs a commercial paper to lend credit to another party to the paper.

accord and satisfaction: an agreement to substitute a different performance for that called for in the contract and the performance of that substitute agreement.

accretion: the acquisition of title to additional land when the owner's land is built up by gradual deposits made by the natural action of water.

acknowledgment: an admission or confirmation, generally of an instrument and usually made before a person authorized to administer oaths, such as a notary public; the purpose being to declare that the instrument was executed by the person making the instrument, or that it was a voluntary act or that that person desires that it be recorded.

action: a proceeding to enforce any right.

action in personam: an action brought to impose liability upon a person, such as a money judgment.

action in rem: an action brought to declare the status of a thing, such as an action to declare the title to property to be forfeited because of its illegal use.

action of assumpsit: a common-law action brought to recover damages for breach of a contract.

action of ejectment: a common-law action brought to recover the possession of land.

action of mandamus: a common-law action brought to compel the performance of a ministerial or clerical act by an officer.

action of quo warranto: a common-law action brought to challenge the authority of an officer to act or to hold office.

action of replevin: a common-law action brought to recover the possession of personal property.

action of trespass: a common-law action brought to recover damages for a tort.

Act of God: a natural phenomenon that is not reasonable foreseeable.

administrative agency: a governmental commission or board given authority to regulate particular matters.

administrator-administratrix: the person (man-woman) appointed to wind up and settle the estate of a person who has died without a will.

adverse possession: the hostile possession of real estate, which when actual, visible, notorious, exclusive, and continued for the required time, will vest the title to the land in the person in such adverse possession.

advisory opinion: an opinion that may be rendered in a few states when there is no actual controversy before the court and the matter is submitted by private persons, or in some instances by the governor of the state, to obtain the court's opinion.

affidavit: a statement of facts set forth in written form and supported by the oath or affirmation of the person making the statement setting forth that such facts are true on the basis of actual knowledge or on information and belief. The affidavit is executed before a notary public or other person authorized to administer oaths.

affinity: the relationship that exists by virtue of marriage.

affirmative covenant: an express undertaking or promise in a contract or deed to do an act.

agency: the relationship that exists between a person identified as a principal and another by virtue of which the latter may make contracts with third persons on behalf of the principal. (Parties—principal, agent, third person)

agency coupled with an interest in the authority: an agency in which the agent has given a consideration or has paid for the right to exercise the authority granted.

agency coupled with an interest in the subject matter: an agency in which for a consideration the agent is given an interest in the property to which the agency relates.

agency shop: a union contract provision requiring that nonunion employees pay to the union the equivalent of union dues in order to retain their employment.

agent: one who is authorized by the principal or by operation of law to make contracts with third persons on behalf of the principal.

allonge: a paper securely fastened to a commercial paper in order to provide additional space for endorsements.

alluvion: the additions made to land by accretion.

alteration: any material change of the terms of a writing fraudulently made by a party thereto.

ambulatory: not effective and therefore may be changed, as in the case of a will that is not final until its maker has died.

amicable action: an action that all parties agree should be brought and one that is begun by the filing of such an agreement, rather than by serving the adverse parties with process. Although the parties agree to litigate, the dispute is real, and the decision is not an advisory opinion.

amicus curiae: literally, a friend of the court; one who is appointed by the court to take part in litigation and to assist the court by furnishing an opinion in the matter.

annexation: attachment of personal property to realty in such a way as to make it become real property and part of the realty.

annuity: a contract by which the insured pays a lump sum to the insurer and later receives fixed annual payments.

anomalous indorser: a person who signs a commercial paper but is not otherwise a party to the instrument.

anticipatory breach: the repudiation by a promisor of the contract prior to the time that performance is required when such repudiation is accepted by the promisee as a breach of the contract.

anti-injunction acts: statutes prohibiting the use of injunctions in labor disputes except under exceptional circumstances; notably the federal Norris-La Guardia Act of 1932.

Anti-Pertrillo Act: a federal statute that makes it a crime to compel a radio broadcasting station to hire musicians not needed, to pay for services not performed, or to refrain from broadcasting music of school children or from foreign countries.

antitrust acts: statutes prohibiting combinations and contracts in restraint of trade, notably the federal Sherman Antitrust Act of 1890, now generally inapplicable to labor union activity.

appeal: taking a case to a reviewing court to determine whether the judgment of the lower court or administrative agency was correct. (Parties—appellant, appellee)

appellate jurisdiction: the power of a court to hear and decide a given class of cases on appeal from another court or administrative agency.

arbitration: the settlement of disputed questions, whether of law or fact, by one or more arbitrators by whose decision the parties agree to be bound. Increasingly used as a procedure for labor dispute settlement.

assignment: transfer of a right. Generally used in connection with personal property rights, as rights under a contract, commercial paper, an insurance policy, a mortgage, or a lease. (Parties—assignor, assignee)

assumption of risk: the common-law rule that an employee could not sue the employer for injuries caused by the ordinary risks of employment on the theory that the employee assumed such risks by undertaking the work. The rule has been abolished in those areas governed by workers' compensation laws and most employers' liability statutes.

attachment: the seizure of property of a debtor to secure satisfaction of a judgment.

attractive nuisance doctrine: a rule imposing liability upon a landowner for injuries sustained by small children playing on the land when the landowner permits a condition to exist or maintains equipment that a reasonable person should realize would attract small children who could not realize the danger. The rule does not apply if an unreasonable burden would be imposed upon the landowner in taking steps to protect the children.

authenticate: make or establish as genuine, official, or final, such as by signing, countersigning, sealing, or performing any other act indicating approval.

B

bad check laws: laws making it a criminal offense to issue a bad check with intent to defraud.

baggage: such articles of necessity or personal convenience as are usually carried for personal use by passengers of common carriers.

bail: variously used in connection with the release of a person or property from the custody of the law, referring (a) to the act of releasing or bailing, (b) to the persons who assume liability in the event that the released person does not appear or that it is held that the property should not be released, and (c) to the bond or sum of money that is furnished the court or other official as indemnity for nonperformance of the obligation.

bailee's lien: a specific, possessory lien of the bailee upon the goods for work done to them. Commonly extended by statute to any bailee's claim for compensation and eliminating the necessity of retention of possession.

bailment: the relationship that exists when personal property is delivered into the possession of another under an agreement, express or implied, that the identical property will be returned or will be delivered in accordance with the agreement. (Parties—bailor, bailee)

bankruptcy: a procedure by which one unable to pay debts may surrender to the court for administration and distribution to creditors all assets in excess of any exemption claim, and the debtor is given a discharge that releases from the unpaid balance due on most debts.

bearer: the person in physical possession of commercial paper payable to bearer, a document of title directing delivery to bearer, or an investment security in bearer form.

beneficiary: the person to whom the proceeds of a life insurance policy are payable, a person for whose benefit property is held in trust, or a person given property by a will.

bequest: a gift of personal property by will.

bill of exchange (draft): an unconditional order in writing by one person upon another, signed by the person giving it, and ordering the person to whom it is directed to pay upon demand or at a definite time a sum certain in money to order or to bearer.

bill of lading: a document issued by a carrier reciting the receipt of goods and the terms of the contract of transportation. Regulated by the federal Bills of Lading Act or the UCC.

bill of sale: a writing signed by the seller reciting that the personal property therein described has been sold to the buyer.

binder: a memorandum delivered to the insured stating the essential terms of a policy to be executed in the future, when it is agreed that the contract of insurance is to be effective before the written policy is executed.

blank indorsement: an indorsement that does not name the person to whom the paper, document of title, or investment security is negotiated.

blue sky laws: state statutes designed to protect the public from the sale of worthless stocks and bonds.

boardinghouse keeper: one regularly engaged in the business of offering living accommodations to permanent lodgers or boarders.

bona fide: in good faith; without any fraud or deceit.

bond: an obligation or promise in writing and sealed, generally of corporations, personal representatives, and trustees; fidelity bonds.

boycott: a combination of two or more persons to cause harm to another by refraining from patronizing or dealing with such other person in any way or inducing others to so refrain; commonly an incident of labor disputes.

bulk sales acts: statutes to protect creditors of a bulk seller. Notice must be given creditors, and the bulk sale buyer is liable to the seller's creditors if the statute is not satisfied. Expanded to bulk transfers under the UCC.

business trust: a form of business organization in which the owners of the property to be devoted to the business transfer the title of the property to trustees with full power to operate the business.

C

cancellation: a crossing-out of a part of an instrument or a destruction of all legal effect of the instrument, whether by act of party, upon breach by the other party, or pursuant to agreement or decree of court.

capital: net assets of a corporation.

capital stock: the declared money value of the outstanding stock of the corporation.

cash surrender value: the sum paid the insured upon the surrender of a policy to the insurer.

cause of action: the right to damages or other judicial relief when a legally protected right of the plaintiff is violated by an unlawful act of the defendant.

caveat emptor: let the buyer beware. This maxim has been nearly abolished by warranty and strict tort liability concepts.

certificate of protest: a written statement by a notary public setting forth the fact that the holder had presented the commercial paper to the primary party and that the latter had failed to make payment.

certiorari: a review by a higher court of the regularity of proceedings before a lower court. Originally granted within the discretion of the reviewing court. The name is derived from the language of the writ, which was in Latin and directed the lower court to certify its record and transfer it to the higher court. In modern practice, the scope of review has often been expanded to include a review of the merits of the case and, also, to review the action of administrative agencies.

cestui que trust: the beneficiary or person for whose benefit the property is held in trust.

charter: the grant of authority from a government to exist as a corporation. Generally replaced today by a certificate of incorporation approving the articles of incorporation.

chattels personal: tangible personal property.

chattels real: leases of land and buildings.

check: an order by a depositor on a bank to pay a sum of money to a payee; a bill of exchange drawn on a bank and payable on demand.

chose in action: intangible personal property in the nature of claims against another, such as a claim for accounts receivable or wages.

chose in possession: tangible personal property.

circumstantial evidence: relates to circumstances surrounding the facts in dispute from which the trier of fact may deduce what has happened.

civil action: in many states a simplified form of action combining all or many of the former common-law actions.

civil court: a court with jurisdiction to hear and determine controversies relating to private rights and duties.

closed shop: a place of employment in which only union members may be employed. Now prohibited.

codicil: a testator's or testatrix's writing executed with all the formality of a will and treated as an addition to or modification of the will.

coinsurance: a clause requiring the insured to maintain insurance on property up to a stated amount and providing that to the extent that this is not done the insured is to be deemed a coinsurer with the insurer, so that the latter is liable only for its proportionate share of the amount of insurance required to be carried.

collateral note: a note accompanied by collateral security.

collective bargaining: the process by which the terms of employment are agreed upon through negotiations between the employer or employers within a given industry or industrial area and the union or the bargaining representative of the employees.

collective bargaining unit: the employment area within which employees are by statute authorized to select a bargaining representative, who is then to represent all the employees in bargaining with the employer.

collusion: an agreement between two or more persons to defraud the government or the courts, as by obtaining a divorce by collusion when no grounds for a divorce exist, or to defraud third persons of their rights.

color of title: circumstances that make a person appear to be the owner when in fact not the owner, as the existence of a deed appearing to convey the property to a given person gives color of title although the deed is worthless because it is in fact a forgery.

commission merchant: a bailee to whom goods are consigned for sale.

common carrier: a carrier that holds out its facilities to serve the general public for compensation without discrimination.

common law: the body of unwritten principles originally based upon the usages and customs of the community that were recognized and enforced by the courts.

common stock: stock that has no right or priority over any other stock of the corporation as to dividends or distribution of assets upon dissolution.

common trust fund: a plan by which the assets of small trust estates are pooled into a common fund, each trust being given certificates representing its proportionate ownership of the fund, and the pooled fund is then invested in investments of large size.

community property: the cotenancy held by husband and wife in property acquired during their marriage under the law of some of the states, principally in the southwestern United States.

complaint: the initial pleading filed by the plaintiff in many actions, which in many states may be served as original process to acquire jurisdiction over the defendant.

composition of creditors: an agreement among creditors that each shall accept a part payment as full payment in consideration of the other creditors doing the same.

concealment: the failure to volunteer information not requested.

conditional estate: an estate that will come into being upon the satisfaction of a condition precedent or that will be terminated upon the satisfaction of a condition subsequent.

confidential relationship: a relationship in which, because of the legal status of the parties or their respective physical or mental conditions or knowledge, one party places full confidence and trust in the other.

conflict of laws: the body of law that determines the law of which state is to apply when two or more states are involved in the facts of a given case.

confusion of goods: the mixing of goods of different owners that under certain circumstances results in one of the owners becoming the owner of all the goods.

consanguinity: relationship by blood.

consideration: the promise or performance that the promisor demands as the price of the promise.

consignment: a bailment made for the purpose of sale by the bailee. (Parties—consignor, consignee)

consolidation of corporations: a combining of two or more corporations in which the corporate existence of each one ceases and a new corporation is created.

constructive: an adjective employed to indicate that the instrument, described by the noun that is modified by the adjective, does not exist but the law disposes of the matter as though it did; as a constructive bailment or a constructive trust.

contingent beneficiary: the person to whom the proceeds of a life insurance policy are payable in the event that the primary beneficiary dies before the insured.

contract: a binding agreement based upon the genuine assent of the parties, made for a lawful object, between competent parties, in the form required by law, and generally supported by consideration.

contract carrier: a carrier that transports on the basis of individual contracts that it makes with each shipper.

contract to sell: a contract to make a transfer of title in the future as contrasted with a present transfer.

contribution: the right of a co-obligor who has paid more than a proportionate share to demand that the other obligor pay the amount of the excess payment made.

contributory negligence: negligence of the plaintiff that contributes to injury and at common law bars from recovery from the defendant although the defendant may have been more negligent than the plaintiff.

conveyance: a transfer of an interest in land, ordinarily by the execution and delivery of a deed.

cooling-off period: a procedure designed to avoid strikes by requiring a specified period of delay before the strike may begin during which negotiations for a settlement must continue.

cooperative: a group of two or more persons or enterprises that acts through a common agent with respect to a common objective, such as buying or selling.

copyright: a grant to an author or artist of an exclusive right to publish and sell the copyrighted work for the life of the author or artist and fifty years thereafter. For a "work made for hire," a grant of an exclusive right to publish and sell the copyrighted work for 100 years from its creation or 75 years from its publication, whichever is shorter.

corporation: an artificial being created by government grant, which for many purposes is treated as a natural person.

cost plus: a method of determining the purchase price or contract price by providing for the payment of an amount equal to the costs of the seller or contractor to which is added a stated percentage as the profit.

costs: the expenses of suing or being sued, recoverable in some actions by the successful party, and in others, subject to allocation by the court. Ordinarily, costs do not include attorney's fees or compensation for loss of time.

counterclaim: a claim that the defendant in an action may make against the plaintiff.

covenants of title: covenants of the grantor in a deed that guarantee such matters as the right to make the conveyance, to ownership of the property, to freedom of the property from encumbrances, or that the grantee will not be disturbed in the quiet enjoyment of the land.

crime: a violation of the law that is punished as an offense against the state or government.

cross complaint: a claim that the defendant may make against the plaintiff.

cross-examination: the examination made of a witness by the attorney for the adverse party.

cumulative voting: a system of voting for directors in which each shareholder has as many votes as the number of voting shares owned multiplied by the number of directors to be elected and such votes can be distributed for the various candidates as desired.

cy pres doctrine: the rule under which a charitable trust will be carried out as nearly as possible in the way the settlor desired, when for any reason it cannot be carried out exactly in the way or for the purposes expressed.

D

damages: a sum of money recovered to redress or make amends for the legal wrong or injury done.

damnum absque injuria: loss or damage without the violation of a legal right, or the mere fact that a person sustains a loss does not mean that legal rights have been violated.

declaratory judgment: a procedure for obtaining the decision of a court on a question before any action has been taken or loss sustained. It differs from an advisory opinion in that there must be an actual, imminent controversy.

dedication: acquisition by the public or a government of title to land when it is given over by its owner to use by the public and such gift is accepted.

deed: an instrument by which the grantor (owner of land) conveys or transfers the title to a grantee.

de facto: existing in fact as distinguished from as of right, as in the case of an officer or a corporation purporting to act as such without being elected to the office or having been properly incorporated.

deficiency judgment: a personal judgment entered against any person liable on the mortgage debt for the amount still remaining due on the mortgage after foreclosure. Statutes generally require the mortgagee to credit the fair value of the property against the balance due when the mortgagee has purchased the property. Also, a similar judgment entered by a creditor against a debtor in a secured transaction under Article 9 of the UCC.

del credere agent: an agent who sells goods for the principal and who guarantees to the principal that the buyer will pay for the goods.

delegation: the transfer to another of the right and power to do an act.

de minimis non curat lex: a maxim that the law is not concerned with trifles. Not always applied, as in the case of the encroachment of a building over the property line, in which case the law will protect the landowner regardless of the extent of the encroachment.

demonstrative evidence: evidence that consists of visible, physical objects, such as a sample taken from the wheat in controversy or a photograph of the subject matter involved.

demonstrative legacy: a legacy to be paid or distributed from a specified fund or property.

demurrage: a charge made by the carrier for the unreasonable detention of cars by the consignor or consignee.

demurrer: a pleading that may be filed to attack the sufficiency of the adverse party's pleading as not stating a cause of action or a defense.

dependent relative revocation: the doctrine recognized in some states that if a testator revokes or cancels a will in order to replace it with a later will, the earlier will is to be deemed revived if for any reason the later will does not take effect or no later will is executed.

deposition: the testimony of a witness taken out of court before a person authorized to administer oaths.

detrimental reliance: see reliance and promissory estoppel.

devise: a gift of real estate made by will.

directed verdict: a direction by the trial judge to the jury to return a verdict in favor of a specified party to the action.

directors: the persons vested with control of the corporation, subject to the elective power of the shareholders.

discharge in bankruptcy: an order of the bankruptcy court discharging the debtor from the unpaid balance of most claims.

discharge of contract: termination of a contract by performance, agreement, impossibility, acceptance of breach, or operation of law.

discovery: procedures for ascertaining facts prior to the time of trial in order to eliminate the element of surprise in litigation.

dishonor by nonacceptance: the refusal of the drawee to accept a draft (bill of exchange).

dishonor by nonpayment: the refusal to pay a commercial paper when properly presented for payment.

dismiss: a procedure to terminate an action by moving to dismiss on the ground that the plaintiff has not pleaded a cause of action entitling the plaintiff to relief.

disparagement of goods: the making of malicious, false statements as to the quality of the goods of another.

distress for rent: the common-law right of the lessor to enter the premises when the rent has not been paid and to seize all personal property found on the premises. Statutes have modified or abolished this right in many states.

distributive share: the proportionate part of the estate of the decedent that will be distributed to an heir or legatee, and also as devisee in those jurisdictions in which real estate is administered as part of the decedent's estate.

domestic bill of exchange: a draft drawn in one state and payable in the same or another state.

domestic corporation: a corporation that has been incorporated by the state in question as opposed to incorporation by another state.

domicile: the home of a person or the state of incorporation, to be distinguished from a place where a person lives but does not regard as home, or a state in which a corporation does business but in which it was not incorporated.

double indemnity: a provision for payment of double the amount specified by the insurance contract if death is caused by an accident and occurs under specified circumstances.

double jeopardy: the principle that a person who has once been placed in jeopardy by being brought to trial at which the proceedings progressed at least as far has having the jury sworn cannot thereafter be tried a second time for the same offense.

draft: see bill of exchange.

draft-varying acceptance: one in which the acceptor's agreement to pay is not exactly in conformity with the order of the instrument.

due care: the degree of care that a reasonable person would exercise to prevent the realization of harm, which under all the circumstances was reasonably foreseeable in the event that such care was not taken.

due process of law: the guarantee by the 5th and 14th Amendments to the U.S. Constitution and the guarantee of many state constitutions that no person shall be deprived of life, liberty, or property without due process of law. As currently interpreted, this process prohibits any law, either state or federal, that sets up an unfair procedure or the substance of which is arbitrary or capricious.

duress: conduct that deprives the victim of free will and that generally gives the victim the right to set aside any transaction entered into under such circumstances.

E

easement: a permanent right that one has in the land of another, as the right to cross another's land or an easement of way.

eleemosynary corporation: a corporation organized for a charitable or benevolent purpose.

embezzlement: a statutory offense consisting of the unlawful conversion of property entrusted to the wrongdoer.

eminent domain: the power of government and certain kinds of corporations to take private property against the objection of the owner, provided the taking is for a public purpose and just compensation is made therefor.

encumbrance: a right held by a third person in or a lien or charge against property, such as a mortgage or judgment lien on land.

equity: the body of principles that originally developed because of the inadequacy of the rules then applied by the common-law courts of England.

erosion: the loss of land through a gradual washing away by tides or currents, with the owner losing title to the lost land.

escheat: the transfer to the state of the title to a decedent's property when the owner of the property dies intestate not survived by anyone capable of taking the property as heir.

escrow: a conditional delivery of property or of a deed to a custodian or escrow holder, who in turn makes final delivery to the grantee or transferee when a specified condition has been satisfied.

estate: the extent and nature of one's interest in land; the assets constituting a decedent's property at the time of death; the assets of a debtor in bankruptcy proceedings.

estate in fee simple: the largest estate possible, in which the owner has absolute and entire property in the land.

estoppel: the principle by which a person is barred from pursuing a certain course of action or of disputing the truth of certain matters.

evidence: that which is presented to the trier of fact as the basis upon which the trier is to determine what happened.

exception: an objection, such as an exception to the admission of evidence on the ground that it is hearsay; a clause excluding particular property from the operation of a deed.

ex contractu: a claim or matter that is founded upon or arises out of a contract.

ex delicto: a claim or matter that is founded upon or arises out of a tort.

execution: the carrying out of a judgment of a court, generally directing that property owned by the defendant be sold and the proceeds first be used to pay the execution or judgment creditor.

exemplary damages: damages, in excess of the amount needed to compensate for the plaintiff's injury, that are awarded in order to punish the defendant for malicious or wanton conduct; also called punitive damages.

exoneration: an agreement or provision in an agreement that one party shall not be held liable for loss; the right of the surety to demand that those primarily liable pay the claim for which the surety is secondarily liable.

expert witness: one who has acquired special knowledge in a particular field as through practical experience or study, or both, whose opinion is admissible as an aid to the trier of fact.

ex post facto law: a law making criminal an act that was lawful when done or that increases the penalty when done. Such laws are generally prohibited by constitutional provisions.

extraordinary bailment: a bailment in which the bailee is subject to unusual duties and liabilities, such as a hotel keeper or common carrier.

F

factor: a bailee to whom goods are consigned for sale.

factors' acts: statutes protecting persons who buy in good faith for value from a factor although the goods had not been delivered to the factor with the consent or authorization of their owner.

fair employment practice acts: statutes designed to eliminate discrimination in employment on the basis of race, religion, national origin, or sex.

fair labor standards acts: statutes, particularly the federal statute, designed to prevent excessive hours of employment and low pay, the employment of young children, and other unsound practices.

featherbedding: the exaction of money for services not performed, which is made an unfair labor practice generally and a criminal offense in connection with radio broadcasting.

Federal Securities Act: a statute designed to protect the public from fraudulent securities.

Federal Securities Exchange Act: a statute prohibiting improper practices at and regulating security exchanges.

Federal Trade Commission Act: a statute prohibiting unfair methods of competition in interstate commerce.

fellow-servant rule: a common-law defense of the employer that barred an employee from suing an employer for injuries caused by a fellow employee.

felony: a criminal offense that is punishable by confinement in prison or by death, or that is expressly stated by statute to be a felony.

financial responsibility laws: statutes that require a driver involved in an automobile accident to prove financial responsibility in order to retain a license, such responsibility may be shown by procuring public liability insurance in a specified minimum amount.

financing factor: one who lends money to manufacturers on the security of goods to be manufactured thereafter.

firm offer: an offer stated to be held open for a specified time, which must be so held in some states even in the absence of an option contract, or under the UCC, with respect to merchants.

fixture: personal property that has become so attached to or adapted to real estate that it has lost its character as personal property and is part of the real estate.

Food, Drug, and Cosmetic Act: a federal statute prohibiting the interstate shipment of misbranded or adulterated foods, drugs, cosmetics, and therapeutic devices.

forbearance: refraining from doing an act.

foreclosure: procedure for enforcing a mortgage resulting in the public sale of the mortgaged property and, less commonly, in merely barring the right of the mortgagor to redeem the property from the mortgage.

foreign (international) bill of exchange: a bill of exchange made in one nation and payable in another.

foreign corporation: a corporation incorporated under the laws of another state.

forgery: the fraudulent making or altering of an instrument that apparently creates or alters a legal liability of another.

franchise: (a) a privilege or authorization, generally exclusive, to engage in a particular activity within a particular geographic area, such as a government franchise to operate a taxi company within a specified city, or a private franchise as the grant by a manufacturer of a right to sell products within a particular territory or for a particular number of years; (b) the right to vote.

fraud: the making of a false statement of a past or existing fact, with knowledge of its falsity or with reckless indifference as to its truth, with the intent to cause another to rely thereon, and such person does rely thereon and is harmed thereby.

freight forwarder: one who contracts to have goods transported and, in turn, contracts with carriers for such transportation.

fructus industriales: crops that are annually planted and raised.

fructus naturales: fruits from trees, bushes, and grasses growing from perennial roots.

fungible goods: goods of a homogeneous nature of which any unit is the equivalent of any other unit or is treated as such by mercantile usage.

future advance mortgage: a mortgage given to secure additional loans to be made in the future as well as to secure an original loan.

G

garnishment: the name given in some states to attachment proceedings.

general creditor: a creditor who has a claim against a debtor but does not have any lien on any of the debtor's property, whether as security for the debt or by way of a judgment or execution upon a judgment.

general damages: damages that in the ordinary course of events follow naturally and probably from the injury caused by the defendant.

general legacy: a legacy to be paid out of the decedent's assets generally without specifying any particular fund or source from which the payment is to be made.

general partnership: a partnership in which the partners conduct as co-owners a business for profit, and each partner has a right to take part in the management of the business and has unlimited liability.

gift causa mortis: a gift, made by the donor in the belief that death was immediate and impending, that is revoked or is revocable under certain circumstances.

grace period: a period generally of 30 or 31 days after the due date of a life insurance premium in which the payment may be made.

grand jury: a jury not exceeding 23 in number that considers evidence of the commission of crime and prepares indictments to bring offenders to trial before a petty jury.

grant: convey real property; an instrument by which such property has been conveyed, particularly in the case of a government.

gratuitous bailment: a bailment in which the bailee does not receive any compensation or advantage.

grievance settlement: the adjustment of disputes relating to the administration or application of existing contracts as compared with disputes over new terms of employment.

guarantor: one who undertakes the obligation of guaranty.

guaranty: an undertaking to pay the debt of another if the creditor first sues the debtor and is unable to recover the debt from the debtor or principal. (In some instances the liability is primary, in which case it is the same as suretyship.)

H

hearsay evidence: statements made out of court that are offered in court as proof of the information contained in the statements, and that, subject to many exceptions, are not admissible in evidence.

hedging: the making of simultaneous contracts to purchase and to sell a particular commodity at a future date with the intention that the loss on one transaction will be offset by the gain on the other.

heirs: those persons specified by statute to receive the estate of a decedent not disposed of by will.

holder: the person in possession of a commercial paper payable to that person as payee or indorsee, or the person in possession of a commercial paper payable to bearer.

holder in due course: a holder of a commercial paper who is favored and is given an immunity from certain defenses.

holder through a holder in due course: a person who is not a holder in due course but is a holder of the paper after it was held by some prior party who was a holder in due course, and who is given the same rights as a holder in due course.

holographic will: an unwitnessed will written by hand.

hotel keeper: one regularly engaged in the business of offering living accommodations to all transient persons.

hung jury: a petty jury that has been unable to agree upon a verdict.

I

ignorantia legis neminem excusat: ignorance of the law excuses no one.

implied contract: a contract expressed by conduct or implied or deduced from the facts. Also used to refer to a quasi contract.

imputed: vicariously attributed to or charged to another; for instance the knowledge of an agent obtained while acting in the scope of authority is imputed to the principal.

incidental authority: authority of an agent that is reasonably necessary to execute express authority.

incontestability clause: a provision that after the lapse of a specified time the insurer cannot dispute the policy on the ground of misrepresentation or fraud of the insured or similar wrongful conduct.

in custodia legis: in the custody of the law.

indemnity: the right of a person secondarily liable to require that a person primarily liable pay for loss sustained when the secondary party discharges the obligation that the primary party should have discharged; the right of an agent to be paid the amount of any loss or damage sustained without fault because of obedience to the principal's instructions; an undertaking by one person for a consideration to pay another person a sum of money to indemnify that person when a specified loss is incurred.

independent contractor: a contractor who undertakes to perform a specified task according to the terms of a contract but over whom the other contracting party has no control except as provided for by the contract.

indictment: a grand jury's formal accusation of crime, from which the accused is then tried by a petty or trial jury.

inheritance: the interest that passes from the decedent to the decedent's heirs.

injunction: an order of a court of equity to refrain from doing (negative injunction) or to do (affirmative or mandatory injunction) a specified act. Its use in labor disputes has been greatly restricted by statute.

in pari delicto: equally guilty; used in reference to a transaction as to which relief will not be granted to either party because both are equally guilty of wrongdoing.

insolvency: an excess of debts and liabilities over assets; or inability to pay debts as they mature.

insurable interest: an interest in the nonoccurrence of the risk insured against, generally because such occurrence would cause financial loss, although sometimes merely because of the close relationship between the insured and the beneficiary.

insurance: a plan of security against risks by charging the loss against a fund created by the payments made by policyholders.

intangible personal property: an interest in an enterprise, such as an interest in a partnership or stock of a corporation, and claims against other persons, whether based upon contract or tort.

interlineation: a writing between the lines or adding to the provisions of a document, the effect thereof depending upon the nature of the document.

interlocutory: an intermediate step or proceeding that does not make a final disposition of the action and from which ordinarily no appeal may be made.

international bill of exchange: a bill or draft made in one nation and payable in another.

interpleader: a form of action or proceeding by which a person against whom conflicting claims are made may bring the claimants into court to litigate their claims between themselves, as in the case of a bailee when two persons each claim to be the owner of the bailed property, or an insurer when two persons each claim to be the beneficiary.

inter se: among or between themselves, such as the rights of partners inter se or as between themselves.

inter vivos: any transaction which takes place between living persons and creates rights prior to the death of any of them.

intestate: the condition of dying without a will as to any property.

intestate succession: the distribution, made as directed by statute, of a decedent's property not effectively disposed of by will.

ipso facto: by the very act or fact in itself without any further action by any one.

irrebuttable presumption: a presumption that cannot be rebutted by proving that the facts are to the contrary; not a true presumption but merely a rule of law described in terms of a presumption.

irreparable injury to property: an injury that would be of such a nature or inflicted upon such an interest that it would not be reasonably possible to compensate the injured party by the payment of money damages because the property in question could not be purchased in the open market with the money damages that the defendant could be required to pay.

J

joint and several contract: a contract in which two or more persons are jointly and separately obligated or under which they are jointly and separately entitled to recover.

joint contract: a contract in which two or more persons are jointly liable or jointly entitled to performance under the contract.

joint stock company: an association in which the shares of the members are transferable and control is delegated to a group or board.

joint tenancy: the estate held by two or more jointly with the right of survivorship as between them, unless modified by statute.

joint venture: a relationship in which two or more persons combine their labor or property for a single undertaking and share profits and losses equally unless otherwise agreed.

judgment: the final sentence, order, or decision entered into at the conclusion of the action.

judgment note: a promissory note containing a clause authorizing the holder of the note to enter judgment against the maker of the note if it is not paid when due; also called a cognovit note.

judgment n.o.v.: a judgment that may be entered after verdict upon the motion of the losing party on the ground that the verdict is so wrong that a judgment should be entered the opposite of the verdict, or non obstante veredicto (notwithstanding the verdict).

judgment on the pleadings: a judgment that may be entered after all the pleadings are filed when it is clear from the pleadings that a particular party is entitled to win the action without proceeding any further.

judicial sale: a sale made under order of court by an officer appointed to make the sale or by an officer having such authority as incident to the office. The sale may have the effect of divesting liens on the property.

jurisdiction: the power of a court to hear and determine a given class of cases; the power to act over a particular defendant.

jurisdictional dispute: a dispute between rival labor unions that may take the form of each claiming that particular work should be assigned to it.

justifiable abandonment by employee: the right of an employee to abandon employment because of nonpayment of wages, wrongful assault, the demand for the performance of services not contemplated, or injurious working conditions.

justifiable discharge of employee: the right of an employer to discharge an employee for nonperformance of duties, fraud, disobedience, disloyalty, or incompetence.

L

laches: the rule that the enforcement of equitable rights will be denied when the party has delayed so long that rights of third persons have intervened or the death or disappearance of witnesses would prejudice any party through the loss of evidence.

land: earth, including all things embedded in or attached thereto, whether naturally or by the act of man.

last clear chance: the rule that a defendant who had the last clear chance to have avoided injuring the plaintiff is liable even though the plaintiff had also been contributorily negligent. In some states also called the humanitarian doctrine.

law of the case: matters decided in the course of litigation that are binding on the parties in the subsequent phases of litigation.

leading questions: questions that suggest the desired answer to the witness, or assume the existence of a fact that is in dispute.

lease: an agreement between the owner of property and a tenant by which the former agrees to give possession of the property to the latter in consideration of the payment of rent. (Parties—landlord or lessor, tenant or lessee)

leasehold: the estate or interest of a tenant in rented land.

legacy: a gift of personal property made by will.

legal tender: such form of money as the law recognizes as lawful and declares that a tender thereof in the proper amount is a proper tender that the creditor cannot refuse.

letter of credit: a written agreement by which the issuer of the letter, usually a bank, agrees with the other contracting party, its customer, that the issuer will honor drafts drawn upon it by the person named in the letter as the beneficiary. Domestic letters are regulated by the UCC, Article 5; international letters by the Customs and Practices for Commercial Documentary Credits. Commercial or payment letter: the customer is the buyer of goods sold by the beneficiary and the letter covers the purchase price of the goods. Standby letter: a letter obtained instead of a suretyship or guaranty contract requiring the issuer to honor drafts drawn by the beneficiary upon the issuer when the customer of the issuer fails to perform a contract between the customer and the beneficiary. Documentary letter: a letter of credit that does not obligate the issuer to honor drafts unless they are accompanied by the documents specified in the letter.

letters of administration: the written authorization given to an administrator of an estate as evidence of appointment and authority.

letters testamentary: the written authorization given to an executor of an estate as evidence of appointment and authority.

levy: a seizure of property by an officer of the court in execution of a judgment of the court, although in many states it is sufficient if the officer is physically in the presence of the property and announces the fact that it is "seized," but then allows the property to remain where it was found.

lex loci: the law of the place where the material facts occurred as governing the rights and liabilities of the parties.

lex loci contractus: the law of the place where the contract was made as governing the rights and liabilities of the parties to a contract with respect to certain matters.

lex loci fori: the law of the state in which the action is brought as determining the rules of procedure applicable to the action.

lex loci sitae rei: the law of the place where land is located as determining the validity of acts done relating thereto.

libel: written or visual defamation without legal justification.

license: a personal privilege to do some act or series of acts upon the land of another, as the placing of a sign thereon, not amounting to an easement or a right of possession.

lien: a claim or right, against property, existing by virtue of the entry of a judgment against its owner or by the entry of a judgment and a levy thereunder on the property, or because of the relationship of the claimant to the particular property, such as an unpaid seller.

life estate: an estate for the duration of a life.

limited jurisdiction: a court's power to hear and determine cases within certain restricted categories.

limited liability: loss of contributed capital or investment as maximum liability.

limited partnership: a partnership in which at least one partner has a liability limited to the loss of the capital contribution made to the partnership, and such a partner neither takes part in the management of the partnership nor appears to the public to be a general partner.

lineal consanguinity: the relationship that exists when one person is a direct descendant of the other.

liquidated damages: a provision stipulating the amount of damages to be paid in the event of default or breach of contract.

liquidation: the process of converting property into money whether of particular items of property or of all the assets of a business or an estate.

lis pendens: the doctrine that certain kinds of pending action are notice to everyone so that if any right is acquired from a party to such action, the transferee takes that right subject to the outcome of the pending action.

lobbying contract (illegal): a contract by which one party agrees to attempt to influence the action of a legislature or Congress, or any members thereof, by improper means.

lottery: any plan by which a consideration is given for a chance to win a prize.

lucri causa: with the motive of obtaining gain or pecuniary advantage.

M

majority: of age, as contrasted with being a minor; more than half of any group, as a majority of stockholders.

malice in fact: an intention to injure or cause harm.

malice in law: a presumed intention to injure or cause harm when there is no privilege or right to do the act in question, such presumption cannot be contradicted or rebutted.

maliciously inducing breach of contract: the wrong of inducing the breach of any kind of contract with knowledge of its existence and without justification.

malum in se: an offense that is criminal because it is contrary to the fundamental sense of a civilized community, such as murder.

malum prohibitum: an offense that is criminal not because inherently wrong but is prohibited for the convenience of society, such as overtime parking.

marshalling assets: the distribution of a debtor's assets in such a way as to give the greatest benefit to all creditors.

martial law: government exercised by a military commander over property and persons not in the armed forces, as contrasted with military law which governs military personnel.

mechanic's lien: protection afforded by statute to various kinds of laborers and persons supplying materials, by giving them a lien on the building and land that has been improved or added to by them.

mens rea: the mental state that must accompany an act to make the act a crime. Sometimes described as the guilty mind, although appreciation of guilt is not required.

merger by judgment: the discharge of a contract through being merged into a judgment that is entered in a suit on the contract.

merger of corporations: a combining of corporations by which one absorbs the other and continues to exist, preserving its original charter and identity while the other corporation ceases to exist.

misdemeanor: a criminal offense that is neither treason nor a felony.

misrepresentation: a false statement of fact although made innocently without any intent to deceive.

mobilia sequuntur personam: the maxim that personal property follows the owner and in the eyes of the law is located at the owner's domicile.

moratorium: a temporary suspension by statute of the enforcement of debts or the foreclosure of mortgages.

mortgage: an interest in land given by the owner to a creditor as security for the payment of the creditor for a debt, the nature of the interest depending upon the law of the state where the land is located. (Parties—mortgagor, mortgagee)

multiple insurers: insurers who agree to divide a risk so that each is only liable for a specified portion.

N

National Labor Management Relations Act: the federal statute, also known as the Taft-Hartley Act, designed to protect the organizational rights of labor and to prevent unfair labor practices by management or labor.

natural and probable consequences: those ordinary consequences of an act that a reasonable person would foresee.

negative covenant: an undertaking in a deed to refrain from doing an act.

negligence: the failure to exercise due care under the circumstances in consequence of which harm is proximately caused to one to whom the defendant owed a duty to exercise due care.

negligence per se: an action that is regarded as so improper that it is declared by law to be negligent in itself without regard to whether due care was otherwise exercised.

negotiable instruments: drafts, promissory notes, checks, and certificates of deposit in such form that greater rights may be acquired thereunder than by taking an assignment of a contract right; called negotiable commercial paper by the UCC.

negotiation: the transfer of a commercial paper by indorsement and delivery by the person to whom then payable in the case of order paper and by physical transfer in the case of bearer paper.

nominal damages: a nominal sum awarded the plaintiff in order to establish that legal rights have been violated although the plaintiff in fact has not sustained any actual loss or damages.

Norris-La Guardia Anti-Injunction Act: a federal statute prohibiting the use of the injunction in labor disputes, except in particular cases.

notice of dishonor: notice given to parties secondarily liable that the primary party to the instrument has refused to accept the instrument or to make payment when it was properly presented for that purpose.

novation: the discharge of a contract between two parties by their agreeing with a third person that such third person shall be substituted for one of the original parties to the contract, who shall thereupon be released.

nudum pactum: a mere promise for which there is not consideration given and which, therefore, is ordinarily not enforceable.

nuisance: any conduct that harms or prejudices another in the use of land or which harms or prejudices the public.

nuisance per se: an activity that is in itself a nuisance regardless of the time and place involved.

nuncupative will: an oral will made and declared to be a will by the testator in the presence of witnesses; generally made during the testator's last illness.

O

obiter dictum: that which is said in the opinion of a court in passing or by the way, but which is not necessary to the determination of the case and is therefore not regarded as authoritative as though it were actually involved in the decision.

obliteration: any erasing, writing upon, or crossing out that makes all or part of a will impossible to read, and which has the effect of revoking such part when done by the maker of the will with the intent of effecting a revocation.

occupation: taking and holding possession of property; a method of acquiring title to personal property after it has been abandoned.

open-end mortgage: a mortgage given to secure additional loans to be made in the future as well as to secure the original loan.

operation of law: the attaching of certain consequences to certain facts because of legal principles that operate automatically, as contrasted with consequences that arise because of the voluntary action of a party designed to create those consequences.

opinion evidence: evidence not of what the witness observed but the conclusion drawn from what the witness has observed; in the case of expert witnesses, what has been observed in tests or experiments or what has been heard in court.

option contract: a contract to hold an offer to make a contract open for a fixed period of time.

P

paper title: the title of a person evidenced only by deeds or matter appearing of record under the recording statutes.

parol evidence rule: the rule that prohibits the introduction in evidence of oral or written statements made prior to or contemporaneously with the execution of a complete written contract, deed, or instrument, in the absence of clear proof of fraud, accident, or mistake causing the omission of the statement in question.

passive trust: a trust that is created without imposing any duty to be performed by the trustee and is therefore treated as an absolute transfer of the title to the trust beneficiary.

past consideration: something that has been performed in the past and which, therefore, cannot be consideration for a promise made in the present.

patent: the grant to an inventor of an exclusive right to make and sell an invention for a nonrenewable period of 17 years; a deed to

land given by a government to a private person.

pawn: a pledge of tangible personal property rather than of documents representing property rights.

pecuniary legacy: a general legacy of a specified amount of money without indicating the source from which payment is to be made.

per autre vie: limitation of an estate. An estate held by A during the lifetime of B is an estate of A per autre vie.

per curiam opinion: an opinion written by the court rather than by a named judge when all the judges of the court are in such agreement on the matter that it is not deemed to merit any discussion and may be simply disposed of.

perpetual succession: a phrase describing the continuing life of the corporation unaffected by the death of any stockholder or the transfer by stockholders of their stock.

perpetuities, rule against: a rule of law that prohibits the creation of an interest in property that will not become definite or vested until a date further away than 21 years after the death of persons alive at the time the owner of the property attempts to create the interest.

per se: in, through, or by itself.

person: a term that includes both natural persons, or living persons, and artificial persons, such as corporations which are created by act of government.

personal defenses: limited defenses that cannot be asserted by the defendant against a holder in due course. This term is not expressly used in UCC.

per stirpes: according to the root or by way of representation. Distribution among heirs related to the decedent in different degrees, the property being divided into lines of descent from the descendent and the share of each line then divided within the line by way of representation.

petit larceny: more commonly, petty larceny. At common law, the larceny of property having the value of 12 pence or less. When the property had a greater value, the crime was grand larceny and the punishment was death. In many states, degrees of larceny have replaced the common-law classification.

petty jury: the trial jury. Also, petit jury.

picketing: the placing of persons outside of places of employment or distribution so that by words or banners they may inform the public of the existence of a labor dispute or may influence employees or customers.

pleadings: the papers filed by the parties in an action in order to set forth the facts and frame the issues to be tried, although under some systems, the pleadings merely give notice or a general indication of the nature of the issues.

pledge: a bailment given as security for the payment of a debt or the performance of an obligation owed to the pledgee. (Parties—pledgor, pledgee)

police power: the power to govern; the power to adopt laws for the protection of the public heath, welfare, safety, and morals.

policy: the paper evidencing the contract of insurance.

polling the jury: the process of inquiring of each juror individually in open court as to whether the verdict announced in court was agreed to.

possession: exclusive dominion and control of property.

possessory lien: a right to retain possession of property of another as security for some debt or obligation owed the lienor, such right continues only as long as possession is retained.

possibility of reverter: the nature of the interest held by the grantor after conveying land outright but subject to a condition or provision that may cause the grantee's interest to become forfeited and the interest to revert to the grantor or heirs.

postdate: to insert or place on an instrument a later date than the actual date on which it was executed.

power of appointment: a power given to another, commonly a beneficiary of a trust, to designate or appoint who shall be beneficiary or receive the fund after the death of the grantor.

power of attorney: a written authorization to an agent by the principal.

precatory words: words indicating merely a desire or a wish that another use property for a particular purpose but which in law will not be enforced in the absence of an express declaration that the property shall be used for the specified purpose.

preemptive offer of shares: shareholder's right upon the increase of a corporation's capital stock to be allowed to subscribe to such a percentage of the new shares as the shareholder's old shares bore to the former total capital stock.

preferred creditor: a creditor who by some statute is given the right to be paid first or before other creditors.

preferred stock: stock that has a priority or preference as to payment of dividends or upon liquidation, or both.

preponderance of evidence: the degree or quantum of evidence in favor of the existence of a certain fact when from a review of all the evidence it appears more probable that the fact exists than that it does not. The actual number of witnesses involved is not material nor is the fact that the margin of probability is very slight.

prescription: the acquisition of a right to use the land of another, as an easement, through the making of hostile, visible, and notorious use of the land, continuing for the period specified by the local law.

presumption: a rule of proof that permits the existence of a fact to be assumed from the proof that another fact exists when there is a logical relationship between the two or when the means of disproving the assumed fact are more readily within the control or knowledge of the adverse party against whom the presumption operates.

presumption of death: the rebuttable presumption that a person has died when that person has been continuously absent and unheard of for a period of 7 years.

presumption of innocence: the presumption of fact that a person accused of crime is innocent until shown guilty of the offense charged.

presumption of payment: a rebuttable presumption that one performing continuing services that would normally be paid periodically, such as weekly or monthly, has in fact been paid when a number of years have passed without any objection or demand for payment having been made.

presumptive heir: a person who would be the heir if the ancestor should die at that moment.

pretrial conference: a conference, held prior to the trial, at which the court and the attorney seek to simplify the issues in controversy and eliminate matters not in dispute.

price: the consideration for sale of goods.

prima facie: evidence that, if believed, is sufficient by itself to lead to a particular conclusion.

primary beneficiary: the person designated as the first one to receive the proceeds of a life insurance policy, as distinguished from a contingent beneficiary who will receive the proceeds only if the primary beneficiary dies before the insured.

primary liability: the liability of a person whose act or omission gave rise to the cause of action and who in all fairness should, therefore, be the one to pay the victim even though others may also be liable for misconduct.

principal: one who employs an agent; the person who, with respect to a surety, is primarily liable to the third person or creditor.

principal in the first degree: one who actually engages in the commission or perpetration of a crime.

principal in the second degree: one who is actually or constructively present at the commission of the crime and who aids and abets in its commission.

private carrier: a carrier owned by the shipper, such as a company's own fleet of trucks.

privileged communication: information that the witness may refuse to testify to because of the relationship with the person furnishing the information, such as husband-wife or attorney-client.

privilege from arrest: the immunity from arrest of parties, witnesses, and attorneys while present within the jurisdiction for the purpose of taking part in other litigation.

privity: a succession or chain of relationship to the same thing or right, such as privity of contract, privity of estate, privity of possession.

probate: the procedure for formally establishing or proving that a given writing is the last will and testament of the person who purportedly signed it.

product liability: liability imposed upon the manufacturer or seller of goods for harm caused by a defect in the goods, comprising liability for (a) negligence, (b) fraud, (c) breach of warranty, and (d) strict tort.

profit prendre: the right to take a part of the soil or produce of another's land, such as timber or water.

promissory estoppel: the doctrine that a promise will be enforced although it is not supported by consideration when the promisor should have reasonably expected that the promise would induce action or forbearance of a definite and substantial character on the part of the promisee, and injustice can only be avoided by enforcement of the promise.

promissory note: an unconditional promise in writing made by one person to another, signed by the maker engaging to pay on demand, or at a definite time, a sum certain in money to order or to bearer. (Parties—maker, payee)

promissory representation: a representation made by the applicant to the insurer as to what is to occur in the future.

promissory warranty: a representation made by the applicant to the insurer as to what is to occur in the future that the applicant warrants will occur.

promoters: the persons who plan the formation of the corporation and sell or promote the idea to others.

proof: the probative effect of the evidence; the conclusion drawn from the evidence as to the existence of particular facts.

property: the rights and interests one has in anything subject to ownership.

pro rata: proportionately, or divided according to a rate or standard.

protest: the formal certificate by a notary public or other authorized person that proper presentment of a commercial paper was made to the primary party and that such party defaulted, the certificate commonly also including a recital that notice was given to secondary parties.

proximate cause: the act that is the natural and reasonably foreseeable cause of the harm or event that occurs and injures the plaintiff.

proximate damages: damages that in the ordinary course of events are the natural and reasonably foreseeable result of the defendant's violation of the plaintiff's rights.

proxy: a written authorization by a shareholder to another person to vote the stock owned by the shareholder; the person who is the holder of such a written authorization.

public charge: a person who because of personal disability or lack of means of support is dependent upon public charity or relief for sustenance.

public domain: public or government-owned lands.

public easement: a right of way for use by members of the public at large.

public policy: certain objectives relating to health, morals, and integrity of government that the law seeks to advance by declaring invalid any contract that conflicts with those objectives even though there is no statute expressly declaring such a contract illegal.

punitive damages: damages, in excess of those required to compensate the plaintiff for the wrong done, that are imposed in order to punish the defendant because of the particularly wanton or willful character of wrongdoing; also called exemplary damages.

purchase-money mortgage: a mortgage given by the purchaser of land to the seller to secure the seller for the payment of the unpaid balance of the purchase price, which the seller purports to lend the purchaser.

purchaser in good faith: a person who purchases without any notice or knowledge of any defect of title, misconduct, or defense.

Q

qualified acceptance: An acceptance of a draft that varies the order of the draft in some way.

qualified indorsement: an indorsement that includes words such as without recourse evidencing the intent that the indorser shall not be held liable for the failure of the primary party to pay the instrument.

quantum meruit: an action brought for the value of the services rendered the defendant when there was no express contract as to the purchase price.

quantum valebant: an action brought for the value of goods sold the defendant when there was no express contract as to the purchase price.

quasi: as if, as though it were, having the characteristics of; a modifier employed to indicate that the subject is to be treated as though it were in fact the noun that follows the word quasi, as in quasi contract, quasi corporation, quasi public corporation.

quid pro quo: literally "what for what." An early form of the concept of consideration by which an action for debt could not be brought unless the defendant had obtained something in return for the obligation sued upon.

quitclaim deed: a deed by which the grantor purports only to give up whatever right or title the grantor may have in the property without specifying or warranting transfer of any particular interest.

quorum: the minimum number of persons, shares represented, or directors who must be present at a meeting in order that business may be lawfully transacted.

R

ratification by minor: a minor's approval of a contract after the minor attains majority.

ratification of agency: the approval of the unauthorized act of an agent or of a person who is not an agent for any purpose. The approval occurs after the act has been done and has the same effect as though the act had been authorized before it was done.

ratio decidendi: the reason or basis for deciding the case in a particular way.

ratio legis: the reason for a principle or rule of law.

real defenses: certain defenses (universal) that are available against any holder of a commercial paper, although this term is not expressly used by the UCC.

real evidence: tangible objects that are presented in the courtroom for the observation of the trier of fact as proof of the facts in dispute or in support of the theory of a party.

real property: land and all rights in land.

reasonable care: the degree of care that a reasonable person would take under all the circumstances then known.

rebate: a refund, made by the seller or the carrier, of part of the purchase price or freight bill.

rebuttable presumption: a presumption that may be overcome or rebutted by proof that the actual facts were different from those presumed.

receiver: an impartial person appointed by a court to take possession of and manage property for the protection of all concerned.

recognizance: an obligation entered into before a court to do some act, such as to appear at a later date for a hearing. Also called a contract of record.

redemption: the buying back of one's property, which has been sold because of a default, upon paying the amount that had been originally due together with interest and costs.

referee: an impartial person selected by the parties or appointed by a court to determine facts or decide matters in dispute.

referee in bankruptcy: a referee appointed by a bankruptcy court to hear and determine various matters relating to bankruptcy proceedings.

reformation: a remedy by which a written instrument is corrected when it fails to express the actual intent of both parties because of fraud, accident, or mistake.

registration of titles: a system generally known as the Torrens system of permanent registration of title to all land within the state.

reimbursement: the right of one paying money on behalf of another, which such other person should have paid, to recover the amount of the payment from such other person.

release of liens: an agreement or instrument by which the holder of a lien of property such as a mortgage lien, releases the property from the lien although the debt itself is not discharged.

reliance: action taken or not taken by a person in the belief that the facts as stated by another are true or that the promise of another will be performed. Detrimental reliance: a term generally used to refer to reliance of such a degree that the person relying would sustain substantial damages that could not be compensated for by the payment of money; the same concept that underlies part performance as taking an oral contract out of the statute of frauds. In some cases, loosely used when merely reliance was present. See promissory estoppel.

remedy: the action or procedure that is followed in order to enforce a right or to obtain damages for injury to a right.

remote damages: damages that were in fact caused by the defendant's act but the possibility that such damages should occur seemed so improbable and unlikely to a reasonable person that the law does not impose liability for such damages.

renunciation of duty: the repudiation of one's contractual duty in advance of the time for performance.

renunciation of right: the surrender of a right or privilege, such as the right to act as administrator or the right to receive a legacy under the will of a decedent.

reorganization of corporation: procedure devised to restore insolvent corporations to financial stability through readjustment of debt and capital structure either under the supervision of a court of equity or of bankruptcy.

repossession: any taking again of possession although generally used in connection with the act of a secured seller in taking back the property upon the default of the credit buyer.

representations: any statements, whether oral or written, made to give the insurer the information that it needs in writing the insurance, and which if false and relating to a material fact will entitle the insurer to avoid the contract.

representative capacity: action taken by one on behalf of another, as the act of a personal representative on behalf of a decedent's estate, or action taken both on one's behalf and on behalf of others, as a shareholder bringing a representative action.

rescission upon agreement: the setting aside of a contract by the action of the parties as though the contract had never been made.

rescission upon breach: the action of one party to a contract to set the contract aside when the other party is guilty of a breach of the contract.

residuary estate: the balance of the decedent's estate available for distribution after all administrative expenses, exemptions, debts, taxes, and legacies have been paid.

res inter alios acta: the rule that transactions and declarations between strangers having no connection with the ending action are not admissible in evidence.

res ipsa loquitur: the permissible inference that the defendant was negligent in that the thing speaks for itself when the circumstances are such that ordinarily the plaintiff could not have been injured had the defendant not been at fault.

res judicata: the principle that once a final judgment is entered in an action between the parties, it is binding upon them and the matter cannot be litigated again by bringing a second action.

respondeat superior: the doctrine that the principal or employer is vicariously liable for the unauthorized torts committed by an agent or employee while acting within the scope of the agency or the course of the employment, respectively.

restraints on alienation: limitations on the ability of the owner to convey freely as the owner chooses. Such limitations are generally regarded as invalid.

restrictive covenants: covenants in a deed by which the grantee agrees to refrain from doing specified acts.

restrictive indorsement: an indorsement that prohibits the further transfer, constitutes the indorsee the agent of the indorser, vests the title in the indorsee in trust for or to the use of some other person, is conditional, or is for collection or deposit.

resulting trust: a trust that is created by implication of law to carry out the presumed intent of the parties.

retaliatory statute: a statute that provides that when a corporation of another state enters the state it shall be subject to the same taxes and restrictions as would be imposed upon a corporation from the retaliating state if it had entered the other state. Also known as reciprocity statutes.

reversible error: an error or defect in court proceedings of so serious a nature that on appeal the appellate court will set aside the proceedings of the lower court.

reversionary interest: the interest that a lessor has in property that is subject to an outstanding lease.

revival of judgment: the taking of appropriate action to preserve a judgment, in most instances to continue the lien of the judgment that would otherwise expire after a specified number of years.

revival of will: the restoration, by the writer, of a will that had previously been revoked.

rider: a slip of paper executed by the insurer and intended to be attached to the insurance policy for the purpose of changing it in some respect.

riparian rights: the right of a person through whose land runs a natural watercourse to use the water free from unreasonable pollution or diversion by upper riparian owners and blocking by lower riparian owners.

risk: the peril or contingency against which the insured is protected by the contract of insurance.

Robinson-Patman Act: a federal statute designed to eliminate price discrimination in interstate commerce.

run with the land: the concept that certain covenants in a deed to land are deemed to "run" or pass with the land so that whoever owns the land is bound by or entitled to the benefit of the covenants.

S

sale or return: a sale in which the title to the property passes to the buyer at the time of the transaction but the buyer is given the option of returning the property and restoring the title to the seller.

scienter: knowledge, referring to those wrongs or crimes that require a knowledge of wrong in order to constitute the offense.

scope of employment: the area within which the employee is authorized to act with the consequence that a tort committed while so acting imposes liability upon the employer.

seal: at common law an impression on wax or other tenacious material attached to the instrument. Under modern law, any mark not ordinarily part of the signature is a seal when so intended, including the letters L.S. and the word seal, or a pictorial representation of a seal, without regard to whether they had been printed or typed on the instrument before its signing.

sealed verdict: a verdict that is rendered when the jury returns to the courtroom during an adjournment of the court, the verdict then being written down and sealed and later affirmed before the court when the court is in session.

secondary evidence: copies of original writings or testimony as to the contents of such writings that are admissible when the original cannot be produced and the inability to do so is reasonably explained.

secured transaction: a credit sale of goods or a secured loan that provides special protection for the creditor.

securities: stock and bonds issued by a corporation. Under some investor protection laws, the term includes any interest in an enterprise that provides unearned income to its owner. Investment securities: under the UCC, Article 8, this term also includes any instrument representing an interest in property or an enterprise that is commonly dealt in or recognized as a medium of investment. Uncertificated securities: under the 1977 version of the UCC rights to securities that are not represented by a certificate but only by a record on a computer of the issuing enterprise.

settlor: one who settles property in trust or creates a trust estate.

severable contract: a contract the terms of which are such that one part may be separated or severed from the other so that a default as to one part is not necessarily a default as to the entire contract.

several contracts: separate or independent contracts made by different persons undertaking to perform the same obligation.

severalty: ownership of property by one person.

severed realty: real property that has been cut off and made movable, as by cutting down a tree, and which thereby loses its character as real property and becomes personal property.

shareholder's action: an action brought by one or more shareholders on behalf of themselves and on behalf of all shareholders generally and of the corporation to enforce a cause of action of the corporation against third persons.

sheriff's deed: the deed executed and delivered by the sheriff to the purchaser at a sale conducted by the sheriff.

Sherman Antitrust Act: a federal statute prohibiting combinations and contracts in restraint of interstate trade, now generally inapplicable to labor union activity.

shop right: the right of an employer to use in business without charge an invention discovered by an employee during working hours and with the employer's material and equipment.

sight draft: a draft or bill of exchange payable on sight or when presented for payment.

sit-down strike: a strike in which the employees remain in the plant and refuse to allow the employer to operate it.

slander: defamation of character by spoken words or gestures.

slander of title: the malicious making of false statements as to a seller's title.

slowdown: a slowing down of production by employees without actual stopping work.

social security acts: statutes providing for assistance for the aged, blind, unemployed, and similar classes of persons in need.

special agent: an agent authorized to transact a specific transaction or to do a specific act.

special damages: damages that do not necessarily result from the injury to the plaintiff but at the same time are not so remote that the defendant should not be held liable therefor provided that the claim for special damages is properly made in the action.

special indorsement: an indorsement that specifies the person to whom the instrument is indorsed.

special jurisdiction: a court with power to hear and determine cases within certain restricted categories.

specific (identified) goods: goods that are so identified to the contract that no other goods may be delivered in performance of the contract.

specific lien: the right of a creditor to hold particular property or assert a lien on particular property of the debtor because of the creditor's having done work on or having some other association with the property, as distinguished from having a lien generally against the assets of the debtor merely because the debtor is indebted to the lien holder.

specific performance: an action brought to compel the adverse party to perform a contract on the theory that merely suing for damages for its breach will not be an adequate remedy.

spendthrift trust: a trust that, to varying degrees, provides that creditors of the beneficiary shall not be able to reach the principal or income held by the trustee and that the beneficiary shall not be able to assign any interest in the trust.

spoliation: an alteration or change made to a written instrument by a person who has no relationship to or interest in the writing. It has no effect as long as the terms of the instrument can still be ascertained.

stare decisis: the principle that the decision of a court should serve as a guide or precedent and control the decision of a similar case in the future.

status quo ante: the original positions of the parties to a contract prior to the making of the contract or the doing of some other act.

Statute of Frauds: a statute that, in order to prevent fraud through the use of perjured testimony, requires that certain kinds of transactions be evidenced in writing in order to be binding or enforceable.

Statute of Limitations: a statute that restricts the period of time within which an action may be brought.

stop delivery: the right of an unpaid seller under certain conditions to prevent a carrier or a bailee from delivering goods to the buyer.

stop payment: an order by a depositor to the bank to refuse to make payment of a check when presented for payment.

strict tort liability: a product liability theory that imposes liability upon the manufacturer, seller, or distributor of goods for harm caused by defective goods.

sublease: a transfer of the premises by the lessee to a third person, the sublessee or subtenant, for a period of less than the term of the original lease.

subpoena: a court order directing a person to appear as a witness. In some states it is also the original process that is to be served on the defendant in order to give the court jurisdiction over the defendant.

subrogation: the right of a party secondarily liable to stand in the place of the creditor after making payment to the creditor and to enforce the creditor's right against the party primarily liable in order to obtain indemnity from such primary party.

subsidiary corporation: a corporation that is controlled by another corporation through the ownership by the latter of a controlling amount of the voting stock of the former.

subsidiary term: a provision of a contract that is not fundamental or does not go to the root of the contract.

substantial performance: the equitable doctrine that a contractor substantially performing a contract in good faith is entitled to recover the contract price less damages for noncompletion or defective work.

substantive law: the law that defines rights and liabilities.

substitution: discharge of a contract by substituting another in its place.

subtenant: one who rents the leased premises from the original tenant for a period of time less than the balance of the lease to the original tenant.

sui generis: in a class by itself, or its own kind.

sui juris: legally competent, possessing capacity.

summary judgment: a judgment entered by the court when no substantial dispute of fact is present, the court acting on the basis of affidavits or depositions that show that the claim or defense of a party is a sham.

summons: a writ by which an action was commenced under the common law.

supersedeas: a stay of proceedings pending the taking of an appeal or an order entered for the purpose of effecting such a stay.

suretyship: an undertaking to pay the debt or be liable for the default of another.

surrender: the yielding up of the tenant's leasehold estate to the lessor in consequence of which the lease terminates.

survival acts: statutes that provide that causes of action shall not terminate on death but shall survive and may be enforced by or against a decedent's estate.

survivorship: the right by which a surviving joint tenant or tenant by the entireties acquires the interest of the predeceasing tenant automatically upon the death of such tenant.

symbolic delivery: the delivery of goods by delivery of the means of control, such as a key or a relevant document of title, such as a negotiable bill of lading.

syndicate: an association of individuals formed to conduct a particular business transaction, generally of a financial nature.

T

tacking: adding together successive periods of adverse possession of persons in privity with each other in order to constitute a sufficient period of continuous adverse possession to vest title thereby.

Taft-Hartley Act: popular name for the Labor Management Relations Act of 1947.

tariff: domestically—a government-approved schedule of charges that may be made by a regulated business, such as a common carrier or warehouser. Internationally—a tax imposed by a country on goods crossing its borders, without regard to whether the purpose is to raise revenue or to discourage the traffic in the taxed goods.

tenancy at sufferance: a tenant's holding over of the rented land after a lease has expired without the permission of the landlord and prior to the time that the landlord has elected to treat such possessor as a trespasser or a tenant.

tenancy at will: the holding of land for an indefinite period that may be terminated at any time by the landlord or by the landlord and tenant acting together.

tenancy for years: a tenancy for a fixed period of time, even though the time is less than a year.

tenancy from year to year: a tenancy that continues indefinitely from year to year until terminated.

tenancy in common: the relationship that exists when two or more persons own undivided interests in property.

tenancy in partnership: the ownership relationship that exists between partners under the Uniform Partnership Act.

tender of payment: an unconditional offer to pay the exact amount of money due at the time and place specified by the contract.

tender of performance: an unconditional offer to perform at the time and in the manner specified by the contract.

tentative trust: a trust that arises when money is deposited in a bank account in the name of the depositor "in trust for" a named person.

terminable fee: an estate that terminates upon the happening of a contingency without any entry by the grantor or heirs, as a conveyance for "so long as" the land is used for a specified purpose.

testamentary: designed to take effect at death, as by disposing of property or appointing a personal representative.

testate: the condition of leaving a will upon death.

testate succession: the distribution of an estate in accordance with the will of the decedent.

testator-testatrix: a man-woman who makes a will.

testimonium clause: a concluding paragraph in a deed, contract, or other instrument, reciting that the instrument has been executed on a specified date by the parties.

testimony: the answers of witnesses under oath to questions given at the time of the trial in the presence of the trier of fact.

theory of the case: the rule that, when a case is tried on the basis of one theory, the appellant in taking an appeal cannot argue a different theory to the appellate court.

third party beneficiary: a third person whom the parties to a contract intend to benefit by the making of the contract and to confer upon such person the right to sue for breach of contract.

tie-in sale: the requirement imposed by the seller that the buyer of particular goods or equipment also purchase certain other goods from the seller in order to obtain the original property desired.

time draft: a bill of exchange payable at a stated time after sight or at a definite time.

title insurance: a form of insurance by which the insurer insures the buyer of real property against the risk of loss should the title acquired from the seller be defective in any way.

toll the statute: stop the running of the period of the Statute of Limitations by the doing of some act by the debtor.

Torrens system: see registration of titles.

tort: a private injury or wrong arising from a breach of a duty created by law.

trade acceptance: a draft or bill of exchange drawn by the seller of goods on the purchase at the time of sale and accepted by the purchaser.

trade fixtures: articles of personal property that have been attached to the freehold by a tenant and that are used for or are necessary to the carrying on of the tenant's trade.

trademark: a name, device, or symbol used by a manufacturer or seller to distinguish goods from those of other persons.

trade name: a name under which a business is carried on and, if fictitious, it must be registered.

trade secrets: secrets of any character peculiar and important to the business of the employer that have been communicated to the employee in the course of confidential employment.

treason: an attempt to overthrow or betray the government to which one owes allegiance.

treasury stock: corporate stock that the corporation has reacquired.

trier of fact: in most cases a jury, although it may be the judge alone in certain classes of cases (as in equity) or in any case when jury trial is waived, or when an administrative agency or commission is involved.

trust: a transfer of property by one person to another with the understanding or declaration that such property be held for the benefit of another; the holding of property by the owner in trust for another, upon a declaration of trust, without a transfer to another person. (Parties—settlor, trustee, beneficiary.)

trust corpus: the fund or property that is transferred to the trustee or held by the settlor as the body or subject matter of the trust.

trust deed: a form of deed that transfers the trust property to the trustee for the purposes therein stated, particularly used when the trustee is to hold the title to the mortgagor's land in trust for the benefit of the mortgage bondholders.

trustee de son tort: a person who is not a trustee but who has wrongly intermeddled with property of another and who is required to account for the property as though an actual trustee.

trustee in bankruptcy: an impartial person elected to administer the debtor's estate.

U

uberrima fides: utmost good faith, a duty to exercise the utmost good faith that arises in certain relationships, such as that between an insurer and the applicant for insurance.

ultra vires: an act or contract that the corporation does not have authority to do or make.

underwriter: an insurer.

undisclosed principal: a principal on whose behalf an agent acts without disclosing to the third person the fact of agency or the identity of the principal.

undue influence: the influence that is asserted upon another person by one who dominates that person.

unfair competition: the wrong of employing competitive methods that have been declared unfair by statute or an administrative agency.

unfair labor practice acts: statutes that prohibit certain labor practices and declare them to be unfair.

unincorporated association: a combination of two or more persons for the furtherance of a common nonprofit purpose.

union contract: a contract between a labor union and an employer or group of employers prescribing the general terms of employment of workers by the latter.

union shop: under present unfair labor practice statutes, a place of employment where nonunion workers may be employed for a trial period of not more than 30 days after which the nonunion workers must join the union or be discharged.

universal agent: an agent authorized by the principal to do all acts that can lawfully be delegated to a representative.

usury: the lending of money at greater than the maximum rate of interest allowed by law.

V

vacating of judgment: the setting aside of a judgment.

valid: legal.

verdict: the decision of the trial or petty jury.

void: of no legal effect and not binding on anyone.

voidable: a transaction that may be set aside by one party thereto because of fraud or similar reason but which is binding on the other party until the injured party elects to avoid.

voidable preference: a preference given by the debtor in bankruptcy to a creditor, but which may be set aside by the trustee in bankruptcy.

voir dire examination: the preliminary examination of a juror or a witness to ascertain fitness to act as such.

volenti non fit injuria: the maxim that the defendant's act cannot constitute a tort if the plaintiff has consented thereto.

voluntary nonsuit: a means of a plaintiff's stopping a trial at any time by moving for a voluntary nonsuit.

voting trust: the transfer by two or more persons of their shares of stock of a corporation to a trustee who is to vote the shares and act for such shareholders.

W

waiver: the release or relinquishment of a known right or objection.

warehouse receipt: a receipt issued by the warehouser for stored goods. Regulated by the UCC, which clothes the receipt with some degree of negotiability.

warranties of indorser of commercial paper: the implied covenants made by an indorser of a commercial paper distinct from any undertaking to pay upon the default of the primary party.

warranties of insured: statements or promises made by the applicant for insurance that, if false, will entitle the insurer to avoid the contract of insurance in many jurisdictions.

warranties of seller of goods: warranties consisting of express warranties that relate to matters forming part of the basis of the bargain; warranties as to title and right to sell; and the implied warranties that the law adds to a sale depending upon the nature of the transaction.

warranty deed: a deed by which the grantor conveys a specific estate or interest to the grantee and makes one or more of the covenants of title.

warranty of authority: an implied warranty of an agent of the authority exercised by the agent.

warranty of principal: an implied warranty of an agent that the agent is acting for an existing principal who has capacity to contract.

watered stock: stock issued by a corporation as fully paid when in fact it is not.

will: an instrument executed with the formality required by law, by which a person makes a disposition of property to take effect upon death or appoints a personal representative.

willful: intentional, as distinguished from accidental or involuntary. In penal statutes, with evil intent or legal malice, or without reasonable ground for believing one's act to be lawful.

Wool Products Labeling Act: a federal statute prohibiting the misbranding of woolen fabrics.

workers' compensation: a system providing for payments to workers because they have been injured from a risk arising out of the course of their employment while they were employed at their employment or who have contracted an occupational disease in that manner, payment being made without consideration of the negligence or lack of negligence of any party.

Y

year and a day: the common-law requirement that death result within a year and a day in order to impose criminal liability for homicide.

Z

zoning restrictions: restrictions imposed by government on the use of property for the advancement of the general welfare.

CASE INDEX

Principal cases are in boldface type; cited cases are in Roman type.

SUBJECT INDEX